TURNER  MOVIES P LEONARD CLA MOVIE GUIDE

LEONARD MALTIN is a respected film critic, historian, and diehard old-movie fan. His first article about classic movies was published in *The 8mm Collector* when he was thirteen years old. At the same time he launched a column in *Film Fan Monthly*, and two years later took over as its editor and publisher. He was hired to edit the first edition of his annual movie guide when he was seventeen. Since then he has written hundreds of articles; interviewed countless Hollywood figures from the golden age to the present day (from Lillian Gish to George Clooney); authored numerous books on subjects ranging from comedy teams to the art of the cinematographer; introduced the work of Harold Lloyd, John Wayne, and Walt Disney on DVD; appeared on innumerable television shows; and provided expertise for a number of documentaries about the movies.

As far back as 1973 he received the Cinephile Award from the Society for Cinephiles. Since then he has been recognized by Anthology Film Archives, the American Society of Cinematographers, and the Telluride Film Festival, which awarded him its Silver Medallion in 2007.

Although he reviews contemporary films on a regular basis, and hasn't lost his enthusiasm for cinema, he firmly believes that "old movies are better than ever."

TURNER CLASSIC MOVIES PRESENTS LEONARD MALTIN'S
CLASSIC MOVIE GUIDE
3rd Edition

Edited by Leonard Maltin

MANAGING EDITOR
Spencer Green

CONTRIBUTING EDITORS
Rob Edelman
Michael Scheinfeld
Tom Weaver

VIDEO EDITOR
Casey St. Charnez

CONTRIBUTORS
Richard W. Bann
Boyd Magers
Bill Warren

A PLUME BOOK

PLUME
An imprint of Penguin Random House LLC
375 Hudson Street
New York, New York 10014
penguin.com

First Plume Printing, 2005
First Plume Printing (2nd edition), 2010
First Plume Printing (3rd edition), 2015

Copyright © 2005, 2010, 2015 by JessieFilm, Inc.
Penguin supports copyright. Copyright fuels creativity, encourages diverse voices, promotes free speech, and creates a vibrant culture. Thank you for buying an authorized edition of this book and for complying with copyright laws by not reproducing, scanning, or
distributing any part of it in any form without permission. You are supporting writers and
allowing Penguin to continue to publish books for every reader.

ISBN 978-0-14-751682-4

Printed in the United States of America
10   9   8   7   6   5   4   3   2   1

LEONARD MALTIN is a respected film critic and historian, best known for his paperback reference *Leonard Maltin's Movie Guide*, which was first published in 1969. He reached an even wider audience during his thirty-year run on television's *Entertainment Tonight*, and has appeared regularly on ReelzChannel since its inception in 2006. He appears on Turner Classic Movies and cohosts the weekly podcast *Maltin on Movies with Baron Vaughn*. He teaches at the USC School of Cinematic Arts in Los Angeles and was a member of the faculty of the New School for Social Research in New York City. His other books include *Leonard Maltin's 151 Best Movies You've Never Seen*, *Leonard Maltin's Movie Crazy*, *The Great Movie Comedians*, *The Disney Films*, *Of Mice and Magic: A History of American Animated Cartoons*, *The Art of the Cinematographer*, *Leonard Maltin's Movie Encyclopedia*, and (as coauthor) *The Little Rascals: The Life and Times of Our Gang*. His articles have appeared in *The New York Times*, *The Los Angeles Times*, *The London Times*, *Premiere*, *Smithsonian*, *TV Guide*, *Esquire*, and the *Village Voice*. He is also a contributor to Oxford University's *Dictionary of American Biography*. For six years he was film critic for *Playboy* magazine. He has been a Guest Curator at the Museum of Modern Art and served two terms as President of the Los Angeles Film Critics Association. In 1997 he was named to the National Film Preservation Board and in 2006 was selected by the Librarian of Congress to sit on the Board of Directors of the National Film Preservation Foundation. For nine years he hosted and coproduced the popular *Walt Disney Treasures* DVD series. He has appeared in many documentaries and has produced, written, and hosted such cable TV and home-video programs as *Young Duke: The Making of a Movie Star* (which debuted on A&E's *Biography*), *Cliffhangers: Adventures from the Thrill Factory*, *The Making of "The Quiet Man," The Making of "High Noon," The Lost Stooges*, and *Cartoons for Big Kids*. He serves as one of the hosts of the annual TCM Classic Film Festival in Hollywood and has been the recipient of awards from the Los Angeles Film Critics Association, American Society of Cinematographers, Telluride Film Festival, George Eastman House, Anthology Film Archives, and San Diego's Comic-Con International. Perhaps the pinnacle of his career was his appearance in a now-classic episode of *South Park*. (Or was it Carmela consulting his *Movie Guide* on an episode of *The Sopranos*?) He lives with his wife and daughter in Los Angeles, and holds court at leonardmaltin.com. You can also follow him on Twitter #leonardmaltin.

About the Editors

ROB EDELMAN has, for the past decade and a half, taught film history courses at the University at Albany (SUNY). He offers film commentary on WAMC (Northeast) Public Radio, and his work appears on the WAMC Web site. His books include *Great Baseball Films* and *Baseball on the Web* (which Amazon.com cited as a Top 10 Internet book), and he often contributes to *Base Ball: A Journal of the Early Game*, edited by John Thorn, the official historian of Major League Baseball. With his wife, Audrey Kupferberg, he has coauthored *Meet the Mertzes*, a double biography of Vivian Vance and William Frawley; *Matthau: A Life*; and *Angela Lansbury: A Life on Stage and Screen*. He is a contributing editor of *Leonard Maltin's Movie Guide*, *Leonard Maltin's Family Film Guide*, and *Leonard Maltin's Movie Encyclopedia*; has edited *Issues on Trial: Freedom of the Press* and written several children's books (on such subjects as Watergate and the Vietnam War); and has presented lectures in the New York State Council for the Humanities' Speakers in the Humanities program. His byline has appeared in many reference books (including *A Political Companion to American Film*, *Total Baseball*, *International Dictionary of Films and Filmmakers*, *The Total Baseball Catalog*, *Women Filmmakers and Their Films*, *Baseball and American Culture: Across the Diamond*, *St. James Encyclopedia of Popular Culture*, and histories of the 1918 Boston Red Sox, 1947 Brooklyn Dodgers, 1947 New York Yankees, and 1960 Pittsburgh Pirates) and dozens of periodicals (including, most recently, *NINE: A Journal of Baseball History and Culture*). He was Director of Programming for Home Film Festival; is the author of a baseball film essay for the Kino International DVD *Reel Baseball: Baseball Films from the Silent Era, 1899–1926*; is an interviewee on several documentaries on the director's cut DVD of *The Natural*; and has been a juror at the National Baseball Hall of Fame and Museum's annual film festival.

Major funding for SPENCER GREEN's bio has been provided by the Chubb Group of Insurance Companies. Mr. Green has written for *In Living Color*, *AAAHH!!! Real Monsters*, *Duckman*, *Mad TV*, *The Fairly Oddparents*, *Denis Leary's Merry F#%$in' Christmas*, and *Americana* for BBC Radio. He was a contributing editor for more than two decades to Leonard Maltin's annual *Movie Guide*, as well as coeditor of *Leonard Maltin's Movie Encyclopedia*, and edited *We'll Never Be Young Again: Remembering the Last Days of John F. Kennedy*. Mr. Green performs at the Los Angeles comedic writers' salon Sit 'n Spin and is coauthor/colyricist of *BUKOWSICAL*, which won Outstanding Musical at the 2007 New York International Fringe Festival and recently played at St. Louis' New Line Theatre. He writes regularly for *The Huffington Post* and created the parody Web site The Parallel Universe Film Guide; his plays have been produced by St. Louis' Theatre Lab, Seattle's Slingshot New Works Series, and Los Angeles' Sci-Fest LA. We hope you have enjoyed this bio. Now, please exit on the right-hand side.

MICHAEL SCHEINFELD is a writer and editor at HBO. As a Senior Writer for *TV Guide*, he wrote film reviews and the popular "Classic Movies" column, as well as a DVD review column. He served as contributing editor of *Leonard Maltin's Movie Guide* and *Leonard Maltin's Family Film Guide*. He also contributed essays for the "City Secrets" book *Movies: The Ultimate Insider's Guide*, and has written for several other books and magazines, including *The Motion Picture Guide*, *The Virgin Film Guide*, *Films in Review*, *The 500 Best British and Foreign Films*, and others. He has also worked for AMC and MTV Films, and has produced and programmed film series for cable channels in New York City and Philadelphia.

CASEY ST. CHARNEZ saw his first motion picture at age two (it was *The Tales of Hoffmann*, in case you wondered). In elementary school, he began a lifelong avocation of writing film reviews for newspapers, moving somewhat later into radio and TV, as well as both print (*American Film*, *The Hollywood Reporter*) and online periodicals (www.SantaFe.com). In junior high he went to the National Spelling Bee twice in a row, and in high school he often sneaked into spicy, forbidden foreign films. He earned a B.A. (English lit) and an M.A. (comparative mythology) at Texas Tech, then another M.A. (Cinema Studies) and a Ph.D. (film and dance history) at New York University, specializing in the movie musical. It was at NYU where he met one Leonard Maltin, his boss at the *Washington Square Journal*. Subsequently a publicity associate with Paramount (*A Separate Peace*, *The Little Prince*) and Fox (*Lucky Lady*), he is also the author of *The Complete Films of Steve McQueen* and wrote about Greer Garson in *100 Years: A Celebration of Filmmaking in New Mexico*. He has been an editor on the various iterations of the Maltin Movie Guides since 1986. Working on the *Classic Guide* is always rewarding for him, as he knows that all the best movies were made before 1965. Except, of course, for *Star Wars*. He continues to waltz in the Sangre de Cristo Mountains with his strawberry blonde bride, Lisa Suzonne Harris.

TOM WEAVER of Sleepy Hollow, New York, has been a fan of old movies, especially monster movies, since he was in short pants. This has led him to conduct interviews with hundreds of cast and crew members from many of his favorite fright films. Most of his thirty books, including the newish *The Creature Chronicles* (the history of the three *Creature from the Black Lagoon* movies), were published by McFarland & Co.; Weaver frequently calls himself McFarland's favorite author, although he admits that he does so without sanction, and in fact with no proof of that statement's accuracy. With equal frequency, he also points out that *The New York Times* once called him "one of the leading scholars in the horror field." Weaver has enjoyed doing dozens of DVD and Blu-ray audio commentaries and riding a Florida roller coaster with Anne Francis. His major life achievement: While being lectured for five minutes by Christopher Lee ("No, no, no, you are not from Sleepy Hollow, there is no such town"), and not allowed to interrupt, he successfully suppressed the urge to shout the *It's a Wonderful Life* line "Idiot! Don't you think I know where I live??" He's now fifty-seven and, sad to say, still wears short pants, just in a vastly larger size.

Introduction

There's nothing I love more than researching and writing about vintage movies, so you can imagine how happy I was when I got the green light for a third edition of this *Classic Movie Guide*. Ever since our last version in 2010, I'd been maintaining a file of titles to add based on recent discoveries, DVD and Blu-ray releases, and the always-interesting Turner Classic Movies schedule. I also realized that many titles that were cut from our annual guide in recent years, because of space limitations, could be restored to this volume.

The new inclusions are incredibly diverse, ranging from European silent films to Hollywood B movies of the 1930s and '40s, from a Mary Pickford vehicle to an early Milos Forman feature from the 1960s. "New" titles featuring Clara Bow, Joe E. Brown, Mary Pickford, Conrad Veidt, and Wheeler and Woolsey share pages with features directed by Fritz Lang, Jules Dassin, Julien Duvivier, Frank Borzage, Paul Fejos, Victor Fleming, and even John Ford.

Some of those titles didn't make the cut in our first two editions because there simply wasn't room for everything (which is still the case). Others have only become accessible in the past five years. A prime example is John Ford's entertaining silent comedy *Upstream* (1927), which was thought lost until a nearly perfect 35mm print was discovered in New Zealand. It's now available on DVD, along with other recently unearthed material, on a disc called *Lost and Found: American Treasures from the New Zealand Film Archive*, produced by the National Film Preservation Foundation. (Full disclosure: I am on the NFPF board. Fuller disclosure: I didn't include another great discovery, an early credit for Alfred Hitchcock called *The White Shadow*, because only three reels of that 1924 feature survive.)

The fact that so much time and effort goes into the preservation—and presentation—of older films is testament to their ongoing value. When I observe the sell-out audiences at the Los Angeles Conservancy's annual "Last Remaining Seats" series, where Angelenos enjoy vintage films in the city's great movie palaces, or the San Francisco Silent Film Festival, where audiences pack the beautiful Castro Theatre, I see people of all ages—not just elderly moviegoers indulging in mere nostalgia. The latter festival's motto says it best: true art transcends time.

That doesn't mean that every old movie is a classic; there were plenty of clinkers and potboilers in the 1920s, '30s, and '40s, but those aren't the ones we cherish and revive. Part of the fun of being an old-movie buff is coming upon a hidden gem, a film that slipped through the cracks or didn't get the attention it deserved when it was new. I hope this book will lead you to some personal discoveries that you can share with like-minded friends.

Since our last *Classic Movie Guide* came out I've been keeping a list of additions and corrections, but until my cohort Spencer Green and I began work in earnest we didn't realize how much there would be to do.

The Philo Vance mystery isn't called *Bishop Murder Case*, but *The Bishop Murder Case*. The Olsen and Johnson comedy isn't *Fifty Million Frenchmen*, but *50 Million Frenchmen*. For his early Hollywood effort *Danger—Love at Work*, the director was credited as Otto L. Preminger; he later dropped the middle initial. We always listed *Thank You, Mr. Moto* as a 1938 movie but it turns out it debuted in December of 1937.

Our primary source for credits is always the film itself. We generally trust whatever it says on-screen, although even here there are exceptions, as when a studio carelessly misspells someone's name. For further corroboration we attempt to find source material from the time of the film's release.

One can easily drown in such details, but detective work can be satisfying when one finds a definitive answer. For my rewrite of *Naughty Marietta* (1935) I wanted to refer to Victor Herbert's famous song (known to a later generation from Mel Brooks' *Young Frankenstein*), "Ah, Sweet Mystery of Life." Or is it "Ah! Sweet Mystery of Life"? Check online and you'll find contradictory references from supposedly reliable sources. In frustration, I turned to eBay and located a piece of sheet music from the song's initial publication in 1910—with an exclamation point, not a comma. And that's that.

Naughty Marietta is also a better movie than I indicated in my earlier write-up. It is just one of many films my colleagues and I have revisited and rerated for this edition. We don't take these changes of heart lightly, be they positive or negative, but when a film looks better than it did the first time around, or hasn't aged well, it seems foolish to stand by an outdated opinion.

As always, determining a film's running time can be exasperating. In some cases, recent restorations change the facts: the latest iteration of Michael Powell and Emeric Pressburger's *Tales of Hoffman* is 133 minutes, which hasn't been the case in decades. There are at least three variants of Orson Welles' *Touch of Evil*. But it can be just as difficult to nail down the facts about movies that aren't as celebrated and haven't been restored. For silent pictures the issue is especially challenging: it depends on the speed at which the film is projected. The same movie may exist in different video editions that can vary as much as an hour in length! If there is an official, licensed version that's the one we cite.

Following the example of our longtime annual *Leonard Maltin's Movie Guide*, we list the year a film was theatrically released in its country of origin. We previously labeled the British import *The Golden Mask* as a 1954 picture. The Internet Movie Database says 1953. Further research proved that it actually opened in the UK in 1952, and we're happy to make that correction.

With the release of the Cinerama films of the 1950s on home video we turned to our Roadshow specialist Michael Scheinfeld and Cinerama maven David Strohmaier to get the complete running times, including overture and intermission. For the 1960 *Scent of Mystery*, recently released on Blu-ray under its reissue title *Holiday in Spain*, Michael explained, "It was actually filmed in a process called 'Todd-70' and advertised as being shown in both 'Cinemiracle' and 'Super Cinerama.' Todd-70 was identical to Todd-AO, but the family had lost the rights to the name so producer Mike Todd, Jr., came up with the new moniker." Accordingly we have added Todd-70 to our Widescreen Glossary.

A book like this is not a one-person endeavor. I am grateful beyond words to the eagle-eyed Spencer Green for overseeing this project and wallowing in minutiae for months on end. Our longtime colleagues Rob Edelman, Michael Scheinfeld, and Casey St. Charnez came through with knowledgeable contributions. Tom Weaver provided changes and clarifications that have made the book more informative and reliable. Many readers sent in useful material, while true-blue friends like Bruce Goldstein and Alan K. Rode came through with facts and details whenever we needed them.

Extra thanks go to Darwyn Carson for pitching in, and of course my family for their love and support. My wonderful wife Alice patiently sat through everything from *To Beat the Band* with Hugh Herbert to *The Cisco Kid* with Warner Baxter. She's been my favorite moviegoing partner for more than forty years. Our daughter Jessie tends to avoid such screenings but provides encouragement in countless other ways.

Finally, I am delighted that Turner Classic Movies has agreed to put its name on my book. I view this as a perfect marriage, as TCM has become the movie buff's best friend over the past twenty years. I hope this guide will become a useful companion for TCM viewers. Leading people to good movies is the most satisfying aspect of my job.

Now, on with the show!

—Leonard Maltin

Memorable Performances—from A to Z

All lists of this kind are arbitrary, but I wanted to recognize a disparate array of performances from classic films and this seemed as good a way as any. These are personal favorites, and I offer no further reason for selecting them. In many cases I have veered 180 degrees from the obvious choice for a given actor, and that's deliberate: I always love Fred Astaire, but I think his comedic efforts (as well as his dancing) in *Broadway Melody of 1940* are vastly underrated. Errol Flynn is an indelible Robin Hood, but there is something special about his evocation of prizefighter James J. Corbett in *Gentleman Jim* that stands out in my mind. So it is, up and down this roster. Some of the titles are well known, some less so, but they are all well worth seeing—and cherishing. That's why we regard these movies as classics.

Fred **ASTAIRE**, Broadway Melody of 1940 (1940)
Lucille **BALL**, Without Love (1945)
Lon **CHANEY,** The Unknown (1927)
Marlene **DIETRICH**, A Foreign Affair (1948)
ERROL Flynn, Gentleman Jim (1942)
Douglas **FAIRBANKS**, Flirting With Fate (1917)
Jean **GABIN**, Touchez Pas au Grisbi (1954)
Jean **HARLOW**, Red-Headed Woman (1932)
Rex **INGRAM**, Sahara (1943)
JANET Gaynor, The Young in Heart (1938)
KIRK Douglas, Ace in the Hole/The Big Carnival (1951)
Angela **LANSBURY**, State of the Union (1948)
MARION Davies, The Patsy (1928)
NINA Foch, My Name Is Julia Ross (1945)
OLIVER Hardy, Sons of the Desert (1933)
Sidney **POITIER**, Cry, the Beloved Country (1951)
John **QUALEN**, The Long Voyage Home (1940)
RONALD Colman, The Talk of the Town (1942)
Barbara **STANWYCK**, The Furies (1950)
Spencer **TRACY**, Bad Day at Black Rock (1955)
UNA Merkel, 42nd Street (1933)
VIVIEN Leigh, Sidewalks of London (1938)
WILL Rogers, Judge Priest (1934)
XAVIER Cugat, You Were Never Lovelier (1942)
Roland **YOUNG**, Ruggles of Red Gap (1935)
Montgomery Clift in Fred **ZINNEMANN'S** The Search (1948)

Key to This book

Alphabetization: Articles of speech—A, An, The—are eliminated. (*The Toast of New York* is listed under *Toast of New York, The.*) Aside from that, film titles are listed in strict letter-by-letter spelling sequence. Separation of words and punctuation are ignored; everything hinges on the letters. So, *The Seekers* is listed before *See My Lawyer* because "k" comes before "m." Titles that begin with *Mister* or *Doctor* will come before the abbreviated *Mr.* or *Dr.* Let the alphabet be your guide, letter-by-letter, and you'll find the title you're looking for.

Each entry lists title and year of release. The letter "C" before a running time indicates that the film was made in color. "D" indicates the name of the director. This is followed by a listing of the principal cast members. Alternate titles (if any) are noted at the end of the entry.

Ratings range from ****, for the very best, to *½. There is no * rating; instead, for bottom-of-the-barrel movies, we use the citation BOMB.

▼ This symbol indicates the title is available on videocassette
● indicates laserdisc availability
◗ indicates DVD availability

(These symbols indicate that a film was released in one or more of these formats at one time; we cannot guarantee current availability.)

Mail-Order Sources for Home Video

When the second edition of our *Classic Movie Guide* came out in February 2010, the film fan's world was a lot different from the way things are now.

To wit: Many theaters still presented motion pictures on 35mm film. Digital projection was a specialized niche instead of the multiplex standard it has become.

On the home front, there were lots of video stores, with industry leader Blockbuster as omnipresent as Starbucks. Now, Big Blue has vanished, and the few remaining independent stores are nostalgic remnants.

Sony's Blu-ray had won its war against Toshiba's HD, but the dramatically improved disc was far from a commercial success, as renters and buyers were reluctant to trade up from standard DVD.

While Warner Bros. had already launched its Warner Archive experiment in manufacturing DVDs on demand, other Golden Age studios were yet to follow suit, waiting to see if the Warner template would last . . . which it certainly did. Now you easily can access Hollywood's finest, including Fox, Columbia, and Universal, from Metro to Monogram, from Paramount to Poverty Row.

And streaming? Back then, Hulu.com only had just begun offering its services. Amazon Prime Instant Video was still unknown. Netflix's business model depended on the U.S. Post Office. Tens of thousands of movies at one's fingertips seemed like science-fiction.

But as *tempus* continues to *fugit*, we continue to remind you that our write-ups have a ▶ for DVD, ● for laserdisc, and ▼ for tape. A title without a symbol hasn't come to home media (but be patient, it probably will). We also notate symbols only on movies under U.S. copyright or in public domain. Further, we reiterate that once a movie comes to home media, it might not be available forever, and we encourage you to peruse the following companies for the out of print, the offbeat, the hard to find.

One can't help but wonder, though, what astonishing changes there will be when the fourth edition of this *Classic Movie Guide* rolls around. What would Edison and Méliès think, much less Steve Jobs? The mind boggles, but one thing that remains constant is that we fervently continue to wish you: Happy Hunting!

Let's go shopping.

Absolute Beta Products, Post Office Box 130, Remington, VA 22734-0130, (540) 439-3259, www.absolutebeta.com, Facebook
Directly addressing a diehard niche, only for U.S. Betamax customers needing repairs and blank tapes. Established 1987.

Best Video, 1842 Whitney Ave., Hamden, CT 06517-1405, (800) 727-3843, (203) 287-9286, www.bestvideo.com, Facebook, Twitter
Blu-ray/DVD/VHS sales. Web site is quite informational. Est. 1985.

Captain Bijou, POB 7307, Houston, TX 77248-7307, (713) 864-8101, www.captainbijou.com, Facebook
Delightful collection of genre titles, B movies, old TV, etc. Also buys/sells memorabilia. Est. 1984.

ClassicFlix, POB 157, Lincoln, CA 95648-0157, (800) 592-6149, (916) 209-8520, www.classicflix.com, Facebook, Twitter
Pre-1970 movies & TV, to buy or rent. Over 8,000 titles. Est. 2007.

Columbia Classics, www.columbia-classics.com, Facebook
On-demand titles from the Columbia Pictures vault, available at Critics' Choice, Amazon, Warner Archive. Est. 2010.

The Criterion Collection, 215 Park Ave. So., New York, NY 10003-1614, www.criterion.com, Facebook, Twitter, YouTube, Tumblr
High-water mark for quality presentation of noteworthy films. "My Criterion" virtual collection service is free. Est. 1984.

Critics' Choice, POB 642, Itasca, IL 60143-0642, (800) 367-7765, www.ccvideo.com, Facebook, Twitter
A kazillion titles. Print catalog for sale, free monthly mailers, e-mail updates. Est. 1987.

Flicker Alley, POB 931762, Los Angeles, CA 90093-1762, (323) 851-1905, www.flickeralley.com, Facebook, Twitter, YouTube, Tumblr
Buff-friendly collection of the offbeat, and the often out of print, in Blu-ray, DVD, streaming. Good section of worthy posts. Est. 2002.

Fox Connect, (877) 369-7867, www.foxconnect.com, Facebook, Twitter, YouTube
Twentieth Century-Fox releases only, with thousands of current titles and vault classics. Est. 2009.

Kino Lorber, Inc., 333 W. 39th St., #503, New York, NY 10018-1380, (800) 562-3330, (212) 629-6880, www.kinolorber.com, Facebook, Twitter
World cinema titles for sale, old and new. Teachers: www.kinolorber-edu.com. Free print catalog in U.S. and Canada. Est. 2009.

LaserDisc Database, www.lddb.com
Another long-gone video format lives on at this 20th-century emporium for devoted collectors. Members-only forum. Est. 2002.

Movies Unlimited, 3015 Darnell Rd., Philadelphia, PA 19154-3201, (800) 466-8437, (215) 637-4444, www.moviesunlimited.com, Facebook, Twitter
Founding father of video sellers is definitive. Doorstopper print catalog is a reference book unto itself. Est. 1978.

NetFlix, (866) 579-7172, www.netflix.com, Facebook, Twitter
Pioneer in mail-order subscription rental also streams and produces its own original programming. Est. 1997.

Olive Films, 312 N. May St. #102, Chicago, IL 60607-1237 (630) 444-1757, www.olivefilms.com, Facebook, Twitter, YouTube
Disc debuts of often neglected titles from studio libraries, on Blu-ray and DVD. Est. 2010.

PBS, POB 609, Melbourne, FL 32902-0609, (800) 531-4727, www. shoppbs.org, Facebook, Twitter, YouTube, Pinterest
Public Broadcasting Service's online store for consumers. Schools: www.teacher.shop.pbs.org, (800) 424-7963. Est. 1969.

Robert's Videos, 107 Tucker Crescent, Saskatoon, SK S7H 3H7 CA, (800) 440-2960 (in North America), (306) 955-3763 (outside N.A.), www.robertsvideos.com
Search service for hard-to-find DVD, VHS, PAL, SECAM, etc. Est. 1998.

Sinister Cinema, POB 4369, Medford, OR 97501-0168, (541) 773-6860, www.sinistercinema.com, Facebook
Fan-pleasing assortment of B-movie discs and tapes, as retro as it gets. Armchair Fiction reprints old pulp novels. Est. 1984.

Something Weird Video, POB 33664, Seattle, WA 98133-0664, (425) 290-5830, www.somethingweird.com, Facebook, Twitter, YouTube
Exploitation-palooza, with dozens of trashy movie categories. New digital downloads. Some material age 18+ only. Est. 1990.

Turner Classic Movies, 1050 Techwood Dr. NW, Atlanta, GA 30318-5604, (404) 885-5535 (messages only), www.tcm.com, Facebook, Twitter
Indispensable site boasts video store, research database, blogs, forums, photo archives, games, more. Est. 1994.

Twilight Time, POB 550, Linden, VA 22642-0550, (888) 345-6335, (540) 635-1154, www1.screenarchives.com, Facebook
Limited-edition releases (Fox, Sony, MGM, Cannon, Polygram, Orion, Protagonist) from restored transfers, on Blu-ray and DVD. Est. 2011.

VCI Entertainment, 11333 E. 60th Pl, Tulsa, OK 74146-6828, (800) 331-4077, (918) 254-6117, www.vcientertainment.com, Facebook, Twitter, YouTube, Pinterest
Video Communications, Inc., is a fine company run by film lovers for film lovers. Exclusive collection of British films from the J. Arthur Rank Organisation. Est. 1976.

Warner Archive, (888) 883-9437, www.warnerarchive.com, Facebook, Twitter, YouTube Buffs may scan the pre-1986 holdings of Warner Bros., MGM, RKO, and Monogram for on-demand DVDs or digital downloads. New titles every week. Est. 2009.

Widescreen Glossary

An aspect ratio is the relationship between the width and height of a screen image. Virtually all sound films until 1953 were 1.37 to 1, that is, slightly wider than they were tall—a modest rectangle. Since television screen size is 1.33:1, little is lost when an older movie is shown on TV. (Even films in the later standard 1.66:1 don't suffer *too* badly.)

In the 1950s, however, Hollywood's attempt to lure people away from TV and back into theaters led to a battle of screen sizes, beginning with CinemaScope, more than twice as wide as it was high.

Today, most films are 1.85:1; since this has become the norm, they are no longer thought of as "widescreen." Our listings only cite films in special widescreen processes, such as the ones below:

CinemaScope—2.35:1 (some early titles 2.66:1 and 2.55:1)
CinemaScope 55—2.35:1 (55mm)
Cinerama—2.6:1 to 2.8:1
Dyaliscope—2.35:1 (France)
Grandeur—2:1 approx. (70mm)
Hammerscope—2.35:1 (England)
Megascope—2.35:1 (England)
MGM Camera 65—2.75:1 (70mm; same as Ultra Panavision)
Natural Vision—2:1 approx. (63.5mm)
Naturama—2.35:1 (Republic studios)
Panavision—2.35:1 (2.4:1 from 1971)
Realife—2:1 approx. (70mm)
Regalscope—2.35:1
RKO-Scope—2.35:1 (same as Super-Scope 235)
Sovscope/Sovscope 70—2.35:1 (U.S.S.R.)
Superama—2.35:1 (same as Super 35)
SuperCinescope—2.35:1 (Italy)

Super Panavision 70—2.2:1 (70mm); 2.35:1 (35mm)
SuperScope—2:1
SuperScope 235—2.35:1 (origin of Super 35)
Super Technirama 70—2.2:1 (70 mm)
SuperTotalscope—2.35:1 (Italy)
Technirama—2.35:1
Todd-AO—2.2:1 (70mm)
Todd-70—2.2:1 (70mm)
Tohoscope—2.35:1 (Japan)
Totalscope—2.35:1 (Italy/France)
Ultra Panavision 70—2.76:1 (70mm)
VistaVision—1.66:1 to 2:1 (1.85:1 recommended)
Vitascope—2:1 approx. (65mm)
WarnerScope—2.35:1

Aaron Slick From Punkin Crick (1952) **C-95m.** ** D: Claude Binyon. Alan Young, Dinah Shore, Adele Jergens, Robert Merrill, Minerva Urecal, Veda Ann Borg. Innocuous musical of dreamy farm widow Shore, obsessed with moving to the city; she's courted by shy-bumpkin neighbor Young, and is taken by on-the-lam crooks Merrill and Jergens. Based on a 1919 play—and it shows. Unmemorable score. Film debut of opera star Merrill.

Abandoned (1949) **79m.** **½ D: Joe Newman. Dennis O'Keefe, Gale Storm, Jeff Chandler, Raymond Burr, Marjorie Rambeau, Will Kuluva, Meg Randall, Mike Mazurki, Jeanette Nolan. Pretty good exposé about a baby-selling racket; reporter O'Keefe tries to help Storm find out what happened to her sister. Good L.A. locations; snappy dialogue by William Bowers.

Abandon Ship (1957-British) **100m.** *** D: Richard Sale. Tyrone Power, Mai Zetterling, Lloyd Nolan, Stephen Boyd, Moira Lister, James Hayter. Tyrone is officer suddenly in command of lifeboat holding survivors from sunken luxury liner. Tense, exciting study of people fighting to stay alive while exposed to savage seas and each other. British title: SEVEN WAVES AWAY.▼

Abbott and Costello Go to Mars (1953) **77m.** *½ D: Charles Lamont. Robert Paige, Mari Blanchard, Martha Hyer, Horace McMahon. Unimaginative vehicle has Bud and Lou sailing through space with escaped gangsters, landing on Venus, a planet populated with scantily clad women. Look quickly for Anita Ekberg.▼❙

Abbott and Costello in Hollywood (1945) **83m.** ** D: S. Sylvan Simon. Frances Rafferty, Robert Stanton, Jean Porter, Warner Anderson, Dean Stockwell. Uneven comedy with A&C as barber and porter in Tinseltown. A few peeks behind the scenes at MGM with Rags Ragland, Lucille Ball, Preston Foster, Butch Jenkins, and director Robert Z. Leonard. Officially titled BUD ABBOTT AND LOU COSTELLO IN HOLLYWOOD.▼❙

Abbott and Costello in the Foreign Legion (1950) **80m.** ** D: Charles Lamont. Patricia Medina, Walter Slezak, Douglass Dumbrille. Unexceptional vehicle pitting A&C against nasty sergeant Slezak. Best scene involves mirages in the desert. ▼❙

Abbott and Costello Meet Captain Kidd (1952) **C-70m.** ** D: Charles Lamont. Charles Laughton, Hillary Brooke, Fran Warren, Bill Shirley, Leif Erickson. Middling pirate spoof with too many lousy songs, worth catching to see Laughton having the time of his life in atypical low comedy.▼❙

Abbott and Costello Meet Dr. Jekyll and Mr. Hyde (1953) **77m.** ** D: Charles Lamont. Boris Karloff, Craig Stevens, Reginald Denny, Helen Westcott, John Dierkes. Disappointing attempt to mix A&C with Jekyll (Karloff) and Hyde (stuntman Eddie Parker), with too few funny scenes. Special effects are film's main asset.▼❙

Abbott and Costello Meet Frankenstein (1948) **83m.** ***½ D: Charles Barton. Lon Chaney, Jr., Bela Lugosi, Lenore Aubert, Jane Randolph, Glenn Strange, Frank Ferguson. Dracula (Lugosi) plans to put Lou's brain in Frankenstein's monster; werewolf Larry Talbot (Chaney) has his paws full convincing the boys they're in danger. All-time great horror-comedy still works beautifully, mainly because the monsters play it straight. Yes, that *is* Vincent Price's voice at the end. Officially titled BUD ABBOTT LOU COSTELLO MEET FRANKENSTEIN. ▼❙

Abbott and Costello Meet the Invisible Man (1951) **82m.** *** D: Charles Lamont. Nancy Guild, Arthur Franz, Adele Jergens, Sheldon Leonard. One of the team's best vehicles, with Bud and Lou as detectives helping boxer (Franz) who's been framed by mobster Leonard, with aid of invisibility formula. The effects are top-notch.▼❙

Abbott and Costello Meet the Keystone Kops (1955) **79m.** ** D: Charles Lamont. Fred Clark, Lynn Bari, Mack Sennett, Maxie Rosenbloom, Frank Wilcox, Henry Kulky, Sam Flint. Low-budget comedy could have been better. Clark is fine as conniving producer in this synthetic period piece of silent-slapstick movie days.▼❙

Abbott and Costello Meet the Killer Boris Karloff (1949) **84m.** **½ D: Charles Barton. Lenore Aubert, Gar Moore, Donna Martell, Alan Mowbray. Pleasant blend of comedy and whodunit with bodies hanging in closets perplexing hotel dick Abbott, and phony mystic Karloff trying to do away with klutzy bellboy Costello.▼❙

Abbott and Costello Meet the Mummy (1955) **79m.** **½ D: Charles Lamont. Marie Windsor, Michael Ansara, Dan Seymour, Kurt Katch, Richard Deacon. Amusing adventure with A&C mixed up with villainess Windsor, a subterranean tomb, and a mummy who's still alive. **▼O●**

ABC Murders, The SEE: **Alphabet Murders, The**

Abductors, The (1957) **80m. *½** D: Andrew McLaglen. Victor McLaglen, George Macready, Fay Spain, Gavin Muir. Boring account of McLaglen and Macready's scheme to steal and hold for ransom the remains of Abraham Lincoln; based on fact. Only time McLaglen was directed by his son. Regalscope.

Abe Lincoln in Illinois (1940) **110m. ****** D: John Cromwell. Raymond Massey, Gene Lockhart, Ruth Gordon, Mary Howard, Dorothy Tree, Minor Watson, Alan Baxter, Howard da Silva. First-rate Americana; sincere story of Lincoln's life and career is beautifully acted by Massey, with top support from Gordon as Mary Todd. Based on Robert Sherwood's Pulitzer Prize–winning play. **▼●**

Abe Lincoln of Ninth Avenue, The SEE: **Streets of New York**

Abie's Irish Rose (1946) **96m.** BOMB D: A. Edward Sutherland. Joanne Dru, Richard Norris, Michael Chekhov, Eric Blore, Art Baker, J. M. Kerrigan. Outmoded remake of 1920s Broadway comedy about a Jewish boy marrying an Irish girl. Filmed before in 1929. Produced by Bing Crosby. Look for Shelley Winters as a bridesmaid.

Abilene Town (1946) **89m. ***** D: Edwin L. Marin. Randolph Scott, Ann Dvorak, Edgar Buchanan, Rhonda Fleming, Lloyd Bridges. Above-average Scott vehicle as patient sheriff tries to straighten out homesteader conflict out West after the Civil War. Also shown in computer-colored version. **▼●**

Abominable Snowman, The (1957-British) **90m. **½** D: Val Guest. Forrest Tucker, Peter Cushing, Richard Wattis, Maureen Connell, Robert Brown. Intelligent tale of good man (Cushing) and corrupt man (Tucker) heading an expedition seeking the elusive title creature, with surprising results. Aka THE ABOMINABLE SNOWMAN OF THE HIMALAYAS. Original U.S. running time 85m. Widescreen Hammerscope. **▼O●**

About Face (1952) **C-94m. *½** D: Roy Del Ruth. Gordon MacRae, Eddie Bracken, Dick Wesson, Phyllis Kirk, Joel Grey. Dull comedy-musical remake of BROTHER RAT, about three friends in military academy, one of them secretly married. Grey's film debut.

About Mrs. Leslie (1954) **104m. ***** D: Daniel Mann. Shirley Booth, Robert Ryan, Marjie Millar, Alex Nicol, Sammy White, James Bell, Eilene Janssen, Henry (Harry) Morgan, Gale Page, Ellen Corby, Amanda Blake, Joan Shawlee, Benny Rubin, Jack Larson, Jerry Paris. Flashbacks reveal romance between chanteuse (Booth) and mysterious, lonely magnate (Ryan). Well-acted soaper; forgivable illogical coupling of stars.

Above and Beyond (1952) **122m. ***** D: Melvin Frank, Norman Panama. Robert Taylor, Eleanor Parker, James Whitmore, Larry Keating, Larry Gates, Marilyn Erskine, Jim Backus. Meaningful account of Paul Tibbets (Taylor), U.S. pilot who flew over Hiroshima with first atomic bomb; film focuses on his training and its effect on his personal life. Story also told in 1980 TVM ENOLA GAY. **▼●**

Above Suspicion (1943) **90m. ***** D: Richard Thorpe. Joan Crawford, Fred MacMurray, Conrad Veidt, Basil Rathbone, Reginald Owen, Richard Ainley. Crawford and MacMurray asked to do spy mission during European honeymoon on the eve of WW2. Pure escapism, with Joan more than a match for the Nazis. **▼●**

Above Us the Waves (1956-British) **92m. ***** D: Ralph Thomas. John Mills, John Gregson, Donald Sinden, James Robertson Justice. Utilizing documentary style, film relates account of unrelenting British attempt to destroy Nazi warship. Fine cast in exciting submarine drama. **▼●**

Abraham Lincoln (1930) **97m. **½** D: D. W. Griffith. Walter Huston, Una Merkel, Edgar Dearing, Russell Simpson, Cameron Prud'homme, Oscar Apfel, Henry B. Walthall. Huston is excellent in this sincere but static biography of Lincoln; can't match Griffith's silent masterpieces. **▼O●**

A Brivele der Mamen (1938-Polish) **100m. **** D: Joseph Green. Lucy Gehrman, Misha Gehrman, Max Bozyk, Edmund Zayenda, Alexander Stein. Overly sentimental Yiddish-language soaper that examines the effect of immigration on the family; the scenario focuses on a Polish-Jewish mother and son, and what happens when the latter heads off to America. The title's English translation is A LETTER TO MOTHER; also known as THE ETERNAL SONG. **▼●**

Abroad With Two Yanks (1944) **80m. **½** D: Allan Dwan. William Bendix, Helen Walker, Dennis O'Keefe, John Loder, John Abbott. Bendix and O'Keefe are Marines on the loose in Australia, both chasing Walker; breezy comedy. **▼**

Absent Minded Professor, The (1961) **97m. ***** D: Robert Stevenson. Fred MacMurray, Nancy Olson, Keenan Wynn, Tommy Kirk, Ed Wynn, Leon Ames, Elliott Reid. MacMurray discovers flubber (flying rubber) in this Disney audience-pleaser, but no one will believe him except Keenan Wynn, who tries to steal the substance. Broad comedy and bright special effects make this a lot of fun. Also shown in computer-colored version. Sequel: SON OF FLUBBER. Remade in 1995 (as a TVM) and in 1997 as FLUBBER. **▼O●**

Absolute Quiet (1936) **70m. ***** D: George B. Seitz. Lionel Atwill, Irene Hervey, Raymond Walburn, Stuart Erwin, Ann Loring, Louis Hayward, Wallace Ford, Bernadene

Hayes, Harvey Stephens, J. Carrol Naish. A great group of character actors portray a planeload of disparate types who make a forced landing on a ranch owned by ruthless financier Atwill, just as he is being held hostage by fugitives. Entertaining potboiler mixes melodrama and comedy quite nicely.

Accattone (1961-Italian) **120m.** ******* D: Pier Paolo Pasolini. Franco Citti, Franca Pasut, Roberto Scaringella, Adele Cambria, Paolo Guidi, Silvana Corsini. Pasolini's first film is a vivid, unsentimental look at the desperate (and depressing) existence of pimps and petty thieves living in the slums of Rome. Bernardo Bertolucci was one of the assistant directors. Released in the U.S. in 1968.▼●)

Accent on Youth (1935) **77m.** ****½** D: Wesley Ruggles. Sylvia Sidney, Herbert Marshall, Phillip Reed, Holmes Herbert, Catharine Doucet, Astrid Allwyn. Trim comedy from Samson Raphaelson's play about middle-aged playwright pursued by his young secretary. A bit talky by modern standards, but quite watchable. Remade as MR. MUSIC and BUT NOT FOR ME.

Accidents Will Happen (1939) **62m.** ****½** D: William Clemens. Ronald Reagan, Gloria Blondell, Sheila Bromley, Dick Purcell, Addison Richards. Good little "B" picture about a young go-getting insurance claims adjuster who tries to blow the whistle on a phony-accident racket.

Accomplices, The (1959-Italian) **93m.** ***½** D: Gianni Vernuccio. Sandro Luporini, Sandro Fizzotro, Annabella Incontrera, Jeannie. Lurid, minor film of love triangle, with resulting murder; unconvincing and pat.

Accused, The (1948) **101m.** ******* D: William Dieterle. Loretta Young, Robert Cummings, Wendell Corey, Sam Jaffe, Douglas Dick. Professor Young is sexually attacked by a student, accidentally kills him in self-defense, and then tries to cover it up. Taut thriller, with good support from Cummings.▼

Accused (1957) SEE: **Mark of the Hawk, The**

Accused of Murder (1956) **C-74m.** ****** D: Joseph Kane. David Brian, Vera Ralston, Sidney Blackmer, Virginia Grey, Warren Stevens, Lee Van Cleef, Claire Carleton, Wally Cassell, Elisha Cook, Jr. Interesting cast in bland murder mystery–melodrama of police detective Brian involved in underworld killing. Naturama.

Ace in the Hole (1951) **112m.** ******* D: Billy Wilder. Kirk Douglas, Jan Sterling, Bob Arthur, Porter Hall, Frank Cady, Richard Benedict, Ray Teal, Gene Evans. An embittered New Mexico reporter looking for the elusive brass ring finds it when he stumbles onto a story of a man trapped in an ancient Indian ruin. Unrelentingly cynical (yet mostly believable) tale of how the reporter exploits the "human interest story" for his own benefit—and how the potential tragedy turns into a three-

ring circus—has a peculiarly contemporary ring to it. Biting and extremely well acted. Originally titled THE BIG CARNIVAL. Inspired by the actual 1925 Floyd Collins case; the real reporter won a Pulitzer Prize.❱

Ace of Aces (1933) **76m.** ****** D: J. Walter Ruben. Richard Dix, Elizabeth Allan, Ralph Bellamy, Theodore Newton, Frank Conroy, William Cagney. Sculptor Dix has no use for flagwaving as America enters WW1; after being admonished by girlfriend Allan, he becomes a fighter pilot . . . and undergoes a personality change. Sincere antiwar tract, but far too melodramatic. Coscripted by John Monk Saunders.▼❱

Ace of Hearts, The (1921) **75m.** ******* D: Wallace Worsley. Lon Chaney, Leatrice Joy, John Bowers, Hardee Kirkland, Raymond Hatton, Edwin Wallock. An anarchist suffers professional and personal crises when he discovers his bomb will slay innocent bystanders dining next to his target . . . who just happens to be "the other man" in a current love affair. Good mid-career Chaney vehicle, a relic of the early Red Scare era, relies more on characterization than on makeup effects.❱

Across the Bridge (1957-British) **103m.** ******* D: Ken Annakin. Rod Steiger, David Knight, Marla Landi, Noel Willman, Bernard Lee, Bill Nagy, Eric Pohlmann. Smug German business magnate flees his home base in England when Scotland Yard investigates his corrupt dealings. His only hope is to get to Mexico through the U.S., but en route he switches identities with a fellow train passenger. Engrossing yarn based on a Graham Greene novella. Shot mostly in Spain. Later remade as DOUBLE TAKE.▼❱

Across the Pacific (1942) **97m.** ****½** D: John Huston. Humphrey Bogart, Mary Astor, Sydney Greenstreet, Victor Sen Yung, Keye Luke, Richard Loo. Three MALTESE FALCON leads reteamed for enjoyable WW2 adventure. Bogart trails spies to Panama, has running battle of wits with Greenstreet, while romancing enticing Astor. Despite title, the movie never gets to the Pacific, much less across it. Also shown in computer-colored version.▼●)

Across the Wide Missouri (1951) **C-78m.** ****½** D: William Wellman. Clark Gable, Ricardo Montalban, John Hodiak, Adolphe Menjou, Maria Elena Marques, J. Carrol Naish, Jack Holt, Alan Napier, George Chandler, Richard Anderson. Rocky Mountain location filming helps pedestrian frontier adventure as beaver trapper Gable and other mountain men contend with Indians. Awful comedy relief during the title trip (an all-male square dance, a slapstick free-for-all, Indian Naish in a suit of armor, etc.) makes the Missouri feel intolerably wide.▼❱

Across to Singapore (1928) **85m.** ****½** D: William Nigh. Ramon Novarro, Joan Crawford, Ernest Torrence, Dan Wolheim, Duke

Martin, Edward Connelly, James Mason. Boisterous seaman Torrence falls for pert Crawford and, without her knowledge, asks her father for permission to marry her . . . but she's really in love with his boyish kid brother (Novarro). Passions collide in this unremarkable though entertaining seafaring yarn, also filmed in 1923 and 1953 as ALL THE BROTHERS WERE VALIANT (the name of the Ben Ames Williams novel on which this is based). Anna May Wong appears prominently, but is unbilled. ▶

Action for Slander (1938-British) **83m.** ****½** D: Tim Whelan. Clive Brook, Ann Todd, Margaretta Scott, Arthur Margetson, Ronald Squire, Athole Stewart, Percy Marmont, Francis L. Sullivan, Felix Aylmer, Googie Withers. Adequate drama about suave, stiff-upper-lip cavalry officer Brook, who feels his life is ruined when he's falsely accused of cheating at cards. Sparked by Sullivan's forceful presence as Brook's lawyer. ▼

Action in Arabia (1944) **72m.** ****½** D: Leonide Moguy. George Sanders, Virginia Bruce, Gene Lockhart, Robert Armstrong, Lenore Aubert, H. B. Warner, Alan Napier, Marcel Dalio, Michael Ansara. OK drama in which troubleshooting reporter Sanders tangles with assorted characters in Damascus, where Nazis and Allies are jockeying for Arab support on the eve of WW2. Desert footage was shot by Merian C. Cooper and Ernest B. Schoedsack for an unmade film. ▼▶

Action in the North Atlantic (1943) **127m.** ******* D: Lloyd Bacon. Humphrey Bogart, Raymond Massey, Alan Hale, Julie Bishop, Ruth Gordon, Sam Levene, Dane Clark. Rousing tribute to WW2 Merchant Marine, with officers Bogart and Massey, seamen Hale and Levene, usual hothead Clark, and Gordon as Massey's wife. Also shown in computer-colored version. ▼▶

Action of the Tiger (1957-British) **C-94m.** ****½** D: Terence Young. Van Johnson, Martine Carol, Herbert Lom, Anna Gerber, Sean Connery. Action-packed, clichéd adventure story with Johnson the virile American rescuing pro-Western refugees from Albania. CinemaScope.

Act of Love (1953) **108m.** ****½** D: Anatole Litvak. Kirk Douglas, Dany Robin, Barbara Laage, Robert Strauss, Gabrielle Dorziat, Serge Reggiani, Brigitte Bardot. Entertaining if unremarkable chronicle of the romance between lonely American soldier Douglas and down-and-out French girl Robin in Paris. Scripted by Irwin Shaw, based on Alfred Hayes' novel *The Girl on the Via Flaminia.*

Act of Murder, An (1948) **91m.** ******* D: Michael Gordon. Fredric March, Florence Eldridge, Edmond O'Brien, Geraldine Brooks. March is excellent as strict jurist who must judge himself for saving his wife the anguish of illness by killing her; absorbing drama.

Act of Violence (1949) **92m.** ******* D: Fred Zinnemann. Van Heflin, Robert Ryan, Janet Leigh, Mary Astor, Phyllis Thaxter, Berry Kroeger, Taylor Holmes. Stark, well-acted drama, with crippled, embittered Ryan stalking former senior officer Heflin, who betrayed his men while a POW. Fine vignette by Astor as a sympathetic call girl. ▶

Act One (1963) **110m.** ****½** D: Dore Schary. George Hamilton, Jason Robards, George Segal, Eli Wallach, Sam Levene, Ruth Ford, Jack Klugman. Interesting for oddball cast, this fabrication of writer Moss Hart's autobiography lacks finesse or any sense of reality, but Robards is ideally cast as George S. Kaufman.

Actors and Sin (1952) **82m.** ****½** D: Ben Hecht, Lee Garmes. Edward G. Robinson, Eddie Albert, Marsha Hunt, Alan Reed, Dan O'Herlihy, Tracey Roberts, Rudolph Anders, Paul Guilfoyle, Jenny Hecht, John Crawford. Uneven two-part film: the overly melodramatic "Actor's Blood" concerns has-been thespian Robinson and his hard-hearted (and murdered) Broadway star daughter Hunt; the more successful "Woman of Sin" details the plight of agent Albert, whose newest client is a 9-year-old (Hecht, Ben's daughter), who's penned a lascivious book. ▼

Actor's Revenge, An (1963-Japanese) **C-114m.** ****½** D: Kon Ichikawa. Kazuo Hasegawa, Ayako Wakao, Fujiko Yamamoto, Ganjiro Nakamura, Raizo Ichikawa. Confusing tale of Kabuki actor Hasegawa getting back at a lord (Nakamura) responsible for the demise of his parents. Unevenly directed. Aka THE REVENGE OF UKENO-JO. Daieiscope. ▶

Actress, The (1953) **91m.** ******* D: George Cukor. Spencer Tracy, Jean Simmons, Teresa Wright, Anthony Perkins, Mary Wickes. Flavorful account based on Ruth Gordon's experiences as a teenager in early 20th-century Massachusetts, determined to become an acting star; Tracy is the irascible father. Jackie Coogan appears in unbilled bit. Perkins' film debut. ▶

Ada (1961) **C-109m.** ******* D: Daniel Mann. Susan Hayward, Dean Martin, Wilfrid Hyde-White, Ralph Meeker, Martin Balsam. Histrionic rags-to-riches soap opera with prostitute Hayward maneuvering easygoing Martin into the governor's mansion, using her iron will to overcome political corruption (in the person of Hyde-White). CinemaScope. ▼

Adam and Evalyn (1949-British) **92m.** ****½** D: Harold French. Jean Simmons, Stewart Granger, Wilfrid Hyde-White, Helen Cherry, Raymond Young. Pleasant but ordinary tale of gambler Granger and the daughter he adopts when a friend dies. British title: ADAM AND EVELYNE. ▼

Adam Had Four Sons (1941) **81m.** ****½** D: Gregory Ratoff. Ingrid Bergman, Warner Baxter, Susan Hayward, Fay Wray, Richard Denning, Johnny Downs, June Lockhart. Handsome but predictable family saga about French governess Bergman watching over Baxter's household after his wife's death. Bergman gives warm performance, and Hayward plays bad girl to the hilt.▼▶

Adam's Rib (1949) **100m. ★★★★** D: George Cukor. Spencer Tracy, Katharine Hepburn, Judy Holliday, Tom Ewell, David Wayne, Jean Hagen, Hope Emerson, Polly Moran, Marvin Kaplan, Paula Raymond, Tommy Noonan. Smart, sophisticated comedy (by Ruth Gordon and Garson Kanin) about husband and wife lawyers on opposing sides of the same attempted-murder case. One of Hollywood's greatest comedies about the battle of the sexes, with peerless Tracy and Hepburn supported by movie newcomers Holliday, Ewell, Hagen, and Wayne. Cole Porter contributed the song "Farewell, Amanda." Remade in Bulgaria in 1956 (in this version the heroine rebels against tradition as a result of her conversion to Marxism-Leninism!). Later a TV series. Also shown in computer-colored version. ▼◉▶

Address Unknown (1944) **72m. ★★** D: William Cameron Menzies. Paul Lukas, Mady Christians, Morris Carnovsky, Carl Esmond, K.T. Stevens, Peter Van Eyck. Longtime American resident Lukas returns to his native Germany, and is all too easily swept up by Naziism. Offbeat visual style of director Menzies doesn't alleviate hollowness of this heavy-handed parable.▶

Admirable Crichton, The (1957-British) **C-94m. ★★** D: Lewis Gilbert. Kenneth More, Diane Cilento, Cecil Parker, Sally Ann Howes, Martita Hunt. Oft-filmed James Barrie classic wears thin: impeccable servant proves to be most resourceful when he and his aristocratic employers are shipwrecked on an island. Retitled PARADISE LAGOON; previously made in 1918 and 1919 (as MALE AND FEMALE). VistaVision.▼▶

Admiral Was a Lady, The (1950) **87m. ★★** D: Albert Rogell. Edmond O'Brien, Wanda Hendrix, Rudy Vallee, Steve Brodie. Ex-WAVE Hendrix encounters quartet of fun-loving, work-hating men, all interested in courting her; weak.▼▶

Adorable Julia (1962-French-Austrian) **94m. ★★★** D: Alfred Weidenmann. Lilli Palmer, Charles Boyer, Jean Sorel, Thomas Fritsch. Charming rendering of Somerset Maugham's novel *Theatre* and the play of the same title he penned with Guy Bolton. Palmer is an aging stage star who becomes the mistress of young Sorel (despite being wed to director-producer Boyer). Bolton also cowrote the script. Remade as BEING JULIA (2004).▼

À Double Tour SEE: **Web of Passion**

Advance to the Rear (1964) **97m. ★★½** D: George Marshall. Glenn Ford, Stella Stevens, Melvyn Douglas, Joan Blondell, Jim Backus, Andrew Prine. During Civil War, Northern soldier rejects are sent to Western territory. Stevens as Reb spy and Blondell as saucy worldly woman add only spice to predictable slapstick comedy. Panavision.

Adventure (1945) **125m. ★★** D: Victor Fleming. Clark Gable, Greer Garson, Joan Blondell, Thomas Mitchell, Tom Tully, John Qualen, Richard Haydn. Footloose, philosophical seaman Gable is drawn to librarian Garson, who might just get him to settle down. Overlong romantic drama has its moments but never quite jells. A famous flop in its day, it marked Gable's return after WW2 service with the ad line "Gable's back and Garson's got him!"▼▶

Adventure, The SEE: **L'Avventura**

Adventure for Two SEE: **Demi-Paradise, The**

Adventure in Baltimore (1949) **89m. ★★** D: Richard Wallace. Shirley Temple, John Agar, Robert Young, Josephine Hutchinson. Mild (and, some might say, reactionary) comedy, set in the horse-and-buggy era. Temple plays a spunky miss whose independent spirit and feminist leanings are depicted as youthful folly. Young, auditioning for *Father Knows Best*, plays Shirley's understanding pastor-father. Temple and Agar were then married.▶

Adventure in Diamonds (1940) **76m. ★★** D: George Fitzmaurice. George Brent, Isa Miranda, John Loder, Nigel Bruce. Tepid formula programmer dealing with jewel robberies in Africa.

Adventure in Iraq (1943) **64m. ★½** D: D. Ross Lederman. John Loder, Ruth Ford, Warren Douglas, Paul Cavanagh, Barry Bernard, Peggy Carson. Yank pilot and two British passengers crash-land in the desert and are taken hostage by a sheik (Cavanagh) who wants to exchange them for brothers being held by the British as Nazi spies. Subpar rehash of 1930's THE GREEN GODDESS. Cavanagh is good but no match for George Arliss in the original.▼▶

Adventure in Manhattan (1936) **73m. ★★½** D: Edward Ludwig. Jean Arthur, Joel McCrea, Reginald Owen, Thomas Mitchell, Herman Bing. Bizarre blend of comedy and melodrama with the stars foiling planned bank robbery. Doesn't always work, but interesting.▶

Adventure in Sahara (1938) **60m. ★★½** D: D. Ross Lederman. Paul Kelly, C. Henry Gordon, Lorna Gray (Adrian Booth), Robert Fiske, Marc Lawrence, Dick Curtis, Stanley Brown, Alan (Al) Bridge, Charles Moore. Kelly joins the French Foreign Legion to avenge his brother's death at the hands of a sadistic commandant (Gordon). Standard-issue stuff, but extremely well crafted, with an expert cast. Story by Sam Fuller.▶

Adventure in Washington (1941) **84m. ★★** D: Alfred E. Green. Herbert Marshall, Virginia Bruce, Gene Reynolds, Samuel S. Hinds, Ralph Morgan, Charles Smith,

Dickie Jones, Tommy Bond. Misleading title for tame account of Senator Marshall and his attempt to reform a delinquent youth who is working as a Senate page boy.

Adventurers, The (1951-British) **86m.** ** D: David MacDonald. Jack Hawkins, Peter Hammond, Dennis Price, Grégoire Aslan, Charles Paton, Siobhan McKenna, Bernard Lee, Ronald Adam. In 1902, in the waning days of the Boer War, a British soldier hides some valuable diamonds he finds on a man's body in South Africa. When he returns to claim them he's forced to take on confederates. Poor man's TREASURE OF THE SIERRA MADRE. Aka THE GREAT ADVENTURE and FORTUNE IN DIAMONDS. ▶

Adventures at Rugby SEE: **Tom Brown's School Days** (1940)

Adventures in Silverado (1948) **75m.** *** D: Phil Karlson. William Bishop, Gloria Henry, Forrest Tucker, Edgar Buchanan, Edgar Barrier, Irving Bacon. Author Robert Louis Stevenson takes a trip to Napa Valley, California, in 1880 and gets involved in the exploits of a stagecoach driver who captures a hooded highwayman called The Monk. Supposedly inspired by a true incident, this offbeat Western based on Stevenson's *The Silverado Squatters* is a dandy, high-spirited adventure yarn. ▶

Adventures of Captain Fabian (1951) **100m.** *½ D: William Marshall. Errol Flynn, Micheline Presle, Agnes Moorehead, Vincent Price. Soggy sea yarn has Flynn involved with accused murderess. Set in 1840 New Orleans but filmed in France; screenplay by Flynn. ▼▶

Adventures of Casanova (1948) **83m.** ** D: Roberto Gavaldon. Arturo de Cordova, Lucille Bremer, Turhan Bey, John Sutton. Very ordinary swashbuckler of Casanova de Córdova leading the oppressed people of Sicily against tyrannical rule; this one cries for color. Filmed entirely in Mexico.

Adventures of Curley and His Gang, The SEE: **Curley**

Adventures of Don Juan (1948) **C-110m.** *** D: Vincent Sherman. Errol Flynn, Viveca Lindfors, Robert Douglas, Alan Hale, Ann Rutherford, Raymond Burr. Handsome tongue-in-cheek swashbuckler has Errol stringing along countless maidens and even enticing the Queen (Lindfors); Oscar winner for Best Costumes. The lady at the end is Flynn's second wife, Nora Eddington. ▼●▶

Adventures of Gallant Bess (1948) **C-73m.** ** D: Lew Landers. Cameron Mitchell, Audrey Long, Fuzzy Knight, James Millican. Mitchell is torn between his girl and his horse in this colorful but routine equestrian drama. ▼▶

Adventures of Hajji Baba, The (1954) **C-94m.** **½ D: Don Weis. John Derek, Elaine Stewart, Thomas Gomez, Amanda Blake,

Paul Picerni. Derek adds spark to OK desert tale of his romancing sheik's daughter, who's out to marry heir of rival kingdom. CinemaScope.

Adventures of Huckleberry Finn, The (1939) **90m.** *** D: Richard Thorpe. Mickey Rooney, Walter Connelly, William Frawley, Rex Ingram, Lynne Carver. Subdued Rooney fine, Ingram excellent as Huck and Jim in classic Mark Twain tale of early 19th-century America; Connelly and Frawley are amusing as riverboat con artists. Also shown in computer-colored version. Aka HUCKLEBERRY FINN. ▼▶

Adventures of Huckleberry Finn, The (1960) **C-107m.** *** D: Michael Curtiz. Tony Randall, Eddie Hodges, Archie Moore, Patty McCormack, Neville Brand. Good version of Twain's story with an appealing Hodges (Huck) and excellent Archie Moore (Jim). Assorted characters played by veterans Buster Keaton, Andy Devine, Judy Canova, John Carradine, Mickey Shaughnessy, and Sterling Holloway. CinemaScope. ▼▶

Adventures of Ichabod and Mr. Toad, The (1949) **C-68m.** *** D: Jack Kinney, Clyde Geronimi, James Algar. Voices of Eric Blore, Pat O'Malley, John Ployardt, Colin Campbell, Claude Allister, The Rhythmaires. Very entertaining animated doubleheader from Disney: a witty adaptation of Kenneth Grahame's *The Wind in the Willows*, about Mr. Toad and his friends, centering on Toad's infatuation with motorcars, narrated by Basil Rathbone; and a broad, cartoony version of Washington Irving's "The Legend of Sleepy Hollow," with a genuinely scary climax, narrated (and sung) by Bing Crosby. ▼●▶

Adventures of Jack London, The SEE: **Jack London**

Adventures of Marco Polo, The (1938) **100m.** **½ D: Archie Mayo. Gary Cooper, Sigrid Gurie, Basil Rathbone, George Barbier, Binnie Barnes, Ernest Truex, Alan Hale. Lighthearted approach to famed explorer's life doesn't always work, but Cooper is pleasant and Rathbone's a good villain; sumptuous production. Look for Lana Turner as one of the handmaidens. ▼▶

Adventures of Mark Twain, The (1944) **130m.** *** D: Irving Rapper. Fredric March, Alexis Smith, Donald Crisp, Alan Hale, C. Aubrey Smith, John Carradine, Percy Kilbride. This Hollywoodized story of Samuel Clemens' colorful life may not be great biography, but it's consistently entertaining—despite some biopic clichés. March is fine in title role. Filmed in 1942. ▼▶

Adventures of Martin Eden, The (1942) **87m.** *** D: Sidney Salkow. Glenn Ford, Claire Trevor, Evelyn Keyes, Stuart Erwin, Dickie Moore. Sturdy Jack London tale of seaman aboard terror of a ship, writing account of sailing, fighting for literary recognition.

[6]

Adventures of Prince Achmed, The (1926-German) **66m.** ***½ D: Lotte Reiniger. Captivating "silhouette film" (often cited as the first animated feature) based on various *Arabian Nights* tales involving the title prince and his experiences during a journey on a flying horse. A treat for children and adults alike, with the plot taking a backseat to the nonstop flow of eye-popping images. The video/DVD is a reconstruction derived from an existing tinted and toned nitrate print. ▼❶

Adventures of Rin Tin Tin, The SEE: **Return of Rin Tin Tin, The**

Adventures of Robin Hood, The (1938) **C-102m.** **** D: Michael Curtiz, William Keighley. Errol Flynn, Olivia de Havilland, Basil Rathbone, Claude Rains, Patric Knowles, Eugene Pallette, Alan Hale, Herbert Mundin, Una O'Connor, Melville Cooper, Ian Hunter, Montagu Love. Dashing Flynn in the definitive swashbuckler, winning hand of de Havilland (never lovelier as Maid Marian), foiling evil prince Rains, dueling wicked Rathbone. Erich Wolfgang Korngold's outstanding score earned an Oscar, as did the art direction and editing. Scripted by Norman Reilly Raine and Seton I. Miller. Arguably Flynn's greatest role. ▼❶❸

Adventures of Robinson Crusoe (1952-Mexican) **C-90m.** ***½ D: Luis Buñuel. Daniel (Dan) O'Herlihy, Jaime Fernandez. Colorful, entertaining adaptation of Daniel Defoe's classic story about a resourceful shipwreck victim, with some distinctive Buñuel touches; vivid performance by O'Herlihy. Screenplay by Philip Ansell Roll (Hugo Butler) and Buñuel. Excellent music score by Anthony Collins. Main title on film is ROBINSON CRUSOE. ▼❶

Adventures of Sadie, The (1954-British) **C-88m.** **½ D: Noel Langley. Joan Collins, George Cole, Kenneth More, Robertson Hare, Hermione Gingold, Walter Fitzgerald, Hattie Jacques. Obvious sex satire relying on premise of Collins stuck on desert isle with love-hungry men. From an Ernest K. Gann novel. Original British title: OUR GIRL FRIDAY. ▼❶

Adventures of Sherlock Holmes, The (1939) **85m.** ***½ D: Alfred Werker. Basil Rathbone, Nigel Bruce, Ida Lupino, Alan Marshal, Terry Kilburn, George Zucco, E. E. Clive, Mary Gordon. The master sleuth faces one of his greatest challenges when the nefarious Professor Moriarty (Zucco) plots to steal the Crown Jewels. The second and last of Fox's excellent Rathbone-Bruce period pieces, which predated Universal's entertaining modern series. ▼❶❸

Adventures of Tartu, The (1943-British) **103m.** *** D: Harold S. Bucquet. Robert Donat, Valerie Hobson, Walter Rilla, Phyllis Morris, Glynis Johns. Well-turned spy drama with intrepid British soldier Donat dispatched incognito into Nazi-occupied Czechoslovakia to blow up a German poison gas plant. Donat's lively performance makes this one worth watching. Retitled: TARTU. Also shown in alternate British release version, SABOTAGE AGENT. ▼❶

Adventures of Three Reporters, The SEE: **Miss Mend**

Adventures of Tom Sawyer, The (1938) **C-77m.** ***½ D: Norman Taurog. Tommy Kelly, Jackie Moran, Ann Gillis, May Robson, Walter Brennan, Victor Jory, Spring Byington, Margaret Hamilton. Entertaining David O. Selznick production of Mark Twain classic with more slapstick than Twain may have had in mind. Cave sequence with Injun Joe is unforgettable. Original running time 93m. Previously filmed in 1930, and again in 1973 (twice that year)—all under the title TOM SAWYER. Refilmed in 1995 as TOM AND HUCK. ▼❶

Adventuress, The (1946-British) **98m.** *** D: Frank Launder. Deborah Kerr, Trevor Howard, Raymond Huntley, Liam Redmond, Harry Webster. A feisty Irish lass is persuaded to help a German agent during WW2—because it will hurt her sworn enemies, the British. Well-made, low-key film with touches of droll humor. British prints were originally 114m., which explains some abruptness in exposition. British title: I SEE A DARK STRANGER. ▼❶

Adventurous Blonde (1937) **60m.** **½ D: Frank McDonald. Glenda Farrell, Barton MacLane, Anne Nagel, Tom Kennedy, George E. Stone, Natalie Moorhead, William Hopper. One of the better *Torchy Blane* entries, with sardonic crime reporter Farrell interrupting her wedding to cantankerous cop MacLane in order to probe the murder of a publicity-seeking actor. ❶

Advice to the Lovelorn (1933) **62m.** **½ D: Alfred Werker. Lee Tracy, Sally Blane, Sterling Holloway, Jean Adair, Paul Harvey. Engaging comedy-drama capitalizing on Tracy's success in BLESSED EVENT; here he parlays a lonelyhearts column into business enterprise, with unexpected results. Loosely based on Nathanael West's *Miss Lonelyhearts*. Holloway excellent in key supporting role. Filmed again as LONELYHEARTS.

Advise & Consent (1962) **139m.** *** D: Otto Preminger. Henry Fonda, Don Murray, Charles Laughton, Walter Pidgeon, Peter Lawford, Gene Tierney, Franchot Tone, Lew Ayres, Burgess Meredith, Paul Ford, George Grizzard, Betty White. Long but engrossing drama of Washington wheeling and dealing, from Allen Drury novel. Cast is fine, with effective underplaying by Ayres and Tone standing out among more flamboyant performances by Laughton (his last film) and Grizzard. Also shown in computer-colored version. Panavision. ▼❶❸

Aelita (1924-Russian) **112m.** **½ D: Yakov Protazanov. U. I. Solnetseva, N. M. Tsereteli, Valentina Kuinzhi, N. P. Batalov, V. G. Orlova. Moscow engineer who suspects his wife of infidelity fantasizes about the title character, the Queen of Mars, who watches him through a telescope. His dream is to construct a spaceship that will take him to the Red Planet, which is about to be embroiled in a workers' uprising. Ambitious combination of sci-fi epic and socialist treatise is occasionally confusing but has eye-popping constructivist sets and costumes. Based on a novel by Alexei Tolstoy, a relative of Leo's. Aka AELITA: QUEEN OF MARS. ▼▶

Aerial Gunner (1943) 78m. ** D: William H. Pine. Richard Arlen, Chester Morris, Lita (Amelita) Ward, Jimmy Lydon, Keith Richards, Dick Purcell. Formula WW2 action propaganda, pitting old rivals Arlen and Morris during basic training and competing for Ward's love. Partially salvaged by some energetic combat scenes. Look quick for Robert Mitchum. ▼▶

Affair in Havana (1957) 77m. *½ D: Laslo Benedek. John Cassavetes, Raymond Burr, Sara Shane, Lila Lazo. Unexciting tale of songwriter in love with crippled man's wife. Filmed in Cuba.

Affair in Monte Carlo (1953-British) C-75m. ** D: Victor Saville. Merle Oberon, Richard Todd, Leo Genn, Peter Illing. Rich widow tries to convince gambler that romance is more rewarding than roulette. Monte Carlo backgrounds don't help. Original British title: 24 HOURS OF A WOMAN'S LIFE. ▶

Affair in Reno (1957) 75m. *½ D: R. G. Springsteen. John Lund, John Archer, Doris Singleton, Alan Hale. Inoffensive little film about detective Singleton falling in love with PR-man Lund. Naturama.

Affair in Trinidad (1952) 98m. **½ D: Vincent Sherman. Rita Hayworth, Glenn Ford, Alexander Scourby, Torin Thatcher, Juanita Moore, Steven Geray. Hayworth and Ford sparkle as cafe singer and brother-in-law seeking her husband's murderer. Hayworth is most enticing. ▼▶

Affairs in Versailles SEE: **Royal Affairs in Versailles**

Affairs of Anatol, The (1921) 117m. *** D: Cecil B. DeMille. Wallace Reid, Gloria Swanson, Bebe Daniels, Wanda Hawley, Theodore Roberts, Elliott Dexter, Theodore Kosloff, Agnes Ayres, Monte Blue. Battle of the sexes is waged in this amusing tale of Anatol De Witt Spencer (Reid), a modern-day knight who naively tries to rescue several ladies-in-distress, much to the consternation of his new wife (Swanson). Daniels is not to be missed as the notorious Satan Synne! William Boyd, Julia Faye, Raymond Hatton, Lucien Littlefield, and Polly Moran have small parts; Elinor Glyn, of "It" girl fame, is one of the bridge players. Scenario by Jeanie Macpherson, suggested by an Arthur Schnitzler novel and play. ▼▶

Affairs of Annabel, The (1938) 68m. **½ D: Ben Stoloff. Jack Oakie, Lucille Ball, Ruth Donnelly, Bradley Page, Fritz Feld, Thurston Hall. Fair film industry satire, with Ball scoring as an actress and Oakie her scheming press agent whose publicity gimmicks always backfire. Followed by ANNABEL TAKES A TOUR. ▼●

Affairs of Cellini, The (1934) 80m. *** D: Gregory La Cava. Constance Bennett, Fredric March, Frank Morgan, Fay Wray, Jessie Ralph. March is excellent as roguish Renaissance artist who falls in love with duchess. Lavish production, fine cast make this most entertaining. Lucille Ball plays a lady in waiting. ▶

Affairs of Dobie Gillis, The (1953) 74m. *** D: Don Weis. Debbie Reynolds, Bobby Van, Hans Conried, Lurene Tuttle, Bob Fosse. Entertaining musicomedy based on Max Shulman's book of college kids. Debbie and Van make a cute couple; Conried is their dour professor. Later a TV series. ▼▶

Affairs of Jimmy Valentine, The (1942) 72m. *** D: Bernard Vorhaus. Dennis O'Keefe, Ruth Terry, Gloria Dickson, Roman Bohnen, George E. Stone, Spencer Charters, Roscoe Ates. A small town is turned upside down when a radio program offers $10,000 to find an infamous safecracker who is hiding there under a new identity. Absorbing little mystery with some snappy dialogue, surprising twists, and noir-ish visuals by cinematographer John Alton.

Affairs of Martha, The (1942) 66m. **½ D: Jules Dassin. Marsha Hunt, Richard Carlson, Marjorie Main, Virginia Weidler, Spring Byington, Allyn Joslyn, Frances Drake, Barry Nelson, Melville Cooper, Sara Haden, Margaret Hamilton. Scandal comes to a quiet, exclusive Long Island town when a maid pens a "kitchen's eye" view of the people she works for. Cute farce holds up for most of the way, with a host of character actors in top form.

Affairs of Susan, The (1945) 110m. **½ D: William A. Seiter. Joan Fontaine, George Brent, Dennis O'Keefe, Don DeFore, Rita Johnson, Walter Abel. Fairly entertaining comedy of actress Fontaine who does more acting for her beaus than she does onstage.

Affair to Remember, An (1957) C-115m. **½ D: Leo McCarey. Cary Grant, Deborah Kerr, Richard Denning, Neva Patterson, Cathleen Nesbitt, Robert Q. Lewis, Charles Watts, Fortunio Bonanova. Middling remake of McCarey's LOVE AFFAIR. Bubbling shipboard comedy in first half, overshadowed by draggy soap-opera clichés and unnecessary musical numbers in N.Y.C. finale. Vic Damone croons title tune on soundtrack. Film was to turn up decades later as a major plot device in 1993 hit SLEEPLESS IN SEATTLE. Remade again as LOVE AFFAIR in 1994. CinemaScope. ▼◐●

Affair With a Stranger (1953) **89m. ★★** D: Roy Rowland. Jean Simmons, Victor Mature, Mary Jo Tarola, Monica Lewis, Jane Darwell, Dabbs Greer, Olive Carey. Bland romantic drama, mostly told in flashback, chronicling relationship between struggling playwright Mature (who is sorely miscast) and model Simmons.

Affectionately Yours (1941) **90m. ★★** D: Lloyd Bacon. Merle Oberon, Dennis Morgan, Rita Hayworth, Ralph Bellamy, George Tobias. Attractive triangle flounders in weak comedy of Morgan trying to win back wife Oberon, with interference from Hayworth. Bellamy is the poor sap again.

Afraid to Talk (1932) **69m. ★★★** D: Edward L. Cahn. Eric Linden, Sidney Fox, Tully Marshall, Louis Calhern, George Meeker, Robert Warwick, Berton Churchill, Edward Arnold, Mayo Methot, Matt McHugh, Gustav von Seyffertitz. Eye-opening pre-Code melodrama about a hotel bellboy who inadvertently witnesses a murder, then finds himself a pawn of a massively corrupt city government. Sparks fly in this unsubtle shocker, adapted from a play cowritten by Albert Maltz. Photographed by the great Karl Freund.

African Lion, The (1955) **C-75m. ★★★½** D: James Algar. Narrated by Winston Hibler. Outstanding True-Life documentary is perhaps Disney's best. Naturalists Alfred and Elma Milotte filmed the African lion in his native habitat through a year's cycle of seasons. Filled with drama, excitement, color, humor. A gem. ◐

African Queen, The (1951) **C-105m. ★★★★** D: John Huston. Katharine Hepburn, Humphrey Bogart, Robert Morley, Peter Bull, Theodore Bikel, Walter Gotell. Superb combination of souse Bogart (who won an Oscar) and spinster Hepburn traveling downriver on his broken-down boat *The African Queen* in Africa during WW1, combating the elements and the Germans, and each other. Script by James Agee and director Huston from C. S. Forester's novel; gorgeously filmed on location in the Belgian Congo by Jack Cardiff. ▼◐●

African Treasure (1952) **70m. ★½** D: Ford Beebe. Johnny Sheffield, Laurette Luez, Lyle Talbot, Arthur Space, Martin Garralaga, Robert "Smoki" Whitfield, Leonard Mudie. Bomba the Jungle Boy vs. diamond smugglers posing as geologists. Formulaic jungle intrigue. Look for Woody Strode as a native mailman. ◐

Africa Screams (1949) **79m. ★★★** D: Charles Barton. Bud Abbott, Lou Costello, Hillary Brooke, Max Baer, Clyde Beatty, Frank Buck, Shemp Howard, Joe Besser, Buddy Baer. A&C go on safari in this funny outing full of wheezy but often hilarious gags and routines. Also shown in computer-colored version. ▼◐●

After Midnight With Boston Blackie (1943) **64m. ★★½** D: Lew Landers. Chester Morris, Ann Savage, George E. Stone, Richard Lane, Cy Kendall, George McKay, Walter Sande, Lloyd Corrigan. Blackie helps a jailbird's daughter retrieve some hidden diamonds and winds up being accused of the old man's murder. Minor but quite enjoyable entry.

After Office Hours (1935) **75m. ★★** D: Robert Z. Leonard. Constance Bennett, Clark Gable, Stuart Erwin, Billie Burke, Harvey Stephens, Henry Travers, William Demarest, Katherine Alexander. Editor Gable tries to manipulate society girl Bennett while investigating shady Stephens. Gable's charm cannot overcome forgettable script (written by Herman J. Mankiewicz). ◐

After the Dance (1935) **60m. ★★** D: Leo Bulgakov. Nancy Carroll, George Murphy, Thelma Todd, Jack La Rue, Arthur Hohl, Wyrley Birch, Thurston Hall, Victor Kilian. Hoofer Murphy is railroaded for manslaughter; he busts out of jail and forms a song-and-dance act with Carroll, until vampish ex-partner Todd blackmails him. Carroll is wasted in this clumsy hybrid of prison yarn and musical.

After the Thin Man (1936) **113m. ★★★½** D: W. S. Van Dyke II. William Powell, Myrna Loy, James Stewart, Elissa Landi, Joseph Calleia, Jessie Ralph, Alan Marshal, Penny Singleton, William Law, Sam Levene, George Zucco. Delightful second entry in the series finds the urbane Charleses in San Francisco and, when not inordinately inebriated, investigating murder charges brought against Loy's unstable cousin (Landi). Slightly overlong but first rate, with a truly surprising culprit. Also shown in computer-colored version. ▼◐●

After Tomorrow (1932) **81m. ★★** D: Frank Borzage. Charles Farrell, Marian Nixon, Minna Gombell, William Collier, Sr., Josephine Hull, William Pawley, Greta Granstedt. Depression-era yarn based (all too obviously) on a stage play about two young people in love who want to get married but face one obstacle after another. Hull is uncomfortably effective as Farrell's suffocating, selfish mother. ◐

After Tonight (1933) **72m. ★★** D: George Archainbaud. Constance Bennett, Gilbert Roland, Edward Ellis, Sam Godfrey, Lucien Prival, Mischa Auer. Russian spy Bennett falls for Austrian captain Roland in this derivative but handsomely mounted WW1 romance in the wake of MATA HARI and DISHONORED. Bennett even sings and does a fan dance! She and Roland later married in real life.

Against All Flags (1952) **C-83m. ★★½** D: George Sherman. Errol Flynn, Maureen O'Hara, Anthony Quinn, Mildred Natwick. Flynn found his forte again as dashing 18th-century naval officer who maneuvers way into pirate fortress, while managing to flirt with O'Hara. Although not Flynn's final swashbuckler, this was his last *good* entry in that genre. Remade as THE KING'S PIRATE.▼●◗

Against the Wind (1948-British) **96m.** *** D: Charles Crichton. Robert Beatty, Simone Signoret, Jack Warner, Gordon Jackson, Paul Dupuis, James Robertson Justice. Taut, engrossing tale of British spies trained for mission inside occupied Belgium during WW2. Documentary-style training scenes complement the dramatic story of resistance fighters.▼

Agent 8¾ (1964-British) **C-98m.** *** D: Ralph Thomas. Dirk Bogarde, Sylva Koscina, Leo McKern, Robert Morley, Roger Delgado, John LeMesurier. Released at height of James Bond craze, this spoof features Bogarde as a bumbling secret agent working in Czechoslovakia. Sometimes witty, bright comedy. Originally released in U.S. at 77m. Original British title: HOT ENOUGH FOR JUNE. ◗

Age of Consent, The (1932) **63m.** *** D: Gregory La Cava. Dorothy Wilson, Arline Judge, Richard Cromwell, Eric Linden, John Halliday, Aileen Pringle, Grady Sutton. Realistic—and still relevant—exploration of flirtations and misunderstandings between the sexes on a college campus, including the hot-and-cold romance between students Wilson and Cromwell. See if you can spot Betty Grable as a coed. Based on a play, *Cross Roads*, by Martin Flavin. ◗

Age of Innocence, The (1934) **81m.** **½ D: Philip Moeller. Irene Dunne, John Boles, Lionel Atwill, Helen Westley, Laura Hope Crews, Julie Haydon. Modest but effective version of Edith Wharton's novel about a thwarted romance between an engaged attorney and a divorcée, in rigid 1870s Manhattan society. Starts off with a terrific Jazz Age montage prologue, then gets bogged down in static, stagy treatment as elderly Boles relates the story of his ill-fated affair to his grandson. Dunne gives a luminous and touching performance. Remade in 1993. ◗

Agony and the Ecstasy, The (1965) **C-140m.** **½ D: Carol Reed. Charlton Heston, Rex Harrison, Diane Cilento, Harry Andrews, Adolfo Celi. Huge spectacle of Michelangelo's artistic conflicts with Pope Julius II has adequate acting overshadowed by meticulous production. Short documentary on artist's work precedes fragmentary drama based on bits of Irving Stone's novel. Includes an intermission/entr'acte, exit music. Todd-AO. ▼●◗

A-Haunting We Will Go (1942) **68m.** *½ D: Alfred Werker. Stan Laurel, Oliver Hardy, Dante the Magician, Sheila Ryan, John Shelton, Don Costello, Elisha Cook, Jr. One of Stan and Ollie's poorest films, involving them with gangsters, a troublesome coffin, and a hokey stage magician. No magic in this turkey. ◗

Ah, Wilderness! (1935) **101m.** ***½ D: Clarence Brown. Wallace Beery, Lionel Barrymore, Aline MacMahon, Eric Linden, Cecilia Parker, Mickey Rooney, Frank Albertson, Bonita Granville. Rich Americana in this adaptation of Eugene O'Neill play about turn-of-the-20th-century small-town life, focusing on boy facing problems of adolescence. Rooney, playing younger brother, took the lead in musical remake SUMMER HOLIDAY. Screenplay by Albert Hackett and Frances Goodrich. ▼◗

Aida (1953-Italian) **C-96m.** **½ D: Clemente Fracassi. Sophia Loren, Lois Maxwell, Luciano Della Marra, Afro Poli, Antonio Cassinelli. Medium adaptation of the Verdi opera, of interest mostly for casting of Loren, in one of her earlier screen appearances, as the tragic Ethiopian princess. Her singing is dubbed by Renata Tebaldi. ◗

Ain't Misbehavin' (1955) **C-82m.** **½ D: Edward Buzzell. Rory Calhoun, Piper Laurie, Jack Carson, Mamie Van Doren, Reginald Gardiner, Barbara Britton. Pleasant musical fluff about rowdy Laurie crashing high society when wealthy Calhoun falls in love with her.

Air Cadet (1951) **94m.** ** D: Joseph Pevney. Stephen McNally, Gail Russell, Alex Nicol, Richard Long, Charles Drake, Robert Arthur, Rock Hudson, Peggie Castle, James Best, Parley Baer. Familiar account of Air Force recruits training to become fighter pilots; McNally plays their tough but troubled flight commander. It's fun to see Hudson barking orders at the recruits.

Air Force (1943) **124m.** *** D: Howard Hawks. John Garfield, John Ridgely, Gig Young, Arthur Kennedy, Charles Drake, Harry Carey, George Tobias, Faye Emerson. Archetypal WW2 movie, focusing on archetypal bomber crew. Tough to stomach at times ("Fried Jap going down," chimes Tobias after scoring a hit), but generally exciting, well done.▼●◗

Air Hawks (1935) **68m.** **½ D: Albert S. Rogell. Ralph Bellamy, Tala Birell, Douglass Dumbrille, Robert Allen, Billie Seward, Victor Kilian, Geneva Mitchell, Edward Van Sloan. Just when you think you know where this movie about barnstorming pilots is headed, it goes completely screwy, bringing in a mad scientist, a disintegration ray, and a mysterious Mr. Big behind all the scheming, and real-life pilot extraordinaire Wiley Post! A fun, fast-paced B movie with plenty of surprises to go along with its expected clichés. Post, of course, died in a crash later that year with Will Rogers. ◗

Air Hostess (1933) **67m.** ** D: Albert (S.) Rogell. Evalyn Knapp, James Murray, Arthur Pierson, Thelma Todd, J. M. Kerrigan,

Jane Darwell, Mike Donlin. Nice-guy airline pilot Pierson loves stewardess Knapp, but she marries daredevil flier Murray, who's seduced by wealthy mantrap Todd. Interesting look at 1930s aviation industry is grounded by the trite story of this routine programmer. ▶

Airmail (1932) 83m. *** D: John Ford. Pat O'Brien, Ralph Bellamy, Russell Hopton, Slim Summerville, Frank Albertson, Gloria Stuart. Routine story of pioneer airmail pilots supercharged by fine aerial scenes and good cast. First-rate. From a Frank "Spig" Wead story. Remade as LEGION OF LOST FLYERS (1939), which uses some of its footage.

Air Raid Wardens (1943) 67m. ** D: Edward Sedgwick. Stan Laurel, Oliver Hardy, Edgar Kennedy, Jacqueline White, Horace (Stephen) McNally, Donald Meek. Weak, later Laurel and Hardy comedy. One potentially good scene with slow-burn expert Kennedy doesn't meet expectations. ▼▶

Aladdin and His Lamp (1952) C-67m. *½ D: Lew Landers. Patricia Medina, Richard Erdman, John Sands, Noreen Nash. Poppycock, based on the juvenile fable, that will bore even the least discriminating children.

Alakazam the Great (1961-Japanese) C-84m. *** D: Taiji Yabushita, Daisaku Shirakawa, Osamu Tezuka. Voices of Frankie Avalon, Jonathan Winters, Arnold Stang, Sterling Holloway, Dodie Stevens, Peter Fernandez. Visually spectacular Japanese-made cartoon, based on a Chinese folktale and a popular Japanese comics adaptation (by Tezuka), is good children's entertainment. Story centers on a magical monkey's ambitious adventures, from a bullfight in the pit of a volcano to an epic battle with Hercules. U.S. voice cast provides an enjoyable English-language track and Les Baxter adds a lively score. Toeiscope.

Alamo, The (1960) C-161m. *** D: John Wayne. John Wayne, Richard Widmark, Laurence Harvey, Richard Boone, Carlos Arruza, Frankie Avalon, Pat Wayne, Linda Cristal, Chill Wills, Ken Curtis, Hank Worden, Denver Pyle, Olive Carey, Veda Ann Borg, John Dierkes, Guinn "Big Boy" Williams. Long, and long-winded, saga of the Alamo, with plenty of historical name-dropping and speechifying. Worthwhile for final attack, a truly memorable movie spectacle. Fine score by Dimitri Tiomkin includes popular "The Green Leaves of Summer." Filmed on location in Brackettville, Texas. Original Roadshow version runs 202m. with an overture, intermission/ entr'acte, exit music; other prints run 193m., 167m., and 140m. Todd-AO. ▼●▶

Alaska Seas (1954) 78m. ** D: Jerry Hopper. Robert Ryan, Jan Sterling, Brian Keith, Gene Barry, Ross Bagdasarian. Crooks will be crooks, in insipid tale of north-country salmon canner who regrets rehiring former partner, now an ex-con. Remake of SPAWN OF THE NORTH.

Albert, R.N. SEE: **Break to Freedom**

Albuquerque (1948) C-91m. **½ D: Ray Enright. Randolph Scott, Barbara Britton, George "Gabby" Hayes, Lon Chaney, Jr., Russell Hayden, Catherine Craig, George Cleveland. Good Western for Scott fans with Randy a tall Texan who arrives in title locale to work for his uncle, unaware that his new employer is corrupt. Based on a novel by Luke Short. Nice showcase for young Karolyn Grimes, of IT'S A WONDERFUL LIFE fame. ▼▶

Al Capone (1959) 105m. **½ D: Richard Wilson. Rod Steiger, Fay Spain, James Gregory, Martin Balsam, Nehemiah Persoff, Murvyn Vye. Good latter-day gangster biography with Steiger tirading as scarfaced Capone; good supporting cast, bringing back memories of Cagney-Robinson-Bogart films of the '30s. ▼▶

Alcatraz Island (1937) 64m. ** D: William McGann. John Litel, Ann Sheridan, Addison Richards, Mary Maguire, George E. Stone, Dick Purcell, Ben Welden. Watchable Warner Bros. prison yarn with Litel a racketeer sent up on a tax rap, trying to keep innocent daughter Sheridan unaware of his criminal activities.

Alexander Hamilton (1931) 73m. **½ D: John Adolfi. George Arliss, Doris Kenyon, Montagu Love, Dudley Digges, June Collyer, Alan Mowbray. Arliss cowrote the story for this vehicle that focuses on one crucial period in the political (and personal) life of the American patriot, who refuses to surrender his ideals. Typical Arliss theatrics, and enjoyable.

Alexander Nevsky (1938-Russian) 107m. **** D: Sergei Eisenstein. Nikolai Cherkassov, Nikolai Okhlopkov, Alexander Abrikossov, Dmitri Orlov, Vassily Novikov. Epic tale of Cherkassov and Russian army repelling German invasion during the 13th century, a disturbing parallel to world situation at time of production. Magnificently visualized battle sequences, wonderful Prokofiev score. A masterpiece. ▼●▶

Alexander's Ragtime Band (1938) 105m. *** D: Henry King. Tyrone Power, Alice Faye, Don Ameche, Ethel Merman, Jack Haley, Jean Hersholt, Helen Westley, John Carradine. Corny but entertaining musical chronicling the professional and romantic ups and downs of hot-headed aristocrat bandleader Power, nice-guy pianist-composer Ameche, and tough-but-vulnerable singer Faye (in one of her best performances). Sparked by Irving Berlin songs "Blue Skies," "Easter Parade," title tune. ▼●▶

Alexander the Great (1956) C-141m. *** D: Robert Rossen. Richard Burton, Fredric March, Claire Bloom, Danielle Darrieux, Harry Andrews, Stanley Baker, Peter Cushing, Michael Hordern, Helmut Dantine. Remarkable cast, intelligent acting, but static, lacking essential sweep to make tale of Greek conqueror moving. CinemaScope.▼●◗

Algiers (1938) **95m.** *** D: John Cromwell. Charles Boyer, Sigrid Gurie, Hedy Lamarr, Joseph Calleia. Alan Hale, Gene Lockhart, Johnny Downs, Paul Harvey. Boyer as Pepe Le Moko falls in love with alluring Lamarr visiting Casbah district of Algiers: Calleia as police official, Lockhart as informer, stand out in well-cast romance. Remake of French PÉPÉ LE MOKO, remade as CASBAH.▼◗

Alias a Gentleman (1948) **76m.** ** D: Harry Beaumont. Wallace Beery, Tom Drake, Dorothy Patrick, Gladys George, Leon Ames. Minor saga of aging jailbird who doesn't want to see his daughter involved with shady characters like himself.

Alias Boston Blackie (1942) **67m.** **½ D: Lew Landers. Chester Morris, Adele Mara, Richard Lane, George E. Stone, Lloyd Corrigan, Walter Sande, Larry Parks. When Blackie stages a magic act as part of a prison Christmas show, an innocent con (Parks) escapes to track down the men who framed him. (Incidentally, Morris was a magic enthusiast in real life.) Look fast for Lloyd Bridges as a bus driver.

Alias Bulldog Drummond SEE: **Bulldog Jack**

Alias Jesse James (1959) **C-92m.** *** D: Norman Z. McLeod. Bob Hope, Rhonda Fleming, Wendell Corey, Jim Davis, Gloria Talbott. One of Hope's funniest has him as tenderfoot insurance salesman out West, ordered to protect Jesse James, to whom he has sold a life insurance policy, being mistaken for sharpshooter. Fleming is a lovely Western belle; the two do a cute song together. Many Western stars cameo at the climax.▼●◗

Alias John Preston (1956-British) **66m.** ** D: David MacDonald. Alexander Knox, Betta St. John, Christopher Lee, Peter Grant, John Longden, Betty Ann Davies, Bill Fraser, Sandra Dorne, Patrick Holt. Wealthy Preston (Lee) buys a business and land in a small English city and soon begins courting St. John, upsetting her longtime beau (Grant). Then psychoanalyst Knox discovers that Lee is hiding a dark secret, even from himself. Low-key, intelligent psychological drama is well played but takes too long to get going. An early starring role for Lee. ▼

Alias Nick Beal (1949) **93m.** *** D: John Farrow. Ray Milland, Audrey Totter, Thomas Mitchell, George Macready, Fred Clark. Allegory of Devil (Milland) corrupting honest politician Mitchell with help of trollop Totter. Interesting drama with unusually sinister Milland.

Alias the Doctor (1932) **62m.** **½ D: Michael Curtiz. Richard Barthelmess, Marian Marsh, Lucille La Verne, Norman Foster, Adrienne Dore, Oscar Apfel, Claire Dodd.

Austrian medical student, in love with his foster sister, wants to be a farmer but takes the rap for ne'er-do-well foster brother's illegal operation. When he gets out of jail, he assumes his brother's identity, then has to operate to save the life of his foster mom! Contrived pre-Code melodrama is notable for stylish display of Teutonic expressionism by Curtiz and art director Anton Grot. Boris Karloff is said to have a small role, but we couldn't find him. ◗

Ali Baba and the Forty Thieves (1944) **C-87m.** *** D: Arthur Lubin. Maria Montez, Jon Hall, Turhan Bey, Andy Devine, Kurt Katch, Frank Puglia, Fortunio Bonanova, Scotty Beckett, Ramsay Ames. Straightforward retelling of classic *Arabian Nights* story, with young Ali (Beckett) pledging his love to young princess, then witnessing his father's betrayal and murder. He hides out with the Forty Thieves and returns years later (now played by Hall) to save the same princess from a forced marriage to Mongol plunderer Hulagu Khan (Katch). Lavish, exquisite production design and costumes in glorious Technicolor. The stars are beautiful, too! Remade (with stock footage) as THE SWORD OF ALI BABA (1965).▼●◗

Ali Baba Goes to Town (1937) **81m.** *** D: David Butler. Eddie Cantor, Tony Martin, Roland Young, June Lang, John Carradine, Louise Hovick (Gypsy Rose Lee). Entertaining musical comedy sends Cantor back in time but retains topical jokes of 1937; nice production with Cantor in top form. Ends with modern-day movie premiere and glimpses of many stars, from Shirley Temple to Tyrone Power. ◗

Alibi (1929) **84m.** ** D: Roland West. Chester Morris, Harry Stubbs, Mae Busch, Eleanor Griffith, Irma Harrison, Regis Toomey, Al Hill. Creaky, early-talkie gangster melodrama about a hood (Morris), just released from jail, who feigns honesty, weds a police sergeant's daughter, and then is suspected of killing a cop. Highly regarded in its time—this earned Oscar nominations for Best Picture and Actor—it pales beside such bona-fide classics as THE PUBLIC ENEMY and LITTLE CAESAR. Still, it's of note for its striking visuals and sets.▼◗

Alibi Ike (1935) **73m.** *** D: Ray Enright. Joe E. Brown, Olivia de Havilland, William Frawley, Ruth Donnelly, Roscoe Karns. Brown is aces as the title character, a brash Chicago Cubs rookie hurler who's always ready with excuses for his mistakes. He becomes involved with pretty de Havilland, and tangles with gamblers who try to bribe him. Based on a story by Ring Lardner; the last of Brown's baseball trilogy, following FIREMAN, SAVE MY CHILD and ELMER THE GREAT. ◗

Alice Adams (1935) **99m.** ***½ D: George

Stevens. Katharine Hepburn, Fred Mac-Murray, Fred Stone, Evelyn Venable, Ann Shoemaker, Frank Albertson, Hattie Mc-Daniel, Charley Grapewin, Grady Sutton, Hedda Hopper. Excellent small-town Americana with social-climbing girl finally finding love in person of unpretentious MacMurray. Booth Tarkington's Pulitzer Prize–winning novel becomes fine film, if not altogether credible. The dinner-table scene is unforgettable. Screenplay by Dorothy Yost, Mortimer Offner, and Jane Murfin. Filmed before in 1923.▼●▮

Alice in Wonderland (1933) 77m. ** D: Norman Z. McLeod. Charlotte Henry, Richard Arlen, Gary Cooper, W. C. Fields, Cary Grant, Edward Everett Horton, Baby LeRoy, Edna May Oliver, Jack Oakie, many others. Top Paramount stars appear, disguised as Lewis Carroll characters, in this slow-moving adaptation of the classic story. Fascinating for its casting—Cooper as White Knight, Fields as Humpty Dumpty, Grant as Mock Turtle—but, overall, a bore. Screenplay by Joseph L. Mankiewicz and William Cameron Menzies. ▮

Alice in Wonderland (1950-British) C-83m. ** D: Dallas Bower. Carol Marsh, Stephen Murray, Pamela Brown, Felix Aylmer, Ernest Milton. Static adaptation of Lewis Carroll classic with gimmick of mixing live action and puppets; most of the wit and charm are missing.▼▮

Alice in Wonderland (1951) C-75m. *** D: Clyde Geronimi, Hamilton Luske, Wilfred Jackson. Voices of Kathryn Beaumont, Ed Wynn, Richard Haydn, Sterling Holloway, Jerry Colonna, Verna Felton, Bill Thompson. Entertaining, if somewhat aloof, rendering of Lewis Carroll's classic, with the Walt Disney animation team at its best bringing the Cheshire Cat, the Queen of Hearts, and the Mad Hatter to life. Episodic film is given major boost by strong personalities of Wynn, Colonna, Holloway, et al., and such tunes as "I'm Late" and "The Unbirthday Song."▼●▮

Alimony (1949) 70m. ** D: Alfred Zeisler. Martha Vickers, John Beal, Hillary Brooke, Laurie Lind, Douglass Dumbrille, James Guilfoyle, Marie Blake, Leonid Kinskey. Final work by a minor German expatriate director typecasts pouty Vickers as a professional schemer who lures, weds, and dumps (formerly) successful men, all for cold cash. Her latest target: tormented songwriter Beal. Sordid but uninspired time killer. ▼▮

Al Jennings of Oklahoma (1951) C-79m. ** D: Ray Nazarro. Dan Duryea, Gale Storm, Dick Foran, Gloria Henry. Modest Western enhanced by Duryea in title role of gangster who serves his time and goes straight; sporadic action.

All About Eve (1950) 138m. **** D: Joseph L. Mankiewicz. Bette Davis, Anne Baxter, George Sanders, Celeste Holm, Gary Mer-

rill, Thelma Ritter, Marilyn Monroe, Hugh Marlowe, Gregory Ratoff. Brilliantly sophisticated (and cynical) look at life in and around the theater, with a heaven-sent script by director Mankiewicz (based on the story "The Wisdom of Eve" by Mary Orr). Davis is absolutely perfect as an aging star who takes in an adoring fan (Baxter) and soon discovers that the young woman is taking over her life. Witty dialogue to spare, especially great when spoken by Sanders and Ritter. Six Oscars include Best Picture, Director, Screenplay, and Supporting Actor (Sanders). Later musicalized on Broadway as *Applause*.▼●▮

All American (1953) 83m. ** D: Jesse Hibbs. Tony Curtis, Lori Nelson, Richard Long, Mamie Van Doren, Gregg Palmer, Stuart Whitman. Ordinary drama in which college football hero Curtis gives up the game after his parents' death, and accepts an architecture scholarship at a snooty Ivy League–type school. Of note for appearances of several all-Americans (including Frank Gifford). Look fast for football great Tom Harmon in the announcing booth.

All-American Chump (1936) 63m. **½ D: Edwin L. Marin. Stuart Erwin, Robert Armstrong, Betty Furness, Edmund Gwenn, Harvey Stephens, Edward Brophy, E. E. Clive, Dewey Robinson. Erwin is funny, in his usual country bumpkin way, as a small-town math whiz known as "the human adding machine" who is exploited by card sharks and hustlers. Fairly diverting.

All-American Co-Ed (1941) 49m. **½ D: LeRoy Prinz. Frances Langford, Johnny Downs, Marjorie Woodworth, Noah Beery, Jr., Esther Dale, Harry Langdon, Alan Hale, Jr., Kent Rogers, The Tanner Sisters. Snappy, amusing Hal Roach Streamliner (a short feature film intended for double bills) about a Quinceton University frat boy (Downs) who dresses in drag to win a beauty queen scholarship at Mar Brynn girls' school. Directorial debut for renowned choreographer Prinz.▼▮

All Ashore (1953) C-80m. *½ D: Richard Quine. Mickey Rooney, Dick Haymes, Peggy Ryan, Ray McDonald. Musical yarn of three gobs on shore leave finding gals, sinks despite Rooney's sprightly spirit.

All at Sea (1957-British) 87m. *** D: Charles Frend. Alec Guinness, Irene Browne, Percy Herbert, Harold Goodwin. Robust comedy that holds its own throughout. Guinness is admirable as seaman who can't bear sight of water but buys rundown house-laden pier, turning it into an amusement palace. Original title: BARNACLE BILL. ▮

Allegheny Uprising (1939) 81m. *** D: William Seiter. John Wayne, Claire Trevor, George Sanders, Brian Donlevy, Robert Barrat, Moroni Olsen, Chill Wills. Wayne leads band of brave men against crooked Donlevy, tyrannical British captain Sanders in pre-Revolutionary colonies. Fine, unpretentious film; Trevor appealing as girl who goes after Wayne. Also shown in computer-colored version. **▼O●**

All Fall Down (1962) **110m. ★★★** D: John Frankenheimer. Warren Beatty, Eva Marie Saint, Karl Malden, Angela Lansbury, Brandon de Wilde. Improbable but absorbing William Inge script about narcissistic young man (Beatty), his admiring younger brother (de Wilde), indulgent parents (Lansbury and Malden), and the older woman (Saint) with whom he becomes involved. Fine performances. Also shown in computer-colored version. **▼O●**

All Hands on Deck (1961) **C-98m. ★★** D: Norman Taurog. Pat Boone, Buddy Hackett, Dennis O'Keefe, Barbara Eden. Innocuous musical comedy of free-wheeling sailors, Boone and Hackett, is lightweight entertainment. CinemaScope. **●**

All I Desire (1953) **79m. ★★½** D: Douglas Sirk. Barbara Stanwyck, Richard Carlson, Lyle Bettger, Lori Nelson, Maureen O'Sullivan, Billy Gray. Actress Stanwyck returns to husband and three children she abandoned years before in this predictable but well-made soap opera set in 1910. Marked by fluid, stylish camerawork (by Carl Guthrie) and Stanwyck's honest performance. Look for young Stuart Whitman in the school play and Guy Williams in the party scene. **▼O●**

Alligator Named Daisy, An (1955-British) **C-88m. ★★** D: J. Lee Thompson. Donald Sinden, Jeannie Carson, James Robertson Justice, Diana Dors, Roland Culver, Stanley Holloway, Margaret Rutherford, Stephen Boyd, Ernest Thesiger. Sinden inadvertently acquires an alligator while sailing home to his family and fiancée. No one understands his attachment to the reptile except a friendly woman he meets on his voyage. Labored farce with incongruous musical numbers by Carson. VistaVision. **●**

Alligator People, The (1959) **74m. ★★½** D: Roy Del Ruth. Beverly Garland, George Macready, Lon Chaney (Jr.), Richard Crane, Frieda Inescort, Bruce Bennett. Garland searches for runaway husband and finds him at his family's Southern mansion—partly transformed into an alligator! Obviously inspired by the success of THE FLY. Strictly routine. CinemaScope. **▼O●**

All in a Night's Work (1961) **C-94m. ★★½** D: Joseph Anthony. Dean Martin, Shirley MacLaine, Charlie Ruggles, Cliff Robertson. Featherweight (and often feather-brained) comedy about innocent office worker caught in compromising position with big-business exec, leading to a series of misunderstandings. Filled with familiar character actors (Gale Gordon, Jerome Cowan, Jack Weston, et al.). **▼O●**

All Mine to Give (1957) **C-102m. ★★½** D: Allen Reisner. Cameron Mitchell, Glynis Johns, Patty McCormack, Hope Emerson. Often touching story of pioneer family

in Wisconsin determined to overcome all obstacles. **▼O●**

All My Sons (1948) **94m. ★★★** D: Irving Reis. Edward G. Robinson, Burt Lancaster, Mady Christians, Louisa Horton, Howard Duff, Arlene Francis, Lloyd Gough, Henry (Harry) Morgan. Arthur Miller's compelling drama of returning soldier (Lancaster) discovering that his father (Robinson) cheated on a war matériel order, with tragic results. Post-WW2 drama is well acted, but verbose and preachy. **▼**

All Night Long (1962-British) **95m. ★★½** D: Basil Dearden. Patrick McGoohan, Marti Stevens, Betsy Blair, Paul Harris, Keith Michell, Richard Attenborough. Fair updating of *Othello,* about an interracial couple, a white singer and black bandleader, and their Iago, a drummer (amusingly played by McGoohan). Guest musicians include Dave Brubeck, Charlie Mingus, John Dankworth. **●**

All of Me (1934) **70m. BOMB** D: James Flood. Fredric March, Miriam Hopkins, George Raft, Helen Mack, William Collier, Sr. Hopkins loves March but refuses to spoil it by marrying him; yet she takes interest in ex-con Raft and his pregnant girlfriend Mack, who very much want to get married. As if it didn't have enough problems, this dreary potboiler is poorly edited.

Allotment Wives (1945) **83m. ★★** D: William Nigh. Kay Francis, Paul Kelly, Otto Kruger, Gertrude Michael, Teala Loring. Mild sensationalism involving women who marry servicemen to collect their military pay; not one of Francis' better films.

All Over Town (1937) **62m. ★★½** D: James W. Horne. Ole Olsen, Chic Johnson, Mary Howard, Harry Stockwell, Franklin Pangborn, James Finlayson. Low-budget shenanigans, with Olsen and Johnson trying to stage a show in a "jinxed" theater. Spotty, but has some funny moments. **▼**

All Quiet on the Western Front (1930) **133m. ★★★★** D: Lewis Milestone. Lew Ayres, Louis Wolheim, John Wray, Slim Summerville, Russell Gleason, Ben Alexander, Beryl Mercer. Vivid, moving adaptation of Erich Maria Remarque's eloquent pacifist novel about German boys' experiences as soldiers during WW1. Time hasn't dimmed its power, or its poignancy, one bit. Scripted by Milestone, Maxwell Anderson, Del Andrews, and George Abbott. Academy Award winner for Best Picture and Director. Originally shown at 140m., then cut many times over the years; restored in 1998. Sequel: THE ROAD BACK. Remade for TV a half century later. Also shown in 131m. silent version, edited separately in 1930, using alternate shots; it offers a different perspective on this classic. **▼O●**

All That Heaven Allows (1955) **C-89m. ★★★** D: Douglas Sirk. Jane Wyman, Rock Hudson, Agnes Moorehead, Conrad Nagel,

Virginia Grey, Gloria Talbott, William Reynolds, Charles Drake, Merry Anders. When upper-class widow Wyman allows gardener Hudson—a younger man—to romance her, she faces the ire of her children, friends, and society. Typically sleek Sirk soaper. Remade by Rainer Werner Fassbinder as ALI—FEAR EATS THE SOUL.▼▶

All That Money Can Buy SEE: **Devil and Daniel Webster, The**

All the Brothers Were Valiant (1953) C-101m. **½ D: Richard Thorpe. Robert Taylor, Stewart Granger, Ann Blyth, Keenan Wynn, James Whitmore, Lewis Stone. Waterlogged adventure based on Ben Ames Williams' novel. Taylor and Granger lack conviction as New Bedford whalers having career and romantic conflicts. Filmed before in 1923 and in 1928 as ACROSS TO SINGAPORE.▼▶

All the Fine Young Cannibals (1960) C-112m. *½ D: Michael Anderson. Robert Wagner, Natalie Wood, Susan Kohner, George Hamilton, Pearl Bailey, Anne Seymour. Clichés abound in this romantic soap opera that was actually inspired by the life of jazz trumpeter Chet Baker (whose role is played here, somewhat improbably, by Wagner). British music group Fine Young Cannibals took its name from this film. CinemaScope.

All the King's Horses (1934) 87m. ** D: Frank Tuttle. Carl Brisson, Mary Ellis, Edward Everett Horton, Katherine DeMille, Eugene Pallette. Mediocre musical about movie star who exchanges places with look-alike king, causing complications for both men, especially where l'amour is concerned.

All the King's Men (1949) 109m. **** D: Robert Rossen. Broderick Crawford, Joanne Dru, John Ireland, Mercedes McCambridge, John Derek, Shepperd Strudwick, Anne Seymour. Brilliant adaptation (by director Rossen) of Robert Penn Warren's Pulitzer Prize–winning novel about the rise and fall of a Huey Long–like senator, played by Crawford in the performance of his career. He and McCambridge (in her first film) won well-deserved Oscars, as did the film, for Best Picture. Campaign montages directed by Don Siegel. Remade in 2006.▼▶

All These Women (1964-Swedish) C-80m. **½ D: Ingmar Bergman. Jarl Kulle, Harriet Andersson, Bibi Andersson, Allan Edwall. Satirical frolic involving woman-chasing cellist. He bargains with music critic to have biography written by agreeing to play writer's composition. Notable only as Bergman's first film in color. Written by Bergman and Erland Josephson. Aka NOW ABOUT THESE WOMEN.

All the Way SEE: **Joker Is Wild, The**

All the Way Home (1963) 97m. ***½ D: Alex Segal. Jean Simmons, Robert Preston, Aline MacMahon, Pat Hingle, Michael Kearney, John Cullum, Thomas Chalmers.

Outstanding filmization of the Tad Mosel play, set in 1915 Tennessee, an adaptation of James Agee's *A Death in the Family*. Preston is subdued in the pivotal role of a father and husband who is accidentally killed, leaving his loved ones to interpret the meaning of their lives before and after his death. Beautifully done, with Simmons offering an award-caliber performance as Preston's wife. Fine script by Philip Reisman, Jr.

All the Young Men (1960) 87m. **½ D: Hall Bartlett. Alan Ladd, Sidney Poitier, James Darren, Glenn Corbett, Mort Sahl. Hackneyed Korean war story with all the stereotypes present, mouthing the same old platitudes.▼

All This, and Heaven Too (1940) 143m. *** D: Anatole Litvak. Bette Davis, Charles Boyer, Jeffrey Lynn, Barbara O'Neil, Virginia Weidler, Helen Westley, Walter Hampden, Henry Daniell, June Lockhart. Nobleman Boyer falls in love with governess Davis, causing scandal and death; stars do very well in elaborate filmization of Rachel Field book set in 19th-century France.▼▶

All Through the Night (1942) 107m. *** D: Vincent Sherman. Humphrey Bogart, Conrad Veidt, Kaaren Verne, Jane Darwell, Frank McHugh, Peter Lorre, Judith Anderson, William Demarest, Jackie Gleason, Phil Silvers, Barton MacLane, Martin Kosleck. Bogart's gang tracks down Fifth Columnists (Veidt, Lorre, Anderson) in WW2 N.Y.C. Interesting blend of spy, gangster, and comedy genres, with memorable double-talk and auction scenes.▼▶▶

Almost a Bride SEE: **Kiss For Corliss, A**

Almost Angels (1962) C-93m. **½ D: Steve Previn. Peter Weck, Hans Holt, Fritz Eckhardt, Bruni Lobel, Vincent Winter, Sean Scully. Schmaltzy but entertaining Disney film about two youngsters who become friends in the Vienna Boys Choir. Pleasant story, fine music.▼▶

Aloma of the South Seas (1941) C-77m. ** D: Alfred Santell. Dorothy Lamour, Jon Hall, Lynne Overman, Philip Reed, Katherine DeMille. Still another sarong saga with native Hall sent to U.S. for education, returning when father dies to stop revolution on once peaceful island. Filmed before in 1927, with Gilda Gray.

Alone on the Pacific (1963-Japanese) C-104m. *** D: Kon Ichikawa. Yûjirô Ishihara, Kinuyo Tanaka, Masayuki Mori, Ruriko Asaoka, Hajime Hana. Stirring, contemplative film based on the real-life story of Kenichi Horie, who made a solo voyage from Osaka Bay to San Francisco; juxtaposes the confines of Japanese society with the vastness (and dangers) of the sea. Well photographed by Yoshihiro Yamazaki. Aka MY ENEMY, THE SEA. CinemaScope.

Along Came Jones (1945) 90m. *** D: Stuart Heisler. Gary Cooper, Loretta Young, William Demarest, Dan Duryea, Frank

Sully, Russell Simpson. Three stars are most ingratiating in very low-key, leisurely Western spoof, with Cooper (who also produced) mistaken for notorious outlaw Duryea.▼▶

Along the Great Divide (1951) 88m. **½ D: Raoul Walsh. Kirk Douglas, Virginia Mayo, John Agar, Walter Brennan. Douglas is appropriately tight-lipped as lawman determined to bring in his man, despite desert storm; some spectacular scenery.▼▶

Along the Navajo Trail (1945) 66m. *** D: Frank McDonald. Roy Rogers, George "Gabby" Hayes, Dale Evans, Estelita Rodriguez, Douglas Fowley, Nestor Paiva, Roy Barcroft, Bob Nolan and the Sons of the Pioneers. Evil rancher Fowley covets the spread owned by Dale's father, as it's in demand by a drilling company that wants to run a pipeline across the property. Great stunts by Yakima Canutt, a wonderful rendition of "Cool Water" by the Sons, and a charming song called "Savin' for a Rainy Day" by Roy and Dale help make this a winner.▼▶

Alphabet Murders, The (1965-British) 90m. **½ D: Frank Tashlin. Tony Randall, Anita Ekberg, Robert Morley, Guy Rolfe, James Villiers. Odd adaptation of Agatha Christie's *The ABC Murders* (the film's original British title), with Hercule Poirot after a killer who seems to be doing in his victims in alphabetical order. Strange casting of Randall as the Belgian sleuth and a little too much slapstick make this more of a curiosity than anything else. Margaret Rutherford makes a gag appearance as Miss Marple. ▼▶

Alphaville (1965-French) 95m. ** D: Jean-Luc Godard. Eddie Constantine, Anna Karina, Akim Tamiroff, Howard Vernon. Constantine, as super private-eye Lemmy Caution, is sent to futuristic city run by electronic brain to rescue scientist trapped there. Jumbled Godard epic, recommended for New Wave disciples only.▼●▶

Always a Bride (1954-British) 83m. ** D: Ralph Smart. Peggy Cummins, Terence Morgan, Ronald Squire, James Hayter. Mild comedy of treasury officer romancing girl, aiding her dad to fleece others.

Always Goodbye (1938) 75m. **½ D: Sidney Lanfield. Barbara Stanwyck, Herbert Marshall, Ian Hunter, Cesar Romero, Lynn Bari, Binnie Barnes. Still another sacrificing mother tale—specifically, a remake of GALLANT LADY. Stanwyck is forced to give up her illicit child. Nicely done, but the same old story. ▶

Always in My Heart (1942) 92m. **½ D: Jo Graham. Kay Francis, Walter Huston, Gloria Warren, Patty Hale, Frankie Thomas, Una O'Connor, Sidney Blackmer, Borrah Minevitch and his Harmonica Rascals. Cast adds zest to this musical soap opera about nice guy ex-con Huston and his ex-wife (Francis), who is about to remarry.

Their son (Thomas) and daughter (Warren, a Deanna Durbin wannabe) think he's dead, and complications arise when he arrives on the scene.

Always Leave Them Laughing (1949) 116m. **½ D: Roy Del Ruth. Milton Berle, Virginia Mayo, Ruth Roman, Bert Lahr, Alan Hale. Berle is at home in tale of cocky comedian's ups and downs. Unfortunately, zesty opening leads into soggy drama. Lahr does his classic "stop in the name of the stationhouse" routine.

Always Together (1947) 78m. **½ D: Frederick de Cordova. Robert Hutton, Joyce Reynolds, Cecil Kellaway, Ernest Truex; guests Humphrey Bogart, Jack Carson, Dennis Morgan, Janis Paige, Alexis Smith. Innocuous fluff of dying millionaire Kellaway giving money to young Reynolds, then discovering he's quite healthy. Worthwhile only for amusing cameos by many Warner Bros. stars throughout film.

Amarilly of Clothes-Line Alley (1918) 67m. **½ D: Marshall Neilan. Mary Pickford, William Scott, Kate Price, Ida Waterman, Norman Kerry, Fred Goodwins, Margaret Landis, Tom Wilson, Gustav von Seyffertitz. Mary is Amarilly, a working-class Irish girl who proudly toils as a "scrub lady." Complications arise when she goes to work for wealthy Kerry. Solid (albeit by-the-numbers) Pickford vehicle teaches us that it's better to be poor and happy than rich and pompous. ▼▶

Amazing Adventure (1936-British) 70m. **½ D: Alfred Zeisler. Cary Grant, Mary Brian, Henry Kendall, Leon M. Lion, Garry Marsh, John Turnbull. Grant inherits a fortune and, feeling guilty, sets out to earn his living instead. One of those The-Poor-Are-Smarter comedies typical of the era, and a rare opportunity to see Cary working on his home turf. Originally titled THE AMAZING QUEST OF ERNEST BLISS in Britain, ROMANCE AND RICHES in the U.S. E. Phillips Oppenheim's novel filmed before in England in 1920.▼▶

Amazing Colossal Man, The (1957) 80m. **½ D: Bert I. Gordon. Glenn Langan, Cathy Downs, James Seay, Larry Thor. Army officer who survives an atomic explosion starts growing; at 60 feet he attacks Las Vegas! Starts well but ends up as your standard monster-on-the-loose flick. Sequel: WAR OF THE COLOSSAL BEAST.▼

Amazing Dr. Clitterhouse, The (1938) 87m. *** D: Anatole Litvak. Edward G. Robinson, Claire Trevor, Humphrey Bogart, Allen Jenkins, Donald Crisp, Gale Page. Amusing film of "method doctor" Robinson trying to discover what makes a crook tick; he joins Bogart's gang and becomes addicted.▼

Amazing Mrs. Holliday, The (1943) 96m. **½ D: Bruce Manning. Deanna Durbin, Edmond O'Brien, Barry Fitzgerald, Arthur

Treacher, Frieda Inescort. Lukewarm WW2 comedy-drama about dedicated missionary Durbin trying to sneak Chinese orphans into U.S. Deanna's song interludes offer respite from silly plot. Much of this was directed by Jean Renoir, but his and Durbin's plans for the film went awry. ▼▶

Amazing Mr. Williams, The (1939) 85m. *** D: Alexander Hall. Melvyn Douglas, Joan Blondell, Clarence Kolb, Ruth Donnelly, Edward S. Brophy, Donald MacBride, Don Beddoe, Jonathan Hale, John Wray. Douglas is a workaholic police detective whose long-suffering girlfriend Blondell (who happens to be the mayor's secretary) runs out of patience and tries to get him canned so he'll settle down and marry her. The two stars have great chemistry in this bright, breezy crime comedy featuring a terrific supporting cast of character actors.

Amazing Mr. X, The (1948) 78m. **½ D: Bernard Vorhaus. Turhan Bey, Lynn Bari, Cathy O'Donnell, Richard Carlson, Donald Curtis, Virginia Gregg. Intriguing little chiller in which wealthy, vulnerable widow Bari desperately misses her late husband. Will she be able to contact him via the powers of psychic Bey? Aka THE SPIRITUALIST. ▼▶▶

Amazing Quest of Ernest Bliss, The SEE: **Amazing Adventure**

Amazing Transparent Man, The (1960) 58m. BOMB D: Edgar G. Ulmer. Douglas Kennedy, Marguerite Chapman, James Griffith, Ivan Triesault. Tawdry cheapie in which a mad scientist makes a convict invisible to steal radioactive materials for him, but the subject is more interested in testing his new power on a nearby bank. Disappointed Ulmer fans will wish they had the formula themselves. ▼▶▶

Ambassador Bill (1931) 70m. *** D: Sam Taylor. Will Rogers, Marguerite Churchill, Greta Nissen, Tad Alexander, Ray Milland, Gustav von Seyffertitz, Arnold Korff. Cattleman-turned-diplomat Rogers takes up his post in Sylvania, where its boy-king is being manipulated by a corrupt prime minister. Naturally, Rogers goes about setting things right. Enjoyable Rogers vehicle written by Guy Bolton. ▶

Ambassador's Daughter, The (1956) C-102m. **½ D: Norman Krasna. Olivia de Havilland, John Forsythe, Myrna Loy, Adolphe Menjou, Edward Arnold, Francis Lederer, Tommy Noonan, Minor Watson. Oomph is missing even though stars give all to uplift sagging comedy of de Havilland out for a fling in Paris, romanced by soldier Forsythe. CinemaScope. ▼▶

Ambush (1939) 62m. **½ D: Kurt Neumann. Gladys Swarthout, Lloyd Nolan, William Henry, William Frawley, Ernest Truex, Broderick Crawford, Rufe Davis, Richard Denning, Antonio Moreno, Polly

Moran. Fast-paced programmer about bank robbers forcing the innocent sister of a gang member to dupe truck driver Nolan into helping them make their getaway. Bang-bang action blends well with lively dialogue, courtesy of writers Laura and S. J. Perelman. Final film (and only nonmusical) for Metropolitan Opera star Swarthout.

Ambush (1949) 89m. **½ D: Sam Wood. Robert Taylor, John Hodiak, Arlene Dahl, Don Taylor, Jean Hagen, Bruce Cowling, Leon Ames, John McIntire, Chief Thundercloud. Cavalrymen embark on a search for Indian raiders who abducted the daughter of an army general; their romantic entanglements with women back at the fort add complications. Rugged New Mexico locations add to the visual interest. ▶

Ambush at Cimarron Pass (1958) 73m. ** D: Jodie Copelan. Scott Brady, Margia Dean, Clint Eastwood, Baynes Barron, William Vaughn. Stranded cowboys and cavalrymen try to protect shipment of guns from Indians—though they disagree strongly on strategy. Post–Civil War Western features young Eastwood, who continually flies into a white-hot rage whenever he hears the word "Yankee." Regalscope. ▶

Ambush at Tomahawk Gap (1953) C-73m. ** D: Fred F. Sears. John Hodiak, John Derek, David Brian, Maria Elena Marques, Ray Teal, John Qualen. Plenty of fisticuffs enliven this otherwise standard oater, in which four men with different agendas are released from prison and set out in search of stolen loot. ▼▶

America (1924) 141m. *** D: D.W. Griffith. Neil Hamilton, Carol Dempster, Erville Alderson, Charles Emmett Mack, Lee Beggs, Frank McGlynn, Lionel Barrymore, Louis Wolheim. Impressive silent-film treatment of Revolutionary War, with fine battle scenes, period flavor, marred somewhat by silly love story; florid villainy by Barrymore. Still quite good. ▼▶

America, America (1963) 168m. **** D: Elia Kazan. Stathis Giallelis, Frank Wolff, Elena Karam, Lou Antonio, John Marley, Estelle Hemsley. The dream of passage to America—as it unfolded for late 19th-century immigrants—is movingly captured by writer-director Kazan in this long, absorbing film, based on his uncle's experiences. Heartfelt and heart-rending, with impressive Oscar-winning art direction/set decoration by Gene Callahan. ▼▶▶

American Empire (1942) 82m. **½ D: William McGann. Richard Dix, Leo Carrillo, Preston Foster, Frances Gifford, Guinn Williams. Dix and Foster join forces to develop cattle empire in Texas after Civil War, but not without problems. Pretty good outdoor actioner. ▼▶

Americaner Schadchen (1940) 87m. ** D: Edgar G. Ulmer. Leo Fuchs, Judith Abarbanel, Yudel Dubinsky, Wolf Mercur, Rosetta Bialis. Slight romantic satire about a movie star (Fuchs) whose fiancées keep breaking their engagements, and who opens a marriage bureau. The last of four Yiddish-language features made by cult director Ulmer. Aka AMERICAN MATCHMAKER. ▼

American Guerrilla in the Philippines (1950) C-105m. **½ D: Fritz Lang. Tyrone Power, Micheline Prelle (Presle), Tom Ewell, Bob Patten, Tommy Cook, Jack Elam, Robert Barrat. Interesting but flawed account of resistance to Japanese after the fall of the Philippines during WW2, focusing on the activities of American naval officer Power. Marred by clichéd, jingoistic script, predictable romantic subplot involving Prelle. On-location filming adds authentic flavor. Based on Ira Wolfert's novel. ▶

American in Paris, An (1951) C-115m. ***½ D: Vincente Minnelli. Gene Kelly, Leslie Caron, Oscar Levant, Georges Guetary, Nina Foch. Joyous, original musical built around Gershwin score; dazzling in color. Plot of artist Kelly torn between gamine Caron and wealthy Foch is creaky, but the songs, dances, production are superb. Oscars include Best Picture, Story and Screenplay (Alan Jay Lerner), Cinematography (Alfred Gilks and John Alton), Scoring (Johnny Green and Saul Chaplin), Art Direction, Costume Design, and a special citation to Kelly. Look fast for Noel Neill as an art student. ▼◉▶

Americanization of Emily, The (1964) 117m. ***½ D: Arthur Hiller. James Garner, Julie Andrews, Melvyn Douglas, James Coburn, Joyce Grenfell, Keenan Wynn, Judy Carne, Liz Fraser, Edward Binns, William Windom, Alan Sues. Garner is fall guy for U.S. admiral's master plan to have American naval officer first Normandy invasion victim, with predictable results. Cynical Garner-Andrews romance blends well with realistic view of life among U.S. military brass. Script by Paddy Chayefsky, from William Bradford Huie's novel. Also shown in computer-colored version.▼◉▶

American Madness (1932) 81m. *** D: Frank Capra. Walter Huston, Pat O'Brien, Kay Johnson, Constance Cummings, Gavin Gordon. Huston is dynamic as a put-upon bank president in the depths of the Great Depression; vivid, upbeat film marred only by idiotic romantic subplot.▼▶

American Matchmaker SEE: **Americaner Schadchen**

Americano, The (1955) C-85m. **½ D: William Castle. Glenn Ford, Cesar Romero, Frank Lovejoy, Ursula Thiess, Abbe Lane. Good guy Ford meets Brazilian bad guys in standard Western, with change of scenery as major asset.▼▶

American Romance, An (1944) C-122m. **½ D: King Vidor. Brian Donlevy, Ann Richards, Walter Abel, John Qualen, Stephen McNally. Long, flavorful story of immigrant steelworker's rise to wealth and power. Might have been a better film with someone more magnetic than Donlevy in the lead. Originally released at 151m.▶

American Tragedy, An (1931) 95m. ** D: Josef von Sternberg. Phillips Holmes, Sylvia Sidney, Frances Dee, Irving Pichel, Frederick Burton, Claire McDowell. Straightforward telling of Theodore Dreiser story about weak young man torn between poor girlfriend and beautiful, wealthy girl who falls in love with him. Sidney is ideally cast, but film is cold and uninvolving; certainly not as florid as remake, A PLACE IN THE SUN.

Among the Living (1941) 68m. **½ D: Stuart Heisler. Albert Dekker, Susan Hayward, Frances Farmer, Harry Carey, Gordon Jones. Intriguing little B film about a deranged man, one of twins, kept isolated for years, who breaks loose and stirs up trouble. Some great moments, but film is a little too hurried and simplistic; Dekker is excellent in dual role.

Among the Missing (1934) 62m. **½ D: Albert S. Rogell. Richard Cromwell, Henrietta Crosman, Billie Seward, Arthur Hohl, Ivan Simpson, Paul Hurst. Minor but interesting programmer about an elderly woman (Crosman) who moves in with a trio of crooks. Naturally, she tries to rehabilitate the youngest member of the gang (Cromwell). Notable for its striking cinematography (by Joseph August) and use of L.A. locations, by day and by night.▶

Amorous Adventures of Moll Flanders, The (1965-British) C-126m. **½ D: Terence Young. Kim Novak, Richard Johnson, Angela Lansbury, George Sanders, Vittorio De Sica, Lilli Palmer, Leo McKern, Cecil Parker. Billed as female Tom Jones, Moll is far from thrilling. Fine cast romps through 18th-century England from bedroom to boudoir, but film needs more spice than Novak can muster. The two leads were married briefly in real life. Panavision. ▼◉

Amorous Mister Prawn (1962-British) 89m. **½ D: Anthony Kimmins. Joan Greenwood, Cecil Parker, Ian Carmichael, Robert Beatty. Diverting fluff finds wife (Greenwood) of general (Parker) devising a scheme to obtain badly needed money so they can retire in style. Original British title: THE AMOROUS PRAWN.

Amorous Prawn, The SEE: **Amorous Mister Prawn**

Anastasia (1956) C-105m. **** D: Anatole Litvak. Ingrid Bergman, Yul Brynner, Helen Hayes, Akim Tamiroff, Martita Hunt, Felix Aylmer, Natalie Schafer, Ivan Desny. Inspired casting makes this film exceptional. Bergman won Oscar as amnesiac refugee selected by Brynner to impersonate surviving daughter of Russia's last czar. High point: confrontation scene in which Hayes as grand duchess must determine if girl is her relative. Screenplay by Arthur Laurents based on Marcelle Maurette's play. CinemaScope. ▼●◗

Anatahan (1953-Japanese) **92m.** **½ D: Josef von Sternberg. Akemi Negishi, Suganuma, Sawamura, Nakayama, Fujikawa, Kondo, Miyashita. Von Sternberg wrote, directed, photographed, and narrates this strange, stylized curio about twelve Japanese soldiers during WW2 who are stranded on a deserted island with an old man and an alluring young woman for seven years, refusing to believe that the war is over. Von Sternberg's last film (but released before JET PILOT), said to be based on an actual incident. Aka THE SAGA OF ANATAHAN.

Anatomist, The (1961-British) **73m.** **
D: Leonard William. Alastair Sim, George Cole, Jill Bennett, Margaret Gordon. Respected surgeon encourages corpse stealing for experiments, causing rash of murders. Sim is wry in tame spooker. ◗

Anatomy of a Murder (1959) **160m.** ****
D: Otto Preminger. James Stewart, Lee Remick, Ben Gazzara, Arthur O'Connell, Eve Arden, Kathryn Grant (Crosby), George C. Scott, Orson Bean, Murray Hamilton. Long, exciting courtroom drama; daring when released, tamer now. Sterling cast: O'Connell as drunken lawyer inspired by Stewart, Scott as prosecuting attorney, Joseph Welch as judge (Welch was the famous Army-McCarthy hearings lawyer who later became a judge in real life). Stewart towers over all as witty, easygoing, but cagy defense lawyer. Script by Wendell Mayes, from novel by Robert Traver (Judge John D. Voelker). Duke Ellington composed the score and also appears on-screen. ▼●◗

Anatomy of a Syndicate SEE: **Big Operator, The**

Anchors Aweigh (1945) **C-140m.** **½
D: George Sidney. Frank Sinatra, Kathryn Grayson, Gene Kelly, Jose Iturbi, Dean Stockwell, Pamela Britton. Popular '40s musical of sailors on leave doesn't hold up storywise, but musical numbers still good: Sinatra's "I Fall in Love Too Easily," Kelly's irresistible dance with Jerry the cartoon mouse. ▼●◗

And Baby Makes Three (1949) **84m.** **
D: Henry Levin. Robert Young, Barbara Hale, Robert Hutton, Billie Burke, Melville Cooper. OK comedy has Hale about to marry for second time, only to discover she's pregnant, and she really does want to stay married to Hubby #1 (Young). ◗

. . . And God Created Woman (1956-French) **C-92m.** **½ D: Roger Vadim. Brigitte Bardot, Curt Jurgens, Jean-Louis Trintignant, Christian Marquand, Georges Poujouly, Jean Tissier. Location shooting (at St. Tropez) and famous Bardot figure on display in simple tale of man-teaser finding it hard to resist temptation. Great cast clicks in Brigitte's best-known vehicle. Beware edited prints. Remade (in name only)

by Vadim in the U.S. in 1987. CinemaScope. ▼●◗

And Now Tomorrow (1944) **85m.** **½
D: Irving Pichel. Alan Ladd, Loretta Young, Susan Hayward, Barry Sullivan, Beulah Bondi, Cecil Kellaway. Poor doctor Ladd falls in love with deaf socialite patient Young in this Rachel Field romance; sticky going at times. Director Pichel appears as a cashier.

And One Was Beautiful (1940) **70m.** **½
D: Robert B. Sinclair. Robert Cummings, Laraine Day, Jean Muir, Billie Burke, Ann Morriss, Esther Dale, Charles Waldron. Spunky tomboy Day grows up fast when she becomes enamored of wealthy, irresponsible Cummings, and finds herself neck-deep in intrigue after a terrible accident. Entertaining drama with a showcase role for Day.

And Quiet Flows the Don (1957-Russian) **C-107m.** *** D: Sergei Gerasimov. Ellina Bystritskaya, Pyotr Glebov, Zinaida Kirienko, Danilo Ilchenko. Faithful realization of Mikhail Sholokhov's novel revolving around life of small village family during WW1 and after. Absorbing study of social upheavals caused by revolution and war. Originally a multipart film; only one segment was released in the West. ◗

Andrews' Raiders SEE: **Great Locomotive Chase, The**

Androcles and the Lion (1952) **98m.** ***
D: Chester Erskine. Jean Simmons, Alan Young, Victor Mature, Maurice Evans, Elsa Lanchester, Robert Newton. Shaw's amusing satire of ancient Rome can't be dampened by dull production retelling fable of Christian and lion he befriends. ▼◗

And So They Were Married (1936) **74m.** **½ D: Elliott Nugent. Melvyn Douglas, Mary Astor, Edith Fellows, Dorothy Stickney, Jackie Moran, Donald Meek. Widower and a divorcée meet at a winter resort, but their children do all they can to prevent romance from blossoming. Predictable fare.

And So They Were Married (1944) SEE: **Johnny Doesn't Live Here Any More**

And the Angels Sing (1944) **96m.** **½ D: George Marshall. Dorothy Lamour, Fred MacMurray, Betty Hutton, Diana Lynn, Mimi Chandler, Raymond Walburn, Eddie Foy, Jr., Frank Albertson. Four small-town sisters have a singing act; bandleader MacMurray sells them a line about giving them their big break and complications ensue. Bright, funny musical comedy (written by Norman Panama and Melvin Frank, from a Claude Binyon story) goes on too long, but there's plenty to enjoy. The best song ("It Could Happen to You") is treated almost as a throwaway!

And Then There Were None (1945) **98m.** **** D: René Clair. Barry Fitzgerald, Walter Huston, Louis Hayward, Roland Young, June Duprez, C. Aubrey Smith,

Judith Anderson, Mischa Auer, Richard Haydn. Highly suspenseful Agatha Christie yarn of ten people invited to lonely island where one by one they're murdered. Great script by Dudley Nichols complemented by superb visual ideas. Famous score by M. Castelnuovo-Tedesco. Remade three times as TEN LITTLE INDIANS.▼●◖

Andy Hardy One of the most popular series of all time, the Hardy family first appeared in A FAMILY AFFAIR (1937) with Lionel Barrymore and Mickey Rooney as father and son. In 1938, YOU'RE ONLY YOUNG ONCE began the official series in the town of Carvel, with Rooney as Andy Hardy, typical American teenager, interested in cars and girls, Lewis Stone as Judge James Hardy, a stern but understanding father, Fay Holden as his "swell" mother, Cecilia Parker as Marian, his older sister striving to be a young lady, Sara Haden as Aunt Millie, and Ann Rutherford as Polly, the girlfriend who was often neglected for other prospects but to whom Andy always returned; George B. Seitz directed most entries in the series. Testament to the series' appeal was the special 1942 Oscar "for its achievement in representing the American Way of Life." MGM used the films to springboard young starlets such as Judy Garland, Lana Turner, Esther Williams, Kathryn Grayson, and Donna Reed. The Andy Hardy films do not always wear well; they serve mainly as reminders of an era that is long gone. Indeed, when the cast, except Stone, was reunited, in 1958 for ANDY HARDY COMES HOME, the formula just didn't jell.

ANDY HARDY

A Family Affair (1937)
You're Only Young Once (1938)
Judge Hardy's Children (1938)
Love Finds Andy Hardy (1938)
Out West With the Hardys (1938)
The Hardys Ride High (1939)
Andy Hardy Gets Spring Fever (1939)
Judge Hardy and Son (1939)
Andy Hardy Meets Debutante (1940)
Andy Hardy's Private Secretary (1941)
Life Begins for Andy Hardy (1941)
The Courtship of Andy Hardy (1942)
Andy Hardy's Double Life (1942)
Andy Hardy's Blonde Trouble (1944)
Love Laughs at Andy Hardy (1946)
Andy Hardy Comes Home (1958)

Andy Hardy Comes Home (1958) **80m. ****
D: Howard W. Koch. Mickey Rooney, Patricia Breslin, Fay Holden, Cecilia Parker, Sara Haden, Joey Forman, Jerry Colonna. Andy, now a middle-aged married man with children, returns to Carvel on business and gets involved in local politics. Belated, undistinguished reunion for the Hardy clan, with a conspicuously absent Lewis Stone.

Teddy Rooney, Mickey's son, plays Andy Hardy, Jr. ◖

Andy Hardy Gets Spring Fever (1939) **85m. **½** D: W. S. Van Dyke II. Lewis Stone, Mickey Rooney, Cecilia Parker, Fay Holden, Ann Rutherford, Sara Haden, Helen Gilbert, Terry Kilburn, Sidney Miller. Amusing series entry as Andy falls for his high school drama teacher and writes a play for himself to star in.▼◖

Andy Hardy Meets Debutante (1940) **89m. **½** D: George B. Seitz. Mickey Rooney, Lewis Stone, Fay Holden, Cecilia Parker, Judy Garland, Sara Haden, Ann Rutherford, Tom Neal, Diana Lewis. Heartache and disillusionment result when Andy is smitten by a Manhattan socialite. Garland sings "Alone" and "I'm Nobody's Baby."▼◖

Andy Hardy's Blonde Trouble (1944) **107m. **½** D: George B. Seitz. Mickey Rooney, Lewis Stone, Fay Holden, Sara Haden, Bonita Granville, Jean Porter, Keye Luke, Herbert Marshall. Starting college, Andy has his hands full with precocious twins (Lee and Lyn Wilde). Well-produced but overlong entry. ◖

Andy Hardy's Double Life (1942) **92m. **½** D: George B. Seitz. Mickey Rooney, Lewis Stone, Cecilia Parker, Ann Rutherford, Sara Haden, Esther Williams, William Lundigan, Susan Peters. Andy, finished with high school, turns his attention to girls, including the aquatic charms of Williams (in her film debut). Look for Bobby (Robert) Blake in a small role.▼◖

Andy Hardy's Private Secretary (1941) **101m. **½** D: George B. Seitz. Mickey Rooney, Lewis Stone, Fay Holden, Ian Hunter, Sara Haden, Kathryn Grayson, Todd Karns, Gene Reynolds. As he's about to graduate from high school, Andy gets a swelled head and hires Grayson (who gets to sing Strauss's "Voices of Spring") to be his social secretary. Grayson's film debut.▼◖

Angel (1937) **91m. **** D: Ernst Lubitsch. Marlene Dietrich, Herbert Marshall, Melvyn Douglas, Edward Everett Horton, Laura Hope Crews. Disappointing film about Marlene leaving husband Marshall for vacation, falling in love with Douglas. Not worthy of star trio.▼◖

Angel and the Badman (1947) **100m. ***** D: James Edward Grant. John Wayne, Gail Russell, Harry Carey, Irene Rich, Bruce Cabot. First-rate Western with Russell humanizing gunfighter Wayne; predictable plot is extremely well handled. Remade for TV in 2009. Also shown in computer-colored version. ▼◖

Angel Baby (1961) **97m. ***** D: Paul Wendkos, Hubert Cornfield. George Hamilton, Salome Jens, Mercedes McCambridge, Joan Blondell, Henry Jones, Burt Reynolds. Penetrating exposé of evangelistic circuit plying backwood country; Jens in title role, Hamilton the promoter, McCambridge his shrewish wife—marvelous cameos by Blondell and Jones. Reynolds' film debut. ▼❶

Angel Face (1952) **91m.** **✶✶½ D:** Otto Preminger. Robert Mitchum, Jean Simmons, Herbert Marshall, Mona Freeman, Leon Ames, Barbara O'Neil, Kenneth Tobey, Jim Backus. Slow-building but engrossing film noir provides uncharacteristic role for Simmons as wealthy Marshall's impulsive daughter, who lures Mitchum away from his job as an ambulance driver (and girlfriend Freeman) and into a job as a chauffeur. But as he falls for her, he's initially unaware that she's nuts and has dark plans for her hated stepmother (O'Neil). Preminger's best movie in this vein after LAURA; its reputation has steadily increased over the decades. ❶

Angel From Texas, An (1940) **69m.** **✶✶½ D:** Ray Enright. Eddie Albert, Wayne Morris, Rosemary Lane, Jane Wyman, Ronald Reagan, Ruth Terry, John Litel. Stage producers Morris and Reagan con innocent Albert into backing their show. Pleasant farce, nicely acted by the stars of BROTHER RAT. Based on George S. Kaufman's *The Butter and Egg Man,* filmed many times under different titles.

Angel in a Taxi (1959-Italian) **95m.** **✶✶½ D:** Antonio Leonviola. Vera Cecova, Vittorio De Sica, Marietto, Gabriele Ferzetti, Roberto Risso. Marietto is the whole show in this cute if predictable comedy-fantasy of a six-year-old orphan who sees a photo of pretty ballerina Cecova—and decides that she's his mother. De Sica appears in three small but important roles. ▼❶

Angel on My Shoulder (1946) **101m.** **✶✶✶ D:** Archie Mayo. Paul Muni, Anne Baxter, Claude Rains, George Cleveland, Onslow Stevens. Entertaining fantasy of murdered convict Muni sent to earth by Devil as respected judge, and his efforts to outwit Satan while still in mortal form. Remade for TV in 1980 with Peter Strauss and Richard Kiley. ▼❶

Angel on the Amazon (1948) **86m.** **✶½ D:** John H. Auer. George Brent, Vera Ralston, Constance Bennett, Brian Aherne, Fortunio Bonanova, Alfonso Bedoya, Gus Schilling, Walter Reed. Ludicrous "romance" with Vera as a mystery woman from the Brazilian jungle who sweeps pilot Brent off his feet after she rescues him and his passengers following a plane crash.

Angels' Alley (1948) **67m.** **✶✶ D:** William Beaudine. Leo Gorcey, Huntz Hall, Gabriel Dell, Billy Benedict, David Gorcey, Frankie Darro, Nestor Paiva, Rosemary La Planche, Bennie Bartlett. Slip's ex-con cousin (Darro) comes to visit and gets the Bowery Boys into predictable scrapes with the law. ❶

Angels in Disguise (1949) **63m.** **✶✶ D:** Jean Yarbrough. Leo Gorcey, Huntz Hall, Billy Benedict, David Gorcey, Gabriel Dell, Bennie Bartlett, Mickey Knox, Jean Dean, Bernard Gorcey. The Bowery Boys go undercover to help catch some Runyonesque gangsters. ❶

Angels in the Outfield (1951) **102m.** **✶✶✶ D:** Clarence Brown. Paul Douglas, Janet Leigh, Keenan Wynn, Donna Corcoran, Spring Byington, Ellen Corby, Lewis Stone, Bruce Bennett; voice of James Whitmore. Cute comedy-fantasy with Douglas ideally cast as the Pittsburgh Pirates' hot-tempered, foul-mouthed manager, whose hard-luck team goes on a winning streak thanks to some heavenly intervention. Amusing cameos from the worlds of baseball and show business. Remade in 1994. ▼❶

Angels of Darkness (1953-Italian) **84m.** **✶✶ D:** Giuseppe Amato. Linda Darnell, Anthony Quinn, Valentina Cortese, Lea Padovani. Aimless account of life and love among unhappy inhabitants of Rome; a waste of stars' abilities.

Angels One Five (1954-British) **98m.** **✶✶ D:** George More O'Ferrall. Jack Hawkins, Michael Denison, Dulcie Gray, John Gregson. Grounded for accidental plane mishap, British war pilot rebels against officers and friends, seeking to fly again. ▼❶

Angels Over Broadway (1940) **80m.** **✶✶½ D:** Ben Hecht, Lee Garmes. Douglas Fairbanks, Jr., Rita Hayworth, Thomas Mitchell, John Qualen, George Watts. Mordant, ahead-of-its-time black comedy in which hustler Fairbanks decides to do "one good deed"—rescuing suicidal embezzler Qualen—aided by chorus girl Hayworth and boozy Mitchell (who spouts reams of sardonic dialogue in a bravura performance). Hecht buffs will undoubtedly rate this higher, but despite impeccable production, it's just too offbeat (and pleased with itself about it) for most viewers. ▼❶

Angel Street SEE: **Gaslight** (1940)

Angels Wash Their Faces, The (1939) **84m.** **✶✶½ D:** Ray Enright. Ann Sheridan, Dead End Kids, Frankie Thomas, Bonita Granville, Ronald Reagan, Margaret Hamilton, Marjorie Main, Eduardo Ciannelli. Protective sister Sheridan tries to clear brother Thomas' police record, but he joins Dead End Kids for more trouble. OK juvenile delinquent drama, sequel to ANGELS WITH DIRTY FACES. ❶

Angels With Dirty Faces (1938) **97m.** **✶✶✶½ D:** Michael Curtiz. James Cagney, Pat O'Brien, Humphrey Bogart, Ann Sheridan, George Bancroft, Billy Halop, Leo Gorcey, Huntz Hall, Gabe Dell, Bobby Jordan, Bernard Punsley. Superior cast in archetypal tale of two playmates; one (Cagney) becomes a gangster, the other (O'Brien) a priest. The Dead End Kids idolize Cagney, much to O'Brien's chagrin. Rowland Brown's story was scripted by John Wexley and Warren Duff. Quintessential Warner

[21]

Bros. melodrama, a favorite of parodists for decades. Followed by THE ANGELS WASH THEIR FACES. Also shown in computer-colored version. ▼◑❙

Angel Who Pawned Her Harp, The (1954-British) **76m. ✱✱** D: Alan Bromly. Felix Aylmer, Diane Cilento, Jerry Desmonde, Joe Linnane, Alfie Bass, David Kossoff, Sheila Sweet. Cilento, in her film debut, stars as an angel who visits earth and becomes involved in various people's lives. Slight, forgettable fare. ❙

Angel Wore Red, The (1960) **99m. ✱✱½** D: Nunnally Johnson. Ava Gardner, Dirk Bogarde, Joseph Cotten, Vittorio De Sica. Sometimes engrossing tale of clergyman who joins the Spanish loyalist cause and his romance with a good-natured entertainer.

Angry Hills, The (1959) **105m. ✱✱½** D: Robert Aldrich. Robert Mitchum, Elisabeth Mueller, Stanley Baker, Gia Scala, Theodore Bikel, Sebastian Cabot. Mitchum shows vim in WW2 actioner as war correspondent plotting escape from Greece with valuable data for Allies.

Angry Red Planet, The (1959) **C-83m. ✱✱** D: Ib Melchior. Gerald Mohr, Nora Hayden, Les Tremayne, Jack Kruschen, Paul Hahn. Martians sic incredible monsters on first Earth expedition to Mars. Lots of wild-eyed effects have given this film cult status. Filmed in odd "Cinemagic" process, which mostly turns everything pink. ▼◑❙

Angry Silence, The (1960-British) **95m. ✱✱✱** D: Guy Green. Richard Attenborough, Pier Angeli, Michael Craig, Bernard Lee, Geoffrey Keen, Oliver Reed. Rewarding, unheralded film about brave stand by a simple British factory worker who refuses to join unofficial strike, the repercussions he and his family endure. Story by Richard Gregson and Michael Craig, screenplay by Bryan Forbes. ❙

Animal Crackers (1930) **98m. ✱✱✱** D: Victor Heerman. Groucho, Harpo, Chico, and Zeppo Marx, Margaret Dumont, Lillian Roth, Louis Sorin, Hal Thompson, Robert Greig. Marx Brothers' second movie, adapted from Broadway success, suffers from staginess and musical comedy plotting, but gives the zany foursome plenty of comic elbow-room. "Story" has to do with stolen painting, but never mind: Groucho performs "Hooray for Captain Spaulding," Chico and Harpo play bridge, Groucho shoots an elephant in his pajamas, etc. ▼◑❙

Animal Farm (1955-British) **C-75m. ✱✱✱** D: John Halas, Joy Batchelor. Good straightforward animated-feature version of George Orwell's political satire. Ending changed from original to make it more upbeat, but trenchant views of government still hold fast. Not a kiddie film. Remade for cable TV in 1999. ▼◑❙

Animal Kingdom, The (1932) **85m. ✱✱✱** D: Edward H. Griffith. Ann Harding, Les-

lie Howard, Myrna Loy, William Gargan, Neil Hamilton, Ilka Chase, Henry Stephenson. Publisher Howard, undergoing a crisis in values, has had a relationship with free-spirited artist Harding but marries manipulative, middle-class Loy. Sophisticated entertainment, still adult by today's standards, adapted from the Philip Barry play. Remade as ONE MORE TOMORROW. ▼❙

Anna (1951-Italian) **95m. ✱✱½** D: Alberto Lattuada. Silvana Mangano, Raf Vallone, Vittorio Gassman, Gaby Morlay. Thoughtful study of confused young woman who enters convent to avoid deciding which man she really loves; fate forces her to decide. Look quick for Sophia Loren.▼

Anna and the King of Siam (1946) **128m. ✱✱✱½** D: John Cromwell. Irene Dunne, Rex Harrison, Linda Darnell, Lee J. Cobb, Gale Sondergaard, Mikhail Rasumny. Sumptuous production chronicling the experiences of a British governess in 19th-century Thailand, and her battle of wits with strong-willed ruler. Based on Margaret Landon's book about real-life Anna Leonowens (renamed Anna L. Owens in the movie). Dunne and Harrison (in his Hollywood debut) are superb; won Oscars for Cinematography (Arthur Miller) and Art Direction/Set Decoration (then known as "Interior Decoration"). Screenplay by Talbot Jennings and Sally Benson. Later musicalized as THE KING AND I; remade as ANNA AND THE KING.▼❙

Annabel Takes a Tour (1938) **67m. ✱✱** D: Lew Landers. Lucille Ball, Jack Oakie, Ruth Donnelly, Bradley Page, Ralph Forbes, Frances Mercer, Donald MacBride. Disappointing follow-up to THE AFFAIRS OF ANNABEL, with actress Ball going on tour with press agent Oakie. Second and last entry in series.▼

Anna Boleyn (1920-German) **118m. ✱✱** D: Ernst Lubitsch. Henny Porten, Emil Jannings, Paul Hartmann, Ludwig Hartau, Aud Egede Nissen, Hilde Müller. Plodding historical drama about Boleyn (Porten), the second wife of England's King Henry VIII (Jannings, whose vivid performance rises above the material). Way-overlong costumer is mainly of historical interest to Lubitsch aficionados. ▼❙

Anna Christie (1930) **90m. ✱✱✱** D: Clarence Brown. Greta Garbo, Charles Bickford, Marie Dressler, Lee Phelps, George Marion. Garbo is effective in her first talkie as girl with shady past finding love with seaman Bickford. Film itself is rather static. From the play by Eugene O'Neill. Beware of 74m. prints. Filmed simultaneously in a German-language version, with Garbo and a different supporting cast. Filmed before in 1923, with Blanche Sweet. ▼◑❙

Anna Christie (1930) **82m. ✱✱✱½** D: Jacques Feyder. Greta Garbo, Hans Junkermann, Salka Steuermann (Viertel), Theo

[22]

Schall, Herman Bing. Garbo always said she preferred this German-language edition of Eugene O'Neill's play to the American version she made at the same time. Filmed in a moody and poetic style, this tale of a prostitute who falls in love with a sailor is treated in a much more frank and adult way than the Hollywood film: grittier and more cinematic (despite being shot on the same sets by the same cameraman, William Daniels), with more natural performances, including that of Garbo's friend Viertel (who later wrote several of her movies) as Marthy. ▶

Anna Karenina (1935) 95m. **** D: Clarence Brown. Greta Garbo, Fredric March, Freddie Bartholomew, Maureen O'Sullivan, May Robson, Basil Rathbone. Tolstoy's tragic love chronicle makes excellent Garbo vehicle, with fine support from March as her lover, Rathbone her husband, and Bartholomew, her adoring son. Filmed before with Garbo as LOVE; remade several times.▼●▶

Anna Karenina (1948-British) 123m. **½ D: Julien Duvivier. Vivien Leigh, Ralph Richardson, Kieron Moore, Sally Ann Howes, Niall MacGinnis, Martita Hunt, Marie Lohr, Michael Gough. Despite its stellar cast, this is a mostly turgid adaptation of the Tolstoy classic about a woman married to stodgy bureaucrat, who falls in love with a dashing Army officer. Duvivier and Jean Anouilh were among the scriptwriters. ▼●▶

Anna Lucasta (1949) 86m. ** D: Irving Rapper. Paulette Goddard, William Bishop, Oscar Homolka, John Ireland, Broderick Crawford, Will Geer, Gale Page, Mary Wickes, Whit Bissell. Sluggish, watered-down version of Philip Yordan's Broadway play (which featured an all-black cast, as does the 1958 remake). Goddard plays the title role, a woman of the Brooklyn streets who was tossed out of her home by her alcoholic father; her oppressive brother-in-law tries to marry her off, in a money-making scheme. Scripted by Yordan (who also produced) and Arthur Laurents.

Anna Lucasta (1958) 97m. ** D: Arnold Laven. Eartha Kitt, Sammy Davis, Jr., Frederick O'Neal, Henry Scott, Rex Ingram, Alvin Childress. Tepid remake of Philip Yordan's play about a prostitute who tries to leave her past behind. Kitt doesn't so much act as pose, but Ingram is excellent as her father.▶

Annapolis Salute (1937) 65m. *½ D: Christy Cabanne. James Ellison, Marsha Hunt, Harry Carey, Van Heflin, Ann Hovey, Arthur Lake. Ho-hum account of rival Navy cadets, with suave Ellison and surly Heflin vying for Hunt, the sister of comically inept Lake.

Annapolis Story, An (1955) C-81m. ** D: Don Siegel. John Derek, Diana Lynn, Kevin McCarthy, Pat Conway. Uninspired reuse of old service-school formula with Derek

and McCarthy undergoing rigid training, both romancing Lynn.▼

Ann Carver's Profession (1933) 71m. **½ D: Edward Buzzell. Fay Wray, Gene Raymond, Claire Dodd, Arthur Pierson, Claude Gillingwater, Frank Albertson, Frank Conroy, Jessie Ralph, Robert Barrat. Law school grad Wray and would-be architect Raymond get married; she agrees to play housewife, until a juicy case lures her into the courtroom. Her career soars while his stalls, leading to marital strife and misunderstandings. Starts out well, with lots of banter, then gets much too soapy and serious. Interesting racial material in this pre-Code film. Screenplay by Robert Riskin, who later married Wray. Remade as THE LADY OBJECTS (1938).

Anne of Green Gables (1934) 79m. *** D: George Nicholls, Jr. Anne Shirley, Tom Brown, O. P. Heggie, Helen Westley, Sara Haden. Utterly charming adaptation of L. M. Montgomery's book (filmed before in 1919) about a spirited orphan with a vivid imagination who endears herself to the older couple who take her in . . . and everyone else around her. Only the conclusion seems hurried and contrived. Anne Shirley took her professional name from the character she played in this film (until then she was known as Dawn O'Day). Followed by ANNE OF WINDY POPLARS. Remade for TV in 1985.▼▶

Anne of the Indies (1951) C-81m. **½ D: Jacques Tourneur. Jean Peters, Louis Jourdan, Debra Paget, Herbert Marshall. Peters isn't always believable as swaggering pirate, but surrounded by professionals and good production, actioner moves along. Built around stock footage from THE BLACK SWAN.

Anne of Windy Poplars (1940) 88m. ** D: Jack Hively. Anne Shirley, James Ellison, Henry Travers, Patric Knowles, Slim Summerville, Elizabeth Patterson, Marcia Mae Jones. Uninspired sequel to ANNE OF GREEN GABLES. Anne has grown up and become a dedicated, kind-hearted schoolteacher, but has to contend with local politics and hypocrisy in the small town where she lives and works. Remade for TV.

Annie Get Your Gun (1950) C-107m. *** D: George Sidney. Betty Hutton, Howard Keel, Louis Calhern, Edward Arnold, Keenan Wynn, Benay Venuta, J. Carrol Naish. Lively filming of Irving Berlin's Wild West show musical about Annie Oakley getting her man—sharpshooter Frank Butler. Songs include "Anything You Can Do," "Doin' What Comes Naturally," "There's No Business Like Show Business."▼▶

Annie Laurie (1927) 97m. *** D: John S. Robertson. Lillian Gish, Norman Kerry, Creighton Hale, Joseph Striker, Hobart Bosworth, Patricia Avery, Russell Simpson, Brandon Hurst, David Torrence. A forbidden romance only fuels the flames of hatred between the warring Macdonald and Campbell clans in Scotland. Gish is quite good in an unusually warm characterization. Film gets better and better as it goes along, climaxed by battle scenes that are forceful and frightening; only a tacked-on ending (in two-color Technicolor) doesn't ring true.

Annie Oakley (1935) **88m.** ******* D: George Stevens. Barbara Stanwyck, Preston Foster, Melvyn Douglas, Pert Kelton, Andy Clyde. Lively biography of female sharpshooter Stanwyck and her on-again off-again romance with fellow performer Foster. Tight direction within episodic scenes gives believable flavor of late 19th-century America. Moroni Olsen plays Buffalo Bill. Also shown in computer-colored version.▼▶

Ann Vickers (1933) **72m.** ****½** D: John Cromwell. Irene Dunne, Walter Huston, Bruce Cabot, Edna May Oliver, Conrad Nagel, Sam Hardy, Mitchell Lewis. Feminist–social worker–prison reformer Dunne has an affair with heel Cabot, eventually finds love with charismatic—and already married—judge Huston. Leads are fine in this cut-down adaptation of the Sinclair Lewis novel. Very pre-Code, but more episodic than any movie has a right to be.▼

Another Dawn (1937) **73m.** ****½** D: William Dieterle. Kay Francis, Errol Flynn, Ian Hunter, Frieda Inescort, Mary Forbes. Francis is torn between devotion to husband Hunter and officer Flynn in well-paced adventure story set at British Army post in African desert.▶

Another Face (1935) **69m.** ****½** D: Christy Cabanne. Brian Donlevy, Wallace Ford, Phyllis Brooks, Erik Rhodes, Molly Lamont, Alan Hale, Hattie McDaniel. Notoriously ugly gangster Donlevy has plastic surgery, heads to Hollywood, and breaks into the movies. Funny premise clicks most of the time and has some real laughs.

Another Language (1933) **77m.** ******* D: Edward H. Griffith. Helen Hayes, Robert Montgomery, Louise Closser Hale, John Beal, Margaret Hamilton, Henry Travers. Vivid, devastating picture of American family life (based on Rose Franken's play), with Hayes as an outsider who marries Montgomery and faces hostility from matriarch Hale and her gossipy offspring.

Another Man's Poison (1951-British) **89m.** ****½** D: Irving Rapper. Bette Davis, Gary Merrill, Emlyn Williams, Anthony Steel, Barbara Murray, Reginald Beckwith. Bette is feisty, man-hungry novelist on isolated Yorkshire farm who won't let her criminal husband, or his crony Merrill, get in her way. Well-paced melodrama can't hide its stage origins, but Davis wrings every drop out of a showy role. Coproduced by Douglas Fairbanks, Jr.▼▶

Another Part of the Forest (1948) **107m.** ******* D: Michael Gordon. Fredric March,

Dan Duryea, Edmond O'Brien, Ann Blyth, Florence Eldridge, John Dall. Lillian Hellman's story predates THE LITTLE FOXES by tracing the Hubbard family's ruthlessness; unpleasant but well-acted movie.

Another Thin Man (1939) **105m.** ******* D: W. S. Van Dyke II. William Powell, Myrna Loy, C. Aubrey Smith, Otto Kruger, Nat Pendleton, Virginia Grey, Tom Neal, Marjorie Main, Ruth Hussey, Sheldon Leonard. Murder strikes at a Long Island estate and the screen's favorite lush-detective couple (along with Asta and newborn son, Nick, Jr.) move in to solve it, although motherhood has slowed down Nora's drinking a bit. Enjoyable third entry in the series and the last to be based on a Dashiell Hammett story.▼▶

Another Time, Another Place (1958) **98m.** ****½** D: Lewis Allen. Lana Turner, Barry Sullivan, Glynis Johns, Sean Connery. Unconvincing melodrama; Turner suffers nervous breakdown when her lover is killed during WW2. Filmed in England. VistaVision.▼▶

À Nous la Liberté (1931-French) **97m.** ******** D: René Clair. Raymond Cordy, Henri Marchand, Rolla France, Paul Olivier, Jacques Shelly, Andre Michaud. Classic satire on machinery and industrialization centering on the adventures of escaped prisoner Cordy, who becomes owner of a phonograph factory, and his former jail friend (Marchand), now a vagrant. Predates and equals MODERN TIMES in poignancy, with groundbreaking use of music. Arguably, Clair's masterpiece. Clair recut film in 1950 to 83m.▼▶

Anthony Adverse (1936) **141m.** *****½** D: Mervyn LeRoy. Fredric March, Olivia de Havilland, Donald Woods, Anita Louise, Edmund Gwenn, Claude Rains, Louis Hayward, Gale Sondergaard, Akim Tamiroff, Billy Mauch, Ralph Morgan, Henry O'Neill, Scotty Beckett, Luis Alberni. Blockbuster filmization of Hervey Allen bestseller (scripted by Sheridan Gibney) of young man gaining maturity through adventures in various parts of early 19th-century Europe, Cuba, and Africa. Sondergaard won Oscar as Best Supporting Actress in her film debut; rousing musical score by Erich Wolfgang Korngold and Tony Gaudio's cinematography also won. ▼▶

Antigone (1960-Greek) **85m.** ****½** D: George Tzavellas. Irene Papas, Manos Katrakis, Maro Kodou, Nikos Kazis, Ilia Livykou, John Argiris, Byron Pallis. In ancient Thebes, Oedipus' daughter Antigone (Papas) risks royal retribution from King Creon (Katrakis) when she loudly demands a hero's funeral for her slain warrior brother. Literal, by-the-numbers rendering of Sophocles' 442 B.C. tragedy.▼▶

Antoine and Antoinette (1947-French) **89m.** ******* D: Jacques Becker. Roger Pigaut, Claire Maffei, Noël Roquevert, Gaston Modot, Made Siamé, Pierre Trabaud, Jacques Meyran. Charming tale of a struggling young couple who win a lottery jackpot and then lose the ticket. Effervescent mix of romantic comedy and neorealism offers evocative glimpses of postwar Paris.

Any Number Can Play (1949) **112m. ** D: Mervyn LeRoy. Clark Gable, Alexis Smith, Wendell Corey, Audrey Totter, Mary Astor, Lewis Stone, Marjorie Rambeau, Darryl Hickman. Low-key drama of gambling-house owner Gable, estranged from wife Smith and son Hickman. Good character roles breathe life into film. ▼▶

Any Number Can Win (1963-French) **108m. **½** D: Henri Verneuil. Jean Gabin, Alain Delon, Viviane Romance, Carla Marlier. Aging ex-con Gabin enlists ne'er-do-well Delon in a plot to rob the impregnable vault of a plush Riviera casino. Some tense climactic moments. Dyaliscope. ▼▶

Anything Can Happen (1952) **107m. ** D: George Seaton. Jose Ferrer, Kim Hunter, Kurt Kasznar, Eugenie Leontovich, Oscar Beregi, Nick Dennis. Intriguingly awful comedy/propaganda piece with Ferrer as a wide-eyed Russian who emigrates to the U.S. Very much a product of its time; based on a true story.

Anything Goes (1936) **92m. **½** D: Lewis Milestone. Bing Crosby, Ethel Merman, Charlie Ruggles, Ida Lupino, Grace Bradley, Arthur Treacher. Pleasant Crosby shipboard musical retains Merman from the cast of the Broadway show, but scuttles much of the plot and most of Cole Porter's songs (except "You're the Top" and "I Get a Kick Out of You"). Remade (again with Bing) in 1956.

Anything Goes (1956) **C-106m. ** D: Robert Lewis. Bing Crosby, Jeanmaire, Donald O'Connor, Mitzi Gaynor, Phil Harris, Kurt Kasznar. Flat musical involving show business partners Crosby and O'Connor each signing a performer for the leading role in their next show. Sidney Sheldon's script bears little resemblance to the original Broadway show, though some Cole Porter songs remain. Crosby fared better in the 1936 film. VistaVision. ▶

Apache (1954) **C-91m. ** D: Robert Aldrich. Burt Lancaster, Jean Peters, John McIntire, Charles (Bronson) Buchinsky. Pacifist Indian (Lancaster) learns might makes right from U.S. cavalry; turns to fighting one man crusade for his tribe's rights. Overacted and improbable (though based on fact). ▼▶

Apache Country (1952) **62m. ** D: George Archainbaud. Gene Autry, Pat Buttram, Carolina Cotton, Harry Lauter, Mary Scott, Sydney Mason, Francis X. Bushman, Gregg Barton, Iron Eyes Cody, The Cass County Boys. Cavalry scout Autry is assigned to break up an outlaw gang that's staging phony Indian raids. Gene sings Hank Williams' "Cold, Cold Heart" and duets with Cotton, but the story stops dead at several points for authentic Indian dances. ▶

Apache Drums (1951) **C-74m. **½** D: Hugo Fregonese. Stephen McNally, Coleen Gray, Willard Parker, Arthur Shields, James Griffith, Georgia Backus, James Best, Clarence Muse. Zesty little Western in which gambler "Sam Slick" (McNally) is kicked out of the town of Spanish Boot. What will happen to him when he returns to warn its citizens of an impending Apache attack? Indians are mostly, eerily, unseen, identifying this as a Val Lewton production.

Apache Rifles (1964) **C-92m. **½** D: William Witney. Audie Murphy, Michael Dante, Linda Lawson, John Archer, J. Pat O'Malley. Audie is stalwart cavalry captain assigned to corral renegading Apaches. Stock footage and plot mar potentials of actioner. ▼▶

Apache Rose (1947) **C-75m. **½** D: William Witney. Roy Rogers, Dale Evans, Olin Howlin, George Meeker, John Laurenz, Russ Vincent, Minerva Urecal, LeRoy Mason, Donna de Mario (Martell), Terry Frost, Bob Nolan and the Sons of the Pioneers. Roy plays an oil prospector seeking drilling rights to a Spanish land grant, but Meeker and his henchmen are trying to gain control of the same property by running up the owners' gambling debts. First of Roy's more serious late-1940s Westerns directed by Witney (in Trucolor) is pretty good, but the best was yet to come. ▼▶

Apache Territory (1958) **C-75m. ** ½ D: Ray Nazarro. Rory Calhoun, Barbara Bates, John Dehner, Carolyn Craig. Calhoun almost single-handedly routs rampaging Apaches and rescues defenseless Bates. ▶

Apache Warrior (1957) **74m. ** D: Elmo Williams. Keith Larsen, Jim Davis, Michael Carr, Eddie Little, Eugenia Paul. When an Indian leader's brother is killed, Apaches go on the warpath. Nothing new. Regalscope.

Apache War Smoke (1952) **67m. ** ½ D: Harold F. Kress. Gilbert Roland, Robert Horton, Glenda Farrell, Gene Lockhart, Bobby (Robert) Blake. Pat Western involving stagecoach robbery and Indian attack on stage-line station. Good supporting cast wasted. Remake of APACHE TRAIL (1942).

Apache Woman (1955) **C-83m. BOMB** D: Roger Corman. Lloyd Bridges, Joan Taylor, Lance Fuller, Morgan Jones, Paul Birch, Dick Miller, Chester Conklin. Government affairs expert Bridges attempts to ease tension between Apaches and whites, tangles with hellcat half-breed Taylor. Sometimes hilariously bad, but mostly a bore. ▼

Aparajito (1956-Indian) **108m. ***½** D: Satyajit Ray. Pinaki Sen Gupta, Smaran Ghosal, Karuna Banerji, Kanu Banerji, Ramani Sen Gupta. The second of Ray's Apu trilogy is a moving, beautifully filmed story of life and death in a poor Indian family, with the son, Apu (Ghosal), trekking off to college in Calcutta. Aka THE UNVANQUISHED.▼▶

Apartment, The (1960) **125m.** ******** D: Billy Wilder. Jack Lemmon, Shirley Mac-Laine, Fred MacMurray, Ray Walston, Jack Kruschen, Edie Adams, David Lewis, Joan Shawlee. Superb comedy-drama that manages to embrace both sentiment and cynicism. Lemmon attempts to climb corporate ladder by loaning his apartment key to various executives for their extramarital trysts, but it backfires when he falls for his boss' latest girlfriend. Fine performances all around, including MacMurray as an uncharacteristic heel. Oscar winner for Best Picture, Director, Screenplay (Wilder and I.A.L. Diamond), Editing (Daniel Mandell), Art Direction–Set Decoration (Alexander Trauner, Edward G. Boyle). Later a Broadway musical, *Promises, Promises*. Panavision.▼▶

Apartment for Peggy (1948) **C-99m.** ******* D: George Seaton. Jeanne Crain, William Holden, Edmund Gwenn, Gene Lockhart. Breezy story of newlyweds trying to live on college campus; old pros Gwenn and Lockhart steal film from young lovers.▶

Ape, The (1940) **62m.** ****** D: William Nigh. Boris Karloff, Maris Wrixon, Gertrude W. Hoffman, Henry Hall. Low-budget shocker with mad small-town doctor Karloff donning pelt of slain circus ape so he can kill his neighbors for their spinal fluid. Based on play of the same name, filmed before as HOUSE OF MYSTERY (1934).▼▶

Ape Man, The (1943) **64m.** ****** D: William Beaudine. Bela Lugosi, Louise Currie, Wallace Ford, Henry Hall, Minerva Urecal. Minor horror effort with Lugosi and cast overacting in story of scientist becoming part ape, embarking on murder spree (accompanied by an ape). Followed by nonsequel RETURN OF THE APE MAN.▼▶

Apology for Murder (1945) **65m.** ****** D: Sam Newfield. Ann Savage, Hugh Beaumont, Russell Hicks, Charles D. Brown, Pierre Watkin, Sarah Padden, Norman Willis. Reporter Beaumont falls for femme fatale Savage and helps bump off her rich, elderly husband; then he's assigned to write a story about the case. Poverty Row rip-off of DOUBLE INDEMNITY is so similar that Paramount sued to get it pulled from theaters. Not too bad in its tawdry, two-bit way, and a prime showcase for noir icon Savage, replete with Stanwyckesque ankle bracelet.

Applause (1929) **78m.** ****½** D: Rouben Mamoulian. Helen Morgan, Joan Peers, Fuller Mellish, Jr., Henry Wadsworth, Dorothy Cumming. Revolutionary early talkie may seem awfully hokey to modern audiences (Morgan plays a fading burlesque queen with a two-timing boyfriend and an innocent young daughter just out of a convent), but Morgan's heart-rending performance and innovative use of camera and sound

by Mamoulian (in his film directing debut) make it a must for buffs.▼▶

Appointment for Love (1941) **89m.** ****½** D: William Seiter. Charles Boyer, Margaret Sullavan, Rita Johnson, Reginald Denny, Ruth Terry, Eugene Pallette. Frothy comedy showcasing delightful stars: husband and wife with careers find happy marriage almost impossible.

Appointment in Berlin (1943) **77m.** ****½** D: Alfred E. Green. George Sanders, Marguerite Chapman, Onslow Stevens, Gale Sondergaard, Alan Napier. Another WW2 intrigue film, better than most, with Sanders joining Nazi radio staff to learn secret plans.▶

Appointment in Honduras (1953) **C-79m.** ****½** D: Jacques Tourneur. Ann Sheridan, Glenn Ford, Zachary Scott, Jack Elam. Idealistic American (Ford) out to save Latin-American country, corrals villainous companions into helping crusade. Sheridan is not focal point, and a pity.▼▶

Appointment in London (1953-British) **96m.** ******* D: Philip Leacock. Dirk Bogarde, Ian Hunter, Dinah Sheridan, William Sylvester, Walter Fitzgerald, Bryan Forbes. Engrossing story of British bomber squadron in WW2 and high-pressured officer Bogarde, who insists on flying dangerous mission in spite of orders to the contrary.

Appointment With a Shadow (1958) **73m.** ****** D: Richard Carlson. George Nader, Joanna Moore, Brian Keith, Virginia Field, Frank De Kova. Former ace reporter swears off alcohol and scoops big story. CinemaScope.

Appointment With Danger (1951) **89m.** ******* D: Lewis Allen. Alan Ladd, Phyllis Calvert, Paul Stewart, Jan Sterling, Jack Webb, Henry (Harry) Morgan. Ladd is a U.S. postal inspector aided by nun Calvert in cracking a case. Forget that part of the story; Webb and Morgan are the *villains* here, and *Dragnet* fans will be extremely amused. Best bit: Ladd "dropping" Webb on a handball court.▶

Appointment With Murder (1948) **67m.** ***½** D: Jack Bernhard. John Calvert, Catherine Craig, Jack Reitzen, Lyle Talbot, Robert Conte. Appointment with boredom is more like it in this quickie *Falcon* mystery centering on international art thieves.

Appointment With Venus SEE: **Island Rescue**

April in Paris (1952) **C-101m.** ****½** D: David Butler. Doris Day, Ray Bolger, Claude Dauphin, Eve Miller, George Givot, Paul Harvey. Diplomatic corps bureaucrat tries to boost Franco-American relations and falls in love with a showgirl mistakenly chosen to appear in the "April in Paris" show he's staging. Mediocre Warner Bros. musical buoyed by the personalities of Day and Bolger—who make an unconvincing romantic couple.▼▶

April Love (1957) **C-97m.** ****½** D: Henry

Levin. Pat Boone, Shirley Jones, Dolores Michaels, Arthur O'Connell, Matt Crowley. Engaging musical with wholesome Boone visiting relatives' Kentucky farm, falling in love with neighbor Jones. Pat had a hit with the title tune. Previously filmed as HOME IN INDIANA. CinemaScope. ▶

April Showers (1948) **94m. **** D: James V. Kern. Jack Carson, Ann Sothern, Robert Alda, S. Z. Sakall, Robert Ellis. Hackneyed backstage vaudeville yarn with Carson-Sothern teaming, splitting, reteaming, etc.

Arabian Nights (1942) **C-86m. **½** D: John Rawlins. Jon Hall, Maria Montez, Sabu, Leif Erickson, Turhan Bey, Billy Gilbert, Shemp Howard, John Qualen, Thomas Gomez. Colorful, corny escapist stuff—beautifully mounted in Technicolor—about a dashing hero, an enslaved Sherazade, and an evil caliph. Shemp also memorable as a retired Sinbad the Sailor. First teaming of Montez, Hall, and Sabu. ▼●

Arch of Triumph (1948) **114m. **½** D: Lewis Milestone. Ingrid Bergman, Charles Boyer, Charles Laughton, Louis Calhern, Ruth Warrick, Roman Bohnen, J. Edward Bromberg, Ruth Nelson, Stephen Bekassy. Sluggish drama of doctor-refugee Boyer becoming involved with Bergman in pre-WW2 Paris. Based on Erich Maria Remarque's novel. William Conrad appears unbilled. Archivally restored to 131m. Remade for British TV in 1984 with Anthony Hopkins and Lesley-Anne Down. ▼

Are Husbands Necessary? (1942) **79m. **** D: Norman Taurog. Ray Milland, Betty Field, Patricia Morison, Eugene Pallette, Cecil Kellaway. And what about this film?

Arena (1953) **C-83m. **½** D: Richard Fleischer. Gig Young, Jean Hagen, Polly Bergen, Henry (Harry) Morgan, Barbara Lawrence, Lee Aaker, Robert Horton, Lee Van Cleef. Colorful if utterly predictable story of rodeo star Young, on the verge of divorce from Bergen, falling under the spell of sexy Lawrence. Morgan is a standout as a onetime star reduced to taking a job as rodeo clown. Action scenes skillfully integrated. Filmed in Tucson, Arizona. Originally in 3-D.

Are Parents People? (1925) **60m. **½** D: Malcolm St. Clair. Betty Bronson, Adolphe Menjou, Florence Vidor, Lawrence Gray. Enjoyable silent with good cast; innocuous story of young Bronson bringing her estranged parents together. ▼●

Are You Listening? (1932) **73m. **** D: Harry Beaumont. William Haines, Madge Evans, Anita Page, Karen Morley, Neil Hamilton, Wallace Ford, Jean Hersholt, Joan Marsh, John Miljan. Dreary tale of radio writer Haines, who loves coworker Evans but can't break away from his harridan of a wife (Morley)—until fate steps in. Subplot involving Evans' naïve kid sister (Marsh) offers some pre-Code fodder. ▶

Are You With It? (1948) **90m. **½** D: Jack

Hively. Donald O'Connor, Olga San Juan, Martha Stewart, Lew Parker. Bright little musical of math-whiz O'Connor joining a carnival.

Argentine Nights (1940) **74m. **½** D: Albert S. Rogell. Ritz Brothers, Andrews Sisters, Constance Moore, George Reeves, Peggy Moran, Anne Nagel. Boisterous musical comedy with the Ritzes fleeing the U.S., hooking up with troupe of entertainers in Argentina. Incoherent plotwise, but diverting.

Arise, My Love (1940) **113m. **½** D: Mitchell Leisen. Claudette Colbert, Ray Milland, Walter Abel, Dennis O'Keefe, Dick Purcell. Reporter Colbert rescues flyer Milland from a Spanish firing squad in the days before WW2 breaks out in Europe. Bright stars make Billy Wilder–Charles Brackett script seem better than it is; Benjamin Glazer and John S. Toldy received Oscars for their original story.

Arizona (1931) **67m. *½** D: George B. Seitz. Laura La Plante, John Wayne, June Clyde, Forrest Stanley, Nina Quartero, Susan Fleming. Despite its title this is not a Western, but one of Wayne's justly forgotten early talkies about a West Point star athlete whose ex-lover (La Plante) marries his guardian and best friend, who is also his commanding officer. Slow, stilted adaptation of an old theatrical warhorse by Augustus Thomas (previously filmed in 1913, and in 1918 with Douglas Fairbanks). ▶

Arizona (1940) **127m. **½** D: Wesley Ruggles. Jean Arthur, William Holden, Warren William, Porter Hall, Paul Harvey. Lively story of determined woman battling corruption and plundering while trying to settle in new Arizona territory. Well done, but seems to go on forever. ▼●▶

Arizona Kid, The (1939) **61m. ***** D: Joseph Kane. Roy Rogers, George "Gabby" Hayes, Sally March, Stuart Hamblen, Dorothy Sebastian, Earl Dwire, David Kerwin. Roy and Gabby track down an outlaw guerrilla leader (Hamblen) in the days of the Civil War. Solid Rogers vehicle captures Civil War atmosphere better than some major Hollywood movies. ▼▶

Arizona Mission SEE: **Gun the Man Down**

Arizona Raiders (1965) **C-88m. **½** D: William Witney. Audie Murphy, Michael Dante, Ben Cooper, Buster Crabbe, Gloria Talbott. Murphy is Confederate army officer heading Arizona rangers after Civil War, battling Quantrill's raiders. Techniscope. ▼▶

Arizona to Broadway (1933) **66m. **** D: James Tinling. James Dunn, Joan Bennett, Herbert Mundin, Sammy Cohen, Theodore von Eltz, J. Carrol Naish. Joan enlists carnival con man Dunn's help in reclaiming money lost to gang of swindlers; predictable tale, remade as JITTERBUGS.

Arizonian, The (1935) **75m. **½** D: Charles Vidor. Richard Dix, Margot Grahame, Preston Foster, Louis Calhern, James Bush, Willie Best, Joseph Sauers (Sawyer),

Ray Mayer, Francis Ford, Etta MacDaniel. Entertaining B-plus Western programmer with marshal Dix teaming with outlaw Foster to rid town of corrupt Calhern. Script by Dudley Nichols.

Arkansas Traveler, The (1938) 85m. ** D: Alfred Santell. Bob Burns, Fay Bainter, Jean Parker, Irvin S. Cobb, John Beal, Lyle Talbot, Dickie Moore, Porter Hall. Burns rambles into small town, keeps the local paper afloat, and plays Cupid. Pleasant entertainment relies on the charm of Bazooka Bob.

Armored Attack SEE: **North Star, The**

Armored Car Robbery (1950) 68m. *** D: Richard Fleischer. Charles McGraw, Adele Jergens, William Talman, Steve Brodie, Douglas Fowley, Don McGuire, Gene Evans. Crackerjack crime drama in which Talman masterminds the title theft; he and his gang are pursued by determined cop McGraw.▼●

Armored Command (1961) 99m. ** D: Byron Haskin. Howard Keel, Tina Louise, Warner Anderson, Burt Reynolds. Bland war film with stars merely going through their paces.▼

Army Mystery SEE: **Criminals Within**

Arnelo Affair, The (1947) 86m. ** D: Arch Oboler. John Hodiak, George Murphy, Frances Gifford, Dean Stockwell, Eve Arden. Neglected wife drawn hypnotically to husband's client finally learns of his involvement in girl's murder.

Around the World (1943) 79m. ** D: Allan Dwan. Kay Kyser and His Band, Mischa Auer, Joan Davis, Marcy McGuire, Wally Brown, Georgia Carroll, Alan Carney, Ish Kabibble, Robert Armstrong, Barbara Hale, Rosemary La Planche. Hokey fare with Kyser and band traveling the globe, putting on shows for soldiers (and, in a silly subplot, battling Nazis).▼●

Around the World in Eighty Days (1956) C-183m. *** D: Michael Anderson. David Niven, Cantinflas, Shirley MacLaine, Robert Newton, Buster Keaton, Jose Greco, John Gielgud, Robert Morley, Marlene Dietrich, all-star cast. Oscar-winning favorite has lost much of its charm over the years, but even so, Mike Todd's version of the Jules Verne tale offers plenty of entertainment, and more than 40 cameo appearances offer plenty of star-gazing for buffs. Great Victor Young score was also an Oscar winner, as was the screenplay (James Poe, John Farrow, S. J. Perelman), cinematography (Lionel Lindon), and editing (Gene Ruggiero, Paul Weatherwax). Wonderful end title sequence by Saul Bass. Includes intermission/entr'acte, exit music; other prints run 167m. and 143m. Remade as a 1989 TV miniseries, and in 2004. Todd-AO.▼●■

Arrest Bulldog Drummond (1939) 57m. **½ D: James Hogan. John Howard, Heather Angel, H. B. Warner, George

Zucco, E. E. Clive, Reginald Denny. Drummond is framed in the murder of a ray-gun inventor and tracks down the real culprits in this zippy entry.▼●

Arrowhead (1953) C-105m. **½ D: Charles Marquis Warren. Charlton Heston, Jack Palance, Katy Jurado, Brian Keith, Milburn Stone. Well-paced account of cavalry scout Heston, who despises Indians, and his response when Apaches return to their reservation and Apache chief Palance arrives on the scene. Watch this, and you will understand why Native Americans have lambasted the manner in which they have been depicted by Hollywood.▼●

Arrow in the Dust (1954) C-80m. ** D: Lesley Selander. Sterling Hayden, Coleen Gray, Keith Larsen, Tom Tully. Deserting horse soldier (Hayden) learns sterling virtues when he assumes identity of dead commanding officer, warding off Indian attack on passing wagon train.●

Arrowsmith (1931) 99m. **½ D: John Ford. Ronald Colman, Helen Hayes, Richard Bennett, A. E. Anson, Claude King, Russell Hopton, Myrna Loy, Beulah Bondi, John Qualen. Seriously flawed and illogical adaptation of Sinclair Lewis' novel about a dedicated young research doctor who spends most of his life facing the temptation of selling out. Worth seeing for some fine performances and stirring moments. Screenplay by Sidney Howard (who fared better with Lewis' *Dodsworth*). Originally 110m.; cut to 101m. for reissue, restored in recent years to 99m.▼●

Arsenal (1928-Russian) 75m. ***½ D: Alexander Dovzhenko. Semyon Svashenko, Amvrosi Buchma, Mykola Nademsky, Dmitri Erdman, Sergei Petrov. Vivid, bone-chilling imagery highlights this powerful account of a 1918 Ukrainian/Bolshevik revolt against antirevolutionary Russians, culminating in the spirited defense of a munitions plant. Packed with symbolism, the film at once glorifies revolutionary action and vividly portrays the violence and human misery resulting from that action.▼●

Arsenal Stadium Mystery, The (1939-British) 85m. *** D: Thorold Dickinson. Leslie Banks, Greta Gynt, Ian MacLean, Liane Linden, Anthony Bushell, Esmond Knight. Who is responsible for the murder of football (soccer) star Bushell—right in the middle of a game? Eccentric, crackerjack Scotland Yard inspector Banks finds out. Neat little whodunit, and very British.▼●

Arsène Lupin (1932) 84m. *** D: Jack Conway. John Barrymore, Lionel Barrymore, Karen Morley, John Miljan, Henry Armetta, Tully Marshall. Ripe detective yarn set in Paris: John is a gentleman, Lionel a detective, Morley a mystery woman. Which one is the title jewel thief? John and Lionel B. make a marvelous team in their first film together.●

[28]

Arsène Lupin Returns (1938) 81m. ★★★ D: George Fitzmaurice. Melvyn Douglas, Virginia Bruce, Warren William, John Halliday, Nat Pendleton, Monty Woolley, E. E. Clive, George Zucco, Vladimir Sokoloff. Douglas takes over John Barrymore's role as the famed Parisian jewel thief. Lupin, now retired as a gentleman farmer, pretends to make a comeback in order to catch a copycat crook. Slick, satisfying comedy-thriller, deftly handled by a fine cast. ▶

Arsenic and Old Lace (1944) 118m. ★★★½ D: Frank Capra. Cary Grant, Priscilla Lane, Raymond Massey, Peter Lorre, Jack Carson, Josephine Hull, Jean Adair, James Gleason, Grant Mitchell, John Alexander, Edward Everett Horton. Hilarious adaptation of Joseph Kesselring's hit play (scripted by the Epstein Brothers) about two seemingly harmless old ladies who poison lonely gentleman callers. Frantic cast is excellent, especially Lorre and Massey as unsuspecting murderers holed up in Brooklyn household. Made in 1941. Hull, Adair, and Alexander repeat their Broadway roles. Also shown in computer-colored version. ▼◑▶

Arson-Inc. (1949) 61m. ★★½ D: William Berke. Robert Lowery, Anne Gwynne, Edward Brophy, Marcia Mae Jones, Douglas Fowley, Maude Eburne, Byron Foulger. L.A. arson squad investigator infiltrates an insurance fraud mob. Rock-solid low-budgeter is hampered by unnecessary comic relief and incessant references to Lowery's good looks. ▶

Artists & Models (1937) 97m. ★★½ D: Raoul Walsh. Jack Benny, Ida Lupino, Judy Canova, Gail Patrick, Richard Arlen, Martha Raye, Connee Boswell, Ethel Clayton. Lupino pretends to be a socialite in flimsy plot with uncharacteristic Benny and songs "Stop You're Breaking My Heart," "Whispers in the Dark." Vintage fun. ▶

Artists and Models (1955) C-109m. ★★★ D: Frank Tashlin. Dean Martin, Jerry Lewis, Shirley MacLaine, Dorothy Malone, Eva Gabor, Anita Ekberg. Cartoonist Martin uses Lewis' far-out dreams as inspiration for his comic strips in this deliciously garish Technicolor outing. VistaVision. ▼◑▶

Artists and Models Abroad (1938) 90m. ★★★ D: Mitchell Leisen. Jack Benny, Joan Bennett, Mary Boland, Charley Grapewin, Yacht Club Boys, Joyce Compton. Breezy, entertaining froth of musical troupe stranded in Paris, perennially saved by conniving boss Benny. Yacht Club Boys sing incredible song, "You're Broke, You Dope."

Art of Love, The (1965) C-99m. ★★ D: Norman Jewison. James Garner, Dick Van Dyke, Elke Sommer, Angie Dickinson, Ethel Merman, Carl Reiner. Ordinary comedy set in France, with a bemused cast headed by Van Dyke as a struggling artist who fakes death to increase the value of his work. Sommer is

his virtuous girl, boisterous Merman a local madam with a yen for singing.

Ashes and Diamonds (1958-Polish) 96m. ★★★½ D: Andrzej Wajda. Zbigniew Cybulski, Ewa Krzyzanowska, Adam Pawlikowski, Bogumil Kobiela, Waclaw Zastrzezynski. Stark, intelligent, perceptive account of the Resistance movement in Poland during the closing days of WW2. Cybulski, the Polish James Dean, came into his own with his portrayal of a young Resistance fighter. The last of Wajda's War trilogy, following A GENERATION and KANAL. ▼◑▶

Ask Any Girl (1959) C-101m. ★★★ D: Charles Walters. David Niven, Shirley MacLaine, Gig Young, Rod Taylor, Jim Backus, Elisabeth Fraser. Effervescent gloss of naive MacLaine coming to N.Y.C., discovering most men have lecherous designs on girls; she wants a husband, however. CinemaScope. ▼

As Long As They're Happy (1957-British) C-76m. ★½ D: J. Lee Thompson. Janette Scott, Jean Carson, Diana Dors, Hugh McDermott, Jack Buchanan. Mini-musical involving daughter of staid British stockholder who falls for visiting song-and-dance man.

Asphalt (1929-German) 93m. ★★★ D: Joe May. Albert Steinrück, Else Heller, Gustav Fröhlich, Betty Amann, Hans Adalbert Schlettow, Hans Albers, Rosa Valetti. A sensuous thief (Amann) attempts to coerce and seduce the proper young policeman (Fröhlich) who nabs her as she steals a diamond from a jewelry store. Atmosphere and interesting characterizations highlight this German Expressionist melodrama, which begins with dazzling images of Berlin. Starts slowly but builds in interest as it goes along; sultry Amann is a memorable presence. ▼▶

Asphalt Jungle, The (1950) 112m. ★★★½ D: John Huston. Sterling Hayden, Louis Calhern, Jean Hagen, James Whitmore, Sam Jaffe, John McIntire, Marc Lawrence, Marilyn Monroe. The plotting of a crime, and the gathering of a gang to pull it off; a taut, realistic film full of fine characterizations (especially Jaffe, and Monroe in a memorable bit). A model of its kind, frequently copied, and remade no less than three times (as THE BADLANDERS, CAIRO, COOL BREEZE). Scripted by Ben Maddow and Huston, from a W. R. Burnett novel. Also shown in computer-colored version. ▼◑▶

Assassin, The (1953-British) SEE: **Venetian Bird**

Assassin, The (1961-Italian) 105m. ★★½ D: Elio Petri. Marcello Mastroianni, Salvo Randone, Micheline Presle, Cristina Gajoni. Engaging study of scoundrel Mastroianni implicated in a murder, broken by the police, proven innocent, with a wry ending.

Assassin of Youth (1937) 80m. ★½ D: Elmer Clifton. Luana Walters, Arthur

Gardner, Dorothy Short, Earl Dwire, Fern Emmett. Another hokey marijuana exposé (this one a notch above the rest), about some fun-loving teens who smoke one too many reefers at one too many reefer parties. An intrepid investigative reporter poses as a soda jerk to expose their decadence. The short film within a film, THE MARIJUANA MENACE, is a hoot.▼❶

Assault of the Rebel Girls SEE: **Cuban Rebel Girls**

Assigned to Danger (1948) **66m.** **½ D: Oscar (Budd) Boetticher. Gene Raymond, Noreen Nash, Robert Bice, Martin Kosleck, Mary Meade, Ralf Harolde, Jack Overman, Gene Evans. Insurance investigator Raymond probes a payroll robbery and tracks the gang to an isolated country lodge, where he is mistaken for a doctor and forced to remove a bullet from the wounded gang leader. Initially intriguing crime drama gets bogged down in static setting and too much talk.

Assignment in Brittany (1943) **96m.** ** D: Jack Conway. Pierre (Jean-Pierre) Aumont, Susan Peters, Richard Whorf, Margaret Wycherly, Signe Hasso, Reginald Owen. Aumont is lookalike for Nazi leader, uses this to his advantage working for French underground; patriotic WW2 melodrama. Aumont's U.S. debut.

Assignment—Paris (1952) **85m.** ** D: Robert Parrish. Dana Andrews, Marta Toren, George Sanders, Audrey Totter. Fitfully entertaining drama of reporter Andrews trying to link together threads of plot between middle European Communist countries against Russia. Filmed in Paris. ❶

Assignment Redhead SEE: **Million Dollar Manhunt**

As the Sea Rages (1960) **74m.** ** D: Horst Haechler. Maria Schell, Cliff Robertson, Cameron Mitchell. Seaman Robertson arrives in Greece planning a sponge-diving business and meets resistance from townfolk and the elements; muddled script.

Astonished Heart, The (1950-British) **92m.** **½ D: Terence Fisher, Anthony Darnborough. Noel Coward, Celia Johnson, Margaret Leighton, Joyce Carey. Drawing-room melodrama about a married psychiatrist who succumbs to the wiles of another woman—an old schoolmate of his wife's—with unhappy results. One of Coward's lesser stories.

Astounding She-Monster, The (1958) **62m.** BOMB D: Ronnie Ashcroft. Robert Clarke, Kenne Duncan, Shirley Kilpatrick, Marilyn Harvey, Jeanne Tatum, Ewing Brown. Awesomely cheap little film about an apparently evil female alien who kills with a touch, interacting with kidnappers and the kidnappees out in the woods. Has developed a kind of perverse fan following. ALIENATOR is a semi-remake.▼❶

As You Desire Me (1932) **71m.** **½ D: George Fitzmaurice. Greta Garbo, Melvyn Douglas, Erich von Stroheim, Hedda Hopper, Owen Moore. OK version of Pirandello play about amnesiac (Garbo) returning to husband she doesn't really remember. Never as compelling as it should be.▼

As You Like It (1936-British) **96m.** *** D: Paul Czinner. Elisabeth Bergner, Laurence Olivier, Sophie Stewart, Henry Ainley, Leon Quartermaine, Felix Aylmer. Olivier is solid (and handsome) as Orlando in his first attempt at the Bard on celluloid; but Bergner's Rosalind is more a matter of taste. Overall, an enjoyable production of this Shakespeare comedy. Kenneth Branagh's 2006 version debuted in the U.S. on cable TV. ▼❶

As Young As You Feel (1951) **77m.** **½ D: Harmon Jones. Monty Woolley, Thelma Ritter, David Wayne, Jean Peters, Constance Bennett, Marilyn Monroe, Allyn Joslyn, Albert Dekker. Printing company employee Woolley is "retired" when he turns 65, and he just won't sit still for it. Amiable satire of corporate bureaucracy, with a first-rate cast, based on a story by Paddy Chayefsky.▼❶

At Gunpoint (1955) **C-81m.** **½ D: Alfred L. Werker. Fred MacMurray, Dorothy Malone, Walter Brennan, Tommy Rettig, Jack Lambert. MacMurray is well suited to role of peace-loving man drawn into gunplay by taunting outlaws. CinemaScope.▼

Athena (1954) **C-96m.** **½ D: Richard Thorpe. Jane Powell, Debbie Reynolds, Edmund Purdom, Vic Damone, Louis Calhern, Evelyn Varden, Ray Collins, Linda Christian, Steve Reeves, Ed Fury. Back Bay lawyer Purdom and singer Damone romance sisters who come from an eccentric family of health and fitness advocates. Ahead of its time in some ways, but a misfire, with songs by Hugh Martin and Ralph Blane (including a gender-switch version of "The Boy Next Door"). ▼❶

Atlantic SEE: **Titanic: Disaster in the Atlantic**

Atlantic Adventure (1935) **68m.** **½ D: Albert S. Rogell. Nancy Carroll, Lloyd Nolan, Harry Langdon, Arthur Hohl, Robert Middlemass, John Wray, E. E. Clive, Dwight Frye. Nolan cracks wise as a hotshot reporter who gets canned and tries to win back his job by catching a killer aboard an ocean liner. Snappy mystery with comic relief provided by Langdon.

Atlantic City (1944) **87m.** **½ D: Ray McCarey. Brad Taylor (Stanley Brown), Constance Moore, Charley Grapewin, Jerry Colonna, Adele Mara, Paul Whiteman & Orchestra, Louis Armstrong & Orchestra, Buck and Bubbles, Belle Baker, Dorothy Dandridge, Joe Frisco. Plethora of good musical numbers compensates for unoriginal plot about promoter who turns the Atlantic City pier into "the playground of America," starting pre-WW1. Taylor, who took his name from this (he was Stanley Brown at

Columbia), and Moore are Republic Pictures' John Payne–Alice Faye counterparts.

Atlantik SEE: **Titanic: Disaster in the Atlantic**

Atlantis, the Lost Continent (1961) C-90m. *½ D: George Pal. Anthony Hall, Joyce Taylor, John Dall, Frank de Kova. Famed sci-fi producer George Pal's worst film is set on the island of Atlantis, in the time of ancient Greece. Heroic young fisherman becomes involved in tedious intrigue "before, finally, the place sinks. Lots of stock footage, poor effects. Occasionally funny—but not on purpose. ▼○)

Atlas (1961) C-80m. ** D: Roger Corman. Michael Forest, Frank Wolff, Barboura Morris, Walter Maslow, Christos Exarchos. Praximedes convinces Olympic champion Atlas to represent him in battle, but Atlas eventually fights for the common folk. Slightly hilarious low-budget nonsense, filmed in Greece. VistaScope. ▼)

Atoll K SEE: **Utopia**

Atom Age Vampire (1960-Italian) 87m. BOMB D: Anton Giulio Majano. Alberto Lupo, Susanne Loret, Sergio Fantoni, Franca Parisi Strahl, Ivo Garrani. Mad professor restores dancer's disfigured face, then kills other women to obtain cells that will maintain her beauty. Hilariously bad; original running time 105m., video version 72m. ▼)

Atomic Brain, The SEE: **Monstrosity**

Atomic City, The (1952) 85m. *** D: Jerry Hopper. Gene Barry, Lydia Clarke, Michael Moore, Nancy Gates, Lee Aaker, Milburn Stone, Bert Freed. Title refers to Los Alamos, New Mexico, home of the Manhattan Project, where the son of a top physicist is kidnapped by spies; the child will be spared only if his father agrees to pass on atomic secrets. Evocative 1950s Cold War thriller builds to a solid climax. ▼)

Atomic Kid, The (1954) 86m. *½ D: Leslie Martinson. Mickey Rooney, Robert Strauss, Elaine Davis, Bill Goodwin. Rooney survives desert atomic blast, discovering he's radioactive. Slight spy comedy. Davis was Mrs. Rooney at the time. Story by Blake Edwards. ▼)

Atomic Man, The (1955-British) 78m. ** D: Ken Hughes. Gene Nelson, Faith Domergue, Joseph Tomelty, Peter Arne. Bland narrative of reporter and girlfriend involved in a mystery in which title character's experiments with radioactive materials have put him a few seconds into the future (allowing him to answer questions before they are asked). Still, this is basically a spy melodrama. Original British title: TIMESLIP. ▼)

Atomic Submarine, The (1959) 72m. ** D: Spencer Bennet. Arthur Franz, Dick Foran, Brett Halsey, Tom Conway, Bob Steele, Victor Varconi, Joi Lansing. Title sub investigates mysterious goings-on in the Arctic Circle. The culprit is an underwater flying saucer

piloted by an alien! Typical Alex Gordon production, boasting lots of familiar character actors, is appealing and atmospheric. Mainly for buffs. ▼○)

Atonement of Gosta Berling, The (1924-Swedish) 91m. *** D: Mauritz Stiller. Lars Hanson, Greta Garbo, Ellen Cederstrom, Mona Martenson, Jenny Hasselquist, Gerda Lundequist. Memorable drama, from the Selma Lagerlof novel, about a defrocked priest (Hanson) and his love for a young married woman (a pleasingly plump Garbo, in the role which brought her to world attention). Stiller was, of course, Garbo's discoverer and mentor. Several longer versions run between 105m. and 165m. Aka GOSTA BERLING'S SAGA, THE SAGA OF GOSTA BERLING, THE LEGEND OF GOSTA BERLING, and THE STORY OF GOSTA BERLING. ▼)

Atragon (1963-Japanese) 96m. ** D: Ishiro Honda. Tadao Takashima, Yoko Fujiyama, Yu Fujiki, Horisho Koizumi. World is threatened by undersea kingdom in this juvenile sci-fi adventure, with enjoyable (if not believable) special effects. Title refers to giant submarine rather than a monster. Tohoscope. ▶

At Sword's Point (1952) C-81m. **½ D: Lewis Allen. Cornel Wilde, Maureen O'Hara, Robert Douglas, Dan O'Herlihy, Alan Hale, Jr., Blanche Yurka. Silly but likable variation on THE THREE MUSKE-TEERS, with Wilde, O'Herlihy, Hale, and O'Hara playing the sons and daughter of the original Musketeers. Energetic cast, vivid Technicolor settings. ▼○)

Attack (1956) 107m. *** D: Robert Aldrich. Jack Palance, Eddie Albert, Lee Marvin, Robert Strauss, Richard Jaeckel, Buddy Ebsen, William Smithers. Reenactment of the Battle of the Bulge, emphasizing a group of American soldiers "led" by cowardly captain Albert; tightly directed, avoids war-movie clichés. ▼○)

Attack of the Crab Monsters (1957) 68m. ** D: Roger Corman. Richard Garland, Pamela Duncan, Russell Johnson, Leslie Bradley, Mel Welles, Ed Nelson. People are trapped on a shrinking island by intelligent, brain-eating giant crabs. Interesting early Corman thriller is hampered by low budget—and some very silly monsters—but Charles B. Griffith's script has many ingenious ideas. ▼)

Attack of the 50 Foot Woman (1958) 66m. BOMB D: Nathan Hertz (Juran). Allison Hayes, William Hudson, Yvette Vickers, Roy Gordon. A harridan with a philandering husband has an alien encounter and grows to mammoth proportions, seeks revenge on hubby. Hilariously awful sci-fi with some of the funniest special effects of all time. Remade for TV in 1993 with Daryl Hannah. ▼○)

Attack of the Giant Leeches (1959) 62m.

*½ D: Bernard L. Kowalski. Ken Clark, Yvette Vickers, Jan Shepard, Michael Emmet, Gene Roth, Bruno Ve Sota. Giant leeches in back waters of a Southern swamp take prisoners and suck their blood. Ludicrous hybrid of white trash and monster genres; screenplay by actor Leo Gordon. Aka THE GIANT LEECHES.▼▶

Attack of the Mayan Mummy (1963) 77m. BOMB D: Jerry Warren, Rafael Portillo. Richard Webb, Nina Knight, John Burton, Steve Conte, George Mitchell, Rosa Arenas, Bruno Vesota. Scientist gets patient to revert to former life and reveal site of ancient tomb. Grade-Z outing, comprised largely of Mexican horror-film footage.

Attack of the Mushroom People SEE: **Matango**

Attack of the Puppet People (1958) 78m. *½ D: Bert I. Gordon. John Agar, John Hoyt, June Kenney, Scott Peters. Low-class shocker about mad dollmaker who shrinks people; good performance by Hoyt, otherwise predictable and amateurish.▼▶

Attack of the Rebel Girls SEE: **Cuban Rebel Girls**

Attention Bandits SEE: **Bandits**

At the Circus (1939) 87m. **½ D: Edward Buzzell. Groucho, Chico and Harpo Marx, Margaret Dumont, Eve Arden, Nat Pendleton, Kenny Baker, Fritz Feld, Florence Rice. Not top-grade Marx Brothers, but some good scenes as they save circus from bankruptcy. Highlight: Groucho singing "Lydia the Tattooed Lady."▼▶

Attila (1954-Italian-French) C-83m. *½ D: Pietro Francisci. Anthony Quinn, Sophia Loren, Henri Vidal, Irene Papas. Inept spectacle with ridiculous script of Attila readying to conquer Rome.▼▶

Attorney for the Defense (1932) 72m. **½ D: Irving Cummings. Edmund Lowe, Evelyn Brent, Constance Cummings, Donald Dillaway, Dorothy Peterson, Bradley Page, Nat Pendleton, Dwight Frye, Clarence Muse. After sending an innocent man to the chair, a heartless D.A. becomes a defense attorney and pays for the dead man's son's education; years later, he has to defend the boy on a murder charge. Fairly absorbing drama despite the convoluted plot.

At War with the Army (1950) 93m. **½ D: Hal Walker. Dean Martin, Jerry Lewis, Polly Bergen, Angela Greene, Mike Kellin. In their first starring feature, Dean and Jerry are in the service, with some funny sequences, including memorable soda machine gag.▼▶

Au Bonheur des Dames (1930-French) 89m. *** D: Julien Duvivier. Dita Parlo, Pierre de Guingand, Armand Bour, Ginette Maddie, Germaine Rouer, Nadia Sibirskaïa. Shy orphan (Parlo) arrives in Paris and moves in with her uncle, whose fabric shop is being devoured by an ever-expanding department store. She becomes a model at the store, where different men with different agendas take interest in her. Updating of an Émile Zola novel is worth a look for its stunning direction and on-location filming at Paris' famed Galeries Lafayette. The sound version of this silent feature no longer exists. Remade in 1943.

▶

Auntie Mame (1958) **C-143m.** ***½ D: Morton DaCosta. Rosalind Russell, Forrest Tucker, Coral Browne, Fred Clark, Roger Smith, Patric Knowles, Peggy Cass, Joanna Barnes, Pippa Scott, Lee Patrick, Willard Waterman, Connie Gilchrist, Robin Hughes, Jan Handzlik. Colorful film version of Patrick Dennis' novel about his eccentric aunt, who believes that "life is a banquet, and most poor suckers are starving to death." Episodic but highly entertaining, sparked by Russell's tour-de-force performance. Betty Comden–Adolph Green script was adapted from the Jerome Lawrence–Robert E. Lee Broadway play. Musicalized as MAME. Technirama. ▼▶

Austerlitz SEE: **Battle of Austerlitz, The**

Autumn Afternoon, An (1962-Japanese) **C-115m.** *** D: Yasujiro Ozu. Chishu Ryu, Shima Iwashita, Shinichiro Mikami, Keiji Sada, Mariko Okada. Contemplative study of loneliness and the fleeting nature of life, about a middle-class widower (Ryu) who dutifully arranges the marriage of his daughter. A series of subplots focus on various characters who are in some way connected to the nuptials. Ozu's final film. ▼▶

Autumn Leaves (1956) 108m. **½ D: Robert Aldrich. Joan Crawford, Cliff Robertson, Vera Miles, Lorne Greene. Middle-aged typist marries younger man (Robertson), only to discover he is mentally disturbed and already married. Stalwart performance by Crawford as troubled woman.▼▶

Avalanche (1946) 70m. *½ D: Irving Allen. Bruce Cabot, Roscoe Karns, Helen Mowery, Veda Ann Borg. Programmer tale of murder and suspense at an isolated ski lodge; shoddy production.

Avenger, The (1960-German) 102m. **½ D: Karl Anton. Ingrid Van Bergen, Heinz Drache, Ina Duscha, Maria Litto. Above-par shocker based on Edgar Wallace tale of bestial villain beheading several people, mailing their severed heads to appropriate recipients.▼▶

Avengers, The (1942) SEE: **Day Will Dawn, The**

Avenging Conscience, The (1914) 84m. *** D: D. W. Griffith. Henry B. Walthall, Spottiswoode Aitken, Blanche Sweet, George Siegmann, Ralph Lewis, Mae Marsh, Robert Harron, George Beranger, Josephine Crowell, Walter Long, Wallace Reid. Complications arise when Walthall is pressured to end his romance with Sweet by his possessive uncle. Still-potent psychological drama, heavily influenced by the writings of Edgar Allan

Poe (several of which are directly referenced on-screen). Full title is THE AVENGING CONSCIENCE: OR, THOU SHALT NOT KILL. ▼▶

Away All Boats (1956) C-114m. **½ D: Joseph Pevney. Jeff Chandler, George Nader, Julie Adams, Lex Barker, Keith Andes, Richard Boone, David Janssen. Strict, aloof captain Chandler must ignite spark of fighting spirit among inexperienced crew aboard WW2 attack transport *Belinda*. Exciting, inspiring story of battle action in Pacific Theater. Look fast for Clint Eastwood as a medical orderly near film's end. VistaVision. ▼▶

Awful Dr. Orlof, The (1962-Spanish-French) 95m. ** D: Jess (Jesus) Franco. Howard Vernon, Conrado Sanmartin, Diana Lorys, Ricardo Valle, Perla Cristal. Medium spooker about deranged surgeon operating on a series of women, trying to find spare parts to revitalize his disfigured daughter. A long, disjointed Orloff series followed. ▼▶

Awful Truth, The (1937) 92m. ***½ D: Leo McCarey. Irene Dunne, Cary Grant, Ralph Bellamy, Cecil Cunningham, Mary Forbes, Alex D'Arcy, Joyce Compton, Molly Lamont. Hilarious screwball comedy; Cary and Irene divorce, she to marry hayseed Bellamy, he to wed aristocratic Lamont. Each does his best to spoil the other's plans. McCarey won an Oscar for his inspired direction. Screenplay by Vina Delmar. Based on a play by Arthur Richman previously filmed in 1925 and 1929; remade in 1953 as the musical LET'S DO IT AGAIN. ▼▶

Babbitt (1934) 74m. ** D: William Keighley. Aline MacMahon, Guy Kibbee, Claire Dodd, Maxine Doyle, Glen Boles, Minor Watson, Minna Gombell, Alan Hale, Hattie McDaniel. Realtor George F. Babbitt manages to get into hot water, personally and professionally at the same time. Sinclair Lewis' landmark book about Midwestern Americans is dumbed down as a vehicle for Kibbee's familiar bombastic-idiot persona, with an artificial happy ending to boot. Filmed before in 1924.

Babe Ruth Story, The (1948) 106m. BOMB D: Roy Del Ruth. William Bendix, Claire Trevor, Charles Bickford, Sam Levene, William Frawley, Mark Koenig, Mel Allen, Harry Wismer, H. V. Kaltenborn. Perfectly dreadful bio of the Sultan of Swat is sugar-coated beyond recognition; the Babe is depicted as an overgrown child whose behavior is constantly misunderstood. Bendix is badly miscast, and the finale is not to be believed. The Babe died one month after film's premiere. ▼▶

Babes in Arms (1939) 96m. **½ D: Busby Berkeley. Mickey Rooney, Judy Garland, Charles Winninger, Guy Kibbee, June Preisser, Douglas McPhail. Rodgers and Hart's musical, minus most of their songs, and one that's left, "Where or When," is trammeled to death. What remains is energetic but standard putting-on-a-show vehicle for Mickey and Judy. Dated fun. Original ending, "My Day," was a production number spoofing Mr. and Mrs. Franklin D. Roosevelt, which was removed for a 1948 reissue and later restored. Also shown in computer-colored version. ▼▶

Babes in Bagdad (1952-U.S.-British-Spanish) C-79m. BOMB D: Edgar G. Ulmer. Paulette Goddard, Gypsy Rose Lee, Richard Ney, John Boles, Sebastian Cabot, Christopher Lee. Embarrassing, hokey costumer made even seedier by miscast veteran performers.

Babes in Toyland (1934) 73m. ***½ D: Gus Meins, Charles R. Rogers. Stan Laurel, Oliver Hardy, Charlotte Henry, Henry Kleinbach (Brandon), Felix Knight, Jean Darling, Johnny Downs, Marie Wilson. L&H version of Victor Herbert operetta looks better all the time, compared to lumbering "family musicals" of recent years. Stan and Ollie are in fine form, and fantasy element of Toyland—especially attack by Bogeymen—is excellent. Video title: MARCH OF THE WOODEN SOLDIERS. Originally released at 79m. Remade in 1961 and for TV in 1986. Also shown in computer-colored version. ▼▶

Babes in Toyland (1961) C-105m. **½ D: Jack Donohue. Ray Bolger, Tommy Sands, Annette Funicello, Henry Calvin, Gene Sheldon, Tommy Kirk, Ed Wynn, Ann Jillian. Colorful but contrived Disneyfication of Victor Herbert operetta has no substance or heart; classic songs, visual gimmicks, clowning of Calvin and Sheldon keep it afloat. Remade for TV in 1986. ▼▶

Babes on Broadway (1941) 118m. **½ D: Busby Berkeley. Mickey Rooney, Judy Garland, Fay Bainter, Virginia Weidler, Richard Quine, Ray McDonald, Donna Reed. Showcase for Mickey and Judy's talents, with duo doing everything from imitations of Carmen Miranda and Bernhardt to minstrel numbers. Standout is Judy's "F.D.R. Jones." Film debut of Margaret O'Brien. Look fast for Ava Gardner in the audience watching the final number. ▼▶

Babes on Swing Street (1944) 69m. **½ D: Edward Lilley. Ann Blyth, Peggy Ryan, Andy Devine, Leon Errol, Anne Gwynne, Kirby Grant, June Preisser, Sidney Miller, Marion Hutton, Freddie Slack and His Orchestra. Young friends have to raise money for music-school tuition; luckily, Devine offers entertainment at his barbershop. Standard Universal B musical with some bright moments: Hutton sings the hit "Take It Easy"; cute "Musical Chairs" number features Ryan and choreographer Louis DaPron. Miller, who plays Corny, also co-wrote some of the film's original songs.

[33]

Babette Goes to War (1959-French) **C-106m.** **½ D: Christian-Jaque. Brigitte Bardot, Jacques Charrier, Francis Blanche, Ronald Howard. Bardot is not in her element playing lighthearted comedy. Flimsy WW2 account of French agent Bardot working for British, being sent back to France to kidnap a Nazi bigwig. CinemaScope.

Baby and the Battleship, The (1956-British) **C-96m.** **½ D: Jay Lewis. John Mills, Richard Attenborough, Andre Morell, Bryan Forbes, Lisa Gastoni, Michael Hordern, Lionel Jeffries, Gordon Jackson. Mildly amusing account of sailor Mills smuggling Italian baby aboard ship and his antics as he tries to keep it hidden from top brass. ▼

Baby Doll (1956) **114m.** ***½ D: Elia Kazan. Karl Malden, Carroll Baker, Eli Wallach, Mildred Dunnock, Lonny Chapman, Rip Torn. Starkly photographed on location in Mississippi, story revolves around a child bride, her witless and blustery husband, and a smarmy business rival bent on using both of them. Condemned by Legion of Decency when released, this Tennessee Williams story, although tame by today's standards, still sizzles. Film debuts of Wallach and Torn. ▼▶

Baby Face (1933) **70m.** **½ D: Alfred E. Green. Barbara Stanwyck, George Brent, Donald Cook, Margaret Lindsay, Douglass Dumbrille, John Wayne. Pre-Code item has Stanwyck bartending at a speakeasy, then literally sleeping her way floor by floor to the top of a N.Y.C. office building. Great first half gives way to sappily moralistic conclusion. Wayne's coat-and-tie bit—as one of the office help used by the heroine—is a hoot. Even harsher version discovered in 2004 runs about 5m. longer. ▼▶

Baby Face Harrington (1935) **61m.** **½ D: Raoul Walsh. Charles Butterworth, Una Merkel, Harvey Stephens, Nat Pendleton, Eugene Pallette. Mild-mannered Butterworth gets mixed up with gangsters in this pleasant comedy vehicle that takes its time getting started.

Baby Face Nelson (1957) **85m.** ** D: Don Siegel. Mickey Rooney, Carolyn Jones, Cedric Hardwicke, Jack Elam, Ted De Corsia. Rooney gives flavorful performance in title role of gun-happy gangster in Prohibition-Depression days; low-budget product, but action-filled.

Baby Take a Bow (1934) **76m.** ** D: Harry Lachman. Shirley Temple, James Dunn, Claire Trevor, Alan Dinehart, Ray Walker. Shirley's first starring vehicle seems one of her weakest today, but helped boost her career nonetheless; in typical little-miss-fixit fashion, she helps her ex-con father beat a bum rap. Also shown in computer-colored version. ▼▶

Baby The Rain Must Fall (1965) **100m.** *** D: Robert Mulligan. Lee Remick, Steve McQueen, Don Murray, Paul Fix, Josephine Hutchinson, Ruth White. Much underrated account of ex-convict McQueen, returning to his wife and daughter, but unable to change his restless ways. Murray is sincere sheriff who tries to help. Screenplay by Horton Foote, from his play *The Traveling Lady*. ▼▶

Bachelor and the Bobby-Soxer, The (1947) **95m.** *** D: Irving Reis. Cary Grant, Myrna Loy, Shirley Temple, Rudy Vallee, Ray Collins, Harry Davenport. Judge Loy orders playboy Grant to wine and dine her sister Temple, so the teenager will forget her infatuation for him. Breezy entertainment earned Sidney Sheldon an Oscar for his original screenplay. Also shown in computer-colored version. ▼▶

Bachelor Apartment (1931) **77m.** **½ D: Lowell Sherman. Lowell Sherman, Irene Dunne, Mae Murray, Claudia Dell, Noel Francis, Bess Flowers. Sophisticated comedy about gay-blade Sherman shuffling his various girls back and forth; ancestor of COME BLOW YOUR HORN, etc. ▼

Bachelor Bait (1934) **74m.** **½ D: George Stevens. Stuart Erwin, Rochelle Hudson, Pert Kelton, "Skeets" Gallagher, Berton Churchill, Grady Sutton. After being fired from his job as a clerk at the marriage bureau, Erwin starts his own successful matchmaking agency and finds himself assailed by gold diggers and a crooked politician . . . but he doesn't even notice that secretary Hudson is in love with him. In his second feature, Stevens demonstrates a deft comic touch and turns a minor trifle into a cute romantic farce. Kelton is hilarious.

Bachelor Father, The (1931) **90m.** **½ D: Robert Z. Leonard. Marion Davies, Ralph Forbes, C. Aubrey Smith, Doris Lloyd, Halliwell Hobbes, Ray Milland. Once dashing bachelor Smith, now old and lonely, wants to know his three grown children. Staid but enjoyable adaptation of Edward Childs Carpenter's stage play. ▶

Bachelor Flat (1962) **C-91m.** ** D: Frank Tashlin. Tuesday Weld, Richard Beymer, Celeste Holm, Terry-Thomas. Weld visits her mother's beach house and finds scientist Thomas at work; she moves in anyway and creates eventual havoc. Thomas has had better material; film's entertainment is all in his lap. CinemaScope. ▶

Bachelor Girls SEE: **Bachelor's Daughters, The**

Bachelor in Paradise (1961) **C-109m.** ** D: Jack Arnold. Bob Hope, Lana Turner, Janis Paige, Jim Hutton, Paula Prentiss, Don Porter, Agnes Moorehead. Hope vehicle about the only bachelor in a community of married couples. Amusing, but not great. Hope has done better; Paige is fun as always. CinemaScope. ▼▶

Bachelor Mother (1939) **81m.** ***½ D: Garson Kanin. Ginger Rogers, David Niven,

Charles Coburn, Frank Albertson, Ernest Truex. Rogers unwittingly becomes guardian for abandoned baby in this delightful comedy by Norman Krasna. Remake of 1935 German film LITTLE MOTHER; remade as BUNDLE OF JOY. Also shown in computer-colored version.▼●▶

Bachelor Party, The (1957) 93m. *** D: Delbert Mann. Don Murray, E. G. Marshall, Jack Warden, Patricia Smith, Carolyn Jones, Larry Blyden, Philip Abbott, Nancy Marchand. Perceptive Paddy Chayefsky drama (originally a TV play) about bachelor party for groom-to-be Abbott, and its emotional effect on other married participants. Jones is exceptional as philosophical nympho. Film debuts of Smith, Blyden, Abbott, and Marchand.▼

Bachelor's Daughters, The (1946) 88m. **½ D: Andrew L. Stone. Claire Trevor, Gail Russell, Ann Dvorak, Adolphe Menjou, Billie Burke, Jane Wyatt, Eugene List, Damian O'Flynn, John Whitney, Russell Hicks. Four Manhattan shopgirls lease a Long Island mansion and enlist Menjou and Burke as temporary parents in an elaborate charade to attract wealthy suitors. Engaging but unremarkable romantic comedy has a far better cast than script. Concert pianist List's only film. Aka BACHELOR GIRLS. ▼

Back at the Front (1952) 87m. **½ D: George Sherman. Tom Ewell, Harvey Lembeck, Mari Blanchard, Richard Long. Followup to UP FRONT, with Bill Mauldin's army goof-offs Willie and Joe scampering around post-WW2 Tokyo. Retitled: WILLIE AND JOE BACK AT THE FRONT.

Back Door to Heaven (1939) 85m. **½ D: William K. Howard. Wallace Ford, Aline MacMahon, Stuart Erwin, Patricia Ellis, Bert Frohman, Van Heflin, George Lewis, Billy (William) Redfield, Iris Adrian, James Lydon. Small-town schoolteacher awaits the arrival of former pupils for a reunion, believing they've all succeeded in life—except for the one boy who went to reform school. The truth is much harsher, however. Ambitious social drama doesn't entirely succeed but has enough originality to make you stick with it to the end. James Lydon is impressive in his screen debut. That's director Howard as the prosecuting attorney in the courtroom scene. ▼▶

Back Door to Hell (1964) 68m. **½ D: Monte Hellman. Jimmie Rodgers, Jack Nicholson, John Hackett, Annabelle Huggins, Conrad Maga. Mildly interesting film about WW2 reconnaissance mission in the Philippines; early collaboration of Nicholson and Hellman, who filmed FLIGHT TO FURY back to back with this.▶

Backfire (1950) 91m. **½ D: Vincent Sherman. Viveca Lindfors, Dane Clark, Virginia Mayo, Edmond O'Brien, Gordon MacRae, Ed Begley, Richard Rober, Sheila Stephens (MacRae). MacRae, just out of a veterans'

hospital, plays detective after learning that his buddy (O'Brien) is wanted for murder. Not-bad mystery-thriller with MacRae in a nonsinging role. ▶

Back From Eternity (1956) 97m. **½ D: John Farrow. Robert Ryan, Anita Ekberg, Rod Steiger, Phyllis Kirk. Moderately engrossing account of victims of plane crash, stranded in South American jungle, and their various reactions to the situation. OK remake of FIVE CAME BACK.▼●▶

Back From the Dead (1957) 79m. BOMB D: Charles Marquis Warren. Peggie Castle, Arthur Franz, Marsha Hunt, Evelyn Scott, James Bell. Castle is earnest as wife possessed by will of husband's dead first spouse, but cliché-ridden production makes everything ridiculous. Regalscope.

Background to Danger (1943) 80m. *** D: Raoul Walsh. George Raft, Brenda Marshall, Sydney Greenstreet, Peter Lorre, Osa Massen, Kurt Katch. Slam-bang WW2 story with Raft swept into Nazi intrigue in Turkey; terrific car chase caps fast-moving tale.▼▶

Back in Circulation (1937) 81m. ** D: Ray Enright. Pat O'Brien, Joan Blondell, Margaret Lindsay, John Litel, Eddie Acuff, Craig Reynolds, George E. Stone, Walter Byron, Ben Welden, Regis Toomey. Formula newspaper yarn has unscrupulous reporter Blondell and conniving editor O'Brien responsible for railroading Lindsay to the death house for poisoning her husband, then scrambling to free her when they learn she's innocent. Watchable, but curiously low on Warner's usual snap, crackle, and pop.

Back in the Saddle (1941) 73m. *** D: Lew Landers. Gene Autry, Smiley Burnette, Mary Lee, Edward Norris, Jacqueline Wells (Julie Bishop), Addison Richards, Arthur Loft. Foreman Autry heads West and deals with a copper mine that is poisoning stock on cattlemen's ranches, while romancing lovely Wells and her sister Lee. Another winner for Gene, with ecological theme, standout badman Richards, and a title tune that became Gene's theme. ▼▶

Backlash (1947) 66m. ** D: Eugene Forde. Jean Rogers, Richard Travis, Larry Blake, John Eldredge, Leonard Strong, Robert Shayne, Louise Currie, Douglas Fowley. OK programmer of man trying to frame his wife for murder he committed. Also shown in computer-colored version.▶

Backlash (1956) C-84m. **½ D: John Sturges. Richard Widmark, Donna Reed, William Campbell, John McIntire, Barton MacLane, Henry (Harry) Morgan, Edward C. Platt. In the aftermath of an Apache ambush, Widmark (who believes his father was in the doomed party) and Reed (whose husband was killed in the massacre) become involved in a serpentine search for the lone survivor and some missing gold. Plotty Western written by Borden Chase.▶

Back Street (1932) 89m. *** D: John M.

Stahl. Irene Dunne, John Boles, George Meeker, ZaSu Pitts, Arlette Duncan, June Clyde, William Bakewell, Doris Lloyd, Jane Darwell. Dunne shines in oft-filmed Fannie Hurst soaper of spirited young woman who becomes the mistress of Boles and must forever remain in the shadows. Dated, to be sure, but still entertaining. Remade in 1941 and 1961.

Back Street (1941) 89m. *** D: Robert Stevenson. Charles Boyer, Margaret Sullavan, Richard Carlson, Frank McHugh, Tim Holt. Fine team of Boyer and Sullavan breathes life into Fannie Hurst perennial soaper of woman whose love for man doesn't die when he marries another. **)**

Back Street (1961) C-107m. **½ D: David Miller. Susan Hayward, John Gavin, Vera Miles, Charles Drake, Virginia Grey, Reginald Gardiner, Natalie Schafer. Lavish, unbelievable third version of Fannie Hurst's story of a woman's love for married man. Doesn't play as well as previous versions but a fashion show for Hayward in Jean Louis designs. Ross Hunter produced. **▼)**

Back to Bataan (1945) 95m. *** D: Edward Dmytryk. John Wayne, Anthony Quinn, Beulah Bondi, Fely Franquelli, Richard Loo, Philip Ahn, Lawrence Tierney. Good, sturdy WW2 action film with officer Wayne leading Filipino guerrillas to victory in the South Pacific. Also shown in computer-colored version. **▼O)**

Back to God's Country (1919-Canadian) 73m. **½ D: David M. Hartford. Nell Shipman, Wheeler Oakman, Wellington Playter, Charles Arling, Roy Laidlaw. Shipman plays a nature and animal lover who happily resides in the Canadian backwoods, where she is loved by one man, lusted after by another, and protected by a Great Dane named Wapi. Atmospheric melodrama offers a pointed story of female and canine empowerment, but it's told in broad strokes, with ludicrous plot coincidences. Partially filmed under harsh conditions in Alberta, Canada. Shipman scripted, based on a story by James Oliver Curwood, which was reworked in 1927 and 1953. **▼)**

Back to God's Country (1953) C-78m. **½ D: Joseph Pevney. Rock Hudson, Marcia Henderson, Steve Cochran, Hugh O'Brian, Chubby Johnson. Sea captain Hudson and wife Henderson face rigors of nature and villainy of Cochran in the Canadian wilds. Competent programmer; from James Oliver Curwood's classic story, filmed before in 1919 and 1927.

Back to the Wall (1959-French) 94m. ** D: Edouard Molinaro. Gerard Oury, Jeanne Moreau, Philippe Nicaud, Claire Maurier, Jean Lefebvre. As the adulterous wife, Moreau spins entertaining web of extortion and murder; satisfactory suspenser. **▼**

Bad and the Beautiful, The (1952) 118m. ***½ D: Vincente Minnelli. Kirk Douglas, Lana Turner, Dick Powell, Gloria Grahame, Barry Sullivan, Walter Pidgeon, Gilbert Roland. Captivating Hollywood story of ambitious producer (Douglas) told via relationships with actress Turner, writer Powell, director Sullivan. Solid, insightful, witty, with Lana's best performance ever. Five Oscars include Supporting Actress (Grahame), Screenplay (Charles Schnee). David Raksin's wonderful score is another asset. Minnelli and Douglas followed this a decade later with TWO WEEKS IN ANOTHER TOWN. Also shown in computer-colored version. **▼O)**

Bad Bascomb (1946) 110m. ** D: S. Sylvan Simon. Wallace Beery, Margaret O'Brien, Marjorie Main, J. Carrol Naish, Marshall Thompson. Overlong Western with fine action scenes, overshadowed by incredibly syrupy ones with Beery and O'Brien.

Bad Blonde (1953-British) 80m. ** D: Reginald Le Borg. Barbara Payton, Tony Wright, Frederick Valk, John Slater, Sidney James. Naive boxer (Wright) is seduced by the sexy young wife (Payton) of his elderly manager and lured into bumping off the rich old man. Drab British imitation of American film noir tries to exploit Payton's then-notorious off-screen reputation but lacks the earnestly sleazy touch of a Hugo Haas. Original British title: THE FLANAGAN BOY. **)**

Bad Boy (1949) 86m. **½ D: Kurt Neumann. Lloyd Nolan, Jane Wyatt, Audie Murphy, James Gleason, Martha Vickers, Stanley Clements, Rhys Williams, James Lydon, Dickie Moore, Selena Royle, Tommy Cook. Slight BOYS TOWN variation in which Murphy, in his first starring role, plays a supposedly incorrigible teen destined to straighten out during his stay at the Variety Clubs Boys Ranch. Also known as THE STORY OF DANNY LESTER. **▼**

Bad Company (1931) 75m. **½ D: Tay Garnett. Helen Twelvetrees, Ricardo Cortez, John Garrick, Paul Hurst, Frank Conroy, Frank McHugh, Kenneth Thomson, Harry Carey. Fair curio with hood Cortez arranging for lawyer underling Garrick to wed naive Twelvetrees, sister of his rival. Deservedly not as famous as the other gangster pictures of its day. Its main curiosity value is the spectacle of Cortez as a crybaby crook with a Napoleon complex. **▼O**

Bad Day at Black Rock (1955) C-81m. ***½ D: John Sturges. Spencer Tracy, Robert Ryan, Anne Francis, Dean Jagger, Walter Brennan, John Ericson, Ernest Borgnine, Lee Marvin. Powerhouse cast in yarn of one-armed man (Tracy) uncovering skeleton in tiny desert town's closet. Borgnine memorable as slimy heavy. Millard Kaufman expertly adapted Howard Breslin's story "Bad Time at Hondo." Excellent use of CinemaScope. **▼O)**

Bad for Each Other (1953) 83m. **½ D:

Irving Rapper. Charlton Heston, Lizabeth Scott, Dianne Foster, Ray Collins, Arthur Franz, Mildred Dunnock, Marjorie Rambeau. Doctor Heston has to choose between the needs of miners in his Pennsylvania home town and big-city bluebloods. Predictable soap opera. ▶

Bad Girl (1931) **90m.** ****½** D: Frank Borzage. James Dunn, Sally Eilers, Minna Gombell, William Pawley, Frank Darien, George Irving, Sarah Padden. Working-stiff Dunn sacrifices his dream of opening a radio shop in order to marry pregnant girlfriend Eilers. Opens on a snappy note, then veers toward soap opera with periodic touches of melancholy—an unusual melange given weight by Borzage's sensitive direction (which earned him an Oscar). Watered-down screenplay by Edwin Burke (who also won an Academy Award) from the novel and play by Viña Delmar. ▶

Bad Girl (1956-British) **100m.** ****** D: Herbert Wilcox. Anna Neagle, Sylvia Syms, Kenneth Haigh, Norman Wooland, Wilfrid Hyde-White, Helen Haye, Julia Lockwood. Widowed mom Neagle becomes distraught when 17-year-old daughter Syms takes up with creep Haigh. Cornball curio which serves as proof that not all bad 1950s movies about teenagers were made in the U.S. Video title: TEENAGE BAD GIRL. Original British title: MY TEENAGE DAUGHTER. ▼▶

Badlanders, The (1958) **C-83m.** ****½** D: Delmer Daves. Alan Ladd, Ernest Borgnine, Katy Jurado, Claire Kelly, Kent Smith, Nehemiah Persoff, Robert Emhardt. Nicely handled reworking of THE ASPHALT JUNGLE, set in 1898 Arizona, with ex-cons Ladd and Borgnine forming bond and becoming involved in gold robbery. CinemaScope. ▼▶

Bad Lands (1939) **70m.** ****½** D: Lew Landers. Noah Beery, Jr., Robert Barrat, Guinn Williams, Douglas Walton, Andy Clyde, Addison Richards, Robert Coote, Paul Hurst. Thinly disguised Western remake of THE LOST PATROL, about a posse stranded in the Arizona wilderness and trapped by Apaches. Painless and forgettable. ▼▶

Badlands of Dakota (1941) **74m.** ****½** D: Alfred E. Green. Robert Stack, Ann Rutherford, Richard Dix, Frances Farmer, Broderick Crawford, Hugh Herbert. Brothers Crawford and Stack fight over Rutherford, while Wild Bill Hickok (Dix) does fighting of another kind.

Badlands of Montana (1957) **75m.** ***½** D: Daniel B. Ullman. Rex Reason, Beverly Garland, Keith Larsen, Jack Kruschen. Unimaginative oater leading up to inevitable climax of former buddies, sheriff and gunslinger, having shoot-out. Regalscope.

Bad Little Angel (1939) **72m.** ****½** D: William Thiele. Virginia Weidler, Gene Reynolds,

Guy Kibbee, Ian Hunter, Elizabeth Patterson, Reginald Owen, Henry Hull, Lois Wilson. Weidler is most appealing as a Bible-reading waif who runs away from an orphanage with her dog (Toto from THE WIZARD OF OZ) and goes to Egypt, New Jersey, where she's befriended by shoeshine boy Reynolds and warms the hearts of everyone in town. Well-made, effective little MGM programmer.

Bad Lord Byron (1951-British) **85m.** ****½** D: David Macdonald. Dennis Price, Joan Greenwood, Mai Zetterling, Sonia Holm. Potentially exciting but static retelling of the life of 19th-century poet and lover, focusing on his many romances. ▼

Bad Man, The (1941) **70m.** ****½** D: Richard Thorpe. Wallace Beery, Lionel Barrymore, Laraine Day, Ronald Reagan, Tom Conway, Henry Travers, Chris-Pin Martin, Chill Wills, Nydia Westman. Slight but amusing modern-day Western with Beery chewing the scenery as a comically murderous Mexican desperado who descends upon Barrymore and Reagan's ranch. Filmed before in 1923 and 1930 and reworked in 1937 (as WEST OF SHANGHAI!). ▶

Bad Man of Brimstone (1938) **90m.** ****** D: J. Walter Ruben. Wallace Beery, Virginia Bruce, Dennis O'Keefe, Joseph Calleia, Lewis Stone, Guy Kibbee, Bruce Cabot, Noah Beery (Sr.), Cliff Edwards. Low-grade Western vehicle is for Beery fans, with star as outlaw who is reformed by family revelation. O'Keefe's debut as a leading man after many years of bit and extra work. ▶

Bad Man of Deadwood (1941) **61m.** ****½** D: Joseph Kane. Roy Rogers, George "Gabby" Hayes, Carol Adams, Henry Brandon, Herbert Rawlinson, Sally Payne, Hal Taliaferro, Ralf Harolde, Jay Novello, Monte Blue. On the lam, Roy joins Gabby's traveling medicine show and becomes involved with a group of honest businessmen who've been driven out of their own town by a so-called Citizen's League led by Harolde (but controlled by a mystery man). Good, intricate, fast-moving script by James R. Webb, who went on to bigger and better things. ▼▶

Badman's Country (1958) **68m.** ****½** D: Fred F. Sears. George Montgomery, Neville Brand, Buster Crabbe, Karin Booth, Gregory Walcott, Malcolm Atterbury, Russell Johnson, Richard Devon, Morris Ankrum. Fictionalized Western history with name-dropping cast of characters. Sheriff Pat Garrett (Montgomery) and Wyatt Earp (Crabbe) join other famous lawmen for a showdown with Butch Cassidy (Brand), the Sundance Kid (Johnson), and other notorious outlaws. Not bad for such a contrivance.

Badman's Territory (1946) **97m.** ******* D: Tim Whelan. Randolph Scott, Ann Richards, George "Gabby" Hayes, Ray Collins, James Warren, Morgan Conway, Virginia Sale, Chief Thundercloud, Lawrence Tierney,

Steve Brodie, Isabel Jewell. Solid Western in which a sheriff (Scott, at his stalwart best) is forced to ride into an outlaws' haven, setting off nonstop fireworks. Rich characterizations, with Hayes fun as the Coyote Kid. Also shown in computer-colored version. Jewell repeated her Belle Starr part in BELLE STARR'S DAUGHTER.▼◗

Bad Men of Missouri (1941) 74m. *** D: Ray Enright. Dennis Morgan, Jane Wyman, Wayne Morris, Arthur Kennedy, Victor Jory, Alan Baxter. Younger brothers, enraged by Southern carpetbaggers, turn to lawless life in fictional Western, with good cast. Morris starred in the semi-remake THE YOUNGER BROTHERS.

Bad Seed, The (1956) 129m. *** D: Mervyn LeRoy. Nancy Kelly, Patty McCormack, Henry Jones, Eileen Heckart, Evelyn Varden, William Hopper. Stagy but spellbinding account of malicious child McCormack whose inherited evil "causes" deaths of several people. Fine performances; Maxwell Anderson's Broadway play was adapted by John Lee Mahin, with McCormack, Jones, and Heckart re-creating their stage roles. The corny "Hollywoodized" postscript is often cut but remains intact on video. Remade for TV in 1985. McCormack later played a bad seed grown up in MOMMY.▼◗

Bad Sister, The (1931) 71m. ** D: Hobart Henley. Conrad Nagel, Sidney Fox, Bette Davis, ZaSu Pitts, Slim Summerville, Charles Winninger, Emma Dunn, Humphrey Bogart, Bert Roach, David Durand. City slicker Bogart seduces small-town girl Fox to swindle her wealthy father in this stilted early-talkie melodrama. Davis, in her film debut, is wasted in the third screen version of Booth Tarkington's *The Flirt*.

Bad Sleep Well, The (1960-Japanese) 150m. *** D: Akira Kurosawa. Toshiro Mifune, Takeshi Kato, Masayuki Mori, Takashi Shimura, Akira Nishimura. Kurosawa effectively captures the spirit of 1940s Warner Bros. crime dramas in this engrossing tale of rising executive Mifune and corruption in the corporate world. Actually, it's a variation on *Hamlet*. Tohoscope.▼◗

Bagdad (1949) C-82m. ** D: Charles Lamont. Maureen O'Hara, Paul Christian, Vincent Price, John Sutton. Costume hijinks with O'Hara fetching if not believable as native chieftain's daughter seeking revenge for father's death in old Turkey.▼

Bahama Passage (1941) **½ D: Edward Griffith. Madeleine Carroll, Sterling Hayden, Flora Robson, Leo G. Carroll, Mary Anderson. Scenery is chief asset of routine tale of lovely Madeleine meeting handsome Sterling in beautiful Bahamas, with much hamming by Carroll and Robson. The stars later married in real life.

Bailiff, The SEE: Sansho the Bailiff
Bailout at 43,000 (1957) 78m. ** D: Francis D. Lyon. John Payne, Karen Steele, Paul Kelly, Richard Eyer, Constance Ford. Dilemma of Air Force pilot Payne whose relief at not having to test new safety device is outweighed by coward-guilt complex. Routine material is not enhanced by flight sequences or romantic relief.▼

Bait (1954) 79m. *½ D: Hugo Haas. Cleo Moore, Hugo Haas, John Agar, Emmett Lynn. A mining-camp ménage à trois. Heavy-handed Haas at his worst, despite intriguing pre-credit prologue with Cedric Hardwicke as the Devil.◗

Baker's Wife, The (1938-French) 124m. ***½ D: Marcel Pagnol. Raimu, Ginette Leclerc, Charles Moulin, Robert Vattier, Robert Brassac, Charpin. Abandoned by his wife for a shepherd, baker Raimu is unable to function; villagers, who love his bread as much as he loves his wife, bring back the wayward woman. Hilarious.▼

Balalaika (1939) 102m. ** D: Reinhold Schunzel. Nelson Eddy, Ilona Massey, Charles Ruggles, Frank Morgan, Lionel Atwill, George Tobias. Plodding operetta of Russian revolution with little to recommend it.▼◗

Balcony, The (1963) 84m. ** D: Joseph Strick. Shelley Winters, Peter Falk, Lee Grant, Ruby Dee, Peter Brocco, Kent Smith, Jeff Corey, Leonard Nimoy. Low-budget, none-too-successful attempt to adapt Jean Genet play to the screen, with Winters as madam who maintains her brothel during a revolution. Grant stands out as Winters' lesbian confidante.▼◗

Ballad of a Soldier (1959-Russian) 89m. *** D: Grigori Chukrai. Vladimir Ivashov, Shanna Prokhorenko, Antonina Maximova, Nikolai Kruchkov. Effectively simple, poetic love story chronicling the plight of Russian soldier who falls in love with country girl while on leave during WW2. Works both as a romantic drama and an allegory about the sadness and stupidity of war.▼◗

Ball of Fire (1941) 111m. ***½ D: Howard Hawks. Gary Cooper, Barbara Stanwyck, Oscar Homolka, Dana Andrews, Dan Duryea, S. Z. Sakall, Richard Haydn, Henry Travers, Tully Marshall, Gene Krupa. Burlesque dancer moves in with eight prissy professors (led by Cooper) to explain "slang" for their new encyclopedia; delightful twist on *Snow White and the Seven Dwarfs* by screenwriters Billy Wilder and Charles Brackett. Remade (by same director) as A SONG IS BORN.▼◗

Bambi (1942) C-69m. **** D: David Hand. Walt Disney's moving and exquisitely detailed animated feature about a deer, and how the phases of its life parallel the cycle of seasons in the forest. An extraordinary achievement, with the memorably endearing character of Thumper stealing every scene he's in. Followed by direct-to-video sequel. ▼◗

Bambole! (1965-Italian) 111m. ** D: Dino

Risi. Luigi Comencini, Franco Rossi, Mauro Bolognini, Virna Lisi, Nino Manfredi, Elke Sommer, Monica Vitti, Gina Lollobrigida, Akim Tamiroff, Jean Sorel. Quartet of stories on Italian life that never sparkles. "The Phone Call," "Treatise on Eugenics," "The Soup," "Monsignor Cupid." Retitled: FOUR KINDS OF LOVE. ▼▐

Bamboo Blonde, The (1946) **68m.** ** D: Anthony Mann. Frances Langford, Ralph Edwards, Russell Wade, Iris Adrian, Richard Martin, Jane Greer, Glenn Vernon, Paul Harvey. Before embarking on his series of stylish film noirs and rugged Westerns, Mann toiled on this piece of musical fluff. Langford plays a nightclub singer who has a brief fling with a B-29 pilot; the crew paints her picture on their plane and she achieves fame as they become the hottest outfit in the Air Corps. ▐

Bamboo Prison, The (1954) **80m.** ** D: Lewis Seiler. Robert Francis, Dianne Foster, Brian Keith, Jerome Courtland, E. G. Marshall, Earle Hyman. Superficial handling of loyal American soldier Francis posing as informer in North Korean P.O.W. camp to outwit enemy. ▐

Banana Peel (1963-French-Italian) **98m.** ** D: Marcel Ophüls. Jeanne Moreau, Jean-Paul Belmondo, Claude Brasseur, Jean-Pierre Marielle, Alain Cuny, Gert Fröbe, Paulette Dubost, Charles Régnier. Lightweight caper film involving jazz musician/conman Belmondo and his revenge-seeking ex-wife (Moreau), who reunite to rip off some shady characters. The actors sleepwalk through the proceedings; an odd credit for Ophüls, who went on to direct Holocaust documentaries. Franscope. ▐

Bandido (1956) **C-92m.** *** D: Richard Fleischer. Robert Mitchum, Zachary Scott, Ursula Thiess, Gilbert Roland, Rodolfo Acosta. Mitchum is gun supplier who tries to play both sides during 1916 Mexican rebellion; constant action, endless cat-and-mouse twists with rival Scott keep this one humming. CinemaScope.

Bandit of Sherwood Forest, The (1946) **C-86m.** **½ D: George Sherman, Henry Levin. Cornel Wilde, Anita Louise, Jill Esmond, Edgar Buchanan. Colorful but standard swashbuckler with Wilde as son of Robin Hood carrying on in faithful tradition with the Merry Men. ▐

Bandit of Zhobe, The (1959-British) **C-80m.** **½ D: John Gilling. Victor Mature, Anthony Newley, Norman Wooland, Anne Aubrey, Walter Gotell, Sean Kelly. Moderate actioner set in 19th-century India with Mature as native chief turned outlaw combatting the British. CinemaScope.

Bandits of Corsica, The (1953) **81m.** ** D: Ray Nazarro. Richard Greene, Paula Raymond, Raymond Burr, Lee Van Cleef. Pat costumer with Greene championing cause of the righteous. ▐

Band of Angels (1957) **C-127m.** **½ D: Raoul Walsh. Clark Gable, Yvonne De Carlo, Sidney Poitier, Efrem Zimbalist, Jr., Patric Knowles. Flat costume epic from Robert Penn Warren's Civil War novel; Gable is Southern gentleman with shady past, in love with high-toned De Carlo who discovers she has Negro ancestors. Poitier is resolute educated slave. ▼▐

Band of Outsiders (1964-French) **97m.** *** D: Jean-Luc Godard. Anna Karina, Sami Frey, Claude Brasseur, Louisa Colpeyn. Karina enlists the aid of two male hoods to swipe her aunt's stash, but as usual the supposed plot is only a jumping-off point for Godard's commentary on Hollywood melodramas and other 20th-century artifacts. Among the more entertaining of the director's output; looks delightfully mellow today. ▼▐

Band Plays On, The (1934) **87m.** ** D: Russell Mack. Robert Young, Stuart Erwin, Leo Carrillo, Betty Furness, Ted Healy, Preston Foster, Russell Hardie. Inconsequential college football yarn about four juvenile delinquents who are sent to a grid-iron coach for counseling. He teaches them about honesty, teamwork, etc., and they grow up to make him proud. MGM production gloss makes it watchable, but it's instantly forgettable.

Band Wagon, The (1953) **C-112m.** **** D: Vincente Minnelli. Fred Astaire, Cyd Charisse, Oscar Levant, Nanette Fabray, Jack Buchanan. Sophisticated backstage musical improves with each viewing. Astaire plays a "washed-up" movie star who tries his luck on Broadway, under the direction of maniacal genius Buchanan. Musical highlights include "Dancing in the Dark," "Shine on Your Shoes," and "That's Entertainment" (all by Howard Dietz and Arthur Schwartz) and Astaire's Mickey Spillane spoof "The Girl Hunt." Written by Betty Comden and Adolph Green, based on the 1931 Broadway musical by Dietz and Schwartz. ▼▐

Bang You're Dead SEE: Game of Danger

Banjo (1947) **67m.** **½ D: Richard Fleischer. Sharyn Moffett, Jacqueline White, Walter Reed, Una O'Connor, Herbert Evans, Louise Beavers. Warm little girl-and-her-dog tale, with young Moffett as a Southern orphan who loses her beloved pet when she has to move to Boston and live with her snooty aunt. Formula stuff, well handled. ▐

Banjo On My Knee (1936) **96m.** *** D: John Cromwell. Barbara Stanwyck, Joel McCrea, Walter Brennan, Buddy Ebsen, Helen Westley, Walter Catlett, Anthony (Tony) Martin, Katherine DeMille, Victor Kilian. Entertaining tale of "land girl" Stanwyck marrying Mississippi River islander McCrea, who's accused of murder on their wedding night. Brennan is tops as McCrea's music-playing father, and Barbara even sings and dances (with Ebsen). ▐

Bank Dick, The (1940) **74m.** **** D: Eddie Cline. W. C. Fields, Cora Witherspoon, Una Merkel, Evelyn Del Rio, Jessie Ralph, Grady Sutton, Franklin Pangborn, Shemp Howard, Russell Hicks, Reed Hadley. Classic of insane humor loosely wound about a no-account who becomes a bank guard; Sutton as nitwit prospective son-in-law, Pangborn as bank examiner match the shenanigans of Fields. Screenplay by "Mahatma Kane Jeeves."▼O▶

Bannerline (1951) **88m. ** D:** Don Weis. Keefe Brasselle, Sally Forrest, Lionel Barrymore, Lewis Stone. Brasselle is optimistic fledgling reporter who sparks civic pride into town fighting corruption; film marred by typecasting and clichéd plotline.

Banshun SEE: **Late Spring**

Barabbas (1961) **C-137m. *** D:** Richard Fleischer. Anthony Quinn, Silvana Mangano, Arthur Kennedy, Jack Palance, Ernest Borgnine, Katy Jurado. Lavish production, coupled with good script (based on Lagerkvist's novel) and generally fine acting by large cast make for engrossing, literate experience. Overly long. Runs 144m. with overture, intermission/entr'acte. Super Technirama 70. ▼▶

Barbados Quest SEE: **Murder on Approval**

Barbarian, The (1933) **82m. ** D:** Sam Wood. Ramon Novarro, Myrna Loy, Reginald Denny, Louise Closser Hale, C. Aubrey Smith, Edward Arnold, Hedda Hopper. Overbaked account of sleazy, superficially charming Arab guide Novarro, who persistently pursues tourist Loy. Set in Egypt; lots of Myrna on display here— including a nude bathing scene. Screenplay by Anita Loos and Elmer Harris. ▶

Barbarian and the Geisha, The (1958) **C-105m. **½ D:** John Huston. John Wayne, Eiko Ando, Sam Jaffe, So Yamamura. Twisting of 19th-century history allows Wayne as Ambassador Townsend Harris to romance Japanese beauty (Ando). Miscasting of Wayne is ludicrous, throwing costumer amuck. CinemaScope.▼▶

Barbarian and the Lady, The SEE: **Rebel Son, The**

Barbarians, The SEE: **Pagans, The**

Barbary Coast (1935) **90m. ***½ D:** Howard Hawks. Miriam Hopkins, Edward G. Robinson, Joel McCrea, Walter Brennan, Frank Craven, Brian Donlevy. Lusty tale of San Francisco in the late 19th century with dance-hall queen Hopkins running head-on into big-shot Robinson. David Niven can be glimpsed as an extra.▼O▶

Barbary Coast Gent (1944) **87m. ** D:** Roy Del Ruth. Wallace Beery, Binnie Barnes, John Carradine, Noah Beery, Sr., Frances Rafferty, Chill Wills, Donald Meek. Typical Beery vehicle, with good supporting cast, about smooth-talking bandit who goes straight.

Barbed Wire (1952) **61m. ** D:** George Archainbaud. Gene Autry, Pat Buttram,

Anne James, William Fawcett, Leonard Penn, Michael Vallon, Clayton Moore, Eddie Parker. Cattle buyer Autry runs into trouble between cattlemen and homesteaders being stirred up by Penn, who is waiting to take advantage of a coming railroad. Standard entry for Gene, with good slugfest between him and Moore. Watch for Stuart Whitman. ▶

Bardelys the Magnificent (1926) **91m. ***½ D:** King Vidor. John Gilbert, Eleanor Boardman, Roy D'Arcy, Karl Dane, George K. Arthur, Arthur Lubin, Lionel Belmore, Emily Fitzroy, Theodore von Eltz. Gilbert is perfectly cast as the title character, a suave swordsman and ladykiller who falls for a fair maiden and tangles with a smarmy villain in the court of Louis XIII. Lively, witty spoof of Douglas Fairbanks swashbucklers is great fun; the love scenes, replete with corny intertitles, are reminiscent of "The Dueling Cavalier" sequence in SINGIN' IN THE RAIN. Impressive visual touches by Vidor and cinematographer William Daniels. Based on a novel by Rafael Sabatini. Restored in 2008, with missing scenes covered by still photos and title cards. ▶

Barefoot Contessa, The (1954) **C-128m. *** D:** Joseph L. Mankiewicz. Humphrey Bogart, Ava Gardner, Edmond O'Brien, Marius Goring, Rossano Brazzi, Valentina Cortesa, Elizabeth Sellars, Warren Stevens. Cynical tale of beautiful Spanish dancer Gardner and how director Bogart makes her a Hollywood star. Mankiewicz's script is full of juicy dialogue, as usual. O'Brien won an Oscar as the press agent. ▼▶

Barefoot Mailman, The (1951) **C-83m. ** D:** Earl McEvoy. Robert Cummings, Terry Moore, Jerome Courtland, Will Geer. Potentially engaging story of a first postal route in Florida bogs down in tale of former con man (Cummings) tempted to fleece citizens of Miami with phony railroad stock; Moore is pert leading lady.

Barkleys of Broadway, The (1949) **C-109m. *** D:** Charles Walters. Fred Astaire, Ginger Rogers, Oscar Levant, Billie Burke, Gale Robbins. Astaire and Rogers reteamed after ten years in this witty Comden-Green script about show biz couple who split, then make up. Songs include "You'd Be Hard to Replace," "They Can't Take That Away from Me." Ginger reading "La Marseillaise" is a definite low point.▼O▶

Barnacle Bill (1941) **98m. ** D:** Richard Thorpe. Wallace Beery, Marjorie Main, Leo Carrillo, Virginia Weidler, Donald Meek, Barton MacLane. Beery and Main support basically run-of-the-mill material as old salt and woman trying to snare him into marriage.

Barnacle Bill (1957) SEE: **All at Sea**

Baroness and the Butler, The (1938) **75m. ** D:** Walter Lang. William Powell, Annabella, Helen Westley, Henry Stephenson,

Joseph Schildkraut, J. Edward Bromberg. Powell leads double life as Annabella's butler and member of Parliament. He's fine as usual but script is rather thin. ◗

Baron Müenchhausen (1943-German) **C-110m. *** D:** Josef von Baky. Hans Albers, Brigitte Horney, Wilhelm Bendow, Leo Slezak, Ferdinand Marian. Lavish, impressive curio which tells of the legendary, free-spirited Baron, his exploits in Russia, Turkey, Venice, and elsewhere, and his quest for beautiful princesses and empresses. While ostensibly an escapist entertainment, the Baron is an heroic German: noble, shrewd, and ever loyal to the Fatherland. Produced on the order of Goebbels, Hitler's Minister of Propaganda and Public Enlightenment, to mark the 25th anniversary of UFA, the German production studio. This would make a fascinating (if overlong) double bill with Terry Gilliam's THE ADVENTURES OF BARON MUNCHAUSEN. ▼◗

Baron of Arizona, The (1950) **96m. **½ D:** Samuel Fuller. Vincent Price, Ellen Drew, Beulah Bondi, Reed Hadley. Price has field day as landgrabbing scoundrel who almost gains control of Arizona in the 19th century. Based on a real-life historical incident. Fuller also scripted. ▼◗

Barretts of Wimpole Street, The (1934) **110m. *** D:** Sidney Franklin. Norma Shearer, Fredric March, Charles Laughton, Maureen O'Sullivan, Katharine Alexander, Una O'Connor, Ian Wolfe. Handsome, well-acted, and most entertaining MGM production of classic romance between Elizabeth Barrett and Robert Browning in 19th-century England. Director Franklin remade this two decades later. Retitled for TV: FORBIDDEN ALLIANCE. ▼◗●

Barretts of Wimpole Street, The (1957-U.S.-British) **C-105m. **½ D:** Sidney Franklin. Jennifer Jones, John Gielgud, Bill Travers, Virginia McKenna. Tame interpretation of the lilting romance between poets Browning and Barrett, with actors bogged down in prettified fluff. Director Franklin fared better with this material in 1934. CinemaScope. ▼●

Barricade (1939) **71m. ** D:** Gregory Ratoff. Alice Faye, Warner Baxter, Charles Winninger, Arthur Treacher, Keye Luke. Faye and Baxter are trapped in Chinese embassy and fall in love; rather tame.

Barricade (1950) **C-75m. ** D:** Peter Godfrey. Dane Clark, Ruth Roman, Raymond Massey, Robert Douglas. Clark pitted against Massey in gold-mining-camp Western lends a spark to usual battle of good vs. evil. Mild rehash of THE SEA WOLF. ◗

Bar Sinister SEE: **It's a Dog's Life**

Bar 20 (1943) **55m. **½ D:** Lesley Selander. William Boyd, Andy Clyde, George Reeves, Dustine Farnum, Victor Jory, Bob (Robert) Mitchum, Betty Blythe. When Wells Fargo stage is held up, Hopalong Cassidy rescues mother and daughter passengers, then helps save their ranch. Supposedly adapted from the same-named 1907 Clarence E. Mulford novel, story is actually an original coauthored by Michael Wilson. Boasts beautiful Lone Pine scenery and strong cast, though Reeves fails to score as Hoppy's newest youthful saddle pal. Only film of Dustine Farnum, daughter of silent Western star Dustin. ▼◗

Bar 20 Justice (1938) **65m. **½ D:** Lesley Selander. William Boyd, George Hayes, Russell Hayden, Gwen Gaze, William Duncan, Pat J. O'Brien, Paul Sutton, Walter Long. Setting off for a vacation, Hopalong Cassidy is recalled to aid the widow of a mine owner who's been killed by a neighbor secretly bent on ore theft. Too much time confined in dark gold mine, but vivid personalities of Bar 20 trio shine through. Adapted from 1912 Clarence E. Mulford novel *Buck Peters, Ranchman*. This O'Brien is not the same-named star of THE FRONT PAGE, et al. ▼◗

Bar 20 Rides Again (1935) **62m. *** D:** Howard Bretherton. William Boyd, Jimmy Ellison, Jean Rouverol, George Hayes, Harry Worth, Frank McGlynn, Jr., Al St. John. When frontier neighbor is victim of cattle rustling, Bar 20 boys combat intellectual villain who has a Napoleonic complex, climaxing in exciting pitched battle. Based on Clarence E. Mulford's 1926 same-named novel. Third film in Hopalong Cassidy series was the first to cast Hayes as sidekick "Windy." Photography of scenic Lone Pine boulder country is exceptional. Music over credits by Chill Wills and His Avalon Boys. ▼◗

Bat, The (1959) **80m. **½ D:** Crane Wilbur. Vincent Price, Agnes Moorehead, Gavin Gordon, John Sutton, Lenita Lane, Elaine Edwards, Darla Hood. Faithful filming of the Mary Roberts Rinehart–Avery Hopwood play, with mystery writer Moorehead renting an eerie mansion for the summer; she and her maid soon are plagued by the title fiend. Filmed before in 1915, 1926 and (as THE BAT WHISPERS) in 1930. ▼◗●

Bataan (1943) **114m. *** D:** Tay Garnett. Robert Taylor, George Murphy, Thomas Mitchell, Lloyd Nolan, Lee Bowman, Robert Walker, Desi Arnaz, Barry Nelson. Realistically made drama of famous WW2 incident on Pacific Island; good combat scenes. Also shown in computer-colored version. ▼◗●

Bathing Beauty (1944) **C-101m. **½ D:** George Sidney. Red Skelton, Esther Williams, Basil Rathbone, Bill Goodwin, Jean Porter, Nana Bryant, Carlos Ramirez, Ethel Smith, Xavier Cugat and His Orchestra, Lina Romay, Harry James and His Music Makers, Helen Forrest, Donald Meek, Margaret Dumont, Janis Paige. Esther's first starring vehicle gives Skelton and musical guest stars the spotlight most of the way, but does have a spectacular aquatic finale. Silly script, with Red a popular songwriter whose marriage to Williams is sabotaged by scheming Rathbone (in a thankless role). ▼○▶

Battle at Apache Pass, The (1952) **C-85m.** **½ D: George Sherman. Jeff Chandler, John Lund, Beverly Tyler, Richard Egan, Hugh O'Brian, Jay Silverheels. Chandler reprises his BROKEN ARROW role as Cochise, who tries to prevent Indian wars but doesn't quite succeed.

Battle at Bloody Beach (1961) **83m.** **½ D: Herbert Coleman. Audie Murphy, Gary Crosby, Dolores Michaels, Alejandro Rey. Sporadically exciting WW2 action with soldier Murphy locating his wife on a Pacific island, involved with partisan cause and its leader. CinemaScope. ▶

Battle Beyond the Sun (1963) **C-75m.** ** D: Thomas Colchart. Edd Perry, Arla Powell, Andy Stewart, Bruce Hunter. Soviet sci-fi film NEBO ZOVYOT (1959) is refashioned into so-so American product by producer Roger Corman; story deals with rival space missions to Mars. The names of the director and actors are all pseudonyms; Francis Ford Coppola, credited as Associate Producer, oversaw the English adaptation. His father, Carmine (billed as "Carmen" Coppola), wrote the music. Aka MONSTERS FROM BEYOND THE SUN. ▼▶

Battle Circus (1953) **90m.** **½ D: Richard Brooks. Humphrey Bogart, June Allyson, Keenan Wynn, Robert Keith, Philip Ahn. OK tale of MASH unit during Korean War is well acted, and occasionally exciting, but hampered by too much emphasis on the romance between surgeon Bogart and nurse Allyson. Surprisingly ordinary, coming from writer-director Brooks. ▼▶

Battle Cry (1955) **C-149m.** *** D: Raoul Walsh. Van Heflin, Aldo Ray, Mona Freeman, Nancy Olson, James Whitmore, Raymond Massey, Tab Hunter, Dorothy Malone, Anne Francis, William Campbell, John Lupton, Fess Parker, Rhys Williams, Allyn (Ann) McLerie. Entertaining version of Leon Uris WW2 Marine novel, with much barracks profanity removed for film, focusing on servicemen in training, wartime romance, and frustrating battle assignments—with Heflin striving to get his men the tough combat action they yearn for. Hunter as wholesome soldier and Malone a love-hungry Navy wife stand out in episodic actioner. Ray gives good performance as rough-hewn gyrene who falls in love with "nice girl" Olson. Film debut of Justus McQueen, who thereafter acted under the name of his character, L.Q. Jones. Musical score by Max Steiner. Screenplay by Uris. CinemaScope. ▼▶

Battle Flame (1959) **78m.** *½ D: R. G. Springsteen. Scott Brady, Elaine Edwards, Robert Blake, Gordon Jones, Wayne Hef-

fley, Richard Harrison. Soldier Brady attempts to rescue five nurses captured by the Communists during the Korean War and romances one of them (Edwards). Undistinguished programmer.

Battleground (1949) **118m.** *** D: William Wellman. Van Johnson, John Hodiak, Ricardo Montalban, George Murphy, Marshall Thompson, Denise Darcel, Don Taylor, Richard Jaeckel, James Whitmore, James Arness, Scotty Beckett. Star-studded replay of Battle of the Bulge: division of American troops, their problems and reactions to war. Robert Pirosh's slick script, which was awarded an Oscar, lacks genuine insight into the characters; Paul C. Vogel also earned a statuette for his cinematography. Also shown in computer-colored version. ▼○▶

Battle Hymn (1957) **C-108m.** *** D: Douglas Sirk. Rock Hudson, Martha Hyer, Anna Kashfi, Dan Duryea, Don DeFore. Hudson gives convincing performance as real-life clergyman Dean Hess who returns to military duty in Korean War to train fighter pilots; expansive production values. CinemaScope. ▼▶

Battle in Outer Space (1959-Japanese) **C-74m.** *½ D: Ishiro Honda. Ryo Ikebe, Kyoko Anzai, Leonard Stanford, Harold Conway. Unexciting sci-fi as Earth prepares for attack from outer space. Plenty of special effects. Tohoscope. ▶

Battle of Algiers, The (1965-Italian-Algerian) **125m.** ***½ D: Gillo Pontecorvo. Yacef Saadi, Jean Martin, Brahim Haggiag, Tommaso Neri, Samia Kerbash. Straightforward drama about revolt against the French by Algerians from 1954–1962. Its impressive pseudo-documentary style helped earn it many awards, and the searing imperialism vs. independence struggle it depicts still resonates today. ▼○▶

Battle of Austerlitz, The (1960-French-Italian-Yugoslavian-Lichtensteiner) **C-123m.** *½ D: Abel Gance. Claudia Cardinale, Martine Carol, Leslie Caron, Vittorio De Sica, Jean Marais, Ettore Manni, Jack Palance, Orson Welles. International cast reenacts the epic of Napoleon's greatest battle in stultifying fashion. Drastic cutting from original 166m. and terrible dubbing doom it. Originally titled AUSTERLITZ. Dyaliscope. ▼▶

Battle of Rogue River (1954) **C-71m.** ** D: William Castle. George Montgomery, Richard Denning, Martha Hyer, John Crawford. Much needed action sequence never comes in lopsided Western of Montgomery negotiating Indian truce as settlers seek statehood for Oregon in 1850s. ▶

Battle of the Bulge (1965) **C-163m.** ** D: Ken Annakin. Henry Fonda, Robert Shaw, Robert Ryan, Telly Savalas, Dana Andrews, George Montgomery, Ty Hardin, Pier Angeli, Charles Bronson. Originally presented in Cinerama, this overinflated war drama about an important event cannot triumph over banal script. Read a good book on the subject instead. Runs 169m. with overture, intermission, exit music. Ultra Panavision 70.▼●〇

Battle of the Coral Sea (1959) **80m. **½** D: Paul Wendkos. Cliff Robertson, Gia Scala, Teru Shimada, Patricia Cutts, Gene Blakely, Gordon Jones. Staunch Robertson is submarine captain on Japanese-held island during WW2, seeking to send vital data to U.S. fleet.〇

Battle of the River Plate, The SEE: **Pursuit of the Graf Spee**

Battle of the Sexes, The (1928) **88m. **** D: D. W. Griffith. Jean Hersholt, Phyllis Haver, Belle Bennett, Sally O'Neil, Don Alvarado, William Bakewell. Griffith attempted to go modern with this stale tale of gold digger Haver and her oily beau (Alvarado), who scheme to filch wealthy, married—and embarrassingly naïve—Hersholt. Haver is inappropriately comical and cute, and the film is, even in its best moments, silly and predictable. Griffith's final silent film (LADY OF THE PAVEMENTS has some dialogue scenes).▼〇

Battle of the Sexes, The (1959-British) **84m. ***** D: Charles Crichton. Peter Sellers, Robert Morley, Constance Cummings, Jameson Clark. Sparkling British comedy with macabre overtones; Sellers is elderly Scotsman contemplating murder. Supporting cast keeps this moving.▼〇

Battle of the Villa Fiorita, The (1965-British) **C-111m. **½** D: Delmer Daves. Maureen O'Hara, Rossano Brazzi, Richard Todd, Phyllis Calvert, Martin Stephens. Unconvincing soaper with O'Hara running off to Italy to carry on with widower Brazzi; predictable interference from each's children. Panavision.

Battle of the V-1 SEE: **Missiles From Hell**

Battle of the Worlds (1961-Italian) **C-84m. *½** D: Anthony Dawson (Antonio Margheriti). Claude Rains, Maya Brent, Bill Carter, Umberto Orsini, Jacqueline Derval. Rains adds some weight to this English-dubbed cheapie about scientists' frantic efforts to stop alien planet from colliding with Earth. Eerie atmosphere also helps a little.▼〇

Battleship Potemkin (1925-Russian) **70m. ****** D: Sergei Eisenstein. Alexander Antonov, Vladimir Barsky, Grigori Alexandrov, Mikhail Goronorov. Landmark film about 1905 Revolution. Unlike many staples of film history classes, this one has the power to grip any audience. Odessa Steps sequence is possibly the most famous movie scene of all time. Aka POTEMKIN. ▼〇

Battle Shock SEE: **Woman's Devotion, A**

Battle Stations (1956) **81m. *½** D: Lewis Seiler. John Lund, William Bendix, Keefe Brasselle, Richard Boone, James Lydon, Claude Akins. Rehash about crew in WW2

Pacific and their preparation for fighting the Japanese.

Battle Stripe SEE: **Men, The**

Battle Taxi (1955) **82m. **** D: Herbert L. Strock. Sterling Hayden, Arthur Franz, Marshall Thompson, Joel Marston, Leo Needham. Ordinary tale of Korean War missions; strictly pedestrian.

Battle Zone (1952) **82m. **** D: Lesley Selander. John Hodiak, Linda Christian, Stephen McNally, Philip Ahn. Hodiak vies with McNally for Christian, with brief time out to fight Commies in static Korean War film.〇

Battling Bellhop SEE: **Kid Galahad** (1937)

Battling Butler (1926) **71m. **½** D: Buster Keaton. Buster Keaton, Sally O'Neil, Snitz Edwards, Francis McDonald, Mary O'Brien, Tom Wilson, Eddie Borden. Pampered young millionaire falls in love with a girl during a camping trip, and then has to pretend he's actually a champion prizefighter. One of Buster's weaker silent features still has its share of funny moments. Based on a stage play. ▼〇

Battling Hoofer SEE: **Something to Sing About**

Bat Whispers, The (1930) **84m. *½** D: Roland West. Chester Morris, Una Merkel, Chance Ward, Richard Tucker, DeWitt Jennings, Maude Eburne, Spencer Charters, William Bakewell, Gustav von Seyffertitz. Excruciatingly archaic "old dark house" thriller about the search for a mysterious killer known as The Bat. Of interest to buffs for its striking visuals, including some eye-popping miniature sets. Filmed in 1915 and 1926 as THE BAT, remade in 1959. Simultaneously filmed in experimental 70mm widescreen process called Magnifilm. ▼〇

Bay of Angels (1963-French) **79m. ***** D: Jacques Demy. Jeanne Moreau, Claude Mann, Paul Guers, Henri Nassiet. Lesser-known but no less rewarding French New Wave drama tells the story of a young man whose chronic gambling leads him into a dangerous affair with a woman he meets in the casino. Their luck at the tables mirrors their own tumultuous relationship. A vividly blonde Moreau is sensational in one of her best, least-seen performances. Z master Costa-Gavras is credited as Assistant to Director. Shot in gorgeous b&w in the South of France; restored for 2002 U.S. reissue. Score by frequent Demy collaborator Michel Legrand is one of his best. CinemaScope.▼〇

Beach Ball (1965) **C-83m. **** D: Lennie Weinrib. Edd Byrnes, Chris Noel, Robert Logan, Gale Gilmore, Aron Kincaid. Different group tries a beach picture, but it's essentially the same. Pretty girls, surfing, Edd in drag, and performances by The Supremes, Four Seasons, Righteous Bros., Hondells, Walker Bros.

Beach Blanket Bingo (1965) **C-98m. ***** D: William Asher. Frankie Avalon, Annette

Funicello, Paul Lynde, Harvey Lembeck, Don Rickles, Linda Evans, Jody McCrea, Marta Kristen, John Ashley, Deborah Walley, Buster Keaton, Bobbi Shaw, Timothy Carey. Fifth BEACH PARTY movie is the best; amid various plot entanglements (parachuting, kidnapped singing idol Evans, mermaid Kristen), Lynde sneers at everybody, Rickles insults everybody, and Lembeck gets to sing before being cut into two halves by Carey's buzzsaw. The ultimate wallow in '60s surfing nostalgia. Sequel: HOW TO STUFF A WILD BIKINI. Panavision. ▼●▶

Beachcomber, The (1938-British) **92m.** *** D: Erich Pommer. Charles Laughton, Elsa Lanchester, Tyrone Guthrie, Robert Newton, Dolly Mollinger. Disheveled bum Laughton, living on island paradise, is reformed by missionary Lanchester. Two stars (married in real life) delightful in filmization of W. Somerset Maugham story originally titled VESSEL OF WRATH. The sole directorial outing of esteemed German producer (and Laughton partner) Pommer. Remade in 1955. ▼

Beachcomber, The (1954-British) **C-82m.** *** D: Muriel Box. Glynis Johns, Robert Newton, Donald Sinden, Michael Hordern, Donald Pleasence. Remake of Somerset Maugham tale of South Sea island bum entangled with strait-laced sister of missionary is still flavorful. ▼

Beach Girls and the Monster, The (1965) **70m.** BOMB D: Jon Hall. Jon Hall, Sue Casey, Arnold Lessing, Elaine DuPont, Walker Edmiston, Read Morgan. Yes, there are girls, a beach, and a (silly-looking) monster, plus some surfing music, talky family problems, and awesomely inept attempts at humor. Crude, badly paced, with awful rear-screen work. Hall also photographed this crude little movie; did he view it as a comeback attempt? If so, a big mistake. A favorite of bad-movie aficionados. Aka MONSTER FROM THE SURF. ▶

Beachhead (1954) **C-89m.** *** D: Stuart Heisler. Tony Curtis, Frank Lovejoy, Mary Murphy, Eduard Franz, Skip Homeier, John Doucette. Tense WW2 drama in which a small group of Marines sets out to locate a French plantation owner, and a critical message, on a Japanese-held island. Filmed in Kauai, Hawaii. ▶

Beach Party (1963) **C-101m.** ** D: William Asher. Frankie Avalon, Annette Funicello, Bob Cummings, Dorothy Malone, Harvey Lembeck, Jody McCrea, John Ashley, Morey Amsterdam, Candy Johnson, Eva Six. Anthropologist Cummings studies teenagers' "wild" behavior, but comes to learn they aren't so bad after all. First in long-running series is typical blend of slapstick and forgettable songs, as well as introduction of Lembeck's dopey Brandobiker takeoff, Eric Von Zipper. Sequel:

MUSCLE BEACH PARTY. Panavision. ▼▶

Beast From Haunted Cave (1960) **64m.** ** D: Monte Hellman. Michael Forest, Sheila Carol, Frank Wolff, Richard Sinatra, Wally Campo. Economically shot (to say the least) by Roger Corman's company on scenic locations near Deadwood, South Dakota, this pits fleeing robbers against a mysterious, spiderlike monster. Charles B. Griffith script has some good dialogue, and Sinatra (Frank's nephew) and Carol showed promise. Monster created and played by actor Chris Robinson. Remake of NAKED PARADISE, with monster added. ▼▶

Beast From 20,000 Fathoms, The (1953) **80m.** **½ D: Eugene Lourie. Paul Christian, (Paul Hubschmid), Paula Raymond, Cecil Kellaway, Kenneth Tobey, Donald Woods, Lee Van Cleef, Ross Elliott. Prehistoric rhedosaurus wreaks havoc when thawed after an atom-bomb blast. Good Ray Harryhausen special effects, especially in amusement park finale. Suggested by the Ray Bradbury short story "The Fog Horn." ▼●▶

Beast of Budapest, The (1958) **72m.** *½ D: Harmon Jones. Gerald Milton, John Hoyt, Greta Thyssen, Michael Mills, John Banner, Robert Blake. Professor clashes with his son over the merits of Communism. Trite family conflict, mostly of interest as an artifact of the 1950s.

Beast of Hollow Mountain, The (1956-Mexican-U.S.) **C-80m.** **½ D: Edward Nassour, Ismael Rodriguez. Guy Madison, Patricia Medina, Eduardo Noriega, Carlos Rivas. Unusual combination of Western and monster-on-the-loose formula works well, with clever ending. From screen story by Willis O'Brien. Filmed in Mexico. CinemaScope. ●▶

Beast of the City, The (1932) **87m.** *** D: Charles Brabin. Walter Huston, Jean Harlow, Wallace Ford, Jean Hersholt, Dorothy Peterson, Tully Marshall, John Miljan, Mickey Rooney. "Instead of the glorification of gangsters, we need the glorification of policemen," reads President Hoover's opening statement, and this film delivers, in W. R. Burnett's solid, surprisingly gritty story, a sort of early DIRTY HARRY with a downbeat ending. Harlow is incredibly sexy as a gang moll. ▶

Beast of Yucca Flats, The (1961) **60m.** BOMB D: Coleman Francis. Douglas Mellor, Tor Johnson, Barbara Francis. Johnson becomes a disfigured monster as a result of exposure to an A-bomb test. One of the worst films ever made, presented as a virtual silent film with voice-over narration. Subplot of a succession of voluptuous women being strangled bears little relation to the main story. ▼▶

Beast with a Million Eyes (1955) **78m.** ** D: David Kramarsky. Paul Birch, Lorna

Thayer, Dona Cole, Leonard Tarver, Dick (Richard) Sargent, Chester Conklin. Imaginative though poorly executed sci-fi melodrama with desert setting; a group of people is forced to confront an alien that can control an unlimited number of animals, hence the title. Early Roger Corman production features Paul Blaisdell's first movie monster.▐

Beast with Five Fingers, The (1946) **88m.** ****½ D:** Robert Florey. Robert Alda, Andrea King, Peter Lorre, Victor Francen, J. Carrol Naish. Intriguing if not entirely successful mood piece about aging pianist and strange doings in his household. Lorre's confrontation with disembodied hand a horror highlight.▼●▐

Beat Generation, The (1959) **95m.** ***½ D:** Charles Haas. Steve Cochran, Mamie Van Doren, Ray Danton, Fay Spain, Louis Armstrong, Maggie Hayes, Jackie Coogan, Ray Anthony, Maxie Rosenbloom, Irish McCalla, Vampira. Exploitation-type story of detective Cochran tracking down insane sexual assaulter; vivid sequences marred by hokey script. Retitled THIS REBEL AGE. CinemaScope.●▐

Beat Girl SEE: **Wild for Kicks**

Beat the Band (1947) **67m.** **** D:** John H. Auer. Frances Langford, Ralph Edwards, Phillip Terry, Gene Krupa and His Band, June Clayworth, Mabel Paige, Donald MacBride. Threadbare B musical about a returning G.I. who finds that his partner squandered their money instead of keeping their band together during his absence. Krupa's "Drum Boogie" is a high spot.▐

Beat the Devil (1954) **89m.** ***** D:** John Huston. Humphrey Bogart, Jennifer Jones, Gina Lollobrigida, Robert Morley, Peter Lorre, Edward Underdown. Huston and Truman Capote concocted this offbeat, very funny satire of MALTESE FALCON-ish movies on location in Italy. Low-key nature of comedy eluded many people in 1954 and it immediately became a cult favorite, which it remains today.▼●▐

Beau Brummell (1924) **128m.** ***** D:** Harry Beaumont. John Barrymore, Mary Astor, Willard Louis, Carmel Myers, Irene Rich, Alec B. Francis. Barrymore has one of his greatest roles in this opulent silent version of the Clyde Fitch play about the rise and fall of a social-climbing 19th-century dandy who befriends the Prince of Wales. Seventeen-year-old Astor plays the beautiful blueblood with whom he has a doomed affair. Remade in 1954.▐

Beau Brummell (1954-U.S.-British) **C-113m.** ****½ D:** Curtis Bernhardt. Stewart Granger, Elizabeth Taylor, Peter Ustinov, Robert Morley. Handsome cast in lavish production from Granger's rash of costume epics. Here, he's the famous 19th-century British Casanova-fop (played by John Barrymore in the 1924 version).▼

Beau Geste (1939) **114m.** ***** D:** William Wellman. Gary Cooper, Ray Milland, Robert Preston, Brian Donlevy, Susan Hayward, J. Carrol Naish, Albert Dekker, Broderick Crawford, Donald O'Connor. Scene-for-scene remake of famous 1926 silent film (with Ronald Colman) isn't quite as good but faithfully retells story of three devoted brothers serving in the Foreign Legion and battling sadistic martinet commander (Donlevy). Nothing can top that opening sequence! Based on the novel by P.C. Wren. Remade in 1966.▼●▐

Beau James (1957) **C-105m.** ***** D:** Melville Shavelson. Bob Hope, Vera Miles, Paul Douglas, Alexis Smith, Darren McGavin; narrated by Walter Winchell. Flavorful recreation of the political career of Mayor Jimmy Walker in 1920s N.Y.C., based on Gene Fowler's book. Hope is fine in basically noncomic performance. Guest appearances by Jimmy Durante, Jack Benny, George Jessel, Walter Catlett. VistaVision.

Beauties of the Night (1952-French) **84m.** ****½ D:** René Clair. Gérard Philipe, Martine Carol, Gina Lollobrigida, Magali Vendeuil. Diverting fantasy involving aspiring composer Philipe with penchant for dreams wandering through various eras of history. ▼

Beautiful Blonde From Bashful Bend, The (1949) **C-77m.** ****½ D:** Preston Sturges. Betty Grable, Cesar Romero, Rudy Vallee, Olga San Juan, Porter Hall, Sterling Holloway, El Brendel. Film was major flop in 1949, looks somewhat better today; broad Western farce has Grable a gun-toting saloon girl mistaken for schoolmarm in hick town. Hugh Herbert hilarious as nearsighted doctor.▼●▐

Beautiful Stranger SEE: **Twist of Fate** (1954)

Beauty and the Beast (1946-French) **95m.** ****** D:** Jean Cocteau. Jean Marais, Josette Day, Marcel André. Cocteau's hauntingly beautiful, visually dazzling masterpiece, detailing what happens when, to save her father, Beauty (Day) gives herself to the Beast (Marais). Great fantasy, great filmmaking—beguiling on any level.●▐

Beauty and the Beast (1963) **C-77m.** ***½ D:** Edward L. Cahn. Joyce Taylor, Mark Damon, Eduard Franz, Michael Pate, Merry Anders, Dayton Lummis, Walter Burke. Curse turns handsome prince into werewolf-like beast every night; princess defends him, while a usurper seeks his throne. Colorful but turgid. Makeup by the fabled Jack P. Pierce.▼

Beauty and the Boss (1932) **66m.** ****½ D:** Roy Del Ruth. Warren William, Marian Marsh, David Manners, Charles Butterworth, Frederick Kerr, Mary Doran, Lilian Bond. William is in his element as a philandering banker who becomes too distracted by all his pretty secretaries, so he hires mousy Marsh . . . but she blossoms into an irresistible beauty.

Saucy pre-Code Cinderella story is a notch below William's best but still amusing. Remade in 1934 as THE CHURCH MOUSE. ▶

Beauty for Sale (1933) **87m. *** D: Richard Boleslawsky. Madge Evans, Alice Brady, Otto Kruger, Una Merkel, May Robson, Phillips Holmes, Eddie Nugent, Hedda Hopper, Florine McKinney, Isabel Jewell, Charles Grapewin. Entertaining soaper about girl whose job at high-society beauty salon leads to liaison with husband of wealthy customer. Evans never looked more beautiful, photographed here by James Wong Howe. Based on a Faith Baldwin story.

Beauty for the Asking (1939) **68m. **½ D: Glenn Tryon. Lucille Ball, Patric Knowles, Frieda Inescort, Donald Woods, Inez Courtney, Leona Maricle. Working girl Ball is jilted by money-hungry Knowles; he comes crawling back after she invents an exclusive beauty cream. Watchable programmer, with an interesting feminist viewpoint and good early Ball performance. ▼

Be Beautiful But Shut Up (1958-French) **94m. ** D: Henri Verneuil. Mylène Demongeot, Roger Hanin, Béatrice Altariba, René Lefèvre, Henri Vidal, Jean-Paul Belmondo, Alain Delon. Sexy Demongeot becomes involved with a band of youthful punks and smugglers. Of interest mainly for its cast; one of the writers is Roger Vadim. ▼

Bebo's Girl (1964-Italian) **106m. **½ D: Luigi Comencini. Claudia Cardinale, George Chakiris, Mario Lupi, Dany Paris. At times memorable love story spotlighting Cardinale's decision to leave her new lover in order to reaffirm her attachment with first love, now serving a prison term.

Because of Him (1946) **88m. **½ D: Richard Wallace. Deanna Durbin, Franchot Tone, Charles Laughton, Helen Broderick, Donald Meek. Contrived comedy recalls Deanna's earlier (and better) vehicles as she schemes to become the protégée of Broadway star Laughton, with interference from playwright Tone. A few songs are shoehorned into the film as arbitrarily as most of the story elements. ▼▶

Because of You (1952) **95m. ** D: Joseph Pevney. Loretta Young, Jeff Chandler, Alex Nicol, Frances Dee, Mae Clarke, Alexander Scourby. Loretta weds Jeff—but fails to inform him that she's a parolee; then she takes up with her ex-boyfriend, a drug smuggler. Trite and forgettable. ▼

Because They're Young (1960) **102m. **½ D: Paul Wendkos. Dick Clark, Michael Callan, Tuesday Weld, Victoria Shaw, Doug McClure, James Darren, Warren Berlinger, Roberta Shore, Duane Eddy and The Rebels. Clark made his screen acting debut in this ho-hum adaptation of John Farris' *Harrison High*. Mr. American Bandstand stars as an understanding do-gooder teacher, who attempts to help his troubled students. ▶

Because You're Mine (1952) **C-103m. ** D: Alexander Hall. Mario Lanza, James Whitmore, Doretta Morrow, Dean Miller, Paula Corday, Jeff Donnell, Spring Byington, Don Porter, Eduard Franz, Bobby Van. Opera star Lanza is drafted and falls in love with Morrow, the sister of his top sergeant (Whitmore). For Lanza fans only. ▼▶

Becket (1964) **C-148m. **** D: Peter Glenville. Richard Burton, Peter O'Toole, John Gielgud, Donald Wolfit, Martita Hunt, Pamela Brown, Felix Aylmer. Stunning film, adapted by Edward Anhalt (who won an Oscar) from the Jean Anouilh play, centers on stormy friendship between Archbishop of Canterbury Thomas à Becket and his English King, Henry II. Superbly acted and magnificently photographed (by Geoffrey Unsworth) on location in England. Panavision. ▼⚫▶

Becky Sharp (1935) **C-83m. **½ D: Rouben Mamoulian. Miriam Hopkins, Frances Dee, Cedric Hardwicke, Billie Burke, Alison Skipworth, Nigel Bruce. Witty but sometimes ponderous adaptation of Thackeray's *Vanity Fair* with Hopkins as self-reliant girl whose sole concern is herself. Historically important as first full-Technicolor (3-color) feature, designed by Robert Edmond Jones (and photographed by Ray Rennahan). Long available only in inferior 67m. Cinecolor reissue prints; archivally restored in 1985. Previously filmed in 1923 and 1932, remade in 2004 (all as VANITY FAIR).▼▶

Bedelia (1946-British) **92m. **½ D: Lance Comfort. Margaret Lockwood, Ian Hunter, Barry K. Barnes, Anne Crawford, Jill Esmond. Naive Hunter marries a woman with a past, including (it turns out) several husbands who met mysterious ends. Absorbing but not terribly suspenseful. Based on a Vera Caspary novel.

Bedevilled (1955) **C-85m. ** D: Mitchell Leisen. Anne Baxter, Steve Forrest, Simone Renant, Victor Francen. Bizarre yarn of chanteuse Baxter fleeing from murder scene, protected by Forrest, who's studying for priesthood; filmed in Paris. CinemaScope. ▶

Bedford Incident, The (1965) **102m. *** D: James B. Harris. Richard Widmark, Sidney Poitier, James MacArthur, Martin Balsam, Wally Cox, Eric Portman, Donald Sutherland. Strong Cold War story of authoritarian Navy captain (Widmark) scouting Russian subs near Greenland and the mental conflicts that develop on his ship. Poitier is reporter too good to be true, Balsam a sympathetic doctor disliked by Widmark. Cast excels in intriguing battle of wits.▼▶

Bedlam (1946) **79m. *** D: Mark Robson. Boris Karloff, Anna Lee, Ian Wolfe, Richard Fraser, Billy House, Jason Robards, Sr. Atmospheric chiller of courageous Lee trying to expose shameful conditions at notorious 18th-century London insane asylum run by corrupt head Karloff. Producer Val Lewton also coscripted under pseudonym Carlos Keith. Robert Clarke appears unbilled. ▼◐▶

Bed of Roses (1933) 67m. *** D: Gregory La Cava. Constance Bennett, Joel McCrea, Pert Kelton, John Halliday, Samuel S. Hinds, Franklin Pangborn. Smart pre-Code comedy-drama with Bennett and Kelton released from reform school and on the make for plenty of "umpchays with ashcay," that is, until Bennett falls for riverboat skipper McCrea. Kelton is hilarious as a slinky, no-holds-barred "bad girl" with an acid tongue.

Bedside (1934) 66m. ** D: Robert Florey. Jean Muir, Warren William, Allen Jenkins, David Landau, Kathryn Sergava, Donald Meek, Henry O'Neill, Louise Beavers. William has one of his sleaziest "rat" roles as an expelled medical student who buys a diploma from a junkie doctor and cons his way to a lucrative career as a high-society quack. Far-fetched from start to finish and not as enjoyable as other cynical Warner Bros. pre-Code movies because the subject matter is too serious to be treated in such a flip manner.

Bedtime for Bonzo (1951) 83m. **½ D: Frederick de Cordova. Ronald Reagan, Diana Lynn, Walter Slezak, Jesse White, Lucille Barkley. Often cited as the pinnacle of absurdity in Reagan's career, but in fact it's a cute, harmless little comedy about a professor who treats a chimp as his child for a heredity experiment. Reagan did not appear in the sequel, BONZO GOES TO COLLEGE. ▼▶

Bedtime Story, A (1933) 87m. **½ D: Norman Taurog. Maurice Chevalier, Helen Twelvetrees, Baby LeRoy, Adrienne Ames, Edward Everett Horton. Breezy Chevalier musical vehicle with Parisian playboy playing father to abandoned baby who interferes with his romancing.

Bedtime Story (1941) 85m. *** D: Alexander Hall. Fredric March, Loretta Young, Robert Benchley, Allyn Joslyn, Eve Arden, Helen Westley, Joyce Compton. Fine cast in entertaining comedy of popular stage actress Young and playwright husband March. She's determined to retire and enjoy life outside the spotlight but he has other ideas.

Bedtime Story (1964) C-99m. **½ D: Ralph Levy. Marlon Brando, David Niven, Shirley Jones, Dody Goodman, Marie Windsor. Offbeat casting of stars provides chief interest in lackluster comedy of con men Brando and Niven competing for Jones' affection. Remade as DIRTY ROTTEN SCOUNDRELS. ▼

Beethoven's Great Love (1936-French) 116m. ***½ D: Abel Gance. Harry Baur, Jean-Louis Barrault, Marcel Dalio, Jany Holt, Annie Ducaux, Jean Debucourt, Sylvie Gance. The life of the great composer told with titanic verve. Beethoven's artistic triumphs and his tragic struggle with deafness are portrayed against the backdrop of his compositions. Gance's bravura use of images and expressionistic use of sound make this a worthy companion piece to his silent masterpiece NAPOLEON. American titles: BEETHOVEN and THE LIFE AND LOVES OF BEETHOVEN. ▼▶

Before Dawn (1933) 60m. **½ D: Irving Pichel. Stuart Erwin, Dorothy Wilson, Warner Oland, Dudley Digges, Gertrude W. Hoffman, Oscar Apfel, Frank Reicher, Jane Darwell. Detective Erwin uses clairvoyant Wilson to solve the case of buried loot hidden in a spooky old mansion, replete with sliding doors and a floating death mask. Oland took a break from Charlie Chan to play a villainous doctor in this minor but interesting mystery-comedy. Based on an original screen story by Edgar Wallace.

Before I Hang (1940) 71m. **½ D: Nick Grinde. Boris Karloff, Evelyn Keyes, Bruce Bennett, Pedro de Cordoba, Edward Van Sloan. Contrived but intriguing tale of prison scientist Karloff having youth serum backfire on him, driving him mad at odd moments. ▼◐▶

Before I Wake SEE: Shadow of Fear

Before the Revolution (1964-Italian) 115m. *** D: Bernardo Bertolucci. Adriana Asti, Francisco Barilli, Alain Midgette, Morando Morandini, Domenico Alpi. Bertolucci's second feature (which he wrote when he was 22 years old) dramatizes the dilemma of young, middle-class Barilli. Will he embrace a life of social and political radicalism, or submit to the bourgeois status quo? Revealing 1960s time capsule, loaded with topical ideas, references, and fervor. ▼

Beggars of Life (1928) 100m. **** D: William A. Wellman. Wallace Beery, Richard Arlen, Louise Brooks, Robert Perry, Roscoe Karns, Edgar (Blue) Washington. Tramp Arlen comes upon a young girl (Brooks) who has just murdered her lecherous foster father. The two hit the road, one step ahead of the law, and soon mix with Oklahoma Red (Beery), a tough, high-spirited hobo. This empathetic, darkly realistic drama is loaded with stunning visuals, and is one of the great late-silent–era features. Originally included a sound sequence in which Beery sings! Jim Tully adapted his own novel with Benjamin Glazer. ▼▶

Beggar's Opera, The (1953-British) C-94m. *** D: Peter Brook. Laurence Olivier, Stanley Holloway, Dorothy Tutin, Daphne Anderson, Mary Clare, Hugh Griffith, Laurence Naismith. Celebrated stage director Brook made his film debut with this vivid, energetic version of John Gay's opera. Coproducer and star Olivier is somewhat miscast but more than makes up for it with his sly portrayal of a jailed highwayman who exaggerates his exploits into a musical revue. ▶

Beginning of the End (1957) **73m.** *½ D: Bert I. Gordon. Peggie Castle, Peter Graves, Morris Ankrum, Thomas Browne Henry. Awful sci-fi outing about giant grasshoppers (thanks to radiation) on the rampage; at the climax, they invade Chicago—but none too convincingly. ▼▶

Beginning or the End, The (1947) **112m.** *** D: Norman Taurog. Brian Donlevy, Robert Walker, Tom Drake, Beverly Tyler, Audrey Totter, Hume Cronyn, Hurd Hatfield, Joseph Calleia, Godfrey Tearle, Victor Francen, Richard Haydn, Henry O'Neill, Barry Nelson, Art Baker, Ludwig Stossel, Norman Lloyd, Jim Davis, Blake Edwards. Talky but engrossing account of the development of the atomic bomb, culminating in its deployment over Hiroshima. Script is a mirror of its era as it deals with the moral issues of the bomb's use as a weapon in war. Fictional characters blend with real ones, including Leslie Groves (Donlevy), Enrico Fermi (Calleia), J. Robert Oppenheimer (Cronyn), Paul Tibbets (Nelson), and Franklin Roosevelt (Tearle).

Behave Yourself! (1951) **81m.** ** D: George Beck. Farley Granger, Shelley Winters, William Demarest, Francis L. Sullivan, Margalo Gillmore, Lon Chaney, Jr., Sheldon Leonard, Marvin Kaplan, Glenn Anders, Allen Jenkins, Elisha Cook, Jr., Hans Conried. Loud, limp black comedy with Granger and Winters miscast as young marrieds who take in a dog trained to act as a link between two gangs in a smuggling scheme. Good supporting cast is wasted. The title song was cowritten by Buddy Ebsen! ▼▶

Behemoth the Sea Monster SEE: **Giant Behemoth, The**

Behind Locked Doors (1948) **62m.** **½ D: Oscar (Budd) Boetticher. Richard Carlson, Lucille Bremer, Douglas Fowley, Thomas Browne Henry, Dickie Moore, Tor Johnson. Pretty good grade-B film noir about a private eye who checks into a sanitarium on a tip that a wanted judge is holed up there. Johnson is put to good use as a former prizefighter kept in solitary confinement. ▼▶

Behind That Curtain (1929) **90m.** *½ D: Irving Cummings. Warner Baxter, Lois Moran, Gilbert Emery, Claude King, Philip Strange, Boris Karloff, E. L. Park. Exceedingly stilted and old-fashioned early-talkie melodrama about heiress Moran victimized by her scoundrel of a husband, fleeing to arms of lover Baxter. Noteworthy only as the first sound film appearance of Charlie Chan (Park), albeit in an irrelevant five-minute part near the end. Long considered lost, this is one "treasure" that could have stayed buried. ▼▶

Behind the Eight Ball (1942) **60m.** ** D: Edward F. Cline. Ritz Brothers, Carol Bruce, Grace McDonald, Dick Foran, William Demarest, Johnny Downs. Entertainers get tangled in murder whodunit, with Demarest as

determined detective. Typical nonsense plot squeezed in between musical numbers.

Behind the Front (1926) **60m.** **½ D: A. Edward Sutherland. Wallace Beery, Mary Brian, Raymond Hatton, Richard Arlen, Tom Kennedy, Chester Conklin, Gertrude Astor. Entertaining silent army comedy, broadly played by buddies Beery and Hatton. Many devices have been reused countless times, but they're handled smoothly here. ▼▶

Behind the Headlines (1937) **58m.** **½ D: Richard Rosson. Lee Tracy, Diana Gibson, Philip Huston, Paul Guilfoyle, Donald Meek, Tom Kennedy, Frank M. Thomas, Doodles Weaver. Compact vehicle for Tracy as a fast-talking, death-defying radio reporter. Famed for scooping his competitors, he tangles with a female rival and becomes involved in a scheme to steal a government gold truck.

Behind the High Wall (1956) **85m.** ** D: Abner Biberman. Tom Tully, Sylvia Sidney, Betty Lynn, John Gavin. Intertwining yarn of grasping prison warden, his crippled wife (nicely played by Sidney), hidden money, and convict escape plan. Remake of THE BIG GUY (1939).

Behind the Iron Curtain SEE: **Iron Curtain, The**

Behind the Mask (1932) **70m.** ** D: John Francis Dillon. Jack Holt, Constance Cummings, Boris Karloff, Edward Van Sloan, Claude King. Secret-service man Holt tries to expose mysterious head of dope ring in this okay thriller, not a horror film despite presence of Karloff and Van Sloan. ▶

Behind the Mask (1946) **67m.** ** D: Phil Karlson. Kane Richmond, Barbara Reed, George Chandler, Dorothea Kent, Joseph Crehan, Pierre Watkin, Robert Shayne, June Clyde. Lamont Cranston, aka The Shadow, springs into action and busts a blackmail ring when he's framed for the murder of a slimy newspaper columnist. Decent low-budget whodunit has some nice visual touches but way too much "comedy" relief. Second of three *Shadow* movies made by Monogram based on the popular pulp fiction and radio character; followed by THE MISSING LADY. ▶

Behind the Rising Sun (1943) **89m.** **½ D: Edward Dmytryk. Margo, Tom Neal, J. Carrol Naish, Robert Ryan, Gloria Holden, Don Douglas, George Givot. Japanese man (Naish) urges his Americanized son (Neal) to become involved in Sino-Japanese war during 1930s, but doesn't like what happens as a result. Interesting for WW2-era point of view.▼

Behold a Pale Horse (1964) **118m.** **½ D: Fred Zinnemann. Gregory Peck, Anthony Quinn, Omar Sharif, Mildred Dunnock, Christian Marquand, Raymond Pellegrin. Peck and Quinn wage an ideological battle in post–Spanish Civil War story of politics and violence that loses focus, becoming confused and talky. Valiant try by all. ▼▶

Behold My Wife! (1934) **78m.** ** D: Mitchell Leisen. Sylvia Sidney, Gene Raymond, Juliette Compton, Laura Hope Crews, Ann Sheridan. Raymond's snobbish family objects to his love for Indian maiden Sidney. Predictable wrong-side-of-the-reservation romance.

Bela Lugosi Meets a Brooklyn Gorilla (1952) **74m.** BOMB D: William Beaudine. Bela Lugosi, Duke Mitchell, Sammy Petrillo, Charlita, Muriel Landers, Ramona the Chimp. One of the all-time greats. Mitchell and Petrillo (the very poor man's Martin and Lewis) are stranded on a jungle island, where Lugosi is conducting strange experiments. Proceed at your own risk. Aka THE BOYS FROM BROOKLYN. ▼▶

Bell'Antonio (1960-Italian-French) **101m.** **½ D: Mauro Bolognini. Marcello Mastroianni, Claudia Cardinale, Pierre Brasseur, Rina Morelli. OK seriocomedy of what happens when Mastroianni is unable to consummate his marriage to Cardinale. Coscripted by Pier Paolo Pasolini. Video title: IL BELL'ANTONIO. ▼

Bell Book and Candle (1958) **C-103m.** **½ D: Richard Quine. James Stewart, Kim Novak, Jack Lemmon, Janice Rule, Ernie Kovacs, Hermione Gingold, Elsa Lanchester. John Van Druten play becomes so-so vehicle to showcase Novak as fetching witch who charms about-to-be-married Manhattan publisher Stewart. Kovacs and Gingold supply their brands of humor. ▼●▶

Bellboy, The (1960) **72m.** *** D: Jerry Lewis. Jerry Lewis, Alex Gerry, Bob Clayton, Sonny Sands. Amusing series of blackouts with Jerry as a bellboy at Fontainebleau in Miami Beach. No plot but a lot of funny gags. Milton Berle and Walter Winchell have guest appearances. Lewis' directorial debut. ▼●▶

Belle Le Grand (1951) **90m.** *½ D: Allan Dwan. Vera Ralston, John Carroll, William Ching, Muriel Lawrence. Weak Ralston vehicle has her a Western gambler willing to play any stakes to win back rambunctious Carroll. Look for James Arness in the fire scene.

Belle of New York, The (1952) **C-82m.** **½ D: Charles Walters. Fred Astaire, Vera-Ellen, Marjorie Main, Keenan Wynn, Alice Pearce. Uninspired musical set in Gay '90s N.Y.C. with Astaire as a rich playboy chasing mission worker Vera-Ellen; Pearce adds comic touches. Songs include "Let a Little Love Come In." ▼●▶

Belle of the Nineties (1934) **73m.** *** D: Leo McCarey. Mae West, Roger Pryor, Johnny Mack Brown, Warren Hymer, Duke Ellington Orchestra. Mae struts, sings "My Old Flame," and heats up a gallery of admirers in amusing example of Western humor. ▼●▶

Belle of the Yukon (1944) **C-84m.** **½ D: William Seiter. Randolph Scott, Gypsy Rose Lee, Bob Burns, Dinah Shore, Charles Winninger, William Marshall, Guinn "Big

Boy" Williams, Robert Armstrong, Florence Bates. Minor musical of saloon owner Scott going straight at insistence of his girl (Lee); fast moving, forgettable. Technicolor is film's best feature. ▼▶

Belles of St. Trinians, The (1954-British) **90m.** *** D: Frank Launder. Alastair Sim, Joyce Grenfell, George Cole, Hermione Baddeley, Beryl Reid. Hilarious filmization of Ronald Searle's cartoons about completely crazy school for girls, run by dotty headmistress whose brother, a bookie, wants to use school to his advantage. Sim plays dual role in delightful madcap farce which spawned several sequels. ▼

Belles on Their Toes (1952) **C-89m.** *** D: Henry Levin. Myrna Loy, Jeanne Crain, Debra Paget, Jeffrey Hunter, Edward Arnold, Hoagy Carmichael, Barbara Bates, Robert Arthur, Verna Felton, Martin Milner. Pleasing follow-up to CHEAPER BY THE DOZEN, with a potent feminist point of view. Here, widowed engineer Loy must struggle to support (as well as raise) her maturing brood. 20th Century-Fox backlot seen at its best in recapturing early 1900s America. Clifton Webb makes a brief appearance at the finale. Scripted by Henry and Phoebe Ephron. ▶

Belle Starr (1941) **C-87m.** **½ D: Irving Cummings. Randolph Scott, Gene Tierney, Dana Andrews, John Sheppard (Shepperd Strudwick), Elizabeth Patterson. Sophisticated Tierney miscast as notorious female outlaw in slowly paced account of her criminal career. Remade for TV in 1980 with Elizabeth Montgomery.

Belle Starr's Daughter (1948) **86m.** ** D: Lesley Selander. George Montgomery, Rod Cameron, Ruth Roman, Wallace Ford, Isabel Jewell. Roman is title character, coming to rough Western town to avenge her mother's murder; fair Western. Jewell repeats her Starr role from BAD MAN'S TERRITORY.

Bell for Adano, A (1945) **103m.** ***½ D: Henry King. Gene Tierney, John Hodiak, William Bendix, Glenn Langan, Richard Conte, Stanley Prager, Henry (Harry) Morgan, Hugo Haas, Fortunio Bonanova, Henry Armetta, Luis Alberni, Eduardo Ciannelli, Grady Sutton. John Hersey's moving narrative of American WW2 occupation of small Italian village; Hodiak is sincere commander, Bendix his aide, blonde Tierney the local girl he is attracted to. Scripted by Lamar Trotti (who also coproduced) and Norman Reilly Raine.

Bellissima (1951-Italian) **112m.** ** D: Luchino Visconti. Anna Magnani, Walter Chiari, Tina Apicella, Gastone Renzelli, Alessandro Blasetti. Obvious drama about pushy, patronizing stage mother Magnani, obsessed to the point of hysteria with getting her cute, obedient little daughter into the movies. Loud when it should be tender, and ultimately tiresome. ▼▶

Bells, The (1926) **67m.** ******* D: James Young. Lionel Barrymore, Caroline Frances Cooke, Gustav von Seyffertitz, Lorimer Johnston, Edward (Eddie) Phillips, Lola Todd, Boris Karloff. Well-told melodrama of greed and guilt. Barrymore is an easygoing innkeeper who's deeply in debt and in danger of losing his business to a scoundrel; in an act of desperation, he commits a heinous crime. Karloff is ideally cast as Caligari-like mesmerist. Based on oft-filmed 1869 play, *Le Juif polonais* (*The Polish Jew*), by Alexandre Chatrian and Emile Erckmann, and inspired by an 1849 Edgar Allan Poe poem. ▼❶

Bells Are Ringing (1960) **C-127m.** ******* D: Vincente Minnelli. Judy Holliday, Dean Martin, Fred Clark, Eddie Foy, Jr., Jean Stapleton, Ruth Storey, Frank Gorshin, Gerry Mulligan. Sprightly adaptation of Broadway musical hit by Betty Comden, Adolph Green, and Jule Styne, with Holliday recreating her starring role as an answering-service operator who falls in love with the man she's known only as a voice on the telephone. Songs include "Just in Time," "The Party's Over." Sadly, Holliday's last film. CinemaScope. ▼❶❶

Bells of Capistrano (1942) **73m.** ******* D: William Morgan. Gene Autry, Smiley Burnette, Virginia Grey, Lucien Littlefield, Morgan Conway, Claire Du Brey, Joe Strauch, Jr., Tristram Coffin. Entertaining story of rival rodeos has a good cast, including one of Gene's best leading ladies. Autry's last movie before he entered the service in WW2 ends rather abruptly with a patriotic ditty, "Don't Bite the Hand That's Feeding You." ▼❶

Bells of Coronado (1950) **C-67m.** ****½** D: William Witney. Roy Rogers, Dale Evans, Pat Brady, Grant Withers, Leo Cleary, Clifton Young, Robert Bice, Stuart Randall, Foy Willing and the Riders of the Purple Sage. Roy tangles with crooked gang that is selling uranium to foreign buyers. Pretty good Rogers adventure from his "serious" period, with exciting chase atop an electrical tower. ▼❶

Bells of Rosarita (1945) **68m.** ******* D: Frank McDonald. Roy Rogers, George "Gabby" Hayes, Dale Evans, Adele Mara, Grant Withers, Addison Richards, Roy Barcroft, Bob Nolan and the Sons of the Pioneers. Fun Western with Roy and the Sons playing themselves, movie stars who must save Dale's ranch from crooked realtor Withers, so they call on other Republic Pictures cowboy stars to help out. Original, winning, with plenty of in-jokes and guest stars Don Barry, Bill Elliott, Allan Lane, Bob Livingston, and Sunset Carson. John Wayne's absence is explained because he is out of town! ▼❶

Bells of San Angelo (1947) **C-78m.** ******* D: William Witney. Roy Rogers, Dale Evans, Andy Devine, John McGuire, Olaf Hytten, David Sharpe, Fritz Leiber, Fred "Snow-flake" Toones, Bob Nolan and the Sons of the Pioneers. First of Roy's hard-edged Westerns casts him as a border patrol investigator going after a treacherous gang of thieves and murderers who are illegally operating a silver mine. Tough, gripping, often surprisingly violent, with Devine coming aboard as Rogers' new sidekick. One of Roy's best. ▼❶

Bells of St. Mary's, The (1945) **126m.** ******* D: Leo McCarey. Bing Crosby, Ingrid Bergman, Henry Travers, William Gargan, Ruth Donnelly, Joan Carroll, Martha Sleeper, Rhys Williams. Amiable if meandering sequel to GOING MY WAY, with Father O'Malley assigned to a run-down parish where Bergman is the Sister Superior. Bing introduces the song "Aren't You Glad You're You?" Also shown in computer-colored version. ▼❶❶

Beloved Enemy (1936) **86m.** ******* D: H. C. Potter. Merle Oberon, Brian Aherne, Karen Morley, Henry Stephenson, Jerome Cowan, David Niven, Donald Crisp. High-class love story set during Irish Rebellion with Britisher Oberon in love with rebel leader Aherne. ▼❶

Beloved Infidel (1959) **C-123m.** ****** D: Henry King. Gregory Peck, Deborah Kerr, Eddie Albert,, Philip Ober, Herbert Rudley, John Sutton, Karin Booth, Ken Scott. Ill-conceived casting of Peck as F. Scott Fitzgerald makes romance with Hollywood columnist Sheilah Graham (Kerr) in late 1930s more ludicrous than real; lush photography is only virtue of blunt look at cinema capital. CinemaScope. ▼

Beloved Rogue, The (1927) **99m.** *****½** D: Alan Crosland. John Barrymore, Conrad Veidt, Marceline Day, Henry Victor, Lawson Butt, Mack Swain, Slim Summerville. Rousing, stunningly filmed story of poet-adventurer François Villon, his battle of wits with Louis XI (Veidt) and his swashbuckling romance with a damsel in distress. Not history, just an eye-filling, spirited, tongue-in-cheek costume tale with Barrymore in great form. ▼❶❶

Below the Deadline (1946) **65m.** ****** D: William Beaudine. Warren Douglas, Ramsay Ames, Jan Wiley, Paul Maxey, Philip Van Zandt, John Harmon, Bruce Edwards. Routine Monogram cheapie concerning G.I. Douglas returning from war and taking over his murdered brother's gambling operation, clashing with rival gangs. What the title has to do with all of this is anybody's guess. ❶

Be My Guest (1965-British) **82m.** ***½** D: Lance Comfort. David Hemmings, Stephen Marriot, Andrea Monet, Avril Angers, Joyce Blair, Jerry Lee Lewis, Nashville Teens. Young Hemmings uncovers attempt to mount a phony music contest, while his family takes over a seaside guest house. Trifling musical. ❶

Be My Wife (1921) **57m.** ******* D: Max Linder. Max Linder, Alta Allen, Caroline

Rankin, Lincoln Stedman, Rose Dione, Charles McHugh, Viora Daniel, Arthur Clayton. Max is determined to wed his lady love but must put up with a host of meddling interlopers, including her crabby aunt and a pudgy suitor. That's just for openers! Linder also scripted this funny slapstick feature that's loaded with clever comic visuals. The second of Linder's American features, following SEVEN YEARS BAD LUCK and followed by THE THREE MUST-GET-THERES.◗

Bend of the River (1952) **C-91m.** *** D: Anthony Mann. James Stewart, Arthur Kennedy, Julia (Julie) Adams, Rock Hudson, Jay C. Flippen, Lori Nelson, Stepin Fetchit, Henry (Harry) Morgan, Frances Bavier, Royal Dano. Compelling Western of 1860s Oregon, with bristling conflict between Stewart, outlaw turned wagon-train scout, and Kennedy, his one-time partner in crime who hijacks settlers' supplies for profit.▼◗

Beneath the 12-Mile Reef (1953) **C-102m.** **½ D: Robert Webb. Robert Wagner, Terry Moore, Gilbert Roland, J. Carrol Naish, Richard Boone, Peter Graves. Romeo-and-Juliet-ish tale of sponge-diving families on Key West, Florida. Scenery outshines all. One of the first CinemaScope films.▼◗

Bengal Brigade (1954) **C-87m.** ** D: Laslo Benedek. Rock Hudson, Arlene Dahl, Ursula Thiess, Torin Thatcher, Arnold Moss, Dan O'Herlihy, Michael Ansara. Low-level costumer with Hudson badly miscast as a British army officer working to thwart a Sepoy rebellion in India.◗

Bengazi (1955) **78m.** *½ D: John Brahm. Richard Conte, Victor McLaglen, Richard Carlson, Mala Powers. Lackluster adventure of crooked treasure hunters Conte, McLaglen, and others entrapped in desert shrine by marauding natives. SuperScope.

Ben-Hur (1925) **141m.** *** D: Fred Niblo. Ramon Novarro, Francis X. Bushman, May McAvoy, Betty Bronson, Claire McDowell, Carmel Myers, Nigel de Brulier. Biggest of all silent spectacles holds up quite well against talkie remake, particularly the exciting chariot race and sea battle (both directed by B. Reeves Eason); Novarro (as Judah) and Bushman (as Messala) give the performances of their careers. Trouble-plagued film was years in production, at a then-record cost of $4,000,000, but final result, despite a slow second half, is worth it. Some sequences filmed in two-color Technicolor. Filmed once before (in one reel!) in 1907.▼◗

Ben-Hur (1959) **C-212m.** ***½ D: William Wyler. Charlton Heston, Jack Hawkins, Stephen Boyd, Haya Harareet, Hugh Griffith, Martha Scott, Sam Jaffe, Cathy O'Donnell, Finlay Currie. Epic-scale rendering of Gen. Lew Wallace's "tale of the Christ." Heston and Boyd are well matched as the proud Jew Ben-Hur and his boyhood friend Messala,

whose blind allegiance to Rome turns him into a bitter enemy. Poky at times, but redeemed by the strength of its convictions. Some of the special effects show their age, though the galley-slave sequence and climactic chariot race (directed by Andrew Marton and staged by the legendary stunt expert Yakima Canutt) are still great. Won 11 Oscars, for Best Picture, Director, Actor (Heston), Supporting Actor (Griffith), Cinematography (Robert L. Surtees), Music Score (Miklos Rozsa), Art Direction, Film Editing, Sound, Costume Design, and Special Effects. Runs 222m. with overture, intermission/entr'acte. MGM Camera 65.▼◗

Benny Goodman Story, The (1955) **C-116m.** **½ D: Valentine Davies. Steve Allen, Donna Reed, Herbert Anderson, Hy Averback, Berta Gersten, Robert F. Simon, Sammy Davis, Sr., Gene Krupa, Lionel Hampton, Teddy Wilson. Typical Hollywood gloss about the bandleader's rise to fame and his romance with Reed; not 100% factual, with cliché dialogue to spare, but the music is great. Additional guest performers include Harry James, Ziggy Elman, and Martha Tilton. Goodman himself dubbed Allen's clarinet playing.▼◗

Benson Murder Case (1930) **69m.** **½ D: Frank Tuttle. William Powell, Natalie Moorhead, Eugene Pallette, Paul Lukas, William (Stage) Boyd, E. H. Calvert, May Beatty, Mischa Auer. An unscrupulous stockbroker is killed at his country estate and Philo Vance (Powell) is on hand to solve whodunit. Neat mystery, but slowly paced, and bearing no relationship whatsoever to the original Van Dine novel.

Berkeley Square (1933) **84m.** *** D: Frank Lloyd. Leslie Howard, Heather Angel, Irene Browne, Beryl Mercer, Samuel S. Hinds. Intriguing fantasy of young American Howard finding himself in 18th-century London, living completely different life. Remade as I'LL NEVER FORGET YOU.

Berlin-Alexanderplatz (1931-German) **84m.** *** D: Phil Jutzi. Heinrich George, Maria Bard, Margarete Schlegel, Bernhard Minetti, Gerhard Bienert, Albert Florath. Ambitious, fascinating early filmization of Alfred Döblin's epic novel of Germany between the wars, centering on the plight of Franz Biberkopf (George), a basically decent but deeply flawed Everyman. Reflects the dreary economic reality of post-WW1 Germany and offers a peek into Berlin street life just before Hitler came to power. Remade by Rainer Werner Fassbinder. Döblin also coscripted. Full title is BERLIN-ALEXANDERPLATZ: THE STORY OF FRANZ BIBERKOPF.◗

Berlin Correspondent (1942) **70m.** **½ D: Eugene Forde. Virginia Gilmore, Dana Andrews, Mona Maris, Martin Kosleck, Sig Ruman. American reporter risks life so that his sweetheart and her professor father can escape Nazi Germany. ▶

Berlin Express (1948) 87m. *** D: Jacques Tourneur. Merle Oberon, Robert Ryan, Charles Korvin, Paul Lukas, Robert Coote, Reinhold Schunzel, Roman Toporow, Fritz Kortner, Charles McGraw. Members of several nations combine efforts to save a German statesman after he is kidnapped by the Nazi underground. Location filming in Berlin, Frankfurt, and Paris adds immeasurably to this taut, suspenseful post-WW2 thriller, which also works as a knowing, hopeful look at pre–Cold War U.S.-Soviet relations. From a story by Curt Siodmak. ▼●▶

Berlin: Symphony of a City (1927-German) 65m. ***½ D: Walter Ruttmann. A vast, artistically rendered panorama of Berlin in the late 1920s, before Hitler came to power: a dazzling array of lights, shadows, shapes, patterns, and movement. Ruttmann and his cinematographers (one of them Karl Freund) capture images of the title city; the filmmaker then personalizes these visuals via rapid-fire editing. Freund and Carl Meyer collaborated on the screenplay. Aka BERLIN: SYMPHONY OF A GREAT CITY. ▼▶

Bermuda Mystery (1944) 65m. ** D: Benjamin Stoloff. Preston Foster, Ann Rutherford, Charles Butterworth, Helene Reynolds. Mild account of strange murder and dead man's heirs' pursuit of criminal.

Bernardine (1957) C-95m. ** D: Henry Levin. Pat Boone, Terry Moore, Janet Gaynor, Dean Jagger, Walter Abel. Very weak look at teenage life (all different now) marked return of Janet Gaynor to films after 20 years. Wholesome Pat Boone (in his film debut) sings and sings and sings. Eh! CinemaScope.

Best Foot Forward (1943) C-95m. *** D: Edward Buzzell. Lucille Ball, William Gaxton, Virginia Weidler, Tommy Dix, Nancy Walker, Gloria DeHaven, June Allyson. Entertaining film of Broadway musical about movie star Ball visiting small-town school for a lark; score includes "Buckle Down Winsockie." Harry James and his band do definitive "Two O'Clock Jump." Walker, as dynamic plain-Jane, and Allyson make their feature film debuts re-creating their stage roles. Future filmmaker Stanley Donen can be glimpsed in "The Three B's" number, holding DeHaven's legs. Runs 99m. with overture, exit music. ▼●▶

Best Man, The (1964) 102m. *** D: Franklin Schaffner. Henry Fonda, Cliff Robertson, Edie Adams, Margaret Leighton, Kevin McCarthy, Shelley Berman, Lee Tracy, Ann Sothern, Gene Raymond, Richard Arlen, Mahalia Jackson. Sharp filmization of Gore Vidal's play about political conventioning with several determined presidential candidates seeking important endorsement at any cost; brittle, engrossing drama. Screenplay by Vidal. ▼●▶

Best of Enemies, The (1961-British-Italian) C-104m. *** D: Guy Hamilton. David Niven, Michael Wilding, Harry Andrews, Alberto Sordi, Noel Harrison, Amedeo Nazzari, David Opatoshu. Nice counterplay between Niven and Sordi, as British and Italian officers who constantly, comically cross each other's paths during WW2. Their growing relationship serves to mirror the idiocy of war. Technirama.

Best of Everything, The (1959) C-121m. *** D: Jean Negulesco. Hope Lange, Stephen Boyd, Suzy Parker, Diane Baker, Martha Hyer, Joan Crawford, Brian Aherne, Robert Evans, Louis Jourdan. Multifaceted fabrication about women seeking success and love in the publishing jungles of N.Y.C., highlighted by Crawford's performance as tough executive with empty heart of gold. Captures the zeitgeist of '50s N.Y.C.; adapted from Rona Jaffee's novel. CinemaScope. ▼▶

Best of the Badmen (1951) C-84m. **½ D: William D. Russell. Robert Ryan, Claire Trevor, Robert Preston, Jack Buetel, Walter Brennan, Bruce Cabot. Band of outlaws (including James and Younger brothers) help former Union colonel Ryan in vendetta against detective Preston. Offbeat Western has more talk than action. ▼▶

Best Things in Life Are Free, The (1956) C-104m. **½ D: Michael Curtiz. Gordon MacRae, Dan Dailey, Ernest Borgnine, Sheree North, Tommy Noonan, Murvyn Vye. Typical of the antiseptic 1950s musicals, this film "re-creates" the careers of Tin Pan Alley writers DeSylva, Brown, and Henderson. Highlight: North and Jacques D'Amboise dancing to "The Birth of the Blues." CinemaScope. ▶

Best Years of Our Lives, The (1946) 168m. **** D: William Wyler. Myrna Loy, Fredric March, Dana Andrews, Teresa Wright, Virginia Mayo, Harold Russell, Hoagy Carmichael, Gladys George, Roman Bohnen, Steve Cochran. American classic of three veterans returning home after WW2, readjusting to civilian life. Robert Sherwood's script from MacKinlay Kantor's book perfectly captured mood of postwar U.S.; still powerful today. Seven Oscars include Best Picture, Wyler, March, Russell, Sherwood, Daniel Mandell's editing, Hugo Friedhofer's score. Russell, an actual veteran who lost his hands, also took home a second Oscar, a special award for bringing hope and courage to other veterans. Remade as 1975 TVM RETURNING HOME, with Tom Selleck and Dabney Coleman. ▼●▶

Betrayal From the East (1945) 82m. ** D: William Berke. Lee Tracy, Nancy Kelly, Richard Loo, Abner Biberman, Regis Toomey, Philip Ahn. Americans vs. Japanese in usual flag-waving espionage film, no better or worse than most. ▼

Betrayed (1944) SEE: **When Strangers Marry**

Betrayed (1954) **C-108m.** ** D: Gottfried Reinhardt. Clark Gable, Lana Turner, Victor Mature, Louis Calhern, O.E. Hasse, Wilfrid Hyde-White, Ian Carmichael. Colonel Gable falls for Dutch Resistance member Turner, who's suspected of being in cahoots with the Nazis. Ho-hum WW2 melodrama, with some nice on-location filming in The Netherlands. Clark and Lana's fourth and final teaming.▼●◐

Betrayed Women (1955) **70m.** *½ D: Edward L. Cahn. Carole Mathews, Beverly Michaels, Peggy Knudsen, Tom Drake, Sara Haden. Low-key filming of potentially volatile subject, sadistic treatment of inmates in women's prison.

Better 'Ole, The (1926) **95m.** ** D: Charles Reisner. Syd Chaplin, Doris Hill, Harold Goodwin, Jack Ackroyd, Edgar Kennedy, Charles Gerrard. Warner's second Vitaphone feature with synchronized music and sound effects is an obviously dated but sometimes amusing silent comedy about the misadventures of a jovial British Army sergeant during WW1. Chaplin (Charlie's half brother) perfectly embodies the famous British cartoon character Ol' Bill, created by Bruce Bairnsfather.◖

Betty Co-ed (1946) **68m.** *½ D: Arthur Dreifuss. Jean Porter, Shirley Mills, William Mason, Rosemary La Planche, John Shelton, Kay Morley, Jackie Moran, Edward Van Sloan, Jan Savitt and His Orchestra. Inexplicably dull grade-B musical about a professional singer who decides to go to college, where she's snubbed by sorority girls. Cute as ever, Porter can't save this turkey.

Between Heaven and Hell (1956) **C-94m.** ** D: Richard Fleischer. Robert Wagner, Terry Moore, Broderick Crawford, Buddy Ebsen, Robert Keith, Brad Dexter, Mark Damon, Harvey Lembeck, Skip Homeier, L.Q. Jones, Carl Switzer, Frank Gorshin. Disjointed psychological drama about thoughtless Southerner Wagner and how he is changed by his experiences in WW2 (especially while under the command of psycho Crawford). CinemaScope▼◖

Between Midnight and Dawn (1950) **89m.** **½ D: Gordon Douglas. Mark Stevens, Edmond O'Brien, Gale Storm, Donald Buka, Gale Robbins, Anthony Ross, Roland Winters. Some smart writing (by Eugene Ling) uplifts this otherwise average film noir about WW2 veterans-turned-L.A.-radio-car-cops Stevens and O'Brien, who are determined to bust a slimy young racketeer (Buka). Storm is the woman with the sexy voice whom both men covet. ◖

Between Time and Eternity (1960-German) **C-98m.** **½ D: Arthur Maria Rabenalt. Lilli Palmer, Willy Birgel, Ellen Schwiers, Carlos Thompson. Palmer makes tearjerker believable in story of middle-aged woman

dying of rare disease, seeking romance and fun while she can.

Between 2 Women (1937) **89m.** ** D: George B. Seitz. Franchot Tone, Maureen O'Sullivan, Virginia Bruce, Leonard Penn, Cliff Edwards, Janet Beecher, Charley Grapewin. Doctor Tone loves nurse O'Sullivan but she can't bring herself to leave her abusive husband, so he marries socialite Bruce. Doesn't know when to quit, with one plot turn after another. Best line: Nurse O'Sullivan tells reporter Edwards, "I could kiss you, but you're not sterile." Based on a story by Erich von Stroheim. No relation to same-named 1944 film.

Between Two Women (1944) **83m.** ** D: Willis Goldbeck. Van Johnson, Lionel Barrymore, Gloria DeHaven, Keenan Wynn, Marilyn Maxwell, Keye Luke, Alma Kruger, Walter Kingsford, Marie Blake, Nell Craig. Dr. Adams (Johnson) gets more screen time than Gillespie himself (Barrymore) in this mild triangle tale involving Johnson, Maxwell, and DeHaven (who finds time to sing "I'm in the Mood for Love"). Late *Dr. Kildare* series entry.◖

Between Two Worlds (1944) **112m.** **½ D: Edward A. Blatt. John Garfield, Eleanor Parker, Sydney Greenstreet, Faye Emerson, Paul Henreid, Sara Allgood, Isobel Elsom, George Tobias, Edmund Gwenn. Updated remake of OUTWARD BOUND, with various deceased individuals aboard a ship that will take each one to heaven or hell. Flawed, but good acting by Warner Bros. star stock company makes it worthwhile.◖

Between Us Girls (1942) **89m.** ** D: Henry Koster. Kay Francis, Diana Barrymore, Robert Cummings, Andy Devine, John Boles, Scotty Beckett. Chic Francis and daughter Barrymore have romances at the same time in this OK comedy.

Beware! (1946) **64m.** ** D: Bud Pollard. Louis Jordan, Frank Wilson, Emory Richardson, Valerie Black, Milton Woods, Joseph Hilliard, Tommy Hix. Bandleader Jordan comes to the rescue of the financially troubled college he once attended. Poorly made, hopelessly clichéd all-black musical is enlivened by Jordan, his musicianship, and such numbers as "Beware, Brother, Beware," "Salt Pork, West Virginia," and "Good Morning, Heartache."▼

Beware, My Lovely (1952) **77m.** **½ D: Harry Horner. Ida Lupino, Robert Ryan, Taylor Holmes, O.Z. Whitehead, Barbara Whiting. Brooding, atmospheric psychological thriller with kindly WW1 widow Lupino hiring wanderer Ryan as a handyman and discovering he's a psychopath.▼●

Beware of Blondie (1950) **66m.** ** D: Edward Bernds. Penny Singleton, Arthur Lake, Larry Simms, Marjorie Kent, Adele Jergens, Dick Wessel, Jack Rice, Emory Parnell, Isabel Withers, Danny Mummert. Mr. Dithers makes the biggest mistake of his life when he takes a vacation and puts Dagwood in charge of the office. Edward Earle plays Dithers in this final series entry, which also features the Bumsteads' comic strip neighbors the Woodleys.▼

Beware of Children (1960-British) **80m.** *½ D: Gerald Thomas. Leslie Phillips, Geraldine McEwan, Julia Lockwood, Noel Purcell. Young married couple transforms an inheritance of land into summer camp for all sorts of children, focusing on tedious, predictable pranks of youngsters. Original British title: NO KIDDING.▶

Beware of Pity (1946-British) **102m.** **½ D: Maurice Elvey. Lilli Palmer, Albert Lieven, Cedric Hardwicke, Gladys Cooper, Linden Travers, Ernest Thesiger. Maudlin but effective drama of young Austrian lieutenant Lieven, who allows himself to become involved with crippled baron's daughter Palmer. Based on a novel by Stefan Zweig.▼

Beware, Spooks! (1939) **68m.** ** D: Edward Sedgwick. Joe E. Brown, Mary Carlisle, Clarence Kolb, Marc Lawrence. Good fun as Brown solves mystery and becomes hero in Coney Island fun house.▼

Bewitched (1945) **65m.** ** D: Arch Oboler. Phyllis Thaxter, Edmund Gwenn, Horace (Stephen) McNally, Henry H. Daniels, Jr., Addison Richards, Kathleen Lockhart, Minor Watson. Ambitious B film based on Oboler's radio play "Alter Ego," about a woman tormented by a second personality locked inside her. Interesting idea, especially for its time, but heavy-handed.▶

Beyond a Reasonable Doubt (1956) **80m.** **½ D: Fritz Lang. Dana Andrews, Joan Fontaine, Sidney Blackmer, Philip Bourneuf, Barbara Nichols. Far-fetched tale of man who pretends to be guilty of murder to get first-hand view of justice system, unable to prove himself innocent later on. Pale production values. Intriguing idea doesn't hold up. Remade in 2009.▼▶

Beyond Glory (1948) **82m.** **½ D: John Farrow. Alan Ladd, Donna Reed, George Macready, George Coulouris. Predictable account of West Point captain Ladd, a WW2 veteran, on trial for misconduct. Audie Murphy's first film.

Beyond Mombasa (1956-U.S.-British) **C-90m.** ** D: George Marshall. Cornel Wilde, Donna Reed, Leo Genn, Ron Randell, Christopher Lee. Tame African adventure tale with Wilde seeking killers of his brother and clues to hidden uranium mine.▶

Beyond the Blue Horizon (1942) **C-76m.** ** D: Alfred Santell. Dorothy Lamour, Richard Denning, Jack Haley, Walter Abel, Elizabeth Patterson, Abner Biberman, Patricia Morison. Sarong queen Lamour turns out to be heiress to great fortune; witless film wastes more talent than usual.

Beyond the Forest (1949) **96m.** ** D: King Vidor. Bette Davis, Joseph Cotten, David Brian, Ruth Roman, Dona Drake, Regis

Toomey. Muddled murder story of grasping Davis, her small-town doctor husband (Cotten), and wealthy neighbor (Brian). Davis' overly mannered performance doesn't help. This is the film in which she utters the immortal line, "What a dump!"▼

Beyond the Purple Hills (1950) **69m.** **½ D: John English. Gene Autry, Pat Buttram, Hugh O'Brian, Jo Dennison, Don Beddoe, James Millican. Sheriff Autry is forced to arrest his friend O'Brian for murder, then prove it's really the fault of crooked banker Beddoe. Gene sings "Dear Hearts and Gentle People" and introduces his new horse, Little Champ, who shows off his bag of tricks. Simple and straightforward.▼▶

Beyond the Rocks (1922) **85m.** ** D: Sam Wood. Gloria Swanson, Rodolph (Rudolph) Valentino, Edythe Chapman, Alec B. Francis, Robert Bolder, Gertrude Astor. Swanson marries an older man with money in order to support her family, then is swept off her feet by a dashing playboy (Valentino). Dull adaptation of Elinor Glyn's novel; the story of how this long-lost film was rescued after 80 years is much more interesting than the picture itself!▶

Beyond the Time Barrier (1960) **75m.** ** D: Edgar G. Ulmer. Robert Clarke, Darlene Tompkins, Arianne Arden, Vladimir Sokoloff. Test pilot zooms into the future to find society decimated by cosmic radiation seeping through damaged ozone layer. Cheap film shot in Texas has a few blinks of inspiration; baddie Arden is director Ulmer's daughter.▼

Beyond Tomorrow (1940) **84m.** **½ D: A. Edward Sutherland. Richard Carlson, Jean Parker, Harry Carey, C. Aubrey Smith, Charles Winninger, Maria Ouspenskaya, Rod LaRocque. Sensitive little drama of three wealthy men sharing Christmas with down-and-out Carlson and Parker, who fall in love.▼▶

Beyond Victory (1931) **70m.** ** D: John S. Robertson. William Boyd, Lew Cody, James Gleason, Marion Shilling, ZaSu Pitts, Lissi Arna, Theodore von Eltz, Mary Carr. WW1 film, told in flashback, about four comrades who go to war and the stories of the girls they leave back home. Incredibly noisy, smoke-clogged film has some good ideas and builds an antiwar sentiment, but gets to be pretty tedious by the fourth episode. Gleason coscripted.▼

Be Yourself! (1930) **77m.** ** D: Thornton Freeland. Fanny Brice, Robert Armstrong, Harry Green, Gertrude Astor, Pat Collins. Contrived vehicle for Fanny as nightclub entertainer who falls in love with punchy prizefighter (Armstrong); silly story, overdose of sentiment leave too few moments for star to be herself.▼

B.F.'s Daughter (1948) **108m.** *½ D: Robert Z. Leonard. Barbara Stanwyck, Van Heflin, Charles Coburn, Richard Hart, Keenan

Wynn, Margaret Lindsay. Disastrous film of J. P. Marquand novel, with Stanwyck the domineering girl ruining marriage to professor Heflin. ▶

Bhowani Junction (1956-U.S.-British) **C-110m. **½ D: George Cukor. Ava Gardner, Stewart Granger, Bill Travers, Abraham Sofaer. Set in post-WW2 India; Gardner is half-caste torn between love of country and love for a British colonel. Based on John Masters novel; strikingly shot on location. CinemaScope. ▼●▶

Bicycle Thieves (1948-Italian) **89m. ****** D: Vittorio De Sica. Lamberto Maggiorani, Lianella Carell, Enzo Staiola, Vittorio Antonucci. A man whose livelihood depends on his bicycle spends a shattering week with his son searching for the men who stole it. Stunning in its simplicity, this was one of the cornerstones of the Italian neo-realist movement, filmed entirely on natural locations with nonprofessional actors. It also vividly captures life in post-WW2 Rome. Story by Cesare Zavattini, based on Luigi Bartolini's novel. Screenplay by Zavattini, De Sica, Oreste Biancoli, Suso D'Amico, Adolfo Franci, Gherardo Gherardi, Gerardo Guerrieri. Winner of a special Academy Award, given before there was a Foreign Language Film category. One of the all-time greats. Originally released in the U.S. as THE BICYCLE THIEF. ▼●▶

Bigamist, The (1953) **80m. **** D: Ida Lupino. Edmond O'Brien, Joan Fontaine, Ida Lupino, Edmund Gwenn, Jane Darwell, Kenneth Tobey. Compassionate look at lonely man who finds himself married to (and in love with) two different women. Extremely well acted; one of Lupino's best directorial efforts and the only time she ever directed herself. ▼▶

Big Beat, The (1958) **C-81m. *** D: Will Cowan. William Reynolds, Andra Martin, Gogi Grant, Rose Marie, Hans Conried, Jeffrey Stone, The Del Vikings, Fats Domino, The Diamonds, The Four Aces, Harry James, The Mills Brothers. Reynolds is a record exec, Martin his secretary. The Big Bore—except for the vintage performances of Domino ("I'm Walkin' "), The Diamonds ("Little Darlin' "), and company.

Big Blockade, The (1942-British) **77m. *** D: Charles Frend. Michael Redgrave, Leslie Banks, Will Hay, John Mills, Frank Cellier, Robert Morley, Alfred Drayton, Bernard Miles, Marius Goring, Michael Rennie, Michael Wilding. Dated propaganda chronicling Britain's economic blockade of Nazi Germany.

Big Bluff, The (1955) **70m. *** D: W. Lee Wilder. John Bromfield, Martha Vickers, Robert Hutton, Rosemarie Bowe, Eve Miller. Ordinary melodrama about suave con man Bromfield, who sets his sights on a wealthy young widow (Vickers) with a short time to live. Remake of THE GLASS ALIBI. ▼▶

Big Boodle, The (1957) **83m. *½ D: Richard Wilson. Errol Flynn, Pedro Armendariz, Rossana Rory, Jacques Aubuchon. Tame caper of gangsters and counterfeit money, set in Havana. Seedy programmer emphasizing Flynn's career decline. ▶

Big Boy (1930) **69m. **½ D: Alan Crosland. Al Jolson, Claudia Dell, Louise Closser Hale, Lloyd Hughes, Eddie Phillips, John Harron, Noah Beery. Jolson energetically re-creates his 1925 stage success as Gus, black stable boy who hopes to ride the title horse in the Kentucky Derby. Jolie appears in blackface until the conclusion, when he sings "Tomorrow Is Another Day." A real curio, extremely dated, but fascinating nonetheless. ●▶

Big Broadcast, The (1932) **87m. *** D: Frank Tuttle. Bing Crosby, Kate Smith, George Burns, Gracie Allen, Stuart Erwin, Leila Hyams, Cab Calloway, The Mills Brothers, Boswell Sisters. Failing radio station owned by Burns is taken over by millionaire Erwin, who presents an all-star show featuring Bing and many radio stars. Many offbeat, bizarre touches in standard love-triangle story make this a delight. Bing sings "Please," "Here Lies Love."

Big Broadcast of 1936, The (1935) **97m. **½ D: Norman Taurog. Jack Oakie, George Burns, Gracie Allen, Lyda Roberti, Henry Wadsworth, Wendy Barrie, C. Henry Gordon, Ethel Merman, Charlie Ruggles, Mary Boland, Bill "Bojangles" Robinson, The Nicholas Brothers. Curious muddle of specialty acts and nonsensical "plot" involving radio station owner Oakie. Vignettes feature everyone from radio's original Amos 'n' Andy (Freeman Gosden and Charles Correll, in blackface) to the Vienna Boys Choir. Bing Crosby sings lovely "I Wished on the Moon."

Big Broadcast of 1937, The (1936) **102m. *½ D: Mitchell Leisen. Jack Benny, George Burns, Gracie Allen, Bob Burns, Martha Raye, Shirley Ross, Ray Milland, Frank Forest. Almost unbearable musical about the competition between small-town discovery Ross and egocentric radio star Forest. Manages to waste the talent of its formidable cast, plus guest stars Benny Goodman, Larry Adler, Benny Fields, and Leopold Stokowski!

Big Broadcast of 1938, The (1938) **90m. *** D: Mitchell Leisen. W. C. Fields, Martha Raye, Dorothy Lamour, Shirley Ross, Lynne Overman, Bob Hope, Ben Blue, Leif Erickson. Hodgepodge of bad musical numbers from Tito Guizar to Kirsten Flagstad, notable only for Fields' few scenes, Hope and Ross' rendition of Oscar-winning "Thanks for the Memory." Hope's first feature. ▼▶

Big Brown Eyes (1936) **77m. **½ D: Raoul Walsh. Joan Bennett, Cary Grant, Walter Pidgeon, Isabel Jewell, Lloyd Nolan. Bennett helps detective Grant trap a gang of thieves in pleasing romantic mystery. ▶

Big Business Girl (1931) **75m.** ** D: William A. Seiter. Loretta Young, Ricardo Cortez, Frank Albertson, Joan Blondell, Frank Darien. Young is cute and perky as a career-minded woman on her way up the corporate ladder, trying to help her singer-boyfriend and keep her amorous boss at arm's length.▼

Big Cage, The (1933) **82m.** **½ D: Kurt Neumann. Clyde Beatty, Anita Page, Mickey Rooney, Andy Devine, Vince Barnett, Raymond Hatton, Wallace Ford. Beatty plays himself in silly but watchable circus story; sappy love angle doesn't help, but supporting cast does, including Mickey as youngster who wants to be Just Like Beatty. Exciting animal footage was reused in countless films.

Big Caper, The (1957) **84m.** **½ D: Robert Stevens. Rory Calhoun, Mary Costa, James Gregory, Robert (H.) Harris, Roxanne Arlen, Corey Allen, Paul Picerni, Patrick McVey. Calhoun and Costa pose as married couple in a California town in order to set up a bank robbery. Uplifted by memorable supporting characters (Harris' alcoholic firebug, Allen's psycho health nut) and the intriguing contrast between life in small-town 1950s America and the criminality of the central characters. Based on a novel by Lionel White.▶

Big Carnival, The SEE: **Ace in the Hole**

Big Cat, The (1949) **C-75m.** **½ D: Phil Karlson. Lon McCallister, Peggy Ann Garner, Preston Foster, Forrest Tucker, Skip Homeier, Sara Haden, Irving Bacon, Gene Reynolds. Above-average modern Western about the hunt for a killer cougar in Depression-era Rocky Mountain country. Well made on a low budget, with one of the best (and longest) fistfights in film history.▶

Big Circus, The (1959) **C-108m.** **½ D: Joseph M. Newman. Victor Mature, Red Buttons, Rhonda Fleming, Kathryn Grant, Vincent Price, Peter Lorre, David Nelson, Gilbert Roland, Howard McNear, Steve Allen. Corny and predictable, but still entertaining hokum under the big top, with Lorre as a sardonic clown and Roland tightrope-walking over Niagara Falls. And what a cast! CinemaScope. ▼●

Big City (1937) **80m.** **½ D: Frank Borzage. Spencer Tracy, Luise Rainer, Eddie Quillan, William Demarest, Regis Toomey, Charley Grapewin, Victor Varconi. Cabdriver Tracy and wife Rainer are pitted against crooked taxi bosses in well-acted but average film. Slick and watchable but just a trifle, lacking the conviction of Frank Capra's not dissimilar LADY FOR A DAY. Schmaltzy story by Norman Krasna. Retitled: SKYSCRAPER WILDERNESS.▶

Big City (1948) **103m.** **½ D: Norman Taurog. Margaret O'Brien, Robert Preston, Danny Thomas, George Murphy, Karin Booth, Edward Arnold, Butch Jenkins, Betty Garrett, Lotte Lehmann. Syrupy Americana in which cantor Thomas, cop Murphy, and reverend Preston collectively adopt abandoned baby, who grows up to be precocious O'Brien. Irving Berlin's "God Bless America" is featured throughout.▶

Big City, The (1963-Indian) **131m.** *** D: Satyajit Ray. Madhabi Mukherjee, Anil Chatterjee, Vicky Redwood, Haren Chatterjee, Jaya Bhaduri, Haradhan Bannerjee. A proud Calcutta man is forced by financial circumstances to let his wife work; soon she is the only one with a job. Warm, humorous, and astutely observed portrait of domestic life and women's roles in Indian society. Long but rewarding. ▼●

Big City Blues (1932) **65m.** **½ D: Mervyn LeRoy. Joan Blondell, Eric Linden, Inez Courtney, Evalyn Knapp, Guy Kibbee, Humphrey Bogart, Ned Sparks. Polished Warner Bros. programmer of hayseed Linden encountering disillusionment and love in N.Y.C.

Big Clock, The (1948) **95m.** *** D: John Farrow. Ray Milland, Charles Laughton, Maureen O'Sullivan, George Macready, Rita Johnson, Dan Tobin, Henry (Harry) Morgan. Tyrannical publisher of crime magazine (Laughton) commits murder; his editor (Milland) tries to solve case and finds all the clues pointing to himself. Vibrant melodrama; taut script by Jonathan Latimer from Kenneth Fearing novel. Elsa Lanchester has hilarious vignette as eccentric artist. Remade as NO WAY OUT (1987).▼▶

Big Combo, The (1955) **89m.** *** D: Joseph (H.) Lewis. Cornel Wilde, Jean Wallace, Brian Donlevy, Richard Conte, Lee Van Cleef, Robert Middleton, Earl Holliman, Helen Walker. Raw, violent film noir about persistent cop Wilde going up against cunning, sadistic racketeer Conte. A cult item, stylishly directed; Donlevy's demise is a highlight.▼▶

Big Country, The (1958) **C-166m.** *** D: William Wyler. Gregory Peck, Burl Ives, Jean Simmons, Carroll Baker, Charlton Heston, Chuck Connors, Charles Bickford. Overblown Western has ex-sea captain Peck arrive to marry Baker, but forced to take sides in battle against Ives and sons over water rights. Heston as quick-tempered ranch foreman and Ives (who won an Oscar) as burly patriarch stand out in energetic cast. Jerome Moross' score has become a classic. Technirama. ▼●

Big Day, The SEE: **Jour De Fete**

Big Deal on Madonna Street (1958-Italian) **106m.** ***½ D: Mario Monicelli. Vittorio Gassman, Marcello Mastroianni, Renato Salvatori, Rossana Rory, Carla Gravina, Totò. Classic account of misadventures of amateurish crooks attempting to rob a store; hilarious satire on all burglary capers. Retitled: BIG DEAL; remade as CRACKERS and in 2002 as WELCOME TO COLLINWOOD, and followed by a sequel, BIG DEAL ON MADONNA STREET . . . 20

YEARS LATER, which was actually released 30 years later! Also adapted for Broadway—unsuccessfully. ▼●▶

Big Fella (1937-British) 73m. ** D: J. Elder Wills. Paul Robeson, Elisabeth Welch, Roy Emerton, James Hayter, Lawrence Brown, Eldon Grant, Marcelle Rogez, Margaret Rutherford. Minor Robeson vehicle about an amiable Marseilles layabout who's enlisted to secretly investigate the disappearance of a boy from a tourist ship. Worth a look primarily for the presence—and voices—of Robeson and Welch and the easy camaraderie between the black and white characters. ▼▶

Big Fisherman, The (1959) C-149m. **½ D: Frank Borzage. Howard Keel, John Saxon, Susan Kohner, Herbert Lom, Martha Hyer, Ray Stricklyn, Alexander Scourby. Sprawling religious epic, from Lloyd Douglas' book about the life of St. Peter; seldom dull, but not terribly inspiring. Borzage's last film. Originally 184m., then cut to 164m. Super Panavision 70.

Big Gamble, The (1961) C-100m. **½ D: Richard Fleischer. Stephen Boyd, Juliette Greco, David Wayne, Sybil Thorndike. Not-too-convincing account of Irish adventurer and bride Greco who dally on the African Ivory Coast seeking to build their future the easy way. CinemaScope.

Bigger Than Life (1956) C-95m. *** D: Nicholas Ray. James Mason, Barbara Rush, Walter Matthau, Robert Simon, Roland Winters. Compelling drama of teacher Mason who becomes hooked on drugs, and its devastating effects on him and his family. Mason also produced the film. Quite bold for its time. CinemaScope.▶

Big Guy, The (1939) 78m. **½ D: Arthur Lubin. Jackie Cooper, Victor McLaglen, Ona Munson, Peggy Moran, Edward Brophy. Fairly interesting story of warden McLaglen given choice between wealth and saving innocent man on death row. Remade as BEHIND THE HIGH WALL.

Big Hangover, The (1950) 82m. ** D: Norman Krasna. Van Johnson, Elizabeth Taylor, Leon Ames, Edgar Buchanan, Rosemary DeCamp, Gene Lockhart. Ambitious but noble war veteran Johnson, whose allergy to alcohol makes him drunk at inopportune moments, joins a staid law firm. How long will he remain there? And will he hook up with wealthy Taylor? Predictable, as well as silly and boring.▼▶

Big Hearted Herbert (1934) 60m. **½ D: William Keighley. Aline MacMahon, Guy Kibbee, Patricia Ellis, Helen Lowell, Philip Reed, Robert Barrat, Henry O'Neill, Marjorie Gateson. Snappy little comedy with Kibbee in top form as a first-class grump who constantly belittles his family, to potentially disastrous effect. MacMahon is aces as Herbert's devoted but shrewd wife.

Big Heat, The (1953) 90m. *** D: Fritz Lang. Glenn Ford, Gloria Grahame, Joc-

elyn Brando, Alexander Scourby, Lee Marvin, Carolyn Jones, Jeanette Nolan. Time has taken the edge off once-searing story of cop determined to bust city crime ring; famous coffee-hurling scene still jolts, and Grahame is excellent as bad girl who helps Ford.▼●▶

Big House, The (1930) 86m. *** D: George Hill. Wallace Beery, Chester Morris, Robert Montgomery, Lewis Stone, Karl Dane, Leila Hyams. The original prison drama, this set the pattern for all later copies; it's still good, hard-bitten stuff with one of Beery's best tough-guy roles. Won Oscars for Writing (Frances Marion) and Sound Recording. Also filmed in French and Spanish-language versions, which survive; Charles Boyer stars in the former. ▼▶

Big House, U.S.A. (1955) 83m. **½ D: Howard W. Koch. Broderick Crawford, Ralph Meeker, Reed Hadley, William Talman, Lon Chaney, Jr., Charles Bronson, Randy (Felicia) Farr, Roy Roberts, Robert Bray. Brutal account of kidnapper-extortionist Meeker and his experiences in prison as he mixes with amoral convict Crawford and his cohorts.

Big Jack (1949) 85m. ** D: Richard Thorpe. Wallace Beery, Marjorie Main, Edward Arnold, Richard Conte, Vanessa Brown. Beery's last film, rather flat; he and Main are vagabond thieves in colonial America, Conte a moralistic doctor.

Big Jim McLain (1952) 90m. **½ D: Edward Ludwig. John Wayne, Nancy Olson, James Arness, Alan Napier, Veda Ann Borg, Hans Conried. Wayne and Arness are HUAC investigators who go Commie-hunting in Hawaii. One of the Duke's few dull films, but fascinating as a relic of its era.▼●▶

Big Knife, The (1955) 111m. *** D: Robert Aldrich. Jack Palance, Ida Lupino, Wendell Corey, Jean Hagen, Rod Steiger, Shelley Winters, Ilka Chase, Everett Sloane, Wesley Addy, Paul Langton, Nick Dennis. Clifford Odets' cynical view of Hollywood comes across in this involving (albeit occasionally overheated) drama, chronicling a string of crises in the life of movie star Charlie Castle (Palance). Fine performances almost overcome stereotypes; Steiger chews the scenery as a despotic studio head. ▼●▶

Big Land, The (1957) C-92m. **½ D: Gordon Douglas. Alan Ladd, Virginia Mayo, Edmond O'Brien, Julie Bishop. Cattle owners and grain farmers join together to bring railroad link to Texas; easygoing, familiar. ▶

Big Leaguer (1953) 70m. **½ D: Robert Aldrich. Edward G. Robinson, Vera-Ellen, Jeff Richards, Richard Jaeckel, William Campbell, Carl Hubbell, Paul Layton, Al Campanis. Robinson uplifts this standard baseball tale as real-life ex-major-leaguer John B. "Hans" Lobert, who runs a baseball tryout camp. The scenario follows a group of hopefuls who dream of professional stardom under his watchful eye. ▶

Big Lift, The (1950) 120m. *** D: George Seaton. Montgomery Clift, Paul Douglas, Cornell Borchers, Bruni Löbel, O. E. Hasse. Thoughtful, revealing drama is a mirror of its era as it spotlights American soldier Clift, his involvement with post-WW2 Berlin airlift, and his romantic feelings for a German woman (Borchers). Fascinating as a depiction of postwar German-American relations and for its on-location filming amid the rubble of Berlin. Except for Clift and Douglas (cast as a justifiably cynical G.I.), all those playing American soldiers are nonprofessionals who then were members of the U.S. military. Seaton also scripted. ▼▶

Big Night, The (1951) 75m. ** D: Joseph Losey. John Barrymore, Jr., Preston Foster, Joan Lorring, Howard St. John, Howland Chamberlin (Chamberlain), Dorothy Comingore, Philip Bourneuf, Myron Healey, Emile Meyer. Long-winded account of confused young Barrymore seeking revenge against the man who beat up his father. ▶

Big Noise, The (1944) 74m. BOMB D: Malcolm St. Clair. Stan Laurel, Oliver Hardy, Arthur Space, Veda Ann Borg, Bobby (Robert) Blake, Jack Norton. L&H's worst film, about them delivering a bomb . . . and they do. ▼▶

Big Operator, The (1959) 91m. ** D: Charles Haas. Mickey Rooney, Steve Cochran, Mamie Van Doren, Mel Tormé, Ray Danton, Jim Backus. Ray Anthony, Jackie Coogan. Rooney tries to add vim and vigor to title role as tough hood who goes on violent rampage when federal agents investigate his business activities. Paul Gallico story filmed before as JOE SMITH, AMERICAN. Retitled: ANATOMY OF A SYNDICATE. CinemaScope. ▶

Big Parade, The (1925) 141m. **** D: King Vidor. John Gilbert, Renée Adorée, Hobart Bosworth, Claire McDowell, Claire Adams, Karl Dane, Tom O'Brien. One of the best WW1 films ever; clean-shaven Gilbert a wonderful hero, Adoree an unforgettable heroine. Filled with memorable vignettes, and some of the most harrowingly realistic battle scenes ever filmed. A gem. ▼▶

Big Pond, The (1930) 75m. **½ D: Hobart Henley. Maurice Chevalier, Claudette Colbert, George Barbier, Nat Pendleton. Claudette brings Maurice to America, where to make good he works in chewing gum factory. Chevalier charm overcomes trivia; song: "You Brought a New Kind of Love to Me." Dialogue by Preston Sturges.

Big Punch, The (1948) 80m. ** D: Sherry Shourds. Wayne Morris, Gordon MacRae, Lois Maxwell, Mary Stuart, Jimmy Ames, Anthony Warde. Boxer MacRae is falsely accused of murder, finds refuge with Morris, who has spurned ring for the pulpit. Serviceable melodrama. MacRae's film debut.

Big Red (1962) C-89m. *** D: Norman Tokar. Walter Pidgeon, Gilles Payant, Emile Genest, Janette Bertrand, Doris Lussier. Charming, understated Disney drama of young boy who goes to work for wealthy dog fancier (Pidgeon) and becomes devoted to prize Irish setter. Fine family fare. Filmed in Canada. From popular novel by Jim Kjelgaard. ▼▶

Big Search, The SEE: East of Kilimanjaro

Big Shakedown, The (1934) 64m. ** D: John Francis Dillon. Bette Davis, Ricardo Cortez, Glenda Farrell, Charles Farrell, Adrian Morris. Inconsequential tale. Davis rejects husband Farrell when he joins forces with mobster Cortez in cosmetic fraud. ▶

Big Shot, The (1942) 82m. **½ D: Lewis Seiler. Humphrey Bogart, Irene Manning, Susan Peters, Minor Watson, Chick Chandler, Richard Travis, Stanley Ridges, Howard da Silva. OK grade-B gangster yarn with Bogey a three-time loser involved in robbery frame-up and prison break. ▶

Big Show, The (1936) 70m. *** D: Mack V. Wright. Gene Autry, Smiley Burnette, Kay Hughes, Sally Payne, William Newell, Max Terhune, Charles Judels, Sons of the Pioneers, The Jones Boys, The Beverly Hillbillies, The Light Crust Doughboys. Highly entertaining show-biz Western, with Gene in dual role as an arrogant cowboy star (who can't sing) and a lookalike stunt double with musical talent who impersonates him, causing trouble with gangsters, girlfriends, and the star's movie studio, which decides to make nothing but musical Westerns! Loaded with action, comedy, music, and in-jokes. One of the few B Westerns about the making of B Westerns. ▼▶

Big Show, The (1961) C-113m. **½ D: James B. Clark. Esther Williams, Cliff Robertson, Nehemiah Persoff, Robert Vaughn. Drama of family conflict, similar to 1949's HOUSE OF STRANGERS, somehow set in a circus with Williams in a rare dramatic role. Glug! CinemaScope. ▶

Big Sky, The (1952) 122m. *** D: Howard Hawks. Kirk Douglas, Dewey Martin, Elizabeth Threatt, Arthur Hunnicutt, Buddy Baer, Steven Geray, Hank Worden, Jim Davis. Camaraderie and conflict as fur-trapper Douglas leads expedition up the Missouri River. Eventful, evocative film adapted from A. B. Guthrie, Jr. book by Dudley Nichols; well directed by Hawks. Originally released at 141m. Also shown in computer-colored version. ▼

Big Sleep, The (1946) 114m. **** D: Howard Hawks. Humphrey Bogart, Lauren Bacall, John Ridgely, Martha Vickers, Louis Jean Heydt, Regis Toomey, Peggy Knudsen, Dorothy Malone, Bob Steele, Elisha Cook, Jr. Classic mystery thriller from Raymond Chandler's first novel; detective Philip Marlowe (Bogart) becomes involved with wealthy Bacall and her uncontrollable little sister Vickers. So convoluted even Chandler didn't know who committed one murder, but so incredibly entertaining that no one has ever cared. Powerhouse direction, unforgettable dialogue; script by William Faulkner, Jules Furthman, and Leigh Brackett. Prerelease version (shown to Armed Forces overseas in 1945) runs 116m., with 18m. of scenes reshot or unused in the official release. This version has less of Bogie and Bacall and a more linear plot, but is somehow less exotic and interesting. Also shown in computer-colored version. ▼●)

Big Sombrero, The (1949) **C-80m.** ***
D: Frank McDonald. Gene Autry, Elena Verdugo, Stephen Dunne, Vera Marshe, George J. Lewis, Martin Garralaga, Gene Roth. Gene woos Verdugo and helps to prevent crooks from evicting her tenants off her Big Sombrero rancho. Gene's second, and last, in color is a treat for the eye and ear. ❱

Big Stampede, The (1932) **55m.** ** D: Tenny Wright. John Wayne, Noah Beery, Paul Hurst, Mae Madison, Luis Alberni, Berton Churchill. Formula sagebrush saga of new deputy sheriff in pursuit of cattle rustlers who dispatched town's lawman predecessor. Reworking of 1927 Ken Maynard Western, remade in 1937 as a Dick Foran vehicle. ▼❱

Big Steal, The (1949) **71m.** *** D: Don Siegel. Robert Mitchum, Jane Greer, William Bendix, Patric Knowles, Ramon Novarro. Mitchum is on the trail of Army payroll thief Knowles; he in turn is chased by Bendix, and becomes involved with enticing Greer. Well-made robbery caper, set in Mexico and shot on location, is full of terrific plot twists. ▼●)

Big Store, The (1941) **80m.** ** D: Charles Riesner. Groucho, Chico and Harpo Marx, Tony Martin, Virginia Grey, Margaret Dumont, Douglass Dumbrille, Henry Armetta. Big comedown for Marxes in weak film of detective Groucho investigating crooked Dumbrille's department store. Low spot is Martin's "The Tenement Symphony." ▼●)

Big Street, The (1942) **88m.** **½ D: Irving Reis. Henry Fonda, Lucille Ball, Barton MacLane, Eugene Pallette, Agnes Moorehead, Sam Levene, Ray Collins, Hans Conried, Ozzie Nelson and Orchestra. Damon Runyon produced this treacly adaptation of his own Collier's magazine story "Little Pinks," about a timid busboy who devotes himself to a self-centered nightclub singer. Odd (and oddly watchable), with very unconventional roles for both Fonda and Ball. ▼●)

Big Timer, The (1932) **72m.** **½ D: Edward Buzzell. Ben Lyon, Constance Cummings, Thelma Todd, Tommy (Tom) Dugan, Robert E. O'Connor, Charles Grapewin, Russell Hopton, Nat Pendleton. Small-time pug (Lyon) makes it to the big time with the help of his manager/wife (Cummings), but gets KO'd when he gets mixed up with a blonde society temptress (Todd) and a

crooked promoter. Enjoyable formula boxing yarn given some oomph by the cast and a tangy script by Robert Riskin.

Big Tip Off, The (1955) **79m.** *½ D: Frank McDonald. Richard Conte, Constance Smith, Bruce Bennett, Cathy Downs, James Millican, Dick Benedict. Forgettable programmer about newspaper columnist Conte and his dealings with hood Bennett and a fund-raising scam.

Big Town (1947) **60m.** ** D: William C. Thomas. Phillip Reed, Hillary Brooke, Robert Lowery, Veda Ann Borg, Byron Barr, Charles Arnt. Forceful Steve Wilson (Reed) shakes things up as the new editor of the Illustrated Press, forcing reporter Lorelei Kilbourne (Brooke) to operate his way or not at all. First in a short-lived series based on the popular Big Town radio show. Retitled GUILTY ASSIGNMENT. Followed by I COVER BIG TOWN. ▼

Big Town After Dark (1947) **70m.** ** D: William C. Thomas. Phillip Reed, Hillary Brooke, Richard Travis, Anne Gillis, Vince Barnett, Joe Sawyer, Charles Arnt. Lorelei (Brooke) quits her job at the Illustrated Press, so Steve Wilson (Reed) hires, and starts wooing, the publisher's niece to make Lorelei jealous. Third in the short-lived series based on the Big Town radio show. Retitled UNDERWORLD AFTER DARK. Followed by BIG TOWN SCANDAL.❱

Big Town Scandal (1948) **61m.** ** D: William C. Thomas. Phillip Reed, Hillary Brooke, Stanley Clements, Darryl Hickman, Carl "Alfalfa" Switzer, Roland Dupree, Tommy Bond, Vince Barnett, Charles Arnt. Reporter Brooke convinces her editor (Reed) to take responsibility for a gang of teenagers—including her nephew—who've been caught looting a store. Final film in short-lived series based on the Big Town radio show reunites Our Gang favorites Alfalfa and Butch (Bond). Retitled UNDERWORLD SCANDAL. ❱

Big Trail, The (1930) **110m.** *** D: Raoul Walsh. John Wayne, Marguerite Churchill, El Brendel, Tully Marshall, Tyrone Power, Sr., David Rollins, Ian Keith. Epic Western may seem creaky to some viewers, but remains one of the most impressive early talkies, with its grand sweep and naturalistic use of sound. John Wayne was "discovered" for starring role, and already shows easygoing charm. Also filmed in pioneer 70mm widescreen process called Grandeur, at 122m., which includes extra footage and exit music. ▼❱

Big Trees, The (1952) **C-89m.** ** D: Felix Feist. Kirk Douglas, Eve Miller, Patrice Wymore, Edgar Buchanan, John Archer, Alan Hale, Jr., Roy Roberts, Ellen Corby. Brutally ambitious lumberman Douglas runs afoul of a religious sect—and practically everybody else around him—in this cornball outdoor melodrama. A remake of VALLEY

OF THE GIANTS with stock footage from that earlier color movie. ▼◉◗

Big Wave, The (1962-Japanese) **60m.** *½ D: Tad Danielewski. Sessue Hayakawa, Ichizo Itami, Mickey Curtis, Koji Shitara. Slowly paced account from Pearl Buck novel involving two boys who are childhood friends but later in life clash over their love for a local girl.

Big Wheel, The (1949) **92m.** **½ D: Edward Ludwig. Mickey Rooney, Thomas Mitchell, Spring Byington, Mary Hatcher, Allen Jenkins, Michael O'Shea. Rooney is determined race-car driver following in father's footsteps despite dad's death on track; familiar plot well done. ▼◗

Bikini Beach (1964) **C-100m.** **½ D: William Asher. Frankie Avalon, Annette Funicello, Keenan Wynn, Martha Hyer, Harvey Lembeck, Don Rickles, John Ashley, Jody McCrea, Meredith MacRae, Donna Loren, Candy Johnson, Timothy Carey, "Little" Stevie Wonder, Michael Nader. Third BEACH PARTY movie is second best, with Avalon in dual role as Frankie and a British singing rage called "The Potato Bug" (get it?). Relic of bygone era. Followed by PAJAMA PARTY. Panavision. ▼◗

Bill and Coo (1947) **C-61m.** *** D: Dean Riesner. Produced and narrated by Ken Murray. Charming, unique live-action film using trained birds in a story situation. A special Oscar winner, later reedited with new introductory material by Murray. ▼◗

Billie (1965) **C-87m.** **½ D: Don Weis. Patty Duke, Jim Backus, Jane Greer, Warren Berlinger, Billy De Wolfe, Charles Lane, Dick Sargent, Susan Seaforth, Ted Bessell, Richard Deacon, Bobby Diamond. Patty sings, runs, and prances in this unintentionally funny mid-1960s time capsule as a tomboyish 15-year-old who raises a ruckus when she goes out for the boys' track team. Techniscope. ▼◉◗

Bill of Divorcement, A (1932) **69m.** *** D: George Cukor. John Barrymore, Katharine Hepburn, Billie Burke, David Manners, Henry Stephenson. Barrymore gives sensitive performance as man released from mental institution who returns to wife Burke and gets to know his daughter for the first time. Dated but worth seeing; notable as Hepburn's screen debut. Originally released at 75m. Remade in 1940. ▼◉

Bill of Divorcement, A (1940) **74m.** **½ D: John Farrow. Maureen O'Hara, Adolphe Menjou, Fay Bainter, Herbert Marshall, Dame May Whitty, C. Aubrey Smith, Patric Knowles. Adequate remake with Menjou as mentally ill man who suddenly regains his sanity and returns home, with resulting dramatic fireworks. Scripted by Dalton Trumbo. Retitled NEVER TO LOVE.

Billy Budd (1962-U.S.-British) **122m.** ***½ D: Peter Ustinov. Robert Ryan, Peter Ustinov, Melvyn Douglas, Terence Stamp, Paul Rogers, David McCallum. Melville's classic good vs. evil novella set in British Navy, 1797. Naive, incorruptible seaman is court-martialed for murder of sadistic master-at-arms. Film deals simply with heavier issues of morality. Sterling performances by all. Ustinov also produced and coscripted with DeWitt Bodeen. Stamp's film debut. CinemaScope. ▼◗

Billy Liar (1963-British) **98m.** ***½ D: John Schlesinger. Tom Courtenay, Julie Christie, Wilfred Pickles, Mona Washbourne, Ethel Griffies, Finlay Currie, Leonard Rossiter. Cast excels in story of ambitious but lazy young man caught in dull job routine who escapes into fantasy world, offering some poignant vignettes of middle-class life. Based on Keith Waterhouse novel and play; scripted by Waterhouse and Willis Hall (who also cowrote stage version). Followed by a TV series and a musical. CinemaScope. ▼◗

Billy Rose's Diamond Horseshoe SEE: **Diamond Horseshoe**

Billy Rose's Jumbo (1962) **C-125m.** *** D: Charles Walters. Doris Day, Stephen Boyd, Jimmy Durante, Martha Raye, Dean Jagger. OK circus picture, at best during Rodgers and Hart songs, well staged by Busby Berkeley. Durante (who had starred in the 1935 Broadway production) and Raye are marvelous. Songs include "The Most Beautiful Girl in the World," "My Romance," "This Can't Be Love." Runs 127m. with overture. Aka JUMBO. Panavision. ▼◉◗

Billy the Kid (1930) **90m.** **½ D: King Vidor. Johnny Mack Brown, Wallace Beery, Kay Johnson, Karl Dane, Roscoe Ates. Realistic early talkie Western with marshal Beery trying to capture outlaw Brown; some performances seem badly dated today. Retitled: THE HIGHWAYMAN RIDES. Originally shown in early Realife 70 mm. widescreen process. ◗

Billy the Kid (1941) **C-95m.** **½ D: David Miller. Robert Taylor, Brian Donlevy, Ian Hunter, Mary Howard, Gene Lockhart, Lon Chaney, Jr. Cast looks uncomfortable in remake of 1930 Western, but plot is sturdy enough for OK viewing, with Taylor in title role and Donlevy as marshal. ▼◗

Billy the Kid Returns (1938) **53m.** *** D: Joseph Kane. Roy Rogers, Smiley Burnette, Mary Hart (Lynne Roberts), Morgan Wallace, Fred Kohler, Wade Boteler, Edwin Stanley, Joseph Crehan. After Pat Garrett kills notorious Billy the Kid (Rogers), he employs a lookalike (Rogers, again) to help find villains, who are unaware Billy is dead and are trying to oust homesteaders from their land. Fast-moving B Western, with Roy singing seven songs, including "Born to the Saddle." ▼◗

Biography of a Bachelor Girl (1935) **82m.** *½ D: Edward Griffith. Ann Harding, Robert Montgomery, Edward Everett Horton,

Edward Arnold, Una Merkel. A notorious woman is persuaded to write her memoirs by an aggressive magazine editor—who falls in love with her in spite of the fact that she represents everything he loathes. Dreary, endlessly talky adaptation of S. N. Behrman play.

Birdman of Alcatraz (1962) **143m.** *** D: John Frankenheimer. Burt Lancaster, Karl Malden, Thelma Ritter, Betty Field, Neville Brand, Edmond O'Brien, Hugh Marlowe, Telly Savalas. Pensive study of prisoner Robert Stroud who during his many years in jail became a world-renowned bird authority. Film becomes static despite imaginative sidelights to enlarge scope of action. 148m. version used for overseas release now turning up here. ▼●▶

Bird of Paradise (1932) **80m.** ** D: King Vidor. Joel McCrea, Dolores Del Rio, John Halliday, Skeets Gallagher, Lon Chaney, Jr. Exotic but empty South Seas romance with McCrea as adventurer who falls in love with native girl Del Rio. Handsome but unmoving; remade in 1951. ▼▶

Bird of Paradise (1951) **C-100m.** ** D: Delmer Daves. Louis Jourdan, Debra Paget, Jeff Chandler, Everett Sloane. Jourdan's marriage to South Sea isle chief's daughter causes native uprising in grandly filmed but vapid tale. Remake of 1932 film. ▶

Birds, The (1963) **C-120m.** ***½ D: Alfred Hitchcock. Rod Taylor, Tippi Hedren, Jessica Tandy, Suzanne Pleshette, Veronica Cartwright, Ethel Griffies, Charles McGraw, Joe Mantell, Elizabeth Wilson, Doodles Weaver, Richard Deacon, Suzanne Cupito (Morgan Brittany). Hitchcock's classic about a woman (Hedren) and mass bird attacks that follow her around isolated coastal California community. Not for the squeamish; a delight for those who are game. Hold on to something and watch. Script by Evan Hunter, loosely based on Daphne du Maurier's story. Followed by a terrible TV sequel in 1994. ▼●▶

Birds and the Bees, The (1956) **C-94m.** ** D: Norman Taurog. George Gobel, Mitzi Gaynor, David Niven, Reginald Gardiner, Fred Clark, Hans Conried. Bland remake of THE LADY EVE about rich playboy who breaks off romance with cardshark girlfriend, but later decides he still loves her. Screenplay by Sidney Sheldon (and Preston Sturges). VistaVision. ▼

Birth of a Nation, The (1915) **186m.** **** D: D. W. Griffith. Lillian Gish, Mae Marsh, Henry B. Walthall, Miriam Cooper, Robert Harron, Wallace Reid, Joseph Henabery. The landmark of American motion pictures. Griffith's epic story of two families during Civil War and Reconstruction is still fascinating. Sometimes the drama survives intact; other times, one must watch from a more historical perspective. Griffith's portrayal of Ku Klux Klan in heroic role has kept this film a

center of controversy to the present day. Running time varies from print to print. ▼●▶

Birth of the Blues (1941) **85m.** *** D: Victor Schertzinger. Bing Crosby, Brian Donlevy, Carolyn Lee, Eddie (Rochester) Anderson, Mary Martin. Fiction about Crosby organizing jazz band in New Orleans has great music like "St. Louis Blues," "St. James Infirmary," "Melancholy Baby," and title tune to uplift fair story. ▼▶

Biscuit Eater, The (1940) **83m.** *** D: Stuart Heisler. Billy Lee, Cordell Hickman, Helene Millard, Richard Lane, Lester Matthews. Warm, winning adaptation of James Street story about two boys—one white, one black—who take unwanted dog from litter and try to turn him into champion bird dog. A B picture that was regarded as the sleeper of the year. Remade in 1972.

Bishop Misbehaves, The (1935) **86m.** **½ D: E. A. Dupont. Edmund Gwenn, Maureen O'Sullivan, Norman Foster, Lucile Watson, Reginald Owen, Dudley Digges, Lilian Bond, Melville Cooper. Tongue-in-cheek mystery with Gwenn (in his first American film) as an English bishop with a taste for detective stories who gets mixed up in a real jewel heist. Enjoyable but slow paced.

Bishop Murder Case, The (1930) **91m.** ** D: Nick Grindé. Basil Rathbone, Leila Hyams, Roland Young, George F. Marion, Alec B. Francis, Zelda Sears, Bodil Rosing, Carroll Nye, Delmer Daves. Philo Vance investigates a crafty killer whose murders are patterned after Mother Goose nursery rhymes. Rathbone is disappointingly ordinary as Vance, and while the story itself is clever, it moves at a snail's pace. ▶

Bishop's Wife, The (1947) **108m.** *** D: Henry Koster. Cary Grant, Loretta Young, David Niven, Monty Woolley, James Gleason, Gladys Cooper, Elsa Lanchester. Christmas fantasy of suave angel (Grant) coming to earth to help Bishop Niven and wife Young raise money for new church. Engaging performances by all—and fun to see children from IT'S A WONDERFUL LIFE, Karolyn Grimes and Bobby Anderson, appearing together. Also shown in computer-colored version. Remade as THE PREACHER'S WIFE. ▼●▶

Bitter Creek (1954) **74m.** *½ D: Thomas Carr. Bill Elliott, Carleton Young, Beverly Garland, Claude Akins, Jim Hayward. Tame happenings as Elliott seeks revenge for his brother's untimely death in the Old West.

Bitter Rice (1948-Italian) **107m.** *** D: Giuseppe De Santis. Silvana Mangano, Vittorio Gassman, Raf Vallone, Doris Dowling, Lia Corelli. Effective portrayal of the dreary, backbreaking existence of women toiling in the Po Valley rice fields, exploited by the rice growers and their go-betweens. The seductive Mangano, as a worker who betrays her comrades, became an international star. ▼

Bitter Sweet (1933-British) **93m.** *** D: Herbert Wilcox. Anna Neagle, Fernand Graavey (Gravet), Miles Mander, Clifford Heatherley, Esme Percy, Ivy St. Helier, Pat Paterson, Kay Hammond. Noel Coward's first major work as a composer, filmed by the team of Wilcox-Neagle. Sentimental operetta creaks a bit, but the story of young love in 1880 Vienna is a must for musical theater buffs. Lovely score includes "If Love Were All" and "I'll See You Again." St. Helier vividly re-creates her London stage role of Manon la Crevette, written for her by Coward. Remade in 1940.▼

Bitter Sweet (1940) **C-92m.** *** D: W.S. Van Dyke II. Jeanette MacDonald, Nelson Eddy, George Sanders, Felix Bressart, Lynne Carver, Ian Hunter, Sig Ruman. Ignore plot, enjoy Noel Coward's songs in lavishly filmed operetta. Wonderful Herman Bing provides funniest scene as shopkeeper who hires Nelson and Jeanette to give his daughter music lessons.▼▶

Bitter Tea of General Yen, The (1933) **89m.** ***½ D: Frank Capra. Barbara Stanwyck, Nils Asther, Gavin Gordon, Toshia Mori, Richard Loo, Lucien Littlefield, Clara Blandick, Walter Connolly. May seem antiquated to modern audiences, but Capra's sensuous story of American woman's strange fascination with a Chinese warlord is still dazzling. A moody, beautifully atmospheric, sensitively performed film.▼▶

Bitter Victory (1957-French) **82m.** *** D: Nicholas Ray. Richard Burton, Curt Jurgens, Ruth Roman, Raymond Pellegrin, Anthony Bushell, Christopher Lee. Strong WW2 story with Jurgens as unfit commander who leads mission against Rommel's desert headquarters; Roman is his wife who's had prior affair with officer Burton. 103m. versions now in circulation are from British release of this film. CinemaScope.▶

Bizarre, Bizarre SEE: **Drôle de drame**

Black Angel (1946) **80m.** *** D: Roy William Neill. Dan Duryea, June Vincent, Peter Lorre, Broderick Crawford, Wallace Ford. First-rate whodunit (by Cornell Woolrich) of Vincent trying to clear husband of charge that he murdered Duryea's wife. Imaginative film will have you glued to the screen all the way.▼▶

Black Arrow, The (1948) **76m.** *** D: Gordon Douglas. Louis Hayward, Janet Blair, George Macready, Edgar Buchanan, Paul Cavanagh. Superior swashbuckler with dashing knight Hayward, lovely heroine Blair, and villain Macready. Truly exciting finale with hero vs. villain in jousting tournament. Based on a Robert Louis Stevenson novel. Remade for TV in 1985.▼▶

Black Bart (1948) **C-80m.** **½ D: George Sherman. Yvonne De Carlo, Dan Duryea, Jeffrey Lynn, Percy Kilbride. Enticing De Carlo steps between outlaws Duryea and Lynn, foiling their attempt to overthrow Wells Fargo company. Remade as THE RIDE TO HANGMAN'S TREE (1967).

Blackbeard, the Pirate (1952) **C-99m.** ** D: Raoul Walsh. Robert Newton, Linda Darnell, William Bendix, Keith Andes, Richard Egan, Irene Ryan. Newton is rambunctious as 17th-century buccaneer, with lovely Darnell his captive; fun for a while, but Newton's hamming soon grows tiresome.▼▶

Black Beauty (1946) **74m.** **½ D: Max Nosseck. Mona Freeman, Richard Denning, Evelyn Ankers, Terry Kilburn, Arthur Space, J. M. Kerrigan. Second sound version of Anna Sewell's tale of little girl and her love for her horse is decent if unspectacular, with pleasing Dimitri Tiomkin score. Previously filmed in 1917, 1921, and 1933, remade in 1971 and 1994, and as a British TV series.▼

Blackboard Jungle (1955) **101m.** ***½ D: Richard Brooks. Glenn Ford, Anne Francis, Vic Morrow, Louis Calhern, Sidney Poitier, Richard Kiley, Warner Anderson, Margaret Hayes, Emile Meyer, John Hoyt, Rafael Campos, Paul Mazursky. Excellent adaptation of Evan Hunter's novel (scripted by the director) of a teacher's harrowing experiences in N.Y.C. school system. Poitier memorable as a troubled youth. Hard-hitting entertainment. This was the first film to feature rock music—Bill Haley's "Rock Around the Clock" is played over the opening credits. Look for a young Jamie Farr (billed as Jameel Farah). Also shown in computer-colored version.▼▶

Black Book, The SEE: **Reign of Terror**

Black Camel, The (1931) **71m.** **½ D: Hamilton MacFadden. Warner Oland, Sally Eilers, Bela Lugosi, Dorothy Revier, Victor Varconi, Robert Young, Dwight Frye, Marjorie White, C. Henry Gordon, Mary Gordon. Interesting early-talkie *Charlie Chan* whodunit, with Oland probing the murders of an actress and a beachcomber on his home turf of Hawaii, with cute scenes of his domestic life with ten kids. Picturesque locations and exceptional cast highlight this entry, based on Earl Derr Biggers novel. Feature debut of Robert Young. Reworked as CHARLIE CHAN IN RIO.▶

Black Castle, The (1952) **81m.** ** D: Nathan Juran. Richard Greene, Boris Karloff, Stephen McNally, Paula Corday, Lon Chaney, Jr., John Hoyt. Uninspired gothic melodrama has Greene investigating disappearance of two friends who were guests of sinister Austrian count (McNally). Karloff reduced to colorless supporting role.▼▶

Black Cat, The (1934) **65m.** ***½ D: Edgar G. Ulmer. Karloff (Boris Karloff), Bela Lugosi, David Manners, Jacqueline Wells (Julie Bishop), Lucille Lund, Henry Armetta, Harry Cording. Polished horror film with bizarre sets, even more bizarre plot. Confrontation of architect/devil-worshiper Karloff and doctor Lugosi is still fascinating. The first of Boris and Bela's many teamings. Look fast for John Carradine as an organist at Satanic Mass. Film bears absolutely no resemblance to eponymous Edgar Allan Poe tale.▼◑

Black Cat, The (1941) 70m. **½ D: Albert S. Rogell. Basil Rathbone, Hugh Herbert, Broderick Crawford, Bela Lugosi, Gale Sondergaard, Anne Gwynne, Gladys Cooper, Alan Ladd. Old-dark-house comedy-mystery has relatives gathering for the reading of a will. Rathbone and Lugosi add authenticity to this minor B, with atmospheric photography by Stanley Cortez.▼◑

Black Cross (1960-Polish) C-175m. ** D: Aleksander Ford. Urszula Modrzynska, Grazyna Staniszewska, Andrzej Szalawski. Sterile, unremarkable account of Teutonic knights raiding Poland is notable only for its detailed medieval settings. Dyaliscope.

Black Dakotas, The (1954) C-65m. ** D: Ray Nazarro. Gary Merrill, Wanda Hendrix, John Bromfield, Noah Beery, Jr. Bland oater of greedy men who try to outwit the redskins and incite a war.◗

Black Devils of Kali, The SEE: **Mystery of the Black Jungle**

Black Dragons (1942) 61m. *½ D: William Nigh. Bela Lugosi, Joan Barclay, Clayton Moore, George Pembroke, Robert Frazer. Nazi doctor Lugosi has been altering the faces of some Japanese, to make them pass as Americans for future terrorist activity. Then-topical chiller is now a sleep-inducing bore.▼◑

Black Fox (1962) 89m. ***½ D: Louis Clyde Stoumen. Narrated by Marlene Dietrich. Exceedingly taut, grim documentary tracing the rise and fall of Adolf Hitler, focusing on his use of power during Third Reich. Academy Award winner as Best Documentary Feature.▼◑

Black Friday (1940) 70m. **½ D: Arthur Lubin. Boris Karloff, Bela Lugosi, Stanley Ridges, Anne Nagel, Anne Gwynne, Virginia Brissac. Well-made little chiller with Karloff putting gangster's brain into a professor's body. Jekyll-Hyde results are fascinating; Ridges excellent as victim. Lugosi has small, thankless role as gangster.▼◑

Black Fury (1935) 92m. *** D: Michael Curtiz. Paul Muni, Karen Morley, William Gargan, Barton MacLane, John Qualen, J. Carrol Naish, Vince Barnett. Hard-hitting Warner Bros. melodrama about union manipulation of coal miners, with Muni as robust "bohunk" who gets in over his head. Realistic, strikingly filmed, if a bit uneven dramatically. Muni's accent makes it tough to understand him at times. Based on a true story.▼◗

Black Gold (1947) C-92m. **½ D: Phil Karlson. Anthony Quinn, Katherine DeMille, Elyse Knox, Ducky Louie, Kane Richmond, Moroni Olsen, Raymond Hat-

ton, Thurston Hall, Darryl Hickman. Effective, if sentimental, tale of Indian Quinn who discovers oil on his land and trains a Chinese orphan (Louie) to be the jockey for his beloved thoroughbred. Low-budget, but warmly acted, with excellent use of Cinecolor process. Quinn and DeMille were then husband and wife.▼

Black Gold (1963) 98m. ** D: Leslie Martinson. Philip Carey, Diane McBain, James Best, Claude Akins, Iron Eyes Cody. Predictable search for oil set in Oklahoma, with standard villain and supposedly ironic outcome.◗

Black Hand (1950) 93m. **½ D: Richard Thorpe. Gene Kelly, J. Carrol Naish, Teresa Celli, Marc Lawrence, Frank Puglia. If you can buy Kelly as an Italian immigrant in N.Y.C. (circa 1908), you'll probably go along with this naive but entertaining story about a young man's attempt to avenge his father's murder by the infamous—and seemingly unstoppable—Italian crime syndicate known as the Black Hand.▼◗

Black Horse Canyon (1954) C-81m. **½ D: Jesse Hibbs. Joel McCrea, Mari Blanchard, Race Gentry, Murvyn Vye. Diverting, gentle Western about rebellious black stallion and those who recapture him.

Blackjack Ketchum, Desperado (1956) 76m. *½ D: Earl Bellamy. Howard Duff, Victor Jory, Maggie Mahoney, Angela Stevens. Former gunslinger must endure another shoot-out before returning to a peaceful way of life.

Black Knight, The (1954-U.S.-British) C-85m. **½ D: Tay Garnett. Alan Ladd, Patricia Medina, Andre Morell, Harry Andrews, Peter Cushing. Ladd lends some bounce to small budgeter about mysterious horseman championing King Arthur's cause in merry old England.

Black Legion (1936) 83m. *** D: Archie Mayo. Humphrey Bogart, Erin O'Brien-Moore, Dick Foran, Ann Sheridan, Joe Sauers (Sawyer), Helen Flint, Dickie Jones, Henry Brandon. Factory worker Bogart, disappointed at losing a promotion to a coworker named Dombrowski (Brandon), becomes involved with a Ku Klux Klan–ish group. Powerful, still-relevant social drama.▼◗

Black Like Me (1964) 107m. *** D: Carl Lerner. James Whitmore, Roscoe Lee Browne, Lenka Petersen, Sorrell Booke, Will Geer, Al Freeman, Jr., Dan Priest, Raymond St. Jacques. Strong drama based on actual history of reporter who took drugs that allowed him to pass for black so he could experience racial prejudice firsthand. Some aspects of presentation are dated, but themes are still timely.▼◗

Black Magic (1944) 67m. *½ D: Phil Rosen. Sidney Toler, Mantan Moreland, Frances Chan, Jacqueline de Wit, Claudia Dell, Edward Earle, Joseph Crehan. Minor *Charlie Chan* mystery involving phony fortune tellers and murder at a seance. Aka MEETING AT MIDNIGHT.▼●◗

Black Magic (1949) 105m. **½ D: Gregory Ratoff. Orson Welles, Akim Tamiroff, Nancy Guild, Raymond Burr, Frank Latimore. Welles is predictably florid in chronicle of famous charlatan Cagliostro who seeks to rise to power in 18th-century Italy. (He codirected this handsome film, uncredited.) Filmed in Rome.▼●◗

Blackmail (1929-British) 86m. *** D: Alfred Hitchcock. Anny Ondra, Sara Allgood, John Longden, Charles Paton, Donald Calthrop, Cyril Ritchard. Young woman kills man who tries to rape her, then finds herself caught between investigating detective (who happens to be her boyfriend) and a blackmailer. Hitchcock's—and England's—first talking picture is still exciting, especially for fans and students of the director's work. Originally shot as a silent; that version, running 75m., also exists (and is significantly better). Leading lady Ondra had a heavy accent, so her voice was dubbed for the talkie by Joan Barry.▼●◗

Blackmail (1939) 81m. **½ D: H. C. Potter. Edward G. Robinson, Ruth Hussey, Gene Lockhart, Bobs Watson, Guinn Williams, John Wray, Arthur Hohl. Well-regarded Robinson, an expert at putting out oil fires, has a secret past: he escaped from jail after being falsely convicted of robbery. Slimy Lockhart shows up and threatens blackmail. Taut, clever drama-thriller, marred only by a pat finale.

Blackmail (1947) 67m. **½ D: Lesley Selander. William Marshall, Adele Mara, Ricardo Cortez, Grant Withers, Stephanie Bachelor, Richard Fraser, Roy Barcroft, George J. Lewis. Gumshoe Marshall is up to his fedora in corpses, fistfights, and double-dealing dames after being hired by playboy Cortez to prove he didn't kill a woman who was blackmailing him. Standard but perversely enjoyable private-eye stuff, from a story by pulp detective author Robert Leslie Bellem. Notable for some of the most hilariously hard-boiled dialogue in film history.

Black Market Babies (1945) 71m. ** D: William Beaudine. Ralph Morgan, Kane Richmond, Jayne Hazard, Teala Loring, Marjorie Hoshelle, George Meeker, Maris Wrixon, Nana Bryant, Addison Richards. Exposé of a racket that preys upon pregnant women, selling their babies to couples with money. Based on a magazine story about a true-life situation, but handled in uninspired B-movie terms.◗

Black Moon (1934) 68m. **½ D: Roy William Neill. Jack Holt, Fay Wray, Dorothy Burgess, Cora Sue Collins, Arnold Korff, Clarence Muse. A woman raised in the West Indies feels an irresistible compulsion to return, becomes immersed in sacrificial voodoo rituals. Very odd, dark, downbeat film is

too sluggish to have the impact it promises early on, but still interesting. Moodily photographed by Joseph August.◗

Black Narcissus (1947-British) C-99m. **** D: Michael Powell, Emeric Pressburger. Deborah Kerr, David Farrar, Sabu, Jean Simmons, Kathleen Byron, Flora Robson, Esmond Knight. Visually sumptuous, dramatically charged movie, from Rumer Godden novel, about nuns trying to establish a mission in a remote mountaintop Himalayan outpost amid formidable physical and emotional challenges. One of the most breathtaking color films ever made (winning Oscars for cinematographer Jack Cardiff and art director Alfred Junge). Scenes in which Mother Superior Kerr recalls her former life, a key plot element, were originally censored from American prints.▼●◗

Black Orchid, The (1959) 96m. **½ D: Martin Ritt. Sophia Loren, Anthony Quinn, Ina Balin, Jimmie Baird, (Peter) Mark Richman, Naomi Stevens, Frank Puglia. Fabricated soaper of bumbling businessman (Quinn) romancing criminal's widow (Loren) and the problem of convincing her children that marriage will make all their lives better. VistaVision.▼◗

Black Orpheus (1959-French-Brazilian) C-103m. ***½ D: Marcel Camus. Breno Mello, Marpessa Dawn, Lea Garcia, Adhemar Da Silva, Lourdes De Oliveira. Street-car conductor Mello and country girl Dawn fall in love in Rio de Janeiro during Carnival. Lyrical updating of the Orpheus and Eurydice legend is beautifully acted and directed. Oscar winner for Best Foreign Film; rhythmic score by Luis Bonfa and Antonio Carlos Jobim. Remade as ORFEU.▼●◗

Blackout (1954-British) 87m. ** D: Terence Fisher. Dane Clark, Belinda Lee, Betty Ann Davies, Eleanor Summerfield. Clark, down on his luck, makes some fast money by agreeing to marry a pretty blonde—and then finds himself the patsy in a murder case. Ordinary programmer. Original British title: MURDER BY PROXY.▼◗

Black Patch (1957) 83m. **½ D: Allen H. Miner. George Montgomery, Diane Brewster, Tom Pittman, Leo Gordon, House Peters, Jr., Lynn Cartwright, Peter Brocco, Strother Martin, Sebastian Cabot. One-eyed Marshal Montgomery has his hands full when a friend moves to town with his wife—the woman Montgomery once loved. Interesting dark-tinged Western written by costar Gordon.◗

Black Peter (1964-Czech) 85m. **½ D: Miloš Forman. Ladislav Jakim, Pavla Martínková, Jan Vostrčil, Vladimir Pucholt, Pavel Sedláček, Zdenek Kulhánek. Winning serio-comedy about quiet teenager Peter's (Jakim) summer in a Czech town. He is dissatisfied with his new job, his parents, and life in general, but trying to catch the eye of pretty Martínková. Forman's feature directorial debut—which he also co-wrote—captures generational tensions and the restlessness of youth to a naturalistic tee (with all roles, except Pucholt as Peter's father, played by nonactors), but the film is often as aimless as its hero. Aka BLACK SHEEP.▶

Black Pirate, The (1926) **C-85m.** *** D: Albert Parker. Douglas Fairbanks, Sr., Billie Dove, Anders Randolf, Donald Crisp, Tempe Pigott, Sam De Grasse. Robust silent swashbuckler with Fairbanks a nobleman who turns pirate after being victimized by cutthroats. Filmed in early Technicolor process.▼◐

Black Pirates, The (1954-Mexican-Salvadoran) **C-72m.** **½ D: Allen H. Miner. Anthony Dexter, Martha Roth, Lon Chaney (Jr.), Robert Clarke, Alfonso Bedoya. Uninspired account of pirates searching for gold.▼

Black Raven, The (1943) **64m.** *½ D: Sam Newfield. George Zucco, Wanda McKay, Noel Madison, Bob Randall (Bob Livingston), Byron Foulger. Paltry (and obvious) whodunit, with various people stranded at Zucco's inn during a storm. Glenn Strange is the comedy relief!▼◐

Black Rebels, The SEE: **This Rebel Breed**

Black Room, The (1935) **67m.** *** D: Roy William Neill. Boris Karloff, Marian Marsh, Robert Allen, Katherine DeMille, John Buckler, Thurston Hall. Excellent, understated thriller of twin brothers (Karloff) and the ancient curse that dominates their lives in 19th-century Hungary. Features one—no, *two*—of Karloff's best performances.▼◐

Black Rose, The (1950) **C-120m.** ** D: Henry Hathaway. Tyrone Power, Cecile Aubry, Orson Welles, Jack Hawkins, Michael Rennie, Herbert Lom, James Robertson Justice, Finlay Currie, Bobby (Robert) Blake, Laurence Harvey. Sweeping pageantry follows Norman-hating Power on Oriental adventures during 1200s; plodding film only somewhat redeemed by dynamic action scenes. Filmed in England and North Africa by Jack Cardiff.▶

Black Sabbath (1963-Italian) **C-99m.** **½ D: Mario Bava. Boris Karloff, Mark Damon, Suzy Anderson, Jacqueline Pierreux. Italian three-part film hosted by Karloff, who appears in final episode about a vampire controlling an entire family. Other sequences are good, atmospheric.▼◐

Black Scorpion, The (1957) **88m.** *½ D: Edward Ludwig. Richard Denning, Carlos Rivas, Mara Corday, Mario Navarro. Outstanding animation by KING KONG's Willis O'Brien is the highlight of this sci-fi thriller about giant arachnids popping out of a volcanic fissure in Mexico. Basically a remake of the superior THEM!▼◐

Black Sheep (1935) **76m.** *** D: Allan Dwan. Edmund Lowe, Claire Trevor, Tom Brown, Eugene Pallette, Adrienne Ames, Herbert Mundin, Ford Sterling, Jed Prouty, Billy Bevan. Lowe eschews his usual wise-cracking persona and gives one of his best performances as a professional gambler who fleeces travelers on ocean liners. He takes pity on a young, naïve man who's been robbed, and then discovers it's his own son. Allen Rivkin's screenplay gives wonderful banter to Lowe and Trevor; Dwan conceived the story.

Black Sheep (1964-Czech) SEE: **Black Peter**

Black Shield of Falworth, The (1954) **C-99m.** **½ D: Rudolph Maté. Tony Curtis, Janet Leigh, David Farrar, Barbara Rush, Herbert Marshall. Juvenile version of Howard Pyle novel *Men of Iron*; Curtis unconvincing as nobility rising through ranks to knighthood in medieval England. Settings, supporting cast bolster production. CinemaScope.▼◐

Black Sleep, The (1956) **81m.** *½ D: Reginald LeBorg. Basil Rathbone, Akim Tamiroff, Lon Chaney (Jr.), John Carradine, Bela Lugosi, Herbert Rudley, Patricia Blake (Blair), Tor Johnson. Big horror cast cannot save dull, unatmospheric tale of doctor doing experimental brain surgery in remote English castle. Laughable. Reissued as DR. CADMAN'S SECRET. ▼◐

Black Spurs (1965) **C-81m.** *½ D: R. G. Springsteen. Rory Calhoun, Terry Moore, Linda Darnell, Scott Brady, Lon Chaney (Jr.), Bruce Cabot, Richard Arlen, Patricia Owens, James Best, Jerome Courtland, DeForest Kelley. Ordinary Western with attraction of one-time movie stars including Darnell (her last film). Standard horse opera. Techniscope.

Black Sunday (1960-Italian) **83m.** **½ D: Mario Bava. Barbara Steele, John Richardson, Ivo Garrani, Andrea Checchi. Intriguing story of the one day each century when Satan roams the earth. Steele is a witch who swears vengeance on the descendants of those who killed her hundreds of years ago. Beautifully atmospheric.▼◐

Black Swan, The (1942) **C-85m.** *** D: Henry King. Tyrone Power, Maureen O'Hara, Laird Cregar, Thomas Mitchell, George Sanders, Anthony Quinn, George Zucco. Power is at his dashing best in this lively swashbuckler from the Rafael Sabatini novel about rival pirate gangs in the Caribbean. Sanders seems to be having fun cast against type as a scurrilous brigand. Enhanced by Alfred Newman's music and Leon Shamroy's Oscar-winning Technicolor cinematography.▼◐

Black Tent, The (1956-British) **C-93m.** ** D: Brian Hurst. Anthony Steel, Donald Sinden, Anna Maria Sandri, Donald Pleasence. Passable mixture of romance and action in the African desert as British soldier Steel romances native chief's daughter, helps tribe fight off Nazi attack. VistaVision.▼◐

[65]

Black Tights (1960-French) **C-120m.** ★★★
D: Terence Young. Cyd Charisse, Moira
Shearer, Zizi Jeanmaire, Dirk Sanders,
Roland Petit; narrated by Maurice Chevalier. Ballet fans will feast on this quartet
of stunning performances, featuring some
of the era's top dance talent. Our favorite:
the ballet of Rostand's *Cyrano de Bergerac,*
with Shearer a lovely Roxanne. Super Technirama 70.▼▶

Black Torment, The (1964-British) **C-
90m.** ★★ D: Robert Hartford-Davis. Heather
Sears, John Turner, Ann Lynn, Peter Arne,
Norman Bird, Raymond Huntley, Joseph
Tomelty. In late 18th-century England,
Sir Richard (Turner) brings his new bride
(Sears) home to his isolated manor. Soon
events become mysterious and sinister,
and it all ends in a lively swordfight. Handsomely made Hammer-like period thriller
suffers from the use of one of the most hackneyed of all "surprises."▶

Black Tuesday (1954) **80m.** ★★★ D: Hugo
Fregonese. Edward G. Robinson, Peter
Graves, Jean Parker, Milburn Stone. Throwback to 1930-ish gangster films, with Robinson and Graves as escaped convicts being
hunted by cops. Nice gunplay, with Parker
good as the moll.

Black Watch, The (1929) **93m.** ★★½ D:
John Ford. Victor McLaglen, Myrna Loy,
David Rollins, Lumsden Hare, Roy D'Arcy,
Mitchell Lewis, Cyril Chadwick, David Tor-
rence, Francis Ford. McLaglen is a British
Army officer who is given a secret mis-
sion to quell a holy war in India, where he
dallies with exotic native "goddess" Loy.
Ford's first talkie contains rousing action
and striking photography by Joseph August,
but suffers from interminable and laughable
love scenes. Look fast for John Wayne and
Randolph Scott. Remade in 1953 as KING
OF THE KHYBER RIFLES.

Blackwell's Island (1939) **71m.** ★★½ D:
William McGann. John Garfield, Rosemary Lane, Dick Purcell, Victor Jory, Stanley Fields, Peggy Shannon, Leon Ames,
Milburn Stone. Peppy little based-on-fact
gangster film with crusading reporter Garfield attempting to nail tough but dimwitted
mobster Fields.▶

Black Whip, The (1956) **77m.** ★½ D: Charles
Marquis Warren. Hugh Marlowe, Coleen
Gray, Angie Dickinson, Sheb Wooley. Only
spice to this oater is bevy of beautiful girls
who are rescued by Marlowe. Regalscope.

Black Widow (1954) **C-95m.** ★★ D: Nunnally Johnson. Ginger Rogers, Van Heflin,
Gene Tierney, George Raft, Peggy Ann
Garner, Reginald Gardiner, Virginia Leith,
Otto Kruger, Cathleen Nesbitt, Skip Homeier. Broadway producer Heflin takes
young writer Garner under his wing, is
naturally suspected when she turns up dead
in his apartment. Glossy but dull adaptation
of Patrick Quentin mystery, with remarkably poor performances by Rogers as bitchy
star and Raft as dogged detective. Johnson
also produced and wrote the screenplay.
CinemaScope.▶

Black Zoo (1963) **C-88m.** ★½ D: Robert
Gordon. Michael Gough, Virginia Grey,
Jerome Cowan, Elisha Cook, Jeanne Cooper. Gough, head of private zoo, doubles as
leader of cult of animal worshipers. Good
cast flounders, but film has a moment or
two. Panavision.▶

Blanche Fury (1948-British) **C-95m.** ★★★
D: Marc Allegret. Stewart Granger, Valerie Hobson, Walter Fitzgerald, Michael
Gough, Maurice Denham. Beautifully
mounted gothic melodrama about a governess who marries into wealthy family and the
headstrong steward (Granger) who aspires
to run the estate.▼

Blast of Silence (1961) **77m.** ★★★ D: Allen
Baron. Allen Baron, Molly McCarthy, Larry
Tucker, Peter H. Clune, Danny Meehan.
Moody, micro-budgeted noir chronicling a
Cleveland hit man's fateful trip to N.Y.C.
during Christmastime to carry out a contract.
Outstanding location work and the jazzy,
omniscient narration (written by Waldo Salt
under a pseudonym and performed by an uncredited Lionel Stander) highlight this cool
cult film, scripted by actor-director Baron.▶

Blaze of Noon (1947) **91m.** ★★½ D: John
Farrow. Anne Baxter, William Holden,
Sonny Tufts, William Bendix, Sterling
Hayden. Hokey story of Holden torn be-
tween his wife (Baxter) and his true love,
flying.

Blazing Arrows SEE: **Fighting Caravans**

Blazing Forest, The (1952) **C-90m.** ★½
D: Edward Ludwig. John Payne, Agnes
Moorehead, Richard Arlen, William Demarest, Susan Morrow. Felling trees and
romancing Moorehead's niece (Morrow)
occupies Payne till big fire diverts him, but
not the bored viewer.

Blazing Sun, The (1950) **70m.** ★★ D: John
English. Gene Autry, Pat Buttram, Lynne
Roberts, Anne Gwynne, Edward Norris,
Kenne Duncan, Alan Hale, Jr., Gregg Barton, Tom London. A couple of exciting action sequences aboard a speeding freight
train and an engaging dual role for Duncan
(as good and bad brothers) liven up this
otherwise routine modern-day Autry Western in which he tracks down a crafty bank
robber. Gene gets to serenade two leading
ladies, Roberts and Gwynne.

Blessed Event (1932) **81m.** ★★★ D: Roy Del
Ruth. Lee Tracy, Mary Brian, Dick Powell,
Emma Dunn, Frank McHugh, Allen Jenkins,
Ned Sparks, Ruth Donnelly. Tracy's most
famous role has him a Walter Winchell prototype whose spicy column makes him famous but also gets him in hot water; Powell
makes film debut as crooner. Fast-moving,
delightful.▼▶

Blind Adventure (1933) **63m.** ★★★ D: Ernest

[66]

B. Schoedsack. Robert Armstrong, Helen Mack, Ralph Bellamy, Roland Young, John Miljan, Laura Hope Crews. Armstrong is an American in London who stumbles into the midst of international intrigue, with Mack an innocent dupe; together they try to unravel the mystery, enlisting the aid of cat burglar Young. Modest but entertaining yarn in the vein of THE THIN MAN and THE 39 STEPS. Overlooked credit for Schoedsack, paired again with Armstrong, from KING KONG and THE SON OF KONG, and Mack, the latter film's leading lady.

Blind Alley (1939) **71m.** ****½** D: Charles Vidor. Chester Morris, Ralph Bellamy, Ann Dvorak, Joan Perry, Melville Cooper, Rose Stradner, John Eldredge. One of Hollywood's first attempts to illustrate psychological ideas. Morris is troubled gangster who holds psychiatrist Bellamy prisoner and allows himself to be analyzed. Dated but interesting. Remade as THE DARK PAST. **)**

Blind Date (1934) **71m.** ****½** D: Roy William Neill. Ann Sothern, Paul Kelly, Neil Hamilton, Mickey Rooney, Jane Darwell, Joan Gale. Sothern has her hands full choosing between mechanic Kelly and wealthy Hamilton in this pleasant little domestic comedy.

Blind Date (1959) SEE: **Chance Meeting**

Blind Husbands (1919) **93m.** ******* D: Erich von Stroheim. Erich von Stroheim, Gibson Gowland, Sam De Grasse, Francelia Billington, Fay Holderness. Von Stroheim plays a decadent Austrian military officer on holiday in the Alps who sets out to seduce the wife of a rich American doctor. Von Stroheim's directorial debut already reveals his predilection toward sexual frustration and moral corruption and still holds interest through arresting visuals and perverse psychological details. **▼)**

Blind Spot (1947) **73m.** ******* D: Robert Gordon. Chester Morris, Constance Dowling, Steven Geray, Sid Tomack. Mystery writer Morris has to extricate himself from charge of murdering his publisher in this tight little mystery.

Blithe Spirit (1945-British) **C-96m.** *****½** D: David Lean. Rex Harrison, Constance Cummings, Kay Hammond, Margaret Rutherford, Hugh Wakefield, Joyce Carey. Delicious adaptation of Noel Coward's comedy-fantasy about a man whose long-dead first wife appears to haunt—and taunt—him in his newly married life. Rutherford is wonderful as Madame Arcati, the spiritual medium; this earned an Oscar for its special effects. Scripted by the director, the producer (Anthony Havelock-Allan), and the cinematographer (Ronald Neame). **▼●)**

Blob, The (1958) **C-86m.** ****** D: Irvin S. Yeaworth, Jr. Steven McQueen, Aneta Corseaut (Corsaut), Earl Rowe, Olin Howlin. Endearingly campy classic of cheap '50s sci-fi has "Steven" (in his first starring role) leading teenagers into battle to save their small town from being swallowed up by giant glop of cherry Jell-O from outer space. Not really all that good, but how can you hate a film like this? (Especially when Burt Bacharach composed the title song.) Filmed in Valley Forge, PA. Later redubbed for comic effect as BLOBERMOUTH. Sequel: BEWARE! THE BLOB. Remade 30 years later. **▼●)**

Blockade (1938) **85m.** ******* D: William Dieterle. Madeleine Carroll, Henry Fonda, Leo Carrillo, John Halliday, Vladimir Sokoloff, Reginald Denny. Vivid romance drama of Spanish Civil War with globetrotting Carroll falling in love with fighting Fonda. **)**

Block Busters (1944) **60m.** ****** D: Wallace Fox. Leo Gorcey, Huntz Hall, Gabriel Dell, Jimmy Strand, Minerva Urecal, Noah Beery, Sr., Billy Benedict, Bernard Gorcey. Muggs fights a new French kid in town, but all is forgiven when he helps the East Side Kids win the big baseball game. Raucous comedy; a sad comedown for silent clown Harry Langdon in a bit part.

Block-Heads (1938) **55m.** ******* D: John G. Blystone. Stan Laurel, Oliver Hardy, Patricia Ellis, Minna Gombell, Billy Gilbert, James Finlayson. Stan's been marching in a trench for 20 years—nobody told him WW1 was over! Ollie brings him home to find he hasn't changed. Top L&H. Also shown in computer-colored version. **▼)**

Blond Cheat (1938) **62m.** ****** D: Joseph Santley. Joan Fontaine, Derrick de Marney, Cecil Kellaway, Lilian Bond, Cecil Cunningham, Robert Coote, Olaf Hytten, John Sutton. Actress Fontaine is hired by the father of heiress Bond to break up her engagement to playboy de Marney. Radiant young Fontaine's charm boosts this harmless romantic-comedy trifle, one of five quickies she made in 1938.

Blonde Bait (1956-British) **70m.** ****** D: Elmo Williams. Beverly Michaels, Jim Davis, Joan Rice, Richard Travis, Paul Cavanagh, Thora Hird, Avril Angers, Gordon Jackson. Cheap, toothy blond bombshell Michaels excels as a Yank showgirl breaking out of a sedate British prison for women. British film, originally titled WOMEN WITHOUT MEN, was retitled, reedited, and reshot (with Davis, Travis, and Cavanagh added to cast) for U.S. release.

Blonde Bombshell SEE: **Bombshell**

Blonde Crazy (1931) **79m.** ****½** D: Roy Del Ruth. James Cagney, Joan Blondell, Louis Calhern, Ray Milland, Polly Walters, Nat Pendleton. Dated fun with Cagney as small-time con man who plays cat-and-mouse with big-time sharpie Calhern. Young Milland appears as businessman who marries Jimmy's girlfriend, Blondell. **▼●)**

Blonde Dynamite (1950) **66m.** ****** D: William Beaudine. Leo Gorcey, Huntz Hall, Gabriel Dell, Adele Jergens, Harry Lewis, Murray Alper, Bernard Gorcey, Billy Benedict, David Gorcey, Jody Gilbert. The Bowery Boys go into the escort service business and predictably get mixed up with crooks. ▶

Blonde Fever (1944) **69m.** ** D: Richard Whorf. Philip Dorn, Mary Astor, Felix Bressart, Gloria Grahame, Marshall Thompson. Astor lends class to this mild account of married woman whose husband (Dorn) is vamped by sultry Grahame. Based on a play by Ferenc Molnár. Look for Ava Gardner in a bit. And yes, that's Jessica Tandy and Hume Cronyn, appearing briefly (without billing).

Blonde for a Day (1946) **67m.** *½ D: Sam Newfield. Hugh Beaumont, Kathryn Adams, Cy Kendall, Marjorie Hoshelle, Richard Fraser, Paul Bryar. Negligible *Michael Shayne* murder mystery, centering on a female crime reporter targeted for death by the crooks she's exposing.

Blonde from Brooklyn (1945) **65m.** ** D: Del Lord. Lynn Merrick, Robert Stanton (Bob Haymes), Thurston Hall, Mary Treen, Hugh Beaumont, Gwen Verdon. Merrick and newly minted WW2 vet Stanton scheme to crack the big time as radio singers. Paper-thin plot serves as an excuse for almost nonstop songs in this B musical.

Blonde Ice (1948) **73m.** **½ D: Jack Bernhard. Robert Paige, Leslie Brooks, Russ Vincent, Michael Whalen, James Griffith, Emory Parnell, Walter Sande, Selmer Jackson. Beautiful Brooks marries for money and can't wait for her honeymoon to be over to plot her husband's demise. Enjoyable noir-ish programmer; Brooks delivers as an icy femme fatale. ▼▶

Blonde in a White Car SEE: **Nude in a White Car**

Blondes at Work (1938) **63m.** ** D: Frank McDonald. Glenda Farrell, Barton MacLane, Tom Kennedy, Rosella Towne, Donald Briggs, John Ridgely, Carole Landis. Farrell is back as indefatigable reporter Torchy Blane, confounding her colleagues with scoops stolen directly from her cop boyfriend MacLane. Reworking of the 1935 Bette Davis FRONT PAGE WOMAN. ▶

Blonde Savage (1947) **62m.** **½ D: S. K. Seeley (Steve Sekely). Leif Erickson, Gale Sherwood, Veda Ann Borg, Douglass Dumbrille, Matt Willis. The perils of a soundstage African jungle and the stock footage library don't deter he-man pilot Erickson as he seeks to protect a white girl raised by natives from wicked diamond miner Dumbrille. As these things go, this one's a small cut above.

Blonde Venus (1932) **97m.** *** D: Josef von Sternberg. Marlene Dietrich, Herbert Marshall, Cary Grant, Dickie Moore, Sidney Toler, Hattie McDaniel. Episodic story of performer Dietrich returning to the stage while her chemist husband is off seeking a cure for his illness; plenty of complications ensue, including her evolving relationship with wealthy, powerful Grant. A triumph of style over content; this is the film where Marlene appears in an ape suit to sing "Hot Voodoo"! ▼▶

Blondie With a vast audience already familiar with the Chic Young comic strip (which had made its debut in 1930), a Blondie movie series seemed like a shoo-in in 1938—and it was. Penny Singleton, the former Dorothy McNulty, bleached her hair blonde and was a perfect choice to play the title character. Arthur Lake found the role of a lifetime as bumbling Dagwood Bumstead. Larry Simms was cast as Baby Dumpling, and an endearing pooch was found to play Daisy. Character actor Jonathan Hale was an inspired choice for Dagwood's irascible boss, J. C. Dithers. Inquisitive Alvin Fuddle was played by Danny Mummert, with Fay Helm as his mother. The series prospered for 12 years and 28 episodes. The first ones were the best—fresh and original, with many clever touches belying the fact that they were low-budget films. By the mid-1940s, however, a formula set in; the films became more predictable, and the humor more contrived. One plus for the series was that there was some continuity from one episode to the next, with Baby Dumpling growing up, starting school in the fourth film, taking the name of Alexander in the eleventh. Cookie is also born in the eleventh film, and Daisy has pups in the following one. Another bonus derives from the fact that Columbia used the series as a proving ground for some of its fledgling stars, including Rita Hayworth in BLONDIE ON A BUDGET, Glenn Ford in BLONDIE PLAYS CUPID, and Larry Parks and Janet Blair in BLONDIE GOES TO COLLEGE. Other future "names" like Lloyd Bridges and Robert Sterling turn up in bit parts. The films were a particular field day for familiar-faced character actors, including Irving Bacon, who created the role of the harassed mailman (later played by Eddie Acuff and then Dick Wessel), Jerome Cowan (who replaced Jonathan Hale as Dagwood's boss), and Jack Rice (best remembered as Edgar Kennedy's obnoxious brother-in-law, playing a not dissimilar role in Dagwood's office).

BLONDIE

Blondie (1938)
Blondie Meets the Boss (1939)
Blondie Takes a Vacation (1939)
Blondie Brings Up Baby (1939)
Blondie on a Budget (1940)
Blondie Has Servant Trouble (1940)
Blondie Plays Cupid (1940)
Blondie Goes Latin (1941)

Blondie in Society (1941)
Blondie Goes to College (1942)
Blondie's Blessed Event (1942)
Blondie for Victory (1942)
It's a Great Life (1943)
Footlight Glamour (1943)
Leave It to Blondie (1945)
Life With Blondie (1946)
Blondie's Lucky Day (1946)
Blondie Knows Best (1946)
Blondie's Big Moment (1947)
Blondie's Holiday (1947)
Blondie in the Dough (1947)
Blondie's Anniversary (1947)
Blondie's Reward (1948)
Blondie's Secret (1948)
Blondie's Big Deal (1949)
Blondie Hits the Jackpot (1949)
Blondie's Hero (1950)
Beware of Blondie (1950)

Blondie (1938) **68m.** ******* D: Frank Strayer. Penny Singleton, Arthur Lake, Larry Simms, Gene Lockhart, Ann Doran, Jonathan Hale, Gordon Oliver, Danny Mummert, Irving Bacon, Fay Helm. First in the series of 28 *Blondie* films, introducing the farcical Bumstead family with a typically amusing plot: Dagwood is sacked from his job and Blondie thinks he's running around on her on the eve of their fifth anniversary.**▼▶**

Blondie and Dagwood—It's a Great Life SEE: **It's a Great Life**

Blondie Brings Up Baby (1939) **67m.** ****½** D: Frank Strayer. Penny Singleton, Arthur Lake, Larry Simms, Danny Mummert, Jonathan Hale, Fay Helm, Peggy Ann Garner, Helen Jerome Eddy, Irving Bacon. Standard screwball antics when Baby Dumpling starts school and promptly disappears, sending bumbling Dagwood in hot pursuit. Robert Sterling and Bruce Bennett have bits.**▼▶**

Blondie for Victory (1942) **70m.** ****** D: Frank Strayer. Penny Singleton, Arthur Lake, Larry Simms, Majelle White, Stuart Erwin, Jonathan Hale, Danny Mummert, Edward Gargan, Renie Riano, Irving Bacon. Dagwood and the other neighborhood husbands suffer when Blondie organizes a housewives' war effort. Cast strains for laughs in this topical series entry.**▼**

Blondie Goes Latin (1941) **69m.** ****½** D: Frank Strayer. Penny Singleton, Arthur Lake, Larry Simms, Tito Guizar, Ruth Terry, Jonathan Hale, Danny Mummert, Irving Bacon, Janet Burston. Silliness on a South American cruise as Dagwood joins Tito Guizar's conga band and Blondie cuts loose in some song-and-dance routines. Look for future "Sky King" Kirby Grant in a small role as a band singer.**▼▶**

Blondie Goes to College (1942) **74m.** ****** D: Frank Strayer. Penny Singleton, Arthur Lake, Larry Simms, Jonathan Hale, Danny Mummert, Larry Parks, Janet Blair,

Lloyd Bridges, Esther Dale, Adele Mara. Predictable complications occur when the Bumsteads go back to school (where most of the students are Columbia's young contract players) and pretend they're not married.**▼▶**

Blondie Has Servant Trouble (1940) **70m.** ****½** D: Frank Strayer. Penny Singleton, Arthur Lake, Larry Simms, Danny Mummert, Jonathan Hale, Arthur Hohl, Esther Dale, Irving Bacon, Fay Helm. Enjoyable haunted-house comedy, as the Bumsteads stay in a creepy mansion replete with strange servants and "ghosts."**▼▶**

Blondie Hits the Jackpot (1949) **66m.** ***½** D: Edward Bernds. Penny Singleton, Arthur Lake, Larry Simms, Jerome Cowan, Lloyd Corrigan, Ann Carter, George Humbert, David Sharpe, Danny Mummert, James Flavin, Dick Wessel. Dagwood is rescued from manual labor at a construction company when Blondie wins a radio quiz show in this threadbare entry.**▼**

Blondie in Society (1941) **75m.** ****½** D: Frank Strayer. Penny Singleton, Arthur Lake, Larry Simms, Jonathan Hale, Danny Mummert, William Frawley, Edgar Kennedy, Chick Chandler, Irving Bacon, Robert Mitchell Boys Choir. Blondie enters a pedigreed Great Dane in a dog show but gets Dagwood into trouble with a client who also has a dog in the running. Pretty funny entry with the added bonus of old pros Frawley and Kennedy.**▼▶**

Blondie in the Dough (1947) **69m.** ****** D: Abby Berlin. Penny Singleton, Arthur Lake, Larry Simms, Marjorie Kent, Jerome Cowan, Hugh Herbert, Clarence Kolb, Danny Mummert, Eddie Acuff. Blondie's in the dough up to her neck when she starts a baking business which attracts the attention of a cookie tycoon (Herbert).**▼**

Blondie Johnson (1933) **68m.** ****** D: Ray Enright. Joan Blondell, Chester Morris, Allen Jenkins, Earle Foxe, Claire Dodd, Mae Busch, Sterling Holloway. When a relief agency turns a deaf ear to Blondell's pleas to help her ailing mother, she vows to make money from that point on, any way she can, and becomes a con artist who even dares to step on the toes of a gangland bigwig. Punchy Warners Depression-era film shifts tone too often, though Blondell and Morris are very good.**▶**

Blondie Knows Best (1946) **69m.** ****** D: Abby Berlin. Penny Singleton, Arthur Lake, Larry Simms, Marjorie Kent, Steven Geray, Shemp Howard, Ludwig Donath, Jerome Cowan, Danny Mummert, Jack Rice. Dagwood pretends to be his boss, Mr. Dithers, causing predictable complications in this minor entry enlivened by Shemp as a myopic process server.**▼**

Blondie Meets the Boss (1939) **75m.** ****½** D: Frank Strayer. Penny Singleton, Arthur Lake, Larry Simms, Dorothy Moore, Jonathan Hale, Stanley Brown, Inez Courtney,

Don Beddoe, Danny Mummert, Irving Bacon. Second entry in the series has Blondie taking over at the office for Dagwood when he goes on a fishing trip. Look for James Craig and Robert Sterling in bits.▼▶

Blondie of the Follies (1932) **90m. **½** D: Edmund Goulding. Marion Davies, Robert Montgomery, Billie Dove, Jimmy Durante, ZaSu Pitts, Sidney Toler, Louise Carter. Davies and Dove vie for the affection of Montgomery, while ascending to stardom in the Follies. Dramatically wobbly, but the musical numbers are fun. James Gleason fine as Marion's dad. Best are Davies and Durante spoofing Garbo and Barrymore in GRAND HOTEL.

Blondie on a Budget (1940) **73m. **½** D: Frank Strayer. Penny Singleton, Arthur Lake, Rita Hayworth, Larry Simms, Danny Mummert, Don Beddoe, John Qualen, Fay Helm, Irving Bacon, Thurston Hall. Columbia ingenue Hayworth drops by as Dagwood's ex-sweetheart, which not surprisingly makes Blondie jealous. Lovely Rita helps perk up this entry.▼

Blondie Plays Cupid (1940) **68m. **½** D: Frank Strayer. Penny Singleton, Arthur Lake, Glenn Ford, Larry Simms, Danny Mummert, Jonathan Hale, Irving Bacon, Luana Walters. Blondie helps a young couple elope, but the course of true love does not run smoothly. Cute entry notable for early appearance by Ford.▼▶

Blondie's Anniversary (1947) **75m. **** D: Abby Berlin. Penny Singleton, Arthur Lake, Larry Simms, Marjorie Kent, Adele Jergens, Jerome Cowan, Grant Mitchell, William Frawley, Jack Rice, Eddie Acuff. Dagwood brings home a fancy watch for a client's wife, which Blondie naturally believes is her anniversary gift.▼

Blondie's Big Deal (1949) **66m. **** D: Edward Bernds. Penny Singleton, Arthur Lake, Larry Simms, Jerome Cowan, Marjorie Kent, Collette Lyons, Ray Walker, Eddie Acuff, Jack Rice, Danny Mummert. Dagwood gets a shellacking when he invents a nonflammable paint and tests it out on his boss's house. Naturally, unscrupulous competitors switch the paint.▼

Blondie's Big Moment (1947) **69m. **** D: Abby Berlin. Penny Singleton, Arthur Lake, Larry Simms, Marjorie Kent, Jerome Cowan, Anita Louise, Danny Mummert, Jack Rice, Eddie Acuff. Dagwood gets into trouble with his new boss, throwing the whole Bumstead household into chaos. Nothing new.▼

Blondie's Blessed Event (1942) **69m. **½** D: Frank Strayer. Penny Singleton, Arthur Lake, Larry Simms, Norma Jean Wayne, Jonathan Hale, Danny Mummert, Hans Conried, Mary Wickes, Stanley Brown, Irving Bacon. Dagwood wreaks havoc at a convention while Baby Dumpling gets a new sister, Cookie, in this typically fran-

tic series entry. Look for a young Arthur O'Connell as an intern.▼

Blondie's Hero (1950) **67m. **** D: Edward Bernds. Penny Singleton, Arthur Lake, Larry Simms, Marjorie Kent, William Frawley, Danny Mummert, Joe Sawyer, Teddy Infuhr, Alyn Lockwood, Frank Jenks, Iris Adrian, Edward Earle, Dick Wessel. Penultimate series entry is a stock service farce, as Dagwood accidentally joins the Army reserve.▼

Blondie's Holiday (1947) **67m. **** D: Abby Berlin. Penny Singleton, Arthur Lake, Larry Simms, Marjorie Kent, Jerome Cowan, Grant Mitchell, Sid Tomack, Jeff York, Alyn Lockwood, Jack Rice, Eddie Acuff. Dagwood gets involved with gamblers and winds up in jail when he decides to play the ponies for some quick money. Bobby Larson replaced Danny Mummert as Alvin for this one entry.▼

Blondie's Lucky Day (1946) **75m. **** D: Abby Berlin. Penny Singleton, Arthur Lake, Larry Simms, Marjorie Kent, Robert Stanton, (Bob Haymes), Angelyn Orr, Frank Jenks, Paul Harvey, Charles Arnt, Jack Rice, Frank Orth. Dagwood gets fired (again), and decides to go into business with the help of a WAC, which naturally makes Blondie nervous.▼

Blondie's Reward (1948) **67m. **** D: Abby Berlin. Penny Singleton, Arthur Lake, Larry Simms, Marjorie Kent, Jerome Cowan, Gay Nelson, Ross Ford, Danny Mummert, Paul Harvey, Frank Jenks, Chick Chandler, Jack Rice, Eddie Acuff, Alyn Lockwood. Dagwood the bonehead is demoted to office boy when he purchases the wrong real estate property. Very mild entry with the gags (and all concerned) showing their age.▼

Blondie's Secret (1948) **68m. **** D: Edward Bernds. Penny Singleton, Arthur Lake, Larry Simms, Marjorie Kent, Jerome Cowan, Thurston Hall, Jack Rice, Danny Mummert, Frank Orth, Alyn Lockwood, Eddie Acuff. Dagwood's boss doesn't want him to take a vacation, so he hires some bumbling crooks to steal the Bumsteads' luggage. Trivial fluff, with the tired series coming into the home stretch.▼

Blondie Takes a Vacation (1939) **68m. **½** D: Frank Strayer. Penny Singleton, Arthur Lake, Larry Simms, Danny Mummert, Donald Meek, Donald MacBride, Elizabeth Dunne, Irving Bacon. Blondie and family take over a mountain lodge to save it from bankruptcy and get into plenty of hot water in this diverting entry.▼▶

Blood Alley (1955) **C-115m. **½** D: William Wellman. John Wayne, Lauren Bacall, Paul Fix, Mike Mazurki, Anita Ekberg. Enjoyable escapism with Wayne, Bacall, and assorted Chinese escaping down river to Hong Kong pursued by Communists. CinemaScope.▼◀▶

Blood and Black Lace (1964-Italian-

French-German) **C-88m.** *½ D: Mario Bava. Cameron Mitchell, Eva Bartok, Mary Arden. Gruesome thriller about a sex murderer doing in fashion models. Wooden script and performances don't help. Fans of the genre will at least enjoy Bava's imaginative direction.▼●❿

Blood and Roses (1961-Italian) **C-74m.** **½ D: Roger Vadim. Mel Ferrer, Elsa Martinelli, Annette Vadim, Marc Allegret. This story of a jealous girl's obsession with her family's history of vampirism was based on Sheridan Le Fanu's *Carmilla*. Despite effective moments, film does not succeed. Same story refilmed as THE VAMPIRE LOVERS and THE BLOOD-SPATTERED BRIDE. Technirama.▼

Blood and Sand (1922) **80m.** **½ D: Fred Niblo. Rudolph Valentino, Lila Lee, Nita Naldi, George Field, Walter Long, Leo White. Dated but still absorbing story of bullfighter Valentino torn between good-girl Lee and vampish Naldi. Scenes of hero being seduced are laughable, but bullfight material holds up well. Remade in 1941 and 1989.▼●❿

Blood and Sand (1941) **C-123m.** *** D: Rouben Mamoulian. Tyrone Power, Linda Darnell, Rita Hayworth, Nazimova, Anthony Quinn, J. Carrol Naish, John Carradine, George Reeves, Laird Cregar. Pastel remake of Valentino's silent film about naive bullfighter who ignores true love (Darnell) for temptress (Hayworth). Slow-paced romance uplifted by Nazimova's knowing performance as Power's mother; beautiful color production earned cinematographers Ernest Palmer and Ray Rennahan Oscars.▼❿

Blood Arrow (1958) **75m.** *½ D: Charles Marquis Warren. Scott Brady, Paul Richards, Phyllis Coates, Don Haggerty. Uninspired tale of Mormon girl Coates trudging through Indian territory to obtain medicine, with usual Indian attacks. Regalscope.

Blood Creature SEE: **Terror Is a Man**

Bloodhounds of Broadway (1952) **C-90m.** **½ D: Harmon Jones. Mitzi Gaynor, Scott Brady, Mitzi Green, Michael O'Shea, Marguerite Chapman, Charles Buchinski (Bronson). Hick Gaynor becomes slick gal in N.Y.C., involved with pseudo-Damon Runyon folk; funny Green has too small a role. Songs include "I Wish I Knew." Runyon stories used as basis for 1989 film of the same name.❿

Blood Money (1933) **65m.** *** D: Rowland Brown. George Bancroft, Frances Dee, Judith Anderson, Chick Chandler, Blossom Seeley. Lively, implausible story of underworld bail-bondsman Bancroft falling for thrill-a-minute socialite Dee, causing friction with Bancroft's female cohort (played by Anderson in incongruously gutsy, glamorous role). Dee's closing scene is a knockout. Feature debut of Anderson. Look fast for Lucille Ball as Chandler's girlfriend at the racetrack.

Blood of a Poet, The (1930-French) **52m.** *** D: Jean Cocteau. Lee Miller, Pauline Carton, Odette Talazac, Enrique Rivero, Jean Desbordes. Cocteau's first feature is a highly personal, poetic, symbolic fantasy, which supposedly transpires in a split second: the time it takes for a chimney to crumble and land. Imaginative, dreamlike, and still a visual delight. The commentary is spoken by Cocteau.▼❿

Blood of Dracula (1957) **68m.** *½ D: Herbert L. Strock. Sandra Harrison, Gail Ganley, Jerry Blaine, Louise Lewis. Inoffensive programmer about troubled teenage girl being hypnotized into a life of vampirism.▼❿

Blood of Jesus, The (1941) **57m.** *** D: Spencer Williams. Cathryn Caviness, Spencer Williams, Juanita Riley, Reather Hardeman, Rogenia Goldthwaite, Jas. (James) B. Jones, Frank H. McClennan. Devoutly religious Caviness is accidentally shot by her sin-embracing husband (Williams). Will she end up in heaven, or will she be enticed by Judas Green (McClennan), an emissary of Satan? Williams also scripted this artful, still provocative morality tale, which also is the first all-black-cast independent production added to the Library of Congress' National Film Registry.▼❿

Blood of the Vampire (1958-British) **C-87m.** ** D: Henry Cass. Donald Wolfit, Barbara Shelley, Vincent Ball, Victor Maddern. Potentially vivid horror film weakened by slack production: doctor sent to prison hospital finds the warden (Wolfit, made up to resemble Bela Lugosi) is an anemic mad scientist. Need more be said?▼❿

Blood on the Arrow (1964) **C-91m.** *½ D: Sidney Salkow. Dale Robertson, Martha Hyer, Wendell Corey, Elisha Cook, Ted de Corsia. Humdrum Western dealing with Apache massacre and survivors' attempt to rescue son who is held captive.

Blood on the Moon (1948) **88m.** *** D: Robert Wise. Robert Mitchum, Barbara Bel Geddes, Robert Preston, Walter Brennan, Phyllis Thaxter, Frank Faylen, Tom Tully, Charles McGraw, Tom Tyler. Straightforward Western tale (from a novel by Luke Short) about a drifter who's hired by his former partner to help him bilk some naive landowners. Mitchum sizes up the situation and decides he doesn't like it; Preston is an unrepentant villain. Watch for that great confrontation scene in a darkened barroom. Also shown in computer-colored version.▼●

Blood on the Sun (1945) **98m.** *** D: Frank Lloyd. James Cagney, Sylvia Sidney, Wallace Ford, Rosemary DeCamp, Robert Armstrong. Newspaper editor Cagney, in Japan during the 1930s, smells trouble coming but is virtually helpless; good melodrama. Also shown in computer-colored version.▼●❿

Bloody Brood, The (1959-Canadian) **80m.**
** D: Julian Roffman. Jack Betts, Barbara
Lord, Peter Falk, Robert Christie, Ronald
Hartmann. Mind-boggling time capsule
with Falk most impressive in his second
screen role as Nico, a deranged "beatnik"
who gets his kicks by feeding a hamburger
laced with broken glass to an unsuspecting
kid! Laughable, thoroughly cynical depiction of the Beat Generation. ▼▶

Bloody Pit of Horror (1965-Italian) **C-
87m.** *½ D: Max Hunter (Massimo Pupillo).
Mickey Hargitay, Walter Brandi (Brandt),
Louise Barret (Luisa Baratto), Rita Klein,
Alfred Rice (Alfredo Rizzo), Barbara Nelli,
Moa Tahi. Reclusive former muscleman
actor (Hargitay) allows some writers and
photographers to use his isolated but well-
lit castle for a book project. But their arrival
drives him insane and he comes to believe
that he's the reincarnation of the Crimson
Executioner, who was too much even for the
Inquisition. Straight-faced thriller makes
no attempt at being scary, simply presenting one inventive torture and death after
another; gruesome, though tame by 21st-
century standards. Hargitay's performance,
all grimaces and flexed stances, makes this
a favorite among devotees of high-camp ho-
moeroticism. ▶

Blossoms in the Dust (1941) **C-100m.** ***
D: Mervyn LeRoy. Greer Garson, Walter
Pidgeon, Felix Bressart, Marsha Hunt, Fay
Holden, Samuel S. Hinds. Slick tearjerker
of Texas orphanage founded by Garson
when she loses her own child; tastefully
acted. ▼▶

Blot, The (1921) **91m.** *** D: Lois Weber.
Claire Windsor, Louis Calhern, Philip Hubbard, Margaret McWade, Marie Walcamp.
Earnest, humanistic account of economic
barriers between the classes, spotlighting
the pretty daughter (Windsor) of a griev-
ously underpaid college professor who is
courted by three men, including wealthy,
spoiled student Calhern. Meanwhile, the
professor's wife has trouble with her nouveau riche immigrant neighbors. Overly
melodramatic at times, but still a notable
work for its long-ignored director. Calhern's film debut. ▼▶

Blowing Wild (1953) **90m.** ** D: Hugo
Fregonese. Gary Cooper, Barbara Stanwyck, Ruth Roman, Anthony Quinn, Ward
Bond. Tempestuous Stanwyck is married
to oil tycoon Quinn, but sets her sights on
wildcatter Cooper, who's fully recovered
from their one-time affair. Heated emotions
can't warm up this plodding story, filmed in
Mexico. ▼▶

Blue Angel, The (1930-German) **106m.**
***½ D: Josef von Sternberg. Marlene Die-
trich, Emil Jannings, Kurt Gerron, Rosa
Valetti, Hans Albers. Ever-fascinating film
classic with Jannings as stuffy professor
who falls blindly in love with cabaret enter-

tainer Lola-Lola (Dietrich), who ruins his
life. Dietrich introduces "Falling in Love
Again"; this role made her an international
star. Robert Liebman scripted, from Heinrich Mann's novel *Professor Unrath.* Simultaneously shot in German and English
versions; the former is obviously superior.
Remade in 1959. ▼▶

Blue Angel, The (1959) **C-107m.** *½ D:
Edward Dmytryk. Curt Jurgens, May Britt,
Theodore Bikel, John Banner, Ludwig
Stossel, Fabrizio Mioni. Disastrous remake
of Josef von Sternberg–Marlene Dietrich
classic, updated to 1950s Germany, from
Heinrich Mann's novel of precise profes-
sor won over by tawdry nightclub singer.
CinemaScope.

Bluebeard (1944) **73m.** *** D: Edgar G.
Ulmer. Jean Parker, John Carradine, Nils
Asther, Ludwig Stossel, Iris Adrian, Emmett Lynn. Surprisingly effective story set
in 19th-century Paris. Incurable strangler
Carradine falls for smart girl Parker, who
senses that something is wrong. ▼▶

Bluebeard (1962-French-Italian) **C-114m.**
**½ D: Claude Chabrol. Charles Denner,
Michele Morgan, Danielle Darrieux, Hildegarde Neff, Stephane Audran, Catherine
Rouvel, Françoise Lugagne. Retelling of
life of French wife-killer, far less witty than
Chaplin's MONSIEUR VERDOUX. Origi-
nal French title: LANDRU. ▼

Bluebeard's Eighth Wife (1938) **80m.**
** D: Ernst Lubitsch. Claudette Colbert,
Gary Cooper, David Niven, Edward Everett Horton, Elizabeth Patterson, Herman
Bing. Contrived comedy about a woman
determined to gain the upper hand over an
oft-married millionaire. One of Lubitsch's
weakest films, notable mainly for the way
its two stars "meet cute." Script by Billy
Wilder and Charles Brackett. Previously
filmed in 1923. ▼▶

Bluebeard's Ten Honeymoons (1960-
British) **93m.** ** D: W. Lee Wilder. George
Sanders, Corinne Calvet, Jean Kent, Patricia Roc. Sanders enlivens OK chronicle of
fortune hunter who decides that marrying
and murdering a series of women is the key
to financial success.

Blue Bird, The (1918) **75m.** **** D: Maurice Tourneur. Tula Belle, Robin Macdougall, Edwin E. Reed, Emma Lowry, William
J. Gross, Florence Anderson, Lillian Cook.
Lavish and exquisite rendering of Maurice
Maeterlinck's fantasy about a fairy who
takes two poor children on a magical journey to search for the Blue Bird of Happiness. Enchanting in every way, and a
milestone in silent-film artistry. Remade in
1940 and 1976. ▼▶

Blue Bird, The (1940) **C-88m.** ** D:
Walter Lang. Shirley Temple, Spring Byington, Nigel Bruce, Gale Sondergaard,
Eddie Collins, Sybil Jason. Released one
year after THE WIZARD OF OZ, this

lavish Technicolor fantasy (based on the famous play by Maurice Maeterlinck) has everything but charm. Even Shirley seems stiff. Filmed before in 1918, remade in 1976.▼❿

Blue Blood (1951) **C-72m.** *½ D: Lew Landers. Bill Williams, Jane Nigh, Arthur Shields, Audrey Long. Lackluster racehorse story with a few good moments by Shields as elderly trainer seeking comeback.

Blue Canadian Rockies (1952) **58m.** ** D: George Archainbaud. Gene Autry, Pat Buttram, Gail Davis, Carolina Cotton, Ross Ford, Tom London, Don Beddoe, John Merton, Gene Roth, The Cass County Boys. Montana rancher unhappy about his daughter's impending marriage sends his foreman (Autry) to Canada to break up the romance, but when Gene arrives he has to solve a murder as well. Strictly routine.❿

Blue Dahlia, The (1946) **99m.** *** D: George Marshall. Alan Ladd, Veronica Lake, William Bendix, Howard da Silva, Hugh Beaumont, Doris Dowling. Exciting Raymond Chandler–scripted melodrama has Ladd returning from military service to find wife unfaithful. She's murdered, he's suspected in well-turned film. Produced by John Houseman. ▼❿

Blue Denim (1959) **89m.** *** D: Philip Dunne. Carol Lynley, Brandon de Wilde, Macdonald Carey, Marsha Hunt, Warren Berlinger, Roberta Shore. De Wilde and Lynley are striking as teenagers faced with Carol's pregnancy. Dated and naive, but well-acted adaptation of Broadway play. CinemaScope.

Blue Eagle, The (1926) **68m.** *** D: John Ford. George O'Brien, Janet Gaynor, William Russell, Robert Edeson, David Butler, Phil Ford, Ralph Sipperly, Margaret Livingston. Waterfront rivals O'Brien and Russell are both in love with Gaynor and continue their feud when they join the Navy. After the war they call a temporary truce to take on dope peddlers who are destroying their neighborhood. Silent Ford film is an enjoyable mix of brawling action and roughhouse comedy that turns into a gritty gangster melodrama.

Blue Gardenia, The (1953) **90m.** *** D: Fritz Lang. Anne Baxter, Richard Conte, Ann Sothern, Raymond Burr, Jeff Donnell, George Reeves, Nat King Cole. Engaging murder caper with 1940s flavor. Baxter is accused of murdering wolfish Burr, decides to take columnist Conte's offer of help. Solid film with twist ending. ▼❿

Blue Grass of Kentucky (1950) **C-71m.** ** D: William Beaudine. Bill Williams, Jane Nigh, Ralph Morgan. Routine account of horse-breeding families, their rivalry and eventual healing of old wounds when romance blooms between the younger generations.

Blue Hawaii (1961) **C-101m.** **½ D: Nor-

man Taurog. Elvis Presley, Joan Blackman, Angela Lansbury, Roland Winters, Iris Adrian. Agreeable Presley vehicle bolstered by Lansbury's presence as mother of ex-G.I. (Presley) returning to islands and working with tourist agency. Elvis performs one of his prettiest hits, "Can't Help Falling in Love." Panavision. ▼◉

Blue Lagoon, The (1949-British) **C-101m.** *** D: Frank Launder. Jean Simmons, Donald Houston, Noel Purcell, Cyril Cusack, Maurice Denham. Idyllic romance of Simmons and Houston, shipwrecked on tropic isle, falling in love as they grow to maturity; slowly paced but refreshing. Remade in 1980.

Blue Lamp, The (1950-British) **84m.** *** D: Basil Dearden. Jack Warner, Jimmy Hanley, Dirk Bogarde, Robert Flemyng, Bernard Lee, Peggy Evans, Patric Doonan, Gladys Henson, Meredith Edwards. Crackerjack police-procedural–thriller involving the lives of various bobbies and their superiors and how they go about maintaining the peace. Unpretentious and exciting. Key British postwar film is enhanced by superior location filming in London and Bogarde's chilling, star-making performance as a thug. Music hall star Tessie O'Shea appears as herself. Screenplay by T.E.B. Clarke. ▼

Blue Light, The (1932-German) **77m.** ** D: Leni Riefenstahl. Leni Riefenstahl, Mathias Weimann, Beni Fuhrer, Max Holzboer. Mysterious mountain maiden Riefenstahl is loved and destroyed by artist Weimann. Slow, pretentious fable, also produced and cowritten by Riefenstahl. She recut film in 1952, and it is this version that's usually shown today.▼❿

Blue Montana Skies (1939) **56m.** ** D: B. Reeves Eason. Gene Autry, Smiley Burnette, June Storey, Harry Woods, Tully Marshall, Al Bridge, Glenn Strange, Dorothy Granger, Edmund Cobb, Walt Shrum and His Colorado Hillbillies. Cattlemen Gene and Frog try to find the fur smugglers who murdered their partner (Marshall), unaware that the smugglers are using Storey's guest ranch as a front for their illegal activities. Rather bland Autry vehicle; even the songs are below par. ▼❿

Blue Murder at St. Trinian's (1957-British) **86m.** **½ D: Frank Launder. Terry-Thomas, George Cole, Joyce Grenfell, Lionel Jeffries, Eric Barker, Lisa Gastoni, Ferdy Mayne, Alastair Sim. OK entry in the series of farces set at the St. Trinian's School for Girls. Ever-mischievous students win a trip to the continent and become immersed in various hijinks. Sim appears too briefly (in drag) as Miss Amelia Fritton, the school's headmistress.▼

Blueprint for Murder, A (1953) **76m.** **½ D: Andrew L. Stone. Joseph Cotten, Jean Peters, Gary Merrill, Catherine McLeod, Jack Kruschen, Barney Phillips,

Freddy Ridgeway, Mae Marsh. Is Peters somehow responsible for the poisoning of her stepdaughter? Her brother-in-law (Cotten) is determined to find out. Neat little whodunit, scripted by Stone. ▶

Blueprint for Robbery (1961) 87m. **½ D: Jerry Hopper. J. Pat O'Malley, Robert Wilke, Robert Gist, Romo Vincent, Tom Duggan. Deliberately offbeat, low-key film of heist engineered by old-timer O'Malley; good moments put this above average, but overall result is unmemorable.

Blues Busters (1950) 67m. **½ D: William Beaudine. Leo Gorcey, Huntz Hall, Adele Jergens, Gabriel Dell, Craig Stevens, Phyllis Coates, Billy Benedict, Bernard Gorcey, David Gorcey. Louie's Sweet Shop is turned into a nightclub when Sach's tonsillectomy turns him into a swooning crooner. Amusing *Bowery Boys* comedy, with Hall a standout. ▼▶

Blues in the Night (1941) 88m. **½ D: Anatole Litvak. Priscilla Lane, Richard Whorf, Betty Field, Lloyd Nolan, Jack Carson, Elia Kazan, Wallace Ford, Billy Halop, Peter Whitney. Intriguing musical drama abandons early promise for soapy, silly melodramatics, in story of self-destructive musician (Whorf) and his band (young Kazan is featured as clarinetist). Good moments, wonderful Warner Bros. montages, but the great title song is never played once in its entirety! ▶

Blue Skies (1946) C-104m. *** D: Stuart Heisler. Fred Astaire, Bing Crosby, Joan Caulfield, Billy De Wolfe, Olga San Juan, Frank Faylen. Astaire and Crosby play onetime show-biz partners and rivals in this paper-thin vehicle kept aloft by lots and lots of Irving Berlin songs. Highlights: Astaire's terrific "Puttin' on the Ritz," star duo's "A Couple of Song and Dance Men." ▼▶

Blue Steel (1934) 54m. ** D: Robert Bradbury. John Wayne, Eleanor Hunt, George Hayes, Edward Peil, Yakima Canutt, Lafe McKee. Routine story of crooks hoping to drive residents out of town in order to claim gold strike only they know about. Wayne is a U.S. marshal operating undercover, Canutt is the Polka Dot Bandit. Too much footage shot in drab, cramped sets betrays budgetary limitations of Wayne's Lone Star Westerns. Also available in computer-colored form as STOLEN GOODS. ▼▶

Blue Veil, The (1951) 113m. *** D: Curtis Bernhardt. Jane Wyman, Charles Laughton, Joan Blondell, Richard Carlson, Agnes Moorehead, Don Taylor, Audrey Totter, Everett Sloane, Cyril Cusack, Natalie Wood, Warner Anderson, Vivian Vance, Philip Ober. Wyman is self-sacrificing nursemaid whose life story is chronicled with intertwined episodes of her charges and their families. Well done.

Blue, White and Perfect (1941) 73m. **½ D: Herbert I. Leeds. Lloyd Nolan, Mary

Beth Hughes, Helene Reynolds, George Reeves, Steven Geray, Curt Bois. Slick espionage action, with tough shamus Michael Shayne (Nolan) turning patriotic to catch enemy agents trying to smuggle industrial diamonds to their countries. Reeves is notable as glib mystery man who may or may not be the ringleader. Title refers to industrial diamonds.

Bobbikins (1960-British) 89m. ** D: Robert Day. Max Bygraves, Shirley Jones, Steven Stocker, Billie Whitelaw. Gimmicky comedy with British singer Bygraves and Jones the parents of an infant who talks like an adult. Not bad . . . but that awful title! CinemaScope. ▶

Bobby Ware Is Missing (1955) 67m. *½ D: Thomas Carr. Neville Brand, Arthur Franz, Kim Charney, John Hamilton, Peter Leeds, Paul Picerni, Walter Reed, William Schallert, Jean Willes. Title tells all in this tedious melodrama of a cop (Brand) helping parents find their kidnapped boy. ▼

Bob Le Flambeur (1955-French) 102m. *** D: Jean-Pierre Melville. Roger Duchesne, Isabel Corey, Daniel Cauchy, Guy Decomble, Andre Garet, Gerard Buhr, Howard Vernon. Witty inversion of THE ASPHALT JUNGLE: hard-luck gambler Duchesne enlists pals in intricate plan to knock over Deauville casino, but everything is so stacked against them that we almost hope he'll call it off. Clever and atmospheric, blessed with eerily sexy Corey and a great closing line. Unreleased in the U.S. until 1982. Remade as THE GOOD THIEF. [PG] ▼▶

Bob Mathias Story, The (1954) 80m. *** D: Francis D. Lyon. Bob Mathias, Ward Bond, Melba Mathias, Paul Bryar, Ann Doran. Agreeable biography of Olympic star athlete, his sports career, military duty, family life. Mathias turns in an engaging portrayal of himself.

Boccaccio '70 (1962-Italian) C-165m. *** D: Vittorio De Sica, Luchino Visconti, Federico Fellini. Anita Ekberg, Sophia Loren, Romy Schneider, Peppino De Filippo, Dante Maggio, Tomas Milian. Trio of episodes: "The Raffle"—timid soul wins a liaison with a girl as prize; "The Job" —aristocrat's wife takes a job as her husband's mistress; "The Temptation of Dr. Antonio"—fantasy of puritanical fanatic and a voluptuous poster picture which comes alive. A fourth episode, directed by Mario Monicelli, was dropped for U.S. release. ▼▶

Body and Soul (1925) 102m. ** D: Oscar Micheaux. Paul Robeson, Mercedes Gilbert, Julia T. Russell, Lawrence Chenault, Marshall Rogers, Lillian Johnson, Madame Robinson, Chester A. Alexander. Set in the Deep, and deeply religious, South, Robeson's screen debut casts him as both an evil preacher and his righteous brother, who clash over a lovely young member of the congregation. Though this is the famed singer-activist's only silent film, his screen presence is palpable in an otherwise routine melodrama. Adapted by Micheaux from his own novel, the film bears no relation to other movies of the same name. ▼◗

Body and Soul (1947) **104m.** **★★★★** D: Robert Rossen. John Garfield, Lilli Palmer, Hazel Brooks, Anne Revere, William Conrad, Joseph Pevney, Canada Lee. Most boxing films pale next to this classic (written by Abraham Polonsky) of Garfield working his way up by devious means, becoming famous champ. Superb photography by James Wong Howe, and Oscar-winning editing by Francis Lyon and Robert Parrish. Remade in 1981 and for TV in 1998. ▼◗

Body Disappears, The (1941) **72m.** **★★½** D: Ross Lederman. Jeffrey Lynn, Jane Wyman, Edward Everett Horton, Marguerite Chapman. Frantic, high-energy sci-fi farce with Lynn made invisible by daffy professor Horton; many comic complications ensue. Wyman and Horton also have "invisible" scenes. Funnier than the same year's similar THE INVISIBLE WOMAN (possibly this film's inspiration).

Bodyguard (1948) **62m.** **★★½** D: Richard Fleischer. Lawrence Tierney, Priscilla Lane, Philip Reed, June Clayworth, Elisabeth Risdon, Steve Brodie. Hard-boiled homicide cop Tierney is suspended; he reluctantly takes a job as a bodyguard and is promptly framed on a murder rap. Solid little B film, strikingly directed. Based on a story coauthored by 23-year-old Robert Altman! ◗

Bodyhold (1949) **63m.** **★½** D: Seymour Friedman. Willard Parker, Lola Albright, Hillary Brooke, Allen Jenkins, Roy Roberts, Iris Adrian, John Dehner, Henry Kulky. Plumber Parker becomes a pro wrestler, rebels when pressured to throw a match. Dull programmer.

Body Snatcher, The (1945) **77m.** **★★★½** D: Robert Wise. Boris Karloff, Bela Lugosi, Henry Daniell, Edith Atwater, Russell Wade, Rita Corday. Fine, atmospheric tale from Robert Louis Stevenson short story of doctor (Daniell) who is forced to deal with scurrilous character (Karloff) in order to get cadavers for experiments in 19th-century Edinburgh. Last film to team Karloff and Lugosi, their scenes together are eerie and compelling. Classic Val Lewton thriller. Screenplay by Philip MacDonald and Carlos Keith (Lewton). ▼◗

Boeing Boeing (1965) **C-102m.** **★★★** D: John Rich. Jerry Lewis, Tony Curtis, Dany Saval, Christiane Schmidtmer, Suzanna Leigh, Thelma Ritter. A surprisingly subdued Lewis is paired with Curtis in story of American newspaperman who runs swinging pad in Paris, constantly stocked with stewardesses, to the chagrin of housekeeper Ritter. Amusing. Based on a play by Marc Camoletti. ▼◗

Bogus Bandits SEE: **Devil's Brother, The**

Bohemian Girl, The (1936) **71m.** **★★★** D: James Horne, Charles R. Rogers. Stan Laurel, Oliver Hardy, Thelma Todd, Antonio Moreno, Darla Hood, Jacqueline Wells (Julie Bishop), Mae Busch. Nifty comic opera with Stan and Ollie part of gypsy caravan. They adopt abandoned girl who turns out to be a princess. Todd's last feature, released posthumously. ▼◗

Bold and the Brave, The (1956) **87m.** **★★★** D: Lewis R. Foster. Wendell Corey, Mickey Rooney, Don Taylor, Nicole Maurey. Routine WW2 study of soldiers fighting in Italy, greatly uplifted by unstereotyped performances; Rooney is outstanding. SuperScope.

Bolero (1934) **83m.** **★★½** D: Wesley Ruggles. George Raft, Carole Lombard, Sally Rand, Gertrude Michael, William Frawley, Ray Milland. Silly, protracted story of cocky dancer's rise to fame is made fun by good stars and production values; dance sequences are first-rate, although much of Raft and Lombard's footwork is "doubled" by professionals. Rand, in a rare film appearance, performs her famous fan dance. Raft and Lombard reteamed for RUMBA.

Bomba the Jungle Boy In 1949 producer Walter Mirisch, who has gone on to far greater things, decided to produce a series of low-budget adventure films based on Roy Rockwood's series of popular juvenile books from the 1920s about a boy who grew up in the jungle. For this road-company Tarzan series he hired Johnny Sheffield, who had played Boy in the Tarzan films, and veteran serial and B-picture director Ford Beebe, an expert at making something out of nothing. With a small studio backlot, and access to the 1930 documentary film AFRICA SPEAKS for stock footage, BOMBA THE JUNGLE BOY emerged, a not-bad little adventure, with talented Peggy Ann Garner playing opposite Sheffield. The subsequent eleven films in the series, however, worked their way into a standard formula that quickly wore thin. Bomba was made for younger audiences, who may still respond to the formula plots.

BOMBA THE JUNGLE BOY

Bomba, The Jungle Boy (1949)
Bomba on Panther Island (1949)
The Lost Volcano (1950)
The Hidden City (1950); aka Bomba and the Hidden City
The Lion Hunters (1951)
Bomba and the Elephant Stampede (1951); Aka The Elephant Stampede
African Treasure (1952)
Bomba and the Jungle Girl (1952)
Safari Drums (1953)
The Golden Idol (1954)
Killer Leopard (1954)
Lord of the Jungle (1955)

Bomba and the Elephant Stampede (1951) **71m.** ** D: Ford Beebe. Johnny Sheffield, Donna Martell, Edith Evanson, Martin Wilkins, Myron Healey, Leonard Mudie. A politically correct Bomba the Jungle Boy combats ivory poachers who are slaughtering elephants. One of the most bearable of this minor series. Also known as THE ELEPHANT STAMPEDE. ▶

Bomba and the Hidden City SEE: Hidden City, The

Bomba and the Jungle Girl (1952) **70m.** *½ D: Ford Beebe. Johnny Sheffield, Karen Sharpe, Walter Sande, Suzette Harbin, Martin Wilkins, Leonard Mudie. Jungle Boy meets Jungle Girl (Sharpe) and Jungle chimp (Kimba) on a quest to discover the true identity of Bomba's parents. ▶

Bomba and the Lost Volcano SEE: Lost Volcano, The

Bomba on Panther Island (1949) **76m.** *½ D: Ford Beebe. Johnny Sheffield, Allene Roberts, Lita Baron, Charles Irwin, Smoki Whitfield. Bomba battles a deadly black panther and superstitious natives in this trite entry. ▶

Bombardier (1943) **99m.** *** D: Richard Wallace. Pat O'Brien, Randolph Scott, Anne Shirley, Eddie Albert, Walter Reed, Robert Ryan, Barton MacLane. Familiar framework of fliers being trained during WW2 comes off well with fast-moving script. Also shown in computer-colored version. ▼▶

Bomba, The Jungle Boy (1949) **70m.** ** D: Ford Beebe. Johnny Sheffield, Peggy Ann Garner, Smoki Whitfield, Onslow Stevens, Charles Irwin. First in the series has Bomba helping a photographer and his daughter on a perilous safari. ▶

Bombers B-52 (1957) **C-106m.** **½ D: Gordon Douglas. Natalie Wood, Karl Malden, Marsha Hunt, Efrem Zimbalist, Jr., Dean Jagger. Ordinary love story between army pilot Zimbalist and Wood, with latter's sergeant father objecting, intertwined with good aerial footage of jet plane maneuvers. CinemaScope. ▼▶

Bombshell (1933) **95m.** ***½ D: Victor Fleming. Jean Harlow, Lee Tracy, Frank Morgan, Franchot Tone, Una Merkel, Pat O'Brien, C. Aubrey Smith, Ted Healy, Isabel Jewell. Devastating satire of 1930s Hollywood, with Harlow a much-abused star, Tracy an incredibly unscrupulous publicity director making her life hell. No holds barred. Scripted by John Lee Mahin and Jules Furthman, from a play by Caroline Francke and Mack Crane. Retitled BLONDE BOMBSHELL. ▼●▶

Bombs Over Burma (1942) **65m.** ** D: Joseph H. Lewis. Anna May Wong, Noel Madison, Leslie Denison, Nedrick Young, Dan Seymour, Frank Lackteen, Judith Gibson (Teala Loring), Dennis Moore, Richard Loo. Interesting if failed attempt to make a hard-hitting, topical film. Wong plays a school-teacher, working as an undercover agent, who accompanies a truckload of international passengers (one of whom is a spy) on their way to Chungking. Director/cowriter Lewis' visual flair can't save a talky, pedestrian script. Wong comes off well, as usual. ▶

Bonjour Tristesse (1958) **C/B&W-94m.** *** D: Otto Preminger. Deborah Kerr, David Niven, Jean Seberg, Geoffrey Horne, Mylene Demongeot. Teenager does her best to break up romance between playboy widowed father and his mistress, with tragic results. Françoise Sagan's philosophy seeps through glossy production; Kerr exceptionally fine in soaper set on French Riviera. CinemaScope. ▼▶

Bonnie Parker Story, The (1958) **81m.** **½ D: William Witney. Dorothy Provine, Jack Hogan, Richard Bakalyan, Joseph Turkel. With the success of BONNIE AND CLYDE, this film takes on added luster, recounting the lurid criminal life of the female crook (Provine)—though Clyde Barrow isn't even mentioned in this low-budget saga. Superama.

Bonnie Prince Charlie (1948-British) **C-118m.** ** D: Anthony Kimmins. David Niven, Margaret Leighton, Jack Hawkins, Judy Campbell, Morland Graham, Finlay Currie. Niven is Prince Charles of 18th-century Scotland in this draggy, overlong historical drama. The battle scenes are well staged and the photography of Robert Krasker is excellent, but when film was first released in England, it was considered a total disaster. Released at 140m., then cut to 118m. U.S. TV prints run 100m. and are in black and white. ▼

Bonnie Scotland (1935) **80m.** **½ D: James Horne. Stan Laurel, Oliver Hardy, June Lang, William Janney, Anne Grey, Vernon Steele, James Finlayson. Plot sometimes gets in the way of L&H, but their material is well up to par; Stan and Ollie inadvertently join a Scottish military regiment stationed in the desert. ▼●▶

Bon Voyage! (1962) **C-130m.** *½ D: James Neilson. Fred MacMurray, Jane Wyman, Michael Callan, Deborah Walley, Tommy Kirk, Kevin Corcoran. Slow, drawn-out Disney comedy about "typical" American family's misadventures on trip to Europe. Aimed more at adults than kids, but too draggy and simple-minded for anyone. ▼▶

Bonzo Goes to College (1952) **80m.** ** D: Frederick de Cordova. Maureen O'Sullivan, Charles Drake, Edmund Gwenn, Gigi Perreau, Gene Lockhart, Irene Ryan, David Janssen. Follow-up to BEDTIME FOR BONZO has brainy chimp lead college football team to victory; good cast takes back seat to monkey-shines.

Boob, The (1926) **61m.** ** D: William A. Wellman. Gertrude Olmstead, George K. Arthur, Joan Crawford, Charles Murray, Antonio D'Algy, Hank Mann, Babe London. A buffoonish yokel hopes to win the dream girl who keeps rejecting him by rescuing her from bootleggers. Silly bit of nonsense notable as an early credit for Wellman and Crawford (playing a revenue agent!).▶

Boogie Man Will Get You, The (1942) **66m.** ****½** D: Lew Landers. Boris Karloff, Peter Lorre, Jeff Donnell, Larry Parks, Slapsie Maxie Rosenbloom, Maude Eburne, Don Beddoe, Frank Puglia. Good cast in lightweight cash-in on ARSENIC AND OLD LACE. Karloff is dotty scientist attempting to make supermen out of traveling salesmen while Donnell tries to turn his home into Colonial tourist trap; Lorre is screwy doctor/sheriff/notary/loan shark. No great shakes, but pleasant.▶

Boomerang! (1947) **88m.** *****½** D: Elia Kazan. Dana Andrews, Jane Wyatt, Lee J. Cobb, Arthur Kennedy, Sam Levene, Robert Keith, Taylor Holmes, Ed Begley, Karl Malden, Cara Williams, Barry Kelley. Minister's murder brings rapid arrest of an innocent man; prosecuting attorney determines to hunt out real facts. Brilliant drama in all respects. Richard Murphy's taut screenplay, from Anthony Abbott's article "The Perfect Case," is based on a factual incident. Playwright Arthur Miller appears as one of the line-up suspects. See if you can spot Brian Keith in the crowd outside the courthouse as Cobb escorts prisoner Kennedy.▼▶

Boom in the Moon (1946-Mexican) **C-83m.** BOMB D: Jaime Salvador. Buster Keaton, Angel Garasa, Virginia Serret, Fernando Soto, Luis Barreiro. Rock-bottom "comedy" vehicle for poor Buster as an innocent thought to be a modern-day Bluebeard, who then gets shanghaied to fly a rocketship to the moon. Filmed as A MODERN BLUEBEARD, and barely seen until its video release in the 1980s.▼▶

Boom Town (1940) **118m.** ******* D: Jack Conway. Clark Gable, Spencer Tracy, Claudette Colbert, Hedy Lamarr, Frank Morgan, Lionel Atwill, Chill Wills. No surprises in tale of get-rich-quick drilling for oil, but star-studded cast gives it life. Also shown in computer-colored version.▼⊙▶

Boots and Saddles (1937) **60m.** ******* D: Joseph Kane. Gene Autry, Smiley Burnette, Judith Allen, Ra Hould (Ronnie Sinclair), Guy Usher, Gordon Elliott. Twofold plot has Gene supplying horses to the Army and holding on to young, spoiled Ra Hould's ranch while teaching him Western ways and tolerance. Ending is a bit mild. One year later Gordon Elliott became a Western star himself, as Bill Elliott.▼▶

Boots Malone (1952) **103m.** ******* D: William Dieterle. William Holden, Johnny Stewart, Ed Begley, Harry Morgan, Whit Bissell. Holden comes alive in role of shady character who reforms when he trains Stewart to become a jockey.▼

Bop Girl (1957) **79m.** ***½** D: Howard W. Koch. Judy Tyler, Bobby Troup, Margo Woode, Lucien Littlefield, Mary Kaye Trio,

Nino Tempo. Psychologist Troup predicts that rock 'n' roll will lose its popularity to calypso. He was wrong. Aka BOP GIRL GOES CALYPSO.

Bop Girl Goes Calypso SEE: **Bop Girl**

Border Café (1937) **67m.** ****½** D: Lew Landers. Harry Carey, John Beal, Armida, George Irving, Leona Roberts, J. Carrol Naish, Marjorie Lord, Lee Patrick, Paul Fix. Rich, irresponsible Beal must grow up fast when he lands in a border town, where he falls for singer Armida. So-so programmer, but it's always great to see Carey (playing rancher Tex Stevens) astride a horse.

Border Incident (1949) **92m.** ******* D: Anthony Mann. Ricardo Montalban, George Murphy, Howard da Silva, Teresa Celli, Charles McGraw. Tension-packed story of U.S. agents cracking down on smuggling of immigrants across Texas-Mexico border. Well directed, and uncompromisingly violent. ▶

Borderland (1937) **82m.** ******* D: Nate Watt. William Boyd, Jimmy Ellison, George Hayes, Stephen Morris (Morris Ankrum), Nora Lane, Al Bridge. A bandit named The Fox is too slick for the Texas Rangers, so they enlist Hopalong Cassidy to go undercover across the Mexican border and apprehend him. Shooting at Joshua Tree in the Mojave Desert adds distinction. Notable as the longest Western ever made for a B cowboy series . . . but sadly, the last entry with Ellison. Followed by sequel IN OLD MEXICO.▼▶

Border Legion, The (1940) **63m.** ******* D: Joseph Kane. Roy Rogers, George "Gabby" Hayes, Carol Hughes, Joe Sawyer, Maude Eburne, Jay Novello, Hal Taliaferro. Roy is an Eastern doctor fleeing west from a robbery charge who lands a job as a saloon singer and gets involved with villainous Sawyer's gang. Clever script (from a Zane Grey novel), expert direction, with humor, action, and Roy's youthful charm. Aka WEST OF THE BADLANDS.▼▶

Borderline (1950) **88m.** ****** D: William A. Seiter. Fred MacMurray, Claire Trevor, Raymond Burr, Jose Torvay, Morris Ankrum, Roy Roberts. Odd thriller-comedy in which L.A. cop Trevor attempts to gather evidence against wily drug smuggler Burr while mixing with tough guy MacMurray in Mexico. Starts out promisingly, but soon bogs down in silliness. Burr makes a vivid villain.▼⊙▶

Border Patrol (1943) **64m.** ******* D: Lesley Selander. William Boyd, Andy Clyde, Jay Kirby, Russell Simpson, Claudia Drake, George Reeves, Duncan Renaldo, Bob (Robert) Mitchum. In this hands-across-the-border saga, Hopalong Cassidy and sidekicks serve as Texas Rangers who work with Mexican authorities to combat outlaw gang there led by American menace Simpson. Strong cast, rapid pace, with fierce retribution for the climax. This story of oppression and revolt was penned by subsequently blacklisted Michael Wilson. ▼▶

Border River (1954) C-80m. ** D: George Sherman. Joel McCrea, Yvonne De Carlo, Pedro Armendariz, Howard Petrie. Mildly intriguing Western about Rebel officer McCrea's mission to buy much-needed weapons from Mexicans to continue fight against Yankees. ▶

Border Street (1949-Polish) 115m. ***½ D: Aleksander Ford. Maria Broniewska, Tadeusz Fijewski, Wladyslaw Godik, Jerzy Leszczynski, Mieczyslawa Cwiklinksa, Wladyslaw Walter, Jerzy Pichelski, Ida Kaminska. Warsaw, 1939: Jews are outsiders and are subjected to anti-Semitic taunts from their fellow Poles. Then Hitler invades Poland and their lot only worsens. Chilling film offers an early portrait of the horrors of the Holocaust, with the emphasis on the impact of the Nazi presence on Jewish—and non-Jewish—children. Deeply humane drama, which includes a vivid depiction of the Warsaw Ghetto uprising, is loaded with stunning imagery and is ripe for rediscovery. ▼▶

Bordertown (1935) 90m. *** D: Archie Mayo. Paul Muni, Bette Davis, Eugene Pallette, Margaret Lindsay. Fine drama of unusual triangle in bordertown cafe, with Davis as flirtatious wife of Pallette with designs on lawyer Muni; her overwrought scene on the witness stand is not easily forgotten. Used as basis for later THEY DRIVE BY NIGHT (1940), but more serious in tone. Also shown in computer-colored version. ▶

Border Vigilantes (1941) 62m. *** D: Derwin Abrahams. William Boyd, Russell Hayden, Andy Clyde, Frances Gifford, Victor Jory, Morris Ankrum, Tom Tyler. Summoned by rancher friend Ankrum, the Bar 20 trio travels to a frontier mining community to aid locals being robbed of their silver, despite supposed efforts of the Border Vigilantes. Interesting role reversal in the casting of Ankrum as a good guy but Jory, Tyler, and former Hopalong Cassidy sidekick Britt Wood as villains. Lots of gunplay and furious action. Scenic exteriors lensed in Lone Pine. Hayden makes a disparaging remark about singing cowboys! ▼▶

Born Reckless (1930) 82m. **½ D: John Ford. Edmund Lowe, Catherine Dale Owen, Lee Tracy, Marguerite Churchill, Warren Hymer, William Harrigan, Frank Albertson. Lowe is a convicted bootlegger sent to war by a judge (where he spends most of his time playing baseball!), then returns to New York and falls for socialite Owen while battling gang rival Hymer. Weird combination of gangster film and war drama is fairly entertaining. Lifelong Ford regulars Ward Bond and Jack Pennick have bits as soldiers. ▶

Born Reckless (1937) 59m. **½ D: Malcolm St. Clair. Rochelle Hudson, Brian Donlevy, Barton MacLane, Robert Kent, Harry Carey, Pauline Moore. Big-shot race car driver Donlevy goes broke and takes a job as a hack to help out pal involved in a taxi war with racketeers. Peppy, minor programmer with lots of two-fisted action. Lon Chaney, Jr., appears as a garage mechanic.

Born Reckless (1959) 79m. *½ D: Howard W. Koch. Mamie Van Doren, Jeff Richards, Arthur Hunnicutt, Carol Ohmart, Tom Duggan, Jeanne Carmen. Rodeo star Richards divides his time between busting broncos and busting heads of lecherous old cowpokes trying to paw Mamie. Not bad enough to be really funny, but it has its moments; Mamie sings five of film's eight songs, including unforgettable "I'm Just a Nice, Sweet, Home-Type of Girl." ▶

Born to Be Bad (1934) 61m. **½ D: Lowell Sherman. Loretta Young, Cary Grant, Jackie Kelk, Henry Travers, Russell Hopton, Harry Green, Marion Burns. Conniving unwed mom Young raises illegitimate son to cheat his way through life; when he has an accident and is adopted by rich Grant and his wife, she schemes to break up their marriage. Sassy, sometimes sappy story by Ralph Graves is notable for pre-Code morals (or lack of them) and two exceptionally good-looking stars. ▶

Born to Be Bad (1950) 94m. **½ D: Nicholas Ray. Joan Fontaine, Robert Ryan, Zachary Scott, Joan Leslie, Mel Ferrer, Harold Vermilyea. "Little fake" Fontaine, despite attraction to writer Ryan, schemes to win wealthy Scott away from fiancée Leslie. And that's just for openers. Good cast in somewhat overwrought, predictable drama. ▼◉▶

Born to Be Loved (1959) 82m. ** D: Hugo Haas. Carol Morris, Vera Vague (Barbara Jo Allen), Hugo Haas, Dick Kallman, Jacqueline Fontaine. Low-key yarn of poor-but-honest Morris and rich widow Vague seeking romance, helped by elderly music instructor Haas.

Born to Dance (1936) 105m. *** D: Roy Del Ruth. Eleanor Powell, James Stewart, Virginia Bruce, Una Merkel, Sid Silvers, Frances Langford, Raymond Walburn, Buddy Ebsen, Reginald Gardiner. Powell bears out title in good Cole Porter musical with sensational footwork and fine songs: "Easy To Love" (introduced by Stewart) and "I've Got You Under My Skin." ▼◉▶

Born to Kill (1947) 92m. *** D: Robert Wise. Claire Trevor, Lawrence Tierney, Walter Slezak, Audrey Long, Elisha Cook, Jr., Phillip Terry. Murderer Tierney marries insecure Long, but can't stay away from her divorced sister Trevor. Super-tough film noir is uncharacteristically mean-spirited for director Wise, but is well put together nonetheless. A cult item. ▼▶

Born to Sing (1942) 82m. **½ D: Edward

Ludwig. Virginia Weidler, Ray McDonald, Leo Gorcey, "Rags" Ragland, Douglas McPhail, Sheldon Leonard, Henry O'Neill, Larry Nunn, Margaret Dumont, Darla Hood, Joe Yule. Second-string let's-put-on-a-show musical about kids who stage a patriotic Broadway revue is fast, funny, and amiable. Busby Berkeley directed the lavish production number finale, "Ballad for Americans."

Born to the West (1937) 52m. **½ D: Charles Barton. John Wayne, Marsha Hunt, Johnny Mack Brown, John Patterson, Monte Blue, Lucien Littlefield, James Craig, Sid Saylor. Boyhood feud is revived after two cousins grow up; dependable cowpuncher Brown foolishly gives less reliable Wayne a trail-boss job. Loosely based on same-named Zane Grey novel, filmed before in 1926. Lots of action and well photographed. Reissued as HELL TOWN with additional stock footage at the outset to extend running time to an hour.▼▶

Born Yesterday (1950) 103m. ***½ D: George Cukor. Judy Holliday, William Holden, Broderick Crawford, Howard St. John. Junk-dealer-made-good Crawford wants girlfriend (Holliday) culturefied, hires Holden to teach her in hilarious Garson Kanin comedy set in Washington, D.C. Priceless Judy repeated Broadway triumph and won Oscar for playing quintessential dumb blonde. Remade in 1993. ▼●▶

Borrowed Trouble (1948) 58m. ** D: George Archainbaud. William Boyd, Andy Clyde, Rand Brooks, Anne O'Neal, John Parrish, Cliff Clark. Spinster teacher who objects when saloon operates near her school is kidnapped; it's up to Hopalong Cassidy to rescue her and solve a related mystery. This unremarkable, slow-paced series entry doesn't have much action and depends on its stars' personalities. Reissued as LAW OF THE TRAIL.▶

Boss, The (1956) 89m. *** D: Byron Haskin. John Payne, William Bishop, Gloria McGehee, Doe Avedon, Roy Roberts, Rhys Williams, Joe Flynn, Gil Lamb. Saga of urban politico has WW1 veteran Payne building a corrupt municipal fief. Perhaps Payne's best performance; scripted by a blacklisted Dalton Trumbo. ▶

Boston Blackie Over a span of nine years, Chester Morris starred in 14 films as Boston Blackie, a former thief now on the right side of the law but preferring to work for himself rather than for the police. He brought to the role a delightful offhand manner and sense of humor that kept the films fresh even when the scripts weren't. (He even got to pursue his hobby—performing magic—in a couple of episodes.) Regulars included Richard Lane as a frustrated police detective convinced that Blackie was up to no good, but always one step behind him; George E. Stone as Blackie's talkative, dim-witted buddy; and Lloyd Corrigan as a dizzy millionaire pal who'd

do anything for a lark. Top-flight directors Robert Florey and Edward Dmytryk got the series started, and when the films fell into less capable hands, Morris and company came to the rescue with consistently ingratiating performances.

BOSTON BLACKIE

Meet Boston Blackie (1941)
Confessions of Boston Blackie (1941)
Alias Boston Blackie (1942)
Boston Blackie Goes Hollywood (1942)
After Midnight With Boston Blackie (1943)
The Chance of a Lifetime (1943)
One Mysterious Night (1944)
Boston Blackie Booked on Suspicion (1945)
Boston Blackie's Rendezvous (1945)
A Close Call for Boston Blackie (1946)
The Phantom Thief (1946)
Boston Blackie and the Law (1946)
Trapped by Boston Blackie (1948)
Boston Blackie's Chinese Venture (1949)

Boston Blackie and the Law (1946) 70m. ** D: D. Ross Lederman. Chester Morris, Trudy Marshall, Constance Dowling, Richard Lane, George E. Stone, Frank Sully. Blackie uses his skill at prestidigitation to catch a killer who escaped from a women's prison during one of his magic shows. Mediocre entry utilizing a distaff version of the ALIAS BOSTON BLACKIE plot.

Boston Blackie Booked on Suspicion (1945) 66m. **½ D: Arthur Dreifuss. Chester Morris, Lynn Merrick, Richard Lane, Frank Sully, Steve Cochran, George E. Stone, Lloyd Corrigan. Blackie becomes a prime suspect when he helps out an auctioneer friend and discovers counterfeit rare books—and murder. Fair mystery brightened by jaunty playing. ▼▶

Boston Blackie Goes Hollywood (1942) 68m. *** D: Michael Gordon. Chester Morris, George E. Stone, Richard Lane, Forrest Tucker, Constance Worth, William Wright, Lloyd Corrigan, Walter Sande. Classy entry with the nimble Blackie transporting $60,000 for a friend to California. The cops follow him in hope of finding the lost Monterey diamond.

Boston Blackie's Appointment With Death SEE: One Mysterious Night

Boston Blackie's Chinese Venture (1949) 59m. ** D: Seymour Friedman. Chester Morris, Joan Woodbury, Maylia, Richard Lane, Don McGuire, Sid Tomack, Frank Sully, Charles Arnt, Philip Ahn, Benson Fong. Last, and least, of the Blackie mysteries finds our hero probing Chinatown murders, which he's naturally been accused of. George E. Stone is sorely missed as sidekick "Runt," replaced by Tomack for this final entry. ▶

Boston Blackie's Rendezvous (1945)

**64m. **½ D: Arthur Dreifuss. Chester Morris, Nina Foch, Steve Cochran, Richard Lane, George E. Stone, Frank Sully, Iris Adrian, Harry Hayden. Fairly tense entry, with Blackie on the trail of Cochran, a psycho killer who escapes from an asylum and goes on a murder spree.

Botany Bay (1953) C-94m. **½ D: John Farrow. Alan Ladd, James Mason, Patricia Medina, Cedric Hardwicke. Based on Charles Nordhoff novel set in 1790s, picturesque yarn tells of convict ship bound for Australia, focusing on conflict between prisoner Ladd and sadistic skipper Mason, with Medina as Ladd's love interest.▼

Both Sides of the Law (1953-British) 94m. *** D: Muriel Box. Peggy Cummins, Terence Morgan, Anne Crawford, Rosamund John. Documentary-style account of London policewomen and their daily activity. Unpretentious production; good performances. Aka STREET CORNER.

Bottom of the Bottle, The (1956) C-88m. **½ D: Henry Hathaway. Van Johnson, Joseph Cotten, Ruth Roman, Jack Carson, Margaret Hayes, Bruce Bennett, Brad Dexter, Jim Davis, Margaret Lindsay, Henry (Harry) Morgan. Hot-and-heavy soaper detailing fireworks after alcoholic fugitive Johnson appears on the doorstep of his respectable lawyer-rancher brother (Cotten). Based on a novel by Georges Simenon. Cinema-Scope.◗

Bottoms Up (1934) 85m. *** D: David Butler. Spencer Tracy, Pat Paterson, John Boles, Sid Silvers, Herbert Mundin, Harry Green, Thelma Todd, Robert Emmett O'Connor. Sharp, knowing comedy with music about a smooth-talking con man (Tracy) and his two cronies, who pass off movie extra Paterson as royalty, allowing her a shot at Hollywood stardom. Great fun, especially for film buffs. If you blink, you'll miss Lucille Ball in a bit. Silvers, who plays Spud, cowrote the story.

Boudu Saved From Drowning (1932-French) 87m. *** D: Jean Renoir. Michel Simon, Charles Granval, Marcelle Hania, Severine Lerczynska. Title tramp is rescued from the Seine and taken home by well-meaning book dealer; he eventually takes over household, then seduces both the wife and maid. Classic attack on complacency still holds up, with ratty-bearded Simon giving the performance of a lifetime. U.S. remake: DOWN AND OUT IN BEVERLY HILLS.▼◗

Bought! (1931) 92m. **½ D: Archie Mayo. Constance Bennett, Ben Lyon, Richard Bennett, Dorothy Peterson, Ray Milland, Doris Lloyd, Maude Eburne, Clara Blandick. Working-class girl dreams of living a better life and forsakes her friends when she has a chance to break into high society. One scene in which Milland comes to Bennett's room at night is fairly explicit for its time. Fairly good soap opera marks the only time Bennett worked with her famous father, playing an older man who takes an interest in her.

Bounty Hunter, The (1954) C-79m. **½ D: Andre de Toth. Randolph Scott, Dolores Dorn, Marie Windsor, Howard Petrie. In a desert town, title character Scott must ferret out the three residents responsible for a bloody holdup. Packed with comin'-at-ya 3-D-type moments; it was shot in that format but never released in 3-D.

Bounty Killer, The (1965) C-92m. **½ D: Spencer G. Bennet. Dan Duryea, Rod Cameron, Audrey Dalton, Richard Arlen, Buster Crabbe, Fuzzy Knight, Johnny Mack Brown, Bob Steele, Bronco Billy Anderson. Chief interest is cast of old-timers from Hollywood Westerns. Unlike their previous vehicles, this is adult, low-key, and minus happy ending as Eastern tenderfoot Duryea morphs into ruthless title character.

Bourbon Street Shadows SEE: **Invisible Avenger**

Bowery, The (1933) 90m. *** D: Raoul Walsh. Wallace Beery, George Raft, Jackie Cooper, Fay Wray, Pert Kelton, Herman Bing. Rowdy, colorful yarn of N.Y.C. in the Gay '90s, with Beery as saloon owner Chuck Connors, Cooper as his adopted son, and Raft as Steve Brodie, who made his name by jumping off the Brooklyn Bridge. This film has something to offend seemingly every racial and ethnic group! Kelton is a hoot as a saloon soubrette.

Bowery at Midnight (1942) 63m. ** D: Wallace Fox. Bela Lugosi, John Archer, Wanda McKay, Tom Neal, Dave O'Brien. Lugosi is kindly psychiatrist who leads double life as criminal mastermind in the Bowery. An inexplicable subplot involves reviving the dead. Mild but atmospheric.▼◗

Bowery Battalion (1951) 69m. ** D: William Beaudine. Leo Gorcey, Huntz Hall, Donald MacBride, Virginia Hewitt, Russell Hicks, William (Billy) Benedict, Bernard Gorcey, David Gorcey. Serviceable service romp, as the Bowery Boys join the Army to catch some spies.

Bowery Blitzkrieg (1941) 62m. *½ D: Wallace Fox. Leo Gorcey, Bobby Jordan, Huntz Hall, Sunshine Sammy Morrison, Donald Haines, David Gorcey, Warren Hull, Charlotte Henry, Keye Luke, Bobby Stone, Dennis Moore. Cliché-ridden *East Side Kids* entry about good kid Jordan torn between boxing and school, mixed up with the requisite gangsters.▼◗

Bowery Bombshell (1946) 65m. **½ D: Phil Karlson. Leo Gorcey, Huntz Hall, Bobby Jordan, Billy Benedict, David Gorcey, Teala Loring, James Burke, Sheldon Leonard, Bernard Gorcey. The boys track down some bank robbers when Sach becomes a suspect in this amusing entry with perennial nightclub gangster Leonard in fine form.◗

The Bowery Boys Sidney Kingsley's Broadway play *Dead End* was a superior drama that cast a critical eye on big-city tenement slums. When Samuel Goldwyn brought it to the screen, he retained the services of the young performers who'd played the street kids on stage: Billy Halop, Bobby Jordan, Gabriel Dell, Huntz Hall, Leo Gorcey, and Bernard Punsley. Though Kingsley never intended to glorify hoodlums, these young actors made a tremendous impact on audiences, much as gangster antiheroes had earlier in the decade . . . and before long, the "Dead End Kids" were stars! Warner Bros. featured them in six films over the next few years with such costars as James Cagney (ANGELS WITH DIRTY FACES), Humphrey Bogart (CRIME SCHOOL), and John Garfield (THEY MADE ME A CRIMINAL). Most of these films maintained the *Dead End* stance of portraying these juvenile delinquents as victims of society, though some of this posturing rang hollow considering their shenanigans. Some of the gang also found work at Universal; a B picture called LITTLE TOUGH GUY launched a series of "Dead End Kids and Little Tough Guys" films, which included both original kids and newcomers. These vehicles were a motley and uneven bunch randomly integrating action, melodrama, and juvenile comedy. Not only wasn't there the pointedness of *Dead End*; there was often no point at all. Universal even featured the group in three Saturday matinee serials, JUNIOR G-MEN, SEA RAIDERS, and JUNIOR G-MEN OF THE AIR. Then, in 1940, producer Sam Katzman launched a low-budget series called *The East Side Kids* for Monogram Pictures, featuring Leo Gorcey and Bobby Jordan, who were later joined by fellow Dead Enders Huntz Hall and Gabriel Dell. These low-budget films stressed (grade-B) drama as much as comedy. Gamblers, boxers, and Nazis figured prominently, along with Bela Lugosi, who costarred in SPOOKS RUN WILD and GHOSTS ON THE LOOSE. The cast members began to hit their stride in these films, developing the camaraderie that was to make them enduringly popular. In 1946, Leo Gorcey took a hand in revamping the films, assumed the official starring role of Slip Mahoney, with Huntz Hall as his sidekick Sach Jones, and the series was rechristened *The Bowery Boys*. For several years' time these films flirted with drama, as in HARD BOILED MAHONEY, IN FAST COMPANY, and JINX MONEY, but then decided to go all-out with broad juvenile comedy. Audiences enjoyed the results, and The Bowery Boys experienced a healthy run right into the 1950s. Leo Gorcey's father, Bernard, played Louie Dumbrowski, proprietor of the gang's ice-cream parlor hangout, and when he died in 1956, Leo left the series. Stanley Clements was brought in to replace him, for seven more generally lackluster comedies (HOT SHOTS, HOLD THAT HYPNOTIST, UP IN SMOKE, etc.) before the series finally breathed its last in 1958.

THE BOWERY BOYS

The Dead End Kids
Dead End (1937)
Crime School (1938)
Angels With Dirty Faces (1938)
They Made Me a Criminal (1939)
Hell's Kitchen (1939)
Angels Wash Their Faces, The (1939)
On Dress Parade (1939)

The Dead End Kids and Little Tough Guys
Little Tough Guy (1938)
Call a Messenger (1939)
You're Not So Tough (1940)
Give Us Wings (1940)
Hit the Road (1941)
Mob Town (1941)
Tough as They Come (1942)
Mug Town (1943)
Keep 'Em Slugging (1943)

East Side Kids
East Side Kids (1940)
Boys of the City (1940)
That Gang of Mine (1940)
Pride of the Bowery (1941)
Flying Wild (1941)
Bowery Blitzkrieg (1941)
Spooks Run Wild (1941)
Mr. Wise Guy (1942)
Let's Get Tough! (1942)
Smart Alecks (1942)
'Neath Brooklyn Bridge (1942)
Kid Dynamite (1943)
Clancy Street Boys (1943)
Ghosts on the Loose (1943)
Mr. Muggs Steps Out (1943)
Million Dollar Kid (1944)
Follow the Leader (1944)
Block Busters (1944)
Bowery Champs (1944)
Docks of New York, The (1945)
Mr. Muggs Rides Again (1945)
Come Out Fighting (1945)

Bowery Boys
Live Wires (1946)
In Fast Company (1946)
Bowery Bombshell (1946)
Spook Busters (1946)
Mr. Hex (1946)
Hard Boiled Mahoney (1947)
News Hounds (1947)
Bowery Buckaroos (1947)
Angels' Alley (1948)
Jinx Money (1948)
Smugglers' Cove (1948)
Trouble Makers (1948)
Fighting Fools (1949)
Hold That Baby! (1949)
Angels in Disguise (1949)

Master Minds (1949)
Blonde Dynamite (1950)
Lucky Losers (1950)
Triple Trouble (1950)
Blues Busters (1950)
Bowery Battalion (1951)
Ghost Chasers (1951)
Let's Go Navy! (1951)
Crazy Over Horses (1951)
Hold That Line (1952)
Here Come the Marines (1952)
Feudin' Fools (1952)
No Holds Barred (1952)
Jalopy (1953)
Loose in London (1953)
Clipped Wings (1953)
Private Eyes (1953)
Paris Playboys (1954)
The Bowery Boys Meet the Monsters (1954)
Jungle Gents (1954)
Bowery to Bagdad (1954)
High Society (1955)
Spy Chasers (1955)
Jail Busters (1955)
Dig That Uranium (1956)
Crashing Las Vegas (1956)
Fighting Trouble (1956)
Hot Shots (1956)
Hold That Hypnotist (1957)
Spook Chasers (1957)
Looking for Danger (1957)
Up in Smoke (1957)
In the Money (1958)

Bowery Boys Meet the Monsters, The (1954) **65m.** **½ D: Edward Bernds. Leo Gorcey, Huntz Hall, Bernard Gorcey, Bennie Bartlett, Lloyd Corrigan, Ellen Corby, John Dehner. Efficient blend of laughs and chills as the gang meets a family of transplant-happy mad scientists. ▶
Bowery Buckaroos (1947) **66m.** ** D: William Beaudine. Leo Gorcey, Huntz Hall, Bobby Jordan, Gabriel Dell, Billy Benedict, David Gorcey, Julie Gibson, Bernard Gorcey, Minerva Urecal, Russell Simpson, Iron Eyes Cody. Mild spoof, with the boys getting into all sorts of trouble out West in Hangman's Hollow. ▼▶
Bowery Champs (1944) **62m.** ** D: William Beaudine. Leo Gorcey, Huntz Hall, Billy Benedict, Jimmy Strand, Bud Gorman, Gabriel Dell, Anne Sterling, Evelyn Brent, Ian Keith. Newshound Muggs (Gorcey) gets embroiled in a murder investigation in this frantic *East Side Kids* outing. Former costar Bobby Jordan appears as himself in an amusing running gag.
Bowery to Bagdad (1954) **64m.** ** D: Edward Bernds. Leo Gorcey, Huntz Hall, David Gorcey, Bennie Bartlett, Bernard Gorcey, Joan Shawlee, Eric Blore, Robert Bice, Rick Vallin, Jean Willes. N.Y. gangsters and Bagdad baddies are on the trail of Slip and Sach after a magic lamp falls into the boys' hands. Unsubtle, to say the least.

Veteran scene-stealer Blore appears as the genie! ▶
Bowery to Broadway (1944) **94m.** **½ D: Charles Lamont. Jack Oakie, Donald Cook, Maria Montez, Louise Allbritton, Susanna Foster, Turhan Bey, Andy Devine, Rosemary DeCamp, Frank McHugh, Ann Blyth, Leo Carrillo, Evelyn Ankers, Peggy Ryan, Donald O'Connor. Film depends solely on its many guest stars for what entertainment it has; limp story of rival theatrical producers (Oakie, Cook) doesn't make it.
Boy and the Laughing Dog, The SEE: **Good-bye, My Lady**
Boy and the Pirates, The (1960) **C-82m.** **½ D: Bert I. Gordon. Charles Herbert, Susan Gordon, Murvyn Vye, Paul Guilfoyle. OK fantasy-adventure for kids about a boy who is magically transported back to the days of pirates on the high seas. Vye is well cast as Blackbeard, the main cutthroat. ▶
Boy From Indiana (1950) **66m.** ** D: John Rawlins. Lon McCallister, Lois Butler, Billie Burke, George Cleveland. Modest horseracing yarn, with McCallister grooming his beloved horse, romancing Butler.
Boy From Oklahoma, The (1954) **C-88m.** **½ D: Michael Curtiz. Will Rogers, Jr., Nancy Olson, Lon Chaney (Jr.), Anthony Caruso, Wallace Ford, Merv Griffin. Quiet Western film with Rogers as pacifist sheriff who manages to keep the town intact and romance Olson; good production values. Spun off as TV series *Sugarfoot.* ▶
Boy from Stalingrad, The (1943) **69m.** ** D: Sidney Salkow. Bobby Samarzich, Conrad Binyon, Mary Lou Harrington, Scotty Beckett, Steven Muller, John Wengraf, Erik Rolf. Least known of Hollywood's pro-Russian propaganda films from WW2 is a dated, and somewhat heavy-handed, drama about brave kids from a burnt-out village who band together to ward off invading Nazis. Interesting as a historical curio. ▶
Boy Meets Girl (1938) **86m.** **½ D: Lloyd Bacon. James Cagney, Pat O'Brien, Marie Wilson, Ralph Bellamy, Frank McHugh, Dick Foran, Penny Singleton, Ronald Reagan. Screwball spoof of Hollywood sometimes pushes too hard, but has enough sharp dialogue, good satire in tale of two sharpster screenwriters to make it worthwhile. Script by Samuel and Bella Spewack, from their Broadway play. ▼▶
Boy of the Streets (1937) **75m.** **½ D: William Nigh. Jackie Cooper, Maureen O'Connor, Kathleen Burke, Robert Emmett O'Connor, Marjorie Main, George Cleveland. Atmospheric little programmer with Cooper a cocky young punk who hero-worships his dad, a slimy political hack. Awfully sentimental at times. ▼▶
Boy on a Dolphin (1957) **C-111m.** **½ D: Jean Negulesco. Alan Ladd, Clifton Webb, Sophia Loren, Laurence Naismith, Alex Minotis, Jorge Mistral. Loren's Hol-

[82]

lywood debut understandably caused a sensation for her initial appearance in a wet, clingy blouse; thereafter, it's an OK adventure about rival teams of divers racing to locate the titular statue, sunk centuries ago off the island of Hydra. Spectacular Greek locations are the real stars; Webb's droll villainy is another asset. CinemaScope.

Boys, The (1962-British) **123m. *** D:** Sidney J. Furie. Richard Todd, Robert Morley, Felix Aylmer, Wilfred Brambell. Engrossing study of attorney who tries to uncover motives for crimes allegedly committed by four teenagers. CinemaScope.

Boys From Brooklyn, The SEE: **Bela Lugosi Meets a Brooklyn Gorilla**

Boys From Syracuse, The (1940) **73m. **½ D:** A. Edward Sutherland. Allan Jones, Joe Penner, Martha Raye, Rosemary Lane, Irene Hervey, Alan Mowbray, Charles Butterworth, Samuel S. Hinds, Eric Blore. Disappointingly ordinary adaptation of Rodgers & Hart's Broadway musical based on Shakespeare's *Comedy of Errors,* but set in ancient Greece. Songs: "This Can't Be Love," "Falling in Love With Love."

Boy Slaves (1939) **70m. **½ D:** P. J. Wolfson. Anne Shirley, Roger Daniel, James McCallion, Walter Ward, Charles Powers, Johnny Fitzgerald, Walter Tetley, Charles Lane. Grim social drama about a gang of impoverished runaways who are promised work by oily businessman Lane, only to end up behind barbed wire in a forced labor camp. Scrappy grade-B hybrid of WILD BOYS OF THE ROAD and I AM A FUGITIVE FROM A CHAIN GANG is dated but still packs a punch.

Boys' Night Out (1962) **C-115m. *** D:** Michael Gordon. Kim Novak, James Garner, Tony Randall, Howard Duff, Janet Blair, Patti Page, Zsa Zsa Gabor, Howard Morris. Trio of married men and bachelor Garner decide to set up an apartment equipped with Novak. Some interesting innuendos, with comic relief from Blair, Page, and Gabor. CinemaScope.▼❶

Boys of the City (1940) **65m. ** D:** Joseph H. Lewis. Leo Gorcey, Bobby Jordan, Sunshine Sammy Morrison, David Gorcey, Dave O'Brien, Vince Barnett, Dennis Moore, Donald Haines, Hally Chester, Frankie Burke. Muggs (Gorcey) and his gang are sent to the country where they get mixed up with murder in a "haunted" house. OK follow-up to EAST SIDE KIDS and the first official entry in the series.▼❶

Boys' Ranch (1946) **96m. **½ D:** Roy Rowland. Jackie "Butch" Jenkins, James Craig, Skippy Homeier, Dorothy Patrick, Ray Collins, Darryl Hickman, Sharon McManus, Minor Watson, Geraldine Wall. Nicely told, fact-based BOYS TOWN–like tale of a just-retired ballplayer (Craig) who establishes and operates the title ranch for homeless, troubled teens. Homeier is the embittered punk who's desperately in need of reform; Jenkins is as lovable as ever, particularly when he attempts to ride a mule.

Boys Town (1938) **96m. *** D:** Norman Taurog. Spencer Tracy, Mickey Rooney, Henry Hull, Gene Reynolds, Leslie Fenton, Addison Richards, Edward Norris, Sidney Miller, Bobs Watson, Frankie Thomas. Tracy won Oscar as Father Flanagan, who develops school for juvenile delinquents; Rooney is his toughest enrolee. Syrupy but well done; Eleanore Griffin and Dore Schary also earned Oscars for their original story. Sequel: MEN OF BOYS TOWN. Almost 60 years later, Rooney played Father Flanagan in the direct-to-video feature THE ROAD HOME. Also shown in computer-colored version.▼❶❶

Boy Ten Feet Tall, A (1963-British) **C-118m. *** D:** Alexander Mackendrick. Edward G. Robinson, Fergus McClelland, Constance Cummings, Harry H. Corbett. Colorful, charming film about orphaned boy traveling through Africa alone to reach his aunt, who lives in Durban. Cut to 88m. for American release. Originally titled SAMMY GOING SOUTH. CinemaScope.

Boy! What a Girl (1946) **70m. *** D:** Arthur Leonard. Tim Moore, Duke Williams, Elwood Smith, Sheila Guyse, Betti Mays, Deek Watson and His Brown Dots, Big Sid Catlett, International Jitterbugs, Slam Stewart, Ann Cornell. Wonderfully entertaining musical comedy featuring all-black cast (with the exception of Gene Krupa). Scenario centers on a couple of producers attempting to win backing for their show. Moore is funny in drag; the jitterbugging is quite X-rated for 1946.▼❶

Boy Who Stole a Million, The (1960-British) **64m. ** D:** Charles Crichton. Maurice Reyna, Virgilio Texera, Marianne Benet, Harold Kasket, George Coulouris. Family-type film of youth who gets involved in bank theft to help father with oppressive debts.

Boy With Green Hair, The (1948) **C-82m. *** D:** Joseph Losey. Pat O'Brien, Robert Ryan, Barbara Hale, Dean Stockwell, Dwayne Hickman. Thought-provoking allegory of war orphan Stockwell, who becomes a social outcast when his hair changes color. Controversial on its release because of its pacifistic point of view. Dale Robertson and Russ Tamblyn appear uncredited.▼❶❶

Brain, The (1962-British-German) **85m. *** D:** Freddie Francis. Anne Heywood, Peter Van Eyck, Cecil Parker, Bernard Lee, Maxine Audley, Jeremy Spenser, Jack MacGowran. Good remake of DONOVAN'S BRAIN, about scientist overtaken by the brain of a vengeance-seeking dead man that is being kept "alive" in his laboratory. Original British title: VENGEANCE.▼❶

Brain Eaters, The (1958) **60m. ** D:** Bruno Ve Sota. Edwin (Ed) Nelson, Alan Frost, Joanna Lee, Jody Fair. Loosely based (without credit) on Robert Heinlein's *Puppet Masters*, this has spongy brain creatures boring up from inner earth in a ship, attaching themselves to people's heads and turning them into mindless zombies. Some mildly scary moments. Look for Leonard Nimoy.▼

Brain From Planet Arous, The (1958) **70m.** ** D: Nathan Juran. John Agar, Joyce Meadows, Robert Fuller, Henry Travis, Morris Ankrum, Tom Browne Henry. Giant floating brain (with eyes) takes over the body of scientist Agar as its first step in conquering Earth; meanwhile, an alien policeman's brain hides out in Agar's dog while waiting for the right moment to make the arrest. Fun in an idiotic sort of way, and Agar is pretty good under the circumstances.▼●▶

Brain Machine, The (1956-British) **72m.** ** D: Ken Hughes. Patrick Barr, Elizabeth Allan, Maxwell Reed, Vanda Godsell. Average yarn about drug smuggling and those involved, one of them as the result of mind-shattering machine.

Brainstorm (1965) **114m.** ** D: William Conrad. Jeff Hunter, Anne Francis, Dana Andrews, Viveca Lindfors, Stacy Harris, Kathie Brown. Fair thriller about a determined man (Hunter) who attempts the perfect crime in order to eliminate Andrews and marry Francis. Contrived. Panavision.▶

Brain That Wouldn't Die, The (1963) **81m.** *½ D: Joseph Green. Herb (Jason) Evers, Virginia Leith, Adele Lamont, Leslie Daniel, Paula Maurice. Poorly produced tale of surgeon trying to find body to attach to fiancée's head (she was decapitated but still lives). Beware of shorter version, which eliminates most of the gore.▼▶

Brainwashed (1961-German) **102m.** ** D: Gerd Oswald. Curt Jurgens, Claire Bloom, Hansjorg Felmy, Albert Lieven. Austrian Jurgens' struggle to retain sanity while undergoing intense Nazi interrogation is basis of this psychological drama. Strong performances but weak story mars film.

Bramble Bush, The (1960) **C-105m.** **½ D: Daniel Petrie. Richard Burton, Barbara Rush, Jack Carson, Angie Dickinson. Charles Mergendahl's potboiler becomes superficial gloss with Burton, totally ill at ease, playing New England doctor returning to Cape Cod, where he falls in love with his dying friend's wife.▼

Branded (1950) **C-95m.** **½ D: Rudolph Maté. Alan Ladd, Mona Freeman, Charles Bickford, Joseph Calleia, Milburn Stone. Outlaws use carefree Ladd to impersonate rancher Bickford's long-missing son, leading to much different outcome than anticipated; action and love scenes balanced OK.▼●▶

Brasher Doubloon, The (1947) **72m.** ** D: John Brahm. George Montgomery, Nancy Guild, Conrad Janis, Roy Roberts, Fritz Kortner. Rare coin seems to be object of several murders in very uneven version of

Philip Marlowe detective mystery. Filmed before as TIME TO KILL.▶

Brass Bottle, The (1964) **C-89m.** ** D: Harry Keller. Tony Randall, Burl Ives, Barbara Eden, Edward Andrews, Ann Doran. Juvenile comedy-fantasy about genie Ives coming out of magic bottle to serve Randall. Eden fared better when she went into a lamp herself on TV.▼▶

Brass Legend, The (1956) **79m.** **½ D: Gerd Oswald. Hugh O'Brian, Nancy Gates, Raymond Burr, Reba Tassell (Rebecca Welles), Donald MacDonald, Robert Burton. Modest oater about the repercussions that follow when young MacDonald comes to the aid of sheriff O'Brian in his pursuit of outlaw Burr.

Brass Monkey, The (1948-British) **81m.** ** D: Thornton Freeland. Carroll Levis, Carole Landis, Herbert Lom, Avril Angers, Ernest Thesiger, Edward Underdown, Henry Edwards, Henry Worthington, Terry-Thomas. A radio personality (Canadian-born BBC host Levis, as himself) gets tangled up in a real-life crime, the theft of the title sculpture. Film interrupts suspense for broadcast skits. Unlikely overlap has Landis near the end of her career and T-T at the start of his. Aka LUCKY MASCOT.▼

Brat, The (1931) **81m.** **½ D: John Ford. Sally O'Neil, Alan Dinehart, Frank Albertson, Virginia Cherrill, June Collyer, J. Farrell MacDonald, William Collier, Sr. Wealthy novelist takes a waif home to stay with him in order to research his next book. Naturally, they fall in love, much to the chagrin of his snooty family and socialite girlfriend. Change of pace for Ford is a stylish, pleasing foray into satire and light comedy. Filmed before in 1919 and again as THE GIRL FROM AVENUE A (1940).

Bravados, The (1958) **C-98m.** *** D: Henry King. Gregory Peck, Joan Collins, Stephen Boyd, Albert Salmi, Henry Silva, Kathleen Gallant, Barry Coe, George Voskovec, Herbert Rudley, Lee Van Cleef. Compelling Western with embittered Peck showing up in a small town to witness a hanging—but there are complications. Joe DeRita (later Curly Joe of The Three Stooges) plays the hangman. CinemaScope.▼▶

Brave Bulls, The (1951) **108m.** *** D: Robert Rossen. Mel Ferrer, Miroslava, Anthony Quinn, Eugene Iglesias. Flavorful account of public and private life of a matador, based on Tom Lea book. Film admirably captures atmosphere of bullfighting. Some prints now available run 114m., with bullfight footage originally deemed too gruesome for U.S. audiences.

Brave One, The (1956) **C-100m.** *** D: Irving Rapper. Michel Ray, Rodolfo Hoyos, Fermin Rivera, Elsa Cardenas, Carlos Navarro, Joi Lansing. Predictable but charming tale of peasant-boy Ray and his love for Gitano, a valiant bull destined to meet his fate in the arena. Filmed in Mexico. "Robert Rich" (a pseudonym for blacklisted Dalton Trumbo) received a Best Original Story Academy Award, which went unclaimed until 1975. CinemaScope. ▼●)

Brave Warrior (1952) **C-73m.** *½ D: Spencer G. Bennet. Jon Hall, Jay Silverheels, Michael Ansara, Christine Larson. Inept yarn, set in 1800s Indiana, has Hall preventing Indian hostilities.)

Bread, Love and Dreams (1954-Italian) **90m.** *** D: Luigi Comencini. Vittorio De Sica, Gina Lollobrigida, Marisa Merlini, Roberto Risso. Peppery comedy with spicy Gina vying for attention of town official De Sica. ▼)

Breakfast at Tiffany's (1961) **C-115m.** ***½ D: Blake Edwards. Audrey Hepburn, George Peppard, Patricia Neal, Buddy Ebsen, Mickey Rooney, Martin Balsam, John McGiver. Charming film from Truman Capote's story, with Hepburn as Holly Golightly, backwoods girl who goes mod in N.Y.C. Dated trappings don't detract from high comedy and winning romance. Screenplay by George Axelrod. Oscar winner for Score (Henry Mancini) and Song, "Moon River" (Mancini and Johnny Mercer). ▼●)

Breakfast for Two (1937) **67m.** **½ D: Alfred Santell. Barbara Stanwyck, Herbert Marshall, Glenda Farrell, Eric Blore, Donald Meek, Frank M. Thomas, Etienne Girardot. Silly but enjoyable screwball comedy about Texas heiress Stanwyck trying to reform womanizing playboy Marshall. Adding to the fun are Blore as a wry butler, Farrell as Marshall's brassy girlfriend, and a humongous Great Dane.)

Breakfast in Hollywood (1946) **91m.** *½ D: Harold Schuster. Tom Breneman, Bonita Granville, Beulah Bondi, Edward Ryan, Raymond Walburn, ZaSu Pitts, Billie Burke, Hedda Hopper. Uninspired film derived from radio series of the same name; romantic plot offset by musical numbers with Spike Jones, The (Nat) King Cole Trio, and others. ▼)

Breaking Point, The (1950) **97m.** ***½ D: Michael Curtiz. John Garfield, Patricia Neal, Phyllis Thaxter, Wallace Ford, Sherry Jackson. High-voltage refilming of Hemingway's TO HAVE AND HAVE NOT, with Garfield as skipper so desperate for money he takes on illegal cargo. Garfield and mate Juano Hernandez give superb interpretations. Screenplay by Ranald MacDougall. Remade again as THE GUN RUNNERS.)

Breaking the Sound Barrier (1952-British) **109m.** ***½ D: David Lean. Ralph Richardson, Ann Todd, Nigel Patrick, John Justin, Dinah Sheridan, Denholm Elliott. Grade-A documentary-style story of early days of jet planes and men who tested them; Richardson particularly good. Written by Terence Rattigan. Oscar winner for Sound Recording. Originally shown in England as THE SOUND BARRIER at 118m.)

Break in the Circle (1957-British) **C-69m.** *½ D: Val Guest. Forrest Tucker, Eva Bartok, Marius Goring, Guy Middleton, Eric Pohlman. Unexciting chase tale has Tucker a brash adventurer hired by greedy Goring to smuggle a Polish physicist out of East Germany. ▼

Break of Hearts (1935) **80m.** ** D: Philip Moeller. Katharine Hepburn, Charles Boyer, John Beal, Jean Hersholt, Sam Hardy, Susan Fleming, Jean Howard. Temperamental orchestra conductor Boyer, who has been spoiled by success, weds unknown composer Hepburn . . . then there are complications. Stars try hard but can do nothing with sappy, sub-par material. ▼●)

Breakout (1959-British) **99m.** **½ D: Don Chaffey. Richard Todd, Richard Attenborough, Michael Wilding, Dennis Price, Bernard Lee, Donald Houston, Michael Caine. Although format is now familiar, this remains an exciting story of British POWs attempting escapes from Axis prison camp during WW2. Fine performances all around. Original title: DANGER WITHIN.

Breakthrough (1950) **91m.** **½ D: Lewis Seiler. David Brian, John Agar, Frank Lovejoy, Paul Picerni, William Self. Saga of men training for combat, their days of fighting and romancing; stark and satisfactory. Highlight is D-day invasion of Normandy beach. ▼)

Break to Freedom (1953-British) **88m.** ** D: Lewis Gilbert. Anthony Steel, Jack Warner, Robert Beatty, William Sylvester, Michael Balfour. Typical POWs escape-from-German-camp, uplifted by restrained acting. Original British title: ALBERT, R.N.

Breathless (1960-French) **89m.** ***½ D: Jean-Luc Godard. Jean Seberg, Jean-Paul Belmondo, Daniel Boulanger, Liliane David. Belmondo is ideally cast as a Parisian hood who, accompanied by American girl (Seberg), is chased by police after stealing a car and killing a cop. Groundbreaking, influential New Wave tale with a classic romanticized gangster-hero and great candid shots of Paris life. Dedicated to Monogram Pictures, with a story by François Truffaut. Remade in 1983. ▼●)

Breath of Scandal, A (1960) **C-98m.** ** D: Michael Curtiz. Sophia Loren, John Gavin, Maurice Chevalier, Isabel Jeans, Angela Lansbury. Molnar's play *Olympia* is limp costume vehicle for Loren, playing a princess romanced by American Gavin. Chevalier and Lansbury vainly try to pump some life into proceedings. Filmed in Vienna. Remake of John Gilbert's notorious HIS GLORIOUS NIGHT (1929). ▼)

Brewster's Millions (1945) **79m.** **½ D: Allan Dwan. Dennis O'Keefe, Helen Walker, Eddie "Rochester" Anderson, June Havoc, Gail Patrick, Mischa Auer, Joe Sawyer, Herbert Rudley. Bright, energetic filming of venerable George Barr McCutcheon comedy about ordinary guy (this time, a returning GI) who must spend $1 million in a month's time in order to receive major inheritance. Previously filmed in 1914, 1921, and 1935; remade in 1985.▼❶

Bribe, The (1949) 98m. ** D: Robert Z. Leonard. Robert Taylor, Ava Gardner, Charles Laughton, Vincent Price, John Hodiak. Taylor looks uncomfortable playing federal man who almost sacrifices all for sultry singer Gardner. ❶

Bridal Path, The (1959-Scottish) **C-95m.** ***½ D: Frank Launder. Bill Travers, Bernadette O'Farrell, Alex MacKenzie, Eric Woodburn, Jack Lambert, John Rae. Charming film of young islander who goes to Scottish mainland in search of a wife. Enhanced by beautiful scenery in color.

Bride and the Beast, The (1958) 78m. BOMB D: Adrian Weiss. Charlotte Austin, Lance Fuller, Johnny Roth, Steve Calvert. A gorilla fancies the wife of an explorer who may have been a gorilla herself in a past life. Screenplay by Edward D. Wood, Jr.; aka QUEEN OF THE GORILLAS.▼❶

Bride Came C.O.D., The (1941) 92m. **½ D: William Keighley. James Cagney, Bette Davis, Stuart Erwin, Eugene Pallette, Jack Carson, George Tobias. Unlikely comedy team in vehicle made enjoyable only by their terrific personalities; he's a flier, she's an abducted bride.▼❶❷

Bride Comes Home, The (1935) 82m. **½ D: Wesley Ruggles. Claudette Colbert, Fred MacMurray, Robert Young, William Collier, Sr., Edgar Kennedy. Breezy fluff with wealthy Young competing against roughneck MacMurray for Claudette's affections in vintage comedy. ❶

Bride Comes to Yellow Sky, The SEE: Face to Face (1952)

Bride for Sale (1949) 87m. **½ D: William D. Russell. Claudette Colbert, Robert Young, George Brent, Max Baer. Veteran star trio carries on despite thin story of female tax expert seeking wealthy spouse.

Bride Goes Wild, The (1948) 98m. ** D: Norman Taurog. Van Johnson, June Allyson, Butch Jenkins, Hume Cronyn, Una Merkel, Arlene Dahl, Richard Derr. Silly, predictable farce in which irresponsible children's book author Johnson pretends to be Jenkins' widowed father in order to keep illustrator Allyson from exposing his shenanigans. ❶

Bride Is Much Too Beautiful, The (1956-French) 85m. ** D: Pierre Gaspard-Huit. Louis Jourdan, Brigitte Bardot, Micheline Presle, Marcel Amont, Jean-Francois Calve. Paper-thin sex farce with Bardot a country girl who becomes a famous model, finds herself the "bride" in a fake marriage. Aka HER BRIDAL NIGHT.▼

Bride of Frankenstein (1935) 75m. **** D: James Whale. Karloff (Boris Karloff), Colin Clive, Valerie Hobson, Ernest Thesiger, Elsa Lanchester, Una O'Connor, E. Clive, Gavin Gordon, Douglas Walton, O. P. Heggie, Dwight Frye, John Carradine. Eye-filling sequel to FRANKENSTEIN is even better, with rich vein of dry wit running through the chills. Inimitable Thesiger plays weird doctor who compels Frankenstein into helping him make a mate for the Monster; Lanchester plays both the "bride" and, in amusing prologue, Mary Shelley. Pastoral interlude with blind hermit and final, riotous creation scene are highlights of this truly classic movie. Scripted by John L. Balderston and William Hurlbut. Marvelous Franz Waxman score, reused for many subsequent films. Followed by SON OF FRANKENSTEIN; reworked in 1985 as THE BRIDE. ▼❶

Bride of the Gorilla (1951) 65m. ** D: Curt Siodmak. Barbara Payton, Lon Chaney, Jr., Raymond Burr, Tom Conway, Paul Cavanagh, Woody Strode. Surprisingly watchable trash set on a South American jungle plantation, where hulking Burr marries sexy Payton—only to find himself the victim of a voodoo curse. Terrible but fun. Scripted by director Siodmak, and somewhat reminiscent of his classic THE WOLF MAN. ▼❶

Bride of the Monster (1955) 69m. BOMB D: Edward D. Wood, Jr. Bela Lugosi, Tor Johnson, Tony McCoy, Loretta King, Harvey B. Dunn, George Becwar, Don Nagel, Bud Osborne. A dissipated Lugosi creates giant rubber octopus that terrorizes woodland stream. Huge Swedish wrestler Johnson provides added laughs as hulking manservant Lobo. Another hilariously inept Grade Z movie from the king of bad cinema. Sequel: REVENGE OF THE DEAD (aka NIGHT OF THE GHOULS).▼❶

Bride of Vengeance (1949) 91m. ** D: Mitchell Leisen. Paulette Goddard, John Lund, Macdonald Carey, Raymond Burr, Albert Dekker, Rose Hobart. Medium-warm costumer of medieval Italy with Goddard as a Borgia sent to do mischief but instead falling in love.

Brides of Dracula, The (1960-British) **C-85m.** *** D: Terence Fisher. Peter Cushing, Martita Hunt, Yvonne Monlaur, Freda Jackson, David Peel, Miles Malleson, Andree Melly. In the Carpathian Mountains, a young teacher (Monlaur) is attracted to a nobleman (Peel) held captive by his own mother (Hunt). When the young woman sets him free, he's revealed as a vampire—and a disciple of Count Dracula. Vampire hunter Van Helsing (Cushing) energetically comes to her aid. Exciting, colorful period horror, this first sequel to HORROR OF DRACULA is one of Hammer's best thrillers. Dracula never turns up—but you won't miss him. ▼❶

Bride Walks Out, The (1936) 81m. ** D: Leigh Jason. Barbara Stanwyck, Gene Raymond, Robert Young, Ned Sparks, Helen Broderick, Hattie McDaniel. Flat comedy

[86]

of model Stanwyck who, against her better instincts, goes domestic and weds brash, struggling engineer Raymond. Buffs will enjoy spotting Ward Bond as a taxi cab-driving extra in the "Fifth Avenue and 45th Street" scene.▼▶

Bride Wore Boots, The (1946) **86m.** ★★ D: Irving Pichel. Barbara Stanwyck, Robert Cummings, Diana Lynn, Peggy Wood, Robert Benchley, Natalie Wood, Willie Best. Witless comedy of horse-loving Stanwyck saddled by Cummings, who does his best to win her total affection; they all try but script is weak.▶

Bride Wore Red, The (1937) **103m.** ★★½ D: Dorothy Arzner. Joan Crawford, Franchot Tone, Robert Young, Billie Burke, Reginald Owen, Lynne Carver, George Zucco, Dickie Moore. Lowly Crawford is thrust into society on the whim of a count and becomes the romantic object of aristocrat-playboy Young and soulful peasant Tone. Glossy soaper based on a play by Ferenc Molnár.▼▶

Bridge, The (1960-German) **100m.** ★★★ D: Bernhard Wicki. Folker Bohnet, Fritz Wepper, Michael Hinz, Frank Glaubrecht. Unrelenting account of teen-age boys drafted into the German army in 1945, as last resort effort to stem Allied invasion.▼▶

Bridge of San Luis Rey, The (1944) **89m.** ★★ D: Rowland V. Lee. Lynn Bari, Nazimova, Louis Calhern, Akim Tamiroff, Francis Lederer, Blanche Yurka, Donald Woods. Thornton Wilder's moody, unusual story of five people meeting doom on a rickety bridge makes a slow-moving film. Previously filmed in 1929 and remade in 2004. ▼▶

Bridge on the River Kwai, The (1957-British) **C-161m.** ★★★★ D: David Lean. William Holden, Alec Guinness, Jack Hawkins, Sessue Hayakawa, Geoffrey Horne, James Donald, Andre Morell, Ann Sears. British soldiers in Japanese prison camp build a bridge as a morale exercise—under single-minded leadership of British colonel Guinness—as Holden and Hawkins plot to destroy it. Psychological battle of wills combined with high-powered action sequences make this a blockbuster. Seven Oscars include Picture, Director, Actor (Guinness), Cinematography (Jack Hildyard), Editing (Peter Taylor), Scoring (Malcolm Arnold—who used the famous WWI whistling tune "Colonel Bogey March"), and Screenplay (by Carl Foreman and Michael Wilson, based on Pierre Boulle's novel). The writers were blacklisted, so Boulle—who spoke no English—was credited with the script! Filmed in Ceylon. CinemaScope. ▼▶

Bridges at Toko-Ri, The (1954) **C-103m.** ★★★½ D: Mark Robson. William Holden, Grace Kelly, Fredric March, Mickey Rooney, Robert Strauss, Earl Holliman. Powerful, thoughtful drama, based on the James Michener best-seller, focusing on the conflicts and exploits of lawyer Holden after he is recalled by the Navy to fly jets in Korea. While the flying sequences are exciting—the special effects earned an Oscar—the ultimate futility of the Korean War is in no way deemphasized. ▼▶

Bridge to the Sun (1961-U.S.-French) **113m.** ★★★ D: Etienne Perier. Carroll Baker, James Shigeta, James Yagi. Well-intentioned telling of Southern girl Baker who marries Japanese diplomat Shigeta and moves to Japan at outbreak of WW2. Based on Gwen Terasaki's autobiography. ▼▶

Brief Encounter (1945-British) **85m.** ★★★★ D: David Lean. Celia Johnson, Trevor Howard, Stanley Holloway, Cyril Raymond, Joyce Carey. Two ordinary strangers, both married, meet at a train station and find themselves drawn into a short but poignant romance. Intense and unforgettable, underscored by perfect use of Rachmaninoff's *Second Piano Concerto*. Adapted by Noel Coward from his one-act play "Still Life" (from *Tonight at Eight-thirty*); screenplay by director Lean and Ronald Neame. A truly wonderful film. Remade as a TV movie in 1974 with Richard Burton and Sophia Loren. Later a stage musical. ▼▶

Brief Moment (1933) **70m.** ★★ D: David Burton. Carole Lombard, Gene Raymond, Monroe Owsley, Donald Cook, Arthur Hohl, Reginald Mason, Irene Ware. Wealthy Raymond marries nightclub singer Lombard against his snobbish family's wishes, but she's the one who objects when he won't stop partying and get a job. Starts as a breezy romance but bogs down into soapy histrionics.▶

Brigadoon (1954) **C-108m.** ★★★ D: Vincente Minnelli. Gene Kelly, Van Johnson, Cyd Charisse, Elaine Stewart, Barry Jones, Hugh Laing. Americans Kelly and Johnson discover magical Scottish village in this entertaining filmization of Lerner & Loewe Broadway hit. Overlooked among 1950s musicals, it may lack innovations but has its own quiet charm, and lovely score, including "The Heather on the Hill." CinemaScope. ▼▶

Brigand, The (1952) **C-94m.** ★★ D: Phil Karlson. Anthony Dexter, Anthony Quinn, Gale Robbins, Jody Lawrance. Dexter is lookalike for king and becomes involved with court intrigue; flat costumer.▶

Brigand of Kandahar, The (1965-British) **C-81m.** ★★½ D: John Gilling. Ronald Lewis, Oliver Reed, Duncan Lamont, Yvonne Romain, Catherine Woodville. Nonsense set on British outpost in 1850s India with rampaging natives. CinemaScope.

Brigham Young (1940) **114m.** ★★ D: Henry Hathaway. Tyrone Power, Linda Darnell, Dean Jagger, Brian Donlevy, John Carradine, Jane Darwell, Jean Rogers, Mary Astor, Vincent Price. Well-intentioned but ineffectual depiction of Mormon leader with Jagger nominally in the lead, focus shifting to tepid romance between Power and Darnell; Astor all wrong as homespun wife. Advertised as BRIGHAM YOUNG, FRONTIERSMAN, in an attempt to widen the appeal of the picture. ▼▶

Bright Eyes (1934) **83m.** **½ D: David Butler. Shirley Temple, James Dunn, Judith Allen, Jane Withers, Lois Wilson, Charles Sellon. Early Shirley, and pretty good, with juvenile villainy from Withers in tale of custody battle over recently orphaned Temple. Includes "On the Good Ship Lollipop." Also shown in computer-colored version. ▼▶

Bright Leaf (1950) **110m.** **½ D: Michael Curtiz. Gary Cooper, Lauren Bacall, Patricia Neal, Jack Carson, Donald Crisp. Loose chronicle of 19th-century tobacco farmer (Cooper) building successful cigarette empire, seeking revenge on old enemies and finding romance. ▶

Bright Lights (1930) **69m.** *** D: Michael Curtiz. Dorothy Mackaill, Frank Fay, Noah Beery, Daphne Pollard, James Murray, Tom Dugan, Inez Courtney, Frank McHugh, Eddie Nugent. Broadway star is about to give up the stage and marry into money but a man from her sordid past arrives to complicate matters. Lively backstage yarn with a good blend of racy comedy and drama interspersed with outrageous production numbers, notably a bizarre ditty called "I'm Crazy for Cannibal Love." Originally released in two-strip Technicolor. ▶

Bright Lights (1935) **83m.** ** D: Busby Berkeley. Joe E. Brown, Ann Dvorak, Patricia Ellis, William Gargan, Joseph Cawthorn, Arthur Treacher. Rags-to-riches show business tale of husband and wife separating while trying to hit it big. Entertaining, but full of clichés.

Brighton Rock (1947-British) **86m.** *** D: John Boulting. Richard Attenborough, Carol Marsh, Hermione Baddeley, William Hartnell, Harcourt Williams, Nigel Stock. Tour-de-force role for young Attenborough as loathsome, baby-faced gangster who finally gets his comeuppance. Notable for incredibly cynical trick ending. Screenplay by Terence Rattigan and Graham Greene from Greene's novel. Remade in 2011. U.S. title: YOUNG SCARFACE. ▼

Brighton Strangler, The (1945) **67m.** **½ D: Max Nosseck. John Loder, June Duprez, Michael St. Angel (Steven Flagg), Miles Mander, Rose Hobart, Gilbert Emery. Eerie little thriller, similar to A DOUBLE LIFE, set in WW2 England. Actor Loder has made a hit as "The Brighton Strangler" on the stage, but when he's conked on the head during an air raid, he begins to live the part. ▼

Bright Road (1953) **69m.** ** D: Gerald Mayer. Dorothy Dandridge, Harry Belafonte, Robert Horton, Philip Hepburn. Well-intentioned but labored tale of black teacher in small Southern town trying to solve her young pupils' problems. Belafonte's film debut. ▶

Bright Victory (1951) **97m.** *** D: Mark Robson. Arthur Kennedy, Peggy Dow, Julia (Julie) Adams, James Edwards, Will Geer, Nana Bryant, Jim Backus, Murray Hamilton, Richard Egan. Touching account of blinded ex-soldier who slowly readjusts to civilian life, even finding love. Potentially sticky subject handled well, with Kennedy excellent in lead role. Rock Hudson can be glimpsed as a soldier.

Brimstone (1949) **C-90m.** ** D: Joseph Kane. Rod Cameron, Adrian Booth, Walter Brennan, Forrest Tucker, Jack Holt, Jim Davis, Guinn (Big Boy) Williams, Jack Lambert. "Brimstone" Courteen (Brennan) and his sons are old-time Western outlaws who find themselves victimized by a ghostlike black-clad bandit. Standard B-plus Western with Brennan rising above the material. ▼

Bring 'Em Back Alive (1932) **65m.** **½ D: Clyde Elliott. Frank Buck plays Great White Hunter (and narrator) in this documentary curio, a great hit in its day and still interesting for its exciting jungle footage, as well as its often blatant phoniness. The inspiration for a same-named TV series 50 years later. ▼▶

Bringing Up Baby (1938) **102m.** **** D: Howard Hawks. Cary Grant, Katharine Hepburn, Charlie Ruggles, May Robson, Barry Fitzgerald, Walter Catlett, Fritz Feld, Ward Bond. In her sole venture into slapstick, Hepburn plays a madcap heiress—"Baby" is her pet leopard—who sets her sights on absentminded zoologist Grant and inadvertently (?) proceeds to make a shambles of his life. Not a hit when first released, this is now considered the definitive screwball comedy and one of the fastest, funniest films ever made; grand performances by all. Screenplay by Dudley Nichols and Hagar Wilde, from Wilde's original story. More or less remade as WHAT'S UP, DOC? Also shown in computer-colored version. ▼●▶

Bring On the Girls (1945) **C-92m.** ** D: Sidney Lanfield. Veronica Lake, Sonny Tufts, Eddie Bracken, Marjorie Reynolds, Alan Mowbray, Grant Mitchell, Frank Faylen, Huntz Hall. Wealthy Bracken is unable to find a girl who isn't a gold-digger, so he joins the Navy. Slight comedy, with music; best are numbers by dancer Johnny Coy and Spike Jones and His City Slickers. That's Yvonne De Carlo as the hat-check girl.

Bring Your Smile Along (1955) **C-83m.** ** D: Blake Edwards. Frankie Laine, Keefe Brasselle, Constance Towers, Lucy Marlow, William Leslie, Jack Albertson. Thin musical comedy of schoolteacher/songwriter Towers coming to N.Y.C. and hooking up with Brasselle both professionally and romantically. Laine records their songs, and he perks up the proceedings. This was Edwards' directing debut; he also wrote the script.

Brink of Life (1958-Swedish) 84m. **½
D: Ingmar Bergman. Eva Dahlbeck, Ingrid Thulin, Bibi Andersson, Barbro Hiort af Ornas, Erland Josephson, Max von Sydow, Gunnar Sjoberg. Realistic, almost documentary-like chronicle of the lives of three women in a maternity ward. Meticulously filmed, but also gloomy and static; one of Bergman's lesser efforts.▼

Britannia Mews SEE: **Forbidden Street, The**

British Agent (1934) 81m. *½ D: Michael Curtiz. Kay Francis, Leslie Howard, William Gargan, Philip Reed, J. Carrol Naish, Cesar Romero. British diplomat Howard falls for staunch Soviet Francis in 1917 Russia; a trite script sinks this turkey, which tries to combine romance and international intrigue.▶

British Intelligence (1940) 62m. **½
D: Terry Morse. Boris Karloff, Margaret Lindsay, Maris Wrixon, Holmes Herbert, Leonard Mudie. Not-bad programmer gives Karloff a good part as Valdar, a scar-faced butler who works for a British cabinet minister during WW1, and who may just be a spy. He tangles with alluring secret agent Lindsay—who may just be a double agent. Filmed before as THREE FACES EAST in 1925 and 1930. ▼▶

Broadminded (1931) 72m. **½ D: Mervyn LeRoy. Joe E. Brown, William Collier, Jr., Margaret Livingston, Thelma Todd, Bela Lugosi, Ona Munson, Holmes Herbert. Pleasant Brown comedy with added spice of lovely Todd and presence of Lugosi in a supporting role.▶

Broadway (1929) 105m. **½ D: Paul Fejos. Glenn Tryon, Evelyn Brent, Merna Kennedy, Thomas Jackson, Robert Ellis, Paul Porcasi, Leslie Fenton, Otis Harlan, Arthur Housman. Atmospheric, Runyonesque tale, based on a 1926 play by Philip Dunning and George Abbott, with song-and-dance man Tryon working in a small nightclub and rehearsing a new act with Kennedy while surrounded by ego-driven producers, tough-talking gangsters, squabbling chorus girls, and nosy cops. All-too-familiar tale is uplifted by dazzling camera movement and stunning, impressive set design. Jackson stands out as Detective Dan McCorn, a role he created onstage. Released in both silent and sound versions, with a Technicolor finale. Remade in 1942.
▶

Broadway (1942) 91m. *** D: William A. Seiter. George Raft, Pat O'Brien, Janet Blair, Broderick Crawford, Marjorie Rambeau, S. Z. Sakall. Raft recalls his days as a nightclub hoofer in this Prohibition yarn (remake of 1929 film), full of colorful characters and incidents but without an eye toward believability. O'Brien is tough copper, Crawford a ruthless gangster.

Broadway Bad (1933) 61m. **½ D:

Sidney Lanfield. Joan Blondell, Ricardo Cortez, Ginger Rogers, Adrienne Ames. Chorus girl Blondell is unjustly maligned by husband, decides to milk bad publicity for all its worth. A 1930s soap given first-class treatment.

Broadway Bill (1934) 102m. *** D: Frank Capra. Warner Baxter, Myrna Loy, Walter Connolly, Helen Vinson, Lynne Overman, Raymond Walburn, Clarence Muse, Douglass Dumbrille, Charles Lane, Ward Bond, Margaret Hamilton, Clara Blandick, Frankie Darro, Jason Robards (Sr.), and Broadway Bill. Baxter, who's "sold out" and married money, risks his marriage and his future on a racehorse; Loy, his wife's sister, seems to be the only one who believes in him. The unremitting good cheer of this Capra concoction overcomes its flaws. Script by Robert Riskin, from the Mark Hellinger story "On the Nose." Remade (by Capra) in 1950 as RIDING HIGH—using some of the same actors, and even some of the same footage. Look fast for a young, blonde Lucille Ball as a telephone operator.▼▶

Broadway Gondolier (1935) 98m. **½ D: Lloyd Bacon. Dick Powell, Joan Blondell, Adolphe Menjou, Louise Fazenda, William Gargan, Grant Mitchell. Powell goes globetrotting so he'll be discovered by famous producer. Songs include: "Lulu's Back in Town."

Broadway Limited (1941) 74m. ** D: Gordon Douglas. Dennis O'Keefe, Victor McLaglen, Marjorie Woodworth, ZaSu Pitts, Patsy Kelly, George E. Stone, Leonid Kinskey. Considering cast, a big disappointment, though innocuous entertainment: florid director Kinskey makes his new star (Woodworth) the center of publicity stunt that backfires.▼▶

Broadway Melody, The (1929) 100m. **½ D: Harry Beaumont. Bessie Love, Anita Page, Charles King, Jed Prouty, Kenneth Thomson, Edward Dillon, Mary Doran. Early talkie musical curio about a pair of stage-struck sisters who seek fame on the Great White Way and fall for a charming song-and-dance man. This was the first musical to win a Best Picture Academy Award. Awfully dated today, but there's still a good score by Arthur Freed and Nacio Herb Brown: Title tune, "You Were Meant for Me," and "The Wedding of the Painted Doll." Some sequences originally in Technicolor; remade as TWO GIRLS ON BROADWAY.▼▶

Broadway Melody of 1936 (1935) 101m. *** D: Roy Del Ruth. Jack Benny, Eleanor Powell, Robert Taylor, Una Merkel, Sid Silvers, Buddy Ebsen. Pleasant musi-comedy with Winchell-like columnist Benny trying to frame producer Taylor via dancer Powell, whose solo spots are pure delight. Arthur Freed–Nacio Herb Brown songs: "You Are My Lucky Star," "Broadway Rhythm,"

[89]

"I've Got a Feelin' You're Foolin'" (which earned an Oscar for Dave Gould's dance direction).▼●◗

Broadway Melody of 1938 (1937) **110m.** **½ D: Roy Del Ruth. Robert Taylor, Eleanor Powell, George Murphy, Binnie Barnes, Buddy Ebsen, Judy Garland, Sophie Tucker, Charles Igor Gorin, Raymond Walburn, Robert Benchley, Willie Howard, Billy Gilbert. Not up to 1936 MELODY, with tuneful but forgettable songs, overbearing Tucker, and elephantine finale. Powell's dancing is great and Garland sings "Dear Mr. Gable." ▼●◗

Broadway Melody of 1940 (1940) **102m.** *** D: Norman Taurog. Fred Astaire, Eleanor Powell, George Murphy, Frank Morgan, Ian Hunter, Florence Rice, Lynne Carver, Ann Morriss. Friendship and rivalry between dance partners Astaire and Murphy spark delightful, underrated MGM musical, with hilarious vignettes, fine performance from Astaire, outstanding Cole Porter songs, and matchless Astaire-Powell numbers like "Begin the Beguine" (danced *twice* in the finale). If only they'd tie up the plot a bit sooner. Douglas McPhail (unbilled) introduces the Porter standard "I Concentrate On You." ▼●◗

Broadway Musketeers (1938) **62m.** **½ D: John Farrow. Margaret Lindsay, Ann Sheridan, Marie Wilson, John Litel, Janet Chapman, Richard Bond. Three women who grew up together in an orphanage meet again as adults, having taken very different paths in life. Snappy remake of the melodramatic THREE ON A MATCH with some interesting plot variations, and a couple of songs from Sheridan.

Broadway Rhythm (1944) **C-114m.** ** D: Roy Del Ruth. George Murphy, Ginny Simms, Charles Winninger, Gloria De Haven, Nancy Walker, Ben Blue, Tommy Dorsey and Orch. Tedious, overlong MGM musical with plot (ex-vaudevillian Winninger at odds with producer-son Murphy) getting in the way of good songs like "Amor," "All the Things You Are." ▼◗

Broadway Serenade (1939) **114m.** ** D: Robert Z. Leonard. Jeanette MacDonald, Lew Ayres, Ian Hunter, Frank Morgan, Rita Johnson, Virginia Grey, William Gargan, Katharine Alexander. Mediocre musical of songwriter Ayres and wife, singer MacDonald, having careers split up their marriage.▼◗

Broadway Thru a Keyhole (1933) **90m.** *** D: Lowell Sherman. Constance Cummings, Paul Kelly, Russ Columbo, Blossom Seeley, Gregory Ratoff, Texas Guinan, Abe Lyman and His Band, Hugh O'Connell, Eddie Foy, Jr. Once-in-a-lifetime cast enlivens this colorful tale of nightclub performer Cummings, who attracts the attention of racketeer Kelly and singer-bandleader Columbo. Based on a story by Walter Winchell, the characters supposedly modeled after Ruby Keeler, Al Jolson, and N.Y.C. gangster Larry Fay; nice showcase for crooner Columbo, who died in 1934. Lucille Ball is noticeable in a bit.

Broadway to Hollywood (1933) **85m.** ** D: Willard Mack. Alice Brady, Frank Morgan, Jackie Cooper, Russell Hardie, Madge Evans, Mickey Rooney, Eddie Quillan. Three generations of show biz (Cooper grows up to be Hardie, whose son, Rooney, grows up to be Quillan) in a story that's for the birds—but the acting is good, and some of the production numbers (lifted from MGM's famous 1930 extravaganza THE MARCH OF TIME) interesting to see.

Broken Arrow (1950) **C-93m.** *** D: Delmer Daves. James Stewart, Jeff Chandler, Debra Paget, Will Geer, Jay Silverheels. Authentic study of 1870s Apache Chief Cochise (Chandler) and ex-Army man (Stewart) trying to seek accord between feuding Indians and settlers. Flavorful and effective; good action sequences. Screenplay, credited to Michael Blankfort, was actually written by Albert Maltz, then a blacklistee. Chandler played Cochise again in THE BATTLE AT APACHE PASS. Later a TV series.▼◗

Broken Blossoms (1919) **95m.** *** D: D. W. Griffith. Lillian Gish, Richard Barthelmess, Donald Crisp, Arthur Howard, Edward Piel. Dated but lovely film of Chinaman Barthelmess protecting frail Gish from clutches of brutal father Crisp; still creates a mood sustained by sensitive performances. One of Griffith's more modest, and more successful, films. Remade in England in 1936.▼●◗

Broken Blossoms (1936-British) **88m.** **½ D: Hans (John) Brahm. Dolly Haas, Emlyn Williams, Arthur Margetson, C. V. France, Basil Radford, Edith Sharpe, Donald Calthrop. Remake of D. W. Griffith's silent film is a fascinating oddity. Actor-playwright Williams wrote the screenplay and plays (none too convincingly) a naïve Chinese man whose spirit—and spirituality—are broken by his mistreatment in England. Then he meets a waif even worse off than he: the innocent daughter of a drunken prizefighter. Archaic in its stereotypes but effective in portraying the seedy milieu of London's Limehouse district. ▶

Broken Lance (1954) **C-96m.** ***½ D: Edward Dmytryk. Spencer Tracy, Robert Wagner, Jean Peters, Richard Widmark, Katy Jurado, Hugh O'Brian, Eduard Franz, Earl Holliman, E. G. Marshall. Tracy is superlative in tight-knit script (by Richard Murphy, from an Oscar-winning Philip Yordan story) about patriarchal rancher who finds he's losing control of his cattle empire and his family is fragmenting into warring factions. Remake of HOUSE OF STRANGERS (although it owes more to *King Lear!*). CinemaScope.▼●◗

Broken Land, The (1962) **C-60m.** ** D: John Bushelman. Kent Taylor, Dianna Darrin, Jody McCrea, Robert Sampson, Jack Nicholson. Routine low-budget Western about a sadistic sheriff who browbeats just about everybody, including his deputy and the harmless son (Nicholson) of a notorious gunman. CinemaScope.

Broken Lullaby (1932) **77m.** *** D: Ernst Lubitsch. Lionel Barrymore, Nancy Carroll, Phillips Holmes, ZaSu Pitts, Lucien Littlefield, Emma Dunn. Excellent drama of French soldier who feels guilty for killing German during war, then falls in love with dead man's sweetheart. Retitled: THE MAN I KILLED.

Broken Strings (1940) **60m.** *½ D: Bernard B. Ray. Clarence Muse, Sybil Lewis, William Washington, Tommiwitta Moore, Stymie Beard, Pete Webster, Edward Thompson, Buck Woods. A celebrated violin virtuoso's life is shattered when his hand is paralyzed after an auto accident, then his violin-playing son veers toward swing instead of the classics. All-black-cast independent is well intentioned but poorly acted and directed, and slow as molasses. ▼▶

Bronco Buster (1952) **C-81m.** **½ D: Budd Boetticher. John Lund, Scott Brady, Joyce Holden, Chill Wills, Casey Tibbs. Minor story of rodeo star Lund helping Brady learn the ropes, forced to fight him for Holden's love. Good rodeo action.

Bronze Buckaroo, The (1939) **58m.** **½ D: Richard C. Kahn. Herbert Jeffrey (Herb Jeffries), Lucius Brooks, Artie Young, F. E. (Flournoy) Miller, Spencer Williams, Jr., Clarence Brooks, The Four Tones. Jeffrey's final appearance as Bob Blake (after TWO GUN MAN FROM HARLEM and HARLEM RIDES THE RANGE) has the singing cowboy arriving at the ranch of a friend in distress, only to find him missing. Agreeable all-black-cast oater-with-music. ▼▶

Bronze Venus, The SEE: **Duke Is Tops, The**

Brother Orchid (1940) **91m.** *** D: Lloyd Bacon. Edward G. Robinson, Ann Sothern, Humphrey Bogart, Ralph Bellamy, Donald Crisp, Allen Jenkins. Farfetched but entertaining yarn of racketeer Robinson who seeks "the real class" in life. When he tries to rejoin his old mob, they throw him out and Robinson joins a monastery to plot his next move! Sothern delightful as his ever-faithful girlfriend. ▼▶●

Brother Rat (1938) **90m.** *** D: William Keighley. Priscilla Lane, Wayne Morris, Johnnie Davis, Jane Bryan, Eddie Albert, Ronald Reagan, Jane Wyman, William Tracy. Comedy of three pals at Virginia Military Institute isn't as fresh as it was in the 1930s, but still remains entertaining, with enthusiastic performances by all. Albert stands out in his screen debut, in a role he played on the stage. Sequel: BROTHER RAT AND A BABY. Remade as ABOUT FACE. ▶

Brother Rat and a Baby (1940) **87m.** **½ D: Ray Enright. Priscilla Lane, Wayne Morris, Eddie Albert, Jane Bryan, Ronald Reagan, Jane Wyman. Sassy follow-up to BROTHER RAT is not the same success, but is still fun. Morris, Reagan, and Albert have graduated the Virginia Military Institute; the first two come to the latter's aid when he's up for VMI baseball coach job. Look quickly for Alan Ladd as a cadet. ▶

Brothers in Law, The (1957-British) **94m.** **½ D: Roy Boulting. Richard Attenborough, Ian Carmichael, Terry-Thomas, Jill Adams, Miles Malleson, Raymond Huntley. Misadventures of a young lawyer (Carmichael) fill this amiable British comedy. ▼

Brothers Karamazov, The (1958) **C-146m.** *** D: Richard Brooks. Yul Brynner, Maria Schell, Claire Bloom, Lee J. Cobb, Richard Basehart, William Shatner, Albert Salmi. Set in 19th-century Russia, film version of Dostoyevsky's tragedy revolving about death of a dominating father (Cobb) and effect on his sons: fun-seeking Brynner, scholarly Basehart, religious Shatner, and epileptic Salmi. Exceptionally well scripted by Brooks. William Shatner's first film. ▼▶

Brothers Rico, The (1957) **92m.** **½ D: Phil Karlson. Richard Conte, Dianne Foster, Kathryn Grant (Crosby), Larry Gates, James Darren. Incisive gangster yarn; Conte comes to N.Y.C. to counteract nationwide criminal gang's plot to eliminate his two brothers. Based on Georges Simenon novel; remade for TV as THE FAMILY RICO in 1972. ▶

Broth of a Boy (1959-Irish) **77m.** **½ D: George Pollock. Barry Fitzgerald, Harry Brogan, Tony Wright, June Thorburn, Eddie Golden. British TV producer hits upon scheme of filming birthday celebration of oldest man in the world, Irish villager Fitzgerald. The latter's battle to get cut of the pie is vehicle for study of human nature; quietly effective. ▼

Browning Version, The (1951-British) **90m.** ***½ D: Anthony Asquith. Michael Redgrave, Jean Kent, Nigel Patrick, Brian Smith, Wilfrid Hyde-White, Ronald Howard, Bill Travers. Redgrave is superb as middle-aged boarding school teacher who realizes he's a failure, with an unfaithful wife and a new teaching position he doesn't want. Cast does full justice to the play by Terence Rattigan; he also scripted. Remade in 1994.▼▶

Brown of Harvard (1926) **85m.** **½ D: Jack Conway. William Haines, Jack Pickford, Mary Brian, David Torrence, Edward Connelly, Guinn "Big Boy" Williams. Prototypical collegiate romance, with brash jock Haines pursuing professor's daughter Brian. Already the screen's third version of Rida Johnson Young's 1906 stage play, it's most notable today for an easily spotted early appearance by a 19-year-old USC football lineman soon to become John Wayne. ▼

Brute, The SEE: **El Bruto**

Brute Force (1947) **98m.** ***½ D: Jules Dassin. Burt Lancaster, Hume Cronyn, Charles Bickford, Yvonne De Carlo, Ann Blyth, Ella Raines, Howard Duff, Whit Bissell, Jeff Corey, Sam Levene, Roman Bohnen, John Hoyt, Anita Colby. Tingling, hard-bitten prison film with its few clichés punched across solidly. Brutal captain Cronyn is utterly despicable, but you *know* he's going to get it in the end. Scripted by Richard Brooks, from Robert Patterson's story. Duff's film debut. ▼●❙

Brute Man, The (1946) **60m.** *½ D: Jean Yarbrough. Tom Neal, Rondo Hatton, Jane Adams, Peter Whitney, Jan Wiley. Loosely based on Hatton's own tragic life (handsome as a youth, he became impaired by acromegaly), this deals with a disfigured man who becomes a mad killer. ▼●❙

Buccaneer, The (1938) **124m.** *** D: Cecil B. DeMille. Fredric March, Franciska Gaal, Margot Grahame, Akim Tamiroff, Walter Brennan, Anthony Quinn. Typically entertaining epic-scale saga from DeMille, with florid performance by March as pirate-hero Jean Lafitte, who aids American cause during Battle of New Orleans. Good storytelling and good fun. Remade in 1958. ❙

Buccaneer, The (1958) **C-121m.** *** D: Anthony Quinn. Yul Brynner, Charlton Heston, Claire Bloom, Charles Boyer, Inger Stevens, Henry Hull, E. G. Marshall, Lorne Greene, Fran Jeffries, Woodrow (Woody) Strode. Starchy swashbuckler retelling events during Battle of New Orleans when Andrew Jackson (Heston) is forced to rely on buccaneer Lafitte (Brynner) to stem the British invasion; action is spotty but splashy. Quinn's only film as director; executive-produced by his then-father-in-law, Cecil B. DeMille, who directed the 1938 original, and whose last film this was. VistaVision. ▼●❙

Buccaneer's Girl (1950) **C-77m.** ** D: Frederick de Cordova. Yvonne De Carlo, Philip Friend, Robert Douglas, Elsa Lanchester, Andrea King, Henry Daniell. Standard pirate-movie elements, plus several songs, can be found in this middling romp with Friend as a Robin Hood of the bounding main and De Carlo as the feisty stowaway who becomes a thorn in his side on land (New Orleans) and sea. No surprises here, mateys. ❙

Buchanan Rides Alone (1958) **C-78m.** *** D: Budd Boetticher. Randolph Scott, Craig Stevens, Barry Kelley, Tol Avery, Peter Whitney, Manuel Rojas, Jennifer Holden. Scott runs afoul of corrupt family in control of border town; taut B Western written by Charles Lang never runs out of plot twists. ❙

Buck Benny Rides Again (1940) **82m.** *** D: Mark Sandrich. Jack Benny, Ellen Drew, Andy Devine, Phil Harris, Virginia Dale, Dennis Day, Eddie "Rochester" Anderson. Amusing Western spoof with Jack trying to convince Drew that he's a 100% cowboy. Radio colleagues help out, with Rochester supplying steady flow of funny dialogue.

Bucket of Blood, A (1959) **66m.** *** D: Roger Corman. Dick Miller, Barboura Morris, Antony Carbone, Julian Burton, Ed Nelson, Burt (Bert) Convy. Wimpy busboy impresses his coffeehouse betters with amazingly lifelike "sculptures." Writer Charles Griffith's predecessor to THE LITTLE SHOP OF HORRORS is nifty semi-spoof of dead-bodies-in-the-wax-museum genre. Nicely captures spirit of beatnik era; cult actor Miller's finest hour (he's reused his character's name, Walter Paisley, several times since). Remade for TV as THE DEATH ARTIST in 1996. ▼❙

Buck Privates (1941) **84m.** **½ D: Arthur Lubin. Bud Abbott, Lou Costello, Lee Bowman, Alan Curtis, The Andrews Sisters, Jane Frazee, Nat Pendleton, Shemp Howard. Dated but engaging Army opus with Bud and Lou accidentally enlisting. Brassy songs (including Andrews Sisters' "Boogie Woogie Bugle Boy") and subplots get in the way, but A&C's routines are among their best; their first starring film. ▼●❙

Buck Privates Come Home (1947) **77m.** *** D: Charles Barton. Bud Abbott, Lou Costello, Tom Brown, Joan Fulton (Shawlee), Nat Pendleton, Beverly Simmons, Don Beddoe. One of A&C's most enjoyable romps has boys returning to civilian life and trying to smuggle a young European orphan into this country. Climactic chase a highlight. ▼●❙

Buckskin Frontier (1943) **74m.** ** D: Lesley Selander. Richard Dix, Jane Wyatt, Albert Dekker, Lee J. Cobb, Victor Jory, Lola Lane, Max Baer, Joe Sawyer, George Reeves. Unusual cast adds interest to this otherwise standard Western about railroad man Dix and his conflicts with proud Cobb (who fears for the demise of his freight company) and slimy Jory. Cobb, who's exactly the same age as Wyatt, is cast here as her father! ▼❙

Bud Abbott Lou Costello in Hollywood SEE: **Abbott and Costello in Hollywood**

Bud Abbott Lou Costello Meet Frankenstein SEE: **Abbott and Costello Meet Frankenstein**

Buffalo Bill (1944) **C-90m.** **½ D: William Wellman. Joel McCrea, Maureen O'Hara, Linda Darnell, Thomas Mitchell, Anthony Quinn, Edgar Buchanan, Chief Thundercloud, Sidney Blackmer. Colorful biography of legendary Westerner should have been much better, but still provides some fun and has good cast. ▼❙

Bugles in the Afternoon (1952) **C-85m.** **½ D: Roy Rowland. Ray Milland, Forrest Tucker, George Reeves, Helena Carter, Gertrude Michael. Standard tale of man branded coward (Milland) during Civil War, with Little Big Horn finale. ▼

Bugle Sounds, The (1941) **101m.** ** D: S. Sylvan Simon. Wallace Beery, Marjorie Main, Lewis Stone, George Bancroft, Henry O'Neill, Donna Reed. Old-time sergeant Beery objects to progress in the army, bails cavalry out of trouble in finale.

Bulldog Drummond Hugh "Bulldog" Drummond, an ex-British army officer who yearned for adventure, was created in 1919 by "Sapper" (Herman Cyril McNeile); the character's film possibilities were realized and Drummond was the subject of several silent films. The definitive BULLDOG DRUMMOND was made in 1929 with dashing Ronald Colman in the lead and Claud Allister as his constant companion Algy; Colman also starred in a delightful sequel, BULLDOG DRUMMOND STRIKES BACK, which unfortunately is not available to TV. No one ever approached Colman's charm—or the wittiness of these first two scripts—in subsequent efforts (though the British spoof called BULLDOG JACK scored a bull's-eye in its own comic way, and other Britishers like Jack Buchanan and Ralph Richardson had a go at the role—like the second Colman film, these interesting-sounding entries cannot be seen on TV). The major series was made in the late 1930s by Paramount, with John Howard as Drummond, John Barrymore as Inspector Neilson of Scotland Yard, Reginald Denny as Algy, and E. E. Clive as the butler Tenny. These were brief (around one hour), entertaining mysteries with such formidable villains as J. Carrol Naish, Anthony Quinn, George Zucco, and Eduardo Ciannelli. In the late 1940s Ron Randell and Tom Conway did two Drummonds each, which weren't bad but didn't catch on. The last one was CALLING BULLDOG DRUMMOND, a 1951 film with Walter Pidgeon in the lead and David Tomlinson as Algy. (One attempt to revive the character was a flop: DEADLIER THAN THE MALE [1967] and SOME GIRLS DO [1969], both with Richard Johnson.) Other older films that still pop up include such Drummonds as John Lodge and Ray Milland.

BULLDOG DRUMMOND

Bulldog Drummond (1929)
The Return of Bulldog Drummond (1934)
Bulldog Jack (1934)
Bulldog Drummond Escapes (1937)
Bulldog Drummond at Bay (1937)
Bulldog Drummond Comes Back (1937)
Bulldog Drummond's Revenge (1937)
Bulldog Drummond's Peril (1938)
Bulldog Drummond in Africa (1938)
Bulldog Drummond's Secret Police (1939)
Bulldog Drummond's Bride (1939)
Arrest Bulldog Drummond (1939)
Bulldog Drummond at Bay (1947)
Bulldog Drummond Strikes Back (1947)
The Challenge (1948)
13 Lead Soldiers (1948)
Calling Bulldog Drummond (1951)

Bulldog Drummond (1929) **89m. ★★★½** D: F. Richard Jones. Ronald Colman, Joan Bennett, Lilyan Tashman, Montagu Love, Lawrence Grant, Claud Allister. Colman is a delight (in his first talking picture) as the bored ex-British Army officer who comes to the rescue of an American girl (Bennett) whose wealthy uncle is being held captive in an asylum by a sadistic doctor and his gang. Sidney Howard's polished script, Gregg Toland and George Barnes' photography, and William Cameron Menzies' stylish sets help make this a classy and sophisticated romp.▼●

Bulldog Drummond at Bay (1937-British) **62m. ★★½** D: Norman Lee. John Lodge, Dorothy Mackaill, Victor Jory, Claud Allister, Hugh Miller, Maire O'Neill. Innocuous British "quota quickie" has Drummond (Lodge) battling foreign agents trying to steal plans for a top-secret British aircraft. Most faithful screen adaptation of character as created by H. C. McNeile.▼

Bulldog Drummond at Bay (1947) **70m. ★½** D: Sidney Salkow. Ron Randell, Anita Louise, Pat O'Moore, Terry Kilburn, Holmes Herbert. Quickie entry with Drummond, now portrayed by Australian Randell, after a murderous diamond thief.▼

Bulldog Drummond Comes Back (1937) **64m. ★★½** D: Louis King. John Barrymore, John Howard, Louise Campbell, Reginald Denny, E. E. Clive, J. Carrol Naish, John Sutton. Naish and his gang kidnap Drummond's fiancée and are pursued by the adventurer and his friend Colonel Nielson. Howard makes an urbane, if bland Drummond, but Barrymore is a hoot as his master-of-disguise pal from Scotland Yard. Adapted from McNeile's *The Female of the Species.*▼▶

Bulldog Drummond Escapes (1937) **65m. ★★** D: James Hogan. Ray Milland, Guy Standing, Heather Angel, Porter Hall, Reginald Denny, E. E. Clive, Fay Holden. Drummond falls for a pretty heiress (Angel) who is being victimized by her own guardian (Hall). Milland had his one shot at portraying Drummond in this lightweight programmer.▼▶

Bulldog Drummond in Africa (1938) **60m. ★★½** D: Louis King. John Howard, Heather Angel, H. B. Warner, J. Carrol Naish, Reginald Denny, Anthony Quinn, Michael Brooke. Scotland Yard Inspector Nielson (Warner, replacing John Barrymore) is abducted, sending Drummond on a deadly trek into the wilds of the jungle. Atmospheric entry with a formidable supporting cast.▼▶

Bulldog Drummond's Bride (1939) **55m. ★★½** D: James Hogan. John Howard, Heather Angel, H. B. Warner, Reginald Denny, Eduardo Ciannelli, Elizabeth Patterson. Bulldog and his fiancée have their wedding plans in France interrupted when Bulldog takes off after villainous Ciannelli and his gang of bank robbers in this high-speed entry.▼❿

Bulldog Drummond's Peril (1938) **66m.** ****½** D: James Hogan. John Barrymore, John Howard, Louise Campbell, Reginald Denny, E. E. Clive, Porter Hall, Nydia Westman. Drummond's wedding is interrupted by murder, sending the sleuth off on an adventure involving synthetic diamonds. Pleasing, swift-moving series entry.▼❿

Bulldog Drummond's Revenge (1937) **60m.** ****½** D: Louis King. John Barrymore, John Howard, Louise Campbell, Reginald Denny, E. E. Clive, Nydia Westman, Lucien Littlefield. Drummond tracks down a gang of spies after a secret bomb formula in this lean entry. ▼❿

Bulldog Drummond's Secret Police (1939) **56m.** ****½** D: James Hogan. John Howard, Heather Angel, H. B. Warner, Reginald Denny, Leo G. Carroll, Elizabeth Patterson. Pared-down entry has Drummond (Howard) making wedding arrangements while villainous Carroll, posing as a butler, plots to steal an ancient treasure hidden beneath Drummond's home. Lengthy dream sequence incorporates footage from earlier series episodes. Remake of TEMPLE TOWER (1930).▼❿

Bulldog Drummond Strikes Back (1947) **65m.** ***½** D: Frank McDonald. Ron Randell, Gloria Henry, Pat O'Moore, Anabel Shaw, Terry Kilburn. Pedestrian entry built around a favorite plot of mystery series writers: the old one about a phony heiress trying to pick up an inheritance.

Bulldog Jack (1935-British) **73m.** ******* D: Walter Forde. Jack Hulbert, Ralph Richardson, Fay Wray, Claude Hulbert, Athole Fleming. British comedian Hulbert finds himself taking the place of ailing Bulldog Drummond on a sinister case. Fast and funny with some first-rate suspense as well; memorable climax set in the London underground system. Originally shown in the U.S. as ALIAS BULLDOG DRUMMOND, with all the comedy cut out!▼

Bullet for a Badman (1964) **C-80m.** ****½** D: R. G. Springsteen. Audie Murphy, Darren McGavin, Ruta Lee, Skip Homeier, George Tobias, Bob Steele. Another revenge tale involving outlaw, his ex-wife, and a friend who married her.

Bullet for Joey, A (1955) **85m.** ****** D: Lewis Allen. Edward G. Robinson, George Raft, Audrey Totter, George Dolenz, Peter Hanson, Peter Van Eyck. Drab crime drama, set in Montreal, involving a Communist agent who hires thug Raft to mastermind the kidnapping of a nuclear scientist. Robinson, playing a police inspector, gives one of his most uninspired performances.▼❿

Bullet for Stefano (1947-Italian) **96m.** ****** D: Duilio Coletti. Rossano Brazzi, Valentina Cortese, Carlo Campanini, Lillian Laine, Alberto Sordi. Uninspired account of carefree young Brazzi falling into a life of crime. Released in the U.S in 1950.

Bullet Is Waiting, A (1954) **C-82m.** ****½** D: John Farrow. Jean Simmons, Rory Calhoun, Stephen McNally, Brian Aherne. Interesting human nature study hinging on sheriff's discovery that his prisoner is really innocent; nice desert locale.▼❿

Bullets for O'Hara (1941) **50m.** ****½** D: William K. Howard. Joan Perry, Roger Pryor, Anthony Quinn, Maris Wrixon, Dick Purcell, Hobart Bosworth, Richard Ainley, DeWolf Hopper (William Hopper), Joan Winfield, Roland Drew. Quinn gives a nice, nasty performance as a gangster who is turned in to the FBI by his wife. Ultra-compact Warner Bros. feature is a rapid-fire, entertaining remake of PUBLIC ENEMY'S WIFE, from which it recycled action footage. Crime addicts with less than an hour to spare could do a lot worse.

Bullets or Ballots (1936) **81m.** ******* D: William Keighley. Edward G. Robinson, Joan Blondell, Barton MacLane, Humphrey Bogart, Frank McHugh. Cop Robinson pretends to leave police force to crack citywide mob ring run by MacLane. Good, tough gangster film.▼❿❿

Bullfighter and the Lady (1951) **87m.** *****½** D: Budd Boetticher. Robert Stack, Joy Page, Gilbert Roland, Katy Jurado, Virginia Grey, John Hubbard. Cocky American visiting Mexico decides that he wants to tackle bullfighting and enlists the aid of the country's leading matador with tragic results. The movies' best treatment of this subject, a fine, mature drama with unforgettable bullfighting scenes and an appealing love story as well. Roland has never been better; only the second leads (Grey, Hubbard) are a detriment. Produced by John Wayne. Boetticher's version, running 124m., has been restored, and it's even better than the shorter print. ▼❿

Bullfighters, The (1945) **61m.** ****** D: Mal St. Clair. Stan Laurel, Oliver Hardy, Margo Woode, Richard Lane, Carol Andrews, Diosa Costello. One of better L&H later works, involving mistaken identity (Stan is lookalike for famous matador; subsequent nonsense in bull ring.▼❿

Bullwhip (1958) **C-80m.** ****** D: Harmon Jones. Guy Madison, Rhonda Fleming, James Griffith, Don Beddoe. Madison is offered the choice of marrying Fleming or being hanged on phony murder charge; expected results. CinemaScope.▼

Bunco Squad (1950) **67m.** ****½** D: Herbert I. Leeds. Robert Sterling, Joan Dixon, Ricardo Cortez, Douglas Fowley, Elisabeth Risdon, Marguerite Churchill, John Kellogg. L.A. police detective Sterling convinces his aspiring actress girlfriend Dixon to go undercover to help smash con man Cortez's phony fortune-telling and séance racket. Fast-paced B movie isn't bad. Famous magician Dante appears as himself. Remake of CRIME RING (1938). ▶

Bundle of Joy (1956) **C-98m.** ** D: Norman Taurog. Eddie Fisher, Debbie Reynolds, Adolphe Menjou, Tommy Noonan. Labored musical remake of BACHELOR MOTHER has Reynolds as salesgirl who takes custody of a baby, causing scandal that boyfriend Fisher (in starring debut) is child's father. Made when Debbie and Eddie were America's favorite couple. ▼▶

Bunny Lake Is Missing (1965) **107m.** *** D: Otto Preminger. Laurence Olivier, Carol Lynley, Keir Dullea, Noel Coward, Martita Hunt, Finlay Currie, The Zombies. American Lynley, newly arrived in London, reports the disappearance of her preschool daughter—but police detective Olivier can't help but notice that Lynley has no proof that the child ever existed at all. Well paced, expertly acted, with some interestingly offbeat characters in the margins. Made in England. Panavision. ▶

Bureau of Missing Persons (1933) **75m.** **½ D: Roy Del Ruth. Bette Davis, Lewis S. Stone, Pat O'Brien, Allen Jenkins, Ruth Donnelly, Hugh Herbert, Glenda Farrell, Alan Dinehart, George Chandler. Typically fast-paced—but strange—Warner Bros. programmer about big-city bureau of missing persons, where benevolent Stone plays God with the losers and hard-luck cases that come before him. Hip-shooting cop O'Brien is transferred there in hopes he'll mellow out, and we'll bet you a dollar six bits he doesn't. Davis is a mystery woman with whom he gets involved. ▼▶

Burglar, The (1957) **90m.** **½ D: Paul Wendkos. Dan Duryea, Jayne Mansfield, Martha Vickers, Peter Capell, Mickey Shaughnessy, Phoebe Mackay. Odd, boldly stylish film noir about robbers Duryea and Mansfield, who've grown up together, and their hotheaded accomplices. Scripted by David Goodis from his novel. Shot in Philadelphia and Atlantic City in 1955, before Mansfield became a star. Remade in France in 1971 as THE BURGLARS. ▶

Burma Convoy (1941) **72m.** **½ D: Noel Smith. Charles Bickford, Evelyn Ankers, Frank Albertson, Cecil Kellaway, Keye Luke, Turhan Bey. Neat little actioner of conflicting trucking interests involved in carrying needed supplies over the Burma Road during hectic days of WW2.

Burmese Harp, The (1956-Japanese) **116m.** ***½ D: Kon Ichikawa. Rentaro Mikuni, Shoji Yasui, Tatsuya Mihashi, Tanie Kitabayashi, Yunosuke Ito. Private Yasui volunteers to persuade a group of mountain fighters to surrender at the end of WW2 and undergoes a religious experience, becoming obsessed with desire to bury war casualties. Extraordinary antiwar drama is affecting and memorable if a bit overlong.

Also known as HARP OF BURMA; remade by Ichikawa in 1985. ▼▶

Burn 'Em Up O'Connor (1939) **70m.** ** D: Edward Sedgwick. Dennis O'Keefe, Cecilia Parker, Nat Pendleton, Harry Carey, Addison Richards, Charley Grapewin, Tom Neal. Formula racing action with O'Keefe energetic as a hick speed demon, determined to become a racing star and joining ruthless Carey's "jinxed" team of midget car drivers. Script and production stuck in cruise control.

Burning Crucible, The (1923-French) **110m.** *** D: Ivan Mosjoukine. Ivan Mosjoukine, Nathalie Lissenko, Nicolas Koline, Camille Bardou, Huguette (Anna) Delacroix. Lissenko, overindulged by her wealthy husband and living a carefree life, is haunted by a disturbing dream. How is this connected to the exploits of a celebrated detective (Mosjoukine) who takes on disguises and solves crimes? Clever, imaginative fable is occasionally over the top but still amusing, if you warm to its sense of humor. Mosjoukine also scripted. Original title: LE BRASIER ARDENT.

Burning Hills, The (1956) **C-94m** ** D: Stuart Heisler. Tab Hunter, Natalie Wood, Skip Homeier, Eduard Franz, Earl Holliman, Claude Akins. Passive Hunter can't spark life into tired script based on a Louis L'Amour novel. Man on run from cattle thieves is sheltered by Wood, miscast as a half-breed Mexican girl. CinemaScope. ▼▶

Burn, Witch, Burn (1962-British) **90m.** *** D: Sidney Hayers. Peter Wyngarde, Janet Blair, Margaret Johnston, Anthony Nicholls. Story of witchcraft entering lives of schoolteacher and his wife builds to shattering suspense, genuinely frightening climax. Fritz Leiber's novel *Conjure Wife* was filmed before as WEIRD WOMAN; this version scripted by Charles Beaumont and Richard Matheson. Later spoofed in WITCHES' BREW. Original British title: NIGHT OF THE EAGLE. ▼▶

Bury Me Dead (1947) **68m.** *** D: Bernard Vorhaus. June Lockhart, Cathy O'Donnell, Hugh Beaumont, Mark Daniels, Greg McClure, Milton Parsons, Virginia Farmer. Woman who supposedly perished in a suspicious fire shows up at her own funeral to find out who set the blaze and who is buried in her place. Intriguing premise is let down by talky treatment and an annoying abundance of light comedy. Noir expert John Alton's cinematography is as stylish as always. ▼▶

Bush Christmas (1947-Australian) **76m.** *** D: Ralph Smart. Chips Rafferty, John Fernside, Stan Tolhurst, Pat Penny, Thelma Grigg. Solid little adventure about some children who set out across the Australian bush in pursuit of horse thieves. Holds up quite nicely; kids should enjoy it. Remade in 1983. ▶

[95]

Busher, The (1919) **63m.** ******* D: Jerome Storm. Charles Ray, Colleen Moore, Jack (John) Gilbert, Jay Morley, Otto Hoffman. Engaging comedy-drama with Ray ideally cast as a country bumpkin with a talent for tossing baseballs who undergoes a personality change when he reaches the major leagues. Of special note are the idyllic country scenes featuring Ray and Moore (who plays his small-town girlfriend). ▼▶

Bushwhackers, The (1952) **70m.** ****** D: Rod Amateau. John Ireland, Wayne Morris, Lawrence Tierney, Dorothy Malone, Lon Chaney, Jr., Myrna Dell, Jack Elam. Standard oater of peace-loving Civil War vet Ireland, who heads west and predictably finds that he must dust off his gun to fight corruption. ▼▶

Busman's Honeymoon SEE: **Haunted Honeymoon**

Bus Riley's Back in Town (1965) **C-93m.** ****½** D: Harvey Hart. Ann-Margret, Michael Parks, Janet Margolin, Brad Dexter, Kim Darby, Jocelyn Brando, Larry Storch, David Carradine. Muddled William Inge script of folksy people in the Midwest. Parks, ex-sailor, returns home, torn by faltering ambitions and taunted by wealthy ex-girlfriend Ann-Margret. Character cameos make the film worthwhile. ▼

Busses Roar (1942) **60m.** ****½** D: D. Ross Lederman. Richard Travis, Julie Bishop, Charles Drake, Eleanor Parker, Elisabeth Fraser, Richard Fraser, Peter Whitney, Willie Best, Bill Kennedy, Harry Lewis. Zippy little programmer set in a California bus station, where Axis agents attempt to plant a bomb aboard a bus that is due to pass by an oil field. Taut suspense and some neat character sketches all in just one hour. Parker's feature film debut.

Bus Stop (1956) **C-96m.** *****½** D: Joshua Logan. Marilyn Monroe, Don Murray, Arthur O'Connell, Betty Field, Eileen Heckart, Hope Lange, Hans Conried, Casey Adams (Max Showalter). The film that finally proved Monroe really could act; excellent comedy-drama about innocent cowboy (Murray) who falls for saloon singer and decides to marry her—without bothering to ask. Fine performances by all, with MM's famed rendition of "(That Old) Black Magic" a highlight; adapted by George Axelrod from the William Inge play. Film debuts of Murray and Lange (who subsequently married). Later a brief TV series. CinemaScope. ▼▶▶

Buster Keaton Story, The (1957) **91m.** ***½** D: Sidney Sheldon. Donald O'Connor, Ann Blyth, Rhonda Fleming, Peter Lorre, Larry Keating. Weak fiction ignores the facts about silent-star Keaton, making up its own. More private life than on-screen moments are detailed with Blyth as his true love and Fleming as a siren. Little comedy in this tale of a great comedian. VistaVision.

But Not for Me (1959) **105m.** ******* D: Walter Lang. Clark Gable, Carroll Baker, Lilli Palmer, Barry Coe, Lee J. Cobb, Thomas Gomez, Charles Lane. Chic remake of Samson Raphaelson's ACCENT ON YOUTH. Twenty-two-year-old secretary/aspiring actress Baker falls for her has-been theatrical-producer boss (Gable), who won't admit he's on the dark side of 50. Palmer is his wily ex-wife, Cobb a faded playwright. VistaVision.▼

BUtterfield 8 (1960) **C-109m.** ****½** D: Daniel Mann. Elizabeth Taylor, Laurence Harvey, Eddie Fisher, Dina Merrill, Mildred Dunnock, Susan Oliver, Betty Field, Jeffrey Lynn, Kay Medford. Adaptation of John O'Hara novel substitutes clichéd ending in tale of high-class prostitute wanting to go straight, convincing herself she's found Mr. Right. Film's major assets: great supporting cast and old-style performance by Taylor, who won Oscar. CinemaScope. ▼▶▶

But the Flesh Is Weak (1932) **77m.** ****** D: Jack Conway. Robert Montgomery, Nora Gregor, Heather Thatcher, Edward Everett Horton, C. Aubrey Smith, Nils Asther. Ivor Novello wrote this talky adaptation of his hit play *The Truth Game*, involving a father and son on the prowl for rich wives among London's upper crust. Swanky MGM fluff barely raises a smile and sorely needed the touch of a Lubitsch. Look fast for Ray Milland in a party scene. Remade as FREE AND EASY. ▶

Buy Me That Town (1941) **70m.** ****½** D: Eugene Forde. Lloyd Nolan, Constance Moore, Albert Dekker, Sheldon Leonard, Barbara Allen (Vera Vague), Warren Hymer, Edward Brophy, Horace McMahon, Russell Hicks. Clever little B comedy-drama about gangster (Nolan) who actually buys a bankrupt little village; he plans to use it as a hideout for lawbreaker pals, but eventually becomes more civic-minded. Amusing and observant, with great cast full of veteran tough guys.

Bwana Devil (1952) **C-79m.** ***½** D: Arch Oboler. Robert Stack, Barbara Britton, Nigel Bruce, Paul McVey. Dud actioner was sparked theatrically as first commercial 3-D feature; man-eating lions set their teeth on railway workers in Africa.

By Candlelight (1933) **70m.** ****** D: James Whale. Paul Lukas, Elissa Landi, Nils Asther, Dorothy Revier, Lawrence Grant, Esther Ralston. Typical Continental fluff about valet who poses as his master to woo woman he believes is a countess. Leaden Lukas is so wrong for the part that he almost sinks the film, but a few Whale touches make it watchable; buffs may find it more to taste.

Bye Bye Birdie (1963) **C-112m.** ******* D: George Sidney. Janet Leigh, Dick Van Dyke, Ann-Margret, Maureen Stapleton, Paul Lynde, Jesse Pearson, Bobby Rydell,

Ed Sullivan. Entertaining version of Broadway musical about drafted rock 'n' roll idol coming to small town to give "one last kiss" to one of his adoring fans. Lynde stands out as Ann-Margret's father. Remade for TV in 1995 with Jason Alexander and Vanessa Williams. Panavision. ▼○●

By Love Possessed (1961) C-115m. **½ D: John Sturges. Lana Turner, Efrem Zimbalist, Jr., Jason Robards, Jr., George Hamilton, Thomas Mitchell, Susan Kohner, Barbara Bel Geddes, Everett Sloane, Carroll O'Connor. Ultraglossy, well-cast but empty soaper, in which neurotic Turner commences an affair with Zimbalist, the law partner of her impotent husband (Robards). Based on—but not true to—the James Gould Cozzens novel. ▼○●

By the Light of the Silvery Moon (1953) C-102m. **½ D: David Butler. Doris Day, Gordon MacRae, Leon Ames, Rosemary DeCamp, Mary Wickes, Billy Gray. Set in post WW1, this Booth Tarkington story finds returning soldier MacRae and fiancée Day readjusting to life. Ames wonderful as father thought to be romancing French actress, and Wickes delightful as family maid. Merv Griffin pops up in the closing scene. This old-fashioned musical was a sequel to ON MOONLIGHT BAY. ▼○●

By Whose Hand? (1932) 63m. *** D: Benjamin Stoloff. Ben Lyon, Barbara Weeks, William V. Mong, Ethel Kenyon, Kenneth Thomson, Tom Dugan, William Halligan, Helene Millard, Dwight Frye, Nat Pendleton. Rock-solid, ingeniously structured whodunit about an escaped killer who may—or may not—be on board a speeding train. At the center of the story is a brash, skirt-chasing reporter (nicely played by Lyon). This works despite some obvious plot holes and Dugan's annoying presence as a drunk.

By Your Leave (1934) 82m. ** D: Lloyd Corrigan. Frank Morgan, Genevieve Tobin, Neil Hamilton, Marian Nixon, Gene Lockhart, Margaret Hamilton, Betty Grable, Glenn Anders. Morgan plays a husband going through a midlife crisis who yearns for extramarital excitement, but wife Tobin finds it first. Unusual subject matter for a '30s film is treated very lightly, though a good cast offers some minor compensation.

Cabinet of Caligari, The (1962) 104m. **½ D: Roger Kay. Dan O'Herlihy, Glynis Johns, Richard Davalos, Lawrence Dobkin, Estelle Winwood, J. Pat O'Malley. Unimaginative remake of the 1919 German classic, removing all the mystery-exotic appeal; Johns tries hard as lady in ornate modern home confronted by O'Herlihy's sinister Caligari; many bizarre scenes. Written by Robert Bloch. CinemaScope. ●

Cabinet of Dr. Caligari, The (1919-German) 69m. ***½ D: Robert Wiene.

Werner Krauss, Conrad Veidt, Lil Dagover. Somewhat stiff but still fascinating German Expressionist film about "magician" Caligari and hypnotic victim who carries out his evil bidding. Landmark film still impresses audiences today. Remade in 1962. ▼○●

Cabin in the Cotton, The (1932) 77m. **½ D: Michael Curtiz. Richard Barthelmess, Dorothy Jordan, Bette Davis, Hardie Albright, David Landau, Berton Churchill, Henry B. Walthall, Tully Marshall. Dated melodrama of sharecroppers, with earnest Barthelmess almost led to ruin by Southern belle Davis; exaggerated, but interesting. Bette's immortal line: "Ah'd like to kiss ya, but Ah jes' washed mah hair." ▼

Cabin in the Sky (1943) 100m. *** D: Vincente Minnelli. Eddie "Rochester" Anderson, Lena Horne, Ethel Waters, Louis Armstrong, Rex Ingram, Duke Ellington and His Orchestra, The Hall Johnson Choir. Stellar black cast in winning (if somewhat racist) musical fable about forces of good and evil vying for the soul of Little Joe (Anderson). John Bubbles' dancing, Waters singing "Happiness Is a Thing Called Joe" (written for the film) among musical highlights. First feature for Minnelli (who, with Waters and Ingram, came from the Broadway production). ▼○●

Cabiria (1914-Italian) 148m. ***½ D: Piero Fosco (Giovanni Pastrone). Italia Almirante Manzini, Lidia Quaranta, Bartolomeo Pagano, Umberto Mozzato, Vitale de Stefano. Still-impressive silent epic, a landmark film for its use of lighting and camera movement, as well as its sheer spectacle. The story chronicles the plight of the title character (Quaranta), a Sicilian slave girl, during the Second Punic War. Pastrone co-scripted with poet Gabriele D'Annunzio, who penned those lushly composed intertitles. This also served as an inspiration to D. W. Griffith, particularly for the Babylonian sequence of INTOLERANCE. ▼○●

Caddy, The (1953) 95m. *½ D: Norman Taurog. Dean Martin, Jerry Lewis, Donna Reed, Fred Clark, Barbara Bates, Joseph Calleia. Weak Martin & Lewis vehicle about golfnut Jerry coaching Dean to be a champion player. Dean sings "That's Amore." ▼●

Caesar and Cleopatra (1946-British) C-134m. ** D: Gabriel Pascal. Claude Rains, Vivien Leigh, Stewart Granger, Flora Robson, Francis L. Sullivan, Cecil Parker. Two fine stars suffer through static, boring rendition of George Bernard Shaw's play, which seems to go on forever. Occasional wit and intrigue can't keep this afloat. ▼●

Café Metropole (1937) 84m. **½ D: Edward H. Griffith. Loretta Young, Tyrone Power, Adolphe Menjou, Gregory Ratoff, Charles Winninger, Helen Westley. Young is courted by penniless playboy Power, who's posing as a Russian prince. OK comedy, from a story by Ratoff. ●

[97]

Cafe Society (1939) **83m.** **½ D: Edward H. Griffith. Madeleine Carroll, Fred MacMurray, Shirley Ross, Jessie Ralph, Claude Gillingwater. This time around Carroll chases MacMurray to win husband on a bet; chic fluff.

Caged (1950) **96m.** *** D: John Cromwell. Eleanor Parker, Agnes Moorehead, Ellen Corby, Hope Emerson, Jan Sterling, Jane Darwell, Gertrude Michael. Remarkable performances in stark record of Parker going to prison and becoming hardened criminal after exposure to brutal jail life. Remade as HOUSE OF WOMEN (1962).▶

Caged Fury (1948) **60m.** ** D: William Berke. Richard Denning, Sheila Ryan, Mary Beth Hughes, Buster Crabbe. Not bad low-budgeter about mad killer on the loose in a circus.▼▶

Cage of Gold (1950-British) **83m.** **½ D: Basil Dearden. Jean Simmons, David Farrar, James Donald, Madeleine Lebeau, Herbert Lom, Bernard Lee. Fair suspense yarn with sleazy Farrar, supposedly dead in a plane crash, attempting to blackmail wife Simmons, now remarried to doctor Donald.

Cain and Mabel (1936) **90m.** ** D: Lloyd Bacon. Marion Davies, Clark Gable, David Carlyle (Robert Paige), Allen Jenkins, Roscoe Karns, Walter Catlett, Hobart Cavanaugh, Ruth Donnelly, Pert Kelton. Publicist concocts phony romance between Broadway star Davies (who's miscast) and heavyweight champ Gable—who happen to despise one another. Gargantuan production numbers add nothing to stale plot. Rescued somewhat by the snappy one-liners delivered by the supporting cast.▶

Caine Mutiny, The (1954) **C-125m.** **** D: Edward Dmytryk. Humphrey Bogart, Jose Ferrer, Van Johnson, Robert Francis, May Wynn, Fred MacMurray, E.G. Marshall, Lee Marvin, Tom Tully, Claude Akins. WW2 Naval officers Johnson and Francis mutiny against paranoid, unpopular Capt. Queeg (Bogart) and are court-martialed in this exciting adaptation (by Stanley Roberts) of Herman Wouk's Pulitzer Prize novel. Wartime mutiny scene during typhoon still packs a wallop. Followed by a TVM in 1988.▼▶

Cairo (1942) **101m.** ** D: W.S. Van Dyke II. Jeanette MacDonald, Robert Young, Ethel Waters, Reginald Owen, Lionel Atwill, Dooley Wilson. Musi-comedy spoof of WW2 spy films is strained, although stars are pleasant and production is well mounted.▼▶

Cairo (1963-British) **91m.** **½ D: Wolf Rilla. George Sanders, Richard Johnson, Faten Hamama, John Meillon, Eric Pohlmann, Walter Rilla. Mediocre remake of THE ASPHALT JUNGLE with the "surefire" caper aiming to steal King Tut's treasures from the Cairo Museum.

Calamity Jane (1953) **C-101m.** *** D: David Butler. Doris Day, Howard Keel, Allyn

(Ann) McLerie, Philip Carey, Gale Robbins, Dick Wesson, Paul Harvey. Doris is irresistible as the bombastic, rootin'-tootin' title character in this lively musical, with Keel as Wild Bill Hickok, who only begins to realize his feelings for her when she makes a stab at becoming more "feminine." Sammy Fain–Paul Francis Webster score includes the Oscar-winning "Secret Love." Jane Alexander later played Calamity in a 1984 TV movie.▼▶●

Calamity Jane and Sam Bass (1949) **C-85m.** *½ D: George Sherman. Yvonne De Carlo, Howard Duff, Dorothy Hart, Lloyd Bridges, Milburn Stone. Tattered retelling of 19th-century cowgirl and Texas outlaw, with De Carlo and Duff a disinterested duo.▶

Calcutta (1947) **83m.** **½ D: John Farrow. Alan Ladd, Gail Russell, William Bendix, June Duprez, Lowell Gilmore. Standard actioner with pilot Ladd avenging friend's murder.

Calendar Girl (1947) **88m.** ** D: Allan Dwan. Jane Frazee, William Marshall, Gail Patrick, Kenny Baker, Victor McLaglen, Irene Rich, James Ellison, Janet Martin, Franklin Pangborn, Gus Schilling, Charles Arnt. Titillating title for a bland tuner about a singer, a composer, and a painter in a turn-of-the-19th-century boardinghouse. Republic Pictures musical has forgettable songs by Harold Adamson and Jimmy McHugh ("Let's Have Some Pretzels and Beer") and proves again that this genre wasn't the studio's strong suit.▼▶

California (1946) **C-97m.** **½ D: John Farrow. Barbara Stanwyck, Ray Milland, Barry Fitzgerald, Albert Dekker, Anthony Quinn, Julia Faye, George Coulouris. Ray is a wagonmaster with a past, Stanwyck a shady gal who makes good in this elaborately ordinary Western.▶

California Conquest (1952) **C-79m.** **½ D: Lew Landers. Cornel Wilde, Teresa Wright, John Dehner, Hank Patterson. Film deals with sidelight of American history. Californian Wilde et al. under Spanish control help their ally against Russian attempt to confiscate the territory.

California Passage (1950) **90m.** **½ D: Joseph Kane. Forrest Tucker, Jim Davis, Adele Mara, Estelita Rodriguez, Peter Miles, Charles Kemper, Bill Williams, Rhys Williams, Paul Fix. Tucker and Davis make an engaging team as uneasy partners in a saloon and rivals for the love of Mara. Davis tries to get Tucker out of the way by framing him for robberies of gold shipments. Action-packed Republic Western hokum moves along at a gallop.

California Straight Ahead (1937) **67m.** ** D: Arthur Lubin. John Wayne, Louise Latimer, Robert McWade, Theodore Von Eltz, Tully Marshall. Good little actioner with Wayne competing in cross-country race between trucks and train.

Call a Messenger (1939) 65m. ** D: Arthur Lubin. Billy Halop, Huntz Hall, William Benedict, David Gorcey, Robert Armstrong, Buster Crabbe, Anne Nagel, Victor Jory, El Brendel, Mary Carlisle. Well-cast *Little Tough Guys* outing. Halop gets a job as a junior mailman and tangles with gangsters in this typical crime yarn. Crabbe makes an impressive heavy, complete with mustache.

Callaway Went Thataway (1951) 81m. **½ D: Norman Panama, Melvin Frank. Fred MacMurray, Dorothy McGuire, Howard Keel, Jesse White, Fay Roope, Natalie Schafer, Stan Freberg. Gentle spoof of early-TV "Hopalong Cassidy" craze, with Keel as lookalike who impersonates veteran cowboy star for promotional purposes; good fun until it starts getting serious. Several MGM stars make cameo appearances.

Call Her Savage (1932) 88m. **½ D: John Francis Dillon. Clara Bow, Gilbert Roland, Thelma Todd, Monroe Owsley, Estelle Taylor, Russell Simpson, Margaret Livingston. Wild comeback vehicle for indefatigable Clara Bow ranges from sharp comedy to teary-eyed soap opera, but it's never dull. Bow is amazingly sensual throughout, matched in brief confrontations with Todd; great fun.▶

Calling Bulldog Drummond (1951-U.S.-British) 80m. **½ D: Victor Saville. Walter Pidgeon, Margaret Leighton, Robert Beatty, David Tomlinson, Peggy Evans, Charles Victor, Bernard Lee. Pidgeon makes a satisfactory Drummond as the sleuth is called out of retirement to help Scotland Yard nab a gang of sophisticated thieves armed with military hardware. Starts well but bogs down in talk.

Calling Dr. Death (1943) 63m. ** D: Reginald LeBorg. Lon Chaney, Jr., Patricia Morison, J. Carrol Naish, David Bruce, Ramsay Ames. Ultra-low-budget mystery about a neurologist (a badly miscast Chaney) who is tormented by the realization that he may have killed his unfaithful wife during a moment of madness. First of the *Inner Sanctum* series. ▼▶

Calling Dr. Gillespie (1942) 84m. **½ D: Harold S. Bucquet. Lionel Barrymore, Philip Dorn, Donna Reed, Phil Brown, Nat Pendleton, Alma Kruger, Mary Nash, Walter Kingsford, Charles Dingle, Nell Craig, Marie Blake, Jonathan Hale. With Lew Ayres gone, the series continues with Gillespie getting a new assistant (Dorn), while the crusty old sawbones himself is the target of a homicidal maniac. Enjoyable melodrama; look sharp for Ava Gardner.▶

Calling Dr. Kildare (1939) 86m. **½ D: Harold S. Bucquet. Lew Ayres, Lionel Barrymore, Laraine Day, Lana Turner, Lynne Carver, Nat Pendleton, Samuel S. Hinds, Emma Dunn, Walter Kingsford, Marie Blake, Donald Barry. Efficient second entry in the series has Kildare in trouble with the police for treating a gangster and getting involved with the hood's cute sister (Turner).▶

Calling Homicide (1956) 61m. *½ D: Edward Bernds. Bill Elliott, Don Haggerty, Jeanne Cooper, Thomas Browne Henry, Lyle Talbot, Kathleen Case, Myron Healey, James Best, Mary Treen. Low-key crime yarn involving homicide detective Elliott's search for a cop killer. Former Western star Elliott played the same character in four other movies.▶

Calling Northside 777 SEE: **Call Northside 777**

Calling Philo Vance (1940) 62m. ** D: William Clemens. James Stephenson, Margot Stevenson, Henry O'Neill, Edward Brophy, Ralph Forbes, Martin Kosleck. Stephenson makes a refined (if sinister) Philo Vance, investigating the death of an aircraft manufacturer by foreign agents. Minor, but watchable, entry is virtually a scene-for-scene remake of THE KENNEL MURDER CASE, updated to wartime.

Call It a Day (1937) 89m. ** D: Archie Mayo. Olivia de Havilland, Ian Hunter, Anita Louise, Alice Brady, Roland Young, Frieda Inescort, Bonita Granville, Peggy Wood, Walter Woolf King. Minor, fluffy domestic comedy set during a 24-hour period and chronicling the various entanglements, romantic and otherwise, of a middle-class British couple (Hunter, Inescort) and their three children.▶

Call It Murder SEE: **Midnight** (1934)

Call Me Bwana (1963) C-103m. ** D: Gordon Douglas. Bob Hope, Anita Ekberg, Edie Adams, Lionel Jeffries, Arnold Palmer. Hope and Adams on jungle safari encounter Ekberg and Jeffries and nothing much happens. The ladies are lovely.▼▶

Call Me Madam (1953) C-117m. *** D: Walter Lang. Ethel Merman, Donald O'Connor, George Sanders, Vera-Ellen, Billy DeWolfe, Walter Slezak, Lilia Skala. Often stagy musical from Irving Berlin tuner based on Perle Mesta's life as Washington, D.C., hostess and Liechtenstein ambassadress. Merman is blowsy delight. Songs include "The Best Thing for You," "It's a Lovely Day Today," "You're Just in Love."▶

Call Me Mister (1951) C-95m. **½ D: Lloyd Bacon. Betty Grable, Dan Dailey, Danny Thomas, Dale Robertson, Benay Venuta, Richard Boone, Frank Fontaine, Jeffrey Hunter. Acceptable plot line helps buoy this musical. Soldier Dailey, based in Japan, goes AWOL to patch up marriage with Grable traveling with USO troupe. Bears little resemblance to the Broadway revue on which it's supposedly based. An unbilled Bobby Short sings "Going Home Train."▶

Call Northside 777 (1948) 111m. ***½ D: Henry Hathaway. James Stewart, Richard Conte, Lee J. Cobb, Helen Walker, Moroni

Olsen, E. G. Marshall. Absorbing drama of reporter Stewart convinced that convicted killer is innocent, trying to prove it; handled in semi-documentary style. Retitled: CALLING NORTHSIDE 777. ▼○●

Call of the Canyon (1942) 71m. *½ D: Joseph Santley. Gene Autry, Smiley Burnette, Sons of the Pioneers, Ruth Terry, Thurston Hall, Joe Strauch, Jr., Cliff Nazarro, Dorothea Kent. Gene deals with the crooked purchasing agent for a packing company and gets roped into doing a Western radio show. Plays like a tired pastiche of Autry's previous movies; even his pairing with the Sons of the Pioneers is lackluster. ▼)

Call of the Flesh (1930) 100m. *½ D: Charles Brabin. Ramon Novarro, Dorothy Jordan, Ernest Torrence, Nance O'Neil, Renée Adorée, Mathilde Comont, Russell Hopton. Jordan is a young novice who leaves the convent after flipping for Latin singer Novarro. Ornate star vehicle moves like molasses and inspires unintentional laughter. Some scenes were originally in two-strip Technicolor.

Call of the Prairie (1936) 65m. **½ D: Howard Bretherton. William Boyd, Jimmy Ellison, Muriel Evans, George Hayes, Chester Conklin, Alan Bridge, Hank Mann, Chill Wills and His Avalon Boys. Following Bar 20 cattle sale, a bad crowd frames unwitting Ellison (who's on a drinking bender) in a scheme to steal Hopalong Cassidy's bankroll. Adapted from Clarence E. Mulford's 1926 novel, *Hopalong Cassidy's Protégé.* Not so slick as other entries; driven by personalities and authentic atmosphere. Boyd uses heavy Southern accent and Hayes plays sinister outlaw leader! ▼)

Call of the Wild, The (1935) 81m. *** D: William Wellman. Clark Gable, Loretta Young, Jack Oakie, Reginald Owen, Frank Conroy. More Hollywood than Jack London, this Yukon adventure/romance is lots of fun, and Owen a fine snarling villain. Original release was 95m. Remade in 1972 and as a TVM in 1976, 1993, and 1997, and in 2009 in 3-D.)

Call Out the Marines (1942) 67m. ** D: Frank Ryan, William Hamilton. Edmund Lowe, Victor McLaglen, Binnie Barnes, Paul Kelly, Dorothy Lovett, Franklin Pangborn. Tepid comedy, Lowe and McLaglen's last starring film together. The boys tangle with waterfront seductress Barnes while on the trail of spies. Several forgettable tunes (like "Zana Zaranda") to boot. ▼

Calm Yourself (1935) 71m. **½ D: George B. Seitz. Robert Young, Madge Evans, Betty Furness, Ralph Morgan, Nat Pendleton, Hardie Albright, Claude Gillingwater. When Young is fired from his advertising agency job, he starts his own company, called Confidential Services, which specializes in calming down clients by handling unpleasant tasks for them. Frothy

filler gets by on its genial cast and some surprising dialogue, as when Young tells Evans, "You're habit forming, like hashish and whiskey."

Caltiki, the Immortal Monster (1959-Italian) 76m. ** D: Robert Hampton (Riccardo Freda). John Merivale, Didi Sullivan, Gerard Herter, Daniela Rocca. Set in Mexico, sci-fi has blob-ish fiend pursuing members of scientific expedition; poorly conceived but amusing. Photographed by Mario Bava.)

Calypso Heat Wave (1957) 86m. ** D: Fred F. Sears. Johnny Desmond, Merry Anders, Paul Langton, Michael Granger, Meg Myles, Joel Grey, The Treniers, The Tarriers, The Hi-Lo's, Maya Angelou, Darla Hood. Trite plot—crooked Granger takes over Langton's record company—takes a back seat to performances by Desmond, Grey, Hi-Lo's, etc. A once-in-a-lifetime cast. Alan Arkin is one of The Tarriers.

Calypso Joe (1957) 76m. *½ D: Edward Dein. Herb Jeffries, Angie Dickinson, Edward Kemmer, Stephen Bekassy, Laurie Mitchell, Lord Flea and His Calypsonians. Thin programmer about stewardess Dickinson and TV star Kemmer quarreling and making up in a South American setting. Jeffries sings seven songs.

Cameo Kirby (1923) 77m. **½ D: John Ford. John Gilbert, Gertrude Olmstead, Alan Hale, Eric Mayne, William E. Lawrence, Richard Tucker, Phillips Smalley, Jean Arthur. Gilbert is dashing as a Mississippi riverboat gambler who inadvertently causes the death of an old man, then falls in love with his daughter. Colorful silent, the first for which Ford was billed as John instead of Jack, with good atmosphere involving card games and duels. Jean Arthur's film debut. Based on a play by Harry Leon Wilson and Booth Tarkington. Previously filmed in 1914; remade in 1930.

Cameraman, The (1928) 76m. *** D: Edward Sedgwick. Buster Keaton, Marceline Day, Harold Goodwin, Sidney Bracy, Harry Gribbon, Edward Brophy. Buster plays a lovesick would-be newsreel cameraman in this entertaining silent comedy, a cut below his masterpieces but still brimming with invention, ingenious set pieces, and big laughs. Remade with Red Skelton as WATCH THE BIRDIE. ▼○●

Camille (1921) 70m. **½ D: Ray C. Smallwood. (Alla) Nazimova, Rudolph Valentino, Rex Cherryman, Arthur Hoyt, Zeffie Tilbury, Patsy Ruth Miller, Elinor Oliver, William Orlamond. "Modernized" version of Alexandre Dumas' oft-filmed tale, set in contemporary Paris, with law student Armand Duval (Valentino) becoming enamored of Marguerite Gautier (Nazimova), "the Lady of the Camellias," a frail, flirtatious, but self-sacrificing beauty. Overbaked melodrama benefits from stunning

Art Deco sets (courtesy of Natasha Rambova, Valentino's eventual wife) and Rudy's presence. Written by June Mathis. ▼▶

Camille (1937) **108m. ***½ D:** George Cukor. Greta Garbo, Robert Taylor, Lionel Barrymore, Elizabeth Allan, Laura Hope Crews, Henry Daniell, Joan Brodel (Leslie). Beautiful MGM production; in one of her most famous roles, Garbo is Dumas' tragic heroine who must sacrifice her own happiness in order to prove her love. Taylor is a bit stiff as Armand, but Daniell is a superb villain. Filmed before in 1915 (with Clara Kimball Young), 1917 (Theda Bara), and 1921 (Nazimova, with Rudolph Valentino as Armand). Remade for TV in 1984 with Greta Scacchi. Also shown in computer-colored version. ▼●▶

Campbell's Kingdom (1957-British) **C-102m. ** D:** Ralph Thomas. Dirk Bogarde, Stanley Baker, Michael Craig, Barbara Murray. Set in Canadian Rockies, big-budget adventure film focuses on landowner Bogarde's conflict with Baker et al., when latter seeks to build large dam near his property. ▶

Camp on Blood Island, The (1958-British) **81m. ** D:** Val Guest. Andre Morell, Carl Mohner, Walter Fitzgerald, Edward Underdown. So-so gore as inhabitants rebel against brutal commander of prison compound. Followed by THE SECRET OF BLOOD ISLAND. Megascope. ▶

Campus Rhythm (1943) **63m. ** D:** Arthur Dreifuss. Johnny Downs, Gale Storm, Robert Lowery, Candy Candido, Gee Gee Pearson, Doug Leavitt, Tom Kennedy, Claudia Drake. By-the-numbers campus musical with radio singing star Storm quitting the biz to realize her dream of attending college.

Canadian Pacific (1949) **C-95m. **½ D:** Edwin L. Marin. Randolph Scott, Jane Wyatt, J. Carrol Naish, Victor Jory, Nancy Olson. Scott is railroad surveyor helping with construction of train link, fighting Indians while romancing Wyatt and Olson.

Canadians, The (1961) **C-85m. ** D:** Burt Kennedy. Robert Ryan, John Dehner, Torin Thatcher, John Sutton, Teresa Stratas. Cornball nonsense about Mounties who pacify war-happy Sioux. Film features Metropolitan Opera singer Stratas to no advantage. Filmed in Canada; Kennedy's first feature as director. CinemaScope.

Canaris Master Spy (1954-German) **92m. ** D:** Alfred Weidenmann. O. E. Hasse, Martin Held, Barbara Rutting, Adrian Hoven. Potentially interesting account of German Intelligence leader during 1930s who tried to depose Hitler; meandering.

Canary Murder Case (1929) **81m. **½ D:** Malcolm St. Clair. William Powell, Louise Brooks, James Hall, Jean Arthur, Charles Lane. Stilted but interesting and well-cast early talkie (originally shot as a silent) with Powell debuting as urbane sleuth Philo Vance, probing the death of scheming nightclub singer Brooks. (She made this right before

her classic German films with G. W. Pabst. When she refused to return for retakes she was doubled, fairly obviously in some scenes, by Margaret Livingston.)

Can-Can (1960) **C-131m. **½ D:** Walter Lang. Frank Sinatra, Shirley MacLaine, Maurice Chevalier, Louis Jourdan, Juliet Prowse. Lackluster version of Cole Porter musical of 1890s Paris involving lawyer Sinatra defending MacLaine's right to perform "daring" dance in her nightclub. Chevalier and Jourdan try to inject charm, but Sinatra is blasé and MacLaine shrill. Songs: "C'est Magnifique," "I Love Paris," "Let's Do It," "Just One of Those Things." Runs 142m. with overture, intermission/entr'acte, exit music. Todd-AO. ▼●▶

Cannibal Attack (1954) **69m. *½ D:** Lee Sholem. Johnny Weissmuller, Judy Walsh, David Bruce, Bruce Cowling. Weissmuller dropped the *Jungle Jim* moniker and used his own name in this juvenile yarn about enemy agents who disguise themselves as crocodiles(!?) to steal cobalt. ▼

Canon City (1948) **82m. *** D:** Crane Wilbur. Scott Brady, Jeff Corey, Whit Bissell, Stanley Clements, DeForest Kelley. Solid crime thriller follows members of a prison break from a Colorado State jail in semi-documentary style. Strong and violent with excellent photography by John Alton.

Canterbury Tale, A (1944-British) **124m. *** D:** Michael Powell, Emeric Pressburger. Eric Portman, Sheila Sim, John Sweet, Dennis Price, Esmond Knight, Charles Hawtrey, Hay Petrie. Curious and disarming film from the Powell-Pressburger writing-and-directing team draws on British eccentricities—and provincial flavor—to flesh out its simple story about three people whose lives cross in a small English village during the war. There's only the slightest tangent with the Chaucer work from which it draws its title. American version with added footage of Kim Hunter runs 95m. and doesn't retain the charm of the original. ▼▶

Canterville Ghost, The (1944) **96m. *** D:** Jules Dassin. Charles Laughton, Robert Young, Margaret O'Brien, William Gargan, Reginald Owen, "Rags" Ragland, Una O'Connor, Mike Mazurki, Peter Lawford. Enjoyable fantasy, loosely adapted from Oscar Wilde's short story, of 17th-century ghost Laughton, spellbound until descendant, WW2 soldier Young, helps him perform heroic deed. Remade for TV in 1986 (with John Gielgud) and 1996 (with Patrick Stewart). ▼●▶

Can't Help Singing (1944) **C-89m. **½ D:** Frank Ryan. Deanna Durbin, Robert Paige, Akim Tamiroff, Ray Collins, Thomas Gomez. Durbin goes West to find her roaming lover; despite good cast and Jerome Kern songs, it's nothing much. ▼●▶

Canyon Crossroads (1955) **83m. ** D:** Alfred L. Werker. Richard Basehart, Phyllis

Kirk, Stephen Elliott, Russell Collins, Richard Hale, Charles Wagenheim, Tommy Cook. Unexceptional account of down-on-his-luck mining engineer Basehart, who's hired by a geology professor to prospect for uranium, with resulting complications. Shot on location in and around Moab, Utah.

Canyon Passage (1946) C-92m. *** D: Jacques Tourneur. Dana Andrews, Brian Donlevy, Susan Hayward, Patricia Roc, Ward Bond, Hoagy Carmichael, Fay Holden, Stanley Ridges, Lloyd Bridges, Andy Devine, Rose Hobart. Intelligent Western, complexly plotted, set in a backwoods Northwest settlement in the 1850s. Among the characters are hardworking shopkeeper Andrews and banker-gambler Donlevy, with Hayward the woman between them. Oregon locations are stunning in Technicolor, and Carmichael introduces "Ole Buttermilk Sky." Adapted from a novel by Ernest Haycox. ▼❶

Canyon River (1956) C-80m. *½ D: Harmon Jones. George Montgomery, Marcia Henderson, Peter Graves, Richard Eyer. Trite Western of Indian and rustler attacks on cattle drive. Remake of 1951 Bill Elliott Western LONGHORN. CinemaScope. ❶

Cape Canaveral Monsters, The (1960) 69m. BOMB D: Phil Tucker. Scott Peters, Linda Connell, Jason Johnson, Katherine Victor, Gary Travis. Aliens, represented by small balls of white light, inhabit slowly decomposing corpses in order to shoot down U.S. rockets; science student Peters, using wallet inserts and Pig Latin, combats the invaders. Astonishing film is almost the equal of writer-director Tucker's legendarily awful ROBOT MONSTER. ▼

Cape Fear (1962) 105m. *** D: J. Lee Thompson. Gregory Peck, Robert Mitchum, Polly Bergen, Martin Balsam, Lori Martin, Jack Kruschen, Telly Savalas, Barrie Chase, Edward Platt. Mitchum is memorably (and believably) creepy as a wily Southern ex-con who blames lawyer Peck for his incarceration and plots an insidious revenge on his family. Dated only in its lack of explicitness, but still daring for its time. Based on John D. MacDonald's novel *The Executioners*. Musical score by Bernard Herrmann is reminiscent of his best work with Hitchcock. Remade in 1991. ▼❶❷

Capital Punishment (1925) 67m. **½ D: James P. Hogan. Elliott Dexter, George Hackathorne, Clara Bow, Margaret Livingston, Alec B. Francis, Mary Carr. Dexter, who is fervently against the death penalty, conducts an experiment by having Hackathorne accused of a murder that did not happen . . . but complications arise. Clever but predictable crime melodrama, predating such films as Fritz Lang's BEYOND A REASONABLE DOUBT. Bow has a supporting role as Hackathorne's fiancée. ▼

Captain Applejack (1931) 63m. ** D: Hobart Henley. Mary Brian, John Halli-

day, Kay Strozzi, Alec B. Francis, Louise Closser Hale, Claud Allister, Julia Swayne Gordon, Arthur Edmund Carewe. Restless English nobleman's thirst for adventure is realized when a clutch of thieves appears at his castle seeking treasure buried by a pirate ancestor. Bizarre pastiche of drawing-room comedy, old-dark-house thriller, and pirate-movie spoof, with a dream sequence that must be seen to be believed.

Captain Blackjack (1951-U.S.-French) 90m. ** D: Julien Duvivier. George Sanders, Herbert Marshall, Patricia Roc, Agnes Moorehead, Marcel Dalio. Tacky tale of derelict ship purchased by suave Sanders to use for drug smuggling, and what happens when all those on board mysteriously die. Moorehead is good as a villainess. Filmed in Spain; released in France at 105m. ▼

Captain Blood (1935) 119m. ***½ D: Michael Curtiz. Errol Flynn, Olivia de Havilland, Lionel Atwill, Basil Rathbone, Ross Alexander, Guy Kibbee, Henry Stephenson, Robert Barrat, Donald Meek, J. Carrol Naish. Flynn's first swashbuckler, based on Rafael Sabatini's novel, scores a broadside. He plays Irish physician Peter Blood who is forced to become a pirate, teaming for short spell with French cutthroat Rathbone, but paying more attention to proper young lady de Havilland. Vivid combination of exciting sea battles, fencing duels, and tempestuous romance provides Flynn with a literally star-making vehicle. First original film score for Erich Wolfgang Korngold. Beware of 99m. reissue version. Also shown in computer-colored version. ▼❶❷

Captain Blood (1960-French) C-95m. ** D: Andre Hunebelle. Jean Marais, Elsa Martinelli, Arnold Foa, Bourvil, Pierrette Bruno. Set in 17th-century France, this juvenile costumer deals with plot to overthrow throne of Louis XIII. Dyaliscope.

Captain Boycott (1947-British) 92m. **½ D: Frank Launder. Stewart Granger, Kathleen Ryan, Cecil Parker, Mervyn Johns, Alastair Sim. Poor Irish farmers band together to combat the abuses of their landlords in early 19th century; interesting but dramatically uneven, with misplaced components of humor and romance. Robert Donat appears briefly as Charles Parnell; Parker has title role. ▼

Captain Carey, U.S.A. (1950) 83m. *** D: Mitchell Leisen. Alan Ladd, Wanda Hendrix, Francis Lederer, Joseph Calleia, Rusty (Russ) Tamblyn. Nicely turned account of WW2 vet Ladd returning to Italy to uncover the informer who cost the lives of villagers, including the woman he loved. Ray Evans–Jay Livingston theme song "Mona Lisa," which plays a key role in the story, won an Oscar. ❶

Captain Caution (1940) 85m. ** D: Richard Wallace. Victor Mature, Louise Platt, Leo Carrillo, Bruce Cabot, Vivienne

Osborne, Robert Barrat. OK action film of spunky Platt commandeering her father's ship into war; no messages, just fast-moving narrative. Look for Alan Ladd as a sailor.▼

Captain China (1949) 97m. ** D: Lewis R. Foster. John Payne, Gail Russell, Jeffrey Lynn, Lon Chaney (Jr.), Edgar Bergen. Often listless sea yarn of Payne, seeking out persons responsible for his losing his ship's command.

Captain Eddie (1945) 107m. **½ D: Lloyd Bacon. Fred MacMurray, Lynn Bari, Charles Bickford, Thomas Mitchell, Lloyd Nolan, James Gleason. Routine aviation film doesn't do justice to exciting life of Eddie Rickenbacker; it's standard stuff.

Captain Fracasse (1929-French) 92m. **½ D: Alberto Cavalcanti, Henry Wulschleger. Pierre Blanchar, Lien Deyers, Charles Boyer. Swashbuckler about a French aristocrat who joins a troupe of traveling players incognito. Based on the oft-filmed novel by Theophile Gautier, this version's silent turn by Boyer as a suavely villainous duke was his last French work before achieving American stardom.◗

Captain From Castile (1947) C-140m. *** D: Henry King. Tyrone Power, Jean Peters, Cesar Romero, Lee J. Cobb, John Sutton, Antonio Moreno, Thomas Gomez, Alan Mowbray, Barbara Lawrence, George Zucco, Roy Roberts, Marc Lawrence, Reed Hadley, Jay Silverheels. Power, driven to avenge the cruel treatment of his family by Spanish Inquisitor (Sutton), eventually serves with Cortez (Romero) during his conquest of Mexico. Color and romance; magnificent location photography by Charles Clarke and Arthur E. Arling; Alfred Newman's majestic score ranks with Hollywood's very best. Peters' film debut.▼◐

Captain Fury (1939) 91m. *** D: Hal Roach. Brian Aherne, Victor McLaglen, Paul Lukas, June Lang, John Carradine, George Zucco, Douglass Dumbrille, Charles Middleton. Australia serves as background in story of illustrious adventurer fighting evil land baron.

Captain Hates the Sea, The (1934) 93m. ** D: Lewis Milestone. Victor McLaglen, John Gilbert, Walter Connolly, Wynne Gibson, Helen Vinson, Alison Skipworth, Leon Errol, Walter Catlett, Akim Tamiroff, Donald Meek, Arthur Treacher, The Three Stooges. Bizarre, seagoing GRAND HOTEL, with accent on comedy; romances and intrigues carry on under bored eye of disgruntled skipper Connolly. Once-in-a-lifetime cast does its best with mediocre script; Gilbert (ironically cast as a heavy drinker) gives a solid performance in his final film.◗

Captain Horatio Hornblower (1951-British) C-117m. *** D: Raoul Walsh. Gregory Peck, Virginia Mayo, Robert Beatty, Denis O'Dea, Christopher Lee,

Stanley Baker, James Robertson Justice. Exciting, well-produced sea epic based on C. S. Forester's British naval hero of the Napoleonic wars. Original British title: CAPTAIN HORATIO HORNBLOWER R.N. ▼◐◗

Captain Is a Lady, The (1940) 63m. ** D: Robert B. Sinclair. Charles Coburn, Beulah Bondi, Virginia Grey, Helen Broderick, Billie Burke, Dan Dailey. Thin little comedy of Coburn pretending to be a woman to accompany wife Bondi to old ladies' home.

Captain January (1936) 75m. **½ D: David Butler. Shirley Temple, Guy Kibbee, Slim Summerville, Buddy Ebsen, June Lang, Sara Haden. Straightforward, sentimental tale of orphaned Shirley, and the new truant officer who tries to separate her from her adoptive father, lighthouse keeper Kibbee. Short and sweet. Shirley and Ebsen sing and dance "At the Codfish Ball."▼◗

Captain John Smith and Pocahontas (1953) C-75m. *½ D: Lew Landers. Anthony Dexter, Jody Lawrance, Alan Hale, Jr., Douglass Dumbrille, Robert Clarke. Title tells all in pedestrian tale set in colonial America.◗

Captain Kidd (1945) 89m. ** D: Rowland V. Lee. Charles Laughton, Randolph Scott, Barbara Britton, Reginald Owen, John Carradine, Gilbert Roland, Sheldon Leonard. Even with Laughton, this is slow-going low-budget stuff.▼◗

Captain Kidd and the Slave Girl (1954) C-83m. ** D: Lew Landers. Anthony Dexter, Eva Gabor, Alan Hale, Jr., James Seay. Modest costumer has Dexter and Gabor in title roles romping the seas to find treasure for their benefactor.◗

Captain Lightfoot (1955) C-91m. *** D: Douglas Sirk. Rock Hudson, Barbara Rush, Jeff Morrow, Finlay Currie, Kathleen Ryan. Fine, flavorful costume adventure about 19th-century Irish rebellion and one of its dashing heroes. Beautifully filmed on location in Ireland in CinemaScope.◗

Captain Newman, M.D. (1963) C-126m. *** D: David Miller. Gregory Peck, Angie Dickinson, Tony Curtis, Eddie Albert, Jane Withers, Bobby Darin, Larry Storch, Bethel Leslie, Robert Duvall. Provocative, well-acted comedy-drama about dedicated Army psychiatrist Peck, battling bureaucracy and the macho military mentality on a stateside air base during WW2. Darin is particularly good as a troubled, ill-fated corporal. Based on Leo Rosten's best-selling novel.▼◗

Captain Pirate (1952) C-85m. **½ D: Ralph Murphy. Louis Hayward, Patricia Medina, John Sutton, Charles Irwin, George Givot, Ted de Corsia. Reformed pirate must return to his renegade ways in order to expose the imposter who is using his name; good-enough programmer based on Sabatini's *Captain Blood Returns.*◗

Captain Scarface (1953) 72m. **½ D:

Paul Guilfoyle. Barton MacLane, Leif Erickson, Virginia Grey, Rudolph Anders, Peter Coe, Don Dillaway, Howard Wendell, Isabel Randolph, Paul Brinegar. Interesting little programmer about a Communist agent who schemes to blow up the Panama Canal. Erickson's world-weary antihero character easily might have been written for Humphrey Bogart.▶

Captain Scarlett (1953) **C-75m.** *½ D: Thomas Carr. Richard Greene, Leonora Amar, Nedrick Young, Edouardo Noriega. Acceptable costumer with Greene properly dashing.▼▶

Captains Courageous (1937) **116m.** **** D: Victor Fleming. Freddie Bartholomew, Spencer Tracy, Lionel Barrymore, Melvyn Douglas, Charley Grapewin, John Carradine, Mickey Rooney, Walter Kingsford. Spoiled rich-boy Bartholomew falls off cruise ship, rescued by Portuguese fisherman Tracy (who won Oscar for role). Boy learns to love seafaring on crusty Barrymore's fishing vessel. Enthusiastic cast in this splendid production of Kipling's story. Scripted by John Lee Mahin, Marc Connelly, and Dale Van Every. Remade as a TV movie in 1977 (with Karl Malden and Ricardo Montalban) and 1996 (with Robert Urich). Also shown in computer-colored version.▼◉▶

Captain Sindbad (1963-U.S.-West German) **C-85m.** **½ D: Byron Haskin. Guy Williams, Heidi Bruhl, Pedro Armendariz, Abraham Sofaer, Bernie Hamilton. Williams is an energetic Sindbad in this elaborate, effects-filled but ponderous fantasy.▼▶

Captain Sirocco SEE: **Pirates of Capri, The**

Captains of the Clouds (1942) **C-113m.** *** D: Michael Curtiz. James Cagney, Dennis Morgan, Brenda Marshall, Alan Hale, George Tobias, Reginald Gardiner. Atmospheric wartime drama charting the shenanigans of cocky bush pilot Cagney, who joins the Canadian air force but refuses to follow regulations.▼▶

Captain's Paradise, The (1953-British) **77m.** *** D: Anthony Kimmins. Alec Guinness, Yvonne De Carlo, Celia Johnson, Bill Fraser. Guinness has field day as carefree skipper who shuttles back and forth between wives in opposite ports. De Carlo and Johnson make a good contrast as the two women. Original British running time: 86m. Later a Broadway musical, *Oh, Captain!*▼◉▶

Captain's Table, The (1960-British) **C-90m.** ** D: Jack Lee. John Gregson, Peggy Cummins, Donald Sinden, Nadia Gray. Satisfactory comedy involving skipper of cargo vessel (Gregson) who is given trial command of luxury liner, and the chaos ensuing trying to keep order among crew and passengers.▼▶

Captain Thunder (1931) **65m.** *½ D: Alan Crosland. Victor Varconi, Fay Wray,

Charles Judels, Robert Elliott, Don Alvarado, Natalie Moorhead, Bert Roach. Dull, technically primitive nonsense from the director of THE JAZZ SINGER chronicling the romantic and criminal exploits of a Robin Hood–like Mexican bandit. Ostensibly performed tongue-in-cheek, but merely obnoxious.

Captain Tugboat Annie (1945) **60m.** ** D: Phil Rosen. Jane Darwell, Edgar Kennedy, Charles Gordon, Mantan Moreland, Pamela Blake, Hardie Albright, H. B. Warner. Annie sails again in low-budget epic which depends entirely on its stars, Darwell and Kennedy, for its flavor.

Captive City, The (1952) **90m.** *** D: Robert Wise. John Forsythe, Joan Camden, Harold J. Kennedy, Marjorie Crosland, Victor Sutherland, Ray Teal, Martin Milner. Small-city newspaper editor Forsythe gradually learns that the Mafia has taken over bookie operations formerly run by corrupt local businessmen. Based-on-fact drama is earnest and intelligent, with fine noir-style photography by Lee Garmes. Sen. Estes Kefauver provides an afterword.▶

Captive Girl (1950) **73m.** ** D: William Berke. Johnny Weissmuller, Buster Crabbe, Anita Lhoest, Rick Vallin, John Dehner. More *Jungle Jim* hokum, this time he's trying to save young Lhoest from a witch doctor, while battling treasure hunter Crabbe. Interesting primarily for pitting two former Tarzans against each other.

Captive Heart, The (1946-British) **108m.** ***½ D: Basil Dearden. Michael Redgrave, Mervyn Johns, Basil Radford, Jack Warner, Jimmy Hanley, Gordon Jackson, Ralph Michael, Rachel Kempson. Compelling examination of British POWs during WW2 and their German captors with controlled, flawless performance by Redgrave and excellent supporting cast. Patrick Kirwan's story was scripted by Angus MacPhail and Guy Morgan. Original British running time: 98m.▼▶

Captive Wild Woman (1943) **61m.** **½ D: Edward Dmytryk. John Carradine, Evelyn Ankers, Milburn Stone, Acquanetta, Martha MacVicar (Vickers), Lloyd Corrigan. Deranged Dr. Carradine surgically transforms a circus ape into a beautiful woman (Acquanetta), who at stressful moments becomes an ape woman (envision a female Wolf Man). Good fun. Stone's animal-training scenes are stock footage of Clyde Beatty from THE BIG CAGE. Sequels: JUNGLE WOMAN, THE JUNGLE CAPTIVE.▼▶

Captive Women (1952) **64m.** *½ D: Stuart Gilmore. Robert Clarke, Margaret Field, Gloria Saunders, Ron Randell, Stuart Randall, William Schallert, Robert Bice. In the year 3000, following nuclear wars, three primitive tribes—some deformed by radiation—vie for supremacy amidst the ruins of Manhattan. Then-novel idea is hampered by tired, routine treatment. Reissue title: 1000 YEARS FROM NOW.

Capture, The (1950) 91m. **½ D: John Sturges. Lew Ayres, Teresa Wright, Victor Jory, Jacqueline White, Jimmy Hunt, Barry Kelley, Duncan Renaldo. Oil field supervisor Ayres begins to ponder whether the payroll robber he shot was really an innocent man. Straightforward, well acted, but slow at times. ▼▶

Captured (1933) 72m. **½ D: Roy Del Ruth. Leslie Howard, Douglas Fairbanks, Jr., Paul Lukas, Margaret Lindsay. Dated drama set in a German POW camp during WW1, where Howard is joined by an old friend (Fairbanks) who—it turns out—had a relationship with his wife. The two leading actors bring some value to this otherwise unmemorable film.

Caravan (1934) 101m. **½ D: Erik Charrell. Loretta Young, Charles Boyer, Jean Parker, Phillips Holmes, Louise Fazenda. Offbeat musical of royal Loretta forced to marry vagabond Boyer; main interest is curiosity in this not altogether successful film.

Carbine Williams (1952) 91m. *** D: Richard Thorpe. James Stewart, Jean Hagen, Wendell Corey, Paul Stewart, James Arness. Sturdy history of the inventor of famed rifle, his problems with the law, and his simple family life. Stewart is most convincing in title role. Also shown in computer-colored version. ▶

Card, The SEE: **Promoter, The**

Cardinal, The (1963) C-175m. **½ D: Otto Preminger. Tom Tryon, John Huston, Romy Schneider, Carol Lynley, Jill Haworth, Raf Vallone, Joseph Meinrad, Burgess Meredith, Ossie Davis, John Saxon, Robert Morse, Dorothy Gish, Tullio Carminati, Maggie McNamara, Bill Hayes, Cecil Kellaway, Murray Hamilton, Patrick O'Neal, Chill Wills, Arthur Hunnicutt. Long, long story of an Irish-American's rise from priesthood to the College of Cardinals. Has some outstanding vignettes by old pros like Meredith, but emerges as an uneven, occasionally worthwhile film. Includes an intermission/ entr'acte. Panavision. ▼▶

Cardinal Richelieu (1935) 83m. **½ D: Rowland V. Lee. George Arliss, Maureen O'Sullivan, Edward Arnold, Cesar Romero. Arliss etches another historical portrayal of France's unscrupulous cardinal who controlled Louis XIII (Arnold). Good cast supports star. ▶

Career (1959) 105m. *** D: Joseph Anthony. Dean Martin, Anthony Franciosa, Shirley MacLaine, Carolyn Jones, Joan Blackman, Robert Middleton, Donna Douglas. Occasionally shrill, generally forceful presentation of an actor's (Franciosa's) tribulations in seeking Broadway fame; Jones is excellent as lonely talent agent. ▼▶

Career Girl (1959) C-61m. *½ D: Harold David. June Wilkinson, Charles Robert

Keane, Lisa Barrie, Joe Sullivan. Sloppy account of Wilkinson going to Hollywood, seeking screen career; sleazy production values. ▶

Carefree (1938) 80m. *** D: Mark Sandrich. Fred Astaire, Ginger Rogers, Ralph Bellamy, Luella Gear, Jack Carson, Franklin Pangborn, Hattie McDaniel. Madcap Rogers is sent to psychiatrist Astaire, and romance naturally blossoms; Fred and Ginger's most comic outing, wacky and offbeat, with good Irving Berlin score including "Change Partners," "I Used to Be Color Blind." ▼▶

Caretakers, The (1963) 97m. **½ D: Hall Bartlett. Robert Stack, Polly Bergen, Diane McBain, Joan Crawford, Janis Paige, Van Williams, Constance Ford, Sharon Hugueny, Herbert Marshall, Barbara Barrie, Ellen Corby, Ana St. Clair, Robert Vaughn, Susan Oliver. Well-intentioned but clichéd account of life in a psychiatric hospital, centering on dedicated, progressive doctor Stack and a patient (Bergen, never better) driven to the brink after the death of her child. Paige also scores as a patient with attitude issues. ▼▶

Cargo to Capetown (1950) 80m. *½ D: Earl McEvoy. Broderick Crawford, John Ireland, Ellen Drew, Edgar Buchanan. Tramp steamer is setting for mild love triangle as Crawford and Ireland vie for Drew.

Caribbean (1952) C-97m. ** D: Edward Ludwig. John Payne, Arlene Dahl, Cedric Hardwicke, Francis L. Sullivan, Woody Strode. 18th-century costume vehicle allows Payne to battle pirates and flirt with Dahl.

Cariboo Trail (1950) C-81m. **½ D: Edwin L. Marin. Randolph Scott, George "Gabby" Hayes, Bill Williams, Karin Booth, Victor Jory, Douglas Kennedy, Jim Davis, Dale Robertson, Mary Stuart, Lee Tung Foo. Sturdy Scott vehicle about a cattleman who brings his herd to the Canadian wilderness, where he takes on corrupt Jory. Filmed in Colorado and British Columbia. ▼▶

Carlton-Browne of the F.O. SEE: **Man in a Cocked Hat**

Carmen (1915) 59m. **½ D: Cecil B. DeMille. Geraldine Farrar, Wallace Reid, Pedro de Cordoba, Horace B. Carpenter, William Elmer, Jeanie Macpherson. Opera diva Farrar, in her screen debut, offers a florid performance as a conniving gypsy seductress, linked with a band of smugglers, who distracts supposedly incorruptible military officer Reid. Farrar sang the role onstage; however, the film is based on Prosper Mérimée's 1845 novella rather than the Bizet opera. One of the earliest versions of an oft-told tale. ▼▶

Carmen Jones (1954) C-105m. ***½ D: Otto Preminger. Dorothy Dandridge, Harry Belafonte, Pearl Bailey, Roy Glenn, Diahann Carroll, Brock Peters. Powerful melodrama adapted from Bizet's opera by Oscar Hammerstein II, with exciting music and equally exciting Dandridge as the ultimate femme fatale. Stars' singing voices are all dubbed—Dandridge's by opera star Marilyn Horne. Film debuts of Carroll and Peters. Cinema-Scope. ▼●▶

Carnegie Hall (1947) 134m. **½ D: Edgar G. Ulmer. Marsha Hunt, William Prince, Frank McHugh, Martha O'Driscoll. Lame story about a pushy mother and her pianist son links magnificent concert performances by the cream of the classical music world: Artur Rubinstein, Leopold Stokowski, Jascha Heifetz, Rise Stevens, Lily Pons, Ezio Pinza, Jan Peerce, Gregor Piatigorsky, Bruno Walter and The New York Philharmonic. Some mediocre pop tunes are shoehorned into the proceedings, along with Vaughn Monroe and Harry James. ▼▶

Carnet de Bal SEE: Un Carnet de Bal

Car 99 (1935) 68m. ** D: Charles Barton. Fred MacMurray, Sir Guy Standing, Ann Sheridan, William Frawley, Dean Jagger, Marina Schubert, Frank Craven. Michigan rookie state trooper MacMurray is suspended when he lets a gang of bank robbers get away but proves his worth when they kidnap his girl. Fair crime filler gave MacMurray one of his first big roles, but it's stolen by Frawley as comical sergeant and Standing as criminal mastermind posing as a kindly old professor.

Carnival Boat (1932) 62m. **½ D: Albert Rogell. William Boyd, Ginger Rogers, Hobart Bosworth, Fred Kohler, Edgar Kennedy. Trifling but enjoyable story of North Woods logger Bosworth, who expects his son to follow in his footsteps, but Boyd's attention is divided between his job and Rogers, the cute entertainer on the carnival boat. Benefits from location shooting and some hair-raising action scenes: one on a runaway locomotive, the other involving planting TNT in the middle of a logjam. ▼

Carnival in Costa Rica (1947) C-95m. ** D: Gregory Ratoff. Dick Haymes, Vera-Ellen, Cesar Romero, Celeste Holm, Anne Revere, J. Carrol Naish. Despite fair cast, boring musical of trip to Costa Rica and the shenanigans of newlyweds and their quarreling parents. ▶

Carnival in Flanders (1935-French) 115m. *** D: Jacques Feyder. Françoise Rosay, Jean Murat, Louis Jouvet, André Alerme, Bernard Lancret. Rollicking farce about Spanish invasion of a small Flemish town in the 17th century. While all the men find excuses to leave, the women stay behind and conquer the warriors with romance and revelry. Amusing costume comedy with outstanding photography by Harry Stradling and striking art direction. American version runs 95m. Original title: LA KERMESSE HEROIQUE. ▼

Carnival of Souls (1962) 83m. **½ D: Herk Harvey. Candace Hilligoss, Sid-ney Berger, Frances Feist, Herk Harvey, Stan Levitt, Art Ellison. Eerie little film of "phantom figure" pursuing Hilligoss after she has seemingly drowned. Imaginative low-budget effort. Filmed mostly in Lawrence, Kansas. Has developed a strong cult reputation in recent years. Original running time: 91m. Computer-colored version also available. Remade in 1998 and 2008 (as YELLA). ▼●▶

Carnival Rock (1957) 75m. ** D: Roger Corman. Susan Cabot, Dick Miller, Brian Hutton, The Platters, David Houston, David J. Stewart. Stewart, owner of a dilapidated nightclub, loves singer Cabot, who in turn loves gambler Hutton. Forgettable melodrama with The Platters, Houston, and others in musical cameos. ▼

Carnival Story (1954) C-95m. ** D: Kurt Neumann. Anne Baxter, Steve Cochran, Lyle Bettger, George Nader, Jay C. Flippen. Hardened Baxter is involved with sleazy Cochran. "Nice guy" high diver Bettger takes her on as a protégée, and there are complications. When this romantic melodrama is not trashy, it's sluggish. Set in Germany (and filmed in Munich), and not unlike E. A. Dupont's classic, VARIETY. A German version was also filmed, with Eva Bartok, Bernhard Wicki, and Curt Jurgens. ▼▶

Carolina Blues (1944) 81m. *½ D: Leigh Jason. Kay Kyser and His Band, Ann Miller, Victor Moore, Jeff Donnell, Howard Freeman, Georgia Carroll, Ish Kabibble, Harry Babbitt, Sully Mason, Harold Nicholas. Excruciating musical about Kyser raising money for war bonds while roguish Moore and daughter Miller try to land her a job singing with his band. Redeemed briefly by a great Harlem-inspired production number, "Mr. Beebe," performed by Nicholas with the Four Step Brothers and, unbilled, dancer Marie Bryant and singer June Richmond. ▶

Carolina Cannonball (1955) 74m. *½ D: Charles Lamont. Judy Canova, Andy Clyde, Jack Kruschen, Ross Elliott. Hicksville hokum with Canova involved with enemy agents and a missile that lands in her backyard.

Carolina Moon (1940) 65m. ** D: Frank McDonald. Gene Autry, Smiley Burnette, June Storey, Mary Lee, Eddy Waller, Hardie Albright. Gene gets involved with horse racing in the Deep South. Ambles along, but Autry seems a bit far away from the range. Gene sings the title tune. ▶

Carousel (1956) C-128m. ***½ D: Henry King. Gordon MacRae, Shirley Jones, Cameron Mitchell, Barbara Ruick, Claramae Turner, Robert Rounseville, Gene Lockhart. Excellent filmization of Rodgers & Hammerstein's memorable adaptation of Ferenc Molnár's Liliom, with MacRae as rowdy carousel barker Billy Bigelow, who tries to change for the better when he falls in love with Jones. Excitement of wide-screen location filming will be minimized on TV, but moving characters, timeless songs remain. Script by Phoebe and Henry Ephron. Filmed before as LILIOM in 1930 and 1934. CinemaScope 55.▼O◗

Carpetbaggers, The (1964) C-150m. **½ D: Edward Dmytryk. George Peppard, Carroll Baker, Alan Ladd, Bob Cummings, Martha Hyer, Elizabeth Ashley, Lew Ayres, Martin Balsam, Ralph Taeger, Archie Moore, Leif Erickson, Tom Tully, Audrey Totter. Blowsy claptrap based on Harold Robbins novel of millionaire plane manufacturer (Peppard) dabbling in movies and lovemaking à la Howard Hughes. Set in 1920s–30s; sexploitation values are tame. Ladd's last film; followed by prequel, NEVADA SMITH. Panavision.▼O◗

Carrie (1952) 118m. **½ D: William Wyler. Jennifer Jones, Laurence Olivier, Miriam Hopkins, Eddie Albert, Mary Murphy, William Reynolds. Jones passively plays the title role in this uneven turn-of-the-20th-century soaper of poor farm girl who comes to Chicago, eventually links up with unhappily married restaurant manager Olivier (who is excellent). David Raksin's score is a plus. Based on Theodore Dreiser's *Sister Carrie*. DVD includes restored "flop house" scene, which runs almost 3m.▼O◗

Carrington, V. C. SEE: **Court Martial**
Carry On Admiral SEE: **Ship Was Loaded, The**
Carry On Cleo (1964-British) C-92m. **½ D: Gerald Thomas. Amanda Barrie, Sidney James, Kenneth Williams, Joan Sims, Kenneth Connor, Charles Hawtrey. Diverting reworking of ancient history to serve as amusing satire on CLEOPATRA epic, sufficiently laced with hijinks by perennial misfits. Aka CALIGULA'S FUNNIEST HOME VIDEOS.▼◗

Carry On Nurse (1959-British) 90m. **½ D: Gerald Thomas. Kenneth Connor, Shirley Eaton, Charles Hawtrey, Hattie Jacques, Terence Longden, Leslie Phillips, Joan Sims, Kenneth Williams, Wilfrid Hyde-White, Joan Hickson, Jill Ireland, Michael Medwin. Occasionally funny but too often silly farce detailing the various hijinks in a hospital ward. Typical entry in the series is crammed with lowbrow humor.▼◗

Carry On Sergeant (1958-British) 88m. ** D: Gerald Thomas. William Hartnell, Bob Monkhouse, Shirley Eaton, Eric Barker, Dora Bryan, Bill Owen, Kenneth Connor. This time around prankish misfits are the bane of Army officer's existence, who swears he'll make these recruits spiffy soldiers or bust.◗

Carry On Spying (1964-British) 88m. **½ D: Gerald Thomas. Kenneth Williams, Barbara Windsor, Bernard Cribbins, Charles Hawtrey, Eric Barker, Victor Maddern. Acceptable James Bond spoof with daffy novice spy-catchers on the hunt for enemy agents who stole secret formula.◗

Carson City (1952) C-87m. ** D: Andre De Toth. Randolph Scott, Lucille Norman, Raymond Massey, Don Beddoe, Richard Webb, James Millican, Larry Keating, George Cleveland. Opposing forces clash when construction engineer Scott commences building a railroad through Nevada in the 1870s. OK of its type.◗

Carson City Kid, The (1940) 57m. *** D: Joseph Kane. Roy Rogers, George "Gabby" Hayes, Bob Steele, Noah Beery, Jr., Pauline Moore, Francis McDonald, Hal Taliaferro, Arthur Loft. Marshall Hayes sets out to capture the title outlaw (Rogers), who seeks to avenge his brother's death at the hands of saloon owner Steele. One of Roy's best from his late '30s–early '40s "historical" period, with Steele a standout. Remade as IN OLD SACRAMENTO (1946), with Bill Elliott.▼◗

Carthage in Flames (1959-Italian) C-96m. ** D: Carmine Gallone. José Suárez, Pierre Brasseur, Anne Heywood, Illaria Occhini, Daniel Gélin, Mario Girotti (Terence Hill). Unremarkable mixture of love and intrigue set against backdrop of Rome-Carthage war of 2nd century B.C.; spirited action scenes. Super Technirama 70.▼

Cartouche (1964-French-Italian) C-115m. ***½ D: Philippe De Broca. Jean-Paul Belmondo, Claudia Cardinale, Odile Versois, Jess Hahn, Jean Rochefort, Philippe Lemaire, Marcel Dalio, Noel Roquevert. Colorful, exciting exploits of 18th-century French Robin Hood who takes over a Parisian crime syndicate. Belmondo is dashing as Cartouche and Cardinale is ravishing as Venus, his gypsy-mistress, in this rousing action-comedy. Dyaliscope.▼◗

Carve Her Name With Pride (1958-British) 119m. *** D: Lewis Gilbert. Virginia McKenna, Paul Scofield, Jack Warner, Maurice Ronet, Bill Owen, Denise Grey, Billie Whitelaw, Michael Caine. McKenna, widowed during WW2, becomes a courageous British secret agent. Solid and inspiring; based on a true story.▼◗

Casablanca (1942) 102m. **** D: Michael Curtiz. Humphrey Bogart, Ingrid Bergman, Paul Henreid, Claude Rains, Conrad Veidt, Peter Lorre, Sydney Greenstreet, Dooley Wilson, Marcel Dalio, S. Z. Sakall, Joy Page, Helmut Dantine, Curt Bois. Everything is right in this WW2 classic of wartorn Morocco with elusive nightclub owner Rick (Bogart) finding old flame (Bergman) and her husband, underground leader Henreid, among skeletons in his closet. Rains is marvelous as dapper police chief, and nobody sings "As Time Goes By" like Dooley Wilson. Three Oscars include Picture, Director, and Screenplay (Julius & Philip

Epstein and Howard Koch). Our candidate for the best Hollywood movie of all time. Spawned short-lived TV series in the 1950s and the 1980s. Also shown in computer-colored version.▼O〉

Casanova Brown (1944) **94m.** **½ D: Sam Wood. Gary Cooper, Teresa Wright, Frank Morgan, Anita Louise, Isobel Elsom. Cooper has divorced Wright, but now she's pregnant; entertaining little comedy with stars outshining material. Filmed in 1930 and 1939 as LITTLE ACCIDENT.▼〉

Casanova in Burlesque (1944) **74m.** **½ D: Leslie Goodwins. Joe E. Brown, June Havoc, Dale Evans, Lucien Littlefield, Marjorie Gateson, Ian Keith, Sugar Geise. Shakespeare professor leads a double life as a burlesque clown in this slight but amusing musical comedy. Evans sings jive numbers like "Mess Me Up" and "Willie the Shake," while Havoc performs a very funny "Who Took Me Home Last Night?"

Casanova's Big Night (1954) **C-86m.** *** D: Norman Z. McLeod. Bob Hope, Joan Fontaine, Audrey Dalton, Basil Rathbone, Raymond Burr. Lavish costumed fun with Bob masquerading as Casanova (Vincent Price in an unbilled cameo role) in Venice and wooing lovely Dalton.▼O〉

Casanova '70 (1965-French-Italian) **C-113m.** **½ D: Mario Monicelli. Marcello Mastroianni, Virna Lisi, Michele Mercier, Marisa Mell, Marco Ferreri, Enrico Maria Salerno. Dashing Major Mastroianni is only interested in seducing women when there is an element of danger involved. Modest, though amusing.▼〉

Casa Ricordi SEE: **House of Ricordi**

Casbah (1948) **94m.** *** D: John Berry. Tony Martin, Yvonne De Carlo, Peter Lorre, Marta Toren, Hugo Haas, Thomas Gomez, Douglas Dick, Katherine Dunham, Herbert Rudley, Virginia Gregg. If you can accept singer Martin as slippery thief Pépé Le Moko (he's actually quite good) you'll enjoy this musical remake of ALGIERS. It's stylishly directed and designed, and features Lorre in one of his best performances as the crafty inspector determined to nail Le Moko. Fine score by Harold Arlen and Leo Robin includes "For Every Man There's a Woman" and "Hooray for Love." Look fast and you'll spot Eartha Kitt, then one of the Katherine Dunham dance troupe. Martin also produced the film.▼

Case Against Brooklyn, The (1958) **82m.** *½ D: Paul Wendkos. Darren McGavin, Maggie Hayes, Warren Stevens, Peggy McCay. Unexciting little exposé yarn involves fledgling cop McGavin combating gambling syndicate in title borough.〉

Case Against Mrs. Ames, The (1936) **85m.** **½ D: William Seiter. Madeleine Carroll, George Brent, Arthur Treacher, Alan Baxter, Beulah Bondi. D.A. Brent finds himself falling in love with beautiful Carroll, suspected of murdering her husband.

Case of Dr. Laurent, The (1958-French) **91m.** ** D: Jean-Paul le Chanois. Jean Gabin, Nicole Courcel, Sylvia Monfort, Michel Barbey. Film was exploited theatrically for its frank birth sequence, only small logical sequence in recounting life of country doctor Gabin who advocates natural childbirth.▼

Case of Mrs. Loring, The SEE: **Question of Adultery, A**

Case of the Black Cat, The (1936) **65m.** **½ D: William McGann. Ricardo Cortez, June Travis, Jane Bryan, Gordon (William) Elliott, Craig Reynolds, Harry Davenport. A trio of murders, a treasure hunt, and a shrieking feline are the ingredients in this enjoyable *Perry Mason* mystery, with Cortez quite adequate in his only crack at the role. One mystery unsolved by Perry: who gave this title to a movie about a *white* cat? 〉

Case of the Curious Bride, The (1935) **80m.** ** D: Michael Curtiz. Warren William, Margaret Lindsay, Donald Woods, Claire Dodd, Allen Jenkins, Wini Shaw. Shrill *Perry Mason* film takes offhanded approach to murder mystery with large doses of humor; Perry (William) is more interested in gourmet food than he is in the case! Errol Flynn has small role as the victim in his first Hollywood film. 〉

Case of the Howling Dog, The (1934) **75m.** ** D: Alan Crosland. Warren William, Mary Astor, Helen Trenholme, Allen Jenkins, Grant Mitchell, Dorothy Tree. First of the *Perry Mason* series is probably the least interesting, centering on the case of feuding neighbors who both claim they're married to the same woman.〉

Case of the Lucky Legs, The (1935) **76m.** **½ D: Archie Mayo. Warren William, Genevieve Tobin, Patricia Ellis, Lyle Talbot, Allen Jenkins, Barton MacLane. Stylish *Perry Mason* whodunit centering on the murder of a crooked beauty contest promoter. The movie is as much a comedy as a mystery, maybe more so, especially with Perry struggling to stay on an anti-alcoholic diet.〉

Case of the Red Monkey (1955-British) **73m.** ** D: Ken Hughes. Richard Conte, Rona Anderson, Colin Gordon, Russell Napier. Acceptable police-on-the-case fare, tracking down murderers of atomic scientists. Original British title: LITTLE RED MONKEY.

Case of the Stuttering Bishop, The (1937) **70m.** ** D: William Clemens. Donald Woods, Ann Dvorak, Anne Nagel, Linda Perry, Craig Reynolds. Woods is a bland Perry Mason in this last series entry, about the murder of an oil millionaire whose granddaughter—now suddenly his heir—may be an imposter.〉

Case of the Velvet Claws, The (1936) **60m.** ** D: William Clemens. Warren William, Claire Dodd, Winifred Shaw, Gordon (William) Elliott, Joseph King. Perry Mason (William) finally weds Della Street (Dodd), but the honeymoon is interrupted by the case of a murdered scandal sheet publisher. Brisk entry marked William's final appearance in the role. ◗

Cash (1933-British) **73m.** *½ D: Zoltan Korda. Robert Donat, Wendy Barrie, Edmund Gwenn, Clifford Heatherley, Morris Harvey. Dull, disappointing comedy about ex-rich boy Donat, now working for a living, who becomes involved with pretty Barrie and scheming father Gwenn. The U.S. title was FOR LOVE OR MONEY; aka IF I WERE RICH. ▼◗

Cash McCall (1959) **C-102m.** **½ D: Joseph Pevney. James Garner, Natalie Wood, Nina Foch, Dean Jagger, E.G. Marshall, Henry Jones, Otto Kruger, Roland Winters. Garner is just right as business tycoon who adopts new set of values as he romances daughter (Wood) of failing businessman Jagger. Superficial film from Cameron Hawley novel. ▼◗

Cash on Delivery (1956-British) **82m.** ** D: Muriel Box. Shelley Winters, John Gregson, Peggy Cummins, Wilfrid Hyde-White. Story with a twist suffers from sloppy execution. Winters seeks to earn inheritance by preventing ex-husband's wife from having a child. Original title: TO DOROTHY A SON.

Casino Murder Case (1935) **85m.** ** D: Edwin L. Marin. Paul Lukas, Alison Skipworth, Donald Cook, Rosalind Russell, Arthur Byron, Ted Healy, Eric Blore, Leo G. Carroll, William Demarest. Polished but perfunctory *Philo Vance* mystery about a series of murders at the mansion of eccentric old lady Skipworth, with Healy and Blore around for comic relief. Stolid, thickly accented Lukas is not very effective as Vance. ◗

Casque d'Or (1952-French) **98m.** **** D: Jacques Becker. Simone Signoret, Serge Reggiani, Claude Dauphin, Raymond Bussières, William Sabatier, Gaston Modot. Signoret is luminous as a seductive underworld beauty who inspires men to die for her love in this tale of rivalry and revenge among Parisian "apache" gangsters in 1898. Much more than just a period crime yarn, this is one of the most physically beautiful and sensuous films ever made. Becker's poetic direction and Robert Le Febvre's shimmering photography are sheer perfection. Aka GOLDEN MARIE and GOLDEN HELMET. ◗

Cassidy of Bar 20 (1938) **58m.** **½ D: Lesley Selander. William Boyd, Russell Hayden, Frank Darien, Nora Lane, Robert Fiske, John Elliott, Gertrude Hoffman. Terrorized by cattle rustlers, former sweetheart sends for Hopalong Cassidy to clean up her town, run by high-handed Fiske. Sequel to HOPALONG RIDES AGAIN, based on 1928 novel *Me an' Shorty* by series creator Clarence E. Mulford. Leisurely paced

Western melodrama is light on action but still entertaining. Alleged comedy relief by sidekick Darien (as "Pappy") proves George Hayes was irreplaceable. ▼◗

Cass Timberlane (1947) **119m.** **½ D: George Sidney. Spencer Tracy, Lana Turner, Zachary Scott, Tom Drake, Mary Astor, Albert Dekker, Margaret Lindsay, John Litel, Mona Barrie, Josephine Hutchinson, Rose Hobart, Selena Royle, Cameron Mitchell. Ordinary adaptation of Sinclair Lewis novel of an upright, upper-crust Minnesota judge (Tracy) whose friends are either corrupt or elitist and his marriage to bright, working-class Turner (in one of her best performances). Walter Pidgeon appears as himself in a cocktail party scene. ▼◗

Cast a Dark Shadow (1955-British) **84m.** *** D: Lewis Gilbert. Dirk Bogarde, Margaret Lockwood, Kathleen Harrison, Kay Walsh, Robert Flemyng, Mona Washbourne. Tense suspenser with Bogarde in fine form as a psychotic Bluebeard who murders rich, aging mate Washbourne. Lockwood and Walsh won't be such easy prey, however. ▼

Cast a Long Shadow (1959) **82m.** *½ D: Thomas Carr. Audie Murphy, Terry Moore, John Dehner, James Best, Rita Lynn, Denver Pyle, Ann Doran. Murphy, troubled by shady past, is reformed by being given a ranch and building a new future; plodding oater. ◗

Castle in the Desert (1942) **62m.** *** D: Harry Lachman. Sidney Toler, Arleen Whelan, Richard Derr, Douglass Dumbrille, Henry Daniell, Edmund MacDonald, Victor Sen Yung, Ethel Griffies. Twentieth Century-Fox's last *Charlie Chan* entry is a first-rate mystery set in a spooky mansion in the Mojave, where mysterious deaths are occurring. ▼◗

Castle of Terror, The (1964-Italian-French) **85m.** ** D: Anthony Dawson (Antonio Margheriti). Barbara Steele, George Riviere, Margarete Robsahm, Henry Kruger, Montgomery Glenn, Sylvia Sorente. On a wager, poet spends the night in haunted castle. Atmospheric chiller. Remade by the same director as WEB OF THE SPIDER. Aka CASTLE OF BLOOD. ▼◗

Castle of the Living Dead (1963-Italian-French) **90m.** ** D: Herbert Wise (Luciano Ricci). Christopher Lee, Gala Germani, Philippe Leroy, Jacques Stanislawski, Donald Sutherland. Lee is suitably cast as sinister Count Drago, who mummifies visitors to his gothic castle. Unexceptional horror fare, notable mainly as Sutherland's film debut in two roles—one an old lady. ▼◗

Castle on the Hudson (1940) **77m.** *** D: Anatole Litvak. John Garfield, Pat O'Brien, Ann Sheridan, Burgess Meredith, Jerome Cowan, Henry O'Neill, Guinn "Big Boy" Williams, John Litel. Faithful but familiar remake of 20,000 YEARS IN SING SING, with tough, stubborn hood Garfield going up against dedicated, reform-minded warden O'Brien.◗

Castles in the Sky SEE: **Yidl Mitn Fidl**

Cat and the Canary, The (1927) **74m.** ******* D: Paul Leni. Laura LaPlante, Tully Marshall, Flora Finch, Creighton Hale, Gertrude Astor, Lucien Littlefield. Delightful silent classic, the forerunner of all "old dark house" mysteries, with nice touch of humor throughout as heiress LaPlante and nervous group spend night in haunted house. Remade several times.▼◗

Cat and the Canary, The (1939) **74m.** ******* D: Elliott Nugent. Bob Hope, Paulette Goddard, Gale Sondergaard, John Beal, Douglass Montgomery, Nydia Westman, Elizabeth Patterson, George Zucco. Entertaining remake of the venerable "old dark house" chiller, spiced with Hope's brand of humor. This film cemented his movie stardom and led to the even more successful scare comedy THE GHOST BREAKERS. Remade again in 1978.◗

Cat and the Fiddle, The (1934) **90m.** ******* D: William K. Howard. Jeanette MacDonald, Ramon Novarro, Frank Morgan, Charles Butterworth, Jean Hersholt. Delightful Jerome Kern–Otto Harbach operetta, filled with sly comedy and clever ideas. Novarro is a struggling composer who forces his attentions on MacDonald; Morgan is "benefactor" who comes between them. Songs include "The Night Was Made for Love," "She Didn't Say Yes." Final sequence is in color.▼◗

Cat Ballou (1965) **C-96m.** *****½** D: Elliot Silverstein. Jane Fonda, Lee Marvin, Michael Callan, Dwayne Hickman, Tom Nardini, John Marley, Reginald Denny, Jay C. Flippen, Arthur Hunnicutt, Bruce Cabot. Funny Western comedy, with Fonda as Cat Ballou, notorious school-teacher-turned-outlaw. Marvin copped an Oscar for his dual role as a drunken gunman and his twin, a desperado with an artificial nose. Nat King Cole and Stubby Kaye appear as strolling minstrels. Roy Chanslor's novel was adapted by Walter Newman and Frank R. Pierson.▼◗

Catch Us If You Can SEE: **Having a Wild Weekend**

Cat Creeps, The (1946) **58m.** ***½** D: Erle C. Kenton. Noah Beery, Jr., Lois Collier, Paul Kelly, Fred Brady, Douglass Dumbrille, Rose Hobart. Shabby B mystery with reporter and various greedy types searching for fortune in old lady's spooky mansion.

Catered Affair, The (1956) **93m.** ******* D: Richard Brooks. Bette Davis, Ernest Borgnine, Debbie Reynolds, Barry Fitzgerald, Rod Taylor. Davis sheds all glamour as Bronx taxi driver's wife wanting to give daughter ritzy wedding. Gore Vidal's script based on Paddy Chayefsky TV play. Also shown in computer-colored version. Later a Broadway musical. ▼◗

Cat Girl (1957-British) **69m.** ***½** D: Alfred Shaughnessy. Barbara Shelley, Robert Ayres, Kay Callard, Paddy Webster. A family curse is passed down to Shelley, who begins to imagine that she's part cat, in this no-chills thriller that shamelessly rips off CAT PEOPLE. Silly, low-grade stuff.▼

Catherine the Great (1934-British) **92m.** ****½** D: Paul Czinner. Douglas Fairbanks, Jr., Elisabeth Bergner, Flora Robson, Joan Gardner, Gerald Du Maurier. Lavish historical drama of Russian czarina whose life is spoiled by rigidly planned marriage. Slow-moving but interesting. Also known as THE RISE OF CATHERINE THE GREAT.▼◗

Catman of Paris, The (1946) **65m.** ***½** D: Lesley Selander. Carl Esmond, Lenore Aubert, Adele Mara, Douglass Dumbrille, Gerald Mohr, Fritz Feld, Francis Pierlot, John Dehner, Anthony Caruso. A werewolf-like catman stalks the streets of fin de siècle Paris and suspicion falls on famous writer Esmond, who's subject to blackouts. Talky, routine horror from Republic. After transformation, the catman is played by an unbilled Robert J. Wilke.

Cat on a Hot Tin Roof (1958) **C-108m.** *****½** D: Richard Brooks. Elizabeth Taylor, Paul Newman, Burl Ives, Jack Carson, Judith Anderson, Madeleine Sherwood, Larry Gates. Southern patriarch Ives learns he is dying; his greedy family, except for son Newman, falls all over itself sucking up to him. Tennessee Williams' classic study of "mendacity" comes to the screen somewhat laundered but still packing a wallop; entire cast is sensational. Adaptation by Brooks and James Poe. Remade for TV in 1976 and 1984.▼◗

Cat People (1942) **73m.** ******* D: Jacques Tourneur. Simone Simon, Kent Smith, Tom Conway, Jack Holt, Jane Randolph. Storyline and plot elements don't hold up, but moments of shock and terror are undiminished in the first of producer Val Lewton's famous horror films. Smith falls in love with strange, shy woman (Simon) who fears ancient curse of the panther inside her. Followed by THE CURSE OF THE CAT PEOPLE. Remade in 1982.▼◗

Cat's-Paw, The (1934) **98m.** ****½** D: Sam Taylor. Harold Lloyd, Una Merkel, George Barbier, Alan Dinehart, Grace Bradley, Nat Pendleton. Harold is a missionary's son, raised in China; he comes to U.S. a babe in the woods, is duped into running for mayor in big city by corrupt politicos who regard him as perfect patsy. Odd Capraesque comedy ends with strange denouement where Lloyd takes law into his own hands. A real curio.◗

Cattle Drive (1951) **C-77m.** ****½** D: Kurt Neumann. Joel McCrea, Dean Stockwell, Leon Ames, Chill Wills, Henry Brandon, Howard Petrie, Bob Steele. What lessons will be learned by bratty Stockwell, the neglected son of a railroad magnate, while in the company of veteran cowhand McCrea? Predictable but agreeable Western. ◗

Cattle Empire (1958) **C-83m.** ** D: Charles Marquis Warren. Joel McCrea, Gloria Talbott, Don Haggerty, Phyllis Coates. McCrea agrees to lead cattle drive, planning revenge on cattle owners who sent him to jail; OK Western. CinemaScope.

Cattle King (1963) **C-88m.** ** D: Tay Garnett. Robert Taylor, Joan Caulfield, Robert Loggia, Robert Middleton, Larry Gates, Malcolm Atterbury. Control of grazing land subject of standard Western confrontation saga, Taylor and Middleton squaring off in forgettable drama. Metroscope. ◗

Cattle Queen of Montana (1954) **C-88m.** **½ D: Allan Dwan. Barbara Stanwyck, Ronald Reagan, Gene Evans, Lance Fuller, Anthony Caruso, Jack Elam. Stanwyck battles to protect her livestock and property from plundering by Indians—and a ruthless villain (Evans). Reagan plays second fiddle to feisty Stanwyck here—but they're both done in by mediocre script. Beautiful scenery (filmed in Glacier National Park, Montana) helps. ▼◗

Cattle Town (1952) **71m.** ** D: Noel Smith. Dennis Morgan, Philip Carey, Amanda Blake, Rita Moreno, Sheb Wooley, Merv Griffin. Both Warner Bros. and Morgan were at low points when this sad echo of a slick Western was churned out. ◗

Cat-Women of the Moon (1954) **64m.** *½ D: Arthur Hilton. Sonny Tufts, Victor Jory, Marie Windsor, Bill Phipps, Douglas Fowley, Susan Morrow. All-star cast in tacky sci-fi entry about a moon expedition that discovers female civilization and its underground empire. Aka ROCKET TO THE MOON. Remade as MISSILE TO THE MOON. 3-D. ▼◗

Caught (1949) **88m.** *** D: Max Opuls (Ophuls). James Mason, Barbara Bel Geddes, Robert Ryan, Frank Ferguson, Curt Bois, Natalie Schafer. Compelling tale of naïve Bel Geddes, from a modest background, who dreams of wedding a wealthy man. She does just that, but life with powerful, sadistic Ryan (a character reportedly based on Howard Hughes) is not what she envisioned. ▼◗

Caught in the Draft (1941) **82m.** *** D: David Butler. Bob Hope, Dorothy Lamour, Lynne Overman, Eddie Bracken. The last thing movie star Hope wants is to get drafted, but he accidentally enlists himself. Very funny service comedy. ▼◗

Caught Plastered (1931) **69m.** **½ D: William Seiter. Bert Wheeler, Robert Woolsey, Dorothy Lee, Lucy Beaumont, Jason Robards (Sr.), DeWitt Jennings, Charles Middleton. Amusing farce loaded with puns, wisecracks, and vaudeville gags. W&W play itinerant song-and-dance men who help save a sweet old lady's drugstore from foreclosure by us-

ing it to stage live radio broadcasts, then try to keep it from falling into the hands of a bootlegging gang. ◗

Caught Short (1930) **75m.** **½ D: Charles F. Riesner. Marie Dressler, Polly Moran, Anita Page, Charles Morton, Thomas Conlin, Greta Mann, T. Roy Barnes. Bickering boardinghouse landladies try to one-up each other as they invest in the stock market, as Marie's daughter and Polly's son fall in love. Typical Dressler-Moran comedy is pleasant enough but has no big slapstick sequences and lacks the punch of such other films as PROSPERITY. Ostensibly based on Eddie Cantor's best-selling book about the stock-market crash.

Cause for Alarm! (1951) **74m.** *** D: Tay Garnett. Loretta Young, Barry Sullivan, Bruce Cowling, Margalo Gillmore, Carl Switzer, Richard Anderson. Simple, effective thriller with Young registering as the panic-stricken wife of psychotic Sullivan. Tension builds, and there's a neat plot twist. ▼◗

Cavalcade (1933) **110m.** **** D: Frank Lloyd. Diana Wynyard, Clive Brook, Herbert Mundin, Ursula Jeans, Margaret Lindsay, Beryl Mercer, Una O'Connor, Billy Bevan, Frank Lawton. Lavish Hollywood adaptation of Noel Coward's London stage success (which may remind many of TV's *Upstairs, Downstairs*) chronicling two English families from eve of the 20th century to early 1930s. Nostalgic, richly atmospheric, but also sharply critical of war and the aftershocks that brought an end to a wonderful way of life. Oscar winner for Best Picture, Best Director, and "Interior Decoration" (it *is* handsome). ▼◗

Cavalry Charge SEE: **Last Outpost, The** (1951)

Cavalry Scout (1951) **C-78m.** ** D: Lesley Selander. Rod Cameron, Audrey Long, Jim Davis, James Millican, James Arness. Routine Western of scout Cameron tracking down stolen army goods and romancing Long. ▼◗

Cave of Outlaws (1951) **C-75m.** ** D: William Castle. Macdonald Carey, Alexis Smith, Edgar Buchanan, Victor Jory. Search for stolen gold leads ex-con, lawman, miner, et al. to title situation; Smith is wasted.

Cease Fire (1953) **75m.** ** D: Owen Crump. Members of an American infantry platoon in Korea embark on a dangerous patrol as delicate peace negotiations are under way in Panmunjon. Documentary produced by Hal Wallis with the U.S. Dept. of Defense is interesting for its glimpses of actual GIs on real battlefield locations, but marred by obvious reenactments and staged situations. Originally shown in 3-D.

Ceiling Zero (1936) **95m.** *** D: Howard Hawks. James Cagney, Pat O'Brien, June Travis, Stuart Erwin, Barton MacLane, Isabel Jewell. Irresponsible mail flier Cagney causes no end of grief for old pal (and boss) O'Brien, especially when he sets his sights on young pilot Travis. Typically machine-gun–paced Hawks drama belies its stage origins; one of the best Cagney-O'Brien vehicles. Based on the play by Frank "Spig" Wead; remade as INTERNATIONAL SQUADRON.▼

Cell 2455 Death Row (1955) 77m. ** D: Fred F. Sears. William Campbell, Kathryn Grant (Crosby), Vince Edwards, Marian Carr. Exploitative retracing of life of notorious criminal, based on real-life Caryl Chessman and his demand, while in prison, for retrials. Alan Alda later played Chessman in KILL ME WHILE YOU CAN.❿

Centennial Summer (1946) C-102m. **½ D: Otto Preminger. Jeanne Crain, Cornel Wilde, Linda Darnell, William Eythe, Walter Brennan, Constance Bennett, Dorothy Gish. Leisurely, plush musical of Philadelphia Exposition of 1876, with sisters Crain and Darnell both after handsome Wilde; nice Jerome Kern score helps.

Central Airport (1933) 75m. **½ D: William A. Wellman. Richard Barthelmess, Sally Eilers, Tom Brown, Grant Mitchell, Willard Robertson, Glenda Farrell. Film's title has nothing to do with its story, a romantic rivalry between pilot brothers Barthelmess and Brown. Some great aerial stunts and impressive miniature special effects help make up for underdeveloped script. Blink and you'll miss John Wayne in a bit part as Brown's copilot in the climactic sequence.❿

Central Park (1932) 61m. **½ D: John Adolfi. Joan Blondell, Guy Kibbee, Wallace Ford, Henry B. Walthall, Patricia Ellis, Charles Sellon. Blondell and Ford uplift this programmer as a pair of small-town kids making their way in the big city who inadvertently become involved with gangsters. Set entirely in N.Y.C.'s Central Park.

Ceremony, The (1963) 105m. **½ D: Laurence Harvey. Laurence Harvey, Sarah Miles, Robert Walker, Jr., John Ireland, Ross Martin, Lee Patterson, Noel Purcell. Mishmash about convicted killer rescued by brother who demands liaison with sister-in-law as reward.❿

Certain Smile, A (1958) C-106m. **½ D: Jean Negulesco. Rossano Brazzi, Joan Fontaine, Bradford Dillman, Christine Carere. Françoise Sagan's novella becomes overblown soap opera. Romance between Parisian students Dillman (in film debut) and Carere interrupted when she is beguiled by roué Brazzi; chic Fontaine is wasted. CinemaScope.

César (1936-French) 134m. ***½ D: Marcel Pagnol. Raimu, Pierre Fresnay, Orane Demazis, Charpin, Andre Fouche, Alida Rouffe. Fanny's son (Fouche), now grown, learns that his father is Marius (Fresnay), not Panisse (Charpin). Raimu steals the film in the title role, particularly when he gives a poignant discourse on death. Third of Pagnol's trilogy, preceded by MARIUS and

FANNY. All three were the basis of the play and movie FANNY (1961).▼●❿

Chad Hanna (1940) C-86m. ** D: Henry King. Henry Fonda, Dorothy Lamour, Linda Darnell, Guy Kibbee, Jane Darwell, John Carradine. Rather flat circus drama set in 19th-century New York; colorful but empty.❿

Chained (1934) 76m. **½ D: Clarence Brown. Joan Crawford, Clark Gable, Otto Kruger, Stuart Erwin, Una O'Connor, Akim Tamiroff. Chic formula MGM love triangle with Crawford torn between love for Gable and married lover Kruger. Watch for Mickey Rooney splashing in a swimming pool.▼❿

Chain Lightning (1950) 94m. ** D: Stuart Heisler. Humphrey Bogart, Eleanor Parker, Raymond Massey, Richard Whorf. After WW2, bomber pilot Bogart becomes a test pilot for jet manufacturer Massey. Some romantic rivalry over Parker with inventor Whorf is as low-key as the rest of this bland, uninvolving movie.▼●❿

Chain of Evidence (1957) 64m. *½ D: Paul Landres. Bill Elliott, Don Haggerty, James Lydon, Claudia Barrett, Tina Carver, Ross Elliott, Dabbs Greer, Hugh Sanders, Timothy Carey, Meg Randall. Programmer has dedicated homicide detective Elliott tracking down the real killer of a businessman. Former Western star Elliott played the same character in four other movies.❿

Chalk Garden, The (1964-British) C-106m. *** D: Ronald Neame. Deborah Kerr, Hayley Mills, John Mills, Edith Evans, Felix Aylmer, Elizabeth Sellars. Very-high-class soap opera with good cast supporting story of teenager set on right path by governess Kerr; colorful production, quite entertaining. From Enid Bagnold play.▼❿

Challenge, The (1948) 68m. ** D: Jean Yarbrough. Tom Conway, June Vincent, Richard Stapley, John Newland, Eily Malyon, Terry Kilburn, Stanley Logan. Conway easily slides into the role of Bulldog Drummond in this fair mystery about a murdered sea captain who knew the whereabouts of hidden gold.

Challenge, The (1960) SEE: **It Takes a Thief**

Challenge to Lassie (1949) C-76m. **½ D: Richard Thorpe. Edmund Gwenn, Donald Crisp, Geraldine Brooks, Reginald Owen, Alan Webb, Ross Ford, Henry Stephenson, Alan Napier, Sara Allgood, Arthur Shields. Based-on-fact story, set in 19th-century Edinburgh, about a dog (actually a Skye terrier but played here by Lassie), who keeps returning to a churchyard where its master (Crisp) is buried. Pleasant film, with a fine character actor cast. Remade as GREYFRIARS BOBBY, which also features Crisp (as the cemetery caretaker).▼

Chamber of Horrors (1940-British) 80m. **½ D: Norman Lee. Leslie Banks, Lilli Palmer, Romilly Lunge, Gina Malo, Richard Bird, Cathleen Nesbitt. Low-budget horror comes over fairly well, with dastardly Banks duplicating his MOST DANGEROUS GAME–Count Zaroff look and accent—even though his character here is Spanish! Based on Edgar Wallace story. Original British title: THE DOOR WITH SEVEN LOCKS.▼●▶

Champ, The (1931) **87m.** ***½ D: King Vidor. Wallace Beery, Jackie Cooper, Irene Rich, Roscoe Ates, Edward Brophy, Hale Hamilton. Superb tearjerker about a washed-up prizefighter and his adoring son, played to perfection by Beery and Cooper (in the first of their several teamings). Simple, sentimental in the extreme, but very effective. Beery won an Oscar for his performance, as did Frances Marion for her original story. Remade in 1953 (as THE CLOWN) and 1979.▼●▶

Champagne (1928-British) **93m.** **½ D: Alfred Hitchcock. Betty Balfour, Jean Bradin, Gordon Harker, Ferdinand von Alten, Clifford Heatherley, Jack Trevor. Romantic escapades of irresponsible socialite Balfour whose father pretends he's broke to teach her a lesson. Overlong silent Hitch is moderately entertaining with the usual quota of striking visuals.▼▶

Champagne Charlie (1944) **107m.** **½ D: Cavalcanti. Tommy Trinder, Betty Warren, Stanley Holloway, Austin Trevor, Jean Kent, Guy Middleton. Splendid evocation of British music halls of the 1860s and their robust entertainers simply hasn't got enough story to last 107m. The songs are still great fun. Look for young Kay Kendall.▶

Champagne for Caesar (1950) **99m.** *** D: Richard Whorf. Ronald Colman, Celeste Holm, Vincent Price, Barbara Britton, Art Linkletter. Genius Colman becomes national celebrity on TV quiz show; sponsor Price sends temptress Holm to distract big winner. Enjoyable spoof; Price hilarious as neurotic soap manufacturer.▼●▶

Champagne Safari (1952) **60m.** **½ D: Jackson Leighter. Documentary on Rita Hayworth and Prince Aly Khan's troubled second honeymoon in colonial Africa is a fascinating curio that combines *National Geographic*-style travelogue with *Photoplay*-esque heartbreak-of-the-stars. Amid stops in Uganda, Kenya, and the former Tanganyika and Belgian Congo, Leighter's camera captures a marriage that is already beginning to unravel. (They were divorced before the film's release.) Originally photographed in color; all current prints are b&w.▼▶

Champagne Waltz (1937) **87m.** ** D: A. Edward Sutherland. Gladys Swarthout, Fred MacMurray, Jack Oakie, Herman Bing, Vivienne Osborne. Flyweight musical about rivalry between Vienna waltz palace and American jazz band next door gets sillier as it goes along; operatic Swarthout is saddled with mediocre songs. Oakie's comedy relief most welcome.

Champ for a Day (1953) **90m.** ** D: William Seiter. Alex Nicol, Audrey Totter, Charles Winninger, Hope Emerson, Henry (Harry) Morgan. Brooklyn boxer tracks down friend's murderer. Standard.

Champion (1949) **99m.** ***½ D: Mark Robson. Kirk Douglas, Marilyn Maxwell, Arthur Kennedy, Ruth Roman, Paul Stewart, Lola Albright. Unscrupulous boxer punches his way to the top, thrusting aside everybody and everything. Douglas perfectly cast in title role; gripping film, with Harry Gerstad's Oscar-winning editing. Also shown in computer-colored version.▼●▶

Chance at Heaven (1933) **70m.** ** D: William Seiter. Ginger Rogers, Joel McCrea, Marian Nixon, Andy Devine, Ann Shoemaker, Betty Furness. Honest, hardworking McCrea leaves fiancée Ginger for spoiled society brat Nixon. Sincere performances and realistic small-town atmosphere are only virtues of this humdrum film.▶

Chance Meeting (1959-British) **96m.** **½ D: Joseph Losey. Hardy Kruger, Stanley Baker, Micheline Presle, Robert Flemyng, Gordon Jackson. Kafkaesque story of painter framed for girlfriend's murder. Intriguing little mystery becomes talky, loses initial momentum. British title: BLIND DATE.▼

Chance of a Lifetime, The (1943) **65m.** **½ D: William Castle. Chester Morris, Erik Rolf, Jeanne Bates, Richard Lane, George E. Stone, Lloyd Corrigan, Walter Sande, Douglas Fowley, Cy Kendall. Director Castle made his debut with this proficient *Boston Blackie* episode about a group of prisoners who are paroled to Blackie's care to work in a war plant—but some of them have larceny and not patriotism in mind.

Chance of a Lifetime, The (1950-British) **89m.** *** D: Bernard Miles, Alan Osbiston. Basil Radford, Niall MacGinnis, Bernard Miles, Geoffrey Keen, Kenneth More, Julien Mitchell, Hattie Jacques. Nearly a landmark film by actor-director Miles, blending comedy and drama when a fed-up factory owner (Radford) agrees to turn over all management duties to his workers. Laborers, led by Miles and More, eventually learn how difficult it is to run a business. Outstanding performances and realistic location filming.

Chances (1931) **72m.** *** D: Allan Dwan. Douglas Fairbanks, Jr., Rose Hobart, Anthony Bushell, Mary Forbes, William Austin. Entertaining, neatly acted drama of love and war, with soldier-brothers Fairbanks and Bushell both falling for Hobart. Fairbanks in particular is a standout.

Chandu the Magician (1932) **70m.** *½ D: William Cameron Menzies, Marcel Varnel. Edmund Lowe, Bela Lugosi, Irene Ware,

Henry B. Walthall, Herbert Mundin. Mystic Chandu battles madman whose death ray threatens to destroy world; not as good as most serials of this genre, and even sillier. Disappointing.▼◗

Chang (1927) **67m.** ***½ D: Merian C. Cooper, Ernest B. Schoedsack. Kru, Chantui, Nah, Ladah, Bimbo. Set in the jungle of Siam (Thailand), this fascinating ethnographic documentary/narrative tells the story of Kru and his family, and their daily struggle for survival amid wild animals and cruel forces of nature—particularly a herd of *chang* (the Siamese word for "elephant"). Some of the shots of animals are truly amazing. The Cooper-Schoedsack team later made KING KONG. ▼◗◗

Change of Heart (1943) **90m.** ** D: Albert S. Rogell. John Carroll, Susan Hayward, Gail Patrick, Eve Arden, Melville Cooper, Walter Catlett, Dorothy Dandridge, Count Basie & Orchestra, Freddy Martin & Orchestra. Forgettable musical numbers abound in this romantic trifle of Carroll stealing songwriter Hayward's work. Of course, they fall in love. Originally titled HIT PARADE OF 1943.

Chaplin Revue, The (1958) **119m.** ***½ D: Charles Chaplin. Charlie Chaplin, Edna Purviance, Sydney Chaplin, Mack Swain. Three of Chaplin's best shorts strung together with his own music, narration, and behind-the-scenes footage: A DOG'S LIFE (1918), one of his loveliest films; SHOULDER ARMS (1918), a classic WW1 comedy; and THE PILGRIM (1923), his underrated gem about a convict who disguises himself as a minister.▼◗

Chapman Report, The (1962) **C-125m.** **½ D: George Cukor. Efrem Zimbalist, Jr., Shelley Winters, Jane Fonda, Claire Bloom, Glynis Johns, Ray Danton, Ty Hardin, Andrew Duggan, John Dehner, Harold J. Stone, Corey Allen, Cloris Leachman, Chad Everett, Henry Daniell, Jack Cassidy. Slick, empty yarn about Kinsey-like sex researchers coming to suburban community to get statistical survey, with repercussions on assorted females. Potboiler material elevated by good performances and direction.◗

Charade (1953-British) **82m.** ** D: Roy Kellino. James Mason, Pamela Mason, Scott Forbes, Paul Cavanagh, Bruce Lester, John Dodsworth, Judy Osborne, Sean McClory. Trilogy of short stories adapted by the then-married Masons (and directed by her ex-husband) for British TV, subsequently reedited for theatrical release. Only the middle piece, Alexandre Dumas' romantic drama "Duel at Dawn," holds up today. The others: a mystery, "Portrait of a Murderer," and a light comedy, "The Midas Touch."▼

Charade (1963) **C-114m.** ***½ D: Stanley Donen. Cary Grant, Audrey Hepburn, Walter Matthau, James Coburn, George Kennedy, Ned Glass, Jacques Marin. Suave comedy-mystery in Hitchcock vein, with Grant aiding widow Hepburn to recover fortune secreted by husband, being sought by trio of sinister crooks; set in Paris. Excellent screenplay by Peter Stone, score by Henry Mancini. Remade in 2002 as THE TRUTH ABOUT CHARLIE.▼◗

Charge at Feather River, The (1953) **C-96m.** **½ D: Gordon Douglas. Guy Madison, Vera Miles, Frank Lovejoy, Dick Wesson, Helen Westcott, Onslow Stevens, Steve Brodie, Neville Brand, Henry Kulky. Pretty good saga of Madison leading ragtag "guardhouse brigade" toward an inevitable clash with the Cheyenne at title location. Subplots involve a SEARCHERS-like rescue of two white girls raised by Indians and a bit too much comedy relief from Wesson and Kulky. Listen for Lt. Wilhelm! Originally in 3D; Lovejoy even spits at the camera.

Charge of the Lancers (1954) **C-74m.** ** D: William Castle. Paulette Goddard, Jean-Pierre Aumont, Richard Stapley, Karin Booth, Charles Irwin. Stilted affair of gypsy Goddard and British officer Aumont finding romance in midst of Crimean War.◗

Charge of the Light Brigade, The (1936) **116m.** *** D: Michael Curtiz. Errol Flynn, Olivia de Havilland, Patric Knowles, Henry Stephenson, Nigel Bruce, Donald Crisp, David Niven, C. Henry Gordon, Robert Barrat, Spring Byington, J. Carrol Naish. Thundering action based on Tennyson's poem, with immortal charge into the valley of death by British 27th Lancers cavalry. Lavish production values accent romantic tale of Flynn and de Havilland at army post in India. Max Steiner's first musical score for Warner Brothers is superb. Balaklava Heights charge directed by action specialist B. Reeves Eason. Remade in 1968. Also shown in computer-colored version.▼◗◗

Charley's Aunt (1930) **88m.** **½ D: Al Christie. Charles Ruggles, June Collyer, Hugh Williams, Doris Lloyd, Halliwell Hobbes. Ruggles shines in this amusing (if occasionally creaky) version of the Brandon Thomas farce. He's a twit who impersonates the title relative and chaperones for a couple of his pals and their girlfriends. Originally filmed in 1925 (with Sydney Chaplin); remade in 1941.▼

Charley's Aunt (1941) **81m.** **½ D: Archie Mayo. Jack Benny, Kay Francis, James Ellison, Anne Baxter, Edmund Gwenn, Reginald Owen. Broad but surefire filming of Brandon Thomas play about Oxford student posing as maiden aunt, joke getting out of hand. Previously filmed six other times! Remade as musical WHERE'S CHARLEY?◗

Charlie Chan Earl Derr Biggers enjoyed great success with a series of novels featuring a detective on the Honolulu police force.

The character first appeared on-screen in 1926, but did not make an impression until Warner Oland took over the role in 1931's CHARLIE CHAN CARRIES ON (one of four early Chan films which no longer exist—except in a Spanish-language version—the others being CHARLIE CHAN'S CHANCE, CHARLIE CHAN'S COURAGE, and CHARLIE CHAN'S GREATEST CASE). Swedish-born Oland seemed born to play the Mandarin-like sleuth, but the series really hit its stride when Keye Luke was cast as his youthful, Americanized "Number One Son" Lee in CHARLIE CHAN IN PARIS; their good-natured parrying gave the series a uniquely human, and humorous, foundation that made them more than mere whodunits. Oland's death in 1937 might have spelled the end of the series, but 20th Century-Fox decided to continue, and found another actor well suited to the part, Sidney Toler. He was soon joined by (Victor) Sen Yung, who was cast as Jimmy Chan, Charlie's Number Two Son. The series became more formulaic, but still benefited from good writing and the best array of character actors in Hollywood to play the various red herrings. Fox retired the series in 1942, but two years later, low-budget Monogram Pictures decided to revive it, with Toler in the lead. These potboilers have little to recommend them. In 1947, after Toler's death, Roland Winters took on the role for a final round before the series expired in 1949. The vintage Chan movies, from the mid-1930s to the early 1940s, remain highly enjoyable today, deftly blending crime solving and comedy, and always punctuated by Charlie's wise sayings, like: "Insignificant molehill sometimes more important than conspicuous mountain."

CHARLIE CHAN

Behind That Curtain (1929)
The Black Camel (1931)
Charlie Chan in London (1934)
Charlie Chan in Paris (1935)
Charlie Chan in Egypt (1935)
Charlie Chan in Shanghai (1935)
Charlie Chan's Secret (1936)
Charlie Chan at the Circus (1936)
Charlie Chan at the Race Track (1936)
Charlie Chan at the Opera (1936)
Charlie Chan at the Olympics (1937)
Charlie Chan on Broadway (1937)
Charlie Chan at Monte Carlo (1938)
Charlie Chan in Honolulu (1938)
Charlie Chan in Reno (1939)
Charlie Chan at Treasure Island (1939)
Charlie Chan in City in Darkness (1939)
Charlie Chan in Panama (1940)
Charlie Chan's Murder Cruise (1940)
Charlie Chan at the Wax Museum (1940)
Murder Over New York (1940)
Dead Men Tell (1941)

Charlie Chan in Rio (1941)
Castle in the Desert (1942)
Charlie Chan in the Secret Service (1944)
The Chinese Cat (1944)
Black Magic (1944); aka Meeting at Midnight
The Jade Mask (1945)
The Scarlet Clue (1945)
The Shanghai Cobra (1945)
The Red Dragon (1945)
Dark Alibi (1946)
Shadows Over Chinatown (1946)
Dangerous Money (1946)
The Trap (1947)
The Chinese Ring (1947)
Docks of New Orleans (1948)
The Shanghai Chest (1948)
The Golden Eye (1948)
The Feathered Serpent (1948)
The Sky Dragon (1949)

Charlie Chan and the Golden Eye SEE: **Golden Eye, The**
Charlie Chan at Monte Carlo (1938) **71m.** ** D: Eugene Forde. Warner Oland, Keye Luke, Virginia Field, Sidney Blackmer, Harold Huber, Kay Linaker, Robert Kent. A casino vacation on the Riviera turns into a murder investigation for the inscrutable detective. Oland's final appearance as Chan is not one of his best.◗
Charlie Chan at the Circus (1936) **72m.** **½ D: Harry Lachman. Warner Oland, Keye Luke, George and Olive Brasno, Francis Ford, Maxine Reiner, John McGuire, Shirley Deane, J. Carrol Naish. Murder strikes under the big top, with Charlie and his 12 kids on hand to investigate. Pleasing entry.◗
Charlie Chan at the Olympics (1937) **71m.** **½ D: H. Bruce Humberstone. Warner Oland, Keye Luke, Katherine DeMille, Pauline Moore, Allan Lane, C. Henry Gordon, Jonathan Hale, Morgan Wallace, Layne Tom, Jr., John Eldredge, Frederick Vogeding. Spies converge on the 1936 Berlin games and kidnap Number One Son Luke from the American swim team. Neat entry featuring well-integrated Olympic newsreel footage, and amusing byplay with plucky Charlie Chan, Jr. (Tom).◗
Charlie Chan at the Opera (1936) **66m.** *** D: H. Bruce Humberstone. Warner Oland, Boris Karloff, Keye Luke, Charlotte Henry, Thomas Beck, Margaret Irving, Gregory Gaye, Nedda Harrigan, Frank Conroy, William Demarest. The series at its peak, a stylish blend of murder and music, with Karloff as the leading suspect, Demarest as a skeptical cop, and a bogus opera written for the film by Oscar Levant. ▼◗●
Charlie Chan at the Race Track (1936) **70m.** **½ D: H. Bruce Humberstone. Warner Oland, Keye Luke, Helen Wood, Thomas Beck, Alan Dinehart, Gavin Muir, Gloria Roy, Jonathan Hale, Junior Coghlan, Frankie Darro. Chan corrals some crooked

gamblers during the investigation of a horse owner's murder, with Number One Son Luke starting to become a regular participant in the series.◗

Charlie Chan at the Wax Museum (1940) **63m. **½** D: Lynn Shores. Sidney Toler, Sen Yung, C. Henry Gordon, Marc Lawrence, Joan Valerie, Marguerite Chapman, Ted Osborn, Michael Visaroff. A gangster put away by Chan escapes and swears vengeance, hiding out at a wax museum run by a madman. Atmospheric entry with an appropriately creepy milieu and a handful of surprises.▼◗

Charlie Chan at Treasure Island (1939) **75m. ***** D: Norman Foster. Sidney Toler, Cesar Romero, Pauline Moore, Sen Yung, Douglas Fowley, June Gale, Sally Blane, Wally Vernon, Donald MacBride, Douglass Dumbrille. One of the best Toler entries, with Charlie getting help from magician Romero in his attempt to prove that a phony psychic was behind the mysterious suicide of his friend. Tight script by John Larkin, set at Golden Gate International Exposition.◗

Charlie Chan in Black Magic SEE: **Black Magic** (1944)

Charlie Chan in City in Darkness (1939) **75m. **** D: Herbert I. Leeds. Sidney Toler, Lynn Bari, Richard Clarke, Harold Huber, Pedro de Cordoba, Dorothy Tree, C. Henry Gordon, Douglass Dumbrille, Noel Madison, Lon Chaney, Jr., Leo G. Carroll, Frederick Vogeding. In Paris, Chan and bumbling inspector Huber investigate the killing of an arms dealer supplying weapons to the Germans. Mediocre entry with a topical angle.◗

Charlie Chan in Dangerous Money SEE: **Dangerous Money**

Charlie Chan in Egypt (1935) **72m. ***** D: Louis King. Warner Oland, "Pat" Paterson, Thomas Beck, Rita Cansino (Hayworth), Jameson Thomas, Frank Conroy, Nigel de Brulier, Paul Porcasi, Stepin Fetchit. Highly enjoyable mystery about the search for a mummified archeologist in the land of the pyramids. Many horror-movie trappings in this one, including music lifted from CHANDU THE MAGICIAN.◗

Charlie Chan in Honolulu (1938) **68m. **½** D: H. Bruce Humberstone. Sidney Toler, Phyllis Brooks, Sen Yung, Eddie Collins, John King, Claire Dodd, George Zucco, Robert Barrat, Marc Lawrence, Richard Lane, Philip Ahn. Toler makes a serviceable Chan in his first outing (with Yung also debuting as Number Two Son Jimmy), probing murder on a ship docked in Hawaii while his daughter is about to give birth to his number one grandchild. Layne Tom, Jr., is fun as the daring young Charlie Chan, Jr. ◗

Charlie Chan in London (1934) **79m. ***** D: Eugene Forde. Warner Oland, Drue Leyton, Douglas Walton, Alan Mowbray, Mona Barrie, Raymond (Ray) Milland, George Barraud, David Torrence, Madge Bellamy,

Murray Kinnell, E. E. Clive. Charlie tries to solve a murder during a foxhunt weekend at a British country estate—while dodging death-dealing darts and interpreting mysterious notes. Solid entry is helped by good portrayal of gentried British types . . . including a young Ray Milland.◗

Charlie Chan in Meeting at Midnight SEE: **Black Magic** (1944)

Charlie Chan in Panama (1940) **67m. **½** D: Norman Foster. Sidney Toler, Jean Rogers, Kane Richmond, Lionel Atwill, Mary Nash, Sen Yung, Chris-Pin Martin, Jack La Rue. They really started to play up the WW2 angle with this one, a slick entry about saboteurs planning to attack Navy ships in the Panama Canal. Strong cast helps. Reworking of MARIE GALANTE.◗

Charlie Chan in Paris (1935) **72m. **½** D: Lewis Seiler. Warner Oland, Mary Brian, Thomas Beck, Erik Rhodes, John Miljan, Ruth Peterson, Minor Watson, Murray Kinnell, John Qualen, Keye Luke, Henry Kolker. Compact early entry has Chan rounding up counterfeiters with the help of Number One Son Luke, making his first appearance as Lee.▼◗

Charlie Chan in Reno (1939) **70m. **½** D: Norman Foster. Sidney Toler, Ricardo Cortez, Phyllis Brooks, Pauline Moore, Slim Summerville, Kane Richmond, Sen Yung, Robert Lowery, Eddie Collins, Kay Linaker, Morgan Conway. Chan heads for the divorce capital to defend a friend charged with murder in this trim episode.◗

Charlie Chan in Rio (1941) **61m. **½** D: Harry Lachman. Sidney Toler, Mary Beth Hughes, Cobina Wright, Jr., Ted (Michael) North, Victor Jory, Harold Huber, Victor Sen Yung, Richard Derr, Kay Linaker. Picturesque Brazil is the backdrop for this entertaining murder mystery, with Chan joining the local police to solve a double homicide. A reworking of THE BLACK CAMEL (1931), which was directed by Hamilton MacFadden, who appears in this film as Bill Kellogg.▼◗

Charlie Chan in Shanghai (1935) **70m. **½** D: James Tinling. Warner Oland, Irene Hervey, Russell Hicks, Keye Luke, Halliwell Hobbes, Charles Locher (Jon Hall), Frederick Vogeding. Charlie tracks down murderous opium smugglers in this one. More physical action than usual.◗

Charlie Chan in the Secret Service (1944) **63m. **** D: Phil Rosen. Sidney Toler, Mantan Moreland, Gwen Kenyon, Benson Fong, Arthur Loft, Marianne Quon. The Oriental sleuth probes the murder of an inventor in this initial *Charlie Chan* film for low-budget Monogram studios, which resulted in an obvious drop in production quality and the addition of Moreland in the stereotyped role of Birmingham, a frightened cab driver.▼◗

Charlie Chan on Broadway (1937) **68m.**

*** D: Eugene Forde. Warner Oland, Keye Luke, Joan Marsh, J. Edward Bromberg, Leon Ames, Joan Woodbury, Douglas Fowley, Louise Henry, Donald Woods, Harold Huber, Marc Lawrence. Slangy entry about a shady chanteuse who's murdered for her little black book containing the names and misdeeds of some highly placed criminals. Try to solve this one—and look fast for Lon Chaney, Jr.◗

Charlie Chan's Murder Cruise (1940) **75m.** ** D: Eugene Forde. Sidney Toler, Sen Yung, Marjorie Weaver, Lionel Atwill, Robert Lowery, Don Beddoe, Leo G. Carroll, Cora Witherspoon, Kay Linaker, Harlan Briggs, Charles Middleton, Layne Tom, Jr. Overly familiar shipboard whodunit centering on the murder of a Scotland Yard inspector. Remake of CHARLIE CHAN CARRIES ON (1931), which no longer exists.◗

Charlie Chan's Secret (1936) **71m.** ** D: Gordon Wiles. Warner Oland, Rosina Lawrence, Charles Quigley, Henrietta Crosman, Edward Trevor, Astrid Allwyn, Herbert Mundin. Hollow mystery about a missing heir believed drowned who turns up alive, only to be killed during a seance. Number One Son is sorely missed.▼◗

Charlie Chaplin Carnival (1938) **100m.** **** Four vintage comedies from Chaplin's 1916–17 peak period: BEHIND THE SCREEN, THE COUNT, THE FIREMAN, THE VAGABOND. First one is best, with leading lady Edna Purviance and oversized villain Eric Campbell. Some prints run 75m. ▼

Charlie Chaplin Cavalcade (1938) **75m.** **** More priceless gems from 1916–17 period: ONE A.M. (Chaplin's famous solo film), THE RINK, THE PAWNSHOP, THE FLOORWALKER. All great. ▼

Charlie Chaplin Festival (1938) **96m.** **** Best of the Chaplin compilations, which all suffer from obtrusive sound effects and music: THE ADVENTURER, THE CURE, EASY STREET, THE IMMIGRANT. Four of the greatest comedies ever made—don't miss them. Some prints run 75m. ▼

Charlie McCarthy, Detective (1939) **65m.** **½ D: Frank Tuttle. Edgar Bergen, Charlie McCarthy, Constance Moore, Robert Cummings, Louis Calhern, John Sutton, Harold Huber, Edgar Kennedy. Good comedy-whodunit with Bergen & McCarthy rivaling Inspector Kennedy's investigation. ◗

Charming Sinners (1929) **85m.** *½ D: Robert Milton. Ruth Chatterton, Clive Brook, William Powell, Mary Nolan, Laura Hope Crews, Florence Eldridge. Obvious, creaky marital drama of Chatterton, whose philandering husband (Brook) has taken up with her best friend. To pique his jealousy, she pretends to become involved with former boyfriend Powell. Based on Somerset Maugham's *The Constant Wife*.

Charterhouse of Parma, The (1948-French-Italian) **170m.** **½ D: Christian-Jaque. Gérard Philipe, Renée Faure, María Casarès, Tullio Carminati, Louis Salou, Lucien Coëdel. Epic-length romantic tragedy from Stendhal's 1839 masterwork about a cleric irredeemably in love with a parish girl and the jealous aunt bent on preserving his purity . . . for herself. Director's assured hand convincingly alternates appropriate reverence with forbidden passion, but the hero's descent is a slow fall. ▼◗

Chartroose Caboose (1960) **C-75m.** ** D: William "Red" Reynolds. Molly Bee, Ben Cooper, Edgar Buchanan, Mike McGreevey. Buchanan, an eccentric retired train conductor, shelters a young couple in his strange house, a converted caboose. Panavision.

Chase, The (1946) **86m.** **½ D: Arthur D. Ripley. Robert Cummings, Michele Morgan, Steve Cochran, Peter Lorre, Lloyd Corrigan, Jack Holt, Don Wilson, James Westerfield. Mildly diverting melodrama with luckless vet Cummings becoming involved with a ruthless racketeer (well played by Cochran) and his melancholy wife (Morgan). Scripted by Philip Yordan, based on a book by Cornell Woolrich.

Chase a Crooked Shadow (1958-British) **87m.** *** D: Michael Anderson. Richard Todd, Anne Baxter, Herbert Lom, Alexander Knox. Heiress Baxter doubts her sanity when allegedly dead brother Todd appears to claim inheritance; exciting, Hitchcock-like melodrama. Epilogue by film's producer, Douglas Fairbanks, Jr. ◗

Chase Me Charlie (1932) **61m.** ** Narrated by Teddy Bergman. Charlie Chaplin, Edna Purviance, Ben Turpin. Inept attempt to string early Chaplin shorts into storyline—1914 material used is often weak.

Chaser, The (1928) **63m.** BOMB D: Harry Langdon. Harry Langdon, Gladys McConnell, Helen Hayward, Bud Jamison, Charles Thurston. Baby-faced Langdon is forced by a judge to take his spouse's place as a housewife—in drag—for thirty days in this embarrassing and unfunny comedy. Langdon's decision to direct himself sent his career plummeting, and it's easy to see why. ▼◗

Chasing Rainbows (1930) **85m.** ** D: Charles F. Riesner. Bessie Love, Charles King, Jack Benny, Marie Dressler, Polly Moran, George K. Arthur, Gwen Lee. Love, laughs, and tears among the members of a touring theatrical company. Benny, Dressler, and Moran provide welcome comic relief in this standard early-talkie backstage musical in the wake of THE BROADWAY MELODY, which also starred Love and King. Songs include "Happy Days Are Here Again." Originally contained two lavish production numbers in two-strip Technicolor; both are now lost. Original running time: 100m. ◗

Chatterbox (1936) 68m. **½ D: George Nicholls, Jr. Anne Shirley, Phillips Holmes, Edward Ellis, Erik Rhodes, Margaret Hamilton, Granville Bates, Allen Vincent, Lucille Ball. Sweetly likable account of enthusiastic but naïve country girl Shirley, who yearns for a career as an actress but must contend with her narrow-minded grandfather. Starts off nicely but fizzles out near the finale.

Chatterbox (1943) 76m. **½ D: Joseph Santley. Joe E. Brown, Judy Canova, Rosemary Lane, John Hubbard, Gus Schilling, Chester Clute, Anne Jeffreys. Entertaining comedy of radio-cowboy Brown (not much of a hero in real life) visiting dude ranch for publicity purposes.

Cheaper by the Dozen (1950) C-85m. *** D: Walter Lang. Clifton Webb, Myrna Loy, Jeanne Crain, Mildred Natwick, Edgar Buchanan. Charming turn-of-the-20th-century story of the Gilbreth children, twelve strong, their exacting father (well played by Webb), and mother (Loy). From the Gilbreth-Carey novel. Loosely remade in 2003. Sequel: BELLES ON THEIR TOES. ▼❶

Cheat, The (1915) 59m. *** D: Cecil B. DeMille. Fannie Ward, Sessue Hayakawa, Jack Dean, James Neill. Once audacious melodrama remains an engrossing curio about a proper, upper-class Long Island lady (Ward) who is exploited by a licentious Asian (Hayakawa). Watch this, and you'll see why Hayakawa was one of the most popular screen actors of the time. Remade in 1923, 1931, and 1937 (in France as FORFAITURE, also with Hayakawa). ▼❶

Cheat, The (1931) 74m. *** D: George Abbott. Tallulah Bankhead, Irving Pichel, Harvey Stephens, Jay Fassett, Ann Andrews. Bankhead gives a standout performance as the flighty wife of a struggling financier who lives beyond her means among Long Island society. When she's desperate for money she succumbs to the advances of wealthy, creepy Pichel, who's spent time in Japan and likes to brand his female conquests! Abbott and cinematographer George Folsey create fluid scenes, with naturalistic use of sound. Pre-Code remake of the notorious 1915 silent film. ❶

Cheaters, The (1945) 87m. *** D: Joseph Kane. Joseph Schildkraut, Billie Burke, Eugene Pallette, Ona Munson, Raymond Walburn, Ruth Terry. Excellent cast in enjoyable tale of wealthy family of snobs humanized by downtrodden actor they invite for Christmas dinner. Aka THE CASTAWAY. ❶

Check and Double Check (1930) 80m. BOMB D: Melville Brown. Freeman Gosden, Charles Correll, Sue Carol, Charles Morton, Ralf Harolde, Duke Ellington and His Band. Movie debut for radio's Amos 'n' Andy is a leaden-paced early talkie with stale script and precious little comedy; not nearly as good as a sample radio (or later TV) episode of the show. ▼❶

Cheers for Miss Bishop (1941) 95m. *** D: Tay Garnett. Martha Scott, William Gargan, Edmund Gwenn, Sterling Holloway, Sidney Blackmer, Mary Anderson, Dorothy Peterson. Sentimental story of Scott devoting her life to teaching in small Midwestern town. Nicely done. ▼❶

Cheers of the Crowd (1935) 60m. ** D: Vin Moore. Russell Hopton, Irene Ware, Harry Holman, Bradley Page, John Dilson. A publicity stunt designed to boost the box office of the Broadway musical *Yes Yes Georgette* results in comical complications. The very low budget prevents us from seeing even a moment of the show, but by movie's end you'll know the lobby and hatcheck room layouts intimately!

Cherokee Strip (1940) 86m. **½ D: Lesley Selander. Richard Dix, Florence Rice, Victor Jory, William Henry, Andy Clyde, George E. Stone. Solid if unsurprising little Western with quiet but determined Dix becoming marshal of small town, hoping to get the goods on crooked Jory and his gang.

Cheyenne (1947) 100m. ** D: Raoul Walsh. Dennis Morgan, Jane Wyman, Janis Paige, Bruce Bennett, Alan Hale, Arthur Kennedy, Barton MacLane. Standard Western as gambler attempts to capture outlaw—instead spends time with outlaw's wife. Later a TV series. Retitled THE WYOMING KID. ❶

Cheyenne Autumn (1964) C-145m. *** D: John Ford. Richard Widmark, Carroll Baker, Karl Malden, Dolores Del Rio, Sal Mineo, Edward G. Robinson, James Stewart, Ricardo Montalban, Gilbert Roland, Arthur Kennedy, Patrick Wayne, Elizabeth Allen, Victor Jory, John Carradine, Mike Mazurki, John Qualen, George O'Brien. Sprawling, uneven, but entertaining John Ford Western (his last) about Cheyenne Indian tribe and its eventful journey back to original settlement after being relocated by the government. Director Ford's last film in Monument Valley. Dodge City sequence (with Stewart as Wyatt Earp) was cut after premiere engagements. Roadshow version on video runs 157m. with overture, intermission/entr'acte, and restored footage. Super Panavision 70. ▼❶

Chicago Calling (1951) 74m. ** D: John Reinhardt. Dan Duryea, Mary Anderson, Gordon Gebert, Ross Elliott. Slim premise has Duryea sitting by telephone awaiting news of estranged family injured in car accident; mild tour de force. ❶

Chicago Confidential (1957) 73m. **½ D: Sidney Salkow. Brian Keith, Beverly Garland, Dick Foran, Beverly Tyler, Elisha Cook. Keith and Garland make good protagonists in their crusade to clean up corruption and crime amid the labor unions of the Windy City. ❶

Chicago Deadline (1949) 87m. **½ D: Lewis Allen. Alan Ladd, Donna Reed, June Havoc, Irene Hervey, Arthur Kennedy, Shepperd Strudwick. Potentially top-notch actioner bogs down in clichés, with Ladd as crusading reporter in corruption-filled city. Remade as FAME IS THE NAME OF THE GAME.

Chicago Syndicate (1955) 83m. ** D: Fred F. Sears. Dennis O'Keefe, Abbe Lane, Paul Stewart, Xavier Cugat. Passable exposé film involving cleanup of Windy City rackets.▼

Chicken Every Sunday (1948) 91m. **½ D: George Seaton. Dan Dailey, Celeste Holm, Colleen Townsend, Alan Young, Natalie Wood. Easygoing turn-of-the-20th-century Americana about get-rich-quick schemer Dailey and understanding wife Holm.❱

Chief, The (1933) 65m. *½ D: Charles Riesner. Ed Wynn, Charles "Chic" Sale, Dorothy Mackaill, William "Stage" Boyd, Effie Ellsler, C. Henry Gordon, Mickey Rooney, George Givot, Nat Pendleton. Designed to cash in on Wynn's radio popularity, this clumsy film has a script problem: no one bothered to write one! After getting Ed involved in a kidnapping plot, and some innocuous love interest, it winds up at Wynn's radio show, where he describes the plot to announcer Graham McNamee . . . and it ends. Not a moment too soon.

Chief Crazy Horse (1955) C-86m. **½ D: George Sherman. Victor Mature, Suzan Ball, John Lund, Ray Danton, Keith Larsen, Paul Guilfoyle, David Janssen, Dennis Weaver. Intelligent if slow-moving Western with Mature perfectly cast as the proud, idealistic Sioux chief who unites the Indian tribes (and defeats Custer at Little Big Horn). CinemaScope.

Chikamatsu Monogatari SEE: **Crucified Lovers, The**

Child Is Born, A (1940) 79m. *** D: Lloyd Bacon. Geraldine Fitzgerald, Jeffrey Lynn, Gladys George, Gale Page, Spring Byington, Eve Arden. Smooth, touching remake of LIFE BEGINS about everyday life in maternity ward, involving prisoner Fitzgerald sent to hospital to have her child.

Child Is Waiting, A (1963) 102m. *** D: John Cassavetes. Burt Lancaster, Judy Garland, Gena Rowlands, Steven Hill, Bruce Ritchey. Poignant story of Lancaster's attempts to treat retarded children with the help of overly sympathetic Garland. Sensitive subject handled with honesty and candor.▼❱

Child of Manhattan (1933) 70m. **½ D: Edward Buzzell. Nancy Carroll, Charles (Buck) Jones, John Boles, Jessie Ralph, Clara Blandick, Luis Alberni, Warburton Gamble, Jane Darwell, Nat Pendleton, Tyler Brooke. Dance-hall girl falls in love with a millionaire, but an unexpected pregnancy complicates the relationship for both of them. Nice little film has a fairly light touch and keeps moving, which covers a multitude of sins. Carroll is excellent, genuinely

touching in her dramatic moments. You'll have to look sharp to spot Betty Grable. Based on a play by Preston Sturges.

Children Are Watching Us, The (1944-Italian) 84m. ***½ D: Vittorio De Sica. Emilio Cigoli, Luciano De Ambrosis, Isa Pola, Adriano Rimoldi, Giovanna Cigoli. Devastating drama about a little boy (De Ambrosis, in a heartbreaking performance) who can't avoid noticing that his mother is carrying on with another man. Even though there is no hint of WW2 on-screen, the events unfolding in Europe when the film was made reverberate throughout. Filmed in 1942; released in the U.S. in 1947. This was the first credited collaboration for De Sica and Cesare Zavattini, who are among the screenwriters.▼❱

Children of Paradise (1945-French) 195m. **** D: Marcel Carné. Jean-Louis Barrault, Arletty, Pierre Brasseur, Albert Remy, Maria Casarés, Leon Larive, Marcel Herrand, Pierre Renoir. Timeless masterpiece of filmmaking (and storytelling), focusing on a rough-and-tumble theatrical troupe in 19th-century France. Barrault plays the mime whose unfulfilled passion for free-spirited Arletty dominates his life, even as he achieves great fame on stage. Wise, witty, and completely captivating. Written by Jacques Prévert. Filming began in 1943 in Nazi-occupied France, but wasn't completed until 1945.▼❱

Children of the Damned (1964-British) 90m. **½ D: Anton Leader. Ian Hendry, Alan Badel, Barbara Ferris, Patrick White, Bessie Love. Follow-up to VILLAGE OF THE DAMNED suffers from unimaginative account of precocious deadly children and their quest for power.▼❱

Children's Hour, The (1961) 107m. **½ D: William Wyler. Audrey Hepburn, Shirley MacLaine, James Garner, Miriam Hopkins, Fay Bainter, Karen Balkin, Veronica Cartwright. Updated version of Lillian Hellman's play is more explicit in its various themes, including lesbianism, than original THESE THREE (also made by Wyler), but not half as good. Impact is missing, despite MacLaine and Hepburn as two teachers, Hopkins as meddling aunt, Bainter as questioning grandmother.▼❱

Chimes at Midnight (1965-Spanish-Swiss) 115m. *** D: Orson Welles. Orson Welles, Jeanne Moreau, Margaret Rutherford, John Gielgud, Marina Vlady, Keith Baxter; narrated by Ralph Richardson. Welles combines parts of five Shakespeare plays with mixed results, but his performance as Falstaff makes it well worth seeing. Gielgud is also magnificent. Despite a modest budget, one key battle scene is a Wellesian tour de force. Aka FALSTAFF.

China (1943) 79m. ** D: John Farrow. Loretta Young, Alan Ladd, William Bendix, Philip Ahn, Iris Wong, Sen Yung. Pat war-

time tale of mercenary Ladd who suddenly realizes his true allegiance while helping enemy.▼◗
China Clipper (1936) 85m. **½ D: Ray Enright. Pat O'Brien, Beverly Roberts, Ross Alexander, Humphrey Bogart, Marie Wilson, Henry B. Walthall. O'Brien stars as man determined to develop trans-Pacific flights; usual plot of initial failure, grim determination, and neglected wife; fairly well done.◗
China Corsair (1951) 67m. *½ D: Ray Nazzaro. Jon Hall, Lisa Ferraday, Ron Randell, Douglas Kennedy, Ernest Borgnine. Tinsel-like adventure of Hall's romancing, combating crooks aboard title ship. Borgnine's film debut.
China Doll (1958) 88m. *½ D: Frank Borzage. Victor Mature, Li Li Hua, Bob Mathias, Stuart Whitman. Bizarre storyline can't boost dull film of Air Force pilot Mature accidentally buying Asian wife whom he grows to love. Romantic story with WW2 backdrop from John Wayne's Batjac unit.◗
China Gate (1957) 97m. *** D: Samuel Fuller. Gene Barry, Angie Dickinson, Nat King Cole, Paul Dubov, Lee Van Cleef, George Givot, Marcel Dalio. International soldiers under French command attack Communist munitions dumps in Indochina. Interesting subplots flesh out Fuller's dynamic action story, with early view of Vietnam's internal strife. CinemaScope.▼◗
China Girl (1942) 95m. ** D: Henry Hathaway. Gene Tierney, George Montgomery, Lynn Bari, Victor McLaglen, Sig Ruman, Bobby (Robert) Blake, Ann Pennington, Philip Ahn. American photographer in mysterious Orient during WW2 is background for unbelievable adventure yarn; Bari best item in film.
China Seas (1935) 90m. *** D: Tay Garnett. Clark Gable, Jean Harlow, Wallace Beery, Lewis Stone, Rosalind Russell, Dudley Digges, Robert Benchley, C. Aubrey Smith, Hattie McDaniel. Impossible to dislike film with that cast, even if the story—about mysterious goings-on and relationships on Gable's Singapore-bound ship—is ludicrous. Also shown in computer-colored version.▼◗
China Sky (1945) 78m. ** D: Ray Enright. Randolph Scott, Ruth Warrick, Ellen Drew, Anthony Quinn, Carol Thurston, Richard Loo. Slow-moving Pearl Buck story of dedicated doctor Scott fighting Japanese with Chinese comrades during WW2.▼◗
China's Little Devils (1945) 74m. ** D: Monta Bell. Harry Carey, Paul Kelly, "Ducky" Louie, Hayward Soo Hoo, Gloria Ann Chew, Ralph Lewis, Philip Ahn. Patriotic WW2 yarn involving Chinese waifs who battle Japanese invaders and come to the aid of downed American pilots.
Chinatown Nights (1929) 82m. ** D: William A. Wellman. Wallace Beery, Florence Vidor, Warner Oland, Jack Oakie, Jack McHugh, Tetsu Komai, Frank Chew. San Francisco socialite Vidor gets caught in the middle of a Tong war in the Chinese quarter and takes up with gang leader Beery. Silent film with some dialogue scenes obviously added at the last minute; awkward but interesting.
China Venture (1953) 83m. **½ D: Don Siegel. Edmond O'Brien, Barry Sullivan, Jocelyn Brando, Richard Loo, Philip Ahn. Exciting WW2 adventure film of marine group on mission to capture Japanese naval commander wanted by U.S. interrogation department.
Chinese Cat, The (1944) 65m. ** D: Phil Rosen. Sidney Toler, Benson Fong, Joan Woodbury, Mantan Moreland, Weldon Heyburn, Ian Keith, John Davidson, Betty Blythe. Formula *Charlie Chan* programmer, with usual assortment of villains literally dying to get their hands on statue containing an uncut diamond.▼◗
Chinese Ring, The (1947) 65m. *½ D: William Beaudine. Roland Winters, Warren Douglas, Victor Sen Yung, Mantan Moreland, Philip Ahn, Louise Currie, Byron Foulger. Charlie Chan probes the murder of a Chinese princess, with Winters debuting as the great detective. Routine entry indistinguishable from the other Monogram cheapies.▼◗
Chip Off the Old Block (1944) 82m. ** D: Charles Lamont. Donald O'Connor, Peggy Ryan, Ann Blyth, Helen Vinson, Helen Broderick, Arthur Treacher, Patric Knowles, Ernest Truex. Innocuous wartime musical of misunderstandings, climaxing in teenage romance and musical show. Blyth's film debut.
Chocolate Soldier, The (1941) 102m. ** D: Roy Del Ruth. Nelson Eddy, Rise Stevens, Nigel Bruce, Florence Bates, Dorothy Gilmore, Nydia Westman. Not the Oscar Straus operetta, but rather a remake of Molnár's THE GUARDSMAN. Eddy and Stevens are husband-wife opera stars; to test her fidelity, he disguises himself as a Cossack and woos her. Much too talky and not enough music; remade as LILY IN LOVE. Film debut of Met Opera star Stevens.
Christmas Carol, A (1938) 69m. *** D: Edwin L. Marin. Reginald Owen, Gene Lockhart, Kathleen Lockhart, Terry Kilburn, Barry MacKay, Lynne Carver, Leo G. Carroll, Ann Rutherford. Nicely done adaptation of Dickens' classic with Owen a well-modulated Scrooge, surrounded by good MGM players and period settings. Young June Lockhart makes her screen debut. Also shown in computer-colored version.▼◗
Christmas Carol, A (1951-British) 86m. **** D: Brian Desmond-Hurst. Alastair Sim, Jack Warner, Kathleen Harrison, Mervyn Johns, Hermione Baddeley, Clifford Mollison, Michael Hordern, George Cole, Carol Marsh, Miles Malleson, Ernest Thesiger, Hattie Jacques, Peter Bull, Hugh Demp-

ster. Superb film is too good to be shown only at Christmastime; always delightful Sim makes Scrooge a three-dimensional character in this faithful, heartwarming rendition of the Dickens classic. Screenplay by Noel Langley. Patrick Macnee plays young Marley. Original British title: SCROOGE. Also shown in computer-colored version. ▼●◗

Christmas Eve (1947) 90m. *½ D: Edwin L. Marin. George Brent, George Raft, Randolph Scott, Joan Blondell, Virginia Field, Ann Harding, Reginald Denny, Joe Sawyer. Slow-moving mixture of comedy and drama as foster sons discover evil intentions of relations to victimize Harding. Retitled: SINNER'S HOLIDAY. ◗

Christmas Holiday (1944) 92m. *** D: Robert Siodmak. Deanna Durbin, Gene Kelly, Gale Sondergaard, Gladys George, Richard Whorf. Somerset Maugham novel reset in America. Crime story with Durbin gone wrong to help killer-hubby Kelly; songs include "Spring Will Be a Little Late This Year."

Christmas in Connecticut (1945) 101m. **½ D: Peter Godfrey. Barbara Stanwyck, Dennis Morgan, Sydney Greenstreet, Reginald Gardiner, S. Z. Sakall, Robert Shayne, Una O'Connor. Airy fluff with Stanwyck, a chic magazine writer who's supposed to be an expert homemaker, forced to entertain a war veteran (Morgan) and her boss (Greenstreet) for the holidays. Standard studio corn it may be, but a wonderful treat for late-night viewing on Christmas Eve. Remade for cable TV in 1992. Also shown in computer-colored version. ▼●◗

Christmas in July (1940) 67m. ***½ D: Preston Sturges. Dick Powell, Ellen Drew, Raymond Walburn, William Demarest, Ernest Truex, Franklin Pangborn. Top Sturges comedy about Powell going on shopping spree after mistakenly believing he has won big contest. Walburn and Demarest are at their best. ▼●◗

Christmas Wish, A SEE: **Great Rupert, The**

Christopher Bean (1933) 87m. ***½ D: Sam Wood. Marie Dressler, Lionel Barrymore, Helen Mack, Beulah Bondi, Jean Hersholt, Russell Hardie, H. B. Warner, George Coulouris. N.Y.C. art dealers pursue a small-town family when they learn that a deceased artist worked as their handyman and gave them one of his now-valuable paintings. Deliciously droll (and still-timely) comedy. Dressler, as a household slavey, and Barrymore, as a not-so-simple country doctor, are at their best. Based on Sidney Howard's play *The Late Christopher Bean*, adapted from the French play *Prenez Garde à la Peinture*, itself filmed in 1932. Dressler's final film. Aka HER SWEETHEART.

Christopher Columbus (1949-British) C-104m. *** D: David Macdonald. Fredric

March, Florence Eldridge, Francis L. Sullivan, Linden Travers, Kathleen Ryan, Derek Bond, James Robertson Justice, Felix Aylmer, Nora Swinburne, Abraham Sofaer. Stark, slowly paced biography of explorer, with earnest portrayal by March in title role; good period setting. ▼●◗

Christopher Strong (1933) 77m. **½ D: Dorothy Arzner. Katharine Hepburn, Colin Clive, Billie Burke, Helen Chandler, Jack LaRue. Hepburn's an aviatrix in love with married Clive. Dated film intriguing for star's performance as headstrong, individualistic woman—and dig that silver lamé costume. Margaret Lindsay appears unbilled. ▼●◗

Chu-Chin-Chow (1934-British) 103m. ** D: Walter Forde. George Robey, Fritz Kortner, Anna May Wong, John Garrick, Pearl Argyle, Laurence Hanray, Dennis Hoey, Malcolm McEachern, Francis L. Sullivan. Elephantine operetta version of *Ali Baba and the Forty Thieves* (more or less), shot on enormous indoor sets, makes THE DESERT SONG seem like cutting-edge entertainment. Labored, hokey, claustrophobic, miscast, but curiously fascinating, with Austrian Kortner as Abu Hassan, Cockney Robey as Ali Baba, and Wong with too little to do as a mistress of intrigue. Sullivan doesn't show up until the end, but livens things up as the bored Caliph. The popular play was filmed before in 1923. ◗

Chump at Oxford, A (1940) 63m. **½ D: Alfred Goulding. Stan Laurel, Oliver Hardy, Wilfred Lucas, Forrester Harvey, James Finlayson, Anita Garvin. So-called feature is more like a series of barely related shorts; film is nearly half over before L&H even get to Oxford. Still quite funny, especially when they settle down in the Dean's quarters. A young Peter Cushing plays one of the boys' tormentors. Also shown in computer-colored version. ▼●◗

Chushingura (1962-Japanese) C-108m. ***½ D: Hiroshi Inagaki. Koshiro Matsumoto, Yuzo Kayama, Chusha Ichikawa, Toshiro Mifune, Yoko Tsukasa. Young lord Kayama is forced to commit hara kiri by corrupt feudal lord Ichikawa, and his 47 samurai retainers (or ronin) seek vengeance. A version of an oft-filmed story, based on a real-life event: sprawling, episodic, exquisitely beautiful, if a bit slow. Sometimes referred to as the GONE WITH THE WIND of Japanese cinema. Originally released in Japan in two parts, running 204m. Tohoscope. ▼●◗

Cimarron (1931) 124m. **½ D: Wesley Ruggles. Richard Dix, Irene Dunne, Estelle Taylor, Nance O'Neil, William Collier, Jr., Roscoe Ates. Edna Ferber's saga about an American family and the effect of empire building on the American West, 1889–1929. Oscar winner for Best Picture and Best Screenplay (Howard Estabrook), it dates badly, particularly Dix's overripe performance—but it's still worth seeing. Remade in 1960.▼▶

Cimarron (1960) **C-147m.** **½ D: Anthony Mann. Glenn Ford, Maria Schell, Anne Baxter, Arthur O'Connell, Russ Tamblyn, Mercedes McCambridge, Vic Morrow, Charles McGraw, Henry (Harry) Morgan, Edgar Buchanan, Robert Keith, Aline MacMahon, David Opatoshu, Mary Wickes. Edna Ferber's chronicle of frontier life in Oklahoma between 1889 and 1929 becomes an indifferent sprawling soap opera unsalvaged by a few spectacular scenes. CinemaScope.▼◑▶

Cimarron Kid, The (1952) **C-84m.** **½ D: Budd Boetticher. Audie Murphy, Beverly Tyler, James Best, Yvette Dugay, Hugh O'Brian, Roy Roberts, Noah Beery (Jr.), Leif Erickson, Rand Brooks. Formulaic but actionful Western with Murphy in title role, reluctantly riding a lawless road alongside the Daltons and other "name value" outlaws. Some fine scenery.▶

Cincinnati Kid, The (1965) **C-113m.** **½ D: Norman Jewison. Steve McQueen, Ann-Margret, Edward G. Robinson, Karl Malden, Tuesday Weld, Joan Blondell, Rip Torn, Jack Weston, Cab Calloway. Roving card-sharks get together in New Orleans for big poker game; side episodes of meaningless romance. Robinson, Blondell, and Malden come off best as vivid members of the playing profession. Script by Ring Lardner, Jr., and Terry Southern; Jewison replaced Sam Peckinpah as director. Ray Charles sings the title song.▼◑▶

Cinderella (1914) **52m.** *** D: James Kirkwood. Mary Pickford, Owen Moore, Isabel Vernon, Georgia Wilson, Lucille Carney, W. N. Cone. Charming version of the beloved fairy tale about the girl who is cruelly treated by her stepmother and stepsisters and whose life changes after a visit from her Fairy Godmother. Mary makes a sweet Cinderella. Contemporary children may not relate to this, but it's a real curio for film buffs. Prince Charming is played by Pickford's real-life husband at the time, Owen Moore.▼▶

Cinderella (1950) **C-74m.** ***½ D: Wilfred Jackson, Hamilton Luske, Clyde Geronimi. Voices of Ilene Woods, William Phipps, Eleanor Audley, Rhoda Williams, Lucille Bliss, Verna Felton. One of Walt Disney's best animated fairy tales spins the traditional story with some delightful comic embellishments, including a couple of mice named Gus and Jaq who befriend the put-upon heroine. Tuneful score includes "A Dream Is a Wish Your Heart Makes" and "Bibbidi Bobbidi Boo." Followed by two DVD sequels.▼◑▶

Cinderella Jones (1946) **88m.** ** D: Busby Berkeley. Joan Leslie, Robert Alda, S. Z. Sakall, Edward Everett Horton, Ruth Donnelly, Elisha Cook, Jr. Silly comedy of girl who must marry brainy husband to collect inheritance; good cast defeated by trivial script.

Cinderfella (1960) **C-91m.** **½ D: Frank Tashlin. Jerry Lewis, Ed Wynn, Judith Anderson, Anna Maria Alberghetti, Henry Silva, Count Basie. Jerry is the poor stepson turned into a handsome prince for a night by fairy godfather Wynn. Fairy tale classic revamped as a pretentious Lewis vehicle, with talky interludes and ineffectual musical sequences.▼▶

Cinerama Holiday (1955) **C-128m.** *** D: Robert L. Bendick, Philippe De Lacy. Three-panel Cinerama travelogue is a captivating relic of its era as it follows a "typical" American couple from Kansas and what they see and experience as they tour Europe, as well as a Swiss couple and their first experience in the U.S. Opens with images of ice-capped Swiss Alps that look as if they might have been filmed last week using state-of-the-art 21st-century technology. 2012 restoration is presented in a curved screen simulation that duplicates the feeling of seeing the film in its original presentation. Cinerama.▶

Circle, The (1959-British) **84m.** **½ D: Gerald Thomas. John Mills, Derek Farr, Roland Culver, Wilfrid Hyde-White. Well-acted, neatly paced murder yarn involving London medico. Retitled: THE VICIOUS CIRCLE.

Circle of Danger (1951-British) **86m.** **½ D: Jacques Tourneur. Ray Milland, Patricia Roc, Marius Goring, Hugh Sinclair. Straightforward account of Milland returning to England to ferret out brother's killers. ▼▶

Circle of Deception, A (1961-British) **100m.** **½ D: Jack Lee. Bradford Dillman, Suzy Parker, Harry Andrews, Robert Stephens, Paul Rogers. At times engaging psychological yarn of WW2 espionage agent Dillman, who breaks under Axis torture; ironic climax. Dillman and Parker later married in real life. CinemaScope.

Circle of Love (1964-French-Italian) **C-105m.** *½ D: Roger Vadim. Jane Fonda, Jean-Claude Brialy, Maurice Ronet, Jean Sorel, Catherine Spaak, Anna Karina, Marie Dubois, Claude Giraud, Françoise Dorléac. Undistinguished remake of Ophuls' classic LA RONDE: A seduces B, B makes love to C, C has an affair with D—circling all the way back to A. Screenplay by Jean Anouilh; original running time: 110m. Other screen version of the Arthur Schnitzler play on which this is based is CHAIN OF DESIRE. Franscope.▼▶

Circumstantial Evidence (1945) **68m.** **½ D: John Larkin. Michael O'Shea, Lloyd Nolan, Trudy Marshall, Billy Cummings, Ruth Ford, Reed Hadley, Roy Roberts, Scotty Beckett. Thoughtful, engaging programmer of O'Shea fighting with a grocer, who is accidentally killed; he then finds himself accused of murder and convicted on the testimony of eyewitnesses who think they saw him commit the crime.▶

Circus, The (1928) **72m.** ***½ D: Charles

Chaplin. Charlie Chaplin, Merna Kennedy, Allan Garcia, Betty Morrissey, Harry Crocker. Not the "masterpiece" of THE GOLD RUSH or CITY LIGHTS, but still a gem; story has Charlie accidentally joining traveling circus, falling in love with bareback rider. Hilarious comedy, with memorable finale. Chaplin won a special Academy Award for "versatility and genius in writing, acting, directing and producing" this.▼◑❿

Circus Clown, The (1934) 63m. ** D: Ray Enright. Joe E. Brown, Dorothy Burgess, Patricia Ellis, Lee Moran, Tom Dugan, William Demarest. Brown mixes comedy and drama in account of circus star whose father objects to his work.

Circus of Horrors (1960-British) C-89m. **½ D: Sidney Hayers. Anton Diffring, Erika Remberg, Yvonne Monlaur, Donald Pleasence. A most unethical plastic surgeon takes over a run-down circus and begins turning scarred female criminals into beautiful star attractions. Fast-moving, rousing horror film. ▼◑❿

Circus Queen Murder, The (1933) 65m. *** D: Roy William Neill. Adolphe Menjou, Greta Nissen, Ruthelma Stevens, Donald Cook, Dwight Frye, Harry Holman. A madman is on the loose in a traveling circus, but vacationing N.Y.C. police commissioner Thatcher Colt (Menjou) happens to be on the scene to investigate. A quick perusal of the cast list pretty much tips off the main suspect, but this is a stylish and enjoyable little whodunit with some clever touches. Circus footage is lifted from Frank Capra's RAIN OR SHINE. Menjou also played Colt in THE NIGHT CLUB LADY (1932). Sidney Blackmer played Colt in THE PANTHER'S CLAW (1942).

Circus World (1964) C-135m. **½ D: Henry Hathaway. John Wayne, Rita Hayworth, Claudia Cardinale, John Smith, Lloyd Nolan, Richard Conte. Made in Spain, film has nothing new to offer, but rehashes usual circus formula quite nicely with the Duke as Big Top boss trying to pull his three-ring Wild West show through various perils during European tour. Climactic fire sequence is truly spectacular. Runs 138m. with intermission/entr'acte, exit music. Super Technirama 70. ▼◑

Cisco Kid, The (1931) 61m. ** D: Irving Cummings. Warner Baxter, Edmund Lowe, Conchita Montenegro, Nora Lane, Frederick Burt, Willard Robertson, Charles Stevens, Chris (Pin) Martin. Barney McGill's fluid camerawork and shots of silhouetted cacti against the Arizona sky are more interesting than the hackneyed screenplay about O. Henry's "romantic bad man" (Baxter) helping a widow and her kids while dodging cocky Army sergeant Lowe. Sequel to IN OLD ARIZONA; followed by THE RETURN OF THE CISCO KID in 1939. ❿

Cisco Kid and the Lady, The (1939) 74m. **½ D: Herbert I. Leeds. Cesar Romero, Marjorie Weaver, Chris-Pin Martin, George Montgomery, Robert Barrat, Virginia Field, Harry Green. Lively B Western has Cisco wooing two women (a dance-hall girl and a schoolmarm) while tangling with Barrat over ownership of a mine and possession of an orphaned baby. First of six *Cisco Kid* movies featuring Romero. ❿

Citadel, The (1938-U.S.-British) 112m. ***½ D: King Vidor. Robert Donat, Rosalind Russell, Ralph Richardson, Rex Harrison, Emlyn Williams, Penelope Dudley-Ward, Francis L. Sullivan. Superb adaptation of A. J. Cronin novel of impoverished doctor Donat eschewing ideals for wealthy life of treating rich hypochondriacs, neglecting wife and friends in the process; tragedy opens his eyes. Weak ending, but fine acting makes up for it. Frank "Spig" Wead, Emlyn Williams, Ian Dalrymple, Elizabeth Hill, and John Van Druten all contributed to the script. Remade in Britain as a TV miniseries.▼❿

Citizen Kane (1941) 119m. **** D: Orson Welles. Orson Welles, Joseph Cotten, Everett Sloane, Agnes Moorehead, Dorothy Comingore, Ray Collins, George Coulouris, Ruth Warrick, William Alland, Paul Stewart, Erskine Sanford. Welles' first and best, a film that broke all the rules and invented some new ones, with fascinating story of Hearst-like publisher's rise to power. The cinematography (by Gregg Toland), music score (by Bernard Herrmann), and Oscar-winning screenplay (by Welles and Herman J. Mankiewicz) are all first-rate. A stunning film in every way . . . and Welles was only 25 when he made it! Incidentally, the reporter with a pipe is Alan Ladd; Arthur O'Connell is another one of the reporters.▼◑❿

City Across the River (1949) 90m. **½ D: Maxwell Shane. Stephen McNally, Thelma Ritter, Luis Van Rooten, Jeff Corey, Anthony (Tony) Curtis, Richard Jaeckel. Watered-down version of Irving Shulman's novel *The Amboy Dukes*, involving tough life in Brooklyn slums, with predictable hoods et al.

City After Midnight (1957-British) 84m. *½ D: Compton Bennett. Phyllis Kirk, Dan O'Herlihy, Petula Clark, Wilfrid Hyde-White, Jack Watling. Tame detective film of private eye O'Herlihy investigating death of antique dealer. British title: THAT WOMAN OPPOSITE.

City Beneath the Sea (1953) C-87m. **½ D: Budd Boetticher. Robert Ryan, Mala Powers, Anthony Quinn, Suzan Ball, Woody Strode. Inconsequential underwater yarn invigorated by Ryan and Quinn as deep-sea divers hunting treasure off Jamaican coast.

City for Conquest (1940) 101m. *** D: Anatole Litvak. James Cagney, Ann Sheridan, Frank Craven, Arthur Kennedy, Donald

Crisp, Frank McHugh, George Tobias, Elia Kazan, Anthony Quinn. Cagney makes this a must as boxer devoted to younger brother Kennedy. Beautiful production overshadows film's pretentious faults. A rare chance to see young Kazan in an acting role, as a neighborhood pal turned gangster. Long-missing prologue was restored in 2006, bringing running time to 104m. ▼●⦆

City Girl (1930) **88m.** ***½ D: F. W. Murnau. Charles Farrell, Mary Duncan, David Torrence, Edith Yorke, Dawn O'Day (Anne Shirley), Tom McGuire, Richard Alexander, Pat Rooney, Roscoe Ates, Guinn "Big Boy" Williams. Minnesota farmer Farrell goes to the big city to sell his family's wheat crop and returns with a wife, a waitress with whom he's fallen in love. His family is unwelcoming, to say the least. Beautifully realized silent drama is simple, eloquent, and exquisitely photographed (by Ernest Palmer). Murnau's final Hollywood production. Talkie version no longer exists. ⦆

City in Darkness SEE: **Charlie Chan in City in Darkness**

City Lights (1931) **86m.** **** D: Charles Chaplin. Charlie Chaplin, Virginia Cherrill, Harry Myers, Hank Mann. Chaplin's masterpiece tells story of his love for blind flower girl and his hot-and-cold friendship with a drunken millionaire. Eloquent, moving, and funny. One of the all-time greats. ▼●⦆

City of Bad Men (1953) **C-82m.** ** D: Harmon Jones. Jeanne Crain, Dale Robertson, Richard Boone, Lloyd Bridges, Carl Betz. Robbers attempt to steal prizefight proceeds in 1890s Nevada; film combines Western with re-creation of Jim Corbett–Bob Fitzsimmons fight bout. ⦆

City of Fear (1959) **81m.** *½ D: Irving Lerner. Vince Edwards, Lyle Talbot, John Archer, Steven Ritch, Patricia Blair. Programmer involving escaped convict Edwards sought by police and health officials; container he stole is filled with radioactive material, not money. ⦆

City of Missing Girls (1941) **74m.** ** D: Elmer Clifton. H. B. Warner, Astrid Allwyn, John Archer, Sarah Padden, Gale Storm. Assistant DA Archer tries to get the goods on a slick racketeer whose "School of Fine Arts" lures wannabe-showgirls into the world of nightclubs—and worse. Tinny organ music score sounds like it's from a 1940s radio soap opera. George Rosener, playing a cop named "Copper," cowrote the screenplay. ⦆

City of Shadows (1955) **70m.** *½ D: William Witney. Victor McLaglen, John Baer, Kathleen Crowley, Anthony Caruso. Mild happenings about crafty newsboys involved with derelict racketeer McLaglen. ⦆

City of the Dead, The SEE: **Horror Hotel**
City on a Hunt SEE: **No Escape** (1953)
City Streets (1931) **82m.** *** D: Rouben Mamoulian. Gary Cooper, Sylvia Sidney,

Paul Lukas, Wynne Gibson, Guy Kibbee, Stanley Fields. Cooper is an unambitious carnival worker who's drawn into the underworld by his love for racketeer's daughter (Sidney). Stylish melodrama is more interesting for Mamoulian's innovative presentation (and the stunning camerawork of Lee Garmes) than for its predictable plot. Lukas and Kibbee stand out in unusually smarmy characterizations. Notable, too, as Dashiell Hammett's only original screen story.

City Streets (1938) **68m.** ** D: Albert S. Rogell. Edith Fellows, Leo Carrillo, Tommy Bond, Mary Gordon, Helen Jerome Eddy. Painless programmer with kindly Carrillo fighting for the interests of crippled orphan Fellows. Likable performances by the leads. ⦆

City That Never Sleeps (1953) **90m.** *** D: John H. Auer. Gig Young, Mala Powers, William Talman, Edward Arnold, Chill Wills, Marie Windsor, Paula Raymond, Otto Hulett, Wally Cassell, Tom Poston. Film noir about one night in the life of Chicago cop Young, who plans to quit his job and leave his wife for nightclub singer Powers. Events centering on criminal Talman and crooked lawyer Arnold interfere. Tense and ethically complex in the noir manner, and well photographed on location. Main misstep: Wills plays Chicago, the city itself, in human form. ⦆

City Under the Sea, The SEE: **War-Gods of the Deep**

City Without Men (1943) **75m.** *½ D: Sidney Salkow. Linda Darnell, Michael Duane, Sara Allgood, Edgar Buchanan, Glenda Farrell, Leslie Brooks, Margaret Hamilton, Sheldon Leonard, Rosemary DeCamp. Very routine lower-berth item about a boardinghouse near a prison where the women wait for their men to get out. ▼●⦆

Civilization (1916) **86m.** **½ D: Thomas H. Ince, Raymond B. West, Reginald Barker. Howard Hickman, Enid Markey, Herschel Mayall, Lola May, George Fisher, J. Frank Burke. Intriguing if drawn-out epic set in a fictitious kingdom, portraying its destiny in time of war. Of interest mostly for historical reasons, as a humanistic, antiwar morality tale intended to champion the foreign policy of President Woodrow Wilson (before America became involved in WW1). ▼●⦆

Clairvoyant, The (1934-British) **80m.** **½ D: Maurice Elvey. Claude Rains, Fay Wray, Jane Baxter, Mary Clare, Athole Stewart, Felix Aylmer, Donald Calthrop. A phony music hall mind-reader suddenly acquires clairvoyant powers—and soon discovers they're more of a curse than a blessing. Intriguing storyline doesn't hold up to the end, though Rains is fine as always. Also known as THE EVIL MIND. ▼●⦆

Clancy Street Boys (1943) **66m.** **½ D: William Beaudine. Leo Gorcey, Huntz Hall, Bobby Jordan, Sunshine Sammy Morrison,

Noah Beery, Sr., Amelita Ward, Bennie Bartlett, Rick Vallin, Billy Benedict. Farcical *East Side Kids* yarn, with Muggs (Gorcey) enlisting the boys to be his siblings for benefit of uncle Beery. Hall in drag is a comic highlight.▼❙

Clarence the Cross-Eyed Lion (1965) **C-98m.** **½ D: Andrew Marton. Marshall Thompson, Betsy Drake, Cheryl Miller, Richard Haydn, Alan Caillou. Basis for *Daktari* TV show is good family entertainment set in Africa with adventure and wholesome comedy well blended. ▼❙

Clash by Night (1952) **105m.** *** D: Fritz Lang. Barbara Stanwyck, Paul Douglas, Robert Ryan, Marilyn Monroe, Keith Andes, J. Carrol Naish. Moody, well-acted Clifford Odets story of drifter Stanwyck settling down, marrying good-natured fisherman Douglas. Cynical friend Ryan senses that she's not happy, tries to take advantage. Andes and Monroe provide secondary love interest.▼❍❙

Clash of the Wolves (1925) **74m.** **½ D: Noel Mason Smith. Rin Tin Tin, June Marlowe, Charles Farrell, "Heinie" Conklin, William Walling, Pat Hartigan. Tenderfoot prospector Farrell rescues and tames a half-breed wolf dog called Lobo; the animal shows his loyalty when his new pal is imperiled by a dastardly claim jumper. Predictable but enjoyable action yarn, made to order for its canine star. Worth a look if only for those majestic shots of Rinty perched atop boulders and racing across the desert. ▼❙

Classe Tous Risques (1960-French) **103m.** *** D: Claude Sautet. Lino Ventura, Jean-Paul Belmondo, Sandra Milo, Marcel Dalio, Stan Krol. Solid crime drama with Ventura as a murderer who's been living in exile in Milan but decides to return to Paris after pulling one last heist. His plans go awry, and while he expects his criminal pals to help him when he arrives in Nice, they send a young guy instead (Belmondo) to pick him up. Tough, ironic tale filled with interesting characters and vivid location work. Great showcase for the young Belmondo, made around the same time as BREATHLESS.

Claudelle Inglish (1961) **99m.** **½ D: Gordon Douglas. Diane McBain, Arthur Kennedy, Will Hutchins, Constance Ford, Claude Akins, Chad Everett, Robert Logan. Trite soaper derived from Erskine Caldwell tale of Southern farm gal who gives all to find excitement, with predictable consequences.❙

Claudia (1943) **91m.** *** D: Edmund Goulding. Dorothy McGuire, Robert Young, Ina Claire, Reginald Gardiner, Olga Baclanova, Jean Howard. Warm comedy of young Claudia suddenly marrying, facing adult problems, learning a lot about life in short period; beautifully acted. McGuire, in film debut, recreates her Broadway role. Sequel: CLAUDIA AND DAVID.❙

Claudia and David (1946) **78m.** *** D:

Walter Lang. Dorothy McGuire, Robert Young, Mary Astor, John Sutton, Gail Patrick, Florence Bates. Enjoyable follow-up to CLAUDIA with McGuire and Young having a baby, adjusting to suburban life; engaging, well acted.

Clay Pigeon, The (1949) **63m.** **½ D: Richard O. Fleischer. Bill Williams, Barbara Hale, Richard Loo, Richard Quine, Frank Fenton, Martha Hyer. Neat little actioner with Williams, a seaman accused of treason and of responsibility in the death of his friend, on the trail of the real culprit, a Japanese prison guard. Written by Carl Foreman, based on a true incident.

Clear All Wires! (1933) **78m.** **½ D: George Hill. Lee Tracy, Benita Hume, Una Merkel, James Gleason, Alan Edwards. Tracy enlivens this so-so story of a manipulative, globe-trotting journalist, who creates as much news as he covers; highlighted are his escapades while in Russia. Script by Bella and Sam Spewack, from their play.❙

Cleo From 5 to 7 (1962-French) **C/B&W-90m.** *** D: Agnés Varda. Corinne Marchand, Antoine Bourseiller, Dorothée Blanck, Michel Legrand, Anna Karina, Eddie Constantine, Jean-Luc Godard. Intelligent, fluid account of Parisian songstress forced to reevaluate her life while awaiting vital medical report on her physical condition. First scene is in color. ▼❍❙

Cleopatra (1934) **100m.** ***½ D: Cecil B. DeMille. Claudette Colbert, Warren William, Henry Wilcoxon, Gertrude Michael, Joseph Schildkraut, C. Aubrey Smith, Claudia Dell, Robert Warwick. Opulent DeMille version of Cleopatra doesn't date badly, stands out as one of his most intelligent films, thanks in large part to fine performances by all. Top entertainment, with Oscar-winning cinematography by Victor Milner.▼❍❙

Cleopatra (1963) **C-243m.** ** D: Joseph L. Mankiewicz. Elizabeth Taylor, Richard Burton, Rex Harrison, Pamela Brown, George Cole, Hume Cronyn, Cesare Danova, Kenneth Haigh, Andrew Keir, Martin Landau, Roddy McDowall, Robert Stephens, Francesca Annis, Herbert Berghof, Michael Hordern, John Hoyt, Carroll O'Connor. Saga of the Nile goes on and on and on. Definitely a curiosity item, but you'll be satisfied after an hour. Good acting, especially by Harrison and McDowall, but it's lost in this flat, four-hour misfire. Nevertheless earned Oscars for cinematography, art direction–set decoration, costumes, special effects. Runs 251m. with overture, intermission/entr'acte, exit music. Todd-AO.▼❍❙

Cleopatra's Daughter (1960-Italian) **C-102m.** ** D: Richard McNamara. Debra Paget, Ettore Manni, Erno Crisa, Robert Alda, Corrado Panni. American actors are lost in this costumer, more intent on playing up sadistic sequences; intrigue at Egyptian court the highlight. Ultrascope.▼❙

[125]

Climax, The (1944) **C-86m.** **½ D: George Waggner. Boris Karloff, Susanna Foster, Turhan Bey, Gale Sondergaard, Thomas Gomez, Scotty Beckett, George Dolenz, Jane Farrar, June Vincent, Ludwig Stossel. Technicolor tale of suave but sinister physician to the Vienna Opera House who takes an unnatural interest in their newest soprano (Foster)—just as he did another singer who disappeared ten years ago. No surprises here, but slickly done. ▼⊙▶

Clinging Vine, The (1926) **71m.** **½ D: Paul Sloane. Leatrice Joy, Tom Moore, Toby Claude, Robert Edeson, Dell Henderson. Handsome fluff about unfeminine executive (Joy) who becomes involved in business swindle and falls in love. ▼▶

Clipped Wings (1953) **65m.** **½ D: Edward Bernds. Leo Gorcey, Huntz Hall, Bernard Gorcey, David (Gorcey) Condon, Bennie Bartlett, Renie Riano, Todd Karns, June Vincent, Mary Treen, Philip Van Zandt. Sach and Slip join the Air Force in a fast and funny *Bowery Boys* entry. ▼▶

Clive of India (1935) **90m.** **½ D: Richard Boleslawski. Ronald Colman, Loretta Young, Colin Clive, Francis Lister, C. Aubrey Smith, Cesar Romero, Montagu Love, Leo G. Carroll, Don Ameche. Colman is ideally cast as Robert Clive, the "man of destiny" who secured British rule in India at the sacrifice of his own personal happiness. More fanciful than factual, but entertaining and lavishly produced. ▶

Cloak and Dagger (1946) **106m.** **½ D: Fritz Lang. Gary Cooper, Lilli Palmer, Robert Alda, Vladimir Sokoloff, J. Edward Bromberg, Marjorie Hoshelle, Ludwig Stossel, Helene Thimig, Dan Seymour, Marc Lawrence. U.S. professor-physicist Cooper heads to Europe to link up with an atomic scientist and becomes involved in assorted intrigue. Spy drama is not among Lang's best, but is still worth a look. Screenplay by Albert Maltz and Ring Lardner, Jr. ▼⊙▶

Cloak Without Dagger SEE: **Operation Conspiracy**

Clock, The (1945) **90m.** ***½ D: Vincente Minnelli. Judy Garland, Robert Walker, James Gleason, Keenan Wynn, Marshall Thompson, Lucille Gleason. Soldier Walker has two-day leave in N.Y.C., meets office worker Judy; they spend the day falling in love, encountering friendly milkman Gleason, drunk Wynn; charming little love story with beguiling Garland. Also shown in computer-colored version.▼⊙▶

Close Call for Boston Blackie, A (1946) **60m.** ** D: Lew Landers. Chester Morris, Lynn Merrick, Richard Lane, Frank Sully, George E. Stone, Claire Carleton, Erik Rolf, Charles Lane. Blackie is framed for murder by a femme fatale in this disappointing entry with a plethora of comedy. ▶

Close Call for Ellery Queen (1942) **65m.**

*½ D: James Hogan. William Gargan, Margaret Lindsay, Charley Grapewin, Ralph Morgan, Kay Linaker, Edward Norris, James Burke, Addison Richards. Gargan picks up the role of Queen in this dreary entry about a missing heirs racket.

Close to My Heart (1951) **90m.** *** D: William Keighley. Ray Milland, Gene Tierney, Fay Bainter, Howard St. John. Superior soaper; Tierney attaches herself to waif in Bainter's orphanage, but husband Milland won't allow adoption until child's background is traced.▶

Cloudburst (1951-British) **83m.** **½ D: Francis Searle. Robert Preston, Elizabeth Sellars, Colin Tapley, Sheila Burrell, Harold Lang, Mary Germaine. Moody, atmospheric drama, set right after WW2, with intelligence officer Preston determined to avenge the death of his beloved wife. ▶

Clouded Yellow, The (1950-British) **85m.** *** D: Ralph Thomas. Jean Simmons, Trevor Howard, Sonia Dresdel, Barry Jones, Kenneth More, Geoffrey Keen, Andre Morell, Maxwell Reed. Entertaining psychological drama/mystery/chase film in which ex-secret serviceman Howard takes a job cataloguing butterflies, and becomes involved with a strange, fragile young girl (Simmons)—and murder.▼

Clouds Over Europe SEE: **Q Planes**

Clown, The (1953) **91m.** **½ D: Robert Z. Leonard. Red Skelton, Tim Considine, Jane Greer, Loring Smith, Philip Ober. Sentimental remake of THE CHAMP about a washed-up, self-destructive comic with a devoted son who looks out for him. Skelton's not bad in rare dramatic role; Considine is so good he overcomes some of the hokiness of script. Charles Bronson has a bit role in dice game scene.▼▶

Club Havana (1945) **62m.** ** D: Edgar G. Ulmer. Tom Neal, Margaret Lindsay, Don Douglas, Gertrude Michael, Isabelita (Lita Baron), Dorothy Morris, Ernest Truex. Roadshow GRAND HOTEL is very cheap production with little of interest.▼

Clue of the New Pin (1960-British) **58m.** *½ D: Allan Davis. Paul Daneman, Bernard Archard, James Villiers, Catherine Woodville, Clive Morton. Old-fashioned Edgar Wallace yarn about "perfect crime," with Villiers a TV interviewer who tangles with murderer; ponderous.

Cluny Brown (1946) **100m.** ***½ D: Ernst Lubitsch. Charles Boyer, Jennifer Jones, Peter Lawford, Helen Walker, Reginald Gardiner, C. Aubrey Smith, Reginald Owen, Richard Haydn, Sara Allgood, Ernest Cossart, Una O'Connor, Florence Bates, Christopher Severn. Delightful comedy which charts the evolving relationship between orphan Jones and penniless Czech refugee professor Boyer in pre-WW2 England. Takes hilarious potshots at the British class system, with the help of a sterling cast of character actors. Screenplay by Samuel Hoffenstein and Elizabeth Reinhardt, from Margery Sharp's novel.

"C" Man (1949) **75m.** **½ D: Joseph Lerner. Dean Jagger, John Carradine, Harry Landers, Lottie Elwen, Rene Paul. Spunky little N.Y.-made programmer in which U.S. Customs agent Jagger sets out to track a stolen necklace and find the killer of another agent, his longtime friend.▼❱

Coast Guard (1939) **72m.** ** D: Edward Ludwig. Randolph Scott, Frances Dee, Ralph Bellamy, Walter Connolly, Warren Hymer, Robert Middlemass, Stanley Andrews. Scott and Bellamy are hard-loving, hard-fighting guardsmen in love with Dee. When one of them is stranded in the snow after a plane crash, the other must decide whether to help or not. Routine but action-filled hokum with similarities to Capra's DIRIGIBLE.

Coast of Skeletons (1964-British) **C-91m.** ** D: Robert Lynn. Richard Todd, Dale Robertson, Heinz Drache, Marianne Koch, Elga Andersen, Derek Nimmo. Edgar Wallace's *Sanders of the River* is basis for largely rewritten tale of ex-officer hired to investigate scuttling of American tycoon's African diamond operation. Todd repeats role he played in SANDERS (DEATH DRUMS ALONG THE RIVER). Techniscope.❱

Cobra (1925) **75m.** *** D: Joseph Henabery. Rudolph Valentino, Nita Naldi, Gertrude Olmstead, Casson Ferguson, Henry Barrows, Lillian Langdon. Valentino produced Martin Brown's play about an aristocratic seducer held in thrall by a female serpent. The star shows acting muscle his peers never noticed in a three-dimensional role as tailor-made for him as a fine Italian suit. Pluses: gowns by MGM's Adrian and handsome art deco direction by William Cameron Menzies.▼❱

Cobra Woman (1944) **C-70m.** *** D: Robert Siodmak. Maria Montez, Jon Hall, Sabu, Lon Chaney (Jr.), Edgar Barrier, Lois Collier, Mary Nash. Deliriously silly camp classic, with island beauty Montez, set to wed Hall, finding herself kidnapped and discovering she has an evil twin sister. Sabu plays Hall's faithful (and ever-so-goofy) companion Kado. Coscripted by Richard Brooks!❱

Cobweb, The (1955) **C-124m.** ** D: Vincente Minnelli. Richard Widmark, Lauren Bacall, Gloria Grahame, Charles Boyer, Lillian Gish, John Kerr, Susan Strasberg, Oscar Levant, Tommy Rettig, Paul Stewart, Adele Jergens. Good cast in static soaper detailing the goings-on in psychiatric clinic headed by Dr. Widmark; of course, some of the personnel are more unbalanced than the patients. Scripted by John Paxton, produced by John Houseman. Film debuts of Strasberg and Kerr. CinemaScope.◗❱

Cocaine Fiends, The (1936) **68m.** BOMB D: William A. O'Connor. Noel Madison, Lois January, Sheila (Bromley) Mannors,

Dean Benton, Lois Lindsay, Eddie Phillips. Dope peddler and mob front man, on the lam, turns a young girl on to cocaine (which she believes is "headache powder") . . . and she's hopelessly addicted. Then her brother is taken "on a sleigh ride with some snow birds." Tawdry, hilariously awful and, in its way, a bit depressing; from the REEFER MADNESS school of filmmaking. Originally shown as THE PACE THAT KILLS.▼❱

Cockeyed Cavaliers (1934) **72m.** *** D: Mark Sandrich. Bert Wheeler, Robert Woolsey, Thelma Todd, Dorothy Lee, Noah Beery, Franklin Pangborn. Colorful costume comedy with Wheeler & Woolsey trying to crash into society by posing as the King's physicians; lively mix of slapstick, puns, and music.▼

Cockeyed Miracle, The (1946) **81m.** ** D: S. Sylvan Simon. Frank Morgan, Keenan Wynn, Cecil Kellaway, Audrey Totter, Marshall Thompson. Good cast carries weak material. Morgan returns from heaven to make up for financial error he made involving family.

Cockeyed World, The (1929) **118m.** *½ D: Raoul Walsh. Victor McLaglen, Edmund Lowe, Lily Damita, El Brendel, Lelia Karnelly, Stuart Erwin. Sequel to WHAT PRICE GLORY with McLaglen and Lowe as battling Marines Flagg and Quirt sent to South Sea island where fiery Damita captures their attention. Smash hit in 1929, it moves like molasses today, and is no match for GLORY.

Cockleshell Heroes, The (1955-British) **C-97m.** ** D: Jose Ferrer. Jose Ferrer, Trevor Howard, Dora Bryan, Anthony Newley, Victor Maddern, Christopher Lee. Special task force is trained in the use of kayaks for WW2 mission. Film never jells. CinemaScope.

Cocktail Hour (1933) **73m.** ** D: Victor Schertzinger. Bebe Daniels, Randolph Scott, Sidney Blackmer, Muriel Kirkland, Jessie Ralph, Barrie Norton, George Nardelli. Successful illustrator Daniels lives life to the fullest but meets her match in Scott, her chauvinistic boss. Opening scenes in Bebe's incredible art deco apartment, and her bantering relationship with Scott, shouldn't lead to such a dull, dreary third act. Director and composer Schertzinger inserts a completely incongruous rhythmic embarkation montage as an ocean liner sets sail.

Cocktails in the Kitchen SEE: **For Better, For Worse**

Cocoanut Grove (1938) **85m.** ** D: Alfred Santell. Fred MacMurray, Harriet Hilliard (Nelson), Yacht Club Boys, Ben Blue, Rufe Davis, Billy Lee, Eve Arden. MacMurray's band just has to make good at Cocoanut Grove audition in flimsy musical with nine songs you'll never hear again.

Cocoanuts, The (1929) **96m.** *** D: Joseph Santley, Robert Florey. Groucho, Harpo, Chico, Zeppo Marx, Kay Francis, Oscar Shaw, Mary Eaton, Margaret Dumont. The Marxes' first film suffers from stagy filming and stale musical subplot, but when the brothers have scenes to themselves it's a riot; highlights include hilarious auction, classic "viaduct" routine.▼◐❙

Code of Scotland Yard (1946-British) **90m.** *** D: George King. Oscar Homolka, Derek Farr, Muriel Pavlov, Kenneth Griffith, Manning Whiley, Kathleen Harrison, Diana Dors. Entertaining melodrama with Homolka most effective as a seemingly respectable London antique dealer who's really an escapee from Devil's Island; Griffith matches him as his slimy assistant. Original British title: THE SHOP AT SLY CORNER.▼

Code of the Secret Service (1939) **58m.** *½ D: Noel Smith. Ronald Reagan, Rosella Towne, Eddie Foy, Jr., Moroni Olsen, Edgar Edwards, Jack Mower. Limp actioner with Lt. Brass Bancroft (Reagan) tangling with counterfeiters in Mexico. Second of a series, following SECRET SERVICE OF THE AIR. ❙

Code Two (1953) **69m.** ** D: Fred Wilcox. Ralph Meeker, Sally Forrest, Keenan Wynn, Robert Horton, Jeff Richards. Three recruits on L.A. motorcycle police force face occupational hazards; when Richards is killed, his partners go after culprits. ❙

Colditz Story, The (1957-British) **97m.** ***½ D: Guy Hamilton. John Mills, Eric Portman, Christopher Rhodes, Lionel Jeffries, Bryan Forbes, Ian Carmichael, Anton Diffring, Theodore Bikel. Supersolid POW saga set in Germany's Colditz Castle, supposedly "escape-proof" but challenged by various European prisoners, and a hardy British group in particular.▼❙

Cold Wind in August, A (1961) **80m.** **½ D: Alexander Singer. Lola Albright, Scott Marlowe, Herschel Bernardi, Joe De Santis. Offbeat account of tenement boy Marlowe having affair with stripper Albright; frank, flavorful tale. ❙

Cole Younger, Gunfighter (1958) **C-78m.** ** D: R. G. Springsteen. Frank Lovejoy, James Best, Abby Dalton, Jan Merlin. Modest actioner has gunfights to perk up trite account of 1870s Texas. CinemaScope. ❙

Collector, The (1965) **C-119m.** *** D: William Wyler. Terence Stamp, Samantha Eggar, Maurice Dallimore, Mona Washbourne. Disturbing story of man who collects more than just butterflies, which is where Eggar fits in. Chilling, if not altogether believable. Based on the novel by John Fowles.▼◐❙

Colleen (1936) **89m.** *** D: Alfred E. Green. Dick Powell, Ruby Keeler, Jack Oakie, Joan Blondell, Hugh Herbert, Paul Draper, Louise Fazenda, Marie Wilson. Neglected Warner Bros. musical is quite good,

with usual boy-meets-girl plot framing tasteful musical numbers. Includes perhaps-definitive Hugh Herbert performance. ❙

College (1927) **65m.** *** D: James W. Horne. Buster Keaton, Anne Cornwall, Flora Bramley, Harold Goodwin, Grant Withers, Snitz Edwards. Highbrow student Buster has to become an all-star athlete to please his girlfriend; episodic gag structure makes this less impressive than other Keaton features, but it's awfully funny.▼◐❙

College Coach (1933) **75m.** **½ D: William Wellman. Dick Powell, Ann Dvorak, Pat O'Brien, Hugh Herbert, Herman Bing, Lyle Talbot. Well-paced tale of ruthless football coach O'Brien, neglected wife Dvorak, star player Powell who also likes chemistry. Look for John Wayne in a bit part. ❙

College Confidential (1960) **91m.** *½ D: Albert Zugsmith. Steve Allen, Jayne Meadows, Mamie Van Doren, Walter Winchell, Herbert Marshall, Cathy Crosby, Conway Twitty, Ziva Rodann, Mickey Shaughnessy. Idiocy involving sociology professor Allen and what happens when he surveys the sexual activities of his students. "Special Guests" include Rocky Marciano, Sheilah Graham, Pamela Mason, and Earl Wilson.

College Holiday (1936) **88m.** **½ D: Frank Tuttle. Jack Benny, George Burns, Gracie Allen, Mary Boland, Martha Raye, Marsha Hunt, Eleanore Whitney. Silly musicomedy about college types arriving at bankrupt hotel where Boland is doing sex experiments.

College Humor (1933) **80m.** *** D: Wesley Ruggles. Bing Crosby, Jack Oakie, Burns and Allen, Richard Arlen, Mary Carlisle, Mary Kornman, Joseph Sauers (Sawyer). College was never like this. Hokey, entertaining rah-rah musical with Bing a professor (!), Arlen and Oakie football stars; Carlisle and Kornman provide love interest. Songs: "Learn to Croon," "Down the Old Ox Road," among others. ❙

College Rhythm (1934) **75m.** **½ D: Norman Taurog. Jack Oakie, Joe Penner, Lanny Ross, Helen Mack, Lyda Roberti, Mary Brian, George Barbier, Franklin Pangborn, Dean Jagger. Brash Oakie, All-American football player and "cupid's gift to coeds," finds himself unemployed and humbled upon graduation. Silly but enjoyable musical/comedy/romance with Mack Gordon–Harry Revel songs. Penner and his duck are even tolerable here.

College Scandal (1935) **75m.** ** D: Elliott Nugent. Arline Judge, Kent Taylor, Wendy Barrie, William Frawley, Benny Baker, William Benedict, Mary Nash, Edward Nugent. Students turn amateur sleuths when murder strikes on campus. Lower-bracket cast fails to add pep to Paramount's seemingly unending series of '30s "College" movies. Formula script manages to find time for a lightweight musical revue. Remade as SWEATER GIRL in 1942.

College Swing (1938) **86m.** ******* D: Raoul Walsh. George Burns, Gracie Allen, Martha Raye, Bob Hope, Edward Everett Horton, Florence George, Ben Blue, Betty Grable, John Payne, Robert Cummings, Jerry Colonna. Gracie hasn't been able to graduate from school in this entertaining collegiate musicomedy with top cast, forgettable songs. Preston Sturges worked (uncredited) on the script.▼❿

Colonel Blimp SEE: **Life and Death of Colonel Blimp, The**

Colonel Effingham's Raid (1945) **70m.** ****½** D: Irving Pichel. Charles Coburn, Joan Bennett, William Eythe, Allyn Joslyn, Elizabeth Patterson, Donald Meek. Entertaining little comedy of ex-officer Coburn fighting to save town's historical landmark; cast supports fair material.▼❿

Colorado (1940) **54m.** ****½** D: Joseph Kane. Roy Rogers, George "Gabby" Hayes, Pauline Moore, Milburn Stone, Maude Eburne, Arthur Loft, Hal Taliaferro, Vester Pegg. Undercover Union officer Rogers is sent to Colorado territory to quell secessionist unrest and finds his brother (Stone) at the bottom of the trouble. Well handled by director Kane, with notable work from Moore and Taliaferro. ▼❿

Colorado Sunset (1939) **65m.** ****½** D: George Sherman. Gene Autry, Smiley Burnette, June Storey, Barbara Pepper, Buster Crabbe, Robert Barrat, Patsy Montana, The Texas Rangers, Purnell Pratt, William Farnum, Kermit Maynard, Elmo Lincoln. When Gene and Smiley mistakenly buy a milk-cow ranch, they are thrust into the middle of a dairy war as racketeers try to drive them out of business. Entertaining blend of action, comedy, and music, with songs "I Want to Be a Cowboy's Sweetheart" and "It Happened in Monterey." ▼❿

Colorado Territory (1949) **94m.** ******* D: Raoul Walsh. Joel McCrea, Virginia Mayo, Dorothy Malone, Henry Hull, John Archer, Frank Puglia. Strong, fast-moving Western with McCrea an outlaw on the lam; remake of director Walsh's HIGH SIERRA, later remade as I DIED A THOUSAND TIMES. Also shown in computer-colored version. ❿

Colossus of New York, The (1958) **70m.** ****** D: Eugene Lourie. John Baragrey, Mala Powers, Otto Kruger, Robert Hutton, Ross Martin. Doctor implants dead son's brain into oversized robot with predictable chaos. Inspired by the ancient Golem legend; eerie piano score. ❿

Colossus of Rhodes, The (1960-Italian) **C-128m.** ****½** D: Sergio Leone. Rory Calhoun, Lea Massari, Georges Marchal, Conrado Sanmartin, Angel Aranda, Mabel Karr. Big-budget sword-and-sandal spectacular about a slave revolt against the corrupt leaders of ancient Rhodes. Though Calhoun looks mighty uncomfortable in a toga and the dubbing is poor, Leone's directorial de-

but is notable for some well-staged battle scenes and impressive sets, including the title edifice. SuperTotalscope. ❿

Colt Comrades (1943) **66m.** ****½** D: Lesley Selander. William Boyd, Andy Clyde, Jay Kirby, George Reeves, Gayle Lord (Teddi Sherman), Victor Jory, Bob (Robert) Mitchum. Average Hopalong Cassidy yarn of cattle ranchers struggling against water rights monopoly. Novel by Bliss Lomax (Harry Sinclair Drago) adapted by Michael Wilson, who went on to bigger and better things. Strong cast, including producer Harry Sherman's daughter; exteriors lensed in scenic Lone Pine.▼❿

Colt .45 (1950) **C-74m.** ****½** D: Edwin L. Marin. Randolph Scott, Ruth Roman, Zachary Scott, Lloyd Bridges, Alan Hale, Chief Thundercloud. In the Old West days of single-shot pistols, gun salesman Randolph Scott hawks the first Colt .45 repeaters—but a pair falls into the hands of a sadist who forms an unstoppable gang. Scott rides out for retribution in a Western that doesn't skimp on gunplay and gore. Hale's final film. Retitled THUNDERCLOUD. ❿

Column South (1953) **C-85m.** ****** D: Frederick de Cordova. Audie Murphy, Joan Evans, Robert Sterling, Ray Collins. OK mixture of Civil War and Indian fighting, as Union officer Murphy champions underdog Indians to prevent hostilities.

Comanche (1956) **C-87m.** ****** D: George Sherman. Dana Andrews, Kent Smith, Linda Cristal, Nestor Paiva, Henry Brandon. Andrews is staunch as Indian scout seeking to patch Indian-cavalry hostilities in this pat Western. CinemaScope.▼

Comancheros, The (1961) **C-107m.** ******* D: Michael Curtiz. John Wayne, Stuart Whitman, Lee Marvin, Ina Balin, Bruce Cabot, Nehemiah Persoff. Well-paced actioner with Duke a Texas Ranger out to bring in gang supplying liquor and firearms to the Comanches. Curtiz's last film. CinemaScope.▼❿

Comanche Station (1960) **C-74m.** ****½** D: Budd Boetticher. Randolph Scott, Nancy Gates, Claude Akins, Skip Homeier, Richard Rust, Rand Brooks. Scott rescues a woman from Indian capture, then runs into an old nemesis who wants to turn her in himself—for a fat reward. Typically interesting Boetticher/Scott Western, with a Burt Kennedy script. CinemaScope.▼❿

Comanche Territory (1950) **C-76m.** ****½** D: George Sherman. Maureen O'Hara, Macdonald Carey, Will Geer, Charles Drake, Pedro de Cordoba, James Best. So-so Western in which Jim Bowie (Carey) tangles with fiery bar owner O'Hara as he aids the Comanches, whose treaty with the U.S. government is about to expire.▼❿

Combat Squad (1953) **72m.** ***½** D: Cy Roth. John Ireland, Lon McAllister, Hal March, Tris Coffin, George E. Stone, Norman Leavitt, Myron Healey, Don Haggerty. Weak study of platoon led by Sgt. Ireland during the Korean War.

Come and Get It (1936) **99m. *** D:** Howard Hawks, William Wyler. Edward Arnold, Joel McCrea, Frances Farmer, Walter Brennan, Andrea Leeds, Frank Shields, Mady Christians, Mary Nash. Arnold plays a self-made empire-builder who fights his way to the top in Wisconsin lumber business, sacrificing the one love of his life. Farmer has best screen showcase of her career, in dual role, as a saloon entertainer and (years later) her own daughter; Brennan won his first Best Supporting Actor Oscar playing Arnold's simple Swedish pal. Typically plotty, two-generation Edna Ferber saga. Reissued as ROARING TIMBER. ▼●▶

Come Back, Little Sheba (1952) **99m. ***½ D:** Daniel Mann. Burt Lancaster, Shirley Booth, Terry Moore, Richard Jaeckel, Philip Ober. William Inge play is emotional tour de force for Booth (who won an Oscar recreating her Tony Award–winning stage role) as slovenly housewife coping with drunken ex-chiropractor husband (Lancaster) and boarder Moore, whose curiosity about her landlords sets drama in motion. Screenplay by Ketti Frings. ▼●▶

Come Blow Your Horn (1963) **C-112m. *** D:** Bud Yorkin. Frank Sinatra, Lee J. Cobb, Molly Picon, Barbara Rush, Jill St. John, Tony Bill. Sinatra is good as a free-swinging bachelor with wall-to-wall girls and a nagging father (Cobb). He also sings the title song, and teaches kid brother (Bill) the ropes. From Neil Simon play. Panavision. ▼▶

Come Dance With Me! (1959-French) **C-91m. **½ D:** Michel Boisrond. Brigitte Bardot, Henri Vidal, Dawn Addams, Noel Roquevert, Dario Moreno, Philippe Nicaud, Serge Gainsbourg. Sometimes amusing mystery-comedy with Bardot a pert dentist's wife who plays detective when her husband is suspected of murder. Video title: DO YOU WANT TO DANCE WITH ME? ▼▶

Comedy of Terrors, The (1963) **C-84m. **½ D:** Jacques Tourneur. Vincent Price, Peter Lorre, Boris Karloff, Basil Rathbone, Joe E. Brown, Joyce Jameson. Medium horror spoof with undertaker Price trying to hasten customers' demise, "helped" by bumbling assistant Lorre. Great cast; Richard Matheson wrote the screenplay. Panavision. ▼●▶

Come Fill the Cup (1951) **113m. **½ D:** Gordon Douglas. James Cagney, Phyllis Thaxter, Raymond Massey, James Gleason, Gig Young. Cagney is quite restrained as ex-newspaperman seeking to conquer alcoholism. Fine performance by Gleason as helpful ex-drunk and by Young as drunken playboy.

Come Fly With Me (1963) **C-109m. **½ D:** Henry Levin. Hugh O'Brian, Pamela Tiffin,

Dolores Hart, Karl Boehm, Lois Nettleton, Karl Malden. Flighty fluff of three stewardesses trying to catch husbands, becoming involved with three men on a trans-Atlantic flight. Glossy, easy to take. Panavision. ▶

Come Live With Me (1941) **86m. *** D:** Clarence Brown. James Stewart, Hedy Lamarr, Ian Hunter, Verree Teasdale, Donald Meek, Barton MacLane, Adeline de Walt Reynolds. Charming romantic comedy with starving writer Stewart marrying Lamarr so she won't be deported. Strong supporting cast, with Reynolds fine as Stewart's grandmother. ▶

Come Next Spring (1956) **C-92m. *** D:** R. G. Springsteen. Ann Sheridan, Steve Cochran, Walter Brennan, Sherry Jackson, Richard Eyer, Edgar Buchanan, Sonny Tufts, Mae Clarke, Roscoe Ates, James Best. Charming slice of Americana, set in 1920s Arkansas. Cochran walked out on his wife and kids nine years ago; now he returns, cold sober and determined to make good (and try to make up for his past transgressions). Appealing performances and a nice feel for the material distinguish this modest film, which Cochran also produced.

Come-On, The (1956) **83m. ** D:** Russell Birdwell. Anne Baxter, Sterling Hayden, John Hoyt, Jesse White. Baxter is dramatically fine as unscrupulous con woman involved with murder, but the story is hackneyed. SuperScope.

Come On, Rangers (1938) **57m. **½ D:** Joseph Kane. Roy Rogers, Mary Hart (Lynne Roberts), Raymond Hatton, J. Farrell MacDonald, Purnell Pratt, Harry Woods. Former Texas Rangers regroup to assist the U.S. cavalry in running down rampaging outlaws who have killed Roy's brother. Emphasis is on action, but Roy still takes time out for songs. ▼▶

Come out Fighting (1945) **62m. *½ D:** William Beaudine. Leo Gorcey, Huntz Hall, Billy Benedict, Gabriel Dell, Mende Koenig, Bud Gorman, Johnny Duncan, Amelita Ward, June Carlson. The police commissioner asks the East Side Kids to toughen up his wimpy son in this grating entry. Last in the series before it was revamped and rechristened *The Bowery Boys.*

Come September (1961) **C-112m. *** D:** Robert Mulligan. Rock Hudson, Gina Lollobrigida, Sandra Dee, Bobby Darin, Walter Slezak, Joel Grey. Frothy comedy about the younger generation (Darin and Dee) vs. the "older" folks (Hudson and Lollobrigida) at an Italian villa. Good fun, with some dated Darin vocals. CinemaScope. ▼▶

Come to the Stable (1949) **94m. *** D:** Henry Koster. Loretta Young, Celeste Holm, Hugh Marlowe, Elsa Lanchester, Regis Toomey, Mike Mazurki. Young and Holm register well as French nuns living in New England, seeking aid from a variety of local characters in building a children's dispensary. Warm, sentimental comedy-drama. Story by Clare Boothe Luce. ▼▶

Comet Over Broadway (1938) **69m. *½** D: Busby Berkeley. Kay Francis, Ian Hunter, John Litel, Donald Crisp, Minna Gombell, Melville Cooper. Sappy, dated soap opera tells risible story of stage star Francis and the tragedy caused by her burning ambition. Not even a musical number to save it.

Coming-Out Party (1934) **79m. *½** D: John G. Blystone. Frances Dee, Gene Raymond, Alison Skipworth, Nigel Bruce, Harry Green. Tired tale of young socialite Dee in love with jazz musician, fighting her mother's ambitions for her to marry within social class.

Coming-Out Party (1961-British) **100m. **½** D: Ken Annakin. James Robertson Justice, Leslie Phillips, Stanley Baxter, Eric Sykes, Richard Wattis. P.O.W. comedy with prisoner Baxter impersonating lookalike Nazi commandant to help peevish scientist Justice escape camp. Original British title: VERY IMPORTANT PERSON.

Comin' Round the Mountain (1936) **60m. *** D: Mack V. Wright. Gene Autry, Smiley Burnette, Ann Rutherford, LeRoy Mason, Raymond Brown, Ken Cooper, Robert McKenzie. Pony Express rider Autry proposes a race between Rutherford's wild mustangs and bad guy Mason's thoroughbreds, the winner to receive a valuable contract to sell horses to the Express company. One of Gene's best early starring films builds up to that remarkable race and makes excellent use of wild-horse footage from Yakima Canutt's 1926 silent film THE DEVIL HORSE. ▶

Comin' Round the Mountain (1951) **77m. *½** D: Charles Lamont. Bud Abbott, Lou Costello, Dorothy Shay, Kirby Grant, Joe Sawyer, Glenn Strange. Bud and Lou invade hillbilly country in this substandard comedy, with far too much footage of singing Shay. ▼▶

Command, The (1954) **C-88m. ** D: David Butler. Guy Madison, Joan Weldon, James Whitmore, Carl Benton Reid. Madison unflinchingly copes with smallpox epidemic and rampaging Indians as he leads troops and civilians through Wyoming. Filmed (but not released) in 3-D. CinemaScope.▶

Command Decision (1948) **112m. ***½** D: Sam Wood. Clark Gable, Walter Pidgeon, Van Johnson, Brian Donlevy, Charles Bickford, John Hodiak, Edward Arnold, Marshall Thompson, Richard Quine, Cameron Mitchell, John McIntire. Taut, engrossing adaptation of the William Wister Haines stage hit, with Gable a flight commander who knows that, to win the war, he must send his men on suicide missions over Germany. Intriguing look at behind-the-scenes politics of the U.S. war effort.

Screenplay by William Laidlaw and George Froeschel. Also shown in computer-colored version.▼▶●

Commandos Strike at Dawn (1942) **96m. **½** D: John Farrow. Paul Muni, Anna Lee, Lillian Gish, Cedric Hardwicke, Robert Coote, Ray Collins, Rosemary DeCamp, Alexander Knox. Well-intentioned drama of Norwegian Muni aiding British commandos in attack on Nazis who have invaded Norway. Dated propaganda angle lessens impact today.▼▶

Common Law, The (1931) **74m. ** D: Paul L. Stein. Constance Bennett, Joel McCrea, Lew Cody, Robert Williams, Hedda Hopper. McCrea falls in love with Bennett, but when he learns she has "known" other men he sends her away. Will true love prevail? Tiresome soap opera is notable only for risqué pre-Code plot elements and an all-too-brief sequence at a huge Beaux Arts ball.▼

Company She Keeps, The (1950) **83m. **½** D: John Cromwell. Lizabeth Scott, Jane Greer, Dennis O'Keefe, Fay Baker, John Hoyt, Don Beddoe. Satisfactory tale of ex-con Greer, who's determined to go straight. She yearns for companionship and makes a play for O'Keefe, the boyfriend of her parole officer (Scott). Produced by John Houseman. Jeff Bridges' screen debut; he's the baby in Greer's arms.

Compulsion (1959) **99m. ***½** D: Richard Fleischer. Orson Welles, Diane Varsi, Dean Stockwell, Bradford Dillman, E. G. Marshall, Martin Milner. Hard-hitting version of Leopold-Loeb thrill murder case of 1920s Chicago. Good characterizations, period decor, and well-edited courtroom scenes. Story also told in earlier ROPE and later SWOON. CinemaScope.▼▶●

Comrade X (1940) **90m. **½** D: King Vidor. Clark Gable, Hedy Lamarr, Felix Bressart, Oscar Homolka, Eve Arden, Sig Ruman. NINOTCHKA-esque plot with American Gable warming up icy Russian Lamarr (a streetcar conductor). Synthetic romance tale never convinces; Bressart has great closing line, though.▼▶

Concrete Jungle, The (1960-British) **86m. *** D: Joseph Losey. Stanley Baker, Margit Saad, Sam Wanamaker, Gregoire Aslan, Jill Bennett, Laurence Naismith, Edward Judd, Patrick Magee. Baker shines in this intense, stunningly directed account of a criminal who must contend with jailer Magee and, most tellingly, hood Wanamaker (with whom he robs a racetrack). More than just a crime drama, it's a story of how greed and lust for money can result in alienation, and the destruction of the spirit. Original title: THE CRIMINAL, released at 97m.▶

Condemned (1929) **86m. ** D: Wesley Ruggles. Ronald Colman, Ann Harding, Louis Wolheim, Dudley Digges, William Elmer. Suave thief Colman is sent to Devil's Island, where he becomes romantically involved with the wife of sadistic warden Digges. Stiff early-talkie melodrama, which attempts to depict social evils of the infamous penal colony. Scripted by Sidney Howard.

Condemned of Altona, The (1962-Italian) **114m. ****½ D: Vittorio De Sica. Sophia Loren, Fredric March, Robert Wagner, Maximilian Schell, Francoise Prevost. Sluggish pseudo-intellectual version of Jean-Paul Sartre play about post-WW2 Germany involving dying magnate (March), his two sons—one a playboy (Wagner) with an actress wife (Loren); the other an insane Nazi war criminal (Schell). CinemaScope.

Condemned to Live (1935) **67m.** *½ D: Frank R. Strayer. Ralph Morgan, Maxine Doyle, Pedro de Cordoba, Mischa Auer, Russell Gleason, Lucy Beaumont. A series of vampirelike murders has plagued a quiet European village. Surely it can't have anything to do with the saintlike Professor Kristan (Morgan) or his hunchbacked assistant (Auer)? Romantic elements complicate slow-moving story. Achingly sincere Poverty Row horror film was shot on familiar Universal sets and in Bronson Caverns. **▼▶**

Condemned Women (1938) **77m.** **½ D: Lew Landers. Louis Hayward, Anne Shirley, Sally Eilers, Esther Dale, Lee Patrick, Leona Roberts, George Irving. Blunt little women-in-prison drama, a precursor of CAGED, with embittered prisoner Eilers becoming romantically linked to penitentiary psychiatrist Hayward. There's a ruthless matron, a naive inmate who's taken the rap for her boyfriend, a prison break. . . .

Coney Island (1943) **C-96m.** *** D: Walter Lang. Betty Grable, George Montgomery, Cesar Romero, Charles Winninger, Phil Silvers, Matt Briggs. Breezy, enjoyable turn-of-the-century musical of saloon entertainer Grable turned into famous musical star by hustling Montgomery. Remade with Grable seven years later as WABASH AVENUE. **▶**

Confess, Dr. Corda (1958-German) **81m.** ** D: Josef von Báky. Hardy Kruger, Elisabeth Mueller, Lucie Mannheim, Hans Nielsen. Tedious handling of story of Kruger circumstantially involved in death of his mistress, with his attempt to prove innocence at trial. **▼▶**

Confession (1937) **86m.** *** D: Joe May. Kay Francis, Basil Rathbone, Ian Hunter, Donald Crisp, Jane Bryan, Dorothy Peterson, Laura Hope Crews, Veda Ann Borg, Robert Barrat. Extremely stylish, well-acted soap opera in the MADAME X vein, with singer Francis recounting events leading up to her murder of oily Rathbone. Visually arresting, this looks more like a 1920s German film than a late 1930s Hollywood product; in fact, director May was a German émigré. Based very closely on the 1935 German film MAZURKA (which starred Pola Negri).

Confession (1956) SEE: **Deadliest Sin, The**

Confessions of a Nazi Spy (1939) **102m.** **½ D: Anatole Litvak. Edward G. Robinson, Francis Lederer, George Sanders, Paul Lukas, Henry O'Neill, James Stephenson, Sig Rumann, Dorothy Tree, Lya Lys, Joe Sawyer. Fast-paced but obvious drama of FBI agent Robinson investigating vast Nazi spy ring operating in the U.S. Of interest mainly as a reflection of its era; Lukas, as a German-American Bund leader, clearly patterns his mannerisms and speeches on those of Hitler. **▶**

Confessions of an Opium Eater (1962) **85m.** *½ D: Albert Zugsmith. Vincent Price, Linda Ho, Richard Loo, June Kim, Philip Ahn, Victor Sen Yung. Bizarre low-budgeter. Price is hammy in tale of slave girls brought to the Chinese section of San Francisco in 1902 and the adventurer who aids them. **▼▶**

Confessions of Boston Blackie (1941) **65m.** *** D: Edward Dmytryk. Chester Morris, Harriet Hilliard (Nelson), Richard Lane, George E. Stone, Lloyd Corrigan, Joan Woodbury, Walter Sande. Delightful second entry in the series finds Blackie, trying to smash a murderous art forgery racket, being chased by the killers as well as the relentless Inspector Farraday. George E. Stone joins the cast as Blackie's sidekick "Runt" (replacing Charles Wagenheim), providing ample comic relief.

Confessions of Felix Krull, The (1958-German) **107m.** **½ D: Kurt Hoffman. Horst Buchholz, Lilo Pulver, Ingrid Andree, Susi Nicoletti. Waggish chronicle of charming rascal Buchholz rising in rank as Parisian hotel employee; based on Thomas Mann novel. **▼**

Confidence Girl (1952) **81m.** **½ D: Andrew L. Stone. Hillary Brooke, Tom Conway, Eddie Marr, Dan Riss, Jack Kruschen, John Gallaudet, Aline Towne. Brooke capably portrays title character, hooking up with slick swindler Conway for a series of clever scams in L.A. that baffle the cops. But she has a change of heart while posing as a mind reader in a nightclub. Absorbing second feature is given a big plus by Stone's use of authentic locales and William Clothier's top-notch camerawork.

Confidential (1935) **67m.** **½ D: Edward L. Cahn. Donald Cook, Evalyn Knapp, Warren Hymer, J. Carrol Naish, Herbert Rawlinson, Theodore von Eltz, Morgan Wallace, Kane Richmond, Reed Howes. Fast-moving gangster programmer with G-man Cook going undercover to bust open a crime syndicate. Knapp is a sassy blonde; Hymer a dumb lug with Brooklyn accent; Naish a cold-blooded killer. Good fun. **▼▶**

Confidential Agent (1945) **118m.** *** D: Herman Shumlin. Charles Boyer, Lauren Bacall, Katina Paxinou, Peter Lorre, Victor Francen, George Coulouris, Wanda Hendrix, John Warburton. Boyer is Graham Greene's hero in engrossing spy yarn of Spanish Civil War; he meets Bacall along the way; they battle enemy agents Lorre and Paxinou. ▶

Confidentially Connie (1953) **74m. **½ D:** Edward Buzzell. Van Johnson, Janet Leigh, Louis Calhern, Walter Slezak, Gene Lockhart. Mild chuckles as pregnant wife Leigh schemes to get underpaid professor hubby (Johnson) to leave academic circles. Calhern as Van's rich Texan father is amusing. ▶

Confidential Report SEE: **Mr. Arkadin**

Confirm or Deny (1941) **73m. **½ D:** Archie Mayo. Don Ameche, Joan Bennett, Roddy McDowall, John Loder, Raymond Walburn. Love in an air-raid shelter with Ameche and Bennett as reporter and wireless operator; pleasant romance. ▶

Conflagration SEE: **Enjo**

Conflict (1945) **86m. **½ D:** Curtis Bernhardt. Humphrey Bogart, Alexis Smith, Sydney Greenstreet, Rose Hobart, Charles Drake, Grant Mitchell. Far-fetched story of husband (Bogart) plotting to murder wife (Hobart) to marry her sister (Smith). Unconvincing plot not salvaged by good cast. ▼▶

Congo Crossing (1956) **C-87m. ** D:** Joseph Pevney. Virginia Mayo, George Nader, Peter Lorre, Michael Pate, Rex Ingram. OK adventure yarn set in Africa, involving wanted criminals and construction engineer's attempt to civilize the Congo territory.

Congo Maisie (1940) **70m. **½ D:** H. C. Potter. Ann Sothern, John Carroll, Shepperd Strudwick, Rita Johnson, J. M. Kerrigan, E. E. Clive. Second *Maisie* entry, in which Brooklyn chorus girl Sothern finds herself involved with doctor Carroll in the middle of an African native revolt. ▶

Conjugal Bed, The (1963-French-Italian) **90m. *** D:** Marco Ferreri. Ugo Tognazzi, Marina Vlady, Walter Giller, Linda Sini. Tognazzi is admirably suited to the role of a middle-aged bachelor who weds beautiful young Vlady and must cope with her sexual demands as she desires to become pregnant. A funny, entertaining sex comedy.

Connecticut Yankee, A (1931) **78m. *** D:** David Butler. Will Rogers, Maureen O'Sullivan, Myrna Loy, Frank Albertson, William Farnum. Mark Twain's classic story of a man who travels back in time to King Arthur's court, rewritten to suit Rogers' genial personality. Full of contemporary wisecracks and funny ideas, though the script gets a bit silly.▼

Connecticut Yankee in King Arthur's Court, A (1949) **C-107m. **½ D:** Tay Garnett. Bing Crosby, Rhonda Fleming, William Bendix, Cedric Hardwicke, Henry Wilcoxon, Murvyn Vye, Virginia Field. Mark Twain's story becomes carefree Crosby musical, with Bing transported into past, branded a wizard. No great songs, but colorful production. Previously filmed in 1921

and 1931 (with Will Rogers); remade in 1979 (as UNIDENTIFIED FLYING ODDBALL); TVMs in 1989 and 1995. ▼▶

Connection, The (1961) **103m. ***½ D:** Shirley Clarke. William Redfield, Warren Finnerty, Garry Goodrow, Jerome Raphael, James Anderson, Carl Lee, Roscoe Lee Browne, Jackie McLean. Searing, admirably acted drama of junkies awaiting arrival of their "connection" with heroin, and a documentary filmmaker (Redfield) filming them. Independently produced, based on Jack Gelber's stage play. Original running time 110m.; some prints run 93m. ▼▶

Conquered City (1962-Italian) **C-87m. **½ D:** Joseph Anthony. David Niven, Ben Gazzara, Michael Craig, Martin Balsam, Lea Massari, Daniela Rocca. Niven and disparate international group are holed up in Athens hotel under siege in waning days of WW2; not-bad programmer released overseas as THE CAPTIVE CITY at 108m.

Conqueror, The (1956) **C-111m. ** D:** Dick Powell. John Wayne, Susan Hayward, Pedro Armendariz, Agnes Moorehead, Thomas Gomez, John Hoyt, William Conrad. Mongols vs. Tartars, and John Wayne vs. the silliest role of his career, Genghis Khan. Expensive epic has camp dialogue to spare. The film had a sobering real-life aftermath, however: it was shot on location in Utah near an atomic test site, and an alarming number of its cast and crew (including the stars) were later stricken by cancer. CinemaScope.▼▶

Conquerors, The (1932) **86m. ** D:** William A. Wellman. Richard Dix, Ann Harding, Edna May Oliver, Guy Kibbee, Julie Haydon, Donald Cook. Unabashed rip-off of CIMARRON with Dix and Harding as newlyweds who go West to make their fortune, and build a banking empire that spans 50 years of ups and downs. Some good scenes lost in clichés in this epic saga. Retitled PIONEER BUILDERS. ▶

Conquest (1937) **112m. *** D:** Clarence Brown. Greta Garbo, Charles Boyer, Reginald Owen, Alan Marshal, Henry Stephenson, Leif Erickson, Dame May Whitty, Maria Ouspenskaya, Vladimir Sokoloff, Scotty Beckett. Boyer as Napoleon and Garbo as Polish countess Walewska in fairly interesting costumer with fine performances making up for not-always-thrilling script. ▼▶

Conquest of Cochise (1953) **C-70m. ** D:** William Castle. John Hodiak, Robert Stack, Joy Page, John Crawford. Unspectacular Indian vs. cavalry, set in 1850s Southwest, as Stack and troops try to calm Cochise's (Hodiak) rampaging braves.▼▶

Conquest of Everest, The (1953-British) **C-78m. *** No director credited. Outstanding, Oscar-nominated documentary chronicle of Edmund Hillary and company's successful expedition to the summit of Mount Everest. As dramatic as the most complexly plotted fiction; breathtaking photography by Thomas Stobart and George Love. ▼▶

Conquest of Space (1955) **C-80m.** **½ D: Byron Haskin. Eric Fleming, William Hopper, Ross Martin, Walter Brooke, Joan Shawlee. Despite some good special effects, this George Pal production about the first trip to Mars is hampered by a pedestrian script and an inappropriate emphasis on religion. A disappointment. ▼▶

Conquest of the Air, The (1936-British) **66m.** **½ D: Alexander Esway, Zoltan Korda, John Monk Saunders, Alexander Shaw, Donald Taylor. Frederick Culley, Laurence Olivier, Franklin Dyall, Henry Victor, Hay Petrie, John Turnbull, Alan Wheatley. Informative history of the evolution of flying, with actors (most notably Olivier) playing men across the ages who attempt to soar through the skies—with varying degrees of success. Updated version, running 71m. and acknowledging the role of air power in the earliest days of WW2, was released in 1940. ▶

Consolation Marriage (1931) **82m.** ** D: Paul Sloane. Irene Dunne, Pat O'Brien, John Halliday, Myrna Loy, Matt Moore, Lester Vail. Dunne and O'Brien are married after they're both jilted by their respective mates but years later must decide what to do when the former lovers return. Standard marital melodrama uplifted by considerably charming cast. ▼

Conspiracy (1939) 58m. **½ D: Lew Landers. Allan Lane, Linda Hayes, Robert Barrat, Charley Foy, Lionel Royce, J. Farrell MacDonald, Lester Matthews, Henry Brandon. Taut little B thriller about a ship's radio operator (Lane), who finds himself immersed in intrigue when his craft pulls into port in a fascist country. Jerome Chodorov's unsubtle script mirrors the world situation at the time of the film's release.

Conspiracy of Hearts (1960-British) 116m. *** D: Ralph Thomas. Lilli Palmer, Sylvia Syms, Yvonne Mitchell, Ronald Lewis. Despite familiar situation of nuns sheltering refugee Jewish youths in Northern Italy, this film is both suspenseful and moving. ▼

Conspirator (1949-British) 85m. ** D: Victor Saville. Robert Taylor, Elizabeth Taylor, Robert Flemyng, Harold Warrender, Honor Blackman, Wilfrid Hyde-White. Innocent Elizabeth is unaware that the dashing soldier (Taylor) with whom she's fallen in love is a Communist spy. Stale melodrama. ▼▶

Conspirators, The (1944) 101m. **½ D: Jean Negulesco. Hedy Lamarr, Paul Henreid, Sydney Greenstreet, Peter Lorre, Victor Francen, Vladimir Sokoloff, George Macready, Monte Blue, Joseph Calleia. WW2 intrigue in Lisbon, with echoes of CASABLANCA; this one's no classic, but with that cast (and Hedy at her most beautiful) how bad can it be? ▶

Constant Husband, The (1955-British) **C-88m.** *** D: Sidney Gilliat. Rex Harrison, Margaret Leighton, Kay Kendall, Cecil Parker, Nicole Maurey, George Cole, Raymond Huntley, Michael Hordern, Robert Coote, Eric Pohlmann. Harrison, recovering from amnesia, realizes he's wed to more than one woman. Entertaining comedy, with sexy Rexy ideally cast (opposite real-life wife Kendall).

Constantine and the Cross (1962-Italian) **C-120m.** *** D: Lionello de Felice. Cornel Wilde, Christine Kaufmann, Belinda Lee, Elisa Cegani, Massimo Serato. Intelligent interpretation of 4th century A.D. Emperor (Wilde) battling Romans for Christianity. Good action. Totalscope. ▼▶

Constant Nymph, The (1943) 112m. ***½ D: Edmund Goulding. Charles Boyer, Joan Fontaine, Alexis Smith, Brenda Marshall, Charles Coburn, Dame May Whitty, Peter Lorre, Joyce Reynolds, Jean Muir, Montague Love, Edward (Eduardo) Ciannelli. Intensely romantic story of a Belgian gamine (Fontaine) who's madly in love with a self-serious and self-absorbed composer (Boyer). He marries a socialite (Smith) without ever realizing the depth of his own feelings for the younger girl. Touching, intelligent, and beautifully realized, with sweeping music by Erich Wolfgang Korngold. Margaret Kennedy's novel and play were adapted by Kathryn Scola. Filmed before in 1928 and 1934. ▶

Contempt (1963-French-Italian) **C-103m.** ***½ D: Jean-Luc Godard. Brigitte Bardot, Jack Palance, Michel Piccoli, Giorgia Moll, Fritz Lang. Perversely funny look at international moviemaking with Piccoli as a dramatist of integrity who gets mixed up with a vulgar producer (Palance) and director (Lang—playing himself) in a film version of *The Odyssey.* Producer Joseph E. Levine didn't seem to understand that Godard, who appears here as Lang's assistant, held *him* in contempt, making this film a highly amusing "in" joke. Bardot's appearance only adds to the fun. Franscope. ▼▶

Contraband (1940-British) 92m. ***½ D: Michael Powell. Conrad Veidt, Valerie Hobson, Hay Petrie, Joss Ambler, Raymond Lovell, Esmond Knight, Peter Bull, Leo Genn. Superior spy yarn from the team of Michael Powell and Emeric Pressburger that's very much in the Hitchcock vein. Veidt is a Danish merchant sea captain, Hobson an enigmatic passenger—both get caught up with London spy ring. Though set in 1939, film hardly seems dated at all! That's Bernard Miles as a disgruntled smoker. Powell and Brock Williams adapted Pressburger's story. P&P had teamed up with Veidt and Hobson the previous year for THE SPY IN BLACK. Original U.S. title: BLACKOUT. ▼▶

Convicted (1950) 91m. **½ D: Henry

Levin. Glenn Ford, Broderick Crawford, Millard Mitchell, Dorothy Malone, Carl Benton Reid, Frank Faylen, Will Geer, Roland Winters, Ed Begley. Above-par reworking of THE CRIMINAL CODE, with Ford a luckless ex-GI who ends up in the slammer after a nightclub mishap and becomes romantically involved with the daughter of district-attorney-turned-warden Crawford. ◗

Convicted Woman (1940) 65m. **½ D: Nick Grinde. Rochelle Hudson, Frieda Inescort, June Lang, Lola Lane, Glenn Ford, Iris Meredith, Esther Dale. Innocent Hudson is wrongfully accused of theft and railroaded to a reformatory, where she is subjected to brutal treatment at the hands of corrupt matron Dale. Crusading reporter (a very young Ford) and reform-minded lawyer (Inescort) fight to free her. Not bad women-in-prison exposé with an ending copied from CRIME SCHOOL.

Convict 99 (1938-British) 88m. *** D: Marcel Varnel. Will Hay, Moore Marriott, Graham Moffatt, Googie Withers, Garry Marsh, Peter Gawthorne, Basil Radford, Kathleen Harrison. Bumbling, disgraced schoolmaster is mistakenly appointed warden of a prison and wins the tough inmates over by letting them run the joint. Pretty funny vehicle for British music-hall comedian Hay, though this has more elements of social criticism than his usual farces. Val Guest was one of the writers. ◗

Convicts 4 (1962) 105m. *** D: Millard Kaufman. Ben Gazzara, Stuart Whitman, Ray Walston, Vincent Price, Rod Steiger, Broderick Crawford, Sammy Davis, Jr., Jack Kruschen. Gazzara gives sincere portrayal as long-term prisoner who becomes professional artist. Oddball supporting cast. Retitled: REPRIEVE. ▼◗

Cookin' Up Trouble (1944) 67m. ** D: D. Ross Lederman. Billy Gilbert, Shemp Howard, Maxie Rosenbloom, Helen Gilbert, June Lang, Buzzy Henry. A fading comic team acts offstage as foster parents to a small boy. Feeble attempt by Monogram Pictures to create its own version of The Three Stooges, including Curly Howard's brother Shemp (a once and future Stooge). Excessively sentimental, but at least the accent is on vintage vaudeville humor and slapstick. Aka THREE OF A KIND. ▼

Cool and the Crazy, The (1958) 78m. *** D: William Witney. Scott Marlowe, Gigi Perreau, Dick Bakalyan, Dick Jones. Fifties equivalent of REEFER MADNESS is a great unsung j.d. melodrama; reform school veteran introduces thirtyish-looking high schoolers to grass, turns them into psychotics. On-location Kansas City photography gives this one an authentic feel. Remade, in name only, in 1994.

Cool World, The (1964) 105m. *** D:

Shirley Clarke. Hampton Clanton, Yolanda Rodríguez, Bostic Felton, Gary Bolling, Carl Lee, Clarence Williams (III), Gloria Foster, Georgia Burke, Antonio Fargas. The streets, rhythms, and populace of Harlem are the stars of this justifiably celebrated cinéma vérité film. While primarily a mood piece, it does feature a gritty, realistic— and very un-Hollywood—storyline, which involves a young black teen gang member (Clanton, in his only screen appearance). Based on a novel by Warren Miller and play by Miller and Robert Rossen. Clarke also coscripted (with Lee) and edited. Produced by Frederick Wiseman.

Copacabana (1947) 92m. ** D: Alfred E. Green. Groucho Marx, Carmen Miranda, Andy Russell, Steve Cochran, Gloria Jean, Louis Sobol, Abel Green, Earl Wilson. Potentially intriguing Marx-Miranda casting can't save this unengrossing musical comedy. Groucho is a Broadway agent attempting to promote Carmen, his only client, resulting in her being hired for two jobs (in two different guises) at the same nightclub. This was Groucho's first film without his brothers. Also shown in computer-colored version. ▼◗◗

Cop Hater (1958) 75m. *** D: William Berke. Robert Loggia, Gerald O'Loughlin, Ellen Parker, Shirley Ballard, Russell Hardie, Hal Riddle, Jerry Orbach, Vincent Gardenia. Stark, low-key crime drama based on an Ed McBain novel about the hunt for a killer who's picking off cops of the 87th Precinct one by one during a Manhattan heat wave. Low budget is more than offset by vivid location photography, gritty feel, and a neat twist ending. Orbach's film debut. ◗

Copper Canyon (1950) C-83m. **½ D: John Farrow. Ray Milland, Hedy Lamarr, Macdonald Carey, Mona Freeman, Harry Carey, Jr., Frank Faylen, Hope Emerson, Percy Helton. OK Western of post–Civil War days, with Confederate vet Milland faced with decision to assist fellow Southerners who are being harassed as they attempt to mine copper. Lamarr plays the femme fatale. ▼◗◗

Coquette (1929) 75m. ** D: Sam Taylor. Mary Pickford, John Mack Brown, Matt Moore, John Sainpolis, William Janney, Henry Kolker, George Irving, Louise Beavers. Pickford's first talkie, for which she won an Oscar playing an ill-tempered flapper who becomes involved with a man who is beneath her station, resulting in tragedy. This stilted, artificial melodrama is a curio at best, notable as a showcase for Pickford's "new," modern screen personality. Based on a play which was a famous vehicle for Helen Hayes. ▼

Corky of Gasoline Alley (1951) 80m. ** D: Edward Bernds. Scotty Beckett, Jimmy Lydon, Don Beddoe, Gordon Jones, Patti Brady, Susan Morrow, Kay Christopher, Madelon Mitchel, Dick Wessel, John Dehner, Ludwig Stossel, Emil Sitka. Second in short-lived B movie series (following GASOLINE ALLEY) based on Frank King's comic strip is completely unlike the first. Broad slapstick comedy has Skeezix (Lydon) running a fix-it shop (repairing television sets, among other things). He and the rest of the family are undone by the arrival of an obnoxious, know-it-all cousin (Jones), who's so insufferable he all but sinks the film.◗

Cornered (1945) **102m. *** D:** Edward Dmytryk. Dick Powell, Walter Slezak, Micheline Cheirel, Nina Vale, Morris Carnovsky, Luther Adler. High-tension drama with determined Canadian flyer Powell in Buenos Aires, tracking down the man responsible for the death of his French bride during WW2. Powell is in peak form. Also shown in computer-colored version. ▼○◗

Corn Is Green, The (1945) **114m. ***½ D:** Irving Rapper. Bette Davis, Nigel Bruce, John Dall, Joan Lorring, Rhys Williams, Rosalind Ivan, Mildred Dunnock. Thoughtful acting in this story of devoted middle-aged teacher Davis in Welsh mining town coming to terms with her prize pupil. Emlyn Williams' play was adapted by Casey Robinson and Frank Cavett. Remade, beautifully, for TV with Katharine Hepburn in 1979. ▼◗

Coronado (1935) **77m. **½ D:** Norman Z. McLeod. Johnny Downs, Betty Burgess, Jack Haley, Andy Devine, Leon Errol, Jacqueline Wells (Julie Bishop), Alice White, Eddy Duchin with His Orchestra, The Nicholas Brothers. Unspectacular but pleasant B musical about wealthy, brash songwriter Downs and his romantic escapades with singer Burgess one summer at a resort hotel. Haley and Devine lend support as a couple of hapless sailors.

Coroner Creek (1948) **C-93m. *** D:** Ray Enright. Randolph Scott, Marguerite Chapman, George Macready, Sally Eilers, Edgar Buchanan, Barbara Reed, Wallace Ford, Forrest Tucker, William Bishop. Single-minded Scott seeks vengeance against the seemingly respectable man responsible for the events leading to a mysterious death. Solid little Western, based on a Luke Short novel; Scott's fisticuffs with henchman Tucker are a highlight. ▼◗

Corpse Came C.O.D., The (1947) **87m. ** D:** Henry Levin. George Brent, Joan Blondell, Adele Jergens, Jim Bannon, Leslie Brooks, Grant Mitchell, Una O'Connor, Marvin Miller. Rival reporters Brent and Blondell attempt to solve the mystery of why movie star Jergens has received a dead body. Passable comedy-mystery, with too much emphasis on the former.

Corpse Vanishes, The (1942) **64m. ** D:** Wallace Fox. Bela Lugosi, Luana Walters, Tristram Coffin, Elizabeth Russell, Vince Barnett, Joan Barclay, Angelo Rossitto. A cut above the average low-grade thrillers Lugosi

made for producer Sam Katzman. Bela is a scientist who kidnaps brides for the purpose of using their body fluids to rejuvenate wife Russell, an elderly countess. ▼◗

Corregidor (1943) **73m. ** D:** William Nigh. Otto Kruger, Elissa Landi, Donald Woods, Frank Jenks, Rick Vallin, Wanda McKay, Ian Keith. Routine WW2 melodrama focusing not so much on the American military's courageous stand against the Japanese at the title locale but on a corny love triangle involving a trio of doctors (one of whom is a woman). Unintentionally funny at times; Eddie Hall and Charles Jordan play characters named "Brooklyn" and "Bronx." Coscripted by Edgar Ulmer. ▼◗

Corridor of Mirrors (1948-British) **105m. *** D:** Terence Young. Eric Portman, Edana Romney, Barbara Mullen, Hugh Sinclair, Joan Maude, Lois Maxwell, Christopher Lee. Underrated "art" film, similar to Jean Cocteau's work of this period, has Portman well cast as an artist who lives in the past, surrounding himself with Renaissance-era objects. Beauteous Romney (whose acting is not so hot) is the woman he falls in love with. Stunning sets, photography, and musical score. ▼◗

Corridors of Blood (1962-British) **86m. **½ D:** Robert Day. Boris Karloff, Betta St. John, Finlay Currie, Christopher Lee, Francis Matthews, Adrienne Corri, Nigel Green. Middling account of 19th-century British doctor who experiments with anesthetics, becomes addicted to the narcotics, and winds up consorting with grave-robbers to continue his experiments. Filmed in 1958. ▼○

Corsair (1931) **73m. **½ D:** Roland West. Chester Morris, Alison Loyd (Thelma Todd), William Austin, Frank McHugh, Emmett Corrigan, Fred Kohler, Frank Rice, Ned Sparks, Mayo Methot. Former college football hero Morris goes to work for a crooked Wall Street tycoon and tries to woo his beautiful, spoiled daughter (Todd), but she's not interested until he becomes a bootlegger! Title refers to the name of the boat he uses to hijack the booze. Stylish but slow-moving crime drama is notable for Ray June's fluid camerawork.◗

Corsican Brothers, The (1941) **112m. *** D:** Gregory Ratoff. Douglas Fairbanks, Jr., Ruth Warrick, Akim Tamiroff, J. Carrol Naish, H. B. Warner, Henry Wilcoxon. Entertaining swashbuckler from Dumas story of twins who are separated, but remain spiritually tied. Fairbanks excellent in the dual lead, with strong support, ingenious photographic effects. Remade for TV in 1985. ▼◗

Corvette K-225 (1943) **99m. *** D:** Richard Rosson. Randolph Scott, James Brown, Ella Raines, Barry Fitzgerald, Andy Devine, Walter Sande, Richard Lane. First-rate war film with Canadian officer Scott fighting to save prominent Navy destroyer from enemy attack; realistic actioner produced by Howard Hawks. Look quickly for Robert Mitchum.

Cosmic Man, The (1959) 72m. *½ D: Herbert Greene. Bruce Bennett, John Carradine, Angela Greene, Paul Langton, Scotty Morrow. Mediocre sci-fi, a pale imitation of THE DAY THE EARTH STOOD STILL, in which the title character (Carradine) arrives on Earth. The military wants to destroy him, while scientists argue that this would result in dire consequences. Well-intentioned message regarding abuse of atomic energy is lost in poorly made film. ▼❙

Cosmic Monster, The (1958-British) 75m. *½ D: Gilbert Gunn. Forrest Tucker, Gaby André, Martin Benson, Alec Mango, Wyndham Goldie, Hugh Latimer. Britain's only Giant Bug movie is talky tale of a mad scientist whose magnetism experiments punch a hole in the ionosphere, letting in cosmic rays which enlarge insects in the woods. Gleefully ghoulish at times. Original British title: THE STRANGE WORLD OF PLANET X. ▼

Cossacks, The (1928) 92m. **½ D: George (W.) Hill. John Gilbert, Renée Adorée, Ernest Torrence, Nils Asther, Paul Hurst, Dale Fuller, Mary Alden. Gilbert is a disgrace to his father, his girlfriend, and his village until he transforms himself into a Cossack warrior. Silly story, slickly made by MGM to reunite Gilbert and Adorée, the romantic stars of THE BIG PARADE, with a rousing action climax. Based on a Leo Tolstoy novel. ❙

Cossacks, The (1959-Italian) C-113m. ** D: Giorgio Rivalta. Edmund Purdom, John Drew Barrymore, Giorgia Moll, Massimo Girotti. Heavy-handed historical tale set in 1850s Russia; Cossack Purdom and son Barrymore clash in loyalties to Czar Alexander II. Totalscope.

Cottage to Let (1941-British) 90m. ** D: Anthony Asquith. Alastair Sim, John Mills, Leslie Banks, Michael Wilding, Carla Lehmann, Catherine Lacey, George Cole. Good cast is wasted in this disappointing thriller about Nazi spies attempting to pilfer the plans for inventor Banks' secret bomb sight. Interesting to see Sim and Cole acting together, ten years before they played Ebenezer Scrooge—old and young—in A CHRISTMAS CAROL. ▼❙

Couch, The (1962) 100m. **½ D: Owen Crump. Shirley Knight, Grant Williams, Onslow Stevens, William Leslie. Bizarre yarn of psychopathic killer on the prowl while under analysis. Script by Robert Bloch from screen story cowritten by Blake Edwards. ❙

Counsel for Crime (1937) 61m. **½ D: John Brahm. Otto Kruger, Douglass Montgomery, Jacqueline Wells (Julie Bishop), Thurston Hall, Nana Bryant, Gene Morgan, Marc Lawrence. Idealistic law school graduate (Montgomery) is given a job by a crafty defense lawyer (who else but Kruger?), quits when he discovers his boss' unscrupulous ways, and later prosecutes him for murder—unaware that the legal eagle is his real father. Kruger's magnetic performance and some clever plotting keep this B film afloat.

Counsellor-at-Law (1933) 82m. **** D: William Wyler. John Barrymore, Bebe Daniels, Doris Kenyon, Onslow Stevens, Isabel Jewell, Melvyn Douglas, Thelma Todd, John Qualen, Mayo Methot. Vivid adaptation of Elmer Rice play about rags-to-riches Jewish lawyer who can't escape his background—and begins to question his success when he learns his wife has been unfaithful. Barrymore gives one of his greatest performances in meaty, colorful role; Wyler keeps this comedy-drama moving at breakneck pace. Scripted by Rice. Cast also includes future directors Vincent Sherman, Richard Quine, and Robert Gordon. ▼❙

Counter-Attack (1945) 90m. **½ D: Zoltan Korda. Paul Muni, Marguerite Chapman, Larry Parks, Philip Van Zandt, George Macready, Roman Bohnen. Satisfactory WW2 movie of Allied fighters going behind enemy lines to sabotage German positions; no classic, but good. ❙

Counter-Espionage (1942) 73m. **½ D: Edward Dmytryk. Warren William, Eric Blore, Hillary Brooke, Thurston Hall, Fred Kelsey, Forrest Tucker. Deftly handled *Lone Wolf* series entry pits the sleuth against Nazi spies in London amidst the brutal German bombing blitz. ❙

Counterfeiters (1948) 73m. **½ D: Peter Stewart (Sam Newfield). John Sutton, Doris Merrick, Hugh Beaumont, Lon Chaney (Jr.), George O'Hanlon, Herbert Rawlinson, Joyce (Joi) Lansing. Not bad little actioner with Scotland Yard cop Sutton going undercover to nab counterfeiter Beaumont and his gang.

Counterfeit Plan, The (1957-British) 80m. ** D: Montgomery Tully. Zachary Scott, Peggie Castle, Mervyn Johns, Sydney Tafler. Scott is appropriately nasty as escaped murderer who sets up international counterfeit syndicate. ❙

Counterfeit Traitor, The (1962) C-140m. ***½ D: George Seaton. William Holden, Lilli Palmer, Hugh Griffith, Erica Beer, Werner Peters, Eva Dahlbeck. Holden is a double agent during WW2, falls in love with Palmer between various dangerous missions. Authentic backgrounds and fine cast. Based on true story. ▼❙

Counterplot (1959) 76m. ** D: Kurt Neumann. Forrest Tucker, Allison Hayes, Gerald Milton, Edmundo Rivera Alvarez. Mundane hide-and-seeker set in Puerto Rico where Tucker is dodging police and his double-dealing attorney. ❙

Counterspy Meets Scotland Yard (1950) 67m. **½ D: Seymour Friedman. Howard St. John, Ron Randell, Amanda Blake,

Lewis Martin, June Vincent, Charles Meredith, Fred Sears, John Dehner, Everett Glass, Gregory Gay (Gaye), John Doucette, Rick Vallin. Scotland Yard agent (Randell) is assigned to work with Counterspy David Harding (St. John) to discover who is leaking government secrets to "the enemy." Slick, efficient B movie yarn based on Phillips H. Lord's radio show, following DAVID HARDING, COUNTERSPY.▶

Countess of Monte Cristo, The (1948) 77m. ** D: Frederick de Cordova. Sonja Henie, Olga San Juan, Dorothy Hart, Michael Kirby, Arthur Treacher. Sonja and Olga pretend to be royal visitors in this limp costume comedy.

Count Five and Die (1958-British) 92m. **½ D: Victor Vicas. Jeffrey Hunter, Nigel Patrick, Ann-Marie Duringer, David Kossoff. WW2 espionage flick has Hunter an American agent working with British to mislead Nazis about Allied landing site. CinemaScope.

Count of Monte Cristo, The (1934) 113m. ***½ D: Rowland V. Lee. Robert Donat, Elissa Landi, Louis Calhern, Sidney Blackmer, Raymond Walburn, O.P. Heggie, Luis Alberni, Irene Hervey. Superb filmization of classic story of Edmond Dantes, who spends years in prison unjustly but escapes to seek revenge on enemies who framed him. Donat leads excellent cast in rousing classic from Dumas' story.▼▶

Count of Monte Cristo, The (1954-French) C-97m. **½ D: Robert Vernay. Jean Marais, Lia Amanda, Roger Piguat. Serviceable rendition of Alexandre Dumas costume classic.

Count of Monte Cristo, The (1961-French) C-90m. **½ D: Claude Autant-Lara. Louis Jourdan, Yvonne Furneaux, Pierre Mondy, Bernard Dheran. Faithful adaptation of Dumas novel, but Jourdan hasn't the zest that Robert Donat gave the role in 1934. Originally 120m. Dyaliscope.

Country Gentlemen (1936) 66m. ** D: Ralph Staub. Ole Olsen, Chic Johnson, Joyce Compton, Lila Lee, Pierre Watkin, Donald Kirke, Ray Corrigan. Slight Olsen & Johnson comedy, with the boys cast as fast-talking con men involved in a variety of shenanigans.▼▶

Country Girl, The (1954) 104m. ***½ D: George Seaton. Bing Crosby, Grace Kelly, William Holden, Anthony Ross. Kelly won an Oscar as wife of alcoholic singer (Crosby) trying for comeback via help of director (Holden). Crosby excels in one of his finest roles. Writer-director Seaton also won Academy Award for adaptation of Clifford Odets play. New songs by Ira Gershwin and Harold Arlen. Remade for cable TV in 1982.▼▶

Country Music Holiday (1958) 81m. ** D: Alvin Ganzer. Ferlin Husky, Zsa Zsa Gabor, Jesse White, Rocky Graziano, Cliff Norton, Clyde Woods, June Carter, The Jordanaires, Drifting Johnny Miller, Patty Duke. A hillbilly's rise to fame; lots of songs and specialties dominate this curio.

Count the Hours (1953) 76m. ** D: Don Siegel. Teresa Wright, Macdonald Carey, Dolores Moran, Adele Mara, Jack Elam. Lawyer Carey takes case of migrant worker falsely accused of a double murder. Trim, well-directed (if implausible) story; Elam is at his slimiest as an alcoholic psycho.

Count Three and Pray (1955) C-102m. **½ D: George Sherman. Van Heflin, Joanne Woodward, Raymond Burr, Nancy Kulp. Atmospheric rural Americana in post-Civil War days, with Heflin exerting influ- ence on townfolk as new pastor with reckless past. Woodward (making film debut) as strong-willed orphan lass and Burr, the perennial villain, are fine. CinemaScope.

Count Your Blessings (1959) C-102m. ** D: Jean Negulesco. Deborah Kerr, Rossano Brazzi, Maurice Chevalier, Martin Stephens, Tom Helmore, Patricia Medina. Unfunny comedy that even Chevalier's smile can't help. Kerr marries French playboy Brazzi during WW2; he goes off philandering for years. Their child conspires to bring them together again. CinemaScope.

Courage of Black Beauty (1957) C-77m. ** D: Harold Schuster. John Crawford, Diane Brewster, J. Pat O'Malley, John Bryant. Wholesome programmer of Crawford and colt he is given.▼

Courage of Lassie (1946) C-92m. **½ D: Fred Wilcox. Elizabeth Taylor, Frank Morgan, Tom Drake, Selena Royle, George Cleveland, Carl (Alfalfa) Switzer. Third of the MGM Lassie movies has a radiant Taylor trying to rehabilitate the collie after his combat experiences during WW2. Despite title, the dog in question is called Bill, not Lassie, though played by the same collie who starred in the other studio films. Filmed on beautiful locations in Canada.▼▶

Courageous Dr. Christian (1940) 67m. ** D: Bernard Vorhaus. Jean Hersholt, Dorothy Lovett, Robert Baldwin, Tom Neal, Maude Eburne. The good doctor battles a town's indifference to its homeless and an epidemic that breaks out in shantytown. Typical entry in Hersholt's B picture series.▼▶

Courageous Mr. Penn (1941-British) 79m. ** D: Lance Comfort. Clifford Evans, Deborah Kerr, Dennis Arundell, Aubrey Mallalieu, D. J. Williams. Repetition overwhelms this sometimes intelligent—but mostly dull—biography of Quaker William Penn, his trial for religious freedom and founding of the Pennsylvania colony. Original British title: PENN OF PENNSYLVANIA.▼

Court Jester, The (1956) C-101m. **** D: Norman Panama, Melvin Frank. Danny Kaye, Glynis Johns, Basil Rathbone, Angela Lansbury, Cecil Parker, Mildred Natwick, Robert Middleton, John Carradine. One of the best comedies ever made has Danny as phony jester who finds himself involved in romance, court intrigue, and a deadly joust. Delightfully complicated comic situations (scripted by the directors), superbly performed. And remember: the pellet with the poison's in the vessel with the pestle. VistaVision. ▼●▋

Court Martial (1955-British) **105m.** ***
D: Anthony Asquith. David Niven, Margaret Leighton, Victor Maddern, Maurice Denham. Tense courtroom story of officer Niven accused of stealing military funds. The trial reveals provocations of grasping wife. A solid drama. Originally released as CARRINGTON, V.C.▼

Court-Martial of Billy Mitchell, The (1955) **C-100m.** *** D: Otto Preminger. Gary Cooper, Charles Bickford, Ralph Bellamy, Rod Steiger, Elizabeth Montgomery, Fred Clark, James Daly, Jack Lord, Peter Graves, Darren McGavin. Low-key drama about trial of military pioneer who in 1925 predicted Japanese attack on U.S. Steiger adds spark to slowly paced film as wily attorney; Montgomery made her movie debut here. CinemaScope. ▼●▋

Courtney Affair, The (1947-British) **112m.** **½ D: Herbert Wilcox. Anna Neagle, Michael Wilding, Gladys Young, Coral Browne, Michael Medwin. Wealthy young man marries housemaid in this family saga tracing the years 1900–1945; amiable but soapy, this was a big hit in England. Originally ran 120m. Original title: THE COURTNEYS OF CURZON STREET.▼

Courtneys of Curzon Street, The SEE: Courtney Affair, The

Courtship of Andy Hardy, The (1942) **93m.** ** D: George B. Seitz. Mickey Rooney, Lewis Stone, Fay Holden, Cecilia Parker, Ann Rutherford, Sara Haden, Donna Reed, William Lundigan. While Judge Hardy handles a divorce case, Andy romances the couple's withdrawn daughter (Reed). Sticky series entry. ▋

Courtship of Eddie's Father, The (1963) **C-117m.** *** D: Vincente Minnelli. Glenn Ford, Ronny Howard, Shirley Jones, Stella Stevens, Dina Merrill, Roberta Sherwood, Jerry Van Dyke. Cute family comedy with Howard trying to find wife for widower father Ford. Look sharp for Lee Meriwether as Glenn's assistant. Later a TV series. Panavision. ▼●▋

Cousins, The (1959-French) **112m.** ***½ D: Claude Chabrol. Jean-Claude Brialy, Gerard Blain, Juliette Mayniel, Claude Cerval, Genevieve Cluny. Complex, depressing, ultimately haunting tale of youthful disillusion, with decadent city boy Brialy and provincial cousin Blain competing for the affection of beauty Mayniel. Superbly directed by Chabrol.▼▋

Covered Wagon, The (1923) **98m.** **½ D: James Cruze. J. Warren Kerrigan, Lois Wilson, Alan Hale, Ernest Torrence. Slow-paced silent forerunner of Western epics, following a wagon train as it combats Indians and the elements; beautifully photographed, but rather tame today.▼●

Cover Girl (1944) **C-107m.** *** D: Charles Vidor. Rita Hayworth, Gene Kelly, Lee Bowman, Phil Silvers, Jinx Falkenburg, Eve Arden, Otto Kruger, Anita Colby. Incredibly clichéd plot is overcome by loveliness of Rita, fine Jerome Kern–Ira Gershwin musical score (including "Long Ago and Far Away"), and especially Kelly's solo numbers. Silvers adds some laughs, but Eve Arden steals the film as Kruger's wisecracking assistant.▼●▋

Cowboy (1958) **C-92m.** *** D: Delmer Daves. Glenn Ford, Jack Lemmon, Anna Kashfi, Brian Donlevy, Dick York. Intelligent, atmospheric Western based on Frank Harris' reminiscences as a tenderfoot. Lemmon is Harris, with Ford as his stern boss on eventful cattle roundup.▼▋

Cowboy and the Indians, The (1949) **70m.** ** D: John English. Gene Autry, Sheila Ryan, Jay Silverheels, Frank Richards, Hank Patterson, Claudia Drake, Iron Eyes Cody, Clayton Moore. With pretensions of social drama, Gene comes to the aid of Navajo Indians being treated badly by crooked Indian agent Richards. Female doctor Ryan aids Autry in his quest to help the starving Indians. Amusing note: Silverheels (the future Tonto) plays a good guy, while Moore (The Lone Ranger) is a villain! ▋

Cowboy and the Lady, The (1938) **91m.** **½ D: H. C. Potter. Gary Cooper, Merle Oberon, Patsy Kelly, Walter Brennan, Fuzzy Knight, Harry Davenport, Henry Kolker. Bored, aristocratic Oberon, whose father is a presidential aspirant, goes slumming at a rodeo and falls for reluctant cowpuncher Cooper. Slight (if sometimes overly cute) comedy. Leo McCarey cowrote the story; the script had contributions from Anita Loos and Dorothy Parker!▼●▋

Cowboy and the Senorita (1944) **77m.** **½ D: Joseph Kane. Roy Rogers, Mary Lee, Dale Evans, John Hubbard, Guinn "Big Boy" Williams, Fuzzy Knight, Dorothy Christy, Lucien Littlefield, Hal Taliaferro, Bob Nolan and the Sons of the Pioneers. Crooked town boss Hubbard tries to cheat teenaged Lee out of a mine she's inherited, convincing her it's worthless; Roy is doubtful and investigates with his pal Teddy Bear (Williams). Significant as the first teaming of Roy and Dale, but big musical numbers don't blend well with the story. Look for Spanky McFarland and Kirk (*Superman*) Alyn in bit parts.▼▋

Cowboy From Brooklyn (1938) **77m.** **½ D: Lloyd Bacon. Dick Powell, Pat O'Brien,

Priscilla Lane, Dick Foran, Ann Sheridan, Johnnie Davis, Ronald Reagan, Emma Dunn. Singing tenderfoot Powell, who has a phobia about animals, hires on at a Wyoming dude ranch, then is mistaken for a cowboy crooner by fast-talking N.Y. agent O'Brien. Silly but enjoyable musicomedy includes songs "Ride, Tenderfoot, Ride" and the title tune. Remade as TWO GUYS FROM TEXAS. ❙

Cowboy Quarterback, The (1939) **56m.** *½ D: Noel M. Smith. Bert Wheeler, Marie Wilson, Gloria Dickson, William Demarest, Eddie Foy, Jr., DeWolf (William) Hopper. Tiresome reworking of Ring Lardner–George M. Cohan's play *Elmer the Great*, with Wheeler (minus Woolsey) miscast as a Montana cowpoke who becomes a gridiron hero and unknowingly gets mixed up with gamblers. Previously made as FAST COMPANY and ELMER, THE GREAT.

Cowboy Serenade (1942) **66m.** **½ D: William Morgan. Gene Autry, Smiley Burnette, Fay McKenzie, Cecil Cunningham, Addison Richards, Rand Brooks, Lloyd "Slim" Andrews, Tristram Coffin, Melinda Leighton. Professional gamblers cheat gullible Brooks out of all the money entrusted to him by Gene and the Cattlemen's Association . . . but there's someone even more powerful behind their dirty deeds. Pretty good Autry outing. ❙

Cow Country (1953) **82m.** ** D: Lesley Selander. Edmond O'Brien, Helen Westcott, Robert Lowery, Barton MacLane, Peggie Castle, Robert Barrat, Raymond Hatton. Earnest Western set in 1880s Texas, with O'Brien coming to the rescue of debt-ridden ranchers struggling against villainous Lowery and his cronies.

Cow Town (1950) **71m.** **½ D: John English. Gene Autry, Gail Davis, Harry Shannon, Jock O'Mahoney (Mahoney), Clark "Buddy" Burroughs. When Gene brings in barbed wire to fence his range, town blacksmith Shannon instigates a range war to further his own ends. Another sober, tough entry from Autry's early 1950s period.▼❙

Cracked Nuts (1931) **65m.** **½ D: Edward Cline. Bert Wheeler, Robert Woolsey, Edna May Oliver, Dorothy Lee, Leni Stengel, Stanley Fields, Boris Karloff, Ben Turpin. The boys get mixed up in a Latin American revolution as Woolsey wins the throne in a crap game. Wheeler wants to be king to impress his girl's aunt. Meanwhile, general Fields plots a coup and cross-eyed Turpin tries to bump them off by dropping bombs from a plane. No DUCK SOUP, but still fun. As usual, Oliver steals every scene she's in. ❙

Crack in the Mirror (1960) **97m.** *** D: Richard Fleischer. Orson Welles, Juliette Greco, Bradford Dillman, Alexander Knox. Welles, Greco, and Dillman enact contrasting dual roles in intertwining love triangles set in contemporary Paris, involving murder, courtroom trial, and illicit love; novelty eventually wears thin, marring Grade-A effort. CinemaScope.

Crack in the World (1965) **C-96m.** **½ D: Andrew Marton. Dana Andrews, Janette Scott, Kieron Moore, Alexander Knox, Peter Damon. Believable sci-fi about scientists trying to harness earth's inner energy but almost causing destruction of the world; realistic special effects. ❙

Crack-Up (1937) **71m.** **½ D: Malcolm St. Clair. Peter Lorre, Brian Donlevy, Helen Wood, Ralph Morgan, Thomas Beck, Kay Linaker. Not-bad espionage tale, with Lorre highly amusing as a spy trying to secure plans for experimental airplane; Donlevy's the test pilot he tries to bribe. ❙

Crack-Up (1946) **93m.** *** D: Irving Reis. Pat O'Brien, Claire Trevor, Herbert Marshall, Wallace Ford, Ray Collins. Art critic O'Brien remembers surviving a train wreck that never took place; it's just the first incident in a growing web of intrigue and murder. Tense, fast-paced Hitchcockian thriller with many imaginative touches. ▼❙

Craig's Wife (1936) **75m.** *** D: Dorothy Arzner. Rosalind Russell, John Boles, Billie Burke, Jane Darwell, Dorothy Wilson, Alma Kruger, Thomas Mitchell. Russell scored first big success as domineering wife who thinks more of material objects than of her husband. Based on George Kelly play, remade as HARRIET CRAIG. ▼

Crainquebille (1922-French) **76m.** ***½ D: Jacques Feyder. Maurice de Féraudy, Marguerite Carré, Charles Mosnier, René Worms, Félix Oudart, Jean Forest, Jeanne Cheirel. Ironic, biting account of the title character (de Féraudy), a kindly, no-nonsense vegetable peddler who's been pushing his cart through the streets of Paris for a half century and is unjustly arrested for insulting a policeman. Vividly atmospheric, with Feyder capturing the pulse of the city and offering pointed commentary on the abuse of power. Feyder adapted Anatole France's novel. Restored in 2005; beware of shorter prints. Remade in 1933 and 1954. ❙

Cranes Are Flying, The (1957-Russian) **94m.** ***½ D: Mikhail Kalatozov. Tatyana Samoilova, Alexei Batalov, Vasili Merkuriev, A. Shvorin. Lilting love story set in WW2 Russia. Doctor's son (Batalov) leaves his sweetheart (Samoilova) to join the army. She is seduced by his cousin, marries him, and from subsequent tragedies tries to rebuild her life. ▼❙

Crash, The (1932) **58m.** ** D: William Dieterle. George Brent, Ruth Chatterton, Paul Cavanagh, Barbara Leonard, Henry Kolker, Lois Wilson. Chatterton is fine in this otherwise plodding drama about a self-centered, materialistic woman whose stockbroker husband (Brent) loses his fortune. ❙

Crash Dive (1943) C-105m. **½ D: Archie Mayo. Tyrone Power, Anne Baxter, Dana Andrews, James Gleason, Dame May Whitty, Henry (Harry) Morgan. Submarine battleground just backdrop for love story; Power and Andrews both love young Baxter. Oscar winner for special effects, film's main asset. ▼❖

Crashing Hollywood (1938) 61m. *** D: Lew Landers. Lee Tracy, Joan Woodbury, Paul Guilfoyle, Lee Patrick, Richard Lane, Bradley Page, Tom Kennedy, George Irving, Frank M. Thomas, Jack Carson. Lively comedy about screenwriter Tracy collaborating with ex-con Guilfoyle on a script based on his last bank robbery. Amusing movie-studio background (shot all around the RKO lot) supports Tracy's usual fast-talking antics.

Crashing Las Vegas (1956) 62m. ** D: Jean Yarbrough. Leo Gorcey, Huntz Hall, Jimmy Murphy, David (Gorcey) Condon, Mary Castle, Nicky Blair. An electric shock enables Sach to predict numbers in this flat *Bowery Boys* entry. A noticeably inebriated Gorcey threw in the towel after this one, claiming he couldn't go on after the death of his father Bernard, who played "Louie Dumbrowski" in the series. ❖

Crash Landing (1958) 76m. *½ D: Fred F. Sears. Gary Merrill, Nancy Davis (Reagan), Irene Hervey, Roger Smith. Insipid revelations of passengers aboard plane facing possible crash landing into the ocean. ❖

Crash of Silence (1953-British) 93m. *** D: Alexander Mackendrick. Phyllis Calvert, Jack Hawkins, Terence Morgan, Mandy Miller. Honest drama of young deaf girl (Miller) and her mother's dilemma: keep her at home or send her to a special school. Originally titled MANDY. ▼

Crashout (1955) 90m. **½ D: Lewis R. Foster. William Bendix, Arthur Kennedy, Luther Adler, William Talman. Low-budget but interesting story of prison break headed by Bendix. Kennedy as humane gang member is fine. ▼❖

Crawling Eye, The (1958-British) 85m. **½ D: Quentin Lawrence. Forrest Tucker, Laurence Payne, Janet Munro, Jennifer Jayne, Warren Mitchell. OK, if predictable, tale (adapted by Jimmy Sangster from British TV series *The Trollenberg Terror*) about cloud hiding alien invaders on Swiss mountaintop. Hampered by low-grade special effects. ▼❖❖

Crawling Hand, The (1963) 89m. *½ D: Herbert L. Strock. Peter Breck, Kent Taylor, Rod Lauren, Arline Judge, Richard Arlen, Allison Hayes, Alan Hale, Jr. Astronaut's disembodied hand instigates rash of stranglings in this amateurish rehash of THE BEAST WITH FIVE FINGERS. Good for a few (unintended) laughs, anyway. ▼❖❖

Crawling Monster, The SEE: **Creeping Terror, The**

Crazy House (1943) 80m. *** D: Edward F. Cline. Ole Olsen, Chic Johnson, Martha O'Driscoll, Patric Knowles, Cass Daley, Percy Kilbride. Olsen & Johnson take over film studio to make epic in frantic musicomedy with guests galore: Basil Rathbone, Count Basie, Allan Jones, Edgar Kennedy, Billy Gilbert, Andy Devine, etc.

Crazylegs (1953) 87m. *½ D: Francis D. Lyon. Elroy Hirsch, Lloyd Nolan, Joan Vohs, Louise Lorimer. Inconclusive fiction based on the football escapades of Elroy "Crazylegs" Hirsch with gridiron star playing himself.

Crazy Over Horses (1951) 65m. ** D: William Beaudine. Leo Gorcey, Huntz Hall, William (Billy) Benedict, Bernard Gorcey, David Gorcey, Bennie Bartlett, Ted de Corsia, Allen Jenkins. The Bowery Boys get mixed up with a race horse (again) and some crooked gamblers (again). ❖

Creation of the Humanoids, The (1962) C-75m. BOMB D: Wesley E. Barry. Don Megowan, Frances McCann, Erica Elliott, Don Doolittle. Years after an atomic war, human beings are about to be outnumbered by their subservient robots; anti-robot Megowan discovers a plot to replace people with robot duplicates. Andy Warhol loved this slow, stagy cheapie. ▼❖

Creature From the Black Lagoon (1954) 79m.** D: Jack Arnold. Richard Carlson, Julia (Julie) Adams, Richard Denning, Antonio Moreno, Whit Bissell, Nestor Paiva, Ricou Browning, Ben Chapman. Archetypal '50s monster movie has been copied so often that some of the edge is gone, but story of Amazon expedition encountering deadly Gill Man is still entertaining, with juicy atmosphere, luminous underwater photography sequences directed by James C. Havens and Scotty Welbourne. Originally in 3-D, but just as good without it. Two sequels: REVENGE OF THE CREATURE and THE CREATURE WALKS AMONG US. 3-D. ▼❖❖

Creature From the Haunted Sea (1961) 74m. *½ D: Roger Corman. Antony Carbone, Betsy Jones-Moreland, Edward Wain, E. R. Alvarez, Robert Bean. Gangster tries to cover crime wave by creating panic with story of sea monster . . . then real sea monster shows up. Roger Corman quickie comedy is not as freakish as his others. Co-star Wain is actually Oscar-winning screenwriter Robert Towne. Remake of NAKED PARADISE. ▼❖

Creature Walks Among Us, The (1956) 78m. ** D: John Sherwood. Jeff Morrow, Rex Reason, Leigh Snowden, Gregg Palmer. Sequel to REVENGE OF THE CREATURE has Gill Man (Ricou Browning in the water, Don Megowan on land) captured by scientists in Florida Everglades and surgically made more human: smooth-skinned, air-breathing, clothes-wearing. Third and final

Creature movie "jumps the shark" by ruining the look of Universal's coolest monster, but his climactic house-wrecking rampage provides an exciting series wrap-up. ▼○▶

Creature With the Atom Brain (1955) **70m. **** D: Edward L. Cahn. Richard Denning, Angela Stevens, Gregory Gaye, Tristram Coffin. Passable hokum: scientist revives the dead via high-charged brain tissue, and these robots are used by gangster seeking revenge.▶

Creeper, The (1948) **64m. **** D: Jean Yarbrough. Onslow Stevens, Eduardo Ciannelli, June Vincent, Ralph Morgan, Janis Wilson. Scientists experimenting with cats start getting bumped off by a fiend with a cat's hand. Indoorsy, talky, sleep-inducing. ▼

Creeping Terror, The (1964) **75m.** BOMB D: Art J. Nelson (Vic Savage). Vic Savage, Shannon O'Neill, William Thourlby, Louise Lawson, Robin James. Awful horror movie, poor on every conceivable (and inconceivable) level. Monster aptly described as a giant carpet absorbs humans into its body. When it's destroyed, another takes its place. Badly shot. Aka THE CRAWLING MONSTER. ▼▶

Creeping Unknown, The SEE: **Quatermass Xperiment, The**

Crest of the Wave (1954-British) **90m. **½** D: John Boulting, Roy Boulting. Gene Kelly, John Justin, Bernard Lee, Jeff Richards. Static account of Navy officer Kelly joining British research group to supervise demolition experiments. Original British title: SEAGULLS OVER SORRENTO. ▶

Crime against Joe (1956) **69m. **** D: Lee Sholem. John Bromfield, Julie London, Henry Calvin, Patricia Blake (Blair), Rhodes Reason, Joyce Jameson. Standard whodunit with struggling artist/Korean War vet Bromfield out on a drunken binge, during which a singer is murdered—and he's the prime suspect. ▶

Crime and Punishment (1935) **88m. **½** D: Josef von Sternberg. Edward Arnold, Peter Lorre, Marian Marsh, Tala Birell, Elisabeth Risdon. Fascinating Hollywoodization of Dostoyevsky's novel about man haunted by murder he committed. Low-budget but full of inventive ideas by von Sternberg.▼○

Crime and Punishment (1956-French) **108m. ***** D: Georges Lampin. Jean Gabin, Marina Vlady, Ulla Jacobsson, Bernard Blier. Perceptive updating of Dostoyevsky novel set in Paris. Retitled: THE MOST DANGEROUS SIN.

Crime and Punishment U.S.A. (1959) **78m. **½** D: Denis Sanders. George Hamilton, Mary Murphy, Frank Silvera, Marian Seldes, John Harding, Wayne Heffley. Trim, updated version of Dostoyevsky novel has Hamilton (film debut) a law student who becomes involved in robbery and murder.▶

Crime By Night (1944) **72m. **½** D: William Clemens. Jane Wyman, Jerome Cowan, Faye Emerson, Eleanor Parker, Creighton Hale. Good little murder mystery with detective Cowan unwittingly walking into murder case.

Crime Doctor In 1943 Columbia Pictures took Max Marcin's successful radio show *Crime Doctor* and initiated a film series of that name with Warner Baxter in the lead. The first film set the premise of an amnesia victim named Dr. Ordway becoming the country's leading criminal psychologist, later discovering that he was a gang leader himself before a blow clouded his memory. This idea served as the basis for ten fairly respectable, enjoyable mysteries. Most of the films followed a standard whodunit formula, but were well acted and directed (by such people as William Castle and George Archainbaud), with competent players rounded up from Columbia's contract list. The films moved along briskly, most of them running barely over an hour.

CRIME DOCTOR

Crime Doctor (1943)
The Crime Doctor's Strangest Case (1943)
Shadows in the Night (1944)
The Crime Doctor's Courage (1945)
The Crime Doctor's Warning (1945)
Crime Doctor's Man Hunt (1946)
Just Before Dawn (1946)
The Millerson Case (1947)
The Crime Doctor's Gamble (1947)
The Crime Doctor's Diary (1949)

Crime Doctor (1943) **66m. **½** D: Michael Gordon. Warner Baxter, Margaret Lindsay, John Litel, Ray Collins, Harold Huber, Don Costello, Leon Ames. Ex-gang leader Baxter loses his memory and becomes a criminal psychologist, only to stand trial when his past is revealed. Slow-starting, but fairly good initial entry. Remake of THE MAN WHO LIVED TWICE, remade in 1953 as MAN IN THE DARK.

Crime Doctor's Courage, The (1945) **70m. **½** D: George Sherman. Warner Baxter, Hillary Brooke, Jerome Cowan, Robert Scott, Lloyd Corrigan, Emory Parnell, Stephen Crane. Dr. Ordway probes the murder of a man whose first two wives died mysteriously in this OK entry.

Crime Doctor's Diary, The (1949) **61m. **** D: Seymour Friedman. Warner Baxter, Lois Maxwell, Adele Jergens, Robert Armstrong. The Crime Doctor's final case, with a lethargic Baxter getting involved with an ex-con who claims he was framed on arson charges.

Crime Doctor's Gamble, The (1947) **66m. **½** D: William Castle. Warner Baxter, Micheline Cheirel, Roger Dann, Steven Geray, Marcel Journet. The doc's vacation in gay Paree is interrupted by murder that involves a case of art theft and a colorful chase across Europe.

Crime Doctor's Man Hunt (1946) **61m.** **½ D: William Castle. Warner Baxter, Ellen Drew, William Frawley, Frank Sully, Claire Carleton, Bernard Nedell. An amnesiac soldier is murdered and Ordway is led into a web of deceit by the man's fiancée in this lively episode with a good script by Leigh Brackett and welcome wisecracks by cop Frawley.

Crime Doctor's Strangest Case, The (1943) **68m.** ** D: Eugene J. Forde. Warner Baxter, Lynn Merrick, Lloyd Bridges, Reginald Denny, Barton MacLane, Jerome Cowan, Rose Hobart. Dr. Ordway analyzes an old lady's dreams, which hold the key to a murder in this sluggish entry.

Crime Doctor's Warning, The (1945) **70m.** **½ D: William Castle. Warner Baxter, John Litel, Dusty Anderson, Coulter Irwin, Miles Mander, John Abbott. Engrossing entry, as Dr. Ordway gets involved in the case of an emotionally unstable artist who suffers from blackouts and is suspected of murder when his models start turning up dead.

Crime, Inc. SEE: Gangs, Inc.

Crime in the Streets (1956) **91m.** **½ D: Donald Siegel. James Whitmore, John Cassavetes, Sal Mineo, Mark Rydell, Virginia Gregg, Denise Alexander, Will Kuluva, Peter Votrian, Malcolm Atterbury. Incisive if overlong drama of angry, alienated teen Cassavetes, who conspires to commit murder. Good performances by Cassavetes, Mineo and future director Rydell as his cronies, and Whitmore as an idealistic social worker. Adapted by Reginald Rose from his 1955 teleplay; Cassavetes, Rydell, and Kuluva repeat their TV performances.▼▶

Crime of Doctor Crespi, The (1935) **63m.** ** D: John H. Auer. Erich von Stroheim, Dwight Frye, Paul Guilfoyle, Harriett Russell, John Bohn, Jean Brooks. Von Stroheim gets even with man who loves his girl by planning unspeakable buried-alive torture for him. Low-grade chiller. Allegedly based on "The Premature Burial" by Edgar Allan Poe; filmed in the Bronx(!).▼▶

Crime of Doctor Hallet, The (1938) **68m.** *½ D: S. Sylvan Simon. Ralph Bellamy, William Gargan, Josephine Hutchinson, Barbara Read, John King. Tedious story of jungle doctor working on fever cure who assumes assistant's identity when the latter dies in experiment. Remade as STRANGE CONQUEST.

Crime of Monsieur Lange, The (1936-French) **90m.** *** D: Jean Renoir. Rene Lefevre, Jules Berry, Florelle, Nadia Sibirskaia, Sylvia Bataille, Jean Daste. Clever (if a bit too talky) tale of an exploited publishing house clerk (Lefevre), who pens stories in his spare time, his evil, lecherous

boss (Berry), and a host of complications. Scripted by Jacques Prévert, with a pointed anticapitalist message.▼▶▶

Crime of Passion (1957) **84m.** **½ D: Gerd Oswald. Barbara Stanwyck, Sterling Hayden, Raymond Burr, Fay Wray, Royal Dano, Virginia Grey. Stanwyck is rough and tough as grasping wife who'll do anything to forward police lieutenant husband's career.▼▶

Crime of the Century, The (1933) **73m.** *** D: William Beaudine. Stuart Erwin, Frances Dee, Jean Hersholt, Wynne Gibson, Robert Elliott, David Landau. Doctor Hersholt invites police captain Elliott to witness a hypnosis session in which he commands a criminal to rob a bank; naturally, things don't go as planned. Snappy, well-plotted whodunit with nice twists and clever touches (introducing the cast in silhouette, reviewing the suspects as a grandfather's clock ticks off one minute).

Crimes at the Dark House (1940-British) **69m.** *** D: George King. Tod Slaughter, Sylvia Marriott, Hilary Eaves, Geoffrey Wardell, Hay Petrie. Slaughter is at his lip-smacking best in this adaptation of Wilkie Collins' *The Woman in White.* Old-fashioned melodrama without a whiff of condescension is not to all tastes, but for those with a liking for this rip-snorting stuff, this is one of the best. Typical line: "I'll feed your entrails to the pigs!"▼▶

Crime School (1938) **86m.** **½ D: Lewis Seiler. Dead End Kids (Billy Halop, Bobby Jordan, Huntz Hall, Leo Gorcey, Bernard Punsley, Gabriel Dell), Humphrey Bogart, Gale Page. Bogart sets out to improve a reform school, but meets his match in the Dead End Kids. OK reworking of THE MAYOR OF HELL, weakened by the Kids' disreputable personalities and Bogart's unlikely casting as a do-gooder. Story rehashed again as HELL'S KITCHEN.▶

Crimes of Dr. Mabuse, The SEE: Testament of Dr. Mabuse, The

Crimes of Stephen Hawke, The (1936-British) **69m.** **½ D: George King. Tod Slaughter, Marjorie Taylor, D. J. Williams, Eric Portman, Ben Soutten. Florid melodrama with Slaughter deliciously ripe as kindly moneylender Hawke, secretly the murderous fiend known as Spine Breaker. Stodgy direction, in this case, seems appropriate. Lower the rating if you can't stand barnstorming thrillers. Aka STRANGLER'S MORGUE.▼▶

Crime Unlimited (1935-British) **71m.** **½ D: Ralph Ince. Esmond Knight, Lilli Palmer, Cecil Parker, George Merritt, Richard Grey, Raymond Lovell, Sara Allgood. Scotland Yard agent Knight goes undercover to infiltrate a gang of jewel thieves and becomes romantically involved with Russian Palmer, a gang member. Standard tale, nicely done; Palmer's first English-language screen role.

Crime Wave (1954) **74m.** **½ D: Andre De Toth. Sterling Hayden, Gene Nelson, Phyllis Kirk, Ted de Corsia, Charles Buchinsky (Bronson), Jay Novello, James Bell, Dub Taylor, Timothy Carey. Neat little B picture about some escaped cons who try to involve a former prisonmate (who's now gone straight) in their latest heist. Actuality-style filming on L.A. locations gives this an extra boost.▶

Crime Without Passion (1934) **72m.** *** D: Ben Hecht, Charles MacArthur. Claude Rains, Margo, Whitney Bourne, Stanley Ridges, Esther Dale, Leslie Adams. Bizarre, fascinating melodrama of callous lawyer Rains, jealous of Margo's escorts, who must establish false alibi after shooting her in lovers' quarrel. Helen Hayes (Mrs. Charles MacArthur) and Fanny Brice have brief cameos in hotel lobby scene, and directors Hecht and MacArthur play reporters! Slavko Vorkapich contributed that incredible opening montage depicting The Furies in night flight over N.Y.C.

Criminal, The SEE: Concrete Jungle, The

Criminal Code, The (1931) **95m.** **½ D: Howard Hawks. Walter Huston, Phillips Holmes, Constance Cummings, Mary Doran, Boris Karloff, De Witt Jennings. Warden Huston—tough but essentially fair—faces a dilemma when his daughter falls in love with prisoner Holmes, who's shielding the killer of a squealer. Creaky in parts, lively in others, but cast and director make this a must for buffs. Remade as PENITENTIARY in 1938 and CONVICTED in 1950.▼▶

Criminal Court (1946) **63m.** ** D: Robert Wise. Tom Conway, Martha O'Driscoll, Robert Armstrong, Addison Richards, June Clayworth, Pat Gleason, Steve Brodie. Disappointingly routine programmer finds O'Driscoll charged with murder of blackmailer Armstrong, defended by wily attorney Conway who is the real killer (by accident). Confusing mystery tale. ▼▶

Criminal Lawyer (1937) **72m.** **½ D: Christy Cabanne. Lee Tracy, Margot Grahame, Eduardo Ciannelli, Erik Rhodes, Betty Lawford, Frank M. Thomas. Tracy's the whole show here, playing a slick, self-confident trial lawyer who becomes district attorney and goes up against crafty Ciannelli, whom he once represented.

Criminal Lawyer (1951) **74m.** *½ D: Seymour Friedman. Pat O'Brien, Jane Wyatt, Carl Benton Reid, Mary Castle. Alcoholic attorney O'Brien sobers up to defend friend saddled with homicide charge.▶

Criminal Life of Archibaldo de la Cruz, The (1955-Mexican) **91m.** ** D: Luis Buñuel. Ernesto Alonso, Miroslava Stern, Rita Macedo, Ariadna Welter, Rodolfo Landa, Andrea Palma. Very minor psychological drama from Buñuel. As a boy, Archibaldo witnesses his governess' death and is fasci-

nated by what he feels; as a man, he's obsessed with murder and dying. Much too talky; it sounds far more interesting than it plays.▼

Criminals Within (1941) **66m.** ** D: Joseph H. Lewis. Eric Linden, Ann Doran, Constance Worth, Donald Curtis, Weldon Heyburn, Ben Alexander, Dudley Dickerson. Pallid Poverty Row spy thriller in which sinister foreign agents murder a scientist to purloin his secret explosives formula. The scientist's kid brother, an Army corporal, tracks the spies to solve the crime and save America from its enemies. Film's pre-WW2 naiveté somewhat dampens the gung-ho attitude. Aka ARMY MYSTERY.▼▶

Crimson Blade, The (1963-British) **C-82m.** **½ D: John Gilling. Lionel Jeffries, Oliver Reed, Jack Hedley, June Thorburn, Duncan Lamont. OK swashbuckler features romance between two young people on opposite sides of Cromwell's struggle for power in 17th century; good-looking Hammer production. Originally titled THE SCARLET BLADE. Megascope.▶

Crimson Canary, The (1945) **64m.** **½ D: John Hoffman. Noah Beery, Jr., Lois Collier, Danny Morton, John Litel, Claudia Drake, Steven Geray. Offbeat murder mystery with nightclub musicians the suspects, nicely done. Jazz fans will enjoy Coleman Hawkins, Howard McGhee, Oscar Pettiford, Sir Charles Thompson, and Denzel Best playing "Hollywood Stampede" ("Sweet Georgia Brown").

Crimson Kimono, The (1959) **82m.** **½ D: Samuel Fuller. Victoria Shaw, Glenn Corbett, James Shigeta, Anna Lee, Paul Dubov, Gloria Pall. Two close-knit L.A. detectives investigate a stripper's murder and its ties to the city's Japanese community. Uniquely odd Fuller film explores racial identity and a seldom-seen facet of L.A.▶

Crimson Pirate, The (1952) **C-104m.** ***½ D: Robert Siodmak. Burt Lancaster, Nick Cravat, Eva Bartok, Torin Thatcher, Christopher Lee, James Hayter. Lancaster and Cravat swashbuckle their way across the Mediterranean in one of the great genre classics of all time. Well-loved film offers loads of thrills and laughs to both children and adults.▼●▶

Crimson Romance (1934) **72m.** *** D: David Howard. Ben Lyon, Sari Maritza, Erich von Stroheim, Hardie Albright, James Bush, William Bakewell, Herman Bing, Jason Robards, Sr. Provocative drama of impetuous American test pilot Lyon, whose German-born pal returns to the Fatherland during WW1—before America's involvement in the fracas. He joins his friend in the German military, and finds himself at odds with a sadistic commandant (who else but von Stroheim?).▼▶

Cripple Creek (1952) **C-78m.** **½ D: Ray Nazarro. George Montgomery, Karin

Booth, Jerome Courtland, Richard Egan. Government agents Montgomery and Courtland track down mining crooks by joining gang in this OK Western.

Crisis (1946-Swedish) **93m. ** D:** Ingmar Bergman. Inga Landgré, Stig Olin, Marianne Löfgren, Dagny Lind, Allan Bohlin, Ernst Eklund, Signe Wirff. A plain, poor, small-town woman lovingly raises a child who was abandoned at birth. When the girl is 18, her manipulative birth mother arrives unexpectedly to take her away to Stockholm. Overwrought melodrama, contrasting idyllic country life with the corruption of the big city; notable mainly as Bergman's directorial debut.▐

Crisis (1950) **95m. **½ D:** Richard Brooks. Cary Grant, Jose Ferrer, Paula Raymond, Signe Hasso, Ramon Novarro, Antonio Moreno, Leon Ames, Gilbert Roland. Melodrama of American doctor (Grant) held in South American country to treat ailing dictator (Ferrer); intriguing but slow. Brooks' first film as director. Also shown in computer-colored version.▐

Criss Cross (1949) **87m. ***** D:** Robert Siodmak. Burt Lancaster, Yvonne De Carlo, Dan Duryea, Stephen McNally. Lancaster returns to hometown, where he crosses path of ex-wife De Carlo, who's taken up with gangster Duryea. Potent film noir look (by cinematographer Franz Planer) and music (by Miklos Rozsa) help compensate for Lancaster's miscasting as easily manipulated husband. Tony Curtis' screen debut; he's briefly seen as De Carlo's dance partner. Remade in 1995 as UNDERNEATH. ▼●▐

Critic's Choice (1963) **C-100m. **½ D:** Don Weis. Bob Hope, Lucille Ball, Marilyn Maxwell, Rip Torn, Jessie Royce Landis, Marie Windsor, John Dehner. An in-joke Broadway play diluted for movie audience consumption. Lucy as a novice playwright outshines Hope who plays her drama critic hubby. Film emerges as tired, predictable comedy, with best moments contributed by supporting players. Based on a play by Ira Levin. Panavision.▼▐

Crooked Circle, The (1932) **70m. ** D:** H. Bruce Humberstone. ZaSu Pitts, James Gleason, Ben Lyon, Irene Purcell, C. Henry Gordon, Raymond Hatton, Roscoe Karns. Creaky comedy-mystery teams jittery housemaid Pitts with excitable motorcycle cop Gleason to figure out who murdered an amateur criminologist. Overstuffed plot with counterfeiters and Secret Service agents running loose in a haunted-house setting ensures every possible genre cliché is present. ▼▐

Crooked Road, The (1965-British) **86m. **½ D:** Don Chaffey. Robert Ryan, Stewart Granger, Nadia Gray, Marius Goring, George Coulouris. OK battle of wits between dictator Granger and newspaperman Ryan, who's got the goods on him. ▐

Crooked Way, The (1949) **90m. ** D:** Robert Florey. John Payne, Sonny Tufts, Ellen Drew, Rhys Williams. Military hero Payne recovers from shellshock to be confronted by criminal past and his old gang seeking to eliminate him.▐

Crooked Web, The (1955) **77m. *½ D:** Nathan Juran. Frank Lovejoy, Mari Blanchard, Richard Denning, Richard Emory. Ponderous unspinning of government officer's ensnaring prime suspect to return to Germany, scene of the crime.▐

Crooks Anonymous (1962-British) **87m. *½ D:** Ken Annakin. Leslie Phillips, Stanley Baxter, Wilfrid Hyde-White, James Robertson Justice, Julie Christie. Cornball comedy with thief Phillips enrolling in Alcoholics Anonymous–type organization for hoods. Christie, in her film debut, plays Babette La Vern, a stripper.

Crook's Tour (1941-British) **81m. **½ D:** John Baxter. Basil Radford, Naunton Wayne, Greta Gynt, Charles Oliver, Gordon McLeod, Abraham Sofaer, Bernard Rebel, Cyril Gardiner. Charters and Caldicott, the scene-stealing characters introduced in Hitchcock's THE LADY VANISHES (and seen again in NIGHT TRAIN TO MUNICH), are reunited in this slight but amiable comedy-mystery in which they're mistaken for spies while touring the Middle East. Based on a radio serial by Frank Launder and Sidney Gilliat, who created the characters.▐

Crooner (1932) **68m. **½ D:** Lloyd Bacon. David Manners, Ann Dvorak, Ken Murray, J. Carrol Naish, Guy Kibbee, Claire Dodd, Allen Vincent, Edward J. Nugent, William Janney. Struggling bandleader Manners inadvertently hits on a gimmick—singing through a megaphone—that makes him a star. Topical Warner Bros. programmer is predictable but still fun to watch.

Crosby Case, The (1934) **60m. **½ D:** Edwin L. Marin. Wynne Gibson, Alan Dinehart, Onslow Stevens, Warren Hymer, Skeets Gallagher. Former lovers have to clear themselves when police suspect them of murder. Good whodunit with interesting plot point—a hint of abortion.

Cross-Country Romance (1940) **69m. **½ D:** Frank Woodruff. Gene Raymond, Wendy Barrie, Hedda Hopper, Billy Gilbert, George P. (G. P.) Huntley, Berton Churchill, Alan Ladd. Flighty heiress Barrie skips out on her arranged marriage, attaches herself to doctor Raymond. Will romance ensue? Moderately amusing variation on IT HAPPENED ONE NIGHT.

Crossed Swords (1954-Italian) **C-86m. *½ D:** Milton Krims. Errol Flynn, Gina Lollobrigida, Cesare Danova, Nadia Gray. Unsuccessful attempt to recapture flavor of swashbucklers of 1930s; set in 16th-century Italy with Flynn out to save Gina and her father's kingdom.

Crossfire (1947) **86m. ***½ D:** Edward

[145]

Dmytryk. Robert Young, Robert Mitchum, Robert Ryan, Gloria Grahame, Paul Kelly, Richard Benedict, Sam Levene, Jacqueline White, Steve Brodie, Lex Barker. Engrossing film of insane ex-soldier leading city police in murderous chase. Anti-Semitic issue handled with taste, intelligence. Script by John Paxton, from Richard Brooks' novel *The Brick Foxhole*. Also shown in computer-colored version.▼●◗

Cross My Heart (1946) **83m.** ** D: John Berry. Betty Hutton, Sonny Tufts, Rhys Williams, Ruth Donnelly, Iris Adrian, Michael Chekhov. Compulsive liar Hutton claims she's a killer so scrupulously honest lawyer husband Tufts can clear her and earn a reputation. Almost as bad as the comedy it's a remake of, TRUE CONFESSION.

Cross of Lorraine, The (1943) **90m.** ***½ D: Tay Garnett. Jean-Pierre Aumont, Gene Kelly, Cedric Hardwicke, Richard Whorf, Joseph Calleia, Peter Lorre, Hume Cronyn. High-grade propaganda of WW2 POW camp with hero Aumont rousing defeated Kelly to battle; Whorf is dedicated doctor, Lorre a despicable Nazi, Cronyn a fickle informer.◗

Crossroads (1942) **82m.** *** D: Jack Conway. William Powell, Hedy Lamarr, Claire Trevor, Basil Rathbone, Margaret Wycherly, Felix Bressart, Reginald Owen, Sig Ruman, H. B. Warner. Smooth, clever tale of respected diplomat Powell, who was once a victim of amnesia; he is accused by an extortionist of having a previous identity as a sly petty crook, causing much grief for him and his new wife (Lamarr).◗

Crosswinds (1951) **C-93m.** ** D: Lewis R. Foster. John Payne, Rhonda Fleming, Forrest Tucker, Robert Lowery. Payne tries to retrieve cargo of gold from plane that crashed in New Guinea, encountering headhunters, crooks, and gorgeous Fleming.

Crowd, The (1928) **104m.** **** D: King Vidor. Eleanor Boardman, James Murray, Bert Roach, Daniel G. Tomlinson, Dell Henderson, Lucy Beaumont. Classic drama about a few happy and many not-so-happy days in the marriage of hard-luck couple. One of the greatest silent films; holds up beautifully. Written by Harry Behn, John V.A. Weaver, and director Vidor, from the latter's original story.▼●

Crowded Sky, The (1960) **C-105m.** **½ D: Joseph Pevney. Dana Andrews, Rhonda Fleming, Efrem Zimbalist, Jr., John Kerr, Troy Donahue, Keenan Wynn, Joe Mantell, Donald May, Louis Quinn, Edward Kemmer, Jean Willes, Patsy Kelly. Slick film focusing on emotional problems aboard jet liner and Navy plane bound for fateful collision; superficial but diverting.◗

Crowd Roars, The (1932) **70m.** **½ D: Howard Hawks. James Cagney, Joan Blondell, Ann Dvorak, Eric Linden, Guy Kibbee, Frank McHugh. Exciting racing-driver tale with Cagney in typically cocky

role, familiar plot devices, but well done by Warner Bros. stock company. Remade as INDIANAPOLIS SPEEDWAY.◗

Crowd Roars, The (1938) **92m.** **½ D: Richard Thorpe. Robert Taylor, Edward Arnold, Frank Morgan, Maureen O'Sullivan, William Gargan, Lionel Stander, Jane Wyman. Tippling Morgan gets son Taylor into fighting game and involved with underworld chief Arnold in well-handled yarn. Remade as KILLER McCOY.◗

Crown v. Stevens (1936-British) **66m.** **½ D: Michael Powell. Beatrix Thomson, Patric Knowles, Glennis Lorimer, Reginald Purdell, Allan Jeayes, Frederick Piper, Googie Withers. Thomson gives an excellent performance as a greedy young wife who murders a money lender and then plots to bump off her stingy husband. Fairly straightforward thriller was one of Powell's several 1930s British "quota quickies."

Crucible, The (1956-French-German) **140m.** *** D: Raymond Rouleau. Simone Signoret, Yves Montand, Mylene Demongeot, Jean Debucourt, Raymond Rouleau. Successful French translation of Arthur Miller's stirring play about the Salem witchcraft trials of the 17th century. Signoret and Montand are excellent, re-creating their stage performances in the leading roles. Adaptation by Jean-Paul Sartre. Originally titled THE WITCHES OF SALEM. Remade in 1996.▼

Crucified Lovers, The (1954-Japanese) **100m.** ***½ D: Kenji Mizoguchi. Kazuo Hasegawa, Kyoko Kagawa, Yoko Minamida, Eitaro Shindo, Sakae Ozawa. Timid scrollmaker Hasegawa loves his master's wife (Kagawa), with tragic results. Superior performances, stunning direction; originally a marionette play written in 1715. Better known by its original Japanese title, CHIKAMATSU MONOGATARI.▼

Cruel Sea, The (1953-British) **126m.** ***½ D: Charles Frend. Jack Hawkins, Donald Sinden, Denholm Elliott, John Stratton, Stanley Baker, Liam Redmond, Virginia McKenna, Moira Lister, Alec McCowen. Poignant drama of life on a British warship as it battles German U-boats and the elements during WW2. Main focus is the effect war has on civilians who've been pressed into military service. Eric Ambler scripted, from Nicholas Monsarrat's novel. Beware edited 121m. version.

Cruel Swamp SEE: **Swamp Women**

Cruel Tower, The (1956) **79m.** **½ D: Lew Landers. John Ericson, Mari Blanchard, Charles McGraw, Steve Brodie, Peter Whitney, Alan Hale, Jr. Friendship, loyalty, jealousy, and fighting among a crew of highriggers; standard stuff, well done.

Crusade Against Rackets SEE: **Slaves in Bondage**

Crusades, The (1935) **123m.** *** D: Cecil B. DeMille. Loretta Young, Henry Wilcoxon, Ian Keith, C. Aubrey Smith, Katherine DeMille, Joseph Schildkraut, Alan Hale, C. Henry Gordon, J. Carrol Naish. Love, action, and great big siege machines in DeMille version of medieval era Holy Crusades spectacle that's good for fun, with Young a luminous queen who's kidnapped by infidels; Wilcoxon as Richard the Lion-Hearted must rescue her. Look fast for Ann Sheridan as a Christian girl.▼▶

Cry Baby Killer, The (1958) 62m. *½ D: Jus Addiss. Harry Lauter, Jack Nicholson, Carolyn Mitchell, Brett Halsey, Lynn Cartwright, Ed Nelson. Nicholson's film debut is a Roger Corman quickie about juvenile delinquent who panics when he thinks he's committed murder. A curio at best, with co-scripter Leo Gordon and Corman himself in bit parts.▶

Cry Danger (1951) 79m. *** D: Robert Parrish. Dick Powell, Rhonda Fleming, Richard Erdman, William Conrad, Regis Toomey, Jean Porter, Joan Banks. Jaded, smart-mouthed ex-con Powell hunts down those responsible for framing him and finds himself neck-deep in a world of sleaze. Taut film noir yarn is Parrish's directorial debut; interesting use of L.A. locations. ▼▶

Cry for Happy (1961) C-110m. **½ D: George Marshall. Glenn Ford, Donald O'Connor, Miiko Taka, Myoshi Umeki. Poor man's TEAHOUSE OF THE AUGUST MOON, involving Navy photography team in Tokyo using a geisha house for their home. CinemaScope. ▼

Cry From the Streets, A (1959-British) 99m. *** D: Lewis Gilbert. Max Bygraves, Barbara Murray, Colin Peterson, Dana Wilson. Kathleen Harrison. Poignant handling of story about homeless London children and social workers who attempt to rehabilitate them; plot is forgivably diffuse and episodic.▼

Cry "Havoc" (1943) 97m. *** D: Richard Thorpe. Margaret Sullavan, Joan Blondell, Ann Sothern, Fay Bainter, Marsha Hunt, Ella Raines, Frances Gifford, Diana Lewis, Heather Angel. Female volunteers join some overworked American nurses on beleaguered island of Bataan during WW2. Reveals its stage origins and incorporates expected clichés, but also presents pretty honest picture of war. Robert Mitchum has a bit part as a dying soldier.▶

Cry in the Night, A (1956) 75m. ** D: Frank Tuttle. Edmond O'Brien, Brian Donlevy, Natalie Wood, Raymond Burr, Richard Anderson. Why is mysterious, psychotic Burr spying on Wood and her boyfriend? And what happens after he kidnaps her? Overwrought drama, but fascinating as a time capsule of its era, and then prevalent attitudes toward cops and victims. Burr is quite good.

Cry of Battle (1963) 99m. **½ D: Irving Lerner. Van Heflin, Rita Moreno, James MacArthur, Leopoldo Salcedo. Uneven actioner set in Philippines with MacArthur as son of wealthy businessman who joins partisan cause, finding romance and sense of maturity.▼▶

Cry of the City (1948) 95m. **½ D: Robert Siodmak. Victor Mature, Richard Conte, Fred Clark, Shelley Winters, Betty Garde, Debra Paget, Hope Emerson. Rehash of MANHATTAN MELODRAMA about childhood pals, one who becomes a cop, the other a criminal—slick but predictable.▶

Cry of the Hunted (1953) 80m. ** D: Joseph H. Lewis. Vittorio Gassman, Barry Sullivan, Polly Bergen, William Conrad. Unnoteworthy chase film involving escaped convict Gassman being sought by lawman Sullivan, with a few atmospheric sequences set in Louisiana marshland.

Cry of the Werewolf (1944) 63m. ** D: Henry Levin. Nina Foch, Stephen Crane, Osa Massen, Blanche Yurka, Fritz Leiber, John Abbott. Young woman raised by gypsies is the daughter of a werewolf and becomes one herself, killing those who have found her out. OK low-grade thriller.▼

Crystal Ball, The (1943) 81m. ** D: Elliott Nugent. Paulette Goddard, Ray Milland, Virginia Field, Gladys George, William Bendix, Ernest Truex. Weak comedy of beauty-contest loser who becomes fortune-teller; good players left stranded by stale material.

Cry Terror! (1958) 96m. *** D: Andrew L. Stone. James Mason, Rod Steiger, Inger Stevens, Neville Brand, Angie Dickinson, Jack Klugman. Tight pacing conceals implausibilities in caper of psychopath Steiger forcing Mason to aid him in master extortion plot, filmed on N.Y.C. locations. Stevens good as Mason's frightened but resourceful wife. Also shown in computer-colored version.

Cry, the Beloved Country (1951-British) 111m. ***½ D: Zoltan Korda. Canada Lee, Charles Carson, Sidney Poitier, Geoffrey Keen, Reginald Ngeabo, Joyce Carey. Simple back-country minister journeys to Johannesburg in search of his son, while fate links his path with that of a wealthy, bigoted white landowner. Heartrending story chronicles racial divisiveness (and its roots) in South Africa without resorting to preachiness. Alan Paton's book was also basis for stage and film musical LOST IN THE STARS. Some prints run 96m. Remade in 1995.▼●

Cry Tough (1959) 83m. ** D: Paul Stanley. John Saxon, Linda Cristal, Joseph Calleia, Arthur Batanides, Joe De Santis, Barbara Luna, Frank Puglia. Saxon emotes well as Puerto Rican ex-con tempted back into criminal life by environment and his old gang. Torrid love scenes shot for foreign markets gave film initial publicity.

Cry Vengeance (1954) 83m. **½ D: Mark

Stevens. Mark Stevens, Martha Hyer, Skip Homeier, Joan Vohs. Stevens lives up to title as innocent ex-con seeking gangsters who sent him to prison.▼❿

Cry Wolf (1947) **83m. **** D: Peter Godfrey. Barbara Stanwyck, Errol Flynn, Geraldine Brooks, Richard Basehart, Jerome Cowan. Static adventure-mystery of Stanwyck attempting to untangle family secrets at late husband's estate.▼❿

Cuban Love Song, The (1931) **80m. **½** D: W.S. Van Dyke. Lawrence Tibbett, Lupe Velez, Ernest Torrence, Jimmy Durante, Karen Morley, Hale Hamilton, Louise Fazenda. Generally enjoyable, if slow-moving, musical-romance with fun-loving marine Tibbett (surprisingly effective as a romantic lead) tangling amorously with hot-tempered peanut vendor Velez in Havana—a cue for the song "The Peanut Vendor." Torrence and Durante are Tibbett's rowdy sidekicks.

Cuban Rebel Girls (1959) **68m.** BOMB D: Barry Mahon. Errol Flynn, Beverly Aadland, John McKay, Marie Edmund, Jackie Jackler. Flynn's last film is an embarrassment: playing himself, he aids Fidel Castro in his overthrow of Batista. Shot on location during the Castro revolution. Of interest only to see Flynn teamed with his final girlfriend, 16-year-old Aadland. Aka ASSAULT OF THE REBEL GIRLS and ATTACK OF THE REBEL GIRLS.▼❿

Cuckoos, The (1930) **97m. **** D: Paul Sloane. Bert Wheeler, Robert Woolsey, June Clyde, Hugh Trevor, Dorothy Lee, Ivan Lebedeff, Marguerita Padula, Mitchell Lewis, Jobyna Howland. Following their success in RIO RITA, RKO quickly reteamed Wheeler and Woolsey for this similar musical comedy about the adventures of two phony fortune tellers who get mixed up with gypsies. Pretty creaky, like a photographed stage play, though W&W are funny and Wheeler has one good song, "I Love You So Much." Some sequences in two-strip Technicolor.

Cult of the Cobra (1955) **82m. **½** D: Francis D. Lyon. Faith Domergue, Richard Long, Marshall Thompson, Jack Kelly, David Janssen. Minor camp masterpiece involves ex-servicemen being killed in post-WW2 N.Y.C. by exotic serpent lady.▼❿

Curley (1947) **C-54m. *½** D: Bernard Carr. Frances Rafferty, Larry Olsen, Gerald Perreau, Eilene Janssen, Dale Belding, Kathleen Howard. Producer Hal Roach's feeble attempt to revive *Our Gang* finds these unappealing little rascals tormenting their new schoolteacher (Rafferty). Almost unwatchable. Followed by WHO KILLED DOC ROBBIN? Reissued as part of HAL ROACH'S COMEDY CARNIVAL. Later retitled THE ADVENTURES OF CURLEY AND HIS GANG for TV.▼❿

Curley and His Gang in the Haunted Mansion SEE: **Who Killed Doc Robbin?**

Curly Top (1935) **75m. **½** D: Irving Cummings. Shirley Temple, John Boles, Rochelle Hudson, Jane Darwell, Rafaela Ottiano, Arthur Treacher. Shirley sings "Animal Crackers In My Soup" as she plays Cupid again, this time for sister Hudson and handsome Boles. Based on Jean Webster's *Daddy Long Legs*. Also shown in computer-colored version.▼❿

Curse of Dracula, The SEE: **Return of Dracula, The**

Curse of Frankenstein, The (1957-British) **C-83m. **½** D: Terence Fisher. Peter Cushing, Christopher Lee, Hazel Court, Robert Urquhart, Valerie Gaunt, Noel Hood. OK retelling of original Shelley tale, with Cushing as Baron von Frankenstein, whose experimentation with creation of life becomes an obsession. First of Hammer Films' long-running horror series, and itself followed by six sequels, starting with THE REVENGE OF FRANKENSTEIN.▼❿

Curse of Simba SEE: **Curse of the Voodoo**

Curse of the Aztec Mummy (1957-Mexican) **65m. *½** D: Rafael Portillo. Ramón Gay, Rosita Arenas, Crox Alvarado, Luis Aceves Castañeda, Jorge Mondragón, Arturo Martinez. Escaped supervillain The Bat tries to force the secret of Aztec gold out of those who faced LA MOMIA AZTECA (1957). A dashing but ineffectual masked, caped hero called the Angel is around, too. Cheap and droning; the Aztec Mummy only shows up for a couple of brief scenes.▼❿

Curse of the Cat People, The (1944) **70m. ***** D: Gunther von Fritsch, Robert Wise. Simone Simon, Kent Smith, Jane Randolph, Elizabeth Russell, Ann Carter, Julia Dean. Follow-up to CAT PEOPLE creates wonderful atmosphere in story of lonely little girl who conjures up vision of Simon, her father's mysterious first wife. Despite title, not a horror film but a fine, moody fantasy. Produced by Val Lewton, written by DeWitt Bodeen. Wise's directing debut. Also available in computer-colored version.▼❿

Curse of the Demon (1957-British) **95m. ***½** D: Jacques Tourneur. Dana Andrews, Peggy Cummins, Niall MacGinnis, Athene Seyler, Liam Redmond, Reginald Beckwith, Maurice Denham. Andrews is a psychologist who doesn't believe that series of deaths have been caused by ancient curse, but film convinces audience right off the bat and never lets up. Charles Bennett and producer Hal E. Chester adapted Montague R. James' story "Casting the Runes." Exceptional shocker, originally called NIGHT OF THE DEMON. Beware of truncated 83m. version.▼❿

Curse of the Faceless Man (1958) **66m.** BOMB D: Edward L. Cahn. Richard Anderson, Elaine Edwards, Adele Mara, Luis Van Rooten. There are echoes of Karloff's THE MUMMY in this silly tale of a gladiator, coated with lava during the eruption of Vesuvius, returning to life in the 20th century and searching for the reincarnation of his Pompeiian love. Written by Jerome Bixby. ◕▶

Curse of the Fly (1965-British) **86m.** *½ D: Don Sharp. Brian Donlevy, Carole Gray, George Baker, Michael Graham, Jeremy Wilkins, Charles Carson, Burt Kwouk. In the third and last of original THE FLY series, young escapee (Gray) from a mental institution winds up involved with the Delambre family, still doggedly trying to make their teleportation machine work. Highly inadequate makeup, weak script, but very atmospheric direction produce oddly mixed results. CinemaScope. ▶

Curse of the Living Corpse (1964) **84m.** ** D: Del Tenney. Helen Warren, Roy R. Sheider (Scheider), Margo Hartman, Hugh Franklin, Candace Hilligoss. Tepid old-darkhouse murder mystery with dead man supposedly returning to "life" and committing series of killings. Scheider's film debut. ▼▶

Curse of the Mummy's Tomb, The (1964-British) **C-81m.** ** D: Michael Carreras. Terence Morgan, Ronald Howard, Fred Clark, Jeanne Roland, George Pastell, Jack Gwillim, Dickie Owen (as the Mummy). Handsomely photographed but routine Hammer thriller featuring vengeful mummy at large in Victorian London, killing the usual profaners of the tomb in foggy surroundings. Most unusual twist: The (human) villain is in fact the Mummy's brother. Follow-up, not sequel, to THE MUMMY (1959). Techniscope. ▶

Curse of the Stone Hand (1965) **72m.** BOMB D: Jerry Warren, Carl Schlieppe. John Carradine, Sheila Bon, Ernest Walch, Katherine Victor, Lloyd Nelson. Americanized version of 1959 Mexican film tries to interweave two separate story elements with incoherent results.

Curse of the Undead (1959) **79m.** ** D: Edward Dein. Eric Fleming, Michael Pate, Kathleen Crowley, John Hoyt, Bruce Gordon, Edward Binns. Once-novel mixture of horror-Western tale hasn't much zing. Mysterious gunslinging stranger has vampirish designs on Crowley. ▼

Curse of the Voodoo (1965-British) **77m.** *½ D: Lindsay Shonteff. Bryant Haliday, Dennis Price, Lisa Daniely, Ronald Leigh-Hunt, Mary Kerridge, Danny Daniels. In Africa, hunter Haliday kills a lion in the area dominated by a lion-worshiping tribe. He follows his fed-up wife to England, where it seems he is stalked by vengeful African natives. Slow-paced and thinly plotted, but not without a few effective moments. "Africa," however, never looks like anything but the English countryside. Original British title: CURSE OF SIMBA. ▶

Curse of the Werewolf, The (1961-British) **C-91m.** **½ D: Terence Fisher. Clifford Evans, Oliver Reed, Yvonne Romain, Anthony Dawson. Reed has wolf's blood and struggles to control the monster within him; it finally erupts when he is denied his girl's love. Eerie atmosphere pervades this good chiller. Loosely based on novel *The Werewolf of Paris* by Guy Endore. ▼◕▶

Curtain Call at Cactus Creek (1950) **C-86m.** **½ D: Charles Lamont. Donald O'Connor, Gale Storm, Vincent Price, Walter Brennan, Eve Arden. Sometimes foolish slapstick as O'Connor, touring with road show, gets involved with bank robbers and irate citizens of Arizona.

Curtain Up (1952-British) **85m.** **½ D: Ralph Smart. Robert Morley, Margaret Rutherford, Kay Kendall, Olive Sloane, Joan Rice, Michael Medwin, Charlotte Mitchell, Liam Gaffney. Mild but amusing look at a repertory troupe in the British provinces that suffers a minor crisis when the amateur playwright of its latest show turns up on the first day of rehearsals. Morley (as the director) and Rutherford (as the playwright) are great fun to watch.

Curucu, Beast of the Amazon (1956) **C-76m.** *½ D: Curt Siodmak. John Bromfield, Beverly Garland, Tom Payne, Harvey Chalk. One of the most infamous disappointments (for monster-loving kids of the 1950s) as Bromfield and Garland go after title monster in South American jungle.

Cyclops, The (1957) **66m.** ** D: Bert I. Gordon. James Craig, Gloria Talbott, Lon Chaney, Jr., Tom Drake. Expedition scours Mexico in search of Talbott's lost fiancé, discovers that radiation has transformed him into an enormous monster. Nothing much in this cheapie. ▼▶

Cynara (1932) **78m.** ** D: King Vidor. Ronald Colman, Kay Francis, Henry Stephenson, Phyllis Barry, Paul Porcasi. Badly dated film about British lawyer who has interlude with working girl while wife is away; Colman is good as usual.

Cynthia (1947) **98m.** *½ D: Robert Z. Leonard. Elizabeth Taylor, George Murphy, S. Z. Sakall, Mary Astor, Gene Lockhart, Spring Byington, Jimmy Lydon. Sugary film of sickly girl Taylor finding outlet in music; good cast wasted. ▶

Cyrano de Bergerac (1925-Italian) **C-114m.** **½ D: Augusto Genina. Pierre Magnier, Linda Moglia, Angelo Ferrari, Alex Bernard, Umberto Casilini. Cyrano, fabled poet-swordsman-philosopher of 17th-century Paris, must conceal his love for his cousin Roxane because of the size of his nose. Adequate retelling of Edmond Rostand's classic lacks the requisite romantic fire. Worth seeing for its use of color, produced by tinting, toning, stencil coloring, and hand-painting. First filmed in 1900; remade in 1945, 1950, 1987 (as ROXANNE), and 1990. ▼▶

Cyrano de Bergerac (1950) **112m.** ***½

D: Michael Gordon. Jose Ferrer, Mala Powers, William Prince, Morris Carnovsky, Elena Verdugo. Ferrer received an Oscar for portraying the tragic 17th-century wit, renowned for his nose but longing for love of a beautiful lady. From Edmond Rostand's play. Previously filmed in 1900, 1925, and 1945; later modernized as ROXANNE, and remade in 1990. Also shown in computer-colored version. ▼●)

Daddy-Long-Legs (1919) **85m.** *** D: Marshall Neilan. Mary Pickford, Milla Davenport, Percy Haswell, Fay Lemport, Mahlon Hamilton, Lillian Langdon, Marshall Neilan. Mary's the whole show in this heartfelt fairy tale about a waif who's cruelly treated in an orphanage; then a new trustee agrees to anonymously finance her college education. Pickford displays her versatility as she is transformed from spunky child to lovely young woman. Remade in 1931, 1935 (as CURLY TOP), in the Netherlands in 1938, and as a musical in 1955. ▼▶

Daddy Long Legs (1955) **C-126m.** **½ D: Jean Negulesco. Fred Astaire, Leslie Caron, Thelma Ritter, Fred Clark, Terry Moore, Larry Keating. Overlong musical remake of oft-filmed story about playboy (Astaire) anonymously sponsoring waif's education—then she falls in love with him. Some good dance numbers, and Johnny Mercer score highlighted by "Something's Got to Give." Previously filmed in 1919, 1931, as CURLY TOP in 1935, and in the Netherlands in 1938. CinemaScope. ▼●)

Daddy-O (1959) **74m.** BOMB D: Lou Place. Dick Contino, Sandra Giles, Bruno VeSota, Gloria Victor, Ron McNeil. Thugs recruit truck driver-singer Contino to drive a getaway car. Like wow, man, this flick's for squares. Aka OUT ON PROBATION. ▼

Daisy Kenyon (1947) **99m.** **½ D: Otto Preminger. Joan Crawford, Dana Andrews, Henry Fonda, Ruth Warrick, Martha Stewart, Peggy Ann Garner, Connie Marshall. Love triangle starts intelligently, bogs down halfway into typical soapy histrionics (with a plot thread about child abuse surprising for its time). Good performances; handsomely filmed. Look sharp in the Stork Club scene for Walter Winchell, John Garfield, and Leonard Lyons.▶

Dakota (1945) **82m.** ** D: Joseph Kane. John Wayne, Vera Hruba Ralston, Walter Brennan, Ward Bond, Mike Mazurki, Ona Munson, Olive Blakeney, Hugo Haas, Nicodemus Stewart, Paul Fix, Bobby (Robert) Blake. Lesser Wayne Western casts him as a gambler who runs off with a Chicago railroad tycoon's daughter (Ralston) and becomes involved in a land dispute with villains Bond and Mazurki. Based on an original story by Carl Foreman. ▼●)

Dakota Incident (1956) **C-88m.** **½ D: Lewis R. Foster. Linda Darnell, Dale Robertson, John Lund, Ward Bond, Regis Toomey, Skip Homeier, Irving Bacon, John Doucette, Whit Bissell. Gritty Western drama-morality tale with diverse group of individuals under Indian attack while stranded in the Southwestern frontier. Bond's pacifistic U.S. senator is a fascinating mirror of 1950s American politics and culture. ▼

Dakota Lil (1950) **C-88m.** ** D: Lesley Selander. George Montgomery, Rod Cameron, Marie Windsor, John Emery, Wallace Ford, Jack Lambert, Marion Martin, Walter Sande. Secret Service agent Montgomery infiltrates the world of Dakota Lil (Windsor) in order to catch vicious railroad bandit Cameron. Sande plays Butch Cassidy in this routine yarn ostensibly about the Hole in the Wall Gang.

Dallas (1950) **C-94m.** **½ D: Stuart Heisler. Gary Cooper, Ruth Roman, Steve Cochran, Raymond Massey, Barbara Payton, Leif Erickson, Antonio Moreno. In post–Civil War Texas, former guerrilla Cooper masquerades as a greenhorn marshal (complete with Eastern dude costume) in order to settle scores with a trio of enemies. Begins almost like a comedy but segues into a more-than-adequate action yarn, with Cooper in good form. ▼▶

Damaged Lives (1933) **61m.** ** D: Edgar G. Ulmer. Diane Sinclair, Lyman Williams, Cecilia Parker, George Irving, Almeda Fowler, Jason Robards, Sr. Earnest melodrama preaching against the perils of extramarital flings which, in this case, leads to venereal disease. Definitely low-budget, but not the exploitation "camp" one would assume. Originally followed by a half-hour medical lecture on VD. ▼▶

Dam Busters, The (1955-British) **124m.** ***½ D: Michael Anderson. Richard Todd, Michael Redgrave, Ursula Jeans, Basil Sydney, Patrick Barr, Ernest Clark, Derek Farr, Robert Shaw, Patrick McGoohan. Sharp-edged WW2 drama with engineer Redgrave devising a special weapon that will allow the British to bomb Germany's hydroelectric dams. Beware edited 105m. version. ▼▶

Dames (1934) **90m.** *** D: Ray Enright. Joan Blondell, Dick Powell, Ruby Keeler, ZaSu Pitts, Hugh Herbert, Guy Kibbee, Phil Regan. Short on plot (let's-back-a-Broadway-musical) but has top Busby Berkeley production ensembles like "I Only Have Eyes For You." Other songs include "When You Were a Smile on Your Mother's Lips and a Twinkle in Your Daddy's Eye," and classic title tune.▼●)

Damn Citizen (1958) **88m.** **½ D: Robert Gordon. Keith Andes, Maggie Hayes, Gene Evans, Lynn Bari. Fact-based, hard-hitting account of WW2 veteran Andes hired to head Louisiana state police, clean up widespread crime and corruption.

Damned Don't Cry, The (1950) **103m.**

**½ D: Vincent Sherman. Joan Crawford, David Brian, Steve Cochran, Kent Smith, Richard Egan. Follow-up to FLAMINGO ROAD formula; Crawford is well cast as lower-class gal rising to wealth via wit and looks, discovering too late that a gangster's moll has no right to love and happiness.◗

Damn the Defiant! (1962-British) **C-101m.** *** D: Lewis Gilbert. Alec Guinness, Dirk Bogarde, Maurice Denham, Nigel Stock, Richard Carpenter, Anthony Quayle. Bogarde vs. Guinness in stalwart tale of British warship during Napoleonic campaign. Production shows great attention to historic detail. Original British title: H.M.S. DEFIANT. CinemaScope.▼●◗

Damn Yankees (1958) **C-110m.** *** D: George Abbott, Stanley Donen. Tab Hunter, Gwen Verdon, Ray Walston, Russ Brown, Jimmie Komack, Jean Stapleton, Nathaniel Frey. Aging, frustrated Washington Senators baseball fan says he'd sell his soul to see the club get one good hitter; a devilish Mr. Applegate appears to fulfill his wish, and transforms *him* into the club's new star. Faithful translation of hit Broadway musical (with Walston, Verdon, and others repeating their original roles) loses something along the way, and has a particularly weak finale, but it's still quite entertaining. Songs include "(You Gotta Have) Heart," "Whatever Lola Wants," and a mambo memorably danced by Verdon and choreographer Bob Fosse.▼●◗

Damon and Pythias (1962-Italian) **C-99m.** ** D: Curtis Bernhardt. Guy Williams, Don Burnett, Ilaria Occhini, Liana Orfei, Arnoldo Foa. Title reveals all in this routine costumer making legendary figures juvenile cardboard heroes.▼◗

Damsel in Distress, A (1937) **101m.** *** D: George Stevens. Fred Astaire, George Burns, Gracie Allen, Joan Fontaine, Constance Collier, Reginald Gardiner, Montagu Love. Bright Gershwin musical set in London, with dancing star Astaire pursuing aristocratic heiress Fontaine. Burns and Allen have never been better—they even get to sing and dance. Songs include "Foggy Day in London Town," "Nice Work If You Can Get It." The clever "Fun House" sequence won an Oscar for Hermes Pan's dance direction. Based on a novel by P. G. Wodehouse, who cowrote the script.▼●◗

Dance, Fools, Dance (1931) **81m.** **½ D: Harry Beaumont. Joan Crawford, Cliff Edwards, Clark Gable, Earl Foxe, Lester Vail, Natalie Moorhead. Crawford, alone in the world, becomes reporter out to expose mobster Gable by winning him over. Interesting for early Gable-Crawford teaming; brisk pre-Code drama.▼◗

Dance, Girl, Dance (1940) **90m.** **½ D: Dorothy Arzner. Maureen O'Hara, Louis Hayward, Lucille Ball, Virginia Field, Ralph Bellamy, Maria Ouspenskaya, Mary Carlisle, Walter Abel, Edward Brophy. Inno-

cent young girl (O'Hara) aspires to be a ballerina, but self-centered Ball steers her toward burlesque instead. Film has won latter-day acclaim for feminist angles, especially for O'Hara's burlesque-hall speech; unfortunately, it's not as good as one would like. Lucy is terrific as Bubbles.▼●◗

Dance Hall (1941) **74m.** *½ D: Irving Pichel. Carole Landis, Cesar Romero, William Henry, June Storey. Mild romantic musical with Romero, who runs a dance hall, falling in love with worker Landis.▼

Dance Hall (1950-British) **78m.** ** D: Charles Crichton. Natasha Parry, Jane Hylton, Diana Dors, Petula Clark, Donald Houston, Bonar Colleano, Sydney Tafler, Kay Kendall, Geraldo, Ted Heath Band. Episodic tale of four factory girls' encounters and adventures at local dance hall. Nothing much.▼

Dance Hall Racket (1953) **60m.** *½ D: Phil Tucker. Lenny Bruce, Honey Harlowe, Timothy Farrell, Sally Marr. This one could be retitled *All in the* (Dysfunctional) *Family*: Lenny plays a hood, real-life wife Harlowe is a bimbo who shows off her cleavage, and mom Marr is along for laughs. Scripted by Bruce; it would make a classy double bill with Tucker's ROBOT MONSTER.▼◗

Dance Little Lady (1955-British) **C-87m.** **½ D: Val Guest. Mai Zetterling, Terence Morgan, Guy Rolfe, Mandy Miller, Eunice Gayson, Reginald Beckwith. Prima ballerina Zetterling is married to heel Morgan; after a car accident ends her career, he exploits the dancing talent of their daughter (Miller). Corny drama is aided by pleasant dance sequences.▼

Dance of Life, The (1929) **108m.** *** D: A. Edward Sutherland, John Cromwell. Nancy Carroll, Hal Skelly, Dorothy Revier, Ralph Theodore, Charles D. Brown, Al St. John, May Boley, Oscar Levant. Skelly gives a moving portrayal of a struggling burlesque entertainer who marries dancer Carroll and makes it big on Broadway but can't handle success. He hits the bottle when she discovers he is having an affair. Adapted from the stage smash *Burlesque* (which starred Skelly and Barbara Stanwyck), this vivid, colorful early talkie really captures the backstage milieu. Levant's film debut; co-directors Cromwell and Sutherland have bit parts. Originally 115m.; some production numbers were shot in two-strip Technicolor. Remade as SWING HIGH, SWING LOW and WHEN MY BABY SMILES AT ME.

Dancers in the Dark (1932) **74m.** **½ D: David Burton. Miriam Hopkins, Jack Oakie, George Raft, William Collier, Jr., Eugene Pallette, Lyda Roberti. Bandleader Oakie tries to kindle romance with taxi-dancer Hopkins, by sending her boyfriend (Collier) out of town, but doesn't reckon with gangster Raft falling for her too. Good stars help murky drama.

Dance With Me, Henry (1956) 79m. *½ D: Charles Barton. Lou Costello, Bud Abbott, Gigi Perreau, Rusty Hamer. Low-grade Abbott and Costello involving the duo's ownership of run-down amusement park and two kids they've adopted; their last film together.▼⊃

Dancing Co-Ed (1939) 84m. **½ D: S. Sylvan Simon. Lana Turner, Richard Carlson, Artie Shaw and His Band, Ann Rutherford, Lee Bowman, Thurston Hall, Leon Errol, Roscoe Karns, Mary Beth Hughes, June Preisser, Monty Woolley. Polished MGM fluff with Lana (girlishly gorgeous) sent to a Midwestern college as part of a stunt to be "discovered" by a Hollywood studio. Shaw's band is at its best, with Buddy Rich on drums; a year later the bandleader married Turner.⊃

Dancing in the Dark (1949) C-92m. **½ D: Irving Reis. William Powell, Betsy Drake, Mark Stevens, Adolphe Menjou, Walter Catlett. Occasionally bubbly musical comedy with Powell hoping to cement good relations with film company by signing Broadway star; he becomes intrigued with talents of unknown girl, who turns out to be his daughter.

Dancing Lady (1933) 94m. **½ D: Robert Z. Leonard. Joan Crawford, Clark Gable, Franchot Tone, May Robson, Nelson Eddy, Fred Astaire, Robert Benchley, Ted Healy and His Stooges. Glossy backstage romance is best remembered for Astaire's film debut (he plays himself), dancing opposite a less-than-inspired Crawford. Show-biz story, three-cornered romance are strictly standard, but cast and MGM gloss add points. Funniest moments belong to The Three Stooges. Look fast for a young Eve Arden.▼⊃

Dancing Masters, The (1943) 63m. *½ D: Mal St. Clair. Oliver Hardy, Stan Laurel, Trudy Marshall, Robert Bailey, Matt Briggs, Margaret Dumont. L&H overcome by routine material, special effects that look phony. Robert Mitchum has bit as a hood.⊃

Dancing Mothers (1926) 60m. **½ D: Herbert Brenon. Clara Bow, Alice Joyce, Dorothy Cumming, Norman Trevor. Sprightly account of Flapper Bow defying conventions as prototype of the Jazz Age. Silent film has simple plot but enthusiastic performances.▼⊃

Dancing on a Dime (1940) 74m. **½ D: Joseph Santley. Grace McDonald, Robert Paige, Virginia Dale, Peter Lind Hayes. Programmer musical with wispy plot allowing for McDonald et al. to do some dancing and vocalizing, such as "I Hear Music" and title tune. Not bad.

Danger Island SEE: **Mr. Moto in Danger Island**

Danger Lights (1930) 73m. ** D: George B. Seitz. Louis Wolheim, Robert Armstrong, Jean Arthur, Hugh Herbert, Robert Edeson. Tough but kindhearted railroad yard supervisor Wolheim is engaged to marry Arthur, but she falls for younger, handsomer tramp turned engineer Armstrong. Predictable, with race-against-the-clock finale. Natural Vision 70mm.▼

Danger—Love at Work (1937) 81m. **½ D: Otto L. Preminger. Ann Sothern, Jack Haley, Mary Boland, John Carradine, Edward Everett Horton, E. E. Clive, Stanley Fields. Wacky comedy of family headed by nutty Boland involved in shotgun wedding of Sothern and Haley.⊃

Dangerous (1935) 78m. **½ D: Alfred E. Green. Bette Davis, Franchot Tone, Margaret Lindsay, Alison Skipworth, John Eldredge, Dick Foran. Former stage star Davis, on the skids, is pulled out of the gutter by architect Tone, who's determined to put her back on Broadway. Syrupy and full of speeches but compelling, with flamboyant Oscar-winning performance by Davis. Remade as SINGAPORE WOMAN.▼⊃

Dangerous Corner (1934) 66m. **½ D: Phil Rosen. Virginia Bruce, Conrad Nagel, Melvyn Douglas, Erin O'Brien Moore, Ian Keith, Betty Furness, Doris Lloyd. Interesting, well-acted adaptation of J. B. Priestley's play about a group of friends whose after-dinner conversation reveals the truth about an alleged suicide and theft committed years before; unique flashback structure and trick ending hold up.

Dangerous Crossing (1953) 75m. **½ D: Joseph M. Newman. Jeanne Crain, Michael Rennie, Casey Adams (Max Showalter), Carl Betz, Mary Anderson, Willis Bouchey. Well-acted suspenser has Crain a bride on ocean liner whose husband mysteriously disappears. Based on a John Dickson Carr story. Remade for cable TV in 1992 as TREACHEROUS CROSSING.⊃

Dangerous Exile (1958-British) C-90m. ** D: Brian Desmond Hurst. Louis Jourdan, Belinda Lee, Keith Michell, Richard O'Sullivan. Jourdan is properly dashing in OK adventurer in which he saves royalty from execution during French revolution, aided by English lass (Lee). VistaVision.

Dangerous Female SEE: **Maltese Falcon, The** (1931)

Dangerous Game, A (1941) 61m. BOMB D: John Rawlins. Richard Arlen, Andy Devine, Jeanne Kelly (Jean Brooks), Edward Brophy, Marc Lawrence. Frequent screen partners Arlen and Devine diverged from their usual run of B actioners to do this appallingly lowbrow mystery-comedy about murder at a sanitarium. Scenes of the entire ad-libbing cast screaming, hollering, and running in circles for minutes at a time are the "lowlights," but not *much* worse than the rest.

Dangerous Liaisons 1960 (1959-French) 106m. *** D: Roger Vadim. Jeanne Moreau, Gérard Philipe, Jeanne Valérie, Annette

(Stroyberg) Vadim, Simone Renant, Jean-Louis Trintignant. Modern-dress version of the 18th-century novel of sexcapades among the debauched . . . and who better to film it than Vadim? Faithful in spirit to its origins, though the leads here are a *married* couple, cavorting in Paris and the Alps. Lots of fun, with gorgeous actors and jazz soundtrack by Thelonious Monk, Art Blakey, and Duke Jordan, who also appear. Don't miss Vadim's priceless prologue, shot for 1961 American audiences. Vadim remade this in 1976 as UNE FEMME FIDÈLE (GAME OF SEDUCTION). French title: LES LIAISONS DANGEREUSES. ▼●▶

Dangerously They Live (1942) 77m. **½ D: Robert Florey. John Garfield, Nancy Coleman, Raymond Massey, Moroni Olsen, Lee Patrick. When spy Coleman is captured by Nazis, doctor Garfield comes to her aid. Tried-and-true WW2 spy tale. ▶

Dangerous Millions (1946) 59m. **½ D: James Tinling. Kent Taylor, Dona Drake, Tala Birell, Leonard Strong, Rex Evans. An American tycoon's potential heirs, converged in China, are taken hostage by a bandit chieftain (Strong) who demands half the inheritance. Unusual story and Strong's wily performance lift this above the expected B level.

Dangerous Mission (1954) C-75m. **½ D: Louis King. Victor Mature, Piper Laurie, William Bendix, Vincent Price, Betta St. John, Harry Cheshire, Walter Reed. Mob hit man is hired to rub out witness in an upcoming murder trial and tracks her to a hotel in Glacier National Park, where another killer is on the loose. Enjoyable thriller boasts a solid cast, lovely locations, and a nifty twist at the halfway point, but the script has too many subplots and surprisingly flat dialogue. That's Dennis Weaver as one of Bendix's deputies. Originally in 3-D. ▼

Dangerous Money (1946) 64m. *½ D: Terry Morse. Sidney Toler, Gloria Warren, Victor Sen Yung, Rick Vallin, Joseph Crehan, Willie Best. Yawnworthy *Charlie Chan* entry about the hunt for a murderer aboard a ship. ▶

Dangerous Moonlight (1941-British) 93m. *** D: Brian Desmond Hurst. Anton Walbrook, Sally Gray, Derrick de Marney, Keneth Kent. Intelligently presented account of concert pianist who becomes a member of a British fighter squadron during WW2; musical interludes (including Richard Addinsell's well-known "Warsaw Concerto") well handled. Look for Michael Rennie in a small role. Retitled: SUICIDE SQUADRON. ▼

Dangerous Paradise (1930) 61m. ** D: William A. Wellman. Nancy Carroll, Richard Arlen, Warner Oland, Gustav von Seyffertitz, Francis McDonald. Lurid early talkie with heroic hermit Arlen rescuing pert musician Carroll from a bunch of sleazeballs

at a South Seas island hotel. Fitfully entertaining melodrama, loosely based on Joseph Conrad's novel *Victory*. Filmed before in 1919 and again in 1940 as VICTORY.

Dangerous Partners (1945) 74m. **½ D: Edward L. Cahn. James Craig, Signe Hasso, Edmund Gwenn, Audrey Totter, Mabel Paige, John Warburton. After surviving a plane crash, a couple tries to unravel the mystery of a fellow passenger who was carrying four million-dollar wills signed by four different people. Not-bad grade-B mystery yarn.

Dangerous Profession, A (1949) 79m. *½ D: Ted Tetzlaff. George Raft, Pat O'Brien, Ella Raines, Jim Backus, Roland Winters. Heavy-handed crime drama-romance lacks only logic, understandable character motivation, pace, and excitement. L.A. bail bondsman Raft carries a torch for the wife (Raines) of one of his clients; murder ensues. ▶

Dangerous to Know (1938) 70m. **½ D: Robert Florey. Akim Tamiroff, Anna May Wong, Gail Patrick, Lloyd Nolan, Harvey Stephens, Anthony Quinn, Roscoe Karns. Slick, class-conscious mobster Tamiroff sets his sights on aristocratic Patrick, while his elegant hostess (Wong) suffers in silence. Interesting B picture never quite delivers.

Dangerous Venture (1947) 59m. ** D: George Archainbaud. William Boyd, Andy Clyde, Rand Brooks, Fritz Leiber, Douglas Evans, Betty Alexander. Hopalong Cassidy combats cattle rustlers masquerading as Indians and a crooked scientist who is plundering riches from ancient Indian burial sites. Weak if fantastic story about lost Indian civilization, but the film's meager budget is all too apparent. Reissued as SIX SHOOTER JUSTICE. ▼▶

Dangerous When Wet (1953) C-95m. *** D: Charles Walters. Esther Williams, Fernando Lamas, Jack Carson, Charlotte Greenwood, Denise Darcel, William Demarest, Donna Corcoran, Barbara Whiting. Cute musical comedy, one of Esther's best, about a health-conscious family whose leading light tries to swim the English Channel. Williams cavorts underwater with the animated Tom and Jerry in one memorable scene. She later married leading-man Lamas in real life. ▼●▶

Danger Patrol (1937) 60m. **½ D: Lew Landers. John Beal, Sally Eilers, Harry Carey, Frank M. Thomas, Crawford Weaver, Lee Patrick, Edward Gargan, Paul Guilfoyle. Beal is an aspiring doctor who earns money for medical school by taking a perilous job as a "nitro shooter," delivering nitroglycerin to oil fields, and falling for daughter of grizzled "soup handler" Carey in the process. No great shakes but quite acceptable action filler that plays like a B-movie precursor to THE WAGES OF FEAR.

Danger Signal (1945) 78m. ** D: Robert Florey. Faye Emerson, Zachary Scott,

Rosemary DeCamp, Bruce Bennett, Mona Freeman. No-account Scott comes between Emerson and her family in this routine drama; Scott is a most convincing heel.

Danger Within SEE: **Breakout**

Daniel Boone (1936) 75m. **½ D: David Howard. George O'Brien, Heather Angel, John Carradine, Ralph Forbes, Clarence Muse. OK action adventure detailing a chapter in the life of the legendary pioneer: his leading some settlers west from North Carolina into Kentucky. O'Brien is well cast in the title role.▼▶

Daniel Boone, Trail Blazer (1956) C-76m. **½ D: Albert C. Gannaway, Ismael Rodriguez. Bruce Bennett, Lon Chaney (Jr.), Faron Young, Kem Dibbs. Generally well-acted low-budget version of life of famous frontier explorer and his skirmishes with Indians. Filmed in Mexico.▼▶

Dante's Inferno (1935) 88m. **½ D: Harry Lachman. Spencer Tracy, Claire Trevor, Henry B. Walthall, Alan Dinehart, Scotty Beckett. No Dante in this yarn of carnival owner who gets too big for his own good; just one elaborate sequence showing Satan's paradise in good Tracy vehicle. Young Rita Hayworth dances in one scene.▶

Darby O'Gill and the Little People (1959) C-90m. ***½ D: Robert Stevenson. Albert Sharpe, Janet Munro, Sean Connery, Jimmy O'Dea, Kieron Moore, Estelle Winwood. Outstanding Disney fantasy about an Irish caretaker (Sharpe) who spins so many tales that no one believes him when he says he's befriended the King of Leprechauns. An utter delight, with dazzling special effects—and some truly terrifying moments along with the whimsy.▼▶❂

Darby's Rangers (1958) 121m. **½ D: William Wellman. James Garner, Etchika Choureau, Jack Warden, Edward Byrnes, Venetia Stevenson, Torin Thatcher, Peter Brown, Corey Allen, Stuart Whitman, Murray Hamilton. Garner does well in WW2 actioner as leader of assault troops in North Africa and Italy, focusing on relationships among his command and their shore romances.▼▶

Daring Young Man, The (1942) 73m. ** D: Frank Strayer. Joe E. Brown, Marguerite Chapman, William Wright, Roger Clark. Brown is able to make this formula Nazi spy chase comedy of passable interest; set in N.Y.C.▼

Dark Alibi (1946) 61m. *½ D: Phil Karlson. Sidney Toler, Benson Fong, Mantan Moreland, Teala Loring, George Holmes, Edward Earle, Russell Hicks, Joyce Compton. Someone's committing crimes and framing innocents by forging their fingerprints in this tedious *Charlie Chan* outing for Karlson completists only.▶

Dark Angel, The (1935) 110m. *** D: Sidney Franklin. Fredric March, Merle Oberon, Herbert Marshall, Janet Beecher,

John Halliday. Effective soaper of love, guilt, and fate. The three leads are lifelong friends; March and Oberon are destined to marry, but he and Marshall head off to WW1—and tragedy. Coscripted by Lillian Hellman; based on a play by H. B. Trevelyan (Guy Bolton). Originally filmed in 1925 with Ronald Colman.▼

Dark at the Top of the Stairs, The (1960) C-123m. ***½ D: Delbert Mann. Robert Preston, Dorothy McGuire, Eve Arden, Angela Lansbury, Shirley Knight, Lee Kinsolving, Frank Overton, Robert Eyer. Simple, eloquent drama, set in 1920s Oklahoma, with Preston in top form as a traveling salesman caught in a passionless marriage. His relationships with wife McGuire, daughter Knight, and "friend" Lansbury are played out in a series of beautifully acted scenes. Poignant script by Irving Ravetch and Harriet Frank, Jr., from William Inge's play.

Dark Avenger, The SEE: **Warriors, The** (1955-British)

Dark City (1950) 98m. **½ D: William Dieterle. Charlton Heston, Lizabeth Scott, Viveca Lindfors, Dean Jagger, Jack Webb, Don DeFore, Ed Begley, Henry (Harry) Morgan. Moody drama of cynical, alienated Heston, and what happens when he and his cronies take sap DeFore in a card game. It's fun to see Webb and Morgan, both of later *Dragnet* fame, cast as a wiseguy and ex-pug at each other's throats. This was Heston's Hollywood debut.▶

Dark Command (1940) 94m. *** D: Raoul Walsh. Claire Trevor, John Wayne, Walter Pidgeon, Roy Rogers, George "Gabby" Hayes, Porter Hall, Marjorie Main. Pidgeon plays character based on 1860s renegade Quantrill, small-town despot who (in this story) launches his terror raids after clashing with new marshal Wayne. Dramatically uneven, but entertaining. Also shown in computer-colored version.▼▶

Dark Corner, The (1946) 99m. *** D: Henry Hathaway. Lucille Ball, Clifton Webb, William Bendix, Mark Stevens, Kurt Kreuger, Cathy Downs, Reed Hadley, Constance Collier. Top-notch mystery with secretary Ball helping moody boss Stevens escape from phony murder charge. Well-acted, exciting film noir.▼▶

Dark Delusion (1947) 90m. ** D: Willis Goldbeck. Lionel Barrymore, James Craig, Lucille Bremer, Jayne Meadows, Warner Anderson, Henry Stephenson, Alma Kruger, Keye Luke, Art Baker, Marie Blake, Nell Craig. The *Dr. Kildare/Dr. Gillespie* series came to an end with this blah entry about Gillespie getting a new protégé (Craig) who's assigned to the case of a neurotic socialite whose family wants her committed.▶

Dark Eyes of London SEE: **Human Monster, The**

Dark Hazard (1934) 72m. ** D: Alfred E. Green. Edward G. Robinson, Genevieve

Tobin, Glenda Farrell, Henry B. Walthall, Sidney Toler. Robinson is bright spot of programmer about his precarious married life to Tobin, endangered by girlfriend Farrell and urge to gamble. ❶

Dark Horse, The (1932) 75m. **½ D: Alfred E. Green. Warren William, Bette Davis, Guy Kibbee, Vivienne Osborne, Frank McHugh. Lively political spoof with nitwit Kibbee running for governor with help from campaign manager William and co-worker Davis.▼❶

Dark Hour, The (1936) 64m. ** D: Charles Lamont. Ray Walker, Berton Churchill, Irene Ware, Hobart Bosworth, Hedda Hopper, E. E. Clive. A wealthy old sorehead is murdered and *every*body's got a motive—even Walker and Churchill, the police detectives on the case. Talky, set-bound Poverty Row meller wears out its welcome, but the final reel is notable for its record number of false endings and twists.

Dark Intruder (1965) 59m. *** D: Harvey Hart. Leslie Nielsen, Judi Meredith, Mark Richman, Werner Klemperer, Gilbert Green, Charles Bolender. Uneven performances major liability in near-flawless supernatural thriller. Occult expert called in by San Francisco police in connection with series of weird murders. Intricate plot and exceptional use of time period blending with suspense make this a one-of-a-kind movie. Busted TV pilot given theatrical release.

Dark Journey (1937-British) 82m. *** D: Victor Saville. Conrad Veidt, Vivien Leigh, Joan Gardner, Anthony Bushell, Ursula Jeans. Engrossing love story, set in WW1 Stockholm, about dress-shop-owner–double agent Leigh, who gets involved with baron Veidt, head of German Intelligence. Young Vivien is radiant.▼❶

Dark Mirror, The (1946) 85m. *** D: Robert Siodmak. Olivia de Havilland, Lew Ayres, Thomas Mitchell, Richard Long, Charles Evans, Garry Owen. De Havilland plays twin sisters—one good, one disturbed—who are implicated in murder. One of Hollywood's post-WW2 forays into psychological drama; no longer fresh, but still entertaining. Remade for TV in 1984 with Jane Seymour.▼

Dark Mountain (1944) 56m. *½ D: William Berke. Robert Lowery, Ellen Drew, Regis Toomey, Eddie Quillan, Elisha Cook, Jr. Throwaway B movie, short on running time *and* plot. After unwittingly marrying a gangster (Toomey), Drew must hide out with him in mountain cabin when he goes on the lam. Movie starts with some action but most of the rest is a lot of talk in a couple of dark rooms. Semi-remake of FEMALE FUGITIVE (1938).

Dark Passage (1947) 106m. *** D: Delmer Daves. Humphrey Bogart, Lauren Bacall, Bruce Bennett, Agnes Moorehead. Engrossing caper of escaped convict (Bogart) undergoing plastic surgery, hiding out at Bacall's apartment till his face heals. Stars outshine far-fetched happenings. Also shown in computer-colored version. ▼❶

Dark Past, The (1948) 75m. *** D: Rudolph Maté. William Holden, Nina Foch, Lee J. Cobb, Adele Jergens, Stephen Dunne. Absorbing narrative of mad killer holding psychologist prisoner and latter's attempts to talk sense into the maniac. Remake of BLIND ALLEY.▼

Dark Sands (1937-British) 77m. ** D: Thornton Freeland. Paul Robeson, Henry Wilcoxon, Wallace Ford, Princess Kouka, John Laurie. Weak drama with American deserter Robeson joining African desert tribe to avoid corporal punishment. Robeson again defeated by his material. Originally titled JERICHO.▼❶

Dark Tower, The (1943-British) 94m. **½ D: John Harlow. Ben Lyon, Anne Crawford, David Farrar, Herbert Lom, Frederick Burtwell, Bill (William) Hartnell. Traveling circus, barely scraping by, is in desperate need of a novelty act. That proves to be a mysterious hypnotist (Lom), whose creepy presence affects one and all. Generally well-done drama, based on a 1933 George S. Kaufman–Alexander Woollcott play.

Dark Victory (1939) 106m. ***½ D: Edmund Goulding. Bette Davis, George Brent, Humphrey Bogart, Geraldine Fitzgerald, Ronald Reagan, Cora Witherspoon, Henry Travers. Definitive Davis performance as spoiled socialite whose life is ending; Brent as brain surgeon husband, Fitzgerald as devoted friend register in good soaper. Bogart as Irish stable master seems out of place. Remade as STOLEN HOURS, and for TV in 1976 with Elizabeth Montgomery and Anthony Hopkins. Also shown in computer-colored version. ▼❶

Dark Waters (1944) 90m. ** D: Andre de Toth. Merle Oberon, Franchot Tone, Thomas Mitchell, Fay Bainter, Rex Ingram, John Qualen, Elisha Cook, Jr. Cast sinks into the bog (some literally) in confused film of traumatized woman recuperating amid the strange occupants of an eerie Louisiana mansion.

Darling (1965-British) 122m. ***½ D: John Schlesinger. Julie Christie, Dirk Bogarde, Laurence Harvey, Roland Curram, Jose Luis de Villalonga, Alex Scott, Basil Henson. Christie won Oscar as girl who rises from commonplace life to marry an Italian noble, with several unsatisfactory love affairs in between. Trendy, influential '60s film—in flashy form and cynical content. Frederic Raphael's script and costume designer Julie Harris also won Oscars.▼❶

Darling, How Could You! (1951) 96m. **½ D: Mitchell Leisen. Joan Fontaine, John Lund, Mona Freeman, Peter Hanson, David Stollery. Doctor Lund and wife Fon-

[155]

taine return from Central America to their three children, with various comical complications. Strictly sitcom stuff, sometimes sweet but mostly silly and stupid. Based on a James M. Barrie play.

Date With Judy, A (1948) **C-113m.** **½ D: Richard Thorpe. Wallace Beery, Jane Powell, Elizabeth Taylor, Carmen Miranda, Xavier Cugat, Robert Stack, Scotty Beckett. Musicomedy of two teenagers involved in family shenanigans; highlight is Beery dancing with Miranda. Songs include "It's a Most Unusual Day."▼○▶

Date With the Falcon, A (1941) 63m. **½ D: Irving Reis. George Sanders, Wendy Barrie, James Gleason, Allen Jenkins, Mona Maris, Frank Moran, Ed Gargan. Sanders interrupts his wedding plans to find a missing scientist who has invented a synthetic diamond formula. Entertaining second entry in the series, with a good deal of comic relief.▶

Daughter of Dr. Jekyll (1957) 71m. *½ D: Edgar G. Ulmer. John Agar, Gloria Talbott, Arthur Shields, John Dierkes. Talbott thinks she is the half-human/half-monster her father was, especially when the village death rate increases. Madly scrambles vampire, werewolf, and Jekyll-Hyde story elements.▼▶

Daughter of Horror SEE: **Dementia**
Daughter of Mata Hari SEE: **Mata Hari's Daughter**
Daughter of Rosie O'Grady, The (1950) C-104m. **½ D: David Butler. June Haver, Gordon MacRae, Debbie Reynolds, Gene Nelson, James Barton, S. Z. Sakall, Jane Darwell. Formula period musical with Haver in title role singing turn-of-the-20th-century favorites. Talented MacRae is her love interest, and Sakall is forced to give another cuddly stereotype.▶

Daughter of Shanghai (1937) 63m. **½ D: Robert Florey. Anna May Wong, Charles Bickford, Larry (Buster) Crabbe, Cecil Cunningham, J. Carrol Naish, Anthony Quinn, Philip Ahn, Fred Kohler, Evelyn Brent, Frank Sully. Good girl Wong seeks to avenge father's death by exposing illegal alien racket in tight-knit B actioner. Beautifully staged and shot.

Daughter of the Dragon (1931) 72m. **½ D: Lloyd Corrigan. Warner Oland, Anna May Wong, Sessue Hayakawa, Bramwell Fletcher, Frances Dade, Holmes Herbert. Oland is Dr. Fu Manchu in opening reels of this entertaining, if familiar, adaptation of a Sax Rohmer story; the good doctor dispatches daughter Wong to commit murder, and she becomes entangled with Scotland Yard sleuth Hayakawa.▼

Daughters Courageous (1939) 107m. *** D: Michael Curtiz. John Garfield, Claude Rains, Fay Bainter, Priscilla Lane, Rosemary Lane, Lola Lane, Gale Page, May Robson, Donald Crisp, Frank McHugh.

Enjoyable reworking of FOUR DAUGHTERS, featuring the same cast and chronicling what happens when wanderer Rains returns to the family he abandoned 20 years before. Garfield is fine as the brash charmer who's romancing Priscilla Lane.▶

Daughters of Destiny (1954-French) 94m. ** D: Marcel Pagliero. Claudette Colbert, Michele Morgan, André Clement, Daniel Ivernel. Overblown, sluggish trio of tales telling of three famous women of history: Elizabeth I, Lysistrata, Joan of Arc.

David and Bathsheba (1951) C-116m. ** D: Henry King. Gregory Peck, Susan Hayward, Raymond Massey, Kieron Moore, James Robertson Justice, Jayne Meadows, John Sutton, George Zucco. Biblical epic with good production values but generally boring script; only fair performances.▼○▶

David and Goliath (1960-Italian) C-95m. ** D: Richard Pottier, Ferdinando Baldi. Orson Welles, Ivo Payer, Edward Hilton, Eleonora Rossi-Drago, Massimo Serato. Juvenile spectacle based on biblical tale, with wooden script, bad acting, Welles as hefty King Saul. Totalscope.▼▶

David and Lisa (1962) 94m. *** D: Frank Perry. Keir Dullea, Janet Margolin, Howard da Silva, Neva Patterson, Clifton James. Independently made film about two disturbed teenagers is excellent, sensitively played by then-newcomers Dullea and Margolin. Da Silva is fine as an understanding doctor. Remade for TV in 1998.▼○▶

David Copperfield (1935) 130m. **** D: George Cukor. Freddie Bartholomew, Frank Lawton, W.C. Fields, Lionel Barrymore, Madge Evans, Roland Young, Basil Rathbone, Edna May Oliver, Maureen O'Sullivan, Lewis Stone, Lennox Pawle, Elsa Lanchester, Una O'Connor, Arthur Treacher. Hollywood does right by Dickens in this lavishly mounted, superbly cast production, following David's exploits from youth to young manhood, with such unforgettable characterizations as Fields' Micawber, Rathbone's Mr. Murdstone, Young's Uriah Heep, and Oliver's Aunt Betsey. A treat from start to finish. Screenplay by Howard Estabrook and Hugh Walpole; the latter also portrays the vicar. Also shown in computer-colored version. ▼○▶

David Harding, Counterspy (1950) 71m. *½ D: Ray Nazarro. Willard Parker, Audrey Long, Howard St. John, Harlan Warde, Alex Gerry, John Dehner, Jimmy Lloyd, Jock Mahoney. Federal bigwig (St. John) in charge of counterespionage recalls a case from WW2: Navy commander Parker joins the team to investigate a torpedo plant infiltrated by enemy spies, which also puts him back in contact with the woman he once loved. Incredibly dull. First of a two-film series based on Phillips H. Lord's radio series; followed by COUNTERSPY MEETS SCOTLAND YARD.▶

[156]

David Harum (1934) **83m.** **½ D: James Cruze. Will Rogers, Louise Dresser, Evelyn Venable, Kent Taylor, Stepin Fetchit, Noah Beery, Charles Middleton. Foxy rancher Rogers plays matchmaker for Venable and Taylor, while spinning his own brand of folksy humor. Filmed before in 1915.▶

Davy Crockett and the River Pirates (1956) **C-81m.** **½ D: Norman Foster. Fess Parker, Buddy Ebsen, Jeff York, Kenneth Tobey, Clem Bevans, Irvin Ashkenazy. Second CROCKETT feature strung together from two Disney TV shows; first half is comic keelboat race with Mike Fink (York), self-proclaimed "King of the River," second half is more serious confrontation with Indians. Lightweight fun.▼●▶

Davy Crockett Indian Scout (1950) **71m.** ** D: Lew Landers. George Montgomery, Ellen Drew, Philip Reed, Noah Beery, Jr., Paul Guilfoyle, Addison Richards, Robert Barrat, Chief Thundercloud. Humdrum wagon train saga has nothing whatsoever to do with the legend of Davy C. Montgomery plays Crockett's nephew and namesake, an Army scout escorting settlers who are under Indian attack. Retitled INDIAN SCOUT.▶

Davy Crockett, King of the Wild Frontier (1955) **C-93m.** *** D: Norman Foster. Fess Parker, Buddy Ebsen, Basil Ruysdael, Hans Conried, William Bakewell, Kenneth Tobey. Originally filmed as three segments for Disney's TV show, this created a nationwide phenomenon in 1955; it's still fun today with Parker as famous Indian scout and Ebsen as his pal George Russel, whose adventures take them from Washington, D.C., to the Alamo.▼▶

Dawn at Socorro (1954) **C-80m.** **½ D: George Sherman. Rory Calhoun, Piper Laurie, David Brian, Kathleen Hughes, Edgar Buchanan, Alex Nicol, Lee Van Cleef, Skip Homeier. Calhoun is gunslinger wishing to reform, but fate forces inevitable shootout.▶

Dawn Patrol, The (1930) **107m.** **½ D: Howard Hawks. Richard Barthelmess, Douglas Fairbanks, Jr., Neil Hamilton, William Janney, James Finlayson, Clyde Cook. John Monk Saunders' Oscar-winning story of a beleaguered aerial squadron in WW1 France. Devotees of director Hawks prefer this to 1938 remake, but it doesn't hold up as well, particularly the stiff, overdrawn performances.▶

Dawn Patrol, The (1938) **103m.** ***½ D: Edmund Goulding. Errol Flynn, Basil Rathbone, David Niven, Donald Crisp, Melville Cooper, Barry Fitzgerald. Remake of 1930 classic is fine actioner of British flyers in WW1 France; Rathbone as stern officer forced to send up green recruits, Flynn and Niven as pilot buddies, all excellent. Insightful study of wartime camaraderie and grueling pressures of battlefront command.▼●▶

Dawn Rider, The (1935) **53m.** **½ D: R. N. Bradbury. John Wayne, Marion Burns, Denny Meadows (Dennis Moore), Reed Howes, Yakima Canutt, Earl Dwire. Returning to town after a long absence, Wayne watches his dad die during an express office holdup, then sets out to find the killer, who is the brother of Wayne's soon-to-be sweetheart. Has all the pluses and minuses of Western quickies, with Archie Stout's outdoor photography covering budgetary limitations. Young Wayne is assured, leisurely, and likable. Monogram producer Paul Malvern used this story three times during the 1930s.▼▶

Day and the Hour, The (1963-French-Italian) **115m.** **½ D: René Clement. Simone Signoret, Stuart Whitman, Genevieve Page, Michel Piccoli, Reggie Nalder, Pierre Dux, Billy Kearns. In Nazi-occupied France, Signoret is a widow who becomes involved in the Resistance movement; Whitman is an American paratrooper trying to escape to Spain. Franscope.▼

Day at the Races, A (1937) **111m.** ***½ D: Sam Wood. Groucho, Harpo, Chico Marx, Allan Jones, Maureen O'Sullivan, Esther Muir, Margaret Dumont, Douglass Dumbrille, Sig Ruman, Dorothy Dandridge. The Marxes wreak havoc at a sanitorium, where wealthy hypochondriac Dumont is the leading patient; often uproarious comedy features some of the trio's funniest set pieces (Chico selling race tips, the seduction scene, etc.). A perfunctory storyline and unmemorable songs keep it from topping its immediate predecessor, A NIGHT AT THE OPERA . . . but the comedy content is sensational.▼●▶

Daybreak (1931) **75m.** *** D: Jacques Feyder. Ramon Novarro, Helen Chandler, Karen Morley, Jean Hersholt, C. Aubrey Smith, Kent Douglass (Douglass Montgomery), William Bakewell, Glenn Tryon. Poignant love story detailing the romance between Austrian lieutenant Novarro and innocent piano teacher Chandler, who becomes the mistress of gambler Hersholt. Polished adaptation of Arthur Schnitzler's novel is glowingly photographed by Merritt B. Gerstad and given a touch of European sophistication by the underrated Feyder.

Daybreak (1939) SEE: **Le Jour Se Lève**

Daybreak (1946-British) **75m.** ** D: Compton Bennett. Eric Portman, Ann Todd, Maxwell Reed, Edward Rigby, Bill Owen, Jane Hylton. Repressed Portman weds sultry Todd. He's out of town once too often . . . while oily, menacing Reed comes on the scene. Contrived film noir is only modestly entertaining.

Day in the Country, A (1946-French) **40m.** **** D: Jean Renoir. Sylvia Bataille, Georges Saint-Saens (Georges Darnoux), Jacques Borel (Jacques Brunius), Jeanne Marken. At a picnic along a river, a bourgeois Parisian mother and daughter find romance while the menfolk try to fish. Nature plays a starring role in this cinematic tone poem about the emotional depth of spiritual love and the sexual high of a romp in the hay. Screenplay by Renoir, from a short story by Guy de Maupassant; among his assistants on this were Yves Allegret, Jacques Becker, Henri Cartier-Bresson, and Luchino Visconti! Renoir cast himself as Poulain the innkeeper. Shot in 1936, only partially completed, and edited in Renoir's absence. Original title: UNE PARTIE DE CAMPAGNE. ▼▶

Day Mars Invaded Earth, The (1962) 70m. *½ D: Maury Dexter. Kent Taylor, Marie Windsor, William Mims, Betty Beall, Lowell Brown, Gregg Shank. On a fancy estate where space scientist Taylor, his wife, and kids are vacationing, unfriendly Martians arrive in the form of Taylor, his wife, and kids. A how-low-can-you-go budget results in a "space invasion" movie shot on one piece of property and with earthlings *and* Martians played by the same few actors! CinemaScope. ▶

Day of Fury, A (1956) C-78m. *** D: Harmon Jones. Dale Robertson, Mara Corday, Jock Mahoney, Carl Benton Reid. Manipulative, silver-tongued desperado Robertson turns neighbor against neighbor in a small Western town with devilish ease. Offbeat and interesting.

Day of Reckoning (1933) 65m. **½ D: Charles Brabin. Richard Dix, Madge Evans, Conway Tearle, Una Merkel, Stuart Erwin, Spanky McFarland, Isabel Jewell. Dix embezzles funds to keep his extravagant wife (Evans) happy and ends up in jail, thanks to the scheming of lecherous tycoon Tearle, who's got designs on Evans. Moderately entertaining crime meller is well suited to Dix's brand of square-jawed dramatics. *Our Gang's* Spanky plays one of Dix's kids. ▶

Day of the Bad Man (1958) C-81m. ** D: Harry Keller. Fred MacMurray, Joan Weldon, John Ericson, Robert Middleton. MacMurray is appropriately stiff in tame account of country judge holding off condemned man's brothers so scheduled hanging can occur. CinemaScope.

Day of the Outlaw (1959) 91m. *** D: Andre de Toth. Robert Ryan, Burl Ives, Tina Louise, Alan Marshal, Nehemiah Persoff, Venetia Stevenson, David Nelson, Jack Lambert, Elisha Cook. Stark Western melodrama of outlaw Ives and gang taking over isolated Western town. ▶

Day of the Triffids, The (1963-British) C-95m. **½ D: Steve Sekely. Howard Keel, Nicole Maurey, Janette Scott, Kieron Moore, Mervyn Johns. Meteor display blinds everyone who watched, while mutating experimental plants into giant, walking maneaters. Based on John Wyndham's classic sci-fi novel. Variable special effects. Remade in 1981 as a British TV miniseries; and in 1997 as a cable TV movie. Cinema-Scope. ▼▶

Day of Wrath (1943-Danish) 110m. ***½ D: Carl Theodor Dreyer. Thorkild Roose, Lisbeth Movin, Sigrid Neiiendam, Preben Lerdorff, Anna Svierker. Strikingly composed drama about an old woman accused of being a witch and the curse that she puts on the pastor who is responsible for her burning. Serious, stark cinema, peerlessly photographed by Carl Andersson. Some prints run 95m. ▼▶

Days of Glory (1944) 86m. **½ D: Jacques Tourneur. Gregory Peck, Alan Reed, Maria Palmer, Lowell Gilmore, Tamara Toumanova. Sincere but plodding WW2 action pitting Russians against Nazis, memorable only as Peck's screen debut. ▼▶

Days of Jesse James (1939) 63m. **½ D: Joseph Kane. Roy Rogers, George "Gabby" Hayes, Don Barry, Pauline Moore, Harry Woods, Arthur Loft, Wade Boteler, Ethel Wales, Scotty Beckett, Harry Worth, Glenn Strange, Olin Howland, Monte Blue. Roy and Gabby infiltrate the James Gang as corrupt railroad detective Woods tries to use Rogers' efforts for his own gain. Solid Western from Roy's early "historical" period. ▼▶

Days of Thrills and Laughter (1961) 93m. **** Compiled by Robert Youngson. Third Youngson silent-film compilation combines comedy clips (with Chaplin, Laurel and Hardy, the Keystone Kops) with serials and action films (featuring Douglas Fairbanks, Pearl White, Harry Houdini). Great fun. ▼▶

Days of Wine and Roses (1962) 117m. ***½ D: Blake Edwards. Jack Lemmon, Lee Remick, Charles Bickford, Jack Klugman, Alan Hewitt, Tom Palmer, Jack Albertson. Modern LOST WEEKEND set in San Francisco, with Lemmon marrying Remick and pulling her into state of alcoholism. Realistic direction and uncompromising writing combine for excellent results; poignant score by Henry Mancini, who also earned an Oscar for the title song with Johnny Mercer. Originally a television play, written by JP Miller. ▼●▶

Day the Earth Caught Fire, The (1961-British) 99m. *** D: Val Guest. Edward Judd, Janet Munro, Leo McKern, Michael Goodliffe, Bernard Braden. Intelligent, absorbing sci-fi drama of gradual chaos that follows when atomic explosions start Earth spiraling toward the sun. Judd is the reporter who first breaks the story, with the assistance of Munro (whom he romances). Watch for Michael Caine as a policeman directing traffic! Dyaliscope. ▼▶

Day the Earth Stood Still, The (1951) 92m. **** D: Robert Wise. Michael Rennie, Patricia Neal, Hugh Marlowe, Sam Jaffe, Billy Gray, Frances Bavier, Lock Martin. Landmark science-fiction drama about dignified alien (Rennie) who comes to Earth to deliver anti-nuclear warning, stays to learn that his peaceful views are shared by most humans—but not all. Brilliantly acted, more timely than ever, with trenchant script by Edmund North, moody score by Bernard Herrmann. And remember: *Klaatu barada nikto!* Remade in 2008. ▼●)

Day the Sky Exploded, The (1958-Italian) 80m. ** D: Paolo Heusch. Paul Hubschmid, Madeleine Fischer, Fiorella Mari, Ivo Garrani. An exploding missile in outer space sends debris to Earth, causing utterly predictable chaos. ▼)

Day the World Ended (1956) 82m. ** D: Roger Corman. Richard Denning, Lori Nelson, Adele Jergens, Touch (Mike) Connors. Modest sci-fi involving survivors of nuclear war and interplay of human nature that causes friction among the group. And yes, there's a monster. Remade as YEAR 2889; also remade (in name only) in 2001 for cable TV. SuperScope. ▼)

Day They Robbed the Bank of England, The (1960-British) 85m. *** D: John Guillermin. Aldo Ray, Elizabeth Sellars, Peter O'Toole, Hugh Griffith, Kieron Moore, Albert Sharpe. IRA members plan to rob the Bank of England in this meticulous caper film. Metroscope.)

Day-time Wife (1939) 71m. ** D: Gregory Ratoff. Tyrone Power, Linda Darnell, Warren William, Binnie Barnes, Wendy Barrie, Joan Davis. Power and Darnell make an engaging couple, even in lightweight fare such as this: wife thinks husband is fooling around with his secretary, so she gets an office job to see why bosses are attracted to their help.)

Day Will Dawn, The (1942-British) 99m. *** D: Harold French. Hugh Williams, Griffiths Jones, Deborah Kerr, Ralph Richardson, Francis L. Sullivan, Roland Culver, Finlay Currie, Niall MacGinnis, Raymond Huntley, Patricia Medina. Solid WW2 adventure about foreign correspondent Williams and his involvement in destroying a German U-boat base in Norway. Kerr is fine in one of her early roles, as a young Norwegian lass who assists him. Written by Terence Rattigan, Anatole de Grunwald, and Patrick Kirwen. Also known as THE AVENGERS. ▼

D-Day the Sixth of June (1956) C-106m. *** D: Henry Koster. Robert Taylor, Richard Todd, Dana Wynter, Edmond O'Brien. Well-executed study of WW2's Normandy invasion, with massive action shots; film focuses on American officer Taylor and British leader Todd, their professional and personal problems. You may like THE LONGEST DAY better. CinemaScope. ▼)

Dead Don't Dream, The (1948) 62m. *½ D: George Archainbaud. William Boyd, Andy Clyde, Rand Brooks, John Parrish, Leonard Penn, Mary Tucker (Mary Ware). Hopalong Cassidy and pal California visit town to attend Lucky's wedding, then bride-to-be's uncle is found slain in gold mine. More a whodunit than a Western, with lots of sleuthing at a frontier desert hotel—

indoors! Reissued with misleading title FIGHTING MAN FROM ARIZONA. ▼)

Dead End (1937) 93m. ***½ D: William Wyler. Sylvia Sidney, Joel McCrea, Humphrey Bogart, Wendy Barrie, Claire Trevor, Marjorie Main, Huntz Hall, Leo Gorcey, Gabriel Dell, Ward Bond, Billy Halop, Bernard Punsley, Allen Jenkins. Grim Sidney Kingsley play of slum life shows vignettes of humanity at breaking point in N.Y.C. tenements; extremely well directed, engrossing. Script by Lillian Hellman; magnificent sets by Richard Day. Introduced the Dead End Kids, who appeared in the original Broadway production (see *Bowery Boys* entry for details). ▼)

Dead Eyes of London (1961-German) 98m. ** D: Alfred Vohrer. Joachim Fuchsberger, Karin Baal, Dieter Borsche, Wolfgang Lukschy, Klaus Kinski, Eddi Arent, Adi Berber. The drownings of rich foreigners in London seem to be linked to a charity for the homeless blind. Acceptable thriller with interlaced plots mostly takes place at night and/or in the fog. Taken from the same Edgar Wallace novel that was the basis of Lugosi's THE HUMAN MONSTER (1939).)

Deadlier Than the Male (1957-French) 104m. ** D: Julien Duvivier. Jean Gabin, Daniele Delorme, Lucienne Bogaert, Gerard Blain. Delorme encamps in exstepfather's home, planning to marry and then murder him; Gabin is stodgy as girl's intended victim.

Deadliest Sin, The (1956-British) 90m. *½ D: Ken Hughes. Sydney Chaplin, Audrey Dalton, John Bentley, Peter Hammond. Flashbacks reveal the story of a man who confesses murder to a priest. Slight, forgettable, and all too familiar. Original British title: CONFESSION.

Deadline at Dawn (1946) 83m. **½ D: Harold Clurman. Susan Hayward, Paul Lukas, Bill Williams, Joseph Calleia, Osa Massen, Lola Lane, Jerome Cowan, Steven Geray. Atmospheric but muddled murder mystery, with aspiring actress Hayward attempting to clear naive sailor Williams, who is suspected of murder. Clurman's only film as director. Screenplay by Clifford Odets, from a novel by William Irish (Cornell Woolrich). ▼)

Deadline U.S.A. (1952) 87m. *** D: Richard Brooks. Humphrey Bogart, Ethel Barrymore, Kim Hunter, Ed Begley, Warren Stevens, Paul Stewart, Martin Gabel, Joe De Santis, Audrey Christie, Jim Backus. Biting account of newspaper's struggle to survive and maintain civic duty. Bogey is tops as the crusading editor; taut, knowing script by director Brooks. Most enjoyable. Don't blink or you'll miss a young James Dean in a silent bit part during a newspaper production montage.

Deadly Companions, The (1961) C-90m. **½ D: Sam Peckinpah. Maureen O'Hara,

Brian Keith, Steve Cochran, Chill Wills. Ex-army officer accidentally kills O'Hara's son and he makes amends by escorting the funeral procession through Indian country. Peckinpah's first feature is decent if unspectacular Western. Panavision.▼●)

Deadly Is the Female SEE: **Gun Crazy**

Deadly Mantis, The (1957) **78m.** ** D: Nathan Juran. Craig Stevens, William Hopper, Alix Talton, Donald Randolph. N.Y.C. is threatened again, here by giant insect heading south after Arctic tour de force; obligatory love story interrupts good special effects.▼●)

Dead Man's Eyes (1944) **64m.** **½ D: Reginald LeBorg. Lon Chaney, Jr., Jean Parker, Paul Kelly, Thomas Gomez, Acquanetta. Interesting *Inner Sanctum* yarn of blind man (Chaney) accused of murdering girlfriend's father, whose announced intention was to bequeath his eyes to Chaney for transplant operation.▼)

Dead Men Tell (1941) **60m.** **½ D: Harry Lachman. Sidney Toler, Sheila Ryan, Robert Weldon, Sen Yung, Don Douglas, Kay Aldridge, George Reeves, Ethel Griffies. Suspenseful *Charlie Chan* mystery, centering on a treasure hunt for $60 million in pirate booty. Clever direction, moody camerawork overcome claustrophobic setting.◗

Dead Men Walk (1943) **67m.** ** D: Sam Newfield. George Zucco, Mary Carlisle, Nedrick Young, Dwight Frye, Fern Emmett. Zucco plays brothers, one good, one evil, in this standard low-budget vampire tale—but it's hard to dismiss any film with Dwight Frye as a maniacal assistant.▼)

Dead of Night (1945-British) **103m.** **** D: Cavalcanti, Basil Dearden, Robert Hamer, Charles Crichton. Mervyn Johns, Roland Culver, Antony Baird, Judy Kelly, Miles Malleson, Sally Ann Howes, Googie Withers, Ralph Michael, Michael Redgrave, Basil Radford, Naunton Wayne, Frederick Valk. Classic chiller of gathering at a country house, where guests trade supernatural stories. One of them (Johns) has been having a nightmare that now seems to be coming true; final sequence with Redgrave as a schizophrenic ventriloquist is a knockout. ▼●)

Dead Reckoning (1947) **100m.** *** D: John Cromwell. Humphrey Bogart, Lizabeth Scott, Morris Carnovsky, William Prince, Wallace Ford. Bogart's fine as tough WW2 veteran solving soldier-buddy's murder. Well-acted drama.▼●)

Dead Ringer (1964) **115m.** **½ D. Paul Henreid. Bette Davis, Karl Malden, Peter Lawford, Jean Hagen, George Macready, Estelle Winwood. A double dose of Davis, playing twin sisters (as she did earlier in A STOLEN LIFE) bearing a long-time grudge over a man, the sinister one trying to get even. Farfetched but fun; Bette's vehicle all the way, directed by her 1940s co-

star Paul Henreid. Remade for TV as THE KILLER IN THE MIRROR (1986, with Ann Jillian).▼●)

Dear Brat (1951) **82m.** **½ D: William A. Seiter. Mona Freeman, Billy DeWolfe, Edward Arnold, Lyle Bettger. This sequel to DEAR RUTH has Freeman in title role involved with a crook trying to reform.

Dear Brigitte (1965) **C-100m.** **½ D: Henry Koster. James Stewart, Fabian, Glynis Johns, Cindy Carol, Billy Mumy, John Williams, Jack Kruschen, Alice Pearce, Jesse White, Ed Wynn. Guest: Brigitte Bardot. Good cast in OK family farce about an 8-year-old genius (Stewart's son, Mumy) with a crush on Brigitte Bardot (who makes a brief appearance near the end). Tries to be whimsical but is contrived instead. Look fast for James Brolin as student spokesman. CinemaScope. ▼

Dear Heart (1964) **114m.** *** D: Delbert Mann. Glenn Ford, Geraldine Page, Michael Anderson, Jr., Barbara Nichols, Angela Lansbury, Patricia Barry, Charles Drake, Alice Pearce, Mary Wickes. Winning romance with gentlemanly traveling salesman Ford coming to N.Y.C., meeting up with sweetly wacky postmistress Page, who's in town for a convention. Excellent characterizations, with fine comic supporting players.▼)

Dear Murderer (1947-British) **90m.** **½ D: Arthur Crabtree. Eric Portman, Greta Gynt, Dennis Price, Maxwell Reed, Jack Warner, Hazel Court. Husband Portman kills wife's lover. All-too-familiar "perfect crime" melodrama sparked by fine Portman performance.▼)

Dear Ruth (1947) **95m.** **½ D: William D. Russell. Joan Caulfield, William Holden, Mona Freeman, Edward Arnold, Billy DeWolfe. Bouncy, naive comedy of errors with young girl pretending to be her older sister to impress soldier she corresponds with. Norman Krasna's Broadway smash was also a Hollywood hit and led to sequels DEAR WIFE and DEAR BRAT.

Dear Wife (1949) **88m.** **½ D: Richard Haydn. Joan Caulfield, William Holden, Edward Arnold, Billy DeWolfe, Mona Freeman. Follow-up to DEAR RUTH focuses on Freeman's antics to get Holden elected to the state senate, although her politician father Arnold is seeking same position.▼

Death Drums Along the River SEE: **Sanders**

Death in Small Doses (1957) **78m.** **½ D: Joseph Newman. Peter Graves, Mala Powers, Chuck Connors, Roy Engel, Merry Anders. Competently made crime meller, based on a *Saturday Evening Post* exposé, with Graves as an FDA undercover man on the trail of the gang selling illegal "stay-awake pills" (bennys) to long-distance truckers. Connors is a scream as a hopped-up driver.

Death in the Garden (1956-French-Mexican) **C-92m.** *** D: Luis Buñuel. Simone

Signoret, Georges Marchal, Charles Vanel, Michele Girardon, Michel Piccoli, Tito Junco. Fleeing an unspecified Fascist state, a ragged group—including a prostitute, a miner, and a priest—embark on a surreal trek through the jungles of South America. This may have merely been a "commercial chore" for the great Buñuel, but it's fascinating nonetheless. Originally titled LA MORT EN CE JARDIN at 97m.▼◗

Death Kiss, The (1933) 75m. *** D: Edwin L. Marin. David Manners, Adrienne Ames, Bela Lugosi, John Wray, Vince Barnett, Alexander Carr, Edward Van Sloan, Barbara Bedford, Wade Boteler. Minor but entertaining whodunit set inside a movie studio, where a leading man is shot dead while filming a scene. The film's scriptwriter (Manners) is determined to nab the culprit. Nice atmosphere of studio at work. Uses hand tinting in two scenes. ▼◗

Death of a Salesman (1951) 115m. ***½ D: Laslo Benedek. Fredric March, Mildred Dunnock, Kevin McCarthy, Cameron Mitchell, Howard Smith, Royal Beal, Jesse White. Arthur Miller's Pulitzer Prize–winning social drama of middle-aged man at end of emotional rope is transformed to the screen intact, with stagy flashbacks. March in title role can't fathom why business and family life failed; Dunnock is patient wife; McCarthy and Mitchell are disillusioned sons. Superb. Dunnock, Mitchell, and Smith re-create their Broadway roles; McCarthy repeats the role he played on the London stage.

Death of a Scoundrel (1956) 119m. **½ D: Charles Martin. George Sanders, Yvonne de Carlo, Zsa Zsa Gabor, Victor Jory. Episodic chronicle of foreigner coming to U.S., ingratiating himself with an assortment of women whom he cons into helping him get ahead. Low-budget but fascinating.▼◗●

Death on the Diamond (1934) 69m. ** D: Edward Sedgwick. Robert Young, Madge Evans, Nat Pendleton, Ted Healy, C. Henry Gordon, David Landau, Paul Kelly. Absurd crime tale in which a mystery man is murdering St. Louis Cardinals ballplayers one by one. It'll be up to rookie hurler Young to discover the culprit. Watch for Mickey Rooney as a clubhouse boy, Walter Brennan selling hot dogs, Ward Bond as a cop.

Death Takes a Holiday (1934) 78m. ***½ D: Mitchell Leisen. Fredric March, Evelyn Venable, Guy Standing, Gail Patrick, Helen Westley, Kent Taylor, Henry Travers, Katherine Alexander. Fascinating allegory about Death (March) entering the human world to discover what makes us tick, and falling in love. Maxwell Anderson, Gladys Lehman, and Walter Ferris adapted Alberto Casella's play. Remade as a TVM in 1971 (with Melvyn Douglas, Myrna Loy, and Monte Markham), and as MEET JOE BLACK in 1998.▼◗

Decameron Nights (1952-British) C-87m.

** D: Hugo Fregonese. Joan Fontaine, Louis Jourdan, Binnie Barnes, Joan Collins, Marjorie Rhodes. Boring tale of Boccaccio (Jourdan), on the run after martial law is declared in Florence; he hides out at Fontaine's villa, where in the company of his hostess and her wards a trio of romantic tales are spun (each of which also stars Jourdan and Fontaine).▼◗

Deception (1946) 112m. *** D: Irving Rapper. Bette Davis, Paul Henreid, Claude Rains, John Abbott. Talky but engrossing drama, set in the world of classical music, about a celebrated composer (a charismatic Rains) who seeks revenge when his lover (Davis) weds her old flame (Henreid).▼◗

Decision Against Time (1957-British) 87m. **½ D: Charles Crichton. Jack Hawkins, Elizabeth Sellars, Eddie Byrne, Lionel Jeffries, Donald Pleasence. Hawkins is effective as test pilot giving all to save troubled craft for boss and to protect job future. Original British title: THE MAN IN THE SKY.

Decision at Sundown (1957) C-77m. **½ D: Budd Boetticher. Randolph Scott, John Carroll, Karen Steele, Noah Beery, Jr., John Litel. Scott tracks down man supposedly responsible for his wife's suicide in this odd but interesting Western.▼◗

Decision Before Dawn (1952) 119m. *** D: Anatole Litvak. Richard Basehart, Gary Merrill, Oskar Werner, Hildegarde Neff, Dominique Blanchar, O. E. Hasse, Wilfried Seyfert. Top-notch WW2 espionage thriller, with Werner an idealistic German medic/POW who agrees to become a spy for his captors. Outstanding work by Werner, Neff (as a sympathetic bar-girl), and the supporting cast. Look quickly for Klaus Kinski as a whining soldier. Perceptive script by Peter Viertel; Litvak coproduced.◗

Decision of Christopher Blake, The (1948) 75m. **½ D: Peter Godfrey. Alexis Smith, Robert Douglas, Cecil Kellaway, Ted Donaldson, John Hoyt, Harry Davenport, Mary Wickes. Insipid drama charting young Donaldson's reaction upon learning that his parents are divorcing. Fantasy sequences that visualize the boy's daydreams are intriguing but overlong. Based on a play by Moss Hart.

Decks Ran Red, The (1958) 84m. **½ D: Andrew L. Stone. James Mason, Dorothy Dandridge, Broderick Crawford, Stuart Whitman. Bizarre but allegedly fact-based sea yarn with strange casting involves sailors' attempt to murder freighter captain and entire crew and use vessel for salvage.

Decoy (1946) 77m. *** D: Jack Bernhard. Jean Gillie, Edward Norris, Herbert Rudley, Robert Armstrong, Sheldon Leonard, Marjorie Woodworth, Phil Van Zandt. Superior low-budget film noir about a gangster's ruthless moll (Gillie) who seduces a sap doctor as part of her outlandish scheme to find $400,000 in buried loot—by reviving her boyfriend after his execution in the gas chamber! Taut B movie, based on a story by Stanley Rubin, doesn't quite live up to its "lost classic" reputation, but the opening and closing scenes are knockouts, and the British Gillie makes an unforgettable femme fatale; Leonard has one of his finest hours as a jaded police detective. ▶

Dédée d'Anvers (1948-French) **85m. **½** D: Yves Allégret. Simone Signoret, Marcel Pagliero, Bernard Blier, Marcel Dalio, Jane Marken, Marcel Dieudonné, Mia Mendelson. On the wharves of Antwerp, lust and wrath boil over when a lady-for-rent falls for an Italian sailor on shore leave. Her pimp is angry, a bartender is sad to see it all . . . somebody will have to do something. Signoret's first major lead, directed by her first husband, made her an international name. Squalid tale from a novel by *Pépé le Moko* author Henri La Barthe. ▼

Deep Blue Sea, The (1955-British) **C-99m. **½** D: Anatole Litvak. Vivien Leigh, Kenneth More, Eric Portman, Emlyn Williams. Terence Rattigan play of marital infidelity and the repercussions on Leigh, frustrated well-married woman; slow moving, but interesting. CinemaScope.

Deep in My Heart (1954) **C-132m. **½** D: Stanley Donen. Jose Ferrer, Merle Oberon, Helen Traubel, Doe Avedon, Tamara Toumanova, Paul Stewart, Douglas Fowley, Jim Backus; guest stars Walter Pidgeon, Paul Henreid, Rosemary Clooney, Gene and Fred Kelly, Jane Powell, Vic Damone, Ann Miller, Cyd Charisse, Howard Keel, Tony Martin. The life of composer Sigmund Romberg is not the stuff of high drama, but film sparkles in production numbers with MGM guest stars. Highlights include Kelly brothers' only film appearance together, Charisse's exquisite and sensual dance number with James Mitchell, and an incredible number featuring Ferrer performing an entire show himself. ▼●

Deep Six, The (1958) **C-105m. **½** D: Rudolph Maté. Alan Ladd, Dianne Foster, William Bendix, Keenan Wynn, James Whitmore, Efrem Zimbalist, Jr., Joey Bishop. Ladd is Quaker naval officer during WW2 who compensates for past inaction by heading dangerous shore mission; Bendix gives able support. ▼▶

Deep Valley (1947) **104m. *** D: Jean Negulesco. Ida Lupino, Dane Clark, Wayne Morris, Fay Bainter, Henry Hull. Into Lupino's humdrum farm life comes an escapee from a nearby prison gang. Odd, artsy film set against real-life building of the Pacific Coast Highway extension in Monterey. Lupino is good, if miscast. ▶

Deep Waters (1948) **85m. ** D: Henry King. Dana Andrews, Jean Peters, Cesar Romero, Dean Stockwell, Anne Revere, Ed Begley. Slick, empty tale of fisherman Andrews and landlubber Peters brought together by cute little Stockwell.

Deerslayer, The (1957) **C-78m. *½** D: Kurt Neumann. Lex Barker, Forrest Tucker, Rita Moreno, Jay C. Flippen, Cathy O'Donnell, Carlos Rivas. James Fenimore Cooper's Leatherstocking novel is given pedestrian treatment, with virtually all indoor sets and rear-screen projection. Barker links up with Chingachgook (Rivas), his Mohican blood-brother, to rescue an ornery hunter and his two daughters from the Hurons. Filmed before, as early as 1913; remade as a TVM. CinemaScope.

Defense Rests, The (1934) **70m. **½** D: Lambert Hillyer. Jack Holt, Jean Arthur, Nat Pendleton, Shirley Grey, Arthur Hohl, Raymond Hatton. Unscrupulous lawyer (Holt) who's never lost a case is goaded into following his conscience by his newest employee, a worshipful law school graduate (Arthur). OK melodrama with lots of familiar faces in small parts (Ward Bond, Donald Meek, J. Carrol Naish). ▶

Defiant Ones, The (1958) **97m. **** D: Stanley Kramer. Tony Curtis, Sidney Poitier, Theodore Bikel, Charles McGraw, Cara Williams, Lon Chaney, Jr. Engrossing story of two escaped convicts—one black, one white— shackled together as they flee from police in the South. Fine performances by Williams and Chaney as people they meet along the way. Academy Award–winning screenplay by Harold Jacob Smith and Nathan E. Douglas (blacklisted actor-writer Nedrick Young) and cinematography by Sam Leavitt. Remade for TV in 1986. ▼●

Delicate Delinquent, The (1957) **100m. *** D: Don McGuire. Jerry Lewis, Martha Hyer, Darren McGavin, Horace McMahon, Milton Frome. Jerry's first solo effort after splitting with Dean Martin has him as delinquent who becomes a cop with McGavin's help. Agreeable blend of sentiment and slapstick. VistaVision. ▼●

Delicious (1931) **106m. *½** D: David Butler. Janet Gaynor, Charles Farrell, El Brendel, Raul Roulien, Virginia Cherrill. Insipid romance; Janet is Scottish lassie who falls in love with wealthy Farrell in N.Y.C. Brief highlights in Gershwin score are bizarre dream sequence of Janet's welcome to America and "New York Rhapsody."

Delightfully Dangerous (1945) **93m. **½** D: Arthur Lubin. Jane Powell, Ralph Bellamy, Constance Moore, Morton Gould, Arthur Treacher, Louise Beavers. Enjoyable fluff with spunky teen Powell unaware that big sister Moore is a burlesque star. Bellamy is kindly Broadway producer who gets immersed in Powell's shenanigans. ▼▶

Delinquent Daughters (1944) **72m. *½** D: Albert Herman. June Carlson, Fifi D'Orsay, Teala Loring, Mary Bovard, Margia Dean, Johnny Duncan. Title tells all in this low-level time-killer involving teens who become involved with racketeers and what happens when one commits suicide. ▶

Delinquents, The (1957) 75m. ** D: Robert Altman. Tom Laughlin, Peter Miller, Richard Bakalyan, Rosemary Howard, Helene Hawley. Intriguingly awful exploitation drama about nice boy who becomes involved with a street gang because girlfriend is too young to go steady. Altman's first film, made in Kansas City, with Julia Lee singing "Dirty Rock Boogie."

Deluge (1933) 70m. ** D: Felix E. Feist. Sidney Blackmer, Peggy Shannon, Lois Wilson, Matt Moore, Edward Van Sloan, Fred Kohler, Sr. Justly famous for its spectacular special effects sequence of N.Y.C. destroyed by tidal wave; unfortunately, the *rest* of the story (about a handful of survivors) is second-rate melodrama. ▼

De Mayerling à Sarajevo (1940-French) 89m. **½ D: Max Ophuls. John Lodge, Edwige Feuillère, Aimé Clariond, Gabrielle Dorziat, Jean Worms, Jean Debucourt, (Raymond) Aimos. Or, "How to Start World War One." After the suicide of Austria's Crown Prince Rudolph, Emperor Franz Joseph reluctantly readies his likable but unprepared nephew to take over the throne. Typically lush Ophuls mounting details the courtly lives and ignoble assassinations of the nephew and his wife, the Archduke Franz-Ferdinand and Czech Countess Sophie Chotek. Drama about the fall of the Hapsburgs subtly mirrors contemporaneous European politics; it was therefore withdrawn and not seen until 1945. Director's last film before emigrating to the U.S. ▼

Dementia (1955) 55m. *** D: John J. Parker. Adrienne Barrett, Bruno Ve Sota, Ben Roseman, Richard Barron, Lucille Howland, Edward Hinkle, Gayne Sullivan, Jebbie Ve Sota, Angelo Rossitto, Shorty Rogers and His Giants. Surreal, fascinating psychological portrait set in a vast urban landscape (and briefly but tellingly in a cemetery) that visualizes the turmoil of a deeply troubled young woman (Barrett). No dialogue, just stark images, a few sound effects, an appropriately dramatic music score by George Antheil, and bizarre, ethereal vocals by Marni Nixon. Completed in 1953 but unreleased because of a battle with the censors. Reissued as DAUGHTER OF HORROR; this version is edited slightly and features unnecessary narration by Ed McMahon! In its own modest way, quite extraordinary. ▼❶

Dementia 13 (1963) 81m. ** D: Francis Ford Coppola. William Campbell, Luana Anders, Bart Patton, Mary Mitchel, Patrick Magee. Gory horror film, set in Ireland, about a series of axe murders. Coppola's directorial debut—excluding his earlier nudie, TONITE FOR SURE—filmed for about 29¢ for Roger Corman; may be worth a look for curiosity's sake. ▼❶❶

Demetrius and the Gladiators (1954) C-101m. **½ D: Delmer Daves. Victor Mature, Susan Hayward, Michael Rennie, Debra Paget, Anne Bancroft, Richard Egan, Ernest Borgnine. Hokey sequel to THE ROBE has Emperor Caligula (Jay Robinson) searching for magic robe of Christ; Mature dallies with royal Hayward. CinemaScope.▼❶❶

Demi-Paradise, The (1943-British) 115m. *** D: Anthony Asquith. Laurence Olivier, Penelope Dudley Ward, Leslie Henson, Marjorie Fielding, Margaret Rutherford, Felix Aylmer, Edie Martin, Joyce Grenfell, Jack Watling, Miles Malleson, John Laurie, Wilfrid Hyde-White, George Cole. Charming romantic comedy-satire with Olivier intriguingly cast as a Russian engineer who skeptically comes to England . . . and promptly becomes involved with Ward. Perceptive and, in its way, still-topical Anatole de Grunwald script gently chides people's prejudice against "foreigners." Marred only by the predictable finale. U.S. title: ADVENTURE FOR TWO.▼❶

Demon Barber of Fleet Street, The SEE: **Sweeney Todd, The Demon Barber of Fleet Street**

Demoniaque (1957-French) 97m. **½ D: Luis Saslavsky. François Périer, Micheline Presle, Jeanne Moreau, Madeleine Robinson, Marc Cassot, Pierre Mondy. Perky yarn of French POW escaping and seeking refuge with girl his dead buddy romanced via the mails; girl believes him to be the letter-writer.

Dentist in the Chair (1960-British) 84m. ** D: Don Chaffey. Peggy Cummins, Bob Monkhouse, Kenneth Connor, Eric Barker. Occasionally amusing shenanigans of dentists involved in crooked dealings, trying to undo their mischievous thefts. ▼❶

Denver & Rio Grande (1952) C-89m. **½ D: Byron Haskin. Edmond O'Brien, Sterling Hayden, Dean Jagger, ZaSu Pitts, J. Carrol Naish, Laura Elliott (Kasey Rogers), Lyle Bettger, Paul Fix. Another railroad rivalry Western as two competing companies battle elements and each other to complete tie-line through title area. Climax features an actual head-on collision between two steam locomotives. ▼

Deported (1950) 80m. **½ D: Robert Siodmak. Marta Toren, Jeff Chandler, Claude Dauphin, Carlo Rizzo. Engaging gangster yarn with Chandler deported to Italy, involved in the black market, but going straight to win Toren's love.

Derby Day (1952-British) 84m. **½ D: Herbert Wilcox. Anna Neagle, Michael Wilding, John McCallum, Googie Withers. Diverting study of human nature, as an assortment of people intermingle at Epsom Downs race track. Retitled: FOUR AGAINST FATE.

Der Purimshpiler (1937-Polish) 90m. *** D: Joseph Green, Jan-Nowina Przybylski. Zygmunt Turkow, Miriam Kressyn, Hymie Jacobson, Max Bozyk. Amusing Yiddish-language musical fable, set in Galicia, about a wandering vaudeville actor; he falls in love with the pretty daughter of a cobbler, who wants to marry her off into a prominent family. The title's English translation is THE PURIM PLAYER; aka THE JESTER and THE JEWISH JESTER. ▼▶

Desert Attack (1958-British) **79m.** ******* D: J. Lee Thompson. John Mills, Sylvia Syms, Anthony Quayle, Harry Andrews, Diane Clare. Well-handled psychological drama of British ambulance officer, two nurses, and a German soldier brought together in African desert. Original British version ICE COLD IN ALEX runs 132 m.

Desert Desperados (1959-U.S.-Italian) **81m.** ***½** D: Steve Sekely. Ruth Roman, Akim Tamiroff, Otello Toso, Gianni Glori. Unsuccessful mishmash about alluring Roman disrupting a caravan headed toward Alexandria, Egypt. Retitled THE SINNER.

Deserter (1933-Russian) **105m.** *****½** D: V. I. Pudovkin. Boris Livanov, Vasili Kovrigin, Aleksandr Chistyakov, Tamara Makarova, Semyon Svashenko. Eye-popping visuals and experimental use of sound mark this chronicle of a dockworkers' strike and its aftermath, focusing on a laborer (Livanov) who challenges his employers and a corrupt union. Plenty of rhetoric involving worker struggles and solidarity, along with characters that are admittedly political symbols, but attention grabbing as a mirror of post-Revolution Russia; an essential visual and aural experience. ▼▶

Desert Fox: The Story of Rommel, The (1951) **88m.** ******* D: Henry Hathaway. James Mason, Cedric Hardwicke, Jessica Tandy, Luther Adler, Everett Sloane, Leo G. Carroll, George Macready, Richard Boone, Robert Coote. Mason standout as Field Marshal Rommel in sensitive account of his military defeat in WW2 Africa and disillusioned return to Hitler Germany. Mason repeated role in THE DESERT RATS. ▼▶●

Desert Fury (1947) **C-95m.** ****½** D: Lewis Allen. John Hodiak, Lizabeth Scott, Burt Lancaster, Mary Astor, Wendell Corey. Mild drama of love and mystery among gamblers, stolen by Astor in bristling character portrayal.

Desert Hawk, The (1950) **C-77m.** ****** D: Frederick de Cordova. Yvonne De Carlo, Richard Greene, Jackie Gleason, Rock Hudson, George Macready, Joe Besser. Pat Arabian desert tale, interesting for Gleason and Hudson in secondary roles.

Desert Hell (1958) **82m.** ****** D: Charles Marquis Warren. Brian Keith, Barbara Hale, Richard Denning, Johnny Desmond. French Foreign Legion battles warring Arabs to save peace; very little of promised action given to viewer. Regalscope.

Desert Legion (1953) **C-86m.** ****** D: Joseph Pevney. Alan Ladd, Richard Conte, Arlene Dahl, Akim Tamiroff. Mild Ladd vehicle of battling French Foreign Legion in a lost city; cowritten by Irving Wallace.

Desert Nights (1929) **62m.** ****½** D: William Nigh. John Gilbert, Ernest Torrence, Mary Nolan. Posing as a British lord and his daughter, thieves (Torrence and Nolan) rob a diamond mine in South Africa and escape into the desert, taking the mine's manager (Gilbert) as a hostage . . . but he turns the tables on the crooks. Steamy histrionics for fading matinee idol Gilbert in his last silent film before a short-lived career in talkies. Good photography by James Wong Howe. ▶

Desert Patrol (1958-British) **78m.** ****½** D: Guy Green. Richard Attenborough, John Gregson, Michael Craig, Vincent Ball. Staunch account of British patrol attempting to blow up Axis fuel dump before pending WW2 battle of El Alamein. Originally titled SEA OF SAND. ▼▶

Desert Rats, The (1953) **88m.** ******* D: Robert Wise. Richard Burton, James Mason, Robert Newton, Chips Rafferty. Fine WW2 actioner with Mason convincing as Field Marshal Rommel (repeating his role from THE DESERT FOX); Burton is British commando trying to ward off Germans in North Africa. ▼▶

Desert Sands (1955) **C-87m.** ****** D: Lesley Selander. Ralph Meeker, Marla English, J. Carrol Naish, John Smith, Ron Randell, John Carradine, Keith Larsen, Lita Milan. Standard actioner with French Foreign Legionnaires battling vengeance-seeking Arabs in North Africa. ▶

Desert Song, The (1929) **125m.** ***½** D: Roy Del Ruth. John Boles, Louise Fazenda, Myrna Loy, Carlotta King, Johnny Arthur, Edward Martindel, John Miljan. First version of the Romberg operetta is an archaic museum piece, despite Boles' fine singing as French general's wimpy son who is secretly the masked "Red Shadow," leading a rebellion against evil Arabs in Morocco. Feels like it will never end and looks like it was shot from a theater stall. Arthur offers bizarre comic relief as an effeminate reporter, and scantily clad Loy gyrates wildly as a half-caste native. Some sequences were filmed in two-strip Technicolor. Remade in 1943 and 1953.

Desert Song, The (1943) **C-90m.** ***½** D: Robert Florey. Dennis Morgan, Irene Manning, Bruce Cabot, Lynne Overman, Gene Lockhart, Fay Emerson, Victor Francen, Curt Bois, Jack La Rue, Gerald Mohr. Wrongheaded remake of the operetta updated to WW2. Riff leader El Khobar turns out to be an American (Morgan) who's fighting a Nazi-backed plan to build a railroad in the Moroccan desert. The much-loved score is downplayed in favor of newly written songs. In spite of Technicolor trappings this is a bad grade-B musical. ▶

Desert Song, The (1953) **C-110m.** ****½** D: H. Bruce Humberstone. Kathryn Grayson, Gordon MacRae, Steve Cochran, Raymond

Massey, William Conrad, Dick Wesson. Third version of Sigmund Romberg operetta set in Africa creaks along on thin plot. American MacRae is secret leader of good natives (Riffs) in battle against evil Arabs. Songs: "The Riff Song," "One Alone."▼▶

Desert Trail, The (1935) 54m. ** D: Cullen Lewis (Lewis D. Collins). John Wayne, Mary Kornman, Paul Fix, Eddy Chandler, Carmen LaRoux, Lafe McKee. Rodeo star Wayne and his bickering gambling buddy flee when they're accused of robbery. One of Wayne's lesser B Westerns, with Chandler badly miscast as his comedy sidekick, but Kornman (*Our Gang*'s original leading lady in the 1920s) is cute, and scenes of Wayne flirting with her are a highlight. One amazing stunt shows action star leap from galloping horse through shattered glass window into a shack.▼▶

Design for Living (1933) 90m. *** D: Ernst Lubitsch. Fredric March, Gary Cooper, Miriam Hopkins, Edward Everett Horton, Franklin Pangborn, Isabel Jewell, Jane Darwell. Ben Hecht adapted Noel Coward's stage comedy about artist Cooper and playwright March, best friends and Americans in Paris, and what happens when they both fall in love with Hopkins. Most of the witty innuendos are left intact (even if the pacing isn't quite right).●▶

Design for Scandal (1941) 85m. **½ D: Norman Taurog. Rosalind Russell, Walter Pidgeon, Edward Arnold, Lee Bowman, Jean Rogers, Mary Beth Hughes, Guy Kibbee. Deft performances in comedy of reporter Pidgeon doing sensational story involving prominent female judge Russell.▶

Designing Woman (1957) C-118m. *** D: Vincente Minnelli. Gregory Peck, Lauren Bacall, Dolores Gray, Sam Levene, Mickey Shaughnessy, Chuck Connors, Ed Platt, Jack Cole. Sportswriter and fashion designer marry and run head-on in this chic comedy reminiscent of the great Hepburn-Tracy vehicles. Bacall and Peck do their best; George Wells won an Oscar for Best Story and Screenplay. CinemaScope.▼●▶

Desire (1936) 96m. *** D: Frank Borzage. Marlene Dietrich, Gary Cooper, John Halliday, William Frawley, Ernest Cossart, Akim Tamiroff, Alan Mowbray, Zeffie Tilbury. American car-designer Cooper falls in love with jewel thief Dietrich. Sophisticated romancer set in Spain; Marlene sings "Awake in a Dream." From the scintillating start to the finish, it bears the stylish stamp of its producer, Ernst Lubitsch.▼▶

Desiree (1954) C-110m. **½ D: Henry Koster. Marlon Brando, Jean Simmons, Merle Oberon, Michael Rennie, Cameron Mitchell, Elizabeth Sellars, Cathleen Nesbitt, Richard Deacon, Carolyn Jones. Tepid, elaborate costumer: Brando plays a confused Napoleon, Simmons his seamstress love who marries another man; Oberon is quite lovely as Empress Josephine. Fiction and fact are muddled backdrop for rise and fall of the Emperor; few action scenes. CinemaScope.▼●▶

Desire in the Dust (1960) 102m. **½ D: William F. Claxton. Raymond Burr, Martha Hyer, Joan Bennett, Ken Scott. Good casting carries this turgid soaper of a Southern aristocrat with a yen for politics, who tries to hide the shady past of some family members. CinemaScope.

Desire Me (1947) 91m. ** D: No director credited. Greer Garson, Robert Mitchum, Richard Hart, George Zucco, Morris Ankrum. Weak melodramatic romance with Garson caught between new love and old husband, presumed dead, who returns to make problems. Familiar story not helped by limp script. Directed mostly by George Cukor, who removed his name after studio tampering; Mervyn LeRoy and Jack Conway also had a hand in it.▶

Desire Under the Elms (1958) 114m. **½ D: Delbert Mann. Sophia Loren, Anthony Perkins, Burl Ives, Frank Overton. Eugene O'Neill stage piece about family hatred and greed for land. Loren miscast as Ives' young wife in love with stepson Perkins, but she sparks some life into brooding account of 19th-century New England farm story. VistaVision.▼●▶

Desk Set (1957) C-103m. ***½ D: Walter Lang. Spencer Tracy, Katharine Hepburn, Gig Young, Joan Blondell, Dina Merrill, Sue Randall, Neva Patterson, Diane Jergens, Merry Anders. Broadway play becomes a vehicle for Hepburn and Tracy, a guarantee for top entertainment. He's an efficiency expert automating her research department at a TV network; they clash, argue, and fall in love. Great fun. Scripted by Phoebe and Henry Ephron, from the stage play by William Marchant. Merrill's film debut. CinemaScope.▼●▶

Desperadoes, The (1943) C-85m. *** D: Charles Vidor. Randolph Scott, Glenn Ford, Claire Trevor, Evelyn Keyes, Edgar Buchanan, Raymond Walburn, Guinn Williams. Pretty good Western; bandit Ford goes straight, joins forces with marshal Scott to clean up town.▼▶

Desperadoes Are in Town, The (1956) 73m. *½ D: Kurt Neumann. Robert Arthur, Kathy Nolan, Rhys Williams, Rhodes Reason, Dave O'Brien, Kelly Thordsen, Mae Clarke. Young Arthur heads West and inadvertently becomes involved with outlaw gang. Bland. Regalscope.

Desperate (1947) 73m. **½ D: Anthony Mann. Steve Brodie, Audrey Long, Raymond Burr, Douglas Fowley, William Challee, Jason Robards, Sr. An honest truck driver is victimized by racketeers and forced to flee with his wife. Well-made little film noir, if not as good as director Mann's follow-ups (RAW DEAL, T-MEN, etc.). Also shown in computer-colored version.▼▶

Desperate Chance for Ellery Queen (1942) **70m.** *½ D: James Hogan. William Gargan, Margaret Lindsay, Charley Grapewin, John Litel, Lilian Bond, James Burke, Jack LaRue, Morgan Conway. Gargan's second shot as Queen is no better than the first; he's hired by a woman to find her husband, a missing banker.

Desperate Hours, The (1955) **112m.** ***½ D: William Wyler. Humphrey Bogart, Fredric March, Arthur Kennedy, Martha Scott, Dewey Martin, Gig Young, Mary Murphy, Robert Middleton. Extremely well acted account of escaped convicts terrorizing family household. From Joseph Hayes' novel and Broadway play, inspired by actual events. Remade in 1990. VistaVision. ▼●▶

Desperate Journey (1942) **107m.** *** D: Raoul Walsh. Errol Flynn, Raymond Massey, Ronald Reagan, Nancy Coleman, Alan Hale, Arthur Kennedy, Albert Basserman. Spirited WW2 drama of American pilots stranded in Germany, struggling to cross border; forgivable propaganda interludes. Wait till you see Reagan doubletalk Nazi. ▼▶

Desperate Man, The (1959-British) **57m.** *½ D: Peter Maxwell. Jill Ireland, Conrad Phillips, William Hartnell, Charles Gray. Dull yarn of reporter Phillips linking up with attractive Ireland to track down a Sussex crook.

Desperate Moment (1953-British) **88m.** **½ D: Compton Bennett. Dirk Bogarde, Mai Zetterling, Philip Friend, Gerard Heinz. Taut melodrama involving displaced person in post-WW2 Berlin falsely accused of homicide; sensibly acted.

Desperate Search (1952) **73m.** **½ D: Joseph H. Lewis. Howard Keel, Jane Greer, Patricia Medina, Keenan Wynn. Trim film of two kids stranded in Canadian wastelands after plane crash, and their father's efforts to find them. ▶

Desperate Siege SEE: **Rawhide**

Destination Gobi (1953) **C-89m.** **½ D: Robert Wise. Richard Widmark, Don Taylor, Casey Adams (Max Showalter), Murvyn Vye, Darryl Hickman, Martin Milner. Unusual WW2 actioner involving U.S. naval men joining forces with natives against Japanese assaults; nice action sequences. ▶

Destination Moon (1950) **C-91m.** **½ D: Irving Pichel. John Archer, Warner Anderson, Tom Powers, Dick Wesson, Erin O'Brien-Moore. One of the pioneer sci-fi films about the first manned expedition to the moon, modestly mounted but still effective. Striking lunar paintings by Chesley Bonestell. Won an Oscar for its special effects. Produced by George Pal; coscripted by Robert Heinlein. Woody Woodpecker makes a "guest appearance." ▼●▶

Destination 60,000 (1957) **65m.** BOMB D: George Waggner. Preston Foster, Pat Conway, Jeff Donnell, Coleen Gray. Worn-out premise: test pilots zoom through space, families wait nervously on the ground.

Destination Tokyo (1943) **135m.** *** D: Delmer Daves. Cary Grant, John Garfield, Alan Hale, John Ridgely, Dane Clark, Warner Anderson, William Prince. Suspenseful WW2 account of U.S. submarine sent into Japanese waters and interaction among crew. Commander Grant, seamen Garfield and Clark ring true. John Forsythe makes his film debut. Also shown in computer-colored version. ▼▶

Destiny (1921-German) **99m.** ***½ D: Fritz Lang. Lil Dagover, Walter Janssen, Bernhard Goetzke, Eduard von Winterstein, Rudolf Klein-Rogge. After her beloved is taken by Death, a woman is given a chance to win him back if she can save the life of another who is about to die in three different periods of history: ancient Arabia, medieval China, and Renaissance Venice. Extraordinarily stylized expressionistic silent fantasy on Lang's favorite subject (the inevitability of fate) that put the great director on the map, with brilliant art direction, photography, and effects that still astonish. Original title: DER MÜDE TOD. ▼▶

Destiny (1944) **65m.** ** D: Reginald LeBorg. Gloria Jean, Alan Curtis, Frank Craven, Grace McDonald. Routine study of man sent to prison on homicide charge and snowballing effects on his life. Expanded from a 30m. sequence originally made by director Julien Duvivier for FLESH AND FANTASY.

Destroyer (1943) **99m.** **½ D: William Seiter. Edward G. Robinson, Glenn Ford, Marguerite Chapman, Edgar Buchanan, Leo Gorcey, Regis Toomey, Ed Brophy, Lloyd Bridges, Larry Parks. Predictable WW2 actioner uplifted by Robinson as a shipyard welder who reenlists in the Navy and butts heads with self-assured young Ford. ▶

Destry (1954) **C-95m.** **½ D: George Marshall. Audie Murphy, Mari Blanchard, Lyle Bettger, Lori Nelson, Thomas Mitchell, Edgar Buchanan, Wallace Ford. Audie is gun-shy sheriff who tames town and dance-hall girl without violence. The 1939 version—DESTRY RIDES AGAIN—is still unsurpassed. Later a TV series.

Destry Rides Again (1939) **94m.** **** D: George Marshall. James Stewart, Marlene Dietrich, Charles Winninger, Brian Donlevy, Una Merkel, Mischa Auer, Allen Jenkins, Irene Hervey, Jack Carson, Billy Gilbert, Samuel S. Hinds. Slam-bang, action-filled Western satire, with Stewart taming rowdy town without violence and tangling with boisterous dance-hall girl Dietrich. Marlene sings "See What the Boys in the Back Room Will Have" in this sequel to Max Brand's story, filmed in 1932, then again in 1950 (as FRENCHIE), and in 1954 (as DESTRY). Screenplay by Felix Jackson, Gertrude Purcell, and Henry Myers. Simply wonderful. ▼●▶

Detective, The (1954-British) **91m.** *** D: Robert Hamer. Alec Guinness, Joan Greenwood, Peter Finch, Cecil Parker, Bernard Lee, Sidney James, Ernest Thesiger. Guinness is in rare form as G. K. Chesterton's clerical sleuth after stolen art treasures; another British gem, superbly cast. British title: FATHER BROWN.▼

Detective Kitty O'Day (1944) **63m.** ** D: William Beaudine. Jean Parker, Peter Cookson, Tim Ryan, Veda Ann Borg. Parker adds bubbly zest as amateur sleuth who sets out to solve a crime; pleasant fluff on low-budget scale. ◗

Detective Story (1951) **103m.** ***½ D: William Wyler. Kirk Douglas, Eleanor Parker, Horace McMahon, William Bendix, Lee Grant, Craig Hill, Cathy O'Donnell, Bert Freed, George Macready, Joseph Wiseman, Gladys George, Frank Faylen, Luis van Rooten, Warner Anderson, Michael Strong, Gerald Mohr. Sidney Kingsley's once-forceful play about life at a N.Y.C. police precinct has lost much of its punch, but is still a fine film. Well cast, with Douglas a bitter detective, Parker his ignored wife, and Bendix, in one of his best roles, a sympathetic colleague. McMahon (the shrewd precinct head), Wiseman (a hysterical thief), Grant (unforgettable as a frightened shoplifter), and Strong (another thief) re-create their Broadway roles. This was Grant's first film—and also her last—before being blacklisted. Screenplay by Philip Yordan and Robert Wyler (the director's brother).◗

Detour (1945) **69m.** *** D: Edgar G. Ulmer. Tom Neal, Ann Savage, Claudia Drake, Edmund MacDonald, Tim Ryan, Esther Howard. Now-legendary B movie, filmed in less than a week, is the quintessence of film noir. Neal is a hitchhiking drifter who has the misfortune to become involved with a formidable femme fatale (Savage, in an unforgettable performance). Ulmer makes the most of his meager budget. Written by Martin Goldsmith. Remade in 1992 with Tom Neal, Jr. ▼●◗

Devil and Daniel Webster, The (1941) **85m.** ***½ D: William Dieterle. Edward Arnold, Walter Huston, James Craig, Anne Shirley, Jane Darwell, Simone Simon, Gene Lockhart, John Qualen, H. B. Warner. Stephen Vincent Benet's story as a visual delight, with Huston's sparkling performance as Mr. Scratch (the Devil) matched by Arnold as the loquacious Webster. Oscar-winning score by Bernard Herrmann, cinematography by Joseph August, and special effects by Vernon L. Walker all superb. Screenplay by the author and Dan Totheroh. Cut for reissue in 1952; restored to 107m. on video, adding interesting material missing from other extant prints. Remade in 2007 as SHORTCUT TO HAPPINESS. Aka ALL THAT MONEY CAN BUY and DANIEL AND THE DEVIL. ▼●◗

Devil and Miss Jones, The (1941) **92m.** ***½ D: Sam Wood. Jean Arthur, Robert Cummings, Charles Coburn, Spring Byington, Edmund Gwenn, S. Z. Sakall, William Demarest. Delightful social comedy by Norman Krasna; millionaire Coburn masquerades as clerk in his own department store to investigate employee complaints. A must.▼◗

Devil and the Deep (1932) **78m.** **½ D: Marion Gering. Tallulah Bankhead, Gary Cooper, Charles Laughton, Cary Grant, Paul Porcasi. Overplayed but lush melodrama of Bankhead, her suitors Grant and Cooper, and jealous husband, submarine commander Laughton. ◗

Devil and the Ten Commandments, The (1962-French) **126m.** ** D: Julien Duvivier. Michel Simon, Fernandel, Danielle Darrieux, Micheline Presle, Mel Ferrer, Claude Dauphin, Marcel Dalio, Charles Aznavour, Lino Ventura, Alain Delon, Jean-Claude Brialy, Louis de Funès. Highly uneven collection of stories and fables related to the Ten Commandments—some amusing, some tragic, some simply ineffectual. All-star cast provides interest throughout, but this is one of Duvivier's weaker efforts. Franscope. ◗

Devil at 4 O'Clock, The (1961) **C-126m.** **½ D: Mervyn LeRoy. Spencer Tracy, Frank Sinatra, Jean-Pierre Aumont, Kerwin Mathews, Barbara Luna. Static production, not saved by volcanic eruption climax, involving priest Tracy helping to evacuate children's hospital in midst of lava flow. Stars are lost in weak film.▼●◗

Devil Bat, The (1941) **69m.** ** D: Jean Yarbrough. Bela Lugosi, Suzanne Kaaren, Dave O'Brien, Guy Usher, Yolande Mallott (Donlan), Donald Kerr. Lugosi raises bats and trains them to suck victims' blood on cue. One of Lugosi's more notorious pictures, and fairly entertaining. Aka KILLER BATS. Reworked as THE FLYING SERPENT. Sequel: DEVIL BAT'S DAUGHTER. ▼●◗

Devil Bat's Daughter (1946) **66m.** ** D: Frank Wisbar. Rosemary La Planche, Molly Lamont, John James, Ed Cassidy. In this sequel to THE DEVIL BAT, La Planche is thought to have inherited the murderous tendencies of her late father, but in a bizarre turn of events, Dad turns out to have been a kindly researcher (contradicting the first film entirely!).▼◗

Devil Commands, The (1941) **65m.** **½ D: Edward Dmytryk. Boris Karloff, Amanda Duff, Richard Fiske, Anne Revere, Ralph Penny, Dorothy Adams, Kenneth MacDonald. Improbable but intriguing chiller of scientist Karloff obsessed with idea of communicating with dead wife. Predictable but fun. Only debit: the absurd narration.◗

Devil Dogs of the Air (1935) **86m.** ** D:

Lloyd Bacon. James Cagney, Pat O'Brien, Margaret Lindsay, Frank McHugh. Tiresome potboiler with Marine Air Corps rivalry between Cagney and O'Brien. Their personalities and good stunt-flying scenes are only saving grace.▼▶

Devil-Doll, The (1936) 79m. *** D: Tod Browning. Lionel Barrymore, Maureen O'Sullivan, Frank Lawton, Robert Greig, Lucy Beaumont, Henry B. Walthall, Grace Ford, Rafaela Ottiano. Very entertaining yarn of Devil's Island escapee Barrymore shrinking humans to doll size to carry out nefarious schemes. Coscripted by Erich von Stroheim.▼●▶

Devil Doll (1964-British) 80m. *** D: Lindsay Shonteff. Bryant Haliday, William Sylvester, Yvonne Romain, Philip Ray. Underrated mystery features an eerily effective Haliday as a hypnotist-ventriloquist trying to transfer Romain's soul into that of a dummy, as he had already done with his onetime assistant. An exquisitely tailored, sharply edited sleeper.▼▶

Devil Girl From Mars (1954-British) 77m. *½ D: David MacDonald. Patricia Laffan, Hugh McDermott, Hazel Court, Adrienne Corri, Peter Reynolds, Joseph Tomelty, John Laurie. Clad in black leather, Laffan lands in remote Scotland with her refrigerator-like robot, hunting for human husbands! Hilariously solemn, high-camp British imitation of U.S. cheapies would be even funnier if it weren't rather dull and setbound.▼▶

Devil Goddess (1955) 70m. *½ D: Spencer Bennet. Johnny Weissmuller, Angela Stevens, Selmer Jackson, William Tannen, Ed Hinton. Weissmuller helps a professor look for an ex-colleague who's set himself up as a "god." The end of the vine for *Jungle Jim* Weissmuller, who retired from the big screen after this.

Devil in the Flesh (1946-French) 110m. ***½ D: Claude Autant-Lara. Gérard Philipe, Micheline Presle, Denise Grey, Jacques Tati. Exquisitely filmed, compassionate story of WW1 love affair between married woman and sensitive high school student. Controversial in its day because of sensual love scenes and cuckolding of soldier husband. Remade in 1986.▼

Devil Is a Sissy, The (1936) 92m. **½ D: W. S. Van Dyke. Freddie Bartholomew, Mickey Rooney, Jackie Cooper, Ian Hunter, Peggy Conklin, Katherine Alexander. Three top juvenile stars outclass their material in this rambling, episodic tale of tenement-district pals and British newcomer (Bartholomew) who tries to join their gang.▶

Devil Is a Woman, The (1935) 83m. *** D: Josef von Sternberg. Marlene Dietrich, Lionel Atwill, Cesar Romero, Edward Everett Horton, Alison Skipworth. Sumptuous-looking film about alluring but heartless woman and the men who all but ruin their lives for her, set against backdrop of 19th-century Spanish revolution. Hypnotic, if dramatically shaky; Luis Buñuel used same source material for THAT OBSCURE OBJECT OF DESIRE.▼▶

Devil Makes Three, The (1952) 96m. ** D: Andrew Marton. Gene Kelly, Pier Angeli, Richard Egan, Claus Clausen. Kelly (none too convincing in one of his rare nonmusicals) plays a soldier returning to Munich to thank family who helped him during WW2; he becomes involved with daughter Angeli and black market gangs.▶

Devil on Horseback (1954-British) 89m. ** D: Cyril Frankel. Googie Withers, John McCallum, Jeremy Spenser, Liam Redmond, Meredith Edwards, Sam Kydd, Vic Wise, George Rose. Inconsequential racing yarn, with talented but cocky teen apprentice jockey Spenser attempting to bully his way to success. Coproduced by John Grierson.▼

Devil Pays Off, The (1941) 56m. ** D: John H. Auer. J. Edward Bromberg, Osa Massen, William Wright, Margaret Tallichet, Martin Kosleck, Abner Biberman. Dishonored ex-Navy man Wright is recruited to track down espionage agents in this minor drama.

Devil's Bait (1959-British) 58m. ** D: Peter Graham Scott. Geoffrey Keen, Jane Hylton, Gordon Jackson, Dermot Kelly. Leisurely paced B film about baker Keen and wife Hylton, who learn that cyanide has been accidentally put in their wares.

Devil's Brother, The (1933) 88m. *** D: Hal Roach, Charles R. Rogers. Stan Laurel, Oliver Hardy, Dennis King, Thelma Todd, James Finlayson, Henry Armetta. Destitute Stan and Ollie become bungling henchmen for notorious singing bandit Fra Diavolo (King) in this adaptation of Auber's 1830 operetta. One of the comedy team's best features. Aka FRA DIAVOLO.▼●▶

Devil's Canyon (1953) C-92m. ** D: Alfred L. Werker. Virginia Mayo, Dale Robertson, Stephen McNally, Arthur Hunnicutt. Former marshal put in prison for shootouts, where he's entangled in prison riot. Photographed in 3-D.▼

Devil's Cargo, The (1948) 61m. *½ D: John F. Link. John Calvert, Rochelle Hudson, Roscoe Karns, Lyle Talbot, Tom Kennedy, Theodore Von Eltz. Poverty Row continuation of *The Falcon* series; mundane murder mystery showcasing Calvert's magic act skills.▼

Devil's Commandment, The (1957-Italian) 78m. **½ D: Riccardo Freda. Gianna Maria Canale, Antoine Balpetre, Paul Muller, Carlo Dangelo, Wandisa Guida. A reporter in Paris investigates a string of murders in which women's bodies are drained of blood. This stylish yarn started the trend of gothic Italian horrors of the 1950s and

1960s. Photographed by Mario Bava (who also codirected, sans credit). Beware of 70m. version which inserts bogus footage shot by the American distributor (featuring Al Lewis!). Originally titled I VAMPIRI. CinemaScope.▼▶

Devil's Daughter, The (1939) 65m. ** D: Arthur Leonard. Nina Mae McKinney, Jack Carter, Ida James, Hamtree Harrington, Willa Mae Lane, Emmett Wallace. A sweet young woman (James) returns to Jamaica from N.Y.C. to take over the banana plantation she inherited from her father. Her embittered stepsister (McKinney) feels she's the rightful owner and plots revenge amid romantic complications. Pleasant-enough all-black-cast independent. ▼▶

Devil's Disciple, The (1959-British) 82m. ***½ D: Guy Hamilton. Burt Lancaster, Kirk Douglas, Laurence Olivier, Janette Scott, Eva LeGallienne, Harry Andrews, Basil Sydney, George Rose, Neil McCallum, David Horne, Mervyn Johns. Sparkling adaptation of George Bernard Shaw's satire, set during American Revolution, with standout performances by star trio (notably Olivier as General Burgoyne, who serves as Shaw's mouthpiece). Shows how, in Shaw's view, the bumbling British managed to lose their colonies. Screenplay by John Dighton and Roland Kibbee.▼

Devil's Doorway (1950) 84m. *** D: Anthony Mann. Robert Taylor, Louis Calhern, Paula Raymond, Marshall Thompson, Edgar Buchanan. Well-turned Western with offbeat casting of Taylor as Indian who served in Civil War, returning home to find that he must fight to right the injustices done against his people. ▶

Devil's Envoys, The SEE: **Les Visiteurs du Soir**

Devil's Eye, The (1960-Swedish) 90m. *** D: Ingmar Bergman. Jarl Kulle, Bibi Andersson, Nils Poppe, Sture Lagerwall. A woman's chastity gives the Devil sty in his eye, so he sends Don Juan back to Earth from Hell to seduce her, but the modern-day woman finds his old-fashioned charm amusing rather than irresistible. Droll Bergman comedy is a bit slow, but witty and playful.▼

Devil's General, The (1956-German) C-120m. ***½ D: Helmut Kautner. Curt Jurgens, Marianne Cook (Koch), Victor De Kowa, Karl John, Eva-Ingeborg Scholz, Albert Lieven. Jurgens is outstanding as a German war hero aviator who becomes disenchanted with Hitler and Nazism. Allegedly based on fact.▼▶

Devil's Hairpin, The (1957) C-82m. **½ D: Cornel Wilde. Cornel Wilde, Jean Wallace, Mary Astor, Arthur Franz. Wilde is reckless sports car champion who learns fair play on the track; obligatory racing scenes are above average. VistaVision.

Devil's Henchman, The (1949) 69m. ** D: Seymour Friedman. Warner Baxter, Mary Beth Hughes, Mike Mazurki, Harry Shannon. In this programmer, Baxter sets out to capture waterfront gang and becomes involved in murder.

Devil-Ship Pirates, The (1964-British) C-89m. **½ D: Don Sharp. Christopher Lee, Andrew Keir, Michael Ripper, John Cairney. Good little movie of stray Spanish ships conquering English coastal village, unaware Armada has been defeated. Megascope.▶

Devil's Holiday, The (1930) 80m. ** D: Edmund Goulding. Nancy Carroll, Phillips Holmes, James Kirkwood, Hobart Bosworth, Ned Sparks, Morgan Farley, Jed Prouty, Paul Lukas, ZaSu Pitts, Morton Downey. Carroll is hired to woo farm boy Holmes to induce him to buy Sparks' line of equipment—but she falls in love with him for real. Predictable from the first scene on, but competently done. Goulding also wrote the story.

Devil's in Love, The (1933) 71m. **½ D: William Dieterle. Loretta Young, Victor Jory, Vivienne Osborne, C. Henry Gordon, David Manners, J. Carrol Naish. Very odd, well-made film about doctor falsely accused of murder, efforts to clear his name. Bela Lugosi has good, small role as prosecuting attorney.

Devil's Island (1940) 62m. **½ D: William Clemens. Boris Karloff, Nedda Harrigan, James Stephenson, Adia Kuznetzoff, Will Stanton, Edward Keane. Above-average Karloff vehicle of innocent doctor exiled to Devil's Island, mistreated by supervisor Stephenson.▶

Devil's Mask, The (1946) 66m. ** D: Henry Levin. Jim Bannon, Anita Louise, Michael Duane, Mona Barrie, Ludwig Donath, Barton Yarborough. OK entry in short-lived I Love a Mystery series with Bannon as Jack Packard, Yarborough as Doc Young. Far-fetched story involving shrunken heads and murder is intriguing but spoiled by obvious identity of killer.

Devil's Messenger, The (1962-U.S.-Swedish) 72m. ** D: Herbert L. Strock. Lon Chaney (Jr.), Karen Kadler, John Crawford, Michael Hinn. Three episodes of an unsold Swedish-made TV series, 13 Demon Street, are combined with U.S.-made framing scenes featuring the Devil (Chaney) and his beautiful but reluctant new emissary. Strock gets directing credit (he helmed the few minutes of Chaney footage), while Curt Siodmak, who directed the three episodes, is unmentioned. ▼▶

Devils of Darkness (1965-British) C-88m. ** D: Lance Comfort. William Sylvester, Hubert Noel, Carole Gray, Tracy Reed, Diana Decker, Rona Anderson, Peter Illing, Victor Brooks. While vacationing in Brittany, the wife of a writer disappears. He takes a medallion connected with her disappearance back to England, unaware that he's followed by a long-lived vampire and his cult in quest of the medallion. Intelligent, with interesting use of color, but flat, slow, and ultimately trivial. Original U.S. release was in b&w.◗

Devil's Party, The (1938) 65m. ** D: Ray McCarey. Victor McLaglen, William Gargan, Paul Kelly, Beatrice Roberts, Frank Jenks, Samuel S. Hinds. So-so melodrama of former Hell's Kitchen pals who reunite once a year . . . except this year one of them is murdered. ▼◗

Devil's Playground (1937) 74m. **½ D: Erle C. Kenton. Richard Dix, Dolores Del Rio, Chester Morris, Pierre Watkin, Ward Bond. Good combination of action and romance with diver Dix discovering wife Del Rio in love with Morris; exciting underwater climax. Remake of 1928 Frank Capra film SUBMARINE. ◗

Devil's Playground, The (1946) 62m. **½ D: George Archainbaud. William Boyd, Andy Clyde, Rand Brooks, Elaine Riley, Robert Elliott. Mysterious young woman searches for gold hidden in the rock-studded Lone Pine terrain by her imprisoned husband. After a 2-year break, Boyd returned to movie screens as Hopalong Cassidy. Slanted more toward adults than kids, this is the best effort of the final dozen Hoppy movies he produced. Reissue title: GUNPOWDER VALLEY. ▼◗

Devil's Wanton, The (1949-Swedish) 72m. **½ D: Ingmar Bergman. Doris Svedlund, Birger Malmsten, Eva Henning, Hasse Ekman. Sober account of desperate girl finding romance with another equally unhappy soul, reaffirming their faith in humanity. Not released in U.S. until 1962. ▼

Devil Thumbs a Ride, The (1947) 62m. **½ D: Felix Feist. Lawrence Tierney, Ted North, Nan Leslie, Betty Lawford, Andrew Tombes, Harry Shannon. Tierney, a "slap-happy bird with a gun," commits robbery and murder, then hitches a ride with friendly, tipsy North. Fast-paced B film. ▼

Devil to Pay!, The (1930) 73m. **½ D: George Fitzmaurice. Ronald Colman, Loretta Young, David Torrence, Myrna Loy, Mary Forbes, Paul Cavanagh. Early talkie shows its age, but Colman is fine in this drawing-room comedy.●

Devil With Women, A (1930) 64m. ** D: Irving Cummings. Victor McLaglen, Mona Maris, Humphrey Bogart, Luana Alcaniz, John St. Polis, Michael Vavitch, Mona Rico. Adventurer tangles with a friendly rival while trying to capture a revolutionary leader in Central American country. Plodding, all-too-typical vehicle for boisterous McLaglen. Bogart, in his second talkie feature, plays the Edmund Lowe–ish, devil-may-care pal.

Devotion (1946) 107m. **½ D: Curtis Bernhardt. Olivia de Havilland, Ida Lupino, Paul Henreid, Sydney Greenstreet, Nancy Cole-

man, Arthur Kennedy, Dame May Whitty. Powerful real-life story of Brontë sisters becomes routine love triangle with Henreid in the middle; worthwhile for intense, dramatic performances. Made in 1943.◗

D. I., The (1957) 106m. **½ D: Jack Webb. Jack Webb, Don Dubbins, Lin McCarthy, Jackie Loughery, Monica Lewis, Virginia Gregg, Barbara Pepper. Ostensibly realistic account of Marine basic training is today a wonderful exercise in high camp. Webb is emotionally empty sergeant trying to whip his raw recruits (most of them played by actual soldiers) into shape; stubborn Dubbins is the chief thorn in his side. Sequence where soldiers search for a "murdered" sand flea is priceless. Story reused 13 years later (but with a different outcome) for a TVM, TRIBES. ▼◗

Diabolical Dr. Mabuse, The SEE: **1,000 Eyes of Dr. Mabuse, The**

Diabolique (1955-French) 114m. ***½ D: Henri-Georges Clouzot. Simone Signoret, Vera Clouzot, Paul Meurisse, Charles Vanel, Michel Serrault. Tyrannical school-master (Meurisse) is bumped off by his long-suffering wife (Clouzot) and mistress (Signoret). Classic chiller builds slowly, surely to final quarter hour that will drive you right up the wall. A must. Older American prints run 107m. Aka LES DIABOLIQUES; remade for U.S. TV as REFLECTIONS OF MURDER (1974) and HOUSE OF SECRETS (1993), and for theaters in 1996. Rereleased theatrically in 1994 with 9m. of footage edited out of original U.S. theatrical version.▼◗

Dial M for Murder (1954) C-105m. *** D: Alfred Hitchcock. Ray Milland, Grace Kelly, Robert Cummings, John Williams, Anthony Dawson. Frederick Knott's suspense play of man plotting wife's murder and subsequent police investigation: stagey at times but slick and entertaining. Remade for TV in 1981 with Angie Dickinson and Christopher Plummer, and in 1998 as A PERFECT MURDER. 3-D. ▼●◗

Dial 999 SEE: **Way Out, The**

Dial 1119 (1950) 75m. ** D: Gerald Mayer. Marshall Thompson, Virginia Field, Andrea King, Sam Levene, Keefe Brasselle, William Conrad. Modest suspenser with mentally unhinged Thompson holding a group of bar patrons hostage, threatening to kill all in 25 minutes if his demands are not met. Takes place in "real time." ◗

Dial Red O (1955) 62m. **½ D: Daniel B. Ullman. Bill Elliott, Keith Larsen, Helene Stanley, Paul Picerni, Jack Kruschen, Elaine Riley, Robert Bice, Rick Vallin. Former cowboy star Elliott plays a just-the-facts-ma'am police detective in this taut tale of an escaped psychiatric patient (Larsen) framed for the murder of his wife. First of a short-lived series of DRAGNET-style crime melodramas, followed by SUDDEN

DANGER. Sam Peckinpah was dialogue coach and plays a small role. ▶

Diamond, The SEE: **Diamond Wizard, The**

Diamond Head (1963) **C-107m.** **½ D: Guy Green. Charlton Heston, Yvette Mimieux, George Chakiris, France Nuyen, James Darren, Aline MacMahon, Elizabeth Allen. Soap opera set in Hawaii with Heston the domineering head of his family, whose dictates almost ruin their lives. Panavision. ▼●▶

Diamond Horseshoe (1945) **C-104m.** **½ D: George Seaton. Betty Grable, Dick Haymes, Phil Silvers, William Gaxton, Beatrice Kay, Carmen Cavallaro, Margaret Dumont. Musical performer Grable has to choose between a long-cherished dream of luxury and life with struggling med student-cum-singer Haymes. Colorful escapism, with good Harry Warren–Mack Gordon songs: "The More I See You," "I Wish I Knew." Original title: BILLY ROSE'S DIAMOND HORSESHOE.

Diamond Jim (1935) **93m.** *** D: A. Edward Sutherland. Edward Arnold, Jean Arthur, Binnie Barnes, Cesar Romero, Eric Blore. Big-budget biography of eccentric millionaire of 19th century whose appetite for money is only matched by love of food and Lillian Russell; Arthur has dual role in re-creation of Gay '90s era. Most entertaining. Screenplay by Preston Sturges.

Diamond Queen, The (1953) **C-80m.** ** D: John Brahm. Fernando Lamas, Arlene Dahl, Gilbert Roland, Michael Ansara. Dahl is dazzling title figure over whom Lamas and Roland fight in costumer set in India.

Diamonds and Crime SEE: **Hi Diddle Diddle**

Diamonds of the Night (1964-Czech) **71m.** ***½ D: Jan Nemec. Ladislav Jansky, Antonin Kumbera, Ilse Bischofova. Nemec's first feature is a landmark of the ill-fated Czech "New Wave": a haunting, startlingly directed chronicle of two Jewish boys' experiences after escaping from a train heading for a Nazi death camp during WW2. Scripted by Nemec and Arnost Lustig (based on the latter's story). ▼

Diamond Wizard, The (1954-British) **83m.** ** D: Dennis O'Keefe, Montgomery Tully. Dennis O'Keefe, Margaret Sheridan, Philip Friend, Alan Wheatley, Francis De Wolff, Eric Berry, Michael Balfour. OK caper of American treasury agent O'Keefe coming to England and hooking up with Scotland Yard inspector Friend to sniff out the makers and smugglers of the perfect synthetic diamond. Various prints credit O'Keefe or Tully as sole director. Filmed in 3-D. Original British title: THE DIAMOND.

Diane (1956) **C-110m.** **½ D: David Miller. Lana Turner, Pedro Armendariz, Roger Moore, Marisa Pavan, Sir Cedric Hardwicke, Henry Daniell. Although predictable, medieval romance has good cast, gorgeous sets and

costumes, and comes off surprisingly well. Lana looks lovely, and Miklos Rozsa's score helps set the mood. CinemaScope. ▼●▶

Diary of a Chambermaid (1946) **87m.** ** D: Jean Renoir. Paulette Goddard, Hurd Hatfield, Francis Lederer, Burgess Meredith, Judith Anderson, Irene Ryan, Florence Bates, Reginald Owen. Uneasy attempt at Continental-style romantic melodrama, with blonde Goddard as outspoken maid who arouses all sorts of emotions in her snooty household. Tries hard, but never really sure of what it wants to be. Meredith as nutsy neighbor and Ryan as timid scullery maid do their best; Meredith also coproduced and wrote the screenplay. Remade in 1964. ▼▶

Diary of a Chambermaid (1964-French) **87m.** ***½ D: Luis Buñuel. Jeanne Moreau, Michel Piccoli, Georges Geret, Francoise Lugagne, Daniel Ivernel, Jean Ozenne. Remake of Jean Renoir's 1946 film concerns fascism in France in 1939 and how the bourgeoisie are viewed by maid Moreau. Sharp, unrelenting film from one of the great directors. Franscope. ▼●▶

Diary of a Country Priest (1950-French) **120m.** ***½ D: Robert Bresson. Claude Laydu, Nicole Ladmiral, Jean Riveyre, Nicole Maurey, Andre Guibert, Martine Lemaire. The life and death of an unhappy young priest attempting to minister to his first parish in rural France. Slow moving but rewarding, with brilliantly stylized direction. Bresson also scripted. ▼●▶

Diary of a Lost Girl (1929-German) **104m.** ***½ D: G. W. Pabst. Louise Brooks, Fritz Rasp, Josef Ravensky, Sybille Schmitz, Valeska Gert. Pabst and Brooks' follow-up to their PANDORA'S BOX is even more sordid, yet in some ways more intriguing: Louise is, in succession, raped, gives birth, is put in a detention home, then a brothel, inherits money, marries, is widowed . . . and writer Rudolf Leonhardt claims only the first half of his script was filmed. Fascinating nonetheless, with an explicitness that's still surprising. ▼●▶

Diary of a Madman (1963) **C-96m.** **½ D: Reginald Le Borg. Vincent Price, Nancy Kovack, Chris Warfield, Ian Wolfe, Nelson Olmstead. 19th-century magistrate Price is possessed by an evil spirit called the Horla, which compels him to murder. Colorful but routine. Based on a story by Guy de Maupassant. ▼●▶

Diary of Anne Frank, The (1959) **170m.** ***½ D: George Stevens. Millie Perkins, Joseph Schildkraut, Shelley Winters, Richard Beymer, Lou Jacobi, Diane Baker, Ed Wynn. Meticulously produced version of Broadway drama dealing with Jewish refugees hiding in WW2 Amsterdam. Unfortunately, Perkins never captures pivotal charm of title character, though Schildkraut is fine as father Frank. Winters won Supporting Actress Oscar as shrill Mrs. Van Daan, ever fearful of Nazi arrest, and the cinematography (William C. Mellor) and Art Direction–Set Decoration also earned Academy Awards. Frances Goodrich and Albert Hackett utilized Anne's diary for their stage play and its screen adaptation. Later cut to 156m. Restored Roadshow version on video runs 179m. with an overture, intermission, exit music. Remade several times. CinemaScope.▼●)

Diary of Oharu SEE: **Life of Oharu, The**

Dick Tracy Chester Gould's immortal comic-strip crimefighter first came to movies in a quartet of Republic Pictures Saturday-matinee serials in the late 1930s and early '40s. Except for the first, these cliffhangers were full of action, excitement, and imagination . . . though they bore little resemblance to the newspaper strip. Leading man Ralph Byrd was born to play Gould's jut-jawed hero. In 1945 RKO decided to revive Tracy for a series of grade-B feature films, but the results were mostly mediocre. Morgan Conway played Tracy in the first two, without distinction, then Byrd returned to the role. None of the four RKO features capitalized on the rich lode of material that Gould had provided in his years of daily detective adventures.

DICK TRACY

Dick Tracy, Detective (1945); aka Dick Tracy
Dick Tracy Versus Cueball (1946)
Dick Tracy's Dilemma (1947)
Dick Tracy Meets Gruesome (1947)

Dick Tracy, Detective (1945) 62m. ** D: William Berke. Morgan Conway, Anne Jeffreys, Mike Mazurki, Jane Greer, Lyle Latell, Joseph Crehan, Tommy Noonan. Chester Gould's square-jawed detective sets out to nab Splitface (Mazurki), a vengeance-seeking killer. Originally titled DICK TRACY.▼●)

Dick Tracy Meets Gruesome (1947) 65m. ** D: John Rawlins. Boris Karloff, Ralph Byrd, Anne Gwynne, Lyle Latell. Karloff is fun as Gruesome, who uses Dr. A. Tomic's experimental gas (which causes people to freeze in place) to commit daring bank robbery. Silly but watchable. Lex Barker has a bit role as ambulance driver. ▼●)

Dick Tracy's Dilemma (1947) 60m. ** D: John Rawlins. Ralph Byrd, Lyle Latell, Kay Christopher, Jack Lambert, Ian Keith. RKO contract players abound in this Tracy series entry, pitting detective against The Claw. Fast pacing makes predictable crime-solving satisfactory.▼●)

Dick Tracy Versus Cueball (1946) 62m. ** D: Gordon Douglas. Morgan Conway, Anne Jeffreys, Lyle Latell, Rita Corday, Dick Wessel. Ex-jailbird goes on a killing spree and Tess may be his next victim. Ralph Byrd is de-

finitive screen Tracy, but he isn't in this one; Conway does his best in OK entry in the Tracy series.▼●)

Dick Turpin (1925) 73m. *** D: John G. Blystone. Tom Mix, Kathleen Myers, Philo McCullough, Alan Hale, Bull Montana. Mix abandoned cowboy clothes to play famous English highwayman, but retained surefire formula of action and comedy in this enjoyable vehicle.▼)

Die! Die! My Darling! (1965-British) C-97m. **½ D: Silvio Narizzano. Tallulah Bankhead, Stefanie Powers, Peter Vaughan, Donald Sutherland, Yootha Joyce. Tallulah, in her last film, has field day as weirdo who keeps Powers under lock and key for personal vengeance against the death of her son. Engaging fun, especially for Bankhead devotees. Script by Richard Matheson. Original British title: FANATIC.▼)

Die, Monster, Die! (1965-U.S.-British) C-80m. ** D: Daniel Haller. Boris Karloff, Nick Adams, Freda Jackson, Suzan Farmer, Terence de Marney, Patrick Magee. Based on H. P. Lovecraft story, this thriller has Karloff a recluse who discovers a meteor which gives him strange powers. Good premise is not carried out well. Filmed in England. Remade as THE CURSE (1987). Original British title: MONSTER OF TERROR. Horrifying Colorscope.▼●)

Die Nibelungen (1924-German) 186m. **** D: Fritz Lang. Paul Richter, Margarete Schon, Theodor Loos, Hanna Ralph, Rudolf Klein-Rogge, Georg John. Lang's epic masterpiece of German mythology is told in two parts, each different in style and theme. In SIEGFRIED, the titanic hero achieves virtual immortality by bathing in the blood of a slain dragon (a landmark scene in silent cinema). After his death, Siegfried's widow seeks vengeance in KRIEMHILD'S REVENGE, in which she marries Attila the Hun in order to carry out her plan. A rich treasure trove of folklore and magic, in which Lang creates a mystical geometric universe where the characters play against vast architectural landscapes. A must-see.▼●)

Different from the Others (1919-German) 50m. **½ D: Richard Oswald. Conrad Veidt, Fritz Schulz, Anita Berber, Reinhold Schünzel, Leo Connard, Magnus Hirschfeld. Landmark melodrama features an early depiction of an openly gay character, a celebrated violin virtuoso (Veidt) who accepts his sexuality and the repercussions he faces when he becomes involved with a young admirer. Preachy at times but fascinating as social history. Much of the action in this reconstruction (by Filmmuseum München) is communicated via intertitles and still photos.▼)

Dig That Uranium (1956) 61m. ** D: Edward Bernds. Leo Gorcey, Huntz Hall, Bernard Gorcey, Bennie Bartlett, Mary Beth

Hughes, Raymond Hatton, Myron Healey, Harry Lauter. Broad Western spoof, as the Bowery Boys get mixed up with crooks and a phony uranium mine. Look for Carl "Alfalfa" Switzer in a bit. ▶

Dillinger (1945) **70m.** *** D: Max Nosseck. Edmund Lowe, Anne Jeffreys, Lawrence Tierney, Eduardo Ciannelli, Elisha Cook, Jr., Marc Lawrence. Solid gangster yarn written by Philip Yordan, one of the best B movies of its kind (though a key bank robbery is comprised of stock footage lifted from Fritz Lang's YOU ONLY LIVE ONCE). ▼▶

Dime With a Halo (1963) **97m.** **½ D: Boris Sagal. Barbara Luna, Roger Mobley, Paul Langton, Rafael Lopez, Manuel Padilla. Five poor Mexican kids steal ten cents from church collection plate and bet on a racehorse. Minor but winning little film.

Dimples (1936) **78m.** **½ D: William Seiter. Shirley Temple, Frank Morgan, Helen Westley, Robert Kent, Stepin Fetchit, Astrid Allwyn. Prime Shirley, with our heroine doing her best to save her destitute father, played by marvelous Morgan. Songs: "Oh Mister Man Up in the Moon," "What Did the Bluebird Say." Also shown in computer-colored version. ▼▶

Dingaka (1965-South African) **C-98m.** **½ D: Jamie Uys. Stanley Baker, Juliet Prowse, Ken Gampu, Siegfried Mynhardt, Bob Courtney. Film focuses on contrasting white-black ways of life and the clashes of the two cultures; production bogs down in stereotypes. CinemaScope. ▼

Dinky (1935) **65m.** ** D: D. Ross Lederman, Howard Bretherton. Jackie Cooper, Mary Astor, Roger Pryor, Henry Armetta. Astor is framed, accused of fraud. She tries to keep it from hurting son Cooper in military school. Nothing special.

Dinner at Eight (1933) **113m.** **** D: George Cukor. Marie Dressler, John Barrymore, Wallace Beery, Jean Harlow, Lionel Barrymore, Lee Tracy, Edmund Lowe, Billie Burke, Madge Evans, Jean Hersholt, Karen Morley, Phillips Holmes, May Robson. Vintage MGM constellation of stars portray various strata of society in N.Y.C., invited to dine and shine; Harlow in fine comedy form, but Dressler as dowager steals focus in filmization of George Kaufman–Edna Ferber play. Scripted by three top writers: Herman Mankiewicz, Frances Marion, and Donald Ogden Stewart. Don't miss this one. Remade for cable TV in 1989 with Lauren Bacall. ▼●▶

Dinner at the Ritz (1937-British) **77m.** **½ D: Harold Schuster. Annabella, Paul Lukas, David Niven, Romney Brent. Diverting murder whodunit with Annabella seeking the killer of her father; classy settings spice film. ▼▶

Dino (1957) **94m.** **½ D: Thomas Carr. Sal Mineo, Brian Keith, Susan Kohner, Joe De

Santis, Penny Santon, Frank Faylen, Richard Bakalyan. Mineo at his rebellious best playing juvenile delinquent befriended by a girl (Kohner) and a social worker (Keith). Reginald Rose adapted his acclaimed TV play, and Mineo recreated his starring role. ▼

Dinosaurus! (1960) **C-85m.** **½ D: Irvin S. Yeaworth, Jr. Ward Ramsey, Paul Lukather, Kristina Hanson, Alan Roberts. Interesting and amusing story of hazards faced by caveman and two prehistoric monsters who are accidentally unearthed and revived on a modern-day tropical island. CinemaScope. ▼▶

Diplomaniacs (1933) **63m.** *** D: William A. Seiter. Bert Wheeler, Robert Woolsey, Marjorie White, Louis Calhern, Edgar Kennedy, Hugh Herbert. Genuinely odd but endearing nonsense musical comedy (cowritten by Joseph L. Mankiewicz!) about barbers from Indian reservation sent to Geneva peace conference. Reminiscent of MILLION DOLLAR LEGS and DUCK SOUP, with memorable comic performances by Herbert—as a Confucius-quoting sage—and Calhern. ▼●▶

Diplomatic Courier (1952) **97m.** *** D: Henry Hathaway. Tyrone Power, Patricia Neal, Stephen McNally, Hildegarde Neff, Karl Malden. Power seeks to avenge friend's death in Trieste, becomes involved in international espionage. Cold War film is exciting, well acted. Look for Lee Marvin, Charles Bronson, and Michael Ansara in small, unbilled roles. ▼▶

Dirigible (1931) **100m.** **½ D: Frank Capra. Jack Holt, Ralph Graves, Fay Wray, Hobart Bosworth, Roscoe Karns. Frank "Spig" Wead story about Navy pilots' experimental use of dirigibles in the Antarctic has plenty of action and guts, but a sappy romantic story to weigh it down. On the whole, an interesting antique.

Dirty Game, The (1965-Italian) **91m.** **½ D: Terence Young, Christian-Jaque, Carlo Lizzani. Henry Fonda, Vittorio Gassman, Annie Girardot, Robert Ryan, Peter Van Eyck. Hodgepodge of stories dealing with espionage in post-WW2 era; none of episodes is convincing, stars don't help much. ▼▶

Disbarred (1939) **59m.** **½ D: Robert Florey. Gail Patrick, Robert Preston, Otto Kruger, Sidney Toler, Helen MacKellar, Virginia Dabney, Edward Marr. Kruger is smooth as ever in his umpteenth turn as a crooked mouthpiece. After being disbarred, he recruits honest lawyer Patrick as an unwitting front, but she falls for straight-arrow prosecutor Preston and learns the truth. Slick little gangster yarn with neat courtroom trimmings.

Disc Jockey Jamboree SEE: **Jamboree!**

Disembodied, The (1957) **65m.** *½ D: Walter Grauman. Paul Burke, Allison

[173]

Hayes, Eugenia Paul, Robert Christopher, John Wengraf. Standard voodoo chiller involving woman (Hayes) who will do just about anything to get out of the jungle where her doctor-husband lives. ▶

Dishonorable Discharge (1958-French) **105m.** ** D: Bernard Borderie. Eddie Constantine, Pascale Roberts, Lino Ventura, Lise Bourdin. Variation on Hemingway's TO HAVE AND HAVE NOT, with Constantine skippering luxury ship loaded with hidden dope; flabby film. Franscope.

Dishonored (1931) **91m.** **½ D: Josef von Sternberg. Marlene Dietrich, Victor McLaglen, Lew Cody, Warner Oland, Gustav von Seyffertitz. Alluring Dietrich makes the most of a creaky script starring her as secret agent X-27 during WW1. Worth seeing for her masquerade as peasant girl. ▼▶

Dishonored Lady (1947) **85m.** ** D: Robert Stevenson. Hedy Lamarr, Dennis O'Keefe, John Loder, William Lundigan, Morris Carnovsky, Natalie Schafer, Paul Cavanagh, Douglass Dumbrille, Margaret Hamilton. Adequate drama of glamorous but neurotic magazine art editor Lamarr, who leaves her job and takes on a new identity. She falls in love with nice guy O'Keefe, and promptly becomes a murder suspect. Lamarr and Loder were married when this was made. ▼▶

Disorderly Orderly, The (1964) **C-90m.** *** D: Frank Tashlin. Jerry Lewis, Glenda Farrell, Susan Oliver, Everett Sloane, Jack E. Leonard, Alice Pearce, Kathleen Freeman, Barbara Nichols, Milton Frome. First-rate slapstick and sight gags (including a wild chase finale) mix with cloying sentiment as Jerry runs amuck in a nursing home. Best scene: Jerry's suffering of "sympathy pains" as patient Pearce complains of her ills. Title tune sung by Sammy Davis, Jr. ▼▶

Dispatch From Reuters, A (1940) **89m.** **½ D: William Dieterle. Edward G. Robinson, Edna Best, Eddie Albert, Albert Basserman, Gene Lockhart, Nigel Bruce, Otto Kruger. Watchable (if not always inspired) Warner Bros. biography of the man who started famous worldwide news agency by using pigeons to transmit information across the European continent.

Disputed Passage (1939) **87m.** **½ D: Frank Borzage. Dorothy Lamour, Akim Tamiroff, John Howard, Victor Varconi, Keye Luke. Elisabeth Risdon, Philip Ahn. Average drama of conflict between scientists in their ideals. One believes that there's no place for marriage in science field.

Disraeli (1929) **89m.** *** D: Alfred E. Green. George Arliss, Joan Bennett, Florence Arliss, Anthony Bushell, David Torrence, Ivan Simpson. Somewhat stagy but effective vehicle for Arliss, who won Oscar as cunning British prime minister—a great statesman, devoted husband, and matchmaker (for Bennett and Bushell). Remake of Arliss' 1921 silent vehicle. ▼

Distant Drums (1951) **C-101m.** **½ D: Raoul Walsh. Gary Cooper, Mari Aldon, Richard Webb, Ray Teal. In 1840 Florida, Army captain Cooper and his men, outflanked by Seminole warriors, must retreat into alligator-and-snake–infested Everglades. Combination of Western-style action and Florida backgrounds (in lush Technicolor) is appealing. A reworking of the central story idea from director Walsh's WW2 saga OBJECTIVE, BURMA! ▼▶

Distant Trumpet, A (1964) **C-117m.** **½ D: Raoul Walsh. Troy Donahue, Suzanne Pleshette, Kent Smith, Claude Akins, James Gregory. Paul Horgan's novel gets short-circuited in stock presentation of Army men in the Old West combatting warring Indians while romancing women on the post; good supporting cast. Panavision. ▶

Dive Bomber (1941) **C-133m.** *** D: Michael Curtiz. Errol Flynn, Fred MacMurray, Ralph Bellamy, Alexis Smith, Robert Armstrong, Regis Toomey, Craig Stevens. Exciting, well-paced aviation film of experiments to eliminate pilot-blackout. Flynn, MacMurray, and Smith perform well in formula story. ▼▶

Divided Heart, The (1954-British) **89m.** *** D: Charles Crichton. Cornell Borchers, Yvonne Mitchell, Armin Dahlen, Alexander Knox, Michel Ray, Geoffrey Keen, Theodore Bikel. Intelligent study of dilemma faced by parents of foster child when real mother, thought dead, returns to claim her son. Set in Europe after WW2.

Divine Lady, The (1929) **100m.** *** D: Frank Lloyd. Corinne Griffith, Victor Varconi, H. B. Warner, Ian Keith, Marie Dressler, Dorothy Cumming, Montagu Love. Lloyd won an Oscar for directing this lavishly appointed if bowdlerized account of the scandalous affair of Lady Emma Hamilton and Lord Nelson. Lloyd, who later made MUTINY ON THE BOUNTY, stages some exciting sea battles, while the sumptuous sets, costumes, and photography create a convincing period look. Silent with some synchronized singing sequences. Same story was later told in THAT HAMILTON WOMAN and THE NELSON AFFAIR. ▶

Divorce (1945) **71m.** ** D: William Nigh. Kay Francis, Bruce Cabot, Helen Mack, Craig Reynolds, Larry Olsen, Mary Gordon. Francis is city girl who returns to home town, enticing Cabot away from Mack and family; satisfactory programmer.

Divorcee, The (1930) **83m** **½ D: Robert Z. Leonard. Norma Shearer, Chester Morris, Conrad Nagel, Robert Montgomery, Florence Eldridge. Stagy but interesting tale of young wife Shearer who puts up with husband Morris' flirtations until she decides to equal him. Shearer won an Oscar for this performance. ▼▶

Divorce—Italian Style (1961-Italian) **104m.** ***½ D: Pietro Germi. Marcello Mastroianni, Daniela Rocca, Stefania Sandrelli, Leopoldo Trieste. Marcello can't stomach wife Rocca, so he schemes to wed sexy young Sandrelli. Hilarious, flavorful comedy, which earned an Oscar for its story and screenplay. The twist ending adds a perfect—and most ironic—touch. ▼▶

Divorce of Lady X, The (1938-British) C-91m. **½ D: Tim Whelan. Merle Oberon, Laurence Olivier, Binnie Barnes, Ralph Richardson, Morton Selten. Cute but extremely dated screwball comedy with lawyer Olivier forced to share a hotel room with mischievous Oberon. He becomes convinced he's the cause of her pending divorce—even though she's not married. ▼●

Dixiana (1930) C/B&W-98m. **½ D: Luther Reed. Bebe Daniels, Everett Marshall, Bert Wheeler, Robert Woolsey, Joseph Cawthorn, Jobyna Howland, Dorothy Lee, Bill "Bojangles" Robinson. Ambitious but dated early-talkie musical set in 1840s New Orleans, with Daniels as a circus star who falls in love with the scion of a wealthy family (Metropolitan Opera star Marshall). Enlivened by Wheeler and Woolsey's comedy relief, and (in restored prints) a beautiful two-color Technicolor Mardi Gras finale, with a showstopping tap dance solo by Bojangles. ▼▶

Dixie (1943) C-89m. *** D: A. Edward Sutherland. Bing Crosby, Dorothy Lamour, Billy DeWolfe, Marjorie Reynolds, Lynne Overman, Raymond Walburn, Eddie Foy, Jr., Grant Mitchell. Atmosphere overshadows plot in this biography of pioneer minstrel Dan Emmett, who wrote title song; Bing also sings "Sunday, Monday or Always."

D.O.A. (1950) 83m. ***½ D: Rudolph Maté. Edmond O'Brien, Pamela Britton, Luther Adler, Beverly Campbell (Garland), Lynn Baggett, William Ching, Henry Hart, Neville Brand. Gripping, original film noir with O'Brien desperately trying to find who has given him a slow-acting poison—and why. Inventively photographed (by Ernest Laszlo) on the streets of San Francisco and L.A. Written by Russell Rouse and Clarence Greene. Music by Dimitri Tiomkin. Remade in 1969 (as COLOR ME DEAD) and 1988. Also shown in computer-colored version. ▼●▶

Dock Brief, The (1962-British) 88m. **½ D: James Hill. Peter Sellers, Richard Attenborough, Beryl Reid, David Lodge. Sellers is aging barrister who incompetently represents accused killer Attenborough with strange results; pleasant comic satire. John Mortimer adapted his own play. U.S. title: TRIAL AND ERROR. ▼▶

Docks of New Orleans (1948) 64m. BOMB D: Derwin Abrahams. Roland Winters, Victor Sen Yung, Mantan Moreland, John Gallaudet, Virginia Dale, Carol Forman, Douglas Fowley. Bottom-of-the-barrel *Charlie Chan*

entry about killers trying to get their hands on a chemical shipment. ▶

Docks of New York, The (1928) 76m. **** D: Josef von Sternberg. George Bancroft, Betty Compson, Olga Baclanova, Mitchell Lewis, Clyde Cook, Gustav von Seyffertitz. Burly ship stoker Bancroft marries the suicidal girl he saved from the drink, first taking her for granted, then coming to love her. A rival to SUNRISE as the visual apogee of silent cinema, though the smoky hues of von Sternberg's waterfront dive can fully be appreciated only on the big screen. ▼▶

Docks of New York, The (1945) 61m. ** D: Wallace Fox. Leo Gorcey, Huntz Hall, Billy Benedict, Gloria Pope, Carlyle Blackwell, Jr., Bud Gorman, George Meeker. The East Side Kids get mixed up in another murder mystery, this time involving a stolen necklace.

Doctor and the Girl, The (1949) 98m. **½ D: Curtis Bernhardt. Glenn Ford, Charles Coburn, Gloria DeHaven, Janet Leigh, Warner Anderson, Nancy Davis (Reagan). Ford is appropriately sterile as idealistic young doctor who married poor girl and practices medicine in N.Y.C. slum. ▶

Doctor at Large (1957-British) C-98m. **½ D: Ralph Thomas. Dirk Bogarde, Muriel Pavlow, Donald Sinden, James Robertson Justice, Shirley Eaton, Derek Farr, Michael Medwin, George Coulouris, Anne Heywood, Lionel Jeffries, Mervyn Johns, Ernest Thesiger. Another entry in pleasing series, with novice doctor Bogarde seeking staff position in wealthy hospital. VistaVision. ▼▶

Doctor At Sea (1955-British) C-93m. **½ D: Ralph Thomas. Dirk Bogarde, Brigitte Bardot, Brenda de Banzie, James Robertson Justice, Maurice Denham, Michael Medwin, Raymond Huntley. Preferring the bachelor life, Bogarde signs on as ship's doctor on passenger-carrying freighter, in second entry of this entertaining series. VistaVision. ▼▶

Doctor Blood's Coffin (1961-British) C-92m. **½ D: Sidney Furie. Kieron Moore, Hazel Court, Ian Hunter, Fred Johnson. In Cornwall, young scientist holes up in an abandoned tin mine to work on his theory that placing a live heart in a corpse will bring it back to life. He's right, as it turns out, but unfortunately he's also crazy.... Crude but lively imitation-Hammer horror opus. ▼●▶

Doctor Bull (1933) 75m. *** D: John Ford. Will Rogers, Marian Nixon, Ralph Morgan, Rochelle Hudson, Berton Churchill, Louise Dresser, Andy Devine. Rogers in fine form as country doctor battling small-town pettiness as much as fighting illness. Stereotyped characters are perfect foils for Rogers' common-sense pronouncements; director Ford provides ideal atmosphere. ▶

Doctor In Clover (1965-British) C-101m.

** D: Ralph Thomas. Leslie Phillips, James Robertson Justice, Shirley Anne Field, John Fraser, Joan Sims. New doctor, same old zany situations in sixth entry of series. Doctor studies nurses more than medicine. Not up to the others' standard. ▶

Doctor In Distress (1963-British) **C-102m.** **½ D: Ralph Thomas. Dirk Bogarde, Samantha Eggar, James Robertson Justice, Mylene Demongeot, Donald Houston, Barbara Murray, Dennis Price, Leo McKern. Pompous chief surgeon falls in love for the first time, and his assistant tries to help the romance along while balancing his own love life. Another entertaining entry in comedy series. Bogarde's last appearance as Dr. Sparrow. ▼▶

Doctor in Love (1960-British) **C-93m.** ** D: Ralph Thomas. Michael Craig, James Robertson Justice, Virginia Maskell, Carole Lesley, Leslie Phillips, Liz Fraser. Craig inherited Bogarde's role in *Doctor* series. This entry centers on young medic's inability to avoid romantic attachments. ▶

Doctor in the House (1954-British) **C-92m.** ***½ D: Ralph Thomas. Dirk Bogarde, Muriel Pavlow, Kenneth More, Donald Sinden, Kay Kendall, James Robertson Justice, Donald Houston, Suzanne Cloutier, Geoffrey Keen, George Coulouris, Shirley Eaton, Joan Hickson, Richard Wattis. Hilarious comedy follows exploits of medical students intent on studying beautiful women and how to become wealthy physicians. This delightful film (from Richard Gordon's stories) spawned six other *Doctor* movies, plus a TV series. Justice memorable as Sir Lancelot Spratt. Scripted by Gordon, Ronald Wilkenson, and costar Nicholas Phipps. ▼▶

Doctor Rhythm (1938) **80m.** **½ D: Frank Tuttle. Bing Crosby, Mary Carlisle, Beatrice Lillie, Andy Devine, Laura Hope Crews, Sterling Holloway. Amiable but second-rate Crosby vehicle about doctor who masquerades as cop and falls in love with woman he's assigned to guard. Lillie adds her distinctive spark.

Doctor's Dilemma (1958-British) **C-99m.** *** D: Anthony Asquith. Leslie Caron, Dirk Bogarde, Alastair Sim, Robert Morley. Bubbly Shaw period play of young wife Caron conniving to convince medical specialists that her scoundrel husband is worth saving. ▶

Doctor's Horrible Experiment, The SEE: Le Testament du Dr. Cordelier

Doctors' Wives (1931) **82m.** ** D: Frank Borzage. Warner Baxter, Joan Bennett, Victor Varconi, Cecilia Loftus, Paul Porcasi, Minna Gombell. Bennett marries Baxter, even though she's been warned that dedicated doctors don't make good husbands because they're consumed by their work. Pretty stale soap opera in which the characters' actions don't make a lot of sense.

Fairly static presentation for a director of Borzage's skill.

Doctor Syn (1937-British) **80m.** **½ D: Roy William Neill. George Arliss, Margaret Lockwood, John Loder, Roy Emerton, Graham Moffatt. Arliss' final film finds aging star somewhat miscast as English vicar who rides at night as a pirate, but director Neill keeps things moving at his usual pace, and the atmosphere is rich. Remade twice in 1962—as NIGHT CREATURES and DR. SYN, ALIAS THE SCARECROW. ▼

Doctor Takes a Wife, The (1940) **89m.** *** D: Alexander Hall. Ray Milland, Loretta Young, Reginald Gardiner, Gail Patrick, Edmund Gwenn, Frank Sully, Gordon Jones. Milland is mistaken for Young's husband, then forced to pretend he is. Stars and material spark each other at a lively pace. ▼▶

Doctor X (1932) **C-80m.** ** D: Michael Curtiz. Lionel Atwill, Fay Wray, Lee Tracy, Preston Foster, Robert Warwick, Mae Busch. Police have tracked the "full-moon strangler" to Atwill's experimental NYC laboratory. Ludicrous Grand Guignol chiller (Wray's entrance has her screaming—for no reason at all) is a must for horror-film buffs because of its Anton Grot sets, special Max Factor makeup, and rich use of two-color Technicolor . . . but it creaks *badly* and seems much longer than it is. ▼▶▶

Doctor Zhivago (1965) **C-197m.** ***½ D: David Lean. Omar Sharif, Julie Christie, Geraldine Chaplin, Tom Courtenay, Alec Guinness, Siobhan McKenna, Ralph Richardson, Rod Steiger, Rita Tushingham, Adrienne Corri, Geoffrey Keen, Jeffrey Rockland, Klaus Kinski, Jack MacGowran, Tarek Sharif. Sumptuous, sprawling epic from Boris Pasternak's acclaimed novel; Sharif is charismatic as Russian poet/doctor, an orphan who marries aristocratic Chaplin but falls in love with politicized nurse Christie. Spans several decades, including WW1 and Bolshevik Revolution, with stirring crowd scenes, gorgeous romantic vistas (set to Maurice Jarre's sweeping music), and a powerful exodus sequence on train. Overlong, but with top production values and superb acting in every role. Won Oscars for screenplay (Robert Bolt), cinematography (Freddie Young), art direction–set decoration (John Box and Terry Marsh; Dario Simoni), costume design (Phyllis Dalton), and score. Reissued at 180m. Restored Roadshow version on video runs 200m. with an overture, intermission, entr'acte. Remade as a cable miniseries in 2003 and a stage musical in 2015. Panavision. ▼▶▶

Dodge City (1939) **C-105m.** *** D: Michael Curtiz. Errol Flynn, Olivia de Havilland, Ann Sheridan, Bruce Cabot, Frank McHugh, Alan Hale, John Litel, Victor Jory, Ward Bond. Errol tames the West and de Havilland, in entertaining large-scale

Western, with Warner Bros. stock company and the granddaddy of all barroom brawls. The principal inspiration for BLAZING SADDLES.▼○◑

Dodsworth (1936) 101m. **** D: William Wyler. Walter Huston, Ruth Chatterton, Paul Lukas, Mary Astor, David Niven, Gregory Gaye, Maria Ouspenskaya, Spring Byington, Harlan Briggs. Superb adaptation of Sinclair Lewis novel about middle-aged American industrialist who retires, goes to Europe, where he and his wife find differing sets of values and new relationships. Intelligently written (by Sidney Howard), beautifully filmed, extremely well acted, with Huston re-creating his Broadway role. John Payne (billed as John Howard Payne) makes screen debut in small role. Won Oscar for Interior Decoration (Richard Day). Unusually mature Hollywood film, not to be missed. ▼○◑

Dog, a Mouse and a Sputnik, A SEE: Sputnik

Dog Eat Dog (1964-U.S.-Italian-German) 84m. BOMB D: Gustav Gavrin. Cameron Mitchell, Jayne Mansfield, Dody Heath, Ivor Salter, Isa Miranda. Unintentionally funny potboiler of lust, greed, and depravity, with various characters intent upon making off with a stolen million dollars. Highlight: Jayne's constant complaining about her need for clean panties. Various sources list Albert Zugsmith and Ray Nazarro as director. ◑

Dog of Flanders, A (1959) C-96m. ** D: James B. Clark. David Ladd, Donald Crisp, Theodore Bikel, Max Croiset, Monique Ahrens. Tearjerker for children about a boy, his dog, and friends they make. Crisp and Bikel have good character roles. Previously made in 1935; remade in 1975 (as a Japanese animated feature) and in 1999. CinemaScope.▼◑

Doll, The (1919-German) 65m. *** D: Ernst Lubitsch. Max Kronert, Hermann Thimig, Victor Janson, Marga Köhler, Ossi Oswalda, Gerhard Ritterband. An unmarried baron, fearing that he will have no heir, orders Lancelot (Thimig), his nephew, to wed and sire a son. Lancelot (who is no Prince Charming) wants to stay single and schemes to fool the baron by marrying a human-sized doll! Lubitsch and Hanns Kräly coscripted this clever, charming fantasy (based on an operetta), filmed on painted sets.◑

Doll Face (1945) 80m. **½ D: Lewis Seiler. Vivian Blaine, Dennis O'Keefe, Perry Como, Carmen Miranda, Martha Stewart, Michael (Stephen) Dunne, Reed Hadley, Lex Barker. Brash promoter O'Keefe schemes to get burlesque queen girlfriend Blaine cast in a "legitimate" Broadway show. Fast-paced, lightly likable musical, based on Gypsy Rose Lee's play *The Naked Genius*, features Como's first big hit, "Dig You Later (A Hubba-Hubba-Hubba)."▼◑

Dolly Sisters, The (1945) C-114m. **½ D: Irving Cummings. Betty Grable, John Payne, June Haver, S. Z. Sakall, Reginald Gardiner, Frank Latimore. Sassy hokum about popular vaudeville sister act with two lovely stars and a bevy of old song favorites, plus newly written "I Can't Begin to Tell You."▼◑

Domino Kid, The (1957) 73m. *½ D: Ray Nazarro. Rory Calhoun, Kristine Miller, Andrew Duggan, Roy Barcroft. Revenge-oater with Calhoun returning to Lone Star State to seek killers of his family.

Dondi (1961) 100m. BOMB D: Albert Zugsmith. David Janssen, Patti Page, David Kory, Walter Winchell, Gale Gordon. Adaptation of sentimental comic strip about a cute war orphan trying to get along in the U.S. Goshes! Watch this film and you'll know why Janssen became a fugitive! ◑

Don Juan (1926) 111m. *** D: Alan Crosland. John Barrymore, Mary Astor, Willard Louis, Estelle Taylor, Helene Costello, Warner Oland, Montagu Love, Myrna Loy, Hedda Hopper. Entertaining swashbuckler, with Barrymore at his amorous best, surrounded by a top cast (including Oland as Cesare Borgia and Taylor as the infamous Lucretia) and lavish settings. Notable as the first silent film released with Vitaphone music and sound effects. ▼◑

Don Juan Quilligan (1945) 75m. **½ D: Frank Tuttle. William Bendix, Joan Blondell, Phil Silvers, Anne Revere, B. S. Pully, Mary Treen. Bendix marries two girls at same time; lightweight comedy.

Do Not Disturb (1965) C-102m. **½ D: Ralph Levy. Doris Day, Rod Taylor, Hermione Baddeley, Sergio Fantoni, Reginald Gardiner, Mike Romanoff, Leon Askin. Mild Day vehicle with Taylor as executive husband who brings her to suburban England. She meets suave Fantoni, enraging jealous hubby. Not up to her earlier fashion romps. CinemaScope.◑

Donovan's Brain (1953) 83m. *** D: Felix Feist. Lew Ayres, Gene Evans, Nancy Davis (Reagan), Steve Brodie. Scientist is dominated by brain of dead industrialist, which he's kept alive in his lab; intriguing story by Curt Siodmak; modest, capable production. Filmed before as THE LADY AND THE MONSTER, again as THE BRAIN.▼◑

Donovan's Reef (1963) C-109m. *** D: John Ford. John Wayne, Lee Marvin, Elizabeth Allen, Jack Warden, Cesar Romero, Dorothy Lamour, Mike Mazurki. Action-comedy bounces along with a good cast. Wayne and his freewheeling friends on a Pacific island are disrupted by Warden's grown daughter (Allen) who comes to visit. Lots of fun in Wayne's last feature film with John Ford. That's Ford's yacht *Araner* in several scenes.▼○◑

Don Q, Son of Zorro (1925) 110m. **½ D: Donald Crisp. Douglas Fairbanks, Mary

Astor, Jack McDonald, Donald Crisp, Stella De Lanti, Warner Oland, Jean Hersholt. Fairbanks in his element in OK sequel to THE MARK OF ZORRO, as Don Cesar de Vega, who romances lovely Astor, clashes with heinous Crisp (and is falsely accused of murder). Doug is both father and son in the rousing finale. ▼O▶

Don't Bet on Blondes (1935) 59m. **½ D: Robert Florey. Warren William, Claire Dodd, Guy Kibbee, William Gargan, Vince Barnett, Hobart Cavanaugh, Clay Clement, Errol Flynn. "Odds" Owen, New York's biggest bookmaker, quits and becomes a speculative insurance broker instead. Light, enjoyable Warners programmer. Clean-shaven Flynn has a small but decent role as one of Claire's boyfriends. Movie drunk Jack Norton appears sober here, promoting the world's champion husband-caller, Maude Eburne ("Hennnnn-reeee!"). ▶

Don't Bother to Knock (1952) 76m. **½ D: Roy (Ward) Baker. Richard Widmark, Marilyn Monroe, Anne Bancroft, Jeanne Cagney, Elisha Cook, Jr., Gloria Blondell. Title has more punch than improbable yarn of airline pilot Widmark getting involved with mentally disturbed Monroe hired as babysitter in large hotel. Bancroft's film debut. Remade for TV as THE SITTER. ▼▶

Don't Bother to Knock (1961-British) SEE: **Why Bother to Knock**

Don't Fence Me In (1945) 71m. *** D: John English. Roy Rogers, George "Gabby" Hayes, Dale Evans, Robert Livingston, Moroni Olsen, Marc Lawrence, Lucile Gleason, Andrew Tombes, Bob Nolan and the Sons of the Pioneers. Nosy magazine reporter Evans travels west to find out the truth about Wildcat Kelly, whose name has been popularized in Cole Porter's hit song (which Roy introduced in 1944's HOLLYWOOD CANTEEN). A particular showcase for Gabby and great fun all the way. ▼▶

Don't Gamble With Strangers (1946) 68m. ** D: William Beaudine. Kane Richmond, Bernadene Hayes, Peter Cookson, Gloria Warren, Charles Trowbridge, Tony (Anthony) Caruso, Phil (Philip) Van Zandt. Card-cheats Richmond and Hayes pretend to be siblings and take control of a crooked gambling den. Strictly routine. ▶

Don't Give Up the Ship (1959) 89m. *** D: Norman Taurog. Jerry Lewis, Dina Merrill, Diana Spencer, Mickey Shaughnessy, Robert Middleton, Gale Gordon, Claude Akins. Top comedy with Jerry as U.S. Navy lieutenant who lost a destroyer escort during war and doesn't remember how. Shaughnessy is pal who helps look for it underwater. One of Lewis' all-time best. VistaVision. ▼▶

Don't Go Near the Water (1957) C-107m. *½ D: Charles Walters. Glenn Ford, Gia Scala, Anne Francis, Fred Clark, Eva Gabor, Earl Holliman, Keenan Wynn, Russ Tamblyn, Jeff Richards, Mickey Shaugh-

nessy, Jack Albertson. Submerged comedy of sailors in the South Pacific of WW2 building a recreation hall. Clark, as a frustrated officer, is best thing in slow film. CinemaScope. ▼▶

Don't Knock the Rock (1956) 84m. ** D: Fred F. Sears. Bill Haley and His Comets, Alan Freed, Little Richard, Alan Dale, The Treniers, Patricia Hardy. Rock 'n' roll star Dale returns to his hometown, encounters adult hostility. Of course, the elders are cheering the rockers by the finale. Little Richard sings "Long Tall Sally" and "Tutti Frutti." ▶

Don't Knock the Twist (1962) 87m. BOMB D: Oscar Rudolph. Chubby Checker, Gene Chandler, Vic Dana, Linda Scott, Mari Blanchard, Lang Jeffries. The Dovells. Television producer Jeffries, with Checker's assistance, coordinates a twist show. Chandler, with cape, monocle, and top hat, sings "Duke of Earl"; otherwise, you may want to twist your way to your remote. ▶

Don't Take It to Heart (1945-British) 89m. *** D: Jeffrey Dell. Richard Greene, Patricia Medina, Richard Bird, Wylie Watson, Ernest Thesiger, Ronald Squire. Pleasant romantic comedy of ghost-ridden castle; Greene helps Medina and her townfolk overcome avaricious landowner.

Don't Trust Your Husband SEE: **Innocent Affair, An**

Doolins of Oklahoma, The (1949) 90m. **½ D: Gordon Douglas. Randolph Scott, George Macready, Louise Allbritton, John Ireland. Action-packed Western with Scott as head of the Doolin gang, who decides to give up his life of crime. ▼▶

Doomed Caravan (1941) 62m. *** D: Lesley Selander. William Boyd, Russell Hayden, Andy Clyde, Minna Gombell, Morris Ankrum, Georgia Hawkins. Hopalong Cassidy aids frontierswoman trying to save her wagon-freighting line in the Mexican-American border region, threatened by slick hombre Ankrum. First-rate in all departments, a model for all series Westerns. Screenplay coauthored by Johnston McCulley, the creator of Zorro. ▼▶

Doomed Cargo SEE: **Seven Sinners** (1936)

Doomed to Die (1940) 57m. *½ D: William Nigh. Boris Karloff, Grant Withers, Marjorie Reynolds, Melvin Lang, Guy Usher. Fifth entry in the *Mr. Wong* series, with the detective on the trail of a shipping tycoon's killer, uncovering the whereabouts of some missing contraband bonds. ▼▶

Door-to-Door Maniac (1961) 80m. *½ D: Bill Karn. Johnny Cash, Donald Woods, Cay Forrester, Pamela Mason, Midge Ware, Victor Tayback, Ronny Howard, Merle Travis. Cash and Tayback plot a bank robbery. Of interest only for the cast; also known as FIVE MINUTES TO LIVE. ▼▶

Doorway to Hell, The (1930) 78m. *½ D:

Archie L. Mayo. Lew Ayres, Charles Judels, Dorothy Matthews, Leon Janney, Robert Elliott, James Cagney, Kenneth Thomson. Antique, early-talkie gangster saga with Ayres improbably cast as ruthless Chicago underworld biggie and Cagney (billed sixth, in his second film) as his henchman.◗

Door With Seven Locks, The (1962-German) **96m. **½ D: Alfred Vohrer. Eddie Arent, Heinz Drache, Klaus Kinski, Adi Berber, Sabina Sesselman. Bizarre account of man who leaves in his will seven keys to treasure vault, with expected friction and murder; from Edgar Wallace story made before as CHAMBER OF HORRORS.

Double Bunk (1960-British) **92m. *½ D: C. M. Pennington-Richards. Ian Carmichael, Janette Scott, Sidney James, Liz Fraser, Dennis Price. Slapstick account of Carmichael and Scott navigating their houseboat down the Thames, with predictable sight gags.

Double Confession (1950-British) **86m. ** D: Ken Annakin. Derek Farr, Joan Hopkins, Peter Lorre, William Hartnell, Kathleen Harrison, Naunton Wayne. Murky melodrama at a seaside resort: an innocent man tries to set someone else up as a murder suspect in his wife's mysterious death, only to get involved with some real killers.▼◗

Double Cross (1941) **66m. *½ D: Albert Kelley. Kane Richmond, Pauline Moore, Wynne Gibson. Mild account of cop seeking to get the goods on criminal gang; nothing unusual.▼◗

Double Cross (1949-Italian) **77m. **½ D: Riccardo Freda. Vittorio Gassman, Amedeo Nazzari, Gianna Maria Canale, Caterina Boratto, Camillo Pilotto. Acceptable account of businessman Nazzari, who's framed for murder and seeks retribution years later.

Double Cross (1956-British) **71m. ** D: Anthony Squire. Donald Houston, Fay Compton, Anton Diffring, Delphi Lawrence, William Hartnell, Frank Lawton, Robert Shaw. Mild account of foreign agents plotting to steal government secrets.

Double Crossbones (1951) **C-75m. ** D: Charles Barton. Donald O'Connor, Helena Carter, Will Geer, Hope Emerson, Glenn Strange, Charles McGraw, James Arness. O'Connor is bumbling store clerk on the lam after being framed by a crooked colonial governor, and now sailing under the Jolly Roger. Light satire that doesn't quite come off.◗

Double Dynamite (1951) **80m. ** D: Irving Cummings. Frank Sinatra, Jane Russell, Groucho Marx, Don McGuire. Sinatra plays a bank clerk falsely accused of robbery. Flat comedy marked a career low point for all three of its stars. Filmed in 1948.▼◗

Double Harness (1933) **74m. *** D: John Cromwell. Ann Harding, William Powell, Lucile Browne, Henry Stephenson, Lilian Bond, George Meeker, Reginald Owen. Harding, believing that marriage is a woman's business, schemes to snare free-living playboy Powell. Will they live happily ever after? Sharp, well-played pre-Code marital tale ably showcases its two stars.◗

Double Indemnity (1944) **106m. **** D: Billy Wilder. Barbara Stanwyck, Fred MacMurray, Edward G. Robinson, Porter Hall, Tom Power, Fortunio Bonanova, Jean Heather, Bess Flowers. Wilder–Raymond Chandler script (from the James M. Cain novel) packs fireworks in account of insurance salesman MacMurray lured into murder plot by alluring Stanwyck and subsequent investigation by Fred's colleague Robinson. An American movie classic, with crackling dialogue throughout. Remade for TV in 1973 with Richard Crenna and Samantha Eggar, and the obvious inspiration for Lawrence Kasdan's BODY HEAT. ▼◗▮

Double Life, A (1947) **104m. ***½ D: George Cukor. Ronald Colman, Signe Hasso, Edmond O'Brien, Shelley Winters, Ray Collins, Millard Mitchell. Colman gives a bravura, Oscar-winning performance as an actor whose stage roles spill over into his life—and now he's about to play Othello. Brilliant melodrama by Ruth Gordon and Garson Kanin, with wonderful New York theater flavor. Miklos Rozsa's fine score also won an Oscar. Watch for playwright Paddy Chayefsky as a crime-scene photographer.

Double or Nothing (1937) **95m. **½ D: Theodore Reed. Bing Crosby, Martha Raye, Andy Devine, Mary Carlisle, William Frawley, Fay Holden, Frances Faye. Entertaining musical about four people given 30 days to double gifts of $5000. Several good specialty acts thrown in for good measure, and Bing sings "The Moon Got in My Eyes."◗

Double Trouble (1962) SEE: **Swingin' Along**

Double Wedding (1937) **87m. **½ D: Richard Thorpe. William Powell, Myrna Loy, Florence Rice, John Beal, Jessie Ralph, Edgar Kennedy, Sidney Toler, Mary Gordon, Donald Meek. Loy's orchestration of her sister's wedding is upset by the presence of free-spirited bohemian Powell. The stars are the whole show in this disappointing adaptation of Ferenc Molnár's play *Great Love.* ▼◗

Doubting Thomas (1935) **78m. *** D: David Butler. Will Rogers, Billie Burke, Alison Skipworth, Sterling Holloway, Andrew Tombes, Gail Patrick, Frank Albertson, John Qualen. Rogers is at his best dealing with a variety of eccentric and pompous characters when his stagestruck wife Burke joins an amateur theatrical troupe. Often hilarious adaptation of George Kelly's play *The Torch Bearers,* with Skipworth in rare form as the play's directress.▼◗

Doughboys (1930) **79m. *½ D: Edward Sedgwick. Buster Keaton, Sally Eilers, Cliff Edwards, Edward Brophy, Victor Potel. One of Buster's worst films; a tiresome Army comedy. Obnoxious sergeant Brophy overrides few comic moments; some bright spots with "Ukulele Ike" Edwards. ▼○◗

Doughgirls, The (1944) **102m.** **½ D: James V. Kern. Ann Sheridan, Alexis Smith, Jane Wyman, Eve Arden, Jack Carson, Charlie Ruggles, Alan Mowbray, Craig Stevens, Regis Toomey. Brittle comedy, still another variation on crowded situation in wartime Washington, with newlyweds Carson and Wyman on hectic honeymoon. Arden stands out as Russian Army officer.

Down Among the Sheltering Palms (1953) **C-87m.** ** D: Edmund Goulding. William Lundigan, Jane Greer, Mitzi Gaynor, David Wayne, Gloria DeHaven, Billy Gilbert, Jack Paar. Poor man's SOUTH PACIFIC recounts love problems of two U.S. Army officers stationed in Pacific after WW2. Look fast for Lee Marvin.

Down Among the Z Men (1952-British) **70m.** ** D: Maclean Rogers. Harry Secombe, Peter Sellers, Carole Carr, Spike Milligan, Clifford Stanton, Graham Stark, Miriam Karlin. Creaky vehicle for radio's The Goons in story of criminals who visit small town to steal a professor's secret scientific formula. Some good bits, especially Sellers doing impressions of Yank soldiers, but overloaded with dull song-and-dance numbers by a female chorus line. ▼○◗

Down Argentine Way (1940) **C-90m.** *** D: Irving Cummings. Don Ameche, Betty Grable, Carmen Miranda, Charlotte Greenwood, J. Carrol Naish, Henry Stephenson, Leonid Kinskey. Enjoyable 20th Century-Fox musical with Grable (in the movie that boosted her to stardom) falling in love with smooth Argentinian horse breeder Ameche. Miranda is terrific in her first American movie, performing infectious Brazilian songs with her own band . . . and look out for the Nicholas Brothers, who do a dynamite specialty number. Picture-postcard color throughout. ▼○◗

Down Dakota Way (1949) **C-67m.** *** D: William Witney. Roy Rogers, Dale Evans, Pat Brady, Elisabeth Risdon, Roy Barcroft, Byron Barr, Foy Willing and the Riders of the Purple Sage. Barcroft (Republic Pictures' best bad guy) plays a rancher who tries to hide the fact that his cattle have hoof-and-mouth disease. Another bull's-eye for Roy and director Witney; this was Brady's first film as Roy's sidekick. ▼◗

Downhill (1927-British) **95m.** **½ D: Alfred Hitchcock. Ivor Novello, Ben Webster, Robin Irvine, Sybil Rhoda, Lillian Braithwaite, Isabel Jeans, Ian Hunter. Schematic silent film charts a man's spiritual slide beginning when, as a schoolboy, he is disowned by his family after an indiscretion with a girl, and later as an adult when his wife fritters away his unexpected inheritance. Major debit: the contrived

happy ending. Lesser Hitchcock boasts the master's visual flair. Cowritten by Novello.

Down in San Diego (1941) **69m.** ** D: Robert B. Sinclair. Ray McDonald, Bonita Granville, Dan Dailey, Leo Gorcey, Henry O'Neill, Stanley Clements, Charles B. Smith, Dorothy Morris. When ex-crook Dailey enlists in the Marines, his old gang frames him into spying for them, so Gorcey (here stretching to play a mug called "Snap" instead of "Slip") springs into action with his pals to save the day. Former Broadway hoofer McDonald makes an inauspicious film debut in this very routine WW2 propaganda yarn.

Down Memory Lane (1949) **72m.** *** D: Phil Karlson (new footage). Steve Allen, Franklin Pangborn, Frank Nelson, Mack Sennett; scenes of W. C. Fields, Bing Crosby, others. Allen decides to show old Sennett comedies on his TV show. OK framework for silent clips of Ben Turpin, Gloria Swanson, etc. Fields' classic THE DENTIST and Crosby's BLUE OF THE NIGHT both shown almost in toto, making silly Allen footage worth watching.

Down Mexico Way (1941) **77m.** *** D: Joseph Santley. Gene Autry, Smiley Burnette, Fay McKenzie, Harold Huber, Sidney Blackmer, Joe Sawyer, Andrew Tombes, Murray Alper, Duncan Renaldo, Julian Rivero, Paul Fix. Gene and Frog (Burnette) go South of the Border to rout some con men who've been convincing people to invest their money in a nonexistent movie production. One of Autry's most enjoyable outings has him reprising some of his biggest hits, including "South of the Border," "Maria Elena," and "The Gay Ranchero." There's a great action finale, too. ◗

Downstairs (1932) **77m.** ***½ D: Monta Bell. John Gilbert, Paul Lukas, Virginia Bruce, Hedda Hopper, Reginald Owen, Olga Baclanova. Crackling, adult drama about a heel who sleeps and cajoles his way from one wealthy household to another—using both the mistresses of the houses upstairs and the servants downstairs. Gilbert delivers an audacious performance that more than any other redeems his maligned reputation as a "talkie" actor; he also gets story credit for the film. Leading lady Bruce was then his wife. Karen Morley appears unbilled in final scene. ◗

Down the Stretch (1936) **66m.** ** D: William Clemens. Mickey Rooney, Dennis Moore, Patricia Ellis, Willie Best, Gordon Hart, Gordon (William) Elliott, Virginia Brissac. Rooney plays a wayward jockey who is taken in by a wealthy couple and given a chance to redeem himself by winning the big race. Naturally, racketeers have other ideas. Formula horse-racing yarn made watchable by the always energetic Rooney and some well-staged racing scenes.

Down Three Dark Streets (1954) 85m. **½ D: Arnold Laven. Broderick Crawford, Ruth Roman, Martha Hyer, Marisa Pavan, Casey Adams (Max Showalter), Kenneth Tobey, Gene Reynolds, Claude Akins. FBI agent is murdered while working on three cases. Colleague Crawford takes them over and has to determine which one is linked to the killing. OK suspense yarn done in semi-documentary style. ▶

Down to Earth (1932) 73m. **½ D: David Butler. Will Rogers, Irene Rich, Dorothy Jordan, Mary Carlisle, Matty Kemp. Homer Croy's sequel to THEY HAD TO SEE PARIS has nouveau riche Midwesterner Rogers putting an end to his family's foolish spending by declaring that he's broke. OK Rogers vehicle, but not up to his best film efforts.

Down to Earth (1947) C-101m. ** D: Alexander Hall. Rita Hayworth, Larry Parks, Marc Platt, Roland Culver, James Gleason, Edward Everett Horton. Terpsichore, the Goddess of Dance (Hayworth), comes to Earth to help Parks with his mythological musical play. Rita's beauty is only asset of this hack musical, which appropriates Gleason, Horton, and Culver characters from HERE COMES MR. JORDAN. Remade as XANADU. ▼●▶

Down to Their Last Yacht (1934) 64m. *½ D: Paul Sloane. Mary Boland, Ned Sparks, Polly Moran, Sidney Blackmer, Sidney Fox, Sterling Holloway. Depression-era comedy involving people of the Social Register who are replaced by people of the Cash Register, and a crew of ex-socialites who play host to a group of nouveau riche passengers on an ocean voyage. Initially clever, but quickly becomes heavy-handed and tiresome, with bizarre musical interludes. A dud.

Down to the Sea in Ships (1922) 83m. **½ D: Elmer Clifton. William Walcott, Marguerite Courtot, Clara Bow, Raymond McKee, J. Thornton Baston. Archaic plot line of romantic conflict in a whaling family enhanced by vivid atmosphere of on-location shooting in New England and on board actual whaling ships at sea. Also notable as Clara Bow's film debut. ▼▶

Down to the Sea in Ships (1949) 120m. *** D: Henry Hathaway. Richard Widmark, Lionel Barrymore, Dean Stockwell, Cecil Kellaway, Gene Lockhart. Young Stockwell fulfills seafaring goal on crusty Barrymore's whaling ship, under guidance of sailor Widmark. Good atmospheric yarn. ▶

Do You Love Me? (1946) C-91m. **½ D: Gregory Ratoff. Maureen O'Hara, Dick Haymes, Harry James, Reginald Gardiner, Alma Kruger. Lightweight musical of band-singer Haymes romancing college dean O'Hara. ▶

Do You Want to Dance With Me? SEE: **Come Dance With Me!**

Dracula (1931) 75m. ***½ D: Tod Browning. Bela Lugosi, David Manners, Helen Chandler, Dwight Frye, Edward Van Sloan, Herbert Bunston, Frances Dade. Classic horror film of Transylvanian vampire working his evil spell on perplexed group of Londoners. Lugosi's most famous role with his definitive interpretation of the Count, ditto Frye as looney Renfield and Van Sloan as unflappable Professor Van Helsing. Reissued on video with a new score by Philip Glass. Sequel: DRACULA'S DAUGHTER. ▼●▶

Dracula (1931) 103m. *** D: George Melford. Carlos Villar (Villarias), Lupita Tovar, Pablo Alvarez Rubio, Barry Norton, Eduardo Arozamena, Carmen Guerrero, Manuel Arbo. Spanish-language adaptation of the horror classic was filmed simultaneously with the Hollywood version—at night, on the very same sets—but much of the staging and camerawork is actually better! Other major difference: the women are dressed more provocatively. All that's missing is an actor with the charisma of Lugosi in the lead. ▼▶

Dracula (1958) SEE: **Horror of Dracula**

Dracula's Daughter (1936) 70m. *** D: Lambert Hillyer. Gloria Holden; Otto Kruger, Marguerite Churchill, Irving Pichel, Edward Van Sloan, Nan Grey, Hedda Hopper. Sequel to the Lugosi classic depicts vampirish activities of Holden; Pichel adds imposing support as her sinister manservant. Hillyer, normally a B-Western director, manages to imbue this chiller with a moody, subtly sensual quality. ▼●▶

Draegerman Courage (1937) 58m. *** D: Louis King. Barton MacLane, Jean Muir, Henry O'Neill, Robert Barrat, Addison Richards, Gordon Oliver, Joseph Crehan. Tense, vividly filmed yarn about a mine cave-in, which is complicated by the antagonism among those trapped inside—including a doctor, the mine owner, and the foreman—and ace rescuer MacLane, who's in love with the doc's daughter and was fired for warning about a previous cave-in. First-rate programmer, reportedly based on a real-life Nova Scotia mine disaster in 1936. ▶

Dragnet (1954) C-89m. *** D: Jack Webb. Jack Webb, Ben Alexander, Richard Boone, Ann Robinson, Stacy Harris, Virginia Gregg, Dennis Weaver. "This is the city . . ." While investigating brutal murder, Sgt. Friday and Officer Frank Smith ignore 57 varieties of civil liberties; feature film version of classic TV show evokes its era better than almost anything. Highly recommended on a nonesthetic level. ▼▶

Dragonfly Squadron (1954) 82m. ** D: Lesley Selander. John Hodiak, Barbara Britton, Bruce Bennett, Jess Barker. Usual Korean War story, alternating between pilots in the air and their romantic problems on the ground. ▼▶

Dragon Murder Case, The (1934) 68m.

** D: H. Bruce Humberstone. Warren William, Margaret Lindsay, Lyle Talbot, Eugene Pallette, Dorothy Tree. An eerie, so-called "dragon pool" is the setting for murder in this *Philo Vance* whodunit, but the suspects are so unpleasant you'll wish someone bumped them all off. William, debuting as Vance, is colorless; Pallette (as Sergeant Heath) has all the good lines. ◗

Dragon Seed (1944) 145m. **½ D: Jack Conway, Harold S. Bucquet. Katharine Hepburn, Walter Huston, Aline MacMahon, Turhan Bey, Hurd Hatfield, Agnes Moorehead, Frances Rafferty, J. Carrol Naish, Akim Tamiroff, Henry Travers. Wellmeant but overlong film of Pearl Buck's tale of Chinese town torn asunder by Japanese occupation; fascinating attempts at Oriental characterization. ▼◗

Dragonwyck (1946) 103m. **½ D: Joseph L. Mankiewicz. Gene Tierney, Walter Huston, Vincent Price, Glenn Langan, Anne Revere, Spring Byington, Henry (Harry) Morgan, Jessica Tandy. Period chiller set at a gloomy mansion on the Hudson, with good cast but episodic presentation. Mankiewicz's directorial debut; he also scripted from the Anya Seton story. ◗

Dragoon Wells Massacre (1957) C-88m. ** D: Harold Schuster. Barry Sullivan, Dennis O'Keefe, Mona Freeman, Katy Jurado, Sebastian Cabot. Marauding Apaches force lawmen and renegades to join forces for self-protection; some action-packed scenes. CinemaScope.

Dragstrip Girl (1957) 70m. *½ D: Edward L. Cahn. Fay Spain, Steven Terrell, John Ashley, Frank Gorshin, Russ Bender, Tommy Ivo, Grazia Narciso, Tito Vuolo, Dorothy Bruce, Don Shelton. Spain is a "car crazy, speed crazy, boy crazy" hottie who revs up the hot-rod rivalry between thrill-hungry rich punk Ashley and honest garage mechanic Terrell, leading to inevitable big race. By-the-numbers AIP drive-in fodder, indistinguishable from scores of others. Remade (in name only) in 1994 as part of Showtime's "Rebel Highway" series.

Dramatic School (1938) 80m. **½ D: Robert B. Sinclair. Luise Rainer, Paulette Goddard, Alan Marshal, Lana Turner, Genevieve Tobin, Anthony Allan (John Hubbard), Henry Stephenson, Gale Sondergaard, Melville Cooper, Erik Rhodes, Virginia Grey, Ann Rutherford, Hans Conried, Margaret Dumont, Dick Haymes. Fascinating cast toplines this so-so drama with Rainer the center of attraction as a fanciful wannabe actress.

Drango (1957) 92m. ** D: Hall Bartlett, Jules Bricken. Jeff Chandler, Joanne Dru, Julie London, Donald Crisp. Chandler is Yankee Civil War veteran assigned to restore order to Southern town his command plundered. OK Western.

Dr. Broadway (1942) 68m. **½ D: Anthony Mann. MacDonald Carey, Jean Phillips, J. Carrol Naish, Richard Lane, Eduardo Ciannelli, Warren Hymer. Anthony Mann's first film is a decent little B mystery centering on Carey as Times Square doc and the assorted crooks and loonies he becomes involved with. Nicely done on a low budget and featuring a rare performance by Phillips, Ginger Rogers's stand-in.

Dr. Cadman's Secret SEE: **Black Sleep, The**

Dr. Christian Responding to the phenomenal worldwide interest in the birth of the Dionne Quintuplets in Canada in 1935, 20th Century-Fox made a movie about the doctor who delivered the babies. Jean Hersholt was cast as Dr. Allan Dafoe in THE COUNTRY DOCTOR (1936) and repeated the role in two successful sequels, REUNION (1936) and FIVE OF A KIND (1938). The role fit the Danish actor like a glove, but attempts to extend the series were dashed when Dafoe refused to sell further rights to his story. Instead, Hersholt helped create a similar character called Dr. Christian, who became the focus of a successful radio series that began in 1937. (It lasted until 1953!) In 1939, RKO released the first of six independently made, low-budget films about the Good Doctor and his neighbors in River's End, Minnesota. Dorothy Lovett appears as Christian's attractive nurse, Judy Price, whose romantic entanglements provide sturdy subplot material. All six films are bucolic, low-key in nature, and heavily sentimental; they don't wear particularly well, although the doctor's efforts to help the homeless in COURAGEOUS DR. CHRISTIAN (cowritten, incidentally, by Ring Lardner, Jr.) give that particular entry a surprisingly contemporary slant.

DR. CHRISTIAN

Meet Dr. Christian (1939)
Courageous Dr. Christian (1940)
Dr. Christian Meets the Women (1940)
Remedy for Riches (1940)
Melody for Three (1941)
They Meet Again (1941)

Dr. Christian Meets the Women (1940) 68m. ** D: William McGann. Jean Hersholt, Dorothy Lovett, Edgar Kennedy, Rod La Rocque, Frank Albertson, Marilyn (Lynn) Merrick, Maude Eburne, Veda Ann Borg. Predictable but harmless series entry, with the good doctor exposing "Professor" La Rocque's diet and physical-culture scam. ▼◗

Dr. Cyclops (1940) C-75m. **½ D: Ernest Schoedsack. Albert Dekker, Thomas Coley, Janice Logan, Victor Kilian, Charles Halton. In South American jungle, title character (Dekker) shrinks humans to doll size; the story is just OK, but the elaborate special effects (in color) are worth seeing. ▼●◗

Dreamboat (1952) **83m.** ******* D: Claude Binyon. Ginger Rogers, Clifton Webb, Jeffrey Hunter, Anne Francis, Elsa Lanchester. Clever romp: silent-star Rogers cashes in on TV showings of her old movies, to chagrin of costar Webb, now a distinguished professor. Scenes showing their old silent films are most enjoyable.◗

Dream Girl (1948) **85m.** ****** D: Mitchell Leisen. Betty Hutton, Macdonald Carey, Virginia Field, Patric Knowles, Walter Abel, Peggy Wood. Hutton stars as female Walter Mitty with constant daydreams; low-brow version of Elmer Rice play.

Dreaming Lips (1937-British) **93m.** ****½** D: Paul Czinner, Lee Garmes. Elisabeth Bergner, Raymond Massey, Romney Brent, Joyce Bland, Charles Carson, Felix Aylmer. Glamorous, pampered Bergner, wife of orchestra conductor Brent, commences a romance with world-famous (but desperately lonely) violinist Massey. A bit overdone, and the ending is a disappointment, but it's entertaining most of the way. Good star vehicle for Bergner. Previously filmed as DER TRÄUMENDE MUND (1932, also with Bergner) and MÉLO (1932); remade as DER TRÄUMENDE MUND (1953) and MÉLO (1986).▼

Dreaming Out Loud (1940) **81m.** ****** D: Harold Young. Lum 'n' Abner (Chester Lauck, Norris Goff), Frances Langford, Frank Craven, Bobs Watson, Phil Harris. Radio comedians Lum 'n' Abner's screen debut is a very slight rural comedy-melodrama with music. The fabled proprietors of the Jot-Em-Down general store in Pine Ridge, Arkansas, get involved in the lives of various local residents.▼◗

Dreams (1955-Swedish) **86m.** ****** D: Ingmar Bergman. Eva Dahlbeck, Harriet Andersson, Gunnar Bjornstrand, Ulf Palme, Inga Landgre. Sometimes fascinating but mostly vague—and, ultimately lesser—Bergman drama, about photo agency head Dahlbeck and model Andersson, and their dreams, torments, crises, oppression, relations with men. Aka JOURNEY INTO AUTUMN.▼

Dream Street (1921) **138m.** ****** D: D. W. Griffith. Carol Dempster, Ralph Graves, Charles Emmett Mack, Edward Peil, Tyrone Power (Sr.), Morgan Wallace. Disappointing silent melodrama about Gypsy Fair (Dempster), a music hall dancer, who is admired by two Irish brothers and an evil Chinese gambling den proprietor. Based on stories from *Limehouse Nights* by Thomas Burke, the book that also spawned Griffith's poetic BROKEN BLOSSOMS. Due to Dempster's limited abilities, this film never flowers. After its N.Y. premiere, it was shown with experimental sound-on-disc sequences by Orlando Kellum.▼

Dream Wife (1953) **101m.** ***½** D: Sidney Sheldon. Cary Grant, Deborah Kerr, Walter Pidgeon, Betta St. John, Buddy Baer, Movita, Steve Forrest. Silly bedroom farce about Grant's engagement to Middle Eastern princess and interference from his former fiancée, Kerr, a State Dept. official. Cast is wasted. Also shown in computer-colored version.▼◗

Dr. Ehrlich's Magic Bullet (1940) **103m.** *****½** D: William Dieterle. Edward G. Robinson, Ruth Gordon, Otto Kruger, Donald Crisp, Maria Ouspenskaya, Montagu Love, Sig Ruman, Donald Meek. Outstanding chronicle of 19th-century German scientist who developed cure for venereal disease. Robinson earnest in superior script by John Huston, Heinz Herald, and Norman Burnside; surprisingly compelling.▼◗

Dressed to Kill (1941) **71m.** ****½** D: Eugene Forde. Lloyd Nolan, Mary Beth Hughes, Sheila Ryan, William Demarest, Ben Carter, Virginia Brissac, Henry Daniell. Hard-boiled P.I. Michael Shayne (Nolan) probes a string of strange murders linked to a play in which the victims are all wearing theatrical costumes. Reasonably absorbing series entry.◗

Dressed to Kill (1946) **72m.** ****½** D: Roy William Neill. Basil Rathbone, Nigel Bruce, Patricia Morison, Edmond Breon, Carl Harbord, Patricia Cameron, Tom Dillon. Music boxes made in prison hold the key to the whereabouts of stolen bank plates in this lively final entry in the Rathbone *Sherlock Holmes* series. Also shown in computer-colored version. Aka PRELUDE TO MURDER.▼◗

Dr. Gillespie's Criminal Case (1943) **89m.** ****½** D: Willis Goldbeck. Lionel Barrymore, Van Johnson, Donna Reed, Keye Luke, John Craven, William Lundigan, Walter Kingsford, Nat Pendleton, Marilyn Maxwell, Alma Kruger, Marie Blake, Henry O'Neill, Nell Craig. Gillespie tries to help a convicted murderer prove his innocence in this unusually serious entry which helped to establish Johnson and Reed, as well as providing an early role for young Margaret O'Brien.◗

Dr. Gillespie's New Assistant (1942) **87m.** ****½** D: Willis Goldbeck. Lionel Barrymore, Van Johnson, Susan Peters, Richard Quine, Keye Luke, Alma Kruger, Stephen McNally, Nat Pendleton, Walter Kingsford, Nell Craig, Marie Blake, Frank Orth, Rose Hobart, Ann Richards. Three young surgeons (Johnson, Luke, and Quine) are put on "trial" by Gillespie to see who gets to replace Dr. Kildare in this satisfying entry stocked with burgeoning MGM talent. Quine and Peters were married in real life the following year.◗

Dr. Goldfoot and the Bikini Machine (1965) **C-90m.** ****** D: Norman Taurog. Vincent Price, Frankie Avalon, Dwayne Hickman, Susan Hart, Fred Clark. Mad scientist tries to make a fortune manufacturing lifelike lady robots to marry wealthy men. Good chase scene, but otherwise just silly. Panavision. ▼▶

Drifting Weeds SEE: **Floating Weeds**

Driftwood (1947) **90m. **½ D: Allan Dwan. Ruth Warrick, Walter Brennan, Natalie Wood, Dean Jagger, Charlotte Greenwood, Jerome Cowan, H. B. Warner, Margaret Hamilton. A scripture-quoting young orphan who's never experienced "civilization" becomes attached to a small-town doctor-researcher and a lost collie. Sweet if somewhat calculated family film features a standout performance by young Wood. ▼

Drive a Crooked Road (1954) **82m. *** D: Richard Quine. Mickey Rooney, Dianne Foster, Kevin McCarthy, Jack Kelly, Harry Landers, Jerry Paris, Paul Picerni, Dick Crockett. Low-key but effective drama about introverted auto mechanic Rooney, who dreams of a career as a race car driver. He's taken in by alluring Foster, who's setting him up as a chump for her gangster boyfriend. Rooney is quietly effective and utterly believable. Screenplay by Blake Edwards. ▶

Dr. Jack (1922) **60m. *** D: Fred Newmeyer. Harold Lloyd, Mildred Davis, John T. Prince, Eric Mayne, C. Norman Hammond, Mickey Daniels, Jackie Condon. Simple, warmhearted comedy with Harold a dedicated country physician who uses horse sense to tend to his flock. He's just what the doctor ordered when it comes to "curing" a wealthy, overprotected Sick-Little-Well-Girl (Davis). Loaded with clever sight gags; Our Gang fans will enjoy seeing Daniels and Condon. ▼▶

Dr. Jekyll and Mr. Hyde (1920) **96m. *** D: John S. Robertson. John Barrymore, Martha Mansfield, Brandon Hurst, Nita Naldi, Charles Lane, Louis Wolheim. One of several silent versions of famous tale, this one can hold its own next to the later March and Tracy filmings; Barrymore is superb as curious doctor who ventures into the unknown, emerging as evil Mr. Hyde. Bravura performance sparks well-made production. ▼●▶

Dr. Jekyll and Mr. Hyde (1932) **97m. *** D: Rouben Mamoulian. Fredric March, Miriam Hopkins, Rose Hobart, Holmes Herbert, Halliwell Hobbes. Exciting, floridly cinematic version of famous story with March in Oscar-winning portrayal of tormented doctor, Hopkins superb as tantalizing Ivy. Beware of 82m. reissue version. ▼●▶

Dr. Jekyll and Mr. Hyde (1941) **114m. *** D: Victor Fleming. Spencer Tracy, Ingrid Bergman, Lana Turner, Donald Crisp, Ian Hunter, Barton MacLane, C. Aubrey Smith, Sara Allgood. Tracy and Bergman are excellent in thoughtful, lush remake of Robert Louis Stevenson's classic, which stresses Hyde's emotions rather than physical horror. Also shown in computer-colored version. ▼●▶

Dr. Kildare From 1938 to 1947, this MGM series, set in Blair General Hospital, was one of the most successful and entertaining of all. INTERNES CAN'T TAKE MONEY (1937, Paramount) was the first film based on Max Brand's characters, with Joel McCrea as Kildare, but it was not part of the series and did not use any of the later familiar roles. The first official entry, MGM's YOUNG DR. KILDARE, starred Lew Ayres as Kildare, Lionel Barrymore as Dr. Gillespie, Laraine Day (Mary Lamont), Alma Kruger (Nurse Molly Byrd), Walter Kingsford (Dr. Carewe, head of the hospital), Nat Pendleton (Joe Wayman, ambulance driver), Emma Dunn and Samuel S. Hinds (Dr. Kildare's benevolent parents), Nell Craig (Nurse Parker), Marie Blake (Sally, switchboard operator), Frank Orth (Mike), and George Reed (Conover). Indeed, the Kildare series has more running characters than most others. Laraine Day left the series after DR. KILDARE'S WEDDING DAY, and the parents left along with Lew Ayres after DR. KILDARE'S VICTORY. Van Johnson and Keye Luke spent several films trying to become Dr. Gillespie's assistant, with Marilyn Maxwell as love interest for Van. Philip Dorn tried out in CALLING DR. GILLESPIE, and James Craig finished the series with DARK DELUSION. Lionel Barrymore appeared in all of them as the crusty Dr. Gillespie, and supported those entries with lesser plots and casts, often by himself.

DR. KILDARE

Internes Can't Take Money (1937)
Young Dr. Kildare (1938)
Calling Dr. Kildare (1939)
The Secret of Dr. Kildare (1939)
Dr. Kildare's Strange Case (1940)
Dr. Kildare Goes Home (1940)
Dr. Kildare's Crisis (1940)
The People vs. Dr. Kildare (1941)
Dr. Kildare's Wedding Day (1941)
Dr. Kildare's Victory (1942)
Calling Dr. Gillespie (1942)
Dr. Gillespie's New Assistant (1942)
Dr. Gillespie's Criminal Case (1943)
Three Men in White (1944)
Between Two Women (1944)
Dark Delusion (1947)

Dr. Kildare Goes Home (1940) **78m. ** D: Harold S. Bucquet. Lew Ayres, Lionel Barrymore, Laraine Day, Samuel S. Hinds, Gene Lockhart, Emma Dunn, Nat Pendleton, Walter Kingsford, Alma Kruger, Nell Craig, Marie Blake. Selfless Kildare gives up chance to become Dr. Gillespie's assistant to help his overworked, smalltown physician dad set up a clinic. One of the internes is a young Arthur O'Connell. ▶

Dr. Kildare's Crisis (1940) **75m. **½ D: Harold S. Bucquet. Lew Ayres, Lionel Barrymore, Laraine Day, Robert Young, Emma

Dunn, Nat Pendleton, Bobs Watson, Walter Kingsford, Alma Kruger, Nell Craig, Frank Orth, Marie Blake, Horace MacMahon. Kildare's impending nuptials are jeopardized by a diagnosis of possible epilepsy in his fiancée's brother (Young). Sleek entry with good production.▶

Dr. Kildare's Strange Case (1940) **76m.** ****½** D: Harold S. Bucquet. Lew Ayres, Lionel Barrymore, Laraine Day, Shepperd Strudwick, Samuel S. Hinds, Emma Dunn, Nat Pendleton, Walter Kingsford, Alma Kruger, Nell Craig, Horace McMahon, Marie Blake, Frank Orth. Kildare utilizes shock therapy and other "modern" techniques to help cure a mental patient. Arresting entry with numerous subplots.▼▶

Dr. Kildare's Victory (1942) **92m.** ****½** D: W.S. Van Dyke II. Lew Ayres, Lionel Barrymore, Ann Ayars, Robert Sterling, Jean Rogers, Alma Kruger, Walter Kingsford, Nell Craig, Marie Blake, Frank Orth, Barry Nelson. Kildare, still heartsick over "Mary Lamont," falls for a socialite patient while fighting a hospital zoning problem in this busy episode. Ayres' last appearance in the series.▶

Dr. Kildare's Wedding Day (1941) **82m.** ****½** D: Harold S. Bucquet. Lew Ayres, Lionel Barrymore, Laraine Day, Red Skelton, Fay Holden, Walter Kingsford, Alma Kruger, Samuel S. Hinds, Emma Dunn, Nils Asther, Miles Mander, Nell Craig, Frank Orth. Tragedy strikes Kildare's fiancée (Day, whom MGM was grooming for bigger roles) in this surprisingly somber episode leavened with comic relief by Skelton. Erstwhile "Dick Tracy" Ralph Byrd plays a cop.▶

Dr. Mabuse, The Gambler (1922) **270m.** *****½** D: Fritz Lang. Rudolph Klein-Rogge, Aud Egede Nissen, Gertrude Welcker, Alfred Abel, Lil Dagover, Paul Richter. Baroque tale of master criminal Mabuse (Klein-Rogge), who gambles with lives and fates, is an allegory of postwar German decadence. Brilliantly directed, designed, and photographed. Originally shown in two parts; the second half, DR. MABUSE, KING OF CRIME, details Mabuse's descent into madness. It isn't as flamboyant as Part One, but still quite good. Adapted by Lang and Thea von Harbou from a novel by Norbert Jacques. Shown as separate films for many years; prints circulate in various lengths. Lang later made THE TESTAMENT OF DR. MABUSE (1932) and THE 1,000 EYES OF DR. MABUSE (1960).▼▶

Dr. Monica (1934) **53m.** ******* D: William Keighley. Kay Francis, Warren William, Jean Muir, Verree Teasdale, Emma Dunn, Phillip Reed, Herbert Bunston, Ann Shoemaker. Francis is very good as a physician who desperately wants to have children but can't conceive. She's stunned to discover that her cad husband (William) is not only

having an affair with her close friend (Muir) but has also gotten her pregnant. Frank, mature treatment of adultery and illegitimacy ran into censorship trouble and was severely cut but is still worthwhile. Original running time: 65m.

Dr. No (1962-British) **C-111m.** *****½** D: Terence Young. Sean Connery, Ursula Andress, Joseph Wiseman, Jack Lord, Bernard Lee, Lois Maxwell. First James Bond film is least pretentious, with meaty story, fine all-round production of Ian Fleming caper. Bond investigates strange occurrences in Jamaica, encounters master-fiend Dr. No (Wiseman).▼▶

Drôle de drame (1937-French) **97m.** ******* D: Marcel Carné. Françoise Rosay, Michel Simon, Jean-Pierre Aumont, Louis Jouvet, Nadine Vogel, Henri Guisol, Jenny Burnay, Jean-Louis Barrault. Rapier-witted satire about botanist Simon, who pens successful, controversial crime novels under a pseudonym and is thought to have murdered his wife (who is very much alive). Carné and screenwriter Jacques Prévert lampoon upper-class elitism, hypocritical religious leaders, inept journalists, overzealous cops, and the ever-fickle masses. Full title is DRÔLE DE DRAME OU L'ÉTRANGE AVENTURE DE DOCTEUR MOLYNEUX. U.S. title: BIZARRE, BIZARRE.▼▶

Dr. Renault's Secret (1942) **58m.** ****½** D: Harry Lachman. J. Carrol Naish, John Shepperd (Shepperd Strudwick), Lynne Roberts, George Zucco, Arthur Shields, Mike Mazurki, Ray Corrigan. Could that secret involve Renault's brutish assistant Noel, who's devoted to the doctor's daughter (Roberts)? Naish is excellent as the sympathetic but murderous semi-simian. Odd, likable almost-horror B movie set in the French countryside. From a novel by Gaston Leroux.▶

Dr. Socrates (1935) **70m.** ******* D: William Dieterle. Paul Muni, Ann Dvorak, Barton MacLane, Raymond Brown, Mayo Methot. Enjoyable film about small-town doctor Muni who unwillingly becomes official doctor for wounded mobsters. Offbeat role for Muni, unusually good one for MacLane as loudmouthed gangster. Remade as KING OF THE UNDERWORLD with Kay Francis in the Muni role!

Dr. Strangelove or: How I Learned to Stop Worrying and Love the Bomb (1964-British) **93m.** ******** D: Stanley Kubrick. Peter Sellers, George C. Scott, Sterling Hayden, Slim Pickens, Keenan Wynn, Peter Bull, James Earl Jones. U.S. President must contend with the Russians and his own political and military leaders when a fanatical general launches A-bomb attack on U.S.S.R. Sellers plays the President, British captain, and mad inventor of the Bomb in this brilliant black comedy, which seems better with each passing year. Sellers' phone conversation with

Soviet premier is classic. Outstanding cast, incredible sets by Ken Adam. Screenplay by Kubrick, Peter George, and Terry Southern, from George's (serious) book *Red Alert*. Jones' film debut. ▼●▶

Dr. Syn, Alias the Scarecrow (1962) C-98m. **½ D: James Neilson. Patrick Mc-Goohan, George Cole, Michael Hordern, Tony Britton, Geoffrey Keen, Kay Walsh, Patrick Wymark. Agreeable Disney production made in England (and originally shown in three parts on the Disney TV show as *The Scarecrow of Romney Marsh*) about country vicar who in reality is a smuggler and pirate. McGoohan is well cast as the mysterious bandit-hero who conducts his nightly raids disguised as a scarecrow. Filmed before in 1937 with George Arliss; another 1962 version, NIGHT CREATURES, stars Peter Cushing. [G]▼▶

Dr. Terror's House of Horrors (1965-British) C-98m. **½ D: Freddie Francis. Peter Cushing, Christopher Lee, Roy Castle, Max Adrian, Michael Gough, Donald Sutherland, Neil McCallum, Edward Underdown, Ursula Howells, Jeremy Kemp, Bernard Lee. Don't let title steer you from this intelligent episodic thriller about a strange doctor (Cushing) who tells five men's fortunes on a train. Enjoyable horror-fantasy. Techniscope.▼

Drum, The (1938) SEE: **Drums**

Drum Beat (1954) C-111m. **½ D: Delmer Daves. Alan Ladd, Audrey Dalton, Marisa Pavan, Robert Keith, Rodolfo Acosta, Charles Bronson, Warner Anderson, Elisha Cook, Jr., Anthony Caruso, Strother Martin. In southern Oregon, former Indian fighter Ladd tries to talk Modoc chief Captain Jack (Bronson) into peace. Director Daves based his script on historical events. Bronson is especially good in an unusual role. CinemaScope.▼▶

Drums (1938-British) C-99m. *** D: Zoltan Korda. Sabu, Raymond Massey, Valerie Hobson, Roger Livesey, David Tree. Fine, colorful adventure with precocious Sabu rescuing British cavalry in early 20th-century India; atmospheric and actionful. Originally titled THE DRUM. Original British running time: 104m.▼▶

Drums Across the River (1954) C-78m. ** D: Nathan Juran. Audie Murphy, Lisa Gaye, Walter Brennan, Lyle Bettger, Hugh O'Brian, Mara Corday, Jay Silverheels, Regis Toomey, Bob Steele. Murphy ties in with gold-jumpers overrunning Indian land, redeems himself by joining forces against these men to achieve peace. ▶

Drums Along the Mohawk (1939) C-103m. ***½ D: John Ford. Claudette Colbert, Henry Fonda, Edna May Oliver, John Carradine, Jessie Ralph, Arthur Shields, Robert Lowery, Ward Bond. John Ford richly captures flavor of Colonial life in this vigorous, courageous story of settlers in upstate New York during Revolutionary War. Action, drama, sentiment, humor deftly in-terwoven in beautiful Technicolor production. From Walter Edmonds' novel. ▼●▶

Drums in the Deep South (1951) C-87m. **½ D: William Cameron Menzies. James Craig, Barbara Payton, Guy Madison, Barton MacLane, Craig Stevens. The Civil War puts friends on opposing sides: Southerner Craig and his detail mount cannons atop an impregnable Georgia peak to bombard a Union supply train route, while Northern officer Madison is assigned to blow them up. THE GUNS OF NAVARONE done Dixie style! Menzies was also production designer. ▼▶

Drums of Africa (1963) C-91m. ** D: James B. Clark. Frankie Avalon, Mariette Hartley, Lloyd Bochner, Torin Thatcher, Hari Rhodes, Michael Pate. Avalon trades in his surfboard for a safari jacket in this trifling account of a young man who comes to Equatorial East Africa in 1897 and, with assorted other characters, tangles with slave traders. Hartley is wasted as a missionary. And yes, Frankie even gets to sing. ▶

Drums of Tahiti (1954) C-73m. *½ D: William Castle. Dennis O'Keefe, Patricia Medina, Francis L. Sullivan, George Keymas. Footloose American aids a Tahitian queen who opposes annexation by the French in the late 1800s. Silly Sam Katzman production whose only novelty (in theaters) was the use of 3-D—as you can tell by flaming torches poked at the camera!

Drums of the Desert (1940) 64m. ** D: George Waggner. Ralph Byrd, Lorna Gray (Adrian Booth), Mantan Moreland, George Lynn, William Costello, Jean Del Val, Ann Codee. En route to a stint in the French Foreign Legion, Byrd enjoys a shipboard romance with Gray, not knowing she's engaged to best friend and fellow Legionnaire Lynn. Arid dramaturgy clogs up the burly action in this Monogram adventure yarn. ▼▶

Drunken Angel (1948) 102m. *** D: Akira Kurosawa. Takashi Shimura, Toshiro Mifune, Reisaburo Yamamoto, Chieko Nakakita, Michiyo Kogure, Norika Sengoku. The first of 16 movies Mifune made with Kurosawa is a humane and affecting story set in the disease-ridden slums of postwar Japan, focusing on the relationship between an embittered, alcoholic doctor (Shimura) and a gangster (Mifune) dying of tuberculosis. Considered Kurosawa's first important work, the film is equally notable as a realistic social drama and a Hollywood-style crime movie. ▼▶

Dr. Who and the Daleks (1965-British) C-85m. **½ D: Gordon Flemyng. Peter Cushing, Roy Castle, Jennie Linden, Roberta Tovey, Barrie Ingham. Pleasing feature inspired by the long-running British TV serial, with the Doctor and his young friends transported to another world where humans are threatened by robotlike Daleks. Followed by DALEKS—INVASION EARTH 2150 A.D. Techniscope. ▼▶

Du Barry Was a Lady (1943) C-101m. *** D: Roy Del Ruth. Red Skelton, Lucille Ball, Gene Kelly, Virginia O'Brien, Rags Ragland, Zero Mostel, Donald Meek, George Givot, Louise Beavers, Tommy Dorsey and His Orchestra. Nightclub worker Skelton pines for beautiful singing star Ball; when he swallows a Mickey Finn, he dreams he's Louis XVI, and has to contend with the prickly Madame DuBarry (Ball). Colorful nonsense, missing most of the songs from Cole Porter's Broadway score, though "Friendship" is used as the finale. Opens like a vaudeville show, with beautiful chorines and specialty acts, including young Mostel, and Dorsey's band—with Buddy Rich on drums—doing a sensational "Well, Git It." They turn up later in powdered wigs, as do The Pied Pipers, with Dick Haymes and Jo Stafford. Lana Turner has a bit part. ▼▶●

Du Barry, Woman of Passion (1930) 90m. ** D: Sam Taylor. Norma Talmadge, William Farnum, Conrad Nagel, Hobart Bosworth, Alison Skipworth. Early sound version of oft-told tale about the life and loves of the famous 18th-century courtesan. Stiff and primitive but with fine art direction by William Cameron Menzies.▼

Duchess of Idaho (1950) C-98m. **½ D: Robert Z. Leonard. Esther Williams, Van Johnson, John Lund, Paula Raymond, Clinton Sundberg, Connie Haines, Mel Tormé, Amanda Blake. Williams vehicle has her going to Sun Valley to assist her lovesick roommate, attracting bandleader Johnson. Guest stars Lena Horne, Eleanor Powell (in her last film), and Red Skelton pep up formula production.▼

Duck Soup (1933) 70m. **** D: Leo McCarey. Groucho, Harpo, Chico, Zeppo Marx, Margaret Dumont, Louis Calhern, Raquel Torres, Edgar Kennedy, Leonid Kinskey, Charles Middleton. The Marx Brothers' most sustained bit of insanity, a flop when first released, but now considered a satiric masterpiece. In postage-stamp–sized Freedonia, Prime Minister Rufus T. Firefly (Groucho) declares war on neighboring Sylvania just for the hell of it. Enough gags for five movies, but our favorite is still the mirror sequence. Zeppo's swan song with his brothers.▼▶●

Dude Goes West, The (1948) 87m. ** D: Kurt Neumann. Eddie Albert, Gale Storm, James Gleason, Binnie Barnes, Gilbert Roland, Barton MacLane. Innocuous little comedy of Easterner Albert becoming a Western hero.▶

Dudes Are Pretty People (1942) 95m. ** D: Hal Roach, Jr. Jimmy Rogers, Noah Beery, Jr., Marjorie Woodworth, Paul Hurst, Marjorie Gateson, Russell Gleason, Grady Sutton. A couple of itinerant cowboys move to a dude ranch when one of them falls for a

flashy blonde. Pretty dull. Originally one of producer Hal Roach's 46m. "Streamliner" featurettes; for TV it's been spliced to its equally dull sequel, CALABOOSE.

Duel at Apache Wells (1957) 70m. *½ D: Joseph Kane. Anna Maria Alberghetti, Ben Cooper, Jim Davis, Bob Steele, Frank Puglia, Harry Shannon. Cooper heads home when he learns that Davis is muscling in on his father's ranch—and on his girl (Alberghetti). Unsatisfying (and slow-moving) Western. Naturama.

Duel at Silver Creek, The (1952) C-77m. **½ D: Don Siegel. Audie Murphy, Faith Domergue, Stephen McNally, Susan Cabot, Gerald Mohr, Eugene Iglesias, Kyle James (James Anderson), Lee Marvin. The "Silver Kid" (Murphy), quick on the draw and with a hidden agenda, joins up with sheriff McNally to take on a gang of claim jumpers who've been brutalizing honest miners. Some nice touches by director Siegel enhance this otherwise standard Western. ▼▶

Duel in Durango SEE: **Gun Duel in Durango**

Duel in the Jungle (1954-British) C-102m. **½ D: George Marshall. Dana Andrews, Jeanne Crain, David Farrar, George Coulouris, Wilfrid Hyde-White. Action-packed adventure of insurance investigator tracking allegedly dead man to Africa. Strong cast.

Duel in the Sun (1946) C-130m. *** D: King Vidor. Jennifer Jones, Joseph Cotten, Gregory Peck, Lionel Barrymore, Lillian Gish, Herbert Marshall, Walter Huston, Butterfly McQueen, Charles Bickford, Tilly Losch, Harry Carey. Producer-writer David O. Selznick's ambitious attempt to duplicate success of GONE WITH THE WIND: big, brawling, engrossing, often stupid sex-Western, with half-breed Jones caught between brothers Peck and Cotten. Great in Technicolor, with some memorable scenes and an unexpectedly bizarre finale. From the novel by Niven Busch. Superb score by Dimitri Tiomkin. Runs 144m. with prelude/overture, exit music. ▼▶●

Duel of Champions (1961-Italian) C-105m. ** D: Ferdinando Baldi. Alan Ladd, Franca Bettoja, Franco Fabrizi, Robert Keith, Luciano Marin. Stodgy epic set in ancient Rome with bored-looking Ladd the Roman leader who challenges forces of Alba. Totalscope.▼▶

Duel of the Titans (1961-Italian) C-88m. ** D: Sergio Corbucci. Steve Reeves, Gordon Scott, Virna Lisi, Massimo Girotti. Reeves is Romulus and Scott is Remus in this fictional account of justice overcoming tyranny in ancient Rome. CinemaScope.▼

Duffy of San Quentin (1954) 78m. **½ D: Walter Doniger. Louis Hayward, Joanne Dru, Paul Kelly, Maureen O'Sullivan, George Macready. Low-keyed account of Warden Duffy's reforms within famed prison. Followed by THE STEEL CAGE. ▶

Duffy's Tavern (1945) **97m.** BOMB D: Hal Walker. Barry Sullivan, Marjorie Reynolds, Bing Crosby, Dorothy Lamour, Alan Ladd, Betty Hutton, Eddie Bracken, Veronica Lake, Robert Benchley, Paulette Goddard, Brian Donlevy. Disastrous "comedy" of radio character Ed Gardner trying to save Duffy's Tavern, Victor Moore trying to save his record company. No redeeming values despite guest appearances by several dozen Paramount stars.

Duke Is Tops, The (1938) **80m. ★★** D: William Nolte. Ralph Cooper, Lena Horne, Lawrence Criner, Monte Hawley, Neva Peoples, Vernon McCallum. Crudely made showbiz saga with Horne, in her screen debut, as a singer nicknamed the "Bronze Nightingale," whose expanding career affects her relationship with a good-hearted boyfriend-manager (Cooper). All-black-cast curiosity is noteworthy for the presence of a pre-Hollywood Horne. The specialty numbers are fun to watch, particularly the appropriately named Rubber Neck Holmes. Reissued as THE BRONZE VENUS.▼❿

Duke of West Point, The (1938) **109m. ★★½** D: Alfred E. Green. Louis Hayward, Joan Fontaine, Tom Brown, Richard Carlson, Alan Curtis, Donald Barry. Predictable West Point saga of honor and love at the Academy is trite but entertaining, with Fontaine winning as the ingenue.▼

Dulcimer Street (1948-British) **112m. ★★½** D: Sidney Gilliat. Richard Attenborough, Alastair Sim, Fay Compton, Stephen Murray, Wylie Watson, Susan Shaw, Joyce Carey, Ivy St. Helier, Hugh Griffith, Maurice Denham. Atmospheric account of a slum area of London and its inhabitants who champion one of their own accused of murder. Original British title: LONDON BELONGS TO ME.▼

Dulcy (1940) **73m. ★½** D: S. Sylvan Simon. Ann Sothern, Ian Hunter, Roland Young, Reginald Gardiner, Billie Burke, Lynne Carver, Dan Dailey, Jr. Pretty bad comedy of Chinese orphan mending new family's problems. Good cast with inferior material. Based on the George S. Kaufman–Marc Connelly play filmed before in 1923 and 1930 (as NOT SO DUMB).

Dumbo (1941) **C-64m. ★★★★** D: Ben Sharpsteen. Voices of Sterling Holloway, Edward Brophy, Verna Felton, Herman Bing, Cliff Edwards. One of Walt Disney's most charming animated films, about pint-sized elephant with giant-sized ears, and how his friend Timothy the Mouse helps build his confidence. Never a dull moment, but pink-elephants dream sequence is special treat. Frank Churchill and Oliver Wallace's scoring earned them Oscars.▼❶❿

Dunkirk (1958-British) **113m. ★★★** D: Leslie Norman. John Mills, Richard Attenborough, Bernard Lee, Robert Urquhart, Ray Jackson, Lionel Jeffries. Near-epic dramatization of the rescue by the Royal Navy and small civilian craft of 300,000 British soldiers trapped on the French beach of the title in 1940. One of the last films of the famed Ealing studios. Very realistic, with a fine cast and good direction. Original British length: 135m. Metroscope.

Dust Be My Destiny (1939) **88m. ★★½** D: Lewis Seiler. John Garfield, Priscilla Lane, Alan Hale, Frank McHugh, John Litel, Billy Halop, Henry Armetta, Stanley Ridges, Bobby Jordan, Charley Grapewin. Garfield is ideally cast as an alienated drifter who finds himself in jail, where he falls for vicious prison foreman's stepdaughter (Lane). The stars rise above their less-than-original material.❶

Dybbuk, The (1938-Polish) **125m. ★★★** D: Michael Waszynsky. Leon Liebgold, Lili Liliana, Max Bozyk, Abraham Morevsky, Dina Halpern. Fascinating, beautifully detailed (and restored) Yiddish-language version of Sholom Anski's famous folktale of a restless, disembodied spirit who enters the body of the woman he was pledged to wed. Of special interest as a look at a culture made extinct by Hitler. One of a dozen or so Yiddish features made in Poland prior to the Holocaust.▼❶

Dynamite (1929) **129m. ★★★** D: Cecil B. DeMille. Conrad Nagel, Kay Johnson, Charles Bickford, Julia Faye, Joel McCrea. Enough plot for seven films in this silly but fascinating early talkie; aristocratic Johnson marries miner Bickford, who's about to be executed, to gain inheritance . . . then Bickford is cleared. Typical DeMille entertainment.

Dynamite (1949) **69m. ★½** D: William H. Pine. William Gargan, Virginia Welles, Richard Crane, Irving Bacon, Frank Ferguson, Mary Newton. Young commercial dynamiter Crane clashes with older colleague Gargan over affections of Welles in standard B opus.▼❶

Each Dawn I Die (1939) **92m. ★★★** D: William Keighley. James Cagney, George Raft, George Bancroft, Jane Bryan, Maxie Rosenbloom, Stanley Ridges, Louis Jean Heydt, Abner Biberman, John Wray, Victor Jory, Thurston Hall. Reporter Cagney is framed, sent to prison, where he meets tough-guy Raft. Good performances all around—Cagney hits a white-hot peak as the embittered, stir-crazy fall guy—but last half of film becomes outrageously improbable. Music score by Max Steiner.▼❶❿

Eagle, The (1925) **77m. ★★★** D: Clarence Brown. Rudolph Valentino, Vilma Banky, Louise Dresser, Albert Conti, James Marcus, George Nichols. Valentino plays a sort of Russian Robin Hood in this entertaining costume picture, winning the hand of Vilma Banky while trying to outwit Czarina Dresser, angry because he snubbed her advances.▼●◗

Eagle and the Hawk, The (1933) 68m. ***½ D: Stuart Walker. Fredric March, Cary Grant, Jack Oakie, Carole Lombard, Guy Standing, Douglas Scott. Well-produced antiwar film with reluctant hero March, bullying gunner-observer Grant, everyone's friend Oakie, sympathetic society girl Lombard. Sobering John Monk Saunders story is still timely. Mitchell Leisen, credited as "associate director," reportedly directed most of the film. Originally 72m.▼◗

Eagle and the Hawk, The (1950) C-104m. **½ D: Lewis R. Foster. John Payne, Rhonda Fleming, Dennis O'Keefe, Thomas Gomez, Fred Clark. Contrived actioner set in 1860s Mexico-Texas with O'Keefe and Payne U.S. law enforcers stifling coup to make Maximilian ruler of Mexico; Fleming is fetching love interest.

Eagle's Brood, The (1935) 59m. **½ D: Howard Bretherton. William Boyd, James Ellison, George Hayes, William Farnum, Addison Richards, Nana Martinez (Joan Woodbury), Dorothy Revier. After notorious "El Toro" saves his life, Bill "Hopalong" Cassidy repays the debt by rescuing the outlaw's orphaned grandson. Depicts several surprisingly brutal murders. Hayes hasn't yet developed his "Windy" persona in this solid, character-driven film, the second Hoppy movie; based on creator Clarence E. Mulford's same-named novel.▼◗

Eagle Squadron (1942) 109m. **½ D: Arthur Lubin. Robert Stack, Eddie Albert, Diana Barrymore, Nigel Bruce, Jon Hall, Evelyn Ankers, Gladys Cooper, Mary Carr. Usual WW2 action and romance as young American fliers fought the war in the RAF. Good action scenes help average script.

Eagle With Two Heads, The (1948-French) 93m. **½ D: Jean Cocteau. Edwige Feuillere, Jean Marais, Sylvia Monfort, Jacques Varennes, Jean Debucourt, Yvonne de Bray. Stuffy, slightly crazed Queen Feuillere's husband was assassinated a decade earlier, on their wedding day. Amid much court intrigue, a poet-anarchist (Marais) who bears a striking resemblance to the deceased monarch stumbles into her quarters. Static romantic drama is Cocteau's least successful film. He scripted, based on his play (which also starred Feuillere and Marais).▼

Earl Carroll Sketchbook (1946) 90m. **½ D: Albert S. Rogell. Constance Moore, William Marshall, Bill Goodwin, Johnny Coy, Vera Vague, Edward Everett Horton, Hillary Brooke, Dorothy Babb. Marshall writes radio jingles but secretary Moore, who's secretly in love with him, thinks his songs belong on Broadway. Enjoyable blend of romantic comedy and backstage musical. Lavish by Republic Pictures standards, with choreography by Nick Castle, songs by Sammy Cahn and Jule Styne.

Earl Carroll Vanities (1945) 91m. **½ D: Joseph Santley. Dennis O'Keefe, Constance Moore, Eve Arden, Otto Kruger, Alan Mowbray, Stephanie Bachelor, Pinky Lee, Mary Forbes, Woody Herman and his Orchestra. A princess (Moore) with unexpected musical talent comes to N.Y.C. and becomes involved with a nightclub owner (O'Keefe). Kruger plays real-life Broadway producer Earl Carroll. Ambitious Republic Pictures musical isn't bad but is nothing to sing about (pun intended). Arden adds her usual pizzazz. Reissued as MOONSTRUCK MELODY.

Earl of Chicago, The (1940) 85m. **½ D: Richard Thorpe. Robert Montgomery, Edward Arnold, Reginald Owen, Edmund Gwenn. Montgomery can't put over farfetched tale of Chicago mobster inheriting English title. His awkward performance strains film's credibility.◗

Early Autumn SEE: **End of Summer, The**

Early Spring (1956-Japanese) 145m. *** D: Yasujiro Ozu. Chikage Awashima, Ryo Ikebe, Teiji Takahashi, Keiko Kishi, Chishu Ryu. Married office drone (Ikebe), dissatisfied with the drudgery of his daily life, becomes involved in an extramarital relationship with a cute, flirtatious coworker. Incisive exploration of isolation and alienation in post-WW2 Japan; the scenes of veterans who come together to reminisce are fascinating. Ozu scripted with Kôgo Noda. Not shown in the U.S. until 1974.◗

Early Summer (1951-Japanese) 125m. *** D: Yasujiro Ozu. Setsuko Hara, Chishu Ryu, Kuniko Miyake, Chikage Awashima, Chiyeko Higashiyama. Stirring tale of a woman (Hara) who, at 28, is aging by her society's standards. She resides with her elderly parents, and must deal with their pressure to marry the man of their choice. A sensitively rendered film about basic human emotions, made by a master filmmaker.▼●◗

Early to Bed (1936) 75m. **½ D: Norman Z. McLeod. Mary Boland, Charlie Ruggles, George Barbier, Gail Patrick, Robert McWade, Lucien Littlefield. Ruggles' sleepwalking involves him in shady adventure with gangsters. Boland and Ruggles are a perfect match.

Earrings of Madame de . . . , The (1953-French-Italian) 105m. **** D: Max Ophuls. Charles Boyer, Danielle Darrieux, Vittorio De Sica, Jean Debucourt, Lia de Léa. Captivating classic detailing the events that unravel after fickle Darrieux pawns the earrings presented her by husband Boyer. A knowing look at the effect of living a shallow, meaningless life. Masterfully acted and directed, with dazzling tracking shots. Screenplay by Marcel Achard, Ophuls, and Annette Wademant, from the novel by Louise de Vilmorin. ▼●◗

Earth (1930-Russian) 90m. **** D: Alexander Dovzhenko. Semyon Svashenko, Stepan Shkurat, Mikola Nademsky, Yelena

Maximova. Lyrical, deservedly famous classic about collective farming in the Ukraine, with peasants opposing a landowner and the arrival of a tractor symbolizing the transformation of Soviet society. This ode to the wonders of nature is loaded with beautiful imagery. Long a staple on all-time-best-film lists.▼▶

Earthbound (1940) **67m.** ****** D: Irving Pichel. Warner Baxter, Andrea Leeds, Lynn Bari, Charley Grapewin, Henry Wilcoxon, Elizabeth Patterson, Russell Hicks, Christian Rub, Ian Wolfe. Murdered Baxter's ghost remains on earth and receives guidance from heavenly emissary Grapewin to help his widow bring his killer to justice. Strange little fantasy is a deadly serious mixture of half-baked philosophy and heavy-handed special effects.

Earth Dies Screaming, The (1964-British) **62m.** ****½** D: Terence Fisher. Willard Parker, Virginia Field, Dennis Price, Vanda Godsell. Grim thriller with invaders taking over remote village; packs great initial suspense but labors.▶

Earth vs. the Flying Saucers (1956) **82m.** ******* D: Fred F. Sears. Hugh Marlowe, Joan Taylor, Donald Curtis, Morris Ankrum, Tom Browne Henry; voice of Paul Frees. Matter-of-fact presentation gives tremendous boost to familiar storyline (alien invaders order us to surrender peaceably—or else). Literate dialogue, subdued performances, and solid Ray Harryhausen effects make this a winner that belies its B origins nearly every step of the way. Also available in computer-colored version.▼▶

Earth vs the Spider (1958) **73m.** ****** D: Bert I. Gordon. Ed Kemmer, June Kenny, Gene Persson, Gene Roth, Hal Torey, Sally Fraser, June Jocelyn, Troy Patterson, Hank Patterson. A spider bigger than a bus is found in a cave; when it's apparently killed, it's put on display in a high school gym—where it is revived by the sounds of rock 'n' roll! Teenager-oriented Bert I. Gordon movie is more watchable than most of his giant-thing-on-the-loose films. Aka THE SPIDER. Remade in name only in 2001.▼▶

Earthworm Tractors (1936) **69m.** ****½** D: Ray Enright. Joe E. Brown, June Travis, Guy Kibbee, Dick Foran, Carol Hughes, Gene Lockhart, Olin Howland. Broad comedy with Joe as *Saturday Evening Post* character Alexander Botts, braggart and tractor salesman extraordinaire.▼▶

Easiest Way, The (1931) **74m.** ****½** D: Jack Conway. Constance Bennett, Adolphe Menjou, Robert Montgomery, Marjorie Rambeau, Anita Page, Clark Gable, Hedda Hopper. Bennett rises from dire poverty to a life of luxury after becoming the mistress of advertising mogul Menjou, but finds heartbreak when she falls for reporter Montgomery. Watered-down adaptation of notorious play about high-priced call girls starts out great, then turns into a standard romantic

triangle melodrama to satisfy the Hays Office. Gable has a small, but strong role in his first film as an MGM contract player.▶

East and West (1923-Austrian) **85m.** ******* D: Sidney M. Goldin, Ivan Abramson. Molly Picon, Jacob Kalich, Sidney M. Goldin, Saul Nathan, Laura Glucksman, Eugen Neufeld, Johannes Roth. Picon is funny and charming as Mollie Brown—formerly Brownstein—a spirited New Yorker who travels with her father to Galicia to attend a family wedding and attracts the attention of a poor, shy Yeshiva scholar (Kalich, Picon's real-life husband). Perceptively observes the clash between religious and secular lifestyles and Old and New World cultures. Also released as GOOD LUCK and MAZEL TOV.▼

East End Chant SEE: **Limehouse Blues**

Easter Parade (1948) **C-103m.** *****½** D: Charles Walters. Judy Garland, Fred Astaire, Peter Lawford, Ann Miller, Jules Munshin. Delightful Irving Berlin musical about Astaire trying to forget ex-dance partner Miller while rising to stardom with Garland. Too good to watch just at Eastertime. Musical highlights include Astaire's solo "Steppin' Out With My Baby," Miller's "Shaking the Blues Away," Fred and Judy's "A Couple of Swells," and the Fifth Avenue finale with Berlin's title song. Oscar winner for musical scoring (Johnny Green and Roger Edens). Story by Frances Goodrich and Albert Hackett; they also scripted with Sidney Sheldon.▼▶

East Meets West (1936-British) **75m.** ****½** D: Herbert Mason. George Arliss, Lucie Mannheim, Godfrey Tearle, Romney Brent, Ballard Berkeley, Ronald Ward, Norma Varden. Arliss is the whole show as a crafty sultan who plots to barter a treaty between England and Japan that will benefit his small, cash-starved country. Political thriller is notable today for presaging future world events. Not top-flight Arliss, but still enjoyable.▼

East of Borneo (1931) **76m.** ****½** D: George Melford. Rose Hobart, Charles Bickford, Georges Renavent, Lupita Tovar, Noble Johnson. Hobart treks to remote kingdom in the title locale in search of runaway husband Bickford, now court physician to a prince whose idea of fun is feeding his subjects to crocodiles. Pre-Code sexual situations highlight this rumble in the jungle, all set in the shadow of a volcano supernaturally set to erupt upon the death of the prince.▼▶

East of Eden (1955) **C-115m.** ******** D: Elia Kazan. James Dean, Julie Harris, Raymond Massey, Jo Van Fleet, Burl Ives, Richard Davalos, Albert Dekker, Lois Smith. Emotionally overwhelming adaptation of the John Steinbeck novel about two brothers' rivalry for the love of their father; affects today's generation as much as those who witnessed Dean's starring debut. Van Fleet (in film debut) won Oscar as boys' mother. Screenplay by Paul Osborn. Runs 118m.

with overture. Remade as TV miniseries. CinemaScope.▼●◗

East of Kilimanjaro (1957-U.S.-British-Italian) **C-75m.** *½ D: Arnold Belgard, Edoardo Capolino. Marshall Thompson, Gaby Andre, Fausto Tozzi, Kris Aschan, Rolf Aschan. Dull story of cameraman Thompson and efforts to halt virus affecting cattle in title region. Filmed in Africa. Originally ran 85m.; some prints 72m. Aka THE BIG SEARCH. Vistarama.

East of Shanghai SEE: **Rich and Strange**

East of Sumatra (1953) **C-82m.** **½ D: Budd Boetticher. Jeff Chandler, Marilyn Maxwell, Anthony Quinn, Suzan Ball, Peter Graves. Satisfactory actioner set on Pacific island. Chandler is mining engineer trying to prevent native uprising while romancing Maxwell; Quinn effective as villain. Based on a Louis L'Amour novel.

East of the River (1940) **73m.** **½ D: Alfred E. Green. John Garfield, Brenda Marshall, Marjorie Rambeau, William Lundigan, George Tobias, Jack LaRue, Douglas Fowley. Another variation of MANHATTAN MELODRAMA, with childhood pals Garfield and Lundigan growing up on opposite sides of the law. Rambeau is fine as Garfield's mother. ◗

East Side Kids (1940) **62m.** *½ D: Robert F. Hill. Harris Berger, Hally Chester, Frankie Burke, Donald Haines, Dave O'Brien, Dennis Moore, Vince Barnett, Leon Ames. Slum kids take on counterfeiters in this cheapie Sam Katzman–Monogram production. Despite title, this has nothing to do with the subsequent Leo Gorcey–Bobby Jordan–Huntz Hall series.▼◗

East Side Kids Meet Bela Lugosi, The SEE: **Ghosts on the Loose**

East Side of Heaven (1939) **90m.** *** D: David Butler. Bing Crosby, Joan Blondell, Mischa Auer, Irene Hervey, C. Aubrey Smith, Baby Sandy. Cute Crosby comedy with songs; Bing becomes guardian of abandoned baby, croons title tune, "Sing a Song of Sunbeams."◗

East Side, West Side (1949) **108m.** **½ D: Mervyn LeRoy. Barbara Stanwyck, James Mason, Ava Gardner, Van Heflin, Cyd Charisse, Gale Sondergaard, William Frawley, Nancy Davis (Reagan). Stanwyck and Mason have pivotal roles as chic N.Y.C. society couple with abundant marital woes, stirred up by alluring Gardner and understanding Heflin. Static MGM version of Marcia Davenport's superficial novel.▼◗

Easy Come, Easy Go (1947) **77m.** **½ D: John Farrow. Barry Fitzgerald, Diana Lynn, Sonny Tufts, Dick Foran, Frank McHugh, Allen Jenkins. Fitzgerald is his usual self as a horseplayer who refuses to let daughter Lynn get married.

Easy Go SEE: **Free and Easy**

Easy Life, The SEE: **Il Sorpasso**

Easy Living (1937) **86m.** *** D: Mitchell

Leisen. Jean Arthur, Edward Arnold, Ray Milland, Franklin Pangborn, William Demarest, Mary Nash, Luis Alberni. Millionaire Arnold throws spoiled wife's mink out the window; it drops on unsuspecting working girl Arthur. Arnold's son Milland, off making his career, falls in love. The girl: Arthur. Highlight: a mêlée in an Automat. Delightful comedy written by Preston Sturges. ▼◗

Easy Living (1949) **77m.** *** D: Jacques Tourneur. Victor Mature, Lizabeth Scott, Lucille Ball, Sonny Tufts, Lloyd Nolan, Paul Stewart, Jeff Donnell, Jack Paar, Art Baker. Mature is aging football star who can't adjust to impending retirement—especially under constant pressure from grasping wife Scott. Intelligent film from Irwin Shaw story, with good performance from Lucy as team secretary in love with Mature.▼◗

Easy to Love (1934) **61m.** **½ D: William Keighley. Genevieve Tobin, Adolphe Menjou, Mary Astor, Edward Everett Horton, Patricia Ellis, Hugh Herbert, Hobart Cavanaugh, Guy Kibbee. While Menjou plays footsie with Astor, his wife (Tobin) pretends to fool around with Horton. Simple but pleasing marital comedy, deftly played by a good cast.

Easy to Love (1953) **C-96m.** **½ D: Charles Walters. Esther Williams, Van Johnson, Tony Martin, John Bromfield, Carroll Baker. Pleasant Williams aquatic vehicle set at Florida's Cypress Gardens, with Johnson and Martin vying for her love. Spectacular production numbers by Busby Berkeley. Baker's first film.▼◗

Easy to Wed (1946) **C-110m.** **½ D: Edward Buzzell. Van Johnson, Esther Williams, Lucille Ball, Keenan Wynn, Cecil Kellaway, June Lockhart. Remake of LIBELED LADY can't hold a candle to original, but remains passable comedy, with Lucy in one of her first major comedy showcases.▼◗

Easy Virtue (1927-British) **89m.** **½ D: Alfred Hitchcock. Isabel Jeans, Franklin Dyall, Eric Bransby Williams, Ian Hunter, Robin Irvine, Violet Farebrother. Jeans suffers nobly as the wife of an alcoholic and the lover of a suicide in this melodramatic silent Hitchcock. Laughable dramatics but imaginatively shot, based on a Noel Coward play. Remade in 2009. ▼◗

Easy Way, The SEE: **Room for One More**

Ebb Tide (1937) **C-94m.** **½ D: James Hogan. Frances Farmer, Ray Milland, Oscar Homolka, Lloyd Nolan, Barry Fitzgerald. Hokey but entertaining outdoors picture with Nolan a madman on strange island. Remade as ADVENTURE ISLAND.

Eclipse (1962-French-Italian) **123m.** *** D: Michelangelo Antonioni. Alain Delon, Monica Vitti, Francisco Rabal, Lilla Brignone, Louis Seigner, Rossana Rory. Obvious but fascinating drama of alienation, Antonioni-style, about a translator (Vitti) who breaks up with her boyfriend and commences an affair with stockbroker Delon. Antonioni strikingly captures Vitti's isolation, and the world (and city of Rome) as filtered through her sensibilities. Third in a trilogy, following L'AVVENTURA and LA NOTTE. Original title: L'ECLISSE. ▼▶

Ecstasy (1933-Czech) **88m. **½ D: Gustav Machatý. Hedy Kiesler (Lamarr), Aribert Mog, Jaromir Rogoz, Leopold Kramer. A young bride discovers her husband is impotent and has an affair. Undistinguished romantic drama was once notorious for scenes of pre-Hollywood Hedy in the buff—and showing her in the throes of sexual passion. ▼▶

Eddie Cantor Story, The (1953) **C-116m.** *½ D: Alfred E. Green. Keefe Brasselle, Marilyn Erskine, Aline MacMahon, Marie Windsor. If Brasselle doesn't turn you off as energetic entertainer Cantor, MacMahon's Grandma Esther or a putty-nosed young actor (Jackie Barnett) playing Jimmy Durante certainly will. ▼▶

Eddy Duchin Story, The (1956) **C-123m.** **½ D: George Sidney. Tyrone Power, Kim Novak, Victoria Shaw, James Whitmore, Shepperd Strudwick, Frieda Inescort, Rex Thompson, Larry Keating. Glossy, largely invented bio of popular pianist-bandleader of the 1930s and '40s (with Carmen Cavallaro dubbing the keyboard tracks). You couldn't ask for two more attractive stars. CinemaScope. ▼▶

Edge of Darkness (1943) **120m.** ***½ D: Lewis Milestone. Errol Flynn, Ann Sheridan, Walter Huston, Nancy Coleman, Helmut Dantine, Judith Anderson, Ruth Gordon, John Beal, Roman Bohnen. Intense, compelling drama of underground movement in Norway during Nazi takeover in WW2. Eye-popping camerawork complements fine performances. Scripted by Robert Rossen, from William Woods' story. Also shown in computer-colored version. ▼▶

Edge of Doom (1950) **90m.** ** D: Mark Robson. Dana Andrews, Farley Granger, Joan Evans, Mala Powers, Paul Stewart, Adele Jergens. Poor but hardworking Granger loses control when his mother dies; only parish priest Andrews understands his torment. Turgid drama.

Edge of Eternity (1959) **C-80m.** ** D: Don Siegel. Cornel Wilde, Victoria Shaw, Mickey Shaughnessy, Edgar Buchanan, Rian Garrick, Jack Elam. Deputy sheriff Wilde tracks killers to Grand Canyon, leading to shoot-out on mining buckets suspended on cables way above canyon. CinemaScope. ▶

Edge of Fury (1958) **77m.** **½ D: Robert Gurney, Jr., Irving Lerner. Michael Higgins, Lois Holmes, Jean Allison, Doris Fesette, Malcolm Beggs, Craig Kelly, John Harvey. Young man released from mental institution takes out his murderous rage on a family that's renting his beach cottage. Very low-budget but genuinely disturbing shocker still packs a punch. First credit for future Oscar winner Conrad Hall, one of three cinematographers responsible for the moody photography. Filmed in 1953.

Edge of Hell (1956) **76m.** *½ D: Hugo Haas. Hugo Haas, Francesca de Scaffa, Ken Carlton, June Hammerstein. Offbeat, minor film of pauper Haas, his beloved dog, and small boy who enters the scene.

Edge of the City (1957) **85m.** **** D: Martin Ritt. John Cassavetes, Sidney Poitier, Jack Warden, Ruby Dee, Kathleen Maguire, Ruth White. Somber, realistic account of N.Y.C. waterfront life and corruption. Friendship of army deserter Cassavetes and dock worker Poitier, both conflicting with union racketeer Warden, provides focus for reflections on integration and integrity in lower-class society. Masterfully acted by all. Ritt's first film as director. Robert Alan Aurthur adapted his own 1955 TV play, *A Man Is Ten Feet Tall* (which was also film's British title), in which Poitier originated his role. Also shown in computer-colored version. ▶

Edge of the World, The (1937-British) **74m.** ***½ D: Michael Powell. Niall MacGinnis, Belle Chrystall, John Laurie, Finlay Currie, Eric Berry. The life and death of an isolated Shetland island as it is evacuated of its citizens. Engrossing drama, filmed on the North Sea isle of Foula. That's Powell playing the yachtsman in opening scene. Powell and those cast and crew still alive revisited the location 40 years later to film the documentary RETURN TO THE EDGE OF THE WORLD. ▼▶

Edison, the Man (1940) **107m.** *** D: Clarence Brown. Spencer Tracy, Rita Johnson, Lynne Overman, Charles Coburn, Gene Lockhart, Henry Travers, Felix Bressart. Sequel to YOUNG TOM EDISON perfectly casts Tracy as earnest inventor with passion for mechanical ingenuity. Facts and MGM fantasy combine well in sentimental treatment. Also shown in computer-colored version. ▼▶

Edmund Kean: Prince Among Lovers SEE: **Kean**

Edward, My Son (1949-British) **112m.** **½ D: George Cukor. Spencer Tracy, Deborah Kerr, Ian Hunter, James Donald, Mervyn Johns, Felix Aylmer, Leueen McGrath. Well-acted but talky, stagy drama in which brash, rags-to-riches Tracy pampers his son, failing to instill within him a sense of responsibility. Gimmicks of Tracy talking to viewer, title character never being shown, come off as forced. Based on a play by Robert Morley and Noel Langley. ▶

Eegah (1962) **C-92m.** BOMB D: Nicholas Merriwether (Arch Hall, Sr.). Arch Hall, Jr., Marilyn Manning, Richard Kiel, William Watters (Arch Hall, Sr.). In the desert near Palm Springs, a prehistoric giant (Kiel) falls in love with teenage Manning. A staple at "All-Time Worst Film" festivals. Arch Hall, Jr., sings the memorable "I Love You, Vickie."▼O◗

Egg and I, The (1947) **108m.** *** D: Chester Erskine. Claudette Colbert, Fred MacMurray, Marjorie Main, Louise Allbritton, Percy Kilbride, Richard Long, Billy House, Ida Moore, Esther Dale, Donald MacBride. Predictable but entertaining comedy from Betty MacDonald's bestseller about a city girl who goes along with her husband's dream of running a chicken farm. First appearance of Ma and Pa Kettle (Main and Kilbride). Later a short-lived TV series and likely inspiration for *Green Acres.*▼O◗

Egyptian, The (1954) **C-140m.** ** D: Michael Curtiz. Jean Simmons, Victor Mature, Gene Tierney, Michael Wilding, Bella Darvi, Peter Ustinov, Edmund Purdom, Judith Evelyn, Henry Daniell, John Carradine, Tommy Rettig. Ponderous, often unintentionally funny biblical-era soaper with Purdom cast as the sensitive, truth-seeking title character, a physician in ancient Egypt. Darvi's performance as a femme fatale is hilariously awful; see how much of her dialogue you can understand. Loosely based on Mika Waltari's novel. CinemaScope.▼O◗

8½ (1963-Italian) **135m.** **** D: Federico Fellini. Marcello Mastroianni, Claudia Cardinale, Anouk Aimée, Sandra Milo, Barbara Steele, Rossella Falk, Madeleine LeBeau, Caterina Boratto, Edra Gale, Mark Herron. Fellini's unique self-analytical movie casts Mastroianni as a filmmaker trying to develop a new project, amid frequent visions and countless subplots. A long, difficult, but fascinating film, overflowing with creative and technical wizardry. Certainly one of the most intensely personal statements ever made on celluloid. Screenplay by Fellini, Tullio Pinelli, Ennio Flaiano, and Brunello Rondi. Oscar winner for Costume Design and as Best Foreign Language Film. Reworked as a Broadway musical, *Nine,* which was filmed in 2009.▼O◗

Eighteen and Anxious (1957) **93m.** ** D: Joe Parker. Mary Webster, Ron Hagerthy, William Campbell, Jackie Loughery, Martha Scott, Jim Backus, Jackie Coogan, Yvonne Craig, Connie Stevens. Dated curio about a pregnant teenager.

Eight Iron Men (1952) **80m.** ** D: Edward Dmytryk. Bonar Colleano, Arthur Franz, Lee Marvin, Richard Kiley, Nick Dennis, James Griffith, Dick (Dickie) Moore, Barney Phillips, Mary Castle. Talky WW2 drama (based on a Broadway play) about a squadron holed up in a war-torn Italian town. Young Marvin stands out in a solid cast. Dreamlike flashbacks enable the film to include some sexy women. ◗

Eight O'Clock Walk (1952-British) **87m.** **½ D: Lance Comfort. Richard Attenborough, Cathy O'Donnell, Derek Farr, Ian Hunter. Courtroom drama manages to create pace and tension, involving murder trial; nicely played by Attenborough.

80,000 Suspects (1963-British) **113m.** ** D: Val Guest. Claire Bloom, Richard Johnson, Yolande Donlan, Cyril Cusack. Capable cast saddled with yarn of doctor (Johnson) and wife (Bloom) finding new love together while combating local small-pox outbreak. CinemaScope.

El (1952-Mexican) **88m.** **** D: Luis Buñuel. Arturo de Córdova, Delia Garcés, Luis Beristáin, José Pidal, Aurora Walker, Carlos Martínez Baena. A wealthy, religious middle-aged virgin marries a beautiful younger woman but becomes insanely jealous and possessive, making her a virtual prisoner. One of Buñuel's great films, demonstrating his genius for tiny, subtle details to depict a pathological personality. Chilling, darkly humorous study of paranoia and obsession, with a classic final shot. Aka THIS STRANGE PASSION. ▼

El Alamein (1953) **67m.** ** D: Fred F. Sears. Scott Brady, Edward Ashley, Rita Moreno, Michael Pate. No surprises in WW2 desert actioner with Brady heading group being attacked by Nazis.

El Bruto (1952-Mexican) **83m.** ** D: Luis Buñuel. Pedro Armendariz, Katy Jurado, Andres Soler, Rosita Arenas. Armendariz is conned by scheming boss into harassing tenants he unfairly wants to evict; seduced by the boss's lusty mistress (Jurado), he then falls in love with a girl whose father he accidentally murdered. Simplistic, quite unsubtle melodrama, a disappointment from a master filmmaker. Aka THE BRUTE. ▼◗

El Cid (1961) **C-184m.** *** D: Anthony Mann. Charlton Heston, Sophia Loren, Raf Vallone, Genevieve Page, John Fraser, Gary Raymond, Hurd Hatfield, Massimo Serato, Herbert Lom, Michael Hordern. Mammoth Samuel Bronston spectacle, shot in Spain, celebrates that country's 11th-century warrior hero. When not clashing with Moors, Heston's Cid romances his equally statuesque wife (Loren). Uneven dramatics are sold by top-scale production values, including Miklos Rozsa's famed score. One of the better historical epics of its time. Runs 188m. with overture, intermission/entr'acte, exit music. Super Technirama 70. ▼◗

Eleanor Roosevelt Story, The (1965) **91m.** ***½ D: Richard Kaplan. Narrated by Archibald Macleish, Eric Sevareid, Francis Cole. Oscar-winning documentary account of the former First Lady, a great American citizen who overcame personal obstacles and became a beacon of human kindness. A most effective music score by Ezra Laderman.▼◗

Electronic Monster, The (1957-British) **72m.** *½ D: Montgomery Tully. Rod Cameron, Mary Murphy, Meredith Edwards, Peter

Illing. Cameron investigates an actor's mysterious death, revealing strange experiments in electronic hypnosis at a clinic. Blah sci-fi programmer. Aka ESCAPEMENT. ▼▶

Elena and Her Men SEE: **Paris Does Strange Things**

Elephant Boy (1937-British) **80m.** *** D: Robert Flaherty, Zoltan Korda. Sabu, W. E. Holloway, Walter Hudd, Allan Jeayes, Bruce Gordon, D. J. Williams. Interesting early-day docudrama about native boy (Sabu, in film debut) who claims he knows location of mythic elephant herd. ▼●▶

Elephant Gun (1958-British) **C-84m.** ** D: Ken Annakin. Belinda Lee, Michael Craig, Patrick McGoohan, Anna Gaylor, Eric Pohlmann, Pamela Stirling. Jungle love triangle has virtue of on-location shooting in Africa. Original British title: NOR THE MOON BY NIGHT.

Elephant Stampede, The SEE: **Bomba and the Elephant Stampede**

Elephant Walk (1954) **C-103m.** ** D: William Dieterle. Elizabeth Taylor, Dana Andrews, Peter Finch, Abraham Sofaer. Overblown melodrama set on Ceylon tea plantation, with Taylor as Finch's new bride who must cope with environment and his father complex. Pachyderm stampede climax comes none too soon. Vivien Leigh, replaced by Taylor, can be seen in long shots. ▼▶

Elevator to the Gallows (1958-French) **91m.** ***½ D: Louis Malle. Jeanne Moreau, Maurice Ronet, Georges Poujouly, Yori Bertin, Jean Wall, Charles Denner, Jean-Claude Brialy, Lino Ventura. Malle's experience making documentaries informs his first fictional feature, as an amorous man and woman attempt to pull off the perfect crime. Filmed by Henri Decaë on the streets of Paris in a bracing style that anticipates the New Wave. Famous score improvised by Miles Davis. Original U.S. title: FRANTIC. ▼▶

Eleven Men and a Girl SEE: **Maybe It's Love**

Elizabeth of Ladymead (1948-British) **C-97m.** *** D: Herbert Wilcox. Anna Neagle, Hugh Williams, Michael Laurence, Bernard Lee, Nicholas Phipps, Isabel Jeans. Engaging comedy-drama in four episodes from husband-wife team of Wilcox-Neagle. Latter charming as English lady-of-the-manor with mind of her own welcoming home four husbands from four different British wars. Star vehicle, unsuccessful when released, quite intriguing today for its depiction of woman's role in English society. Some prints run 90m. ▼▶

Elizabeth the Queen SEE: **Private Lives of Elizabeth and Essex, The**

Ella Cinders (1926) **60m.** *** D: Alfred E. Green. Colleen Moore, Lloyd Hughes, Vera Lewis, Doris Baker, Emily Gerdes, Jed Prouty. Moore is in top form as the much-abused stepdaughter of crotchety old Lewis,

who wins a contest and treks off to Hollywood to seek fame in the movies. Bright and peppy, with Harry Langdon on hand in a most amusing cameo. Based on a popular comic strip. ▼▶

Ellery Queen Perhaps the most successful series of detective stories ever written, the Ellery Queen mysteries rank as one of the least successful film series. A few scattered attempts to film Queen stories in the 1930s with Donald Cook and Eddie Quillan never aroused much interest. Then in 1940, Columbia began a series starring Ralph Bellamy as Ellery Queen, Charley Grapewin as his Inspector father, Margaret Lindsay as his Girl Friday Nikki, and James Burke as Inspector Queen's dim-witted aide. The very first entry, ELLERY QUEEN, MASTER DETECTIVE, belied its title by making Bellamy an incredible "comic" bumbler, an inexplicable characterization that lasted through all of Bellamy's films in the series. Heavy doses of comedy relief in entries like ELLERY QUEEN AND THE MURDER RING were not offset by solid mystery angles, and the films, though only one hour long, moved like molasses. Making William Gargan the lead character in 1942 did not help matters, with the actual suspects becoming more obvious than ever. Gargan's three efforts as Queen were undistinguished, and his last episode, ENEMY AGENTS MEET ELLERY QUEEN, was also the last in the short-lived series.

ELLERY QUEEN

The Spanish Cape Mystery (1935)
The Mandarin Mystery (1936)
Ellery Queen, Master Detective (1940)
Ellery Queen's Penthouse Mystery (1941)
Ellery Queen and the Perfect Crime (1941)
Ellery Queen and the Murder Ring (1941)
Close Call for Ellery Queen (1942)
Desperate Chance for Ellery Queen (1942)
Enemy Agents Meet Ellery Queen (1942)

Ellery Queen and the Murder Ring (1941) **65m.** *½ D: James Hogan. Ralph Bellamy, Margaret Lindsay, Charley Grapewin, Mona Barrie, Paul Hurst, James Burke, Blanche Yurka, George Zucco, Tom Dugan, Leon Ames. Queen (stupider than ever!) helps Pop when murder strikes, this time in a private hospital. Bellamy's final appearance in this disappointing series. Loosely adapted from *The Dutch Shoe Mystery.*

Ellery Queen and the Perfect Crime (1941) **68m.** *½ D: James Hogan. Ralph Bellamy, Margaret Lindsay, Charley Grapewin, Spring Byington, H. B. Warner, James Burke, Douglass Dumbrille, John Beal, Linda Hayes, Sidney Blackmer, Walter Kingsford, Charles Lane. Nothing perfect at all in this entry about the murder of a shady stockbroker.

Ellery Queen, Master Detective (1940)

66m. ** D: Kurt Neumann. Ralph Bellamy, Margaret Lindsay, Charley Grapewin, James Burke, Michael Whalen, Marsha Hunt, Fred Niblo, Charles Lane, Douglas Fowley, Katherine DeMille. The "master" sleuth is turned into a buffoon in this initial series entry, centering on the murder of a millionaire at a health spa. Lindsay has some good moments as Nikki Porter. Too much talk and too little intrigue.

Ellery Queen's Penthouse Mystery (1941) **69m.** ** D: James Hogan. Ralph Bellamy, Margaret Lindsay, Charley Grapewin, Anna May Wong, James Burke, Eduardo Ciannelli, Frank Albertson, Ann Doran, Charles Lane, Russell Hicks, Tom Dugan, Mantan Moreland. Detective Queen helps out his police inspector father (Grapewin) in the case of a murdered Chinese entertainer who was smuggling jewels. Wong is good as always, but wasted here. Slow going.

Elmer Gantry (1960) **C-145m.** ***½ D: Richard Brooks. Burt Lancaster, Jean Simmons, Dean Jagger, Arthur Kennedy, Shirley Jones, Patti Page, Edward Andrews, Hugh Marlowe, John McIntire, Rex Ingram. Lancaster gives a vibrant Oscar-winning performance as the salesman with the gift of gab who joins evangelist Simmons' barnstorming troupe in the 1920s Midwest. Jones won Academy Award as his jilted girlfriend turned prostitute; Brooks also won an Oscar for his sprawling screenplay from Sinclair Lewis's trenchant novel.▼●▶

Elmer, the Great (1933) **74m.** *** D: Mervyn LeRoy. Joe E. Brown, Patricia Ellis, Frank McHugh, Claire Dodd, Preston S. Foster, Russell Hopton, Sterling Holloway, Emma Dunn, J. Carrol Naish. Brown is at his best as the home-run–hitting title character, a loud-mouthed rube who arrives in the major leagues with the Chicago Cubs. Based on a play by Ring Lardner and George M. Cohan. The second in Brown's baseball trilogy, following FIREMAN, SAVE MY CHILD and followed by ALIBI IKE. Originally made as FAST COMPANY; reworked as THE COWBOY QUARTERBACK.▶

Elopement (1951) **82m.** ** D: Henry Koster. Clifton Webb, Anne Francis, Charles Bickford, William Lundigan, Reginald Gardiner. Tame proceedings despite Webb's arch performance as Francis' father, who disapproves of her marriage to Lundigan.

El Paso (1949) **C-103m.** ** D: Lewis R. Foster. John Payne, Gail Russell, Sterling Hayden, George "Gabby" Hayes, Dick Foran, Eduardo Noriega, Henry Hull, Mary Beth Hughes, H. B. Warner, Arthur Space. Good cast boosts this otherwise routine Western set in post–Civil War Texas, with lawyer Payne coming to title locale, locking horns with corrupt bully Hayden and his henchmen.

Elusive Corporal, The (1962-French) **108m.** **½ D: Jean Renoir. Jean-Pierre Cassel, Claude Brasseur, Claude Rich, O. E. Hasse, Jean Carmet. Pointed if predictable chronicle of French corporal who attempts to escape with his pals from a German prison camp during WW2. Sobering look at friendship and freedom, which Renoir explored more successfully in other, earlier films. The wry comic touches are an asset.▼●▶

Elusive Pimpernel, The (1950-British) **C-109m.** *** D: Michael Powell, Emeric Pressburger. David Niven, Margaret Leighton, Cyril Cusack, Jack Hawkins, Arlette Marchal, Robert Coote, Patrick Macnee. Colorful remake of THE SCARLET PIMPERNEL. Niven is British fop who secretly aids victims of Reign of Terror; lively fun. This was filmed as a musical—you can tell where the numbers were cut! Released in U.S. in 1954 as THE FIGHTING PIMPERNEL.▼

Embraceable You (1948) **80m.** ** D: Felix Jacoves. Dane Clark, Geraldine Brooks, S. Z. Sakall, Wallace Ford. Tough-guy Clark injures young girl, then falls in love with her, in this sentimental romance.

Emergency Call (1933) **61m.** ** D: Edward L. Cahn. William Boyd, Wynne Gibson, William Gargan, Betty Furness, Reginald Mason, George E. Stone. Boyd (pre-Hopalong Cassidy) is a naïve young surgeon who teams with sassy ambulance driver Gargan to battle racketeers trying to muscle in on hospital business. Minor programmer co-written by Joseph L. Mankiewicz does have a certain cheesy appeal.

Emergency Wedding (1950) **78m.** ** D: Edward Buzzell. Barbara Hale, Larry Parks, Una Merkel, Jim Backus, Queenie Smith. Sterile remake of YOU BELONG TO ME detailing jealous Parks who thinks new wife, doctor Hale, spends too much time with her male patients.

Emil and the Detectives (1964) **C-99m.** *½ D: Peter Tewksbury. Walter Slezak, Bryan Russell, Roger Mobley, Heinz Schubert, Peter Erlich, Cindy Cassell. Turgid Disney version of Erich Kastner's children's book about a young boy who is robbed and determines to nail the thief with the help of young detective friends. Filmed in Germany, where it was made before in 1931.▼▶

Emma (1932) **73m.** *** D: Clarence Brown. Marie Dressler, Richard Cromwell, Jean Hersholt, Myrna Loy, John Miljan, Leila Bennett. Dressler is at her best, as down-to-earth woman who works as housemaid-nanny for family and eventually marries widowed father (Hersholt). Sentimental movie never cloys, thanks to wonderful Marie. Frances Marion's story was scripted by Leonard Praskins and Zelda Sears.▶

Emperor Jones, The (1933) **72m.** **½ D: Dudley Murphy. Paul Robeson, Dudley Digges, Frank Wilson, Fredi Washington,

Ruby Elzy. Robeson plays Pullman porter who escapes from chain gang and improbably becomes king of a Caribbean island. Pretentious adaptation of Eugene O'Neill play derives its chief interest and value from Robeson himself. Look for Moms Mabley in bit part. ▼●◗

Emperor's Candlesticks, The (1937) 89m. **½ D: George Fitzmaurice. William Powell, Luise Rainer, Robert Young, Maureen O'Sullivan, Frank Morgan, Emma Dunn, Douglass Dumbrille. Powell and Rainer play cat-and-mouse as spies on opposite sides of the fence who (naturally) fall in love, in this enjoyable but wildly far-fetched story set in Czarist Russia and Vienna. Based on a novel by Baroness Orczy (who also wrote *The Scarlet Pimpernel*). ◗

Emperor Waltz, The (1948) **C-106m.** **½ D: Billy Wilder. Bing Crosby, Joan Fontaine, Roland Culver, Lucile Watson, Richard Haydn, Sig Ruman. Lavish but lackluster musical set in Franz Joseph Austria with Bing selling record players to royalty. Awfully schmaltzy material for writer-director Wilder. Filmed in 1946. Jasper National Park in Alberta, Canada, fills in for Tyrolean Alps. ▼◗

Employees' Entrance (1933) 75m. *** D: Roy Del Ruth. Warren William, Loretta Young, Wallace Ford, Alice White, Allen Jenkins. Zesty pre-Code look at life in a department store and its ruthless, amoral manager. Gripping, funny, outrageous, racy. Based on a stage play. ▼●◗

Empty Canvas, The (1963-French-Italian) 118m. *½ D: Damiano Damiani. Bette Davis, Horst Buchholz, Catherine Spaak, Isa Miranda, Lea Padovani, Daniela Rocca, Georges Wilson. Artist Buchholz is obsessed with model Spaak, eventually decorates her naked body with bank notes. Davis is his wealthy mother; hopefully, she was well paid for her time. Based on an Alberto Moravia novel. ▼

Enchanted April (1935) 66m. **½ D: Harry Beaumont. Ann Harding, Frank Morgan, Katharine Alexander, Reginald Owen, Jane Baxter, Ralph Forbes, Jessie Ralph, Charles Judels, Rafaela Ottiano. Nicely realized adaptation of Elizabeth von Arnim's novel about two repressed Englishwomen who leave their husbands to rent an Italian villa for a month—and blossom in the rarefied atmosphere. Harding is ideal in the lead, but Owen is way over the top as a British blowhard. Improved upon by the 1991 remake.

Enchanted Cottage, The (1945) 92m. **½ D: John Cromwell. Dorothy McGuire, Robert Young, Herbert Marshall, Mildred Natwick, Spring Byington, Hillary Brooke. Adaptation of Arthur Pinero play about two misfits, a homely woman and a disfigured man, who find each other beautiful in the enchanted cottage. Never quite as good

as you'd like it to be. Previously filmed in 1924. Some prints run 78m. ▼●◗

Enchanted Forest (1945) **C-78m.** **½ D: Lew Landers. Edmund Lowe, Brenda Joyce, Billy Severn, Harry Davenport, John Litel. Nicely done story of young boy who learns about life from old man who lives amid nature in the forest. ▼◗

Enchanted Island (1958) **C-94m.** *½ D: Allan Dwan. Dana Andrews, Jane Powell, Don Dubbins, Arthur Shields. Miscast, low-budget version of Herman Melville's *Typee*. Andrews is deserter from American whaling ship who finds love with native girl Powell on South Sea island; some minor uprisings by local cannibals for good measure. ▼

Enchantment (1948) 102m. *** D: Irving Reis. David Niven, Teresa Wright, Evelyn Keyes, Farley Granger, Jayne Meadows, Leo G. Carroll. Weepy romancer with elderly Niven recalling his tragic love as he watches great-niece Keyes' romance with Granger. ▼●◗

Encore (1952-British) 85m. *** D: Pat Jackson, Anthony Pelissier, Harold French. Nigel Patrick, Roland Culver, Kay Walsh, Glynis Johns, Terence Morgan. Entertaining trilogy of Somerset Maugham stories: brothers try to outdo one another over money; busybody matron almost ruins ship cruise; apprehensive circus performer faces a crisis.

End of Summer, The (1961-Japanese) **C-103m.** *** D: Yasujiro Ozu. Ganjiro Nakamura, Setsuko Hara, Yôko Tsukasa, Michiyo Aratama, Keiju Kobayashi, Masahiko Shimazu, Daisuke Katô, Reiko Dan, Chishu Ryu. Astute, deliberately paced slice of life about a Japanese family whose relationships reflect changing times in the "new" Japan. Set during a hot summer that refuses to end, as the characters constantly observe. Along the way, Ozu (who scripted with Kôgo Noda) ruminates on the inevitability of death and the importance of having a happy life. Aka EARLY AUTUMN. ◗

End of the Affair, The (1955-British) 106m. **½ D: Edward Dmytryk. Deborah Kerr, Van Johnson, John Mills, Peter Cushing, Michael Goodliffe. Graham Greene's mystic-religious novel about a wartime love affair in London loses much in screen version, especially from mismatched stars. Remade in 1999. ▼◗

End of the River, The (1947-British) 80m. ** D: Derek Twist. Sabu, Bibi Ferreira, Esmond Knight, Torin Thatcher, Robert Douglas. Native boy Sabu fights for acceptance in white world; ambitious drama suffers from mediocre casting.

End of the Road, The (1936-British) 72m. *** D: Alex Bryce. Harry Lauder, Ruth Haven, Ethel Glendinning, Bruce Seton, Margaret Moffatt, Campbell Gullan. Lauder survives various misfortunes as he travels the countryside in his caravan, entertaining people wherever he goes. Utterly charming vehicle for the great Scottish entertainer, filled with wonderful songs; he's an absolute natural on camera. Released in U.S. as SONG OF THE ROAD.

Enemy Agents Meet Ellery Queen (1942) **64m. *½ D:** James Hogan. William Gargan, Margaret Lindsay, Charley Grapewin, Gale Sondergaard, Gilbert Roland, Sig Rumann, James Burke. Queen takes on Nazi spies in this final entry to an undistinguished series.

Enemy Below, The (1957) **C-98m. *** D:** Dick Powell. Robert Mitchum, Curt Jurgens, Theodore Bikel, Doug McClure, Russell Collins, David Hedison. Fine submarine chase tale, which manages to garner interest from usual crew interaction of U.S. vs. Germany in underwater action; the special effects for this earned Walter Rossi an Academy Award. CinemaScope. ▼●)

Enemy From Space SEE: **Quatermass II**
Enemy General, The (1960) **74m. **½ D:** George Sherman. Van Johnson, Jean-Pierre Aumont, Dany Carrel, John Van Dreelen. OSS officer Johnson and French resistance leader Aumont join forces to rescue Nazi general Van Dreelen who wants to defect to Allies; satisfactory handling of middling material.

Enforcer, The (1951) **87m. *** D:** Bretaigne Windust. Humphrey Bogart, Zero Mostel, Ted de Corsia, Everett Sloane, Roy Roberts. When informer de Corsia dies, D.A. Bogart has to find another way to prove that Sloane is the head of a murder-for-hire ring. Loosely based on the true story of Murder, Inc., this is a generally effective, moody thriller. Mostel is particularly good as a frightened crook. ▼●)

English Without Tears SEE: **Her Man Gilbey**

Enjo (1958-Japanese) **96m. ***½ D:** Kon Ichikawa. Raizo Ichikawa, Tatsuya Nakadai, Ganjiro Nakamura, Yoko Uraji, Tanie Kitabayashi. Troubled young novice priest Ichikawa cannot handle corruption around him and burns down a temple. Perceptive psychological study of a human being's destruction; based on a Yukio Mishima novel, fashioned around a true story. Aka CONFLAGRATION. Daieiscope. ▼

Ensign Pulver (1964) **C-104m. ** D:** Joshua Logan. Robert Walker, Jr., Burl Ives, Walter Matthau, Tommy Sands, Millie Perkins, Kay Medford. Flat sequel to MISTER ROBERTS has Walker sinking in Jack Lemmon role amid synthetic seaboard and coral-isle shenanigans. Worth noting for its large cast of future stars: Larry Hagman, Gerald O'Loughlin, Al Freeman, Jr., James Farentino, James Coco, Diana Sands, and Jack Nicholson. Panavision. ▼●)

Enter Arsene Lupin (1944) **72m. ** D:** Ford Beebe. Charles Korvin, Ella Raines,

J. Carrol Naish, George Dolenz, Gale Sondergaard. Good supporting cast of villains gives zest to tame tale of naive heroine possessing a wealth of jewels.

Enter Madame (1935) **83m. **½ D:** Elliott Nugent. Elissa Landi, Cary Grant, Lynne Overman, Sharon Lynne, Frank Albertson. Grant marries opera star Landi and winds up taking back seat to her career; pleasant romantic comedy.

Entertainer, The (1960-British) **104m. ***½ D:** Tony Richardson. Laurence Olivier, Brenda De Banzie, Roger Livesey, Joan Plowright, Daniel Massey, Alan Bates, Shirley Anne Field, Albert Finney, Thora Hird. Seedy vaudevillian (Olivier, re-creating his stage role) ruins everyone's life and won't catch on. Film captures flavor of chintzy seaside resort, complementing Olivier's brilliance as egotistical song-and-dance man. Coscripted by John Osborne, from his play. Film debuts of Bates and Finney. Olivier and Plowright married the following year. Remade as a 1976 TVM starring Jack Lemmon. ▼●)

Equinox Flower (1958-Japanese) **C-118m. *** D:** Yasujiro Ozu. Shin Saburi, Fujiko Yamamoto, Kinuyo Tanaka, Ineko Arima, Chishu Ryu. One of Ozu's final films, and his first in color, is a moving story of a young woman who clashes with her father when she rejects an arranged marriage and chooses a man of her own to wed. Another gentle and quietly observant study of parents and children from Ozu, this time imbued with a sense of melancholy over traditional ways being supplanted by impersonal modern society. Original title: HIGANBANA. ▼)

Erik the Conqueror (1961-Italian) **C-81m. ** D:** Mario Bava. Cameron Mitchell, Alice Kessler, Ellen Kessler, Françoise Christophe. Unexceptional account of 10th-century Viking life, with Mitchell fighting for virtue and love. Released on video as THE INVADERS at 88m. Dyaliscope. ▼)

Erotikon (1920-Swedish) **97m. *** D:** Mauritz Stiller. Tora Téje, Lars Hanson, Karin Molander, Anders De Wahl, Vilhelm Bryde, Torsten Hammarén. Satirical, sophisticated drawing room comedy (based on a play) about attraction and flirtation, involving a stuffy, well-heeled entomology professor, his chic adulterous wife, his sweetly devoted niece, a sculptor who is his loyal best friend, and an amorous baron. Stiller (who also cowrote the screenplay) pokes fun at proper Swedish society.)

Errand Boy, The (1961) **92m. **½ D:** Jerry Lewis. Jerry Lewis, Brian Donlevy, Howard McNear, Sig Ruman, Fritz Feld, Iris Adrian, Kathleen Freeman, Doodles Weaver, Renee Taylor. Jerry on the loose in a movie studio has its moments. Long string of gags provide the laughter; veteran character actors produce the sparkle. ▼●)

[197]

Escapade (1935) **89m.** **✶✶** D: Robert Z. Leonard. William Powell, Luise Rainer, Frank Morgan, Virginia Bruce, Reginald Owen, Mady Christians, Laura Hope Crews, Henry Travers. Married woman is persuaded to pose for a roguish Viennese artist, but when the semi-nude illustration is printed, it causes a potential scandal. Sophisticated comedy/drama was Rainer's Hollywood debut film; she and Powell are charming, but the film's initial sparkle eventually goes flat—as the picture goes on. Remake of the much superior (and sexier) Austrian film MASKERADE (1934).

Escapade (1955-British) **87m.** **✶✶✶** D: Philip Leacock. John Mills, Yvonne Mitchell, Alastair Sim, Jeremy Spenser, Andrew Ray, Marie Lohr, Peter Asher. Mills is a professional pacifist whose life is anything but tranquil; his three sons, fearing that their parents are about to be divorced, react in a most unusual manner. Ambitious, insightful, solidly acted drama about the cynicism and hypocrisy of adults and the idealism of youth. Stick with this. Roger MacDougall's play was adapted by Donald Ogden Stewart (under the pseudonym Gilbert Holland). ▼

Escapade in Japan (1957) **C-93m.** **✶✶** D: Arthur Lubin. Cameron Mitchell, Teresa Wright, Jon Provost, Roger Nakagawa, Philip Ober, Kuniko Miyake, Susumu Fujita. Stunning location filming in Japan is the prime asset of this forgettable adventure about two young boys, one American and the other Japanese, and their search for the former's parents. Clint Eastwood appears briefly as a pilot. Technirama. ▼

Escape (1940) **104m.** **✶✶✶** D: Mervyn LeRoy. Norma Shearer, Robert Taylor, Conrad Veidt, Nazimova, Felix Bressart, Albert Basserman, Philip Dorn, Bonita Granville, Blanche Yurka. Countess Shearer, mistress of Nazi general Veidt, helps Taylor get his mother (Nazimova) out of German concentration camp before WW2; polished, with sterling cast. Based on Ethel Vance's 1939 best-seller. ▶

Escape (1948) **78m.** **✶✶✶** D: Joseph L. Mankiewicz. Rex Harrison, Peggy Cummins, William Hartnell, Norman Wooland, Jill Esmond, Frederick Piper, Marjorie Rhodes, Betty Ann Davies, Cyril Cusack. Intelligent, well-paced story of law-abiding man for whom a chance encounter leads to a prison sentence; morally outraged, he determines to escape. Harrison is excellent as the cerebral hero of this John Galsworthy story (which was filmed before in 1930). Shot on natural locations around England. Screenplay by Philip Dunne.

Escape From East Berlin (1962) **94m.** **✶✶** D: Robert Siodmak. Don Murray, Christine Kaufmann, Werner Klemperer, Ingrid van Bergen, Karl Schell. East German chauffeur becomes determined to tunnel to West Berlin, to allow his family and new girlfriend to escape Communist domination. Dated and propagandistic but based on true events. ▶

Escape From Fort Bravo (1953) **C-98m.** **✶✶✶** D: John Sturges. William Holden, Eleanor Parker, John Forsythe, Polly Bergen, William Demarest, William Campbell, Richard Anderson. Well-executed Civil War–era Western with Holden a hard-nosed cavalry captain at an Arizona fort where Confederate prisoners are held; both sides end up tangling with Indians. ▼▶

Escape From Red Rock (1958) **75m.** **✶½** D: Edward Bernds. Brian Donlevy, Jay C. Flippen, Eilene Janssen, Gary Murray. Modest oater of rancher and girl involved in theft, being chased into Indian country by pursuing posse. Regalscope.

Escape From San Quentin (1957) **81m.** BOMB D: Fred F. Sears. Johnny Desmond, Merry Anders, Richard Devon, Roy Engel. Drab film has Desmond as runaway convict who decides to give himself and buddy up to police. ▶

Escape From Yesterday SEE: **La Bandera**

Escape From Zahrain (1962) **C-93m.** **✶½** D: Ronald Neame. Yul Brynner, Sal Mineo, Madlyn Rhue, Jack Warden, James Mason, Jay Novello. Plodding film of five prisoners escaping from jail in Mideastern country, being chased across desert. Nice photography at least. Panavision. ▶

Escape in the Desert (1945) **81m.** **✶✶** D: Edward A. Blatt. Jean Sullivan, Philip Dorn, Irene Manning, Helmut Dantine, Alan Hale, Samuel S. Hinds, Bill Kennedy. Tame reworking of THE PETRIFIED FOREST, updated to WW2. Dutch flyer Dorn and others confront a quartet of escaped Nazi prisoners-of-war at an isolated desert hotel.

Escape in the Fog (1945) **65m.** **✶✶** D: Oscar (Budd) Boetticher. Nina Foch, William Wright, Otto Kruger, Konstantin Shayne. Capable but unexceptional programmer of girl who has strange dream of murder being committed and encounters the dream victim in real life. Look fast for Shelley Winters.

Escape Me Never (1947) **104m.** **✶½** D: Peter Godfrey. Errol Flynn, Ida Lupino, Eleanor Parker, Gig Young, Reginald Denny, Isobel Elsom. Sappy remake of 1935 Elisabeth Bergner vehicle, with Lupino as an itinerant waif (!) and Flynn as struggling composer who marries her but takes up with his brother's aristocratic fiancée (Parker). Forget it. ▼▶

Escapement SEE: **Electronic Monster, The**

Escape Route SEE: **I'll Get You**

Escape to Burma (1955) **C-87m.** **✶✶** D: Allan Dwan. Barbara Stanwyck, Robert Ryan, David Farrar, Murvyn Vye, Lisa Montell, Reginald Denny. Stanwyck rides herd over a tea plantation—and a pack of wild animals—but doesn't quite know how to deal with a wanted man who seeks refuge. Cast does what it can with pulp material. SuperScope. ▼▶

Escape to Glory (1940) **74m.** ******* D: John Brahm. Constance Bennett, Pat O'Brien, John Halliday, Alan Baxter, Melville Cooper. British ship is attacked by German sub at outbreak of WW2, giving pause to various passengers on-board—including a German doctor. Thoughtful, atmospheric B picture with minimal amount of clichés.

Escort for Hire (1960-British) **C-66m.** ****** D: Godfrey Grayson. June Thorburn, Noel Trevarthan, Peter Murray, Jill Melford, Guy Middleton. Clichéd murder yarn, with Trevarthan an out-of-work actor joining escort service, becoming involved in murder.

Escort West (1959) **75m.** ****½** D: Francis D. Lyon. Victor Mature, Elaine Stewart, Faith Domergue, Reba Waters, Noah Beery (Jr.), Leo Gordon, Rex Ingram. Fairly good Western with Confederate soldier and 10-year-old daughter heading West, encountering two women who survived renegade attack and saved Army payroll. CinemaScope.▼▶

Eskimo (1933) **113m.** ******* D: W. S. Van Dyke. Mala, Lotus Long, Joe Sawyer. After filming WHITE SHADOWS IN THE SOUTH SEAS and going to Africa for TRADER HORN, Van Dyke took an expedition to the Arctic for this raw and sexually frank anthropological docudrama about an Eskimo hunter who is wanted by the police for killing the white trader who raped his wife. Dramatic episodes are well integrated with beautifully photographed landscapes and wildlife scenes. Mostly native cast speaks in their natural language with subtitles translating the dialogue. Based on two books by Peter Freuchen, who plays the villainous captain of the trading ship; Van Dyke appears as a Canadian Mountie. Conrad Nervig's editing won an Oscar.

Espionage (1937) **67m.** ****½** D: Kurt Neumann. Edmund Lowe, Madge Evans, Paul Lukas, Ketti Gallian, Skeets Gallagher, Leonid Kinskey, Billy Gilbert. Slick, fast-paced MGM B pic. Lowe and Evans are rival reporters on the trail of arms tycoon Lukas aboard the Orient Express.

Espionage Agent (1939) **83m.** ****** D: Lloyd Bacon. Joel McCrea, Brenda Marshall, George Bancroft, Jeffrey Lynn, James Stephenson, Martin Kosleck. Formula spy caper with McCrea and Marshall tracking down the head of notorious spy ring.

Esther and the King (1960-U.S.-Italian) **C-109m.** ****** D: Raoul Walsh. Joan Collins, Richard Egan, Denis O'Dea, Sergio Fantoni. Cardboard biblical costumer pretends to recreate 4th-century B.C. Persia, with stony performances by Egan and Collins as the king and the Jewish maiden he wants to replace murdered queen. Filmed in Italy. CinemaScope.▼▶

Esther Waters (1948-British) **108m.** ****½** D: Ian Dalrymple. Kathleen Ryan, Dirk Bogarde, Cyril Cusack, Ivor Barnard, Fay Compton, Mary Clare. Well-appointed account of rogue Bogarde (in starring debut) involved with lovely damsels frequenting the racetracks; set in 19th-century England. Film bogs down into soaper of gloomy married life, marring initial zest.▶

Eternal Love (1929) **71m.** ****½** D: Ernst Lubitsch. John Barrymore, Camilla Horn, Victor Varconi, Hobart Bosworth, Bodil Rosing, Mona Rico. In the early 19th century, a small Swiss town is overrun by the invading French Army, inciting rebellion and igniting souls on both sides. Silent film has a bit of the famed Lubitsch touch but functions primarily as a mountain adventure. "Alpine" scenery is really the spectacular Canadian Rockies near Banff, Alberta. From the novel *Der Koenig der Bernina* by Jakob Christoph Heer. Remade in 1957.▼▶

Eternally Yours (1939) **95m.** ****½** D: Tay Garnett. Loretta Young, David Niven, Hugh Herbert, C. Aubrey Smith, Billie Burke, Broderick Crawford, ZaSu Pitts, Eve Arden. Wayout idea comes off fairly well; Young is married to magician Niven, thinks his tricks are taking precedence to their married life. Also shown in computer-colored version.▼▶

Eternal Return, The SEE: **Love Eternal**

Eternal Sea, The (1955) **103m.** ****½** D: John H. Auer. Sterling Hayden, Alexis Smith, Dean Jagger, Virginia Grey. Well-played biography of Admiral John Hoskins' efforts to retain active command despite WW2 injury. Hayden is restrained in lead role; modest production values.▶

Eternal Song, The SEE: **A Brivele der Mamen**

Étoile sans Lumière SEE: **Star Without Light**

Eureka Stockade (1949-British-Australian) **103m.** ******* D: Harry Watt. Chips Rafferty, Jane Barrett, Gordon Jackson, Jack Lambert, Peter Illing, Ralph Truman, Peter Finch. Stirring period drama, set in the 1850s upon the discovery of gold in Australia, chronicling the conflict between workingmen intent on panning for gold and their former employers (and government) intent on restricting their freedom. One of the former (Rafferty, in a forceful performance) attempts to mediate between the opposing groups. Aka MASSACRE HILL.▼

Europa '51 SEE: **Greatest Love, The**

Eva (1962-French-British) **103m.** ******* D: Joseph Losey. Jeanne Moreau, Stanley Baker, Virna Lisi, Giorgio Albertazzi, James Villiers. Complex psychological drama involving outwardly successful (albeit guilt-ridden and self-destructive) writer Baker and his obsession with amoral seductress Moreau. Losey disowned this version; the DVD includes director's cut, titled EVE, which runs 119m.; in it, the characters and their motivations are more fleshed out. Based on a novel by James Hadley Chase.▼▶

Evangeline (1929) **87m.** ******* D: Edwin Carewe. Dolores Del Rio, Roland Drew, Alec B. Francis, Donald Reed, Paul McAllister, James A. Marcus, George F. Marion, Sr. Acadian lovers in 1740s Nova Scotia are torn asunder by evil British soldiers but vow to meet again though they be a continent apart. Robust adaptation of Longfellow's 1847 narrative poem is a curious silent/sound hybrid and was the last of seven collaborations between glamorous Del Rio and her devoted director. Some location shooting in Louisiana. Previously filmed in 1908, 1914, and 1919. **▼▶**

Eve Knew Her Apples (1945) **64m.** ****½** D: Will Jason. Ann Miller, William Wright, Robert Williams, Ray Walker. Sprightly musical variation of IT HAPPENED ONE NIGHT, with Miller on the lam from her marriage-minded fiancé.

Evelyn Prentice (1934) **80m.** ****½** D: William K. Howard. William Powell, Myrna Loy, Una Merkel, Rosalind Russell, Isabel Jewell, Harvey Stephens, Edward Brophy, Cora Sue Collins. Story of successful attorney who doesn't know his own wife is in trouble is too drawn out, and ultimately implausible. Cast rises above the material. Russell's first film. Remade as STRONGER THAN DESIRE. **▼▶**

Eve of St. Mark, The (1944) **96m.** ******* D: John M. Stahl. Anne Baxter, William Eythe, Michael O'Shea, Vincent Price, Dickie Moore. Human focus on WW2 in tale of soldier Eythe and girl friend Baxter at outset of war; not always successful Maxwell Anderson story. Title refers to a premonition of death. One of Price's best performances.

Evergreen (1934-British) **94m.** ******* D: Victor Saville. Jessie Matthews, Sonnie Hale, Betty Balfour, Barry Mackay, Ivor MacLaren. British musical-comedy star's best-known film is enjoyable fluff about young girl who becomes a stage sensation masquerading as her long-retired mother. Score includes Rodgers and Hart's "Dancing on the Ceiling." **▼●**

Ever in My Heart (1933) **68m.** ****½** D: Archie Mayo. Barbara Stanwyck, Otto Kruger, Ralph Bellamy, Ruth Donnelly, Frank Albertson. New Englander Stanwyck, a Daughter of the American Revolution, weds German-born college professor Kruger. He becomes an American citizen—and then WW1 comes. Well-meaning soaper reflects the mood of the period, but is too hurried and simplistic to really score.

Ever Since Eve (1937) **79m.** ***½** D: Lloyd Bacon. Marion Davies, Robert Montgomery, Frank McHugh, Patsy Kelly, Allen Jenkins, Louise Fazenda, Barton MacLane. Davies makes herself homely in order to avoid being harassed on the job; dreary comedy tests the mettle of Warner Bros. stock cast. This was Marion's last film.

Everybody Does It (1949) **98m.** *****½** D:

Edmund Goulding. Paul Douglas, Linda Darnell, Celeste Holm, Charles Coburn, Millard Mitchell, Lucile Watson, John Hoyt, George Tobias. Exceptionally amusing yarn of aspiring singer Holm, harried husband Douglas, and prima donna Darnell. Celeste wants vocal career, Douglas gets one instead. Remake of WIFE, HUSBAND, AND FRIEND; Nunnally Johnson adapted his earlier screenplay (based on a James M. Cain story). **▶**

Everybody's Hobby (1939) **55m.** ****½** D: William C. McGann. Irene Rich, Henry O'Neill, Jackie Moran, Aldrich Bowker, Jean Sharon, John Ridgely, Peggy Stewart. Lightly likable *Andy Hardy*–ish comedy-drama about a small-town family and its hobbies. A rare leading role for prolific character actor O'Neill as the clan's newspaper-editor patriarch. Intended as the first in a series that never materialized.

Everybody Sing (1938) **91m.** ****** D: Edwin L. Marin. Allan Jones, Judy Garland, Fanny Brice, Reginald Owen, Billie Burke, Reginald Gardiner. Shrill musical with stupid plot, unmemorable songs; good cast fighting weak material about nutty family involved in putting on a show. After loud finale you'll be waiting for a sequel called EVERYBODY SHUT UP. **▼●▶**

Everybody's Woman SEE: **La Signora di Tutti**

Every Day's a Holiday (1937) **80m.** ******* D: A. Edward Sutherland. Mae West, Edmund Lowe, Charles Butterworth, Charles Winninger, Walter Catlett, Lloyd Nolan, Louis Armstrong. Mae sells Herman Bing the Brooklyn Bridge, so police detective Lowe orders her to leave N.Y.C. She returns to help expose crooked police chief Nolan. Gay '90s setting for fast-moving West vehicle. Scripted by the star herself. **▼▶**

Every Day's a Holiday (1964-British) SEE: **Seaside Swingers**

Every Girl Should Be Married (1948) **85m.** ****½** D: Don Hartman. Cary Grant, Franchot Tone, Diana Lynn, Betsy Drake, Alan Mowbray, Eddie Albert. Airy comedy of girl (Drake) setting out to trap bachelor (Grant) into marriage; Tone has thankless "other man" role. Drake also "captured" Grant in real life; they were married soon after this film came out. Also shown in computer-colored version. **▼●▶**

Every Night at Eight (1935) **81m.** ****½** D: Raoul Walsh. George Raft, Alice Faye, Frances Langford, Patsy Kelly, Herman Bing, Walter Catlett. Forgettable trifle about Faye, Langford, and Kelly singing their way to fame with bandleader Raft. Dorothy Fields–Jimmy McHugh score includes "I Feel a Song Comin' On" and "I'm in the Mood for Love."

Everything But the Truth (1956) **C-83m.** ****** D: Jerry Hopper. Maureen O'Hara, John Forsythe, Tim Hovey, Frank Faylen. When youngster Hovey joins truth pledge crusade at school, repercussions to his family and townfolk grow; cutesy.

Everything Happens at Night (1939) 77m. **½ D: Irving Cummings. Sonja Henie, Ray Milland, Robert Cummings, Maurice Moscovich, Alan Dinehart, Fritz Feld, Jody Gilbert, Victor Varconi. Rival journalists Cummings and Milland come to Swiss village in search of supposedly assassinated "peace leader," but find themselves sidetracked by pert Henie (who gets to do plenty of skiing and ice-skating). Uneven comedy/drama/romance/thriller. ▼●

Everything I Have Is Yours (1952) C-92m. ** D: Robert Z. Leonard. Marge and Gower Champion, Dennis O'Keefe, Eduard Franz. Champions play dance team who finally get Broadway break, only to discover she's pregnant. Mild musical helped by stars' multitalents. ▼●

Everything's Ducky (1961) 81m. ** D: Don Taylor. Mickey Rooney, Buddy Hackett, Jackie Cooper, Roland Winters. Nonsense of Rooney-Hackett teaming up with talking duck, with trio ending up on Navy missile orbiting earth; strictly for kids. ▶

Evil Eye, The (1962-Italian) 92m. **½ D: Mario Bava. Leticia Roman, John Saxon, Valentina Cortese, Dante Di Paolo. Incredible but enjoyable chiller set in Rome, with Roman involved in a series of unsolved brutal murders. Aka THE GIRL WHO KNEW TOO MUCH. ▼●

Evil Mind, The SEE: **Clairvoyant, The**

Evil of Frankenstein (1964-British) C-84m. ** D: Freddie Francis. Peter Cushing, Duncan Lamont, Peter Woodthorpe, James Maxwell, Sandor Eles. Dr. F. thaws out his monster, with all-too-predictable consequences in this Hammer Films potboiler, a sequel to REVENGE OF FRANKENSTEIN. Followed by FRANKENSTEIN CREATED WOMAN. ▼●

Ex-Champ (1939) 64m. ** D: Phil Rosen. Victor McLaglen, Tom Brown, Nan Grey, William Frawley, Constance Moore, Donald Briggs, Samuel S. Hinds, Marc Lawrence. Ex-boxer McLaglen is shunned by his social-climbing son but comes to his aid when he's in a fix. No surprises here.

Exclusive (1937) 85m. **½ D: Alexander Hall. Fred MacMurray, Frances Farmer, Charlie Ruggles, Lloyd Nolan, Fay Holden, Ralph Morgan, Horace McMahon. Lively newspaper story has Farmer joining tabloid in direct competition with her father (Ruggles) and boyfriend (MacMurray), who are also reporters. Uneasy mix of comedy, romance, and melodrama.

Exclusive Story (1936) 75m. **½ D: George B. Seitz. Franchot Tone, Madge Evans, Stuart Erwin, Joseph Calleia, Robert Barrat, J. Farrell MacDonald, Louise Henry. Fast-paced B picture with Tone as newspaper attorney trying to get the goods on Calleia and falling in love with Evans. ▶

Excuse My Dust (1951) C-82m. **½ D: Roy Rowland. Red Skelton, Sally Forrest, Macdonald Carey, Monica Lewis, William Demarest. Amiable Skelton musicomedy. Red invents automobile which almost costs him his sweetheart; her father owns town livery stable. ▶

Executive Suite (1954) 104m. *** D: Robert Wise. William Holden, June Allyson, Barbara Stanwyck, Fredric March, Walter Pidgeon, Louis Calhern, Shelley Winters, Paul Douglas, Nina Foch, Dean Jagger. Slick, multifaceted story of company power struggle with top cast, from Cameron Hawley novel . . . though similar film PATTERNS is much better. Later a TV series. ▼●

Exile, The (1947) 95m. **½ D: Max Ophuls. Douglas Fairbanks, Jr., Maria Montez, Paule Croset (Rita Corday), Henry Daniell, Nigel Bruce, Robert Coote. OK swashbuckler with exiled king Fairbanks falling in love with common girl; guest appearance by Montez.

Exiles, The (1961) 73m. ***½ D: Kent Mackenzie. Yvonne Williams, Homer Nish, Tommy Reynolds, Rico Rodriguez, Clifford Ray Sam, Clydean Parker. Compelling, often harrowing documentary-style portrait of a community of American Indians in downtown L.A. during the late 1950s. Away from the reservation and their traditions, with drink as their only escape, these outsiders try the best they can to get through the night. A searing true-life drama, and an unforgettable b&w snapshot of L.A. before the area called Bunker Hill was torn down and rebuilt. Unreleased theatrically until 2009. ▶

Exit Smiling (1926) 77m. *** D: Sam Taylor. Beatrice Lillie, Jack Pickford, Doris Lloyd, DeWitt Jennings, Harry Myers, Tenen Holtz, Louise Lorraine, Franklin Pangborn. Lillie, in her screen debut (and lone silent film), is the whole show in this likable comedy, as a wannabe leading actress who does odd jobs for a traveling theater company and falls for a bank-employee-turned-actor (Pickford) who's been falsely accused of embezzlement. Story by Marc Connelly. ▶

Ex-Lady (1933) 65m. **½ D: Robert Florey. Bette Davis, Gene Raymond, Frank McHugh, Claire Dodd, Ferdinand Gottschalk. Davis, looking sensational, plays an independent-minded woman who loves Raymond but doesn't believe in marriage. Provocative and sexy, stylishly filmed, but begins to drag and become conventional by the second half. A remake of ILLICIT, filmed just two years earlier! ▼▶

Ex-Mrs. Bradford, The (1936) 80m. *** D: Stephen Roberts. William Powell, Jean Arthur, James Gleason, Eric Blore, Robert Armstrong. Chic à la THIN MAN comedy-mystery, with Powell teaming with ex-wife Arthur to crack a case. ▼●▶

Exodus (1960) **C-207m.** ******* D: Otto Preminger. Paul Newman, Eva Marie Saint, Ralph Richardson, Peter Lawford, Lee J. Cobb, Sal Mineo, John Derek, Hugh Griffith, Gregory Ratoff, Felix Aylmer, Jill Haworth, David Opatoshu, Marius Goring, George Maharis. Leon Uris' sprawling history of Palestinian war for liberation becomes sporadic action epic. Newman as Israeli resistance leader, Saint as non-Jewish army nurse aren't a convincing duo; supporting roles offer stereotypes. Best scene shows refugees escaping Cyprus detention center, running British blockade into homeland. Ernest Gold won an Oscar for his score. Runs 213m. with intermission/entr'acte. Super Panavision 70.▼O●

Expensive Husbands (1937) 62m. **½ D: Bobby Connolly. Patric Knowles, Beverly Roberts, Allyn Joslyn, Gordon Oliver, Vladimir Sokoloff, Eula Guy, Fritz Feld. Hollywood actress Roberts, frustrated with her career, travels to Vienna, where she sparks the interest of a mischievous waiter (Knowles) who's harboring a secret. Formulaic but generally enjoyable Lubitsch-inspired romantic comedy-with-music.

Experiment in Evil SEE: **Le Testament du Dr. Cordelier**

Experiment in Terror (1962) 123m. *** D: Blake Edwards. Glenn Ford, Lee Remick, Stefanie Powers, Ross Martin, Roy Poole, Ned Glass. Taut suspense with bank clerk Remick terrorized by murderous extortionist Martin . . . but FBI agent Ford is on the case. Realistic, unsentimental, with convincing performances by Remick and Martin. Great Henry Mancini score, good use of San Francisco locations.▼O●

Experiment Perilous (1944) 91m. ** D: Jacques Tourneur. Hedy Lamarr, George Brent, Paul Lukas, Albert Dekker, Margaret Wycherly, Julia Dean. Static melodrama in the GASLIGHT tradition, with doctor Brent coming to the aid of—and falling in love with—fearful Lamarr, who's being terrorized by crazed husband Lukas.▼●

Explosive Generation, The (1961) 89m. ** D: Buzz Kulik. William Shatner, Patty McCormack, Billy Gray, Steve Dunne, Lee Kinsolving, Virginia Field, Phillip Terry, Edward Platt, Beau Bridges. High school teacher Shatner causes an uproar when he has his students write essays on their attitudes about sex. Based-on-fact account is an intriguing relic of its era (both for its subject and cast).●

Exposed (1947) 59m. **½ D: George Blair. Adele Mara, Robert Scott (Mark Roberts), Adrian Booth, Robert Armstrong, William Haade, Bob Steele, Harry Shannon. Tough-talking private eye Mara takes on a wealthy client who wants her to tail his stepson, as he's been acting strange. OK programmer with some good L.A. location scenes.

Expresso Bongo (1959-British) 108m. **½

D: Val Guest. Laurence Harvey, Sylvia Syms, Yolande Donlan, Cliff Richard, Ambrosine Phillpotts, Eric Pohlmann, Hermione Baddeley, Wilfrid Lawson, Kenneth Griffith, Susan Hampshire. Atmospheric but dated drama with Harvey shining as a high-energy, jive-spouting London hustler who thinks he's found his version of Elvis in poor young bongo-playing rocker Richard. Written by Wolf Mankowitz. DyaliScope.▼●

Exterminating Angel, The (1962-Mexican) 95m. ***½ D: Luis Buñuel. Silvia Pinal, Enrique Rambal, Jacqueline Andere, Jose Baviera, Augusto Benedico. Guests at elegant dinner party cannot bring themselves to leave, begin to starve and die after several days. Wry assault on bourgeois manners by master surrealist Buñuel.▼●

Extra Girl, The (1923) 69m. **½ D: F. Richard Jones. Mabel Normand, Ralph Graves, George Nichols, Anna Hernandez, Vernon Dent. Mack Sennett silent feature is far from prime, but still has its moments, thanks to classic comedienne Normand and an obliging lion. Dramatic interludes in Hollywood rags-to-riches saga don't really work. Look for Sennett in Mabel's screen test scene.▼●

Eye Creatures, The (1965) 80m. *½ D: Larry Buchanan. John Ashley, Cynthia Hull, Warren Hammack, Chet Davis, Bill Peck. Gory horror film about title creatures and the intrepid band that tries to fight them off. Remake of INVASION OF THE SAUCER MEN. Aka ATTACK OF THE THE EYE CREATURES (sic).▼

Eyes in the Night (1942) 80m. **½ D: Fred Zinnemann. Edward Arnold, Ann Harding, Donna Reed, Stephen McNally, Reginald Denny, Rosemary DeCamp, Mantan Moreland, Barry Nelson. Above-par mystery with Arnold as blind detective Duncan Maclain protecting Harding from Nazi agents. The dog steals the picture. Zinnemann's feature directing debut.▼●

Eyes of Hell (1961-Canadian) 83m. *½ D: Julian Roffman. Paul Stevens, Claudette Nevins, Bill Walker, Anne Collings, Martin Lavut, Jim Moran. Low-budget shocker about an ancient Aztec mask that causes wearer to hallucinate and murder. 3-D scenes were put together by famed montage expert Slavko Vorkapich. Originally released as THE MASK.●

Eyes of Texas (1948) **C-70m.** *** D: William Witney. Roy Rogers, Lynne Roberts, Andy Devine, Nana Bryant, Roy Barcroft, Francis Ford, Danny Morton, Bob Nolan and the Sons of the Pioneers. One of Roy's best films is also one of his toughest, as cold-blooded female lawyer Bryant uses a pack of killer dogs to do her dirty work, murdering ranch owner Ford and arranging for his "son" (Morton) to suddenly turn up and claim his rights. Just the right blend of story, suspense, action, and music. Only b&w prints survive.▼)

Eyes of the Underworld (1942) **61m.** ✶✶ D: Roy William Neill. Richard Dix, Wendy Barrie, Lon Chaney, Jr., Lloyd Corrigan, Don Porter, Billy Lee. Police chief Dix busts an auto theft and car-stripping ring, but blackmailers expose his secret criminal past and he resigns to battle crooks on his own. Title and director promise more than they deliver in draggy second feature with too much sentiment and romance.

Eyes Without a Face (1960-French-Italian) **88m.** ✶✶✶ D: Georges Franju. Pierre Brasseur, Alida Valli, Edith Scob. Moody horror film, a classic in some circles, about a brilliant but crazed scientist/surgeon/researcher (Brasseur) and his fate after disfiguring his daughter. Aka THE HORROR CHAMBER OF DR. FAUSTUS. ▼●)

Eye Witness (1950-British) **104m.** ✶✶½ D: Robert Montgomery. Robert Montgomery, Felix Aylmer, Leslie Banks, Michael Ripper, Patricia Wayne (Cutts). Unpretentious yarn of American attorney Montgomery in London to defend friend accused of homicide, coping with contrasting British legal system while hunting title figure. Originally titled YOUR WITNESS.▼)

Fabiola (1948-Italian-French) **96m.** ✶✶✶ D: Alessandro Blasetti. Michele Morgan, Michel Simon, Henri Vidal, Massimo Girotti, Louis Salou, Gino Cervi. Confusing but impressive epic of persecution against Christians in 4th-century Rome. Simon is the powerful, forward-thinking Fabius Severus; Morgan is Fabiola, his cavalier offspring; Vidal is Rhual, steadfast Christian gladiator. Originally released in Europe at 150m.; English-dubbed version, adapted by Marc Connelly and Fred Pressburger and featuring an altogether different storyline, opened in the U.S. in 1951.▼)

Fabulous Baron Munchausen, The (1961-Czech) **C-84m.** ✶✶½ D: Karel Zeman. Milos Kopecky, Jana Brejchova, Rudolph Jelinek, Jan Werich. Filmmaker Zeman (FABULOUS WORLD OF JULES VERNE) provides another visual delight here, but his episodic fantasy—which takes his hero from the inside of a whale to the surface of the moon—is stilted and uninvolving. Aka THE ORIGINAL FABULOUS ADVENTURES OF BARON MUNCHAUSEN.▼●)

Fabulous Dorseys, The (1947) **88m.** ✶✶ D: Alfred E. Green. Tommy Dorsey, Jimmy Dorsey, Janet Blair, Paul Whiteman, William Lundigan. Limp "biography" of bandleading brothers, constantly arguing in between "Marie," "Green Eyes," and other hit songs. Musical highlight: a jam session with Art Tatum, Charlie Barnet, Ziggy Elman, and Ray Bauduc.▼●)

Fabulous Joe, The (1947) **C-60m.** ✶✶ D:

Bernard Carr, Harve Foster. Marie Wilson, Walter Abel, Margot Grahame, Donald Meek. Abel is typecast in this segment from THE HAL ROACH COMEDY CARNIVAL. He's harassed husband who gains moral support from talking dog.▼

Fabulous Suzanne, The (1946) **71m.** ✶✶ D: Steve Sekely. Barbara Britton, Rudy Vallee, Bill (William) Henry, Otto Kruger, Richard Denning, Veda Ann Borg. Not-so-fabulous account of Britton, whose lucky pin allows her to pick winning racehorses and profitable stocks.

Fabulous Texan, The (1947) **96m.** ✶✶ D: Edward Ludwig. William Elliott, John Carroll, Catherine McLeod, Albert Dekker, Andy Devine, Patricia Knight, Ruth Donnelly, Johnny Sands, Harry Davenport, Robert Barrat, Douglass Dumbrille, Reed Hadley, Jim Davis. Elliott and Carroll return home to Texas after the Civil War and tangle with carpetbaggers who have turned it into a police state; McLeod supplies the requisite love interest. Standard story, though production is more lavish than usual for Republic Pictures.

Fabulous World of Jules Verne, The (1958-Czech) **83m.** ✶✶½ D: Karel Zeman. Lubor Tokos, Arnost Navratil, Miroslav Holub, Jana Zatloukalova. Zeman's ingenious visual effects, reproducing the look of 19th-century engravings, outshine leaden enactment of fanciful sci-fi story by Verne. Released here in 1961 with Americanized names in credits and pointless introduction by Hugh Downs.▼)

Face at the Window, The (1939-British) **65m.** ✶✶½ D: George King. Tod Slaughter, Marjorie Taylor, John Warwick, Robert Adair, Harry Terry. A fiendish killer known as "The Wolf" strikes terror in 1880s Paris. Who can it be? Surely not the Chevalier del Gardo (Slaughter), respected nobleman! And who is the hideous, drooling face at the window? Charming, well-produced blood-and-thunder melodrama, based on the frequently filmed play by F. Brooke Warren. The blessedly hammy Slaughter is in great form here.▼)

Face Behind the Mask, The (1941) **69m.** ✶✶✶ D: Robert Florey. Peter Lorre, Evelyn Keyes, Don Beddoe, George E. Stone, John Tyrrell. Model B film of immigrant Lorre having face disfigured in fire, donning mask, bitterly turning to life of crime. Extremely well done on slim budget.

Face in the Crowd, A (1957) **125m.** ✶✶✶½ D: Elia Kazan. Andy Griffith, Patricia Neal, Anthony Franciosa, Walter Matthau, Lee Remick, Kay Medford. Perceptive script by Budd Schulberg about homespun hobo (Griffith) discovered by Neal and promoted into successful—and unscrupulous—TV star. Cast gives tale of fascinating story. Film debuts of Griffith and Remick. Look for young Rip Torn and Lois Nettleton. Many celebrities also appear as themselves, including Burl Ives, Mike Wallace, Betty Furness, Bennett Cerf, Faye Emerson, and Walter Winchell.▼▶

Face in the Night SEE: **Menace in the Night**

Face in the Rain, A (1963) 91m. **½ D: Irvin Kershner. Rory Calhoun, Marina Berti, Niall MacGinnis, Massimo Giuliani. At times tense melodrama of Calhoun, U.S. spy, being hidden in Italy by partisan whose wife has been associating with Axis.

Face in the Sky (1933) 74m. *** D: Harry Lachman. Spencer Tracy, Marian Nixon, Stuart Erwin, Sam Hardy, Lila Lee, Sarah Padden, Russell Simpson. Fairy-tale–like yarn about an outdoor sign painter, a self-styled artist who believes "if you live in the clouds, everybody's got to look up to you." Sweet, highly original film that goes in unexpected directions, enhanced by unusual, showy camera angles and continuous music track. Tracy is dynamic, cocky, and funny. Photographed by Lee Garmes.

Face of a Fugitive (1959) **C-81m. ** D: Paul Wendkos. Fred MacMurray, Lin McCarthy, Dorothy Green, James Coburn, Alan Baxter, Myrna Fahey. OK Western about MacMurray forced to start over again in a new town when he's falsely accused of murder; his past still haunts him.

Face of Fire (1959) 83m. *** D: Albert Band. Cameron Mitchell, James Whitmore, Bettye Ackerman, Royal Dano, Robert Simon, Richard Erdman. Unique adaptation of Stephen Crane short story "The Monster" about man disfigured while saving child from fire. Uneven cast, good direction.▶

Face of Fu Manchu, The (1965-British) **C-96m. *** D: Don Sharp. Christopher Lee, Nigel Green, James Robertson Justice, Howard Marion-Crawford, Tsai Chin, Walter Rilla. First of new series with Emperor Fu bent on conquering West. Great 1920s atmosphere, good international cast. Followed by THE BRIDES OF FU MANCHU. Techniscope.▼▶

Face of Marble, The (1946) 70m. *½ D: William Beaudine. John Carradine, Claudia Drake, Robert Shayne, Maris Wrixon. Another screwy doctor with new technique for bringing dead back to life—including a dog who turns vampire! Ludicrous.▶

Face of the Frog (1959-German) 92m. ** D: Harald Reinl. Joachim Fuchsberger, Fritz Rasp, Siegfried Lowitz, Joachen Brochmann. Lowitz is Inspector Elk tracking down the "Frog" in this routine Edgar Wallace actioner; serial-like techniques utilized. Retitled: FELLOWSHIP OF THE FROG.▼▶

Face of the Screaming Werewolf (1964-Mexican-U.S.) 60m. BOMB D: Gilberto Martinez Solares, Jerry Warren, Rafael Lopez Portillo. Lon Chaney (Jr.), Yerye Beirute, George Mitchell, Fred Hoffman, Rosa Arenas, Ramón Gay. Two mummies are retrieved from a Yucatan pyramid. One wanders off (carrying a woman) and is hit by a car; the other (Chaney) is stolen by a scientist, subjected to electrical treatments, and turns out to be a werewolf. Oops. Greatly altered from the 1960 Mexican original (LA CASA DEL TERROR, a comedy). A total stinker.

Face That Launched a Thousand Ships, The SEE: **Loves of Three Queens**

Face to Face (1952) 92m. **½ D: John Brahm, Bretaigne Windust. James Mason, Michael Pate, Robert Preston, Marjorie Steele. Quiet two-part film: Joseph Conrad's "Secret Sharer" faithfully filmed with Mason as captain, Pate as fugitive; Stephen Crane's "Bride Comes to Yellow Sky" bland with Preston bringing bride Steele out West.▼

Facts of Life, The (1960) 103m. *** D: Melvin Frank. Bob Hope, Lucille Ball, Ruth Hussey, Don DeFore. Sophisticated comedy with Bob and Lucy leaving their spouses for an interlude together. The two stars make a good team worth watching.▼▶

Fail-Safe (1964) 111m. ***½ D: Sidney Lumet. Henry Fonda, Walter Matthau, Fritz Weaver, Dan O'Herlihy, Sorrell Booke, Larry Hagman, Frank Overton, Dom DeLuise. U.S. bomber is accidentally ordered to nuke Moscow, plunging heads of American and Russian governments into crisis of decision making as time runs out. High-tension drama done with taste and intelligence. Walter Bernstein adapted the Eugene Burdick–Harvey Wheeler bestseller. Remade in 2000 for TV.▼▶

Fair Warning (1937) 70m. **½ D: Norman Foster. J. Edward Bromberg, Betty Furness, John (Howard) Payne, Victor Kilian, Billy Burrud, Gavin Muir, Gloria Roy, Andrew Tombes, Ivan Lebedeff, John Eldredge. A mine owner is murdered while staying at a Death Valley dude ranch; the deputy sheriff enlists a precocious kid who's a chemistry whiz to help solve the crime. Absorbing little Fox whodunit with comic touches plays like a discarded script for the studio's *Charlie Chan* series.

Fair Wind to Java (1953) **C-92m. **½ D: Joseph Kane. Fred MacMurray, Vera Ralston, Victor McLaglen, Robert Douglas, Philip Ahn. Hard-boiled skipper goes after treasure in the South Seas. Pretty good adventure yarn with Ralston acceptable as native love interest. Great climactic volcano explosion—though accompanying process-screen work is awful.

Faithful in My Fashion (1946) 81m. ** D: Sidney Salkow. Donna Reed, Tom Drake, Edward Everett Horton, Spring Byington, Sig Ruman, Harry Davenport, William "Bill" Phillips, Margaret Hamilton, Hobart Cavanaugh, Warner Anderson. Tired comedy-romance with soldier-on-leave Drake paying a surprise visit to his girl (Reed), unaware that she's never loved him . . . and is engaged to someone else. Good cast hampered by stale material.

Faithless (1932) **76m. **½ D:** Harry Beaumont. Tallulah Bankhead, Robert Montgomery, Hugh Herbert, Louise Closser Hale, Henry Kolker. Impoverished Bankhead tries to start life fresh after dismal past; polished soaper. ▶

Fake, The (1953-British) **80m. ** D:** Godfrey Grayson. Dennis O'Keefe, Coleen Gray, Hugh Williams, Guy Middleton, John Laurie, Billie Whitelaw. Leonardo da Vinci painting is pilfered while being shipped to London's Tate Gallery. Investigator O'Keefe quickly recovers it, but his problems are only beginning. Uninspired whodunit, filmed largely on location inside the Tate.

The Falcon Michael Arlen's debonair trouble-shooter, the Falcon, served as the basis for 16 above-average mysteries in the 1940s, and while the series cannot be called unusual, one of its entries presented a perhaps-unique situation. George Sanders had played the character in three films when, in 1942, he decided to leave the series. In THE FALCON'S BROTHER it was arranged to put him out of the way so his brother could take over for him. Sanders' real-life brother, Tom Conway, was the replacement; he carried on for nine subsequent films. John Calvert played the character in three final low-budget films which aren't really part of the main series. Various character actors came in and out of the series playing cronies of the Falcon, such as Allen Jenkins, Ed Brophy, Eddie Dunn, and Ed Gargan. James Gleason played a thick-witted inspector in the first few films, and Cliff Clark took over for the rest. In fact, some of the films had so much comedy relief, one yearned for some mystery relief from the comedy! One interesting gimmick in several films had a beautiful girl enter near the end of the picture to alert the Falcon to danger in a new location; this would lead into the next film in which the Falcon and the girl would embark upon the new mystery. One entry, THE FALCON TAKES OVER, was from a Raymond Chandler novel, FAREWELL, MY LOVELY, which was remade as MURDER, MY SWEET with Dick Powell as Philip Marlowe.

THE FALCON

Falcon and the Co-eds, The (1943) **68m. **½ D:** William Clemens. Tom Conway, Jean Brooks, Rita Corday, Amelita Ward, Isabel Jewell, George Givot, Cliff Clark, Ed Gargan. There's a slew of sinister suspects when murder strikes at a girls' school, with playboy Falcon called in to investigate. Amusing entry features Dorothy Malone(y) in a bit part as a student.

Falcon in Danger, The (1943) **70m. ** D:** William Clemens. Tom Conway, Jean Brooks, Elaine Shepard, Amelita Ward, Cliff Clark, Ed Gargan, Clarence Kolb, Richard Martin. Minor entry about disappearance of passengers and $100,000 from a downed airplane. ▶

Falcon in Hollywood, The (1944) **67m. **½ D:** Gordon Douglas. Tom Conway, Barbara Hale, Veda Ann Borg, John Abbott, Sheldon Leonard, Konstantin Shayne, Emory Parnell, Frank Jenks, Rita Corday, Jean Brooks. While on vacation in Tinseltown, the Falcon probes the murder of an actor, allowing for an entertaining tour of RKO studio's back lot. Borg shines as a brassy cab driver. ▶

Falcon in Mexico, The (1944) **70m. **½ D:** William Berke. Tom Conway, Mona Maris, Martha MacVicar (Vickers), Nestor Paiva, Mary Currier, Emory Parnell, Pedro de Cordoba. Suspenseful entry takes the Falcon from Manhattan to Mexico City to solve the murder of an art gallery owner over a new painting by a supposedly dead artist. Scenic exteriors of Mexico are rumored to be from Orson Welles' unfinished film IT'S ALL TRUE. ▼▶

Falcon in San Francisco, The (1945) **66m. **½ D:** Joseph H. Lewis. Tom Conway, Rita Corday, Edward Brophy, Sharyn Moffett, Fay Helm, Robert Armstrong, Myrna Dell. The Falcon, sidekick Brophy, and moppet Moffett take on a gang of silk smugglers in this leisurely but well-directed entry. ▶

Falcon Out West, The (1944) **64m. **½ D:** William Clemens. Tom Conway, Barbara Hale, Don Douglas, Carole Gallagher, Joan Barclay, Cliff Clark, Ed Gargan, Minor Watson, Lyle Talbot. The Falcon heads to Texas to catch the killer of a millionaire rancher who died in a N.Y.C. nightclub. Future leading man Lawrence Tierney plays an orchestra leader. ▶

Falcon's Adventure, The (1946) **61m. ** D:** William Berke. Tom Conway, Madge Meredith, Edward S. Brophy, Robert Warwick, Myrna Dell, Steve Brodie, Carol Forman, Ian Wolfe. Stale rehash of A DATE WITH THE FALCON, about imperiled inventor of synthetic diamonds. Last *Falcon* entry featuring Conway. ▼▶

Falcon's Alibi, The (1946) **62m.** ** D: Ray McCarey. Tom Conway, Rita Corday, Vince Barnett, Jane Greer, Elisha Cook, Jr., Emory Parnell, Al Bridge, Jason Robards, Sr., Jean Brooks, Myrna Dell. Basically a retread of initial entry, THE GAY FALCON, about society matron's stolen jewels. Tepid, despite a good supporting cast. ◗

Falcon's Brother, The (1942) **63m.** **½ D: Stanley Logan. George Sanders, Tom Conway, Jane Randolph, Don Barclay, Amanda Varela, George Lewis, Cliff Clark, Edward Gargan. Enemy agents plan to assassinate a South American diplomat to sabotage U.S.-Latin American relations and the Falcon calls in his brother Tom (real-life brother Conway) to help out. Sanders' last film in the series. ◗

Falcon Strikes Back, The (1943) **66m.** **½ D: Edward Dmytryk. Tom Conway, Harriet Hilliard (Nelson), Jane Randolph, Edgar Kennedy, Cliff Edwards, Rita Corday, Wynne Gibson, Cliff Clark, Ed Gargan. The Falcon is framed for murdering a banker as part of a war-bond racket and tracks down the real culprits in this breezy entry. A plum role for Kennedy. ◗

Falcon Takes Over, The (1942) **62m.** *** D: Irving Reis. George Sanders, Lynn Bari, James Gleason, Allen Jenkins, Helen Gilbert, Ward Bond, Edward Gargan, Anne Revere, George Cleveland, Hans Conried, Turhan Bey. Substantial, well-meshed mystery based on Chandler's *Farewell, My Lovely*, with Sanders up to his neck in corpses and double-crossing clients, aided by reporter Bari. Bond is a memorable Moose Malloy. Remade just two years later as MURDER, MY SWEET. ▼◗

Fallen Angel (1945) **97m.** **½ D: Otto Preminger. Alice Faye, Dana Andrews, Linda Darnell, Charles Bickford, Anne Revere, Bruce Cabot, John Carradine. Andrews, hard up and bitter, stops in a small California town and falls for sultry waitress Darnell. To get money to marry her, he plans to first wed mousy heiress Faye and fleece her. Slow-paced (if good-looking) film noir was an ill-fated change of pace for musical star Faye, in her last starring movie. ◗

Fallen Idol, The (1948-British) **94m.** ***½ D: Carol Reed. Ralph Richardson, Michele Morgan, Bobby Henrey, Sonia Dresdel, Jack Hawkins, Bernard Lee. Young boy idolizes a household servant who is suspected of murdering his wife. Exceptional realization of Graham Greene story "The Basement Room," told in large part from the child's point of view. Scripted by Greene, Lesley Storm, and William Templeton. Also shown in computer-colored version. ▼◗

Fallen Sparrow, The (1943) **94m.** **½ D: Richard Wallace. John Garfield, Maureen O'Hara, Walter Slezak, Patricia Morison, Martha O'Driscoll, Bruce Edwards, John Miljan, John Banner, Hugh Beaumont. En-

tertaining if somewhat vague WW2 thriller with Garfield returning to N.Y.C. after fighting in the Spanish Civil War, only to find himself hunted by undercover Nazis. Promising material never really pans out. ▼◗

Fall Guy (1947) **64m.** **½ D: Reginald Le Borg. Clifford (Leo) Penn, Robert Armstrong, Teala Loring, Elisha Cook, Jr., Douglas Fowley, Charles Arnt, Virginia Dale, Iris Adrian. Poor sap wakes up from a blackout with blood on his hands and is questioned by the police about a murder. With only a foggy memory of attending a wild party the night before, he escapes and tries to find out what really happened. Low-budget noir, based on Cornell Woolrich's story "Cocaine," with appropriately seedy atmosphere and a few nice touches. Debut for leading man Penn, who became a prolific TV director and the father of Sean Penn. ◗

Fall of the House of Usher SEE: **House of Usher**

Fall of the Roman Empire, The (1964) C-**180m.** ***½ D: Anthony Mann. Sophia Loren, Stephen Boyd, Alec Guinness, James Mason, Christopher Plummer, Anthony Quayle, John Ireland, Omar Sharif, Mel Ferrer, Eric Porter. Intelligent scripting, good direction, and fine acting place this far above the usual empty-headed spectacle. Mason and Guinness are superb; several action sequences are outstanding. A winner all the way. Screenplay by Philip Yordan, Ben Barzman, and Basilio Franchina. Runs 185m. with overture, intermission/entr'acte, exit music. Ultra Panavision 70. ▼◗

False Colors (1943) **65m.** **½ D: George Archainbaud. William Boyd, Andy Clyde, Jimmy Rogers, Douglass Dumbrille, Tom Seidel, Claudia Drake, Bob (Robert) Mitchum, Glenn Strange, Roy Barcroft. Bar 20 cowpuncher, heir to a ranch with valuable water rights, is murdered so that an impostor can claim ownership on behalf of a crooked banker. Handsome production features Clyde in rare form, and the series debut for Will Rogers' son Jimmy as Hopalong Cassidy's newest (and least interesting) young sidekick. It's fun watching 47-year-old Boyd pulverize 25-year-old Mitchum in a slam-bang fight. ▼◗

False Paradise (1948) **59m.** **½ D: George Archainbaud. William Boyd, Andy Clyde, Rand Brooks, Elaine Riley, Cliff Clark, Kenneth R. MacDonald. Slick banker holding a mortgage cons retired professor and his daughter to obtain silver-rich real estate. Second-to-last Hopalong Cassidy feature builds to nice action finish and is one of the better efforts produced by Boyd, though disappointing when he doesn't wear dark outfit fans expect. Reissued as THE FIGHTING TEXAN. ▼◗

Falstaff SEE: **Chimes at Midnight**

Fame Is the Spur (1946-British) **116m.** **✱✱½** D: John and Roy Boulting. Michael Redgrave, Rosamund John, Anthony Wager, Brian Weske. Thoughtful if slow-moving chronicle of a noted politician-diplomat who rises from poverty to fame.▼

Family Affair, A (1937) **69m.** ✱✱✱ D: George B. Seitz. Lionel Barrymore, Mickey Rooney, Spring Byington, Cecilia Parker, Eric Linden, Julie Haydon, Charley Grapewin, Sara Haden. Amiable first entry in the *Andy Hardy* series centers on Judge Hardy (Barrymore) solving various family problems while trying to be reelected. A good intro to the sentimental charm of life in Louis B. Mayer's idealized vision of small-town America. Byington and Barrymore's roles were taken over by Fay Holden and Lewis Stone for the rest of the series. Based on the play *Skidding* by Aurania Rouverol. ▶

Family Honeymoon (1948) **90m.** **✱✱½** D: Claude Binyon. Claudette Colbert, Fred MacMurray, Rita Johnson, Gigi Perreau. What could have been fine comedy turns out to be uneven farce as widow takes children on second honeymoon. Very good cast does its best. Also shown in computer-colored version. ▶

Family Jewels, The (1965) **C-100m.** **✱✱½** D: Jerry Lewis. Jerry Lewis, Donna Butterworth, Sebastian Cabot, Robert Strauss, Milton Frome. Depending on your taste for Lewis, you'll either be in ecstasy or writhing on the floor in pain because he plays seven parts—all of them as potential guardians of little girl who is inheriting several million dollars. ▼

Family Secret, The (1951) **85m.** **✱✱½** D: Henry Levin. John Derek, Lee J. Cobb, Jody Lawrance, Erin O'Brien-Moore, Santos Ortega, Henry O'Neill, Carl Benton Reid. Law student Derek, a child of privilege who's been indulged by his parents, accidentally kills his best friend. What will he do? Quietly effective drama explores issues of guilt, innocence, and responsibility. ▼▶

Fan, The (1949) **89m.** **✱✱** D: Otto Preminger. Jeanne Crain, Madeleine Carroll, George Sanders, Richard Greene. Oscar Wilde's comedy of manners *Lady Windermere's Fan*, involving marital indiscretion and social-climbing in Victorian England, loses much of its wit in this version. Madeleine Carroll's last film. Previously filmed in 1916, 1925, 1935 (in Germany), and 1944 (in Mexico), and remade in 2004 as A GOOD WOMAN. ▶

Fanatics, The (1957-French) **85m.** **✱✱** D: Alex Joffé. Pierre Fresnay, Michel Auclair, Gregoire Aslan, Betty Schneider. Occasionally taut tale of two revolutionaries (Fresnay, Auclair) with very different ideas about assassinating a South American dictator.

Fancy Pants (1950) **C-92m.** ✱✱✱ D: George

Marshall. Mr. Robert Hope (formerly Bob), Lucille Ball, Bruce Cabot, Jack Kirkwood, Lea Penman, Eric Blore. Amusing musical remake of RUGGLES OF RED GAP with English valet Hope accompanying nouveau riche wildcat Lucy to her Western home. ▼▶

Fanfan La Tulipe (1952-French) **99m.** ✱✱✱ D: Christian-Jaque. Gérard Philipe, Gina Lollobrigida, Noel Roquevert, Olivier Hussenot, Marcel Herrand, Sylvie Pelayo, Genevieve Page. Delightful satire of swashbuckling epics, with Philipe ideal as the sword-wielding, love-hungry 18th-century Frenchman joining Louis XV's army.▶

Fanny (1932-French)**120m.** ✱✱✱½ D: Marc Allegret. Raimu, Pierre Fresnay, Charpin, Orane Demazis, Alida Rouffe. Marius (Fresnay) abandons Fanny (Demazis) with his child; with César (Raimu) playing Cupid, she marries Panisse (Charpin). Second of Marcel Pagnol's charming trilogy, preceded by MARIUS and followed by CÉSAR. All three were the basis of the play and movie FANNY (1961). Remade in 2013 by Daniel Auteuil. ▼▶

Fanny (1961) **C-133m.** ✱✱✱ D: Joshua Logan. Leslie Caron, Maurice Chevalier, Charles Boyer, Horst Buchholz, Baccaloni, Lionel Jeffries. Gorgeously photographed and beautifully scored dramatic version of Marcel Pagnol's trilogy involving young girl left with child by adventure-seeking sailor. Chevalier and Boyer give flavorful performances.▼▶

Fanny by Gaslight SEE: **Man of Evil**

Fantasia (1940) **C-120m.** ✱✱✱½ D: Ben Sharpsteen (production supervisor). Leopold Stokowski and the Philadelphia Orchestra; narrated by Deems Taylor. Walt Disney's eight-part marriage of music and animated images remains an amazing achievement; Taylor's narration dates it more than the content. "The Sorcerer's Apprentice" (with Mickey Mouse), "The Dance of the Hours" (with dancing hippos and alligators), "Rite of Spring" (dinosaurs stalking the earth), and "A Night on Bald Mountain" (with Chernobog, the personification of evil) are so stunning that they make up for the less compelling sequences. Also notable for groundbreaking use of multichannel stereophonic sound. DVD (with newly filmed credits) runs 124m. Followed by FANTASIA 2000. ▼▶

Fantômas (1964-French-Italian) **C-105m.** **✱✱½** D: André Hunebelle. Jean Marais, Louis de Funès, Mylène Demongeot, Jacques Dynam, Robert Dalban, Marie-Hélène Arnaud. French cinema's arch-criminal and master of disguise (first seen in a 1913 serial) is updated for the James Bond era in the first of three lavish, campy 1960s films. Marais has a dual role as Fantômas and an intrepid reporter on his trail, while de Funès fumes frantically as a bumbling police chief who's always one step behind. Followed by FANTÔMAS STRIKES BACK. Franscope.

[207]

Fantômas Strikes Back (1965-French-Italian) **C-100m.** **½ D: André Hunebelle. Jean Marais, Louis de Funès, Mylène Demongeot, Jacques Dynam, Christian Toma, Michel Duplaix, Robert Dalban. Fantômas kidnaps scientists working on a mind-control device as part of a nefarious plot to take over the world. Silly but fun romp filled with gadgets galore and some strikingly stylized sets. Followed by FANTÔMAS VS. SCOTLAND YARD. Franscope.

Far Country, The (1955) **C-97m.** *** D: Anthony Mann. James Stewart, Ruth Roman, Corinne Calvet, Walter Brennan, Jay C. Flippen, John McIntire, Harry Morgan, Jack Elam, Robert Wilkie, Connie Gilchrist, Kathleen Freeman. Cattleman Stewart, a confirmed loner, brings his herd through Alaska to Canada and finds nothing but trouble. Solid Canadian-made Western set against colorful backdrop of mining camp towns. Story and screenplay by Borden Chase. ▼●▶

Farewell Again (1937-British) **81m.** **½ D: Tim Whelan. Leslie Banks, Flora Robson, Sebastian Shaw, Patricia Hilliard. Neatly handled minor film detailing events in the lives of British soldiers on short leave before embarking for the front again. U.S. Title: TROOPSHIP.

Farewell to Arms, A (1932) **78m.** *** D: Frank Borzage. Helen Hayes, Gary Cooper, Adolphe Menjou, Mary Philips, Jack LaRue, Blanche Frederici. Lushly romantic adaptation of Hemingway novel about ill-fated WW1 romance between American soldier and British nurse; dated but well done. Charles Lang's exquisite cinematography won an Oscar. Remade in 1951 (as FORCE OF ARMS) and in 1957. Also shown in computer-colored version. ▼●▶

Farewell to Arms, A (1957) **C-152m.** **½ D: Charles Vidor. Rock Hudson, Jennifer Jones, Vittorio De Sica, Alberto Sordi, Mercedes McCambridge, Elaine Stritch, Oscar Homolka. Overblown, padded remake has unconvincing leads, static treatment of WW1 story so romantically told in Hemingway novel. Hudson is American ambulance driver wounded in WW1 Italy who falls in love with nurse Jones. Last film produced by David O. Selznick. CinemaScope. ▼▶

Far Frontier (1948) **C-67m.** *** D: William Witney. Roy Rogers, Gail Davis, Andy Devine, Francis Ford, Roy Barcroft, Clayton Moore, Robert Strange, Holly Bane, Lane Bradford, Foy Willing and the Riders of the Purple Sage. Hard-hitting Rogers Western, with Roy up against vicious gangsters who smuggle deported criminals back into the country. Tough storyline, good direction, one of Roy's best late-'40s outings. Only b&w prints seem to survive. ▼▶

Far Horizons, The (1955) **C-108m.** **½ D: Rudolph Maté. Fred MacMurray, Charlton Heston, Donna Reed, Barbara Hale,

William Demarest. Movie fiction about Lewis and Clark expedition, beautifully photographed; sporadic action; implausible love interest. VistaVision. ▶

Farmer's Daughter, The (1940) **60m.** ** D: James Hogan. Martha Raye, Charlie Ruggles, Richard Denning, Gertrude Michael, William Frawley, Inez Courtney, William Demarest. Not to be confused with later film, this one is about a Broadway huckster who transforms a barn into a theater. Worthwhile only for Raye, playing the title character.

Farmer's Daughter, The (1947) **97m.** ***½ D: H. C. Potter. Loretta Young, Joseph Cotten, Ethel Barrymore, Charles Bickford, Rose Hobart, Harry Davenport, Lex Barker, James Aurness (Arness), Keith Andes, Rhys Williams, Art Baker. Young won an Oscar for her irresistible performance as a naïve but straight-thinking farm girl who goes to work for a senator—and winds up running for a congressional seat against his party. Delightful comedy with an excellent cast. Allen Rivkin and Laura Kerr adapted Juhani Tervapää's play *Hulda, Daughter of Parliament*. Later a TV series. ▼

Farmer's Wife, The (1928-British) **97m.** **½ D: Alfred Hitchcock. Jameson Thomas, Lillian Hall-Davies, Gordon Harker. A Hitchcock silent comedy. Farmer Thomas, unsuccessful at finding a bride, is secretly loved by devoted housekeeper Davies. Enjoyable rustic comedy; written by the director. Based on a play by Eden Philpotts. ▼▶

Farmer Takes a Wife, The (1935) **91m.** **½ D: Victor Fleming. Janet Gaynor, Henry Fonda, Charles Bickford, Slim Summerville, Jane Withers, Andy Devine, Margaret Hamilton, George "Gabby" Hayes. Leisurely paced tale, set in the mid-19th century, with wannabe farmer Fonda (in his screen debut, re-creating a role he played on Broadway) working on a boat that traverses the Erie Canal in upstate New York, becoming romantically involved with spirited Gaynor. Remade as a musical in 1953. ▶

Farmer Takes a Wife, The (1953) **C-81m.** ** D: Henry Levin. Betty Grable, Dale Robertson, Thelma Ritter, John Carroll, Eddie Foy, Jr., Gwen Verdon. Musical remake of 1935 film is slow-paced account of life in 1800s along the Erie Canal. ▼●

Fashions of 1934 (1934) **78m.** *** D: William Dieterle. William Powell, Bette Davis, Verree Teasdale, Reginald Owen, Frank McHugh, Phillip Reed, Hugh Herbert. Trivial but enjoyable romp of con man Powell and designer Davis conquering the Paris fashion world. Fine cast glides along with dapper Powell; Busby Berkeley's "Spin a Little Web of Dreams" number is great fun. Aka FASHIONS. ▼▶

Fast and Furious (1939) **73m.** **½ D: Busby Berkeley. Franchot Tone, Ann Sothern, Ruth Hussey, John Miljan, Allyn Joslyn, Bernard Nedell, Mary Beth Hughes. Tone and Sothern are well matched as Joel and Garda Sloane, rare-book dealers who get involved in a murder at a seaside beauty pageant. Last of three MGM B movies about these characters written by Harry Kurnitz. ▶

Fast and Loose (1930) **75m.** *½ D: Fred Newmeyer. Miriam Hopkins, Carol(e) Lombard, Frank Morgan, Ilka Chase, Charles Starrett. Stiff adaptation of a Broadway comedy about a society girl falling in love with an ordinary guy. Preston Sturges is credited with the dialogue. Hopkins' film debut; Lombard has a smallish role.

Fast and Loose (1939) **80m.** **½ D: Edwin L. Marin. Robert Montgomery, Rosalind Russell, Reginald Owen, Ralph Morgan, Etienne Girardot, Alan Dinehart, Jo Ann Sayers, Joan Marsh, Sidney Blackmer. Montgomery and Russell are engaging as Joel and Garda Sloane, Nick & Nora–ish rare-book dealers who become involved in solving the murder of a wealthy bibliophile. Goes on a bit too long, but still fun. Second of three MGM films about this duo, written by Harry Kurnitz. Followed by FAST AND FURIOUS. ▶

Fast and Sexy (1958-Italian) **C-98m.** **½ D: Reginald Denham. Gina Lollobrigida, Dale Robertson, Vittorio De Sica, Carla Macelloni. Lollobrigida is fun-loving widow who returns to her village seeking new husband. Technirama.

Fast and the Furious, The (1954) **73m.** ** D: Edwards Sampson, John Ireland. John Ireland, Dorothy Malone, Iris Adrian, Bruce Carlisle, Jean Howell, Larry Thor. Ireland is fugitive on the lam from murder frameup who jockeys Malone's sports car, with uninspired romantic interludes and cops-on-the-chase sequences. Produced and written by Roger Corman, this was the first film for American Releasing Corporation—soon to be the fabled AIP (American-International Pictures). ▼▶

Fast Company (1938) **73m.** ** D: Edward Buzzell. Melvyn Douglas, Florence Rice, Claire Dodd, Louis Calhern, George Zucco, Shepperd Strudwick, Dwight Frye, Nat Pendleton. Lighthearted mystery about snappily married couple who find their rare-book business a springboard for sleuthing—especially when a fellow dealer is murdered and a friend of theirs is the key suspect. Based on a novel by Marco Page (a pseudonym for Harry Kurnitz, who also co-scripted the film). Followed by FAST AND LOOSE (1939). TV title: THE RARE-BOOK MURDER.

Fast Company (1953) **67m.** ** D: John Sturges. Howard Keel, Polly Bergen, Marjorie Main, Nina Foch, Robert Burton, Carol Nugent, Joaquin Garay, Horace McMahon, Iron Eyes Cody. Silly horse-racing yarn with hot-tempered Bergen inheriting a

nag and tangling with (and falling for) horse trainer Keel.

Fastest Gun Alive, The (1956) **92m.** *** D: Russell Rouse. Glenn Ford, Jeanne Crain, Broderick Crawford, Russ Tamblyn. Sincere Western with a moral. Ford is a peace-loving storekeeper trying to live down renown as gunslinger, but there's always someone waiting to challenge him. Tamblyn has an impressive solo dance feature. Also shown in computer-colored version. ▼▶

Fast Lady, The (1963-British) **C-95m.** **½ D: Ken Annakin. James Robertson Justice, Leslie Phillips, Stanley Baxter, Kathleen Harrison, Julie Christie, Eric Barker. Enjoyable, modest farce of naive Baxter, a Scotsman living in England, learning to drive an antique car—and to woo Christie in the process. Julie, in second film role, is thoroughly charming.

Fast Life (1932) **82m.** **½ D: Harry Pollard. William Haines, Madge Evans, Conrad Nagel, Arthur Byron, Cliff Edwards, Warburton Gamble. Vintage action farce stars Haines as the smart-aleck designer of a high-speed boat engine who competes with wealthy Nagel and his snobbish friends. Breezy but dated frolic must have seemed pretty snappy at the time. Buffs will note a rare on-screen appearance by short-subject producer/narrator Pete Smith as the announcer during the big race finale. ▶

Fast Workers (1933) **68m.** *½ D: Tod Browning. John Gilbert, Robert Armstrong, Mae Clarke, Muriel Kirkland, Vince Barnett, Virginia Cherrill, Sterling Holloway. Abysmal film based on a play called *Rivets*, about construction workers who are friendly romantic rivals. Starts out snappy, then turns to turgid dramatics. Odd material for horror director Browning, too. ▶

Fatal Desire (1954-Italian) **80m.** ** D: Carmine Gallone. Anthony Quinn, Kerima, May Britt, Ettore Manni, Umberto Spadaro; voice of Tito Gobbi. Nonmusical version of Mascagni's opera *Cavalleria Rusticana*, about love, adultery, and revenge in small Sicilian town. Originally filmed in color and 3-D, not released in U.S. until 1963 in b&w.

Fatal Hour, The (1940) **67m.** *½ D: William Nigh. Boris Karloff, Marjorie Reynolds, Grant Withers, Charles Trowbridge, John Hamilton, Frank Puglia, Jason Robards, Sr. Slight mystery, fourth in the *Mr. Wong* series, with the detective becoming involved in the investigation of a cop's death. ▼▶

Fatal Witness, The (1945) **59m.** *½ D: Lesley Selander. Evelyn Ankers, Richard Fraser, George Leigh, Barbara Everest, Frederick Worlock. Quickie mystery yarn with obvious plot about wealthy matron's murder, capture of culprit.

Fate Is the Hunter (1964) **106m.** **½ D: Ralph Nelson. Glenn Ford, Nancy Kwan, Rod

Taylor, Suzanne Pleshette, Jane Russell, Wally Cox, Nehemiah Persoff, Mark Stevens, Max Showalter, Mary Wickes. One-note drama of investigation into cause of controversial plane crash. Good cast works with routine script. Dorothy Malone appears unbilled in one key scene. CinemaScope. ▶

Father Brown SEE: **Detective, The** (1954)

Father Goose (1964) **C-115m.** *** D: Ralph Nelson. Cary Grant, Leslie Caron, Trevor Howard, Jack Good, Nicole Felsette. Grant goes native as shiftless bum on a South Seas island during WW2, who's persuaded to become a lookout for the Australian Navy—and finds himself sheltering Caron and a gaggle of schoolgirls fleeing the Japanese. Lightweight and enjoyable. Oscar-winning script by Peter Stone and Frank Tarloff. ▼▶

Father Is a Bachelor (1950) **84m.** ** D: Norman Foster, Abby Berlin. William Holden, Coleen Gray, Mary Jane Saunders, Stuart Erwin, Sig Ruman. Vagabond Holden with five "adopted" kids meets Gray who wants to marry him; "cute" comedy. ▶

Father Makes Good (1950) **61m.** *½ D: Jean Yarbrough. Raymond Walburn, Walter Catlett, Barbara Brown, Gertrude Astor. Mild little film in Walburn series about smalltown man who purchases a cow to show his contempt for new milk tax.

Father of the Bride (1950) **93m.** **** D: Vincente Minnelli. Spencer Tracy, Elizabeth Taylor, Joan Bennett, Billie Burke, Leo G. Carroll, Don Taylor, Rusty (Russ) Tamblyn. Liz is marrying Don Taylor, but Dad (Tracy) has all the aggravation. Perceptive view of American life, witty script by Frances Goodrich and Albert Hackett (based on Edward Streeter's book), and peerless Tracy performance. Sequel: FATHER'S LITTLE DIVIDEND. Later a TV series. Remade in 1991. Also shown in computer-colored version. ▼▶

Father's Little Dividend (1951) **82m.** *** D: Vincente Minnelli. Spencer Tracy, Joan Bennett, Elizabeth Taylor, Don Taylor, Billie Burke, Rusty (Russ) Tamblyn. Delightful sequel to FATHER OF THE BRIDE with same cast. Now Tracy is going to be a grandfather and he doesn't look forward to it. Also shown in computer-colored version. ▼▶

Father's Wild Game (1950) **61m.** *½ D: Herbert I. Leeds. Raymond Walburn, Walter Catlett, Jane Darwell, Roscoe Ates, Ann Tyrrell. In this entry, Walburn is protesting inflation at the meat market and decides to hunt wild game himself.

Father Takes a Walk (1935-British) **82m.** *** D: William Beaudine. Paul Graetz, Violet Farebrother, Chili Bouchier, Mickey Brantford, Ralph Truman, Barry Livesey, Kenneth Villiers. Lovely little sleeper about an aging department store entrepreneur (Graetz) who feels he no longer fits in now

that his son is running the business. Fascinating "quota quickie" curio is loaded with heart. Based on a Mary Roberts Rinehart story. Aka MR. COHEN TAKES A WALK.

Father Takes a Wife (1941) **79m.** **½ D: Jack Hively. Adolphe Menjou, Gloria Swanson, John Howard, Desi Arnaz, Helen Broderick, Florence Rice, Neil Hamilton. Pleasant little comedy about glamorous stage star (Swanson) who "settles down" and marries Menjou, but takes on opera singer Arnaz as her protégé.

Father Takes the Air (1951) **61m.** *½ D: Frank McDonald. Raymond Walburn, Walter Catlett, Florence Bates, Gary Gray. Walburn is involved with local flying school and accidentally captures a crook.

Father Was a Fullback (1949) **84m.** **½ D: John M. Stahl. Fred MacMurray, Maureen O'Hara, Betty Lynn, Rudy Vallee, Thelma Ritter, Natalie Wood. Wholesome comedy with most engaging cast. MacMurray is football coach with as many household problems as on the gridiron. ▼▶

Fat Man, The (1951) **77m.** **½ D: William Castle. J. Scott Smart, Rock Hudson, Julie London, Clinton Sundberg, Jayne Meadows, Emmett Kelly. The star of radio's popular series of the same name appeared in this one-shot film adaptation as the corpulent gourmet/detective (created by Dashiell Hammett) whose investigation of a murder leads him to a circus for whodunit showdown. Only dramatic film role for top clown Kelly.

Fat Spy, The (1965) **C-75m.** *½ D: Joseph Cates. Phyllis Diller, Jack E. Leonard, Brian Donlevy, Jayne Mansfield, Jordan Christopher, The Wild Ones, Johnny Tillotson. Once-in-a-lifetime cast makes this a must for camp followers—and a sure thing to avoid for most others. Fat Jack plays dual roles, in a story of a search for the Fountain of Youth. Shot in Florida. ▼▶

Faust (1926-German) **116m.** *** D: F. W. Murnau. Emil Jannings, Gosta Ekman, Camilla Horn, Wilhelm (William) Dieterle, Yvette Guilbert, Eric Barclay. Oft-told story of the eternal, earthly conflict between good and evil, in which the title character bargains away his soul to Mephistopheles (Jannings). Not a classic like Murnau's THE LAST LAUGH or SUNRISE, but still a compelling, inventively directed, visually sumptuous film, highlighted by clever special effects and impressive use of light and shadow. Based on the play by Goethe. Dieterle, then an actor, later directed THE DEVIL AND DANIEL WEBSTER. ▼▶

Fazil (1928) **88m.** ** D: Howard Hawks. Charles Farrell, Greta Nissen, Mae Busch, Vadim Uraneff, Tyler Brooke, John Boles. Strange casting of Farrell as desert sheik is just one oddity in this opulent romance. Visually stunning but dramatically far-fetched silent film. ▼

FBI Code 98 (1964) **104m.** ****½** D: Leslie H. Martinson. Jack Kelly, Ray Danton, Andrew Duggan, Philip Carey, William Reynolds, Peggy McCay, Kathleen Crowley, Merry Anders, Jack Cassidy, Vaughn Taylor, Robert Ridgely. Efficient, no-frills procedural utilizing documentary footage and a stentorian narrator singing the glories of the FBI during a hunt for the culprit who planted a bomb aboard a plane carrying three executives of an electronics company working on the U.S. missile program. Made for TV but released to theaters instead. ▶

F.B.I. Girl (1951) **74m.** ****** D: William Berke. Cesar Romero, George Brent, Audrey Totter, Tom Drake, Raymond Burr, Raymond Greenleaf, Margia Dean, Tom Noonan, Pete (Peter) Marshall, Joy (Joi) Lansing. Standard fare involving G-men Romero and Brent's investigation of the "accidental" death of a Bureau clerk. Burr is a standout as a quietly menacing thug. ▼▶

FBI Story, The (1959) **C-149m.** ******* D: Mervyn LeRoy. James Stewart, Vera Miles, Murray Hamilton, Larry Pennell, Nick Adams, Diane Jergens, Joyce Taylor. Well-mounted fabrication of history of FBI as seen through career of agent Stewart, allowing for episodic sidelights into action-packed capers and view of his personal life. The real J. Edgar Hoover appears briefly, seated at his desk, in a narrated scene without dialogue. ▼▶

Fear (1946) **68m.** ****** D: Alfred Zeisler. Peter Cookson, Warren William, Anne Gwynne, Francis Pierlot, Nestor Paiva, Darren McGavin. Impoverished student Cookson murders a pawnbroking college professor in a robbery attempt, then is hounded by police investigator William, in this low-budget modern-dress takeoff on Dostoyevsky's *Crime and Punishment*. ▼▶

Fear (1954-German-Italian) **84m.** ****½** D: Robert Rossellini. Ingrid Bergman, Mathias Wieman, Renate Mannhardt, Kurt Kreuger, Elise Aulinger, Edith Schultze-Westrum. Bergman gives an intense performance as the wife of a German scientist who breaks off an extramarital affair but is blackmailed by her lover's former mistress. Minor but compelling Rossellini film given an extra dimension by a surprise twist. Rossellini and Bergman's final film together before their divorce. Based on a novella by Stefan Zweig.

Fear and Desire (1953) **68m.** ****** D: Stanley Kubrick. Frank Silvera, Kenneth Harp, Paul Mazursky, Steve Coit, Virginia Leith; narrated by David Allen. Kubrick's elusive, shoestring-budget feature-film debut is an existential antiwar allegory centering on four GIs (including a very green Mazursky, in his film debut) stranded behind the lines of an unknown enemy and fighting a fictitious war in an unidentified country. Long suppressed by Kubrick himself—who also photographed, edited, and cowrote with poet/

playwright Howard Sackler—the movie contains some striking imagery and shows the germs of budding talent, but generally comes off as an arty and pretentious student film. ▶

Fear in the Night (1947) **72m.** ******* D: Maxwell Shane. Paul Kelly, DeForest Kelley, Kay Scott, Ann Doran, Robert Emmett Keane. Nifty chiller in which bank teller Kelley dreams he has killed a man in a mirrored room—and wakes up to be confronted by evidence that his fantasy was in fact reality. Based on the story "Nightmare" by William Irish (Cornell Woolrich); remade under that title in 1956. ▼▶

Fearless Fagan (1952) **79m.** ****** D: Stanley Donen. Carleton Carpenter, Janet Leigh, Keenan Wynn, Richard Anderson, Ellen Corby, Barbara Ruick. Title character is circus lion who accompanies his dimwitted master (Carpenter) into the Army, with predictable results. Inconsequential comedy. ▶

Fearmakers, The (1958) **83m.** ****½** D: Jacques Tourneur. Dana Andrews, Dick Foran, Marilee Earle, Veda Ann Borg, Mel Tormé. Brainwashed ex-POW Andrews comes home from the Korean War to discover that his PR firm has been overrun by subversives. Crisply told, low-budget Cold War thriller. While it's very much of its time, it anticipates contemporary ideas about the way politicians and political ideas are sold to the public. ▼▶

Fear Strikes Out (1957) **100m.** ******* D: Robert Mulligan. Anthony Perkins, Karl Malden, Norma Moore, Adam Williams, Perry Wilson. Stark account of baseball star Jimmy Piersall and his bout with mental illness; Perkins is properly intense, with Malden superb as his domineering father. VistaVision. ▼▶

Feathered Serpent, The (1948) **68m.** ***½** D: William Beaudine. Roland Winters, Keye Luke, Victor Sen Yung, Mantan Moreland, Carol Forman, Robert Livingston, Martin Garralaga, Nils Asther, Jay Silverheels. Even the return of Number One Son Luke can't revive this moribund *Charlie Chan* entry about the search for a priceless Mexican statue. Scripter Oliver Drake pilfered this from his own RIDERS OF THE WHISTLING SKULL (1937), which starred Livingston. ▼

Feather in Her Hat, A (1935) **72m.** ****½** D: Alfred Santell. Pauline Lord, Basil Rathbone, Louis Hayward, Billie Burke, Wendy Barrie, Nydia Westman, Victor Varconi, Thurston Hall, Nana Bryant, David Niven. Poor widow (stage actress Lord, in her second and final screen role after MRS. WIGGS OF THE CABBAGE PATCH) schemes to brighten the prospects of her son (Hayward), who aspires to be a playwright. Not exactly profound, but worth seeing for its cast.

Feet First (1930) **91m.** ****½** D: Clyde Bruckman. Harold Lloyd, Barbara Kent,

Robert McWade, Lillian Leighton, Henry Hall. Lloyd talkie tries to rekindle spirit of his silent comedies with middling results. Episodic film has some very funny moments, but Harold's building-ledge routine doesn't quite come off. ▼▶

Fellowship of the Frog SEE: **Face of the Frog**

Female (1933) **60m.** *** D: Michael Curtiz. Ruth Chatterton, George Brent, Ferdinand Gottschalk, Philip Faversham, Ruth Donnelly, Johnny Mack Brown, Lois Wilson, Gavin Gordon. Chatterton runs a major auto company with an iron hand—and tries to conduct her love life the same way—until independent-minded Brent comes along. (The two stars were then married in real life.) Funny, fascinating role-reversal yarn with incredibly lavish set design—watch for the organist perched in Ruth's entrance foyer! ▼●▶

Female (1956) SEE: **Violent Years, The**

Female and the Flesh SEE: **Light Across the Street, The**

Female Animal, The (1958) **84m.** **½ D: Harry Keller. Hedy Lamarr, Jane Powell, Jan Sterling, George Nader. Sad waste of Lamarr as mature Hollywood star who grapples with adopted daughter Powell over Nader. CinemaScope.

Female Jungle (1956) **56m.** ** D: Bruno VeSota. Jayne Mansfield, Lawrence Tierney, John Carradine, Kathleen Crowley, Rex Thorsen, Burt Carlisle, Bruno VeSota. Lukewarm melodrama of cop Tierney seeking the killer of an actress. Mansfield costars as a nymphomaniac; also known as THE HANGOVER. ▼

Female on the Beach (1955) **97m.** ** D: Joseph Pevney. Joan Crawford, Jeff Chandler, Jan Sterling, Cecil Kellaway, Judith Evelyn, Natalie Schafer, Charles Drake. Hot, heavy—and very tacky—melodrama, in which fisherman-stud Chandler attempts to put the make on wealthy widow Crawford. Outrageously trashy script is crammed with sexual double entendres. A must for Crawford fans—but don't expect anything resembling a good movie. ▶

Feminine Touch, The (1941) **97m.** **½ D: W. S. Van Dyke II. Rosalind Russell, Don Ameche, Kay Francis, Van Heflin, Donald Meek, Gordon Jones, Robert Ryan. Brittle comedy of author Ameche writing book on jealousy, finding himself a victim when he brings wife Russell to N.Y.C.; she suspects he's carrying on with glamorous Francis.

Feminine Touch, The (1956-British) **C-91m.** ** D: Pat Jackson. George Baker, Belinda Lee, Delphi Lawrence, Adrienne Corri, Diana Wynyard. Undistinguished look at student nurses' experiences as they graduate to full-time hospital jobs. Also known as THE GENTLE TOUCH.

Fernandel the Dressmaker (1957-French) **84m.** **½ D: Jean Boyer. Fernandel, Suzy

Delair, Françoise Fabian, Georges Chamarat. Undemanding plot has Fernandel wanting to be high-fashion designer rather than drab man's tailor. ▼

Ferry Cross the Mersey (1965-British) **88m.** ** D: Jeremy Summers. Gerry and The Pacemakers, Cilla Black, The Fourmost, Jimmy Saville. Gerry Marsden and The Pacemakers perform eight songs in this musical made to cash in on their popularity; most appropriately, they appear as a Liverpool band attempting to compete in a music contest.

Ferry to Hong Kong (1959-British) **C-103m.** **½ D: Lewis Gilbert. Orson Welles, Curt Jurgens, Sylvia Syms, Jeremy Spenser. Welles and Jurgens have field day as straight-faced ferry boat skipper and drunken Austrian on trip to Macao. Otherwise just routine. CinemaScope. ▼▶

Feudin' Fools (1952) **63m.** ** D: William Beaudine. Leo Gorcey, Huntz Hall, Bennie Bartlett, David Gorcey, Bernard Gorcey, Dorothy Ford, Lyle Talbot, Benny Baker, Russell Simpson, Bob Easton. Sach inherits a farm in Kentucky and gets caught in the crossfire of a family feud. Formula *Bowery Boys* slapstick for the sticks. ▶

Feudin', Fussin' and a-Fightin' (1948) **78m.** **½ D: George Sherman. Donald O'Connor, Marjorie Main, Percy Kilbride, Penny Edwards, Joe Besser. Pleasant musical comedy about a traveling salesman who is "recruited" by a rural town to represent them in an annual footrace. Title derives from a pop hit of the day. O'Connor also performs his famous "Me and My Shadow" number with Louis DaPron. ▼

Fever in the Blood, A (1961) **117m.** **½ D: Vincent Sherman. Efrem Zimbalist, Jr., Angie Dickinson, Herbert Marshall, Don Ameche, Jack Kelly, Carroll O'Connor. Turgid dramatics focusing on murder trial which various candidates for governor use to further political ambitions. ▶

Fever Mounts at El Pao SEE: **La Fièvre Monte à El Pao**

Fiancés, The (1963-Italian) **77m.** ***½ D: Ermanno Olmi. Carlo Cabrini, Anna Canzi. Young man accepts a welding job in Sicily that will take him away from his fiancée for a year and a half; neither is sure if their relationship will survive the strain of the time apart. Quietly piercing study of love and loneliness in the modern era, told—often in flashbacks—with graceful ease. Writerdirector Olmi uses locations and sounds to create a mood that is as expressive and suggestive as the faces of his two lead actors. Italian title: I FIDANZATI. ▶

Fiendish Ghouls, The SEE: **Mania**

Fiend Who Walked the West, The (1958) **101m.** **½ D: Gordon Douglas. Hugh O'Brian, Robert Evans, Dolores Michaels, Linda Cristal, Stephen McNally. Interesting if not altogether successful transposition of

KISS OF DEATH to Western setting, with Evans ludicrous in the Widmark psycho role. CinemaScope. ▼▶

Fiend Without a Face (1958-British) **74m.** *½ D: Arthur Crabtree. Marshall Thompson, Kim Parker, Terence Kilburn, Michael Balfour, Gil Winfield. Scientist materializes thoughts in form of invisible brain-shaped creatures which kill people for food. Horrific climax; good special effects. ▼▶●

Fiercest Heart, The (1961) **C-91m.** ** D: George Sherman. Stuart Whitman, Juliet Prowse, Ken Scott, Raymond Massey, Geraldine Fitzgerald. Good cast and action-packed skirmishes with Zulus can't raise this programmer to any heights. Set in Africa. CinemaScope.

Fiesta (1947) **C-104m.** ** D: Richard Thorpe. Esther Williams, Akim Tamiroff, Ricardo Montalban, John Carroll, Mary Astor, Cyd Charisse. Williams trades in her bathing suit for a toreador outfit in this weak musical opus. ▶

15 Maiden Lane (1936) **65m.** ** D: Allan Dwan. Claire Trevor, Cesar Romero, Douglas Fowley, Lloyd Nolan, Lester Matthews. Trevor lures Romero in order to crack his underworld gang in this satisfactory programmer.

5th Ave. Girl (1939) **83m.** ** D: Gregory LaCava. Ginger Rogers, Walter Connolly, Verree Teasdale, James Ellison, Tim Holt, Kathryn Adams, Franklin Pangborn, Louis Calhern, Jack Carson. Tiresome social comedy with Rogers as homeless girl taken in by unhappy millionaire Connolly; even Ginger is lifeless in this film that purports to show that poor is better than rich if you've got a head on your shoulders. ▼▶

55 Days at Peking (1963) **C-150m.** *** D: Nicholas Ray. Charlton Heston, Ava Gardner, David Niven, Flora Robson, John Ireland, Paul Lukas, Jacques Sernas. Stars provide most of the interest in confusing historical account of Boxer Rebellion in 1900s China. Runs 159m. with overture, intermission/entr'acte, exit music. Super Technirama 70. ▼●

50 Million Frenchmen (1931) **68m.** ** D: Lloyd Bacon. William Gaxton, Claudia Dell, Ole Olsen, Chic Johnson, John Halliday, Helen Broderick, Lester Crawford. An American (Gaxton) in Paris bets $50,000 that he can woo and win Dell in two weeks without spending any money. Flat early-talkie farce adapted from the Broadway hit musical inexplicably cuts out all the songs by Cole Porter! Olsen & Johnson try to add some life to the proceedings. Look for Bela Lugosi as a sinister magician. Originally released in two-strip Technicolor.

Fifty Roads to Town (1937) **81m.** **½ D: Norman Taurog. Don Ameche, Ann Sothern, Slim Summerville, Jane Darwell, John Qualen, Stepin Fetchit, Oscar Apfel. Above-par comedy of Ameche and Soth-

ern, both on the lam for different reasons, snowbound together in small inn.

52nd Street (1937) **80m.** ** D: Harold Young. Ian Hunter, Leo Carrillo, Pat Paterson, Kenny Baker, Ella Logan, ZaSu Pitts. Fictionalized story of how 52nd St. became nightclub row in the 1930s; soggy drama punctuated by appearances of some 52nd St. entertainers like Jerry Colonna, Georgie Tapps, Pat Harrington, Sr.

Fighter, The (1952) **78m.** **½ D: Herbert Kline. Richard Conte, Vanessa Brown, Lee J. Cobb, Roberta Haynes. Absorbing tale set in Mexico with Conte a boxer who uses winnings to buy arms to seek revenge for family's murder. ▼▶

Fighter Attack (1953) **C-80m.** ** D: Lesley Selander. Sterling Hayden, J. Carrol Naish, Joy Page, Paul Fierro. Modest film uses flashback to recount Hayden's last important mission in WW2 Italy. ▼

Fighter Squadron (1948) **C-96m.** ** D: Raoul Walsh. Edmond O'Brien, Robert Stack, John Rodney, Tom D'Andrea, Henry Hull. OK WW2 drama of dedicated flier O'Brien, has abundance of clichés weighing against good action sequences. Rock Hudson's first film. ▶

Fight For Your Lady (1937) **67m.** **½ D: Ben Stoloff. John Boles, Jack Oakie, Ida Lupino, Margot Grahame, Gordon Jones, Erik Rhodes, Billy Gilbert. Wrestling trainer Oakie takes over singer Boles' love life when he's jilted by tony Grahame in this fluffy but funny musical comedy. Rhodes is hilarious, as usual, as Spadissimo.

Fighting Caravans (1931) **92m.** ** D: Otto Brower, David Burton. Gary Cooper, Lili Damita, Ernest Torrence, Tully Marshall, Eugene Pallette, Fred Kohler, Charles Winninger. Cooper is a wagon train scout romancing pretty Damita while thwarting an Indian attack stirred up by evil trader Kohler. Good cast is only point of interest in this unexciting, would-be prestige Western based on a Zane Grey tale. TV title: BLAZING ARROWS. ▼▶

Fighting Chance, The (1955) **70m.** ** D: William Witney. Rod Cameron, Julie London, Ben Cooper, Taylor Holmes, Bob Steele. Standard fare. Horse trainer and jockey friend both fall in love with London and are soon at odds with each other.

Fighting Coast Guard (1951) **86m.** **½ D: Joseph Kane. Brian Donlevy, Forrest Tucker, Ella Raines, John Russell, Richard Jaeckel, William Murphy, Martin Milner, Steve Brodie, Hugh O'Brian. Better than usual entry in training-for-war film, mixing romance with WW2 military action.

Fighting Cowboy, The SEE: **Hoppy's Holiday**

Fighting Father Dunne (1948) **93m.** **½ D: Ted Tetzlaff. Pat O'Brien, Darryl Hickman, Charles Kemper, Una O'Connor, Arthur Shields, Anna Q. Nilsson, Billy Gray. Road company BOYS TOWN with determined priest O'Brien devoting his life to easing the plight of poor, homeless newsboys in St. Louis. ▼

Fighting Fools (1949) 69m. ** D: Reginald LeBorg. Leo Gorcey, Huntz Hall, Gabriel Dell, Frankie Darro, Billy Benedict, David Gorcey, Benny Bartlett, Lyle Talbot, Evelynne Eaton, Bernard Gorcey. Familiar fisticuffs as the Bowery Boys team with boxer Darro to break up a fight fixing racket. ▶

Fighting Guardsman (1945) 84m. ** D: Henry Levin. Willard Parker, Anita Louise, Janis Carter, John Loder, Edgar Buchanan, George Macready. OK costumer of oppressed Frenchmen rising against tyranny in days before French Revolution.

Fighting Kentuckian, The (1949) 100m. **½ D: George Waggner. John Wayne, Vera Ralston, Philip Dorn, Oliver Hardy, Marie Windsor. Frontierland around 1810 is setting for two-fisted saga of Kentuckian (Wayne) combating land-grabbing criminals and courting Ralston, French general's daughter. Hardy makes rare solo appearance in character role. Also shown in computer-colored version. ▼▶

Fighting Lawman, The (1953) 71m. *½ D: Thomas Carr. Wayne Morris, Virginia Grey, Harry Lauter, John Kellogg, Myron Healey, Dick Rich. Lackluster account of a woman determined to grab loot from robbers. Grey tries but is defeated by flimsy script.

Fighting Man From Arizona SEE: **Dead Don't Dream, The**

Fighting Man of the Plains (1949) C-94m. **½ D: Edwin L. Marin. Randolph Scott, Bill Williams, Jane Nigh, Victor Jory, Douglas Kennedy, Joan Taylor. Scott seeks to avenge brother's murder, but kills the wrong man. OK Western, with Dale Robertson in his first prominent role (as Jesse James).

Fighting O'Flynn, The (1949) 94m. **½ D: Arthur Pierson. Douglas Fairbanks, Jr., Richard Greene, Helena Carter, Patricia Medina. Enjoyable swashbuckler set in 1800s Ireland with Fairbanks and Greene vying in love and intrigue. Cowritten by Fairbanks and Robert Thoeren.

Fighting Pimpernel, The SEE: **Elusive Pimpernel, The**

Fighting Seabees, The (1944) 100m. *** D: Edward Ludwig. John Wayne, Susan Hayward, Dennis O'Keefe, William Frawley, Leonid Kinskey, J. M. Kerrigan, Ben Welden, Paul Fix, Grant Withers, Duncan Renaldo. Spirited WW2 saga of construction company boss Wayne and naval officer O'Keefe tangling professionally and personally, with journalist Hayward the love interest. The scenario charts the manner in which the "Seabees" (or battalion of construction worker–soldiers) came to be established. Screenplay by Borden

Chase and Aeneas MacKenzie. Action-packed second unit direction by Howard Lydecker. ▼▶

Fighting 69th, The (1940) 90m. **½ D: William Keighley. James Cagney, Pat O'Brien, George Brent, Jeffrey Lynn, Alan Hale, Frank McHugh, Dennis Morgan, Dick Foran, John Litel, George Reeves, Frank Coghlan, Jr. Overripe (but tough to dislike) WW1 tale mixes roughneck comedy, exciting battle action, sloppy sentiment, incredible characterizations (especially Cagney's) detailing exploits of famed Irish regiment. Also shown in computer-colored version. ▼▶

Fighting Sullivans, The SEE: **Sullivans, The**

Fighting Texan, The SEE: **False Paradise**

Fighting Trouble (1956) 61m. *½ D: George Blair. Huntz Hall, Stanley Clements, Adele Jergens, Joseph Downing, Queenie Smith, David Gorcey. With Leo Gorcey gone (replaced by Clements, as "Duke"), Hall became top banana in the *Bowery Boys* series, starting with this underdeveloped crime photographers tale. ▶

Fighting Wildcats, The (1957-British) 74m. ** D: Arthur Crabtree. Keefe Brasselle, Kay Callard, Karel Stepanek, Ursula Howells. Innocuous intrigue set in London and Middle East involving gangsters. Original title: WEST OF SUEZ.

Fighting Youth (1935) 85m. **½ D: Hamilton MacFadden. Charles Farrell, June Martel, Andy Devine, J. Farrell MacDonald, Ann Sheridan, Edward Nugent. Commies vs. College Football! A genuinely bizarre bit of kitsch with subversive student Sheridan squaring off against antiradical quarterback Farrell. Definitely one for the time capsule.

File on Thelma Jordon, The (1949) 100m. **½ D: Robert Siodmak. Barbara Stanwyck, Wendell Corey, Joan Tetzel, Stanley Ridges, Richard Rober, Paul Kelly. Assistant D.A. Corey's secret fling with Stanwyck ends when she's accused of her wealthy aunt's murder. He gets himself assigned to prosecute her in order to throw the case . . . but *is* she the killer, and was the fling just part of her long-range plan? You haven't seen enough films noir if you're not one step ahead of this plot. Handsomely photographed by George Barnes. Aka THELMA JORDON. ▶

Final Edition, The (1932) 65m. **½ D: Howard Higgin. Pat O'Brien, Mae Clarke, Mary Doran, Bradley Page, Morgan Wallace, James Donlan, Phil Tead. Big-city reporter Clarke tries to get the goods on racketeers to impress her hot-tempered editor (O'Brien), who also happens to be her on-again, off-again boyfriend. Enjoyable little newspaper yarn is peppered with snappy dialogue and captures the seamy underworld milieu.

Final Lie, The SEE: **Matter of Dignity, A**

Final Test, The (1953-British) **84m.** **½
D: Anthony Asquith. Jack Warner, Robert
Morley, George Relph, Adrianne Allen.
Droll, minor comedy of father-son rivalry
over charming Allen.

Finances of the Grand Duke, The (1924-
German) **78m.** **½ D: F. W. Murnau. Harry
Liedtke, Mady Christians, Alfred Abel,
Julius Falkenstein, Walter Rilla, Adolphe
Engers, Guido Herzfeld, Ilka Grüning, Max
Schreck. Kindhearted dictator of a small
island nation is wallowing in debt. What's
a benevolent despot to do? Perhaps marry
a Russian princess (Christians) who is rolling in wealth. Trivial but lightly likable
dramatic farce; unusual fare for Murnau.
Schreck (of NOSFERATU fame) plays one
of a quartet of creepy conspirators. Scripted
by Thea von Harbou, from a novel by Frank
Heller.▶

Finders Keepers (1951) **74m.** **½ D:
Frederick de Cordova. Tom Ewell, Julia (Julie) Adams, Evelyn Varden, Dusty
Henley. Scatterbrained comedy that chugs
down at end. Ewell and Varden enliven proceedings about a little boy who comes home
with a cartful of money.

Finger Man (1955) **82m.** ** D: Harold
Schuster. Frank Lovejoy, Forrest Tucker,
Peggie Castle, Timothy Carey, Glenn Gordon, Evelynne Eaton. Convincing performances uplift account of federal agents
capturing liquor gang.▼

Finger of Guilt (1956-British) **85m.** **½
D: Joseph Losey. Richard Basehart, Mary
Murphy, Constance Cummings, Roger
Livesey, Mervyn Johns, Faith Brook.
Film director Basehart is blackmailed by
woman claiming to be his mistress, which
threatens his career and marriage. Intriguing film with disappointing resolution;
good look inside British film studio, however. Directed by blacklistee Losey under
pseudonyms Alec Snowden/Joseph Walton.
Originally released in England as THE IN-
TIMATE STRANGER at 95m.

Finger on the Trigger (1965) **C-87m.**
BOMB D: Sidney Pink. Rory Calhoun,
James Philbrook, Todd Martin, Silvia
Solar, Brad Talbot. Reb and Yankee vets
join forces to secure buried treasure while
holding off hostile Indians. Made in Spain.
Techniscope.▼

Finger Points, The (1931) **88m.** **½ D:
John Francis Dillon. Richard Barthelmess,
Fay Wray, Regis Toomey, Robert Elliott,
Clark Gable. Vivid though meandering
melodrama about crime reporter Barthelmess on the payroll of the mob. Wray
is a newspaperwoman who urges him to go
straight; Gable scores as a gang boss. One
of the writers was W. R. Burnett.

Fingerprints Don't Lie (1951) **57m.** ** D:
Sam Newfield. Richard Travis, Sheila
Ryan, Sid Melton, Tom Neal, Margia Dean,
Lyle Talbot. It's science vs. crime decades

before TV's famed forensic series as police
lab man Travis checks into the possibility of
faked fingerprints, examines hair samples,
etc., to determine if a convicted man was
intricately framed. Production values are on
a 1950s TV level, there's an organ score,
and comic relief Melton is relentless.

Fingers at the Window (1942) **80m.** **½
D: Charles Lederer. Lew Ayres, Laraine Day,
Basil Rathbone, Walter Kingsford, Miles
Mander, James Flavin. Entertaining mystery
of Ayres and Day tracking down maniac killer
masterminding repeated axe murders.

Finishing School (1934) **73m.** **½ D:
Wanda Tuchock, George Nicholls, Jr.
Frances Dee, Bruce Cabot, Ginger Rogers,
Beulah Bondi, Billie Burke, John Halliday.
Interesting look at exclusive girls' school
where hypocrisy reigns; wealthy Dee falls
in love with struggling hospital intern Cabot.
▼▶

Finnegans Wake (1965) **97m.** ***½ D:
Mary Ellen Bute. Page Johnson, Martin
J. Kelly, Jane Reilly, Peter Haskell. James
Joyce's classic story of Irish tavern-keeper
who dreams of attending his own wake is
brought to the screen with great energy and
control.

Fire and Ice SEE: Le Combat dans L'ile

Fireball, The (1950) **84m.** *** D: Tay Garnett. Mickey Rooney, Pat O'Brien, Beverly
Tyler, Marilyn Monroe, Milburn Stone,
Glenn Corbett. Rooney's energetic performance carries this film. Orphan boy devotes
himself to becoming big-time roller-skating
champ.▼▶

Fire Down Below (1957-British) **C-116m.**
**½ D: Robert Parrish. Rita Hayworth, Rob-
ert Mitchum, Jack Lemmon, Herbert Lom,
Bernard Lee, Anthony Newley. Contrived
but entertaining melodrama of Mitchum
and Lemmon, owners of tramp boat, falling
in love with shady Hayworth on voyage between islands. CinemaScope.▼▶

Firefly, The (1937) **129m.** **½ D: Robert Z.
Leonard. Jeanette MacDonald, Allan Jones,
Warren William, Billy Gilbert, Henry Dani-
ell, Douglass Dumbrille, George Zucco.
MacDonald plays a spy working in France
on behalf of Spain during the Napoleonic
wars in this rewrite of the Rudolf Friml–
Otto Harbach operetta. Goes on much too
long, but fans of Jeanette won't mind, and
Jones introduces "The Donkey Serenade."
▼▶

Fire Maidens of Outer Space (1956-
British) **80m.** BOMB D: Cy Roth. Anthony
Dexter, Susan Shaw, Paul Carpenter, Harry
Fowler, Sydney Tafler. Ultracheap space
opera about astronauts who land on Jupiter's
13th moon and discover a society of young
lovelies in need of male companionship.
Another in the So Bad It's Good Sweepstakes; you haven't lived until you've seen
the Fire Maidens perform their ritual dance
to "Stranger in Paradise." Original British

[215]

title: FIRE MAIDENS FROM OUTER SPACE. ▼▶

Fireman, Save My Child (1932) 67m. **½ D: Lloyd Bacon. Joe E. Brown, Evalyn Knapp, Lillian Bond, Guy Kibbee, Virginia Sale. Amusing Brown romp with Joe dividing his time between fire-fighting and baseball. The first in his baseball trilogy, followed by ELMER THE GREAT and ALIBI IKE.

Fireman Save My Child (1954) 80m. *½ D: Leslie Goodwins. Spike Jones, The City Slickers, Buddy Hackett, Hugh O'Brian, Adele Jergens. Sloppy slapstick with Spike Jones et al. manning fire station in 1900s San Francisco, running amuck when they receive a new fire engine. Originally intended for Abbott and Costello, who are still visible in some long shots.

Fire Over Africa (1954) C-84m. ** D: Richard Sale. Maureen O'Hara, Macdonald Carey, Binnie Barnes, Guy Middleton. O'Hara makes a pretty law enforcer traveling to Africa to track down dope-smuggling syndicate. Filmed on location.

Fire Over England (1937-British) 89m. *** D: William K. Howard. Laurence Olivier, Flora Robson, Leslie Banks, Raymond Massey, Vivien Leigh, Tamara Desni, Morton Selten, Robert Newton, Donald Calthrop. Satisfying historical drama of British-Spanish conflict in 1500s with flawless performance by Robson (Queen Elizabeth), fine villainy by Massey, romantic support by Olivier and Leigh. Watch for James Mason in a small (unbilled) role. ▼▶

Fires on the Plain (1959-Japanese) 105m. ***½ D: Kon Ichikawa. Eiji Funakoshi, Mantaro Ushio, Yoshihiro Hamaguchi, Osamu Takizawa. Japanese soldiers struggle to survive at the finale of the Philippine campaign during WW2; focus is on travails of tubercular Funakoshi, separated from his unit. Graphically realistic, disturbing, and depressing vision of damnation on earth, with a sobering antiwar message. Daieiscope. ▼●▶

Fire Within, The (1963-French) 108m. ***½ D: Louis Malle. Maurice Ronet, Lena Skerla, Yvonne Clech, Hubert Deschamps, Jeanne Moreau, Alexandra Stewart. Shattering study of alcoholism, as wealthy Ronet, released from a sanitarium after a breakdown, visits his old friends in Paris one last time. Probably Malle's best early film—photographed, scored (with the music of Erik Satie), and acted to maximum effect—and with a minimum of self-pity. ▼▶

First Auto, The (1927) 77m. *** D: Roy Del Ruth. Russell Simpson, Patsy Ruth Miller, Charles Emmett Mack, Frank Campeau, William Demarest, Gibson Gowland. Humor, history, and sentiment are well blended in story (by Darryl F. Zanuck) of the clash between the stubborn old owner of a livery stable and his race-car–loving son at the turn of the 20th century. Legendary racer Barney Oldfield appears as himself in this silent film featuring synchronized sound effects, music, and a few words.▶

First Comes Courage (1943) 88m. **½ D: Dorothy Arzner. Merle Oberon, Brian Aherne, Carl Esmond, Isobel Elsom, Fritz Leiber, Erik Rolf, Larry Parks. Arzner's final feature is a fairly good wartime drama, with Norwegian Oberon using her feminine wiles to extract secrets from Nazi officer Esmond. Complications arise when British commando Aherne enters the scene.

First Hundred Years, The (1938) 73m. *** D: Richard Thorpe. Robert Montgomery, Virginia Bruce, Warren William, Binnie Barnes, Harry Davenport, Alan Dinehart, Nydia Westman. Chic comedy finds married couple Montgomery and Bruce at a crossroads: should she give up her successful career as a theatrical agent in N.Y.C. when he finally gets a big promotion that necessitates moving to New England? Ahead of its time, though the frivolity peters out before the end. Produced and written by Norman Krasna.

First Lady (1937) 82m. *** D: Stanley Logan. Kay Francis, Anita Louise, Verree Teasdale, Preston Foster, Walter Connolly, Victor Jory, Louise Fazenda. Witty adaptation of the acerbic George S. Kaufman–Katherine Dayton play, with Francis as the ambitious wife of the Secretary of State (Foster), whom she's pushing into presidential campaign against corrupt judge Connolly. Not very cinematic, but brightly acted by fine ensemble.

First Legion, The (1951) 86m. *** D: Douglas Sirk. Charles Boyer, William Demarest, Lyle Bettger, Barbara Rush. Engrossing low-key account of Jesuit priest who is dubious about an alleged miracle occurring in his town. Boyer gives one of his best performances.▼

First Love (1939) 84m. *** D: Henry Koster. Deanna Durbin, Robert Stack, Helen Parrish, Eugene Pallette, Leatrice Joy, Marcia Mae Jones, Frank Jenks. Charming Cinderella story of orphaned girl (Durbin) going to live with uncle and finding romance with Stack (in his film debut). Durbin sings "Amapola" and other songs; her first screen kiss (courtesy Stack) made headlines around the world. ▼▶

First Love (1958-Italian) 103m. ** D: Mario Camerini. Carla Gravina, Raf Mattioli, Lorella DeLuca, Luciano Marin. Ettore Scola coscripted this simple—and all-too-familiar—account of the pangs of adolescent love.

First Man Into Space (1959-British) 77m. ** D: Robert Day. Marshall Thompson, Marla Landi, Robert Ayres, Bill Nagy, Carl Jaffe, Bill Edwards. Daring pilot, brother of hero, disobeys orders and becomes the title character, returning to Earth a dust-encrusted, blood-drinking monster. Better than it sounds.▼▶

First Men in the Moon (1964-British) **C-103m.** *** D: Nathan Juran. Edward Judd, Martha Hyer, Lionel Jeffries, Erik Chitty. Lavish adaptation of H. G. Wells novel is heavy-handed at times, overloaded with comic relief, but still worthwhile; good Ray Harryhausen special effects. Cameo appearance by Peter Finch. Panavision.▼●▶

First of the Few, The SEE: **Spitfire** (1942)

First Spaceship on Venus (1960-German) **C-78m.** ** D: Kurt Maetzig. Yoko Tani, Oldrich Lukes, Ignacy Machowski, Julius Ongewe. Expedition goes to Venus following clues left by alien ship that exploded on Earth years before. They discover war-blasted landscape and still operating machines. Well produced but stilted. International coproduction was cut by an hour in the U.S., explaining the incoherent storyline. From novel by Europe's most significant sci-fi writer, Stanislaw Lem, who repudiated the film. Totalvision.▼▶

First Texan, The (1956) **82m.** **½ D: Byron Haskin. Joel McCrea, Felicia Farr, Jeff Morrow, Wallace Ford. McCrea is forceful as Sam Houston, leading Texans in fight against Mexico for independence; good action sequences. CinemaScope.▶

First Time, The (1952) **89m.** ** D: Frank Tashlin. Robert Cummings, Barbara Hale, Jeff Donnell, Mona Barrie, Cora Witherspoon. Predictable comedy pegged on young couple's many problems with raising a baby.▶

First Traveling Saleslady, The (1956) **C-92m.** ** D: Arthur Lubin. Ginger Rogers, Barry Nelson, Carol Channing, David Brian, James Arness, Clint Eastwood. Rogers and Channing try to elevate this plodding comedy of girdle-sellers in the old West, but barely succeed. Carol and Clint make one of the oddest couples in screen history.

First Yank Into Tokyo (1945) **82m.** ** D: Gordon Douglas. Tom Neal, Barbara Hale, Marc Cramer, Richard Loo, Keye Luke, Leonard Strong, Benson Fong. Low-budget quickie made to be topical isn't so anymore, and it's not too good either; Neal undergoes plastic surgery, poses as Japanese soldier to help captured American atomic scientist escape. Of note as the first Hollywood film to acknowledge the existence of nuclear firepower.▼

First Year, The (1926) **67m.** *** D: Frank Borzage. Matt Moore, Kathryn Perry, John Patrick, Frank Currier, Frank Cooley, Virginia Madison, J. Farrell MacDonald. Sensitive and perceptive comedy-drama about the problems that befall newlyweds Moore and Perry during their first year of marriage. A disastrous dinner party scene is a gem. Sweet silent film is one of its director's minor works, but charming nonetheless. From a play by Frank Craven. Remade in 1932.

Fistful of Dollars (1964-Italian) **C-100m.** *** D: Sergio Leone. Clint Eastwood, Gian Maria Volonté, Marianne Koch, Wolfgang Lukschy, Mario Brega, Carol Brown. Sagebrush remake of YOJIMBO single-handedly invented the "spaghetti Western," made an international superstar of Eastwood, and boosted the careers of Leone and composer Ennio Morricone as well. Clint plays the laconic Man With No Name, a tough gunslinger manipulating (and manipulated by!) two rival families warring over small frontier town. Amusing, violent, and very stylish. Released in the U.S. in 1967. Sequel: FOR A FEW DOLLARS MORE. Techniscope. ▼●▶

Fist in His Pocket (1965-Italian) **105m.** **** D: Marco Bellochio. Lou Castel, Paola Pitagora, Marino Mase, Liliana Gerace, Pier Luigi Troglio. Brilliant one-of-a-kind about a mad family of epileptics whose protagonist kills his mother and drowns his younger brother, while his sis merely settles for repressed incest. One of the great, if largely unheralded, foreign films of the '60s, with Castel more than up to the demands of the difficult role. Aka FISTS IN HIS POCKET.▶

Fit for a King (1937) **73m.** **½ D: Edward Sedgwick. Joe E. Brown, Helen Mack, Paul Kelly, Harry Davenport, Halliwell Hobbes, John Qualen. Somewhat better than usual vehicle for Brown, as a *N.Y. Blade* office boy who plays cub reporter and covers a royal assassination plot against a visiting archduke. Among the set pieces are Brown in frilly drag as a maid and a big chase finale. Good supporting cast elevates silly material. Remake of I'LL TELL THE WORLD (1933).▼▶

Five (1951) **93m.** *** D: Arch Oboler. William Phipps, Susan Douglas, James Anderson, Charles Lampkin, Earl Lee. Intriguing, offbeat film by famed radio writer-director Oboler about the survivors of an atomic holocaust. Talky (and sometimes given to purple prose) but interesting. Filmed in and around Oboler's Frank Lloyd Wright house.▶

5 Against the House (1955) **84m.** **½ D: Phil Karlson. Guy Madison, Kim Novak, Brian Keith, Alvy Moore, Kerwin Mathews, William Conrad, Kathryn Grant. On a lark, a bored college rich boy plans a Reno, Nevada, casino heist. He doesn't realize that one of his pals (Keith), a mentally scarred war veteran, is a loose cannon. Interesting (if sometimes overpraised) film has its moments; noteworthy for sympathetic portrayal of the Keith character. Stirling Silliphant, William Bowers, and John Barnwell adapted Jack Finney's story.▶

Five and Ten (1931) **89m.** *** D: Robert Z. Leonard. Marion Davies, Leslie Howard, Richard Bennett, Irene Rich, Kent Douglass (Douglass Montgomery), Mary Duncan. Self-made mogul and his family move to N.Y.C. from Kansas City. He's too busy running his business empire to note that his wife is straying, his son is frustrated, and his daughter (Davies) is setting her sights on architect Howard, who's engaged to someone else. Snappy dialogue and nice Davies-Howard chemistry add oomph to this entertaining pre-Code soap opera. Based on a book by Fannie Hurst.

Five Angles on Murder SEE: **Woman in Question, The**

5 Branded Women (1960) **106m.** ** D: Martin Ritt. Van Heflin, Silvana Mangano, Jeanne Moreau, Vera Miles, Barbara Bel Geddes, Richard Basehart, Harry Guardino, Carla Gravina, Alex Nicol, Steve Forrest. Overambitious production, badly miscast, set in WW2 Middle Europe. Five girls scorned by partisans for consorting with Nazis prove their patriotism.

Five Came Back (1939) **75m.** *** D: John Farrow. Chester Morris, Lucille Ball, Wendy Barrie, John Carradine, Allen Jenkins, Joseph Calleia, C. Aubrey Smith, Patric Knowles. This sleeper shows its age a bit, but remains interesting for colorful character studies among passengers on plane downed in headhunter-infested Amazon jungle. Remade by Farrow as BACK FROM ETERNITY. ▼●)

Five Day Lover (1961-French-Italian) **86m.** *** D: Philippe De Broca. Jean Seberg, Micheline Presle, Jean-Pierre Cassel, François Perier. Perceptive, flavorful bedroom comedy featuring Seberg as a bored housewife-mother who has an affair with Cassel, who's being kept by her friend (Presle).

Five Finger Exercise (1962) **109m.** **½ D: Daniel Mann. Rosalind Russell, Jack Hawkins, Maximilian Schell, Richard Beymer, Lana Wood, Annette Gorman. Peter Shaffer's play suffers from change of locale and alteration of original ideas; now it becomes embarrassing soap opera of possessive mother in love with daughter's tutor. Stars are miscast but try their best. ●

5 Fingers (1952) **108m.** *** D: Joseph L. Mankiewicz. James Mason, Danielle Darrieux, Michael Rennie, Walter Hampden, Oscar Karlweis, Herbert Berghof, John Wengraf, Michael Pate. Exceptionally intelligent spy thriller with Mason as a cool customer selling high-priced secrets right under the noses of his British government employers during WW2. Based on true-life events! Followed by a short-lived TV series. ▼●)

Five Gates to Hell (1959) **98m.** *½ D: James Clavell. Neville Brand, Benson Fong, Shirley Knight, Ken Scott, John Morley, Dolores Michaels, Nancy Kulp, Irish McCalla. Overly melodramatic plot of American nurses captured by Chinese mercenaries and the various ordeals they undergo. CinemaScope.

Five Golden Hours (1961-British-Italian) **90m.** ** D: Mario Zampi. Ernie Kovacs, Cyd Charisse, George Sanders, Kay Hammond, Dennis Price, Finlay Currie, Ron Moody. Con man Kovacs fleeces wealthy widows, but his luck is sure to change after falling for Charisse, whose husband has just died. Limp comedy wastes the talents of its cast. ▼●

Five Graves to Cairo (1943) **96m.** ***½ D: Billy Wilder. Franchot Tone, Anne Baxter, Akim Tamiroff, Erich von Stroheim, Peter Van Eyck, Fortunio Bonanova. WW2 intrigue situated in Sahara oasis hotel run by Tamiroff and Baxter; Tone attempts to obtain secrets from visiting Field Marshal Rommel (von Stroheim). Billy Wilder-Charles Brackett script manages to incorporate wit and humor into genuinely exciting wartime yarn. A remake of HOTEL IMPERIAL. ▼●

Five Guns West (1955) **C-78m.** ** D: Roger Corman. John Lund, Dorothy Malone, Touch (Mike) Connors, Jack Ingram. Fair Corman Western, which he coscripted, about a group of Rebel soldiers who hold up a Yankee stagecoach. This was Corman's first film as director. ▼●

Five Little Peppers and How They Grew (1939) **58m.** **½ D: Charles Barton. Edith Fellows, Clarence Kolb, Dorothy Peterson, Ronald Sinclair, Charles Peck, Tommy Bond, Jimmy Leake, Dorothy Ann Seese. An impoverished family left with half ownership of a copper mine by their late father become partners with a crusty old financier (Kolb) and his grandson. First in a four-film series based on Margaret Sidney's book is a genial blend of wholesome humor and homespun sentiment. Followed by FIVE LITTLE PEPPERS AT HOME.

Five Little Peppers at Home (1940) **67m.** ** D: Charles Barton. Edith Fellows, Dorothy Ann Seese, Clarence Kolb, Dorothy Peterson, Ronald Sinclair, Charles Peck, Tommy Bond, Bobby Larson. Second of the series centers on family's efforts to help save "Grandpa" King (Kolb) from bankruptcy by discovering copper, leading to a mine cave-in climax. Syrupy entry emphasizes the comic antics of cute moppet Seese. Followed by OUT WEST WITH THE PEPPERS.

Five Little Peppers in Trouble (1940) **64m.** *½ D: Charles Barton. Edith Fellows, Dorothy Ann Seese, Dorothy Peterson, Pierre Watkin, Ronald Sinclair, Charles Peck, Tommy Bond, Bobby Larson, Rex Evans. Treacly finale to the sentimental series finds the Pepper siblings having a hard time fitting in with the snooty students when they enroll in a private boarding school.

Five Miles to Midnight (1962) **110m.** **½ D: Anatole Litvak. Tony Perkins, Sophia Loren, Gig Young, Jean-Pierre Aumont, Pascale Roberts. Jumbled murder mystery with Perkins convincing wife Loren to collect insurance money when it's thought he's been killed, with ironic results.▼

Five Pennies, The (1959) **C-117m.** **½ D: Melville Shavelson. Danny Kaye, Barbara Bel Geddes, Tuesday Weld, Louis Armstrong, Bob Crosby, Harry Guardino, Ray Anthony, Shelley Manne, Bobby Troup. Danny plays jazz trumpeter Red Nichols in this sentimental biography. Only bright spots are musical numbers, especially duets with Kaye and Armstrong. VistaVision.▼●◗

Five Star Final (1931) **89m.** *** D: Mervyn LeRoy. Edward G. Robinson. H. B. Warner, Marian Marsh, George E. Stone, Ona Munson, Boris Karloff, Aline MacMahon. Powerful drama of sensationalist newspaper sometimes falls apart with bad acting by second leads, but editor Robinson and unscrupulous reporter Karloff make it a must. Remade as TWO AGAINST THE WORLD.◗

5 Steps To Danger (1957) **81m.** ** D: Henry S. Kesler. Ruth Roman, Sterling Hayden, Werner Klemperer, Richard Gaines, Charles Davis, Jeanne Cooper, Ken Curtis. Vacationer Hayden becomes entangled in a web of intrigue involving mystery woman Roman. Far-fetched mystery/spy melodrama.

5,000 Fingers of Dr. T., The (1953) **C-88m.** *** D: Roy Rowland. Peter Lind Hayes, Mary Healy, Tommy Rettig, Hans Conried. A boy who hates to practice the piano has a vivid nightmare about a land where his officious teacher Dr. Terwilliger (Conried) rules over hundreds of boys and a gigantic keyboard. Imaginative fantasy conceived by Dr. Seuss, with clever songs by Seuss and Frederick Hollander. Major weakness: conventional "grown-up" leads played by then-popular performers Healy and Hayes. Look for George Chakiris among the dancers. ▼●◗

Five Weeks in a Balloon (1962) **C-101m.** **½ D: Irwin Allen. Red Buttons, Barbara Eden, Fabian, Cedric Hardwicke, Peter Lorre, Richard Haydn, Barbara Luna. Innocuous entertainment with formula script from Jules Verne tale of balloon expedition to Africa. Buoyed by fine cast, including veterans Billy Gilbert, Herbert Marshall, Reginald Owen, Henry Daniell. CinemaScope.▼●◗

Fixed Bayonets! (1951) **92m.** **½ D: Samuel Fuller. Richard Basehart, Gene Evans, Michael O'Shea, Richard Hylton, Craig Hill. Taut Korean War drama of platoon cut off from the rest of its outfit; typical tough Fuller production. James Dean is one of the soldiers.◗

Fixer Dugan (1939) **69m.** **½ D: Lew Landers. Lee Tracy, Virginia Weidler, Peggy Shannon, Bradley Page, William Edmunds, Edward Gargan. Predictable but enjoyable fluff centering on fast-talking circus manager Tracy and his involvement with spunky or-

phan Weidler. Lion-taming scenes are especially well done, and Weidler steals every scene she's in.

Flame, The (1947) **97m.** ** D: John H. Auer. Vera Ralston, John Carroll, Robert Paige, Broderick Crawford, Henry Travers, Constance Dowling. Routine story of woman falling in love with intended victim of blackmail plot.

Flame and the Arrow, The (1950) **C-88m.** *** D: Jacques Tourneur. Burt Lancaster, Virginia Mayo, Robert Douglas, Aline MacMahon, Nick Cravat. Bouncy, colorful action with Lancaster romping through his gymnastics as rebel leader in medieval Italy leading his people on to victory. Mayo is gorgeous heroine.▼●◗

Flame and the Flesh (1954) **C-104m.** ** D: Richard Brooks. Lana Turner, Pier Angeli, Carlos Thompson, Bonar Colleano, Charles Goldner, Peter Illing. Pointless Turner vehicle filmed in Europe involving brunette Lana being romanced by continental Thompson, which causes a lot of misery.

Flame Barrier, The (1958) **70m.** *½ D: Paul Landres. Arthur Franz, Kathleen Crowley, Robert Brown, Vincent Padula. A satellite downed in jungle is discovered embedded in an ultra-hot alien organism. Fair cast tries hard in ineffectual story.

Flame of Araby (1951) **C-77m.** **½ D: Charles Lamont. Maureen O'Hara, Jeff Chandler, Maxwell Reed, Susan Cabot. O'Hara, looking fetching as ever, rides through this costumer of the Far East, involving battle over a prize horse.▼◗

Flame of Barbary Coast (1945) **91m.** **½ D: Joseph Kane. John Wayne, Ann Dvorak, Joseph Schildkraut, William Frawley, Virginia Grey. Hick rancher Wayne competes with slick Schildkraut for savvy saloon singer Dvorak; undemanding fluff, with Republic Pictures' version of the San Francisco earthquake. Also shown in computer-colored version. ▼◗

Flame of Calcutta (1953) **C-69m.** ** D: Seymour Friedman. Denise Darcel, Patric Knowles, Paul Cavanagh, George Keymas, Joseph Mell, Ted Thorpe, Leonard Penn. Cut-rate Sam Katzman kitsch chronicling the exploits of sexy Zorro-like freedom fighter Darcel and her quest for revenge against the evil prince who killed her father. Garish Technicolor helps a little.

Flame of New Orleans, The (1941) **78m.** *** D: René Clair. Marlene Dietrich, Bruce Cabot, Roland Young, Laura Hope Crews, Mischa Auer, Andy Devine. Dietrich can have her pick of any man in New Orleans, can't decide between wealthy Young or hard-working Cabot. Picturesque, entertaining. Clair's first American film.▼◗

Flame of Stamboul (1951) **68m.** *½ D: Ray Nazarro. Richard Denning, Lisa Ferraday, Norman Lloyd, Nestor Paiva, George Zucco. U.S. spy Denning tries to nab villain Zucco in this substandard programmer about espionage in the ancient title city.

Flame of the Islands (1955) **C-90m.** ** D: Edward Ludwig. Yvonne De Carlo, Howard Duff, Zachary Scott, Kurt Kasznar, Barbara O'Neil. Caribbean scenery and sultry De Carlo provide most of the spice in this tale of a cafe singer and the men who fall in love with her. ▼

Flame Over India (1959-British) **C-130m.** *** D: J. Lee Thompson. Lauren Bacall, Kenneth More, Herbert Lom, Wilfrid Hyde-White. Fast-paced actioner set on northern frontier of India as British soldiers and governess Bacall seek to speed an Indian prince to safety aboard a run-down train. Originally titled NORTHWEST FRONTIER. CinemaScope. ▼▶

Flame Within, The (1935) **71m.** ** D: Edmund Goulding. Ann Harding, Herbert Marshall, Maureen O'Sullivan, Louis Hayward. Tired story of unrequited love. Young woman psychiatrist falls in love with patient, despite fact that she knows that it could never succeed.

Flaming Feather (1951) **C-77m.** *** D: Ray Enright. Sterling Hayden, Forrest Tucker, Barbara Rush, Arleen Whelan. Rousing Western as vigilantes rescue white woman from renegade Indians.

Flaming Frontier (1958-Canadian) **70m.** *½ D: Sam Newfield. Bruce Bennett, Jim Davis, Paisley Maxwell, Cecil Linder, Peter Humphreys. Indian war is averted by half-breed Army officer; very cheap Western. Regalscope.

Flamingo Road (1949) **94m.** *** D: Michael Curtiz. Joan Crawford, Zachary Scott, Sydney Greenstreet, David Brian, Gertrude Michael, Gladys George. Crawford is excellent as tough carnival dancer ditched in small town where she soon is loving Scott and Brian and matching wits with corrupt politician Greenstreet. Remade as TVM in 1980, which later spun off a TV series. ▼▶▶

Flaming Star (1960) **C-91m.** *** D: Don Siegel. Elvis Presley, Barbara Eden, Steve Forrest, Dolores Del Rio, John McIntire. Elvis is excellent as a half-breed Indian who must choose sides when his mother's people go on the warpath. No songs after the first ten minutes but lots of action; arguably Presley's best film. CinemaScope. ▼▶

Flanagan Boy, The SEE: **Bad Blonde**

Flapper, The (1920) **88m.** ** D: Alan Crosland. Olive Thomas, Warren Cook, Theodore Westman, Jr., Katherine Johnston, Arthur Housman, Louise Lindroth, Norma Shearer. Meandering comedy about the misadventures of a teen (Thomas) who becomes innocently infatuated with an older man and mingles with a pair of crooks while away at boarding school. Of interest primarily as a vehicle for the radiant Thomas, who died under mysterious circumstances at age 25, four months after the film's release.▶

Flat Top (1952) **C-83m.** ** D: Lesley Selander. Sterling Hayden, Richard Carlson, Bill Phipps, Keith Larsen. WW2 combat footage of Navy flyers vs. Japanese Zeros provides the high points in this otherwise rudimentary yarn of an aircraft carrier's young fighter pilots taking to the skies under the watchful eye of their disciplinarian commander (Hayden). ▼▶

Flaxy Martin (1949) **86m.** **½ D: Richard Bare. Virginia Mayo, Zachary Scott, Dorothy Malone, Tom D'Andrea, Helen Westcott, Elisha Cook, Jr. Smooth melodrama of lawyer framed by client on a murder charge.

Fleet's In, The (1942) **93m.** *** D: Victor Schertzinger. Dorothy Lamour, William Holden, Eddie Bracken, Betty Hutton, Betty Jane Rhodes, Leif Erickson, Cass Daley, Gil Lamb, Barbara Britton, Rod Cameron, Lorraine and Rognan, Jimmy Dorsey Orchestra with Bob Eberly and Helen O'Connell. Bouncy wartime musical with reputed romeo Holden trying to melt iceberg Lamour. Sensational score (composed by director Schertzinger and Johnny Mercer) includes "Tangerine," "I Remember You," and "Arthur Murray Taught Me Dancing in a Hurry." Feature debuts of Hutton (in a hilarious performance that made her an instant star) and Daley. Previously filmed as TRUE TO THE NAVY and LADY BE CAREFUL; remade as SAILOR BEWARE.

Flesh (1932) **95m.** *** D: John Ford. Wallace Beery, Karen Morley, Ricardo Cortez, Jean Hersholt, Herman Bing, John Miljan. Unusual, melancholy drama with Beery as simple-minded German wrestler in love with Morley—who tries to hide her shady relationship with no-good Cortez. ▶

Flesh & Blood (1951-British) **102m.** ** D: Anthony Kimmins. Richard Todd, Glynis Johns, Joan Greenwood, Andre Morell, Freda Jackson, James Hayter, George Cole, Michael Hordern. Turbulent study of generations of family life, focusing on clashes and romances of parents and children. Set in Scotland.

Flesh and Desire (1954-French) **94m.** ** D: Jean Josipovici. Rossano Brazzi, Viviane Romance, Peter Van Eyck, Jean-Paul Roussillon. Turgid melodrama involving jealousy, murder, and other assorted goings-on caused by the presence of virile Brazzi.

Flesh and Fantasy (1943) **93m.** *** D: Julien Duvivier. Charles Boyer, Edward G. Robinson, Barbara Stanwyck, Robert Benchley, Betty Field, Robert Cummings, Thomas Mitchell, Charles Winninger. Three-part film of supernatural linked by Benchley; Field is ugly girl turned beauty by Cummings' love; Robinson's life is changed by fortune-teller Mitchell; Boyer is psychic circus star haunted by Stanwyck. Robinson sequence, based on Oscar Wilde's "Lord

Arthur Saville's Crime," is the most interesting. Coproduced by Duvivier and Boyer. Look for Peter Lawford as a Mardi Gras reveler in the first sequence. Fourth episode, dropped before release, subsequently expanded into feature titled DESTINY.▶

Flesh and Flame SEE: **Night of the Quarter Moon**

Flesh and Fury (1952) 82m. **½ D: Joseph Pevney. Tony Curtis, Jan Sterling, Mona Freeman, Wallace Ford, Harry Guardino. Curtis gives presentable performance as deaf prizefighter who seeks to regain hearing and love of decent girl.

Flesh and the Devil (1927) 112m. *** D: Clarence Brown. John Gilbert, Greta Garbo, Lars Hanson, Barbara Kent, William Orlamond, George Fawcett, Eugenie Besserer. Garbo at her most seductive as temptress who comes between old friends Gilbert and Hanson. Pulsatingly romantic, beautifully filmed, probably the best Garbo-Gilbert love match. But talk about surprise endings!▼▶

Flesh and the Fiends, The SEE: **Mania**

Flesh and the Woman (1953-French-Italian) C-102m. ** D: Robert Siodmak. Gina Lollobrigida, Jean-Claude Pascal, Arletty, Raymond Pellegrin, Peter Van Eyck. Whole film is Lollobrigida, who plays dual roles: a Parisienne whose corrupt ways cause her husband to join the Foreign Legion and a lookalike prostitute in Algiers. Remake of Jacques Feyder's 1934 French film LE GRAND JEU.

Flesh Eaters, The (1964) 87m. *½ D: Jack Curtis. Martin Kosleck, Rita Morley, Byron Sanders, Barbara Wilkin. Group trapped on island with deranged scientist is menaced by tiny but plentiful sea creatures that eventually mass to make one giant monster. Occasionally tense, but gruesome and generally boring. Longer version on video.▼▶

Flight (1929) 116m. **½ D: Frank Capra. Jack Holt, Ralph Graves, Lila Lee, Alan Roscoe, Harold Goodwin, Jimmy de la Cruze. Dated story of battling buddies in the Marine flying corps, with some still-impressive aerial sequences. Costar Graves wrote the original story.

Flight Command (1940) 116m. ** D: Frank Borzage. Robert Taylor, Ruth Hussey, Walter Pidgeon, Paul Kelly, Nat Pendleton, Shepperd Strudwick, Red Skelton, Dick Purcell. Hackneyed story with good cast as upstart Taylor tries to make the grade in naval flight squadron. Look fast for John Raitt as a cadet.▶

Flight for Freedom (1943) 99m. ** D: Lothar Mendes. Rosalind Russell, Fred MacMurray, Herbert Marshall, Eduardo Ciannelli, Walter Kingsford. Stilted tale of dedicated aviatrix Russell (loosely based on Amelia Earhart), who gains worldwide fame, and is romanced by self-centered flier MacMurray.▶

Flight From Ashiya (1964) C-100m. ** D: Michael Anderson. Yul Brynner, Richard Widmark, George Chakiris, Suzy Parker, Shirley Knight. Slow movie dealing with three aviators in rescue attempt over Pacific. Big name cast will attract; stiff script. Panavision.▶

Flight From Destiny (1941) 73m. *** D: Vincent Sherman. Geraldine Fitzgerald, Thomas Mitchell, Jeffrey Lynn, James Stephenson, Mona Maris, Jonathan Hale. Well-acted tale of Mitchell, with short time to live, helping young couple (Fitzgerald and Lynn) by murdering the woman who is blackmailing Lynn.

Flight From Glory (1937) 67m. **½ D: Lew Landers. Chester Morris, Whitney Bourne, Onslow Stevens, Van Heflin, Richard Lane, Paul Guilfoyle. Above-average programmer involving pilots who fly dangerous missions over the Andes. Trouble comes when suspended aviator Heflin arrives on the scene with wife Bourne. ▼

Flight Lieutenant (1942) 80m. *½ D: Sidney Salkow. Pat O'Brien, Glenn Ford, Evelyn Keyes, Minor Watson, Larry Parks, Lloyd Bridges, Hugh Beaumont. Commander Watson has sore memories of Ford's father (O'Brien), making life difficult; tired programmer.

Flight Nurse (1953) 90m. ** D: Allan Dwan. Joan Leslie, Forrest Tucker, Arthur Franz, Jeff Donnell, Ben Cooper. Leslie's sincere performance as Air Force nurse involved with pilots Franz and Tucker during the Korean War lifts this serviceable service yarn that's heavy on sentiment and anti-Red propaganda.

Flight of the Phoenix, The (1965) C-147m. ***½ D: Robert Aldrich. James Stewart, Richard Attenborough, Peter Finch, Hardy Kruger, Ernest Borgnine, Ian Bannen, Ronald Fraser, Christian Marquand, Dan Duryea, George Kennedy. A plane crash leaves a group of men stranded in the Sahara desert; film avoids clichés as tension mounts among the men. Stewart as the captain, Attenborough as the navigator stand out in uniformly fine cast. Remade in 2004. ▼▶

Flight to Hong Kong (1956) 88m. ** D: Joseph M. Newman. Rory Calhoun, Barbara Rush, Dolores Donlon, Soo Yong. Standard fare of gangster in Far East preferring Rush to his smuggler friends; it almost costs him his life.

Flight to Mars (1951) C-72m. ** D: Lesley Selander. Marguerite Chapman, Cameron Mitchell, Virginia Huston, Arthur Franz. Adequate sci-fi about scientists and newspapermen who land on Mars and discover an advanced civilization. Effects hampered by modest budget.▼▶

Flight to Nowhere (1946) 75m. BOMB D: William Rowland. Evelyn Ankers, Alan Curtis, Jack Holt, Jerome Cowan, Micheline Cheirel, John Craven, Inez Cooper, Hoot Gibson. Ultracheap, ultraboring account of former federal agent Curtis, who against his will becomes involved in an effort to recover a map of uranium deposits. ▼▶

Flight to Tangier (1953) **C-90m.** **½ D: Charles Marquis Warren. Joan Fontaine, Jack Palance, Corinne Calvet, Robert Douglas. Fast-paced drama involving a cache of money aboard plane that has crashed, and the assorted people chasing after the loot. Originally in 3-D.

Flipper (1963) **C-90m.** **½ D: James Clark. Chuck Connors, Luke Halpin, Kathleen Maguire, Connie Scott. Typical wholesome family fare about a boy who befriends a dolphin. Spun off into a TV series in 1964 (with Halpin) and another in 1995. Remade in 1996. ▼▶

Flipper's New Adventure (1964) **C-103m.** ** D: Leon Benson. Luke Halpin, Pamela Franklin, Helen Cherry, Tom Helmore, Brian Kelly. Further exploits of everybody's favorite dolphin: Flipper and Halpin thwart escaped convicts' efforts to blackmail millionaire Helmore. Pleasant, inoffensive fare for kids, filmed in the Bahamas and Key Biscayne. ▼▶

Flirtation Walk (1934) **97m.** **½ D: Frank Borzage. Dick Powell, Ruby Keeler, Pat O'Brien, Ross Alexander, Guinn Williams, Henry O'Neill, Tyrone Power. West Point plot is clichéd and trivial as cadet Powell falls in love with officer's daughter Keeler; some fairly good numbers highlighted by "Mr. and Mrs. Is the Name."▼▶

Flirting Widow, The (1930) **71m.** *½ D: William A. Seiter. Dorothy Mackaill, Basil Rathbone, Leila Hyams, William Austin, Claude Gillingwater, Anthony Bushell. Gillingwater won't let his young daughter get married before her older sister (Mackaill) does, so Mackaill invents a fictitious fiancé, only to have him actually show up in the suave personage of Rathbone. Stilted drawing-room antique must have seemed dated even in 1930.

Flirting With Fate (1916) **50m.** *** D: Christy Cabanne. Douglas Fairbanks, W. E. Lawrence, Jewel Carmen, Dorothy Haydel, George Beranger, Lillian Langdon. Cute comedy with Fairbanks well cast as a hard-luck starving artist who thinks he's been rebuffed by the pretty society girl (Carmen) with whom he's smitten. He offers professional assassin Automatic Joe (nicely played by Beranger) his last $50 to bump him off, but then his luck changes and he no longer wants to die. ▼▶

Flirting With Fate (1938) **69m.** ** D: Frank McDonald. Joe E. Brown, Leo Carrillo, Beverly Roberts, Wynne Gibson, Steffi Duna, Stanley Fields, Charles Judels. Juvenile slapstick with Joe heading a vaudeville troupe stranded in South America. Carrillo fun as influential bandit, Duna's off-key singing good for a few laughs, but basically a weak comedy. ▶

Floating Weeds (1959-Japanese) **C-119m.** ***½ D: Yasujiro Ozu. Ganjiro Nakamura, Machiko Kyo, Haruko Sugimura, Ayako Wakao. Struggling acting troupe visits remote island, where its leader (Nakamura) visits his illegitimate son and the boy's mother, with whom he had an affair years before. Powerful drama is meticulously directed, solidly acted. Ozu previously made this as A STORY OF FLOATING WEEDS (1934). Aka DRIFTING WEEDS. ▼▶

Floods of Fear (1959-British) **82m.** ** D: Charles Crichton. Howard Keel, Anne Heywood, Cyril Cusack, Harry H. Corbett, John Crawford. Adequate drama about prisoner Keel on the lam, performing heroic deeds during flood, later proving innocence and winning girl's love.

Flood Tide (1958) **82m.** **½ D: Abner Biberman. George Nader, Cornell Borchers, Michel Ray, Judson Pratt. Nicely done drama in which an innocent man is convicted of murder on the say-so of a crippled, emotionally scarred 10-year-old boy. Nice-guy Nader falls for the boy's widowed mother, and attempts to elicit the truth. CinemaScope.

Florentine Dagger, The (1935) **69m.** *** D: Robert Florey. Donald Woods, Margaret Lindsay, C. Aubrey Smith, Henry O'Neill, Robert Barrat, Florence Fair, Frank Reicher, Charles Judels, Rafaela Ottiano, Paul Porcasi. Neat little "Clue Club" whodunit, from a Ben Hecht novel, with Woods, who is obsessed by the Borgias, becoming involved in solving a murder. Barrat is a delight as a cunning police inspector.

Florian (1940) **91m.** ** D: Edwin L. Marin. Robert Young, Helen Gilbert, Charles Coburn, Lee Bowman, Reginald Owen, Lucile Watson. Young and Gilbert, poor man and rich woman, marry, united by their love of horses.

Florida Special (1936) **70m.** ** D: Ralph Murphy. Jack Oakie, Sally Eilers, Kent Taylor, Frances Drake, J. Farrell MacDonald, Sam (Schlepperman) Hearn, Claude Gillingwater, Sidney Blackmer. Romance, mystery, and murder aboard southbound train. Song: "It's You I'm Talking About."

Florodora Girl, The (1930) **80m.** *** D: Harry Beaumont. Marion Davies, Lawrence Gray, Walter Catlett, Louis John Bartels, Ilka Chase, Vivien Oakland, Jed Prouty, Sam Hardy. Charming piece of nostalgia with Marion only one of famed Florodora Sextette of Gay '90s to spurn wealthy admirers and seek true love. Some scenes originally in color.

Flower Drum Song (1961) **C-133m.** *** D: Henry Koster. Nancy Kwan, James Shigeta, Miyoshi Umeki, Benson Fong, Jack Soo, Juanita Hall, Reiko Sato, Patrick Adiarte, Victor Sen Yung. Rodgers and Hammerstein's Broadway musical becomes a bright Technicolor confection about life and love in San Francisco's Chinatown, where Old World traditions clash with modern American sensibilities. Songs include "I Enjoy Being a Girl." All-Asian cast was a rarity in Hollywood at that time. Opera singer Marilyn Horne dubs Sato's voice on "Love, Look Away."▼●◗

Flowers of St. Francis, The SEE: **Francesco—Giullare di Dio**

Flowing Gold (1940) 82m. **½ D: Alfred E. Green. John Garfield, Frances Farmer, Pat O'Brien, Raymond Walburn, Cliff Edwards, Tom Kennedy. Dynamic Garfield in story that doesn't flow; standard fare in which he and O'Brien drill for oil and fight over Farmer. ◗

Fluffy (1965) C-92m. ** D: Earl Bellamy. Tony Randall, Shirley Jones, Edward Andrews, Ernest Truex, Howard Morris, Dick Sargent. Silly film dealing with professor Randall experimenting with a lion; he can't shake the beast, causing all sorts of repercussions, even winning Jones' affection. ◗

Fly, The (1958) C-94m. *** D: Kurt Neumann. Al (David) Hedison, Patricia Owens, Vincent Price, Herbert Marshall, Kathleen Freeman. Improbable but diverting sci-fi (screenplay by James Clavell!) about scientist who experiments with teleportation machine and has his atomic pattern mingled with that of a fly. "Help me! Help me!" Two sequels—RETURN OF THE FLY and CURSE OF THE FLY. Remade in 1986. CinemaScope. ▼●◗

Fly-Away Baby (1937) 60m. ** D: Frank McDonald. Glenda Farrell, Barton MacLane, Gordon Oliver, Hugh O'Connell, Marcia Ralston, Tom Kennedy, Harry Davenport. Episode two in the *Torchy Blane* reporter series, serving mainly as a showcase for the wisecracking charms of Farrell as she takes to the air in pursuit of killers. ◗

Fly by Night (1942) 74m. **½ D: Robert Siodmak. Richard Carlson, Nancy Kelly, Albert Basserman, Walter Kingsford, Martin Kosleck, Miles Mander. Carlson is young doctor accused of murdering scientist who tracks down a Nazi spy ring in effort to clear himself. Fairly entertaining WW2 B propaganda, which aims for the Hitchcock style.

Flying Aces SEE: **Flying Deuces, The**

Flying Deuces, The (1939) 65m. *** D: A. Edward Sutherland. Stan Laurel, Oliver Hardy, Jean Parker, Reginald Gardiner, Charles Middleton, James Finlayson. Stan and Ollie join the Foreign Legion so Ollie can forget Parker; usual complications result. Good fun, faster paced than most L&H films, includes charming song and dance to "Shine On, Harvest Moon."▼●◗

Flying Down to Rio (1933) 89m. *** D: Thornton Freeland. Dolores Del Rio, Gene Raymond, Raul Roulien, Ginger Rogers, Fred Astaire, Blanche Frederici, Eric Blore,

Franklin Pangborn. Slim Del Rio vehicle memorable for its scene of dancing girls cavorting on plane wings, plus Astaire and Rogers doing "The Carioca" in their first screen teaming. Also shown in computer-colored version.▼●◗

Flying Fontaines, The (1959) C-84m. **½ D: George Sherman. Michael Callan, Evy Norlund, Joan Evans, Joe De Santis, Roger Perry, Rian Garrick. Circus yarn involving egocentric high-wire artist Callan who covets one of the showgirls, and the repercussions involved.

Flying High (1931) 80m. **½ D: Charles F. Riesner. Bert Lahr, Charlotte Greenwood, Pat O'Brien, Kathryn Crawford, Charles Winninger, Hedda Hopper, Guy Kibbee. Dated, oddball comedy about harebrained inventor Lahr concocting an "aerocopter" machine; Lahr (in Hollywood debut) and Greenwood are fun together. Some DeSylva-Brown-Henderson songs carried over from Broadway production. ◗

Flying Irishman, The (1939) 72m. ** D: Leigh Jason. Douglas Corrigan, Paul Kelly, Robert Armstrong, Gene Reynolds. Routine biog, largely fictional, dealing with life of Douglas "Wrong Way" Corrigan.

Flying Leathernecks (1951) C-102m. *** D: Nicholas Ray. John Wayne, Robert Ryan, Jay C. Flippen, Janis Carter, Don Taylor, William Harrigan. Major Wayne is exceedingly tough on his Marines; executive officer Ryan thinks he should be a little nicer. Guess who wins this argument. Solid, if not especially original, WW2 actioner, with good aerial scenes and nice turn by Flippen as crafty sergeant.▼●◗

Flying Missile, The (1950) 93m. ** D: Henry Levin. Glenn Ford, Viveca Lindfors, Henry O'Neill, Jerry Paris, Richard Quine. Clichéd WW2 story of commander Ford's attempt to modernize his fighting ship, with predictable results.

Flying Saucer, The (1950) 69m. *½ D: Mikel Conrad. Mikel Conrad, Pat Garrison, Russell Hicks, Denver Pyle. Pedestrian espionage tale set in Alaska; the lone flying saucer, disappointingly, is from Earth.▼◗

Flying Scot, The SEE: **Mailbag Robbery**

Flying Serpent, The (1946) 59m. ** D: Sherman Scott (Sam Newfield). George Zucco, Ralph Lewis, Hope Kramer, Eddie Acuff, Milton Kibbee. Zucco sole interest in serial-like B movie. Doctor protects Aztec treasure with prehistoric bird. Basically a reworking of THE DEVIL BAT.▼◗

Flying Tigers (1942) 102m. **½ D: David Miller. John Wayne, John Carroll, Anna Lee, Paul Kelly, Mae Clarke, Gordon Jones, James "Jimmie" Dodd. Good war film in which Wayne commands the volunteer Flying Tigers in China prior to Pearl Harbor while contending with egotistical ace pilot Carroll. Exciting dog-fight scenes. Also shown in computer-colored version.▼●◗

Flying Wild (1941) **62m.** ** D: William West. Leo Gorcey, Bobby Jordan, Donald Haines, Joan Barclay, Dave O'Brien, David Gorcey, Bobby Stone, Sunshine Sammy Morrison, Dennis Moore. The East Side Kids tackle airborne spies in this lightweight entry. Love the flipping-car blooper in the opening reel. ▼▶

Flying With Music (1942) **46m.** ** D: George Archainbaud. Marjorie Woodworth, George Givot, William Marshall, Edward Gargan, Jerry Bergen, Norma Varden, Marie Windsor. A man (Givot) on the run from making alimony payments impersonates a tour guide for a group of socialites in South America. Innocuous Hal Roach mini-musical crams in five songs in less than an hour, including the Oscar-nominated "Pennies for Peppino."

Fog Island (1945) **72m** *½ D: Terry Morse. George Zucco, Lionel Atwill, Veda Ann Borg, Jerome Cowan, Sharon Douglas. Grade-B chiller situated at eerie mansion with usual gathering of people suspecting one another of murder and intrigue; Zucco and Atwill are potentially terrific team. ▼▶

Fog Over Frisco (1934) **68m.** **½ D: William Dieterle. Bette Davis, Lyle Talbot, Margaret Lindsay, Donald Woods, Henry O'Neill, Arthur Byron, Hugh Herbert, Alan Hale, William Demarest. Snappy melodrama of deceitful, thrill-a-minute partygirl Davis involved in stolen-securities scheme; stepsister Lindsay tries to help. ▶

Folies Bergère de Paris (1935) **84m.** *** D: Roy Del Ruth. Maurice Chevalier, Ann Sothern, Merle Oberon, Eric Blore, Ferdinand Munier. Entertainer Chevalier is asked to pose as aristocratic businessman, forcing him to temporarily desert fiery Sothern for elegant Oberon. Delightful musical is highlighted by Busby Berkeleyish "Straw Hat" finale which won Dave Gould an Oscar for dance direction. Remade as THAT NIGHT IN RIO and ON THE RIVIERA.

Folies Bergère (1956-French) **C-90m** ** D: Henri Decoin. Jeanmaire, Eddie Constantine, Nadia Gray, Yves Robert. Slim plot boasts expansive cafe production numbers in tale of American crooner in Paris who almost loses wife when she becomes more successful in show biz than he.

Follow a Star (1959-British) **93m.** *½ D: Robert Asher. Norman Wisdom, June Laverick, Jerry Desmonde, Hattie Jacques, John Le Mesurier, Richard Wattis, Ron Moody. Flabby slapstick musical involving zany Wisdom as a cleaning store worker who is stagestruck. ▶

Follow Me Quietly (1949) **59m.** *** D: Richard O. Fleischer. William Lundigan, Dorothy Patrick, Jeff Corey, Nestor Paiva, Charles D. Brown, Paul Guilfoyle. Solid little film noir about police manhunt for self-righteous psychopathic killer called The Judge. Packs style and substance into just 59 minutes. ▼▶

Follow That Dream (1962) **C-110m.** **½ D: Gordon Douglas. Elvis Presley, Arthur O'Connell, Anne Helm, Joanna Moore, Jack Kruschen, Simon Oakland. Presley and family move to southern Florida where they intend to homestead, despite all opposition. Easygoing comedy from Richard Powell's book *Pioneer Go Home.* Elvis sings "Home Is Where the Heart Is" and "On Top of Old Smokey"! Panavision. ▼●▶

Follow That Woman (1945) **69m.** ** D: Lew Landers. Nancy Kelly, William Gargan, Regis Toomey, Ed Gargan, Byron Barr, Pierre Watkin. Predictable crime yarn, notable only for Kelly's sincere performance as a woman innocently implicated in a murder.

Follow the Boys (1944) **110m.** *** D: A. Edward Sutherland. Marlene Dietrich, George Raft, Orson Welles, Vera Zorina, Dinah Shore, W. C. Fields, Jeanette MacDonald, Maria Montez, Andrews Sisters, Sophie Tucker, Nigel Bruce, Gale Sondergaard. Universal Pictures' entry in all-star WW2 series has Raft organizing USO shows, Welles sawing Dietrich in half, MacDonald singing "Beyond the Blue Horizon," Fields doing classic pool-table routine, etc. Lots of fun. ▼

Follow the Boys (1963) **C-95m.** ** D: Richard Thorpe. Connie Francis, Paula Prentiss, Ron Randell, Janis Paige, Russ Tamblyn, Dany Robin. Dumb comedy unspiked by Francis' singing or antics as quartet of girls chase around the French Riviera seeking husbands. Panavision.●▶

Follow the Fleet (1936) **110m.** **** D: Mark Sandrich. Fred Astaire, Ginger Rogers, Randolph Scott, Harriet Hilliard (Nelson), Astrid Allwyn, Betty Grable. Delightful musical with sailors Astaire and Scott romancing sisters Rogers and Hilliard. Irving Berlin songs include "Let's Face the Music and Dance," "Let Yourself Go," "We Saw the Sea." A reworking of SHORE LEAVE, a 1925 Richard Barthelmess silent, and the 1930 musical HIT THE DECK. That's Lucille Ball as Kitty. ▼●▶

Follow the Leader (1930) **76m.** **½ D: Norman Taurog. Ed Wynn, Ginger Rogers, Stanley Smith, Lou Holtz, Lida Kane, Ethel Merman, Bobby Watson, Preston Foster, Jack La Rue. Waiter tries to help his boss' daughter launch a stage career. First attempt to fashion a decent talkie vehicle for stage and radio star Wynn, "The Perfect Fool." His wacky inventions provide the comedy highlights. Monologist Holtz has as much screen time as Wynn! Based on the Broadway musical *Manhattan Mary,* minus most of its songs.

Follow the Leader (1944) **64m.** ** D: William Beaudine. Leo Gorcey, Huntz Hall, Dave Durand, Bud Gorman, Bobby Stone, Gabriel Dell, Jimmy Strand, Jack LaRue, Billy Benedict, Bernard Gorcey, Joan Marsh. WW2 vets Muggs (Gorcey) and Glimpy (Hall) try to weed out a rotten apple from their ranks to clear a pal in this repetitive *East Side Kids* entry.

Follow the Sun (1951) **93m.** ****½** D: Sidney Lanfield. Glenn Ford, Anne Baxter, Dennis O'Keefe, June Havoc. Fictionalized biopic of golfer Ben Hogan with hokey dramatics to fill in lean spots. ▼⫐

Follow Thru (1930) **C-92m.** ****½** D: Lloyd Corrigan, Lawrence Schwab. Charles "Buddy" Rogers, Nancy Carroll, Zelma O'Neal, Jack Haley, Eugene Pallette, Thelma Todd. Love and rivalry on the golf links, with all the archaic conventions of a 1920s Broadway musical. Carroll was born to appear in two-color Technicolor, but O'Neal gets the best songs (by DeSylva, Brown, and Henderson), "Button Up Your Overcoat" and the irresistible "I Want to Be Bad," which cues the film's only big production number. Look fast for young Frances Dee and Virginia Bruce.

Folly to Be Wise (1952-British) **91m.** ******* D: Frank Launder. Alastair Sim, Elizabeth Allan, Roland Culver, Martita Hunt. Generally amusing nonsense with Sim an Army chaplain trying to enliven service life with various unique entertainment programs.

Foolish Wives (1922) **107m.** ******* D: Erich von Stroheim. Erich von Stroheim, Maud George, Mae Busch, Cesare Gravina, Malvine Polo. Von Stroheim's third film as director is a typically sophisticated, fascinating tale of seduction, fake counts, blackmail, suicide, lechery, and murder. Great photography by William Daniels and Ben Reynolds, and an incredible set depicting the Monte Carlo casino designed by von Stroheim and Richard Day. ▼⫐◗

Fool Killer, The (1965) **100m.** ******* D: Servando Gonzalez. Anthony Perkins, Edward Albert, Dana Elcar, Henry Hull, Salome Jens, Arnold Moss. Set in post–Civil War South, film relates unusual adventures of runaway orphan (Albert) and his meeting with strange young man (Perkins). Interesting and offbeat. ▼

Fools for Scandal (1938) **81m.** ****½** D: Mervyn LeRoy. Carole Lombard, Fernand Gravet, Ralph Bellamy, Allen Jenkins, Isabel Jeans, Marie Wilson. Generally a misfire, despite lovely Lombard as movie star who meets impoverished Paris nobleman Gravet; Bellamy plays the sap again.

Fool's Gold (1947) **63m.** ****** D: George Archainbaud. William Boyd, Andy Clyde, Rand Brooks, Robert Emmett Keane, Jane Randolph, Earle Hodgins. When young man flees court-martial to join outlaws, Hopalong Cassidy pretends to be a cattle rancher and invades dangerous territory, where he finds mad scientist with collection of deadly spiders and designs on Army gold shipment. Second entry in the revived series produced by Boyd is short on action; slightly substandard Hoppy fare. Reissued as THE MAN FROM BUTTE. ▼⫐

Fool There Was, A (1915) **67m.** ****½** D: Frank Powell. Theda Bara, Edward José, Mabel Fremyear, May Allison, Runa Hodges, Clifford Bruce, Frank Powell. Will wealthy lawyer-statesman—and happy family man—José be driven to the depths of ruin by sultry, devilish "vampire" Bara? Watch this and you'll see why Bara was considered the screen's premier sex symbol of her day. Inspired by a Rudyard Kipling poem. Remade in 1922. ▼⫐

Footlight Glamour (1943) **75m.** ****½** D: Frank Strayer. Penny Singleton, Arthur Lake, Larry Simms, Ann Savage, Jonathan Hale, Danny Mummert, Thurston Hall, Marjorie Ann Mutchie. Amusing *Blondie* entry finds the Bumsteads mixed up with the stage-struck daughter of one of Dagwood's clients. ▼

Footlight Parade (1933) **104m.** *****½** D: Lloyd Bacon. James Cagney, Joan Blondell, Ruby Keeler, Dick Powell, Guy Kibbee, Ruth Donnelly, Hugh Herbert, Frank McHugh. Cagney plays a stage director who tries to outdo himself with spectacular musical numbers. Fast-paced Warner Bros. opus winds up with three incredible Busby Berkeley numbers back-to-back: "Honeymoon Hotel," "By a Waterfall," and "Shanghai Lil." ▼◗

Footlight Serenade (1942) **80m.** ******* D: Gregory Ratoff. Betty Grable, Victor Mature, John Payne, Jane Wyman, Phil Silvers, James Gleason, Mantan Moreland, Cobina Wright, Jr. Cute backstage musical with cocky boxer Mature turning to Broadway and trying to woo Grable, who's secretly engaged to Payne. Good fun. ▼⫐

Footlight Varieties (1951) **61m.** ****½** D: Hal Yates. Leon Errol, The Sportsmen, Liberace, Jerry Murad's Harmonicats, Frankie Carle Orchestra, Red Buttons, Inesita, Grace Romanos. Jack Paar is master of ceremonies for a vaudeville-style revue of musical numbers, comedy skits, and specialty acts combined with clips culled from old RKO shorts. Highlights include Errol in the short HE FORGOT TO REMEMBER. Paar also dances a little.

Footloose Heiress, The (1937) **59m.** ****½** D: William Clemens. Ann Sheridan, Craig Reynolds, William Hopper, Anne Nagel, Hugh O'Connell, Teddy Hart. Sheridan is perky and sexy as a tycoon's madcap daughter who elopes on her 18th birthday in order to win a $5,000 bet. Hobo Reynolds complicates matters by befriending her outraged father and throwing a monkey wrench into her plans. Pretty funny screwball comedy bubbles along at a dizzy pace.

Footsteps in the Dark (1941) **96m.** ****½** D: Lloyd Bacon. Errol Flynn, Brenda Marshall, Ralph Bellamy, Alan Hale, Lee Patrick, Allen Jenkins. Flynn leads double life as happily married businessman and mystery writer. Silly but genial. ▼⫐

Footsteps in the Fog (1955-British) **C-90m.** *** D: Arthur Lubin. Stewart Granger, Jean Simmons, Finlay Currie, Bill Travers, Ronald Squire. Cat-and-mouse battle involving servant girl who blackmails her employer for having murdered his wife. Fine acting, rich Victorian atmosphere. ▶

Footsteps in the Night (1957) **62m.** *½ D: Jean Yarbrough. Bill Elliott, Don Haggerty, Eleanore Tanin, Zena Marshall. Programmer with homicide detective Elliott attempting to solve the motel murder of a friend. Former Western star Elliott played the same character in four other movies.

For a Few Dollars More (1965-Italian) **C-132m.** *** D: Sergio Leone. Clint Eastwood, Lee Van Cleef, Gian Maria Volonté, Josef Egger, Mara Krup, Rosemarie Dexter, Klaus Kinski, Mario Brega. Sequel to FISTFUL OF DOLLARS finds two gunslingers forming an uneasy alliance in their quest for outlaw Indio (Volonté)—although their reasons for chasing him are markedly different. Slightly draggy but still fun; don't miss the scene where Van Cleef strikes a match on the back of Kinski's neck! Trademark atmospheric score by Ennio Morricone. Released in the U.S. in 1967. Followed by THE GOOD, THE BAD AND THE UGLY. Techniscope. [R—originally rated M] ▼●▶

For Better, For Worse (1954-British) **C-83m.** **½ D: J. Lee Thompson. Dirk Bogarde, Susan Stephen, Cecil Parker, Dennis Price, Eileen Herlie, Athene Seyler, Thora Hird, Sidney James. Intelligently handled account of young married couple harassed by bills, in-laws, and marital adjustment. U.S. title: COCKTAILS IN THE KITCHEN.

Forbidden (1932) **81m.** ** D: Frank Capra. Barbara Stanwyck, Adolphe Menjou, Ralph Bellamy, Dorothy Peterson, Henry Armetta. A spinster librarian takes a cruise and falls in love with a man who can never marry her. Fine performances and stunning Joseph Walker photography buoy this BACK STREET soap opera until its ridiculous conclusion. ▶

Forbidden (1953) **85m.** **½ D: Rudolph Maté. Tony Curtis, Joanne Dru, Lyle Bettger, Marvin Miller, Victor Sen Yung. OK suspenser in which two-fisted Curtis arrives in Macao, hired by a gangland chief to uncover the whereabouts of Dru (who just so happens to be Curtis' ex-girlfriend).

Forbidden Adventure SEE: **Newly Rich**
Forbidden Alliance SEE: **Barretts of Wimpole Street, The** (1934)

Forbidden Cargo (1954-British) **83m.** **½ D: Harold French. Nigel Patrick, Elizabeth Sellars, Terence Morgan, Jack Warner, Greta Gynt, Joyce Grenfell, Theodore Bikel. Modest drama about customs agent Patrick clashing with dope-smuggling syndicate, enlivened by a solid cast.

Forbidden Fruit (1959-French) **97m.** **½ D: Henri Verneuil. Fernandel, Francoise Arnoul, Claude Nollier, Sylvie, Jacques Castelot. Unpretentious little film of Fernandel's touching love affair with a young maiden.

Forbidden Games (1952-French) **87m.** ***½ D: René Clement. Brigitte Fossey, Georges Poujouly, Louis Herbert. During WW2, young Parisian girl is orphaned and taken in by simple peasant family; she develops friendship with their youngest son, and shares with him a private world which the grown-ups cannot understand. Sad, intensely moving drama earned a Best Foreign Film Oscar. ▼●▶

Forbidden Island (1959) **C-66m.** *½ D: Charles B. Griffith. Jon Hall, Nan Adams, John Farrow, Jonathan Haze, Greigh Phillips. Sleazy film with Hall a skindiver seeking to find sunken treasure before a gang of crooks uncovers the loot.

Forbidden Planet (1956) **C-98m.** ***½ D: Fred McLeod Wilcox. Walter Pidgeon, Anne Francis, Leslie Nielsen, Warren Stevens, Jack Kelly, Richard Anderson, Earl Holliman, George Wallace, James Drury. Sci-fi version of Shakespeare's *The Tempest* remains one of the most ambitious and intelligent films of its genre; only slow, deliberate pacing works against it, as Nielsen and fellow space travelers visit planet where expatriate Pidgeon has built a one-man empire with daughter Francis and obedient Robby the Robot. Great effects, eerie electronic score. Beware 95m. reissue prints. Cinema-Scope. ▼●▶

Forbidden Street, The (1949-British) **91m.** ** D: Jean Negulesco. Dana Andrews, Maureen O'Hara, Sybil Thorndike, Wilfrid Hyde-White, Fay Compton. Fanciful Victorian melodrama of wealthy O'Hara defying her family by marrying beneath her class; Andrews has a dual role, as a down-and-out artist (with his voice dubbed) and an ex-barrister. Scripted by Ring Lardner, Jr. Originally titled BRITANNIA MEWS.

Force of Arms (1951) **100m.** **½ D: Michael Curtiz. William Holden, Nancy Olson, Frank Lovejoy, Gene Evans, Dick Wesson. Updating of Hemingway's A FAREWELL TO ARMS to WW2 Italy, with unmemorable results. Reissued as A GIRL FOR JOE. ▼●▶

Force of Evil (1948) **78m.** *** D: Abraham Polonsky. John Garfield, Beatrice Pearson, Thomas Gomez, Roy Roberts, Marie Windsor, Howland Chamberlin, Beau Bridges. Rock-solid film noir about a racketeer's lawyer (Garfield, in a stunning performance), whose ideals have been obscured by his greed. Beautifully photographed (by George Barnes) and lit; this has become something of a cult item. Polonsky, who coscripted with Ira Wolfert, was blacklisted and didn't make another film until 1969's TELL THEM WILLIE BOY IS HERE. ▼●▶

Foreign Affair, A (1948) **116m.** ***½ D: Billy Wilder. Jean Arthur, Marlene Dietrich, John Lund, Millard Mitchell, Peter Von Zerneck, Stanley Prager. Staid Arthur is sent to Berlin to investigate post-WW2 conditions, finds romance instead, with hot competition from Dietrich. Marlene sings "Black Market," "Ruins of Berlin," but Jean Arthur's Iowa State Song equally memorable in great Wilder comedy. Written by Charles Brackett, Billy Wilder, and Richard Breen.▼❿

Foreign Agent (1942) **64m.** ** D: William Beaudine. John Shelton, Gale Storm, Ivan Lebedeff, George Travell, Patsy Moran, Lyle Latell. Passable bargain-basement B film involving movie actors battling German and Japanese spies who are plotting to bomb L.A. Highlight: Gale singing the less-than-memorable "Taps for the Japs."

Foreign Correspondent (1940) **119m.** ****
D: Alfred Hitchcock. Joel McCrea, Laraine Day, Herbert Marshall, George Sanders, Albert Basserman, Robert Benchley, Edmund Gwenn, Eduardo Ciannelli, Harry Davenport, Martin Kosleck. McCrea in title role caught in middle of spy ring with reporters Sanders and Benchley, innocent Day, suspicious father Marshall. Tremendously entertaining film with several vintage Hitchcock showpieces. Scripted by Charles Bennett and Joan Harrison; dialogue by James Hilton and Benchley.▼❿

Foreign Intrigue (1956) **C-100m.** ** D: Sheldon Reynolds. Robert Mitchum, Genevieve Page, Ingrid Thulin, Frederick O'Brady. Colorful location filming throughout Europe enlivens this otherwise plodding suspenser, with stolid press agent Mitchum investigating the death of his wealthy, mysterious employer. Based on a syndicated TV series of the same name. ❿

Foreman Went to France, The (1941-British) **88m.** **½ D: Charles Frend. Tommy Trinder, Clifford Evans, Constance Cummings, Robert Morley, Mervyn Johns, Gordon Jackson, Ernest Milton. Documentary-style tale of industrial engineer who journeys to France during WW2 to help save secret machinery from being confiscated by the Axis. Adapted from a J.B. Priestley story based on a true incident. ▼

Forest Rangers, The (1942) **C-87m.** **½ D: George Marshall. Fred MacMurray, Paulette Goddard, Susan Hayward, Albert Dekker, Rod Cameron, Lynne Overman, Eugene Pallette. Hayward tries to show ranger MacMurray that he's made a mistake marrying wealthy Goddard in this OK romance with good action scenes. Introduced the hit song "I've Got Spurs That Jingle, Jangle, Jingle."

Forever Amber (1947) **C-140m.** *** D: Otto Preminger. Linda Darnell, Cornel Wilde, Richard Greene, George Sanders, Jessica Tandy, Anne Revere, Leo G. Carroll. "Musical beds" costumer, taken from Kathleen Winsor's once-scandalous novel, about blonde Darnell's ascension to the court of Charles II. Lengthy but colorful and entertaining, with David Raksin's outstanding score.▼❿

Forever and a Day (1943) **104m.** *** D: René Clair, Edmund Goulding, Cedric Hardwicke, Frank Lloyd, Victor Saville, Robert Stevenson, Herbert Wilcox. Brian Aherne, Robert Cummings, Ida Lupino, Charles Laughton, Herbert Marshall, Ray Milland, Anna Neagle, Merle Oberon, Claude Rains, Victor McLaglen, Buster Keaton, Jessie Matthews, Roland Young, C. Aubrey Smith, Edward Everett Horton, Elsa Lanchester, Edmund Gwenn. Eighty-odd British (and American) stars contributed their services to this episodic film, about a house and its inhabitants over the years, to raise funds for British War Relief. Uneven result, but has many fine moments and star-gazing galore; once-in-a-lifetime cast.▼❿

Forever, Darling (1956) **C-91m.** **½ D: Alexander Hall. Lucille Ball, Desi Arnaz, James Mason, Louis Calhern. Ball's madcap antics nearly drive husband Arnaz to divorce, but guardian angel Mason saves the day. Contrived but enjoyable.▼❿

Forever Female (1953) **93m.** ** D: Irving Rapper. Ginger Rogers, William Holden, Paul Douglas, Pat Crowley, James Gleason, Jesse White, Marjorie Rambeau, George Reeves, King Donovan, Marion Ross. Slick but hollow tale of Broadway show people: cynical producer Douglas (who has all the best lines), his glamorous leading lady and ex-wife Rogers, newly minted playwright Holden, and frightfully ambitious young actress Crowley (featured here in a bid for movie stardom). Julius J. and Philip G. Epstein based their screenplay on James M. Barrie's play *Rosalind*. Best thing about the film is the elaborate set re-creating Sardi's Restaurant.▼❿

Forever My Love (1962-German) **C-147m.** **½ D: Ernest Marischka. Romy Schneider, Karl Boehm, Magda Schneider, Vilma Degischer. Typical German confection dealing with 19th-century Austrian Emperor Franz Josef and Empress Elizabeth.

Forgiven Sinner, The SEE: **Leon Morin, Priest**

Forgotten Woman (1939) **63m.** **½ D: Harold Young. Sigrid Gurie, William Lundigan, Eve Arden, Elizabeth Risdon, Virginia Brissac. Overnight star (and overnight fade-out) Gurie is helpless woman, framed by influential gangsters, suffering on trial.

For Heaven's Sake (1926) **86m.** ****
D: Sam Taylor. Harold Lloyd, Jobyna Ralston, Noah Young, James Mason, Paul Weigel. Screamingly funny silent comedy has Lloyd a blase young millionaire whose crush on Ralston inspires him to help attract

"customers" for her father's Bowery Mission. Even THE FRENCH CONNECTION hasn't dimmed the luster of Lloyd's chase climax on L.A. streets.◗

For Heaven's Sake (1950) **92m. **½** D: George Seaton. Clifton Webb, Joan Bennett, Robert Cummings, Edmund Gwenn, Joan Blondell. Droll fantasy with Webb and Gwenn two angels sent to earth to speed along the arrival of Bennett and Cummings' heavenly baby.

For Love or Money (1933) SEE: **Cash**

For Love or Money (1963) **C-108m. **½** D: Michael Gordon. Kirk Douglas, Mitzi Gaynor, Gig Young, Thelma Ritter, William Bendix, Julie Newmar. Comedy strains to be funnier than it is. Widow Ritter hires lawyer Douglas to find spouses for her three daughters.◗

For Me and My Gal (1942) **104m. **½** D: Busby Berkeley. Judy Garland, George Murphy, Gene Kelly, Marta Eggerth, Ben Blue, Horace (Stephen) McNally, Keenan Wynn, Richard Quine. Music sustains old-hat plot of vaudeville couple determined to play Palace, circa WW1. In his film debut, Kelly sings title tune with Garland. Also shown in computer-colored version.▼●◗

For Men Only (1952) **93m. *** D: Paul Henreid. Paul Henreid, Kathleen Hughes, Russell Johnson, James Dobson, Margaret Field, Vera Miles, Douglas Kennedy, O. Z. Whitehead. Sincere if obvious study of fraternity hazing that gets out of hand on a college campus. Retitled: THE TALL LIE.▼◗

Forsaking All Others (1934) **84m. **½** D: W. S. Van Dyke II. Clark Gable, Joan Crawford, Robert Montgomery, Charles Butterworth, Billie Burke, Frances Drake, Rosalind Russell, Arthur Treacher. Gable, just back from Spain, is about to propose to Crawford but learns she's set to wed flaky Montgomery. Star trio sparkles in this so-so romantic comedy, scripted by Joseph L. Mankiewicz. Butterworth is a treat, as always.▼●◗

Fort Algiers (1953) **78m. *** D: Lesley Selander. Yvonne De Carlo, Carlos Thompson, Raymond Burr, Leif Erickson. De Carlo romps through this adventure set in Algiers, dealing with villainous Arab leader inciting the natives to rebel.◗

Fort Apache (1948) **127m. *** D: John Ford. John Wayne, Henry Fonda, Shirley Temple, Pedro Armendariz, John Agar, Ward Bond, George O'Brien, Victor McLaglen, Anna Lee, Irene Rich, Dick Foran, Guy Kibbee, Mae Marsh, Hank Worden. Fonda is effectively cast against type as stubborn martinet who rubs his own men—as well as neighboring Indians—the wrong way. First of Ford's cavalry trilogy tells its story slowly, deliberately, with time for comedy and telling characterizations. Followed by SHE WORE A YELLOW RIBBON. Also shown in computer-colored version.▼●◗

Fort Defiance (1951) **C-81m. **½** D: John Rawlins. Dane Clark, Ben Johnson, Peter Graves, Tracey Roberts, George Cleveland, Iron Eyes Cody, Dennis Moore. In the wake of the Civil War, Johnson seeks out the man he blames for his brother's death. Instead he finds the man's brother, who is blind and waiting for his sibling to return to run their ranch in Arizona. Interesting Western yarn.◗

Fort Dobbs (1958) **90m. **½** D: Gordon Douglas. Clint Walker, Virginia Mayo, Brian Keith, Richard Eyer, Russ Conway, Michael Dante. Walker rescues Mayo and her son after an Indian attack and escorts them to the safety of a fort, but their troubles are far from over in this pretty good Western. Keith has the most colorful role as a gun supplier. Written by Burt Kennedy and George W. George. Stock footage was lifted from CHARGE AT FEATHER RIVER.◗

For the Defense (1930) **63m. *** D: John Cromwell. William Powell, Kay Francis, Scott Kolk, William B. Davidson, Thomas E. Jackson, Harry Walker, James Finlayson. Well-made vintage courtroom drama with Powell excellent as a slick criminal lawyer (supposedly inspired by William Fallon) who discovers that his actress girlfriend (Francis) is involved in a manslaughter case he's taken on.◗

For the First Time (1959) **C-97m. **½** D: Rudolph Maté. Mario Lanza, Johanna Von Koszian, Kurt Kasznar, Zsa Zsa Gabor, Hans Sohnker. Lanza is typecast as fiery opera singer who falls in love with beautiful deaf girl in Capri. Not bad, with plenty of music to satisfy Lanza fans; this was his last film. Technirama.▼●◗

For the Love of Mary (1948) **90m. **½** D: Frederick de Cordova. Deanna Durbin, Edmond O'Brien, Don Taylor, Jeffrey Lynn. Airy fluff with Durbin a White House switchboard operator getting political figures and her own romance tangled up. Deanna's final film.▼◗

For the Love of Mike (1960) **C-84m. **½** D: George Sherman. Richard Basehart, Stuart Erwin, Arthur Shields, Armando Silvestre. Mild happenings as Indian boy trains a horse, hoping to use prize money for a village shrine. Another intelligent Robert B. Radnitz production. CinemaScope.

For Those Who Think Young (1964) **C-96m. *** D: Leslie H. Martinson. James Darren, Pamela Tiffin, Paul Lynde, Tina Louise, Bob Denver, Robert Middleton, Nancy Sinatra, Claudia Martin, Ellen McRae (Burstyn), Woody Woodbury, Louis Quinn, Sammee Tong, Addison Richards, Mousie Garner, Benny Baker, Anna Lee, Jack La Rue, Allen Jenkins, Robert Armstrong, Lada Edmund, Jr. Great time-capsule cast in a silly time-waster about college high jinks. Notable for taking its title from a

Pepsi slogan at the time—making this a milestone in the history of product placement! George Raft and Roger Smith appear unbilled. Techniscope.

Fort Massacre (1958) **C-80m. **** D: Joseph M. Newman. Joel McCrea, Forrest Tucker, Susan Cabot, John Russell. McCrea is leader of troop which constantly is entangled with Indian skirmishes. CinemaScope. ▶

Fort Osage (1952) **C-72m.** BOMB D: Lesley Selander. Rod Cameron, Jane Nigh, Douglas Kennedy, Iron Eyes Cody, Morris Ankrum, John Ridgely, William Phipps, Myron Healey. Inept Grade-D Western involving perennial Indian uprisings. ▶

Fort Ti (1953) **C-73m. **** D: William Castle. George Montgomery, Joan Vohs, Irving Bacon, James Seay. Best facet of this oater set during French-Indian war of 1760s is its 3-D gimmickry; otherwise, standard stuff.

Fortune in Diamonds SEE: **Adventurers, The**

Fortune Is a Woman SEE: **She Played with Fire**

Fortunes of Captain Blood (1950) **91m. **** D: Gordon Douglas. Louis Hayward, Patricia Medina, George Macready, Terry Kilburn. This filming of Sabatini novel lacks flair and scope of the Flynn version. Costumer recounts tale of Irish doctor (Hayward) who becomes notorious pirate to revenge wrongdoings. ▶

Fort Vengeance (1953) **C-75m. **** D: Lesley Selander. James Craig, Rita Moreno, Keith Larsen, Reginald Denny, Morris Ankrum, Michael Granger. Two brothers—one good, one incorrigible—join the Royal Canadian Mounted Police and wind up fighting Chief Sitting Bull. Routine Western with a change of scenery. ▶

Fort Worth (1951) **C-80m. **** D: Edwin L. Marin. Randolph Scott, David Brian, Phyllis Thaxter, Helena Carter. Scott learns that pen is not mightier than the sword; he's a gunslinger who becomes newspaper editor but can only rid town of outlaws via six-shooter. ▶

Forty Guns (1957) **80m. **½** D: Samuel Fuller. Barbara Stanwyck, Barry Sullivan, Dean Jagger, John Ericson, Gene Barry, Robert Dix, Jidge Carroll, Ziva Rodann, Hank Worden, Eve Brent. Strong direction and clever double entendres highlight this florid, wildly dramatic Western with Stanwyck as the self-appointed land baroness of Tombstone Territory—until gunslinger-turned-lawman Sullivan shows up. Fuller also scripted. CinemaScope. ▶

Forty Little Mothers (1940) **90m. **½** D: Busby Berkeley. Eddie Cantor, Judith Anderson, Ralph Morgan, Rita Johnson, Martha O'Driscoll, Bonita Granville, Diana Lewis. Second-rate Cantor vehicle with Eddie as unemployed college professor who becomes reluctant protector of an abandoned baby, as well as a teacher in a girls' school. Veronica Lake (then known as Constance Keane) is one of his charges.

Forty Naughty Girls (1937) **63m.** BOMB D: Edward Cline. James Gleason, ZaSu Pitts, Marjorie Lord, George Shelley, Joan Woodbury, Frank M. Thomas, Tom Kennedy. Final *Hildegarde Withers* mystery-comedy is just plain awful, with Pitts and Gleason getting involved in a backstage murder. ▶

49th Man, The (1953) **73m. **** D: Fred F. Sears. John Ireland, Richard Denning, Suzanne Dalbert, Robert Foulk, Touch Conners (Mike Connors), Richard Avonde, Peter Marshall. Cold War espionage thriller with Ireland and Denning trying to track down smugglers who are bringing A-bomb parts into the U.S. Decent but unexceptional, this Sam Katzman production makes the most of its low budget. ▶

49th Parallel (1941-British) **123m. ***½** D: Michael Powell. Anton Walbrook, Eric Portman, Leslie Howard, Raymond Massey, Laurence Olivier, Glynis Johns, Niall MacGinnis, Finlay Currie. Taut, exciting WW2 yarn of Nazi servicemen whose U-boat is sunk off the Canadian coast. Top-notch cast, rich suspense and characterizations. Oscar winner for Best Story (Emeric Pressburger); screenplay by Pressburger and Rodney Ackland. U.S. title: THE INVADERS. ▼ ⬤

40 Pounds of Trouble (1963) **C-106m. **½** D: Norman Jewison. Tony Curtis, Phil Silvers, Suzanne Pleshette, Larry Storch, Howard Morris, Stubby Kaye, Claire Wilcox, Jack La Rue. "Cute" Curtis comedy of casino manager who "adopts" little girl with endless complications occurring. Disneyland locations and fine character actors pep it up. Carbon copy of LITTLE MISS MARKER. Panavision. ▼ ⬤

42nd Street (1933) **89m. ****** D: Lloyd Bacon. Warner Baxter, Ruby Keeler, George Brent, Bebe Daniels, Dick Powell, Guy Kibbee, Una Merkel, Ginger Rogers, Ned Sparks, George E. Stone. The definitive backstage musical still has plenty of sass—along with its clichés. Ailing director Baxter puts everything into what may be his final show, then leading lady Daniels twists her ankle! Good thing Ruby Keeler's on hand. Harry Warren–Al Dubin songs include title tune, "Young and Healthy," "You're Getting to Be a Habit with Me," "Shuffle Off to Buffalo." Busby Berkeley's ground-breaking production numbers are sensational. Scripted by Rian James and James Seymour, from Bradford Ropes' story. Adapted for the Broadway stage 50 years later. Also shown in computer-colored version. ▼ ⬤

47 Ronin, Part I, The (1941-Japanese) **112m. ***½** D: Kenji Mizoguchi. Chojuro Kawarazaki, Yoshizaburo Arashi, Utaemon Ichikawa, Mieko Takamine. Legendary samurai warriors scheme to gain revenge for the death of their leader, who was tricked and forced to commit suicide. Based on a famous Japanese story, and fascinating as both cinema and as propaganda (remember, this was made during WW2). First of Mizoguchi's two-part epic, also known as THE LOYAL 47 RONIN. Several dozen versions of this same story have been filmed in Japan. Remade in 2013. ▼▶

47 Ronin, Part II, The (1942-Japanese) 113m. ***½ D: Kenji Mizoguchi. Chojuro Kawarazaki, Yoshizaburo Arashi, Utaemon Ichikawa, Mieko Takamine. The 47 Ronin gain vengeance for their master's death. Together with its predecessor, this was the most impressive Japanese film produced during WW2; the finale is especially stirring and revealing. ▼▶

Forty Thieves (1944) 61m. **½ D: Lesley Selander. William Boyd, Andy Clyde, Jimmy Rogers, Douglass Dumbrille, Louise Currie, Kirk Alyn. Boyd loses reelection as sheriff when malefactors pad the polls. Satisfactory Hopalong Cassidy effort, with Alyn (later the first screen incarnation of Superman) here a saloonkeeper with no backbone. The last Hoppy film produced by Harry Sherman; Boyd himself assumed production reins when series resumed two and a half years later. ▼▶

Fort Yuma (1955) C-78m. ** D: Lesley Selander. Peter Graves, Joan Taylor, Addison Richards, Joan Vohs. Indians go on warpath when their chief is killed. Occasionally good combat sequences. ▼▶

For Whom the Bell Tolls (1943) C-130m. ***½ D: Sam Wood. Gary Cooper, Ingrid Bergman, Akim Tamiroff, Arturo de Córdova, Joseph Calleia, Katina Paxinou, Vladimir Sokoloff, Mikhail Rasumny, Fortunio Bonanova. Hemingway story of U.S. mercenary Cooper fighting for Spain with motley crew of peasants, including Bergman; tense action, beautiful color, great love scenes, marvelous Victor Young score. Paxinou won Best Supporting Actress Oscar. Originally released at 170m.; archivally restored version runs 156m. Restored DVD version is 165m., with an overture, intermission/entr'acte. ▼●▶

Fountain, The (1934) 83m. **½ D: John Cromwell. Ann Harding, Brian Aherne, Paul Lukas, Jean Hersholt, Ian Wolfe. WW1 romance with Harding torn between former sweetheart Aherne and husband Lukas. Handsome but tedious.

Fountainhead, The (1949) 114m. **½ D: King Vidor. Gary Cooper, Patricia Neal, Raymond Massey, Kent Smith, Robert Douglas, Henry Hull, Ray Collins, Jerome Cowan. Ambitious but confused version of Ayn Rand philosophic novel, spotlighting an idealistic architect's clash with compromises of society; cast does what it can with the script. ▼●▶

Four Against Fate SEE: **Derby Day**

Four Around the Woman (1921-German) 84m. **½ D: Fritz Lang. Hermann Böttcher,

Carola Tolle, Lilli Lohrer, Ludwig Hartau, Anton Edthofer, Robert Forster-Larrinaga, Rudolph Klein-Rogge. Complications arise when wealthy Hartau suspects that, once upon a time, his wife (Tolle) was romantically involved with Edthofer (who also plays the man's look-alike brother, a jewel thief). Little-seen early Lang melodrama is generally entertaining but cannot compare to his later work. Original title: VIER UM DIE FRAU. ▶

Four Bags Full SEE: **La Traversée de Paris**

Four Dark Hours SEE: **Green Cockatoo, The**

Four Daughters (1938) 90m. ***½ D: Michael Curtiz. Claude Rains, Rosemary Lane, Lola Lane, Priscilla Lane, Gale Page, John Garfield, Jeffrey Lynn, Frank McHugh, May Robson, Dick Foran. Believable, beautifully acted soaper of small-town life; four young women with musical father Rains have lives altered by four young men. Garfield is superb in first film, matched by fine cast. Followed immediately by DAUGHTERS COURAGEOUS and sequels FOUR WIVES and FOUR MOTHERS. Remade as YOUNG AT HEART. ▼▶

Four Days Leave (1950) 98m. ** D: Leopold Lindtberg. Cornel Wilde, Josette Day, Simone Signoret, Alan Hale, Jr. Rather tame account of GI Wilde finding romance while on leave in Switzerland.

Four Desperate Men (1960-Australian) 104m. **½ D: Harry Watt. Aldo Ray, Heather Sears. Stark study of human nature as quartet of hardened thugs decide whether or not to set off huge bomb that would destroy Sydney harbor. Original title: THE SIEGE OF PINCHGUT.

4D Man (1959) C-85m. **½ D: Irvin S. Yeaworth, Jr. Robert Lansing, Lee Meriwether, James Congdon, Robert Strauss, Patty Duke, Guy Raymond. Well-handled sci-fi of scientist who learns art of transposing matter, thus giving him power to pass through any barrier—but each time ages him horribly. ▼▶

Four Faces West (1948) 90m. **½ D: Alfred E. Green. Joel McCrea, Frances Dee, Charles Bickford, Joseph Calleia, William Conrad. Quiet, fact-based Western with McCrea a reluctant bank robber who becomes involved with nurse Dee while being pursued by sheriff Pat Garrett (Bickford). ▼▶

Four Fast Guns (1959) 72m. *½ D: William J. Hole, Jr. James Craig, Martha Vickers, Edgar Buchanan, Brett Halsey, Paul Richards. Undistinguished oater with Craig playing a man on the run who becomes unofficial marshal in the lawless town of Purgatory, Arizona, in the 1870s. CinemaScope. ▶

Four Feathers, The (1929) 81m. *** D: Lothar Mendes, Merian C. Cooper, Ernest B. Schoedsack. Richard Arlen, Fay Wray,

Clive Brook, William Powell, Theodore von Eltz, Noah Beery, Noble Johnson. David O. Selznick produced this exciting silent version (with synchronized music and sound effects) of the classic A. E. W. Mason adventure story. Well shot, partially on location in Africa with an excellent cast, it still impresses with several rip-roaring action scenes, including a rousing hippo stampede. Codirectors Cooper and Schoedsack later teamed up with Selznick for KING KONG. Previously filmed in 1921; remade in 1939, as STORM OVER THE NILE, as a TVM in 1978 with Beau Bridges, and in 2002.

Four Feathers, The (1939-British) C-115m. **** D: Zoltan Korda. John Clements, Ralph Richardson, C. Aubrey Smith, June Duprez, Allan Jeayes, Jack Allen, Donald Gray, Clive Baxter. Grand adventure from A. E. W. Mason story of tradition-bound Britisher who must prove he's not a coward by helping Army comrades quell Sudan uprising. Smith is just wonderful as tale-spinning Army veteran. Screenplay by R. C. Sherriff, Lajos Biro, and Arthur Wimperis. Score by Miklos Rozsa. Original release ran 130m. ▼●〗

4 for Texas (1963) C-114m. *** D: Robert Aldrich. Frank Sinatra, Dean Martin, Anita Ekberg, Ursula Andress, Charles Bronson, Victor Buono, Richard Jaeckel, Mike Mazurki, Jack Elam, The Three Stooges, Yaphet Kotto. Nonsensical Sinatra-Martin romp set in the old West, with their antics only outdone by Buono as villainous banker. Ekberg and Andress both outstanding scenery attractions. ▼●〗

Four Frightened People (1934) 78m. **½ D: Cecil B. DeMille. Claudette Colbert, Herbert Marshall, William Gargan, Mary Boland, Leo Carrillo. Four shipwrecked souls try to survive in the jungle, while the two men become increasingly interested in the plain-Jane schoolteacher who's the most frightened of the lot. DeMille's quietest movie (and a somewhat notorious flop in its day) is entertaining malarkey, with Colbert getting more glamorous in each successive scene. Filmed on the island of Hawaii.〗

Four Girls in Town (1956) C-85m. *** D: Jack Sher. George Nader, Julie Adams, Gia Scala, Marianne Cook (Koch), Elsa Martinelli, Sydney Chaplin, Grant Williams, John Gavin. Clichéd but absorbing account of four contrasting would-be stars coming to Hollywood seeking fame and romance; excellent musical score by Alex North. CinemaScope.

Four Guns to the Border (1954) C-82m. **½ D: Richard Carlson. Rory Calhoun, Colleen Miller, George Nader, Walter Brennan, Nina Foch. Better than usual handling of outlaws vs. Indians, with slight morality lesson for finale. From a Louis L'Amour novel.

Four Horsemen of the Apocalypse, The (1921) 131m. *** D: Rex Ingram. Rudolph Valentino, Alice Terry, Alan Hale, Jean Hersholt, Nigel de Brulier, Wallace Beery. Famous silent spectacle cemented Valentino's popularity via legendary tango scene, but aside from that it's a relentlessly grim antiwar story of cousins who end up fighting on opposite sides during WW1. Extremely well made, with imagery that still staggers and message that cannot be overlooked. Based on the Blasco Ibanez novel. Remade in 1962. ▼●

Four Horsemen of the Apocalypse, The (1962) C-153m. **½ D: Vincente Minnelli. Glenn Ford, Ingrid Thulin, Charles Boyer, Lee J. Cobb, Paul Henreid, Paul Lukas, Yvette Mimieux, Karl Boehm. Glossy, padded trash, losing all sense of reality in its telling of a family whose members fight on opposite sides during WW2. Loose remake of the 1921 silent film based on a novel by Vincent Blasco Ibanez. Angela Lansbury dubbed in Thulin's lines. Great André Previn score. CinemaScope. ▼●〗

Four Hours to Kill! (1935) 71m. *** D: Mitchell Leisen. Richard Barthelmess, Joe Morrison, Helen Mack, Gertrude Michael, Dorothy Tree, Ray Milland, Roscoe Karns, John Howard, Noel Madison, Charles Wilson. Ingenious structure has film taking place entirely in a vaudeville theater (and lobby) where a killer (Barthelmess) escapes from the detective escorting him to execution, hoping to kill the stoolie who ratted on him. Norman Krasna's snappy script juggles numerous subplots à la GRAND HOTEL. Watch for director Leisen in a cameo as the orchestra leader.

Four Hundred Blows, The (1959-French) 99m. **** D: François Truffaut. Jean-Pierre Léaud, Patrick Auffay, Claire Maurier, Albert Remy, Jeanne Moreau, Jean-Claude Brialy, Jacques Demy, François Truffaut. Captivating study of Parisian youth who turns to life of small-time crime as a reaction to derelict parents. First of Truffaut's autobiographical Antoine Doinel series; followed by the "Antoine et Colette" episode in LOVE AT TWENTY. Dyaliscope. ▼●〗

Four in a Jeep (1951-Swiss) 97m. **½ D: Leopold Lindtberg. Viveca Lindfors, Ralph Meeker, Joseph Yadin, Michael Medwin, Dinan, Paulette Dubost. Revealing drama, set in a postwar Vienna occupied by American, Russian, French, and British forces. American M.P. Meeker takes an interest in troubled Lindfors, whose husband has just escaped from a Russian prison camp. On-location filming helps. ▼〗

Four in the Morning (1965-British) 94m. **½ D: Anthony Simmons. Ann Lynn, Judi Dench, Norman Rodway, Brian Phelan, Joe Melia. Grim kitchen sink drama, centering on two unhappy women going nowhere in working-class London. Worth a look for Dench's vivid performance as an impatient young mother with marital woes.〗

Four Jacks and a Jill (1942) 68m. ** D: Jack Hively. Ray Bolger, Desi Arnaz, Anne Shirley, June Havoc, Eddie Foy, Jr., Jack Durant, Henry Daniell, Fritz Feld. Struggling hoofer/pianist Bolger and his musician pals take in singing waif Shirley in this lackluster musical. Bolger's dancing is always a pleasure to watch, but Arnaz is wasted as an exiled king turned taxi driver. Remake of STREET GIRL and THAT GIRL FROM PARIS.▼

Four Jills in a Jeep (1944) 89m. **½ D: William A. Seiter. Kay Francis, Carole Landis, Martha Raye, Mitzi Mayfair, Phil Silvers, Dick Haymes, Jimmy Dorsey and His Orchestra; guest stars Betty Grable, Alice Faye, Carmen Miranda, George Jessel. Contrived wartime entertainment with four leading ladies reenacting their actual experiences entertaining soldiers overseas (which Landis turned into a popular book of the same name). Some good musical moments but nothing to shout about.▼▶

Four Men and a Prayer (1938) 85m. *** D: John Ford. Loretta Young, Richard Greene, George Sanders, David Niven, C. Aubrey Smith, William Henry, J. Edward Bromberg, Alan Hale, Reginald Denny, John Carradine. Compelling story of four brothers determined to unravel mystery behind their father's murder; handsome, well-paced production. Remade as FURY AT FURNACE CREEK.▶

Four Mothers (1941) 86m. **½ D: William Keighley. Priscilla Lane, Rosemary Lane, Lola Lane, Gale Page, Claude Rains, Jeffrey Lynn, Eddie Albert, May Robson, Frank McHugh, Dick Foran. Warmhearted but formulaic second sequel to FOUR DAUGHTERS. This time around, an unexpected family crisis affects the lives of the title quartet and their loved ones.▶

Four Poster, The (1952) 103m. ***½ D: Irving Reis. Rex Harrison, Lilli Palmer. Jan de Hartog play is tour de force for stars who enact various phases of married couple's life; warm, witty script; superb performances enhanced by ingenious animated interludes by UPA studio. Later became the stage musical *I Do! I Do!*

Four's a Crowd (1938) 91m. **½ D: Michael Curtiz. Errol Flynn, Olivia de Havilland, Rosalind Russell, Patric Knowles, Hugh Herbert, Lana Turner. Lightheaded romance in which everyone loves another; straight comedy's a switch for Flynn. Pleasant.▶

Four Sided Triangle (1953-British) 81m. BOMB D: Terence Fisher. James Hayter, Barbara Payton, Stephen Murray, John Van Eyssen, Percy Marmont. Scientist invents a duplicating machine; hoping to solve romantic triangle, he duplicates the woman he and his best friend both love. Silly programmer.▼▶

Four Skulls of Jonathan Drake, The (1959) 70m. ** D: Edward L. Cahn. Edu-

ard Franz, Valerie French, Henry Daniell, Grant Richards, Paul Cavanagh, Howard Wendell. Acceptable horror fare involving centuries-old voodoo curse upon family and contemporary scientist who puts an end to the weird goings-on.●▶

Four Sons (1928) 100m. *** D: John Ford. James Hall, Margaret Mann, Earle Foxe, Charles Morton, Francis X. Bushman, Jr., George Meeker. Famous silent tearjerker about a Bavarian widow whose four beloved sons fight in WW1—one of them on the American side. Simple and obvious but still effective. Remade in 1940.▼▶

Four Sons (1940) 89m. **½ D: Archie Mayo. Don Ameche, Eugenie Leontovich, Mary Beth Hughes, Alan Curtis, George Ernest, Robert Lowery. Czech family affected by Nazi rise to power, with sons choosing different allegiances. Remake of 1928 silent.▼▶

Four Steps in the Clouds (1942-Italian) 91m. *** D: Alessandro Blasetti. Gino Cervi, Adriana Benetti, Giuditta Rissone, Carlo Romano, Guido Celano, Margherita Seglin. Unwed mother-to-be Benetti convinces unhappily married traveling salesman Cervi to pose as her husband when she goes home to see her parents. Warm, sensitive, and charming tale presents a surprisingly nonideological depiction of life in WW2 Italy. Original title: QUATTRO PASSI FRA LE NUVOLE. Remade in France as THE VIRTUOUS BIGAMIST starring Fernandel, and as A WALK IN THE CLOUDS with Keanu Reeves.

Fourteen Hours (1951) 92m. *** D: Henry Hathaway. Paul Douglas, Richard Basehart, Barbara Bel Geddes, Debra Paget, Agnes Moorehead, Robert Keith, Howard da Silva, Jeffrey Hunter, Martin Gabel, Grace Kelly, Jeff Corey. Well-made suspense drama about a man threatening to jump off the ledge of a building, told in semidocumentary fashion. Look for Harvey Lembeck and Ossie Davis as cabbies, Joyce Van Patten as Paget's girlfriend. Grace Kelly's film debut.▶

Four Ways Out (1951-Italian) 77m. **½ D: Pietro Germi. Gina Lollobrigida, Renato Baldini, Cosetta Greco, Paul Muller, Enzo Maggio. Engrossing if unoriginal drama of a robbery at a soccer stadium, and the motives and fates of the various thieves. Federico Fellini worked on the original story; he and Germi were among the scriptwriters. Released in the U.S. in 1955.▼

Four Wives (1939) 110m. **½ D: Michael Curtiz. Claude Rains, Eddie Albert, Priscilla Lane, Rosemary Lane, Lola Lane, Gale Page, John Garfield, May Robson, Frank McHugh, Jeffrey Lynn. Sentimental but well-acted sequel to FOUR DAUGHTERS, further chronicling the lives and loves of the title quartet. Garfield appears briefly in flashback. Max Steiner's score includes his *Symphonie Moderne*. Followed by FOUR MOTHERS. ▶

Foxes of Harrow, The (1947) **117m. **½ D: John M. Stahl. Rex Harrison, Maureen O'Hara, Richard Haydn, Victor McLaglen, Vanessa Brown, Patricia Medina, Gene Lockhart. Lavish but lumbering tale of philanderer breaking up his marriage to seek affluence and fame in New Orleans in 1820. Pretty stale despite the trimmings. ▶

Foxfire (1955) **C-92m. **½ D: Joseph Pevney. Jane Russell, Jeff Chandler, Dan Duryea, Mara Corday, Barton MacLane. Russell battles cultural barriers when she impulsively marries Indian mining engineer Chandler while vacationing in Arizona. Not bad; the stars are well matched. Incidentally, that's Chandler singing the title song; he also wrote the lyrics.

Foxhole in Cairo (1960-British) **79m. **½ D: John Moxey. James Robertson Justice, Adrian Hoven, Peter Van Eyck, Neil McCallum, Michael Caine. Sensibly told account of counterintelligence at work in Egypt during WW2.

Foxiest Girl in Paris (1956-French) **100m. **½ D: Roger De Broin. Martine Carol, Michel Piccoli, Mischa Auer. Sultry Carol, a fashion model, becomes amateur sleuth to solve a robbery and a murder.

Fra Diavolo SEE: **Devil's Brother, The**

Framed (1947) **82m. ** D: Richard Wallace. Glenn Ford, Janis Carter, Barry Sullivan, Edgar Buchanan, Karen Morley. Rootless patsy Ford falls for scheming Carter but is kept in the dark as she hatches a robbery plan with banker Sullivan. Not especially stylish but efficient noir-ish melodrama. ▶

Francesco—Giullare di Dio (1950-Italian) **75m. *** D: Roberto Rossellini. Aldo Fabrizi, Brother Nazario Gerardi, Arabella Lemaitre. Assisi's favorite 13th-century saint is venerated in this austere biopic about a man of peace who has forsaken his family's wealth to lead a circle of believers into poverty, and into grace. Sincere, humble approach; acted by nonprofessionals and cowritten by Rossellini, Federico Fellini, and two Italian priests. Aka THE FLOWERS OF ST. FRANCIS and FRANCIS, JESTER OF GOD. ▶

Francis (The Talking Mule) Never hailed as an artistic triumph, the Francis series made up for that in box-office receipts from 1949 to 1956. Based on a book by David Stern, each of the seven films dealt with a sincere but stupid young man (at West Point he is 687th in a class of 687) led into and out of trouble by a canny talking mule. The off-screen voice was Chill Wills, the on-screen bumbler was Donald O'Connor in all but the last film, which starred Mickey Rooney. O'Connor once explained, "When you've made six pictures and the mule still gets more fan mail than you do..." Universal worked their contract starlets (Piper Laurie, Martha Hyer, Julie Adams, etc.) into the series

as love interests, but the center of attraction was always the mule. The films, except the last one, were all about on a par: silly but amusing. The first six films were directed by Arthur Lubin, who went on to create a similar TV series called *Mr. Ed*, about a talking horse.

FRANCIS (THE TALKING MULE)

Francis (1949)
Francis Goes to the Races (1951)
Francis Goes to West Point (1952)
Francis Covers the Big Town (1953)
Francis Joins the Wacs (1954)
Francis in the Navy (1955)
Francis in the Haunted House (1956)

Francis (1949) **91m. **½ D: Arthur Lubin. Donald O'Connor, Patricia Medina, ZaSu Pitts, Ray Collins, John McIntire, Eduard Franz, Anthony (Tony) Curtis. G.I. O'Connor becomes a war hero with the help of his talking mule, but is thought to be crazy when he tries to convince his superiors of the animal's ability. Initial entry sets the tone for the rest. Video title: FRANCIS THE TALKING MULE. ▼●▶

Francis Covers the Big Town (1953) **86m. **½ D: Arthur Lubin. Donald O'Connor, Nancy Guild, Yvette Dugay, Gene Lockhart, William Harrigan, Gale Gordon. O'Connor and his talking mule join a big city newspaper and get mixed up in a murder trial. ▼▶

Francis Goes to the Races (1951) **88m. **½ D: Arthur Lubin. Donald O'Connor, Piper Laurie, Cecil Kellaway, Jesse White, Barry Kelley, Hayden Rorke, Larry Keating. O'Connor falls for horsebreeder Kellaway's niece (Laurie) and foils some crooks when Francis coaches a sorry nag to win the big race. ▼●▶

Francis Goes to West Point (1952) **81m. **½ D: Arthur Lubin. Donald O'Connor, Lori Nelson, Alice Kelley, William Reynolds, Palmer Lee (Gregg Palmer), James Best, Les Tremayne, David Janssen. Francis helps O'Connor get in and out of trouble during basic training at the military school. Look for Leonard Nimoy and Paul Burke as cadets. ▼▶

Francis in the Haunted House (1956) **80m. ** D: Charles Lamont. Mickey Rooney, Virginia Welles, James Flavin, Paul Cavanagh, Mary Ellen Kaye, David Janssen, Richard Deacon, Timothy Carey. Rooney took over the reins from O'Connor for this final entry, a simplistic "spooky" comedy. Paul Frees also replaced Chill Wills as the voice of Francis. ▼▶

Francis in the Navy (1955) **80m. **½ D: Arthur Lubin. Donald O'Connor, Martha Hyer, Richard Erdman, Jim Backus, David Janssen, Clint Eastwood, Martin Milner, Paul Burke. For his last outing in the series, O'Connor plays a dual role. Typical service farce, notable for appearance of Eastwood, in his second film. Director Lubin also quit after this one and went on to produce TV's *Mr. Ed.*▼❚

Francis, Jester of God SEE: **Francesco—Giullare di Dio**

Francis Joins the Wacs (1954) **94m. **½** D: Arthur Lubin. Donald O'Connor, Julia (Julie) Adams, Mamie Van Doren, Chill Wills, Lynn Bari, ZaSu Pitts, Mara Corday, Allison Hayes, Joan Shawlee. An Army snafu sends Francis and O'Connor to a WAC base, causing all sorts of problems. More amiable nonsense, but then, you know you're not dealing with reality when Van Doren is cast as "Corporal Bunky Hilstrom." Wills, the voice of Francis, also appears on screen.▼❚

Francis of Assisi (1961) **C-111m. **½** D: Michael Curtiz. Bradford Dillman, Dolores Hart, Stuart Whitman, Cecil Kellaway, Finlay Currie, Pedro Armendariz. Lavish religious epic dealing with story of founder of school of monks with sympathetic performance by Dillman. Good cast and atmosphere. Script tends to sag at wrong moments. CinemaScope.▼❚

Frankenstein (1931) **70m. ***½** D: James Whale. Colin Clive, Mae Clarke, Boris Karloff, John Boles, Edward Van Sloan, Dwight Frye, Frederick Kerr, Lionel Belmore. Definitive monster movie, with Clive as the ultimate mad scientist, creating a man-made being (Karloff) but inadvertently giving him a criminal brain. It's creaky at times, and cries for a music score, but it's still impressive . . . as is Karloff's performance in the role that made him a star. Long-censored footage, restored in 1987, enhances the impact of several key scenes, including the drowning of a little girl. Based on Mary Shelley's novel. Followed by BRIDE OF FRANKENSTEIN.▼❚●

Frankenstein Conquers the World (1965-Japanese) **C-87m. **** D: Ishiro Honda. Nick Adams, Tadao Takashima, Kumi Mizuno. Grade-C horror film, with Adams a scientist in Tokyo trying to combat giant, newly grown Frankenstein monster terrorizing the countryside; poor special effects. Tohoscope.▼❚

Frankenstein Meets the Spacemonster (1965) **78m.** BOMB D: Robert Gaffney. Marilyn Hanold, Jim Karen, Lou Cutell, Nancy Marshall, David Kerman. Low-grade horror entry dealing with interplanetary robot that goes berserk. Bizarre, Flash Gordon–esque aliens also involved. Has gained a peculiar cult reputation. Aka MARS INVADES PUERTO RICO.▼❚

Frankenstein Meets the Wolf Man (1943) **72m. **** D: Roy William Neill. Lon Chaney, Jr., Patric Knowles, Ilona Massey, Bela Lugosi, Maria Ouspenskaya, Lionel Atwill, Dennis Hoey, Rex Evans, Dwight Frye. Sequel to both THE GHOST OF

FRANKENSTEIN and THE WOLF MAN finds werewolf Chaney seeking Dr. Frankenstein, hoping to be put out of his misery. He finds the scientist is dead—but the Monster isn't. Slick, atmospheric, fast-paced fun; Lugosi's only stint as the Monster. Followed by HOUSE OF FRANKENSTEIN.▼❚●

Frankenstein 1970 (1958) **83m.** BOMB D: Howard W. Koch. Boris Karloff, Tom Duggan, Jana Lund, Donald Barry. As last of the Frankenstein scientists, Karloff uses money from TV production shooting in his castle to revive original monster with atomic energy. Film is slow, monster unexciting, and Karloff hammy. CinemaScope.▼❚

Frankenstein's Daughter (1959) **85m.** BOMB D: Richard Cunha. John Ashley, Sandra Knight, Donald Murphy, Sally Todd, Harold Lloyd, Jr. Low-grade descendant of famed monster series with a new female horror-robot being created with typical results; tinsel sets.▼❚

Frankie and Johnny (1936) **66m.** BOMB D: Chester Erskine. Helen Morgan, Chester Morris, Lilyan Tashman, Florence Reed, Walter Kingsford. Dismally bad, cheaply made costume musical drama based on the old love-triangle song; even the great Morgan is undone. Made in 1934.▼

Frantic SEE: **Elevator to the Gallows**

Fraulein (1958) **C-98m. **** D: Henry Koster. Dana Wynter, Mel Ferrer, Dolores Michaels, Maggie Hayes. Bizarre post-WW2 Berlin tale of German girl helping U.S. soldier, then being held by the Communists. Wynter miscast. CinemaScope.❚

Freaks (1932) **64m. ***½** D: Tod Browning. Wallace Ford, Olga Baclanova, Leila Hyams, Harry Earles, Roscoe Ates, Johnny Eck, Daisy and Violet Hilton, Prince Randian, Zip and Pip, Schlitze. A unique movie about a traveling sideshow and the camaraderie of its unusual performers, goaded to vengeance by cruel trapeze star Baclanova. Horror-film master Tod Browning gathered an incredible cast of real-life sideshow freaks for this bizarre and fascinating film. Severely cut in U.S. during release and banned in the U.K. for 30 years, some reissue prints are missing brief epilogue; aka NATURE'S MISTAKES.▼❚●

Free and Easy (1930) **92m. **½** D: Edward Sedgwick. Buster Keaton, Anita Page, Robert Montgomery, Edgar Dearing, Lionel Barrymore, Dorothy Sebastian, Trixie Friganza. Interesting early-talkie musicomedy about Keaton becoming movie star; many guest appearances by Cecil B. DeMille, William Haines, et al. to boost uneven film. Keaton also filmed a Spanish-language version, ESTRELLADOS. Retitled: EASY GO.▼❚

Free and Easy (1941) **56m. **** D: George Sidney. Robert Cummings, Ruth Hussey, Judith Anderson, C. Aubrey Smith, Nigel Bruce, Reginald Owen, Tom Conway.

Short, sweet bauble about a high-class but penniless father-son duo (Cummings, Bruce) and what happens when the younger man is offered a choice between love and money. Spins out of control at the finale (literally), but otherwise a solid effort with a good cast. Based on a play by Ivor Novello; previously filmed as BUT THE FLESH IS WEAK.

Free, Blonde and 21 (1940) 67m. *½ D: Ricardo Cortez. Lynn Bari, Mary Beth Hughes, Joan Davis, Henry Wilcoxon. Low-grade hokum about gold-digging gals on the make for wealthy men.

Free for All (1949) 83m. ** D: Charles Barton. Robert Cummings, Ann Blyth, Percy Kilbride, Ray Collins. Mild froth about Cummings inventing instant gasoline.

Free Soul, A (1931) 91m. **½ D: Clarence Brown. Norma Shearer, Lionel Barrymore, Clark Gable, Leslie Howard, James Gleason. A hard-drinking, free-swinging attorney successfully defends gangster Gable on a murder rap—then finds to his dismay that his equally free-spirited daughter has fallen in love with him. Dated morality play–melodrama retains interest because of its cast and Barrymore's famous courtroom finale, which clinched him an Oscar. Based on Adela Rogers St. Johns' book about her father. Remade as THE GIRL WHO HAD EVERYTHING. ▼▶

Free to Love (1925) 60m. **½ D: Frank O'Connor. Clara Bow, Donald Keith, Raymond McKee, Winter Hall, Hallam Cooley, Charles (Hill) Mailes. Tailor-made vehicle has Clara an embittered young woman who is unable to carry out her plan to murder the judge who unjustly sent her to a reformatory. She becomes his ward, but her past comes to haunt her. ▼▶

French Cancan (1955-French) C-93m. *** D: Jean Renoir. Jean Gabin, Francoise Arnoul, Maria Felix, Edith Piaf. Not top-drawer Renoir, but still an impressive, enjoyable fiction about beginnings of the Moulin Rouge and impresario Gabin's revival of the cancan. Originally released in the U.S. in 1956; a brilliantly beautiful restored version, with approximately 10m. of additional footage, opened theatrically in 1985. Originally released in France as ONLY THE FRENCH CAN at 102m. ▼●▶

Frenchie (1950) C-81m. **½ D: Louis King. Joel McCrea, Shelley Winters, John Russell, John Emery, George Cleveland, Elsa Lanchester, Marie Windsor. A Western town's new saloon queen (Winters) has actually arrived to avenge the death of her father, murdered when she was a small girl; the quiet, no-guns sheriff (McCrea) wants her to mend her ways. OK Western vaguely based on DESTRY RIDES AGAIN. Winters-Windsor catfight is a highlight.

French Key, The (1946) 64m. **½ D: Walter Colmes. Albert Dekker, Mike Mazurki, Evelyn Ankers, John Eldredge, Frank Fen-

ton, Richard Arlen, Byron Foulger. Dekker and pal Mazurki accidentally discover a corpse; Dekker gives this OK mystery drama some class.

French Line, The (1954) C-102m. ** D: Lloyd Bacon. Jane Russell, Gilbert Roland, Arthur Hunnicutt, Mary McCarty, Craig Stevens, Steven Geray, Joyce McKenzie, Paula Corday, Scott Elliot. Russell's bust in 3-D was the gimmick to sell this dull musical. All that's left is flat tale of wealthy Texas girl in Paris being romanced by Parisian. McCarty's wisecracking is a blessing. If you blink, you'll miss Kim Novak modeling a gown. ▼

Frenchman's Creek (1944) C-113m. *** D: Mitchell Leisen. Joan Fontaine, Arturo de Córdova, Basil Rathbone, Nigel Bruce, Cecil Kellaway, Ralph Forbes, George Kirby. Colorful female fantasy escapism of Fontaine romanced by dashing pirate de Córdova; good supporting cast. Based on a Daphne du Maurier novel. ▼▶

French, They Are a Funny Race, The (1956-French) 83m. ** D: Preston Sturges. Jack Buchanan, Noel-Noel, Martine Carol, Genevieve Brunet. Director-writer Sturges' last film is a misfire, with Buchanan as veddy-British major whose marriage to Frenchwoman sparks continuing nationalistic arguments. Original title: LES CARNETS DU MAJOR THOMPSON at 105m.

Frenzy SEE: **Torment**

Fresh From Paris (1955) C-70m. *½ D: Leslie Goodwins. Forrest Tucker, Margaret Whiting, Martha Hyer. Grade-C musical filmed at Moulin Rouge cafe in Hollywood, with tiresome musical interludes. Original title: PARIS FOLLIES OF 1956. ▶

Freshman, The (1925) 70m. **** D: Sam Taylor, Fred Newmeyer. Harold Lloyd, Jobyna Ralston, Brooks Benedict, James Anderson, Hazel Keener. One of Lloyd's best-remembered films casts him as collegiate patsy who'll do anything to be popular on campus, unaware that everyone is making fun of him. Football game finale is one of several comic highlights. A real audience-rouser. ▼▶

Freud (1962) 120m. ***½ D: John Huston. Montgomery Clift, Susannah York, Larry Parks, David McCallum, Susan Kohner, Eileen Herlie. Intelligent, unglamorous account of Sigmund Freud as young doctor, focusing on his early psychiatric theories and treatments and his struggle for their acceptance among Viennese medical colleagues. Fascinating dream sequence. Originally released at 139m. Also known as FREUD: THE SECRET PASSION.

Frieda (1947-British) 97m. *** D: Basil Dearden. David Farrar, Glynis Johns, Mai Zetterling, Flora Robson, Albert Lieven. Interesting study of Farrar bringing German wife Zetterling back home to England, and bigotry they encounter. ▼

Friendly Enemies (1942) **95m.** **½ D: Allan Dwan. Charles Winninger, Charlie Ruggles, James Craig, Nancy Kelly. Hoary WW1 play about a conflict between German immigrant friends, one of whom has assimilated and one who has not. Simplistic in the extreme, and torpedoed by its stars' burlesque accents. ▼

Friendly Persuasion (1956) **C-140m.** **** D: William Wyler. Gary Cooper, Dorothy McGuire, Marjorie Main, Anthony Perkins, Richard Eyer, Robert Middleton, (Peter) Mark Richman, Walter Catlett, William Schallert. Charming account (from Jessamyn West novel) of Quaker family struggling to maintain its identity amid confusion and heartbreak of Civil War. Warm, winning performances in this beautifully made film. Music by Dimitri Tiomkin. Though no screenplay credit appears, film was written by blacklisted Michael Wilson; he received posthumous credit in 1996. Remade for TV in 1975 with Richard Kiley and Shirley Knight. ▼●▶

Friends and Lovers (1931) **68m.** **½ D: Victor Schertzinger. Adolphe Menjou, Laurence Olivier, Lili Damita, Erich von Stroheim, Hugh Herbert. Unexceptional film interesting only for its cast. Menjou and Olivier are British officers stationed in India, both in love with Damita. Von Stroheim is fun to watch as Damita's sly, conniving husband. ●

Friends of Mr. Sweeney (1934) **68m.** *** D: Edward Ludwig. Charlie Ruggles, Ann Dvorak, Eugene Pallette, Robert Barrat, Berton Churchill, Dorothy Burgess. Ruggles is a delight in a hand-tailored role as a meek, browbeaten writer for a conservative paper who reluctantly gives in to his editor's orders to write a favorable piece about a corrupt politician. A visit from a college chum and a wild, drunken night on the town completely transform his personality. Hilarious support by Pallette as the old friend and Barrat as a Communist agitator. Humor, sentiment, and warmth are perfectly blended in this small but satisfying film.

Frightened Bride, The (1952-British) **75m.** ** D: Terence Young. Andre Morell, Flora Robson, Mai Zetterling, Michael Denison, Mervyn Johns. Murder haunts a family when the youngest son becomes involved in homicide. Original British title: TALL HEADLINES.

Frightened City, The (1961-British) **97m.** **½ D: John Lemont. Herbert Lom, John Gregson, Sean Connery, Alfred Marks, Yvonne Romain. Interesting inside look at a London racketeer amalgamating various city gangs for master plan syndicate. ▼▶

Frightened Man, The (1952-British) **69m.** **½ D: John Gilling. Dermot Walsh, Barbara Murray, Charles Victor, John Blythe, Michael Ward, Thora Hird, Martin Benson. Arrogant young man, just booted out of Oxford, will do anything for a quick buck, in-

cluding exploiting his loved ones. Gilling also scripted this entertaining no-frills melodrama. ▶

Frisco Jenny (1933) **70m.** **½ D: William Wellman. Ruth Chatterton, Louis Calhern, Helen Jerome Eddy, Donald Cook, James Murray, Hallam Cooley, Pat O'Malley, Harold Huber, J. Carrol Naish. Pregnant Chatterton's lover is killed in the San Francisco earthquake, but her problems have only begun. Loose retelling of MADAME X is a tailor-made Chatterton vehicle. Good atmosphere and smart dialogue overcome film's tendency to meander. ▶

Frisco Kid (1935) **77m.** ** D: Lloyd Bacon. James Cagney, Margaret Lindsay, Ricardo Cortez, Lili Damita, Fred Kohler, George E. Stone, Donald Woods. Routine drama of Barbary Coast with Cagney fighting his way to the top, almost dethroned by local gangs but saved by blueblood Lindsay. ▶

Frisco Sal (1945) **94m.** ** D: George Waggner. Susanna Foster, Turhan Bey, Alan Curtis, Andy Devine, Thomas Gomez, Samuel S. Hinds. Tepid costume drama of New England choir singer Foster journeying to San Francisco's Barbary Coast in the Gay '90s on the trail of her long-missing brother.

Frisky (1954-Italian) **98m.** **½ D: Luigi Comencini. Gina Lollobrigida, Vittorio De Sica, Roberto Risso, Marisa Merlini. Lollobrigida provides sufficient sex appeal to carry simple tale of flirtatious village girl who beats out competition in winning heart of police official De Sica.

Frogmen, The (1951) **96m.** *** D: Lloyd Bacon. Richard Widmark, Dana Andrews, Gary Merrill, Jeffrey Hunter, Robert Wagner, Jack Warden. Intriguing look at underwater demolition squads in action in the Pacific during WW2. ▶

From Hell It Came (1957) **71m.** *½ D: Dan Milner. Tod Andrews, Tina Carver, Linda Watkins, John McNamara, Gregg Palmer, Robert Swan. Monstrous tree rises from grave of native chief's son, causing terror in South Seas village. As walking-tree movies go, this is at the top of the list. ▶

From Hell to Borneo (1964) **C-96m.** ** D: George Montgomery. George Montgomery, Julie Gregg, Torin Thatcher, Lisa Moreno. Filmed in the Philippines, tale recounts Montgomery's efforts to maintain sanctity of his private island against aggressive crooks and smugglers. ▼

From Hell to Heaven (1933) **67m.** **½ D: Erle C. Kenton. Carole Lombard, Jack Oakie, Adrienne Ames, David Manners, Sidney Blackmer, Verna Hillie, James Eagles, Shirley Grey. Another GRAND HOTEL clone, this time tracing the fortunes of guests at a racetrack hotel, all of whom have varying reasons for betting on an upcoming race. Lombard and Oakie are always fun to watch, and there's some interesting camerawork by Henry Sharp utilizing zoom lenses, which were rarely used in the '30s.

From Hell to Texas (1958) **C-100m.** **½ D: Henry Hathaway. Don Murray, Diane Varsi, Chill Wills, Dennis Hopper. Sincere Western with Murray on the run with posse on his trail for accidentally killing a man. CinemaScope. ▶

From Here to Eternity (1953) **118m.** ****
D: Fred Zinnemann. Burt Lancaster, Montgomery Clift, Deborah Kerr, Donna Reed, Frank Sinatra, Philip Ober, Ernest Borgnine, Mickey Shaughnessy, Jack Warden, Claude Akins, George Reeves. Toned-down but still powerful adaptation of James Jones' novel of Army life in Hawaii just before Pearl Harbor. Depiction of Japanese sneak attack combines unforgettable action scenes with actual combat footage. Brilliantly acted by entire cast, including Sinatra in his "comeback" role as the ill-fated soldier Maggio. Eight Oscars include Best Picture, Director, Screenplay (Daniel Taradash), Cinematography (Burnett Guffey), and Supporting Actors Sinatra and Reed. Remade in 1979 as a TV miniseries, which in turn spun off a brief series. ▼●▶

From Russia With Love (1963-British) **C-118m.** ***½ D: Terence Young. Sean Connery, Daniela Bianchi, Lotte Lenya, Pedro Armendariz, Robert Shaw, Bernard Lee, Lois Maxwell. Second James Bond film is one of the best; plenty of suspense and action, and one of the longest, most exciting fight scenes ever staged. Lenya makes a very sinister spy. ▼●▶

From the Earth to the Moon (1958) **C-100m.** **½ D: Byron Haskin. Joseph Cotten, George Sanders, Debra Paget, Don Dubbins, Patric Knowles, Melville Cooper, Carl Esmond, Henry Daniell. Jules Verne's fiction doesn't float well in contrived sci-fi of early rocket flight to the moon. Veteran cast looks most uncomfortable. ▼●▶

From the Manger to the Cross (1912) **71m.** **½ D: Sidney Olcott. Robert Henderson-Bland, Percy Dyer, Gene Gauntier, Alice Hollister, Sidney Olcott, Robert G. Vignola. Years before DeMille's THE KING OF KINGS—and decades before Mel Gibson—came this well-intentioned but pedestrian reenactment of the life of Christ. Extremely dated but still of interest as the first biblical epic filmed "on the original locations" in the Middle East. ▼▶

From the Terrace (1960) **C-144m.** *** D: Mark Robson. Paul Newman, Joanne Woodward, Myrna Loy, Ina Balin, Leon Ames, Elizabeth Allen, Barbara Eden, George Grizzard, Patrick O'Neal, Felix Aylmer, Mae Marsh. John O'Hara novel of WW2 vet Newman's rise to financial and social success makes for an engrossing soaper. Woodward is chic as his wife, with Loy superb as his alcoholic mother and Ames fine as his bitter dad. CinemaScope. ▼●▶

From This Day Forward (1946) **95m.**

*** D: John Berry. Joan Fontaine, Mark Stevens, Rosemary DeCamp, Henry (Harry) Morgan, Arline Judge, Bobby Driscoll, Mary Treen. Agreeable soaper of Fontaine and Stevens readjusting their lives when he returns from war, and their struggle to get on in the world.

Frontier Gal (1945) **C-84m.** **½ D: Charles Lamont. Yvonne De Carlo, Rod Cameron, Andy Devine, Fuzzy Knight, Andrew Tombes, Sheldon Leonard, Clara Blandick. Sex in the West as saloon queen De Carlo falls in love with outlaw Cameron; no sympathy from villain Leonard in OK Western-comedy. ▶

Frontier Gun (1958) **70m.** ** D: Paul Landres. John Agar, Robert Strauss, Barton MacLane, Morris Ankrum. Agar is honest sheriff who discovers that gunplay is only solution to town's crooks. Regalscope.

Frontier Horizon SEE: New Frontier

Frontier Marshal (1939) **71m.** *** D: Allan Dwan. Randolph Scott, Nancy Kelly, Cesar Romero, Binnie Barnes, John Carradine, Lon Chaney, Jr., Chris-Pin Martin, Eddie Foy, Jr. Colorful retelling of events leading to legendary gunfight at the O.K. Corral. Scott is fine as Tombstone's new marshal, Wyatt Earp; Romero is more moody than cold-blooded as Doc *Halliday*, and Kelly is the girl from his past who reminds Doc of his earlier, saner days as—an obstetrician! Many scenes and bits of dialogue were used in the 1946 remake, MY DARLING CLEMENTINE. Ward Bond, who plays Earp's brother in the later film, appears briefly as a cowardly town marshal. ▶

Frontier Pony Express (1939) **58m.** *** D: Joseph Kane. Roy Rogers, Mary Hart (Lynne Roberts), Raymond Hatton, Edward Keane, Noble Johnson, Monte Blue, Donald Dillaway, William Royle. Pony Express rider Roy falls in love with Hart, whose brother is a Confederate spy posing as a reporter. A perfect example of the formula that made Rogers' early films so popular, with a fast-moving story of the Civil War, Pony Express, spies, and outlaw raids, with time out for romance, a pair of songs, and even a moment for Trigger to shine on his own. Look for young George Montgomery as a Union cavalry soldier. ▼▶

Frontiersmen, The (1938) **72m.** **½ D: Lesley Selander. William Boyd, George Hayes, Russell Hayden, Evelyn Venable, Charles A. Hughes, William Duncan, Dickie Jones. Prairie schoolmarm is snubbed by Bar 20 owner's unruly son; while Hopalong Cassidy is busy acting as truant officer, she falls for crooked mayor, who secretly operates cattle-rustling ring. Venable's charming performance as the teacher is a big plus, along with robust action windup. Adapted from 1906 novel *Bar-20* by series creator Clarence E. Mulford. Without a single mention of it, classroom is integrated. ▼▶

Front Page, The (1931) **103m.** ***½ D: Lewis Milestone. Adolphe Menjou, Pat O'Brien, Mary Brian, Edward Everett Horton, Walter Catlett, Mae Clarke, George E. Stone. First filming of Hecht-MacArthur play is forceful, funny, and flamboyantly directed, with Menjou and O'Brien a good pair as battling editor and reporter in Chicago. Stands up quite well alongside remake HIS GIRL FRIDAY. Remade again in 1974 and as SWITCHING CHANNELS (1988).▼●

Front Page Story (1954-British) **99m.** **½ D: Gordon Parry. Jack Hawkins, Elizabeth Allan, Eva Bartok, Martin Miller, Derek Farr. Solid performances enhance story of many problems confronting newspaper editor: pending divorce, murder, lost children, and a rebellious staff.

Front Page Woman (1935) **82m.** **½ D: Michael Curtiz. Bette Davis, George Brent, Winifred Shaw, Roscoe Karns, Joseph Crehan. Breezy yarn of rival reporters Davis and Brent trying to outdo each other covering unusual murder and trial. Prime ingenue Davis fare.▶

Frozen Ghost, The (1945) **61m.** **½ D: Harold Young. Lon Chaney (Jr.), Evelyn Ankers, Milburn Stone, Douglass Dumbrille, Martin Kosleck, Elena Verduzo, Tala Birell. Entertaining *Inner Sanctum* yarn with Chaney as a stage mentalist who blames himself for a man's death, and seeks refuge (!) in a creepy wax museum run by Birell.▼●

Fugitive, The (1947) **104m.** ***½ D: John Ford. Henry Fonda, Dolores Del Rio, Pedro Armendariz, J. Carrol Naish, Leo Carrillo, Ward Bond. Brooding drama set in Mexico with revolutionist priest turned in by man who once sheltered him. Based on Graham Greene's novel *The Power and the Glory*. Superbly shot by Gabriel Figueroa. Also shown in computer-colored version.▼●

Fugitive Kind, The (1959) **121m.** **½ D: Sidney Lumet. Marlon Brando, Anna Magnani, Joanne Woodward, Maureen Stapleton, Victor Jory, R. G. Armstrong. Uneven filming of Tennessee Williams' *Orpheus Descending*, with strange casting. Wandering bum (Brando) arrives in Southern town, sparking romances with middle-aged married woman (Magnani) and spunky Woodward. Movie goes nowhere. Remade for cable TV in 1990 as ORPHEUS DESCENDING.▼●

Fugitive Lovers (1934) **84m.** ** D: Richard Boleslawski. Robert Montgomery, Madge Evans, Nat Pendleton, Ted Healy, C. Henry Gordon, The Three Stooges. Genially preposterous tale of runaway chorus girl and prison escapee who are drawn together during cross-country bus trip (all of it shot with "arty" camera angles). Moves like lightning to even *more* preposterous climax in snowbound Colorado.▼

Full Confession (1939) **73m.** ** D: John Farrow. Victor McLaglen, Sally Eilers, Joseph Calleia, Barry Fitzgerald, Elizabeth Risdon. Well-meaning but unbearably preachy melodrama in which Fitzgerald is falsely accused of murder. McLaglen confesses the crime to priest Calleia, but what can the father do?

Fuller Brush Girl, The (1950) **85m.** ** D: Lloyd Bacon. Lucille Ball, Eddie Albert, Jeff Donnell, Jerome Cowan, Lee Patrick. Low-grade slapstick with energetic Lucy as door-to-door salesgirl, mixed up with thieves.▼●

Fuller Brush Man, The (1948) **93m.** **½ D: S. Sylvan Simon. Red Skelton, Janet Blair, Don McGuire, Adele Jergens, Ross Ford, Hillary Brooke. Usual Skelton slapstick, with Red involved in murder while valiantly trying to succeed as a door-to-door salesman.▼●

Full of Life (1956) **91m.** *** D: Richard Quine. Judy Holliday, Richard Conte, Salvatore Baccaloni, Esther Minciotti. Holliday's pregnant wife antics almost matched by Baccaloni's as excitable father-in-law with his own way of running things.▼●

Full Treatment, The SEE: **Stop Me Before I Kill!**

Fun & Fancy Free (1947) **C-73m.** **½ D: William Morgan, Jack Kinney, Bill Roberts, Hamilton Luske. Edgar Bergen, Luana Patten; voices of Dinah Shore, Anita Gordon, Cliff Edwards, Billy Gilbert, Clarence Nash, The Kings Men, The Dinning Sisters. Disney feature comprised of two cartoon segments, Sinclair Lewis' so-so story "Bongo," about a circus bear, and the lively Mickey/Donald/Goofy "Mickey and the Beanstalk." Bergen's live-action interludes with Charlie McCarthy and Mortimer Snerd are also amusing. Second feature appearance of Jiminy Cricket has him singing a song intended for use in PINOCCHIO, "I'm a Happy-Go-Lucky Fellow."▼●

Fun in Acapulco (1963) **C-97m.** **½ D: Richard Thorpe. Elvis Presley, Ursula Andress, Paul Lukas, Alejandro Rey. Scenery outshines story of Presley working as lifeguard and entertainer in Mexican resort city and performing the likes of "No Room to Rhumba in a Sports Car" and "You Can't Say No in Acapulco." Lukas is amusing as temperamental chef.▼

Funny Face (1957) **C-103m.** ***½ D: Stanley Donen. Audrey Hepburn, Fred Astaire, Kay Thompson, Michel Auclair, Suzy Parker, Ruta Lee. Stylish and highly stylized musical with Astaire as fashion photographer who turns Hepburn into chic Paris model. Top Gershwin score ("How Long Has This Been Going On," "He Loves and She Loves," "S'Wonderful," title tune), striking use of color, entertaining performance by Thompson as magazine editor. Cinematography by Ray June and John P. Fulton. Leonard Gershe based his screenplay on an unproduced stage musical—and

Astaire's role was based on Richard Avedon, who's credited as visual consultant. VistaVision.**▼O●**

Fun on a Weekend (1947) 93m. ****** D: Andrew L. Stone. Eddie Bracken, Priscilla Lane, Tom Conway, Allen Jenkins, Arthur Treacher, Alma Kruger. Scatterbrain fluff as Bracken and Lane maneuver their way from penniless fortune to love and riches, all in the course of a day.

Furies, The (1950) 109m. ****½** D: Anthony Mann. Barbara Stanwyck, Walter Huston, Wendell Corey, Gilbert Roland, Judith Anderson, Beulah Bondi, Thomas Gomez, Albert Dekker, Blanche Yurka, Wallace Ford. Fiery Stanwyck has always been able to sweet-talk her cattle-baron father, who presides over a vast New Mexico ranch called The Furies—but lately he isn't listening, and she locks horns with him. Operaticstyle Western saga of love and hate, adapted by Charles Schnee from a Niven Busch novel and directed with flair by Mann. Striking cinematography by Victor Milner. This was Huston's final film.**▶**

Fury (1936) 94m. *****½** D: Fritz Lang. Sylvia Sidney, Spencer Tracy, Walter Abel, Bruce Cabot, Edward Ellis, Walter Brennan, Frank Albertson. Still timely drama of lynch mobs and mob rule in small town, making an embittered man of innocent Tracy, spoiling his love for sweetheart Sidney. Lang's first American film; he also scripted with Bartlett Cormack, from a Norman Krasna story. Also shown in computer-colored version.**▼▶**

Fury at Furnace Creek (1948) 88m. ****** D: H. Bruce Humberstone. Victor Mature, Coleen Gray, Glenn Langan, Reginald Gardiner, Albert Dekker. Ordinary Western tale of Mature erasing mar on father's career against formidable opposition. Remake of FOUR MEN AND A PRAYER.**▶**

Fury at Gunsight Pass (1956) 68m. ****½** D: Fred F. Sears. David Brian, Neville Brand, Richard Long, Lisa Davis, Katherine Warren, Percy Helton, Morris Ankrum. Brian tries to double-cross cohort Brand in carrying out plans for a bank robbery, with unexpected complications (including a ferocious sandstorm), in this fast-moving Western.

Fury at Showdown (1957) 75m. ***½** D: Gerd Oswald. John Derek, John Smith, Carolyn Craig, Nick Adams, Gage Clarke, Robert Griffin, Malcolm Atterbury, Rusty Lane. It's assumed that justifiably embittered Derek is the "mad-dog killer" who deliberately gunned a man down over a woman. Too much chatter and too little action sink this minor Western.

Fury at Smuggler's Bay (1961-British) 92m. ****** D: John Gilling. Peter Cushing, Michele Mercier, Bernard Lee, George Coulouris, Liz Fraser. Sea yarn of pirates scavenging passing ships and reaping rewards off the English coastline. Panascope.

Fury of the Congo (1951) 69m. ***½** D:

William Berke. Johnny Weissmuller, Sherry Moreland, William Henry, Lyle Talbot. Jungle Jim nonsense about a gang of smugglers who are out to capture strange animals called Okongos whose secretions form a potent narcotic.**▼▶**

Fuzzy Pink Nightgown, The (1957) 87m. ****** D: Norman Taurog. Jane Russell, Ralph Meeker, Adolphe Menjou, Keenan Wynn, Fred Clark, Una Merkel. Mediocre comedy. When movie star is kidnapped, everyone thinks it's a publicity gag.**▼**

Gabriel Over the White House (1933) 87m. ******* D: Gregory La Cava. Walter Huston, Karen Morley, Franchot Tone, C. Henry Gordon, Samuel S. Hinds, Jean Parker, Dickie Moore. Dizzying Depression fantasy of crooked Huston elected President, experiencing mysterious change that turns him into Superpresident, determined to eliminate racketeers, find world peace. Bizarre, fascinating.**▼O●**

Gaby (1956) C-97m. ****½** D: Curtis Bernhardt. Leslie Caron, John Kerr, Sir Cedric Hardwicke, Taina Elg. Remake of WATERLOO BRIDGE, telling of ballerina Caron and her romance with soldier Kerr in WW2 England. Not bad, but not up to original. CinemaScope.

Gallant Bess (1946) C-101m. ****** D: Andrew Marton. Marshall Thompson, George Tobias, Jim Davis, Clem Bevans, Donald Curtis, Chill Wills. Blah MGM B movie is a grown-up version of concurrent THE YEARLING—soldier takes army horse home with him; it eventually saves his life. The first MGM film produced in Cinecolor, if that's your idea of a milestone.**▶**

Gallant Blade, The (1948) C-81m. ****** D: Henry Levin. Larry Parks, Marguerite Chapman, Victor Jory, George Macready. Colorful, standard swashbuckler with dashing Parks protecting French general from villainous plot.

Gallant Hours, The (1960) 111m. ******* D: Robert Montgomery. James Cagney, Dennis Weaver, Ward Costello, Richard Jaeckel. Sincere, low-key bio of WW2 Admiral "Bull" Halsey played documentary-style. Cagney is reserved and effective, but production needs livening.**▼▶**

Gallant Journey (1946) 85m. ****½** D: William Wellman. Glenn Ford, Janet Blair, Charles Ruggles, Henry Travers, Arthur Shields, Selena Royle. Ford pioneers glider plane development in 19th century. OK, but not as stirring as it's meant to be.

Gallant Lady (1934) 86m. ****** D: Gregory LaCava. Ann Harding, Clive Brook, Otto Kruger, Tullio Carminati, Dickie Moore, Janet Beecher. Handsome but standard soaper about unwed Harding giving up baby for adoption, later hoping for second chance when adopted mother dies. Remade as ALWAYS GOODBYE.

Gallant Legion, The (1948) 88m. *** D: Joe Kane. William Elliott, Adrian Booth, Joseph Schildkraut, Bruce Cabot, Andy Devine, Jack Holt, Grant Withers, Adele Mara, James Brown. Superior "Wild Bill" Elliott vehicle is an action-packed semi-historical yarn of how the Texas Rangers stopped a crooked politician and various lawless factions from breaking up the Lone Star State into separate pieces. Fast paced and exciting.

Galloping Major (1950-British) 82m. ** D: Henry Cornelius. Basil Radford, Jimmy Hanley, Janette Scott, A. E. Matthews, Rene Ray, Joyce Grenfell, Hugh Griffith, Sidney James. Crackerjack cast enlivens this so-so comedy about a retired major (Radford) who raises the funds to purchase a racehorse, with assorted comical complications.▼

Gal Who Took the West, The (1949) C-84m. ** D: Frederick de Cordova. Yvonne De Carlo, Charles Coburn, Scott Brady, John Russell. De Carlo is attractive as singer in 1890s Arizona who allows Brady and Russell to court her.

Gambler and the Lady, The (1952-British) 72m. **½ D: Patrick Jenkins, Sam Newfield. Dane Clark, Kathleen Byron, Naomi Chance, Meredith Edwards, Anthony Forwood, Eric Pohlmann, Mona Washbourne. Clark earns his junior John Garfield credentials in this entertaining character study as an up-by-his-bootstraps American-born gambler who yearns for entrée into British high society.◗

Gambler From Natchez, The (1954) C-88m. ** D: Henry Levin. Dale Robertson, Debra Paget, Thomas Gomez, Lisa Daniels, Kevin McCarthy, Douglas Dick, Woody Strode. Set in 1840s, film focuses on Robertson's plot to eliminate trio of men who shot his father, a gambler caught cheating. ◗

Gambler's Choice (1944) 66m. ** D: Frank McDonald. Chester Morris, Nancy Kelly, Russell Hayden, Lee Patrick, Lyle Talbot, Sheldon Leonard. Another variation of MANHATTAN MELODRAMA— three kids grow up; one becomes a lawman, the other a shady gambler, the third the nice girl they both love.▼◗

Gambling House (1950) 80m. **½ D: Ted Tetzlaff. Victor Mature, Terry Moore, William Bendix, Zachary A. Charles, Basil Ruysdael, Cleo Moore, Ann Doran, Jack Kruschen. Intriguing period piece about gambling syndicate underling Mature, threatened with deportation as an undesirable alien, and how he (predictably) comes to learn the value of being an American.

Gambling Lady (1934) 66m. **½ D: Archie Mayo. Barbara Stanwyck, Joel McCrea, Pat O'Brien, Claire Dodd, C. Aubrey Smith. Honest professional gambler Stanwyck weds society boy McCrea; her motives are suspect because, after all, she's from "the

other side of the tracks." So-so drama picks up in its second half. And isn't that Tyrone Power in a bit in the Park Avenue gambling scene?

Gambling Ship (1933) 70m. ** D: Louis Gasnier, Max Marcin. Cary Grant, Benita Hume, Jack La Rue, Glenda Farrell, Roscoe Karns, Arthur Vinton. Cary seems a little stiff in this early assignment, acting tough as a reformed gambler posing as a businessman; he falls for gangster's moll Hume, who's pretending to be a socialite. This leads to a clash with nasty former cohort La Rue. Lots of talk and romantic complications before a bullet-ridden finale.

Game of Danger (1954-British) 88m. **½ D: Lance Comfort. Jack Warner, Veronica Hurst, Derek Farr. Offbeat study of two youngsters involved in homicide, with strange effects on their lives. Original title: BANG YOU'RE DEAD.

Game of Death, A (1946) 72m. *½ D: Robert Wise. John Loder, Audrey Long, Edgar Barrier, Russell Wade, Russell Hicks, Jason Robards (Sr.), Noble Johnson. Second official version of THE MOST DANGEROUS GAME—madman Barrier hunts humans shipwrecked on his island. Moves well, but indifferently acted; nowhere nearly as exciting as the 1932 original. Next remake: RUN FOR THE SUN.

Gamma People, The (1956-British) 79m. ** D: John Gilling. Paul Douglas, Eva Bartok, Leslie Phillips, Walter Rilla. Douglas and Phillips happen upon comic-opera country ruled by scientists trying to create geniuses; they do, but sometimes brainless "goons" also. Worse, the geniuses have no emotions. Peculiar Ruritanian sci-fi adventure.▼

Gang Busters (1954) 78m. **½ D: Bill Karn. Myron Healey, Don C. Harvey, Sam Edwards, Frank Gerstle. Standard but tough, fast-moving crime drama with lawmen on the trail of brainy, brutal Public Enemy #4 (Healey). Pasted together from episodes of the TV series.▼◗

Gang's All Here, The (1943) C-103m. **½ D: Busby Berkeley. Alice Faye, Carmen Miranda, Phil Baker, Benny Goodman and Orchestra, Eugene Pallette, Charlotte Greenwood, Edward Everett Horton, Tony DeMarco, James Ellison, Sheila Ryan. Corny but visually dazzling wartime musical, with soldier Ellison going off to battle while both Faye and Ryan believe they're engaged to him. Two socko musical numbers courtesy of Berkeley: "The Lady with the Tutti-Frutti Hat" (featuring Miranda at her best) and the finale, "The Polka Dot Polka." Faye does "No Love, No Nothin'." And, as an added kitsch treat, Benny Goodman sings! Watch for June Haver as a hat-check girl, Jeanne Crain by the swimming pool.●◗

Gangs, Inc. (1941) 72m. **½ D: Phil Rosen. Joan Woodbury, Jack LaRue, Linda

Ware, John Archer, Vince Barnett, Allan (Alan) Ladd, Gavin Gordon. Fast-paced programmer with innocent Woodbury seeking revenge after shielding her boyfriend and finding herself incarcerated on a hit-and-run rap. Of note for Ladd's supporting role as a reporter. Originally titled PAPER BULLETS, then CRIME, INC.▼)

Gangs of New York (1938) **67m.** ****½** D: James Cruze. Charles Bickford, Ann Dvorak, Alan Baxter, Wynne Gibson, Harold Huber, Willard Robertson, Maxie Rosenbloom. With imprisoned Public Enemy #1 "Rocky" Thorpe (Bickford) secretly stashed in solitary, a look-alike undercover cop (also Bickford) takes over his gang in order to smash it from the inside. Improbable but fun Republic programmer, "suggested" by 1928 Herbert Asbury book that also influenced Martin Scorsese's 2002 GANGS OF NEW YORK. Cowritten by Sam Fuller. Remade in 1955 as I COVER THE UNDERWORLD.

Gangster, The (1947) **84m.** ******* D: Gordon Wiles. Barry Sullivan, Belita, Joan Lorring, Akim Tamiroff, Harry Morgan, John Ireland, Fifi D'Orsay, Shelley Winters. Sullivan gives strong performance as man who falls victim to his slum environment and ends up a vengeful crook.▼)

Gangster at Bay SEE: **Gunman in the Streets**

Gangster Story (1959) **65m.** ***½** D: Walter Matthau. Walter Matthau, Carol Grace, Bruce McFarlan, Gerrett Wallberg. Matthau's lone film as director is a low-quality, ultra-low-budget chronicle of the plight of a bank robber and killer. Grace, as a librarian who falls for the thug, is real-life Mrs. Matthau.▼)

Gang War (1958) **75m.** ****½** D: Gene Fowler, Jr. Charles Bronson, Kent Taylor, Jennifer Holden, John Doucette. Grade-B film tracing the savage events resulting from a teacher testifying against gang brutality. Regalscope.

Gangway for Tomorrow (1943) **69m.** ****** D: John H. Auer. Margo, John Carradine, Robert Ryan, Amelita Ward, William Terry, Harry Davenport, James Bell, Charles Arnt, Wally Brown, Alan Carney. Lives of five workers in wartime munitions plant told in flashbacks; dated wartime fare with occasional bright moments. Written by Arch Oboler.

Garden Murder Case, The (1936) **62m.** ****½** D: Edwin L. Marin. Edmund Lowe, Virginia Bruce, Benita Hume, Douglas Walton, Nat Pendleton, Gene Lockhart, H. B. Warner. Philo Vance (Lowe) tracks a cunning killer who uses hypnosis to induce his victims to do themselves in. Fast-moving programmer.)

Garden of Allah, The (1936) **C-80m.** ****** D: Richard Boleslawski. Marlene Dietrich, Charles Boyer, Tilly Losch, Basil Rathbone, Joseph Schildkraut, Henry Kleinbach (Henry Brandon), John Carradine.

Flagrantly silly romance set in the Algerian desert; full of ripe dialogue, troubled glances, beauty shots of Marlene in a variety of gorgeous sheaths and flowing gowns, and some wonderful Technicolor scenery (which helped win its cameramen, W. Howard Greene and Harold Rosson, a special Oscar). It just isn't very good. ▼)

Garden of Eden, The (1928) **78m.** ******* D: Lewis Milestone. Corinne Griffith, Lowell Sherman, Louise Dresser, Maude George, Charles Ray, Edward Martindel. Delicate beauty Griffith (the movies' onetime "Orchid Lady") is enchanting in a smart late silent about an Austrian girl whose dreams of stardom come true, more or less, thanks to an unlikely fairy godmother. Sophisticated production—part fable, part farce—is set in Vienna, Budapest, and Monte Carlo, with art direction by the great William Cameron Menzies. From a play by Rudolph Bernauer and Rudolf Osterreicher. ▼)

Garden of Evil (1954) **C-100m.** ****½** D: Henry Hathaway. Gary Cooper, Susan Hayward, Richard Widmark, Hugh Marlowe, Cameron Mitchell, Rita Moreno. Meandering adventure set in 1850s Mexico, with trio escorting Hayward through bandit territory to save her husband. CinemaScope.)

Garden of the Moon (1938) **94m.** ****½** D: Busby Berkeley. Pat O'Brien, Margaret Lindsay, John Payne, Johnnie Davis, Melville Cooper, Isabel Jeans, Penny Singleton. Nightclub owner O'Brien and bandleader Payne have running feud; plot is pleasant excuse to work in Berkeley numbers: "Girlfriend of the Whirling Dervish," "Love Is Where You Find It," title tune. Look for Jerry Colonna in the band.)

Garment Jungle, The (1957) **88m.** ****½** D: Vincent Sherman. Lee J. Cobb, Kerwin Mathews, Gia Scala, Richard Boone, Valerie French, Robert Loggia, Joseph Wiseman, Harold J. Stone. Pretty good programmer based on newspaper articles about gangland infiltration in the garment business. Cobb is a proud dress manufacturer who uses paid hoodlums (led by Boone) to keep the union out of his shop . . . until his son (Mathews) arrives on the scene.

Gaslight (1940-British) **84m.** *****½** D: Thorold Dickinson. Anton Walbrook, Diana Wynyard, Frank Pettingell, Cathleen Cordell, Robert Newton, Jimmy Hanley. First version of Patrick Hamilton's play about an insane criminal who drives his wife crazy in order to discover hidden jewels. Electrifying atmosphere, delicious performances, and a succinctly conveyed sense of madness and evil lurking beneath the surface of the ordinary. MGM supposedly tried to destroy the negative of this original when they filmed the remake. Screenplay by A. R. Rawlinson and Bridget Boland. U.S. title: ANGEL STREET.▼)

Gaslight (1944) **114m.** ******* D: George

Cukor. Ingrid Bergman, Charles Boyer, Joseph Cotten, Dame May Whitty, Angela Lansbury, Terry Moore. The bloom has worn off this classic chiller about a man trying to drive his wife insane, but lush production, Victorian flavor, and fine performances remain intact. Bergman won Oscar; Lansbury's film debut. Filmed before in 1940. Also shown in computer-colored version. ▼●)

Gaslight Follies (1945) **77m.** *½ D: Joseph E. Levine. Charlie Chaplin, Harold Lloyd, Mary Pickford, Douglas Fairbanks, Jr., Marie Dressler, William S. Hart, Lillian Gish, Rudolph Valentino. Pointless hodgepodge of clips from scores of silent films and newsreels. ▼

Gasoline Alley (1951) **76m.** **½ D: Edward Bernds. Scotty Beckett, Jimmy Lydon, Susan Morrow, Don Beddoe, Patti Brady, Madelon Mitchel, Dick Wessel, Gus Schilling, Byron Foulger, Jimmy Lloyd, Christine McIntyre. First of two B movies based on Frank King's long-running comic strip is an agreeable domestic comedy in which Corky (Beckett) tries to make good by starting a diner with money borrowed from his brother Skeezix (Lydon). The whole family gets involved in this likable, low-key film with many familiar faces in the cast. Followed by CORKY OF GASOLINE ALLEY. ❱

Gate of Hell (1953-Japanese) **C-86m.** ***½ D: Teinosuke Kinugasa. Machiko Kyo, Kazuo Hasegawa, Isao Yamagata, Koreya Senda. Stark, stunning historical drama, set in 12th-century Japan, about a Samurai who falls in love with—and then tragically shames—a married woman. This beautiful production earned Oscars for Costume Design and Best Foreign Film. ▼❱

Gates of Paris (1957-French-Italian) **96m.** *** D: René Clair. Pierre Brasseur, Georges Brassens, Henri Vidal, Dany Carrel. Sweet, human story of a souse (Brasseur), and what happens when he begins looking after a gangster (Vidal) who has taken refuge in the house of his friend (Brassens).

Gateway (1938) **73m.** ** D: Alfred L. Werker. Don Ameche, Arleen Whelan, Gregory Ratoff, Binnie Barnes, Gilbert Roland, Raymond Walburn, John Carradine, Harry Carey. Silly story of naive Irish immigrant Whelan pursued by reporter Ameche and various other men during ocean crossing; redeemed only by interesting Ellis Island background. ❱

Gathering of Eagles, A (1963) **C-115m.** *** D: Delbert Mann. Rock Hudson, Rod Taylor, Mary Peach, Barry Sullivan, Kevin McCarthy, Henry Silva, Leif Erickson. Crisp Strategic Air Command drama with novelty of peacetime setting; Hudson gives one of his best performances as less than likable colonel whose wife struggles to adjust to being a military spouse. Good script

by Robert Pirosh. The song "The SAC Song" that Rod Taylor sings was written by Tom Lehrer. Look for Louise Fletcher as a patient's wife. ▼

Gaucho, The (1927) **96m.** *** D: F. Richard Jones. Douglas Fairbanks, Lupe Velez, Eve Southern, Gustav von Seyffertitz, Nigel De Brulier, Geraine Greear (Joan Barclay). Fairbanks swaggers through this lavish star vehicle as a famed, egocentric Argentine cowboy who leads a rebel band and romances fiery tavern girl Velez. Religious backdrop of the story is most unusual for a Fairbanks film, but it's still great fun to watch him in action. Mary Pickford, Fairbanks' wife, appears as "Our Lady of the Shrine." ▼❱

Gaucho Serenade (1940) **66m.** *** D: Frank McDonald. Gene Autry, Smiley Burnette, June Storey, Duncan Renaldo, Mary Lee, Clifford Severn, Jr., Lester Matthews, Smith Ballew, Joseph Crehan. Gene and Frog take to the road and have a series of adventures as they travel across the country, helping a British boy who hopes to be reunited with his father, picking up a runaway bride and her little sister, stopping off at a Mexican cantina, etc. Great fun all the way in one of Autry's best movies, with an enthusiastic cast of costars. Gene introduces his hit song "The Singing Hills." ▼❱

Gay Adventure, The (1952-British) **87m.** *** D: Gordon Parry. Burgess Meredith, Jean-Pierre Aumont, Paul Valenska, Kathleen Harrison. Interesting yarn, with three men concocting romantic fantasies about beautiful Harrison. Made in 1949. Original British title: GOLDEN ARROW.

Gay Bride, The (1934) **80m.** ** D: Jack Conway. Carole Lombard, Chester Morris, ZaSu Pitts, Leo Carrillo, Nat Pendleton. Unsatisfying blend of comedy and melodrama with gold-digging Lombard hitching herself to succession of gangsters.

Gay Deception, The (1935) **77m.** **½ D: William Wyler. Francis Lederer, Frances Dee, Benita Hume, Alan Mowbray, Lennox Pawle, Akim Tamiroff, Luis Alberni, Lionel Stander. Romantic trifle of working girl (Dee) on spree in N.Y.C., pursued by proletarian-posing prince (Lederer). A slight comedy engagingly handled by Wyler. The song "Paris in the Evening" was written by Preston Sturges! ❱

Gay Desperado, The (1936) **85m.** ** D: Rouben Mamoulian. Nino Martini, Ida Lupino, Leo Carrillo, Harold Huber, James Blakely, Stanley Fields, Mischa Auer. Jovial Mexican bandido Carrillo and his gang (who've learned how to be tough from Grade B gangster movies) recruit reluctant singer Martini and kidnap Lupino and her rich, wimpy boyfriend. Outlandishly silly, and pretty hard to take. ▼●)

Gay Divorcee, The (1934) **107m.** ***½ D: Mark Sandrich. Fred Astaire, Ginger Rogers, Alice Brady, Edward Everett Horton,

Erik Rhodes, Eric Blore, Betty Grable. Top Astaire-Rogers froth with usual needless plot and unusual musical numbers, including Oscar-winning "Continental" and Cole Porter's "Night and Day." Rhodes is memorable as would-be corespondent in divorce case. Incidentally, the Broadway hit on which this was based was called *The Gay Divorce,* but the Hollywood Production Code disapproved. ▼○▶

Gay Falcon, The (1941) 67m. **½ D: Irving Reis. George Sanders, Wendy Barrie, Allen Jenkins, Anne Hunter, Gladys Cooper, Edward S. Brophy, Arthur Shields, Turhan Bey. In the first *Falcon* entry, the blithe amateur sleuth and ladies' man is called on to break up a phony jewelry insurance scam. Very similar to Sanders' *The Saint* series, but still enjoyable. Incidentally, the title refers to the Falcon's first name, not his inclination. ▶

Gay Lady, The (1949-British) C-95m. **½ D: Brian Desmond Hurst. Jean Kent, James Donald, Hugh Sinclair, Lana Morris, Bill Owen, Michael Medwin. Lightweight costume picture about saucy entertainer who marries nobility; most notable aspect of film is its stunning use of Technicolor. Look fast for Christopher Lee as a dapper stage-door Johnnie. Original British title: TROTTIE TRUE. ▼

Gay Purr-ee (1962) C-86m. **½ D: Abe Levitow. Voices of Judy Garland, Robert Goulet, Red Buttons, Hermione Gingold, Paul Frees, Morey Amsterdam. A naive cat's misadventures in Paris. Stylish cartoon from UPA studio, written by Chuck and Dorothy Jones, lacks storytelling oomph. Chief assets are Garland and Goulet performing original songs by Harold Arlen and E. Y. Harburg, who wrote THE WIZARD OF OZ score for Judy years earlier. ▼○▶

Gay Ranchero, The (1948) C-72m. ** D: William Witney. Roy Rogers, Jane Frazee, Tito Guízar, Andy Devine, Estelita Rodriguez, George Meeker, LeRoy Mason, Dennis Moore, Bob Nolan and the Sons of the Pioneers. Sheriff Rogers fights to stop a gang of hoods trying to gain control of Frazee's airline by sabotage. Not much of a story, but Republic Pictures' "Hands Across the Border" policy is strongly in evidence with Latin stars Guízar and Rodriguez. ▼▶

Gay Sisters, The (1942) 108m. ** D: Irving Rapper. Barbara Stanwyck, George Brent, Geraldine Fitzgerald, Gig Young, Nancy Coleman, Donald Crisp, Gene Lockhart, Anne Revere. Stanwyck secretly marries Brent to gain inheritance money in thin soaper, immensely aided by Fitzgerald and Coleman as her sisters. Young took his name from the character he plays in this.

Gazebo, The (1959) 100m. *** D: George Marshall. Glenn Ford, Debbie Reynolds, Carl Reiner, Doro Merande, John McGiver, Mabel Albertson. Offbeat comedy involv-

ing murder and a backyard gazebo that covers up crime. Character actors McGiver and Merande wrap this up, but stars are competent. Also shown in computer-colored version. CinemaScope. ▼▶

Geisha, A (1953-Japanese) 87m. *** D: Kenji Mizoguchi. Michiyo Kogure, Ayako Wakao, Seizaburô Kawazu, Chieko Naniwa, Eitarô Shindô. Mizoguchi's remake of his own SISTERS OF THE GION relates the story of a young girl who is groomed to be a geisha but realizes that the Japanese symbol of feminine beauty has become nothing more than a glorified prostitute. Beautiful photography by the great Kazuo Miyagawa complements Mizoguchi's usual biting social critique. Aka GION FESTIVAL MUSIC. ▼

Geisha Boy, The (1958) C-98m. **½ D: Frank Tashlin. Jerry Lewis, Marie McDonald, Sessue Hayakawa, Nobu McCarthy, Suzanne Pleshette, Barton MacLane, Robert Hirano. Jerry, an inept magician, travels to Japan with disastrous consequences. Imaginative visual gags; there's a cute sequence featuring the Los Angeles Dodgers (and, in particular, Gil Hodges). Pleshette's film debut. VistaVision. ▼▶

Gene Autry and the Mounties (1951) 71m. **½ D: John English. Gene Autry, Pat Buttram, Elena Verdugo, Carleton Young, Richard Emory, Gregg Barton. Montana marshal Autry works with the Mounties to break a gang of bank robbers who cross over into Canada and redeems an angry French Canadian boy, whose uncle is one of the criminals. Gene sings "Blue Canadian Rockies" in this satisfactory outing. ▶

Gene Krupa Story, The (1959) 101m. **½ D: Don Weis, Sal Mineo, Susan Kohner, James Darren, Susan Oliver, Yvonne Craig, Lawrence Dobkin, Red Nichols, Buddy Lester. Hackneyed version of great jazz drummer's life, his ups and downs, his siege of dope addiction. ▼○▶

General, The (1927) 74m. **** D: Buster Keaton, Clyde Bruckman. Buster Keaton, Marion Mack, Glen Cavender, Jim Farley, Joseph Keaton. One of Keaton's best silent features, setting comedy against true Civil War story of stolen train, Union spies. Not as fanciful as other Keaton films, but beautifully done; Disney did same story in 1956 as THE GREAT LOCOMOTIVE CHASE. ▼○▶

General Died at Dawn, The (1936) 97m. ***½ D: Lewis Milestone. Gary Cooper, Madeleine Carroll, Akim Tamiroff, Dudley Digges, Porter Hall, William Frawley. Fine, atmospheric, often tense drama of intrigue in China, with freedom fighter Cooper opposing bandit general Tamiroff, falling in love with Carroll. Author John O'Hara has cameo as reporter on train. Another celebrated writer, Clifford Odets, scripted from John Booth's novel. ▼▶

General Spanky (1936) **71m. **** D: Fred Newmeyer, Gordon Douglas. George "Spanky" McFarland, Billie "Buckwheat" Thomas, Carl "Alfalfa" Switzer, Phillips Holmes, Ralph Morgan, Irving Pichel, Rosina Lawrence, Louise Beavers. Sluggish Civil War story, balancing kiddie antics against an adult romance, was intended to showcase three *Our Gang* stars in a feature-film format; it's easy to see why there wasn't an encore. Buckwheat's role as a slave in search of a master may displease contemporary audiences.▼●

Generation, A (1954-Polish) **88m. ***** D: Andrzej Wajda. Ursula Modrzinska, Tadevsz Lomnicki, Zbigniew Cybulski. Strong, necessarily downbeat drama about the Polish Resistance during World War 2 and what happens when a young man falls in love with the woman who leads the Resistance group. Wajda's first film and the first of a trilogy that includes the even better KANAL and ASHES AND DIAMONDS. Young Roman Polanski is featured in the cast.▼▶

Genevieve (1953-British) **C-86m. ***½** D: Henry Cornelius. Dinah Sheridan, John Gregson, Kay Kendall, Kenneth More, Geoffrey Keen, Joyce Grenfell, Michael Medwin. Lively, colorful comedy (by William Rose) pits two couples and their vintage roadsters against one another in a cross-country race. Uniquely British, brimming with charm and humor; a huge success in its day. Music score by harmonica virtuoso Larry Adler.▼▶

Genghis Khan (1965) **C-124m. *½** D: Henry Levin. Omar Sharif, Stephen Boyd, James Mason, Eli Wallach, Françoise Dorleac, Telly Savalas, Robert Morley, Yvonne Mitchell, Woody Strode. Laughable epic with gross miscasting and juvenile script, loosely based on legend of Mongol leader. No sweep or spectacle, but radiant Dorleac and earnest Sharif. Panavision.▶

Genius at Work (1946) **61m. *½** D: Leslie Goodwins. Wally Brown, Alan Carney, Lionel Atwill, Anne Jeffreys, Bela Lugosi, Marc Cramer. Radio detectives get involved in real-life murder schemes of Atwill. Brown & Carney's last film as Abbott & Costello-like team is pretty weak; Lugosi is wasted. Remake of SUPER-SLEUTH.▶

Gentle Annie (1944) **80m. **** D: Andrew Marton. Donna Reed, Marjorie Main, Harry Morgan, James Craig, Barton MacLane. Main vehicle about female outlaw with heart of gold.

Gentle Gunman, The (1952-British) **86m. ***** D: Basil Dearden. Dirk Bogarde, John Mills, Elizabeth Sellars, Robert Beatty. Unpretentious actioner of Irish revolution and enthusiast whose attempt to prove his patriotism backfires.

Gentleman After Dark (1942) **77m. **** D: Edwin L. Marin. Brian Donlevy, Miriam Hopkins, Preston Foster, Harold Huber.

Hodgepodge yarn of man escaping prison to redeem honor of his daughter by killing his shady wife; good cast stifled by sloppy script. Remake of FORGOTTEN FACES.▼

Gentleman at Heart, A (1942) **66m. **½** D: Ray McCarey. Cesar Romero, Carole Landis, Milton Berle, J. Carrol Naish, Richard Derr. Modest little comedy about bookie Romero discovering there's money in art forgery.

Gentleman Jim (1942) **104m. ***½** D: Raoul Walsh. Errol Flynn, Alexis Smith, Jack Carson, Alan Hale, John Loder, William Frawley, Minor Watson, Ward Bond, Arthur Shields. Sassy biography of polished boxer Jim Corbett in fight game's early days. Flynn is dynamic in title role (reportedly his favorite), supported by colorful cast—especially Bond in larger-than-life role as legendary champ John L. Sullivan. Scripted by Vincent Lawrence and Horace McCoy. Also shown in computer-colored version.▼▶

Gentleman's Agreement (1947) **118m. ***** D: Elia Kazan. Gregory Peck, Dorothy McGuire, John Garfield, Celeste Holm, Anne Revere, June Havoc, Albert Dekker, Jane Wyatt, Dean Stockwell, Sam Jaffe. Sincere Oscar-winning adaptation of Laura Z. Hobson's novel of writer (Peck) pretending to be Jewish, discovering rampant anti-Semitism. Holm won Supporting Actress Oscar as chic but lonely fashion editor, as did Kazan for his direction. Then-daring approach to subject matter is tame now. Screenplay by Moss Hart. ▼▶

Gentleman's Fate (1931) **94m. **½** D: Mervyn LeRoy. John Gilbert, Louis Wolheim, Leila Hyams, Anita Page, Marie Prevost, John Miljan. Happy-go-lucky orphan Gilbert is in for quite a shock as he learns his father is still alive and his brother (Wolheim) is a notorious bootlegger. So-so crime melodrama.

Gentlemen Are Born (1934) **75m. **½** D: Alfred E. Green. Franchot Tone, Jean Muir, Margaret Lindsay, Ann Dvorak, Ross Alexander, Nick (Dick) Foran, Charles Starrett, Henry O'Neill. Four college pals graduate together but find it tough going at the depth of the Depression. Forgotten film takes a surprisingly grim look at the realities of life in the 1930s—and that alone makes it worth seeing.

Gentlemen Marry Brunettes (1955) **C-97m. **** D: Richard Sale. Jane Russell, Jeanne Crain, Alan Young, Rudy Vallee, Scott Brady. Anita Loos' follow-up to GENTLEMEN PREFER BLONDES has Russell and Crain, two sisters in show biz in Paris, trying to avoid romances. Not up to original. CinemaScope.

Gentlemen Prefer Blondes (1953) **C-91m. ***** D: Howard Hawks. Jane Russell, Marilyn Monroe, Charles Coburn, Elliott Reid, Tommy Noonan, George "Foghorn"

Winslow. Slick, colorful bauble of entertainment with two sassy leading ladies tantalizing the men of two continents; Marilyn is at her best as fortune-hunter Lorelei Lee, and Russell gives a sly, knowing comic performance as her pal. Based on the Broadway adaptation of Anita Loos' venerable story, with sprightly Leo Robin–Jule Styne songs including "Diamonds Are a Girl's Best Friend." Sequel: GENTLEMEN MARRY BRUNETTES. ▼●▶

Gentle Touch, The SEE: **Feminine Touch, The** (1956-British)

Geordie SEE: **Wee Geordie**

George Raft Story, The (1961) 106m. **½ D: Joseph M. Newman. Ray Danton, Jayne Mansfield, Barrie Chase, Julie London, Neville Brand, Frank Gorshin. Danton is good in title role of fast-moving account of Raft's rise from Broadway dancer to top Hollywood star. How much is true, who can say? ▶

George Washington Slept Here (1942) 93m. **½ D: William Keighley. Jack Benny, Ann Sheridan, Charles Coburn, Percy Kilbride, Hattie McDaniel, William Tracy, Joyce Reynolds, Lee Patrick, Charles Dingle, John Emery. Sheridan (never more beautiful) surprises her city-dweller husband Benny by buying a dilapidated country house, and pouring all their money—and patience—into the process of fixing it up. Pleasant but predictable adaptation of the Kaufman-Hart play, with Benny in good form, and Kilbride re-creating his Broadway role as the hayseed contractor. ▼●▶

George White's Scandals (1934) 80m. **½ D: George White, Thornton Freeland, Harry Lachman. Rudy Vallee, Jimmy Durante, Alice Faye, Adrienne Ames, Gregory Ratoff, Cliff Edwards, Dixie Dunbar, Gertrude Michael, George White. Idiotic backstage romance plot propels entertaining, expensive musical; Faye, in film debut, sings "Oh, You Nasty Man," one of several big production numbers.

George White's Scandals (1935) 83m. ** D: George White. Alice Faye, James Dunn, Ned Sparks, Lyda Roberti, Cliff Edwards, Arline Judge, Eleanor Powell, George White, Benny Rubin. Tired show biz story of producer White seeing talented Alice in small-town show, bringing her (and her pals) to N.Y.C. where success poses problems. Story, songs all routine, but good cast gives it some life; Powell's dancing film debut. Retitled GEORGE WHITE'S 1935 SCANDALS. ▶

George White's Scandals (1945) 95m. ** D: Felix E. Feist. Joan Davis, Jack Haley, Phillip Terry, Martha Holliday, Bettejane (Jane) Greer, Margaret Hamilton, Glenn Tryon. Mild musical centering around the mounting of a "Scandals" stageshow, and chronicling the romances of Davis-Haley and Holliday-Terry. Tryon

plays George White; the real impresario produced. ▼▶

Germany Year Zero (1948-Italian) 73m. ***½ D: Roberto Rossellini. Edmund Meschke, Ernst Pittschau, Ingetraud Hinze, Franz Grüger (Franz-Otto Krüger), Erich Gühne. Shattering neorealist masterpiece, filmed amid the rubble of post-WW2 Berlin, charting the plight of a 12-year-old boy whose family is starving, battling for survival in a society drowning in corruption and cruelty. Heartbreaking story of a childhood tragically, irrevocably tainted, with a devastating finale. Screenplay by Rossellini, Max Colpet (Kolpé), and Carlo Lizzani. Final entry in Rossellini's war trilogy, following OPEN CITY and PAISAN. ▼▶

Geronimo (1939) 89m. ** D: Paul H. Sloane. Preston Foster, Ellen Drew, Andy Devine, Gene Lockhart, William Henry, Ralph Morgan, Marjorie Gateson, Chief Thundercloud. Run-of-the-mill Western marred by overuse of stock footage and bad process shots to simulate outdoor scenes. Lockhart getting just deserts is best item in trivial Indian vs. cavalry contest. Remake of THE LIVES OF A BENGAL LANCER.

Geronimo (1962) C-101m. **½ D: Arnold Laven. Chuck Connors, Kamala Devi, Pat Conway, Armando Silvestre, Lawrence Dobkin, Ross Martin, Denver Pyle, Adam West. Connors fares well as the noble Apache warrior who refuses to submit to the U.S. Army. Connors later married leading lady Devi. Panavision. ▼●▶

Gertrud (1964-Danish) 117m. **½ D: Carl Th. Dreyer. Nina Pens Rode, Bendt Rothe, Ebbe Rode, Baard Owe, Axel Strøbye. Dreyer's final film (and first in a decade) charts the dilemma of the title character, trapped in a loveless marriage, who leaves her husband to find emotional fulfillment and happiness. Her problem: the men in her life all are accomplished professionals who value their work more than relationships. Slow-moving, deliberately paced drama is not for all tastes. Dreyer also scripted, from a play by Hjalmar Söderberg. Poetic finale seems to be summarizing Dreyer's life and worldview. ▼▶

Gervaise (1956-French) 116m. *** D: René Clement. Maria Schell, Francois Perier, Suzy Delair, Armand Mestral. Splendidly acted version of Emile Zola tale of Schell struggling to keep her family going but finally succumbing to tawdry life of her drunken husband. ▼▶

Get-Away, The (1941) 89m. ** D: Edward Buzzell. Robert Sterling, Charles Winninger, Donna Reed, Henry O'Neill, Dan Dailey, Don Douglas, Grant Withers. To solve a series of bank robberies, stalwart G-man Sterling goes undercover in prison and befriends gangster Dailey. Virtually a shot-for-shot remake of PUBLIC HERO #1, this one is thoroughly mediocre, despite being produced by the director of the original, J. Walter Ruben. Reed's film debut.

Get Hep to Love (1944) 71m. *½ D: Charles Lamont. Gloria Jean, Donald O'Connor, Jane Frazee, Robert Paige. Weak musical with precocious musical personality Jean running away to find happier home and singing career.

Get On With It (1961-British) 88m. ** D: C. M. Pennington-Richards. Bob Monkhouse, Kenneth Connor, Shirley Eaton, Eric Barker, Ronnie Stevens, Richard Wattis, Reginald Beckwith. Dental school graduates Monkhouse and Stevens promote a new toothpaste. Intermittently funny. Aka DENTIST ON THE JOB.

Getting Gertie's Garter (1945) 72m. **½ D: Allan Dwan. Dennis O'Keefe, Marie McDonald, Barry Sullivan, Binnie Barnes, Sheila Ryan, J. Carrol Naish, Jerome Cowan. Similar to UP IN MABEL'S ROOM, a funny little comedy of O'Keefe trying to retrieve embarrassing memento without wife's knowledge.▼❙

Get Yourself A College Girl (1964) C-88m. *½ D: Sidney Miller. Chad Everett, Nancy Sinatra, Mary Ann Mobley, Dave Clark Five, The Animals. Songwriter who is undergraduate at a staid girls' school falls in love with a music publisher at resort hotel. Strictly for dropouts.❙

Ghidrah, The Three-Headed Monster (1964-Japanese) C-85m. **½ D: Ishiro Honda. Yosuke Natsuki, Yunko Hoshi, Hiroshi Koizumi, Akiko Wakabayashi, Takashi Shimura, Emi Ito, Yumi Ito. Beautiful princess, feared killed in a plane crash, reappears, claiming to be from Mars and warning that we're about to be attacked by a space dragon. Darned if she isn't right. Debut of King Ghidorah (whose name was misspelled by the original U.S. distributor) is one of the better Toho monster rallies, with Godzilla, Rodan, and Mothra calling a truce to battle this new foe. Akira Ifukube's dynamic score is a plus, as is the warm presence of the illustrious Shimura. Japanese running time is 92m. Tohoscope.▼❙

Ghost, The (1963-Italian) C-96m. **½ D: Robert Hampton (Riccardo Freda). Barbara Steele, Peter Baldwin, Leonard Elliott (Elio Jotta), Harriet White. In 1910 Scotland, adulterous wife Steele and doctor-lover are seemingly haunted by the vengeful ghost of her crippled husband, whom they murdered. Measured, moody horror, let down by routine plot; still atmospheric and watchable. Follow-up to THE HORRIBLE DR. HICHCOCK.▼❙

Ghost and Mrs. Muir, The (1947) 104m. ***½ D: Joseph L. Mankiewicz. Gene Tierney, Rex Harrison, George Sanders, Edna Best, Vanessa Brown, Anna Lee, Robert Coote, Natalie Wood. A lonely widow is romanced by the ghost of a sea captain in her "haunted" English cottage. Charming,

beautifully made fantasy, a distant cousin to later TV sitcom; lovely score by Bernard Herrmann. Philip Dunne scripted, from the R.A. Dick novel.▼●❙

Ghost Breakers, The (1940) 85m. *** D: George Marshall. Bob Hope, Paulette Goddard, Richard Carlson, Paul Lukas, Anthony Quinn, Willie Best, Noble Johnson, Tom Dugan, Lloyd Corrigan. More plot than usual for a Hope film as Bob and Paulette investigate eerie Cuban castle that she's inherited. Some real chills as well as laughs in this first-rate film. Robert Ryan has bit as ambulence attendant. Remade as SCARED STIFF (1953).▼●❙

Ghost Catchers (1944) 67m. *** D: Edward F. Cline. Ole Olsen, Chic Johnson, Gloria Jean, Martha O'Driscoll, Leo Carrillo, Andy Devine, Walter Catlett, Lon Chaney, Jr. One of Olsen and Johnson's wackiest comedies, with duo as nightclub owners who help Southern colonel Catlett and his daughters, who have just moved into the haunted house next door. Try to spot Mel Tormé as a drummer in the band.

Ghost Chasers (1951) 69m. **½ D: William Beaudine. Leo Gorcey, Huntz Hall, William (Billy) Benedict, David Gorcey, Buddy Gorman, Jan Kayne, Bernard Gorcey, Lloyd Corrigan. Spirited supernatural spoof, as the Bowery Boys try to expose a fake medium.▼❙

Ghost Comes Home, The (1940) 79m. ** D: William Thiele. Frank Morgan, Billie Burke, Ann Rutherford, John Shelton, Reginald Owen, Donald Meek, Nat Pendleton, Frank Albertson. Morgan, thought dead, returns to his family—which has been doing fine without him. Fine cast does its best with mediocre comedy material. Based on a German play that was filmed before in 1935.

Ghost Goes West, The (1936) 82m. **½ D: René Clair. Robert Donat, Eugene Pallette, Jean Parker, Everly Gregg, Elsa Lanchester, Hay Petrie, Morton Selten. Bombastic American purchases a Scottish castle, unaware that it's haunted by the ghost of the current owner's fast-living ancestor. Genial but bland comedy written by Robert E. Sherwood and filmed by Clair in an oddly aloof fashion—with barely any close-ups of its leading actors!▼❙

Ghost of Dragstrip Hollow (1959) 65m. BOMB D: William Hole, Jr. Jody Fair, Russ Bender, Henry McCann, Martin Braddock, Elaine DuPont, Leon Tyler, Jack Ging. Square, law-abiding teenage hot-rodders throw a party in a "haunted" house. Annoying, plotless excuse for a scare comedy. Paul Blaisdell wears his SHE-CREATURE costume in humiliating cameo.❙

Ghost of Frankenstein, The (1942) 68m. **½ D: Erle C. Kenton. Cedric Hardwicke, Lon Chaney, Jr., Lionel Atwill, Ralph Bellamy, Bela Lugosi, Evelyn Ankers, Dwight Frye. Sequel to SON OF FRANKENSTEIN.

Ygor (Lugosi) tries to convince Dr. Frankenstein (Hardwicke) to put his brain into the Monster. Good cast manages to save stale plot. Followed by FRANKENSTEIN MEETS THE WOLF MAN.▼●◗

Ghost Ship, The (1943) 69m. *** D: Mark Robson. Richard Dix, Russell Wade, Edith Barrett, Ben Bard, Lawrence Tierney. Offbeat Val Lewton melodrama about young man who signs on merchant ship run by power-crazy captain (Dix) who's obsessed with "authority." Absorbing mood piece with unfortunately abrupt conclusion.▼●◗

Ghost Ship (1952-British) 69m. ** D: Vernon Sewell. Dermot Walsh, Hazel Court, Hugh Burden, John Robinson, Joss Ambler. Small-budget yarn about young couple (real-life husband and wife Walsh and Court) purchasing a haunted yacht.▼◗

Ghosts of Berkeley Square, The (1947-British) 85m. **½ D: Vernon Sewell. Robert Morley, Felix Aylmer, Yvonne Arnaud, Claude Hulbert, Abraham Sofaer, Ernest Thesiger, Martita Hunt, Ronald Frankau, Wilfrid Hyde-White. In 1708, fuddy-duddy generals Morley and Aylmer accidentally kill themselves and are forced to haunt their Berkeley Square home until it is visited by reigning royalty; we see their escapades through the centuries. Morley plays two roles and leads a sterling cast. Almost a working definition of "droll," this dry British comedy never quite coalesces, though it's fun to watch.▼

Ghosts of Rome (1961-Italian) C-105m. **½ D: Antonio Pietrangeli. Marcello Mastroianni, Belinda Lee, Sandra Milo, Vittorio Gassman, Franca Marzi. Scatterbrain antics of oddball characters inhabiting run-down house soon to be demolished, with prospects of finding new quarters frightening them all.

Ghosts on the Loose (1943) 65m. ** D: William Beaudine. Leo Gorcey, Huntz Hall, Bobby Jordan, Bela Lugosi, Sunshine Sammy Morrison, Billy Benedict, Stanley Clements, Bobby Stone, Ava Gardner, Rick Vallin. Gorcey and his gang take on Nazi spies (led by Lugosi) in this misleadingly titled entry. Notable only for early appearance of ingenue Gardner. Retitled THE EAST SIDE KIDS MEET BELA LUGOSI.▼●◗

Ghost Walks, The (1934) 66m. **½ D: Frank Strayer. John Miljan, June Collyer, Richard Carle, Henry Kolker, Spencer Charters, Johnny Arthur. Life (and murder) imitate art when a Broadway playwright's newest thriller starts coming true while he and his producer are stranded in an odd, out-of-the-way mansion brimming with odd, out-of-the-way guests. Story lynchpins need oil in this rusting antique, but it's lightly humorous and it does have enough plot for six other movies.▼◗

Ghoul, The (1933-British) 73m. **½ D: T. Hayes Hunter. Boris Karloff, Cedric Hardwicke, Ernest Thesiger, Dorothy Hyson, Anthony Bushell, Ralph Richardson, Kathleen Harrison. England's answer to Hollywood's horror films: Egyptologist Karloff wishes to be buried with a jewel he believes will allow him eternal life. It's stolen, and he rises from the dead in search of the culprit. Slow going until Karloff's resurrection; then it really hums. Richardson's film debut. Remade as 1962 comedy NO PLACE LIKE HOMICIDE! Original 79m. version is available on video.▼◗

Giant (1956) C-201m. **** D: George Stevens. Elizabeth Taylor, Rock Hudson, James Dean, Carroll Baker, Jane Withers, Chill Wills, Mercedes McCambridge, Dennis Hopper, Sal Mineo, Rodney (Rod) Taylor, Earl Holliman. Near-legendary epic based on Edna Ferber's novel about two generations of larger-than-life Texans holds up beautifully although still very much of its time. Hudson's best performance, close to Taylor's best, and Dean's last film. Stevens won Oscar for direction. Screenplay by Fred Guiol and Ivan Moffat.▼●◗

Giant Behemoth, The (1959-British) 80m. ** D: Eugene Lourie. Gene Evans, Andre Morell, John Turner, Leigh Madison, Jack MacGowran. Enormous radioactive dinosaur menaces England, finally invades London. Animation effects directed by Willis O'Brien are fine, but film is turgid. Original British title: BEHEMOTH THE SEA MONSTER. ▼●◗

Giant Claw, The (1957) 76m. *½ D: Fred F. Sears. Jeff Morrow, Mara Corday, Morris Ankrum, Edgar Barrier. Lack of decent special effects ruins the running battle between colossal bird and fighter jets. Big bird is laughable.▼◗

Giant From the Unknown (1958) 77m. *½ D: Richard E. Cunha. Edward Kemmer, Sally Fraser, Bob Steele, Morris Ankrum, Buddy Baer, Joline Brand, Billy Dix. Giant, depraved conquistador Baer, in suspended animation for centuries, is revived in California mountains, wreaking minor havoc. Cheap and silly.▼◗

Giant Gila Monster, The (1959) 74m. *½ D: Ray Kellogg. Don Sullivan, Lisa Simone, Shug Fisher, Jerry Cortwright, Beverly Thurman, Don Flourney, Pat Simmons. Big, beaded lizard menaces small Texas town. Not as good as it sounds. Has a couple of wildly inappropriate songs.▼◗

Giant Leeches, The SEE: **Attack of the Giant Leeches**

Giants of Thessaly, The (1960-Italian) C-86m. ** D: Riccardo Freda. Roland Carey, Ziva Rodann, Massimo Girotti, Alberto Farnese. Episodic sword-and-sandal account of Jason (Carey) and Orpheus (Girotti) seeking golden fleece, with expected clashes with monsters, evil women, etc. Totalscope.▼◗

G.I. Blues (1960) C-104m. **½ D: Norman Taurog. Elvis Presley, Juliet Prowse,

Robert Ivers, Leticia Roman, Ludwig Stossel. Prowse's versatile performance as a cabaret dancer uplifts this standard Presley fare about a guitar-playing G.I. in West Germany. Elvis sings "Tonight Is So Right for Love," "Wooden Heart," "Blue Suede Shoes," and title song. ▼●)

Gideon of Scotland Yard (1958-British) **C-91m.** *½ D: John Ford. Jack Hawkins, Dianne Foster, Cyril Cusack, Andrew Ray, James Hayter, Ronald Howard, Anna Massey, Anna Lee, Laurence Naismith. A typical day in the life of a Scotland Yard inspector; Hawkins is likable but the film is unbelievably dull. A surprising dud from director Ford. British version, titled GIDEON'S DAY, runs 118m. Originally released theatrically in the U.S. in b&w.)

Gideon's Day SEE: **Gideon of Scotland Yard**

Gidget (1959) **C-95m.** **½ D: Paul Wendkos. Sandra Dee, James Darren, Cliff Robertson, Arthur O'Connell, Joby Baker, Yvonne Craig, Doug McClure, Tom Laughlin. California teenage girl hits the beach one summer and falls in love with two surfer boys. Dee is spirited in the title role of this hit movie (based on Frederick Kohner's novel about his daughter), which is credited with firing Southern California's surfing craze. It also led to a number of sequels and two different TV series! CinemaScope. ▼●)

Gidget Goes Hawaiian (1961) **C-102m.** ** D: Paul Wendkos. James Darren, Michael Callan, Deborah Walley, Carl Reiner, Peggy Cass, Eddie Foy, Jr. Inane follow-up has teenager off to the Islands, with embarrassing results for all. ▼)

Gidget Goes to Rome (1963) **C-101m.** ** D: Paul Wendkos. Cindy Carol, James Darren, Jessie Royce Landis, Cesare Danova, Jeff Donnell. Mild follow-up has fetching teenager off to Italy, involved in predictable romancing. ▼)

Gift for Heidi, A (1958) **C-71m.** ** D: George Templeton. Douglas Fowley, Sandy Descher, Van Dyke Parks. Heidi learns the meaning of faith, hope, and charity. OK entertainment for youngsters. Inspired by Johanna Spyri's story.

Gift Horse, The (1952-British) **100m.** *** D: Compton Bennett. Trevor Howard, Richard Attenborough, Sonny Tufts, James Donald, Joan Rice, Bernard Lee, Dora Bryan, Hugh Williams, Sidney James. Solid WW2 drama with Howard as a troublesome ship's captain, disliked by his crew, who comes into his own while battling a German U-boat. Also known as GLORY AT SEA. ▼

Gift of Gab (1934) **71m.** *½ D: Karl Freund. Edmund Lowe, Gloria Stuart, Alice White, Victor Moore, Hugh O'Connell, Helen Vinson; guest stars Gene Austin, Ruth Etting, Ethel Waters, Paul Lukas, Chester Morris, Roger Pryor, Binnie Barnes, Karloff (Boris Karloff), Bela Lugosi, June Knight,

Gus Arnheim and His Orchestra, The Beale Street Boys, Alexander Woollcott. Fast-talking egomaniac Lowe becomes a radio star, but success goes to his head. Dumb movie with cardboard characters and a silly plot; even the songs by such greats as Etting and Waters are second-rate. Karloff has an amusing bit in a murder-mystery skit. So static it's hard to believe this was directed by legendary cinematographer Freund.

Gift of Love, The (1958) **C-105m.** ** D: Jean Negulesco. Lauren Bacall, Robert Stack, Evelyn Rudie, Lorne Greene, Anne Seymour. If you could put up with SENTIMENTAL JOURNEY you might bear this remake, which isn't even as good. Bacall dies but returns to earth as guiding spirit for her husband and daughter. Remade again for TV as SENTIMENTAL JOURNEY. CinemaScope.

Gigantis, the Fire Monster (1959-Japanese) **78m.** ** D: Motoyoshi Oda, Hugo Grimaldi. Hiroshi Koizumi, Setsuko Makayama. A new Godzilla, here called Gigantis, battles spiny Angorous, trashing another Japanese city. First sequel to GODZILLA KING OF THE MONSTERS!, retitled: GODZILLA RAIDS AGAIN. ▼)

Gigi (1949-French) **83m.** **½ D: Jacqueline Audry. Daniele Delorme, Frank Villard, Yvonne de Bray, Gaby Morlay, Jean Tissier, Madeleine Rousset. Original version of Colette's novel is not a musical but a drolly amusing (if talky and uncinematic) comedy of manners. Delorme, who starred in two more films based on Colette stories, is delightful as Gigi, the girl trained to be a courtesan by her aunt and grandmother in fin de siècle Paris. Originally 109m.)

Gigi (1958) **C-116m.** **** D: Vincente Minnelli. Leslie Caron, Maurice Chevalier, Louis Jourdan, Hermione Gingold, Jacques Bergerac, Eva Gabor. Joyful turn-of-the-20th-century musical based on Colette's story of a French girl who's groomed to be a courtesan. Exquisitely filmed, perfectly cast, with memorable Lerner & Loewe score: title tune, "Thank Heaven for Little Girls," "I Remember It Well." Winner of nine Academy Awards including Best Picture, Director, Writing (Alan Jay Lerner), Cinematography (Joseph Ruttenberg), Costumes (Cecil Beaton), Song ("Gigi"), and Scoring (Andre Previn). Chevalier received an honorary Oscar. Later a Broadway musical. CinemaScope. ▼●)

Gigot (1962) **C-104m.** *** D: Gene Kelly. Jackie Gleason, Katherine Kath, Gabrielle Dorziat, Albert Remy, Yvonne Constant. Sentimental, well-acted tale of a deaf mute (Gleason) and a young girl in Paris. Simple film, well done; Gleason is excellent. Remade for TV as THE WOOL CAP MAN (2004).)

Gilda (1946) **110m.** *** D: Charles Vidor. Rita Hayworth, Glenn Ford, George

Macready, Joseph Calleia, Steven Geray. Highly charged story of emotional triangle—mysterious South American casino owner Macready, his new man-Friday Ford, and Macready's alluring wife (Hayworth)—unfortunately cops out with silly resolutions. Rita has never been sexier, especially when singing "Put the Blame on Mame."▼●▶

Gilded Lily, The (1935) 80m. *** D: Wesley Ruggles. Claudette Colbert, Fred MacMurray, Ray Milland, C. Aubrey Smith, Edward Craven, Luis Alberni, Grace Bradley. Colbert has to choose between aristocratic Milland and down-to-earth MacMurray. Fine romantic fluff. MacMurray's breezy performance here made a strong impression and boosted him to stardom.▶

Gildersleeve's Ghost (1944) 64m. ** D: Gordon Douglas. Harold Peary, Marion Martin, Richard LeGrand, Amelita Ward. Programmer entry in the *Great Gildersleeve* series, involving mixture of spooks and gangsters, with predictable results.

Gion Festival Music SEE: **Geisha, A**

Girl, a Guy, and a Gob, A (1941) 91m. **½ D: Richard Wallace. George Murphy, Lucille Ball, Edmond O'Brien, Henry Travers, Franklin Pangborn, George Cleveland. The girl is zany stenographer Ball; the guy is shy lawyer O'Brien; the gob is happy-go-lucky Murphy. Wacky, silly three-cornered romance; plenty of slapstick and pantomime, not surprising, since film was produced by Harold Lloyd.▼

Girl Can't Help It, The (1956) C-99m. **½ D: Frank Tashlin. Tom Ewell, Jayne Mansfield, Edmond O'Brien, Julie London. One-joke film about press agent Ewell trying to hype gangster's girlfriend (Mansfield) to stardom. Some good Tashlin sight gags; classic performances by Fats Domino ("Blue Monday"), The Platters ("You'll Never Know"), Gene Vincent and His Blue Caps ("BeBop A Lula"), Little Richard ("She's Got It," "Ready Teddy," and "The Girl Can't Help It"). CinemaScope.▼▶

Girl Crazy (1932) 74m. **½ D: William A. Seiter. Bert Wheeler, Robert Woolsey, Dorothy Lee, Eddie Quillan, Mitzi Green, Brooks Benedict, Kitty Kelly, Arline Judge, Stanley Fields, Chris Pin Martin. First screen version of the Gershwin musical comedy is a strange hybrid—neither a faithful rendition of the show nor a really good Wheeler & Woolsey vehicle. But it's not *bad*, with W&W as city slickers out West, clashing with Arizona heavy Fields. Best song, "You've Got What Gets Me," was written for the film. Perennial Marx Brothers foil Margaret Dumont has a funny uncredited cameo. Remade in 1943.▶

Girl Crazy (1943) 99m. ***½ D: Norman Taurog. Mickey Rooney, Judy Garland, Gil Stratton, Robert E. Strickland, "Rags" Ragland, June Allyson, Nancy Walker, Guy Kibbee, Tommy Dorsey and His Orchestra. Rooney sent to small Southwestern school to forget girls, but meets Garland and that's that. Great Gershwin score includes "I Got Rhythm," "Embraceable You," "But Not for Me." Busby Berkeley (the original director) staged the finale. Filmed before in 1932; remade as WHEN THE BOYS MEET THE GIRLS.▼●▶

Girl for Joe, A SEE: **Force of Arms**

Girl Friend, The (1935) 67m. **½ D: Edward Buzzell. Ann Sothern, Jack Haley, Roger Pryor, Thurston Hall, Victor Kilian, Ray Walker, Inez Courtney. Failed playwright Pryor, who's penned a musical about Napoleon, poses as a Broadway producer and convinces farmer Haley that he's going to put on the hick's tragic play about Bonaparte. Winning little musical with good songs by Gus Kahn and Arthur Johnston, all reprised as part of the finale. Title has absolutely nothing to do with the film!

Girl Friends, The SEE: **Le Amiche**

Girl From Chicago, The (1932) 69m. ** D: Oscar Micheaux. Carl Mahon, Starr Calloway, Grace Smith, Eunice Brooks, John Everett, Frank Wilson, Juano Hernandez. A T-man discovers the murder case he's working on involves a woman with whom he fell in love while sleuthing down in Mississippi. Routine all-black meller was adapted by Micheaux from his own short story.▼▶

Girl From Jones Beach, The (1949) 78m. **½ D: Peter Godfrey. Ronald Reagan, Virginia Mayo, Eddie Bracken, Dona Drake, Henry Travers, Lois Wilson, Florence Bates. Breezy comedy about an artist trying to find living embodiment of the perfectly proportioned female in his illustrations. Capable romantic-comedy performance by Reagan.▶

Girl from Manhattan, The (1948) 81m. ** D: Alfred E. Green. Dorothy Lamour, George Montgomery, Charles Laughton, Ernest Truex, Hugh Herbert, Constance Collier, William Frawley, Sara Allgood. Forgettable tale of celebrated N.Y.C. model Lamour returning to her hometown, coming to the aid of her kindhearted uncle, who has not been keeping up his mortgage payments.

Girl From Mexico, The (1939) 71m. **½ D: Leslie Goodwins. Lupe Velez, Donald Woods, Leon Errol, Linda Hayes, Donald MacBride. Advertising man Woods goes to Mexico to find a star for his radio show and bumps (literally!) into Velez. Lupe's sex appeal is unleashed in this hectic comedy which led to the *Mexican Spitfire* series. Errol is very funny as her comic cohort.▶

Girl From Missouri, The (1934) 75m. *** D: Jack Conway. Jean Harlow, Lionel Barrymore, Franchot Tone, Lewis Stone, Patsy Kelly, Alan Mowbray. Delightful fluff about good-girl Harlow trying to win a millionaire without sacrificing her integrity. Wise-cracking Kelly as her girlfriend is a treat.▼▶

Girl From Scotland Yard, The (1937) 62m. *½ D: Robert Vignola. Karen Morley, Robert Baldwin, Katherine Alexander, Eduardo Ciannelli. Story of girl trying to track down mysterious madman with destruction ray is poorly handled; not nearly as much fun as it might have been.

Girl from 10th Avenue, The (1935) 69m. *** D: Alfred E. Green. Bette Davis, Ian Hunter, Colin Clive, Alison Skipworth, John Eldredge, Phillip Reed, Katharine Alexander. Honest working girl Davis marries alcoholic, recently jilted society lawyer Hunter and gets him back on his feet. Then his ex-girlfriend decides she wants him back. Davis shines in this engrossing soaper. Based on a play filmed three times in the silent era. ▶

Girl Happy (1965) C-96m. **½ D: Boris Sagal. Elvis Presley, Shelley Fabares, Harold J. Stone, Gary Crosby, Joby Baker, Nita Talbot, Mary Ann Mobley, Chris Noel, Jackie Coogan. Formula Presley musical with tiresome plot of Elvis in Fort Lauderdale chaperoning Fabares, daughter of Chicago mobster. Teri Garr is one of the dancers. Panavision. ▼▶

Girl He Left Behind, The (1956) 103m. **½ D: David Butler. Tab Hunter, Natalie Wood, Jessie Royce Landis, Jim Backus, Henry Jones, Murray Hamilton, Alan King, James Garner, David Janssen. Hunter is new recruit in Army. Reminiscent of SEE HERE, PRIVATE HARGROVE, without any of the warmth or humor. ▶

Girl Hunters, The (1963-British) 103m. **½ D: Roy Rowland. Mickey Spillane, Lloyd Nolan, Shirley Eaton, Hy Gardner. Spillane plays his own fictional detective Mike Hammer in this rugged murder mystery. Since the disappearance of his devoted secretary, Hammer has been wallowing in alcohol; he sobers up, and goes into action, upon learning she might be alive. Panavision. ▼▶

Girl in a Million, A (1946-British) 81m. ** D: Francis Searle. Joan Greenwood, Hugh Williams, Yvonne Owen, Edward Lexy, Jane Hylton, Michael Hordern. Sometimes wacky comedy focusing on deaf mute who uses her charm to reform several cantankerous gentlemen.

Girl in Black Stockings, The (1957) 73m. ** D: Howard W. Koch. Lex Barker, Anne Bancroft, Mamie Van Doren, Ron Randell, Marie Windsor. Minor murder mystery with some nice touches and good performances; set at chic Utah resort. ▶

Girl in Danger (1934) 57m. *** D: D. Ross Lederman. Ralph Bellamy, Shirley Grey, Arthur Hohl, Charles Sabin, (J.) Carrol Naish, Ward Bond, Ed Le Saint, Vincent Sherman, Edward Keane. Thrill-seeking socialite Grey gets more than she bargained for when she gets mixed up with a jewel thief who has stolen a priceless emerald. Zippy, quite enjoyable little mystery featuring some fascinating glimpses of downtown L.A. (including the original Egyptian Theatre). Fourth and final entry in Columbia's *Inspector Trent* series.

Girl in Distress SEE: **Jeannie**

Girl in Every Port, A (1928) 62m. **½ D: Howard Hawks. Victor McLaglen, Robert Armstrong, Louise Brooks, Marcia Cassajuana, Myrna Loy, William Demarest, Sally Rand. Lusty silent comedy about two swaggering sailor pals who travel the world brawling over anything—especially women. Pretty dated, but enthusiasm still puts it over; of special interest to Hawks buffs as the earliest example of his "buddy-buddy" films. Remade as GOLDIE. ▶

Girl in Every Port, A (1952) 86m. ** D: Chester Erskine. Groucho Marx, Marie Wilson, William Bendix, Don DeFore, Gene Lockhart, George E. Stone. Nonsense of two gobs who become involved with a lame racehorse. Good cast is wasted. ▼●

Girl in His Pocket (1957-French) C-82m. **½ D: Pierre Kast. Jean Marais, Geneviève Page, Jean-Claude Brialy, Amédée, Joëlle Janin, Agnès Laurent, Régine Lovi, Pasquali. Scientist Marais invents a liquid that can simultaneously shrink live things and turn them into figurines. His fiancée (Page) becomes suspicious of his relationship with his new lab assistant (Laurent), and soon the newcomer is turned back and forth into a tiny statue. Unlikely combination of science fiction and romantic comedy is briskly paced but stalls halfway through. Released in b&w in the U.S. Aka NUDE IN HIS POCKET. ▼▶

Girl in the Kremlin, The (1957) 81m. ** D: Russell Birdwell. Lex Barker, Zsa Zsa Gabor, Jeffrey Stone, William Schallert. Espionage hokum involving Gabor in dual role as twins, one of whom is Stalin's mistress.

Girl in the News (1940-British) 78m. *** D: Carol Reed. Margaret Lockwood, Barry K. Barnes, Emlyn Williams, Roger Livesey, Margaretta Scott, Wyndham Goldie, Basil Radford, Irene Handl, Mervyn Johns, Betty Jardine, Kathleen Harrison, Felix Aylmer. Clever Hitchcockian thriller, scripted by Sidney Gilliat, involving a young nurse (Lockwood) who's found innocent of murdering a patient—and is promptly framed on another, similar charge. ▶

Girl in the Painting (1948-British) 89m. *** D: Terence Fisher. Mai Zetterling, Robert Beatty, Guy Rolfe, Herbert Lom, Patrick Holt. Intriguing drama of serviceman involved in strange case of amnesiac girl seeking her lost past in Germany. Retitled: PORTRAIT FROM LIFE.

Girl in the Red Velvet Swing, The (1955) C-109m. **½ D: Richard Fleischer. Ray Milland, Joan Collins, Farley Granger, Cornelia Otis Skinner, Glenda Farrell, Luther Adler. Glossy, fictionalized account of Evelyn Nesbit–Stanford White–Harry Thaw escapade of early 20th-century N.Y.C. Showgirl falls in love with prominent architect, which upsets mentally disturbed millionaire. CinemaScope. ◗

Girl in the Street SEE: **London Melody**

Girl in the Woods (1958) 71m. *½ D: Tom Gries. Forrest Tucker, Maggie Hayes, Barton MacLane, Diana Francis, Murvyn Vye, Paul Langton, Joyce Compton, Kim Charney. Lumbering tale of lumbermen challenging the ownership of valuable woodlands.

Girl in White, The (1952) 93m. ** D: John Sturges. June Allyson, Arthur Kennedy, Gary Merrill, Mildred Dunnock, James Arness. Humdrum biography of Emily Dunning, the first woman to work as a doctor in a N.Y.C. public hospital. ◗

Girl Missing (1933) 69m. *** D: Robert Florey. Glenda Farrell, Ben Lyon, Mary Brian, Lyle Talbot, Guy Kibbee, Harold Huber, Edward Ellis, Peggy Shannon, Louise Beavers. Gold-digging chorines Farrell and Brian get mixed up in murder and kidnapping while plying their wares in Palm Beach. Amusing comedy-mystery done in zippy Warners Bros. style. Opening scene with Brian rebuffing lecherous sugar daddy Kibbee is a riot. ◗

Girl Most Likely, The (1957) C-98m. *** D: Mitchell Leisen. Jane Powell, Cliff Robertson, Keith Andes, Tommy Noonan, Kaye Ballard, Una Merkel. Musical remake of TOM, DICK AND HARRY comes off as bright, cheerful entertainment. A girl must decide which one of the trio she'll wed; Kaye Ballard does very well in supporting role. Choreography by Gower Champion. ▼◗

Girl Named Tamiko, A (1962) C-110m. **½ D: John Sturges. Laurence Harvey, France Nuyen, Martha Hyer, Gary Merrill, Michael Wilding. Miyoshi Umeki, Lee Patrick. Overblown soaper set in Tokyo. Harvey charms Hyer into proposing marriage so he can get U.S. citizenship. Nuyen is sweet Asian he really loves. Panavision.

Girl Next Door, The (1953) C-92m. *** D: Richard Sale. Dan Dailey, June Haver, Dennis Day, Billy Gray, Cara Williams, Natalie Schafer. Minor but cheerful musical about a chorus-girl-turned-star who moves next door to a widower and his son and threatens to break up their buddy relationship. Great set design, clever use of animation (by the UPA studio), bright Harry Warren–Josef Myrow songs, and eye-popping film noir production number "Nowhere Guy" spark this likable confection. Haver's last film. ◗

Girl of the Golden West, The (1938) 120m. **½ D: Robert Z. Leonard. Jeanette MacDonald, Nelson Eddy, Walter Pidgeon, Leo Carrillo, Buddy Ebsen, Leonard Penn. Oft-produced tale of love affair of good girl MacDonald and bandit Eddy, with tuneful Gus Kahn–Sigmund Romberg score that didn't produce any hits. ◗

Girl of the Night (1960) 93m. **½ D: Joseph Cates. Anne Francis, Lloyd Nolan,

Kay Medford, John Kerr. Francis gives a vivid performance as prostitute undergoing psychoanalysis. ◗

Girl of the Rio (1932) 69m. BOMB D: Herbert Brenon. Dolores Del Rio, Norman Foster, Leo Carrillo, Ralph Ince, Lucile Gleason, Stanley Fields. Hoary stage play was passé even in 1932, which is all too evident in this preposterous film in which Del Rio tells Foster, "My heart she is thumthump-thumping when I see you," and Carrillo proclaims himself "the best caballero in all Mexico." Pidgin English reigns supreme in this appallingly awful film.

Girl O' My Dreams (1934) 65m. ** D: Ray (Raymond) McCarey. Mary Carlisle, Sterling Holloway, Eddie (Edward J.) Nugent, Arthur Lake, Creighton Chaney (Lon Chaney, Jr.). College track team members Nugent, Lake, and, believe it or not, Chaney cope with silly romantic dilemmas while preparing for the big meet. Embarrassingly lightweight Monogram college comedy is enlivened by the spectacle of future horror luminary Chaney as the callow shot-put star. Highlight: Chaney's lying-atop-apiano crooning of "Thou Art My Baby"!

Girl on the Bridge (1951) 77m. **½ D: Hugo Haas. Hugo Haas, Beverly Michaels, Robert Dane, Johnny Close, Anthony Jochim. Kindly shopkeeper saves young woman from suicide and takes her in—along with her baby. Typical Haas melodrama but better than most. ▼◗

Girl on the Front Page, The (1936) 75m. ** D: Harry Beaumont. Edmund Lowe, Gloria Stuart, Reginald Owen, Spring Byington, Gilbert Emery, David Oliver. Stuart inherits her father's big-city newspaper, which puts her at odds with headstrong, smart-alecky editor Lowe. Fun for a while, but becomes utterly preposterous; buoyed only by Stuart's natural appeal.

Girl Rush (1944) 65m. *½ D: Gordon Douglas. Alan Carney, Wally Brown, Frances Langford, Paul Hurst, Vera Vague, Robert Mitchum. Dim-witted comedy with Carney and Brown starring as vaudeville troupers stranded in San Francisco during the gold rush. Langford is always good, but the film isn't. ▼◗

Girl Rush, The (1955) C-85m. **½ D: Robert Pirosh. Rosalind Russell, Fernando Lamas, Eddie Albert, Gloria DeHaven, Marion Lorne. Russell inherits a Las Vegas casino and determines to make it go, romanced by Lamas. Minor musical numbers and forced gaiety are all too evident. VistaVision.

Girls About Town (1931) 82m. *** D: George Cukor. Kay Francis, Joel McCrea, Lilyan Tashman, Eugene Pallette, Alan Dinehart, Louise Beavers. Title tells all in this pre-Code comedy that stops just short of calling Francis and Tashman tarts. The latter (who died three years later) is likable in her best screen role, and gorgeous Travis

Banton costumes add to the film. One of the best of the early Cukor films.

Girls Can Play (1937) **59m. ** D: Lambert Hillyer. Jacqueline Wells (Julie Bishop), Charles Quigley, Rita Hayworth, John Gallaudet, George McKay, Gene Morgan, Patricia Farr, Guinn "Big Boy" Williams. By-the-numbers programmer with crooked Gallaudet forming a girls' ball team as a front for his nefarious activities. Worth seeing primarily for Hayworth, as the squad's catcher-captain.▼

Girls' Dormitory (1936) **66m. **½ D: Irving Cummings. Herbert Marshall, Ruth Chatterton, Simone Simon, Constance Collier, J. Edward Bromberg, Dixie Dunbar, Tyrone Power. Fairly standard tale of girl's infatuation for school head Marshall spotlights newcomer Simon and young leading man Power in featured role.❿

Girls! Girls! Girls! (1962) **C-106m. **½ D: Norman Taurog. Elvis Presley, Stella Stevens, Laurel Goodwin, Jeremy Slate, Benson Fong, Robert Strauss, Ginny Tiu. Elvis tries to mend his womanizing ways in order to purchase his retiring boss' boat and fishing-guide business. Along the way, he sings "Return to Sender" and some other less memorable numbers (like "Song of the Shrimp").▼❿

Girl Shy (1924) **81m. *** D: Fred Newmeyer, Sam Taylor. Harold Lloyd, Jobyna Ralston, Richard Daniels, Carlton Griffin. Enjoyable Lloyd vehicle mixes comedy and sentiment with a spectacular chase finale. Harold is a small-town boy who's petrified of women but writes book on lovemaking secrets! Fantasy scenes of his love life mark highlight.▼❿

Girls in Prison (1956) **87m. *½ D: Edward L. Cahn. Richard Denning, Joan Taylor, Adele Jergens, Helen Gilbert, Lance Fuller, Jane Darwell, Raymond Hatton, Mae Marsh. Tawdry study of prison life with usual female stereotype prisoners. Remade (in name only) for cable TV in 1994.▼

Girls in the Night (1953) **83m. ** D: Jack Arnold. Joyce Holden, Glenda Farrell, Harvey Lembeck, Patricia Hardy, Jaclynne Greene. Compact account of young people seeking to better their lives, blighted by N.Y.C. tenement existence.

Girls of Pleasure Island, The (1953) **C-95m. ** D: F. Hugh Herbert, Alvin Ganzer. Leo Genn, Don Taylor, Gene Barry, Elsa Lanchester, Audrey Dalton. Unfunny comedy involving Genn and brood of daughters combating swarm of G.I.s who establish a base on their island.

Girls of the Night (1959-French) **114m. **½ D: Maurice Cloche. Georges Marchal, Nicole Berger, Claus Holm, Kay Fischer, Gil Vidal. Sensible telling of plight of group of prostitutes and clergyman who tries to help them.

Girls of the Road (1940) **61m. ** D: Nick

Grinde. Ann Dvorak, Helen Mack, Lola Lane, Ann Doran, Bruce Bennett, Don Beddoe. Interesting B movie about daughter of a governor who goes incognito to learn first-hand about the way young women who've taken to the hobo life are being treated. Conventional, barely believable, but starts out with some real punch.

Girls on Probation (1938) **63m. *½ D: William McGann. Jane Bryan, Ronald Reagan, Anthony Averill, Sheila Bromley, Henry O'Neill, Elisabeth Risdon, Sig Rumann, Susan Hayward. Uninspired B picture about a young woman (Bryan) who can't seem to stay out of trouble with the law; Reagan is a lawyer who defends her and falls in love with her.

Girls on the Beach, The (1965) **C-80m. *½ D: William N. Witney. Martin West, Noreen Corcoran, Peter Brooks, Lana Wood, The Beach Boys, Lesley Gore, Dick Miller. Three coeds promise they'll get The Beatles to make a personal appearance and then have a mite of trouble delivering. The Beach Boys sing two tunes in this predictable comedy. Reissued as SUMMER OF '64.

Girls on the Loose (1958) **77m. ** D: Paul Henreid. Mara Corday, Lita Milan, Barbara Bostock, Mark Richman, Joyce Barker, Abby Dalton, Jon Lormer. All-female gang of thieves falls out after pulling off a $200,000 payroll robbery in this routine crime caper. Some camp value provided by man-eater Corday as the ruthless leader, who likes to have hunky delivery boys deliver more than groceries and tells her pretty partners things like "thinking takes brains, just forget you've got 'em."

Girls' School (1938) **71m. *** D: John Brahm. Anne Shirley, Nan Grey, Ralph Bellamy, Dorothy Moore, Gloria Holden, Marjorie Main, Margaret Tallichet, Peggy Moran, Kenneth Howell, Noah Beery, Jr., Cecil Cunningham, Marjorie Lord, Martha O'Driscoll. Cop-out finale is all that mars this attention-grabbing curio involving hypocrisy and class distinctions at all levels of a snooty all-girls school. Shirley is the working-class scholarship student who suffers a variety of indignities from her classmates.

Girls Town (1959) **92m. *½ D: Charles Haas. Mamie Van Doren, Mel Tormé, Paul Anka, Ray Anthony, Maggie Hayes, Cathy Crosby, Gigi Perreau, Gloria Talbott, Jim Mitchum, Elinor Donahue, Sheilah Graham, The Platters, Harold Lloyd, Jr. Wisecracking bad girl Van Doren is sent to title correctional institution, where she learns that she doesn't have all the answers. Absurd in the extreme, but has definite camp value just for the cast alone . . . plus, Anka sings "Ave Maria"! As Mamie says, it's "cool, crazy, fantabulous." Retitled INNOCENT AND THE DAMNED.▼

Girl Trouble (1942) **82m. ** D: Harold

[252]

Schuster. Don Ameche, Joan Bennett, Billie Burke, Frank Craven, Vivian Blaine. Pleasant frou-frou with Ameche and Bennett involved in business and romancing, with fine support from the adept scatter-brain Burke. ▶

Girl Who Had Everything, The (1953) 69m. **½ D: Richard Thorpe. Elizabeth Taylor, Fernando Lamas, William Powell, Gig Young, James Whitmore, Robert Burton. Good cast uplifts murky remake of A FREE SOUL. Independent-minded Taylor is attracted to gambling kingpin Lamas, the client of her trial lawyer father (Powell). Young has another of his thankless "other man" roles. ▼▶

Girl Who Stayed at Home, The (1919) 60m. **½ D: D. W. Griffith. Carol Dempster, Richard Barthelmess, Clarine Seymour, Robert Harron, Adolph Lestina. Oft-cast Griffith leading lady Dempster is ideally paired with Barthelmess in a short but bittersweet trifle about the fates of two sets of wartime lovers. Second leads Seymour and Harron were poised for imminent top billing, but sadly both died suddenly the next year. ▼▶

Girl With a Suitcase (1960-Italian) 111m. ***½ D: Valerio Zurlini. Claudia Cardinale, Jacques Perrin, Luciana Angelillo, Corrado Pani. Impressive film of devoted but shady girl Cardinale following her ex-lover to Parma, only to fall in love with his adolescent brother. Confusing at times, but extremely well acted. ▼▶

Girl With Green Eyes (1964-British) 91m. *** D: Desmond Davis. Rita Tushingham, Peter Finch, Lynn Redgrave, T. P. McKenna, Marie Kean, Julian Glover. Moving drama of young farm girl falling in love with writer Finch, highlighted by winning Tushingham performance. Redgrave scores as her roommate. Filmed in Dublin. ▼▶

Git Along Little Dogies (1937) 68m. **½ D: Joseph Kane. Gene Autry, Smiley Burnette, Maple City Four, Judith Allen, Weldon Heyburn, William Farnum, Willie Fung, Carleton Young, Will and Gladys Ahern, The Cabin Kids. Cattleman Autry locks horns with Allen, then teams up with her to dig an oil well in cattle territory and thwart villain Heyburn, who's waiting for her dead father's option on the fields to expire. Interesting story, some surprise twists, and 15—count 'em, 15—songs, including a community sing, with lyrics superimposed on-screen. ▼▶

Give a Girl a Break (1953) C-82m. **½ D: Stanley Donen. Marge and Gower Champion, Debbie Reynolds, Helen Wood, Bob Fosse, Kurt Kasznar, Richard Anderson, William Ching, Larry Keating. Innocuous musical fluff about three young women competing for the starring role in a Broadway musical. Watching Marge and Gower dance is always a treat, but the real highlight is seeing two of the greatest choreographers of all time (Champion and Fosse) dancing together. Undistinguished score by Ira Gershwin and Burton Lane. ▼●▶

Give 'Em Hell (1955-French) 90m. **½ D: John Berry. Eddie Constantine, Mai Britt, Jean Danet, Jean Carmet. If not taken seriously, amusing gangster yarn of Johnny Jordan (Constantine), with usual amount of fisticuffs and gunplay.

Give Me a Sailor (1938) 80m. **½ D: Elliott Nugent. Martha Raye, Bob Hope, Betty Grable, Jack Whiting, Clarence Kolb, J. C. Nugent. Fast-moving comedy with Raye an ugly duckling constantly upstaged by her prettier, self-centered sibling (Grable); Hope and Whiting are Navy brothers who play out a comic/romantic scenario involving the sisters. ▼▶

Give Me Your Heart (1936) 87m. **½ D: Archie Mayo. Kay Francis, George Brent, Roland Young, Patric Knowles, Henry Stephenson, Frieda Inescort. Francis has a child by a married man, weds Brent yet still pines for her baby. Well made but all-too-familiar drama, highlighted by Kay's glamorous wardrobe. ▶

Give My Regards to Broadway (1948) C-89m. ** D: Lloyd Bacon. Dan Dailey, Charles Winninger, Nancy Guild, Charles Ruggles, Fay Bainter. Blah musical of old-time vaudevillian Winninger refusing to admit that the family act should break up.

Give Out, Sisters (1942) 65m. ** D: Edward F. Cline. The Andrews Sisters, Grace McDonald, Dan Dailey, Jr., Charles Butterworth, Walter Catlett, William Frawley, The Jivin' Jacks and Jills (including Donald O'Connor, Peggy Ryan, Tommy Rall). Silly B musical about McDonald's three old biddy aunts disapproving of her dancing in a nightclub. The Andrews Sisters are well featured and finish the picture with "The Pennsylvania Polka."

Give Us Wings (1940) 62m. ** D: Charles Lamont. Billy Halop, Huntz Hall, Bernard Punsley, Gabriel Dell, Bobby Jordan, Victor Jory, Wallace Ford, Anne Gwynne, Shemp Howard, Milburn Stone, William (Billy) Benedict. The Little Tough Guys become pilots for a shady crop-dusting firm in this routine meller.

Gladiator, The (1938) 70m. **½ D: Edward Sedgwick. Joe E. Brown, Man Mountain Dean, June Travis, Dickie Moore, Lucien Littlefield. Timid boy (Brown) takes serum, becomes all-star hero at college. Simple, sincere, enjoyable. ▼▶

Glamour Boy (1941) 80m. **½ D: Ralph Murphy. Jackie Cooper, Susanna Foster, Walter Abel, Darryl Hickman, Ann Gillis, William Demarest, Jackie Searl, John Gallaudet. Cooper plays a has-been child actor who's called back to Hollywood to coach a remake of SKIPPY. Given the art-imitates-life concept, this promises more than it delivers, though it's still of interest. Foster is given ample vocal ops, from Loesser and Schertzinger's "Love Is Such an Old-Fashioned Thing" to a high F above C in Verdi's "Sempre Libera." Cecil B. DeMille cameos as himself, plugging his upcoming REAP THE WILD WIND.

Glass Alibi, The (1946) **70m.** ** D: W. Lee Wilder. Paul Kelly, Douglas Fowley, Anne Gwynne, Maris Wrixon, Jack Conrad. Satisfactory drama involving con man who thinks marrying a dying heiress is a sure bet, till he discovers she's recovering. Remade as THE BIG BLUFF.

Glass Cage, The SEE: **Glass Tomb, The**

Glass Key, The (1935) **80m.** *** D: Frank Tuttle. George Raft, Claire Dodd, Edward Arnold, Rosalind Keith, Ray Milland, Guinn Williams. Solid Dashiell Hammett story about politician Arnold getting involved in mysterious murder, Raft trying to dig out the facts. Drags during second half, but still quite good. Remade in 1942.

Glass Key, The (1942) **85m.** ***½ D: Stuart Heisler. Brian Donlevy, Veronica Lake, Alan Ladd, Joseph Calleia, William Bendix, Bonita Granville, Richard Denning. Fast-moving remake of 1935 film, with wardheeler Donlevy accused of murder, henchman Ladd bailing him out. Lake fine as mysterious love interest, Bendix effective as brutal bodyguard. Akira Kurosawa claims this was his inspiration for YOJIMBO. Dashiell Hammett novel neatly adapted by Jonathan Latimer. Dane Clark appears unbilled. ▼●▶

Glass Menagerie, The (1950) **107m.** **½ D: Irving Rapper. Jane Wyman, Kirk Douglas, Gertrude Lawrence, Arthur Kennedy. More notable for its cast and intention than results. Slow-moving version of Tennessee Williams' drama of lame girl, her faded Southern belle mother, and idealistic brother, all living in their own fragile dream worlds. Remade twice.

Glass Mountain, The (1950-British) **94m.** *** D: Henry Cass. Valentina Cortese, Michael Denison, Dulcie Gray, Sebastian Shaw. Beautifully made film of a British composer who writes an opera, inspired by majestic Italian Alps. A treat for music lovers, with many singers from La Scala appearing in opera sequence. ▶

Glass Slipper, The (1955) **C-94m.** **½ D: Charles Walters. Leslie Caron, Michael Wilding, Keenan Wynn, Estelle Winwood, Elsa Lanchester, Amanda Blake. Silky musical of Cinderella story with talky plot bogging down lilting fantasy dance and song sequences. ▼▶

Glass Tomb, The (1955-British) **59m.** ** D: Montgomery Tully. John Ireland, Honor Blackman, Geoffrey Keen, Eric Pohlmann, Sydney Tafler, Liam Redmond, Sam Kydd. Bizarre carnival backgrounds give this typical murder tale some spice. Original British title: THE GLASS CAGE. ▼▶

Glass Tower, The (1957-German) **92m.** **½ D: Harold Braun. Lilli Palmer, O. E. Hasse, Peter Van Eyck, Brigitte Horney, Hannes Messemer. Interesting study of overly jealous husband keeping beautiful wife Palmer a prisoner so she won't be tempted by other men; well acted.

Glass Wall, The (1953) **80m.** ** D: Maxwell Shane. Vittorio Gassman, Gloria Grahame, Ann Robinson, Jerry Paris, Kathleen Freeman. Drama of refugee Gassman who illegally came to N.Y.C. and, rather than accept deportation, goes on the lam. ▶

Glass Web, The (1953) **81m.** *** D: Jack Arnold. Edward G. Robinson, John Forsythe, Kathleen Hughes, Marcia Henderson, Richard Denning, Hugh Sanders. Robinson is fine as criminal research authority for TV mystery show, who's caught up in murder utilized as basis for one of the programs. Originally shot in 3-D.

Glenn Miller Story, The (1954) **C-116m.** *** D: Anthony Mann. James Stewart, June Allyson, Charles Drake, George Tobias, Harry Morgan, Frances Langford, Louis Armstrong, Gene Krupa. Stewart is convincingly cast as the popular bandleader in this extremely sentimental (and largely fictitious) account of his life. Music's the real star here, with most of Miller's hit records re-created. Oscar winner for Sound Recording. ▼●▶

Glen or Glenda (1953) **61m.** BOMB D: Edward D. Wood, Jr. Bela Lugosi, Dolores Fuller, Daniel Davis, Lyle Talbot, Timothy Farrell, "Tommy" Haynes, Charles Crafts, Conrad Brooks. Sensational but sincere "docu-fantasy" about transvestism could well be the worst movie ever made. Legendarily awful director Wood stars (under the name Daniel Davis) as Glen, who can't decide how to tell his fiancée he wants to wear her clothes. Dizzying hodgepodge of stock footage, demented dream sequences, and heartfelt plea for tolerance linked by campy Lugosi narrating from haunted house. "Beware!" Even more inept and hilarious than Wood's infamous PLAN 9 FROM OUTER SPACE. Also released as I CHANGED MY SEX, I LED 2 LIVES, and HE OR SHE. Reissued at 67m. ▼●▶

Global Affair, A (1964) **84m.** **½ D: Jack Arnold. Bob Hope, Lilo Pulver, Michele Mercier, Elga Andersen, Yvonne De Carlo, Miiko Taka, Robert Sterling, Nehemiah Persoff, John McGiver, Jacques Bergerac, Mickey Shaughnessy. Unwitty Hope vehicle has Bob in charge of a baby found at U.N., with female representative from each nation demanding the child. Also shown in computer-colored version. Metroscope. ▼▶

Glorifying the American Girl (1929) **87m.** **½ D: Millard Webb, John Harkrider. Mary Eaton, Edward Crandall; and as themselves: Eddie Cantor, Helen Morgan, Rudy Vallee, Florenz Ziegfeld, Adolph

Zukor, Otto Kahn, Texas Guinan, Mayor & Mrs. James Walker, Ring Lardner, Noah Beery, Johnny Weissmuller. Early talkie musical revue produced by Ziegfeld himself is a routine chorus-girl-trying-to-break-into-show-biz plot, overshadowed by the novelty of seeing a dazzling and sometimes bizarre array of talent appearing as themselves (best of all: Helen Morgan). Originally released with some two-color Technicolor sequences. Archivally restored to 96m. ▼▶

Glory (1956) C-100m. ** D: David Butler. Margaret O'Brien, Walter Brennan, Charlotte Greenwood, John Lupton. Bland horseracing story, with grown-up O'Brien as woman who owns champion horse. SuperScope. ▼

Glory Alley (1952) 79m. **½ D: Raoul Walsh. Ralph Meeker, Leslie Caron, Gilbert Roland, Louis Armstrong, John McIntire. Just before the championship bout, boxer Meeker quits the fight game, then goes from skid row to war hero. New Orleans backgrounds allow for some good musical interludes.

Glory at Sea SEE: **Gift Horse, The**

Glory Brigade, The (1953) 81m. ** D: Robert D. Webb. Victor Mature, Alexander Scourby, Lee Marvin, Richard Egan, Nick Dennis, Roy Roberts, Alvy Moore, Henry Kulky. Passable Korean War drama with Mature leading a platoon of American GIs assigned to escort some Greek soldiers into enemy territory. ▶

Glory Guys, The (1965) C-112m. ** D: Arnold Laven. Tom Tryon, Harve Presnell, Michael Anderson, Jr., Senta Berger, James Caan, Slim Pickens, Wayne Rogers. Lumbering cavalry Western with a love triangle thrown in. Screenplay by Sam Peckinpah. Panavision. ▼▶

"G" Men (1935) 85m. ***½ D: William Keighley. James Cagney, Ann Dvorak, Margaret Lindsay, Robert Armstrong, Barton MacLane, Lloyd Nolan, William Harrigan. Although raised by an underworld figure, Cagney joins F.B.I. when a pal is killed by gangsters, puts his first-hand knowledge to use. Exciting film, beautifully shot by Sol Polito; prologue with David Brian added for 1949 reissue. Also shown in computer-colored version. ▼▶

Go Chase Yourself (1938) 70m. ** D: Edward F. Cline. Joe Penner, Lucille Ball, Richard Lane, June Travis, Fritz Feld, Tom Kennedy, Bradley Page, Jack Carson. Penner is a milquetoast bank clerk who gets mixed up with robbers and a runaway heiress. Lucy and the supporting cast supply a few chuckles but can't quite overcome the insipid plot and radio star Penner's imbecilic screen persona. ▶

Goddess, The (1958) 105m. *** D: John Cromwell. Kim Stanley, Lloyd Bridges, Steven Hill, Betty Lou Holland, Patty Duke. Absorbing biography of an ambitious girl seeking Hollywood fame. Author Paddy Chayefsky based his story on Marilyn Monroe; the film captures tragedy of the real-life Monroe with fine acting by Stanley and Bridges, among others. Film debuts of Stanley and Duke. ▼▶▶

Goddess of Love, The (1958-Italian) C-68m. *½ D: Fernando Cerchio, Viktor Tourjansky. Belinda Lee, Jacques Sernas, Massimo Girotti, Maria Frau. Drivel concerning country girl who becomes prostitute when her lover is killed. Set in ancient times. Released in the U.S. in 1960. Totalscope.

God Is My Co-Pilot (1945) 90m. **½ D: Robert Florey. Dennis Morgan, Raymond Massey, Andrea King, Alan Hale, Dane Clark, John Ridgely, Stanley Ridges, Donald Woods. Well-intentioned drama of WW2 pilots bogs down in clichés, still has many good scenes. ▼▶

God Is My Partner (1957) 80m. ** D: William F. Claxton. Walter Brennan, John Hoyt, Marion Ross, Jesse White, Nancy Kulp. Sincere, hokey film of old-timer who feels he owes a spiritual obligation which he can redeem by giving away his money. Regalscope.

Godless Girl, The (1929) 128m. **½ D: Cecil B. DeMille. Lina Basquette, Marie Prevost, George Duryea (Tom Keene), Noah Beery, Eddie Quillan, Mary Jane Irving, Kate Price, Julia Faye. Proselytizing atheist high school student Basquette, her new recruit (Quillan), and her ideological opposite (Duryea) are all sent to a reformatory after a tragic event. DeMille's final silent film is a provocative look at warring ideologies, then becomes a melodramatic exposé of juvenile prisons. Well made but endless, with an especially silly resolution. But it's never dull! Beery is perfectly cast as a sadistic guard. Originally released with a talking sequence tacked on at the last minute. ▶

God's Country (1946) C-62m. ** D: Robert E. Tansey. Buster Keaton, Robert Lowery, Helen Gilbert, William Farnum. Chief virtue of this flabby Western is Keaton trying to recreate some of his better pantomime skits. ▼

God's Country and the Woman (1936) C-80m. ** D: William Keighley. George Brent, Beverly Roberts, Barton MacLane, Robert Barrat, Alan Hale, Joseph King. Routine tale of Brent and Roberts running rival lumber companies; color is only asset.

God's Gift to Women (1931) 72m. *** D: Michael Curtiz. Frank Fay, Laura La Plante, Joan Blondell, Charles Winninger, Alan Mowbray, Yola d'Avril, Louise Brooks. Incorrigible philanderer has trouble adjusting his swinging lifestyle after being told he has a bad heart and must give up wine and women, or, as the doctor puts it, "Live like a clam, or die!" Wild pre-Code sex farce with lots of racy humor. Legendary silent screen siren Brooks has a small part as one of Fay's lovers. ❚

God's Little Acre (1958) 117m. *** D: Anthony Mann. Robert Ryan, Tina Louise, Aldo Ray, Buddy Hackett, Jack Lord, Fay Spain, Michael Landon, Vic Morrow, Rex Ingram. Picaresque Americana from Erskine Caldwell's best-selling book about a lusty, eccentric Georgia family. Amusing, passionate, and highly charged; quite sexy for its time. Some censored moments were restored years after its original release. Wonderful score by Elmer Bernstein. ▼❚

Godzilla (1954-Japanese) 96m. *** D: Ishirô Honda. Takashi Shimura, Momoko Kôchi, Akira Takarada, Akihiko Hirata. Granddaddy of Japanese monster movies, with the radiation-breathing title behemoth terrorizing Tokyo. Much more complex and nuanced than the Americanized GODZILLA KING OF THE MONSTERS! (see below), the so-called Raymond Burr version, which used only an hour of the original's footage. Released uncut in the U.S. in 2004. Remade in 1985, 1998, and 2014. Original title: GOJIRA. ❚

Godzilla King of the Monsters! (1956-Japanese-U.S.) 80m. **½ D: Terry Morse, Ishirô Honda. Raymond Burr, Takashi Shimura, Momoko Kôchi, Akira Takarada, Akihiko Hirata. U.S. version of the fabled Japanese monster movie is reedited and rearranged, with Burr inserted into the action as a reporter (named Steve Martin!) reacting to Godzilla's rampage. Fun to watch, but pales in comparison to the Japanese original. ▼❚

Godzilla Raids Again SEE: **Gigantis, the Fire Monster**

Godzilla vs the Thing (1964-Japanese) C-90m. **½ D: Ishirô Honda. Okira Takarada, Yuriko Hoshi, Hiroshi Koizumi, Yu Fujiki. Vivid special effects highlight battle between reptile Godzilla and Mothra, giant moth. Aka GODZILLA VS. MOTHRA. Tohoscope. ▼❚

Go for Broke! (1951) 92m. *** D: Robert Pirosh. Van Johnson, Lane Nakano, Henry Nakamura, George Miki, Henry Oyasato, Warner Anderson. Fine WW2 drama with Johnson, a bigoted Texan, assigned to train and lead the 442nd Regimental Combat Team, composed mostly of Japanese-Americans (Nisei). Crammed with ironic touches, and uncompromising in its point of view (reflecting the Nisei's collective heroic war record). Pirosh also scripted. ▼❚

Gog (1954) C-85m. ** D: Herbert L. Strock. Richard Egan, Constance Dowling, Herbert Marshall, John Wengraf. Is a series of deaths at scientific installation the result of equipment malfunction or sabotage? Title refers to one of a pair of nonhumanoid robots. OK sci-fi, originally in 3-D. ❚

Going Highbrow (1935) 67m. **½ D: Robert Florey. Guy Kibbee, ZaSu Pitts, Edward Everett Horton, Ross Alexander, June Martel, Gordon Westcott, Judy Canova, Arthur Treacher. Ingratiating lunacy with Kibbee and Pitts as nouveaux riches trying to crash New York society with Horton's help by throwing a lavish coming-out party for their debutante daughter . . . except they don't have a daughter, so they hire a waitress to pose as her. Funny showcase for trio of wonderful character actors.

Going Hollywood (1933) 80m. *** D: Raoul Walsh. Marion Davies, Bing Crosby, Fifi D'Orsay, Stuart Erwin, Ned Sparks, Patsy Kelly. Enjoyable fluff with Davies following crooner Crosby to Hollywood determined to win him away from tempestuous screen star D'Orsay. Kelly all but steals film from stars. Songs include "Temptation," "We'll Make Hay While the Sun Shines," and the title tune. ▼❍❚

Going My Way (1944) 126m. **** D: Leo McCarey. Bing Crosby, Barry Fitzgerald, Risë Stevens, Frank McHugh, James Brown, Gene Lockhart, Jean Heather, Porter Hall, Fortunio Bonanova, Stanley Clements, Carl (Alfalfa) Switzer. Sentimental story of down-to-earth priest Father O'Malley (Crosby) winning over aging superior (Fitzgerald) and sidewalk gang of kids is hard to resist—thanks to the skills of writer-director McCarey, who won two Oscars. Academy Awards also went to Crosby, Fitzgerald, Best Picture, and Best Song: "Swinging on a Star." Sequel: THE BELLS OF ST. MARY'S. ▼❍

Going Places (1938) 84m. *** D: Ray Enright. Dick Powell, Anita Louise, Allen Jenkins, Ronald Reagan, Walter Catlett, Harold Huber, Louis Armstrong, Maxine Sullivan, Eddie Anderson, The Dandridge Sisters. Sprightly nonsense comedy from Warner Bros. about a sporting goods salesman who tries to pass himself off as a member of the horsey set—and a jockey. Many ingenious, funny scenes plus musical numbers from Armstrong (who introduces "Jeepers Creepers"), Sullivan, et al.

Going Steady (1958) 79m. *½ D: Fred F. Sears. Molly Bee, Bill Goodwin, Alan Reed, Jr., Irene Hervey. Uninspired happenings involving secretly married teenagers and repercussions when in-laws discover fact. ▼

Going Wild (1930) 66m. ** D: William A. Seiter. Joe E. Brown, Lawrence Gray, Laura Lee, Walter Pidgeon, Frank McHugh, Ona Munson, May Boley, Johnny Arthur. Brown mugs shamelessly as a down-and-out reporter mistaken for a famous aviator at a beach resort, resulting in typical romantic mix-ups and a slapstick airplane race. Stagy, warmed-over rehash of elements from Brown's superior TOP SPEED. ▼

Goin' to Town (1935) 74m. *** D: Alexander Hall. Mae West, Paul Cavanagh,

Ivan Lebedeff, Marjorie Gateson, Tito Coral, Gilbert Emery. Good West vehicle of dance-hall girl trying to crash society, highlight: Mae doing "Samson and Delilah" scenes. West wrote the screenplay. ▼▶

Go Into Your Dance (1935) 89m. **½ D: Archie L. Mayo. Al Jolson, Ruby Keeler, Glenda Farrell, Helen Morgan, Patsy Kelly, Benny Rubin, Phil Regan, Barton MacLane. Flimsy backstage plot allows real-life husband and wife Jolson and Keeler (in their only film together) to sing and dance through seven listenable Harry Warren–Al Dubin tunes, including "About a Quarter to Nine" and "A Latin From Manhattan."●▶

Gojira SEE: Godzilla

Go, Johnny, Go! (1958) 75m. ** D: Paul Landres. Jimmy Clanton, Alan Freed, Sandy Stewart, Chuck Berry, Jo-Ann Campbell, The Cadillacs, Ritchie Valens, Eddie Cochran, Harvey (Fuqua), The Flamingos, Jackie Wilson. Orphan Clanton, booted out of church choir for playing rock 'n' roll, is transformed by Freed into "Johnny Melody," teen idol. Not very good, but an artifact of its era. Berry, who acts as well as sings, performs "Memphis, Tennessee," "Little Queenie," and "Johnny Be Good," Cochran performs "Teenage Heaven," and Wilson does "You'd Better Know It."▼●

Goldbergs, The (1950) 83m. **½ D: Walter Hart. Gertrude Berg, Philip Loeb, Eli Mintz, Betty Walker, David Opatoshu, Barbara Rush. Warm, human story of famous radio-TV Bronx family and their everyday problems. Retitled: MOLLY.

Gold Diggers in Paris (1938) 97m. **½ D: Ray Enright. Rudy Vallee, Rosemary Lane, Hugh Herbert, Allen Jenkins, Gloria Dickson, Mabel Todd, Freddie "Schnickelfritz" Fisher. Lively musical has Vallee and his nightclub troupe going to Paris. Storyline is negligible, but the songs (like "Latin Quarter") and Busby Berkeley production numbers are fun to watch. Carole Landis is one of the chorus girls.▶

Gold Diggers of 1933 (1933) 96m. ***½ D: Mervyn LeRoy. Joan Blondell, Ruby Keeler, Aline MacMahon, Dick Powell, Guy Kibbee, Warren William, Ned Sparks, Ginger Rogers, Sterling Holloway. Another spectacular Busby Berkeley dance outing with familiar let's-produce-a-Broadway-show plot. Highlights: Blondell's "Forgotten Man," Rogers' "We're In the Money" (partly singing in pig Latin!), chorus girls' "Shadow Waltz." ▼●▶

Gold Diggers of 1935 (1935) 95m. *** D: Busby Berkeley. Dick Powell, Adolphe Menjou, Gloria Stuart, Alice Brady, Glenda Farrell, Frank McHugh, Winifred Shaw. Big-scale Berkeley musical with stereotypes providing plot line and laughs between fantastic precision production numbers, including "The Words Are in My Heart," and classic, Oscar-winning "Lullaby of Broadway," sung by Wini Shaw.▼●▶

Gold Diggers of 1937 (1936) 100m. *½ D: Lloyd Bacon. Dick Powell, Joan Blondell, Glenda Farrell, Victor Moore, Lee Dixon, Osgood Perkins. Insufferable Warner Bros. musical about insurance salesmen getting involved in show business. The usual players try their hardest but this is tough sledding. Only bright spot is bizarre Busby Berkeley number, "All's Fair in Love and War."▶

Gold Dust Gertie (1931) 66m. **½ D: Lloyd Bacon. Ole Olsen, Chic Johnson, Winnie Lightner, Dorothy Christy, Claude Gillingwater, Arthur Hoyt, Charley Grapewin. Olsen & Johnson are bathing-suit salesmen trying to elude their mutual ex-wife. Lightner is energetic as always in this absurd knockabout comedy with plenty of sexual innuendo.

Golden Age of Comedy, The (1957) 78m. **** D: Compiled by Robert Youngson. Laurel and Hardy, Carole Lombard, Ben Turpin, Will Rogers, Harry Langdon. Peerless grouping of some of silent comedy's greatest moments, including Rogers' classic spoofs of silent stars, and ending with Laurel and Hardy's legendary pie fight from BATTLE OF THE CENTURY.▼●▶

Golden Arrow, The (1936) 68m. **½ D: Alfred E. Green. Bette Davis, George Brent, Eugene Pallette, Dick Foran, Carol Hughes, Catherine Doucet. Pleasant but featherweight comedy of "heiress" Davis and down-to-earth reporter Brent establishing marriage of convenience.▶

Golden Arrow (1952-British) SEE: **Gay Adventure, The**

Golden Blade, The (1953) C-81m. **½ D: Nathan Juran. Rock Hudson, Piper Laurie, Gene Evans, George Macready, Kathleen Hughes, Steven Geray. Hudson, with the help of the magical Sword of Damascus, helps Baghdad princess Laurie battle her caliph father's grand vizier (Macready) and his strong-arm son (Evans). Typical but entertaining Arabian Nights adventure.▶

Golden Boy (1939) 99m. *** D: Rouben Mamoulian. Barbara Stanwyck, Adolphe Menjou, William Holden, Lee J. Cobb, Joseph Calleia, Sam Levene, Don Beddoe. Italian immigrant's son is torn between his love of the violin—instilled by his insistent father—and his passion for prizefighting. Clifford Odets' story may seem like one giant cliché by now, but it's played with gusto (perhaps too much gusto by Cobb as the Henry Armetta–ish father) and benefits from Stanwyck's heartfelt performance. This role propelled an unknown Holden to stardom. ▼●▶

Golden Coach, The (1952-Italian) C-101m. ***½ D: Jean Renoir. Anna Magnani, Odoardo Spadaro, Nada Fiorelli, Dante Rino, Duncan Lamont, Jean Debucourt. Delightful film about an acting troupe touring South America in the 18th

[257]

century and the amorous adventures of its leading lady. Theatrical and stylized, this is one of the great films about acting— and a stunning achievement in the use of color. Ironically, it was a flop when first released, then critically rediscovered. Photographed by Claude Renoir; music by Vivaldi. ▼◐

Golden Dawn (1930) **C-81m.** BOMB D: Ray Enright. Noah Beery, Dick Henderson, Walter Woolf (King), Vivienne Segal, Alice Gentle, Lupino Lane. Oh, *no!* A white woman abducted by natives in WW1 British East Africa is about to be married to a wooden image of the god Mulungu! Will stalwart captain King rescue her from this dreadful fate (and film)? Staggering racism overshadows amusing hokum of Broadway's 1927 underdressed and overcooked operetta. "Camp" seems to have been coined for such compositions as "My Bwana" and "The Whip Song." Lane does his usual comedy acrobatic turn while Rita Hayworth's father, Eduardo Cansino, plays the dancing instructor. ◐

Golden Earrings (1947) **95m. **½ D: Mitchell Leisen. Ray Milland, Marlene Dietrich, Murvyn Vye, Dennis Hoey, Quentin Reynolds. Incredible yet enjoyable escapism set in WW2 Europe has Milland joining gypsy Dietrich for espionage work; Dietrich most convincing. Gypsy Vye sings the title song. ▼◐

Golden Eye, The (1948) **69m. *½ D: William Beaudine. Roland Winters, Victor Sen Yung, Tim Ryan, Wanda McKay, Bruce Kellogg, Evelyn Brent. Charlie Chan investigates the mystery of a supposedly barren mine that miraculously begins to yield gold in this poor entry. Aka THE MYSTERY OF THE GOLDEN EYE and CHARLIE CHAN AND THE GOLDEN EYE. ◐

Golden Fleecing, The (1940) **68m. **½ D: Leslie Fenton. Lew Ayres, Rita Johnson, Lloyd Nolan, Virginia Grey, Leon Errol, Nat Pendleton, Richard Carle, Ralph Byrd, Marc Lawrence, Thurston Hall, William Demarest. Sprightly little screwball yarn about insurance agent Ayres getting a big raise for selling a $50,000 policy to Nolan, only to learn he's a gangster with a price on his head. Complications mount as Ayres struggles to keep Nolan alive. Written by S. J. Perelman, Laura Perelman, and Marion Parsonnet. ◐

Golden Girl (1951) **C-108m. **½D: Lloyd Bacon. Mitzi Gaynor, Dale Robertson, Dennis Day, Una Merkel. Undistinguished musical set in California during Civil War, with Gaynor portraying entertainer Lotta Crabtree who's intrigued by Rebel officer Robertson.

Golden Gloves (1940) **69m. ** D: Edward Dmytryk. Richard Denning, Jeanne Cagney, Robert Paige, J. Carrol Naish, William Frawley, Edward Brophy, Robert Ryan, George

Ernst, Sidney Miller, Frank Coghlan, Jr. Featherweight boxing exposé about a sportswriter organizing an honest amateur tournament to compete against a crooked promoter, who counters by entering a ringer in the competition. Formulaic programmer. Ryan, an undefeated collegiate boxer in real life, is quite convincing as a pug in one of his first roles.

Golden Gloves Story, The (1950) **76m. *½ D: Felix E. Feist. James Dunn, Dewey Martin, Kay Westfall, Kevin O'Morrison. OK fare of two boxers and effects of pending championship bout on their lives.

Golden Hawk, The (1952) **C-83m. ** D: Sidney Salkow. Rhonda Fleming, Sterling Hayden, John Sutton, Raymond Hatton. Frank Yerby's novel of Spanish-English fight against France in 17th century, set in Caribbean seas. ◐

Golden Helmet SEE: **Casque d'Or**

Golden Hoofs (1941) **68m. **½ D: Lynn Shores. Jane Withers, Charles "Buddy" Rogers, Kay Aldridge, George Irving, Buddy Pepper, Cliff Clark, Philip Hurlic, Sheila Ryan. Jane's grandfather is forced to sell his horse farm, but the plucky girl determines to persuade the new buyer (Rogers) that he should stick with her beloved trotters instead of breeding racehorses. Formula-bound B movie is politically incorrect but still enjoyable. ◐

Golden Horde, The (1951) **C-77m. ** D: George Sherman. Ann Blyth, David Farrar, George Macready, Henry Brandon, Richard Egan. Typical Arabian adventure set in 13th century, with Blyth using her brains to outwit invaders of her people's city.

Golden Idol, The (1954) **71m. *½ D: Ford Beebe. Johnny Sheffield, Anne Kimbell, Paul Guilfoyle, Leonard Mudie, Smoki Whitfield, Rick Vallin. Bomba the Jungle Boy (with the help of some "talking" drums) recovers a priceless Watusi statue stolen by evil Arabs.

Golden Madonna, The (1949-British) **88m. **½ D: Ladislas Vajda. Phyllis Calvert, Michael Rennie, Tullio Carminati. Lively romantic yarn of Yankee lass inheriting an Italian villa and, aided by Rennie, seeking to retrieve a holy painting.

Golden Marie SEE: **Casque d'Or**

Golden Mask, The (1952-British) **C-88m. **½ D: Jack Lee. Van Heflin, Wanda Hendrix, Eric Portman, Charles Goldner. Intelligent adventure yarn of people seeking fabulous treasure mask in Egyptian desert. Original British title: SOUTH OF ALGIERS.

Golden Mistress, The (1954) **C-82m. ** D: Joel Judge (Abner Biberman). John Agar, Rosemarie Bowe, Abner Biberman, Andre Narcisse. Agar comes to Bowe's rescue in hunting out alleged voodoo killers of her father. Filmed in Haiti. ▼

Golden Salamander (1950-British) **96m. *** D: Ronald Neame. Trevor Howard,

Anouk Aimée, Walter Rilla, Herbert Lom, Wilfrid Hyde-White. Courting a Tunisian girl, Howard becomes involved in gun smuggling; taut actioner.▼❶

Golden Stallion, The (1949) **C-67m.** ★★★ D: William Witney. Roy Rogers, Dale Evans, Estelita Rodriguez, Pat Brady, Douglas Evans, Frank Fenton, Foy Willing and the Riders of the Purple Sage. Smugglers use wild horses to sneak their contraband diamonds across the border, then Trigger gets blamed for a murder. Roy takes responsibility, goes to jail, and the smugglers buy Trigger at auction, training the horse to smuggle diamonds. One of Rogers' best "serious" Westerns directed by Witney.▼❶

Goldfinger (1964-British) **C-111m.** ★★★½ D: Guy Hamilton. Sean Connery, Gert Frobe, Honor Blackman, Shirley Eaton, Bernard Lee, Lois Maxwell, Harold Sakata, Tania Mallet. Entertaining, exciting James Bond adventure, third in the series. Full of ingenious gadgets and nefarious villains, with hair-raising climax inside Fort Knox. Frobe (Goldfinger) and Sakata (Oddjob) are villains in the classic tradition.▼❶⬤

Gold for the Caesars (1964-French-Italian) **C-86m.** ★½ D: Andre de Toth. Jeffrey Hunter, Mylene Demongeot, Ron Randell, Massimo Girotti, Giulio Bosetti, Ettore Manni. Still another Roman slave epic starring an American actor who'd look more at home in David and Ricky Nelson's fraternity. Nothing special. Original French running time: 95m. CinemaScope.❶

Gold Is Where You Find It (1938) **C-90m.** ★★½ D: Michael Curtiz. George Brent, Olivia de Havilland, Claude Rains, Margaret Lindsay, John Litel, Barton MacLane. And gold-rush miners find it on California farmland, starting bitter feud in brisk film, perked by good cast.❶

Gold Mine in the Sky (1938) **60m.** ★★★ D: Joseph Kane. Gene Autry, Smiley Burnette, Carol Hughes, LeRoy Mason, Craig Reynolds, J. L. Frank's Golden West Cowboys. Classic Autry vehicle has Gene teaching stuck-up city girl Hughes the ways of the West while battling Chicago gangsters, led by Mason. Irresistible combination of cowboys, gangsters, music, and action. Gene sings "There's a Gold Mine in the Sky."❶

Gold of Naples (1954-Italian) **107m.** ★★★ D: Vittorio De Sica. Sophia Loren, Vittorio De Sica, Totò, Silvana Mangano, Paolo Stoppa. Four vignettes—poignant, perceptive, hilarious in turn: Loren as philandering wife of pizza baker; De Sica as avid cardplayer upstaged by 8-year-old; Totò as Milquetoast family man; Mangano as prostitute involved in unusual marriage.▼❶

Gold of the Seven Saints (1961) **88m.** ★★½ D: Gordon Douglas. Clint Walker, Roger Moore, Leticia Roman, Robert Middleton, Chill Wills, Gene Evans, Roberto Contreras. Fur-trappers Walker and Moore (the lat-

ter sporting blond hair and an Irish brogue) find 125 lbs. of gold nuggets and are pursued across the desert by several parties who want to pry it loose from them. Enjoyable Western knockoff of THE TREASURE OF THE SIERRA MADRE, featuring some striking Utah scenery and a tangy script co-written by Leigh Brackett. WarnerScope.❶

Gold Raiders (1951) **56m.** ★½ D: Edward Bernds. George O'Brien, The Three Stooges, Sheila Ryan, Clem Bevans, Lyle Talbot. Stooges add the only life to this flabby Western, with their usual shenanigans foiling the crooks and saving the day.▼❶

Gold Rush, The (1925) **82m.** ★★★★ D: Charlie Chaplin. Charlie Chaplin, Georgia Hale, Mack Swain, Tom Murray. Immortal Chaplin classic, pitting Little Tramp against Yukon, affections of dance-hall girl, whims of a burly prospector. Dance of the rolls, eating leather shoe, cabin tottering over cliff—all highlights of wonderful, timeless comedy. Chaplin reedited film in 1942; that version, with his narration and music, runs 72m.▼❶⬤

Gold Rush Maisie (1940) **82m.** ★★ D: Edwin L. Marin. Ann Sothern, Lee Bowman, Virginia Weidler, John F. Hamilton, Mary Nash, Slim Summerville, Scotty Beckett. Innocuous *Maisie* entry involving a poor family's attempt to find gold.❶

Goldstein (1965) **85m.** ★★½ D: Benjamin Manaster, Philip Kaufman. Lou Gilbert, Ellen Madison, Thomas Erhart, Benito Carruthers, Severn Darden, Nelson Algren. The prophet Elijah (Gilbert) emerges from Lake Michigan, is pursued by sculptor Erhart. Quirky, inventive film made on a shoestring in Chicago. Based on a story by Martin Buber. Original running time: 115m.❶

Gold Strike Fever SEE: **Lucky Texan, The**

Goldtown Ghost Riders (1953) **57m.** ★★★ D: George Archainbaud. Gene Autry, Smiley Burnette, Kirk Riley, Carleton Young, Neyle Morrow, John Doucette, Denver Pyle, Blackie Whiteford. Rancher-turned-circuit-court-judge Autry tries a murderer who claims the man he is accused of killing is still alive. Intricate, somber story with plenty of action and thrills; one of Gene's best latter-day films.❶

Goldwyn Follies, The (1938) **C-120m.** ★½ D: George Marshall. Adolphe Menjou, Andrea Leeds, Kenny Baker, The Ritz Brothers, Zorina, Helen Jepson, Bobby Clark, Edgar Bergen & Charlie McCarthy. Dreadful hodgepodge as producer Menjou hires Leeds as "Miss Humanity," to judge his movies from average person's point of view. She probably would have skipped this one. Ritz Bros. come off best, while Baker sings "Love Walked In" about 30 times. George Balanchine's ballet is a matter of taste. Look for Alan Ladd as an auditioning singer.▼❶⬤

Golem, The (1920-German) **75m.** ★★★½

D: Paul Wegener, Carl Boese. Paul Wegener, Albert Steinruck, Ernst Deutsch, Lyda Salmonova. Chilling, visually dazzling story of the supernatural, based on a famous Jewish folktale of the 16th century. Rudolph of Hapsburg has exiled the Jews, blaming them for a plague; a rabbi conjures up a golem (a clay monster, played by Wegener) in order to convince the king to repeal the edict. This classic of German Expressionist cinema is also a forerunner of FRANKENSTEIN, from the way the golem is brought to life to his attraction to a child. The sets were designed by famed architect Hans Poelzig. The story has been filmed many times; Wegener also codirected versions in 1914 and 1917, and Julien Duvivier filmed it in 1938, with Harry Baur. Aka THE GOLEM: HOW HE CAME INTO THE WORLD. ▼▶

Goliath Against the Giants (1961-Italian) **C-90m.** *½ D: Guido Malatesta. Brad Harris, Gloria Milland, Fernando Rey, Barbara Carrol. Juvenile cartoon characterizations in this sword-and-sandal, with Harris overcoming sea creatures, Amazons, and his people's enemies. SuperTotalscope. ▶

Goliath and the Barbarians (1960-Italian) **C-86m.** ** D: Carlo Campogalliani. Steve Reeves, Bruce Cabot, Giulia Rubini, Chelo Alonso, Arturo Dominici, Gino Scotti. Muscleman Reeves comes to the rescue of Italy by holding off rampaging hordes pressing down from the Alps. Totalscope. ▶

Goliath and the Dragon (1960-Italian) **C-87m.** BOMB D: Vittorio Cottafavi. Mark Forest, Broderick Crawford, Gaby Andre, Leonora Ruffo. Fantasy costumer with embarrassing performances by all; poor special effects, with Forest challenging villainous Crawford. Totalscope. ▼▶

Goliath and the Vampires (1961-Italian) **C-91m.** *½ D: Giacomo Gentilomo. Gordon Scott, Jacques Sernas, Gianna Maria Canale. Cloak-and-sandal nonsense; spotty special effects add only color to film. U.S. release 1964. Totalscope. ▼▶

Go, Man, Go! (1954) **82m.** **½ D: James Wong Howe. Dane Clark, Pat Breslin, Sidney Poitier, Edmon Ryan. Imaginative telling of the formation of Harlem Globetrotters and their rise as famed basketball team. A rare directorial effort by celebrated cinematographer Howe.

Go Naked in the World (1961) **C-103m.** ** D: Ranald MacDougall. Gina Lollobrigida, Anthony Franciosa, Ernest Borgnine, Luana Patten. Turgid melodrama badly cast. Easy-loving Lollobrigida hooks Franciosa, much to his father's (Borgnine's) dismay. CinemaScope.

Gone Are the Days (1963) **97m.** *** D: Nicholas Webster. Ossie Davis, Ruby Dee, Sorrell Booke, Godfrey Cambridge, Alan Alda, Beah Richards. Davis' satiric fable *Purlie Victorious* survives cheap adaptation,

thanks to buoyant performances and basic story: self-appointed preacher schemes to undo a despotic plantation owner, as a symbolic freeing of his people from ways of the Old South. Alda's film debut. ▼▶

Gone to Earth SEE: **Wild Heart, The**

Gone With the Wind (1939) **C-222m.** **** D: Victor Fleming. Clark Gable, Vivien Leigh, Leslie Howard, Olivia de Havilland, Thomas Mitchell, Barbara O'Neil, Victor Jory, Laura Hope Crews, Hattie McDaniel, Ona Munson, Harry Davenport, Ann Rutherford, Evelyn Keyes, Carroll Nye, Paul Hurst, Isabel Jewell, Cliff Edwards, Ward Bond, Butterfly McQueen, Rand Brooks, Eddie Anderson, Oscar Polk, Jane Darwell, William Bakewell, L. Kemble-Cooper, Eric Linden, George Reeves. If not the greatest movie ever made, certainly one of the greatest examples of storytelling on film, maintaining interest for nearly four hours. Margaret Mitchell's story is, in effect, a Civil War soap opera, focusing on vixenish Southern belle Scarlett O'Hara, brilliantly played by Leigh; she won Oscar, as did the picture, McDaniel, director Fleming, screenwriter Sidney Howard (posthumously), many others. Memorable music by Max Steiner in this one-of-a-kind film meticulously produced by David O. Selznick. Runs 233m. with overture, intermission/entr'acte, exit music. Followed over five decades later by a TV miniseries, *Scarlett.* ▼▶●

Good Bad Girl, The (1931) **70m.** **½ D: Roy William Neill. Mae Clarke, James Hall, Marie Prevost, Robert Ellis, Nance O'Neill, James Donlan, Paul Porcasi, Paul Fix. Clarke is a gangster's moll who dumps him to marry a rich and respectable man (Hall); then the hood busts out of the big house, seeking revenge. More of a "woman's picture" (replete with happy complications) than a hard-boiled gangster film, but entertaining nonetheless.

Goodbye Again (1933) **66m.** **½ D: Michael Curtiz. Warren William, Joan Blondell, Genevieve Tobin, Hugh Herbert, Wallace Ford, Helen Chandler, Hobart Cavanaugh, Ruth Donnelly. Frantic antics about philandering romance novelist William being pursued by a married ex-flame who thinks she's the inspiration for his latest book. Blondell is a joy as William's sassy secretary, secretly in love with him. Deftly played farce, remade in 1941 as HONEYMOON FOR THREE.

Goodbye Again (1961) **120m.** *** D: Anatole Litvak. Ingrid Bergman, Tony Perkins, Yves Montand, Jessie Royce Landis, Diahann Carroll. Françoise Sagan's chic soaper becomes teary Bergman vehicle of middle-aged woman having affair with Perkins, still craving playboy Montand. Set in Paris. ▼

Goodbye Charlie (1964) **C-117m.** *½ D: Vincente Minnelli. Tony Curtis, Deb-

[260]

bie Reynolds, Pat Boone, Walter Matthau, Martin Gabel, Ellen McRae (Burstyn). Tasteless, flat version of George Axelrod's play; crude gangster dies and comes back to earth as Reynolds. Even Matthau struggles for laughs. James Brolin is an extra in big party scene. CinemaScope.▼◗

Goodbye, Mr. Chips (1939-U.S.-British) 114m. ***½ D: Sam Wood. Robert Donat, Greer Garson, Paul von Hernreid (Henreid), Terry Kilburn, John Mills. Donat won well-deserved Oscar for memorable portrayal of shy schoolmaster who devotes his life to "his boys," only coming out of his shell when he meets Garson. Extreme length works against film's honest sentiment, but Donat makes it all worthwhile. Garson's film debut made her a star overnight. Based on James Hilton's novel; scripted by R. C. Sherriff, Claudine West, and Eric Maschwitz. Remade as a musical in 1969. Also shown in computer-colored version. ▼◗

Goodbye, My Fancy (1951) 107m. *** D: Vincent Sherman. Joan Crawford, Robert Young, Frank Lovejoy, Eve Arden. Congresswoman Crawford returns to her old college, more to see former boyfriend Young than to receive honorary degree. Lovejoy is callous newsman. Film debut of Janice Rule.◗

Good-bye, My Lady (1956) 95m. **½ D: William A. Wellman. Walter Brennan, Phil Harris, Brandon de Wilde, Sidney Poitier, William Hopper, Louise Beavers. A little boy (de Wilde), growing up in rural Mississippi with his elderly uncle (Brennan), finds and trains a small dog, which brings joy into his life. Easygoing, poignant coming-of-age tale, based on a James H. Street novel. Reissued as THE BOY AND THE LAUGHING DOG. ▼◗

Good Companions, The (1933-British) 113m. *** D: Victor Saville. Jessie Matthews, Edmund Gwenn, John Gielgud, George Zucco, Dennis Hoey, Mary Glynne, Finlay Currie, Jack Hawkins, Max Miller. J. B. Priestley's novel about a group of strangers who form traveling theatrical company turns into a delightful film. Matthews is given full rein to display her considerable musical and comedic charms; Gielgud is equally humorous and surprising. He even sings! Remade in 1956.▼◗

Good Companions, The (1956-British) C-104m. *** D: J. Lee Thompson. Eric Portman, Celia Johnson, Hugh Griffith, Janette Scott, John Fraser, Joyce Grenfell, Bobby Howes, Rachel Roberts, Thora Hird, Mona Washbourne, Alec McCowen, John Le Mesurier, Anthony Newley, Shirley Anne Field. Fabulous cast adds luster to this entertaining chronicle of a group of individuals who combine their resources to save a failing "concert party" (musical troupe). Based on a novel by J. B. Priestley; first filmed in 1933. CinemaScope.

Good Dame (1934) 74m. *½ D: Marion Gering. Fredric March, Sylvia Sidney, Jack LaRue, Helene Chadwick, Noel Francis, Russell Hopton. March and Sidney deserve better than this: tired story of carnival huckster redeemed by the love of a good woman.

Good Day for a Hanging (1958) C-85m. **½ D: Nathan Juran. Fred MacMurray, Maggie Hayes, Robert Vaughn, Joan Blackman, James Drury, Denver Pyle. Straightforward account of MacMurray taking over for slain sheriff and bringing in killer, only to find townspeople don't care if murderer is sentenced. ▼◗

Good Die Young, The (1954-British) 100m. ** D: Lewis Gilbert. Laurence Harvey, Gloria Grahame, Richard Basehart, Stanley Baker, Margaret Leighton, John Ireland, Joan Collins. Solid cast fails to enhance standard robbery tale, with a quartet of strangers coming together to commit a holdup.

Good Earth, The (1937) 138m. **** D: Sidney Franklin. Paul Muni, Luise Rainer, Walter Connolly, Charley Grapewin, Jessie Ralph, Tilly Losch, Keye Luke, Harold Huber. Mammoth Pearl Buck novel re-created in detail, telling story of greed ruining lives of simple Chinese farming couple. Rainer won Oscar as the ever-patient wife of Muni, as did Karl Freund for his cinematography. Screenplay by Talbot Jennings, Tess Slesinger, and Claudine West. The special effects are outstanding. ▼◗

Good Fairy, The (1935) 97m. ***½ D: William Wyler. Margaret Sullavan, Herbert Marshall, Frank Morgan, Reginald Owen, Alan Hale, Beulah Bondi, Cesar Romero. Sparkling romantic comedy, adapted from Molnár play by Preston Sturges; wide-eyed Sullavan tries to act as "good fairy" to struggling lawyer Marshall, while hotly pursued by wealthy Morgan. Hilarious, charming; movie spoof near beginning is priceless. Remade as I'LL BE YOURS.▼◗

Good Girls Go to Paris (1939) 75m. **½ D: Alexander Hall. Melvyn Douglas, Joan Blondell, Walter Connolly, Alan Curtis, Isabel Jeans, Clarence Kolb. Spunky waitress will do anything to visit France; she sees a meal ticket in wealthy Curtis, but really loves professor Douglas. OK comedy.

Good Humor Man, The (1950) 79m. **½ D: Lloyd Bacon. Jack Carson, Lola Albright, Jean Wallace, George Reeves, Richard Egan. Broad slapstick comedy about ice-cream vendor Carson, who stumbles into a crime ring. Written by Frank Tashlin.▼

Good Luck SEE: **East and West**

Good Morning (1959-Japanese) C-93m. *** D: Yasujiro Ozu. Keiji Sada, Yoshiko Kuga, Masahiko Shimazu, Chishu Ryu, Kuniko Miyake, Haruko Sugimura. Perceptive comedy about life from the perspective of two spoiled children who take a vow of silence when their father refuses to buy them a TV set. Brightly hued remake of Ozu's own equally sharp I WAS BORN, BUT . . . updates the material but retains his wry take on the Westernization of Japanese society. ▼▶

Good Morning, Miss Dove (1955) C-107m. *** D: Henry Koster. Jennifer Jones, Robert Stack, Kipp Hamilton, Robert Douglas, Peggy Knudsen, Marshall Thompson, Chuck Connors, Biff Elliot, Jerry Paris, Mary Wickes, Richard Deacon. For several generations, small town spinster schoolteacher has touched and helped shape lives of her students. Now hospitalized, her past is revealed through flashbacks. Sentimental, warm, and wonderful. CinemaScope. ▶

Good Neighbor Sam (1964) C-130m. *** D: David Swift. Jack Lemmon, Romy Schneider, Edward G. Robinson, Michael Connors, Dorothy Provine, Neil Hamilton, Joyce Jameson, Robert Q. Lewis. Good comedy of Lemmon's adventures pretending he's not married to his real wife but to luscious neighbor Schneider. Plenty of sight gags and chase scenes make this a lot of fun. Based on a novel by Jack Finney. ▼

Good News (1930) 90m. *** D: Nick Grinde. Mary Lawlor, Stanley Smith, Bessie Love, Cliff Edwards, Gus Shy, Lola Lane, Dorothy McNulty (Penny Singleton), Delmer Daves, Ann Dvorak, Kane Richmond, Harry Earles, Abe Lyman and His Band. Quintessential college song-and-dance fest asks Flaming Youth's burning questions: Can a comely coed help the Tait campus football hero pass his astronomy exam? And then, gosh, will he ask her to the dance? Based on the 1927 Broadway hit, this early talkie is expectedly stagy but boosted by its memorable DeSylva-Brown-Henderson score and genuinely peppy period-piece staging. That's Al Norman doing the eccentric dance solo. Technicolor finale is missing in surviving prints. Remade in 1947. ●

Good News (1947) C-95m. *** D: Charles Walters. June Allyson, Peter Lawford, Patricia Marshall, Joan McCracken, Ray McDonald, Mel Tormé, Donald MacBride, Tom Dugan, Clinton Sundberg. Spirited remake of the 1920s collegiate musical (by DeSylva, Brown, and Henderson), given a new coat of varnish by screenwriters Betty Comden and Adolph Green. Lawford is Tait College's cocky football hero, and Allyson is the brainy girl who catches him on the rebound. Vintage songs include "The Best Things in Life Are Free," "Just Imagine," "Varsity Drag"; new numbers include "The French Lesson" and "Pass That Peace Pipe." Filmed previously in 1930. ▼●▶

Good Old Soak, The (1937) 67m. **½ D: J. Walter Ruben. Wallace Beery, Una Merkel, Eric Linden, Judith Barrett, Betty Furness, Ted Healy, Janet Beecher, George Sidney, Margaret Hamilton. Beery is the lovable small-town drunkard of the title, who sobers up in time to put a crooked banker in his place and straighten out the

financial mess son Linden got in to impress a big-city showgirl. Typical Beery vehicle.

Good Sam (1948) 113m. ** D: Leo McCarey. Gary Cooper, Ann Sheridan, Ray Collins, Edmund Lowe, Joan Lorring, Ruth Roman. Almost complete misfire, despite cast and director. Cooper is an incurable good Samaritan in this lifeless comedy. Some prints run 128m. ▼▶

Good Time Girl (1950-British) 81m. *½ D: David MacDonald. Jean Kent, Dennis Price, Herbert Lom, Flora Robson. Inoffensive trivia about young girl steered away from wayward life by a judge's recounting the tragic fate of another teenager.

Goose and the Gander, The (1935) 65m. ** D: Alfred E. Green. Kay Francis, George Brent, Genevieve Tobin, John Eldredge, Claire Dodd, Ralph Forbes, Helen Lowell. Forgettable fluff involving spiraling events that occur as Francis schemes against Tobin, who stole husband Forbes away from her. ▶

Gorgeous Hussy, The (1936) 102m. **½ D: Clarence Brown. Joan Crawford, Robert Taylor, Lionel Barrymore, Franchot Tone, Melvyn Douglas, James Stewart, Alison Skipworth, Beulah Bondi, Louis Calhern, Melville Cooper, Sidney Toler, Gene Lockhart. Star-studded cast in strained, fictionalized historical drama of Peggy O'Neal, President Andrew Jackson's controversial confidante. Crawford et al. are beautifully costumed in well-appointed settings. Based on the novel by Samuel Hopkins Joyce. ▼▶

Gorgo (1961-British) C-78m. *** D: Eugene Lourie. Bill Travers, William Sylvester, Vincent Winter, Bruce Seton, Joseph O'Conor. Good sci-fi story of captured baby sea monster put into London circus and gigantic parent coming to rescue it. Exciting special effects. ▼●▶

Gorgon, The (1964-British) C-83m. **½ D: Terence Fisher. Peter Cushing, Christopher Lee, Richard Pasco, Barbara Shelley, Michael Goodliffe. In 19th-century Balkan village, one of the snake-headed Gorgons still survives, turning her victims to stone—but who is she by day? Good Hammer production. ▼●▶

Gorilla, The (1939) 66m. ** D: Allan Dwan. The Ritz Brothers, Anita Louise, Patsy Kelly, Lionel Atwill, Bela Lugosi, Joseph Calleia. Disappointing comedy-whodunit with the Ritz Brothers as fumbling detectives prowling around old-dark-house in search of murderer. Lugosi is wasted. Filmed before in 1927 and 1930. ▼●▶

Gorilla (1944) SEE: **Nabonga**

Gorilla at Large (1954) C-84m. *** D: Harmon Jones. Cameron Mitchell, Anne Bancroft, Lee J. Cobb, Raymond Burr, Peter Whitney, Lee Marvin, Warren Stevens. Offbeat murder mystery at amusement park, with exceptionally able cast. Filmed in 3-D. ▶

Gorilla Man, The (1942) 64m. ** D: D. Ross Lederman. John Loder, Ruth Ford,

Marian Hall, Richard Fraser, Creighton Hale. Title is misleading. Pro-Nazis try to discredit RAF pilot by linking him with series of brutal murders. Grade-B material with adequate acting.

Gospel According to St. Matthew, The (1964-Italian-French) 135m. ******** D: Pier Paolo Pasolini. Enrique Irazoqui, Margherita Caruso, Susanna Pasolini, Marcello Morante, Mario Socrate. Unconventional, austere film on life and teachings of Christ, based solely on writings of the Apostle Matthew. Amateur cast (including director's mother) is expressive and moves with quiet dignity. Ironically, director of this masterpiece was a Marxist. **▼●**

Gosta Berling's Saga SEE: **Atonement of Gosta Berling, The**

Government Girl (1943) 94m. ****½** D: Dudley Nichols. Olivia de Havilland, Sonny Tufts, Anne Shirley, Jess Barker, James Dunn, Paul Stewart, Agnes Moorehead. Production expert Tufts comes to Washington to build airplanes for the war effort; he spars with (and, of course, falls for) secretary de Havilland. Frantic comedy with serious (and still timely) overtones about government bureaucracy. Scripted by Nichols; adapted by Budd Schulberg from a story by Adela Rogers St. Johns. **▶**

Go West (1925) 69m. ****½** D: Buster Keaton. Buster Keaton, Howard Truesdale, Kathleen Myers, Brown Eyes. Buster plays a greenhorn named Friendless who winds up working on a cattle ranch out West, and finding his soulmate in a cow named Brown Eyes. Not one of Buster's best silents, this still has plenty of good scenes, especially the climactic stampede, executed with typically Keatonesque comic skill. **▼●**

Go West (1940) 81m. ****** D: Edward Buzzell. Groucho, Chico, and Harpo Marx, John Carroll, Diana Lewis, Walter Woolf King, Robert Barrat. Big letdown from Marxes, until hilarious train-ride climax. Occasional bits sparkle through humdrum script. **▼●**

Go West, Young Lady (1941) 70m. ****½** D: Frank Strayer. Penny Singleton, Glenn Ford, Ann Miller, Charles Ruggles, Allen Jenkins, Jed Prouty, Onslow Stevens, Edith Meiser, Bob Wills and His Texas Playboys, The Foursome. Slapstick Western musical has Singleton as a prim Easterner facing a hard new life in the rugged town of Headstone, where she's courted by ladies' man Ford but out-vamped by sequined showgirl Miller. Standout in Sammy Cahn–Saul Chaplin score is the ordinarily nonmusical Jenkins' "I Wish I Could Be a Singing Cowboy." Title song performed by Miller in stiletto-heeled cowboy boots atop a saloon bar.

Go West, Young Man (1936) 82m. ******* D: Henry Hathaway. Mae West, Randolph Scott, Warren William, Alice Brady, Elizabeth Patterson, Lyle Talbot, Isabel Jewell.

Movie queen Mae is stuck in the Pennsylvania sticks, but passes time nicely with handsome mechanic. Not top-notch West, but still fun. Mae wrote the screenplay. **▼▶**

Gracie Allen Murder Case, The (1939) 74m. ****½** D: Alfred E. Green. Gracie Allen, Warren William, Ellen Drew, Kent Taylor, Jerome Cowan, Judith Barrett, Donald MacBride, William Demarest, H. B. Warner. Fitfully amusing screwball mystery with the scatterbrained Allen as herself, constantly annoying Philo Vance in his investigation of a murdered convict. This was written for the screen first, *then* as a novel by S. S. Van Dine.

Graft (1931) 54m. ****** D: Christy Cabanne. Regis Toomey, Sue Carol, Dorothy Revier, Boris Karloff, George Irving, Richard Tucker, William B. Davidson, Willard Robertson, Harold Goodwin, Carmelita Geraghty. Cub reporter Toomey tries to impress his editor by getting the scoop on local racketeer Davidson. Karloff plays Davidson's henchman, and every one of his scenes is lit and staged to emphasize his menacing personality. Supposedly this is what inspired James Whale to cast Karloff in FRANKENSTEIN . . . though the film itself is thoroughly forgettable.

Grand Canyon Trail (1948) C-67m. ****½** D: William Witney. Roy Rogers, Andy Devine, Jane Frazee, Robert Livingston, Roy Barcroft, Charles Coleman, Emmett Lynn, Ken Terrell, James Finlayson, Foy Willing and the Riders of the Purple Sage. Crooked mining engineer Livingston convinces Eastern mine owner Coleman that his silver mine is worthless so he can buy it cheap. Coleman's secretary (Frazee) comes West to investigate. Roy and friends lend a hand as they're heavily invested in mining stock. Enjoyable Rogers Western, his first with Foy Willing and Co. Filmed in Red Rock Canyon, California. Only b&w prints seem to survive. **▼▶**

Grand Central Murder (1942) 73m. ****½** D: S. Sylvan Simon. Van Heflin, Patricia Dane, Cecilia Parker, Virginia Grey, Samuel S. Hinds, Sam Levene, Horace (Stephen) McNally, Tom Conway. Slick, fast-moving B whodunit, with Heflin investigating actress' murder on private train car at Grand Central Station. **▶**

Grand Duchess and the Waiter, The (1926) 85m. ******* D: Malcolm St. Clair. Adolphe Menjou, Florence Vidor, Lawrence Grant, André Beranger, Dot Farley, Barbara Pierce, Brandon Hurst. Millionaire Menjou (perfectly cast) pretends to be a waiter in order to get closer to a Grand Duchess with whom he's become infatuated. Charming comedy in the Lubitsch vein, adapted from a French play. Remade as HERE IS MY HEART. **▼**

Grand Exit (1935) 68m. ******* D: Erle C. Kenton. Edmund Lowe, Ann Sothern, Onslow Stevens, Robert Middlemass, Wyrley Birch, Selmer Jackson, Guy Usher. Adroit blend of detective mystery and screwball comedy starring Lowe as a dapper, hard-drinking insurance investigator who hooks up with daffy socialite Sothern while tracking a cunning arsonist. Fun B movie offers witty banter and nifty plotting.

Grand Hotel (1932) **113m.** ******** D: Edmund Goulding. Greta Garbo, John Barrymore, Joan Crawford, Wallace Beery, Lionel Barrymore, Lewis Stone, Jean Hersholt, Ferdinand Gottschalk, Tully Marshall, Mary Carlisle. Vicki Baum's novel and play of plush Berlin hotel where "nothing ever happens." Stars prove the contrary: Garbo as lonely ballerina, John B. her jewel-thief lover, Lionel B. a dying man, Crawford an ambitious stenographer, Beery a hardened businessman, Stone the observer. Scripted by William A. Drake. Best Picture Oscar winner; a must. Plot reworked many times (in HOTEL BERLIN, WEEK-END AT THE WALDORF, etc.). Later a Broadway musical. ▼●▶

Grand Illusion (1937-French) **117m.** ******** D: Jean Renoir. Jean Gabin, Pierre Fresnay, Erich von Stroheim, (Marcel) Dalio, Dita Parlo, (Julien) Carette, Gaston Modot, Jean Dasté. Renoir's classic treatise on war, focusing on French prisoners during WW1 and their cultured German commandant. Beautiful performances enhance an eloquent script (by Renoir and Charles Spaak). Edited to 94m. for U.S. release in 1938. Beware of other versions with variant running times. Original French title: LA GRANDE ILLUSION. ▼●▶

Grand Maneuver, The SEE: **Les Grandes Manoeuvres**

Grandma's Boy (1922) **81m.** ******* D: Fred Newmeyer. Harold Lloyd, Mildred Davis, Anna Townsend, Charles Stevenson, Noah Young, Dick Sutherland. Lloyd's first great success casts him as a mousy small-town type inspired to fight for his girl—and his honor—by his grandma's tales of family heritage. Very entertaining.▶

Grand National Night (1953-British) **81m.** ****** D: Bob McNaught. Nigel Patrick, Moira Lister, Beatrice Campbell, Betty Ann Davies, Michael Hordern, Noel Purcell. Melodramatic murder yarn involving the horsey set in northern England. Hordern, as a police inspector, gives the most interesting performance. Pay close attention to the surname of leading man Patrick's character. Aka WICKED WIFE.▶

Grand Old Girl (1935) **71m.** ****½** D: John Robertson. May Robson, Mary Carlisle, Fred MacMurray, Alan Hale, Etienne Girardot, Ward Bond. Robson is the centerpiece of this tug-at-your-heartstrings programmer as a gruff but lovable and dedicated high school teacher who solves everyone's problems—and takes on her town's shifty power brokers.

Grand Slam (1933) **67m.** ****½** D: William Dieterle. Paul Lukas, Loretta Young, Frank McHugh, Glenda Farrell, Helen Vinson, Roscoe Karns, Ferdinand Gottschalk. When waiter Lukas beats a bridge expert, entrepreneurial McHugh ghostwrites a book under Lukas' name and turns him into an overnight sensation. Made at a time when the U.S. was bridge-crazy, this satire (laced with silliness) gets broader as it goes along. Lukas is very likable and amusing.

Granny Get Your Gun (1940) **56m.** ****½** D: George Amy. May Robson, Harry Davenport, Margot Stevenson, Hardie Albright, Clem Bevans, William Davidson. Robson is a hoot as a rough-riding Nevadan who straps on her six-shooters and turns sleuth to clear her granddaughter of a trumped-up murder charge. Cute comic mystery based on Erle Stanley Gardner's Perry Mason story "The Case of the Dangerous Dowager."

Grapes of Wrath, The (1940) **129m.** ******** D: John Ford. Henry Fonda, Jane Darwell, John Carradine, Charley Grapewin, Dorris Bowdon, Russell Simpson, John Qualen, O. Z. Whitehead, Eddie Quillan, Zeffie Tilbury, Darryl Hickman, Ward Bond, Charles Middleton, Tom Tyler, Mae Marsh, Jack Pennick. One of the great American films, an uncompromising adaptation of John Steinbeck's novel about impoverished Okie farmers making the trek to California during the Depression, where the good life they've hoped for is well out of reach. Fonda is great in his defining role as an ex-con whose social conscience is aroused; Darwell is unforgettable as the matriarch Ma Joad. She and Ford won well-deserved Oscars. Screenplay by Nunnally Johnson.▼●▶

Grass (1925) **70m.** *****½** D: Merian C. Cooper, Ernest B. Schoedsack, Marguerite Harrison. Landmark ethnographic documentary, right up with NANOOK OF THE NORTH and MOANA in its impact. The highlight: Cooper, Schoedsack, and Harrison accompany the Bakhityari, a tribe of 50,000 Persian (Iranian) nomads, on their annual journey across hazardous terrain to bring their herds to pasture. Cooper and Schoedsack went on to make CHANG and then KING KONG. ▼●▶

Grass Is Greener, The (1961) **C-105m.** ******* D: Stanley Donen. Cary Grant, Deborah Kerr, Robert Mitchum, Jean Simmons. Chic drawing-room fare that suffers from staginess. Grant-Kerr marriage is threatened by Simmons and Mitchum romancing the two, respectively. Technirama. ▼●▶

Grave Robbers From Outer Space SEE: **Plan 9 From Outer Space**

Great Adventure, The (1953-Swedish) **73m.** *****½** D: Arne Sucksdorff. Anders Norberg, Kjell Sucksdorff, Arne Sucksdorff. Outstanding story told in semidocumentary style covering four seasons of a boy's life on a farm. Written, directed, edited, and photographed by an Oscar-winning filmmaker with a special gift for capturing animal life.▼

Great Adventure, The SEE: **Adventurers, The**

Great American Broadcast, The (1941) 92m. **½ D: Archie Mayo. Alice Faye, John Payne, Jack Oakie, Cesar Romero, The Four Ink Spots, James Newill, Mary Beth Hughes. Fictional fun of development of radio industry, with such musical guests as zany Wiere Brothers. Entertaining.◗

Great American Pastime, The (1956) 89m. ** D: Herman Hoffman. Tom Ewell, Anne Francis, Ann Miller, Dean Jones, Rudy Lee. Suburbanite Ewell doesn't know what he's getting into when he begins managing his son's Little League team. Slight, forgettable programmer.◗

Great Caruso, The (1951) C-109m. *** D: Richard Thorpe. Mario Lanza, Ann Blyth, Jarmila Novotna, Dorothy Kirsten. Biographical fiction about the legendary singer, entertainingly done. Fine music makes clichés endurable.▼◗

Great Chase, The (1963) 81m. ***½ Narrated by Frank Gallop. Buster Keaton, Douglas Fairbanks, Sr., Pearl White, Richard Barthelmess, Lillian Gish. Entertaining silent-film compilation of great chase scenes from THE MARK OF ZORRO, WAY DOWN EAST, etc., with most of film devoted to Keaton's classic THE GENERAL. Score composed by harmonica virtuoso Larry Adler.

Great Dan Patch, The (1949) 94m. **½ D: Joe (Joseph M.) Newman. Dennis O'Keefe, Gail Russell, Ruth Warrick, Charlotte Greenwood. Henry Hull, John Hoyt, Arthur Hunnicutt, Clarence Muse. Acceptable yarn about the legendary pacing horse Dan Patch and his phenomenal harness-racing career. O'Keefe is Dan's owner, Warrick and Russell (in a nicely modulated performance) the two very different women in his life.▼◗

Great Day (1945-British) 94m. **½ D: Lance Comfort. Eric Portman, Flora Robson, Sheila Sim, Isabel Jeans, Walter Fitzgerald, Philip Friend. English village readies itself for visit by Eleanor Roosevelt. Despite soap-opera plot, film works as a wartime curio, capturing a particular place and time.▼

Great Day in the Morning (1956) C-92m. **½ D: Jacques Tourneur. Virginia Mayo, Robert Stack, Ruth Roman, Alex Nicol, Raymond Burr. Good cast, beautiful color scenery help so-so story of pre–Civil War Colorado, when gold rush fever and separationist sentiments clashed. SuperScope.▼

Great Diamond Robbery, The (1953) 69m. ** D: Robert Z. Leonard. Red Skelton, Cara Williams, James Whitmore, Dorothy Stickney, Steven Geray. Limp vehicle buoyed by Skelton. Red is hoodwinked by jewel thief who wants him to recut huge diamond.◗

Great Dictator, The (1940) 128m. ***½ D: Charles Chaplin. Charles Chaplin, Paulette Goddard, Jack Oakie, Reginald Gardiner, Maurice Moscovich, Billy Gilbert, Henry Daniell. Chaplin's first full talkie; unusual comedy combines slapstick, satire, and social commentary, as he plays dual role of Jewish ghetto barber and dictator Adenoid Hynkel of Tomania. Unique, surprisingly effective film also features Oakie in unforgettable portrayal of Benzino Napaloni of rival country Bacteria.▼◗

Great Escape, The (1963) C-168m. **** D: John Sturges. Steve McQueen, James Garner, Richard Attenborough, Charles Bronson, James Coburn, David McCallum, Donald Pleasence, James Donald, Gordon Jackson, John Leyton, Angus Lennie, Nigel Stock. Allied POWs plot massive escape from Nazi prison camp. Based on true story, this blockbuster was beautifully photographed by Daniel Fapp on location in Germany. Rip-roaring excitement with marvelous international cast; script by James Clavell and W. R. Burnett, from Paul Brickhill's book. Rousing score by Elmer Bernstein. Followed by a TV sequel 25 years later. Panavision.▼◗

Greatest Love, The (1951-Italian) 110m. *½ D: Roberto Rossellini. Ingrid Bergman, Alexander Knox, Giulietta Masina, Teresa Pellati, Ettore Giannini. Bergman plays a wealthy American living in Rome, who feels compelled to help people in order to restore meaning to her own life after her son's suicide. Obvious, slow-moving story. Originally titled EUROPA '51.▼

Greatest Show on Earth, The (1952) C-153m. ***½ D: Cecil B. DeMille. Betty Hutton, Charlton Heston, Cornel Wilde, Dorothy Lamour, Gloria Grahame, James Stewart, Henry Wilcoxon, Lawrence Tierney, Lyle Bettger. Big package of fun from DeMille, complete with hokey performances, clichés, big-top excitement, and a swell train wreck. Stewart well cast as circus clown with mysterious past. Some funny surprise guests appear. Oscar winner for Best Picture and Story (Fredric M. Frank, Theodore St. John, Frank Cavett).▼◗

Greatest Story Ever Told, The (1965) C-199m. **½ D: George Stevens. Max von Sydow, Charlton Heston, Carroll Baker, Angela Lansbury, Sidney Poitier, Shelley Winters, John Wayne, Ed Wynn, Jose Ferrer, Van Heflin, Claude Rains, Telly Savalas, many others. Some of the most spectacular scenes ever filmed lose all validity because of incessant cameos that run throughout film. Would *you* believe John Wayne as a Roman centurion supervising Christ's crucifixion? Carl Sandburg is listed in credits as a Creative Associate. Includes overture, intermission/entr'acte, exit music. Originally released at 225m., other prints run 141m. Ultra Panavision 70.▼◗

Great Expectations (1934) 102m. **½ D:

Stuart Walker. Jane Wyatt, Phillips Holmes, George Breakston, Henry Hull, Florence Reed, Alan Hale, Francis L. Sullivan. Acceptable version of Dickens' story about a young boy and unknown benefactor is dwarfed by 1946 classic. Sullivan plays Jaggers in both films. ▼

Great Expectations (1946-British) **118m. **** D: David Lean. John Mills, Valerie Hobson, Bernard Miles, Francis L. Sullivan, Finlay Currie, Martita Hunt, Anthony Wager, Jean Simmons, Alec Guinness, Ivor Barnard, Freda Jackson, Torin Thatcher, Eileen Erskine, Hay Petrie. One of the greatest films ever made, a vivid adaptation of Dickens' tale of a mysterious benefactor making poor young orphan a gentleman of means. Opening graveyard sequence is a gem. Oscars went to cinematographer Guy Green and art director John Bryan. Lean, Kay Walsh, Cecil McGivern, and producers Anthony Havelock-Allan and Ronald Neame all contributed to script. Filmed in 1934, 1974, and 2012, and updated in 1998. Jean Simmons played Miss Havisham in a 1989 miniseries. ▼○▶

Great Flamarion, The (1945) **78m. **½ D: Anthony Mann. Erich von Stroheim, Mary Beth Hughes, Dan Duryea, Stephen Barclay, Lester Allen, Esther Howard. Better than most von Stroheim cheapies, this one casts him as a vaudeville trick shot artist who becomes romantically entangled with his scheming married assistant. ▼▶

Great Gabbo, The (1929) **95m. ** D: James Cruze. Erich von Stroheim, Don Douglas, Betty Compson, Margie Kane. The idea of von Stroheim as an egomaniacal ventriloquist is irresistible, but the story is slim, predictable, and stiffly done— padded out by lots of big and unintentionally hilarious musical numbers. A curio for film buffs. Based on Ben Hecht story; some sequences originally in color. ▶

Great Gambini, The (1937) **70m. **½ D: Charles Vidor. Akim Tamiroff, Marian Marsh, Genevieve Tobin, William Demarest, Reginald Denny. Nightclub mindreader Tamiroff predicts a murder, then becomes involved in the investigation. Interesting B-movie fluff, with added novelty of a "mystery minute" to give you a chance to guess the killer.

Great Garrick, The (1937) **91m. *** D: James Whale. Brian Aherne, Olivia de Havilland, Edward Everett Horton, Melville Cooper, Lionel Atwill, Lana Turner, Marie Wilson. Members of the Comédie Française perpetrate a hoax to deflate the ego of pompous David Garrick (Aherne) in this entertaining, fictionalized yarn about real-life British actor. ▶

Great Gatsby, The (1949) **92m. **½ D: Elliott Nugent. Alan Ladd, Betty Field, Macdonald Carey, Barry Sullivan, Ruth Hussey, Shelley Winters, Howard da Silva. Misguided adaptation of F. Scott Fitzger-ald's book about a mysterious young millionaire who crashes Long Island society in the 1920s. Too talky and much too literal-minded. Ladd is pretty good, but Field (as Daisy Buchanan) gives a strangely petulant performance. Filmed before in 1926, again in 1974 and 2013, and for TV in 2001.

Great Gilbert and Sullivan, The (1953-British) **C-105m. *** D: Sidney Gilliat. Robert Morley, Maurice Evans, Eileen Herlie, Peter Finch, Martyn Green. Agreeable production is only a superficial biography of the legendary operetta composers, but does offer many highlights from their wonderful works. Their lives are probed more incisively in TOPSY-TURVY. Original British title: THE STORY OF GILBERT AND SULLIVAN.

Great Gildersleeve, The (1943) **62m. ** D: Gordon Douglas. Harold Peary, Nancy Gates, Freddie Mercer, Mary Field, Jane Darwell, Thurston Hall. First of series based on famous radio character Throckmorton P. Gildersleeve is moderately amusing nonsense, as Gildy enters local politics and avoids spinster Field. ▼▶

Great Guns (1941) **74m. ** D: Monty Banks. Stan Laurel, Oliver Hardy, Sheila Ryan, Dick Nelson, Edmund MacDonald. Later L&H Army comedy is weak, not as bad as some but far below their classic films. Look quickly for Alan Ladd. ▼▶

Great Guy (1936) **75m. ** D: John G. Blystone. James Cagney, Mae Clarke, James Burke, Edward Brophy, Henry Kolker, Bernadene Hayes, Edward McNamara. Second-rate Cagney in low-budget production about inspector crusading against corruption in meat business. ▼▶

Great Impostor, The (1961) **112m. **½ D: Robert Mulligan. Tony Curtis, Karl Malden, Raymond Massey, Edmond O'Brien, Arthur O'Connell, Gary Merrill, Frank Gorshin. Incredible story of Ferdinand Demara, who succeeded in a variety of professional guises. Film is episodic and pat. ▼▶

Great Jasper, The (1933) **85m. ** D: J. Walter Ruben. Richard Dix, Florence Eldridge, Edna May Oliver, Wera Engels, Bruce Cabot. Turn-of-the-20th-century tale of ne'er-do-well streetcar conductor Dix, who goes to Atlantic City in search of success and finds it as a glib fortune-teller who appeals to the feminine trade. Oliver, as a veteran boardwalk palm reader, almost makes the film worth watching, but tired soap-opera plotting and dialogue weigh down a potentially colorful story.

Great Jesse James Raid, The (1953) **C-74m. **½ D: Reginald LeBorg. Willard Parker, Barbara Payton, Tom Neal, Wallace Ford. Jesse (Parker) and his gang plot to steal miners' gold but mostly fight among themselves. The one-time-only Payton-Neal pairing makes this a must for "Hollywood scandal" fans. ▼▶

Great John L., The (1945) **96m. **½ D:
Frank Tuttle. Greg McClure, Linda Darnell,
Barbara Britton, Lee Sullivan, Otto Kruger,
Wallace Ford, George Matthews, Rory Calhoun. Not bad little biography of famous
boxer John L. Sullivan's rise and fall, his
two loves and unhappy end.
Great K&A Train Robbery, The (1926)
53m. ***½ D: Lewis Seiler. Tom Mix,
Dorothy Dwan, William Walling, Harry
Grippe, Tony. Silent screen's most popular
cowboy star in one of his greatest films: rollicking fun, filmed on magnificent locations
in Colorado. ▼)
Great Lie, The (1941) **107m. *** D:** Edmund Goulding. Mary Astor, Bette Davis,
George Brent, Lucile Watson, Hattie Mc-
Daniel, Grant Mitchell, Jerome Cowan. Brent
marries Davis when alliance with Astor is an-
nulled. He is lost in plane crash, leaving Davis
and pregnant Astor to battle each other and the
elements. Well-mounted soaper won Astor an
Oscar as fiery concert pianist. ▼●)
Great Locomotive Chase, The (1956) **C-
85m. *** D:** Francis D. Lyon. Fess Parker,
Jeffrey Hunter, Jeff York, John Lupton, Eddie Firestone, Kenneth Tobey. True story of
Andrews' Raiders (filmed before by Buster
Keaton as THE GENERAL) comes to life in
colorful Disney film; Parker is famous Union
spy who leads a rowdy band in capturing and
"kidnapping" a Confederate railroad train
during Civil War. Retitled ANDREWS'
RAIDERS. CinemaScope. ▼)
Great Lover, The (1949) **80m. *** D:** Alexander Hall. Bob Hope, Rhonda Fleming, Roland Young, Roland Culver, George
Reeves, Jim Backus. Vintage Hope; Bob's
a boy scout leader on ship filled with his
troop, luscious Fleming, and murderer
Young. ▼)
Great Madcap, The (1949-Mexican)
90m. * D:** Luis Buñuel. Fernando Soler,
Rosario Granados, Ruben Rojo, Gustavo
Rojo, Maruja Grifell. One of Buñuel's earliest Mexican films, this surprisingly lighthearted romp is like a Hollywood screwball
comedy of the '30s. Soler plays a Walter
Connolly type, a drunken millionaire
whose lazy family tries to get their hands
on his money by convincing him that he's
broke. Then he learns of the plan and turns
the tables on them. An amusing diversion
from the surrealist master. Original title: EL
GRAN CALAVERA. ▼
Great Man, The (1956) **92m. ***½ D:** Jose
Ferrer. Jose Ferrer, Dean Jagger, Keenan
Wynn, Julie London, Jim Backus, Ed
Wynn. Well-loved TV star dies and Ferrer
prepares memorial show, only to discover
star was a despicable phony. Hard-bitten
look at TV industry; top performances by
senior and junior Wynns. Ferrer and Al
Morgan adapted Morgan's thinly veiled
novel about Arthur Godfrey.
Great Manhunt, The SEE: State Secret

Great Man's Lady, The (1942) **90m. **½ D:**
William Wellman. Barbara Stanwyck, Joel
McCrea, Brian Donlevy, Thurston Hall,
K. T. Stevens, Lucien Littlefield. Saga of the
West is no great shakes as McCrea dreams
of oil wells, Donlevy takes his girl. Stanwyck ages to 100 years to frame story. ▼)
Great Man Votes, The (1939) **72m.
***½ D:** Garson Kanin. John Barrymore,
Peter Holden, Virginia Weidler, Donald
MacBride, William Demarest. Simple,
sincere, delightful film of Barrymore,
once a professor, now a souse, fighting
for custody of his children, suddenly elevated to new stature when election-time
rolls around. MacBride fun as small-time
politico, Demarest an energetic campaign
promoter. ▼
Great McGinty, The (1940) **81m. *** D:**
Preston Sturges. Brian Donlevy, Muriel Angelus, Akim Tamiroff, Allyn Joslyn, William Demarest, Louis Jean Heydt, Arthur
Hoyt. Sturges' directorial debut (and Oscar-
winning screenplay) isn't up to his later
comedy classics, but Donlevy is excellent
as bum who is manipulated into governor's
chair by crooked political machine—then
blows it all when he tries to be honest.
Typically sharp dialogue, plus fine work by
Sturges' stock company of character actors.
Donlevy and Tamiroff reprised their roles
as a gag in Sturges' THE MIRACLE OF
MORGAN'S CREEK. ▼●)
Great Meadow, The (1931) **78m. **½ D:**
Charles Brabin. John Mack Brown, Eleanor
Boardman, Lucille LaVerne, Anita Louise,
Gavin Gordon, Guinn Williams, Russell
Simpson, John Miljan. Naive and primitive
but still compelling story of Virginians who
undertake mountainous trek to settle new
land in Kentucky, circa 1777. Fairly authentic drama gives a real sense of the hardship
these pioneers endured. Filmed in Realife
70mm.
Great Mike, The (1944) **70m. ** D:** Wallace W. Fox. Stuart Erwin, Robert (Buzzy)
Henry, Marion Martin, Carl (Alfalfa) Switzer, Pierre Watkin, Gwen Kenyon. Slight
tale of young Henry and his love for a horse
who, predictably and after various complications, is destined to become a racing
champ. ▼)
Great Missouri Raid, The (1950) **C-83m.
** D:** Gordon Douglas. Wendell Corey,
Macdonald Carey, Ellen Drew, Ward Bond,
Anne Revere, Bruce Bennett, Bill Williams,
Edgar Buchanan. By-the-numbers account
of Frank and Jesse James (played by Corey
and Carey, respectively) and the Younger
brothers, who are forced to become outlaws
after the Civil War by a conniving Army
major (Bond). ▼
Great Moment, The (1944) **83m. ** D:**
Preston Sturges. Joel McCrea, Betty Field,
Harry Carey, William Demarest, Franklin
Pangborn, Grady Sutton, Louis Jean Heydt.

Confused biography of anesthesia pioneer wavers from comedy to drama; ineffectual, filled with frustrating flashbacks. Very offbeat for writer-director Sturges, although film was taken out of his hands and reedited. Filmed in 1942. ▼●▶

Great Morgan, The (1946) 57m. ** D: Nat Perrin. Frank Morgan, Leon Ames. MGM stalwart Morgan gets a chance to produce a picture, but his grand opus turns out to be a shambles consisting of outtakes from the studio's musicals and clips from short subjects. Oddity was never released theatrically in the U.S. and is mostly a mess, but interesting for film buffs. Cute closing bit with Leo the Lion. Famed art director Cedric Gibbons, costume designer Irene, and sound department head Douglas Shearer appear as themselves.

Great Mr. Nobody, The (1941) 71m. **½ D: Benjamin Stoloff. Eddie Albert, Joan Leslie, Alan Hale, William Lundigan, John Litel, Charles Trowbridge, Paul Hurst, Dickie Moore, John Ridgely, Alexis Smith. Dogooder Albert sells classified ads for a newspaper and never earns credit for his ideas or acts of kindness. Formulaic but painless and agreeable.

Great O'Malley, The (1937) 71m. *½ D: William Dieterle. Pat O'Brien, Humphrey Bogart, Ann Sheridan, Donald Crisp, Mary Gordon, Frieda Inescort, Sybil Jason. Syrupy film of ruthless cop O'Brien and poor man Bogart who has lame daughter and turns to crime to support her. Pretty sticky. ▶

Great Profile, The (1940) 82m. **½ D: Walter Lang. John Barrymore, Mary Beth Hughes, Gregory Ratoff, John Payne, Anne Baxter, Lionel Atwill, Edward Brophy. Barrymore on downslide provides some laughs in self-parodying tale of aging, conceited actor. ▶

Great Race, The (1965) C-150m. **½ D: Blake Edwards. Tony Curtis, Natalie Wood, Jack Lemmon, Peter Falk, Keenan Wynn, Larry Storch, Dorothy Provine, Arthur O'Connell, Vivian Vance, Ross Martin, George Macready. Long, sometimes funny, often labored comedy, not the greatest ever made, as advertised. Duel sequence and barroom brawl are highlights, but pie fight falls flat, other gimmicks don't work. Definitely a mixed bag (although Natalie never looked better); one good song, "The Sweetheart Tree." Runs 160m. with overture, intermission/entr'acte, exit music. Panavision. ▼●▶

Great Rupert, The (1950) 86m. **½ D: Irving Pichel. Jimmy Durante, Terry Moore, Tom Drake, Queenie Smith, Frank Orth, Jimmy Conlin, Chick Chandler. Agreeable comedy-fantasy about a trained squirrel who finds a cache of money and gives it to impoverished vaudevillian Durante and his family. Durante is at his best, but story runs out of steam before it's through. Produced

by George Pal; director Pichel appears in a brief bit. Later colorized and retitled A CHRISTMAS WISH. ▼▶

Great Sinner, The (1949) 110m. **½ D: Robert Siodmak. Gregory Peck, Ava Gardner, Melvyn Douglas, Walter Huston, Ethel Barrymore, Frank Morgan, Agnes Moorehead. Lavishly produced but murky, talky costumer of writer Peck falling for beautiful Gardner and becoming obsessed with gambling. Screenplay by Christopher Isherwood. ▶

Great Sioux Uprising, The (1953) C-80m. **½ D: Lloyd Bacon. Jeff Chandler, Faith Domergue, Lyle Bettger, Glenn Strange. Chandler as ex-Yankee officer is adequate in formula Western about threatened Indian war. ▼

Great St. Louis Bank Robbery, The (1959) 86m. *½ D: Charles Guggenheim, John Stix. Steve McQueen, David Clarke, Crahan Denton, Molly McCarthy, James Dukas. Modest robbery caper with virtue of McQueen in cast. Fact-based and shot on location in Missouri, with police officers recreating their true-life actions on the day of the heist. ▼●▶

Great Victor Herbert, The (1939) 91m. **½ D: Andrew L. Stone. Allan Jones, Mary Martin, Walter Connolly, Lee Bowman, Susanna Foster, Jerome Cowan. Music overshadows plot in lightweight romance about two young singers and the famed composer. Many of Herbert's most popular songs ("Ah, Sweet Mystery of Life," "March of the Toys," etc.) included.

Great Waltz, The (1938) 102m. **½ D: Julien Duvivier. Luise Rainer, Fernand Gravet, Miliza Korjus, Hugh Herbert, Lionel Atwill, Curt Bois. Music outdoes drama in this elaborately produced biography of composer Johann Strauss, with plenty of waltzes covering up a standard triangle tale. Joseph Ruttenberg's lovely cinematography earned an Oscar. ▼●▶

Great War, The (1959-Italian-French) 118m. ** D: Mario Monicelli. Vittorio Gassman, Alberto Sordi, Silvana Mangano, Folco Lulli. Uneven, episodic comedy-drama of two gold-bricking pals during WW1, somewhat reminiscent of WHAT PRICE GLORY? but not nearly as good. Released in U.S. in 1961. CinemaScope. ▼

Great Ziegfeld, The (1936) 176m. ***½ D: Robert Z. Leonard. William Powell, Myrna Loy, Luise Rainer, Frank Morgan, Fanny Brice, Virginia Bruce, Reginald Owen, Ray Bolger, Stanley Morner (Dennis Morgan). Spectacular, immensely entertaining biography of flamboyant impresario Florenz Ziegfeld, with Powell quite dashing in the title role. However, Rainer (as Anna Held) is stunning, and won an Academy Award; her telephone scene is a classic. Also won Oscars for Best Picture and Dance Direction (the "A Pretty Girl Is Like a Melody" number, supervised by Seymour Felix). Runs 185m. with overture, intermission/entr'acte, exit music. ▼○●

Greed (1925) 117m. **** D: Erich von Stroheim. Gibson Gowland, ZaSu Pitts, Jean Hersholt, Chester Conklin, Dale Fuller. Powerful adaptation of Frank Norris' novel *McTeague,* about a simple man whose wife's obsession with money eventually drives him to madness. Even though von Stroheim's version was taken from him and severely cut by the studio (it originally ran eight hours), this remains a stunning work, one of the greatest of all silent films. The final sequences in Death Valley are unforgettable. Reconstructed in 1999, using stills to cover long-lost footage; this version runs 242m. ▼●

Greed of William Hart, The (1948-British) 80m. BOMB D: Oswald Mitchell. Tod Slaughter, Henry Oscar, Ann Trego, Jenny Lynn, Patrick Addison, Arnold Bell, Aubrey Woods. Another variation on the tale of "resurrectionists" Burke and Hare. This time Slaughter and a partner steal bodies for a doctor, killing when necessary. Cheap, tawdry, and dull, the worst of Slaughter's barnstormers, and one of the last. Only he and Woods (as a victim) provide any entertainment. Filmed using the real names, then rerecorded when censors objected. Aka HORROR MANIACS.●

Greeks Had a Word for Them, The (1932) 79m. *** D: Lowell Sherman. Joan Blondell, Ina Claire, Madge Evans, David Manners, Lowell Sherman. Vintage comedy of three gold-digging girls looking for husbands; still entertaining although redone several times, including HOW TO MARRY A MILLIONAIRE. Video title: THREE BROADWAY GIRLS.▼●

Green Cockatoo, The (1937-British) 65m. ** D: William Cameron Menzies. John Mills, Rene Ray, Robert Newton, Charles Oliver, Bruce Seton. Considering credentials of this film (story by Graham Greene, director Menzies, etc.) the results are particularly disappointing: song-and-dance man Mills tries to unravel mystery surrounding murder of his brother (Newton). Originally titled FOUR DARK HOURS.▼●

Green Dolphin Street (1947) 141m. **½ D: Victor Saville. Lana Turner, Van Heflin, Donna Reed, Richard Hart, Frank Morgan, Edmund Gwenn, Dame May Whitty, Reginald Owen, Gladys Cooper, Moyna MacGill, Linda Christian, Gigi Perreau. If only for its glossy production and Oscar-winning special effects (earthquake and resultant tidal wave), this plodding costumer has merit. Story of two sisters (Turner, Reed) after the same man in 19th-century New Zealand is tedious. ▼●

Greene Murder Case, The (1929) 69m. **½ D: Frank Tuttle. William Powell, Florence Eldridge, Ulrich Haupt, Jean Arthur, Eugene Pallette. Despite creaky early-talkie technique, this is a generally satisfying *Philo*

Vance mystery about the murder of a penurious Manhattan matron. Unfortunately, the killer's identity becomes painfully obvious around the halfway mark.

Green-Eyed Blonde, The (1957) 76m. ** D: Bernard Girard. Susan Oliver, Linda Plowman, Beverly Long, Norma Jean Nilsson. Illegitimate mother Plowman is sent to reformatory, where she encounters tough-as-nails Oliver (who's quite good). Written by Dalton Trumbo, though credited to Sally Stubblefield.

Green Eyes (1934) 68m. ** D: Richard Thorpe. Shirley Grey, Charles Starrett, Claude Gillingwater, John Wray, William Bakewell. After a tyrannical millionaire is murdered at a costume party, detective-story writer Starrett butts in on the police investigation. No-frills whodunit with a shortage of likable characters (even the leads are annoying). Wray steals the show with rat-a-tat delivery as a no-nonsense police inspector.

Green Fields (1937) 95m. *** D: Edgar G. Ulmer, Jacob Ben-Ami. Michael Goldstein (Gorrin), Helen Beverly, Isidore Cashier, Anna Appel, Dena Drute, Herschel Bernardi. Lovely, lyrical adaptation of Peretz Hirschbein's Yiddish stage classic about an orphaned, wandering scholar (Goldstein) who's searching for a meaningful life, and what happens when he's taken in by a peasant family. Filmed in upstate New York; codirector Ben-Ami, respected actor-director in both the Yiddish and American theater, starred in this on the stage.▼

Green Fire (1954) C-100m. **½ D: Andrew Marton. Grace Kelly, Stewart Granger, Paul Douglas, John Ericson, Murvyn Vye. Hokum about love and conflict between emerald prospector (Granger) and coffee-plantation owner (Kelly), set in Colombia, South America. Attractive stars, hot love scenes, slimy villain (Vye). Cinema-Scope. ▼●

Green for Danger (1946-British) 93m. **** D: Sidney Gilliat. Alastair Sim, Sally Gray, Trevor Howard, Rosamund John, Leo Genn, Judy Campbell, Megs Jenkins, George Woodbridge. Exciting whodunit set in a rural English emergency hospital during WW2. Tension neatly counterbalanced by droll wit of Sim as implacable Scotland Yard inspector; a must-see classic. Written by Gilliat and Claude Guerney.▼●

Green Glove, The (1952) 88m. **½ D: Rudolph Maté. Glenn Ford, Geraldine Brooks, Cedric Hardwicke, George Macready, Jany Holt, Juliette Greco. Occasionally interesting tale of ex-paratrooper Ford returning to France after WW2 to find medieval, gem-laden religious artifact, becoming involved in murder and mayhem.▼●

Green Goddess, The (1930) 80m. ** D: Alfred E. Green. George Arliss, Alice Joyce, H. B. Warner, Ralph Forbes, Reginald Sheffield, Nigel de Brulier, Ivan

Simpson. Campy early talkie, with Arliss as a self-righteous potentate who holds innocent Britishers prisoner. The closing line is a gem. A remake of Arliss' 1923 silent film. Reworked as ADVENTURE IN IRAQ.

Green Grass of Wyoming (1948) **C-89m.** ****½** D: Louis King. Peggy Cummins, Robert Arthur, Charles Coburn, Lloyd Nolan. Atmospheric tale of rival horse-breeding families; the usual, but nicely done. Sequel to THUNDERHEAD—SON OF FLICKA, based on a novel by Mary O'Hara. ▶

Green Grow the Rushes (1951-British) **80m.** ****** D: Derek Twist. Richard Burton, Honor Blackman, Roger Livesey, Geoffrey Keen, Archie Duncan. Talky, fitfully funny comedy of a Kent community involved in brandy smuggling. Of interest solely for the presence of Burton, in his last British film before going Hollywood. ▼▶

Green Hell (1940) **87m.** ****½** D: James Whale. Douglas Fairbanks, Jr., Joan Bennett, John Howard, George Sanders, Alan Hale, George Bancroft, Vincent Price. Diverse group of men, led by stalwart Fairbanks, head into unexplored South American jungle in search of a temple of ancient treasures. Hokey but entertaining.

Green Light, The (1937) **85m.** ****½** D: Frank Borzage. Errol Flynn, Anita Louise, Margaret Lindsay, Cedric Hardwicke, Henry O'Neill, Spring Byington, Erin O'Brien-Moore. Genuinely odd blend of melodrama, religion, purple prose, and medical drama with Flynn as an idealistic doctor who makes a career sacrifice and then tries to understand the larger meaning of his life. Adaptation of a Lloyd C. Douglas novel is entertaining enough but awfully hard to swallow seriously. ▶

Green Man, The (1957-British) **80m.** ******* D: Robert Day. Alastair Sim, George Cole, Terry-Thomas, Jill Adams, Avril Angers, Colin Gordon. Droll comedy of a seemingly timid clockmaker who prefers his part-time job as paid assassin.

Green Mansions (1959) **C-104m.** ****½** D: Mel Ferrer. Audrey Hepburn, Anthony Perkins, Lee J. Cobb, Sessue Hayakawa, Henry Silva, Nehemiah Persoff. W. H. Hudson's romance set in South America suffers from miscast Hepburn as Rima the Bird Girl, whom fate decrees shall not leave her sanctuary. Perkins properly puzzled as male lead. CinemaScope. ▼▶

Green Pastures, The (1936) **92m.** *****½** D: William Keighley, Marc Connelly. Rex Ingram, Oscar Polk, Eddie Anderson, Frank Wilson, George Reed, Abraham Gleaves, Myrtle Anderson. All-black cast in Marc Connelly fable of life in heaven, and biblical stories which give more meaning to Adam, Noah, and Moses than many so-called biblical films. Ingram is fine as "de Lawd."▼▶

Green Promise, The (1949) **93m.** ****½** D: William D. Russell. Marguerite Chapman, Walter Brennan, Robert Paige, Natalie Wood, Ted Donaldson, Connie Marshall, Milburn Stone. Thoughtful drama of stubborn, manipulative Brennan, who lords it over his children while attempting to eke out a living on a farm. Watch this and you'll learn all you'll ever need to know about 4-H Clubs!▼▶

Green Scarf, The (1955-British) **96m.** ******* D: George More O'Ferrall. Michael Redgrave, Ann Todd, Kieron Moore, Leo Genn. Imaginative handling of blind man accused of homicide, defended by aging attorney; set in Paris.

Greenwich Village (1944) **C-82m.** ****½** D: Walter Lang. Carmen Miranda, Don Ameche, William Bendix, Vivian Blaine, Felix Bressart, Tony and Sally DeMarco, The Four Step Brothers. Silly but amiable musical about a "serious" composer (Ameche) persuaded to adapt his songs for a Broadway revue starring Blaine. When it's supposed to be 1922 N.Y.C. and Carmen Miranda turns up, you know not to expect stark realism. Look fast in both party scenes to spot The Revuers (Betty Comden, Adolph Green, Judy Holliday, Alvin Hammer). ▶

Green Years, The (1946) **127m.** ****½** D: Victor Saville. Charles Coburn, Tom Drake, Hume Cronyn, Gladys Cooper, Dean Stockwell, Jessica Tandy, Norman Lloyd, Wallace Ford. Sentimental A. J. Cronin weeper of orphaned Irish lad and his experiences growing up with his mother's family in Scotland. Coburn is wonderful as his great-grandfather, an irascible teller of tall tales. Tandy plays Cronyn's *daughter* here. ▶

Gretchen the Greenhorn (1916) **58m.** ****½** D: C. M. (Chester) and S. A. (Sidney) Franklin. Dorothy Gish, Ralph Lewis, Frank Bennett, Eugene Pallette, Kate Bruce, Elmo Lincoln, George Stone. Old-fashioned, tug-at-your-heartstrings melodrama about a Dutch girl who emigrates to the U.S., where her tenement neighbors are like a U.N. delegation and she is wooed by a young Italian (Bennett). Meanwhile, her unsuspecting father is duped into engraving counterfeit money. Nostalgic, romanticized ode to the American immigrant experience and melting pot ideal. ▶

Greyfriars Bobby (1961) **C-91m.** ****½** D: Don Chaffey. Donald Crisp, Laurence Naismith, Alex Mackenzie, Kay Walsh, Duncan Macrae, Gordon Jackson. British Disney film based on true story of a Skye terrier who became "neighborhood pet" in Edinburgh during 19th century through unusual circumstances. Great charm, fine performances offset by slow pacing. A remake of CHALLENGE TO LASSIE, which also features Crisp (who played the dog's master in the earlier film). Remade in England in 2006. ▼▶

Gribiche (1926-French) **112m.** ******* D: Jacques Feyder. Jean Forest, Françoise Rosay, Cécile Guyon, Rolla Norman, Andrée Canti. A kind act on the part of a working-class boy (Forest) who's being raised by his widowed mother brings him in contact with a well-meaning millionairess who offers to adopt him. A world of privilege is opened up for him, but there are complications. Feyder also scripted this potent ode to the value of parent-child bonds. Forest is a real scene stealer. Aka MOTHER OF MINE. ◗

Grip of the Strangler SEE: **Haunted Strangler, The**

Grisbi SEE: **Touchez Pas au Grisbi**

Grissly's Millions (1945) **54m.** **½ D: John English. Paul Kelly, Virginia Grey, Don Douglas, Elisabeth Risdon, Robert Barrat, Clem Bevans, Adele Mara. Smoothly done programmer about greedy relatives converging on the mansion of a wealthy man who has been murdered.

Groom Wore Spurs, The (1951) **80m.** **½ D: Richard Whorf. Ginger Rogers, Jack Carson, Joan Davis, Stanley Ridges. Lightly likable comedy of attorney Rogers marrying cowboy actor Carson, divorcing him, but coming to his defense in criminal case. ▼◗

Grounds for Marriage (1950) **91m.** **½ D: Robert Z. Leonard. Van Johnson, Kathryn Grayson, Paula Raymond, Barry Sullivan, Lewis Stone. Cutesy musicomedy of opera star Grayson and her ex-husband, physician Johnson.

Guadalcanal Diary (1943) **93m.** **½ D: Lewis Seiler. Preston Foster, Lloyd Nolan, William Bendix, Richard Conte, Anthony Quinn, Richard Jaeckel, Lionel Stander. WW2 actioner based on Richard Tregaskis' best-selling account of the Marines taking a Pacific island stronghold. This hasn't aged especially well, with archetypes instead of characters, from Bendix's Brooklyn cabbie to Jaeckel (in his film debut) as the ultimate mama's boy. Still watchable, but for an overload of racial slurs. ▼◗

Guardsman, The (1931) **89m.** *** D: Sidney Franklin. Alfred Lunt, Lynn Fontanne, Roland Young, ZaSu Pitts, Maude Eburne, Herman Bing. The Lunts' only starring film is charming tour de force from Molnar's comedy of jealous husband testing his wife's fidelity. Remade as THE CHOCOLATE SOLDIER and LILY IN LOVE. ▼

Guerillas in Pink Lace (1964) **C-96m.** *½ D: George Montgomery. George Montgomery, Valerie Varda, Roby Grace, Joan Shawlee. Poorly produced yarn filmed in Philippines about Montgomery and group of showgirls on the lam from Manila and the Japanese. ◗

Guest, The (1964-British) **105m.** *** D: Clive Donner. Alan Bates, Donald Pleasence, Robert Shaw. Derelict Pleasence invades the world of mentally ill Shaw and his sadistic brother Bates. Superior cast and superb performances, but claustrophobically directed by Donner. Screenplay by Harold Pinter, based on his play *The Caretaker,* which was also this film's title in Britain.

Guest in the House (1944) **121m.** *** D: John Brahm. Anne Baxter, Ralph Bellamy, Aline MacMahon, Ruth Warrick, Scott McKay, Marie McDonald, Jerome Cowan, Margaret Hamilton, Percy Kilbride. Atmospheric, occasionally gripping melodrama about neurotic young Baxter and her effect on the family of her betrothed. Bellamy is extremely attractive in a rare romantic lead, and Anne goes all out in this Eve Harrington–like characterization. ▼◗

Guest Wife (1945) **90m.** **½ D: Sam Wood. Claudette Colbert, Don Ameche, Dick Foran, Charles Dingle, Grant Mitchell, Wilma Francis. Breezy comedy depends on stars for flair; they do just fine, with Claudette posing as Ameche's wife to husband Foran's chagrin. ▼◗

Guilt of Janet Ames, The (1947) **83m.** *** D: Henry Levin. Rosalind Russell, Melvyn Douglas, Sid Caesar, Betsy Blair, Nina Foch, Charles Cane, Harry Von Zell. Good casting highlights well-done film of Russell at the end of her rope when husband dies and she seeks the cause. ◗

Guilty, The (1947) **70m.** **½ D: John Reinhardt. Bonita Granville, Don Castle, Wally Cassell, Regis Toomey. At times engaging murder yarn; twin sisters clash over their love for Castle.

Guilty as Hell (1932) **78m.** *** D: Erle C. Kenton. Edmund Lowe, Victor McLaglen, Richard Arlen, Adrienne Ames, Henry Stephenson, Ralph Ince, Noel Francis. Doctor strangles his unfaithful young wife, frames her lover, and manipulates the cops as they send innocent man to the gallows, only to see his perfect crime unravel at the last moment. Entertaining thriller with stylishly mobile camerawork (by Karl Struss), strong injections of black comedy, and wisecracking banter from reporter Lowe and police captain McLaglen. Remade in 1937 as NIGHT CLUB SCANDAL.

Guilty Assignment SEE: **Big Town**

Guilty Bystander (1950) **92m.** **½ D: Joseph Lerner. Zachary Scott, Faye Emerson, Mary Boland, Sam Levene, Kay Medford. Down-and-out ex-house detective finds new zest for life when estranged wife reports their child kidnapped.

Guilty Generation, The (1931) **81m.** *** D: Rowland V. Lee. Leo Carrillo, Constance Cummings, Robert Young, Boris Karloff, Emma Dunn, Leslie Fenton. *Romeo and Juliet* is transposed to the underworld, as a bootlegger's son (Young) changes his name and disavows his father (Karloff), then falls for the daughter (Cummings) of his father's vicious rival (Carrillo). Well-acted, little-known gangster film with a powerful climax. ◗

Guilty Hands (1931) **71m.** *** D: W. S. Van Dyke. Lionel Barrymore, Kay Francis, Madge Evans, William Bakewell, C. Aubrey Smith, Polly Moran, Alan Mowbray.

Former D.A. Barrymore tells unscrupulous lothario Mowbray that he'll kill him—and get away with it—if he dares to go through with his plan to marry Lionel's daughter. First-rate whodunit-style drama with imaginative camerawork, a solid script, some real plot twists, and an unusually lively performance from Barrymore.

Guilty of Treason (1950) **86m.** ** D: Felix E. Feist. Charles Bickford, Paul Kelly, Bonita Granville, Richard Derr, Roland Winters, John Banner. Grim, preachy Red Scare time capsule about a foreign correspondent (Kelly) in Hungary, where the commies are painting liberty-loving Josef Cardinal Mindszenty (Bickford) as an anti-Semite and traitor. Granville is fatally miscast as a Hungarian schoolteacher.▼▶

Gulliver's Travels (1939) **C-74m.** **½ D: Dave Fleischer. Singing voices of Lanny Ross, Jessica Dragonette. Max Fleischer's feature-length cartoon version of Jonathan Swift tale suffers from weak scripting, never getting audience involved in story. Towncrier Gabby is obnoxious, but he's got film's most memorable song, "All's Well."▼●▶

Gun Battle at Monterey (1957) **67m.** *½ D: Carl G. Hittleman, Sidney A. Franklin, Jr. Sterling Hayden, Pamela Duncan, Mary Beth Hughes, Lee Van Cleef, Byron Foulger, Ted de Corsia. Unremarkable oater with stern Hayden the gunslinger out for revenge against former friend.

Gun Belt (1953) **C-77m.** **½ D: Ray Nazarro. George Montgomery, Tab Hunter, Helen Westcott, John Dehner, William Bishop, Jack Elam, Douglas Kennedy, James Millican. Fairly tense Western programmer about Dehner trying to persuade his brother (Montgomery) to join him on the wrong side of the law. Wyatt Earp and his brother and the Ringo clan are all character names but this is strictly Hollywood fodder. Remade as FIVE GUNS TO TOMBSTONE (1961)▶

Gun Brothers (1956) **79m.** ** D: Sidney Salkow. Buster Crabbe, Ann Robinson, Neville Brand, Michael Ansara. Innocuous Western of two brothers, one who becomes a rancher, the other an outlaw who wants to go straight.▶

Gun Crazy (1949) **86m.** ***½ D: Joseph H. Lewis. Peggy Cummins, John Dall, Berry Kroeger, Morris Carnovsky, Anabel Shaw, Harry Lewis, Nedrick Young, Rusty (Russ) Tamblyn. Knockout of a sleeper in the BONNIE AND CLYDE tradition, stylishly (and sometimes startlingly) directed. Cummins is femme fatale who leads guncrazy Dall into life of crime. Screenplay credited to MacKinlay Kantor and Millard Kaufman (who was "fronting" for then-blacklisted writer Dalton Trumbo), from Kantor's *Saturday Evening Post* story. Aka DEADLY IS THE FEMALE. Loosely remade in 1992.▼▶

Gun Duel in Durango (1957) **73m.** ** D: Sidney Salkow. George Montgomery, Ann Robinson, Steve Brodie, Bobby Clark, Frank Ferguson, Donald Barry. Montgomery tries to go straight—and look after a young boy—but his old gang won't let him. Adequate Montgomery vehicle.▶

Gun Fever (1958) **83m.** ** D: Mark Stevens. Mark Stevens, John Lupton, Larry Storch, Jana Davi (Maureen Hingert), Aaron Saxon, Iron Eyes Cody. Stevens also co-scripted this dusty, atmospheric little Western about a prospector who seeks revenge against the lout who's been agitating the Sioux and is also responsible for the murder of his parents.

Gunfight at Comanche Creek (1964) **C-90m.** *½ D: Frank McDonald. Audie Murphy, Colleen Miller, Ben Cooper, DeForest Kelley, Jan Merlin, John Hubbard. Undistinguished Western. Detective Murphy infiltrates gang of outlaws forcing wanted men to participate in robberies, then killing them to collect reward money. Panavision.▶

Gunfight at Dodge City, The (1959) **C-81m.** ** D: Joseph M. Newman. Joel McCrea, Julie Adams, John McIntire, Nancy Gates, Richard Anderson, James Westerfield. McCrea plays Bat Masterson, who cleans up outlaw-ridden town with ironic results. CinemaScope.▶

Gunfight at the O.K. Corral (1957) **C-122m.** *** D: John Sturges. Burt Lancaster, Kirk Douglas, Rhonda Fleming, Jo Van Fleet, John Ireland, Lee Van Cleef, Frank Faylen, Kenneth Tobey, DeForest Kelley, Earl Holliman, Dennis Hopper, Martin Milner, Olive Carey. Stimulating Western filled with tense action sequences in recreation of Doc Holliday–Wyatt Earp battle in streets of Tombstone with Clanton gang. Written by Leon Uris. Frankie Laine sings title song. VistaVision.▼●▶

Gunfighter, The (1950) **84m.** ***½ D: Henry King. Gregory Peck, Helen Westcott, Millard Mitchell, Jean Parker, Karl Malden, Skip Homeier, Verna Felton, Ellen Corby, Richard Jaeckel, Alan Hale, Jr. Peck is most impressive as gunslinger trying to overcome his bloody past. Classic psychological Western scripted by William Bowers and William Sellers; story by Bowers and Andre de Toth. Exteriors shot in Lone Pine, California. Catch this one! ▼●▶

Gunfighters (1947) **C-87m.** **½ D: George Waggner. Randolph Scott, Barbara Britton, Dorothy Hart, Bruce Cabot, Charles Grapewin, Forrest Tucker. Strictly average story of gunfighter who vows never again to spill blood. Good cast, but there must be 50 like this one.

Gunfighters of Casa Grande (1964-U.S.-Spanish) **C-92m.** ** D: Roy Rowland. Alex Nicol, Jorge Mistral, Dick Bentley, Steve Rowland, Phil Posner. After the Civil

War, outlaw Nicol rustles up some cattle in Mexico and leads the herd to beef-starved Texas, but faces opposition from rival banditos and members of his own gang. Talky Western helped by scenic locations in Spain. Based on a story by Borden and Patricia Chase. CinemaScope. ▶

Gunfire at Indian Gap (1958) 70m. ** D: Joseph Kane. Vera Ralston, Anthony George, George Macready, John Doucette, Barry Kelley, Glenn Strange. Ralston falls in love with stagecoach robbery suspect George, while the real culprit (Macready) hatches his plans. Blah cast in tolerable widescreen B Western. Naturama.

Gun for a Coward (1957) C-73m. **½ D: Abner Biberman. Fred MacMurray, Jeffrey Hunter, Janice Rule, Chill Wills, Dean Stockwell, Josephine Hutchinson. MacMurray is rancher whose two younger brothers have contrasting personalities; predictable results. CinemaScope. ▶

Gun Fury (1953) C-83m. *** D: Raoul Walsh. Rock Hudson, Donna Reed, Phil Carey, Roberta Haynes, Leo Gordon, Lee Marvin, Neville Brand. Hudson seeks revenge after being left for dead by cynical outlaw Carey, who's also kidnapped his fiancée (Reed). Action-packed Western, shot on beautiful Arizona locations. Originally shown in 3-D. ▼●▶

Gunga Din (1939) 117m. **** D: George Stevens. Cary Grant, Victor McLaglen, Douglas Fairbanks, Jr., Joan Fontaine, Sam Jaffe, Eduardo Ciannelli, Montagu Love, Abner Biberman, Robert Coote, Lumsden Hare, Cecil Kellaway. *The* Hollywood action-adventure yarn, vaguely based on Rudyard Kipling's famous poem, about three soldier-comrades in 19th-century India battling the savage thuggee cult when they aren't busy carousing and getting into trouble. Water boy Jaffe saves the day in rousing climax. Splendid comic adventure whose story is credited to Ben Hecht and Charles MacArthur (who based the relationships of the central characters on the same marriage/rivalry device used in *The Front Page*); scripted by Joel Sayre and Fred Guiol. For years most prints ran 96m., until film was archivally restored. Shot on location in Lone Pine, California. Also shown in computer-colored version. Remade as SERGEANTS THREE. ▼●▶

Gung Ho! (1943) 88m. **½ D: Ray Enright. Randolph Scott, Grace McDonald, Alan Curtis, Noah Beery, Jr., J. Carrol Naish, David Bruce, Robert Mitchum, Sam Levene. Typical WW2 action film is marked by outrageous jingoism, celebrating the bloodthirsty misfits of the "gung ho" squadron as great American patriots. A jaw-dropping experience. Also shown in computer-colored version. ▼▶

Gun Glory (1957) C-89m. ** D: Roy Rowland. Stewart Granger, Rhonda Flem-

ing, Chill Wills, James Gregory. Granger is reformed gunslinger rejected by his community until outlaw rampage allows him to redeem himself. CinemaScope. ▼▶

Gun Hawk, The (1963) C-92m. **½ D: Edward Ludwig. Rory Calhoun, Rod Cameron, Ruta Lee, John Litel, Rod Lauren, Morgan Woodward, Robert J. Wilke. Outlaw Calhoun attempts to reform Lauren, who's heading for criminal life. ▶

Gunman in the Streets (1950-French-U.S.) 86m. *** D: Frank Tuttle. Dane Clark, Simone Signoret, Fernand Gravet, Robert Duke, Michel Andre. Interesting film noir about a gangster on the lam in France who turns to his girlfriend for money—and a way out of the country. Notable for Eugen Schüfftan's cinematography, which makes great use of Paris locations, and an early appearance by sultry Signoret. Never released theatrically in the U.S. Aka GANGSTER AT BAY and TIME RUNNING OUT. ▶

Gunman's Walk (1958) C-97m. *** D: Phil Karlson. Van Heflin, Tab Hunter, Kathryn Grant (Crosby), James Darren. Rancher Heflin tries to train sons Hunter and Darren to be respectable citizens, but clashing personalities cause outburst of violence. Tight-knit Western. CinemaScope. ▼

Gun Moll SEE: **Jigsaw**

Gunpowder Valley SEE: **Devil's Playground, The** (1946)

Gun Runners, The (1958) 83m. ** D: Don Siegel. Audie Murphy, Eddie Albert, Patricia Owens, Everett Sloane, Jack Elam. Murphy is involved with gun-smuggling to Cuba in this bland remake of TO HAVE AND HAVE NOT. ▶

Guns and Guitars (1936) 58m. *** D: Joseph Kane. Gene Autry, Smiley Burnette, Dorothy Dix, Earle Hodgins, J. P. McGowan, Harrison Greene. Gene and Smiley, members of Hodgins' medicine show, get mixed up in a battle for sheriff and control of a valley's cattle herds as McGowan and Greene mastermind a plot to get their diseased cattle through to market over Dix's property. A fan favorite among Autry's early Westerns. Gene sings the title tune. ▶

Guns at Batasi (1964-British) 103m. **½ D: John Guillermin. Richard Attenborough, Jack Hawkins, Mia Farrow, Flora Robson, John Leyton. Acting is all in this intelligent if predictable account of British military life in present-day Africa. CinemaScope. ▼▶

Guns, Girls and Gangsters (1959) 70m. ** D: Edward L. Cahn. Mamie Van Doren, Gerald Mohr, Lee Van Cleef, Grant Richards, Elaine Edwards, John Baer, Carlo Fiore, Paul Fix. Classic 1950s trash, with the pneumatic Mamie in her prime as a Vegas nightclub singer drawn into scheme to rip off an armored truck carrying casino winnings. Vigorous direction and diverting cast.

Gunsight Ridge (1957) 85m. **½ D: Francis D. Lyon. Joel McCrea, Mark Stevens, Joan Weldon, Addison Richards, Darlene Fields, Carolyn Craig, Slim Pickens, Jody McCrea, L. Q. Jones, Morgan Woodward. McCrea is an undercover agent tracking outlaw Stevens (a onetime concert pianist!) in this above-average Western programmer. ▶

Gunslinger (1956) C-83m. *½ D: Roger Corman. John Ireland, Beverly Garland, Allison Hayes, Martin Kingsley. Strange little Western of female marshal trying to maintain law and order in outlaw-ridden town. ▼▶

Gun Smoke (1931) 71m. *** D: Edward Sloman. Richard Arlen, Mary Brian, William "Stage" Boyd, Eugene Pallette, Charles Winninger, Louise Fazenda, Brooks Benedict, Dawn O'Day (Anne Shirley). Big-city crooks descend on a Western town, where they're mistaken for investors and welcomed by everyone but rancher Arlen, who sees through them right away. Unusually tough, violent Western for its day; Arlen even gives a contemporary-sounding pro-ecology speech opposing development!

Gunsmoke (1953) C-79m. **½ D: Nathan Juran. Audie Murphy, Susan Cabot, Paul Kelly, Charles Drake, Jack Kelly. Compact Western with Murphy reforming to run a ranch and marry his employer's daughter. ▼

Gunsmoke in Tucson (1958) C-80m. **½ D: Thomas Carr. Mark Stevens, Forrest Tucker, Gale Robbins, Vaughn Taylor, John Ward, Kevin Hagen, John Cliff, Gail Kobe. Two sons of a hanged horse thief grow up on opposite sides of the law, leading to the inevitable showdown (albeit with a twist). Formulaic plot given a boost by strong performances and vigorous action. CinemaScope. ▶

Guns of August, The (1964) 99m. *** D: Nathan Kroll. Straightforward documentary about World War 1 spans the period from Edward VII's funeral (1910) through the final Armistice eight years later. Highly competent, if not exceptional, adaptation of Barbara Tuchman's best-seller utilizes lots of rare combat footage from the time. Well worth a look. ▼▶

Guns of Darkness (1962-British) 95m. **½ D: Anthony Asquith. David Niven, Leslie Caron, David Opatoshu, James Robertson Justice, Eleanor Summerfield, Ian Hunter. Civilized drama of Niven searching for life's meaning, set in South America. ▶

Guns of Fort Petticoat, The (1957) C-82m. *** D: George Marshall. Audie Murphy, Kathryn Grant (Crosby), Hope Emerson, Jeff Donnell, Isobel Elsom. Most enjoyable Western, with Army deserter Murphy supervising a group of Texas women in the art of warfare against impending Indian attack.

Guns of Navarone, The (1961) C-157m. ***½ D: J. Lee Thompson. Gregory Peck,

David Niven, Anthony Quinn, Stanley Baker, Anthony Quayle, James Darren, Irene Papas, Gia Scala, James Robertson Justice, Richard Harris, Albert Lieven, Bryan Forbes, Walter Gotell. Explosive action film about Allied commandos during WW2 plotting to destroy German guns; high-powered adventure throughout this first-rate production, highlighted by Oscar-winning special effects. Script by Carl Foreman from the Alistair MacLean novel. Sequel: FORCE 10 FROM NAVARONE. CinemaScope. ▼▶

Gun That Won the West, The (1955) C-71m. ** D: William Castle. Dennis Morgan, Paula Raymond, Richard Denning, Robert Bice. Harmless Grade-B Western of cavalry's use of Springfield rifles to put down Indian uprising. ▶

Gun the Man Down (1956) 78m. ** D: Andrew V. McLaglen. James Arness, Angie Dickinson, Robert Wilke, Emile Meyer, Harry Carey, Jr. Wounded Arness swears revenge on the cohorts (and his fiancée!) who abandoned him when a holdup went wrong. Sleepy Western drama produced by John Wayne's Batjac company. ▶

Guy Named Joe, A (1943) 120m. **½ D: Victor Fleming. Spencer Tracy, Irene Dunne, Van Johnson, Ward Bond, James Gleason, Lionel Barrymore, Barry Nelson, Esther Williams, Don DeFore. Good cast flounders in meandering fantasy about WW2 pilot Tracy coming back to Earth to give young serviceman Johnson a hand in his romance with Tracy's girlfriend Dunne. Remade in 1989 as ALWAYS. ▼▶

Guys and Dolls (1955) C-150m. *** D: Joseph L. Mankiewicz. Marlon Brando, Jean Simmons, Frank Sinatra, Vivian Blaine, Stubby Kaye, B. S. Pully, Veda Ann Borg, Sheldon Leonard, Regis Toomey. Lavish Hollywoodization of classic Broadway musical based on Damon Runyon's colorful characters with Blaine, Kaye, Pully, and Johnny Silver reprising their stage performances and Brando making a not-bad musical debut as gambler Sky Masterson. Tuneful Frank Loesser score includes "Fugue for Tinhorns," "If I Were a Bell," "Luck Be a Lady," Blaine's memorable "Adelaide's Lament," and Stubby's showstopping "Sit Down, You're Rockin' the Boat." CinemaScope. ▼▶

Guy Who Came Back, The (1951) 91m. ** D: Joseph M. Newman. Paul Douglas, Linda Darnell, Joan Bennett, Don DeFore, Zero Mostel. Cast is above such material but does well by it: ex-football star tries to "find himself."

Guy With a Grin SEE: **No Time for Comedy**

Gypsy (1962) C-149m. *** D: Mervyn LeRoy. Rosalind Russell, Natalie Wood, Karl Malden, Paul Wallace, Betty Bruce, Parley Baer, Harvey Korman. Entertaining screen version of bittersweet Broadway musical about the ultimate stage mother, Mama Rose, and her daughters Baby June (Havoc) and Gypsy Rose Lee. Can't lose with that Stephen Sondheim–Jule Styne score. Suzanne Cupito (Morgan Brittany) and Ann Jilliann (Jillian) both play young June. Remade as a TVM in 1993 with Bette Midler. Technirama. ▼◐▷

Gypsy and the Gentleman, The (1958-British) **C-107m.** **½ D: Joseph Losey. Melina Mercouri, Keith Michell, Patrick McGoohan, Flora Robson. Mercouri as fiery gypsy makes a spicy drama of her love affair with a member of the nobility.

Gypsy Colt (1954) **C-72m.** **½ D: Andrew Marton. Donna Corcoran, Ward Bond, Frances Dee, Larry Keating. Tender film of faithful horse who returns to mistress after parents sell it to racing stable. Remake of LASSIE COME HOME. ▼▷

Gypsy Fury (1949-Swedish-French) **63m.** ** D: Christian-Jaque. Viveca Lindfors, Christopher Kent (Alf Kjellin), Edvin Adolphson, Lauritz Falk, Naima Wifstrand, Michel Auclair. Fable about a gypsy (Lindfors) and the aristocratic knight who becomes smitten with her—even though (gasp!) he's set to wed another. So-so. Released in the U.S. in 1951.

Gypsy Wildcat (1944) **C-75m.** ** D: Roy William Neill. Maria Montez, Jon Hall, Nigel Bruce, Leo Carrillo, Gale Sondergaard, Douglass Dumbrille. Lowbrow saga of princess raised by gypsies; colorful, splashy, but routine. James M. Cain was one of the writers! ▷

Hail! Mafia. (1965) **89m.** **½ D: Raoul Levy. Henry Silva, Jack Klugman, Eddie Constantine, Elsa Martinelli, Micheline Presle. Fairly interesting melodrama about hired killers going after a witness to gangland mayhem; has some good European players and nice photography by Raoul Coutard. ▼▷

Hail the Conquering Hero (1944) **101m.** **** D: Preston Sturges. Eddie Bracken, Ella Raines, Raymond Walburn, William Demarest, Bill Edwards, Elizabeth Patterson, Jimmy Conlin, Franklin Pangborn, Jack Norton, Paul Porcasi, Al Bridge. Frail Bracken, rejected by Marine Corps, is mistaken for war hero by home town. Satirical Sturges at his best, with Demarest and Pangborn stealing much of the crazed proceedings. ▼◐▷

Hairy Ape, The (1944) **90m.** ** D: Alfred Santell. William Bendix, Susan Hayward, John Loder, Alan Napier, Dorothy Comingore, Eddie Kane. One-note drama of bestial ship stoker Bendix's obsession with wealthy, bitchy passenger Hayward. Disappointing version of Eugene O'Neill play. ▼▷

Half a Hero (1953) **71m.** ** D: Don Weis. Red Skelton, Jean Hagen, Charles Dingle, Willard Waterman, Mary Wickes, Polly Bergen. Subdued Skelton vehicle written

by Max Shulman casts him in situation-comedy mold, as N.Y. magazine writer who tries suburban life. Pretty bland. ▷

Half Angel (1951) **C-77m.** **½ D: Richard Sale. Loretta Young, Joseph Cotten, Cecil Kellaway, Basil Ruysdael, Jim Backus, Irene Ryan, John Ridgely. Pleasant comedy of Young blessed with sleepwalking troubles, leading to romantic complications. ▷

Half-Breed, The (1952) **C-81m.** ** D: Stuart Gilmore. Robert Young, Janis Carter, Jack Buetel, Barton MacLane, Reed Hadley, Porter Hall, Connie Gilchrist. Unexceptional Western with slimy Hadley scheming to agitate Apaches whose reservation sits atop some valuable ore. Caught in the middle are gambler Young, entertainer Carter, and half-breed Buetel. Young's character is named Daniel Craig! ▼▷

Half Human (1955-Japanese) **70m.** *½ D: Ishiro Honda, Kenneth Crane. John Carradine, Morris Ankrum, Russ Thorson, Robert Karnes. Americans Carradine, Karnes, Ankrum, et al. are spliced into Japanese film about an abominable snowmanlike monster and his son(!). There are indications that the original Japanese film might be OK. This version isn't. Almost no dubbing, just Carradine's narration. Full title on-screen is HALF HUMAN: THE STORY OF THE ABOMINABLE SNOWMAN. ▼▷

Half Naked Truth, The (1932) **77m.** *** D: Gregory LaCava. Lupe Velez, Lee Tracy, Eugene Pallette, Frank Morgan. Delightful comedy about wiseguy carnival pitchman (Tracy) scheming to make Velez an instant celebrity; plenty of laughs, and wonderful performance by Morgan as neurotic Ziegfeld-ish producer. ▷

Half Shot at Sunrise (1930) **78m.** **½ D: Paul Sloane. Bert Wheeler, Robert Woolsey, Edna May Oliver, Dorothy Lee, George MacFarlane. Pretty funny Wheeler and Woolsey comedy (their first starring vehicle) has them as WW1 soldiers AWOL in Paris and featured in a variety of misogynistic episodes as the military police close in. Best of all: the mock ballet. ▼▷

Halfway House, The (1943-British) **95m.** **½ D: Basil Dearden. Mervyn Johns, Glynis Johns, Françoise Rosay, Tom Walls, Alfred Drayton, Sally Ann Howes. Pleasant but low-key fantasy of disparate people brought together at mysterious country inn run by quiet but all-seeing Johns and his daughter (father and daughter in real life). ▼

Hallelujah (1929) **106m.** ***½ D: King Vidor. Daniel L. Haynes, Nina Mae McKinney, William Fountaine, Everett McGarrity, Victoria Spivey. King Vidor's early talkie triumph, a stylized view of black life focusing on a Southern cotton-picker who becomes a preacher but retains all-too-human weaknesses. Dated in some aspects and

[275]

unabashedly melodramatic, but still quite moving. Beautifully filmed on location, with outstanding musical sequences.▼●▶
Hallelujah I'm a Bum (1933) 82m. ***½ D: Lewis Milestone. Al Jolson, Madge Evans, Frank Morgan, Harry Langdon, Chester Conklin, Tyler Brooke, Edgar Connor. Fascinating Depression curio about a hobo who tries to "reform" for the sake of a beautiful woman. Provocative, politically savvy script by Ben Hecht and S. N. Behrman, rhyming dialogue and lovely songs by Rodgers and Hart (who also make cameo appearances as a photographer and a bank clerk, respectively), and winning performances all around. Beware edited prints (reissue title: THE HEART OF NEW YORK) and the frequently screened British version, cut and redubbed as HALLELUJAH I'M A TRAMP.▼●▶

Hallelujah Trail, The (1965) C-165m. **½ D: John Sturges. Burt Lancaster, Lee Remick, Jim Hutton, Brian Keith, Martin Landau, Donald Pleasence, Pamela Tiffin; narrated by John Dehner. Remick is rambunctious temperance leader out to stop cavalry-guarded shipment of whiskey en route to thirsting Denver miners; amiable but lumbering Western satire goes on and on. Includes an overture, intermission/entr'acte, exit music; other prints run 159m. Ultra Panavision 70.▼●▶

Halliday Brand, The (1957) 77m. **½ D: Joseph H. Lewis. Joseph Cotten, Viveca Lindfors, Betsy Blair, Ward Bond. Brooding Western about rancher whose domination of family and workers leads to gunplay and revenge. Weak script; strong performances.▶

Halls of Montezuma (1951) C-113m. *** D: Lewis Milestone. Richard Widmark, Karl Malden, Walter (Jack) Palance, Reginald Gardiner, Richard Wagner, Richard Hylton, Richard Boone, Skip Homeier, Jack Webb, Bert Freed, Neville Brand, Martin Milner, Philip Ahn. Gung-ho salute to the U.S. Marines as a squadron embarks on a typically rugged WW2 Pacific island invasion, with flashbacks to various men's civilian lives. Especially notable for a cast filled with future stars . . . including real-life ex-Marine Brand.▼▶

Hal Roach Comedy Carnival SEE: **Curley** and **Fabulous Joe, The**

Hamlet (1948-British) 153m. **** D: Laurence Olivier. Laurence Olivier, Eileen Herlie, Basil Sydney, Felix Aylmer, Jean Simmons, Stanley Holloway, Peter Cushing. Brilliant adaptation of Shakespeare's play about Danish prince "who just couldn't make up his mind." Won Oscars for Best Picture, Best Actor (Olivier), Art Direction–Set Decoration, and Costumes.▼●▶

Hand, The (1960-British) 60m. *½ D: Henry Cass. Derek Farr, Ronald Leigh Hunt, Reed De Rouen, Ray Cooney. Odd, infuriatingly muddled mystery in which a Scotland Yard inspector investigates the amputation of an old drunk's hand and in so doing uncovers a fiendish plot.▼▶

Hand in Hand (1960-British) 75m. **½ D: Philip Leacock. Loretta Parry, Philip Needs, John Gregson, Sybil Thorndike. Good film with a moral for children, about a Jewish girl and a Catholic boy who become friends and learn about each other. Adults may find it hard to take at times.▶

Handle With Care (1958) 82m. **½ D: David Friedkin. Dean Jones, Joan O'Brien, Thomas Mitchell, John Smith, Walter Abel. Earnest minor film about law student Jones investigating crime within the town where classmates are assigned mock grand-jury work.

Hands Across the Border (1944) 72m. *½ D: Joseph Kane. Roy Rogers, Ruth Terry, Guinn "Big Boy" Williams, Onslow Stevens, Mary Treen, Joseph Crehan, Duncan Renaldo, LeRoy Mason, Roy Barcroft, The Wiere Brothers, Bob Nolan and the Sons of the Pioneers. Roy and his pals help the daughter (Terry) of a murdered rancher find the killer. This was the first Rogers film to go way overboard on singing, dancing, and specialty acts at the expense of story. One of Rogers' worst starring vehicles.▼▶

Hands Across the Table (1935) 80m. *** D: Mitchell Leisen. Carole Lombard, Fred MacMurray, Ralph Bellamy, Astrid Allwyn, Marie Prevost. Lombard sparkles as fortune-hunting manicurist who has to choose between glib gigolo MacMurray and wheelchair-bound Bellamy.▼▶

Hands of a Stranger (1962) 86m. **½ D: Newton Arnold. Paul Lukather, Joan Harvey, James Stapleton, Irish McCalla, Barry Gordon, Sally Kellerman. Entertaining and well-directed little chiller is an unacknowledged fourth version of THE HANDS OF ORLAC. Brilliant young pianist's hands are injured in a car accident; idealistic surgeon replaces them with those of a just-deceased criminal.▼▶

Hands of Orlac, The (1924-Austrian) 81m. *** D: Robert Wiene. Conrad Veidt, Fritz Kortner, Carmen Cartellieri, Alexandra Sorina, Fritz Strassny. Veidt is an eerie presence as Paul Orlac, a celebrated pianist whose hands are crushed in a train wreck; a strange doctor replaces them with those of an executed killer. Genuinely spooky chiller, adapted from the Maurice Renard story and made by the director of THE CABINET OF DR. CALIGARI. Remade in 1935 (as MAD LOVE) and 1961.▼▶

Hands of Orlac, The (1960-British-French) 95m. ** D: Edmond T. Greville. Mel Ferrer, Lucile Saint-Simon, Christopher Lee, Dany Carrel, Felix Aylmer, Basil Sydney, Donald Wolfit, Donald Pleasence. Pianist gets hand transplant from a strange doctor—and finds he has the impulse to kill. Flat remake of Maurice Renard's famous story, filmed before in 1925 and (as MAD LOVE) in 1935. French-language version runs 105m. Also known as HANDS OF THE STRANGLER.▼▶

Hands over the City (1963-Italian) **101m. *** D: Francesco Rosi. Rod Steiger, Salvo Randone, Guido Alberti, Marcello Cannavale, Dante Di Pinto, Alberto Conocchia, Carlo Fermariello, Terenzio Cordova. The collapse of a building in a Naples slum triggers a series of shady political schemes and backroom deals, as a ruthless land developer (Steiger) uses his position as a city councilman to manipulate the investigation to his advantage. Fiery critique of civic corruption and capitalist greed in the name of "progress" is vividly filmed on location, using many real-life Neapolitan politicians in the cast.▶

Hanging Tree, The (1959) **C-106m. *** D: Delmer Daves. Gary Cooper, Maria Schell, Karl Malden, George C. Scott, Karl Swenson, Ben Piazza, Virginia Gregg. Literate, low-key Western with outstanding performance by Schell as a blind girl nursed by Cooper, a frontier doctor with a past. Not for all tastes. Scott's first film.▼▶

Hangman, The (1959) **86m. ** D: Michael Curtiz. Robert Taylor, Tina Louise, Fess Parker, Jack Lord, Mickey Shaughnessy, Shirley Harmer. Rugged Taylor is the lawman who must buck the entire Western town defending a man wanted for murder. ▶

Hangman's House (1928) **72m. *** D: John Ford. June Collyer, Larry Kent, Earle Foxe, Victor McLaglen, Hobart Bosworth. Florid melodrama of frustrated romance and family honor, with Collyer acceding to her father's wishes and marrying blackguard Foxe despite her love for Kent. Elevated by sumptuous production and Ford's sure direction, with McLaglen playing a character who is the polar opposite of his role in THE INFORMER. Steeplechase scene predates the one in THE QUIET MAN and you can spot young John Wayne as one of the animated spectators along the racetrack railing!▼▶

Hangman's Knot (1952) **C-81m. *** D: Roy Huggins. Randolph Scott, Donna Reed, Claude Jarman, Jr., Frank Faylen, Glenn Langan, Richard Denning, Lee Marvin, Jeanette Nolan, Clem Bevans, Ray Teal, Guinn "Big Boy" Williams. Above-par Western involving Rebels, led by officer Scott, robbing Union gold shipment, unaware that the Civil War has ended. Nifty Western offers a potent (and still-timely) exploration of hypocrisy and greed. Written by Huggins. ▼▶

Hangmen Also Die! (1943) **135m. **½ D: Fritz Lang. Brian Donlevy, Walter Brennan, Anna Lee, Gene Lockhart, Dennis O'Keefe, Lionel Stander. OK WW2 drama, loosely based on fact and spotlighting the resistance by Czech citizens against their Nazi occupiers and the plight of Donlevy after he assassinates Reinhard Heydrich, Nazi governor of Prague. Based on a story by Lang and Bertolt Brecht, which is also told in HITLER'S MADMAN. Newest restoration includes a one-minute coda long missing from U.S. prints. ▼▶

Hangover, The SEE: **Female Jungle**

Hangover Square (1945) **77m. *** D: John Brahm. Laird Cregar, Linda Darnell, George Sanders, Glenn Langan, Faye Marlowe, Alan Napier, Frederic Worlock. Cregar (in his final film) is delicious as unhinged composer who goes off his top and kills women whenever he hears loud, discordant noises. Barre Lyndon's script bears little relation to the Patrick Hamilton novel, but result is still entertaining, with superb Victorian London sets and evocative Bernard Herrmann score.▶

Hannah Lee SEE: **Outlaw Territory**

Hannibal (1960-U.S.-Italian) **C-103m. ** D: Edgar G. Ulmer. Victor Mature, Rita Gam, Gabriele Ferzetti, Milly Vitale. Cardboard costume saga follows Hannibal and his elephants across the Alps and into Rome . . . but *you* may not last that long. SuperCinescope.▼▶

Hans Christian Andersen (1952) **C-112m. **½ D: Charles Vidor. Danny Kaye, Farley Granger, Jeanmaire, Roland Petit, John Qualen. Melodic Frank Loesser score ("Inchworm," "Ugly Duckling," "Thumbelina," etc.) can't save musical biography of vagabond tale-teller. Glossy and completely fabricated—has no relation to real Andersen's life story. ▼▶

Hans Le Marin SEE: **Wicked City**

Happiest Days of Your Life, The (1950-British) **84m. *** D: Frank Launder. Alastair Sim, Margaret Rutherford, Guy Middleton, Joyce Grenfell, Edward Rigby, Muriel Aked, John Bentley, Bernadette O'Farrell, Richard Wattis, Pat (Patricia) Owens. Funny comedy involving a boys' school sharing quarters with a displaced girls' academy, with frantic situations resulting. Launder and John Dighton scripted, from the latter's play.▼

Happiness (1965) SEE: **Le Bonheur**

Happiness Ahead (1934) **86m. **½ D: Mervyn LeRoy. Dick Powell, Josephine Hutchinson, Frank McHugh, John Halliday, Allen Jenkins, Ruth Donnelly. Pleasant little film about wealthy heiress pretending to be poor when she meets likable working-stiff Powell. No production numbers, really, but several nice songs, including "Pop Goes Your Heart."▶

Happy Anniversary (1959) **81m. **½ D: David Miller. David Niven, Mitzi Gaynor, Carl Reiner, Loring Smith, Monique Van Vooren, Patty Duke, Elizabeth Wilson. Funny but strained comedy of married couple Niven and Gaynor being embarrassed by daughter Duke telling nation on TV that father was indiscreet in his younger days.

Happy Days (1930) **84m.** ** D: Benjamin Stoloff. Charles E. Evans, Marjorie White, Richard Keene, Stuart Erwin, Janet Gaynor, Charles Farrell, Will Rogers, Victor McLaglen, Edmund Lowe, Warner Baxter, El Brendel, William Collier, Sr., Tom Patricola, George Jessel, Dixie Lee, Nick Stuart, Rex Bell, Frank Albertson, Walter Catlett, Ann Pennington, James J. Corbett, George Olsen and His Orchestra. Yet another all-star early talkie, this one from Fox uses—p.c. alert!—a minstrel show as its centerpiece. Special material is less than inspired (Baxter does card tricks), though Rogers and especially Jessel are very funny in a scene at an actors' club. Big musical numbers substitute size for ingenuity. Also filmed in 70mm Grandeur.

Happy Ever After SEE: **Tonight's the Night**

Happy Go Lovely (1951-British) **C-87m.** ** D: Bruce Humberstone. David Niven, Vera-Ellen, Cesar Romero, Bobby Howes, Diane Hart, Gordon Jackson. The charm of its three stars uplifts this otherwise minor musical-romance, set in Edinburgh, with chorus girl Vera-Ellen getting the lead in a show when the director (Romero) thinks she's about to wed a millionaire (Niven) she's never met.▼❚

Happy Go Lucky (1943) **C-81m.** **½ D: Curtis Bernhardt. Mary Martin, Dick Powell, Eddie Bracken, Betty Hutton, Rudy Vallee, Mabel Paige, Eric Blore. Happy little musical has Martin chasing millionaire Vallee on Caribbean cruise. Songs include "Murder He Says."❚

Happy Is the Bride (1957-British) **84m.** ** D: Roy Boulting. Ian Carmichael, Janette Scott, Cecil Parker, Terry-Thomas, Joyce Grenfell, John Le Mesurier, Eric Barker, Athene Seyler. Remake of 1940's QUIET WEDDING, a mild farce about a young couple's headaches as their families prepare for their nuptials. Seyler repeats her role from the original as a helpful aunt.

Happy Land (1943) **73m.** **½ D: Irving Pichel. Don Ameche, Frances Dee, Harry Carey, Ann Rutherford, Cara Williams, Richard Crane, Henry (Harry) Morgan, Dickie Moore. Sincere but not always successful Americana of grieving father learning meaning of war as he questions his son's death in WW2. Five-year-old Natalie Wood's first feature.❚

Happy Landing (1938) **102m.** **½ D: Roy Del Ruth. Sonja Henie, Don Ameche, Cesar Romero, Ethel Merman, Jean Hersholt, Billy Gilbert. Predictable Henie vehicle is not up to her other musicals. Pilot Ameche lands near her home; romance blossoms instantly.▼❚

Happy Road, The (1957) **100m.** **½ D: Gene Kelly. Gene Kelly, Barbara Laage, Michael Redgrave, Bobby Clark, Brigitte Fossey. Two single parents—American Kelly and Frenchwoman Laage—are drawn together when their children run away from school together. Pleasant but minor family fare, enhanced by location filming in French countryside.❚

Happy Thieves, The (1962) **88m.** **½ D: George Marshall. Rex Harrison, Rita Hayworth, Joseph Wiseman, Gregoire Aslan, Alida Valli. Sad pairing of star duo, out of place in museum theft caper, set in Spain.❚

Happy Time, The (1952) **94m.** ***½ D: Richard Fleischer. Charles Boyer, Louis Jourdan, Bobby Driscoll, Marsha Hunt, Kurt Kasznar, Linda Christian, Marcel Dalio, Jeanette Nolan, Richard Erdman. Charming film about a boy's coming of age in 1920s Ottawa, Canada, amidst a colorful and eccentric family. Driscoll is the adolescent who develops a crush on pretty magician's assistant Christian. Boyer is his understanding father, eternally forgiving of his two wayward brothers (Jourdan and Kasznar, recreating his Broadway role). Earl Felton adapted Samuel A. Taylor's play, based in turn on Robert Fontaine's autobiographical stories.

Happy Years, The (1950) **C-110m.** *** D: William Wellman. Dean Stockwell, Scotty Beckett, Darryl Hickman, Leo G. Carroll, Margalo Gillmore, Leon Ames. High-spirited boy in turn-of-the-20th-century prep school finds he has trouble fitting in. Familiar comedy-drama, adapted from Owen Johnson's *Lawrenceville Stories*, is hardly typical Wellman fare, but well done. Robert Wagner makes his film debut.❚

Harakiri (1919-German) **87m.** **½ D: Fritz Lang. Paul Biensfeldt, Lil Dagover, Georg John, Meinhart Maur, Rudolf Lettinger, Niels Prien. Young Japanese woman (Dagover) is manipulated by an evil, lustful monk, while Europeans and European culture have a considerable impact on her life. Offbeat, little-seen early Lang melodrama, based on *Madame Butterfly* and set in Japan but filmed in Berlin, with German actors.❚

Harakiri (1962-Japanese) **133m.** ***½ D: Masaki Kobayashi. Tatsuya Nakadai, Rentarô Mikuni, Akira Ishihama, Shima Iwashita, Tetsurô Tamba, Masao Mishima, Ichirô Nakaya, Kei Sato, Yoshio Inaba, Yoshiro Aoki. In 1630 Edo, an unemployed Hiroshima samurai begs the Iyi clan to permit his ritual suicide in their courtyard. But is this piteous ronin who he says he is, or just another poverty-stricken mercenary hoping for a handout during peacetime? Potent display of Asian machismo is a tale of desperation and a lesson in honor that plays like a courtroom drama. Scalding angry indictment of noble hypocrisy, rendered in monochromatic imagery, is far too bloody for color. Screenplay by Shinobu Hashimoto, from a story by Yasuhiko Takiguchi. Remade in 2011 as HARA-KIRI: DEATH OF A SAMURAI. Grandscope.❚

Harbor Lights (1963) **68m.** BOMB D:

[278]

Maury Dexter. Kent Taylor, Jeff Morrow, Miriam Colon, Allan Sague. Cheap film of intrigue, with B picture perennial Taylor. Congratulations to anyone who can find some relation between title and what goes on in film. CinemaScope.

Harbor of Missing Men (1950) **60m.** *½ D: R. G. Springsteen. Richard Denning, Barbara Fuller, Steven Geray, George Zucco, Ray Teal, Percy Helton. Unsparkling Republic Pictures programmer with Denning innocently involved with jewel smuggling.

Hard Boiled Mahoney (1947) **63m.** **½ D: William Beaudine. Leo Gorcey, Huntz Hall, Bobby Jordan, Gabriel Dell, Billy Benedict, David Gorcey, Teala Loring, Dan Seymour, Bernard Gorcey, Betty Compson. The Bowery Boys do the sleuth bit, probing a phony fortune-teller racket in this mix of farce and mystery. ▼)

Hard Day's Night, A (1964-British) **85m.** **** D: Richard Lester. John Lennon, Paul McCartney, George Harrison, Ringo Starr, Wilfrid Brambell, Norman Rossington, John Junkin, Victor Spinetti, Anna Quayle. First Beatles film is director Lester's idea of a typical day in the group's life. He lets his imagination run wild; result is a visual delight, with many Beatles songs on the soundtrack (including "Can't Buy Me Love," "And I Love Her," "I Should Have Known Better," and the title tune). Original screenplay by Alun Owen. Reissued in 1982 with a short prologue. ▼○)

Hard Drivin' SEE: **Thunder in Carolina**

Harder They Fall, The (1956) **109m.** ***½ D: Mark Robson. Humphrey Bogart, Rod Steiger, Jan Sterling, Mike Lane, Max Baer, Edward Andrews. Bogart's last feature casts him as cynical sportswriter-turned-press agent who realizes for the first time how badly prizefighters are manipulated by their unfeeling managers. Powerful drama by Budd Schulberg. ▼)

Hard, Fast and Beautiful (1951) **79m.** ** D: Ida Lupino. Claire Trevor, Sally Forrest, Carleton Young, Robert Clarke, Kenneth Patterson. Domineering mother pushes daughter into world of competitive tennis. Straightforward story, awkwardly filmed (and acted) at times. Director Lupino and Robert Ryan make cameo appearances.)

Hard Man, The (1957) **C-80m.** ** D: George Sherman. Guy Madison, Lorne Greene, Valerie French, Trevor Bardette, Barry Atwater, Robert Burton, Rudy Bond. Madison is earnest sheriff who falls in love with murdered rancher's widow.

Hard to Get (1938) **80m.** *** D: Ray Enright. Dick Powell, Olivia de Havilland, Charles Winninger, Allen Jenkins, Bonita Granville, Penny Singleton. Good variation on spoiled-rich-girl-meets-poor-but-hardworking-boy idea. Winninger, as Olivia's wealthy father, and Singleton, as their maid, are hilarious. Film is full of great

supporting comics (Grady Sutton, Thurston Hall, Arthur Housman, etc.), and includes "You Must Have Been a Beautiful Baby.")

Hard to Handle (1933) **78m.** **½ D: Mervyn LeRoy. James Cagney, Mary Brian, Ruth Donnelly, Allen Jenkins, Emma Dunn, Claire Dodd, Robert McWade. Cagney sparkles in this otherwise so-so Depression-era comedy as a fast-talking promoter/hustler who courts pretty Brian; Donnelly is aces as her mom. The "Grapefruit Acres" and diet schemes are homages of sorts to Cagney's legendary scene with Mae Clarke in THE PUBLIC ENEMY.)

Hard to Hold SEE: **Paid to Dance**

Hard Way, The (1943) **109m.** *** D: Vincent Sherman. Ida Lupino, Dennis Morgan, Joan Leslie, Jack Carson, Gladys George, Julie Bishop. Intriguing but artificial story of strong-willed Lupino pushing younger sister Leslie into show business career. Holds up until improbable finale, although it seems unlikely that Broadway would cheer Leslie as the greatest discovery of the age. Morgan and Carson (in first of several teamings) match Lupino's fine performance. ▼○)

Hardys Ride High, The (1939) **80m.** **½ D: George B. Seitz. Lewis Stone, Mickey Rooney, Cecilia Parker, Fay Holden, Ann Rutherford, Sara Haden, Virginia Grey, Marsha Hunt. Financial troubles abound when the family inherits a large estate and enters the world of the nouveau riche. Haden gets some juicy scenes in this *Andy Hardy* series entry.)

Harem Girl (1952) **70m.** ** D: Edward Bernds. Joan Davis, Peggie Castle, Arthur Blake, Minerva Urecal. Wacky Davis does her best to enliven slim vehicle about her substituting for a princess.)

Harlem Globetrotters, The (1951) **80m.** ** D: Phil Brown. Thomas Gomez, Dorothy Dandridge, Bill Walker, Angela Clarke. Vehicle built around famed basketball team, with a few romantic interludes.

Harlem on the Prairie (1937) **57m.** **½ D: Sam Newfield. Herbert Jeffries (Jeffrey), Flournoy E. Miller, Mantan Moreland, Connie Harris, Maceo B. Sheffield, Spencer Williams, Jr., George Randol, The Four Tones. Jeffries is tall in the saddle in this, the first of his four all-black-cast Westerns (followed by TWO GUN MAN FROM HARLEM, HARLEM RIDES THE RANGE, and THE BRONZE BUCKAROO, in which he plays a different character). Likable, by-the-numbers oater has singing cowboy Jeffries searching for a cache of gold stolen years before by now-reformed Williams.

Harlem Rides the Range (1939) **56m.** **½ D: Richard C. Kahn. Herbert Jeffrey (Herb Jeffries), Lucius Brooks, F. E. (Flournoy) Miller, Artie Young, Clarence Brooks, Spencer Williams, Jr., Tom Southern, Leonard Christmas, The Four Tones. The second of three amiable low-budget all-black-cast Westerns featuring singing cowboy Jeffrey as Bob Blake. Here, Blake and his sidekick become immersed in murder, mayhem, and romance on a ranch. Released after TWO GUN MAN FROM HARLEM and followed by THE BRONZE BUCKAROO. ▼❒

Harlow (1965) **C-125m.** **½ D: Gordon Douglas. Carroll Baker, Peter Lawford, Red Buttons, Michael Connors, Raf Vallone, Angela Lansbury, Martin Balsam, Leslie Nielsen. Slick, colorful garbage will hold your interest, but doesn't ring true. Baker could never match the real Harlow, but Vallone and Lansbury are good as her stepfather and mother. Rushed through production to compete with the slipshod Carol Lynley version. Panavision. ▼❒

Harlow (1965) **109m.** ** D: Alex Segal. Carol Lynley, Efrem Zimbalist, Jr., Barry Sullivan, Hurd Hatfield, Ginger Rogers, Hermione Baddeley, Lloyd Bochner, Audrey Totter, John Williams, Robert Strauss. Amateurish off-the-cuff tedium loosely based on screen star of the 1930s. Rogers as Mama Harlow is best. This quickie production made news in 1965 because it was produced in an unusual manner: staged as a live television show and recorded as a kinescope. ❒

Harold Lloyd's World of Comedy (1962) **94m.** *** Compiled by Harold Lloyd. Harold Lloyd, Bebe Daniels, Mildred Davis. Delightful comedy scenes show why Lloyd was so popular in the 1920s. Highlights include classic building-climbing episode and other great sight gags. A real gem. ❒

Harp of Burma SEE: **Burmese Harp, The**

Harriet Craig (1950) **94m.** *** D: Vincent Sherman. Joan Crawford, Wendell Corey, Lucile Watson, Allyn Joslyn, Ellen Corby. Remake of CRAIG'S WIFE is well cast, with Crawford in title role of perfectionist wife who'll stop at nothing to have her house and life run as she wishes. ▼❒

Harry Black SEE: **Harry Black and the Tiger**

Harry Black and the Tiger (1958-British) **C-107m.** BOMB D: Hugo Fregonese. Stewart Granger, Barbara Rush, Anthony Steel, I. S. Johar. Moldy jungle film tangled in the underbrush, with confusing flashbacks. Filmed in India. Sorry, Harry. Original British title: HARRY BLACK. CinemaScope.▼

Harum Scarum (1965) **C-86m.** **½ D: Gene Nelson. Elvis Presley, Mary Ann Mobley, Fran Jeffries, Michael Ansara, Jay Novello, Philip Reed, Theo Marcuse, Billy Barty. Visiting the Middle East gives usual Presley musical formula a change of scenery, via back-lot desert locations.▼❒

Harvest (1937-French) **127m.** **** D: Marcel Pagnol. Gabriel Gabrio, Orane Demazis, Fernandel, Edouard Delmont, Henri Poupon. Simple, stark tale of peasants Gabrio and Demazis struggling against all odds to till the land and give life to the earth. Magnificent, with Fernandel memorable as Demazis' comical husband.▼

Harvey (1950) **104m.** ***½ D: Henry Koster. James Stewart, Josephine Hull, Peggy Dow, Charles Drake, Cecil Kellaway, Victoria Horne, Jesse White, Wallace Ford, Ida Moore. Stewart gives one of his best performances as tippler Elwood P. Dowd, whose companion is a six-foot invisible rabbit named Harvey (actually, he's 6 feet, 3½ inches). Hull won Oscar as distraught sister. Mary Chase and Oscar Brodney adapted Chase's Pulitzer Prize–winning play. Hull and White recreate their Broadway roles. Remade for TV in 1998.▼❍

Harvey Girls, The (1946) **C-101m.** *** D: George Sidney. Judy Garland, Ray Bolger, John Hodiak, Angela Lansbury, Preston Foster, Virginia O'Brien, Marjorie Main, Kenny Baker, Cyd Charisse, Catherine McLeod. Westward expansion brings with it Fred Harvey's railroad station restaurants, and proper young waitresses who have civilizing influence on rowdy communities. Silly script made entertaining by good cast and a few musical highlights (like Oscar-winning "On the Atchison, Topeka, and the Santa Fe").▼❍

Harvey Middleman, Fireman (1965) **C-75m.** ** D: Ernest Pintoff. Gene Troobnick, Hermione Gingold, Patricia Harty, Arlene Golonka, Will MacKenzie, Charles Durning. Low-key comedy about mild-mannered fireman trying to coordinate fantasy and real life; amiable but unfocused film was animator Pintoff's first live-action feature.

Has Anybody Seen My Gal (1952) **C-89m.** **½ D: Douglas Sirk. Charles Coburn, Piper Laurie, Rock Hudson, Gigi Perreau, Lynn Bari, William Reynolds, Larry Gates, Skip Homeier. Pleasant, lightweight 1920s nostalgia about rich old Coburn planning to leave his fortune to the family of a woman who turned down his marriage proposal years earlier. Coburn's performance is the whole show; look fast for James Dean. ❒

Hasty Heart, The (1949-British) **99m.** ***½ D: Vincent Sherman. Ronald Reagan, Patricia Neal, Richard Todd, Anthony Nicholls, Howard Crawford. Sensitive film version of John Patrick play, focusing on proud Scottish soldier who discovers he has short time to live and friendships he finally makes among his hospital mates. Remade in 1983 for cable TV.▼❒

Hatari! (1962) **C-159m.** ***½ D: Howard Hawks. John Wayne, Elsa Martinelli, Red Buttons, Hardy Kruger, Gerard Blain, Bruce Cabot. Marvelous lighthearted action film of wild-animal trappers in Africa, with just-right mixture of adventure and comedy. Wayne is at his best. Notable Henry Mancini score. Filmed in Tanganyika; title is Swahili for "Danger!"▼❍

Hat Check Girl (1932) **65m.** **½ D: Sidney

Lanfield. Sally Eilers, Ben Lyon, Ginger Rogers, Monroe Owsley, Arthur Pierson, Noel Madison, Henry Armetta. Nightclub hatcheck girl Eilers is surrounded by men on the make—and assorted lowlifes—but falls in love with millionaire Lyon. Minor but entertaining pre-Code romantic comedy with underworld spice. Some clever visual touches and funny wisecracks, mostly from best friend Ginger. Look for Dennis O'Keefe and Eddie "Rochester" Anderson in bits.

Hatchet Man, The (1932) 74m. **½ D: William Wellman. Edward G. Robinson, Loretta Young, Dudley Digges, Blanche Frederici, Leslie Fenton. Fascinating yarn about Chinatown tongs, and Robinson's attempts to Americanize himself. Potent melodrama, once you get past obvious barrier of Caucasian cast. ▶

Hatful of Rain, A (1957) **109m.** *** D: Fred Zinnemann. Eva Marie Saint, Don Murray, Anthony Franciosa, Lloyd Nolan, Henry Silva, Gerald S. O'Loughlin, William Hickey. Realistic melodrama of the living hell dope addict Murray undergoes, and the effects on those around him; fine performances. Scripted by Michael V. Gazzo, Alfred Hayes, and Carl Foreman from Gazzo's play. CinemaScope. ▶

Hats Off (1936) 70m. ** D: Boris Petroff. Mae Clarke, John Payne, Helen Lynd, Luis Alberni, Skeets Gallagher, Franklin Pangborn. Minor musical about the travails of rival press agents. The supporting actors, particularly Alberni and Gallagher, fare best here. Payne's first starring film. ▼▶

Hatter's Castle (1941-British) 90m. **½ D: Lance Comfort. Deborah Kerr, James Mason, Robert Newton, Emlyn Williams. Fine cast must support fair material in tale of poor man who relentlessly pursues his dream of social acceptance; from A. J. Cronin's novel.

Haunted Castle, The (1921-German) 82m. *** D: F. W. Murnau. Arnold Korff, L. Kyser-Korff, Lothar Mehnert, Paul Hartmann, Paul Bildt, Olga Tschechowa, Victor Blütner, Hermann Vallentin. The upbeat mood among the guests at the Castle Vogelöd is irrevocably tainted by the arrival of an uninvited visitor (Mehnert), a count who allegedly murdered his brother. Despite its title, this subtly eerie tale is more mystery than chiller. Adapted by Carl Mayer from a novel by Rudolf Stratz. Full title is THE HAUNTED CASTLE: THE EXPOSURE OF A SECRET. Beware various versions and running times. Remade in 1936. ▼▶

Haunted Gold (1932) 59m. **½ D: Mack V. Wright. John Wayne, Sheila Terry, Harry Woods, Erville Alderson, Martha Mattox, Blue Washington. Wayne's best early Warners Western is a fast-paced yarn about dispute over rights to an abandoned gold mine haunted by a character known as The Phan-

tom. Miracle horse Duke gets star billing with Wayne above spooky main title sporting animated owls. Mystery fans in search of the original Maltese Falcon statue will find it atop the heroine's piano. ▼▶

Haunted Honeymoon (1940-British) 83m. **½ D: Arthur B. Woods. Robert Montgomery, Constance Cummings, Leslie Banks, Seymour Hicks, Robert Newton, Googie Withers. Famed amateur criminologist Lord Peter Wimsey (Montgomery) marries mystery writer (Cummings) and settles down to quiet honeymoon—until murder enters the picture and demands their involvement. Montgomery miscast as Dorothy L. Sayers' witty sleuth. Originally titled BUSMAN'S HONEYMOON.

Haunted Palace, The (1963) C-85m. **½ D: Roger Corman. Vincent Price, Debra Paget, Lon Chaney, Jr., Frank Maxwell, Leo Gordon, Elisha Cook, Jr., John Dierkes. When a man arrives in New England town to claim family castle, he discovers the town populated by mutants and the castle under an ancestor's evil spell, which soon possesses him. Good-looking but minor film from Corman's Edgar Allan Poe cycle, although based mainly on H. P. Lovecraft's *The Strange Case of Charles Dexter Ward.* Script by Charles Beaumont. Panavision. ▼▶

Haunted Strangler, The (1958-British) 81m. **½ D: Robert Day. Boris Karloff, Anthony Dawson, Elizabeth Allan, Jean Kent, Derek Birch. Offbeat story set in 1880; socially conscious author Karloff investigates the case of a man who was executed twenty years earlier. Original British title: GRIP OF THE STRANGLER. ▼▶

Haunting, The (1963) 112m. ***½ D: Robert Wise. Julie Harris, Claire Bloom, Richard Johnson, Russ Tamblyn, Lois Maxwell, Fay Compton. 90-year-old New England haunted house is setting for chosen group being introduced to the supernatural, with hair-raising results. Don't see this one alone! Filmed in England; Nelson Gidding adapted Shirley Jackson's *The Haunting of Hill House.* Remade in 1999. Panavision. ▼▶

Havana Widows (1933) 62m. **½ D: Ray Enright. Joan Blondell, Glenda Farrell, Guy Kibbee, Allen Jenkins, Lyle Talbot, Frank McHugh, Ruth Donnelly, Hobart Cavanaugh. Perennial gold diggers Blondell and Farrell are brassy showgirls on the prowl in Cuba, looking to trap millionaire Kibbee in a breach of promise suit. Raunchy pre-Code farce lets the Warner Bros. stock players do what they do best in a fast-paced, forgettable film. ▶

Have a Heart (1934) 82m. ** D: David Butler. Jean Parker, James Dunn, Una Merkel, Stuart Erwin, Willard Robertson, Samuel S. Hinds, Muriel Evans. Hokey tearjerker about a dance teacher (Parker) who's crippled in an accident, loses her fiancé, and finds true love with ice cream vendor Dunn, until heartbreak strikes again. Smoothly made soaper, but it's all a bit too much.

Have Rocket—Will Travel (1959) **76m.** **✶✶½** D: David Lowell Rich. The Three Stooges, Jerome Cowan, Anna Lisa, Bob Colbert. Good slapstick as The Stooges accidentally launch into space, meet a unicorn, and go on to become national heroes. This was the trio's first starring feature after being rediscovered on TV, though Joe DeRita had, by this time, filled the Curly/Shemp slot.▼▶

Having a Wild Weekend (1965-British) **91m.** **✶✶½** D: John Boorman. Dave Clark Five, Barbara Ferris, Lenny Davidson, Rick Huxley, Mike Smith, Denis Payton, David Lodge. Just as The Dave Clark Five tried to steal some of the Beatles' thunder, this fast-paced trifle tried to capture success of A HARD DAY'S NIGHT. The Five star as stuntmen who, along with a model (Ferris), search for a dream island. Songs include "Having a Wild Weekend," "Catch Us If You Can," "I Can't Stand It." Director Boorman's first film. Originally titled CATCH US IF YOU CAN.▼▶

Having Wonderful Crime (1945) **70m.** **✶✶½** D: A. Edward Sutherland. Pat O'Brien, George Murphy, Carole Landis, Lenore Aubert, George Zucco. Lively mystery-comedy in which a trio of friends—brash lawyer O'Brien and wise-cracking newlyweds Murphy and Landis—become involved with a magician who disappears and his mysterious assistant. Based on characters created by Craig Rice, though the film bears no relation to Rice's novel of the same name.▼▶

Having Wonderful Time (1938) **71m.** **✶✶½** D: Alfred Santell. Ginger Rogers, Douglas Fairbanks, Jr., Peggy Conklin, Lucille Ball, Lee Bowman, Eve Arden, Dorothea Kent, Richard (Red) Skelton, Donald Meek, Jack Carson, Allan Lane, Grady Sutton. OK film about Catskills resort hotel; Ginger wants culture on summer vacation but gets Doug instead. Arthur Kober adapted his own Broadway comedy, but the original's satiric depiction of Jewish New Yorkers is completely homogenized. Skelton sparkles in his feature debut; Dean Jagger plays Ginger's brother and Ann Miller is visible among the campers. ▼▶

Häxan SEE: **Witchcraft Through the Ages**

Hazard (1948) **95m.** **✶✶** D: George Marshall. Paulette Goddard, Macdonald Carey, Fred Clark, Stanley Clements. Routine comedy of private eye Carey following Goddard, falling in love in the process.

Head, The (1959-German) **92m.** **✶✶** D: Victor Trivas. Horst Frank, Karin Kernke, Michel Simon, Helmut Schmid, Dieter Eppler. Old-fashioned chiller involving head-transplants, with obligatory murders and blood-drenched revenge; extremely eerie but not very convincing.▼▶

Heading for Heaven (1947) **71m.** **✶½** D: Lewis D. Collins. Stuart Erwin, Glenda

Farrell, Irene Ryan, Milburn Stone, Selmer Jackson, Janis Wilson. Soggy account of well-meaning Erwin trying to build model middle-income-bracket community, but being fleeced by racketeers.▶

Headin' Home (1920) **73m.** **✶✶** D: Lawrence Windom. Babe Ruth, Ruth Taylor, William Sheer, Margaret Seddon, Frances Victory, James A. Marcus. The Sultan of Swat makes his screen debut in this cornball comedy-drama about a wholesome small-town boy who becomes a baseball star. Even though his character is called Babe, this ode to the simple joys of rural America is not to be confused with the Bambino's own life story. A curio to be sure, and a must for baseball fans. ▼▶

Headless Ghost, The (1959-British) **61m.** BOMB D: Peter Graham Scott. Richard Lyon, Liliane Sottane, David Rose, Clive Revill, Carl Bernard, Trevor Barnett. Brainless horror-comedy with students investigating a haunted castle. Dyaliscope.▼◉▶

Headline Hunters (1955) **70m.** **✶✶** D: William Witney. Rod Cameron, Julie Bishop, Ben Cooper, Raymond Greenleaf. Uninspired tale of fledgling reporter tracking down big-city racketeers. Remake of 1940 BEHIND THE NEWS.

Headline Shooter (1933) **61m.** **✶✶✶** D: Otto Brower. William Gargan, Frances Dee, Ralph Bellamy, Jack La Rue, Gregory Ratoff, Wallace Ford, Robert Benchley, Betty Furness, Hobart Cavanaugh, June Brewster, Franklin Pangborn, Dorothy Burgess. Vigorous, fast-paced yarn about a brash newsreel cameraman skillfully integrates real-life footage of fire, flood, and the 1933 Long Beach earthquake into its B-movie script. Bellamy's role as reporter Dee's hometown fiancée—and her ultimate response—anticipates HIS GIRL FRIDAY. Good fun.

Headlines of Destruction (1955-French) **85m.** **✶✶** D: John Berry. Eddie Constantine, Bella Darvi, Paul Frankeur, Walter Chiari. Interesting concept poorly executed; Darvi is defense attorney involved with Constantine in trial of man accused of murder.

Hear Me Good (1957) **80m.** **✶½** D: Don McGuire. Hal March, Joe E. Ross, Merry Anders, Jean Willes. Trivia concerning a fixed beauty contest. VistaVision.

Heartbeat (1946) **102m.** **✶✶** D: Sam Wood. Ginger Rogers, Jean Pierre Aumont, Adolphe Menjou, Basil Rathbone, Melville Cooper, Mikhail Rasumny, Eduardo Ciannelli, Mona Maris, Henry Stephenson. Boring remake of the French film BATTEMENT DE COEUR, with Rogers sorely miscast as an 18-year-old reform school escapee who becomes a pickpocket and ends up falling for one of her victims, a handsome young diplomat (Aumont).▼▶

Heart of a Nation, The (1943-French) **82m.** **✶✶½** D: Julien Duvivier. Raimu, Michèle Morgan, Louis Jouvet, Suzy Prim, Lucien Nat, Renèe Devillers, (Robert) Le Vigan, Fernand Ledoux, Louis Jourdan. Episodic soaper recounting the plight of one French family across the decades, from 1871 (with their country under attack by Germany during the Franco-Prussian War) to the beginning of WW2. A patriotic love letter to France. Completed in 1940, just before the Germans marched into Paris; a print was smuggled out of Occupied France and reedited for U.S. release with introductory commentary by Charles Boyer. Released in France in 1945. ▶

Heart of Arizona (1938) **68m. **½** D: Lesley Selander. William Boyd, George Hayes, Russell Hayden, John Elliott, Natalie Moorhead, Dorothy Short, Alden (Stephen) Chase. Hopalong Cassidy exposes crooked foreman in cattle-rustling scheme. Well-plotted yarn with some unusual twists, including a leading lady fresh from 5 years in prison falling for Hoppy. Makes good use of the so-called Hoppy Cabin nestled high in Alabama Hills' giant rocks in Lone Pine, California. ▼▶

Heart of New York, The (1932) **74m. **½** D: Mervyn LeRoy. George Sidney, Joe Smith, Charles Dale, Ruth Hall, Anna Appel, Aline MacMahon, Marion Byron, Oscar Apfel, Donald Cook. Raucous ethnic comedy with Sidney as a poor Lower East Side Jewish plumber who invents a washing machine and becomes rich overnight. Vaudeville stars Smith & Dale costar as Hester Street residents Shtrudel and Schnaps. Based on the play *Mendel, Inc.* by David Freedman.

Heart of the Golden West (1942) **65m.** ***** D: Joseph Kane. Roy Rogers, George "Gabby" Hayes, Smiley Burnette, Ruth Terry, Walter Catlett, Paul Harvey, Edmund MacDonald, Leigh Whipper, William Haade, Hal Taliaferro, Hall Johnson Choir, Sons of the Pioneers. The star's most ambitious film yet, with *two* sidekicks (Smiley's usual partner, Gene Autry, had gone off to war). Roy and his pals outwit greedy trucking company owner MacDonald by moving their cattle on Catlett's steamboat line. Exciting climax in a storm-ridden swamp is followed by a finale featuring the catchy tune "River Robin." ▼▶

Heart of the Matter, The (1953-British) **105m.** **** D: George More O'Ferrall. Trevor Howard, Elizabeth Allan, Maria Schell, Denholm Elliott. Graham Greene's novel of inner and outward conflict set in Sierra Leone, with Howard as police officer on verge of mental collapse.

Heart of the North (1938) **C-83m. **½** D: Lewis Seiler. Dick Foran, Gloria Dickson, Gale Page, Allen Jenkins, Patric Knowles, Janet Chapman, James Stephenson, Joe Sawyer. Foran leads the Royal Canadian Mounted Police on a manhunt for a gang of fur and gold thieves who killed a Mountie.

Ordinary "northern" Western adventure is decked out in splendid early Technicolor and given a fairly vigorous treatment on eye-catching backwoods locations.

Heart of the Rio Grande (1942) **68m. **½** D: William Morgan. Gene Autry, Smiley Burnette, Fay McKenzie, Edith Fellows, Pierre Watkin, Joe Strauch, Jr., Jean Porter, William Haade, Sarah Padden, Jimmy Wakely Trio. Dude ranch foreman Autry has to contend with spoiled teenage guest Fellows and the resentment of the man he replaced. Amiable Autry vehicle features Gene singing "Deep in the Heart of Texas" and promoting the purchase of war bonds and stamps to his ranch hands. ▼▶

Heart of the Rockies (1951) **56m.** ***** D: William Witney. Roy Rogers, Penny Edwards, Gordon Jones, Ralph Morgan, Fred Graham, Robert (Buzz) Henry, Rand Brooks, Foy Willing and the Riders of the Purple Sage. Roy tries to help youthful first-offenders by having them work on a road-building project, but rancher Morgan doesn't want the highway built on his land. Meanwhile, his foreman (out to cheat Morgan) plots against him and makes it seem as if the boys are guilty of his mischief. Roy's dog Bullet plays a major role in this entertaining story, and his master has one of his all-time best fight scenes. ▼▶

Heart of the West (1936) **63m.** **** D: Howard Bretherton. William Boyd, James Ellison, George Hayes, Sidney Blackmer, Lynn Gabriel, Fred Kohler, Warner Richmond. Polished heavy Blackmer tries hiring Bar 20 boys to trail-herd some cattle, but they soon switch allegiance to neighboring rancher who seeks to erect a protective fence. Sixth, last, and least entry in first, strong season of the *Hopalong Cassidy* series, shot mostly in Kernville, California. ▼▶

Heart o' the Hills, The (1919) **77m. **½** D: Sidney A. Franklin. Mary Pickford, Harold Goodwin, Allan Sears, Fred Huntley, Claire McDowell, Sam De Grasse, Jack (John) Gilbert. Picturesque but overly familiar yarn about low-down skunks who conspire to rob rural Kentucky mountainfolk of their land; high-spirited Mary is determined to halt the scheme and avenge her father's murder. Pickford's the entire show and convincingly matures from rambunctious 13-year-old to lovely young woman. Of special note is the brief appearance of the KKK-ish "Night Riders" and the context in which they are presented. ▼▶

Hearts Divided (1936) **87m.** **** D: Frank Borzage. Marion Davies, Dick Powell, Charlie Ruggles, Claude Rains, Edward Everett Horton, Arthur Treacher. Napoleon's younger brother (Powell) woos and weds an American (Davies). This lackluster musical is based on a true story, though you'd never know it. A remake of the silent GLORIOUS BETSY.

Hearts in Bondage (1936) **72m. **½** D:

Lew Ayres. James Dunn, Mae Clarke, David Manners, Charlotte Henry, Henry B. Walthall, Fritz Leiber, George Irving, Irving Pichel, J. M. Kerrigan, Frank McGlynn, Sr., Ben Alexander, George Hayes. Saga of the *Monitor* and the *Merrimac* is fascinating, but personal story surrounding it in this film is less than thrilling. Still, a worthy attempt to bring this chapter of American history to life, with a stalwart cast of character actors. Battle scenes are first-rate, with what was then state-of-the-art use of miniatures. Ayres' only attempt at directing a Hollywood feature.▶

Hearts of the World (1918) **122m.** **½ D: D. W. Griffith. Lillian Gish, Dorothy Gish, Robert Harron, Kate Bruce, Ben Alexander, George Fawcett, George Siegmann. Griffith's epic of WW1, shot in England and France. Melodramatic story, conceived as anti-German propaganda, spotlights a young American (Harron) living in a French village, where he is engaged to be married; he fights for France once war is declared. Dorothy Gish has fine comedy role, young Noel Coward a small part as villager with wheelbarrow, Erich von Stroheim a lusty German. For these highlights, other good moments, worth seeing.▼◐

Heat Lightning (1934) **64m.** *** D: Mervyn LeRoy. Aline MacMahon, Ann Dvorak, Preston Foster, Lyle Talbot, Glenda Farrell, Frank McHugh, Ruth Donnelly, Jane Darwell, Edgar Kennedy. Archetypal Warner Bros. melodrama—spiced with the usual racy wisecracks—centering on jaded mechanic MacMahon and her naive younger sister (Dvorak), who run a gas-station/cafe/motel in the middle of the desert and tangle with crooks and other assorted quirky characters. Atmospheric and very well acted, with MacMahon a standout as a tough-as-nails dame who's repressed her femininity. Based on a play by George Abbott and Leon Abrams. Remade as HIGHWAY WEST (1941).▶

Heat's On, The (1943) **80m.** **½ D: Gregory Ratoff. Mae West, Victor Moore, William Gaxton, Lester Allen, Mary Roche, Hazel Scott, Xavier Cugat, Lloyd Bridges. Mae's last starring vehicle (for several decades) is a routine show-biz musical about a star involved with conniving producers. Befuddled Moore and colorful Cugat are fun, but there isn't enough of West in this film; when she's on-screen, she's just as funny as ever.▼◐

Heat Wave (1954-British) **68m.** *½ D: Ken Hughes. Alex Nicol, Hillary Brooke, Sidney James, Susan Stephen, Paul Carpenter, Alan Wheatley, Peter Illing, Joan Hickson. Hack novelist Nicol becomes intrigued by greedy, alluring (and married) neighbor Brooke. Barely adequate programmer; Hughes scripted, based on his novel. Original British title: THE HOUSE ACROSS THE LAKE.▼◐

Heaven Can Wait (1943) **C-112m.** ***½ D: Ernst Lubitsch. Gene Tierney, Don Ameche, Charles Coburn, Marjorie Main,

Laird Cregar, Spring Byington, Allyn Joslyn, Eugene Pallette, Signe Hasso, Louis Calhern. Excellent comedy-fantasy told in flashback. Ameche, who believes he's lived a life of sin, recalls his past as he requests admission to Hades. Witty Samson Raphaelson script helps make this a delight. Based on the play *Birthdays* by Laszlo Bus-Fekete.▼◐

Heaven Knows, Mr. Allison (1957) **C-107m.** *** D: John Huston. Deborah Kerr, Robert Mitchum. Marvelous, touching tale of nun Kerr and Marine Mitchum stranded together on a Japanese-infested Pacific island during WW2. Solid performances by the stars. CinemaScope.

Heavenly Body, The (1943) **95m.** ** D: Alexander Hall. Hedy Lamarr, William Powell, James Craig, Fay Bainter, Henry O'Neill, Spring Byington. Hedy is heavenly, but script is silly; astronomer Powell suspects neglected wife Lamarr of being unfaithful with air-raid warden Craig.▶

Heavenly Days (1944) **71m.** ** D: Howard Estabrook. Fibber McGee and Molly (Jim and Marion Jordan), Barbara Hale, Eugene Pallette, Gordon Oliver. Mild entry in famed radio comedians' series, with the lovable married couple off to Washington to help run the Senate.▶

Heaven Only Knows (1947) **95m.** **½ D: Albert S. Rogell. Robert Cummings, Brian Donlevy, Jorja Curtwright, Marjorie Reynolds, Bill Goodwin, John Litel, Stuart Erwin. Oddball Western with fantasy touches as angel Cummings descends to earth to help soulless gambler. Retitled: MONTANA MIKE.▶

Heavens Above! (1963-British) **105m.** *** D: John Boulting. Peter Sellers, Cecil Parker, Isabel Jeans, Eric Sykes, Bernard Miles, Ian Carmichael, Irene Handl, Brock Peters, William Hartnell, Roy Kinnear, Joan Hickson. Wry satire on British clergy life; Sellers top-notch as the reverend who becomes bishop in outer space. Originally ran 118m. Produced by Roy Boulting.▼◐

Heaven With a Barbed Wire Fence (1939) **62m.** **½ D: Ricardo Cortez. Jean Rogers, Raymond Walburn, Marjorie Rambeau, Glenn Ford, Nicholas (Richard) Conte, Ward Bond. Spunky little road movie with Rogers, Ford, and Conte linking up and riding the rails to California. Ford's feature debut, as well as Conte's. Coscripted by Dalton Trumbo and based on his story.▶

He Couldn't Say No (1938) **57m.** **½ D: Lewis Seiler. Frank McHugh, Jane Wyman, Cora Witherspoon, Berton Churchill, Diana Lewis, Ferris Taylor, Tom Kennedy. McHugh is a meek clerk who tangles with gangsters when he impulsively buys a nude statue modeled by a senator's daughter and winds up romancing her. Disarming nonsense gives character actor McHugh a rare starring role.

Heidi (1937) **88m.** **½ D: Allan Dwan.

Shirley Temple, Jean Hersholt, Arthur Treacher, Helen Westley, Mady Christians, Sidney Blackmer, Sig Ruman, Marcia Mae Jones, Mary Nash. Classic children's story set in 19th-century Switzerland is good vehicle for Shirley, playing girl taken from grandfather (Hersholt) to live with cruel Nash. Nice tearjerker for children. Also shown in computer-colored version.▼●▶

Heidi (1952-Swiss) **98m.** *** D: Luigi Comencini. Elsbeth Sigmund, Heinrich Gretler, Thomas Klameth, Elsie Attenhofer. Faithful, flavorful retelling of Johanna Spyri's children's classic, filmed in the story's actual locales. Sigmund is well cast in the title role. Followed by HEIDI AND PETER.▼

Heidi (1965-Austrian-German) **C-95m.** *** D: Werner Jacobs. Eva Marie Singhammer, Gertraud Mittermayr, Gustav Knuth, Lotte Ledi. Fine retelling of classic children's story about young girl who leaves her cozy home in the Swiss Alps for adventures in the world below.▼

Heidi and Peter (1955-Swiss) **C-89m.** **½ D: Franz Schnyder. Heinrich Gretler, Elsbeth Sigmund, Thomas Klameth, Anita Mey. So-so follow-up to HEIDI (1952), involving her adventures with Peter and a flood that threatens their village.

Heiress, The (1949) **115m.** **** D: William Wyler. Olivia de Havilland, Ralph Richardson, Montgomery Clift, Miriam Hopkins, Vanessa Brown, Mona Freeman, Ray Collins, Selena Royle. Henry James' novel *Washington Square* receives superlative screen treatment with Oscar-winning de Havilland as spinster wooed by fortune-hunter Clift in 19th-century N.Y.C., despite warnings from her cruel father, Richardson. Aaron Copland's music score also won an Oscar. Adapted by Ruth and Augustus Goetz from their stage play. Remade in 1997 as WASHINGTON SQUARE.▼●▶

Heir to Genghis Khan, The SEE: **Storm Over Asia**

He Laughed Last (1956) **C-77m.** **½ D: Blake Edwards. Frankie Laine, Lucy Marlow, Anthony Dexter, Richard Long, Alan Reed, Jesse White, Florenz Ames, Henry Slate. Marlow is a 1920s flapper who inherits a gangster's nightclub in this colorful spoof of Prohibition era crime stories. Laine even gets to croon a couple of songs.

Heldorado (1946) **70m.** ** D: William Witney. Roy Rogers, George "Gabby" Hayes, Dale Evans, Paul Harvey, Barry Mitchell (Brad Dexter), John Bagni, LeRoy Mason, Eddie Acuff, Clayton Moore, Bob Nolan and the Sons of the Pioneers. Park Ranger Rogers and Gabby team up with Dale to stop counterfeiters at the Las Vegas Helldorado Days celebration. Not enough action, and somewhat stifled by downtown Vegas locations, despite some scenes being shot at Boulder Dam and Lake Mead.▼▶

Helen Morgan Story, The (1957) **118m.**

**½ D: Michael Curtiz. Ann Blyth, Paul Newman, Richard Carlson, Gene Evans, Alan King, Cara Williams. Fiction about dynamic 1920s and '30s torch singer, dwelling on her romances and alcoholism; Blyth never captures the star's pathos or greatness. She's dubbed by Gogi Grant. CinemaScope.▼▶

Helen of Troy (1956) **C-118m.** ** D: Robert Wise. Stanley Baker, Rossana Podesta, Brigitte Bardot, Jacques Sernas, Cedric Hardwicke, Harry Andrews. Sweeping pageantry, but empty script spoils this version of story about the woman who caused the Trojan War. Filmed in Italy. Runs 121m. with overture. CinemaScope.▼●▶

Hell and High Water (1954) **C-103m.** **½ D: Samuel Fuller. Richard Widmark, Bella Darvi, Victor Francen, Cameron Mitchell, Gene Evans, David Wayne, Stephen Bekassy, Richard Loo. Uneven mixture of romance, espionage, and a demolition caper, stemming from U.S. sub's mission to Arctic. Tame film got a boost from being shot in CinemaScope.▶

Hell Below (1933) **105m.** **½ D: Jack Conway. Robert Montgomery, Walter Huston, Madge Evans, Jimmy Durante, Robert Young, Sterling Holloway, Eugene Pallette. Vintage submarine drama surpasses many more elaborate efforts; Huston is captain, Montgomery his seaman nemesis.

Hell Below Zero (1954) **C-91m.** ** D: Mark Robson. Alan Ladd, Joan Tetzel, Basil Sydney, Stanley Baker. Tepid adventure yarn casting Ladd as helper of Tetzel, who commands a whaling vessel while searching for her dad's killer. Made in England.▼

Hell Bent for Leather (1960) **C-82m.** **½ D: George Sherman. Audie Murphy, Felicia Farr, Stephen McNally, Robert Middleton, Rad Fulton, Jan Merlin, Herbert Rudley, Allan Lane, John Qualen, Bob Steele. Adequate Western with Murphy a horse trader accused of murder; greedy sheriff McNally knows he's innocent, but still heads the posse on his trail. CinemaScope.

Hell Canyon Outlaws (1957) **72m.** ** D: Paul Landres. Dale Robertson, Brian Keith, Rossana Rory, Dick Kallman, Buddy Baer. Triumph against outlaw forces in the Old West; that's it.

Hellcats of the Navy (1957) **82m.** **½ D: Nathan Juran. Ronald Reagan, Nancy Davis (Reagan), Arthur Franz, Harry Lauter, Selmer Jackson. Satisfactory actioner of WW2 exploits of U.S. submarine and its crew. Ronald and Nancy Reagan's only screen appearance together.▼▶

Hell Divers (1932) **113m.** ** D: George Hill. Wallace Beery, Clark Gable, Conrad Nagel, Dorothy Jordan, Marjorie Rambeau, Marie Prevost, Cliff Edwards. Beery and Gable are boisterous rivals in the Naval Air Force in this often lively but overlong MGM effort, with some still-exciting aerial action. Watch for young Robert Young as a sailor.▶

Hell Drivers (1957-British) **108m.** ★★★ D: C. Raker (Cy) Endfield. Stanley Baker, Herbert Lom, Peggy Cummins, Patrick McGoohan, William Hartnell, Wilfred Lawson, Sidney James, Jill Ireland, Alfie Bass, Gordon Jackson, David McCallum, Sean Connery. Taut account of ex-con joining trucking company that encourages reckless competition among the drivers making their daily rounds. What a cast! VistaVision.

Heller in Pink Tights (1960) **C-100m.** ★★½ D: George Cukor. Sophia Loren, Anthony Quinn, Margaret O'Brien, Steve Forrest, Edmund Lowe. Colorful tale of theatrical troupe that travels throughout the Old West—with the law often in pursuit. Based on a Louis L'Amour novel. ▼◗

Hellfire (1949) **C-90m.** ★★½ D: R. G. Springsteen. William Elliott, Marie Windsor, Forrest Tucker, Jim Davis, H. B. Warner, Paul Fix, Grant Withers, Emory Parnell, Esther Howard, Jody Gilbert, Denver Pyle. Fast-moving B Western with an unusual plot: gambler Elliott changes his ways and attempts to build a church in order to honor a minister who gave up his own life to save Elliott's. Windsor is fetching in Trucolor, playing a bandit-turned-saloon-singer Elliott falls for and tries to reform. ▼◗

Hellfire Club, The (1961-British) **C-93m.** ★★★ D: Robert S. Baker, Monty Berman. Keith Michell, Adrienne Corri, Peter Cushing, Peter Arne, Kai Fischer, David Lodge, Martin Stephens, Miles Malleson, Francis Matthews. Lively, entertaining 18th-century swashbuckler with familiar rightful- vs. wrongful-heir plot; acrobatic Michell makes a dashing hero. The depraved, powerful, real-life club of the title serves as backdrop. DyaliScope. ▼◗

Hellgate (1952) **87m.** ★★ D: Charles Marquis Warren. Sterling Hayden, Joan Leslie, Ward Bond, James Arness, Peter Coe, Robert Wilke, Sheb Wooley, Timothy Carey. Offbeat story about Kansas veterinarian Hayden, who's wrongly accused of aiding a murderer and sent to hellish prison. Interesting ingredients in this story based on real events; hampered by ineffectual treatment. ◗

Hell in Korea (1956-British) **81m.** ★★½ D: Julian Amyes. Ronald Lewis, Stephen Boyd, Victor Maddern, George Baker, Robert Shaw, Stanley Baker, Harry Andrews, Michael Medwin, Michael Caine, Percy Herbert. Standard drama about small U.N. patrol tangling with Chinese; interesting to see Caine in his first film, Shaw in his second. Aka A HILL IN KOREA. ▼

Hellions, The (1962-British) **C-87m.** ★★½ D: Ken Annakin. Richard Todd, Anne Aubrey, Lionel Jeffries, Zena Walker, Jamie Uys, Marty Wilde. Western revenge plot transferred to 19th-century South Africa; inevitable shoot-out intact. Technirama.

Hell Is a City (1960-British) **96m.** ★★★ D: Val Guest. Stanley Baker, John Crawford, Donald Pleasence, Maxine Audley, Billie Whitelaw, Joseph Tomelty, George A. Cooper. Tough, exciting crime thriller from Hammer Films featuring Baker as a morally ambiguous police inspector dealing with marital troubles while chasing ruthless escaped murderer Crawford. Vividly filmed on location in Manchester with a fine cast. Hammerscope. ▼◗

Hell Is for Heroes (1962) **90m.** ★★★ D: Donald Siegel. Steve McQueen, Bobby Darin, Fess Parker, Harry Guardino, James Coburn, Mike Kellin, Nick Adams, Bob Newhart. Tough, taut WW2 film about a small squadron forced to hold off a German attack by pretending they're larger—and more powerful—than they really are. Takes its time getting started but builds in intensity to a riveting climax. Only incongruous note: young Newhart, who even interpolates a variation on one of his telephone monologues into the story! Cowritten by WW2 specialist Robert Pirosh. ▼●◗

Hello Elephant (1952-Italian) **78m.** ★½ D: Gianni Franciolini. Vittorio De Sica, Sabu, Maria Mercader, Nando Bruno. Misfire of comedy-satire involving royalty who bestows an elephant on one of his subjects. Retitled: PARDON MY TRUNK. ▼

Hello Frisco, Hello (1943) **C-98m.** ★★ D: H. Bruce Humberstone. Alice Faye, John Payne, Jack Oakie, Lynn Bari, Laird Cregar, June Havoc, Ward Bond. Hackneyed musicomedy of Payne getting too big for his britches as Barbary Coast entrepreneur; Oscar-winning song, "You'll Never Know." Big comedown from earlier musicals with star trio. ▼◗

Hell on Devil's Island (1957) **74m.** ★★ D: Christian Nyby. Helmut Dantine, William Talman, Donna Martell, Jean Willes, Rex Ingram, Robert Cornthwaite, Mel Welles. Former reporter Dantine, released after serving eight years on Devil's Island, battles crooked law enforcement officials and an unscrupulous plantation owner in this OK programmer. Regalscope.

Hell on Frisco Bay (1955) **C-98m.** ★★½ D: Frank Tuttle. Alan Ladd, Edward G. Robinson, Joanne Dru, William Demarest, Paul Stewart, Fay Wray, Rodney (Rod) Taylor, Jayne Mansfield. Thirties-style gangster film recounting the exposure of crime syndicate and its head; actionful, with good cast. CinemaScope. ▼

Hello, Sister! (1933) **62m.** ★★½ D: Erich von Stroheim, Alfred Werker. James Dunn, Boots Mallory, ZaSu Pitts, Minna Gombell. Innocuous boy-meets-girl story of special interest to film buffs. Originally filmed by von Stroheim as WALKING DOWN BROADWAY; later reedited, partially refilmed; enough bizarre touches remain to reveal von Stroheim's touch, however.

Hello Sucker (1941) **60m.** ★½ D: Edward Cline. Peggy Moran, Tom Brown, Walter Catlett, Hugh Herbert. Dingy little film of

Moran and Brown acquiring vaudeville booking agency, making it a success, and finding love with one another.

Hell's Angels (1930) **127m.** ***½ D: Howard Hughes. Ben Lyon, James Hall, Jean Harlow, John Darrow, Lucien Prival, Roy Wilson. Hughes' expensive, indulgent WW1 aviation film is in a class by itself; slow-moving and sometimes corny storywise, but unmatched for aerial spectacle. Also the film that launched Harlow ("Would you be shocked if I put on something more comfortable?") to stardom. Two-color Technicolor party scene and tinted night sequences were restored in 1989. James Whale, credited as dialogue director, actually wrote and directed much of the film. Beware shorter prints. Runs 131m. with intermission/entr'acte. The making of this is depicted in Martin Scorsese's THE AVIATOR. ▼▶

Hell's Crossroads (1957) **73m.** ** D: Franklin Adreon. Stephen McNally, Peggie Castle, Robert Vaughn, Barton MacLane, Harry Shannon, Henry Brandon, Myron Healey. Predictable oater involving the outlaw James Brothers, with McNally a gang member who wishes to go straight. Naturama.

Hell's Five Hours (1958) **73m.** ** D: Jack L. Copeland. Stephen McNally, Coleen Gray, Vic Morrow, Maurice Manson. Several people are held prisoners at missile depot by Morrow, bent on blowing the place sky-high. ▶

Hell's Half Acre (1954) **91m.** *½ D: John H. Auer. Wendell Corey, Evelyn Keyes, Elsa Lanchester, Nancy Gates, Jesse White, Philip Ahn, Keye Luke, Marie Windsor. Woman seeks her long-missing husband in Honolulu, where he's established a new identity. Badly acted, written, and directed. Only value is Hawaiian location footage shot especially for the film. ▶

Hell's Heroes (1929) **68m.** ***½ D: William Wyler. Charles Bickford, Raymond Hatton, Fred Kohler, Fritzi Ridgeway. After robbing a bank in New Jerusalem ("A Bad Town . . . for Bad Men"), three outlaws try to flee across the sweltering, windswept desert but eventually wind up caring for a baby when its mother dies. First sound version of Peter B. Kyne's *Three Godfathers* is probably the most satisfying, and certainly the least sentimental; beautifully directed, tersely acted, and vividly atmospheric. ▶

Hell's Highway (1932) **62m.** **½ D: Rowland Brown. Richard Dix, Tom Brown, C. Henry Gordon, Charles Middleton, Rochelle Hudson, Oscar Apfel, Stanley Fields, Fuzzy Knight, Clarence Muse. Dix, serving time on a blatantly misrun chain gang, has to change his escape plans when his kid brother is brought in as prisoner. Though it pales alongside I AM A FUGITIVE FROM A CHAIN GANG (released just a few months later), this highly melodramatic tale is tough, raw (touching on everything from racial prejudice to homosexuality), and pictorially striking. Biggest disappointment: the finale.

Hell's Hinges (1916) **64m.** ***½ D: Charles Swickard. William S. Hart, Clara Williams, Jack Standing, Alfred Hollingsworth, Robert McKim, J. Frank Burke, Louise Glaum. Hart is Blaze Tracey, a rough cowboy in a wide-open Wild West town; he changes his ways as he falls for the good-hearted sister of a weak-willed parson. This unambiguous morality tale of good versus evil still has powerful moments. One of the most famous silent Westerns, and a perfect vehicle for Hart (who directed most of the film without credit). See if you can spot Jean Hersholt and John Gilbert as townsmen. ▼▶

Hell Ship Mutiny (1957) **66m.** *½ D: Lee Sholem, Elmo Williams. Jon Hall, John Carradine, Peter Lorre, Roberta Haynes, Mike Mazurki, Stanley Adams. Hall looks bored in rehash of South Sea tale of ship captain overcoming sinister forces exploiting the natives. ▼▶

Hell's Horizon (1955) **80m.** ** D: Tom Gries. John Ireland, Marla English, Bill Williams, Hugh Beaumont, Jerry Paris, Kenneth Duncan. Interaction among men of bombing squad in the Korean War.

Hell's House (1932) **72m.** ** D: Howard Higgin. Junior Durkin, Pat O'Brien, Bette Davis, Junior Coghlan, Charley Grapewin, Emma Dunn. Low-budget quickie about naive kid who takes rap for bootlegger and goes to poorly run boys' reformatory. Interesting mainly for early appearances of O'Brien and Davis. ▼▶

Hell's Island (1955) **C-84m.** **½ D: Phil Karlson. John Payne, Mary Murphy, Francis L. Sullivan, Eduardo Noriega, Paul Picerni. Tough-talking melodrama about Payne's pursuit of stolen gem and relationship with deceitful former girlfriend; script has echoes of THE MALTESE FALCON, and even a Sydney Greenstreet figure in the person of Sullivan. VistaVision. ▼▶

Hell's Kitchen (1939) **81m.** **½ D: Lewis Seiler, E. A. Dupont. Ronald Reagan, Stanley Fields, Grant Mitchell, Margaret Lindsay, Dead End Kids. Ex-con Fields goes straight, tries to bail Dead End Kids out of trouble, sets them on the right road. Remake of THE MAYOR OF HELL. ▶

Hell's Long Road (1963-Italian) **C-89m.** **½ D: Charles Roberti. Elena Brazzi, Kay Nolandi, Berto Frankis, Bela Kaivi, Marcello Charli. Offbeat costume sudser set in ancient Rome during rule of Nero (Frankis), focusing on personal life of arch senator (Charli) and romance with splendiferous Brazzi; vivid settings.

Hell's Outpost (1954) **90m.** ** D: Joseph Kane. Rod Cameron, Joan Leslie, Chill Wills, John Russell. Cameron is ambitious miner in this sturdy little film; Leslie is the fetching love interest.

Hell to Eternity (1960) **132m.** ****½** D: Phil Karlson. Jeffrey Hunter, David Janssen, Vic Damone, Patricia Owens, Sessue Hayakawa. Straightforward drama based on true story of WW2 hero Guy Gabaldon, who was raised by Japanese foster parents; battle scenes galore. **▼❶**

Hell Town SEE: **Born to the West**

Hellzapoppin' (1941) **84m.** ******* D: H. C. Potter. Ole Olsen, Chic Johnson, Martha Raye, Mischa Auer, Jane Frazee, Hugh Herbert, Robert Paige, Shemp Howard, Elisha Cook, Jr. Famous madcap Broadway show is conventionalized by Hollywood, with romantic subplot and too many songs, but still has many inspired moments of lunacy, from a throwaway CITIZEN KANE gag to the mutterings of Hugh Herbert.

He Loved an Actress SEE: **Mad About Money**

Help! (1965-British) **C-90m.** *****½** D: Richard Lester. John Lennon, Paul McCartney, George Harrison, Ringo Starr, Leo McKern, Eleanor Bron, Victor Spinetti, Roy Kinnear, Patrick Cargill. Crazy, funny film, the Beatles' second. Lots of wild gags, many songs (including "Ticket to Ride," "Another Girl," "You've Got to Hide Your Love Away," title tune). The story: a religious sect attempts to recover a sacrificial ring from Ringo. Written by Charles Wood and Marc Behm. **▼❶❶**

He Married His Wife (1940) **83m.** ****** D: Roy Del Ruth. Joel McCrea, Nancy Kelly, Roland Young, Mary Boland, Cesar Romero, Lyle Talbot, Mary Healy, Elisha Cook, Jr. Obvious, talky comedy in which McCrea, tired of paying alimony to ex-wife Kelly, schemes to get her remarried. John O'Hara was one of the writers.

Hemingway's Adventures of a Young Man (1962) **C-145m.** ****** D: Martin Ritt. Richard Beymer, Diane Baker, Paul Newman, Corinne Calvet, Fred Clark, Dan Dailey, James Dunn, Juano Hernandez, Arthur Kennedy, Ricardo Montalban, Susan Strasberg, Jessica Tandy, Eli Wallach, Simon Oakland, Michael (J.) Pollard. Loosely based on autobiographical data from his stories, this pretentious, drawn-out memory of the famed author is overblown, cornball, and embarrassing. Fine cast mostly wasted. Aka ADVENTURES OF A YOUNG MAN. CinemaScope. **❶**

Henry Aldrich Teenaged Henry Aldrich was Paramount's answer to MGM's *Andy Hardy* series, and while the Aldrich films were less popular, less prestigious, and shorter-lived, they were then, and remain today, well-crafted, entertaining little B movies, without any of the pretentiousness and calculated coyness that marred the *Hardy* series. Henry and group were the invention of Clifford Goldsmith, whose play

What a Life opened in 1938 on Broadway, spawning a radio series with Ezra Stone repeating his stage role of Henry. In 1939, Paramount turned the hit play into a pleasant film, retaining Betty Field (as Henry's plain-jane girlfriend) and Vaughan Glaser (as dour principal Mr. Bradley) from the original cast, but bypassing Ezra Stone in favor of Jackie Cooper. Best of all, Paramount assigned their writing team of Billy Wilder and Charles Brackett to provide the script—an unlikely pair for such Middle American doings, but welcome nonetheless. In 1941, Jackie Cooper repeated his role in a second outing, LIFE WITH HENRY, a typically silly but likable effort. Then Paramount cast a newcomer, Jimmy Lydon, in the key role of Henry and surrounded him with a new supporting cast for a string of actual series films: Charles Smith as his laconic but shifty pal Dizzy, John Litel as his stern father, Olive Blakeney as his forgiving mother, and welcome Vaughan Glaser as the forever-pouting principal. A new director, ex-film editor Hugh Bennett, was added to comprise the working unit that turned out nine films over the next four years. The Aldrich films, timed around 70 minutes, fell into a pattern that proved generally successful: putting hopelessly blundering Henry into an increasingly complicated series of mishaps which would alienate him from his parents, sometimes his friends, and often the entire town, before culminating in a major action and/or slapstick climax in which Henry would be vindicated. The films are consistently well paced and slickly filmed, never belying their modest budgets, and filled with engaging players: Mary Anderson as Henry's girlfriend in several entries (later replaced by Diana Lynn, and other less notable starlets); Frances Gifford as a movie star who accepts Henry's prom invitation as a publicity stunt in HENRY ALDRICH GETS GLAMOUR, Fritz Feld as a famous musician whose Stradivarius is accidentally "borrowed" by Henry in HENRY ALDRICH SWINGS IT; Lucien Littlefield as an antagonistic teacher in two of the episodes; June Preisser as a vamp in HENRY ALDRICH FOR PRESIDENT; and Vera Vague as a potential wife for Mr. Bradley in HENRY ALDRICH PLAYS CUPID. Best of all is Francis Pierlot as a character called Nero Smith, a pyromaniac who announces his intentions to Henry, leading to suspicions and troubles galore in perhaps the best series entry, HENRY ALDRICH, EDITOR. HENRY ALDRICH'S LITTLE SECRET is the last and easily the weakest film of the nine Lydon pictures, but the other eight maintain a surprisingly good standard of filmmaking quality and good, lightweight entertainment.

HENRY ALDRICH

What a Life (1939)
Life With Henry (1941)

Henry Aldrich for President (1941)
Henry and Dizzy (1942)
Henry Aldrich, Editor (1942)
Henry Aldrich Gets Glamour (1943)
Henry Aldrich Swings It (1943)
Henry Aldrich Haunts a House (1943)
Henry Aldrich, Boy Scout (1944)
Henry Aldrich Plays Cupid (1944)
Henry Aldrich's Little Secret (1944)

Henry Aldrich, Boy Scout (1944) **66m.** ****½** D: Hugh Bennett. Jimmy Lydon, Charles Smith, John Litel, Olive Blakeney, Joan Mortimer, Darryl Hickman, Minor Watson, Richard Haydn. Henry as a Scout Leader? Just a jumping-off point for him to get into more jams than usual—including a literal cliffhanger.

Henry Aldrich, Editor (1942) **71m.** ******* D: Hugh Bennett. Jimmy Lydon, Charles Smith, John Litel, Olive Blakeney, Rita Quigley, Vaughan Glaser, Francis Pierlot. When a pyromaniac tells Henry where he plans to strike next—and Henry prints the news—he becomes the prime suspect! Solid series entry with a truly exciting climax, and memorable performance by Pierlot as Nero Smith.

Henry Aldrich for President (1941) **73m.** ****½** D: Hugh Bennett. Jimmy Lydon, Charles Smith, June Preisser, Mary Anderson, Martha O'Driscoll, Dorothy Peterson, John Litel, Rod Cameron, Lucien Littlefield, Kenneth Howell. Henry's race for the presidency of the Centerville High School student council gets him into the usual hot water. Particularly attractive cast of young Hollywood hopefuls supports Lydon in his series debut.

Henry Aldrich Gets Glamour (1943) **75m.** ****½** D: Hugh Bennett. Jimmy Lydon, Charles Smith, John Litel, Olive Blakeney, Diana Lynn, Frances Gifford, Gail Russell, Bill Goodwin, Vaughan Glaser. Henry wins first prize in a *Movieplay* magazine contest: a date with glamorous Hilary Dane (Gifford). Entertaining (if typically farfetched) entry with appealing distaff cast.

Henry Aldrich Haunts a House (1943) **73m.** ****½** D: Hugh Bennett. Jimmy Lydon, Charles Smith, John Litel, Olive Blakeney, Joan Mortimer, Vaughan Glaser, Jackie Moran, Lucien Littlefield, Mike Mazurki. Henry gets into more trouble than usual when he swallows a test tube full of experimental strength serum, and stumbles into a "haunted" house. Contrived, to say the least, but fun.

Henry Aldrich Plays Cupid (1944) **65m.** ****½** D: Hugh Bennett. Jimmy Lydon, Charles Smith, John Litel, Olive Blakeney, Diana Lynn, Vaughan Glaser, Vera Vague (Barbara Jo Allen), Paul Harvey, Barbara Pepper. Henry tries to marry off the school principal Mr. Bradley in this enjoyable outing which features Vera Vague as the other half of the match.

Henry Aldrich's Little Secret (1944)

75m. ****** D: Hugh Bennett. Jimmy Lydon, Charles Smith, Joan Mortimer, John Litel, Olive Blakeney, Ann Doran, John David Robb, Tina Thayer, Noel Neill. Henry tries to help out a troubled young mother by taking care of her infant in this so-so entry that brought the series to a close.

Henry Aldrich Swings It (1943) **64m.** ****½** D: Hugh Bennett. Jimmy Lydon, Charles Smith, John Litel, Olive Blakeney, Mimi Chandler, Vaughan Glaser, Marion Hall, Fritz Feld, Bernard Nedell. Henry is smitten with his pretty music teacher (Hall); his Dad likes her too, but Mrs. Aldrich misunderstands, thinks her husband is unfaithful. Meanwhile, Henry forms his own band and gets into trouble with gamblers and crooks. Amusing comedy of errors.

Henry and Dizzy (1942) **71m.** ****½** D: Hugh Bennett. Jimmy Lydon, Charles Smith, Mary Anderson, John Litel, Olive Blakeney, Maude Eburne, Vaughan Glaser, Shirley Coates. Typical comic misadventures of Henry and his pal Basil A. "Dizzy" Stevens, with a great climax at Lake Wopacotapotalong. Look for future "Lois Lane" Noel Neill as Dizzy's girlfriend, and former Little Rascal Carl "Alfalfa" Switzer as a bratty kid.

Henry V (1945-British) **C-137m.** ******** D: Laurence Olivier. Laurence Olivier, Robert Newton, Leslie Banks, Renee Asherson, Esmond Knight, Leo Genn, Ralph Truman, Harcourt Williams, Ivy St. Helier, Ernest Thesiger, Max Adrian, George Cole, Felix Aylmer, Robert Helpmann, Freda Jackson, Jimmy Hanley, John Laurie. Olivier's masterful rendition of Shakespeare play is a cinematic treat, filmed in rich color and framed by ingenious presentation of a typical performance at the Globe theater during 1500s. This earned Olivier a special Academy Award "for his outstanding achievement as actor, producer, and director in bringing HENRY V to the screen." ▼●◗

Henry Goes Arizona (1939) **69m.** ****½** D: Edwin L. Marin. Frank Morgan, Virginia Weidler, Guy Kibbee, Slim Summerville, Douglas Fowley, Owen Davis, Jr., Porter Hall. Modest but charming vehicle for Morgan, perfectly cast as a blustery vaudevillian who inherits a ranch and proceeds to rout the crooks responsible for his half-brother's murder. Good showcase for young Weidler, too.

Henry, the Rainmaker (1949) **64m.** ***½** D: Jean Yarbrough. Raymond Walburn, Walter Catlett, William Tracy, Mary Stuart. Mild comedy of homey Walburn, who develops a "scientific" way to make rain. First in short-lived "Father" series; followed by LEAVE IT TO HENRY.

Her Adventurous Night (1946) **76m.** ****½** D: John Rawlins. Dennis O'Keefe, Helen Walker, Scotty Beckett, Fuzzy Knight, Milburn Stone, Tom Powers. Beckett is a youngster with a wild imagination whose fanciful tale of murder and crime causes untold problems for his parents. Occasionally diverting crime comedy.

He Ran All the Way (1951) 77m. **½ D: John Berry. John Garfield, Shelley Winters, Wallace Ford, Selena Royle, Gladys George, Norman Lloyd. Taut but predictable thriller with on-the-lam cop killer Garfield hiding out in Winters' home. Garfield's final film. ◗

Her Bridal Night SEE: **Bride Is Much Too Beautiful, The**

Her Brother (1960-Japanese) C-98m. **½ D: Kon Ichikawa. Keiko Kishi, Hiroshi Kawaguchi, Kinuyo Tanaka, Masayuki Mori. Troublesome family is brought together when immature brother-son Kawaguchi contracts tuberculosis; central to the scenario is his warm relationship with his older sister (Kishi). Sentimental drama. Daieiscope.

Her Cardboard Lover (1942) 93m. *½ D: George Cukor. Norma Shearer, Robert Taylor, George Sanders, Frank McHugh, Elizabeth Patterson, Chill Wills. Shearer is as chic as ever (in her final screen appearance), but neither she nor a miscast Taylor can salvage this tired romantic comedy about a flighty socialite who becomes the love object of a songwriter. Filmed before in 1928 as THE CARDBOARD LOVER and in 1932 as THE PASSIONATE PLUMBER. ◗

Hercules (1959-Italian) C-107m. **½ D: Pietro Francisci. Steve Reeves, Sylva Koscina, Gianna Maria Canale, Fabrizio Mioni, Ivo Garrani, Gina Rovere, Luciana Paoluzzi (Paluzzi). This Italian import became a surprise U.S. hit, and served as the prototype of all cloak-and-sandal pictures to come: Reeves is musclebound mythical hero in essentially a retelling of the story of Jason and the Golden Fleece. Sequel: HERCULES UNCHAINED. Dyaliscope. ▼●◗

Hercules Against Rome (1960-Italian) C-87m. ** D: Piero Pierott. Alan Steel, Wandisa Guida, Livio Lorenzon, Daniele Vargas. Steel fights a series of unconvincing villains to protect the late emperor's daughter. Totalscope.

Hercules in the Haunted World (1961-Italian) C-83m. ** D: Mario Bava. Reg Park, Christopher Lee, Leonora Ruffo, Giorgio Ardisson, Ida Galli. Occasionally sparked by atmospheric settings, this sword-and-sandal epic narrates adventures of Park in the devil's kingdom. Totalscope Super/100. ▼◗

Hercules Unchained (1960-Italian) C-101m. ** D: Pietro Francisci. Steve Reeves, Sylva Koscina, Primo Carnera, Sylvia Lopez. Par-for-the-course entry featuring the muscleman hero and his princess bride setting off for the city of Thebes; along the way he will bid to prevent a war and tangle with a sinister queen. Dyaliscope. ▼●◗

Here Comes Cookie (1935) 65m. **½ D:
Norman Z. McLeod. George Burns, Gracie Allen, George Barbier, Betty Furness, Andrew Tombes, Rafael Storm. An heiress converts the family mansion into a haven for down-on-their-luck vaudevillians. In their third of three Paramount pictures, Burns and Allen play characters named Burns and Allen. Inconsequential (and improbable) screwball comedy/variety show is watchable mainly for the numerous specialty acts. ▼◗

Here Comes Mr. Jordan (1941) 93m. **** D: Alexander Hall. Robert Montgomery, Evelyn Keyes, Claude Rains, Rita Johnson, Edward Everett Horton, James Gleason, John Emery. Excellent fantasy-comedy of prizefighter Montgomery accidentally sent to heaven before his time, forced to occupy a new body on earth. Hollywood moviemaking at its best, with first-rate cast and performances; Harry Segall won an Oscar for his original story, as did Sidney Buchman and Seton I. Miller for their screenplay. Characters used again in DOWN TO EARTH (1947); film remade as HEAVEN CAN WAIT in 1978 and DOWN TO EARTH (2001). Look for a young Lloyd Bridges. ▼●◗

Here Comes the Band (1935) 86m. ** D: Paul Sloane. Ted Lewis and His Orchestra, Virginia Bruce, Harry Stockwell, Ted Healy, Nat Pendleton, Addison Richards, Donald Cook, George "Spanky" McFarland. Cheerfully incoherent musical-comedy vehicle for "the high-hatted tragedian of song" about WW1 vets with a yen for show business. Story comes and goes (like Lewis himself, who's off-screen a lot). Comedy buffs will want to see Healy poke Pendleton as if he were a Stooge and an unbilled Billy Gilbert do his hilarious sneezing routine. The leading man is Guy and Dean Stockwell's father.

Here Comes the Groom (1951) 113m. *** D: Frank Capra. Bing Crosby, Jane Wyman, Franchot Tone, Alexis Smith, James Barton, Anna Maria Alberghetti. Crosby contrives to keep former fiancée Wyman from marrying millionaire Tone in this lightweight musical outing. Guest appearances by Louis Armstrong, Dorothy Lamour, Phil Harris, and Cass Daley, plus Oscar-winning song, "In the Cool, Cool, Cool of the Evening." ▼●◗

Here Comes the Navy (1934) 86m. **½ D: Lloyd Bacon. James Cagney, Pat O'Brien, Gloria Stuart, Dorothy Tree, Frank McHugh. Enjoyable but standard tale of cocky Cagney who becomes Navy hero; nothing new, but well done. ◗

Here Come the Co-Eds (1945) 87m. **½ D: Jean Yarbrough. Bud Abbott, Lou Costello, Peggy Ryan, Martha O'Driscoll, June Vincent, Lon Chaney (Jr.), Donald Cook. Pretty zany Abbott and Costello comedy of two wacky caretakers turning formerly staid girls' school on its ear. ▼◗

Here Come the Girls (1953) C-78m. **½

D: Claude Binyon. Bob Hope, Arlene Dahl, Rosemary Clooney, Tony Martin, Fred Clark, Robert Strauss, the Four Step Brothers. At times amusing romp with Hope a naive show biz-ite who becomes involved with killer on the loose.▼●

Here Come the Marines (1952) **66m.** *½ D: William Beaudine. Leo Gorcey, Huntz Hall, David Gorcey, Bennie Bartlett, Bernard Gorcey, Gil Stratton, Jr., Murray Alper, Hanley Stafford, Myrna Dell, Arthur Space, Tim Ryan. The Bowery Boys are drafted and probe a murder in this tired rehash. ▶

Here Come the Nelsons (1952) **76m.** ** D: Frederick de Cordova. Ozzie, Harriet, David, Ricky Nelson, Rock Hudson, Ann Doran, Jim Backus, Barbara Lawrence, Sheldon Leonard, Gale Gordon. Expanded version of radio's *Adventures of Ozzie & Harriet,* spotlighting a series of typical, comical situations. Light, predictable fare that paved the way for the long-running TV series. ▼

Here Come the Waves (1944) **99m.** *** D: Mark Sandrich. Bing Crosby, Betty Hutton, Sonny Tufts, Ann Doran, Gwen Crawford, Noel Neill, Catherine Craig, Mae Clarke. Zippy wartime music-comedy with Crosby cleverly cast as a Sinatra-like crooner, the idol of bobby-soxers, who joins the Navy, and becomes involved with twin sisters (played by Hutton—and one's even demure!). Harold Arlen–Johnny Mercer score includes "Let's Take the Long Way Home," "(That Old) Black Magic" (reprised from STAR SPANGLED RHYTHM), and "Accent-u-ate the Positive," which is performed in blackface! Yvonne De Carlo and Mona Freeman have bit parts. ▼▶

Here Is My Heart (1934) **77m.** **½ D: Frank Tuttle. Bing Crosby, Kitty Carlisle, Roland Young, Alison Skipworth, Reginald Owen, William Frawley, Cecilia Parker, Akim Tamiroff. Crooner Crosby pretends to be a waiter in order to woo Russian princess Carlisle in this elegant romantic comedy, a remake of the 1926 silent film THE GRAND DUCHESS AND THE WAITER. Pleasant, but the stars lack chemistry. Songs include "Love Is Just Around the Corner" and "June in January." ▶

Her Enlisted Man SEE: **Red Salute**

Here We Go Again (1942) **76m.** ** D: Allan Dwan. Edgar Bergen and Charlie McCarthy, Jim and Marian Jordan (Fibber McGee and Molly), Harold Peary (The Great Gildersleeve), Ginny Simms, Bill Thompson, Isabel Randolph, Gale Gordon, Mortimer Snerd. Follow-up to LOOK WHO'S LAUGHING finds Fibber and Molly on a cross-country trip for their 20th anniversary, getting involved in mild antics at resort hotel with rest of radio gang. Easy-to-take comedy, but nothing special. ▶

Her First Romance (1951) **73m.** *½ D: Seymour Friedman. Margaret O'Brien, Allen Martin, Jr., Jimmy Hunt, Sharyn Moffett.

O'Brien's first grown-up role and her first screen kiss are only assets of this plodding summer camp story.

Her Highness and the Bellboy (1945) **112m.** **½ D: Richard Thorpe. Hedy Lamarr, Robert Walker, June Allyson, Carl Esmond, Agnes Moorehead, Rags Ragland. Sentimental fluff of N.Y.C. bellboy Walker, crippled girlfriend Allyson, captivating Princess (Lamarr) he escorts; a bit creaky. ▶

Her Husband's Affairs (1947) **83m.** *½ D: S. Sylvan Simon. Lucille Ball, Franchot Tone, Edward Everett Horton, Mikhail Rasumny, Gene Lockhart, Nana Bryant. Pretty sterile comedy: Ball learns not to poke into husband's business affairs.▼▶

Her Jungle Love (1938) **C-81m.** **½ D: George Archainbaud. Dorothy Lamour, Ray Milland, Lynne Overman, J. Carrol Naish, Dorothy Howe (Virginia Vale). Flyers Milland and Overman stranded on tropical isle with Lamour; Ray teaches her how to kiss, Naish tries to destroy everyone in this escapist fare. ▶

Her Kind of Man (1946) **79m.** ** D: Frederick De Cordova. Dane Clark, Janis Paige, Zachary Scott, Faye Emerson, George Tobias, Howard Smith, Harry Lewis, Sheldon Leonard. Lukewarm crime drama with music, spotlighting the life and times of thuggish gambler Scott; Paige is his nightclub singer girlfriend, Clark a savvy newspaper columnist.

Her Lucky Night (1945) **63m.** ** D: Edward Lilley. The Andrews Sisters, Martha O'Driscoll, Noah Beery, Jr., George Barbier, Grady Sutton, Ida Moore. Minor comedy with singing trio desperately seeking love, becoming involved with an astrologer whom they hope will predict their romantic destinies.

Her Majesty, Love (1931) **75m.** *½ D: William Dieterle. Marilyn Miller, W. C. Fields, Leon Errol, Ford Sterling, Chester Conklin, Ben Lyon, Virginia Sale. Unbearable musical with sweet Miller in love with Lyon in old Berlin. Errol as persistent suitor, Fields as juggling father, provide only uplifting moments.

Her Man Gilbey (1944-British) **89m.** **½ D: Harold French. Michael Wilding, Penelope (Dudley) Ward, Lilli Palmer, Claude Dauphin, Albert Lieven, Peggy Cummins, Margaret Rutherford, Martin Miller, Roland Culver, Guy Middleton. Moderately pleasing yarn with upper-crust Ward and butler Wilding falling for each other. Screenplay by Terence Rattigan and Anatole de Grunwald. Original British title: ENGLISH WITHOUT TEARS.

Her Night of Romance (1924) **85m.** *** D: Sidney Franklin. Constance Talmadge, Ronald Colman, Jean Hersholt, Albert Gran, Sidney Bracey. American heiress Talmadge, sailing to England with her father, makes herself look unattractive to ward off suitors who are after her money. Who should she meet on the ship but Colman, an impoverished lord. Charming comedy vehicle for Talmadge written by frequent Lubitsch collaborator Hanns (Hans) Kräly. **)**

Herod the Great (1960-Italian) **C-93m.** *½ D: Arnaldo Genoino. Edmund Purdom, Sylvia Lopez, Sandra Milo, Alberto Lupo. Juvenile account of ruler of ancient Judea, his warring and his jealousy of wife's admirers. Totalscope. **▼)**

Heroes for Sale (1933) **73m.** *** D: William A. Wellman. Richard Barthelmess, Loretta Young, Aline MacMahon, Robert Barrat, Grant Mitchell, Douglass Dumbrille, Charles Grapewin, Ward Bond. Potent melodrama with Barthelmess as an American Everyman who manages to survive one calamity after another—from morphine addiction (as a result of a WW1 injury) to job-hunting during the Depression—and continues to endure, like the country itself. Ambitious script by Wilson Mizner and Robert Lord tackles everything from the hypocrisy of hero worship to Communism! A fascinating social document of the early 1930s. **▼)**

Heroes of Telemark, The (1965-British) **C-131m.** **½ D: Anthony Mann. Kirk Douglas, Richard Harris, Michael Redgrave, Mervyn Johns, Eric Porter. Douglas and Harris spend more time battling each other than the Nazis overrunning Norway in this pictorially striking (filmed on location), predictable blow-up-the-German-factory yarn. Panavision. **▼)**

Hero's Island (1962) **C-94m.** **½ D: Leslie Stevens. James Mason, Kate Manx, Neville Brand, Rip Torn, Warren Oates, Brendan Dillon, (Harry) Dean Stanton. Peculiar mixture of adventure and soap opera set in 18th-century on island near North Carolina, involving pirates and homesteaders. Mason coproduced. Panavision. **)**

Her Panelled Door (1950-British) **84m.** *** D: Ladislas Vajda. Phyllis Calvert, Edward Underdown, Helen Cherry, Richard Burton. During an air raid Calvert is shellshocked, forgetting her past, leading to dramatic results. Original British title: THE WOMAN WITH NO NAME.

Her Primitive Man (1944) **79m.** *½ D: Charles Lamont. Robert Paige, Louise Allbritton, Robert Benchley, Edward Everett Horton. Grade-C flick with Paige pretending to be a savage to win love of anthropologist Allbritton.

Her Sister from Paris (1925) **74m.** **½ D: Sidney Franklin. Constance Talmadge, Ronald Colman, George K. Arthur, Gertrude Claire. Twin sisters switch places so the worldly one can help her humdrum sibling win back the affection of her husband. Lighthearted Talmadge vehicle is amusing for a while but awfully predictable. Screenplay by Hanns (Hans) Kräly from a play by Ludwig Fulda. Remade as TWO-FACED WOMAN. **)**

Her Sister's Secret (1946) **86m.** **½ D: Edgar G. Ulmer. Nancy Coleman, Margaret Lindsay, Felix Bressart, Regis Toomey, Philip Reed, Henry Stephenson. Young woman discovers she's pregnant after brief affair. Fair weeper with competent cast.

Hers to Hold (1943) **94m.** ** D: Frank Ryan. Deanna Durbin, Joseph Cotten, Charles Winninger, Nella Walker, Gus Schilling, Ludwig Stossel, Irving Bacon. Grown-up Durbin is in love with serviceman Cotten in undistinguished romance, brightened by Deanna's singing. Songs: "Begin the Beguine," etc.

Her Sweetheart SEE: **Christopher Bean**

Her Twelve Men (1954) **C-91m.** ** D: Robert Z. Leonard. Greer Garson, Robert Ryan, Barry Sullivan, Richard Haydn, James Arness, Tim Considine, David Stollery, Frances Bergen. Maudlin script has Greer as dedicated teacher in boys' school. A failed attempt to repeat the success of GOODBYE, MR. CHIPS.

He's a Cockeyed Wonder (1950) **77m.** *½ D: Peter Godfrey. Mickey Rooney, Terry Moore, William Demarest, Ross Ford, Mike Mazurki. Bland Rooney film has him as energetic young man who captures a gang of robbers and gets to marry his boss' daughter.

He Stayed for Breakfast (1940) **89m.** ** D: Alexander Hall. Loretta Young, Melvyn Douglas, Una O'Connor, Eugene Pallette, Alan Marshal. NINOTCHKA and COMRADE X in reverse, as Russian Douglas is Americanized by Young; trivial.

He Walked by Night (1948) **79m.** *** D: Alfred L. Werker. Richard Basehart, Scott Brady, Roy Roberts, Whit Bissell, Jack Webb. Grade-A drama of killer hunted by police; told in semi-documentary style (and partially directed by Anthony Mann). Great climax in L.A. storm drains; photographed by the great John Alton. This clearly inspired Webb's creation of *Dragnet*. **▼●)**

He Was Her Man (1934) **70m.** ** D: Lloyd Bacon. James Cagney, Joan Blondell, Victor Jory, Frank Craven, Sarah Padden. Disappointing drama of safecracker Cagney on the lam, meeting Blondell, who's engaged to fisherman Jory. One of Cagney's weakest Warner Bros. vehicles.

He Who Gets Slapped (1924) **85m.** *** D: Victor Seastrom. Lon Chaney, Norma Shearer, John Gilbert, Tully Marshall, Marc McDermott, Ford Sterling. Brilliant scientist tries to bury personal tragedy under mask of circus clown, who falls in love with beautiful bareback rider (Shearer). Famous story becomes Pagliacci-type vehicle for Chaney. **▼●)**

Hey Boy! Hey Girl! (1959) **81m.** *½ D: David Lowell Rich. Louis Prima, Keely Smith, James Gregory, Henry Slate, Asa Maynor, Sam Butera and The Witnesses. Minor low-budget musical about a singer (Smith) who will join Prima and The Witnesses only if they appear at a church bazaar. Louis sings the unforgettable "A Banana Split for My Baby (And a Glass of Water for Me)."

Hey, Let's Twist! (1961) **80m. BOMB D:** Greg Garrison. Joey Dee, The Starliters, Peppermint Loungers, Jo Ann Campbell, Zohra Lampert, Teddy Randazzo, Allan Arbus. Let's not. This minor film about the rise, decline, and rise of the Peppermint Lounge nightclub came out at the height of the Twist dance rage and wasn't very good then . . . now it's just a bad way to kill 80 minutes. Try spotting a young Joe Pesci (then a Starliters guitarist, making his film debut) as an extra.

Hey, Rookie (1944) **77m. **½ D:** Charles Barton. Larry Parks, Ann Miller, The Condos Brothers, Joe Sawyer, Jack Gilford, Selmer Jackson. Typical let's-put-on-a-show-for-the-servicemen, with Miller's dancing and several specialty acts.

Hey There It's Yogi Bear (1964) **C-89m. **½ D:** William Hanna, Joseph Barbera. Voices of: Mel Blanc, J. Pat O'Malley, Julie Bennett, Daws Butler, Don Messick. First full-length cartoon from Hanna-Barbera studio stars Yogi Bear in amusing musical tale for younger folk. ▼○)

H. G. Wells' New Invisible Man SEE: **New Invisible Man, The**

Hiawatha (1952) **C-80m. **½ D:** Kurt Neumann. Vincent Edwards, Keith Larsen, Michael Tolan, Yvette Dugay. Juvenile low-budget version of the Longfellow classic. ▶

Hidden City, The (1950) **71m. **½ D:** Ford Beebe. Johnny Sheffield, Sue England, Paul Guilfoyle, Damian O'Flynn, Leon Belasco, Smoki Whitfield. Bomba the Jungle Boy comes to the aid of a jungle orphan (England) who's actually a princess. Aka BOMBA AND THE HIDDEN CITY. ▶

Hidden Eye, The (1945) **69m. **½ D:** Richard Whorf. Edward Arnold, Frances Rafferty, Ray Collins, Paul Langton, Raymond Largay, William Phillips. Follow-up to EYES IN THE NIGHT, with blind detective Arnold making good use of other senses to solve murder mystery; fast-moving, entertaining mystery.

Hidden Fear (1957) **83m. *½ D:** Andre de Toth. John Payne, Alexander Knox, Conrad Nagel, Natalie Norwick. On-location filming in Copenhagen is chief virtue of mild hunt-down-the-murderer plot.

Hidden Fortress, The (1958-Japanese) **126m. ***½ D:** Akira Kurosawa. Toshiro Mifune, Misa Uehara, Minoru Chiaki, Kamatari Fujiwara, Susumu Fujita, Takashi Shimura. Autocratic young Princess Uehara and loyal general Mifune must make dangerous journey to their homeland with royal fortune, with only bare minimum of help from two bumbling misfits hoping to make off with a share of the gold. Solid comedy-adventure with great deadpan performance by Mifune; one of Kurosawa's personal favorites. Acknowledged by George Lucas as a primary inspiration for STAR WARS. Some U.S. prints cut to 90m.; released in Japan at 139m., and reissued in the U.S. in 1984 at that length. Tohoscope. ▼○)

Hidden Gold (1940) **61m. **½ D:** Lesley Selander. William Boyd, Russell Hayden, Minor Watson, Ruth Rogers, Britt Wood, Ethel Wales. Mine owner Watson is helpless against crowd of outlaws stealing gold ore from stage line, until Hopalong Cassidy, as express company agent, lends a hand. Enough hard riding, fisticuffs, and gunplay to satisfy. Alleged comedy relief offered by Wood underscores value of such sidekicks as George Hayes and Andy Clyde. ▼)

Hidden Homicide (1959-British) **70m. *½ D:** Anthony Young. Griffith Jones, James Kenney, Patricia Laffan, Bruce Seton, Charles Farrell. Circumstantial evidence makes writer think he's a murderer.

Hidden Room, The (1949-British) **98m. *** D:** Edward Dmytryk. Robert Newton, Sally Gray, Naunton Wayne, Phil Brown, Michael Balfour, Olga Lindo. Very effective suspenser involving Newton's plan to eliminate a man threatening his marriage; nifty climax. Retitled: OBSESSION. ▼)

Hi De Ho (1947) **64m. **½ D:** Josh Binney. Cab Calloway and His Orchestra, Ida James, Jeni Le Gon, William Campbell, Virginia Girvin, George Wiltshire, James Dunmore. Bandleader Calloway is bored with his jealous, scheming girlfriend Minnie (Le Gon); she's convinced he's romancing his pert manager (James) and conspires with a gangster to rub him out. Limp dramatics take a backseat to an endless stream of sparkling musical numbers, with charismatic Cab performing "Hi De Ho Man," "Minnie's a Hepcat Now," "St. James Infirmary Blues," and many others. Calloway also appeared in two similarly titled 1930s short subjects. ▼)

Hideous Sun Demon, The (1959) **74m. *½ D:** Robert Clarke, Tom Boutross. Robert Clarke, Patricia Manning, Nan Peterson, Patrick Whyte, Fred La Porta. Doctor exposed to radiation discovers that sunlight turns him into ghastly lizard creature. Hideously low-budget production stars codirector Clarke himself as demon of title. ▼)

Hide-Out (1934) **83m. **½ D:** W. S. Van Dyke. Robert Montgomery, Maureen O'Sullivan, Edward Arnold, Elizabeth Patterson, Whitford Kane, Mickey Rooney, C. Henry Gordon, Edward Brophy. Big-city racketeer recovers from gunshot wound on idyllic farm where he falls in love (of course) with fetching O'Sullivan. Opens and closes great, with some humdrum stuffing in between; wonderful supporting cast (including Henry Armetta and Herman Bing as nightclub co-owners!). Remade in 1941 as I'LL WAIT FOR YOU. ▼

Hideout (1949) **61m.** ****** D: Philip Ford. Adrian Booth, Lloyd Bridges, Ray Collins, Sheila Ryan, Alan Carney, Jeff Corey. Con man Collins and his cronies settle in a small Midwestern town, where they tangle with nosy city attorney/mayoralty candidate Bridges. Innocuous crime melodrama.

Hi Diddle Diddle (1943) **72m.** ****** D: Andrew L. Stone. Adolphe Menjou, Martha Scott, Pola Negri, Dennis O'Keefe, Billie Burke, June Havoc. Strained screwball comedy about a sailor (O'Keefe) on shore leave whose wedding is repeatedly postponed, while his con-man father (Menjou) tries to win back the money his future mother-in-law (Burke) gambled away. Tries awfully hard, with a multitude of gimmicks (even animated footage by Leon Schlesinger studios) but only modest results . . . though the demonstration of double-takes is pretty swell. Silent screen vamp Negri plays an egotistical opera star.▼▶

High and Dry (1954-British) **93m.** ****½** D: Alexander Mackendrick. Paul Douglas, Alex Mackenzie, James Copeland, Abe Barker. Satisfactory, minor yarn about U.S. financier Douglas in conflict with the captain of broken-down ship carrying valuable cargo; static at times. Originally titled THE 'MAGGIE.'▶

High and Low (1963-Japanese) **142m.** ******* D: Akira Kurosawa. Toshiro Mifune, Tatsuya Mihashi, Yutaka Sada, Tatsuya Nakadai, Kyoko Kagawa. Carefully paced study of business executive Mifune, who is financially ruined when he nobly pays ransom money to kidnappers who mistakenly stole his chauffeur's son. Based on an Ed McBain story; one color sequence. Tohoscope.▼▶●

High and the Mighty, The (1954) **C-147m.** ******* D: William A. Wellman. John Wayne, Claire Trevor, Laraine Day, Robert Stack, Jan Sterling, Phil Harris, Robert Newton, David Brian, Paul Kelly, John Howard, Sidney Blackmer, Julie Bishop, Wally Brown, Doe Avedon, Karen Sharpe, John Smith, William Campbell, Douglas Fowley, (Pedro) Gonzales Gonzales, John Qualen, Ann Doran, Paul Fix, Joy Kim, Carl Switzer, William Hopper, Regis Toomey. Granddaddy of all airborne disaster films and more fun than most of them put together: a GRAND HOTEL cast of characters boards a flight from Honolulu to San Francisco, little dreaming of the trouble in store, or the tensions in the cockpit. Corny at times, but still entertaining; bolstered by Dimitri Tiomkin's Oscar-winning music (including the title song, which became a big hit). Written by Ernest K. Gann, from his novel. CinemaScope.▼▶

High Barbaree (1947) **91m.** ****** D: Jack Conway. Van Johnson, June Allyson, Thomas Mitchell, Marilyn Maxwell, Cameron Mitchell. Navy flier's life story told in flashback as he awaits rescue in plane in ocean. Good cast in inferior story.▶

High Command, The (1937-British) **90m.** ****½** D: Thorold Dickinson. Lionel Atwill, Lucie Mannheim, Steven Geray, James Mason, Allan Jeayes, Wally Patch. Crime melodrama set at an African military outpost. Atwill is a general caught up in a blackmailing scheme that leads to murder. An early role for Mason.▼

High Cost of Loving, The (1958) **87m.** ****½** D: Jose Ferrer. Jose Ferrer, Gena Rowlands, Joanne Gilbert, Jim Backus, Bobby Troup, Edward Platt, Werner Klemperer, Nancy Kulp, Abby Dalton. Lots of familiar faces in this very mild romantic comedy about tensions that threaten marriage of Ferrer and Rowlands. Enjoyable but innocuous semi-satire. Rowlands' film debut. CinemaScope.

Higher and Higher (1943) **90m.** ****½** D: Tim Whelan. Michele Morgan, Jack Haley, Frank Sinatra, Leon Errol, Marcy McGuire, Victor Borge, Mary Wickes, Mel Tormé. Bright, breezy, generally witless musical, with good cheer compensating for lack of material, as once-wealthy Errol schemes with his own servants to raise money. Sinatra's songs are fine: "The Music Stopped," "I Couldn't Sleep a Wink Last Night." This was his starring debut.▼▶●

High Flight (1957-British) **C-89m.** ***½** D: John Gilling. Ray Milland, Bernard Lee, Kenneth Haigh, Anthony Newley. Stale British drama of recruits in training for the RAF—not as good as Milland's I WANTED WINGS. Last reel, in the air, only exciting part. CinemaScope.

High Flyers (1937) **70m.** ****** D: Edward Cline. Bert Wheeler, Robert Woolsey, Lupe Velez, Marjorie Lord, Margaret Dumont, Jack Carson, Paul Harvey, Charles Judels. Wheeler and Woolsey's last movie together finds them going through the motions as dimwit carny performers duped into a jewel-smuggling scheme. Pretty tired, apart from a scene where Wheeler accidentally sniffs some cocaine! Dumont works just as well with W&W as she does with the Marx Brothers.▶

High Fury (1947-British) **71m.** ****** D: Harold French. Madeleine Carroll, Ian Hunter, Michael Rennie, Michael McKeag, Anne Marie Blanc. Nice location filming in Switzerland uplifts this otherwise standard drama about the plight of war orphans. Carroll wants to adopt young McKeag against the wishes of philandering husband Rennie. Original British title: WHITE CRADLE INN.▼

High Hell (1958-British) **87m.** ****½** D: Burt Balaban. John Derek, Elaine Stewart, Rodney Burke, Patrick Allen. Mine owner's wife has an affair with husband's partner; trio snowbound for winter fight about it.

High Lonesome (1950) **C-81m.** ****** D: Alan LeMay. John Barrymore, Jr., Chill

Wills, John Archer, Lois Butler, Kristine Miller, Basil Ruysdael, Jack Elam. Odd, unsatisfying Texas-made Western with an unusual mystery twist: Sullen teenage drifter Barrymore swears that two men known to be long dead are responsible for recent killings. Ghosts? Young Barrymore's performance is often unintentionally funny. Sole directing credit for LeMay, prolific Western author best remembered for writing *The Searchers*. ▼▶

Highly Dangerous (1950-British) **88m.** ****½** D: Roy Baker. Dane Clark, Marius Goring, Margaret Lockwood, Wilfrid Hyde-White, Olaf Pooley, Eric Pohlmann. American reporter (Clark) accompanies scientist (Lockwood) on secret mission; well paced. ▶

High Noon (1952) **84m.** ******** D: Fred Zinnemann. Gary Cooper, Thomas Mitchell, Lloyd Bridges, Katy Jurado, Grace Kelly, Otto Kruger, Lon Chaney (Jr.), Henry (Harry) Morgan, Lee Van Cleef, Robert Wilke, Sheb Wooley. On his wedding—and retirement—day, marshal Cooper learns that a gunman is coming seeking revenge. Though he has good excuses for leaving, he feels a responsibility to stay and face the gunman—but no one in town is willing to help. The story appears to unfold in "real time," as the many on-screen clocks will verify. Legendary Western drama about a crisis of conscience, written by Carl Foreman, underscored by Tex Ritter's performance of Oscar-winning Dimitri Tiomkin–Ned Washington song, "Do Not Forsake Me, Oh My Darlin'." Oscars also went to Cooper, Tiomkin's score, and Elmo Williams' and Harry Gerstad's editing. Followed by 1980 TV sequel with Lee Majors; remade for TV in 2000. Also shown in computer-colored version. ▼▶

High Pressure (1932) **74m.** ******* D: Mervyn LeRoy. William Powell, Evelyn Brent, Frank McHugh, George Sidney, Guy Kibbee, Evalyn Knapp, Ben Alexander. Slam-bang conman caper stars Powell as hilarious scheming promotor trying to sell artificial rubber. Typical nonstop Warner Bros. early talkie farce. ▶

High School Caesar (1960) **72m.** ****** D: O'Dale Ireland. John Ashley, Gary Vinson, Lowell Brown, Steve Stevens, Judy Nugent, Daria Massey. Rich kid Ashley, whose parents are too busy for him, gets a chip on his shoulder the size of the Rock of Gibraltar . . . and sets up his own little crime empire in school. Actually, not bad of its type. ▼▶

High School Confidential! (1958) **85m.** ***½** D: Jack Arnold. Russ Tamblyn, Jan Sterling, John Drew Barrymore, Mamie Van Doren, Diane Jergens, Ray Anthony, Jerry Lee Lewis, Jackie Coogan, Charles Chaplin, Jr., Lyle Talbot, William Wellman, Jr., Michael Landon. Amateurish, hilariously awful marijuana exposé, with young undercover agent Tamblyn obtaining evidence against dope pushers. A most fascinating

cast. Retitled YOUNG HELLIONS; followed by COLLEGE CONFIDENTIAL! CinemaScope. ▼▶

High Sierra (1941) **100m.** ******* D: Raoul Walsh. Ida Lupino, Humphrey Bogart, Alan Curtis, Arthur Kennedy, Joan Leslie, Henry Hull, Henry Travers, Barton MacLane, Jerome Cowan, Cornel Wilde, Donald MacBride, John Eldredge, Isabel Jewell, Willie Best. Bogey is Mad Dog Earle, killer with a soft heart on the lam from police, in rousing (if not exactly credible) gangster caper. Lupino as the moll and Leslie as the lame innocent Bogart befriends offer interesting contrast. Screenplay by John Huston and W. R. Burnett based on Burnett's novel. Remade as I DIED A THOUSAND TIMES, and in Western garb as COLORADO TERRITORY. Also shown in computer-colored version. ▼▶

High Society (1955) **61m.** ****** D: William Beaudine. Leo Gorcey, Huntz Hall, Bernard Gorcey, Amanda Blake, David (Gorcey) Condon, Addison Richards, Gavin Gordon, Paul Harvey, Bennie Bartlett. The Bowery Boys go from a greasy garage to an aristocrat's mansion when Sach is mistakenly believed to be heir to a fortune. OK, but nothing new. ▶

High Society (1956) **C-107m.** ******* D: Charles Walters. Bing Crosby, Grace Kelly, Frank Sinatra, Celeste Holm, John Lund, Louis Calhern, Louis Armstrong, Sidney Blackmer. Fluffy remake of THE PHILADELPHIA STORY is enjoyable, but has lost all the bite of the original. Kelly is about to marry Lund when ex-hubby Crosby arrives, along with reporters Sinatra and Holm. Cole Porter songs include "True Love," "Did You Evah?," "You're Sensational," plus Bing and Satchmo's "Now You Has Jazz." Grace Kelly's last acting role. Runs 111m. with overture. VistaVision. ▼▶

High Terrace (1956-British) **77m.** ****** D: Henry Cass. Dale Robertson, Lois Maxwell, Derek Bond, Eric Pohlmann. Fledgling actress is implicated in murder in minor drama.

High Tide (1947) **72m.** ****½** D: John Reinhardt. Lee Tracy, Don Castle, Julie Bishop, Regis Toomey, Anabel Shaw, Francis Ford. L.A. newspaperman Tracy attempts to stifle a gambling syndicate's efforts to take control of the city. Solid low-budget crime drama.

High Time (1960) **C-103m.** ****½** D: Blake Edwards. Bing Crosby, Fabian, Tuesday Weld, Nicole Maurey. Middling Crosby vehicle has Bing a widower resuming college career and trying to be one of the boys; forced comedy. CinemaScope. ▶

High Treason (1951-British) **93m.** ****½** D: Roy Boulting. Andre Morell, Liam Redmond, Mary Morris. Well-handled drama involving complex caper to instigate chaos in English industrial life via high-explosive bomb.

High Voltage (1929) **57m.** ***½** D: Howard Higgin. William Boyd, Owen Moore, Carol(e) Lombard, Diane Ellis, Phillips Smalley, Billy Bevan. Main attraction in this deadening, laughably predictable antique is a very young Lombard (who was then billed as "Carol," without the final "e"), as one of a diverse group stranded in the wilderness after a snowstorm; she's a prisoner, in the custody of sheriff (Moore), who falls for tough guy (Boyd). ▼▶

High Wall (1947) 99m. *** D: Curtis Bernhardt. Robert Taylor, Audrey Totter, Herbert Marshall, Dorothy Patrick, H. B. Warner, Warner Anderson. Well-paced thriller in which ex-bomber-pilot-war-hero Taylor thinks he has murdered his two-timing wife and attempts to piece together the facts with the help of psychiatrist Totter. ▶

Highway Dragnet (1954) 71m. ** D: Nathan Juran. Richard Conte, Joan Bennett, Wanda Hendrix, Reed Hadley, Mary Beth Hughes. Tawdry caper of accused killer Conte on the lam in the desert with hostages Bennett and Hendrix. This was Roger Corman's first film, as cowriter and coproducer.

Highwayman, The (1951) C-82m. **½ D: Lesley Selander. Charles Coburn, Wanda Hendrix, Philip Friend, Cecil Kellaway, Victor Jory. Filmization of famous poem, involving innkeeper's daughter in love with nobleman who masquerades as bandit to help the oppressed; set in 1760s England.

Highwayman Rides, The SEE: **Billy the Kid** (1930)

Highways by Night (1942) 62m. ** D: Peter Godfrey. Richard Carlson, Jane Randolph, Jane Darwell, Barton MacLane, Ray Collins, Gordon Jones, Jack La Rue. Reclusive millionaire ventures out into the world to get in touch with the common man before entering the Navy, falls in love, and helps his girlfriend's grandma battle racketeers who want to take over her family trucking business. Negligible time-passer.

Highway 13 (1948) 58m. ** D: William Berke. Robert Lowery, Pamela Blake, Clem Bevans, Michael Whalen, Gaylord (Steve) Pendleton, Lyle Talbot, Maris Wrixon, Mary Gordon. Truck driver Lowery is falsely accused when a series of "accidents" threaten his company's vehicles. So-so crime drama. ▶

Highway 301 (1950) 83m. ** D: Andrew L. Stone. Steve Cochran, Virginia Grey, Robert Webber, Richard Egan. Good little gangster film relating robbery capers in straightforward manner. ▶

Highway to Battle (1960-British) 71m. ** D: Ernest Morris. Gerard Heinz, Margaret Tyzack, Peter Reynolds, Richard Shaw. Trim little film set in 1935 England involving Nazi diplomats who try to defect, chased by Gestapo agents.

High, Wide, and Handsome (1937) 112m. **½ D: Rouben Mamoulian. Irene Dunne,

Randolph Scott, Dorothy Lamour, Elizabeth Patterson, Charles Bickford, Raymond Walburn, Alan Hale, Akim Tamiroff, William Frawley. Jerome Kern–Oscar Hammerstein old-time musical of determined Scott drilling for oil in 19th-century Pennsylvania, fighting corrupt Hale. Corny plot put over by energetic cast; result is entertaining. Songs include "The Folks Who Live on the Hill." ▶

High Wind in Jamaica, A (1965-British) C-104m. *** D: Alexander Mackendrick. Anthony Quinn, James Coburn, Dennis Price, Gert Frobe, Lila Kedrova, Nigel Davenport, Kenneth J. Warren, Deborah Baxter. Excellent cast and intelligent script about group of children who reveal their basic natures when left adrift aboard a pirate vessel. Score composed by harmonica virtuoso Larry Adler. CinemaScope. ▶

Hi, Good Lookin' (1944) 62m. ** D: Edward Lilley. Harriet Hilliard, Eddie Quillan, Kirby Grant, Betty Kean, Roscoe Karns, Ozzie Nelson and His Orchestra, Jack Teagarden and His Orchestra, Delta Rhythm Boys, Tip, Tap and Toe. Lightweight musical programmer serves as a showcase for Hilliard as she attempts to become a radio star with help of Grant.

Hilda Crane (1956) C-87m. ** D: Philip Dunne. Jean Simmons, Guy Madison, Jean-Pierre Aumont, Judith Evelyn, Evelyn Varden. Twice-divorced Simmons returns to the college town that used to be her home, starts the local gossips to fluttering with her behavior. Not much overall, but title character is surprisingly liberated for her time, making her one of the '50s' more interesting screen heroines. Based on a play by Samuel Raphaelson. CinemaScope. ▶

Hildegarde Withers In 1932, RKO Radio Pictures purchased the rights to a story by Stuart Palmer about Hildegarde Withers, a schoolteacher with a yen for sleuthing who becomes involved with Inspector Oscar Piper of the Police Department. The role of the stubborn and occasionally thick-witted New York cop went to James Gleason, while Hildegarde found her perfect personification in character actress Edna May Oliver. When Piper gruffly asks who she is, she replies archly, "I'm a schoolteacher, and I might have done wonders with you if I'd caught you early enough." PENGUIN POOL MURDER is a first-rate mystery in every respect, but it's the relationship between Hildegarde and Oscar, which builds to a level of grudging respect and even affection, that makes it special. It took RKO more than a year to produce a sequel, which ignored the fact that the two lead characters had gotten married at the end of the first picture (clearly, it made for better material to maintain them as friendly adversaries). MURDER ON THE BLACKBOARD reunited Gleason and Oliver with the same writer

(Willis Goldbeck) and director (George Archainbaud) who fashioned the original film, and yielded similarly pleasing results. Returning too were Edgar Kennedy, as one of Gleason's cops, and Gustav von Seyffertitz, as a lab technician. Another year passed before Hildegarde would call on Oscar to help solve a mystery on picturesque Catalina Island in MURDER ON A HONEYMOON, which was cowritten by Seton I. Miller and famed humorist Robert Benchley. Unfortunately, Miss Oliver left RKO just when the studio (finally) committed itself to making a more regular series with these characters. Oliver was replaced by Helen Broderick for MURDER ON A BRIDLE PATH, a terribly slow-moving mystery which gave the usually jaunty actress no material to work with, and Gleason's character the stupidest lines of the series. Then RKO cast ZaSu Pitts as Hildegarde for THE PLOT THICKENS, and things took a turn for the better. Pitts and Gleason are well teamed, and the mystery is engaging. Unfortunately, the stars' follow-up did not maintain that standard. FORTY NAUGHTY GIRLS is more comic than mysterious, and more heavy-handed than hilarious. With that obvious failure, RKO gave up. One of Stuart Palmer's Withers stories was later adapted as MGM feature called MR. O'MALLEY AND MRS. MALONE, with Marjorie Main and James Whitmore; later still, Eve Arden starred as Hildegarde in a rather freely rewritten TV movie, 1972's A VERY MISSING PERSON, with James Gregory as Oscar Piper. With only a handful of films on its roster, and only half of them worthwhile, this may not be the most significant series in Hollywood history, but at its best it remains one of the most enjoyable.

HILDEGARDE WITHERS

Penguin Pool Murder (1932)
Murder on the Blackboard (1934)
Murder on a Honeymoon (1935)
Murder on a Bridle Path (1936)
The Plot Thickens (1936)
Forty Naughty Girls (1937)

Hill, The (1965) **122m.** ***½ D: Sidney Lumet. Sean Connery, Harry Andrews, Ian Hendry, Michael Redgrave, Ian Bannen, Alfred Lynch, Ossie Davis, Roy Kinnear, Jack Watson. Powerful drama of military prison camp, with superb performances by all. One problem: British actors bark at each other and much dialogue is unintelligible to American ears (though if you can make it through the first reel, hang on). Written by Ray Rigby. Also shown in computer-colored version. ▼◗❙
Hill in Korea, A SEE: **Hell in Korea**
Hills of Home (1948) **C-97m.** *** D: Fred M. Wilcox. Edmund Gwenn, Donald Crisp,

Tom Drake, Rhys Williams, Janet Leigh. Fine Lassie movie about doctor convincing Scottish father to urge son to study medicine. ▼◗
Hills of Old Wyoming (1937) **78m.** *** D: Nate Watt. William Boyd, George Hayes, Russell Hayden, Gail Sheridan, Clara Kimball Young, Earle Hodgins. After ranchers start missing cattle, Hopalong Cassidy looks to nearby Indian reservation for answers and finds a shady deputy. Strong scenic values; tinny incidental music score the only drawback. This marked Hayden's acting debut, replacing Jimmy Ellison as Hoppy's impetuous young sidekick. ▼◗
Hills of Utah (1951) **70m.** *** D: John English. Gene Autry, Pat Buttram, Elaine Riley, Donna Martell, Onslow Stevens, Denver Pyle, William Fawcett, Harry Lauter, Kenne Duncan, Tom London, Tommy Ivo, Teddy Infuhr. Gene returns to his hometown of Coffin Gap as a doctor and lands smack in the middle of a bitter feud between copper miners and big cattle outfits; it doesn't take him long to figure out why cattle are dying from mining waste water. Gene sings his hit song "Peter Cottontail." One of Autry's better 1950s outings. ▼
Hill 24 Doesn't Answer (1955-Israeli) **102m.** *** D: Thorold Dickinson. Edward Mulhare, Haya Harareet, Michael Wager, Michael Shillo, Arieh Lavi. Evocative if occasionally schmaltzy drama, played in flashbacks, of the fight for modern Israel, centering on the stories of four soldiers defending a hill outside Jerusalem during the 1948 war. ▼◗
Hindle Wakes (1927-British) **117m.** ***½ D: Maurice Elvey. Estelle Brody, John Stuart, Norman McKinnel, Marie Ault, Humberston Wright, Gladys Jennings, Irene Rooke, Peggy Carlisle, Cyril McLaglen. Young Lancashire mill worker (Brody) is romanced by a mill owner's playboy son (Stuart), even though he is engaged to wed a daughter of wealth. A surprise turn of events alters their lives and those of their families and neighbors. Complex, vividly etched drama offers thoughtful, three-dimensional characterizations and a memorable portrait of a feisty heroine who is in firm control of her life. Stunningly visual late-silent film is a pleasure to watch for its imagery alone. Stanley Houghton's then-controversial 1912 stage play was previously filmed by Elvey in 1918; remade in 1931 and 1952.◗
Hindu, The SEE: **Sabaka**
Hi, Nellie! (1934) **75m.** **½ D: Mervyn LeRoy. Paul Muni, Glenda Farrell, Ned Sparks, Robert Barrat, Kathryn Sergava, Hobart Cavanaugh, Berton Churchill, Douglass Dumbrille. Minor but enjoyable newspaper yarn with Muni as hard-hitting editor who's punished by being assigned to advice-to-the-lovelorn column. Loses initial mo-

mentum with gangland subplot, but it's still entertaining. Remade as LOVE IS ON THE AIR, YOU CAN'T ESCAPE FOREVER, and THE HOUSE ACROSS THE STREET. ▶

Hips, Hips, Hooray! (1934) 68m. *** D: Mark Sandrich. Bert Wheeler, Robert Woolsey, Dorothy Lee, Thelma Todd, Ruth Etting, George Meeker. One of Wheeler & Woolsey's best vehicles is a lavish, risqué musical comedy about their attempts to save Todd's ailing beauty business. Wild production numbers, plus a nice song from Etting, "Keep Romance Alive." ▼○▶

Hired Gun, The (1957) 63m. **½ D: Ray Nazarro. Rory Calhoun, Anne Francis, Vince Edwards, John Litel, Chuck Connors. Francis is fetching as condemned killer Calhoun determines to prove innocent. CinemaScope. ▶

Hired Wife (1940) 96m. *** D: William A. Seiter. Rosalind Russell, Brian Aherne, Virginia Bruce, Robert Benchley, John Carroll. Secretary Russell marries boss Aherne for business reasons; then the fun begins. Hilarious trifle with cast of comedy experts.

Hiroshima, Mon Amour (1959-French-Japanese) 91m. ***½ D: Alain Resnais. Emmanuele (Emmanuelle) Riva, Eiji Okada, Stella Dassas, Pierre Barbaud, Bernard Fresson. Resnais' first feature is a thoughtful, complex study of a French film actress (Riva) and Japanese architect (Okada), each with a troubled past, who have a brief affair in postwar Hiroshima. Scripted by Marguerite Duras. ▼▶

His Brother's Wife (1936) 90m. ** D: W. S. Van Dyke, II. Barbara Stanwyck, Robert Taylor, Jean Hersholt, Joseph Calleia, John Eldredge, Samuel S. Hinds. Glossy soaper of dedicated scientist Taylor scorning Stanwyck, who marries his brother Eldredge for spite. Stanwyck and Taylor married in real life three years later.

His Butler's Sister (1943) 94m. ** D: Frank Borzage. Deanna Durbin, Franchot Tone, Pat O'Brien, Evelyn Ankers, Elsa Janssen, Akim Tamiroff, Walter Catlett, Alan Mowbray. Great opening (Iris Adrian and Robin Raymond as the Sunshine Twins) and moving finale (Deanna's stunning rendition of "Nessun Dorma" from *Turandot*), but in between, a tired Durbin vehicle with Tone as an aloof Broadway composer. ▼

His Double Life (1933) 67m. **½ D: Arthur Hopkins. Roland Young, Lillian Gish, Montague Love, Lucy Beaumont, Lumsden Hare. Slight, moderately entertaining tale about a shy but famous artist (Young), who is more than pleased to settle down with middle-class spinster Gish when he is thought dead. Based on Arnold Bennett's play *Buried Alive*, filmed three times in the silent era. Remade far more successfully as HOLY MATRIMONY. ▼▶

His First Command (1929) 61m. ** D:

Gregory La Cava. William Boyd, Dorothy Sebastian, Gavin Gordon, Helen Parrish, Alphonse Ethier. Slow-moving romantic drama with Boyd offering an awkward performance as a playboy who enlists in the army to win the affection of colonel's daughter Sebastian. Forgettable. ▼

His Girl Friday (1940) 92m. **** D: Howard Hawks. Cary Grant, Rosalind Russell, Ralph Bellamy, Gene Lockhart, Helen Mack, Ernest Truex, Clarence Kolb, Porter Hall, Roscoe Karns, Abner Biberman, Cliff Edwards, John Qualen, Frank Jenks, Billy Gilbert. Splendid comedy remake of THE FRONT PAGE with Grant as conniving editor, Russell as star reporter (and his ex-wife), Bellamy as mama's boy she's trying to marry amid hot murder story. Terrific character actors add sparkle to must-see film, scripted by Ben Hecht and Charles Lederer. Remade (with the same gender twist) in 1988 as SWITCHING CHANNELS. ▼○▶

His Greatest Gamble (1934) 72m. **½ D: John Robertson. Richard Dix, Dorothy Wilson, Bruce Cabot, Erin O'Brien-Moore, Edith Fellows, Shirley Grey. Idealistic gambler Dix takes it on the lam with his beloved daughter; then a horrible accident separates the two. Above-average soaper is distinguished by Dix's performance, as well as his character's worldview.

His Kind of Woman (1951) 120m. *** D: John Farrow. Robert Mitchum, Jane Russell, Vincent Price, Tim Holt, Raymond Burr, Charles McGraw, Marjorie Reynolds, Jim Backus. Mitchum blindly goes to Mexico for a payoff of 50 grand, discovers he's the soon-to-be-dead chump whose identity will help deported gangster Burr re-enter the country. Cult film is overlong, but its spoofing of he-man heroics predates the more celebrated BEAT THE DEVIL by three years; Price is hilarious as a ham actor. ▼▶

His Majesty O'Keefe (1953) C-92m. **½ D: Byron Haskin. Burt Lancaster, Joan Rice, Benson Fong, Philip Ahn, Grant Taylor. Another athletic Lancaster buccaneer romp, set in the South Seas. ▼▶

His Picture in the Papers (1916) 62m. *** D: John Emerson. Douglas Fairbanks, Clarence Handysides, Loretta Blake, Charles Butler, Homer Hunt, Rene Boucicault, Jean Temple. Hoping to win approval to wed his beloved, Fairbanks concocts a series of harebrained schemes to publicize the vegetarian products his father markets. (It doesn't help that he prefers a good beefsteak to prunes and lentils.) Doug is typically effervescent and athletic in this lightly likable satire, scripted by Emerson and Anita Loos. An unbilled Erich von Stroheim is prominently featured as a gangster. ▶

His Private Secretary (1933) 61m. *½ D: Phil Whitman. John Wayne, Evelyn Knapp, Reginald Barlow, Alec B. Francis, Arthur

[298]

Hoyt, Natalie Kingston, Al St. John. In the big wicked city, a straitlaced young lady straightens out a debonair but reckless playboy who's squandering his life on wine, women, song, and more women. Unlikely low-budget Wayne vehicle miscasts him as what his dad calls a "worthless, dissolute, girl-crazy young squirt." ▼▶

History Is Made at Night (1937) 97m. ***½ D: Frank Borzage. Charles Boyer, Jean Arthur, Leo Carrillo, Colin Clive, Ivan Lebedeff, George Meeker, Lucien Prival, George Davis. Arthur, fleeing from a jealous husband she doesn't love, falls in love with Parisian headwaiter Boyer. Elegant, adult romantic drama, seamlessly directed by Borzage, with incredible shipboard climax and flawless performances by the two leads. ▼●

History of Mr. Polly, The (1949-British) 96m. *** D: Anthony Pelissier. John Mills, Sally Ann Howes, Finlay Currie, Betty Ann Davies, Edward Chapman, Megs Jenkins, Juliet Mills. Worthy adaptation of H. G. Wells novel about timid draper's clerk (Mills) and his relationships with women—notably a shrewish cousin and a jolly innkeeper. Amusing and enjoyable Victorian comedy. ▶

His Woman (1931) 80m. ** D: Edward Sloman. Gary Cooper, Claudette Colbert, Douglass Dumbrille, Harry Davenport. Stiff, early-talkie romance between skipper Cooper and passenger, nurse Colbert.

Hit and Run (1957) 84m. BOMB D: Hugo Haas. Hugo Haas, Cleo Moore, Vince Edwards. Trash involving Haas' efforts to rid himself of wife's young boyfriend.

Hitch Hike Lady (1935) 76m. **½ D: Aubrey Scotto. Alison Skipworth, Mae Clarke, Arthur Treacher, Jimmy (James) Ellison, Warren Hymer, Beryl Mercer, J. Farrell MacDonald, Christian Rub, George ("Gabby") Hayes. British widow Skipworth treks to the U.S. to visit her son, not knowing that he's doing a stretch in San Quentin. Likable Depression-era comedy, with Clarke and Ellison attractively cast as lovebirds.

Hitch-Hiker, The (1953) 71m. **½ D: Ida Lupino. Edmond O'Brien, Frank Lovejoy, William Talman, Jose Torvay. Well-made suspense yarn about two men on a hunting trip whose car is commandeered by a murderous fugitive. Good performances, especially by a venal Talman in the title role, but the film's once-powerful impact has been muted by decades of more graphic and imaginative films. ▼●▶

Hitler (1962) 107m. **½ D: Stuart Heisler. Richard Basehart, Cordula Trantow, Maria Emo, Martin Kosleck, John Banner, Carl Esmond. Basehart gives a cerebral interpretation to the career of the leader of the Third Reich. ▼▶

Hitler—Beast of Berlin (1939) 69m. **½ D: Sherman Scott (Sam Newfield). Roland

Drew, Steffi Duna, Alan Ladd, Greta Granstedt, Lucien Prival, Vernon Dent. Anti-Nazi resistance group members discover the true horrors of the Third Reich after they are arrested and tortured at a concentration camp. Ladd received his first screen credit for this once-controversial and still fairly hard-hitting propaganda piece from poverty row studio PRC. Reissued under various titles. ▶

Hitler—Dead or Alive (1943) 70m. ** D: Nick Grinde. Ward Bond, Dorothy Tree, Warren Hymer, Paul Fix, Russell Hicks, Felix Basch, Bobby Watson. Low-budget nonsense, with con men shooting for high stakes by attempting to kill Hitler. ▼▶

Hitler Gang, The (1944) 101m. **½ D: John Farrow. Robert (Bobby) Watson, Martin Kosleck, Victor Varconi, Luis Van Rooten, Sig Ruman, Tonio Selwart, Ludwig Donath. Historical drama of Hitler's rise to power had greatest impact on WW2 audiences but is still fairly interesting, though dwarfed by recent documentaries.

Hitler's Children (1943) 83m. *** D: Edward Dmytryk, Irving Reis. Tim Holt, Bonita Granville, Kent Smith, Otto Kruger, H. B. Warner, Lloyd Corrigan. Engrossing exploitation film of young people forced to live life of horror in Nazi Germany. Quite sensational in its day. ▼

Hitler's Madman (1943) 84m. **½ D: Douglas Sirk. Patricia Morison, John Carradine, Alan Curtis, Ralph Morgan, Howard Freeman, Ludwig Stossel, Edgar Kennedy. Vintage WW2 propaganda of citizens in small Czech village and their fate against their Nazi tormentors. Carradine is appropriately depraved as Reinhard Heydrich, Nazi governor of Prague. Coscripted by Yiddish playwright Peretz Hirschbein; look for Ava Gardner in a small part. Loosely based on fact; the story is also told in HANGMEN ALSO DIE!

Hit Parade of 1943 SEE: **Change of Heart**

Hit the Deck (1955) C-112m. **½ D: Roy Rowland. Jane Powell, Tony Martin, Debbie Reynolds, Ann Miller, Vic Damone, Russ Tamblyn, Walter Pidgeon, Kay Armen, Gene Raymond. Second-string MGM musical of sailors on shore leave is pleasant time-filler, with nice Vincent Youmans songs like "Hallelujah," "Sometimes I'm Happy," "More Than You Know." Filmed before in 1930. CinemaScope. ▼●▶

Hit the Hay (1945) 62m. ** D: Del Lord. Judy Canova, Ross Hunter, Fortunio Bonanova, Doris Merrick, Gloria Holden, Grady Sutton, Luis Alberni. Destitute opera company believes that cornpone Canova (whose mother was a famous diva) can rescue their new season. Mild comedy shows off Judy's surprisingly versatile voice and has one plot point that anticipates SINGIN' IN THE RAIN.

Hit the Ice (1943) 82m. **½ D: Charles Lamont. Bud Abbott, Lou Costello, Ginny Simms, Patric Knowles, Elyse Knox, Sheldon Leonard, Marc Lawrence, Joseph Sawyer. Bud and Lou are newspaper photographers involved with gang of thugs in zany comedy with good gags on skating rink. ▼O▶

Hit the Road (1941) 61m. ** D: Joe May. Billy Halop, Huntz Hall, Gabriel Dell, Bernard Punsley, Gladys George, Barton MacLane, Bobs Watson, Evelyn Ankers, Charles Lang, Shemp Howard. Halop, Hall, and the other boys are turned into vengeful orphans when their dads are all rubbed out in a mob war. Uninteresting *Little Tough Guys* entry.▼

Hitting a New High (1937) 85m. **½ D: Raoul Walsh. Lily Pons, Jack Oakie, Edward Everett Horton, Eric Blore, Eduardo Ciannelli. Title refers to Pons' voice, not the film per se; fluffy musical romance relies on supporting cast for entertainment. ▶

Hi'ya, Chum (1943) 61m. *½ D: Harold Young. The Ritz Brothers, Jane Frazee, Robert Paige, June Clyde, Edmund MacDonald. Entertainers find themselves in small boomtown, and open a restaurant there. Weak B musical comedy.

H-Man, The (1958-Japanese) C-79m. ** D: Ishiro Honda. Kenji Sahara, Yumi Shirakawa, Akihiko Hirata, Koreya Senda. Good special effects marred by dumb script involving radioactive liquid causing havoc in Tokyo, subplot of cops vs. underworld. Tohoscope. ▼▶

H. M. Pulham, Esq. (1941) 120m. ***½ D: King Vidor. Hedy Lamarr, Robert Young, Ruth Hussey, Charles Coburn, Van Heflin, Fay Holden, Bonita Granville, Leif Erickson, Sara Haden. Intelligent, mature, and witty film (based on John P. Marquand story) about a man who's lived his life as he was supposed to—not as he chose to. Lamarr is excellent as the spirited career woman who coaxes proper Bostonian Young out of his shell, ever so briefly. Scripted by Elizabeth Hill and director Vidor. Anne Revere has unbilled bit as a secretary in flashback scenes. Look fast for Ava Gardner on the dance floor behind Lamarr and Young.

H.M.S. Defiant SEE: **Damn the Defiant!**

Hobson's Choice (1954-British) 107m. *** D: David Lean. Charles Laughton, John Mills, Brenda De Banzie, Daphne Anderson, Prunella Scales, Richard Wattis, Helen Haye. Laughton is selfish, overbearing owner of bootshop in 1890s who's used to being tended to by his three subservient daughters; then his eldest (De Banzie) decides to take matters into her own hands. Beautifully staged and photographed (by Jack Hildyard), with Laughton having a field day in the lead. Loses momentum along the way, but still entertaining. Filmed before in 1920 and 1931; remade as a TVM in 1983. ▼O▶

Hold Back the Dawn (1941) 115m. ***½ D: Mitchell Leisen. Charles Boyer, Olivia de Havilland, Paulette Goddard, Victor Francen, Walter Abel, Rosemary DeCamp. First-rate soaper with Billy Wilder–Charles Brackett script of gigolo Boyer marrying spinsterish Olivia to get into U.S. That's director Leisen in the Hollywood soundstage sequence, directing Veronica Lake and Brian Donlevy in I WANTED WINGS. Catch this one.

Hold Back the Night (1956) 80m. **½ D: Allan Dwan. John Payne, Mona Freeman, Peter Graves, Chuck Connors. Korean War officer Payne recounts facts about bottle of liquor he always has with him.

Hold Back Tomorrow (1955) 75m. ** D: Hugo Haas. Cleo Moore, John Agar, Frank de Kova, Harry Guardino, Jan Englund. Another of writer-director-producer Haas' oddball low-budget dramas, this one about a condemned murderer who marries a girl on the night before his execution. Fairly ambitious for a film clearly made on a shoestring.

Hold 'Em Jail (1932) 74m. **½ D: Norman Taurog. Bert Wheeler, Robert Woolsey, Betty Grable, Edgar Kennedy, Edna May Oliver, Roscoe Ates, Robert Armstrong, Paul Hurst, Warren Hymer. Silly comedy in which Wheeler and Woolsey are framed, sent to jail, and play on Warden Kennedy's football team. The climactic big game is the highlight. ▼▶

Hold 'Em Navy (1937) 64m. ** D: Kurt Neumann. Lew Ayres, Mary Carlisle, John Howard, Benny Baker, Elizabeth Patterson. Ayres and Howard on the gridiron, with Carlisle the love interest. Boolah, boolah! Look for Alan Ladd in a bit part.

Hold That Baby! (1949) 64m. ** D: Reginald LeBorg. Leo Gorcey, Huntz Hall, Billy Benedict, David Gorcey, Bennie Bartlett, Gabriel Dell, Frankie Darro, John Kellogg, Anabel Shaw, Bernard Gorcey. The Bowery Boys find a bouncing bundle of joy in a laundromat and get mixed up in an inheritance swindle; standard series shenanigans ▶

Hold That Blonde (1945) 76m. ** D: George Marshall. Eddie Bracken, Veronica Lake, Albert Dekker, Frank Fenton, George Zucco, Donald MacBride. OK comedy, sometimes strained, of kleptomaniac Bracken tangling with sultry thief Lake.

Hold That Co-Ed (1938) 80m. *** D: George Marshall. John Barrymore, George Murphy, Marjorie Weaver, Joan Davis, Jack Haley, George Barbier. Good musicomedy supercharged by Barrymore as windy politician; he makes the whole film. ▶

Hold That Ghost (1941) 86m. *** D: Arthur Lubin. Bud Abbott, Lou Costello, Richard Carlson, Joan Davis, Mischa Auer, Evelyn Ankers, Marc Lawrence, Shemp Howard, Ted Lewis, The Andrews Sisters. Prime A&C, with the boys inheriting a haunted house. Fine cast includes hilarious Davis as professional radio screamer. Highlight: the moving candle. ▼▶

Hold That Hypnotist (1957) **61m.** ** D: Austen Jewell. Huntz Hall, Stanley Clements, Jane Nigh, David (Gorcey) Condon, Robert Foulk, James Flavin, Queenie Smith, Jimmy Murphy. Hypnotized Sach regresses to a past life in the 17th century, where he gets mixed up with Blackbeard the pirate. Adequate *Bowery Boys* time passer. ▶

Hold That Line (1952) **64m.** ** D: William Beaudine. Leo Gorcey, Huntz Hall, Gil Stratton, Jr., David Gorcey, Bennie Bartlett, Bernard Gorcey, John Bromfield, Veda Ann Borg, Taylor Holmes, Pierre Watkin. The Bowery Boys go to college and bring along some old vaudeville gags as Sach becomes a gridiron hero. ▶

Hold Your Man (1933) **86m.** *** D: Sam Wood. Jean Harlow, Clark Gable, Stuart Erwin, Elizabeth Patterson, Blanche Friderici. Delightful film that effectively makes the transition from comedy to drama with Harlow falling for jailbound Gable. The stars are at their best here. ▼▶

Hole, The SEE: **Le Trou**

Hole in the Head, A (1959) **C-120m.** ** D: Frank Capra. Frank Sinatra, Edward G. Robinson, Eleanor Parker, Carolyn Jones, Thelma Ritter, Eddie Hodges, Keenan Wynn, Joi Lansing. Sticky story of a ne'er-do-well (Sinatra) and his son (Hodges) doesn't seem sincere. Only distinction is Oscar-winning song, "High Hopes." Later a Broadway musical titled *Golden Rainbow*. CinemaScope. ▼▶

Hole in the Wall, The (1929) **65m.** **½ D: Robert Florey. Edward G. Robinson, Claudette Colbert, David Newell, Nelly Savage, Donald Meek, Alan Brooks, Louise Closser Hale. Dynamic stars elevate this standard tale of crooks using a phony medium to fleece rich clients. Interesting relic with stylish sets and photography, made at Paramount's East Coast studio in Astoria, N.Y. Notable only for performances of Robinson and Colbert, who are completely natural in their talkie debuts.

Holiday (1930) **96m.** *** D: Edward H. Griffith. Ann Harding, Robert Ames, Mary Astor, Edward Everett Horton, Hedda Hopper, Monroe Owsley. First version of Philip Barry's play about nonconformity is a pleasant surprise; an unstodgy early talkie with casting that in some cases (Astor, Owsley) even tops the more famous 1938 version (Horton plays the same role in both movies).

Holiday (1938) **93m.** ***½ D: George Cukor. Katharine Hepburn, Cary Grant, Doris Nolan, Lew Ayres, Edward Everett Horton, Henry Kolker, Binnie Barnes, Jean Dixon, Henry Daniell. Fine, literate adaptation of Philip Barry's play (filmed before in 1930) about nonconformist Grant confronting stuffy N.Y.C. society family, finding his match in Hepburn (who had understudied the role in the original Broadway company a decade earlier). Screenplay by Donald Ogden Stewart and Sidney Buchman. Delightful film. ▼▶

Holiday Affair (1949) **87m.** *** D: Don Hartman. Robert Mitchum, Janet Leigh, Wendell Corey, Gordon Gebert, Griff Barnett, Esther Dale, Henry O'Neill, Henry (Harry) Morgan. Well-done Christmastime story of war widow Leigh, with a young son, who's courted by nice-guy Corey. Fate intervenes when she meets articulate, kindly rolling stone Mitchum. Remade for TV in 1997. ▼▶

Holiday Camp (1947-British) **97m.** **½ D: Ken Annakin. Dennis Price, Flora Robson, Jack Warner, Diana Dors, Patricia Roc, Hazel Court. Pleasant account of life and love at British summer resort; atmospheric, with good characterizations.

Holiday for Lovers (1959) **C-103m.** **½ D: Henry Levin. Clifton Webb, Jane Wyman, Jill St. John, Carol Lynley, Paul Henreid, Gary Crosby, Jose Greco. Arch Dr. Webb and Wyman escort attractive daughters on South American vacation, with predictable mating. CinemaScope. ▶

Holiday for Sinners (1952) **72m.** **½ D: Gerald Mayer. Gig Young, Janice Rule, Keenan Wynn, William Campbell. Strange goings-on at Mardi Gras as several people try to forget their troublesome lives and have a good time.

Holiday in Havana (1949) **73m.** ** D: Jean Yarbrough. Desi Arnaz, Mary Hatcher, Ann Doran, Steven Geray, Minerva Urecal, Sig Arno. Bargain-basement musical, with Arnaz and Hatcher playing pair of Cuban love birds. Of interest solely for Desi's presence.

Holiday in Mexico (1946) **C-127m.** *** D: George Sidney. Walter Pidgeon, Jose Iturbi, Roddy McDowall, Ilona Massey, Xavier Cugat and His Orchestra, Jane Powell, Hugo Haas, Linda Christian. Complications arise when mischievous, precocious teen Powell, daughter of the U.S. ambassador to Mexico, falls for an "older" man; meanwhile, her widowed father (Pidgeon) rekindles romance with a Hungarian countess who sings with Cugat's band. Powell is billed as "your young singing star" in this engaging, well-cast musical comedy. ▼▶

Holiday Inn (1942) **101m.** ***½ D: Mark Sandrich. Bing Crosby, Fred Astaire, Marjorie Reynolds, Virginia Dale, Walter Abel, Louise Beavers. Entertaining musical built on paper-thin plot about a romantic triangle, and the establishment of a country inn that's open only on holidays. That's the cue for a raft of Irving Berlin holiday songs (there's even one for George Washington's birthday!) including the timeless Oscar winner "White Christmas." Good fun, and snappier than partial remake WHITE CHRISTMAS. Bing's original Rhythm Boys partner, Harry Barris, plays the orchestra leader. Also available in computer-colored version. ▼▶

Holiday in Spain (1960) **C-108m.** ** D: Jack Cardiff. Denholm Elliott, Peter Lorre, Beverly Bentley, Paul Lukas, Liam Redmond, Leo McKern, Peter Arne, Diana Dors. Mystery writer stumbles onto a real-life crime scene and finds himself tracking an elusive woman around Spain, with a sardonic cab driver (Lorre) as his companion. Scenic travelogue serves as backdrop for a boring tale. Of interest primarily because it was originally released in Mike Todd, Jr.'s Smell-O-Vision as SCENT OF MYSTERY and features a surprise star cameo at the end. Later presented in "Cinemiracle." Roadshow version on Blu-ray & DVD includes overture, intermission/entr'acte, exit music. Todd-70. ▶

Hollow Point SEE: **Wild Pair, The**

Hollow Triumph (1948) **83m.** *** D: Steve Sekely. Paul Henreid, Joan Bennett, Eduard Franz, Leslie Brooks. Tense melodrama of killer assuming identity of lookalike doctor. Jack Webb's film debut. Retitled: THE SCAR.▼▶

Holly and the Ivy, The (1952-British) **80m.** *** D: George More O'Ferrall. Ralph Richardson, Celia Johnson, Margaret Leighton, Denholm Elliott, Hugh Williams, Roland Culver. Straightforward adaptation of Wynyard Browne play revolving around Christmas holiday with Richardson, a small-town cleric, learning about his three grown-up children; nicely acted.

Hollywood and Vine (1945) **58m.** BOMB D: Alexis Thurn-Taxis. Jimmy Ellison, Wanda McKay, June Clyde, Ralph Morgan, Franklin Pangborn, Leon Belasco, Billy Benedict, Charles Middleton. Threadbare PRC production about two young Hollywood hopefuls, aspiring actress McKay and screenwriter Ellison. Patently awful, with no redeeming qualities; looks as if it were shot in a closet.▼▶

Hollywood Boulevard (1936) **70m.** **½ D: Robert Florey. John Halliday, Marsha Hunt, Robert Cummings, Mae Marsh, C. Henry Gordon, Esther Ralston, Frieda Inescort, Esther Dale, Albert Conti, Charles Ray, Francis X. Bushman, Maurice Costello, Betty Compson. Halliday is vain former star who writes his memoirs for *Confidential*-type magazine, affecting lives of daughter Hunt, ex-girlfriend Ralston. Slow-moving drama is saved by sometimes crisp, perceptive dialogue, presence of silent stars Marsh, Bushman, Ray, etc. Gary Cooper appears briefly as himself.

Hollywood Canteen (1944) **124m.** **½ D: Delmer Daves. Bette Davis, John Garfield, Joan Leslie, Robert Hutton, Dane Clark, Janis Paige; many guest stars including Joan Crawford, Ida Lupino, Barbara Stanwyck, Eddie Cantor, Jack Carson, Eleanor Parker, Alexis Smith, S. Z. Sakall. Amiable all-star silliness set in Hollywood's real-life haven for WW2 servicemen, featuring cofounders Davis and Garfield. Hutton plays G.I. with a crush on lovely Leslie. Best bits: Peter Lorre and Sydney Greenstreet; Jack Benny and violinist Joseph Szigeti. Roy Rogers introduces "Don't Fence Me In," later reprised by the Andrews Sisters.▼●

Hollywood Cavalcade (1939) **C-96m.** **½ D: Irving Cummings. Alice Faye, Don Ameche, J. Edward Bromberg, Al Jolson, Mack Sennett, Stuart Erwin, Buster Keaton, Rin-Tin-Tin, Jr., Alan Curtis. Colorful saga of pioneering days in Hollywood (based, very loosely, on Mack Sennett and Mabel Normand) starts out fun, with lively re-creations of silent slapstick comedies, but gets bogged down in clichéd dramatics.▶

Hollywood Hotel (1937) **109m.** **½ D: Busby Berkeley. Dick Powell, Rosemary Lane, Lola Lane, Ted Healy, Johnnie "Scat" Davis, Alan Mowbray, Frances Langford, Louella Parsons, Hugh Herbert, Glenda Farrell, Edgar Kennedy. Silly, paper-thin plot about Powell winning Hollywood talent contest but finding stardom elusive, buoyed by bright Johnny Mercer–Richard Whiting score, including "Hooray for Hollywood" and historic numbers by the Benny Goodman band ("Sing Sing Sing") and quartet (with Gene Krupa, Lionel Hampton, Teddy Wilson). Ronald Reagan has brief bit as radio announcer.▶

Hollywood or Bust (1956) **C-95m.** **½ D: Frank Tashlin. Dean Martin, Jerry Lewis, Anita Ekberg, Pat Crowley. Starstruck Lewis teams up with gambler Martin on trek to crash the movie capital; typical comedy by the frantic team. Dean and Jerry's last film together opens with Jerry's "tribute" to movie fans around the world. VistaVision.▼▶

Hollywood Party (1934) **68m.** **½ No director credited. Jimmy Durante, Laurel and Hardy, Lupe Velez, Polly Moran, Charles Butterworth, Eddie Quillan, June Clyde, George Givot, Jack Pearl, Ted Healy and The Three Stooges, many others. Musical comedy hodgepodge built around screen star Durante throwing a gala party. Romantic subplot is for the birds, but Stan and Ollie battling fiery Velez, Durante as Schnarzan, befuddled Butterworth and opening title tune make it worthwhile. Richard Boleslawski, Allan Dwan, Roy Rowland directed various scenes without credit; some prints run 63m., and are missing appearance by Mickey Mouse and color Disney cartoon HOT CHOC-LATE SOLDIERS.▼▶

Hollywood Revue of 1929, The (1929) **130m.** ** D: Charles Riesner. Conrad Nagel, Jack Benny, John Gilbert, Norma Shearer, Joan Crawford, Laurel and Hardy, Bessie Love, Lionel Barrymore, Marion Davies, Buster Keaton, Marie Dressler, Polly Moran, many others. MGM's all-star revue introducing its silent-film stars as talkie personalities, cohosted by Benny and Nagel. Definitely a curio for film buffs, rough sledding for others. Surviving 116m. print is missing material; several scenes originally filmed in color.◐▮

Hollywood Round-Up (1937) 63m. **½ D: Ewing Scott. Buck Jones, Helen Twelvetrees, Grant Withers, Shemp Howard, Dickie Jones, Eddie Kane, Monty Collins. Likable little B Western looks at the making of B Westerns, as stunt man Jones puts obnoxious cowboy "hero" Withers in his place and falls for leading lady Twelvetrees while foiling real-life bank robbers.

Hollywood Stadium Mystery! (1938) 66m. **½ D: David Howard. Neil Hamilton, Evelyn Venable, Jimmy Wallington, Barbara Pepper, Lucien Littlefield, Lynne Roberts. Breezy B mystery with D.A. and lady mystery writer competing to unravel the conundrum of a boxer inexplicably dropping dead in the ring. Smiley Burnette has an amusing cameo as himself, imitating race car noises!

Hollywood Story (1951) 77m. **½ D: William Castle. Richard Conte, Julia (Julie) Adams, Richard Egan, Henry Hull, Fred Clark, Jim Backus. Orson Welles–like producer Conte arrives in Hollywood to shoot his first feature, based on the unsolved 1929 murder of a top silent film director. Loaded with potential that's mostly unrealized. Strongest asset is location filming around Hollywood and the old Chaplin studio. Features guest appearances by aging silent screen luminaries, as well as Joel McCrea.
▮

Holy Matrimony (1943) 87m. *** D: John M. Stahl. Monty Woolley, Gracie Fields, Laird Cregar, Una O'Connor, Alan Mowbray, Melville Cooper, Franklin Pangborn. Delightful tale of artist Woolley assuming late butler's identity to avoid publicity, finding many complications. Remake of 1933 film HIS DOUBLE LIFE. ▮

Holy Mountain, The (1926-Germany) 105m. *** D: Arnold Fanck. Leni Riefenstahl, Luis Trenker, Ernst Petersen, Frida Richard, Friedrich Schneider. Fascinating curio, a "mountain film" played out against the majestic German Alps, with Riefenstahl a beguiling presence as a beautiful dancer who is practically a force of nature. A tale of romantic love and yearning, spotlighting the dancer's involvement with two men and a fateful misunderstanding. Story is secondary to Riefenstahl's eye-catching beauty and the stark footage of crashing waves, soaring mountain peaks, and glistening snow. ▼▮

Holy Terror, A (1931) 53m. **½ D: Irving Cummings. George O'Brien, Sally Eilers, James Kirkwood, Rita La Roy, Humphrey Bogart, Stanley Fields, Robert Warwick. After his father is murdered, O'Brien heads West to check out a family mystery. Flying his own plane, he crashes into Eilers' bathroom while she's taking a shower! Entertaining Western is notable for presence of young Bogart as a heavy. Based on Max

Brand's novel *Trailin'*, which was filmed under that name in 1921 with Tom Mix.

Home at Seven (1952-British) 85m. *** D: Ralph Richardson. Ralph Richardson, Margaret Leighton, Jack Hawkins, Campbell Singer. Taut thriller of club treasurer who can't account for a day in his life when a murder and a robbery occurred. Aka MURDER ON MONDAY. ▼

Home Before Dark (1958) 136m. *** D: Mervyn LeRoy. Jean Simmons, Dan O'Herlihy, Rhonda Fleming, Efrem Zimbalist, Jr. Shiny but poignant telling of Simmons' readjustment to life after nervous breakdown; on-location shooting in Massachusetts. ▮

Homecoming (1948) 113m. ** D: Mervyn LeRoy. Clark Gable, Lana Turner, Anne Baxter, John Hodiak, Ray Collins, Cameron Mitchell. Gable and Turner have exciting WW2 romance in the trenches, but that can't support 113 minutes of dreary drama; one of Gable's lesser efforts. ▼▮

Home From the Hill (1960) C-150m. *** D: Vincente Minnelli. Robert Mitchum, Eleanor Parker, George Peppard, George Hamilton, Luana Patten, Everett Sloane, Constance Ford. Strong drama, set in southeastern Texas, centering on most prominent family in a small town. Patriarch Mitchum is estranged from wife Parker and takes over raising their son Hamilton when he comes of age. Peppard is a likable, fatherless local important to both the older man and his son. Low-key, involving, and intelligent; well directed by Minnelli, handling uncharacteristic material. Cast is very good, including Peppard and Hamilton in what may be career-best performances for both. From the best-selling novel by William Humphrey. ▼◐▮

Home in Indiana (1944) C-103m. *** D: Henry Hathaway. Walter Brennan, Jeanne Crain, June Haver, Charlotte Greenwood, Lon McCallister, Ward Bond, Willie Best, George Cleveland. Typical horse-racing saga gets a good rehashing here with colorful production and sincere performances; climactic race is well handled. Remade as APRIL LOVE. ▮

Home in Oklahoma (1946) 72m. **½ D: William Witney. Roy Rogers, George "Gabby" Hayes, Dale Evans, Carol Hughes, George Meeker, Lanny Rees, Ruby Dandridge, Bob Nolan and the Sons of the Pioneers. Newspaper editor Rogers suspects foul play in the death of a rancher who's left his property to 12-year-old Rees, much to the displeasure of his niece (Hughes) and foreman (Meeker). Tough murder story, given top production by Republic. ▼▮

Home in Wyomin' (1942) 68m. *** D: William Morgan. Gene Autry, Smiley Burnette, Fay McKenzie, Olin Howland, Chick Chandler, Joe Strauch, Jr., Forrest Taylor, James Seay. Gene returns home to help an old friend whose rodeo operation is being hurt by his son's bad behavior. As if that weren't enough trouble to deal with, gamblers on the lam from a Chicago mob turn up in town. Well-plotted musical Western. Gene introduces "Tweedle-O-Twill," which he cowrote, and Irving Berlin's timely "Any Bonds Today?" Look for Spade Cooley in the band.▼▶

Home Is the Hero (1959-Irish) **83m.** **½ D: Fielder Cook. Walter Macken, Eileen Crowe, Arthur Kennedy, Joan O'Hara. Modest yarn with Abbey Theatre group, telling story of ex-con (Macken) trying to pick up pieces of home life.

Home of the Brave (1949) **85m.** *** D: Mark Robson. James Edwards, Douglas Dick, Steve Brodie, Jeff Corey, Lloyd Bridges, Frank Lovejoy. More daring when made than now, but still hard-hitting account of black soldier Edwards suffering more abuse from fellow G.I.'s than the enemy while on a mission during WW2. From an Arthur Laurents play.▼▶

Home on the Prairie (1939) **59m.** ** D: Jack Townley. Gene Autry, Smiley Burnette, June Storey, George Cleveland, Walter Miller, Gordon Hart, Earle Hodgins. Crooked rancher Miller and cattle broker Hart try to ship their cattle—infected with hoof-and-mouth disease—to market before inspectors Gene and Smiley catch on. Meanwhile, Gene romances Storey and Smiley fools around with medicine-show man Hodgins and his elephant. Not up to Gene's usual standards.▼▶

Homestretch, The (1947) **C-96m.** ** D: H. Bruce Humberstone. Cornel Wilde, Maureen O'Hara, Glenn Langan, Helen Walker, James Gleason. Harmless film of romance between young girl and horse-owner suffers from uneven acting and script.

Home, Sweet Homicide (1946) **90m.** ** D: Lloyd Bacon. Peggy Ann Garner, Randolph Scott, Lynn Bari, Dean Stockwell. Nothing-special comedy-mystery, as children of mystery writer solve local murder and find husband for their mother.

Home Town Story (1951) **61m.** ** D: Arthur Pierson. Jeffrey Lynn, Donald Crisp, Marjorie Reynolds, Alan Hale, Jr., Marilyn Monroe, Barbara Brown, Glenn Tryon. Obvious programmer of recently defeated pol Lynn, who blames big business for his loss and tries to defame manufacturer Crisp. Of interest mostly for Monroe's supporting role as one of Lynn's employees.▼▶

Homicidal (1961) **87m.** **½ D: William Castle. Jean Arless, Joan Marshall, Patricia Breslin, Glenn Corbett, Eugenie Leontovitch, Alan Bunce, Richard Rust. One of Castle's less gimmicky shockers, about pretty but rather strange young nurse who presides over creepy household consisting of mute stroke victim and decidedly meek young man. Shamelessly steals a great deal from PSYCHO, and much of the dialogue is

ludicrous, but still manages to deliver some shudders.▶

Homicide Bureau (1939) **58m.** *½ D: C. C. Coleman, Jr. Bruce Cabot, Rita Hayworth, Robert Paige, Marc Lawrence, Richard Fiske, Moroni Olsen. Cabot plays a brash detective who's in perennial hot water with his superiors in this humdrum B picture. Rita's role as a lab technician is small—and dull.

Homicide for Three (1948) **60m.** **½ D: George Blair. Audrey Long, Warren Douglas, Grant Withers, Lloyd Corrigan, Stephanie Bachelor, Tala Birell, Billy Curtis. Agreeable mystery-comedy with honeymooners Long and Douglas, desperate to find a hotel room in L.A., becoming immersed in multiple-murder plot.

Hondo (1953) **C-84m.** *** D: John Farrow. John Wayne, Geraldine Page, Ward Bond, Michael Pate, James Arness, Rodolfo Acosta, Leo Gordon, Lee Aaker, Lassie. Rousing, well-done Western with Wayne the tough, wily cavalry scout who comes upon Page and her young son living in the wilderness, unalarmed about a pending Apache uprising. Wayne is in top form here. Good script by James Edward Grant, from a story by Louis L'Amour. Later a short-lived TV series. 3-D.▼▶

Honeychile (1951) **C-90m.** *½ D: R. G. Springsteen. Judy Canova, Eddie Foy, Jr., Alan Hale, Jr., Walter Catlett. Cornball stuff involving Canova in the music-publishing business.

Honeymoon (1947) **74m.** ** D: William Keighley. Shirley Temple, Franchot Tone, Guy Madison, Lina Romay, Gene Lockhart, Grant Mitchell. A silly script does in this romantic comedy in which G.I. Madison and fiancée Temple race around Mexico City trying to get hitched.▶

Honeymoon (1959-Spanish) **C-90m.** ** D: Michael Powell. Anthony Steel, Ludmilla Tcherina, Antonio, Rosita Segovia. Muddled romancer intertwined with ballet sequences, from the director of THE RED SHOES. Steel, on wedding trip with Tcherina, encounters Antonio who tries to court the ex-ballerina. Excerpts from ballets *Los Amantes de Teruel* and *El Amor Brujo*. Technirama.

Honeymoon Ahead (1945) **60m.** ** D: Reginald LeBorg. Allan Jones, Raymond Walburn, Grace McDonald, Vivian Austin. Kindly Orpheus (Jones) has been leading a convict's choir; what's he to do when he's released from prison? Silly Universal B musical.

Honeymoon for Three (1941) **77m.** **½ D: Lloyd Bacon. Ann Sheridan, George Brent, Charlie Ruggles, Osa Massen, Walter Catlett, Jane Wyman. Breezy remake of GOODBYE AGAIN (1933) with novelist Brent warding off female admirers by pretending to be married; Sheridan is his witty, amorous secretary.

Honeymoon Hotel (1964) **C-89m.** *½
D: Henry Levin. Robert Goulet, Jill St.
John, Nancy Kwan, Robert Morse, Elsa
Lanchester, Keenan Wynn. Asinine shenanigans with bachelors Goulet and Morse arriving at resort for newlyweds. Lanchester
is fun despite all. Panavision. ◗

Honeymoon in Bali (1939) **95m.** *** D:
Edward H. Griffith. Fred MacMurray, Madeleine Carroll, Allan Jones, Osa Massen,
Helen Broderick, Akim Tamiroff, Astrid Allwyn, Carolyn Lee, Monty Woolley. Pleasant
romantic comedy about a career woman (Carroll) who is determined never to marry—until
she meets easy-to-take MacMurray. Video
title: MY LOVE FOR YOURS. ▼◗

Honeymoon Lodge (1943) **63m.** ** D:
Edward Lilley. David Bruce, Harriet Hilliard (Nelson), June Vincent, Rod Cameron,
Franklin Pangborn, Andrew Tombes,
Ozzie Nelson and His Orchestra, Veloz and
Yolanda, Tip, Tap and Toe. Innocuous musical centers on Bruce and Vincent's romantic
complications at a country resort. Slim pretext for some amusing songs and dances by
Ozzie & Harriet and others.

Honeymoon Machine, The (1961) **C-87m.** **½ D: Richard Thorpe. Steve McQueen, Jim Hutton, Paula Prentiss, Brigid
Bazlen, Dean Jagger, Jack Weston. Pleasant comedy with a spirited cast about two
sailors who find a way to beat the roulette
table in Venice. Easy to take, easy to forget.
CinemaScope. ▼◗

Hong Kong (1951) **C-92m.** ** D: Lewis R.
Foster. Ronald Reagan, Rhonda Fleming,
Nigel Bruce, Marvin Miller, Lee Marvin.
Mediocre account of Reagan trying to heist
a valuable antique from orphaned boy but
going straight before finale. Strictly backlot
Hong Kong.

Hong Kong Affair (1958) **79m.** *½ D: Paul
F. Heard. Jack Kelly, May Wynn, Richard
Loo, Lo Lita Shek. Kelly is the Yank who
comes to the Orient to investigate his property holdings, getting more than he bargained for.

Hong Kong Confidential (1958) **67m.** **½
D: Edward L. Cahn. Gene Barry, Beverly
Tyler, Allison Hayes, Noel Drayton. Harmless B film about Anglo-American agents
rescuing a kidnapped Arabian prince. ◗

Honky Tonk (1941) **105m.** **½ D: Jack
Conway. Clark Gable, Lana Turner, Frank
Morgan, Claire Trevor, Marjorie Main, Albert Dekker, Chill Wills, Veda Ann Borg.
Good-gal Lana loves gambler Gable in romantic Western that's fun for a spell, then
drags into talky marathon. Morgan and
Wills offer fine character performances.
Remade for TV in 1974. Also shown in
computer-colored version. ▼◗●

Honolulu (1939) **83m.** **½ D: Edward
Buzzell. Eleanor Powell, Robert Young,
George Burns, Gracie Allen, Rita Johnson,
Willie Fung, Sig Rumann, Ruth Hussey,
Eddie Anderson, The King's Men. Pleasant
musical fluff with Young in a dual role, as
a movie star who, seeking peace and quiet,
trades places with his lookalike, a Hawaiian
plantation owner. Powell has several dance
features (including a tap hula!), but many of
the best moments belong to Gracie. Oddly
enough, this was Burns and Allen's final
film together. ▼◗

Honolulu Lu (1941) **67m.** **½ D: Charles
Barton. Lupe Velez, Leo Carrillo, Bruce
Bennett, Marjorie Gateson, Don Beddoe,
Forrest Tucker. Con artist Carrillo schemes
to fleece rich widows in Hawaii, but his
niece—and erstwhile partner—Velez tries
to reform him while posing as a cabaret
singer. Frantic farce performed with zeal by
all concerned and given a lustrous sheen by
cinematographer Franz Planer.

Hoodlum, The (1951) **61m.** **½ D: Max
Nosseck. Lawrence Tierney, Allene Roberts, Marjorie Riordan, Lisa Golm, Edward
Tierney. Real-life Tierney brothers star as
siblings: Lawrence an unregenerate parolee
planning an armored car robbery, Edward
as his square, disapproving sibling. Tough,
compact, entirely predictable low-budget
crime saga. ▼◗

Hoodlum Empire (1952) **98m.** **½ D:
Joseph Kane. Brian Donlevy, Claire Trevor,
Forrest Tucker, Vera Ralston, Luther Adler.
Cast is sufficiently versed in format to make
this exposé of a crime syndicate better than
average. ▼◗

Hoodlum Priest, The (1961) **101m.** ***
D: Irvin Kershner. Don Murray, Larry
Gates, Keir Dullea, Logan Ramsey, Cindi
Wood. Based on real-life clergyman who
devoted himself to trying to help would-be
criminals, focusing on Murray's efforts to
rehabilitate delinquent Dullea (in film debut); splendidly acted. Murray coproduced
and cowrote (latter under pseudonym Don
Deer). ▼◗

Hoodlum Saint, The (1946) **91m.** ** D:
Norman Taurog. William Powell, Esther
Williams, Angela Lansbury, James Gleason, Lewis Stone, "Rags" Ragland, Frank
McHugh, Slim Summerville. Confusing
mishmash with Powell a cynical, money-obsessed WW1 vet who, between schemes,
falls for pretty Williams. This one squeaks
by solely on Powell's charm.

Hoodoo Ann (1916) **65m.** *** D: Lloyd
Ingraham. Mae Marsh, Robert Harron,
William H. Brown, Wilbur Higby, Loyola
O'Connor, Mildred Harris, Anna Hernandez, Charles Lee, Elmo Lincoln, Carl
Stockdale. Marsh is an ill-treated orphan
whose life brightens when she's taken in by
a childless couple and befriended by a wannabe cartoonist (Harron). Then a shocking
event threatens to disrupt her world. Formulaic but fun, with Marsh oozing charm. A
highlight: Marsh and Harron attend a silent
movie, and respond to the on-screen action.

D. W. Griffith scripted (using the name Granville Warwick) and produced.▶

Hook, The (1963) 98m. *** D: George Seaton. Kirk Douglas, Robert Walker, Jr., Nick Adams, Nehemiah Persoff. Film examines men at war (Korean) and the taking of one life, face-to-face, as opposed to killing many in battle. Earnest, thought-provoking. Music by harmonica virtuoso Larry Adler. Panavision. ▶

Hook, Line and Sinker (1930) 72m. **½ D: Edward F. Cline. Bert Wheeler, Robert Woolsey, Dorothy Lee, Jobyna Howland, Ralf Harolde, Natalie Moorhead, George Marion, Sr., Hugh Herbert. W&W play ex–insurance men running a dilapidated hotel for heiress Lee, having to fend off the inevitable crooks. Herbert is funny as the house dick. Verbal gags abound in this above-average Wheeler and Woolsey vehicle. ▼▶

Hoopla (1933) 85m. *** D: Frank Lloyd. Clara Bow, Richard Cromwell, Preston Foster, Herbert Mundin, James Gleason, Minna Gombell. Carnival pitchman hires an "older" woman (Bow at 28) to turn his "boy" (Cromwell was 23) into a man. Corny, predictable story is made special by Bow's winning, sincere performance; hard to believe this was her final film. Midway milieu adds a trashy aroma to this pre-Code adaptation of Kenyon Nicholson's play *The Barker,* filmed before in 1928. Contains atmospheric footage of the 1933 Chicago "Century of Progress" Exposition.

Hooray for Love (1935) 72m. *** D: Walter Lang. Ann Sothern, Gene Raymond, Bill Robinson, Maria Gambarelli, Pert Kelton, Fats Waller, Jeni Le Gon, Thurston Hall, Lionel Stander. Modest but very entertaining musical with aspiring show-biz hotshot Raymond romancing reluctant singer Sothern. Robinson shines in "I'm Living in a Great Big Way" specialty number, ably assisted by Waller and Le Gon; Kelton adds laughs as an inept soprano. ▶

Hoosier Schoolboy (1937) 62m. **½ D: William Nigh. Mickey Rooney, Anne Nagel, Frank Shields, Edward Pawley, William Gould. Perceptive little Depression-era melodrama detailing the myriad problems of the title character (Rooney). Scenario depicts everything from the plight of forgotten WW1 veterans to greedy capitalists who cause strikes and strife. ▼▶

Hootenanny Hoot (1963) 91m. ** D: Gene Nelson. Peter Breck, Joby Baker, Ruta Lee, Pam Austin, Johnny Cash, Sheb Wooley, The Brothers Four, Judy Henske. Predictable comedy about college hootenanny show brought to TV is made bearable only by presence of Cash and other country/folk performers. One of producer Sam Katzman's "topical" low-budgeters.

Hop-Along Cassidy (1935) 59m. *** D: Howard Bretherton. William Boyd, Jimmy Ellison, Paula Stone, George Hayes, Kenneth Thomson, Robert Warwick, Frank McGlynn, Jr., Charles Middleton. Competing cattle ranchers feud over water rights and fencing of open range. First and best entry in a series of 66 with vivid portrayals by Boyd, Ellison, Hayes, and Middleton (in a rare sympathetic part). Features warm comedy, scenic tumbled terrain of Lone Pine, two memorable songs, and a driving action finish. Loosely adapted from Clarence E. Mulford's 1910 novel titled *Hopalong Cassidy.* Reissued as HOPALONG CASSIDY ENTERS. ▼▶

Hopalong Cassidy Enters SEE: Hop-Along Cassidy

Hopalong Cassidy Returns (1936) 71m. *** D: Nate Watt. William Boyd, George Hayes, Gail Sheridan, Evelyn Brent, Stephen Morris (Morris Ankrum), William Janney, Al St. John, Ray Whitley. Before he is murdered, crusading editor sends for Hoppy to restore law and order in cow town run by dance hall operator and brutal thugs. Brent makes strong impression as model, rare romantic interest for Boyd. Janney is weak substitute for Jimmy Ellison in Bar 20 trio. Based on same-named 1923 novel by Clarence E. Mulford. Remade five years later as WIDE OPEN TOWN. ▼▶

Hopalong Rides Again (1937) 63m. *** D: Lesley Selander. William Boyd, George Hayes, Russell Hayden, Nora Lane, Harry Worth, Lois Wilde. Hoppy has a new love interest (rare in this series); her brother is a professor of paleontology, but also a ruthless killer behind cattle thievery who employs dynamite as a weapon. Top grade in all departments, with memorable treachery by Worth. Benefits from spectacular Lone Pine scenery and great use of Paramount music library. Based on 1923 novel *Black Buttes* by series creator Clarence E. Mulford. ▼▶

Hoppity Goes to Town (1941) C-77m. **½ D: Dave Fleischer. Pleasant animated feature about residents of bug-ville and their various problems—living in a human world, and threatened by villainous C. Bagley Beetle. Good-looking but uncompelling story-wise, with unmemorable Frank Loesser–Hoagy Carmichael score. Originally titled MR. BUG GOES TO TOWN. ▼⊙▶

Hoppy Serves a Writ (1943) 67m. *** D: George Archainbaud. William Boyd, Andy Clyde, Jay Kirby, Victor Jory, George Reeves, Jan Christy, Hal Taliaferro. Texas sheriff Hopalong Cassidy's task: lure known band of brigands across Oklahoma border and serve warrant of arrest. Based on the same-named final novel penned by series creator Clarence E. Mulford. Story and action are well paced, with a good slugfest between Boyd and Jory (who was once a prizefighter). Debut of Robert Mitchum. ▼▶

Hoppy's Holiday (1947) **60m.** ****** D: George Archainbaud. William Boyd, Andy Clyde, Rand Brooks, Andrew Tombes, Leonard Penn, Jeff Corey, Mary Ware. On vacation, the Bar 20 trio stops in Mesa City for the town festival, where they become implicated in a bank robbery. Five credited writers, including actress Ellen Corby, failed to fix this Hopalong Cassidy entry. Slow, played too much for laughs. Hoppy for once calls his horse Topper by name. Reissued as THE FIGHTING COWBOY. ▼❙

Horizons West (1952) **C-81m.** ****½** D: Budd Boetticher. Robert Ryan, Julia (Julie) Adams, Rock Hudson, Raymond Burr, James Arness, John McIntire, Dennis Weaver. Standard Western of brothers Ryan and Hudson on opposite sides of the law; the latter attempts to block the former's efforts to ruthlessly acquire power in post–Civil War Texas. ▼❙

Horizontal Lieutenant, The (1962) **C-90m.** ****** D: Richard Thorpe. Jim Hutton, Paula Prentiss, Miyoshi Umeki, Jim Backus, Jack Carter, Marty Ingels, Charles McGraw. Artificial service comedy about inept army intelligence officer Hutton and his misadventures in the Pacific during WW2. CinemaScope. ▼❙

Horn Blows at Midnight, The (1945) **78m.** ******* D: Raoul Walsh. Jack Benny, Alexis Smith, Dolores Moran, Allyn Joslyn, Reginald Gardiner, Guy Kibbee, John Alexander, Margaret Dumont, Franklin Pangborn, Bobby (Robert) Blake. Enjoyable, original comedy-fantasy about an angel (Benny) sent to destroy earth with a blast from Gabriel's horn. Broad, funny, no classic, but not the turkey Benny so often joked about either. Franklin Pangborn is especially funny as a flustered hotel detective. ▼❙

Horrible Dr. Hichcock, The (1962-Italian) **C-76m.** ****½** D: Robert Hampton (Riccardo Freda). Robert Flemyng, Barbara Steele, Teresa Fitzgerald, Maria Teresa Vianello. Unaware her doctor husband is a (gulp!) necrophiliac, woman accompanies him to the mansion where his first wife apparently died 12 years earlier during sexual games. Eerie, handsome horror, with undertones of Poe. British version, TERROR OF DR. HICHCOCK, runs 88m. and is also available on tape. Followed by THE GHOST (1963). Panoramic. ▼❙

Horror Castle (1963-Italian) **C-83m.** ***½** D: Anthony Dawson (Antonio Margheriti). Christopher Lee, Rossana Podesta, George Riviere, Jim Nolan, Anny Belli Uberti. Chiller about a demented WW2 victim running rampant in a Rhine castle, using assorted torture chamber devices on unsuspecting people. Effect is numbing. Aka THE VIRGIN OF NUREMBERG and TERROR CASTLE. ▼❙

Horror Chamber of Dr. Faustus, The SEE: **Eyes Without a Face**

Horror Hotel (1960-British) **76m.** ****½** D: John Moxey. Dennis Lotis, Christopher Lee, Betta St. John, Patricia Jessel, Venetia Stevenson. Seventeenth-century New England witch (Jessel) burned at the stake returns from the dead, maintains an inn to lure victims for blood sacrifice to the devil. Not bad of its type. Original British title: THE CITY OF THE DEAD. ▼❙)

Horror Island (1941) **60m.** ****½** D: George Waggner. Dick Foran, Leo Carrillo, Peggy Moran, Fuzzy Knight, John Eldredge, Lewis Howard, Iris Adrian. Fast-paced, diverting B-thriller comedy has various colorful types converging at isolated manor; one by one, they're stalked and murdered. ❙

Horror Maniacs SEE: **Greed of William Hart, The**

Horror of Dracula (1958-British) **C-82m.** ******* D: Terence Fisher. Peter Cushing, Christopher Lee, Melissa Stribling, Michael Gough, Carol Marsh, John Van Eyssen, Valerie Gaunt, Miles Malleson. Probably Hammer Films' best shocker, a handsomely mounted retelling of the Stoker tale, with fantasy elements deemphasized. Lee is smooth as the Count, and Cushing perfect as tireless Professor Van Helsing. Script by Jimmy Sangster; full-blooded score by James Bernard. Released in Britain as DRACULA; followed by numerous sequels, the first of which was DRACULA— PRINCE OF DARKNESS. ▼❙)

Horror of It All, The (1963-British) **75m.** ***½** D: Terence Fisher. Pat Boone, Erica Rogers, Dennis Price, Andree Melly, Valentine Dyall, Jack Bligh, Erik Chitty, Archie Duncan. Young American visits the family of his British fiancée at their spooky, isolated manor, learns they're macabre weirdos—and being killed one by one. Standard horror-comedy setup gets dismayingly ordinary treatment, considering it was written by genre veteran Ray Russell. Not scary and not funny. Boone sings one song.

Horror of Party Beach, The (1964) **72m.** BOMB D: Del Tenney. John Scott, Alice Lyon, Allen Laurel, Marilyn Clark, Eulabelle Moore. Radioactive waste is dumped off-shore, resulting in scaly monsters who disrupt the fun of a bunch of Connecticut beach bunnies. One of the earliest anti-nuclear warning films, although for some strange reason the message fails to come across. Billed as "The First Horror Musical" by its producers, who evidently never saw Liberace in SINCERELY YOURS. ▼❙

Horrors of Spider Island (1960-German) **89m.** ***½** D: Jamie Nolan (Fritz Bottger). Harald Maresch, Helga Franck, Alex D'Arcy, Helga Neuner, Rainer Brandt, Elfie Wagner, Barbara Valentin. After a plane wreck, one guy (D'Arcy) and eight statuesque dancers are washed ashore on a South Pacific island. A large spider bites the guy and transforms him into a hairy-faced monster. Two other guys show up, and there is a lot of dancing and catfighting. Well-photographed sex film, typical of the period (i.e., no nudity), almost casually tosses in sci-fi elements. Aka IT'S HOT IN PARADISE, a more fitting title. ▼▶

Horrors of the Black Museum (1959-British) **C-95m.** **½ D: Arthur Crabtree. Michael Gough, June Cunningham, Graham Curnow, Shirley Ann Field, Geoffrey Keen. Gruesome sequences highlight chiller about writer who uses his hypnotized helper to commit murders. Originally released in Britain at 81m.; prologue was added later. Cinema-Scope. ▼▶▶

Horse Feathers (1932) **68m.** ***½ D: Norman Z. McLeod. Groucho, Harpo, Chico, and Zeppo Marx, Thelma Todd, David Landau, Robert Greig, Nat Pendleton. Groucho is head of Huxley College, building up football team to play rival Darwin U. in crazy Marx nonsense. The password is "swordfish." Originally released at 70m. ▼▶▶

Horsemasters, The (1961) **C-87m.** ** D: William Fairchild. Annette Funicello, Janet Munro, Tommy Kirk, Donald Pleasence, Tony Britton, Jean Marsh, John Fraser, Millicent Martin. Minor family fare (originally shown on Disney TV show) about Annette learning horsemanship—and to overcome her fear of jumping—at exclusive British riding school. Filmed in England; released as a feature in Europe. ▼

Horse Named Comanche, A SEE: **Tonka**

Horse's Mouth, The (1958-British) **C-93m.** ***½ D: Ronald Neame. Alec Guinness, Kay Walsh, Renee Houston, Mike Morgan, Michael Gough, Ernest Thesiger. Guinness adapted Joyce Cary's story into this droll screenplay about a brilliant, eccentric, egocentric—and perpetually starving—artist whom some consider a genius. Many others, who know him more intimately, think of him as a major irritant. Score makes ideal use of Prokofiev's "Lieutenant Kije" suite. ▼▶▶

Horse Soldiers, The (1959) **C-119m.** **½ D: John Ford. John Wayne, William Holden, Constance Towers, Althea Gibson, Hoot Gibson, Anna Lee, Russell Simpson, Ken Curtis, Denver Pyle, Strother Martin, Hank Worden. Ford's only feature set during the Civil War, based on actual incidents. Union Colonel Wayne leads sabotage party deep into Rebel territory, accompanied by somewhat pacifistic doctor Holden. Large-scale actioner rates only a "medium" by Ford buffs; others may like it better. ▼▶▶

Horse Without a Head, The (1963) **C-89m.** *** D: Don Chaffey. Leo McKern, Jean-Pierre Aumont, Herbert Lom, Pamela Franklin, Vincent Winter. Excellent cast in entertaining British-made Disney film (first shown on the Disney TV show) about kids mixed up with bad guys on the trail of stolen loot. First-rate family fare. ▼▶

Hostages (1943) **88m.** ** D: Frank Tuttle.

Luise Rainer, William Bendix, Roland Varno, Oscar Homolka, Katina Paxinou, Paul Lukas. Routine tale of underground movement in WW2; Bendix outshines Rainer acting-wise. Rainer's last starring film.

Hot Blood (1956) **C-85m.** *½ D: Nicholas Ray. Jane Russell, Cornel Wilde, Luther Adler, Joseph Calleia. Jane Russell shakes her tambourines and drives Cornel Wilde, in this supremely silly (not to mention unbelievable) gypsy yarn. CinemaScope. ▶

Hot Car Girl SEE: **Hot Rod Girl**

Hotel Berlin (1945) **98m.** **½ D: Peter Godfrey. Helmut Dantine, Andrea King, Raymond Massey, Faye Emerson, Peter Lorre, Alan Hale. GRAND HOTEL author Vicki Baum tries again with sundry characters based in hotel during decline of Nazi Germany; good cast makes it generally interesting.

Hotel for Women (1939) **83m.** ** D: Gregory Ratoff. Linda Darnell, Ann Sothern, Elsa Maxwell, Lynn Bari, Sidney Blackmer, Alan Dinehart. Weak film about group of manhunting girls, noteworthy only as Darnell's film debut. Originally titled ELSA MAXWELL'S HOTEL FOR WOMEN.

Hotel Imperial (1927) **84m.** *** D: Mauritz Stiller. Pola Negri, James Hall, George Siegmann, Max Davidson, Michael Vavitch, Otto Fries, Nicholas Soussanin. As WW1 floods over the map of Europe, a squad of Austrian soldiers seeks sanctuary in a small village inn, only to find it occupied by enemy Russians. Chambermaid Negri holds the key to their survival. One of Paramount's most polished continental productions, made in Hollywood, U.S.A. Remade in 1939 and 1943 (as FIVE GRAVES TO CAIRO).

Hotel Imperial (1939) **67m.** ** D: Robert Florey. Isa Miranda, Ray Milland, Reginald Owen, Gene Lockhart, Albert Dekker. Miranda encounters intrigue while searching for man responsible for her sister's death; fairly entertaining drama. Troubled film was years in production, with numerous cast, director, and title changes. A remake of 1927 silent, this was in turn remade as FIVE GRAVES TO CAIRO. ▶

Hotel Reserve (1944-British) **79m.** *** D: Lance Comfort, Max Greene, Victor Hanbury. James Mason, Lucie Mannheim, Herbert Lom, Patricia Medina, Anthony Shaw, David Ward. Innocent Austrian medical student (Mason) who's accused of espionage while on holiday in pre-WW2 France must unmask the real spy . . . or else. Based on an Eric Ambler novel. ▶

Hotel Sahara (1951-British) **96m.** **½ D: Ken Annakin. Yvonne De Carlo, Peter Ustinov, David Tomlinson, Roland Culver. Pleasant fluff about North African hotel owner and beautiful fiancée who must shift "loyalties" every time new army marches into town during WW2. ▶

Hot Enough for June SEE: **Agent 8¾**

Hot Heiress, The (1931) **80m.** ** D: Clarence Badger. Ben Lyon, Ona Munson, Walter Pidgeon, Tom Dugan, Holmes Herbert, Inez Courtney, Thelma Todd. Riveter Lyon and debutante Munson "meet cute" when he invades her penthouse to retrieve a stray bolt. Naturally, they fall in love, and she passes him off as an architect to trick her snobby parents and friends. Amiable but uninspired musical comedy with Rodgers and Hart songs, including the unforgettable "Nobody Loves a Riveter (but His Mother)."

Hot Lead SEE: **Run of the Arrow**

Hot News (1953) **68m. *½** D: Edward Bernds. Stanley Clements, Gloria Henry, Ted de Corsia, Veda Ann Borg. Programmer tale of dedicated newspaperman cleaning up crime syndicate involved in sporting events. ▶

Hot Pepper (1933) **76m. **½** D: John G. Blystone. Victor McLaglen, Edmund Lowe, Lupe Velez, El Brendel. Another reprise of feud between Flagg (McLaglen) and Quirt (Lowe) from WHAT PRICE GLORY?, now civilians involved in nightclub, with spitfire Velez the woman they fight over. Constant wisecracks are a bit forced, but stars milk script for all its worth.

Hot Rod Gang (1958) **72m. *½** D: Lew Landers. John Ashley, Gene Vincent, Jody Fair, Steve Drexel. Low-budget relic of its era, about hot-rod-happy Ashley joining Vincent's band to earn money to enter big race. ▶

Hot Rod Girl (1956) **75m.** BOMB D: Leslie H. Martinson. Lori Nelson, Chuck Connors, John Smith, Frank Gorshin, Roxanne Arlen, Dabbs Greer. Blah juvenile delinquency potboiler, with sympathetic cop Connors establishing drag strip to keep hot-rodding teens off the streets. Aka HOT CAR GIRL.▶

Hot Rod Rumble (1957) **79m. *½** D: Leslie Martinson. Brett Halsey, Richard Hartunian, Joey Forman, Leigh Snowden. Title tells all in this formula programmer of juvenile delinquents.

Hot Saturday (1932) **72m. *** D: William A. Seiter. Cary Grant, Nancy Carroll, Randolph Scott, Edward Woods, Lilian Bond, William Collier, Sr., Jane Darwell, Grady Sutton. Popular girl is accused of spending the night with playboy Grant, which reveals the jealousies and pettiness of her community. Plenty of sparks in this pre-Code drama, with authentic (and surprisingly acerbic) small-town atmosphere and a nifty song, "I'm Burning for You." ▶

Hot Shots (1956) **61m. *½** D: Jean Yarbrough. Huntz Hall, Stanley Clements, Joi Lansing, Jimmy Murphy, David Gorcey, Queenie Smith, Robert Shayne. The Bowery Boys become caretakers to an unhappy child TV star in this threadbare entry from the tail end of the series. ▶

Hot Spell (1958) **86m. ** D: Daniel Mann. Shirley Booth, Anthony Quinn, Shirley MacLaine, Earl Holliman, Eileen Heckart, Warren Stevens. Quinn—not just a pig but a blue-ribbon hog—cheats on wife Booth, who spouts irritating platitudes like Hazel on speed. Well-acted but dated drama about the breakup's effect on their children; MacLaine shines as their daughter. Set in New Orleans. VistaVision ▼

Hot Spot SEE: **I Wake Up Screaming**

Hot Summer Night (1957) **86m. **½** D: David Friedkin. Leslie Nielsen, Colleen Miller, Edward Andrews, Claude Akins, Paul Richards. Offbeat story about reporter seeking an interview with leader of robbery gang.

Hot Water (1924) **60m. *** D: Sam Taylor, Fred Newmeyer. Harold Lloyd, Jobyna Ralston, Josephine Crowell, Charles Stevenson, Mickey McBan, Pat Harmon. Typically entertaining silent comedy feature with Lloyd, atypically, as a put-upon husband. Not as strong as Lloyd's best comedies; built instead on three lengthy set pieces, but they're very funny indeed—especially the ride on the trolley and a trouble-prone automobile outing with the family. ▼▶

Houdini (1953) **C-106m. **½** D: George Marshall. Tony Curtis, Janet Leigh, Torin Thatcher, Ian Wolfe, Sig Ruman. Fanciful biography of famed escape artist; more fiction than fact, but entertaining.▼●▶

Hound-Dog Man (1959) **C-87m. *** D: Don Siegel. Fabian, Carol Lynley, Stuart Whitman, Arthur O'Connell, Dodie Stevens, Betty Field, Royal Dano, Margo Moore, Claude Akins, Edgar Buchanan, Jane Darwell, L.Q. Jones. Pleasant tale of Southern country boys Fabian (in film debut) and Whitman courting Stevens and Lynley. Fabian is surprisingly good; of course, he also sings. CinemaScope.

Hound of the Baskervilles, The (1939) **80m. *** D: Sidney Lanfield. Basil Rathbone, Nigel Bruce, Richard Greene, Wendy Barrie, Lionel Atwill, John Carradine, Beryl Mercer, Mary Gordon, E. E. Clive. Rathbone made his first appearance as Sherlock Holmes in this grade-A production based on Conan Doyle's story about mysterious murders taking place at a creepy mansion on the moors (though he's off-screen for a good part of the story). Fairly faithful to the source material with the now classic closing line from cocaine-user Holmes: "Oh Watson, the needle!" (This was the fourth screen version of the oft-filmed novel.)▼●▶

Hound of the Baskervilles, The (1959-British) **C-84m. *** D: Terence Fisher. Peter Cushing, Christopher Lee, Andre Morell, Marla Landi, Miles Malleson, John LeMesurier. Cushing is well cast as Sherlock Holmes and Lee is fine as Sir Henry Baskerville in this atmospheric Hammer Films adaptation of the Conan Doyle classic. ▼●▶

Hour Before the Dawn, The (1944) **75m. ** D: Frank Tuttle. Franchot Tone, Veronica Lake, John Sutton, Binnie Barnes, Henry

Stephenson, Mary Gordon, Nils Asther. Polished, empty WW2 romance-espionage, with Tone falling for Nazi spy Lake; unlikely casting doesn't help.

Hour of Decision (1957-British) **81m.** ** D: C.M. Pennington Richards. Jeff Morrow, Hazel Court, Anthony Dawson, Lionel Jeffries, Carl Bernard, Mary Laura Wood. Morrow is newspaperman who tracks down murderer of fellow columnist, discovering his wife was involved with the man. ▼

Hour of Glory SEE: **Small Back Room, The**

Hour of 13, The (1952) **79m.** **½ D: Harold French. Peter Lawford, Dawn Addams, Roland Culver, Colin Gordon. Mystery yarn set in 1890s London, with Lawford a ritzy thief who develops a heart of gold in order to do a good deed for society. Remake of 1934 film THE MYSTERY OF MR. X. ▶

House Across the Bay, The (1940) **86m.** **½ D: Archie Mayo. George Raft, Joan Bennett, Lloyd Nolan, Gladys George, Walter Pidgeon, June Knight. Raft's out to get Pidgeon, who has taken wife Bennett from him while he's been in jail. Familiar but exciting film. ▼▶

House Across the Lake, The SEE: **Heat Wave**

House Across the Street, The (1949) **69m.** ** D: Richard Bare. Wayne Morris, Janis Paige, James Mitchell, Alan Hale, Bruce Bennett. Routine remake of Paul Muni's HI, NELLIE, with Morris as newspaperman on the scent of a murder. Paige is peppery as love interest. ▶

Houseboat (1958) **C-110m.** ***½ D: Melville Shavelson. Cary Grant, Sophia Loren, Martha Hyer, Harry Guardino, Eduardo Ciannelli, Murray Hamilton. Loren becomes Grant's housekeeper and takes his three motherless kids in hand. Predictable romance ensues, in this delightful comedy. Guardino hilarious as houseboat handyman. VistaVision. ▼▶

House by the River (1950) **84m.** *** D: Fritz Lang. Louis Hayward, Jane Wyatt, Lee Bowman, Ann Shoemaker, Kathleen Freeman. Strange, moody tale of larcenous husband (Hayward) who spins web of evil that involves his wife (Wyatt) and brother (Bowman). Overwrought at times—particularly near the end—but full of fascinating touches, striking atmosphere. ▶

House Divided, A (1931) **70m.** *** D: William Wyler. Walter Huston, Kent Douglass (Douglass Montgomery), Helen Chandler, Mary Foy, Lloyd Ingraham, Charles Middleton, Walter Brennan. Huston gives a tour-de-force performance as a recently widowed, ultra-macho fisherman whose young mail-order bride (Chandler) falls for his sensitive son (Douglass). Shades of Eugene O'Neill in a powerful, fluidly directed early talkie featuring dialogue written by the star's son, John Huston.

Householder, The (1963-U.S.-Indian) **100m.** **½ D: James Ivory. Shashi Kapoor, Leela Naidu, Durga Khote, Hariendernath Chattopadaya. Fair comedy about perplexed schoolteacher Kapoor, coping with his arranged marriage and new obligations. Ivory's first fiction feature, and initial collaboration with longtime producer Ismail Merchant and scriptwriter Ruth Prawer Jhabvala; from her novel. ▼▶

House in Marsh Road, The SEE: **Invisible Creature, The**

House in the Square, The SEE: **I'll Never Forget You**

House Is Not a Home, A (1964) **98m.** ** D: Russell Rouse. Shelley Winters, Robert Taylor, Cesar Romero, Ralph Taeger, Kaye Ballard, Broderick Crawford, Mickey Shaughnessy, Lisa Seagram, Jesse White. Mediocre film based on the memoirs of notorious madam Polly Adler, who thrived in the 1920s. The subject matter was still considered notorious in 1964! Title song by Burt Bacharach and Hal David (sung by Brook Benton) is more memorable than the picture. Look for Raquel Welch and Edy Williams as call girls.

Housekeeper's Daughter, The (1939) **79m.** ** D: Hal Roach. Joan Bennett, Victor Mature, Adolphe Menjou, William Gargan. Pleasant murder mystery enhanced by chic Bennett, who helps crack a homicide case. Mature's film debut.

House of Bamboo (1955) **C-102m.** **½ D: Samuel Fuller. Robert Ryan, Robert Stack, Shirley Yamaguchi, Cameron Mitchell, Sessue Hayakawa. Picturesque if not credible story of Army officers and Japanese police tracking down a gang of former soldiers working for a well-organized syndicate. CinemaScope. ▶

House of Dracula (1945) **67m.** **½ D: Erle C. Kenton. Onslow Stevens, Lon Chaney, Jr., John Carradine, Martha O'Driscoll, Jane Adams, Lionel Atwill, Glenn Strange, Skelton Knaggs. Sequel to HOUSE OF FRANKENSTEIN takes different tack: Stevens tries "real" science to cure various Universal monsters, but finds that some of their bad habits begin to rub off. Acting, direction, eerie set design compensate for overambitious script, hasty resolution. ▼▶

House of Fear, The (1939) **67m.** **½ D: Joe May. William Gargan, Irene Hervey, Alan Dinehart, Walter Woolf King, Dorothy Arnold, El Brendel, Harvey Stephens, Robert Coote. Murderer stalks N.Y.C. theater; offbeat show business characters in pretty good whodunit. Remake of 1929 film THE LAST WARNING.

House of Fear, The (1945) **69m.** *** D: Roy William Neill. Basil Rathbone, Nigel Bruce, Dennis Hoey, Aubrey Mather, Paul Cavanagh, Holmes Herbert, Gavin Muir. Sherlock Holmes is called in to investigate when members of an eccentric Scottish gentleman's club are knocked off one by one.

Liberal, but ingenious, adaptation of Conan Doyle's "The Five Orange Pips."▼●▶

House of Frankenstein (1944) 71m. **½ D: Erle C. Kenton. Boris Karloff, J. Carrol Naish, Lon Chaney, Jr., John Carradine, Elena Verdugo, Anne Gwynne, Lionel Atwill, Peter Coe, George Zucco, Glenn Strange, Sig Rumann. Episodic all-star monster opus linked by evil scientist Karloff and hunchback Naish posing as traveling horror show operators. First third has them dealing with Dracula (wonderfully played by Carradine), the rest picks up where FRANKENSTEIN MEETS THE WOLF MAN left off. Contrived, to say the least, but tough to dislike. Strange's first appearance as the Frankenstein Monster. Sequel: HOUSE OF DRACULA.▼●▶

House of Fright SEE: **Two Faces of Dr. Jekyll, The**

House of Horrors (1946) 65m. ** D: Jean Yarbrough. Bill Goodwin, Robert Lowery, Virginia Grey, Rondo Hatton, Martin Kosleck. Slightly below average horror meller. Frustrated artist (Kosleck) uses fiend The Creeper to knock off critics. Laughable script, OK acting.▼●▶

House of Intrigue, The (1956-Italian) C-94m. **½ D: Duilio Coletti. Curt Jurgens, Dawn Addams, Folco Lulli, Dario Michaelis, Philippe Hersent. Nazis capture a high-level British spy in this moderately entertaining WW2 espionage caper. Released in the U.S. in 1959. CinemaScope.

House of Mystery (1961-British) 56m. **½ D: Vernon Sewell. Jane Hylton, Peter Dyneley, Nanette Newman, Maurice Kaufman, John Merivale. Nifty little story of haunted house, with its new owners learning the mysterious history of the premises; supernatural played up well.▼

House of Numbers (1957) 92m. **½ D: Russell Rouse. Jack Palance, Barbara Lang, Harold J. Stone, Edward Platt. Palance plays dual role as man seeking to spring gangster brother from prison and take his place. CinemaScope.

House of Ricordi (1954-Italian) C-117m. ** D: Carmine Gallone. Paolo Stoppa, Roland Alexandre, Marta Toren, Roldano Lupi, Marcello Mastroianni. Passable biography of well-known music-publishing house, set in the 18th century, with many musical interludes. Retitled: CASA RICORDI.

House of Rothschild, The (1934) 88m. *** D: Alfred L. Werker. George Arliss, Boris Karloff, Loretta Young, Robert Young, Florence Arliss, C. Aubrey Smith. Elaborate, entertaining chronicle of famed banking family, with Arliss as Nathan Rothschild at time of Napoleonic Wars, Loretta his daughter, R. Young her suitor, Karloff as civilized villain. Finale shot in color.

House of Strangers (1949) 101m. *** D: Joseph L. Mankiewicz. Edward G. Robinson, Susan Hayward, Richard Conte,

Luther Adler, Efrem Zimbalist, Jr., Debra Paget, Hope Emerson, Esther Minciotti. Dynamic drama of ruthless financier Robinson who uses his four sons to suit his own schemes. Unique plotline has been utilized in various disguises for many subsequent films—most memorably, five years later in the Western BROKEN LANCE and as THE BIG SHOW (1961).▼▶

House of the Black Death (1965) 80m. *½ D: Harold Daniels. Lon Chaney, Jr., John Carradine, Andrea King, Tom Drake, Dolores Faith, Sabrina. Warlock holds people captive in a creepy old house; terribly dragged out, grade-Z stuff.▼

House of the Damned (1963) 63m. ** D: Maury Dexter. Ron Foster, Merry Anders, Richard Crane, Erika Peters, Dal McKennon, Richard Kiel. Young architect, hired to rehabilitate a disused mansion near the California coast, goes there with his wife and mysterious things begin happening. Modestly suspenseful, with unusual, and surprisingly wistful, ending. A thriller, not a horror film. CinemaScope.▶

House of the Seven Gables, The (1940) 89m. *** D: Joe May. George Sanders, Margaret Lindsay, Vincent Price, Nan Grey, Alan Napier, Cecil Kellaway, Dick Foran. Good adaptation of Hawthorne's classic novel. Set in 19th-century New England; conniving Sanders frames his brother, Price, for murder of their father in effort to cheat him out of inheritance. Fine performances from all. Price also appeared in TWICE-TOLD TALES, which includes abbreviated version of *Seven Gables* novel.▼▶

House of the Seven Hawks, The (1959) 92m. **½ D: Richard Thorpe. Robert Taylor, Nicole Maurey, Linda Christian, Donald Wolfit, David Kossoff, Eric Pohlmann. Diverting account of skipper Taylor involved in shipboard murder and hunt for long-lost Nazi loot. Made in England.▶

House of Usher (1960) C-85m. ***½ D: Roger Corman. Vincent Price, Mark Damon, Myrna Fahey, Harry Ellerbe. First-rate horror film based on classic tale by Edgar Allan Poe. When beautiful young girl's suitor arrives to ask her hand in marriage, the doors of the house of Usher fling open, and terror begins. Filmed several times before and since, but never this effectively; a great tour de force for Price. First of Corman's eight Poe adaptations. Aka FALL OF THE HOUSE OF USHER. CinemaScope.▼●▶

House of Wax (1953) C-88m. *** D: Andre de Toth. Vincent Price, Frank Lovejoy, Phyllis Kirk, Paul Picerni, Carolyn Jones, Paul Cavanagh, Charles Buchinsky (Bronson). Remake of MYSTERY OF THE WAX MUSEUM stars Price as vengeful sculptor who rebuilds his fire-destroyed showplace by using human victims as wax figures. Jones excellent as an early victim. Most popular of the era's 3-D films, a status it retains today. This is the film that launched Price on his horror film cycle after 15 years of "straight" roles. Love that paddleball man! Remade in 2005. 3-D. ▼●▶

House of Women (1962) 85m. **½ D: Walter Doniger. Shirley Knight, Andrew Duggan, Constance Ford, Barbara Nichols, Margaret Hayes, Virginia Gregg. Trite rendition of conditions in a women's prison elevated by good cast and fast pacing. Remake of CAGED. ▶

House on 56th Street, The (1933) 68m. ** D: Robert Florey. Kay Francis, Margaret Lindsay, Ricardo Cortez, Gene Raymond, John Halliday, Frank McHugh, Sheila Terry, William "Stage" Boyd, Hardie Albright. Sprawling chronicle of 25 years in the life of a house, as Francis spends two decades in jail for a crime she didn't commit. The residence is now a speakeasy/gambling joint, where Francis returns to save her daughter from the same situation she was in. Offbeat but nothing special. ▶

House on Haunted Hill (1958) 75m. *** D: William Castle. Vincent Price, Carol Ohmart, Richard Long, Alan Marshal, Elisha Cook, Jr., Carolyn Craig, Leona Anderson. Zillionaire Price offers group of people $10,000 each if they'll spend a night in spooky old mansion with murderladen history; he even provides loaded guns as party favors. Campy fun. Originally presented theatrically with flying skeleton gimmick "Emergo." Remade in 1999. ▼●▶

House on Marsh Road, The SEE: Invisible Creature, The

House on 92nd Street, The (1945) 88m. ***½ D: Henry Hathaway. William Eythe, Lloyd Nolan, Signe Hasso, Gene Lockhart, Leo G. Carroll, Lydia St. Clair; narrated by Reed Hadley. Exciting, trend-setting documentary-style drama—based on fact and staged on actual locations—about FBI counterespionage activities during WW2: Nazi agents, operating in N.Y.C., attempt to pilfer part of the atom bomb formula. Charles G. Booth earned an Oscar for his original story. Screenplay by Booth, Barre Lyndon, and John Monks, Jr. Look for E. G. Marshall, in film debut. Followed by THE STREET WITH NO NAME (1948). ▼▶

House on Telegraph Hill, The (1951) 93m. **½ D: Robert Wise. Richard Basehart, Valentina Cortese, William Lundigan, Fay Baker. Good cast in intriguing tale of WW2 refugee assuming dead woman's identity so that she can come to San Francisco where wealthy relatives reside. ▶

Housewife (1934) 69m. ** D: Alfred E. Green. Bette Davis, George Brent, Ann Dvorak, John Halliday, Ruth Donnelly. Little punch in story of struggling copywriter Brent deserting wife Dvorak for old-flame Davis (playing unsubtle vamp). ▶

Houston Story, The (1956) 79m. **½ D: William Castle. Gene Barry, Barbara Hale,

Edward Arnold, Jeanne Cooper, Paul Richards, Frank Jenks, John Zaremba. Barry gives a terrific performance as a Texas oil worker who ruthlessly works his way up the ranks of Arnold's mob. Gritty Sam Katzman production is efficient if unremarkable. Notable for casting Hale as the femme fatale and Cooper as the nice girl. ▶

Howards of Virginia, The (1940) 122m. **½ D: Frank Lloyd. Cary Grant, Martha Scott, Cedric Hardwicke, Alan Marshal, Richard Carlson, Paul Kelly, Irving Bacon. Historical account of Revolutionary War is OK, but too long for such standard retelling. Look for young Peter Cushing. ▼▶

How Green Was My Valley (1941) 118m. **** D: John Ford. Walter Pidgeon, Maureen O'Hara, Donald Crisp, Anna Lee, Master Roddy McDowall, John Loder, Sara Allgood, Barry Fitzgerald, Patric Knowles, Rhys Williams, Arthur Shields, Ann (E.) Todd, Mae Marsh. Narrated by Irving Pichel; United Kingdom version narrated by Rhys Williams. Moving drama from Richard Llewellyn's story of Welsh coal miners, centering on Crisp's large, close-knit family. Beautifully filmed, lovingly directed, winner of five Academy Awards: Best Picture, Director, Supporting Actor (Crisp), Cinematography (Arthur Miller), Art Direction. Screenplay by Philip Dunne. ▼●▶

How the West Was Won (1962) C-155m. ***½ D: John Ford ("The Civil War"), Henry Hathaway ("The Rivers, The Plains, The Outlaws"), George Marshall ("The Railroad"). Carroll Baker, Henry Fonda, Gregory Peck, George Peppard, Carolyn Jones, Eli Wallach, Robert Preston, Debbie Reynolds, James Stewart, John Wayne, Richard Widmark, All-Star Cast; narrated by Spencer Tracy. Blockbuster epic about three generations of Western pioneers isn't same experience seen at home as it is on a Cinerama screen, but great cast, first-rate photography and lovely Alfred Newman score still make it top entertainment. Peppard stands out with excellent portrayal. This won Oscars for Story and Screenplay (James R. Webb) and Editing (Harold F. Kress). Runs 164m. with overture, intermission/entr'acte, exit music. Cinerama. ▼●▶

How to Be Very, Very Popular (1955) C-89m. **½ D: Nunnally Johnson. Betty Grable, Robert Cummings, Charles Coburn, Sheree North, Fred Clark, Alice Pearce, Orson Bean. Grable and North on the lam hide in a college fraternity in this semi-remake of SHE LOVES ME NOT. Sheree does wild "Shake, Rattle and Roll" number, stealing Grable's spotlight. This was Betty's last movie. CinemaScope.

How to Make a Monster (1958) 74m. BOMB D: Herbert L. Strock. Robert H. Harris, Gary Conway, Gary Clarke, Paul

Brinegar. Dismal chiller involving studio makeup artist who goes berserk and turns his creations into zombielike killers. Final 11m. of film are in color. Remade (in name only) for cable TV in 2001. Superama. ▼▶

How to Marry a Millionaire (1953) C-95m. *** D: Jean Negulesco. Marilyn Monroe, Betty Grable, Lauren Bacall, William Powell, Rory Calhoun, David Wayne, Alex D'Arcy, Fred Clark, Cameron Mitchell. Terrific ensemble work in dandy comedy of three man-hunting females pooling resources to trap eligible bachelors. Nunnally Johnson scripted and produced this remake of THE GREEKS HAD A WORD FOR THEM, which is preceded by Alfred Newman conducting his famed "Street Scene" theme (a prologue designed to show off stereophonic sound). Look for George Chakiris in the chorus. CinemaScope. ▼▶●

How to Murder a Rich Uncle (1957-British) 80m. **½ D: Nigel Patrick. Charles Coburn, Nigel Patrick, Wendy Hiller, Anthony Newley, Katie Johnson, Athene Seyler. Amusing cash-in on THE LADYKILLERS, with nouveau poor British family deciding to knock off visiting American relative Coburn for his money, succeeding only in doing themselves in. No classic, but entertaining. Script by John Paxton; Michael Caine has a tiny bit. CinemaScope.

How to Murder Your Wife (1965) C-118m. *** D: Richard Quine. Jack Lemmon, Virna Lisi, Terry-Thomas, Eddie Mayehoff, Claire Trevor, Sidney Blackmer, Max Showalter, Jack Albertson, Mary Wickes. Engaging comedy that almost holds up to finale. Cartoonist Lemmon marries Lisi while drunk and spends rest of film devising ways to get rid of her. Mayehoff is standout as Lemmon's lawyer friend. ▼▶●

How to Stuff a Wild Bikini (1965) C-93m. ** D: William Asher. Annette Funicello, Dwayne Hickman, Brian Donlevy, Buster Keaton, Mickey Rooney, Harvey Lembeck, Beverly Adams, Jody McCrea, John Ashley, Bobbi Shaw. The fatigue is palpable in this sixth BEACH PARTY movie, which tries out another new leading man (with Frankie Avalon again shunted to a cameo role). As usual, the veterans—especially Rooney—liven things a little, but overall, pretty mediocre. Followed by GHOST IN THE INVISIBLE BIKINI. Panavision. ▼▶

Huckleberry Finn (1931) 80m. **½ D: Norman Taurog. Jackie Coogan, Mitzi Green, Junior Durkin, Eugene Pallette, Jackie Searl, Clarence Muse, Jane Darwell. Life on the Mississippi with Huck, Tom Sawyer, and Becky Thatcher. Charming but very, very dated; a follow-up to previous year's TOM SAWYER, with same cast.

Huckleberry Finn (1939) SEE: **Adventures of Huckleberry Finn, The** (1939)

Hucksters, The (1947) 115m. *** D: Jack

Conway. Clark Gable, Deborah Kerr, Sydney Greenstreet, Adolphe Menjou, Ava Gardner, Keenan Wynn, Edward Arnold. Glossy dig at advertising and radio industries, with Gable battling for integrity among yes-men. Greenstreet memorable as despotic head of soap company; Kerr's first American movie. Also shown in computer-colored version. ▼▶●

Hud (1963) 112m. **** D: Martin Ritt. Paul Newman, Patricia Neal, Melvyn Douglas, Brandon de Wilde, John Ashley. Excellent story of moral degradation set in modern West, with impeccable performances by all. Neal won Best Actress Oscar as family housekeeper who doesn't want to get involved with no-account Newman. Douglas received Best Supporting Oscar as Newman's ethical, uncompromising father, and James Wong Howe's cinematography also earned a statuette. Irving Ravetch and Harriet Frank, Jr. scripted from Larry McMurtry's novel *Horseman, Pass By*. Panavision. ▼▶●

Huddle (1932) 104m. ** D: Sam Wood. Ramon Novarro, Madge Evans, Una Merkel, Ralph Graves, John Arledge, Frank Albertson, Kane Richmond, Martha Sleeper, Henry Armetta. Novarro is a working-class Italian American who wins a football scholarship to Yale and comes up against snobbery and class distinction. Fatuous, overlong star vehicle bolstered by grade-A MGM production values. European version substituted soccer for football. ▶

Hudson's Bay (1940) 95m. **½ D: Irving Pichel. Paul Muni, Gene Tierney, Laird Cregar, John Sutton, Virginia Field, Vincent Price, Nigel Bruce. Muni's good, but life of founder of Hudson Bay fur-trading company lacks punch. Expansive production. ▶

Hue and Cry (1947-British) 82m. *** D: Charles Crichton. Alastair Sim, Jack Warner, Valerie White, Harry Fowler, Jack Lambert, Frederick Piper, Joan Dowling. Snappy romp as young Fowler suspects that details in the stories published in his favorite weekly pulp magazine are being used as a code by a gang of crooks. Nicely filmed on location on the streets of post-WW2 London. The first of many good Ealing comedies; written by T.E.B. Clarke. Released in the U.S. in 1950. ▼

Huk (1956) C-84m. *½ D: John Barnwell. George Montgomery, Mona Freeman, John Baer, James Bell. Philippine-made hokum about Montgomery returning to the Islands to revenge his dad's murder.

Hula (1927) 64m. **½ D: Victor Fleming. Clara Bow, Clive Brook, Arlette Marchal, Arnold Kent, Maude Truax, Albert Gran. Daughter of a Hawaiian plantation owner sets her sights on a British engineer but soon discovers she's out of her league. Typical silent vehicle for the irrepressible and uninhibited Bow; a forerunner of Jean Harlow's RED DUST, silly and simplistic but fun to watch. First shot of the star shows her luxuriating—ostensibly naked—in a lagoon! ▼❭

Hullabaloo (1940) 78m. **½ D: Edwin L. Marin. Frank Morgan, Virginia Grey, Dan Dailey, Jr., Billie Burke, Nydia Westman, Ann Morriss, Donald Meek, Reginald Owen, Virginia O'Brien, Curt Bois, Sara Haden, Leo Gorcey, Arthur O'Connell. Easy-to-take comedy/musical with Morgan cast as a wannabe radio star. Highlights include a parody of Orson Welles' *War of the Worlds* radio broadcast and Morgan's "impersonations" of A-list MGM stars. ❭

Human Beast, The SEE: **La Bête Humaine**

Human Comedy, The (1943) 118m. ***½ D: Clarence Brown. Mickey Rooney, Frank Morgan, Jackie "Butch" Jenkins, James Craig, Marsha Hunt, Fay Bainter, Ray Collins, Darryl Hickman, Donna Reed, Van Johnson. Memorable Americana, faithfully adapted from William Saroyan's sentimental Oscar-winning story of life in a small town during WW2. Unfolds like a novel, with many lovely vignettes, and one of Rooney's best performances as a teenager with growing responsibilities. Screenplay by Howard Estabrook. P.S.: Keep an eye out for those three soldiers on leave: Barry Nelson, Don DeFore, and Robert Mitchum! Also shown in computer-colored version. ▼❬❭

Human Condition SEE: **No Greater Love**, **Road to Eternity**, and **Soldier's Prayer, A**

Human Desire (1954) 90m. **½ D: Fritz Lang. Glenn Ford, Gloria Grahame, Broderick Crawford, Edgar Buchanan, Kathleen Case, Diana DeLaire. Lang's follow-up to THE BIG HEAT is a well-directed but muddled account of railroad engineer Ford, just back from Korea, who becomes mixed up with married Grahame and murder. Based on Zola's *La Bête Humaine*, filmed in 1938 in France by Jean Renoir. ▼❭

Human Duplicators, The (1965) C-82m. ** D: Hugo Grimaldi. George Nader, Barbara Nichols, Richard Kiel, George Macready, Dolores Faith, Hugh Beaumont, Richard Arlen. An alien giant paves the way for a major invasion by duplicating people— but then falls in love. Some imagination here, but low-budget production sinks it. ▼❭

Human Gorilla, The SEE: **Behind Locked Doors**

Human Jungle, The (1954) 82m. **½ D: Joseph M. Newman. Gary Merrill, Jan Sterling, Paula Raymond, Emile Meyer, Regis Toomey, Chuck Connors, Lamont Johnson, Claude Akins. Documentary-style account of a typical day at a busy police precinct house; nicely done.

Human Monster, The (1939-British) 73m. ** D: Walter Summers. Bela Lugosi, Hugh Williams, Greta Gynt, Edmon Ryan, Wilfred Walter. Absurd, sometimes engaging Edgar Wallace tale of evil Lugosi using

blind men as pawns in elaborate murder scheme. Original British title: DARK EYES OF LONDON. Remade in West Germany as DEAD EYES OF LONDON. ▼❬❭

Human Vapor, The (1960-Japanese) C-92m. **½ D: Ishirô Honda. Tatsuya Mihashi, Kaoru Yachigusa, Yoshio Tsuchiya, Keiko Sata, Fuyuki Murakami, Bokuzen Hidari. A series of puzzling bank robberies seem linked to a reclusive dancer (Yachigusa), who's loved from afar by a shy, bookish librarian (Tsuchiya). Police learn he has somehow been given the ability to turn into a smoky vapor and back again—and has turned homicidal. Handsome, low-key Japanese science-fiction thriller with an odd, interesting performance by Tsuchiya. Original U.S. release was in b&w and ran 81m. ▼

Human Wreckage SEE: **Sex Madness**

Humoresque (1946) 125m. ***½ D: Jean Negulesco. Joan Crawford, John Garfield, Oscar Levant, J. Carrol Naish, Craig Stevens, Tom D'Andrea, Peggy Knudsen, Paul Cavanagh. Ambitious violinist Garfield gets involved with wealthy, unstable patroness Crawford. No cardboard soap opera this; superb performances, handsome production, hilarious support from Levant, and a knockout finale. Perhaps Crawford's finest hour. Young Robert Blake plays Garfield as a child, and that's Isaac Stern's violin on the soundtrack. Filmed before in 1920. ▼❬❭

Hunchback of Notre Dame, The (1923) 93m. *** D: Wallace Worsley. Lon Chaney, Patsy Ruth Miller, Ernest Torrence, Tully Marshall, Norman Kerry. Lavish filming of Hugo classic, capturing flair of medieval Paris and strange attraction of outcast Chaney for dancing girl (Miller). Silent classic holds up well, with Chaney's makeup still incredible. ▼❬❭

Hunchback of Notre Dame, The (1939) 115m. ***½ D: William Dieterle. Charles Laughton, Sir Cedric Hardwicke, Thomas Mitchell, Maureen O'Hara, Edmond O'Brien, Alan Marshal, Walter Hampden, Harry Davenport, George Zucco, Curt Bois, George Tobias, Rod La Rocque. Superb remake of Lon Chaney silent is even better than the original. Laughton, as Victor Hugo's misshapen bell-ringer Quasimodo, is haunting and unforgettable. Magnificently atmospheric studio re-creation of 15th-century Paris also a big plus. Film debut of O'Brien, and U.S. debut of O'Hara. Also shown in computer-colored version. ▼❬❭

Hunchback of Notre Dame, The (1956-French) C-104m. **½ D: Jean Delannoy. Gina Lollobrigida, Anthony Quinn, Jean Danet, Alain Cuny. Quinn makes a valiant try in lead, but film misses scope and flavor of Hugo novel. CinemaScope. ▼❬❭

Hungry Hill (1947-British) 92m. ** D: Brian Desmond Hurst. Margaret Lockwood, Dennis Price, Cecil Parker, Jean Simmons,

Eileen Herlie, Siobhan McKenna. Based on Daphne Du Maurier's book focusing on 19th-century Irish family with their vices and virtues highlighted; capable cast, with Herlie and McKenna making their film debuts.

Hunted, The (1948) **86m. **** D: Jack Bernhard. Preston Foster, Belita, Pierre Watkin, Larry Blake, Russell Hicks, Frank Ferguson, Charles McGraw. Detective sends lover to jail for robbery, even though she says she was framed; when she gets out on parole, he can't stay away from her, even though she promised to kill him and her double-crossing lawyer. Low-budget noir has a hard-boiled sheen but a prosaic, overlong treatment; it even finds time for one of Belita's ice skating routines! ▶

Hunted (1952) SEE: **Stranger in Between**
Hunters, The (1958) **C-108m. **½** D: Dick Powell. Robert Mitchum, Robert Wagner, Richard Egan, Mai Britt, Lee Phillips. Veteran pilot falls for wife of younger flyer—who crashes behind enemy lines. Fair of its type. CinemaScope. ▼▶

Hunt the Man Down (1950) **68m. **** D: George Archainbaud. Gig Young, Lynne Roberts, Willard Parker, Gerald Mohr, Paul Frees. Ordinary whodunit: public defender Young trying to solve a murder. ▼

Hurricane, The (1937) **102m. ***½** D: John Ford. Dorothy Lamour, Jon Hall, Mary Astor, C. Aubrey Smith, Raymond Massey, Thomas Mitchell, John Carradine, Jerome Cowan. First-rate escapism on isle of Manikoora, where idyllic native life of Hall and Lamour is disrupted by vindictive governor Massey. Climactic hurricane effects have never been equaled. Lovely score by Alfred Newman. Screenplay by Dudley Nichols and Oliver H. P. Garrett, from the novel by Charles Nordhoff and James Norman Hall. Remade in 1979. ▼▶

Hurricane Island (1951) **C-70m. *½** D: Lew Landers. Jon Hall, Marie Windsor, Marc Lawrence, Edgar Barrier. Ponce de Leon's expedition and a female pirate's cutthroats clash while seeking the Fountain of Youth. Colorful nonsense with a LOST HORIZON twist.

Hurricane Smith (1952) **C-90m. **** D: Jerry Hopper. Yvonne De Carlo, John Ireland, James Craig, Forrest Tucker. Romance and a search for gold as a ship is beached on a South Sea island.

Hush ... Hush, Sweet Charlotte (1964) **133m. ***** D: Robert Aldrich. Bette Davis, Olivia de Havilland, Joseph Cotten, Agnes Moorehead, Cecil Kellaway, Victor Buono, Mary Astor, Bruce Dern. Macabre story of a family with a skeleton in its closet, confusing at times but worth watching for its cast. Bette is Olivia's victimized cousin; Cotten is Olivia's boyfriend. ▼▶

Hustler, The (1961) **135m. ****** D: Robert Rossen. Paul Newman, Jackie Gleason, Piper Laurie, George C. Scott, Myron Mc-

Cormick, Murray Hamilton, Michael Constantine, Jake LaMotta, Vincent Gardenia. Newman is outstanding as disenchanted drifter and pool hustler who challenges legendary Minnesota Fats (Gleason). Dingy pool-hall atmosphere vividly realized in this incisive film. Cinematographer Eugen Shuftan won an Oscar. Walter Tevis novel adapted by Sidney Carroll and director Rossen. Followed years later by THE COLOR OF MONEY. CinemaScope. ▼▶

Hypnotic Eye, The (1960) **79m. **** D: George Blair. Jacques Bergerac, Merry Anders, Marcia Henderson, Allison Hayes. Partially successful chiller of theatrical mesmerizer with penchant for having female victims disfigure themselves. ▶

Hysteria (1965-British) **85m. **½** D: Freddie Francis. Robert Webber, Anthony Newlands, Jennifer Jayne, Maurice Denham, Lelia Goldoni, Peter Woodthorpe, Sandra Boize. After a car accident, an amnesiac Yank in London finds himself entangled in a complex murder plot that may or may not be a figment of his imagination. Twisty, reasonably intriguing Hammer thriller starts out promisingly, but gets bogged down. ▼▶

I Accuse! (1958-British) **99m. **½** D: Jose Ferrer. Jose Ferrer, Anton Walbrook, Emlyn Williams, Viveca Lindfors, David Farrar, Leo Genn, Herbert Lom, Harry Andrews, Felix Aylmer, George Coulouris, Donald Wolfit. Sincere but pretentious treatment of the treason trial of Alfred Dreyfus (Ferrer), with Williams as his defender, Emile Zola. Screenplay by Gore Vidal. CinemaScope.

I Aim at the Stars (1960) **107m. ***** D: J. Lee Thompson. Curt Jurgens, Victoria Shaw, Herbert Lom, Gia Scala. Low-key fictional history of Nazi missile scientist Wernher von Braun and his problems adjusting to life in America.

I Am a Camera (1955-British) **98m. ***½** D: Henry Cornelius. Julie Harris, Laurence Harvey, Shelley Winters, Ron Randell, Anton Diffring, Patrick McGoohan, Peter Prowse. Intelligent adaptation of John van Druten's play (based on Christopher Isherwood stories) about prewar Berlin, with Harris a delight as a fun-loving young woman who'll accept anything from anyone. Screenplay by John Collier. Basis of Broadway musical and film CABARET.▼

I Am a Fugitive from a Chain Gang (1932) **93m. ****** D: Mervyn LeRoy. Paul Muni, Glenda Farrell, Helen Vinson, Preston Foster, Edward Ellis, Allen Jenkins. Still packs a wallop after all these years, with Muni as innocent man brutally victimized by criminal justice system. Haunting finale is justly famous. Scripted by Sheridan Gibney and Brown Holmes, from Robert E. Burns' autobiographical story. Also dramatized in the cable TVM THE MAN WHO BROKE 1,000 CHAINS. ▼▶

I Am a Thief (1934) **64m.** ** D: Robert Florey. Mary Astor, Ricardo Cortez, Dudley Digges, Robert Barrat, Irving Pichel. Stilted adventure of jewel thieves and insurance fraud set on Orient Express. Good cast can't save indifferent script.

I Am Cuba (1964-Russian-Cuban) **141m.** ***½ D: Mikhail Kalatozov. Sergio Corrieri, Salvador Vud, Jose Gallardo, Raul Garcia. Luz Maria Collazo, Jean Bouise. Sweeping, eye-popping ode to Cuba and the Castro revolution. Vignettes idealize hardworking but exploited peasants and Castro's staunch, freedom-loving revolutionaries, depicting Americans as decadent, sexist swine. And the images are consistently dazzling; the film demands to be seen and savored by any lover of pure cinema. Scripted by Yevgeny Yevtushenko and Enrique Pineda Barnet; released in the U.S. in 1995. ▼○●

I Am Suzanne! (1933) **100m.** *** D: Rowland V. Lee. Lilian Harvey, Gene Raymond, Leslie Banks, Georgia Caine, Geneva Mitchell, Halliwell Hobbes, Murray Kinnell, Edward Keane. Über-bizarre musical set in a Parisian marionette theater, where evil baron Banks manipulates his stars like puppets. British-born German dance and stage star Harvey, in one of her very few American films, plays a performer who tries to snip her strings, assisted by an appealing Raymond. Darn close to a psychological horror movie, with a nightmare sequence not to be missed.

I Am the Law (1938) **83m.** **½ D: Alexander Hall. Edward G. Robinson, Otto Kruger, Wendy Barrie, John Beal, Louis Jean Heydt, Fay Helm, Barbara O'Neil. No surprises in this story of D.A. Robinson fighting corrupt city government, but it's done so smoothly you forget you've seen it before. Don't miss E.G. dancing the Big Apple at the beginning. ▼○●

I Became a Criminal SEE: **They Made Me a Fugitive**

I Believe in You (1952-British) **93m.** **½ D: Michael Relph, Basil Dearden. Cecil Parker, Celia Johnson, Harry Fowler, Godfrey Tearle, Laurence Harvey, Joan Collins. Intelligent study of methods used by probation officers to reform their charges.

I Bury the Living (1958) **76m.** *** D: Albert Band. Richard Boone, Theodore Bikel, Peggy Maurer, Herbert Anderson. Crisp little chiller about cemetery manager who finds he may have power of life and death by sticking white (or black) pins into a map of the graveyard. ▼○●

I Can Get It for You Wholesale (1951) **90m.** *** D: Michael Gordon. Susan Hayward, Dan Dailey, Sam Jaffe, George Sanders, Randy Stuart, Marvin Kaplan, Harry Von Zell. Hayward is aces as a model-turned-dress-designer determined to make it in N.Y.C.'s garment industry. Jerome Weidman's flavorful novel was adapted by Vera

Caspary and scripted by Abraham Polonsky. Aka: ONLY THE BEST. ▶

Ice Cold in Alex SEE: **Desert Attack**

Ice Follies of 1939, The (1939) **93m.** ** D: Reinhold Schunzel. Joan Crawford, James Stewart, Lew Ayres, Lewis Stone, Bess Ehrhardt, Lionel Stander, Roy Shipstad, Eddie Shipstad, Oscar Johnson. Stewart and Ayres are skating partners who split after Jimmy marries Joan; rather than risk hurting their act and getting in the way of Jimmy's dream to start a musical ice revue, she goes off on her own and becomes a movie star overnight! Strange pastiche obviously concocted by MGM to showcase Shipstad and Johnson's Ice Follies show—complete with a (boring) Technicolor finale. ○●

Iceland (1942) **79m.** ** D: H. Bruce Humberstone. Sonja Henie, John Payne, Jack Oakie, Felix Bressart, Osa Massen, Joan Merrill. Labored love story defeats this Henie musical, although skating and singing interludes are pleasant; song hit, "There Will Never Be Another You." ▼▶

Ice Palace (1960) **C-143m.** **½ D: Vincent Sherman. Richard Burton, Robert Ryan, Carolyn Jones, Martha Hyer, Jim Backus, Ray Danton, Shirley Knight, Diane McBain, Karl Swenson, George Takei. Typically sprawling (and silly) Edna Ferber saga of two men whose friendship turns to bitter rivalry, and whose lives parallel the development of Alaska. Watchable, to be sure, but hokey from start to finish. ▼▶

I Confess (1953) **95m.** **½ D: Alfred Hitchcock. Montgomery Clift, Anne Baxter, Karl Malden, Brian Aherne, Dolly Haas, O. E. Hasse. A priest hears a murderer's confession and is himself accused of the crime. Lesser Hitchcock film, made in Quebec, is nevertheless intriguing for its stark photography and symbolism. The shooting of the film plays a key role in LE CONFESSIONNAL (1995). ▼○●

I Could Go on Singing (1963-British) **C-99m.** **½ D: Ronald Neame. Judy Garland, Dirk Bogarde, Jack Klugman, Aline MacMahon, Gregory Phillips. Garland is famed singer returning to England to claim illegitimate son living with father (Bogarde). Garland is exceptional in singing sequences revealing the true Judy; sadly, this was her last film. Panavision. ▼○●

I Cover Big Town (1947) **63m.** ** D: William C. Thomas. Philip Reed, Hillary Brooke, Robert Lowery, Robert Shayne, Mona Barrie, Louis Jean Heydt, Vince Barnett. Uninspired mystery has reporter Lorelei Kilbourne (Brooke) convincing editor Steve Wilson (Reed) to let her work on a complicated murder case. Based on the popular *Big Town* radio series. Followed by BIG TOWN AFTER DARK. Retitled I COVER THE UNDERWORLD.

I Cover the Underworld (1947) SEE: **I Cover Big Town**

I Cover the Underworld (1955) 70m. *½ D: R. G. Springsteen. Sean McClory, Ray Middleton, Lee Van Cleef, Joanne Jordan. Republic Pictures programmer of clergyman whose twin brother is an about-to-be released gangster. Remake of GANGS OF NEW YORK (1938), based on the same book that inspired Martin Scorsese's 2002 film of the same name!

I Cover the War (1937) 68m. ** D: Arthur Lubin. John Wayne, Gwen Gaze, Major Sam Harris, James Bush, Don Barclay. Second-rate pulp fiction about correspondent Wayne tangling with Arab rebel leader.

I Cover the Waterfront (1933) 70m. **½ D: James Cruze. Ben Lyon, Claudette Colbert, Ernest Torrence, Hobart Cavanaugh, Maurice Black, Purnell Pratt, Wilfred Lucas. Dated but still entertaining yarn about tired but persistent waterfront reporter Lyon, who romances free-spirited Colbert to trap her father (Torrence), who has been smuggling Chinese immigrants. How long will it take for him to actually fall in love? Considered pretty raw in its day. ▼❿

Idaho (1943) 70m. **½ D: Joseph Kane. Roy Rogers, Smiley Burnette, Virginia Grey, Harry Shannon, Ona Munson, Dick Purcell, Onslow Stevens, Arthur Hohl, Hal Taliaferro, Robert Mitchell Boy Choir, Bob Nolan and the Sons of the Pioneers. Local judge (Shannon) wants to clean up the community for the sake of his Boys' Town, but outlaws passing through know a secret from his past and use it against him. Meanwhile, Roy has competition for the attentions of the judge's daughter. Lots of music but too little action in this Rogers vehicle.▼❿

I'd Climb the Highest Mountain (1951) C-88m. *** D: Henry King. Susan Hayward, William Lundigan, Rory Calhoun, Gene Lockhart, Ruth Donnelly, Barbara Bates, Lynn Bari, Alexander Knox. Simple good-hearted slice of Americana filmed on location in Georgia, with Lundigan as a preacher whose bride must learn a new way of life in Southern hill country. ▼❿

Ideal Husband, An (1948-British) C-96m. **½ D: Alexander Korda. Paulette Goddard, Michael Wilding, Diana Wynyard, C. Aubrey Smith, Glynis Johns, Michael Medwin. Oscar Wilde's drawing room comedy receives classy presentation but is slow moving. Remade in 1999.▼

Identity Unknown (1945) 71m. **½ D: Walter Colmes. Richard Arlen, Cheryl Walker, Roger Pryor, Bobby Driscoll, Lola Lane, Ian Keith, John Forrest, Sarah Padden. Occasionally moving but uneven psychological drama about a soldier with amnesia, who treks around the country attempting to discover his identity. The scenes with young Driscoll, who thinks Arlen's his dad, are a highlight. ▼❿

I Died a Thousand Times (1955) C-109m. ** D: Stuart Heisler. Jack Palance, Shelley Winters, Lori Nelson, Lee Marvin, Earl Holliman, Lon Chaney (Jr.), Dennis Hopper. Overblown remake of Bogart's HIGH SIERRA with Palance as mad killer with soft spot for crippled girl (Nelson). Winters is his moll in this gangster run-through. CinemaScope. ▼❿

Idiot, The (1951-Japanese) 166m. *** D: Akira Kurosawa. Toshiro Mifune, Masayuki Mori, Setsuko Hara, Takashi Shimura. Kurosawa coscripted this updated version of the Dostoyevsky novel, about a prince and his friend who both love the same woman. Dramatically uneven (because the release version was edited down from Kurosawa's original cut), but there are enough flashes of brilliance to make it worthwhile.▼❿

Idiot, The (1960-Russian) C-122m. **½ D: Ivan Pyrlev. Julia Borisova, Yuri Yakovlev, N. Podgorny, L. Parkhomenko, R. Maximova, N. Pazhitnov. Faithful if not inspired adaptation of Dostoyevsky novel of tormented soul and his peculiar interactions with others.

Idiot's Delight (1939) 105m. *** D: Clarence Brown. Norma Shearer, Clark Gable, Edward Arnold, Charles Coburn, Joseph Schildkraut, Burgess Meredith, Virginia Grey. Disparate characters—including a tacky vaudevillian and his one-time flame, who's come up in the world—are forced to share each other's company in a hotel near the Italian border as WW2 is about to erupt. Robert E. Sherwood's Pulitzer Prize–winning play is badly dated, an interesting period piece, notable for its pacifist ideals . . . but frankly more interesting for Gable's famous song-and-dance routine to "Puttin' on the Ritz." Alternate ending for European release was added to U.S. laserdisc. ▼❿

I Don't Care Girl, The (1953) C-78m. **½ D: Lloyd Bacon. Mitzi Gaynor, David Wayne, Oscar Levant, Warren Stevens. Premise of George Jessel preparing film bio of Eva Tanguay is vehicle to re-create facets in life of the vaudeville star. Gwen Verdon is a lead dancer. ❿

I Don't Want to Be a Man (1920-German) 45m. *** D: Ernst Lubitsch. Ossi Oswalda, Kurt Götz, Ferry Sikla, Margarete Kupfer, Victor Janson. Charming, gender-bending romantic comedy in which a mischievous young tomboy (Oswalda) fantasizes about what life would be like as a male, and then dresses in men's clothes and spends a night on the town. Short, sweet little gem was written by Lubitsch and Hanns Kräly.❿

I Dood It (1943) 102m. ** D: Vincente Minnelli. Red Skelton, Eleanor Powell, Richard Ainley, Patricia Dane, Lena Horne, Hazel Scott, Sam Levene, Butterfly McQueen, John Hodiak, Jimmy Dorsey and Orchestra. Strained, overlong musicomedy about a tailor's assistant obsessively in love with a stage star; good songs include "Star Eyes" and "Taking a Chance on Love," but patchwork film lifts its big finale from Powell's earlier BORN TO DANCE! A remake (more or less) of Buster Keaton's SPITE MARRIAGE.▼🅓

I'd Rather Be Rich (1964) C-96m. **½ D: Jack Smight. Sandra Dee, Maurice Chevalier, Andy Williams, Robert Goulet, Gene Raymond, Charles Ruggles, Hermione Gingold, Allen Jenkins, Rip Taylor. Airy remake of IT STARTED WITH EVE. Dee finds substitute fiancé to please dying grandfather who wants to see her happy. Only Chevalier-Gingold scenes have spice.

I Dream of Jeanie (1952) C-90m. ** D: Allan Dwan. Ray Middleton, Bill Shirley, Muriel Lawrence, Eileen Christy, Lynn Bari, Richard Simmons, Rex Allen, Louise Beavers, James Kirkwood, Carl "Alfalfa" Switzer. Blah biography of famed 19th-century American composer Stephen Foster (Shirley), who pines over Lawrence (even though Christy, the "Jeanie" of the title, really is the girl for him). Foster's "story" also is told in HARMONY LANE and SWANEE RIVER.▼🅓

I Dream Too Much (1935) 95m. **½ D: John Cromwell. Lily Pons, Henry Fonda, Eric Blore, Osgood Perkins, Lucien Littlefield, Esther Dale. Opera star Pons' Hollywood debut casts her as a singer whose fame leads to marital woes with her more ambitious composer-husband (Fonda). Look for Lucille Ball as an American tourist in Paris. ▼

I Escaped from the Gestapo (1943) 75m. ** D: Harold Young. Dean Jagger, John Carradine, Mary Brian, William Henry, Sidney Blackmer, Ian Keith. Forger-engraver Jagger is sprung from prison so he can work for a secret Gestapo cell that operates a boardwalk arcade in L.A. Unusually good cast in this routine B picture that gets sillier as it goes along. Look for Spanky McFarland as a newsboy. Retitled: NO ESCAPE. 🅓

If a Man Answers (1962) C-102m. **½ D: Henry Levin. Sandra Dee, Bobby Darin, Micheline Presle, John Lund, Cesar Romero, Stefanie Powers, Christopher Knight, Charlene Holt. Trite pap of Dee and Darin (then married in real life) trying to outdo each other with jealousy-baiting antics.🅓

I Fidanzati SEE: **Fiancés, The**

If I Had a Million (1932) 83m. ***½ D: James Cruze, H. Bruce Humberstone, Stephen Roberts, William A. Seiter, Ernst Lubitsch, Norman Taurog, Norman Z. McLeod. Gary Cooper, George Raft, Mary Boland, Charles Laughton, W. C. Fields, Wynne Gibson, Gene Raymond, Charlie Ruggles, Alison Skipworth, Jack Oakie, Frances Dee, Richard Bennett. Wealthy Bennett gives that sum to various people; all the episodes are good, but the most famous are Laughton's worm-turning and Fields' revenge on road hogs.●

If I Had My Way (1940) 94m. **½ D:

David Butler. Bing Crosby, Gloria Jean, Charles Winninger, El Brendel, Allyn Joslyn, Claire Dodd. Title tune is chief asset of pleasant but standard Crosby vehicle in which he helps little Gloria find her guardian, vaudevillian Winninger.🅓

If I'm Lucky (1946) 79m. ** D: Lewis Seiler. Vivian Blaine, Perry Como, Harry James, Carmen Miranda, Phil Silvers, Edgar Buchanan, Reed Hadley. James' band is broke and unemployed, and becomes involved with politician Buchanan's "common man" campaign. Paper-thin remake of THANKS A MILLION, occasionally uplifted by Silvers' and Miranda's spunk.🅓

If I Were Free (1933) 66m. **½ D: Elliott Nugent. Irene Dunne, Clive Brook, Nils Asther, Henry Stephenson, Vivian Tobin, Tempe Pigott, Lorraine MacLean, Laura Hope Crews, Halliwell Hobbes. Dunne and Brook shine as lovers trying to break away from their respective failing marriages. First-rate cast and production do wonders with tearjerker material. 🅓

If I Were King (1938) 101m. *** D: Frank Lloyd. Ronald Colman, Frances Dee, Basil Rathbone, Ellen Drew, C. V. France, Henry Wilcoxon, Heather Thatcher, Sidney Toler. Colman (with that inimitable voice) is ideally cast as the French poet-rogue François Villon, who matches wits with the crafty King Louis XI (Rathbone) and falls hopelessly in love with a lady-in-waiting (Dee). Forget historical accuracy; this is just good entertainment. Scripted by Preston Sturges. Filmed before in 1920 and, as the operetta THE VAGABOND KING, in 1930 and again in 1956. Villon was also played by John Barrymore in THE BELOVED ROGUE (1927).▼🅓

If I Were Rich SEE: **Cash**

I Found Stella Parish (1935) 84m. ** D: Mervyn LeRoy. Kay Francis, Ian Hunter, Paul Lukas, Sybil Jason, Jessie Ralph, Barton MacLane. Mild soaper in which London stage star Francis harbors a secret and mysteriously disappears; cynical newshound Hunter determines to find her.

If This Be Sin (1949-British) 98m. ** D: Gregory Ratoff. Roger Livesey, Myrna Loy, Peggy Cummins, Richard Greene, Elizabeth Allan. Maudlin multi-love-affair story set on isle of Capri. Original British title: THAT DANGEROUS AGE.▼

If Winter Comes (1947) 97m. ** D: Victor Saville. Walter Pidgeon, Deborah Kerr, Angela Lansbury, Binnie Barnes, Janet Leigh, Dame May Whitty, Reginald Owen. Good cast fails to enliven wooden drama about a crisis in the life of kindly, highly principled Pidgeon, living in a stuffy small town outside London and trapped in a marriage to coldhearted Lansbury.🅓

If You Could Only Cook (1935) 70m. *** D: William A. Seiter. Herbert Marshall, Jean Arthur, Leo Carrillo, Lionel Stander, Alan

Edwards. Arthur and Marshall are superb team in this delightful comedy of wealthy automobile tycoon/inventor and penniless woman who, for complex reasons, become mobster Carrillo's maid and butler. This film wrongly carried Frank Capra's name as director in many European prints as a fraudulent studio effort to exploit his massive popularity.▶

If You Knew Susie (1948) **90m.** ****½** D: Gordon Douglas. Eddie Cantor, Joan Davis, Allyn Joslyn, Charles Dingle. Weak film of show biz couple is a delight for Cantor-Davis fans but pointless for others.▼▶

I, Jane Doe (1948) **85m.** ***½** D: John H. Auer. Ruth Hussey, John Carroll, Vera Ralston, Gene Lockhart, John Howard, John Litel. Ludicrous courtroom "drama" of murderess Ralston, with the victim's wife (Hussey) defending her.

Ikiru (1952-Japanese) **143m.** ******** D: Akira Kurosawa. Takashi Shimura, Nobuo Kaneko, Kyoko Seki, Miki Odagiri, Yunosuke Ito. Minor bureaucrat Shimura, dying of cancer, searches for meaning in his life. Thoughtful, poignant examination of loneliness, with a brilliant performance by Shimura. Served as inspiration for LIFE AS A HOUSE. ▼▶

I Know Where I'm Going! (1945-British) **91m.** ******** D: Michael Powell, Emeric Pressburger. Wendy Hiller, Roger Livesey, Finlay Currie, Pamela Brown, Valentine Dyall, Petula Clark. Simple film of headstrong girl (Hiller) who plans to marry for money, stranded in Scottish seacoast town for a week, where she meets and slowly falls in love with Livesey. Very little plot, but an abundance of charm and wit. A quiet gem. Beautifully scripted by the filmmakers. ▼▶

Il Bell'Antonio SEE: **Bell'Antonio**
Il Bidone SEE: **Swindle, The**
Il Generale Della Rovere (1959-Italian) **129m.** *****½** D: Roberto Rossellini. Vittorio De Sica, Hannes Messemer, Sandra Milo, Giovanna Ralli, Anne Vernon. De Sica is brilliant as a con man forced by the Nazis to impersonate a just-deceased Italian general and find out the identity of a Resistance leader. Will this charade somehow transform a coward into a hero? Extended versions run 132m. and 138m. ▼▶

Il Grido (1957-Italian) **115m.** ****½** D: Michelangelo Antonioni. Steve Cochran, Alida Valli, Dorian Gray, Betsy Blair, Lyn Shaw. Leisurely paced yet compelling study of Cochran's mental disintegration due to lack of communication with those he loves; Cochran is quite good. Aka THE OUTCRY. ▼▶

I Like It That Way (1934) **67m.** ****½** D: Harry Lachman. Gloria Stuart, Roger Pryor, Marian Marsh, Shirley Grey, Onslow Stevens, Noel Madison, Lucile Webster Gleason, Clarence Wilson, Mickey Rooney. Super-salesman Pryor falls in love

with chance acquaintance Stuart and tries to change his wayward ways for her sake; then he learns she works as a singer in a nightclub/speakeasy. Flyweight musical built around lovely Stuart, who couldn't sing or dance. Pleasant enough time-filler.

I Like Money (1961-British) **C-97m.** ****½** D: Peter Sellers. Peter Sellers, Nadia Gray, Herbert Lom, Leo McKern, Martita Hunt, John Neville, Michael Gough, Billie Whitelaw. Subdued satirical remake of TOPAZE, with Sellers the timid schoolteacher who becomes an unscrupulous businessman. British title: MR. TOPAZE. CinemaScope.

I Like Your Nerve (1931) **69m.** ***½** D: William McGann. Douglas Fairbanks, Jr., Loretta Young, Henry Kolker, Edmund Breon, Boris Karloff. Devil-may-care Fairbanks breezes into Latin country and sets his sights on Loretta—even though she's engaged. Tiresome comic romance. Karloff has tiny role as a butler named Luigi!

I Live for Love (1935) **64m.** ****½** D: Busby Berkeley. Dolores Del Rio, Everett Marshall, Guy Kibbee, Allen Jenkins, Berton Churchill. Lesser Berkeley musical concerns backstage romance between Del Rio and Marshall. A couple of OK songs, but unfortunately no dancing.

I Live in Fear (1955-Japanese) **105m.** ******* D: Akira Kurosawa. Toshiro Mifune, Eiko Miyoshi, Yutaka Sada, Minoru Chiaki, Haruko Togo, Kyoko Aoyama. The ordinary lives of a modern-day Tokyo patriarch's family are fundamentally shaken upon his sudden decision that they must all move to Brazil to avoid the H-bomb. Mifune is remarkable, as always, here assaying a character twice his own age. Complex effort starts as satire and ends as tragedy. Original Japanese prints run 113m. Aka RECORD OF A LIVING BEING and WHAT THE BIRDS KNEW. ▼▶

I Live My Life (1935) **92m.** ****** D: W. S. Van Dyke II. Joan Crawford, Brian Aherne, Frank Morgan, Aline MacMahon, Eric Blore, Fred Keating, Jessie Ralph, Arthur Treacher, Frank Conroy, Sterling Holloway, Vince Barnett, Hedda Hopper, Lionel Stander. Crawford and Aherne are in love, but she's flighty and he's an archeologist. Glossy and empty. Scripted by Joseph L. Mankiewicz.▼▶

I'll Be Seeing You (1945) **85m.** ****½** D: William Dieterle. Ginger Rogers, Joseph Cotten, Shirley Temple, Spring Byington, Tom Tully, Dare Harris (John Derek). Overblown David Selznick schmaltz. Rogers, convict home on parole, meets disturbed soldier Cotten; they fall in love.▶

I'll Be Yours (1947) **93m.** ****½** D: William A. Seiter. Deanna Durbin, Tom Drake, Adolphe Menjou, William Bendix, Franklin Pangborn. Pleasant but undistinguished remake of THE GOOD FAIRY with Deanna in hot water after telling white lie to wealthy and amorous Menjou. ▼

I'll Cry Tomorrow (1955) **117m.** *****½**
D: Daniel Mann. Susan Hayward, Richard
Conte, Jo Van Fleet, Ray Danton, Eddie
Albert, Margo. Superlative portrayal by
Hayward of star Lillian Roth, her assorted
marriages and alcoholic problems. Everything
a movie biography should be. Helen Rose
won an Oscar for her costumes. Also shown in
computer-colored version. ▼●▶

Illegal (1932-British) **71m.** ***½** D: William
McGann. Isobel Elsom, D. A. Clarke-
Smith, Margot Grahame, Edgar Norfolk,
Moira Lynd, Ivor Barnard. A woman's
worthless husband wastes all her money,
so she's forced to open a shady nightclub in
order to provide a comfortable existence for
her daughters. Trivial Warner Bros. "quota
quickie" made in England. Synopsis may
bring to mind MILDRED PIERCE but film
certainly doesn't.

Illegal (1955) **88m.** ****½** D: Lewis Allen.
Edward G. Robinson, Nina Foch, Hugh
Marlowe, Jayne Mansfield, Albert Dekker,
Ellen Corby, DeForest Kelley, Howard
St. John. Former D.A. Robinson becomes
criminal attorney with gangster client, but
lays reputation—and life—on the line to
defend former assistant Foch for homicide. Valiant attempt to recapture spark of
earlier Robinson vehicles; remake of THE
MOUTHPIECE. ▼▶

Illegal Entry (1949) **84m.** ****½** D: Frederick de Cordova. Howard Duff, Marta Toren,
George Brent, Gar Moore. Harsh narrative
of federal agent assigned to uncover smuggling racket.

Illegal Traffic (1938) **66m.** ******* D: Louis
King. J. Carrol Naish, Mary Carlisle, Robert
Preston, Judith Barrett, Pierre Watkin, Larry
(Buster) Crabbe, Richard Denning, Richard
Stanley (Dennis Morgan). Federal agent
Preston goes undercover to get the goods on
Naish, who runs a transport company that
specializes in smuggling criminals out of
danger in exchange for a hefty cut of their
loot. Crackling cops-and-robbers stuff is
one of the best of Paramount's G-men films
of the period.

I'll Get By (1950) **C-83m.** ****½** D: Richard
Sale. June Haver, William Lundigan, Glo-
ria DeHaven, Dennis Day, Thelma Ritter.
Remake of TIN PAN ALLEY, involving
songwriter and his girlfriend; Jeanne Crain,
Victor Mature, and Dan Dailey make guest
appearances.

I'll Get You (1953-British) **79m.** ****** D:
Seymour Friedman, Peter Graham Scott.
George Raft, Sally Gray, Clifford Evans,
Reginald Tate, Patricia Laffan. OK gangster
yarn of Raft (FBI man) and Gray (British
Intelligence) cracking a kidnapping syn-
dicate. Original British title: ESCAPE
ROUTE. ▼▶

I'll Give a Million (1938) **75m.** ******* D: Walter Lang. Warner Baxter, Marjorie Weaver,
Peter Lorre, Jean Hersholt, John Carradine,

J. Edward Bromberg, Lynn Bari, Fritz Feld,
Sig Rumann, Luis Alberni. Residents of
a French town learn that one of the many
local hobos is actually a millionaire who's
prepared to give a million francs to the first
person who is kind to him with no thought
of reward—but *which* hobo? The Riviera
becomes a vagrants' paradise in this charming comedy with European flavor. Remake
of 1935 Italian film DARO UN MILIONE
with Vittorio De Sica.

Illicit (1931) **81m.** ***½** D: Archie Mayo.
Barbara Stanwyck, James Rennie, Ricardo
Cortez, Joan Blondell, Charles Butterworth,
Natalie Moorhead. Independent-minded
Stanwyck loves Rennie, but doesn't want
marriage to taint her happiness. Boring,
badly directed, overly talky "talkie." Re-
made two years later as EX-LADY. ▼▶

Illicit Interlude (1951-Swedish) **94m.** ****½**
D: Ingmar Bergman. Maj-Britt Nilsson, Alf
Kjellin, Birger Malmsten, Georg Funkquist.
Moody film using flashback retells Nilsson's
romance with now-dead lover and its relation-
ship to her present frame of mind. Original
title: SUMMERPLAY; video title: SUMMER
INTERLUDE. ▼▶

Ill Met by Moonlight SEE: **Night Ambush**

I'll Never Forget You (1951) **C-90m.** ****½**
D: Roy (Ward) Baker. Tyrone Power, Ann
Blyth, Michael Rennie, Dennis Price, Beatrice Campbell. American (Power) working in London is transported back to 18th
century, where he falls in love with Blyth.
Remake of BERKELEY SQUARE. Opens
in b&w, switches to color. Original British
title: THE HOUSE IN THE SQUARE. ▶

I'll See You in My Dreams (1951) **110m.**
**½ D: Michael Curtiz. Doris Day, Danny
Thomas, Frank Lovejoy, Patrice Wymore,
James Gleason. Warner Bros. formula
musical biography at its hokiest: trite telling of Gus Kahn's life and times; songs
include "Ain't We Got Fun," "It Had to Be
You." ▼●▶

I'll Take Romance (1937) **85m.** ****½** D:
Edward H. Griffith. Grace Moore, Mel-
vyn Douglas, Stuart Erwin, Helen Westley,
Margaret Hamilton. Silly story of opera star
Moore kidnapped by agent Douglas has
lovely title tune, operatic arias to keep it
moving along.

I'll Take Sweden (1965) **C-96m.** ****** D:
Frederick de Cordova. Bob Hope, Dina
Merrill, Tuesday Weld, Frankie Avalon, Jeremy Slate. Pseudo-sexy Hope vehicle, with
everyone frantic over life and love; witless
proceedings. ▼▶

I'll Tell the World (1934) **77m.** ****½** D: Edward Sedgwick. Lee Tracy, Gloria Stuart,
Roger Pryor, Onslow Stevens, Alec Francis, Lawrence Grant, Herman Bing, Leon
Waycoff (Ames), Willard Robertson, Walter
Brennan, Ward Bond. Tracy plays a devil-
may-care reporter, working in Europe, who
loves scooping his rivals. Then he falls in love

with a woman who turns out to be a deposed princess! Story starts out in a light, comic vein, then turns serious; Tracy and Stuart are very good. Tracy starred in an unrelated film of the same name in 1945. Remade as FIT FOR A KING.

I'll Tell the World (1945) 61m. ** D: Leslie Goodwins. Lee Tracy, Brenda Joyce, Raymond Walburn, June Preisser, Thomas Gomez, Howard Freeman, Lorin Raker. Minor musical comedy with idea-man Tracy saving Walburn's failing radio station.

Illusion Travels by Streetcar (1953-Mexican) 90m. **½ D: Luis Buñuel. Lilia Prado, Carlos Navarro, Domingo Soler, Fernando Soto, Agustin Isunza. Two transit workers steal a streetcar destined for the scrap heap, take it on one last run, picking up odd assortment of passengers. Agreeable (if lesser) Buñuel fable.▼▶

I Love a Bandleader (1945) 70m. ** D: Del Lord. Phil Harris, Leslie Brooks, Walter Catlett, Eddie Anderson, Frank Sully, Pierre Watkin. Formula claptrap about meek Harris, who becomes a swinging bandleader; stars' personalities rise above material.

I Love a Mystery (1945) 70m. **½ D: Henry Levin. Jim Bannon, Nina Foch, George Macready, Barton Yarborough, Carole Mathews, Lester Matthews. Bizarre, entertaining whodunit based on popular radio show, with Bannon as Jack Packard, Yarborough as Doc Young. Involves strange Oriental cult and a prophecy of doom for bewildered Macready. First in a short-lived series.

I Love a Soldier (1944) 106m. ** D: Mark Sandrich. Paulette Goddard, Sonny Tufts, Beulah Bondi, Mary Treen, Barry Fitzgerald. Reteaming of Goddard and Tufts after their hit in SO PROUDLY WE HAIL! doesn't match original; story examines problems of wartime marriages.

I Loved a Woman (1933) 91m. BOMB D: Alfred E. Green. Edward G. Robinson, Kay Francis, Genevieve Tobin, J. Farrell MacDonald, Robert Barrat. Robinson plays meat-packing plant owner whose life is destroyed by enticing, ambitious opera singer Francis. Absurd story moves like molasses; dialogue yields (unintended) laughs.

I Love Melvin (1953) C-76m. **½ D: Don Weis. Donald O'Connor, Debbie Reynolds, Una Merkel, Allyn Joslyn, Richard Anderson, Noreen Corcoran, Jim Backus, Robert Taylor. N.Y.C. location filming enhances this cute musical, spotlighting lowly photo assistant O'Connor's attempt to impress ambitious dancer Reynolds by pretending that he can get her picture in *Look* magazine.▼▶

I Love Trouble (1948) 94m. *** D: S. Sylvan Simon. Franchot Tone, Janet Blair, Janis Carter, Adele Jergens, Glenda Farrell, Steven Geray, Tom Powers, Lynn Merrick, John Ireland, Donald Curtis, Eduardo Ciannelli, Robert Barrat, Raymond Burr. Fine cast enlivens this solid noir with L.A. gumshoe Stuart Bailey (Tone) hired by a well-heeled older man to spy on his young wife. The Bailey character was later played by Efrem Zimbalist, Jr., on TV's *77 Sunset Strip*. Written by Roy Huggins, from his book *The Double Take*.

I Love You Again (1940) 99m. ***½ D: W. S. Van Dyke II. William Powell, Myrna Loy, Frank McHugh, Edmund Lowe, Donald Douglas, Nella Walker. Hilarious story of amnesiac Powell—solid citizen in a small town—reverting to former life as con man, but trying to forestall divorce proceedings by "his" wife (Loy). Ingenious script by Charles Lederer, George Oppenheimer, and Harry Kurnitz.▼▶

Il Posto (1961-Italian) 93m. ***½ D: Ermanno Olmi. Sandro Panseri, Loredana Detto, Tullio Kezich, Mara Revel. This early Olmi feature has something of the feel of early Truffaut and Milos Forman in its portrayal of everyday life with its tiny triumphs and failures. Simple story concerns a teenaged boy getting his first job and meeting a girl, but the beauty of the film is in the loving and perceptive observation of human behavior. A small-scale gem.▶

Il Sorpasso (1962-Italian) 105m. ***½ D: Dino Risi. Vittorio Gassman, Jean Louis Trintignant, Catherine Spaak, Claudio Gora, Luciano Angelillo, Linda Sini. After meeting by chance, irresponsible, middle-aged lothario Gassman takes shy, repressed law student Trintignant on a wild weekend car trip from Rome to Tuscany. Funny, insightful character study; superbly acted and vividly filmed. Only the ending leaves a sour taste. Screenplay by Risi, Ettore Scola, and Ruggero Maccari. U.S. title: THE EASY LIFE.▶

I'm All Right Jack (1959-British) 104m. ***½ D: John Boulting. Ian Carmichael, Terry-Thomas, Peter Sellers, Richard Attenborough, Margaret Rutherford, Dennis Price, Irene Handl, Miles Malleson. Carmichael works for his uncle and unwittingly upsets an elaborate and crooked business scheme in this memorable comedy. Sellers wonderful as labor leader. Scripted by Frank Harvey, John Boulting, and Alan Hackney, from Hackney's novel *Private Life*. Sequel to PRIVATE'S PROGRESS (1956). Produced by Roy Boulting.▼▶

I Married a Communist (1950) 73m. ** D: Robert Stevenson. Laraine Day, Robert Ryan, John Agar, Thomas Gomez, Janis Carter, Richard Rober, William Talman. Cornball acting and a "better-dead-than-Red" scenario sink this noirish melodrama, which has become a relic of its era. Ryan is a shipping executive and former political radical whose past comes back to haunt him. The "commies" (headed by Gomez) are depicted as two-bit gangsters, but Talman is especially good as a killer-for-hire. Retitled THE WOMAN ON PIER 13.▶

I Married a Doctor (1936) **83m.** ******* D: Archie Mayo. Pat O'Brien, Josephine Hutchinson, Ross Alexander, Guy Kibbee, Louise Fazenda, Olin Howland, Robert Barrat. Effective, if somewhat diluted, adaptation of Sinclair Lewis' *Main Street*, with O'Brien as a complacent small-town doctor who returns home from Chicago with a big-city wife (Hutchinson). Incisive portrayal of jumbled emotions and small-town American narrow-mindedness. Fazenda, cast as a Swedish housekeeper, played the same role in the 1923 version of Lewis' novel, called MAIN STREET.

I Married a Monster from Outer Space (1958) **78m.** ****½** D: Gene Fowler, Jr. Tom Tryon, Gloria Talbott, Ken Lynch, John Eldredge, Jean Carson, Maxie Rosenbloom. One of the silliest titles in film history obscures pretty good little rehash of INVASION OF THE BODY SNATCHERS: Talbott notices that husband Tryon (as well as some of his friends) has been behaving very peculiarly of late. Some nice, creepy moments in chiller which has slowly developed a cult following. Remade for TV in 1998. ▼○◐

I Married an Angel (1942) **84m.** ****** D: W. S. Van Dyke II. Jeanette MacDonald, Nelson Eddy, Edward Everett Horton, Binnie Barnes, Reginald Owen, Douglass Dumbrille. Playboy Eddy dreams he marries angel MacDonald in this bizarre adaptation of Rodgers and Hart musical. MacDonald and Eddy's last film together. Songs include "Spring Is Here," title tune. ▼◐

I Married a Witch (1942) **76m.** ******* D: René Clair. Fredric March, Veronica Lake, Robert Benchley, Susan Hayward, Cecil Kellaway, Elizabeth Patterson. Witch burned in Salem centuries ago (Lake) comes back to haunt descendants of Puritan (March) who sent her to her death. Saucy comedy-fantasy based on a story by Thorne (*Topper*) Smith. Good special effects, too. ▼○◐

I Married a Woman (1958) **84m.** ****** D: Hal Kanter. George Gobel, Diana Dors, Adolphe Menjou, Jessie Royce Landis. Lackluster events concerning harassed ad man Gobel who'd rather spend time with his gorgeous wife than overtime at the office. Look fast for young Angie Dickinson and an amusing movie-star cameo. ▼○

I Met Him in Paris (1937) **86m.** ****½** D: Wesley Ruggles. Claudette Colbert, Melvyn Douglas, Robert Young, Lee Bowman, Mona Barrie, Fritz Feld. Prolonged romantic comedy dependent entirely on charm of its stars. Vacationing Colbert, in Paris, then Switzerland, has to choose from Bowman, Young, and Douglas (you guess who wins out). ◐

I Met My Love Again (1938) **77m.** ****½** D: Arthur Ripley, Joshua Logan. Joan Bennett, Henry Fonda, Dame May Whitty, Alan Marshal, Louise Platt, Alan Baxter, Tim Holt.

Familiar soaper of young girl Bennett running off with amorous author, with tragic consequences; acting surpasses script. ▼

I'm From Missouri (1939) **80m.** ****** D: Theodore Reed. Bob Burns, Gladys George, Gene Lockhart, William Henry, George P. Huntley, Judith Barrett, Patricia Morison. Homespun Burns sails to England with a load of Army mules and encounters London society. Episodic, occasionally funny comedy.

Imitation General (1958) **88m.** ****** D: George Marshall. Glenn Ford, Red Buttons, Taina Elg, Dean Jones, Kent Smith, Tige Andrews. Tepid, occasionally tasteless WW2 comedy defeats its game cast. Ford is a sergeant who impersonates superior officer. CinemaScope. ◗

Imitation of Life (1934) **109m.** ****½** D: John M. Stahl. Claudette Colbert, Warren William, Rochelle Hudson, Louise Beavers, Fredi Washington, Ned Sparks, Alan Hale, Henry Armetta. Believable but dated first version of Fannie Hurst's soaper of working-girl Colbert who makes good with Beavers' pancake recipe; Washington is fine as latter's daughter who passes for white. Ultrasentimental. Adapted for screen by Preston Sturges. ▼◐

Imitation of Life (1959) **C-124m.** *****½** D: Douglas Sirk. Lana Turner, John Gavin, Sandra Dee, Dan O'Herlihy, Susan Kohner, Robert Alda, Juanita Moore, Mahalia Jackson, Troy Donahue, Jack Weston. Plush remake of Fannie Hurst story, with Turner as career-driven actress; Moore is the good-hearted black woman who shares her life, and whose troubled daughter (Kohner) passes for white. Fine performances and direction overcome soap-opera trappings to make this quite credible and moving. ▼◐

Immediate Disaster (1954-British) **75m.** ***½** D: Burt Balaban. Patricia Neal, Helmut Dantine, Derek Bond, Cyril Luckham, Willoughby Gray, Marigold Russell. Tame rehash of THE DAY THE EARTH STOOD STILL (with the same leading actress) as friendly Venusian (Dantine) arrives hoping to curtail our nuclear ambitions. Slow and dry but achingly sincere. Original British title: STRANGER FROM VENUS. ▼◐

Immortal Battalion, The SEE: **Way Ahead, The**

Immortal Monster, The SEE: **Caltiki, the Immortal Monster**

Immortal Sergeant, The (1943) **91m.** ****½** D: John M. Stahl. Henry Fonda, Maureen O'Hara, Thomas Mitchell, Allyn Joslyn, Reginald Gardiner, Melville Cooper. OK wartime drama of inexperienced corporal who is forced to take command of patrol in Africa after sergeant dies. Look for a young Peter Lawford. ▼◐

I'm No Angel (1933) **87m.** *****½** D: Wesley Ruggles. Mae West, Cary Grant, Edward

Arnold, Gertrude Michael, Kent Taylor. West is in rare form as star of Arnold's sideshow who chases after playboy Grant. Builds to a hilarious courtroom climax. Mae gets sole screenplay credit for this, one of her all-time best. ▼◐

I Mobster (1958) **80m.** **½ D: Roger Corman. Steve Cochran, Lita Milan, Robert Strauss, Celia Lovsky, Lili St. Cyr. Rugged account of gangster Cochran and events in his crime-filled life. Full title: I MOBSTER . . . THE LIFE OF A GANGSTER. CinemaScope. ▼◗

Impact (1949) **111m.** *** D: Arthur Lubin. Brian Donlevy, Ella Raines, Helen Walker, Charles Coburn, Anna May Wong, Robert Warwick, Mae Marsh. Nice guy Donlevy's wife is cheating on him. She and her lover plot to do him in . . . but there are complications. Entertaining, thoughtful drama will keep you guessing at every turn. ▼◗

Impatient Maiden, The (1932) **72m.** **½ D: James Whale. Lew Ayres, Mae Clarke, Una Merkel, Andy Devine, John Halliday, Oscar Apfel, Ethel Griffies, Helen Jerome Eddy, Bert Roach, Hattie McDaniel, Walter Brennan. Young woman forsakes true love to become her wealthy boss' mistress. Slight but interesting Depression yarn is worth seeing for Clarke's fine performance and Whale's trademark moving-camera shots. Lengthy opening sequence was shot at L.A. landmark Angels Flight.

Impatient Years, The (1944) **91m.** **½ D: Irving Cummings. Jean Arthur, Lee Bowman, Charles Coburn, Edgar Buchanan, Harry Davenport, Grant Mitchell, Jane Darwell. Thin comedy of soldier Bowman returning to civilian life with wife Arthur, finding trouble readjusting. ◗

Imperfect Lady, The (1947) **97m.** ** D: Lewis Allen. Teresa Wright, Ray Milland, Cedric Hardwicke, Virginia Field, Anthony Quinn, Reginald Owen. Undistinguished drama of Parliament member falling in love with ballerina in London during 1890s.

Imperial Venus (1962-French-Italian) **C-120m.** ** D: Jean Delannoy. Gina Lollobrigida, Stephen Boyd, Raymond Pellegrin, Micheline Presle, Gabriele Ferzetti, Massimo Girotti. Lumpy spectacle about how Paolina Bonaparte, Napoleon's hot-blooded sister, spread her charms around practically his entire army in her lust for power. Super Technirama 70. ◗

Importance of Being Earnest, The (1952-British) **C-95m.** *** D: Anthony Asquith. Michael Redgrave, Michael Denison, Richard Wattis, Edith Evans, Margaret Rutherford, Joan Greenwood, Dorothy Tutin. Oscar Wilde's peerless comedy of manners set in Victorian England is given admirable treatment. Remade in 2002. ▼◐

Impostor, The (1944) **92m.** **½ D: Julien Duvivier. Jean Gabin, Richard Whorf, Allyn Joslyn, Ellen Drew, Peter Van Eyck, Ralph Morgan, Eddie Quillan, John Qualen, Dennis Moore, Milburn Stone. In WW2 France, a German bombing enables prisoner Gabin to escape his own guillotining. Stealing the uniform of a dead French soldier, he assumes the man's identity and winds up in North Africa, waging war and bonding with the men of his unit. Interesting but somehow misses the mark. Duvivier's last film in Hollywood. Retitled STRANGE CONFESSION.

In a Lonely Place (1950) **91m.** ***½ D: Nicholas Ray. Humphrey Bogart, Gloria Grahame, Frank Lovejoy, Robert Warwick, Jeff Donnell, Martha Stewart. Mature, powerful drama about a feisty, self-destructive screenwriter (Bogart) who has an affair with starlet Grahame while trying to clear himself of a murder rap. Excellent performances in this study of two turbulent characters set against realistic and cynical Hollywood backdrop. Written by Andrew Solt. ▼◗

In Caliente (1935) **84m.** ** D: Lloyd Bacon. Dolores Del Rio, Pat O'Brien, Edward Everett Horton, Leo Carrillo, Glenda Farrell. Pedestrian romantic comedy filmed in Agua Caliente, with fast-talking magazine editor O'Brien wooing dancer Del Rio. Horton's comic relief is the saving grace, along with Busby Berkeley's production numbers for "Muchacha" and "The Lady in Red" (sung by Wini Shaw, with a novelty chorus by Judy Canova). ◗

Incendiary Blonde (1945) **C-113m.** *** D: George Marshall. Betty Hutton, Arturo de Cordova, Charlie Ruggles, Albert Dekker, Barry Fitzgerald, Mary Phillips, Bill Goodwin. Hollywoodized biography of 1920s nightclub queen Texas Guinan is Hutton all over. Plenty of old-time songs.

Incident (1949) **69m.** **½ D: William Beaudine. Jane Frazee, Warren Douglas, Robert Osterloh, Joyce Compton, Harry Lauter, Anthony Caruso. Stock salesman (Douglas) mistaken for a notorious crook by rival gangsters is brutally beaten one night, then turns amateur sleuth by posing as his look-alike to catch the thugs. Obscure Monogram noir delivers on its offbeat premise but could have done without the comedy relief from dizzy dame Compton. ◗

Incident at Midnight (1963-British) **58m.** ** D: Norman Harrison. Anton Diffring, William Sylvester, Tony Garnett, Martin Miller. Based on Edgar Wallace short story, film deals with drugstore hangout of dope addicts and gangsters who ply their trade there; trim yarn.

Incredible Journey, The (1963) **C-80m.** *** D: Fletcher Markle. Emile Genest, John Drainie, Tommy Tweed, Sandra Scott. Entertaining, well-made Disney story of three pets—two dogs and a cat—who make 250-mile journey across Canada on their own to be with their family of humans. Remade by

Disney in 1993 as HOMEWARD BOUND: THE INCREDIBLE JOURNEY. ▼●▶

Incredible Mr. Limpet, The (1964) C-102m. ** D: Arthur Lubin. Don Knotts, Jack Weston, Carole Cook, Andrew Duggan, Larry Keating. Knotts plays a milquetoast who dreams of becoming a fish—and miraculously gets his wish (turning into an animated cartoon figure). What's more, he helps the Navy spot Nazi submarines during WW2. Innocuous family fare goes on too long. ▼●▶

Incredible Petrified World, The (1957) 78m. BOMB D: Jerry Warren. John Carradine, Robert Clarke, Allen Windsor, Phyllis Coates, Lloyd Nelson, George Skaff. Four people explore the ocean depths in Dr. Carradine's diving bell and are plunged into land of catacombed tunnels. Not uninteresting sci-fi entry, but ultimately defeated by poor acting, leaden pacing. ▼▶

Incredible Shrinking Man, The (1957) 81m. ***½ D: Jack Arnold. Grant Williams, Randy Stuart, April Kent, Paul Langton, William Schallert, Billy Curtis. Accident results in Williams shrinking ever smaller; trapped in his own basement, he has memorable encounters with a cat and (even smaller) a spider. Intelligent, serious approach, exceptional effects for the period, and a vigorous leading performance result in a genuine sci-fi classic, unsurpassed by later attempts. No dialogue in the last third, just Williams' occasional narration. Director Arnold's best movie. Screenplay by Richard Matheson, from his own novel. ▼●▶

Incredibly Strange Creatures Who Stopped Living and Became Mixed-Up Zombies!!?, The (1963) C-82m. **½ D: Ray Dennis Steckler. Cash Flagg (Ray Dennis Steckler), Brett O'Hara, Atlas King, Sharon Walsh, Madison Clarke, Son Hooker. Legendary (thanks to that title) low-budget horror film about hideous goings-on at a carny sideshow, with lots of rock numbers thrown in. Truly bizarre film features gorgeously saturated color, awful acting, hideous dialogue, haunting atmosphere and little plot. Cinematography by Joe Micelli (author of *American Cinematographers' Manual*) with very young Laszlo Kovacs and Vilmos Zsigmond helping. Aka THE TEENAGE PSYCHO MEETS BLOODY MARY. ▼▶

Indestructible Man (1956) 70m. ** D: Jack Pollexfen. Lon Chaney, Jr., Casey Adams (Max Showalter), Marion Carr, Ross Elliott, Stuart Randall, Robert Shayne, Joe Flynn. Scientist is able to return from the dead a just-executed criminal, "Butcher Benton" (Chaney), who goes on to seek revenge against his shyster lawyer and others. Not-bad sci-fi/horror entry will entertain fans of the genre. ▼▶

Indianapolis Speedway (1939) 82m. ** D: Lloyd Bacon. Pat O'Brien, Ann Sheridan, John Payne, Gale Page, Frank McHugh,

John Ridgely, Regis Toomey. Routine but watchable remake of Howard Hawks' THE CROWD ROARS, about the rivalry between brothers O'Brien and Payne on the racetrack. James Cagney's patented cockiness, the best thing about the original, is what's missing here.

Indian Fighter, The (1955) C-88m. *** D: Andre de Toth. Kirk Douglas, Walter Matthau, Elsa Martinelli, Walter Abel, Lon Chaney. Exciting account of Douglas leading wagon train through rampaging Indian country. CinemaScope. ▼▶

Indian Love Call SEE: **Rose Marie** (1936)

Indian Paint (1964) C-91m. ** D: Norman Foster. Johnny Crawford, Jay Silverheels, Pat Hogan, Robert Crawford, Jr., George J. Lewis. Fifteen-year-old Arikara (Crawford), his foal, and his coming-to-manhood. Harmless, forgettable. ▼▶

Indian Scout SEE: **Davy Crockett Indian Scout**

Indian Territory (1950) 70m. ** D: John English. Gene Autry, Pat Buttram, Gail Davis, Kirby Grant, James Griffith, Phil Van Zandt, Pat Collins, Roy Gordon. Government agent Autry is working undercover for the Chief of Indian Affairs to stop Indian uprisings perpetrated by renegade white gunrunners Van Zandt and Griffith. OK Western with good action but a shaky script. ▶

Indian Tomb, The (1921-German) 212m. **½ D: Joe May. Conrad Veidt, Paul Richter, Olaf Fonss, Mia May, Bernard Goetzke, Lya de Putti, Erna Morena. Sumptuous claptrap, set in the India of the British Empire, about illicit lovers fleeing the grasp of her understandably vengeful husband, the maharajah of Bengal. Two-part epic silent ("The Mission of the Yogi" and "The Tiger of Eschnapur") is just as corny as can be, but it sure looks pretty and is guaranteed to have no subtext whatsoever. Mia May is the director's wife. From Thea von Harbou's 1917 novella, adapted by her husband, Fritz Lang, who helmed the 1959 color remake (known as JOURNEY TO THE LOST CITY in its truncated U.S. edition). ▼▶

Indian Tomb, The (1959-German) C-97m. **½ D: Fritz Lang. Debra Paget, Paul Hubschmid, Walther Reyer, Claus Holm, Sabine Bethmann, René Deltgen. The pace picks up a bit in this second of Lang's Indian diptych, chronicling the events leading up to lovers Paget and Hubschmid's escape from the clutches of maharajah Reyer. Paget's exotic dance is a highlight. This and Part One (THE TIGER OF ESCHNAPUR) were originally dubbed, edited down to 95m., and released in the U.S. as JOURNEY TO THE LOST CITY. ▶

Indian Uprising (1952) C-75m. ** D: Ray Nazarro. George Montgomery, Audrey Long, Carl Benton Reid, Eugene Iglesias, John Baer, Joe Sawyer, Douglas Kennedy,

Robert Shayne. Captain Montgomery of the U.S. Army tries to maintain the fragile peace between white settlers and Chief Geronimo in Arizona in the late 1800s. Routine Western programmer. ▼

Indiscreet (1931) **81m.** *½ D: Leo McCarey. Gloria Swanson, Ben Lyon, Barbara Kent, Arthur Lake, Monroe Owsley. Tiresome romantic comedy-drama with Swanson trying to keep her scarlet past from Lyon. Art deco sets, and Gloria's rendition of two DeSylva-Brown-Henderson songs, aren't compensation enough for sitting through this one. Original running time 92m. ▼▶

Indiscreet (1958) **C-100m.** *** D: Stanley Donen. Cary Grant, Ingrid Bergman, Cecil Parker, Phyllis Calvert, David Kossoff, Megs Jenkins. Bergman is renowned actress whom American playboy Grant romances and can't forget. Delightful comedy from Norman Krasna play *Kind Sir.* Made in England. Remade as a 1988 TVM with Robert Wagner and Lesley-Anne Down. ▼▶

Indiscretion of an American Wife (1953-U.S.-Italian) **63m.** **½ D: Vittorio De Sica. Jennifer Jones, Montgomery Clift, Gino Cervi, Richard Beymer. Turgid melodrama set in Rome's railway station, with Jones the adulterous wife meeting lover Clift for one more clinch. De Sica's original 87m. version, titled TERMINAL STATION, was restored in 1983. Remade in 1998 for TV. ▼▶

Infamous Crimes SEE: **Philo Vance Returns**

In Fast Company (1946) **61m.** *½ D: Del Lord. Leo Gorcey, Huntz Hall, Bobby Jordan, Billy Benedict, Jane Randolph, Judy Clark, David Gorcey, Douglas Fowley. The Bowery Boys get mixed up in a full-scale taxicab war in this substandard entry. ▶

Inferno (1953) **C-107m.** **½ D: Roy (Ward) Baker. Robert Ryan, Rhonda Fleming, William Lundigan, Henry Hull, Carl Betz, Larry Keating. Fleming plots rich husband Ryan's demise, with surprising results. Good desert sequences. Originally in 3-D. Remade as a TV movie, ORDEAL. ▶

Informer, The (1929-British) **82m.** **½ D: Arthur Robison. Lya de Putti, Lars Hanson, Warwick Ward, Carl Harbord, Dennis Wyndham. Intriguing curio, part-silent and part-talkie, about Gypo Nolan (Hanson), Irish Republican Army member who, in a fit of jealousy, betrays his best friend to the police. Pales beside the more famous 1935 version of the Liam O'Flaherty novel, but not without its own merits. Silent sequences are far more effective than the talking ones. ▼▶

Informer, The (1935) **91m.** ***½ D: John Ford. Victor McLaglen, Heather Angel, Preston Foster, Margot Grahame, Wallace Ford, Una O'Connor, J. M. Kerrigan, Joseph Sauers (Sawyer), Donald Meek. Dated but still potent study of human nature tells of hard-drinking McLaglen, who informs on buddy to collect reward during Irish Rebellion of 1922. Powerful drama, based on Liam O'Flaherty's novel, with a memorable Max Steiner score. McLaglen's performance won the Oscar, as did Ford, Steiner, and Dudley Nichols (for Best Screenplay). Filmed before in England in 1929. Remade as UP TIGHT. ▼▶

Informers, The (1965-British) SEE: **Underworld Informers**

In Harm's Way (1965) **165m.** **½ D: Otto Preminger. John Wayne, Kirk Douglas, Patricia Neal, Tom Tryon, Paula Prentiss, Henry Fonda, Brandon de Wilde, Jill Haworth, Dana Andrews, Stanley Holloway, Burgess Meredith, Franchot Tone, Patrick O'Neal, Carroll O'Connor, Slim Pickens, Barbara Bouchet, Hugh O'Brian, George Kennedy, Bruce Cabot, Larry Hagman. Overlong, melodramatic account of warfare in the South Pacific at the outset of WW2, focusing on the exploits of larger-than-life naval officer Wayne (whose character is nicknamed "Rock"). Most interesting for its cast of old-timers and up-and-coming stars. Panavision. ▼▶

Inheritance, The (1947-British) **98m.** *** D: Charles Frank. Jean Simmons, Derrick De Marney, Derek Bond, Katina Paxinou, Esmond Knight. Well-appointed chiller, with Simmons as innocent preyed upon by corrupt uncle; situated in Victorian London and Paris. Based on a novel by Sheridan Le Fanu. Original British title: UNCLE SILAS. ▼▶

Inherit the Wind (1960) **127m.** ***½ D: Stanley Kramer. Spencer Tracy, Fredric March, Gene Kelly, Florence Eldridge, Dick York, Harry Morgan, Donna Anderson, Elliott Reid, Claude Akins, Noah Beery, Jr., Norman Fell. Vocals by Leslie Uggams. Absorbing adaptation of Jerome Lawrence–Robert E. Lee play based on notorious Scopes Monkey Trial of 1925, when Clarence Darrow defended and William Jennings Bryan prosecuted a schoolteacher arrested for teaching Darwin's Theory of Evolution. Names are changed (Kelly's character is based on acid-tongued H. L. Mencken), but the issue is real and still relevant. An acting tour de force, with solid support from Morgan as the judge, Reid as a lawyer, Eldridge as March's devoted wife. Only offbeat casting of Kelly doesn't quite come off. Screenplay by Nathan E. Douglas (Nedrick Young) and Harold Jacob Smith. Remade as 1988 TVM with Kirk Douglas and Jason Robards. Also remade as a TVM in 1999 with Jack Lemmon and George C. Scott. ▼▶

In Love and War (1958) **C-111m.** **½ D: Philip Dunne. Robert Wagner, Dana Wynter, Jeffrey Hunter, Hope Lange, Bradford Dillman, Sheree North, France Nuyen, Mort Sahl. Moderately involving WW2 drama spotlighting three soldiers—troubled Wagner, wealthy Dillman, working-class Hunter—and the women in their lives. Handsome cast uplifts so-so soaper. CinemaScope. ▶

In Name Only (1939) **94m.** ******* D: John Cromwell. Carole Lombard, Cary Grant, Kay Francis, Charles Coburn, Helen Vinson, Peggy Ann Garner. Solid soaper with wealthy, married Grant falling for widowed Lombard, trying desperately to obtain a divorce from bitchy, manipulative social climber Francis. Beautifully acted. ▼●)

Inner Sanctum (1948) **62m.** ****** D: Lew Landers. Charles Russell, Mary Beth Hughes, Lee Patrick, Nana Bryant, Billy House, Roscoe Ates. Not-bad little film noir. A man kills his wife in the dark of night at a train station. A boy witnesses the crime, finds his life in jeopardy. "Inspired by" the radio series of the same name. ▼)

Innocent Affair, An (1948) **90m.** ****** D: Lloyd Bacon. Fred MacMurray, Madeleine Carroll, Charles "Buddy" Rogers, Rita Johnson, Alan Mowbray, Louise Allbritton, Anne Nagel. Outmoded marital sex comedy with adman MacMurray scurrying to woo a client, while wife Carroll thinks he's having an affair. This was the fifth and final pairing of MacMurray and Carroll. Retitled DON'T TRUST YOUR HUSBAND and UNDER SUSPICION.)

Innocent and the Damned SEE: **Girls Town**

Innocent Man, An SEE: **Sagebrush Trail**

Innocents, The (1961-British) **100m.** *****½** D: Jack Clayton. Deborah Kerr, Michael Redgrave, Peter Wyngarde, Megs Jenkins, Pamela Franklin, Martin Stephens. First-rate thriller based on Henry James' "The Turn of the Screw," with Kerr as governess haunted by specters that may or may not be real. Script by William Archibald and Truman Capote, brilliantly realized on film. Photographed by Freddie Francis. Remade in 1992 as THE TURN OF THE SCREW. CinemaScope. ▼●)

Innocents in Paris (1953-British) **93m.** ******* D: Gordon Parry. Alastair Sim, Ronald Shiner, Claire Bloom, Margaret Rutherford, Claude Dauphin, Laurence Harvey, Jimmy Edwards, Richard Wattis, Louis de Funès, Christopher Lee. Engaging comedy about seven diverse types crossing the Channel to France, each having wacky adventures. Original British running time 102m.

Innocents of Paris (1929) **78m.** ****½** D: Richard Wallace. Maurice Chevalier, Sylvia Beecher, Russell Simpson, George Fawcett, John Miljan, Margaret Livingston, David Durand, Jack Luden, Johnnie Morris. An antiques vendor fosters a boy whose mother drowned herself in the Seine and becomes involved with his aunt (Beecher, in her only talkie). Already a major figure in French cinema for 20 years, Chevalier literally introduces himself to an American audience in his first talkie. Sentimental star showcase features one of his trademark songs, Leo Robin and Richard Whiting's "Louise." From the play *Flea Market* by Charles E.

Andrews; originally produced in both silent and sound editions.

Inn of the Sixth Happiness, The (1958) **C-158m.** ******* D: Mark Robson. Ingrid Bergman, Curt Jurgens, Robert Donat, Ronald Squire, Athene Seyler, Richard Wattis. True story of English servant (Bergman) who, despite her lack of credentials, realizes her dream of becoming a missionary in China. Bergman is wonderful and Donat memorable in final screen performance. Simple, effective score by Malcolm Arnold. CinemaScope. ▼●)

In Old Amarillo (1951) **67m.** ****½** D: William Witney. Roy Rogers, Estelita Rodriguez, Penny Edwards, Pinky Lee, Roy Barcroft, Pierre Watkin, Kenneth Howell, Elisabeth Risdon, William Holmes, The Roy Rogers Riders. Edwards and her grandmother are brought to the brink of ruin by drought; rancher Watkin tries to help, but unscrupulous Barcroft schemes against their plans at every turn. Solid Western yarn marred only by the series debut of a badly miscast Lee as Roy's newest sidekick.)

In Old Arizona (1929) **97m.** ****** D: Raoul Walsh, Irving Cummings. Warner Baxter, Edmund Lowe, Dorothy Burgess, J. Farrell MacDonald, Fred Warren, Henry Armetta. Novelty of first major sound Western and first talkie to take microphones outdoors has long since worn off, leaving only stilted performances led by Baxter's dubious Oscar winner as the Cisco Kid. Burgess tops him for broken-English dialect honors as Mexican vamp who betrays him to Army sergeant Lowe. Earthy scenes alternate with acres of talk during which the camera is bolted to the floor. Walsh began filming as both star and solo director before an accident in which he was blinded in one eye.)

In Old Caliente (1939) **57m.** ******* D: Joseph Kane. Roy Rogers, Mary Hart (Lynne Roberts), George "Gabby" Hayes, Jack La Rue, Katherine DeMille, Frank Puglia, Harry Woods. Gringo Rogers makes peace between settlers and Old California Mexican landholders when renegades led by Woods steal precious gold. One of Roy's best early starring films blends story, romance, action, and music in just the right proportions. ▼)

In Old California (1942) **88m.** ****½** D: William McGann. John Wayne, Binnie Barnes, Albert Dekker, Helen Parrish, Patsy Kelly, Edgar Kennedy, Dick Purcell, Harry Shannon. Atypical Wayne Western with Duke cast as a Boston pharmacist who comes to California and tangles with shifty Dekker. Kennedy and Kelly add enjoyable comedy relief. Also shown in computer-colored version. ▼)

In Old Cheyenne (1941) **58m.** ****** D: Joseph Kane. Roy Rogers, George "Gabby" Hayes, Joan Woodbury, J. Farrell MacDonald, Sally Payne, George Rosener, William Haade, Hal Taliaferro, Iron Eyes Cody.

When Gabby is forced to become an outlaw by cattle baron Rosener, young Eastern news reporter Rogers travels West to get the real story. This one never quite comes together.▼❙

In Old Chicago (1938) **95m. ***½** D: Henry King. Tyrone Power, Alice Faye, Don Ameche, Alice Brady, Andy Devine, Brian Donlevy, Phyllis Brooks, Tom Brown, Berton Churchill, Sidney Blackmer, Gene Reynolds, Bobs Watson. Lavish period piece building up to Chicago fire of 1871; Oscar-winning Brady is Mrs. O'Leary, whose sons Power, Ameche, and Brown find their own adventures in the Windy City. Scripted by Lamar Trotti and Sonya Levien, based on a story by Niven Busch. Roadshow version on DVD runs 111m. with restored footage. ▼❙

In Old Colorado (1941) **67m. **½** D: Howard Bretherton. William Boyd, Russell Hayden, Andy Clyde, Margaret Hayes (Dana Dale), Morris Ankrum, Cliff Nazarro. Crooked foreman pits ranchers against one another over water rights in hopes of rustling their cattle. Story packs punch, borrowing many elements from the debut series film, HOP-ALONG CASSIDY, though stock footage and indoor sets betray cost cutting. Hayden, without credit, coauthored the screenplay. Russell Harlan's cinematography of Lone Pine's snowcapped skyline is superb. Attractive heroine Hayes was featured the next year in SULLIVAN'S TRAVELS.▼❙

In Old Kentucky (1935) **86m. **½** D: George Marshall. Will Rogers, Dorothy Wilson, Bill "Bojangles" Robinson, Russell Hardie, Louise Henry, Charles Sellon. Story is as old as the hills—a family feud—but Rogers' natural charm and Bojangles' fantastic footwork make it most enjoyable.❙

In Old Mexico (1938) **68m. **½** D: Edward Venturini. William Boyd, George Hayes, Russell Hayden, Paul Sutton, Betty Amann, Jane (Jan) Clayton, Allan Garcia. Escaping prison, notorious bandit "El Zorro" (The Fox), aided by his treacherous sister, seeks to even the score against captors Colonel Gonzales and Hopalong Cassidy. Much detective work by Hoppy to unravel the mystery confines too much of this film to rancho interiors. Based on Clarence E. Mulford's 1927 novel *Corson of the JC*. A sort-of sequel to BORDERLAND, later remade as UNDERCOVER MAN. Clayton was then Mrs. Russell Hayden.▼❙

In Old Monterey (1939) **73m. ***** D: Joseph Kane. Gene Autry, Smiley Burnette, June Storey, George "Gabby" Hayes, Jonathan Hale, Hoosier Hot Shots, Stuart Hamblen, Billy Lee. Republic upped the budget and running time for this Autry Western. Gene works for the Army and is assigned to purchase land for training. Unpatriotic types try to profit from the situation but are thwarted by Gene, Smiley, and Gabby (who was added for extra box-office clout).❙

In Old Oklahoma (1943) **102m. **½** D: Albert S. Rogell. John Wayne, Martha Scott, Albert Dekker, Gabby Hayes, Marjorie Rambeau, Sidney Blackmer, Dale Evans. Slugger Wayne brooks no nonsense in this oil-drilling yarn; good action, obligatory romance. Rhonda Fleming's film debut. Aka WAR OF THE WILDCATS. ▼❙

In Old Santa Fe (1934) **64m. ***** D: David Howard. Ken Maynard, Evalyn Knapp, H. B. Warner, Kenneth Thomson, Wheeler Oakman, George Hayes, Gene Autry, Lester (Smiley) Burnette. Maynard takes a shine to Knapp, whose father (Warner) owns a dude ranch. Slick Eastern gangster Thomson blackmails Warner but senses that Ken is a threat. Entertaining B Western marked the beginning of the end for Maynard—arguably the first singing cowboy, though his voice here is dubbed by Bob Nolan—and launched Autry's career with a musical interlude featuring him and his pal Burnette. Hayes also solidified his old-codger character here before joining Hopalong Cassidy.▼❙

In Our Time (1944) **110m. **½** D: Vincent Sherman. Ida Lupino, Paul Henreid, Nazimova, Nancy Coleman, Mary Boland, Victor Francen, Michael Chekhov. Lupino and Henreid try to save Poland from Nazi takeover in plush soaper that seeks to be meaningful propaganda; Nazimova is touching as Henreid's aristocratic mother. Never quite hits the mark.

In Person (1935) **85m. **½** D: William Seiter. Ginger Rogers, George Brent, Alan Mowbray, Grant Mitchell, Samuel S. Hinds, Joan Breslau. In between TOP HAT and FOLLOW THE FLEET, Rogers made this formula comedy about a movie star who's had a nervous breakdown; while recuperating, she spars romantically with Brent. Trivial, but pleasant.▼●

In Search of the Castaways (1962) C-100m. ****½** D: Robert Stevenson. Hayley Mills, Maurice Chevalier, George Sanders, Wilfrid Hyde-White, Michael Anderson, Jr., Keith Hamshire. Expedition tries to locate missing sea captain, in journey that encounters fire, flood, earthquake and other disasters. Disney adaptation of Jules Verne suffers from muddled continuity; good cast does its best.▼●❙

Inside Daisy Clover (1965) C-128m. ****½** D: Robert Mulligan. Natalie Wood, Robert Redford, Christopher Plummer, Roddy McDowall, Ruth Gordon, Katherine Bard. Potentially biting account of Wood's rise as Hollywood star in 1930s misfires; pat situations with caricatures instead of people. Gavin Lambert adapted his own novel. Panavision.▼●❙

Inside Detroit (1955) **82m. **** D: Fred F. Sears. Dennis O'Keefe, Pat O'Brien,

Margaret Field, Mark Damon. Ordinary exposé-style narrative of corruption in automobile industry.

Inside Job (1946) 65m. ** D: Jean Yarbrough. Preston Foster, Ann Rutherford, Alan Curtis, Jimmy Moss. Sensible minor film of struggling young marrieds tempted to enter life of crime to solve their financial problems.

Inside Story, The (1948) 87m. ** D: Allan Dwan. Marsha Hunt, William Lundigan, Charles Winninger, Gail Patrick. Warm, minor film set in Depression days in Vermont, involving sudden circulation of large amount of money.

Inside Straight (1951) 89m. **½ D: Gerald Mayer. David Brian, Arlene Dahl, Barry Sullivan, Mercedes McCambridge, Lon Chaney, Jr., Claude Jarman, Jr. Study of greed and corruption as ambitious man rises to fortune in 1870s San Francisco only to find life empty.

Inside the Mafia (1959) 72m. **½ D: Edward L. Cahn. Cameron Mitchell, Elaine Edwards, Robert Strauss, Jim L. Brown, Ted de Corsia, Grant Richards. Gun-blasting account of the Black Hand organization, with cast having field-day.

Inside the Walls of Folsom Prison (1951) 87m. **½ D: Crane Wilbur. Steve Cochran, David Brian, Philip Carey, Ted de Corsia, Dick Wesson, Paul Picerni, William Campbell. Straightforward prison saga set in the 1920s was actually shot at Folsom, and is narrated by the prison itself! De Corsia plays a vicious warden. ❱

In Society (1944) 75m. ** D: Jean Yarbrough. Bud Abbott, Lou Costello, Marion Hutton, Arthur Treacher, Thomas Gomez, Thurston Hall, Kirby Grant. Minor A&C, with the boys as plumbers mistaken for members of society; hectic slapstick finale. Includes chase footage lifted from NEVER GIVE A SUCKER AN EVEN BREAK. ▼❱

Inspector, The SEE: **Lisa**

Inspector Calls, An (1954-British) 80m. *** D: Guy Hamilton. Alastair Sim, Arthur Young, Olga Lindo, Eileen Moore. J. B. Priestley play detailing British police detective Sim's investigation of girl's suicide. Via flashbacks he learns a family's responsibility for her fate. Clever plot finale.

Inspector General, The (1949) C-102m. *** D: Henry Koster. Danny Kaye, Walter Slezak, Barbara Bates, Elsa Lanchester, Gene Lockhart, Alan Hale, Walter Catlett. Kaye plays a buffoon who pretends to be a visiting bureaucrat in an Eastern European village. Entertaining musical adaptation of the Gogol story. ▼❱

Inspector Maigret (1958-French) 110m. **½ D: Jean Delannoy. Jean Gabin, Annie Girardot, Oliver Hussenot, Jeanne Boitel. Famed French detective must track down notorious woman-killer. Retitled: WOMAN-BAIT.

Inspiration (1931) 74m. **½ D: Clarence

Brown. Greta Garbo, Robert Montgomery, Lewis Stone, Marjorie Rambeau, Beryl Mercer. Lesser Garbo vehicle about beautiful Parisian woman whose past makes her decide to leave Montgomery, even though she still loves him. A modern version of Alphonse Daudet's *Sappho.* ▼●

Intent to Kill (1958-British) 89m. **½ D: Jack Cardiff. Richard Todd, Betsy Drake, Herbert Lom, Warren Stevens, Carlo Justini, Alexander Knox, Lisa Gastoni, Jackie Collins. OK thriller about South American president Lom, who's been shot, and who arrives in Montreal incognito for brain surgery—where assassins plot to do him in. Scripted by Jimmy Sangster. CinemaScope. ▼●❱

Interlude (1957) C-90m. **½ D: Douglas Sirk. June Allyson, Rossano Brazzi, Marianne Cook (Koch), Jane Wyatt, Françoise Rosay. Adequate tearjerker of Allyson falling in love with Continental composer Brazzi, whose wife refuses to accept the situation. Remake of WHEN TOMORROW COMES, and remade in 1968 under same title. CinemaScope.

Intermezzo (1936-Swedish) 92m. *** D: Gustaf Molander. Gosta Ekman, Inga Tidblad, Ingrid Bergman, Bullen Berglund, Britt Hagman. Young pianist Bergman and famous—but married—violinist Ekman fall in love. Ingrid is ravishing in her sixth Swedish film; its remake, three years later, was to be her Hollywood debut. Coscripted by Molander. ▼●❱

Intermezzo (1939) 70m. ***½ D: Gregory Ratoff. Leslie Howard, Ingrid Bergman, Edna Best, Cecil Kellaway, John Halliday. One of the best love stories ever filmed, as married Howard, renowned violinist, has an affair with musical protégée Bergman (in her first English-speaking film). Short and sweet, highlighted by Robert Henning–Heinz Provost love theme. Original title: INTERMEZZO, A LOVE STORY; Bergman played same role in Gustav Molander's Swedish version. Remade, after a fashion, as HONEYSUCKLE ROSE. ▼●❱

International Crime (1938) 61m. **½ D: Charles Lamont. Rod La Rocque, Astrid Allwyn, Thomas E. Jackson, Oscar O'Shea, Lou Hearn, William von Brincken. Lamont Cranston, host of a true-crime radio show (sometimes identifying himself as The Shadow), and eager would-be radio star Allwyn investigate a murder, but the plot, involving international criminals, is not the point. Breezy, entertaining quickie is graced with snappy dialogue and the presence of witty, urbane La Rocque, who at one point wryly admits, "the Shadow doesn't know." Far better than his first *Shadow* outing, THE SHADOW STRIKES. ▼❱

International House (1933) 70m. ***½ D: A. Edward Sutherland. W. C. Fields, Peggy Hopkins Joyce, Stuart Erwin, George Burns, Gracie Allen, Bela Lugosi, Franklin

Pangborn, Rudy Vallee, Sterling Holloway, Cab Calloway, Baby Rose Marie. Offbeat, delightful film with early television experiment bringing people from all over the world to large hotel in China. Spotlight alternates between Fields and Burns & Allen, all in rare form, with guest spots by various radio entertainers. Short and sweet, a must-see film. Calloway sings the memorable "Reefer Man."▼●◗

International Lady (1941) 102m. **½ D: Tim Whelan. Ilona Massey, George Brent, Basil Rathbone, Gene Lockhart, Martin Kosleck, Clayton Moore. Massey is a femme fatale spy, Brent the U.S. government agent involved in cracking espionage ring. Superficial but entertaining.▼

International Settlement (1938) 75m. ** D: Eugene Forde. George Sanders, Dolores Del Rio, June Lang, Dick Baldwin, Leon Ames, John Carradine, Harold Huber. Mediocre tale of Shanghai intrigue with Sanders masquerading as notorious smuggler, pursued by various crooks and sultry Del Rio.◗

International Squadron (1941) 87m. **½ D: Lothar Mendes. Ronald Reagan, James Stephenson, Olympe Bradna, William Lundigan, Joan Perry, Julie Bishop, Cliff Edwards. Air Force straightens out no-account Reagan and turns him into fighting ace. Standard war story, a remake of CEILING ZERO.

Internes Can't Take Money (1937) 77m. **½ D: Alfred Santell. Barbara Stanwyck, Joel McCrea, Lloyd Nolan, Stanley Ridges, Lee Bowman, Irving Bacon, Pierre Watkin, Charles Lane, Fay Holden. Fairly successful hybrid of medical drama and gangster tale, with a bit of mother-love sentiment thrown in for good measure. Young intern McCrea helps ex-con Stanwyck rescue her daughter from crooks in the first film to be adapted from the *Dr. Kildare* stories by Max Brand.▼◗

Interns, The (1962) 120m. *** D: David Swift. Michael Callan, Cliff Robertson, James MacArthur, Nick Adams, Suzy Parker, Haya Harareet, Stefanie Powers, Buddy Ebsen, Telly Savalas. Glossy, renovated DR. KILDARE soap opera, kept afloat by an interesting young cast. Followed by sequel THE NEW INTERNS.▼◗

Interpol SEE: **Pickup Alley**

Interrupted Journey (1949-British) 80m. **½ D: Daniel Birt. Richard Todd, Valerie Hobson, Christine Norden, Tom Walls, Ralph Truman. Eerie film about Todd, who runs off with another woman, finds himself caught in a living nightmare. OK thriller is hampered by a cornball finale.▼◗

Interrupted Melody (1955) C-106m. *** D: Curtis Bernhardt. Eleanor Parker, Glenn Ford, Roger Moore, Cecil Kellaway, Ann Codee, Stephen Bekassy. True biography of Marjorie Lawrence, Australian opera star, who made a comeback after being

crippled by polio. Eileen Farrell sings for Parker. William Ludwig and Sonya Levien won Oscars for their story and screenplay. CinemaScope.▼●◗

In the Cool of the Day (1963-British) C-89m. ** D: Robert Stevens. Peter Finch, Jane Fonda, Angela Lansbury, Arthur Hill, Constance Cummings, Alexander Knox, Nigel Davenport, Alec McCowen. Good cast flounders in turgid soaper, with Finch (who is married to bitchy Lansbury) mediating marital rift between Hill and his emotionally and physically fragile wife Fonda; soon Finch and Fonda fall in love. Location filming in Greece helps. Panavision.◗

In the French Style (1963) 105m. **½ D: Robert Parrish. Jean Seberg, Stanley Baker, Addison Powell, James Leo Herlihy, Philippe Forquet, Claudine Auger. Two short stories by Irwin Shaw are basis for this overlong account of American girl who discovers transient affairs are marring her life.◗

In the Good Old Summertime (1949) C-102m. *** D: Robert Z. Leonard. Judy Garland, Van Johnson, S. Z. "Cuddles" Sakall, Spring Byington, Clinton Sundberg, Buster Keaton. Musical remake of THE SHOP AROUND THE CORNER, with Garland and Johnson the pen pals who fall in love. Not up to most MGM Garland vehicles, but pleasant. Judy's daughter Liza Minnelli appears in the finale.▼●◗

In the Meantime, Darling (1944) 72m. ** D: Otto Preminger. Jeanne Crain, Frank Latimore, Eugene Pallette, Mary Nash, Cara Williams, Reed Hadley, Stanley Prager, Gale Robbins. Predictable period piece about wealthy child-bride Crain, who learns duty and humility when forced to rough it after marrying G.I. Latimore. That's young Blake Edwards jitterbugging with Jeanne.

In the Money (1958) 61m. ** D: William Beaudine. Huntz Hall, Stanley Clements, David Gorcey, Eddie LeRoy, Patricia Donahue, Paul Cavanagh, Leonard Penn. The final *Bowery Boys* outing, with Sach and the gang escorting a poodle on a cruise, and the ubiquitous thieves after diamonds concealed on the pooch.◗

In the Navy (1941) 85m. **½ D: Arthur Lubin. Bud Abbott, Lou Costello, Dick Powell, The Andrews Sisters, Claire Dodd, Dick Foran. Bud and Lou are somehow in the Navy; Lou has hallucinations and nearly wrecks the entire fleet. Powell and Andrews Sisters provide songs, and Costello shows Abbott how 7 × 13 = 28. ▼●◗

In the Wake of a Stranger (1959-British) 69m. ** D: David Eady. Tony Wright, Shirley Eaton, Danny Green, Harry H. Corbett, Willoughby Goddard, Barbara Archer, David Hemmings. Sailor implicated in murder tries to clear himself; just fair.

In the Wake of the Bounty (1933-Australian) **70m. **** D: Charles Chauvel. Mayne Lynton, Errol Flynn, Victor Gouriet, John Warwick, Patricia Penman. Lackluster hybrid of documentary on contemporary Pitcairn Island and staging of highlights from the *Mutiny on the Bounty* story. Of note as the screen debut of a pre-Hollywood Flynn, cast as Fletcher Christian. Given his performance, it's difficult to fathom that he would soon become a mega-movie star. A real curio. ▼▶

In This Our Life (1942) **97m. *** D: John Huston. Bette Davis, Olivia de Havilland, George Brent, Dennis Morgan, Charles Coburn, Frank Craven, Billie Burke, Hattie McDaniel, Lee Patrick, Ernest Anderson. Southern Gothic drama of neurotic family with husband-stealing Davis ruining sister de Havilland's life and eventually her own; Davis at histrionic height. Based on Ellen Glasgow novel. Walter Huston has cameo role as bartender. Also shown in computer-colored version. ▼●▶

Intimate Lighting (1965-Czech) **72m. *** D: Ivan Passer. Vera Kresadlova, Zdenek Brezusek, Karel Blazek, Jaroslava Stedra, Jan Vostrcil, Vlastmila Vlkova, Karel Uhlik. Unpretentious, day-in-the-life story of two old friends, professional musicians, reuniting after long absence at country home. Excellent performances. ▼

Intimate Stranger, The SEE: **Finger of Guilt**

Intolerance (1916) **178m. **** D: D. W. Griffith. Lillian Gish, Robert Harron, Mae Marsh, Constance Talmadge, Bessie Love, Seena Owen, Alfred Paget, Eugene Pallette, many others. Landmark American epic interweaves four stories of prejudice and inhumanity, from the Babylonian era to the modern day. Melodramatic, to be sure, but gains in momentum and power as it moves toward its stunning climax. That's Lillian Gish as the mother rocking the cradle; Constance Talmadge gives a most appealing and contemporary performance as the sprightly Mountain Girl. Shown in a variety of prints with variant running times—as long as 208m. ▼●▶

Into the Blue (1950-British) **83m. *½ D: Herbert Wilcox. Michael Wilding, Odile Versois, Jack Hulbert, Constance Cummings, Edward Rigby. Dreary comedy about stowaway Wilding and his adventures on a yacht. Retitled MAN IN THE DINGHY. ▼

Intrigue (1947) **90m. ** D: Edwin L. Marin. George Raft, June Havoc, Helena Carter, Tom Tully, Marvin Miller, Dan Seymour, Philip Ahn, Michael Ansara. Predictable Raft vehicle of ex-military man with mar on his record turning Shanghai crime ring over to cops to clear himself.

Intruder, The (1954-British) **84m. **½ D: Guy Hamilton. Jack Hawkins, Hugh Williams, Michael Medwin, Dennis Price, Dora Bryan. Hawkins is resolute army vet-

eran who digs into past to discover why one of his old military group went astray.

Intruder, The (1962) **80m. *** D: Roger Corman. William Shatner, Frank Maxwell, Beverly Lunsford, Robert Emhardt, Leo Gordon, Jeanne Cooper, Charles Beaumont, George Clayton Johnson, William F. Nolan. Racist Shatner drifts from one small Southern town to another inciting townspeople to riot against court-ordered school integration. Corman's only "message" film—and one of his few box-office flops—still packs a punch; low budget and location filming aid authenticity. Script by Charles Beaumont. Reissued as I HATE YOUR GUTS! and SHAME. ▼▶

Intruder in the Dust (1949) **87m. *** D: Clarence Brown. David Brian, Claude Jarman, Jr., Juano Hernandez, Porter Hall, Elizabeth Patterson. Black man (Hernandez, in a solid performance) is accused of murder in a Southern town, and a gathering mob wants to lynch him. First-rate adaptation of William Faulkner novel. Surprisingly strong for a mainstream Hollywood film of that period; good use of locations, superbly photographed by Robert Surtees. Biggest problem: Brian's character is always speechifying and moralizing. Screenplay by Ben Maddow. ▼▶

Invader, The SEE: **Old Spanish Custom, An**

Invaders, The SEE: **49th Parallel**

Invaders From Mars (1953) **C-78m. *** D: William Cameron Menzies. Helena Carter, Arthur Franz, Jimmy Hunt, Leif Erickson, Hillary Brooke, Bert Freed. Starkly stylish sci-fi told from little boy's point of view, as he alone witnesses arrival of aliens who capture and brainwash residents of average small town. Remade in 1986. Alternate British version runs 83m.—and changes the ending! ▼●▶

Invasion of the Animal People (1962) **73m. *½ D: Virgil Vogel, Jerry Warren. Robert Burton, Barbara Wilson, Sten Gester, Bengt Bomgren. John Carradine is narrator and American link for Swedish-made 1958 production about rampaging monster who escapes from spaceship and terrorizes Lapland. Low-grade nonsense. Original Swedish version, TERROR IN THE MIDNIGHT SUN, available on DVD. ▼▶

Invasion of the Body Snatchers (1956) **80m. ***½ D: Don Siegel. Kevin McCarthy, Dana Wynter, Larry Gates, King Donovan, Carolyn Jones, Virginia Christine. Classic, influential, and still very scary science-fiction (with McCarthy-era subtext) about small-town residents who are being replaced by duplicates hatched from alien "pods." Tense script by Daniel Mainwaring from Jack Finney's *The Body Snatchers*; Sam Peckinpah can be glimpsed as a meter reader. Appropriately frightening musical score by Carmen Dragon. Reissued in 1979 at 76m., minus unnecessary, studio-imposed prologue and epilogue with Whit Bissell and Richard Deacon. Remade in 1978 and 1994 (as BODY SNATCHERS) and in 2007 as THE INVASION. Also shown in computer-colored version. SuperScope.▼○◗

Invasion of the Saucer Men (1957) **69m.** *½ D: Edward L. Cahn. Steve Terrell, Gloria Castillo, Frank Gorshin, Raymond Hatton, Ed Nelson. Slow-paced, minor sci-fi comedy about bulbous-headed aliens trying to pin the death of one of them on a teenager. Cheap, but has some atmosphere and Paul Blaisdell's outlandish aliens. Remade as THE EYE CREATURES.▼

Invasion USA (1952) **74m.** *½ D: Alfred E. Green. Gerald Mohr, Peggie Castle, Dan O'Herlihy, Phyllis Coates, Robert Bice, Tom Kennedy, Noel Neill. Red Scare movie depicting full-fledged invasion of America by "The Enemy" —while Mohr romances Castle. Hopelessly cheap and ineffectual, using tons of stock footage showing actual air battles and bombings. Trivia note: Both women who played Lois Lane on TV's *Superman* series appear in the cast.▼◗

Invisible Agent (1942) **81m.** ** D: Edwin L. Marin. Ilona Massey, Jon Hall, Peter Lorre, Cedric Hardwicke, J. Edward Bromberg, John Litel. Hall plays agent fighting Nazis with invisibility. Fun for the kids; dialogue is witless.▼◗

Invisible Avenger (1958) **60m.** *½ D: James Wong Howe, John Sledge. Richard Derr, Jeanne Neher, Dan Mullin, Mark Daniels, Lee Edwards, Helen Westcott, Leo Bruno. Lamont Cranston, the invisible Shadow (Derr), comes to New Orleans to investigate the murder of a jazz musician friend. Episodes of unsold *Shadow* TV series grafted together; mildly interesting, but no feather in the cap of great cinematographer Howe. Derr is quite good. Also known as BOURBON STREET SHADOWS.▼◗

Invisible Boy, The (1957) **89m.** *** D: Herman Hoffman. Richard Eyer, Philip Abbott, Diane Brewster, Harold J. Stone, Robert H. Harris; voice of Marvin Miller. The movies' first supercomputer not only helps scientist Abbott's lonely son Eyer become invisible (briefly) but also makes him smarter, so he can reassemble FORBIDDEN PLANET's Robby the Robot. However, the computer wants to use Robby to control the world. Robot-loving kids will take this straight, but it's an amusing, intelligent, low-key spoof of itself.▼○◗

Invisible Creature, The (1959-British) **70m.** ** D: Montgomery Tully. Sandra Dorne, Patricia Dainton, Tony Wright. Oddball little film of ghost interfering with homicide plot in eerie English mansion. Retitled: THE HOUSE IN MARSH ROAD.▼

Invisible Ghost (1941) **64m.** ** D: Joseph H. Lewis. Bela Lugosi, John McGuire, Polly Ann Young, Clarence Muse, George Pembroke, Betty Compson, Ernie Adams. Whenever Lugosi catches sight of his insane wife, who he thinks is dead, he goes into a trance and commits another unsolvable murder. Better written and directed than most of Bela's 1940s cheapies, but still a far cry from DRACULA.▼◗

Invisible Invaders (1959) **67m.** *½ D: Edward L. Cahn. John Agar, Jean Byron, Robert Hutton, Philip Tonge, John Carradine, Hal Torey. Invisible aliens from the moon possess corpses and attack the living; holed up in a cave, scientists race against time to stop them. Cheap, silly, and boring.▼○◗

Invisible Man, The (1933) **71m.** ***½ D: James Whale. Claude Rains, Gloria Stuart, Una O'Connor, William Harrigan, E. E. Clive, Dudley Digges, Dwight Frye. H. G. Wells' fantasy brilliantly materializes on screen in tale of mad scientist who makes himself invisible, wreaking havoc on British country village. Rains' starring debut is dated but still enjoyable. Look fast for John Carradine phoning in a "sighting"; that's Walter Brennan whose bicycle is stolen. ▼○◗

Invisible Man Returns, The (1940) **81m.** *** D: Joe May. Cedric Hardwicke, Vincent Price, John Sutton, Nan Grey, Cecil Kellaway, Alan Napier. Fine follow-up, with Price going invisible to clear himself of murder charge. Considered by many to be Price's first horror film.▼◗

Invisible Man's Revenge, The (1944) **77m.** ** D: Ford Beebe. Jon Hall, Alan Curtis, Evelyn Ankers, Leon Errol, John Carradine, Gale Sondergaard, Ian Wolfe, Billy Bevan. Hall allows unsuspecting scientist Carradine to make him invisible so he can seek vengeance on former business partners. Mixed-up script, unfunny comic relief (Errol), and slightly below par special effects add up to weakest INVISIBLE MAN sequel.▼○◗

Invisible Menace, The (1938) **55m.** ** D: John Farrow. Boris Karloff, Marie Wilson, Regis Toomey, Henry Kolker, Eddie Craven, Eddie Acuff, Charles Trowbridge. Not a horror/fantasy film, as the title implies, but a Grade-B whodunit set at a military installation, with Karloff as the woebegone prime suspect. Wilson and Craven supply incongruous comedy relief, while the FBI is rather poorly represented by Cy Kendall. Remade as MURDER ON THE WATERFRONT.◗

Invisible Ray, The (1936) **81m.** **½ D: Lambert Hillyer. Boris Karloff, Bela Lugosi, Frances Drake, Frank Lawton, Walter Kingsford, Beulah Bondi. Scientist Karloff contracts radiation poisoning that gives him touch of death (and makes him glow in the dark). Interesting yarn, but a notch below other Karloff-Lugosi vehicles.▼○◗

Invisible Stripes (1939) **82m.** ******* D: Lloyd Bacon. George Raft, Jane Bryan, William Holden, Flora Robson, Humphrey Bogart, Paul Kelly, Moroni Olsen, Tully Marshall. Earnest account of parolee Raft trying to go straight, protecting brother Holden from gangster Bogart; subdued acting is effective.▶

Invisible Woman, The (1941) **72m.** ******* D: A. Edward Sutherland. John Barrymore, Virginia Bruce, John Howard, Charlie Ruggles, Oscar Homolka, Margaret Hamilton, Donald MacBride, Edward Brophy, Shemp Howard, Charles Lane, Thurston Hall. Great cast in likable comedy about screwy professor Barrymore turning model Bruce invisible, arousing the curiosity of playboy sponsor Howard, as well as the more monetary interests of gangster Homolka. Slick and sprightly, with Ruggles terrific as Howard's long-suffering butler; Maria Montez has a bit as one of Bruce's fellow models.▼▶

Invitation (1952) **84m.** ****½** D: Gottfried Reinhardt. Van Johnson, Dorothy McGuire, Louis Calhern, Ray Collins, Ruth Roman. Society tearjerker decked out in MGM gloss about invalid McGuire; her father (Calhern) tries to buy Johnson to romance dying daughter. Memorable theme by Bronislau Kaper (which was originally used in A LIFE OF HER OWN).▶

Invitation to a Gunfighter (1964) **C-92m.** ****½** D: Richard Wilson. Yul Brynner, George Segal, Janice Rule, Pat Hingle, Brad Dexter. Cast surpasses turgid, talky script about town that hires gunslinger to kill an outcast, with surprising results.▼▶

Invitation to Happiness (1939) **95m.** ****½** D: Wesley Ruggles. Irene Dunne, Fred MacMurray, Charles Ruggles, William Collier, Sr., Eddie Hogan. Ordinary story, well acted: society girl marries fighter, but marriage can't survive because of his driving ambition in boxing ring.

Invitation to the Dance (1956) **C-93m.** ****½** D: Gene Kelly. Gene Kelly, Igor Youskevitch, Claire Sombert, David Paltenghi, Daphne Dale, Claude Bessy, Tommy Rall, Carol Haney, Tamara Toumanova, Belita. Kelly's ambitious film tells three stories entirely in dance. Earnest but uninspired, until final "Sinbad" segment with Kelly in Hanna-Barbera cartoon world. Music by Jacques Ibert, Andre Previn, and Rimsky-Korsakov. Filmed in 1952.▼▶

In Which We Serve (1942-British) **115m.** ******** D: Noel Coward, David Lean. Noel Coward, John Mills, Bernard Miles, Celia Johnson, Kay Walsh, Joyce Carey, Michael Wilding, James Donald, Richard Attenborough. Unlike many WW2 films, this masterpiece doesn't date one bit; superb film about men on a British fighting ship, told through flashback. Written, codirected, and scored by costar Coward (who was given a special Oscar "for his outstanding produc-

tion achievement"). Lean's first directing credit. Film debuts of Johnson, Attenborough, young Daniel Massey, and infant Juliet Mills.▼▶

I Passed for White (1960) **93m.** ****** D: Fred M. Wilcox. Sonya Wilde, James Franciscus, Pat Michon, Elizabeth Council, Griffin Crafts, Isabelle Cooley. Exploitation film handled with slight dignity involving light-skinned black woman and her rich white boyfriend.

Ipcress File, The (1965-British) **C-108m.** *****½** D: Sidney J. Furie. Michael Caine, Nigel Green, Guy Doleman, Sue Lloyd, Gordon Jackson. First and best of Len Deighton's Harry Palmer series, with Caine as unemotional Cockney crook turned secret agent, involved in grueling mental torture caper. Eerie score by John Barry. Followed by two sequels—FUNERAL IN BERLIN and BILLION DOLLAR BRAIN —and a pair of cable TV follow-ups in 1997, BULLET TO BEIJING and MIDNIGHT IN ST. PETERSBURG. Techniscope.▼▶

I Promise to Pay (1937) **65m.** ****½** D: D. Ross Lederman. Chester Morris, Helen Mack, Leo Carrillo, Thomas Mitchell, John Gallaudet, Wallis Clark. Snappy little programmer about likable, scrupulously honest family man Morris who's taken in by loan sharks. Enjoyable (if not quite credible).

I Remember Mama (1948) **134m.** *****½** D: George Stevens. Irene Dunne, Barbara Bel Geddes, Oscar Homolka, Philip Dorn, Cedric Hardwicke, Edgar Bergen, Rudy Vallee, Barbara O'Neil, Florence Bates, Ellen Corby. Beautifully realized, exquisitely detailed filming of John Van Druten's play, based on Kathryn Forbes' memoirs about growing up with her Norwegian immigrant family in San Francisco. A bit long, but richly rewarding, with top performances in each and every role. Screenplay by DeWitt Bodeen. Followed by the TV series *Mama.* Also shown in computer-colored version.▼▶

Irene (1940) **104m.** ****½** D: Herbert Wilcox. Anna Neagle, Ray Milland, Roland Young, Alan Marshal, May Robson, Billie Burke, Marsha Hunt, Arthur Treacher, Tommy Kelly. Pleasant remake of venerable musical (done as a silent film with Colleen Moore) minus most of the songs. Wealthy playboy Milland romances working-girl Neagle; some offbeat touches make it pleasing. "Alice Blue Gown" sequence originally filmed in color.▼▶

Irish Eyes Are Smiling (1944) **C-90m.** ****½** D: Gregory Ratoff. Monty Woolley, June Haver, Dick Haymes, Anthony Quinn, Maxie Rosenbloom, Veda Ann Borg, Maeve McGrail. Colorful corn about Ernest R. Ball, composer of famous Irish songs, with pleasant cast and familiar tunes like "When Irish Eyes Are Smiling," "Mother Machree," and a lavish non-Ball number: "Bessie

With a Bustle" (by Mack Gordon and James V. Monaco). ▶

Irish in Us, The (1935) 84m. **✶✶** D: Lloyd Bacon. James Cagney, Pat O'Brien, Olivia de Havilland, Frank McHugh, Allen Jenkins. Pretty stale comedy about rivalry between policemen and prizefighters, with good cast to hold one's interest.

Irma la Douce (1963) C-142m. **✶✶½** D: Billy Wilder. Shirley MacLaine, Jack Lemmon, Lou Jacobi, Herschel Bernardi, Joan Shawlee, Hope Holiday, Bill Bixby. Wilder's straight comedy adaptation of Broadway musical is a Parisian fairy tale for adults. Gendarme Lemmon falls for prostitute MacLaine and will do anything to keep her for himself. Red Light District is vividly re-created, but reteaming of stars and director can't equal THE APARTMENT. André Previn won an Oscar for his scoring. Look fast for young James Caan in walk-on. Panavision.▼●▶

Iron Crown, The (1941-Italian) 99m. **✶✶✶** D: Alessandro Blasetti. Gino Cervi, Elisa Cegani, Massimo Girotti, Luisa Ferida, Osvaldo Valenti, Rina Morelli, Paolo Stoppa. Lavish medieval spectacle about a ruthless king who murders his own brother in pursuit of a magical iron crown. Stylish and sometimes campy "Fascist" pageantry blends elements from Robin Hood, Hercules, Tarzan, and Shakespeare. Not released in the U.S. until 1949.

Iron Curtain, The (1948) 87m. **✶✶✶** D: William Wellman. Dana Andrews, Gene Tierney, June Havoc, Berry Kroeger, Edna Best. Well-made, based-on-fact "anti-commie" saga of Igor Gouzenko (Andrews), who with wife Tierney attempts to defect to the West with top-secret documents. Filmed on location in Canada. Retitled: BEHIND THE IRON CURTAIN.

Iron Duke, The (1934-British) 88m. **✶✶✶** D: Victor Saville. George Arliss, Gladys Cooper, Ellaline Terriss, A. E. Matthews, Allan Aynesworth, Lesley Wareing, Emlyn Williams, Felix Aylmer, Norma Varden. Arliss is his usual sterling self as the Duke of Wellington, seemingly the only man who can make peace between England, its allies, and France in 1815. Entertaining history lesson gets better and better as it draws us into international and political intrigues. Cooper is outstanding as the Duchess of Angouleme (vengeful daughter of Marie Antoinette); young Williams is fun as a malicious newspaperman.▼

Iron Glove, The (1954) C-77m. **✶✶½** D: William Castle. Robert Stack, Ursula Thiess, Richard Stapley, Charles Irwin, Alan Hale, Jr. Typical swashbuckler about 18th-century England and Prince James, pretender to the throne.

Iron Horse, The (1924) 119m. **✶✶✶** D: John Ford. George O'Brien, Madge Bellamy, Cyril Chadwick, Fred Kohler, Gladys Hulette, J. Farrell MacDonald. Epic-scale silent film about building of transcontinental railroad, intertwined with predictable human-interest subplots involving surveyor O'Brien, sweetheart Bellamy, traitor Kohler, etc. May seem hackneyed today, but it's important to note that this movie *invented* what later became clichés. ▼▶

Iron Major, The (1943) 85m. **✶✶½** D: Ray Enright. Pat O'Brien, Ruth Warrick, Robert Ryan, Leon Ames, Russell Wade, Bruce Edwards, Barbara Hale. O'Brien goes through the paces as Frank Cavanaugh, famed football coach/WW1 hero, in this ultra-patriotic, by-the-numbers biography. Based on a story by Cavanaugh's wife Flo (played by Warrick).▼

Iron Man (1931) 73m. **✶✶** D: Tod Browning. Lew Ayres, Jean Harlow, Robert Armstrong, John Miljan, Eddie Dillon. Routine early talkie of prizefighter Ayres and gold-digging wife Harlow (who hadn't clicked yet in films). Manager-pal Armstrong is only one who sees through her. Remade in 1937 (as SOME BLONDES ARE DANGEROUS) and 1951.

Iron Man (1951) 82m. **✶✶½** D: Joseph Pevney. Jeff Chandler, Evelyn Keyes, Stephen McNally, Joyce Holden, Rock Hudson, Jim Backus, Jim Arness. Reworking of 1931 film focuses on Chandler as a poor, well-intentioned Pennsylvania coal miner who can't control his killer instinct once he steps into the boxing ring.

Iron Mask, The (1929) 87m. **✶✶✶** D: Allan Dwan. Douglas Fairbanks, Belle Bennett, Marguerite De La Motte, Dorothy Revier, Vera Lewis, William Bakewell, Nigel de Brulier, Ullrich Haupt. Entertaining Dumas tale (later filmed as THE MAN IN THE IRON MASK) told from point of view of D'Artagnan (Fairbanks), who becomes Louis XIV's protector from birth to later time when scheming Rochefort (Haupt) tries to pass off twin brother as heir to throne. Lavish silent swashbuckler originally had talkie sequences. Final scenes are especially poignant as this was Doug's farewell to the swashbuckling genre. Most current prints are of the 1940 reissue with narration by Douglas Fairbanks, Jr.▼●▶

Iron Mistress, The (1952) C-110m. **✶✶½** D: Gordon Douglas. Alan Ladd, Virginia Mayo, Joseph Calleia, Phyllis Kirk, Alf Kjellin, Douglas Dick, Tony (Anthony) Caruso, Ned (Nedrick) Young, George Voskovec. Ordinary Ladd vehicle is more soap opera than biopic; he's Jim Bowie, backwoodsman who comes to New Orleans and mixes with shrewish Mayo. Title doesn't refer to a woman, but rather the knife that Bowie designs. ▶

Iron Petticoat, The (1956-British-U.S.) C-83m. **✶✶½** D: Ralph Thomas. Bob Hope, Katharine Hepburn, James Robertson Justice, Robert Helpmann, David Kossoff.

Curious comedy made in England tries to update NINOTCHKA theme with Hepburn as humorless Russian and Hope as American military man who tries to win her over. Stars' surprising rapport is film's chief value; mediocre script and direction kill the rest. British version runs 95m. VistaVision. ▶

Iron Sheriff, The (1957) 73m. *½ D: Sidney Salkow. Sterling Hayden, Constance Ford, John Dehner, Kent Taylor, Darryl Hickman. Marshal Hayden sets out to prove son is not guilty of murder. ▶

Iroquois Trail, The (1950) 86m. ** D: Phil Karlson. George Montgomery, Brenda Marshall, Glenn Langan, Paul Cavanagh, Monte Blue, Sheldon Leonard, Reginald Denny, Dan O'Herlihy, John Doucette. Uninspired programmer about the French and Indian Wars, inspired by James Fenimore Cooper stories, with Montgomery as Hawkeye and Blue as his Indian blood brother Chief Sagamore.

I Saw What You Did (1965) 82m. *** D: William Castle. Sara Lane, Andi Garrett, John Ireland, Joan Crawford, Leif Erickson, Patricia Breslin. Tense, gimmick-free Castle shocker about two teenage girls who dial phone numbers at random and whisper film's title; one of their "victims" is Ireland—who's just murdered his wife! Look out! Remade for TV in 1988.▼▶

I See a Dark Stranger SEE: **Adventuress, The**

I Sell Anything (1934) 71m. **½ D: Robert Florey. Pat O'Brien, Ann Dvorak, Claire Dodd, Roscoe Karns, Hobart Cavanaugh, Russell Hopton, Robert Barrat. Snappy yarn with O'Brien perfectly cast as "Spot Cash" Cutler, a fast-talking—and highly unscrupulous—auctioneer whose life is affected by two women—one wealthy, one poor.

I Shot Jesse James (1949) 81m. ** D: Samuel Fuller. Preston Foster, Barbara Britton, John Ireland, Reed Hadley, J. Edward Bromberg. Flamboyant directorial touches (in Fuller's first film) cannot redeem essential dullness of story about Bob Ford (Ireland),the man who plugged Jesse (Hadley) in the back.▼▶

Island, The (1961-Japanese) 96m. *** D: Kaneto Shindo. Nobuko Otowa, Taiji Tonoyama, Shinji Tanaka, Masanori Horimoto. Engrossing documentary-style study of peasant family living on rocky island near Japan, struggling to survive. Visually stunning film contains not a single word of dialogue.▼

Island in the Sky (1938) 61m. **½ D: Herbert I. Leeds. Gloria Stuart, Michael Whalen, Paul Kelly, Robert Kellard, June Storey, Paul Hurst, Leon Ames, Willard Robertson, Regis Toomey. Honeymooner Stuart persuades her new husband (Whalen), who works for the District Attorney, to prove the innocence of a man accused of

murder. Good little B movie with plenty of plot twists. Title refers to a 70th-story nightclub decorated with palm trees. ▶

Island in the Sky (1953) 109m. ***½ D: William A. Wellman. John Wayne, Lloyd Nolan, Walter Abel, James Arness, Andy Devine, Allyn Joslyn, Jimmy Lydon, Harry Carey, Jr., Hal Baylor, Sean McClory, Wally Cassell, Regis Toomey, Louis Jean Heydt, Bob Steele, Darryl Hickman, Touch (Mike) Connors, Gordon Jones, Frank Fenton, Paul Fix, Carl ("Alfalfa") Switzer, Ann Doran. Transport plane goes down in snowy Labrador, and the crew's flying buddies devote all their energies to locating them. Meanwhile, pilot Wayne has to keep his crew's spirits up as they try to survive in frigid weather with little food and no heat. Moving drama with a striking score by Hugo Friedhofer and Emil Newman. Ernest K. Gann based his screenplay (and novel) on a real-life incident from WW2. Gann, Wellman, and Wayne reteamed a year later for THE HIGH AND THE MIGHTY. Look fast for Fess Parker. ▼▶

Island in the Sun (1957) C-119m. ** D: Robert Rossen. James Mason, Joan Fontaine, Dorothy Dandridge, Joan Collins, Michael Rennie, Diana Wynyard, John Williams, Stephen Boyd, Harry Belafonte. Misfire adaptation of Alec Waugh's book about idyllic West Indies island torn by racial struggle. Good cast can't do much with unconvincing script. CinemaScope.▼▶

Island of Desire (1952-British) C-103m. *½ D: Stuart Heisler. Linda Darnell, Tab Hunter, Donald Gray, John Laurie, Sheila Chong. Sun-drenched, romantic WW2 drama of nurse, Marine, and injured pilot all washed ashore on tropical desert island. Parched performances. British title: SATURDAY ISLAND.▼▶

Island of Doomed Men (1940) 67m. ** D: Charles Barton. Peter Lorre, Robert Wilcox, Rochelle Hudson, George E. Stone, Don Beddoe, Kenneth MacDonald. Sadistic Lorre turns parolees into slave labor for his island diamond mine. Stock characters, stale melodramatics. ▶

Island of Lost Men (1939) 63m. *½ D: Kurt Neumann. Anna May Wong, J. Carrol Naish, Eric Blore, Ernest Truex, Anthony Quinn, Broderick Crawford. In Malaysia, half-caste sadist Naish, who has a slave-labor jungle workforce (and a "What Is Home Without Mother" sign in his house!), is opposed by beautiful Wong. Remake of WHITE WOMAN, complete with stock footage; a few atmospheric scenes, but stilted.

Island of Lost Souls (1933) 70m. ***½ D: Erle C. Kenton. Charles Laughton, Bela Lugosi, Richard Arlen, Kathleen Burke, Stanley Fields, Leila Hyams. Strong adaptation of H. G. Wells' novel of a mad scientist isolated on a remote island, where he transforms jungle beasts into half-human abominations ("... are we not men?"). Laughton hams it up a bit, but despite more explicit horror films of late, this retains its frightening aura, particularly in the grisly finale. Remade as THE ISLAND OF DR. MOREAU in 1977 and 1996.▼●❭

Island of Lost Women (1959) **71m.** ** D: Frank W. Tuttle. Jeff Richards, Venetia Stevenson, John Smith, Diane Jergens, June Blair, Alan Napier. Richards and Smith crash-land their plane on the title isle, which is inhabited by a reclusive atomic scientist and his three comely daughters. Cornball dialogue and silly romantic pairings make this one a guilty pleasure. It's also educational: did you know that hiding behind a boulder a few steps from an atomic explosion will save you?❭

Island of Love (1963) **C-101m.** *½ D: Morton Da Costa. Robert Preston, Tony Randall, Giorgia Moll, Walter Matthau, Betty Bruce, Michael Constantine. Con artist Preston sets out to transform a Greek isle into a tourist trap while evading the clutches of vengeful gangster Matthau. Silly, unfunny comedy wastes the talents of all concerned. Panavision.❭

Island of the Blue Dolphins (1964) **C-93m.** *½ D: James B. Clark. Celia Kaye, George Kennedy, Ann Daniel, Carlos Romero, Larry Domasin. True story of Indian girl (Kaye) abandoned on small island, befriended only by wild dogs. Set in early 19th century. Well meaning but not very good. Based on the novel by Scott O'Dell.▼

Island Princess, The (1954-Italian) **C-98m.** ** D: Paolo Moffa. Marcello Mastroianni, Silvana Pampanini, Gustavo Rojo. Rather hackneyed yarn set in 1500s, with Mastroianni a Spanish captain falling in love with princess of the Canary Islands.

Island Rescue (1951-British) **87m.** ** D: Ralph Thomas. David Niven, Glynis Johns, George Coulouris, Barry Jones, Kenneth More, Noel Purcell, Bernard Lee, Jeremy Spenser, Anton Diffring. Lukewarm comedy involving rescue of cows from German-occupied island during WW2. Original British title: APPOINTMENT WITH VENUS.

Island Woman (1958) **72m.** *½ D: William Berke. Marie Windsor, Vincent Edwards, Marilee Earle, Leslie Scott, Maurine Duvalier, George Symonette. Sailboat captain Edwards falls for tourist Earle, while her aunt (Windsor) connives to win him for herself. Dull; spiced with calypso music.

Isle of Forgotten Sins (1943) **82m.** ** D: Edgar G. Ulmer. John Carradine, Gale Sondergaard, Sidney Toler, Frank Fenton, Rita Quigley, Veda Ann Borg, Rick Vallin, Betty Amann, Tala Birell. Standard programmer with deep sea divers Carradine and Fenton going up against conniving ship captain Toler over a gold treasure. As usual, Ulmer's direction is much better than the

material. Based on his short story; retitled MONSOON.▼❭

Isle of Fury (1936) **60m.** ** D: Frank McDonald. Humphrey Bogart, Margaret Lindsay, Donald Woods, Paul Graetz, Gordon Hart, E. E. Clive. Mild remake of Somerset Maugham novel *The Narrow Corner*, involving love triangle on South Sea island.

Isle of the Dead (1945) **72m.** *** D: Mark Robson. Boris Karloff, Ellen Drew, Marc Cramer, Katherine Emery, Helene Thimig, Jason Robards (Sr.). Eerie horror tale of assorted characters stranded on Greek island during quarantine—one of them possibly a vampire. Good Val Lewton production.▼●❭

Is My Face Red? (1932) **66m.** **½ D: William A. Seiter. Ricardo Cortez, Helen Twelvetrees, Jill Esmond, Robert Armstrong, Sidney Toler, ZaSu Pitts. Cortez does well as a wisecracking, Walter Winchell–like columnist. Some snappy dialogue, but film really goes nowhere—and main character is such a total heel that our sympathies aren't with him when script demands they should be. That's director Seiter as the ship's purser.❭

Isn't It Romantic? (1948) **87m.** ** D: Norman Z. McLeod. Veronica Lake, Mary Hatcher, Mona Freeman, Billy DeWolfe, Patric Knowles, Roland Culver, Pearl Bailey. No.

Isn't Life Wonderful (1924) **115m.** **½ D: D. W. Griffith. Carol Dempster, Neil Hamilton, Erville Alderson, Helen Lowell, Marcia Harris, Frank Puglia, Lupino Lane. Combination grim drama and tender love story about a family of Polish refugees in inflation-laden post-WW1 Germany. The spotlight is on Inge (Dempster) and her sweetheart Paul (Hamilton), a veteran who suffers from gas poisoning, and their attempt to build a life together. A perfect example of how the style and substance of Griffith had become dated by 1924. Nonetheless, a fascinating curio, with some stark and powerful sequences. Filmed on location in Germany.▼●

Istanbul (1957) **C-84m.** ** D: Joseph Pevney. Errol Flynn. Cornell Borchers, John Bentley, Torin Thatcher, Leif Erickson, Martin Benson, Nat "King" Cole, Werner Klemperer. Dull drama of flyer Flynn returning to Istanbul, discovering his lady love (whom he believed had perished in a fire) to be alive and an amnesiac. Sole bright spot: Cole singing "When I Fall in Love." Remake of SINGAPORE. CinemaScope.▼

I Stand Condemned (1935-British) **75m.** **½ D: Anthony Asquith. Harry Baur, Laurence Olivier, Penelope Dudley Ward, Robert Cochran, Morton Selten, Athene Seyler. Inconsequential story of jealous Russian framing young officer as a spy, to eliminate him from rivalry over woman. Worth seeing for young, dashing Olivier. British title: MOSCOW NIGHTS.▼

I Stole a Million (1939) 78m. **½ D: Frank Tuttle. George Raft, Claire Trevor, Dick Foran, Henry Armetta, Victor Jory, Joe Sawyer, John Hamilton, Stanley Ridges. Cabdriver Raft turns to crime when his life savings are stolen; he tries to go straight after marrying Trevor, but society just won't let him. Familiar stuff, smoothly done, with appealing performances and standout photography by Milton Krasner. Nathanael West wrote the screenplay. ▼

it (1927) 72m. **½ D: Clarence Badger. Clara Bow, Antonio Moreno, William Austin, Jacqueline Gadsdon (Jane Daly), Priscilla Bonner. Bow is dazzling in this otherwise ordinary tale of a spirited, gold-digging department-store salesgirl with designs on her handsome boss (Moreno). Based on Elinor Glyn's trendy story of the same title; Madame Glyn appears briefly as herself. Look for Gary Cooper in a walk-on as a reporter. ▼●◗

It Ain't Hay (1943) 80m. **½ D: Erle C. Kenton. Bud Abbott, Lou Costello, Patsy O'Connor, Grace McDonald, Leighton Noble, Cecil Kellaway, Eugene Pallette, Eddie Quillan. Pretty good A&C from Damon Runyon story, "Princess O'Hara," for racehorse Teabiscuit; good supporting cast helps. ◗

I Take This Woman (1940) 97m. ** D: W. S. Van Dyke II. Spencer Tracy, Hedy Lamarr, Verree Teasdale, Kent Taylor, Laraine Day, Mona Barrie, Louis Calhern, Marjorie Main, Frances Drake, Jack Carson. Disappointing soaper with dedicated doctor Tracy sacrificing all for Lamarr, who at first isn't grateful. Long in production, with innumerable behind-the-scenes changes, this was a notorious dud in 1940. ◗

Italiano Brava Gente (1965-Italian) 156m. *** D: Giuseppe De Santis. Arthur Kennedy, Peter Falk, Tatyana Samoilova, Rafaelle Pisu, Andrea Checchi. Expansive chronicle of Italian-Russian war front during WW2, focusing on a variety of strata of soldiers and civilians. Much edited since European opening. Retitled: ATTACK AND RETREAT.

Italian Straw Hat, The (1927-French) 105m. ***½ D: René Clair. Albert Préjean, Geymond Vital, Olga Tschechowa, Paul Ollivier, Alex Allin, Jim Gérald. Clair's masterful rendering of a 19th-century stage farce also serves as an homage to early moviemaking. The story involves a man whose horse eats a lady's expensive, imported chapeau, which he must replace while heading to his own wedding ceremony. The comedy grows with each new complication. Beware of shorter prints. ▼◗

It All Came True (1940) 97m. **½ D: Lewis Seiler. Ann Sheridan, Humphrey Bogart, Jeffrey Lynn, ZaSu Pitts, Jessie Busley, Una O'Connor, Grant Mitchell, Felix Bressart. Offbeat story combines comedy, drama, music, and sentiment as gangster Bogart hides out in quaint boarding-house. Fine

showcase for Sheridan, who sings "Angel in Disguise" and "The Gaucho Serenade." ◗

It Always Rains on Sunday (1947-British) 92m. ***½ D: Robert Hamer. Googie Withers, Jack Warner, John McCallum, Edward Chapman, Jimmy Hanley, John Carol, John Slater, Susan Shaw, Sydney Tafler, Alfie Bass, Betty Ann Davies, Jane Hylton, Hermione Baddeley. Excellent mosaic of characters whose lives intertwine in a drab London neighborhood. McCallum is escaped convict seeking refuge with his ex-lover, Withers. (In real life, the two stars married the following year.) Arthur La Bern's novel was scripted by Henry Cornelius, Angus MacPhail, and Hamer.

It Came From Beneath the Sea (1955) 80m. *** D: Robert Gordon. Kenneth Tobey, Faith Domergue, Donald Curtis, Ian Keith, Harry Lauter. Breathtaking special effects highlight this sci-fi thriller. Huge octopus emerges from Pacific Ocean and wreaks havoc on San Francisco. First film made by the team of Ray Harryhausen and producer Charles H. Schneer. Also available in computer-colored version. ▼●◗

It Came From Outer Space (1953) 81m. *** D: Jack Arnold. Richard Carlson, Barbara Rush, Charles Drake, Russell Johnson, Joe Sawyer, Kathleen Hughes. Intriguing science-fiction based on a Ray Bradbury story. An alien ship crashes in the Arizona desert; its passengers assume the identities of nearby townspeople so they can effect repairs unnoticed—they think. Remarkably sober for its era, with crisp performances and real restraint, even in its use of 3-D. The 1996 TV movie IT CAME FROM OUTER SPACE II is a much inferior remake, rather than the sequel the title suggests. 3-D. ▼●◗

It Conquered the World (1956) 68m. **½ D: Roger Corman. Peter Graves, Beverly Garland, Lee Van Cleef, Sally Fraser, Jonathan Haze, Dick Miller. Low-budget sci-fi which intelligently attempts to create atmospheric excitement in yarn of carrot-shaped monster from Venus, Paul Blaisdell's finest creation. One of Corman's best early quickies, well acted and interesting but awkwardly plotted. Remade as ZONTAR, THE THING FROM VENUS. ▼

It Could Happen to You (1937) 65m. **½ D: Phil Rosen. Alan Baxter, Andrea Leeds, Owen Davis, Jr., Astrid Allwyn, Walter Kingsford, Al Shean, Jack Carson. Offbeat story of immigrant brothers; one aspires to become an educator, the other has recently graduated from law school. The lawyer must come to the defense of his sibling, who gets tangled in a web of blackmail and murder. Primarily interesting as one of the first films to deal with the impending threat of European fascism. Cowritten by Nathanael West from his own story. Jack Carson has a bit. ▼◗

It Grows on Trees (1952) 84m. ** D: Arthur Lubin. Irene Dunne, Dean Jagger, Joan Evans, Richard Crenna, Les Tremayne. Dunne's last feature is slim vehicle of daffy Connecticut housewife with $5 and $10 bills growing on her backyard trees.

It Had To Be You (1947) 98m. **½ D: Don Hartman, Rudolph Maté. Ginger Rogers, Cornel Wilde, Percy Waram, Spring Byington, Ron Randell. Rogers has severe indecision before every scheduled marriage, until dream lover Wilde appears. Airy, fanciful comedy.

It Had to Happen (1936) 79m. ** D: Roy Del Ruth. George Raft, Leo Carrillo, Rosalind Russell, Alan Dinehart, Arline Judge. Italian immigrant Raft working his way to political power in N.Y.C., trying to romance upper-class Russell.

I Thank a Fool (1962-British) C-100m. ** D: Robert Stevens. Susan Hayward, Peter Finch, Diane Cilento, Cyril Cusack, Kieron Moore, Athene Seyler. Dreary, farfetched story about Hayward spending a year and a half in prison for mercy-killing, then becoming involved with lawyer Finch, who prosecuted her case, with bizarre results. CinemaScope. ❱

It Happened at the World's Fair (1963) C-105m. *** D: Norman Taurog. Elvis Presley, Joan O'Brien, Gary Lockwood, Yvonne Craig. Entertaining Presley vehicle set at Seattle World's Fair, with Elvis and O'Brien brought together by little Ginny Tiu. Listenable tunes (including "One Broken Heart for Sale," "A World of Our Own" and "Happy Ending") help make this most enjoyable. Young Kurt Russell, who later played Elvis in a TV movie, makes his film debut in a small role. Panavision. ▼❱

It Happened in Athens (1962) C-92m. ** D: Andrew Marton. Jayne Mansfield, Trax Colton, Lili Valenty, Maria Xenia, Bob Mathias, Nico Minardos. Silly, juvenile charade made somewhat watchable by Mansfield in a variety of revealing costumes as an actress who agrees to marry the winner of the marathon at the 1896 Olympics. CinemaScope. ❱

It Happened in Brooklyn (1947) 105m. ** D: Richard Whorf. Frank Sinatra, Kathryn Grayson, Jimmy Durante, Peter Lawford, Gloria Grahame. Hokey musical with Brooklynite Sinatra returning to his beloved borough after WW2; complications follow as he falls for music teacher Grayson. Some good songs, including "Time After Time" and wonderful Sinatra-Durante duet, "The Song's Gotta Come From the Heart." ▼❱

It Happened in Hollywood (1937) 67m. *** D: Harry Lachman. Richard Dix, Fay Wray, Victor Kilian, Charles Arnt, Granville Bates, William B. Davidson, Franklin Pangborn, Billy Burrud. Funny and touching tale of a silent screen cowboy (Dix) whose career fades out with the advent of

talkies, while his leading lady and sweetheart (Wray) becomes a bigger star. But a young fan (Burrud) never loses faith in his screen hero. Fascinating Tinseltown fable features the stand-ins for such stars as Garbo, Dietrich, Chaplin, W. C. Fields, Mae West, and others in a party scene. Sam Fuller was one of the screenwriters. Aka ONCE A HERO.

It Happened One Night (1934) 105m. **** D: Frank Capra. Clark Gable, Claudette Colbert, Walter Connolly, Roscoe Karns, Alan Hale, Ward Bond. Legendary romantic comedy doesn't age a bit. Still as enchanting as ever, with reporter Gable and runaway heiress Colbert falling in love on rural bus trip. Hitch-hiking travails, the Walls of Jericho, other memorable scenes remain fresh and delightful. First film to win all five major Oscars: Picture, Actor, Actress, Director, and Screenplay (Robert Riskin). Based on Samuel Hopkins Adams' story "Night Bus," originally published in *Cosmopolitan.* Remade as musicals EVE KNEW HER APPLES and YOU CAN'T RUN AWAY FROM IT (1956). ▼❱

It Happened One Summer SEE: State Fair (1945)

It Happened on 5th Avenue (1947) 115m. ** D: Roy Del Ruth. Don DeFore, Ann Harding, Charlie Ruggles, Victor Moore, Gale Storm, Grant Mitchell. Overlong comedy about elegant N.Y.C. mansion taken over by thoughtful bum, who invites horde of friends and real owner in disguise to be his guests. ▼❱

It Happened to Jane (1959) C-98m. **½ D: Richard Quine. Doris Day, Jack Lemmon, Ernie Kovacs, Steve Forrest, Teddy Rooney, Russ Brown, Mary Wickes, Parker Fennelly. Breezy, likable comedy: Doris runs a Maine lobstery, and Jack is her lawyer; together they tangle with ultracheap villain Kovacs (who hams mercilessly). Aka TWINKLE AND SHINE. ❱

It Happened Tomorrow (1944) 84m. *** D: René Clair. Dick Powell, Linda Darnell, Jack Oakie, Edgar Kennedy, John Philliber, Edward Brophy, George Cleveland, Sig Ruman, Paul Guilfoyle. Diverting if somewhat static fantasy yarn about a turn-of-the-20th-century reporter who gets inside track on *tomorrow's* headlines, leading to unexpected complications. Low key, often charming. ▼❱

It Happens Every Spring (1949) 87m. ***½ D: Lloyd Bacon. Ray Milland, Jean Peters, Paul Douglas, Ed Begley, Ted de Corsia, Ray Collins, Jessie Royce Landis, Alan Hale, Jr., Debra Paget. Clever little comedy of chemistry professor (Milland) accidentally discovering a chemical mixture which causes baseballs to avoid all wooden surfaces, namely baseball bats. He takes leave from academia and embarks on meteoric pitching career. A most enjoyable, unpretentious picture. Story by Shirley W.

Smith and Valentine Davies; scripted by Davies.▼◗

It Happens Every Thursday (1953) **80m.** ******* D: Joseph Pevney. Loretta Young, John Forsythe, Frank McHugh, Edgar Buchanan, Jane Darwell, Dennis Weaver. Warm comedy about married couple who buy small-town newspaper and try every method conceivable to make it click. Young's final theatrical film.

I, The Jury (1953) **87m.** ****½** D: Harry Essex. Biff Elliot, Preston Foster, Peggie Castle, Margaret Sheridan, Alan Reed, Mary Anderson, Tom Powers, Joe Besser, Paul Dubov, Elisha Cook, Jr., John Qualen. Screen debut of Mickey Spillane's Mike Hammer (and Elliot as well) finds the thuggish sleuth spending his Christmas holidays hunting down the killer of a close pal. Naturally, more corpses ensue. Dark-humored fun, with a moody Franz Waxman score and stunning 3-D photography by John Alton, including some eye-popping shots inside L.A.'s famed Bradbury Building. Screenplay by Essex. Remade in 1982. 3-D.

It's a Big Country (1951) **89m.** ****½** D: Charles Vidor, Richard Thorpe, John Sturges, Don Hartman, Don Weis, Clarence Brown, William Wellman. Ethel Barrymore, Keefe Brasselle, Gary Cooper, Nancy Davis (Reagan), Gene Kelly, Keenan Wynn, Fredric March, Van Johnson, James Whitmore; narrated by Louis Calhern. Dore Schary's plug for America uses several pointless episodes about the variety of people and places in U.S. Other segments make up for it in very uneven film.◗

It's a Date (1940) **103m.** ****½** D: William A. Seiter. Deanna Durbin, Walter Pidgeon, Kay Francis, Eugene Pallette, Lewis Howard, S. Z. Sakall, Samuel S. Hinds, Cecilia Loftus. Durbin faces unique growing pains when she's offered a Broadway role intended for her mother (Francis) and then is courted by a man her mother's age (Pidgeon). Star trio shines brightly in this enjoyable contrivance, which unfortunately goes on too long and ends (incongruously) with Deanna singing "Ave Maria"! Remade as NANCY GOES TO RIO.▼

It's a Dog's Life (1955) **C-88m.** ****½** D: Herman Hoffman. Jeff Richards, Edmund Gwenn, Dean Jagger, Sally Fraser. Film uses gimmick of having the canine star tell his life story from slums to luxury. Retitled: BAR SINISTER. CinemaScope.▼◗

It's a Gift (1934) **68m.** ******** D: Norman Z. McLeod. W. C. Fields, Baby LeRoy, Kathleen Howard, Tommy Bupp, Morgan Wallace. Fields is a grocery store owner who goes West with his family. Beautiful comedy routines in one of the Great Man's unforgettable films. Charles Sellon as a blind man, T. Roy Barnes as a salesman looking for Carl LaFong, contribute some hilarious moments. A remake of Fields' silent film IT'S THE OLD ARMY GAME.▼◗

It's a Great Feeling (1949) **C-85m.** ****½** D: David Butler. Dennis Morgan. Doris Day, Jack Carson, Bill Goodwin. Gentle spoof of Hollywood with Carson's ego making filming difficult for himself and partner Morgan; guest appearances by many Warner Bros. players and directors, including Joan Crawford, Gary Cooper, Michael Curtiz, Jane Wyman, Sydney Greenstreet, Danny Kaye, Edward G. Robinson, King Vidor, Eleanor Parker, Patricia Neal, Raoul Walsh, Ronald Reagan—and even Reagan and Wyman's daughter Maureen!▼◗

It's a Great Life (1929) **89m.** ****½** D: Sam Wood. Rosetta Duncan, Vivian Duncan, Lawrence Gray, Jed Prouty, Benny Rubin. Sisters develop a successful stage act but split up when one of them gets married. Real-life headliners The Duncan Sisters failed to click as movie stars in their only talkie, but film is a surprisingly sprightly showcase for their singing and clowning and presents a vivid look at theatrical milieu. Some surviving scenes in two-strip Technicolor add pizzazz.◗

It's a Great Life (1943) **75m.** ****½** D: Frank Strayer. Penny Singleton, Arthur Lake, Larry Simms, Hugh Herbert, Jonathan Hale, Danny Mummert, Alan Dinehart, Irving Bacon, Marjorie Ann Mutchie. Dagwood is sent to buy a house and comes back with a horse, if you can believe it, eventually winding up in a fox hunt. Elementary *Blondie* farce raises a few laughs. Video title: BLONDIE AND DAGWOOD—IT'S A GREAT LIFE.▼

It's a Joke, Son (1947) **63m.** ****** D: Ben Stoloff. Kenny Delmar, Una Merkel, June Lockhart, Kenneth Farrell, Douglass Dumbrille. Folksy comedy featuring further exploits of Senator Claghorn (Delmar) from the Fred Allen radio show.▼◗

It's Always Fair Weather (1955) **C-102m.** ******* D: Gene Kelly, Stanley Donen. Gene Kelly, Dan Dailey, Michael Kidd, Cyd Charisse, Dolores Gray, David Burns. Three WW2 buddies meet ten years after their discharge and find they have nothing in common. Pungent Comden and Green script falls short of perfection but still has wonderful moments, and some first-rate musical numbers (like Cyd's "Baby, You Knock Me Out" and Dolores' "Thanks a Lot But No Thanks"). Best: the ash-can dance in widescreen. CinemaScope.▼◗

It's a Mad Mad Mad Mad World (1963) **C-154m.** ****½** D: Stanley Kramer. Spencer Tracy, Edie Adams, Milton Berle, Sid Caesar, Buddy Hackett, Ethel Merman, Mickey Rooney, Dick Shawn, Dorothy Provine, Phil Silvers, Jonathan Winters, Peter Falk, Jimmy Durante, Terry-Thomas, Eddie "Rochester" Anderson, William Demarest, many guest stars. Supercomedy cast in attempt at supercomedy, about group of people racing to find hidden bank loot under watchful eye of detective Tracy. Big, splashy, generally funny, but bigness doesn't equal greatness. Restored on video to 175m. Ultra Panavision 70. ▼●▶

It's a Pleasure! (1945) **C-90m.** ** D: William A. Seiter. Sonja Henie, Michael O'Shea, Bill Johnson, Marie McDonald, Gus Schilling, Iris Adrian. Skater Henie and hockey player O'Shea get married but can't seem to break the ice; pretty weak. ▼▶

It's a Small World (1950) **68m.** ** D: William Castle. Paul Dale, Lorraine Miller, Will Geer, Steve Brodie, Todd Karns. Truly strange B movie stars Dale (a deejay in real life) as a midget who suffers a succession of life's hard knocks until finally becoming "adjusted" and even finding romance in a circus. Director Castle (who appears in a cameo as a cop) makes it interesting but unnecessarily nasty for the little guy. ▶

It's a Wonderful Life (1946) **129m.** ★★★★ D: Frank Capra. James Stewart, Donna Reed, Lionel Barrymore, Thomas Mitchell, Henry Travers, Beulah Bondi, Frank Faylen, Ward Bond, Gloria Grahame, H.B. Warner, Frank Albertson, Todd Karns, Samuel S. Hinds, Mary Treen, Sheldon Leonard, Ellen Corby. Sentimental tale of Stewart, who works all his life to make good in small town, thinking he's failed and trying to end his life. Guardian angel Travers comes to show him his mistake. Only Capra and this cast could pull it off so well; this film seems to improve with age. Capra, Frances Goodrich, Albert Hackett, and Jo Swerling expanded Philip Van Doren Stern's short story "The Greatest Gift" (which had originally been written by Stern as a Christmas card!). Remade for TV as IT HAPPENED ONE CHRISTMAS. Also shown in computer-colored version. ▼●▶

It's a Wonderful World (1939) **86m.** ★★★ D: W. S. Van Dyke II. Claudette Colbert, James Stewart, Guy Kibbee, Nat Pendleton, Frances Drake, Edgar Kennedy, Ernest Truex, Sidney Blackmer, Hans Conried. Screwball comedy with Colbert a runaway poetess, Stewart a fugitive chased by cops Pendleton and Kennedy. Very, very funny, with Stewart having a field day. Scripted by Ben Hecht, from his and Herman J. Mankiewicz' story. We swear by our eyes! ▶

It's Hot in Paradise SEE: **Horrors of Spider Island**

It Should Happen to You (1954) **87m.** ★★★ D: George Cukor. Judy Holliday, Peter Lawford, Jack Lemmon, Michael O'Shea, Vaughn Taylor. Holliday is Gladys Glover of Binghamton, N.Y., who has come to N.Y.C. to make a name for herself—and does so, by plastering her moniker across a Columbus Circle billboard. Judy is radiant in this charming romantic comedy/satire, scripted by Garson Kanin. Lemmon's first film. ▼●▶

It Shouldn't Happen to a Dog (1946) **70m.** ★★½ D: Herbert I. Leeds. Carole Landis, Allyn Joslyn, Margo Woode, Henry (Harry) Morgan, Reed Hadley, John Alexander, Jean Wallace, John Ireland. Fluff about reporter Joslyn, who erroneously thinks policewoman Landis and a Doberman pinscher named Rodney robbed a bar. ▶

It's in the Air (1935) **80m.** ** D: Charles Riesner. Jack Benny, Una Merkel, Ted Healy, Nat Pendleton, Mary Carlisle, Grant Mitchell. Benny plays it mostly straight as a con artist who woos, weds, then loses Merkel. Dull comedy leads to a climax involving a hot-air balloon that's patently phony—and consequently not funny.

It's in the Bag! (1945) **87m.** ★★★ D: Richard Wallace. Fred Allen, Binnie Barnes, Robert Benchley, Sidney Toler, Jack Benny, Don Ameche, Victor Moore, Rudy Vallee, William Bendix. Story similar to THE TWELVE CHAIRS with flea-circus promoter Allen entitled to inheritance; plot soon goes out the window in favor of unrelated but amusing episodes, including hilarious encounter between Allen and Benny, and great movie-going sequence. ▼

It's Love Again (1936-British) **83m.** ★★★ D: Victor Saville. Robert Young, Jessie Matthews, Sonnie Hale, Ernest Milton, Robb Wilton, Sara Allgood. Lighter-than-air musical-comedy vehicle for Matthews following her success with Saville on EVERGREEN. Young is wise-guy publicity man who dreams up idea of creating an imaginary socialite, until Matthews steps out of the chorus line to fill the role. Funny, charming and imaginatively done, with several pleasant songs. ▼▶

It's Love I'm After (1937) **90m.** ★★★ D: Archie Mayo. Bette Davis, Leslie Howard, Olivia de Havilland, Patric Knowles, Eric Blore, Bonita Granville, Spring Byington, Veda Ann Borg. Delightful, witty comedy of ego-struck actor Howard and his fiancée/costar Davis, who explodes when he becomes involved with infatuated admirer de Havilland. Reminiscent in spirit of TWENTIETH CENTURY; Blore is marvelous as Howard's ultra-dedicated valet. ▶

It's Never Too Late (1956-British) **C-95m.** ★★½ D: Michael McCarthy. Phyllis Calvert, Guy Rolfe, Sarah Lawson, Peter Illing, Patrick Barr. Pleasant frou-frou about Calvert becoming famed writer, caught between choice of being good mother or living a celebrity's life.

It's Never Too Late to Mend (1937-British) **70m.** ★★★ D: David MacDonald. Tod Slaughter, Jack Livesey, Marjorie Taylor, Ian Colin, Lawrence Hanray, D. J. Williams, Roy Russell. Ruthless squire Slaughter feigns kindness but is eager to snare beautiful neighbor Taylor; he also runs the local prison with a brutal hand. Fast-paced, entertaining barnstorming melodrama, one of

Slaughter's best. Based on Charles Reade's 1856 novel that led to British prison reform. Aka NEVER TOO LATE.◗

It'$ Only Money (1962) **84m.** *** D: Frank Tashlin. Jerry Lewis, Joan O'Brien, Zachary Scott, Jack Weston, Jesse White, Mae Questel. TV repairman Jerry wants to be a detective like his idol (White!), so he sets out to locate a missing heir—and guess who it turns out to be? Slick mystery-comedy is one of Lewis' best vehicles, thanks to solid script (by John Fenton Murray) and direction, fine cast, and memorable climax involving robot lawn mowers.◗

It Started in Naples (1960) **C-100m.** **½ D: Melville Shavelson. Clark Gable, Sophia Loren, Vittorio De Sica, Marietto, Paolo Carlini, Claudio Ermelli. Gable is American lawyer, in Italy to bring nephew back to America, but sexy Aunt Sophia won't agree. Star duo never clicks, but they try. Attractive fluff. VistaVision.▼◗

It Started With a Kiss (1959) **C-104m.** **½ D: George Marshall. Glenn Ford, Debbie Reynolds, Eva Gabor, Fred Clark, Edgar Buchanan, Harry Morgan. Airy comedy about wacky Reynolds and her Army officer husband Ford, trying to make a go of marriage; set in Spain. Incidentally, the Lincoln Futura that figures so prominently in this film was later modified to become the Batmobile in the 1960s. CinemaScope.▼◗

It Started With Eve (1941) **90m.** *** D: Henry Koster. Deanna Durbin, Charles Laughton, Robert Cummings, Guy Kibbee, Margaret Tallichet, Walter Catlett. Delightful romantic comedy; Deanna poses as Cummings' fiancée to please his dying father (Laughton). Trouble starts when Laughton shows signs of recovery. Remade as I'D RATHER BE RICH.▼◗

It's the Old Army Game (1926) **104m.** *** D: Edward Sutherland. W. C. Fields, Louise Brooks, Blanche Ring, William Gaxton, Mary Foy, Mickey Bennett, Josephine Dunn. Fields is a small-town druggist, constantly harassed by the world, who gets mixed up in a phony Florida real estate deal. Very funny silent comedy, a string of the Great Man's best routines (dealing with idiotic customers, naps constantly interrupted by cacophonous noises, etc.). Revamped as IT'S A GIFT.

It's Tough to Be Famous (1932) **79m.** *** D: Alfred E. Green. Douglas Fairbanks, Jr., Mary Brian, Walter Catlett, Lilian Bond, Terrence Ray, David Landau. Pungent story of naval hero who becomes a much-manipulated media celebrity against his wishes. Done with usual Warner Bros. pizazz—and still surprisingly timely.◗

It's Trad, Dad! SEE: **Ring-a-Ding Rhythm!**

It Takes a Thief (1960-British) **90m.** ** D: John Gilling. Jayne Mansfield, Anthony Quayle, Carl Mohner, Peter Reynolds, Barbara Mullen, Edward Judd. Mansfield is

gangland leader with big heist in the workings; supporting cast uplifts flick. Original title: THE CHALLENGE.▼◗

It! The Terror From Beyond Space (1958) **69m.** **½ D: Edward L. Cahn. Marshall Thompson, Shawn Smith, Kim Spalding, Ann Doran, Dabbs Greer. The second spaceship to Mars heads for Earth with the sole survivor of the *first* expedition, accused of murdering his crewmates—but the real killer is a Martian monster (Ray "Crash" Corrigan), which has crept aboard the returning ship. ALIEN owes a lot to this tidy, suspenseful, but underproduced movie, scripted by sci-fi writer Jerome Bixby. ▼◗

I Vampiri SEE: **Devil's Commandment, The**

Ivanhoe (1952) **C-106m.** *** D: Richard Thorpe. Robert Taylor, Joan Fontaine, Elizabeth Taylor, Emlyn Williams, George Sanders, Robert Douglas, Finlay Currie, Felix Aylmer, Francis de Wolff, Guy Rolfe, Norman Wooland, Basil Sydney. Visually impressive epic, based on Sir Walter Scott's novel of England in the Middle Ages. The title character returns from the Crusades and battles evil Sanders and Rolfe, who want to usurp the throne of King Richard. Beautifully photographed by F. A. Young on location in Great Britain; marred only by draggy scripting. Remade as a TVM in 1982. ▼◗

Ivan's Childhood SEE: **My Name Is Ivan**

Ivan the Terrible, Part One (1945-Russian) **99m.** **** D: Sergei Eisenstein. Nikolai Cherkassov, Ludmila Tselikovskaya, Serafima Birman. Film spectacle of the highest order. Eisenstein's incredibly lavish, detailed chronicle of Czar Ivan IV's life from coronation to defeat to reinstatement, forging fascinating image of the man and his country. Enhanced by Prokofiev's original score. Heavy going, but worthwhile; the story continues in IVAN THE TERRIBLE, PART TWO.▼◗

Ivan the Terrible, Part Two (1946-Russian) **88m.** ***½ D: Sergei Eisenstein. Nikolai Cherkassov, Serafima Birman, Mikhail Nazvanov, Pavel Kadochnikov, Andrei Abrikosov. Czar Ivan IV takes on the boyars in a battle for power. Impressive film is just a shade below its predecessor. Banned by Stalin because of controversial depiction of Ivan's secret police, and not released until 1958. (The director had planned to shoot Part Three—which, needless to say, he never did.) Banquet-dance sequence was originally in color.▼◗

I've Always Loved You (1946) **C-117m.** *** D: Frank Borzage. Philip Dorn, Catherine McLeod, Bill Carter, Maria Ouspenskaya, Felix Bressart, Elizabeth Patterson, Vanessa Brown, Lewis Howard, Adele Mara, Stephanie Bachelor. Heartfelt romantic drama (from the master of the genre, Borzage) about a young woman who studies to be a concert pianist with a brilliant but harsh taskmaster—and falls in love with him. Beautifully photographed in Technicolor, with Artur Rubinstein providing the actual piano renditions on the soundtrack. That's young Andre Previn as a piano student in the opening scene. ▼○▶

I've Lived Before (1956) **82m.** **½ D: Richard Bartlett. Jock Mahoney, Leigh Snowden, Ann Harding, John McIntire. Strange small-budget film from the 1950s era of the Bridey Murphy (reincarnation) fad, about pilot who thinks he is an aviator who died in WW1.

I Vitelloni (1953-Italian) **107m.** **** D: Federico Fellini. Alberto Sordi, Franco Interlenghi, Franco Fabrizi, Leopoldo Trieste, Riccardo Fellini. Magnificent comedy-drama—arguably Fellini's masterpiece—about five shiftless male adolescents in a small Adriatic town who have to cope with emerging adulthood. Film's episodic structure brings to mind AMERICAN GRAFFITI; its love of humanity anticipates the director's own AMARCORD two decades later. In any event, a lovely film. ▼○▶

Ivory Hunter (1951-British) **C-107m.** **½ D: Harry Watt. Anthony Steel, Dinah Sheridan, Harold Warrender, Meredith Edwards, William Simons. Documentary-ish account of establishment of Mount Kilimanjaro Game Preserve Park in Africa. Retitled: WHERE NO VULTURES FLY.

Ivory Hunters SEE: **Last Elephant, The**
Ivy (1947) **99m.** **½ D: Sam Wood. Joan Fontaine, Patric Knowles, Herbert Marshall, Richard Ney, Cedric Hardwicke, Lucile Watson. Average drama of murderess snared in her own seemingly faultless plans. Good cast gives film added boost.

I Wake Up Screaming (1941) **82m.** *** D: H. Bruce Humberstone. Betty Grable, Victor Mature, Carole Landis, Laird Cregar, William Gargan, Alan Mowbray, Allyn Joslyn, Elisha Cook, Jr. Entertaining whodunit with Grable and Mature implicated in murder of Betty's sister (Landis), pursued by determined cop Cregar. Twist finish to good mystery. Remade as VICKI; originally titled HOT SPOT. ▼▶

I Walk Alone (1947) **98m.** ** D: Byron Haskin. Burt Lancaster, Lizabeth Scott, Kirk Douglas, Wendell Corey, Kristine Miller, George Rigaud, Marc Lawrence. A prison term changes Lancaster's outlook on life, and return to outside world makes him bitter. Good cast, weak film.

I Walked with a Zombie (1943) **69m.** ***½ D: Jacques Tourneur. Frances Dee, Tom Conway, James Ellison, Edith Barrett, Christine Gordon, Theresa Harris, James Bell. Nurse Dee comes to Caribbean island to treat zombielike wife of troubled Conway, finds skeletons in family closet, plus local voodoo rituals and legends that cannot be ignored. Exceptional Val Lewton chiller with rich atmosphere, mesmerizing story.

Loosely adapted from *Jane Eyre*! Read small-print disclaimer in opening credits carefully. Remade as RITUAL. ▼○▶

I Want a Divorce (1940) **75m.** **½ D: Ralph Murphy. Joan Blondell, Dick Powell, Gloria Dickson, Frank Fay, Dorothy Burgess, Jessie Ralph, Harry Davenport, Conrad Nagel. Powell and Blondell have just gotten married but already they're beginning to wonder in this light comedy. The two stars were married at the time in real life, too.

I Wanted Wings (1941) **131m.** ** D: Mitchell Leisen. Ray Milland, William Holden, Wayne Morris, Brian Donlevy, Constance Moore, Veronica Lake, Hedda Hopper. Stale plot of three men undergoing Air Force training served to introduce Lake as star material; that remains only real point of interest. However, the special effects for this did garner an Oscar.

I Want to Live! (1958) **120m.** ***½ D: Robert Wise. Susan Hayward, Simon Oakland, Virginia Vincent, Theodore Bikel, John Marley, Dabbs Greer, Gavin MacLeod. Hayward won an Oscar for her gutsy performance as prostitute-crook Barbara Graham who (according to the film) is framed for murder and goes to gas chamber. Smart presentation, fine acting, memorable jazz score by Johnny Mandel. Nelson Gidding and Don Mankiewicz based script on articles about Graham. Look fast for Jack Weston, Brett Halsey. Remade as a 1983 TVM with Lindsay Wagner. ▼○▶

I Want You (1951) **102m.** *** D: Mark Robson. Dana Andrews, Dorothy McGuire, Farley Granger, Peggy Dow, Robert Keith, Mildred Dunnock, Martin Milner, Ray Collins, Jim Backus. Dated yet still touching Americana detailing effects of the Korean War on a small-town family. An artifact of its era, with fine performances all around. Screenplay by Irwin Shaw. ▼

I Was a Communist for the F.B.I. (1951) **83m.** **½ D: Gordon Douglas. Frank Lovejoy, Dorothy Hart, Philip Carey, James Millican, Richard Webb, Konstantin Shayne, Paul Picerni, Roy Roberts, Eddie (Edward) Norris. Low-key, effective documentary-style relic of its era spotlights Matt Cvetic (Lovejoy), a real-life Slovenian-American who posed as a Communist Party member while gathering information on subversive activities for the F.B.I. Based on "I Posed as a Communist for the F.B.I.," an article penned by Cvetic. ▶

I Was a Male War Bride (1949) **105m.** *** D: Howard Hawks. Cary Grant, Ann Sheridan, Marion Marshall, Randy Stuart, William Neff, Ken Tobey. Delightful comedy of errors has French Army officer Grant trying to accompany WAC wife Sheridan back to U.S. with hilarious results. Grant in drag makes this one worth watching. ▼▶

I Was an Adventuress (1940) **81m.** **½ D: Gregory Ratoff. Vera Zorina, Erich von

Stroheim, Richard Greene, Peter Lorre, Sig Ruman. Jewel thief Zorina goes straight, marries Greene, but can't shake off former associates von Stroheim, Lorre. With that cast, it should have been better. Remake of 1938 French film J'ÉTAIS UNE AVENTURIÈRE. ▶

I Was an American Spy (1951) 85m. **½ D: Lesley Selander. Ann Dvorak, Gene Evans, Douglas Kennedy, Richard Loo, Philip Ahn, Lisa Ferraday. Dvorak is chanteuse in Manila who helps combat Japanese attack in WW2 spy story, elevated by veteran star. Song: "Because of You." ▶

I Was a Shoplifter (1950) 82m. **½ D: Charles Lamont. Scott Brady, Mona Freeman, Charles Drake, Andrea King, Anthony (Tony) Curtis. Fair programmer with cop Brady going undercover to bust open a shoplifting gang. Look for Rock Hudson as a department-store detective.

I Was a Spy (1933-British) 83m. ***½ D: Victor Saville. Madeleine Carroll, Conrad Veidt, Herbert Marshall, Gerald du Maurier, Edmund Gwenn, Donald Calthrop, Nigel Bruce. First-rate account of espionage agent Carroll, a Belgian nurse who aids the British after her country is overrun by the Germans during WW1. Veidt is perfectly cast as a German commandant. ▼▶

I Was a Teenage Frankenstein (1957) 72m. *½ D: Herbert L. Strock. Whit Bissell, Gary Conway, Phyllis Coates, Robert Burton. Campy junk about mad scientist who pulls young Conway from an auto wreck and "repairs" him. Doesn't live up to that title; worth catching only for Bissell's immortal line, "Speak! You've got a civil tongue in your head. I know you have because I sewed it back myself." One sequence is in color. ▼

I Was a Teenage Werewolf (1957) 75m. *** D: Gene Fowler, Jr. Michael Landon, Yvonne Lime, Whit Bissell, Vladimir Sokoloff, Guy Williams. Landon plays a hair-trigger-temper teen who's got a nut (Bissell) for a psychotherapist with dangerous ideas about hypnotic regression and man's prehistoric past. Result: a werewolf in a high school jacket. As good as a low-budget drive-in monster movie gets; it launched Landon's career. ▼

I Was Born, But ... (1932-Japanese) 89m. *** D: Yasujiro Ozu. Tatsuo Saito, Tokkanikozo (Tomio Aoki), Mitsuko Yoshikawa, Takeshi Sakamoto, Teruyo Hayami. Two little brothers go on a hunger strike to force their father to stand up to his boss and to increase their own stature as new kids in a neighborhood gang (one of whose members is the boss' son). Amusing satire of cultural mores has a serious underside about the personal sacrifices one must make to get ahead in business and the power of peer group pressure. Ozu remade in color in 1959 as GOOD MORNING. ▼▶

I Was Monty's Double (1958-British)

100m. ***½ D: John Guillermin. M. E. Clifton-James, John Mills, Cecil Parker, Marius Goring, Michael Hordern, Leslie Phillips, Bryan Forbes. Exciting, true WW2 story of actor persuaded to pose as Gen. Montgomery in order to divert German intelligence in North Africa. Cast is first-rate. ▼

I Wonder Who's Kissing Her Now (1947) C-104m. **½ D: Lloyd Bacon. June Haver, Mark Stevens, Martha Stewart, Reginald Gardiner, Lenore Aubert, William Frawley. Innocuous re-creation of life and loves of 1890s songwriter Joseph E. Howard. As usual, music is better than script. ▶

I Wouldn't Be in Your Shoes (1948) 70m. **½ D: William Nigh. Don Castle, Elyse Knox, Regis Toomey, Charles D. Brown, Rory Mallinson, Robert Lowell, Bill Kennedy. Knox teams up with cop Toomey to save her tap-dancing husband, who was railroaded after throwing a pair of shoes out the window to silence a wailing cat, only to be convicted of murder after police find his shoe prints near the corpse of a rich man. Minor film noir based on a Cornell Woolrich story has good shabby atmosphere and fairly engrossing story; twist ending is pretty obvious, but still satisfying.

J'accuse! (1919-French) 166m. ***½ D: Abel Gance. Romuald Joubé, Maxime Desjardins, Séverin-Mars, Angèle Guys, Maryse Dauvray. Vividly filmed classic, one of the earliest cinematic indictments of war, as a gentle poet (Joubé) is thrust into combat during WW1. Filled with innovative, stunningly artful imagery; the highlight comes near the finale, when the poet imagines the ghosts of his dead comrades rising up, returning to their homes, and observing the impact of their sacrifices. Gance remade this in 1938. ▼▶

J'Accuse (1938-French) 95m. *** D: Abel Gance. Victor Francen, Jean Max, Delaitre, Renee Devillers. Very good—but not great—antiwar film, focusing on exploited war veteran Francen; in a vivid sequence, he calls on war casualties to rise from their graves. Previously filmed by Gance in 1919. ▼

Jack and the Beanstalk (1952) C/B&W-78m. **½ D: Jean Yarbrough. Bud Abbott, Lou Costello, Dorothy Ford, Barbara Brown, Buddy Baer. A&C version of fairy tale OK for kids, but not as funny as their earlier films. Begins in sepiatone, then changes to color, like THE WIZARD OF OZ. ▼▶

Jackass Mail (1942) 80m. ** D: Norman Z. McLeod. Wallace Beery, Marjorie Main, J. Carrol Naish, Darryl Hickman, William Haade, Dick Curtis. Easygoing Beery vehicle about fugitive who accidentally becomes a hero. Take it or leave it; no harm done either way.

Jackie Robinson Story, The (1950) 76m.

*** D: Alfred E. Green. Jackie Robinson, Ruby Dee, Minor Watson, Louise Beavers, Richard Lane, Harry Shannon, Ben Lessy, Joel Fluellen. Straightforward bio of Robinson, the first black man to play major-league baseball. Fascinating as a social history; pointed in its presentation of the racial issues involved. Interestingly, Robinson's Negro League ball club is called the Black Panthers! Dee plays Robinson's wife; 40 years later, she was cast as his mother in the TV movie THE COURT-MARTIAL OF JACKIE ROBINSON. Robinson's story is also told in 42. ▼❱

Jack London (1943) 94m. *½ D: Alfred Santell. Michael O'Shea, Susan Hayward, Osa Massen, Harry Davenport, Frank Craven, Virginia Mayo. Hokey, episodic "biography" of famed writer spends too much time maligning Japanese—which was supposed to give topical slant to this period drama in 1943. O'Shea and Mayo later wed in real life. Aka THE ADVENTURES OF JACK LONDON and THE LIFE OF JACK LONDON. ▼❱

Jack McCall, Desperado (1953) C-76m. ****** D: Sidney Salkow. George Montgomery, Angela Stevens, Douglas Kennedy, James Seay, Eugene Iglesias, Jay Silverheels. During the Civil War, Union soldier is framed by Confederates posing as Yankees, and seeks revenge. Standard Western programmer shoehorns McCall and Wild Bill Hickok into far-fetched story. ▼

Jackpot, The (1950) 87m. ****½** D: Walter Lang. James Stewart, Barbara Hale, James Gleason, Fred Clark, Natalie Wood. Dated, minor comedy, uplifted by stars; Stewart is winner of radio contest but can't pay taxes on winnings. ▼❱

Jack Slade (1953) 90m. ****** D: Harold Schuster. Mark Stevens, Dorothy Malone, Barton MacLane, John Litel. Oater programmer of Stevens turning criminal with tragic results; Malone is wasted.

Jack the Giant Killer (1962) C-94m. ******* D: Nathan Juran. Kerwin Mathews, Judi Meredith, Torin Thatcher, Walter Burke. Marvelous Fantascope special effects make this costume adventure yarn (in the SINBAD tradition) great fun. Beware reissue, which was dubbed into an ersatz musical! ▼❱

Jack the Ripper (1960-British) 88m. ****** D: Robert Baker, Monty Berman. Lee Patterson, Eddie Byrne, George Rose, Betty McDowall. Middling retelling of notorious knife-wielder, with alternating scenes of Scotland Yard and fiend at work in London. Sometimes hits the mark with gory sensationalism. ▼❱

Jacqueline (1956-British) C-92m. ******* D: Roy Baker. John Gregson, Kathleen Ryan, Jacqueline Ryan, Noel Purcell, Cyril Cusack. Captivating drama of lovable little Irish girl

(Jacqueline Ryan) and how she helps her tippler father (Gregson) find work. Lots of warmth.

Jade Mask, The (1945) 66m. *½ D: Phil Rosen. Sidney Toler, Mantan Moreland, Edwin Luke, Janet Warren, Edith Evanson, Hardie Albright, Frank Reicher, Alan Bridge, Ralph Lewis. Curmudgeonly old scientist is murdered in an isolated country house and there isn't a relative or servant in the place without a motive. Only the greenest of armchair sleuths will fail to guess whodunit in this subpar Monogram *Charlie Chan* mystery. ▼❍❱

Jaguar (1956) 66m. *½ D: George Blair. Sabu, Chiquita, Barton MacLane, Jonathan Hale, Touch (Mike) Connors. Presence of former elephant boy Sabu is only virtue of ridiculous programmer about mysterious murders on an oilfield.

Jail Bait (1954) 70m. *½ D: Edward D. Wood, Jr. Timothy Farrell, Lyle Talbot, Steve Reeves, Herbert Rawlinson, Dolores Fuller, Clancey Malone, Theodora Thurman, Mona McKinnon. Farrell leads young Malone into life of crime; when the law closes in, he forces Malone's plastic surgeon father to change his face. Misleadingly titled thriller is less inept than Wood's "classics," and thus less funny, but inspired teaming of Talbot and Reeves (in his first speaking part) as cops is good for a few giggles. ▼❍❱

Jailbreakers, The (1960) 64m. *½ D: Alexander Grasshoff. Robert Hutton, Mary Castle, Michael O'Connell, Gabe Delutri, Anton Van Stralen. Escaped prisoners harass a young couple in a deserted town. Tepid programmer.

Jail Busters (1955) 61m. ****** D: William Beaudine. Leo Gorcey, Huntz Hall, Bernard Gorcey, Barton MacLane, Anthony Caruso, Percy Helton, David Gorcey, Bennie Bartlett, Murray Alper, Fritz Feld, Lyle Talbot. The Bowery Boys go up the river to settle the score with convicts who beat up David Gorcey, an undercover reporter. ❱

Jailhouse Rock (1957) 96m. ******* D: Richard Thorpe. Elvis Presley, Judy Tyler, Vaughn Taylor, Dean Jones, Mickey Shaughnessy. Elvis learns to pick a guitar in the Big House, later becomes a surly rock star. Presley's best film captures the legend in all his nostril-flaring, pre-Army glory. Great Leiber-Stoller score, including "Treat Me Nice," "Don't Leave Me Now," and terrific title song. Also shown in computer-colored version. CinemaScope. ▼❍❱

Jalna (1935) 78m. ****** D: John Cromwell. Kay Johnson, Ian Hunter, Nigel Bruce, C. Aubrey Smith, David Manners, Peggy Wood, Jessie Ralph. Moderately interesting filmization of an old-fashioned novel about a city girl marrying into a tight-knit family that lives on a remote farm in Canada. Hackneyed plot situations interfere with some fine performances and fluid camera-work. Johnson and director Cromwell were married.

Jalopy (1953) **62m.** ** D: William Beaudine. Leo Gorcey, Huntz Hall, David Gorcey, Bennie Bartlett, Bernard Gorcey, Robert Lowery, Murray Alper, Jane Easton, Richard Benedict. Sputtering laughs as the Bowery Boys enter an auto race with the help of a supercharged gas formula invented by Sach. ▶

Jamaica Inn (1939-British) **98m.** ** D: Alfred Hitchcock. Charles Laughton, Maureen O'Hara, Leslie Banks, Robert Newton, Emlyn Williams, Mervyn Johns. Stodgy Victorian costumer of cutthroat band headed by nobleman Laughton; O'Hara is lovely, but plodding Hitchcock film is disappointing. Based on Daphne du Maurier novel; Hitch had far more success a year later with du Maurier's *Rebecca.* Remade for British TV in 1985 with Jane Seymour and Patrick McGoohan. ▼●▶

Jamaica Run (1953) **C-92m.** ** D: Lewis R. Foster. Ray Milland, Arlene Dahl, Wendell Corey, Patric Knowles. Milland works for Dahl's nutty family, salvage diving in the Caribbean. Dull production.

Jamboree! (1957) **71m.** ** D: Roy Lockwood. Kay Medford, Robert Pastine, Paul Carr, Freda Halloway, Slim Whitman, Jodie Sands, Frankie Avalon, Fats Domino, Jerry Lee Lewis, Carl Perkins, Lewis Lymon and The Teen Chords, Buddy Knox, Count Basie, Joe Williams, Sandy Singer, Dick Clark, Connie Francis. Slight plot—singers Carr and Halloway fall in love, are manipulated by ambitious manager Medford—highlighted by rock, rockabilly, and jazz vignettes. Avalon looks about 12 years old, and Lewis sings "Great Balls of Fire." Aka DISC JOCKEY JAMBOREE. ▼▶

James Dean Story, The (1957) **82m.** ** D: George W. George, Robert Altman. Narrated by Martin Gabel. Uninspired use of available material makes this a slow-moving documentary on life of 1950s movie star. ▼●▶

Jam Session (1944) **77m.** ** D: Charles Barton. Ann Miller, Jess Barker, Charles D. Brown, Eddie Kane, Louis Armstrong, Duke Ellington and His Band, Glen Gray and His Band, Teddy Powell and His Band, Charlie Barnet Orchestra, Nan Wynn, Pied Pipers. Mild musical of showgirl Miller trying to crash Hollywood; notable for many musical guests doing enjoyable specialty numbers.

Jane Eyre (1934) **67m.** ** D: Christy Cabanne. Virginia Bruce, Colin Clive, Beryl Mercer, Aileen Pringle, David Torrence, Lionel Belmore. Thin version of the oft-filmed Brontë novel, produced by Monogram, of all studios, with Bruce in the title role and Clive as Mr. Rochester. Still, it's not uninteresting as a curio. ▼▶

Jane Eyre (1944) **96m.** *** D: Robert Stevenson. Orson Welles, Joan Fontaine, Margaret O'Brien, Henry Daniell, John Sutton, Agnes Moorehead, Elizabeth Taylor, Peggy Ann Garner, Sara Allgood, Aubrey Mather, Hillary Brooke. Artistically successful if slow-moving version of Charlotte Brontë novel about orphan girl who grows up to become a governess in mysterious household. Young Taylor appears unbilled. ▼●▶

Janie (1944) **106m.** **½ D: Michael Curtiz. Joyce Reynolds, Edward Arnold, Ann Harding, Robert Benchley, Robert Hutton, Alan Hale, Hattie McDaniel. Naive (now) but pleasant comedy about small-town teenage girl falling in love with serviceman despite father's objections to love-hungry soldiers. From the Broadway play by Josephine Bentham and Herschel Williams. Followed by JANIE GETS MARRIED.

Janie Gets Married (1946) **89m.** **½ D: Vincent Sherman. Joan Leslie, Robert Hutton, Edward Arnold, Ann Harding, Robert Benchley, Dorothy Malone, Hattie McDaniel, Mel Tormé. Pleasant follow-up to JANIE, with bright-eyed Leslie helping soldier-hubby Hutton readjust to civilian life.

Japanese War Bride (1952) **91m.** **½ D: King Vidor. Don Taylor, Shirley Yamaguchi, Cameron Mitchell, Marie Windsor, Philip Ahn. Penetrating study of WW2 veterans who return to life in U.S.A. with Asian brides.

Jason and the Argonauts (1963-British) **C-104m.** *** D: Don Chaffey. Todd Armstrong, Gary Raymond, Nancy Kovack, Honor Blackman, Nigel Green. Great special effects (by Ray Harryhausen) and colorful backgrounds in fable about Jason's search for golden fleece. Encounters with mythic monsters and gods highlight this sweeping adventure. Rich score by Bernard Herrmann. Remade for TV in 2000. ▼●▶

Jassy (1947-British) **C-96m.** **½ D: Bernard Knowles. Margaret Lockwood, Patricia Roc, Dennis Price, Dermot Walsh, Basil Sydney, Nora Swinburne. Brooding drama of gypsy girl accused of causing her husband's death; well-mounted 19th-century yarn.

Java Head (1934-British) **70m.** *** D: J. Walter Ruben. Anna May Wong, Elizabeth Allan, Edmund Gwenn, John Loder, Ralph Richardson, Herbert Lomas. Perceptive, literate account of 19th-century sea captain Loder, whose roots are in a puritanical English port city, and his marriage to a Mandarin princess (Wong). Based on the Joseph Hergesheimer best-seller (which was set in Massachusetts). ▼

Jayhawkers!, The (1959) **C-100m.** ** D: Melvin Frank. Jeff Chandler, Fess Parker, Nicole Maurey, Henry Silva, Herbert Rudley. Turgid Western set in 1850s Kansas, where Chandler schemes to become its Napoleonic "emperor." VistaVision. ▼◗

Jazz Boat (1960-British) **90m.** **½ D: Ken Hughes. Anthony Newley, Anne Aubrey, Lionel Jeffries, David Lodge, Bernie Winters, James Booth. Energetic caper of handyman Newley pretending to be a crook and then having to carry through, with dire results. CinemaScope.

Jazz on a Summer's Day (1959) **C-85m.** ***½ D: Bert Stern. Louis Armstrong, Big Maybelle, Chuck Berry, Dinah Washington, Gerry Mulligan, Thelonious Monk, Anita O'Day, Mahalia Jackson, Sonny Stitt, Jack Teagarden. Candid, enjoyable filmed record of the 1958 Newport Jazz Festival. A must for jazz aficionados. ▼◗

Jazz Singer, The (1927) **89m.** **½ D: Alan Crosland. Al Jolson, May McAvoy, Warner Oland, Eugenie Besserer, Otto Lederer, William Demarest, Roscoe Karns. Legendary first talkie is actually silent with several sound musical and talking sequences. Story of Cantor Oland's son (Jolson) going into show business is creaky, but this movie milestone should be seen once. Songs: "My Mammy," "Toot Toot Tootsie Goodbye," "Blue Skies," etc. Look fast for Myrna Loy as a chorus girl. Runs 96m. with overture, exit music. Remade twice (so far!). ▼◗◗

Jazz Singer, The (1953) **C-107m.** **½ D: Michael Curtiz. Danny Thomas, Peggy Lee, Mildred Dunnock, Eduard Franz, Tom Tully, Allyn Joslyn. Slick remake benefits from Curtiz' no-nonsense direction and presence of Lee and Dunnock . . . but it's still just *so* schmaltzy. ▼◗

Jealousy (1945) **71m.** ** D: Gustav Machaty. John Loder, Nils Asther, Jane Randolph, Karen Morley, Hugo Haas. Whodunit set in L.A. that, after a promising start, descends into mediocrity. Machaty's touch is still evident in unusual camera shots and montages. Based on a story by Dalton Trumbo.

Jeanne Eagels (1957) **109m.** **½ D: George Sidney. Kim Novak, Jeff Chandler, Agnes Moorehead, Gene Lockhart, Virginia Grey. Novak tries but can't rise to demands of portraying famed actress of 1920s. Chandler is her virile love interest. ◗

Jeannie (1941-British) **101m.** *** D: Harold French. Michael Redgrave, Barbara Mullen, Wilfrid Lawson, Kay Hammond, Albert Lieven, Edward Chapman, Googie Withers, Rachel Kempson, Ian Fleming. Enjoyable comedy-romance with Scottish lass Mullen vacationing in Vienna and becoming involved with washing machine salesman Redgrave and gigolo Lieven. Anatole de Grunwald was one of the writers. Aka GIRL IN DISTRESS. Remade as LET'S BE HAPPY.

Jeepers Creepers (1939) **69m.** ** D: Frank McDonald. The Weaver Brothers and Elviry, Roy Rogers, Thurston Hall, Billy Lee, Johnny Arthur, Lucien Littlefield, Loretta Weaver, Maris Wrixon. Crooked Hall tries to cheat the Weavers out of their coal-rich land, no matter what it takes. Roy has a supporting role as town sheriff in this OK musical vehicle for the popular cornpone stars. ▼

Jennie Gerhardt (1933) **85m.** *** D: Marion Gering. Sylvia Sidney, Donald Cook, Mary Astor, Edward Arnold, Louise Carter, Cora Sue Collins, H. B. Warner. Meticulously produced version of Theodore Dreiser saga of poor girl Sidney finding kind benefactor Arnold, losing him, and living as Cook's back-street lover. Actors and elaborate production lend credibility to episodic soaper set at turn of the century.

Jennifer (1953) **73m.** ** D: Joel Newton. Ida Lupino, Howard Duff, Robert Nichols, Mary Shipp, Ned Glass, Kitty McHugh, Russ Conway. Emotionally fragile woman takes a job as caretaker at a huge, empty California mansion and becomes obsessed with the unexplained disappearance of her predecessor, a "mystery woman" named Jennifer. Unsatisfying chamber piece with loose ends and red herrings galore. Matt Dennis (incongruously) introduces his great song "Angel Eyes" in a scene set at a dance. Stylishly photographed by James Wong Howe. Director Newton is apparently a pseudonym for Bernard Girard.

Jeopardy (1953) **69m.** *** D: John Sturges. Barbara Stanwyck, Barry Sullivan, Ralph Meeker, Lee Aaker. Stanwyck struggles to save husband Sullivan from drowning after an accident at a remote Mexican beach during a family vacation. Taut, fast-paced yarn with Meeker making a strong impression as a killer on the lam. ◗

Jericho SEE: **Dark Sands**

Jerrico, The Wonder Clown SEE: **Three Ring Circus**

Jesse James (1939) **C-105m.** *** D: Henry King. Tyrone Power, Henry Fonda, Nancy Kelly, Randolph Scott, Henry Hull, Brian Donlevy, John Carradine, Jane Darwell. Sprawling, glamorous Western with Power and Fonda as Jesse and Frank James; movie builds a case that the Old West's most notorious outlaw was misguided. Shot in Missouri. Sequel: THE RETURN OF FRANK JAMES. ▼◗◗

Jesse James at Bay (1941) **56m.** ** D: Joseph Kane. Roy Rogers, George "Gabby" Hayes, Sally Payne, Pierre Watkin, Ivan Miller, Hal Taliaferro, Gale Storm, Roy Barcroft. Roy's last historical Western casts him as Jesse James, who steals from crooked railroad magnate Watkin to aid farmers, and an evil lookalike, hired by Watkin to sully Jesse's "good" name. Complex script from future Oscar winner James Webb is not given the time required to do it justice. Payne and Storm play two of the dumbest newspaper reporters ever seen. ▼◗

Jesse James vs. the Daltons (1954) **C-**

65m. ** D: William Castle. Brett King, Barbara Lawrence, James Griffith, Bill Phipps, John Cliff. Prairie pariah King hooks up with the Dalton gang to try and verify that he really is the son of the notorious outlaw—who may still be alive. Blah Sam Katzman quickie lacks even a colorful supporting cast. Originally in 3-D.

Jesse James' Women (1954) **C-83m.** *½ D: Donald Barry. Don Barry, Jack Buetel, Peggie Castle, Lita Baron. Romancing a variety of women leaves James little time for outlaw activities; cute premise doesn't work out.▼▶

Jessica (1962) **C-112m.** **½ D: Jean Negulesco. Angie Dickinson, Maurice Chevalier, Noel-Noel, Gabriele Ferzetti, Sylva Koscina, Agnes Moorehead. Dickinson is an Italian midwife who has men in her village lusting for her, with Chevalier as the local priest. Malarkey. Panavision.

Jester, The SEE: **Der Purimshpiler**

Jet Attack (1958) **68m.** BOMB D: Edward L. Cahn. John Agar, Audrey Totter, Gregory Walcott, James Dobson. Sloppy Korean War programmer about rescue of U.S. scientist caught behind North Korean lines.▼

Jet Over the Atlantic (1960) **95m.** ** D: Byron Haskin. Guy Madison, Virginia Mayo, George Raft, Ilona Massey, Margaret Lindsay, George Macready, Anna Lee, Venetia Stevenson, Mary Anderson, Bret Halsey. Capable cast in clichéd situation of plane with bomb on board. Madison's the former Air Force pilot saving the day; predictable plot line.▼

Jet Pilot (1957) **C-112m.** ** D: Josef von Sternberg. John Wayne, Janet Leigh, Jay C. Flippen, Paul Fix, Richard Rober, Roland Winters, Hans Conried. One of Howard Hughes' movie curios, updating his HELL'S ANGELS interest in aviation with cold war theme, as American pilot Wayne falls in love with Russian jet ace Leigh. Ridiculous, to say the least, though some of its humor seems to have been intentional. Completed in 1950, unreleased for seven years! Incidentally, some of the stunt flying was done by Chuck Yeager.▼▶

Jewel Robbery (1932) **70m.** ***½ D: William Dieterle. William Powell, Kay Francis, Hardie Albright, Henry Kolker, Spencer Charters, Alan Mowbray, Helen Vinson. Lubitsch-like bauble with wealthy, married Francis (who aches for excitement in her life) being captivated by debonair burglar Powell. Breathlessly paced, witty and charming. Screenplay by Erwin Gelsey, based on a play by Ladislaus Fodor.▶

Jewish Jester, The SEE: **Der Purimshpiler**

Jew Süss (1934-British) **105m.** *** D: Lothar Mendes. Conrad Veidt, Benita Hume, Frank Vosper, Cedric Hardwicke, Gerald du Maurier, Paul Graetz, Pamela Ostrer (Mason), Dennis Hoey. Powerful drama about Joseph "Jew Süss" Oppenheimer (Veidt),

an 18th-century Jewish businessman who becomes financial advisor to a pompous nobleman. Oppenheimer is depicted as a savior of his people and the film is a pointed exposé of anti-Semitism through the ages. An altogether different take on Oppenheimer may be found in Veit Harlan's notoriously anti-Semitic JUD SÜSS (1940), produced in Nazi Germany.

Jezebel (1938) **103m.** ***½ D: William Wyler. Bette Davis, Henry Fonda, George Brent, Margaret Lindsay, Donald Crisp, Fay Bainter, Spring Byington, Richard Cromwell, Henry O'Neill. Davis won her second Oscar as tempestuous Southern belle who goes too far to make fiancé Fonda jealous; Bainter also received Oscar as Davis' sympathetic aunt. Fine production, entire cast excellent. John Huston was one of the writers. Also shown in computer-colored version.▼▶

Jigsaw (1949) **70m.** ** D: Fletcher Markle. Franchot Tone, Jean Wallace, Myron McCormick, Marc Lawrence, Betty Harper (Doe Avedon). Pedestrian caper of assistant D.A. Tone on the trail of a journalist's killer, uncovering a racist hate group. Sparked by unbilled appearances of Marlene Dietrich, Henry Fonda, John Garfield, Burgess Meredith, Marsha Hunt. Retitled: GUN MOLL.▼▶

Jimmy and Sally (1933) **68m.** **½ D: James Tinling. James Dunn, Claire Trevor, Harvey Stephens, Lya Lys, Jed Prouty. Gogetter Dunn lets his ambition cloud his devotion to Trevor in amiable little film of no consequence whatsoever.

Jimmy the Gent (1934) **67m.** **½ D: Michael Curtiz. James Cagney, Bette Davis, Alice White, Allen Jenkins, Philip Reed, Mayo Methot. Crooked businessman Cagney pretends to refine himself to impress Davis in this bouncy comedy.▶

Jim Thorpe—All-American (1951) **107m.** **½ D: Michael Curtiz. Burt Lancaster, Charles Bickford, Steve Cochran, Phyllis Thaxter, Dick Wesson. The life of the famed American Indian athlete who was stripped of his Olympic medals for playing professional baseball. Lancaster lends dignified vigor to title role; Bickford is especially outstanding as Thorpe's mentor, legendary coach Pop Warner.▼▶

Jinx Money (1948) **68m.** ** D: William Beaudine. Leo Gorcey, Huntz Hall, Gabriel Dell, Billy Benedict, David Gorcey, Bennie Bartlett, Sheldon Leonard, Donald MacBride, Wanda McKay, John Eldredge. The Bowery Boys stumble upon $50,000 of a dead gangster's loot and spend a slow hour being chased by his cohorts.▶

Jitterbugs (1943) **74m.** ** D: Mal St. Clair. Stan Laurel, Oliver Hardy, Vivian Blaine, Robert Bailey, Douglas Fowley, Noel Madison. One of the team's better later efforts, with Blaine sharing the spotlight and doing quite nicely. Ollie's scene with Southern belle Lee Patrick is a gem. Previously filmed as ARIZONA TO BROADWAY.▶

Jivaro (1954) **C-91m.** ** D: Edward Ludwig. Fernando Lamas, Rhonda Fleming, Brian Keith, Lon Chaney (Jr.), Richard Denning, Rita Moreno. Cornball adventure with beautiful Fleming arriving in the Amazon to search for her missing fiancé; promptly and predictably, she hooks up with Lamas.

Jive Junction (1943) **62m.** **½ D: Edgar G. Ulmer. Tina Thayer, Dickie Moore, Johnny Michaels, Jan Wiley, Jack Wagner, Gerra Young, Beverly Boyd, Johnny Duncan. Classical music student braves his disapproving teachers to organize an all-girl orchestra that plays for soldiers. Though ex–child star Moore is a bit geeky as the bandleader, this WW2 musical's home front setting (with no men around) feels genuine, and Ulmer's direction is a textbook example of how to make something out of nothing. Script cowritten by Irving Wallace. Sole film by soprano Young, who sings Delibes' "Bell Song."

Joan of Arc (1948) **C-100m.** **½ D: Victor Fleming. Ingrid Bergman, Jose Ferrer, Francis L. Sullivan, J. Carrol Naish, Ward Bond, Shepperd Strudwick, Hurd Hatfield, Gene Lockhart, John Emery, Cecil Kellaway, George Coulouris, John Ireland. Bergman is staunchly sincere in this overlong, faithful adaptation of Maxwell Anderson's play. Not enough spectacle to balance talky sequences. Originally released theatrically at 145m.▼●▶

Joan of Ozark (1942) **80m.** ** D: Joseph Santley. Judy Canova, Joe E. Brown, Eddie Foy, Jr., Jerome Cowan, Alexander Granach, Anne Jeffreys. Hillbilly Canova hunts down Nazi underground ring in U.S. Brainless propaganda comedy.▶

Joan of Paris (1942) **92m.** ***½ D: Robert Stevenson. Michele Morgan, Paul Henreid, Thomas Mitchell, Laird Cregar, May Robson, Alexander Granach, Alan Ladd, Hans Conried, Marie Windsor. Excellent WW2 tale of five RAF flyers shot down over Occupied France, with Henreid their nominal leader and Morgan the young café worker who becomes involved with him. Cregar is perfectly cast as a slimy Nazi. U.S. debuts for both Morgan and Henreid. ▼▶

Joan the Woman (1917) **138m.** *** D: Cecil B. DeMille. Geraldine Farrar, Raymond Hatton, Hobart Bosworth, Theodore Roberts, Wallace Reid, Charles Clary, James Neill, Tully Marshall, Lillian Leighton, Walter Long. DeMille's first historical epic is nicely mounted, spotlighting the heroism and sacrifice of Joan of Arc (a miscast Farrar) as she evolves from peasant girl to saintlike figure and becomes involved with Englishman Reid. Fashioned as an accolade to France, with the story bookended by sequences set during WW1 involving a soldier who is inspired by Joan's bravery. Some of the effects are in color. ▼▶

Joe and Ethel Turp Call on the President (1939) **70m.** **½ D: Robert Sinclair. Ann Sothern, Lewis Stone, Walter Brennan, William Gargan, Marsha Hunt, Tom Neal. Cute little B film from Damon Runyon story about Brooklynites Sothern and Gargan who go all the way to the White House to see the President (Stone) when their favorite mailman (Brennan) is jailed for destroying a registered letter.

Joe Butterfly (1957) **C-90m.** **½ D: Jesse Hibbs. Audie Murphy, Burgess Meredith, George Nader, Kieko Shima, Keenan Wynn, Fred Clark. Mildly amusing variation on THE TEAHOUSE OF THE AUGUST MOON, set in post-WW2 Japan. American soldiers at mercy of wily Japanese Meredith to get needed supplies. CinemaScope.

Joe Dakota (1957) **C-79m.** **½ D: Richard Bartlett. Jock Mahoney, Luana Patten, Charles McGraw, Barbara Lawrence, Claude Akins, Lee Van Cleef. Folksy oater of Mahoney arriving in a small town where oil-drilling locals give him a BAD DAY AT BLACK ROCK–style reception.

Joe Louis Story, The (1953) **88m.** ** D: Robert Gordon. Coley Wallace, Paul Stewart, Hilda Simms, James Edwards, John Marley, Dots Johnson. Biopic of the heavyweight champ is interesting historically but dramatically hokey; Wallace looks the part of Louis, but is no actor.▼▶

Joe Macbeth (1955-British) **90m.** **½ D: Ken Hughes. Paul Douglas, Ruth Roman, Bonar Colleano, Gregoire Aslan, Sidney James. Occasionally amusing variation on Shakespeare's *Macbeth*, with Douglas a 1930s gangster whose wife (Roman) nags him into murdering his way to the top of his "profession."

Joe Palooka SEE: **Palooka**

Joe Smith, American (1942) **63m.** ** D: Richard Thorpe. Robert Young, Marsha Hunt, Harvey Stephens, Darryl Hickman. Dated WW2 morale booster about munitions worker Young and what happens when he is kidnapped by enemy spies. Paul Gallico story later remade as THE BIG OPERATOR. Watch for Ava Gardner in a bit, and Robert Blake in the flashback, as Young's son.

John Goldfarb, Please Come Home (1965) **C-96m.** *½ D: J. Lee Thompson. Shirley MacLaine, Peter Ustinov, Richard Crenna, Scott Brady, Jim Backus, Charles Lane, Jerome Cowan, Wilfrid Hyde-White, Fred Clark, Harry Morgan, Telly Savalas, Richard Deacon, Jackie Coogan, Jerome (Jerry) Orbach, Barbara Bouchet. Trapped in desert kingdom, two Americans (pilot, woman reporter) conspire to help Arabian chief Ustinov's football team beat Notre Dame. Notre Dame University found this spoof so offensive it sued in court; the viewer has an easier alternative. Screenplay by William Peter Blatty. Look for Teri Garr. CinemaScope.

John Loves Mary (1949) **96m.** **½ D: David Butler. Ronald Reagan, Jack Carson, Patricia Neal, Wayne Morris, Edward Arnold, Virginia Field. Genial adaptation of Norman Krasna's Broadway hit about a soldier (Reagan) who does his pal a favor by marrying the fellow's British girlfriend, so she can come to the U.S.—intending to get divorce upon arrival. Naive fluff was Neal's film debut.▼▶

John Meade's Woman (1937) **87m.** ** D: Richard Wallace. Edward Arnold, Gail Patrick, Francine Larrimore, George Bancroft, Aileen Pringle, Sidney Blackmer. Arnold plays another Great American Businessman, marrying one girl to spite another. Idea backfires; so does film.

Johnny Allegro (1949) **81m.** **½ D: Ted Tetzlaff. Nina Foch, George Raft, George Macready, Will Geer. Seamy gangster melodrama of ex-racketeer Raft going undercover to help federal agents capture counterfeiters. Last part of story imitates THE MOST DANGEROUS GAME.▶

Johnny Angel (1945) **79m.** *** D: Edwin L. Marin. George Raft, Claire Trevor, Signe Hasso, Lowell Gilmore, Hoagy Carmichael, Marvin Miller, Margaret Wycherly, J. Farrell MacDonald. Tough, well-done melodrama, with Raft cleaning up notorious mob, solving mystery of father's murder. Trevor lends good support.▼▶

Johnny Apollo (1940) **93m.** *** D: Henry Hathaway. Tyrone Power, Dorothy Lamour, Edward Arnold, Lloyd Nolan, Charles Grapewin, Lionel Atwill, Marc Lawrence. Good-natured Power turns crook, resentful of father Arnold, white-collar thief. Good acting, especially by Lamour as the girlfriend.▼▶

Johnny Belinda (1948) **103m.** ***½ D: Jean Negulesco. Jane Wyman, Lew Ayres, Charles Bickford, Jan Sterling, Agnes Moorehead, Stephen McNally, Rosalind Ivan, Alan Napier, Dan Seymour. Sensitively acted, atmospheric drama of young deaf-mute girl (Wyman) and doctor (Ayres) who works with her. Setting of provincial fishing-farming community vividly realized. Wyman won an Oscar for her fine performance. Elmer Harris play was scripted by Irmgard von Cube and Allen Vincent. Remade for TV in 1982 with Rosanna Arquette. Also shown in computer-colored version.▼▶

Johnny Come Lately (1943) **97m.** **½ D: William K. Howard. James Cagney, Grace George, Marjorie Main, Marjorie Lord, Hattie McDaniel, Ed McNamara. Tame but amusing Cagney vehicle, with Jimmy as wandering newspaperman who helps elderly editor George in small-town political battle.▼▶

Johnny Concho (1956) **84m.** **½ D: Don McGuire. Frank Sinatra, Keenan Wynn, William Conrad, Phyllis Kirk, Wallace Ford, Dorothy Adams, Jean Byron, Claude Akins, John Qualen. Plodding Western with

novelty of Sinatra as cowardly soul who must build courage for inevitable shoot-out. Adapted from a *Studio One* TV play.

Johnny Cool (1963) **101m.** *** D: William Asher. Henry Silva, Elizabeth Montgomery, Sammy Davis, Jr., Richard Anderson, Jim Backus, Wanda Hendrix, Brad Dexter, Joey Bishop, Marc Lawrence, John McGiver, Mort Sahl, Telly Savalas, Elisha Cook, Jr. Sadistic study of vicious gangster seeking revenge. Brutal account, realistically told.
▶

Johnny Dark (1954) **C-85m.** **½ D: George Sherman. Tony Curtis, Piper Laurie, Don Taylor, Paul Kelly, Ilka Chase, Sidney Blackmer. Curtis is energetic as auto designer who enters big race.

Johnny Doesn't Live Here Any More (1944) **77m.** **½ D: Joe May. Simone Simon, James Ellison, Minna Gombell, Alan Dinehart, Robert Mitchum, Grady Sutton. WW2 ancestor of THE APARTMENT, with Simon's flat becoming a madhouse. Retitled: AND SO THEY WERE MARRIED.▶

Johnny Doughboy (1942) **64m.** **½ D: John H. Auer. Jane Withers, Henry Wilcoxon, William Demarest, Ruth Donnelly, Etta McDaniel. Jane plays an adolescent movie star who wants to break out of her little-girl roles and a lookalike fan who switches places with her. Most interesting aspect of this B-movie musical is its casting of former child actors as themselves, including Bobby Breen, Cora Sue Collins, Robert Coogan, Baby Sandy, and *Our Gang*'s Spanky McFarland and "Alfalfa" Switzer, who sing a Sammy Cahn–Jule Styne song about being all washed up!

Johnny Eager (1941) **107m.** *** D: Mervyn LeRoy. Robert Taylor, Lana Turner, Edward Arnold, Van Heflin, Robert Sterling, Patricia Dane, Glenda Farrell, Barry Nelson. Slick MGM melodrama with convoluted plot about sociology student (and daughter of D.A. Arnold) Turner falling in love with unscrupulous racketeer Taylor. Heflin won Best Supporting Actor Oscar as Taylor's alcoholic friend.▼▶

Johnny Guitar (1954) **C-110m.** ***½ D: Nicholas Ray. Joan Crawford, Sterling Hayden, Scott Brady, Mercedes McCambridge, Ward Bond, Ben Cooper, Ernest Borgnine, Royal Dano, John Carradine, Paul Fix, Frank Ferguson. The screen's great kinky Western, a memorable confrontation between saloonkeeper Crawford and righteous hellion McCambridge, who wants her run out of town and/or hanged. Simply fascinating with symbolism rampant throughout. Script by Philip Yordan. Later a stage musical.▼▶

Johnny Holiday (1949) **92m.** *** D: Willis Goldbeck. William Bendix, Allen Martin, Jr., Stanley Clements, Jack Hagen, Hoagy Carmichael, Buddy Cole. Remarkably sincere study of juvenile delinquent torn between friends from dishonest past and those trying to help him at reform farm. Filmed in Indiana.▼

Johnny in the Clouds SEE: **Way to the Stars, The**

Johnny Nobody (1961-British) **88m. ***** D: Nigel Patrick. Nigel Patrick, Yvonne Mitchell, Aldo Ray, William Bendix, Cyril Cusack. Irish priest suspects murder when drunken author is killed. Unusual plot twists with religious overtones. Neat, well-made little thriller. Warwickscope. ▼

Johnny O'Clock (1947) **95m. **½** D: Robert Rossen. Dick Powell, Evelyn Keyes, Lee J. Cobb, Ellen Drew, Nina Foch, S. Thomas Gomez, John Kellogg, Jim Bannon, Mabel Paige, Phil Brown, Jeff Chandler. Title character (Powell), a slick gambling club overseer and night owl, finds himself a prime suspect in a couple of murders. Slightly above-average noir is distinguished by Powell's solid presence and some sharp, tough dialogue by screenwriter Rossen, making his directing debut.▶

Johnny One-Eye (1950) **78m. **** D: Robert Florey. Pat O'Brien, Wayne Morris, Dolores Moran, Gayle Reed. Schmaltzy Damon Runyon yarn of O'Brien, a gangster with a heart of gold, on the lam.▼▶

Johnny Rocco (1958) **84m. **** D: Paul Landres. Richard Eyer, Stephen McNally, Coleen Gray, Russ Conway. Gangster's son (Eyer) is focal point of gangland hunt because he witnessed a killing; OK drama.

Johnny Shiloh (1963) **C-90m. **½** D: James Neilson. Kevin Corcoran, Brian Keith, Darryl Hickman, Skip Homeier. Young Corcoran leaves his family and tags along with Civil War Army led by Keith. Set-bound adventure, but well acted and easy to watch. Originally shown in two parts on the Disney TV show.▶

Johnny Stool Pigeon (1949) **76m. **½** D: William Castle. Howard Duff, Shelley Winters, Dan Duryea, Anthony (Tony) Curtis. Standard drama of convict being sprung from prison so he can lead federal agents to former gang members.

Johnny Tremain (1957) **C-80m. ***** D: Robert Stevenson. Hal Stalmaster, Luana Patten, Jeff York, Sebastian Cabot, Dick Beymer, Walter Sande. Excellent Disney film, from Esther Forbes' novel about a young boy who gets involved in the Revolutionary War; sprinkles fiction with fact to bring history to life.▼▶

Johnny Trouble (1957) **80m. **½** D: John H. Auer. Ethel Barrymore, Cecil Kellaway, Carolyn Jones, Stuart Whitman, Jesse White, Jack Larson. Tender story of elderly Barrymore, convinced that her long-missing son will return and that he wasn't a bad boy. Ethel's final film. Remake of SOMEONE TO REMEMBER.

John Paul Jones (1959) **C-126m. **½** D: John Farrow. Robert Stack, Marisa Pavan, Charles Coburn, Erin O'Brien, Macdonald Carey, Jean-Pierre Aumont, Peter Cushing, Bruce Cabot, Bette Davis. Empty spectacle of 18th-century American naval hero, with cameo by Davis as Russian empress, Catherine the Great. Look for Mia Farrow (daughter of film's director and Maureen O'Sullivan) in film debut. Technirama.▼▶

Johnstown Flood, The (1926) **70m. **½** D: Irving Cummings. George O'Brien, Florence Gilbert, Janet Gaynor, Anders Randolf. Silent-era disaster film, and no worse than a lot of newer ones; compactly told, with still-dazzling special effects. Gaynor's first feature-length movie. Look fast for Carole Lombard as a bridesmaid, and look closely for Clark Gable in the bar scene.

Joker Is Wild, The (1957) **126m. ***** D: Charles Vidor. Frank Sinatra, Mitzi Gaynor, Jeanne Crain, Eddie Albert, Beverly Garland, Jackie Coogan, Sophie Tucker. Sinatra is fine in biography of nightclub performer Joe E. Lewis, with Crain and Gaynor diverting as his two loves. Cahn and Van Heusen song "All the Way" won an Oscar; in fact, the film was reissued as ALL THE WAY. VistaVision.

Jolly Bad Fellow, A (1964-British) **94m. **** D: Don Chaffey. Leo McKern, Janet Munro, Maxine Audley, Duncan MacRae. Peculiar yarn of college professor who plays God by trying to kill those people whom he feels are evil parasites; strange blend of drama-satire. Retitled: THEY ALL DIED LAUGHING.

Jolson Sings Again (1949) **C-96m. **½** D: Henry Levin. Larry Parks, Barbara Hale, William Demarest, Ludwig Donath, Tamara Shayne. Attempt to continue THE JOLSON STORY only partially succeeds, and is a curio at best . . . especially when Parks (playing Jolson) meets Parks (playing Parks). Jolson standards ("Baby Face," "Sonny Boy," "Back in Your Own Back Yard," and many others) are still great.▼▶

Jolson Story, The (1946) **C-128m. ***½** D: Alfred E. Green. Larry Parks, Evelyn Keyes, William Demarest, Bill Goodwin, Ludwig Donath, Tamara Shayne. Hokey but very entertaining biography of all-time great Al Jolson, with Parks giving his all in story of brash vaudeville performer's rise in the show biz world. Songs: "April Showers," "Avalon," "You Made Me Love You," "My Mammy" plus many others, all dubbed by Jolson; that's the real Jolson in long shot on the runway during the "Swanee" sequence. Morris Stoloff earned an Oscar for his scoring. Sequel: JOLSON SINGS AGAIN.▼▶

Joseph and His Brethren (1962) **C-103m. **** D: Irving Rapper. Marietto, Geoffrey Horne, Belinda Lee, Finlay Currie, Antonio Segurini, Charles Borromel, Carlo Giustini. Juvenile biblical tale, lavishly produced but empty-headed. Totalscope.▼▶

Josette (1938) **73m. *½** D: Allan Dwan. Don Ameche, Simone Simon, Robert Young,

Bert Lahr, Joan Davis, Tala Birell, Paul Hurst, William Collier, Sr., Lynn Bari, William Demarest. Idiotic romance about two very different brothers (Ameche and Young); they become involved with virtuous Simon, who's been forced to impersonate a famous chanteuse. Lahr and Davis are wasted. Among the forgettable songs: "May I Drop a Petal in Your Glass of Wine."

Jour de Fete (1949-French) **70m.** ***½ D: Jacques Tati. Jacques Tati, Guy Decomble, Paul Frankeur, Santa Relli, Maine Vallee, Roger Rafal. In this exquisite feature-film directorial debut French comedian/mime Tati plays a postman whose attempts to modernize delivery link up a series of delightful gags built around a small town's Bastille Day celebration. Tati's cleverness and timing make him one of the most accomplished cinematic comedians since Buster Keaton. Originally filmed in color, but released in b&w with color tinting. Restored to its original color version in 1997. Some prints run 87m. Aka THE BIG DAY. ▼○)

Journal of a Crime (1934) **65m.** **½ D: William Keighley. Ruth Chatterton, Adolphe Menjou, Claire Dodd, George Barbier, Douglass Dumbrille, Henry O'Neill, Walter Pidgeon. Chatterton shoots hubby Menjou's mistress in a jealous rage and an innocent man is arrested for the crime. Then she loses her memory in an accident while en route to make a confession. Outlandish but quite watchable melodrama with a most unusual pre-Code ending.

Journey, The (1959) C-**125m.** *** D: Anatole Litvak. Deborah Kerr, Yul Brynner, Jason Robards, Jr., Robert Morley, E. G. Marshall, Anne Jackson, Ronny Howard, Kurt Kasznar, Gérard Oury, Anouk Aimée. Colorful and unexpected events (including romance) surround a group of Westerners as they attempt to leave Budapest after the Soviet uprising in 1956. Glossy drama marked feature-film debuts of Robards and young Howard. ▶)

Journey Beneath the Desert (1961-French-Italian) C-**105m.** **½ D: Edgar G. Ulmer. Haya Harareet, Jean-Louis Trintignant, Rad Fulton, Amedeo Nazzari, Georges Riviere, Giulia Rubini. Enjoyable hokum in which three mining engineers find themselves trapped in the Lost City of Atlantis, located beneath the Sahara Desert (as well as smack dab in the middle of a nuclear testing site). Aka L'ATLANTIDE. Previously filmed in 1921, 1932, and 1948 (as SIREN OF ATLANTIS). Technirama. ▶)

Journey for Margaret (1942) **81m.** *** D: W. S. Van Dyke II. Robert Young, Laraine Day, Fay Bainter, Nigel Bruce, Margaret O'Brien, William Severn. Heartfelt WW2 drama about American journalist Young developing an attachment to children orphaned in London bombings. ▼)

Journey into Autumn SEE: **Dreams**

Journey into Fear (1942) **69m.** *** D: Norman Foster. Orson Welles, Joseph Cotten, Dolores Del Rio, Ruth Warrick, Agnes Moorehead, Everett Sloane, Jack Moss, Hans Conried. Often baffling WW2 spy drama started by Welles, taken out of his hands. Much of tale of smuggling munitions into Turkey still exciting. Cotten and Welles scripted this adaptation of the Eric Ambler novel. Remade in 1975. Also shown in computer-colored version. ▼○

Journey into Light (1951) **87m.** **½ D: Stuart Heisler. Sterling Hayden, Viveca Lindfors, Thomas Mitchell, H. B. Warner, Ludwig Donath. Thought-provoking theme, poorly paced; Hayden is clergyman who finds his belief in God again with aid of blind Lindfors.

Journey's End (1930-British-U.S.) **125m.** **½ D: James Whale. Colin Clive, Ian MacLaren, David Manners, Billy Bevan, Anthony Bushell, Robert Adair, Charles Gerrard. Whale's first film is a stagy early-talkie adaptation of R. C. Sherriff's play set in the British trenches behind enemy lines during WW1, as a group of stiff-upper-lip officers crack up while waiting for the next big attack. Historically valuable as a record of a famous theater piece, but extremely slow and veddy British. Whale evidently saved all his visual bravado for his next film with Clive, FRANKENSTEIN.

Journey to Freedom (1957) **60m.** *½ D: Robert C. Dertano. Jacques Scott, Geneviève Aumont, Morgan Lane, Fred Kohler, Jr., Don Marlowe, Tor Johnson. Lukewarm spy hunt, with Communist agents tracking down pro-American Scott, a refugee who's come to the U.S. ▶

Journey Together (1945-British) **95m.** **½ D: John Boulting. Richard Attenborough, Jack Watling, Edward G. Robinson, Bessie Love, David Tomlinson, John Justin, George Cole, Ronald Squire, Hugh Wakefield, Sebastian Shaw. Documentary-like chronicle of wannabe R.A.F. pilots Attenborough and Watling, and their training in England and the U.S. during WW2. Robinson is on hand in a supporting role as one of the flight instructors. Most of those involved with the film's production were then R.A.F. members. Boulting also scripted, based on a story by Terence Rattigan. ▼

Journey to Italy SEE: **Strangers**

Journey to the Center of the Earth (1959) C-**132m.** *** D: Henry Levin. James Mason, Pat Boone, Arlene Dahl, Diane Baker, Thayer David, Alan Napier. Entertaining, old-fashioned fantasy-adventure, from Jules Verne's story of daring expedition headed by Mason; long in telling, with silly digressions, but generally fun. Remade in 1999 (for TV), 2008, and as WHERE TIME BEGAN. Best enjoyed in CinemaScope. ▼○)

Journey to the Lost City SEE: **Indian Tomb, The** and **Tiger of Eschnapur, The**

Journey to the Seventh Planet (1961-Danish) **C-83m.** *½ D: Sidney Pink. John Agar, Greta Thyssen, Ann Smyrner, Mimi Heinrich, Carl Ottosen. In year 2001, expedition to Uranus discovers hostile alien brain that can turn thoughts into reality. Cheap, clumsy, dull, with just a smidge of imagination. ▼●)

Joy House (1964-French) **98m.** **½ D: René Clement. Jane Fonda, Alain Delon, Lola Albright, Sorrell Booke. Living on his looks, a playboy on the run seeks refuge in gloomy French mansion run by two American women. Fate and quicker wits than his control this brooding tale of irony. Aka THE LOVE CAGE. Franscope. ▼●

Joy in the Morning (1965) **C-103m.** ** D: Alex Segal. Richard Chamberlain, Yvette Mimieux, Arthur Kennedy, Sidney Blackmer. Betty Smith's gentle novel of struggling law student and his marital problems becomes mild vehicle for Chamberlain, who crusades for human dignity amid stereotypes of a college town.

Joyless Street, The (1925-German) **96m.** *** D: G.W. Pabst. Asta Nielsen, Greta Garbo, Werner Krauss, Valeska Gert, Jaro Furth, Agnes Esterhazy, Einar Hanson. Fascinating, expressionistic account of economic and moral decay, focusing on the inhabitants of one sorry Viennese street after WW1. Garbo, in her third feature, plays a professor's daughter who attempts to keep her family from starving. Many varied versions of this oft-edited title exist. Aka THE STREET OF SORROW. ▼●

Joy of Living (1938) **90m.** *** D: Tay Garnett. Irene Dunne, Douglas Fairbanks, Jr., Alice Brady, Guy Kibbee, Jean Dixon, Eric Blore, Lucille Ball. Delightful screwball musicomedy with gay-blade Fairbanks wooing singing star Dunne. ▼●

Joy of Loving SEE: School for Love

Joy Ride (1958) **60m.** *½ D: Edward Bernds. Rad Fulton, Ann Doran, Regis Toomey, Nicholas King, Robert Levin. Minor account of middle-aged man trying to reform hot-rod gang members; occasionally bristling.

Juarez (1939) **132m.** *** D: William Dieterle. Paul Muni, Bette Davis, Brian Aherne, Claude Rains, John Garfield, Gale Sondergaard, Donald Crisp, Gilbert Roland, Louis Calhern, Grant Mitchell. Interesting biography of Mexican leader (Muni), with unforgettable performance by Rains as Napoleon III; also notable is Garfield's offbeat casting as Mexican General Diaz. Elaborately done, but never as inspiring as it's intended to be. ▼●

Jubal (1956) **C-101m.** *** D: Delmer Daves. Glenn Ford, Ernest Borgnine, Rod Steiger, Valerie French, Felicia Farr, Noah Beery, Jr., Charles Bronson. It's Bard in the Saddle with this Western *Othello*: when jealous rancher Borgnine seeks some love-making advice from cowhand Ford, along comes Steiger hinting that Ford's giving Borgnine's wife (French) a few "lessons" as well. Brooding, intense drama is pretty good on its own terms, more intriguing if you know the original. CinemaScope. ▼●

Jubilee Trail (1954) **C-103m.** **½ D: Joseph Inman Kane. Vera Ralston, Joan Leslie, Forrest Tucker, John Russell, Ray Middleton, Pat O'Brien, Buddy Baer, Jim Davis, Barton MacLane, Richard Webb, Jack Elam. Expansive Republic Western vehicle for Ralston as on-the-lam chanteuse who heads for California and becomes involved in the lives of an assortment of characters. ▼

Judas Was a Woman SEE: La Bête Humaine

Judge, The (1949) **69m.** ** D: Elmer Clifton. Milburn Stone, Katherine de Mille, Paul Guilfoyle, Stanley Waxman, Norman Budd, Jonathan Hale, John Hamilton. Well-intentioned but muddled low-budget melodrama chronicling the fate of Stone, a clever criminal attorney who gets his clients off on legal technicalities. Dreadful musical accompaniment is no help. ▼●

Judge Hardy and Son (1939) **91m.** **½ D: George B. Seitz. Lewis Stone, Mickey Rooney, Cecilia Parker, Fay Holden, Sara Haden, Ann Rutherford, Maria Ouspenskaya, June Preisser, Martha O'Driscoll. Rather somber Andy Hardy series entry, as the Judge tries to help an elderly couple threatened with eviction while dealing with the personal problems of his wife's illness. Joe Yule, Rooney's father, plays a garageman. ●

Judge Hardy's Children (1938) **78m.** **½ D: George B. Seitz. Lewis Stone, Mickey Rooney, Cecilia Parker, Fay Holden, Ann Rutherford, Betty Ross Clarke, Ruth Hussey. The good Judge has duties in Washington, D.C., where Andy falls for a French diplomat's daughter. Average Andy Hardy entry. ●

Judge Priest (1934) **80m.** ***½ D: John Ford. Will Rogers, Tom Brown, Anita Louise, Henry B. Walthall, Stepin Fetchit, Hattie McDaniel. Exceptional slice of Americana with Rogers as commonsensical yet controversial judge in small town; full of warm and funny character vignettes, including Walthall's stirring courtroom scene. Ford remade it in 1953 as THE SUN SHINES BRIGHT. ▼●

Judge Steps Out, The (1949) **91m.** **½ D: Boris Ingster. Alexander Knox, Ann Sothern, George Tobias, Sharyn Moffett, Frieda Inescourt. Judge Knox runs away from his job and shrewish wife (Inescourt), hides out as a short-order cook, falls in love with Sothern. Cowritten by Alexander Knox and Boris Ingster. ▼●

Judgment at Nuremberg (1961) **178m.** **** D: Stanley Kramer. Spencer Tracy,

Burt Lancaster, Richard Widmark, Marlene Dietrich, Judy Garland, Maximilian Schell, Montgomery Clift, William Shatner. Superior production revolving around U.S. judge Tracy presiding over German war-criminal trials. Schell, who originated the role in Abby Mann's 1959 TV play, won Oscar as defense attorney, as did Mann for his screenplay. Fine performances by Dietrich as widow of German officer, Garland as hausfrau, Clift as unbalanced victim of Nazi atrocities. Runs 186m. with overture, exit music. Later a Broadway play. ▼●

Judith of Bethulia (1914) 47m. *** D: D. W. Griffith. Blanche Sweet, Henry Walthall, Mae Marsh, Robert Harron, Lillian Gish, Dorothy Gish, Kate Bruce, Harry Carey. Considered the first feature-length American movie, this Old Testament story tells the tale of a widow who tries to save her people when Assyrians attack the Judean fortress city of Bethulia. Fairly lavish biblical mini-epic looks like a dry run for parts of INTOLERANCE, with Griffith honing his narrative technique and cinematic style. Running time varies. ●

Juggler, The (1953) 86m. **½ D: Edward Dmytryk. Kirk Douglas, Milly Vitale, Paul Stewart, Alf Kjellin, Beverly Washburn. Sentimental account of Jewish refugee Douglas going to Israel to rebuild his life, overcoming bitterness from life in a concentration camp. Filmed in Israel. ●

Juke Box Rhythm (1959) 81m. *½ D: Arthur Dreifuss. Jo Morrow, Jack Jones, Brian Donlevy, George Jessel, Hans Conried, Karin Booth, Marjorie Reynolds, Fritz Feld, Johnny Otis, The Treniers, The Earl Grant Trio. Perfectly awful minor musical focusing on various schemes of clean-cut young singer Jones. However, Otis does sing "Willie and the Hand Jive."

Juke Girl (1942) 90m. **½ D: Curtis Bernhardt. Ann Sheridan, Ronald Reagan, Richard Whorf, Gene Lockhart, Betty Brewer, Faye Emerson, George Tobias, Alan Hale, Howard da Silva, Donald MacBride, William B. Davidson, Fuzzy Knight, Willie Best. Exploitation of farmers is the subject of this robust Warner Bros. film, which is spoiled by typecasting of the bad guys and a melodramatic script that veers way off-course. It does provide Reagan with one of his most interesting parts, however, as an itinerant worker who becomes a farmers' rights activist(!), battling for underdog Tobias against fat-cat Lockhart. ●

Jules and Jim (1961-French) 104m. **** D: François Truffaut. Jeanne Moreau, Oskar Werner, Henri Serre, Marie Dubois, Vanna Urbino. Truffaut's memorable tale of three people in love, and how the years affect their interrelationships. A film of rare beauty and charm. Screenplay by Truffaut and Jean Gruault, based on novel by Henri-Pierre Roché. Americanized by

Paul Mazursky in WILLIE AND PHIL. Franscope. ▼●

Julia Misbehaves (1948) 99m. *** D: Jack Conway. Greer Garson, Walter Pidgeon, Peter Lawford, Elizabeth Taylor, Cesar Romero, Mary Boland, Nigel Bruce. Bouncy account of showgirl Garson returning to dignified husband Pidgeon when daughter Taylor is about to marry; Romero is fun as bragging acrobat. Stars seem right at home with slapstick situations. ▼●

Julie (1956) 99m. ** D: Andrew L. Stone. Doris Day, Louis Jourdan, Barry Sullivan, Frank Lovejoy, Jack Kelly, Ann Robinson, Jack Kruschen, Mae Marsh. Overbaked soaper in which Day contends with jealous, psychopathic spouse Jourdan, who strangled her first husband and now threatens to kill her. Sometimes tense, but too often unintentionally funny. Also shown in computer-colored version. ▼●

Juliet of the Spirits (1965-Italian) C-148m. *** D: Federico Fellini. Giulietta Masina, Sandra Milo, Mario Pisu, Valentina Cortese, Lou Gilbert, Sylva Koscina. Surrealistic fantasy triggered by wife's fears that her well-to-do husband is cheating on her. A film requiring viewer to delve into woman's psyche via a rash of symbolism; counterbalanced with rich visual delights. ▼●

Julietta (1953-French) 96m. **½ D: Marc Allegret. Jean Marais, Jeanne Moreau, Dany Robin, Denise Grey, Nicole Berger. Frilly comedy in which pert Robin dallies with handsome Marais—even though he's engaged to wed Moreau.

Julius Caesar (1953) 120m. ***½ D: Joseph L. Mankiewicz. Marlon Brando, James Mason, John Gielgud, Louis Calhern, Edmond O'Brien, Greer Garson, Deborah Kerr, George Macready, Michael Pate, Alan Napier, Ian Wolfe, Douglass Dumbrille, Edmund Purdom. Superior adaptation of William Shakespeare's play of political power and honor in ancient Rome. Lavishly produced (by John Houseman), with an excellent cast and Oscar-winning art direction–set decoration. Screenplay by director Mankiewicz. ▼●

July 14th SEE: **Quatorze Juillet**

Jumbo SEE: **Billy Rose's Jumbo**

Jump for Glory (1937-British) 90m. ** D: Raoul Walsh. Douglas Fairbanks, Jr., Valerie Hobson, Alan Hale, Jack Melford, Anthony Ireland, Barbara Everest, Edward Rigby, Esme Percy, Basil Radford, Leo Genn. Fairbanks is suave as a cat burglar who decides to reform after becoming romantically involved with one of his victims (Hobson), unaware that she's engaged to his ex-partner, with whom he still has a score to settle. Disappointingly slow, genteel crime caper, considering it was directed by American action-movie maestro Walsh. U.S. title: WHEN THIEF MEETS THIEF.

Jumping Jacks (1952) **96m.** ****½** D: Norman Taurog. Dean Martin, Jerry Lewis, Mona Freeman, Don DeFore, Robert Strauss. Daffy duo has good opportunity for plenty of sight gags when they join military paratroop squad.▼●▶

Jump Into Hell (1955) **93m.** ****½** D: David Butler. Jacques Sernas, Kurt Kasznar, Peter Van Eyck, Pat Blake. Neatly paced actioner of paratroopers involved in Indochina war. ▶

June Bride (1948) **97m.** ******* D: Bretaigne Windust. Bette Davis, Robert Montgomery, Fay Bainter, Tom Tully, Barbara Bates, Jerome Cowan, Mary Wickes. Flippant comedy of magazine writers Davis and Montgomery inspired by story they are doing on June brides. Breezy script by Ranald MacDougall. Don't blink or you'll miss Debbie Reynolds in her film debut.▼▶

June Moon (1931) **71m.** ****½** D: A. Edward Sutherland. Jack Oakie, Frances Dee, Wynne Gibson, Harry Akst, June MacCloy, Sam Hardy. Oakie is well cast as a country chump in N.Y.C. trying to make it as a lyricist while romancing Dee. Cowritten by Joseph L. Mankiewicz, this version of the Ring Lardner–George S. Kaufman play is an odd but generally amusing mix of naiveté and sophistication, with a colorful depiction of Tin Pan Alley. Real-life songwriter Akst is hilarious as wisecracking pianist Maxie Schwartz. Remade as BLONDE TROUBLE (1937).

June Night (1940-Swedish) **86m.** ****½** D: Per Lindberg. Ingrid Bergman, Olof Widgren, Gunnar Sjöberg, Carl Ström, Marianne Löfgren, Lill-Tollie Zellman, Alf Kjellin. Generally fine performances compensate for melodramatic nature of this soaper, detailing the plight of small-town girl Bergman after she becomes involved with sailor Sjoberg. Bergman's final film before coming to Hollywood.▼●▶

Jungle, The (1952) **74m.** ***½** D: William Berke. Rod Cameron, Cesar Romero, Marie Windsor, Sulochana. Romantic triangle burdens tale of expedition in India that encounters still living mammoths. Shot on location but still dull and pedestrian.

Jungle Book (1942) **C-105m.** ******* D: Zoltan Korda. Sabu, Joseph Calleia, John Qualen, Frank Puglia, Rosemary DeCamp, Noble Johnson. Colorful Kipling fantasy of boy (Sabu) raised by wolves. Exciting family fare, fine Miklos Rozsa score. Remade twice (by Disney).▼●▶

Jungle Captive, The (1945) **63m.** BOMB D: Harold Young. Otto Kruger, Amelita Ward, Phil Brown, Vicky Lane, Jerome Cowan, Rondo Hatton. Sloppy sequel to JUNGLE WOMAN deals with yet another mad scientist's attempt to transform apewoman into beautiful girl. Three strikes and you're out.▼

Jungle Cat (1960) **C-70m.** ****½** D: James Algar. Narrated by Winston Hibler. One of Disney's weaker True-Life Adventures suffers from script and presentation, not raw material: wildlife footage of the title character, a jaguar, is excellent.▼▶

Jungle Cavalcade (1941) **76m.** ****½** D: Clyde Elliot, Armand Denis, Frank Buck. A compilation film of Buck capturing and caging a zooful of wild animals, edited from his first three features (BRING 'EM BACK ALIVE, WHITE CARGO, FANG AND CLAW). Buck's narration is laughably hokey and self-serving, and his attitude will not endear him to animal rights activists . . . but there's still plenty of exciting footage.▼▶

Jungle Fighters SEE: **Long and the Short and the Tall, The**

Jungle Gents (1954) **64m.** ****** D: Edward Bernds. Leo Gorcey, Huntz Hall, David Gorcey, Bennie Bartlett, Patrick O'Moore, Laurette Luez, Bernard Gorcey, David (Gorcey) Condon, Joel Fluellen, Woody Strode. Sach develops the ability to smell diamonds, so the Boys go to Africa to strike it rich in this low-grade romp, shot on leftover sets from BOMBA, THE JUNGLE BOY. Look for a young Clint Walker as Tarzan.▶

Jungle Girl SEE: **Bomba and the Jungle Girl**

Jungle Goddess (1948) **65m.** ***½** D: Lewis D. Collins. Ralph Byrd, George Reeves, Wanda McKay, Armida. Very low-budget jungle saga is good only for laughs.▼▶

Jungle Jim When athletic Johnny Weissmuller left the Tarzan series after 16 years in the role, enterprising producer Sam Katzman proposed a new series that would enable the more mature but still rugged star to cavort in familiar surroundings. It was Jungle Jim, presold to an anxious audience via a successful comic strip and radio show. One critic accurately summed it up as "Tarzan with clothes on." The series was considered sure-fire and performed well at the box office for seven years, despite its almost consistent mediocrity. Aimed primarily at juvenile audiences, most efforts had Jungle Jim helping some Columbia Pictures heroine in distress (a lady scientist seeking a rare drug, a WAC captain lost in the jungle, etc.) and getting tangled up with hostile natives, voodoo curses, and nefarious villains (often all three at once). In the last three films of the series (CANNIBAL ATTACK, JUNGLE MOON MEN, DEVIL GODDESS) the name Jungle Jim was dropped and Weissmuller played himself, but the format remained the same, with Johnny's ever-faithful chimpanzee friend Tamba at his side. (Tamba became Kimba for the last three films when they lost the Jungle Jim name and rights.) Perhaps the highlight of the series was CAPTIVE GIRL, an average entry which had the distinction of Buster Crabbe, whose career

[353]

paralleled Weissmuller's in many ways, as the villain.

JUNGLE JIM

Jungle Jim (1948)
The Lost Tribe (1949)
Captive Girl (1950)
Mark of the Gorilla (1950)
Pygmy Island (1950)
Fury of the Congo (1951)
Jungle Manhunt (1951)
Jungle Jim in the Forbidden Land (1952)
Voodoo Tiger (1952)
Savage Mutiny (1953)
Killer Ape (1953)
Valley of Head Hunters (1953)
Jungle Man-Eaters (1954)
Cannibal Attack (1954)
Jungle Moon Men (1955)
Devil Goddess (1955)

Jungle Jim (1948) **73m.** ** D: William Berke. Johnny Weissmuller, Virginia Grey, George Reeves, Lita Baron, Rick Vallin, Holmes Herbert. Weissmuller leads a perilous expedition to find a miracle drug, accompanied by scientist Grey and pre-*Superman* Reeves in this initial adventure. Not as bizarre as what would follow.▼▶
Jungle Jim in the Forbidden Land (1952) **65m.** *½ D: Lew Landers. Johnny Weissmuller, Angela Greene, Jean Willes, Lester Matthews, William Tannen. Weissmuller unwillingly leads an anthropologist to the land of the giant people (with the aid of some cheap stock footage) in this ridiculous entry.
Jungle Man-Eaters (1954) **68m.** *½ D: Lee Sholem. Johnny Weissmuller, Karin Booth, Richard Stapley, Bernard (Bernie) Hamilton, Gregory Gay, Lester Matthews. Jungle Jim vs. diamond smugglers. Hohum. Last of the official *Jungle Jim* entries, with Weissmuller using his real name in the final three adventures.▶
Jungle Manhunt (1951) **66m.** *½ D: Lew Landers. Johnny Weissmuller, Bob Waterfield, Sheila Ryan, Rick Vallin, Lyle Talbot. Real-life gridiron hero Waterfield plays a footballer who has become leader of a small jungle tribe besieged by marauding "skeleton men." Never fear, *Jungle Jim* Weissmuller is on the case.▶
Jungle Moon Men (1955) **70m.** *½ D: Charles S. Gould. Johnny Weissmuller, Jean Byron, Helene Stanton, Bill Henry, Myron Healey, Billy Curtis. Enjoyably bad grade-Z ripoff of SHE, about an eternally young high priestess (Stanton).▶
Jungle Princess, The (1936) **85m.** *** D: William Thiele. Dorothy Lamour, Ray Milland, Akim Tamiroff, Lynne Overman, Molly Lamont, Mala, Hugh Buckler. Lamour (in her first sarong role) grows up Tarzan-style in the Malayan wilds, falls in love with lost tiger hunter Milland. Ro-

mantic jungle adventure is nicely juiced-up action-wise with stock footage from CHANG et al.
Jungle Woman (1944) **60m.** *½ D: Reginald LeBorg. Acquanetta, Evelyn Ankers, J. Carrol Naish, Samuel S. Hinds. Psychiatrist fails to cure killer-ape tendencies of Acquanetta in this sorry sequel to CAPTIVE WILD WOMAN. Tries to emulate the style of Val Lewton's classy horror movies, even keeps ape-woman off-camera (until final shot). Followed by THE JUNGLE CAPTIVE.▼▶
Junior Miss (1945) **94m.** **½ D: George Seaton. Peggy Ann Garner, Allyn Joslyn, Michael Dunne, Faye Marlowe, Mona Freeman, Sylvia Field, Barbara Whiting, Mel Tormé. Naive but entertaining comedy of teenager Garner and harried father Joslyn, based on Broadway play by Jerome Chodorov and Joseph Fields (from Sally Benson's stories).▶
Juno and the Paycock (1930-British) **96m.** ** D: Alfred Hitchcock. Sara Allgood, Edward Chapman, Sidney Morgan, Maire O'Neill, John Laurie, Dennis Wyndham, John Longden. Faithful but dull, stagebound adaptation (by Hitchcock and Alma Reville) of Sean O'Casey's play about a poor Dublin family's travails during the civil war. The straightforward material defeats the director; however, Allgood is a standout as Juno. That's Barry Fitzgerald as "The Orator," in his screen debut.▼▶
Jupiter's Darling (1955) **C-96m.** **½ D: George Sidney. Esther Williams, Howard Keel, George Sanders, Marge and Gower Champion, Norma Varden. Lavish musical of Robert Sherwood's *Road to Rome*, which bogs down in tedium: Williams is temptress who dallies with Hannibal (Keel) to prevent attack on Rome. CinemaScope.▼◉▶
Just Across the Street (1952) **78m.** ** D: Joseph Pevney. Ann Sheridan, John Lund, Cecil Kellaway, Natalie Schafer, Harvey Lembeck. Mild shenanigans with working-woman Sheridan being mistaken for wealthy estate owner.
Just a Gigolo (1931) **66m.** ** D: Jack Conway. William Haines, Irene Purcell, C. Aubrey Smith, Charlotte Granville, Lilian Bond, Maria Alba, Ray Milland. Haines is a philandering British lord who pretends to be a gigolo in order to see if he can seduce the woman whom his rich uncle has chosen for him to marry. Would-be sophisticated froth whose attempts at "naughtiness" mainly fall flat.
Just Around the Corner (1938) **70m.** ** D: Irving Cummings. Shirley Temple, Joan Davis, Charles Farrell, Amanda Duff, Bill Robinson, Bert Lahr, Claude Gillingwater. Simpleminded corn with Shirley single-handedly ending the Depression, manipulating pessimistic tycoon Gillingwater into creating new jobs. But the musical numbers with Robinson are still a delight. Also shown in computer-colored version.▼▶

Just Before Dawn (1946) 66m. **½ D: William Castle. Warner Baxter, Adelle Roberts, Martin Kosleck, Mona Barrie, Marvin Miller, Charles D. Brown, Craig Reynolds. Dr. Ordway (Baxter) is tricked into giving a fatal injection to one of his patients and won't rest until he catches the real culprits in this dark and moody *Crime Doctor* entry.

Just for Fun (1963-British) 85m. *½ D: Gordon Flemyng. Mark Wynter, Cherry Roland, Richard Vernon, Reginald Beckwith, John Wood, Bobby Vee, The Crickets, Freddie Cannon, Johnny Tillotson, Ketty Lester, The Tremeloes. A wisp of a plot—teens establish their own political party to run a pop election—surrounds this forgettable musical trifle. Among the more recognizable tunes are "The Night Has a Thousand Eyes" (Bobby Vee) and "Keep on Dancin'" (The Tremeloes). ▶

Just for You (1952) C-104m. *** D: Elliott Nugent. Bing Crosby, Jane Wyman, Ethel Barrymore, Bob Arthur, Natalie Wood, Cora Witherspoon, Regis Toomey. Zesty musical of producer Crosby who can't be bothered with his growing children, till Wyman shows him the way. Pleasant Harry Warren–Leo Robin score, highlighted by "Zing a Little Zong." Based on Stephen Vincent Benet novel *Famous*. ▼●▶

Just Imagine (1930) 109m. *½ D: David Butler. El Brendel, Maureen O'Sullivan, John Garrick, Marjorie White, Frank Albertson, Hobart Bosworth. Famous but utterly disappointing sci-fi musical set in 1980, with Brendel, officially dead since 1930, suddenly revived and unable to get used to phenomenal changes in living. Futuristic sets, gags, costumes made tremendous impression on everyone who saw film in 1930, but alas, it doesn't wear well at all. Songs by DeSylva-Brown-Henderson.

Just Off Broadway (1942) 66m. ** D: Herbert I. Leeds. Lloyd Nolan, Marjorie Weaver, Phil Silvers, Janis Carter. Acceptable Michael Shayne caper, with swanky dame on trial for murder; outcome is easy for mystery fans. ▶

Just Pals (1920) 55m. *** D: Jack (John) Ford. Buck Jones, Helen Ferguson, George (E.) Stone, Duke R. Lee, William Buckley, Edwin Booth Tilton. Jones plays the town loafer who's so lazy and shiftless that, as one title card puts it, "just watching people makes him tired." He changes his ways when he falls in love and befriends a troubled young boy who drifts into town. Genial, charming silent film shows why Jones became a star. ▶

Just This Once (1952) 90m. **½ D: Don Weis. Janet Leigh, Peter Lawford, Lewis Stone, Marilyn Erskine, Richard Anderson. Cute little comedy of stern Leigh in charge of playboy Lawford's dwindling fortunes, and their inevitable romance.

Just Tony (1922) 58m. **½ D: Lynn Reynolds. Tom Mix, Claire Adams, J. P. Lockney, Duke Lee, Frank Campeau. Amiable Tom Mix Western sheds spotlight on his beloved horse Tony, tracing his life from mistreated mustang to benevolent protector of cowboy Mix. ▼▶

Juvenile Jungle (1958) 69m. *½ D: William Witney. Corey Allen, Rebecca Welles, Richard Bakalyan, Anne Whitfield, Joe Di Reda, Joe Conley, Walter Coy. Plodding crime caper with hep-cat punk Allen planning to kidnap wealthy Welles but going straight when he falls for her, which doesn't sit too well with his cohorts. Humdrum attempt by Republic to crash the sex-and-sin 1950s teen market. Naturama.

Kameradschaft (1931-German) 93m. ***½ D: G. W. Pabst. Fritz Kampers, Alexander Granach, Ernst Busch, Elisabeth Wendt, Gustav Püttjer, Andrée Ducret. Heartfelt, ultra-realistic account of a mining accident that occurred near the Franco-German perimeter in 1906, and what happens when German miners dig underneath the border in an attempt to rescue their French brethren. Filled with drama, irony, symbolism, and a huge dose of humanity. It should be contrasted to the content of Pabst's WEST-FRONT 1918. ▼

Kanal (1956-Polish) 97m. ***½ D: Andrzej Wajda. Teresa Izewska, Tadeusz Janczar, Wienczylaw Glinski, Wladyslaw (Vladek) Sheybal. Intense, almost unrelentingly graphic account of the final days of the September, 1944, Warsaw uprising in Nazi-occupied Poland. This is the second of Wajda's war trilogy, after A GENERATION and before ASHES AND DIAMONDS. Aka THEY LOVED LIFE. Not shown in U.S. until 1961. ▼▶

Kangaroo: The Australian Story (1952) C-84m. ** D: Lewis Milestone. Maureen O'Hara, Peter Lawford, Finlay Currie, Richard Boone. Uninspired blend of romance and adventure, salvaged by good on-location Australian landscapes and fetching O'Hara. Released as KANGAROO. ▼▶

Kansan, The (1943) 79m. **½ D: George Archainbaud. Richard Dix, Jane Wyatt, Victor Jory, Albert Dekker, Eugene Pallette, Robert Armstrong. Zippy Western, with Dix becoming town hero, taming outlaws, but facing more trouble with corrupt town official. ▼▶

Kansas City Confidential (1952) 98m. *** D: Phil Karlson. John Payne, Coleen Gray, Preston Foster, Neville Brand, Lee Van Cleef, Jack Elam, Dona Drake. Tough action drama with hard-luck ex-con Payne implicated in a bank heist, determined to quite literally unmask the real culprits. Quentin Tarantino must have seen this one prior to scripting RESERVOIR DOGS! ▼▶

Kansas City Kitty (1944) **71m.** ** D: Del Lord. Joan Davis, Bob Crosby, Jane Frazee, Erik Rolf. Programmer sparked by Davis, involved in purchase of song-publishing company on the skids.

Kansas Pacific (1953) **C-73m.** ** D: Ray Nazarro. Sterling Hayden, Eve Miller, Barton MacLane, Reed Hadley, Irving Bacon. Inoffensive account of building of title railway during 1860s, with Reb soldiers trying to prevent its completion.▼●▶

Kansas Raiders (1950) **C-80m.** ** D: Ray Enright. Audie Murphy, Brian Donlevy, Marguerite Chapman, Scott Brady, Tony Curtis, Richard Arlen, Richard Long, James Best, Dewey Martin, Richard Egan. Fair Civil War Western with young Jesse James and company joining Quantrill's Raiders, who are portrayed as a vigilante group more concerned with killing and looting than fighting Northern soldiers. Most interesting are the depictions of Jesse (Murphy) as a good-boy-gone-bad and Quantrill (Donlevy) as a megalomaniac.▶

Kathleen (1941) **88m.** ** D: Harold S. Bucquet. Shirley Temple, Herbert Marshall, Laraine Day, Gail Patrick, Felix Bressart. Predictable story of neglected daughter Temple bringing widower father Marshall and Day together. ▶

Kathy O' (1958) **C-99m.** **½ D: Jack Sher. Dan Duryea, Jan Sterling, Patty McCormack, Mary Fickett, Sam Levene, Mary Jane Croft, Walter Woolf King, Joseph Sargent. Sluggish frolic of temperamental child star McCormack and her desperate public relations agent Duryea. CinemaScope.

Katie Did It (1951) **81m.** **½ D: Frederick de Cordova. Ann Blyth, Mark Stevens, Cecil Kellaway, Jesse White. Blyth is perkier than usual as square New England librarian who becomes hep when romanced by swinging New Yorker Stevens.

Kean (1924-French) **136m.** ** D: Alexandre Volkoff. Ivan Mosjoukine, Nicolas Koline, Nathalie Lissenko, Kenelm Foss, Mary Odette, Georges Deneubourg, Otto Detlefsen. Overlong, melodramatic biopic of flamboyant, egocentric Edmund Kean (Mosjoukine), England's premier Shakespearean actor during the early 19th century, spotlighting the trouble he encounters when he falls for a Danish countess of a higher social rank. Comic asides are more silly than funny and the endless quotes from Shakespeare quickly lose their power. Partially based on an Alexandre Dumas play. Full title is: KEAN, OR WILDNESS AND GENIUS. Aka EDMUND KEAN: PRINCE AMONG LOVERS.▶

Keep 'Em Flying (1941) **86m.** **½ D: Arthur Lubin. Bud Abbott, Lou Costello, Carol Bruce, Martha Raye, William Gargan, Dick Foran. Good A&C mixed in with clichéd plot of stunt pilot Foran unable to accustom himself to Air Force discipline. Raye is fun playing twins.▼●▶

Keep 'Em Rolling (1934) **69m.** **½ D: George Archainbaud. Walter Huston, Frances Dee, Minna Gombell, Frank Conroy, G. Pat Collins, Robert Shayne. Effective, sentimental tale about hell-raising soldier Huston's devotion to a wild stallion he tames, which later saves his life during WW1. Hokey material is greatly enhanced by Huston's performance and comes off as oddly touching and memorable.

Keep 'Em Slugging (1943) **60m.** ** D: Christy Cabanne. Bobby Jordan, Huntz Hall, Gabriel Dell, Norman Abbott, Evelyn Ankers, Elyse Knox, Frank Albertson, Don Porter, Shemp Howard. Jordan takes over the Little Tough Guys from Billy Halop, as a clerk in a shipping company beset by hijackers.▼

Keeper of the Flame (1943) **100m.** *** D: George Cukor. Spencer Tracy, Katharine Hepburn, Richard Whorf, Margaret Wycherly, Forrest Tucker, Frank Craven, Audrey Christie, Horace (Stephen) McNally, Darryl Hickman, Howard da Silva, Donald Meek. Reporter Tracy sets out to write the true story of a beloved, just-deceased American patriot. Dated, somewhat heavy-handed treatment of a still-timely theme: the pitfalls of blind hero worship. Scripted by Donald Ogden Stewart, with some interesting echoes of CITIZEN KANE.▼●▶

Keep It Cool SEE: **Let's Rock!**

Keep Your Powder Dry (1945) **93m.** ** D: Edward Buzzell. Lana Turner, Laraine Day, Susan Peters, Agnes Moorehead, Bill Johnson, Natalie Schafer, Lee Patrick, Jess Barker, June Lockhart. Hackneyed tale of playgirl Turner, by-the-book Day, and soldier's wife Peters, and their exploits as they join the WACS during WW2.▶

Kelly and Me (1957) **C-86m** ** D: Robert Z. Leonard. Van Johnson, Piper Laurie, Martha Hyer, Onslow Stevens. Johnson is unsuccessful hoofer who hits movie big-time with talented dog for partner. Mild musical. CinemaScope.

Kelly the Second (1936) **70m.** **½ D: Gus Meins. Patsy Kelly, Guinn "Big Boy" Williams, Charley Chase, Pert Kelton, Edward Brophy, Harold Huber, Maxie Rosenbloom, Billy Gilbert, Syd Saylor, Carl "Alfalfa" Switzer. Kelly attempts to turn brawny truck driver Williams into a championship boxer. Amiable if unmemorable slapstick farce marked comedy producer Hal Roach's attempt to create a feature-film showcase for his short-subject stars Kelly and Chase.

Kennel Murder Case, The (1933) **73m.** ***½ D: Michael Curtiz. William Powell, Mary Astor, Eugene Pallette, Ralph Morgan, Helen Vinson, Jack LaRue, Robert Barrat, Arthur Hohl, Paul Cavanagh. The definitive *Philo Vance* mystery, about an apparent suicide which Vance believes was really murder, tied to intrigue among rivals competing in a

Long Island dog show. Stylish direction and photography and a fine cast make this top-notch by any standard.▼●◗

Kentuckian, The (1955) **C-104m.** **½ D: Burt Lancaster. Burt Lancaster, Diana Lynn, Dianne Foster, Walter Matthau, John McIntire, Una Merkel, John Carradine. Minor but spirited frontier adventure set in 1820s with Lancaster (doing double duty as star and director) traveling to Texas with his son, hoping to start new life. Based on Felix Holt's novel *The Gabriel Horn.* Matthau's film debut. CinemaScope.▼●◗

Kentucky (1938) **C-95m.** *** D: David Butler. Loretta Young, Richard Greene, Walter Brennan, Douglass Dumbrille, Karen Morley, Moroni Olsen, Russell Hicks. Lushly filmed story of rival horsebreeding families in blue-grass country, with lovers Young and Greene clinching at finale. Brennan won Best Supporting Actor Oscar.▼◗

Kentucky Kernels (1934) **75m.** *** D: George Stevens. Bert Wheeler, Robert Woolsey, Mary Carlisle, Spanky McFarland, Noah Beery, Lucille LaVerne. Wheeler & Woolsey take little Spanky into the deep South to collect inheritance, but find themselves in the midst of a family feud. Good vehicle for the team with great slapstick finale.▼●◗

Kentucky Moonshine (1938) **85m.** ** D: David Butler. Tony Martin, Marjorie Weaver, The Ritz Brothers, Slim Summerville, John Carradine. Radio singer Martin's ratings are slipping, so he travels Down South to find new talent; show-biz hopefuls Weaver and The Ritz Brothers pose as hillbillies in order to be discovered. Occasionally zany but mostly thin musical comedy.◗

Kettles in the Ozarks, The (1956) **81m.** **½ D: Charles Lamont. Marjorie Main, Arthur Hunnicutt, Una Merkel, Ted de Corsia, Richard Eyer, David O'Brien, Joe Sawyer, Richard Deacon, Sid Tomack. With Pa now gone, Ma Kettle takes the clan to visit her hillbilly brother-in-law (Hunnicutt). Percy Kilbride is sorely missed, but the cast is peppered with familiar character faces, and Ma's showdown with the backwoods moonshiners is pretty funny.▼◗

Kettles on Old Macdonald's Farm, The (1957) **80m.** *½ D: Virgil Vogel. Marjorie Main, Parker Fennelly, Gloria Talbott, John Smith, Claude Akins, Roy Barcroft, Pat Morrow. Ma Kettle plays matchmaker for a spoiled debutante and a poor lumberman in this weak final series entry, with Fennelly taking over the role of Pa.▼◗

Key, The (1934) **71m.** *** D: Michael Curtiz. William Powell, Edna Best, Colin Clive, Hobart Cavanaugh, Halliwell Hobbes, Donald Crisp, J. M. Kerrigan, Arthur Treacher, Dawn O'Day (Anne Shirley). Atmospheric story set in 1920 as a love triangle unfolds against the backdrop of Ireland under martial law, with England's "Black and Tan" unit dispatched to main-

tain the peace. Good little film with some understated but lovely visual moments.◗

Key, The (1958-British) **125m.** **½ D: Carol Reed. William Holden, Sophia Loren, Trevor Howard, Oscar Homolka, Kieron Moore, Bernard Lee. Jan de Hartog novel becomes pointless romance tale. Loren is disillusioned woman passing out key to her room to series of naval captains during WW2, hoping to make their dangerous lives a little happier. Michael Caine has a small role. CinemaScope.▼●◗

Keyhole, The (1933) **69m.** **½ D: Michael Curtiz. Kay Francis, George Brent, Glenda Farrell, Allen Jenkins, Monroe Owsley, Helen Ware, Henry Kolker. Francis' wealthy older husband suspects her of being unfaithful and hires private eye Brent to shadow her . . . but he falls in love with her and discovers she's being blackmailed by her sleazy first husband. Seedy romantic drama with Francis anguishing in a variety of elegant Orry-Kelly gowns.

Key Largo (1948) **101m.** ***½ D: John Huston. Humphrey Bogart, Edward G. Robinson, Lauren Bacall, Lionel Barrymore, Claire Trevor, Thomas Gomez, Jay Silverheels, Marc Lawrence, Dan Seymour, Harry Lewis. Dandy cast in adaptation of Maxwell Anderson's play about tough gangster (Robinson) holding people captive in Florida hotel during tropical storm. Trevor won Best Supporting Actress Oscar as Robinson's boozy moll. Script by Huston and Richard Brooks. Score by Max Steiner. Also shown in computer-colored version.▼●◗

Key Man (1954) **78m.** **½ D: Paul Guilfoyle. Angela Lansbury, Keith Andes, Brian Keith. Competent little picture about illicit love affair leading to mysterious accidents involving Lansbury's architect husband.

Keys of the Kingdom, The (1944) **137m.** *** D: John M. Stahl. Gregory Peck, Thomas Mitchell, Vincent Price, Edmund Gwenn, Roddy McDowall, Cedric Hardwicke, Peggy Ann Garner. Peck is fine in this long but generally good film about missionary's life (played as boy by McDowall); from A. J. Cronin novel.▼●◗

Key to the City (1950) **101m.** **½ D: George Sidney. Clark Gable, Loretta Young, Frank Morgan, Marilyn Maxwell, Raymond Burr, James Gleason. Bland romance between Gable and Young, two mayors who meet at convention in San Francisco.▼◗

Key Witness (1947) **67m.** **½ D: D. Ross Lederman. John Beal, Trudy Marshall, Jimmy Lloyd, Helen Mowery, Wilton Graff, Barbara Reed, Charles Trowbridge. Henpecked hubby goes out with a pal and two dames, one of whom turns up dead. On the lam, he poses as a tycoon's long-lost son, and is eventually accused of killing him, too! Minor flashback-noir manages to keep one watching as it careens from one crazy twist to another.◗

Key Witness (1960) **82m.** **½ D: Phil Karlson. Jeffrey Hunter, Pat Crowley, Dennis Hopper, Joby Baker, Susan Harrison, Johnny Nash, Corey Allen. Overlong but effective narrative of pressures from street gang on Hunter's family to prevent his wife from testifying in criminal case. CinemaScope. ◗

Khyber Patrol (1954) **C-71m.** ** D: Seymour Friedman. Richard Egan, Dawn Addams, Patric Knowles, Raymond Burr. Cast is above pedestrian film of British officers fighting in India, with usual love conflicts.

Kid, The (1921) **60m.** ***½ D: Charles Chaplin. Charlie Chaplin, Jack (Jackie) Coogan, Edna Purviance, Chuck Reisner, Lita Grey. Chaplin's first real feature mixes slapstick and sentiment in a winning combination, as the Tramp raises a streetwise orphan. Wonderful film launched Coogan as major child star, and it's easy to see why. ▼◗ ◗

Kid Brother, The (1927) **83m.** **** D: Ted Wilde, J. A. Howe. Harold Lloyd, Jobyna Ralston, Walter James, Leo Willis, Olin Francis. Delightfully winning, beautifully filmed silent comedy with Harold as Cinderella-type kid brother in robust all-male family, who gets to prove his mettle in exciting finale where he subdues beefy villain. One of Lloyd's all-time best. ▼◗

Kid Dynamite (1943) **73m.** ** D: Wallace Fox. Leo Gorcey, Huntz Hall, Bobby Jordan, Sunshine Sammy Morrison, Bobby Stone, Gabriel Dell, Pamela Blake, Bennie Bartlett, Dave Durand. Rambunctious *East Side Kids* entry, basically an extended fight between Muggs (Gorcey) and Danny (Jordan). ▼◗

Kid for Two Farthings, A (1955-British) **C-96m.** *** D: Carol Reed. Celia Johnson, Diana Dors, David Kossoff, Jonathan Ashmore, Brenda De Banzie, Primo Carnera, Sidney Tafler, Lou Jacobi. Imaginative fable of a poor little London boy (Ashmore) with a vivid imagination; he looks for a unicorn he believes will work miracles, and finds instead a sick, one-horned goat. Script by Wolf Mankowitz, based on his novel. ▼◗

Kid From Brooklyn, The (1946) **C-113m.** *** D: Norman Z. McLeod. Danny Kaye, Virginia Mayo, Vera-Ellen, Steve Cochran, Eve Arden, Walter Abel, Lionel Stander, Fay Bainter. Comedy of milkman accidentally turned into prizefighter is often overdone but still a funny Kaye vehicle; remake of Harold Lloyd's THE MILKY WAY. ▼◗ ◗

Kid From Cleveland, The (1949) **89m.** *½ D: Herbert Kline. George Brent, Lynn Bari, Rusty (Russ) Tamblyn, Tommy Cook, Ann Doran, Bill Veeck, the Cleveland Indians. Sports reporter Brent becomes involved with troubled (but baseball-crazy) youth Tamblyn. Numbingly awful; of interest solely for the presences of Satchel Paige,

Bob Feller, Tris Speaker, Hank Greenberg, and other baseball immortals.

Kid From Kansas, The (1941) **66m.** *½ D: William Nigh. Leo Carrillo, Andy Devine, Dick Foran, Ann Doran. When a fruit buyer offers ridiculously low prices for planters' crops, competitors take drastic measures; low budget, low quality.

Kid From Kokomo, The (1939) **93m.** *** D: Lewis Seiler. Pat O'Brien, Wayne Morris, Joan Blondell, May Robson, Jane Wyman, Stanley Fields, Maxie Rosenbloom, Sidney Toler, Ed Brophy, Ward Bond. Hayseed boxer Morris won't fight until he finds the mother who abandoned him as a baby; O'Brien is scheming manager who gets him into the ring by hiring gin-soaked kleptomaniac Robson to pose as the old dame. Disarmingly silly riff on LADY FOR A DAY, with Robson once again stealing the show. Based on a story by Dalton Trumbo!

Kid From Left Field, The (1953) **80m.** ** D: Harmon Jones. Dan Dailey, Anne Bancroft, Billy Chapin, Lloyd Bridges, Ray Collins, Richard Egan. Homey little film with Dailey as ex-baseball star turned ballpark vendor who uses his son as cover while trying to turn a losing team around. Remade as 1979 TV movie with Gary Coleman. ◗

Kid From Spain, The (1932) **96m.** *** D: Leo McCarey. Eddie Cantor, Lyda Roberti, Robert Young, Ruth Hall, John Miljan, Stanley Fields. Lavish Cantor musical with Eddie mistaken for famed bullfighter; Roberti is his vivacious leading lady. Striking Busby Berkeley musical numbers; look for Paulette Goddard and Betty Grable in the chorus line. ▼◗

Kid From Texas, The (1950) **C-78m.** ** D: Kurt Neumann. Audie Murphy, Gale Storm, Albert Dekker, Shepperd Strudwick, Will Geer, William Talman, Paul Ford. Slapdash Western, Murphy's first, in which he plays Billy the Kid. He's hired by kindly New Mexico rancher Strudwick, and becomes a victim of circumstance—and an outlaw.

Kid Galahad (1937) **101m.** *** D: Michael Curtiz. Edward G. Robinson, Bette Davis, Humphrey Bogart, Wayne Morris, Jane Bryan, Harry Carey, Veda Ann Borg. Well-paced yarn with promoter Robinson making naive bellhop Morris a boxing star, tangling with mobster Bogart at every turn. Remade in 1941 (as THE WAGONS ROLL AT NIGHT) and in 1962. Shown on TV for years as BATTLING BELLHOP. ▼◗

Kid Galahad (1962) **C-95m.** **½ D: Phil Karlson. Elvis Presley, Gig Young, Lola Albright, Joan Blackman, Charles Bronson, Ned Glass. This remake lacks wallop of the original. Elvis stars as a boxer who wins championship—and sings six forgettable songs—but prefers quiet life as garage mechanic. ▼◗

Kid Glove Killer (1942) **74m.** *** D: Fred Zinnemann. Van Heflin, Lee Bowman, Marsha Hunt, Samuel S. Hinds, Cliff Clark, Eddie Quillan. Solid B film about police chemist Heflin uncovering the killer of a mayor, with taut direction by Zinnemann. Look for Ava Gardner as a car hop. ◗

Kid Millions (1934) 90m. *** D: Roy Del Ruth. Eddie Cantor, Ethel Merman, Ann Sothern, George Murphy, Warren Hymer, The Nicholas Brothers. Elaborate Cantor musical about Eddie inheriting a fortune. Musical numbers (including one by The Nicholas Brothers) and comedy set pieces boost a weak script. Color segment in ice-cream factory a delight. Songs include "When My Ship Comes In." Lucille Ball is one of the Goldwyn Girls. ▼◗

Kid Monk Baroni (1952) 80m. ** D: Harold Schuster. Richard Rober, Bruce Cabot, Allene Roberts, Mona Knox, Leonard Nimoy, Jack Larson, Budd Jaxon, Kathleen Freeman. Coached by a priest, an amateur pugilist tries to fight his way out of New York's mean streets but winds up badly scarred instead. After plastic surgery, he seeks a comeback but may now be thwarted by an avaricious woman. Passable boxing-ring drama is remembered (if at all) for Nimoy's only pre–*Star Trek* leading movie role. ▼◗

Kidnapped (1938) 90m. **½ D: Alfred L. Werker. Warner Baxter, Freddie Bartholomew, Arleen Whelan, C. Aubrey Smith, Reginald Owen, John Carradine, Nigel Bruce. Good adventure yarn of 1750s Scotland and England but not Robert Louis Stevenson; fine cast in generally entertaining script. ◗

Kidnapped (1948) 80m. ** D: William Beaudine. Roddy McDowall, Sue England, Dan O'Herlihy, Roland Winters, Jeff Corey. Disappointing low-budget adaptation of Robert Louis Stevenson novel. Look for Hugh O'Brian as a sailor. ◗

Kidnapped (1960) C-97m. **½ D: Robert Stevenson. Peter Finch, James MacArthur, Bernard Lee, Niall MacGinnis, John Laurie, Finlay Currie, Peter O'Toole. Disney feature filmed in England is faithful to Robert Louis Stevenson's classic novel, but surprisingly dull. Good cast and vivid atmosphere are its major assets. ▼◗

Kiki (1926) 108m. **½ D: Clarence Brown. Norma Talmadge, Ronald Colman, Gertrude Astor, Marc McDermott, George K. Arthur, William Orlamond, Frankie Darro, Mack Swain. Change of pace for drama queen Talmadge, cast as a vivacious Parisienne who wheedles her way into the life of Follies manager Colman. Are we the only ones who find her character annoying? Mary Pickford adopted the same persona in her 1931 remake. Hanns (Hans) Kräly adapted the play by André Picard. ◗

Killer Ape (1953) 68m. *½ D: Spencer Bennet. Johnny Weissmuller, Carol Thurston, Ray Corrigan, Max Palmer, Nestor Paiva, Nick Stuart. *Jungle Jim* Weissmuller takes on evil white hunters who are using animals to test their germ warfare weapons. Former cowboy star Corrigan, who frequently worked in an ape suit for jungle cheapies, appears here sans costume.

Killer Bait SEE: **Too Late for Tears**

Killer Bats SEE: **Devil Bat, The**

Killer Is Loose, The (1956) 73m. *** D: Budd Boetticher. Joseph Cotten, Rhonda Fleming, Wendell Corey, Alan Hale (Jr.), Michael Pate. Cop Cotten accidentally kills the wife of quiet bank-clerk-turned-robber Corey, who later escapes from prison with eye-for-an-eye revenge in mind. Fast-paced suspenseful sleeper, with excellent L.A. location photography and perhaps Corey's best performance: he's both scary and pathetic. ◗

Killer Leopard (1954) 70m. *½ D: Ford Beebe, Edward Morey, Jr. Johnny Sheffield, Beverly Garland, Barry Bernard, Donald Murphy, Leonard Mudie, Smoki Whitfield. Bomba the Jungle Boy guides a Hollywood starlet through the bush to find her missing husband. Did this next-to-last series entry really require two directors? ◗

Killer McCoy (1947) 104m. *** D: Roy Rowland. Mickey Rooney, Brian Donlevy, Ann Blyth, James Dunn, Tom Tully, Sam Levene. Good drama of fighter Rooney accidentally involved in murder, with fine supporting cast of promoters and racketeers. Remake of THE CROWD ROARS (1938). ◗

Killers, The (1946) 105m. **** D: Robert Siodmak. Burt Lancaster, Ava Gardner, Edmond O'Brien, Albert Dekker, Sam Levene, Virginia Christine, William Conrad, Charles McGraw. Compelling crime drama (based on Hemingway story) of ex-fighter found murdered, subsequent investigation. Film provides fireworks, early success of Lancaster (in film debut) and Gardner. Miklos Rozsa's dynamic score features the familiar dum-da-dum-dum theme later utilized by *Dragnet*. Screenplay by Anthony Veiller (and, uncredited, John Huston). Reworked in 1964. On-screen title is ERNEST HEMINGWAY'S THE KILLERS. ▼◗

Killers, The (1964) C-95m. **½ D: Don Siegel. Lee Marvin, John Cassavetes, Angie Dickinson, Ronald Reagan, Clu Gulager, Claude Akins, Norman Fell. Two inquisitive hit men piece together the story of the man they've just murdered, in this free adaptation of Hemingway's short story. Originally shot for TV, it was rejected as "too violent" and released to theaters instead. Some latter-day notoriety derives from Reagan's casting as a brutal crime kingpin; it was his last movie role. Marvin has a great closing line. On-screen title is ERNEST HEMINGWAY'S THE KILLERS. ▼◗

Killers From Space (1954) 71m. BOMB D: W. Lee Wilder. Peter Graves, James Seay, Steve Pendleton, Barbara Bestar, Frank Gerstle. Scientist Graves, killed in a plane crash, is brought back to life by aliens from the planet Astron Delta. They're planning to invade Earth and want him to pilfer atomic data. Poor in all departments—and too dull to be funny. ▼◗

Killer Shark (1950) **76m.** *½ D: Oscar (Budd) Boetticher. Roddy McDowall, Laurette Luez, Roland Winters, Edward Norris, Douglas Fowley, Dick Moore. Back Bayite McDowall learns new values as skipper of shark-hunting vessel; cheapie film.▼

Killer Shrews, The (1959) **70m.** **½ D: Ray Kellogg. James Best, Ingrid Goude, Ken Curtis, Baruch Lumet, Gordon McLendon. No, this isn't about an attack of nagging wives, it's an inventive but silly sci-fi tale of people isolated on a Texas island, menaced by title creatures created by well-intentioned scientist. Followed by RETURN OF THE KILLER SHREWS (2012), also with James Best, and parodied in ATTACK OF THE KILLER SHREWS! (2015). ▼◗

Killer's Kiss (1955) **67m.** ** D: Stanley Kubrick. Frank Silvera, Jamie Smith, Irene Kane, Jerry Jarret. Meandering account of revenge when boxer's courting of working girl causes her boss to commit murder. Interesting early Kubrick; the inspiration for the film-within-a-film of STRANGERS KISS. Leading lady Kane became TV and newspaper journalist Chris Chase.▼◗●

Killers of Kilimanjaro (1959-British) **C-91m.** ** D: Richard Thorpe. Robert Taylor, Anthony Newley, Anne Aubrey, Gregoire Aslan, Alan Cuthbertson, Donald Pleasence. Spotty adventure yarn of railroad-building in East Africa. CinemaScope. ◗

Killer That Stalked New York, The (1950) **75m.** **½ D: Earl McAvoy. Evelyn Keyes, Charles Korvin, William Bishop, Dorothy Malone, Lola Albright, Barry Kelley, Carl Benton Reid, Ludwig Donath, Art Smith, Whit Bissell, Roy Roberts, Jim Backus, Richard Egan. N.Y.C. locations boost this OK thriller in which diamond smuggler Keyes, in cahoots with Korvin, returns to the U.S. from Cuba, unknowingly bringing with her a deadly case of smallpox. ◗

Kill Her Gently (1957-British) **73m.** ** D: Charles Saunders. Marc Lawrence, Maureen Connell, George Mikell, Griffith Jones, John Gayford. Brutal B film of supposedly cured mental patient hiring two convicts-at-large to kill his wife.

Killing, The (1956) **83m.** ***½ D: Stanley Kubrick. Sterling Hayden, Coleen Gray, Vince Edwards, Jay C. Flippen, Ted de Corsia, Marie Windsor, Joe Sawyer, Elisha Cook, Timothy Carey. The film that really put Kubrick on the map—a case study of a racetrack heist, with a colorful cast of characters, including the ultimate nebbish (Cook, married to vixenish Windsor) and a sinister sniper for hire (Carey). Major flaw is the *Dragnet*-style narration. Kubrick scripted from Lionel White's novel *Clean Break.*▼◗●

Kill Me Tomorrow (1957-British) **80m.** ** D: Terence Fisher. Pat O'Brien, Lois Maxwell, George Coulouris, Robert Brown, Tommy Steele. Adequate B film about newspaperman cracking murder case leading to arrest of diamond-smuggling syndicate. ◗

Kill or Be Killed (1950) **67m.** *½ D: Max Nosseck. Lawrence Tierney, George Coulouris, Marissa O'Brien, Rudolph Anders. Pedestrian account of man on lam hunted down in jungle by law enforcers. Filmed in Portugal.

Kill or Cure (1962-British) **98m.** **½ D: George Pollock. Terry-Thomas, Eric Sykes, Dennis Price, Lionel Jeffries, Moira Redmond, Katya Douglas, Ronnie Barker. Eccentric private investigator is hired by an older woman to join her at a health spa where she suspects someone is up to no good. Amusing whodunit/farce. ◗

Kill the Umpire (1950) **78m.** **½ D: Lloyd Bacon. William Bendix, Una Merkel, Ray Collins, Gloria Henry, William Frawley, Tom D'Andrea, Richard Taylor (Jeff Richards). Lightweight comedy about baseball lover who becomes the sport's most hated man, the umpire. Ends with spectacular slapstick chase. Screenplay by Frank Tashlin.◗

Kilroy Was Here (1947) **68m.** *½ D: Phil Karlson. Jackie Cooper, Jackie Coogan, Wanda McKay, Frank Jenks. Topical comedy (then) is pretty limp now, with innocent victim of "Kilroy Was Here" joke trying to lead normal life despite his name. ◗

Kim (1950) **C-113m.** ***½ D: Victor Saville. Errol Flynn, Dean Stockwell, Paul Lukas, Thomas Gomez, Cecil Kellaway. Rousing actioner based on Kipling classic, set in 1880s India, with British soldiers combatting rebellious natives. Flavorful production. Remade for TV in 1984.▼◗

Kimberley Jim (1965-South African) **C-82m.** ** D: Emil Nofal. Jim Reeves, Madeleine Usher, Clive Parnell, Arthur Swemmer, Mike Holt. Minor musical of two carefree gamblers who win diamond mine in fixed poker game, and then have a change of heart. Rare screen appearance by late country singer Reeves. Scanoscope.

Kind Hearts and Coronets (1949-British) **104m.** ***½ D: Robert Hamer. Dennis Price, Alec Guinness, Valerie Hobson, Joan Greenwood, Miles Malleson, Hugh Griffith, Jeremy Spenser, Arthur Lowe. Peerless black comedy of castoff member of titled family setting out to eliminate them all. Guinness plays all eight victims! Hamer and John Dighton adapted Roy Horniman's novel *Israel Rank.*▼◗●

Kind Lady (1935) **76m.** **½ D: George B. Seitz. Aline MacMahon, Basil Rathbone, Mary Carlisle, Frank Albertson, Dudley Digges, Doris Lloyd, Donald Meek. MacMahon is being blackmailed and held prisoner in her own house by Rathbone and his cronies; fairly entertaining, but not as good as the remake. Adapted from the Edward Chodorov play, which was based on a Hugh Walpole story. Doris Lloyd, who plays the victim's sister here, took the role of her housemaid in the 1951 version.

Kind Lady (1951) 78m. *** D: John Sturges. Ethel Barrymore, Maurice Evans, Angela Lansbury, Betsy Blair, Keenan Wynn, John Williams, Doris Lloyd. Creepy little chiller about a genteel older woman (Barrymore) who is victimized by a charmer (Evans), who takes over her home—and her life. Wynn is particularly effective as a thug/butler. Coscripted by Edward Chodorov, and based on his play; filmed previously in 1935.

Kind of Loving, A (1962-British) 112m. *** D: John Schlesinger. Alan Bates, June Ritchie, Thora Hird, Bert Palmer, Gwen Nelson, Malcolm Patton, Leonard Rossiter, Peter Madden. Intelligent account of young couple forced to marry when girl becomes pregnant, detailing their home life; well acted.▼

King & Country (1964-British) 90m. ***½ D: Joseph Losey. Dirk Bogarde, Tom Courtenay, Leo McKern, Barry Foster, James Villiers, Peter Copley. Vivid antiwar treatise beautifully acted by strong supporting cast. Bogarde is detached Army captain lawyer assigned to defend deserter private Courtenay during WW1. Score composed by harmonica virtuoso Larry Adler.▼●

King and Four Queens, The (1956) C-86m. **½ D: Raoul Walsh. Clark Gable, Eleanor Parker, Jo Van Fleet, Jean Willes, Barbara Nichols, Sara Shane, Jay C. Flippen. Static misfire with Gable on the search for money hidden by husbands of four women he encounters. CinemaScope.▼●

King and I, The (1956) C-133m. ***½ D: Walter Lang. Deborah Kerr, Yul Brynner, Rita Moreno, Martin Benson, Terry Saunders, Rex Thompson, Alan Mowbray. Excellent film adaptation of Rodgers and Hammerstein Broadway musical, based on book filmed in 1946 as ANNA AND THE KING OF SIAM (and remade as ANNA AND THE KING). Kerr plays widowed English schoolteacher who travels to Siam to teach the King's many children, and finds dealing with His Highness her greatest challenge. Brynner gives the performance of a lifetime, and won an Oscar re-creating his Broadway role. Kerr is charming; her singing voice was dubbed by Marni Nixon. Songs include "Hello, Young Lovers," "Getting to Know You," "Shall We Dance." Also won Oscars for art direction–set decoration, Irene Sharaff's costumes, Alfred Newman and Ken Darby's scoring. Screenplay by Ernest Lehman. Includes an overture, intermission/entr'acte, exit music. CinemaScope 55.▼●

King and the Chorus Girl, The (1937) 94m. **½ D: Mervyn LeRoy. Joan Blondell, Fernand Gravet, Edward Everett Horton, Jane Wyman. Gravet is nobleman on a lark, finding true love with beautiful chorine Blondell. Lively production. Written by Norman Krasna and Groucho Marx!

King Creole (1958) 116m. **½ D: Michael Curtiz. Elvis Presley, Carolyn Jones, Dolores Hart, Dean Jagger, Liliane Montevecchi, Walter Matthau, Paul Stewart, Vic Morrow. Elvis is quite good as young New Orleans nightclub singer who is eventually dragged into the criminal underworld. Toned-down adaptation of Harold Robbins' *A Stone For Danny Fisher* (which was set in Chicago), coscripted by Michael V. Gazzo. Songs include "Trouble," title number. VistaVision.▼●

King Dinosaur (1955) 63m. BOMB D: Bert I. Gordon. Bill Bryant, Wanda Curtis, Douglas Henderson, Patricia Gallagher. A wandering planet enters the solar system, so an expedition is launched to explore it; they happen upon an island full of dinosaurs (clearly portrayed by lizards). First and worst of director Gordon's many 1950s sci-fi films, usually featuring supersized creatures. Boring, silly, and awesomely cheap, with a cast that defines the word "bland."❱

King in New York, A (1957-British) 100m. **½ D: Charles Chaplin. Charles Chaplin, Dawn Addams, Oliver Johnston, Maxine Audley, Harry Green, Michael Chaplin. Unseen in U.S. until 1973, supposedly anti-American film is rather mild satire of 1950s sensibilities, witch hunts, and technology. Chaplin overindulges himself, and film lacks focus, but there are good moments, and interesting performance by son Michael as young malcontent.▼●

King in Shadow (1956-German) 87m. ** D: Harald Braun. O. W. Fischer, Horst Buchholz, Odile Versois, Günther Hadank. Buchholz is mentally disturbed young King of Sweden in 1760s; court intrigue encouraged by his domineering mother (Versois) makes for tepid costume tale.

King Kong (1933) 104m. **** D: Merian C. Cooper, Ernest B. Schoedsack. Fay Wray, Robert Armstrong, Bruce Cabot, Frank Reicher, Sam Hardy, Noble Johnson, James Flavin. Classic version of beauty-and-beast theme is a moviegoing must, with Willis O'Brien's special effects and animation of monster ape Kong still unsurpassed. Final sequence atop Empire State Building is now cinema folklore; Max Steiner music score also memorable. Followed immediately by THE SON OF KONG. Remade in 1976 and 2005. Restored version on DVD and Blu-ray includes an overture; other prints run 100m. Also shown in computer-colored version.▼●

King Kong Vs. Godzilla (1963-Japanese) C-90m. ** D: Ishirô Honda, Thomas Montgomery. Tadao Takashima, Kenji Sahara, Yu Fujiki, Ichiro Arishima, Mie Hama, Akihiko Hirata, Jun Tazaki. Essentially a KONG remake, with Tokyo subbing for N.Y.C. and Godzilla showing up to make that mess even bigger. (Oh yes, there's also a gigantic octopus.) Third Godzilla movie—the first in color and widescreen—was originally a clever satire of the worst excesses of TV journalism, but the U.S. version eliminates most of this (as well as Akira Ifukube's thrilling score), and adds awful new scenes with Michael Keith, Harry Holcombe, Byron Morrow, and Victor Milian. Still worth a look. (P.S.: Despite urban legend, only one ending was shot.) Japanese running time 98m. Tohoscope. ▼◐

King Murder, The (1932) **67m.** *½ D: Richard Thorpe. Conway Tearle, Natalie Moorhead, Marceline Day, Dorothy Revier, Don Alvarado. It's murder most dull as homicide detective Tearle, investigating a gold digger's death, questions suspect after suspect . . . after suspect. For a small-time indie it's nicely mounted (shot at Universal) but the torrents of polite talk are exhausting.

King of Alcatraz (1938) **56m.** **½ D: Robert Florey. J. Carrol Naish, Gail Patrick, Lloyd Nolan, Harry Carey, Robert Preston, Anthony Quinn. Alcatraz escapee Naish takes over passenger ship, encountering rough-and-tumble seamen Nolan and Preston. Film moves like lightning, with outstanding cast making you forget this is just a B picture.

King of Burlesque (1935) **90m.** **½ D: Sidney Lanfield. Warner Baxter, Jack Oakie, Alice Faye, Mona Barrie, Dixie Dunbar. Dumb but enjoyable musical; cliché-ridden story of burlesque producer who risks all on ambitious Broadway show. Faye, Fats Waller (used all too briefly), hit song "I'm Shootin' High" provide highspots. ◐

King of Chinatown (1939) **60m.** **½ D: Nick Grinde. Anna May Wong, Sidney Toler, Akim Tamiroff, J. Carrol Naish, Anthony Quinn, Roscoe Karns, Philip Ahn. Interesting little B movie with good cast, about underworld racketeers trying to gain power in Chinatown.

King of Jazz (1930) **C-93m.** *** D: John Murray Anderson. Paul Whiteman and His Orchestra, John Boles, Jeanette Loff, The Rhythm Boys (Bing Crosby, Al Rinker, Harry Barris). Million-dollar musical revue, shot in two-color Technicolor process, is filled with larger-than-life production numbers and wonderful songs. Highlights include Walter Lantz's cartoon sequence, Joe Venuti's swing violin, young Bing Crosby with the Rhythm Boys, and, of course, Gershwin's "Rhapsody in Blue" (which in early Technicolor is more a rhapsody in turquoise). Uneven, to be sure, but a lot of fun. Originally released at 105m. ▼

King of Kings, The (1927) **155m.** *** D: Cecil B. DeMille. H. B. Warner, Ernest Torrence, Jacqueline Logan, Joseph Schild-kraut, Victor Varconi, Robert Edeson, William Boyd. Lavish silent film holds up rather well, benefits from DeMille's superb storytelling skills and reverence for the subject. The Resurrection sequence is in two-color Technicolor. Some prints run 112m. Remade in 1961. ▼◐

King of Kings (1961) **C-168m.** ***½ D: Nicholas Ray. Jeffrey Hunter, Siobhan McKenna, Robert Ryan, Hurd Hatfield, Viveca Lindfors, Rita Gam, Rip Torn; narrated by Orson Welles. The life of Christ, intelligently told and beautifully filmed; full of deeply moving moments, such as the Sermon on the Mount, Christ's healing of the lame, and many others. Memorable Miklos Rozsa score. Not without flaws, but well worthwhile; grandly filmed in widescreen. Runs 171m. with overture, intermission/entr'acte, exit music. SuperTechnirama 70. ▼◐

King of the Coral Sea (1956-Australian) **74m.** **½ D: Lee Robinson. Chips Rafferty, Charles Tingwell, Ilma Adey, Rod Taylor, Lloyd Berrell, Reginald Lye. On-location filming in Australia aids this account of wetback smuggling into the mainland.

King of the Cowboys (1943) **67m.** *** D: Joseph Kane. Roy Rogers, Smiley Burnette, Peggy Moran, Gerald Mohr, Dorothea Kent, Lloyd Corrigan, Stuart Hamblen, Eddie Dean, Sons of the Pioneers. Roy works undercover to trap a band of WW2 saboteurs who are blowing up government warehouses. Title indicates how popular Rogers had become, and this musical Western thriller shows the cowboy at his very best.▼◐

King of the Jungle (1933) **72m.** **½ D: H. Bruce Humberstone, Max Marcin. Buster Crabbe, Frances Dee, Sidney Toler, Nydia Westman, Robert Barrat, Irving Pichel, Douglass Dumbrille. Imitation Tarzan yarn comes off well, with South African "Lion Man" Crabbe being dragged into civilization and a circus job against his will. Good fun.

King of the Khyber Rifles (1953) **C-100m.** **½ D: Henry King. Tyrone Power, Terry Moore, Michael Rennie, John Justin. Power is half-caste British officer involved in native skirmishes, Moore the general's daughter he loves. Film version of Talbot Mundy's novel lacks finesse or any sense of Kipling-style reality-fantasy. CinemaScope. ◐

King of the Newsboys (1938) **65m.** **½ D: Bernard Vorhaus. Lew Ayres, Helen Mack, Alison Skipworth, Victor Varconi, Sheila Bromley, Alice White, Horace McMahon, William "Billy" Benedict, Jack Pennick, Mary Kornman. Ayres promises a newspaper editor a circulation boost by spotlighting "stuffed shirts in trouble . . . beautiful girls in trouble . . . hangings, fires, and legs." Pretty good B movie about tabloid journalism. Unbilled Marjorie Main plays essentially the same role she did in DEAD END. Story cowritten by Horace McCoy.◐

King of the Pecos (1936) **54m.** **½ D: Joseph Kane. John Wayne, Muriel Evans, Cy Kendall, Jack Clifford, Arthur Aylesworth, Herbert Heywood. Boy watches homesteader parents viciously murdered by Texas claim jumper; a decade later he returns as lawyer for retribution against the killer, who is now a powerful, corrupt figure controlling water rights ranchers depend on. Slick production values, continuous action, and beautifully photographed Lone Pine exteriors elevate this early Republic effort.▼▶

King of the Range SEE: **Marauders, The**

King of the Roaring 20's—The Story of Arnold Rothstein (1961) **106m.** **½ D: Joseph M. Newman. David Janssen, Dianne Foster, Jack Carson, Diana Dors, Mickey Rooney. Slow-paced narrative of famous gambler's rise and fall miscasts lead role (real Rothstein was short and fat), slightly whitewashes him, and gets most of the facts wrong. Stray gangster-movie elements are inappropriately added.▼▶

King of the Underworld (1939) **69m.** ** D: Lewis Seiler. Humphrey Bogart, Kay Francis, James Stephenson, John Eldredge, Jessie Busley. Far-fetched tale of doctor Francis, falsely linked to gangster Bogart, the "last of the public enemies," setting out to prove her innocence. Remake of DR. SOCRATES.▶

King of the Wild Horses (1947) **79m.** *½ D: George Archainbaud. Preston Foster, Gail Patrick, Bill Sheffield, Guinn "Big Boy" Williams. Mild Western about 10-year-old Sheffield's devotion to a fierce stallion.

King of the Wild Stallions (1959) **C-75m.** ** D: R. G. Springsteen. George Montgomery, Diane Brewster, Edgar Buchanan, Emile Meyer, Byron Foulger, Denver Pyle. Widow and her boy may lose their ranch unless foreman Montgomery can capture a wild horse who's actually been protecting them. Mild Western fare. CinemaScope.▶

King of the Zombies (1941) **67m.** ** D: Jean Yarbrough. Dick Purcell, Joan Woodbury, Mantan Moreland, Henry Victor, John Archer. American aviators crash-land on Caribbean Island, where mad scientist Victor uses voodoo and hypnotism to uncover key military secrets. Stiff-necked zombies are incidental, but pop-eyed Moreland is a delight.▼●▶

King Rat (1965) **133m.** *** D: Bryan Forbes. George Segal, Tom Courtenay, James Fox, Patrick O'Neal, Denholm Elliott, James Donald, John Mills, Alan Webb. James Clavell novel of WW2 Japanese POW camp, focusing on effect of captivity on Allied prisoners. Thoughtful presentation rises above clichés; many exciting scenes.▼▶

King Richard and the Crusaders (1954) **C-114m.** *½ D: David Butler. Rex Harrison, Virginia Mayo, George Sanders, Laurence Harvey, Robert Douglas. Cardboard

costumer of Middle Ages, with laughable script. Indeed, Sanders as The Lion Heart and Harrison as a Saracen warrior do appear to be having a good time. CinemaScope. ▼▶

Kings Go Forth (1958) **109m.** *** D: Delmer Daves. Frank Sinatra, Tony Curtis, Natalie Wood, Leora Dana, Karl Swenson. Soapy but well-done three-cornered romance, set in WW2 France. Two GI buddies both fall for same girl, unaware that she is half-black. Script by Merle Miller; several jazz greats, including Red Norvo and Pete Candoli, put in appearances.▼●▶

Kings of the Sun (1963) **C-108m.** **½ D: J. Lee Thompson. Yul Brynner, George Chakiris, Shirley Anne Field, Richard Basehart, Brad Dexter. Skin-deep spectacle, badly cast, telling of Mayan leader who comes to America with surviving tribesmen and encounters savage Indians. Filmed in Mexico. Panavision.▶

King Solomon's Mines (1937-British) **80m.** *** D: Robert Stevenson. Paul Robeson, Cedric Hardwicke, Roland Young, John Loder, Anna Lee. Robust adventure given full-blooded treatment by fine cast, exploring Africa in search of treasure-filled mines. One of Robeson's best screen roles even allows him to sing. H. Rider Haggard story remade in 1950, 1985, and for TV in 2004.▼▶

King Solomon's Mines (1950) **C-102m.** ***½ D: Compton Bennett, Andrew Marton. Deborah Kerr, Stewart Granger, Richard Carlson, Hugo Haas. Remake of H. Rider Haggard story is given polished production, with Granger-Kerr-Carlson trio leading safari in search for legendary diamond mines. Scripted by Helen Deutsch. This won Oscars for Cinematography (Robert Surtees) and Editing; excess footage used in WATUSI and other later jungle films. Remade in 1985. ▼●▶

Kings Row (1942) **127m.** ***½ D: Sam Wood. Ann Sheridan, Robert Cummings, Ronald Reagan, Betty Field, Charles Coburn, Claude Rains, Judith Anderson, Maria Ouspenskaya. Forerunner of PEYTON PLACE still retains its sweep of life in pre-WW1 Midwestern town, with the fates of many townsfolk intertwined. Beautiful Erich Wolfgang Korngold music score backs up plush production, fine characterizations. Notable, too, as Reagan's finest performance. Screenplay by Casey Robinson, from Henry Bellamann's best-selling book. Also shown in computer-colored version.▼●▶

King's Story, A (1965-British) **C-100m.** *** D: Harry Booth. With the voices of Orson Welles, Flora Robson, Patrick Wymark, David Warner. Strong documentary focusing on early life of Duke of Windsor and his ultimate abdication from throne of England to marry the woman he loved.

King Steps Out, The (1936) **85m.** *** D: Josef von Sternberg. Grace Moore, Franchot Tone, Walter Connolly, Raymond Walburn, Elizabeth Risdon, Nana Bryant, Victor Jory. Fanciful musical romance with fine cast supporting Moore's lovely voice; direction big asset to otherwise average musical. ▼

King's Thief, The (1955) **C-78m.** *** D: Robert Z. Leonard. Ann Blyth, Edmund Purdom, David Niven, George Sanders, Roger Moore, John Dehner, Sean McClory. The king is England's Charles II (Sanders) and the thief is brash Purdom, whose pilfering of a valuable book sets off plenty of intrigue in this lavish costumer. Niven makes a fine villain. CinemaScope. ▼❶

King's Vacation, The (1933) **60m.** **½ D: John G. Adolfi. George Arliss, Dudley Digges, Dick Powell, Patricia Ellis, Marjorie Gateson, Florence Arliss. Refreshing story of monarch Arliss returning to ex-wife Gateson in search for "the simple life," only to find she's living even better than he is! Typical of Arliss' lighter vehicles. ❶

Kino-Eye (1924-Russian) **74m.** *** D: Dziga Vertov. Celebrated experimental film is a visual newsmagazine that extols the virtues of everyday life in a post-Revolutionary Russian village, centering on a group of "young pioneers" and their work on a cooperative. Vertov augments this with sequences in a slaughterhouse and an insane asylum (among other locations), and explores the language of cinema by playfully running footage backward. Photographed by the filmmaker's brother, Mikhail Kaufman. ▼❶

Kipps (1941-British) **82m.** *** D: Carol Reed. Michael Redgrave, Diana Wynyard, Arthur Riscoe, Phyllis Calvert, Max Adrian, Helen Haye, Michael Wilding, Hermione Baddeley. Meticulous adaptation of H. G. Wells' story about a shopkeeper who inherits money and tries to crash Society. Faithfully scripted by Sidney Gilliat, but a bit stodgy overall. Basis for musical HALF A SIXPENCE. Originally released in U.S. as THE REMARKABLE MR. KIPPS. Original British running time 108m. ▼

Kismet (1944) **C-100m.** **½ D: William Dieterle. Ronald Colman, Marlene Dietrich, Edward Arnold, Florence Bates, James Craig, Joy Ann Page, Harry Davenport. Colman tries a change of pace playing the "king of beggars," a wily magician whose daughter is wooed by the handsome young Caliph in this plot-heavy Arabian Nights-type tale. Passably entertaining but nothing special, despite opulent MGM production. Best of all is Dietrich, with tongue in cheek and body painted gold for one famous dance scene. Filmed before in 1920 and 1930; remade in 1955 after the Broadway musical version. Retitled ORIENTAL DREAM. ▼❶

Kismet (1955) **C-113m.** **½ D: Vincente Minnelli. Howard Keel, Ann Blyth, Dolores Gray, Monty Woolley, Sebastian Cabot, Vic Damone. Handsome but uninspired filming of the Broadway musical of this Arabian Nights–type tale. Robert Wright–George Forrest songs (based on Borodin themes) include "Stranger in Paradise," "Baubles, Bangles, and Beads." CinemaScope. ▼❶

Kiss, The (1929) **89m.** *** D: Jacques Feyder. Greta Garbo, Conrad Nagel, Anders Randolf, Holmes Herbert, Lew Ayres, George Davis. Married Garbo gives young Ayres, who is smitten with her, an innocent goodnight kiss, which leads to misunderstanding and tragedy. Sleek, fluidly filmed Garbo vehicle was her last silent and Ayres' first starring role. Farfetched but very enjoyable. ▼❶

Kiss and Make-Up (1934) **78m.** ** D: Harlan Thompson. Cary Grant, Genevieve Tobin, Helen Mack, Edward Everett Horton, Lucien Littlefield, Mona Maris, Toby Wing, Clara Lou (Ann) Sheridan, Henry Armetta. Risqué trifle, primarily set in Paris, with Grant as a celebrity "beauty doctor" who hawks facial crèmes on the radio and services an array of clients. The cast of this third-tier Lubitsch imitation is liberally sprinkled with WAMPAS Baby Stars, including Jacqueline Wells (Julie Bishop) and Helene Cohan, George M.'s daughter. Grant even sings; it's not his finest hour on-screen. ❶

Kiss and Tell (1945) **90m.** **½ D: Richard Wallace. Shirley Temple, Jerome Courtland, Walter Abel, Katherine Alexander, Robert Benchley, Porter Hall. Film of successful Broadway play about wacky teenager Corliss Archer is a bit forced but generally funny; one of Temple's better grown-up roles. Sequel: A KISS FOR CORLISS.

Kiss Before Dying, A (1956) **C-94m.** *** D: Gerd Oswald. Robert Wagner, Virginia Leith, Jeffrey Hunter, Joanne Woodward, Mary Astor, George Macready. Effective chiller with Wagner superb as psychopathic killer and Astor his devoted mother; well paced. Based on an Ira Levin novel. Remade in 1991. CinemaScope. ▼❶

Kiss Before the Mirror, The (1933) **67m.** **½ D: James Whale. Frank Morgan, Paul Lukas, Nancy Carroll, Jean Dixon, Gloria Stuart, Walter Pidgeon, Donald Cook, Charles Grapewin. While defending Lukas for killing his adulterous wife, attorney Morgan begins to see the entire chain of events recurring in his own home! Strange romantic melodrama is made even stranger by being shot on leftover FRANKENSTEIN sets; good performances and typical Whale stylistics keep one watching. Remade by the director as WIVES UNDER SUSPICION.

Kisses for My President (1964) **113m.** **½ D: Curtis Bernhardt. Fred MacMurray,

Polly Bergen, Arlene Dahl, Edward Andrews, Eli Wallach. Thirties-style comedy of Bergen becoming President of the U.S., with MacMurray her husband caught in unprecedented protocol. Sometimes funny, often witless. ▼●❙

Kiss for Corliss, A (1949) 88m. ** D: Richard Wallace. Shirley Temple, David Niven, Tom Tully, Virginia Welles. Puffed-up comedy of teenager Temple convincing everyone that she and playboy Niven are going together; naïve fluff. Limp follow-up to KISS AND TELL with Shirley as Corliss Archer; this was her final film. Retitled ALMOST A BRIDE. ▼❙

Kissin' Cousins (1964) C-96m. **½ D: Gene Nelson. Elvis Presley, Arthur O'Connell, Glenda Farrell, Jack Albertson, Pamela Austin, Yvonne Craig, Donald Woods. Elvis has a dual role as military officer trying to convince yokel relative to allow missile site to be built on homestead; good supporting cast, usual amount of singing—mostly forgettable—and dancing. Teri Garr is one of the dancers. Panavision. ▼❙

Kissing Bandit, The (1948) C-102m. ** D: Laslo Benedek. Frank Sinatra, Kathryn Grayson, Ann Miller, J. Carrol Naish, Ricardo Montalban, Mildred Natwick, Cyd Charisse, Billy Gilbert. Frail Sinatra vehicle about son of Western kissing bandit who picks up where Dad left off; song "Siesta" sums it up. ▼❙

Kiss in the Dark, A (1949) 87m. ** D: Delmer Daves. David Niven, Jane Wyman, Victor Moore, Wayne Morris, Broderick Crawford, Joseph Buloff, Maria Ouspenskaya. One-note farce about uptight concert pianist Niven, who loosens up when his business manager uses his savings to purchase an apartment building—where one of the residents is perky model Wyman. ❙

Kiss Me Again (1931) 75m. ** D: William A. Seiter. Bernice Claire, Walter Pidgeon, Edward Everett Horton, June Collyer, Frank McHugh, Claude Gillingwater. Faded version of Victor Herbert operetta *Mlle. Modiste*, centering on amorous mix-ups between a French lieutenant and a dress shop model-turned-singer. Pretty stiff, though the charming Claire has a nice voice. Originally shown in two-strip Technicolor.

Kiss Me Deadly (1955) 105m. ***½ D: Robert Aldrich. Ralph Meeker, Albert Dekker, Paul Stewart, Cloris Leachman, Wesley Addy, Nick Dennis, Maxine Cooper, Gaby Rodgers, Jack Elam, Strother Martin, Jack Lambert. Meeker is a perfect Mike Hammer in moody, fast, and violent adaptation of Mickey Spillane novel. Years ahead of its time, a major influence on French New Wave directors, and one of Aldrich's best films. Leachman's film debut. Some video versions have 82 seconds of additional footage which completely change the finale. ▼●❙

Kiss Me Kate (1953) C-109m. ***½ D:

George Sidney. Kathryn Grayson, Howard Keel, Ann Miller, Bobby Van, Keenan Wynn, James Whitmore, Bob Fosse, Tommy Rall, Kurt Kasznar, Ron Randell. Bright filmization of Cole Porter's Broadway musical, adapted from Shakespeare's *The Taming of the Shrew*. Grayson and Keel are erstwhile married couple whose off-stage and on-stage lives intertwine. Songs include "So in Love," "Always True to You in My Fashion," "Brush Up Your Shakespeare" (delightfully performed by Wynn and Whitmore); the "From This Moment On" number, highlighting Fosse and Carol Haney, is outstanding. 3-D. ▼●❙

Kiss Me, Stupid (1964) 122m. ** D: Billy Wilder. Dean Martin, Ray Walston, Kim Novak, Felicia Farr, Cliff Osmond, Barbara Pepper, Doro Merande, Henry Gibson, John Fiedler, Mel Blanc. Martin plays womanizing crooner named "Dino" whose interest in unsuccessful songwriter Walston might increase if he gets a crack at his wife. Lewd farce (by Wilder and I. A. L. Diamond) was condemned as "smut" when first released, and hasn't improved very much—although it does have its defenders. DVD features the alternate European ending. Panavision. ▼●❙

Kiss of Death (1947) 98m. *** D: Henry Hathaway. Victor Mature, Brian Donlevy, Coleen Gray, Richard Widmark, Karl Malden, Taylor Holmes, Mildred Dunnock. Famous gangster saga is showing its age, with both the cops and robbers a little too polite—except, of course, for Widmark, in his notorious film debut as giggling, psychopathic killer who shoves a wheelchair-bound old woman (Dunnock) down a flight of stairs! Mature is solid as thief who turns state's evidence. Scripted by Ben Hecht and Charles Lederer; filmed on authentic N.Y.C. locations. Remade in 1995. ▼❙

Kiss of Fire (1955) C-87m. **½ D: Joseph M. Newman. Barbara Rush, Jack Palance, Rex Reason, Martha Hyer. Run-of-the-mill costumer. Rush gives up Spanish throne to remain in America with true love.

Kiss of the Vampire, The (1963-British) C-88m. **½ D: Don Sharp. Clifford Evans, Edward De Souza, Noel Willman, Jennifer Daniel. Luckless honeymooners run out of petrol in eastern Europe and take refuge in the castle of Count Ravna, leader of a vampire cult. Ornate masked ball anticipates Polanski's FEARLESS VAMPIRE KILLERS. Intelligent Hammer production with many chilling sequences. ▼●❙

Kiss the Blood off My Hands (1948) 80m. ** D: Norman Foster. Joan Fontaine, Burt Lancaster, Robert Newton. Disappointing romance-thriller follows the plight of two lost souls, lonely nurse–war widow Fontaine and deeply troubled ex-POW Lancaster, who's on the lam for murder in London. Some potent scenes and good

Miklos Rozsa score cannot salvage tepid film.

Kiss the Boys Goodbye (1941) **85m.** **½ D: Victor Schertzinger. Mary Martin, Don Ameche, Oscar Levant, Virginia Dale, Barbara Jo Allen (Vera Vague), Raymond Walburn, Elizabeth Patterson, Connee Boswell. Enjoyable backstage musical of aspiring actress and director, with good support from Levant and bright Frank Loesser–Victor Schertzinger score based on a play by Clare Boothe Luce.

Kiss Them for Me (1957) **C-105m.** **½ D: Stanley Donen. Cary Grant, Jayne Mansfield, Leif Erickson, Suzy Parker, Larry Blyden, Ray Walston. Forced comedy about romantic entanglements of Navy officers on shore leave. CinemaScope.◗

Kiss the Other Sheik (1965-Italian-French) **C-85m.** BOMB D: Luciano Salce, Eduardo De Filippo. Marcello Mastroianni, Pamela Tiffin, Virna Lisi, Luciano Salce. Off-color and off-base comedy of crazy man and his sexy wife. Panavision.

Kiss Tomorrow Goodbye (1950) **102m.** **½ D: Gordon Douglas. James Cagney, Barbara Payton, Luther Adler, Ward Bond, Helena Carter, Steve Brodie, Barton MacLane, Rhys Williams, Frank Reicher, John Litel, William Frawley, Neville Brand, Kenneth Tobey. Violent thriller in the wake of WHITE HEAT, with Cagney as criminal so ruthless he even blackmails crooked cops! Despite impressive cast, Jimmy's practically the whole show; only Adler as shyster lawyer gives him any competition. Cagney's brother William produced—and also plays his brother.▼●◗

Kit Carson (1940) **97m.** *** D: George B. Seitz. Jon Hall, Lynn Bari, Dana Andrews, Harold Huber, Ward Bond, Renie Riano, Clayton Moore. Sturdy Western with Hall in title role, Andrews as cavalry officer, Bari the woman they fight over; plenty of action in Indian territory. Also shown in a computer-colored version.▼◗

Kitten With a Whip (1964) **83m.** ** D: Douglas Heyes. Ann-Margret, John Forsythe, Patricia Barry, Peter Brown, Ann Doran. Uninspired account of delinquent (Ann-Margret) and friends victimizing wannabe senator Forsythe and forcing him to drive to Mexico.▼◗

Kitty (1945) **104m.** *** D: Mitchell Leisen. Paulette Goddard, Ray Milland, Patric Knowles, Reginald Owen, Cecil Kellaway, Constance Collier. Overlong but entertaining costumer of girl's rise from guttersnipe to lady in 18th-century England with help of impoverished rake Milland; one of Goddard's best roles.

Kitty Foyle (1940) **107m.** ***½ D: Sam Wood. Ginger Rogers, Dennis Morgan, James Craig, Eduardo Ciannelli, Ernest Cossart, Gladys Cooper. Tender love story won Rogers an Oscar as Christopher Mor-

ley's working-girl heroine; Ciannelli memorable as speakeasy waiter.▼●◗

Kliou (The Killer) (1936) **50m.** **½ D: Henri de la Falaise. Dhi, Bhat, Nyan, Kham. A deadly tiger has been terrorizing a Moi village in Indochina and Bhat, a brave young tribesman, is determined to hunt it down. Long-lost silent drama is predictable but validated by striking jungle footage. De la Falaise (the husband of Gloria Swanson and Constance Bennett) appears in a prologue and relates the story. Originally in Technicolor; surviving prints are in b&w.▼◗

Klondike Annie (1936) **80m.** *** D: Raoul Walsh. Mae West, Victor McLaglen, Philip Reed, Helen Jerome Eddy, Harry Beresford, Harold Huber, Soo Young, Lucille Webster Gleason. West and McLaglen are rugged team, with Mae on the lam from police, going to the Yukon and masquerading as Salvation Army worker. West chants "I'm an Occidental Woman in an Oriental Mood For Love," and other hits.▼●◗

Klondike Kate (1943) **64m.** *½ D: William Castle. Ann Savage, Tom Neal, Glenda Farrell, Constance Worth, Sheldon Leonard, Lester Allen. Low-budget humdrum of innocent Neal accused of murder in Alaska, fighting for his life and his girl.◗

Knack . . . and How to Get It, The (1965-British) **84m.** ***½ D: Richard Lester. Rita Tushingham, Ray Brooks, Michael Crawford, Donal Donnelly. One of the funniest comedies ever imported from Britain. One man's a whiz with the ladies, and his buddy simply wants to learn his secret. Fast-moving, constantly funny. Charles Wood adapted Ann Jellicoe's play. Look sharp for Charlotte Rampling (as a water skier) and Jacqueline Bisset.▼●◗

Knave of Hearts SEE: **Lovers, Happy Lovers!**

Knickerbocker Holiday (1944) **85m.** ** D: Harry Brown. Nelson Eddy, Charles Coburn, Constance Dowling, Shelley Winters, Percy Kilbride, Chester Conklin. Plodding film of Kurt Weill–Maxwell Anderson musical of N.Y.C.'s early days; score includes "September Song."▼

Knife in the Water (1962-Polish) **94m.** **** D: Roman Polanski. Leon Niemczyk, Jolanta Umecka, Zygmunt Malanowicz. Absorbing drama grows out of the tensions created when a couple off for a sailing weekend pick up a student hitchhiker. Polanski's first feature film is a brilliant piece of cinematic storytelling, and a must-see movie.▼●◗

Knights of the Round Table (1953) **C-115m.** **½ D: Richard Thorpe. Robert Taylor, Ava Gardner, Mel Ferrer, Stanley Baker, Felix Aylmer. MGM's first widescreen film (made in England) was excuse for this pretty but empty mini-spectacle of King Arthur's Court, revealing famous love triangle. CinemaScope.▼●◗

Knight Without Armour (1937-British) 101m. *** D: Jacques Feyder. Marlene Dietrich, Robert Donat, Irene Vanbrugh, Herbert Lomas (Lom), Miles Malleson, David Tree. Secret agent Donat helps countess Dietrich flee Russian revolutionaries. Sumptuous production, charismatic stars.▼●

Knock on Any Door (1949) 100m. **½ D: Nicholas Ray. Humphrey Bogart, John Derek, George Macready, Allene Roberts, Susan Perry. More a showcase for young Derek—as a "victim of society" who turns to crime—than a vehicle for Bogart, as conscience-stricken attorney who defends him. Serious but dated drama. Sequel: LET NO MAN WRITE MY EPITAPH.▼●)

Knock on Wood (1954) C-103m. *** D: Norman Panama, Melvin Frank. Danny Kaye, Mai Zetterling, Torin Thatcher, David Burns, Leon Askin, Abner Biberman. Superior Kaye vehicle, with ventriloquist Danny involved with beautiful Zetterling and international spies; good Kaye routines.●

Knockout (1941) 73m. **½ D: William Clemens. Arthur Kennedy, Olympe Bradna, Virginia Field, Anthony Quinn, Cliff Edwards, Cornel Wilde. Slick little programmer in which cocky prizefighter Kennedy seesaws between fame and folly as he is manipulated by slimy promoter Quinn.

Knute Rockne All American (1940) 96m. *** D: Lloyd Bacon. Pat O'Brien, Gale Page, Donald Crisp, Ronald Reagan, Albert Bassermann, John Qualen. Corny but entertaining bio of famed Notre Dame football coach (O'Brien, in a standout performance), with Reagan as his star player, George Gipp. Several long-excised scenes, including O'Brien's famous locker-room pep talk and Reagan's "win just one for the Gipper" speech have now been restored to most TV prints. You *can* see it all on homevideo in any case. Also shown in computer-colored version.▼●

Konga (1961-British) C-90m. *½ D: John Lemont. Michael Gough, Margo Johns, Jess Conrad, Claire Gordon. *Very* mad scientist Gough, intent on creating a plant-animal hybrid, occasionally enlarges his chimpanzee friend to gorilla size, then sends the ape out to kill his enemies. A climactic overdose makes Konga king-sized for an exceptionally dull rampage. Brassy, silly Herman Cohen–produced knockoff of KING KONG has only Gough's juicy, hammy performance to recommend it.▼●

Kongo (1932) 85m. *** D: William Cowen. Walter Huston, Lupe Velez, Conrad Nagel, Virginia Bruce, C. Henry Gordon. Bizarre, fascinating melodrama of crippled madman Huston ruling African colony, seeking revenge on man who paralyzed him by torturing his daughter. Not for the squeamish. Remake of WEST OF ZANZIBAR.●

Kon-Tiki (1950) C-68m. *** D: No director credited. Narrated by Ben Grauer, Thor Heyerdahl. Oscar-winning documentary based on Heyerdahl's best-selling book about his raft trip from Peru to Tahiti, which substantiated his theory that ancient sailing boats crossed the Pacific Ocean. Revised and rescored in 1995; that version runs 58m.▼●

Kriemhild's Revenge SEE: **Die Nibelungen**

Kronos (1957) 78m. **½ D: Kurt Neumann. Jeff Morrow, Barbara Lawrence, John Emery, George O'Hanlon, Morris Ankrum. Diverting science-fiction with unique monster: an enormous metallic walking machine capable of absorbing the Earth's energy. Occasionally shaky special effects are compensated for by nice touch of mysterioso and convincing performances, especially by Emery as the alien's catspaw. Regalscope.▼●

Kwaidan (1964-Japanese) C-164m. ***½ D: Masaki Kobayashi. Rentaro Mikuni, Michiyo Aratama, Keiko Kishi, Tatsuya Nakadai, Takashi Shimura. Four tales of the supernatural, based on works by Lafcadio Hearn, focusing on samurais, balladeers, monks, spirits. Subtle, moody, well staged; stunning use of color and widescreen. Released in U.S. in 1965 at 125m., with the second episode (featuring Kishi and Nakadai) deleted. Tohoscope.▼●

La Bandera (1935-French) 96m. *** D: Julien Duvivier. Jean Gabin, Annabella, Robert Le Vigan, Raymond Aimos, Pierre Renoir, Gaston Modot, Viviane Romance. French criminal on the lam in Africa takes time to find love with an Arab girl, even though he knows he's being pursued by a detective, Javert-style. Old-fashioned in the best sense, this Foreign Legion adventure shot in southern Morocco made Gabin a star and is redolent with the director's poetic realism. Cowritten by Pierre (MacOrlan) Dumarchais from his 1931 novel. Aka ESCAPE FROM YESTERDAY.▼●

La Bête Humaine (1938-French) 99m. ***½ D: Jean Renoir. Jean Gabin, Julien Carette, Simone Simon, Fernand Ledoux, Blanchette Brunoy, Gerard Landry. Locomotive engineer Gabin displays fits of uncontrollable violence against women. When he forms a liaison with the flirtatious wife of a deputy stationmaster, he becomes entangled in a plot to kill the husband. Sublimely atmospheric adaptation of Emile Zola's novel suited the fatalistic mood of Europe in 1938, as the Nazis overran Czechoslovakia. That's Renoir himself in the role of Cabuche; he also scripted. Aka THE HUMAN BEAST and JUDAS WAS A WOMAN. Fritz Lang remade it in the U.S. as HUMAN DESIRE.▼●

La Bohème (1926) 94m. ***½ D: King Vidor. Lillian Gish, John Gilbert, Renee Adoree, George Hassell, Roy D'Arcy, Edward Everett Horton, Karl Dane, Gino Corrado. Charming, floridly romantic silent vehicle for Gish and Gilbert (at their very best) as the star-crossed lovers who live among the starving artists in Paris' Latin Quarter. Gilbert and director Vidor had just made THE BIG PARADE together; this was a worthy follow-up. Based on an 1851 novel, by the way, and quite different from Puccini's famous opera. ❱

La Chienne (1931-French) **95m.** ******** D: Jean Renoir. Michel Simon, Janie Mareze, Georges Flamant, Madeleine Berubet. Renoir's first sound film, and first sound-film masterpiece: a terse, somber drama of mild-mannered bank cashier Simon, with an overbearing wife, who plays into the hands of prostitute Mareze and her scheming pimp. Renoir coscripted; Mareze died in a car accident a couple of weeks after filming was completed. Fritz Lang redid this as SCARLET STREET; what a double bill they would make! ▼◑❱

Lad: A Dog (1962) **C-98m.** ****½** D: Aram Avakian, Leslie H. Martinson. Peter Breck, Peggy McCay, Carroll O'Connor, Angela Cartwright, Maurice Dallimore. Genuine if schmaltzy version of Albert Payson Terhune novel of dog who brings new zest for life to lame child. ▼❱

Ladies Courageous (1944) **88m.** ****** D: John Rawlins. Loretta Young, Geraldine Fitzgerald, Diana Barrymore, Evelyn Ankers, Frank Jenks, Ruth Roman, Anne Gwynne, Phillip Terry, Lois Collier, Kane Richmond. Well-meant idea fails because of hackneyed script and situations; saga of the WAFs during WW2 who played a vital part in air warfare.

Ladies' Day (1943) **62m.** ****** D: Leslie Goodwins. Lupe Velez, Eddie Albert, Patsy Kelly, Max Baer, Jerome Cowan, Iris Adrian, Joan Barclay. Slight baseball farce with Albert a top hurler with an eye for the ladies whose athletic skills disappear each time he gets a new girlfriend. The latest to catch his eye is movie star Velez.

Ladies in Love (1936) **97m.** ****½** D: Edward Griffith. Janet Gaynor, Loretta Young, Constance Bennett, Simone Simon, Don Ameche, Paul Lukas, Tyrone Power. Man-hunting girls in Budapest stick together to find likely victims. Large cast makes it entertaining; young Power seen to good advantage.

Ladies in Retirement (1941) **92m.** ******* D: Charles Vidor. Ida Lupino, Louis Hayward, Evelyn Keyes, Elsa Lanchester, Edith Barrett, Isobel Elsom, Emma Dunn. Static but well-made gothic melodrama about housekeeper Lupino's attempt to cover up murder in eccentric British household. Not as potent—or as shocking—as it must have been in 1941, but still good. Remade as THE MAD ROOM. ❱

Ladies' Man (1931) **70m.** ***½** D: Lothar Mendes. William Powell, Kay Francis, Carole Lombard, Gilbert Emery, John Holland. Lifeless story of gigolo Powell becoming involved with society mother (Olive Tell) and daughter (Lombard), trying to find true happiness with Francis. Strange, downbeat film.

Ladies' Man (1947) **91m.** ****** D: William D. Russell. Eddie Bracken, Cass Daley, Virginia Welles, Spike Jones and His City Slickers. Brassy comedy of hayseed inheriting a fortune, coming to N.Y.C. to paint the town.

Ladies' Man, The (1961) **C-96m.** ******* D: Jerry Lewis. Jerry Lewis, Helen Traubel, Kathleen Freeman, Hope Holiday, Pat Stanley, Jack Kruschen, Doodles Weaver, Harry James and His Band. Pretty funny comedy with Jerry the handyman in a girls' boardinghouse run by Miss Wellenmelon (Traubel). Enormous set is the real star; Buddy Lester and George Raft have amusing cameo appearances. ▼◑❱

Ladies of Leisure (1930) **98m.** ****½** D: Frank Capra. Barbara Stanwyck, Ralph Graves, Lowell Sherman, Marie Prevost, Nance O'Neill, George Fawcett. Stanwyck falls in love with playboy-artist Graves, but cannot shake her reputation as gold digger. Creaky story made worthwhile by Stanwyck's believable performance and Capra's fluent filmmaking technique. Remade as WOMEN OF GLAMOR. ▼❱

Ladies of the Big House (1931) **76m.** ****½** D: Marion Gering. Sylvia Sidney, Gene Raymond, Wynne Gibson, Purnell Pratt, Louise Beavers, Jane Darwell, Noel Francis, Marjorie Main. Sidney is framed and imprisoned while husband Raymond is sent to Death Row; a tearful, well-acted prison drama. Remade as WOMEN WITHOUT NAMES.

Ladies of the Chorus (1949) **61m.** ****** D: Phil Karlson. Adele Jergens, Rand Brooks, Marilyn Monroe, Eddie Garr, Nana Bryant. Cheapie musical about mother/daughter burlesque chorines, with young Monroe seemingly headed for the same romantic blunder that mom Jergens made. Worth a look for MM in her first sizable role. Garr (who plays a burlesque clown) is the father of Teri. ▼

Ladies of the Jury (1932) **65m.** ****½** D: Lowell Sherman. Edna May Oliver, Jill Esmond, Roscoe Ates, Ken Murray, Kitty Kelly, Cora Witherspoon, Florence Lake. Oliver shines as society matron evaluating a murder trial who makes a shambles of courtroom and jury room. Unfortunately, surrounding production is static and unimaginative. Title is odd misnomer, since jury is coed; Guinn Williams appears unbilled as juror with French wife. Remade in 1937 as WE'RE ON THE JURY.

Ladies of the Park SEE: **Les Dames du Bois du Boulogne**

Ladies Should Listen (1934) **62m.** ****** D: Frank Tuttle. Cary Grant, Frances Drake, Edward Everett Horton, Nydia Westman, Ann Sheridan. Grant's life is manipulated by telephone operator Drake in flimsy comedy, no great shakes.

Ladies They Talk About (1933) **69m.** ****½** D: Howard Bretherton, William Keighley. Barbara Stanwyck, Preston Foster, Lyle Talbot, Dorothy Burgess, Maude Eburne, Lillian Roth, Ruth Donnelly. Stanwyck is terrific in this punchy but occasionally silly pre-Code women's prison picture. She's a tough cookie who's sent up the river after participating in a bank heist. ▼●)

Ladies Who Do (1963-British) **85m.** ****½** D: C. M. Pennington-Richards. Peggy Mount, Robert Morley, Harry H. Corbett, Nigel Davenport, Carol White, Miriam Karlin. When a charwoman discovers that wastepaper scraps contain valuable stock market tips, a mild satire on British financial world unfolds.

La Dolce Vita (1960-Italian) **175m.** *****½** D: Federico Fellini. Marcello Mastroianni, Anita Ekberg, Anouk Aimée, Yvonne Furneaux, Magali Noel, Alain Cuny, Annibale Ninchi, Walter Santesso, Lex Barker, Jacques Sernas, Nadia Gray. Lengthy trend-setting film, not as ambiguous as other Fellini works—much more entertaining, with strong cast. Mastroianni stars as tabloid reporter who sees his life in shallow Rome society as worthless but can't change. Story and screenplay by Fellini, Ennio Flaiano, and Tullio Pinelli, with Brunello Rondi. Piero Gherardi's costumes won an Oscar. Totalscope. ▼●)

Lady and the Bandit, The (1951) **79m.** ****** D: Ralph Murphy. Louis Hayward, Patricia Medina, Suzanne Dalbert, Tom Tully. Harmless costumer about career and love of highwayman Dick Turpin.

Lady and the Mob, The (1939) **66m.** ****½** D: Ben Stoloff. Fay Bainter, Lee Bowman, Ida Lupino, Henry Armetta. Bainter gives dignity to mini-tale of eccentric rich lady involved with gangster mob.

Lady and the Monster, The (1944) **86m.** ****** D: George Sherman. Vera Hruba Ralston, Richard Arlen, Erich von Stroheim, Helen Vinson, Sidney Blackmer. In a horror-movie–style castle in the Arizona desert, surgeons Arlen and von Stroheim are unable to save the life of a plane crash victim but secretly steal his brain and keep it alive in a glass tank. The dead man turns out to be a ruthless financier whose brain telepathically takes control of Arlen. Gloomy, minor entry in the "brain swap" school of sci-fi, based on Curt Siodmak's novel *Donovan's Brain*. Later versions: DONOVAN'S BRAIN and THE BRAIN.

Lady and the Tramp (1955) **C-75m.** *****½** D: Hamilton Luske, Clyde Geronimi, Wilfred Jackson. Voices of Peggy Lee, Barbara Luddy, Bill Thompson, Bill Baucon, Stan Freberg, Verna Felton, Alan Reed. One of Walt Disney's most endearing animated features, based on Ward Greene's story about a rakish dog named Tramp who helps pedigreed canine named Lady out of a jam—and into a romance. Elements of adventure and drama are masterfully blended with comedy and music in this stylish film, the Disney studio's first feature cartoon in CinemaScope. Songs by Sonny Burke and Peggy Lee (who's the voice of Peg, Darling, Si and Am, the Siamese cats). Followed in 2001 by a direct-to-video sequel. CinemaScope. ▼●)

Lady at Midnight (1948) **62m.** ****½** D: Sherman Scott (Sam Newfield). Richard Denning, Frances Rafferty, Lora Lee Michel, Ralph Dunn, Nana Bryant, Jack Searle, Harlan Warde, Sid Melton. Entertaining B mystery with married couple Denning and Rafferty finding themselves in turmoil after a murder takes place on their doorstep.

Lady Be Good (1941) **111m.** ******* D: Norman Z. McLeod. Eleanor Powell, Ann Sothern, Robert Young, Lionel Barrymore, John Carroll, Red Skelton, Virginia O'Brien, Dan Dailey, Jimmy Dorsey and His Orchestra. Spunky musical of married songwriters Sothern and Young, with Powell and Skelton along for good measure. Fine score: title tune, "Fascinating Rhythm," "You'll Never Know," Oscar-winning "Last Time I Saw Paris." ▼●)

Ladybug Ladybug (1963) **84m.** ******* D: Frank Perry. Jane Connell, William Daniels, James Frawley, Richard Hamilton, Kathryn Hays, Jane Hoffman, Elena Karam, Judith Lowry, Nancy Marchand, Estelle Parsons, Miles Chapin, Alice Playten. Ambitious and provocative (if a bit too obvious) account of some rural schoolchildren and their reactions when a civil defense system warns of an impending nuclear attack. Screenplay by Eleanor Perry; a follow-up of sorts to DAVID AND LISA. Based on an actual incident.

Lady by Choice (1934) **78m.** ****½** D: David Burton. Carole Lombard, May Robson, Roger Pryor, Walter Connolly, Arthur Hohl. Enjoyable follow-up to LADY FOR A DAY; dancer Lombard takes in scraggly Robson, makes her proper lady. ▼●)

Lady Confesses, The (1945) **64m.** ****** D: Sam Newfield. Mary Beth Hughes, Hugh Beaumont, Edmund MacDonald, Claudia Drake. After seven years of mysterious absence, a bitchy, unmissed wife turns up just in time to prevent husband Beaumont from declaring her dead and remarrying; her subsequent strangulation prompts Beaumont's fiancée Hughes to go undercover to find the killer. A dearth of suspects detracts from the fun in somber Poverty Row noir.

Lady Consents, The (1936) **75m.** ****½** D: Stephen Roberts. Ann Harding, Herbert Marshall, Margaret Lindsay, Walter Abel.

[369]

Pat triangle with married Marshall discovering that he still loves his ex-wife.

Lady Dances, The SEE: **Merry Widow, The** (1934)

Lady Doctor (1956-Italian) **90m. **½** D: Camillo Mastrocinque. Abbe Lane, Vittorio De Sica, Toto, Titina De Filippo, German Cobos, Teddy Reno. Pungent nonsense as Toto and De Sica try to con doctor Lane out of a fortune hidden in her house.

Lady Eve, The (1941) **94m. ***½** D: Preston Sturges. Barbara Stanwyck, Henry Fonda, Charles Coburn, Eugene Pallette, William Demarest, Eric Blore, Melville Cooper. Stanwyck is a con artist who sets her eyes on wealthy Fonda—the dolt to end all dolts, who proclaims "snakes are my life." Sometimes silly and strident, this film grows funnier with each viewing— thanks to Sturges' script, breathless pace, and two incomparable stars. Remade as THE BIRDS AND THE BEES. ▼○▶

Lady for a Day (1933) **96m. ****** D: Frank Capra. Warren William, May Robson, Guy Kibbee, Glenda Farrell, Jean Parker, Walter Connolly, Ned Sparks, Nat Pendleton. Wonderful Damon Runyon fable of seedy apple vendor Robson transformed into perfect lady by softhearted racketeer William. Robert Riskin adapted Runyon's story "Madame La Gimp." Sequel: LADY BY CHOICE. Remade by Capra as POCKETFUL OF MIRACLES. ▼○▶

Lady for a Night (1942) **87m. **** D: Leigh Jason. Joan Blondell, John Wayne, Ray Middleton, Philip Merivale, Blanche Yurka, Edith Barrett, Hattie Noel. Plodding costume drama of wealthy, status-seeking gambling queen Blondell and her plight upon marrying impoverished society drunk Middleton. Good cast seems out of place. ▼▶

Lady From Cheyenne (1941) **87m. **½** D: Frank Lloyd. Loretta Young, Robert Preston, Edward Arnold, Frank Craven, Gladys George. Average fare of schoolteacher Young (in 1869 Wyoming) striking a blow for women's rights about a century too early, as she fights for the opportunity to sit on a jury. Good supporting cast helps.

Lady From Chungking (1942) **66m. *** D: William Nigh. Anna May Wong, Harold Huber, Mae Clarke, Rick Vallin, Paul Bryar, Ted Hecht, Louis (Ludwig) Donath. Charismatic, dignified Wong is the only reason to wade through this plodding, heavy-handed film about a Chinese freedom fighter who poses as a courtesan to a warlord (Huber) and has to endure the scorn of her followers. ▶

Lady From Louisiana (1941) **82m. **½** D: Bernard Vorhaus. John Wayne, Ona Munson, Ray Middleton, Henry Stephenson, Helen Westley, Jack Pennick, Dorothy Dandridge. Wayne and Munson fall in love, then discover they're on opposite sides of gambling controversy; so-so period piece. ▼▶

Lady From Shanghai, The (1948) **87m. **** D: Orson Welles. Rita Hayworth, Orson Welles, Everett Sloane, Glenn Anders, Ted de Corsia, Erskine Sanford, Gus Schilling. The camera's the star of this offbeat thriller, with the cast incidental in bizarre murder mystery about an Irish adventurer (Welles) who joins seductive Hayworth and her husband (Sloane) on a Pacific cruise. The famous hall of mirrors climax is riveting. Cinematography by Charles Lawton, Jr. Based on novel by Sherwood King; scripted and produced by Welles. That's Errol Flynn's yacht, *Zaca*, in the seagoing scenes. ▼○▶

Lady From Texas, The (1951) **C-77m.** D: Joseph Pevney. Howard Duff, Mona Freeman, Josephine Hull, Gene Lockhart, Craig Stevens. Strange minor film of eccentric old lady Hull; Duff and Freeman come to her rescue.

Lady Gambles, The (1949) **98m. *** D: Michael Gordon. Barbara Stanwyck, Robert Preston, Stephen McNally, Edith Barrett, John Hoyt, Leif Erickson. The LOST WEEKEND of gambling films, a well-acted drama chronicling Stanwyck's decline from respectable writer's wife to desperate, addicted gambler and all-around screwup. Look for Tony Curtis—then billed as "Anthony"—as a bellboy. ▶

Lady Gangster (1942) **62m. **½** D: Florian Roberts (Robert Florey). Faye Emerson, Julie Bishop, Frank Wilcox, Roland Drew, Jackie C. Gleason, Ruth Ford, Virginia Brissac, DeWolf (William) Hopper. Fast-paced B film with girl-gone-bad Emerson linked to a gang of hoods (with the "sensitive" one played by young Gleason). Will crusading investigative radio reporter Wilcox be able to reform her? ▼▶

Lady Godiva (1955) **C-89m. *** D: Arthur Lubin. Maureen O'Hara, George Nader, Victor McLaglen, Rex Reason, Torin Thatcher, Eduard Franz, Leslie Bradley, Henry Brandon, Arthur Shields. Cardboard costumer about famed 11th-century Englishwoman rising from humble origins, interceding in royal affairs, and, of course, taking her underdressed horseback ride—and what a dull ride it is! Look fast for Clint Eastwood in an unbilled bit. Full title on-screen is LADY GODIVA OF COVENTRY. ▼▶

Lady Godiva of Coventry SEE: **Lady Godiva**

Lady Godiva Rides Again (1951-British) **90m. *** D: Frank Launder. Dennis Price, John McCallum, Stanley Holloway, Pauline Stroud, Diana Dors, George Cole, Kay Kendall, Sidney James, Dagmar (Dana) Wynter, Googie Withers, Alastair Sim. Intriguing cast keeps one watching this OK comedy about a simple lass who wins a beauty contest and is exposed to the seamy side of glamour. Joan Collins' film debut, as one of the contestants.

Lady Hamilton SEE: **That Hamilton Woman**

Lady Has Plans, The (1942) 77m. ** D: Sidney Lanfield. Paulette Goddard, Ray Milland, Roland Young, Albert Dekker, Margaret Hayes, Cecil Kellaway. Jumbled spy comedy with innocent Goddard suspected of being agent and Milland tailing her in Lisbon.

Lady in a Cage (1964) 93m. *** D: Walter Grauman. Olivia de Havilland, Ann Sothern, Jeff Corey, James Caan, Jennifer Billingsley, Rafael Campos, Scatman Crothers. Bone-chilling psychological drama in which incapacitated widow de Havilland finds herself stuck in an elevator in her home, then is terrorized by thugs. Allegorical tale of alienation and mindless cruelty in an impersonal society; unpleasant to watch, but undeniably truthful and prophetic. Starkly directed and well acted.▼⫸

Lady in a Jam (1942) 78m. **½ D: Gregory La Cava. Irene Dunne, Patric Knowles, Ralph Bellamy, Eugene Pallette, Queenie Vassar. Thirties-type screwball comedy doesn't really hit bull's-eye, with wacky Dunne convincing psychiatrist Knowles to marry her to cure her ills. ⫸

Lady in Distress (1939-British) 76m. *** D: Herbert Mason. Paul Lukas, Sally Gray, Michael Redgrave, Patricia Roc, Hartley Power. Redgrave falls for wife of jealous magician after witnessing what looked like her murder. Original British title: A WINDOW IN LONDON.▼⫸

Lady in Question, The (1940) 81m. **½ D: Charles Vidor. Brian Aherne, Rita Hayworth, Glenn Ford, Irene Rich, George Coulouris, Lloyd Corrigan. Aherne plays a juror interested in defendant Hayworth. He manages to save her, but later falls prey to jealousy. Varies awkwardly from comedy to drama.▼⫸

Lady in Scarlet, The (1935) 65m. ** D: Charles Lamont. Reginald Denny, Patricia Farr, Jameson Thomas, Dorothy Revier, James Bush. Who killed the ornery Manhattan art dealer? The tension is bearable as barflies Denny and Farr, sleuth and secretary, respectively, run down the list of suspects. No-frills Poverty Row takeoff on THE THIN MAN doesn't come off because the leads' relationship is more nasty (he calls her Stupid, she's no nicer) than witty.

Lady in the Dark (1944) C-100m. **½ D: Mitchell Leisen. Ginger Rogers, Ray Milland, Jon Hall, Warner Baxter, Barry Sullivan, Gail Russell, Mischa Auer. Overproduced Technicolor adaptation of the groundbreaking Moss Hart Broadway show (minus most of the Kurt Weill–Ira Gershwin songs) about a career woman who undergoes psychoanalysis to find the root of her problems. Intriguing but ultimately ponderous.

Lady in the Fog SEE: **Scotland Yard Inspector**

Lady in the Iron Mask (1952) C-78m. ** D: Ralph Murphy. Louis Hayward, Patricia Medina, Alan Hale (Jr.), John Sutton. Varia-

tion of Dumas tale, with Three Musketeers still about; moderate costumer.

Lady in the Lake (1946) 103m. **½ D: Robert Montgomery. Robert Montgomery, Audrey Totter, Lloyd Nolan, Tom Tully, Leon Ames, Jayne Meadows. Raymond Chandler whodunit has novelty of camera taking first-person point of view of detective Philip Marlowe (Montgomery); unfortunately, confusing plot is presented in more prosaic (and dated) manner.▼⫸

Lady Is Willing, The (1942) 92m. *** D: Mitchell Leisen. Marlene Dietrich, Fred MacMurray, Aline MacMahon, Arline Judge, Stanley Ridges, Roger Clark. Agreeable comedy; glamorous Dietrich wants to adopt a baby, so she marries pediatrician MacMurray. Dramatic segment near the end spoils lively mood.▼

Lady Killer (1933) 74m. *** D: Roy Del Ruth. James Cagney, Mae Clarke, Leslie Fenton, Margaret Lindsay, Henry O'Neill, Raymond Hatton, George Chandler. Vintage Cagney, with tangy tale of mobster becoming Hollywood actor, torn between two professions; Cagney repeats his Clarke slapfest.▼⫸

Ladykillers, The (1955-British) C-90m. ***½ D: Alexander Mackendrick. Alec Guinness, Katie Johnson, Cecil Parker, Herbert Lom, Peter Sellers, Danny Green, Frankie Howerd, Jack Warner. Droll black comedy of not-so-bright crooks involved with seemingly harmless old lady. Guinness scores again (even his *teeth* are funny) with top-notch supporting cast in this little Ealing Studios gem, written by William Rose. Original British running time: 97m. Remade in 2004.▼⫸

Lady L (1965-British) C-107m. **½ D: Peter Ustinov. Sophia Loren, Paul Newman, David Niven, Claude Dauphin, Philippe Noiret, Michel Piccoli. Stars and sets are elegant, but this wacky comedy set in early 20th-century London and Paris fizzles, despite Ustinov's writing, directing, and cameo appearance. Panavision.▼⫸

Lady Luck (1946) 97m. *** D: Edwin L. Marin. Robert Young, Barbara Hale, Frank Morgan, James Gleason. Hale marries gambler Young with hopes of reforming him but meets more problems than she bargained for.

Lady of Burlesque (1943) 91m. *** D: William Wellman. Barbara Stanwyck, Michael O'Shea, J. Edward Bromberg, Iris Adrian, Marion Martin, Pinky Lee, Frank Conroy, Gloria Dickson. Stanwyck attempts to uncover—no pun intended—killer of strippers in this amusing adaptation of Gypsy Rose Lee's *G-String Murders.*▼⫸

Lady of Chance, A (1928) 78m. **½ D: Robert Z. Leonard. Norma Shearer, Lowell Sherman, John (Johnny) Mack Brown, Gwen Lee, Eugenie Besserer, Buddie (Buddy) Messinger, Polly Moran. Shearer (in her last silent film) rises way above her material, a so-so comedy-drama-romance in which she plays a gold-digging dame with a criminal past who hustles money from wealthy men. With fellow con artists Sherman and Lee watching over her, she sets her sights on businessman Brown. Originally released with added talking sequences, but none featured Shearer. ◗

Lady of Secrets (1936) **73m.** **✶✶½** D: Marion Gering. Ruth Chatterton, Otto Kruger, Lionel Atwill, Marian Marsh, Lloyd Nolan, Robert Allen. Smooth but soapy story of woman whose one unhappy love affair has made her live a life of seclusion. Good cast makes standard film worth seeing.

Lady of the Dugout, The (1918) **64m.** **✶✶½** D: W. S. Van Dyke. Al Jennings, Frank Jennings, Corinne Grant, Ben Alexander, Joseph Singleton, Carl Stockdale. Al Jennings, real-life Western bandit-turned-movie-actor-producer, relates a tale in which he and his brother Frank are stranded in a desert wasteland. After robbing a bank in a dreary little town, they come upon the downtrodden title character. Jennings' company produced this grimly realistic look at the harshness of life in the American West. ◗

Lady of the Night (1925) **61m.** **✶✶½** D: Monta Bell. Norma Shearer, Malcolm MacGregor, Dale Fuller, George K. Arthur, Fred Esmelton, Lew Harvey, Gwen Lee. A young inventor is torn between two lookalike women who come from very different backgrounds: one is a dance hall dame whose father was a crook, the other a wealthy judge's privileged daughter. Shearer's convincing performance in a dual role distinguishes this minor silent melodrama. ◗

Lady of the Tropics (1939) **92m.** **✶✶** D: Jack Conway. Hedy Lamarr, Robert Taylor, Joseph Schildkraut, Frederick Worlock, Natalie Moorhead. Sad love affair between playboy Taylor and half-breed Lamarr in exotic setting; slow-moving.

Lady of Vengeance (1957-British) **73m.** **✶✶** D: Burt Balaban. Dennis O'Keefe, Ann Sears, Patrick Barr, Vernon Greeves. Tedious account of man hiring killer to avenge a girl's death, becoming embroiled in further murder.

Lady on a Train (1945) **93m.** **✶✶✶** D: Charles David. Deanna Durbin, Ralph Bellamy, Edward Everett Horton, George Coulouris, Allen Jenkins, David Bruce, Patricia Morison, Dan Duryea, William Frawley. Excellent comedy/murder-mystery with Deanna witnessing a murder, then getting involved with nutty family of the deceased tycoon. You'll never guess killer's identity in neatly plotted yarn which even allows Deanna to sing a few tunes. Based on a Leslie Charteris story. ◗◗

Lady Pays Off, The (1951) **80m.** **✶✶½** D: Douglas Sirk. Linda Darnell, Stephen McNally, Gigi Perreau, Virginia Field. Fanciful drama of schoolteacher Darnell who must pay off gambling debts in Reno by tutoring casino owner's daughter.

Lady Possessed (1952-British) **87m.** **✶✶** D: William Spier, Roy Kellino. James Mason, June Havoc, Pamela Kellino (Mason), Fay Compton, Odette Myrtil. Bizarre film of ill woman thinking she is controlled by will of Mason's dead wife.

Lady Says No, The (1952) **80m.** **✶✶** D: Frank Ross. David Niven, Joan Caulfield, Lenore Lonergan, James Robertson Justice. Lightweight comedy of fickle Caulfield, who won't decide if marriage is for her. ▼◗

Lady Scarface (1941) **69m.** **✶✶** D: Frank Woodruff. Dennis O'Keefe, Judith Anderson, Frances Neal, Mildred Coles, Eric Blore, Marc Lawrence. Anderson tries to elevate this episodic yarn of police hunting for dangerous gunwoman and her gang. ▼

Lady's From Kentucky, The (1939) **67m.** **✶✶½** D: Alexander Hall. George Raft, Ellen Drew, Hugh Herbert, ZaSu Pitts, Louise Beavers, Stanley Andrews. Regardless of title, Raft's horse takes precedence over his lady in this well-done horse-racing saga.

Lady's Morals, A (1930) **75m.** **✶✶** D: Sidney Franklin. Grace Moore, Reginald Denny, Wallace Beery, Jobyna Howland. First attempt to make star of opera singer Moore doesn't click. She plays Jenny Lind, who learns value of love from devoted Denny.

Lady Surrenders, A SEE: **Love Story** (1944)

Lady Takes a Chance, A (1943) **86m.** **✶✶✶** D: William A. Seiter. Jean Arthur, John Wayne, Charles Winninger, Phil Silvers, Mary Field, Don Costello. Wayne and Arthur make fine comedy team as burly rodeo star and wide-eyed city girl who falls for him; Silvers adds zip as bus-tour guide. ▼◗

Lady Takes a Flyer, The (1958) **C-94m.** **✶✶½** D: Jack Arnold. Lana Turner, Jeff Chandler, Richard Denning, Andra Martin. Different-type Turner fare. Lana is lady flier who marries pilot Chandler, each finds it hard to settle down to married life. CinemaScope.

Lady Takes a Sailor, The (1949) **99m.** **✶✶** D: Michael Curtiz. Jane Wyman, Dennis Morgan, Eve Arden, Robert Douglas, Allyn Joslyn, Tom Tully, Lina Romay, William Frawley, Fred Clark, Craig Stevens. Featherweight fluff about Morgan inadvertently ruining career woman Wyman's reputation as a consumer watchdog. Sheer silliness.

Lady to Love, A (1930) **92m.** **✶✶** D: Victor Seastrom (Sjostrom). Edward G. Robinson, Vilma Banky, Robert Ames, Richard Carle, Lloyd Ingraham. Stilted early talkie version of Sidney Howard's play *They Knew What They Wanted*, previously filmed in 1928, and remade in 1940 under its original title. Robinson is miscast as an Italian vintner in San Francisco who gets a young mail-order bride (Banky) by sending her a picture of his hunky foreman (Ames). Between Robinson's heavy-handed Chico Marx–like dialect and Banky's Budapest accent, subtitles might have helped.

Lady Vanishes, The (1938-British) **97m. ****** D: Alfred Hitchcock. Margaret Lockwood, Michael Redgrave, Paul Lukas, Dame May Whitty, Googie Withers, Cecil Parker, Linden Travers, Catherine Lacey. An old woman's disappearance during a train ride leads baffled young woman into a dizzying web of intrigue. Delicious mystery-comedy; Hitchcock at his best, with a witty script by Frank Launder and Sidney Gilliat, and wonderful performances by Naunton Wayne and Basil Radford, who scored such a hit as a pair of twits that they repeated those roles in several other films! Based on Ethel Lina White's novel *The Wheel Spins*. Remade in 1979 and as a 2013 BBC TVM. ▼●▶

Lady Wants Mink, The (1953) **C-92m. ***** D: William A. Seiter. Eve Arden, Ruth Hussey, Dennis O'Keefe, William Demarest, Gene Lockhart. Most diverting little film of wife Hussey breeding mink to get the coat she's always wanted.

Lady Windermere's Fan (1925) **89m. ***½** D: Ernst Lubitsch. Ronald Colman, May McAvoy, Bert Lytell, Irene Rich, Edward Martindel, Mme. Daumery. Smart, elegant adaptation of Oscar Wilde's comedy of manners, in which Lord Darlington (Colman) announces his love for married Lady Windermere (McAvoy); meanwhile, the calculating Mrs. Erlynne (a superb Rich) drifts into London and reveals a secret. Lubitsch captures the essence of Wilde's play in this absorbing tale of love, desire, deception, and misunderstanding, while brilliantly satirizing upper-class mores. Previously filmed in England in 1916; remade in Germany in 1935, in Mexico in 1944, in 1949 (as THE FAN), and in 2004 (as A GOOD WOMAN). ▼●▶

Lady With a Lamp, The (1951-British) **112m. ***** D: Herbert Wilcox. Anna Neagle, Michael Wilding, Felix Aylmer, Maureen Pryor, Gladys Young, Julian D'Albie. Methodical recreation of 19th-century nurse-crusader Florence Nightingale, tastefully enacted by Neagle.

Lady With a Past (1932) **80m. **½** D: Edward H. Griffith. Constance Bennett, Ben Lyon, David Manners, Astrid Allwyn, Merna Kennedy, Nella Walker, Blanche Frederici. Chic fluff about rich "good girl" Bennett who discovers that she's much more popular with men when she acts "bad."

Lady Without Passport, A (1950) **72m. **½** D: Joseph H. Lewis. Hedy Lamarr, John Hodiak, James Craig, George Macready. Turgid melodrama as Lamarr seeks to leave Havana, former romantic and business associations behind her. ▶

Lady With Red Hair (1940) **81m. **½** D: Curtis Bernhardt. Miriam Hopkins, Claude Rains, Richard Ainley, Laura Hope Crews, Helen Westley, John Litel, Victor Jory. Breathless pace, likable cast make up for silliness in story of actress Mrs. Leslie Carter and her colorful mentor David Belasco. Look fast for young Cornel Wilde at boardinghouse.

Lady With the Dog, The (1960-Russian) **88m. **½** D: Iosif Heifitz. I. Savvina, A. Batalov. While vacationing in Yalta, a man and a woman—both married—meet and fall in love. Sensitive, deliberately paced tale of loneliness, guilt, and longing, based on a short story by Anton Chekhov, which also is partly the basis of DARK EYES (1987). ▶

Lafayette (1962-French) **C-110m. **** D: Jean Dreville. Jack Hawkins, Orson Welles, Howard St. John, Edmund Purdom, Vittorio De Sica, Michel Le Royer. Overblown, badly scripted costumer of famed 18th-century Frenchman; an episodic minor spectacle. Super Technirama 70. ▶

Lafayette Escadrille (1958) **93m. **** D: William Wellman. Tab Hunter, Etchika Choureau, William Wellman, Jr., Jody McCrea, Dennis Devine, Marcel Dalio, David Janssen, Paul Fix, Will Hutchins, Clint Eastwood, Tom Laughlin, Brett Halsey. Wellman's final film is a well-intentioned but flat account of the celebrated French flying legion of WW1, spotlighting the coming to maturity of wayward Hunter. Mostly of interest for its cast, with Wellman, Jr., playing his father (who actually was a pilot during the war). Wellman, Sr., wrote the story and narrates. ▶

La Fièvre Monte à El Pao (1959-French-Mexican) **97m. ***** D: Luis Buñuel. Gérard Philipe, Maria Felix, Jean Servais, Raoul Dantes, Miguel Ángel Ferriz, Domingo Soler, Victor Junco. Incisive look at life in a tiny Latin American dictatorship filled with political prisoners, where corruption and sexual deviance run rampant. Idealistic but cowardly official Philipe tries to make a difference. Lesser-known Buñuel, a ripe, steamy mixture of melodrama, satire, and pure star power. Philipe's final film. Mexican title: LOS AMBICIOSOS. Known in the U.S. as REPUBLIC OF SIN and FEVER MOUNTS AT EL PAO. ▶

L'Age d'Or (1930-French) **63m. ****** D: Luis Buñuel. Gaston Modot, Lya Lys, Max Ernst, Pierre Prévert. Bishops turn into skeletons and the cow wanders into the bedroom in Buñuel's first feature, a surrealistic masterpiece coscripted by Salvadore Dali. Right-wing agitators caused a riot at the film's first (and for a long time, only) public screening; its anticlericalism put it into the "banned film" category for decades. Still has the power to delight, if no longer shock. ▼●▶

La Grande Illusion SEE: **Grand Illusion**

La Habañera (1937-German) **93m. **½**

D: Detlev Sierk (Douglas Sirk). Zarah Leander, Ferdinand Marian, Karl Martell, Julia Serda, Boris Alekin, Paul Bildt. Swedish tourist in Puerto Rico impulsively marries a captivating nobleman. A decade later, virtually her husband's prisoner, she discovers he's deliberately suppressing news of an epidemic sweeping the island nation. Feverish melodrama—with Sirk's florid imagery floating the implausibilities—was one of the German-born director's best-appreciated pictures abroad, made just prior to his flight from Hitler to the U.S. ▼▶

Lake Placid Serenade (1944) 85m. ** D: Steve Sekely. Vera Hruba Ralston, Robert Livingston, Vera Vague (Barbara Jo Allen), Eugene Pallette, Stephanie Bachelor, Walter Catlett, John Litel; guest star, Roy Rogers. Flimsy musical romance about an ice skater, played by real-life skating queen Ralston. Supporting cast does its best.

La Kermesse Heroique SEE: **Carnival in Flanders**

La Marseillaise (1938-French) 130m. ***½ D: Jean Renoir. Pierre Renoir, Louis Jouvet, Julien Carette, Lisa Delamare. Renoir scripted this stirring account of the French Revolution, featuring dialogue extracted from documents of the 1790s. Begins with news of the fall of the Bastille reaching Louis XVI, ends with the Marseilles Battalion of the French Revolutionary Army storming the Tuilleries and marching to Valmy. Renoir opted for a humanist approach to history, avoiding what he considered the false solemnity of most historical epics. ▼▶

La Maternelle (1932-French) 86m. *** D: Jean Benoit-Levy. Madeleine Renaud, Alice Tissot, Paulette Elambert, Sylvette Fillacier, Mady Berri, Henri Debain. Insightful, compassionate drama about the plight of slum children in Montmartre day nursery. The focus is on little Elambert's pain, confusion, and attachment to nurse Renaud. Its observations about children's perceptions have dated not one bit. ▼

Lancer Spy (1937) 84m. *** D: Gregory Ratoff. Dolores Del Rio, George Sanders, Peter Lorre, Joseph Schildkraut, Virginia Field, Sig Ruman, Fritz Feld. Sanders disguises himself as German officer to get information in this taut thriller; Del Rio has to choose between love and loyalty to her country. ▶

Land of Fury SEE: **Seekers, The**

Land of Liberty (1939) 80m. **½ No director credited. All-star salute to the heroes of American history was cobbled together from a slew of Hollywood films, silent and sound. Produced at 138m. for both the New York World's Fair and San Francisco's Golden Gate Exposition, it was cut in 1941 for theatrical release to benefit the Red Cross. Finally ended up as a 16mm staple in classrooms, where baby boomers learned that Jean Lafitte and Wild Bill Hickok looked like Frederic March and Gary Cooper. Supervised and narrated by Cecil B. DeMille.

Land of the Pharaohs (1955) C-106m. **½ D: Howard Hawks. Jack Hawkins, Joan Collins, James Robertson Justice, Dewey Martin, Alexis Minotis, Sydney Chaplin, James Hayter. Entertaining, if fruity spectacle about building of the Great Pyramid, filmed on an epic scale. Hawks claimed neither he nor his writers (including William Faulkner and Harry Kurnitz) "knew how a pharaoh talked" . . . and it shows. Still worth catching for great revenge ending and now-campy villainy by Collins. CinemaScope. ▼▶

Landru SEE: **Bluebeard** (1962)

Land Unknown, The (1957) 78m. ** D: Virgil Vogel. Jock Mahoney, Shawn Smith, Henry Brandon, Douglas Kennedy. Naval helicopter exploring Antarctica is forced down in tropical subterranean valley of prehistoric animals. Monsters are clumsily done but film is OK. CinemaScope. ▼▶

La Notte (1961-French-Italian) 120m. **½ D: Michelangelo Antonioni. Jeanne Moreau, Marcello Mastroianni, Monica Vitti, Bernhard Wicki. Moreau is bored and troubled by one-dimensional husband Mastroianni in this study of noncommunication. Moody, introverted, abstract—and superficial—filled with "empty, hopeless images." The second of a trilogy, preceded by L'AVVENTURA and followed by L'ECLISSE. Aka THE NIGHT. ▼▶

La Nuit Fantastique (1942-French) 91m. *** D: Marcel L'Herbier. Fernand Gravey, Micheline Presle, Saturnin Fabre, Charles Granval, Bernard Blier, Marcel Levesque. Witty fantasy centering on a student (Gravey) who, while working at night, continually dreams of adventures with a mysterious beauty dressed in white (Presle). Then he meets her in real life and tries to save her from a plot hatched by her evil magician father. Or does he? Don't look for normal narrative logic in this delightfully surreal look at illusion and reality. ▼▶

La Parisienne (1957-French-Italian) C-85m. ** D: Michel Boisrond. Brigitte Bardot, Charles Boyer, Henri Vidal, Andre Luguet, Nadia Gray, Noel Roquevert, Claire Maurier. Flimsy comedy with Bardot the daughter of the Premier of France. To get back at her Don Juan husband (Vidal), she has an affair with married prince Boyer. Aka UNE PARISIENNE. ▼

La Pointe-courte (1954-French) 81m. ***½ D: Agnès Varda. Silvia Monfort, Philippe Noiret. Superlative debut feature from Varda is a snapshot of life in a small, rubble-strewn Mediterranean fishing village. The spotlight is on a young man, a village native who has returned for a visit; his Parisian wife joins him, and they sort out their rocky relationship. Their story blends with the sorrows, joys, and crises of the townsfolk. Deceptively simple, quietly powerful film is both a precursor of the French New Wave and an offshoot of Italian Neorealism. Coedited by Alain Resnais. ▶

Larceny (1948) 89m. **½ D: George Sherman. John Payne, Joan Caulfield, Dan Duryea, Shelley Winters, Dorothy Hart. Slick but ordinary underworld tale, with roguish Payne deciding to help lovely Caulfield; Duryea is slimy villain.

Larceny, Inc. (1942) 95m. ***½ D: Lloyd Bacon. Edward G. Robinson, Jane Wyman, Broderick Crawford, Jack Carson, Anthony Quinn, Edward Brophy. Hilarious little comedy of ex-cons Robinson, Crawford, and Brophy using luggage store as front for shady activities; villain Quinn tries to horn in. Look for Jackie Gleason in a small role as a soda jerk. ▶

Larceny in Her Heart (1946) 68m. ** D: Sam Newfield. Hugh Beaumont, Cheryl Walker, Ralph Dunn, Paul Bryar, Charles Wilson, Douglas Fowley. Sleuth Michael Shayne (Beaumont) gets mixed up with a femme fatale during a murder investigation in this passable minor entry, though seeing the Beaver's future TV dad in the lead may be the chief point of interest today.

La Revue des Revues (1927-French) 103m. **½ D: Joé Francis (Francys). Hélène Hallier, André Luguet. Slight, trite plot—a much-abused young woman dreams of (and predictably finds) show business stardom—is secondary to the parade of routines featuring Parisian stage luminaries that are sprinkled throughout this curio. The numbers, which collectively celebrate Paris nightlife 1920s-style, are statically filmed but beautifully color-tinted. Highlight: two eccentric dances featuring leggy 21-year-old Josephine Baker. ▶

La Ronde (1950-French) 97m. ***½ D: Max Ophuls. Anton Walbrook, Serge Reggiani, Simone Simon, Simone Signoret, Daniel Gelin, Danielle Darrieux, Fernand Gravet, Odette Joyeux, Jean-Louis Barrault, Isa Miranda, Gérard Philipe. Wise, witty account of various people having affairs, forming a chain that eventually comes full circle, all held together by sarcastic Walbrook. A film of style and charm, based on an Arthur Schnitzler play. Screenplay by Jacques Natanson and director Ophuls. Remade as CIRCLE OF LOVE and CHAIN OF DESIRE. ▼●▶

La Roue (1923-French) 273m. ***½ D: Abel Gance. Séverin-Mars, Ivy Close, Gabriel de Gravone, Pierre Magnier, Max Maxudian, Georges Térof. A railroad conductor (Séverin-Mars) rescues a young girl from a train wreck and raises her as his daughter. He keeps this adoption secret, which has a powerful effect on his son . . . and himself. What might have been a corny soap opera with over-the-top performances becomes

an epic tragedy in the hands of Gance, who makes dazzling (and groundbreaking) use of cinematic technique to tell the story. Originally screened in a longer version, then edited for theatrical distribution. ▶

Lash, The (1930) 75m. ** D: Frank Lloyd. Richard Barthelmess, James Rennie, Mary Astor, Marian Nixon, Fred Kohler, Barbara Bedford, Robert Edeson, Arthur Stone. Barthelmess is miscast as a Spanish cattle rancher in 1800s California who becomes a Robin Hood–type bandit to avenge his people against unscrupulous American land agents. Dated early-talkie Western adventure features some sweeping spectacle, especially an impressive cattle stampede. Filmed both in 35mm and in a pioneering 65mm widescreen process called Vitascope.

La Signora di Tutti (1934-Italian) 89m. *** D: Max Ophuls. Isa Miranda, Memo Benassi, Tatiana Pavlova, Federico Benfer, Nelly Corradi, Franco Coop. Ophuls' only film made in Italy is an intricately structured flashback tale about the tragic life of a beautiful peasant girl who becomes a movie star (a radiant Miranda). Superbly photographed and elegantly directed; a moving study of love, loss, and illusion that not only feels like a warm-up for Ophuls' own 1955 masterpiece, LOLA MONTES, but also bears similarities to Joseph L. Mankiewicz's THE BAREFOOT CONTESSA. Aka EVERYBODY'S WOMAN. ▼

Lassie Come Home (1943) C-88m. ***½ D: Fred M. Wilcox. Roddy McDowall, Donald Crisp, Dame May Whitty, Edmund Gwenn, Nigel Bruce, Elsa Lanchester, Elizabeth Taylor. Winning, wonderful film from Eric Knight's book about a poor family forced to sell their beloved dog, who undertakes several tortuous journeys to return to them. A tearjerker of the first order, and one of the all-time great family films. Lassie is played—quite remarkably—by a male collie named Pal. Sequel: SON OF LASSIE. Remade as GYPSY COLT, THE MAGIC OF LASSIE, and LASSIE (2005). ▼●▶

Last Angry Man, The (1959) 100m. *** D: Daniel Mann. Paul Muni, David Wayne, Betsy Palmer, Luther Adler, Joby Baker, Joanna Moore, Godfrey Cambridge, Billy Dee Williams. Sentimental story of an old, dedicated family doctor in Brooklyn whose life is going to be portrayed on TV. Muni (in his last film) makes it worth seeing. Adapted by Gerald Green from his novel. Remade as 1974 TVM with Pat Hingle. ▼

Last Blitzkrieg, The (1958) 84m. ** D: Arthur Dreifuss. Van Johnson, Kerwin Mathews, Dick York, Larry Storch. WW2 actioner trying to focus on German point of view.

Last Bridge, The (1954-Austrian-Yugoslavian) 95m. ***½ D: Helmut Kautner. Maria Schell, Bernhard Wicki, Barbara

Rutting, Carl Mohner. Schell gives well-modulated performance as German doctor captured by Yugoslavian partisans during WW2, first administering medical aid reluctantly, then realizing all people deserve equal attention. Released in the U.S. in 1957.▼

Last Command, The (1928) **88m. ****** D: Josef von Sternberg. Emil Jannings, Evelyn Brent, William Powell, Nicholas Soussanin, Michael Visaroff, Jack Raymond, Fritz Feld. Stunning silent drama of refugee Russian general Jannings, who is now reduced to working as a Hollywood extra—and destined to appear in a movie depicting the Russian revolution. A fascinating story laced with keen perceptions of life and work in Hollywood. Lajos Biros' story was based on an actual person; Jannings' gripping performance won him an Oscar (shared for his work in THE WAY OF ALL FLESH).▼)

Last Command, The (1955) **C-110m. **½** D: Frank Lloyd. Sterling Hayden, Anna Maria Alberghetti, Richard Carlson, Arthur Hunnicutt, Ernest Borgnine, J. Carrol Naish, Ben Cooper, John Russell, Virginia Grey, Jim Davis, Eduard Franz, Otto Kruger, Slim Pickens. Elaborate, sweeping account of the battle of the Alamo, hampered by tedious script. Story centers on wandering adventurer Jim Bowie (Hayden), who is galvanized by Mexican threats against Texas. All the historical Alamo set pieces are here, with Hunnicutt a refreshingly rustic Davy Crockett. Music by Max Steiner; "Jim Bowie" sung by Gordon MacRae.▼

Last Days of Dolwyn, The (1949-British) **95m. **½** D: Emlyn Williams. Edith Evans, Emlyn Williams, Richard Burton, Anthony James, Hugh Griffith. A dowager is called upon for help when her Welsh village is slated for extinction as part of a reservoir project; well acted but somewhat aloof. Written by actor-director Williams; Burton's first film. Aka WOMAN OF DOLWYN.▼

Last Days of Pompeii, The (1913-Italian) **88m. **½** D: Mario Caserini. Fernanda Negri Pouget, Eugenia Tettoni Fior, Ubaldo Stefani, Antonio Grisanti, Cesare Gani-Carini, Vitale Di Stefano. Melodramatic account of the lives, loves, and fates of various characters in A.D. 79 Pompeii, before and during the eruption of Mount Vesuvius. Back in 1913, this was an impressive, state-of-the-art disaster film; today, it's primarily a curio. Based on Edward George Bulwer-Lytton's oft-filmed novel. ▼)

Last Days of Pompeii, The (1935) **96m. ***** D: Ernest B. Schoedsack. Preston Foster, Basil Rathbone, Dorothy Wilson, David Holt, Alan Hale, John Wood, Louis Calhern. Former blacksmith Foster aspires to wealth and power as gladiator. Plays like a dramatic pageant but comes to life in climactic spectacle, with effects by the team that did KING KONG. Also shown in computer-colored version. ▼○)

Last Days of Pompeii, The (1960-Italian) **C-105m. **½** D: Mario Bonnard. Steve Reeves, Christine Kaufmann, Barbara Carroll, Anne Marie Baumann, Mimmo Palmara. New version of venerable tale focuses on muscleman Reeves and synthetic account of Christian martyrs. Very little spectacle. SuperTotalscope. ▼)

Last Flight, The (1931) **80m. ***** D: William Dieterle. Richard Barthelmess, John Mack Brown, Helen Chandler, Walter Byron, Elliott Nugent, David Manners. Piquant film about an ex-WW1 flying ace (Barthelmess) and his flippant friends in 1920s Paris. Written by John Monk Saunders (of WINGS fame), and based on his novel, this focuses on the same "lost generation" that Hemingway wrote about in *The Sun Also Rises*. Not a perfect film, but an interesting and unusual one. German director Dieterle's English-language debut.)

Last Frontier, The (1956) **C-98m. **½** D: Anthony Mann. Victor Mature, Guy Madison, Robert Preston, James Whitmore, Anne Bancroft. Three wilderness scouts see their lives change with the coming of cavalry outpost and military martinet (Preston). Offbeat characterizations in this cavalry drama. Aka SAVAGE WILDERNESS. CinemaScope.▼

Last Gangster, The (1937) **81m. ***** D: Edward Ludwig. Edward G. Robinson, James Stewart, Rosa Stradner, Lionel Stander, Douglas Scott, John Carradine, Sidney Blackmer, Louise Beavers, Edward Brophy, Grant Mitchell. Robinson's dynamic performance, and slick MGM production, elevate this tale of an underworld chief who's sent away for ten years, obsessed by the thought of the son he's never met. Entertaining story by William Wellman and Robert Carson was originally to have been called *Another Public Enemy*. U.S. film debut of Stradner.)

Last Gentleman, The (1934) **80m. ***** D: Sidney Lanfield. George Arliss, Edna May Oliver, Charlotte Henry, Janet Beecher, Ralph Morgan, Edward Ellis, Donald Meek. Delightful comedy with Arliss as dying millionaire whose family descends on him in hopes of carting away a piece of his fortune. Ingenious denouement gives Arliss last laugh.

Last Holiday (1950-British) **89m. ***** D: Henry Cass. Alec Guinness, Beatrice Campbell, Kay Walsh, Bernard Lee, Wilfrid Hyde-White, Sidney James, Ernest Thesiger. Ordinary man is told he is dying and decides to live it up at a swank resort. A droll, biting script by J. B. Priestley (who also coproduced), with sterling performances by all. Remade in 2006.▼)

Last Hunt, The (1956) **C-108m. **½**

D: Richard Brooks. Robert Taylor, Stewart Granger, Lloyd Nolan, Debra Paget, Russ Tamblyn, Constance Ford. In the Old West, Granger and Taylor form an uneasy partnership to hunt the last remaining herds of buffalo; Granger is sick of killing, Taylor likes it all too well. Complex characters and good dialogue help, but overlength and slow pace damage this serious Western drama. CinemaScope. ▼❒

Last Hurrah, The (1958) 121m. ***½ D: John Ford. Spencer Tracy, Jeffrey Hunter, Dianne Foster, Basil Rathbone, Pat O'Brien, Donald Crisp, James Gleason, Ed Brophy, John Carradine, Ricardo Cortez, Frank McHugh, Jane Darwell, Anna Lee, Charles FitzSimmons, Ken Curtis, O. Z. Whitehead, Jack Pennick, Dan Borzage. Sentimental version of Edwin O'Connor novel of politics, loosely based on life of Boston's mayor James Curley who in this story is mounting his final election campaign. Top-notch veteran cast makes film sparkle. Remade for TV in 1977 by (and with) Carroll O'Connor. ▼❍❒

Last Laugh, The (1924-German) 87m. ***½ D: F. W. Murnau. Emil Jannings, Maly Delschaft, Max Hiller, Hans Unterkirchen. Silent-film classic told entirely by camera, without title cards. Jannings plays proud doorman at posh hotel who is suddenly demoted; film details his utter and grievous humiliation. Brilliantly filmed by pioneer cameraman Karl Freund, with towering performance by Jannings. Remade in Germany in 1955. ▼❍❒

Last Man on Earth, The (1964-U.S.-Italian) 86m. ** D: Sidney Salkow. Vincent Price, Franca Bettoia, Emma Danieli, Giacomo Rossi-Stuart, Tony Cerevi. Often crude chiller with Price the sole survivor of plague, besieged by victims who arise at night thirsting for his blood; erratic production. Based on Richard Matheson's *I Am Legend*; remade as THE OMEGA MAN and I AM LEGEND. CinemaScope. ▼❍❒

Last Man to Hang, The (1956-British) 75m. ** D: Terence Fisher. Tom Conway, Elizabeth Sellars, Eunice Gayson, Freda Jackson, Raymond Huntley, Anthony Newley. Forthright courtroom film of man on trial for alleged murder of wife.

Last Mile, The (1932) 70m. *** D: Sam Bischoff. Howard Phillips, Preston S. Foster, George E. Stone, Noel Madison, Alan Roscoe, Paul Fix. Stark, atmospheric drama about life on death row, with Killer Mears (Foster) leading a takeover of the cellblock. Based on John Wexley's play. Remade in 1959. ▼❒

Last Mile, The (1959) 81m. **½ D: Howard W. Koch. Mickey Rooney, Clifford David, Harry Millard, Don "Red" Barry, Ford Rainey, Leon Janney. The "big house" oldie dusted off as a dramatic vehicle for Rooney. ❒

Last Millionaire, The (1934-French) 90m. *** D: René Clair. Max Dearly, Renée Saint-Cyr, Jose Noguero, Raymond Cordy, Paul Olivier. Light, mildly funny satire about the world's wealthiest man (Dearly), who is asked to govern a bankrupt, mythical kingdom; he is knocked on the head, and his idiotic rulings are interpreted as acts of genius. Not bad, but not up to Clair's best films of the period.

Last of Mrs. Cheyney, The (1929) 94m. **½ D: Sidney Franklin. Norma Shearer, Basil Rathbone, George Barraud, Herbert Bunston, Hedda Hopper, George K. Arthur. Young woman who has charmed a group of British society types turns out to be involved with a ring of jewel thieves. Very much an early-talkie stage play, with some terribly arch performances, but still quite watchable. Based on the play by Frederick Lonsdale. Remade in 1937 and 1951 (as THE LAW AND THE LADY). ❍❒

Last of Mrs. Cheyney, The (1937) 98m. *** D: Richard Boleslawski. Joan Crawford, William Powell, Robert Montgomery, Frank Morgan, Jessie Ralph, Nigel Bruce. Glossy remake of Norma Shearer's 1929 success, from Frederick Lonsdale's play about a chic American jewel thief in England. Great fun for star watchers, though it was considered dated when it came out. Remade in 1951 as THE LAW AND THE LADY. ▼❒

Last of the Badmen (1957) C-79m. ** D: Paul Landres. George Montgomery, Meg Randall, James Best, Michael Ansara, Keith Larsen. Unexceptional documentary-style Western about Chicago detectives in 1880s chasing after killers of their fellow-worker. Remade as GUNFIGHT AT COMANCHE CREEK. CinemaScope.

Last of the Buccaneers (1950) C-79m. *½ D: Lew Landers. Paul Henreid, Jack Oakie, Mary Anderson, John Dehner. Quickie costumer tainting the legendary name of Jean Lafitte with plodding account of his post–Battle of New Orleans exploits.

Last of the Comanches (1952) C-85m. **½ D: Andre de Toth. Broderick Crawford, Barbara Hale, Lloyd Bridges, Martin Milner, John War Eagle, William Andrews (Steve Forrest). Capable rehash of cavalrymen fighting off Indian attack. Western remake of SAHARA. ▼

Last of the Fast Guns, The (1958) C-82m. ** D: George Sherman. Jock Mahoney, Gilbert Roland, Linda Cristal, Eduard Franz. Adequately told Western of search for missing man, and obstacles the hired gunslinger must overcome. CinemaScope.

Last of the Mohicans, The (1920) 75m. *** D: Maurice Tourneur, Clarence Brown. Wallace Beery, Barbara Bedford, Albert Roscoe, Lillian Hall, Henry Woodward, James Gordon, Harry Lorraine. Colorful retelling of the oft-filmed James Fenimore Cooper classic, pitting the villainous Magua (Beery, who's well cast) against Hawkeye, Uncas, Chingachgook, and the story's other characters. First-rate silent drama. Look for Boris Karloff in a bit part as an Indian. Brown took over directing when Tourneur was injured during production. ▼O●

Last of the Mohicans, The (1936) **91m.** *** D: George B. Seitz. Randolph Scott, Binnie Barnes, Heather Angel, Hugh Buckler, Henry Wilcoxon, Bruce Cabot, Phillip Reed, Robert Barrat. Effective and exciting adaptation of James Fenimore Cooper novel about conflicts between British Army and Colonial settlers during the French and Indian War. Scott is a stout Hawkeye, Cabot an appropriately hissable Magua. Screenplay by Philip Dunne. Also shown in computer-colored version. ▼O●

Last of the Pagans (1935) **72m.** **½ D: Richard Thorpe. Mala, Lotus Long, Telo A. Tematua, Ae A Faaturia, Rangapo A Taipoo. MGM reteamed Mala and Long (who were discovered for the 1933 docudrama ESKIMO) as South Seas island lovers whose idyllic existence is shattered when he is forced to become a mine digger for slimy white slavers. Picturesque melodrama very loosely based on Herman Melville's *Typee*, with a shark fight, a cave-in, and a hurricane adding thrills to beautiful Tahiti locations. Photographed by Clyde De Vinna, who also shot WHITE SHADOWS IN THE SOUTH SEAS, TRADER HORN, and ESKIMO.

Last of the Pony Riders (1953) **59m.** **½ D: George Archainbaud. Gene Autry, Smiley Burnette, Dick Jones, Kathleen Case, John Downey, Gregg Barton, Arthur Space. Gene's setting up a stage line during the waning days of the Pony Express; Jones is a young pony rider with a romantic interest in Case. Autry's last feature film is a good one with an interesting storyline. ▶

Last of the Redmen (1947) **C-77m.** **½ D: George Sherman. Jon Hall, Michael O'Shea, Evelyn Ankers, Julie Bishop, Buster Crabbe. OK adaptation of THE LAST OF THE MOHICANS, with Hall cast as Major Hayward, O'Shea as Hawkeye, and Crabbe as Magua. Story focuses on Hawkeye's attempt to escort a British general's children through dangerous Indian country. ▼

Last of the Vikings, The (1961-Italian) **C-102m.** ** D: Giacomo Gentilomo. Cameron Mitchell, Edmund Purdom, Isabelle Corey, Helene Remy. Filmed with gusto, elaborate epic deals with Mitchell out to punish the Norse for devastating his homelands; poorly acted. Dyaliscope. ▼▶

Last Outlaw, The (1936) **72m.** *** D: Christy Cabanne. Harry Carey, Hoot Gibson, Henry B. Walthall, Tom Tyler, Margaret Callahan. Delightful blend of comedy and Western ingredients with Carey as a once notorious bandit released from prison after 25 years, only to find the Old West gone. Carey is wonderful (along with entire cast). There's even a

hilarious dig at singing cowboys! John Ford coauthored the story. ▼

Last Outpost, The (1935) **70m.** *** D: Louis Gasnier, Charles Barton. Cary Grant, Claude Rains, Gertrude Michael, Kathleen Burke, Colin Tapley, Akim Tamiroff. Exciting action-adventure with British troops in Africa, along lines of THE LOST PATROL, THE LIVES OF A BENGAL LANCER, etc. ▶

Last Outpost, The (1951) **C-88m.** **½ D: Lewis R. Foster. Ronald Reagan, Rhonda Fleming, Bruce Bennett, Bill Williams, Peter Hanson, Noah Beery, Jr. Burst of action saves wornout yarn of two brothers on opposite sides of Civil War, teaming up to fight off Indian attack. This was Reagan's first starring Western. Video title: CAVALRY CHARGE. ▼▶

Last Performance, The (1929) **60m.** **½ D: Paul Fejos. Conrad Veidt, Mary Philbin, Leslie Fenton, Fred MacKaye, Gustav Partos, Eddie Boland, Anders Randolph, Sam de Grasse. Celebrated magician/hypnotist Erik the Great (Veidt) is obsessed with his young assistant (Philbin); then another altogether different man enters the picture. Predictable story is redeemed somewhat by Veidt's commanding presence. Filmed in 1927 as a silent, with talking sequences added for its 1929 release. ▶

Last Posse, The (1953) **73m.** ** D: Alfred L. Werker. Broderick Crawford, John Derek, Charles Bickford, Wanda Hendrix, Warner Anderson. Sheriff's men track down robbers, not without surprising results. ▶

La Strada (1954-Italian) **115m.** **** D: Federico Fellini. Anthony Quinn, Giulietta Masina, Richard Basehart, Aldo Silvani, Marcella Rovere, Livia Venturini. Deceptively simple tale of brutish strongman Quinn taking simple-minded Masina with him as he tours countryside, where he encounters gentle acrobat Basehart. Best Foreign Film Oscar winner; stunning performances, haunting Nino Rota score. Story and screenplay by Fellini and Tullio Pinelli. ▼▶

Last Round-Up, The (1947) **77m.** *** D: John English. Gene Autry, Jean Heather, Ralph Morgan, Carol Thurston, Mark Daniels, Bobby (Robert) Blake, Russ Vincent, The Texas Rangers, Jay Silverheels, Iron Eyes Cody. Government agent Autry tries to relocate an Indian tribe so an aqueduct can be built to irrigate their land, but crooked Morgan wants that land and attempts to incite an Indian uprising to get it. A bit long, with more drama than music, but still good and one of Gene's favorites; it was the first film produced under his banner for Columbia Pictures. Naturally, he sings the title song. ▼▶

Last Stagecoach West (1957) **67m.** *½ D: Joseph Kane. Jim Davis, Victor Jory, Mary Castle, Lee Van Cleef. Fair cast cannot save bland Western about stage driver who loses government contracts and goes out of business. Filmed in Naturama.

Last Sunset, The (1961) **C-112m.** ******* D: Robert Aldrich. Rock Hudson, Kirk Douglas, Dorothy Malone, Joseph Cotten, Carol Lynley, Neville Brand, Regis Toomey, Jack Elam. Strange on the range, courtesy of Aldrich and scriptwriter Dalton Trumbo. Philosophical outlaw Douglas and vengeance-seeking Hudson play cat and mouse with each other during lengthy cattle drive. A key revelation near the finale adds resonance to the story. ▶

Last Ten Days, The (1956-German) **113m.** ******* D: G. W. Pabst. Albin Skoda, Oskar Werner, Lotte Tobisch, Willy Krause, Helga Kennedy-Dohrn. Finely etched study of downfall of leader of Third Reich. Retitled: LAST TEN DAYS OF ADOLPH HITLER.

Last Time I Saw Archie, The (1961) **98m.** ****** D: Jack Webb. Robert Mitchum, Jack Webb, Martha Hyer, France Nuyen, Louis Nye, Richard Arlen, Don Knotts, Joe Flynn, Robert Strauss. Webb's sole attempt at comedy is less funny than some of his more serious films; a pity, because William Bowers' script—based on his own Army experiences—had real potential, and Mitchum nicely underplays as the titular con man. (By the way, the real Archie Hall sued for invasion of privacy!)

Last Time I Saw Paris, The (1954) **C-116m.** ******* D: Richard Brooks. Elizabeth Taylor, Van Johnson, Donna Reed, Walter Pidgeon, Eva Gabor, George Dolenz, Roger Moore. Updated version of F. Scott Fitzgerald story, set in post-WW2 Paris, of ruined marriages and disillusioned people. MGM gloss helps. Moore's U.S. film debut. ▼●▶

Last Trail, The (1927) **58m.** ******* D: Lewis Seiler. Tom Mix, Carmelita Geraghty, William B. Davidson, Jerry Madden, Frank Hagney, Lee Shumway. Mix rides his horse Tony to the rescue once more in this silent saga set during the Nevada gold rush. An old friend, now the Carson City sheriff, entreats his help to halt a plague of stagecoach robberies. This was one of Mix's biggest hits; the fast and furious stagecoach race may remind you of BEN-HUR. Based on a Zane Grey novel; filmed before in 1921 and again in 1933. ▼

Last Train From Gun Hill (1959) **C-94m.** ******* D: John Sturges. Kirk Douglas, Anthony Quinn, Carolyn Jones, Earl Holliman, Brad Dexter, Brian Hutton, Ziva Rodann. Superior Western of staunch sheriff determined to leave Gun Hill with murder suspect, despite necessity for shoot-out. VistaVision. ▼▶

Last Train From Madrid, The (1937) **77m.** ******* D: James Hogan. Dorothy Lamour, Lew Ayres, Gilbert Roland, Anthony Quinn, Lee Bowman, Karen Morley, Helen Mack, Evelyn Brent, Robert Cummings, Lionel Atwill, Olympe Bradna. Imitation

GRAND HOTEL linking vignettes of various people escaping from wartorn Spain during 1930s. Modest but well-made film, with impressive cast.

Last Voyage, The (1960) **C-91m.** ******* D: Andrew L. Stone. Robert Stack, Dorothy Malone, George Sanders, Edmond O'Brien, Woody Strode. Engrossing drama of luxury ship that goes down at sea, and the ways the crew and passengers are affected. (To heighten the realism of the film, they really sank a ship.) Sanders is ill-fated captain, Stack and Malone a married couple in jeopardy. ▼●▶

Last Wagon, The (1956) **C-99m.** ******* D: Delmer Daves. Richard Widmark, Felicia Farr, Susan Kohner, Tommy Rettig, Stephanie Griffin, Ray Stricklyn, Nick Adams, Timothy Carey. Widmark is condemned killer who saves remnants of wagon train after Indian attack, leading them to safety. Clichéd plot well handled. CinemaScope. ▶

Last Warning, The (1929) **89m.** ****½** D: Paul Leni. Laura La Plante, Montagu Love, Roy D'Arcy, Margaret Livingston, John Boles, Burr McIntosh, Mack Swain, Bert Roach, Slim Summerville. A theater is reopened five years after a murder was committed there during a performance; will the killer strike again? Leni's last film before his untimely death; it's the flamboyant camera moves and opulent production design that make this worth watching, not the silly story. Originally released in both silent and part-talkie versions. Remade as THE HOUSE OF FEAR in 1939. ▼

Last Will of Dr. Mabuse, The SEE: Testament of Dr. Mabuse, The

Last Woman on Earth, The (1960) **C-71m.** BOMB D: Roger Corman. Antony Carbone, Edward Wain, Betsy Jones-Moreland. Dull three-cornered romance involving last survivors on Earth after unexplained disaster. Screenplay by Robert Towne—his first. He also costars, using acting pseudonym Edward Wain. Shot in Puerto Rico. Vistascope. ▼▶

Last Year at Marienbad (1961-French-Italian) **93m.** ******* D: Alain Resnais. Delphine Seyrig, Giorgio Albertazzi, Sacha Pitoeff. Murky, difficult but oddly fascinating tale in which Albertazzi confronts bewildered Seyrig, claiming they'd had an affair "last year at Frederiksbad, or perhaps at Marienbad." An art-house film in its day, beautifully photographed (by Sacha Vierny); scripted by Alain-Robbe Grillet. Dyaliscope. ▼▶

Las Vegas Nights (1941) **86m.** ****** D: Ralph Murphy. Constance Moore, Bert Wheeler, Phil Regan, Lillian Cornell, Virginia Dale, Hank Ladd, Betty Brewer. Minor musical fluff about a family of vaudevillians who inherit a rundown club in Vegas (depicted as a quaint cow town!). Worth seeing for some good numbers by Tommy Dorsey and His Orchestra, including the Oscar-nominated "Dolores" and "I'll Never Smile Again," featuring Frank Sinatra in his first screen appearance. Buddy Rich also does some mean drum solos. Subtitle on-screen: THE LAST FRONTIER TOWN.

Las Vegas Shakedown (1955) 79m. ** D: Sidney Salkow. Dennis O'Keefe, Coleen Gray, Charles Winninger, Thomas Gomez, Elizabeth Patterson, Robert Armstrong. Improbable yet diverting account of O'Keefe's effort to run an honest gambling house, with on-location filming in Las Vegas.▼

Las Vegas Story, The (1952) 88m. ** D: Robert Stevenson. Jane Russell, Victor Mature, Vincent Price, Hoagy Carmichael, Brad Dexter. Synthetic murder yarn supposedly set in gambling capital, sparked by Russell's vitality.▼)

La Symphonie Pastorale (1946-French) 105m. ***½ D: Jean Delannoy. Pierre Blanchar, Michele Morgan, Jean Desailly, Line Noro, Andree Clement. Quietly powerful classic about pastor Blanchar's all-consuming passion for blind girl Morgan, whom he takes under his wing and educates. This sensitive study of moral and spiritual corruption was coscripted by the director, and based on an André Gide novel.▼

L'Atalante (1934-French) 89m. **** D: Jean Vigo. Michel Simon, Dita Parlo, Jean Dasté, Gilles Margaritis, Louis Lefèvre, Diligent Raya. Naturalism and surrealist fantasy blend beautifully in all-time masterpiece about a young couple who begin their life together sailing down the Seine on a barge. Ultimate in romantic cinema also anticipated neorealist movement by more than a decade; Vigo died at 29, just as film premiered. Restored in 1990 to its full length; avoid 82m. version, which circulated for years.▼)

Late Autumn (1960-Japanese) C-127m. *** D: Yasujiro Ozu. Setsuko Hara, Yoko Tsukasa, Mariko Okada, Keiji Sada, Shin Saburi. Widowed Hara seeks a husband for unmarried daughter Tsukasa. Solid Ozu drama reworking his LATE SPRING.)

Late Chrysanthemums (1954-Japanese) 101m. ***½ D: Mikio Naruse. Haruko Sugimura, Sadako Sawamura, Chikako Hosokawa, Yûko Mochizuki, Ken Uehara, Hiroshi Koizumi. Subtle character study about a quartet of retired, middle-aged geishas. Once celebrated for their beauty and elegance, each now must face the grind of daily life. A superbly made saga of aging, memory, solitude, and disappointment. Naruse (who deserves to be better known in the West) infuses the film with an authentic sense of everyday life. ▼

Late George Apley, The (1947) 98m. *** D: Joseph L. Mankiewicz. Ronald Colman, Peggy Cummins, Vanessa Brown, Richard Haydn, Charles Russell, Richard Ney, Percy Waram, Mildred Natwick, Edna Best. John P. Marquand's gentle satire of Boston bluebloods is smoothly entertaining. Colman is

perfectly cast as the stuffy patriarch who strives to uphold his family's social status.▶

Late Mathias Pascal, The (1926-French) 171m. *** D: Marcel L'Herbier. Ivan Mosjoukine, Marcelle Pradot, Lois Moran, Marthe Mellot, Pauline Carton, Irma Perrot, (Mireille) Barsac, Michel Simon. Mathias Pascal (Mosjoukine) is a free-thinking young man who yearns to be the master of his fate but exists in a world of rampant greed. How will he react when he learns that he's been reported dead and now can take on a false identity and begin life anew? Absorbing mixture of realism and illusion. L'Herbier scripted, from a novel by Luigi Pirandello. Alberto Cavalcanti and Lazare Meerson are among the film's art directors. Original title: FEU MATHIAS PASCAL. Aka THE LIVING DEAD MAN. Remade in France in 1937.▶

La Terra Trema (1947-Italian) 154m. **** D: Luchino Visconti. Narrated by Luchino Visconti, Antonio Pietrangeli. Powerful, lyrical neorealist classic about a poor family in a Sicilian fishing village, exploited by fish wholesalers and boat owners. Filmed on location, and in Sicilian dialect, with a nonprofessional cast. Francesco Rosi and Franco Zeffirelli were Visconti's assistant directors. Beware of severely edited versions.▼)

Late Spring (1949-Japanese) 108m. **** D: Yasujiro Ozu. Setsuko Hara, Chishu Ryu, Haruko Sugimura, Jun Usamai, Yumeji Tsukioka. A widower pretends he is going to be remarried in order to get his devoted daughter to leave home and get married herself. One of Ozu's personal favorites, this serene, acutely observed examination of filial relationships and middle-class life is a transcendent and profoundly moving work rivaling TOKYO STORY as the director's masterpiece. Reworked by Ozu as LATE AUTUMN. Original title: BANSHUN.▼)

Latin Lovers (1953) C-104m. **½ D: Mervyn LeRoy. Lana Turner, Ricardo Montalban, John Lund, Louis Calhern, Jean Hagen, Rita Moreno. Hokey romance yarn set in South America, with Turner seeking true love; pointless script.▼

La Traversée de Paris (1956-French) 80m. *** D: Claude Autant-Lara. Jean Gabin, Bourvil, Louis de Funès, Jeannette Batti, Georgette Anys, Robert Arnoux, Laurence Badie. Black-marketer Bourvil recruits a total stranger (Gabin) to help him transport a freshly butchered pig across town one night, dodging both gendarmes and Nazis. Vivid portrait of life in Paris under German Occupation in WW2, told with a sardonic sense of humor. Originally released in U.S. as FOUR BAGS FULL, reissued in 2014 as A PIG ACROSS PARIS.▶

Laugh, Clown, Laugh (1928) 73m. ***

D: Herbert Brenon. Lon Chaney, Bernard Siegel, Loretta Young, Cissy Fitzgerald, Nils Asther, Gwen Lee. In this touching silent drama, circus clown Chaney adopts an orphan who grows to be a beautiful young woman (15-year-old Young, in her first major role). When she learns he is in love with her, she must choose between her devotion to him and the wealthy nobleman who has asked her to marry him. Perfect example of Chaney's unmatched talent for turning tearjerking melodrama into heartbreaking tragedy.▶

Laughing at Life (1933) **70m. **½ D: Ford Beebe. Victor McLaglen, Conchita Montenegro, William "Stage" Boyd, Lois Wilson, Henry B. Walthall, Regis Toomey, Guinn "Big Boy" Williams, Noah Beery, Sr., Tully Marshall, Henry Armetta, Frankie Darro. No comedy this, with a rough-'n'-ready ex–civil engineer gunrunning, fighting in WW1, and spearheading a South American revolution, all while searching for his lost son. Preposterous tale spans the years and roams the globe as twists strain credibility, but it's never less than entertaining, thanks to McLaglen's generously oversized performance. ▼▶

Laughing Sinners (1931) **72m. ** D: Harry Beaumont. Joan Crawford, Clark Gable, Neil Hamilton, John Mack Brown, Marjorie Rambeau, Guy Kibbee, Roscoe Karns. Crawford attempts suicide after Hamilton dumps her; Salvation Army preacher Gable (!) stops her. The rest is predictable. ▼▶

Laughter (1930) **77m. **½ D: Harry D'Arrast. Nancy Carroll, Fredric March, Frank Morgan, Leonard Carey. Lumpy film with a few bright sequences about Follies girl Carroll marrying millionaire but finding life empty, unhappy.

Laughter in Paradise (1951-British) **95m. **½ D: Mario Zampi. Alastair Sim, Joyce Grenfell, Hugh Griffith, Fay Compton, John Laurie. Notorious practical joker dies, and leaves hefty sum to four relatives if they will carry out his devilish instructions. Pleasant little comedy. Audrey Hepburn appears fleetingly as cigarette girl. Remade in 1969 as SOME WILL, SOME WON'T.

Laura (1944) **85m. **** D: Otto Preminger. Gene Tierney, Dana Andrews, Clifton Webb, Vincent Price, Judith Anderson, Grant Mitchell, Lane Chandler, Dorothy Adams. Classic mystery with gorgeous Tierney subject of murder plot; detective Andrews trying to assemble crime puzzle. Fascinating, witty, classic, with Webb a standout as cynical columnist Waldo Lydecker and Price in his finest nonhorror performance as suave Southern gigolo. Based on the Vera Caspary novel; also features David Raksin's theme. Rouben Mamoulian started directing film, Preminger took over. Screenplay by Jay Dratler,

Samuel Hoffenstein, and Betty Reinhardt. Joseph LaShelle's cinematography earned an Oscar. ▼▶

Laurel and Hardy's Laughing 20's (1965) **90m. ***½ Compiled by Robert Youngson. Stan Laurel, Oliver Hardy, Charley Chase, Edgar Kennedy, James Finlayson, Anita Garvin. Some of L&H's best moments on film are included, with everything from pie-throwing to pants-ripping. Also some excellent sequences of Charley Chase, adding to the fun. ▼▶

Lavender Hill Mob, The (1951-British) **82m. ***½ D: Charles Crichton. Alec Guinness, Stanley Holloway, Sidney James, Alfie Bass, Marjorie Fielding, John Gregson, Edie Martin. Excellent comedy with droll Guinness a timid bank clerk who has perfect scheme for robbing a gold bullion truck, with a madcap chase climax. Won an Oscar for Best Story and Screenplay (T. E. B. Clarke); look for Audrey Hepburn in opening scene. ▼▶

La Viaccia (1962-Italian) **103m. **½ D: Mauro Bolognini. Jean-Paul Belmondo, Claudia Cardinale, Pietro Germi, Romolo Valli, Gabriella Pallotta, Gina Sammarco. Zesty yarn of country youth finding romance in the city with prostitute. Retitled: THE LOVEMAKERS.

L'Avventura (1960-French-Italian) **145m. ***½ D: Michelangelo Antonioni. Monica Vitti, Gabriele Ferzetti, Lea Massari, Dominique Blanchar, James Addams. Massari mysteriously disappears on an uninhabited island after arguing with boyfriend Ferzetti, impelling him and her friend Vitti to look for her. Subtle, incisive allegory of spiritual and moral decay makes for demanding viewing. Antonioni's first international success was also the first of a trilogy (followed by LA NOTTE and L'ECLISSE). ▼▶

Law, The SEE: **Where the Hot Wind Blows!**

Law and Disorder (1958-British) **76m. **½ D: Charles Crichton. Michael Redgrave, Robert Morley, Ronald Squire, Elizabeth Sellars, Jeremy Burnham. Brisk comedy of con man (Redgrave) who gives up crime to avoid embarrassment of making up stories to tell prim son (Burnham).

Law and Jake Wade, The (1958) **C-86m. *** D: John Sturges. Robert Taylor, Richard Widmark, Patricia Owens, Robert Middleton, Henry Silva, DeForest Kelley. Robust Western drama in which Taylor, a lawman with a past, tangles with nasty Widmark over some buried loot. The two stars make good adversaries. CinemaScope. ▼▶

Law and Order (1932) **70m. ***½ D: Edward L. Cahn. Walter Huston, Harry Carey, Raymond Hatton, Russell Hopton, Ralph Ince, Andy Devine, Walter Brennan. Exceptional Western that takes a familiar story (Wyatt Earp and Doc Holliday vs. the Clantons) and reworks it with style but no flourishes. Huston plays Saint Johnson, gunslinger and lawman. Stark, realistic, with a knockout finale. Coscripted by John Huston. Remade in 1953.

Law and Order (1953) **C-80m.** ****** D: Nathan Juran. Ronald Reagan, Dorothy Malone, Alex Nicol, Preston Foster, Ruth Hampton, Russell Johnson, Dennis Weaver, Jack Kelly. Lawman Reagan wants to retire to marry Malone, but first must tame bad guy Foster. Standard Western was filmed far more successfully in 1932. ▼▶

Law and the Lady, The (1951) **104m.** ****½** D: Edwin H. Knopf. Greer Garson, Michael Wilding, Fernando Lamas, Marjorie Main, Hayden Rorke, Margalo Gillmore. Stylish if standard remake of THE LAST OF MRS. CHEYNEY with Garson (gowned by Cecil Beaton) teaming up with Wilding for slick society jewel robberies. ▶

Law Is the Law, The (1959-French) **103m.** ****½** D: Christian-Jaque. Fernandel, Totò, Mario Besozzi, René Genin. Two top Continental comedians work well together in yarn of French customs official and his pal who smuggle items over the border.

Lawless, The (1950) **83m.** ****** D: Joseph Losey. Gail Russell, Macdonald Carey, Lalo Rios, Lee Patrick, John Sands, Martha Hyer, Tab Hunter. Vaguely interesting study of Mexican-American fruit-pickers in Southern California, with facets of racial discrimination pointed out. ▶

Lawless Breed, The (1952) **C-83m.** ******* D: Raoul Walsh. Rock Hudson, Julia (Julie) Adams, John McIntire, Mary Castle, Hugh O'Brian, Lee Van Cleef, Dennis Weaver, Michael Ansara. Solid Western drama that recounts the life and times of legendary (and misunderstood) outlaw John Wesley Hardin (well played by Hudson, in his starring debut). ▼▶

Lawless Eighties, The (1957) **70m.** ****** D: Joe Kane. Buster Crabbe, John Smith, Marilyn Saris, Ted de Corsia, Anthony Caruso, John Doucette, Frank Ferguson, Walter Reed. Gunman Crabbe comes to the rescue of circuit rider Smith, who's run afoul of crooked Indian agent de Corsia in this OK post–Civil War Western. Naturama.

Lawless Frontier, The (1934) **56m.** ***½** D: R. N. Bradbury. John Wayne, Sheila Terry, Jack Rockwell, George Hayes, Jay Wilsey (Buffalo Bill, Jr.), Yakima Canutt. After a Mexican outlaw kills young Wayne's parents, he joins forces with Hayes for retribution. Substandard B Western made in 5-plus days in California's Red Rock Canyon. Also shown in computer-colored version. ▼▶

Lawless Nineties, The (1936) **56m.** ****** D: Joe Kane. John Wayne, Ann Rutherford, Harry Woods, George Hayes, Al Bridge, Fred "Snowflake" Toones, Etta McDaniel. Government dispatches undercover federal agent Wayne to lawless 1890s Wyoming in hopes of restoring order before a vote on statehood. Hayes and bad guy Woods boost this ordinary B Western. ▼▶

Lawless Range (1935) **59m.** ***½** D: R. N. Bradbury. John Wayne, Sheila Mannors (Bromley), Frank McGlynn, Jr., Jack Curtis, Wallace Howe, Yakima Canutt. Stock Western tale of cattle rustling and villainous banker grabbing gold mines. Holds few surprises, save one: weak warbling by Wayne. Several frontier skullduggery scenes filmed at the picturesque Vasquez Rocks. ▼▶

Lawless Street, A (1955) **C-78m.** ****½** D: Joseph H. Lewis. Randolph Scott, Angela Lansbury, Warner Anderson, Jean Parker, Wallace Ford, Ruth Donnelly, Michael Pate. Hard-bitten marshal Scott tries to eliminate evil forces from western town, then confronts his bittersweet past when musical star Lansbury comes to town. Entertaining Western with disappointing resolution. ▼▶

Law of the Lawless (1964) **C-88m.** ****½** D: William F. Claxton. Dale Robertson, Yvonne De Carlo, William Bendix, Bruce Cabot, Richard Arlen, John Agar, Lon Chaney (Jr.), Kent Taylor. Veteran cast is chief interest here, with Robertson an ex-gunman turned judge. Techniscope.

Law of the Pampas (1939) **71m.** ****½** D: Nate Watt. William Boyd, Russell Hayden, Sidney Toler, Steffi Duna, Sidney Blackmer, Pedro de Cordoba, William Duncan. Range hero Hopalong Cassidy journeys to South America, delivering prize cattle to a ranch beset by a shifty foreman who's been arranging murders so as to marry the heir and get rich. Average Hoppy outing with good action scenes, Lone Pine passing for Argentina. Sidney Toler, on leave from *Charlie Chan* series, offers comedy relief during post–George Hayes and pre–Andy Clyde era. Unfortunately, The King's Men sing but Eddie Dean doesn't. ▼▶

Law of the Trail SEE: **Borrowed Trouble**

Law of the Tropics (1941) **76m.** ****** D: Ray Enright. Constance Bennett, Jeffrey Lynn, Regis Toomey, Mona Maris, Hobart Bosworth, Craig Stevens. Lynn, toiling on a South American rubber plantation, becomes involved with on-the-lam singer Bennett. Strictly routine; a loose reworking of OIL FOR THE LAMPS OF CHINA.

Lawrence of Arabia (1962-British) **C-216m.** ******** D: David Lean. Peter O'Toole, Alec Guinness, Anthony Quinn, Jack Hawkins, Claude Rains, Anthony Quayle, Arthur Kennedy, Omar Sharif, Jose Ferrer. Blockbuster biography of enigmatic adventurer T. E. Lawrence is that rarity, an epic film that is also literate. Loses some momentum in the second half, but still a knockout—especially in 1989 reissue version, which restored many cuts made over the years (and made a few judicious trims in the process). Still, the only way to really appreciate this film is on a big screen. Screenplay by Robert Bolt and Michael Wilson, based on Lawrence's book *The Seven Pillars of Wisdom.* Seven Oscars include Best Picture, Director, Cinematography (F. A. Young), Score (Maurice Jarre), Editing, and Art Direction. O'Toole's first leading role made him an instant star. Beware of shorter prints. Originally 222m. Restored Roadshow version on video runs 227m. with an overture, intermission/entr'acte, exit music. Super Panavision 70. ▼◐●

Law vs. Billy the Kid, The (1954) **C-73m.** **½ D: William Castle. Scott Brady, Betta St. John, James Griffith, Alan Hale, Jr., Paul Cavanagh. A self-defense killing forces Billy (a too-old-for-the-part Brady) to ride the outlaw trail in this romanticized version of his life and times. Originally in 3-D.

Law West of Tombstone, The (1938) **73m.** **½ D: Glenn Tryon. Harry Carey, Tim Holt, Evelyn Brent, Jean Rouverol, Clarence Kolb, Allan Lane, Esther Muir, Ward Bond. Tall-tale spinner Carey heads to a frontier town and dispenses law and order with the aid of a local gunslinger (Holt, making like Billy the Kid). Enjoyable, lighthearted B-plus oater based on the exploits of Judge Roy Bean. ◐

Lawyer Man (1932) **72m.** *** D: William Dieterle. William Powell, Joan Blondell, Claire Dodd, Sheila Terry, Alan Dinehart, David Landau, Helen Vinson, Allen Jenkins, Roscoe Karns, Sterling Holloway. Powell is aces in this amusing pre-Code drama as an ambitious lawyer—with a near-fatal eye for the ladies—who tangles with crooked politicians. Blondell is his loyal, lovesick secretary. Powell even speaks Yiddish in this one. ◐

Lay That Rifle Down (1955) **71m.** *½ D: Charles Lamont. Judy Canova, Robert Lowery, Jacqueline de Wit, Jil Jarmyn, Richard Deacon, Tweeny Canova. Mild Cinderella story featuring Canova as an overworked drudge who finds herself contending with a nasty aunt, a greedy banker, and a pair of swindlers. ▼◐

Lazybones (1925) **86m.** *** D: Frank Borzage. Charles "Buck" Jones, Madge Bellamy, Virginia Marshall, Edythe Chapman, Leslie Fenton, ZaSu Pitts. Story of endearing but aimless character, his romances, and the path life takes him down as years go by. Poignant evocation of small-town life from turn of the century into the 1920s. Unusual role for Jones, better known as cowboy hero. ◐

Lazy River (1934) **76m.** ** D: George B. Seitz. Jean Parker, Robert Young, Ted Healy, C. Henry Gordon, Nat Pendleton, Ruth Channing, Maude Eburne, Raymond Hatton. Aimless story of escaped convicts led by Young who ingratiate themselves into Parker's Louisiana Bayou family, intending to fleece them but predictably having a change of heart. Pleasant, though nothing special, apart from Gregg Toland's cinematography.

League of Frightened Men, The (1937) **65m.** ** D: Alfred E. Green. Walter Connolly, Lionel Stander, Eduardo Ciannelli, Irene Hervey, Victor Kilian, Walter Kingsford. Second Nero Wolfe film casts relatively amiable Connolly in the role of Rex Stout's sleuth for a none-too-inscrutable mystery about a band of former college chums who are being killed off one by one.

League of Gentlemen, The (1960-British) **114m.** ***½ D: Basil Dearden. Jack Hawkins, Nigel Patrick, Roger Livesey, Richard Attenborough, Bryan Forbes, Kieron Moore, Robert Coote, Nanette Newman. Ex-army colonel enlists the aid of former officers (through blackmail) to pull off big bank heist. High-class British humor makes this tale of crime a delight. Forbes also wrote the script. Look for Oliver Reed as a ballet dancer! ▼◐

Le Amiche (1955-Italian) **104m.** *** D: Michelangelo Antonioni. Eleonora Rossi Drago, Valentina Cortese, Gabriele Ferzetti, Yvonne Furneaux, Madeleine Fischer, Franco Fabrizi. Early work by Antonioni (and one of his most accessible films) takes a penetrating look at a group of women in Turin—including a fashion designer, a model, an artist, and a socialite—and the pressures that drive one of them to attempt suicide. Sensitive direction and highly capable cast make the most of a potentially soapy story. Aka THE GIRL FRIENDS.

Lease of Life (1954-British) **C-94m.** **½ D: Charles Frend. Robert Donat, Kay Walsh, Denholm Elliott, Adrienne Corri, Cyril Raymond. Donat makes anything worth watching, even this mild tale of poor-but-honest country vicar with one year to live, struggling to make ends meet and maintain his integrity.

Leather Boys, The (1963-British) **105m.** *** D: Sidney J. Furie. Rita Tushingham, Colin Campbell, Dudley Sutton, Gladys Henson. Uncompromising study of impulsive Tushingham's incompatible marriage to motorcycle-loving mechanic, focusing on their opposing viewpoints and sleazy environment. CinemaScope. ▼◐

Leather Burners (1943) **66m.** **½ D: Joseph E. Henabery. William Boyd, Andy Clyde, Jay Kirby, Victor Jory, George Givot, Shelley Spencer, George Reeves, Bob (Robert) Mitchum. Rustlers use abandoned gold mine to store stolen cattle, but Hopalong Cassidy discovers secret entrance. Comedian Givot is cast against type as an insane villain. Fine script and action, and well directed by Henabery, who played Lincoln in THE BIRTH OF A NATION. ▼◐

Leather Gloves (1948) **75m.** ** D: Richard Quine, William Asher. Cameron Mitchell, Virginia Grey, Sam Levene, Jane Nigh, Henry O'Neill, Blake Edwards. Fight flick about on-the-skids boxer Mitchell lacks sufficient punch to push over clichés.

Leathernecks Have Landed, The (1936)

68m. **½ D: Howard Bretherton. Lew Ayres, Isabel Jewell, Jimmy Ellison, James Burke, J. Carrol Naish, Ward Bond, Henry Mowbray. Enjoyable B-picture fare about Marinc (Ayres) who, with help of beauty Jewell, starts running guns to rebel forces in Shanghai. Written by Seton I. Miller.

Leather Saint, The (1956) **86m.** **½ D: Alvin Ganzer. Paul Douglas, John Derek, Jody Lawrance, Cesar Romero, Ernest Truex. Forthright account of clergyman who becomes a boxer to earn money to help congregation. VistaVision.

Leave Her to Heaven (1945) **C-110m.** *** D: John M. Stahl. Gene Tierney, Cornel Wilde, Jeanne Crain, Vincent Price, Mary Philips, Ray Collins, Darryl Hickman, Gene Lockhart. Tierney's mother says, "There's nothing wrong with Ellen. It's just that she loves too much." In fact, she loves some people to death! Slick trash, expertly handled all around with Tierney breathtakingly photographed in Technicolor by Oscar winner Leon Shamroy. And how about those incredible homes in New Mexico and Maine! Remake for TV as TOO GOOD TO BE TRUE in 1988.▼●❙

Leave It to Blondie (1945) **75m.** ** D: Abby Berlin. Penny Singleton, Arthur Lake, Larry Simms, Jonathan Hale, Chick Chandler, Marjorie Ann Mutchie (Kent), Danny Mummert, Eddie Acuff, Jack Rice. The Bumsteads enter a songwriting contest in this trivial *Blondie* entry.▼

Leave It to Henry (1949) **57m.** *½ D: Jean Yarbrough. Raymond Walburn, Walter Catlett, Gary Gray, Mary Stuart. Quickie film has Walburn destroying the town bridge when son is fired as toll-booth collector. Second in a B-picture series, followed by FATHER MAKES GOOD.

Leaves from Satan's Book (1920-Danish) **121m.** *** D: Carl Theodor Dreyer. Helge Nissen, Halvard Hoff, Jacob Texiere, Hallander Helleman, Ebon Strandin, Johannes Meyer. After being banished from Heaven, the Devil tries to tempt and corrupt mankind at four different points in history: during the life of Jesus, the Spanish Inquisition, the French Revolution, and the Russo-Finnish War of 1918. Dreyer's third film is a poetic exploration of spirituality and the nature of evil.❙

Le Beau Serge (1958-French) **97m.** *** D: Claude Chabrol. Jean-Claude Brialy, Gérard Blain, Michele Meritz, Bernadette Lafont, Edmond Beauchamp. Considered to be the first French New Wave film, this rural tale also marked the feature directing debut of *Cahiers du Cinéma* film critic Claude Chabrol. When Brialy returns to his tiny hometown, he is stunned to find how drastically his old school chum (Blain) has changed. Perceptive examination of the trials of life in a poor farming community and the moral questions raised by how one treats a friend. Brialy, Blain, and young Lafont (a teenaged nymphet) continued to collaborate with Chabrol (who also wrote and produced) for three decades.▼❙

Le Bonheur (1965-French) **C-80m.** **½ D: Agnès Varda. Jean-Claude Drouot, Claire Drouot, Sandrine Drouot, Oliver Drouot, Marie-France Boyer. Happily married carpenter Drouot falls for postal clerk Boyer, feels he can love both her and wife and they will share him. Intriguing, but emotionally uninvolving and unbelievable. Drouot's real wife and children portray his cinematic spouse and offspring. Aka HAPPINESS. ▼❙

Le ciel est à vous (1944-French) **107m.** *** D: Jean Grémillon. Madeleine Renaud, Charles Vanel, Jean Debucourt, Raymonde Vernay, Léonce Corne, Raoul Marco, Albert Rémy. Heartfelt, crowd-pleasing tale of an honest, hardworking blue-collar French family and what happens when Renaud, the wife and mother, becomes involved in aviation. Fact-based story dates from before WW2, but the film pays homage to the perseverance of the French citizenry during the Occupation. Aka THE WOMAN WHO DARED.❙

L'Eclisse SEE: Eclipse (1962-French-Italian)

Le Combat dans L'ile (1962-French) **104m.** *** D: Alain Cavalier. Romy Schneider, Jean-Louis Trintignant, Henri Serre, Diana Lepvrier, Robert Bousquet, Jacques Berlioz, Armand Meffre, Maurice Garrel, Jean-Pierre Melville. Noir-influenced drama of a seemingly ordinary married couple. The extroverted wife (Schneider) is unaware that her coldly serious husband (Trintignant) is a member of a right-wing political organization that's plotting a political assassination. Engrossing tale of passion and betrayal; jarringly contemporary in its depiction of a misguided fringe organization that's intent on maintaining the status quo through violent means. Produced by Louis Malle. Aka FIRE AND ICE.❙

Le Corbeau (1943-French) **92m.** ***½ D: Henri-Georges Clouzot. Pierre Fresnay, Ginette Leclerc, Helena Manson, Noel Roquevert, Sylvie, Louis Seigner. Ingenious suspenser detailing what happens when a series of mysterious poison pen letters begins circulating in a small French town. Quite controversial in its day, because it was financed by a German movie company and considered to be anti-French propaganda. Remade in Hollywood as THE 13TH LETTER. Aka THE RAVEN.▼❙

Leda SEE: Web of Passion

Le Doulos (1962-French) **108m.** *** D: Jean-Pierre Melville. Jean-Paul Belmondo, Serge Reggiani, Jean Desailly, Fabienne Dali, Michel Piccoli, René Lefèvre, Monique Hennessy. Hard-boiled crime tale centering on the search for hidden loot stolen by Reggiani and whether or not fellow crook Belmondo ratted him out to the cops. Slick Melville imitation of an American film noir is a notch below his best, but still an entertaining study of duplicity and honor among thieves. Aka DOULOS—THE FINGER MAN. ▼▶

Leech Woman, The (1960) 77m. *½ D: Edward Dein. Coleen Gray, Grant Williams, Phillip Terry, Gloria Talbott, John Van Dreelen. In Africa, an aging woman obtains power that restores her youth, but requires her to murder—including her rotten husband. Back in L.A. it's more of the same. Gray is very good; the movie isn't. ▼⊙▶

Left Handed Gun, The (1958) 102m. **½ D: Arthur Penn. Paul Newman, Lita Milan, John Dehner, Hurd Hatfield. Faltering psychological Western dealing with Billy the Kid's career, method-acted by Newman. Penn's first feature, based on a 1955 *Philco Playhouse* TV play by Gore Vidal in which Newman starred. ▼▶

Left Hand of God, The (1955) C-87m. *** D: Edward Dmytryk. Humphrey Bogart, Gene Tierney, Lee J. Cobb, Agnes Moorehead, E. G. Marshall, Benson Fong. Bogart manages to be convincing as American caught in post-WW2 China, posing as clergyman with diverting results. CinemaScope. ▼▶

Left Right and Center (1959-British) 95m. **½ D: Sidney Gilliat. Ian Carmichael, Patricia Bredin, Alastair Sim, Eric Barker. Simple, entertaining comedy about opponents in political campaign falling in love. Sim is hilarious, as always, as Carmichael's conniving uncle.

Legend of Gosta Berling, The SEE: Atonement of Gosta Berling, The

Legend of Lobo, The (1962) C-67m. **½ No director credited. Narrated by Rex Allen, with songs by Sons of the Pioneers. Disney film follows a wolf named Lobo from birth to adulthood, as he learns the ways of life in the West. Well done, if unmemorable, with bright soundtrack. ▶

Legend of the Lost (1957) C-109m. ** D: Henry Hathaway. John Wayne, Sophia Loren, Rossano Brazzi, Kurt Kasznar, Sonia Moser. Incredibly insipid hodgepodge interesting as curio: Wayne and Brazzi on treasure hunt in Sahara battle over rights to Loren. Technirama. ▼▶

Legend of Tom Dooley, The (1959) 79m. ** D: Ted Post. Michael Landon, Jo Morrow, Jack Hogan, Richard Rust, Dee Pollock. Landon is pleasing in title role of Rebel soldier who robs a stage for the cause, only to discover war is over and he's now an outlaw. Based on the hit song. ▼

Legong (Dance of the Virgins) (1935) C-56m. **½ D: Henri de la Falaise. In a Balinese village, a "chaste maiden and sacred dancer of the Temple" falls for a carefree young musician. He, in turn, is at-

tracted to her half sister. Silent film is shot on location in two-strip Technicolor with an all-native cast. Its slight story is secondary to the eye-opening footage of Balinese customs. ▼▶

Le Jour Se Lève (1939-French) 93m. ***½ D: Marcel Carné. Jean Gabin, Jacqueline Laurent, Jules Berry, Arletty, Mady Berry. A staple of French cinema, from the writer-director team that later created CHILDREN OF PARADISE; factory worker Gabin, trapped in a building, flashes back on events that drove him to murder. Generally holds up, while going a long way toward defining Gabin's screen persona. Written by Jacques Prévert, from Jacques Viot's story. U.S. title: DAYBREAK. Later remade here as THE LONG NIGHT. ▼▶

Lem Hawkins' Confession SEE: **Murder in Harlem**

Le Million (1931-French) 85m. ***½ D: René Clair. Annabella, René Lefevre, Vanda Greville, Paul Olivier, Louis Allibert. A chase after a lost lottery ticket propels this charming, whimsical, innovative gem from Clair. The actors sing some of their dialogue; as much fun today as when first released. ▼⊙▶

Lemonade Joe (1964-Czech) 84m. *** D: Oldrich Lipsky. Carl Fiala, Olga Schoberova, Veta Fialova, Miles Kopeck, Rudy Dale, Joseph Nomaz. Sometimes repetitious but often quite funny spoof of the American Western; title refers to hero, who drinks Kola Loca lemonade instead of booze. Original running time is 99m. CinemaScope. ▼▶

Lemon Drop Kid, The (1934) 71m. ** D: Marshall Neilan. Lee Tracy, Helen Mack, William Frawley, Minna Gombell, Baby LeRoy, Robert McWade, Henry B. Walthall, Kitty Kelly, Eddie Peabody. Racetrack con man flees to quiet burg, falls in love, and settles down. Drifts from comedy to sentiment to melodrama, killing off best Damon Runyon elements. Frawley is fun as silver-tongued tout called The Professor. Look for Ann Sheridan in bit part at the track. Remade with Bob Hope.

Lemon Drop Kid, The (1951) 91m. *** D: Sidney Lanfield. Bob Hope, Marilyn Maxwell, Lloyd Nolan, Jane Darwell, William Frawley. Hope is hilarious as racetrack tout who owes big money to gangster (Nolan) and must pay or else. Adapted from Damon Runyon story, filmed before in 1934. Film introduced Livingston-Evans Christmas hit "Silver Bells." ▼⊙▶

Le Notti Bianche SEE: **White Nights** (1957-Italian)

Leon Morin, Priest (1961-French) 116m. **½ D: Jean-Pierre Melville. Jean-Paul Belmondo, Emmanuele Riva, Patricia Gozzi, Irene Tunc. Belmondo gives subdued, offbeat performance as clergyman trying to set shady woman onto the path of righteousness. Aka THE FORGIVEN SINNER. ▼◗

Leopard, The (1963-French-Italian) **C-187m. ****** D: Luchino Visconti. Burt Lancaster, Alain Delon, Claudia Cardinale, Rina Morelli, Paolo Stoppa. Magnificent spectacle, set in 1860 Sicily, about an aristocrat who tries coming to terms with the unification of Italy. Originally screened at 195m., then released in the U.S. in a badly dubbed 165m. version. Visconti tinkered with the film repeatedly over the years, finally pronouncing the 187m. print "definitive" (although Lancaster's voice is still dubbed by another actor in the original *foreign* version). Delon and Cardinale are close to the final word in romantic pairings; concluding hour-long banquet scene is among the great set pieces in movie history. Technirama.◗

Leopard Man, The (1943) **66m. **½** D: Jacques Tourneur. Dennis O'Keefe, Margo, Jean Brooks, Isabel Jewell, James Bell, Margaret Landry, Abner Biberman. Intriguing but flawed Val Lewton thriller about series of murders in small New Mexico town blamed on escaped leopard. Based on novel *Black Alibi* by Cornell Woolrich. ▼◗◗

Le Petit Soldat (1960-French) **88m. **** D: Jean-Luc Godard. Michel Subor, Anna Karina, Henri-Jacques Huet, Paul Beauvais, László Szabó, Georges de Beauregard. Godard's second feature concerns the terrorist activities of Algerian rebels who capture French army deserter Subor and blackmail him into committing an assassination. Godard's future wife Karina makes her feature debut as a leftist activist with whom Subor falls in love. Featuring an unforgettable torture scene, this powerful film was banned in France until 1963; less about politics than personal freedom and the banality of evil. ▼◗

Le Plaisir (1952-French) **97m. ***½** D: Max Ophuls. Jean Gabin, Danielle Darrieux, Simone Simon, Claude Dauphin, Gaby Morlay, Pierre Brasseur, Pauline Dubost, Madeleine Renaud, Daniel Gelin. The joy and heartache of *l'amour* and the pursuit of pleasure are explored with subtlety and sophistication in a trilogy of stories by Guy de Maupassant: in "Le Masque," a vain old man tries to regain his youth by donning a mask at a ball; in "Le Maison Tellier," a group of prostitutes travels to the country to attend the first communion of the madam's niece; in "Le Modele," a free-living artist's affair with a model takes a tragic turn. Brilliantly acted by a superb cast and directed with customary virtuosity and a dazzlingly fluid style. Jean Marais narrates the French version of the film as de Maupassant (Peter Ustinov narrates the English version; Anton Walbrook narrates the German version). ▼◗

Le Quai des Brumes SEE: **Port of Shadows**
Le Rouge et le Noir (1954-French-Italian)

C-145m. ** D: Claude Autant-Lara. Gérard Philipe, Danielle Darrieux, Antonella Lualdi, Jean Martinelli. Solidly acted, handsomely produced historical drama based on the Stendahl novel about a man of the lower classes (Philipe) and his obsession with making it in society in 1830 France; Darrieux and Lualdi are the women in his life. Released in the U.S. in 1958; European running time 170m. Remade for French TV in 1997. Aka THE RED AND THE BLACK.▼

Les Bonnes Femmes (1960-French) **93m. *** D: Claude Chabrol. Bernadette Lafont, Clotilde Joano, Stephane Audran, Lucile Saint-Simon, Pierre Bertin, Jean-Louis Maury, Claude Berri, Mario David. Offbeat, intriguing Chabrol concoction, an important film of the early French New Wave, about a quartet of French shopgirls and their varied hopes and dreams. The most interesting storyline spotlights dreamy Joano and her fascination with a mysterious motorcyclist who appears to be following her. The finale is a real knockout.▼◗

Les Carabiniers (1963-French-Italian) **80m. *** D: Jean-Luc Godard. Albert Juross, Marino Masé, Genevieve Galea, Catherine Ribeiro, Gérard Poirot, Jean Brassat, Alvaro Gheri, Barbet Schroeder. In an unspecified time and place, two peasants are offered money and the promise of great adventures if they fight for the king; they accept, but are executed when a peace treaty is signed. Critically lambasted upon its release, this (intentionally) crudely made and anachronistic fable remains one of the few honest films about the insanity and immorality of war: it refuses to romanticize its subject. Written by Godard, Jean Gruault, and Roberto Rossellini. ▼◗

Les Dames du Bois du Boulogne (1945-French) **90m. **½** D: Robert Bresson. Maria Casarès, Elina Labourdette, Paul Bernard, Jean Marchat. A woman schemes to avenge herself on the man who rejected her by making him fall for a femme whom he doesn't know was a prostitute. Early piece by this most austere of all French realisateurs proves again that Hell hath no fury, etc. Cowritten by Jean Cocteau (but bereft of his personal touch) from an episode in the determinist philosopher Denis Diderot's 1796 novel *Jacques le Fataliste*. Aka LADIES OF THE PARK. ▼◗

Les Diaboliques SEE: **Diabolique** (1955)
Les Enfants Terribles (1949-French) **105m. *** D: Jean-Pierre Melville. Nicole Stéphane, Edouard Dermithe, Renée Cosima, Jacques Bernard, Melvyn Martin, Maria Cyliakus, Jean-Marie Robain. Jean Cocteau (who also narrates) chose Melville to direct this adaptation of his daring play detailing the perverse, fantasy-filled relationship between a brother and sister and the tragedy that ensues when their private world is shattered by outsiders. Handsomely crafted, well acted, and

[386]

beautifully shot by Henri Decaë. U.S. title: THE STRANGE ONES. ▼▋

Les Girls (1957) **C-114m.** ***½ D: George Cukor. Gene Kelly, Mitzi Gaynor, Kay Kendall, Taina Elg, Jacques Bergerac, Leslie Phillips, Henry Daniell, Patrick Macnee. Charming, sprightly musical involving three showgirls who (via flashback) reveal their relationship to hoofer Kelly; chicly handled in all departments, with Cole Porter tunes and Oscar-winning Orry-Kelly costumes. John Patrick adapted Vera Caspary's novel. CinemaScope. ▼●▋

Les Grandes Manoeuvres (1955-French-Italian) **C-106m.** *** D: René Clair. Gérard Philipe, Michele Morgan, Brigitte Bardot, Yves Robert, Pierre Dux, Jean Desailly, Jacques Fabri. In a pre-WW1 garrison town, soldier Philipe wagers he can seduce and abandon divorced beauty Morgan, but the tables are turned when the Don Juan finds himself succumbing to a new emotion: love. Entertaining Clair confection (his first in color) is amusing, if not quite as witty or imaginative as his finest films. Aka THE GRAND MANEUVER; SUMMER MANEUVERS. ▼

Le Silence de la Mer (1947-French) **86m.** *** D: Jean-Pierre Melville. Howard Vernon, Nicole Stéphane, Jean-Marie Robain, Ami Aroe, Denis Sadier. During the Occupation, a patrician German officer is assigned lodging with a provincial family who is unwilling even to speak to him. Nevertheless, each evening he reminisces about life and war in the face of their stubborn silence. Melville's intimately contained first feature clearly reflects postwar attitudes, particularly concerning what defines an enemy. From a 1942 novella by Vercors (Jean Bruller), a classic of Resistance literature. ▼▋

Les Misérables (1935) **108m.** ***½ D: Richard Boleslawski. Fredric March, Charles Laughton, Cedric Hardwicke, Rochelle Hudson, Frances Drake, John Beal, Florence Eldridge, Jessie Ralph, Leonid Kinskey. Meticulous production of Victor Hugo's oft-filmed classic tale. Minor thief March tries to bury past and become respectable town mayor, but police inspector Javert (Laughton) won't let him. John Carradine has bit part as student radical. Screenplay by W. P. Lipscomb. ▼●▋

Les Miserables (1947-Italian) **118m.** *** D: Riccardo Freda. Gino Cervi, Valentina Cortesa, John Hinrich, Aldo Nicodemi, Duccia Giraldi, Marcello Mastroianni. Intelligent, handsomely mounted version of the oft-filmed Victor Hugo story, with Cervi making a fine Jean Valjean. Mario Monicelli was one of the scripters. Originally made 140m. ▼▋

Les Miserables (1952) **104m.** *** D: Lewis Milestone. Michael Rennie, Debra Paget, Robert Newton, Sylvia Sidney, Edmund Gwenn, Cameron Mitchell, Elsa Lanchester, Florence Bates. Glossy but thoughtful remake of the venerable Victor Hugo classic. ▋

Les Misérables (1958-French-German-Italian) **C-210m.** **½ D: Jean-Paul Le Chanois. Jean Gabin, Daniele Delorme, Bernard Blier, Bourvil, Gianni Esposito, Serge Reggiani. Victor Hugo tale, with Gabin as Jean Valjean, Blier as Javert. Respectful but uninspiring. Often shown in two parts. Technirama. ▼▋

Les Parents Terribles (1948-French) **98m.** *** D: Jean Cocteau. Jean Marais, Josette Day, Yvonne de Bray, Marcel Andre, Gabrielle Dorziat. Absorbing drama of a dysfunctional middle-class family, with in-experienced young Marais falling in love with Day, unaware that she's been his father's mistress. De Bray is outstanding as Marais' neurotic mother, who subtly expresses incestuous feelings toward her son. Cocteau scripted based on his play (which featured these same actors). Remade in England as INTIMATE RELATIONS. ▼●

Lesson in Love, A (1954-Swedish) **95m.** *** D: Ingmar Bergman. Gunnar Bjornstrand, Eva Dahlbeck, Yvonne Lombard, Harriet Andersson, Ake Gronberg. Obstetrician Bjornstrand, happily married for 15 years to Dahlbeck, has an affair with a patient; Dahlbeck then returns to *her* former lover—the husband's best friend. Medium Bergman. ▼

Les Visiteurs du Soir (1942-French) **120m.** **½ D: Marcel Carné. Arletty, Jules Berry, Marie Déa, Fernand Ledoux, Alain Cuny, Marcel Herrand. In the Middle Ages, the Devil sends two envoys disguised as minstrels to a chateau to break up a love affair, but one of them falls for the woman he is trying to seduce. Celebrated but somewhat disappointing French fantasy made during the Nazi occupation, intended by writers Jacques Prévert and Pierre Laroche as an allegory, with the Devil representing Hitler. Beautiful to look at but rather cold and artificial. Aka THE DEVIL'S ENVOYS. ▼▋

Let 'Em Have It (1935) **90m.** **½ D: Sam Wood. Richard Arlen, Virginia Bruce, Alice Brady, Bruce Cabot, Harvey Stephens, Eric Linden, Joyce Compton, Gordon Jones. Predictable gangster saga is interesting for depiction of newly formed FBI at work. Some strong action scenes. ▼▋

Le Testament du Dr. Cordelier (1959-French) **100m.** *** D: Jean Renoir. Jean-Louis Barrault, Michel Vitold, Teddy Billis, Jean Topart, Micheline Gary, Gaston Modot. Barrault gives a marvelous, swaggering performance in this adaptation of *Dr. Jekyll and Mr. Hyde* set in contemporary Paris. Eschewing elaborate makeup or special effects, Renoir directs in a deceptively simple style, stripping the story down to its basics to present stinging social satire and a sympathetic but unflinching portrait of the dark side of human nature. Originally made for TV. Aka EXPERIMENT IN EVIL and THE DOCTOR'S HORRIBLE EXPERIMENT. ▼▋

Let Freedom Ring (1939) 87m. *** D: Jack Conway. Nelson Eddy, Virginia Bruce, Victor McLaglen, Lionel Barrymore, Edward Arnold, Guy Kibbee, Charles Butterworth, H. B. Warner, Raymond Walburn, George F. (Gabby) Hayes. Ben Hecht scripted this fascinating Western drama with music about a singing lawyer (Eddy) who returns to his hometown and battles corrupt Arnold. Sermonizes a bit, but its points about the power of the press and a citizen's responsibilities in a free society are as relevant as ever. ▼▶

Let No Man Write My Epitaph (1960) 106m. *** D: Philip Leacock. Burl Ives, Shelley Winters, James Darren, Jean Seberg, Ricardo Montalban, Ella Fitzgerald. Bizarre account of slum life, focusing on Darren and his dope-addicted mother involved with a variety of corrupt individuals. Sequel to KNOCK ON ANY DOOR. ▼

Le Trou (1960-French-Italian) 120m. ***½ D: Jacques Becker. Michel Constantin, Jean Keraudy, Philippe Leroy, Raymond Meunier, Marc Michel, André Bervil, Catherine Spaak. Four prisoners in Paris' La Santé jail, though suspicious of a newly arrived convict in their cell, have no choice but to involve him in their slow, agonizingly laborious escape attempt. Acted by nonactors, all but plotless and without music, this harrowing near-documentary thriller is riveting in its detail and holds one in thrall to the bitter end. From the 1947 autobiographical (!) novel by future director José Giovanni. Becker's last film. Aka THE HOLE. ▼▶

Let's Be Happy (1957-British) C-93m. **½ D: Henry Levin. Tony Martin, Vera-Ellen, Zena Marshall, Guy Middleton. Featherweight musical of girl going to Scotland to claim a castle she's inherited. Remake of JEANNIE. CinemaScope.

Let's Dance (1950) C-112m. **½ D: Norman Z. McLeod. Betty Hutton, Fred Astaire, Roland Young, Ruth Warrick, Shepperd Strudwick, Lucile Watson, Barton MacLane, Melville Cooper. Lesser-known Astaire vehicle is still fun, with war widow Hutton attempting to shield her young son from the clutches of his wealthy, stuffy great-grandmother. Astaire is the man who loves her, and his dancing (particularly in the "Piano Dance" number) is wonderful. Songs by Frank Loesser. ▼▶

Let's Do It Again (1953) C-95m. *** D: Alexander Hall. Jane Wyman, Ray Milland, Aldo Ray, Leon Ames, Tom Helmore. Musical remake of THE AWFUL TRUTH with Milland in Cary Grant's role, Wyman in Irene Dunne's, and Ray in Ralph Bellamy's. Songs add to spicy plot, but no classic like original '37 film. ▶

Let's Face It (1943) 76m. ** D: Sidney Lanfield. Bob Hope, Betty Hutton, ZaSu Pitts, Phyllis Povah, Dave Willock, Eve Arden. Brassy comedy with loud Hutton competing with Hope for laughs in forced

wartime comedy of soldiers hired as male companions.

Let's Fall in Love (1933) 75m. **½ D: David Burton. Edmund Lowe, Ann Sothern, Miriam Jordan, Gregory Ratoff, Greta Meyer, Betty Furness, Arthur Jarrett, Anderson Lawler. Sothern shines in her first credited role as a carnival performer discovered by Hollywood director Lowe, who grooms her to be a star and convinces dyspeptic studio boss Ratoff that she's from Sweden. Amusing romantic comedy with songs by Harold Arlen and Ted Koehler, including the repeatedly heard title tune. Remade as SLIGHTLY FRENCH (1949).

Let's Get Tough! (1942) 62m. ** D: Wallace Fox. Leo Gorcey, Bobby Jordan, Huntz Hall, Sunshine Sammy Morrison, Bobby Stone, David Gorcey, Tom Brown, Florence Rice, Robert Armstrong, Gabriel Dell. The East Side Kids take on Japanese spies in this rampantly jingoistic entry. The kids ad lib shamelessly, with frequently amusing results. ▼▶

Let's Go Native (1930) 75m. **½ D: Leo McCarey. Jack Oakie, Jeanette MacDonald, Skeets Gallagher, James Hall, William Austin, Kay Francis, David Newell, Eugene Pallette, Grady Sutton. Fashion designer MacDonald, hoping to stage a musical revue, sails for South America but is shipwrecked on a tropical isle ("It was one of the Virgin Islands, but it drifted"). Strange film plays like an elongated two-reel comedy with gags both old-hat and wildly ingenious. Musical numbers are haphazard, the best a shipboard novelty with Oakie and chorus girls that uses "arty" camera angles and even a kaleidoscope effect.

Let's Go Navy! (1951) 68m. **½ D: William Beaudine. Leo Gorcey, Huntz Hall, William Benedict, David Gorcey, Bernard Gorcey, Allen Jenkins, Buddy Gorman, Charlita, Dorothy Ford, Tom Neal, Frank Jenks. The Bowery Boys sign up and ship out to catch some crooks who are posing as gobs. One of their funniest outings. ▶

Let's Live a Little (1948) 85m. **½ D: Richard Wallace. Hedy Lamarr, Robert Cummings, Anna Sten, Robert Shayne, Mary Treen. Amusing but unspectacular romantic comedy, with Lamarr and Cummings falling in love. ▶

Let's Make It Legal (1951) 77m. ** D: Richard Sale. Claudette Colbert, Macdonald Carey, Zachary Scott, Robert Wagner, Barbara Bates, Marilyn Monroe. Trifling comedy in which Colbert divorces Carey and is tempted to wed ex-beau Scott. Monroe is wasted as a bathing beauty. ▼▶

Let's Make Love (1960) C-118m. *** D: George Cukor. Marilyn Monroe, Yves Montand, Tony Randall, Frankie Vaughan, Wilfrid Hyde-White, David Burns. Billionaire Montand hears of show spoofing him, wants to stop it, then meets the show's star, Monroe. To charm her, he hires Bing Crosby to teach him to sing, Milton Berle to coach on comedy, Gene Kelly to make him dance. Bubbly cast, snappy musical numbers. CinemaScope.▼◑❶

Let's Make Music (1940) **85m. **½ D: Leslie Goodwins. Bob Crosby, Jean Rogers, Elisabeth Risdon, Joseph Buloff. Nathanael West wrote this entertaining B musical about bandleader Crosby turning prim schoolteacher's football victory song into a hit. Good fun; other songs include "Big Noise from Winnetka."

Let's Make Up (1954-British) **C-94m.** ** D: Herbert Wilcox. Errol Flynn, Anna Neagle, David Farrar, Kathleen Harrison, Peter Graves. Froth about overimaginative Neagle trying to decide between suitors Flynn and Farrar. Sean Connery has a bit in his film debut. Original title: LILACS IN THE SPRING.▼

Let's Rock! (1958) **79m.** ** D: Harry Foster. Julius La Rosa, Phyllis Newman, Conrad Janis, Della Reese, Joy Harmon, Royal Teens, Paul Anka, Danny and the Juniors, Roy Hamilton, Wink Martindale. Balladeer La Rosa resists changing his singing style with the popularity of rock 'n' roll. KING LEAR it isn't. Danny and the Juniors sing "At the Hop"; the Royal Teens do "Short Shorts." Aka KEEP IT COOL.

Let's Talk About Men (1965-Italian) **93m.** *** D: Lina Wertmuller. Nino Manfredi, Luciana Paluzzi, Margaret Lee, Milena Vukotic, Patrizia DeClara, Alfredo Baranchini. Amusing episodic film (four stories tied to a fifth): Manfredi competently and comically plays five different men involved with different women and situations. Made right after Ettore Scola's LET'S TALK ABOUT WOMEN, this took 11 years to cross the ocean but was worth the wait.

Let's Talk About Women (1964-Italian-French) **108m.** **½ D: Ettore Scola. Vittorio Gassman, Maria Fiore, Donatella Mauro, Giovanna Ralli, Antonella Lualdi, Slyva Koscina, Heidi Stroh, Rosanna Ghevardi, Walter Chiari, Eleonora Rossi-Drago, Jean Valerie. Nine-episode comedy with Gassman starring in each, and encountering a variety of women. Some segments better than others; one of the best has Gassman discovering that the prostitute he's hired is married to an old friend of his! Lina Wertmuller's LET'S TALK ABOUT MEN came a year later.

Letter, The (1929) **65m.** **½ D: Jean de Limur. Jeanne Eagels, Reginald Owen, Herbert Marshall, Irene Brown (Browne), O. P. Heggie. First screen version of W. Somerset Maugham's play, set in Singapore, about a woman who murders her lover, then trades on her unsuspecting husband's name and reputation to bolster her claim of self-defense. Unseen for decades, this is the first—and only surviving—talkie appearance of the legendary Eagels, who died later that year. Hampered by primitive sound techniques, it still exerts a strange fascination, and her performance justifies her reputation. (It's also more frank than the 1940 remake in which Marshall, who plays the lover here, is cast as the husband.) Producer Monta Bell also had a hand in script.❶

Letter, The (1940) **95m.** ***½ D: William Wyler. Bette Davis, Herbert Marshall, James Stephenson, Frieda Inescort, Gale Sondergaard. Lushly photographed Somerset Maugham drama set in Malaya, with Davis pleading self-defense after fatally shooting a man . . . but was it? Davis quite appealing in her unsympathetic role. DVD offers an alternate ending. Previously filmed in 1929 (also with Herbert Marshall in cast); remade as THE UNFAITHFUL, then again for TV in 1982 with Lee Remick.▼◑❶

Letter for Evie, A (1945) **89m.** ** D: Jules Dassin. Marsha Hunt, John Carroll, Hume Cronyn, Spring Byington, Pamela Britton, Norman Lloyd, Donald Curtis. Inconsequential romancer in which insecure G.I. Cronyn begins pen-pal relationship with pretty Hunt; complications arise when she asks for a photo, and he sends her one of playboy buddy Carroll.

Letter From an Unknown Woman (1948) **90m.** *** D: Max Opuls (Ophuls). Joan Fontaine, Louis Jourdan, Mady Christians, Marcel Journet, Art Smith. Lush romantic flavor of direction and performances obscures clichés and improbabilities in story of Fontaine's lifelong infatuation with musician Jourdan. Based on a Stefan Zweig story filmed in 1929 in Germany as NARKOSE.▼◑❶

Letter of Introduction (1938) **104m.** **½ D: John M. Stahl. Adolphe Menjou, Andrea Leeds, Edgar Bergen (and Charlie McCarthy), George Murphy, Rita Johnson, Eve Arden, Ann Sheridan. Aspiring actress Leeds calls on her father, faded matinee idol Menjou, who hasn't seen her since she was a baby. Bergen and McCarthy add laughs to this slick concoction.▼❶

Letters From My Windmill (1954-French) **140m.** **½ D: Marcel Pagnol. Henri Velbert, Daxely, Yvonne Gamy, Rellys, Robert Vattier, Roger Crouzet. A trio of delights from Pagnol: "The Three Low Masses," "The Elixir of Father Gaucher," "The Secret of Master Cornille." The second is best, with monk Rellys leading his monastery into liquor business. Pagnol scripted, and the English subtitles were penned by Preston Sturges!▼

Letter to Mother, A SEE: **A Brivele der Mamen**

Letter to Three Wives, A (1949) **103m.** **** D: Joseph L. Mankiewicz. Jeanne

Crain, Linda Darnell, Ann Sothern, Kirk Douglas, Paul Douglas, Jeffrey Lynn, Barbara Lawrence, Connie Gilchrist, Florence Bates, Thelma Ritter. Delicious Americana showing reactions of three women who receive a letter from town flirt who has run off with one of their husbands. Celeste Holm provides the voice of the letter's authoress. Mankiewicz won Oscars for his terrific script and direction. Based on a novel by John Klempner, adapted by Vera Caspary. Remade as a TVM in 1985.▼●◗

Letty Lynton (1932) **84m.** ****½** D: Clarence Brown. Joan Crawford, Robert Montgomery, Nils Asther, Lewis Stone, May Robson, Louise Closser Hale, Emma Dunn, Walter Walker. Once she meets Montgomery on a romantic ocean liner, Crawford realizes she has to end her relationship with Asther, whom she left behind in Montevideo. Slick Crawford vehicle with a nifty pre-Code finale; the star has never looked more glamorous. Inspired by a notorious 1857 case in Glasgow, Scotland, as was DISHONORED LADY and MADELEINE (1950). Film was also subject of a plagiarism suit that went all the way to the U.S. Supreme Court.

Let Us Be Gay (1930) **79m.** ****** D: Robert Z. Leonard. Norma Shearer, Marie Dressler, Rod LaRocque, Gilbert Emery, Hedda Hopper, Raymond Hackett, Sally Eilers, Dickie Moore. Frumpy (and barely recognizable) Shearer, a devoted wife, divorces husband LaRocque after learning that he's been unfaithful. Three years pass, and they meet again under completely different circumstances. Talky, one-note comedy-drama is worth a look solely for Shearer's presence and startling transformation. Based on a play by Rachel Crothers.◗

Let Us Live (1939) **68m.** ****½** D: John Brahm. Maureen O'Sullivan, Henry Fonda, Ralph Bellamy, Alan Baxter, Stanley Ridges, Henry Kolker. Working man Fonda dreams of a bright future with the woman he loves . . . but he's in the wrong place at the wrong time and finds himself accused of murder. Impassioned but formulaic Depression-era tale.◗

Libel (1959-British) **100m.** ****½** D: Anthony Asquith. Dirk Bogarde, Olivia de Havilland, Robert Morley, Paul Massie, Wilfrid Hyde-White, Anthony Dawson, Richard Wattis, Millicent Martin. Engrossing if uninspired filming of Edward Wooll's vintage play about a baronet (and former prisoner of war) who is challenged in court to prove his identity—which turns out to be unusually difficult. Metroscope.◗

Libeled Lady (1936) **98m.** ******** D: Jack Conway. Jean Harlow, William Powell, Myrna Loy, Spencer Tracy, Walter Connolly, Charley Grapewin, Cora Witherspoon. Wonderful comedy with the four stars working at full steam: conniving newspaper editor Tracy uses his fiancée (Harlow) and

ex-employee (Powell) to get the goods on hot-headed heiress Loy—but everything goes wrong. Sit back and enjoy. Screenplay by Maurine Watkins, Howard Emmett Rogers, and George Oppenheimer. Remade as EASY TO WED.▼●◗

Liebelei (1932-German) **82m.** *****½** D: Max Ophuls. Wolfgang Leibeneiner, Magda Schneider, Luise Ullrich, Gustaf Grundgens, Olga Tschechowa, Willy Eichberger. Haunting, exquisitely filmed adaptation of Arthur Schnitzler's play about a tragic love affair between a worldly army officer (Leibeneiner) and an innocent fraulein (Schneider) in turn-of-the-20th-century Austria. Ophuls' lyrical direction and Franz Planer's glistening photography create an evocative picture of old Vienna, with nocturnal sleigh rides through snowy woods and duels at twilight. Schneider's daughter Romy played the fraulein role in a 1958 remake called CHRISTINE. ▼

Lieutenant Wore Skirts, The (1956) **C-99m.** ****½** D: Frank Tashlin. Tom Ewell, Sheree North, Rita Moreno, Rick Jason, Les Tremayne, Jean Willes. Ewell makes nonsense acceptable as he chases after wife who reenlisted in service thinking he'd been drafted again. CinemaScope.◗

Life and Adventures of Nicholas Nickleby, The SEE: **Nicholas Nickleby** (1947-British)

Life and Death of Colonel Blimp, The (1943-British) **C-163m.** ******** D: Michael Powell, Emeric Pressburger. Roger Livesey, Deborah Kerr, Anton Walbrook, John Laurie, James McKechnie, Neville Mapp. Superb, sentimental story of a staunch British soldier, and incidents that dovetail in his long, eventful life. Opens in WW2 and flashes back as far as the Boer War. Kerr charming as three different women in the Colonel's life. (Title character bears no relation to famous David Low caricature buffoon on whom he's supposedly based.) Heavily cut for various reissues; often shown in b&w.▼●◗

Life at the Top (1965-British) **117m.** ****½** D: Ted Kotcheff. Laurence Harvey, Jean Simmons, Honor Blackman, Michael Craig, Donald Wolfit, Robert Morley, Margaret Johnston, Nigel Davenport. Follow-up to ROOM AT THE TOP picks up the account a decade later; film lacks flavor or life—best moments are flashbacks to Signoret-Harvey romance.▼

Life Begins (1932) **71m.** ******* D: James Flood, Elliott Nugent. Loretta Young, Aline MacMahon, Glenda Farrell, Vivienne Osborne, Eric Linden, Preston Foster, Elizabeth Patterson, Dorothy Tree. Offbeat film of maternity ward, with fine Warner Bros. cast depicting nurses, mothers, and others involved in life-giving process. Remade as A CHILD IS BORN.

Life Begins at College SEE: **Life Begins in College**

Life Begins at 8:30 (1942) **85m.** **½ D: Irving Pichel. Monty Woolley, Ida Lupino, Cornel Wilde, Sara Allgood, Melville Cooper, J. Edward Bromberg. Lupino has sacrificed her own happiness in order to care for her father, a once-great, now washed-up, drunken actor. Opens with a great scene of Woolley as a drunken department store Santa, but develops in fits and starts after that; an odd little film redeemed by fine performances. Nunnally Johnson adapted Emlyn Williams' play. ▼▶

Life Begins at Forty (1935) **85m.** *** D: George Marshall. Will Rogers, Rochelle Hudson, Richard Cromwell, Jane Darwell, Slim Summerville, George Barbier, Thomas Beck, Sterling Holloway. Delightful Americana, with newspaper editor Rogers trying to clear name of Cromwell, who was framed for bank robbery years ago. Rogers' comments on American life remain surprisingly contemporary. ▶

Life Begins at 17 (1958) **75m.** *½ D: Arthur Dreifuss. Mark Damon, Dorothy Johnson, Edd Byrnes, Luana Anders, Ann Doran, Hugh Sanders. Rich punk Damon is dating plain Anders, but is only using her to get to her beauty-queen sister. Demented specimen of producer Sam Katzman's low-budget (albeit successful) 1950s teenpics.

Life Begins for Andy Hardy (1941) **100m.** *** D: George B. Seitz. Mickey Rooney, Lewis Stone, Judy Garland, Fay Holden, Ann Rutherford, Sara Haden, Patricia Dane, Ray McDonald. Andy decides to get a job in the Big Apple before starting college and is confronted with the harsh realities of life and love. Unusually adult and cynical addition to the series. Garland's third and final appearance; her songs were cut(!) from the finished film. ▼▶

Life Begins in College (1937) **94m.** **½ D: William A. Seiter. Joan Davis, Tony Martin, The Ritz Brothers, Gloria Stuart, Nat Pendleton, Fred Stone. Sis-boom-bah college nonsense with zany Ritz trio helping the school team win the big game. Pendleton is fun as an Indian who comes to college. ▶

Lifeboat (1944) **96m.** ***½ D: Alfred Hitchcock. Tallulah Bankhead, William Bendix, Walter Slezak, Mary Anderson, John Hodiak, Henry Hull, Heather Angel, Hume Cronyn, Canada Lee. Penetrating revelations about shipwreck survivors adrift in lonely lifeboat during WW2. Bankhead remarkable as spoiled journalist, Slezak fine as Nazi taken aboard. Only Hitchcock would take on the challenge of such a film—and succeed. Jo Swerling adapted John Steinbeck's original story. Remade as a 1993 TVM, LIFEPOD. ▼▶

Life in the Balance, A (1955) **74m.** ** D: Harry Horner. Ricardo Montalban, Anne Bancroft, Lee Marvin, Jose Perez. Lukewarm narrative set in a Latin American city, about a series of woman-killings; the police hunt for guilty person. ▶

Life of Emile Zola, The (1937) **116m.** **** D: William Dieterle. Paul Muni, Gale Sondergaard, Joseph Schildkraut, Gloria Holden, Donald Crisp, Erin O'Brien-Moore, Morris Carnovsky, Louis Calhern, Harry Davenport, Marcia Mae Jones, Dickie Moore, Ralph Morgan. Sincere biography of famed 19th-century French writer who rose to cause of wrongly exiled Captain Dreyfus (Schildkraut); detailed production filled with fine vignettes. Won Oscars for Best Picture, Screenplay (Norman Reilly Raine, Geza Herczeg, and Heinz Herald), Supporting Actor (Schildkraut). ▼▶

Life of Her Own, A (1950) **108m.** **½ D: George Cukor. Lana Turner, Ray Milland, Tom Ewell, Louis Calhern, Ann Dvorak, Margaret Phillips, Jean Hagen, Barry Sullivan, Phyllis Kirk. Turner is at the center of three-cornered romance leading to heartbreak for all. MGM fluff; Dvorak wraps it up with her expert portrayal of an aging model. Bronislau Kaper's musical theme was later reused for his classic INVITATION. ▼▶

Life of Jack London, The SEE: **Jack London**

Life of Jimmy Dolan, The (1933) **89m.** *** D: Archie Mayo. Douglas Fairbanks, Jr., Loretta Young, Guy Kibbee, Fifi D'Orsay, Aline MacMahon, Lyle Talbot. Fast-moving account of boxer Fairbanks, on the run after he thinks he killed a reporter, winding up at a home for crippled children. Look for Mickey Rooney as one of the kids, John Wayne in boxing trunks. Remade as THEY MADE ME A CRIMINAL.

Life of Oharu, The (1952-Japanese) **146m.** **½ D: Kenji Mizoguchi. Kinuyo Tanaka, Toshiro Mifune, Hisako Yamane, Yuriko Hamada, Ichiro Sugai. Clichéd account of beautiful Tanaka, banished for loving a samurai (Mifune, in a small role) below her station, ending up an aged prostitute. Also shown at 118m. and known as DIARY OF OHARU. ▼▶

Life of Riley, The (1949) **87m.** **½ D: Irving Brecher. William Bendix, James Gleason, Rosemary DeCamp, Bill Goodwin, Beulah Bondi, Meg Randall, Richard Long, John Brown. Adaptation of the popular radio comedy series about hard-luck working stiff Chester A. Riley. More bittersweet than the subsequent TV series but enjoyable, with the black comedy of Brown's Digger O'Dell a real novelty.

Life of the Party, The (1937) **77m.** ** D: William Seiter. Gene Raymond, Harriet Hilliard (Nelson), Ann Miller, Joe Penner, Parkyakarkas, Victor Moore, Billy Gilbert, Helen Broderick, Franklin Pangborn, Margaret Dumont. Young Raymond will forfeit $3 million if he weds Hilliard before he turns 30. Second-rate musical comedy.

Life of Vergie Winters, The (1934) **82m.** **½ D: Alfred Santell. Ann Harding, John Boles, Helen Vinson, Betty Furness, Lon

Chaney, Jr., Bonita Granville. Successful adaptation of Louis Bromfield weeper chronicling life of Harding, who defies small-town gossip, following her own instincts.

Life With Blondie (1946) **64m.** **½ D: Abby Berlin. Penny Singleton, Arthur Lake, Larry Simms, Marjorie Kent, Jonathan Hale, Ernest Truex, Marc Lawrence, Veda Ann Borg, Jack Rice, Bobby Larson, Eddie Acuff. Genial nonsense about the Bumsteads' dog, Daisy, winning a Navy pinup contest and being kidnapped by gangsters.▼

Life With Father (1947) **C-118m.** **** D: Michael Curtiz. William Powell, Irene Dunne, Elizabeth Taylor, Edmund Gwenn, ZaSu Pitts, Jimmy Lydon, Martin Milner. Rich adaptation of long-running Broadway play (by Howard Lindsay and Russel Crouse) based on Clarence Day's story of growing up in turn-of-the-20th-century N.Y.C. with his loving but eccentric father. Utterly delightful, and a handsome production as well. Screenplay by Donald Ogden Stewart.▼●

Life With Henry (1941) **80m.** **½ D: Ted Reed. Jackie Cooper, Leila Ernst, Eddie Bracken, Fred Niblo, Hedda Hopper, Kay Stewart, Moroni Olsen, Rod Cameron, Pierre Watkin, Lucien Littlefield, Frank M. Thomas. Follow-up to WHAT A LIFE brings Cooper back to role of Henry Aldrich, the perpetual foul-up who this time wants to win a trip to Alaska. Bracken is fun as his comic pal.

Light Across the Street, The (1956-French) **76m.** **½ D: Georges Lacombe. Brigitte Bardot, Raymond Pellegrin, Roger Pigaut, Claude Romain. Above-par Bardot fare: she's wed to jealous Pellegrin, who begins to suspect she's fooling around with the new next-door neighbor. Original running time: 99m. Retitled: FEMALE AND THE FLESH.

Light Ahead, The (1939) **94m.** *** D: Edgar G. Ulmer. Isidore Cashier, Helen Beverly, David Opatoshu, Rosetta Bialis, Tillie Rabinowitz. Heartfelt, pleasingly sentimental saga, based on the writings of Mendele Mocher Sforim (Mendele the bookseller), detailing the plight of poor, luckless lovers Beverly and Opatoshu, and how they are helped by wise old bookseller Cashier in a provincial Russian town during the 1880s. Yiddish-language gem was shot in Newton, New Jersey!▼

Light Fingers (1957-British) **90m.** ** D: Terry Bishop. Guy Rolfe, Eunice Gayson, Roland Culver, Lonnie Donegan, Hy Hazell, Ronald Howard. Miserly husband (Culver) thinks wife is kleptomaniac; hires bodyguard butler who is really a thief. Adequate production.

Light in the Forest, The (1958) **C-93m.** *** D: Herschel Daugherty. James MacArthur, Carol Lynley, Fess Parker, Wendell Corey, Joanne Dru, Jessica Tandy, Joseph Calleia, John McIntire. Absorbing Disney for young people, from Conrad Richter's story of a white boy, raised by Indians, who has difficulty readjusting to life with his real parents. Lynley's film debut.▼●

Light in the Piazza (1962) **C-101m.** ***½ D: Guy Green. Olivia de Havilland, Rossano Brazzi, Yvette Mimieux, George Hamilton, Barry Sullivan. Splendid soaper about mother who's anxious to marry off retarded daughter but isn't sure she's being fair to suitor. Beautifully filmed on location in Italy. Screenplay by Julius Epstein, from Elizabeth Spencer's novel. Later a Broadway musical. CinemaScope.▶

Lightnin' (1925) **104m.** *** D: John Ford. Jay Hunt, Madge Bellamy, Wallace MacDonald, J. Farrell MacDonald, Ethel Clayton, James Marcus, Edythe Chapman, Otis Harlan. Swindlers learn that a hotel straddling the California-Nevada state line (where women come for quickie divorces) stands on a proposed railroad site and try to cheat the owners, a lazy old boozehound (Hunt) and his kindly wife (Chapman). Amusing silent comedy, full of folksy humor, adapted by Frances Marion from the play by Frank Baron and Winchell Smith. Remade in 1930 with Will Rogers.

Lightning Strikes Twice (1934) **63m.** ** D: Ben Holmes. Ben Lyon, Thelma Todd, Skeets Gallagher, Pert Kelton, Walter Catlett, John Davidson. Engaging cast makes the most of an oddball script, which opens as a whodunit, segues into a comedy of errors, and only returns to the mystery near the end. Kelton and Catlett as vaudevillians offer the funniest scenes.

Lightning Strikes Twice (1951) **91m.** **½ D: King Vidor. Richard Todd, Ruth Roman, Mercedes McCambridge, Zachary Scott. Muddled yet engaging yarn of ex-con returning home to start new life, finding actual killer of his wife.▶

Lights of New York (1928) **57m.** **½ D: Bryan Foy. Helene Costello, Cullen Landis, Gladys Brockwell, Mary Carr, Wheeler Oakman, Eugene Pallette, Robert Elliott, Tom Dugan. Country boy opens a barber shop in the big city and gets mixed up with crooks. Story may be routine, production crude, and acting laughable, but all that is overshadowed by the fact that this fascinating artifact was the first "100% All-Talking Picture" and created the template for future Warner Bros. crime movies.

Lights of Old Santa Fe (1944) **78m.** ** D: Frank McDonald. Roy Rogers, George "Gabby" Hayes, Dale Evans, Lloyd Corrigan, Richard Powers (Tom Keene), Claire Du Brey, Arthur Loft, Roy Barcroft, Lucien Littlefield, Bob Nolan and the Sons of the Pioneers. Roy must save rodeo company owner Dale from competitor Powers, who wants to marry her and combine their shows. Music and romance dominate this unexciting entry, with title tune, "Cowboy Jubilee," and "Ride 'Em Cowboy." ▼▶

Light That Failed, The (1939) 97m. ******* D: William Wellman. Ronald Colman, Walter Huston, Ida Lupino, Dudley Digges, Muriel Angelus, Fay Helm, Francis McDonald. Fine cast in Kipling melodrama of London artist Colman going blind, determined to finish portrait of Lupino, whose florid Cockney performance steals film. Filmed before in 1916 and 1923.

Light Touch, The (1951) 110m. ****½** D: Richard Brooks. Stewart Granger, Pier Angeli, George Sanders, Kurt Kasznar. On-location shooting in Europe perks up lukewarm drama of art thief Granger and his innocent girlfriend Angeli.

Likely Story, A (1947) 88m. ***½** D: H. C. Potter. Bill Williams, Barbara Hale, Sam Levene, Lanny Rees, Dan Tobin, Nestor Paiva. Williams and Hale, then real-life newlyweds, star in this inane comedy about a deluded, shellshocked ex-GI who thinks he's dying and the determined young artist who rescues him. Levene adds the only spark as a Runyonesque crook.

Li'l Abner (1940) 78m. ***½** D: Albert S. Rogell. Granville Owen, Martha O'Driscoll, Mona Ray, Johnnie Morris, Buster Keaton, Kay Sutton. Actors in grotesque makeup bring Al Capp's Dogpatch comic strip characters to life, but despite the presence of many silent comedy veterans (Keaton, Edgar Kennedy, Chester Conklin, Billy Bevan, Al St. John, to name a few) there's nary a laugh in sight. Later musical is much better. ▼▶

Li'l Abner (1959) C-113m. ******* D: Melvin Frank. Peter Palmer, Leslie Parrish, Stubby Kaye, Howard St. John, Julie Newmar, Stella Stevens, Billie Hayes, Robert Strauss. Lively Gene DePaul–Johnny Mercer musical based on Broadway version of Al Capp's comic strip; loud and brassy, with corny comedy, some good songs. Stubby Kaye is fine as Marryin' Sam; other Dogpatch characters vividly enacted. Look sharp for young Valerie Harper and Beth Howland among the chorus girls. VistaVision. ▼▶

Lilacs in the Spring SEE: **Let's Make Up**

Lilac Time (1928) 90m. ****½** D: George Fitzmaurice. Colleen Moore, Gary Cooper, Burr McIntosh, Cleve Moore, Kathryn McGuire, Eugenie Besserer, Emile Chautard, Jack Stone, Arthur Lake. Rickety aviation yarn a la WINGS, with WW1 biplane pilots aloft over France, raring to survive the mission and return to their mamzelles on the ground. In truth, it's a weepy star vehicle for Moore and a showcase for up-and-comer Cooper. Based on a 1917 play by Jane Cowl and Jane Murfin, this late silent introduced the song "Jeannine, I Dream of Lilac Time." Whiteknuckle dogfights in the sky are a reminder that stunt pilot Frank Baker was killed during production. ▼

Lili (1953) C-81m. ******** D: Charles Wal-

ters. Leslie Caron, Mel Ferrer, Zsa Zsa Gabor, Jean-Pierre Aumont, Amanda Blake, Kurt Kasznar. Enchanting fable with Leslie as French orphan who attaches herself to carnival and self-pitying puppeteer Ferrer. Bronislau Kaper's Oscar-winning score includes "Hi Lili, Hi Lo." Helen Deutsch scripted, from Paul Gallico's story, and provided the lyrics for the title song. ▼▶

Lilies of the Field (1963) 93m. ******* D: Ralph Nelson. Sidney Poitier, Lilia Skala, Lisa Mann, Isa Crino, Stanley Adams. A "little" film that made good, winning Poitier an Oscar as handyman who helps build chapel for Skala and her German-speaking nuns. Quiet, well acted, enjoyable. Director Nelson followed this with a TV movie, CHRISTMAS LILIES OF THE FIELD. ▼▶

Liliom (1930) 94m. ****½** D: Frank Borzage. Charles Farrell, Rose Hobart, Estelle Taylor, H. B. Warner, Lee Tracy, Walter Abel, Guinn Williams, Dawn O'Day (Anne Shirley). Early talkie curio, adapted by S. N. Behrman and Sonya Levien from the Molnár play, involving Julie (Hobart), a sweet young servant girl, and her passionate love for Liliom (Farrell), a wayward carnival barker. Slow going at times and Farrell is sorely miscast, but Hobart is fine, Tracy (as The Buzzard) is superb, and Harry Oliver's sets are dazzling. Originally filmed in 1919 (by Michael Curtiz); remade in 1934, and later musicalized as CAROUSEL. ▶

Liliom (1934-French) 116m. *****½** D: Fritz Lang. Charles Boyer, Madeleine Ozeray, Florelle, Robert Arnoux, Roland Toutain. After fleeing Nazi Germany in 1933, Lang went to France and made this version of Molnár's celebrated fantasy, previously filmed in the U.S. in 1919 and 1930 and subsequently musicalized as CAROUSEL. Boyer stars as the brutish carnival barker who is killed while committing a robbery to support his pregnant girlfriend and returns to Earth years later to visit his now-grown daughter. Dreamily romantic yet appropriately dark, with superbly stylish sets and photography, particularly in the imaginative sequences depicting heaven. ▼▶

Lilith (1964) 114m. ****½** D: Robert Rossen. Warren Beatty, Jean Seberg, Peter Fonda, Kim Hunter, Jessica Walter, Anne Meacham, Gene Hackman, Rene Auberjonois. Fairly faithful version of controversial J. R. Salamanca novel about a novice therapist who falls in love with a troubled patient. A probing if not altogether satisfying look at the many facets of madness—and love. Director-writer Rossen's last film. ▼▶

Lillian Russell (1940) 127m. ****** D: Irving Cummings. Alice Faye, Don Ameche, Henry Fonda, Edward Arnold, Warren William, Leo Carrillo, Nigel Bruce. Strained bio of early 20th-century star; lavish backgrounds and weak plotline diminish Faye's vehicle; Arnold repeats his Diamond Jim Brady role with gusto. ▶

Lilli Marlene (1950-British) **75m.** ****** D: Arthur Crabtree. Lisa Daniely, Hugh McDermott, Richard Murdoch, Leslie Dwyer, John Blythe, Stanley Baker. Potentially exciting film is middling fare, with Daniely the girl used by the Nazis to broadcast pessimistic news to British army. Followed by THE WEDDING OF LILLI MARLENE. ▶

Lilly Turner (1933) **65m.** ****½** D: William A. Wellman. Ruth Chatterton, George Brent, Frank McHugh, Guy Kibbee, Robert Barrat, Ruth Donnelly, Marjorie Gateson. Wildly melodramatic tale following the sorrows of carnival performer Chatterton, who gets mixed up with one worthless man after another. Then she meets nice guy Brent, but can their happiness last? Redeemed by the acting and Wellman's typically pungent touches.

Limehouse Blues (1934) **65m.** ****** D: Alexander Hall. George Raft, Jean Parker, Anna May Wong, Kent Taylor, Billy Bevan, Robert Loraine, Eric Blore. Atmospheric but predictable melodrama of race and class differences, set in London's Limehouse district, where brutalized "white girl" Parker is taken in by half-American/half-Chinese saloonkeeper Raft. Watch for Ann Sheridan in a bit. Retitled: EAST END CHANT.

Limelight (1952) **145m.** ******* D: Charles Chaplin. Charles Chaplin, Claire Bloom, Nigel Bruce, Buster Keaton, Sydney Chaplin, Norman Lloyd. Sentimental story of aging, washed-up music hall clown (Chaplin) who saves ballerina Bloom from suicide and regains his own confidence while building her up. Overlong, indulgent Chaplin effort still has many moving scenes, historic teaming of Chaplin and Keaton in comedy skit. Young Geraldine Chaplin (the director's daughter) makes her film debut as a street urchin. This won an Oscar for its score in 1972, the year in which it was first eligible for the competition—because it had not been shown in an L.A. theater until then! ▼●▶

Limping Man, The (1953-British) **76m.** ****** D: Charles de Lautour (Cy Endfield). Lloyd Bridges, Moira Lister, Leslie Phillips, Hélène Cordet, Alan Wheatley, Rachel Roberts, Jean Marsh. Passable mystery with ex-GI Bridges returning to London to rekindle romance with actress Lister, and finding himself embroiled in murder and mayhem. ▼▶

Lineup, The (1958) **86m.** ****½** D: Don Siegel. Eli Wallach, Robert Keith, Richard Jaeckel, Mary LaRoche, William Leslie, Emile Meyer, Marshall Reed, Raymond Bailey, Vaughn Taylor, Warner Anderson. Expanded version of TV series set (and filmed) in San Francisco focuses on psychotic hood Wallach, his equally warped pal (Keith, in one of his best performances), and their efforts to score a cache of dope. Cult favorite with fans of director Siegel, despite the fact

that it's a pretty ordinary police procedural. Anderson reprises his role as Lieutenant Guthrie from the TV series, with Meyer replacing Tom Tully as his partner. Script by Stirling Silliphant. ▶

Lion, The (1962) **C-96m.** ****** D: Jack Cardiff. William Holden, Trevor Howard, Capucine, Pamela Franklin, Samuel Romboh, Christopher Agunda. Beautiful scenery of Kenya is far better than melodrama about young girl attached to pet lion, with family concerned it is turning her into a savage. CinemaScope.

Lion and the Horse, The (1952) **C-83m.** ****** D: Louis King. Steve Cochran, Bob Steele, Sherry Jackson, Ray Teal. Warm B film of valiant horse who combats a fierce African lion; geared for children.

Lion Has Wings, The (1939?-British) **76m.** ****½** D: Michael Powell, Brian Desmond-Hurst, Adrian Brunel. Merle Oberon, Ralph Richardson, June Duprez, Robert Douglas, Anthony Bushell, Derrick de Marney, Brian Worth, Austin Trevor, Ivan Brandt. Dated British WW2 morale-builder, produced by Alexander Korda in a (then) unique "docudrama" style. Top-notch cast and technical credits boost the propagandist elements dramatizing England's entry into the war and the strength of the RAF. ▼

Lion Hunters, The (1951) **75m.** ***½** D: Ford Beebe. Johnny Sheffield, Morris Ankrum, Ann B. Todd, Douglas Kennedy, Smoki Whitfield, Robert Davis, Woodrow (Woody) Strode. It's Bomba the Jungle Boy to the rescue when a hunting expedition is slaughtering lions on sacred Masai grounds. Typical juvenile adventure with even lower production values than usual for this cut-rate series. ▼▶

Lion Is in the Streets, A (1953) **C-88m.** ****½** D: Raoul Walsh. James Cagney, Barbara Hale, Anne Francis, Warner Anderson, John McIntire, Jeanne Cagney, Lon Chaney, Jr., Frank McHugh. Cagney, in a Huey Long take-off, is lively as a swamp peddler turned politician, but rambling screenplay prevents film from having much impact. Well photographed by Harry Stradling. ▼▶

Lisa (1962-U.S.-British) **C-112m.** ****½** D: Philip Dunne. Stephen Boyd, Dolores Hart, Leo McKern, Hugh Griffith, Donald Pleasence, Harry Andrews, Robert Stephens, Marius Goring, Finlay Currie. Jan de Hartog's suspenseful novel of Dutch-Jewish girl in post-WW2 Europe trying to get to Palestine. Exciting film despite gaps in story logic. Stylishly photographed on location by Arthur Ibbetson. Released in England as THE INSPECTOR. ▶

Lisbon (1956) **C-90m.** ****½** D: Ray Milland. Ray Milland, Maureen O'Hara, Claude Rains, Yvonne Furneaux, Francis Lederer, Percy Marmont, Jay Novello. On-location tale of international thief Rains hiring skipper Milland to rescue Maureen's husband from Communist imprisonment. Nice scenery, nothing special. Naturama. ▼

Listen, Darling (1938) 70m. **½ D: Edwin L. Marin. Judy Garland, Freddie Bartholomew, Mary Astor, Walter Pidgeon, Alan Hale, Scotty Beckett. Judy and Freddie try to land mother (Astor) a husband; Garland sings "Zing Went The Strings Of My Heart." ▼●〗

List of Adrian Messenger, The (1963) 98m. *** D: John Huston. George C. Scott, Clive Brook, Dana Wynter, Herbert Marshall, Tony Curtis, Kirk Douglas, Burt Lancaster, Robert Mitchum, Frank Sinatra, John Huston, Bernard Fox. Good murder mystery has a gimmick: Curtis, Douglas, Lancaster, Mitchum, and Sinatra are all heavily disguised in character roles. All that trouble wasn't necessary; the mystery is good on its own. The director's son Tony (billed as Anthony Walter Huston) plays Wynter's son. ▼●〗

Little Annie Rooney (1925) 97m. ** D: William Beaudine. Mary Pickford, William Haines, Walter James, Gordon Griffith, Carlo Schippa. One of Mary's weaker starring vehicles mixes comedy, sentiment, melodrama, and blarney in uneven doses, as ragamuffin girl and her brother set out to avenge their father's murder. ▼●〗

Little Big Horn (1951) 86m. **½ D: Charles Marquis Warren. Lloyd Bridges, John Ireland, Marie Windsor, Reed Hadley, Hugh O'Brian. Small-budget film manages to generate excitement in its account of Custer's Last Stand. ▼〗

Little Big Shot (1935) 71m. **½ D: Michael Curtiz. Sybil Jason, Glenda Farrell, Robert Armstrong, Edward Everett Horton, Jack LaRue, Arthur Vinton, J. Carrol Naish, Edgar Kennedy. Warners' first attempt to create their own Shirley Temple (see LITTLE MISS THOROUGHBRED) stars 5-year-old South African–born Jason playing a gangster's orphaned daughter who is taken in by a pair of Broadway con men. Engaging cast and swift direction make it painless. Jason's impressions of Garbo, Mae West, and Jimmy Durante are pretty cute.

Little Bit of Heaven, A (1940) 87m. ** D: Andrew Marton. Gloria Jean, Robert Stack, Hugh Herbert, C. Aubrey Smith, Stuart Erwin, Nan Grey. Jean has vocal outing as 12-year-old singer supporting family; OK vehicle.

Little Boy Lost (1953) 95m. *** D: George Seaton. Bing Crosby, Claude Dauphin, Nicole Maurey, Gabrielle Dorziat. Synthetic tearjerker set in post-WW2 France, where newspaperman Crosby is trying to locate his son, not knowing which boy at orphanage is his. ▼

Little Caesar (1930) 80m. ***½ D: Mervyn LeRoy. Edward G. Robinson, Douglas Fairbanks, Jr., Glenda Farrell, Stanley Fields, Sidney Blackmer, Ralph Ince, George E.

Stone. Small-time hood becomes underworld big-shot; Robinson as Caesar Enrico Bandello gives star-making performance in classic gangster film, still exciting. Francis Faragoh and Robert E. Lee adapted W. R. Burnett's novel. ▼●〗

Little Colonel, The (1935) 80m. *** D: David Butler. Shirley Temple, Lionel Barrymore, Evelyn Venable, John Lodge, Sidney Blackmer, Bill Robinson. Even nonfans should like this, one of Shirley's best films, as she mends broken ties between Grandpa Barrymore and Mama Venable in the Reconstruction South . . . and does that famous step dance with Robinson. Final scene was filmed in Technicolor. Also shown in computer-colored version. ▼●〗

Little Egypt (1951) C-82m. **½ D: Frederick de Cordova. Mark Stevens, Rhonda Fleming, Nancy Guild, Charles Drake, Tom D'Andrea, Verna Felton, John Litel, Fritz Feld. Chicago Fair in the 1890s is setting for tale of entrepreneurs who popularized the later-famous belly dancer.

Little Foxes, The (1941) 116m. ***½ D: William Wyler. Bette Davis, Herbert Marshall, Teresa Wright, Richard Carlson, Patricia Collinge, Dan Duryea, Charles Dingle. Outstanding filmization of Lillian Hellman's play of greed and corruption within a crumbling Southern family on the financial outs, headed by majestic Davis as ruthless Regina. Collinge, Duryea, Dingle, Carl Benton Reid, and John Marriott all re-create their Broadway roles, with Collinge, Duryea, Reid, and Teresa Wright making their film debuts. Scripted by Hellman. Prequel: ANOTHER PART OF THE FOREST. ▼●〗

Little Fugitive (1953) 75m. *** D: Ray Ashley, Morris Engel, Ruth Orkin. Richie Andrusco, Rickie Brewster, Winifred Cushing, Will Lee. A young boy who thinks he has killed his brother wanders lost through Coney Island. A lyrical little comedy-drama, produced independently and on a threadbare budget. A minor classic. ▼●〗

Little Giant, The (1933) 74m. *** D: Roy Del Ruth. Edward G. Robinson, Mary Astor, Helen Vinson, Kenneth Thomson, Russell Hopton. Just three years after LITTLE CAESAR, Robinson spoofed his own gangster image in this bright comedy about a bootlegger who decides to better himself and crash high society. ●〗

Little Giant (1946) 91m. ** D: William A. Seiter. Bud Abbott, Lou Costello, Brenda Joyce, Jacqueline de Wit, George Cleveland, Elena Verdugo, Mary Gordon, Margaret Dumont. Bud and Lou don't work as a team in this atypical comedy with Lou becoming a vacuum cleaner salesman; filled with amusing, tried-and-true routines. ▼〗

Little Hut, The (1957-British) C-90m. ** D: Mark Robson. Ava Gardner, Stewart Granger, David Niven, Finlay Currie, Walter Chiari. Busy husband Granger takes sexy wife Gardner for granted. Will her friendship with Niven stay platonic when all three are stranded on an island? Static, flat, talky sex farce, from the Andre Roussin play.

Little Kidnappers, The (1953-British) **95m. ***½** D: Philip Leacock. Jon Whiteley, Vincent Winter, Adrienne Corri, Duncan Macrae, Jean Anderson, Theodore Bikel. Splendid children's story set in Nova Scotia, 1900. Two orphan youngsters "adopt" abandoned baby when strict grandfather forbids them having a dog. Whiteley and Winter won special Oscars for outstanding juvenile performances. British title: THE KIDNAPPERS. Remade for cable TV in 1990 with Charlton Heston.

Little Lord Fauntleroy (1921) **111m. ★★★** D: Alfred E. Green, Jack Pickford. Mary Pickford, Claude Gillingwater, Joseph J. Dowling, Colin Kenny, James Marcus, Kate Price, Fred M. Malatesta. Pickford offers a gender-bending dual performance in this heartwarming adaptation of the Frances Hodgson Burnett story as a likable, rough-and-tumble N.Y.C. street boy, as well as his widowed mother. The boy's life is inexorably altered when he learns he's heir to his grandfather's fortune. Mary is as charming as ever; her brother codirected. Previously filmed in England in 1914; remade in 1936 and in Russia in 2003. ▼❂

Little Lord Fauntleroy (1936) **98m. ★★★** D: John Cromwell. Freddie Bartholomew, C. Aubrey Smith, Guy Kibbee, Dolores Costello, Mickey Rooney, Jessie Ralph. Young New Yorker Bartholomew suddenly finds himself a British lord in this charming film from classic story. Handsome, well-cast production. Previously filmed in England in 1914 and in 1921; remade for TV in 1980 with Ricky Schroder and Alec Guinness, and in Russia in 2003. Also shown in computer-colored version.▼❂

Little Man, What Now? (1934) **91m. ★★★½** D: Frank Borzage. Margaret Sullavan, Douglass Montgomery, Alan Hale, Catherine Doucet, Mae Marsh, Alan Mowbray, Hedda Hopper. Impoverished German newlyweds are further strapped when wife becomes pregnant. Splendid romance was also the first Hollywood film to deal even peripherally with conditions that resulted in Hitler's rise to power. Sullavan is luminous. William Anthony McGuire scripted, from the novel by Hans Fallada.❂

Little Men (1940) **84m. ★★** D: Norman Z. McLeod. Kay Francis, Jack Oakie, George Bancroft, Jimmy Lydon, Ann Gillis, Charles (Carl) Esmond, William Demarest. Occasionally cute but slight, predictable adaptation of the Louisa May Alcott novel, focusing on

rough adolescent Lydon "learning the ways" at Francis' school. Oakie easily steals the film as an irrepressible con man. Remade in 1998.▼❂

Little Minister, The (1934) **110m. ***½** D: Richard Wallace. Katharine Hepburn, John Beal, Donald Crisp, Andy Clyde, Beryl Mercer. Charming film of James M. Barrie story about Scottish pastor falling in love, with Hepburn radiant in period romance. ▼❂

Little Miss Broadway (1938) **70m. ★★** D: Irving Cummings. Shirley Temple, George Murphy, Jimmy Durante, Phyllis Brooks, Edna May Oliver, George Barbier. Not bad Temple, with Shirley bringing Oliver's theatrical boardinghouse to life; Shirley and Durante are good together. Songs include "Be Optimistic." Also shown in computer-colored version.▼❂

Little Miss Marker (1934) **80m. ★★★** D: Alexander Hall. Adolphe Menjou, Shirley Temple, Dorothy Dell, Charles Bickford, Lynne Overman, Warren Hymer. Winning Damon Runyon tale of bookie Menjou and N.Y.C. gambling colony reformed by adorable little Shirley, left as IOU for a debt. Remade as SORROWFUL JONES and 40 POUNDS OF TROUBLE, and again in 1980. Also shown in computer-colored version. ▼❂

Little Miss Nobody (1936) **65m. ★★½** D: John G. Blystone. Jane Withers, Jane Darwell, Ralph Morgan, Sara Haden, Harry Carey, Thomas E. Jackson, Jed Prouty, Clarence Wilson. Likable if formulaic vehicle for Withers as the resident troublemaker (and fixer-upper) at an orphanage. Many familiar faces, young and old, in the cast; Carey is especially good as a stranger who helps Jane out of a jam. Filmed before in 1929 as BLUE SKIES. ❂

Little Miss Thoroughbred (1938) **63m. ★★** D: John Farrow. John Litel, Ann Sheridan, Janet Chapman, Frank McHugh, Eric Stanley, Robert Homans, John Ridgely. Litel is a hard-boiled gambler named "Nails" Morgan who adopts moppet Chapman and reforms. Pretty sappy attempt to copy LITTLE MISS MARKER as Warner Bros. tried to turn 6-year-old Chapman (in her film debut) into another Shirley Temple.

Little Mister Jim (1946) **92m. ★★** D: Fred Zinnemann. Jackie "Butch" Jenkins, James Craig, Frances Gifford, Luana Patten, Spring Byington, Ching Wah Lee, Laura La Plante, Henry O'Neill. Sentimental story of young Army brat Jenkins, whose officer father hits the bottle when his pregnant wife dies; family's philosophizing Chinese cook Lee helps set things straight. Early commercial chore for Zinnemann is an OK family film that starts as light comedy then takes a tearjerking turn to melodrama.

Little Mother SEE: **Mamele**

Little Nellie Kelly (1940) **100m. ★★½** D: Norman Taurog. Judy Garland, George

Murphy, Charles Winninger, Douglas McPhail. Lightweight musical based on George M. Cohan play about Judy patching up differences between father Murphy and grandfather Winninger. Garland sings "It's a Great Day for the Irish."▼○●

Little Old New York (1940) **100m.** **½ D: Henry King. Alice Faye, Brenda Joyce, Fred MacMurray, Richard Greene, Henry Stephenson. Claims to be story of Robert Fulton and his steamboat; merely serves as framework for standard romance.●

Little Princess, A (1917) **62m.** **½ D: Marshall Neilan. Mary Pickford, Norman Kerry, Katherine Griffith, Ann Schaefer, ZaSu Pitts, William E. Lawrence, Theodore Roberts, Gertrude Short, Gustav von Seyffertitz. Mary is a delight as Sara Crewe, the beloved heroine from Frances Hodgson Burnett's oft-filmed novel, a little girl whose soldier-father travels with her from Bombay to London and enrolls her in "Miss Minchin's school for select young ladies." It's also a treat to see 23-year-old Pitts in one of her first screen appearances as Sara's pal Becky. However, an extended fantasy sequence, set in India and involving Ali Baba, is little more than filler. Remade in 1939 (with Shirley Temple), twice in 1995, again in 1997, and for television.▼●

Little Princess, The (1939) **C-91m.** *** D: Walter Lang. Shirley Temple, Richard Greene, Anita Louise, Ian Hunter, Cesar Romero, Arthur Treacher, Marcia Mae Jones, Sybil Jason. Shirley stars as a Victorian waif who makes good in this lavishly mounted, colorful production. Remade (twice) in 1995, again in 1997, and for television.▼○●

Little Red Monkey SEE: **Case of the Red Monkey**

Little Shepherd of Kingdom Come, The (1961) **C-108m.** **½ D: Andrew V. McLaglen. Jimmie Rodgers, Luana Patten, Chill Wills, George Kennedy, Neil Hamilton. Bland family-type film of boy who fought for the North during Civil War and his return to rural life. Based on the 1903 novel by John William Fox. Kennedy's film debut. CinemaScope.

Little Shop of Horrors, The (1960) **70m.** ***½ D: Roger Corman. Jonathan Haze, Jackie Joseph, Mel Welles, Dick Miller, Myrtle Vail, Jack Nicholson. Classic black comedy about young schnook who develops bloodthirsty plant and is forced to kill in order to feed it. Initially infamous as The Film Shot In Two Days, but now considered one of Corman's best pictures. Nicholson has hilarious bit as masochist who thrives on dental pain; delightful screenplay by Charles Griffith (who also plays the hold-up man and is the voice of "Audrey, Jr."). Later a stage musical, which was filmed in 1986, and also a short-lived animated children's TV series. Also shown in computer-colored version.▼○●

Littlest Outlaw, The (1955) **C-75m.** *** D: Roberto Gavaldon. Pedro Armendariz, Joseph Calleia, Rodolfo Acosta, Andres Velasquez, Pepe Ortiz. Unpretentious little Disney film about Mexican boy (Velasquez) who runs away with a horse rather than see it killed for its misdeeds; filmed on location.▼●

Littlest Rebel, The (1935) **73m.** *** D: David Butler. Shirley Temple, John Boles, Jack Holt, Karen Morley, Bill Robinson, Stepin Fetchit, Guinn "Big Boy" Williams. One of Shirley's best films, a Civil War saga set in the Old South, with our heroine managing to wrap Union officer Holt around her little finger and protect her Confederate officer father (Boles). Temple and Robinson do some delightful dancing as well. Also shown in computer-colored version.▼●

Little Tough Guy (1938) **80m.** ** D: Harold Young. Billy Halop, Huntz Hall, Gabriel Dell, Bernard Punsly, David Gorcey, Hally Chester, Helen Parrish, Robert Wilcox, Jackie Searl, Marjorie Main, Peggy Stewart. When his dad is railroaded into jail, young Halop rounds up his refined pals (you know—Pig, Ape, Dopey, et al.) and tears up the town. First entry of a minor series spun off from the *Dead End Kids* (see *Bowery Boys* entry for further details).▼●

Little Tough Guys in Society (1938) **76m.** *½ D: Erle Kenton. Mischa Auer, Mary Boland, Edward Everett Horton, Helen Parrish, Jackie Searl, Peggy Stewart, Harold Huber, David Oliver, Frankie Thomas. Paper-thin tale of title delinquents—junior Dead End Kids—and their escapades. Auer, Boland, and Horton can't save it.

Little Women (1933) **115m.** **** D: George Cukor. Katharine Hepburn, Joan Bennett, Paul Lukas, Frances Dee, Jean Parker, Edna May Oliver, Douglass Montgomery, Spring Byington. Film offers endless pleasure no matter how many times you've seen it; a faithful, beautiful adaptation of Alcott's book by Victor Heerman and Sarah Y. Mason, who deservedly received Oscars. The cast is uniformly superb. Remade in 1949, 1978 (for TV), and 1994.▼●

Little Women (1949) **C-121m.** **½ D: Mervyn LeRoy. June Allyson, Peter Lawford, Margaret O'Brien, Elizabeth Taylor, Janet Leigh, Mary Astor. Glossy remake of Louisa May Alcott's gentle account of teenage girls finding maturity and romance—patly cast.▼●

Little World of Don Camillo, The (1951-French-Italian) **96m.** **½ D: Julien Duvivier. Fernandel, Sylvie, Gino Cervi, Vera Talqui, Franco Interlenghi, Saro Urzi. Fernandel is the whole show in this comic tale of a small-town priest who's outraged when the Communists are elected to local office. Moderately funny satire of religion and politics, coscripted by Duvivier and based on the novel by Giovanni Guareschi.

English-language version is narrated by Orson Welles. Followed by several sequels.▼

Live Fast, Die Young (1958) **82m.** ** D: Paul Henreid. Mary Murphy, Norma Eberhardt, Michael Connors. Turgid B film of runaway girl and her sister who prevents her from starting a life of crime.

Live, Love and Learn (1937) **78m.** **½ D: George Fitzmaurice. Robert Montgomery, Rosalind Russell, Robert Benchley, Mickey Rooney, Helen Vinson, Monty Woolley, Al Shean, Billy Gilbert. Stars glide through this formula MGM fluff, with ritzy Russell marrying nonconformist artist Montgomery. ▶

Lively Set, The (1964) **C-95m.** **½ D: Jack Arnold. James Darren, Pamela Tiffin, Doug McClure, Marilyn Maxwell, Charles Drake, Greg Morris. Empty-headed account of cocky Darren, quitting college to become a champion sports car racer. Several forgettable songs—including The Surfaris' "Boss Barracuda."

Lives of a Bengal Lancer, The (1935) **109m.** **** D: Henry Hathaway. Gary Cooper, Franchot Tone, Richard Cromwell, Sir Guy Standing, C. Aubrey Smith, Monte Blue, Kathleen Burke, Noble Johnson, Lumsden Hare, Akim Tamiroff, J. Carrol Naish, Douglass Dumbrille. Delightful Hollywood foray into empire building in Northwest India. Cooper and Tone are pals in famed British regiment, Cromwell the callow son of commander Standing whom they take under their wing. Top story, action, repartee—and wonderful snake-charming scene. Grover Jones, William Slavens McNutt, Achmed Abdullah, Waldemar Young, and John Balderston coscripted; from the novel by Major Francis Yeats-Brown. Remade, with obvious changes, as GERONIMO (1939).▼▶●

Live Wires (1946) **64m.** **½ D: Phil Karlson. Leo Gorcey, Huntz Hall, Bobby Jordan, Billy Benedict, William Frambes, Claudia Drake, Pamela Blake, Mike Mazurki. Gorcey tangles with gangsters in this first official *Bowery Boys* entry, a smooth mix of crime and slapstick. Remake of HE COULDN'T TAKE IT (1933). ▶

Living Dead Man, The SEE: **Late Mathias Pascal, The**

Living Desert, The (1953) **C-69m.** *** D: James Algar. Narrated by Winston Hibler. Disney's first True-Life Adventure feature has dazzling footage of the American desert and its inhabitants, but attracted justifiable criticism for its gimmicky treatment of some material like the famous "scorpion dance." Still worthwhile. Academy Award winner.▼▶

Living Ghost, The (1942) **61m.** BOMB D: William Beaudine. James Dunn, Joan Woodbury, Paul McVey, Norman Willis, J. Farrell MacDonald, Jan Wiley. Dunn hams outrageously as a detective trying to find a murderer in a houseful of suspects. Grade Z comedy-mystery-thriller. Video title: A WALKING NIGHTMARE. ▼▶

Living in a Big Way (1947) **103m.** ** D: Gregory La Cava. Gene Kelly, Marie McDonald, Charles Winninger, Phyllis Thaxter, Spring Byington. Kelly returns from WW2 to get to know his war bride for the first time and clashes with her nouveau riche family. A notorious flop in its day, but not all that bad; Kelly does a couple of first-rate dance numbers.▼▶

Living It Up (1954) **C-95m.** *** D: Norman Taurog. Dean Martin, Jerry Lewis, Janet Leigh, Edward Arnold, Fred Clark, Sheree North, Sig Ruman. Bright remake of NOTHING SACRED. Jerry has Carole Lombard's role as supposed radiation victim brought to N.Y.C. as publicity stunt by reporter Leigh; Martin is Jerry's doctor. Scene at Yankee Stadium is a classic. That's sexy Sheree North, in her film debut, doing what was billed as "the first rock 'n' roll dance on the screen."▶

Living on Love (1937) **60m.** **½ D: Lew Landers. James Dunn, Whitney Bourne, Joan Woodbury, Solly Ward, Tom Kennedy, Franklin Pangborn. Starving artist Dunn and newly employed Bourne reluctantly agree to share a room; he'll occupy it during the day, while she'll do so at night. Modest but appealing remake of RAFTER ROMANCE.▶

Living on Velvet (1935) **80m.** ** D: Frank Borzage. Kay Francis, George Brent, Warren William, Russell Hicks, Maude Turner Gordon, Samuel S. Hinds. Amateur pilot Brent, sole survivor of a crash in which his parents and sister died, becomes reckless and irresponsible in the wake of the tragedy; upper-class Francis marries him, thinking she can turn him around. Offbeat romantic drama never rings true. ▶

Lizzie (1957) **81m.** **½ D: Hugo Haas. Eleanor Parker, Richard Boone, Joan Blondell, Hugo Haas, Ric Roman, Marion Ross, Johnny Mathis. Interesting, if ultimately pedantic, adaptation of Shirley Jackson's *The Bird's Nest*, with Parker as a mousy woman who turns out to have three distinct personalities. Boone is a psychiatrist trying to help her. A project of rare distinction for cultish director Haas, though he injects his familiar personality by playing a kibitzing neighbor. Parker is excellent. Eclipsed by release of similar (and superior) THE THREE FACES OF EVE soon after.

Lloyd's of London (1936) **115m.** ***½ D: Henry King. Freddie Bartholomew, Madeleine Carroll, Sir Guy Standing, Tyrone Power, C. Aubrey Smith, Virginia Field, George Sanders. Handsomely mounted fiction of rise of British insurance company; young messenger boy Bartholomew grows up to be Power, who competes with Sanders for affection of Carroll. ▶

Loaded Pistols (1949) **70m.** **½ D: John English. Gene Autry, Barbara Britton, Chill Wills, Jack Holt, Russell Arms, Robert

Shayne, Vince Barnett, Leon Weaver, Fred Kohler, Clem Bevans. A man is killed during a blackout in a dice game and Gene must figure out the real culprit. Leisurely paced effort with interesting mystery angle. Gene sings title song and "When the Bloom Is on the Sage." ▼▶

Loan Shark (1952) **80m.** ** D: Seymour Friedman. George Raft, Dorothy Hart, Paul Stewart, John Hoyt, Helen Westcott, Henry Slate, Russell Johnson, Margia Dean. Raft tries to instill life into this unexceptional thriller about an ex-fighter smashing the brutal loan-shark racket that killed his brother-in-law. Also brutal: Hotcha Hart's love scenes with silver-haired, twice-her-age Raft!

Local Boy Makes Good (1931) **67m.** **½ D: Mervyn LeRoy. Joe E. Brown, Dorothy Lee, Ruth Hall, Robert Bennett, Edward Woods. Entertaining Brown vehicle, with mousy Joe turning into a track-and-field star. ▶

Locked Door, The (1929) **74m.** **½ D: George Fitzmaurice. Rod La Rocque, Barbara Stanwyck, William (Stage) Boyd, Betty Bronson, Harry Stubbs, Harry Mestayer, Mack Swain, ZaSu Pitts. Happily married Stanwyck (in her debut film) learns that her sister-in-law's new boyfriend is a cad who once tried to seduce her. Not-bad early talkie, based on the play *The Sign on the Door* by Channing Pollock, filmed under that title in 1921. See if you can spot Paulette Goddard on the rum boat in the film's opening sequence.

Locket, The (1946) **86m.** ** D: John Brahm. Laraine Day, Brian Aherne, Robert Mitchum, Gene Raymond, Sharyn Moffet, Ricardo Cortez. Another of those post-WW2 psychological dramas, with Day as a woman who makes men fall in love with her—blinding them to her true personality (and problems). Famed for its flashback within a flashback within a flashback ... but not very good. Look for young brunette Martha Hyer as a party guest and Ellen Corby as a household servant. ●▶

Lodger, The (1926-British) **75m.** *** D: Alfred Hitchcock. Ivor Novello, Malcolm Keen, June, Marie Ault, Arthur Chesney. The director's first suspense thriller, with a classic Hitchcockian theme: lodger Novello is accused by jealous detective Keen of being a killer. Memorable finale: Novello chased by bloodthirsty mob. Remade in 1932 (again with Novello), 1944, in 1953 as MAN IN THE ATTIC, and in 2008. Look for Hitchcock's first cameo. Full title on-screen is THE LODGER: A STORY OF THE LONDON FOG. ▼▶

Lodger, The (1944) **84m.** *** D: John Brahm. Merle Oberon, George Sanders, Laird Cregar, Sir Cedric Hardwicke, Sara Allgood, Aubrey Mather, Queenie Leonard, Doris Lloyd, Billy Bevan. That new lodger at a turn-of-the-20th-century London boardinghouse may be Jack the Ripper. Good, at-

mospheric chiller with fine performances. Remade as MAN IN THE ATTIC (1953). Again remade as THE LODGER (2008), reset in Los Angeles. ▶

Lola (1961-French) **90m.** *** D: Jacques Demy. Anouk Aimée, Marc Michel, Jacques Harden, Alan Scott, Elina Labourdette. Contemporary fable of love, with several disparate people's lives intertwining in port city of Nantes. Aimée is enchanting as cabaret dancer and carefree single mother; Michel is young man looking for life's meaning—and romance. Demy's first feature successfully links coincidence and Hollywood-movie fantasy with '60s realism and sexual frankness. References to Lola pop up in Demy's later films. Music score by Michel Legrand; film is dedicated to Max Ophuls. Franscope. ▼▶

Lola Montès (1955-French) **C-115m.** *** D: Max Ophuls. Martine Carol, Peter Ustinov, Anton Walbrook, Oskar Werner, Ivan Desny. Legendary film about beautiful circus performer and her effect on various men nonetheless suffers from Carol's lack of magnetism in title role. Ophuls makes superb use of widescreen and color; the celebrated director's last film. Aka THE SINS OF LOLA MONTÈS. CinemaScope. ▼●▶

Lolita (1962-British) **152m.** *** D: Stanley Kubrick. James Mason, Shelley Winters, Peter Sellers, Sue Lyon, Marianne Stone, Diana Decker. Sexually precocious Lyon becomes involved with stolid professor Mason, and bizarre Sellers provides peculiar romance leading to murder and lust. Screenplay for this genuinely strange film is credited to Vladimir Nabokov, who wrote the novel of the same name, but bears little relation to his actual script, later published. Winters is outstanding as Lyon's sex-starved mother. Reissued in U.S. with 1m. of additional dialogue from British version. Remade in 1997. ▼●▶

London Belongs to Me SEE: **Dulcimer Street**

London Melody (1937-British) **75m.** ** D: Herbert Wilcox. Anna Neagle, Tullio Carminati, Robert Douglas, Horace Hodges, Grizelda Hervey. Static account of Cockney street entertainer Neagle—made up to look like a movie queen despite her character's station in life—who is taken under the wing of diplomat Carminati. Released in the U.S. a year later as GIRL IN THE STREET. ▼

Lone Gun, The (1954) **C-78m.** ** D: Ray Nazarro. George Montgomery, Dorothy Malone, Frank Faylen, Neville Brand, Skip Homeier, Douglas Kennedy, Douglas Fowley, Robert Wilke. Three rustler brothers take advantage of Malone and her brother Homeier, and Marshal Montgomery has to step in. Pretty good Western with a first-rate cast. Remade as THE GAMBLER WORE A GUN (1961). ▶

Lone Hand (1953) **C-80m.** ****½** D: George Sherman. Joel McCrea, Barbara Hale, Alex Nicol, Charles Drake, Jimmy Hunt, Jim (James) Arness, Roy Roberts. Sturdy Western with widower McCrea and son settling down on a farm; the boy suspects that his dad has fallen in with some outlaws. Interesting to see Arness playing a character who might be described as the anti–Matt Dillon.

Loneliness of the Long Distance Runner, The (1962-British) **103m.** ******** D: Tony Richardson. Michael Redgrave, Tom Courtenay, Avis Bunnage, Peter Madden, Alec McCowen, James Fox, Julia Foster, John Thaw. Engrossing story of rebellious young man chosen to represent reform school in track race. Superbly acted film confronts society, its mores and institutions. Screenplay by Alan Sillitoe, from his own story. Key British film of 1960s.**▼O▷**

Lonely Are the Brave (1962) **107m.** ******* D: David Miller. Kirk Douglas, Gena Rowlands, Walter Matthau, Michael Kane, Carroll O'Connor, William Schallert, George Kennedy, Bill Bixby. Penetrating study of rebellious cowboy Douglas escaping from jail, pursued by posse utilizing modern means of communications and transportation. Script by Dalton Trumbo, from Edward Abbey's novel, *Brave Cowboy*. Panavision.**▼O▷**

Lonely Heart Bandits (1950) **60m.** ****** D: George Blair. Dorothy Patrick, John Eldredge, Barbara Fuller, Robert Rockwell, Ann Doran, Richard Travis, Kathleen Freeman, William Schallert. First of four films (so far) inspired by the notorious 1940s crime spree of a con-artist couple who swindled and murdered wealthy widows. Bland Republic B picture given a sinister edge by Eldredge's cold-blooded portrayal. Story later filmed as THE HONEYMOON KILLERS, DEEP CRIMSON, and LONELY HEARTS.

Lonelyhearts (1958) **101m.** ****½** D: Vincent J. Donehue. Montgomery Clift, Robert Ryan, Myrna Loy, Dolores Hart, Maureen Stapleton, Frank Maxwell, Jackie Coogan, Mike Kellin. Superior cast in interesting adaptation of Nathanael West's book and Howard Teichmann's play, both titled *Miss Lonelyhearts*. Clift is would-be reporter assigned to title column and becomes too deeply involved in the problems of his readers. A bit dated by today's standards, but watchable; scripted and produced by Dore Schary. West's book had previously been filmed as ADVICE TO THE LOVELORN. Film debuts of Stapleton and director Donehue.**▼**

Lonely Man, The (1957) **87m.** ******* D: Henry Levin. Anthony Perkins, Jack Palance, Elaine Aiken, Neville Brand, Claude Akins. Solid acting and taut direction remove sting of hackneyed gunslinger-trying-to-reform plot. VistaVision.**▼▷**

Lonely Trail, The (1936) **57m.** ****** D: Joseph Kane. John Wayne, Ann Rutherford, Cy Kendall, Bob Kortman, Fred "Snowflake" Toones, Denny Meadows (Dennis Moore), Yakima Canutt. OK historical Western, with a nondescript title, set in Texas following the Civil War tells of carpetbaggers exploiting the South. Wayne is adequate as ex-Union officer; the story does have some interesting turns.**▼▷**

Lonely Woman, The SEE: **Strangers**

Lone Ranger, The (1956) **C-86m.** ****½** D: Stuart Heisler. Clayton Moore, Jay Silverheels, Lyle Bettger, Bonita Granville, Perry Lopez, Robert J. Wilke. Action-packed feature version of the popular TV series, focusing on the Masked Man and Tonto as they tangle with scheming rancher Bettger, who has been stirring up trouble with the Indians.**▼▷**

Lone Ranger and the Lost City of Gold, The (1958) **C-80m.** ****** D: Lesley Selander. Clayton Moore, Jay Silverheels, Douglas Kennedy, Charles Watts. Typical Lone Ranger Western is fine for younger audiences, involving hooded killers and mysterious clues to a hidden treasure city.**▼▷**

Lonesome (1929) **69m.** *****½** D: Paul Fejos. Glenn Tryon, Barbara Kent, Fay Holderness, Gustav Partos, Eddie Phillips, Andy Devine. Two lonely New Yorkers (a factory worker and a switchboard operator) meet one day among the masses in Coney Island, and it's love at first sight. Stunningly directed romantic comedy-drama may be a bit corny by today's standards but is still sweet and poignant. Emotions build slowly but surely toward a highly satisfying finale. Color-tinted Luna Park shots are dazzling. One weakness: several awkward sound sequences, interpolated into this silent film at the last minute.**▷**

Lonesome Gun SEE: **Stranger on the Run**

Lone Star (1952) **94m.** ****½** D: Vincent Sherman. Clark Gable, Ava Gardner, Broderick Crawford, Lionel Barrymore, Beulah Bondi, Ed Begley, James Burke, William Farnum, Moroni Olsen, William Conrad. Glossy MGM Western about conflict over Texas joining the Union. Sam Houston (Olsen) wins wealthy, powerful Gable to his cause, which pits him against state senator Crawford (and his crusading newspaper-editor girlfriend Gardner). Also shown in computer-colored version.**▼▷**

The Lone Wolf Michael Lanyard, better known as the Lone Wolf, was a jewel thief who would always sacrifice his own ambitions to help a lady in distress. Created by Louis Joseph Vance in 1914, his impact was such that Lanyard's nickname became a part of our language. The character was featured in a number of silent films, portrayed by such formidable actors as Henry B. Walthall and Jack Holt. Columbia Pictures starred Bert Lytell in a series of *Lone Wolf* outings that spanned the early talkie era. When the studio made THE LONE

WOLF RETURNS, in 1935, it was a chance for moviegoers to reacquaint themselves with an already familiar character (and for Columbia a chance to dust off the script of its same-named 1926 production). Melvyn Douglas played the dapper character in this stylish and delightful film; three years later the studio cast Francis Lederer in THE LONE WOLF IN PARIS, with Frances Drake as a rival thief. Then in 1939, Warren William took over the role and played a reformed Lanyard in a series of nine low-budget, fast-moving, enjoyable films which lacked the class of the first two entries but had a certain charm of their own. There was a heavy accent on comedy, and Eric Blore was added to the cast as Lanyard's light-fingered valet Jamison, who not only served as comic relief but usually got tangled up in the plot as well. William's best effort by far was his first, THE LONE WOLF SPY HUNT, a reworking of 1929's THE LONE WOLF'S DAUGHTER by mystery writer Jonathan Latimer, in which the leading man was aided by a delightfully screwball Ida Lupino as his girlfriend, Virginia Weidler as his curious daughter, an alluring Rita Hayworth as a slinky spy, and Ralph Morgan as the spy leader. Subsequent films in the series couldn't match that cast—or that script—but they were generally entertaining grade-B fare. After a respite of a few years, Gerald Mohr took up the role for several fair-to-middling efforts like 1947's THE LONE WOLF IN LONDON, which brought back valet Eric Blore. Ron Randell played Lanyard in the final entry, THE LONE WOLF AND HIS LADY (1949).

THE LONE WOLF

The Lone Wolf Returns (1935)
The Lone Wolf in Paris (1938)
The Lone Wolf Spy Hunt (1939)
The Lone Wolf Strikes (1940)
The Lone Wolf Meets a Lady (1940)
The Lone Wolf Takes a Chance (1941)
The Lone Wolf Keeps a Date (1941)
Secrets of the Lone Wolf (1941)
Counter-Espionage (1942)
One Dangerous Night (1943)
Passport to Suez (1943)
The Notorious Lone Wolf (1946)
The Lone Wolf in London (1947)
The Lone Wolf in Mexico (1947)
The Lone Wolf and His Lady (1949)

Lone Wolf and His Lady, The (1949) **60m.** *½ D: John Hoffman. Ron Randell, June Vincent, Alan Mowbray, William Frawley, Colette Lyons, Douglass Dumbrille. The Wolf turns newshound to cover the exhibition of a famous gem, and of course it's stolen, and of course he's suspected. Randell previously helped kill the *Bulldog Drummond* series, and does the same here in this final

entry. Mowbray inherits Eric Blore's role as Jamison the valet.
Lone Wolf in London, The (1947) **68m.** ** D: Leslie Goodwins. Gerald Mohr, Nancy Saunders, Eric Blore, Evelyn Ankers, Richard Fraser, Queenie Leonard, Alan Napier. Some valuable jewels are stolen and Scotland Yard naturally suspects the Wolf. Glib entry not helped by Mohr's lack of charm.
Lone Wolf in Mexico, The (1947) **69m.** ** D: D. Ross Lederman. Gerald Mohr, Sheila Ryan, Jacqueline de Wit, Eric Blore, Nestor Paiva, John Gallaudet. Mohr's third and final appearance as the Wolf, as the series was becoming increasingly prosaic. This time he's accused of both robbery and murder down Mexico way.
Lone Wolf in Paris, The (1938) **66m.** ** D: Albert S. Rogell. Francis Lederer, Frances Drake, Walter Kingsford, Leona Maricle, Olaf Hytten, Albert Van Dekker. Lederer takes over for this one entry, becomes mixed up in political intrigue when he's hired by a princess to steal back her mother's crown jewels from a greedy duke.
Lone Wolf Keeps a Date, The (1941) **65m.** ** D: Sidney Salkow. Warren William, Frances Robinson, Bruce Bennett, Eric Blore, Thurston Hall, Jed Prouty, Don Beddoe. Listless episode has the Lone Wolf mixed up with a kidnapped millionaire and stolen ransom money in Miami.
Lone Wolf Meets a Lady, The (1940) **71m.** ** D: Sidney Salkow. Warren William, Eric Blore, Jean Muir, Victor Jory, Roger Pryor, Warren Hull, Thurston Hall, Fred A. Kelsey, Bruce Bennett. The nonchalant reformed crook comes to the aid of a socialite (Muir) whose $100,000 necklace is lifted on the eve of her wedding. Standard entry with a plethora of complications. ▶
Lone Wolf Returns, The (1935) **69m.** *** D: Roy William Neill. Melvyn Douglas, Gail Patrick, Tala Birell, Arthur Hohl, Thurston Hall, Raymond Walburn, Douglass Dumbrille. Urbane jewel thief Douglas wants to retire but is blackmailed by gangsters into helping them pull a heist. Stylish and delightfully lighthearted caper; filmed before in 1926.
Lone Wolf Spy Hunt, The (1939) **67m.** *** D: Peter Godfrey. Warren William, Ida Lupino, Rita Hayworth, Virginia Weidler, Ralph Morgan, Tom Dugan, Don Beddoe, Marc Lawrence, James Craig. Highly satisfactory blend of screwball comedy and genuine suspense as spies in Washington, D.C., kidnap Lanyard in an attempt to steal military secrets. William's first effort as the Lone Wolf, and certainly his best, with a top-notch cast worthy of a bigger budget. Script by ace mystery writer Jonathan Latimer (his first), based on 1929's THE LONE WOLF'S DAUGHTER. Hayworth, not yet a star, makes a sultry femme fatale.
Lone Wolf Strikes, The (1940) **67m.** **½

D: Sidney Salkow. Warren William, Joan Perry, Eric Blore, Alan Baxter, Astrid Allwyn, Montagu Love, Robert Wilcox, Don Beddoe, Fred A. Kelsey. Nimble entry focusing on an heiress' stolen string of pearls which the Lone Wolf is trying to return to its owner.

Lone Wolf Takes a Chance, The (1941) 76m. **½ D: Sidney Salkow. Warren William, June Storey, Henry Wilcoxon, Eric Blore, Thurston Hall, Don Beddoe, Evalyn Knapp, Fred Kelsey, Regis Toomey. The Lone Wolf is framed for murder and uncovers a counterfeiting racket in an attempt to prove his innocence. Well-paced entry; early appearance by Lloyd Bridges.

Long and the Short and the Tall, The (1961-British) 105m. *** D: Leslie Norman. Richard Todd, Laurence Harvey, Richard Harris, David McCallum, Ronald Fraser. Well-delineated account of British patrol unit during WW2, focusing on their conflicting personalities and raids on Japanese. Retitled: JUNGLE FIGHTERS.

Long Arm, The SEE: Third Key, The

Long Dark Hall, The (1951-British) 86m. **½ D: Anthony Bushell, Reginald Beck. Rex Harrison, Lilli Palmer, Tania Held, Henrietta Barry. Sturdy melodrama of man accused of killing girlfriend, with wife remaining loyal to him. ▼▶

Long Day's Journey Into Night (1962) 174m. ***½ D: Sidney Lumet. Katharine Hepburn, Ralph Richardson, Jason Robards, Jr., Dean Stockwell, Jeanne Barr. Faithful, stagy adaptation of Eugene O'Neill's detailed study of family in the 1910s. Superb performances from Hepburn as dope-addicted wife, Richardson her pompous actor husband, Stockwell the son dying of TB, and Robards the alcoholic son. Later cut to 136m. Remade for TV in 1987 with Jack Lemmon. ▼▶●

Longest Day, The (1962) 180m. **** D: Ken Annakin, Andrew Marton, Bernhard Wicki. John Wayne, Rod Steiger, Robert Ryan, Peter Lawford, Henry Fonda, Robert Mitchum, Richard Burton, Richard Beymer, Jeffrey Hunter, Sal Mineo, Roddy McDowall, Eddie Albert, Curt Jurgens, Gert Frobe, Sean Connery, Robert Wagner, Red Buttons, Mel Ferrer, many others. One of the all-time great epic WW2 films. Brilliant retelling of the Allied invasion of Normandy, complete with all-star international cast, re-creation of historical events on a grand scale; Oscar-winning special effects and cinematography. Also shown in computer-colored version. CinemaScope. ▼▶●

Longest Night, The (1936) 50m. **½ D: Errol Taggart. Robert Young, Florence Rice, Ted Healy, Julie Haydon, Catharine Doucet, Janet Beecher, Leslie Fenton, Sidney Toler. Owner of a department store finds romance, mystery, and murder all in one night as he teams up with a pretty female employee to

track down a gang of thieves hiding in the store. Slick, enjoyable MGM mini-feature, with an abbreviated running time working to its advantage.

Long Gray Line, The (1955) C-138m. *** D: John Ford. Tyrone Power, Maureen O'Hara, Robert Francis, Ward Bond, Donald Crisp, Betsy Palmer, Phil Carey, Harry Carey, Jr. Lengthy sentimental melodrama of West Point athletic trainer Power and his many years at the Academy. O'Hara is radiant as his wife. CinemaScope. ▼▶

Long Haul, The (1957-British) 88m. **½ D: Ken Hughes. Victor Mature, Diana Dors, Patrick Allen, Gene Anderson. Truck driver Mature gets mixed up with crooked doings and sexy Dors. Alternately pulpy and provocative; action climax is a doozy. ▼▶

Long Hot Summer, The (1958) C-117m. *** D: Martin Ritt. Paul Newman, Joanne Woodward, Anthony Franciosa, Orson Welles, Lee Remick, Angela Lansbury. Well-blended William Faulkner short stories make a flavorful, brooding drama of domineering Southerner (Welles) and a wandering handyman (Newman), who decides to stick around and marry daughter Woodward. Excellent Alex North score, weak finish to strong film; the Newmans' first film together. Remade for TV with Don Johnson. CinemaScope. ▼▶●

Long John Silver (1954-Australian) C-109m. **½ D: Byron Haskin. Robert Newton, Connie Gilchrist, Kit Taylor, Grant Taylor. Newton reprises title role from TREASURE ISLAND (with same director as the Disney film) and chews the scenery in this loose adaptation of Robert Louis Stevenson. Look for Rod Taylor in a small role. Aka RETURN TO TREASURE ISLAND. CinemaScope. ▼▶

Long, Long Trailer, The (1954) C-96m. **½ D: Vincente Minnelli. Lucille Ball, Desi Arnaz, Marjorie Main, Keenan Wynn, Gladys Hurlbut. Lucy and Desi decide to spend their honeymoon visiting scenic spots in the West, traveling and living in the 50-foot house trailer of the title. Though based on the popular novel by Clinton Twiss, this enduringly popular slapstick comedy is almost an *I Love Lucy* episode on wheels. ▼▶●

Long Lost Father (1934) 63m. **½ D: Ernest B. Schoedsack. John Barrymore, Helen Chandler, Donald Cook, Alan Mowbray, Claude King. Minor Barrymore vehicle casts him as man who deserted daughter Chandler years ago, tries to make up for it when she gets in a jam.

Long Memory, The (1952-British) 91m. *** D: Robert Hamer. John Mills, John McCallum, Elizabeth Sellars, Geoffrey Keen, John Chandos, Vida Hope. Mills is framed for murder by girlfriend Sellars. When released from prison 12 years later, he sets out to prove his innocence. Well-done drama. ▶

Long Night, The (1947) 101m. ** D: Anatole Litvak. Henry Fonda, Barbara Bel Geddes, Vincent Price, Ann Dvorak, Howard Freeman, Elisha Cook, Jr., Queenie Smith, Charles McGraw. Factory worker Fonda kills Price, then holes up in his boardinghouse (besieged by police) and relives in flashbacks, and flashbacks within flashbacks, the events leading up to his predicament. Plodding and sullen; a long night indeed. Remake of Jean Gabin film LE JOUR SE LEVE.▼▶

Long Pants (1927) 61m. ** D: Frank Capra. Harry Langdon, Gladys Brockwell, Al Roscoe, Alma Bennett, Frankie Darro, Priscilla Bonner. Langdon's follow-up to THE STRONG MAN is one of the most curious silent comedies ever made: a dark, mostly unfunny story of a boy in knickers who fantasizes about being a great lover (based on books he's read), and gets his chance when a sexy femme fatale passes through town. However, this does require that he murder his hometown bride first! For what it's worth, Capra didn't complete the film, and didn't like what was done with it. ▼◉

Long Ships, The (1964-British-Yugoslavian) C-125m. ** D: Jack Cardiff. Richard Widmark, Sidney Poitier, Rosanna Schiaffino, Russ Tamblyn, Oscar Homolka, Colin Blakely. Fairly elaborate but comic-book–level costume adventure of Vikings battling Moors for fabled treasure. Good cast deserves better. Super Technirama 70.▼▶

Long Voyage Home, The (1940) 105m. ***½ D: John Ford. John Wayne, Thomas Mitchell, Ian Hunter, Ward Bond, Barry Fitzgerald, Wilfrid Lawson, Mildred Natwick, John Qualen, Arthur Shields, Joe Sawyer, J. M. Kerrigan. Evocative look at men who spend their lives at sea, adapted (by Dudley Nichols) from four short O'Neill plays. Richly textured drama with many beautiful vignettes; exquisitely photographed by Gregg Toland. ▼◉

Long Wait, The (1954) 93m. ** D: Victor Saville. Anthony Quinn, Charles Coburn, Gene Evans, Peggie Castle, Dolores Donlon, Mary Ellen Kay. Meandering, actionless account of man with loss of memory discovering he's been framed for several crimes.

Look Back in Anger (1959-British) 99m. ***½ D: Tony Richardson. Richard Burton, Claire Bloom, Edith Evans, Mary Ure, Gary Raymond, Glen Byam Shaw, Donald Pleasence. John Osborne's trend-setting angry-young-man play, with Burton rebelling against life and wife, realistically filmed and acted; dialogue bristles. Remade for British TV in 1989.▼◉

Look for the Silver Lining (1949) C-100m. **½ D: David Butler. June Haver, Ray Bolger, Gordon MacRae, Charles Ruggles, Rosemary DeCamp. Superficial biography of Marilyn Miller's career in show business, with vintage vaudeville numbers bolstering trivial plot line.▼▶

Look In Any Window (1961) 87m. ** D: William Alland. Paul Anka, Ruth Roman, Alex Nicol, Gigi Perreau, Carole Mathews, George Dolenz, Jack Cassidy. Suburban teen Anka, coming of age with dysfunctional parents, acts out his angst by donning a mask and becoming a peeping Tom. Ho-hum drama is producer-sometime-actor Alland's lone film as director.▶

Looking for Danger (1957) 62m. ** D: Austen Jewell. Huntz Hall, Stanley Clements, Eddie LeRoy, David (Gorcey) Condon, Jimmy Murphy, Otto Reichow, Lili Kardell, Percy Helton. Genial *Bowery Boys* caper, relating a flashback adventure in North Africa to trap some Nazis during WW2.▶

Looking for Love (1964) C-83m. BOMB D: Don Weis. Connie Francis, Susan Oliver, Jim Hutton, Barbara Nichols, Danny Thomas, Johnny Carson, George Hamilton, Paula Prentiss. They should have looked for a script instead. Plastic show-biz romance with little help from various guest stars, including Carson (who wound up making HORN BLOWS AT MIDNIGHT–type jokes about this—his first film appearance).▶

Looking for Trouble (1934) 76m. *** D: William A. Wellman. Spencer Tracy, Constance Cummings, Jack Oakie, Morgan Conway, Arline Judge, Judith Wood, Paul Harvey, Joe Sauers (Sawyer). Tracy and Oakie click as telephone linemen troubleshooters who find the time to track down a wiretapping and bank-robbing gang while trading wisecracks and kisses with phone operators Cummings and Judge. Highly enjoyable yarn is packed with crackling dialogue and serial-like thrills; it even incorporates real footage of the 1933 Long Beach, California, earthquake.

Looking Forward (1933) 82m. **½ D: Clarence Brown. Lionel Barrymore, Lewis Stone, Benita Hume, Elizabeth Allan, Phillips Holmes, Colin Clive, Doris Lloyd. Stone gives one of his best performances as a man trying to keep his London department store (founded by his family 200 years ago) afloat during the depths of the Depression; Barrymore is a mousy clerk who's been with the store for 40 years. Superficial but pleasant drama boasts that its title came from a speech by F.D.R.

Look-Out Sister (1947) 65m. **½ D: Bud Pollard. Louis Jordan, Suzette Harbin, Monte Hawley, Bob Scott, Glenn Allen, Tommy Southern, Jack Clisby, Maceo Sheffield. Overworked bandleader Jordan dreams that he's on an Arizona dude ranch, where he becomes immersed in typical B-Western shenanigans. Above-average all-black-cast entertainment is loaded with musical numbers, including a lively performance of Jordan's hit "Caledonia."▼▶

Look Who's Laughing (1941) 78m. ** D: Allan Dwan. Edgar Bergen, Jim and Marion Jordan (Fibber McGee and Molly),

Lucille Ball, Harold Peary (The Great Gildersleeve), Lee Bonnell. Bergen's plane inadvertently lands in Wistful Vista, where he becomes involved in a municipal squabble with Fibber and Molly. Slim vehicle for radio favorites only comes alive when Charlie McCarthy takes the spotlight.▼●▮

Loophole (1954) **80m.** **½ D: Harold D. Schuster. Barry Sullivan, Charles McGraw, Dorothy Malone, Don Haggerty, Mary Beth Hughes, Don Beddoe. Imaginative handling of oft-told tale of bank employee accused of theft, catching actual crooks. ▮

Loose Ankles (1930) **67m.** *** D: Ted Wilde. Loretta Young, Douglas Fairbanks, Jr., Louise Fazenda, Ethel Wales, Otis Harlan, Daphne Pollard, Inez Courtney. Young and her greedy family will inherit a fortune if she stays scandal-free and marries a man whom her prissy aunts approve of. She decides to teach her relatives a lesson by advertising for a gigolo, who shows up in the person of love-struck Fairbanks. Giddy early-talkie farce performed with zeal, boasting some smart lines and a fine sense of the absurd. ▮

Loose in London (1953) **63m.** **½ D: Edward Bernds. Leo Gorcey, Huntz Hall, David Gorcey, Bernard Gorcey, John Dodsworth, Norma Varden, Angela Greene, Walter Kingsford, Joan Shawlee. When Sach is thought to be related to a dying British earl, the Bowery Boys head to England and expose some scheming heirs in this enjoyable romp. ▮

Looters, The (1955) **87m.** **½ D: Abner Biberman. Rory Calhoun, Julie Adams, Ray Danton, Thomas Gomez. OK drama of survivors of plane crash fighting amongst themselves for money aboard wreckage. ▮

Lord Byron of Broadway (1930) **C/B&W-77m.** ** D: Harry Beaumont, William Nigh. Charles Kaley, Ethelind Terry, Marion Shilling, Cliff Edwards, Gwen Lee, Benny Rubin. Kaley uses personal relationships as fodder for the songs he writes, fancying himself a modern-day Lord Byron. Swell songs and wisecracks from "Ukulele Ike" Edwards are the only compensation for a hackneyed script, terrible performances by short-lived film stars Kaley and Terry, and dull two-color Technicolor musical numbers. ▮

Lord Jeff (1938) **86m.** ** D: Sam Wood. Freddie Bartholomew, Mickey Rooney, Charles Coburn, Herbert Mundin, Terry Kilburn, Gale Sondergaard, Peter Lawford, Monty Woolley. Acceptable family film about good-boy Bartholomew led astray, sent to straighten out at naval school.

Lord Jim (1965) **C-154m.** **½ D: Richard Brooks. Peter O'Toole, James Mason, Curt Jurgens, Eli Wallach, Jack Hawkins, Paul Lukas, Daliah Lavi, Akim Tamiroff. Overlong, uneven adaptation of Joseph Conrad's story about idealistic young man in British

Merchant Marine in the 19th century discredited as a coward who lives with scar for the rest of his life. Film's great moments provided by outstanding supporting cast. Super Panavision 70.▼▮

Lord of the Flies (1963-British) **90m.** *** D: Peter Brook. James Aubrey, Tom Chapin, Hugh Edwards, Roger Elwin, Tom Gaman. Unique story of a group of British schoolboys stranded on remote island. Their gradual degeneration into a savage horde is compelling. Adapted from William Golding's novel. Remade in 1990.▼●▮

Lord of the Jungle (1955) **69m.** *½ D: Ford Beebe. Johnny Sheffield, Wayne Morris, Nancy Hale, Paul Picerni, William Phipps, Smoki Whitfield, Leonard Mudie, Harry Lauter, Joel Fluellen, Juanita Moore. Bomba the Jungle Boy tries to weed out a rogue elephant to save the entire herd from extinction; final entry of this shoddy series. ▮

Lorna Doone (1935-British) **89m.** *** D: Basil Dean. John Loder, Margaret Lockwood, Victoria Hopper, Roy Emerson, Edward Rigby, Mary Clare, Roger Livesey. Well-photographed tale of 17th-century love affair between farmer and outlaw's daughter (though she is hiding her true identity). Lovely locations, fine acting. Also a 1922 silent with Madge Bellamy; remade in 1951 and for TV in 1990. ▮

Lorna Doone (1951) **C-88m.** **½ D: Phil Karlson. Barbara Hale, Richard Greene, Carl Benton Reid, William Bishop. Middling screen version of Richard D. Blackmore's novel of 1680s England, with farmers rebelling against oppressive landlords. Done on small budget, but not bad.

Loser Takes All (1956-British) **C-88m.** ** D: Ken Annakin. Rossano Brazzi, Glynis Johns, Robert Morley, Tony Britton, Geoffrey Keen, Peter Illing. Brazzi and Johns celebrate their honeymoon in Monte Carlo and try out their "perfect system" for winning at roulette, with unusual effect on their marriage. On-location filming helps. Remade in 1990 as STRIKE IT RICH. CinemaScope.

Los Olvidados (1950-Mexican) **88m.** ***½ D: Luis Buñuel. Alfonso Mejia, Roberto Cobo, Stella Inda, Miguel Inclan. Gripping story of juvenile delinquency among slums of Mexico, with surreal dream sequences interspersed. An offbeat winner from Buñuel. Buñuel shot an alternate, "happy" ending which was rediscovered in 2005 for reissue and video release. Aka THE YOUNG AND THE DAMNED.▼●

Loss of Innocence (1961-British) **C-99m.** **½ D: Lewis Gilbert. Kenneth More, Danielle Darrieux, Susannah York, Maurice Denham. York gives poignant performance as teenager who, through love affair, becomes a woman; events leave her and younger sister and brother stranded on the

Continent. Original title: THE GREEN-GAGE SUMMER.

Lost (1955-British) **C-89m.** **½ D: Guy Green. David Farrar, David Knight, Julia Arnall, Anthony Oliver, Marjorie Rhodes. Offbeat account of effects of a child kidnapping on parents, police, press, and crooks.

Lost Angel (1944) **91m.** **½ D: Roy Rowland. Margaret O'Brien, James Craig, Marsha Hunt, Philip Merivale, Henry O'Neill, Donald Meek, Keenan Wynn, Bobby (Robert) Blake. O'Brien is winning as precocious child—trained as a genius by scientists—who learns life's simple pleasures when she moves in with reporter Craig. Look for Ava Gardner as a hat-check girl. ▶

Lost Boundaries (1949) **99m.** *** D: Alfred L. Werker. Beatrice Pearson, Mel Ferrer, Richard Hylton, Susan Douglas, Canada Lee, Rev. Robert Dunn, Carleton Carpenter. Penetrating, well-meaning if slow-moving account of a dedicated, light-skinned Negro doctor (Ferrer, in his screen debut) who (with his family) passes for white in a small New Hampshire town. A clear-eyed look at segregated America. ▼▶

Lost Canyon (1942) **61m.** ** D: Lesley Selander. William Boyd, Andy Clyde, Jay Kirby, Lola Lane, Doug Fowley, Herbert Rawlinson. Hopalong Cassidy's young sidekick is wrongly accused of bank robbery, so the Bar 20 boys must nab the real culprit, a lawyer who is also behind a band of land-grabbing outlaws. Routine remake of 1937 Hoppy entry RUSTLER'S VALLEY draws extensive stock footage from that film (including clear shots of Lee J. Cobb!). Clyde is funny, Fowley weak in the Cobb role. Contemporary song hit "Jingle, Jangle, Jingle" is shoehorned into proceedings. ▼▶

Lost Continent (1951) **86m.** ** D: Samuel Newfield. Cesar Romero, Hillary Brooke, John Hoyt, Whit Bissell, Sid Melton, Acquanetta. Lavish production values are obviously lacking as Romero leads expedition to prehistoric mountaintop to recover missing rocket, encounters stop-motion dinosaurs. Some scenes are tinted. ▼▶

Lost Honeymoon (1947) **71m.** ** D: Leigh Jason. Franchot Tone, Ann Richards, Tom Conway, Frances Rafferty, Una O'Connor, Clarence Kolb. Trivial comedy of ex-GI Tone aware that he had amnesia while stationed in London during WW2, but unaware that he had married and fathered two children. ▼▶

Lost Horizon (1937) **132m.** **** D: Frank Capra. Ronald Colman, Jane Wyatt, John Howard, Edward Everett Horton, Margo, Sam Jaffe, H. B. Warner, Isabel Jewell, Thomas Mitchell. James Hilton's classic story about five people stumbling into strange Tibetan land where health, peace, and longevity reign. A rare movie experience, with haunting finale. Screenplay by Robert

Riskin. After being shown in edited reissue prints for years, this classic has been restored to its original length—though several scenes are still missing, and are represented by dialogue only, illustrated with stills. Won Oscars for Art Direction (Stephen Goosson) and Film Editing (Gene Havlick, Gene Milford). Remade with music in 1973. ▼▶●

Lost in a Harem (1944) **89m.** **½ D: Charles Riesner. Bud Abbott, Lou Costello, Marilyn Maxwell, John Conte, Douglass Dumbrille, Lottie Harrison, Jimmy Dorsey Orchestra. Slicker-than-usual A&C (made on infrequent trip to MGM), but strictly routine. Some good scenes here and there with sultan Dumbrille; Maxwell is perfect harem girl. ▼▶●

Lost in Alaska (1952) **76m.** *½ D: Jean Yarbrough. Bud Abbott, Lou Costello, Mitzi Green, Tom Ewell, Bruce Cabot. Unremarkable slapstick set in 1890s, with A&C off to the wilds to help a friend but doing more hindering. ▼▶

Lost Missile, The (1958) **70m.** ** D: Lester Berke. Robert Loggia, Ellen Parker, Larry Kerr, Philip Pine. Super-hot alien missile circles Earth, setting fires and melting cities. Loggia races against time to destroy it before it reaches N.Y.C. Too cheap for its ideas, but Loggia is good. Ending is surprisingly downbeat. ▶

Lost Moment, The (1947) **88m.** *** D: Martin Gabel. Robert Cummings, Susan Hayward, Agnes Moorehead, Joan Lorring, Eduardo Ciannelli, John Archer, Frank Puglia. American publisher Cummings travels to Venice to secure the love letters of a famous 19th-century poet and rents a room in the villa where the poet's aged lover still resides with her protective niece (Hayward). Interesting if not altogether convincing. Based on Henry James' *The Aspern Papers* and filmed on a breathtaking interior set. Actor Gabel's only film as director. ▼▶●

Lost One, The (1951-German) **97m.** ** D: Peter Lorre. Peter Lorre, Karl John, Renate Mannhardt, Johanna Hofer. Lorre's only film as director is a talky, grim, but not uninteresting drama about the downfall of a German researcher (played by Peter himself, with appropriate weariness) whose girlfriend is thought to have been passing on his discoveries to the British during WW2. Of interest mostly as a footnote to Lorre's career; based on a true story. ▼

Lost Patrol, The (1934) **73m.** **** D: John Ford. Victor McLaglen, Boris Karloff, Wallace Ford, Reginald Denny, Alan Hale, J. M. Kerrigan, Billy Bevan. McLaglen's small British military group lost in Mesopotamian desert, as Arabs repeatedly attack the dwindling unit. Classic actioner filled with slice-of-life stereotypes, headed by religious fanatic Karloff. Fast-moving fun, great Max Steiner score. Scripted by Dudley Nichols, from Philip MacDonald's novel *Patrol*. Previously filmed in 1929, as a British silent starring Victor McLaglen's brother, Cyril, in the lead role; reworked many times (BAD LANDS, SAHARA, BATAAN, etc.). ▼●❶

Lost Squadron, The (1932) 79m. **½ D: George Archainbaud. Richard Dix, Mary Astor, Erich von Stroheim, Joel McCrea, Dorothy Jordan, Robert Armstrong. WW1 pilots forced to find work as stunt fliers for movies; interesting idea boosted by von Stroheim's overacting as director "Arthur von Furst." ▼●

Lost Tribe, The (1949) 72m. ** D: William Berke. Johnny Weissmuller, Myrna Dell, Elena Verdugo, Joseph Vitale, Ralph Dunn, George J. Lewis. Action-packed *Jungle Jim* romp, with Weissmuller fighting lions, crocodiles, and sharks to help save an African city from plunderers.

Lost Volcano, The (1950) 76m. *½ D: Ford Beebe. Johnny Sheffield, Donald Woods, Marjorie Lord, John Ridgely, Robert Lewis, Elena Verdugo, Tommy Ivo. Bomba the Jungle Boy fights greedy African guides who are after buried treasure. ▼❶

Lost Weekend, The (1945) 101m. **** D: Billy Wilder. Ray Milland, Jane Wyman, Phillip Terry, Howard da Silva, Doris Dowling, Frank Faylen, Mary Young. An unsuccessful novelist battles the bottle. Unrelenting drama of alcoholism—and a landmark of adult filmmaking in Hollywood. Milland's powerful performance won him an Oscar; there's fine support from bartender da Silva, sanitarium aide Faylen. Won Academy Awards for Best Picture, Director, Actor, Screenplay (Wilder and Charles Brackett). ▼●❶

Lost World, The (1925) 93m. **½ D: Harry Hoyt. Bessie Love, Wallace Beery, Lewis Stone, Lloyd Hughes. Silent film version of A. Conan Doyle adventure yarn is remarkable for special effects re-creating prehistoric beasts encountered on scientific expedition to remote plateau. Interesting as precursor to KING KONG—in story structure and in Willis O'Brien's special effects. Shown in severely truncated prints for years; two restored versions now exist. Remade twice. ▼●❶

Lost World, The (1960) C-98m. ** D: Irwin Allen. Michael Rennie, Jill St. John, David Hedison, Claude Rains, Fernando Lamas, Richard Haydn. Despite cinematic advances, this remake of the 1925 film doesn't match original's special effects. OK juvenile entry of an expedition into remote territory hopefully inhabited by prehistoric monsters ("played" by photographically enlarged lizards). CinemaScope. ▼❶

Lottery Bride, The (1930) 80m. **½ D: Paul Stein. Jeanette MacDonald, John Garrick, Joe E. Brown, ZaSu Pitts, Robert Chisholm, Max Davidson. Delightfully creaky musical with Norwegian setting; Jeanette must deny her true love when she becomes lottery bride for his older brother. Impressive

sets, forgettable music, enjoyable comic relief from Brown and Pitts. ▼❶

Louisa (1950) 90m. *** D: Alexander Hall. Ronald Reagan, Charles Coburn, Ruth Hussey, Edmund Gwenn, Spring Byington, Piper Laurie, Scotty Beckett, Martin Milner. Delightful romantic yarn of Byington seeking to become a December bride, undecided between Coburn and Gwenn; most disarming. Film debut of Piper Laurie.

Louisiana Purchase (1941) C-98m. **½ D: Irving Cummings. Bob Hope, Vera Zorina, Victor Moore, Irene Bordoni, Dona Drake. Brassy Irving Berlin musicomedy about an investigation of graft in the state government of . . . Louisiana! Hope's comedy very funny, especially famous filibuster scene in Congress. Zorina, Moore, and Bordoni re-create their Broadway roles. Opening scene of chorus girls (including Barbara Britton, Margaret Hayes, and Jean Wallace) singing lines about characters being fictitious is probably a movie first . . . and last. ▼❶

Louisiana Story (1948) 77m. **** D: Robert Flaherty. Classic, influential documentary set in the Louisiana bayous, with a young boy observing oil drillers at work. Beautifully made; produced by the Standard Oil Company. Music by Virgil Thomson. ▼❶

Lovable Cheat, The (1949) 75m. ** D: Richard Oswald. Charlie Ruggles, Peggy Ann Garner, Richard Ney, Alan Mowbray, Fritz Feld, Ludwig Donath, Buster Keaton, Curt Bois. Interesting more for cast and credits than actual achievement, this rather odd independent production (based on a Balzac play) centers on the comic antics of Ruggles battling against his creditors. ▼

Love (1927) 82m. **½ D: Edmund Goulding. Greta Garbo, John Gilbert, George Fawcett, Emily Fitzroy, Brandon Hurst, Philippe De Lacy. Silent version of *Anna Karenina* in modern setting, as married Garbo falls in love with dashing military guard Gilbert, an affair doomed from start. Lesser entry for famed screen lovers, with Gilbert's eyebrow-raising gestures at their worst. Garbo's 1935 remake (ANNA KARENINA) is much better. MGM actually filmed two endings—one happy, one sad. ▼●❶

Love Affair (1932) 68m. ** D: Thornton Freeland. Dorothy Mackaill, Humphrey Bogart, Jack Kennedy, Barbara Leonard, Astrid Allwyn. Romance between a spoiled heiress and a dedicated aircraft engineer; pretty tired stuff, even with the curiosity value of a clean-cut Bogart as leading man. ❶

Love Affair (1939) 87m. ***½ D: Leo McCarey. Irene Dunne, Charles Boyer, Maria Ouspenskaya, Lee Bowman, Astrid Allwyn, Maurice Moscovich, Joan Brodel (Leslie). Superior comedy-drama about shipboard romance whose continuation on-shore is interrupted by unforseen circumstances. Dunne and Boyer are a marvelous match. Screenplay by Delmer Daves and Donald Ogden Stewart, from story by Mildred Cram and Leo McCarey. Remade by McCarey as AN AFFAIR TO REMEMBER, and a second time (by Warren Beatty). Beware public-domain copy with entirely new music score.▼🅳

Love Among the Millionaires (1930) 74m. *½ D: Frank Tuttle. Clara Bow, Stanley Smith, Stuart Erwin, Mitzi Green, Skeets Gallagher, Charles Sellon, Claude King, Barbara Bennett, Theodor von Eltz. Fiery Bow's trackside cafe is the center of life for local railroaders, two of whom compete for her attentions. Limp demi-musical shows off Bow's surprisingly good voice, but penny-dreadful script demonstrates all too clearly how her studio allowed her career to languish.

Love and Hisses (1937) 82m. **½ D: Sidney Lanfield. Walter Winchell, Ben Bernie and His Orchestra, Simone Simon, Bert Lahr, Joan Davis, Dick Baldwin, Ruth Terry, Douglas Fowley, The Peters Sisters, The Brewster Twins, Raymond Scott Quintet. Bandleader Bernie concocts a sneaky strategy to get his songbird (Simon) written up in the papers. Lahr and Davis' solid supporting turns are better than this aptly titled musical. Gordon-Revel score includes "Broadway's Gone Hawaiian" and the reflexive "I Want to Be in Winchell's Column." Scott group performs its classic "Power House."

Love and Kisses (1965) C-87m. **½ D: Ozzie Nelson. Rick Nelson, Kristin Nelson, Jack Kelly, Jerry Van Dyke, Pert Kelton, Madelyn Hines. Harmless fare. Rick gets married, disrupting his family's life.

Love and Larceny (1963-Italian) 94m. **½ D: Dino Risi. Vittorio Gassman, Anna Maria Ferrero, Dorian Gray, Peppino De Filippo. Saucy comedy of exuberant con-man Gassman making no pretense about his carefree life and pleasures. Totalscope. ▼🅳

Love and Learn (1947) 83m. ** D: Frederick de Cordova. Jack Carson, Robert Hutton, Martha Vickers, Janis Paige, Otto Kruger. Overdone idea of songwriters Carson and Hutton waiting for their big break; young girl comes to their aid, but she doesn't save film.

Love at Twenty (1962-International) 113m. **½ D: François Truffaut, Renzo Rossellini, Shintaro Ishihara, Marcel Ophuls, Andrzej Wajda. Jean-Pierre Léaud, Eleonora Rossi-Drago, Zbigniew Cybulski, Nami Tamura, Marie-France Pisier, Barbara Lass. Quintet of middling stories produced in France, Germany, Italy, Japan, Poland; variations on theme of LOVE among younger generation. Truffaut's ANTOINE ET CO-LETTE is a sequel to THE FOUR HUNDRED BLOWS (the first of his Antoine Doinel films). Original French running time: 123m. Totalscope.

Love Before Breakfast (1936) 70m. **½ D:

Walter Lang. Carole Lombard, Preston Foster, Cesar Romero, Janet Beecher, Betty Lawford, Douglas Blackley (Robert Kent). Fast-starting comedy slows down to obvious ending, but Lombard (as object of Foster's and Romero's attention) is always worth watching. Preston Sturges worked uncredited on the script.🅳

Love Crazy (1941) 99m. **½ D: Jack Conway. William Powell, Myrna Loy, Gail Patrick, Jack Carson, Florence Bates, Sidney Blackmer, Sig Ruman. One misunderstanding leads to another in this energetic marital farce that loses steam halfway through. Highlighted by Powell's attempts to prove himself insane and Carson's hilarious characterization as Ward Willoughby. ▼🅳

Loved One, The (1965) 121m. ***½ D: Tony Richardson. Robert Morse, Jonathan Winters, Anjanette Comer, Rod Steiger, Dana Andrews, Milton Berle, James Coburn, John Gielgud, Tab Hunter, Margaret Leighton, Liberace, Roddy McDowall, Robert Morley, Lionel Stander, Ayllene Gibbons, Bernie Kopell, Alan Napier, Jamie Farr. Correctly advertised as the picture with something to offend everyone. Britisher Morse attends to uncle's burial in California, encountering bizarre aspects of funeral business. Often howlingly funny, and equally gross. Once seen, Mrs. Joyboy can never be forgotten. Based on the Evelyn Waugh novel, adapted by Terry Southern and Christopher Isherwood.▼🅾🅳

Love Eternal (1943-French) 100m. *** D: Jean Delannoy. Jean Marais, Madeleine Sologne, Jean Murat, Piéral, Alexandre Rignault, Junie Astor, Roland Toutain, Jeanne Marken, Jean d'Yd, Yvonne de Bray. Modern-dress retelling of the Welsh legend of Tristan and Isolde, in which a man under the spell of a love potion cannot help but fall for his uncle's wife. Screenplay by Jean Cocteau delineates the tragic consequences of honor and is characteristically full of his poetry from a higher plane. Released in U.S. in 1948. Aka THE ETERNAL RETURN. ▼

Love Finds Andy Hardy (1938) 90m. *** D: George B. Seitz. Lewis Stone, Mickey Rooney, Judy Garland, Cecilia Parker, Fay Holden, Ann Rutherford, Betsy Ross Clark, Lana Turner, Gene Reynolds. One of the best of the series finds young Andrew frantically trying to juggle two girlfriends at the same time. Classy support by ingenues Garland and Turner. Judy sings three songs, including "Meet the Beat of My Heart."▼🅾🅳

Love Flower, The (1920) 70m. **½ D: D. W. Griffith. Carol Dempster, Richard Barthelmess, George McQuarrie, Anders Randolf, Florence Short, Crauford Kent. After he has murdered his wife's lover, a man escapes to a West Indian isle and finds forgiveness in his daughter's adoration. Then a detective catches up with him. Griffith's best collaboration with Dempster still falls overboard, but has glorious cinematography by Paul H. Allen and G. W. Bitzer), shimmering underwater scenes, and contributes much to the myth of the sultry tropics. ▼▶

Love From a Stranger (1937-British) **90m. ** D:** Rowland V. Lee. Ann Harding, Basil Rathbone, Binnie Hale, Bruce Seton, Bryan Powley, Jean Cadell. Working girl Harding wins fortune in a lottery, is swept off her feet by suave Rathbone, but after their marriage she begins to suspect he's not quite what he seemed. Stagy but interesting thriller features Rathbone's most unbridled performance, quite a sight to see. From Frank Vosper's play of a story by Agatha Christie. Joan Hickson, later TV's shrewd Miss Marple, plays a scatterbrained maid. Remade in 1947. ▼▶

Love From a Stranger (1947) **81m. **½** D: Richard Whorf. Sylvia Sidney, John Hodiak, John Howard, Isobel Elsom, Ernest Cossart. Capable cast goes through familiar paces in SUSPICION-like story of woman who learns her new husband may be a murderer. Filmed before in 1937. ▼

Love Goddesses, The (1965) **87m. ***** Compiled by Saul J. Turell and Graeme Ferguson. Marilyn Monroe, Mae West, Jean Harlow, Theda Bara, Rita Hayworth, Claudette Colbert, Dorothy Lamour, many others. Compilation covers a lot of ground, featuring many major female stars from silent days to the present. Not always the ideal clips, but well done, with many welcome classic scenes. Some color sequences. Revised for 1972 theatrical reissue. ▶

Love Happy (1949) **91m. ** D:** David Miller. Harpo, Chico, and Groucho Marx, Ilona Massey, Vera-Ellen, Marion Hutton, Raymond Burr, Eric Blore. No NIGHT AT THE OPERA, but even diluted Marx Brothers are better than none. Putting on a musical forms background for Harpo's antics, with Chico in support, Groucho in a few unrelated scenes. Marilyn Monroe has a brief bit. Among the writers were Ben Hecht and Frank Tashlin. ▼▶

Love Has Many Faces (1965) **C-105m. **½** D: Alexander Singer. Lana Turner, Cliff Robertson, Hugh O'Brian, Ruth Roman, Stefanie Powers, Virginia Grey. Timid attempt at lurid soaper; playgirl Turner's costume changes are the highlights. O'Brian and Robertson are gigolos. Filmed in Acapulco. ▼▶

Love in a Goldfish Bowl (1961) **C-88m.** BOMB D: Jack Sher. Tommy Sands, Fabian, Jan Sterling, Edward Andrews. Film is as bad as its title, a worthless, boring trifle about teenagers taking over a beach house. Forget it. Panavision. ▼

Love in Bloom (1935) **75m. ** D:** Elliott Nugent. George Burns, Gracie Allen, Joe Morrison, Dixie Lee, J. C. Nugent, Lee Kohlmar. Burns and Allen are forced to take back seat to sappy romantic story about

struggling songwriter and his girlfriend; George and Gracie give this minor film its only value. ▼▶

Love in the Afternoon (1957) **130m. ***½** D: Billy Wilder. Gary Cooper, Audrey Hepburn, Maurice Chevalier, John McGiver. Forget age difference between Cooper and Hepburn and enjoy sparkling romantic comedy, with Chevalier as Audrey's private-eye dad. McGiver lends good support in witty comedy set in Paris. Wilder's first film cowritten with I.A.L. Diamond, and a tribute to his idol, Ernst Lubitsch. Remake of 1931 German film ARIANE. ▼▶

Love in the City (1953-Italian) **90m. ** D:** Michelangelo Antonioni, Federico Fellini, Dino Risi, Carlo Lizzani, Alberto Lattuada, Francesco Maselli, Cesare Zavattini. Ugo Tognazzi, Maresa Gallo, Caterina Rigoglioso, Silvio Lillo, Angela Pierro. The title tells all in this episodic, six-part neorealist chronicle—filmed cinéma vérité style—of various aspects of romance in Rome. This was supposed to be the first edition of a film journal, known as "The Spectator." Originally 110m.; the Lizzani-directed sequence, about prostitution, was deleted from foreign-release prints. ▼▶

Love in the Rough (1930) **84m. ** D:** Charles F. Riesner. Robert Montgomery, Dorothy Jordan, Benny Rubin, J. C. Nugent, Dorothy McNulty (Penny Singleton), Allan Lane. Montgomery is a shipping clerk who gives the boss tips on the links while romancing his daughter in this fluffy, forgettable addition to that extremely obscure subgenre: Golf Musicals. Rubin easily steals the movie as a Yiddish-speaking caddy from Brooklyn. Remake of 1927's SPRING FEVER with William Haines and Joan Crawford.

Love Is a Ball (1963) **C-111m. **½** D: David Swift. Glenn Ford, Hope Lange, Charles Boyer, Ricardo Montalban, Telly Savalas. Forced froth trying hard to be chic; gold-digging and romance on the Riviera. Panavision. ▶

Love Is a Headache (1938) **68m. ** D:** Richard Thorpe. Gladys George, Franchot Tone, Ted Healy, Mickey Rooney, Frank Jenks, Ralph Morgan, Virginia Weidler, Jessie Ralph, Fay Holden. Fading Broadway diva adopts a pair of bratty orphans as a publicity stunt, which leads to a fake kidnapping plot and the usual amorous complications. Frantic romantic trifle is good for a few chuckles but strains for screwball zaniness.

Love Is a Many Splendored Thing (1955) **C-102m. **** D: Henry King. William Holden, Jennifer Jones, Murray Matheson, Torin Thatcher, Jorja Curtright, Virginia Gregg, Isobel Elsom, Richard Loo, Soo Yong, Philip Ahn, James Hong, Keye Luke. Well-mounted soaper set in Hong Kong at time of Korean War. Eurasian doctor Jones falls in love with war correspondent Holden. Effective telling of true story, beautifully executed, with Oscar-winning costumes (Charles LeMaire), scoring (Alfred Newman), and title song (Sammy Fain and Paul Francis Webster). CinemaScope.▼○❍

Love Is a Racket (1932) 72m. ** D: William A. Wellman. Douglas Fairbanks, Jr., Ann Dvorak, Frances Dee, Lee Tracy, Lyle Talbot, Andre Luguet, Warren Hymer. Attractive cast in curiously unappealing story of a Broadway columnist and his private intrigues. Tracy, who portrayed Winchell types so often, here plays the columnist's legman. ❭

Love Is Better Than Ever (1952) 81m. **½ D: Stanley Donen. Elizabeth Taylor, Larry Parks, Josephine Hutchinson, Tom Tully, Ann Doran, Elinor Donahue, Kathleen Freeman. Forgettable froth involving talent agent Parks and dance teacher Taylor. Mild MGM musical, but Liz looks terrific. Gene Kelly has an unbilled cameo.▼○

Love Is News (1937) 78m. **½ D: Tay Garnett. Tyrone Power, Loretta Young, Don Ameche, Slim Summerville, George Sanders, Jane Darwell, Stepin Fetchit, Pauline Moore, Elisha Cook, Jr., Dudley Digges, Walter Catlett. Heiress Young decides to get even with relentless reporter Power by announcing she's going to marry him—so he'll see what it's like to be in the spotlight for a change. Middling comedy about media celebrity was remade more successfully as THAT WONDERFUL URGE, with Power repeating his starring role. ❭

Love Is on the Air (1937) 61m. ** D: Nick Grinde. Ronald Reagan, June Travis, Eddie Acuff, Ben Welden, Robert Barrat, Addison Richards. Reagan's first film casts him as a brash headline-making radio personality who goes after corrupt city officials—but is sidetracked by his cautious boss. Passable B picture with meaningless title; one of several remakes of Paul Muni's HI, NELLIE! ❭

Love Laughs at Andy Hardy (1946) 94m. **½ D: Willis Goldbeck. Mickey Rooney, Lewis Stone, Sara Haden, Bonita Granville, Fay Holden, Lina Romay, Dorothy Ford, Addison Richards, Hal Hackett. Andy (played by a 26-year-old Rooney) returns to college after serving in WW2 to find that his sweetheart is engaged to someone else. The naive Hardy sentimentality was out of tune with the postwar mood and the series came to a close after this (although a reunion film was made 12 years later).▼❭

Love Letters (1945) 101m. ** D: William Dieterle. Jennifer Jones, Joseph Cotten, Ann Richards, Anita Louise, Cecil Kellaway, Gladys Cooper, Reginald Denny. Artificial soaper of amnesiac Jones cured by Cotten's love; only real asset is Victor Young's lovely title song. Ayn Rand adapted Chris Massie's book, *Pity My Simplicity.*▼❭

Love Light, The (1921) 89m. ** D: Frances Marion. Mary Pickford, Evelyn Dumo,

Raymond Bloomer, Fred Thomson, Albert Prisco, Georges Rigas (George Regas), Edward (Eddie) Phillips. Ambitious but disappointing Pickford vehicle casts Mary as a humble young Italian woman whose boyfriend and brothers head off to war. She becomes a lighthouse keeper, and then a mysterious stranger washes ashore. Pickford is excellent, but the film is far too melodramatic. One of screenwriter Marion's rare directorial efforts; she also scripted. ▼❭

Love Lottery, The (1954-British) C-89m. ** D: Charles Crichton. David Niven, Peggy Cummins, Anne Vernon, Herbert Lom, Hugh McDermott. Niven is movie star involved in international lottery; the winner gets him! Vernon is girl he really loves. Potential satire never comes off. Humphrey Bogart has guest bit in finale.

Lovely To Look At (1952) C-105m. **½ D: Mervyn LeRoy. Kathryn Grayson, Red Skelton, Howard Keel, Ann Miller, Marge & Gower Champion, Zsa Zsa Gabor. Second screen version of ROBERTA is a lesser MGM musical, but definitely has its moments as American comic Skelton inherits half-interest in a Paris dress salon run by Grayson and Marge Champion. Miller and the Champions add punch to the musical sequences; Vincente Minnelli directed the fashion show sequence. Songs include "Smoke Gets in Your Eyes," "I Won't Dance," and title tune.▼❭

Love Me Forever (1935) 90m. **½ D: Victor Schertzinger. Grace Moore, Leo Carrillo, Robert Allen, Spring Byington, Douglass Dumbrille. Entertaining musical of down-and-out singer who miraculously rises to top and becomes star. Good cast helped make Moore become star in real life too.

Love Me or Leave Me (1955) C-122m. ***½ D: Charles Vidor. Doris Day, James Cagney, Cameron Mitchell, Robert Keith, Tom Tully. Engrossing musical bio (from an Oscar-winning story by Daniel Fuchs) of singer Ruth Etting, whose life and career were dominated by a gangster called the Gimp. Day and Cagney give strong performances. Score includes Doris' hit "I'll Never Stop Loving You," plus oldies like "Ten Cents a Dance," "Shaking the Blues Away." CinemaScope.▼○❍

Love Me Tender (1956) 89m. **½ D: Robert D. Webb. Richard Egan, Debra Paget, Elvis Presley, Robert Middleton, William Campbell, Neville Brand, Mildred Dunnock. Presley's film debut is Civil War yarn of conflicting politics among sons in a Southern family, and their mutual love for Paget. Elvis' singing ("Let Me," "We're Gonna Move (to a Better Home)," "Poor Boy," and the title tune) highlights so-so Western. Elvis' swivel hips *might* not be authentic period detail! CinemaScope.▼❭

Love Me Tonight (1932) 96m. **** D:

Rouben Mamoulian. Maurice Chevalier, Jeanette MacDonald, Charlie Ruggles, Myrna Loy, C. Aubrey Smith, Charles Butterworth, Robert Greig. One of the best musicals ever made; Chevalier plays a tailor who falls in love with a princess (MacDonald). Along the way they get to sing Rodgers and Hart's "Lover," "Mimi," "Isn't It Romantic?," among others. Mamoulian's ingenious ideas, and mobile camera, keep this fresh and alive. Screenplay by Samuel Hoffenstein, Waldemar Young, and George Marion, Jr., from a play by Leopold Marchand and Paul Armont. Originally released at 104m. ▼❚

Love Nest (1951) **84m.** ****** D: Joseph M. Newman. June Haver, William Lundigan, Frank Fay, Marilyn Monroe, Jack Paar, Leatrice Joy. Cheerful but bland comedy about an Army returnee whose wife has bought a broken-down brownstone apartment, and whose tenants become part of their lives. Interesting only for early looks at Monroe and future TV host Paar. ▼❚

Love of Jeanne Ney, The (1927-German) **105m.** *****½** D: G. W. Pabst. Edith Jehanne, Uno Henning, Fritz Rasp, Brigitte Helm, Adolph Edgar Licho, Eugen Jensen, Hans Jaray, Siegfried Arno, Vladimir Sokoloff. Alfred Ney, a "foreign observer" in the Crimea, is murdered by a Bolshevik who is the lover of his daughter, Jeanne (Jehanne). Her past follows her as she settles in Paris, where she finds herself immersed in intrigue and betrayal. One of the near-classics of late-1920s German cinema, this piercing drama mirrors the disarray of post–WW1 Europe. Helm (of METROPOLIS fame) is a striking presence as a victimized blind girl. ▼❚

Love of Sunya, The (1927) **77m.** ******* D: Albert Parker. Gloria Swanson, John Boles, Anders Randolph, Andres de Segurola, Hugh Miller, Pauline Garon. Lavish vehicle for silent-star Swanson has Eastern yogi enabling her to envision her life with two potential husbands—neither of whom is the man she truly loves. Soap opera deluxe, remake of earlier EYES OF YOUTH. ▼❚

Love on a Pillow (1962-French) **C-102m.** ****** D: Roger Vadim. Brigitte Bardot, Robert Hossein, James Robertson Justice, Jean-Marc Bory. Charitable Bardot bestows her pleasures on young man, hoping to divert his intended suicide; saucy little comedy. Franscope. ▼❚

Love on the Dole (1941-British) **100m.** ******* D: John Baxter. Deborah Kerr, Clifford Evans, Mary Merrall, George Carney, Geoffrey Hibbert, Joyce O'Neill. Serious, well-acted study of struggling Manchester family during Depression. From Walter Greenwood novel. ▼❚

Love on the Run (1936) **80m.** ****** D: W. S. Van Dyke II. Joan Crawford, Clark Gable, Franchot Tone, Reginald Owen, Mona Barrie, Ivan Lebedeff, Charles Judels, William Demarest, Donald Meek. Roving newspaper correspondent Gable takes it on the lam with frustrated heiress Crawford and becomes involved with international spies. This stale IT HAPPENED ONE NIGHT variation relies solely on its star power. ▼❂❚

Love Parade, The (1929) **110m.** ******* D: Ernst Lubitsch. Maurice Chevalier, Jeanette MacDonald, Lillian Roth, Lionel Belmore, Lupino Lane, Ben Turpin. Initial teaming of Chevalier and MacDonald is enjoyable operetta with chic Lubitsch touch, about love among the royalty of Sylvania. Acrobatic comedian Lane and personality performer Roth make wonderful second leads. Virginia Bruce is one of Jeanette's ladies-in-waiting. "Dream Lover" is film's best song. Score by Victor Schertzinger (later a film director himself) and Clifford Grey. MacDonald's film debut. Jean Harlow is an extra. ❂❚

Lover Boy SEE: **Lovers, Happy Lovers!**

Lover Come Back (1946) **90m.** ****½** D: William A. Seiter. Lucille Ball, George Brent, Vera Zorina, Carl Esmond, William Wright, Charles Winninger. Bright little comedy of Lucy suing Brent for divorce when she sees his companion during war, photographer Zorina. Retitled WHEN LOVERS MEET.

Lover Come Back (1961) **C-107m.** *****½** D: Delbert Mann. Rock Hudson, Doris Day, Tony Randall, Edie Adams, Jack Oakie, Jack Kruschen, Ann B. Davis, Joe Flynn, Jack Albertson, Howard St. John, Donna Douglas. Early Day-Hudson vehicle is one of the best. Funny, fast-moving comedy has ad exec Doris trying to get account away from rival Rock—unaware that the product doesn't exist! Edie Adams stands out in fine supporting cast. ▼❂❚

Lovers, The (1958-French) **88m.** ******* D: Louis Malle. Jeanne Moreau, Alain Cuny, Jose Luis de Villalonga, Jean-Marc Bory, Gaston Modot. Chic, once-controversial tale of wealthy, married, spiritually empty Moreau and her two very different extramarital involvements. Malle's first major international success, and one of Moreau's most important early credits. Dyaliscope. ▼❚

Lovers and Lollipops (1955) **80m.** ****½** D: Morris Engel, Ruth Orkin. Lori March, Gerald O'Loughlin, Cathy Dunn, William Ward. Sweet but flawed little film about 7-year-old Dunn becoming jealous when her widowed mother begins dating a nice guy. The story rambles, and the music score is intrusive, but the N.Y.C. location footage is exceptional, as it was in Engel and Orkin's landmark film LITTLE FUGITIVE. ▼❚

Lovers Courageous (1932) **77m.** ****** D: Robert Z. Leonard. Robert Montgomery, Madge Evans, Roland Young, Frederick Kerr, Reginald Owen, Beryl Mercer, Alan Mowbray. Working-class dreamer Montgomery, traveling the world in search of himself, meets and falls for wealthy Evans . . . but there are complications. Well-intentioned but predictable, melodramatic saga of love and sacrifice. ▶

Lovers, Happy Lovers! (1954-British) 103m. *** D: René Clement. Gérard Philipe, Valerie Hobson, Joan Greenwood, Margaret Johnston, Natasha Parry. Philipe is wed to Hobson but tries to seduce her friend (Parry) in this witty, deftly ironic sex comedy. Original title: KNAVE OF HEARTS. Retitled: LOVER BOY.

Lovers of Paris (1957-French) 115m. **½ D: Julien Duvivier. Gérard Philipe, Danielle Darrieux, Dany Carrel. Spirited drama of Philipe coming to Paris bent on success and marriage; Darrieux is his perfect choice. Original title: POT-BOUILLE.

Love Slaves of the Amazons (1957) C-81m. ** D: Curt Siodmak. Don Taylor, Eduardo Ciannelli, Gianna Segale, Harvey Chalk. Programmer about a city of women and their male captives offers no more surprises than the title. Shot in Brazil.

Loves of a Blonde (1965-Czech) 88m. ***½ D: Milos Forman. Hana Brejchova, Josef Sebanek, Vladimir Pucholt, Jan Vostrell, Vladimir Mensik. Sweet, poignant tale of idealistic shoe-factory worker Brejchova, and what happens after she spends the night with—and falls in love with—womanizing pianist Pucholt. Gentle comedy-drama is both entertaining and revealing. ▼▶●

Loves of Carmen (1927) 94m. *** D: Raoul Walsh. Dolores Del Rio, Victor McLaglen, Don Alvarado, Nancy Nash, Rafael Valverde, Mathilde Comont, Fred Kohler. Del Rio is a fiery Carmen in spirited silent adaptation of the famous story. McLaglen is his usual swaggering self as the toreador seduced by the gypsy spitfire. Walsh treats the story in a pleasantly tongue-in-cheek manner, packing the film with typically lusty touches.

Loves of Carmen, The (1948) C-99m. **½ D: Charles Vidor. Rita Hayworth, Glenn Ford, Ron Randell, Victor Jory, Luther Adler. Hayworth's beauty is all there is in this colorful but routine retelling of the story of a gypsy man-killer, minus Bizet's music. ▼▶●

Loves of Edgar Allan Poe, The (1942) 67m. ** D: Harry Lachman. Linda Darnell, John Shepperd (Shepperd Strudwick), Virginia Gilmore, Jane Darwell, Mary Howard, Henry (Harry) Morgan. Plodding biography of 19th-century writer and women who influenced him. ▶

Loves of Three Queens (1953-Italian) C-90m. ** D: Marc Allegret. Hedy Lamarr, Massimo Serato, Cathy O'Donnell, Luigi Tosi, Guido Celano, Robert Beatty. Three-part film involving lives and loves of Genevieve of Brabant, Empress Josephine, and Helen of Troy (Lamarr). Originally three-hour meandering epic, now chopped down; still lacks continuity or interest. Retitled:

THE FACE THAT LAUNCHED A THOUSAND SHIPS.▼

Love Story (1944-British) 108m. ** D: Leslie Arliss. Margaret Lockwood, Stewart Granger, Patricia Roc, Tom Walls, Reginald Purdell, Moira Lister. No relation to later, more famous film has Lockwood as a concert pianist with a heart condition who tries to get away from it all at a summer resort in Cornwall. There she falls in love with Granger, who's losing his sight. Rather drippy romantic drama. Originally released in the U.S. as A LADY SURRENDERS. ▶

Love That Brute (1950) 85m. **½ D: Alexander Hall. Paul Douglas, Jean Peters, Cesar Romero, Joan Davis, Arthur Treacher, Keenan Wynn, Peter Price, Jay C. Flippen. Douglas is well cast as a loud-talking, good-natured prohibition racketeer with a yen for innocent Peters. Romero, who's the heavy here, had the lead in TALL, DARK AND HANDSOME, of which this is a remake. ▶

Love Thy Neighbor (1940) 82m. ** D: Mark Sandrich. Jack Benny, Fred Allen, Mary Martin, Verree Teasdale, Eddie "Rochester" Anderson, Virginia Dale, Theresa Harris. Contrived attempt to capitalize on Benny-Allen radio feud. Martin still good, though, and Rochester has some sprightly scenes, but disappointment for fans of both Benny and Allen.

Love Trap, The (1929) 70m. **½ D: William Wyler. Laura La Plante, Neil Hamilton, Robert Ellis, Rita La Roy, Jocelyn Lee, Norman Trevor. Pleasant if unremarkable silent-talkie hybrid has former dancer La Plante marrying well, only to be recognized by her new husband's uncle from a long-ago wild party. Early Wyler effort is mainly a vehicle for its likable star, La Plante. ▼▶

Love Under Fire (1937) 75m. **½ D: George Marshall. Loretta Young, Don Ameche, Frances Drake, Walter Catlett, Sig Ruman, John Carradine, Holmes Herbert. Romance and adventure as detective Ameche has to arrest alleged thief Young in Madrid amid Spanish Civil War. Disjointed but enjoyable.

Love With the Proper Stranger (1963) 100m. *** D: Robert Mulligan. Natalie Wood, Steve McQueen, Edie Adams, Herschel Bernardi, Tom Bosley. Nifty, cynical romance tale of working girl Wood and trumpet player McQueen. Much N.Y.C. on-location filming, nice support from Adams. Written by Arnold Schulman. Good bit: the title tune. ▼●

Loving You (1957) C-101m. **½ D: Hal Kanter. Elvis Presley, Lizabeth Scott, Wendell Corey, Dolores Hart, James Gleason. Publicist Liz and country-western musician Corey discover gas station attendant Presley and promote him to stardom. Elvis' second movie is highlighted by his performance of "Teddy Bear" and the title tune. VistaVision.▼▶●

Lovin' the Ladies (1930) **66m.** ****½** D: Melville W. Brown. Richard Dix, Lois Wilson, Allen Kearns, Rita La Roy, Renée Macready, Virginia Sale, Selmer Jackson, Anthony Bushell, Henry Armetta. Amusing (if stagebound) trifle in which two wealthy boors bet each other to see if erudite electrician Dix can charm an ice-cold socialite. ▶

Lower Depths, The (1936-French) **92m.** ****½** D: Jean Renoir. Jean Gabin, Louis Jouvet, Suzy Prim, Vladimir Sokoloff, Junie Astor, Robert Le Vignan. Sordid drama about assorted characters in a squalid home for derelicts. Pepel (Gabin), a professional thief, loves the younger sister of his mistress, and commits murder to save her from the clutches of a police officer to whom she has been "given" as a bribe. Loose adaptation of the 1902 Maxim Gorki play changes the setting from Czarist Russia to an imaginary land. Renoir scripted with Charles Spaak. Remade 21 years later by Akira Kurosawa, who was more faithful to the play. Original title: LES BAS-FONDS. ▼▶

Lower Depths, The (1957-Japanese) **125m.** ******* D: Akira Kurosawa. Toshiro Mifune, Isuzu Yamada, Ganjiro Nakamura, Kyoko Kagawa. Well-directed and acted but endlessly talky drama of tortured, poverty-stricken souls, with Mifune a thief who becomes involved with Kagawa. Based on a Maxim Gorki play. ▼▶

Loyal 47 Ronin, The SEE: **47 Ronin, Part I** and **Part II, The**

L-Shaped Room, The (1963-British) **125m.** ******* D: Bryan Forbes. Leslie Caron, Tom Bell, Brock Peters, Avis Bunnage, Emlyn Williams, Cicely Courtneidge, Bernard Lee, Patricia Phoenix, Nanette Newman. French woman crosses the Channel to face pregnancy alone, comes to meet interesting assortment of characters in shabby London boarding house. Caron is superb in the lead. ▼

Luck of Ginger Coffey, The (1964-Canadian-U.S.) **100m.** ******* D: Irvin Kershner. Robert Shaw, Mary Ure, Liam Redmond, Tom Harvey, Libby McClintock. Effective kitchen-sink drama with Shaw in one of his best performances as an out-of-work Irish-born dreamer, approaching middle age, who moves to Montreal with wife Ure and their teenage daughter, hoping to find success. Scripted by Brian Moore, based on his novel. ▼

Luck of the Irish, The (1948) **99m.** ****½** D: Henry Koster. Tyrone Power, Anne Baxter, Cecil Kellaway, Lee J. Cobb, Jayne Meadows. Leprechaun Kellaway becomes reporter Power's conscience in this "cute" but unremarkable romance. ▶

Lucky Devils (1933) **64m.** ****** D: Ralph Ince. William Boyd, Dorothy Wilson, William Gargan, Bob Rose, Bruce Cabot, Creighton Chaney (Lon Chaney, Jr.), Roscoe Ates, William Bakewell, Julie Haydon,

Betty Furness. Stuntman Gargan likes extra Wilson, but she loves stuntman Boyd. Hokey programmer, but great opening scene; Hollywood-on-film buffs will surely want to see it. Veteran stuntman Rose cowrote screenplay. ▶

Lucky Jim (1957-British) **95m.** ****½** D: John Boulting. Ian Carmichael, Terry-Thomas, Hugh Griffith, Sharon Acker, Jean Anderson. Comic misadventures of puckish history professor at provincial British university; amusing adaptation of Kingsley Amis book, though not up to Boulting Brothers standard. ▼

Lucky Jordan (1942) **84m.** ****½** D: Frank Tuttle. Alan Ladd, Helen Walker, Marie McDonald, Mabel Paige, Sheldon Leonard, Lloyd Corrigan. Far-fetched story of smart-mouthed hood Ladd reluctantly drafted into the Army, becoming entangled with U.S.O. worker Walker (in her feature debut) and Nazi spies.

Lucky Legs (1942) **64m.** ****½** D: Charles Barton. Jinx Falkenburg, Leslie Brooks, Kay Harris, Elizabeth Patterson, Russell Hayden, William Wright, Don Beddoe. Leggy chorus girl Falkenburg unexpectedly inherits a million dollars from a Broadway bookkeeper—except the money was stolen from his gangster boss, who wants it back! Amusing little musical comedy with some witty dialogue.

Lucky Losers (1950) **69m.** ****** D: William Beaudine. Leo Gorcey, Huntz Hall, Hillary Brooke, Gabriel Dell, Lyle Talbot, Bernard Gorcey, Billy Benedict, Joseph Turkel, Frank Jenks, David Gorcey. Stale *Bowery Boys* comedy, with Slip and Sach trading their overalls for pinstripes when they land jobs as stockbrokers.

Lucky Mascot SEE: **Brass Monkey, The**

Lucky Me (1954) **C-100m.** ****** D: Jack Donohue. Doris Day, Robert Cummings, Phil Silvers, Eddie Foy, Nancy Walker, Martha Hyer, Bill Goodwin. Bright-faced but doggedly mediocre musical set in Miami, with Doris as star of Silvers' third-rate theatrical troupe who attracts the attention of Broadway songwriter Cummings. Look for young Angie Dickinson in first film appearance. CinemaScope. ▼▶

Lucky Nick Cain (1951) **87m.** ****½** D: Joseph M. Newman. George Raft, Coleen Gray, Charles Goldner, Walter Rilla. Acceptable gangster yarn of Raft involved with counterfeiting gang, accused of murder; filmed in Italy.

Lucky Night (1939) **82m.** ***½** D: Norman Taurog. Myrna Loy, Robert Taylor, Henry O'Neill, Joseph Allen, Douglas Fowley, Charles Lane, Marjorie Main. Incoherent, interminable mess, in which magnate's daughter Loy and down-and-out gambler Taylor meet, get drunk, and get married—all in one evening. Sounds far more promising than it plays.

Lucky Partners (1940) 99m. ** D: Lewis Milestone. Ronald Colman, Ginger Rogers, Jack Carson, Spring Byington, Cecilia Loftus, Harry Davenport. Far-fetched comedy about Colman and Rogers winning sweepstakes together, then taking "imaginary" honeymoon. Stars try to buoy mediocre script.▼)

Lucky Star (1929) 100m. ***½ D: Frank Borzage. Janet Gaynor, Charles Farrell, Guinn ("Big Boy") Williams, Hedwiga Reicher, Paul Fix. Simple, tender love story about the evolving relationship between beleaguered, ill-educated farm girl Gaynor and spirited telephone lineman Farrell, who goes off to war and returns a "cripple." A cruel, gullible mother and slimy villain play key roles in this tremendously moving film that is definitely not for the jaded. Adapted from Tristram Tupper's *Three Episodes in the Life of Timothy Osborn.*)

Lucky Stiff, The (1949) 99m. ** D: Lewis R. Foster. Dorothy Lamour, Brian Donlevy, Claire Trevor, Irene Hervey, Marjorie Rambeau. Sturdy cast in slim vehicle of lawyer setting trap for actual killer after girl suspect has death sentence reprieved. Produced by, of all people, Jack Benny!

Lucky Texan, The (1934) 55m. **½ D: Robert N. Bradbury. John Wayne, Barbara Sheldon, Lloyd Whitlock, George Hayes, Yakima Canutt. Pleasing treatment of trite story: Wayne teams up with likable Hayes, a friend of his deceased father, discovers gold, and gets cheated by crooked assayers who try to steal their claim and ranch. Canutt doubles both Wayne and the villain (Whitlock), so in one hard-riding scene chases himself out of town. Also available in computer-colored form as GOLD STRIKE FEVER.▼)

Lucy Gallant (1955) C-104m. **½ D: Robert Parrish. Charlton Heston, Jane Wyman, Thelma Ritter, Claire Trevor, William Demarest, Wallace Ford. Spiritless soaper of success-bent Wyman rejecting suitors Heston et al., wanting to get ahead instead; set in Western oil town. Wyman plays dressmaker, and veteran Hollywood costume designer Edith Head makes a rare on-screen appearance near the end. VistaVision.

Lullaby of Broadway (1951) C-92m. **½ D: David Butler. Doris Day, Gene Nelson, Gladys George, S. Z. Sakall, Billy de Wolfe, Florence Bates, Anne Triola. Musical comedy star Day returns to N.Y.C., unaware that her singer mother has hit the skids. Warner Bros. musical is decent but no big deal; good cast and lots of great old songs keep it moving.▼●)

Lulu Belle (1948) 87m. ** D: Leslie Fenton. Dorothy Lamour, George Montgomery, Albert Dekker, Otto Kruger, Glenda Farrell. Hackneyed drama of singer stepping on anyone and everyone to achieve fame.

Lumberjack (1944) 65m. **½ D: Les-

ley Selander. William Boyd, Andy Clyde, Jimmy Rogers, Douglass Dumbrille, Ellen Hall, Francis McDonald, Hal Taliaferro. When a friend of Hopalong Cassidy's is murdered, he not only helps the widow fulfill her logging contracts but also nabs the killer. Rare series entry emphasizing almost continuous brawling action and gunplay. Exciting, holds up well.▼)

Lumiére d'Eté (1943-French) 110m. *** D: Jean Grémillon. Madeleine Renaud, Pierre Brasseur, Madeleine Robinson, Paul Bernard, Georges Marchal, Léonce Corne. Pretty Parisian fashion illustrator (Robinson) arrives at a rural resort hotel to rendezvous with her new boyfriend, setting off a series of emotional fireworks involving unrequited love, jealousy, and plenty of secrets and lies. Talky but engaging allegorical drama effectively contrasts modest, hardworking blue-collar types and their self-centered upper-class "betters" who wallow in decadence. Coscripted by Jacques Prévert and Pierre Laroche.)

Lured (1947) 102m. **½ D: Douglas Sirk. George Sanders, Lucille Ball, Charles Coburn, Alan Mowbray, Cedric Hardwicke, Boris Karloff, George Zucco. Ball turns detective in this melodrama, encounters strange characters and harrowing experiences while tracking murderer; pretty good, with top cast. Remake of Robert Siodmak's 1939 French film PIÈGES.▼)

Lure of the Wilderness (1952) C-92m. **½ D: Jean Negulesco. Jeffrey Hunter, Jean Peters, Constance Smith, Walter Brennan, Jack Elam. Remake of SWAMP WATER doesn't match earlier version's atmosphere of Southern swamps where murderer holds young man hostage to keep his whereabouts secret. Brennan repeats his SWAMP WATER role.)

Lust for Gold (1949) 90m. **½ D: S. Sylvan Simon. Ida Lupino, Glenn Ford, Gig Young, William Prince, Edgar Buchanan, Will Geer, Paul Ford, Jay Silverheels, Eddy Waller. Lupino gets overly dramatic as grasping woman stopping at nothing to obtain riches of gold-laden mine. Remade as SECRET OF TREASURE MOUNTAIN. ▼)

Lust for Life (1956) C-122m. **** D: Vincente Minnelli. Kirk Douglas, Anthony Quinn, James Donald, Pamela Brown, Everett Sloane, Niall MacGinnis, Noel Purcell, Henry Daniell, Jill Bennett, Lionel Jeffries, Eric Pohlmann. Brilliant adaptation of Irving Stone's biography of painter Van Gogh, vividly portraying his anguished life. Quinn won well-deserved Oscar for performance as painter friend Gauguin, in this exquisite color production. Script by Norman Corwin. Produced by John Houseman. Fine music score by Miklos Rozsa. CinemaScope.▼●)

Lusty Men, The (1952) 113m. *** D:

[413]

Nicholas Ray. Susan Hayward, Robert Mitchum, Arthur Kennedy, Arthur Hunnicutt, Frank Faylen. Intelligent, atmospheric rodeo drama, with ex-champ Mitchum becoming mentor of novice Kennedy—and finding himself attracted to Kennedy's no-nonsense wife (Hayward). Solid going most of the way—until that hokey finale. Well directed by Ray.▼○●

Luxury Liner (1948) **C-98m.** ** D: Richard Whorf. George Brent, Jane Powell, Lauritz Melchior, Frances Gifford, Xavier Cugat. MGM fluff aboard a cruise ship, with Powell singing her heart out.○●

Lydia (1941) **104m.** *** D: Julien Duvivier. Merle Oberon, Edna May Oliver, Alan Marshal, Joseph Cotten, Hans Yaray, George Reeves. Sentimental tale of elderly woman (Oberon) meeting her former beaux and recalling their courtship. Remake of Duvivier's own French classic, UN CARNET DE BAL.▼

Lydia Bailey (1952) **C-89m.** **½ D: Jean Negulesco. Dale Robertson, Anne Francis, Luis Van Rooten, Juanita Moore, William Marshall. Handsome but empty version of Kenneth Roberts actioner of 1800s Haiti and revolt against French rulers.

Lying Lips (1939) **68m.** ** D: Oscar Micheaux. Edna Mae Harris, Carman Newsome, (Robert) Earl Jones, Frances Williams, Cherokee Thornton, "Slim" Thompson, Gladys Williams, Juano Hernandez, Amanda Randolph. Nightclub singer Harris is framed on a murder rap; her manager-boyfriend and a policeman set out to prove her innocence. Low-grade Micheaux effort, primarily of note for its cast.▼)

M (1931-German) **111m.** **** D: Fritz Lang. Peter Lorre, Ellen Widmann, Inge Landgut, Gustav Grundgens. Harrowing melodrama about psychotic child murderer brought to justice by Berlin underworld. Riveting and frighteningly contemporary; cinematically dazzling, especially for an early talkie. Lorre's performance is unforgettable. Restored prints feature a brief courtroom coda that subtly changes film's final message. Older 99m. prints still circulate. Lorre also filmed a 96m. English-language version. Remade in 1951.

M (1951) **88m.** *** D: Joseph Losey. David Wayne, Howard da Silva, Luther Adler, Karen Morley, Jorja Curtright, Martin Gabel, Norman Lloyd. Interesting, intelligent rethinking of Fritz Lang classic set in L.A., with Wayne as child-killer hunted down by community of criminals.

Ma and Pa Kettle Betty MacDonald's best-selling book *The Egg and I* told of the hardships a city girl faced moving with her husband to a rural chicken farm. Among the problems were the incredible local characters, two of whom, Ma and Pa Kettle, were given prime footage in the screen version of

THE EGG AND I. Played by veterans Marjorie Main and Percy Kilbride, the "hillbilly" duo (who actually resided in Cape Flattery, Washington) created a hit—Main even earned an Oscar nomination—and became the stars of their own series. The Kettle movies, shot on the Universal back lot for a relative pittance, and seldom praised by critics, earned millions and millions of dollars for the studio. Rambunctious Ma and hesitant Pa's adventures were not exactly out of Noel Coward, but they knew how to please their audience with gags that were tried and true. What's more, Main and Kilbride were absolutely perfect in the leads. Lori Nelson played the eldest daughter in the Kettles' tremendous brood (ranging somewhere from twelve to fifteen children). Ray Collins and Barbara Brown were introduced as the snobby Bostonian in-laws the Parkers in MA AND PA KETTLE BACK ON THE FARM, and various actors took turns playing Pa's Indian farmhands, with Oliver Blake winning the best showcase as Geoduck in MA AND PA KETTLE AT HOME (also the series' funniest entry). In 1955 Percy Kilbride left the series. Arthur Hunnicutt played a backwoods brother-in-law in THE KETTLES IN THE OZARKS, and Parker Fennelly (best remembered as Titus Moody on Fred Allen's radio show) took on the role of Pa in THE KETTLES ON OLD MACDONALD'S FARM, but neither actor caught on, and the series came to an end in 1957. Some Hollywood pundits concluded that such cornball humor had run its course, but in the 1960s a TV series called *The Beverly Hillbillies* came along to prove them wrong.

MA AND PA KETTLE

Ma and Pa Kettle (1949)
Ma and Pa Kettle Go to Town (1950)
Ma and Pa Kettle Back on the Farm (1951)
Ma and Pa Kettle at the Fair (1952)
Ma and Pa Kettle On Vacation (1953)
Ma and Pa Kettle at Home (1954)
Ma and Pa Kettle at Waikiki (1955)
The Kettles in the Ozarks (1956)
The Kettles on Old Macdonald's Farm (1957)

Ma and Pa Kettle (1949) **75m.** **½ D: Charles Lamont. Marjorie Main, Percy Kilbride, Richard Long, Meg Randall, Patricia Alphin, Esther Dale. The Kettles and their fifteen kids are threatened with eviction, but Pa wins a tobacco slogan contest and they all move into a luxurious "home of the future." First in the series of lowbrow bread-and-butter programmers. The futuristic home is a lot of fun. Video title: FURTHER ADVENTURES OF MA AND PA KETTLE.▼○●

Ma and Pa Kettle at Home (1954) **81m.**

*** D: Charles Lamont. Marjorie Main, Percy Kilbride, Alan Mowbray, Ross Elliott, Alice Kelley, Brett Halsey, Mary Wickes, Irving Bacon, Emory Parnell, Oliver Blake. Sixth and best entry in the series has the Kettles trying to impress an Eastern magazine editor (Mowbray) in order to win a scholarship prize. One slapstick gag follows another, leading to a wild climactic chase; there's some homespun sentiment, too, as we spend Christmas with the Kettles (and, at last count, fifteen kids).▼▶

Ma and Pa Kettle at the Fair (1952) **78m.** **½ D: Charles Barton. Marjorie Main, Percy Kilbride, Lori Nelson, James Best, Esther Dale, Russell Simpson, Emory Parnell. Standard entry centering on the Kettles' efforts to win money at a country fair (with Ma's cooking) to send their daughter to college. Funny finale features Pa in a hectic horse race.▼▶

Ma and Pa Kettle at Waikiki (1955) **79m.** ** D: Lee Sholem. Marjorie Main, Percy Kilbride, Lori Nelson, Byron Palmer, Loring Smith, Lowell Gilmore, Mabel Albertson, Esther Dale, Ida Moore. To help out a relative, the Kettles travel to Hawaii where Pa immediately blows up the family pineapple factory and gets himself kidnapped. Pretty weak. Kilbride's last film.▼▶

Ma and Pa Kettle Back on the Farm (1951) **80m.** ** D: Edward Sedgwick. Marjorie Main, Percy Kilbride, Richard Long, Meg Randall, Barbara Brown, Ray Collins, Emory Parnell, Peter Leeds. The Kettles have to contend with their snobby in-laws while dealing with crooks who think there are uranium deposits on their land. Typical cornball entry.▼▶

Ma and Pa Kettle Go to Town (1950) **70m.** **½ D: Charles Lamont. Marjorie Main, Percy Kilbride, Richard Long, Meg Randall, Gregg Martell, Charles McGraw, Jim Backus, Elliott Lewis, Bert Freed, Hal March. The Kettles get mixed up with crooks on a trip to New York, and their country smarts naturally subdue the city slickers. One of the series' best.▼▶

Ma and Pa Kettle on Vacation (1953) **75m.** ** D: Charles Lamont. Percy Kilbride, Marjorie Main, Ray Collins, Bodil Miller, Sig Ruman, Barbara Brown, Oliver Blake, Teddy Hart. The formula's wearing thin, as Ma and Pa travel to Paris as the guests of the Parkers and get mixed up with spies and femmes fatales. Look fast for a young Rita Moreno.▼▶

Ma Barker's Killer Brood (1960) **90m.** ** D: Bill Karn. Lurene Tuttle, Tristram Coffin, Paul Dubov, Nelson Leigh. Energetic performance by Tuttle and surprisingly sadistic violence hoist this programmer gangster yarn above tedium.▼▶

Macabre (1958) **73m.** ** D: William Castle. William Prince, Jim Backus, Christine White, Jacqueline Scott. Weird goings-on in small town where doctor's young daughter mysteriously vanishes—and an anonymous phone caller announces that the child has been buried alive. Film promises much, delivers little. Famous for Castle's gimmick of handing out policies insuring moviegoers for $1,000 against death by fright.▶

Macao (1952) **80m.** ** D: Josef von Sternberg. Robert Mitchum, Jane Russell, William Bendix, Gloria Grahame, Thomas Gomez, Philip Ahn. Flat yarn supposedly set in murky title port, with Russell a singer and Mitchum the action-seeking man she loves.▼▶▶

Macbeth (1948) **89m.** *** D: Orson Welles. Orson Welles, Jeanette Nolan, Dan O'Herlihy, Edgar Barrier, Roddy McDowall, Robert Coote, Erskine Sanford, Alan Napier, Peggy Webber, John Dierkes. Welles brought the Bard to Republic Pictures with this moody, well-done adaptation, filmed entirely on bizarre interiors (which deliberately emphasize its theatricality). Welles' original version, which runs 105m., has the actors speaking with authentic Scot accents.▼▶▶

Machine-Gun Kelly (1958) **80m.** **½ D: Roger Corman. Charles Bronson, Susan Cabot, Barboura Morris, Morey Amsterdam, Wally Campo, Jack Lambert, Connie Gilchrist. With typical efficiency, Corman gives this gangster chronicle pacing and more than passing interest. Bronson is fine in title role. Superama.▼

Machine to Kill Bad People (1952-Italian) **80m.** **½ D: Roberto Rossellini. Gennaro Pisano, Giovanni Amato, Marilyn Buferd, Pietro Carloni. Eye-catching title for a sober postwar parable about a demonic camera that assassinates the villagers whose pictures it snaps. While the photographer's imagination is initially piqued by the political and societal potential inherent in such a device, he soon learns how hard it can be for a god to discern between good and evil. Filmed in 1948. Original title: LA MACCHINA AMMAZZACATTIVI.▼

Macomber Affair, The (1947) **89m.** ***½ D: Zoltan Korda. Gregory Peck, Joan Bennett, Robert Preston, Reginald Denny, Carl Harbord. Penetrating, intelligent filmization of Hemingway story about conflicts that develop when hunter Peck takes married couple (Preston, Bennett) on safari. Bristling performances help make this one of the most vivid screen adaptations of a Hemingway work. Based on "The Short Happy Life of Francis Macomber"; scripted by Casey Robinson and Seymour Bennett.

Macumba Love (1960) **C-86m.** *½ D: Douglas Fowley. Walter Reed, Ziva Rodann, William Wellman, Jr., June Wilkinson. Trivia of supernatural debunker Reed delving into voodoo practices in Haiti. Shot in Brazil.▼

Mad About Men (1954-British) **C-90m.**

[415]

** D: Ralph Thomas. Glynis Johns, Donald Sinden, Anne Crawford, Margaret Rutherford, Dora Bryan, Noel Purcell. Mermaid and young woman look-alike change places in this pleasant fantasy, and love takes its course. Sequel to MIRANDA.▐

Mad About Money (1937-British) **74m.** ** D: Melville Brown. Lupe Velez, Ben Lyon, Wallace Ford, Harry Langdon, Mary Cole, Cyril Raymond, Ronald Ward. Nifty cast sparks hoary plot of motion-picture entrepreneurs attempting to milk a cattle baroness who's actually a showgirl in mufti trying to get into their movie. Bland on every level, but likable cast and a few lively songs help. Original title: STARDUST. U.S. title: HE LOVED AN ACTRESS.▐

Mad About Music (1938) **98m.** *** D: Norman Taurog. Deanna Durbin, Herbert Marshall, Gail Patrick, Arthur Treacher, Helen Parrish, Marcia Mae Jones, William Frawley. Excellent Durbin vehicle; busy mother Patrick leaves Deanna in Swiss girls' school, where she pretends Marshall is her father. Holds up better than remake, TOY TIGER.▼▐

Madame (1961-French) **C-104m.** **½ D: Christian-Jaque. Sophia Loren, Robert Hossein, Julien Bertheau, Marina Berti. Uninspired remake of MADAME SANS-GENE (filmed in 1925) with Loren, who uses looks and wits to rise from laundress to nobility in Napoleonic France. Super Technirama 70.▐

Madame Bovary (1934-French) **102m.** ** D: Jean Renoir. Valentine Tessier, Pierre Renoir, Max Dearly, Daniel Lecourtois, Fernand Fabre, Alice Tissot, Helena Manson. Uneven, unsatisfying version of the oft-filmed Flaubert story, about the romantic, ill-fated title character. Originally three hours long, Renoir (who also scripted) was forced to drastically edit it. While the first version may have been more compelling than the existing film, the fact remains that Tessier is miscast as Emma Bovary.▼

Madame Bovary (1949) **115m.** ***½ D: Vincente Minnelli. Jennifer Jones, James Mason, Van Heflin, Louis Jourdan, Christopher Kent (Alf Kjellin), Gene Lockhart, Gladys Cooper, George Zucco, Henry (Harry) Morgan. Gustave Flaubert's 19th-century heroine sacrifices her husband and their security for love, meets a horrible end. Once-controversial adaptation looks better every year, despite an odd "framing" device involving Flaubert's morals trial. Justifiably celebrated ball sequence is among the greatest set pieces of Minnelli's—or anyone else's—career. Screenplay by Robert Ardrey. Previously filmed in 1932 (as UNHOLY LOVE) and 1934 (in France, by Jean Renoir); remade in France in 1991.▼●▐

Madame Butterfly (1932) **86m.** **½ D: Marion Gering. Sylvia Sidney, Cary Grant, Charlie Ruggles, Irving Pichel, Helen Je-

rome Eddy. Puccini opera (minus music) of Oriental woman in love with American (Grant) is sensitive, tragic romance, dated but well handled.

Madame Curie (1943) **124m.** *** D: Mervyn LeRoy. Greer Garson, Walter Pidgeon, Henry Travers, Albert Basserman, Robert Walker, C. Aubrey Smith. Despite stretches of plodding footage, bio of famed female scientist is generally excellent. Garson and Pidgeon team well, as usual.▼●▐

Madame Du Barry (1934) **77m.** ** D: William Dieterle. Dolores Del Rio, Reginald Owen, Victor Jory, Osgood Perkins, Verree Teasdale, Ferdinand Gottschalk, Dorothy Tree, Anita Louise, Henry O'Neill. Intriguing cast can't do much with this superficial historical charade about the life and loves of the infamous courtesan during the wicked reign of King Louis XV. At least it looks good, with lavish costumes and sets.

Madame Racketeer (1932) **70m.** *** D: Alexander Hall, Harry Wagstaff Gribble. Alison Skipworth, Richard Bennett, George Raft, John Breeden, Evalyn Knapp, Gertrude Messinger, Robert McWade, J. Farrell MacDonald. Charming con artist posing as a countess visits her estranged husband (Bennett) and hides true identity from her two daughters, keeping coin-flipping gangster Raft away from one of them and fixing up the other with a banker's son. Droll showcase for the wonderful character actress Skipworth.

Madame X (1929) **90m.** ** D: Lionel Barrymore. Ruth Chatterton, Lewis Stone, Raymond Hackett, Holmes Herbert, Eugenie Besserer, Sidney Toler. Leaden weeper, filmed previously in 1906, 1916, and 1920, about cold, cruel husband Stone forcing wife Chatterton onto the streets. Their son comes of age believing she's dead . . . and then gets to defend her on a murder charge. A curio at best; the remakes are better.●▐

Madame X (1937) **71m.** **½ D: Sam Wood. Gladys George, John Beal, Warren William, Reginald Owen, William Henry, Henry Daniell, Phillip Reed, Ruth Hussey. Alexandre Bisson's stalwart soap opera gets polished MGM treatment and a fine performance by Gladys George as the woman whose ultimate sacrifice is never detected by her son. Goes astray toward the end (with Beal a bit much), but worth a look.▼▐

Madam Satan (1930) **115m.** *** D: Cecil B. DeMille. Kay Johnson, Reginald Denny, Roland Young, Lillian Roth, Elsa Peterson, Tyler Brooke. Bizarre semimusical extravaganza with placid Johnson posing as wicked Madam Satan to win back errant husband Denny. Mad party scene on Zeppelin is certainly an eye-popper.▼▐

Mad at the World (1955) **72m.** *½ D: Harry Essex. Frank Lovejoy, Keefe Brasselle, Cathy O'Donnell, Karen Sharpe. Pointless study of Brasselle seeking vengeance on teenage slum gang who harmed his baby; Lovejoy is detective on case. The "teens" (Stanley Clements, Joe Turkel, Paul Dubov) are played by actors long out of adolescence.

Mad Checkmate SEE: **It's Your Move**

Mädchen in Uniform SEE: **Mäedchen in Uniform** (1931)

Mad Doctor, The (1941) 90m. ****** D: Tim Whelan. Basil Rathbone, Ellen Drew, John Howard, Barbara Jo Allen (Vera Vague), Ralph Morgan, Martin Kosleck. Not a horror film, but a polished B about suave medico who marries women and murders them for their money. Interesting for a while, but misses the mark.

Mad Doctor of Market Street, The (1942) 61m. ** D: Joseph H. Lewis. Lionel Atwill, Una Merkel, Claire Dodd, Nat Pendleton, Anne Nagel. Mini-chiller from Universal about insane scientist (Atwill) marooned on Pacific isle, worshipped by its natives, and using fellow castaways for strange experiments. ▶

Mad Dog Coll (1961) 86m. *½ D: Burt Balaban. John Davis Chandler, Brooke Hayward, Kay Doubleday, Jerry Orbach, Telly Savalas. Minor crime melodrama about the career of Vincent "Mad Dog" Coll, the most vicious killer in all gangland. Hayward is the daughter of Margaret Sullavan and the author of *Haywire*; that's Vincent Gardenia as Dutch Schultz, Gene Hackman (in his film debut) as a cop. ▶

Made For Each Other (1939) 93m. ******* D: John Cromwell. Carole Lombard, James Stewart, Charles Coburn, Lucile Watson, Alma Kruger, Esther Dale, Ward Bond, Louise Beavers. First-rate soaper of struggling young marrieds Stewart and Lombard battling illness, lack of money, Stewart's meddling mother Watson. Fine acting makes this all work. Also shown in computer-colored version. ▼▶

Madeleine (1950-British) 114m. **½ D: David Lean. Ann Todd, Leslie Banks, Elizabeth Sellars, Ivor Barnard. Superior cast improves oft-told drama of woman accused of murdering her lover. A vehicle for Lean's then wife, Ann Todd, and one of the filmmaker's few disappointments. Retitled: STRANGE CASE OF MADELEINE. ▼▶

Madeleine (1958-German) 86m. *½ D: Kurt Meisel. Eva Bartok, Sabina Sesselmann, Ilse Steppat, Alexander Kerst. Unsensational study of prostitutes, with a witless plot of Bartok trying to shed her shady past. Aka NAKED IN THE NIGHT. ▶

Mademoiselle Fifi (1944) 69m. **½ D: Robert Wise. Simone Simon, John Emery, Kurt Kreuger, Alan Napier, Jason Robards, Sr., Helen Freeman. A laundress reveals more integrity and patriotic spirit than her condescending fellow passengers on an eventful coach ride during the Franco-Prussian war. Uneven Val Lewton production (with allegorical implications about WW2), adapted from two Guy de Maupassant stories. ▼●

Mademoiselle Striptease SEE: **Please! Mr. Balzac**

Made on Broadway (1933) 68m. ******* D: Harry Beaumont. Robert Montgomery, Sally Eilers, Madge Evans, Eugene Pallette, C. Henry Gordon, Jean Parker, Ivan Lebedeff. Montgomery deftly plays a slick press agent (and political fixer) who rescues street waif Eilers from a suicide attempt and transforms her into a refined sophisticate. She promptly uses her newfound celebrity to beat a murder rap. Breezy pre-Code riff on *Pygmalion* has a surprisingly modern view of male-female relationships and how spin doctors manipulate the media. ▶

Mad Genius, The (1931) 81m. ******* D: Michael Curtiz. John Barrymore, Marian Marsh, Donald Cook, Carmel Myers, Charles Butterworth, Mae Madison, Frankie Darro, Luis Alberni, Boris Karloff. Follow-up to SVENGALI has Barrymore a deranged entrepreneur who lives vicariously through Cook's dancing career. Bizarre, entertaining film with hilarious Butterworth as Barrymore's crony, Alberni as a dope fiend. Karloff has small role near the beginning as Darro's sadistic father.

Mad Ghoul, The (1943) 65m. **½ D: James Hogan. David Bruce, Evelyn Ankers, George Zucco, Turhan Bey, Charles McGraw, Robert Armstrong, Milburn Stone, Rose Hobart. Strong cast buoys grim story of scientist Zucco turning assistant Bruce into a zombie in order to clear the path to romance with Bruce's girl. ▼▶

Mad Holiday (1936) 71m. **½ D: George B. Seitz. Edmund Lowe, Elissa Landi, ZaSu Pitts, Ted Healy, Edmund Gwenn, Edgar Kennedy, Walter Kingsford. Mildly amusing blend of mystery and comedy with Lowe as a movie detective who's fed up with his tired cinematic adventures and takes a cruise to escape. Naturally he becomes embroiled in a real-life murder, with pulp novelist Landi and studio press agent Healy aboard for the ride.

Madison Avenue (1962) 94m. **½ D: H. Bruce Humberstone. Dana Andrews, Eleanor Parker, Jeanne Crain, Eddie Albert, Howard St. John, Henry Daniell. Tightly produced programmer centering on machinations in N.Y.C.'s advertising jungle. CinemaScope. ▶

Madison Sq. Garden (1932) 74m. **½ D: Harry Joe Brown. Jack Oakie, Marian Nixon, Thomas Meighan, William (Stage) Boyd, ZaSu Pitts, Lew Cody, William Collier, Sr., Warren Hymer. Minor-league prizefighting drama with Oakie a rising middleweight boxer is nonetheless a sports buff's find as it features a host of the era's best-known athletes and sportswriters appearing as themselves. The footage featuring a bug-eyed Jack "The Great White Hope" Johnson is especially revealing. ▶

Mad Little Island (1957-British) C-94m.

**½ D: Michael Relph. Jeannie Carson, Donald Sinden, Roland Culver, Noel Purcell, Ian Hunter, Duncan MacRae, Catherine Lacey, Jean Cadell, Gordon Jackson. Sequel to TIGHT LITTLE ISLAND finds that little Scottish isle's tranquility disturbed again, this time by imminent installation of missile base. Not up to its predecessor, but on its own terms, decent enough. Original title: ROCKETS GALORE!

Mad Love (1935) 70m. *** D: Karl Freund. Peter Lorre, Frances Drake, Colin Clive, Ted Healy, Sara Haden, Edward Brophy, Keye Luke. Famous *Hands of Orlac* story refitted for Lorre as mad Paris surgeon in love with married Drake. He agrees to operate on her pianist husband's injured hands, with disastrous results. Stylishly directed by legendary cameraman Freund; only debit is unwelcome comedy relief by Healy.▼●◗

Mad Magician, The (1954) 72m. **½ D: John Brahm. Vincent Price, Mary Murphy, Patrick O'Neal, Eva Gabor, John Emery, Lenita Lane, Donald Randolph, Jay Novello. Amusing knockoff of HOUSE OF WAX, made by many of the same hands (and also shot in 3-D). This time Price is an illusionist, but otherwise the plots are pretty much alike. Much better than it has any right to be; Brahm, no stranger to Victorian-era melodrama, keeps it moving swiftly, with Lane upstaging the stars as a nosy crime novelist. Lyle Talbot appears unbilled as a program hawker.◗

Mad Miss Manton, The (1938) 80m. **½ D: Leigh Jason. Barbara Stanwyck, Henry Fonda, Sam Levene, Frances Mercer, Stanley Ridges, Vicki Lester, Whitney Bourne, Hattie McDaniel, Penny Singleton, Grady Sutton. Socialite Stanwyck involves her friends in murder mystery; trivial but enjoyable film, with sleuthing and slapstick combined.▼●◗

Mad Monster, The (1942) 72m. *½ D: Sam Newfield. Johnny Downs, George Zucco, Anne Nagel, Glenn Strange, Sarah Padden, Gordon DeMain. Dull, low-budget mad-scientist thriller drags heavy feet for unintended laughs. Zucco effortlessly steals show as crazed doctor changing man into beast in bargain-basement WOLF MAN knockoff.▼◗

Madonna of the Seven Moons (1946-British) 105m. *** D: Arthur Crabtree. Phyllis Calvert, Stewart Granger, Patricia Roc, Jean Kent, John Stuart, Peter Glenville. Calvert is pushed in two directions because of strange gypsy curse; she is wife, mother, and mistress at same time. Taut melodrama, may be considered camp in some circles.◗

Madonna's Secret, The (1946) 79m. ** D: William Thiele. Francis Lederer, Gail Patrick, Ann Rutherford, Linda Stirling, John Litel. OK whodunit involving hunt for killer of artist's model.

Mad Wednesday SEE: **Sin of Harold Diddlebock, The**

Mäedchen in Uniform (1931-German) 98m. ***½ D: Leontine Sagan. Dorothea Wieck, Hertha Thiele, Emilia Unda, Hedwig Schlichter, Ellen Schwannecke. Winning drama about sensitive student Thiele forming lesbian relationship with teacher Wieck in oppressive girls boarding school. Simply, sympathetically handled by Sagan; this highly acclaimed and once-controversial film was based on a novel written by a woman, Christa Winsloe, who also co-scripted. Beware of edited prints. Title sometimes is listed as MAØDCHEN IN UNIFORM. Remade in 1958.▼

Mäedchen in Uniform (1958-German) C-91m. **½ D: Geza von Radvanyi. Lilli Palmer, Romy Schneider, Christine Kaufmann, Therese Giehse. Rather talky story of girls' school and one particularly sensitive youngster (Schneider) who is attracted to her teacher (Palmer). Remake of famous 1931 movie is a shade above average.◗

Mafioso (1962-Italian) 99m. *** D: Alberto Lattuada. Alberto Sordi, Norma Bengell, Gabriella Conti, Ugo Attanasio, Cinzia Bruno, Katiusca Piretti, Armando Tine. Sicilian Sordi has a good job in Milan and is about to embark on his first vacation in years: a visit home to show off his Northern Italian wife and children to his skeptical family and friends. He soon learns that the village Mafia don, now a grandfatherly figure, has lost none of his power. You'll never guess where this story is headed! Fascinating blend of comedy and drama and a tailor-made vehicle for Sordi, who personifies the Italian working-class hero. Released in the U.S. in 1964; a restored version was released theatrically in 2007.◗

Maggie, The SEE: **High and Dry**

Magic Bow, The (1947-British) 105m. **½ D: Bernard Knowles. Stewart Granger, Phyllis Calvert, Jean Kent, Dennis Price, Cecil Parker. As usual, music overshadows weak plot in biography of violinist Paganini.▼

Magic Box, The (1951-British) C-103m. **** D: John Boulting. Robert Donat, Maria Schell, Margaret Johnston, Robert Beatty; guests Laurence Olivier, Michael Redgrave, Eric Portman, Glynis Johns, Emlyn Williams, Richard Attenborough, Stanley Holloway, Margaret Rutherford, Peter Ustinov, Bessie Love, Cecil Parker, etc. Practically every British star appears in this superb biography of William Friese-Greene, the forgotten inventor of movies. Beautifully done; one scene where Donat perfects the invention, pulling in a cop off the street (Olivier) to see it, is a gem.

Magic Boy (1959) C-83m. *** D: Taiji Yabushita, Akira Daikuhara. Wonderfully designed widescreen anime about a boy living in the forest with his animal friends who embarks on a quest to see a wizard to master his magical powers and defeat an evil witch. Delightful and exciting adventure was the first Japanese animated feature to be shown in the U.S. when it was released here in 1961. Toeiscope. ◗

Magic Carpet, The (1951) C-84m. ** D: Lew Landers. Lucille Ball, John Agar, Patricia Medina, George Tobias, Raymond Burr, Gregory Gaye, Rick Vallin, William Fawcett. Run-of-the-mill Arabian Nights tale with Agar attempting to reclaim the throne that was stolen from him. Of note only for Ball's presence as a villainous princess. ◗

Magic Face, The (1951) 89m. ** D: Frank Tuttle. Luther Adler, Patricia Knight, William L. Shirer, Ilka Windish. Low-key study of impersonator who murders Hitler and assumes his place; Adler rises above material.

Magic Fire (1956) C-95m. ** D: William Dieterle. Yvonne De Carlo, Carlos Thompson, Rita Gam, Valentina Cortese, Alan Badel. Uninspired musical biography of 19th-century German composer Richard Wagner.

Magician, The (1958-Swedish) 102m. *** D: Ingmar Bergman. Max von Sydow, Ingrid Thulin, Gunnar Bjornstrand, Naima Wifstrand, Bibi Andersson, Erland Josephson. Complex, provocative account of Albert Emanuel Vogler (von Sydow), a 19th-century hypnotist-magician who has studied with Mesmer but finds himself debt-ridden and charged with blasphemy. A thoughtful (and too-long underrated) portrait of a man who is part-faker, part-genius. ▼◗

Magic Sword, The (1962) C-80m. **½ D: Bert I. Gordon. Basil Rathbone, Estelle Winwood, Gary Lockwood, Anne Helm, Liam Sullivan, Jacques Gallo. Entertaining, often (unintentionally) hilarious adventure. Young knight Lockwood sets out to rescue beautiful princess Helm, who's been kidnapped by evil sorcerer Rathbone. In their better moments, Lockwood and Helm seem like refugees from a Beach Party movie; Rathbone and Winwood offer knowingly hammy performances. ▼◗

Magic Town (1947) 103m. *** D: William Wellman. James Stewart, Jane Wyman, Kent Smith, Regis Toomey, Donald Meek. Intriguing satire of pollster Stewart finding perfect average American town, which ruins itself when people are told his discovery. Doesn't always hit bull's-eye but remains engrossing throughout; written by Frank Capra's frequent scripter, Robert Riskin. Also shown in computer-colored version. ▼◗

Magnetic Monster, The (1953) 76m. **½ D: Curt Siodmak. Richard Carlson, King Donovan, Jean Byron, Byron Foulger. Magnetic isotope is stolen, grows in size and creates havoc; stunning climax features special effects lifted from 1930s German film GOLD. ▼◗

Magnificent Ambersons, The (1942) 88m. **** D: Orson Welles. Tim Holt, Joseph Cotten, Dolores Costello, Anne Baxter, Agnes Moorehead, Ray Collins, Richard Bennett, Erskine Sanford. Brilliant drama from Booth Tarkington novel of family unwilling to change its way of life with the times; mother and son conflict over her lover. Welles' follow-up to CITIZEN KANE is equally exciting in its own way, though film was taken out of his hands, recut and reshot by others. Previously filmed in 1925 as PAMPERED YOUTH. Also shown in computer-colored version. Remade for cable TV in 2001. ▼◗

Magnificent Brute, The (1936) 80m. ** D: John G. Blystone. Victor McLaglen, Binnie Barnes, William Hall, Jean Dixon. Pertly acted love triangle, with McLaglen the roughneck blast furnace boss, involved in romance and stolen money.

Magnificent Doll (1946) 95m. ** D: Frank Borzage. Ginger Rogers, Burgess Meredith, David Niven, Horace (Stephen) McNally, Peggy Wood. Rogers just isn't right as Dolley Madison, and historical drama with Meredith as President Madison and Niven as Aaron Burr falls flat. ▼

Magnificent Dope, The (1942) 83m. *** D: Walter Lang. Henry Fonda, Lynn Bari, Don Ameche, Edward Everett Horton, Hobart Cavanaugh, Pierre Watkin. Entertaining comedy of hopeless hayseed Fonda who shows up sharper Ameche in big city; Bari is the girl between them. ▼◗

Magnificent Fraud, The (1939) 78m. **½ D: Robert Florey. Akim Tamiroff, Lloyd Nolan, Patricia Morison, Mary Boland, George Zucco, Steffi Duna, Robert Warwick. Actor who's a master of disguise is recruited to take the place of a recently assassinated Latin American dictator. Good premise is hampered by an unconvincing romantic subplot involving gangster Nolan. Still, it's a great showcase for Tamiroff. Supposedly this was the inspiration for MOON OVER PARADOR.

Magnificent Matador, The (1955) C-94m. **½ D: Budd Boetticher. Anthony Quinn, Maureen O'Hara, Manuel Rojas, Thomas Gomez, Richard Denning, Lola Albright. Another of director Boetticher's bullfighting films has Quinn an aging matador who re-examines his commitment to bullfighting, while protecting his young "protégé" (Rojas) and being romanced by American O'Hara. CinemaScope. ▼

Magnificent Obsession (1935) 101m. *** D: John M. Stahl. Irene Dunne, Robert Taylor, Betty Furness, Charles Butterworth, Sara Haden, Ralph Morgan, Arthur Treacher. Dated but sincere adaptation of Lloyd Douglas' story about drunken playboy who mends his ways, becomes respected surgeon in order to restore the eyesight of a woman (Dunne) he blinded in an auto accident. Soap opera gave Taylor his first important lead—and made him a star. Original running time was 112m. Remade in 1954.▶

Magnificent Obsession (1954) **C-108m.** *** D: Douglas Sirk. Jane Wyman, Rock Hudson, Barbara Rush, Otto Kruger, Agnes Moorehead, Gregg Palmer. Director Sirk pulls out all the stops in this baroque, melodramatic remake of 1935 film which remains faithful to original story. Like its predecessor, a smash hit which (once again) boosted its male lead to stardom.▼▶

Magnificent Rebel, The (1962) **C-95m.** **½ D: Georg Tressler. Karl Boehm, Ernst Nadhering, Ivan Desny, Gabriele Porks. Boehm makes an intense Beethoven in this rather serious Disney film, not really for kids at all. Great musical sequences and very good German location photography, though romantic angle of story never really compels attention. Released theatrically in Europe, shown in U.S. as two-part Disney TV show.▶

Magnificent Roughnecks (1956) 73m. BOMB D: Sherman A. Rose. Jack Carson, Mickey Rooney, Nancy Gates, Jeff Donnell. Allied Artists disaster with the two stars as partners trying to wildcat oilfields.

Magnificent Seven, The (1960) **C-126m.** ***½ D: John Sturges. Yul Brynner, Steve McQueen, Eli Wallach, Horst Buchholz, James Coburn, Charles Bronson, Robert Vaughn, Brad Dexter. Enduringly popular Western remake of SEVEN SAMURAI, about paid gunslingers who try to rout the bandits who are devastating a small Mexican town. Great cast of stars-to-be; memorable Elmer Bernstein score. Followed by three sequels, starting with RETURN OF THE SEVEN, and a TV series. Remade as a TVM in 1998. Panavision.▼▶●

Magnificent Sinner (1959-French) **C-97m.** ** D: Robert Siodmak. Romy Schneider, Curt Jurgens, Pierre Blanchar, Monique Melinand. Lackluster proceedings of Schneider as mistress to Russian Czar, involved in court intrigue. Remake of 1938 French film KATIA with Danielle Darrieux.

Magnificent Yankee, The (1950) 89m. *** D: John Sturges. Louis Calhern, Ann Harding, Eduard Franz, James Lydon, Philip Ober, Richard Anderson, Hayden Rorke, John Hamilton. Genteel, entertaining saga of Oliver Wendell Holmes and his devoted wife, spanning many decades from the day they arrive in Washington, D.C., in 1902 so he may join the Supreme Court. A pleasure from start to finish, with Calhern recreating his triumphant Broadway role.▼▶

Maid in Paris (1956-French) 84m. ** D: Pierre Gaspard-Huit. Dany Robin, Daniel Gélin, Marie Daëms, Tilda Thamar. Bland story of country girl Robin heading to the City of Light in search of romance.

Maid of Salem (1937) 86m. *** D: Frank Lloyd. Claudette Colbert, Fred MacMurray, Louise Dresser, Gale Sondergaard, Beulah Bondi, Bonita Granville, Virginia Weidler,

Donald Meek, Harvey Stephens, Edward Ellis, Mme. Sul-te-wan. Colonial witch-hunting era is backdrop for fine drama with many similarities to Arthur Miller's *The Crucible* (minus the philosophy).▶

Maid's Night Out (1938) 64m. ** D: Ben Holmes. Joan Fontaine, Allan Lane, Hedda Hopper, George Irving, William Brisbane, Billy Gilbert, Cecil Kellaway. On a wager, Lane (who wants to study the home life of fish) delivers milk for his father's company and mistakes debutante Fontaine for a servant. Inane screwball comedy with one clever bit: Hopper's in the cast, and one of Lane's projects involves a fish that eats its young—named Louella! Look for Jack Carson as a roller coaster operator. ▼

Mailbag Robbery (1957-British) 70m. ** D: Compton Bennett. Lee Patterson, Kay Callard, Alan Gifford, Kerry Jordan. Title explains full contents of programmer. Original British title: THE FLYING SCOT. ▼

Mail Order Bride (1964) **C-83m.** **½ D: Burt Kennedy. Buddy Ebsen, Keir Dullea, Lois Nettleton, Warren Oates, Marie Windsor, Barbara Luna. Harmless—and plotless—Western with rambunctious young rancher Dullea marrying widow Nettleton to satisfy his late father's old friend (Ebsen). Climactic shoot-out is virtual duplicate of the one in RIDE THE HIGH COUNTRY. Panavision.▶

Main Attraction, The (1962) **C-90m.** *½ D: Daniel Petrie. Pat Boone, Mai Zetterling, Nancy Kwan, Yvonne Mitchell, Kieron Moore. Boone is fatally out of his depth as a guitar-playing drifter in Europe who causes romantic complications when he falls in with a traveling circus. Filmed in England. Metroscope.

Main Street After Dark (1944) 57m. **½ D: Edward L. Cahn. Edward Arnold, Audrey Totter, Dan Duryea, Hume Cronyn, Selena Royle. Offbeat drama of family pickpocket gang put out of business by civic clean-up campaign.

Main Street to Broadway (1953) 102m. **½ D: Tay Garnett. Tom Morton, Mary Murphy, Clinton Sundberg, Rosemary De-Camp, guest stars Ethel Barrymore, Lionel Barrymore, Shirley Booth, Rex Harrison, Lilli Palmer, Helen Hayes, Henry Fonda, Tallulah Bankhead, Mary Martin, others. Very slight story of romance, struggle, and success on the Great White Way; chief interest is large cast of Broadway stars in cameo appearances. Rodgers & Hammerstein appear on camera and contribute a song, "There's Music in You."▼

Maisie *Maisie* was a middling series of ten MGM features made between 1939 and 1947, starring lively Ann Sothern as a brassy showgirl involved in a progression of topical if trivial situations encompassing the changing role of American women during WW2 America. The series never rose above the B category; all were filmed in black and white and ran about 85 minutes. Production values were too often static, utilizing rear projection and indoor sets to establish the varied locales of the episodes. The *Maisie* series relied almost exclusively on Miss Sothern's vivacious personality to carry the slight tales of the conventional tough-girl-with-a-heart-of-gold. Her costars were competent contract players such as Robert Sterling (Sothern's then-husband), Lew Ayres, John Hodiak, and George Murphy. Unlike the Andy Hardy series, few fledgling starlets appeared in these features, although guests like Red Skelton helped out from time to time. In general the series lacked a basic continuity and flavor; and earlier entries such as MAISIE and CONGO MAISIE, while no classics, had more punch than later efforts such as UNDERCOVER MAISIE.

MAISIE

Maisie (1939)
Congo Maisie (1940)
Gold Rush Maisie (1940)
Maisie Was a Lady (1941)
Ringside Maisie (1941)
Maisie Gets Her Man (1942)
Swing Shift Maisie (1943)
Maisie Goes to Reno (1944)
Up Goes Maisie (1946)
Undercover Maisie (1947)

Maisie (1939) **74m.** ****½** D: Edwin L. Marin. Ann Sothern, Robert Young, Ruth Hussey, Ian Hunter, Anthony Allan (John Hubbard), Cliff Edwards, George Tobias. First entry in the series is a mild romantic comedy, centering on the sassy showgirl's adventures on a Wyoming ranch where she falls for foreman Young and clears him of a murder charge. ▶

Maisie Gets Her Man (1942) **85m.** ****½** D: Roy Del Ruth. Ann Sothern, Red Skelton, Leo Gorcey, Pamela Blake, Allen Jenkins, Donald Meek, Walter Catlett, Fritz Feld, Rags Ragland, Frank Jenks. Maisie joins a theatrical agency in Chicago and starts a stage act with hick Skelton. Amusing entry brightened by a strong supporting cast of veteran comics. ▶

Maisie Goes to Reno (1944) **90m.** ****½** D: Harry Beaumont. Ann Sothern, John Hodiak, Tom Drake, Marta Linden, Paul Cavanagh, Ava Gardner, Bernard Nedell, Donald Meek. OK series entry with Maisie taking a trip to Reno where she has her hands full intervening in the divorce of a soldier and his wife (a young Gardner). ▶

Maisie Was a Lady (1941) **79m.** ****½** D: Edwin L. Marin. Ann Sothern, Lew Ayres, Maureen O'Sullivan, C. Aubrey Smith, Edward Ashley, Joan Perry, Paul Cavanagh. Maisie gets a job as maid to a family of bluebloods and straightens out their sorry personal lives in this well-cast entry with Ayres taking a break from *Dr. Kildare.* ▶

Major and the Minor, The (1942) **100m.** *****½** D: Billy Wilder. Ginger Rogers, Ray Milland, Rita Johnson, Robert Benchley, Diana Lynn, Frankie Thomas, Jr., Charles Smith, Larry Nunn, Norma Varden. Memorable comedy of working girl Rogers disguised as 12-year-old to save train fare, becoming involved with Milland's military school. Wilder's first directorial effort in Hollywood (written with Charles Brackett) is still amusing. Story suggested by Edward Childs Carpenter's play *Connie Goes Home* and *Saturday Evening Post* story "Sunny Goes Home" by Fannie Kilbourne. That's Ginger's real-life mom playing her mother near the end of the film. Remade as YOU'RE NEVER TOO YOUNG. ▼▶

Major Barbara (1941-British) **121m.** ******** D: Gabriel Pascal. Wendy Hiller, Rex Harrison, Robert Morley, Robert Newton, Emlyn Williams, Sybil Thorndike, Deborah Kerr, David Tree, Stanley Holloway. Topnotch adaptation of Shaw play about wealthy girl who joins Salvation Army; Harrison is a professor who woos her. Excellent cast in intelligent comedy (scripted by Anatole de Grunwald and Shaw), Kerr's film debut. Also shown at 115m. ▼▶

Major Dundee (1965) **C-124m.** ****½** D: Sam Peckinpah. Charlton Heston, Richard Harris, Jim Hutton, James Coburn, Michael Anderson, Jr., Senta Berger, Mario Adorf, Brock Peters, Warren Oates, Slim Pickens, Ben Johnson, R.G. Armstrong, L.Q. Jones, Michael Pate, Dub Taylor. Obsessive Union officer Heston leads a ragtag brigade (including recently sprung Confederate prisoner Harris) to Mexico to rescue three children who've been kidnapped by Apaches. Sweeping, violent, epic-scale Western with an Ahab-like protagonist was severely cut prior to release; Peckinpah disowned the film and its score. In 2005 it was reconstituted to 136m., 6m. shy of its intended length, with a supportive new score by Christopher Caliendo. This version is more meaningful if no less flawed. Panavision. ▼◐▶

Majority of One, A (1962) **C-153m.** ****½** D: Mervyn LeRoy. Rosalind Russell, Alec Guinness, Ray Danton, Madlyn Rhue, Mae Questel. Compared to Broadway play, this is overblown, overacted account of Jewish matron Russell falling in love with Japanese widower Guinness. Written by Leonard Spiegelgass. ▼▶

Make a Wish (1937) **76m.** ****** D: Kurt Neumann. Basil Rathbone, Bobby Breen, Marion Claire, Ralph Forbes, Henry Armetta, Leon Errol, Donald Meek, Billy Lee. Inconsequential musical about a summer camp for boys where singing prodigy Breen encounters composer Rathbone. Supporting comedians offer the film's best moments. ▼

Make Haste to Live (1954) **90m.** ****½** D: William A. Seiter. Dorothy McGuire, Stephen McNally, Mary Murphy, Edgar Buchanan, John Howard, Carolyn Jones. McGuire gives believable performance as woman faced with criminal husband who's returned to seek vengeance.▼

Make Me an Offer (1955-British) **C-88m.** ****½** D: Cyril Frankel. Peter Finch, Adrienne Corri, Rosalie Crutchley, Finlay Currie. Satisfactory highbrow shenanigans in the antique-buying field, with Finch after priceless vase.▼

Make Me a Star (1932) **86m.** ****** D: William Beaudine. Joan Blondell, Stuart Erwin, ZaSu Pitts, Ben Turpin, Ruth Donnelly, Sam Hardy, Oscar Apfel. All the comedy has been drained from the George S. Kaufman–Marc Connelly play *Merton of the Movies* (based on Harry Leon Wilson's novel) about an earnest but clueless small-town sap who pursues his dream of becoming a movie actor in Hollywood. Of minor interest for fleeting cameos by Paramount stars Maurice Chevalier, Gary Cooper, Tallulah Bankhead, Clive Brook, Claudette Colbert, Fredric March, and Sylvia Sidney. Filmed before in 1924 and again in 1947 as MERTON OF THE MOVIES.❭

Make Mine Mink (1960-British) **100m.** ******* D: Robert Asher. Terry-Thomas, Athene Seyler, Hattie Jacques, Billie Whitelaw, Elspeth Duxbury, Raymond Huntley, Ron Moody, Jack Hedley, Kenneth Williams, Sidney Tafler. Former military man Terry-Thomas organizes unlikely band of fur thieves in this delightful British farce. Beware of shorter version on tape.▼❭

Make Mine Music (1946) **C-74m.** ****½** D: Joe Grant (production supervisor). Voices of Nelson Eddy, Dinah Shore, Jerry Colonna, The Andrews Sisters, Andy Russell, Sterling Holloway, and music by The Benny Goodman Quartet. Ten-part Walt Disney animated feature with such segments as "Peter and the Wolf," "Johnny Fedora and Alice Blue Bonnet," and "Casey at the Bat." At its worst when it tries to be "arty," and at its best when it offers bright, original pieces like "The Whale Who Wanted to Sing at the Met," and the dazzling Benny Goodman number "After You've Gone." A mixed bag, to be sure. Video version is missing "The Martins and the Coys" segment.▼❭

Make Way for a Lady (1936) **65m.** ****** D: David Burton. Herbert Marshall, Anne Shirley, Gertrude Michael, Margot Grahame, Clara Blandick, Frank Coghlan, Jr. Routine comedy of Shirley playing matchmaker for her widowed father Marshall; pleasant enough.

Make Way For Tomorrow (1937) **92m.** *****½** D: Leo McCarey. Victor Moore, Beulah Bondi, Fay Bainter, Thomas Mitchell, Porter Hall, Barbara Read, Louise Beavers. Sensitive film of elderly couple in financial difficulty, shunted aside by their children, unwanted and unloved; shatteringly true, beautifully done. Screenplay by Vina Delmar, based on Josephine Lawrence's novel *The Years Are So Long* and a play adaptation by Helen and Nolan Leary.❭

Make Your Own Bed (1944) **82m.** ***½** D: Peter Godfrey. Jack Carson, Jane Wyman, Alan Hale, Irene Manning, George Tobias, Ricardo Cortez. Forced comedy of detective Carson disguised as butler, Wyman as maid, to get lowdown on racketeer.

Malaga (1960-British) **97m.** ****½** D: Laslo Benedek. Trevor Howard, Dorothy Dandridge, Edmund Purdom, Michael Hordern. Bizarre casting in routine robbery tale is primary diversion. Originally titled MOMENT OF DANGER.

Malaya (1949) **98m.** ****½** D: Richard Thorpe. Spencer Tracy, James Stewart, Valentina Cortese, Sydney Greenstreet. Routine WW2 melodrama set in the Pacific, about Allies' efforts to smuggle out rubber. Good cast let down by so-so script.▼❭

Male and Female (1919) **117m.** *****½** D: Cecil B. DeMille. Gloria Swanson, Thomas Meighan, Lila Lee, Theodore Roberts, Raymond Hatton, Mildred Reardon, Robert Cain, Bebe Daniels, Julia Faye. Swanson and Meighan are perfectly cast as a spoiled lady and her worldly-wise butler. Will their class differences evaporate when they, along with her snooty family, find themselves shipwrecked? Eloquent story is extremely well told, with Lee adorable as a scullery maid. This is the film in which Swanson takes her famously risqué rosewater bath. And what would a DeMille film be without a Babylonian fantasy sequence? Based on J. M. Barrie's *The Admirable Crichton*, which was previously filmed in 1918 and remade in 1957. ▼

Male Animal, The (1942) **101m.** *****½** D: Elliott Nugent. Henry Fonda, Olivia de Havilland, Joan Leslie, Jack Carson, Herbert Anderson, Don DeFore, Hattie McDaniel, Eugene Pallette. Intelligent, entertaining Elliott Nugent–James Thurber comedy of college professor Fonda defending his rights, while losing wife de Havilland to old flame Carson. Excellent performances in this fine, contemporary film, with spoof on typical football rallies a highlight. Remade as SHE'S WORKING HER WAY THROUGH COLLEGE.▼❭

Male Hunt (1964-French) **92m.** ******* D: Edouard Molinaro. Jean-Paul Belmondo, Jean-Claude Brialy, Catherine Deneuve, Francoise Dorleac, Marie Laforet. Spicy romp about trio of Frenchmen avoiding the clutches of marriage-minded women.

Malibu (1934) SEE: **Sequoia**

Malta Story (1953-British) **98m.** ****½** D: Brian Desmond Hurst. Alec Guinness, Jack Hawkins, Anthony Steel, Muriel Pavlow. On-location filming of this WW2 British-air-force-in-action yarn is sparked by underplayed acting. ▼◗

Maltese Falcon, The (1931) **80m.** *** D: Roy Del Ruth. Bebe Daniels, Ricardo Cortez, Dudley Digges, Robert Elliott, Thelma Todd, Una Merkel, Dwight Frye. First film version of Dashiell Hammett story is quite good, with Cortez more of a ladies' man than Bogart; otherwise very similar to later classic. Remade in 1936 (as SATAN MET A LADY) and 1941. ▼◗

Maltese Falcon, The (1941) **100m.** **** D: John Huston. Humphrey Bogart, Mary Astor, Peter Lorre, Sydney Greenstreet, Ward Bond, Gladys George, Barton MacLane, Elisha Cook, Jr., Lee Patrick, Jerome Cowan. Outstanding detective drama improves with each viewing; Bogey is Dashiell Hammett's "hero" Sam Spade, Astor his client, Lorre the evasive Joel Cairo, Greenstreet (in his talkie film debut) the Fat Man, and Cook the neurotic gunsel Wilmer. Huston's first directorial effort (which he also scripted) moves at lightning pace, with cameo by his father Walter Huston as Captain Jacobi. Previously filmed in 1931 and in 1936 (as SATAN MET A LADY). Also shown in computer-colored version. ▼◗◗

Mama Loves Papa (1945) **61m.** ** D: Frank R. Strayer. Leon Errol, Elisabeth Risdon, Edwin Maxwell, Emory Parnell, Charles Halton, Paul Harvey, Lawrence Tierney. Errol is a small-town nobody goaded by his social-climbing wife to get some ambition. He ends up being appointed park commissioner and exposes political corruption. Errol has to strain for laughs in routine RKO farce, a partial remake of a 1933 movie of the same name (with Charles Ruggles and Mary Boland).

Mambo (1954-U.S.-Italian) **94m.** **½ D: Robert Rossen. Silvana Mangano, Michael Rennie, Shelley Winters, Vittorio Gassman, Eduardo Ciannelli, Mary Clare, Katherine Dunham. Offbeat romance set in Venice; young saleswoman, her love life complicated by a penniless gambler and a sickly count, becomes a famous dancer. Strong cast keeps it watchable. Original Italian running time 107m. ▼

Mamele (1938-Polish) **100m.** **½ D: Joseph Green, Konrad Tom. Molly Picon, Edmund Zayenda, Max Bozyk, Gertrude Bullman, Simcha Fostel. Picon shines in this otherwise all-too-obvious Yiddish-language musical comedy as the youngest daughter of a widower who's forced to play Mama to the rest of her family. Based on a play which starred Picon over a decade earlier. The title's English-language translation is LITTLE MOTHER. ▼◗

Mamma Roma (1962-Italian) **110m.** ***½ D: Pier Paolo Pasolini. Anna Magnani, Ettore Garofolo, Franco Citti, Silvana Corsini, Luisa Orioli, Paolo Volponi. Magnani dominates the screen as the title character,

an earthy, larger-than-life woman attempting to abandon her career as a prostitute and enter the middle class. The scenario charts her complex relationship with (and high hopes for) her adolescent son, with whom she is reunited after many years. Pasolini scripted this fascinating, intensely involving drama, which is loaded with cinematic references; Mamma Roma would be the same character Magnani played in Rossellini's OPEN CITY, only older! Watch for Lamberto Maggiorani, the star of De Sica's BICYCLE THIEVES, in a small but pivotal role. Released theatrically in the U.S. in 1994. ▼◗

Mammy (1930) **84m.** ** D: Michael Curtiz. Al Jolson, Lois Moran, Louise Dresser, Lowell Sherman, Hobart Bosworth. Story of backstage shooting in a minstrel troupe is only tolerable during musical numbers; Jolson sings "Let Me Sing and I'm Happy," "To My Mammy," and "The Call of the South." Some sequences in two-color Technicolor. ◗◗

Mam'zelle Pigalle (1956-French) **C-77m.** ** D: Michel Boisrond. Brigitte Bardot, Jean Bretonniere, Françoise Fabian, Bernard Lancret, Mischa Auer. Dull doings with Bardot as a schoolgirl who pursues crooner Bretonniere and becomes mixed up with counterfeiters. Scripted by Boisrond and Roger Vadim. Retitled: NAUGHTY GIRL and THAT NAUGHTY GIRL. CinemaScope. ▼◗

Man About the House, A (1947-British) **83m.** **½ D: Leslie Arliss. Kieron Moore, Margaret Johnston, Dulcie Gray, Guy Middleton, Felix Aylmer. Murky drama of repressed Victorian sisters Johnston and Gray, who travel to the Italian villa they have inherited and contend with earthy but manipulative Moore. ▼◗

Man About Town (1939) **85m.** **½ D: Mark Sandrich. Jack Benny, Dorothy Lamour, Edward Arnold, Binnie Barnes, Phil Harris, Betty Grable, Monty Woolley, Eddie "Rochester" Anderson. Jack tries to crash London society; lively but undistinguished musical.

Man About Town (1947-French-U.S.) **89m.** ** D: René Clair. Maurice Chevalier, Francois Perier, Marcelle Derrien, Dany Robin, Raymond Cordy, Paul Olivier. Minor Clair farce with Chevalier a middle-aged film director in 1906 Paris who takes on sensitive young Derrien as his protégée. Originally titled LE SILENCE EST D'OR, running 106m. U.S. version is neither dubbed nor subtitled: Chevalier narrates the goings-on on the soundtrack— which doesn't quite work. It also includes a special prologue, filmed under the supervision of Robert Pirosh, in which Chevalier sings "Place Pigalle."

Man Afraid (1957) **84m.** **½ D: Harry Keller. George Nader, Phyllis Thaxter, Tim Hovey, Reta Shaw, Martin Milner. Well-acted story of clergyman Nader protecting family against father of boy he killed in self-defense. CinemaScope.

Man Alive (1945) **70m. **½ D: Ray Enright. Pat O'Brien, Adolphe Menjou, Ellen Drew, Rudy Vallee, Fortunio Bonanova, Joseph Crehan, Jonathan Hale, Minna Gombell, Jason Robards, Sr. Amusing comedy of O'Brien, supposedly dead, playing ghost to scare away wife's new love interest; moves along at brisk pace.

Man Alone, A (1955) **C-96m. **½ D: Ray Milland. Ray Milland, Mary Murphy, Ward Bond, Raymond Burr, Lee Van Cleef. Intelligent oater of fugitive from lynch mob (Milland) hiding with sheriff's daughter (Murphy) in small town. Milland's first directorial attempt isn't bad. ▼

Man and the Monster, The (1959-Mexican) **78m. **½ D: Rafael Baledón. Abel Salazar, Enrique Rambal, Martha Roth, Ofelia Guilmáin, María Roth, Carlos Suárez. Rambal, the greatest pianist in the world, has hidden himself away; we learn that he was a failure who sold his soul to the devil to be a virtuoso, but whenever he plays he becomes a werewolf-like monster. Aimed at an adult audience, this mixes horror and music in a novel way, but despite its Gothic style it's hampered by monster makeup that's unintentionally funny (and poor dubbing as well). ▶

Man Bait (1952-U.S.-British) **78m. **½ D: Terence Fisher. George Brent, Marguerite Chapman, Diana Dors, Raymond Huntley, Peter Reynolds. British-made suspense programmer has Brent a book dealer entangled in blackmail and murder. British title: THE LAST PAGE. ▼▶

Man Beast (1955) **72m. BOMB** D: Jerry Warren. Rock Madison, Virginia Maynor, George Skaff, Lloyd Nelson, Tom Maruzzi. An expedition goes in search of the abominable snowman but comes up with this turkey instead. Star "Rock Madison" is nonexistent; director Warren simply made up a name that would look good in publicity! ▼▶

Man Behind the Gun, The (1952) **C-82m. ** D: Felix E. Feist. Randolph Scott, Patrice Wymore, Philip Carey, Dick Wesson, Lina Romay. Army man Scott goes undercover to investigate southern California secessionist movement in 1850s. Formula stuff. ▶

Man Behind the Mask, The (1936-British) **79m. **½ D: Michael Powell. Hugh Williams, Jane Baxter, Maurice Schwartz, Donald Calthrop, Henry Oscar, Peter Gawthorne, Kitty Kelly. Schwartz is a megalomaniacal astronomer, holed up in a futuristic, art deco mansion with a giant telescope, who kidnaps the daughter of a lord to serve his evil plans. Like THE 39 STEPS, film alternates serious whodunit elements with sly humor, but it eventually goes overboard in its outlandishness.

Man Betrayed, A (1941) **83m. ** D: John

H. Auer. John Wayne, Frances Dee, Edward Ellis, Wallace Ford, Ward Bond, Harold Huber, Alexander Granach. Country lawyer crusades against father of girlfriend to prove that he's crooked politician. Minor melodrama with the Duke in one of his oddest roles. Retitled: WHEEL OF FORTUNE. ▼▶

Man Between, The (1953-British) **101m. *** D: Carol Reed. James Mason, Claire Bloom, Hildegarde Neff, Geoffrey Toone, Aribert Waescher (Wäscher), Ernst Schroeder (Schröder). Naïve Londoner Bloom visits her brother and sister-in-law in post-WW2 Berlin and becomes involved with worldly, mysterious Mason. Taut, moody, well-acted drama benefits from location filming.

Man Called Peter, A (1955) **C-119m. *** D: Henry Koster. Richard Todd, Jean Peters, Marjorie Rambeau, Doris Lloyd, Emmett Lynn. Moving account of Scotsman Peter Marshall who became clergyman and U.S. Senate chaplain; sensitively played by Todd, with fine supporting cast. CinemaScope. ▼▶

Manchurian Candidate, The (1962) **126m. ***½ D: John Frankenheimer. Frank Sinatra, Laurence Harvey, Janet Leigh, Angela Lansbury, Henry Silva, James Gregory, John McGiver, Leslie Parrish, Khigh Dhiegh. Tingling political paranoia thriller about strange aftermath of a Korean war hero's decoration and his mother's machinations to promote her Joseph McCarthy–like husband's career. Harrowing presentation of Richard Condon story (adapted by George Axelrod). Score by David Amram. Rereleased theatrically in 1987; remade in 2004. ▼▶

Mandalay (1934) **65m. ** D: Michael Curtiz. Kay Francis, Ricardo Cortez, Lyle Talbot, Warner Oland, Rafaela Ottiano, Ruth Donnelly. Abandoned in Burma by her gun-runner boyfriend, Russian girl Francis is forced to become notorious cafe hostess Spot White (who "should be called Spot Cash," according to one observer); reformation comes hard. Shirley Temple is supposed to be in this film, but *we* can't find her. ▶

Mandarin Mystery, The (1936) **63m. *½ D: Ralph Staub. Eddie Quillan, Charlotte Henry, Rita La Roy, Wade Boteler, Franklin Pangborn, George Irving. Famous sleuth Ellery Queen solves locked-room murder puzzle and recovers stolen stamp worth $50,000. Hopelessly muddled script and fatal miscasting of diminutive Quillan as EQ sabotages this low-budget mystery. TV version cut to 54m. ▼▶

Mandy SEE: **Crash of Silence**

Man-Eater of Kumaon (1948) **79m. **½ D: Byron Haskin. Sabu, Wendell Corey, Joanne Page, Morris Carnovsky, Argentina Brunetti. Good adventure tale of hunter determined to kill deadly tiger on the loose.

Man Escaped, A (1956-French) **99m. ***½ D: Robert Bresson. François Leterrier,

[424]

Charles Le Clainche, Maurice Beerblock, Roland Monod, Jacques Ertaud. Spellbinding drama about French resistance fighter Leterrier, who is jailed by the Gestapo during WW2 and condemned to die. Bresson masterfully explores the character's inner turmoil and struggle to maintain his humanity under the most trying conditions. The director scripted, from a memoir by André Devigny. ▼)

Manfish (1956) **C-76m.** ** D: W. Lee Wilder. John Bromfield, Lon Chaney (Jr.), Victor Jory, Barbara Nichols. Variation of Edgar Allan Poe stories "The Gold-Bug" and "The Tell-Tale Heart"; mild account of treasure hunt in Jamaica. ▼)

Man from Beyond, The (1922) **68m.** ** D: Burton L. King. Harry Houdini, Arthur Maude, Albert Tavernier, Erwin Connelly, Frank Montgomery, Luis Alberni, Yale Benner, Jane Connelly, Nita Naldi. Survivors of an arctic exhibition come upon a ship that's been missing for a century, as well as a man (Houdini) who is frozen in ice. Incredibly, he is still alive. How is he linked to a young woman in the present who is about to wed? Potentially provocative tale touches on ideas relating to reincarnation, but the result is stiff and muddled (despite some eye-opening footage of an imperiled Houdini at Niagara Falls). Of interest solely for the presence of Houdini, the legendary escape artist, in his best-known feature. He also scripted and produced. Available in various versions and with different running times; the most viewable is the one preserved by the Library of Congress. ▼)

Man From Bitter Ridge, The (1955) **C-80m.** **½ D: Jack Arnold. Lex Barker, Mara Corday, Stephen McNally, Trevor Bardette. Peppy oater of Barker tracking down outlaws by tying in with local banker.

Man From Button Willow, The (1965) **C-84m.** ** D: David Detiege. Cartoon Western featuring the voices of Dale Robertson, Edgar Buchanan, Howard Keel, Herschel Bernardi, Ross Martin and others is only for small kiddies; story deals with America's first undercover agent in 1869 who prevents crooks from forcing settlers to get rid of their land. ▼)

Man from Cairo, The (1953-Italian-British-U.S.) **81m.** ** D: Ray Enright. George Raft, Gianna Maria Canale, Massimo Serato, Alfredo Varelli, Mino Doro, Irene Papas. Disappointing mishmash in which Raft finds himself in Algiers, where he becomes immersed in a hunt for a cache of gold. ▼)

Man From Cheyenne (1942) **60m.** *** D: Joseph Kane. Roy Rogers, George "Gabby" Hayes, Sally Payne, Lynne Carver, William Haade, James Seay, Gale Storm, Sons of the Pioneers. Roy tries to get the goods on a cattle-rustling gang and discovers that the unlikely

ringleader is pretty, flirtatious Carver. Unusually good screenplay by Winston Miller, who went on to work on such A Westerns as MY DARLING CLEMENTINE. ▼)

Man From Colorado, The (1948) **C-99m.** *** D: Henry Levin. Glenn Ford, William Holden, Ellen Drew, Ray Collins, Edgar Buchanan. Unusual Western of brutal Ford appointed Federal judge, taking tyrannical hold of the territory. ▼)

Man From Dakota, The (1940) **75m.** **½ D: Leslie Fenton. Wallace Beery, John Howard, Dolores Del Rio, Donald Meek, Robert Barrat. Above-average Beery vehicle set in Civil War times, with glamorous Del Rio helping him and Howard, Union spies, cross Confederate lines.

Man From Del Rio (1956) **82m.** ** D: Harry Horner. Anthony Quinn, Katy Jurado, Peter Whitney, Douglas Fowley, John Larch, Whit Bissell. Dank Western of Mexican gunslinger Quinn saving a town from outlaws.)

Man From Down Under, The (1943) **103m.** **½ D: Robert Z. Leonard. Charles Laughton, Binnie Barnes, Richard Carlson, Donna Reed, Christopher Severn, Clyde Cook. Overblown, overplotted vehicle for Laughton, who's delightful as a bluff, bragging Aussie who raises two French orphans from WW1 as his own. Look for young Peter Lawford as an Australian soldier toward the end of the film.

Man From Frisco, The (1944) **91m.** **½ D: Robert Florey. Michael O'Shea, Anne Shirley, Dan Duryea, Gene Lockhart, Stephanie Bachelor, Ray Walker. O'Shea is pushy shipbuilding genius who meets resistance from residents of small town where he wants to build a new plant. Fairly entertaining action hokum with a little too much romance.

Man From Galveston, The (1963) **57m.** ** D: William Conrad. Jeffrey Hunter, Preston Foster, James Coburn, Joanna Moore, Edward Andrews, Kevin Hagen, Martin West, Ed Nelson. Unsatisfying little Western with lawyer Hunter defending ex-girlfriend Moore on a murder charge in a frontier town.)

Man from God's Country (1958) **C-72m.** ** D: Paul Landres. George Montgomery, Randy Stuart, Gregg Barton, Kim Charney, Susan Cummings, James Griffith, House Peters, Jr., Phillip Terry. Former sheriff Montgomery moves to Montana to join an old friend, only to find that he and everyone else in the community is in the grip of a power-hungry businessman who's fighting the railroad. Humdrum Western programmer.)

Man From Laramie, The (1955) **C-104m.** *** D: Anthony Mann. James Stewart, Arthur Kennedy, Donald Crisp, Cathy O'Donnell, Alex Nicol, Aline MacMahon, Wallace Ford. Taut action tale of revenge, with Stewart seeking those who killed his brother. CinemaScope. ▼❱

Man From Monterey, The (1933) 57m. *½ D: Mack V. Wright. John Wayne, Ruth Hall, Luis Alberni, Donald Reed, Francis Ford, Nina Quartaro. U.S. military officer Wayne brandishes sword and aids 1848 Monterey locals trying to safeguard Spanish land-grant homes from a swindler. Pretty stiff, short on action. The last of six in Wayne's series of Ken Maynard remakes for Warner Bros. ▼❱

Man From Music Mountain, The (1938) 58m. ** D: Joseph Kane. Gene Autry, Smiley Burnette, Carol Hughes, Sally Payne, Ivan Miller, Ed Cassidy, Lew Kelly, Howard Chase, Polly Jenkins and Her Plowboys. Gene and pal Smiley must foil swindlers who are selling worthless ghost-town land with the promise of water and power to come. Mediocre film features newsreel footage of actual Boulder Dam opening in 1936. Not to be confused with the same-named Roy Rogers movie. ▼❱

Man From Music Mountain (1943) 71m. ** D: Joseph Kane. Roy Rogers, Ruth Terry, Paul Kelly, Ann Gillis, George Cleveland, Pat Brady, Paul Harvey, Jay Novello, Hal Taliaferro, Bob Nolan and the Sons of the Pioneers. Roy returns to his hometown and investigates the murder of an old friend while causing sparks between two sisters. Average Rogers Western with good finale; Pat Brady got elevated here to comic foil. Renamed TEXAS LEGIONNAIRES for TV so as not to be confused with the same-named Autry movie. ▼❱

Man From Oklahoma, The (1945) 68m. **½ D: Frank McDonald. Roy Rogers, George "Gabby" Hayes, Dale Evans, Sons of the Pioneers, Roger Pryor, Arthur Loft, Maude Eburne. Roy and the Sons get involved in a feud between Gabby and a rival rancher who happens to be Dale's grandmother (Eburne). One of Roy's bigger-budgeted mid-1940s vehicles with a greater emphasis on musical numbers still offers a wild-and-woolly wagon race/land rush scene. ❱

Man From Planet X, The (1951) 70m. **½ D: Edgar G. Ulmer. Robert Clarke, Margaret Field, Raymond Bond, William Schallert. Scottish Highlands are visited by alien from wandering planet; at first he is benign, but evil designs of Schallert turn him against human race. Extremely cheap, but atmospheric; script is stilted but story is strong and somewhat unusual. ▼❍❱

Man From Tangier SEE: **Thunder Over Tangier**

Man From the Alamo, The (1953) C-79m. *** D: Budd Boetticher. Glenn Ford, Julia (Julie) Adams, Chill Wills, Hugh O'Brian, Victor Jory, Neville Brand, Jeanne Cooper, Dennis Weaver. Ford leaves the Alamo to protect his family and others but is branded a coward and is forced to prove his hero-

ism while battling lawless Jory. Typically offbeat Boetticher Western, well acted and exciting. ▼❱

Man from the Diner's Club, The (1963) 90m. ** D: Frank Tashlin. Danny Kaye, Martha Hyer, Cara Williams, Telly Savalas, George Kennedy, Ann Morgan Guilbert. Labored slapstick comedy about a bungling credit-card company clerk who inadvertently OKs an account for gangster Savalas. Look for Harry Dean Stanton as a beatnik. Cowritten by Bill (William Peter) Blatty. Title song sung (and cowritten) by Steve Lawrence.

Man From Utah, The (1934) 55m. ** D: Robert N. Bradbury. John Wayne, Polly Ann Young, Anita Campillo, Edward Peil, George Hayes, Yakima Canutt. Town marshal Hayes offers young Wayne assignment as undercover agent to investigate crooked rodeo racket draining locals' loot. Routine sagebrusher burdened by obvious rodeo stock footage. Remade as Tex Ritter's TROUBLE IN TEXAS and Hoot Gibson's UTAH KID. ▼❱

Man From Yesterday, The (1932) 71m. *** D: Berthold Viertel. Claudette Colbert, Clive Brook, Charles Boyer, Andy Devine, Alan Mowbray. WW1 nurse Colbert hears that husband Brook has died in battle, falls hard for Boyer . . . and then Brook returns. Surprisingly well done, thanks mainly to top performances.

Manhandled (1949) 97m. ** D: Lewis R. Foster. Dorothy Lamour, Dan Duryea, Sterling Hayden, Irene Hervey, Philip Reed. Crooked private eye Duryea tries to pin robbery-murder rap on innocent Lamour. Turgid drama that reliable cast can't salvage.

Manhattan Melodrama (1934) 93m. *** D: W. S. Van Dyke II. Clark Gable, William Powell, Myrna Loy, Leo Carrillo, Isabel Jewell, Mickey Rooney, Nat Pendleton. Boyhood pals remain adult friends though one is a gangster and the other a D.A. (a plot device reused many times). What might be unbearably corny is top entertainment, thanks to this star trio and a director with gusto. Arthur Caesar's original story won an Oscar. Footnoted in American history as the film John Dillinger saw just before being gunned down at the Biograph Theatre in Chicago, as illustrated in 2009's PUBLIC ENEMIES. Reworked as a 1942 B movie, NORTHWEST RANGERS. Also shown in computer-colored version. ▼❍❱

Manhattan Merry-Go-Round (1937) 80m. ** D: Charles Riesner. Phil Regan, Ann Dvorak, Leo Carrillo, James Gleason. Gangster Carrillo takes over a record company. Flimsy script, with romantic subplot, is just an excuse for none-too-thrilling specialty numbers by Gene Autry, Cab Calloway, Ted Lewis, Louis Prima, The Kay Thompson Singers, and Joe DiMaggio (!), to name just a few. ▼❱

[426]

Manhattan Parade (1931) 78m. **½ D: Lloyd Bacon. Winnie Lightner, Charles Butterworth, (Joe) Smith and (Charles) Dale, Dickie Moore, Bobby Watson, Frank Conroy, Walter Miller. Lightner is the harried but kindly general manager of a costume supply company; her husband, who runs the business, is carrying on with her secretary. So-so pre-Code soaper highlighted by the appearance of comedy stars Smith and Dale. Originally a musical, but all the numbers were cut prior to the film's release. Filmed in two-color Technicolor, but surviving prints are in b&w.

Man Hunt (1941) 105m. ***½ D: Fritz Lang. Walter Pidgeon, Joan Bennett, George Sanders, John Carradine, Roddy McDowall. Farfetched yet absorbing drama of man attempting to kill Hitler, getting into more trouble than he bargained for. Tense, well done. Screenplay by Dudley Nichols, from Geoffrey Household's novel. Remade as ROGUE MALE.▶

Mania (1959-British) 87m. *** D: John Gilling. Peter Cushing, Donald Pleasence, George Rose, June Laverick, Dermot Walsh, Billie Whitelaw. Deliciously lurid shocker with Cushing going all out as an Edinburgh scientist who employs graverobbers Pleasence and Rose to supply him with corpses for his experiments. Originally titled THE FLESH AND THE FIENDS (and released at 97m.). Aka PSYCHO KILLERS and THE FIENDISH GHOULS; the latter runs 74m. Dyaliscope.▼▶

Maniac (1934) 51m. BOMB D: Dwain Esper. Bill Woods, Horace Carpenter, Ted Edwards, Phyllis Diller (not the comedienne), Theo Ramsey, Jenny Dark. Typically delirious Esper schlockfest—filmed mostly in somebody's basement—about a lunatic who murders a mad doctor and assumes his identity. High points include a passionate soliloquy on insanity, pulling out a cat's eye and eating it, and a climactic fight between two women armed with hypodermic needles!▼▶

Maniac (1962-British) 86m. **½ D: Michael Carreras. Kerwin Mathews, Nadia Gray, Donald Houston, Justine Lord. One of the better British thrillers made in wake of PSYCHO, with Mathews as vacationing artist in France arousing hatred of girlfriend's sick father. Good plot twists. Written by Jimmy Sangster. Megascope.▼▶

Man I Killed, The SEE: **Broken Lullaby**

Manila Calling (1942) 81m. ** D: Herbert I. Leeds. Lloyd Nolan, Carole Landis, Cornel Wilde, James Gleason, Martin Kosleck, Ralph Byrd, Elisha Cook, Jr., Louis Jean Heydt. Pat WW2 drama of Allied radio technicians trapped in Manila after the Japanese invasion heroically battling the enemy.▶

Man I Love, The (1929) 74m. ** D: William A. Wellman. Richard Arlen, Mary Brian, (Olga) Baclanova, Harry Green, Jack Oakie, Leslie Fenton. Stop us if you've heard this one before: a prizefighter struggles to become champ and is torn between his love for a good girl and his fascination with a slinky society beauty. Arlen's energetic performance and some vivid ring scenes in Madison Square Garden add punch to this early talkie written by Herman J. Mankiewicz.

Man I Love, The (1946) 96m. *** D: Raoul Walsh. Ida Lupino, Robert Alda, Bruce Bennett, Andrea King, Dolores Moran, Martha Vickers, Alan Hale. Slick, well-acted melodrama casts Ida as nightclub singer pursued by no-good mobster Alda. Forget logic and just enjoy. This film inspired Scorsese's NEW YORK NEW YORK.▼●▶

Man I Married, The (1940) 77m. *** D: Irving Pichel. Joan Bennett, Francis Lederer, Lloyd Nolan, Anna Sten, Otto Kruger. Strong story of German Lederer taken in by Nazi propaganda while American wife Bennett tries to stop him. Taut, exciting script.▶

Man in a Cocked Hat (1959-British) 88m. *** D: Jeffrey Dell, Roy Boulting. Terry-Thomas, Peter Sellers, Luciana Paluzzi, Thorley Walters, Ian Bannen, John Le Mesurier, Miles Malleson. Screwball farce about Island of Gallardia, a British protectorate forgotten for 50 years; when rediscovered, bumbling Terry-Thomas of the Foreign Office is left in charge. British title: CARLTON-BROWNE OF THE F.O.▼▶

Man in Black (1949-British) 80m. **½ D: Francis Searle. Betty Ann Davies, Sheila Burrell, Sid James, Anthony Forwood, Hazel Penwarden, Courtney Hope, Valentine Dyall. A wealthy dabbler in yoga (James) dies during a trance, leaving his estate to his meek daughter (Penwarden). His scheming widow (Davies) and her daughter (Burrell) plot to get the money for themselves. Clever little thriller with some surprises and a rare noncomic role for James. Based on the British radio series *Appointment with Fear* that featured the title character (Dyall) as the "Story-Teller."▶

Man in Grey, The (1943-British) 116m. *** D: Leslie Arliss. Margaret Lockwood, James Mason, Phyllis Calvert, Stewart Granger, Helen Haye, Martita Hunt. Wealthy Calvert befriends impoverished schoolmate Lockwood; years later, Lockwood repays the kindness by trying to steal her husband. Elaborate costume drama, told in flashback, is entertaining, and notable for boosting Mason (as Calvert's hateful husband) to stardom. Originally shown in the U.S. at 93m.▼▶

Man in Half Street, The (1944) 92m. **½ D: Ralph Murphy. Nils Asther, Helen Walker, Brandon Hurst, Reginald Sheffield. Not-bad horror tale of scientist Asther experimenting with rejuvenation; done on better scale than many of these little epics. Remade as THE MAN WHO COULD CHEAT DEATH.

Man in Hiding (1953-British) 79m. *½ D: Terence Fisher. Paul Henreid, Lois Maxwell, Kieron Moore, Hugh Sinclair. Tame detective-capturing-elusive-killer plot. Original British title: MANTRAP.

Man in Possession, The (1931) 84m. **½ D: Sam Wood. Robert Montgomery, Irene Purcell, Charlotte Greenwood, C. Aubrey Smith, Beryl Mercer, Reginald Owen, Alan Mowbray, Maude Eburne. English bailiff Montgomery takes possession of more than debt-ridden Purcell's home when he poses as her butler and falls in love with her. Saucy light comedy benefits from polished cast and a double-entendre–laden script, cowritten by P. G. Wodehouse. Remade as PERSONAL PROPERTY. ▶

Man Inside, The (1958-British) 90m. *½ D: John Gilling. Jack Palance, Anita Ekberg, Nigel Patrick, Anthony Newley, Sidney James, Donald Pleasence, Eric Pohlmann. Shoddy robbery caper with private investigator hunting jewel thieves throughout Europe. CinemaScope.▼

Man in the Attic (1953) 82m. **½ D: Hugo Fregonese. Jack Palance, Constance Smith, Byron Palmer, Frances Bavier, Rhys Williams, Sean McClory, Isabel Jewell, Leslie Bradley. Flavorful account of notorious Jack the Ripper, with Palance going full-blast. Remake of THE LODGER.▼▶

Man in the Dark (1953) 70m. **½ D: Lew Landers. Edmond O'Brien, Audrey Totter, Ruth Warren, Ted de Corsia, Horace McMahon, Nick Dennis. Convict O'Brien undergoes brain surgery to eliminate criminal bent and loses memory in the process; his old cohorts only care that he remember where he stashed their stolen loot. OK remake of THE MAN WHO LIVED TWICE and CRIME DOCTOR. Originally shown in 3-D. ▶

Man in the Dinghy SEE: **Into the Blue**

Man in the Gray Flannel Suit, The (1956) C-153m. ***½ D: Nunnally Johnson. Gregory Peck, Jennifer Jones, Fredric March, Marisa Pavan, Lee J. Cobb, Ann Harding, Keenan Wynn, Gene Lockhart, Gigi Perreau, Arthur O'Connell, Henry Daniell. Top-notch adaptation of Sloan Wilson's bestseller is an incisive time capsule of the mid-1950s. Harried suburbanite Peck, drowning in debt, with workplace and marital pressures, recalls his experiences in Italy during WW2. Scripted by the director; music by Bernard Herrmann. CinemaScope. ▼●▶

Man in the Iron Mask, The (1939) 110m. *** D: James Whale. Louis Hayward, Joan Bennett, Warren William, Joseph Schildkraut, Alan Hale, Walter Kingsford, Marion Martin. Rousing adventure of twin brothers: one becomes King of France, the other a carefree gay blade raised by D'Artagnan (William) and the Three Musketeers. Fine swashbuckler. Filmed in 1929 with Douglas Fairbanks as THE IRON MASK; remade in 1998 with Leonardo DiCaprio and for TV in 1977. ▼▶

Man in the Middle (1964-British) 94m. ** D: Guy Hamilton. Robert Mitchum, France Nuyen, Barry Sullivan, Keenan Wynn, Alexander Knox, Trevor Howard. Unconvincing, confusing film of Howard Fast novel *The Winston Affair*, about American military officer accused of homicide; static courtroom sequences. CinemaScope.▶

Man in the Moon (1961-British) 98m. *** D: Basil Dearden. Kenneth More, Shirley Anne Field, Norman Bird, Michael Hordern, John Phillips. Top comedy satirizing space race. Government recruits man unaffected by cold, heat, speed, etc., to be perfect astronaut.

Man in the Net, The (1959) 97m. *½ D: Michael Curtiz. Alan Ladd, Carolyn Jones, Diane Brewster, Charles McGraw, John Lupton, Tom Helmore. Inane drama of artist Ladd suspected of wife Jones' murder and in hiding, enlisting the help of all local kids to trap the real killer. Jones' performance is an undisguised Bette Davis imitation throughout. ▶

Man in the Raincoat, The (1957-French-Italian) 97m. ** D: Julien Duvivier. Fernandel, John McGiver, Bernard Blier, Claude Sylvain, Jean Rigaux, Rob Murray. Middling comedy-mystery with Fernandel as a bumbling musician who accidentally becomes involved with murder. Tries hard and has its moments but simply doesn't jell. ▼

Man in the Saddle (1951) C-87m. ** D: Andre de Toth. Randolph Scott, Joan Leslie, Ellen Drew, Alexander Knox. Scott is involved in romantic triangle causing death on the range; justice triumphs.▼▶

Man in the Shadow (1957) 80m. **½ D: Jack Arnold. Jeff Chandler, Orson Welles, Colleen Miller, James Gleason. Welles chomps his way through role of rancher responsible for helper's death. Chandler is the earnest sheriff. CinemaScope.▼▶

Man in the Shadow (1957-British) SEE: **Violent Stranger**

Man in the Sky, The SEE: **Decision Against Time**

Man in the Vault (1956) 73m. *½ D: Andrew V. McLaglen. William Campbell, Karen Sharpe, Anita Ekberg, Berry Kroeger, Mike Mazurki, Paul Fix. Programmer of drab locksmith Campbell, who unwillingly becomes involved in a safe-deposit box robbery. Drab is right.▶

Man in the White Suit, The (1951-British) 84m. ***½ D: Alexander Mackendrick. Alec Guinness, Joan Greenwood, Cecil Parker, Michael Gough, Ernest Thesiger, Vida Hope, George Benson, Edie Martin. Guinness is inventor who discovers a fabric that can't wear out or soil; dismayed garment manufacturers set out to bury his formula. Most engaging comedy. Screenplay by Roger Macdougall, John Dighton, and Mackendrick, from Macdougall's play.▼▶

Man Made Monster (1941) 59m. **

D: George Waggner. Lionel Atwill, Lon Chaney, Jr., Anne Nagel, Frank Albertson, Samuel S. Hinds, William Davidson, Ben Taggart, Connie Bergen. Sci-fi yarn of scientist Atwill making Chaney invulnerable to electricity and able to kill with his touch; fairly well done. ▼▶

Mannequin (1937) 95m. **½ D: Frank Borzage. Joan Crawford, Spencer Tracy, Alan Curtis, Ralph Morgan, Leo Gorcey, Elisabeth Risdon. Prototype rags-to-riches soaper, with working girl Crawford getting ahead via wealthy Tracy. Predictable script, but nice job by stars, usual MGM gloss (even in the tenements!). ▼●▶

Man of Aran (1934-British) 73m. **** D: Robert Flaherty. Colman (Tiger) King, Maggie Dillane. Superb, classic documentary about day-to-day existence, and constant fight for survival, of fisherman in remote Irish coastal community. Scenes at sea are breathtaking. ▼▶

Man of a Thousand Faces (1957) 122m. ***½ D: Joseph Pevney. James Cagney, Dorothy Malone, Jane Greer, Marjorie Rambeau, Jim Backus, Jeanne Cagney, Robert J. Evans, Roger Smith, Jack Albertson, Snub Pollard. Surprisingly good, well-acted biography of silent star Lon Chaney. Cagney as Chaney, Malone as disturbed first wife, Greer as wife who brings him happiness, are all fine. Chaney's life and career are re-created with taste (if not accuracy). Touching portrayal of movie extra by Rambeau. Ralph Wheelwright's story was adapted by R. Wright Campbell, Ivan Goff, and Ben Roberts. CinemaScope. ▼●▶

Man of Conflict (1953) 72m. ** D: Hal Makelim. Edward Arnold, John Agar, Susan Morrow, Russell Hicks. Lukewarm drama of generation clash between father and son over business and philosophy of life. ▼▶

Man of Conquest (1939) 105m. **½ D: George Nicholls, Jr. Richard Dix, Gail Patrick, Edward Ellis, Joan Fontaine, George (Gabby) Hayes. Sprawling but superficial, speech-laden bio of Sam Houston (a well-cast Dix) covers a lot of history—including the battle of the Alamo. ▶

Man of Evil (1944-British) 90m. ** D: Anthony Asquith. Phyllis Calvert, James Mason, Stewart Granger, Wilfrid Lawson, Jean Kent. Elaborate but ponderous costumer of maniac who tries to run people's lives to suit his fancy; overdone and not effective. Original title: FANNY BY GASLIGHT. ▼▶

Man of Iron (1935) 62m. *** D: William (C.) McGann. Barton MacLane, Mary Astor, John Eldredge, Dorothy Peterson, Joseph Crehan, Craig Reynolds, Joseph (Joe) Sawyer, John Qualen. Problems arise when a likable steel mill foreman (MacLane, in a rare starring role) is promoted to general manager of his plant. Thoughtful B movie offers keen insight into the impact of upward mobility, American-style.

Man of Iron (1956-Italian) 116m. *** D: Pietro Germi. Pietro Germi, Luisa Della Noce, Sylva Koscina, Carlo Giuffre. Somber account of Germi, railroad engineer, whose life takes a tragic turn, affecting his whole family; realistically presented. Original title: THE RAILROAD MAN. [PG] ▼●▶

Man of the Moment (1935-British) 81m. ** D: Monty Banks. Douglas Fairbanks, Jr., Laura La Plante, Claude Hulbert, Margaret Lockwood, Peter Gawthorne, Donald Calthrop, Martita Hunt. Trifling Depression-era romantic comedy, with secretary La Plante despondent when she realizes her boss doesn't love her; then handsome Fairbanks enters the picture. Director (and former silent-comedy star) Banks plays a flirtatious doctor.

Man of the West (1958) C-100m. *** D: Anthony Mann. Gary Cooper, Julie London, Lee J. Cobb, Arthur O'Connell, Jack Lord, John Dehner, Royal Dano. Dismissed in 1958, this powerful story deserves another look. Cooper plays a reformed outlaw who is forced to rejoin his ex-boss (Cobb) to save himself and other innocent people from the gang's mistreatment. Strong, epic-scale Western, with script by Reginald Rose. CinemaScope. ▼▶

Man of the World (1931) 71m. ** D: Richard Wallace. William Powell, Carole Lombard, Wynne Gibson, Guy Kibbee, George Chandler. Intriguing vehicle for Powell, a sophisticated spin on a formula story that doesn't wind up as you think it will. Written by Herman J. Mankiewicz. Gibson is vivid as Powell's jealous ex, Lombard (the future Mrs. Powell in real life) is just adequate; this was before she came into her own. ▶

Man of Two Worlds (1934) 97m. *** D: J. Walter Ruben. Francis Lederer, Elissa Landi, Henry Stephenson, J. Farrell MacDonald, Steffi Duna. Thoughtful tale of conflicting cultures, with Eskimo hunter Lederer brought to England by explorer Stephenson. He comes to think of himself as a "white man" and becomes infatuated with the explorer's high-toned daughter (Landi). Based on a novel by Ainsworth Morgan, who also coscripted.

Man on a String (1960) 92m. *** D: Andre de Toth. Ernest Borgnine, Kerwin Mathews, Colleen Dewhurst, Alexander Scourby, Glenn Corbett. Fictionalized account of counterspy Boris Morros, involved in Russian-U.S. Cold War conflict. Taut action sequences. ▶

Man on a Tightrope (1953) 105m. **½ D: Elia Kazan. Fredric March, Gloria Grahame, Terry Moore, Cameron Mitchell, Adolphe Menjou, Richard Boone, Robert Beatty. Passable based-on-fact account of an obscure, downtrodden little circus troupe and its escape from Communist-ruled Czechoslovakia to freedom in Bavaria. Has its moments, but the characters are far too broadly drawn. Scripted by Robert E. Sherwood. ▶

Man on Fire (1957) 95m. **½ D: Ranald MacDougall. Bing Crosby, Mary Fickett, Inger Stevens, E. G. Marshall, Malcolm Broderick, Anne Seymour, Richard Eastham. Divorced father (Crosby) refuses to grant his remarried ex-wife partial custody of their son in this modest domestic drama.

Man on the Eiffel Tower, The (1949) C-97m. ** D: Burgess Meredith. Charles Laughton, Franchot Tone, Burgess Meredith, Robert Hutton, Jean Wallace, Patricia Roc, Wilfrid Hyde-White, Belita. Tiresome adaptation of a Georges Simenon thriller with Laughton as Inspector Maigret and Tone as a madman who thinks he can carry out a perfect crime. Meredith's directorial debut, filmed entirely in Paris. Shot in experimental AnscoColor process; most surviving prints don't look very good. ▶

Man on the Flying Trapeze (1935) 65m. ***½ D: Clyde Bruckman. W. C. Fields, Mary Brian, Kathleen Howard, Grady Sutton, Vera Lewis, Walter Brennan. Hilarious Fieldsian study in frustration, with able assistance from hardboiled wife Howard, good-for-nothing Sutton. Best sequence has W. C. receiving four traffic tickets in a row! ▶

Man or Gun (1958) 79m. ** D: Albert Gannaway. Macdonald Carey, Audrey Totter, James Craig, James Gleason. Bland Western with Carey cleaning up the town. Filmed in Naturama.

Manpower (1941) 102m. *** D: Raoul Walsh. Edward G. Robinson, Marlene Dietrich, George Raft, Alan Hale, Walter Catlett, Frank McHugh, Eve Arden. Lively, typical Warner Bros. film, with nightclub "hostess" Dietrich coming between high-voltage power line workers Robinson and Raft. Scene in a diner is worth the price of admission. ▶

Man-Proof (1938) 74m. ** D: Richard Thorpe. Myrna Loy, Franchot Tone, Rosalind Russell, Walter Pidgeon, Nana Bryant, Rita Johnson, Ruth Hussey. Flimsy plot with bright stars: Loy and Russell both love Pidgeon, but Tone is ready to step in any time.

Man's Castle (1933) 69m. ***½ D: Frank Borzage. Spencer Tracy, Loretta Young, Marjorie Rambeau, Arthur Hohl, Walter Connolly, Glenda Farrell, Dickie Moore. Typically lovely Borzage romance; penniless Young moves in with shantytown tough guy Tracy, hoping to develop a real relationship in spite of his reluctance. Tracy's ultra-macho character is a bit tough to stomach at times, but film's enormous heart conquers all, bolstered by appealing performances. Originally released at 75m.

Man's Favorite Sport? (1964) C-120m. **½ D: Howard Hawks. Rock Hudson, Paula Prentiss, John McGiver, Maria Perschy, Roscoe Karns, Charlene Holt. Amusing, often labored variation on Hawks' own BRINGING UP BABY. Fishing "expert" Hudson, who in reality has never fished, is forced to enter big tournament by pushy Prentiss (in her best performance). Loaded with slapstick and sexual innuendo; Norman Alden is hilarious as wisecracking Indian guide. ▼▶

Manslaughter (1922) 100m. **½ D: Cecil B. DeMille. Thomas Meighan, Leatrice Joy, Lois Wilson, John Miltern, George Fawcett, Julia Faye, Edythe Chapman, Jack Mower, Raymond Hatton. Melodramatic account of wealthy, self-centered jazz baby Joy and her fate after causing the death of a motorcycle cop; Meighan is the district attorney who loves yet prosecutes her. Meant to condemn 1920s-style debauchery, but not without its titillating images; the Roman orgy fantasy sequence is vintage DeMille. Remade in 1930. ▼▶

Man They Could Not Hang, The (1939) 65m. **½ D: Nick Grinde. Boris Karloff, Lorna Gray (Adrian Booth), Robert Wilcox, Roger Pryor, Ann Doran. One of five Karloff films with the same basic premise; hanged man brought back to life seeks revenge on judge, jury, et al. Good of its type. ▼▶

Man to Man Talk (1958-French) 89m. ** D: Louis Saslavsky. Yves Montand, Nicole Berger, Yves Nöel, Georges Chamarat, Bernadette Lange, Laurent Terzieff, Walter Chiari. Muddled account of pregnant Berger and husband Montand, who is forced to explain the facts of life to their son. Done in by several confusing subplots. Original title: PREMIER MAY.

Man to Remember, A (1938) 80m. **½ D: Garson Kanin. Anne Shirley, Edward Ellis, Lee Bowman, William Henry, Granville Bates, Harlan Briggs, Frank M. Thomas, Charles Halton, John Wray, Gilbert Emery, Dickie Jones. Dalton Trumbo scripted this B-movie remake of the superior ONE MAN'S JOURNEY about a dedicated small-town doctor (Ellis) who labors in anonymity while butting heads with the burg's cheap, greedy businessmen. Kanin's directing debut won major kudos in 1938. Only surviving print of this is subtitled in Dutch! ▶

Mantrap (1926) 71m. **½ D: Victor Fleming. Clara Bow, Percy Marmont, Ernest Torrence, Eugene Pallette, Tom Kennedy, Josephine Crowell, William Orlamond, Charles Stevens. Weary big city divorce lawyer Marmont heads off to God's Country for rest and relaxation and promptly mixes with flirtatious (but married) Bow. Pleasant silent comedy, based on a novel by Sinclair Lewis, is a nice showcase for the effervescent Bow. ▶

Mantrap (1953-British) SEE: **Man in Hiding**

Man-Trap (1961) 93m. **½ D: Edmond

O'Brien. Jeffrey Hunter, David Janssen, Stella Stevens, Elaine Devry, Virginia Gregg, Hugh Sanders, Frank Albertson, Perry Lopez, Bob Crane. Korean War hero Hunter, neck-deep in financial and marital woes, becomes involved in shady scheme with war buddy Janssen. Generally entertaining melodrama with Stevens an eye-opener as Hunter's bitchy wife. Based on a story by John D. MacDonald; rare fling at directing for O'Brien. Panavision. ◗

Manuela SEE: **Stowaway Girl**

Man Upstairs, The (1958-British) **88m. *** D: Don Chaffey. Richard Attenborough, Bernard Lee, Donald Houston, Virginia Maskell. Compact study, excellently acted, of Attenborough, a man gone berserk much to everyone's amazement.

Man Wanted (1932) **62m. **½ D: William Dieterle. Kay Francis, David Manners, Una Merkel, Andy Devine, Kenneth Thomson, Claire Dodd, Elizabeth Patterson, Edward Van Sloan. Francis is a workaholic magazine editor who puts up with the philandering ways of her playboy husband but yearns for a little excitement of her own after she hires a young hunk to be her secretary. Dated look at sexual equality and gender stereotypes is uplifted by chic Francis and exudes a sophisticated, sensuous quality. ◗

Man Who Broke the Bank at Monte Carlo, The (1935) **66m. **½ D: Stephen Roberts. Ronald Colman, Joan Bennett, Colin Clive, Nigel Bruce, Montagu Love. Flimsy film carried by Colman charm, translating famous title song into story of man who calculates to clean out treasury of Riviera gambling establishment.

Man Who Came Back, The (1931) **87m. *½ D: Raoul Walsh. Janet Gaynor, Charles Farrell, Kenneth MacKenna, William Holden, Mary Forbes. Perfectly dreadful early talkie for a duo who were tremendously popular in silent romantic dramas. Here, they're given an insipid change-of-image tale with Farrell as an alcoholic playboy who drives Gaynor to prostitution and drug addiction in a Shanghai opium den. Sounds juicy but consists of endless monologues and stilted histrionics.

Man Who Came to Dinner, The (1941) **112m. ***½ D: William Keighley. Bette Davis, Ann Sheridan, Monty Woolley, Billie Burke, Jimmy Durante, Richard Travis, Grant Mitchell, Mary Wickes, Elizabeth Fraser, Reginald Gardiner. Acerbic radio commentator Woolley (re-creating his Broadway role) is forced to stay with Burke's Midwestern family for the winter, driving them crazy with assorted wacky friends passing through. Delightful adaptation of George S. Kaufman–Moss Hart play, inspired by the celebrated critic and columnist Alexander Woollcott. Scripted by the Epstein brothers. Also shown in computer-colored version. ▼◗

Man Who Changed His Mind, The SEE: **Man Who Lived Again, The**

Man Who Cheated Himself, The (1950) **81m. **½ D: Felix E. Feist. Lee J. Cobb, Jane Wyatt, John Dall, Lisa Howard, Harlan Warde. Cop Cobb has fallen for married Wyatt. How will he respond when she accidentally kills her husband? Generally absorbing murder yarn. ▼◗

Man Who Could Cheat Death, The (1959-British) **C-83m. **½ D: Terence Fisher. Anton Diffring, Hazel Court, Christopher Lee, Arnold Marle, Delphi Lawrence. OK remake of THE MAN IN HALF MOON STREET, about sculptor with somewhat messy method of retarding the aging process; typical Hammer production. ◗

Man Who Could Work Miracles, The (1936-British) **82m. ***½ D: Lothar Mendes. Roland Young, Ralph Richardson, Edward Chapman, Ernest Thesiger, Joan Gardner, George Zucco, Wallace Lupino, Joan Hickson, George Sanders, Torin Thatcher. H. G. Wells' fantasy of timid British department store clerk (Young) endowed with power to do anything he wants. Special effects are marvelous, supported by good cast, in charming film. ▼◗

Man Who Cried Wolf, The (1937) **66m. **½ D: Lewis R. Foster. Lewis Stone, Tom Brown, Barbara Read, Robert Gleckler, Forrester Harvey. Hammy actor Stone confesses to various murders, convinces cops he's crazy, planning perfect alibi for real killing. Cheaply filmed; Stone is mainstay of film, with Marjorie Main in good supporting role as society woman.

Man Who Dared, The (1933) **75m. **½ D: Hamilton MacFadden. Preston Foster, Zita Johann, Joan Marsh, Frank Sheridan. Modest but engrossing biography of Anton Cermak, Bohemian immigrant who became Chicago mayor and died when hit by bullet intended for FDR. Foster is excellent.

Man Who Died Twice, The (1958) **70m. ** D: Joseph Kane. Rod Cameron, Vera Ralston, Mike Mazurki, Gerald Milton, Richard Karlan, Louis Jean Heydt, Don Megowan, Paul Picerni, Luana Anders. When a nightclub owner is killed in a car wreck, his cop brother comforts widowed Ralston while helping local authorities investigate the dead man's drug racket. Well-written B movie has few surprises, but is competently made. Naturama.

Man Who Finally Died, The (1962-British) **100m. ** D: Quentin Lawrence. Stanley Baker, Peter Cushing, Mai Zetterling, Eric Portman, Niall MacGinnis, Nigel Green, Barbara Everest. Tepid attempt at Hitchcock-like thriller: Baker returns to German home town and tries to discover what happened to his father during WW2. CinemaScope.

Man Who Found Himself, The (1937) **67m. **½ D: Lew Landers. John Beal, Joan Fontaine, Phillip Huston, Jane Walsh,

George Irving, Jimmy Conlin, Frank M. Thomas, Dwight Frye. Society doctor Beal, through no fault of his own, becomes immersed in a scandal; Fontaine is the fetching nurse who comes to his rescue. Lightly entertaining if predictable programmer.

Man Who Knew Too Much, The (1934-British) **75m. *** D:** Alfred Hitchcock. Leslie Banks, Edna Best, Peter Lorre, Nova Pilbeam, Frank Vosper, Pierre Fresnay. Film buffs argue which version of exciting story is better. We vote this one, with Hitchcock in fine form weaving dry British humor into a story of heart-pounding suspense; young girl is kidnapped to prevent her parents from revealing what they've learned about assassination plot.▼●▌

Man Who Knew Too Much, The (1956) **C-120m. **½ D:** Alfred Hitchcock. James Stewart, Doris Day, Brenda De Banzie, Bernard Miles, Ralph Truman, Daniel Gelin, Alan Mowbray, Carolyn Jones, Hillary Brooke. Hitchcock's remake of his 1934 film is disappointing. Even famous Albert Hall assassination sequence rings flat in tale of American couple accidentally involved in international intrigue. Doris' "Que Sera, Sera" won Jay Livingston and Ray Evans Best Song Oscar. Composer Bernard Herrmann is conducting orchestra at the climax. VistaVision.▼●▌

Man Who Laughs, The (1928) **110m. *** D:** Paul Leni. Conrad Veidt, Mary Philbin, Olga Baclanova, Brandon Hurst, Cesare Gravina, Stuart Holmes, Sam De Grasse, George Siegmann, Josephine Crowell. Visually dazzling adaptation of the Victor Hugo novel with Veidt well cast as the title character, a man whose smile has been carved into his face. Because of this freakish look, it's almost impossible for him to express his true feelings, even to the love of his life. More striking than moving, this is typical of the European influence on Hollywood filmmaking at the end of the silent era. ▼▌

Man Who Lived Again, The (1936-British) **61m. *** D:** Robert Stevenson. Boris Karloff, Anna Lee, John Loder, Frank Cellier, Lyn Harding, Cecil Parker. Mad doctor Karloff has been transferring personalities from one monkey to another. How soon will he be experimenting with human subjects? Solid, above-par chiller. Original British title: THE MAN WHO CHANGED HIS MIND.▼▌

Man Who Lived Twice, The (1936) **73m. **½ D:** Harry Lachman. Ralph Bellamy, Marian Marsh, Thurston Hall, Isabel Jewell, Nana Bryant, Ward Bond. Killer (Bellamy) ditches his cohorts, undergoes brain surgery which literally changes him into a new man. Interesting premise should have made for better film. Remade as CRIME DOCTOR and MAN IN THE DARK.

Man Who Loved Redheads, The (1955-British) **C-103m. *** D:** Harold French.

John Justin, Moira Shearer, Roland Culver, Denholm Elliott, Harry Andrews, Patricia Cutts. Delightful British comedy written by Terence Rattigan about a man with lifelong crush on redheads, dating back to boyhood meeting with beautiful Shearer. American print runs 89m.

Man Who Never Was, The (1956-British) **C-103m. *** D:** Ronald Neame. Clifton Webb, Gloria Grahame, Robert Flemyng, Josephine Griffin, Stephen Boyd. Good WW2 spy yarn based on true story of Allies planting elaborate red herring to divert attention from invasion of Sicily. CinemaScope.▼▌

Man Who Played God, The (1932) **81m. **½ D:** John G. Adolfi. George Arliss, Bette Davis, Violet Heming, Louise Closser Hale, Donald Cook, Ray Milland. Well-acted tale of musician Arliss going deaf, infatuated student Davis sticking by him. Not as stagy as other Arliss films, with Bette getting her first big break and young Milland in a small role. Remake of Arliss' silent vehicle; later remade as SINCERELY YOURS.▌

Man Who Reclaimed His Head, The (1934) **80m. *** D:** Edward Ludwig. Claude Rains, Lionel Atwill, Joan Bennett, Baby Jane, Henry O'Neill, Wallace Ford. Odd drama adapted from Jean Bart stage play, told in flashback. Struggling writer and advocate of world peace used by capitalists (led by Atwill) to their own, selfish ends. Unusual story well acted, especially by Rains, but too slowly paced.

Man Who Shot Liberty Valance, The (1962) **123m. **** D:** John Ford. James Stewart, John Wayne, Vera Miles, Lee Marvin, Edmond O'Brien, Andy Devine, Woody Strode, Jeanette Nolan, Ken Murray, John Qualen, Strother Martin, Lee Van Cleef, John Carradine, Carleton Young. Tenderfoot lawyer Stewart helps civilize the West, but needs help from he-man Wayne to do so. Panned and patronized upon original release, but now regarded as an American classic; one of the great Westerns. Producer Willis Goldbeck and James Warner Bellah adapted Dorothy Johnson's story.▼●▌

Man Who Talked Too Much, The (1940) **75m. **½ D:** Vincent Sherman. George Brent, Virginia Bruce, Brenda Marshall, Richard Barthelmess, William Lundigan, George Tobias. Good courtroom drama with D.A. Brent and lawyer Lundigan, brothers fighting same case. Remake of THE MOUTHPIECE, made again as ILLEGAL (1955).

Man Who Turned to Stone, The (1957) **71m. BOMB D:** Leslie Kardos. Victor Jory, Ann Doran, Charlotte Austin, William Hudson, Paul Cavanagh, Jean Willes, Victor Varconi. Women's detention home wardens Jory et al. stay immortal by siphoning off the life forces of inmates. If they don't get renewed, they petrify. So does the movie. ▼▌

Man Who Understood Women, The (1959) **C-105m. **½ D:** Nunnally John-

[432]

son. Leslie Caron, Henry Fonda, Cesare Danova, Myron McCormick, Marcel Dalio, Conrad Nagel. Unsatisfactory narrative of movie-maker genius Fonda who hasn't slightest notion of how to treat wife Caron. CinemaScope.

Man Who Wagged His Tail, The (1957-Spanish-Italian) **91m.** **½ D: Ladislao Vajda. Peter Ustinov, Pablito Calvo, Aroldo Tieri, Silvia Marco. Scrooge-like slumlord Ustinov is transformed into a dog. OK fantasy filmed in Madrid and Brooklyn. Released in the U.S. in 1961.▼

Man Who Watched Trains Go By SEE: **Paris Express, The**

Man Who Wouldn't Die, The (1942) **65m.** ** D: Herbert I. Leeds. Lloyd Nolan, Marjorie Weaver, Helene Reynolds, Henry Wilcoxon. Nolan is efficient as wisecracking detective Mike Shayne with a tougher caper than usual.▶

Man Who Wouldn't Talk, The (1940) **72m.** ** D: David Burton. Lloyd Nolan, Jean Rogers, Onslow Stevens, Eric Blore, Mae Marsh. Routine drama with Nolan refusing to defend himself on murder charge; silly ending. Based on one-act play *The Valiant*, filmed in 1929 with Paul Muni.

Man Who Wouldn't Talk, The (1958-British) **97m.** *½ D: Herbert Wilcox. Anna Neagle, Anthony Quayle, Zsa Zsa Gabor, Katherine Kath, Dora Bryan. Britain's foremost female lawyer (Neagle) defends Quayle on murder charge, even though he cannot speak, for fear of revealing top-secret information. Dreadful.

Man With a Cloak, The (1951) **81m.** **½ D: Fletcher Markle. Barbara Stanwyck, Joseph Cotten, Louis Calhern, Leslie Caron, Jim Backus, Margaret Wycherly, Joe DeSantis. Intriguing little mystery, set in 19th-century N.Y.C.; housekeeper Stanwyck plots to kill Calhern for his money and romances Cotten, whose identity is kept secret until the climax. Not bad, with spooky David Raksin score, but having Barbara sing was a mistake.▶

Man With a Million (1954-British) **C-92m.** ** D: Ronald Neame. Gregory Peck, Jane Griffiths, Ronald Squire, A. E. Matthews, Wilfrid Hyde-White, Reginald Beckwith. Often tedious telling of Mark Twain story "The Million Pound Bank Note," in which penniless American Peck is given the title sum of money on a wager, leading to various complications. Original title: THE MILLION POUND NOTE. Remade as A MILLION TO JUAN.

Man With a Movie Camera (1929-Russian) **68m.** **** D: Dziga Vertov. Visually dazzling landmark film that straddles the line between documentary and experimental cinema. Via editing, special effects, and cinematography (by Mikhail Kaufman, the director's brother), Vertov offers a dawn-to-dusk view of the city of Moscow. A visual feast and a stimulating exploration of the visual language of film.▼▶

Man With My Face, The (1951) **86m.** ** D: Edward J. Montagne. Barry Nelson, Lynn Ainley, John Harvey, Jim Boles, Carole Mathews, Jack Warden. Good plot idea isn't well realized: businessman Nelson discovers con man look-alike has taken over his life completely. Nice location filming in Puerto Rico.

Man With Nine Lives, The (1940) **74m.** **½ D: Nick Grinde. Boris Karloff, Roger Pryor, Jo Ann Sayers, Stanley Brown, John Dilson, Hal Taliaferro. Scientist Karloff seeks cure for cancer by freezing bodies in suspended animation. Hokey, but fun when Karloff himself thaws out.▼▶

Man Without a Body, The (1957-British) **80m.** *½ D: W. Lee Wilder, Charles Saunders. George Coulouris, Robert Hutton, Julia Arnall, Nadja Regin, Sheldon Lawrence, Michael Golden. Tyrannical industrialist Coulouris, dying of brain cancer, hopes to preserve his mind by convincing the living, disembodied head of Nostradamus that it is actually he, the industrialist. Hutton is a scientist working with living monkey heads, eyes on wall plaques, and whatnot. Confused? Not half as much as this sober but deranged little epic.

Man Without a Star (1955) **C-89m.** *** D: King Vidor. Kirk Douglas, Jeanne Crain, Claire Trevor, Richard Boone, Jay C. Flippen, William Campbell. Boisterous Western with drifter Douglas befriending young Campbell, tangling with manipulative rancher Crain. Kirk gets to sing and play the banjo in this one. Remade as A MAN CALLED GANNON.▼▶

Man With the Balloons, The (1965-Italian-French) **85m.** ** D: Marco Ferreri. Marcello Mastroianni, Catherine Spaak. Mastroianni plays successful businessman who loses his girl, eventually goes mad because he becomes obsessed with finding out how much air a balloon needs before it bursts. Offbeat idea, to be sure, but result is just plain silly. Panoramica.

Man With the Golden Arm, The (1955) **119m.** *** D: Otto Preminger. Frank Sinatra, Kim Novak, Eleanor Parker, Darren McGavin, Arnold Stang, Doro Merande. Nelson Algren's novel, the first to win the National Book Award, was presumed to be unfilmable until Preminger ignored and thus busted Hollywood's Production Code. The taboo subject was heroin addiction, and Sinatra's performance is still provocative, especially in the actor's famed gets-the-shakes withdrawal scene. Otherwise, the film (which appears to have been shot on the cheap) has lost some, though hardly all, of its power. Two other landmarks: Saul Bass' trendsetting opening credits and Elmer Bernstein's jazz score, which put the composer on the map.▼▶▶

Man With the Gun (1955) **83m.** **½ D: Richard Wilson. Robert Mitchum, Jan Sterling, Angie Dickinson, Barbara Lawrence, Karen Sharpe, Henry Hull. Mitchum as lawman who brings peace to a Western town is the whole show.▶

Man With Two Faces, The (1934) **72m.** **½ D: Archie Mayo. Edward G. Robinson, Mary Astor, Ricardo Cortez, Mae Clarke, Louis Calhern, Arthur Byron, John Eldredge, David Landau. Minor but entertaining yarn (from a play by Alexander Woollcott and George S. Kaufman) with Robinson well cast as a brilliant actor who tries to protect actress sister Astor from her sinister husband.▶

Manxman, The (1929-British) **90m.** **½ D: Alfred Hitchcock. Carl Brisson, Malcolm Keen, Anny Ondra, Randle Ayrton. Fisherman Brisson and lawyer Keen, best friends since childhood, both love Ondra. OK melodrama was Hitchcock's last silent film.▼▶

Many Rivers to Cross (1955) **C-92m.** **½ D: Roy Rowland. Robert Taylor, Eleanor Parker, Victor McLaglen, James Arness, Josephine Hutchinson, Rosemary DeCamp. Parker shows more vim and vigor than Taylor in this 1800s Western, centering on her yen for him. Raucous, energetic frontier comedy. CinemaScope.▶

Maracaibo (1958) **C-88m.** **½ D: Cornel Wilde. Cornel Wilde, Jean Wallace, Abbe Lane, Francis Lederer, Michael Landon. Wilde is expert firefighter who goes to Venezuela to combat oil blaze, romancing ex-girlfriend between action scenes. VistaVision.

Mara Maru (1952) **98m.** **½ D: Gordon Douglas. Errol Flynn, Ruth Roman, Raymond Burr, Richard Webb, Nestor Paiva. Turgid adventure pits Flynn against Burr as they vie for sunken treasure, with Roman the love interest.▶

Marauders, The (1947) **63m.** ** D: George Archainbaud. William Boyd, Andy Clyde, Rand Brooks, Ian Wolfe, Dorinda Clifton, Earle Hodgins. During a storm, Hopalong Cassidy and Bar 20 cowpunchers seek refuge in deserted but secretly oil-rich frontier town where a mother and daughter have determined not to be driven out. Eerie, on the slow side, redeemed only by personalities of Boyd and sidekick Clyde. Reissue title: KING OF THE RANGE.▼▶

Marauders, The (1955) **C-81m.** ** D: Gerald Mayer. Dan Duryea, Jeff Richards, Keenan Wynn, Jarma Lewis. OK story of rancher fighting against greedy cattle ranchers.▶

March of the Wooden Soldiers SEE: **Babes in Toyland** (1934)

Marco Polo (1962-Italian) **C-90m.** **½ D: Hugo Fregonese. Rory Calhoun, Yoko Tani, Robert Hundar, Camillo Pilotto, Pierre Cressoy, Michael Chow. Unspectacular epic about medieval adventurer and his journey to China. Calhoun and film lack needed vigor. CinemaScope.

Marco the Magnificent (1965) **C-100m.** **½ D: Denys De La Patelliere, Noel Howard. Horst Buchholz, Anthony Quinn, Omar Sharif, Elsa Martinelli, Akim Tamiroff, Orson Welles. Laughable mini-epic, extremely choppy, with episodic sequences pretending to recount events in life of medieval adventurer. Franscope.

Mardi Gras (1958) **C-107m.** **½ D: Edmund Goulding. Pat Boone, Christine Carere, Tommy Sands, Sheree North, Gary Crosby. Perky, unpretentious musical with energetic cast. Boone wins military school raffle date with movie star Carere. CinemaScope.▶

Margie (1946) **C-89m.** *** D: Henry King. Jeanne Crain, Glenn Langan, Lynn Bari, Alan Young, Barbara Lawrence, Conrad Janis, Esther Dale, Hobart Cavanaugh, Ann Todd, Hattie McDaniel. Sweet nostalgia about ultra-sensitive teen (Crain) in 1920s who gets more than a crush on her handsome new French teacher. The manner in which the teacher relates to Margie is innocent enough, but it surely would get him thrown in jail today! Loaded with snippets of period songs ("April Showers," "My Time Is Your Time," the title tune, etc.).

Margin for Error (1943) **74m.** ** D: Otto Preminger. Joan Bennett, Milton Berle, Otto Preminger, Carl Esmond, Howard Freeman, Ed McNamara. Dated, awkward "comedy" of Jewish cop Berle assigned to guard German consul in N.Y.C. during WW2. Director Preminger should have told actor Preminger to stop overacting.▶

Maria Marten, or The Murder in the Red Barn (1935-British) **70m.** **½ D: Milton Rosmer. Tod Slaughter, Sophie Stewart, D.J. Williams, Eric Portman, Claire Greet, Gerard Tyrell. A secretly corrupt squire (Slaughter) impregnates a country girl (Stewart) then murders her, burying her body in his barn. First of Slaughter's authentic, old-style melodramas, the sort he performed on stage for years. If you dislike this kind of thing, drop a star from the rating. Loosely based on a real event.▼▶

Marianne (1929) **112m.** *** D: Robert Z. Leonard. Marion Davies, George Baxter, Lawrence Gray, Cliff Edwards, Benny Rubin. Davies' first talkie also one of her best; fine vehicle for her charm and comic talent as French girl pursued by two American soldiers during WW1.

Marie Antoinette (1938) **149m.** **½ D: W. S. Van Dyke II. Norma Shearer, Tyrone Power, John Barrymore, Robert Morley, Gladys George, Anita Louise, Joseph Schildkraut. Opulent MGM production of life of 18th-century French queen lacks pace but has good acting, with great performance by Morley as Louis XVI. Shearer captures essence of title role as costumer retells her life from Austrian princess to doomed queen of crumbling empire. Roadshow version runs 157m. with overture, intermission/entr'acte, exit music. ▼◑

Marie Antoinette (1955-French) **C-108m.** **½ D: Jean Delannoy. Michele Morgan, Richard Todd, Jean Morel. Epic on life of famed 18th-century French queen has marvelous Morgan in title role but lacks perspective and scope.

Marie Galante (1934) **88m.** ** D: Henry King. Spencer Tracy, Ketti Gallian, Ned Sparks, Helen Morgan, Sig Rumann, Leslie Fenton, Jay C. Flippen, Stepin Fetchit. So-so adventure in which down-on-her-luck Gallian links up with good guy Tracy to thwart a scheme to blow up the Panama Canal. French actress Gallian's first American film; she's attractive, but her career went nowhere. Morgan sings two forgettable songs. Reworked as CHARLIE CHAN IN PANAMA. ▼◑

"Marihuana" (1936) **58m.** BOMB D: Dwain Esper. Harley Wood, Hugh McArthur, Pat Carlyle, Paul Ellis, Dorothy Dehn, Richard Erskine. Some naive, fun-loving kids puff on the title weed, offered them by a man you know is evil incarnate because he has a mustache, and the result is nude swimming, a drowning . . . and worse! This exploitation fare is a real scream, almost mind-boggling in its dopiness. And don't forget that it was researched "with the help of federal, state and police narcotic officers." A companion piece to REEFER MADNESS. Originally titled "MARIJUANA"—THE DEVIL'S WEED. ▼◑

Marine Raiders (1944) **91m.** ** D: Harold D. Schuster. Pat O'Brien, Robert Ryan, Ruth Hussey, Frank McHugh, Barton MacLane. Typical RKO WW2 film, this time focusing on Marine training. ▼

Marines, Let's Go (1961) **C-104m.** *½ D: Raoul Walsh. Tom Tryon, David Hedison, Barbara Stuart, William Tyler. Tedium about four soldiers, their comic adventures on leave in Tokyo, and their dramatic encounters on Korean battlefield. CinemaScope. ◑

Marius (1931-French) **125m.** *** D: Alexandre (Alexander) Korda. Raimu, Pierre Fresnay, Charpin, Alida Rouffe, Orane Demazis. Amusing, flavorful if a bit too theatrical satire of provincial life, centering on the love of Marius (Fresnay) for Fanny (Demazis). Raimu is wonderful as César, cafe owner and father of Marius. Screenplay by Marcel Pagnol; first of a trilogy, followed by FANNY and CÉSAR. All three were the basis of the play and movie FANNY (1961). Remade in 2013 by Daniel Auteuil. ▼◑

Marjorie Morningstar (1958) **C-123m.** **½ D: Irving Rapper. Gene Kelly, Natalie Wood, Claire Trevor, Ed Wynn, Everett Sloane, Carolyn Jones, Martin Milner, George Tobias, Martin Balsam, Ruta Lee, Edward (Edd) Byrnes, Shelley Fabares. Diluted adaptation of Herman Wouk's bestseller about a well-to-do Jewish girl, conflicted about her religion and background, who's swept off her feet by a musical theater director-performer at a Catskills resort one summer. Kelly is perfectly cast. ▼◑

Mark, The (1961-British) **127m.** ***½ D: Guy Green. Stuart Whitman, Maria Schell, Rod Steiger, Brenda De Banzie, Maurice Denham, Donald Wolfit, Paul Rogers, Donald Houston. Whitman is excellent in his portrayal of emotionally broken sex criminal who has served time, now wants to make new start. Thoughtful, well-acted adult drama written by Sidney Buchman and Stanley Mann. CinemaScope. ▼◑

Marked Woman (1937) **99m.** *** D: Lloyd Bacon. Bette Davis, Humphrey Bogart, Lola Lane, Isabel Jewell, Jane Bryan, Eduardo Ciannelli, Allen Jenkins, Mayo Methot. Bristling gangster drama of D.A. Bogart convincing Bette and four girlfriends to testify against their boss, underworld king Ciannelli. ▼◑

Mark of the Gorilla (1950) **68m.** *½ D: William Berke. Johnny Weissmuller, Trudy Marshall, Suzanne Dalbert, Onslow Stevens, Selmer Jackson, Robert Purcell, Pierce Lyden. A ruthless gang in search of gold disguise themselves as apes in this ludicrous *Jungle Jim* entry. ◑

Mark of the Hawk, The (1957-British) **C-83m.** *** D: Michael Audley. Eartha Kitt, Sidney Poitier, Juano Hernandez, John McIntire. Unusual tale intelligently acted, set in contemporary Africa, with peaceful vs. violent means for racial equality the main theme. Originally titled ACCUSED. Aka SHAKA ZULU. SuperScope 235. ◑

Mark of the Renegade, The (1951) **C-81m.** **½ D: Hugo Fregonese. Ricardo Montalban, Cyd Charisse, J. Carrol Naish, Gilbert Roland, Antonio Moreno, George Tobias, Andrea King, Armando Silvestre, Georgia Backus, Robert Warwick, Robert Cornthwaite. Colorful adventure, based on a story by *Zorro* creator Johnston McCulley, set in 1820s California, then part of Mexico. Dashing Montalban is sent to Los Angeles, which has been besieged by pirates, on a mission that requires him to romance the gorgeous Charisse. Forget the plot and just enjoy the fine cast, gorgeous costumes, Charisse's fiery dance number, and the novelty (for 1951) of a Latino as a leading man.

Mark of the Vampire (1935) **61m.** *** D: Tod Browning. Lionel Barrymore, Elizabeth Allan, Bela Lugosi, Lionel Atwill, Carol (Carroll) Borland, Jean Hersholt, Donald Meek. Delightful, intriguing tale of vampires terrorizing European village; inspector Atwill, vampire expert Barrymore investigate. Beautifully done, with an incredible ending. Remake of Browning's silent LONDON AFTER MIDNIGHT. ▼◑

Mark of the Vampire (1957) SEE: Vampire, The

Mark of the Whistler, The (1944) 61m. *** D: William Castle. Richard Dix, Janis Carter, Porter Hall, Paul Guilfoyle, John Calvert. Dix is a tramp who pretends to be the long-lost owner of a dormant trust fund in this compelling entry of *The Whistler* series, based on a story by Cornell Woolrich.

Mark of Zorro, The (1920) 90m. ***½ D: Fred Niblo. Douglas Fairbanks, Sr., Marguerite De La Motte, Noah Beery, Robert McKim, Charles Mailes. Silent classic with Fairbanks as the masked hero of old California; perhaps Doug's best film—his first swashbuckler. Nonstop fun. Remade in 1940. ▼●▶

Mark of Zorro, The (1940) 93m. ***½ D: Rouben Mamoulian. Tyrone Power, Linda Darnell, Basil Rathbone, Gale Sondergaard, Eugene Pallette, J. Edward Bromberg, Montagu Love. Lavish swashbuckler with Power as son of California aristocrat in 1800s, alternately a foppish dandy and a dashing masked avenger of evil: climactic swordplay with Rathbone a swashbuckling gem. Great score by Alfred Newman. Remake of 1920 classic. Remade for TV in 1974. ▼●▶

Marnie (1964) C-129m. *** D: Alfred Hitchcock. Sean Connery, Tippi Hedren, Diane Baker, Martin Gabel, Louise Latham, Alan Napier. This story of a habitual thief (Hedren) whose employer (Connery) is determined to understand her illness was considered a misfire in 1964 . . . but there's more than meets the eye, especially for Hitchcock buffs. Script by Jay Presson Allen. Look for Bruce Dern, Mariette Hartley, and Melody Thomas Scott in small roles. ▼●▶

Marriage Circle, The (1924) 90m. *** D: Ernst Lubitsch. Florence Vidor, Monte Blue, Marie Prevost, Creighton Hale, Adolphe Menjou, Harry Myers, Dale Fuller, Esther Ralston. Classic, influential silent comedy about the flirtations and infidelities of several well-to-do characters in Vienna, the "city of laughter and romance." Lubitsch's initial American comedy of manners, inspired by Chaplin's A WOMAN OF PARIS. Remade as the musical ONE HOUR WITH YOU. ▼▶

Marriage-Go-Round, The (1960) C-98m. **½ D: Walter Lang. Susan Hayward, James Mason, Julie Newmar, Robert Paige, June Clayworth. Film version of Leslie Stevens' saucy play about marriage: Mason is professor attracted to free-love–oriented Newmar. Amusing, but lacks real bite. CinemaScope. ▶

Marriage Is a Private Affair (1944) 116m. *** D: Robert Z. Leonard. Lana Turner, James Craig, John Hodiak, Frances Gifford, Hugh Marlowe, Keenan Wynn. Somewhat dated, glossy MGM yarn of man-chasing Turner, not about to be stopped just because she's married.

Marriage-Italian Style (1964-Italian) C-102m. *** D: Vittorio De Sica. Sophia Loren, Marcello Mastroianni, Aldo Puglisi, Pia Lindstrom, Vito Moriconi, Marilu Tolo. Spicy account of Loren's efforts to get long-time lover Mastroianni to marry her and stay her husband. Based on Eduardo De Filippo's 1946 play *Filumena*. ▼▶

Marriage on the Rocks (1965) C-109m. ** D: Jack Donohue. Frank Sinatra, Deborah Kerr, Dean Martin, Cesar Romero, Hermione Baddeley, Tony Bill, Nancy Sinatra, John McGiver, Trini Lopez. Frank and Deborah have marital spat, get quickie Mexican divorce, she ends up married to his best pal, Dino. A waste of real talent. Panavision. ▼▶

Married Bachelor (1941) 81m. **½ D: Edward Buzzell. Robert Young, Ruth Hussey, Felix Bressart, Lee Bowman, Sam Levene, Sheldon Leonard. Needing cash to pay off a gambling debt to a gangster (who else but Sheldon Leonard?), Young finds a manuscript of a bachelor's guide to marriage and pretends to be the author, which brings him fame and fortune. Wife Hussey is understandably miffed. Pleasant comic fluff, written by Dore Schary.

Married Before Breakfast (1937) 71m. **½ D: Edwin L. Marin. Robert Young, Florence Rice, June Clayworth, Barnett Parker, Warren Hymer, Hugh Marlowe. Zany fluff about carefree inventor Young, who sells his hair-removing cream to a razor company for $250,000 and spends a crazy night out on the town, during which he gets mixed up with thieves, loses his fiancée, and gains a new one. Breezy and painless.

Married Woman, A (1964-French) 94m. ** D: Jean-Luc Godard. Macha Meril, Philippe Leroy, Bernard Noel. Turgid three-cornered romance, with Meril unable to decide between husband Leroy and lover Noel; then, she finds herself pregnant. Godard narrates this pretentious allegory of middle-class alienation. ▼▶

Marrying Kind, The (1952) 93m. *** D: George Cukor. Judy Holliday, Aldo Ray, Madge Kennedy, Sheila Bond, John Alexander, Rex Williams, Phyllis Povah, Peggy Cass, Mickey Shaughnessy, Griff Barnett. Bittersweet drama of young couple on verge of divorce recalling their life together via flashbacks; sensitive performers outshine talky script—but story and situations haven't dated one bit. Look for Charles Bronson as postal worker. ▼▶

Marry Me Again (1953) 73m. ** D: Frank Tashlin. Robert Cummings, Marie Wilson, Mary Costa, Jess Barker. Mild shenanigans of aviator Cummings and beauty contest winner Wilson's on-again, off-again romance.

Marshal's Daughter, The (1953) 71m. *½ D: William Berke. Ken Murray, Laurie Anders, Preston Foster, Hoot Gibson. Cornpone oater with Murray and Anders ridding their town of outlaws; Tex Ritter even sings a song, with veteran Gibson in supporting role. ▼❚

Marty (1955) 91m. ***½ D: Delbert Mann. Ernest Borgnine, Betsy Blair, Joe Mantell, Joe De Santis, Esther Minciotti, Augusta Ciolli, Karen Steele, Jerry Paris, Frank Sutton. Borgnine shines as a Bronx butcher who unexpectedly finds love. Paddy Chayefsky adapted his TV play for the screen. Oscar winner for Borgnine, Chayefsky, Mann, and Best Picture. Some prints include a scene with Blair and her parents that's inexplicably missing from other versions. ▼●❚

Marx Brothers at the Circus SEE: **At the Circus**

Marx Brothers Go West SEE: **Go West**

Mary Burns, Fugitive (1935) 84m. *** D: William K. Howard. Sylvia Sidney, Melvyn Douglas, Pert Kelton, Alan Baxter, Wallace Ford, Brian Donlevy. Fine gangster melodrama. Sidney is dragged into underworld, valiantly tries to escape her gangster lover (Baxter).

Maryland (1940) C-92m. **½ D: Henry King. Walter Brennan, Fay Bainter, Brenda Joyce, John Payne, Charles Ruggles, Marjorie Weaver. Predictable story given elaborate treatment. Bainter refuses to let son Payne ride horses since his father was killed that way. Beautiful color scenery. ❚

Mary, Mary (1963) C-126m. **½ D: Mervyn LeRoy. Debbie Reynolds, Barry Nelson, Michael Rennie, Diane McBain, Hiram Sherman. Unremarkable, stagy adaptation of Jean Kerr's sex comedy about divorced couple trying to screw up each other's new romances. Stick with THE AWFUL TRUTH.❚

Mary of Scotland (1936) 123m. ***½ D: John Ford. Katharine Hepburn, Fredric March, Florence Eldridge, Douglas Walton, Moroni Olsen, John Carradine, Robert Barrat, Ian Keith, Ralph Forbes, Alan Mowbray, Donald Crisp. Lavish historical drama in which Mary, Queen of Scots (Hepburn), returns to her homeland from France, to rule "fairly and justly." She falls in love with Lord March, and contends with various treacheries. Based on a play by Maxwell Anderson.▼●❚

Mary Poppins (1964) C-140m. **** D: Robert Stevenson. Julie Andrews, Dick Van Dyke, David Tomlinson, Glynis Johns, Ed Wynn, Hermione Baddeley, Karen Dotrice, Matthew Garber, Arthur Treacher, Reginald Owen. There's charm, wit, and movie magic to spare in Walt Disney's adaptation of P. L. Travers' book about a "practically perfect" nanny who brings profound change to the Banks family of London, circa 1910. Oscars went to Richard and Robert Sherman for their tuneful score, the song "Chim-Chim-Cheree," the formidable

Visual Effects team, Cotton Warburton for his editing, and Andrews, in her film debut (though Van Dyke is equally good as Bert, the whimsical jack of all trades). That's Jane Darwell, in her last screen appearance, as the bird lady. A wonderful movie. Scripted by coproducer Bill Walsh and Donald Da Gradi. Adapted for the stage in 2004. For an interesting backstory about this movie, see SAVING MR. BANKS (2013). ▼●❚

Mary Ryan, Detective (1949) 67m. **½ D: Abby Berlin. Marsha Hunt, John Litel, June Vincent, Harry Shannon, Wm. "Bill" Phillips, Katharine Warren, Victoria Horne, John Dehner. Policewoman Hunt goes undercover in a women's prison to uncover a clever gang of jewel thieves and their slippery fence, leading to an unexpected mastermind behind the operation. Fairly absorbing cops-and-robbers programmer, with some surprisingly tough and violent bits. ❚

Mary Stevens, M.D. (1933) 72m. **½ D: Lloyd Bacon. Kay Francis, Lyle Talbot, Glenda Farrell, Thelma Todd, Harold Huber, Una O'Connor. Francis' and Talbot's lives and careers take different paths upon their graduation from medical school. Solid soaper, noteworthy for its depiction of a female doctor's struggles in a man's world.

Mask, The (1961) SEE: **Eyes of Hell**

Mask of Diijon, The (1946) 73m. ** D: Lewis Landers. Erich von Stroheim, Jeanne Bates, Denise Vernac, William Wright, Edward Van Sloan. Stroheim is hypnotist who has delusions of grandeur, and schemes to commit murder; exciting finish. ▼❚

Mask of Dimitrios, The (1944) 95m. *** D: Jean Negulesco. Peter Lorre, Sydney Greenstreet, Zachary Scott, Faye Emerson, Victor Francen, George Tobias, Steve Geray, Eduardo Ciannelli, Florence Bates. Fine, offbeat melodrama with mild-mannered mystery writer Lorre reviewing life of notorious scoundrel Scott (in film debut). Frank Gruber adapted Eric Ambler's novel *A Coffin for Dimitrios.* As always, Lorre and Greenstreet make a marvelous team.▼❚

Mask of Dust SEE: **Race for Life**

Mask of Fu Manchu, The (1932) 68m. **½ D: Charles Brabin. Boris Karloff, Lewis Stone, Karen Morley, Myrna Loy, Charles Starrett, Jean Hersholt. Elaborate chiller of Chinese madman Karloff menacing expedition that plundered the tomb of Genghis Khan. Adaptation of Sax Rohmer novel is ornate and hokey, but fun; Loy is terrific as Fu's deliciously evil daughter.▼

Mask of the Avenger (1951) C-83m. ** D: Phil Karlson. John Derek, Anthony Quinn, Jody Lawrance, Arnold Moss. Not up to snuff; man posing as Count of Monte Cristo is involved in swordplay. ▼

Mask of the Dragon (1951) 53m. *½ D: Sam Newfield. Richard Travis, Sheila

Ryan, Sid Melton, Michael Whalen, Lyle Talbot. A U.S. serviceman in Korea is duped into bringing a jade dragon home to L.A., where a smuggler's knife in the back is his reward; his private eye pal Travis gets right on the case. This surreal B-movie experience includes an organ music score, Melton's nonstop clowning as the killer's henchman Manchu Murphy, and a mid-movie break for two cowboy songs!

Masque of the Red Death, The (1964) C-86m. ***½ D: Roger Corman. Vincent Price, Hazel Court, Jane Asher, David Weston, Patrick Magee, Skip Martin, Nigel Green, John Westbrook. The most Bergman-like of Corman's films, an ultrastylish adaptation of the Poe tale (with another, *Hop Frog,* worked in as a subplot), starring Price as evil Prince Prospero, living it up in eerie, timeless castle while plague ravages the countryside. Beautifully photographed in England by Nicolas Roeg. Remade in 1989. Panavision. ▼O◗

Masquerade (1965-British) C-101m. **½ D: Basil Dearden. Cliff Robertson, Jack Hawkins, Marisa Mell, Michel Piccoli, Bill Fraser, John LeMesurier. Above-average spy satire highlighted by Robertson's portrayal of recruited agent. Good support casting with good location shooting to give Arabic atmosphere.

Masquerade in Mexico (1945) 96m. ** D: Mitchell Leisen. Dorothy Lamour, Arturo de Cordova, Patric Knowles, Ann Dvorak, George Rigaud, Natalie Schafer, Billy Daniels. Frivolous plot, forgettable songs combine in this limp musicomedy of bullfighters, romance, and Mexican intrigue. Remake of MIDNIGHT (1939) by the same director.

Masquerader, The (1933) 78m. **½ D: Richard Wallace. Ronald Colman, Elissa Landi, Halliwell Hobbes, Helen Jerome Eddy. Dated but enjoyable film goes on the ory that two Colmans are better than one; journalist pretends he is his drug-addict cousin, a member of Parliament. Hobbes is splendid as loyal and long-suffering butler.

Massacre (1934) 70m. **½ D: Alan Crosland. Richard Barthelmess, Ann Dvorak, Dudley Digges, Claire Dodd, Henry O'Neill, Robert Barrat. Unusual story about college-educated Sioux (Barthelmess) who tries to fight injustice and discrimination against his people back on the reservation. Interesting attempt to show an enlightened view of contemporary Indians, in the context of typical Warner Bros. melodramatic fodder. ◗

Massacre Hill SEE: **Eureka Stockade**

Master Minds (1949) 64m. ** D: Jean Yarbrough. Leo Gorcey, Huntz Hall, Gabriel Dell, Alan Napier, Jane Adams, Billy Benedict, Bennie Bartlett, David Gorcey, Bernard Gorcey, Glenn Strange, Skelton Knaggs. Temporarily psychic Sach (Hall) is kidnapped by mad scientist Napier, who swaps his personality with that of hulking, hairy Strange. Strange, acting like the goofy Sach, is a daunting and occasionally funny sight. Standard *Bowery Boys* stuff, with Leo Gorcey's malaprops particularly outrageous. ◗

Master of Ballantrae, The (1953) C-89m. **½ D: William Keighley. Errol Flynn, Roger Livesey, Anthony Steel, Yvonne Furneaux. Robert Louis Stevenson's historical yarn has Flynn involved in plot to make Bonnie Prince Charles king of England; on-location filming in Scotland, Sicily, and England adds scope to costumer. Remade for TV in 1984. ▼O◗

Master of the House (1925-Danish) 81m. *** D: Carl Theodor Dreyer. Johannes Meyer, Astrid Holm, Karin Nellemose, Mathilde Nielsen, Clara Schønfeld. Solid domestic comedy-drama about a haughty brute who criticizes and humiliates his wife and children until his elderly nanny steps in to teach him a lesson in obedience. Scenario by Dreyer and Svend Rindom, from Rindom's play. ▼◗

Master of the World (1961) C-104m. *** D: William Witney. Vincent Price, Charles Bronson, Mary Webster, Henry Hull, Richard Harrison. Sci-fi adventure adapted from two Jules Verne novels about a 19th-century genius (Price) seeking to stop war from his ingenious flying machine, a cross between a zeppelin and a helicopter. Bronson (oddly cast) admires his ends, deplores his methods, and sets out to stop him. Very well done. Screenplay by Richard Matheson. ▼O◗

Master Race, The (1944) 96m. **½ D: Herbert J. Biberman. George Coulouris, Stanley Ridges, Osa Massen, Nancy Gates, Lloyd Bridges, Carl Esmond, Morris Carnovsky, Helen Beverly. The Germans are losing WW2 and Nazi Colonel Coulouris goes incognito in a Belgian village, schemes to keep the "Master Race" alive. Thoughtful if overly melodramatic account; the character of the heroic Russian doctor/POW (Esmond) is most intriguing. ▼◗

Masterson of Kansas (1954) C-73m. ** D: William Castle. George Montgomery, Nancy Gates, James Griffith, Jean Willes, Benny Rubin, William Henry, David Bruce, Bruce Cowling, Gregg Barton, Jay Silverheels. Sheriff Bat Masterson (Montgomery) and Doc Holliday (Griffith) face a lynch mob and an Indian uprising in this routine B Western bolstered by Griffith's colorful performance. ◗

Mata Hari (1931) 90m. *** D: George Fitzmaurice. Greta Garbo, Ramon Novarro, Lionel Barrymore, Lewis Stone, C. Henry Gordon, Karen Morley. Garbo is the alluring spy of WW1, beguiling everyone from Novarro to Barrymore. Highlights: Garbo's exotic dance sequence, Morley stalked by gang executioner. That's an unbilled Mischa Auer in opening scene as condemned man who won't betray Garbo's love. ▼O◗

Mata Hari's Daughter (1954-Italian) **C-102m.** ** D: Renzo Meruis. Frank Latimore, Ludmilla Tcherina, Erno Crisa. Humdrum account of alleged daughter of famed WW1 spy in 1940 Java involved in espionage; sterile dubbing. Retitled: DAUGHTER OF MATA HARI.

Matango (1963-Japanese) **C-89m.** **½ D: Ishirô Honda. Akira Kubo, Kumi Mizuno, Hiroshi Koizumi, Kenji Sahara, Hiroshi Tachikawa, Yoshio Tsuchiya, Miki Yashiro. Seven survivors of a storm-crippled yacht end up on a Pacific island, where an uninhabited shipwreck from a year before leads them to realize the mushrooms that grow in profusion everywhere will, if eaten, gradually turn people into walking fungi—and they're running out of food. Initially slow-paced but grows into a disturbing, peculiarly intimate kind of horror, unusual for director Honda. More serious and better than suggested by its original U.S. title, ATTACK OF THE MUSHROOM PEOPLE.▶

Match King, The (1932) **80m.** **½ D: Howard Bretherton, William Keighley. Warren William, Lili Damita, Glenda Farrell, Harold Huber, John Wray, Hardie Albright. Clever, ambitious man will stop at nothing to succeed, becomes a multimillionaire buying exclusive rights to manufacture matches around the world! Interesting if uneven, story is doubly compelling because it's mostly true, based on life of Ivar Kreuger.

Matchmaker, The (1958) **101m.** *** D: Joseph Anthony. Shirley Booth, Anthony Perkins, Shirley MacLaine, Paul Ford, Robert Morse, Wallace Ford. Endearing Thornton Wilder comedy about middle-aged widower deciding to re-wed . . . but the matchmaker he consults has plans of her own. Solid performances, fine period detail; later musicalized as HELLO, DOLLY! VistaVision.▼●

Matinee Idol, The (1928) **56m.** *** D: Frank Capra. Johnnie Walker, Bessie Love, Lionel Belmore, Ernest Hilliard, Sidney D'Albrook. Delightful farce about Broadway star Walker who, while stranded in the country, appears incognito in Love's local play, then brings her amateur theater group to N.Y. to put on a hilariously bad Civil War show. Long-lost Capra silent is an expert mixture of comedy, romance, and sentiment.▼●

Mating Call, The (1928) **70m.** **½ D: James Cruze. Thomas Meighan, Evelyn Brent, Renée Adorée, Alan Roscoe, Gardner James, Helen Foster, Cyril Chadwick. Very odd silent film about a WW1 soldier (Meighan) who comes home to find his small-town sweetheart married to another man—but she's still as amorous as ever. This riles up the no-account husband, who's the power behind a secret KKK-like society! Meanwhile, Meighan "buys" himself a wife straight off the boat at Ellis Island. After all that plot, the film ends rather abruptly; still strangely compelling. Based

on a Rex Beach novel; produced by Howard Hughes.

Mating Game, The (1959) **C-96m.** *** D: George Marshall. Debbie Reynolds, Tony Randall, Paul Douglas, Fred Clark, Una Merkel, Philip Ober, Charles Lane. Zippy comedy romp of tax agent Randall falling in love with farm girl Reynolds, with Douglas rambunctious as Debbie's father. CinemaScope.▼▶

Mating of Millie, The (1948) **87m.** **½ D: Henry Levin. Glenn Ford, Evelyn Keyes, Ron Randell, Willard Parker, Virginia Hunter. Ford tries to help Keyes trap a husband so she can adopt a child, but falls in love with her himself. Predictable but pleasant.

Mating Season, The (1951) **101m.** ***½ D: Mitchell Leisen. Gene Tierney, John Lund, Miriam Hopkins, Thelma Ritter, Jan Sterling, Larry Keating, James Lorimer. Excellent, underrated comedy with cynical undertones about the American dream. Hardworking Lund marries socialite Tierney, suffers embarrassment when his plain-talking mother (Ritter) comes to town and is mistaken for servant. Ritter is simply superb. Written by Walter Reisch, Richard Breen, and producer Charles Brackett.

Matrimaniac, The (1916) **46m.** **½ D: Paul Powell. Douglas Fairbanks, Constance Talmadge, Wilbur Higby, Fred Warren, Clyde Hopkins, Winifred Westover, Monte Blue, Mildred Harris, Carmel Myers. By-the-numbers farce by Anita Loos about comical complications that result when lovesick (and ever-resourceful) Fairbanks attempts to elope with girlfriend Talmadge. Doug's boundless enthusiasm and athleticism make this worth watching.▼▶

Matter of Dignity, A (1958-Greek) **101m.** **½ D: Michael Cacoyannis. Ellie Lambeti, George Pappas, Athena Michaelidou, Eleni Zafirou, Michaelis Nikolinakos, Dimitris Papamichael. Affluent Athenian family, jolted by the threat of impending bankruptcy, pins all its hopes on the ring finger of the most eligible daughter, though the intended groom could not be more boring or the bride-to-be less willing. Meanwhile, their resentful maid—unpaid for months—tends to her injured son. Clash of the classes is *Upstairs/Downstairs* as Greek tragedy. Aka THE FINAL LIE.▼▶

Matter of Life and Death, A (1946-British) **C/B&W-104m.** **** D: Michael Powell, Emeric Pressburger. David Niven, Kim Hunter, Raymond Massey, Roger Livesey, Robert Coote, Marius Goring, Richard Attenborough. Powell and Pressburger manage to straddle reality and fantasy in a most disarming manner in this unusual story of a pilot during WW2 who claims he was accidentally chosen to die, and must now plead for his life in a Heavenly court. Like most films by this writer-director team, an absolute original—and a gem, too. Original U.S. title: STAIRWAY TO HEAVEN. ▼❱

Matter of WHO, A (1961-British) **90m. **½ D: Don Chaffey. Terry-Thomas, Alex Nicol, Sonja Ziemann, Guy Deghy, Richard Briers, Carol White, Honor Blackman. Occasionally entertaining mystery with Thomas in a rare straight role as a World Health Organization bureaucrat who turns detective to trace a smallpox carrier. ▼❱

Mauvaise Graine (1933-French) **77m. *** D: Billy Wilder, Alexandre Esway. Pierre Mingand, Danielle Darrieux, Raymond Galle, Paul Escoffier, Michel Duran, Jean Wall. Sweet comedy-drama about a disinherited layabout (Mingand) who becomes involved with a band of professional thieves while falling for a seemingly innocent 17-year-old (Darrieux). Wilder cowrote and took his first directorial credit for this film, made during the brief time he spent in Paris before coming to the U.S. Freewheeling shooting style in Paris and Marseilles and use of jump cuts prefigure the French New Wave of the '50s. ▼❱

Maverick Queen, The (1956) **C-92m. **½ D: Joseph Kane. Barbara Stanwyck, Barry Sullivan, Scott Brady, Mary Murphy, Wallace Ford. Stanwyck is peppy as outlaw who's willing to go straight for lawman Sullivan. Filmed in Naturama. ▼

Maxime (1958-French) **93m. **½ D: Henri Verneuil. Michele Morgan, Charles Boyer, Arletty, Felix Marten. Morgan is good match for Parisian scoundrel Boyer in this love tale set in 1910s.

Maybe It's Love (1930) **72m. ** D: William A. Wellman. All-American Football Eleven, Joan Bennett, Joe E. Brown, James Hall, Laura Lee, Anders Randolf, Stuart Erwin. Bennett vamps real-life all-American football stars to recruit them to join a third-rate college football squad. Not much of a film, but a must for football buffs. Based on a story by Darryl F. Zanuck (credited as Mark Canfield). Aka ELEVEN MEN AND A GIRL. ❱

Mayerling (1936-French) **92m. *** D: Anatole Litvak. Charles Boyer, Danielle Darrieux, Suzy Prim, Jean Dax, Vladimir Sokoloff. Touching, well-made romantic tragedy based on true story of Austrian Crown Prince Rudolph, who dared to fall in love with a commoner. Good performances spark international hit; miles ahead of 1968 remake. ▼❱

Mayor of 44th Street, The (1942) **86m. ** D: Alfred E. Green. George Murphy, Anne Shirley, William Gargan, Richard Barthelmess, Joan Merrill, Rex Downing, Millard Mitchell, Mary Wickes. Weird but watchable mix of music and mobsters stars Murphy as the head of a big-band booking agency harassed by ex-con Barthelmess and teenage gangs trying to muscle in on his biz. Real-life bandleader Freddy Martin is on hand with his orchestra to provide swing tunes. ❱

Mayor of Hell, The (1933) **90m. *** D: Archie Mayo. James Cagney, Madge Evans, Allen Jenkins, Dudley Digges, Arthur Byron, Frankie Darro, Allen "Farina" Hoskins. Fascinating, somewhat strange melodrama with political-machine appointee Cagney taking a genuine interest in the way kids are being mistreated at reform school run by slimy Digges. Climax is both unexpected and bizarre. Remade as CRIME SCHOOL and HELL'S KITCHEN. ❱

Maytime (1937) **132m. *** D: Robert Z. Leonard. Jeanette MacDonald, Nelson Eddy, John Barrymore, Herman Bing, Tom Brown, Lynne Carver, Rafaela Ottiano, Paul Porcasi, Sig Ruman, Walter Kingsford, Harry Davenport. One of singing duo's best films, despite occasional heavy-handedness and piercing operatic sequence near the end (composed especially for film, based on Tchaikovsky's Fifth Symphony). Exquisite filming of simple story: opera star and penniless singer fall in love in Paris, but her husband/mentor (Barrymore) interferes. Only song retained from Sigmund Romberg's hit Broadway score is "Will You Remember (Sweetheart)." ▼●❱

Maytime in Mayfair (1949-British) **C-96m. **½ D: Herbert Wilcox. Anna Neagle, Michael Wilding, Peter Graves, Tom Walls, Nicholas Phipps, Thora Hird. Pleasant, light-as-a-soufflé romantic trifle in which Wilding inherits a London dress shop which he intends to sell . . . until he meets the manager (Neagle).

Maze, The (1953) **81m. ** D: William Cameron Menzies. Richard Carlson, Veronica Hurst, Michael Pate, Katherine Emery, Hillary Brooke. Mysterious doings at a Scottish castle; a low-budgeter with a ludicrous (and unsatisfying) payoff. Stylishly composed as a 3-D movie by designer-director Menzies.

Mazel Tov SEE: **East and West**

McConnell Story, The (1955) **C-107m. *** D: Gordon Douglas. Alan Ladd, June Allyson, James Whitmore, Frank Faylen. Weepy yet effective fictional biography of jet test pilot, with Allyson as his understanding wife. CinemaScope. ▼●❱

McGuire, Go Home! (1965-British) **C-101m. **½ D: Ralph Thomas. Dirk Bogarde, George Chakiris, Susan Strasberg, Denholm Elliott. Set in 1954 Cyprus; peppy account of terrorist campaign against British occupation, with side plot of officer Bogarde in love with American girl Strasberg. Video titles: A DATE WITH DEATH; THE HIGH BRIGHT SUN. ▼

McHale's Navy (1964) **C-93m. **½ D: Edward J. Montagne. Ernest Borgnine, Joe Flynn, Tim Conway, George Kennedy, Claudine Longet, Bob Hastings, Carl Ballantine, Billy Sands, Gavin MacLeod, Jean

Willes. Theatrical feature inspired by popular TV series finds the PT-73 crew doing everything possible to try and raise money to pay off gambling debts. Usual blend of slapstick and snappy dialogue; entertaining for fans. Remade (more or less) in 1997. ▼❱

McHale's Navy Joins the Air Force (1965) **C-90m.** ****½** D: Edward J. Montagne. Tim Conway, Joe Flynn, Bob Hastings, Ted Bessell, Susan Silo, Henry Beckman, Billy Sands, Gavin MacLeod, Tom Tully, Jacques Aubuchon. Rather unusual comedy with little relation to either the first feature or the TV series (including no Borgnine). Ensign Parker (Conway) is mistaken for an Air Force hot shot, and the more he screws up, the higher he's promoted! John Fenton Murray's intricate script adds some mild satire to normal quota of slapstick; a genuine curio. ▼

McLintock! (1963) **C-127m.** ******* D: Andrew V. McLaglen. John Wayne, Maureen O'Hara, Patrick Wayne, Stefanie Powers, Yvonne De Carlo, Chill Wills, Bruce Cabot, Jack Kruschen, Jerry Van Dyke, Perry Lopez, Strother Martin. Brawling cattle baron G. W. McLintock (Wayne) locks horns with his feisty, estranged wife (O'Hara) who has returned home to get a divorce; their daughter visiting from college only complicates matters. Rowdy slapstick seldom stops—a giant mud pit free-for-all and a public spanking for O'Hara are just a few of the stops along the way in this Western version of *The Taming of the Shrew.* Not recommended for feminists. Produced by Michael Wayne. Panavision. ▼❱❳

Me and My Gal (1932) **78m.** ******* D: Raoul Walsh. Spencer Tracy, Joan Bennett, Marion Burns, George Walsh, J. Farrell MacDonald, Noel Madison. Wholly entertaining film blending comedy, romance, melodrama in one neat package; cop Tracy falls in love with waitress Bennett, whose sister and father become involved with a gangster. Stars at their most charming, with bottomless reserve of snappy dialogue. ❱

Me and the Colonel (1958) **109m.** ****½** D: Peter Glenville. Danny Kaye, Curt Jurgens, Nicole Maurey, Françoise Rosay. Franz Werfel's *Jacobowsky and the Colonel* is source for spotty satire; Jacobowsky is played by Kaye, and Jurgens is the anti-Semitic military officer, both brought together during crisis in WW2. Filmed in France. ▼

Meanest Gal in Town, The (1934) **62m.** ******* D: Russell Mack. ZaSu Pitts, Pert Kelton, El Brendel, James Gleason, Skeets Gallagher. Sleepy little town is disrupted by arrival of a hotshot dame (Kelton) who's been stranded by a theatrical troupe. When barber Brendel hires her as a manicurist, he incurs the wrath of longtime sweetheart Pitts. A fine cast of pros milks every possibility from a clever script, full of good laughs.

Meanest Man in the World, The (1943) **57m.** ******* D: Sidney Lanfield. Jack Benny, Priscilla Lane, Eddie "Rochester" Anderson, Edmund Gwenn, Matt Briggs, Anne Revere. Snappy yarn of good-natured lawyer Benny discovering that he can only succeed in business by being nasty. Benny-Rochester repartee is hilarious; film is a must for Benny devotees. That's cult figure Tor Johnson as a wrestler. ❱

Medal for Benny, A (1945) **77m.** *****½** D: Irving Pichel. Dorothy Lamour, Arturo de Cordova, J. Carrol Naish, Mikhail Rasumny, Fernando Alvarado, Charles Dingle, Frank McHugh. Small town hypocritically honors one of its war dead. Excellent comedy-drama scripted by Frank Butler from a story by John Steinbeck and Jack Wagner.

Medicine Man, The (1930) **66m.** ***½** D: Scott Pembroke. Jack Benny, Betty Bronson, Eva Novak, E. Alyn Warren, Billy Butts, Adolph Milar, George (E.) Stone, Tommy (Tom) Dugan. Smooth-talking carny medicine man comes to the aid of Bronson and her brother, who live with possibly the most abusive father in screen history! Dull melodrama would be worthless if not for curiosity value of Benny in the lead. ▼

Medium, The (1951) **84m.** ****½** D: Gian-Carlo Menotti. Marie Powers, Anna Maria Alberghetti, Leo Coleman, Belva Kibler. Murky filmization of Gian-Carlo Menotti opera about eccentric spiritualist, the girl living in her seedy apartment, the outcast mute boy in love with girl. ▼❱

Meet Boston Blackie (1941) **61m.** ******* D: Robert Florey. Chester Morris, Rochelle Hudson, Richard Lane, Charles Wagenheim, Constance Worth. First in the *Boston Blackie* series is a slick and fast-paced mystery-comedy, introducing Morris as the whimsical ex-thief tracking down spies hiding out at Coney Island. Franz Planer's stylish cinematography enhances this solid programmer.

Meet Danny Wilson (1952) **86m.** ****½** D: Joseph Pevney. Frank Sinatra, Shelley Winters, Alex Nicol, Raymond Burr. Minor but engaging musical about a young singer and his piano-playing pal, who make the mistake of signing a contract with nightclub owner/racketeer Burr—then moving in on his "girl." No original songs, but Sinatra does sing plenty of old favorites and even does a winning duet with Winters on "A Good Man Is Hard to Find." ▼

Meet Dr. Christian (1939) **63m.** ****** D: Bernard Vorhaus. Jean Hersholt, Dorothy Lovett, Robert Baldwin, Enid Bennett, Paul Harvey, Marcia Mae Jones, Jackie Moran. Typically folksy entry in film series of small-town doctor who solves everyone's difficulties. ▼❱

Meeting at Midnight SEE: **Black Magic** (1944)

Meet John Doe (1941) **132m.** ******* D: Frank Capra. Gary Cooper, Barbara Stanwyck, Edward Arnold, Walter Brennan, Spring Byington, James Gleason, Gene Lockhart. Overlong but interesting social commentary, with naive Cooper hired to spearhead national goodwill drive benefitting corrupt politician Arnold. Wordy idealism can't bury good characterizations; usual Capra touches exulting populism. Virtually all existing prints (from reissue) run 123m. Also shown in computer-colored version.▼●◗

Meet Me After the Show (1951) **C-86m.** ****½** D: Richard Sale. Betty Grable, Macdonald Carey, Rory Calhoun, Eddie Albert, Lois Andrews, Irene Ryan, Gwen Verdon. Undistinguished Grable musical lacking bounce of her other vehicles, with usual show biz storyline.◗

Meet Me at the Fair (1953) **C-87m.** ****½** D: Douglas Sirk. Dan Dailey, Diana Lynn, Hugh O'Brian, Carole Mathews, Rhys Williams, Chet Allen, Scatman Crothers. Dailey is good as a sideshow medicine man who helps a young orphan and courts Lynn; pleasant musical.

Meet Me in Las Vegas (1956) **C-112m.** ****** D: Roy Rowland. Dan Dailey, Cyd Charisse, Agnes Moorehead, Lili Darvas, Jim Backus; guest stars Jerry Colonna, Paul Henreid, Lena Horne, Frankie Laine, Mitsuko Sawamura. Rancher Dailey finds that haughty ballerina Charisse is his good luck charm in the casinos of Las Vegas. Lumbering, overlong MGM musical features songs by Horne, Laine, and Colonna with no attempt to integrate them into the already contrived storyline. ▼●◗

Meet Me in St. Louis (1944) **C-113m.** ******** D: Vincente Minnelli. Judy Garland, Margaret O'Brien, Lucille Bremer, Tom Drake, Mary Astor, Leon Ames, Marjorie Main, June Lockhart, Harry Davenport, Joan Carroll, Hugh Marlowe. Captivating musical based on Sally Benson's slice of Americana about a family's experiences during the years 1903 and 1904, leading up to the St. Louis World's Fair. Judy sings wonderful Ralph Blane–Hugh Martin songs "The Boy Next Door," "Have Yourself a Merry Little Christmas," "The Trolley Song," while Margaret O'Brien steals every scene she's in as little sister Tootie. (In fact, she won a special Oscar, as the year's best child actress.) Screenplay by Irving Brecher and Fred F. Finklehoffe. Years later adapted for Broadway.▼●◗

Meet Me on Broadway (1946) **78m.** ****** D: Leigh Jason. Marjorie Reynolds, Fred Brady, Jinx Falkenburg, Spring Byington, Allen Jenkins, Gene Lockhart, Loren Tindall. Cocky Broadway director (Brady) gets fired and takes a job staging a country club charity production, much to the chagrin of his wisecracking songwriter (Jenkins) and long-suffering girlfriend/ac-

tress (Reynolds). Minor musical fluff made watchable by the fine supporting cast.

Meet Me Tonight SEE: **Tonight at 8:30**

Meet Miss Bobby Socks (1944) **68m.** ****½** D: Glenn Tryon. Bob Crosby, Lynn Merrick, Louise Erickson, Robert White, Howard Freeman, Mary Currier, Louis Jordan and His Tympany Five. "Typical" teen Erickson has been writing pen-pal letters to lonely G.I. Crosby. Complications arise when he shows up on her family's doorstep and she schemes to hype his singing career. Lightly likable programmer.

Meet Mr. Lucifer (1953-British) **83m.** ****** D: Anthony Pelissier. Stanley Holloway, Peggy Cummins, Jack Watling, Barbara Murray, Joseph Tomelty, Gordon Jackson, Jean Cadell, Kay Kendall, Ian Carmichael. Meek little satire on the evils of television, with Holloway in dual role as Devil and his earthly helper.

Meet Nero Wolfe (1936) **73m.** ****½** D: Herbert Biberman. Edward Arnold, Lionel Stander, Joan Perry, Victor Jory, Nana Bryant, Dennie Moore. Rex Stout's corpulent detective makes his screen debut, with Arnold faithfully playing him as demanding and difficult—in short, none too endearing (though he laughs a bit too much); Stander is his legman, Archie. The mystery itself (with two seemingly unrelated murders) is not bad. Bonus: a young and beautiful Rita Cansino (later Hayworth) in a minor role. Followed by THE LEAGUE OF FRIGHTENED MEN.

Meet the Baron (1933) **68m.** ****½** D: Walter Lang. Jack Pearl, Jimmy Durante, ZaSu Pitts, Ted Healy and His Stooges, Edna May Oliver. Comic hodgepodge was an attempt to fashion a movie vehicle for radio comedian Pearl, in character as the tale-spinning, malaprop-laden Baron Munchausen. Supporting comics steal the show, especially Healy and his (Three) Stooges. There's also—out of left field—a Busby Berkeleyish musical number with nearly nude coeds singing "Clean as a Whistle" while taking a shower!◗

Meet the Chump (1941) **60m.** ****** D: Edward Cline. Hugh Herbert, Lewis Howard, Jeanne Kelly (Brooks), Anne Nagel, Kathryn Adams, Shemp Howard, Richard Lane. Wacky Herbert plays inept trustee of estate due young Lewis Howard, desperate to find a way to cover the fact that he's dissipated $10 million. Mildly amusing, but generally routine.

Meet the People (1944) **100m.** ****½** D: Charles Riesner. Lucille Ball, Dick Powell, Virginia O'Brien, Bert Lahr, Rags Ragland, June Allyson, Vaughn Monroe and His Orchestra, Spike Jones and His City Slickers, Bobby (Robert) Blake. Complications follow when shipyard worker Powell convinces stage star Ball to bring to Broadway the "common man" musical he's coauthored. OK musicomedy; so-so score.◗

Meet the Stewarts (1942) **73m.** ****½** D:

[442]

Alfred E. Green. William Holden, Frances Dee, Grant Mitchell, Anne Revere, Mary Gordon, Marjorie Gateson, Margaret Hamilton, Don Beddoe. Wealthy girl marries hard-working Holden, can't adjust to new financial arrangement; not earthshaking, but enjoyable. ▶

Mein Kampf (1961-Swedish) **117m. ***** D: Erwin Leiser. Narrated by Claude Stephenson. Technically smooth, impressive documentary chronicle of the horrors of Nazi Germany. Restrained narration allows the visuals to speak for themselves. ▼●▶

Melba (1953-British) **C-113m. **½** D: Lewis Milestone. Patrice Munsel, Robert Morley, Sybil Thorndike, Martita Hunt, John McCallum. Occasionally interesting biography of Australian opera star Nellie Melba.

Melody Cruise (1933) **76m. **½** D: Mark Sandrich. Charlie Ruggles, Phil Harris, Helen Mack, Greta Nissen, Chick Chandler, June Brewster. Sexy (pre-Production Code) musical comedy with Harris romancing Mack and Ruggles providing the laughs. Notable for its imaginative use of photography and optical effects, which virtually steal the show. Director Sandrich went on to do the Astaire-Rogers musicals. Look for Betty Grable in a bit. ▼

Melody for Three (1941) **67m. ** ** D: Erle C. Kenton. Jean Hersholt, Fay Wray, Walter Woolf King, Astrid Allwyn, Schuyler Standish, Irene Ryan. Adequate entry in Hersholt's *Dr. Christian* series. Wray is a music teacher and mother of violin prodigy Standish, divorced from orchestra conductor King. You can be sure that, by the final reel, the kindly doctor will reunite them. ▼

Melody Ranch (1940) **84m. ***** D: Joseph Santley. Gene Autry, Jimmy Durante, Ann Miller, Barton MacLane, Barbara Allen (Vera Vague), George "Gabby" Hayes, Mary Lee, Joe Sawyer, Jerome Cowan. Radio star Autry goes back to his hometown to get more authentic Western experience. Entertaining attempt to put Gene into a larger-scale musical, but with Durante, Vera Vague, and Gabby dominating so much of the footage it seems like even the comedy relief has comedy relief. Not aimed at Autry purists. Gene sings "We Never Dream the Same Dream Twice." ▼▶

Melody Time (1948) **C-75m. ***** D: Clyde Geronimi, Hamilton Luske, Jack Kinney, Wilfred Jackson. Roy Rogers, Bob Nolan and The Sons of the Pioneers, Bobby Driscoll, Luana Patten, The Andrews Sisters, Ethel Smith, The Dinning Sisters, Freddy Martin and His Orchestra, Fred Waring and His Pennsylvanians. Alternately cute and arty mélange of Disney cartoon shorts lines up several winners in a row: the greeting-card charm of "Once Upon a Wintertime," the surreally frenetic "Bumble Boogie," a jaunty "Johnny Appleseed," the prairie saga of "Pecos Bill," the return of Jose Carioca in

"Blame It on the Samba," the somber Joyce Kilmer poem "Trees," and more. ▼▶

Melody Trail (1935) **60m. **½** D: Joseph Kane. Gene Autry, Ann Rutherford, Smiley Burnette, Wade Boteler, Willy Costello, Al Bridge, Fern Emmett, Marie Quillan, Gertrude Messinger. Autry's second starring film for Republic is essentially a comedy involving mistaken identities, with a baby-stealing dog, Smiley's antics, and a fast-paced action climax. Nothing special, but it did set the tone for Gene's—and other similar cowboys'—future Westerns. ▼

Member of the Wedding, The (1952) **91m. ***** D: Fred Zinnemann. Ethel Waters, Julie Harris, Brandon de Wilde, Arthur Franz, Nancy Gates, James Edwards. Carson McCullers' sensitive account of child Harris prodded into growing up by her brother's forthcoming marriage. Waters, Harris, and de Wilde movingly re-create their Broadway roles, the latter two making their film debuts. Slow but worthwhile. Remade for cable TV in 1997. ▼▶

Men, The (1950) **85m. ***½** D: Fred Zinnemann. Marlon Brando, Teresa Wright, Everett Sloane, Jack Webb, Richard Erdman, Dorothy Tree, Howard St. John, DeForest Kelley. Brando excels in film debut as ex-GI adjusting to life in wheelchair after wartime injury; low-key acting is most effective. Story and screenplay by Carl Foreman. Retitled: BATTLE STRIPE. ▼●▶

Menace, The (1932) **64m. ** ** D: Roy William Neill. H. B. Warner, Bette Davis, Walter Byron, Natalie Moorhead, William B. Davidson, Crauford Kent. Man seeks revenge on his stepmother and her cohorts, who framed him for his father's murder. Based on an Edgar Wallace story; handsome, but stodgy, and pretty obvious. Davis plays a demure British ingenue.

Menace in the Night (1957-British) **78m. *½** D: Lance Comfort. Griffith Jones, Lisa Gastoni, Vincent Ball, Eddie Byrne. Tired tale of witness to murder being pressured by gang not to testify. Original British title: FACE IN THE NIGHT.

Men Against the Sky (1940) **75m. *½** D: Leslie Goodwins. Richard Dix, Wendy Barrie, Kent Taylor, Edmund Lowe, Granville Bates, Grant Withers. Dix is a defamed ex-pilot who becomes involved with the invention of a state-of-the-art wing design at an aircraft factory. Uninspired and uninspiring drama. ▶

Men Are Not Gods (1936-British) **90m. **½** D: Walter Reisch. Miriam Hopkins, Gertrude Lawrence, Sebastian Shaw, Rex Harrison, A. E. Matthews. Talky predecessor to A DOUBLE LIFE, with Harrison et al. almost making their play-acting *Othello* come true. ▼

Men Are Such Fools (1938) **69m. ** ** D: Busby Berkeley. Wayne Morris, Priscilla Lane, Humphrey Bogart, Hugh Herbert,

Johnnie Davis, Penny Singleton. Smooth advertising exec Bogart does his best to break up the marriage of ambitious career woman Lane and her nice-guy hubby Morris. Formula romantic dramedy—a rare nonmusical for Berkeley—offers a sociologically interesting portrait of working women in the '30s. Adapted from a Faith Baldwin novel. ◗

Men in Her Life, The (1941) 90m. **½ D: Gregory Ratoff. Loretta Young, Conrad Veidt, Dean Jagger, Eugenie Leontovich, John Shepperd (Shepperd Strudwick), Otto Kruger. Ballerina Young marries her dancing teacher but recalls many suitors she's known in the past. Fairly interesting lovelife saga.

Men in War (1957) 102m. *** D: Anthony Mann. Robert Ryan, Aldo Ray, Robert Keith, Phillip Pine, Nehemiah Persoff, Vic Morrow, James Edwards, L. Q. Jones. In Korea, an American platoon, separated from the main force, joins with a sergeant and nearly comatose general in an effort to rejoin the main group. Grim, low-key, and psychologically valid, this well-acted film is devoid of stereotypes and clichés; deserves to be better known. ▼◗

Men in White (1934) 80m. **½ D: Richard Boleslawski. Clark Gable, Myrna Loy, Jean Hersholt, Elizabeth Allan, Otto Kruger, Wallace Ford, Henry B. Walthall, Samuel S. Hinds. Sterling cast in sterile filming of Sidney Kingsley's play; Gable is doctor torn between study with Hersholt and marriage to society girl Loy. ◗

Men Must Fight (1933) 72m. *** D: Edgar Selwyn. Diana Wynyard, Lewis Stone, Phillips Holmes, May Robson, Ruth Selwyn, Robert Young, Hedda Hopper. Topnotch drama in which nurse Wynyard falls for ill-fated flyer Young during WW1 and becomes pregnant; the scenario eventually jumps ahead to 1940, with the world on the brink of a new Great War. This powder keg of a film is fascinating on many levels, particularly as it looks into the "future" and uncannily depicts the world at war and the mainstream popularity of television.

Men of America (1932) 57m. *** D: Ralph Ince. William Boyd, Charles "Chic" Sale, Dorothy Wilson, Ralph Ince, Henry Armetta, Alphonse Ethier, Theresa Maxwell Conover, Eugene Strong, Fatty Layman. Interesting Depression-era Western has rancher Boyd the object of suspicion when gangsters on the lam murder a local farmer. Boyd must avoid a lynching by rounding up the gang. Pre-"Hopalong Cassidy" Boyd, wearing a black shirt but a white hat here, fills the role nicely. Produced by David O. Selznick. ◗

Men of Boys Town (1941) 106m. **½ D: Norman Taurog. Spencer Tracy, Mickey Rooney, Bobs Watson, Larry Nunn, Darryl Hickman, Henry O'Neill, Lee J. Cobb. If you liked BOYS TOWN . . . ▼◗

Men of Chance (1931) 67m. **½ D: George Archainbaud. Ricardo Cortez, Mary Astor, John Halliday, Ralph Ince, Kitty Kelly, James Donlan, George Davis. Suave gambler Halliday picks up broke Astor on the streets of Paris and palms her off as a countess, in order to seduce and destroy his gambling rival Cortez . . . but falling in love wasn't part of the plan. Well-acted, smoothly done horse-racing yarn with an exciting climactic race.

Men of Sherwood Forest (1954-British) C-77m. ** D: Val Guest. Don Taylor, Reginald Beckwith, Eileen Moore, David King Wood. Yet another Robin Hood yarn, with Taylor properly sword-wielding and cavalier. ▼

Men of the Fighting Lady (1954) C-80m. *** D: Andrew Marton. Van Johnson, Walter Pidgeon, Louis Calhern, Dewey Martin, Keenan Wynn, Frank Lovejoy, Robert Horton, Bert Freed. Above-par Korean War actioner, focusing on lives of men on U. S. aircraft carrier. ▼◗

Men of Two Worlds (1946-British) C-107m. ** D: Thorold Dickinson. Phyllis Calvert, Eric Portman, Robert Adams, Cathleen Nesbitt, Orlando Martins, Cyril Raymond. Unhappy conglomeration of clichés about well-meaning British officials trying to protect natives in Africa. Retitled WITCH DOCTOR. ▼

Men Who Tread on the Tiger's Tail, The (1945-Japanese) 60m. **½ D: Akira Kurosawa. Denjiro Okochi, Susumu Fujita, Kenichi Enomoto, Suhu Nishina, Masayuki Mori, Takashi Shimura. Lyrical, humanistic (if modestly produced) fable, set in the 12th century and based on a Kabuki play about a lord who is being hunted by his brother; he and six generals dress as monks and set out on a journey across a heavily fortified barrier. Banned first by Japanese censors, who alleged it was not true to its source material, then by the country's post-WW2 military occupiers because of its depiction of feudal militarism; released in 1953. Enomoto is especially good as a porter. ▼◗

Men Without Souls (1940) 62m. ** D: Nick Grinde. Barton MacLane, John Litel, Rochelle Hudson, Glenn Ford, Don Beddoe, Cy Kendall. Strictly standard prison film, with young Ford caught up in prison scandal. MacLane repeats role from dozens of other big-house epics.

Men Without Women (1930) 73m. *** D: John Ford. Kenneth MacKenna, Frank Albertson, Paul Page, Walter McGrail, Warren Hymer, J. Farrell MacDonald, Stuart Erwin. Accomplished early talkie is the granddaddy of all submarine-trapped-on-the-bottom-of-the-ocean movies; subplot involves a disgraced British naval officer posing as an American on board the sub. Starts as a slam-bang action comedy and turns into a tense study of courage, cowardice, and grace under pressure. Keep an eye out for John Wayne as a member of the rescue crew. Surviving prints blend some talkie sequences with silent footage, music, and sound effects.

Men With Wings (1938) **C-105m.** ****½** D: William A. Wellman. Fred MacMurray, Louise Campbell, Ray Milland, Andy Devine, Walter Abel, Virginia Weidler. Fictional tale of the epic of flight, with usual love triangle. After good start, it drags on. Donald O'Connor is one of the kids in the opening scenes. ▶

Merrill's Marauders (1962) **C-98m.** ****½** D: Samuel Fuller. Jeff Chandler, Ty Hardin, Peter Brown, Andrew Duggan, Will Hutchins, Claude Akins, John Hoyt. Gritty war film; a WW2 actioner with Chandler (his last screen role) cast as Brig. Gen. Frank Merrill, leader of a band of GIs battling the Japanese in the Burmese jungle. Fuller coscripted. CinemaScope. ▼●▶

Merrily We Go to Hell (1932) **84m.** ****½** D: Dorothy Arzner. Sylvia Sidney, Fredric March, Adrianne Allen, Skeets Gallagher, George Irving, Esther Howard, Cary Grant, Kent Taylor. Heiress Sidney marries reporter March, even though she's aware of his drinking problem. Early exploration of the impact of alcoholism on family relationships benefits from solid performances by March and Sidney; she's never looked lovelier. ▶

Merrily We Live (1938) **90m.** ******* D: Norman Z. McLeod. Constance Bennett, Brian Aherne, Alan Mowbray, Billie Burke, Bonita Granville, Tom Brown, Ann Dvorak, Patsy Kelly. It's all been done before, but fluttery Burke hires suave Aherne as butler to tame spoiled Bennett. Engaging fun. ▶

Merry Andrew (1958) **C-103m.** ****½** D: Michael Kidd. Danny Kaye, Pier Angeli, Baccaloni, Robert Coote. Danny is a British teacher-archeologist with a yen for the circus and one of its performers (Angeli) in this bright musicomedy. Not as wacky as earlier Kaye efforts, but good. CinemaScope. ▶

Merry Frinks, The (1934) **67m.** ******* D: Alfred E. Green. Aline MacMahon, Guy Kibbee, Hugh Herbert, Allen Jenkins, Helen Lowell, Joan Wheeler, Frankie Darro, Ivan Lebedeff, Harold Huber, Louise Beavers. Warm, wacky portrait of an eccentric family living in a tiny N.Y.C. apartment, including drunk sportswriter Herbert, hardworking wife MacMahon, and their three annoying kids. Long-lost uncle Kibbee leaves MacMahon a fortune on the condition she leaves the crazy clan. Endearing mix of sentiment and screwball comedy. ▶

Merry-Go-Round (1923) **114m.** ****½** D: Rupert Julian. Norman Kerry, Mary Philbin, George Siegmann, Dale Fuller, Maude George, Cesare Gravina, Edith Yorke, George Hackathorne. In Old Vienna, a pretty girl who works as an organ grinder is pursued by several men, including a count who keeps his identity a secret. Written and directed by Erich von Stroheim, with all of his signature ingredients (including a painstaking re-creation of Vienna), but completed and reshaped by others. Still interesting, though it doesn't quite work, especially its absurd plot resolutions. Philbin is downright amateurish at times. ▶

Merry Go Round of 1938 (1937) **87m.** ****½** D: Irving Cummings. Bert Lahr, Jimmy Savo, Billy House, Mischa Auer, Alice Brady, Joy Hodges, Louise Fazenda. Disappointing backstage story with sentimental overtones as comedy foursome adopts little girl. Good specialty acts, great cast make tired tale endurable.

Merry Monahans, The (1944) **91m.** ****½** D: Charles Lamont. Donald O'Connor, Peggy Ryan, Jack Oakie, Ann Blyth, Rosemary De Camp, John Miljan. Spirited cast does its best with bland, utterly predictable vaudeville saga, filled with period tunes like "When You Wore a Tulip."

Merry Widow, The (1925) **137m.** ******* D: Erich von Stroheim. Mae Murray, John Gilbert, Roy D'Arcy, Tully Marshall, Josephine Crowell. A playboy prince (Gilbert) falls in love with an American showgirl (Murray). Lavish, well-produced silent version of the Franz Lehar operetta is probably von Stroheim's most "normal" film, though he still manages to inject his usual bizarre touches (including a character with a foot fetish). See if you can spot young Clark Gable as an extra. Remade twice. ▶

Merry Widow, The (1934) **99m.** ******* D: Ernst Lubitsch. Maurice Chevalier, Jeanette MacDonald, Una Merkel, Edward Everett Horton, George Barbier, Herman Bing. Chevalier (as Count Danilo) is sent to Paris to lure a wealthy widow (MacDonald) back to her homeland of Marshovia, where her taxes keep the tiny country afloat. Charming reinvention of the famous operetta gets the fabled Lubitsch touch. Many of the original Franz Lehar songs remain, with new lyrics by Lorenz Hart and Gus Kahn. Chevalier and MacDonald also filmed a French-language version. Remade in 1952. ▼●▶

Merry Widow, The (1952) **C-105m.** ****½** D: Curtis Bernhardt. Lana Turner, Fernando Lamas, Una Merkel, Richard Haydn. Franz Lehar's operetta has been rewritten (the widow is now a glamorous American who poses as a Parisian chorus girl) and the production is sumptuous, but there's no zing in this glossy remake. ▼

Merry Wives of Reno (1934) **64m.** ******* D: H. Bruce Humberstone. Guy Kibbee, Glenda Farrell, Donald Woods, Margaret Lindsay, Hugh Herbert, Frank McHugh, Ruth Donnelly, Roscoe Ates, Hobart Cavanaugh, Hattie McDaniel. Sexy fun and games revolving around three couples at a hotel in Reno, Nevada, the quickie divorce capital. A pet sheep also figures prominently in the plot. Breezy Warner Bros. farce in the wake of their notorious (lost) film CONVENTION CITY (1933) from the same writer (Robert Lord), with many of the same cast members. ▶

Merton of the Movies (1947) **82m.** ** D: Robert Alton. Red Skelton, Virginia O'Brien, Gloria Grahame, Leon Ames, Alan Mowbray, Hugo Haas. Lifeless remake of George S. Kaufman–Marc Connelly play (filmed before in 1924 and 1932) about movie-struck simpleton's adventures in Hollywood. A real disappointment. Choreographer Alton's directing debut. ▼▶

Mesa of Lost Women (1953) **70m.** BOMB D: Herbert Tevos, Ron Ormond. Jackie Coogan, Allan Nixon, Richard Travis, Mary Hill, Robert Knapp, Tandra Quinn, Chris-Pin Martin, Harmon Stevens; narrated by Lyle Talbot. In Mexico on the title mesa, mad scientist Coogan tries to infuse women with the ferocity of spiders. Why? Why not? Deranged but dull, with occasionally striking photography by Karl Struss; Coogan is a long way from THE KID. Weirdly complicated plot is the result of an unfinished film being completed by other hands after the fact. ▼▶

Message to Garcia, A (1936) **77m.** *** D: George Marshall. Wallace Beery, Barbara Stanwyck, John Boles, Alan Hale, Mona Barrie, Herbert Mundin. Historical fiction about agent Boles trying to reach General Garcia during Spanish-American war, with dubious help of roguish Beery and well-bred Stanwyck. Very entertaining. ▶

Meteor Monster SEE: **Teenage Monster**

Metropolis (1927-German) **124m.** **** D: Fritz Lang. Brigitte Helm, Alfred Abel, Gustav Froelich, Rudolf Klein-Rogge, Fritz Rasp. Classic silent-film fantasy of futuristic city and its mechanized society, with upper-class young man abandoning his life of luxury to join oppressed workers in a revolt. Heavy going at times, but startling set design and special effects command attention throughout. Innumerable shorter versions of this film exist, including a 1984 reissue with color tints and a Giorgio Moroder score. Major 2010 restoration, with much long-missing footage, runs 153m. ▼●▶

Metropolitan (1935) **75m.** **½ D: Richard Boleslawski. Lawrence Tibbett, Virginia Bruce, Alice Brady, Cesar Romero, Thurston Hall, Luis Alberni, Ruth Donnelly, Jane Darwell. Enjoyable (if predictable) musical with Tibbett ideally cast as a talented but struggling opera singer who yearns for stardom. Tibbett's many songs include "Road to Mandalay" and "Figaro," which he performs most impressively.

Mexicali Rose (1939) **60m.** *** D: George Sherman. Gene Autry, Smiley Burnette, Noah Beery, Luana Walters, William Farnum, William Royle, LeRoy Mason, Wally Albright, Roy Barcroft. When Gene discovers his radio sponsor is fronting a stock promotion fraud, he sets out to save one of its victims, Walters' orphanage, with the help of a Mexican Robin Hood (a hammy Beery). Nothing terribly original here, but great fun just the same. Gene sings "Cielito Lindo," "El Rancho Grande," "You're the Only Star in My Blue Heaven," and the title tune. ▼▶

Mexican Bus Ride (1951-Mexican) **85m.** *** D: Luis Buñuel. Lilia Prado, Carmen (Carmelita) Gonzáles, Esteban Marquez, Leonor Gómez, Luis Aceves Castañeda. A newlywed has to postpone his honeymoon to make a two-day journey to see his dying mother so that his brothers don't steal his inheritance. During the trip he is seduced by a local tart and the bus gets stuck in a river, among other bizarre incidents. Plot merely serves as a pretext for Buñuel to indulge in erotically charged dream sequences in a darkly comical parable about birth, love, and death. Not one of Buñuel's major works, but quite enjoyable all the same. Original title: SUBIDA AL CIELO. ▼

Mexican Hayride (1948) **77m.** ** D: Charles Barton. Bud Abbott, Lou Costello, Virginia Grey, Luba Malina, John Hubbard, Pedro de Cordoba, Fritz Feld. Lackluster A&C vehicle, with the boys on a wild goose chase with a mine deed in Mexico. Based on a Cole Porter Broadway musical, but without the songs! ▼▶

Mexican Manhunt (1953) **71m.** *½ D: Rex Bailey. George Brent, Hillary Brooke, Morris Ankrum, Karen Sharpe. Actors walk through thin script about solving of old crime.

Mexican Spitfire Fiery Mexican beauty Lupe Velez had personality to burn, but by the late 1930s Hollywood had seemingly run out of ideas to showcase her talent. Then in 1939 RKO cast her in a grade-B comedy called THE GIRL FROM MEXICO, with Donald Woods as an American who falls in love with her, and veteran comic Leon Errol as Woods' Uncle Matt, who becomes her soulmate. The combination of slapstick-style farce and the charisma of Velez clicked with audiences, and before year's end the studio had a follow-up film in theaters called MEXICAN SPITFIRE, which launched the official series. The second film expanded Errol's comic opportunities by introducing a second character for him to play, a tippling British visitor called Lord Epping. As Uncle Matt's wife, Elisabeth Risdon doesn't approve of his friendship with Lupe—but as a social climber, she's forced to kowtow to the aristocratic Epping. Two-reel comedy writers stitched the stories together from this foundation, and Errol was in his element. His routines are often hilarious; what's more, he and Lupe have a great screen rapport. Once the formula was set, however, it never varied, and at times it's hard to distinguish one Spitfire film from another. If ever a series

[446]

was carried by the sheer force of its stars' personalities, this is it; when the surrounding material is good, the Spitfire films are very funny indeed, but too often a sense of déjà vu hangs over the proceedings, and even Lupe's hundred-watt star power can't take it very far.

MEXICAN SPITFIRE

The Girl From Mexico (1939)
Mexican Spitfire (1939)
Mexican Spitfire Out West (1940)
Mexican Spitfire's Baby (1941)
Mexican Spitfire at Sea (1942)
Mexican Spitfire Sees a Ghost (1942)
Mexican Spitfire's Elephant (1942)
Mexican Spitfire's Blessed Event (1943)

Mexican Spitfire (1939) **67m. ***** D: Leslie Goodwins. Lupe Velez, Leon Errol, Donald Woods, Linda Hayes, Cecil Kellaway, Elisabeth Risdon. First official entry in the series is a retread of THE GIRL FROM MEXICO, but shifts focus from bland leading man Woods to hilarious Errol in dual role of Uncle Matt and the tipsy Lord Epping. Meanwhile, Matt's wife (Risdon) attempts to break up her nephew's marriage to the fiery Carmelita. Some solid belly laughs here.▼▶
Mexican Spitfire at Sea (1942) **73m. **** D: Leslie Goodwins. Lupe Velez, Leon Errol, Charles "Buddy" Rogers, ZaSu Pitts, Elisabeth Risdon, Florence Bates, Marion Martin, Lydia Bilbrook. Protracted shipboard antics as the Spitfire causes chaos on an ocean liner in pursuit of a business deal. Series was simply repeating itself by now. ▶
Mexican Spitfire Out West (1940) **76m. **½** D: Leslie Goodwins. Lupe Velez, Leon Errol, Donald Woods, Elisabeth Risdon, Cecil Kellaway. The tempestuous Latin bombshell decides that her hubby isn't paying enough attention to her, so she goes to Reno for a divorce. Lively farce repeats many gags from first Spitfire film, but they're still funny. ▶
Mexican Spitfire's Baby (1941) **69m. **** D: Leslie Goodwins. Lupe Velez, Leon Errol, Charles "Buddy" Rogers, Elisabeth Risdon, Lydia Bilbrook, ZaSu Pitts, Fritz Feld. The Spitfire and her husband (Rogers, replacing Donald Woods) get more than they bargained for when their newly adopted French war orphan turns out to be a very grown-up (and very sexy) blonde, nicely played by Marion Martin. ▶
Mexican Spitfire's Blessed Event (1943) **63m. **½** D: Leslie Goodwins. Lupe Velez, Leon Errol, Walter Reed, Elisabeth Risdon, Lydia Bilbrook, Hugh Beaumont, Alan Carney, Wally Brown. Last entry in the frantic series revolves around the Spitfire's often riotous masquerade of motherhood in an effort to help her husband clinch a big business deal. ▶

Mexican Spitfire Sees a Ghost (1942) **70m. **** D: Leslie Goodwins. Lupe Velez, Leon Errol, Charles "Buddy" Rogers, Elisabeth Risdon, Donald MacBride, Minna Gombell, Mantan Moreland. Errol's riotous turn in three roles fails to save this weak "haunted" house comedy. ▶
Mexican Spitfire's Elephant (1942) **64m. **½** D: Leslie Goodwins. Lupe Velez, Leon Errol, Walter Reed, Elisabeth Risdon, Marion Martin, Lydia Bilbrook, Lyle Talbot, Luis Alberni. Smugglers on a ship use Errol to unwittingly smuggle a gem through customs in a miniature elephant in this frenetic farce. ▶
MGM's The Big Parade of Comedy (1964) **90m. **½** Compiled by Robert Youngson. Fifty of the greatest stars of all time appear in this compilation, but too briefly. Still worthwhile for many priceless sequences with Garbo, Laurel and Hardy, Keaton, Gable, Robert Benchley, Jean Harlow, Marion Davies, Marx Brothers, et al.▼
Miami Expose (1956) **73m. *½** D: Fred F. Sears. Lee J. Cobb, Patricia Medina, Edward Arnold, Michael Granger. Boring round-up of criminal syndicate in Sunshine State.
Miami Story, The (1954) **75m. **** D: Fred F. Sears. Barry Sullivan, Luther Adler, John Baer, Adele Jergens, Beverly Garland. Stern ex-con Sullivan redeems himself in Florida resort city. ▶
Michael (1924-Danish) **86m. ***** D: Carl Theodor Dreyer. Walter Slezak, Benjamin Christensen, Nora Gregor, Max Auzinger, Robert Garrison, Didier Aslan. Michael (played by a young, svelte Slezak), a wannabe artist, is the model and adopted son of master painter Claude Zoret (Christensen), who becomes inconsolably jealous when Michael is attracted to a pretty countess. Complex, provocative drama of desire and manipulation; Zoret's sexual feelings for Michael are obvious but never clearly spelled out. Dreyer and Thea von Harbou scripted from a novel by Herman Bang. Karl Freund, who shot the film (with Rudolph Maté), plays an art dealer.▶
Michael Shayne Having enjoyed considerable success with the Charlie Chan and Mr. Moto films, the B-picture unit of 20th Century-Fox was on the lookout for another detective to head his own series. In 1940 the studio purchased the rights to Brett Halliday's contemporary private eye character Michael Shayne, and cast reliable supporting actor Lloyd Nolan in the role. The kickoff film, MICHAEL SHAYNE, PRIVATE DETECTIVE, was based on Halliday's novel *Dividend on Death,* and (like the Chans and Motos) surrounded the starring sleuth with seasoned character actors and attractive ingenues from the contract roster. Oddly enough, none of the subsequent Shayne films utilized Halliday stories for their source material, though

they *did* turn to other prominent authors of mystery and pulp fiction, including (on one occasion) no less than Raymond Chandler, whose Philip Marlowe tale *The High Window* was turned into the Shayne vehicle TIME TO KILL. Historically, the Shayne series is significant because it presented a self-assured (and down-to-earth) private investigator on the screen *before* the vogue for Sam Spade/Philip Marlowe–type hard-boiled detectives flourished in the 1940s. And if Lloyd Nolan hasn't quite the charisma of Bogart, he was certainly adequate in the role, more so than Hugh Beaumont, who portrayed Shayne in a series of forgettable low-budgeters made for PRC later in the 1940s.

MICHAEL SHAYNE

Michael Shayne, Private Detective (1940)
Sleepers West (1941)
Dressed to Kill (1941)
Blue, White and Perfect (1941)
The Man Who Wouldn't Die (1942)
Just Off Broadway (1942)
Time to Kill (1942)
Murder Is My Business (1946)
Larceny in Her Heart (1946)
Blonde for a Day (1946)
Three on a Ticket (1947)
Too Many Winners (1947)

Michael Shayne, Private Detective (1940) **77m. **½ D:** Eugene Forde. Lloyd Nolan, Marjorie Weaver, Joan Valerie, Walter Abel, Elizabeth Patterson, Donald MacBride. Nolan gives vivid portrayal of detective Shayne, keeping an eye on heavy gambler Weaver in average private-eye thriller.▶
Michael Strogoff SEE: **Soldier and the Lady, The**
Michigan Kid (1947) **C-69m. ** D:** Ray Taylor. Jon Hall, Victor McLaglen, Rita Johnson, Andy Devine, Byron Foulger. Colorful but routine refilming of Rex Beach story of female ranch owner Johnson falling victim to corrupt town government.▼
Mickey One (1965) **93m. **½ D:** Arthur Penn. Warren Beatty, Hurd Hatfield, Alexandra Stewart, Franchot Tone, Teddy Hart, Jeff Corey, Kamatari Fujiwara, Donna Michelle. Nightclub comic in trouble with mob takes it on the lam and assumes a new identity. Offbeat, to say the least; Penn's version of a French New Wave film; heavy with visual symbols but we're not quite sure what it's all about. Fine jazz score by Eddie Sauter with solos by Stan Getz.▼●▶
Middle of the Night (1959) **118m. **½ D:** Delbert Mann. Kim Novak, Fredric March, Glenda Farrell, Lee Grant, Effie Afton, Martin Balsam, Albert Dekker. Slow-moving screen version of Paddy Chayefsky play, with March a middle-aged man about to marry much younger Novak.▶

Midnight (1934) **80m. **½ D:** Chester Erskine. Sidney Fox, O. P. Heggie, Henry Hull, Margaret Wycherly, Lynne Overman, Richard Whorf, Humphrey Bogart. Jury foreman is persecuted by the press—and even his family—after sending woman to the electric chair. Dated but interesting theatrical piece, reissued as CALL IT MURDER to capitalize on Bogart's later stardom.▼●▶
Midnight (1939) **94m. ***½ D:** Mitchell Leisen. Claudette Colbert, Don Ameche, John Barrymore, Francis Lederer, Mary Astor, Hedda Hopper, Monty Woolley. Penniless Colbert masquerades as Hungarian countess in chic Parisian marital mixup; near-classic comedy written by Billy Wilder and Charles Brackett. Barrymore's antics are especially memorable. Remade as MASQUERADE IN MEXICO.▼▶
Midnight Club, The (1933) **64m. *** D:** Alexander Hall, George Somnes. Clive Brook, George Raft, Helen Vinson, Alison Skipworth, Sir Guy Standing, Alan Mowbray, Ferdinand Gottschalk, Ethel Griffies, Billy Bevan. Clever crime yarn about a gang of crooks with impeccable alibis—because they all have lookalikes! Coscripted by Leslie Charteris. Title on-screen is E. PHILLIPS OPPENHEIM'S MIDNIGHT CLUB, in recognition of the then-popular author.
Midnight Lace (1960) **C-108m. *** D:** David Miller. Doris Day, Rex Harrison, John Gavin, Myrna Loy, Roddy McDowall, Herbert Marshall, Natasha Parry, Anthony Dawson. Shrill murder mystery; unbelievable plotline, but star cast and decor smooth over rough spots. Set in London; redone as a TVM in 1980.▼▶
Midnight Mary (1933) **74m. *** D:** William A. Wellman. Loretta Young, Ricardo Cortez, Franchot Tone, Andy Devine, Una Merkel, Frank Conroy, Warren Hymer. Visually arresting story, told in flashback, of hard luck Young, orphaned at nine, seduced at sixteen, sent to prison. Loaded with Wellman flourishes, and Loretta is mesmerizingly beautiful. Story by Anita Loos.▶
Midnight Phantom (1935) **63m. *½ D:** B. B. (Bernard) Ray. Reginald Denny, Claudia Dell, Lloyd Hughes, James Farley, Al St. John. A too-obvious D-grade mystery about the murder of a police chief with enemies on the streets and even more on the force. There's comical circus music as the main title theme, lots of silent-vintage stock footage, and a scene in which a voice comes from off-screen to remind an actor to speak a forgotten line!
Midnight Story, The (1957) **89m. **½ D:** Joseph Pevney. Tony Curtis, Marisa Pavan, Gilbert Roland, Ted de Corsia, Kathleen Freeman. Atmospheric murder yarn with Curtis an ex-cop seeking the culprit who killed neighborhood priest. CinemaScope.

[448]

Midsummer Night's Dream, A (1935) **133m.** ******* D: Max Reinhardt, William Dieterle. James Cagney, Dick Powell, Joe E. Brown, Jean Muir, Hugh Herbert, Olivia de Havilland, Ian Hunter, Frank McHugh, Victor Jory, Ross Alexander, Verree Teasdale, Anita Louise, Mickey Rooney, Arthur Treacher, Billy Barty. Hollywood-Shakespeare has good and bad points; Cagney as Bottom and the Mendelssohn music are among good parts; Hugh Herbert and other incongruous cast members make up the latter. After a while Rooney (as Puck) gets to be a bit too much. Hal Mohr's glistening cinematography won an Oscar—the only one ever awarded on a write-in. This was the only sound film of esteemed European stage director Reinhardt. Film debut of Olivia de Havilland (who had appeared in Reinhardt's Hollywood Bowl production of the play a year earlier). Restored Roadshow version runs 142m. with overture, intermission, exit music; other prints run 117m. ▼●◗

Mighty Barnum, The (1934) **87m.** ****½** D: Walter Lang. Wallace Beery, Adolphe Menjou, Virginia Bruce, Rochelle Hudson, Janet Beecher, Herman Bing. Fanciful biography of the famed showman is strung together by unlikely plot turns, coincidences, etc. While based on Gene Fowler's biography (and a subsequent play), the film admits it isn't truthful! There's more Beery than Barnum here; Menjou plays his reluctant partner, Bailey.

Mighty Joe Young (1949) **94m.** ******* D: Ernest B. Schoedsack. Terry Moore, Ben Johnson, Robert Armstrong, Mr. Joseph Young, Frank McHugh. Updating of KING KONG theme has comparable (and Oscarwinning) stop-motion special effects by Willis O'Brien and Ray Harryhausen, but no matching story line, and Moore is no Fay Wray. Mr. Young is good, though. Last sequence was originally shown with color tints, which have been restored for most prints. Also shown in computer-colored version. Remade in 1998. ▼●◗

Mighty McGurk, The (1946) **85m.** ***½** D: John Waters. Wallace Beery, Dean Stockwell, Dorothy Patrick, Edward Arnold, Aline MacMahon, Cameron Mitchell. Formula Beery vehicle with the star a punchy prizefighter and Stockwell as adorable boy he adopts.

Mikado, The (1939) **C-90m.** ******* D: Victor Schertzinger. Kenny Baker, John Barclay, Martyn Green, Jean Colin, Constance Wills. Baker may not be the ideal Nanki-Poo, but this color film of Gilbert and Sullivan's operetta is still worthwhile, with the marvelous G&S songs intact. ▼◗

Mildred Pierce (1945) **109m.** *****½** D: Michael Curtiz. Joan Crawford, Jack Carson, Zachary Scott, Eve Arden, Ann Blyth, Bruce Bennett, Lee Patrick, Butterfly McQueen.

Crawford won an Oscar as housewife-turned-waitress who finds success in business but loses control of ungrateful daughter Blyth—especially when she finds they're competing for the love of the same man. Solid adaptation (scripted by Ranald Mac-Dougall) of James M. Cain's novel with top supporting cast. Also shown in computer-colored version. Remade as a cable miniseries in 2011. ▼●◗

Milkman, The (1950) **97m.** ****** D: Charles T. Barton. Donald O'Connor, Jimmy Durante, Piper Laurie, Joyce Holden, William Conrad, Henry O'Neill, Jess Barker, Frank Nelson. War vet O'Connor's dad owns a dairy; when father refuses to hire him, he takes a job with the rival company, which employs his pal Durante. Mindless comedy, worth watching only for Durante and his irrepressible personality.

Milky Way, The (1936) **89m.** ******* D: Leo McCarey. Harold Lloyd, Adolphe Menjou, Verree Teasdale, Helen Mack, William Gargan, George Barbier, Dorothy Wilson, Lionel Stander. Milquetoasty milkman is recruited by scheming fight promoter Menjou after inadvertently knocking out the middleweight champion! Bland but entertaining film is one of Lloyd's best talkies. Remade, almost scene for scene, as THE KID FROM BROOKLYN, with Danny Kaye, but they couldn't top the hilarious ducking scene with Lloyd and matron Marjorie Gateson. Some prints run 83m. ▼●◗

Millerson Case, The (1947) **72m.** ****½** D: George Archainbaud. Warner Baxter, Nancy Saunders, Barbara Pepper, Clem Bevans, Paul Guilfoyle. The Crime Doctor (Baxter) probes the death of a physician and battles typhoid in the backwoods of Virginia in this entry that's par for the series.

Millionaire, The (1931) **80m.** ****½** D: John Adolfi. George Arliss, Evalyn Knapp, David Manners, Noah Beery, Florence Arliss, J. Farrell MacDonald, James Cagney. One of Arliss' audience-proof formula films, about a Henry Ford-like industrialist who's forced to retire—but can't stay idle for long. Pleasant fluff, with Cagney memorable in a one-scene appearance as a go-getting insurance salesman. Based on a story by Earl Derr Biggers—with dialogue by Booth Tarkington! Remade as THAT WAY WITH WOMEN.

Millionaire for Christy, A (1951) **91m.** ******* D: George Marshall. Fred MacMurray, Eleanor Parker, Richard Carlson, Una Merkel, Chris-Pin Martin, Douglass Dumbrille, Kay Buckley. Breezy 1930s-style screwball comedy with Parker a harried, gold-digging secretary who schemes to lasso radio personality MacMurray into marriage when she learns he's inherited $2 million. ◗

Millionaires in Prison (1940) **64m.** ****½** D: Ray McCarey. Lee Tracy, Linda Hayes, Raymond Walburn, Morgan Conway, Truman Bradley, Virginia Vale, Cliff Edwards, Shemp Howard. Agreeable programmer with an unusual premise: five millionaires head off to prison, where they mix with convict-with-a-heart-of-gold Tracy.

Millionairess, The (1960-British) **C-90m. **½** D: Anthony Asquith. Sophia Loren, Peter Sellers, Alastair Sim, Vittorio De Sica, Dennis Price. Loren is an heiress who thinks money can buy anything, until she meets Indian doctor Sellers, who won't sell his principles, or his love. Sophia is stunning, but this adaptation of G. B. Shaw's play is heavy-handed comedy. CinemaScope. **▼❶**

Million Dollar Baby (1941) **102m. **½** D: Curtis Bernhardt. Priscilla Lane, Jeffrey Lynn, Ronald Reagan, May Robson, Lee Patrick, Helen Westley. The sudden acquisition of a million dollars causes strain between wide-eyed Lane and her boyfriend (Reagan), a poor but proud pianist. Innocuous comedy sparked by Robson's patented performance as gruff but good-hearted millionairess.

Million Dollar Kid (1944) **65m. *** D: Wallace Fox. Leo Gorcey, Huntz Hall, Billy Benedict, Al Stone, Bobby Stone, Dave Durand, Gabriel Dell, Louise Currie, Noah Beery, Sr., Iris Adrian, Johnny Duncan. Fair *East Side Kids* entry about a rich kid who's leading a life of crime and taken in by the boys in an attempt to reform him. **▼❶**

Million Dollar Legs (1932) **61m. ***½** D: Edward Cline. W. C. Fields, Jack Oakie, Susan Fleming, Lyda Roberti, Andy Clyde, Ben Turpin, Dickie Moore, Billy Gilbert, Hugh Herbert. Wacky nonsense with Fields as President of Klopstokia, a nutty country entering the Olympics. Oakie is a young American pursuing W. C.'s daughter (Fleming). Joseph Mankiewicz was one of the writers of this little gem. Title on-screen is MILLION $ LEGS. **▼❶**

Million Dollar Legs (1939) **65m. **½** D: Nick Grinde. Betty Grable, Jackie Coogan, Donald O'Connor, Larry (Buster) Crabbe, Peter Lind Hayes, Richard Denning. Title supposedly refers to winning horse, but Grable is star so draw your own conclusions. Pleasant college comedy of school trying to keep on its feet. Look fast for William Holden. **▼**

Million Dollar Manhunt (1956-British) **79m.** BOMB D: Maclean Rogers. Richard Denning, Carole Mathews, Ronald Adam, Danny Green, Brian Worth, Hugh Moxey. Drab account of American agent Denning on the tail of counterfeiters and $12 million printed in Nazi Germany. Aka ASSIGNMENT REDHEAD.

Million Dollar Mermaid (1952) **C-115m. **½** D: Mervyn LeRoy. Esther Williams, Victor Mature, Walter Pidgeon, David Brian, Donna Corcoran, Jesse White, Maria Tallchief. Williams does OK as real-life aquatic star Annette Kellerman, alternating

her swimming with romancing Mature. Some typically elaborate production numbers by Busby Berkeley. **▼❶❷**

Million Dollar Weekend (1948) **72m. *** D: Gene Raymond. Gene Raymond, Francis Lederer, Stephanie Paull (Osa Massen), Robert Warwick, James Craven. Average mystery yarn with veteran cast. Stockbroker steals firm's money and heads for Hawaii, where complications snowball. **▼❶**

Million Pound Note, The SEE: **Man With a Million**

Millions Like Us (1943-British) **103m. ****** D: Frank Launder, Sidney Gilliat. Eric Portman, Patricia Roc, Gordon Jackson, Anne Crawford, Megs Jenkins, Basil Radford, Naunton Wayne, Irene Handl, Brenda Bruce. Memorable depiction of ordinary people coping with war. Roc is an airplane-factory worker during WW2, rooming in nearby hostel with women from varied social classes. Boasts realistic approach sorely missing from SWING SHIFT 40 years later.

Million to One, A (1937) **60m. *½** D: Lynn Shores. Herman Brix (Bruce Bennett), Joan Fontaine, Monte Blue, Kenneth Harlan, Suzanne Kaaren, Reed Howes. Static account of athlete preparing for the Olympic decathlon; a showcase for Brix's abilities—in fact, he competed in the 1932 games as a shotputter. Fontaine is the society girl who falls for him. **▼❶**

Mill of the Stone Women (1960-French-Italian) **C-94m. *** D: Giorgio Ferroni. Pierre Brice, Scilla Gabel, Wolfgang Preiss, Robert Boehme, Dany Carrel, Marco Guglielmi, Liana Orfei. Young writer (Brice) comes to the misty canal area of Flanders to write about an old windmill now converted into an attraction featuring statues of women in a carousel-like display. But the artist (Boehme) who owns the mill and his doctor companion (Preiss) share a dark secret about the owner's mysterious daughter (Gabel). Beautifully shot in Technicolor on fog-wreathed locations and handsome sets, this deliberately paced horror film is among the best of the wave of often-elegant "Eurohorror" that crested in the 1960s. **▼❶**

Mill on the Floss, The (1937-British) **94m. *** D: Tim Whelan. Frank Lawton, Victoria Hopper, Fay Compton, Geraldine Fitzgerald, Griffith Jones, Mary Clare, James Mason. Disappointing, dramatically uneven adaptation of George Eliot novel about a feud between a mill owner and solicitor; the latter's crippled son (Lawton) falls for the former's daughter (Fitzgerald), and various complications and tragedies ensue. Remade for TV in 1997 with Emily Watson. **▼❶**

Mills of the Gods (1934) **66m. **½** D: Roy William Neill. May Robson, Fay Wray, Victor Jory, Raymond Walburn, James Blakeley, Mayo Methot, Samuel S. Hinds, Willard Robertson. Robson inherited a plow-manufacturing company from her late husband and ran it for years, so she's not going to stand by and let her good-for-nothing children shut it down and put an entire town out of work. Diverting Depression fable with spoiled rich girl Wray falling in love with labor organizer Jory.

Mimi (1935-British) **98m.** *½ D: Paul Stein. Gertrude Lawrence, Douglas Fairbanks, Jr., Diana Napier, Harold Warrender, Carol Goodner, Austin Trevor. Lawrence is badly miscast as the tragic heroine in this straight adaptation of *La Boheme*, set in Paris' Latin Quarter, though she does get to perform one song. Incredibly sluggish, even in current 62m. prints.▼

Min and Bill (1930) **70m.** **½ D: George Hill. Marie Dressler, Wallace Beery, Dorothy Jordan, Marjorie Rambeau, Frank McGlynn. Sentimental early talkie with unforgettable team of Beery and Dressler as waterfront characters trying to protect Jordan from her alcoholic mother (Rambeau). Dressler won an Academy Award for her performance.▼❙

Mind Benders, The (1963-British) **101m.** *** D: Basil Dearden. Dirk Bogarde, Mary Ure, John Clements, Michael Bryant, Wendy Craig, Edward Fox. Top cast in slow-moving but compelling account of experiments in sensory deprivation, with espionage theme worked into plot.❙

Mind Reader, The (1933) **69m.** *** D: Roy Del Ruth. Warren William, Constance Cummings, Allen Jenkins, Natalie Moorhead, Mayo Methot, Clarence Muse. William is at his slimy peak as a medicine-show grifter who excels in the highly lucrative world of phony clairvoyants with partner Jenkins, then moves into high society selling info to rich wives about their cheating spouses. A consistently witty treat, capped by a great closing line by Jenkins.❙

Mine Own Executioner (1947-British) **108m.** *** D: Anthony Kimmins. Burgess Meredith, Dulcie Gray, Kieron Moore, Christine Norden, Barbara White, John Laurie, Michael Shepley. Engrossing drama about a brilliant, dedicated psychoanalyst (Meredith), who can't seem to sort out his own problems, and his efforts to help a schizophrenic ex-POW (Moore). Perceptive screenplay by Nigel Balchin, from his novel; solid performances all around, and some arresting visual highlights.▼

Minesweeper (1943) **67m.** ** D: William Berke. Richard Arlen, Jean Parker, Russell Hayden, Guinn "Big Boy" Williams, Chick Chandler, Douglas Fowley, Frank Fenton, Dub Taylor. Self-hating Navy man Arlen has gone AWOL and is riding the rails. What will he do now that the Japanese have attacked Pearl Harbor? By-the-numbers WW2 flag-waver is primarily of note for the presence of an unbilled Robert Mitchum as a sailor.▼❙

Ministry of Fear (1944) **85m.** *** D: Fritz Lang. Ray Milland, Marjorie Reynolds, Carl Esmond, Hillary Brooke, Percy Waram, Dan Duryea, Alan Napier, Erskine Sanford. Atmospheric thriller of wartime England with Milland, just released from a rural asylum, wanting to head for London and get back into the flow of life. But in a Hitchcockian twist, he winds up in the wrong place at the wrong time and tangles with enemy agents. Good cast, fine touches by director Lang. From the Graham Greene novel.▼❙

Miniver Story, The (1950) **104m.** **½ D: H. C. Potter. Greer Garson, Walter Pidgeon, John Hodiak, Leo Genn, Cathy O'Donnell, Henry Wilcoxon, Reginald Owen, Peter Finch. Sequel to MRS. MINIVER (filmed this time in England) doesn't work as well, but Garson and Pidgeon have some poignant scenes as family reunited in post-WW2 England. Young James Fox, billed as William, makes his film debut.▼❙

Minnesota Clay (1964-Italian-Spanish-French) **C-91m.** **½ D: Sergio Corbucci. Cameron Mitchell, Georges Riviere, Ethel Rojo, Diana Martin, Anthony Ross, Fernando Sancho, Antonio Casas, Gino Pernice. After escaping from a prison labor camp for a murder he didn't commit, gunman Mitchell's plan to seek revenge against the man who framed him is complicated by the fact that he is slowly going blind. Minor early Corbucci effort has much more of the feel of a traditional American oater than a spaghetti Western, but is enjoyable nonetheless. The DVD includes an alternate ending.❙

Minotaur, The (1961-Italian) **C-92m.** *½ D: Silvio Amadio. Bob Mathias, Rosanna Schiaffino, Alberto Lupo, Rik Battaglia. Occasional atmosphere and Schiaffino's appearance still cannot elevate story of mythological hero thwarting attempt of evil queen to subjugate city dwellers with hideous monster. Totalscope.

Minstrel Man (1944) **67m.** ** D: Joseph H. Lewis. Benny Fields, Gladys George, Alan Dinehart, Roscoe Karns, Judy Clark, Jerome Cowan, Molly Lamont, John Raitt, Lee "Lasses" White. Sappy story of a minstrel singer who abandons his daughter after wife dies in childbirth but reunites with the girl years later. Notable only as a vehicle for famed vaudevillian Fields, this low-budget musical received Oscar nominations for Best Score and Best Original Song ("Remember Me to Carolina").❙

Miracle, The (1959) **C-121m.** **½ D: Irving Rapper. Carroll Baker, Roger Moore, Walter Slezak, Vittorio Gassman, Katina Paxinou, Dennis King, Isobel Elsom. Claptrap vehicle resurrected as glossy, empty spectacle of 1810s Spain, with Baker the would-be nun unsure of her decision, Moore the soldier she romances. Technirama.▼

Miracle Can Happen, A SEE: **On Our Merry Way**

Miracle in Milan (1951-Italian) **95m. ***½** D: Vittorio De Sica. Francesco Golisano, Paolo Stoppa, Emma Gramatica, Guglielmo Barnabo. Toto the Good (Golisano) brings cheer to a dreary village of poor people, aided by the old lady who raised him, who is now in heaven. Bitingly comic condemnation of the manner in which displaced Europeans were treated after WW2.▼●

Miracle in the Rain (1956) **107m. **½** D: Rudolph Maté. Jane Wyman, Van Johnson, Peggie Castle, Fred Clark, Eileen Heckart, Josephine Hutchinson, Barbara Nichols, William Gargan, Alan King, Arte Johnson. Above-par soaper of two lost souls, Wyman and Johnson, falling in love in N.Y.C. during WW2.◗

Miracle Man, The (1932) **87m. *** D:** Norman McLeod. Sylvia Sidney, Chester Morris, Robert Coogan, John Wray, Ned Sparks, Hobart Bosworth, Lloyd Hughes, Virginia Bruce, Boris Karloff, Irving Pichel. On the lam, Chinatown-based crook Morris settles in a small town; when he meets faith healer Bosworth he sees an opportunity for a major scam. Offbeat, effective film with strong performances, including Wray as Frog, the part Lon Chaney played in the 1919 silent film. Karloff is an improbable Asian character with an awful accent. Based on a novel later turned into a play by George M. Cohan.

Miracle of Fatima SEE: **Miracle of Our Lady of Fatima, The**

Miracle of Morgan's Creek, The (1944) **99m. **** D:** Preston Sturges. Eddie Bracken, Betty Hutton, William Demarest, Diana Lynn, Brian Donlevy, Akim Tamiroff, Porter Hall, Almira Sessions, Jimmy Conlin. Frantic, hilarious comedy of Betty attending all-night party, getting pregnant and forgetting who's the father. Bracken and Demarest have never been better than in this daring wartime farce. Filmed in 1942; sort of remade as ROCK-A-BYE BABY. ▼●◗

Miracle of Our Lady of Fatima, The (1952) **C-102m. *** D:** John Brahm. Gilbert Roland, Angela Clarke, Frank Silvera, Jay Novello, Sherry Jackson. Thoughtful account of religious miracle witnessed by farm children in 1910s; intelligent script. Retitled: MIRACLE OF FATIMA.▼●◗

Miracle of the Bells, The (1948) **120m. *½** D: Irving Pichel. Fred MacMurray, Valli, Frank Sinatra, Lee J. Cobb, Charles Meredith. Contrived story of miracle occurring when movie star is laid to rest in coal-mining home town; often ludicrous, despite sincere cast. Screenplay by Ben Hecht and Quentin Reynolds. Also shown in computer-colored version.▼◗

Miracle of the Hills (1959) **73m. *½** D: Paul Landres. Rex Reason, Theona Bryant, Jay North, Gilbert Smith, Tracy Stratford, Gene Roth. Timid little Western of town-

running gal who bucks new clergyman. CinemaScope.

Miracle of the White Stallions (1963) **C-117m. *½** D: Arthur Hiller. Robert Taylor, Lilli Palmer, Curt Jurgens, Eddie Albert, James Franciscus, John Larch. Long, talky, confusing drama about evacuation of prized Lippizan show-horses from Vienna during WW2. A most un-Disneylike Disney film.▼◗

Miracle on Main Street (1939) **68m. *** D: Steve Sekely. Margo, Walter Abel, Jane Darwell, Lyle Talbot, William Collier, Sr. Limp drama about depressed carnival dancer Margo, and what happens after she finds an abandoned baby on Christmas Eve. Artistically ambitious B movie that doesn't work.

Miracle on 34th Street (1947) **96m. ***½** D: George Seaton. Maureen O'Hara, John Payne, Edmund Gwenn, Gene Lockhart, Natalie Wood, Porter Hall, William Frawley, Jerome Cowan. Classic Valentine Davies fable of Kris Kringle (Gwenn) working in Macy's, encountering an unbelieving child (Wood), and going on trial to prove he's Santa. Delightful comedy-fantasy won Oscars for Gwenn, Davies, and screenwriter Seaton. Thelma Ritter's auspicious screen debut; an amusing bit for young Jack Albertson, as a postal employee. Remade in 1973 (for TV) and 1994. Also shown in computer-colored version.▼●◗

Miracles for Sale (1939) **71m. **½** D: Tod Browning. Robert Young, Florence Rice, Frank Craven, Henry Hull, Lee Bowman, Cliff Clark, Astrid Allwyn, Walter Kingsford. Young is an ex-magician who now devises elaborate illusions for a living and tries to expose fake spiritualists. When murder rears its head and Rice is threatened, he has his hands full. Browning's last movie is a slick whodunit that cheats its audience a bit too often and features a red herring character who's painfully obvious.◗

Miracle Woman, The (1931) **90m. *** D: Frank Capra. Barbara Stanwyck, David Manners, Sam Hardy, Beryl Mercer, Russell Hopton. Stanwyck plays an evangelist (patterned after Aimee Semple McPherson) whose splashy sermons become big business. Manners is a blind man who falls in love with her. Story contrivances overcome by fine performances, direction, and camerawork (by Joseph Walker).▼◗

Miracle Worker, The (1962) **107m. ***½** D: Arthur Penn. Anne Bancroft, Patty Duke, Victor Jory, Inga Swenson, Andrew Prine, Beah Richards, Kathleen Comegys. Austerely beautiful treatment of William Gibson's play about Annie Sullivan (Bancroft), the remarkable woman who accepts the challenge of getting through to blind, deaf Helen Keller (Duke). There is absolutely no sentiment, which only increases the emotional power of the piece. Bancroft and Duke had been playing these parts on Broadway for over a year, but you'd never know it from their spontaneous and totally compelling performances, which earned them both Oscars. Originally staged as a 1957 *Playhouse 90* on TV, also directed by Penn. Remade for TV in 1979, with Duke in the role of Sullivan, and again in 2000. ▼●◗

Miraculous Journey (1948) **C-83m.** *½ D: Peter Stewart (Sam Newfield). Rory Calhoun, Andrew Long, Virginia Grey, George Cleveland. Substandard psychological study of victims of plane crash in jungle. ◗

Mirage (1965) **109m.** *** D: Edward Dmytryk. Gregory Peck, Diane Baker, Walter Matthau, Kevin McCarthy, Jack Weston, Leif Erickson, Walter Abel, George Kennedy. Fine Hitchcock-like thriller, with Peck the victim of amnesia, and everyone else out to get him. Matthau steals film as easygoing private-eye; interesting on-location footage in N.Y.C. Remade as JIGSAW (1968). ▼●◗

Miranda (1948-British) **80m.** *** D: Ken Annakin. Googie Withers, Glynis Johns, Griffith Jones, John McCallum, David Tomlinson, Margaret Rutherford, Maurice Denham. Cute movie (adapted by Peter Blackmore from his play) about a happily married doctor who's abducted by a mermaid; she agrees to send him back to dry land only if she can accompany him to see what the human world is like. Charming fluff. Amusing to see Johns and Tomlinson together years before they were husband and wife in MARY POPPINS. Title song by Jean Sablon. Followed by a sequel, MAD ABOUT MEN. ◗

Mirror Has Two Faces, The (1958-French) **98m.** **½ D: André Cayatte. Michele Morgan, Bourvil, Gerald Oury, Ivan Desny, Elizabeth Manet, Sylvie, Sandra Milo. Morgan is quite good as woman who begins life anew after plastic surgery. Remade in U.S. in 1996. ▼

Misadventures of Merlin Jones, The (1964) **C-88m.** *½ D: Robert Stevenson. Tommy Kirk, Annette Funicello, Leon Ames, Stuart Erwin, Alan Hewitt, Connie Gilchrist. Skimpy Disney comedy about college brain (Kirk) and his misadventures with mind-reading and hypnotism. Sequel: THE MONKEY'S UNCLE. ▼◗

Misbehaving Husbands (1940) **65m.** *½ D: William Beaudine. Harry Langdon, Betty Blythe, Ralph Byrd, Byron Barr (Gig Young), Gayne Whitman, Vernon Dent. Hapless department store owner forgets his wedding anniversary and, worse, is mistakenly accused of infidelity (with a mannequin!). Painful to watch the two aging leads straining to prolong their careers in this rock-bottom comedy. Young's film debut. ◗

Misfits, The (1961) **124m.** *** D: John Huston. Clark Gable, Marilyn Monroe, Montgomery Clift, Thelma Ritter, Eli Wallach, James Barton, Estelle Winwood,

Kevin McCarthy. Unsatisfying but engrossing parable authored by Arthur Miller, involving disillusioned divorcée Monroe and her brooding cowboy friends. Both Monroe's and Gable's last film. ▼●◗

Miss Annie Rooney (1942) **84m.** ** D: Edwin L. Marin. Shirley Temple, William Gargan, Guy Kibbee, Dickie Moore, Peggy Ryan, Gloria Holden, Selmer Jackson, June Lockhart. Moore gives Shirley her first screen kiss in slight tale of girl from wrong side of tracks in love with rich boy. Also shown in computer-colored version. ▼

Miss Europe SEE: **Prix de Beauté**

Miss Grant Takes Richmond (1949) **87m.** **½ D: Lloyd Bacon. Lucille Ball, William Holden, Janis Carter, James Gleason, Frank McHugh. Ball is wacky secretary innocently involved with crooks; she's the whole show. ▼◗

Missiles From Hell (1958-British) **72m.** ** D: Vernon Sewell. Michael Rennie, Patricia Medina, Milly Vitale, David Knight, Christopher Lee. British work with Polish partisans during WW2 to obtain projectile weapon held by Nazis; choppy editing. Original British title: BATTLE OF THE V-1. ◗

Missile to the Moon (1959) **78m.** *½ D: Richard Cunha. Richard Travis, Cathy Downs, K.T. Stevens, Tommy Cook. Preposterous low-budget sci-fi about lunar expedition finding sinister female presiding over race of moon-women. Lots of laughs, for all the wrong reasons. Remake of CAT-WOMEN OF THE MOON (ROCKET TO THE MOON). ▼◗

Missing Corpse, The (1945) **62m.** *½ D: Albert Herman. J. Edward Bromberg, Isabel Randolph, Frank Jenks, Eric Sinclair, Paul Guilfoyle. Slight, silly comedy-melodrama in which newspaper publisher Bromberg finds himself implicated in the murder of a slimy rival. ▼◗

Missing Guest, The (1938) **68m.** *½ D: John Rawlins. Paul Kelly, Constance Moore, William Lundigan, Edwin Stanley, Selmer Jackson, Billy Wayne. As in many 1930s B melodramas, a newspaper reporter (named "Scoop," no less) is on hand when a murder is committed, this time in a Long Island haunted house. Routine. Filmed before as SECRET OF THE BLUE ROOM, later as MURDER IN THE BLUE ROOM.

Missing Juror, The (1944) **66m.** *** D: Oscar (Budd) Boetticher. Jim Bannon, Janis Carter, George Macready, Jean Stevens, Joseph Crehan, Carole Mathews. Brisk, engrossing drama of unknown killer taking revenge on jury that sent innocent man to his death; low budget, but quite good. ◗

Missing Lady, The (1946) **60m.** **½ D: Phil Karlson. Kane Richmond, Barbara Reed, George Chandler, James Flavin, Pierre Watkin, Dorothea Kent, Claire Carleton, Jo Carroll Dennison. "The Shadow" tangles with thugs and the police while hunting down a "missing lady," which is actually a stolen jade statuette that leaves a trail of murder and numerous suspects in its wake. Last of three Monogram *Shadow* movies from 1946 is the best of the series, played like a straight film noir and offering a few surprise twists.

Mission Over Korea (1953) **85m.** *½ D: Fred F. Sears. John Hodiak, John Derek, Maureen O'Sullivan, Audrey Totter. Substandard Korean War tale. ▼

Mission to Moscow (1943) **123m.** ***½ D: Michael Curtiz. Walter Huston, Ann Harding, Oscar Homolka, George Tobias, Gene Lockhart, Frieda Inescort, Eleanor Parker. Fascinating propaganda of real-life ambassador Joseph Davies (played by Huston) in then-peaceful Russia. Well done, giving interesting insights to American concepts of USSR at the time. Davies himself introduces the film. ▶

Mississippi (1935) **73m.** ***½ D: A. Edward Sutherland. Bing Crosby, W. C. Fields, Joan Bennett, Queenie Smith, Gail Patrick, Claude Gillingwater. Fine cast in musicomedy of riverboat captain Fields and singer Crosby, with Rodgers-Hart score including "It's Easy To Remember But So Hard to Forget." Unforgettable poker game with Fields. Based on Booth Tarkington's *Magnolia*, filmed before as THE FIGHTING COWARD. Look quickly for Ann Sheridan. ▶

Mississippi Gambler, The (1953) **C-98m.** **½ D. Rudolph Maté. Tyrone Power, Piper Laurie, Julia (Julie) Adams, John McIntire, Dennis Weaver. Power is title figure with ambitions of establishing a gambling business in New Orleans. Gwen Verdon in blackface does a voodoo dance. ▶

Miss Julie (1950-Swedish) **87m.** ***½ D: Alf Sjoberg. Anita Bjork, Ulf Palme, Marta Dorff, Anders Henrikson. Masterful adaptation of August Strindberg's tragic play about the love affair between an aristocratic young woman and a commoner. Superbly acted and photographed, with imaginative use of flashbacks. A milestone in Swedish cinema. Remade in 1999, 2009, and 2014. ▼▶

Miss Lulu Bett (1921) **71m.** *** D: William deMille. Theodore Roberts, Lois Wilson, Milton Sills, Helen Ferguson, Mabel Van Buren, May (Mae) Giraci, Clarence Burton, Ethel Wales, Taylor Graves. Sad-sack housekeeper Lulu Bett (Wilson) quietly suffers while slaving away for and putting up with the tantrums and hypocrisies of the family that's taken her in. Complications arise when she "accidentally" marries a man who might be a bigamist. Pointed, pungent drama of small-town small-mindedness, adapted from Zona Gale's novel and Pulitzer Prize–winning play.

Miss Mend (1926-Russian) **250m.** *** D: Feodor Ozep, Boris Barnet. Natalia Glan, Boris Barnet, Vladimir Fogel, Igor Ilyinsky,

Sergei Komarov, Ivan Koval Samborsky. Fiery office worker Vivian Mend (Glan) and a trio of comrades battle an organization of fat-cat capitalists plotting to destroy Russia by spreading a plague. Ambitious, fast-paced serial-style thriller, in three lengthy parts, is designed to mirror German Expressionism and satirize popular American films of the era while offering a distinct anti-capitalist point of view. Supposedly based on pulp novels penned by "Jim Dollar," an American, but actually written by a Russian, Marietta Shaginian. Controversial in its day among political ideologues in its home country for being too trivial and mindlessly entertaining, despite its clear political stance. Aka THE ADVENTURES OF THREE REPORTERS; this easily could be retitled THE PERILS OF VIVIAN. ▶

Missouri Traveler, The (1958) **C-104m.** **½ D: Jerry Hopper. Brandon de Wilde, Lee Marvin, Gary Merrill, Mary Hosford, Paul Ford. Folksy, minor account of orphaned youth (de Wilde) finding new roots in Southern country town in 1910s; earnest but predictable. ▼▶

Miss Pacific Fleet (1935) **66m.** **½ D: Ray Enright. Joan Blondell, Glenda Farrell, Hugh Herbert, Allen Jenkins, Warren Hull, Eddie Acuff, Marie Wilson, Minna Gombell, Guinn Williams. The fleet's in, and hard-boiled dames Blondell and Farrell join Navy boxer Jenkins to hatch a scheme to win Blondell the title popularity contest. Fast-paced, enjoyable Warner Bros. programmer. ▶

Miss Pinkerton (1932) **66m.** ** D: Lloyd Bacon. Joan Blondell, George Brent, John Wray, Ruth Hall, C. Henry Gordon. Elizabeth Patterson, Holmes Herbert. Nurse Blondell has sixth sense for mysteries, decides to go after one in easy-to-take story. ▶

Miss Robin Crusoe (1954) **C-75m.** *½ D: Eugene Frenke. Amanda Blake, George Nader, Rosalind Hayes. Awful female version of *Robinson Crusoe*, with Blake (who's never without lipstick) surviving a shipwreck and battling savage natives. Anna Sten (wife of director Frenke) is credited as the film's "advisor"; what she knew about Crusoe or 17th-century tropical life is anybody's guess.

Miss Robin Hood (1952-British) **78m.** ** D: John Guillermin. Margaret Rutherford, Richard Hearne, Edward Lexy, Frances Rowe. OK mixture of fantasy and farce, Rutherford an elderly nut seeking retrieval of family whiskey formula; Hearne is meek girl's-magazine writer aiding her.

Miss Sadie Thompson (1953) **C-91m.** *** D: Curtis Bernhardt. Rita Hayworth, Jose Ferrer, Aldo Ray, Russell Collins, Charles Bronson. Rita gives a provocative performance in musical of Somerset Maugham's

RAIN, previously made as SADIE THOMPSON and DIRTY GERTIE FROM HARLEM U.S.A. 3-D. ▼●◗

Miss Susie Slagle's (1945) **88m.** ** D: John Berry. Veronica Lake, Sonny Tufts, Joan Caulfield, Lillian Gish, Ray Collins, Billy DeWolfe, Lloyd Bridges. Mild tale of turn-of-the-century boardinghouse for aspiring doctors and nurses.

Miss Tatlock's Millions (1948) **101m.** **½ D: Richard Haydn. John Lund, Wanda Hendrix, Barry Fitzgerald, Monty Woolley, Robert Stack, Ilka Chase, Dorothy Stickney. Original comedy of Hollywood stuntman Lund hired to masquerade as a wealthy nitwit; offbeat, to say the least. Haydn, billed as "Richard Rancyd," appears as a lawyer; watch for cameos by Ray Milland and director Mitchell Leisen.▼

Mister Big (1943) **63m.** ** D: Charles Lamont. Donald O'Connor, Gloria Jean, Peggy Ryan, Robert Paige, Elyse Knox, Florence Bates, Samuel S. Hinds, Ray Eberle, Ben Carter Choir, The Jivin' Jacks and Jills. The hepcat kids at a high-toned drama school ditch plans to perform *Antigone* to do a swing musical instead (with a blackface minstrel number thrown in for good measure). O'Connor is fun to watch, especially in his knockabout numbers with Ryan, and the jitterbugging is sprightly in this thin B musical.

Mister Cory (1957) **C-92m.** **½ D: Blake Edwards. Tony Curtis, Charles Bickford, Martha Hyer, Kathryn Grant (Crosby). Curtis does OK as poor-boy-turned-rich-gambler who returns to home town to show off his wealth. CinemaScope.

Mister Drake's Duck (1950-British) **76m.** *** D: Val Guest. Douglas Fairbanks, Jr., Yolande Donlan, Howard Marion-Crawford, Reginald Beckwith. American newlyweds Fairbanks and Donlan (wife of director Guest) buy a small English farm, then run into maddening military bureaucracy when one—but *which* one?—of their 60 ducks lays uranium eggs. Mild but diverting spoof of postwar red tape, with good performances.▼

Mister Dynamite (1935) **67m.** *** D: Alan Crosland. Edmund Lowe, Jean Dixon, Victor Varconi, Esther Ralston, Verna Hillie, Minor Watson, Matt McHugh. Peppy B movie with Lowe at his smart-aleck best as T. N. Thompson, a San Francisco private eye known as Mr. Dynamite who always seems to be one step ahead of the police. That's why he's hired to investigate a murder that's caused Watson's gambling club to be shuttered. Based on a story by Dashiell Hammett.

Mister 880 (1950) **90m.** *** D: Edmund Goulding. Dorothy McGuire, Burt Lancaster, Edmund Gwenn, Millard Mitchell, Minor Watson. Easygoing comedy, with Gwenn an elderly N.Y.C. counterfeiter tracked down by federal agent Lancaster. Script by Robert Riskin, based on a true story. ◗

Mister Moses (1965-British) **C-113m.** **½ D: Ronald Neame. Robert Mitchum, Carroll Baker, Ian Bannen, Alexander Knox, Raymond St. Jacques, Reginald Beckwith. Malarkey of rugged Mitchum and virtuous Baker leading African native tribe to their new homeland. Panavision.

Mister Roberts (1955) **C-123m.** **** D: John Ford, Mervyn LeRoy. Henry Fonda, James Cagney, William Powell, Jack Lemmon, Betsy Palmer, Ward Bond, Nick Adams, Philip Carey, Harry Carey, Jr., Ken Curtis, Martin Milner, Jack Pennick, Perry Lopez, Pat Wayne. Superb comedy-drama with Fonda recreating his favorite stage role as restless officer on WW2 cargo ship who yearns for combat action but has to contend with an irascible and eccentric captain (Cagney) instead. Fonda, Cagney, Powell (in his last screen appearance) as a philosophical doctor, and Lemmon (in an Oscar-winning performance) as the irrepressible Ensign Pulver, are all terrific. Thomas Heggen and Joshua Logan's Broadway hit was adapted for film by Logan and Frank Nugent. LeRoy replaced Ford as director sometime during production . . . but it certainly doesn't show. Sequel: ENSIGN PULVER. CinemaScope. ▼●◗

Mister Scoutmaster (1953) **87m.** *** D: Henry Levin. Clifton Webb, Edmund Gwenn, George Winslow, Frances Dee, Veda Ann Borg. Child-hater Webb becomes scoutmaster in this airy film which will appeal mainly to kids. ◗

Mister Universe (1951) **89m.** *½ D: Joseph Lerner. Jack Carson, Janis Paige, Vincent (Vince) Edwards, Bert Lahr, Robert Alda, Slapsie Maxie Rosenbloom, Joyce Matthews. Quickie comedy with good cast wasted on inferior material. Young, blond Edwards plays a bodybuilder whom Carson tries to turn into a wrestling star.

Mister V SEE: **Pimpernel Smith**

Misty (1961) **C-92m.** *** D: James B. Clark. David Ladd, Pam Smith, Arthur O'Connell, Anne Seymour. Marguerite Henry's popular children's book is nicely realized, with Ladd and Smith as children on island off Virginia coast who fall in love with a wild horse. CinemaScope.▼●◗

Mix Me a Person (1962-British) **116m.** *½ D: Leslie Norman. Anne Baxter, Donald Sinden, Adam Faith, Jack MacGowran, Topsy Jane, Walter Brown. Unexceptional drama of psychiatrist Baxter proving teenager Faith innocent of murdering a policeman.

M'Liss (1918) **73m.** *** D: Marshall Neilan. Mary Pickford, Theodore Roberts, Thomas Meighan, Tully Marshall, Charles Ogle, Monte Blue, Winnifred Greenwood. Pickford does a delightful Annie Oakley imitation in this entertaining Western set in the mining town of Red Gulch. The spunky daughter of an old geezer, she attracts the town's new schoolmaster (Meighan) while drawn into a murder case and a plot to pilfer an inheritance. Plenty of comic shtick enlivens this adaptation (by Frances Marion) of a Bret Harte story, filmed before in 1915 and again in 1936. ▼▶

Moana (1925) **85m.** ***½ D: Robert Flaherty. Ta'avale, Fa'amgase, Tu'ugaita, Moana, Pe'a. Flaherty's follow-up to NANOOK OF THE NORTH is at once a realistic yet poetic look at life in the South Seas, focusing on a young Polynesian (Moana) and his family. Filmed over a two-year period on the island of Savai'i, in the Somoas. A classic, influential film (although not as highly regarded as NANOOK or LOUISIANA STORY). ▼▶

Mob, The (1951) **87m.** *** D: Robert Parrish. Broderick Crawford, Betty Buehler, Richard Kiley, Otto Hulett, Neville Brand, Ernest Borgnine, John Marley, Charles Bronson. Crawford is tough as nails as undercover cop on the trail of waterfront racketeers and their mystery boss. Sharp dialogue (by William Bowers), good suspense in this combination crime drama-whodunit. ▶

Mob Town (1941) **70m.** *½ D: William Nigh. Billy Halop, Huntz Hall, Gabriel Dell, Bernard Punsly, Dick Foran, Anne Gwynne, Darryl Hickman, Samuel S. Hinds. Cop Foran tries to reform Halop after his gangster brother is sent to the death house, but Halop and his gang have other ideas. Insubstantial *Little Tough Guys* entry.

Moby Dick (1930) **75m.** **½ D: Lloyd Bacon. John Barrymore, Joan Bennett, Walter Long, Nigel de Brulier, Noble Johnson, Virginia Sale. Barrymore is a vivid Captain Ahab, though film is more Hollywood than Melville. Pointless love story added to original narrative, as in Barrymore's earlier silent-film version, THE SEA BEAST. Remade in 1956.

Moby Dick (1956) **C-116m.** *** D: John Huston. Gregory Peck, Richard Basehart, Friedrich Ledebur, Leo Genn, Orson Welles, James Robertson Justice, Harry Andrews, Bernard Miles, Royal Dano. Moody version of Herman Melville sea classic, with Peck lending a deranged dignity to the role of Captain Ahab. Fine scenes throughout, including second-unit camera work by the great Freddie Francis. Screenplay by Huston and Ray Bradbury. Francis Ford Coppola executive-produced 1998 remake as a TV miniseries with Patrick Stewart. ▼●▶

Mockery (1927) **70m.** *** D: Benjamin Christensen. Lon Chaney, Ricardo Cortez, Barbara Bedford, Mack Swain, Emily Fitzroy, Charles Puffy, John Mack Brown. A simple-minded peasant (Chaney) in Siberia protects a countess (Bedford) during the Russian Revolution, but later comes to resent her when she falls in love with an Army officer (Cortez). Chaney masterfully

conveys hurt, jealousy, rejection, and redemption in this compelling silent drama. ▶

Model and the Marriage Broker, The (1951) **103m.** *** D: George Cukor. Jeanne Crain, Scott Brady, Thelma Ritter, Zero Mostel, Michael O'Shea, Frank Fontaine, Nancy Kulp. Poignant, perceptive little comedy-drama chronicling the affairs of marriage broker Ritter, who plays Cupid for model Crain and X-ray technician Brady. However, most of her clients don't have pretty faces: they're shy, lonely, desperate for companionship. A winner. ▶

Model For Murder (1958-British) **75m.** ** D: Terry Bishop. Keith Andes, Hazel Court, Jean Aubrey, Michael Gough. Andes is American in England seeking late brother's girlfriend, becoming involved in jewel robbery. Adequate yarn.

Model Wife (1941) **78m.** **½ D: Leigh Jason. Joan Blondell, Dick Powell, Lee Bowman, Charlie Ruggles, Lucile Watson, Ruth Donnelly, Billy Gilbert. Joan's boss won't let her get married, but she does, to Powell, and has to keep it a secret. Fairly amusing comedy.

Modern Hero, A (1934) **71m.** *** D: G. W. Pabst. Richard Barthelmess, Jean Muir, Marjorie Rambeau, Verree Teasdale, Florence Eldridge, Dorothy Burgess, Hobart Cavanaugh. Barthelmess is excellent in one of his best roles as an ambitious circus performer who claws his way to the top of the business world as an automobile tycoon and munitions manufacturer, only to suffer tragedies in his personal and professional life. Fascinating and compelling social drama was the only American film made by famed German director Pabst.

Modern Musketeer, A (1917) **69m.** *** D: Allan Dwan. Douglas Fairbanks, Marjorie Daw, Kathleen Kirkham, Eugene Ormonde, Edythe Chapman, Frank Campeau, Tully Marshall. In a warm-up for his later swashbucklers, Fairbanks briefly appears as D'Artagnan in this entertaining comedy-melodrama, but his primary role is a chivalrous modern-day hero who leaves his Kansas hometown in search of adventure. Dwan also scripted, from E. P. Lyle, Jr.'s, short story "D'Artagnan of Kansas." An unbilled ZaSu Pitts plays a small-town damsel. ▶

Modern Times (1936) **89m.** **** D: Charlie Chaplin. Charlie Chaplin, Paulette Goddard, Henry Bergman, Chester Conklin, Stanley "Tiny" Sandford. Charlie attacks the machine age in inimitable fashion, with sharp pokes at other social ills and the struggle of modern-day survival. Goddard is the gamin who becomes his partner in life. Chaplin's last silent film (with his own music—including "Smile"—sound effects and gibberish song) is consistently hilarious, and unforgettable. Final shot is among

Chaplin's most famous and most poignant. One of Goddard's sisters early on is young Gloria DeHaven (daughter of Chaplin's assistant director). ▼●▶

Modigliani of Montparnasse SEE: **Montparnasse 19**

Mogambo (1953) C-115m. ***½ D: John Ford. Clark Gable, Ava Gardner, Grace Kelly, Donald Sinden, Philip Stainton, Eric Pohlmann, Laurence Naismith, Denis O'Dea. Lusty remake of RED DUST. Gable repeats his role, Ava replaces Harlow, Kelly has Mary Astor's part. John Lee Mahin reworked his 1932 screenplay. Romantic triangle in Africa combines love and action; beautifully filmed by Robert Surtees and F. A. Young. Title is Swahili for "passion." ▼●▶

Mohawk (1956) C-79m. **½ D: Kurt Neumann. Scott Brady, Rita Gam, Neville Brand, Lori Nelson, Allison Hayes, John Hoyt, Vera Vague (Barbara Jo Allen), Mae Clarke, Ted de Corsia. Unintentionally hilarious hokum of devil-may-care painter Brady attempting to thwart Iroquois uprising in early colonial times while tangling with squaw Gam, among other femmes. There's plenty of heavy breathing, 1950s-style, here. Includes lengthy chase scene lifted from DRUMS ALONG THE MOHAWK. ▼●▶

Mokey (1942) 88m. ** D: Wells Root. Dan Dailey, Donna Reed, Bobby (Robert) Blake, William "Buckwheat" Thomas, Cordell Hickman, Matt Moore, Etta McDaniel. Reed has problems with her stepson, who almost winds up in reform school. Typical of genre. ▶

Mole People, The (1956) 78m. ** D: Virgil Vogel. John Agar, Cynthia Patrick, Hugh Beaumont, Alan Napier. Agar and others find lost underground civilization of albino Sumerians, who have half-human creatures as their slaves. Probably the worst of Universal-International's '50s sci-fi movies. ▼●▶

Molly (1950) SEE: **Goldbergs, The**

Molly and Me (1945) 76m. *** D: Lewis Seiler. Gracie Fields, Monty Woolley, Roddy McDowall, Reginald Gardiner, Natalie Schafer, Edith Barrett, Doris Lloyd. Unemployed actress-turned-housekeeper Fields goes about brightening the life (and solving the problems) of her new boss, a dour and snippy disgraced politician (Woolley). Well played by a fine cast, with Gardiner almost stealing the film as Woolley's butler. ▶

Mollycoddle, The (1920) 86m. *** D: Victor Fleming. Douglas Fairbanks, Ruth Renick, Wallace Beery, Paul Burns, Morris Hughes, George Stewart, Charles Stevens. Amusing, cleverly devised comedy that begins with Fairbanks satirizing himself as a pampered boob who's been softened by a life of leisure in Monte Carlo. He's transformed into an all-American hero after being mistaken for a Secret Service agent and tangles with a shifty diamond smuggler (Beery). Great fun. ▼▶

Mom and Dad (1945) 97m. **½ D: William Beaudine. Hardie Albright, Lois Austin, George Eldredge, Joan Blake (Carlson), Jimmy Clarke. The saga of pretty, innocent Blake, whose repressive mother neglects to inform her about the birds and bees; she does "it," and finds herself "in trouble." Even though this notorious film opens with the National Anthem, and is a "vital educational production, appealing to all true-Americans," it was banned as obscene in some communities. Today, it's pretty tame; a fascinating curio. ▼▶

Moment of Danger SEE: **Malaga**

Mondo Cane (1963-Italian) C-105m. **½ Producer: Gualtiero Jacopetti. First and best of Italian shockumentaries, with dubbed American narration; focuses on bizarre peculiarities of man in various parts of the world. Features hit song "More." ▼●▶

Money and the Woman (1940) 67m. ** D: William K. Howard. Jeffrey Lynn, Brenda Marshall, John Litel, Lee Patrick, Henry O'Neill, Roger Pryor, Guinn "Big Boy" Williams. Convoluted quickie based on a James M. Cain story about a bank executive who falls in love with the wife of an embezzling employee. Minor programmer from a once-major director.

Money From Home (1953) C-100m. ** D: George Marshall. Dean Martin, Jerry Lewis, Marjie Millar, Pat Crowley, Richard Haydn, Robert Strauss, Gerald Mohr, Sheldon Leonard, Jack Kruschen. One of Dean and Jerry's weakest outings is slickly made but wanders all over the place, with Jerry as an aspiring veterinarian who gets involved with gangsters, steeplechase racing, an Arab ruler and his harem. Based on a Damon Runyon story. Originally in 3-D. ▶

Money, Women and Guns (1958) C-80m. ** D: Richard Bartlett. Jock Mahoney, Kim Hunter, Tim Hovey, Gene Evans. Modest Western about lawman sent to track down killers and to find heirs to victim's will. CinemaScope.

Mongols, The (1961-Italian) C-102m. ** D: Andre de Toth, Leopoldo Savona. Jack Palance, Anita Ekberg, Antonella Lualdi, Franco Silva. Unimaginative spectacle set in 13th century, with Palance the son of Genghis Khan on the rampage in Europe, Ekberg his girl. CinemaScope. ▼▶

Monika SEE: **Summer With Monika**

Monkey Business (1931) 77m. ***½ D: Norman Z. McLeod. Groucho, Harpo, Chico, Zeppo Marx, Thelma Todd, Ruth Hall, Harry Woods. Four brothers stow away on luxury liner; Groucho goes after gangster's wife Thelma Todd, all four pretend to be Maurice Chevalier to get off ship. Full quota of sight gags and puns in typically wacky comedy, coscripted by S. J. Perelman; their first film written directly for the screen. ▼●▶

Monkey Business (1952) 97m. *** D:

Howard Hawks. Ginger Rogers, Cary Grant, Charles Coburn, Marilyn Monroe, Hugh Marlowe. Grant discovers rejuvenation serum, which affects him, wife Rogers, boss Coburn, and secretary Monroe in this zany comedy. Coburn's classic line to MM: "Find someone to type this." Written by Ben Hecht, Charles Lederer, and I.A.L. Diamond; that's Hawks' voice during the opening credits.▼●▌

Monkey on My Back (1957) 93m. **½ D: Andre de Toth. Cameron Mitchell, Paul Richards, Dianne Foster, Jack Albertson, Kathy Garver. Mitchell as fighter Barney Ross, who became a dope addict, turns in sincere performance. Well-meant, engrossing little film.▐

Monkey's Uncle, The (1965) C-87m. ** D: Robert Stevenson. Tommy Kirk, Annette Funicello, Leon Ames, Frank Faylen, Arthur O'Connell, Norman Grabowski. Juvenile Disney comedy has Kirk again as Merlin Jones, college whiz-kid who first tries sleep-learning method on monkey, then sets himself up in makeshift flying machine. Flight sequences provide brightest moments. Unforgettable title song warbled by Annette and The Beach Boys. Sequel to THE MISADVENTURES OF MERLIN JONES.▼▌

Monolith Monsters, The (1957) 77m. **½ D: John Sherwood. Lola Albright, Grant Williams, Les Tremayne, Trevor Bardette. Engrossing sci-fi mystery set in desert town. When exposed to water, fragments of shattered meteorites grow and reproduce—wreaking havoc on innocent bystanders. ▼●▌

Mon Oncle (1958-French) C-126m. **** D: Jacques Tati. Jacques Tati, Jean-Pierre Zola, Adrienne Servantie, Alain Bercourt. Tati's first color film is a masterpiece. M. Hulot's simple, uncluttered life is sharply contrasted to that of his sister and brother-in-law, who live in an ultramodern, gadget-laden home reminiscent of those in Buster Keaton's silent classics. Continuous flow of sight gags (including the funniest fountain you'll ever see) makes this easygoing, nearly dialogue-less comedy a total delight. Oscar winner as Best Foreign Film. Also available in 115m. English-language version called MY UNCLE. Original U.S. release ran 110m.▼●▌

Monsieur Beaucaire (1946) 93m. *** D: George Marshall. Bob Hope, Joan Caulfield, Patric Knowles, Marjorie Reynolds, Cecil Kellaway, Joseph Schildkraut, Reginald Owen, Constance Collier. Pleasing Hope vehicle with Bob in costume as barber sent on mission as dead duck sure to be murdered. Plush settings, funny gags. Remake of 1924 Valentino drama.▼●▌

Monsieur Verdoux (1947) 123m. ***½ D: Charles Chaplin. Charles Chaplin, Martha Raye, Isobel Elsom, Marilyn Nash, Irving Bacon, William Frawley. Chaplin's controversial black comedy about a Parisian Bluebeard who murders wives for their money was years ahead of its time; its wry humor and pacifist sentiments make it quite contemporary when seen today. Broad comic sequence with Raye is particular highlight.▼●▌

Monsieur Vincent (1947-French) 114m. *** D: Maurice Cloche. Pierre Fresnay, Aimé Clariond, Jean Debucourt, Lise Delamare, Germaine Dermoz, Gabrielle Dorziat, Pierre Dux, Yvonne Gaudeau. Absorbing biography of Vincent de Paul (Fresnay), the selfless 17th-century French priest who earned fame (and sainthood) for his devotion to and advocacy of the poor. Occasionally slow moving but not without powerful dramatic moments; film mirrors the time in which it was made as it offers the point of view that the wealthy should take responsibility for those less fortunate in a war-torn world. Coscripted by Jean Anouilh and Jean Bernard-Luc. Winner of a special Academy Award, given before there was a Best Foreign Language Film category.▼▌

Monsoon (1943) SEE: **Isle of Forgotten Sins**

Monsoon (1953) C-79m. *½ D: Rodney Amateau. Ursula Thiess, Diana Douglas, George Nader, Ellen Corby. Trite drama of several people destroyed by their passions; set in India.

Monster, The (1925) 86m. ** D: Roland West. Lon Chaney, Gertrude Olmstead, Hallam Cooley, Johnny Arthur, Charles Sellon. Overdose of comedy relief hampers moody Chaney mad-doctor doings; still OK, though, as whole film has tongue-in-cheek. From Crane Wilbur's play.▼▌

Monster and the Girl, The (1941) 65m. **½ D: Stuart Heisler. Ellen Drew, Robert Paige, Paul Lukas, Joseph Calleia, George Zucco, Rod Cameron, Phillip Terry. Unusual B film starts off with story of gangsters dragging Drew into life of prostitution, then veers off into horror as Zucco transfers her dead brother's brain into body of a gorilla! White slavery angle more original than the mad-scientist stuff.▼▌

Monster From Green Hell (1957) 71m. *½ D: Kenneth Crane. Jim Davis, Robert E. Griffin, Barbara Turner, Joel Fluellen, Vladimir Sokoloff, Eduardo Ciannelli. Laboratory wasps are sent into orbit, crash-land in Africa as giant mutations. Standard 1950s sci-fi formula stuff, with lots of talk, little action. Uses ample stock footage from STANLEY AND LIVINGSTONE. Climax originally filmed in color.▼▌

Monster From Mars SEE: **Robot Monster**

Monster From the Ocean Floor (1954) 64m. BOMB D: Wyott Ordung. Anne Kimball, Stuart Wade, Wyott Ordung. Producer Roger Corman's first monster movie is a dreadful yarn about a squidlike creature pursued by a mini-submarine off the Mexican coast; 20,000 yawns under the sea. ▼▌

Monster From the Surf SEE: **Beach Girls and the Monster, The**

Monster Maker, The (1944) **62m.** ** D: Sam Newfield. J. Carrol Naish, Ralph Morgan, Tala Birell, Wanda McKay, Terry Frost, Glenn Strange. Naish lusts after McKay and she's repulsed, so, mad scientist that he is, he infects her father with a disfiguring disease and then proposes a trade: her hand in marriage for a cure! Ick factor is high in this Poverty Row horror yarn. ▼O▶

Monster of Piedras Blancas, The (1961) **71m.** *½ D: Irvin Berwick. Les Tremayne, Don Sullivan, Forrest Lewis, Jeanne Carmen, John Harmon, Frank Arvidson. Sluggish chiller with humanoid sea monster thirsting for blood on a desolate seacoast; obvious and amateurish. ▼

Monster of Terror SEE: **Die, Monster, Die!**

Monster on the Campus (1958) **76m.** **½ D: Jack Arnold. Arthur Franz, Joanna Moore, Judson Pratt, Nancy Walters, Troy Donahue. Mild-mannered college prof Franz, experimenting with the body of a fish long thought to be extinct, is unaware that its blood occasionally turns him into a murderous Neanderthal man. Silly script saved by Arnold's efficient direction and Franz's sensitive performance. ▼O▶

Monsters From Beyond the Sun SEE: **Battle Beyond the Sun**

Monster That Challenged the World, The (1957) **83m.** **½ D: Arnold Laven. Tim Holt, Audrey Dalton, Hans Conried, Casey Adams (Max Showalter). Above-average giant-creature-on-the-loose film is set in the Salton Sea, where colossal mollusks (like big caterpillars in snail shells) menace locals. Intelligent, low-key, with good monsters. ▼O▶

Monster Walks, The (1932) **63m.** **½ D: Frank Strayer. Rex Lease, Vera Reynolds, Mischa Auer, Sheldon Lewis, Sleep 'N' Eat (Willie Best). The reading of a will takes place in a mansion where hairy hands reach out of bed headboards and a caged ape screams in the cellar; sinister servant Auer even strikes Frankenstein poses! Poverty Row dark-and-stormy chiller, slow-going in spots but still corny fun. ▼▶

Monstrosity (1963) **75m.** *½ D: Joseph Mascelli. Marjorie Eaton, Frank Gerstle, Erika Peters, Judy Bamber. An elderly millionairess imports three beautiful girls to the U.S. to serve as housekeepers of her creepy mansion—and secretly plans to have her brain transplanted into one of them. Rock-bottom cheap and lurid; truly a disasterpiece. Oscar-winning film preservationist Kemp Niver plays a hairy animal-man and Bradford Dillman narrates. Dillman's brother Dean cowrote and coproduced the film. Aka THE ATOMIC BRAIN.

Montana (1950) **C-77m.** ** D: Ray Enright. Errol Flynn, Alexis Smith, S. Z.

Sakall, Douglas Kennedy, James Brown, Ian MacDonald. Strictly minor-league Western with Flynn determined to raise sheep in Montana cattle country. Odd musical interludes are no help. ▼▶

Montana Belle (1952) **C-81m.** ** D: Allan Dwan. Jane Russell, George Brent, Scott Brady, Andy Devine, Forrest Tucker. Mildly interesting Western with Russell as Belle Starr, involved with fellow outlaws, the Dalton Brothers. Filmed in 1948. ▼

Montana Mike SEE: **Heaven Only Knows**

Montana Moon (1930) **89m.** ** D: Mal St. Clair. Joan Crawford, John Mack Brown, Dorothy Sebastian, Ricardo Cortez, Benny Rubin, Cliff Edwards, Karl Dane. OUR DANCING DAUGHTERS goes west, with hot jazz baby Joan marrying down-to-earth cowboy Brown. Dated, and stiff as a board. ▶

Montana Territory (1952) **C-64m.** ** D: Ray Nazarro. Lon McCallister, Wanda Hendrix, Preston Foster, Jack Elam, Clayton Moore. McCallister is deputized cowboy who's out to bring in the outlaws.

Monte Carlo (1930) **90m.** *** D: Ernst Lubitsch. Jeanette MacDonald, Jack Buchanan, ZaSu Pitts, Claude Allister. Dated but enjoyable musical froth with Jeanette an impoverished countess wooed by royal Buchanan, who's incognito, of course. Lubitsch's methods of integrating songs into the film were innovations in 1930; most memorable is "Beyond the Blue Horizon." O▶

Montecarlo Story, The (1956-Italian-U.S.) **C-96m.** **½ D: Samuel A. Taylor. Marlene Dietrich, Vittorio De Sica, Arthur O'Connell, Mischa Auer, Natalie Trundy. Count De Sica, a suave but penniless compulsive gambler, becomes romantically involved with Dietrich, who has secrets of her own. Thin story is enhanced by location filming and stunning cinematography (by Giuseppe Rotunno). Technirama.

Monte Cristo (1922) **107m.** **½ D: Emmett J. Flynn. John Gilbert, Estelle Taylor, Robert McKim, William V. Mong, Virginia Brown Faire, George Seigmann, Spottiswoode Aitken, Renée Adorée. Edmond Dantes (Gilbert), a Marseilles seaman who is about to wed his beloved, is framed by his enemies for a crime he did not commit and spends two decades imprisoned in a chateau dungeon. He then escapes and plots revenge. Solid if uninspired version of Alexandre Dumas' oft-filmed *The Count of Monte Cristo*. ▶

Montparnasse 19 (1958-French-Italian) **120m.** **½ D: Jacques Becker. Gérard Philipe, Lilli Palmer, Anouk Aimée, Gerard Sety, Lila Kedrova, Lino Ventura. Unusual biography of Modigliani, with Philipe as the struggling early-20th-century painter; plays up the women in his life but at the same time presents a harshly realistic view of the Parisian art world and its denizens. Philipe is fine as the impoverished, boozing—and romantic—lead (the French star died in 1959, at age 36). Film was prepared by (and is dedicated to) director Max Ophuls, who died prior to shooting. Aka MODIGLIANI OF MONTPARNASSE and MODIGLIANI. ▼

Moon and Sixpence, The (1942) 89m. *** D: Albert Lewin. George Sanders, Herbert Marshall, Doris Dudley, Eric Blore, Albert Bassermann, Molly Lamont, Elena Verdugo, Florence Bates, Heather Thatcher. Surprisingly adult adaptation of W. Somerset Maugham's novel based on the life of Paul Gauguin, with Sanders as the restless (and selfish) spirit who turns his back on his family, and society, to become a painter. A postscript, tacked on to satisfy Hollywood's moral code, weakly tries to undermine the character that Sanders and writer-director Lewin have just portrayed so well! Climactic scene of paintings originally shown in color. ▼◗

Moonfleet (1955) C-87m. **½ D: Fritz Lang. Stewart Granger, George Sanders, Joan Greenwood, Viveca Lindfors, Jon Whiteley, Melville Cooper, Liliane Montevecchi. Moderately entertaining costumer, set in southern England, with suave gentleman bootlegger Granger forging a father-son relationship with orphaned Whiteley amid much intrigue. CinemaScope. ◗◗

Moon Is Blue, The (1953) 99m. **½ D: Otto Preminger. William Holden, David Niven, Maggie McNamara, Tom Tully, Dawn Addams, Gregory Ratoff. Once-saucy sex comedy about a young woman who flaunts her virginity now seems tame, too much a filmed stage play, with most innuendos lacking punch. Adapted by F. Hugh Herbert from his stage hit. Hardy Kruger (who has a small part here) played the lead in a German-language version that Preminger filmed simultaneously. ▼◗◗

Moon Is Down, The (1943) 90m. *** D: Irving Pichel. Cedric Hardwicke, Henry Travers, Lee J. Cobb, Dorris Bowdon, Margaret Wycherly, Peter Van Eyck, William Post, Jr. Fine drama from Steinbeck novel of Norway's invasion by Nazis, tracing local effect and reactions. ◗

Moonlight and Cactus (1944) 60m. *½ D: Edward Cline. The Andrews Sisters, Elyse Knox, Leo Carrillo, Eddie Quillan, Shemp Howard. Singing trio find themselves out West running a ranch and chasing romance. Lightweight production.

Moonlighter, The (1953) 75m. ** D: Roy Rowland. Barbara Stanwyck, Fred MacMurray, Ward Bond, William Ching, John Dierkes, Jack Elam. Drifter MacMurray returns home to find that sweetheart Stanwyck is about to marry his brother. Complications ensue but there are no sparks, though Stanwyck is convincing as a rugged woman of the West. Mediocre Western written by Niven Busch. Originally in 3-D. ◗

Moonlight in Havana (1942) 63m. ** D: Anthony Mann. Allan Jones, Jane Frazee, Marjorie Lord, William Frawley, Don Terry, Sergio Orta, Wade Boteler, Hugh O'Connell, Jack Norton, The Jivin' Jacks and Jills. Baseball player Jones is on suspension from his team (which is in spring training in Havana) so he accepts an offer from agent Frawley to sing with his nightclub troupe in the tropical city—but doesn't reveal his identity. Resulting mix-ups become repetitive and tiresome in this B musical, though Jones is always good.

Moonlight Murder (1936) 66m. *½ D: Edwin L. Marin. Chester Morris, Madge Evans, Leo Carrillo, Frank McHugh, Benita Hume, Grant Mitchell, Katharine Alexander, J. Carrol Naish, H. B. Warner, Duncan Renaldo. Stupid murder yarn about an egotistical tenor (Carrillo) who is killed while performing *Il Trovatore* at the Hollywood Bowl. Silly in the extreme. Screenwriters Florence Ryerson and Edgar Allan Woolf fared much better in 1939 with THE WIZARD OF OZ. Carrillo and supporting player Renaldo later teamed up on TV as the Cisco Kid and his sidekick Pancho. ◗

Moonlight Sonata (1937-British) 80m. **½ D: Lothar Mendes. Ignace Jan Paderewski, Charles Farrell, Marie Tempest, Barbara Greene, Eric Portman. Well-made but stodgy romance, set in household of Swedish baroness, is excuse for screen appearance by famous concert pianist. ▼

Moon Over Burma (1940) 76m. ** D: Louis King. Dorothy Lamour, Preston Foster, Robert Preston, Doris Nolan, Albert Basserman, Frederick Worlock. Island setting tries to cover up for same old triangle with Foster and Preston fighting over Lamour.

Moon Over Harlem (1939) 70m. **½ D: Edgar G. Ulmer. Bud Harris, Cora Green, Izinetta Wilcox, Earl Gough, Zerritta Stepteau, Petrina Moore, Christopher Columbus and His Swing Band, Sidney Bechet and His Clarinet. Fascinating all-black melodrama with music, about a wealthy widow who marries a heel, and the daughter she unjustly accuses of trying to seduce him. Oh yes, there's a subplot about gangsters preying on pushcart vendors. Possibly the cheapest of Ulmer's fabled ultra-low-budget projects; shot in just four days, but retains a real sense of time and place. ▼◗

Moon Over Miami (1941) C-91m. *** D: Walter Lang. Don Ameche, Betty Grable, Robert Cummings, Carole Landis, Charlotte Greenwood, Jack Haley. Grable, sister Landis, and Greenwood go fortune-hunting in Miami, come up with more than they bargained for in smoothly entertaining musical romance, especially nice in Technicolor. Tuneful songs include title number, "You Started Something." Remake of THREE BLIND MICE, also remade as THREE LITTLE GIRLS IN BLUE. ▼◗

Moon Pilot (1962) **C-98m.** ******* D: James Neilson. Tom Tryon, Brian Keith, Edmond O'Brien, Dany Saval, Tommy Kirk, Bob Sweeney, Kent Smith. Dated but enjoyable Disney comedy about astronaut Tryon who meets mysterious girl from another planet (Saval) just before his mission. ▼❶

Moonraker, The (1958-British) **C-82m.** ******* D: David MacDonald. George Baker, Sylvia Syms, Marius Goring, Peter Arne, Gary Raymond. Colorful action-packed adventure, set in 1650s England. The Earl of Dawlish (Baker) leads a double life as the dashing and mysterious hero known as The Moonraker, who sides with the royalists and protects Prince Charles Stuart against Oliver Cromwell. ▼

Moonrise (1948) **90m.** ****½** D: Frank Borzage. Dane Clark, Gail Russell, Ethel Barrymore, Allyn Joslyn, Henry (Harry) Morgan, Lloyd Bridges, Selena Royle, Rex Ingram, Harry Carey, Jr. Unieven script does in this psychological melodrama of angry, alienated Clark and his plight after accidentally killing the banker's son who's been taunting him for years. But it's beautifully directed; check out stunning opening shot, and opening sequence. ▼❶

Moon's Our Home, The (1936) **83m.** ****** D: William A. Seiter. Margaret Sullavan, Henry Fonda, Charles Butterworth, Beulah Bondi, Walter Brennan. Flyweight comedy about turbulent courtship and marriage of movie star and N.Y. novelist; too silly to matter, though stars do their best. (Footnote: Fonda and Sullavan had already been married and divorced when this film was made.) ▼❶

Moon-Spinners, The (1964) **C-118m.** ****½** D: James Neilson. Hayley Mills, Eli Wallach, Pola Negri, Peter McEnery, Joan Greenwood, Irene Papas. Disney's attempt at Hitchcock-like intrigue with a light touch has Hayley a vacationer in Crete who becomes involved with jewelry-smuggling ring. Too long and muddled, but still entertaining, with Negri (off-screen since 1943) an enjoyable villainess. ▼❶❶

Moontide (1942) **94m.** ****½** D: Archie Mayo. Jean Gabin, Ida Lupino, Thomas Mitchell, Claude Rains, Jerome Cowan, Helene Reynolds, Ralph Byrd, (Victor) Sen Yung, Tully Marshall. Jean Gabin's portrayal of rough seaman who cares for potential suicide (Lupino) saves an otherwise average "realistic" movie. ❶

More Than a Secretary (1936) **77m.** ****** D: Alfred E. Green. Jean Arthur, George Brent, Lionel Stander, Ruth Donnelly, Reginald Denny, Dorothea Kent. Arthur's charm gives distinction to routine comedy of secretary in love with handsome boss Brent. ❶

More the Merrier, The (1943) **104m.** ******* D: George Stevens. Jean Arthur, Joel McCrea, Charles Coburn, Richard Gaines, Bruce Bennett, Ann Savage, Ann Doran, Frank Sully, Grady Sutton. The wartime housing shortage forces Arthur to share a Washington, D.C., apartment with McCrea and crafty old codger Coburn (who won an Oscar for this comic performance). Highly entertaining, with Arthur at her peerless best. Remade as WALK, DON'T RUN. ▼❶

Morgan the Pirate (1961-Italian) **C-95m.** ****** D: Andre de Toth. Steve Reeves, Valerie Lagrange, Lydia Alfonsi, Chelo Alonso. Considering cast and Reeves' career, fairly lively and interesting swashbuckler based on life of illustrious pirate. Original Italian running time: 105m. CinemaScope. ▼●

Morituri (1965) **123m.** ****½** D: Bernhard Wicki. Marlon Brando, Yul Brynner, Janet Margolin, Trevor Howard, Wally Cox, William Redfield, Carl Esmond. Brando highlights great cast in study of anti-Nazi German who helps British capture cargo ship. Cast and Conrad Hall's photography are only assets; script degenerates. Aka THE SABOTEUR, CODE NAME MORITURI. ▼❶

Morning Departure (1950-British) **C-102m.** ******* D: Roy (Ward) Baker. John Mills, Richard Attenborough, Kenneth More, Nigel Patrick, James Hayter, Andrew Crawford, Bernard Lee, Peter Hammond, George Cole, Helen Cherry, Lana Morris. Solid, stiff-upper-lip naval drama about a submarine commander (Mills) whose routine mission turns unexpectedly perilous. The crisis brings out the true character of both the leader and his men. Based on a stage play. Aka OPERATION DISASTER. ❶

Morning Glory (1933) **74m.** ******* D: Lowell Sherman. Katharine Hepburn, Adolphe Menjou, Douglas Fairbanks, Jr., C. Aubrey Smith, Mary Duncan. Dated but lovely film from Zoe Akins' play about stagestruck young girl called Eva Lovelace who tries to succeed in N.Y.C. Good cast, sharp script, but it's magically compelling Hepburn who makes this memorable; she won her first Oscar for her work. Remade in 1958 as STAGE STRUCK. ▼❶

Morocco (1930) **92m.** ******* D: Josef von Sternberg. Gary Cooper, Marlene Dietrich, Adolphe Menjou, Francis McDonald, Eve Southern, Paul Porcasi. Dietrich is alluring and exotic in her first Hollywood film, as a cabaret singer (improbably stuck in Morocco) who must choose between wealthy Menjou and Foreign Legionnaire Cooper. A treat. Marlene sings three numbers, including "What Am I Bid." ▼❶

Mortal Storm, The (1940) **100m.** *****½** D: Frank Borzage. Margaret Sullavan, James Stewart, Robert Young, Frank Morgan, Robert Stack, Bonita Granville, Irene Rich, Maria Ouspenskaya, Gene Reynolds, Ward Bond. Nazi takeover in Germany splits family, ruins life of father, professor Morgan; Stewart tries to leave country with professor's daughter (Sullavan). Sincere filming of Phyllis Bottome's novel is beautifully acted, with one of

Morgan's finest performances. Screenplay by Claudine West, Andersen Ellis, and George Froeschel. Film debut of Dan Dailey (billed as Dan Dailey, Jr.); look sharp in second classroom scene for Tom Drake.▼▶

Moscow Nights SEE: **I Stand Condemned**

Moss Rose (1947) **82m.** **½ D: Gregory Ratoff. Peggy Cummins, Victor Mature, Ethel Barrymore, Vincent Price, Margo Woode. OK period piece of ambitious chorus girl who blackmails her way into high society; scheme nearly backfires on her.▶

Most Beautiful, The (1944-Japanese) **85m.** ** D: Akira Kurosawa. Takashi Shimura, Ichiro Sugai, Soji Kiyokawa, Takako Irie, Yoko Yaguchi. One of Kurosawa's earliest features includes considerable WW2 propaganda; young women factory workers are exhorted by foreman Shimura (star of Kurosawa's IKIRU and SEVEN SAMURAI) to become production warriors by increasing output of optical weaponry. Tearful young girl Yaguchi later married Kurosawa. Not released in America until 1987.▶

Most Dangerous Game, The (1932) **63m.** *** D: Ernest B. Schoedsack, Irving Pichel. Joel McCrea, Fay Wray, Leslie Banks, Robert Armstrong, Noble Johnson. Vivid telling of Richard Connell's famous, oft-filmed story about a megalomaniac named Count Zaroff who hunts human beings on his remote island. Banks is a florid, sometimes campy villain. Made at the same time as KING KONG by many of the same people. Remade as A GAME OF DEATH and RUN FOR THE SUN, and ripped off many other times.▼▶

Most Dangerous Man Alive (1961) **76m.** *½ D: Allan Dwan. Ron Randell, Debra Paget, Elaine Stewart, Anthony Caruso, Gregg Palmer, Morris Ankrum. Exposed to mutating rays, a criminal's body becomes like steel and he goes on the hunt for the crooks on his enemies list. Practically a remake of INDESTRUCTIBLE MAN. Veteran director Allan Dwan called it quits after this made-in-Mexico sci-fi turkey.

Most Dangerous Sin, The SEE: **Crime and Punishment** (1958)

Most Precious Thing in Life, The (1934) **67m.** ** D: Lambert Hillyer. Jean Arthur, Richard Cromwell, Donald Cook, Anita Louise, Mary Forbes, Jane Darwell, Ben Alexander, Ward Bond. Working girl Arthur has a child out of wedlock with the son of an Important Man and lives out the rest of her years keeping an eye on her boy. Sappy soaper opens in 1910; by 1916 Arthur is old and gray, and 25 years later she looks worse than Darwell!▶

Most Wanted Man SEE: **Most Wanted Man in the World, The**

Most Wanted Man in the World, The (1953-French) **85m.** ** D: Henri Verneuil. Fernandel, Zsa Zsa Gabor, Nicole Maurey, Alfred Adam. Fernandel vehicle is heavy-handed buffoonery, with bucolic comic mistaken for arch-criminal. Retitled: THE MOST WANTED MAN.

Mother (1926-Russian) **84m.** ***½ D: V. I. Pudovkin. Vera Baranovskaya, Nikolai Batalov, Ivan Koval-Samborsky, Anna Zemtsova, Aleksandr Chistyakov. Pudovkin's first feature is the vividly realized account of an apolitical working-class woman (memorably played by Baranovskaya) and how she is radicalized by the plight of her worker son during the 1905 Revolution. At once a by-the-numbers exercise in Soviet propaganda and a stirring drama of clashing ideas and unconditional love. Stunningly directed. Loosely based on a novel by Maxim Gorky, which was filmed in 1920 and remade in 1941, 1955, and 1989. Pudovkin appears briefly as a police officer.▼▶

Mother Carey's Chickens (1938) **82m.** ** D: Rowland V. Lee. Fay Bainter, Anne Shirley, Ruby Keeler, James Ellison, Walter Brennan, Frank Albertson, Virginia Weidler, Ralph Morgan, Margaret Hamilton, Donnie Dunagan. Pleasant if predictable, sentimental soaper of the Carey family and its attempt to set down roots despite poverty and tragedy. Based on the novel by Kate Douglas Wiggin and play by Wiggin and Rachel Crothers. Remade as SUMMER MAGIC by Disney.

Mother Didn't Tell Me (1950) **88m.** **½ D: Claude Binyon. Dorothy McGuire, William Lundigan, June Havoc, Gary Merrill, Jessie Royce Landis. Naive young woman marries a doctor, not contemplating demands of being a professional man's wife. McGuire brightens this lightweight comedy.

Mother Is a Freshman (1949) **C-81m.** **½ D: Lloyd Bacon. Loretta Young, Van Johnson, Rudy Vallee, Barbara Lawrence, Robert Arthur, Betty Lynn. Refreshing, wholesome confection; Young and daughter Lynn both attend college, vying for Van's affection.▶

Mother Machree (1928) **75m.** **½ D: John Ford. Belle Bennett, Neil Hamilton, Victor McLaglen, Constance Howard, Philippe De Lacy, Ted McNamara. Recently widowed Irishwoman heads to America with her young son to seek a better life . . . but there are complications. Soapy and loaded with Irish blarney, particularly when McLaglen is on-screen, but not without charm. Some nice visual touches foreshadow Ford's later work. Silent with music and synchronized sound effects; only incomplete prints of this exist. John Wayne appears as an extra.

Mother of Mine SEE: **Gribiche**

Mother Riley Meets the Vampire (1952-British) **74m.** ** D: John Gilling. Bela Lugosi, Arthur Lucan, Dora Bryan, Richard Wattis, Philip Leaver, Judith Furse. Overbearing vampire satire with Lugosi cast as Von Housen, crazed criminal who tangles with Old Mother Riley, a comical store-keeper. Last entry in the *Old Mother Riley* series of British farces, with Lucan playing the series title character in drag. Aka VAMPIRE OVER LONDON and MY SON, THE VAMPIRE. ▼▶

Mother Wore Tights (1947) **C-107m.** *** D: Walter Lang. Betty Grable, Dan Dailey, Mona Freeman, Connie Marshall, Vanessa Brown, Veda Ann Borg; narrated by Anne Baxter. One of Grable's most popular films, about a vaudeville family. Colorful production, costumes, nostalgic songs, and an Oscar-winning Alfred Newman score, plus specialty act by the great Señor Wences. ▼▶

Mothra (1961-Japanese) **C-100m.** **½ D: Ishirô Honda, Lee Kresel. Franky Sakai, Hiroshi Koizumi, Kyoko Kagawa, Emi Itoh, Yumi Itoh, Jelly Itoh. Colorful Japanese monster movie about a giant caterpillar who invades Tokyo to rescue tiny twin girls, who are guiding it with their supernatural powers. Caterpillar then turns into a giant moth (natch), which carries on the destruction. Mothra (or its descendants) turned up in later films too. Japanese version runs 101m. Tohoscope. ▼

Motorcycle Gang (1957) **78m.** *½ D: Edward L. Cahn. Anne Neyland, Steve Terrell, John Ashley, Carl ("Alfalfa") Switzer, Raymond Hatton, Edmund Cobb. Semi-remake of DRAGSTRIP GIRL (then a six-month-old movie!) with the same stars, Ashley and Terrell, as identical characters, this time competing on motorcycles rather than in hot rods. It was better the first time. Remade, in name only, in 1994.

Motor Patrol (1950) **67m.** ** D: Sam Newfield. Don Castle, Jane Nigh, Bill Henry, Gwen O'Connor, Reed Hadley, Onslow Stevens, Sid Melton, Frank Jenks, Margia Dean. Passable crime drama with LAPD traffic department cops investigating a hit-and-run death, uncovering a stolen car racket. ▶

Moulin Rouge (1952) **C-119m.** ***½ D: John Huston. Jose Ferrer, Zsa Zsa Gabor, Suzanne Flon, Eric Pohlmann, Colette Marchand, Christopher Lee, Michael Balfour, Peter Cushing. Rich, colorful film based on life of Henri de Toulouse-Lautrec, the 19th-century Parisian artist whose growth was stunted by childhood accident. Huston brilliantly captures the flavor of Montmartre, its characters, and Lautrec's sadly distorted view of life. Excellent cast; memorable theme song by Georges Auric. Oscar winner for its stunning art direction–set decoration and costumes. ▼▶

Mountain, The (1956) **C-105m.** **½ D: Edward Dmytryk. Spencer Tracy, Robert Wagner, Claire Trevor, William Demarest, Richard Arlen, E. G. Marshall. Turgid tale of brothers Tracy and Wagner climbing Alpine peak to reach plane wreckage, for different reasons. VistaVision. ▼▶

Mountain Justice (1937) **82m.** *** D: Michael Curtiz. George Brent, Josephine Hutchinson, Guy Kibbee, Margaret Hamilton, Mona Barrie, Robert McWade, Fuzzy Knight. Backwoods story of Hutchinson struggling to break away from abusive hillbilly father Barrat and become a nurse; lawyer Brent becomes her ally when the situation gets out of hand. Surprisingly realistic melodrama, stylishly shot by Ernest Haller.

Mountain Rhythm (1939) **61m.** ** D: B. Reeves Eason. Gene Autry, Smiley Burnette, June Storey, Maude Eburne, Ferris Taylor, Walter Fenner, Jack Pennick, Hooper Atchley, Jack Ingram, Tom London. Gene comes to the aid of Smiley's aunt and other ranchers in danger of losing their land to Eastern promoter Fenner, who is intent on developing a resort and health farm. Autry formula is wearing a bit thin here, with too much emphasis on music and comedy; Gene introduces "It Makes No Difference Now." ▶

Mountain Road, The (1960) **102m.** **½ D: Daniel Mann. James Stewart, Lisa Lu, Glenn Corbett, Henry (Harry) Morgan, Frank Silvera, James Best. Stewart is always worth watching, but this saga of American squadron working in China during waning days of WW2 is pretty flat. ▼

Mourning Becomes Electra (1947) **173m.** **½ D: Dudley Nichols. Rosalind Russell, Michael Redgrave, Raymond Massey, Katina Paxinou, Nancy Coleman, Leo Genn, Kirk Douglas. Eugene O'Neill's play set in New England and adapted from the Greek tragedy *Oresteia.* Civil War general is killed by wife and their children seek revenge. Heavy, talky drama, even in 105m. version. British version runs 159m. ▼▶

Mouse on the Moon, The (1963-British) **C-82m.** ***½ D: Richard Lester. Margaret Rutherford, Bernard Cribbins, Ron Moody, Terry-Thomas, Michael Crawford. Hilarious sequel to THE MOUSE THAT ROARED, about Duchy of Grand Fenwick. Tiny country enters space race, with little help from its befuddled Grand Duchess, Margaret Rutherford. ▼▶

Mouse That Roared, The (1959-British) **C-83m.** ***½ D: Jack Arnold. Peter Sellers, Jean Seberg, David Kossoff, William Hartnell, Monty Landis, Leo McKern. Hilarious satire about the Duchy of Grand Fenwick declaring war on the U. S. Sellers stars in three roles, equally amusing. Gag before opening titles is a masterpiece. Roger Macdougall and Stanley Mann adapted Leonard Wibberley's novel. Sequel: THE MOUSE ON THE MOON. ▼▶

Mouthpiece, The (1932) **90m.** ***½ D: Elliott Nugent, James Flood. Warren William, Sidney Fox, Mae Madison, Aline MacMahon, John Wray, Guy Kibbee. Solid story based on life of flamboyant attorney William Fallon; up-and-coming prosecutor in D.A.'s office turns to defending people instead, becomes slick and successful, leaving morals behind. First-rate all the way. Scripted by Joseph Jackson and Earl Baldwin. Remade as THE MAN WHO TALKED TOO MUCH and ILLEGAL (1955).

Move Over, Darling (1963) **C-103m. **½** D: Michael Gordon. Doris Day, James Garner, Polly Bergen, Chuck Connors, Thelma Ritter, Fred Clark, Don Knotts, Elliott Reid, John Astin, Pat Harrington, Jr. Woman long thought dead returns from desert island sojourn, to find her husband has remarried. Slick, amusing remake of MY FAVORITE WIFE, with strong cast of character actors milking every laugh. Film was intended to star Marilyn Monroe and Dean Martin, under the title SOMETHING'S GOT TO GIVE, but production was halted early on, and Marilyn died shortly thereafter. CinemaScope.▼❙

Movie Crazy (1932) **84m. *** D: Clyde Bruckman. Harold Lloyd, Constance Cummings, Kenneth Thomson, Sydney Jarvis, Eddie Fetherston. Lloyd's best talkie recaptures the spirit of his silent-comedy hits, telling story of small-town boy who goes to Hollywood with stars in his eyes, gets rude awakening but finally makes good. Includes his famous magician's coat scene. Cummings is a charming leading lady.❙

Movie Struck SEE: **Pick a Star**

Movietone Follies of 1929 (1929) **80m. *** D: David Butler. John Breeden, Lola Lane, Sue Carol, Dixie Lee, David Rollins, De Witt Jennings, Sharon Lynn, Arthur Stone, Stepin Fetchit. Rattletrap backstage musical centers on a gentlemanly investor from Virginia who tries to close down a new show on the Great White Way because he doesn't want his ambitious fiancée to be in it. Book was old hat even then, but there's a pretty good score. Originally presented with Multicolor sequences and shot in 70mm Grandeur, Hollywood's first true widescreen system. Official title on-screen is WILLIAM FOX MOVIETONE FOLLIES OF 1929.

Movietone Follies of 1930 (1930) **84m. *½** D: Benjamin Stoloff. El Brendel, Marjorie White, Frank Richardson, Noel Francis, William Collier, Jr., Miriam Seegar, Yola d'Avril. Mistaken identity misfire about a ladies' man and a butler with eyes on a prize stageful of showgirls, all emoting arthritically. Numbers range from the winning "Cheer Up and Smile" to the humiliating blackface "Here Comes Emily Brown." All-talking, all-singing, all-dancing, all-boring. An unbilled Betty Grable is one of the chorines.

Mr. Ace (1946) **84m. **½** D: Edwin L. Marin. George Raft, Sylvia Sidney, Stanley Ridges, Sara Haden, Jerome Cowan. Ordinary dirty-politics drama of office-seeking Sidney using Raft to achieve her goals.▼❙

Mr. and Mrs. North (1941) **67m. **½** D:

Robert B. Sinclair. Gracie Allen, William Post, Jr., Paul Kelly, Rose Hobart, Virginia Grey, Tom Conway. Radio characters come to screen in comedy involving dead bodies being discovered; sometimes funny, sometimes forced, though it's interesting to see Gracie without George. Later a TV series.

Mr. & Mrs. Smith (1941) **95m. *** D: Alfred Hitchcock. Carole Lombard, Robert Montgomery, Gene Raymond, Jack Carson, Philip Merivale, Betty Compson, Lucile Watson. Madcap comedy of Lombard and Montgomery discovering their marriage wasn't legal. One of Hitchcock's least typical films, but bouncy nonetheless; written by Norman Krasna.▼❙

Mr. Arkadin (1955-Spanish-French) **99m. **½** D: Orson Welles. Orson Welles, Michael Redgrave, Patricia Medina, Akim Tamiroff, Mischa Auer, Katina Paxinou, Robert Arden. Overblown Welles curiosity (thematically similar to CITIZEN KANE) in which he stars as a famed tycoon with a shady past; the scenario follows his actions after being threatened with blackmail by his daughter's suitor. Filmed in English and Spanish-language versions. Various prints run 98m. and 105m. Aka CONFIDENTIAL REPORT.▼❙

Mr. Belvedere Goes to College (1949) **83m. *** D: Elliott Nugent. Clifton Webb, Shirley Temple, Tom Drake, Alan Young, Jessie Royce Landis, Kathleen Hughes. The sharp-tongued character from SITTING PRETTY enrolls in college, with predictable results. Nothing special. Jeff Chandler has bit as a policeman.

Mr. Belvedere Rings the Bell (1951) **87m. **½** D: Henry Koster. Clifton Webb, Joanne Dru, Hugh Marlowe, Zero Mostel, Doro Merande, Billy Lynn. Another follow-up to SITTING PRETTY isn't as witty. Webb enters old folks' home to prove his theory that age has nothing to do with leading a full life.❙

Mr. Blandings Builds His Dream House (1948) **94m. *** D: H. C. Potter. Cary Grant, Myrna Loy, Melvyn Douglas, Reginald Denny, Sharyn Moffett, Connie Marshall, Louise Beavers, Ian Wolfe, Lurene Tuttle, Lex Barker. Slick comedy of city couple attempting to build a house in the country; expertly handled, with Grant at his peak. And no one ever described room colors better than Loy! Norman Panama and Melvin Frank scripted, from Eric Hodgins' novel. Also shown in computer-colored version. Remade in 2007 as ARE WE DONE YET?▼❙

Mr. Bug Goes to Town SEE: **Hoppity Goes to Town**

Mr. Cohen Takes a Walk SEE: **Father Takes a Walk**

Mr. Deeds Goes to Town (1936) **115m. **** D: Frank Capra. Gary Cooper, Jean Arthur, George Bancroft, Lionel Stander, Douglass Dumbrille, Mayo Methot, Raymond Walburn, Walter Catlett, H. B. Warner. Cooper is Longfellow Deeds, who inherits 20 million dollars and wants to give it all away to needy people. Arthur is appealing as the hard-boiled big-city reporter who tries to figure out what makes him tick. Capra won his second Oscar for this irresistible film, written by Robert Riskin (from Clarence Budington Kelland's story "Opera Hat"). Later a short-lived TV series. Remade in 2002.▼●▶

Mr. Denning Drives North (1953-British) **93m.** **½ D: Anthony Kimmins. John Mills, Phyllis Calvert, Eileen Moore, Sam Wanamaker. Cast's sincerity makes this murder yarn palatable, the biggest hunt being for the corpus delicti.

Mr. District Attorney (1941) **69m.** **½ D: William Morgan. Dennis O'Keefe, Florence Rice, Peter Lorre, Stanley Ridges, Minor Watson, Charles Arnt. O'Keefe tries to prove his mettle as he joins the District Attorney's staff but bumbles at every turn, which provides plenty of opportunity for reporter Rice to needle him. Lively comedy with a mystery running through it; Lorre is wasted in his few scenes as a bad guy. This has nothing to do with the popular radio show by Phillips H. Lord on which it's supposedly based. Another so-called adaptation followed in 1947.▶

Mr. District Attorney (1947) **81m.** *½ D: Robert B. Sinclair. Dennis O'Keefe, Adolphe Menjou, Marguerite Chapman, Michael O'Shea, George Coulouris, Jeff Donnell, Steven Geray, Ralph Morgan. Menjou plays a hard-hitting D.A. who hires disaffected lawyer O'Keefe to join his team and bring wrongdoers to justice. Chapman is a wily femme fatale. Clumsy, plot-heavy potboiler is loosely based on Phillips H. Lord's popular radio series (filmed before in 1941), although it's got an unusually strong cast.▶

Mr. Hex (1946) **63m.** **½ D: William Beaudine. Leo Gorcey, Huntz Hall, Bobby Jordan, Gabriel Dell, Billy Benedict, David Gorcey, Gale Robbins, Ian Keith, Bernard Gorcey. Satisfying *Bowery Boys* silliness, as Sach is turned into a pugilistic powerhouse with the help of a hypnotist.▼▶

Mr. Hobbs Takes a Vacation (1962) **C-116m.** **½ D: Henry Koster. James Stewart, Maureen O'Hara, Fabian, John Saxon, Marie Wilson, Reginald Gardiner, Lauri Peters, John McGiver. Glossy Hollywood family fare, '60s-style, about various misadventures as Stewart and O'Hara's clan rent a house by the ocean for the summer. Based on a novel by Edward Streeter, the same man who wrote *Father of the Bride.* CinemaScope.▼▶

Mr. Hulot's Holiday (1953-French) **86m.** ***½ D: Jacques Tati. Jacques Tati, Nathalie Pascaud, Michelle Rolla, Valentine Camax, Louis Perrault. Tati introduced his delightful Hulot character in this amusing excursion to a French resort town; a fond throwback to the days of silent-screen comedy. Original French title: LES VACANCES DE MONSIEUR HULOT.▼●▶

Mr. Imperium (1951) **C-87m.** **½ D: Don Hartman. Lana Turner, Ezio Pinza, Marjorie Main, Barry Sullivan, Cedric Hardwicke, Debbie Reynolds. Threadbare romance between Turner and Pinza, now a monarch; colorful but paper-thin.▼▶

Mr. Lucky (1943) **100m.** *** D: H. C. Potter. Cary Grant, Laraine Day, Charles Bickford, Gladys Cooper, Alan Carney, Henry Stephenson, Paul Stewart, Kay Johnson, Florence Bates. Gambling-ship owner Grant intends to fleece virtuous Day, instead falls in love and goes straight. Basis for later TV series has spirited cast, engaging script. Love that rhyming slang!▼●▶

Mr. Moto With the Charlie Chan films going strong, John P. Marquand's character of a seemingly timid but cunning and intelligent sleuth named Mr. Moto seemed a natural for the movies. Twentieth Century-Fox, the same studio that was making the Chans, inaugurated the series in 1937 with THINK FAST, MR. MOTO, with the offbeat casting of Peter Lorre in the lead. Lorre fell into the role of the cagily Moto quite well, and played the character in all eight Moto films, through 1939. The series was entertaining, but somehow lacked the heart of the Chan films. Fortunately, they were endowed with slick productions and fine casts of character actors, which tended to overshadow the films' shortcomings. Moto globe-trotted from country to country, solving various mysteries with and without the help of police authorities, and confronted such formidable villains as Sig Ruman, Sidney Blackmer, John Carradine, Leon Ames, Ricardo Cortez, Jean Hersholt, and Lionel Atwill. Needless to say, the diminutive Lorre was victorious in every encounter, with the negligible help of such "assistants" as dim-witted Warren Hymer in MR. MOTO IN DANGER ISLAND. Many consider THANK YOU, MR. MOTO the best of the series, with our hero hunting for a valuable map leading to an ancient treasure. In 1965 Fox decided to revive the long-dormant Moto character in a very low-budget second feature called, appropriately enough, THE RETURN OF MR. MOTO. Movie villain Henry Silva starred as Moto, but the film was cheaply done and completely unfaithful to the original conception of the character.

MR. MOTO

Think Fast, Mr. Moto (1937)
Thank You, Mr. Moto (1938)
Mr. Moto's Gamble (1938)
Mr. Moto Takes a Chance (1938)
Mysterious Mr. Moto (1938)

Mr. Moto's Last Warning (1939)
Mr. Moto in Danger Island (1939)
Mr. Moto Takes a Vacation (1939)
The Return of Mr. Moto (1965)

Mr. Moto in Danger Island (1939) **63m.**
**½ D: Herbert I. Leeds. Peter Lorre, Jean
Hersholt, Amanda Duff, Warren Hymer,
Richard Lane, Leon Ames. Moto faces
death at every turn as he tracks a diamond
smuggling ring to Puerto Rico. Minor entry highlighted by Hymer as the dim-witted
"Twister McGurk." Remake of MURDER
IN TRINIDAD (1934) with Moto character
grafted onto original plot. Aka DANGER
ISLAND.◗

Mr. Moto's Gamble (1938) **71m.** ****½** D:
James Tinling. Peter Lorre, Keye Luke,
Dick Baldwin, Lynn Bari, Douglas Fowley,
Jayne Regan, Harold Huber. Moto probes
the death of a boxer and discovers a crooked
gambling racket. *Charlie Chan* fans will
note a guest appearance by Number One Son
(Luke) assisting Moto. In fact, it was originally scripted for the Chan series.◗

Mr. Moto's Last Warning (1939) **71m.**
*** D: Norman Foster. Peter Lorre, Ricardo Cortez, Virginia Field, John Carradine,
George Sanders, Robert Coote, John Davidson. Moto battles a fine rogues' gallery
of character villains, as murderous saboteurs
converge on the Suez Canal and do their best
to dispose of the pesky sleuth.▼◗

Mr. Moto Takes a Chance (1938) **63m.**
**½ D: Norman Foster. Peter Lorre, Rochelle Hudson, Robert Kent, J. Edward
Bromberg, Chick Chandler, George Regas.
Moto teams up with a British spy (Hudson)
to uncover a munitions site in the jungles of
Indochina. Bromberg is improbably but effectively cast as potentate.◗

Mr. Moto Takes a Vacation (1939) **63m.**
**½ D: Norman Foster. Peter Lorre, Joseph
Schildkraut, Lionel Atwill, Virginia Field,
Iva Stewart, Victor Varconi. A pleasure trip
becomes business for Moto as he tries to
thwart criminal mastermind after the Queen
of Sheba's crown as it's being transported
to a museum. Brisk final entry in the Lorre
series.◗

Mr. Muggs Rides Again (1945) **63m.** ***½**
D: Wallace Fox. Leo Gorcey, Huntz Hall,
Billy Benedict, Johnny Duncan, Bud Gorman, Nancy Brinkman, Minerva Urecal,
George Meeker, Mende Koenig, Pierre Watkin, Bernard Gorcey. Jockey Gorcey is suspended after being framed by some crooked
gamblers, but (surprise!) redeems himself in
the end. Lame *East Side Kids* romp.

Mr. Muggs Steps Out (1943) **63m.** ****½** D:
William Beaudine. Leo Gorcey, Huntz Hall,
Billy Benedict, Bobby Stone, Bud Gorman,
Dave Durand, Jimmy Strand, Joan Marsh,
Gabriel Dell, Noah Beery, Sr. Gorcey gets
a job as chauffeur to a society lady and ends

up catching some jewel thieves. Some good
laughs as crude Gorcey and the East Side Kids
crash snooty high society.

Mr. Music (1950) **113m.** ****½** D: Richard
Haydn. Bing Crosby, Nancy Olson, Charles
Coburn, Ruth Hussey, Marge and Gower
Champion, Peggy Lee, Groucho Marx.
Easygoing vehicle for crooner Crosby as
Broadway songwriter who wants to live
the easy life. Remake of ACCENT ON
YOUTH.▼●

Mr. Peabody and the Mermaid (1948)
89m. ****½** D: Irving Pichel. William Powell, Ann Blyth, Irene Hervey, Andrea King,
Clinton Sundberg. Mild comedy-fantasy by
Nunnally Johnson has its moments, with
unsuspecting Powell coming across a lovely
mermaid while fishing. Powell makes anything look good.▼◗

Mr. Perrin and Mr. Traill (1948-British)
90m. ****** D: Lawrence Huntington. Marius
Goring, David Farrar, Greta Gynt, Raymond Huntley. Lukewarm study of progressive vs. conservative schoolteaching.

Mr. Robinson Crusoe (1932) **76m.** *******
D: Edward Sutherland. Douglas Fairbanks,
Sr., William Farnum, Earle Browne, Maria
Alba. An aging but agile Doug is up to his
old tricks, betting that he can survive on
a South Sea island à la Robinson Crusoe.
Great fun; lovely score by Alfred Newman.
Also released in silent version.▼◗

Mr. Rock and Roll (1957) **86m.** ****** D:
Charles Dubin. Alan Freed, Little Richard,
Clyde McPhatter, Frankie Lymon and the
Teenagers, Teddy Randazzo, Chuck Berry,
Rocky Graziano, Lois O'Brien, Lionel
Hampton, Ferlin Husky, The Moonglows,
Brook Benton, LaVern Baker. The saga of
how Alan Freed "discovered" rock 'n' roll.
In AMERICAN HOT WAX, Berry played
opposite Tim McIntire portraying Freed;
here, he acts with the real McCoy. Vintage
footage of McPhatter, Lymon, Little Rich-
ard; Rocky Graziano is along for comic
relief. Also of note: The 1999 TVM MR.
ROCK 'N' ROLL: THE ALAN FREED
STORY.

Mr. Sardonicus (1961) **89m.** ****** D: William Castle. Ronald Lewis, Audrey Dalton,
Guy Rolfe, Oscar Homolka. Recluse count
with face frozen in hideous grin lures wife's
boyfriend/doctor to castle to cure him. Minor fare despite good ending; Castle gave
the theatrical audiences the option of voting
"thumbs up" or "thumbs down" via a "Punishment Poll" (but only one conclusion was
filmed). Screenplay by Ray Russell from
his novella *Sardonicus.*▼◗

Mr. Skeffington (1944) **146m.** ******* D:
Vincent Sherman. Bette Davis, Claude
Rains, Walter Abel, Richard Waring, Jerome Cowan, Charles Drake, Gigi Perreau.
Grand soap opera spanning several decades
of N.Y.C. life from 1914 onward. Davis is
vain society woman who marries stockbro-

ker Rains for convenience, discovering his true love for her only after many years. Lavish settings, bravura Davis performance. ▼⦿⦆

Mr. Skitch (1933) 70m. **½ D: James Cruze. Will Rogers, Rochelle Hudson, ZaSu Pitts, Eugene Pallette, Harry Green, Charles Starrett. Airy Rogers vehicle follows family's adventures driving to California. Pure fluff, highlighted by British entertainer Florence Desmond's comic impressions of costar Pitts and Greta Garbo. ▼⦆

Mrs. Mike (1949) 99m. **½ D: Louis King. Dick Powell, Evelyn Keyes, J. M. Kerrigan, Angela Clarke. Powell and Keyes are pleasing duo, as Canadian mountie indoctrinates his urban wife to rural life. ▼

Mrs. Miniver (1942) 134m. ***½ D: William Wyler. Greer Garson, Walter Pidgeon, Dame May Whitty, Teresa Wright, Reginald Owen, Henry Travers, Richard Ney, Henry Wilcoxon, Helmut Dantine, Peter Lawford. Moving drama about middle-class English family learning to cope with war. Winner of six Academy Awards—for Garson, Wright, director Wyler, and Best Picture, among others—this film did much to rally American support for our British allies during WW2, though its depiction of English life was decidedly Hollywoodized. Screenplay by Arthur Wimperis, George Froeschel, James Hilton, and Claudine West; based on Jan Struther's short stories. Sequel: THE MINIVER STORY. Also shown in computer-colored version. ▼⦿⦆

Mr. Smith Goes to Washington (1939) 129m. **** D: Frank Capra. James Stewart, Jean Arthur, Claude Rains, Edward Arnold, Guy Kibbee, Thomas Mitchell, Eugene Pallette, Beulah Bondi, Harry Carey, H. B. Warner, Charles Lane, Porter Hall, Jack Carson. Stewart is young idealist who finds nothing but corruption in U.S. Senate. Fine Capra Americana, with Stewart's top performance bolstered by Arthur as hard-boiled dame won over by earnest Mr. Smith, and a stellar supporting cast; Carey is magnificent as the Vice President. Brilliant script by Sidney Buchman; however, Lewis R. Foster's Original Story received the Oscar. Later a brief TV series. Remade as BILLY JACK GOES TO WASHINGTON. ▼⦿⦆

Mr. Soft Touch (1949) 93m. ** D: Henry Levin, Gordon Douglas. Glenn Ford, Evelyn Keyes, John Ireland, Beulah Bondi, Percy Kilbride, Ted de Corsia. Ford and Keyes are mild romantic duo in unimportant story of ex-G.I. involved with social worker and gangster-run nightclub. ⦆

Mrs. O'Malley and Mr. Malone (1950) 69m. ** D: Norman Taurog. Marjorie Main, James Whitmore, Ann Dvorak, Fred Clark, Dorothy Malone, Phyllis Kirk. Main is rambunctious but can't elevate film about

small-towner winning prize contest, involved with murder on a N.Y.C-bound train. Whitmore is most enjoyable. ⦆

Mrs. Parkington (1944) 124m. **½ D: Tay Garnett. Greer Garson, Walter Pidgeon, Edward Arnold, Gladys Cooper, Agnes Moorehead, Frances Rafferty, Selena Royle, Dan Duryea, Lee Patrick, Rod Cameron, Tom Drake, Cecil Kellaway, Peter Lawford. Overlong but well-mounted soaper involving poor, naive Garson and how she changes after marrying wealthy, charismatic Pidgeon. ▼⦆

Mrs. Wiggs of the Cabbage Patch (1934) 80m. *** D: Norman Taurog. W. C. Fields, Pauline Lord, ZaSu Pitts, Evelyn Venable, Kent Taylor, Donald Meek, Virginia Weidler. Venerable melodrama about a good-hearted woman and her ever-growing brood gets a shot of comic adrenalin from Fields, who's perfectly matched with Pitts. Not a typical Fields vehicle by any means. Based on the 1901 novel by Alice Hegan Rice; filmed before in 1914 and 1919; remade in 1942. ▼⦆

Mr. Winkle Goes to War (1944) 80m. **½ D: Alfred E. Green. Edward G. Robinson, Ruth Warrick, Ted Donaldson, Robert Armstrong, Bob Haymes, Richard Lane. Wilbert Winkle (Robinson) is timid, henpecked, physically unfit, and past 40, yet he's drafted into WW2. Clever, insightful little comedy. ▼⦆

Mr. Wise Guy (1942) 70m. *½ D: William Nigh. Leo Gorcey, Huntz Hall, Bobby Jordan, David Gorcey, Sunshine Sammy Morrison, Guinn Williams, Bill Lawrence, Joan Barclay, Gabriel Dell, Bobby Stone, Billy Gilbert, Benny Rubin, Douglas Fowley, Ann Doran, Jack Mulhall, Warren Hymer. Trivial (but well cast) *East Side Kids* romp, about corruption at a reform school, from which they break out to catch a killer. ▼⦆

Mr. Wong Author Hugh Wiley created a distinguished, gentlemanly Oriental detective named Mr. Wong for a *Collier's* magazine story in 1935. Three years later, inspired no doubt by the success of the Charlie Chan and Mr. Moto films, Poverty Row studio Monogram Pictures decided to bring Mr. Wong to life on screen. In what was considered a casting coup, the studio managed to sign Boris Karloff for the part, and it is his presence that lends these films what meager distinction they have. The mysteries themselves aren't bad (particularly in the first entry, MR. WONG, DETECTIVE), but there's far too much talk, and no production niceties whatsoever. Running characters, like the gruff and skeptical Captain Street, played by Grant Withers, and an obnoxious reporter played by Marjorie Reynolds, are heavy-handed, to say the least. When Karloff left the series in 1940, Monogram experimented by hiring Charlie Chan's former Number One Son, Keye Luke, to play a younger version of Wong, in PHANTOM

OF CHINATOWN. It was an interesting idea that didn't come off.

MR. WONG

Mr. Wong Detective (1938)
Mystery of Mr. Wong (1939)
Mr. Wong in Chinatown (1939)
The Fatal Hour (1940)
Doomed to Die (1940)
Phantom of Chinatown (1941)

Mr. Wong Detective (1938) **69m.** ** D: William Nigh. Boris Karloff, Grant Withers, Maxine Jennings, Evelyn Brent, Lucien Prival, William Gould. First and best of five films in which Karloff portrays Hugh Wiley's Chinese detective Mr. Wong. The murder is neatly carried out—and the murderer's identity is a real surprise. Monogram Pictures' attempt to emulate the success of the *Charlie Chan* and *Mr. Moto* series. ▼●▶

Mr. Wong in Chinatown (1939) **70m.** *½ D: William Nigh. Boris Karloff, Grant Withers, William Royle, Marjorie Reynolds, Peter George Lynn, Lotus Long, Richard Loo. Blah Mr. Wong mystery, third in the series, with the sleuth becoming involved in the case of a Chinese princess' murder. ▼▶

Mudlark, The (1950) **99m.** *** D: Jean Negulesco. Irene Dunne, Alec Guinness, Finlay Currie, Anthony Steel, Andrew Ray, Beatrice Campbell, Wilfrid Hyde-White. Offbeat drama of Queen Victoria (Dunne), a recluse since her husband's death, coming back to reality after meeting waif who stole into her castle. Dunne does quite well as Queen, with Guinness a joy as Disraeli. Filmed in England. ▶

Mug Town (1943) **60m.** ** D: Ray Taylor. Billy Halop, Huntz Hall, Bernard Punsly, Gabriel Dell, Grace McDonald, Edward Norris, Murray Alper, Tommy Kelly. The Little Tough Guys take on racketeers in this "patriotic" series entry.

Mule Train (1950) **69m.** *** D: John English. Gene Autry, Pat Buttram, Sheila Ryan, Robert Livingston, Frank Jacquet, Vince Barnett, Syd Saylor, Gregg Barton. Buttram's "natural cement" claim is threatened by a crooked contractor (Livingston) and a shady female sheriff (Ryan) until Gene, a U.S. marshal, interferes. The music—including the title song, right off the Hit Parade—makes this one. ▼▶

Mummy, The (1932) **72m.** ***½ D: Karl Freund. Boris Karloff, Zita Johann, David Manners, Arthur Byron, Edward Van Sloan, Bramwell Fletcher, Noble Johnson. Horror classic stars Karloff as Egyptian mummy, revived after thousands of years, believing Johann is reincarnation of ancient mate. Remarkable makeup and atmosphere make it chills ahead of many follow-ups. ▼●▶

Mummy, The (1959-British) **C-88m.** **½ D: Terence Fisher. Peter Cushing, Christopher Lee, Yvonne Furneaux, Eddie Byrne, Felix Aylmer, Raymond Huntley. Against warnings of severe consequences, archeologists desecrate ancient tomb of Egyptian Princess Ananka. They return to England and those consequences. Stylish Hammer resurrection of Universal's Kharis series. ▼●▶

Mummy's Boys (1936) **68m.** ** D: Fred Guiol. Bert Wheeler, Robert Woolsey, Barbara Pepper, Moroni Olsen, Frank M. Thomas, Willie Best. Slackly developed comedy about two moronic ditch diggers, recruited for an archeology expedition, getting mixed up with jewel thieves and an ancient Egyptian "curse." One of the duo's lesser vehicles, filled with lame puns and moldy mummy gags. ▶

Mummy's Curse, The (1944) **62m.** **½ D: Leslie Goodwins. Lon Chaney, Jr., Peter Coe, Virginia Christine, Kay Harding, Dennis Moore, Martin Kosleck, Kurt Katch. Kharis and the reincarnated Ananka, last seen slipping into a New England swamp in THE MUMMY'S GHOST, are unaccountably dug up in a Louisiana bayou, where he's soon strangling people again. Surprisingly eerie and effective, with a good performance by Christine. Silent star William Farnum has a bit role as a caretaker. Last of the series. ▼●▶

Mummy's Ghost, The (1944) **60m.** *½ D: Reginald LeBorg. Lon Chaney, Jr., John Carradine, Ramsay Ames, Robert Lowery, Barton MacLane, George Zucco. Sequel to THE MUMMY'S TOMB finds seemingly unkillable Kharis and his mentor (Carradine) on the trail of a woman who is the reincarnation of Princess Ananka. Least interesting of the series, with nothing new or different to offer. Followed by THE MUMMY'S CURSE. ▼●▶

Mummy's Hand, The (1940) **67m.** *** D: Christy Cabanne. Dick Foran, Wallace Ford, Peggy Moran, Cecil Kellaway, George Zucco, Tom Tyler, Eduardo Ciannelli, Charles Trowbridge. Archeologists seeking lost tomb of Egyptian princess get more than they bargained for when they find it guarded by a living—and very deadly—mummy (Tyler). First of the "Kharis" series is entertaining blend of chills and comedy, with good cast, flavorful music and atmosphere. Not a sequel to THE MUMMY (1932), although it does utilize flashback footage; itself followed by three sequels, starting with THE MUMMY'S TOMB. ▼●▶

Mummy's Tomb, The (1942) **61m.** ** D: Harold Young. Lon Chaney, Jr., Elyse Knox, John Hubbard, Turhan Bey, Dick Foran, Wallace Ford, George Zucco, Mary Gordon. Sequel to THE MUMMY'S HAND finds Kharis (now played by Chaney) transported to America to kill off surviving members of the expedition. Weak script and too much stock footage are the real villains. Followed by THE MUMMY'S GHOST. ▼●▶

Murder! (1930-British) **104m.** *** D: Alfred Hitchcock. Herbert Marshall, Norah Baring, Phyllis Konstam, Edward Chapman. Good early Hitchcock casts Marshall as actor who serves on jury at murder trial and believes accused woman innocent. Some prints run as short as 92m. Hitchcock also made a German-language version called MARY starring Alfred Abel. ▼●

Murder Ahoy (1964-British) **93m.** ***½ D: George Pollock. Margaret Rutherford, Lionel Jeffries, Charles Tingwell, William Mervyn, Joan Benham, Stringer Davis, Miles Malleson. This time out, Miss Marple investigates murder on a naval cadet training-ship. Original screenplay (by David Persall and Jack Seddon) based on wonderful Agatha Christie character. ▼●●

Murder at Dawn (1932) **62m.** **½ D: Richard Thorpe. Josephine Dunn, Jack Mulhall, Eddie Boland, Martha Mattox, Mischa Auer. A solar-powered electric generator is developed in (where else?) an eerie mansion overpopulated by hero Mulhall, ingénues, a comic relief drunk, sinister servants ad absurdum, all searching for the kidnapped inventor. Mystery cheapie suffers from repetition and obnoxious comedy but works up some excitement in the closing minutes.

Murder at 45 R.P.M. (1959-French) **105m.** ** D: Etienne Perier. Danielle Darrieux, Michel Auclair, Jean Servais, Henri Guisol. Darrieux is a popular singer who publicly professes her love for her songwriter husband, while having an affair with her accompanist; after dying in a car "accident," the husband seemingly returns from his grave. Neat plot twists cannot uplift this slow-moving suspenser. ▼●

Murder at the Baskervilles SEE: **Silver Blaze**

Murder at the Gallop (1963-British) **81m.** ***½ D: George Pollock. Margaret Rutherford, Robert Morley, Flora Robson, Charles Tingwell, Duncan Lamont, Stringer Davis, James Villiers, Robert Urquhart. Amateur sleuth Miss Marple suspects foul play when wealthy old recluse dies. Based on Agatha Christie's *After the Funeral*. ▼●●

Murder at the Vanities (1934) **89m.** **½ D: Mitchell Leisen. Carl Brisson, Victor McLaglen, Jack Oakie, Kitty Carlisle, Dorothy Stickney, Gertrude Michael, Jessie Ralph, Charles Middleton, Gail Patrick, Donald Meek, Toby Wing, Duke Ellington's Orchestra. Arguably the smuttiest Hollywood musical ever made (filled with near-nudity and risqué dialogue), this offbeat pre-Code murder mystery is set backstage at *Earl Carroll's Vanities*, with detective McLaglen holding everyone under suspicion when someone is killed backstage on opening night. Songs include "Cocktails for Two" and bizarre "Sweet Marijuana." Look for Ann Sheridan and Lucille Ball as Earl Carroll girls. ▼●

Murder by Contract (1958) **81m.** ** D: Irving Lerner. Vince Edwards, Philip Pine, Herschel Bernardi, Caprice Toriel. Intriguing little film about a hired killer and what makes him tick; ultimately sabotaged by pretentious dialogue and posturing. ●

Murder by Invitation (1941) **67m.** **½ D: Phil Rosen. Wallace Ford, Marian Marsh, Sarah Padden, Gavin Gordon, Minerva Urecal, Dave O'Brien. A kooky old millionairess invites her greedy heirs-in-waiting to a midnight get-together in her secret-passage-filled mansion; murder ensues. Lively Monogram comedy whodunit is so CAT AND THE CANARY that one character mentions CAT AND THE CANARY, while others break character to make cracks about being in this movie!

Murder by Proxy SEE: **Blackout** (1954)

Murder by Television (1935) **60m.** *½ D: Clifford Sandforth. Bela Lugosi, June Collyer, Huntley Gordon, George Meeker, Claire McDowell. A professor who perfects the technology of television is murdered; Lugosi, his assistant, is a prime suspect. Grade Z production holds some interest as a curio. ▼●

Murder by the Clock (1931) **76m.** **½ D: Edward Sloman. William "Stage" Boyd, Lilyan Tashman, Irving Pichel, Regis Toomey, Blanche Frederici, Sally O'Neil, Lester Vail. Creepy, creaky mystery designed and played like a horror film. Complicated plot involves elderly woman who installs a horn in her crypt in case she's buried alive, a mysterious reincarnation drug, and drooling half-wit Pichel. Plenty of atmosphere if not much sense.

Murderers Are Among Us, The (1946-German) **84m.** ***½ D: Wolfgang Staudte. Hildegard Knef, Ernst Wilhelm Borchert, Erna Sellmer, Arno Paulsen, Wolfgang Dohnberg. Riveting post-WW2 propaganda, filmed on location among the ruins of Berlin, about the evolving relationship between a young German ex–concentration camp inmate (Knef) and an embittered former surgeon-soldier (Borchert). Grim story of the survivors of war is of special note for its sympathetic point of view of German citizens who also suffered during WW2. ▼●

Murder, He Says (1945) **93m.** *** D: George Marshall. Fred MacMurray, Helen Walker, Marjorie Main, Jean Heather, Porter Hall, Peter Whitney, Barbara Pepper, Mabel Paige. Zany slapstick of pollster MacMurray encountering Main's family of hayseed murderers. Too strident at times, but generally funny; clever script by Lou Breslow. ▼●

Murder, Inc. (1960) **103m.** *** D: Burt Balaban, Stuart Rosenberg. Stuart Whitman, May Britt, Henry Morgan, Peter Falk, David J. Stewart, Simon Oakland, Morey Amsterdam, Sarah Vaughan, Joseph Campanella. Solid little fact-based chronicle of the title crime organization, with Falk in particular scoring as Abe Reles, the syndicate's ill-fated number-one killer. Lots of familiar faces (Vincent Gardenia, Sylvia Miles, Seymour Cassel) in supporting roles. CinemaScope.◗

Murder in Greenwich Village (1937) **68m.** ** D: Albert S. Rogell. Richard Arlen, Fay Wray, Raymond Walburn, Wyn Cahoon, Scott Colton, Thurston Hall. Dated romantic mystery comedy with heiress Wray using photographer Arlen as alibi for whereabouts when murder took place. Mystery is secondary, solved only as an afterthought.

Murder in Harlem (1935) **102m.** **½ D: Oscar Micheaux. Clarence Brooks, Dorothy Van Engle, Andrew Bishop, Alec Lovejoy, Laura Bowman, Bee Freeman, "Slick" Chester, Oscar Micheaux. Better-than-average all-black-cast independent is the fact-based account of a night watchman who is falsely accused of murdering a white woman. His sister (Van Engle) and a lawyer (Brooks) set out to prove his innocence. Also known as LEM HAWKINS' CONFESSION; previously made by Micheaux as THE GUN-SAULUS MYSTERY (1922).▼◗

Murder in the Air (1940) **55m.** ** D: Lewis Seiler. Ronald Reagan, John Litel, James Stephenson, Eddie Foy, Jr., Lya Lys. The fourth and final Ronald Reagan Brass Bancroft film, with the Secret Service agent assigned to stop enemy spies from stealing government plans.◗

Murder in the Blue Room (1944) **61m.** ** D: Leslie Goodwins. Anne Gwynne, Donald Cook, John Litel, Grace McDonald, Betty Kean, June Preisser, Regis Toomey, Bill Williams. Film has distinction of being an Old Dark House musical, but otherwise has nothing to recommend it. Typical brassy songs against OK whodunit background; filmed before as SECRET OF THE BLUE ROOM and THE MISSING GUEST.

Murder in the Music Hall (1946) **84m.** **½ D: John English. Vera Hruba Ralston, William Marshall, Helen Walker, Nancy Kelly, William Gargan, Ann Rutherford, Julie Bishop, Jerome Cowan, Edward Norris, Jack LaRue. Neat little mystery in which troubled "ballet on ice" performer Ralston finds herself in the wrong place at the wrong time, and is accused of murder. To the rescue comes bandleader boyfriend Marshall.▼

Murder in the Private Car (1934) **63m.** ** D: Harry Beaumont. Charles Ruggles, Una Merkel, Mary Carlisle, Russell Hardie, Snowflake (Fred Toones), Porter Hall, Berton Churchill. An heiress' life is at stake during an eventful railroad trip. Bizarre, incredibly silly, and incoherent, with an exciting runaway-car finale that offers too little too late. Ruggles, as a "crime deflector," spouts a stream of non sequiturs that are meant to be funny but mostly aren't. Walter

Brennan and Akim Tamiroff have bit parts. Remake of RED LIGHTS (1923).

Murder in Times Square (1943) **67m.** **½ D: Lew Landers. Edmund Lowe, Marguerite Chapman, John Litel, William Wright, Bruce Bennett, Esther Dale, Veda Ann Borg, Gerald Mohr, Sidney Blackmer. Lowe hams it up as a conceited, arrogant playwright-actor who's suspected of a series of murders in which all the victims died from poisonous snake venom—just as in his latest play. Minor but well-plotted B mystery.

Murder Is My Beat (1955) **77m.** ** D: Edgar G. Ulmer. Paul Langton, Barbara Payton, Robert Shayne, Selena Royle. Standard B treatment of police detective Langton risking all to clear Payton of murder charge. Painless, even though all twists can be seen far in advance.◗

Murder Is My Business (1946) **64m.** ** D: Sam Newfield. Hugh Beaumont, Cheryl Walker, Lyle Talbot, George Meeker, Pierre Watkin. Programmer Mike Shayne caper, with Beaumont a tame shamus on prowl for killer.

Murder Man, The (1935) **70m.** *** D: Tim Whelan. Spencer Tracy, Virginia Bruce, Lionel Atwill, Harvey Stephens, Robert Barrat, James Stewart. Tracy is good as usual playing a hard-drinking newspaper reporter who specializes in covering murders. Snappy little film also offers Stewart in his first feature appearance (playing a fellow reporter named Shorty).◗

Murder Most Foul (1964-British) **90m.** *** D: George Pollock. Margaret Rutherford, Ron Moody, Charles Tingwell, Andrew Cruickshank, Stringer Davis, Francesca Annis, Dennis Price, James Bolam. When Miss Marple is lone jury member who believes defendant is innocent, she sets out to prove it. Based on Agatha Christie's *Mrs. McGinty's Dead.*▼◗

Murder, My Sweet (1944) **95m.** ***½ D: Edward Dmytryk. Dick Powell, Claire Trevor, Anne Shirley, Otto Kruger, Mike Mazurki, Miles Mander. Adaptation of Raymond Chandler's book *Farewell My Lovely* gave Powell new image as hard-boiled detective Philip Marlowe, involved in homicide and blackmail. Still packs a wallop. Scripted by John Paxton. Story previously used for THE FALCON TAKES OVER; remade again as FAREWELL, MY LOVELY in 1975. Also shown in computer-colored version.▼◗

Murder of Dr. Harrigan, The (1936) **67m.** **½ D: Frank McDonald. Ricardo Cortez, Kay Linaker, John Eldredge, Mary Astor, Joseph Crehan, Frank Reicher. Fast-paced mystery with intern Cortez turning detective to find out who bumped off the title character, who's just invented a new type of anesthesia. Based on a Mignon Eberhart novel.

Murder on a Bridle Path (1936) **65m.** *½

[470]

D: Edward Killy, William Hamilton. James Gleason, Helen Broderick, Louise Latimer, Owen Davis, Jr., John Arledge, John Carroll, Leslie Fenton, Christian Rub, Gustav von Seyffertitz. Broderick takes over the role of Hildegarde Withers for this extremely unsatisfying series mystery about a socialite who's killed during an early morning horseback ride. A terrific finale can't make up for 60 minutes of deadly dullness. Look for young Tony Martin. ▶

Murder on a Honeymoon (1935) 74m. *** D: Lloyd Corrigan. Edna May Oliver, James Gleason, Lola Lane, Chick Chandler, George Meeker, Dorothy Libaire, Morgan Wallace, Leo (G.) Carroll. After a murder takes place on a seaplane ride to Catalina Island, Hildegarde Withers (who happened to be on the plane) gets Inspector Oscar Piper to come there and solve the crime. Entertaining entry in the Withers series, cowritten by Robert Benchley and actually filmed on the picturesque island. ▶

Murder on Approval (1956-British) 90m. ** D: Bernard Knowles. Tom Conway, Delphi Lawrence, Brian Worth, Michael Balfour. Humdrum thriller with private eye Conway hired to determine the authenticity of a rare stamp. Original British title: BARBADOS QUEST. ▼▶

Murder on Monday SEE: **Home at Seven**

Murder on the Blackboard (1934) 72m. *** D: George Archainbaud. Edna May Oliver, James Gleason, Bruce Cabot, Gertrude Michael, Regis Toomey, Tully Marshall, Edgar Kennedy, Jackie Searle, Fredrik Vogeding, Gustav von Seyffertitz. A young female schoolteacher is murdered, and fellow teacher Hildegarde Withers (Oliver) becomes involved in solving the case with Inspector Oscar Piper. Enjoyable entry in the brief Withers series. ▶

Murder Over New York (1940) 65m. **½ D: Harry Lachman. Sidney Toler, Marjorie Weaver, Robert Lowery, Ricardo Cortez, Donald MacBride, Melville Cooper, (Victor) Sen Yung. Charlie Chan (Toler) uncovers a gang of saboteurs while in Manhattan for a police convention. Briskly paced, well-directed entry. Shemp Howard has a brief but funny bit as a fake fakir. ▼▶

Murder She Said (1961-British) 87m. *** D: George Pollock. Margaret Rutherford, Arthur Kennedy, Muriel Pavlow, James Robertson Justice, Charles Tingwell, Thorley Walters, Joan Hickson. Miss Marple takes a job as a domestic in order to solve a murder she witnessed. Based on Agatha Christie's *4:50 From Paddington*; first of four films starring Rutherford as Marple. Trivia note: Rutherford has several scenes with Hickson, later to play Miss Marple herself in a fine British TV series. ▼▶

Murders in the Rue Morgue (1932) 62m. **½ D: Robert Florey. Bela Lugosi, Sidney Fox, Leon Waycoff (Ames), Bert Roach, Noble Johnson, Brandon Hurst, Arlene Francis. Expressionistic horror film based on Poe story, with Lugosi as fiendish Dr. Mirakle, with eyes on lovely Fox as the bride of his pet ape in 1845 Paris. Considered strong stuff back then. John Huston was one of the writers. Remade as PHANTOM OF THE RUE MORGUE, and twice more (once for TV in 1986) under original title. ▼▶

Murders in the Zoo (1933) 62m. *** D: A. Edward Sutherland. Lionel Atwill, Charles Ruggles, Randolph Scott, Gail Patrick, John Lodge, Kathleen Burke. Astonishingly grisly horror film about an insanely jealous zoologist and sportsman (Atwill) who dispatches his wife's suitors (genuine and otherwise). Pretty potent, right from the opening scene of Atwill sewing a victim's mouth shut! ▼▶

Murder Will Out (1952-British) 83m. *** D: John Gilling. Valerie Hobson, Edward Underdown, James Robertson Justice, Henry Kendall. Underplayed suspenser with creditable red herrings to engage the viewer. Retitled: THE VOICE OF MERRILL. ▶

Murder With Pictures (1936) 71m. **½ D: Charles Barton. Lew Ayres, Gail Patrick, Joyce Compton, Paul Kelly, Onslow Stevens, Ernest Cossart, Benny Baker. Newsroom/courtroom murder mystery, with a dash of comedy, about skirmishes between determined photojournalists and the racketeers they chase off the streets into jail. Ayres delivers a dizzying array of rat-tat-tat dialogue in this briskly paced B. ▼▶

Muriel (1963-French-Italian) C-115m. *** D: Alain Resnais. Delphine Seyrig, Jean-Pierre Kérien, Nita Klein, Claude Sainval, Jean-Baptiste Thierée. Poignant drama of alienation, about a widow (Seyrig) and her stepson (Thierée); she's haunted by the memory of her first love, he by his involvement in the torture and death of a woman named Muriel during the Algerian War. ▼▶

Muscle Beach Party (1964) C-94m. **½ D: William Asher. Frankie Avalon, Annette Funicello, Buddy Hackett, Luciana Paluzzi, Don Rickles, John Ashley, Jody McCrea, Morey Amsterdam, Peter Lupus, Candy Johnson, Dan Haggerty. Follow-up to BEACH PARTY picks up the pace as the gang finds the beach has been invaded by Rickles and his stable of body-builders. Usual blend of surf, sand, and corn; Rickles' first series appearance and the screen debut of "Little" Stevie Wonder. Sequel: BIKINI BEACH. Panavision. ▼▶

Music for Madame (1937) 81m. *** D: John Blystone. Nino Martini, Joan Fontaine, Alan Mowbray, Billy Gilbert, Lee Patrick, Grant Mitchell, Alan Hale, Erik Rhodes, Romo Vincent, Frank Conroy, Jack Carson. Enjoyable musical-comedy vehicle for opera star Martini as an Italian immigrant trying to make good as a singer in Hollywood, used as a patsy by a jewel thief, and turned into a wanted man. Silly plot serves as a showcase for Martini's charm, with some pretty good songs and a colorful array of character comedians.

Music for Millions (1944) **120m. **½ D:** Henry Koster. Margaret O'Brien, Jimmy Durante, June Allyson, Marsha Hunt, Hugh Herbert, Jose Iturbi, Connie Gilchrist, Harry Davenport, Marie Wilson, Larry Adler, Ethel Griffies. Teary tale of warbride Allyson, a cellist in Iturbi's orchestra, gallantly waiting to have a baby—and for husband's return. O'Brien is her precocious kid sister. While there's plenty of Chopin and Debussy, Durante steals film with "Umbriago." Watch for Ava Gardner in a bit. ▶

Music in Darkness SEE: **Night Is My Future**

Music in Manhattan (1944) **80m. ** D:** John H. Auer. Anne Shirley, Phillip Terry, Dennis Day, Raymond Walburn, Jane Darwell, Patti Brill, Charlie Barnet and His Orchestra, Nilo Menendez and His Rhumba Band. Song-and-dance team partners Shirley and Day are engaged, but circumstances force her to pretend she's married to war hero Terry. Three guesses what happens next. Competent, thoroughly innocuous wartime musical, indistinguishable from scads of others.

Music in My Heart (1940) **70m. ** D:** Joseph Santley. Tony Martin, Rita Hayworth, Edith Fellows, Alan Mowbray, Eric Blore, George Tobias. Routine musical of Continental Martin cast in show where he meets lovely Hayworth. One good song, "It's a Blue World." ▶▶

Music in the Air (1934) **85m. *** D:** Joe May. Gloria Swanson, John Boles, Douglass Montgomery, June Lang, Reginald Owen, Al Shean. Quarrelsome leading lady Swanson and lyricist Boles are both distracted by the arrival of young songwriter Montgomery and pretty Lang. Predictable plot given chic treatment; good Jerome Kern–Oscar Hammerstein score enhances bright production.

Music Is Magic (1935) **65m. **½ D:** George Marshall. Alice Faye, Ray Walker, Bebe Daniels, Frank Mitchell, Jack Durant, Rosina Lawrence, Thomas Beck, Hattie McDaniel. Limp musical with Faye as a struggling vaudevillian who heads for Hollywood. Will she find stardom? Daniels is outstanding as a vain, aging movie star; her young boyfriend (Beck) is named Tony Bennett!

Music Man, The (1962) **C-151m. ***½ D:** Morton Da Costa. Robert Preston, Shirley Jones, Buddy Hackett, Hermione Gingold, Paul Ford, Pert Kelton, Ronny Howard. Peerless Preston reprises his Broadway performance as super salesman/con man Prof. Harold Hill, who mesmerizes Iowa town with visions of uniformed marching band. Faithful filmization of Meredith Willson's affectionate slice of Americana. Score includes "76 Trombones," "Till

There Was You," and showstopping "Trouble." Remade for TV in 2003. Technirama. ▼●▶

Mutineers, The (1949) **60m. **½ D:** Jean Yarbrough. Jon Hall, Adele Jergens, George Reeves, Noel Cravat. Sloppy account of sailor Hall, who becomes immersed in shipboard intrigue. Retitled PIRATE SHIP.

Mutiny (1952) **C-77m. **½ D:** Edward Dmytryk. Mark Stevens. Angela Lansbury, Patric Knowles, Gene Evans, Rhys Williams. Sleep-inducing actioner set amidst the War of 1812, with rival sailors Stevens and Knowles vying for adventuress Lansbury. ▼▶

Mutiny on the Bounty (1935) **132m. ****** D:** Frank Lloyd. Charles Laughton, Clark Gable, Franchot Tone, Herbert Mundin, Eddie Quillan, Dudley Digges, Donald Crisp, Movita, Henry Stephenson, Spring Byington, Ian Wolfe, Mamo. Storytelling at its best, in this engrossing adaptation of the Nordhoff-Hall book about mutiny against tyrannical Captain Bligh (Laughton) on voyage to the South Seas. Whole cast is good, but Laughton is unforgettable. Scripted by three top writers: Talbot Jennings, Jules Furthman, and Carey Wilson. Oscar winner for Best Picture; leagues ahead of its 1962 remake and the 1984 film THE BOUNTY. Also shown in computer-colored version. ▼●▶

Mutiny on the Bounty (1962) **C-179m. **½ D:** Lewis Milestone. Marlon Brando, Trevor Howard, Richard Harris, Hugh Griffith, Richard Haydn, Tim Seely, Percy Herbert, Tarita, Gordon Jackson. Lavish remake of 1935 classic can't come near it, although visually beautiful; Howard good as Captain Bligh, but Brando is all wrong as Fletcher Christian. Best thing about this version is spectacular score by Bronislau Kaper. Roadshow version runs 186m. with overture, intermission/entr'acte. Ultra Panavision 70. ▼●▶

My Best Girl (1927) **80m. *** D:** Sam Taylor. Mary Pickford, Charles "Buddy" Rogers, Sunshine Hart, Lucien Littlefield, Carmelita Geraghty, Hobart Bosworth, Evelyn Hall, Mack Swain. Pickford's final silent feature is a slick (if strictly formulaic) romantic comedy about a five-and-dime stock girl who's attracted to the handsome new stock boy; he's the boss' son, working in disguise. Crowd-pleasing star vehicle was the only Pickford-Rogers screen pairing; they later married. ▼▶

My Bill (1938) **64m. **½ D:** John Farrow. Kay Francis, Bonita Granville, Anita Louise, Bobby Jordan, John Litel, Dickie Moore, Elisabeth Risdon. Heart-tugging soaper about well-meaning, poverty-stricken small-town widow Francis and her four children; three are ingrates, but the youngest, Bill (Moore), is extra-special. Originally filmed in 1930 as COURAGE.

My Blood Runs Cold (1965) **104m. **½ D:** William Conrad. Troy Donahue, Joey

Heatherton, Barry Sullivan, Jeanette Nolan. Young man thinks girl is long-dead ancestor, and recalls love affair from generations before. Not all that bad, but not worth missing *I Love Lucy* for, either. Panavision.◗

My Blue Heaven (1950) **C-96m.** **½ D: Henry Koster. Betty Grable, Dan Dailey, David Wayne, Jane Wyatt, Mitzi Gaynor, Una Merkel. Pleasing musicomedy with Grable and Dailey as radio stars who try to adopt a child.◗

My Boy (1921) **43m.** **½ D: Albert Austin, Victor Heerman. Jackie Coogan, Claude Gillingwater, Mathilde Brundage, Patsy Marks. A little refugee who's about to be deported escapes from Ellis Island to confront his uncertain future in America. A crusty old sea captain and the boy's desperate (and wealthy) grandmother figure significantly. Silent cinema's most revered child star, age 7, is appealing as ever. Sentimental almost to a fault, but it works. ▼

My Brother's Keeper (1948-British) **96m.** ** D: Alfred Roome. Jack Warner, Jane Hylton, George Cole, Bill Owen, David Tomlinson, Christopher Lee. Hunt-the-escaped-convicts film has gimmick of the two escaped prisoners being handcuffed together.

My Brother Talks to Horses (1946) **93m.** ** D: Fred Zinnemann. "Butch" Jenkins, Peter Lawford, Beverly Tyler, Edward Arnold, Charlie Ruggles, Spring Byington. Gimmick comedy that's fun at the start but drags to slow finish.◗

My Cousin Rachel (1952) **98m.** *** D: Henry Koster. Olivia de Havilland, Richard Burton, Audrey Dalton, John Sutton, Ronald Squire. Successful filmization of Daphne du Maurier mystery, with Burton (in his American debut) trying to discover if de Havilland is guilty or innocent of murder and intrigue.◗

My Darling Clementine (1946) **97m.** **** D: John Ford. Henry Fonda, Linda Darnell, Victor Mature, Walter Brennan, Cathy Downs, Tim Holt, Ward Bond, Alan Mowbray, John Ireland, Jane Darwell, Grant Withers, J. Farrell MacDonald. Beautifully directed, low-key Western about Wyatt Earp (Fonda) and Doc Holliday (Mature), leading to inevitable gunfight at O.K. Corral. Full of wonderful details and vignettes; exquisitely photographed by Joseph P. MacDonald. One of director Ford's finest films, and an American classic. Screenplay by Samuel G. Engel and Winston Miller, from a story by Sam Hellman. Based on a book by Stuart N. Lake. Remake of FRONTIER MARSHAL (1939). In 1994 an archival print was found of the 104m. preview version, containing a number of minor differences and a slightly different finale.▼◗

My Daughter Joy SEE: **Operation X**

My Dear Secretary (1948) **94m.** **½ D: Charles Martin. Laraine Day, Kirk Douglas, Keenan Wynn, Helen Walker, Rudy Vallee,

Florence Bates, Alan Mowbray. Entertaining (if trivial) comedy of wannabe writer Day hiring on as secretary to best-selling author Douglas. Wynn steals the show as Douglas' comical pal.▼◗

My Dream Is Yours (1949) **C-101m.** **½ D: Michael Curtiz. Jack Carson, Doris Day, Lee Bowman, Adolphe Menjou, Eve Arden. Carson makes Day a radio star in standard musicomedy; highlights are Bugs Bunny dream sequence, Edgar Kennedy's performance as Day's uncle. Remake of TWENTY MILLION SWEETHEARTS, with Doris stepping into Dick Powell's role (and reprising the 1934 hit "I'll String Along With You").▼◗

My Enemy, the Sea SEE: **Alone on the Pacific**

My Fair Lady (1964) **C-170m.** ***½ D: George Cukor. Rex Harrison, Audrey Hepburn, Stanley Holloway, Wilfrid Hyde-White, Gladys Cooper, Jeremy Brett, Theodore Bikel, Henry Daniell, Mona Washbourne, Isobel Elsom. Ultrasmooth filmization of Lerner and Loewe's enchanting musical from Shaw's *Pygmalion*, with Prof. Henry Higgins (Harrison) transforming guttersnipe Hepburn into regal lady, to win a bet. Sumptuously filmed, with "The Rain in Spain," Harrison's soliloquys among highlights. Eight Oscars include Picture, Actor, Director, Cinematography (Harry Stradling), Costumes (Cecil Beaton), Score Adaptation (Andre Previn), Art Direction (Beaton and Gene Allen). Roadshow version runs 173m. with overture, intermission/entr'acte, exit music. Super Panavision 70. ▼◗

My Favorite Blonde (1942) **78m.** *** D: Sidney Lanfield. Bob Hope, Madeleine Carroll, Gale Sondergaard, George Zucco, Victor Varconi. Bob and his trained penguin become sitting ducks when spy Madeleine uses them to help deliver secret orders; very funny WW2 Hope vehicle.▼

My Favorite Brunette (1947) **87m.** *** D: Elliott Nugent. Bob Hope, Dorothy Lamour, Peter Lorre, Lon Chaney, John Hoyt, Reginald Denny. Better-than-usual Hope nonsense with Bob as a photographer mixed up with mobsters; Lorre and Chaney add authenticity. Two very funny surprise cameos at beginning and end of film. Also shown in computer-colored version.▼◗

My Favorite Spy (1942) **86m.** ** D: Tay Garnett. Kay Kyser, Ellen Drew, Jane Wyman, Robert Armstrong, William Demarest, Una O'Connor, Helen Westley, George Cleveland, Ish Kabibble. How did we win WW2 with bandleader Kyser as spy? Nonsensical musicomedy tries to explain.●

My Favorite Spy (1951) **93m.** *** D: Norman Z. McLeod. Bob Hope, Hedy Lamarr, Francis L. Sullivan, Mike Mazurki, John Archer, Iris Adrian, Arnold Moss. Bob resembles murdered spy, finds himself thrust into international intrigue. Fast-moving fun, with glamorous Hedy aiding Bob on all counts. ▶

My Favorite Wife (1940) 88m. *** D: Garson Kanin. Irene Dunne, Cary Grant, Gail Patrick, Randolph Scott, Ann Shoemaker, Scotty Beckett, Donald MacBride. Dunne, supposedly dead, returns to U.S. to find hubby Grant remarried to Patrick, in familiar but witty marital mixup, remade as MOVE OVER, DARLING. Inspired by *Enoch Arden*; Grant's character even has the same name. Produced and cowritten (with Sam and Bella Spewack) by Leo McCarey. Also shown in computer-colored version. ▼◑▶

My Foolish Heart (1949) 98m. *** D: Mark Robson. Dana Andrews, Susan Hayward, Kent Smith, Lois Wheeler, Jessie Royce Landis, Robert Keith, Gigi Perreau. Deftly handled sentimental WW2 romance tale between soldier Andrews and Hayward; Victor Young's lovely theme helps. Based on J. D. Salinger's story "Uncle Wiggily in Connecticut," the only one of the author's works ever adapted to film. ▼●

My Forbidden Past (1951) 81m. **½ D: Robert Stevenson. Robert Mitchum, Ava Gardner, Melvyn Douglas, Janis Carter. Silly tripe about Gardner, who's got a skeleton in her family closet, seeking revenge on Mitchum for jilting her. Fast-moving, watchable nonsense set in antebellum New Orleans. ▼▶

My Friend Flicka (1943) C-89m. *** D: Harold Schuster. Roddy McDowall, Preston Foster, Rita Johnson, Jeff Corey, James Bell. Sentimental story of boy who loves rebellious horse; nicely done, beautifully filmed in color. Followed by sequel THUNDERHEAD, SON OF FLICKA and a TV series. Remade in 2006 as FLICKA. ▼▶

My Friend Irma (1949) 103m. ** D: George Marshall. Marie Wilson, John Lund, Diana Lynn, Don DeFore, Dean Martin, Jerry Lewis, Hans Conried. Based on radio series, movie concerns Wilson in title role as dumb blonde, Lynn as her level-headed pal, encountering wacky Martin and Lewis in their film debut. Followed by a sequel. Later a TV series. ▼◑▶

My Friend Irma Goes West (1950) 90m. **½ D: Hal Walker. John Lund, Marie Wilson, Dean Martin, Jerry Lewis, Corinne Calvet, Diana Lynn, Lloyd Corrigan, Don Porter, Kenneth Tobey. Daffy Irma (Wilson) and pals join Martin and Lewis on their trek to Hollywood. ▶

My Gal Sal (1942) C-103m. *** D: Irving Cummings. Rita Hayworth, Victor Mature, John Sutton, Carole Landis, James Gleason, Phil Silvers, Mona Maris, Walter Catlett. Nostalgic Gay '90s musical about songwriter Paul Dresser (Mature) in love with beautiful singer Hayworth. Includes Dresser's songs, such as title tune and

other old-time numbers. The two stars (and knockout Technicolor) really put this one across. That's co-choreographer Hermes Pan featured with Rita in the "Gay White Way" number. Based on the story *My Brother Paul* by Theodore Dreiser.

My Geisha (1962) C-120m. **½ D: Jack Cardiff. Shirley MacLaine, Yves Montand, Edward G. Robinson, Bob Cummings, Yoko Tani. Occasionally amusing comedy. MacLaine is movie star who tries the hard way to convince husband-director Montand that she's right for his movie. Loosely based on MacLaine's relationship with husband Steve Parker (who produced the film). Filmed in Japan. Technirama. ▼◑▶

My Girl Tisa (1948) 95m. **½ D: Elliott Nugent. Lilli Palmer, Sam Wanamaker, Akim Tamiroff, Alan Hale, Hugo Haas, Gale Robbins, Stella Adler. Sincere but uninspiring tale of devoted immigrant girl Palmer working to bring her father to the U.S. Palmer is fine as usual in lead. ▼

My Gun Is Quick (1957) 88m. *½ D: George A. White, Phil Victor. Robert Bray, Whitney Blake, Donald Randolph, Fred Essler, Booth Colman, Pamela Duncan. Drab Mickey Spillane yarn with Mike Hammer (Bray) meeting a down-on-her-luck dame who immediately turns up dead. Result is everything a noirish detective film should not be; the best thing about this is its title. ▶

My Kingdom for a Cook (1943) 83m. *** D: Richard Wallace. Charles Coburn, Marguerite Chapman, Bill Carter, Isobel Elsom, Edward Gargan, Mary Wickes. A caustic British author and gourmet who can't bring his personal chef with him on a U.S. lecture tour creates a stir when he steals a New England socialite's cook. Very funny showcase for the wonderful Coburn in a rare, tailor-made starring role (following his Oscar-winning performance in THE MORE THE MERRIER).

My Lady of Whims (1925) 42m. *½ D: Dallas M. Fitzgerald. Clara Bow, Donald Keith, Carmelita Geraghty, Francis McDonald, Lee Moran, Betty Baker. Underweight comedy about a flapper debutante and the fellow her stern father hires to keep her out of mischief. Slim effort is too short, not sweet at all, and utterly devoid of wit. One of 14 pictures Bow made that year, and it shows. ▼▶

My Life to Live (1962-French) 85m. *** D: Jean-Luc Godard. Anna Karina, Saddy Rebbot, Andre S. Labarthe, Guylaine Schlumberger. Complex, fascinating 12-chapter portrait of a prostitute (Karina, who was then wed to Godard), told in documentary style. Probing look at the manner in which women and men view one another—and a celluloid valentine to Karina, upon whose mere presence Godard seems to be transfixed. Aka VIVRE SA VIE. ▼◑▶

My Life With Caroline (1941) 81m. **½ D: Lewis Milestone. Ronald Colman, Anna

[474]

Lee, Charles Winninger, Reginald Gardiner, Gilbert Roland. Colman's charm sustains this frothy comedy of man suspecting his wife of having a lover.

My Little Chickadee (1940) 83m. **½ D: Edward Cline. Mae West, W. C. Fields, Joseph Calleia, Dick Foran, Ruth Donnelly, Margaret Hamilton, Donald Meek. Team of West and Fields out West is good, but should have been funnier; W. C.'s saloon scenes are notable. The two stars also wrote screenplay. ▼○●

My Love Came Back (1940) 81m. **½ D: Curtis Bernhardt. Olivia de Havilland, Jeffrey Lynn, Eddie Albert, Jane Wyman, Charles Winninger, Spring Byington, Grant Mitchell. Entertaining little romance of violinist de Havilland looking for husband. ▶

My Love for Yours SEE: **Honeymoon in Bali**

My Lucky Star (1938) 84m. **½ D: Roy Del Ruth. Sonja Henie, Richard Greene, Cesar Romero, Buddy Ebsen, Joan Davis, Arthur Treacher, Billy Gilbert, Louise Hovick (Gypsy Rose Lee), George Barbier. Typical Henie vehicle with the skating star becoming the belle of a college campus—and helping department-store heir Romero score a hit with his dad. Finale is an imaginative "Alice in Wonderland" ice ballet. ▼▶

My Man and I (1952) 99m. **½ D: William A. Wellman. Shelley Winters, Ricardo Montalban, Wendell Corey, Claire Trevor, Robert Burton, Jack Elam. Interesting curio about cheerful, kindly Mexican-born Montalban, who despite his trials and struggles is fiercely proud of his American citizenship. ▶

My Man Godfrey (1936) 95m. **** D: Gregory La Cava. William Powell, Carole Lombard, Gail Patrick, Alice Brady, Eugene Pallette, Alan Mowbray, Mischa Auer, Franklin Pangborn. Delightful romp with Lombard and crazy household hiring Powell as butler thinking he's a tramp who needs a job; he teaches them that money isn't everything. Auer is impressive as starving artist, sheltered by patroness Brady. But Pallette—as harried head of household—has some of the best lines. Screenplay by Morrie Ryskind and Eric Hatch, from Hatch's novel. Jane Wyman is an extra in the party scene. Classic screwball comedy; remade in 1957. ▼▶

My Man Godfrey (1957) C-92m. **½ D: Henry Koster. June Allyson, David Niven, Martha Hyer, Eva Gabor, Jeff Donnell. Shallow compared to original, but on its own a harmless comedy of rich girl Allyson finding life's truths from butler Niven. CinemaScope. ▼

My Name Is Ivan (1962-Russian) 94m. *** D: Andrei Tarkovsky. Kolya Burlaiev, Valentin Zubkov, Ye Zharikov, Nikolai Grinko. Taut, poignant account of 12-year-old Burlaiev, whose family is slaughtered during WW2, and his plight as he's sent as a spy into Nazi territory. Tarkovsky's first feature.

Retitled: THE YOUNGEST SPY. Original title: IVAN'S CHILDHOOD. ▼▶

My Name Is Julia Ross (1945) 65m. *** D: Joseph H. Lewis. Nina Foch, Dame May Whitty, George Macready, Roland Varno, Anita Bolster, Doris Lloyd. An unsuspecting young woman answers newspaper ad for a job and winds up the prisoner of a crazy family. Often cited as a model B movie, it does go a long way on a low budget, though it's a bit more obvious now than it must have been in 1945. Foch's performance is still a standout. Later the inspiration for DEAD OF WINTER. ▶

My Outlaw Brother (1951) 82m. ** D: Elliott Nugent. Mickey Rooney, Wanda Hendrix, Robert Preston, Robert Stack, Jose Torvay. Texas Ranger Preston takes on villainous Stack, the brother of dude Rooney. Strictly conventional south-of-the-border oater. ▼▶

My Own True Love (1949) 84m. ** D: Compton Bennett. Melvyn Douglas, Phyllis Calvert, Wanda Hendrix, Philip Friend, Binnie Barnes. Calvert is placed in the awkward position of choosing between two suitors, a father and son; drama lacks ring of truth.

My Pal Gus (1952) 83m. **½ D: Robert Parrish. Richard Widmark, Joanne Dru, Audrey Totter, George Winslow, Regis Toomey. Wholesome film of Widmark coming to realize importance of son Winslow, finding romance with teacher Dru. ▶

My Pal Trigger (1946) 79m. *** D: Frank McDonald. Roy Rogers, George "Gabby" Hayes, Dale Evans, Jack Holt, LeRoy Mason, Roy Barcroft, Kenne Duncan, Bob Nolan and the Sons of the Pioneers. Roy wants to breed his mare to the prize palomino stud on Gabby's ranch, but gambler Holt has similar plans and frames Roy for the death of Gabby's horse. Roy gives one of his best performances in this solid Western saga that features his famous horse. ▼▶

My Reputation (1946) 94m. *** D: Curtis Bernhardt. Barbara Stanwyck, George Brent, Warner Anderson, Lucile Watson, John Ridgely, Eve Arden, Jerome Cowan, Esther Dale, Scotty Beckett, Bobby Cooper. Well-mounted soaper with Stanwyck excellent as a long-stifled recent widow who causes scandal in her conservative community when she begins dating Major Brent. Completed in 1944. ▶

Myrt and Marge (1934) 62m. ** D: Al Boasberg. Myrtle Vail, Donna Damerel, Eddie Foy, Jr., Grace Hayes, Ted Healy, Howard, Fine, and Howard (The 3 Stooges), Bonnie Bonnell. Lackluster backstage musical, based on popular radio show of the same name. Mainly a curio for fans of the Stooges, who get to sing as well as clown.

My Sin (1931) 78m. **½ D: George Abbott. Tallulah Bankhead, Fredric March, Harry Davenport, Scott Kolk, Anne Sutherland, Margaret Adams, Joseph Calleia, Eric

Blore. Bankhead is a nightclub singer in Panama who shoots a man and is defended by alcoholic lawyer March. After acquittal, she flees to N.Y.C. and becomes a successful interior decorator but is haunted by her shady past. Bankhead's second talkie failed to make her a genuine movie star, but March is quite good. Interesting film was one of a handful directed by theatre legend Abbott.

My Sister Eileen (1942) **96m. **½** D: Alexander Hall. Rosalind Russell, Brian Aherne, Janet Blair, George Tobias, Allyn Joslyn, Elizabeth Patterson, June Havoc. Amusing tale of two Ohio girls trying to survive in Greenwich Village apartment; strained at times. Belongs mainly to Russell as older sister of knockout Blair. Ruth McKinney, Joseph Fields, and Jerome Chodorov adapted their Broadway hit (based on McKinney's autobiographical book). Remade as a musical in 1955 (and musicalized on Broadway as *Wonderful Town*). Finale features a gag cameo. **▼●)**

My Sister Eileen (1955) **C-108m. ***½** D: Richard Quine. Betty Garrett, Janet Leigh, Jack Lemmon, Kurt Kasznar, Dick York, Horace McMahon, Robert (Bob) Fosse, Tommy Rall. Delightful, unpretentious musical version of 1942 movie about Ohio girls seeking success in the big city, moving into nutty Greenwich Village apartment. Especially interesting to see young Lemmon singing and equally young Fosse dancing; this was the first film he choreographed on his own. Not to be confused with the Broadway musical *Wonderful Town*, based on the same source. CinemaScope. **▼●)**

My Six Convicts (1952) **104m. ***** D: Hugo Fregonese. Millard Mitchell, Gilbert Roland, John Beal, Marshall Thompson, Alf Kjellin, Henry (Harry) Morgan, Jay Adler, Regis Toomey, John Marley, Charles Buchinsky (Bronson). Unusual comedy of prison life centering on title group who manage to make jail routine tolerable, egged on by prison psychiatrist.

My Six Loves (1963) **C-101m. **½** D: Gower Champion. Debbie Reynolds, Cliff Robertson, David Janssen, Eileen Heckart, Hans Conried, Alice Pearce, Jim Backus. Syrupy fluff of theater star Reynolds "adopting" six waifs. VistaVision.

My Son John (1952) **122m. **½** D: Leo McCarey. Helen Hayes, Robert Walker, Dean Jagger, Van Heflin, Frank McHugh, Richard Jaeckel. Archetypal apple-pie parents (Hayes, Jagger) suspect their son (Walker) of being a Communist in this reactionary period piece. Dramatically overwrought, but fascinating as social history. Walker (who's superb) died before film was finished; most shots of him in final reel are cribbed from STRANGERS ON A TRAIN. **❙**

My Son, My Son (1940) **115m. **** D: Charles Vidor. Madeleine Carroll, Brian Aherne, Louis Hayward, Laraine Day,

Henry Hull, Josephine Hutchinson, Scotty Beckett. Drawn-out, unconvincing tale of rags-to-riches Aherne who spoils his son and lives to regret it. Some good performances wasted on banal script. **▼**

My Son, the Hero (1962-Italian) **C-122m. **** D: Duccio Tessari. Pedro Armendariz, Jacqueline Sassard, Antonella Lualdi, Giuliano Gemma. Costume picture about evil King Cadmus of Thebes, who defies the gods and faces the wrath of the Titans. Originally released in the U.S. at 111m., with comic dubbing à la WHAT'S UP, TIGER LILY?, which it preceded.

My Son, the Vampire SEE: **Mother Riley Meets the Vampire**

Mysterians, The (1957-Japanese) **C-85m. **½** D: Ishiro Honda. Kenji Sahara, Yumi Shirakawa, Momoko Kochi, Akihiko Hirata. Centuries after the destruction of their planet, the title aliens land on Earth, install an impregnable dome by a lake, and demand women. The world does not take this well. Colorful special effects and fast pace make this one of the better Japanese sci-fis. Tohoscope. **▼❙**

Mysterious Doctor, The (1943) **57m. **½** D: Ben Stoloff. John Loder, Eleanor Parker, Bruce Lester, Lester Matthews, Forrester Harvey. A headless ghost terrorizes tin miners in a foggy English village. Moor locations interesting; cast adequate.

Mysterious Dr. Fu Manchu, The (1929) **81m. **½** D: Rowland V. Lee. Warner Oland, Neil Hamilton, Jean Arthur, O. P. Heggie, William Austin, Claude King, Noble Johnson. Fu Manchu's wife and child are inadvertently killed by British troops during the Boxer Rebellion. Years later, he comes to London and uses his hypnotized white ward (Arthur) as part of a diabolical plan of vengeance. The first talkie about Sax Rohmer's Chinese supervillain is an enjoyably hokey guilty pleasure, with striking sets, tongue-in-cheek humor, and lurid, serial-like thrills.

Mysterious Intruder (1946) **61m. **½** D: William Castle. Richard Dix, Barton MacLane, Nina Vale, Regis Toomey, Pamela Blake, Charles Lane, Helen Mowery, Mike Mazurki. Dix is an unscrupulous private eye who resorts to murder in an attempt to find some rare Jenny Lind wax recordings in this atmospheric *Whistler* series entry.

Mysterious Island (1961-British) **C-101m. ***** D: Cy Endfield. Michael Craig, Joan Greenwood, Michael Callan, Gary Merrill, Herbert Lom. Deliberately paced fantasy adventure based on two-part Jules Verne novel, a sequel to his *20,000 Leagues Under the Sea*. Confederate prison escapees hijack observation balloon and are blown off course; find uncharted island with gigantic animals. Great special effects by Ray Harryhausen; rousing Bernard Herrmann score. Filmed before in 1929. Remade for cable TV in 2005. **▼●)**

Mysterious Lady, The (1928) 96m. **½
D: Fred Niblo. Greta Garbo, Conrad Nagel, Gustav von Seyffertitz, Albert Pollet, Edward Connelly. During WW1, Austrian military officer Nagel falls in love with Garbo, unaware that she's a Russian spy. She steals secret papers from him and he's charged with treason. The luminous Garbo and grade-A production values elevate a contrived storyline. ▼❿

Mysterious Mr. Moto (1938) 62m. **½
D: Norman Foster. Peter Lorre, Henry Wilcoxon, Mary Maguire, Erik Rhodes, Harold Huber, Leon Ames, Forrester Harvey. The Oriental sleuth travels to London, where a secret assassination society has Scotland Yard baffled.❿

Mysterious Mr. Wong, The (1935) 63m. ** D: William Nigh. Bela Lugosi, Wallace Ford, Arline Judge, Fred Warren, Lotus Long, Robert Emmett O'Connor. Lugosi, complete with Hungarian accent, plays the title character: a power-mad Chinaman obsessed with possessing 12 coins that were once the property of Confucius. He's also cast as Wong's shy, quiet alter-ego in this campy programmer. Not related in any way to Boris Karloff's *Mr. Wong* series.▼❿

Mystery House (1938) 56m. ** D: Noel Smith. Dick Purcell, Ann Sheridan, Anne Nagel, William Hopper, Dennie Moore. Crackerjack detective Purcell investigates the death of a financier, which has been ruled a suicide but actually is murder. OK mystery; Sheridan, cast as the detective's nurse friend, played the same role in THE PATIENT IN ROOM 18 (which featured Patric Knowles as the gumshoe). The characters also appear in WHILE THE PATIENT SLEPT.❿

Mystery in Mexico (1948) 66m. ** D: Robert Wise. William Lundigan, Jacqueline White, Ricardo Cortez, Tony Barrett, Jacqueline Dalya, Walter Reed. Competent but overly familiar second-feature mystery about insurance investigator Lundigan who goes to Mexico City to find out what happened to White's brother.❿

Mystery Liner (1934) 62m. ** D: William Nigh. Noah Beery, Astrid Allyn (Allwyn), Cornelius Keefe, Gustav von Seyffertitz, Edwin Maxwell, Ralph Lewis, Zeffie Tilbury. A mysterious secret radio-control weapon being developed aboard a cruise ship is sought by various parties in this intriguing but slow-paced B picture. Gabby Hayes is billed as Watchman. Based on an Edgar Wallace novel. ▼❿

Mystery Man (1944) 58m. **½ D: George Archainbaud. William Boyd, Andy Clyde, Jimmy Rogers, Don Costello, Eleanor Stewart, Francis McDonald, Forrest Taylor. Epic battles ensue when Bar 20 cowhands drive a herd to market and come up against notorious outlaw and his desperadoes seeking to rustle cattle. Costello as master heavy

and lovely Stewart are strong, but Rogers is wooden as Hopalong Cassidy's young sidekick. Still enjoyable, with the series' usual first-rate production values.▼❿

Mystery of Edwin Drood, The (1935) 87m. **½ D: Stuart Walker. Claude Rains, Douglass Montgomery, Heather Angel, David Manners, E. E. Clive, Francis (L.) Sullivan, Valerie Hobson. Seemingly respectable English choirmaster Rains is actually responsible for horrible murder. Pretty good Hollywood adaptation of Charles Dickens' unfinished novel, which inspired a Broadway musical in the 1980s. Remade in 1993.▼❿

Mystery of Marie Roget (1942) 60m. **½ D: Phil Rosen. Maria Montez, Maria Ouspenskaya, John Litel, Patric Knowles, Charles Middleton. Poe story provides basis for fairly good murder mystery. Detective tries to unravel mystery of actress' strange disappearance in 1880s Paris.▼❿

Mystery of Mr. Wong (1939) 67m. *½ D: William Nigh. Boris Karloff, Grant Withers, Dorothy Tree, Lotus Long, Morgan Wallace, Holmes Herbert. Modest *Mr. Wong* mystery, second entry in the series, has Oriental sleuth becoming embroiled in mystery surrounding a rare gem and a suspiciously changed will.▼❿

Mystery of Mr. X, The (1934) 85m. *** D: Edgar Selwyn. Robert Montgomery, Elizabeth Allan, Lewis Stone, Ralph Forbes, Henry Stephenson, Forrester Harvey, Ivan Simpson, Leonard Mudie. Stylish, highly enjoyable mixture of suspense and light comedy, with urbane London jewel thief Montgomery suspected of a string of police murders and trying to clear himself while romancing Scotland Yard chief's daughter.

Mystery of Picasso, The (1956-French) C-85m. ***½ D: Henri-Georges Clouzot. Fascinating documentary about Pablo Picasso, who discusses his work and creates a number of paintings before the camera (all of which were destroyed after shooting ended, meaning that they exist only on film). Photographed by Claude (nephew of Jean and grandson of Auguste) Renoir. CinemaScope (part).▼❶❿

Mystery of the Black Jungle (1956-German) 72m. *½ D: Ralph Murphy. Lex Barker, Jane Maxwell, Luigi Tosi, Paul Muller. Embarrassing lowjinks set in India involving idol-worshiping natives. Retitled: THE BLACK DEVILS OF KALI.▼❶❿

Mystery of the Golden Eye SEE: **Golden Eye, The**

Mystery of the Leaping Fish, The (1916) 27m. *** D: John Emerson. Douglas Fairbanks, Bessie Love, Alma Reubens, A. D. Sears, Charles Stevens, Tom Wilson. Doug is Coke Ennyday, a master of disguises and the world's greatest scientific detective, who investigates the activities of a mysterious wealthy gentleman. Fairbanks cavorts outrageously in this loopy farce, which cleverly satirizes detective stories (and Sherlock Holmes in particular). His character's comical consumption of cocaine is a running gag throughout! Story by Tod Browning. ▼▶

Mystery of the Mary Celeste, The SEE: **Phantom Ship**

Mystery of the Wax Museum (1933) C-77m. **½ D: Michael Curtiz. Lionel Atwill, Fay Wray, Glenda Farrell, Allen Vincent, Frank McHugh, Arthur Edmund Carewe. Vintage horror film strays somewhat into excess "comic relief" and contrivances, but plot of madman Atwill encasing victims in wax, with Wray next on his list, is still exciting. Filmed in early two-color Technicolor; noteworthy as a rare 1930s horror film with contemporary urban setting. Remade as HOUSE OF WAX. ▼●

Mystery of the White Room (1939) 58m. *** D: Otis Garrett. Bruce Cabot, Helen Mack, Constance Worth, Joan Woodbury, Mabel Todd, Tom Dugan. Very good *Crime Club* mystery of murders in an operating room; modest but nicely done.

Mystery Street (1950) 93m. **½ D: John Sturges. Ricardo Montalban, Sally Forrest, Bruce Bennett, Elsa Lanchester, Marshall Thompson, Jan Sterling, Edmon Ryan, Betsy Blair. The skeleton of a murdered B girl is studied by Cape Cod cop Montalban and Harvard doctor Bennett in an early movie depiction of forensic science. Intelligent, realistic mystery is well acted and engrossing, if slow paced.▶

Mystery Submarine (1950) 78m. **½ D: Douglas Sirk. Macdonald Carey, Marta Toren, Carl Esmond, Ludwig Donath. Involved plot of military officer Carey being instrumental in destruction of Nazi sub in South America.

Mystery Submarine (1963-British) 90m. *½ D: C. M. Pennington-Richards. Edward Judd, James Robertson Justice, Laurence Payne, Arthur O'Sullivan, Albert Lieven. Tame WW2 espionage tale of German sub manned by British crew—captured by English fleet. Aka DECOY.

My Teenage Daughter SEE: **Bad Girl**

My True Story (1951) 67m. ** D: Mickey Rooney. Helen Walker, Willard Parker, Elisabeth Risdon, Emory Parnell, Aldo Ray, Wilton Graff. A convicted jewel thief (Walker) is paroled as part of a scheme to steal a rare perfume oil owned by a wealthy widow. Routine melodrama was a curious choice for Rooney's directorial debut. Ray is billed under real name of Aldo DaRe in his first released film.

My Uncle SEE: **Mon Oncle**

My Wife's Best Friend (1952) 87m. ** D: Richard Sale. Anne Baxter, Macdonald Carey, Cecil Kellaway, Leif Erickson, Frances Bavier. Unexceptional film of married couple confessing their past indiscretions when their plane seems about to crash. ▶

My Wild Irish Rose (1947) C-101m. ** D: David Butler. Dennis Morgan, Andrea King, Arlene Dahl, Alan Hale, George Tobias. Irish songs galore support limp biography of songwriter Chauncey Olcott.▶

My Woman (1933) 73m. **½ D: Victor Schertzinger. Helen Twelvetrees, Victor Jory, Wallace Ford, Claire Dodd, Hobart Cavanaugh, Harry Holman, Charles Levison (Lane), Raymond Brown. Song-and-dance man Ford becomes a big radio star thanks to the efforts of wife Twelvetrees, but success goes to his head and he leaves her for a Park Avenue socialite. Formulaic rags-to-riches showbiz yarn boosted by zesty performances and a colorful depiction of the radio station milieu. Look fast for Walter Brennan.

My World Dies Screaming (1958) 85m. *½ D: Harold Daniels. Gerald Mohr, Cathy O'Donnell, Bill (William) Ching, John Qualen, Barry Bernard. Newlywed O'Donnell suffers from recurrent nightmares about a spooky house, then husband Mohr takes her to that very house. Looks for a while like GASLIGHT, JR., but veers off in a different direction. Thin, cheap thriller, not quite a horror movie, was notorious for featuring one-frame subliminal images (skulls, monsters) in the would-be scary sections; they were removed when the title was changed to TERROR IN THE HAUNTED HOUSE but restored for the video release under that title. ▼▶

Nabonga (1944) 75m. *½ D: Sam Newfield. Buster Crabbe, Julie London, Fifi D'Orsay, Barton MacLane, Bryant Washburn. Incredible cheapie of little girl who survives jungle plane crash and makes friends with a local gorilla; she grows up (now played by London) to become a jungle goddess. Good for laughs, anyway. London's film debut. Retitled: GORILLA.▼▶

Naked Alibi (1954) 86m. **½ D: Jerry Hopper. Sterling Hayden, Gloria Grahame, Gene Barry, Marcia Henderson, Casey Adams (Max Showalter), Chuck Connors. Dismissed from force because of "police brutality," ex-cop Hayden continues to stalk cop-killer suspect Barry.

Naked and the Dead, The (1958) C-131m. *** D: Raoul Walsh. Aldo Ray, Cliff Robertson, Raymond Massey, William Campbell, Richard Jaeckel, James Best, Joey Bishop, L. Q. Jones, Robert Gist, Lili St. Cyr, Barbara Nichols. Norman Mailer's intense novel about WW2 soldiers in the Pacific gets superficial but rugged filmization. Ray is the tough sergeant, Robertson the rich-kid lieutenant, Bishop the comic Jew, Jones the hick, Gist the loner, etc. RKO-Scope/WarnerScope.▼

Naked City, The (1948) 96m. *** D: Jules Dassin. Barry Fitzgerald, Howard Duff, Don Taylor, Dorothy Hart, Ted de Corsia, House Jameson, Frank Conroy, David Opatoshu,

Celia Adler, Molly Picon. Time (and decades of TV cop shows) have dulled the edge of this once-trendsetting crime drama, produced by columnist Mark Hellinger on the streets of N.Y.C., following the investigation of a murder case step by step. Fitzgerald is still first-rate, cast against type as the detective in charge, and the cast is peppered with soon-to-be-familiar character actors (Arthur O'Connell, Paul Ford, James Gregory, et al.). Cinematographer William Daniels and editor Paul Weatherwax won Oscars for their work. Screenplay by Albert Maltz and Malvin Wald. Later a TV series. ▼●▶

Naked Dawn, The (1955) **C-82m.** **½ D: Edgar G. Ulmer. Arthur Kennedy, Betta St. John, Roy Engel, Eugene Iglesias, Charita. Modern Western about a snowballing series of crimes. Based on a story by Gorky, and much admired by Ulmer buffs.

Naked Earth (1958-British) **96m.** *½ D: Vincent Sherman. Juliette Greco, Richard Todd, John Kitzmiller, Finlay Currie. Misguided soap opera set in 1890s Africa, trying to build up aspiring star Greco. CinemaScope.

Naked Edge, The (1961) **99m.** **½ D: Michael Anderson. Gary Cooper, Deborah Kerr, Eric Portman, Diane Cilento, Hermione Gingold, Michael Wilding, Peter Cushing. Uneven suspenser of Kerr thinking husband Cooper is guilty of murder. Cooper's last film, made in London. ▼

Naked Heart, The (1950-British) **96m.** ** D: Marc Allegret. Michele Morgan, Kieron Moore, Françoise Rosay, Jack Watling. Little of consequence happens in this sad story based on book *Maria Chapdelaine* by Louis Hémon. Filmed before in 1935 (in France) and again in 1983 (in Canada).

Naked Hills, The (1956) **C-73m.** *½ D: Josef Shaftel. David Wayne, Keenan Wynn, James Barton, Marcia Henderson, Jim Backus. Raggedy account of Wayne who has gold fever and spends life searching for ore, ignoring wife and family. ▼▶

Naked in the Night SEE: **Madeleine** (1958-German)

Naked Jungle, The (1954) **C-95m.** *** D: Byron Haskin. Eleanor Parker, Charlton Heston, Abraham Sofaer, William Conrad. High-class South American jungle adventure, with Heston and wife Parker surrounded on their plantation by advancing army of red ants. Produced by George Pal. ▼●▶

Naked Kiss, The (1964) **93m.** *** D: Samuel Fuller. Constance Towers, Anthony Eisley, Michael Dante, Virginia Grey, Patsy Kelly, Betty Bronson. In-your-face melodrama opens with a bang and never lets up, as prostitute Towers arrives in a small town hoping to start a new life. By turns lurid, sentimental, romantic, surprising; a mélange that could only have been concocted by writer-director Fuller. ▼●▶

Naked Maja, The (1959) **C-111m.** ** D:

Henry Koster. Ava Gardner, Anthony Franciosa, Amedeo Nazzari, Gino Cervi, Massimo Serato, Lea Padovani, Carlo Rizzo. Mishmash involving 18th-century Spanish painter Goya and famed model for title painting. Filmed in Italy. Technirama. ▼

Naked Night, The SEE: **Sawdust and Tinsel**

Naked Paradise (1957) **C-68m.** BOMB D: Roger Corman. Richard Denning, Beverly Garland, Lisa Montell, Richard (Dick) Miller, Leslie Bradley. On-location filming in Hawaii can't salvage this balderdash about crooks using cruise boat to rob a local plantation. Retitled: THUNDER OVER HAWAII. Remade as BEAST FROM HAUNTED CAVE and CREATURE FROM THE HAUNTED SEA.

Naked Spur, The (1953) **C-91m.** ***½ D: Anthony Mann. James Stewart, Janet Leigh, Ralph Meeker, Robert Ryan, Millard Mitchell. One of the best Westerns ever made: a tough, hard little film about self-styled bounty hunter Stewart trying to capture Ryan, who stirs tension among Stewart's newly acquired "partners." Strikingly directed and photographed (by William Mellor) on location in the Rockies. Written by Sam Rolfe and Harold Jack Bloom. ▼▶

Naked Street, The (1955) **84m.** ** D: Maxwell Shane. Farley Granger, Anthony Quinn, Anne Bancroft, Peter Graves, Else Neft, Sara Berner, Jerry Paris, Jeanne Cooper, Sid Melton, Lee Van Cleef. Good cast wasted in bland crime drama of Brooklyn mobster Quinn, who is overly protective of his kid sister (Bancroft). How will he respond when she becomes pregnant and the father-to-be (Granger) is a convicted murderer in the death house at Sing Sing?

Naked Truth, The SEE: **Your Past Is Showing**

Naked Youth (1959) **69m.** BOMB D: John F. Schreyer. Carol Ohmart, Robert Hutton, Steve Rowland, Jan Brooks, Robert Arthur, John Goddard. Awful potboiler about drug smuggling, murder and some youths who escape from the "State Boys Honor Farm." That "Switch"—short for switchblade—is a real peach. Plenty of blasting saxophones and bongo drums on the soundtrack. Aka WILD YOUTH. ▼▶

Nana (1926-French-German) **130m.** **½ D: Jean Renoir. Catherine Hessling, Jean Angelo, Werner Krauss, Raymond Guérin-Catelain, Claude Moore (Claude Autant-Lara), Pierre Champagne, Valeska Gert, Pierre Philippe (Pierre Lestringuez), Marie Prevost, Jacqueline Forzane. Emile Zola's oft-filmed novel of decadence and despair centers on the coquettish title character (Hessling), who manipulates her admirers and is "the golden fly that poisons everything she touches." Often dramatically potent but hindered by Hessling's overbaked performance. This was an enormous failure in its day. Coscripted by Renoir and Lestringuez. Autant-Lara (who plays Fauchery) was also the art director and costume designer.▶

Nana (1934) 89m. **½ D: Dorothy Arzner. Anna Sten, Phillips Holmes, Lionel Atwill, Muriel Kirkland, Richard Bennett, Mae Clarke. Initially interesting adaptation of Emile Zola story of luxury-loving woman in tragic love affair runs out of steam towards the middle. Producer Samuel Goldwyn's first attempt to make a new Garbo out of exotic but wooden Sten.

Nancy Drew Carolyn Keene's series of juvenile mystery novels debuted in 1930 and immediately captured the fancy of young readers. In 1938 Warner Bros. purchased the screen rights, and found the perfect actress to bring Nancy to life: Bonita Granville. Her Nancy is brainy, feisty, resourceful, and full of energy—boundless energy. Frankie Thomas plays her boyfriend and crime-solving cohort, and John Litel is (type)cast as her attorney father. Other characters and incidents were combined or compressed from Keene's books, but only two scripts were actually adapted from novels: NANCY DREW, DETECTIVE and NANCY DREW AND THE HIDDEN STAIRCASE, the best in the series and ironically the last. All four films were directed by William Clemens with typical Warner Bros. zip and pace; they're more densely plotted than one might expect for B pictures, and though they're aimed at a younger audience, they seldom skirt the grim realities of crime and murder. The four films are very much of a piece, and hew to a Hollywood formula; if they're not quite as good as the books, they're still fun to watch.

NANCY DREW

Nancy Drew, Detective (1938)
Nancy Drew—Reporter (1939)
Nancy Drew—Troubleshooter (1939)
Nancy Drew and the Hidden Staircase (1939)

Nancy Drew and the Hidden Staircase (1939) 60m. **½ D: William Clemens. Bonita Granville, Frankie Thomas, John Litel, Frank Orth, Renie Riano, Vera Lewis, John Ridgely. Nancy comes to the aid of two aging sisters plagued by mysterious occurrences in their old mansion; best of the short-lived series, and only one of two actually based on a Carolyn Keene novel, *The Hidden Staircase.*▶

Nancy Drew . . . Detective (1938) 66m. **½ D: William Clemens. Bonita Granville, John Litel, James Stephenson, Frankie Thomas, Frank Orth, Renie Riano, Dick Purcell. Nancy investigates a wealthy woman's disappearance in the series' debut film, with Granville's energetic performance scoring a bull's-eye. Based on *The Password to Larkspur Lane.*▶

Nancy Drew . . . Reporter (1939) 68m. **½ D: William Clemens. Bonita Granville, John Litel, Frankie Thomas, Mary Lee, Dickie Jones. One of the series' best entries has school newspaper reporter Nancy determined to prove a girl innocent of murder charges.▼▶

Nancy Drew . . . Trouble Shooter (1939) 69m. ** D: William Clemens. Bonita Granville, Frankie Thomas, John Litel, Aldrich Bowker, Renie Riano. More emphasis on comedy than mystery in this potboiler with Nancy helping to clear a friend of her Dad's who's been accused of murder.▶

Nancy Goes to Rio (1950) C-99m. **½ D: Robert Z. Leonard. Ann Sothern, Jane Powell, Barry Sullivan, Carmen Miranda, Louis Calhern, Fortunio Bonanova, Hans Conried. Agreeable if artificial MGM musical (remake of Deanna Durbin's IT'S A DATE), with Sothern and Powell as mother and daughter who compete for a plum acting role and, through misunderstanding, the same man.▼▶

Nancy Steele Is Missing! (1937) 85m. **½ D: George Marshall. Victor McLaglen, Walter Connolly, Peter Lorre, June Lang, Jane Darwell, John Carradine. McLaglen is so opposed to war he abducts the baby daughter of a WW1 munitions king; many complications ensue. Offbeat *sympathetic* portrayal of a kidnapper.

Nanny, The (1965-British) 93m. *** D: Seth Holt. Bette Davis, Wendy Craig, Jill Bennett, James Villiers, Pamela Franklin, William Dix, Maurice Denham. Twisting, scary plot plus fine direction reap results. Suspects of child murder narrowed to governess Davis and disturbed youngster Dix. Unusual Hammer production, written by Jimmy Sangster. From the novel by Evelyn Piper.▼▶

Nanook of the North (1922) 79m. ***½ D: Robert Flaherty. Pioneer documentary of Eskimos' daily life withstands the test of time quite well, remains as absorbing saga, well filmed. Set the standard for many documentaries to follow. Soundtrack added in 1939. The film's production is re-created in KABLOONAK.▼▶

Napoleon (1927-French) 235m. **** D: Abel Gance. Albert Dieudonné, Antonin Artaud, Pierre Batcheff, Armand Bernard, Harry Krimer, Albert Bras, Abel Gance. Hard to put into words the impact of this monumental silent epic. Dieudonné mesmerizingly plays the famed emperor; notable sequences include snowball fight, the Reign of Terror, and eye-popping three-screen Polyvision finale. Recut and shortened many times over the years (often by Gance himself), finally painstakingly pieced together by historian Kevin Brownlow and reissued in 1981 with a serviceable music score by Carmine Coppola. Not the kind of film one can best appreciate on TV. Filmed in part-widescreen triptych.▼●

Narcotic (1933) **57m.** BOMB D: Dwain Esper. Harry Cording, Joan Dix, Patricia Farley, Jean Lacey, J. Stuart Blackton, Jr. Another gloriously awful Esper epic, presented as a case history of a doctor's decline into hopeless drug addiction. Includes plenty of stock footage, astoundingly wooden acting, and laughable Asian stereotypes. A hoot if you're in the right mood. . . . ▼⃟

Narrow Corner, The (1933) **71m.** ***
D: Alfred E. Green. Douglas Fairbanks, Jr., Patricia Ellis, Ralph Bellamy, Dudley Digges, William V. Mong, Sidney Toler, Henry Kolker, Willie Fung. Fairbanks is on the lam, and winds up on an East Indies island where he finds friendship—and illicit romance. Remarkably adult adaptation of W. Somerset Maugham novel (made in the pre–Production Code era), with only minor flaws. Remade as ISLE OF FURY.

Narrow Margin, The (1952) **70m.** ***½
D: Richard Fleischer. Charles McGraw, Marie Windsor, Jacqueline White, Queenie Leonard. Hard-boiled cop, transporting a gangster's widow to the trial in which she'll testify, must dodge hit men aboard their train who are trying to silence her. One of the best B's ever made—fast paced, well acted, impressively shot in claustrophobic setting. Photographed by George E. Diskant; scripted by Earl Fenton, from a story by Martin Goldsmith and Jack Leonard. Remade in 1990. Also shown in computer-colored version.▼●⃟

Nasty Rabbit, The (1964) **C-85m.** ** D: James Landis. Arch Hall, Jr., Micha Terr, Melissa Morgan, John Akana. Weak spoof with serious overtones involving Russian attempt to set loose a disease-infected rabbit in the U. S. Retitled: SPIES A GO GO. Techniscope.▼⃟

National Velvet (1944) **C-125m.** **** D: Clarence Brown. Mickey Rooney, Elizabeth Taylor, Donald Crisp, Anne Revere, Angela Lansbury, Reginald Owen, Norma Varden, Jackie "Butch" Jenkins, Terry Kilburn. Outstanding family film about a girl who determines to enter her horse in the famed Grand National Steeplechase. Taylor is irresistible, Rooney was never better, and they're surrounded by a perfect supporting cast. Revere won a Best Supporting Actress Oscar as Taylor's mother. Screenplay by Theodore Reeves and Helen Deutsch, from Enid Bagnold's novel. Followed years later by INTERNATIONAL VELVET and a TV series.▼●⃟

Native Son (1950) **91m.** **½ D: Pierre Chenal. Richard Wright, Jean Wallace, Gloria Madison, Nicholas Joy, Charles Cane, George Rigaud. Well-meaning but superficial, ultimately disappointing filming of Richard Wright's milestone novel and play, with the author himself starring as Bigger Thomas, frightened black chauffeur who unintentionally kills a white woman. De-

feated by its low budget, but still a curio. Filmed in Argentina, Chicago's South Side. Remade in 1986.▼

Nature's Mistakes SEE: **Freaks**

Naughty Arlette SEE: **Romantic Age, The**

Naughty But Nice (1939) **90m.** **½ D: Ray Enright. Dick Powell, Ann Sheridan, Gale Page, Helen Broderick, Ronald Reagan, Allen Jenkins, ZaSu Pitts, Jerry Colonna. Stuffy music professor Powell unwittingly writes popular song hit, leading to various complications and gradual personality change. Silly but fun; songs adapted from Wagner, Liszt, Mozart, Bach.

Naughty Flirt, The (1931) **56m.** *½ D: Edward Cline. Alice White, Paul Page, Myrna Loy, Robert Agnew, Douglas Gilmore, George Irving. A wild young socialite (White) is tamed by a hardworking lawyer, but a fortune hunter and his sister scheme to break up the happy couple. Dated jazz-baby flapper stuff notable only for Loy's early appearance as a seductress and the scene where Page puts the annoyingly perky White over his knee for a good spanking. You may wish to do the same.▶

Naughty Girl SEE: **Mam'zelle Pigalle**

Naughty Marietta (1935) **106m.** *** D: W. S. Van Dyke II. Jeanette MacDonald, Nelson Eddy, Frank Morgan, Elsa Lanchester, Douglass Dumbrille, Walter Kingsford, Cecilia Parker, Akim Tamiroff, Harold Huber, Edward Brophy. Charming update of Victor Herbert's 1910 operetta about a French princess fleeing to New Orleans to escape an arranged marriage, falling in love with an Indian scout. First teaming of MacDonald and Eddy is bright and tuneful, with such Herbert classics as "The Italian Street Song," "Tramp, Tramp, Tramp," and "Ah! Sweet Mystery of Life."▼●⃟

Naughty Nineties, The (1945) **76m.** ** D: Jean Yarbrough. Bud Abbott, Lou Costello, Alan Curtis, Rita Johnson, Henry Travers, Lois Collier, Joe Sawyer, Joe Kirk. Ordinary A&C comedy of riverboat gamblers, sparked by duo's verbal exchanges (including "Who's on First?") and slapstick finale.▼●⃟

Navigator, The (1924) **69m.** **½ D: Buster Keaton, Donald Crisp. Buster Keaton, Kathryn McGuire, Frederick Vroom. Buster plays (yet again) a pampered millionaire who—by sheer circumstance, with a dash of stupidity—winds up on a huge, deserted ship with the woman he wants to marry. Many great gags and amusing sequences, but this silent doesn't have the momentum of Buster's best comedies.▼●⃟

Navy Blue and Gold (1937) **94m.** **½ D: Sam Wood. Robert Young, James Stewart, Florence Rice, Billie Burke, Lionel Barrymore, Tom Brown, Samuel S. Hinds, Paul Kelly. Hackneyed but entertaining saga of three pals (one rich and innocent [Brown],

[481]

one a cynic [Young], and one mysterious "with a past" [Stewart]) going to Annapolis. Predictable football game climax is fun. That's Dennis Morgan (billed under his real name, Stanley Morner) dancing with Billie Burke.▼◗

Navy Blues (1929) 75m. ** D: Clarence Brown. William Haines, Anita Page, Karl Dane, J. C. Nugent, Edythe Chapman, Wade Boteler, Mary Brian. Standard gobs-on-shore-leave antics centering on the whirlwind affair of wisecracking sailor Haines and good-girl Page. Moderately amusing until treacle takes over. Haines takes his go-getter character to an overbearing extreme in his first talkie.◗

Navy Blues (1941) 108m. *** D: Lloyd Bacon. Ann Sheridan, Jack Oakie, Martha Raye, Jack Haley, Herbert Anderson, Jack Carson. Brassy musical with fine cast (including young Jackie Gleason), with Raye stealing most of the film.◗

Navy Comes Through, The (1942) 82m. **½ D: A. Edward Sutherland. Pat O'Brien, George Murphy, Jane Wyatt, Jackie Cooper, Carl Esmond, Max Baer, Desi Arnaz, Ray Collins. Ultrapatriotic time capsule with U.S. Navy (led by O'Brien), stationed aboard a Merchant Marine ship, heroically battling the Nazis.▼

Navy Wife (1956) 83m. *½ D: Edward Bernds. Joan Bennett, Gary Merrill, Shirley Yamaguchi, Maurice Manson, Judy Nugent, Martin Milner, Dennis Weaver. Trivial tale of Japanese women revolting to obtain equal treatment from their men as they observe American military and their wives.

Nazarin (1958-Mexican) 92m. *** D: Luis Buñuel. Francisco Rabal, Rita Macedo, Marga Lopez, Ignacio Lopez Tarso, Ofelia Guilmain. Powerful and pointed (if relentlessly grim) drama about saintly priest Rabal, and how hypocritical peasants deal with him as he tries to interpret the lessons of Christ.▼●

Nazi Agent (1942) 83m. ** D: Jules Dassin. Conrad Veidt, Anne Ayars, Dorothy Tree, Frank Reicher, Sidney Blackmer, Martin Kosleck, Marc Lawrence, William Tannen. Veidt plays twin brothers: one a peaceful American; the other a Nazi official. When the latter blackmails the former into spying, the good Veidt kills the bad Veidt and impersonates him. Slow-moving, rather arid tale. Dassin's first feature; good photography by Harry Stradling.

Neanderthal Man, The (1953) 78m. *½ D: E. A. Dupont. Robert Shayne, Richard Crane, Doris Merrick, Joy Terry. Shayne turns a tiger into a sabertooth and himself into a murderous caveman in this below-par '50s entry. Colorless and cheap; director Dupont was a long way from his German classic VARIETY.●◗

Nearly a Nasty Accident (1962-British) 86m. ** D: Don Chaffey. Jimmy Edwards,

Kenneth Connor, Shirley Eaton, Richard Wattis, Ronnie Stevens, Jon Pertwee, Eric Barker. Minor comedy of mechanic who innocently puts the touch of disaster on everyone.

'Neath Brooklyn Bridge (1942) 61m. ** D: Wallace Fox. Leo Gorcey, Huntz Hall, Bobby Jordan, Sunshine Sammy Morrison, Stanley Clements, Bobby Stone, Anne Gillis, Noah Beery, Jr., Marc Lawrence, Gabriel Dell, Dave O'Brien. The East Side Kids band together when Jordan is framed for murder in this terse entry.▼◗

'Neath the Arizona Skies (1934) 53m. *½ D: Harry Fraser. John Wayne, Sheila Terry, Shirley Jean Rickert, Jack Rockwell, Yakima Canutt, Jay Wilsey, George Hayes. Wayne serves as guardian for young Indian girl who, as heiress to an oil fortune, becomes a kidnap target for outlaws. Tattered, uninspired direction of story filmed the year before as CIRCLE CANYON. Worthwhile only for Hayes' dry run of subsequent "Windy" and "Gabby" characterizations. Also shown in computer-colored version.▼◗

Nebraskan, The (1953) C-68m. ** D: Fred F. Sears. Philip Carey, Roberta Haynes, Wallace Ford, Richard Webb, Lee Van Cleef, Maurice Jara, Pat Hogan, Regis Toomey, Dennis Weaver. Six characters trapped at a desolate outpost try to hold off surrounding Sioux. OK little oater features strong early performance by Van Cleef as a psychotic cavalryman . . . not to mention Jay Silverheels as an evil Indian chief! 3-D.◗

Nefertite, Queen of the Nile SEE: **Queen of the Nile**

Nell Gwyn (1934-British) 85m. *** D: Herbert Wilcox. Anna Neagle, Cedric Hardwicke, Jeanne De Casalis, Muriel George, Miles Malleson, Esme Percy, Moore Marriott. Neagle has one of her best roles as the sassy title character, who is cold-shouldered by Britain's aristocracy while attracting the attention of King Charles II, thereby incurring the wrath of the monarch's mistress. Hardwicke's sly wit matches Neagle's feistiness in this entertaining historical yarn written by actor Malleson. Ten minutes of bawdy humor and sexual innuendo were deleted from U.S. version. Wilcox directed Dorothy Gish in NELL GWYNNE (1926).

Neptune's Daughter (1949) C-93m. *** D: Edward Buzzell. Esther Williams, Red Skelton, Keenan Wynn, Betty Garrett, Ricardo Montalban, Mel Blanc. Musical romance with Esther a bathing-suit designer, Skelton a no-account mistaken for polo star by Garrett. Bubbly fun, with Academy Award–winning song: "Baby It's Cold Outside."▼●◗

Nevada (1944) 62m. ** D: Edward Killy. Robert Mitchum, Anne Jeffreys, Guinn "Big Boy" Williams, Nancy Gates, Harry Woods. Standard Zane Grey Western of good-guy Mitchum mopping up gang of outlaws. Filmed before in 1935.◗

Nevada City (1941) **56m.** ******* D: Joseph Kane. Roy Rogers, George "Gabby" Hayes, Sally Payne, George Cleveland, Billy Lee, Joseph Crehan, Fred Kohler, Jr., Pierre Watkin, Jack Ingram. Lively B Western has Roy as a stagecoach driver who tries to intervene in a dispute between railroad owner Crehan and stage line boss Cleveland, while the man behind a riverboat company (Watkin) and his sidekick Black Bart (Kohler) stay busy sabotaging both sides! Written by James R. Webb, who went on to do such Westerns as THE BIG COUNTRY and HOW THE WEST WAS WON.▼▶

Nevadan, The (1950) **C-81m.** ****** D: Gordon Douglas. Randolph Scott, Dorothy Malone, Forrest Tucker, Frank Faylen, George Macready, Charles Kemper, Jeff Corey, Jock O'Mahoney (Mahoney). So-so Western with mystery man Scott befriending crook Tucker, who has hidden away a stash of stolen gold, and courting spunky Malone, the daughter of greedy Macready.▼▶

Never a Dull Moment (1950) **89m.** ****** D: George Marshall. Irene Dunne, Fred MacMurray, William Demarest, Andy Devine, Gigi Perreau, Natalie Wood, Philip Ober, Ann Doran. Chic Park Avenue songwriter Dunne weds rancher MacMurray, and adjusts to life in rural Wyoming. Silly, predictable comedy is only of interest for its cast; you'll find this especially annoying if you're a feminist or an Indian.▼▶

Never Fear (1950) **82m.** ****½** D: Ida Lupino. Sally Forrest, Keefe Brasselle, Hugh O'Brian, Eve Miller, Lawrence Dobkin. Young dancer Forrest's life comes apart when she develops polio. Sincere drama scripted by Lupino and her then-husband, Collier Young. Aka THE YOUNG LOVERS. ▼▶

Never Give a Sucker an Even Break (1941) **71m.** *****½** D: Edward Cline. W. C. Fields, Gloria Jean, Leon Errol, Susan Miller, Franklin Pangborn, Margaret Dumont. Completely insane comedy with Fields (in his last starring film) playing himself; no coherent plot, but a lot of funny scenes. Dumont plays "Mrs. Hemoglobin." Climactic chase is a classic, reused by Abbott and Costello in IN SOCIETY. Story by "Otis Criblecoblis."▼▶

Never Let Go (1960-British) **90m.** ****** D: John Guillermin. Richard Todd, Peter Sellers, Elizabeth Sellars, Carol White, Mervyn Johns. Sellers gives heavy-handed performance as ruthless and sadistic racketeer in weak story about car thievery. Billed as his first dramatic role, it was a poor choice.▼▶

Never Let Me Go (1953) **94m.** ****½** D: Delmer Daves. Clark Gable, Gene Tierney, Bernard Miles, Richard Haydn, Kenneth More, Belita, Theodore Bikel. Unconvincing yet smooth account of Gable trying to smuggle ballerina-wife Tierney out of Russia.▼▶

Never Love a Stranger (1958) **91m.** ****½** D: Robert Stevens. John Drew Barrymore, Lita

Milan, Robert Bray, Steve McQueen, Salem Ludwig, R. G. Armstrong. Cliché-ridden tale of the rise and fall of orphan-turned-hoodlum Barrymore features intense performances. Of interest for its portrayal of urban anti-Semitism and its casting of McQueen as a Jew who is bullied. Harold Robbins adapted his own novel. ▼▶

Never on Sunday (1960-Greek) **91m.** *****½** D: Jules Dassin. Melina Mercouri, Jules Dassin, Georges Foundas, Titos Vandis, Mitsos Liguisos, Despo Diamantidou. Charming idyll of intellectual boob coming to Greece, trying to make earthy prostitute Mercouri cultured. Grand entertainment, with Oscar-winning title song by Manos Hadjidakis. Later a Broadway musical, *Illya Darling.*▼▶

Never Put It in Writing (1964) **93m.** ***½** D: Andrew Stone. Pat Boone, Milo O'Shea, Fidelma Murphy, Reginald Beckwith, Harry Brogan. Grade-B comedy, set in London, with Pat trying to retrieve a letter that will get him fired from his job if the boss sees it. Not much.

Never Say Die (1939) **80m.** ******* D: Elliott Nugent. Martha Raye, Bob Hope, Andy Devine, Gale Sondergaard, Sig Ruman, Alan Mowbray, Monty Woolley. Bob marries Martha at Swiss spa of Bad Gaswasser, thinking he has only two weeks to live. Good cast in lively, trivial romp. Cowritten by Preston Sturges.▼▶

Never Say Goodbye (1946) **97m.** ****½** D: James V. Kern. Errol Flynn, Eleanor Parker, Lucile Watson, S. Z. Sakall, Forrest Tucker, Donald Woods, Peggy Knudsen, Hattie McDaniel, Patti Brady. Light, predictable comedy with Flynn, the doting father of seven-year-old Brady, attempting to win back her mother (Parker) on the first anniversary of their divorce. ▼▶

Never Say Goodbye (1956) **C-96m.** ****½** D: Jerry Hopper. Rock Hudson, Cornell Borchers, George Sanders, Ray Collins, David Janssen, Shelley Fabares. Spotty tearjerker of Hudson and Borchers, long separated, discovering one another again and creating fit home for their child. Remake of THIS LOVE OF OURS. Clint Eastwood is cast as Rock's lab assistant.

Never So Few (1959) **C-124m.** ****½** D: John Sturges. Frank Sinatra, Gina Lollobrigida, Peter Lawford, Steve McQueen, Richard Johnson, Paul Henreid, Brian Donlevy, Dean Jones, Charles Bronson. WW2 action/romance tale; salty performances which make one forget the clichés and improbabilities. CinemaScope. ▼▶

Never Steal Anything Small (1959) **C-94m.** ****½** D: Charles Lederer. James Cagney, Shirley Jones, Roger Smith, Cara Williams, Nehemiah Persoff, Royal Dano, Horace McMahon. Odd musical comedy-drama, with Cagney a waterfront union racketeer who'll do anything to win union

[483]

election. From Maxwell Anderson–Rouben Mamoulian play *The Devil's Hornpipe.* CinemaScope.▼

Never the Twain Shall Meet (1931) 79m. *½ D: W. S. Van Dyke. Leslie Howard, Conchita Montenegro, C. Aubrey Smith, Karen Morley, Mitchell Lewis, Clyde Cook. Rich, proper Howard loves rich, proper Morley . . . and then he becomes the guardian of beautiful, uninhibited Montenegro. Wooden soaper of clashing cultures.

Never to Love (1937) SEE: **Bill of Divorcement, A** (1940)

Never Too Late (1932) SEE: **It's Never Too Late to Mend**

Never Too Late (1965) C-105m. **½ D: Bud Yorkin. Paul Ford, Connie Stevens, Maureen O'Sullivan, Jim Hutton, Jane Wyatt, Henry Jones, Lloyd Nolan. Occasionally amusing film version of hit Broadway play about impending parenthood of middle-agers Ford and O'Sullivan. Older performers are funny; Hutton, Stevens, script, and direction are not. Panavision.▼▶

Never Trust a Gambler (1951) 79m. *½ D: Ralph Murphy. Dane Clark, Cathy O'Donnell, Tom Drake, Jeff Corey, Myrna Dell. Hackneyed account of man on the run, seeking shelter from ex-wife who has fallen in love with detective seeking him.

Never Wave at a WAC (1952) 87m. **½ D: Norman Z. McLeod. Rosalind Russell, Marie Wilson, Paul Douglas, Arleen Whelan, Hillary Brooke, Louise Beavers, Frieda Inescort. Expanded from a TV play, this farce involves socialite Russell joining the WACs, forced to buckle down to hard work; Wilson as dumb comrade-at-arms is most diverting.▼▶

New Adventures of Get Rich Quick Wallingford (1931) 94m. *** D: Sam Wood. William Haines, Jimmy Durante, Ernest Torrence, Leila Hyams, Guy Kibbee, Hale Hamilton, Robert McWade, Clara Blandick. Breezy crime comedy centering on capers of bon vivant con man J. Rufus Wallingford (Haines) and his crew, Blackie (Torrence) and Schnozzle (Durante). Moves at a brisk clip; singing and wisecracking Durante is a riot. Witty script by Charles MacArthur based on magazine stories by George Randolph Chester, which inspired a George M. Cohan play as well as some silent films.

New Adventures of Tarzan, The (1935) 75m. *½ D: Edward Kull, W. F. McGaugh. Herman Brix (Bruce Bennett), Ula Holt, Don Castello, Frank Baker, Lewis Sargent, Dale Walsh. Feature version of the serial about the search for priceless Mayan idol in Guatemala. Strictly for the kiddies. Shot on location by Edgar Rice Burroughs' own company, but no threat to Johnny Weissmuller and MGM. TV print of this feature is completely redubbed by voices other than the actors on-screen!▼▶

New Faces (1954) C-99m. **½ D: Harry

Horner. Ronny Graham, Robert Clary, Eartha Kitt, Alice Ghostley, Paul Lynde, Carol Lawrence. Vaudeville hodgepodge of variety numbers, based on Leonard Sillman's popular Broadway revue, which was springboard for much new talent. One of the writers was Melvin (Mel) Brooks. CinemaScope.▼▶

New Faces of 1937 (1937) 100m. ** D: Leigh Jason. Joe Penner, Milton Berle, Parkyakarkus, Harriet Hilliard (Nelson), Jerome Cowan. Silly movie with same initial premise as THE PRODUCERS, as Berle is patsy left as owner of unwatchable Broadway show. Comic highlight is Berle's stockbroker skit with Richard Lane; Ann Miller featured in finale as one of the New Faces.●▶

New Frontier, The (1935) 54m. *½ D: Carl L. Pierson. John Wayne, Muriel Evans, Warner Richmond, Alan Bridge, Sam Flint, Glenn Strange. After trail herder Wayne's father is murdered, he agrees to serve as sheriff of the town of Frontier, Oklahoma, vanquishing all vice and lawlessness. Wayne's second Republic Western falls flat; only the finale is good. Features footage from Ken Maynard's silent THE RED RAIDERS. No relation to 1939 Wayne movie of the same name.

New Frontier (1939) 57m. ** D: George Sherman. John Wayne, Ray Corrigan, Raymond Hatton, Phylis Isley (Jennifer Jones), Eddy Waller, Sammy McKim, LeRoy Mason. When crooked land grabbers threaten to flood the condemned valley homes of ranchers in order to construct an unwanted dam, the Three Mesquiteers ride to the rescue. Wayne's post-STAGECOACH swan song as Stony Brooke marked his final B picture and Jones' feature debut. No relation to 1935 Wayne movie of the same name. Reissue title: FRONTIER HORIZON.▼

New Gentlemen, The (1929-French) 124m. *** D: Jacques Feyder. Gaby Morlay, Henri Roussell, Albert Préjean, Guy Ferrant, Henry Valbel, Léon Arvel, Gustave Hamilton. During a transport workers strike, a beautiful ballerina (Morlay) is pursued by two suitors: an energetic electrician/union leader (Préjean) and an older aristocrat (Roussell) who holds high political office. Pointed, engrossing tale puts forth the view that the rich and powerful control all aspects of daily life. Original title: LES NOUVEAUX MESSIEURS.▶

New Interns, The (1964) 123m. **½ D: John Rich. Michael Callan, Dean Jones, Telly Savalas, Inger Stevens, George Segal, Greg Morris, Stefanie Powers, Lee Patrick, Barbara Eden. Follow-up to THE INTERNS contains unusual hospital soap opera with better than average cast and a nifty party sequence.

New Invisible Man, The (1957-Mexican) 89m. ** D: Alfredo B. Crevenna. Arturo de Córdova, Ana Luisa Peluffo, Augusto

[484]

Benedico, Rául Meraz. OK updating of the classic story, with de Córdova falsely convicted of murder; he's rendered invisible so he can prove his innocence. A remake of THE INVISIBLE MAN RETURNS. Aka H. G. WELLS' NEW INVISIBLE MAN. ▼▶

New Kind of Love, A (1963) C-110m. **½ D: Melville Shavelson. Paul Newman, Joanne Woodward, Thelma Ritter, Eva Gabor, Maurice Chevalier, George Tobias, Marvin Kaplan, Robert Clary. Silly but enjoyable fluff with sportswriter Newman and fashion buyer Woodward tangling, and then falling in love, in Paris. The stars really put this one over; Chevalier appears as himself, title song sung by Frank Sinatra. ▼▶

Newly Rich (1931) 77m. **½ D: Norman Taurog. Mitzi Green, Edna May Oliver, Jackie Searl, Louise Fazenda, Bruce Line, Virginia Hammond, Dell Henderson, Lawrence Grant. Amusing semisatirical look at child stars and early '30s Hollywood, with Oliver and Fazenda funny as rival stage mothers competing through their kids. Somehow, they all end up in London and have adventures with a runaway boy king. Cowritten by Joseph L. Mankiewicz, from a story by Sinclair Lewis. Aka FORBIDDEN ADVENTURE.

New Mexico (1951) C-76m. **½ D: Irving Reis. Lew Ayres, Marilyn Maxwell, Robert Hutton, Andy Devine, Raymond Burr. Moderately exciting Western of cavalry vs. Indians. ▶

New Moon (1930) 78m. **½ D: Jack Conway. Grace Moore, Lawrence Tibbett, Adolphe Menjou, Roland Young, Gus Shy, Emily Fitzroy. While sailing the Caspian Sea on board the good ship *New Moon*, a previously engaged princess meets a dashing Army officer whom she can't resist. MGM's first version of Oscar Hammerstein–Sigmund Romberg operetta jettisons the libretto and shifts the setting to Russia, but at least it retains the score. Powerfully vocalized by the two Metropolitan Opera leads, and packed full of sexual innuendo with no pretense of propriety.

New Moon (1940) 105m. **½ D: Robert Z. Leonard. Jeanette MacDonald, Nelson Eddy, Mary Boland, George Zucco, H. B. Warner, Grant Mitchell, Stanley Fields. Nelson and Jeanette in old Louisiana, falling in love, singing "One Kiss," "Softly as in a Morning Sunrise," "Lover Come Back to Me," "Stout-Hearted Men." Oscar Hammerstein–Sigmund Romberg score sung before in 1930 filming with Lawrence Tibbett and Grace Moore. ▼▶▶

New Morals for Old (1932) 75m. **½ D: Charles Brabin. Robert Young, Margaret Perry, Lewis Stone, Laura Hope Crews, Myrna Loy, David Newell, Jean Hersholt. Amiable generation gap soaper spotlights independent-minded Young and Perry and their issues with their overprotective par-

ents. Loy is alluring in her brief scenes as a sexpot. Coscripted by John Van Druten.

New Orleans (1947) 89m. **½ D: Arthur Lubin. Arturo de Córdova, Dorothy Patrick, Billie Holiday, Louis Armstrong, Woody Herman & Band, Meade Lux Lewis, other jazz stars. Hackneyed fictionalization of the birth of jazz, spanning 40 years, but there's plenty of good music. Holiday (cast as a maid!) does "Do You Know What It Means to Miss New Orleans" with Armstrong and all-star band, and it's sublime. Shelley Winters appears briefly as de Córdova's secretary. ▼▶

New Orleans After Dark (1958) 69m. *½ D: John Sledge. Stacy Harris, Louis Sirgo, Ellen Moore, Tommy Pelle. Location filming in the Crescent City adds some value to this drab programmer about the hunt for a band of dope smugglers. ▼

New Orleans Uncensored (1955) 76m. *½ D: William Castle. Arthur Franz, Beverly Garland, Helene Stanton, Michael Ansara. Weak exposé account of racketeer-busting in Louisiana, with competent cast trying to overcome script. ▶

News Hounds (1947) 68m. ** D: William Beaudine. Leo Gorcey, Huntz Hall, Bobby Jordan, Billy Benedict, David Gorcey, Gabriel Dell, Bernard Gorcey, Tim Ryan, Bill Kennedy, Robert Emmett Keane, Christine McIntyre, Anthony Caruso. Scoop Mahoney and Shutterbug Sach vs. sportsfixing mobsters. The usual *Bowery Boys* hokum. ▶

New York Confidential (1955) 87m. **½ D: Russell Rouse. Broderick Crawford, Richard Conte, Marilyn Maxwell, Anne Bancroft, J. Carrol Naish, Onslow Stevens, Barry Kelley, Mike Mazurki, Celia Lovsky. Supposed "inside" story of an N.Y.C. mob family, told in semi-documentary style, doesn't wear well, but Bancroft is terrific as mob boss Crawford's daughter. ▶

New York Town (1941) 76m. **½ D: Charles Vidor. Fred MacMurray, Mary Martin, Robert Preston, Akim Tamiroff, Lynne Overman, Eric Blore, Fuzzy Knight. Bright little comedy of wide-eyed Martin manhunting in N.Y.C., assisted by photographer MacMurray. Songs include "Love in Bloom." Preston Sturges worked uncredited on the script.

Next Time I Marry (1938) 65m. **½ D: Garson Kanin. Lucille Ball, James Ellison, Lee Bowman, Granville Bates, Mantan Moreland, Elliott Sullivan. Silly, likable nonsense about a spoiled heiress who must dump her fortune-hunting foreign beau and marry a regular American guy in order to gain her inheritance. Unjustly maligned screwball comedy is one of Lucy's better programmers of the '30s.

Next Time We Love (1936) 87m. *** D: Edward H. Griffith. Margaret Sullavan, James Stewart, Ray Milland, Grant Mitchell, Robert McWade, Hattie McDaniel. Trim romantic soaper with Milland in love with actress Sullavan, who is married to struggling reporter Stewart. Preston Sturges worked uncredited on the script.◗

Next to No Time (1958-British) **C-93m.** ******* D: Henry Cornelius. Kenneth More, Betsy Drake, Bessie Love, Harry Green, Patrick Barr, Roland Culver. Whimsical comedy from Paul Gallico story, about mild-mannered engineer (More) who loses inhibitions on ocean voyage where he's trying to put over important business deal.

Next Voice You Hear . . . , The (1950) **83m.** ****½** D: William Wellman. James Whitmore, Nancy Davis (Reagan), Lillian Bronson, Jeff Corey, Gary Gray. The voice of God is heard nightly on the radio (but not by the audience) and has a profound impact on average American Whitmore, his wife, and son. Ambitious if not terribly successful message film produced by Dore Schary.▼◗

Niagara (1953) **C-89m.** ******* D: Henry Hathaway. Marilyn Monroe, Joseph Cotten, Jean Peters, Casey Adams (Max Showalter), Don Wilson, Richard Allan. Black murder tale of couple staying at Niagara Falls, the wife planning to kill husband. Produced and cowritten by Charles Brackett; good location work. ▼◗

Nice Girl? (1941) **95m.** ******* D: William A. Seiter. Deanna Durbin, Franchot Tone, Walter Brennan, Robert Stack, Robert Benchley. Little Deanna grows up in this cute comedy, with Tone and Stack developing amorous ideas about her. Songs: "Love At Last," "Thank You America." Video includes alternate ending. ▼

Nice Little Bank That Should Be Robbed, A (1958) **87m.** ****** D: Henry Levin. Tom Ewell, Mickey Rooney, Mickey Shaughnessy, Dina Merrill. Cast is game, but story is pure cornball about goofy crooks using their gains to buy a racehorse. CinemaScope.

Nicholas Nickleby (1947-British) **108m.** ******* D: Alberto Cavalcanti. Derek Bond, Cedric Hardwicke, Alfred Drayton, Bernard Miles, Sally Ann Howes, Mary Merrall, Sybil Thorndike, Cathleen Nesbitt. Dickens' classic tale of young man's struggle to protect his family from scheming uncle and a cruel world is vividly brought to life. Can't compare with the Royal Shakespeare Company's 8½-hour stage version—but still quite good. Some American prints run 95m. Remade in 2002. ▼

Nick Carter Detective Nick Carter was created in 1886 and became the busiest crime solver in American literature, being featured in hundreds of short stories in magazines and books. He was the hero of a number of silent films both here and in France, but for all his durability on the printed page he never enjoyed great success on-screen. MGM launched a series in 1939 which cast urbane Walter Pidgeon

as the detective, but only three films resulted. All of them are fast paced, flippant, and somewhat outlandish (like the original stories), with typical MGM polish distinguishing them from other studios' grade-B product, but their chief distinction is the casting of Donald Meek as Bartholomew, The Bee-Man, an off-center oddball who foists himself upon Nick. Nothing about Pidgeon, or the characterization of Carter, created any compelling reason to want to see more. Carter was later played in France by Eddie Constantine, and in a short-lived series, but his most striking screen appearance came in a 1978 Czech film called, variously, NICK CARTER IN PRAGUE and DINNER FOR ADELE, which finally attempted to reproduce the time and atmosphere of the original pulp stories.

NICK CARTER

Nick Carter, Master Detective (1939)
Phantom Raiders (1940)
Sky Murder (1940)

Nick Carter, Master Detective (1939) **60m.** ****** D: Jacques Tourneur. Walter Pidgeon, Rita Johnson, Henry Hull, Donald Meek, Addison Richards, Milburn Stone, Sterling Holloway. Pidgeon is good, tracking down industrial spy in slickly done detective film. Starts out very snappy, then slows to a crawl and loses its way. Memorable for some striking aerial shots. ◗

Night After Night (1932) **70m.** ****** D: Archie Mayo. George Raft, Mae West, Constance Cummings, Wynne Gibson, Roscoe Karns, Louis Calhern, Alison Skipworth. Story of nightclub owner Raft's infatuation with "classy" Cummings is a crashing bore, but when Mae West comes on the screen lights up. It's her film debut, and she's in rare form. ▼◗

Night Ambush (1957-British) **93m.** ******* D: Michael Powell, Emeric Pressburger. Dirk Bogarde, Marius Goring, David Oxley, Cyril Cusack, Christopher Lee. Taut WW2 actioner set in Crete, with fine British cast. Originally released in England as ILL MET BY MOONLIGHT at 104m. VistaVision.▼◗

Night and Day (1946) **C-128m.** ****** D: Michael Curtiz. Cary Grant, Alexis Smith, Monty Woolley, Ginny Simms, Jane Wyman, Eve Arden, Mary Martin, Victor Francen, Alan Hale, Dorothy Malone. Music only worthy aspect of fabricated biography of songwriter Cole Porter, stiffly played by Grant, who even sings "You're the Top." Martin re-creates "My Heart Belongs to Daddy" in film's highlight. Look for Mel Tormé as a drummer. An altogether different perspective on Porter may be found in DELOVELY (2004). ▼◗

Night and the City (1950) **96m.** *****½** D: Jules Dassin. Richard Widmark, Gene Tierney, Googie Withers, Hugh Marlowe,

Francis L. Sullivan, Herbert Lom, Mike Mazurki, Kay Kendall. Frenetic nightclub tout (Widmark) maneuvers himself into a big score by promoting a London wrestling match that results in tragedy. Film noir gem features a memorable turn by Widmark as a quintessential noir loser, with stellar support from slimy nightclub owner Sullivan and his duplicitous mate Withers. Superb location work in London is another asset. Jo Eisinger adapted Gerald Kersh's novel. At 101m., British version has a different music score and additional scenes with Tierney. Remade in 1992. ▼●)

Night at the Opera, A (1935) 92m. **** D: Sam Wood. Groucho, Chico, Harpo Marx, Kitty Carlisle, Allan Jones, Walter Woolf King, Margaret Dumont, Sigfried Rumann. The Marx Brothers invade the world of opera with devastating results. Arguably their finest film (a close race with DUCK SOUP), with tuneful music and appealing romance neatly interwoven. One priceless comedy bit follows another: the stateroom scene, the Party of the First Part contract, etc. This is as good as it gets. ▼●)

Night Caller, The SEE: **Night Caller from Outer Space**

Night Caller from Outer Space (1965-British) 84m. **½ D: John Gilling. John Saxon, Maurice Denham, Patricia Haines, Alfred Burke, Jack Watson, Aubrey Morris. Well-done sci-fi thriller of alien kidnapping humans to take back to his home, a moon of Jupiter. U.S. theatrical title: BLOOD BEAST FROM OUTER SPACE. Original British title: THE NIGHT CALLER. ▼●)

Night Club Scandal (1937) 70m. **½ D: Ralph Murphy. John Barrymore, Lynne Overman, Louise Campbell, Charles Bickford, Evelyn Brent, Elizabeth Patterson, J. Carrol Naish. Doctor Barrymore murders his wife and tries to frame her boyfriend. OK thriller carried by a first-rate cast. Remake of GUILTY AS HELL (1932).

Night Court (1932) 90m. ** D: W.S. Van Dyke. Phillips Holmes, Walter Huston, Anita Page, Lewis Stone, Mary Carlisle, John Miljan, Jean Hersholt. Slimy, crooked night court judge Huston will stop at nothing to avoid being pinned by city watchdog Stone; that includes framing an innocent young couple. Watchable but far from subtle, or surprising, until final twist.

Night Creatures (1962-British) C-81m. **½ D: Peter Graham Scott. Peter Cushing, Yvonne Romain, Patrick Allen, Oliver Reed, Michael Ripper, Martin Benson, David Lodge. In 18th century England, country parson is also the notorious "dead" pirate leader of smugglers who pose as ghosts. Good fun with some scary moments. Remake of DR. SYN. Original British title: CAPTAIN CLEGG.)

Night Editor (1946) 67m. ** D: Henry

Levin. William Gargan, Janis Carter, Jeff Donnell, Coulter Irwin, Charles D. Brown. Minor B movie with a needlessly complicated structure. Married cop Gargan, involved in an affair with sluttish Carter, compromises himself after witnessing a murder. Based on the radio show of the same name; first in a proposed series that never materialized.)

Nightfall (1957) 78m. *** D: Jacques Tourneur. Aldo Ray, Brian Keith, Anne Bancroft, Jocelyn Brando, James Gregory, Frank Albertson, Rudy Bond. Ray plays an innocent man who's being hunted by an insurance investigator and two deadly holdup men who think he has their money. Rock-solid cast in a taut thriller written by Stirling Silliphant, from a novel by David Goodis. Great location work in L.A. and snowy Utah by cinematographer Burnett Guffey. ▼)

Night Fighters (1960-British) 85m. **½ D: Tay Garnett. Robert Mitchum, Anne Heywood, Dan O'Herlihy, Cyril Cusack, Richard Harris, Marianne Benet. Sporadically actionful tale of Irish Revolution, with Mitchum joining the cause against his will. Original title: A TERRIBLE BEAUTY.

Night Flight (1933) 85m. *** D: Clarence Brown. John Barrymore, Helen Hayes, Clark Gable, Lionel Barrymore, Robert Montgomery, Myrna Loy, William Gargan, C. Henry Gordon. During the inaugural 24 hours of a night airmail service in South America, the hard-nosed boss (John Barrymore) pushes pilots to fly over treacherous mountains in the fog and rain to deliver serum to a hospital, while their women anxiously wait for their return. Absorbing, well made, with a poetic and arty quality rare for MGM, yet somehow falls short of greatness. All-star cast rarely share screen time together. Based on a novel by Antoine de Saint Exupery.)

Night Freight (1955) 79m. **½ D: Jean Yarbrough. Forrest Tucker, Barbara Britton, Keith Larsen, Thomas Gomez, George Sanders. Straightforward tale about the bitter rivalry between railroad operator Tucker and trucker Gomez, who compete for business.

Night Has a Thousand Eyes (1948) 80m. **½ D: John Farrow. Edward G. Robinson, Gail Russell, John Lund, Virginia Bruce, William Demarest. Intriguing story of magician who has uncanny power to predict the future; script is corny at times. Based on a story by Cornell Woolrich.

Night Has Eyes, The (1942-British) 79m. **½ D: Leslie Arliss. James Mason, Joyce Howard, Mary Clare, Wilfrid Lawson, Tucker McGuire. OK mystery of schoolteacher Howard discovering why a friend disappeared in the Yorkshire Moors; Mason is a shellshocked composer she loves. Aka TERROR HOUSE. ▼)

Night Heaven Fell, The (1958-French-Italian) **C-90m.** ** D: Roger Vadim. Brigitte Bardot, Alida Valli, Stephen Boyd, Pepe Nieto. Convent girl Bardot falls for ne'er-do-well Boyd, who accidentally kills her uncle. Turgid. CinemaScope.▼▶

Night Holds Terror, The (1955) **86m.** ** D: Andrew L. Stone. Jack Kelly, Hildy Parks, Vince Edwards, John Cassavetes, Jack Kruschen, Joel Marston, Jonathan Hale. Somber little film of family being held captive for ransom.▶

Night in Casablanca, A (1946) **85m.** *** D: Archie Mayo. Groucho, Harpo, Chico Marx, Lisette Verea, Charles Drake, Lois Collier, Dan Seymour, Sig Ruman. No classic, but many funny sequences in latter-day Marx outing, ferreting out Nazi spies in Casablanca hotel.▼▶

Night in New Orleans, A (1942) **75m.** *½ D: William Clemens. Preston Foster, Patricia Morison, Albert Dekker, Charles Butterworth, Dooley Wilson, Cecil Kellaway. Thin yarn of Morison trying to clear husband Foster of murder charge.

Night in Paradise (1946) **C-84m.** **½ D: Arthur Lubin. Merle Oberon, Turhan Bey, Thomas Gomez, Gale Sondergaard, Ray Collins, Ernest Truex. Tongue-in-cheek costumer of Aesop wooing lovely princess Oberon in ancient times; colorful, at least.

Night Into Morning (1951) **86m.** *** D: Fletcher Markle. Ray Milland, John Hodiak, Nancy Davis (Reagan), Lewis Stone, Jean Hagen, Rosemary DeCamp. Small-town professor loses family in fire, almost ruins own life through drink and self-pity. Realistic settings in modest production, with fine performance by Milland.

Night Is My Future (1948-Swedish) **87m.** **½ D: Ingmar Bergman. Mai Zetterling, Birger Malmsten, Olof Winnerstrand, Naima Wifstrand, Hilda Borgstrom. Somber, brooding tale of young Malmsten, blinded while in military service; he struggles for self-respect, and is befriended by housemaid Zetterling. Early, minor Bergman. Aka MUSIC IN DARKNESS.▼▶

Night Is the Phantom SEE: **Whip and the Body, The**

Night Is Young, The (1935) **81m.** BOMB D: Dudley Murphy. Ramon Novarro, Evelyn Laye, Charles Butterworth, Una Merkel, Edward Everett Horton, Donald Cook, Rosalind Russell, Henry Stephenson, Herman Bing. Novarro, wretchedly miscast and mugging mercilessly, brings his 10-year MGM career to a pitiful end playing a Viennese archduke who spurns his royal fiancée for a fling with ballerina Laye (who bolted back to England after this disaster). Oscar Hammerstein–Sigmund Romberg score includes "When I Grow Too Old to Dream."

Night Key (1937) **67m.** ** D: Lloyd Corrigan. Boris Karloff, Warren Hull, Jean Rogers, Hobart Cavanaugh, Ward Bond. Middling yarn about crooks forcing el-

derly inventor to help them with their crimes.▶

Night Life of the Gods (1935) **73m.** **½ D: Lowell Sherman. Alan Mowbray, Florine McKinney, Peggy Shannon, Richard Carle, Theresa Maxwell Conover, Phillips Smalley, Wesley Barry, Henry Armetta, Geneva Mitchell, Robert Warwick. Mowbray dreams that he can turn people (like his annoying family) into statues and bring statues (like the Greek gods at the local museum) to life. Amusing if watered-down version of Thorne Smith's risqué novel doesn't make the most of its premise but remains a fascinating curio. John Fulton's special effects are impressive. Title on-screen is THORNE SMITH'S NIGHT LIFE OF THE GODS.

Nightmare (1942) **81m.** **½ D: Tim Whelan. Diana Barrymore, Brian Donlevy, Gavin Muir, Henry Daniell, Hans Conried, Arthur Shields. Occasionally flavorful mystery with gambler Donlevy breaking into Barrymore's home on the night husband Daniell is murdered and their subsequent flight from both the police and Nazi spies.

Nightmare (1956) **89m.** **½ D: Maxwell Shane. Edward G. Robinson, Kevin McCarthy, Connie Russell, Virginia Christine, Rhys Williams, Meade "Lux" Lewis, Billy May. Location filming in New Orleans is a major asset of this moody psychological drama about musician McCarthy, who has an all-too-real nightmare in which he commits murder. Robinson sparks the proceedings as a crafty homicide detective. Remake of FEAR IN THE NIGHT, based on a story by William Irish (Cornell Woolrich).

Nightmare (1964-British) **83m.** **½ D: Freddie Francis. David Knight, Moira Redmond, Jennie Linden, Brenda Bruce, George A. Cooper, Clytie Jessop, Irene Richmond. Linden returns to her family mansion, plagued by nightmares, and fears that she may be turning into an insane killer, like her mother before her. Typical Hammer Films it's-all-a-plot plot in DIABOLIQUE vein is heightened by elegant camerawork, good performances. Hammerscope. ▼◉▶

Nightmare Alley (1947) **111m.** ***½ D: Edmund Goulding. Tyrone Power, Joan Blondell, Coleen Gray, Helen Walker, Taylor Holmes, Mike Mazurki, Ian Keith, Julia Dean. Morbid but fascinating story of carnival heel Power entangled with mind-reading Blondell, blackmailing psychiatrist Walker, other assorted sideshow weirdos in highly original melodrama. Compelling look at carny life. Jules Furthman scripted, from William Lindsay Gresham's novel.▶

Nightmare Castle (1965-Italian) **104m.** ** D: Allen Grünewald (Mario Caiano). Barbara Steele, Paul Muller, Helga Liné, Laurence Clift, John McDouglas (Giuseppe Addobbati), Rik Battaglia. In early 20th-century Italy, a cold-blooded scientist, Dr. Arrowsmith, no less, murders his evil wife (brunette Steele) and her lover, then marries the wife's kind-natured stepsister (blonde Steele) and tries to drive her insane in order to get her inheritance. But there are also supernatural powers at work. Atmospheric horror thriller diminished by overly familiar plotline, but Steele does her exotic best. ▶

Nightmare in the Sun (1964) C-80m. *½ D: Marc Lawrence. John Derek, Aldo Ray, Arthur O'Connell, Ursula Andress, Sammy Davis, Jr., Allyn Joslyn, Keenan Wynn. Turgid account of what happens when sexy Andress picks up hitchhiker Derek. Look for Richard Jaeckel and Robert Duvall as motorcyclists!

Night Monster (1942) 73m. **½ D: Ford Beebe. Bela Lugosi, Irene Hervey, Don Porter, Nils Asther, Lionel Atwill, Leif Erickson, Ralph Morgan. Intriguing grade-B thriller about creepy figure stalking country estate, murdering doctors who are treating crippled Morgan. ▼▶

Night Must Fall (1937) 117m. *** D: Richard Thorpe. Robert Montgomery, Rosalind Russell, Dame May Whitty, Alan Marshal, Kathleen Harrison, E. E. Clive, Beryl Mercer. Famous film of Emlyn Williams' suspenseful play. Young woman (Russell) slowly learns identity of mysterious brutal killer terrorizing the countryside. Montgomery has showy role in sometimes stagy but generally effective film, with outstanding aid from Russell and Whitty. Screenplay by John Van Druten. Remade in 1964. ▼▶

Night Must Fall (1964-British) 105m. **½ D: Karel Reisz. Albert Finney, Susan Hampshire, Mona Washbourne, Sheila Hancock, Michael Medwin, Joe Gladwin, Martin Wyldeck. Cerebral attempt to match flair of 1937 original, but this remake is too obvious and theatrical for any credibility. Reisz and Finney produced. ▶

Night My Number Came Up, The (1955-British) 94m. **** D: Leslie Norman. Michael Redgrave, Sheila Sim, Alexander Knox, Denholm Elliott, Ursula Jeans, Michael Hordern, George Rose, Alfie Bass. First-rate suspense film will have you holding your breath as it recounts tale of routine military flight, the fate of which may or may not depend on a prophetic dream. Screenplay by R. C. Sherriff, from an article by Victor Goddard. ▼

Night Nurse (1931) 72m. *** D: William Wellman. Barbara Stanwyck, Ben Lyon, Joan Blondell, Clark Gable, Charlotte Merriam, Charles Winninger. Excellent, hard-bitten tale of nurse (Stanwyck) who can't ignore strange goings-on in home where she works. Blondell adds zingy support; one of Gable's most impressive early appearances. Still potent today. ▼▶▸

Night of Adventure, A (1944) 65m. **½ D: Gordon Douglas. Tom Conway, Audrey Long, Nancy Gates, Emory Parnell, Jean Brooks, Louis Borell, Edward Brophy, Addison Richards. Entertaining little drama with lawyer Conway attempting to exonerate bored wife Long's suitor on a murder rap, all the while avoiding scandal. A remake of HAT, COAT AND GLOVE.

Night of Mystery (1937) 66m. ** D: E. A. Dupont. Grant Richards, Roscoe Karns, Helen Burgess, Ruth Coleman, Elizabeth Patterson, Harvey Stephens, June Martel. Tedious remake of THE GREENE MURDER CASE with Richards no match for William Powell as detective Philo Vance.

Night of Terror (1933) 65m. **½ D: Ben Stoloff. Sally Blane, Wallace Ford, Tully Marshall, Bela Lugosi, George Meeker, Gertrude Michael, Bryant Washburn. There's mayhem in the titular a.m. on a walled estate where heirs bicker, a scientist arranges his own premature burial, and turbaned servant Lugosi participates in a séance—with everyone secretly observed at all times by a hairy, fanged knife murderer known as the Maniac. Lively mix of frights and fun. Name another movie with a curtain speech complete with a death threat to audience members! ▼▶

Night of the Blood Beast (1958) 65m. *½ D: Bernard L. Kowalski. Michael Emmet, Angela Greene, John Baer, Ed Nelson, Tyler McVey. Astronaut returns from space apparently dead; when he awakens, he's found to have alien embryos within him—a pregnant man! The alien also turns up murderously. Well directed but too low budget to succeed. ▼▶

Night of the Demon SEE: **Curse of the Demon**

Night of the Ghouls SEE: **Revenge of the Dead**

Night of the Hunter, The (1955) 93m. ***½ D: Charles Laughton. Robert Mitchum, Shelley Winters, Lillian Gish, Evelyn Varden, Peter Graves, James Gleason, Billy Chapin, Sally Jane Bruce. Atmospheric allegory of innocence, evil, and hypocrisy, with psychotic religious fanatic Mitchum chasing orphaned siblings for money stolen by their father. Mitchum is marvelously menacing, matched by Gish as wise matron who takes in the kids. Starkly directed by Laughton; his only film behind the camera. Screenplay credited to James Agee, from the Davis Grubb novel. Remade as a TVM in 1991 with Richard Chamberlain. ▼▶▸

Night of the Iguana, The (1964) 118m. **½ D: John Huston. Richard Burton, Deborah Kerr, Ava Gardner, Sue Lyon, Skip Ward, Grayson Hall, Cyril Delevanti. Plodding tale based on Tennessee Williams' play; alcoholic former clergyman Burton, a bus-tour guide in Mexico, is involved with Kerr, Gardner, and Lyon. Dorothy Jeakins won an Oscar for her costumes. Also shown in computer-colored version. ▼▶▸

Night of the Quarter Moon (1959) 96m. *½ D: Hugo Haas. Julie London, John Drew Barrymore, Nat King Cole, Dean

Jones, James Edwards, Anna Kashfi, Agnes Moorehead, Jackie Coogan. Trite handling of miscegenation theme; good cast wasted. Retitled: FLESH AND FLAME. CinemaScope.

Night Parade (1929) **71m.** *½ D: Malcolm St. Clair. Aileen Pringle, Hugh Trevor, Dorothy Gulliver, Robert Ellis, Ann Pennington, Lloyd Ingraham. Innocent prizefighter is seduced by a "dirty Broadway tramp" and a racketeer, who pay him to take a dive. Crudely filmed early talkie enlivened by climactic bout in a thunderstorm but otherwise a compendium of boxing genre clichés. Based on a play cowritten by George Abbott. Look for Oscar Levant as a piano player in a party scene.

Night Passage (1957) **C-90m.** *** D: James Neilson. James Stewart, Audie Murphy, Dan Duryea, Brandon de Wilde, Dianne Foster. Sound Western of Stewart working for railroad, brother Murphy belonging to gang planning to rob train payroll; exciting climactic shoot-out. Technirama.▶

Night People (1954) **C-93m.** **½ D: Nunnally Johnson. Gregory Peck, Broderick Crawford, Anita Bjork, Rita Gam, Walter Abel, Buddy Ebsen, Casey Adams (Max Showalter), Jill Esmond, Peter Van Eyck. Peck tries to rescue an American soldier who's been abducted to East Germany. Intelligent if not particularly inspired Cold War thriller filmed on location in Berlin. CinemaScope.▶

Night Plane From Chungking (1943) **69m.** **½ D: Ralph Murphy. Ellen Drew, Robert Preston, Otto Kruger, Steven Geray, (Victor) Sen Yung, Tamara Geva, Soo Yong. Adequate adventure yarn about a plane shot down in the jungle, with captain Preston falling for Drew while going up against the Japanese.

Night Riders, The (1939) **58m.** **½ D: George Sherman. John Wayne, Ray Corrigan, Max Terhune, Doreen McKay, Ruth Rogers, Tom Tyler, Kermit Maynard, Sammy McKim. The Three Mesquiteers are uncharacteristically transposed back into the 19th century, where they wear hoods and capes to combat a megalomaniac with a forged land grant. Some scenes uncomfortably (though unintentionally) suggest parallels to the Ku Klux Klan. Based on a true incident. Slick Western with throbbing action throughout. Minor complaint: too many interiors.▶

Night Runner, The (1957) **79m.** ** D: Abner Biberman. Ray Danton, Colleen Miller, Merry Anders, Eddy Waller. Violent B film of insane Danton on killing spree, about to gun down his girlfriend.

Nights of Cabiria (1957-Italian) **117m.** **** D: Federico Fellini. Giulietta Masina, Francois Perier, Amedeo Nazzari, Franca Marzi, Dorian Gray. Masina is a joy as waifish prostitute dreaming of rich, wonderful life but always finding sorrow. Basis for Broadway musical and film SWEET CHARITY. One of Fellini's best, and a most deserving Oscar winner as Best Foreign Film. Restored in 1998 to put back a 7m. sequence Fellini was forced to cut after the premiere.▼▶

Nights of Rasputin (1960-French-Italian) **87m.** ** D: Pierre Chenal. Edmund Purdom, Gianna Maria Canale, John Drew Barrymore, Jany Clair. Purdom is miscast as Rasputin in this plodding biography of the conniving, libidinous hypnotist who gained influence in Czarina Alexandra's court prior to WW1. European version runs 93m., and is in color. Aka THE NIGHT THEY KILLED RASPUTIN.▼▶

Night Song (1947) **101m.** ** D: John Cromwell. Dana Andrews, Merle Oberon, Ethel Barrymore, Hoagy Carmichael, Jacqueline White. Overlong, soapy drama of socialite Oberon falling in love with blind pianist Andrews. Barrymore is very good in the unusual role of comic relief. Artur Rubinstein and conductor Eugene Ormandy appear in the climactic concert sequence, playing the concerto composed especially for the film by Leith Stevens.▶

Night Spot (1938) **60m.** *½ D: Christy Cabanne. Parkyakarkus, Allan Lane, Gordon Jones, Joan Woodbury, Lee Patrick, Bradley Page, Jack Carson, Cecil Kellaway. Comedy, music, and melodrama are an uneasy mix in this trifle in which policeman-musician Lane goes undercover to expose the machinations of an unsavory nightclub owner. Top-billed Parkyakarkus (real name Harry Einstein) is the father of Albert Brooks.

Night Stage to Galveston (1952) **62m.** *½ D: George Archainbaud. Gene Autry, Pat Buttram, Virginia Huston, Thurston Hall, Judy Nugent, Robert Livingston, Clayton Moore, Harry Lauter. Weak outing as Gene and his pal Pat reform the disbanded Texas Rangers to fight corrupt state police while looking after orphan Nugent. Poor pacing, ineffectual villains scuttle this latter-day Autry.▼▶

Night the World Exploded, The (1957) **64m.** ** D: Fred F. Sears. Kathryn Grant, William Leslie, Tris Coffin, Raymond Greenleaf, Marshall Reed. Scientists discover a strange, exploding mineral that threatens to bring about title catastrophe and rush to prevent it. OK idea hampered by low budget.▶

Night They Killed Rasputin, The SEE: **Nights of Rasputin**

Night Tide (1963) **84m.** **½ D: Curtis Harrington. Dennis Hopper, Linda Lawson, Gavin Muir, Luana Anders, Marjorie Eaton, Tom Dillon, H. E. West, Cameron. Lonely sailor Hopper falls for Lawson, who works as a mermaid at the Santa Monica pier, but learns she may be a killer—and a descendant of the sirens. Odd, dreamy little drama is strangely compelling, though not a horror film, as often promoted. Written by the director.▼●▶

Night Time in Nevada (1948) **C-67m.** *** D: William Witney. Roy Rogers, Adele Mara, Andy Devine, Grant Withers, Marie Harmon, Joseph Crehan, George Carleton, Holly Bane, Bob Nolan and the Sons of the Pioneers. Years after her father is murdered by unscrupulous miner Withers, Mara comes to claim her inheritance and becomes a target of bad men ... until Roy steps in. Top-notch screenplay, with Withers a memorably despicable villain. Good example of one of Rogers' later, hard-edged Westerns. Only b&w prints seem to survive. ▼▶

Night to Remember, A (1943) **91m.** ***½ D: Richard Wallace. Loretta Young, Brian Aherne, Jeff Donnell, William Wright, Sidney Toler, Gale Sondergaard, Donald MacBride, Blanche Yurka. Sparkling comedy-mystery of whodunit author Aherne and wife Young trying to solve murder. ▼▶●

Night to Remember, A (1958-British) **123m.** **** D: Roy (Ward) Baker. Kenneth More, David McCallum, Jill Dixon, Laurence Naismith, Frank Lawton, Honor Blackman, Alec McCowen, George Rose. Meticulously produced documentary-style account of sinking of the "unsinkable" passenger liner *Titanic*. Superb combination of disaster spectacle and emotional byplay; a notable contrast to Hollywood's *Titanic* films. Vivid adaptation by Eric Ambler of Walter Lord's book. ▼▶●

Night Train (1940-British) SEE: **Night Train to Munich**

Night Train (1959-Polish) **90m.** ** D: Jerzy Kawalerowicz. Lucyna Winnicka, Leon Niemczyk, Teresa Szmigielowna, Zbigniew Cybulski. Murky account of young woman on a train, forced to share compartment with a doctor; their lack of communication and presence of killer on train are film's focal points. ▶

Night Train to Munich (1940-British) **93m.** *** D: Carol Reed. Rex Harrison, Margaret Lockwood, Paul Von Hernried (Henreid), Basil Radford, Naunton Wayne, Felix Aylmer, Roland Culver. Expert Hitchcockian thriller about British intelligence agent Harrison trying to rescue Czech scientist who escaped from the Nazis to London only to be kidnapped back to Berlin. Stylishly photographed (by Otto Kanturek), sharply scripted by Frank Launder and Sidney Gilliat, who also wrote Hitchcock's THE LADY VANISHES (which introduced the comic characters reprised here by Radford and Wayne). Based on Gordon Wellesley's novel *Report on a Fugitive*. Originally released in U.S. as NIGHT TRAIN. ▼▶●

Night Unto Night (1949) **85m.** ** D: Don Siegel. Ronald Reagan, Viveca Lindfors, Broderick Crawford, Rosemary DeCamp, Osa Massen, Art Baker, Craig Stevens. Somber, unconvincing film about relationship of dying scientist and mentally disturbed widow. Finished in 1947 and shelved

for two years. Reagan's performance isn't bad, but script is against him. ▶

Night Waitress (1936) **57m.** **½ D: Lew Landers. Margot Grahame, Gordon Jones, Vinton Hayworth, Marc Lawrence, Billy Gilbert, Donald Barry, Anthony Quinn. Waitress Grahame, who's out on probation, finds herself neck-deep in murder and mayhem. Adequate programmer features very young Quinn as a hoodlum.

Night Walker, The (1964) **86m.** *** D: William Castle. Barbara Stanwyck, Robert Taylor, Lloyd Bochner, Rochelle Hudson, Judi Meredith, Hayden Rorke. One of the better Castle horror films has Stanwyck as wealthy widow discovering cause of recurring dreams about lost husband. Effective psychological thriller with good cast, unusual script by Robert Bloch. Title on-screen is WILLIAM CASTLE'S THE NIGHT WALKER. ▼

Night Without Sleep (1952) **77m.** ** D: Roy (Ward) Baker. Linda Darnell, Gary Merrill, Hildegarde Neff, Hugh Beaumont, Mae Marsh. Pat treatment of man thinking he's committed murder.

Night Without Stars (1951-British) **86m.** **½ D: Anthony Pelissier. David Farrar, Nadia Gray, Maurice Teynac, June Clyde, Gerard Landry. Adequate mystery with partially blind lawyer Farrar becoming involved with Gray and a murder.

Night World (1932) **56m.** *** D: Hobart Henley. Lew Ayres, Mae Clarke, Boris Karloff, Dorothy Revier, Russell Hopton, Clarence Muse, Hedda Hopper, Bert Roach, George Raft. Outrageous little pre-Code item about the various goings-on in a Prohibition-era nightclub. Karloff is its corrupt owner; Ayres a troubled young man whose mother has murdered his father; Clarke a wisecracking chorus girl; Muse a philosophical doorman; Raft (in a small role) a Broadway tinhorn. Add to this some vintage Busby Berkeley choreography ... and the result is a real curio.

Nikki, Wild Dog of the North (1961) **C-74m.** *** D: Jack Couffer, Don Haldane. Jean Coutu, Emile Genest, Uriel Luft, Robert Rivard. Wolfdog Nikki is separated from his master, a Canadian trapper, and fends for himself in a variety of adventures. Exciting Disney film. ▼▶

Nine Girls (1944) **78m.** **½ D: Leigh Jason. Ann Harding, Evelyn Keyes, Jinx Falkenburg, Anita Louise, Jeff Donnell, Nina Foch, Marcia Mae Jones, Leslie Brooks, Lynn Merrick, Shirley Mills, William Demarest. Wisecrack-laden comedy-mystery about murder at a sorority house.

Nine Hours to Rama (1963) **C-125m.** **½ D: Mark Robson. Horst Buchholz, Jose Ferrer, Robert Morley, Diane Baker, Harry Andrews. Ambitious attempt to make meaningful story of events leading up to assassination of Mahatma Gandhi; bogs down in trite script. Filmed on location in India. CinemaScope.

Nine Lives Are Not Enough (1941) **63m.** **½ D: A. Edward Sutherland. Ronald Reagan, Joan Perry, James Gleason, Peter Whitney, Faye Emerson, Howard da Silva. Reagan is an aggressive newspaperman who solves a murder case. Enjoyable, fast-paced Warner Bros. B comedy-mystery.

1984 (1956-British) **91m.** *** D: Michael Anderson. Edmond O'Brien, Michael Redgrave, Jan Sterling, David Kossoff, Mervyn Johns, Donald Pleasence. Thought-provoking version of George Orwell's futuristic novel. Lovers O'Brien and Sterling trapped in all-powerful state, try valiantly to rebel against "Big Brother." Remade in 1984.▼

Ninety Degrees in the Shade (1964-Czech) **90m.** **½ D: Jiri Weiss. Anne Heywood, James Booth, Donald Wolfit, Ann Todd. Turgid account of Heywood, who works in food store, accused of theft; intertwined with passionate love episodes. Czech-made, with British stars. CinemaScope.

99 River Street (1953) **83m.** *** D: Phil Karlson. John Payne, Evelyn Keyes, Brad Dexter, Peggie Castle, Ian Wolfe, Frank Faylen. Rugged crime caper with Payne caught up in tawdry surroundings, trying to prove himself innocent of murder charge. Unpretentious film really packs a punch. ▶

Ninotchka (1939) **110m.** ***½ D: Ernst Lubitsch. Greta Garbo, Melvyn Douglas, Ina Claire, Bela Lugosi, Sig Ruman, Felix Bressart, Alexander Granach, Richard Carle. Amid much outdated sociological banter, a lighthearted Garbo still shines. Lubitsch's comedy pegged on tale of cold Russian agent Garbo coming to Paris, falling in love with gay-blade Douglas. Supporting cast shows fine comedy flair. Script by Billy Wilder, Charles Brackett, and Walter Reisch was basis for Broadway musical and film SILK STOCKINGS.▼▶

Ninth Guest, The (1934) **67m.** **½ D: R. (Roy) William Neill. Donald Cook, Genevieve Tobin, Hardie Albright, Edward Ellis, Edwin Maxwell, Helen Flint, Vince Barnett, Samuel S. Hinds, Nella Walker. Not-bad adaptation of Owen Davis's play, a kissin' cousin to Agatha Christie's *Ten Little Indians*. Eight people with shady pasts are invited to a swanky penthouse party, but no one knows the identity of the host—a disembodied voice who reveals that "the ninth guest is Death."

Nitwits, The (1935) **81m.** *** D: George Stevens. Bert Wheeler, Robert Woolsey, Betty Grable, Fred Keating, Evelyn Brent, Erik Rhodes, Hale Hamilton, Willie Best. Enjoyable comedy-musical-mystery with Wheeler and Woolsey seeking to uncover the identity of the Black Widow, a blackmailer-killer. Grable plays Wheeler's girlfriend, a murder suspect. Based on a story by Stuart Palmer. ●▶

Noah's Ark (1929) **100m.** **½ D: Michael Curtiz. Dolores Costello, George O'Brien, Noah Beery, Louise Fazenda, Gwynn (Guinn "Big Boy") Williams, Paul McAllister, Myrna Loy. Hokey and derivative story (by Darryl F. Zanuck) has devil-may-care O'Brien, gallivanting through Europe, falling in love with German girl Costello on the eve of WW1, and finally realizing his duty and enlisting in the U.S. Army. Somehow all this is paralleled to the days of Noah in a lengthy flashback sequence. Biblical segment is dazzlingly elaborate and full of great special effects. Silent film with somewhat awkward talking sequences; originally 135m., restored in 1989; beware of 1957 reissue prints running 75m. ▶

Nob Hill (1945) **C-95m.** **½ D: Henry Hathaway. George Raft, Joan Bennett, Vivian Blaine, Peggy Ann Garner, Alan Reed, B. S. Pully, Emil Coleman, Smith and Dale, Rory Calhoun. Gold Coast saloon owner Raft has his head turned when socialite Bennett shows an interest in him. Predictable formula musical given handsome Technicolor production. ▶

Nobody Lives Forever (1946) **100m.** *** D: Jean Negulesco. John Garfield, Geraldine Fitzgerald, Walter Brennan, Faye Emerson, George Coulouris, George Tobias. Well-done but familiar yarn of con man Garfield fleecing rich widow Fitzgerald, then falling in love for real. ▶

Nobody's Baby (1937) **68m.** **½ D: Gus Meins. Patsy Kelly, Lyda Roberti, Lynne Overman, Robert Armstrong, Rosina Lawrence, Don Alvarado, Jimmie Grier's Orchestra. After washing out of show business, Kelly and Roberti become nurses and wind up taking care of an infant for a nightclub dancer who has kept her marriage a secret. Agreeable (if unmemorable) vehicle for two talented comediennes who were teamed by producer Hal Roach. ▶

Nobody's Darling (1943) **71m.** ** D: Anthony Mann. Mary Lee, Louis Calhern, Gladys George, Jackie Moran, Lee Patrick, Bennie Bartlett, Marcia Mae Jones. The neglected daughter of a famous Hollywood couple tries to get their attention by auditioning for the school play. Minor Republic Pictures musical is competently staged (with choreography by Nick Castle) but shows no signs whatsoever of Mann's future brilliance with Westerns and noirs.

Nobody Waved Goodbye (1965-Canadian) **80m.** *** D: Don Owen. Peter Kastner, Julie Biggs, Claude Rae, Toby Tarnow, Charmion King, Ron Taylor. Straightforward, perceptive account of alienated teenager Kastner. A sequel, UNFINISHED BUSINESS, is set 20 years later, and details the plight of Kastner and Biggs's own teen offspring.

Nocturne (1946) **88m.** **½ D: Edwin L. Marin. George Raft, Lynn Bari, Virginia Huston, Joseph Pevney, Myrna Dell. A ladykiller-songwriter is murdered, the police think it's suicide, but stubborn tough-guy cop Raft knows otherwise. Moderately entertaining mystery. Highlight: Raft's investigation takes him to RKO and the set of SINBAD THE SAILOR!▼●▶

No Down Payment (1957) **105m.** *** D: Martin Ritt. Joanne Woodward, Jeffrey Hunter, Sheree North, Tony Randall, Cameron Mitchell, Patricia Owens, Barbara Rush, Pat Hingle. Topical suburban soaper of intertwining problems of several young married couples. CinemaScope.▶

No Escape (1943) SEE: **I Escaped From the Gestapo**

No Escape (1953) **76m.** *½ D: Charles Bennett. Lew Ayres, Marjorie Steele, Sonny Tufts, Gertrude Michael. Modest narrative about couple seeking actual killer to clear themselves of homicide charge. Retitled: CITY ON A HUNT.▶

No Greater Glory (1934) **77m.** *** D: Frank Borzage. George Breakston, Jimmy Butler, Jackie Searl, Frankie Darro, Donald Haines, Rolf Ernest, Samuel S. Hinds, Ralph Morgan, Christian Rub. Rival gangs of street kids engage in deadly war games as they vie for control of a vacant lot in 1914 Hungary. Deeply felt antiwar allegory, based on Molnár's *The Paul Street Boys*, strikingly photographed by Joseph August and passionately acted by its juvenile cast. Filmed before in Hungary in 1929 and remade several times, notably as THE BOYS OF PAUL STREET (1969).▶

No Greater Love (1959-Japanese) **208m.** ***½ D: Masaki Kobayashi. Tatsuya Nakadai, Michiyo Aratama, Ineko Arima, Chikage Awashima, Keiji Sada, Sô Yamamura, Akira Ishihama, Eitarô Ozawa, Shinji Nambara. South Manchuria, 1943: Kaji (Nakadai), a humane, married Japanese steel company employee who is about to be conscripted into the military, is assigned to supervise a rural ore-mining operation whose workers are Chinese POWs. Stirring epic mirrors age-old enmity between Japanese, Chinese, and Koreans while offering a deeply felt portrait of a man who must play a deadly balancing act as he struggles to maintain his values. Scripted by Kobayashi and Zenzo Matsuyama, based on a six-volume novel by Junpei Gomikawa. Aka HUMAN CONDITION I; followed by THE ROAD TO ETERNITY and A SOLDIER'S PRAYER.

No Highway in the Sky (1951) **98m.** *** D: Henry Koster. James Stewart, Marlene Dietrich, Glynis Johns, Jack Hawkins, Janette Scott, Elizabeth Allan, Ronald Squire, Niall MacGinnis, Kenneth More, Maurice Denham, Wilfrid Hyde-White. Offbeat, engrossing drama with Stewart as an engineer who desperately tries to convince others that aircraft can suffer from metal fatigue, and should be grounded after a given time.

Dietrich is a glamorous passenger on the fateful flight. Based on a novel by Nevil Shute. Made in England, where it was released as NO HIGHWAY.▼▶

No Holds Barred (1952) **65m.** ** D: William Beaudine. Leo Gorcey, Huntz Hall, Leonard Penn, Marjorie Reynolds, Bernard Gorcey, David Gorcey, Tim Ryan, Bennie Bartlett, Henry Kulky. Freak-of-nature Sach develops some amazing physical attributes and becomes a wrestling star in this unsurprising *Bowery Boys* match.▶

No Leave, No Love (1946) **119m.** ** D: Charles Martin. Van Johnson, Keenan Wynn, Pat Kirkwood, Guy Lombardo, Edward Arnold, Marie Wilson. No script, no laughs; Johnson and Wynn are sailors on the town in this overlong romantic comedy.

No Limit (1931) **72m.** ** D: Frank Tuttle. Clara Bow, Norman Foster, Stuart Erwin, Dixie Lee, Harry Green, Thelma Todd. Manhattan movie-palace usherette is courted by a Park Avenue suitor but falls instead for a jewel thief who operates a floating gambling den. Improbable light comedy turns serious toward the end. Clumsy at times, though futuristic art deco sets and N.Y.C. location filming are assets. Bow seems miscast as a troubled but virtuous character.

No Love for Johnnie (1961-British) **110m.** *** D: Ralph Thomas. Peter Finch, Stanley Holloway, Mary Peach, Mervyn Johns, Donald Pleasence, Dennis Price, Oliver Reed. Civilized study of politician who cares only about winning the election. CinemaScope.▼

No Man Is an Island (1962) **C-114m.** **½ D: John Monks, Jr., Richard Goldstone. Jeffrey Hunter, Marshall Thompson, Barbara Perez, Ronald Remy, Paul Edwards, Jr., Rolf Bayer, Vicente Liwanag. Spotty production values mar true story of serviceman Hunter trapped on Guam during the three years Japanese controlled area.▼▶

No Man of Her Own (1932) **85m.** **½ D: Wesley Ruggles. Clark Gable, Carole Lombard, Dorothy Mackaill, Grant Mitchell, Elizabeth Patterson, Lillian Harmer, George Barbier. Snappy story of heel reformed by good girl, noteworthy for only co-starring of Gable and Lombard (then not married).▼▶

No Man of Her Own (1950) **98m.** **½ D: Mitchell Leisen. Barbara Stanwyck, John Lund, Jane Cowl, Phyllis Thaxter, Richard Denning, Milburn Stone. Turgid drama based on Cornell Woolrich tale of Stanwyck assuming another's identity, later being blackmailed by ex-boyfriend. Remade in 1982 as I MARRIED A SHADOW and in 1996 as MRS. WINTERBOURNE.▶

No Minor Vices (1948) **96m.** ** D: Lewis Milestone. Dana Andrews, Lilli Palmer, Louis Jourdan, Jane Wyatt, Norman Lloyd, Bernard Gorcey, Beau Bridges. Pretentious comedy in which stereotypically eccentric artist Jourdan attempts to come between pediatrician Andrews and wife Palmer. Starts off well but bogs down.

No More Ladies (1935) **81m.** **½ D: Edward H. Griffith. Joan Crawford, Robert Montgomery, Charlie Ruggles, Franchot Tone, Edna May Oliver, Gail Patrick. Crawford marries playboy Montgomery, tries to settle him down by making him jealous over her attention to Tone. Airy comedy. Joan Burfield (Fontaine) made her film debut here. ▶

No More Orchids (1932) **68m.** *** D: Walter Lang. Carole Lombard, Walter Connolly, Louise Closser Hale, Lyle Talbot, C. Aubrey Smith, Allen Vincent, Ruthelma Stevens. Lombard sparkles as a spoiled heiress who falls for "nobody" Talbot, but agrees to marry a fatuous prince in order to save her father's (Connolly) failing bank. Hale steals every scene she's in as Lombard's tippler grandmother in this smart and sophisticated blend of romantic comedy and drama. ▶

No My Darling Daughter (1961-British) **97m.** **½ D: Ralph Thomas. Michael Redgrave, Michael Craig, Juliet Mills, Roger Livesey, Rad Fulton, Renee Houston. Generally funny film with Mills, rich industrialist's daughter, torn between two suitors, playboy and hard-working businessman.

No Name on the Bullet (1959) **C-77m.** *** D: Jack Arnold. Audie Murphy, Charles Drake, Joan Evans, Virginia Grey, Warren Stevens, Edgar Stehli, R. G. Armstrong, Willis Bouchey, Karl Swenson, Charles Watts, Jerry Paris, Whit Bissell. A quiet, cultured gunman (Murphy, in a fine performance) rides into a small town to kill someone, though no one but he knows who his target is. Guilt and paranoia create their own victims. Slow, philosophical, and intelligent, this is the best of sci-fi director Arnold's several Westerns. CinemaScope. ▼▶

None But the Brave (1965) **C-105m.** **½ D: Frank Sinatra. Frank Sinatra, Clint Walker, Tommy Sands, Tony Bill, Brad Dexter. Taut war drama focusing on crew of cracked-up plane and Japanese army patrol who make peace on a remote island during WW2. Panavision. ▼●▶

None But the Lonely Heart (1944) **113m.** **½ D: Clifford Odets. Cary Grant, Ethel Barrymore, Barry Fitzgerald, Jane Wyatt, Dan Duryea, George Coulouris, June Duprez. Odets' moody drama of a Cockney drifter features one of Grant's most ambitious performances and some fine moments, but suffers from censorship restrictions of the time and misplaced WW2 rhetoric. Barrymore won Supporting Actress Oscar as Grant's dying mother. Also shown in computer-colored version. ▼●▶

None Shall Escape (1944) **85m.** *** D: Andre de Toth. Marsha Hunt, Alexander Knox, Henry Travers, Richard Crane,

Dorothy Morris, Eric Rolf, Ruth Nelson, Kurt Kreuger. Trial of Nazi officer reviews his savage career, in taut drama that retains quite a punch. Released before, but set after, the end of WW2.

No, No, Nanette (1940) **96m.** *½ D: Herbert Wilcox. Anna Neagle, Richard Carlson, Victor Mature, Roland Young, Helen Broderick, ZaSu Pitts, Eve Arden, Billy Gilbert. Lumbering adaptation of the Broadway musical with the title character coming to the aid of her philandering uncle, while an artist (Carlson) and a theatrical producer (Mature) both fall in love with her. British star Neagle (during her brief stay in Hollywood) seems a bit long in the tooth to play Nanette. Previously filmed in 1930; later reworked as TEA FOR TWO (1950). Pitts, cast as a wisecracking servant, played the same role in 1930, while Arden appears in the 1950 version (albeit in a different role). ▼▶

Non-Stop New York (1937-British) **71m.** *** D: Robert Stevenson. John Loder, Anna Lee, Francis L. Sullivan, Frank Cellier, Desmond Tester. Fast-paced, tongue-in-cheek Hitchcock-like yarn about a woman who can provide alibi for innocent man accused of murder—but no one believes her. Love that luxury airplane! ▼▶

No One Man (1932) **73m.** ** D: Lloyd Corrigan. Carole Lombard, Ricardo Cortez, Paul Lukas, George Barbier. Another tired love triangle, with spoiled rich girl Lombard caught between suave but heartless Cortez and earnest doctor Lukas. Becomes laughable before long.

No Orchids for Miss Blandish (1948-British) **104m.** ** D: St. John Legh Clowes. Linden Travers, Jack La Rue, Walter Crisham, MacDonald Parke, Lili Molnar, Danny Green, Percy Marmont, Richard Neilson. Heiress is kidnapped and ultimately finds herself at the mercy of a gang led by an out-and-out psycho (played by American gangster-movie veteran La Rue). Genuinely odd, micro-budget British film aspires to be a Hollywood film noir and misses by a mile. Travers originated the role of Miss Blandish onstage in London. Considered perverse by British critics and censors and badly cut for original U.S. release. Based on a novel by James Hadley Chase, later remade as THE GRISSOM GANG. ▶

Noose Hangs High, The (1948) **77m.** **½ D: Charles Barton. Bud Abbott, Lou Costello, Joseph Calleia, Leon Errol, Cathy Downs, Mike Mazurki, Fritz Feld. Mistaken identity leads to complications with the boys robbed of a large sum of money; typical A&C, bolstered by presence of Errol. Highlight: "Mudder and Fodder." ▼▶

No Other Woman (1933) **58m.** **½ D: J. Walter Ruben. Irene Dunne, Charles Bickford, Gwili Andre, Eric Linden, Christian

Rub, Leila Bennett, J. Carrol Naish. Miningtown couple Dunne and Bickford go from rags to riches with young Linden's great chemical discovery but sacrifice their happiness in the process. OK soap opera dignified by solid performances. Impressive montages by the great Slavko Vorkapich.

No Place Like Homicide! (1962-British) **87m.** ****** D: Pat Jackson. Kenneth Connor, Sidney James, Shirley Eaton, Donald Pleasence, Dennis Price, Michael Gough. At times strained satire about group of people gathered at haunted house for the reading of a will. Remake of THE GHOUL. British title: WHAT A CARVE UP!▼▶

No Place to Hide (1956) **C-71m.** ****½** D: Josef Shaftel. David Brian, Marsha Hunt, Hugh Corcoran, Ike Jarioga, Jr., Celia Flor. Tense account of search for two children who accidentally have disease-spreading pellets in their possession; filmed in Philippines.

No Questions Asked (1951) **81m.** ****½** D: Harold F. Kress. Barry Sullivan, Arlene Dahl, Jean Hagen, George Murphy, William Reynolds, Mari Blanchard. Snappy little film of insurance company lawyer Sullivan seeking easy road to success via crime rackets.

Nora Prentiss (1947) **111m.** ****½** D: Vincent Sherman. Ann Sheridan, Kent Smith, Bruce Bennett, Robert Alda, Rosemary DeCamp, John Ridgely, Robert Arthur, Wanda Hendrix. Proper married doctor Smith falls for kicked-around singer Sheridan, leading to plenty of complications. Entertaining, albeit predictable, drama.▶

No Regrets for Our Youth (1946-Japanese) **111m.** ******* D: Akira Kurosawa. Denjiro Okochi, Eiko Miyoshi, Setsuko Hara, Susumu Fujita, Kuninori Kodo, Haruko Sugimura, Aritake Kono, Takashi Shimura. In prewar Kyoto, a well-bred university student's frivolous world quakes when her professor father is arrested as a political criminal. Then, when her lover is executed as a spy, she moves to the country home of her would-have-been inlaws, who reveal themselves as nothing more than malicious peasants. Feminist drama, portraying a sturdy heroine's victory over governmental oppression and emotional abuse, still rings true.▼▶

No Road Back (1957-British) **83m.** ****** D: Montgomery Tully. Sean Connery, Skip Homeier, Paul Carpenter, Patricia Dainton, Norman Wooland, Margaret Rawlings. Blind and deaf woman sacrifices everything for son, becomes involved with criminals—who then try to pin robbery on the innocent son. Plodding melodrama.

No Room for the Groom (1952) **82m.** ****½** D: Douglas Sirk. Tony Curtis, Piper Laurie, Spring Byington, Don DeFore, Jack Kelly. Harmless shenanigans of ex-G.I. Curtis returning home to find it filled with in-laws.▶

North by Northwest (1959) **C-136m.** ******** D: Alfred Hitchcock. Cary Grant, Eva Marie Saint, James Mason, Leo G. Carroll, Martin Landau, Jessie Royce Landis, Philip Ober, Adam Williams, Josephine Hutchinson, Edward Platt. Quintessential Hitchcock comedy-thriller, with bewildered ad-man Grant chased cross country by both spies (who think he's a double agent) and the police (who think he's an assassin). One memorable scene after another, including now-legendary crop-dusting and Mount Rushmore sequences; one of the all-time great entertainments. Witty script by Ernest Lehman, exciting score by Bernard Herrmann. VistaVision.▼▶

Nor the Moon By Night SEE: **Elephant Gun**

Northern Pursuit (1943) **94m.** ****½** D: Raoul Walsh. Errol Flynn, Julie Bishop, Helmut Dantine, John Ridgely, Gene Lockhart, Tom Tully. Flynn, a Mountie of German descent, pretends to have Nazi sympathies in order to learn the objectives of Nazis operating in Canada, in this standard but slickly done drama.▼▶

North of the Great Divide (1950) **C-67m.** ******* D: William Witney. Roy Rogers, Penny Edwards, Gordon Jones, Roy Barcroft, Jack Lambert, Douglas Evans, Noble Johnson, Riders of the Purple Sage. Indian agent Rogers is sent into Canada to quell trouble between Indians and a ruthless salmon-cannery owner (Barcroft) who's starving them out. Solid story in this Trucolor outing.▼▶

North of the Rio Grande (1937) **72m.** ****½** D: Nate Watt. William Boyd, George Hayes, Russell Hayden, Stephen Morris (Morris Ankrum), Bernadene Hayes, John Rutherford. When his brother is killed in a railroad holdup, Hopalong Cassidy poses as a desperado to solve the mystery and administer retribution to the dual-identity culprit, masked villain "The Lone Wolf." Good series entry climaxes with an exciting train chase. Based on 1924 novel *Cottonwood Gulch* by series creator Clarence E. Mulford. Feature debut of Lee J. Cobb, fresh from N.Y.C.'s Group Theater.▼▶

North Star, The (1943) **105m.** ****½** D: Lewis Milestone. Anne Baxter, Dana Andrews, Walter Huston, Ann Harding, Erich von Stroheim, Jane Withers, Farley Granger, Walter Brennan. Dramatic battle sequences in WW2 Russia marred by uninteresting stretches until German von Stroheim matches wits with village leader Huston. Good performances all around; script by Lillian Hellman. Later edited to 82m. to deemphasize the good Russians and retitled ARMORED ATTACK. Also shown in computer-colored version.▼▶

North to Alaska (1960) **C-122m.** ******* D: Henry Hathaway. John Wayne, Stewart Granger, Ernie Kovacs, Fabian, Capucine, Mickey Shaughnessy, Joe Sawyer, John Qualen. Fast-moving actioner with delightful tongue-in-cheek approach; prospectors Wayne and Granger have their hands full dealing with latter's kid brother Fabian, con artist Kovacs, and gold-digging (in the other sense) Capucine. CinemaScope.▼O◗

Northwest Frontier SEE: **Flame Over India**

North West Mounted Police (1940) C-125m. **½ D: Cecil B. DeMille. Gary Cooper, Madeleine Carroll, Preston Foster, Paulette Goddard, Robert Preston, George Bancroft, Akim Tamiroff, Lon Chaney, Jr., Robert Ryan. DeMille at his most ridiculous, with Cooper as Dusty Rivers, Goddard a fiery half-breed in love with Preston, Lynne Overman as Scottish philosopher in superficial tale of Texas Ranger searching for fugitive in Canada. Much of outdoor action filmed on obviously indoor sets.

Northwest Outpost (1947) 91m. *½ D: Allan Dwan. Nelson Eddy, Ilona Massey, Hugo Haas, Elsa Lanchester, Lenore Ulric. Rudolf Friml operetta of California calvarymen lumbers along pretty lamely. Eddy's last film.▼

Northwest Passage (Book I—Rogers' Rangers) (1940) C-125m. ***½ D: King Vidor. Spencer Tracy, Robert Young, Walter Brennan, Ruth Hussey, Nat Pendleton, Robert Barrat, Addison Richards. Gritty, evocative filming of Kenneth Roberts' book about Rogers' Rangers and their stoic leader (Tracy), enduring hardships and frustrations while opening up new territory in Colonial America. Young and Brennan are greenhorns who learn hard knocks under taskmaster Tracy. The river-fording sequence is a knockout.▼O◗

Northwest Rangers (1943) 64m. **½ D: Joseph M. Newman. James Craig, William Lundigan, Patricia Dane, John Carradine, Jack Holt, Keenan Wynn, Grant Withers, Darryl Hickman. Orphaned after an Indian attack, two boys are raised by a Canadian Mountie but grow up on opposite sides of the law. Lively Western programmer boosted by MGM production gloss.

Northwest Stampede (1948) C-79m. **½ D: Albert S. Rogell. Joan Leslie, James Craig, Jack Oakie, Chill Wills, Victor Kilian, Stanley Andrews, Lane Chandler. Rodeo star Craig returns to the family ranch after his father's death, tangles with cute but tough female foreman Leslie. A coveted white stallion also comes into play in this formulaic oater.

No Sad Songs for Me (1950) 89m. *** D: Rudolph Maté. Margaret Sullavan, Wendell Corey, Viveca Lindfors, Natalie Wood, Ann Doran. Moving account of dying mother Sullavan preparing her family to go on without her. Ironically, Sullavan's last film.◗

Nosferatu (1922-German) 94m. ***½ D: F. W. Murnau. Max Schreck, Alexander Granach, Gustav von Wangenheim, Greta Schroeder. Early film version of *Dracula* is brilliantly eerie, full of imaginative touches that none of the later films quite recaptured. Schreck's vampire is also the ugliest in film history. The making of this film is dramatized in SHADOW OF THE VAMPIRE. Remade in 1979. Aka NOSFERATU, A SYMPHONY OF HORROR. ▼O◗

Not as a Stranger (1955) 135m. *** D: Stanley Kramer. Olivia de Havilland, Frank Sinatra, Robert Mitchum, Charles Bickford, Gloria Grahame, Broderick Crawford, Lee Marvin, Lon Chaney, Henry (Harry) Morgan, Virginia Christine, Jerry Paris. Morton Thompson novel of Mitchum marrying nurse de Havilland who supports him through medical school despite oft-strained relationship. Glossy tribute to medical profession contains excellent performances by all. Producer Kramer's directorial debut. ▼◗

Nothing but a Man (1964) 92m. ***½ D: Michael Roemer. Ivan Dixon, Abbey Lincoln, Julius Harris, Gloria Foster, Martin Priest, Leonard Parker, Yaphet Kotto, Stanley Greene. Quietly powerful look at blacks in the South, with Dixon as a railroad worker who tries to settle down for the first time in his life with schoolteacher Lincoln, and has to deal with a level of prejudice—and self-denial—he's never faced before. Perceptive and honest, this film manages to make its points without melodrama. A small gem. Look for Esther Rolle and Moses Gunn in small roles.▼O◗

Nothing but the Best (1964-British) C-99m. ***½ D: Clive Donner. Alan Bates, Denholm Elliott, Harry Andrews, Millicent Martin, Pauline Delany. Biting look at social-climbing playboy Bates who commits murder to get ahead in the world. Written by Frederic Raphael.

Nothing But the Truth (1941) 90m. *** D: Elliott Nugent. Bob Hope, Paulette Goddard, Edward Arnold, Leif Erickson, Helen Vinson, Willie Best. Entertaining comedy based on sure-fire idea: Bashful stockbroker Hope wagers that he can tell the absolute truth for 24 hours. Good fun. Filmed before in 1920 (with Taylor Holmes) and 1929 (with Richard Dix); also an ancestor of Jim Carrey's LIAR LIAR. ◗

Nothing But Trouble (1944) 69m. ** D: Sam Taylor. Stan Laurel, Oliver Hardy, Mary Boland, Philip Merivale, David Leland, Henry O'Neill. Lesser L&H vehicle with duo hired as servants, meeting young boy king whose life is in danger. Boland is amusing as usual.▼◗

Nothing Sacred (1937) C-75m. ***½ D: William Wellman. Carole Lombard, Fredric March, Walter Connolly, Charles Winninger, Sig Rumann, Frank Fay. Classic comedy about hotshot reporter (March) who exploits Vermont girl's "imminent" death from radium poisoning for headline value in N.Y.C. Ben Hecht's cynical script vividly enacted by

March and Lombard (at her best). Gershwinesque music score by Oscar Levant. Trivia note: Connolly's character is named Oliver Stone! Later a Broadway musical called *Hazel Flagg*. Remade as LIVING IT UP. ▼●▶

No Time for Comedy (1940) 98m. **½ D: William Keighley. James Stewart, Rosalind Russell, Genevieve Tobin, Charles Ruggles, Allyn Joslyn, Louise Beavers. Slick but dated adaptation of S. N. Behrman play about actress who tries to keep her playwright-husband from taking himself too seriously. Smoothly done but artificial. Aka GUY WITH A GRIN. ▶

No Time for Flowers (1952) 83m. ** D: Don Siegel. Viveca Lindfors, Paul Christian, Ludwig Stossel, Manfred Ingor. Low-grade version of NINOTCHKA set in Prague; a pale shadow of its ancestor.

No Time for Love (1943) 83m. **½ D: Mitchell Leisen. Claudette Colbert, Fred MacMurray, Ilka Chase, Richard Haydn, Paul McGrath, June Havoc. Cute but obvious romance between famous magazine photographer Colbert and down-to-earth MacMurray. The stars give this a lift. ▶

No Time for Sergeants (1958) 119m. ***½ D: Mervyn LeRoy. Andy Griffith, Myron McCormick, Nick Adams, Murray Hamilton, Don Knotts. Funny military comedy based on Ira Levin's Broadway play (which got its start as a 1955 *U.S. Steel Hour* TV play). Griffith and McCormick repeat roles as hayseed inducted into service and his harried sergeant. Griffith's best comedy, with good support from Adams, and, in a small role as a noncommissioned officer, Knotts. Script by John Lee Mahin. Followed years later by a TV series. ▼●▶

No Time to Be Young (1957) 82m. ** D: David Lowell Rich. Robert Vaughn, Roger Smith, Merry Anders, Kathy Nolan, Tom Pittman. Pedestrian programmer about a trio of troubled young men: arrogant Vaughn's just been booted out of college; confused Smith is hung up on older woman; and insecure Pittman lies to his girlfriend. Skip it. ▶

No Time to Die SEE: **Tank Force**
Not of This Earth (1957) 67m. **½ D: Roger Corman. Paul Birch, Beverly Garland, Morgan Jones, William Roerick. Above-par low-budget entry from Roger Corman with blank-eyed Birch as an alien vampire here to get blood for his atomic war–ravaged home world. Good supporting cast; great bit by Dick Miller. Remade in 1988, 1996 (for TV), and 1997 (as STAR PORTAL). ▶

Notorious (1946) 101m. ***½ D: Alfred Hitchcock. Cary Grant, Ingrid Bergman, Claude Rains, Louis Calhern, Leopoldine Konstantin, Reinhold Schunzel, Moroni Olsen. Top-notch espionage tale by Ben Hecht, set in post-WW2 South America, with Ingrid marrying spy Rains to aid U.S.

and agent Grant. Frank, tense, well acted, with amazingly suspenseful climax (and one memorably passionate love scene). Remade for cable TV in 1992. ▼●▶

Notorious Affair, A (1930) 69m. ** D: Lloyd Bacon. Billie Dove, Basil Rathbone, Kay Francis, Montagu Love, Kenneth Thomson, Philip Strange, Gino Corrado. Rathbone is uncomfortably cast as a neurotic violinist married to Dove; she finds out he is having an affair but dutifully nurses him back to health when he has a breakdown. Plush production can't save this stagy soap opera.

Notorious Gentleman (1945-British) 123m. *** D: Sidney Gilliat. Rex Harrison, Lilli Palmer, Godfrey Tearle, Griffith Jones, Margaret Johnston, Guy Middleton, Jean Kent. Philandering life of irresponsible playboy is told with wit and style in this handsome production. British title: THE RAKE'S PROGRESS.

Notorious Landlady, The (1962) 123m. **½ D: Richard Quine. Kim Novak, Jack Lemmon, Fred Astaire, Lionel Jeffries, Estelle Winwood, Maxwell Reed. Lemmon entranced by houseowner Novak, decides to find out if she really did kill her husband; set in London. Offbeat comedy-mystery written by Blake Edwards and Larry Gelbart. ▶

Notorious Lone Wolf, The (1946) 64m. ** D: D. Ross Lederman. Gerald Mohr, Janis Carter, Eric Blore, John Abbott, William B. Davidson, Don Beddoe, Adele Roberts, Peter Whitney. The Lone Wolf returns from WW2 and is embroiled in a museum jewel theft. Mohr replaced Warren William for this humdrum entry.

Notorious Sophie Lang, The (1934) 64m. **½ D: Ralph Murphy. Gertrude Michael, Paul Cavanagh, Arthur Byron, Alison Skipworth, Leon Errol, Arthur Hoyt. N.Y.C. police detective Byron is determined to catch jewel thief Michael, who's just returned from London. She's awfully slick, but then, so is her rival (Cavanagh). Amusing vehicle for Michael with a top supporting cast. Followed by THE RETURN OF SOPHIE LANG.

No Trees in the Street (1958-British) 108m. ** D: J. Lee Thompson. Sylvia Syms, Stanley Holloway, Herbert Lom, Ronald Howard, Joan Miller. Lower-class British life examined for its strengths and weaknesses; too sterile a human document.

Not So Dumb (1930) 76m. *** D: King Vidor. Marion Davies, Elliott Nugent, Raymond Hackett, Franklin Pangborn, Julia Faye, William Holden, Donald Ogden Stewart, Sally Starr. Davies is delightful as a well-meaning scatterbrain who throws a big weekend bash to advance the career of her aspiring businessman beau, only to turn it into a disaster. Deft precursor to screwball farces of the 1930s and '40s, with celebrated playwright Stewart very funny in a rare acting role. Based on the play *Dulcy* by George S. Kaufman and Marc Connelly. Previously filmed in 1923 and remade in 1940 under that title.

Not Wanted (1949) **94m. **½ D:** Elmer Clifton. Sally Forrest, Keefe Brasselle, Leo Penn, Dorothy Adams. Well-intentioned account of unwed mother seeking affection and understanding; produced and co-scripted by Ida Lupino (who also apparently directed most of the film). Later expanded with unrelated material (including child-birth footage) and released as an exploitation film THE WRONG RUT. ▼▶

Novel Affair, A (1957-British) **C-83m. ***** D: Muriel Box. Ralph Richardson, Margaret Leighton, Patricia Dainton, Carlo Justini, Marjorie Rhodes, Megs Jenkins. Amusing tale of Leighton who writes a sexy novel, finding the fantasy come true. Nearly everyone plays dual roles, in real life and scenes from the novel! Original British title: THE PASSIONATE STRANGER.

Now and Forever (1934) **81m. **½ D:** Henry Hathaway. Gary Cooper, Carole Lombard, Shirley Temple, Sir Guy Standing, Charlotte Granville. Standard jewel-thief-going-straight yarn; Lombard overshadowed by Cooper and Temple. On tape only in a computer-colored version. ▼▶

No Way Out (1950) **106m. ***** D: Joseph L. Mankiewicz. Richard Widmark, Linda Darnell, Stephen McNally, Sidney Poitier, Ruby Dee, Ossie Davis, Bill Walker. Violent tale of racial hatred involving bigot Widmark, who has gangster pals avenge his brother's death by creating race riots. Once-provocative film is still engrossing but seems a bit artificial at times. Film debuts of Poitier and Davis. ▼▶

Nowhere to Go (1958-British) **87m. ***** D: Seth Holt. George Nader, Maggie Smith, Bernard Lee, Geoffrey Keen, Bessie Love. Unsung, beautifully realized film noir stars Nader as a smooth Canadian con man in England who hides out with Smith while on the run. Brilliant deep-focus photography by Paul Beeson and a moody score by jazz trumpeter Dizzy Reece stand out. Smith's film debut. Metroscope.

Now, Voyager (1942) **117m. ***½ D:** Irving Rapper. Bette Davis, Paul Henreid, Claude Rains, Gladys Cooper, Bonita Granville, John Loder, Ilka Chase, Lee Patrick, Mary Wickes, Janis Wilson. Vintage, first-class soaper with Bette as sheltered spinster brought out of her shell by psychiatrist Rains, falling in love with suave Henreid, helping shy girl Wilson. All this set to beautiful, Oscar-winning Max Steiner music makes for top entertainment of this kind. Olive Higgins Prouty's bestseller was adapted by Casey Robinson. ▼●▶

Nude in a White Car (1958-French) **87m. **½ D:** Robert Hossein. Marina Vlady, Robert Hossein, Odile Versois, Helena Manson, Henri Cremieux. Hossein's only clue to a crime is title person; suspenser set on French Riviera. Vlady and Hossein were married in real life. Retitled: BLONDE IN A WHITE CAR.

Nude in His Pocket SEE: **Girl in His Pocket**

Nuisance, The (1933) **83m. ***** D: Jack Conway. Lee Tracy, Madge Evans, Frank Morgan, Charles Butterworth, John Miljan, Virginia Cherrill, David Landau. Fast-talker extraordinaire Tracy gives one of his quintessential wiseguy performances as a conniving ambulance chaser who falls in love with Evans, unaware she's a special investigator for a streetcar company he's repeatedly victimized. Laugh-a-minute caper only slows down a bit toward the end for romance. Sparkling script by Samuel and Bella Spewack. Remade as THE CHASER (1938). ▶

Numbered Men (1930) **65m. ***** D: Mervyn LeRoy. Conrad Nagel, Bernice Claire, Raymond Hackett, Ralph Ince, Ivan Linow, George Cooper, Tully Marshall. After being framed for counterfeiting, Hackett tries to prove his innocence while working on a road gang that lets him visit sweetheart Claire at a nearby farmhouse. Starchy prison picture with most of the action taking place outside the walls of the big house. LeRoy fared better when he directed I AM A FUGITIVE FROM A CHAIN GANG two years later.

Number Seventeen (1932-British) **63m. ***** D: Alfred Hitchcock. Leon M. Lion, Anne Grey, John Stuart, Donald Calthrop, Barry Jones, Garry Marsh. Entertaining comedy-thriller has tramp Lion stumbling upon a jewel thieves' hideout. Exciting chase sequence involves a train and bus (though the "special effects" are pretty obvious). Screenplay by Hitchcock. ▼▶

Nun's Story, The (1959) **C-149m. ***½ D:** Fred Zinnemann. Audrey Hepburn, Peter Finch, Edith Evans, Peggy Ashcroft, Dean Jagger, Mildred Dunnock. Tasteful filming of Kathryn Hulme book, with Hepburn the nun who serves in Belgian Congo and later leaves convent. Colleen Dewhurst, as a homicidal patient, is electrifying. Screenplay by Robert Anderson. ▼●▶

Nurse Edith Cavell (1939) **108m. ***** D: Herbert Wilcox. Anna Neagle, Edna May Oliver, George Sanders, ZaSu Pitts, May Robson, H. B. Warner, Robert Coote. Neagle is fine as dedicated WW1 nurse who worked with the Brussels underground to aid wounded soldiers. Sturdy production. ▼▶

Nurse on Wheels (1963-British) **86m. ***** D: Gerald Thomas. Juliet Mills, Ronald Lewis, Joan Sims, Noel Purcell, Raymond Huntley, Jim Dale. The trials of nurse Mills, who settles down to practice in a rural community. Entertaining, often touching.

Nut, The (1921) **74m. ***½ D:** Ted Reed. Douglas Fairbanks, Marguerite De La Motte, William Lowery, Gerald Pring, Morris Hughes, Barbara La Marr. Fairbanks is charming as a Greenwich Village romantic who adores a progressive-minded damsel (De La Motte) and must compete for her with a no-account gambler. There's one funny sight gag after another in this enormously entertaining comedy, one of Fairbanks' best. Highlight: Doug's "impersonations" of Napoleon Bonaparte, Ulysses S. Grant, Abraham Lincoln, and Tom Thumb. Cowritten by Fairbanks (under the pseudonym Elton Thomas). ▼▶

Nutty, Naughty Chateau (1964-French) **C-100m.** ****½** D: Roger Vadim. Monica Vitti, Curt Jurgens, Jean-Claude Brialy, Sylvie, Jean-Louis Trintignant, Françoise Hardy. Bizarre minor comedy involving the strange inhabitants of a castle romping about in 1750s styles; most diverting cast. Based on a Françoise Sagan play. Franscope.

Nutty Professor, The (1963) **C-107m.** ******* D: Jerry Lewis. Jerry Lewis, Stella Stevens, Del Moore, Kathleen Freeman, Med Flory, Howard Morris, Elvia Allman, Henry Gibson. Jerry's wildest (and most narcissistic) comedy casts him as chipmunk-faced college professor who does Jekyll-and-Hyde transformation into swaggering Buddy Love (whom some have interpreted as a Dean Martin caricature). More interesting than funny, although "Alaskan Polar Bear Heater" routine with Buddy Lester is a riot; Lewis buffs regard this as his masterpiece. Remade in 1996. Later a stage musical. ▼▶

Oasis (1955-French) **C-84m.** ****** D: Yves Allegret. Michele Morgan, Pierre Brasseur, Cornell Borchers, Carl Raddatz. Morgan's radiance brightens this oft-told story of gold-smuggling in Africa. CinemaScope.

Objective, Burma! (1945) **142m.** *****½** D: Raoul Walsh. Errol Flynn, William Prince, James Brown, George Tobias, Henry Hull, Warner Anderson. Zestful WW2 action film with Flynn and company as paratroopers invading Burma to wipe out important Japanese post; top excitement. Screenplay by Ranald MacDougall and Lester Cole. Reworked as DISTANT DRUMS, also directed by Walsh. Some prints cut to 127m. Also shown in computer-colored version. ▼▶

Obliging Young Lady (1941) **80m.** ****½** D: Richard Wallace. Eve Arden, Edmond O'Brien, Ruth Warrick, Joan Carroll, Franklin Pangborn, George Cleveland. Agreeable comedy about youngster, center of custody fight, finding herself the focal point at a country resort.

Obsessed (1951-British) **78m.** ****** D: Maurice Elvey. David Farrar, Geraldine Fitzgerald, Roland Culver, Jean Cadell. A schoolteacher (Farrar) and the paid companion (Fitzgerald) of his long-ill and mean-spirited wife have fallen in love. Both become murder suspects when the wife is poisoned. Lackluster mystery, based on a hit stage play. Original British title: THE LATE EDWINA BLACK. ▼

Obsession (1949) SEE: **Hidden Room, The**

Ocean's Eleven (1960) **C-127m.** ****½** D: Lewis Milestone. Frank Sinatra, Dean Martin, Sammy Davis, Jr., Peter Lawford, Angie Dickinson, Richard Conte, Cesar Romero, Patrice Wymore, Joey Bishop, Akim Tamiroff, Henry Silva, Ilka Chase, Norman Fell. Fanciful crime comedy about 11-man team headed by Danny Ocean (Sinatra) attempting to rob five Vegas casinos simultaneously. Entire Rat Pack's in it, but no one does much, including some surprise guests. There is a clever twist ending, though. Remade in 2001. Panavision. ▼▶

October (1928-Russian) **103m.** ******* D: Sergei Eisenstein, Grigori Alexandrov. Nikandrov, N. Popov, Boris Livanov. Brilliant reconstruction of the Russian Revolution contains some of Eisenstein's most striking use of montage, though most impressive sequences—such as the masterful massacre around the bridges of St. Petersburg—are in the film's first half. Based on John Reed's *Ten Days That Shook the World*, the film's alternate title. ▼▶

October Man, The (1947-British) **98m.** ******* D: Roy (Ward) Baker. John Mills, Joan Greenwood, Edward Chapman, Joyce Carey, Kay Walsh, Felix Aylmer, Juliet Mills. Stranger with history of mental disorders is suspected of murder and must prove innocence, even to himself. Strong character study and good local atmosphere enhance suspenseful mystery written by Eric Ambler. British running time 110m. ▼

October Moth (1959-British) **54m.** ***½** D: John Kruse. Lee Patterson, Lana Morris, Peter Dyneley, Robert Crawdon. Turgid melodrama set on lonely farm, with Morris trying to cope with dim-witted brother who has injured a passerby.

Odd Man Out (1947-British) **115m.** ******** D: Carol Reed. James Mason, Robert Newton, Kathleen Ryan, Robert Beatty, Cyril Cusack, F.J. McCormick, William Hartnell, Fay Compton, Denis O'Dea, Dan O'Herlihy. Incredibly suspenseful tale of Irish rebel leader hunted by police after daring robbery. Watch this one! Scripted by R. C. Sherriff and F. L. Green, from the latter's novel. Remade as THE LOST MAN. ▼▶

Odd Obsession (1959-Japanese) **C-96m.** ****½** D: Kon Ichikawa. Machiko Kyo, Ganjiro Nakamura, Tatsuya Nakadai, Junko Kano. Elderly, vain Nakamura tempts beautiful wife (Kyo) into an affair with his young doctor (Nakadai). Uneven soap opera; a few bright moments, but disappointing overall. Original running time 107m. Remade in Italy in 1984 as THE KEY, which is also this film's alternative title (a literal translation of the Japanese title, KAGI). Daieiscope. ▼

Odds Against Tomorrow (1959) **95m.** ******* D: Robert Wise. Harry Belafonte, Robert Ryan, Shelley Winters, Ed Begley, Gloria Grahame. A smorgasbord trio of "types" plots to rob an upstate N.Y. bank, but one of them (Belafonte) is black and another (Ryan) is a racist—one of those prime sociopath portrayals on which the actor held the patent. Tough, brutal, and a window to Wise's versatility, half a dozen years before he directed THE SOUND OF MUSIC. John Lewis did the jazz score and familiar faces turn up in small parts, including Wayne Rogers, Robert Earl Jones, Zohra Lampert, and a young Cicely Tyson as a bartender. Written by Nelson Gidding and Abraham Polonsky (who was blacklisted at the time; credit was properly awarded to him years later). ▼○▶

Odette (1950-British) **100m.** ******* D: Herbert Wilcox. Anna Neagle, Trevor Howard, Marius Goring, Peter Ustinov, Bernard Lee. Neagle is excellent in true story of Odette Churchill, undercover British agent imprisoned by Nazis during WW2.

Odongo (1956-British) **C-85m.** BOMB D: John Gilling. Rhonda Fleming, Macdonald Carey, Juma, Eleanor Summerfield, Francis De Wolff. Juvenile jungle flick about search for missing native boy. CinemaScope. ▶

Oedipus Rex (1957-Canadian) **C-87m.** ****½** D: Tyrone Guthrie. Douglas Rain, Douglas Campbell, Eric House, Eleanor Stuart. Restrained, professional rendering of Sophocles' Greek tragedy. ▼▶

Office Wife, The (1930) **58m.** ****½** D: Lloyd Bacon. Dorothy Mackaill, Lewis Stone, Natalie Moorhead, Hobart Bosworth, Joan Blondell, Blanche Frederici. Sexy secretary (Mackaill) at a publishing company sets a trap for her wealthy older boss (Stone), who resists her charms until he learns his young new bride (Moorhead) is cheating. Charmingly dated piece of "naughty" fluff, with sassy support by Blondell as Mackaill's impudent sister and Frederici in a bizarre bit as an ultramasculine, cigar-smoking authoress. ▶

Of Flesh and Blood (1962-French) **C-92m.** ****½** D: Christian Marquand. Robert Hossein, Renato Salvatori, Anouk Aimée, André Bervil, Jean Lefebvre. Murky account of passerby Salvatori having an affair with Aimée, involved with card-cheat-turned-murderer Hossein. Franscope.

Off Limits (1953) **87m.** ****½** D: George Marshall. Bob Hope, Mickey Rooney, Marilyn Maxwell, Eddie Mayehoff, Stanley Clements, Jack Dempsey, Marvin Miller, Tom Harmon, Carolyn Jones. Peppy but predictable comedy with fight manager Hope finding himself in the Army; he attempts to romance Maxwell (whose nephew, Rooney, wants Hope to train him as a boxer). ▼▶

Off the Record (1939) **71m.** ****½** D: James Flood. Pat O'Brien, Joan Blondell, Bobby Jordan, Alan Baxter, William Davidson, Morgan Conway, Clay Clement. Columnist Blondell and reporter husband O'Brien become guardians of delinquent Jordan after she writes an exposé of mobsters who use kids for a gambling racket. Plot thickens when the boy gets mixed up in his brother's jailbreak. Fairly entertaining B movie bogs down in sentimental domestic scenes. Dead End Kid Jordan goes solo here, but we do get David Gorcey (Leo's brother) and Cagney imitator extraordinaire Frankie Burke.

Of Human Bondage (1934) **88m.** ******* D: John Cromwell. Leslie Howard, Bette Davis, Frances Dee, Kay Johnson, Reginald Denny, Alan Hale, Reginald Owen. Smoothly filmed, well-acted version of W. Somerset Maugham's story of doctor Howard's strange infatuation with a vulgar waitress (Davis). Many find Davis' performance overdone, but by any standards it's powerfully impressive, and put her on the map in Hollywood. Howard, lovely Johnson, others are superb. Remade in 1946 and 1964. Also shown in computer-colored version. ▼○▶

Of Human Bondage (1946) **105m.** ****** D: Edmund Goulding. Paul Henreid, Eleanor Parker, Alexis Smith, Edmund Gwenn, Janis Paige, Patric Knowles, Henry Stephenson, Marten Lamont, Isobel Elsom, Una O'Connor. Henreid and Parker give it the old college try but are fatally miscast in this bowdlerized adaptation of Somerset Maugham's steamy novel about the sadomasochistic relationship between a club-footed artist/medical student and a sluttish waitress. Plush production can't compensate for the dearth of erotic heat, which was plentiful in the 1934 Bette Davis version.

Of Human Bondage (1964-British) **98m.** ****** D: Ken Hughes. Kim Novak, Laurence Harvey, Siobhan McKenna, Robert Morley, Roger Livesey, Nanette Newman, Brenda Fricker. Third and least successful filming of Maugham novel of doctor's passion for lowbrow waitress, marred by miscasting and general superficiality. ▼▶

Of Human Hearts (1938) **100m.** ****½** D: Clarence Brown. Walter Huston, James Stewart, Gene Reynolds, Beulah Bondi, Guy Kibbee, Charles Coburn, John Carradine, Ann Rutherford, Charley Grapewin, Gene Lockhart, Sterling Holloway, Ward Bond. Odd blend of potent 19th-century Americana and mile-high corn, in tale of dedicated preacher Huston who never established rapport with his son. When Abraham Lincoln (Carradine) lectures Stewart about neglecting his mother, it gets to be a bit much. ▼▶

Of Life and Love (1957-Italian) **103m.** ****½** D: Aldo Fabrizi, Luchino Visconti, Mario Soldati, Giorgio Pastina. Anna Magnani, Walter Chiari, Natale Cirino, Turi Pandolfini, Myriam Bru, Lucia Bose. Four satisfactory episodes, three of which are based on Pirandello tales; fourth is actual event in Magnani's life ("The Lapdog"). Actually distilled from two Italian episodic features from 1953 and 1954.

Of Love and Desire (1963) **C-97m.** ***½** D:

Richard Rush. Merle Oberon, Steve Cochran, Curt Jurgens, John Agar, Steve Brodie. Beautiful settings (including Oberon's lavish Mexican home) offset overwrought sexual drama of neurotic woman who plays with the affection of several men—including her own stepbrother.

Of Mice and Men (1939) 107m. **** D: Lewis Milestone. Lon Chaney, Jr., Burgess Meredith, Betty Field, Charles Bickford, Bob Steele, Noah Beery, Jr. Chaney gives best performance of his career as feeble-brained Lennie who, with migrant-worker Meredith, tries to live peacefully on ranch. John Steinbeck's morality tale remains intact in sensitive screen version. The film's action begins *before* the main title credits—an arty innovation for 1939. Script by Eugene Solow. Music by Aaron Copland. Remade in 1992 and for TV in 1968 and 1981. ▼●▶

O. Henry's Full House (1952) 117m. **½ D: Henry Hathaway, Howard Hawks, Henry King, Henry Koster, Jean Negulesco. Fred Allen, Anne Baxter, Charles Laughton, Marilyn Monroe, Gregory Ratoff, Jeanne Crain, Oscar Levant, Jean Peters, Richard Widmark, Farley Granger. Five varying stories by O. Henry, introduced by John Steinbeck; cast better than script. "The Clarion Call," "Last Leaf," "Ransom of Red Chief," "Gift of the Magi," and "Cop and the Anthem." ▶

Oh, Men! Oh, Women! (1957) C-90m. **½ D: Nunnally Johnson. Dan Dailey, Ginger Rogers, David Niven, Tony Randall, Barbara Rush. Often bouncy sex farce revolving around psychiatrist and his assorted patients. Randall's feature debut. CinemaScope. ▶

Oh, Mr. Porter! (1937-British) 85m. ***½ D: Marcel Varnel. Will Hay, Moore Marriott, Graham Moffatt, Sebastian Smith, Agnes Lauchlan, Percy Walsh. Delightful vehicle for British music hall comedian Hay and his usual screen sidekicks: toothless old codger Marriott and cheeky, chubby lad Moffatt. Hay plays an incompetent railway worker who is sent to a rundown station in Northern Ireland and winds up catching a gang of gunrunners posing as ghosts. Val Guest was one of the screenwriters, working from Frank Launder's story. ▶

Oh ... Rosalinda!! (1955-British) C-101m. **½ D: Michael Powell, Emeric Pressburger. Michael Redgrave, Ludmilla Tcherina, Anton Walbrook, Mel Ferrer, Dennis Price, Anthony Quayle, Annelise Rothenberger; singing voices of Sari Barabas, Alexander Young, Dennis Dowling, Walter Berry. Johann Strauss' opera *Die Fledermaus* is updated to contemporary Vienna but retains its elements of a masked ball, mistaken identity, flirtation, etc. Not entirely successful, but still stylish, witty, and colorful, as you'd expect from the team that brought you THE RED SHOES and TALES OF HOFFMAN. Redgrave, Quayle, and Rothenberger use their own singing voices, by the way. CinemaScope.

Oh, Sailor, Behave! (1930) 68m. ** D: Archie Mayo. (Ole) Olsen & (Chic) Johnson, Irene Delroy, Charles King, Lowell Sherman, Noah Beery, Lotti Loder, Charles Judels, Vivien Oakland. Archaic musical comedy set in Venice, where amorous King and Delroy are separated by a series of misunderstandings. Olsen and Johnson ("America's Craziest Clowns"), in their screen debut, add sporadic comedy relief, which is all a matter of taste. They also cowrote the script, based on Elmer Rice's play *See Naples and Die.* ▶

Oh, Susanna! (1936) 59m. *** D: Joseph Kane. Gene Autry, Smiley Burnette, Frances Grant, Earle Hodgins, Donald Kirke, Boothe Howard, The Light Crust Doughboys, Ed Peil, Sr. Gene is mistaken for outlaw Howard (and vice versa) in this fast-moving early Autry Western, the first to employ country music groups with regional radio fame. The Doughboys sing "Ride On, Vaquero" and Gene does "I'll Go Ridin' Down That Texas Trail" (which he wrote with Burnette). ▼▶

Oh! Susanna (1951) C-90m. ** D: Joseph Kane. Rod Cameron, Forrest Tucker, Adrian Booth, Chill Wills. Too much feuding between cavalry officers and too little real action mar this Western.

Oh, You Beautiful Doll (1949) C-93m. **½ D: John M. Stahl. June Haver, Mark Stevens, S. Z. Sakall, Charlotte Greenwood, Gale Robbins, Jay C. Flippen. Chipper period musical about song plugger who turns serious composer's works into popular songs. Based on true story of Fred Fisher. Songs include title tune, "Peg o' My Heart," "Dardanella."

Oil for the Lamps of China (1935) 97m. *** D: Mervyn LeRoy. Pat O'Brien, Josephine Hutchinson, Jean Muir, Lyle Talbot, Arthur Byron, John Eldredge, Henry O'Neill, Donald Crisp, Keye Luke. Dated but absorbing saga (from best-selling book by Alice Tisdale Hobart) about a man who dedicates his life to working in China for big oil company, which shows little regard for him in return. Hutchinson's role, as his dedicated wife, is particularly interesting today in light of her comments about a woman's place in a man's life ... while the film's foreword (and *deus ex machina* ending) indicates an uneasiness about attacking powerful oil companies too harshly! ▶

Okay America (1932) 78m. **½ D: Tay Garnett. Lew Ayres, Maureen O'Sullivan, Louis Calhern, Edward Arnold, Walter Catlett, Alan Dinehart, Henry Armetta. Ayres is good but hopelessly miscast as an embittered, hard-boiled newspaperman in the Walter Winchell vein. Promising at first

[501]

but doesn't maintain the punch of its opening sequences. Where is Lee Tracy when you really need him?

Okinawa (1952) 67m. ** D: Leigh Jason. Pat O'Brien, Cameron Mitchell, James Dobson, Richard Denning, Richard Benedict, Alvy Moore. Adequate programmer about men on a warship during the Pacific campaign of WW2.

Oklahoma! (1955) C-145m. ***½ D: Fred Zinnemann. Gordon MacRae, Shirley Jones, Charlotte Greenwood, Rod Steiger, Gloria Grahame, Eddie Albert, James Whitmore, Gene Nelson, Barbara Lawrence, Jay C. Flippen. Expansive film version of Rodgers and Hammerstein's landmark 1943 Broadway musical, filled with timeless songs (and the beautiful voices of MacRae and Jones to sing them) . . . plus a fine supporting cast led by incomparable Grahame as Ado Annie. Enough fine ingredients to make up for overlength of film. Songs include "Oh, What a Beautiful Mornin' " and show-stopping title tune. This was filmed in two versions, one in Todd-AO and the other in CinemaScope (made from entirely separate "takes"). Both appear on DVD: Todd-AO Roadshow version runs 148m. with overture, intermission/entr'acte, exit music; CinemaScope version runs 140m. ▼○◗

Oklahoma Annie (1952) C-90m. *½ D: R. G. Springsteen. Judy Canova, John Russell, Grant Withers, Allen Jenkins, Almira Sessions. Rambunctious Canova is involved with mopping up corruption in her Western town. ▼◗

Oklahoma Kid, The (1939) 80m. *** D: Lloyd Bacon. James Cagney, Humphrey Bogart, Rosemary Lane, Donald Crisp, Harvey Stephens, Charles Middleton, Ward Bond. Cagney's the hero, Bogey's the villain in this sturdy Western about a cowboy seeking redress for the lynching of his father. Classic scene has Cagney singing "I Don't Want to Play in Your Yard." ▼◗

Oklahoman, The (1957) C-80m. **½ D: Francis D. Lyon. Joel McCrea, Barbara Hale, Brad Dexter, Gloria Talbott, Verna Felton, Douglas Dick, Michael Pate. Town doc McCrea tries to keep Indian Pate from getting rooked out of his land. Pretty routine, though Talbott cultists may want to see her play an Indian maiden the same year she had the title role in DAUGHTER OF DR. JEKYLL. Laundry note: Hale wears the same outfit in a disturbingly high number of scenes. CinemaScope. ▼◗

Oklahoma Territory (1960) 67m. ** D: Edward L. Cahn. Bill Williams, Gloria Talbott, Ted de Corsia, Grant Richards, Walter Sande. Western concentrating on Williams' effort to find actual killer of local Indian agent. ◗

Oklahoma Woman, The (1956) 72m.

BOMB D: Roger Corman. Richard Denning, Peggie Castle, Cathy Downs, Touch (Mike) Connors, Tudor Owen, Richard (Dick) Miller. Grade Z Corman quickie Western about ex-con Denning attempting to stay clean but tangling instead with the title character, who is "queen of the outlaws." SuperScope.

Old Acquaintance (1943) 110m. *** D: Vincent Sherman. Bette Davis, Miriam Hopkins, Gig Young, John Loder, Dolores Moran, Phillip Reed, Roscoe Karns, Anne Revere. Well-matched stars of THE OLD MAID are reunited as childhood friends who evolve personal and professional rivalry that lasts 20 years. Davis is noble and Hopkins is bitchy in this entertaining film. John Van Druten and Lenore Coffee scripted, from the former's play. Remade as RICH AND FAMOUS.◗

Old Barn Dance, The (1938) 60m. *** D: Joseph Kane. Gene Autry, Smiley Burnette, Joan Valerie, Sammy McKim, Walt Shrum and His Colorado Hillbillies, The Stafford Sisters, The Maple City Four, Ivan Miller, Earle Dwire, Hooper Atchley, Carleton Young, Earle Hodgins. Horse trainers Gene and Smiley aid farmers who are being cheated by a company selling tractors and unwittingly get involved with a radio station owned by that same company. Autry's easygoing, bashful charm is on full display here, along with action and plenty of music. Roy Rogers (using the name Dick Weston) appears as a square-dance caller! ▼◗

Old Corral, The (1936) 57m. *** D: Joseph Kane. Gene Autry, Smiley Burnette, Hope (Irene) Manning, Cornelius Keefe, Lon Chaney, Jr., John Bradford, Oscar and Elmer, Sons of the Pioneers. Fearing for her life after she witnesses a Chicago gangland murder, Manning travels west and hides out in Turquoise City, where Gene is sheriff. Entertaining B Western is also historically important as one of three Autry films in which Roy Rogers also appears. ▼◗

Old Curiosity Shop, The (1935-British) 95m. ** D: Thomas Bentley. Hay Petrie, Elaine Benson, Ben Webster, Beatrix Thompson, Gibb McLaughlin, Lily Long. Eccentric Scots character actor Petrie is the very portrait of evil as Charles Dickens' avaricious Mr. Quilp, a moneylender and landlord who has lately narrowed his filthy, lustful gaze onto poor pure little Nell. Already the fifth adaptation of the 1841 classic, its villain-still-pursued-her histrionics play far too quaintly to take seriously today. Recommended only to those who have to read the book for school. ▼

Old Dark House, The (1932) 71m. ***½ D: James Whale. Boris Karloff, Melvyn Douglas, Charles Laughton, Gloria Stuart, Lilian Bond, Ernest Thesiger, Raymond Massey, Eva Moore. Outstanding melodrama (with tongue-in-cheek) gathers stranded travelers in mysterious Welsh household, where brutish butler Karloff is just one of many strange characters. A real gem, based on J. B. Priestley's *Benighted*; screenplay by Benn W. Levy and R. C. Sherriff. Remade in England in 1963. ▼●▌

Old Dark House, The (1963-British) **C-86m.** **½ D: William Castle. Tom Poston, Robert Morley, Janette Scott, Joyce Grenfell, Mervyn Johns, Fenella Fielding, Peter Bull. Uneven blend of comedy and chiller, with Poston at loose ends in eerie mansion. Released theatrically in b&w. Check out the 1932 version instead.▌

Old English (1930) **86m.** *** D: Alfred E. Green. George Arliss, Doris Lloyd, Harrington Reynolds, Reginald Sheffield, Betty Lawford, Murray Kinnell, Ivan Simpson, Leon Janney, Ethel Griffies. Aged shipping magnate Arliss, known as Old English, is deep in debt and wants to help the widow of his illegitimate son with money for her children, whom he loves. Ripe Arliss performance, full of stage business, in this entertaining star vehicle based on a John Galsworthy story and play. ▌

Old Fashioned Way, The (1934) **74m.** ***½ D: William Beaudine. W. C. Fields, Judith Allen, Joe Morrison, Baby LeRoy, Jack Mulhall, Oscar Apfel. Fields is in fine form managing troupe of old-time melodrama *The Drunkard,* encountering various troubles as they travel from town to town. Baby LeRoy has memorable scene throwing W. C.'s watch into a jar of molasses; also contains Fields' classic juggling routine.▌

Old Heidelberg SEE: **Student Prince in Old Heidelberg, The**

Old Hutch (1936) **80m.** ** D: J. Walter Ruben. Wallace Beery, Eric Linden, Cecilia Parker, Elizabeth Patterson, Robert McWade. Cute story of shiftless bum discovering $100,000, trying to use it without arousing suspicion. Filmed before in 1920 with Will Rogers as HONEST HUTCH.

Old Ironsides (1926) **111m.** *** D: James Cruze. Charles Farrell, Esther Ralston, Wallace Beery, George Bancroft, Charles Hill Mailes, Johnnie Walker. Elaborate, expansive hokum based on the American Merchant Marine's run-ins with Mediterranean pirates in the early 19th century. Full of rollicking, boisterous seamen—and in their midst, a prim leading lady and leading man. Subtle it ain't, but certainly entertaining, especially with Gaylord Carter's rousing organ score on the homevideo release. Boris Karloff has small role as a Saracen sailor.▼

Old Maid, The (1939) **95m.** *** D: Edmund Goulding. Bette Davis, Miriam Hopkins, George Brent, Donald Crisp, Jane Bryan, Louise Fazenda, James Stephenson, Jerome Cowan, William Lundigan, Rand Brooks, DeWolf (William) Hopper. Solid if subdued soap opera based on Zoe Akins play and Edith Wharton novel about rivalry

and sacrifice in the Old South, focusing on cousins Davis and Hopkins. Builds to a poignant finale. Exquisitely designed and detailed production. ▼●▌

Old Man and the Sea, The (1958) **C-86m.** *** D: John Sturges. Spencer Tracy, Felipe Pazos, Harry Bellaver. Well-intentioned but uneven parable of aging fisherman's daily battle with the elements. Tracy is the whole film, making the most of Hemingway's unfilmic story; Dimitri Tiomkin's expressive score won an Oscar. Remade as a TVM in 1990 with Anthony Quinn.▼●▌

Old Man Rhythm (1935) **75m.** **½ D: Edward Ludwig. Charles "Buddy" Rogers, George Barbier, Barbara Kent, Grace Bradley, Betty Grable, Eric Blore. Business tycoon Barbier goes back to college to keep an eye on his playboy son (Rogers) in this light, fluffy musical; songwriter Johnny Mercer appears as one of the students. ▌

Old San Francisco (1927) **88m.** **½ D: Alan Crosland. Dolores Costello, Warner Oland, Charles Emmett Mack, Josef Swickard, John Miljan, Anders Randolf, Sojin, Angelo Rossitto, Anna May Wong. Spanish flower Costello is abducted and enslaved by evil Oland, the czar of Chinatown's underworld, who is plotting to steal her family's land. Politically incorrect Asian stereotypes abound in this wildly melodramatic silent (from a story by Darryl Zanuck), with an impressively staged climax depicting the great San Francisco earthquake of 1906.▌

Old Spanish Custom, An (1936-British) **61m.** BOMB D: Adrian Brunel. Buster Keaton, Lupita Tovar, Esme Percy, Lyn Harding, Hilda Moreno. Depressing, bottom-of-the-barrel comedy, with Buster a wealthy yachtsman who docks in Spain and is duped by temptress Tovar. Only for terminally curious Keaton fans. Original title: THE INVADER.▼

Old West, The (1952) **61m.** *** D: George Archainbaud. Gene Autry, Pat Buttram, Gail Davis, Lyle Talbot, Louis Jean Heydt, House Peters, Sr., House Peters, Jr., Dick Jones. Gene is shot by a rival (Talbot), who sells horses to Davis' stagecoach line, and is nursed back to health by the new town parson (silent-film matinee idol Peters, Sr.). Entertaining Autry Western.▼▌

Old Yeller (1957) **C-83m.** *** D: Robert Stevenson. Dorothy McGuire, Fess Parker, Tommy Kirk, Kevin Corcoran, Jeff York, Beverly Washburn, Chuck Connors. Disney's first film about a boy and his dog, from Fred Gipson's popular novel, is still one of the best. Atmospheric recreation of farm life in 1869 Texas, where Kirk becomes attached to a yellow hunting dog. Sequel: SAVAGE SAM.▼●▌

Oliver Twist (1922) **77m.** *** D: Frank Lloyd. Jackie Coogan, Lon Chaney, Gladys Brockwell, George Siegmann, Esther Ralston. Entertaining silent version of the oft-filmed

Charles Dickens classic, geared as a vehicle for Coogan, who was then at the height of his juvenile stardom. Chaney, that master of makeup, is ideally cast as Fagin. ▼●▶

Oliver Twist (1933) 77m. ** D· William Cowen. Dickie Moore, Irving Pichel, William "Stage" Boyd, Doris Lloyd, Barbara Kent. Superficial, low-budget version of Dickens' story is mediocre by any standards, but pales particularly in comparison to the later British classic. ▼▶

Oliver Twist (1948-British) 116m. **** D: David Lean. Alec Guinness, Robert Newton, John Howard Davies, Kay Walsh, Francis L. Sullivan, Anthony Newley, Henry Stephenson. Superlative realization of Dickens tale of ill-treated London waif involved with arch-fiend Fagin (Guinness) and his youthful gang, headed by the Artful Dodger (Newley). Later musicalized as OLIVER! ▼●▶

Olympia (1936-German) 220m. **** D: Leni Riefenstahl. Two-part record of the 1936 Berlin Olympics, highlighted by truly eyepopping cinematography, camera movement, and editing. Of course, it's all supposed to be a glorification of the Nazi state. Various edited versions exist (some of which omit all footage of Hitler, who appears throughout the original print). ▼▶

Omaha Trail, The (1942) 62m. **½ D: Edward Buzzell. James Craig, Pamela Blake, Dean Jagger, Edward Ellis, Chill Wills, Donald Meek, Howard Da Silva, Henry (Harry) Morgan. Satisfying actioner concerning Craig's attempts to lay railroad tracks in the Old West while contending with ruthless ox train business tycoon Jagger and marauding Indians. A couple of songs are thrown in for good measure, one of them written by director Buzzell.

Omar Khayyam (1957) C-101m. **½ D: William Dieterle. Cornel Wilde, Debra Paget, John Derek, Raymond Massey, Michael Rennie, Yma Sumac, Sebastian Cabot. Childish but spirited costumer set in medieval Persia; cast defeated by juvenile script. VistaVision.▼

On Again—Off Again (1937) 68m. *½ D: Edward Cline. Bert Wheeler, Robert Woolsey, Marjorie Lord, Patricia Wilder, Esther Muir, Paul Harvey, Russell Hicks, George Meeker, Jack Carson. W&W are feuding operators of a pill factory who agree to settle their differences by having a wrestling match, with the winner taking control of the business and the loser becoming his servant for a year. One of the team's all-time worst. ▶

On an Island With You (1948) C-107m. **½ D: Richard Thorpe. Esther Williams, Peter Lawford, Ricardo Montalban, Jimmy Durante, Cyd Charisse, Xavier Cugat, Leon Ames, Marie Windsor. Splashy musical with Navy man Lawford working as technical advisor on movie star Williams' latest

film; he's hopelessly in love with her, but she's engaged to costar Montalban. Durante easily steals the show. ▼▶

On Approval (1943-British) 80m. *** D: Clive Brook. Beatrice Lillie, Clive Brook, Googie Withers, Roland Culver. Minor British gem showcasing the hilarious Bea Lillie as woman who decides to give her prospective husband a trial run, with unexpected results. Drawing-room comedy par excellence. Leading-man Brook also directed, produced, and cowrote script (from Frederick Lonsdale's play)—the only time he ever worked behind the camera! Filmed before in 1930. ▼●▶

On Borrowed Time (1939) 99m. *** D: Harold S. Bucquet. Lionel Barrymore, Cedric Hardwicke, Beulah Bondi, Una Merkel, Ian Wolfe, Phillip Terry, Eily Malyon. Engrossing fable of Death, Mr. Brink (Hardwicke), coming for grandpa Barrymore, finding himself trapped in tree by Lionel and grandson Bobs Watson. Engaging whimsy from the play by Lawrence Edward Watkin. ▼●▶

Once a Hero SEE: **It Happened in Hollywood**

Once a Thief (1950) 88m. ** D: W. Lee Wilder. June Havoc, Cesar Romero, Marie McDonald, Lon Chaney, Jr., Iris Adrian. OK little film of shoplifter Havoc and her tawdry romance with Romero.

Once a Thief (1965-U.S.-French) 107m. ** D: Ralph Nelson. Ann-Margret, Alain Delon, Van Heflin, Jack Palance, John Davis Chandler, Jeff Corey, Tony Musante. When young ex-con tries to go straight, he finds himself the pawn in another crime. Not at all interesting. Panavision. ▶

Once Before I Die (1965) C-97m. **½ D: John Derek. Ursula Andress, John Derek, Rod Lauren, Richard Jaeckel, Ron Ely. Brutal, offbeat story of band of American soldiers in Philippines during WW2, trying to survive Japanese attack. Andress is only woman in group, and you can guess the rest. ▼▶

Once in a Blue Moon (1936) 67m. *½ D: Ben Hecht, Charles MacArthur. Jimmy Savo, Nikita Balieff, Cecelia Loftus, Whitney Bourne, Edwina Armstrong, Sandor Szabo. Attempt by writer-producer-directors Hecht and MacArthur to create a stylized fable for Broadway comedian Savo falls flat; he doesn't register well on-screen, especially in this heavy-handed film about a family of Russian refugees who joins up with a traveling circus clown. Overbearing music score by George Antheil doesn't help. Cinematographer Lee Garmes is credited as associate director. Look for young Howard da Silva in his film debut.

Once in a Lifetime (1932) 91m. *** D: Russell Mack. Jack Oakie, Sidney Fox, Aline MacMahon, Russell Hopton, ZaSu Pitts, Louise Fazenda, Onslow Stevens, Gregory Ratoff. Stagebound but still hilarious adaptation of Kaufman-Hart play about a trio of connivers who take advantage of Hollywood's state of panic when talkies arrive by pretending to be vocal coaches. Oakie is great as a simpleton, Ratoff in his element as a bombastic studio chief. Reissue print runs 75m.

Once More My Darling (1949) **94m.** ****½** D: Robert Montgomery. Robert Montgomery, Ann Blyth, Jane Cowl, Taylor Holmes, Charles McGraw. Satisfying comedy of young girl infatuated with middle-aged movie star.

Once More, With Feeling (1960-British) **C-92m.** ****½** D: Stanley Donen. Yul Brynner, Kay Kendall, Maxwell Shaw, Mervyn Johns. Despite sparkling Kendall (her last film) as musical conductor Brynner's dissatisfied wife, this marital sex comedy fizzles. ▶

Once Upon a Honeymoon (1942) **117m.** ****½** D: Leo McCarey. Ginger Rogers, Cary Grant, Walter Slezak, Albert Dekker, Albert Basserman, Ferike Boros, Harry Shannon, Hans Conried. Strange but intriguing curio with status-seeking ex-burlesque queen Rogers marrying secret Nazi bigwig Slezak . . . and radio commentator Grant coming to her rescue. Some boring stretches do it in; however, the scenes in which the star duo are mistaken for Jews and almost sent to a concentration camp are fascinating. ▼●▶

Once Upon a Horse . . . (1958) **85m.** ****½** D: Hal Kanter. Dan Rowan, Dick Martin, Martha Hyer, Leif Erickson, Nita Talbot, John McGiver, David Burns, James Gleason. Oddball Western spoof runs hot and cold, with some nutty gags and enough spark to make it worth watching. Old-time Western stars Bob Steele, Kermit Maynard, Tom Keene, Bob Livingston appear briefly as themselves. CinemaScope.

Once Upon a Time (1944) **89m.** ****½** D: Alexander Hall. Cary Grant, Janet Blair, James Gleason, Ted Donaldson, Art Baker. Amusing comedy-fantasy of entrepreneur Grant promoting a dancing caterpillar; trivial fun. Based on a Norman Corwin radio play, from Lucille Fletcher short story. ▶

On Dangerous Ground (1952) **82m.** ******* D: Nicholas Ray. Ida Lupino, Robert Ryan, Ward Bond, Charles Kemper, Anthony Ross, Ed Begley, Ian Wolfe, Cleo Moore, Olive Carey. Effective mood-piece with hardened city cop Ryan softened by blind-girl Lupino, whose brother is involved in rural manhunt. Bernard Herrmann's score was reportedly his favorite work. Produced by John Houseman. ▼●▶

On Dress Parade (1939) **62m.** ****** D: William Clemens. Billy Halop, Leo Gorcey, Bobby Jordan, Huntz Hall, Gabriel Dell, Bernard Punsly, Frankie Thomas, Selmer Jackson, John Litel. Last of the official *Dead End Kids* movies sends the young punks off to military school where they're (unconvincingly) turned into squeaky-clean, well-behaved little cadets. Simple programmer; also known as THE DEAD END KIDS ON DRESS PARADE.

One Arabian Night SEE: **Sumurun**

One Big Affair (1952) **80m.** ****** D: Peter Godfrey. Evelyn Keyes, Dennis O'Keefe, Mary Anderson, Connie Gilchrist. On-location filming in Mexico highlights this lightweight romance yarn.

One Body Too Many (1944) **75m.** ****** D: Frank McDonald. Jack Haley, Jean Parker, Bela Lugosi, Blanche Yurka, Lyle Talbot, Douglas Fowley. Old dark house comedy about the reading of a will. Haley is carefree salesman mistaken for private eye, forced to solve caper. ▼▶

One Dangerous Night (1943) **77m.** ****½** D: Michael Gordon. Warren William, Marguerite Chapman, Eric Blore, Mona Barrie, Tala Birell, Margaret Hayes, Ann Savage, Thurston Hall, Fred Kelsey. Solid entry in *The Lone Wolf* series about a murdered blackmailing gigolo, with the Wolf suspected by both cops and crooks of the crime. Gerald Mohr, who later played the Lone Wolf, plays the gigolo here.

One Desire (1955) **C-94m.** ****½** D: Jerry Hopper. Anne Baxter, Rock Hudson, Julie Adams, Natalie Wood, Betty Garde. Baxter's strong performance as woman in love with gambler Hudson elevates standard soaper. ▶

One-Eyed Jacks (1961) **C-141m.** ******* D: Marlon Brando. Marlon Brando, Karl Malden, Pina Pellicer, Katy Jurado, Ben Johnson, Slim Pickens, Timothy Carey, Elisha Cook, Jr., Margarita Cordova. Fascinating but flawed psychological Western with outlaw Brando seeking revenge on former friend Malden, now a sheriff. Visually striking, and a rich character study, but overlong. Brando's only directorial effort. VistaVision. ▼●▶

One Fatal Hour SEE: **Two Against the World**

One Foot in Heaven (1941) **108m.** *****½** D: Irving Rapper. Fredric March, Martha Scott, Beulah Bondi, Gene Lockhart, Elisabeth Fraser, Harry Davenport, Laura Hope Crews, Grant Mitchell. Superior acting in honest, appealing story of minister and wife facing various problems as church life and 20th-century America clash. Very entertaining, with memorable scene of minister March going to his first movie (a William S. Hart silent). ▶

One Foot in Hell (1960) **C-90m.** ****½** D: James B. Clark, Alan Ladd, Don Murray, Dan O'Herlihy, Dolores Michaels, Barry Coe, Larry Gates, Karl Swenson. Ambitious but peculiar production of sheriff seeking retribution against small town for negligent death of his wife; cowritten by Aaron Spelling. CinemaScope.

One for the Book SEE: **Voice of the Turtle, The**

One Frightened Night (1935) 65m. **½ D: Christy Cabanne. Charley Grapewin, Mary Carlisle, Arthur Hohl, Wallace Ford, Lucien Littlefield, Regis Toomey, Hedda Hopper, Evalyn Knapp, Rafaela Ottiano. Fast-moving, intricately plotted little chiller about crusty old millionaire Grapewin, who wishes to give away his fortune so as to avoid a new inheritance tax. ▼

One Girl's Confession (1953) 74m. ** D: Hugo Haas. Cleo Moore, Hugo Haas, Glenn Langan, Russ Conway. Cleo steals from her loutish guardian, then serves jail sentence knowing the loot is waiting for her. Typical Hugo Haas production, with intriguing premise but flimsy development. Moore is presented as (unbelievably) chaste—but our first look at her is in an alluring low-cut bathing suit. Thanks, Hugo. ▶

One Good Turn (1954-British) 78m. ** D: John Paddy Carstairs. Norman Wisdom, Joan Rice, Shirley Abicair, William Russell, Thora Hird. Minor musical vehicle for man-on-the-street comedian Wisdom, putting forth such homey tunes as "Take a Step in the Right Direction." ●▶

One Heavenly Night (1931) 82m. ** D: George Fitzmaurice. Evelyn Laye, John Boles, Leon Errol, Lilyan Tashman, Hugh Cameron. Lesser Goldwyn musical features Laye as a Budapest flower girl posing as a famous singer in order to trap Count Boles. OK for fanciers of old-fashioned romantic nonsense. Elegant photography by Gregg Toland and George Barnes.

One Hour With You (1932) 80m. ***½ D: Ernst Lubitsch, George Cukor. Maurice Chevalier, Jeanette MacDonald, Genevieve Tobin, Roland Young, Charlie Ruggles. Chic romance of happily married couple upset by arrival of flirtatious Tobin. Chevalier is delightful as always, talking (and singing) directly to the camera. Remake of Lubitsch's 1924 THE MARRIAGE CIRCLE; started by Cukor, completed by Lubitsch with Cukor as his assistant. ●▶

One Hundred and One Dalmatians (1961) C-79m. *** D: Wolfgang Reitherman, Hamilton Luske, Clyde Geronimi. Voices of Rod Taylor, Lisa Davis, Cate Bauer, Ben Wright, Fred Worlock, J. Pat O'Malley, Betty Lou Gerson. Likable, low-key Disney cartoon feature set in England, about the theft and recovery of some adorable dalmatian puppies by a flamboyant villainess named Cruella De Vil. The story's told from a doggy point-of-view, which is just one ingredient of the film's great appeal. Followed 42 years later by a direct-to-video sequel. Remade in 1996. Later a Broadway musical. ▼●▶

One Hundred Men and a Girl (1937) 84m. ***½ D: Henry Koster. Deanna Durbin, Leopold Stokowski, Adolphe Menjou, Alice Brady, Eugene Pallette, Mischa Auer, Frank Jenks, Billy Gilbert. Superior blend of music and comedy as Deanna pesters conductor Stokowski to give work to her unemployed father and musician friends. Brimming with charm—and beautiful music, with Charles Previn's score earning an Oscar. ▼●

One in a Million (1936) 95m. *** D: Sidney Lanfield. Sonja Henie, Adolphe Menjou, Don Ameche, Ned Sparks, Jean Hersholt, The Ritz Brothers, Arline Judge, Borrah Minevitch and His Harmonica Rascals. Debut vehicle for skating star Henie was built around then-timely Winter Olympics. Sonja plays a competitor who may get in trouble by having compromised her amateur status. Still fun; fine supporting cast. ▼

One Last Fling (1949) 74m. ** D: Peter Godfrey. Alexis Smith, Zachary Scott, Douglas Kennedy, Ann Doran, Ransom Sherman, Veda Ann Borg, Jim Backus, Helen Westcott. Limp marital farce involving bored wife Smith, who's eager to return to work at wimpy husband Scott's music store . . . but he's planning to hire another woman.

One Man's Journey (1933) 72m. *** D: John S. Robertson. Lionel Barrymore, May Robson, Dorothy Jordan, Joel McCrea, Frances Dee, David Landau, Buster Phelps, Sam (Samuel S.) Hinds. Doctor Barrymore, who's experienced tough times in the big city, opens a practice in his rural hometown, where he heroically toils in obscurity while facing various life-altering crises. Potent drama about a man who chooses ethics over ambition. Remade as A MAN TO REMEMBER. ▶

One Man's Way (1964) 105m. *** D: Denis Sanders. Don Murray, Diana Hyland, Veronica Cartwright, Ian Wolfe, Virginia Christine, Carol Ohmart, William Windom. Tasteful fictionalized biography of Norman Vincent Peale, his religious convictions and preaching; Murray is earnest in lead role. ▼

One Million B.C. (1940) 80m. **½ D: Hal Roach, Hal Roach, Jr. Victor Mature, Carole Landis, Lon Chaney, Jr., John Hubbard, Mamo Clark, Jean Porter. Bizarre caveman saga told in flashback is real curio, made on a big scale. Excellent special effects—from prehistoric monsters to an erupting volcano—which have turned up as stock footage in countless cheapies. Longtime rumors that D. W. Griffith directed parts are not true. Remade in 1966 as ONE MILLION YEARS B.C.

One Minute to Zero (1952) 105m. ** D: Tay Garnett. Robert Mitchum, Ann Blyth, William Talman, Richard Egan, Charles McGraw, Margaret Sheridan, Eduard Franz. Romance and war combine uneasily in this muddled Korean War melodrama. Mitchum is a colonel attempting to do his job despite the intrusions of girlfriend Blyth, a United Nations envoy. ▼▶

One More River (1934) 90m. *** D: James Whale. Diana Wynyard, Colin Clive, Frank Lawton, Mrs. Patrick Campbell, Jane Wyatt, Reginald Denny, C. Aubrey Smith, Henry Stephenson, Lionel Atwill, Alan Mowbray. Heartfelt but dated drama chronicling a divorce: ruthless husband Clive accuses wife Wynyard of indiscretion with young Lawton. From John Galsworthy's last novel. Film debut of Jane Wyatt.

One More Spring (1935) 88m. *** D: Henry King. Janet Gaynor, Warner Baxter, Walter (Woolf) King, Jane Darwell, Roger Imhof, Grant Mitchell, Lee Kohlmar, Stepin Fetchit, Dick Foran, Rosemary Ames, John Qualen. Warm, heartfelt comedy-drama about two men and a woman who have fallen on tough times and camp out in Central Park, helping each other cope with the travails of daily existence during the Depression. Remarkably honest treatment of such subjects as bank failures, homelessness, poverty, and suicide, yet filled with good humor that holds out hope for the future. Based on Robert Nathan's novel.

One More Tomorrow (1946) 88m. ** D: Peter Godfrey. Ann Sheridan, Dennis Morgan, Jack Carson, Alexis Smith, John Loder, Jane Wyman, Reginald Gardiner. Light-comedy players flounder in reworking of Philip Barry's THE ANIMAL KINGDOM, about a wealthy playboy (Morgan) and a radical magazine photographer (Sheridan) who fall in love but *don't* get married—to their eventual regret.

One Mysterious Night (1944) 61m. *** D: Oscar (Budd) Boetticher. Chester Morris, Janis Carter, Richard Lane, William Wright, George E. Stone, Robert Williams, George McKay. Brisk and breezy *Boston Blackie* entry, with the capricious ex-thief jolted into action when he's accused of stealing a precious gem from a museum. Nineteen-year-old Dorothy Malone (billed as Maloney) appears in one of her first roles as Eileen. TV title: BOSTON BLACKIE'S APPOINTMENT WITH DEATH.▶

One Night at Susie's (1930) 62m. ** D: John Francis Dillon. Billie Dove, Douglas Fairbanks, Jr., Helen Ware, Tully Marshall, James Crane, John Loder. Chorus girl Dove kills a lecherous producer in self-defense and boyfriend Fairbanks takes the rap. His tough foster mother (Ware), who owns a boarding house for mobsters, makes sure Dove does what she has to do to get Fairbanks out . . . even if that means sleeping with the next sleazy producer! Ware steals the show in this creaky early-talkie melodrama.▶

One Night in Lisbon (1941) 97m. ** D: Edward H. Griffith. Fred MacMurray, Madeleine Carroll, Patricia Morison, Billie Burke, John Loder, Edmund Gwenn. Odd, overlong mix of espionage and comedy. Carroll falls for MacMurray after they meet

in a London air-raid shelter. They don't even get to Lisbon until late in the film!

One Night in the Tropics (1940) 82m. **½ D: A. Edward Sutherland. Allan Jones, Nancy Kelly, Bud Abbott, Lou Costello, Robert Cummings, Leo Carrillo, Mary Boland. Ambitious but unmemorable musical with songs by Jerome Kern, Oscar Hammerstein, and Dorothy Fields, from Earl Derr Biggers' gimmicky story "Love Insurance" (filmed before in 1919 and 1924). Abbott and Costello, in film debut, have secondary roles to Jones-Kelly-Cummings love triangle, but get to do a portion of their "Who's on First?" routine.▼▶

One Night of Love (1934) 84m. ***½ D: Victor Schertzinger. Grace Moore, Tullio Carminati, Lyle Talbot, Mona Barrie, Luis Alberni, Jessie Ralph. Classic musical, with an Oscar-winning Louis Silvers score, of aspiring opera star Moore and her demanding teacher Carminati. A delight from start to finish, and a must for music lovers; remains remarkably fresh and entertaining. Unquestionably Moore's best film.▼●

One Night With You (1948-British) 90m. ** D: Terence Young. Nino Martini, Patricia Roc, Bonar Colleano, Guy Middleton, Stanley Holloway, Miles Malleson, Christopher Lee. Diluted musical with socialite Roc intrigued by singer Martini.

' . . . . . . one of our aircraft is missing' (1942-British) 106m. ***½ D: Michael Powell, Emeric Pressburger. Godfrey Tearle, Eric Portman, Hugh Williams, Bernard Miles, Hugh Burden, Emrys Jones, Googie Withers, Joyce Redman, Pamela Brown, Peter Ustinov, Hay Petrie, Roland Culver, Robert Helpmann, John Longden. Thoughtful study of R.A.F. bomber crew who bail out over the Netherlands and seek to return to England. Powell and Pressburger scripted, from the latter's story. Powell makes an appearance as a dispatcher. Some U.S. prints run 82m.▼▶

One Potato, Two Potato (1964) 92m. ***½ D: Larry Peerce. Barbara Barrie, Bernie Hamilton, Richard Mulligan, Robert Earl Jones, Harry Bellaver, Faith Burwell, Tom Ligon. Frank study of interracial marriage, beautifully acted by Barrie and Hamilton. Perceptive script by Raphael Hayes and Orville H. Hampton.

One Rainy Afternoon (1936) 79m. **½ D: Rowland V. Lee. Francis Lederer, Ida Lupino, Roland Young, Hugh Herbert, Erik Rhodes, Mischa Auer. Silly but likable froth about a charming, impetuous young man who causes a stir by kissing a young woman in a movie theater. The song "Sweet Rendezvous" was written by Preston Sturges!▼▶

One Romantic Night (1930) 73m. **½ D: Paul L. Stein. Lillian Gish, Rod La Rocque, Conrad Nagel, Marie Dressler, O. P. Heggie, Albert Conti. Gish is charming in her first talkie as a princess who is wooed by two very different men. Dressler is great fun as her mother. Low-key but likable film based on Ferenc Molnár play; remade with Grace Kelly as THE SWAN. ▶

One Sunday Afternoon (1933) **69m. ***** D: Stephen Roberts. Gary Cooper, Fay Wray, Neil Hamilton, Frances Fuller, Roscoe Karns, Jane Darwell. Cooper is at boyish best in this original version of James Hagan's play about a turn-of-the-20th-century dentist and how his infatuation with a sexy vamp (Wray) who weds his rival almost ruins his marriage and his life. Touching and lovingly made piece of Americana, exuding period charm and atmosphere, though darker in tone than the two Warner Bros. remakes by Raoul Walsh: as THE STRAWBERRY BLONDE in 1941, then under the original title as a 1948 Technicolor musical. ▶

One Sunday Afternoon (1948) **C-90m. **½** D: Raoul Walsh. Dennis Morgan, Janis Paige, Don DeFore, Dorothy Malone, Ben Blue. Musical remake of the 1933 Gary Cooper feature (and 1941's THE STRAWBERRY BLONDE) set in 1910, about a dentist who wonders if he married the right girl; pleasant but nothing more. Attractive cast, unmemorable songs. ▶

One That Got Away, The (1958-British) **106m. ***** D: Roy (Ward) Baker. Hardy Kruger, Colin Gordon, Michael Goodliffe, Terence Alexander. Kruger gives sincere performance as Nazi prisoner in England who believes it is his duty to escape and get back to Germany. Many exciting moments. ▼▶

One Third of a Nation (1939) **79m. **½** D: Dudley Murphy. Sylvia Sidney, Leif Erickson, Myron McCormick, Hiram Sherman, Sidney Lumet, Iris Adrian, Byron Russell. Sidney is a poor girl yearning to escape from the N.Y.C. tenements; young Lumet is her troubled brother, Erickson an unknowing slumlord who falls for her. Still timely social document. ▼

1001 Arabian Nights (1959) **C-75m. **½** D: Jack Kinney. Voices of Jim Backus, Kathryn Grant (Crosby), Dwayne Hickman, Hans Conried, Herschel Bernardi, Alan Reed. Elaborate updating of Arabian Nights tales featuring nearsighted Mr. Magoo has a nice score, pleasing animation. ▼▶

1,000 Eyes of Dr. Mabuse, The (1960-West German-French-Italian) **105m. ***** D: Fritz Lang. Dawn Addams, Peter van Eyck, Gert Frobe, Wolfgang Preiss, Werner Peters, Andrea Checchi. Fast-paced, witty thriller, intricately plotted but crystal clear: using the secrets of the original Dr. Mabuse, a modern-day criminal genius blackmails the wealthy, resorting to murder as necessary. Lang's last film as director, marking a strong return to form. Beware of alternate versions still in circulation: THE SECRET

OF DR. MABUSE and THE DIABOLICAL DR. MABUSE. ▼▶

1000 Years from Now SEE: **Captive Women**

One Touch of Venus (1948) **81m. **½** D: William A. Seiter. Ava Gardner, Robert Walker, Dick Haymes, Eve Arden, Olga San Juan, Tom Conway. Young man in love with department-store window statue of Venus doesn't know what to do when she magically comes to life. Amusing, but misses the bull's-eye, despite its having been a hit on Broadway. Lovely Kurt Weill–Ogden Nash score includes "Speak Low." Also shown in computer-colored version. ▼▶

One, Two, Three (1961) **108m. ****** D: Billy Wilder. James Cagney, Horst Buchholz, Pamela Tiffin, Arlene Francis, Howard St. John, Hanns Lothar, Leon Askin, Ralf Wolter, Lilo Pulver. Hilarious Wilder comedy about Coke executive in contemporary West Berlin freaking out when the boss' visiting 17-year-old daughter secretly weds a Communist. Cagney is a marvel to watch in this machine-gun–paced comedy, his last film appearance until 1981's RAGTIME. Andre Previn's score makes inspired use of Khachaturian's "Sabre Dance." The script, by Wilder and I.A.L. Diamond, was inspired by a Ferenc Molnar one-act play. Red Buttons appears in an unbilled cameo. Panavision. ▼▶

One Way Passage (1932) **69m. ***½** D: Tay Garnett. Kay Francis, William Powell, Aline MacMahon, Warren Hymer, Frank McHugh, Herbert Mundin. Tender shipboard romance of fugitive Powell and fatally ill Francis, splendidly acted, with good support by MacMahon and McHugh as con artists. Robert Lord won an Oscar for his original story. Remade as TILL WE MEET AGAIN. ▶

One-Way Street (1950) **79m. **½** D: Hugo Fregonese. James Mason, Marta Toren, Dan Duryea, William Conrad, Jack Elam, King Donovan. Turgid crime drama chronicling what happens after doctor Mason strips hood Duryea of $200,000—and his moll (Toren). Look for Rock Hudson as a truck driver.

One-Way Ticket to Hell SEE: **Teenage Devil Dolls**

One Way to Love (1945) **83m. **** D: Ray Enright. Chester Morris, Janis Carter, Marguerite Chapman, Willard Parker. Pleasant programmer about two radio writers finding romance and new program ideas on cross-country train trip.

One Woman's Story SEE: **Passionate Friends, The**

One Wonderful Sunday (1947-Japanese) **108m. ***** D: Akira Kurosawa. Isao Numasaki, Chieko Nakahita, Ichiro Sugai, Midori Ariyama, Masao Shimizu. A Tokyo factory worker, disillusioned by the recent war, and his indefatigably optimistic fiancée, herself a war orphan, go out on a weekend date. How they fill what turns out to be a splendid day, though given limited funds, is the episodic, tightly time-constrained script's entire substance. Uplifting and compassionate. Original title: SUBARASHIKI NICHIYOBI. ▼▶

Onibaba (1964-Japanese) **103m. ***** D: Kaneto Shindô. Nobuko Otowa, Jitsuko Yoshimura, Kei Sato, Jukichi Uno. In war-torn medieval Japan, a widow and her mother-in-law ambush and kill soldiers to sell their armor, until the younger woman falls for one of them. Visceral, erotic, and genuinely creepy folk tale is not for the squeamish, but is expertly made, highlighted by stunning Tohoscope cinematography. ▼▶

Onionhead (1958) **110m. **** D: Norman Taurog. Andy Griffith, Felicia Farr, Walter Matthau, Erin O'Brien, Joe Mantell, Ray Danton, James Gregory, Joey Bishop, Roscoe Karns, Claude Akins, Peter Brown, Tige Andrews. Muddled mishmash with Griffith joining the Coast Guard pre-WW2 and becoming a ship's cook. Tries desperately to be a comedy, romance, and drama all at once, with elements of NO TIME FOR SERGEANTS and MISTER ROBERTS, but is only sentimental and silly. ▼▶

—Only Angels Have Wings (1939) **121m. ***½** D: Howard Hawks. Cary Grant, Jean Arthur, Richard Barthelmess, Rita Hayworth, Thomas Mitchell, Sig Ruman, John Carroll, Allyn Joslyn, Noah Beery, Jr. Quintessential Howard Hawks movie, full of idealized men and women (and what men and women!) in this look at relationships among mail pilots stationed in South America—and how things heat up when a showgirl (Arthur) is tossed into the stew. An important star-boosting showcase for Hayworth, too. Jules Furthman scripted, from a story by Hawks. ▼▶

Only the Best SEE: **I Can Get It for You Wholesale**

Only the French Can SEE: **French Cancan**

Only the Valiant (1951) **105m. **** D: Gordon Douglas. Gregory Peck, Barbara Payton, Ward Bond, Gig Young, Lon Chaney, Jr., Neville Brand, Jeff Corey. Unusually brutal Western tale of hard-bitten Army officer Peck assembling a detail of misfit cavalrymen to hold off rampaging Indians. ▼▶

Only Two Can Play (1962-British) **106m. ***** D: Sidney Gilliat. Peter Sellers, Mai Zetterling, Virginia Maskell, Richard Attenborough, Kenneth Griffith. Well-intentioned filming of Kingsley Amis novel *That Uncertain Feeling* (adapted by Bryan Forbes), striving for quick laughs rather than satire. Sellers is librarian flirting with society woman Zetterling. ▼

Only Yesterday (1933) **105m. ***** D: John M. Stahl. Margaret Sullavan, John Boles, Billie Burke, Reginald Denny, Edna May Oliver, Benita Hume. Though Boles is a

drag, Sullavan's performance in her screen debut is still luminous enough to carry this familiar, flashbacked unwed mother saga spanning from the end of WW1 to the Depression. Opening scenes, depicting effect of the stock market crash on a group of partying high-rollers, are extremely evocative but tend to overshadow the rest of the film.

On Moonlight Bay (1951) **C-95m. **½** D: Roy Del Ruth. Doris Day, Gordon MacRae, Billy Gray, Mary Wickes, Leon Ames, Rosemary DeCamp. Turn-of-the-20th-century, folksy musical based on Booth Tarkington's *Penrod* stories with tomboy (Day) and next door neighbor (MacRae) the wholesome young lovers. Sequel: BY THE LIGHT OF THE SILVERY MOON. ▼●▶

On Our Merry Way (1948) **107m. **** D: King Vidor, Leslie Fenton. Burgess Meredith, Paulette Goddard, Henry Fonda, James Stewart, Fred MacMurray, William Demarest, Dorothy Lamour, Victor Moore, Harry James, Eduardo Ciannelli, Dorothy Ford, Hugh Herbert. Silly multi-episode comedy, with a buoyant Meredith posing as an inquiring reporter and asking people what impact a baby has had on their life. Strained slapstick throughout. Protracted sequence, with Stewart and Fonda as laconic musician pals, was written by John O'Hara. Aka A MIRACLE CAN HAPPEN. ▼▶

On Stage Everybody (1945) **65m. **** D: Jean Yarbrough. Jack Oakie, Peggy Ryan, Johnny Coy, Otto Kruger, Esther Dale, Milburn Stone, Wallace Ford, Julie London, The King Sisters. Run-of-the-mill Universal B musical, with frantic Oakie helping to put on a big radio variety program.

On the Avenue (1937) **89m. ***** D: Roy Del Ruth. Dick Powell, Madeleine Carroll, Alice Faye, Ritz Brothers, Alan Mowbray, Billy Gilbert, Cora Witherspoon, Joan Davis, Sig Rumann. Tasteful, intelligent musical of socialite Carroll getting involved with stage star Powell. One good Irving Berlin song after another: "I've Got My Love To Keep Me Warm," "This Year's Kisses," "Let's Go Slumming," "The Girl on the Police Gazette." ▼▶

On the Beach (1959) **133m. ****** D: Stanley Kramer. Gregory Peck, Ava Gardner, Fred Astaire, Anthony Perkins, Donna Anderson, John Tate, Guy Doleman. Thoughtful version of Nevil Shute's novel about Australians awaiting effects of nuclear fallout from explosion that has depopulated the rest of the world. Good performances by all, including Astaire in his first dramatic role. Screenplay by John Paxton. Remade for cable TV in 2000. ▼●▶

On the Double (1961) **C-92m. ***** D: Melville Shavelson. Danny Kaye, Dana Wynter, Wilfrid Hyde-White, Margaret Rutherford, Diana Dors. Danny's resemblance to English general makes him valuable as a WW2 spy. At one point he does a Marlene Dietrich imitation! Repeats dual-identity gimmick from Kaye's earlier ON THE RIVIERA with equally entertaining results. Panavision. ▶

On the Fiddle SEE: **Operation Snafu**

On the Isle of Samoa (1950) **65m.** *½ D: William Berke. Jon Hall, Susan Cabot, Raymond Greenleaf, Henry Marco. Sloppy little story of Hall finding love with native girl, inspiring him to clear up his shady past.

On the Loose (1951) **78m.** *½ D: Charles Lederer. Joan Evans, Melvyn Douglas, Lynn Bari, Robert Arthur, Hugh O'Brian. Lurid melodrama of teen Evans, who's alienated from her self-absorbed parents and finds herself awash in adolescent angst. Pretty awful, but a relic of its era.

On the Old Spanish Trail (1947) **C-75m.** **½ D: William Witney. Roy Rogers, Tito Guízar, Jane Frazee, Andy Devine, Estelita Rodriguez, Charles McGraw, Fred Graham, Bob Nolan and the Sons of the Pioneers. Roy joins the Sons' destitute tent show to ensure its success and comes up against the show's manager (McGraw), who is secretly running a robbery ring. Fairly entertaining, with flair from Guízar and a wild, stunt-laden stagecoach chase. ▼▶

On the Riviera (1951) **C-90m.** *** D: Walter Lang. Danny Kaye, Gene Tierney, Corinne Calvet, Marcel Dalio, Jean Murat. Bouncy musicomedy with Danny in dual role as entertainer and French military hero. "Ballin' the Jack," other songs in lively film. Gwen Verdon is one of chorus girls. Remake of Maurice Chevalier's FOLIES BERGÈRE and also THAT NIGHT IN RIO. ▶

On the Threshold of Space (1956) **C-98m.** **½ D: Robert D. Webb. Guy Madison, Virginia Leith, John Hodiak, Dean Jagger, Warren Stevens. Capable cast merely bridges the span between sequences of astronaut endurance tests and other space-flight maneuvers. CinemaScope.

On the Town (1949) **C-98m.** **** D: Gene Kelly, Stanley Donen. Gene Kelly, Frank Sinatra, Vera-Ellen, Betty Garrett, Ann Miller, Jules Munshin, Alice Pearce, Florence Bates. Three sailors have 24 hours to take in the sights and sounds of N.Y.C. Exuberant MGM musical, innovatively shot on location all over the City, isn't much in terms of plot and discards some of the best songs from the Betty Comden–Adolph Green–Leonard Bernstein show on which it's based . . . but it's still terrific entertainment. Highlight: "New York, New York." Oscar winner for Roger Edens and Lennie Hayton's musical scoring. An impressive directing debut for Kelly and Donen. ▼▶

On the Waterfront (1954) **108m.** **** D: Elia Kazan. Marlon Brando, Karl Malden, Lee J. Cobb, Rod Steiger, Pat Henning, Eva Marie Saint, Leif Erickson, Tony Galento, John Hamilton, Nehemiah Persoff. Budd Schulberg's unflinching account of N.Y.C. harbor unions (suggested by articles by Malcolm Johnson), with Brando unforgettable as misfit, Steiger his crafty brother, Cobb his waterfront boss, and Saint the girl he loves. That classic scene in the back of a taxicab is just as moving as ever. Winner of eight Oscars: Best Picture, Director, Actor (Brando), Supporting Actress (Saint), Story & Screenplay, Cinematography (Boris Kaufman), Art Direction-Set Decoration (Richard Day), and Editing (Gene Milford). Leonard Bernstein's music is another major asset. Film debuts of Saint, Martin Balsam, Fred Gwynne, and Pat Hingle. Adapted as a Broadway show decades later. ▼▶

On Top of Old Smoky (1953) **59m.** ** D: George Archainbaud. Gene Autry, Smiley Burnette, Gail Davis, Grandon Rhodes, Sheila Ryan, Kenne Duncan, Cass County Boys. Optician and rock collector Rhodes harasses Davis because her land contains valuable isinglass. Enter Gene . . . Standard fare, with the ending a particular letdown. Gene sings the title tune and duets with Smiley on Hank Williams' "I Hang My Head and Cry." ▼

On Trial (1954-French) **70m.** ** D: Julien Duvivier. Madeleine Robinson, Daniel Gelin, Eleonora Rossi-Drago, Charles Vanel, Anton Walbrook, Jacques Chabassol. Chabassol, son of D.A. Vanel, investigates conviction of Gelin, discovering disparity between justice and truth; well-intentioned film gone astray.

On With the Show (1929) **C-103m.** *½ D: Alan Crosland. Betty Compson, Arthur Lake, Sally O'Neil, Joe E. Brown, Louise Fazenda, Ethel Waters, William Bakewell, Sam Hardy, Lee Moran, Wheeler Oakman. Warner Bros.' answer to MGM's BROADWAY MELODY depicts the troubled out-of-town tryouts of Broadway-bound *The Phantom Sweetheart*. Clunky backstage musical in two-color Technicolor boasts a leading lady who doesn't do her own singing or dancing. Waters introduces "Am I Blue," but we also have to listen to "Lift the Juleps to Your Two Lips." ▶

On Your Toes (1939) **94m.** **½ D: Ray Enright. Vera Zorina, Eddie Albert, Frank McHugh, Alan Hale, James Gleason, Donald O'Connor. Long-winded backstage story about jealousy and attempted murder has little to do with George Abbott's Broadway hit; even the Rodgers and Hart songs are gone, relegated to background music! Fortunately, Zorina's dancing of "Slaughter on Tenth Avenue" remains, with choreography by George Balanchine.

Open City (1945-Italian) **105m.** **** D: Roberto Rossellini. Aldo Fabrizi, Anna Magnani, Marcello Pagliero, Maria Michi, Vito Annicchiarico, Nando Bruno, Harry Feist. Classic Rossellini account of Italian underground movement during Nazi occupation of Rome; powerful moviemaking gem with excellent performances from a memorable cast. Cowritten by Rossellini,

Federico Fellini, and Sergio Amidei. Aka ROME, OPEN CITY. The first in Rossellini's war trilogy, followed by PAISAN and GERMANY YEAR ZERO. ▼◐◗

Operation Amsterdam (1959-British) **105m.** **½ D: Michael McCarthy. Peter Finch, Eva Bartok, Tony Britton, Alexander Knox, Malcolm Keen. Standard wartime suspense fare as British expedition tries to sneak a cache of diamonds out of Holland before Nazis can get to them. ▼◗

Operation Bikini (1963) **83m.** ** D: Anthony Carras. Tab Hunter, Frankie Avalon, Eva Six, Scott Brady, Gary Crosby, Jim Backus. Occasionally perky cast livens tame WW2 narrative of attempt to destroy sunken treasure before enemy grabs it. Some color sequences. ◗

Operation C.I.A. (1965) **90m.** **½ D: Christian Nyby. Burt Reynolds, Kieu Chinh, Danielle Aubry, John Hoyt, Cyril Collack. Burt attempts to thwart an assassination in Saigon. Neat little actioner, and an intriguing look at a Vietnam of politics and spies, where innocent old men and children die. ◗

Operation Conspiracy (1955-British) **69m.** *½ D: Joseph Sterling. Philip Friend, Mary Mackenzie, Leslie Dwyer, Allan Cuthbertson, John G. Heller. Timid little espionage film involving a former British major (Friend), whose involvement with Mackenzie during WW2 resulted in his failure to nab a spy. Will that mistake be rectified a decade later? Will you care? Released in the U.S. in 1957. Original British title: CLOAK WITHOUT DAGGER.

Operation Crossbow (1965) **C-116m.** ***½ D: Michael Anderson. George Peppard, Sophia Loren, Trevor Howard, Tom Courtenay, Jeremy Kemp, Anthony Quayle, John Mills, Sylvia Syms, Richard Todd, Lilli Palmer. Fine "impossible mission" tale of small band of commandos out to destroy Nazi secret missile stronghold during WW2. Sensational ending, and the pyrotechnics are dazzling. Scripted by Robert Imrie (Emeric Pressburger), Derry Quinn, and Ray Rigby. Retitled THE GREAT SPY MISSION. Panavision. ▼◐◗

Operation Disaster SEE: **Morning Departure**

Operation Eichmann (1961) **93m.** **½ D: R. G. Springsteen. Werner Klemperer, Ruta Lee, Donald Buke, Barbara Turner, John Banner. Fairly intriguing account of the Nazi leader's postwar life and his capture by Israelis. ◗

Operation Haylift (1950) **75m.** ** D: William Berke. Bill Williams, Ann Rutherford, Jane Nigh, Tom Brown. Minor account of Air Force assisting farmers to save stranded cattle during snowstorm. ◗

Operation Mad Ball (1957) **105m.** ** D: Richard Quine. Jack Lemmon, Kathryn Grant (Crosby), Mickey Rooney, Ernie Kovacs, Arthur O'Connell, James Darren, Roger Smith. Weak service comedy about crafty soldiers planning wild party off base. Dull stretches, few gags. O'Connell comes off best. ◗

Operation Pacific (1951) **111m.** *** D: George Waggner. John Wayne, Patricia Neal, Ward Bond, Scott Forbes. Overzealous submariner Wayne is ultradedicated to his Navy command; the WW2 action scenes are taut, and Neal makes a believable love interest. ▼◗

Operation Petticoat (1959) **C-124m.** ***½ D: Blake Edwards. Cary Grant, Tony Curtis, Dina Merrill, Gene Evans, Arthur O'Connell, Richard Sargent, Virginia Gregg, Robert F. Simon, Gavin MacLeod, Madlyn Rhue, Marion Ross, Nicky Blair. Hilarious comedy about submarine captain Grant who's determined to make his injured ship seaworthy again, and con artist Curtis who wheels and deals to reach that goal. Some truly memorable gags; Grant and Curtis are a dynamite team in this happy film. Remade for TV in 1977. ▼◐◗

Operation Secret (1952) **108m.** ** D: Lewis Seiler. Cornel Wilde, Steve Cochran, Phyllis Thaxter, Karl Malden, Dan O'Herlihy Tame WW2 actioner involving a traitor in midst of Allied division. ◗

Operation Snafu (1961-British) **97m.** **½ D: Cyril Frankel. Alfred Lynch, Sean Connery, Cecil Parker, Stanley Holloway, Alan King, Wilfrid Hyde-White, Eric Barker, Kathleen Harrison. Sluggish WW2 account of two buddies becoming heroes unintentionally; most capable cast. Retitled: OPERATION WARHEAD. Originally titled ON THE FIDDLE. ◗

Operation Snatch (1962-British) **83m.** ** D: Robert Day. Terry-Thomas, George Sanders, Lionel Jeffries, Jackie Lane, Lee Montague. Fitfully funny satire involving British attempt to keep "their flag flying" on Gibraltar during WW2.

Operation Warhead SEE: **Operation Snafu**

Operation X (1950-British) **79m.** ** D: Gregory Ratoff. Edward G. Robinson, Peggy Cummins, Richard Greene, Nora Swinburne. Heady yarn with Robinson overly ambitious businessman forgetting his scruples. Original title: MY DAUGHTER JOY.

Operator 13 (1934) **86m.** **½ D: Richard Boleslavsky. Marion Davies, Gary Cooper, Katharine Alexander, Jean Parker, Ted Healy, Russell Hardie, The Four Mills Brothers, Sidney Toler. Davies plays an actress who's recruited as a Union spy during the Civil War; she spends the first half of the film in blackface disguise, the second half falling in love with Confederate officer Cooper. Absurd but entertaining. ◗

Opposite Sex, The (1956) **C-117m.** *** D: David Miller. June Allyson, Joan Collins, Dolores Gray, Ann Sheridan, Ann Miller, Leslie Nielsen, Jeff Richards, Agnes Moorehead, Charlotte Greenwood, Joan Blondell, Sam Levene, Alice Pearce, Barbara Jo Allen (Vera Vague), Carolyn Jones, Alan Marshal, Dick Shawn, Jim Backus, Harry James, Art Mooney, Dean Jones. Well-heeled musical remake of Clare Boothe Luce's THE WOMEN has stellar cast, but still pales next to brittle original (Shearer, Crawford, Russell, etc.). Major difference: music and men appear in this expanded version. CinemaScope.▼●)

Orchestra Wives (1942) **98m. **½ D: Archie Mayo. George Montgomery, Ann Rutherford, Glenn Miller and his Band, Lynn Bari, Carole Landis, Cesar Romero, Virginia Gilmore, Mary Beth Hughes, The Nicholas Brothers, Jackie Gleason, Henry (Harry) Morgan. Hokey storyline (with hotshot trumpeter Montgomery impetuously marrying moony-eyed fan Rutherford) serves as a nice showcase for Miller's band, and features such hits as "Serenade in Blue," "At Last," and "I've Got a Gal in Kalamazoo," featuring Tex Beneke, The Modernaires, and a snazzy dance routine by The Nicholas Brothers. That's young Jackie Gleason as the band's bass player . . . and look fast for Dale Evans as Rutherford's soda-fountain pal.▼●)

Orchid for the Tiger, An (1965-French-Spanish-Italian) **C-85m. *** D: Claude Chabrol. Roger Hanin, Margaret Lee, Michel Bouquet, Roger Dumas, Micaela Cendali, Carlos Casaravilla, Georges Rigaud. Stolen shipments of gold and uranium lead French secret agent The Tiger (Hanin) to Latin America, where he discovers a group of ex-Nazis plotting a revolution. Chabrol has a cameo as a scientist in this droll and entertaining follow-up to THE TIGER LIKES FRESH BLOOD.

Orders Are Orders (1954-British) **78m. ** D: David Paltenghi. Margot Grahame, Maureen Swanson, Peter Sellers, Tony Hancock, Sidney James. Hancock as befuddled lieutenant is best item in this slapstick yarn of movie company using an Army barracks for headquarters. Based on a 1932 play, filmed once before.▼●)

Orders to Kill (1958-British) **93m. **½ D: Anthony Asquith. Eddie Albert, Paul Massie, Lillian Gish, James Robertson Justice. American undercover agent Massie gladly accepts an assignment to kill a Paris lawyer with suspected Nazi ties—then meets and grows to like his future victim. Low-key psychological study with a memorable Gish cameo. Screenplay by Paul Dehn.

Ordet. (1955-Danish) **125m. **** D: Carl Dreyer. Henrik Malberg, Emil Hass Christensen, Preben Lerdorff Rye. Two rural families, at odds with each other over religious differences, are forced to come to grips with their children's love for each other. Arguably Dreyer's greatest film, but certainly the movies' final word on the struggle between conventional Christianity

and more personalized religious faith. Truly awe-inspiring, with a never-to-be-forgotten climactic scene. Based on a play by Kaj Munk, filmed before in 1943.▼●)

Oregon Passage (1957) **C-80m. **½ D: Paul Landres. John Ericson, Lola Albright, Toni Gerry, Edward Platt, Judith Ames, H. M. Wynant, John Shepodd, Walter Barnes. Standard cavalry vs. Indians adventure, with Ericson chasing elusive warrior Black Eagle (Wynant) while clashing with martinet Platt, who's married to Ericson's flirty ex-flame Albright. Fine location filming in Oregon's picturesque Deschutes National Forest is slow-moving film's major asset. CinemaScope.●)

Oregon Trail, The (1959) **C-86m. ** D: Gene Fowler, Jr. Fred MacMurray, William Bishop, Nina Shipman, Gloria Talbott, Henry Hull, John Carradine, John Dierkes, Elizabeth Patterson, James Bell. Dandified New York reporter MacMurray travels west with an 1846 wagon train to get a story on the British-American dispute over the Oregon Territory. Low-budget Western with many "outdoor" scenes economically filmed on a soundstage in front of an embarrassingly obvious "distant-hills-and-sky" backdrop, but the climactic Indian attack scene is worth the wait. CinemaScope.●)

Organizer, The (1963-Italian) **126m. *** D: Mario Monicelli. Marcello Mastroianni, Annie Girardot, Renato Salvatori, Bernard Blier. Serious look at labor union efforts in Italy, with Mastroianni giving low-keyed performance in title role.▼●)

Oriental Dream SEE: **Kismet** (1944)

Orphans of the Storm (1921) **125m. *** D: D. W. Griffith. Lillian Gish, Dorothy Gish, Joseph Schildkraut, Morgan Wallace, Lucille LaVerne, Sheldon Lewis, Frank Puglia, Creighton Hale, Monte Blue, Louis Wolheim. Griffith's epic about sisters cruelly separated, one blind and raised by thieves, one innocent and plundered by lecherous aristocrats. Implausible plot segues into French Revolution, with lavish settings and race-to-the-rescue climax. For all its creaky situations, and extreme length, still dazzling. Based on a 19th-century French play, *The Two Orphans*, which was filmed before in 1915 and again in 1933 and 1955.▼●)

Orpheus (1950-French) **95m. *** D: Jean Cocteau. Jean Marais, Francois Perier, Maria Casarés, Marie Dea, Juliette Greco, Roger Blin. Compelling cinematic allegory set in modern times with poet Marais encountering Princess of Death, exploring their mutual fascination. Heavy-handed at times, but still quite special. Remade by Jacques Demy as PARKING. Original French running time: 112m. Original French title: ORPHÉE.▼)

Osaka Elegy (1936-Japanese) **71m. *** D: Kenji Mizoguchi. Isuzu Yamada, Seiichi Takegawa, Chiyoko Okura, Shinpachiro

Asaka, Benkei Shiganoya, Yôko Umemura. Early Mizoguchi gem deals with big-city life in Japan and its corrupting effect on an innocent young girl. She becomes her boss' mistress in order to help her debt-ridden family but falls into prostitution when she is fired. Moving and highly cinematic critique of an oppressive society and the subordination of women. ▼▶

Oscar Wilde (1960-British) **96m.** ******* D: Gregory Ratoff. Robert Morley, Phyllis Calvert, John Neville, Ralph Richardson, Dennis Price, Alexander Knox. Morley is ideally cast as famed 19th-century playwright and wit, in film that focuses on his traumatic trials and eventual conviction for sodomy. Released at the same time as THE TRIALS OF OSCAR WILDE with Peter Finch.

O'Shaughnessy's Boy (1935) **88m.** ****½** D: Richard Boleslawski. Wallace Beery, Jackie Cooper, Spanky McFarland, Henry Stephenson, Leona Maricle, Sara Haden. Sentimental tale of Beery searching for his son, taken from him by cruel wife.

O.S.S. (1946) **107m.** ******* D: Irving Pichel. Alan Ladd, Geraldine Fitzgerald, Patric Knowles, Richard Benedict, Richard Webb, Don Beddoe, Onslow Stevens. Brisk WW2 espionage film; Ladd is part of the Office of Strategic Services team sent to demolish France's railroad—and one key tunnel. ▼

Ossessione (1942-Italian) **140m.** *****½** D: Luchino Visconti. Massimo Girotti, Clara Calamai, Juan deLanda, Elio Marcuzzo. Visconti's first feature triggered the great era of Italian neorealism, transplanting James Cain's *The Postman Always Rings Twice* quite successfully to Fascist Italy; however, as an unauthorized version of the book, it was not permitted to be shown in the U.S. until 1975. Heavy going at times, but fascinating nonetheless. Filmed earlier in France, twice later in the U.S. ▼▶

Othello (1922-German) **80m.** ******* D: Dimitri Buchowetzki. Emil Jannings, Werner Krauss, Lya de Putti, Ica von Lenkeffy, Theodor Loos, Friedrich Kühne. Shakespeare's oft-filmed, age-old epic of jealousy and intrigue in 16th-century Venice is impressive (although markedly abridged from the original), with Jannings and particularly Krauss offering towering performances as a blindly trusting Othello and duplicitous Iago. Von Lenkeffy is mostly decorative as Desdemona. ▼▶

Othello (1952-Italian) **92m.** *****½** D: Orson Welles. Orson Welles, Micheál MacLiammoir, Suzanne Cloutier, Robert Coote, Michael Lawrence, Fay Compton, Doris Dowling. Riveting, strikingly directed version of the Shakespeare play with Welles in the title role, lied to by Iago (MacLiammoir) into thinking that wife Desdemona

(Cloutier) has been unfaithful. Shot, incredibly, between 1949 and 1952, because of budget difficulties; one of the most fascinating (and underrated) attempts at Shakespeare ever filmed. Joseph Cotten appears as a Senator, Joan Fontaine as a Page. Reconstructed (with its music score rerecorded) for 1992 reissue. Aka THE TRAGEDY OF OTHELLO: THE MOOR OF VENICE. ▼▶

Othello (1965-British) **C-166m.** ******** D: Stuart Burge. Laurence Olivier, Frank Finlay, Maggie Smith, Joyce Redman, Derek Jacobi, Edward Hardwicke, Mike Gambon, John McEnery. Brilliant transferral to the screen of Shakespeare's immortal story of the Moor of Venice. Burge directed the filming, Olivier staged the production. Panavision. ▼▶

Other Love, The (1947) **95m.** ****½** D: Andre de Toth. Barbara Stanwyck, David Niven, Richard Conte, Maria Palmer, Joan Lorring, Gilbert Roland, Richard Hale, Lenore Aubert. Classical pianist Stanwyck, suffering from an unnamed disease, develops a relationship with her doctor (Niven) while being tempted by freewheeling race car driver Conte. Not convincing, but worth seeing for Stanwyck's strong performance. Title on-screen is ERICH MARIA REMARQUE'S THE OTHER LOVE. ▶

Other Men's Women (1931) **70m.** ****½** D: William A. Wellman. Grant Withers, Mary Astor, Regis Toomey, James Cagney, Joan Blondell. Love triangle set in the world of railroad men; interesting melodrama, dated in some ways, but vivid in its atmosphere, with great action finale. Cagney and Blondell have supporting roles. ▶

Other Woman, The (1954) **81m.** BOMB D: Hugo Haas. Hugo Haas, Cleo Moore, Lance Fuller, Lucille Barkley, Jack Macy, John Qualen. Typical Hugo Haas fare involving a girl's plot for revenge on her former boss.

Our Betters (1933) **83m.** ****½** D: George Cukor. Constance Bennett, Gilbert Roland, Charles Starrett, Anita Louise, Alan Mowbray, Minor Watson, Violet Kemble Cooper. Dated but enjoyable film of Somerset Maugham drawing-room comedy about British lord marrying rich American girl. Costars Bennett and Roland later married in real life.

Our Blushing Brides (1930) **104m.** ****½** D: Harry Beaumont. Joan Crawford, Anita Page, Dorothy Sebastian, Robert Montgomery, Raymond Hackett, John Miljan, Hedda Hopper, Edward Brophy, Albert Conti. Level-headed department-store worker Crawford and flighty roommates Page and Sebastian try to nab rich husbands. Crawford shines in this otherwise unconvincing drama. ▶

Our Daily Bread (1934) **74m.** ****½** D: King Vidor. Karen Morley, Tom Keene, John Qualen, Barbara Pepper, Addison Richards, Harry Holman. Landmark experiment by always innovative filmmaker Vidor, who stepped outside the studio system to make this bold, back-to-the-soil drama about communal living. Unfortunately, the acting—especially by leading man Keene—is so pedestrian as to sabotage the film. Climactic irrigation sequence is justly famous, however.▼●▶

Our Dancing Daughters (1928) 83m. *** D: Harry Beaumont. Joan Crawford, Johnny Mack Brown, Dorothy Sebastian, Nils Asther, Anita Page, Kathlyn Williams, Edward Nugent. One of the best Jazz Age silents, with absurdly melodramatic story: flapper Joan loses Johnny to Anita Page, who's been pushed into marriage against her will. Crystallization of the Roaring '20s. Silent film with synchronized music track (and even an occasional bit of off-screen dialogue).▼●▶

Our Girl Friday SEE: **Adventures of Sadie, The**

Our Hearts Were Growing Up (1946) 83m. **½ D: William D. Russell. Gail Russell, Diana Lynn, Brian Donlevy, James Brown, Bill Edwards, William Demarest. Follow-up to enjoyable OUR HEARTS WERE YOUNG AND GAY doesn't match it, with girls on their own at Princeton.

Our Hearts Were Young and Gay (1944) 81m. *** D: Lewis Allen. Gail Russell, Diana Lynn, Charlie Ruggles, Dorothy Gish, James Brown, Bill Edwards, Beulah Bondi. Extremely pleasant fluff from Cornelia Otis Skinner's book, detailing her travels to Europe during 1920s with her girlfriend Emily Kimbrough. Sequel: OUR HEARTS WERE GROWING UP.

Our Hospitality (1923) 74m. **** D: Buster Keaton, Jack Blystone. Buster Keaton, Natalie Talmadge, Joe Keaton, Joe Roberts. Buster goes to the South to claim a family inheritance, and falls in love with the daughter of a longtime rival clan. Sublime silent comedy, one of Buster's best, with a genuinely hairraising finale. Incidentally, Buster married his leading lady in real life.▼●▶

Our Little Girl (1935) 63m. **½ D: John Robertson. Shirley Temple, Rosemary Ames, Joel McCrea, Lyle Talbot, Erin O'Brien-Moore. Usual Temple plot of Shirley bringing separated parents McCrea and Ames together again. Also shown in computer-colored version.▼

Our Man in Havana (1960-British) 107m. **½ D: Carol Reed. Alec Guinness, Burl Ives, Maureen O'Hara, Ernie Kovacs, Noel Coward, Ralph Richardson, Jo Morrow. Weak satirical spy spoof, adapted by Graham Greene from his novel. Guinness is vacuum cleaner salesman who becomes British secret agent in Cuba. CinemaScope.

▶

Our Miss Brooks (1956) 85m. **½ D: Al Lewis. Eve Arden, Gale Gordon, Nick Adams, Robert Rockwell, Richard Crenna,

Don Porter, Jane Morgan. Fairly amusing feature based on beloved TV series has Arden's Brooks trying to snag Rockwell's Mr. Boynton and interest Adams in journalism. Crenna's screeching serenade, "It's Magic," is a high point.▼▶

Our Modern Maidens (1929) 75m. *** D: Jack Conway. Joan Crawford, Rod La Rocque, Douglas Fairbanks, Jr., Anita Page, Josephine Dunn, Edward Nugent, Albert Gran. Entertaining silent jazz-age saga about a young "modern" (Crawford) who disdains conventional morality and tries to help the career of her fiancé (Fairbanks) by coming on to worldly diplomat La Rocque. Special treat for film buffs: Doug Jr. does impressions of John Barrymore, John Gilbert, and his own father! This late-silent release has a synchronized music score, with crowd noises and sound effects. Crawford and Fairbanks were married in real life at this time.▼●▶

Our Relations (1936) 74m. *** D: Harry Lachman. Stan Laurel, Oliver Hardy, Alan Hale, Sidney Toler, Daphne Pollard, Betty Healy, James Finlayson, Arthur Housman, Iris Adrian, Lona Andre. Stan and Ollie get into snowballing comedy of errors with their long-lost twins. Lots of fun; best scenes in Hale's beer garden.▼●

Our Town (1940) 90m. ***½ D: Sam Wood. William Holden, Martha Scott, Frank Craven, Fay Bainter, Beulah Bondi, Thomas Mitchell, Guy Kibbee, Stuart Erwin. Sensitive adaptation of Thornton Wilder's Pulitzer Prize–winning play about small New England town with human drama and conflict in every family. Splendid score by Aaron Copland and production design by William Cameron Menzies. Screenplay by Wilder, Harry Chandlee, and Frank Craven. Craven, Doro Merande, Arthur Allen, and Scott (in her film debut) recreate their Broadway roles.▼▶

Our Very Own (1950) 93m. **½ D: David Miller. Ann Blyth, Farley Granger, Jane Wyatt, Donald Cook, Ann Dvorak, Natalie Wood, Martin Milner. Melodramatic account of Blyth's shock upon discovering she's an adopted child.▼

Our Vines Have Tender Grapes (1945) 105m. ***½ D: Roy Rowland. Edward G. Robinson, Margaret O'Brien, James Craig, Frances Gifford, Agnes Moorehead, Jackie "Butch" Jenkins, Morris Carnovsky. Excellent view of American life in Wisconsin town with uncharacteristic Robinson as O'Brien's kind, understanding Norwegian father.▼▶

Out All Night (1933) 68m. ** D: Sam Taylor. ZaSu Pitts, Slim Summerville, Laura Hope Crews, Shirley Grey, Alexander Carr, Shirley Temple. OK film from long-run teaming of Pitts and Summerville; this time, Slim is dominated by his mother (Crews); she's not pleased when he falls in love with ZaSu.

Outcast (1937) **77m.** ******* D: Robert Florey. Warren William, Karen Morley, Lewis Stone, Jackie Moran, John Wray, Esther Dale, Christian Rub, Virginia Sale. Somber and compelling drama about a doctor who is acquitted of killing a patient. He takes refuge in a small town, but the dead woman's sister-in-law tracks him down and stirs up trouble, leading to a powerful conclusion. William is good in rare sympathetic role and Stone is marvelous as a wise old country lawyer in a moving tale of redemption, written by Dore Schary and Doris Malloy.

Outcast, The (1954) **C-90m.** ****½** D: William Witney. John Derek, Joan Evans, Jim Davis, Catherine McLeod, Ben Cooper. Simply told Western of Derek battling to win his rightful inheritance.▼

Outcast, The (1962-Japanese) **118m.** *****½** D: Kon Ichikawa. Raizo Ichikawa, Shiho Fujimura, Hiroyuki Nagato, Rentaro Mikuni. Schoolteacher Ichikawa hides his identity as member of an outcast class until a writer he greatly respects is murdered. Intense drama is well made, fascinating.

Outcast of the Islands (1951-British) **102m.** ******* D: Carol Reed. Ralph Richardson, Trevor Howard, Robert Morley, Wendy Hiller, Kerima, George Coulouris, Wilfrid Hyde-White. Compelling adaptation of Joseph Conrad story set on Malayan island, where a desperate, misguided man turns to crime and soon becomes the object of massive manhunt. Screenplay by William Fairchild. Good job all around. Some prints run 94m.

Outcasts of Poker Flat, The (1937) **68m.** ****½** D: Christy Cabanne. Preston Foster, Jean Muir, Van Heflin, Virginia Weidler, Margaret Irving, Frank M. Thomas, Si Jenks, Dick Elliott, Al St. John, Bradley Page, Monte Blue, Billy Gilbert. Flavorful, well-acted Western based on two Bret Harte stories about the relationships of gambler Foster, teacher Muir, and preacher Heflin in a California gold mining town in the 1850s. Oft-filmed tale was done by John Ford in 1919 and remade in 1952.

Outcasts of Poker Flat, The (1952) **81m.** ****** D: Joseph M. Newman. Anne Baxter, Miriam Hopkins, Dale Robertson, Cameron Mitchell, John Ridgely. Obvious, uninspired remake of Bret Harte tale of social rejects trapped together in cabin during snowstorm. ❿

Outcry, The SEE: **Il Grido**

Outlaw, The (1943) **116m.** ******* D: Howard Hughes. Jane Russell, Jack Buetel, Walter Huston, Thomas Mitchell, Mimi Aguglia, Joe Sawyer. Notorious "sex Western" (and Russell's ballyhooed screen debut) is actually compelling—if offbeat—story of Billy the Kid, with principal honors going to Huston as Doc Holliday. Filmed in 1941 and directed mostly by Howard Hawks, though Hughes' interest in Russell's bosom is more

than evident. Some prints run 95m. and 103m.▼❿

Outlaw and His Wife, The (1917-Swedish) **73m.** *****½** D: Victor Sjostrom. Victor Sjostrom, Edith Erastoff, John Ekman, Nils Arehn, Jenny Tschernichin-Larsson. Stunningly filmed love story set in 19th-century Iceland concerning an outlaw who goes to work on a farm and falls in love with the wealthy widow who owns it. Pursued by the law, the two flee to the mountains for a brief period of happiness. A landmark of Swedish cinema, this beautifully made silent drama uses the environment with great subtlety and power, and features a fine lead performance by the director. ▼

Outlaw's Daughter, The (1954) **C-75m.** ***½** D: Wesley Barry. Bill Williams, Kelly Ryan, Jim Davis, George Cleveland, Elisha Cook, Jr. Tired B-movie fare about the title character (Ryan), offspring of the notorious James Dalton, and her involvement with a thief-murderer (Williams) and a marshal (Davis).

Outlaws Is Coming, The (1965) **89m.** ****½** D: Norman Maurer. The Three Stooges, Adam West, Nancy Kovack, Mort Mills, Don Lamond, Emil Sitka, Joe Bolton, Henry Gibson. The Stooges' last feature is one of their best, with some sharp satire and good Western atmosphere as the boys, their cowardly friend (West), and Annie Oakley (Kovack) combat an army of gunslingers and a genteel crook. Local TV kiddie-show hosts cast as outlaws, Gibson as a hip Indian.▼❿

Outlaws of the Desert (1941) **67m.** ***½** D: Howard Bretherton. William Boyd, Andy Clyde, Brad King, Duncan Renaldo, Jean Phillips, Forrest Stanley. Bar 20 trio accompanies horse breeder and family to sands of Arabia, where they buy mounts from a sheik. Producer Harry Sherman relocated the Hopalong Cassidy adventures "from their traditional western background" to . . . the Middle East! Dull (and unbelievable) story renders other shortcomings (obvious interiors for exteriors) meaningless. Hoppy demonstrates previously unsuspected fluency in Arabic.▼❿

Outlaw's Son (1957) **89m.** ****** D: Lesley Selander. Dane Clark, Ben Cooper, Lori Nelson, Ellen Drew, Eddie Foy III. Clark is most earnest in modest Western about outlaw and the son he deserted years before. ❿

Outlaw Stallion, The (1954) **C-64m.** ***½** D: Fred F. Sears. Phil Carey, Dorothy Patrick, Billy Gray, Roy Roberts, Gordon Jones. Programmer of horse thieves conning ranch woman and her son to get their herd.

Outlaw Territory (1953) **C-79m.** ****½** D: John Ireland, Lee Garmes. Macdonald Carey, Joanne Dru, John Ireland, Don Haggerty, Peter Ireland, Frank Ferguson. Carey is hired killer who runs afoul of marshal Ireland, and arouses the interest of cafe-owner Dru, against her better judgment. (Ireland and Dru were married in real life.) Routine Western shot in 3-D; original title: HANNAH LEE.▼

Out of the Blue (1947) **84m.** **½ D: Leigh Jason. Virginia Mayo, George Brent, Turhan Bey, Ann Dvorak, Carole Landis, Hadda Brooks. Naive Brent is in trouble when far-from-innocent young woman is discovered unconscious in his apartment; fluffy fun. Dvorak is a delight in an offbeat role.▼●

Out of the Clouds (1957-British) **C-88m.** ** D: Michael Relph, Basil Dearden. Anthony Steel, James Robertson Justice, Gordon Harker, Bernard Lee, Megs Jenkins. Work and play among commercial pilots; nothing special.

Out of the Fog (1941) **93m.** *** D: Anatole Litvak. Ida Lupino, John Garfield, Thomas Mitchell, Eddie Albert, George Tobias, Leo Gorcey, John Qualen, Aline MacMahon. Fine filmization of Irwin Shaw play *The Gentle People*, with racketeer Garfield terrorizing Brooklyn fishermen Qualen and Mitchell—and falling in love with the latter's daughter (Lupino). Scripted by Robert Rossen, Jerry Wald, and Richard Macauley. ❘

Out of the Frying Pan SEE: **Young and Willing**

Out of the Past (1947) **97m.** ***½ D: Jacques Tourneur. Robert Mitchum, Jane Greer, Kirk Douglas, Rhonda Fleming, Richard Webb, Steve Brodie, Virginia Huston, Paul Valentine, Dickie Moore. Mitchum finds he can't escape former life when one-time employer (gangster Douglas) and lover (Greer) entangle him in web of murder and double-dealings. Classic example of 1940s film noir, with dialogue a particular standout. Script by Geoffrey Homes (Daniel Mainwaring), from his novel *Build My Gallows High*. Remade as AGAINST ALL ODDS. Also shown in computer-colored version.▼●❘

Out of this World (1945) **96m.** **½ D: Hal Walker. Eddie Bracken, Veronica Lake, Diana Lynn, Cass Daley, Parkyakarkus, Donald MacBride, Florence Bates, Gary, Philip, Dennis and Lindsay Crosby. Bracken becomes pop crooner (with a very familiar-sounding voice); a cute idea mercilessly padded with loud musical specialties by Daley, Lynn, and guest stars.

Out on Probation SEE: **Daddy-O**

Outpost in Malaya (1952-British) **88m.** **½ D: Ken Annakin. Claudette Colbert, Jack Hawkins, Anthony Steel, Jeremy Spencer. Mostly about marital disharmony on a rubber plantation. Original title: PLANTER'S WIFE.

Outpost in Morocco (1949) **92m.** ** D: Robert Florey. George Raft, Marie Windsor, Akim Tamiroff, John Litel, Eduard Franz. Cardboard adventure yarn with French Foreign Legionnaire Raft attempting to quell tribal revolt, becoming romantically involved with emir's daughter Windsor (who looks to be as Moroccan as Maureen O'Hara).▼❘

Outrage (1950) **75m.** **½ D: Ida Lupino. Mala Powers, Tod Andrews, Robert Clarke, Raymond Bond, Lillian Hamilton, Hal March, Jerry Paris. Innocent young Powers is sexually molested and then further victimized by her gossipy, narrow-minded neighbors. The scenario's sugary optimism—specifically relating to a sympathetic preacher—is much too pat, but Lupino (who also coscripted) deserves an A for effort in tackling a then-touchy theme.

Outrage, The (1964) **97m.** **½ D: Martin Ritt. Paul Newman, Edward G. Robinson, Claire Bloom, Laurence Harvey, William Shatner, Albert Salmi. Western remake of RASHOMON is pretentious fizzle, with Newman hamming it as Mexican bandit who allegedly rapes Bloom while husband Harvey stands by. Robinson as philosophical narrator is best thing about film. Also shown in computer-colored version. Panavision.▼❘

Outriders, The (1950) **C-93m.** ** D: Roy Rowland. Joel McCrea, Arlene Dahl, Barry Sullivan, Claude Jarman, Jr., Ramon Novarro, James Whitmore. Standard account of Reb soldiers trying to capture gold shipment for Confederate cause. ❘

Outsider, The (1961) **108m.** *** D: Delbert Mann. Tony Curtis, James Franciscus, Bruce Bennett, Gregory Walcott, Vivian Nathan. Thoughtful biopic with Curtis giving one of his best performances as a reluctant American hero: Ira Hamilton Hayes, the Pima Indian who was one of the marines to raise the U.S. flag at Iwo Jima. Hayes' plight is also recounted in FLAGS OF OUR FATHERS.

Outside the Law (1930) **76m.** *½ D: Tod Browning. Mary Nolan, Edward G. Robinson, Owen Moore, Rockcliffe Fellowes, Delmar Watson. When Moore arrives in California to rob a bank, local crook Robinson demands they split 50-50. Half the movie is set in the apartment hideout of Moore and moll Nolan and blends their bickering, a bratty kid neighbor who barges in and out, Nolan's reformation by a kite's shadow that looks like a cross, the story of the birth of Jesus, and the shooting of a cop! The longest 76 minutes on Earth. Remake of a 1920 film also directed by Browning.

Outside the Law (1956) **81m.** *½ D: Jack Arnold. Ray Danton, Leigh Snowden, Grant Williams, Onslow Stevens. Half-baked yarn of Danton proving his worth by snaring counterfeiters.

Outside the Wall (1950) **80m.** **½ D: Crane Wilbur. Richard Basehart, Dorothy Hart, Marilyn Maxwell, Signe Hasso, Harry Morgan. Excellent cast carries off this tale of former convict snafuing a robbery syndicate.

Outward Bound (1930) **84m.** *** D: Robert Milton. Leslie Howard, Douglas Fairbanks, Jr., Helen Chandler, Beryl Mercer, Alec B. Francis, Alison Skipworth, Montagu Love. Illicit lovers Fairbanks and Chandler, "half-way" persons who have attempted suicide, find themselves aboard a mysterious ocean liner. Well-acted allegory, from Sutton Vane's play. Remade as BETWEEN TWO WORLDS.

Out West With the Hardys (1938) **84m.** ****½** D: George B. Seitz. Lewis Stone, Mickey Rooney, Cecilia Parker, Fay Holden, Ann Rutherford, Sara Haden, Don Castle, Virginia Weidler, Gordon Jones. Adventures on a ranch where a friend of the family is having water rights problems. OK *Andy Hardy* outing. **)**

Out West with the Peppers (1940) **62m.** ***½** D: Charles Barton. Edith Fellows, Dorothy Ann Seese, Dorothy Peterson, Charles Peck, Tommy Bond, Bobby Larson, Ronald Sinclair, Victor Kilian, Pierre Watkin. When Ma Pepper (Peterson) gets sick, the family heads west to stay with her sister and grumpy lumberjack husband, whose cold heart is quickly melted by the cloying clan. Saccharine third entry in the four-film series. Followed by FIVE LITTLE PEPPERS IN TROUBLE.

Overcoat, The (1959-Russian) **73m.** ******** D: Alexei Batalov. Roland Bykov, Y. Tolubeyev. Charming, fully realized rendition of Gogol's oft-filmed story about lowly clerk and the effect a new overcoat has on his life. Runs full gamut of emotions in simple, moving style; not shown here until 1965.▼

Over-Exposed (1956) **80m.** ****** D: Lewis Seiler. Cleo Moore, Richard Crenna, Isobel Elsom, Raymond Greenleaf, Shirley Thomas (Constance Towers), Jack Albertson, Jeanne Cooper. Hard-bitten drifter (Moore, vacationing from Hugo Haas) stumbles onto a job as an apprentice photographer, then heads to N.Y.C. to start life anew. Begins promisingly but collapses into a predictable tale of corruption and blackmail. Moore and Crenna make a highly unlikely couple. **)**

Overlanders, The (1946-Australian-British) **91m.** *****½** D: Harry Watt. Chips Rafferty, John Nugent Hayward, Daphne Campbell, John Fernside, Jean Blue, Peter Pagan, Helen Grieve. Riveting account of Australian cattle drovers, headed by indomitable Rafferty, bringing their herds across the continent during WW2. Based on actual events. Simple, straightforward, and enormously entertaining.▼

Overland Pacific (1954) **C-73m.** ****** D: Fred F. Sears. Jock Mahoney, Peggie Castle, Adele Jergens, William Bishop. Mahoney is staunch railroad investigator trying to round up the white men behind Indian attacks on the track-layers. Forgettable programmer.

Overland Stage Raiders (1938) **55m.** ****½** D: George Sherman. John Wayne, Ray Corrigan, Max Terhune, Louise Brooks, Anthony

Marsh, Ralph Bowman (John Archer). In modern-day Western, mining company shipping gold on buses is plagued by robberies until the Three Mesquiteers get involved and arrange transportation by air. Train chase and fistfights are among the other action highlights, with a fast pace masking some sloppy direction. Silent star and cult favorite Brooks sports different look (minus bangs) in her final film appearance.▼**)**

Over My Dead Body (1942) **68m.** ****½** D: Malcolm St. Clair. Milton Berle, Mary Beth Hughes, Reginald Denny, Frank Orth, William Davidson. Berle gives peppery performance in farfetched yarn about amateur sleuth who accidentally frames himself for murder.

Over the Goal (1937) **64m.** ****** D: Noel M. Smith. June Travis, William Hopper, Johnnie Davis, Gordon Oliver, William Harrigan, Willard Parker, Eric Stanley, Raymond Hatton, Eddie Anderson, Hattie McDaniel. College alum leaves his entire estate to his alma mater, with one proviso: they must beat their chief rival on the gridiron. Will football star Hopper play in the Big Game, even though one more knee injury may cripple him for life? Typical rah-rah 1930s college football shenanigans. Try to spot Jane Wyman, Carole Landis, and Marie Wilson as coeds.

Over the Hill (1931) **89m.** ****½** D: Henry King. Mae Marsh, James Dunn, Sally Eilers, Edward Crandall, Claire Maynard, Olin Howland, Joan Peers. Story of a mother who sacrifices everything for her children, who go their separate ways as adults, unaware of her terrible fate. This story was an old warhorse even in 1931, but by the time Mae utters the film's closing line it's hard not to shed a tear. Based on a pair of famous poems by Will Carleton; filmed before in 1920.

Over the Moon (1937-British) **C-78m.** ***½** D: Thornton Freeland, William K. Howard. Merle Oberon, Rex Harrison, Ursula Jeans, Robert Douglas, Louis Borell, Zena Dare, David Tree, Elisabeth Welch, Wilfrid Hyde-White, Evelyn Ankers. Disappointingly bad comedy of country girl squandering inherited fortune. Interesting cast cannot save clinker. Beware black-and-white prints.

Overture to Glory (1940) **77m.** ****½** D: Max Nosseck. Moishe Oysher, Helen Beverly, Florence Weiss, Baby Winkler, Maurice Krohner, Lazar Freed, Benjamin Fishbein, Jack Mylong Münz. Yiddish-language variation of THE JAZZ SINGER, with Oysher a Vilna cantor who forsakes his synagogue and community to sing opera. Oysher's voice is the entire show.▼

Over 21 (1945) **102m.** ******* D: Charles Vidor. Irene Dunne, Alexander Knox, Charles Coburn, Jeff Donnell, Lee Patrick, Phil Brown. Zesty comedy of middle-aged

Knox trying to survive in officer's training for WW2 service, with help of wife Dunne; from Ruth Gordon's play. ▶

Ox-Bow Incident, The (1943) 75m. **** D: William A. Wellman. Henry Fonda, Dana Andrews, Mary Beth Hughes, Anthony Quinn, William Eythe, Henry (Harry) Morgan, Jane Darwell, Frank Conroy, Harry Davenport. The irony and terror of mob rule are vividly depicted in this unforgettable drama about a lynch mob taking the law into its own hands, despite protests of some level-headed onlookers. Based on Walter Van Tilburg Clark's book; superb script by Lamar Trotti. ▼▶

Oyster Princess, The (1919-German) 60m. *** D: Ernst Lubitsch. Victor Janson, Ossi Oswalda, Harry Liedtke, Julius Falkenstein, Max Kronert, Kurt (Curt) Bois. Spoiled daughter (Oswalda) of the filthy-rich American Oyster King (Janson) is irate because a rival magnate's offspring has just married a count. Complications arise when the King asks a matchmaker to hook his daughter up with a prince. Delightfully nonsensical Lubitsch farce, scripted by the director and Hanns Kräly. ▶

Pacific Destiny (1956-British) C-97m. ** D: Wolf Rilla. Denholm Elliott, Susan Stephen, Michael Hordern, Gordon Jackson, Inia Te Wiata. Boring (but true) story of Arthur Grimble, who serves in South Seas for British Colonial service circa 1912, and tries to quell native disputes. CinemaScope.

Pacific Liner (1939) 75m. ** D: Lew Landers. Chester Morris, Wendy Barrie, Victor McLaglen, Barry Fitzgerald, Alan Hale, Halliwell Hobbes, Cy Kendall, Paul Guilfoyle. Formula programmer focusing on breakout of epidemic and mutiny aboard a ship; cast is better than the material.

Pacific Rendezvous (1942) 76m. ** D: George Sidney. Lee Bowman, Jean Rogers, Mona Maris, Carl Esmond, Paul Cavanagh, Blanche Yurka. Bowman is a Navy code expert who helps break up a spy ring while getting amorous with Rogers. Lackluster propaganda piece weighed down by too many romantic distractions. Remake of 1935's RENDEZVOUS, which was set in WW1.

Pack Train (1953) 57m. ** D: George Archainbaud. Gene Autry, Smiley Burnette, Gail Davis, Kenne Duncan, Sheila Ryan, Tom London, Harry Lauter. Gene leads a pack train bringing supplies to starving settlers and comes up against greedy storekeeper Duncan and cohort Ryan. Conventional Autry vehicle. ▶

Pack Up Your Troubles (1932) 68m. **½ D: George Marshall, Ray McCarey. Stan Laurel, Oliver Hardy, Mary Carr, James Finlayson, Charles Middleton, Grady Sutton, Billy Gilbert. Daffy duo are drafted during WW1; after some Army shenani-

gans they try to locate relatives of late pal's daughter. Good fun. ▼▶

Pack Up Your Troubles (1939) 75m. ** D: H. Bruce Humberstone. The Ritz Brothers, Jane Withers, Lynn Bari, Joseph Schildkraut, Stanley Fields, Leon Ames. Watch the Ritz Brothers' opening routine, then forget the rest of this WW1 hodgepodge, especially when Jane is focus of the film.

Paddy O'Day (1936) 73m. **½ D: Lewis Seiler. Jane Withers, Pinky Tomlin, Rita Cansino (Hayworth), Jane Darwell, George Givot, Francis Ford, Vera Lewis, Louise Carter, Russell Simpson, Michael Visaroff. Jane plays a plucky Irish girl who befriends a Russian family while sailing to America, where she learns her mother has died. Too much time given over to mediocre musical numbers and Givot's malapropisms, but Jane is fun to watch and young Rita is beautiful. ▶

Pagan, The (1929) 78m. **½ D: W. S. Van Dyke. Ramon Novarro, Renée Adorée, Donald Crisp, Dorothy Janis. Van Dyke's follow-up to WHITE SHADOWS IN THE SOUTH SEAS stars matinee idol Novarro as a carefree island native who incurs the wrath of evil white trader Crisp when he falls in love with the supposedly devout man's adopted "daughter" (after singing "Pagan Love Song" about a thousand times). Flowery silent romance with synchronized musical sequences, sumptuously photographed in the Tuamotu Islands. ▶

Pagan Love Song (1950) C-76m. ** D: Robert Alton. Esther Williams, Howard Keel, Minna Gombell, Rita Moreno. Keel inherits land in Tahiti, falls in love with Williams. Mediocre MGM musical made in Hawaii. ▼▶

Pagans, The (1953-Italian) 80m. *½ D: Ferrucio Cereo. Pierre Cressoy, Hélène Rémy, Vittorio Sanipoli, Luigi Tosi, Franco Fabrizi. Uninspired costumer about a conflict between two wealthy clans during a 16th-century Spanish incursion into Rome. Aka THE BARBARIANS. ▼▶

Page Miss Glory (1935) 90m. **½ D: Mervyn LeRoy. Marion Davies, Pat O'Brien, Dick Powell, Mary Astor, Frank McHugh, Lyle Talbot, Patsy Kelly, Allen Jenkins, Barton MacLane. Fine cast overshadows Davies in this amiable spoof of publicity stunts, with con man O'Brien winning beauty contest with composite photograph of nonexistent girl.

Paid (1931) 80m. **½ D: Sam Wood. Joan Crawford, Kent Douglass (Douglass Montgomery), Robert Armstrong, Marie Prevost, John Miljan, Polly Moran. Not-bad early Crawford. Innocent girl sent to prison; she hardens and seeks revenge. Remade as WITHIN THE LAW. ▶

Paid in Full (1950) 105m. **½ D: William Dieterle. Robert Cummings, Lizabeth Scott, Diana Lynn, Eve Arden, Ray Collins,

Stanley Ridges, John Bromfield, Frank McHugh. Kind-hearted Scott loves nice-guy Cummings, but keeps her feelings to herself because he naively desires to wed her selfish kid sister (Lynn). Turgid soaper, with a based-on-fact scenario. Film debut of Carol Channing, playing a dress-shop patron.

Paid to Dance (1937) **55m.** ****½** D: Charles C. Coleman. Don Terry, Jacqueline Wells (Julie Bishop), Rita Hayworth, Arthur Loft, Paul Fix, Paul Stanton, Louise Stanley, Ralph Byrd, Bess Flowers, Ann Doran. Pretty good, tight little B about a dance-hall racket that is a front for white slavery ring. Terry sets up a rival operation and gets unusual cooperation from the city and the courts. Hmmm. . . . Retitled HARD TO HOLD, with Rita as top-billed star.

Paid to Love (1927) **76m.** ****** D: Howard Hawks. George O'Brien, Virginia Valli, J. Farrell MacDonald, William Powell, Thomas Jefferson, Hank Mann, Sally Eilers, Henry Armetta. American banker MacDonald tries to find a suitable wife for the Crown Prince (O'Brien) of a European kingdom and unexpectedly finds her in a nightclub. Starts out snappy, then slows up, adding an unexpectedly serious complication to its simple story, which throws the film a bit off balance.

Painted Desert, The (1931) **75m.** ****½** D: Howard Higgin. William Boyd, Helen Twelvetrees, William Farnum, J. Farrell MacDonald, Clark Gable. Conflict and romance between the adopted son (Boyd) and daughter of two long-feuding Westerners. A bit stiff, though the scenery is beautiful; notable mainly for Gable's talkie debut. Some action shots are missing, abruptly cut out to use in 1938 remake.▼❿

Painted Faces (1929) **74m.** ****** D: Albert S. Rogell. Joe E. Brown, Helen Foster, Barton Hepburn, Dorothy Gulliver, Lester Cole, Richard Tucker, Purnell Pratt, William B. Davidson. Brown is cast in a largely serious role as a circus clown on a murder trial jury, inexplicably holding out for a not guilty verdict. The man with the spandex grin gives quite a performance as a thickly accented German immigrant with heart, soul, and guilt, but comedy fans will be disappointed. Alas, nobody's perfect.▼❿

Painted Hills, The (1951) **C-65m.** ****½** D: Harold F. Kress. Lassie, Paul Kelly, Bruce Cowling, Gary Gray, Art Smith, Ann Doran. Nicely photographed adventure drama set in the West during the 1870s. Lassie stars as Shep, a collie who is ever-loyal to her prospector owner, with the story involving greed and a gold strike.▼❿

Painted Veil, The (1934) **83m.** ****½** D: Richard Boleslawski. Greta Garbo, Herbert Marshall, George Brent, Warner Oland, Jean Hersholt, Cecilia Parker, Keye Luke. Set in mysterious Orient, film tells Som-erset Maugham's story of unfaithful wife mending her ways. Mundane script uplifted by Garbo's personality, supported by Marshall as her husband, Brent as her lover. Remade in 1957 (as THE SEVENTH SIN) and in 2006.▼❿

Painted Woman, The (1932) **73m.** ****½** D: John G. Blystone. Spencer Tracy, Peggy Shannon, William "Stage" Boyd, Irving Pichel, Raul Roulien, Murray Kinnell, Paul Porcasi, Stanley Fields. While singing in a sleazy South Seas nightclub, Shannon accidentally murders a man who's trying to maul her. She flees to another island, where Tracy falls in love with her, ignorant of her past. Young Tracy is brash and irresistible; outdoor filming adds zest to this predictable but entertaining yarn.

Painting the Clouds With Sunshine (1951) **C-87m.** ****** D: David Butler. Dennis Morgan, Virginia Mayo, Gene Nelson, Lucille Norman, Virginia Gibson, Tom Conway. Lukewarm musical of trio of gold-diggers in Las Vegas searching for rich husbands, a mild reworking of an old musical formula.

❿

Paisan (1946-Italian) **90m.** *****½** D: Roberto Rossellini. Carmela Sazio, Gar Moore, Bill Tubbs, Harriet White, Maria Michi, Robert van Loon, Dale Edmonds, Carla Pisacane, Dots Johnson. Early Rossellini classic, largely improvised by a mostly nonprofessional cast. Six vignettes depict life in Italy during WW2; best has American nurse White searching for her lover in battle-torn Florence. Written by Rossellini and Federico Fellini; Giulietta Masina has a bit part. Italian running time 115m. The second in Rossellini's war trilogy, following OPEN CITY, and followed by GERMANY YEAR ZERO.▼❿

Pajama Game, The (1957) **C-101m.** *****½** D: George Abbott, Stanley Donen. Doris Day, John Raitt, Carol Haney, Eddie Foy, Jr., Barbara Nichols, Reta Shaw. Adaptation of the Broadway musical hit—with much of its original cast intact—virtually defines the word "exuberance." Day is a joy as the head of a factory grievance committee who unexpectedly falls in love with the new foreman (Raitt, in his only starring film). Richard Adler and Jerry Ross' songs include "Hey, There." Dancer Haney stands out in her "Steam Heat" feature and in the energetic "Once a Year Day" picnic number. Choreography by Bob Fosse.▼❿❿

Pajama Party (1964) **C-85m.** ****** D: Don Weis. Tommy Kirk, Annette Funicello, Dorothy Lamour, Elsa Lanchester, Harvey Lembeck, Jody McCrea, Buster Keaton, Susan Hart, Donna Loren. Fourth BEACH PARTY movie moves indoors, changes director and star (although Frankie Avalon and Don Rickles do have cameos). Kirk plays Martian teenager who drops in and is understandably perplexed. Just fair, though it's always nice to see Keaton at work. Teri Garr is one of the dancers buried in the sand. Went back outside for BEACH BLANKET BINGO. Panavision. ▼◗

Paleface, The (1948) **C-91m.** ******* D: Norman Z. McLeod. Bob Hope, Jane Russell, Robert Armstrong, Iris Adrian, Robert (Bobby) Watson. Enjoyable comedy-Western, a spoof of THE VIRGINIAN, has timid Bob backed up by sharpshooting Russell in gunfighting encounters; Oscar-winning song "Buttons and Bows." Remade as THE SHAKIEST GUN IN THE WEST. Sequel: SON OF PALEFACE. ▼◗◗

Pal Joey (1957) **C-111m.** ******* D: George Sidney. Rita Hayworth, Frank Sinatra, Kim Novak, Barbara Nichols, Hank Henry, Bobby Sherwood. Sinatra is in peak form as a cocky nightclub singer who makes a move on every "dame" he meets—including innocent showgirl Novak—but meets his Waterloo when wealthy, demanding Hayworth agrees to bankroll his dream of running his own club. Almost complete rewrite of the 1940 Broadway show based on John O'Hara's short stories, but entertaining just the same, with a great Rodgers and Hart score including "Bewitched, Bothered, and Bewildered" (with sanitized lyrics), "The Lady Is a Tramp." Look fast for Robert Reed. ▼◗◗

Palm Beach Story, The (1942) **87m.** *****½** D: Preston Sturges. Claudette Colbert, Joel McCrea, Rudy Vallee, Mary Astor, Sig Arno, Robert Dudley, William Demarest, Jack Norton, Franklin Pangborn, Jimmy Conlin. Hilarious screwball comedy with Claudette running away from hubby McCrea, landing in Palm Beach with nutty millionairess Astor and her bumbling brother Vallee; overflowing with Sturges madness—from the mystifying title sequence to the arrival of the Ale & Quail Club (not to mention the Wienie King!). ▼◗◗

Palm Springs Weekend (1963) **C-100m.** ****½** D: Norman Taurog. Troy Donahue, Connie Stevens, Stefanie Powers, Robert Conrad, Ty Hardin, Jack Weston, Andrew Duggan, Carole Cook, Jerry Van Dyke, Billy Mumy. Cast tries to play teenagers; yarn of group on a spree in resort town is mostly predictable. ▼◗◗

Palmy Days (1931) **77m.** ****½** D: A. Edward Sutherland. Eddie Cantor, Charlotte Greenwood, Charles Middleton, George Raft, Walter Catlett. Cantor is the patsy for a shady fortune-teller in this so-so musical, hampered by silly comic scenes which don't quite work. Notable mostly for Busby Berkeley overhead shots and Cantor performing "My Baby Said Yes, Yes" and "There's Nothing Too Good for My Baby." ▼◗◗

Palooka (1934) **86m.** ******* D: Benjamin Stoloff. Jimmy Durante, Stu Erwin, Lupe Velez, Marjorie Rambeau, Robert Armstrong, Mary Carlisle, William Cagney,

Thelma Todd. Not much relation to Ham Fisher's comic strip, but delightful entertainment with Erwin as naive young man brought into fight game by flashy promoter Knobby Walsh (Durante). Fine cast includes James Cagney's lookalike brother William, and has Schnozzola in top form. Aka JOE PALOOKA. ▼◗

Pals of the Golden West (1951) **68m.** ****½** D: William Witney. Roy Rogers, Dale Evans, Estelita Rodriguez, Pinky Lee, Anthony Caruso, Roy Barcroft, Pat Brady, The Roy Rogers Riders. Working for the U.S. Border Patrol, Roy tracks down the culprits responsible for sending diseased cattle over the Mexican border. Roy's last big-screen Western (before turning to TV) is pretty good.

Pals of the Saddle (1938) **55m.** ******* D: George Sherman. John Wayne, Ray Corrigan, Max Terhune, Doreen McKay, Ted Adams. Modern-day Western where Wayne, framed for murder, tangles with tough government agent McKay in combating munitions ring trying to smuggle illegal chemicals to foreign enemies. First entry in third season of popular *Three Mesquiteers* series based on characters created by William Colt MacDonald, with Wayne replacing debonair Bob Livingston as Stony Brooke. Prime prairie picture with pulsating action, unusually strong femme interest, and rousing Cy Feuer score. ▼◗

Panama Hattie (1942) **79m.** ****½** D: Norman Z. McLeod. Ann Sothern, Red Skelton, Rags Ragland, Ben Blue, Marsha Hunt, Virginia O'Brien, Alan Mowbray, Lena Horne, Dan Dailey, Carl Esmond. Cole Porter's Broadway musical (which starred Ethel Merman) about nightclub owner in Panama falls flat on screen. Porter's score mostly absent, but Lena sings "Just One of Those Things," and sprightly Sothern sings "I've Still Got My Health." ▼◗

Panama Lady (1939) **64m.** ***½** D: Jack Hively. Lucille Ball, Allan Lane, Steffi Duna, Evelyn Brent, Donald Briggs, Bernadene Hayes, Abner Biberman. Routine bungle in the jungle, as Panama cabaret gal Lucy tries to rob customer Lane but winds up accompanying him to South America, where he strikes oil and she tangles with his girlfriend, as well as her own sleazy ex. At least it's short. Remake of 1932's PANAMA FLO (with Helen Twelvetrees). ▼

Panama Sal (1957) **70m.** BOMB D: William Witney. Elena Verdugo, Carlos Rivas, Joe Flynn, Edward Kemmer. A gentleman-playboy (Kemmer) tries to teach "class" to an ill-bred singer (Verdugo). Not to be confused with PYGMALION. Naturama.

Pan Americana (1945) **84m.** ****** D: John H. Auer. Phillip Terry, Eve Arden, Robert Benchley, Audrey Long, Bettejane (Jane) Greer; narrated by Robert Benchley. Another '40s gesture toward Latin-American goodwill. Magazine staff visits Latin America, with writer Long becoming involved with photographer Terry. Crammed with Latin-American musical and specialty numbers.

Pandora and the Flying Dutchman (1951-British) **C-123m.** ** D: Albert Lewin. James Mason, Ava Gardner, Nigel Patrick, Sheila Sim, Harold Warrender, Marius Goring, Pamela Kellino (Mason). Sorry to say, a big Technicolor bore, one of writer-director Lewin's misfires, about a woman who destroys the lives of all the men around her; then mystical, otherwordly Mason materializes. Intriguing but unconvincing tale, inspired by the legend of The Flying Dutchman, a man cursed to live for all eternity until he can find a woman capable of loving him. Only real attribute is Gardner's breathtaking beauty.▼●◗

Pandora's Box (1928-German) **133m.** **** D: G. W. Pabst. Louise Brooks, Fritz Kortner, Franz (Francis) Lederer, Carl Goetz. Hypnotic silent film stars legendary Brooks as flower girl who becomes protégée—then wife—of editor, with bizarre and unexpected consequences. Striking sexuality and drama, with Brooks an unforgettable Lulu. Scripters Pabst and Laszlo Wajda adapted two plays by Franz Wedekind. ▼◗

Panhandle (1948) **84m.** **½ D: Lesley Selander. Rod Cameron, Cathy Downs, Reed Hadley, Anne Gwynne, Blake Edwards, Dick Crockett. Reformed gunslinger Cameron is forced into one last showdown to avenge the murder of his brother at the hands of Hadley and his gang of land grabbers. Tough B Western, coproduced and cowritten by a young Blake Edwards (in his first work behind the camera), who also does a memorable turn as a vicious hired gun. Originally released in sepiatone.◗

Panic SEE: **Panique**

Panic Button (1964) **90m.** BOMB D: George Sherman. Maurice Chevalier, Eleanor Parker, Jayne Mansfield, Michael Connors, Akim Tamiroff. Good cast is wasted in this amateurish, pathetically unfunny production involving the making of a TV pilot in Italy that's supposed to flop so gangster producers will have legitimate tax loss. Wait for a rerun of THE PRODUCERS. Totalscope.◗

Panic in the Parlor (1956-British) **81m.** **½ D: Gordon Parry. Peggy Mount, Shirley Eaton, Gordon Jackson, Ronald Lewis. Broad but diverting humor about sailor Lewis coming home to get married, and the chaos it causes all concerned. Look for Michael Caine in a bit as a sailor. Originally titled: SAILOR BEWARE!

Panic in the Streets (1950) **93m.** ***½ D: Elia Kazan. Richard Widmark, Paul Douglas, Barbara Bel Geddes, (Walter) Jack Palance, Zero Mostel. Taut drama involving gangsters, one of whom is a carrier of pneumonic

plague, and the manhunt to find him. Makes fine use of New Orleans locale; Edward and Edna Anhalt won an Oscar for their story. Screenplay by Richard Murphy. ▼●◗

Panic in Year Zero! (1962) **95m.** **½ D: Ray Milland. Ray Milland, Jean Hagen, Frankie Avalon, Mary Mitchel, Joan Freeman, Richard Garland. Intriguing film about L.A. family that escapes atomic bomb explosion to find a situation of every-man-for-himself. Loud, tinny music spoils much of film's effectiveness. CinemaScope.●◗

Panique (1946-French) **91m.** ***½ D: Julien Duvivier. Viviane Romance, Michel Simon, Paul Bernard, Max Dalban, Emile Drain, Guy Favières. Sizzling thriller, beautifully directed, about a nondescript middle-aged man (Simon) who becomes obsessed with a young woman despite the presence of her boyfriend; all this transpires during a murder investigation. Based on a Georges Simenon novel; remade in 1989 as MONSIEUR HIRE. Screenplay by Duvivier and Charles Spaak. Aka PANIC.

Pantaloons (1956-French) **C-93m.** **½ D: John Berry. Fernandel, Carmen Sevilla, Christine Carrere, Fernando Rey. Fernandel is peppy in this brisk little period piece as a phony gay blade intent on female conquests. ▼

Panther Island SEE: **Bomba on Panther Island**

Papa's Delicate Condition (1963) **C-98m.** **½ D: George Marshall. Jackie Gleason, Glynis Johns, Charlie Ruggles, Laurel Goodwin, Charles Lane, Elisha Cook, Juanita Moore, Murray Hamilton. Amusing nostalgia of Corinne Griffith's childhood; Gleason dominates everything as tipsy father; set in 1900s. Oscar-winning song, "Call Me Irresponsible."▼●◗

Paper Bullets SEE: **Gangs, Inc.**

Parachute Jumper (1933) **65m.** **½ D: Alfred E. Green. Douglas Fairbanks, Jr., Bette Davis, Frank McHugh, Claire Dodd, Leo Carrillo. Ex-Marine flyers Fairbanks and McHugh and stenographer Davis, all jobless and broke in N.Y.C., get tangled up with gangster Carrillo. Fast-moving programmer with an entertaining mix of comedy, romance, and adventure.◗

Paradine Case, The (1948) **116m.** **½ D: Alfred Hitchcock. Gregory Peck, (Alida) Valli, Ann Todd, Charles Laughton, Charles Coburn, Ethel Barrymore, Louis Jourdan, Leo G. Carroll, John Williams. Talk, talk, talk in complicated, stagy courtroom drama, set in England. Below par for Hitchcock; producer David O. Selznick also wrote the script. Originally 132m., then cut to 125m. and finally 116m.▼◗

Paradise Alley (1961) **85m.** *½ D: Hugo Haas. Marie Windsor, Hugo Haas, Billy Gilbert, Carol Morris, Chester Conklin, Margaret Hamilton, Corinne Griffith. Grade-D mishmash about elderly bit player who charmingly deceives the denizens of a slum neighborhood into believing he's directing a movie there. Interesting only for the veteran cast. Originally made in 1957.

Paradise Canyon (1935) **53m.** *½ D: Carl L. Pierson. John Wayne, Marion Burns, Reed Howes, Earle Hodgins, Yakima Canutt, Gino Corrado. Federal agent Wayne goes undercover working for medicine show to round up counterfeit ring. The last, languid entry in Wayne's Lone Star series. Pierson was an editor with few directing credits, and rough edges here tear credibility in this Western quickie. Also shown in computer-colored version. ▼●)

Paradise Lagoon SEE: **Admirable Crichton, The**

Paramount on Parade (1930) **77m.** **½ D: Dorothy Arzner, Otto Brower, Edmund Goulding, Victor Heerman, Edwin Knopf, Rowland V. Lee, Ernst Lubitsch, Lothar Mendes, Victor Schertzinger, A. Edward Sutherland, Frank Tuttle. Jean Arthur, Clara Bow, Maurice Chevalier, Gary Cooper, Nancy Carroll, Leon Errol, Stuart Erwin, Kay Francis, Fredric March, Helen Kane, Jack Oakie, William Powell, Buddy Rogers, many others. Early-talkie variety revue designed to show off Paramount's roster of stars. Some amusing songs and skits, but a lot of dry spots in between. Highlights include Nancy Carroll's "Dancing to Save Your Sole" and Chevalier's two numbers. Film originally ran 102m. with several sequences in color; current prints feature director Edmund Goulding and such stars as Gary Cooper and Jean Arthur "introducing" a sequence that never comes!

Paranoiac (1963-British) **80m.** **½ D: Freddie Francis. Janette Scott, Oliver Reed, Liliane Brousse, Alexander Davion, Sheila Burrell, Maurice Denham. Murder, impersonation, insanity all part of thriller set in large English country estate. CinemaScope. ▼●)

Paratrooper (1953-British) **C-87m.** ** D: Terence Young. Alan Ladd, Leo Genn, Susan Stephen, Harry Andrews, Donald Houston, Anthony Bushell, Stanley Baker, Anton Diffring. Minor Ladd vehicle involving special tactical forces and Ladd's guilt-ridden past. Original title: THE RED BERET.

Pardners (1956) **C-90m.** **½ D: Norman Taurog. Dean Martin, Jerry Lewis, Lori Nelson, Jackie Loughery, John Baragrey, Agnes Moorehead, Jeff Morrow, Lon Chaney, Jr. Ironically titled M&L vehicle (they were already on the road to their breakup) is pleasant remake of RHYTHM ON THE RANGE, with Jerry as Manhattan millionaire who cleans up Western town in his own inimitable fashion. Written by Sidney Sheldon. VistaVision. ▼●)

Pardon My French (1951-U.S.-French) **81m.** **½ D: Bernard Vorhaus. Paul Henreid, Merle Oberon, Paul Bonifas, Maximiliene, Jim Gerald. Fluff of Oberon inheriting a mansion in France occupied by charming composer Henreid.

Pardon My Past (1945) **88m.** *** D: Leslie Fenton. Fred MacMurray, Marguerite Chapman, Akim Tamiroff, William Demarest, Rita Johnson, Harry Davenport. Excellent tale of unsuspecting lookalike for famous playboy, incurring his debts and many enemies; fine comedy-drama.

Pardon My Rhythm (1944) **62m.** ** D: Felix E. Feist. Gloria Jean, Evelyn Ankers, Patric Knowles, Marjorie Weaver, Mel Tormé, Bob Crosby. Naive minor musical set in ultra-wholesome high school, with Gloria the singing belle of the ball.

Pardon My Sarong (1942) **84m.** *** D: Erle C. Kenton. Lou Costello, Bud Abbott, Lionel Atwill, Virginia Bruce, Robert Paige, William Demarest, Leif Erickson, Samuel S. Hinds, Nan Wynn, Four Ink Spots, Tip, Tap, Toe. A&C in good form as bus drivers who end up on tropical island, involved with notorious jewel thieves. ▼●)

Pardon My Trunk SEE: **Hello Elephant** ▼

Pardon Us (1931) **55m.** **½ D: James Parrott. Stan Laurel, Oliver Hardy, Wilfred Lucas, Walter Long, James Finlayson, June Marlowe. L&H's first starring feature film is amusing spoof of THE BIG HOUSE and prison films in general; slow pacing is its major debit, but many funny bits make it a must for fans of Stan and Ollie. ▼●)

Parent Trap, The (1961) **C-124m.** *** D: David Swift. Hayley Mills, Maureen O'Hara, Brian Keith, Charlie Ruggles, Una Merkel, Leo G. Carroll, Joanna Barnes, Cathleen Nesbitt, Nancy Kulp, Frank DeVol. Hayley plays twins who've never met until their divorced parents send them to the same summer camp; after initial rivalry they join forces to reunite their mom and dad. Attempt to mix slapstick and sophistication doesn't work, but overall it's fun. Erich Kastner's story filmed before as 1954 British film TWICE UPON A TIME. Hayley starred—as mom—in 1986 and 1989 TV sequels. Remade in 1998. ▼●)

Paris After Dark (1943) **85m.** **½ D: Leonide Moguy. George Sanders, Philip Dorn, Brenda Marshall, Madeleine LeBeau, Marcel Dalio. Preachy but effective melodrama of French patriot Dorn, who returns to Paris from concentration camp where he was coerced into accepting Nazi domination. Look for Peter Lawford as a young Resistance fighter. ▶)

Paris Blues (1961) **98m.** *** D: Martin Ritt. Paul Newman, Joanne Woodward, Diahann Carroll, Sidney Poitier, Louis Armstrong, Serge Reggiani. Film improves with each viewing; offbeat account of musicians Newman and Poitier in Left Bank Paris, romancing tourists Woodward and Carroll. Great Duke Ellington score, including explosive "Battle Royal" number; a must for jazz fans. ▼●)

Paris Calling (1941) **95m.** ******* D: Edwin L. Marin. Elisabeth Bergner, Randolph Scott, Basil Rathbone, Gale Sondergaard, Eduardo Ciannelli, Lee J. Cobb. Exciting story of underground movement in Paris to destroy Nazis occupying France. Bergner's only U.S. film.

Paris Does Strange Things (1956-French) **C-98m.** ****** D: Jean Renoir. Ingrid Bergman, Jean Marais, Mel Ferrer, Jean Richard, Magali Noel, Juliette Greco, Pierre Bertin. Claude Renoir's exquisite cinematography highlights this otherwise so-so account of impoverished Polish princess Bergman's romantic intrigues with Marais and Ferrer. Overrated by some; far from Renoir's (or Bergman's) best. French-language version, called ELENA AND HER MEN, is better, and runs 95m.**▼❙**

Paris Express, The (1953-British) **C-80m.** ****½** D: Harold French. Claude Rains, Marta Toren, Marius Goring, Anouk (Aimée), Herbert Lom, Lucie Mannheim, Felix Aylmer, Ferdy Mayne, Eric Pohlmann. A clerk embezzles money, hoping to use it for travel, but gets into more of an adventure than he bargained for. Middling crime yarn based on a Georges Simenon novel. Original British title: THE MAN WHO WATCHED TRAINS GO BY.**▼❙**

Paris Follies of 1956 SEE: **Fresh From Paris**

Paris Holiday (1958) **C-100m.** ****½** D: Gerd Oswald. Bob Hope, Fernandel, Anita Ekberg, Martha Hyer, Preston Sturges. Mixture of French and American farce humor makes for uneven entertainment, with Hope in France to buy a new screenplay. Features writer-director Sturges in a small acting role. Technirama.**▼❙**

Paris Honeymoon (1939) **92m.** ****½** D: Frank Tuttle. Bing Crosby, Shirley Ross, Edward Everett Horton, Akim Tamiroff, Ben Blue, Rafaela Ottiano, Raymond Hatton. Texan Crosby visits France planning to marry Ross, but meets native Franciska Gaal and falls in love with her.

Parisian Love (1925) **62m.** ****** D: Louis Gasnier. Clara Bow, Donald Keith, Lillian Leighton, James Gordon Russell, Hazel Keener, Lou Tellegen, Jean De Briac. Hackneyed silent melodrama of Apache dancer Bow, a member of a band of Parisian thieves. When a prominent scientist, one of their intended victims, "steals" her lover, she seeks revenge.**▼❙**

Paris Interlude (1934) **72m.** ****** D: Edwin L. Marin. Robert Young, Madge Evans, Otto Kruger, Una Merkel, Ted Healy, Louise Henry, Edward Brophy. In post-WWI Paris, world-weary American reporter Kruger and irresponsible protégé Young are both in love with Yank tourist Evans, and spend most of their time drowning their sorrows in bars until Kruger goes off to China. Slow-moving melodrama, cleaned up from a play

by S. J. and Laura Perelman. Aims in vain for sophisticated "lost generation" feeling.

Paris Model (1953) **81m.** ***½** D: Alfred E. Green. Eva Gabor, Tom Conway, Paulette Goddard, Marilyn Maxwell, Cecil Kellaway, Barbara Lawrence, Florence Bates. Lackluster vehicle for veteran actors, revolving around a dress and four women who purchase copies of same.

Paris Playboys (1954) **62m.** ***½** D: William Beaudine. Leo Gorcey, Huntz Hall, Bernard Gorcey, Veola Vonn, Steven Geray, David (Gorcey) Condon, Bennie Bartlett. Sach impersonates a missing French professor and gets mixed up in a spy ring. Feeble *Bowery Boys* slapstick.**❙**

Paris Underground (1945) **97m.** ****½** D: Gregory Ratoff. Constance Bennett, Gracie Fields, George Rigaud, Kurt Kreuger, Leslie Vincent, Charles Andre. Well-acted story of American Bennett and Britisher Fields working in underground movement even while imprisoned in Nazi POW camp. Fields' last film.**❙**

Paris—When It Sizzles (1964) **C-110m.** ***½** D: Richard Quine. William Holden, Audrey Hepburn, Noel Coward, Gregoire Aslan. Labored, unfunny comedy defeats a game cast, in story of screenwriter and secretary who act out movie fantasies in order to finish script. Paris locations, cameos by Marlene Dietrich and other stars don't help. Remake of Julien Duvivier's LA FÊTE À HENRIETTE (1952). **▼❙**

Park Row (1952) **83m.** ******* D: Samuel Fuller. Gene Evans, Mary Welch, Herbert Heyes, Tina Rome, Forrest Taylor. Good, tough little film with newsman Evans starting his own paper, rivaling newspaper magnate Welch in 1880s N.Y.C. Written by the director, a former newspaperman. Typically gutsy, in-your-face Fuller fare.**❙**

Parlor, Bedroom and Bath (1931) **75m.** ****** D: Edward Sedgwick. Buster Keaton, Charlotte Greenwood, Reginald Denny, Cliff Edwards, Dorothy Christy, Joan Peers, Sally Eilers, Natalie Moorhead, Edward Brophy. Buster plays a poor sap who's hired to pose as a great lover in this adaptation of a venerable stage farce filmed before in 1920. Great moments with Buster are few and far between in this contrived vehicle, but at least he's surrounded by compatible costars. Partly filmed in and around Keaton's "italian villa" home. **▼●❙**

Parnell (1937) **119m.** ***½** D: John Stahl. Clark Gable, Myrna Loy, Edna May Oliver, Edmund Gwenn, Alan Marshal, Donald Crisp, Billie Burke, Donald Meek. Biography of popular and powerful Irish nationalist leader of the late 1800s whose career was destroyed by the exposure of adulterous affair. Plodding film fails to realize great story potential; this was (understandably) a notorious flop in 1937.**❙**

Parole Fixer (1940) **58m.** ******* D: Robert

Florey. William Henry, Virginia Dale, Robert Paige, Gertrude Michael, Richard Denning, Fay Helm, Anthony Quinn, Harvey Stephens, Marjorie Gateson, Lyle Talbot, Louise Beavers, Jack Carson. Zippy exposé of crooked lawyers and prison officials who take payoffs to give hardened criminals early paroles. The FBI moves in when one of the cons kills an agent and kidnaps a socialite. Quinn is at his nastiest as a cold-blooded killer. Based on J. Edgar Hoover's book *Persons in Hiding*, with one chilling moment that predates THE BIG HEAT.

Parole Girl (1933) **68m. **½ D: Edward F. Cline. Mae Clarke, Ralph Bellamy, Marie Prevost, Hale Hamilton, Ferdinand Gottschalk, Ernest Wood, Sam Godfrey. Good girl Clarke gets mixed up with con man Hamilton in a department store pickpocket scam and winds up in jail, thanks to coldhearted store manager Bellamy. After getting out, she vows revenge and tricks Bellamy into marrying her. Likable cast and evocative atmosphere overcome the highly contrived plot of this pre-Code melodrama written by Norman Krasna.

Parole, Inc. (1948) **71m. ** D: Alfred Zeisler. Michael O'Shea, Turhan Bey, Evelyn Ankers, Virginia Lee, Lyle Talbot, Michael Whelan. By-the-numbers programmer in which federal agent O'Shea goes undercover to determine why dangerous convicts are mysteriously being granted paroles. ▼❒

Parrish (1961) **C-140m. **½ D: Delmer Daves. Claudette Colbert, Troy Donahue, Karl Malden, Dean Jagger, Connie Stevens, Diane McBain, Sharon Hugueny, Sylvia Miles, Madeleine Sherwood. Slurpy soaper is so bad that at times it's funny; emotionless Donahue lives with his mother (Colbert, in her last theatrical film) on Jagger's tobacco plantation and falls in love with three girls there. Malden overplays tyrannical tobacco czar to the nth degree. Carroll O'Connor and Vincent Gardenia have small roles. ▼❒

Parson and the Outlaw, The (1957) C-71m. *½ D: Oliver Drake. Anthony Dexter, Sonny Tufts, Marie Windsor, Buddy Rogers, Jean Parker, Bob Steele. Minor version of life and times of Billy the Kid.

Parson's Widow, The (1920-Swedish) **71m. ***½ D: Carl Th. (Theodor) Dreyer. Hildur Carlberg, Einar Röd, Greta Almroth. A young man bests two rivals to become parson of a small parish, but there's a catch: he must wed his predecessor's elderly, grim-faced widow (a witch, rumor has it) instead of his pretty, patient fiancée. Simple, stark drama potently explores the impact of religious ritual on the human spirit. Early directorial credit for Dreyer, who adapted a story by Kristofer Janson. Originally titled PRÄSTÄNKAN; aka THE WITCH WOMAN. ❒

Partners of the Plains (1938) **68m. ** D: Lesley Selander. William Boyd, Russell Hayden, Harvey Clark, Gwen Gaze, Hilda Plowright, John Warburton, Al Bridge. Strong-willed absentee owner arrives from England to inspect her ranch, leading to battle of the sexes with foreman Hopalong Cassidy. Subpar Hoppy film has Clark subbing for George Hayes as (alleged) comedy relief and imperious leading lady Gaze suggesting a slimmed-down Charles Laughton in drag. Nominally adapted from Clarence E. Mulford's novel *The Man From Bar-20*, but drawn more from *Buck Peters, Ranchman*. Location scenes shot in San Jacinto National Forest. ▼❒

Party Crashers, The (1958) **78m. *½ D: Bernard Girard. Connie Stevens, Robert (Bobby) Driscoll, Mark Damon, Frances Farmer, Doris Dowling, Walter Brooke, Cathy Lewis, Denver Pyle, Gary Gray. Low-rent curio about a group of bored, mischief-making middle-class teens who are victims of irresponsible parenting. Both Driscoll's and Farmer's last film; they play mother and son.

Party Girl (1958) **C-99m. *** D: Nicholas Ray. Robert Taylor, Cyd Charisse, Lee J. Cobb, John Ireland, Kent Smith. Crooked lawyer (Taylor) and showgirl (Charisse) try to break free from early 1930s Chicago mob life. Charisse has a couple of torrid dance numbers; Ray's stylish treatment has won this film a cult following. Tony Martin (the star's husband) sings the title song. CinemaScope. ▼❍❒

Party Girls for Sale SEE: **They Were So Young**

Party Wire (1935) **70m. **½ D: Erle C. Kenton. Jean Arthur, Victor Jory, Helen Lowell, Robert Allen, Charley Grapewin, Clara Blandick, Geneva Mitchell, Maude Eburne. Fairly vicious look at small-town life and how gossip can ruin a person's reputation, in this case Arthur's, who's falsely thought to be pregnant without benefit of a husband. Far from subtle, but Arthur is as appealing as ever. ❒

Passage to Marseille (1944) **110m. **½ D: Michael Curtiz. Humphrey Bogart, Claude Rains, Michele Morgan, Philip Dorn, Sydney Greenstreet, Peter Lorre, George Tobias, Helmut Dantine, John Loder, Victor Francen, Vladimir Sokoloff, Edward (Eduardo) Ciannelli, Hans Conried. WW2 Devil's Island escape film marred by flashback-within-flashback confusion. Not a bad war film, just too talky; a disappointment considering the cast. Also shown in computer-colored version. ▼❍❒

Passage West (1951) **C-80m. *½ D: Lewis R. Foster. John Payne, Dennis O'Keefe, Arleen Whelan, Mary Beth Hughes, Frank Faylen, Dooley Wilson. Outlaws join up with wagon train with predictable results.

Passing Fancy (1933-Japanese) **101m.

***½ D: Yasujiro Ozu. Takeshi Sakamoto, Nobuko Fushimi, Den Obinata, Choko Iida, Tokkan Kozo (Tomio Aoki), Reiko Tani. Heartrending tale of compassion, sacrifice, and human connection is set into motion when a genial, uneducated single father (Sakamoto, in a magnificent performance) performs an act of kindness toward a young woman (Fushimi) who is all alone in the world. With deep insight, Ozu explores the complexities of human relationships and, in particular, the inexorable bond between father and son.▶

Passion (1954) **C-84m.** ** D: Allan Dwan. Cornel Wilde, Yvonne De Carlo, Raymond Burr, Lon Chaney, Jr., Rodolfo Acosta, John Qualen, Anthony Caruso, Stuart Whitman. By-the-numbers Western set in Old California, with Wilde seeking vengeance against the murderers of his loved ones. Name another Western that climaxes atop a Mexican glacier! ▼▶

Passionate Friends, The (1949-British) **91m.** **½ D: David Lean. Ann Todd, Claude Rains, Trevor Howard, Betty Ann Davies, Isabel Dean, Wilfrid Hyde-White. Second-tier Lean (albeit extremely well crafted), which occasionally recalls BRIEF ENCOUNTER. Todd is in love with Howard but marries wealthy banker Rains for security. Will their romance be rekindled when they accidentally meet years later while on a Swiss vacation? Scripted by Eric Ambler, adapted by Lean and Stanley Haynes from an H. G. Wells novel. Previously filmed in 1923. Originally released in U.S. as ONE WOMAN'S STORY. ▼▶

Passionate Plumber, The (1932) **73m.** ** D: Edward Sedgwick. Buster Keaton, Jimmy Durante, Irene Purcell, Polly Moran, Gilbert Roland, Mona Maris. Stilted adaptation of HER CARDBOARD LOVER as vehicle for Keaton, hired by Parisienne Purcell to make lover Roland jealous. Not enough laughs. Filmed before in 1928 as THE CARDBOARD LOVER and remade as HER CARDBOARD LOVER. ▼▶

Passionate Sentry, The (1952-British) **84m.** ** D: Anthony Kimmins. Nigel Patrick, Peggy Cummins, Valerie Hobson, George Cole, A. E. Matthews, Anthony Bushell. Wispy romantic comedy about madcap gal who falls in love with a guard at Buckingham Palace. Retitled: WHO GOES THERE?

Passionate Stranger, The SEE: **Novel Affair, A**

Passionate Thief, The (1960-Italian) **106m.** *** D: Mario Monicelli. Anna Magnani, Totò, Ben Gazzara, Fred Clark, Edy Vessel, Gina Rovere. Uniquely Italian comedy, populated with comically contradictory characters, unfolds over a long New Year's Eve in Rome. Magnani is a movie extra whose pride and stubbornness involve her in a series of misadventures with aged performer Totò and pickpocket Gazzara.

Passion Flower (1930) **79m.** **½ D: William de Mille. Kay Francis, Kay Johnson, Charles Bickford, Winter Hall, Lewis Stone, ZaSu Pitts, Dickie Moore. Heiress Johnson defies her father by marrying the family chauffeur (Bickford), only to lose him to her glamorous cousin (Francis). Well-acted, effective triangle tale with some touching moments.

Passion of Joan of Arc, The (1928-French) **117m.** **** D: Carl Theodor Dreyer. Maria Falconetti, Eugene Sylvain, Maurice Schutz. Joan of Arc's inquisition, trial, and burning at the stake; the scenario is based on transcript of historical trial. Masterfully directed, with groundbreaking use of close-ups; Falconetti glows in the title role. Photographed by Rudolph Maté.▼▶

Passport to Adventure SEE: **Passport to Destiny**

Passport to Destiny (1944) **64m.** ** D: Ray McCarey. Elsa Lanchester, Gordon Oliver, Lloyd Corrigan, Gavin Muir, Lenore Aubert, Fritz Feld. Tidy programmer with Elsa a patriotic scrubwoman determined to eliminate the Fuehrer. Retitled: PASSPORT TO ADVENTURE.

Passport to Hell, A (1932) **76m.** *½ D: Frank Lloyd. Elissa Landi, Paul Lukas, Warner Oland, Alexander Kirkland, Donald Crisp, Earle Foxe, Yola d'Avril. A tainted woman catches the eye of a naïve young lieutenant, much to the dismay of his father, a commandant in German West Africa in the days leading up to WW1. Aptly named film (from audience's point of view), a plodding RED DUST–like triangle about people one couldn't possibly care about.

Passport to Pimlico (1949-British) **85m.** ***½ D: Henry Cornelius. Stanley Holloway, Margaret Rutherford, Betty Warren, Hermione Baddeley, Barbara Murray, Basil Radford, Naunton Wayne, Paul Dupuis, Michael Hordern. Salty farce of ancient treaty enabling small group of Brits to form their own bounded territory in the middle of London. Screenplay by Cornelius and T.E.B. Clarke.▼▶

Passport to Suez (1943) **71m.** **½ D: Andre De Toth. Warren William, Ann Savage, Eric Blore, Robert Stanford, Sheldon Leonard, Lloyd Bridges, Gavin Muir. Nazi spies lead sleuth William on a wild goose chase as part of a plan to blow up the Suez Canal in this well-made *Lone Wolf* entry with more comedy relief from Blore than usual. ▶

Passport to Treason (1955-British) **70m.** *½ D: Robert S. Baker. Rod Cameron, Lois Maxwell, Clifford Evans, John Colicos. Minor drama, with Cameron trying to solve homicide case for sake of friend.

Password Is Courage, The (1963-British) **116m.** *** D: Andrew L. Stone. Dirk Bogarde, Maria Perschy, Alfred Lynch, Nigel Stock, Reginald Beckwith, Richard Marner. Bogarde tops a fine cast in droll account of

British soldier's plot to escape from WW2 prison camp. Metroscope. ◗

Pat and Mike (1952) **95m.** ******* D: George Cukor. Spencer Tracy, Katharine Hepburn, Aldo Ray, William Ching, Jim Backus, Carl ("Alfalfa") Switzer, Charles Buchinski (Bronson), William Self, Chuck Connors. Hepburn is Pat, top female athlete; Tracy is Mike, her manager, in pleasing comedy, not up to duo's other films. Ray is good as thick-witted sports star. Written by Ruth Gordon and Garson Kanin; many sports notables appear briefly. Also shown in computer-colored version. ▼◗

Patch of Blue, A (1965) **105m.** ******* D: Guy Green. Sidney Poitier, Shelley Winters, Elizabeth Hartman, Wallace Ford, Ivan Dixon, John Qualen, Elisabeth Fraser. Sensitive drama of blind girl (Hartman) falling in love with black man (Poitier); well acted, not too sticky. Winters won Oscar as Hartman's harridan mother. Panavision. ▼◗

Pather Panchali (1955-Indian) **112m.** *****½** D: Satyajit Ray. Kanu Banerji, Karuna Banerji, Subir Banerji, Runki Banerji, Uma Das Gupta, Chunibala Devi. Unrelenting study of a poverty-stricken Indian family in Bengal. Grippingly realistic, with Karuna and Subir Banerji outstanding as the mother and her young son Apu. Ray's feature debut, and the first of his "Apu" trilogy. Music by Ravi Shankar. ▼◗

Pathfinder, The (1952) **C-78m.** ***½** D: Sidney Salkow. George Montgomery, Helena Carter, Jay Silverheels, Elena Verdugo, Chief Yowlachie. Low-budget version of James Fenimore Cooper tale of 1750s Great Lakes area, with Indian and French attacks on Americans. Remade for TV in 1996.

Paths of Glory (1957) **86m.** ******** D: Stanley Kubrick. Kirk Douglas, Ralph Meeker, Adolphe Menjou, George Macready, Wayne Morris, Richard Anderson, Timothy Carey, Suzanne Christian, Bert Freed. During WW1, French general Macready orders his men on a suicidal charge; when they fail, he picks three soldiers to be tried and executed for cowardice. Shattering study of the insanity of war has grown even more profound with the years; stunningly acted and directed. Calder Willingham, Jim Thompson, and Kubrick adapted Humphrey Cobb's novel—based on fact. ▼◗

Patient in Room 18, The (1938) **59m.** ****** D: Bobby Connolly, Crane Wilbur. Patric Knowles, Ann Sheridan, Eric Stanley, John Ridgely, Rosella Towne. A hospital nurse teams up with her detective boyfriend to find out who killed a wealthy patient and stole the radium that was being used to treat him. Sheridan's verve and sassy appeal single-handedly make this watchable. ◗

Patsy, The (1928) **77m.** ******* D: King Vidor. Marion Davies, Orville Caldwell, Marie Dressler, Lawrence Gray, Dell Henderson,

Jane Winton. Davies gives an inspired comedic performance as the ignored youngest child of bossy mom Dressler and henpecked father Henderson. She transforms herself into a vivacious flapper to woo her sophisticated older sister's boyfriend. One of Davies' best silents; her impersonations of Mae Murray, Pola Negri, and Lillian Gish are a riot. ◗

Patsy, The (1964) **C-101m.** ****** D: Jerry Lewis. Jerry Lewis, Ina Balin, Everett Sloane, Keenan Wynn, Peter Lorre, John Carradine, Neil Hamilton, Nancy Kulp. When a top comedian is killed in a plane crash, his sycophants try to groom a bellhop (guess who?) into taking his place. Forced, unfunny combination of humor and pathos, much inferior to somewhat similar ERRAND BOY. Lorre's last film. ▼◗

Patterns (1956) **83m.** *****½** D: Fielder Cook. Van Heflin, Everett Sloane, Ed Begley, Beatrice Straight, Elizabeth Wilson. Trenchant, masterfully acted drama of greed and abuse of power in corporate America, about an all-powerful company head (Sloane) who makes life miserable for humanistic underling Begley. Much better than the similar EXECUTIVE SUITE. Scripted by Rod Serling from his 1956 *Kraft TV Theatre* production (which also starred Sloane and Begley). ▼◗

Paula (1952) **80m.** ****½** D: Rudolph Maté. Loretta Young, Kent Smith, Alexander Knox, Tommy Rettig. Young gives credence to role of otherwise happily married woman who's distraught upon learning she cannot have children and comes to the aid of injured orphan Rettig. Marred only by a cop-out ending. ◗

Pawnbroker, The (1965) **116m.** ******** D: Sidney Lumet. Rod Steiger, Geraldine Fitzgerald, Brock Peters, Jaime Sanchez, Thelma Oliver, Juano Hernandez, Raymond St. Jacques. Important, engrossing film; Steiger is excellent as Sol Nazerman, a Jewish pawnbroker in Harlem who lives in a sheltered world with haunting memories of Nazi prison camps. Notable editing by Ralph Rosenblum and music by Quincy Jones. Edward Lewis Wallant's novel was adapted by David Friedkin and Morton Fine. ▼◗

Pawnee (1957) **C-80m.** ****** D: George Waggner. George Montgomery, Bill Williams, Lola Albright, Francis J. McDonald, Raymond Hatton. Pat Western about Indian-raised white man with conflicting loyalties.

Payment Deferred (1932) **81m.** ******* D: Lothar Mendes. Charles Laughton, Maureen O'Sullivan, Dorothy Peterson, Verree Teasdale, Ray Milland, Billy Bevan. Very theatrical yet engrossing little film about a milquetoast who finds himself tangled up in murder. Laughton is at his most idiosyncratic, with all manner of facial grimaces and gestures.

Payment on Demand (1951) **90m.** ******* D:

Curtis Bernhardt. Bette Davis, Barry Sullivan, Peggie Castle, Jane Cowl, Kent Taylor, Betty Lynn, John Sutton, Frances Dee, Otto Kruger. Well-handled chronicle of Davis-Sullivan marriage, highlighting events which lead to divorce.▶

Pay Off, The (1942) 70m. ** D: Arthur Dreifuss. Lee Tracy, Tom Brown, Tina Thayer, Evelyn Brent, Jack La Rue, Ian Keith. Later, lesser Tracy vehicle has him mugging outrageously as a hotshot newspaper reporter who springs into action upon the murder of a special prosecutor. ▼▷

Pay or Die (1960) 111m. **½ D: Richard Wilson. Ernest Borgnine, Zohra Lampert, Al Austin, John Duke, Robert Ellenstein, Franco Corsaro, John Marley, Mario Siletti. Flavorful account of Mafia activities in 1910s N.Y.C.; sturdy performances. ▼▷

Payroll (1961-British) 94m. **½ D: Sidney Hayers. Michael Craig, Françoise Prevost, Billie Whitelaw, William Lucas, Kenneth Griffith, Tom Bell. Well-handled account involving widow of payroll guard killed in robbery tracking down culprits.

Peach-O-Reno (1931) 63m. **½ D: William A. Seiter. Bert Wheeler, Robert Woolsey, Dorothy Lee, Zelma O'Neal, Joseph Cawthorn, Cora Witherspoon, Sam Hardy. The boys are shyster lawyers who run a quickie divorce service in Reno by day, then transform their office into a casino after dark! Lavish musical numbers, pre-Code banter, and racy gags highlight this typical Wheeler and Woolsey vehicle. ▶

Pearl, The (1948) 77m. *** D: Emilio Fernandez. Pedro Armendariz, Maria Elena Marques. Mexican-filmed John Steinbeck tale of poor fisherman whose life is unhappily altered by finding valuable pearl; a bit heavy-handed. Beautifully photographed by Gabriel Figueroa.▼

Pearl of Death, The (1944) 69m. *** D: Roy William Neill. Basil Rathbone, Nigel Bruce, Evelyn Ankers, Miles Mander, Rondo Hatton, Dennis Hoey, Richard Nugent. Deft *Sherlock Holmes* entry has the sleuth searching for six busts of Napoleon, one of which contains the Borgia pearl, before all the owners are murdered by "The Creeper" (Hatton). Suspenseful story inspired Universal to recast Hatton in two more films as "The Creeper."▼▷

Pearl of the South Pacific (1955) C-86m. *½ D: Allan Dwan. Virginia Mayo, Dennis Morgan, David Farrar, Murvyn Vye. Greedy fortune hunters mix with island natives as they search for a hidden temple and untold riches. A so-bad-it's-funny relic of its era. SuperScope.▼▷

Peck's Bad Boy (1921) 51m. *** D: Sam Wood. Jackie Coogan, Wheeler Oakman, Doris May, Raymond Hatton, Lillian Leighton. Still-fresh and enjoyable vehicle for Coogan as young mischief-maker; clever card-titles written by humorist Irvin S. Cobb.▼▷

Peck's Bad Boy (1934) 70m. **½ D: Edward Cline. Jackie Cooper, Thomas Meighan, Jackie Searl, O. P. Heggie. Cooper is ideally cast as the title character, who enjoys an idyllic relationship with widowed dad Meighan. Trouble comes when his obnoxious aunt and bratty cousin arrive on the scene.▼▷

Peck's Bad Boy With the Circus (1938) 78m. ** D: Edward Cline. Tommy Kelly, Ann Gillis, Edgar Kennedy, Billy Gilbert, Benita Hume, Spanky McFarland, Grant Mitchell. Standard circus story slanted for kiddies. Kennedy and Gilbert wrap this one up.▼▷

Peeping Tom (1960-British) C-101m. *** D: Michael Powell. Carl Boehm, Moira Shearer, Anna Massey, Maxine Audley, Brenda Bruce, Martin Miller. Sensational film—denounced in 1960—went on to develop a fervent following; personal feelings will dictate your reaction to story of psychopathic murderer who photographs his victims at the moment of death. Originally released in the U.S. at 86m. Director Powell plays the father of Boehm in the home-movie sequences.▼●▷

Peggy (1950) C-77m. **½ D: Frederick de Cordova. Diana Lynn, Charles Coburn, Charlotte Greenwood, Rock Hudson, Jerome Cowan, Barbara Lawrence. Lightweight comedy of sisters Lynn and Lawrence entered in Rose Bowl Parade beauty contest.

Peg o' My Heart (1933) 89m. *** D: Robert Z. Leonard. Marion Davies, Onslow Stevens, J. Farrell MacDonald, Irene Browne, Juliette Compton, Alan Mowbray. Sweet, old-fashioned vehicle for Davies as spunky Irish lass who's separated from her father and brought to ritzy English manor, to fulfill terms of inheritance. Corny but fun. Filmed in 1923 with Laurette Taylor.

Peking Express (1951) 95m. **½ D: William Dieterle. Joseph Cotten, Corinne Calvet, Edmund Gwenn, Marvin Miller, Benson Fong. Remake of SHANGHAI EXPRESS lacks flavor or distinction. Cotten is the doctor and Calvet the shady lady he encounters on train.

Penalty, The (1920) 82m. *** D: Wallace Worsley. Lon Chaney, Ethel Grey Terry, Charles Clary, Claire Adams, Kenneth Harlan, James Mason, Cesare Gravina. Chaney is something to see as Blizzard, a cunning, sadistic crime lord, embittered because his legs were amputated by a negligent surgeon in childhood. Terry is the government operative assigned to infiltrate his den of iniquity. Melodramatic at times, but worth seeing for Chaney's bravura performance. ▼▷

Penalty, The (1941) 81m. ** D: Harold S. Bucquet. Edward Arnold, Lionel Barrymore, Marsha Hunt, Robert Sterling, Gene Reynolds, Emma Dunn, Veda Ann Borg, Richard Lane, Gloria DeHaven. Young

Reynolds' loyalties are divided between his notorious killer–bank-robber father (Arnold) and an honest, hardworking farm family. Slick, predictable potboiler. Phil Silvers appears briefly as a hobo.

Penguin Pool Murder (1932) **65m.** ******* D: George Archainbaud. Edna May Oliver, James Gleason, Mae Clarke, Robert Armstrong, Donald Cook, Clarence Wilson, Edgar Kennedy, Rochelle Hudson, Gustav von Seyffertitz, Sidney Miller, Edith Fellows. Schoolteacher Hildegarde Withers (Oliver) helps cigar-chomping cop Oscar Piper (Gleason) solve a grisly murder in an aquarium. First of the short-lived but entertaining *Hildegarde Withers* series based on the stories of Stuart Palmer. **O)**

Pennies From Heaven (1936) **81m.** ****½** D: Norman Z. McLeod. Bing Crosby, Edith Fellows, Madge Evans, Donald Meek, Louis Armstrong. Minor but pleasant Crosby vehicle about a self-styled troubadour and drifter who befriends orphaned girl (Fellows) and her grandfather (Meek). Bing's rendition of title tune is classic. **▼)**

Penn of Pennsylvania SEE: **Courageous Mr. Penn**.

Penny Princess (1951-British) **C-91m.** ******* D: Val Guest. Dirk Bogarde, Yolande Donlan, Kynaston Reeves. Charming froufrou of American Donlan (wife of director Guest) going to Europe to collect inheritance of small principality, and Bogarde who courts her. **)**

Penny Serenade (1941) **118m.** *****½** D: George Stevens. Irene Dunne, Cary Grant, Beulah Bondi, Edgar Buchanan, Ann Doran, Eva Lee Kuney. Quintessential soap opera, with Dunne and Grant as couple who adopt baby after their unborn baby dies. A wonderful tearjerker; scripted by Morrie Ryskind, from Martha Cheavens' story. Also shown in computer-colored version. **▼O)**

Penrod and His Twin Brother (1938) **63m.** ****** D: William McGann. Billy Mauch, Bobby Mauch, Frank Craven, Spring Byington, Charles Halton, Claudia Coleman. Penrod gets blamed for something he didn't do; it's his look-alike who's really responsible. Second in a short-lived series of juvenile tales.

Penrod and Sam (1937) **64m.** ****½** D: William McGann. Billy Mauch, Frank Craven, Spring Byington, Craig Reynolds, Harry Watson, Bernice Pilot, Philip Hurlic. In this agreeable update of Booth Tarkington's famous trio of books (filmed before in 1923 and 1931), Penrod and his pals play Junior G-men to go after some bank robbers. Yes, one of those kids is an older Matthew "Stymie" Beard from *Our Gang*. First of a short-lived B movie series. **)**

Penrod's Double Trouble (1938) **61m.** ****** D: Lewis Seiler. Billy Mauch, Bobby Mauch, Dick Purcell, Gene Lockhart, Kathleen Lockhart, Hugh O'Connell, Charles Halton, Philip Hurlic. There's a reward for Penrod's return but a look-alike is turned in instead. Final entry in short-lived series featuring the Mauch Twins is forgettable B movie fare. Look sharp for Peter Lind Hayes, Carole Landis. **)**

Penthouse (1933) **90m.** *****½** D: W. S. Van Dyke. Warner Baxter, Myrna Loy, Charles Butterworth, Mae Clarke, C. Henry Gordon. Terrific comedy-melodrama, with Baxter as criminal lawyer who enlists the help of sprightly call-girl Loy to nail a crime kingpin (Gordon). A neglected gem. Remade as SOCIETY LAWYER. **O)**

People Against O'Hara, The (1951) **102m.** ****½** D: John Sturges. Spencer Tracy, Pat O'Brien, Diana Lynn, John Hodiak, Eduardo Ciannelli, Jay C. Flippen, James Arness, Arthur Shields, William Campbell. Middling drama, with Tracy a noted criminal lawyer who repents for unethical behavior during a case. Look fast for Charles Bronson as one of Campbell's brothers. **O)**

People on Sunday (1929-German) **73m.** ******* D: Robert Siodmak. Brigitte Borchert, Christl Ehlers, Annie Schreyer, Wolfgang von Waltershausen, Erwin Splettstosser. Landmark silent docudrama notable for the dazzling group of young filmmakers who made it: Siodmak was assisted by Edgar G. Ulmer; Billy Wilder wrote it based on an idea by Curt Siodmak; and it was shot by future Oscar-winning cinematographer Eugen Schüfftan, whose assistant was Fred Zinnemann. Story follows the romantic adventures of a taxi driver and his married friend as they spend one Sunday trying to pick up two women before returning to their dreary lives. A lyrical portrait of pre-WW2 Berlin and the German countryside, filmed in a style that prefigures the Italian neorealist movement of the 1940s, with amateur actors playing themselves. Original title: MENSCHEN AM SONNTAG. **)**

People's Enemy SEE: **Prison Train**

People vs. Dr. Kildare, The (1941) **78m.** ****** D: Harold S. Bucquet. Lew Ayres, Lionel Barrymore, Laraine Day, Bonita Granville, Alma Kruger, Red Skelton, Tom Conway, Walter Kingsford, Chick Chandler, Diana Lewis, Marie Blake, Nell Craig, Frank Orth. Verbose Kildare entry finds the medic being sued for malpractice after operating on ice skater Granville's leg. Skelton's comic relief is more annoying than amusing. **)**

People Will Talk (1935) **67m.** ****½** D: Alfred Santell. Mary Boland, Charles Ruggles, Leila Hyams, Dean Jagger, Ruthelma Stevens, Hans Steinke. Slim comedy about married couple pretending to fight to teach daughter a lesson. Boland and Ruggles could read a newspaper and make it funny.

People Will Talk (1951) **110m.** *****½** D: Joseph L. Mankiewicz. Cary Grant, Jeanne Crain, Finlay Currie, Walter Slezak, Hume Cronyn, Sidney Blackmer, Margaret

Hamilton. Genuinely offbeat, absorbing comedy-drama of philosophical doctor Grant, who insists on treating his patients as human beings; a small-minded colleague (Cronyn) is intimidated by his radical approach to doctoring and sets out to defame him. Fine cast in talky but most worthwhile film, which features obvious parallels to the then-current HUAC investigation and McCarthy witchhunt.▼▶

Pepe (1960) **C-157m.** BOMB D: George Sidney. Cantinflas, Dan Dailey, Shirley Jones, 35 guest stars. Incredibly long, pointless film wastes talents of Cantinflas and many, many others (Edward G. Robinson, Maurice Chevalier, etc.). This one's only if you're desperate. Originally released at 195m. with overture, intermission/entr'acte. CinemaScope.

Pépé Le Moko (1937-French) **95m.** ******** D: Julien Duvivier. Jean Gabin, Mireille Balin, Gabriel Gabrio, Lucas Gridoux. Gabin is magnetic (in role that brought him international prominence) as gangster who eludes capture in Casbah section of Algiers, until he is lured out of hiding by a beautiful woman. Exquisitely photographed and directed; faithfully remade the following year as ALGIERS, later musicalized as CASBAH. 9m. originally cut from U.S. release have now been restored.▼▶

Perfect Clue, The (1935) **64m.** ***½** D: Robert G. Vignola. David Manners, "Skeets" Gallagher, Dorothy Libaire, Betty Blythe, Ralf Harolde, Robert Gleckler. Down-and-out Manners, embittered after doing time for a crime he didn't commit, meets scatterbrained rich girl Libaire; when he's jailed on a murder charge, she turns sleuth to clear him. Once the story *finally* gets going (around the two-thirds mark!), everything happens just the way you know it will.

Perfect Furlough, The (1958) **C-93m.** ****½** D: Blake Edwards. Tony Curtis, Janet Leigh, Keenan Wynn, Linda Cristal, Elaine Stritch, King Donovan, Troy Donahue. Diverting comedy of soldier Curtis winning trip to France, romancing military psychiatrist Leigh. CinemaScope.▼▶

Perfect Gentleman, The (1935) **72m.** ****½** D: Tim Whelan. Frank Morgan, Cicely Courtneidge, Heather Angel, Herbert Mundin, Una O'Connor, Richard Waring, Henry Stephenson. Slight but likable yarn set in England about a blustering old scoundrel who is constantly embarrassing his vicar son, so he takes to the road and teams up with a female musical hall performer. Pleasant showcase for Morgan and delightful British comedienne Courtneidge in her first and only American film.

Perfect Marriage, The (1946) **87m.** ****½** D: Lewis Allen. Loretta Young, David Niven, Eddie Albert, Charles Ruggles, Virginia Field, Rita Johnson, ZaSu Pitts. Niven's tired of wife Young; Young's tired of husband

Niven. Sharply observed, if talky, marital comedy. Scripted by Leonard Spiegelgass, based on a play by Samson Raphaelson.▼

Perfect Specimen, The (1937) **97m.** ****½** D: Michael Curtiz. Errol Flynn, Joan Blondell, Hugh Herbert, Edward Everett Horton, Dick Foran, May Robson, Beverly Roberts, Allen Jenkins. Fairly amusing whimsy about super-rich Flynn, who's kept locked up and sheltered by grandmother Robson until vivacious Blondell comes crashing through his fence and they go off on a whirlwind courtship.

Perfect Strangers (1945) SEE: **Vacation From Marriage**

Perfect Strangers (1950) **88m.** ****½** D: Bretaigne Windust. Ginger Rogers, Dennis Morgan, Thelma Ritter, Margalo Gillmore, Paul Ford, Alan Reed. Rogers and Morgan are jury members who fall in love; engaging romance story.▶

Perfect Understanding (1933-British) **81m.** ****½** D: Cyril Gardner. Gloria Swanson, Laurence Olivier, John Halliday, Nigel Playfair, Michael Farmer, Genevieve Tobin, Nora Swinburne, Miles Malleson. Swanson and Olivier make a marriage pact "never to be husband and wife but lover and mistress," but of course things don't go that smoothly. Romantic comedy trifle is filled with clever transition shots and montages. Swanson (who produced the film) also gets to sing. Interesting to see these two stars at this point in their respective careers.▶

Perfect Woman, The (1949-British) **89m.** ****½** D: Bernard Knowles. Patricia Roc, Stanley Holloway, Miles Malleson, Nigel Patrick, Irene Handl. Screwy scientist tries to improve on nature by making a "perfect" robot woman, modeled on his niece. Mixups follow in this OK British comedy.

Perilous Holiday (1946) **89m.** ******* D: Edward H. Griffith. Pat O'Brien, Ruth Warrick, Alan Hale, Edgar Buchanan, Audrey Long, Willard Robertson, Eduardo Ciannelli. Good O'Brien vehicle casts him as a troubleshooter encountering dangerous counterfeiting gang south of the border.

Perilous Journey, A (1953) **90m.** ****** D: R. G. Springsteen. Vera Ralston, David Brian, Scott Brady, Virginia Grey, Charles Winninger, Ben Cooper, Hope Emerson, Veda Ann Borg, Leif Erickson. Predictable but diverting Western of a ship manned by women who are heading to California to find husbands.

Perils From the Planet Mongo (1940) **91m.** ****½** D: Ford Beebe, Ray Taylor. Buster Crabbe, Carol Hughes, Charles Middleton, Frank Shannon, Anne Gwynne. Truncated version of FLASH GORDON CONQUERS THE UNIVERSE serial. On Mongo, Flash, Dale Arden, and Dr. Zarkov contend with the planet's civilizations, eventually restore Prince Barin as rightful ruler and return to Earth. Uninspired handling of footage from this great serial.▶

Perils of Pauline, The (1947) **C-96m.** ***
D: George Marshall. Betty Hutton, John Lund, Constance Collier, Billy de Wolfe, William Demarest. Lively, entertaining musical-comedy purports to be biography of silent-screen heroine Pearl White, but isn't; energetic Hutton, good Frank Loesser songs, colorful atmosphere, and presence of silent-film veterans make up for it . . . until sappy denouement.▼▶

Period of Adjustment (1962) **112m.** ***
D: George Roy Hill. Tony Franciosa, Jane Fonda, Jim Hutton, Lois Nettleton, John McGiver, Jack Albertson. Newlyweds (Fonda and Hutton) try to help troubled marriage of Nettleton and Franciosa in this heartwarming comedy based on a Tennessee Williams play. Engaging performers make the most of both comic and tender moments.▼▶

Perri (1957) **C-75m.** *** D: N. Paul Kenworthy, Jr., Ralph Wright; narrated by Winston Hibler. Unusual Disney film combines elements of BAMBI with True-Life nature photography, in a romanticized look at a squirrel through the cycle of four seasons in the forest. Based on Felix Salten's book.▶

Perry Mason Long before Raymond Burr made the part of Perry Mason his own on television, Erle Stanley Gardner's crusading attorney was featured in a half-dozen screen adventures. Created in 1933, Perry made his film debut just one year later in THE CASE OF THE HOWLING DOG, based on one of Gardner's best-selling novels. (In fact, all of the Mason films were adaptations of books from the series, which was not the norm for Hollywood.) Leading man Warren William had played both detectives and lawyers before, but the screenwriters (and possibly, directors) of these films kept changing their minds about the way Perry should be portrayed. He was definitely flashier than the Mason depicted on the printed page (with plush offices that could have been created only in Hollywood), and overall spent less time in the courtroom, but in THE CASE OF THE LUCKY LEGS he's portrayed as a constant tippler (à la Nick Charles) and in THE CASE OF THE CURIOUS BRIDE he's positively giddy. Continuity was further undermined by recasting Perry's secretary Della Street from one film to the next; only Claire Dodd managed to play the role twice in succession, winning Perry's marriage proposal at the end of THE CURIOUS BRIDE and honeymooning in THE VELVET CLAWS. After just a couple of films, Warner Bros. downgraded the series from A status to B, and after four pictures, William left. Ricardo Cortez succeeded him, but just for one picture; by the time Donald Woods inherited the role, it was clear that Warners had lost all interest. It remained for television to really capitalize on Erle Stanley Gardner's durable character some 20 years later.

PERRY MASON

The Case of the Howling Dog (1934)
The Case of the Curious Bride (1935)
The Case of the Lucky Legs (1935)
The Case of the Velvet Claws (1936)
The Case of the Black Cat (1936)
The Case of the Stuttering Bishop (1937)

Personal Affair (1953-British) **82m.** **½
D: Anthony Pelissier. Gene Tierney, Leo Genn, Pamela Brown, Walter Fitzgerald, Megs Jenkins, Michael Hordern, Thora Hird, Glynis Johns, Nanette Newman. Seventeen-year-old Johns has a schoolgirl crush on her married Latin teacher (Genn). When she goes missing, he's the subject of gossip and innuendo. Thoughtful drama is at its best when accentuating the consequences of small-town small-mindedness. Fitzgerald is a standout as Johns' father. ▼

Personality Kid, The (1934) **68m.** **½ D: Alan Crosland. Pat O'Brien, Glenda Farrell, Claire Dodd, Robert Gleckler, Henry O'Neill, Thomas Jackson, Arthur Vinton, Clarence Muse. Brash, flashy club fighter O'Brien rises in the boxing world, but not without complications. Minor but snappy Warner Bros. B melodrama with some interesting story twists.

Personal Property (1937) **84m.** **½ D: W. S. Van Dyke II. Jean Harlow, Robert Taylor, Una O'Connor, Reginald Owen, Cora Witherspoon. Taylor stiffly maneuvers through a series of masquerades, and finally courts Harlow in this MGM fluff. Remake of 1931 film THE MAN IN POSSESSION.▼▶

Persons in Hiding (1939) **69m.** *** D: Louis King. Lynne Overman, Patricia Morison, J. Carrol Naish, William Henry, Helen Twelvetrees, William Frawley, Judith Barrett, Richard Stanley (Dennis Morgan), Richard Denning. Coldhearted, materialistic small-town beautician (Morison) hooks up with a petty gunman (Naish) and pushes him into the criminal big leagues. Swift, suspenseful gangster tale patterned after the exploits of Bonnie and Clyde; the first in a series of four Paramount B movies based on a book by F.B.I. chief J. Edgar Hoover.

Pete Kelly's Blues (1955) **C-95m.** ** D: Jack Webb. Jack Webb, Janet Leigh, Edmond O'Brien, Peggy Lee, Andy Devine, Lee Marvin, Ella Fitzgerald, Martin Milner, Than Wynenn, Herb Ellis, Jayne Mansfield. Tedious roaring '20s yarn about a cornet player at a Kansas City speakeasy who tries to shield himself and his band from bootlegger/mobster O'Brien. Webb is strictly one-note here, as actor and director, but the candy-colored production design and the music are strong assets. Lee is notable in a rare dramatic role. Based on Webb's flop radio series, which he later revived for TV. CinemaScope. ▼◕)

Peter Ibbetson (1935) **88m.** ******* D: Henry Hathaway. Gary Cooper, Ann Harding, John Halliday, Ida Lupino, Douglass Dumbrille, Virginia Weidler, Dickie Moore, Doris Lloyd. Most unusual fantasy-romance, based on George du Maurier novel about sweethearts who are separated in childhood but whose destinies draw them together years later, and for all eternity. Someone more ethereal than Harding might have put this over better, but it's still a moving and strikingly artistic endeavor. Beautifully photographed by Charles Lang.◗

Peter Pan (1924) **102m.** ******* D: Herbert Brenon. Betty Bronson, Ernest Torrence, Anna May Wong, Mary Brian, Virginia Browne Faire, Esther Ralston, Cyril Chadwick, Philippe De Lacey. Delightful adaptation of the James M. Barrie classic about the boy who can fly and never wants to grow up, and his adventures as he soars away with Wendy Darling and her brothers to Never Never Land. Bronson makes the role of Peter all her own in this charming fantasy. ▼◗

Peter Pan (1953) **C-77m.** ******* D: Hamilton Luske, Clyde Geronimi, Wilfred Jackson. Voices of Bobby Driscoll, Kathryn Beaumont, Hans Conried, Bill Thompson, Heather Angel, Paul Collins, Candy Candido, Tom Conway. Delightful Walt Disney cartoon feature of the classic James M. Barrie story, with Peter leading Wendy, Michael, and John Darling to Never Land, where they do battle with Captain Hook and his band of pirates. Musical highlight: "You Can Fly," as the children sail over the city of London. Followed in 2002 by RETURN TO NEVER LAND. ▼◕)

Peterville Diamond, The (1943-British) **85m.** ****** D: Walter Forde. Anne Crawford, Donald Stewart, Renee Houston, Oliver Wakefield, Charles Heslop, Bill (William) Hartnell, Felix Aylmer. Bored wife of ever-busy businessman schemes to make her mate jealous by hinting that she's involved with another man. Slight, silly, way-overlong comedy.

Petrified Forest, The (1936) **83m.** *****½** D: Archie Mayo. Leslie Howard, Bette Davis, Dick Foran, Humphrey Bogart, Genevieve Tobin, Charley Grapewin, Porter Hall. Solid adaptation of Robert Sherwood play, focusing on ironic survival of the physically fit in civilized world. Bogart is Duke Mantee, escaped gangster, who holds writer Howard, dreamer Davis, and others hostage at roadside restaurant in Arizona. Stagy, but extremely well acted and surprisingly fresh. Howard and Bogart re-create their Broadway roles. Scripted by Charles Kenyon and Delmer Daves. Remade as ESCAPE IN THE DESERT. Also shown in computer-colored version. ▼◕)

Petticoat Fever (1936) **81m.** ****** D: George Fitzmaurice. Robert Montgomery, Myrna Loy, Reginald Owen, Irving Bacon. Limp farce set in Labrador, with patronizing Montgomery romancing Loy (despite presence of stuffed-shirt fiancé Owen). The stars are defeated by their one-note material.

Petticoat Larceny (1943) **61m.** ****½** D: Ben Holmes. Ruth Warrick, Joan Carroll, Walter Reed, Wally Brown, Tom Kennedy, Jimmy Conlin, Vince Barnett, Paul Guilfoyle. Entertaining Runyonesque yarn involving precocious child actress Carroll, who stars on radio as the "Underworld Angel." Determined to pen her own scripts, she conducts research by consorting with real criminals.

Petty Girl, The (1950) **C-87m.** ****½** D: Henry Levin. Robert Cummings, Joan Caulfield, Elsa Lanchester, Melville Cooper, Mary Wickes, Tippi Hedren. Mild comedy of pin-up artist George Petty (Cummings) falling for prudish Caulfield; Lanchester steals every scene she's in.

Peyton Place (1957) **C-157m.** *****½** D: Mark Robson. Lana Turner, Hope Lange, Arthur Kennedy, Lloyd Nolan, Lee Philips, Terry Moore, Russ Tamblyn, Betty Field, David Nelson, Mildred Dunnock, Diane Varsi, Barry Coe, Leon Ames, Lorne Greene. Grace Metalious' once-notorious novel receives Grade A filming. Soap opera of life behind closed doors in a small New England town boasts strong cast, fine Franz Waxman score. Original running time: 162m. Sequel: RETURN TO PEYTON PLACE. Later a hit TV series. CinemaScope. ▼◕)

Phaedra (1962-U.S.-French-Greek) **115m.** ******* D: Jules Dassin. Melina Mercouri, Anthony Perkins, Raf Vallone, Elizabeth Ercy. Mercouri, wife of shipping magnate Vallone, has an affair with stepson Perkins. Well acted and directed; inspired by Euripides' *Hippolytus.* ◗

Phantom (1922-German) **117m.** ******* D: F. W. Murnau. Alfred Abel, Lil Dagover, Lya de Putti, Frieda Richard, Aud Egede Nissen, H. H. von Twardowski, Karl Etlinger, Adolf Klein. Dreamlike silent film about a young clerk (Abel) who dreams of becoming a rich and famous writer after he is accidentally struck by a passing carriage driven by a wealthy beauty (de Putti), with whom he becomes hopelessly obsessed. Poetic psychodrama featuring some superb bits of German expressionist cinema. ◗

Phantom Creeps, The (1939) **79m.** ****** D: Ford Beebe, Saul A. Goodkind. Bela Lugosi, Robert Kent, Regis Toomey, Dorothy Arnold, Edward Van Sloan, Edward Norris. U.S. government and hostile spies vie for control of mad scientist Lugosi's inventions, including an invisibility belt and a king-sized robot. So bad it's actually entertaining; the whole kettle of fish is thrown in here, including stock footage of the Hindenburg disaster! Edited down from a 12-episode Universal serial of the same title. ▼

Phantom Express, The (1932) **66m.** **
D: Emory Johnson. William Collier, Jr., Sally Blane, J. Farrell MacDonald, Hobart Bosworth, Axel Axelson, Lina Basquette. Melodramatic, ever-so-obvious account of some villains attempting to sabotage a railroad . . . and it's the company president's son (Collier) to the rescue. Notice those violins after engineer Smokey North (MacDonald) is sacked from his job! ▼)

Phantom From Space (1953) **72m.** *½
D: W. Lee Wilder. Ted Cooper, Rudolph Anders, Noreen Nash, Harry Landers, Jim Bannon. An invisible alien crash-lands near L.A., wreaks accidental havoc as he makes his way across the city. OK idea hampered by low budget—and lack of talent. ▼)

Phantom From 10,000 Leagues, The (1956) **72m.** BOMB D: Dan Milner. Kent Taylor, Cathy Downs, Michael Whalen, Helene Stanton, Philip Pine, Rodney Bell, Vivi Janiss. Oceanographer Taylor investigates deaths caused by a monster created by radiation from an undersea rock, which is now guarded by the creature. Lots of spy stuff and a lousy monster fail to enliven this deadly dull early American-International effort. ▼)

Phantom in the House, The (1929) **64m.** ** D: Phil Rosen. Ricardo Cortez, Nancy Welford, Henry B. Walthall, Grace Valentine. For early-talkie fans and the Henry B. Walthall Appreciation Society. After taking the rap for a killing his wife committed, saintly Henry B. returns from prison to find she's put him behind her and kept their daughter clueless. Cortez's casting as a bland nice guy and some hokey acting sink what's left of the ship.

Phantom Lady (1944) **87m.** ***½ D: Robert Siodmak. Ella Raines, Franchot Tone, Alan Curtis, Thomas Gomez, Elisha Cook, Jr., Fay Helm, Andrew Tombes, Regis Toomey. First-rate suspense yarn of innocent man (Curtis) framed for murder of his wife. Secretary Raines seeks real killer with help of Curtis' best friend (Tone) and detective (Gomez). Sexual innuendo in drumming scene with Cook is simply astonishing—the solo was reportedly dubbed by Buddy Rich. Based on a Cornell Woolrich novel; screenplay by Bernard C. Schoenfeld. ▼)

Phantom Light, The (1935-British) **73m.** **½ D: Michael Powell. Binnie Hale, Gordon Harker, Donald Calthrop, Milton Rosmer, Ian Hunter, Herbert Lomas (Lom). The new chief lighthouse keeper in a coastal Welsh village must contend with rumors that his lighthouse is haunted. Some zippy directorial touches enliven this overly talky mystery, one of Powell's early-career "quota quickies." ▼)

Phantom of Chinatown (1941) **61m.** BOMB D: Phil Rosen. Keye Luke, Lo-

tus Long, Grant Withers, Paul McVey, Charles Miller. Sixth and final mystery in the *Mr. Wong* series is bottom-of-the-barrel fare, with Luke replacing Boris Karloff as a younger version of the Oriental sleuth. He's on the trail of a killer out to obtain an ancient scroll and locate an oil deposit. ▼)

Phantom of Crestwood, The (1932) **77m.** *** D: J. Walter Ruben. Ricardo Cortez, Karen Morley, Anita Louise, Pauline Frederick, H. B. Warner, Sam Hardy, Skeets Gallagher. First-rate old-dark-house whodunit with crafty Morley calling together the men in her life for mass-blackmail scheme, resulting in murder. Eye-riveting flashback technique highlights solid mystery. ▼)

Phantom of Paris, The (1931) **72m.** *** D: John S. Robertson. John Gilbert, Leila Hyams, Lewis Stone, Jean Hersholt, C. Aubrey Smith, Natalie Moorhead, Ian Keith. Paris escape artist Gilbert, arrested on a murder charge, escapes—naturally!—and goes to extraordinary lengths to prove his innocence. Far-out to say the very least, but nicely buoyed by arch dialogue and several clever touches. Based on a novel by Gaston Leroux (who wrote *The Phantom of the Opera*), *Chéri-Bibi et Cécily*; remade as CHÉRI-BIBI in 1937 and 1955.

Phantom of the Opera, The (1925) **98m.** ***½ D: Rupert Julian. Lon Chaney, Mary Philbin, Norman Kerry, Snitz Edwards, Gibson Gowland. Classic melodrama with Chaney as the tortured composer who lives in the catacombs under the Paris Opera House and kidnaps young Philbin as his singing protégée. Famous unmasking scene still packs a jolt, and the Bal Masque is especially impressive in two-color Technicolor. One of Chaney's finest hours. Most prints are of the 1929 reissue version, but the original is available on DVD; running times vary. Remade several times, and transformed into a Broadway musical. ▼●)

Phantom of the Opera (1943) **C-92m.** *** D: Arthur Lubin. Claude Rains, Susanna Foster, Nelson Eddy, Edgar Barrier, Jane Farrar, Miles Mander, J. Edward Bromberg, Hume Cronyn, Fritz Leiber, Leo Carrillo, Steven Geray, Fritz Feld. First talkie version of venerable melodrama often has more opera than Phantom, but Rains gives fine, sympathetic performance as disfigured composer worshipping young soprano Foster. Oscar winner for Cinematography (Hal Mohr and W. Howard Greene) and Art Direction. ▼●)

Phantom of the Opera, The (1962-British) **C-84m.** ** D: Terence Fisher. Herbert Lom, Heather Sears, Thorley Walters, Edward DeSouza, Michael Gough, Miles Malleson. Lom stars in this third screen version of the story. It's more elaborate than most Hammer horror films, but also more plodding, with only occasional moments of terror. ▼○◗

Phantom of the Rue Morgue (1954) C-84m. ** D: Roy Del Ruth. Karl Malden, Claude Dauphin, Patricia Medina, Steve Forrest, Allyn Ann McLerie, Erin O'Brien-Moore. Remake of MURDERS IN THE RUE MORGUE suffers from Malden's hamminess in the equivalent of Lugosi's role, plus little real atmosphere. On the other hand, there *is* Merv Griffin as a college student! 3-D. ▼

Phantom Planet, The (1961) 82m. *½ D: William Marshall. Dean Fredericks, Coleen Gray, Tony Dexter, Dolores Faith, Francis X. Bushman. Astronaut crash-lands on an asteroid, is shrunken to the tiny size of its inhabitants, and becomes involved in their war with silly-looking aliens. Bushman plays tiny folks' leader Sesom, but he's no Moses, backward or forward. Fascinatingly terrible movie. Also available in a computer-colored version. ◗

Phantom President, The (1932) 80m. ** D: Norman Taurog. George M. Cohan, Claudette Colbert, Jimmy Durante, Sidney Toler. Musical antique about presidential candidate, with lookalike entertainer (Cohan) falling in love with former's girl (Colbert). Interesting only as a curio, with forgettable Rodgers-Hart score.

Phantom Raiders (1940) 70m. **½ D: Jacques Tourneur. Walter Pidgeon, Donald Meek, Joseph Schildkraut, Florence Rice, Nat Pendleton, John Carroll. Slick, fast-paced Nick Carter detective entry has our hero investigating sabotage in the Panama Canal after Allied ships are sunk. ◗

Phantom Ship (1935-British) 80m. ** D: Denison Clift. Bela Lugosi, Shirley Grey, Arthur Margetson, Edmund Willard, Dennis Hoey, Ben Welden, Gibson Gowland. Slow-paced "explanation" of one of the great unsolved maritime mysteries, the disappearance of the crew of the *Mary Celeste,* in 1872. Routine but holds interest. Lugosi is broad but entertaining as superstitious one-armed seaman. All exteriors filmed on a real ship. Original title: THE MYSTERY OF THE MARY CELESTE. ▼◗

Phantom Speaks, The (1945) 69m. ** D: John English. Richard Arlen, Lynne Roberts, Stanley Ridges, Tom Powers, Charlotte Wynters, Jonathan Hale. Strong-willed spirit of executed killer Powers can take control of psychic researcher Ridges to avenge himself on those he hated. Arlen is a reporter sweet on the scientist's daughter. Understated horror melodrama never rises above its B-movie origins but is simple and efficient; ending is unusually grim. Ridges' role resembles his part in BLACK FRIDAY. ▼

Phantom Stagecoach, The (1957) 69m. **½ D: Ray Nazarro. William Bishop, Kathleen Crowley, Richard Webb, Hugh Sanders, John Doucette, Frank Ferguson, Ray Teal, Percy Helton. Stage line operator tries to corner the market by robbing his rival, utilizing an iron-plated, driverless stagecoach with snipers hiding inside. Enter brawny stranger Bishop, hired to ride shotgun to round up the varmints. Brisk, compact B Western with plenty of action. ◗

Phantom Thief, The (1946) 65m. **½ D: D. Ross Lederman. Chester Morris, Jeff Donnell, Richard Lane, Dusty Anderson, George E. Stone, Frank Sully, Marvin Miller. Murder strikes at a seance and Boston Blackie is called in to investigate. Neat series entry with plenty of haunted-house comic relief from Stone.

Pharaoh's Curse (1957) 66m. *½ D: Lee Sholem. Mark Dana, Ziva Rodann, Diane Brewster, George Neise, Kurt Katch, Terence de Marney. 1903 Egyptian expedition is menaced by a rapidly aging vampiric reincarnate and his mysterious sister. Pompous, slow moving; more supernatural melodrama than horror. ▼◗

Phenix City Story, The (1955) 100m. *** D: Phil Karlson. John McIntire, Richard Kiley, Kathryn Grant (Crosby), Edward Andrews. Fast-paced exposé film, compactly told, with realistic production, fine performances as lawyer returns to corrupt hometown, tries to do something about it. Sometimes shown without 13-minute prologue. ◗

PHFFFT (1954) 91m. *** D: Mark Robson. Judy Holliday, Jack Lemmon, Jack Carson, Kim Novak, Donald Curtis. Saucy sex romp by George Axelrod, with Holliday and Lemmon discovering that they were better off before they divorced. ▼◗

Philadelphia Story, The (1940) 112m. **** D: George Cukor. Cary Grant, Katharine Hepburn, James Stewart, Ruth Hussey, John Howard, Roland Young, John Halliday, Virginia Weidler, Mary Nash, Henry Daniell, Hillary Brooke. Talky but brilliant adaptation of Philip Barry's hit Broadway comedy about society girl who yearns for down-to-earth romance; Grant is her ex-husband, Stewart a fast-talking (!) reporter who falls in love with her. Entire cast is excellent, but Stewart really shines in his offbeat, Academy Award–winning role. Donald Ogden Stewart's script also earned an Oscar. Later musicalized as HIGH SOCIETY. Also shown in computer-colored version. ▼◗

Philo Vance Debonair detective Philo Vance, created by master novelist S. S. Van Dine (real name Willard Wright) enjoyed a long and varied screen career, in the guise of many different actors, in films made over a span of some 20 years by several different studios. The man most closely identified with the role was William Powell, who starred in the first three mysteries for Paramount: THE CA-

NARY MURDER CASE, THE GREENE MURDER CASE, and BENSON MURDER CASE. While these very early talkies are somewhat stilted (particularly CANARY, which was completed as a silent film, then hastily adapted for sound), the whodunit angles are first-rate, as urbane Powell solves the bizarre N.Y.C.-based murders. Eugene Pallette was a fine foil as skeptical Sergeant Heath of the homicide squad, with E. H. Calvert as the N.Y.C. D.A. MGM interrupted this series with one of its own, BISHOP MURDER CASE, casting Basil Rathbone as Vance; though a clever whodunit, with the villain matching his crimes to Mother Goose rhymes, the film was all but done in by a snail-like pacing. Powell's last appearance as Vance was in Warner Bros.' THE KENNEL MURDER CASE, probably the best film in the series, brilliantly directed by Michael Curtiz, and also one of the most complex cases of all. None of the later Vance outings reached this peak of ingenuity and sophisticated filmmaking, and Warren William simply marked time in THE DRAGON MURDER CASE at Warners. MGM's next duo cast Paul Lukas in THE CASINO MURDER CASE, and Edmund Lowe in THE GARDEN MURDER CASE; slickly done, they suffered from formula scripting, acting, and direction. Wilfrid Hyde-White starred in a British production of THE SCARAB MURDER CASE in 1936, but this one never found its way to America. Meanwhile, Paramount remade THE GREENE MURDER CASE as NIGHT OF MYSTERY, a routine B with Grant Richards, and Warren William returned for THE GRACIE ALLEN MURDER CASE, with Vance taking a backseat to the comedienne, whose stupidity became a bit overpowering in this story written for her by Van Dine. Warners then redid THE KENNEL MURDER CASE as CALLING PHILO VANCE, another forgettable B with James Stephenson in the role. Philo Vance went into retirement until 1947, when cheapie company PRC brought him back for three final outings, all surprisingly good little whodunits: William Wright starred in PHILO VANCE RETURNS, and Alan Curtis was a deadpan hero in PHILO VANCE'S GAMBLE and the best of all, PHILO VANCE'S SECRET MISSION, with perky Sheila Ryan as his sleuthing girlfriend. The character of Philo Vance, sophisticated and aloof, did not really fit the hard-boiled detective image of the 1940s and 1950s, so the character never appeared again on-screen, but his better outings, from the beginning and end of his film career, remain first-rate murder mysteries today.

PHILO VANCE

Canary Murder Case (1929)
The Greene Murder Case (1929)
Bishop Murder Case (1930)

Benson Murder Case (1930)
The Kennel Murder Case (1933)
The Dragon Murder Case (1934)
Casino Murder Case (1935)
The Garden Murder Case (1936)
Night of Mystery (1937)
The Gracie Allen Murder Case (1939)
Calling Philo Vance (1940)
Philo Vance Returns (1947)
Philo Vance's Gamble (1947)
Philo Vance's Secret Mission (1947)

Philo Vance Returns (1947) **64m.** ** D: William Beaudine. William Wright, Terry Austin, Leon Belasco, Clara Blandick, Iris Adrian, Frank Wilcox, Damian O'Flynn. Vance (Wright) tries to solve the murder of a philandering Casanova (O'Flynn) in this first of three not-bad entries by Poverty-Row studio PRC. Ignoring the Van Dine books, Vance is now a hard-boiled, wise-cracking private eye.▼

Philo Vance's Gamble (1947) **62m.** ** D: Basil Wrangell. Alan Curtis, Terry Austin, Frank Jenks, Tala Birell, Gavin Gordon. Vance (Curtis) is up to his neck in corpses when he takes on a gang of jewel thieves in this acceptable mystery given a (low-budget) film noir mood.

Philo Vance's Secret Mission (1947) **58m.** **½ D: Reginald LeBorg. Alan Curtis, Sheila Ryan, Tala Birell, Frank Jenks, James Bell. Not-bad little mystery (last in the series) has Vance joining a detective magazine as technical advisor, only to see the publisher get bumped off.

Phone Call From a Stranger (1952) **96m.** *** D: Jean Negulesco. Bette Davis, Shelley Winters, Gary Merrill, Michael Rennie, Keenan Wynn, Evelyn Varden, Warren Stevens, Beatrice Straight, Craig Stevens. Engrossing narrative of Merrill, survivor of a plane crash, visiting families of various victims.▼🄳

Phony American, The (1962-German) **72m.** **½ D: Akos Rathony. William Bendix, Christine Kaufmann, Michael Hinz, Ron Randell. Strange casting is more interesting than tale of a German WW2 orphan, now grown up, wishing to become an American, and a U.S. Air Force pilot.

Photo Finish (1957-French) **110m.** ** D: Norbert Carbonnaux. Fernand Gravet, Jean Richard, Micheline, Louis de Funes. Strained comedy about con-men at work at the racetrack.

Picasso Mystery, The SEE: **Mystery of Picasso, The**

Piccadilly (1929-British) **108m.** **½ D: E. A. Dupont. Gilda Gray, Anna May Wong, Jameson Thomas, Cyril Ritchard, King Ho-Chang, Charles Laughton, Hannah Jones. Sensuous (and ambitious) scullery maid (Wong) attracts London nightclub owner Thomas, who casts aside his current flame and dancing star (Gray). Slick, oozing with atmosphere, but supremely silly, this silent film is redeemed by Wong, who is an unforgettable presence in her all-time best part. Laughton is memorable as an angry diner; look for Ray Milland as a Piccadilly Club patron. ▼▶

Piccadilly Incident (1946-British) **88m.** *** D: Herbert Wilcox. Anna Neagle, Michael Wilding, Michael Laurence, Reginald Owen, Frances Mercer. Familiar Enoch Arden theme of supposedly dead wife appearing after husband has remarried. Good British cast gives life to oft-filmed plot.

Piccadilly Jim (1936) **100m.** **½ D: Robert Z. Leonard. Robert Montgomery, Madge Evans, Frank Morgan, Eric Blore, Billie Burke. Fine light-comedy players in P. G. Wodehouse story of father and son's romantic pursuits; overlong.

Pick a Star (1937) **70m.** **½ D: Edward Sedgwick. Jack Haley, Rosina Lawrence, Patsy Kelly, Mischa Auer, Tom Dugan, Stan Laurel, Oliver Hardy. Mistaken as L&H vehicle, actually a Hal Roach production about small-town girl (Lawrence) hoping for stardom in Hollywood. Sappy story, bizarre musical production numbers, but guest stars Stan and Ollie have two very funny scenes. Retitled: MOVIE STRUCK. ▼●▶

Pickpocket (1959-French) **75m.** ***½ D: Robert Bresson. Martin Lasalle, Marika Green, Kassagi, Pierre Leymarie, Jean Pélégri, Dolly Scal, Pierre Étaix. A petty thief finds himself inexorably attracted to a life of crime and spurns a woman's love to become a professional pickpocket. One of Bresson's great films, a brilliantly shot and edited minimalist portrait of the criminal as an existentialist. Paul Schrader borrowed the moving finale for the end of AMERICAN GIGOLO. ▼▶

Pick-up (1933) **80m.** **½ D: Marion Gering. Sylvia Sidney, George Raft, Lillian Bond, William Harrigan, Clarence Wilson, Brooks Benedict, Robert McWade, Louise Beavers. Mildly entertaining drama about ex-con Sidney, who's down on her luck. She conceals her identity and becomes involved with cab driver Raft.

Pickup (1951) **78m.** *½ D: Hugo Haas. Beverly Michaels, Hugo Haas, Allan Nixon, Howland Chamberlin, Jo Carroll Dennison. First of writer-producer-director-actor Haas' tawdry low-budget melodramas is a kind of poor man's THE POSTMAN ALWAYS RINGS TWICE, with gold-digger Michaels marrying aging railroad inspector thinking he's got lots of dough. Not as enjoyably bad as Hugo's later efforts.

Pickup Alley (1957-British) **92m.** *½ D: John Gilling. Victor Mature, Anita Ekberg, Trevor Howard, Eric Pohlmann. Lackluster account of federal agent's trackdown of dope-smuggling syndicate. Original British title: INTERPOL. CinemaScope. ▶

Pickup on South Street (1953) **80m.** ***½

D: Samuel Fuller. Richard Widmark, Jean Peters, Thelma Ritter, Richard Kiley, Murvyn Vye, Milburn Stone. Pickpocket Widmark inadvertently acquires top-secret microfilm and becomes target for espionage agents. Tough, brutal, well-made film, with superb performance by Ritter as street peddler who also sells information. Story by Dwight Taylor; screenplay by the director. Remade as THE CAPE TOWN AFFAIR. ▼▶

Pickwick Papers, The (1952-British) **109m.** *** D: Noel Langley. James Hayter, James Donald, Hermione Baddeley, Kathleen Harrison, Hermione Gingold, Joyce Grenfell, Alexander Gauge, Lionel Murton, Nigel Patrick, Harry Fowler, Donald Wolfit. Flavorful adaptation of Dickens' classic about observations of English society by members of the Pickwick Club. ▼▶

Picnic (1955) **C-115m.** ***½ D: Joshua Logan. William Holden, Rosalind Russell, Kim Novak, Betty Field, Cliff Robertson, Arthur O'Connell, Verna Felton, Susan Strasberg, Nick Adams, Phyllis Newman, Elizabeth W. Wilson. Excellent film of William Inge's Pulitzer Prize–winning play about drifter (Holden) who stops over in Kansas, stealing alluring Novak from his old buddy Robertson (making his film debut). Russell and O'Connell almost walk away with the film in second leads, and supporting roles are expertly filled; adapted by Daniel Taradash. Remade in 2000 for TV. CinemaScope. ▼●▶

Picnic on the Grass (1959-French) **C-91m.** *** D: Jean Renoir. Paul Meurisse, Catherine Rouvel, Fernand Sardou, Jacqueline Morane, Ingrid Nordine, Jean-Pierre Granval. Enchanting romantic comedy depicting the intoxicating effect of Mother Nature and the charms of a sensual peasant girl on an uptight professor who's running for political office on a platform of artificial insemination! Warm, colorful, irreverent satire; gorgeous Impressionistic visual style pays homage to Renoir's famous artist father. ▼

Picture of Dorian Gray, The (1945) **110m.** ***½ D: Albert Lewin. George Sanders, Hurd Hatfield, Donna Reed, Angela Lansbury, Peter Lawford, Lowell Gilmore; narrated by Cedric Hardwicke. Haunting Oscar Wilde story of man whose painting ages while he retains youth. Young Lansbury is poignant, singing "The Little Yellow Bird" (and her real-life mother Moyna MacGill is the Duchess). Sanders leaves indelible impression as elegant heavy. Several color inserts throughout the film. Harry Stradling's cinematography won an Oscar. Remade in 1970 and 2009 as DORIAN GRAY and for TV in 1974, with Nigel Davenport. ▼●▶

Picture Snatcher (1933) **77m.** *** D: Lloyd Bacon. James Cagney, Ralph Bellamy, Alice White, Patricia Ellis, Ralf Harolde. Fast, funny, exciting little film based on true story of daring photographer who got taboo photo of woman in electric chair. Remade as ESCAPE FROM CRIME. ▶

Pied Piper, The (1942) 86m. *** D: Irving Pichel. Monty Woolley, Roddy McDowall, Otto Preminger, Anne Baxter, Peggy Ann Garner. Woolley, not very fond of children, finds himself leading a swarm of them on chase from the Nazis. Entertaining wartime film scripted by Nunnally Johnson from a Nevil Shute novel. Remade for TV as CROSSING TO FREEDOM (1990, with Peter O'Toole).

Pièges (1939-French) 115m. **½ D: Robert Siodmak. Maurice Chevalier, Marie Déa, Pierre Renoir, Erich von Stroheim, Jean Témerson, André Brunot, Jacques Varennes. Someone is bumping off Parisian women who answer personal column ads; a victim's roommate poses as a decoy but falls in love with a nightclub entertainer who becomes the prime suspect. Change of pace for Chevalier is a fairly absorbing and stylish mystery that dissipates its suspense with time-outs for musical numbers. Siodmak's last European film before he came to Hollywood. Remade in the U.S. as LURED.

Pierre of the Plains (1942) 66m. ** D: George B. Seitz. John Carroll, Ruth Hussey, Bruce Cabot, Phil Brown, Reginald Owen, Henry Travers, Evelyn Ankers, Sheldon Leonard. Carroll is a happy-go-lucky French-Canadian trapper who romances Hussey while getting into scrapes with the Northwest Mounted Police and Brooklynesque bad guys Cabot and Leonard. He also has a habit of regularly bursting into his favorite song, "Saskatchewan." Cheerfully simple-minded B remake of a story filmed before in 1918 and 1922.

Pierrot le Fou (1965-French-Italian) C-110m. *** D: Jean-Luc Godard. Jean-Paul Belmondo, Anna Karina, Dirk Sanders, Raymond Devus, Samuel Fuller, Jean-Pierre Léaud. Belmondo and Karina run away together to the South of France; he is leaving his rich wife, she is escaping her involvement with gangsters. Complex, confusing, but engrossing drama, which exudes an intriguing sense of spontaneity. Allegedly shot without a script; also shown at 90m. and 95m. Techniscope. ▼●

Pig Across Paris, A SEE: **La Traversée de Paris**

Pigeon That Took Rome, The (1962) 101m. **½ D: Melville Shavelson. Charlton Heston, Elsa Martinelli, Harry Guardino, Baccaloni, Marietto, Gabriella Pallotta, Debbie Price, Brian Donlevy. Sometimes amusing WW2 comedy of Heston, behind enemy lines, using pigeons to send message to Allies, romancing local girl in whose home he is based. Panavision.

Pigskin Parade (1936) 93m. *** D: David Butler. Stuart Erwin, Patsy Kelly, Jack Haley, Johnny Downs, Betty Grable, Arline Judge, Dixie Dunbar, Judy Garland,

Anthony (Tony) Martin, Elisha Cook, Jr., Grady Sutton, The Yacht Club Boys. Entertaining college football musicomedy with Erwin the hayseed who becomes a gridiron hero, Kelly the coach's wife who knows more about the game than the coach (Haley). Cook appears as an anarchy-spouting campus radical! Garland plays Erwin's kid sister, in her feature debut, and she swings "It's Love I'm After." Alan Ladd appears as a student, and sings with The Yacht Club Boys. ▼●

Pilgrimage (1933) 95m. **½ D: John Ford. Henrietta Crosman, Heather Angel, Norman Foster, Marian Nixon, Lucille La Verne, Hedda Hopper, Charles Grapewin. Unusual film, beautifully directed by Ford, about old woman who breaks up son's romance by sending him off to war (WW1), living to regret it, but finding solace on visit to France. Delicately sentimental, it works up to a point, then goes overboard, but still has some memorable sequences. ▶

Pillars of the Sky (1956) C-95m. **½ D: George Marshall. Jeff Chandler, Dorothy Malone, Ward Bond, Keith Andes, Lee Marvin, Sydney Chaplin. Chandler is aptly cast as swaggering Army officer fighting Indians, courting Malone. CinemaScope. ▶

Pillow of Death (1945) 66m. ** D: Wallace Fox. Lon Chaney, Jr., Brenda Joyce, J. Edward Bromberg, Rosalind Ivan, Clara Blandick. The final *Inner Sanctum* finds lawyer Chaney mixed up with spiritualists after the murder of his wife. The must-miss movie of 1945. ▼▶

Pillow Talk (1959) C-102m. ***½ D: Michael Gordon. Doris Day, Rock Hudson, Tony Randall, Thelma Ritter, Nick Adams, Julia Meade, Allen Jenkins, Lee Patrick, William Schallert, Frances Sternhagen. Rock pursues Doris, with interference from Randall and sideline witticisms from Ritter. Imaginative sex comedy has two stars sharing a party line without knowing each other's identity. Fast-moving; plush sets, gorgeous fashions. Oscar-winning story and screenplay by Stanley Shapiro, Russell Rouse, Clarence Greene, and Maurice Richlin. CinemaScope. ▼●

Pillow to Post (1945) 92m. ** D: Vincent Sherman. Ida Lupino, Sydney Greenstreet, William Prince, Stuart Erwin, Ruth Donnelly, Barbara Brown, Willie Best, Louis Armstrong, Dorothy Dandridge, Bobby (Robert) Blake, William Conrad. Cornball WW2 comedy of oil supplies saleswoman Lupino having soldier Prince pose as her husband so she can get a room; good cast saddled with predictable script. A highlight: Armstrong and Dandridge's all-too-brief appearance performing "What D'ya Say?"

Pilot #5 (1943) 70m. **½ D: George Sidney. Franchot Tone, Marsha Hunt, Gene Kelly, Van Johnson, Alan Baxter, Dick Simmons. GI pilot Tone volunteers to take off from Java on a suicide mission. As he flies to his death, his buddies recall his troubled past (including his involvement with a Huey Long–like governor). Good cast uplifts so-so curio; it's intriguing to see Kelly in a supporting part, as a morally bankrupt hothead. Watch for Peter Lawford at the opening, and see if you can spot Ava Gardner. ▶

"Pimpernel" Smith (1941-British) 122m. *** D: Leslie Howard. Leslie Howard, Mary Morris, Francis L. Sullivan, Hugh McDermott. Zesty updating of THE SCARLET PIMPERNEL to WW2, with Howard replaying the role of the savior of Nazi-hounded individuals. Retitled: MISTER V. ▼

Pink Panther, The (1964) C-113m. ***½ D: Blake Edwards. Peter Sellers, David Niven, Capucine, Robert Wagner, Claudia Cardinale, Brenda DeBanzie, John LeMesurier, Fran Jeffries. Delightful caper comedy introduced bumbling Inspector Clouseau to the world (as well as the cartoon character featured in the opening titles), so obsessed with catching notorious jewel thief "The Phantom" that he isn't aware his quarry is also his wife's lover! Loaded with great slapstick and especially clever chase sequence; beautiful European locations, memorable score by Henry Mancini. Remade in 2006. Followed by A SHOT IN THE DARK. Technirama. ▼◉▶

Pinky (1949) 102m. *** D: Elia Kazan. Jeanne Crain, Ethel Barrymore, Ethel Waters, Nina Mae McKinney, William Lundigan. Pioneer racial drama of black girl passing for white, returning to Southern home; still has impact, with fine support from Mmes. Waters and Barrymore. ▼▶

Pinocchio (1940) C-88m. **** D: Ben Sharpsteen, Hamilton Luske. Voices of Dickie Jones, Christian Rub, Cliff Edwards, Evelyn Venable, Walter Catlett, Frankie Darro. Walt Disney's brilliant, timeless animated cartoon feature, based on the Collodi story about an inquisitive, tale-spinning wooden puppet who wants more than anything else to become a real boy. Technically dazzling, emotionally rich, with unforgettable characters and some of the scariest scenes ever put on film (Lampwick's transformation into a jackass, the chase with Monstro the whale). A joy, no matter how many times you see it. Songs include Oscar-winning "When You Wish Upon a Star." ▼◉▶

Pinocchio in Outer Space (1964-U.S.-French) C-65m. ** D: Ray Goossens. Voices of Arnold Stang, Jess Cain. Watchable cartoon adventure for kids, with unmemorable songs. ▼▶

Pin Up Girl (1944) C-83m. **½ D: Bruce Humberstone. Betty Grable, Martha Raye, John Harvey, Joe E. Brown, Eugene Pallette, Mantan Moreland, Charlie Spivak Orchestra. One of Grable's weaker vehicles,

despite support from Raye and Brown; songs are nil, so is plot. ▼◉▶

Pioneer Builders SEE: **Conquerors, The**

Pirate, The (1948) C-102m. *** D: Vincente Minnelli. Judy Garland, Gene Kelly, Walter Slezak, Gladys Cooper, Reginald Owen, George Zucco, The Nicholas Brothers. Judy thinks circus clown Kelly is really Caribbean pirate; lavish costuming, dancing and Cole Porter songs (including "Be a Clown") bolster stagy plot. Kelly's dances are exhilarating, as usual. Based on S. N. Behrman play. ▼◉▶

Pirate Ship SEE: **Mutineers, The**

Pirates of Blood River, The (1962-British) C-87m. ** D: John Gilling. Kerwin Mathews, Glenn Corbett, Christopher Lee, Marla Landi, Oliver Reed, Andrew Keir, Peter Arne. Earnest but hackneyed account of Huguenots fighting off buccaneers. Hammerscope. ▶

Pirates of Capri, The (1949) 94m. ** D: Edgar G. Ulmer. Louis Hayward, Binnie Barnes, Alan Curtis, Rudolph (Massimo) Serato. Below-average adventure film has Neapolitan natives revolting against tyrant. Lots of action but not much else. Filmed in Italy. Retitled: CAPTAIN SIROCCO. ▼▶

Pirates of Monterey (1947) C-77m. ** D: Alfred L. Werker. Maria Montez, Rod Cameron, Mikhail Rasumny, Philip Reed, Gilbert Roland, Gale Sondergaard. Dull film of exciting period in history, the fight against Mexican control of California in the 1800s.

Pirates of Tripoli (1955) C-72m. ** D: Felix E. Feist. Paul Henreid, Patricia Medina, Paul Newland, John Miljan, William Fawcett. Veteran cast in tired costumer, with colorful scenery the only virtue. ▶

Pirates on Horseback (1941) 69m. *** D: Lesley Selander. William Boyd, Russell Hayden, Andy Clyde, Eleanor Stewart, Morris Ankrum, William Haade, Dennis Moore, Britt Wood. Grizzled miner is murdered for his strike and relative Clyde journeys to claim inheritance, but no one, including shrewd, obsequious heel Ankrum, can locate prospector's lost lode. Suspenseful film also makes time for comedy interludes. A wonderful showcase for the majestic Sierras and the Hoppy Cabin, where Boyd and his wife bunked while on location in Lone Pine. ▼▶

Pistol for Ringo, A (1965-Italian-Spanish) C-99m. **½ D: Duccio Tessari. Montgomery Wood (Giuliano Gemma), Fernando Sancho, Hally Hammond (Lorella De Luca), Nieves Navarro, George Martin, Antonio Casas, José Manuel Martin. Former stuntman Gemma (billed here under his Anglicized pseudonym) became a star in this popular early spaghetti Western. Captured outlaw Ringo is set free to infiltrate a gang of Mexican bandidos who have robbed a bank and taken refuge on a ranch where the sheriff's fiancée is among the hostages. Relatively lighthearted for the genre, but has some exciting action scenes and a good Ennio Morricone score. Followed by THE RETURN OF RINGO. Techniscope.

Pistol Packin' Mama (1943) **64m.** ****½** D: Frank Woodruff. Ruth Terry, Robert Livingston, Wally Vernon, Jack La Rue, Kirk Alyn, Eddie Parker, Helen Talbot. After being cheated out of all her money by gambler Livingston, Terry moves to N.Y.C. and gets a job singing in his nightclub. Then she takes it over—at gunpoint! Terry is appealing in this grade-B fluff, which features the (Nat) King Cole Trio.▼

Pit and the Pendulum (1961) **C-80m.** *****½** D: Roger Corman. Vincent Price, John Kerr, Barbara Steele, Luana Anders, Antony Carbone. Slick horror tale set right after Spanish Inquisition. Price thinks he is his late father, the most vicious torturer during bloody inquisition. Beautifully staged; watch out for that incredible pendulum . . . and bear with slow first half. The second of Corman's Poe adaptations, scripted by Richard Matheson. Panavision.▼◑

Pitfall (1948) **84m.** ******* D: Andre de Toth. Dick Powell, Lizabeth Scott, Jane Wyatt, Raymond Burr, John Litel, Byron Barr. Married man's brief extramarital fling may cost him his job and marriage. Intriguing film noir look at the American dream gone sour, typefied by Powell's character, who's got a house, a little boy, and a perfect wife— but feels bored and stifled.▼◑

Pittsburgh (1942) **90m.** ****** D: Lewis Seiler. Marlene Dietrich, John Wayne, Randolph Scott, Frank Craven, Louise Allbritton, Thomas Gomez, Shemp Howard. Big John loves the coal and steel business more than he does Marlene, which leaves field open for rival Scott. Slow-moving.▼◑

Place in the Sun, A (1951) **122m.** ******* D: George Stevens. Montgomery Clift, Elizabeth Taylor, Shelley Winters, Keefe Brasselle, Raymond Burr, Anne Revere. Ambitious remake of Theodore Dreiser's AN AMERICAN TRAGEDY derives most of its power from Clift's brilliant performance, almost matched by Winters as plain girl who loses him to alluring Taylor. Depiction of the idle rich, and American morals, seems outdated, and Burr's scenes as fiery D.A. are downright absurd. Everyone gets A for effort; six Oscars included Best Direction, Screenplay (Michael Wilson, Harry Brown), Score (Franz Waxman), Cinematography (William C. Mellor), Film Editing, and Costume Design.▼◑

Place of One's Own, A (1945-British) **92m.** ****½** D: Bernard Knowles. James Mason, Margaret Lockwood, Barbara Mullen, Dennis Price, Helen Haye, Ernest Thesiger. Well-made film about couple who buy "haunted" house, and young woman who becomes possessed by spirit of former owner. Well acted but low key. Mason plays unusual role of older, retired man.

Plainsman, The (1936) **113m.** ******* D: Cecil B. DeMille. Gary Cooper, Jean Arthur, James Ellison, Charles Bickford, Porter Hall, Victor Varconi, Helen Burgess, John Miljan, Gabby Hayes, Paul Harvey, Frank McGlynn, Sr. Typical DeMille hokum, a big, outlandish Western which somehow manages to involve Wild Bill Hickok, Calamity Jane, Buffalo Bill, George Custer, and Abraham Lincoln in adventure of evil Bickford selling guns to the Indians. About as authentic as BLAZING SADDLES, but who cares—it's still good fun. Look for Anthony Quinn as a Cheyenne warrior. Remade in 1966.▼◑

Plainsman and the Lady (1946) **87m.** ****** D: Joseph Kane. William Elliott, Vera Ralston, Gail Patrick, Joseph Schildkraut, Andy Clyde. Uninspiring saga of pony express pioneer battling slimy villains and winning lovely Ralston.▼

Planet of the Vampires (1965-Italian) **C-86m.** ****½** D: Mario Bava. Barry Sullivan, Norma Bengell, Angel Aranda, Evi Marandi, Fernando Villena. Eerily photographed, atmospheric science-fantasy of spaceship looking for missing comrades in misty planet where strange power controls their minds. Shown on TV as THE DEMON PLANET.▼◑

Plan 9 From Outer Space (1959) **79m.** BOMB D: Edward D. Wood, Jr. Gregory Walcott, Tom Keene, Duke Moore, Mona McKinnon, Dudley Manlove, Joanna Lee, Tor Johnson, Lyle Talbot, Bela Lugosi, Vampira, Criswell. Hailed as the worst movie ever made; certainly one of the funniest. Pompous aliens believe they can conquer Earth by resurrecting corpses from a San Fernando Valley cemetery. Lugosi died after two days' shooting in 1956; his remaining scenes were played by a taller, younger man holding a cape over his face! So mesmerizingly awful it actually improves (so to speak) with each viewing. And remember: it's all based on sworn testimony! Followed by REVENGE OF THE DEAD.▼◑

Planter's Wife SEE: **Outpost in Malaya**

Plastic Age, The (1925) **73m.** ****½** D: Wesley Ruggles. Clara Bow, Donald Keith, Gilbert Roland, Mary Alden, Henry B. Walthall, David Butler. Athletic Keith heads off to Prescott College, where he's diverted by campus "hotsy-totsy" Bow. Vintage fun, albeit ever-so-predictable. Young Clark Gable is prominently featured as a student.▼◑

Platinum Blonde (1931) **90m.** ******* D: Frank Capra. Jean Harlow, Loretta Young, Robert Williams, Louise Closser Hale, Donald Dillaway, Walter Catlett. Snappy comedy about wisecracking reporter who marries wealthy girl (Harlow) but can't stand confinement of life among high society. Despite engaging presence of Harlow and Young, it's Williams' show all the way.▼▶

Platinum High School (1960) 93m. ** D: Charles Haas. Mickey Rooney, Terry Moore, Dan Duryea, Yvette Mimieux, Conway Twitty, Jimmy Boyd. Limp attempt at sensationalism, with Rooney a father discovering that his son's death at school wasn't accidental. Retitled: TROUBLE AT 16.▼

Playboy of the Western World, The (1962-Irish) C-100m. *** D: Brian Desmond Hurst. Gary Raymond, Siobhan McKenna, Elspeth March, Michael O'Brian, Liam Redmond, Niall MacGinnis. Simple and eloquent, if a bit stagy, version of J. M. Synge's classic satire. Boyish, boastful Christy Mahon (Raymond) charms a small Irish village with his tale of how he did in his dad.▼

Play-Girl (1932) 60m. **½ D: Ray Enright. Winnie Lightner, Loretta Young, Norman Foster, Guy Kibbee, Dorothy Burgess, Noel Madison, James Ellison, Edward Van Sloan. Sassy pre-Code soaper about ambitious department store clerk Young, who's determined not to fall in love. Brash Foster has other ideas—although he's not what he appears to be.

Play Girl (1940) 75m. ** D: Frank Woodruff. Kay Francis, Nigel Bruce, James Ellison, Margaret Hamilton, Mildred Coles, Katharine Alexander. Contrived programmer with Francis playing an aging gold digger who takes pretty but destitute Coles under her wing, but doesn't count on her protégée falling in love.

Playgirl (1954) 85m. **½ D: Joseph Pevney. Shelley Winters, Barry Sullivan, Gregg Palmer, Richard Long, Kent Taylor. Winters is most comfortable in drama about girl involved with gangsters.

Playgirl After Dark SEE: **Too Hot to Handle** (1959)

Playmates (1941) 94m. *½ D: David Butler. Kay Kyser, Lupe Velez, John Barrymore, May Robson, Patsy Kelly, Peter Lind Hayes. Poor musical "comedy" about a has-been Shakespearean actor who teams up with bandleader Kyser in order to pay back taxes. Crude and tasteless; this was Barrymore's last film.▼▶

Please Believe Me (1950) 87m. **½ D: Norman Taurog. Deborah Kerr, Robert Walker, James Whitmore, Peter Lawford, Mark Stevens, Spring Byington. Pleasant fluff of Britisher Kerr aboard liner headed for America, wooed by assorted bachelors aboard, who think she's an heiress.

Please Don't Eat the Daisies (1960) C-111m. *** D: Charles Walters. Doris Day, David Niven, Janis Paige, Spring Byington, Richard Haydn, Patsy Kelly, Jack Weston, Margaret Lindsay. Bright film based on Jean Kerr's stories about a drama critic and his family. Doris sings title song; her kids are very amusing, as are Byington (the mother-in-law),

Kelly (housekeeper), and especially Paige as a temperamental star. Later a TV series. CinemaScope.▼●▶

Please! Mr. Balzac (1956-French) 99m. ** D: Marc Allegret. Daniel Gelin, Brigitte Bardot, Robert Hirsch, Darry Cowl. Lowbrow THEODORA GOES WILD variation, following Bardot's plight after she pens an anonymous, scandalous book. Scripted by Allegret and Roger Vadim. Aka MADEMOISELLE STRIPTEASE and PLUCKING THE DAISY. ▼▶

Please Murder Me (1956) 78m. **½ D: Peter Godfrey. Angela Lansbury, Raymond Burr, Dick Foran, John Dehner, Lamont Johnson, Denver Pyle. Just before signing on as Perry Mason, Burr played a lawyer in this moderately intriguing mystery. He's become romantically involved with Lansbury, the wife of his best pal, and represents her when she kills her hubby. Paging Della Street and Paul Drake! ▼▶

Please Turn Over (1960-British) 86m. **½ D: Gerald Thomas. Ted Ray, Jean Kent, Leslie Phillips, Joan Sims, Julia Lockwood, Tim Seely. OK froth about teen daughter's lurid novel-writing and the repercussions it causes.

Pleasure Cruise (1933) 72m. **½ D: Frank Tuttle. Roland Young, Genevieve Tobin, Ralph Forbes, Una O'Connor, Herbert Mundin, Minna Gombell. Husband and wife take separate vacations, but he jealously follows her on board ocean liner. Chic Lubitsch-like comedy runs out of steam halfway through.

Pleasure Garden, The (1925-British) 75m. ** D: Alfred Hitchcock. Virginia Valli, Carmelita Geraghty, Miles Mander, John Stuart, George Snell. Hitchcock's first feature, shot in Munich; uneven account of a pair of chorus girls, one (Valli) sweet and knowing, the other (Geraghty) a waif who becomes a glamorous bitch. Forgettable silent melodrama.▶

Pleasure of His Company, The (1961) C-115m. ***½ D: George Seaton. Fred Astaire, Lilli Palmer, Debbie Reynolds, Tab Hunter, Gary Merrill, Charlie Ruggles. Delightful fluff, from Samuel Taylor and Cornelia Otis Skinner's play about charming ex-husband who comes to visit, enchanting his daughter and hounding his wife's new husband. Entire cast in rare form. Taylor also scripted.

Pleasure Seekers, The (1964) C-107m. **½ D: Jean Negulesco. Ann-Margret, Pamela Tiffin, Tony Franciosa, Carol Lynley, Gene Tierney, Brian Keith, Gardner McKay, Isobel Elsom. Glossy, semi-musical remake of THREE COINS IN THE FOUNTAIN (by same director) about three girls seeking fun and romance in Spain. CinemaScope.▶

Plot Thickens, The (1936) 67m. **½ D: Ben Holmes. James Gleason, ZaSu Pitts, Oscar Apfel, Owen Davis, Jr., Arthur Aylesworth,

Paul Fix, Barbara Barondess. Pitts takes on the role of sleuthing schoolteacher Hildegarde Withers for this amiable comic whodunit with a plot that (as the title indicates) grows more elaborate as it goes along. ▶

Plough and the Stars, The (1936) **78m. **** D: John Ford. Barbara Stanwyck, Preston Foster, Barry Fitzgerald, Una O'Connor, J. M. Kerrigan, Bonita Granville, Arthur Shields. Dreary, theatrical filmization of Sean O'Casey's play with Foster as Irish revolutionary leader and Stanwyck as longsuffering wife who fears for his life; script by Dudley Nichols.

Plucking the Daisy SEE: **Please! Mr. Balzac**

Plunderers, The (1948) **C-87m. **** D: Joseph Kane. Rod Cameron, Ilona Massey, Adrian Booth, Forrest Tucker. OK Republic Western involving outlaws and Army joining forces against rampaging redskins: clichés are there.

Plunderers, The (1960) **93m. **½** D: Joseph Pevney. Jeff Chandler, John Saxon, Dolores Hart, Marsha Hunt, Jay C. Flippen, Ray Stricklyn, James Westerfield. Above-par study of outlaws interacting with honest townsfolk. ▶

Plunderers of Painted Flats (1959) **77m. *½** D: Albert C. Gannaway. Corinne Calvet, John Carroll, Skip Homeier, George Macready, Edmund Lowe, Bea Benadaret, Madge Kennedy, Joe Besser. Flabby Western of cowpoke seeking his father's killer. Filmed in widescreen Naturama.

Plunder of the Sun (1953) **81m. **½** D: John Farrow. Glenn Ford, Diana Lynn, Patricia Medina, Francis L. Sullivan, Sean McClory. Competent cast in above-average goings-on. Ford is down-and-out American involved with treasure hunt and murder in Mexico. ▶

Plunder Road (1957) **71m. **½** D: Hubert Cornfield. Gene Raymond, Jeanne Cooper, Wayne Morris, Elisha Cook (Jr.), Stafford Repp, Steven Ritch. Unusual, atmospheric crime tale involving an elaborate train heist and the dreams, frustrations, personalities, and fates of the perpetrators, led by cold-blooded Raymond. Regalscope. ▼▶

Plymouth Adventure (1952) **C-105m. **½** D: Clarence Brown. Spencer Tracy, Gene Tierney, Van Johnson, Leo Genn, Dawn Addams, Lloyd Bridges, Barry Jones. Superficial soap opera, glossily done, of the cynical captain of the *Mayflower* (Tracy) and the settlers who sailed from England to New England in the 17th century. This won an Oscar for its special effects. ▼▶

Poacher's Daughter, The (1960-Irish) **74m. **½** D: George Pollock. Julie Harris, Harry Brogan, Tim Seeley, Marie Keen, Brid Lynch, Noel Magee. Harris lends authenticity in title role as simple girl who straightens out her philandering boyfriend. Originally titled SALLY'S IRISH ROGUE.

Pocketful of Miracles (1961) **C-136m. **½** D: Frank Capra. Bette Davis, Glenn Ford, Hope Lange, Arthur O'Connell, Thomas Mitchell, Peter Falk, Edward Everett Horton, Ann-Margret, Mickey Shaughnessy, David Brian, Sheldon Leonard, Barton MacLane, John Litel, Jerome Cowan, Fritz Feld, Jack Elam, Ellen Corby. Capra's final film, a remake of his 1933 LADY FOR A DAY, is just as sentimental, but doesn't work as well. Bette is Apple Annie, a Damon Runyon character; Ford is Dave the Dude, the racketeer who turns her into a lady. Ann-Margret is appealing in her first film. Panavision. ▼▶

Poil de Carotte (1925-French) **108m. ***½** D: Julien Duvivier. Henry Krauss, Charlotte Barbier-Krauss, André Heuzé, Fabien Haziza, Renée Jean, Lydia Zaréna, Suzanne Talba. Heart-tugging, stunningly visual portrait of a young boy (Heuzé) who suffers a Dickensian existence in rural France. Scenario (by Duvivier from Jules Renard's novel) spotlights his fears and travails, and his complex relationship with his oblivious father (Krauss) and abusive mother (mustachioed Barbier-Krauss, who resembles a young Leo G. Carroll). Duvivier remade this in 1932; also remade in 1952 and 1972, as an animated TV series, and for French TV. ▶

Poil de Carotte (1932-French) **91m. ***½** D: Julien Duvivier. Harry Baur, Robert Lynen, Catherine Fonteney, Louis Gauthier, Simone Aubry, Christiane Dor, Maxime Fromiot. Lynen is impressive as a dejected young boy who's saddled with an unfeeling mother (Fonteney) and self-absorbed father (superbly played by Baur). Heartbreaking and unforgettable; imaginatively directed, with a flair for the poetic. Duvivier also scripted, from Jules Renard's novel; he previously filmed this in 1925. Remade in 1952 and 1972, as an animated TV series, and for French TV. ▼▶

Politics (1931) **71m. **½** D: Charles Riesner. Marie Dressler, Polly Moran, Roscoe Ates, Karen Morley, William Bakewell, John Miljan, Joan Marsh, Kane Richmond. Dressler runs for mayor (with Moran as her campaign manager) when a young girl is killed in a speakeasy, but then discovers her own daughter is in love with one of the crooks involved. Sociologically fascinating comedy-drama for the crowd-pleasing team of Dressler and Moran. Ates is hilarious as a stuttering barber. ▶

Pollyanna (1920) **60m. ***** D: Paul Powell. Mary Pickford, Katherine Griffith, Herbert Ralston, Helen Jerome Eddy, William Courtleigh, Herbert Prior. Delightful silent-film adaptation of Eleanor Porter's book about "the glad girl," who smiles through adversity and brings cheer even to the crabby old aunt who takes her in when she's orphaned. Pickford is at her most charming; neat blend of sentiment, slapstick, and wholesome ideals. Remade by Disney in 1960. ▼O▶

Pollyanna (1960) **C-134m.** ***½ D: David Swift. Hayley Mills, Jane Wyman, Richard Egan, Karl Malden, Nancy Olson, Adolphe Menjou, Donald Crisp, Agnes Moorehead. Disney's treatment of Eleanor Porter story is first-rate, as "the glad girl" spreads cheer to misanthropes of a New England town, including her own Aunt Polly (Wyman). Fine direction and script by Swift, excellent performances all around. Mills was awarded a special Oscar for Outstanding Juvenile Performance. First filmed in 1920 with Mary Pickford. Remade for TV in 1989 as POLLY. ▼O▶

Polly of the Circus (1932) **69m.** ** D: Alfred Santell. Clark Gable, Marion Davies, Raymond Hatton, C. Aubrey Smith, David Landau, Maude Eburne. Ill-conceived vehicle for Davies as sexy trapeze artist who falls in love with minister Gable. Ray Milland has bit part as church usher. ▶

Polo Joe (1936) **62m.** ** D: William McGann. Joe E. Brown, Carol Hughes, Skeets Gallagher, Joseph King, Gordon (Bill) Elliott, George E. Stone. Typical Brown comedy in which Joe's got to learn polo fast to impress his girl.

Pontius Pilate (1962-Italian-French) **C-100m.** ** D: Irving Rapper. Jean Marais, Jeanne Crain, Basil Rathbone, John Drew Barrymore, Massimo Serato, Leticia Roman. Adequate retelling of events before and after Christ's crucifixion from viewpoint of Roman procurator. Dubbing and confused script hamper good intentions. Barrymore plays Christ *and* Judas. CinemaScope.

Pony Express (1953) **C-101m.** *** D: Jerry Hopper. Charlton Heston, Rhonda Fleming, Jan Sterling, Forrest Tucker, Michael Moore, Porter Hall. Exuberant action Western (set in 1860s) about the founding of mail routes from Missouri to California, with Buffalo Bill (Heston) and Wild Bill Hickok (Tucker) attempting to scuttle plot to destroy east-west communications and have California secede from the Union. ▼▶

Pony Soldier (1952) **C-82m.** **½ D: Joseph M. Newman. Tyrone Power, Cameron Mitchell, Robert Horton, Thomas Gomez, Penny Edwards. Power is sturdy in actioner about Canadian mounties and their efforts to stave off Indian war. ▼▶

Poor Little Rich Girl, The (1917) **75m.** **½ D: Maurice Tourneur. Mary Pickford, Madlaine Traverse, Charles Wellesley, Gladys Fairbanks, Frank McGlynn, Sr. Mary plays the good-hearted titular character, who is ignored by her wealthy, money-driven father and social-climbing mother. Unsubtle, to put it mildly, but generally entertaining morality tale provides a custom-made role for the charming Pickford (then 25, playing an 11-year-old) as well as a

strange, surreal dream sequence. Frances Marion adapted the play by Eleanor Gates. ▶

Poor Little Rich Girl (1936) **72m.** ***½ D: Irving Cummings. Shirley Temple, Alice Faye, Jack Haley, Gloria Stuart, Michael Whalen, Jane Darwell, Claude Gillingwater, Henry Armetta. One of Shirley's best films, a top musical on any terms, with Temple running away from home, joining vaudeville team of Haley and Faye, winning over crusty Gillingwater, eventually joining her father (Whalen) and lovely Stuart. Best of all is closing "Military Man" number. Also shown in computer-colored version. ▼▶

Poor Rich, The (1934) **76m.** ** D: Edward Sedgwick. Edward Everett Horton, Edna May Oliver, Andy Devine, Leila Hyams, Grant Mitchell, Thelma Todd, Una O'Connor, E. E. Clive, John Miljan. Impoverished Oliver urges her equally threadbare cousin Horton to marry money, so they try to fix up their run-down family mansion to impress the potential bride's family. Slack-paced grade-B comedy with a cast of old pros, including young Ward Bond and Walter Brennan in bit parts.

Poppy (1936) **75m.** **½ D: A. Edward Sutherland. W. C. Fields, Rochelle Hudson, Richard Cromwell, Catherine Doucet, Lynne Overman. Fields re-creates his stage role as ever-conniving carnival man traveling with daughter Hudson. Too much romantic subplot, not enough of W.C.'s antics. The Great Man also starred in a silent version, SALLY OF THE SAWDUST.

Porgy and Bess (1959) **C-138m.** **½ D: Otto Preminger. Sidney Poitier, Dorothy Dandridge, Pearl Bailey, Sammy Davis, Jr., Brock Peters, Diahann Carroll, Ivan Dixon, Clarence Muse. Classic Gershwin folk opera about love, dreams, and jealousy among poor folk of Catfish Row; a bit stiff, but full of incredible music: "Summertime," "It Ain't Necessarily So," "I Got Plenty of Nothin'." Davis shines as Sportin' Life. Music arrangers Andre Previn and Ken Darby won Oscars. Final film of producer Samuel Goldwyn. Originally released at 146m. with overture, intermission/entr'acte, exit music. Todd-AO.

Pork Chop Hill (1959) **97m.** *** D: Lewis Milestone. Gregory Peck, Harry Guardino, Rip Torn, George Peppard, James Edwards, Bob Steele, George Shibata, Biff Elliot, Woody Strode, Robert Blake, Norman Fell, Martin Landau, Bert Remsen, (Harry) Dean Stanton, Gavin MacLeod. Gritty Korean War combat film about the taking of a seemingly worthless hill, and the political (and communications) problems that interfere with lieutenant Peck's efforts to get the job done. Impressive cast of stars-to-be. Based on a true story. ▼O▶

Port Afrique (1956-British) **C-92m.** ** D:

Rudolph Maté. Pier Angeli, Phil Carey, Eugene Deckers, James Hayter, Rachel Gurney, Anthony Newley, Christopher Lee. Bernard Dyer's picaresque actioner gets middling screen version; adulterous wife's past comes to light when husband investigates her death.

Portland Exposé (1957) 71m. *** D: Harold Schuster. Edward Binns, Carolyn Craig, Virginia Gregg, Russ Conway, Lawrence Dobkin, Frank Gorshin, Joseph Marr, Rusty Lane. Family man vows to nail the ruthless mobsters who turned his neighborhood tavern into a den of iniquity and assaulted his teenage daughter. Taut, trim, and quite nasty entry in the string of '50s true-life crime exposés, well shot on real locations. Gorshin is memorably creepy as a thug with a weakness for jailbait.▶

Port of Call (1948-Swedish) 95m. ** D: Ingmar Bergman. Nine-Christine Jonsson, Bengt Eklund, Erik Hell, Berta Hall, Mimi Nelson. Slim, minor early Bergman drama about troubled young outcast Jonsson and her relationship with seaman Eklund. Setting is a grim harbor slum, and film's ultimately hopeful, upbeat tone just doesn't ring true.▼▶

Port of Hell (1954) 80m. **½ D: Harold D. Schuster. Dane Clark, Carole Mathews, Wayne Morris, Marshall Thompson, Marjorie Lord, Hal (Harold) Peary, Otto Waldis, Tom Hubbard. Tensions mount when Clark, warden of the Port of Los Angeles, imposes tough new rules and falls for tug captain Morris' sister (Mathews). Then it's learned a nuclear bomb is set to explode in one of the harbor's ships. Trim thriller with an unusual premise features extensive location shooting.

Port of New York (1949) 86m. ** D: Laslo Benedek. Scott Brady, Richard Rober, K. T. Stevens, Yul Brynner. Gloomy tale of customs agents cracking down on narcotics smuggling; Brynner's film debut . . . with hair!▼▶

Port of Seven Seas (1938) 81m. ** D: James Whale. Wallace Beery, Frank Morgan, Maureen O'Sullivan, John Beal, Jessie Ralph. Marcel Pagnol's FANNY isn't quite suitable Beery material, but he and good cast try their best as O'Sullivan falls in love with adventuresome sailor in Marseilles. Script by Preston Sturges.

Port of Shadows (1938-French) 91m. *** D: Marcel Carné. Jean Gabin, Michel Simon, Michèle Morgan, Pierre Brasseur, (René) Génin, (Marcel) Perez (Pérès), (Roger) Legris. Atmospheric, poetic-realist account of a loner, world-weary Army deserter Gabin (perfectly cast), who wanders into the port city of Le Havre and comes in contact with various characters, including Morgan, who is lusted after by her seemingly erudite guardian (Simon) and a wimpy petty thug (Brasseur). Jacques Prévert's script, from Pierre Mac Orlan's novel, is crammed with grim philosophizing

and cynicism, as if the film's makers smell the coming of WW2 and can only stand aside and shrug their shoulders in despair.▼▶

Portrait in Black (1960) C-112m. **½ D: Michael Gordon. Lana Turner, Anthony Quinn, Sandra Dee, John Saxon, Richard Basehart, Lloyd Nolan, Ray Walston, Anna May Wong. Average murder/blackmail mystery filled with gaping holes that producer Ross Hunter tried to hide with glamorous decor and offbeat casting.▼▶

Portrait of Alison SEE: **Postmark for Danger**

Portrait of a Mobster (1961) 108m. **½ D: Joseph Pevney. Vic Morrow, Leslie Parrish, Peter Breck, Ray Danton, Norman Alden, Ken Lynch. Pretty good gangster movie following the career of Dutch Schultz (Morrow), centering on his relationship with a woman who marries a crooked cop. Danton reprises his role as Legs Diamond from THE RISE AND FALL OF LEGS DIAMOND.

Portrait of an Assassin (1949-French) 86m. **½ D: Bernard-Roland. Maria Montez, Erich von Stroheim, Arletty, Pierre Brasseur, (Marcel) Dalio, Marcel Dieudonné, Jules Berry. Carnival motorcycle stunt rider Brasseur, determined to murder wife Arletty, accidentally shoots another woman and finds himself involved with sultry Montez and crippled von Stroheim. Diverting tale of twisted love will interest fans of Montez and von Stroheim.▶

Portrait of a Sinner (1959-British) 96m. **½ D: Robert Siodmak. William Bendix, Nadja Tiller, Tony Britton, Donald Wolfit, Adrienne Corri, Joyce Carey. Tiller is effective in leading role as corrupting female who taints all in her path. Based on Robin Maugham story. Original British title: THE ROUGH AND THE SMOOTH.▼▶

Portrait of Clare (1951-British) 94m. ** D: Lance Comfort. Margaret Johnston, Richard Todd, Robin Bailey, Ronald Howard. Unpretentious little film, pegged on gimmick of woman telling granddaughter about her past romances.

Portrait of Jennie (1948) 86m. *** D: William Dieterle. Jennifer Jones, Joseph Cotten, Ethel Barrymore, Lillian Gish, Cecil Kellaway, David Wayne, Albert Sharpe, Henry Hull, Florence Bates, Felix Bressart. Strange otherworldly girl (Jones) inspires penniless artist Cotten. David O. Selznick craftsmanship and a fine cast work wonders with foolish story based on the Robert Nathan novella. Originally released with last reel tinted green and final shot in Technicolor; the special effects earned an Academy Award.▼▶

Port Sinister (1953) 65m. ** D: Harold Daniels. James Warren, Lynne Roberts, Paul Cavanagh, William Schallert, House Peters, Jr., Eric Colmar. Sunken pirate stronghold island Port Royal rises again from Caribbean depths. Modest, somewhat dull B movie with stilted dialogue and a few giant crabs; unusual premise keeps it watchable, but little more. ▼

Posse From Hell (1961) **C-89m.** **½ D: Herbert Coleman. Audie Murphy, John Saxon, Zohra Lampert, Vic Morrow, Lee Van Cleef. Gunslinger Murphy, a loner, agrees to pursue four deadly outlaws after they've robbed a bank and kidnapped a young woman, but he's saddled with an inexperienced posse. Murphy vehicle is surprisingly thoughtful and well written.

Possessed (1931) **76m.** *** D: Clarence Brown. Joan Crawford, Clark Gable, Wallace Ford, Skeets Gallagher, John Miljan. Factory girl Crawford becomes the mistress of Park Avenue lawyer Gable. Fascinating feminist drama, crammed with symbolism and featuring a radiant Crawford. Outrageous pre-Code script by Lenore Coffee. ▼▶

Possessed (1947) **108m.** *** D: Curtis Bernhardt. Joan Crawford, Van Heflin, Raymond Massey, Geraldine Brooks, Stanley Ridges. Crawford gives fine performance in intelligent study of woman whose subtle mental problems lead to ruin. Heflin and Massey are the men in her life; Brooks, as Massey's daughter, is radiant in her film debut. Also shown in computer-colored version. ▼▶

Postal Inspector (1936) **58m.** ** D: Otto Brower. Ricardo Cortez, Patricia Ellis, Michael Loring, Bela Lugosi, David Oliver, Wallis Clark. A real-life postal inspector's life could never be this unusual: a novel romantic tale, a big robbery, and a major flood are all worked into this routine B picture. Lugosi plays a nightclub owner forced into crime by gambling debts. Oh, yes, there's also a song titled "Let's Have Bluebirds on All Our Wallpaper." ▼▶

Postman Always Rings Twice, The (1946) **113m.** **** D: Tay Garnett. Lana Turner, John Garfield, Cecil Kellaway, Hume Cronyn, Audrey Totter, Leon Ames, Alan Reed, Wally Cassell. Garfield and Turner ignite the screen in this bristling drama of lovers whose problems just begin when they do away with her husband (Kellaway). Despite complaints of changes in James M. Cain's original story (mostly for censorship purposes), the film packs a real punch and outshines the more explicit 1981 remake. Harry Ruskin and Niven Busch scripted (from Cain's novel). Filmed twice before, in France and Italy. Also shown in computer-colored version. ▼▶

Postman's Knock (1962-British) **87m.** ** D: Robert Lynn. Spike Milligan, Barbara Shelley, John Wood, Miles Malleson, Ronald Adam, Wilfrid Lawson. Milligan is an overly efficient postal worker who upsets the equilibrium of the London post office—and some ambitious thieves. Scattered laughs in this heavy-handed comedy. ▶

Postmark for Danger (1955-British) **84m.** *½ D: Guy Green. Terry Moore, Robert

Beatty, William Sylvester, Geoffrey Keen, Josephine Griffin, Allan Cuthbertson. Hokey, overbaked murder mystery about what happens when an artist's journalist brother is "accidentally" killed in a car crash, and the actress who supposedly died with him mysteriously appears. Original British title: PORTRAIT OF ALISON. ▼▶

Potemkin SEE: **Battleship Potemkin**

Pot o' Gold (1941) **86m.** ** D: George Marshall. James Stewart, Paulette Goddard, Horace Heidt, Charles Winninger, Mary Gordon, Jed Prouty. Very minor item about harmonica-playing, music-mad Stewart, and his experiences with a band of struggling musicians. Stewart called this his worst movie! Look briefly for Art Carney as a radio announcer. ▼▶

Powder River (1953) **C-78m.** ** D: Louis King. Rory Calhoun, Corrine Calvet, Cameron Mitchell, Carl Betz. Straightforward minor Western, with Calhoun becoming town sheriff and clearing up a friend's murder. ▶

Powdersmoke Range (1935) **72m.** ** D: Wallace Fox. Harry Carey, Hoot Gibson, Guinn "Big Boy" Williams, Tom Tyler, Bob Steele, Sam Hardy, Boots Mallory, Sam Hardy, Buzz Barton, Wally Wales, Art Mix, Buffalo Bill, Jr. (Jay Wilsey), Buddy Roosevelt, Franklyn Farnum, William Farnum. Partners Carey, Gibson, and Williams come to the aid of ex-con Steele, who's run up against town boss Hardy. Likable stars are lost in this snail-like story with bad dialogue and a paucity of action. Tyler steals the show as a hired gun. Touted as "the Barnum and Bailey of Westerns," this was the first film based on William Colt MacDonald's *Three Mesquiteers* characters. ▼

Powder Town (1942) **79m.** ** D: Rowland V. Lee. Victor McLaglen, Edmond O'Brien, June Havoc, Dorothy Lovett, Eddie Foy, Jr., Damian O'Flynn, Marten Lamont, Marion Martin. O'Brien is an eccentric scientist working to develop a secret explosive, clashing with plant foreman McLaglen, who's assigned to keep watch and ferret out spies. Humdrum, talky WW2 propaganda is, curiously, played mainly for laughs.

Power and the Glory, The (1933) **76m.** *** D: William K. Howard. Spencer Tracy, Colleen Moore, Ralph Morgan, Helen Vinson. Considered by many a precursor to CITIZEN KANE, Preston Sturges' script tells rags-to-riches story of callous industrialist (Tracy) in flashback. Silent-star Moore gives sensitive performance as Tracy's wife.

Power and the Prize, The (1956) **98m.** **½ D: Henry Koster. Robert Taylor, Elisabeth Mueller, Burl Ives, Charles Coburn, Cedric Hardwicke, Mary Astor. Sporadically effective study of big men in corporation and their private lives. CinemaScope. ▶

Power of the Press (1943) **64m.** ** D: Lew Landers. Guy Kibbee, Gloria Dickson, Otto Kruger, Lee Tracy, Victor Jory,

Minor Watson, Larry Parks. Hard-hitting but dramatically clumsy B movie about small-town newspaperman Kibbee, who challenges N.Y.C. publisher Kruger, a power-hungry isolationist out to foment dissent amongst the public. Sam Fuller's story is more intriguing for its ambition than its execution. ▶

Power of the Whistler (1945) **66m.** **½ D: Lew Landers. Richard Dix, Janis Carter, Jeff Donnell, Loren Tindall, Tala Birell, John Abbott. Carter tries to help amnesiac Dix recall his identity, only to discover that he's an escaped psycho killer. Third *Whistler* entry is a little padded but still genuinely eerie. ▶

Powers Girl, The (1942) **93m.** ** D: Norman Z. McLeod. George Murphy, Anne Shirley, Dennis Day, Benny Goodman, Carole Landis, Alan Mowbray. Trifling plot revolving about Shirley's attempt to become member of famed modeling school, with musical numbers tossed in.

Practically Yours (1944) **90m.** ** D: Mitchell Leisen. Claudette Colbert, Fred MacMurray, Gil Lamb, Robert Benchley, Rosemary DeCamp, Cecil Kellaway. Stars' expertise redeems contrived story of girl intercepting pilot's message to his dog.

Prairie Moon (1938) **58m.** ** D: Ralph Staub. Gene Autry, Smiley Burnette, Shirley Deane, Tommy Ryan, Walter Tetley, David Gorcey, Stanley Andrews, William Pawley, Warner Richmond. Gangster Pawley is gunned down, but before he dies he makes childhood friend Gene swear to take care of his three tough sons. They soon learn the ways of the West and help bring rustlers to justice. Odd combo of Autry and would-be Dead End Kids adds only spark to standard B Western, with Gene singing (and yodeling) "He's in the Jailhouse Now." ▶▌

Prehistoric Women (1950) **C-74m.** BOMB D: Gregg Tallas. Laurette Luez, Allan Nixon, Joan Shawlee, Judy Landon, Jo Carroll Dennison. Sexy, lonely cavewomen (who have their hair permed and faces made up!) set out to find some cave-hunks. Incredibly silly—and incredibly boring—programmer. ▶▌

Prehistoric World SEE: **Teenage Cave Man**

Prelude to Murder SEE: **Dressed to Kill** (1946)

Premature Burial (1962) **C-81m.** ** D: Roger Corman. Ray Milland, Hazel Court, Richard Ney, Heather Angel, Alan Napier, John Dierkes. Title tells the story in another of Corman's Poe adaptations, with Milland oddly cast as medical student with phobia of accidental entombment. Lavish (for this series), but not one of director's best. Panavision. ▶▶●▌

Premier May SEE: **Man to Man Talk**

Presenting Lily Mars (1943) **104m.** ** D: Norman Taurog. Judy Garland, Van Heflin, Fay Bainter, Richard Carlson, Spring By-

ington, Marta Eggerth, Marilyn Maxwell, Ray McDonald, Leonid Kinskey, Connie Gilchrist, Bob Crosby, Tommy Dorsey. Well, there she is, and there lies the script. Stale story of determined girl getting big chance on Broadway only comes alive when Judy sings. From a Booth Tarkington novel. ▼●▌

President's Lady, The (1953) **96m.** *** D: Henry Levin. Charlton Heston, Susan Hayward, John McIntire, Fay Bainter, Carl Betz. Heston as Andrew Jackson and Hayward the lady with a past he marries work well together in this fictional history of 1800s America, based on the Irving Stone novel. Heston would again play "Old Hickory" five years later in THE BUCCANEER. ▼

President's Mystery, The (1936) **80m.** *** D: Phil Rosen. Henry Wilcoxon, Betty Furness, Sidney Blackmer, Evelyn Brent, Barnett Parker. Utterly fascinating Depression-era curio about a prominent lawyer/lobbyist (Wilcoxon) who reluctantly helps greedy capitalists kill some pro–labor/small business legislation. Believing his life empty, he liquidates his assets and "reinvents" himself—but not without murderous complications. This would make a great double bill with King Vidor's OUR DAILY BREAD. Based on an idea by F.D.R., developed as a magazine article by six writers (including S. S. Van Dine)! Screenplay by Lester Cole and Nathanael West. Beware 53m. version. ▼▌

President Vanishes, The (1934) **83m.** *** D: William A. Wellman. Edward Arnold, Arthur Byron, Paul Kelly, Peggy Conklin, Andy Devine, Janet Beecher, Osgood Perkins, Sidney Blackmer, Edward Ellis, Irene Franklin, Charles Grapewin, Rosalind Russell. The American president fakes his own kidnapping in order to thwart an avaricious group of business tycoons who use propaganda and a fascist group called the Grey Shirts to force the U.S. into taking part in a European war. Utterly fascinating and still-timely political fable, if not always believable. Based on a novel by an anonymous author who was later revealed to be Rex Stout.

Pressure Point (1962) **91m.** *** D: Hubert Cornfield. Sidney Poitier, Bobby Darin, Peter Falk, Carl Benton Reid, Mary Munday, Barry Gordon, Howard Caine. Intelligent drama, with Poitier the prison psychiatrist trying to ferret out the problems of his Nazi patient (Darin). Based on a true case from Dr. Robert M. Lindner's *The Fifty-Minute Hour.* ▼▌

Prestige (1932) **71m.** **½ D: Tay Garnett. Ann Harding, Melvyn Douglas, Adolphe Menjou, Clarence Muse, Ian MacLaren. Flamboyant direction and solid performances elevate hackneyed melodrama about life at French Army outpost in the Far East where White Supremacy—and Douglas' sanity—are threatened.

Pretender, The (1947) **69m. **½ D: W. Lee Wilder. Albert Dekker, Catherine Craig, Linda Stirling, Charles Drake, Charles Middleton, Alan Carney. Dekker gives sharply etched performance as N.Y.C. financier trying to do in a competitor, discovering he may be the victim instead. ▶

Pretty Baby (1950) **92m.** ** D: Bretaigne Windust. Dennis Morgan, Betsy Drake, Zachary Scott, Edmund Gwenn, Barbara Billingsley. Coy minor comedy involving working girl Drake, who snowballs a gimmick to get a subway seat on the morning train into a good job and romance. ▶

Pretty Boy Floyd (1960) **96m.** ** D: Herbert J. Leder. John Ericson, Barry Newman, Joan Harvey, Herb (Jason) Evers, Carl York, Peter Falk, Roy Fant, Shirley Smith. Average chronicle of infamous 1930s gangster, played energetically by Ericson. ▶

Preview Murder Mystery, The (1936) **62m.** *** D: Robert Florey. Reginald Denny, Frances Drake, Gail Patrick, Rod La Rocque, Ian Keith, George Barbier. A murderer stalks a movie studio preying on the cast and director of a new production. Stylish, lightning-paced B movie from Florey, with a nifty mystery and good studio atmosphere. Cast features former silent-film stars, including Conway Tearle, Jack Mulhall, Bryant Washburn, Franklyn Farnum, and Chester Conklin.

Price of Fear, The (1956) **79m. **½ D: Abner Biberman. Merle Oberon, Lex Barker, Charles Drake, Gia Scala, Warren Stevens. Middling account of Oberon involved in hit-and-run accident which snowballs her life into disaster. ▶

Pride and Prejudice (1940) **118m.** **** D: Robert Z. Leonard. Greer Garson, Laurence Olivier, Edna May Oliver, Edmund Gwenn, Mary Boland, Maureen O'Sullivan, Karen Morley, Melville Cooper, E. E. Clive, Ann Rutherford, Marsha Hunt. Outstanding adaptation of Jane Austen's novel about five husband-hunting sisters in 19th-century England. Excellent cast, fine period flavor in classic comedy of manners; Aldous Huxley was one of the screenwriters. Cedric Gibbons and Paul Groesse's art direction deservedly earned an Oscar. Also shown in computer-colored version.▼●▶

Pride and the Passion, The (1957) **C-132m. **½ D: Stanley Kramer. Cary Grant, Frank Sinatra, Sophia Loren, Theodore Bikel, John Wengraf. Miscast actioner involving capture of huge cannon by British naval officer (Grant) in 19th-century Spain. Spectacle scenes—filmed on location—are impressive; but most of the film is ridiculous. From the C. S. Forester novel. VistaVision.▼●▶

Pride of St. Louis, The (1952) **93m. **½ D: Harmon Jones. Dan Dailey, Joanne Dru,

Richard Crenna, Hugh Sanders, Richard Hylton, James Brown. Dailey does well in this otherwise formula biography of brash, colorful Hall of Fame pitcher Dizzy Dean. Watch for Chet Huntley as a baseball broadcaster.▼▶

Pride of the Blue Grass (1954) **C-71m.** ** D: William Beaudine. Lloyd Bridges, Vera Miles, Margaret Sheridan, Arthur Shields, Joan Shawlee. Familiar racetrack story; competent production.

Pride of the Bowery (1941) **61m.** ** D: Joseph H. Lewis. Leo Gorcey, Bobby Jordan, Sunshine Sammy Morrison, Donald Haines, Bobby Stone, Carleton Young, Kenneth Howell, David Gorcey, Mary Ainslee. The East Side Kids are sent to a Civilian Conservation Corps. camp where Muggs is in training for a big boxing match; some well-shot ring scenes.▼▶

Pride of the Marines (1945) **119m. ***½ D: Delmer Daves. John Garfield, Eleanor Parker, Dane Clark, John Ridgely, Rosemary DeCamp, Ann Doran, Ann Todd, Warren Douglas. Ensemble acting by Warner Bros. stock company enhances true account of Marine blinded during Japanese attack, with Garfield as injured Al Schmid, Clark as sympathetic buddy. Screenplay by Albert Maltz.▶

Pride of the West (1938) **55m. **½ D: Lesley Selander. William Boyd, George Hayes, Russell Hayden, Earle Hodgins, Charlotte Field, Billy King. After stage holdup, Hopalong Cassidy rides to rescue Bar 20 pals and determines town banker is behind wrongdoing. Compact, well mounted, if a bit slow; adapted from series creator Clarence E. Mulford's 1920 novel *Johnny Nelson.* In tribute to Russell Harlan's picturesque photography, extraordinary credit line reads, "Photographed near Lone Pine, California, in the shadow of majestic Mt. Whitney."▼▶

Pride of the Yankees, The (1942) **127m. **** D: Sam Wood. Gary Cooper, Teresa Wright, Babe Ruth, Walter Brennan, Dan Duryea, Ludwig Stossel, Addison Richards, Hardie Albright. Superb biography of baseball star Lou Gehrig, with Cooper giving excellent performance; fine support from Wright as devoted wife. Truly memorable final sequence. Script by Jo Swerling and Herman J. Mankiewicz, with Oscar-winning editing by Daniel Mandell. Also shown in computer-colored version.▼●▶

Prime Minister, The (1941-British) **109m. **½ D: Thorold Dickinson. John Gielgud, Diana Wynyard, Will Fyffe, Owen Nares, Fay Compton, Pamela Standish, Frederick Leister, Lyn Harding. Episodic account of the life and works of Benjamin Disraeli. Gielgud at 37 ages from a budding novelist of 30 to an elder statesman of 70, painting the Tory leader as a man of noble principle who proves invaluable to Queen Victoria (a credible Compton) and her expanding British Empire. Gielgud is at least equal to George Arliss' 1929 portrayal, but the movie's budget doesn't begin to support the script's intentions. ▼❱

Primrose Path, The (1925) **53m.** **½ D: Harry O. Hoyt. Wallace MacDonald, Clara Bow, Arline Pretty, Stuart Holmes, Pat Moore, Tom Santschi, Lydia Knott. MacDonald is a reckless lout who drinks, gambles, writes bad checks, becomes involved in diamond smuggling—and more. What will it take to reform him? So-so programmer is worth a look for Bow's radiant presence as a Broadway beauty. ▼❱

Primrose Path (1940) **93m.** **½ D: Gregory La Cava. Ginger Rogers, Joel McCrea, Marjorie Rambeau, Miles Mander, Henry Travers. Girl from wrong side of the tracks falls in love with ambitious young McCrea; starts engagingly, drifts into dreary soap opera and melodramatics. Rambeau is excellent as Ginger's prostitute mother. ▼❱

Prince and the Pauper, The (1937) **120m.** ***½ D: William Keighley. Errol Flynn, Billy and Bobby Mauch, Claude Rains, Alan Hale, Montagu Love, Henry Stephenson, Barton MacLane. Rousing filmization of Mark Twain's story of young look-alikes, one a mistreated urchin, the other a prince, exchanging places. Top-billed Flynn, cast as the boys' rescuer, doesn't appear until around the midway point. Great music score by Erich Wolfgang Korngold. Remade as CROSSED SWORDS. Also available in computer-colored version. ▼❱●

Prince and the Showgirl, The (1957) **C-117m.** **½ D: Laurence Olivier. Marilyn Monroe, Laurence Olivier, Sybil Thorndike, Jeremy Spenser, Richard Wattis. Thoughtful but slow-moving comedy of saucy American showgirl Monroe being romanced by Prince Regent of Carpathia (Olivier) during the 1911 coronation of George V. Filmed in England, with delightful performances by Monroe and Olivier. Script by Terence Rattigan from his play *The Sleeping Prince*. The film's troubled production was later dramatized in MY WEEK WITH MARILYN. ▼❱●

Prince of Foxes (1949) **107m.** **½ D: Henry King. Tyrone Power, Wanda Hendrix, Orson Welles, Marina Berti, Everett Sloane, Katina Paxinou. Lavish, incredibly handsome costume epic of Renaissance-era Italy (filmed on location), with adventurer Power defying all-powerful Cesare Borgia. Story elements—from Samuel Shellabarger novel—don't match impact of Leon Shamroy's sumptuous cinematography. ❱

Prince of Pirates (1953) **C-80m.** **½ D: Sidney Salkow. John Derek, Barbara Rush, Whitfield Connor, Edgar Barrier. Enjoyable little costumer involving French-Spanish wars.

Prince of Players (1955) **C-102m.** **½

D: Philip Dunne. Richard Burton, Maggie McNamara, Raymond Massey, Charles Bickford, John Derek, Eva Le Gallienne, Mae Marsh, Sarah Padden. Burton is 19th-century actor Edwin Booth, embroiled in more offstage drama than on. Shakespearean excerpts thrown in; well performed by earnest cast. Derek plays John Wilkes Booth. Script by Moss Hart. CinemaScope.

Prince of Thieves, The (1948) **C-72m.** ** D: Howard Bretherton. Jon Hall, Patricia Morison, Adele Jergens, Alan Mowbray, Michael Duane. Colorful swashbuckler of Robin Hood and Maid Marian, aimed at juvenile audiences. ▼❱

Princess and the Pirate, The (1944) **C-94m.** *** D: David Butler. Bob Hope, Virginia Mayo, Walter Slezak, Walter Brennan, Victor McLaglen, Hugo Haas, Marc Lawrence. One of Bob's wackiest; he and glamorous Virginia are on the lam from pirate McLaglen, trapped by potentate Slezak. Brennan is hilarious as a pirate; great closing gag, too. ▼❱●

Princess Comes Across, The (1936) **76m.** *** D: William K. Howard. Carole Lombard, Fred MacMurray, Douglass Dumbrille, Alison Skipworth, William Frawley, Porter Hall, Sig Ruman, Mischa Auer. Lombard, posing as royalty on ocean voyage, meets romantic MacMurray; together they are involved in whodunit. And Fred sings "My Concertina." Delightful blend of comedy and mystery. ▼❱

Princesse Tam Tam (1935-French) **77m.** *** D: Edmond T. Greville. Josephine Baker, Albert Prejean, Robert Arnoux, Germaine Aussey, Georges Peclet, Viviane Romance, Jean Galland. Baker lives up to her legend in this disarming reworking of *Pygmalion*: a poor, beautiful, wild African lass is polished and educated by writer Prejean, then passed off as an Indian princess—much to the consternation of his snobbish, two-timing wife. Charming story (by Pepito Abatino, then Baker's husband), lavish Busby Berkeley–ish musical numbers. Partially filmed in Tunisia. ▼❱●

Princess of the Nile (1954) **C-71m.** **½ D: Harmon Jones. Debra Paget, Jeffrey Hunter, Michael Rennie, Dona Drake, Wally Cassell, Jack Elam, Lee Van Cleef. Hokey script diverts any potential this costumer may have had. ❱

Princess O'Rourke (1943) **94m.** **½ D: Norman Krasna. Olivia de Havilland, Robert Cummings, Charles Coburn, Jack Carson, Jane Wyman, Harry Davenport, Gladys Cooper. Very dated comedy starts charmingly with pilot Cummings falling in love with Princess de Havilland, bogs down in no longer timely situations, unbearably coy finale involving (supposedly) F.D.R. himself. Krasna won Best Screenplay Oscar. ❱

Princess Yang Kwei Fei (1955-Japanese) **C-91m.** **** D: Kenji Mizoguchi. Machiko

Kyo, Masayuki Mori, So Yamamura, Eitaro Shindo, Sakae Ozawa. Emperor Mori takes country girl Kyo as his concubine. He is forced out of power by his greedy family: she is killed, and he worships her statue. Breathtakingly beautiful, poetic love story/fable/tragedy.▼

Prince Valiant (1954) **C-100m.** ****½** D: Henry Hathaway. James Mason, Janet Leigh, Robert Wagner, Debra Paget, Sterling Hayden, Victor McLaglen, Donald Crisp, Brian Aherne. Hal Foster's famed comic-strip character is the hero of this cardboard costumer decked out in 20th Century-Fox splendor, battling and loving in Middle Ages England. Script by Dudley Nichols. CinemaScope.▼▶

Prince Who Was a Thief, The (1951) **C-88m.** ****½** D: Rudolph Maté. Tony Curtis, Piper Laurie, Everett Sloane, Jeff Corey, Betty Garde. Juvenile costumer with Curtis fighting to regain his rightful seat on the throne; sparked by enthusiastic performances.

Priorities on Parade (1942) **79m.** ****** D: Albert S. Rogell. Ann Miller, Johnny Johnston, Betty Rhodes, Jerry Colonna, Vera Vague, Eddie Quillan, Harry Barris, Rod Cameron. Swing bandleader Johnston and his septet sign up at a defense plant where they entertain the workers, but vocalist-dancer Miller won't sacrifice her career for Uncle Sam. Then welding boss Rhodes turns out to have a nice voice. Topical (if inconsequential) B musical was cowritten by songwriter Frank Loesser.

Prisoner, The (1955-British) **91m.** ******* D: Peter Glenville. Alec Guinness, Jack Hawkins, Raymond Huntley, Wilfrid Lawson. Grim account of cardinal in Iron Curtain country undergoing grueling interrogation. Guinness-Hawkins interplay is superb.▼▶

Prisoner of Shark Island, The (1936) **95m.** *****½** D: John Ford. Warner Baxter, Gloria Stuart, Claude Gillingwater, John Carradine, Harry Carey, Arthur Byron, Ernest Whitman, Francis McDonald. Excellent film based on true story of Dr. Samuel Mudd, who innocently treated John Wilkes Booth's broken leg after Lincoln assassination, and was sentenced to life imprisonment. Gripping story; Baxter superb, Carradine memorable as villainous sergeant, Whitman fine as Baxter's black comrade. Scripted by Nunnally Johnson. Remade as HELLGATE and the TV movie THE ORDEAL OF DR. MUDD.▶

Prisoner of the Iron Mask, The (1962-Italian) **C-80m.** ****½** D: Francesco De Feo. Michael Lemoine, Wandisa Guida, Andrea Bosic, Jany Clair, Giovanni Materassi. Usual costume shenanigans: an evil count imprisons a man who has proof of the nobleman's treachery. Based not on the expected Dumas novel, but on his *Ten Years After*. D'Artagnan and The Three Musketeers do not appear. Techniscope.

Prisoner of the Volga (1960-Yugoslavian) **C-102m.** ****** D: W. Tourjansky. John Derek, Elsa Martinelli, Dawn Addams, Wolfgang Preiss, Gert Frobe. Well-mounted but ordinary costume drama of soldier who suffers when he seeks revenge on general who impregnated his wife. Totalscope.

Prisoner of War (1954) **80m.** ****** D: Andrew Marton. Ronald Reagan, Steve Forrest, Dewey Martin, Oscar Homolka, Robert Horton, Paul Stewart, Harry Morgan, Stephen Bekassy, Darryl Hickman, Jerry Paris. G.I. Reagan parachutes into North Korea to observe the manner in which the Commies are brainwashing American P.O.W.s. By-the-numbers Korean War drama, primarily of interest as a reflection of its era.

Prisoner of Zenda, The (1922) **113m.** ******* D: Rex Ingram. Ramon Novarro, Lewis Stone, Alice Terry, Robert Edeson, Stuart Holmes, Malcolm McGregor, Barbara La Marr, Snitz Edwards. Entertaining version of the Anthony Hope novel (and play by Edward E. Rose), with Stone, light-years away from Judge Hardy, offering a charismatic performance as Rudolf Rassendyll, a commoner forced to impersonate his double, the heir to the throne of Ruritania. Novarro matches him as Rupert of Hentzau. Great fun! Previously filmed in 1914, then again in 1937, 1952 (with Stone in a supporting role), and 1979.▼▶

Prisoner of Zenda, The (1937) **101m.** ******** D: John Cromwell. Ronald Colman, Madeleine Carroll, Douglas Fairbanks, Jr., C. Aubrey Smith, Raymond Massey, Mary Astor, David Niven, Montagu Love, Alexander D'Arcy. Lavish costume romance/adventure with excellent casting; Colman is forced to substitute for lookalike cousin, King of Ruritanian country, but commoner Colman falls in love with regal Carroll. Fairbanks nearly steals the show as villainous Rupert of Hentzau. Screenplay by John L. Balderston, from Anthony Hope's novel. Remade in 1952 and 1979. Also shown in computer-colored version.▼▶

Prisoner of Zenda, The (1952) **C-101m.** ****½** D: Richard Thorpe. Stewart Granger, Deborah Kerr, Jane Greer, Louis Calhern, Lewis Stone, James Mason, Robert Douglas, Robert Coote. Plush but uninspired remake of the Anthony Hope novel, chronicling the swashbuckling adventures of Granger, a dead ringer for a small European country's king. Stick with the Ronald Colman version; this one copies it scene for scene.▼▶

Prisoners of the Casbah (1953) **C-78m.** ***½** D: Richard Bare. Gloria Grahame, Turhan Bey, Cesar Romero, Nestor Paiva. Low-budget costumer with diverting cast in stale plot of princess and her lover fleeing killers in title locale. Turhan Bey's last movie—for 40 years.

Prison Farm (1938) **69m.** ****½** D: Louis King. Shirley Ross, Lloyd Nolan, John

Howard, J. Carrol Naish, Porter Hall, Esther Dale, May Boley, Marjorie Main. Innocent Ross gets involved with no-good Nolan; they both end up in a brutal prison, where she falls for compassionate doctor Howard. Formula jailhouse melodrama, smoothly done, with memorable performances by Naish as a corrupt sheriff and Main in atypical serious role as a matron.

Prison Train (1938) 63m. **½ D: Gordon Wiles. Fred Keating, Linda Winters (Dorothy Comingore), Clarence Muse, Faith Bacon, Alexander Leftwich, Nestor Paiva. Stylized, atmospheric little chronicle of racketeer Keating, who's convicted of murder and is traveling cross-country to begin doing time at Alcatraz. Hampered by its ultra-low budget but still a nice surprise. Aka PEOPLE'S ENEMY.▼▶

Prison Warden (1949) 62m. ** D: Seymour Friedman. Warner Baxter, Anna Lee, James Flavin, Harlan Warde, Charles Cane, Reginald Sheffield. A public health official is recruited to take over a brutal prison and enact reforms, unaware that his new wife is plotting to break out her former boyfriend. Baxter looks tired in his penultimate film, a standard big house yarn with a few unusual angles.

Private Affairs of Bel Ami, The (1947) 112m. ***½ D: Albert Lewin. George Sanders, Angela Lansbury, Ann Dvorak, Frances Dee, Albert Basserman, Warren William, John Carradine. Delicious, literate adaptation (by Lewin) of Guy de Maupassant's "story of a rogue." Sanders, who gets ahead by using his charm on prominent women, denies himself the real love of Lansbury. Fine performances; beautifully photographed by Russell Metty.▼

Private Buckaroo (1942) 68m. ** D: Edward Cline. The Andrews Sisters, Dick Foran, Joe E. Lewis, Donald O'Connor, Peggy Ryan, Jennifer Holt. Mini-musical from Universal Pictures is vehicle for 1940s favorite sister trio, accompanied by Harry James et al. in Army camp show.▼▶

Private Detective (1939) 55m. **½ D: Noel Smith. Jane Wyman, Dick Foran, Gloria Dickson, Maxie Rosenbloom, John Ridgely, Morgan Conway, John Eldredge, Willie Best, Leo Gorcey. Homicide inspector Foran is continually upstaged by private eye Wyman when the two are forced to team up to solve the case of a murdered millionaire. Snappy, enjoyable mystery-comedy with Warners basically rehashing the formula of their defunct *Torchy Blane* series.

Private Detective 62 (1933) 67m. **½ D: Michael Curtiz. William Powell, Margaret Lindsay, Ruth Donnelly, Arthur Hohl, Natalie Moorhead, Arthur Byron. Powell accepts job with shady private detective Hohl and agrees to dupe wealthy Lindsay, but falls in love with her instead. Warner Bros. programmer picks up after a slow start.▶

Private Eyes (1953) 64m. **½ D: Edward Bernds. Leo Gorcey, Huntz Hall, David (Gorcey) Condon, Bennie Bartlett, Rudy Lee, William Phillips, Joyce Holden, Bernard Gorcey, Chick Chandler, Myron Healey. Good *Bowery Boys* entry, as they open a detective agency when Sach develops the ability to read minds.▶

Private Hell 36 (1954) 81m. **½ D: Don Siegel. Ida Lupino, Steve Cochran, Howard Duff, Dean Jagger, Dorothy Malone. Well-balanced account of guilt overcoming two cops who retrieve stolen money but keep some for themselves. Interesting low-budgeter with first-rate cast, but gets awfully talky in the second half. Lupino also wrote and produced the film with Collier Young.▼▶

Private Life of Don Juan, The (1934-British) 80m. ** D: Alexander Korda. Douglas Fairbanks, Merle Oberon, Binnie Barnes, Joan Gardner, Benita Hume, Athene Seyler, Melville Cooper. Lifeless costumer with aging Fairbanks in title role, pursuing a bevy of beauties in his final film.▼▶

Private Life of Henry VIII, The (1933-British) 97m. **** D: Alexander Korda. Charles Laughton, Binnie Barnes, Robert Donat, Elsa Lanchester, Merle Oberon, Miles Mander, Wendy Barrie, John Loder. Sweeping historical chronicle of 16th-century English monarch, magnificently captured by Oscar-winning Laughton in a multifaceted performance. Lanchester fine as Anne of Cleves, with top supporting cast. Also shown in computer-colored version.▼▶

Private Lives (1931) 84m. *** D: Sidney Franklin. Norma Shearer, Robert Montgomery, Una Merkel, Reginald Denny, Jean Hersholt. Sparkling, witty adaptation of the Noel Coward comedy about a divorced couple (Shearer and Montgomery) who marry others and find themselves honeymooning at the same hotel.▼▶

Private Lives of Adam and Eve, The (1960) C/B&W-87m. BOMB D: Albert Zugsmith, Mickey Rooney. Mickey Rooney, Mamie Van Doren, Fay Spain, Mel Tormé, Martin Milner, Tuesday Weld, Cecil Kellaway, Paul Anka, Ziva Rodann. Perfectly awful fantasy about a stranded Nevada couple, Ad (Milner) and Evie (Van Doren), who dream that they are back in the Garden of Eden. Rooney chews the scenery as the Devil.

Private Lives of Elizabeth and Essex, The (1939) C-106m. ***½ D: Michael Curtiz. Bette Davis, Errol Flynn, Olivia de Havilland, Donald Crisp, Alan Hale, Vincent Price, Henry Stephenson, Henry Daniell, James Stephenson, Ralph Forbes, Robert Warwick, Leo G. Carroll. Colorful, elaborate costume drama with outstanding performance by Davis as queen whose love for dashing Flynn is thwarted. Not authentic history, but good drama. Norman Reilly Raine and Aeneas MacKenzie adapted Maxwell Anderson's play *Elizabeth the Queen*. Adult film debut of Nanette Fabray (Fabares). Aka ELIZABETH THE QUEEN. ▼▶

Private Number (1936) **80m.** **½ D: Roy Del Ruth. Robert Taylor, Loretta Young, Basil Rathbone, Patsy Kelly, Marjorie Gateson, Paul Harvey, Joe (E.) Lewis. Young is charming as a maid who becomes romantically involved with her employers' son (Taylor), causing various complications. Rathbone is effective as the villain butler in this otherwise OK melodrama. Filmed previously in 1919 (with Fannie Ward) and 1931 (with Constance Bennett), as COMMON CLAY. ▶

Private's Affair, A (1959) **C-92m.** **½ D: Raoul Walsh. Sal Mineo, Christine Carere, Barry Coe, Barbara Eden, Gary Crosby, Terry Moore, Jim Backus, Jessie Royce Landis. Energetic young cast involved in putting on the "big Army show" on TV. CinemaScope. ▶

Private's Progress (1956-British) **99m.** *** D: John Boulting. Richard Attenborough, Jill Adams, Dennis Price, Terry-Thomas, Ian Carmichael, Peter Jones, Christopher Lee. Prize collection of funny men, splendidly played by cast, involved in Army shenanigans. Sequel: I'M ALL RIGHT JACK. ▼▶

Private War of Major Benson, The (1955) **C-105m.** **½ D: Jerry Hopper. Charlton Heston, Julie Adams, William Demarest, Tim Hovey, Sal Mineo, David Janssen, Tim Considine, Milburn Stone. Hovey is the little boy at military school who charms rugged commander-turned-schoolmaster Heston into sympathetic person. Remade as MAJOR PAYNE (1995). ▼

Private Worlds (1935) **84m.** **½ D: Gregory La Cava. Claudette Colbert, Charles Boyer, Joan Bennett, Joel McCrea, Helen Vinson, Esther Dale, Jean Rouverol. Dated but engrossing tale of mental institution, with doctors Boyer and Colbert giving restrained performances; noteworthy support by Bennett.

Prix de Beauté (1930-French) **94m.** **½ D: Augusto Genina. Louise Brooks, Jean Bradin, Georges Charlia, Gaston Jacquet, A. Nicolle. Brooks is the whole show in this, her first sound film (and last major screen role). The story may be clichéd—a melodrama in which she's cast as a typist who becomes a beauty queen—but Brooks is as lovely and sensuous as ever. The final sequence is truly memorable. René Clair, originally scheduled to direct, had a hand in the script. Aka MISS EUROPE. ▼▶

Prize, The (1963) **C-136m.** *** D: Mark Robson. Paul Newman, Elke Sommer, Edward G. Robinson, Diane Baker, Kevin McCarthy, Micheline Presle, Leo G. Carroll. Irving Wallace novel is mere stepping stone for glossy spy yarn set in Stockholm, involving participants in Nobel Prize ceremony. Newman and Sommer make handsome leads; Robinson has dual role.

Fast-moving fun; script by Ernest Lehman. Panavision. ▼▶

Prizefighter and the Lady, The (1933) **102m.** *** D: W. S. Van Dyke. Myrna Loy, Max Baer, Otto Kruger, Walter Huston, Jack Dempsey, Primo Carnera, Jess Willard, James J. Jeffries. Entertaining film breathes life into potential clichés; real-life boxing champ Baer plays a prizefighter who falls for high-class gangster's moll Loy. Many boxing and wrestling greats cameo in extended, exciting prize-fight finale. ●▶

Prize of Arms, A (1961-British) **105m.** **½ D: Cliff Owen. Stanley Baker, Tom Bell, Helmut Schmid, John Phillips. Hindered by heavy British accents ruining much dialogue, tale unfolds methodical plan for big heist of Army funds.

Prize of Gold, A (1955-British) **C-98m.** *** D: Mark Robson. Richard Widmark, Mai Zetterling, Nigel Patrick, Donald Wolfit, Eric Pohlmann. Taut caper in post-WW2 Berlin involving a planned heist of gold from the air lift circuit.

Problem Girls (1953) **71m.** *½ D: E. A. Dupont. Helen Walker, Ross Elliott, Susan Morrow, Anthony Jochim, James Seay, Marjorie Stapp, Roy Regnier, Beverly Garland, Joyce Jameson, Nan Leslie, Mara Corday. Doctor Elliott hires on as psychologist at a school for warped rich girls. The students are collectively certifiable, the faculty even more so; the romance languages professor did 20 years for murdering his wife with a meat cleaver! Positively weird and hilariously awful, with a great B-movie cast. Also known as THE VELVET CAGE.

Prodigal, The (1931) **76m.** ** D: Harry Pollard. Lawrence Tibbett, Esther Ralston, Roland Young, Cliff Edwards, Purnell Pratt, Hedda Hopper, Emma Dunn, Stepin Fetchit. The ne'er-do-well scion of an aristocratic Southern family returns home after years of kicking around the country as a hobo, only to fall in love with his brother's wife. Easygoing drama for famed opera star Tibbett allows him to perform a few songs, but the stereotyped portrayal of black plantation workers may make you cringe.

Prodigal, The (1955) **C-114m.** **½ D: Richard Thorpe. Lana Turner, Edmund Purdom, James Mitchell, Louis Calhern, Audrey Dalton, Neville Brand, Taina Elg, Cecil Kellaway, Henry Daniell, Walter Hampden, Joseph Wiseman. Juvenile biblical semi-spectacle, with Turner the evil goddess of love corrupting Purdom; glossy MGM vehicle. CinemaScope. ▼●▶

Professional Soldier (1936) **78m.** **½ D: Tay Garnett. Victor McLaglen, Freddie Bartholomew, Gloria Stuart, Constance Collier, Michael Whalen. McLaglen is hired to kidnap young king Bartholomew, but mutual friendship gets in the way. Good teaming supports average script, based on a Damon Runyon story. ▶

Professional Sweetheart (1933) **68m.** ****** D: William A. Seiter. Ginger Rogers, ZaSu Pitts, Norman Foster, Frank McHugh, Edgar Kennedy, Betty Furness, Gregory Ratoff, Sterling Holloway, Franklin Pangborn. Good cast can't put over weak radio spoof, with Rogers as airwaves star who becomes engaged to hick Foster in publicity stunt.

Professor Beware (1938) **87m.** ****½** D: Elliott Nugent. Harold Lloyd, Phyllis Welch, William Frawley, Etienne Girardot, Raymond Walburn, Lionel Stander, Thurston Hall. One of Lloyd's last vehicles has good moments, but tale of archeologist searching for rare tablet is thin.

Project Moon Base (1953) **63m.** ****** D: Richard Talmadge. Donna Martell, Hayden Rorke, Ross Ford, Larry Johns, Herb Jacobs. In the near future, three people make the first trip to the Moon from the American space station circling the Earth, but one of them is an enemy spy. Mediocre acting in this routine but scientifically accurate story. Famed sci-fi writer Robert A. Heinlein cowrote the movie; the low budget shows.**▼●**

Promises! Promises! (1963) **75m.** BOMB D: King Donovan. Jayne Mansfield, Marie McDonald, Tommy Noonan, Mickey Hargitay, Fritz Feld, T. C. Jones, Claude Stroud, Marjorie Bennett, Eddie Quillan, Eileen Barton, Imogene Coca. Dreadful comedy about couples Mansfield-Noonan and McDonald-Hargitay, and their sexual shenanigans on a cruise. Notorious in its day for Jayne's baring her bod, a first for its time. Still, beware: it *is* a truly bad movie. Mansfield was in real life married to Hargitay; Noonan coproduced and coscripted.**▼●**

Promoter, The (1952-British) **88m.** ******* D: Ronald Neame. Alec Guinness, Glynis Johns, Valerie Hobson, Petula Clark, Edward Chapman. Charming comedy about a likable but penniless young man who sees how to get ahead in the world—and seizes his opportunity. Script by Eric Ambler from Arnold Bennett's story *The Card,* also its title in England.**▼**

Prosperity (1932) **87m.** ******* D: Sam Wood. Marie Dressler, Polly Moran, Anita Page, Norman Foster, Jacquie Lyn, Jerry Tucker, Henry Armetta, John Miljan. In the last of their several popular teamings, Dressler and Moran sock over lots of belly laughs as longtime friends who become feuding mothers-in-law when their kids marry. Fascinating Depression-era banking subplot enhances this genuinely funny film.

Proud and Profane, The (1956) **111m.** ****½** D: George Seaton. William Holden, Deborah Kerr, Thelma Ritter, Dewey Martin, William Redfield, Ross Bagdasarian, Marion Ross. Spotty WW2 romance story has many parallels to FROM HERE TO ETERNITY, but Kerr-Holden romance is never believable. VistaVision.

Proud and the Beautiful, The SEE: **Proud Ones, The** (1953)

Proud Ones, The (1953-French-Mexican) **94m.** *****½** D: Yves Allegret. Michele Morgan, Gérard Philipe, Victor Manuel Mendoza, Michele Cordoue. Well-bred Morgan and down-and-out doctor Philipe cross paths in Vera Cruz, Mexico, in this absorbing tale of love, religion, and the effects of a deadly plague on the impoverished populace. Striking and atmospheric; based on Jean-Paul Sartre novel *L'Amour Redempteur* (set in China!). Original title: LES ORGUEILLEUX. Aka THE PROUD AND THE BEAUTIFUL.**▼**

Proud Ones, The (1956) **C-94m.** ****½** D: Robert D. Webb. Robert Ryan, Virginia Mayo, Jeffrey Hunter, Robert Middleton, Walter Brennan. Staunch acting involving the inevitable showdown between disabled sheriff and outlaws perks up this Western. CinemaScope.**●**

Proud Rebel, The (1958) **C-103m.** ******* D: Michael Curtiz. Alan Ladd, Olivia de Havilland, Dean Jagger, David Ladd, Cecil Kellaway, Henry Hull, John Carradine, (Harry) Dean Stanton. Well-presented post–Civil War study of two-fisted Southerner Ladd seeking medical help for mute son (played by Ladd's real-life son); de Havilland is the woman who tames him. **▼●**

Proud Valley (1940-British) **77m.** ****½** D: Pen Tennyson. Paul Robeson, Edward Chapman, Simon Lack, Rachel Thomas, Edward Rigby. Mild drama of Welsh coalmining village beset by mine shutdown; uplifted only by Robeson's commanding presence and fine voice.**▼●**

Prowler, The (1951) **92m.** *****½** D: Joseph Losey. Van Heflin, Evelyn Keyes, John Maxwell, Katharine Warren. Stark, sinuous film noir about a (literal) bad cop (Heflin) who seduces a vulnerable married woman. Opens with a bang and never lets up. Unusually nasty and utterly unpredictable. Striking camerawork (by Arthur Miller) and production design. Screenplay by Dalton Trumbo, who was blacklisted at the time and received no credit, though he is heard as the voice of Keyes' husband on the radio.**●**

Psyche '59 (1964-British) **94m.** ****½** D: Alexander Singer. Patricia Neal, Curt Jurgens, Samantha Eggar, Ian Bannen, Elspeth March. Turgid melodrama involving infidelity, with good cast doing their best.**●**

Psycho (1960) **109m.** ******** D: Alfred Hitchcock. Anthony Perkins, Janet Leigh, Vera Miles, John Gavin, Martin Balsam, John McIntire, Lurene Tuttle, Simon Oakland, John Anderson, Mort Mills, Frank Albertson, Patricia Hitchcock. The Master's most notorious film is still terrifying after all these years, as larcenous Leigh picks the wrong place to spend a night: The Bates Motel (12 cabins, 12 vacancies . . . and 12 showers), run by a peculiar young man and his crotchety old "mother." Hitchcock's murder set pieces are so potent, they can galvanize (and frighten) even a viewer who's seen them before! Bernard Herrmann's legendary (and endlessly imitated) score adds much to the excitement. Script by Joseph Stefano from the Robert Bloch novel. Followed by three sequels (the last for cable TV), a TV movie (BATES MOTEL), a remake in 1998, and a cable TV series, also called *Bates Motel*. ▼●❙

Psycho Killers, The SEE: **Mania**

Psychomania (1963) 93m. *½ D: Richard Hilliard. Lee Philips, Shepperd Strudwick, Jean Hale, Lorraine Rogers, Margot Hartman, Kaye Elhardt, James Farentino, Dick Van Patten, Sylvia Miles. War hero turned painter, suspected of murdering two beautiful young women, undertakes his own investigation. Exploitive independent production filmed in Connecticut. Originally titled VIOLENT MIDNIGHT.▼❙

PT 109 (1963) **C-140m.** ** D: Leslie H. Martinson. Cliff Robertson, Ty Hardin, James Gregory, Robert Culp, Grant Williams, Lew Gallo, Errol John, Michael Pate, Robert Blake, Biff Elliot, Norman Fell. Gung-ho WW2 action yarn based on President John F. Kennedy's experiences in the Pacific as a PT boat captain. Very much of its time; it was released in June of the year JFK died. Panavision.▼●❙

PT Raiders SEE: **Ship That Died of Shame, The**

Public Be Damned SEE: **World Gone Mad, The**

Public Cowboy No. 1 (1937) **60m.** *** D: Joseph Kane. Gene Autry, Smiley Burnette, Ann Rutherford, William Farnum, Arthur Loft, Frankie Marvin, House Peters, Jr. The Old West meets the New as deputy sheriff Gene battles truck rustlers who use shortwave radio and airplanes to divert cattle on their way to a meatpacking plant. Good Autry vehicle with one song ("The West Ain't What It Used To Be") that even makes fun of singing cowboys!▼❙

Public Defender, The (1931) **69m.** ** D: J. Walter Ruben. Richard Dix, Shirley Grey, Purnell Pratt, Ruth Weston, Edmund Breese, Frank Sheridan, Alan Roscoe, Boris Karloff, Nella Walker. Dix is a society gentleman who works undercover as The Reckoner in a crusade against unscrupulous banking executives who framed an innocent man and defrauded customers. Disappointingly static treatment of an intriguing premise. Karloff's role is unmemorable. ❙

Public Enemy, The (1931) **84m.** ***½ D: William Wellman. James Cagney, Jean Harlow, Eddie Woods, Beryl Mercer, Donald Cook, Joan Blondell, Mae Clarke. Prohibition gangster's rise and fall put Cagney on the map, and deservedly so; he makes up for film's occasional flaws and dated notions. Still pretty powerful, this is the one where Cagney smashes a grapefruit in Clarke's face.

Screened for decades at 82m., restored to full length for DVD. ▼●❙

Public Enemy's Wife (1936) **69m.** **½ D: Nick Grinde. Pat O'Brien, Margaret Lindsay, Robert Armstrong, Cesar Romero, Dick Foran. Romero is good as mobster serving life whose insane jealousy over wife (Lindsay) makes her a perfect pawn for G-man O'Brien. Not-bad Warner Bros. B. Remade as BULLETS FOR O'HARA.

Public Hero #1 (1935) **91m.** **½ D: J. Walter Ruben. Lionel Barrymore, Jean Arthur, Chester Morris, Joseph Calleia, Paul Kelly, Lewis Stone. Interesting but uneven hybrid of gangster yarn (with jailhouse theatrics dominating the first half) and romantic comedy. Arthur is always a pleasure to watch. Remade in 1941 as THE GET-AWAY.

Public Menace, The (1935) **72m.** **½ D: Erle C. Kenton. Jean Arthur, George Murphy, Douglass Dumbrille, George McKay, Robert Middlemass, Victor Kilian. Wacky manicurist Arthur somehow loses her American citizenship and cons cocky reporter Murphy into marrying her in exchange for a phony scoop about a gangster. Pretty amusing bit of froth blending screwball comedy, romance, and crime. ❙

Public Pigeon No. One (1957) **C-79m.** ** D: Norman Z. McLeod. Red Skelton, Vivian Blaine, Janet Blair, Allyn Joslyn, Jay C. Flippen. Bland Skelton vehicle with Red accidentally exposing gang of crooks; typical slapstick. Based on a 1956 *Climax* TV episode in which Skelton starred. ❙

Public Wedding (1937) **58m.** **½ D: Nick Grinde. Jane Wyman, William Hopper, Dick Purcell, Marie Wilson, Berton Churchill, James Robbins, Raymond Hatton, Veda Ann Borg, Horace McMahon, Eddie Anderson. To avoid the hoosegow, down-on-their-luck carny hustlers scheme to raise some dough by staging a fake public wedding. Fast-paced, generally enjoyable comedy.

Pumpkin Eater, The (1964-British) **110m.** *** D: Jack Clayton. Anne Bancroft, Peter Finch, James Mason, Cedric Hardwicke, Alan Webb, Richard Johnson, Maggie Smith, Eric Porter. Intelligent if overlong drama chronicling the plight of the mother of eight children, who discovers her third husband has been unfaithful. Fine performances all around, with Bancroft a standout. Script by Harold Pinter, from the Penelope Mortimer novel. ▼❙

Purchase Price, The (1932) **68m.** ** D: William A. Wellman. Barbara Stanwyck, George Brent, Lyle Talbot, Hardie Albright, David Landau, Murray Kinnell, Leila Bennett, Dawn O'Day (Anne Shirley). Pre-Code Warner Bros. film about nightclub singer Stanwyck, who's seen and done it all, taking it on the lam and becoming—of all things—a mail-order bride for a naive North Dakota farmer. Starts out snappy, winds up silly, though Stanwyck is always worth watching. ▼❙

Pure Hell of St. Trinian's, The (1960-British) **94m.** ** D: Frank Launder. Cecil Parker, Joyce Grenfell, George Cole, Thorley Walters. Absence of Alastair Sim from series lessens glow; outrageous girls' school is visited by sheik seeking harem.▼

Purim Player, The SEE: **Der Purimshpiler**

Purple Gang, The (1960) **85m.** ** D: Frank McDonald. Barry Sullivan, Robert Blake, Elaine Edwards, Marc Cavell, Jody Lawrance, Suzy Marquette, Joseph Turkel. Capable cast, limp police-vs.-gangster yarn.◗

Purple Heart, The (1944) **99m.** *** D: Lewis Milestone. Dana Andrews, Farley Granger, Sam Levene, Richard Conte, Donald Barry, Trudy Marshall, Tala Birell, Nestor Paiva, Benson Fong, Marshall Thompson, Richard Loo. Absorbing drama of U.S. Air Force crew shot down during Tokyo raid, held prisoner and put on trial. Receives strong performances by good cast. Produced and cowritten by Darryl F. Zanuck.▼◗

Purple Mask, The (1955) **C-82m.** ** D: H. Bruce Humberstone. Tony Curtis, Colleen Miller, Gene Barry, Dan O'Herlihy, Angela Lansbury, George Dolenz, Allison Hayes. Wooden historical adventure with Curtis as a Scarlet Pimpernel–like swashbuckling hero who goes up against Napoleon in 1803 France. CinemaScope.

Purple Noon (1960-French-Italian) **C-118m.** *** D: René Clement. Alain Delon, Marie Laforet, Maurice Ronet, Frank Latimore, Ave Ninchi. Marvelously photographed (in southern Italy, by Henri Decaë), tautly directed suspenser about Delon, who envies playboy-friend Ronet and schemes to murder him and assume his identity. Based on Patricia Highsmith's *The Talented Mr. Ripley.* That's Romy Schneider among the friends stopping by cafe in opening scene. Remade as THE TALENTED MR. RIPLEY; also see THE AMERICAN FRIEND and RIPLEY'S GAME. ▼◗

Purple Plain, The (1954-British) **C-102m.** *** D: Robert Parrish. Gregory Peck, Win Min Than, Bernard Lee, Maurice Denham, Brenda De Banzie, Lyndon Brook. Absorbing Eric Ambler–scripted drama of love, loss, and survival during WW2, charting the plight of disaffected pilot Peck, whose wife was killed on the night of their wedding during a London air raid.◗

Pursued (1947) **101m.** *** D: Raoul Walsh. Teresa Wright, Robert Mitchum, Judith Anderson, Dean Jagger, Alan Hale, Harry Carey, Jr., John Rodney. Grim, passionate Western noir, a family saga of love, hate, revenge, and a hint of incest. Mitchum is an orphan raised by Anderson; he falls in love with foster sister Wright, complicated by his having killed her murderous brother. Stunning photography by James Wong Howe. ▼◗▶

Pursuit (1935) **61m.** ** D: Edwin L. Marin. Chester Morris, Sally Eilers, Scotty Beckett, Henry Travers, C. Henry Gordon, Dorothy Peterson. Morris and Eilers are chased by plane, car, and on foot while helping a little boy escape his nasty custody-claiming relatives and delivering him to his mother in Mexico. Briskly paced but routine B movie with too much comic-romantic banter.

Pursuit of the Graf Spee (1956-British) **C-119m.** **½ D: Michael Powell, Emeric Pressburger. John Gregson, Anthony Quayle, Peter Finch, Ian Hunter, Bernard Lee, Patrick Macnee, Christopher Lee. Taut documentary-style account of WW2 chase of German warship by British forces. Original title: THE BATTLE OF THE RIVER PLATE. VistaVision.▼◗

Pursuit to Algiers (1945) **65m.** **½ D: Roy William Neill. Basil Rathbone, Nigel Bruce, Marjorie Riordan, Rosalind Ivan, Martin Kosleck, John Abbott. Lesser *Sherlock Holmes* entry is still diverting tale of heir to an Eastern throne on a perilous Mediterranean voyage.▼◗

Pushover (1954) **88m.** **½ D: Richard Quine. Fred MacMurray, Kim Novak, Phil Carey, Dorothy Malone, E. G. Marshall. MacMurray is cop who falls in love with Novak, moll of a bank heist artist; he plots with her to rob the robber, and complications ensue. Good cast covers familiar ground.▼◗

Puttin' on the Ritz (1930) **88m.** ** D: Edward Sloman. Harry Richman, Joan Bennett, James Gleason, Aileen Pringle, Lilyan Tashman. Famed nightclub entertainer Richman made his film debut in this primitive early talkie about vaudevillian who can't handle success and turns to drink. You may do the same after watching Richman's performance—though he does introduce the title song by Irving Berlin. Partially redeemed by a few production numbers originally filmed in Technicolor, including a charming "Alice in Wonderland." Sets by William Cameron Menzies.

Puzzle of the Red Orchid, The (1962-German) **94m.** ** D: Helmut Ashley. Christopher Lee, Marisa Mell, Klaus Kinski, Fritz Rasp, Adrian Hoven. Moderate Edgar Wallace entry; Scotland Yard and F.B.I. track down international crime syndicate. Retitled: THE SECRET OF THE RED ORCHID.▼◗

Pygmalion (1938-British) **95m.** **** D: Anthony Asquith, Leslie Howard. Leslie Howard, Wendy Hiller, Wilfrid Lawson, Marie Lohr, David Tree. Superlative filmization of the witty G. B. Shaw play which became MY FAIR LADY. Howard excels as the professor, with Hiller his Cockney pupil. Shaw's screenplay won an Oscar, as did its adaptation by Ian Dalrymple, Cecil Lewis, and W. P. Lipscomb. Edited by David Lean.▼◗▶

Pygmy Island (1950) **69m.** *½ D: William Berke. Johnny Weissmuller, Ann Savage, David Bruce, Tristram Coffin, Steven Geray, William Tannen, Billy Curtis, Billy Barty, Pierce Lyden. *Jungle Jim* Weissmuller leads a search party to find missing Savage in this silly entry exemplified by having famous white midget Curtis as the leader of the pygmy tribe. ◗

Pyro (1964-Spanish) **C-99m.** **½ D: Julio Coll. Barry Sullivan, Martha Hyer, Sherry Moreland, Soledad Miranda. Strange chiller of man burned in fire seeking revenge on ex-girlfriend who started it. ▼◗

Q Planes (1939-British) **78m.** *** D: Tim Whelan. Laurence Olivier, Ralph Richardson, Valerie Hobson, George Curzon, David Tree, George Merritt, Gus McNaughton. Delightful tongue-in-cheek espionage tale, with masterminds stealing British aircraft secrets. Richardson is a joy as lighthearted inspector who cracks the case. Retitled: CLOUDS OVER EUROPE. ▼●

Quai des Orfèvres (1947-French) **106m.** ***½ D: Henri-Georges Clouzot. Louis Jouvet, Suzy Delair, Bernard Blier, Simone Renant, Charles Dullin, Henri Arius, Pierre Larquey. When a wealthy "dirty old man" is murdered, there is no shortage of suspects. A police procedural layered with telling character portraits, from a poor simp (Blier) who's suspicious of his coquettish wife, a music-hall singer (Delair), to a dour police detective (Jouvet). Clouzot's staging of key scenes—an argument during a musical rehearsal, a long scene in the back of a theater while chorus girls are dancing—is masterful, as is the overall look of this b&w gem. Title refers to the location of Paris' police headquarters. Originally shown in the U.S. as JENNY LAMOUR. ▼◗

Quality Street (1937) **84m.** *** D: George Stevens. Katharine Hepburn, Franchot Tone, Fay Bainter, Eric Blore, Cora Witherspoon, Estelle Winwood, Bonita Granville, Joan Fontaine, William Bakewell. Hepburn is radiant in delicate adaptation of James Barrie's whimsical play: "old maid" masquerades as her own niece in order to win back the love of a man who hasn't seen her in ten years. Filmed before in 1927, with Marion Davies. ▼◗

Quantez (1957) **C-80m.** **½ D: Harry Keller. Fred MacMurray, Dorothy Malone, Sydney Chaplin, John Gavin, John Larch, Michael Ansara. Above-par Western involving robbery gang heading for Mexico border, encountering stiff opposition along the way. CinemaScope. ◗

Quantrill's Raiders (1958) **C-68m.** ** D: Edward Bernds. Steve Cochran, Diane Brewster, Leo Gordon, Gale Robbins. Predictable Civil War account of the outlaw's planned attack on a Kansas arsenal. CinemaScope. ◗

Quare Fellow, The (1962-Irish) **85m.** ***½ D: Arthur Dreifuss. Patrick McGoohan, Sylvia Syms, Walter Macken, Dermot Kelly, Jack Cunningham, Hilton Edwards. Irish-made adaptation of Brendan Behan play deals with new prison guard, well played by McGoohan, who changes mind about capital punishment. Finely acted; excellent script by director Dreifuss. ◗

Quartet (1948-British) **120m.** **** D: Ken Annakin, Arthur Crabtree, Harold French, Ralph Smart. Basil Radford, Naunton Wayne, Mai Zetterling, Ian Fleming, Jack Raine, Dirk Bogarde, Cecil Parker, Honor Blackman. Superb movie with Somerset Maugham introducing four of his tales, each with different casts and moods. Its success prompted a sequel, TRIO. ▼

Quatermass II (1957-British) **82m.** *** D: Val Guest. Brian Donlevy, Michael Ripper, Sidney James, Bryan Forbes, John Longden, Vera Day, William Franklyn. Even better than the original, THE QUATERMASS XPERIMENT, this tense, scary science-fiction thriller concerns a secret alien invasion and BODY SNATCHERS–like takeovers of human beings. Donlevy is stern as Prof. Quatermass. U.S. title: ENEMY FROM SPACE. Followed by QUATERMASS AND THE PIT. ▼◗

Quatermass Xperiment, The (1955-British) **82m.** *** D: Val Guest. Brian Donlevy, Margia Dean, Jack Warner, Richard Wordsworth. A spaceship returns to Earth with only one man left on board; infested by an alien entity, he gradually transforms into a hideous monster. Tense, imaginative, adult; well acted by all concerned. Based on hit BBC-TV serial by Nigel Kneale. U.S. title: THE CREEPING UNKNOWN. Followed by three sequels, beginning with QUATERMASS II. ▼◗

Quatorze Juillet (1932-French) **98m.** *** D: René Clair. Annabella, Georges Rigaud, Pola Illery, Paul Olivier, Raymond Cordy. Delightful comedy about life in Paris on Bastille Day, centering on the adventures of flower girl Annabella and her taxi driver boyfriend. Filled with fresh, funny touches; Clair at his best. Aka JULY 14TH. ◗

Quebec (1951) **C-85m.** ** D: George Templeton. John Barrymore, Jr., Corinne Calvet, Barbara Rush, Patric Knowles. Historical nonsense set in 1830s Canada during revolt against England. Filmed on location. ▼◗

Queen Bee (1955) **95m.** *** D: Ranald MacDougall. Joan Crawford, Barry Sullivan, Betsy Palmer, John Ireland, Fay Wray, Tim Hovey. Crawford in title role has field day maneuvering the lives of all in her Southern mansion, with husband Sullivan providing the final ironic twist. ▼◗

Queen Christina (1933) **97m.** **** D: Rouben Mamoulian. Greta Garbo, John Gilbert, Ian Keith, Lewis Stone, C. Aubrey

Smith, Gustav von Seyffertitz, Reginald Owen. Probably Garbo's best film, with a haunting performance by the radiant star as 17th-century Swedish queen who relinquishes her throne for her lover, Gilbert. Garbo and Gilbert's love scenes together are truly memorable, as is the famous final shot. Don't miss this one. ▼●▶

Queen Kelly (1928) **96m.** ***½ D: Erich von Stroheim. Gloria Swanson, Seena Owen, Walter Byron, Tully Marshall, Madame Sul Te Wan. A convent girl is swept off her feet by a roguish prince—then sent to live in East Africa where her aunt runs a brothel! Fascinating, extravagantly decadent von Stroheim melodrama that was never completed; this restored version wraps up story with stills and subtitles. A must for film buffs; exquisitely photographed, with scene-stealing performance by Owen as the mad queen. The European-release version, in which the girl meets with an entirely different fate, is also available. ▼●▶

Queen of Babylon, The (1954-Italian) **C-98m.** *½ D: Carlo Bragaglia. Rhonda Fleming, Ricardo Montalban, Roldano Lupi, Carlo Ninchi. American stars can't elevate elephantine study of ancient Babylonia.

Queen of Burlesque (1946) **70m.** *½ D: Sam Newfield. Evelyn Ankers, Carleton G. Young, Marion Martin, Rose La Rose, Alice Fleming. Low-budget suspenser unstrung backstage at burlesque theater. ▼

Queen of Destiny SEE: **Sixty Glorious Years**

Queen of Outer Space (1958) **C-79m.** ** D: Edward Bernds. Zsa Zsa Gabor, Eric Fleming, Laurie Mitchell, Patrick Waltz, Paul Birch, Lisa Davis, Dave Willock. Manned rocketship from Earth is abducted to Venus, where the planet is ruled entirely by women. Silly, to say the least, but at least some of the laughs were intentional. Zsa Zsa, incidentally, does *not* play the title character! CinemaScope. ▼▶

Queen of Spades, The (1949-British) **95m.** ***½ D: Thorold Dickinson. Anton Walbrook, Edith Evans, Ronald Howard, Mary Jerrold, Yvonne Mitchell, Anthony Dawson. Exquisite production of an unusual, macabre Alexander Pushkin story about an impoverished Russian officer (Walbrook, in a rich performance) who will do anything to learn the mystical secret of winning at cards known only by an imperious old woman (Evans). Brilliant use of chiaroscuro lighting and atmosphere in this British sleeper set in 1806. ▼▶

Queen of Spades (1960-Russian) **C-100m.** ***½ D: Roman Tikhomirov. Oleg Strizhenov, Zurab Anzhaparidze, Olga Krasina, Tamara Milashkina. Stark version of Tchaikovsky opera *Pikovaya Dama*, performed by Bolshoi Theater company; deals with young man consumed by gambling urge, leading to his and girlfriend's destruction. ▼▶

Queen of the Gorillas SEE: **Bride and the Beast, The**

Queen of the Jungle (1935) **87m.** BOMB D: Robert Hill. Mary Kornman, Reed Howes, Dickie Jones, Marilyn Spinner, Lafe McKee. Hilariously awful feature adapted from cheapie serial that rivals anything ever made by Edward Wood. A little girl is accidentally cast off in a balloon; she lands in the middle of the African jungle and grows up to become the title monarch. A laugh riot. ▼▶

Queen of the Mob (1940) **61m.** **½ D: James Hogan. Blanche Yurka, Ralph Bellamy, Jack Carson, Richard Denning, James Seay, Paul Kelly, William Henry, Jeanne Cagney, J. Carrol Naish, Hedda Hopper, Billy Gilbert. J. Edgar Hoover's bestselling book *Persons in Hiding* was the basis for this thinly veiled account of the exploits of mobster Ma Barker and her boys. Yurka is outstanding as Ma Webster; Bellamy and Carson are the G-Men hot on her trail. Lively crime programmer. Look for a bit by Robert Ryan in his first film. Cowritten by Horace McCoy.

Queen of the Nile (1962-Italian) **C-85m.** ** D: Fernando Cerchio. Jeanne Crain, Vincent Price, Edmund Purdom, Amedeo Nazzari. Dull account of court life in 2000 B.C. Egypt. Not even campy. Aka NEFERTITE, QUEEN OF THE NILE. SuperCinescope. ▼▶

Queen's Guards, The (1961-British) **C-110m.** ** D: Michael Powell. Daniel Massey, Robert Stephens, Raymond Massey, Ursula Jeans. Tedious, patriotic chronicle of young Massey distinguishing himself in service, saving family name; humdrum film. CinemaScope.

Quentin Durward (1955) **C-101m.** **½ D: Richard Thorpe. Robert Taylor, Kay Kendall, Robert Morley, George Cole, Alec Clunes, Duncan Lamont, Marius Goring. Taylor plays Sir Walter Scott's dashing Scots hero in this handsome but static costume about Louis XI's reign in 15th-century France. CinemaScope.

Question of Adultery, A (1959-British) **86m.** **½ D: Don Chaffey. Julie London, Anthony Steel, Basil Sydney, Donald Houston, Anton Diffring, Andrew Cruickshank. Tepid drama involving pros and cons of artificial insemination. Retitled: THE CASE OF MRS. LORING.

¡Qué Viva México! (1931-1932/1979-Russian-U.S.-Mexican) **88m.** **** D: Sergei Eisenstein. Introduced by Grigori Alexandrov; narrated by Sergei Bondarchuk. Legendary film, presented as a series of vignettes and crammed with dazzling visuals, offering an intimate (and highly political) look at Mexico past and present, and the diversity of its people, landscape, and culture. Most are metaphorical slices of life but one, involving a peasant revolt, features a full storyline. Shot by Eisenstein with colleagues Alexandrov and Eduard Tisse in the early 1930s, but never completed. Truncated versions were cobbled together and released as THUNDER OVER MEXICO and TIME IN THE SUN. This, the most definitive version, was put together decades later by Alexandrov, based on Eisenstein's notes and drawings. Powerful stuff! ▼▶

Quick Before It Melts (1964) **C-98m. **½** D: Delbert Mann. George Maharis, Robert Morse, Anjanette Comer, James Gregory, Yvonne Craig, Doodles Weaver, Howard St. John, Michael Constantine. Trivia involving Maharis and Morse in the Antarctic; they have bright idea of bringing in a planeload of girls, with predictable results. Panavision. ▶

Quick Gun, The (1964) **C-87m. **** D: Sidney Salkow. Audie Murphy, Merry Anders, James Best, Ted de Corsia, Frank Ferguson, Raymond Hatton. Formula Murphy Western, with Audie redeeming himself by combating town outlaws. Technicolor. ▶

Quick Millions (1931) **72m. **½** D: Rowland Brown. Spencer Tracy, Marguerite Churchill, Sally Eilers, Robert Burns, John Wray, George Raft. OK gangster film with Tracy as ambitious truck driver who climbs to top of the rackets. Nothing special, except to see dynamic early Tracy.

Quicksand (1950) **79m. **½** D: Irving Pichel. Mickey Rooney, Jeanne Cagney, Barbara Bates, Peter Lorre, Taylor Holmes, Wally Cassell, Jimmy Dodd. Minor film noir about auto mechanic Rooney, who is hot for trampy Cagney, and what happens when he "borrows" $20 from his boss's cash register. Lorre is wonderfully menacing as a sleazy penny arcade owner. ▼▶

Quiet American, The (1958) **120m. **½** D: Joseph L. Mankiewicz. Audie Murphy, Michael Redgrave, Claude Dauphin, Giorgia Moll, Bruce Cabot. Sanitized version of the Graham Greene novel, with the book's "un-American" feeling eliminated; naive American Murphy arrives in Saigon with his own plan to settle country's conflicts. More a murder mystery than the political thriller intended. Remade in 2002. ▶

Quiet Duel, The (1949-Japanese) **95m. **½** D: Akira Kurosawa. Toshiro Mifune, Takashi Shimura, Miki Sanjo, Kenjiro Uemura, Chieko Nakakita, Noriko Sengoku. Dedicated doctor accidentally contracts syphilis from a scalpel cut during surgery. Years later, he cannot bring himself to reveal the truth of his infection to his confused fiancée. Grim, adult drama is the director's only work to be adapted from the modern Japanese stage (a popular play by Kazuo Kikuta). Lesser Kurosawa, but still has its great moments; wait for the music box scene. Aka A SILENT DUEL. ▼▶

Quiet Man, The (1952) **C-129m. ****** D:

John Ford. John Wayne, Maureen O'Hara, Barry Fitzgerald, Victor McLaglen, Mildred Natwick, Arthur Shields, Ward Bond, Ken Curtis, Mae Marsh, Jack MacGowran, Sean McClory, Francis Ford. American boxer Wayne returns to his native Ireland and falls in love with a spirited lass (O'Hara) —but has to deal with local customs (including the payment of a dowry) and the young woman's bullheaded brother (McLaglen). Boisterous blarney, with beautiful Technicolor scenery, and equally beautiful music by Victor Young. This film was clearly a labor of love for Ford and his Irish-American stars. Maurice Walsh's story was scripted by Frank Nugent. Oscar winner for Best Director and Cinematography (Winton C. Hoch and Archie Stout). Later a Broadway musical, *Donnybrook!* ▼◉▶

Quiet Please Murder (1942) **70m. **½** D: John Larkin. George Sanders, Gail Patrick, Richard Denning, Sidney Blackmer, Lynne Roberts, Kurt Katch, Minerva Urecal, Theodore von Eltz. Offbeat, intriguing yarn of master forger Sanders stealing priceless Shakespeare volume, passing off his copies as the original. Murder and romance expertly woven into story.

Quincannon, Frontier Scout (1956) **C-83m. *½** D: Lesley Selander. Tony Martin, Peggie Castle, John Bromfield, John Smith, Ron Randell. Martin is miscast in title role of programmer. ▶

Quo Vadis (1951) **C-171m. ***** D: Mervyn LeRoy. Robert Taylor, Deborah Kerr, Peter Ustinov, Leo Genn, Patricia Laffan, Finlay Currie, Abraham Sofaer, Buddy Baer. Gargantuan MGM adaptation of Henryk Sienkiewicz' novel set during the reign of Nero; Roman soldier Taylor has to figure out how to romance Christian Kerr without both of them ending up as lunch for the lions. Meticulous production includes fine location shooting and Miklos Rozsa score based on music of the era. Video version runs 175m. with overture and exit music. Remade for Italian TV in 1985. ▼◉▶

Rabbit Trap, The (1959) **72m. **½** D: Philip Leacock. Ernest Borgnine, David Brian, Bethel Leslie, Kevin Corcoran, June Blair, Jeanette Nolan, Don Rickles. Intelligent if slow-moving study of motivational factors behind Borgnine's compulsive work life and ignoring of his family. Script by JP Miller, from his TV play.

Race for Life (1954-British) **68m. *½** D: Terence Fisher. Richard Conte, Mari Aldon, George Coulouris, Peter Illing, Alec Mango. Formula programmer with Conte as an American racing his way around some of Europe's fastest tracks against wishes of wife Aldon. Competent stock-car footage in this pre-horror Hammer production. Original British title: MASK OF DUST. ▶

Racers, The (1955) **C-87m. **½** D:

Henry Hathaway. Kirk Douglas, Bella Darvi, Gilbert Roland, Lee J. Cobb, Cesar Romero, Katy Jurado. Hackneyed sports-car racing yarn, not salvaged by Douglas' dynamics or European location shooting. CinemaScope. ▼

Race Street (1948) 79m. ** D: Edwin L. Marin. George Raft, William Bendix, Marilyn Maxwell, Frank Faylen, Henry (Harry) Morgan, Gale Robbins. Ordinary crime story of San Francisco bookie-turned nightclub owner Raft, who "likes to do things his own way." He plays footsie with cop Bendix while going up against the protection racket responsible for his best friend's murder. ●▶

Rachel and the Stranger (1948) 79m. *** D: Norman Foster. Loretta Young, William Holden, Robert Mitchum, Tom Tully, Sara Haden, Gary Gray. Charming pioneer love story of a farmer (Holden), his indentured servant wife (Young), and the farmer's wandering minstrel friend (Mitchum) who visits their homestead. Three attractive stars at their prime. Originally reviewed at 93m. Also shown in computer-colored version. ▼●

Racing Lady (1937) 59m. ** D: Wallace Fox. Ann Dvorak, Smith Ballew, Harry Carey, Berton Churchill, Frank M. Thomas, Willie Best, Hattie McDaniel. Spirited cast enlivens this by-the-numbers account of Dvorak, the daughter of horse breeder Carey, who becomes the nation's only female trainer. Partially based on a Damon Runyon story.

Rack, The (1956) 100m. *** D: Arnold Laven. Paul Newman, Wendell Corey, Walter Pidgeon, Edmond O'Brien, Anne Francis, Lee Marvin, Cloris Leachman. Newman is pensively convincing as Korean War veteran—brainwashed as a P.O.W.—now on trial for treason, with Pidgeon as his overbearing father and Francis his friend. Slick production adapted from Rod Serling teleplay. Robert Blake, Dean Jones, and Rod Taylor have small roles. ▶

Racket, The (1928) 83m. **½ D: Lewis Milestone. Thomas Meighan, Louis Wolheim, Marie Prevost, Pat Collins, Henry Sedley, George (E.) Stone, Sam De Grasse, Skeets Gallagher. A steely eyed police captain and a tough-as-nails crime boss play cat and mouse, each determined to do the other in, in Bartlett Cormack's adaptation of his Broadway play, which foreshadows the gangster films of the early 1930s. A handful of potent scenes, well shot and staged, stand out in an otherwise routine silent film. Produced by Howard Hughes. Remade in 1951.

Racket, The (1951) 88m. **½ D: John Cromwell. Robert Mitchum, Robert Ryan, Lizabeth Scott, Ray Collins, William Talman, Robert Hutton, William Conrad, Don Porter. Police official Mitchum and gang-ster Ryan spend almost as much time fighting their corrupt superiors as they do each other. Story is painted in broad strokes, with Mitchum miscast as a straight-arrow police captain. Based on a play previously filmed by producer Howard Hughes in 1928, and shows it, although much was changed for this remake. Coscripted by W. R. Burnett. Also shown in computer-colored version. ▼●

Racket Busters (1938) 71m. ** D: Lloyd Bacon. George Brent, Humphrey Bogart, Gloria Dickson, Allen Jenkins, Walter Abel, Henry O'Neill, Penny Singleton. Mobster Bogie's going to take over the trucking business, but Brent doesn't want to cooperate. Standard programmer moves along well; cowritten by Robert Rossen.

Racketeer, The (1929) 66m. *½ D: Howard Higgin. Robert Armstrong, Carol(e) Lombard, Roland Drew, Jeanette Loff, John Loder, Paul Hurst, Hedda Hopper. Mobster-with-a-heart-of-gold Armstrong runs the N.Y.C. rackets, becomes enamored of down-on-her-luck Lombard after helping her alcoholic musician boyfriend. Lumbering early talkie is worth a peek for the presence of Lombard before she blossomed as a star. ▼▶

Racket Man, The (1944) 64m. ** D: D. Ross Lederman. Tom Neal, Hugh Beaumont, Larry Parks, Jeanne Bates, Douglas Fowley, Anthony Caruso, Mary Gordon. Gangster Neal gets drafted, goes straight, and goes undercover to break up a black market ring. Predictable WW2 morale booster is watchable, despite—or perhaps because of—its copious clichés.

Radar Secret Service (1950) 59m. *½ D: Sam Newfield. John Howard, Adele Jergens, Tom Neal, Myrna Dell, Sid Melton, Ralph Byrd, Robert Kent, Tristram Coffin, Kenne Duncan. Slapdash account of secret agents employing state-of-the-art radar technology to track down gang intent on stealing atomic energy material. ▶

Radio Stars on Parade (1945) 70m. **½ D: Leslie Goodwins. Wally Brown, Alan Carney, Frances Langford, Sheldon Leonard, Rufe Davis, Robert Clarke. Flimsy plot about inept talent agents (the highly resistible comedy team of Brown & Carney) who get mixed up with a gangster serves as framework for a fun revue featuring radio stars Ralph Edwards and his *Truth or Consequences* troupe, Don Wilson, Skinnay Ennis and His Band, The Town Criers, The Cappy Barra Boys, and Tony Romano. ▶

Raffles (1930) 72m. *** D: George Fitzmaurice. Ronald Colman, Kay Francis, Ernest Torrence, Frederick Kerr, Bramwell Fletcher, Alison Skipworth. Colman is his usual charming self in a breezy tale of gentleman thief who constantly eludes Scotland Yard. Good fun all the way. Screenplay by Sidney Howard, based on E. W. Hornung's novel *The Amateur Cracksman*, filmed in 1917 with John Barrymore, in 1925 with House Peters, remade in 1940 with David Niven. ▼●▶

Raffles (1940) 72m. **½ D: Sam Wood. David Niven, Olivia de Havilland, Dudley Digges, Dame May Whitty, Douglas Walton, Lionel Pape. Niven is good but can't match Ronald Colman in this nearly scene-for-scene remake of the 1930 film about a gentleman thief (with a notably different finale). Medium-grade fluff. ●▶

Raffles, The Amateur Cracksman (1917) 65m. *** D: George Irving. John Barrymore, Christine Mayo, H. Cooper Cliffe, Frank Morgan, Dudley S. Hill, Kathryn Adams, Evelyn Brent, Mathilde Brundage, Mike Donlin, Frederick Perry. Entertaining early version of the E. W. Hornung story with Barrymore perfectly cast as A. J. Raffles, champion cricketer who doubles as a jewel thief. The scenes featuring The Great Profile and twentysomething Morgan (cast as Bunny Manders, Raffles' pal) are fascinating. ▼▶

Rafter Romance (1933) 72m. **½ D: William A. Seiter. Ginger Rogers, Norman Foster, George Sidney, Robert Benchley, Laura Hope Crews, Sidney Miller, Guinn "Big Boy" Williams. Cute if predictable romantic comedy about roommates who share a Greenwich Village garret but never meet: he works nights, she works days. Benchley is fun as befuddled executive with designs on employee Rogers. Remake of a 1932 German musical; remade as LIVING ON LOVE. ▶

Rage at Dawn (1955) C-87m. ** D: Tim Whelan. Randolph Scott, Forrest Tucker, Mala Powers, J. Carrol Naish, Edgar Buchanan, Myron Healey. Ever-so-familiar Western about a secret agent (Scott) who goes undercover to ferret out the Reno brothers, a notorious outlaw gang, in post–Civil War Indiana. ▼●▶

Rage in Heaven (1941) 83m. ** D: W. S. Van Dyke II. Robert Montgomery, Ingrid Bergman, George Sanders, Lucile Watson, Oscar Homolka, Philip Merivale, Matthew Boulton. Disappointing adaptation of James Hilton novel about mentally disturbed steel mill owner who plots unusual murder-revenge scheme; set in England. ▶

Rage of Paris, The (1938) 75m. *** D: Henry Koster. Danielle Darrieux, Douglas Fairbanks, Jr., Mischa Auer, Louis Hayward, Helen Broderick. Fast-talkers team up to use lovely Darrieux to snare rich husband; fast-paced comedy is fun, Darrieux a delight. Same team that Hollywoodized neophyte Deanna Durbin concocted this winsome image for the French actress. Look quickly for Mary Martin. ▼▶

Rage to Live, A (1965) 101m. ** D: Walter Grauman. Suzanne Pleshette, Bradford Dillman, Ben Gazzara, Peter Graves,

Bethel Leslie, James Gregory, Carmen Mathews, Ruth White. Turgid adaptation of John O'Hara novel charting the premarital and extramarital affairs of emotionally and physically needy Pleshette. Panavision. ▶

Raging Tide, The (1951) 93m. **½ D: George Sherman. Richard Conte, Shelley Winters, Stephen McNally, Alex Nicol, Charles Bickford. Stereotyped script, typecast acting make this murderer-on-the-run yarn tame. Adapted by Ernest K. Gann from his novel.

Rag Man, The (1925) 68m. *** D: Edward F. Cline. Jackie Coogan, Max Davidson, Robert Edeson, Ethel Wales, Lydia Yeamans Titus, William Conklin. Runaway orphan Coogan hides out with junk dealer Davidson and helps him recover his claim to a patent that was stolen years earlier by crooked lawyers. Sentimental silent charmer chockfull of amazing location footage of 1920s Manhattan. Followed by a sequel, OLD CLOTHES, the same year. ▶

Raid, The (1954) C-83m. *** D: Hugo Fregonese. Van Heflin, Anne Bancroft, Richard Boone, Lee Marvin, Tommy Rettig, James Best, Peter Graves, Claude Akins. Well-handled (and true) story of Confederate prisoners escaping from jail in upper New England, with Bancroft and Rettig on their trail. ▶

Raiders, The (1952) C-80m. **½ D: Lesley Selander. Richard Conte, Viveca Lindfors, Barbara Britton, Morris Ankrum, Hugh O'Brian, Richard Martin, William Reynolds. OK Western about miners standing up to land-grabbing Ankrum during California gold rush days. Retitled: RIDERS OF VENGEANCE.

Raiders, The (1963) C-75m. **½ D: Herschel Daugherty. Robert Culp, Brian Keith, Judi Meredith, James McMullan, Alfred Ryder, Simon Oakland. Enthusiastic cast helps this story of cattle drives and the railroad expansion westward.

Raiders of Old California (1957) 72m. ** D: Albert C. Gannaway. Jim Davis, Arleen Whelan, Faron Young, Marty Robbins, Lee Van Cleef, Louis Jean Heydt, Harry Lauter, Douglas Fowley. Minor Western involving a duplicitous cavalry officer who attempts to coerce the proprietor of a hacienda into relinquishing his land. Main point of interest is music stars Young and Robbins in supporting roles. ▶

Raiders of the Seven Seas (1953) C-88m. **½ D: Sidney Salkow. John Payne, Donna Reed, Gerald Mohr, Lon Chaney, Jr. Pirate leader Barbarossa (Payne) abducts countess Reed and crosses swords with her fiancé Mohr, a ruthless Spanish officer. No surprises in highly ordinary swashbuckling tale. ▶

Railroaded! (1947) 72m. *** D: Anthony Mann. John Ireland, Sheila Ryan, Hugh Beaumont, Ed Kelly, Jane Randolph, Keefe Brasselle. Another tight, well-made, low-budget film noir by Anthony Mann. Ireland is a ruthless gangster who framed Ryan's brother for murder; Beaumont is a cop searching for answers. ▼●)

Railroad Man, The SEE: **Man of Iron**

Rails Into Laramie (1954) C-81m. ** D: Jesse Hibbs. John Payne, Mari Blanchard, Dan Duryea, Joyce MacKenzie, Barton MacLane, Lee Van Cleef. Pat movie of Payne's efforts to clean up title town and keep railroad construction moving westward.

Rain (1932) 93m. **½ D: Lewis Milestone. Joan Crawford, Walter Huston, William Gargan, Guy Kibbee, Walter Catlett, Beulah Bondi. Considered a flop in 1932, this version of Maugham's story looks better today. Crawford is good as South Seas island trollop confronted by fire-and-brimstone preacher Huston. Director Milestone does gymnastics with camera during stagier scenes; an interesting antique. Previously filmed as SADIE THOMPSON, then again as DIRTY GERTIE FROM HARLEM U.S.A. and MISS SADIE THOMPSON. Some prints run 77m. ▼▶

Rainbow Island (1944) C-97m. **½ D: Ralph Murphy. Dorothy Lamour, Eddie Bracken, Gil Lamb, Barry Sullivan, Anne Revere, Olga San Juan, Elena Verdugo, Yvonne De Carlo, Reed Hadley, Marc Lawrence. Good cast main asset in musical comedy of Merchant Marines stranded on island with beautiful natives. Lamour, in her umpteenth sarong, wisely keeps her tongue in her cheek.

Rainbow Jacket, The (1954-British) C-99m. ** D: Basil Dearden. Kay Walsh, Bill Owen, Fella Edmonds, Robert Morley, Wilfrid Hyde-White, Honor Blackman. Colorful racetrack sequences spark this predictable study of Owen, veteran jockey gone wrong, who teaches Edmonds how to race properly.

Rainbow Over Texas (1946) 65m. **½ D: Frank McDonald. Roy Rogers, George "Gabby" Hayes, Dale Evans, Sheldon Leonard, Robert Emmett Keane, Gerald Oliver Smith, Minerva Urecal, George J. Lewis, Kenne Duncan, Pierce Lyden, Bob Nolan and the Sons of the Pioneers. Dale has run away (and disguised herself as a boy) to join Roy's traveling Western troupe; complications arise when they stop in his hometown, where her father is the leading citizen, Leonard is the local gambling boss, and Gabby is the sheriff! Amiable musical comedy downplays action elements. Based on a short story by Max Brand. ▼▶

Rainbow 'Round My Shoulder (1952) C-78m. ** D: Richard Quine. Frankie Laine, Billy Daniels, Charlotte Austin, Ida Moore, Arthur Franz, Barbara Whiting, Lloyd Corrigan. Young girl wants to be a movie star, her socialite grandma forbids it, and no surprises ensue. Blah musical written by Quine and Blake Edwards.

Rainbow Trail, The (1925) 58m. *** D: Lynn Reynolds. Tom Mix, Anne Cornwall, George Bancroft, Lucien Littlefield, Mark Hamilton, Vivien Oakland. Sequel to RIDERS OF THE PURPLE SAGE, another robust Zane Grey tale about man who determines to penetrate isolated Paradise Valley, where his uncle trapped himself with a young woman. Handsome production of oft-filmed story.

Rainbow Valley (1935) 52m. *½ D: Robert N. Bradbury. John Wayne, Lucile Browne, George Hayes, LeRoy Mason, Lloyd Ingraham. Wayne acts as undercover agent inside prison, then spoils plans of lawbreakers in an isolated mining hamlet who need an access road built to connect with civilization. Despite some flashes of action, poor direction spoils the suspense in this lackluster low-budget Lone Star Western. Hayes' mail-carrying comedy is only bright spot. ▼▶

Rainmaker, The (1956) C-121m. *** D: Joseph Anthony. Burt Lancaster, Katharine Hepburn, Wendell Corey, Lloyd Bridges, Earl Holliman, Cameron Prud'homme, Wallace Ford. Lancaster is in top form as a charismatic con man who offers hope to a Southwestern town beset by drought, and a woman whose life is at a crossroads. Hepburn is wonderful. N. Richard Nash play was later musicalized on Broadway as *110 in the Shade*. VistaVision. ▼●)

Rainmakers, The (1935) 78m. **½ D: Fred Guiol. Bert Wheeler, Robert Woolsey, Dorothy Lee, Berton Churchill, George Meeker, Edgar Dearing, Clarence H. Wilson. The boys come to the rescue of a drought-plagued bean farmer with a fake rain machine that somehow manages to work. Middling Wheeler and Woolsey vehicle with some amusing gags and a wild train chase finale that precedes—and sometimes equals—a very similar one in the Marx Brothers movie GO WEST. ▶

Rain or Shine (1930) 92m. **½ D: Frank Capra. Joe Cook, Louise Fazenda, Joan Peers, Dave Chasen, William Collier, Jr., Tom Howard. Curious little circus film spotlights puckish Broadway clown Cook (and his stooges Chasen and Howard) in a storyline so thin it's hardly there. Personality and Capra's early talkie technique make this worth seeing for film buffs. ▶

Rains Came, The (1939) 104m. **½ D: Clarence Brown. Myrna Loy, Tyrone Power, George Brent, Brenda Joyce, Nigel Bruce, Maria Ouspenskaya, Joseph Schildkraut, Mary Nash, Jane Darwell, Marjorie Rambeau, Henry Travers, H. B. Warner, Laura Hope Crews. Louis Bromfield novel reduced to Hollywood hokum, with married socialite Loy setting out to seduce dedicated Indian surgeon Power. Outstanding earthquake and flood scenes; the special effects earned an Academy Award. Remade as THE RAINS OF RANCHIPUR. ▼▶

Rains of Ranchipur, The (1955) **C-104m.** ****½** D: Jean Negulesco. Lana Turner, Richard Burton, Fred MacMurray, Joan Caulfield, Michael Rennie, Eugenie Leontovich. Superficial remake of THE RAINS CAME; story of wife of Englishman having affair with Hindu doctor. CinemaScope.

Raintree County (1957) **C-168m.** ******* D: Edward Dmytryk. Elizabeth Taylor, Montgomery Clift, Eva Marie Saint, Lee Marvin, Nigel Patrick, Rod Taylor, Agnes Moorehead, Walter Abel, DeForest Kelley. Humongous MGM attempt to outdo GWTW, with Taylor as spoiled Civil War-era belle who discovers marriage isn't all it's cracked up to be. Solid acting and memorable Johnny Green score help compensate for rambling, overlong script; Clift was disfigured in near-fatal car accident during production, and his performance understandably suffers for it. Roadshow version runs 188m. with overture, intermission/entr'acte, and restored footage. MGM Camera 65. ▼●

Raising a Riot (1954-British) **C-90m.** ****** D: Wendy Toye. Kenneth More, Ronald Squire, Mandy Miller, Shelagh Fraser, Bill Shine. Predictable situation comedy of More, on vacation in countryside, trying to cope with his rambunctious children.

Raising the Wind (1961-British) **C-91m.** ****½** D: Gerald Thomas. James Robertson Justice, Leslie Phillips, Sidney James, Paul Massie, Kenneth Williams. Zany shenanigans of eccentric group of students at a London school of music; well paced.

Raisin in the Sun, A (1961) **128m.** ******** D: Daniel Petrie. Sidney Poitier, Claudia McNeil, Ruby Dee, Diana Sands, Ivan Dixon, John Fiedler, Louis Gossett. Lorraine Hansberry play receives perceptive handling by outstanding cast in drama of black Chicago family's attempts to find sense in their constrained existence. Remade for TV in 1989 and in 2008. ▼●

Rake's Progress, The SEE: **Notorious Gentleman**

Rally 'Round the Flag, Boys! (1958) **C-106m.** ****½** D: Leo McCarey. Paul Newman, Joanne Woodward, Joan Collins, Jack Carson, Dwayne Hickman, Tuesday Weld, Gale Gordon. Disappointing film of Max Shulman's book about small community in uproar over projected missile base. CinemaScope.●

Ramona (1936) **C-90m.** ****** D: Henry King. Loretta Young, Don Ameche, Kent Taylor, Pauline Frederick, Jane Darwell, Katherine DeMille. Oft-told tale doesn't wear well, with aristocratic Spanish girl Young and outcast Indian Ameche in love and shunned by society. Settings are picturesque. ●

Rampage (1963) **C-98m.** ****½** D: Phil Karlson. Robert Mitchum, Elsa Martinelli, Jack Hawkins, Sabu, Cely Carillo, Emile Genest. German gamehunter (Hawkins), his mistress (Martinelli), and hunting guide (Mitchum) form love triangle, with men battling for Elsa. Elmer Bernstein's score is memorable.●

Ramrod (1947) **94m.** ****½** D: Andre de Toth. Veronica Lake, Joel McCrea, Arleen Whelan, Don DeFore, Preston Foster, Charles Ruggles, Donald Crisp, Lloyd Bridges. Fairly good Western of territorial dispute between ranch-owner Lake and her father (Ruggles). Good supporting cast.▼

Rancho Grande (1940) **68m.** ****½** D: Frank McDonald. Gene Autry, Smiley Burnette, June Storey, Mary Lee, Ferris Taylor, Dick Hogan. Another taming-of-the-shrew Autry Western as sassy Eastern gal Storey takes over a ranch sought by crooked attorney Taylor. Emphasis here is on music, Gene's friendly nature, Smiley's comedy, sweet charms of Storey and young singer Lee.●

Rancho Notorious (1952) **C-89m.** ******* D: Fritz Lang. Marlene Dietrich, Arthur Kennedy, Mel Ferrer, Lloyd Gough, Gloria Henry, William Frawley, Jack Elam, George Reeves. Entertaining, unusual Western with Kennedy looking for murderer of his sweetheart, ending up at Marlene's bandit hideout. Colorful characters spice up routine story by Daniel Taradash.▼●

Random Harvest (1942) **126m.** *****½** D: Mervyn LeRoy. Ronald Colman, Greer Garson, Philip Dorn, Susan Peters, Henry Travers, Reginald Owen, Bramwell Fletcher, Margaret Wycherly, Ann Richards. Colman is left an amnesiac after WW1, and saved from life in a mental institution by vivacious music-hall entertainer Garson. James Hilton novel given supremely entertaining MGM treatment, with Colman and Garson at their best. Screenplay by Claudine West, George Froeschel, and Arthur Wimperis.▼●

Randy Rides Alone (1934) **54m.** ***½** D: Harry Fraser. John Wayne, Alberta Vaughn, George Hayes, Yakima Canutt, Earl Dwire. Wayne is jailed for robbery and murder, but heroine releases him to infiltrate and round up gang of brigands responsible. Hayes plays notorious "Matt the Mute." B Western is crudely made and not much fun; notable only for casting Wayne as a singing cowboy (dubbed by Western star Bob Steele's twin brother, Bill Bradbury, son of the Lone Star series' usual director).▼●

Range Feud, The (1931) **58m.** ******* D: D. Ross Lederman. Buck Jones, John Wayne, Susan Fleming, Ed Le Saint, William Walling, Wallace MacDonald, Harry Woods. Jones is fearless sheriff pledged to resolving range rights war among his fiery stepfather, his young stepbrother Wayne, and a rival ranch. In his first Western after THE BIG TRAIL, Wayne romances neighbor's daughter Fleming. Well written, directed, photographed, and acted, with plenty of gunplay, hard riding, and chase scenes. Whirlwind mystery marred only by dubbed hoofbeats and sped-up action.▼

Ranger and the Lady, The (1940) **59m.** **½ D: Joseph Kane. Roy Rogers, George "Gabby" Hayes, Jacqueline Wells (Julie Bishop), Harry Woods, Henry Brandon, Noble Johnson, Si Jenks, Yakima Canutt. Roy deals with a corrupt chief of the Texas Rangers who is imposing an illegal toll on freighters using the Santa Fe Trail. Good story with big action finish. ▼▶

Rangers of Fortune (1940) **80m.** **½ D: Sam Wood. Fred MacMurray, Albert Dekker, Gilbert Roland, Patricia Morison, Dick Foran, Joseph Schildkraut. Smartly-whipped-together yarn of trio fleeing Mexicans, stopping off in Southwestern town to offer assistance.

Range War (1939) **64m.** **½ D: Lesley Selander. William Boyd, Russell Hayden, Willard Robertson, Matt Moore, Betty Moran, Britt Wood, Jason Robards (Sr.). Hopalong Cassidy intervenes to restore peace in dispute among angry cattle ranchers and an extortionist trying to sabotage a new railroad line's completion. Makes use of rail track set built for UNION PACIFIC. Victor Young score is a plus, Britt Wood a minus in comedy sidekick role, attempting to replace the departed George Hayes. Future singing cowboy Eddie Dean has small role. ▼▶

Ransom! (1956) **109m.** **½ D: Alex Segal. Glenn Ford, Donna Reed, Leslie Nielsen, Juano Hernandez, Alexander Scourby, Juanita Moore, Robert Keith. Brooding narrative of business tycoon Ford's efforts to rescue his son who's been kidnapped. Remade in 1996. ▶

Rape of Malaya SEE: **Town Like Alice, A**

Rapture (1965-French) **104m.** *** D: John Guillermin. Melvyn Douglas, Dean Stockwell, Patricia Gozzi, Gunnel Lindblom, Leslie Sands. Intensive, sensitive account of Gozzi's tragic romance with Stockwell, a man on the run. CinemaScope. ▶

Rare-Book Murder, The SEE: **Fast Company** (1938)

Rascals (1938) **77m.** **½ D: H. Bruce Humberstone. Jane Withers, Rochelle Hudson, Robert Wilcox, Borrah Minevitch, Steffi Duna, Katharine Alexander. Pleasant (if politically incorrect) B-movie musical vehicle for Withers, who lives happily with a band of gypsies; when they come upon a young woman suffering from amnesia, they take her in, little dreaming that she's an heiress. Lively music includes numbers by Minevitch's Harmonica Rascals (including Johnny Puleo). ▶

Rashomon (1950-Japanese) **88m.** **** D: Akira Kurosawa. Toshiro Mifune, Machiko Kyo, Masayuki Mori, Takashi Shimura. Kurosawa's first huge international success is superlative study of truth and human nature; four people involved in a rape-murder tell varying accounts of what happened. The film's very title has become part of our language. Oscar winner as Best Foreign Film. Remade as THE OUTRAGE. ▼▶

Rasputin and the Empress (1932) **123m.** *** D: Richard Boleslavsky. John, Ethel, and Lionel Barrymore, Ralph Morgan, Diana Wynyard, Tad Alexander, C. Henry Gordon, Edward Arnold, Jean Parker. Good drama that should have been great, with all three Barrymores in colorful roles, unfolding story of mad monk's plotting against Russia. Contrary to expectations, it's Lionel, not John, who plays Rasputin. The three Barrymores' only film together; Ethel's talkie debut. Wynyard's first film. ▼▶

Rationing (1944) **93m.** **½ D: Willis Goldbeck. Wallace Beery, Marjorie Main, Donald Meek, Gloria Dickson, Henry O'Neill, Connie Gilchrist. Butcher in small town is main character in story of problems during WW2; typical Beery vehicle.

Raton Pass (1951) **84m.** *** D: Edwin L. Marin. Dennis Morgan, Patricia Neal, Steve Cochran, Scott Forbes, Dorothy Hart, Basil Ruysdael, Louis Jean Heydt, Roland Winters. Scheming seductress Neal marries rancher Morgan and tries to swindle his family out of their cattle empire with the aid of gunslinger Cochran. Smoothly directed, entertaining Western with Neal at her alluring best. ▶

Rat Race, The (1960) **C-105m.** *** D: Robert Mulligan. Tony Curtis, Debbie Reynolds, Jack Oakie, Kay Medford, Don Rickles, Joe Bushkin. Comedy-drama of would-be musician (Curtis) and dancer (Reynolds) coming to N.Y.C., platonically sharing an apartment, and falling in love. Nice comic cameos by Oakie and Medford. Script by Garson Kanin, from his play.

Rattle of a Simple Man (1964-British) **96m.** *** D: Muriel Box. Harry H. Corbett, Diane Cilento, Thora Hird, Michael Medwin. Pleasant saucy sex comedy of timid soul Corbett spending the night with Cilento to win a bet; set in London. ▼

Raven, The (1935) **62m.** *** D: Louis Friedlander (Lew Landers). Karloff (Boris Karloff), Bela Lugosi, Irene Ware, Lester Matthews, Samuel S. Hinds. Momentous teaming of horror greats with Lugosi as doctor with Poe obsession, Karloff a victim of his wicked schemes. Hinds is subjected to torture from "The Pit and the Pendulum" in film's climax. Great fun throughout. ▼▶

Raven, The (1943-French) SEE: **Le Corbeau**

Raven, The (1963) **C-86m.** *** D: Roger Corman. Vincent Price, Peter Lorre, Boris Karloff, Hazel Court, Olive Sturgess, Jack Nicholson. Funny horror satire finds magicians Price and Lorre challenging power-hungry colleague Karloff. Climactic sorcerers' duel is a highlight. Screenplay by Richard Matheson, "inspired" by the Poe poem. Panavision. ▼▶

Ravishing Idiot, A (1964-French-Italian) **110m. **** D: Edouard Molinaro. Anthony Perkins, Brigitte Bardot, Gregoire Aslan, André Luguet. Perkins, disenchanted with capitalism, is recruited by a Soviet spy to pilfer a secret NATO file. Silly, mostly unfunny Cold War comedy. ▼▶

Raw Deal (1948) **78m. ***** D: Anthony Mann. Dennis O'Keefe, Claire Trevor, Marsha Hunt, Raymond Burr, John Ireland. Beautifully made, hard-boiled story of O'Keefe escaping from jail and taking out revenge on slimy Burr, who framed him; what's more, he gets caught between love of two women. Tough and convincing, with Burr a sadistic heavy. ▶

Raw Edge (1956) **C-76m. **** D: John Sherwood. Rory Calhoun, Yvonne De Carlo, Mara Corday, Rex Reason, Neville Brand, Emile Meyer, Herbert Rudley, Robert Wilke, John Gilmore (Gavin). In Oregon Territory in the mid-1800s any man can claim a widow as his own—which has some locals rooting for outlaw boss Rudley to buy the farm so they can fight over his wife, De Carlo. Calhoun arrives on the scene to avenge the lynching of his brother, who was wrongly accused of molesting her. Highly offbeat story routinely told.

Rawhide (1938) **58m. **½** D: Ray Taylor. Smith Ballew, Lou Gehrig, Evalyn Knapp, Arthur Loft, Cy Kendall, Dick Curtis, Si Jenks, Lafe McKee. Agreeable oater with Gehrig, cast as himself, retiring from the New York Yankees, moving out West and joining with singing lawyer Ballew to battle a racketeer who's bilking money from ranchers. The Iron Horse isn't bad in his only starring film. He easily could have made the grade as a B-Western star. ▼▶

Rawhide (1951) **86m. ***** D: Henry Hathaway. Tyrone Power, Susan Hayward, Hugh Marlowe, Dean Jagger, Edgar Buchanan, Jack Elam, George Tobias, Jeff Corey. Taut Western saga about a motley gang of no-goods holding Power and Hayward prisoner at a stagecoach way station. Straightforward and unspectacular but well done, with a crackerjack cast and striking use of Lone Pine locations. Remake of 1935 gangster saga SHOW THEM NO MERCY! ▼▶

Rawhide Trail, The (1958) **67m. *½** D: Robert Gordon. Rex Reason, Nancy Gates, Richard Erdman, Ann Doran, Rusty Lane. Humdrum tale of a pair of wagon masters, unfairly blamed for leading their party toward a surprise Comanche attack, who set out to establish their innocence.

Rawhide Years, The (1956) **C-85m. **** D: Rudolph Maté. Tony Curtis, Colleen Miller, Arthur Kennedy, William Demarest, William Gargan. Youthful Curtis perks this routine fare of gambler trying to clear himself of murder charge.

Raw Wind in Eden (1958) **C-89m. **½** D: Richard Wilson. Esther Williams, Jeff Chandler, Rossana Podesta, Carlos Thompson, Rik Battaglia. Plane carrying rich couple on way to yachting party crashes on isolated island. Entertaining adventure yarn is mixed with romance and jealousy. Filmed in Italy. CinemaScope.

Raymie (1960) **72m. **** D: Frank McDonald. David Ladd, Julie Adams, John Agar, Charles Winninger, Richard Arlen, Frank Ferguson. Quiet little film about youngster (Ladd) whose greatest ambition is to catch the big fish that always eludes him. Jerry Lewis sings the title song.

Razor's Edge, The (1946) **146m. ***½** D: Edmund Goulding. Tyrone Power, Gene Tierney, John Payne. Anne Baxter, Clifton Webb, Herbert Marshall, Lucile Watson, Frank Latimore. Slick adaptation of Maugham's philosophical novel, with Marshall as the author, Power as hero seeking true meaning of life, Baxter in Oscar-winning role as a dipsomaniac, Elsa Lanchester sparkling in bit as social secretary. Screenplay by Lamar Trotti. Long but engrossing; remade in 1984. ▼▶

Reach for the Sky (1956-British) **123m. **½** D: Lewis Gilbert. Kenneth More, Muriel Pavlow, Alexander Knox, Sydney Tafler, Nigel Green. Sensibly told account of British pilot Douglas Bader, who overcomes the loss of his legs in a crash to continue his flying career. British running time: 135m. ▼▶

Reaching for the Moon (1917) **69m. ***** D: John Emerson. Douglas Fairbanks, Eileen Percy, Richard Cummings, Millard Webb, Eugene Ormonde, Frank Campeau. Doug is Alexis Caesar Napoleon Brown, an ambitious dreamer who toils in a button factory and yearns to be as celebrated as his namesakes. What will happen when he learns he is heir to the throne of the nation of Vulgaria, and finds himself in great danger? Nifty satire, with an especially sweet finale. Emerson and Anita Loos' scenario is unrelated to the 1931 Fairbanks feature of the same title. See if you can spot Erich von Stroheim as Prince Badinoff's aide. ▶

Reaching for the Moon (1931) **74m. **½** D: Edmund Goulding. Douglas Fairbanks, Bebe Daniels, Edward Everett Horton, Claud Allister, Jack Mulhall, Walter Walker, June MacCloy, Helen Jerome Eddy, Bing Crosby. Doug plays a fast-talking "modern financial wizard" who has no interest in women or love. Will that change when conniving Daniels sets out to vamp him in order to win a bet? Enjoyable Depression-era romantic comedy has Bing singing one Irving Berlin song, "When the Folks High Up Do the Mean Low-Down." Originally 91m. ▼▶

Reaching for the Sun (1941) **90m. **½** D: William Wellman. Joel McCrea, Ellen Drew, Eddie Bracken, Albert Dekker, Billy

Gilbert, George Chandler. OK comedy of North Woods clam-digger who journeys to Detroit to earn money for outboard motor by working on auto assembly line.
Ready, Willing and Able (1937) **95m.** ** D: Ray Enright. Ruby Keeler, Lee Dixon, Allen Jenkins, Louise Fazenda, Carol Hughes, Ross Alexander, Winifred Shaw, Teddy Hart. Undistinguished Warner Bros. musical about college girl (Keeler), who impersonates British star (Shaw) in order to land Broadway role. Notable only for introduction of "Too Marvelous for Words," with a production number featuring a giant typewriter!▶
Real Glory, The (1939) **95m.** *** D: Henry Hathaway. Gary Cooper, David Niven, Andrea Leeds, Reginald Owen, Kay Johnson, Broderick Crawford, Vladimir Sokoloff, Henry Kolker. Cooper's fine as Army medic who solves all of Philippines' medical and military problems almost single-handedly after destructive Spanish-American War. Excellent action scenes.▼▶
Reap the Wild Wind (1942) **C-124m.** *** D: Cecil B. DeMille. Ray Milland, John Wayne, Paulette Goddard, Raymond Massey, Robert Preston, Susan Hayward, Charles Bickford, Hedda Hopper, Louise Beavers, Martha O'Driscoll, Lynne Overman. Brawling DeMille hokum of 19th-century salvagers in Florida, with Goddard as fiery Southern belle, Milland and Wayne fighting for her, Massey as odious villain. Exciting underwater scenes, with the special effects earning an Oscar. Milland good in off-beat characterization. ▼▶
Rear Window (1954) **C-112m.** **** D: Alfred Hitchcock. James Stewart, Grace Kelly, Wendell Corey, Thelma Ritter, Raymond Burr, Judith Evelyn, Ross Bagdasarian. One of Hitchcock's most stylish thrillers has photographer Stewart confined to wheelchair in his apartment, using binoculars to pass the time "spying" on courtyard neighbors, and discovering a possible murder. Inventive Cornell Woolrich story adapted by John Michael Hayes. Stewart, society girlfriend Kelly, and no-nonsense nurse Ritter make a wonderful trio. Remade for TV in 1998 with Christopher Reeve. ▼▶
Rebecca (1940) **130m.** **** D: Alfred Hitchcock. Laurence Olivier, Joan Fontaine, George Sanders, Judith Anderson, Nigel Bruce, Reginald Denny, C. Aubrey Smith, Gladys Cooper, Florence Bates, Leo G. Carroll, Melville Cooper. Hitchcock's first American film is sumptuous David O. Selznick production of Daphne du Maurier novel of girl who marries British nobleman but lives in shadow of his former wife. Stunning performances by Fontaine and Anderson; haunting score by Franz Waxman. Screenplay by Robert E. Sherwood and Joan Harrison. Academy Award winner for

Best Picture and Cinematography (George Barnes). ▼▶
Rebecca of Sunnybrook Farm (1917) **71m.** **½ D: Marshall Neilan. Mary Pickford, Eugene O'Brien, Josephine Crowell, Mayme Kelso, Marjorie Daw, Helen Jerome Eddy. Formulaic Pickford vehicle about spunky girl who's sent to live with her two harsh aunts; mixes sentiment, melodrama, and comedy, but lacks the spontaneity and spark of other Pickford films. Look for young ZaSu Pitts, in her film debut, as a spectator at Mary's circus. Kate Douglas Wiggin's 1903 story was remade in 1932 and 1938 (in name only).▼▶
Rebecca of Sunnybrook Farm (1938) **80m.** **½ D: Allan Dwan. Shirley Temple, Randolph Scott, Jack Haley, Gloria Stuart, Phyllis Brooks, Helen Westley, Slim Summerville, William Demarest. Contrived but entertaining, with surefire elements from earlier Temple movies tossed into simple story of Scott trying to make Shirley a radio star. No relation to Kate Douglas Wiggin's famous story. Also shown in computer-colored version.▼▶
Rebel in Town (1956) **78m.** ** D: Alfred L. Werker. John Payne, Ruth Roman, J. Carrol Naish, Ben Cooper, John Smith. In post–Civil War Arizona, settler Payne swears revenge on a family of renegade Rebels, one of whom recklessly killed Payne's young son. Minor Western with some good performances and action highlights. ▶
Rebel Set, The (1959) **72m.** *½ D: Gene Fowler, Jr. Gregg Palmer, Kathleen Crowley, Edward Platt, Ned Glass, John Lupton, Don Sullivan, Robert Shayne. Perfectly dreadful crime drama is not without interest as an artifact of its time, with its message that "intellectuals" are inherently corrupt and not to be trusted. Platt *is* hilariously cast as a bearded coffee-house owner who recruits an out-of-work actor, a failed novelist, and a rich brat to participate in a robbery.▼▶
Rebel Son, The (1938-British) **88m.** ** D: Alexis Granowsky, Adrian Brunel, Albert de Courville. Harry Baur, Anthony Bushell, Roger Livesey, Patricia Roc, Joan Gardner, Frederick Culley, Joseph Cunningham. Ineffectual English-language version of 1936 French film TARASS BOULBA (which also starred the legendary Baur) makes liberal use of action footage from the original, highlighting tale of 16th-century battle between Cossacks and Poles. Remade as TARAS BULBA. (Absurdly) retitled THE BARBARIAN AND THE LADY, and cut to 70m.
Rebel Without a Cause (1955) **C-111m.** **** D: Nicholas Ray. James Dean, Natalie Wood, Sal Mineo, Jim Backus, Ann Doran, William Hopper, Rochelle Hudson, Corey Allen, Edward Platt, Dennis Hopper, Nick Adams. This portrait of youthful alienation spoke to a whole generation and remains

wrenchingly powerful, despite some dated elements. The yearning for self-esteem, the barrier to communication with parents, the comfort found in friendships, all beautifully realized by director Ray, screenwriter Stewart Stern, and a fine cast (far too many of whom met early ends). This was Dean's seminal performance and an equally impressive showcase for young Mineo. CinemaScope.▼●❍

Rebound (1931) **89m. *** D:** Edward H. Griffith. Ina Claire, Robert Ames, Myrna Loy, Hedda Hopper, Robert Williams, Hale Hamilton. After being jilted by Loy (whom he really loves), Ames marries Claire on the rebound, but they almost break up when he runs into Loy again and she meets up with an old admirer. Smooth and sophisticated adaptation of Donald Ogden Stewart's witty, adult play; cast hits all the right notes, especially Williams, who died shortly after the film was released.

Reckless (1935) **96m. ** D:** Victor Fleming. Jean Harlow, William Powell, Franchot Tone, May Robson, Ted Healy, Nat Pendleton, Rosalind Russell, Henry Stephenson, Leon Waycoff (Ames), Allan Jones, Mickey Rooney, Farina (Allen Hoskins). Big cast, big production, musical numbers—all can't save script of chorus girl tangling up several people's lives. Tired and phony.▼●❍

Reckless Hour, The (1931) **72m. *** D:** John Francis Dillon. Dorothy Mackaill, Conrad Nagel, H. B. Warner, Joan Blondell, Walter Byron, Joe Donahue, Dorothy Peterson, Helen Ware. Solid drama of nice girl Mackaill, of the working class, and her two wealthy suitors. One (Nagel) is sincere but trapped in a bad marriage, while the other (Byron) is a suave creep. Blondell scores as Mackaill's smart-mouthed kid sister.❍

Reckless Moment, The (1949) **82m. ***½ D:** Max Opuls (Ophuls). James Mason, Joan Bennett, Geraldine Brooks, Henry O'Neill, Shepperd Strudwick. Mason blackmails protective mother Bennett, whose teenage daughter has been involved in a man's death. Noir-ish melodrama is also a slyly subversive look at a "typical" American family. Henry Garson and R. W. Soderberg adapted Elisabeth S. Holding's novel *The Blank Wall*. Remade as THE DEEP END (2001).▼

Record of a Living Being SEE: **I Live in Fear**

Red and the Black, The SEE: **Le Rouge et le Noir**

Red Badge of Courage, The (1951) **69m. ***½ D:** John Huston. Audie Murphy, Bill Mauldin, Douglas Dick, Royal Dano, John Dierkes, Arthur Hunnicutt, Tim Durant, Andy Devine; narrated by James Whitmore. Yankee soldier Murphy flees under fire and is guilt stricken over his apparent lack of courage. Stephen Crane's Civil War novel receives both epic and personal treatment by director Huston. Sweeping battle scenes and some truly frightening Rebel cavalry charges highlight this study of the fine line between cowardice and bravery. Many memorable vignettes: scene of Yankee general promising to share supper with half a dozen *different* platoons after the upcoming battle is a classic. Heavily re-edited after oddly negative previews; the film's troubled production is recounted in Lillian Ross' book *Picture*. Remade for TV in 1974.▼●

Red Ball Express (1952) **83m. **½ D:** Budd Boetticher. Jeff Chandler, Alex Nicol, Charles Drake, Hugh O'Brian, Jack Kelly, Jacqueline Duval, Sidney Poitier, Jack Warden. Pretty good WW2 story about real-life truck convoy that was hurriedly created to bring supplies to Patton's Army deep inside German-held territory in France. Screenplay by John Michael Hayes.▼

Red Beard (1965-Japanese) **185m. **½ D:** Akira Kurosawa. Toshiro Mifune, Yuzo Kayama, Yoshio Tsuchiya, Reiko Dan, Kyoko Kagawa, Terumi Niki. Tough but kind doctor Mifune takes intern Kayama under his wing in charity clinic. Unoriginal drama is also way overlong. Tohoscope.▼●❍

Red Beret, The SEE: **Paratrooper**

Red Canyon (1949) **C-82m. ** D:** George Sherman. Ann Blyth, Howard Duff, George Brent, Edgar Buchanan, Chill Wills, Jane Darwell, Lloyd Bridges. Routine Zane Grey Western of wild horses being tamed.

Red Danube, The (1949) **119m. **½ D:** George Sidney. Walter Pidgeon, Ethel Barrymore, Peter Lawford, Angela Lansbury, Janet Leigh. Louis Calhern, Francis L. Sullivan. Meandering drama of ballerina Leigh pursued by Russian agents, aided by amorous Lawford; heavy-handed at times.❍

Red Desert (1964-French-Italian) **C-118m. ** D:** Michelangelo Antonioni. Monica Vitti, Richard Harris, Rita Renoir, Carlo Chionetti. Vague, boring tale of Vitti alienated from her surroundings and on the verge of madness. Antonioni's first color film does have its followers, though. ▼●❍

Red Dragon, The (1945) **64m. *½ D:** Phil Rosen. Sidney Toler, Fortunio Bonanova, Benson Fong, Robert Emmett Keane, Willie Best, Carol Hughes. Assembly-line *Charlie Chan* mystery centering on the search for a secret bomb formula.

Red Dust (1932) **83m. ***½ D:** Victor Fleming. Clark Gable, Jean Harlow, Mary Astor, Donald Crisp, Gene Raymond, Tully Marshall, Willie Fung. Robust romance of Indochina rubber worker Gable, his floozie gal Harlow, and visiting Astor, who is married to Raymond, but falls for Gable. Harlow has fine comic touch. Tart script by John Lee Mahin. Remade as MOGAMBO. Also shown in computer-colored version. ▼●❍

Redemption (1930) **66m.** *½ D: Fred Niblo. John Gilbert, Renée Adorée, Conrad Nagel, Eleanor Boardman, Claire McDowell, Agostino Borgato, Nigel De Brulier, Tully Marshall, Mack Swain. Boardman is set to wed nice-guy Nagel, but charming, irresponsible Gilbert gets in the way; Adorée is a gypsy girl whom Gilbert toys with. Stilted soaper didn't do Gilbert's career any good. Based on an Arthur Hopkins play and a Leo Tolstoy novel.

Red Garters (1954) **C-91m.** **½ D: George Marshall. Rosemary Clooney, Jack Carson, Guy Mitchell, Pat Crowley, Gene Barry, Cass Daley, Frank Faylen, Reginald Owen, Buddy Ebsen. Musical Western spoof gets A for effort—with strikingly stylized color sets, offbeat casting—but falls short of target.▼●]

Redhead and the Cowboy, The (1950) **82m.** **½ D: Leslie Fenton. Glenn Ford, Edmond O'Brien, Rhonda Fleming, Alan Reed, Morris Ankrum, Ray Teal, King Donovan. Action-packed Civil War Western with apolitical cowpoke Ford lured into Union-Confederate conflict by scheming, alluring Fleming.

Red-Headed Woman (1932) **79m.** *** D: Jack Conway. Jean Harlow, Chester Morris, Una Merkel, Lewis Stone, May Robson, Leila Hyams, Charles Boyer. Harlow has never been sexier than in this wild pre-Code movie (by Anita Loos) of a gold-digging secretary who sets out to corral her married boss (Morris).▼●]

Redhead From Wyoming, The (1952) **C-80m.** **½ D: Lee Sholem. Maureen O'Hara, Alexander Scourby, Alex Nicol, Jack Kelly, William Bishop, Dennis Weaver. Saucy Western pepped up by exuberant O'Hara as girl who falls in love with sheriff while protecting local cattle rustler.▼]

Red, Hot and Blue (1949) **84m.** ** D: John Farrow. Betty Hutton, Victor Mature, June Havoc, Jane Nigh, William Demarest, William Talman, Art Smith, Raymond Walburn. Strained Hutton musical-comedy about an ambitious girl trying to make it in showbiz, clashing with boyfriend Mature, a "serious" theater director. The gangster who frames the story is played by songwriter Frank Loesser, who also contributed the score.

Red Hot Tires (1935) **61m.** **½ D: D. Ross Lederman. Lyle Talbot, Mary Astor, Roscoe Karns, Frankie Darro, Gavin Gordon, Mary Treen, Henry Kolker. Good cast enlivens this entertaining (albeit by-the-numbers) programmer involving nice-guy race car mechanic-driver Talbot, who's falsely accused of murder.

Red House, The (1947) **100m.** *** D: Delmer Daves. Edward G. Robinson, Lon McCallister, Allene Roberts, Judith Anderson, Rory Calhoun, Julie London. Ona Munson. Title refers to strange old house containing many mysteries, providing con-

stant fear for farmer Robinson. Exciting melodrama with fine cast.▼]

Red Inn, The (1951-French) **100m.** **½ D: Claude Autant-Lara. Fernandel, Françoise Rosay, (Julien) Carette, Gregoire Aslan, Marie-Claire Olivia. Bizarre, ironic black comedy about what happens when stagecoach passengers seek refuge at an inn run by murderous thieves Rosay and Carette. Fernandel is the dissipated monk who intercedes on the travelers' behalf.

Red Light (1949) **83m.** ** D: Roy Del Ruth. George Raft, Virginia Mayo, Gene Lockhart, Barton MacLane, Henry (Harry) Morgan, Raymond Burr, Arthur Franz, William Frawley. Turgid drama of innocent Raft seeking revenge when freed from prison, hunting brother's killer.]

Red Lily, The (1924) **81m.** ** D: Fred Niblo. Ramon Novarro, Enid Bennett, Frank Currier, Wallace Beery, Gibson Gowland, Mitchell Lewis, Dick Sutherland, Risita (Rosita) Marstini, Sidney Franklin. In a small town in Brittany, the son of a coldhearted mayor and daughter of an ill-fated cobbler have been sweethearts since childhood. What they hope will be a happy future is compromised by cruel fate. Over-the-top soap opera about the corruption of innocence is based on an original story by Niblo.]

Red Line 7000 (1965) **C-110m.** **½ D: Howard Hawks. James Caan, Laura Devon, Gail Hire, Charlene Holt, John Robert Crawford, Marianna Hill, James Ward, Norman Alden, George Takei. Attempt by director Hawks to do same kind of expert adventure pic he'd done for 40 years is sabotaged by overly complex script and indifferent acting, but is a faster and less pretentious racing-car drama than GRAND PRIX. Originally ran 127m.▼●

Red Menace, The (1949) **87m.** *½ D: R. G. Springsteen. Robert Rockwell, Hanne Axman, Betty Lou Gerson, Barbara Fuller. War vet Rockwell is duped by the Commies. McCarthyesque propaganda is now an unintentionally funny antique. Narrated by "Lloyd G. Davies, member of the City Council, Los Angeles, California."▼●]

Red Mill, The (1927) **74m.** **½ D: William Goodrich. Marion Davies, Owen Moore, Louise Fazenda, George Siegmann, Karl Dane, J. Russell Powell, Snitz Edwards. Davies is cute as a Dutch barmaid whose love for a visiting Irishman is thwarted by her cruel boss. Frivolous Cinderella-like silent notable for some deft bits of physical comedy staged by the scandalized Roscoe "Fatty" Arbuckle under the Goodrich pseudonym. Adapted from the musical comedy by Victor Herbert and Henry Blossom.]

Red Mountain (1951) **C-84m.** **½ D: William Dieterle. Alan Ladd, Lizabeth Scott, John Ireland, Arthur Kennedy. When Confederate raider Quantrill (Ireland) tries to establish his own empire in the West during the Civil War, it's up to Southern rebel Ladd and neutral Kennedy to stop him.

Red Planet Mars (1952) **87m.** ****½** D: Harry Horner. Peter Graves, Andrea King, Marvin Miller, Herbert Berghof, House Peters, Jr., Vince Barnett. Outrageous sci-fi of scientist deciphering messages from Mars which turn out to be from God. Hilariously ludicrous anti-Communist propaganda (*Red* Planet Mars, get it?).▼●▶

Red Pony, The (1949) **C-89m.** ******* D: Lewis Milestone. Myrna Loy, Robert Mitchum, Peter Miles, Louis Calhern, Shepperd Strudwick, Margaret Hamilton, Beau Bridges. John Steinbeck adapted his own stories into this warmhearted screenplay about a farm boy who learns about responsibility when he's given his own pony. Keen observations of family dynamics (with Calhern a delight as Loy's garrulous father) make this a standout, along with Tony Gaudio's Technicolor camerawork and a justly famous score by Aaron Copland. Remade for TV in 1973.▼●▶

Red River (1948) **133m.** ******** D: Howard Hawks. John Wayne, Montgomery Clift, Walter Brennan, Joanne Dru, John Ireland, Noah Beery, Jr., Paul Fix, Coleen Gray, Harry Carey, Jr., Harry Carey, Sr., Chief Yowlachie, Hank Worden. One of the greatest American adventures is really a Western MUTINY ON THE BOUNTY: Clift (in his first film, though it was released after THE SEARCH) rebels against tyrannical guardian Wayne (brilliant in an unsympathetic role) during crucial cattle drive. Spellbinding photography by Russell Harlan, rousing Dimitri Tiomkin score; an absolute must. Alternate 125m. version uses Brennan's narration in place of diary pages, which Hawks preferred. Screenplay by Borden Chase and Charles Schnee, from Chase's *Saturday Evening Post* story. If you blink, you'll miss Shelley Winters dancing with Ireland around a campfire. Remade for TV in 1988 with James Arness.▼●▶

Red River Range (1938) **56m.** ****½** D: George Sherman. John Wayne, Ray Corrigan, Max Terhune, Polly Moran, Lorna Gray (Adrian Booth), Kirby Grant, Sammy McKim. When governor deputizes the Three Mesquiteers, Wayne masquerades as lawbreaker to infiltrate modern-day cattle rustlers operating in environs of dude ranch. No moral complexity here, just plenty of hard riding and fighting action. Emphasizes Wayne at the expense of his two saddlemates.▼▶

Red River Valley (1936) **60m.** ****½** D: B. Reeves Eason. Gene Autry, Smiley Burnette, Frances Grant, Boothe Howard, Jack Kennedy, Sam Flint, George Chesebro, Charles King, Frank LaRue, Ken Cooper. Ditch riders Gene and Smiley uncover banker LaRue's

plot to sabotage an irrigation system and secure water rights for himself. Plenty of action and music, although Gene forcing Chesebro at gunpoint to lead workmen in singing "Red River Valley" may be pushing things a bit. Filmed partly at Laguna Dam on the Colorado River and at Yuma Prison.▼▶

Red River Valley (1941) **62m.** ****½** D: Joseph Kane. Roy Rogers, George "Gabby" Hayes, Sally Payne, Trevor Bardette, Gale Storm, Hal Taliaferro, Robert Homans, Sons of the Pioneers. Roy and Gabby do everything they can to prove to the Red River Valley Dam stockholders that they're being manipulated by swindlers. They even kidnap the sheriff and his daughter to prevent a crucial transaction from going through. Light, enjoyable Rogers vehicle. Musical highlights: the Sons performing "When Payday Rolls Around" and "Chant of the Wanderer."▼▶

Red Salute (1935) **78m.** ****½** D: Sidney Lanfield. Barbara Stanwyck, Robert Young, Hardie Albright, Cliff Edwards, Ruth Donnelly, Gordon Jones. Runaway screwball Stanwyck meets no-nonsense soldier Young in this imitation IT HAPPENED ONE NIGHT with wild sociopolitical wrinkle: Barbara's boyfriend (Albright) is a student radical who makes Communist speeches. A real oddity. Aka HER ENLISTED MAN and RUNAWAY DAUGHTER.▼

Red Shoes, The (1948-British) **C-133m.** ******** D: Michael Powell, Emeric Pressburger. Anton Walbrook, Marius Goring, Moira Shearer, Robert Helpmann, Leonide Massine, Albert Basserman, Ludmilla Tcherina, Esmond Knight. A superb, stylized fairy tale. Young ballerina is torn between two creative, possessive men, one a struggling composer, the other an autocratic dance impresario. Landmark film for its integration of dance in storytelling, and a perennial favorite of balletomanes. Brian Easdale's score and Hein Heckroth and Arthur Lawson's art direction-set decoration won Oscars, and Jack Cardiff's cinematography *should* have. Shearer is exquisite in movie debut. Later a Broadway musical.▼●▶

Red Skies of Montana (1952) **C-99m.** ****½** D: Joseph M. Newman. Richard Widmark, Jeffrey Hunter, Constance Smith, Richard Boone, Richard Crenna, Charles Buchinsky (Bronson). Trite account of forest-fire fighters, salvaged by spectacular fire sequences. ▶

Redskin (1929) **C/B&W-82m.** ******* D: Victor Schertzinger. Richard Dix, Gladys Belmont (Julie Carter), Tully Marshall, George Rigas, Noble Johnson, Jane Novak. Heartfelt drama of Wing Foot, a Navajo chief's son, who is taken from the reservation and educated in a white man's world. He grows into adulthood caught between two distinctly different cultures, while fitting into neither. What's more, he falls in love with Corn Blossom, a Pueblo, even though the Navajo and Pueblo are traditional enemies. Partially filmed on location on tribal lands in Arizona and New Mexico; these sequences are in two-strip Technicolor.▶

Red Stallion in the Rockies (1949) **C-85m.** ****** D: Ralph Murphy. Arthur Franz, Wallace Ford, Ray Collins, Jean Heather, Leatrice Joy. OK outdoor drama of Franz and Ford being hired by a rancher for the harvest season and becoming immersed in local conflicts and jealousies.

Red Sundown (1956) **C-81m.** ****½** D: Jack Arnold. Rory Calhoun, Martha Hyer, Dean Jagger, Robert Middleton, Grant Williams, James Millican. Standard yarn of bad guy gone good (Calhoun) pinning on a deputy's badge and enforcing law without using his gun. Lita Baron (Mrs. Calhoun in real life) has a small part.▼

Reducing (1931) **77m.** ****½** D: Charles F. Riesner. Marie Dressler, Polly Moran, Anita Page, Lucien Littlefield, Buster Collier, Jr., Sally Eilers, William Bakewell. Typical comedy vehicle for the two earthy stars, as Dressler and her Depression-struck family move to N.Y.C., where she goes to work for her snooty sister (Moran) at her beauty parlor and reducing salon. Fans of the duo will enjoy the mix of slapstick and sentiment.▶

Reefer Madness (1936) **67m.** BOMB D: Louis Gasnier. Dave O'Brien, Dorothy Short, Warren McCollum, Lillian Miles, Carleton Young, Thelma White. The granddaddy of all "Worst" movies; one of that era's many low-budget "Warning!" films depicts (in now-hilarious fashion) how one puff of pot can lead clean-cut teenagers down the road to insanity and death. Miles' frenzied piano solo is a highlight, but in this more enlightened age, overall effect is a little sad. Originally titled THE BURNING QUESTION, then TELL YOUR CHILDREN; beware shorter prints. Later a stage musical, which became a cable TV movie in 2005.▼●▶

Reet, Petite and Gone (1947) **69m.** ****** D: William Forest Crouch. Louis Jordan, June Richmond, Milton Woods, Bea Griffith, David Bethea, Lorenzo Tucker, Vanita Smythe, Mabel Lee, Dots Johnson. Plenty of vintage music (including Jordan's "Let the Good Times Roll," "Ain't That Just Like a Woman," and the title number) enlivens this so-so all-black musical romance. Jordan plays two characters, a wealthy musical performer on his deathbed and his bandleader offspring, with the father plotting to match the son with the daughter of his lost love.▼▶

Reformer and the Redhead, The (1950) **90m.** ****½** D: Norman Panama, Melvin Frank. June Allyson, Dick Powell, David Wayne, Cecil Kellaway, Ray Collins, Robert Keith, Marvin Kaplan. Sassy shenanigans with lawyer–mayoral candidate Powell becoming involved with spunky, idealistic zookeeper's daughter Allyson during controversial political campaign. Powell and Allyson were real-life Mr. and Mrs. at this time. Spring Byington provides the voice of Allyson's mother.

Reform School Girl (1957) **71m.** BOMB D: Edward Bernds. Gloria Castillo, Ross Ford, Edward Byrnes, Ralph Reed, Luana Anders, Jack Kruschen, Sally Kellerman. Hokey time-capsule about a pretty teen from "the other side of the tracks" (Castillo). After a fatal car mishap, she ends up in reform school. Will she or won't she squeal on the party responsible for her dilemma? Remade for cable TV in 1994.▼

Regeneration (1915) **72m.** *****½** D: Raoul Walsh. Rockcliffe Fellowes, Anna Q. Nilsson, William Sheer, Carl Harbaugh, James Marcus, Maggie Weston. Still stirring and cinematically impressive early gangster film (and social tract) charting the plight and fate of Owen (Fellowes), a surly, charismatic Irish hood, and how his life is affected by Mamie Rose (Nilsson), a young woman who deserts her upper-class roots for life as "a settlement worker in the gangster's district." This vividly realistic melodrama, which portrays the effect of poverty on the human spirit, was filmed on location in N.Y.C.'s Bowery.▼●▶

Registered Nurse (1934) **63m.** ****** D: Robert Florey. Bebe Daniels, Lyle Talbot, John Halliday, Irene Franklin, Sidney Toler, Gordon Westcott, Minna Gombell, Beulah Bondi, Vince Barnett, Mayo Methot, Louise Beavers. Life and love in a big-city hospital, Warner Bros. style. Pretty raw pre-Code yarn, more interesting for its hard-boiled characters and dialogue than its story.▶

Reg'lar Fellers (1941) **66m.** ****** D: Arthur Dreifuss. Billy Lee, Carl "Alfalfa" Switzer, Buddy Boles, Janet Dempsey, Sarah Padden, Roscoe Ates. Extremely dated comedy, based on Gene Byrnes' popular comic strip, chronicling the escapades of typically all-American youngsters who help soften miserable, kid-hating Padden. "Alfalfa" fans will not be disappointed.▼

Reign of Terror (1949) **89m.** ******* D: Anthony Mann. Robert Cummings, Arlene Dahl, Richard Hart, Richard Basehart, Arnold Moss, Beulah Bondi. Vivid costume drama set during French Revolution, with valuable diary eluding both sides of battle. Moss is particularly good as the elegantly, eloquently evil Foucher. Stunningly photographed by John Alton; every shot is a painting! Aka THE BLACK BOOK.▼▶

Relentless (1948) **C-93m.** ******* D: George Sherman. Robert Young, Marguerite Chapman, Willard Parker, Barton MacLane, Akim Tamiroff, Mike Mazurki. Good, solid Western

[566]

story of a man who must catch a wily horse thief in order to prove his own innocence. Young produced this, uncredited, with his *Father Knows Best* partner Eugene Rodney.

Reluctant Debutante, The (1958) **C-94m.** ****½** D: Vincente Minnelli. Rex Harrison, Kay Kendall, John Saxon, Sandra Dee, Angela Lansbury. Bright drawing-room comedy which Harrison, Kendall, and Lansbury make worthwhile: British parents must present their Americanized daughter to society. Harrison and Kendall were real-life husband and wife at this time. Remade as WHAT A GIRL WANTS. CinemaScope. ▼◐❶

Reluctant Dragon, The (1941) **C/B&W-72m.** ******* D: Alfred L. Werker (live-action). Robert Benchley gets a tour of the Walt Disney studio in this pleasant feature that incorporates a number of first-rate cartoon sequences (*Baby Weems, The Reluctant Dragon*), offers some interesting glimpses of studio at work. Clarence "Ducky" Nash and Florence Gill do cartoon voices, Ward Kimball animates Goofy, Frances Gifford shows Benchley around, and young Alan Ladd appears as one of the story men. Opens in b&w, turns to beautiful Technicolor hues. ▼❶

Reluctant Saint, The (1962-U.S.-Italian) **105m.** ****½** D: Edward Dmytryk. Maximilian Schell, Ricardo Montalban, Lea Padovani, Akim Tamiroff, Harold Goldblatt, Mark Damon. Loosely biographical account of St. Joseph of Cupertino, a 17th-century Franciscan whose modest upbringing and simple intellect would never have foretold the religious life he would lead (or the great number of miracles he would perform). Unusual fare; worth a look. ❶

Reluctant Widow, The (1951-British) **86m.** ***½** D: Bernard Knowles. Jean Kent, Guy Rolfe, Kathleen Byron, Paul Dupuis. Mild drama set in late 18th century, of governess Kent marrying rogue Rolfe.

Remains to Be Seen (1953) **89m.** ******* D: Don Weis. Van Johnson, June Allyson, Angela Lansbury, Louis Calhern, Dorothy Dandridge. Disarming comedy based on Howard Lindsay–Russel Crouse play, with Allyson a singer and Johnson the apartment-house manager involved in swank East Side N.Y.C. murder; script by Sidney Sheldon.

Remarkable Andrew, The (1942) **80m.** ****½** D: Stuart Heisler. William Holden, Ellen Drew, Brian Donlevy, Montagu Love, George Watts, Brandon Hurst, Gilbert Emery, Rod Cameron, Richard Webb, Frances Gifford. Far-fetched but well-played fantasy in which small-town bookkeeper Holden is falsely accused of embezzlement; the ghost of Pres. Andrew Jackson (Donlevy), among other pillars of U.S. history, comes to his rescue. Script by Dalton Trumbo, based on his novel.

Remarkable Mr. Pennypacker, The (1959) **C-87m.** ****½** D: Henry Levin. Clifton Webb, Dorothy McGuire, Charles Co-

burn, Ray Stricklyn, Jill St. John, Ron Ely, David Nelson. Broadway play is tailored to Webb's arch screen persona, as he plays a man in early 20th-century Philadelphia who leads a double life—with two separate families. CinemaScope. ❶

Rembrandt (1936-British) **84m.** *****½** D: Alexander Korda. Charles Laughton, Elsa Lanchester, Gertrude Lawrence, Edward Chapman, Roger Livesey, Raymond Huntley, John Clements, Marius Goring, Abraham Sofaer. Handsome bio of Dutch painter, full of visual tableaux and sparked by Laughton's excellent performance. One of Gertrude Lawrence's rare film appearances. ▼◐❶

Remedy for Riches (1940) **60m.** ****** D: Erle C. Kenton. Jean Hersholt, Dorothy Lovett, Edgar Kennedy, Jed Prouty, Walter Catlett, Maude Eburne, Robert Baldwin, Warren Hull. There's more comedy than drama in this typical *Dr. Christian* series entry. A swindler "uncovers" oil in dear old River's End, and the townsfolk line up to invest their hard-earned savings. ▼

Remember? (1939) **83m.** ****** D: Norman Z. McLeod. Robert Taylor, Greer Garson, Lew Ayres, Billie Burke, Reginald Owen, Laura Hope Crews, Henry Travers, Sig Ruman. Blah comedy about bickering couple taking potion which gives them amnesia—whereupon they fall in love all over again. Nice try, but no cigar.

Remember Last Night? (1935) **81m.** ****½** D: James Whale. Edward Arnold, Constance Cummings, Robert Young, Sally Eilers, Robert Armstrong, Reginald Denny, Monroe Owsley, Gustav von Seyffertitz, Arthur Treacher. Freewheeling, perpetually tipsy couple find themselves—and their society friends—involved with multiple murders; detective Arnold tries to get them to take matters seriously enough to solve the mystery. Lightheaded comedy-whodunit is more shrill than funny, though stellar cast of character actors and Whale's trademarked stylistics make it worth watching. ❶

Remember the Day (1941) **85m.** ******* D: Henry King. Claudette Colbert, John Payne, John Shepperd (Shepperd Strudwick), Ann Todd, Douglas Croft, Jane Seymour, Anne Revere. Pleasant, tug-at-your-heartstrings Americana, told in flashback, about the effect teacher Colbert has on a student (Croft, who grows up to be presidential nominee Shepperd). Payne is the fellow teacher with whom Colbert falls in love. ❶

Remember the Night (1940) **94m.** *****½** D: Mitchell Leisen. Barbara Stanwyck, Fred MacMurray, Beulah Bondi, Elizabeth Patterson, Sterling Holloway. Beautifully made, sentimental story of prosecutor MacMurray falling in love with shoplifter Stanwyck during Christmas court recess; builds masterfully as it creates a very special mood. Script by Preston Sturges. ▼❶

[567]

Remorques (1941-French) **84m.** ***½ D: Jean Grémillon. Jean Gabin, Madeleine Renaud, Michéle Morgan, (Charles) Blavette, Jean Marchat, Nane Germon, Jean Daste, Fernand Ledoux. Darkly poetic, subtly powerful drama of tough-but-fair tugboat captain Gabin, who must contend with personality issues at work and the two women in his life: his secretly ailing wife (Renaud), who wishes he would find less dangerous work, and captivating yet desperate Morgan, whose presence is a threat to his marriage. Written by Jacques Prévert and André Cayatte. Filming began in 1939 but was temporarily halted when France fell to Germany. Aka STORMY WATERS.▌

Remote Control (1930) **65m.** **½ D: No director credited. William Haines, Mary Doran, John Miljan, Polly Moran, J. C. Nugent, Edward Nugent. Haines, brash as ever, plays a radio station program director who unmasks a bank robber posing as a clairvoyant, who uses the airwaves to broadcast coded messages to his gang. Radio station backdrop is fun, and so are unbilled cameos by Cliff Edwards, Roscoe Ates, and Benny Rubin, who plays a cowboy actor called Dangerous Dan the Jew! Nick Grinde, Malcolm St. Clair, and Edward Sedgwick were among the uncredited directors.▌

Rendezvous (1935) **91m.** ** D: William K. Howard. William Powell, Rosalind Russell, Binnie Barnes, Lionel Atwill, Cesar Romero. OK WW1 intrigue, with Powell assigned to office work instead of combat during war, running into notorious spy ring. Russell's "comedy" character is only obtrusive here. Remade as PACIFIC RENDEZVOUS.▌

Rendezvous at Midnight (1935) **64m.** ** D: Christy Cabanne. Ralph Bellamy, Valerie Hobson, Catherine Doucet, Irene Ware, Helen Jerome Eddy. Fair whodunit of city commissioner being murdered just as his replacement (Bellamy) begins to investigate his corrupt administration.

Rendez-vous de Juillet (1949-French) **112m.** *** D: Jacques Becker. Daniel Gélin, Brigitte Auber, Nicole Courcel, Pierre Trabaud, Maurice Ronet, Philippe Mareuil, Gaston Modot, Louis Seigner. Lively portrait of young Parisians who reject bourgeois conventions and embrace movies, theater, and *le jazz hot* while becoming enmeshed in love affairs and searching to establish their identities. Perhaps the first film to portray the emerging youth culture of postwar Europe. Watching it, one gets a vivid sense of time and place. Watch closely for an unbilled 18-year-old Capucine. U.S. jazz trumpeter Rex Stewart has a specialty as himself. Becker coscripted; photographed by Claude Renoir.▼

Rendezvous With Annie (1946) **89m.** **½ D: Allan Dwan. Eddie Albert, Faye Marlowe, Gail Patrick, Phillip Reed, C. Aubrey Smith, Raymond Walburn, William Fraw-

ley. Frantic comedy concerning G.I. Albert, who is stationed in England and goes AWOL for a few days to see his wife back in the States. Engaging cast and some funny moments.

Renegades (1930) **84m.** ** D: Victor Fleming. Warner Baxter, Myrna Loy, Noah Beery, Gregory Gaye, George Cooper, C. Henry Gordon, Bela Lugosi. Stodgy story of renegades from Foreign Legion outpost in Morocco, one of whom (Baxter) has been betrayed by seductive spy Loy. Complex story builds to offbeat, and downbeat, ending.

Renegades (1946) **C-88m.** **½ D: George Sherman. Evelyn Keyes, Willard Parker, Larry Parks, Edgar Buchanan, Jim Bannon, Forrest Tucker, Ludwig Donath. Hokey Western has Keyes torn between a good doctor and member of an outlaw family. Soapy scenes offset by good action and Buchanan's standout portrayal of a Bible-spouting bandit. Keyes' garish, Technicolored hair has to be seen to be believed.

Renegade Trail, The (1939) **61m.** **½ D: Lesley Selander. William Boyd, Russell Hayden, George Hayes, Charlotte Wynters, Russell Hopton, Roy Barcroft. Escaped convict seeks refuge with estranged wife and son; it remains for Hopalong Cassidy to rescue the lady and subdue con men, in a fine climactic chase. Hampered only by mawkish scenes involving the boy, Sonny Bupp (who would play Charles Foster Kane III two years later). Eddie Dean joins The King's Men for two satisfactory songs. First Hoppy not even nominally derived from a story by Clarence E. Mulford; last entry for Hayes as "Windy."▼▌

Reno (1939) **73m.** ** D: John Farrow. Richard Dix, Gail Patrick, Anita Louise, Paul Cavanagh, Laura Hope Crews, Louis Jean Heydt, Frank Faylen. Talky drama spotlighting the plight of lawyer-turned-gambling-house-proprietor Dix, with his story paralleling the rise of Reno, Nevada, as the divorce capital of America.

Repeat Performance (1947) **93m.** *** D: Alfred L. Werker. Louis Hayward, Joan Leslie, Tom Conway, Benay Venuta, Richard Basehart, Virginia Field; narrated by John Ireland. On New Year's Eve, woman gets chance to relive the past year, leading up to the moment she murdered her husband. Fine premise smoothly executed in this B production; Basehart's first film. Remade for TV in 1989 as TURN BACK THE CLOCK.▌

Reprisal! (1956) **C-74m.** **½ D: George Sherman. Guy Madison, Felicia Farr, Kathryn Grant, Michael Pate, Edward Platt. Madison has to clear himself of murder charge when a powerful rancher is killed. Decent cast in ordinary grade-B Western drama.

Reptilicus (1961-U.S.-Danish) **C-90m.** BOMB D: Poul Bang, Sidney W. Pink. Carl Ottosen, Ann Smyrner, Mimi Hein-

[568]

rich, Asbjorn Andersen, Marla Behrens. The tail of a prehistoric monster—recently discovered—spawns the full-sized beast. Only good for laughs as script hits every conceivable monster-movie cliché, right to the final shot. ▼▶

Republic of Sin SEE: **La Fièvre Monte à El Pao**

Repulsion (1965-British) **105m.** **** D: Roman Polanski. Catherine Deneuve, Ian Hendry, John Fraser, Patrick Wymark, Yvonne Furneaux, James Villiers. Polanski's first English-language film is excellent psychological shocker depicting mental deterioration of sexually repressed girl left alone in her sister's apartment for several days. Hasn't lost a bit of its impact; will leave you feeling uneasy for days afterward. Screenplay by Polanski and Gerard Brach. ▼◑▶

Requiem for a Gunfighter (1965) **C-91m.** *½ D: Spencer G. Bennet. Rod Cameron, Stephen McNally, Mike Mazurki, Olive Sturgess, Tim McCoy, John Mack Brown, Bob Steele, Lane Chandler, Raymond Hatton. Veteran cast is sole virtue of low-budget Western. Cameron impersonates a judge to ensure that justice is done at murder trial. Techniscope.

Requiem for a Heavyweight (1962) **100m.** *** D: Ralph Nelson. Anthony Quinn, Jackie Gleason, Mickey Rooney, Julie Harris, Nancy Cushman, Madame Spivy, Cassius Clay (Muhammad Ali). Grim account of fighter (Quinn), whose ring career is over, forcing him into corruption and degradation. His sleazy manager Gleason, sympathetic trainer Rooney, and Harris as unrealistic social worker are all fine. Adapted by Rod Serling from his great teleplay; original running time 87m. ▼▶

Restless Breed, The (1957) **C-81m.** ** D: Allan Dwan. Scott Brady, Anne Bancroft, Jim Davis, Scott Marlowe, Evelyn Rudie. Usual Western fare of Brady out to get his father's killer. ▼◑▶

Restless Years, The (1958) **86m.** ** D: Helmut Kautner. John Saxon, Sandra Dee, Margaret Lindsay, Teresa Wright, James Whitmore, Luana Patten, Virginia Grey, Jody McCrea. Overblown relic of its era, an Edward Anhalt–scripted PEYTON PLACE clone, in which illegitimate Dee is overprotected by neurotic mom Wright. Trouble comes when sensitive outsider Saxon—from "the wrong side of the tracks"—takes an interest in her. CinemaScope. ▶

Retreat, Hell! (1952) **95m.** **½ D: Joseph H. Lewis. Frank Lovejoy, Richard Carlson, Russ Tamblyn, Anita Louise. Grim drama chronicling the Marine withdrawal from Korea's Changjin Reservoir in the wake of a massive Chinese offensive. ▼▶

Return From the Ashes (1965-British) **105m.** *** D: J. Lee Thompson. Maximilian Schell, Samantha Eggar, Ingrid Thu-

lin, Herbert Lom, Talitha Pol. Engrossing melodrama of a philandering husband taking up with his stepdaughter when his wife is supposedly killed. Stars lend credibility to far-fetched proceedings. Panavision. ▶

Return From the Sea (1954) **80m.** ** D: Lesley Selander. Jan Sterling, Neville Brand, John Doucette, Paul Langton, John Pickard. Career Navy man marries a waitress and tries to settle down on a farm in California. Brand and Sterling do their best.

Return of Bulldog Drummond, The (1934-British) **71m.** *** D: Walter Summers. Ralph Richardson, Ann Todd, Francis L. Sullivan, Claud Allister, Joyce Kennedy. Richardson gives a full-blooded performance as Drummond in this serial-like account of the ex-Army officer on a bloody vigilante campaign to end crime in England by eliminating all foreigners! Wildly entertaining, and a revelation to those only familiar with genteel British cinema. ▶

Return of Doctor X, The (1939) **62m.** ** D: Vincent Sherman. Humphrey Bogart, Rosemary Lane, Wayne Morris, Dennis Morgan, John Litel, Huntz Hall. Only Bogart as a creepy lab assistant makes this low-grade sci-fi yarn worth viewing. Despite the title, not a sequel to DOCTOR X. ▶

Return of Don Camillo, The (1965-Italian) **115m.** **½ D: Julien Duvivier. Fernandel, Gino Cervi, Charles Vissieres, Edouard Delmont. Fernandel is again the irresponsible smalltown Italian priest involved in more projects of goodwill.

Return of Dracula, The (1958) **77m.** ** D: Paul Landres. Francis Lederer, Norma Eberhardt, Ray Stricklyn, Jimmie Baird. Low-budget flick about the Count (Lederer) killing a European man, taking his papers, and coming to America to stay with smalltown family. Lederer thwarted by mediocre script. TV title: THE CURSE OF DRACULA. ▼◑▶

Return of Dr. Fu Manchu, The (1930) **73m.** ** D: Rowland V. Lee. Warner Oland, Jean Arthur, Neil Hamilton, O. P. Heggie, William Austin, Evelyn Hall. Supposedly dead Fu Manchu (Oland) escapes from his own coffin to continue his nefarious vengeance against the British families he holds responsible for the death of his wife and child. Quickie sequel to THE MYSTERIOUS DR. FU MANCHU is just as creaky but not as campy—or as much fun.

Return of Frank James, The (1940) **C-92m.** *** D: Fritz Lang. Henry Fonda, Gene Tierney, Jackie Cooper, Henry Hull, John Carradine, J. Edward Bromberg, Donald Meek. Fonda reprises role from 1939 JESSE JAMES in story of attempt to avenge his brother Jesse's death; colorful production was Tierney's film debut. ▼◑▶

Return of Jack Slade, The (1955) **79m.** ** D: Harold Schuster. John Ericson, Mari

Blanchard, Neville Brand, Angie Dickinson. To redeem his father's wrongdoings, Ericson joins the law to fight outlaws; adequate Western. SuperScope.

Return of Jesse James, The (1950) 75m. **½ D: Arthur Hilton. John Ireland, Ann Dvorak, Henry Hull, Hugh O'Brian, Reed Hadley. Compact budget Western dealing with rumors that lookalike for outlaw is notorious gunslinger.▼❚

Return of Monte Cristo, The (1946) 91m. ** D: Henry Levin. Louis Hayward, Barbara Britton, George Macready, Una O'Connor, Henry Stephenson. Rather ordinary swashbuckler of original count's young descendant, thwarted in attempt to claim inheritance by dastardly villain.

Return of Mr. Moto, The (1965-British) 71m. *½ D: Ernest Morris. Henry Silva, Terrence Longdon, Suzanne Lloyd, Marne Maitland, Martin Wyldeck. Silva is miscast as the Oriental sleuth in a drab, lifeless update involving an international crime syndicate out to control world oil production (no, it's not OPEC).❚

Return of October, The (1948) C-98m. ** D: Joseph H. Lewis. Glenn Ford, Terry Moore, Albert Sharpe, James Gleason, Steve Dunne. Moore is wholesome girl who thinks her horse (October) is a reincarnation of her favorite uncle, much to her relatives' consternation. Weird comedy written by Norman Panama and Melvin Frank.

Return of Peter Grimm, The (1935) 82m. **½ D: George Nicholls, Jr. Lionel Barrymore, Helen Mack, Edward Ellis, Donald Meek, Allen Vincent. Patriarch of a close-knit family returns from the dead to make amends for all he did wrong in his lifetime. Hoary old David Belasco play gets full-blooded treatment from Barrymore and a cast of pros.▼

Return of Ringo, The (1965-Italian-Spanish) C-96m. *** D: Duccio Tessari. Montgomery Wood (Giuliano Gemma), Fernando Sancho, Hally Hammond (Lorella De Luca), Nieves Navarro, George Martin, Antonio Casas, "Pajarito" (Manuel Muniz). Follow-up to A PISTOL FOR RINGO finds Wood returning from the Civil War, when he was reportedly killed, to find that Mexican bandidos have taken over his home and his fiancée is being forced to marry the gang's leader. Taut, well-crafted spaghetti Western spin on *The Odyssey* is an entertaining example of the genre, boosted in no small part by a terrific score by Ennio Morricone. Techniscope.

Return of Rin Tin Tin, The (1947) C-65m. **½ D: Max Nosseck. Bobby (Robert) Blake, Donald Woods, Rin Tin Tin (III), Claudia Drake, Gaylord Pendleton, Earl Hodgins. Easy-to-take low-budget tale of young boy who comes out of his shell whenever he's with Rin Tin Tin, but bad man takes the dog away. Filmed in ultracheap Vita-

color process. Aka THE ADVENTURES OF RIN TIN TIN.▼❚

Return of Sophie Lang, The (1936) 65m. **½ D: George Archainbaud. Gertrude Michael, Sir Guy Standing, Ray Milland, Elizabeth Patterson, Colin Tapley, Paul Harvey. Jewel-thief-gone-straight Michael seeks Milland's help in staying out of public eye. OK sequel to THE NOTORIOUS SOPHIE LANG.

Return of the Ape Man (1944) 60m. ** D: Philip Rosen. Bela Lugosi, John Carradine, Judith Gibson (Teala Loring), Michael Ames (Tod Andrews), Frank Moran, Mary Currier. Scientist Lugosi transplants Carradine's brain into body of recently discovered Missing Link (Moran!). Typical Monogram fare; no relation to THE APE MAN. Despite an on-screen credit, George Zucco does not appear.

Return of the Bad Men (1948) 90m. **½ D: Ray Enright. Randolph Scott, Robert Ryan, Anne Jeffreys, George "Gabby" Hayes, Jacqueline White, Steve Brodie, Lex Barker. Newly settled Oklahoman Scott gets one female outlaw (Jeffreys) to go straight, but has a tougher time dealing with Billy the Kid, The Dalton Gang, The Younger Brothers, and a particularly nasty Sundance Kid (Ryan) in this routine Western. Also shown in computer-colored version.▼❚

Return of the Cisco Kid, The (1939) 70m. ** D: Herbert I. Leeds. Warner Baxter, Lynn Bari, Cesar Romero, Henry Hull, Kane Richmond, Chris-Pin Martin, Robert Barrat, C. Henry Gordon. Baxter reprises his Oscar-winning role from IN OLD ARIZONA in this slick but routine B movie. Having miraculously healed his own death by firing squad, Cisco helps a pretty maiden and her grandfather reclaim the deed to their ranch from swindler Barrat. Romero plays the hero's scruffy pal Lopez; later that year he inherited the role of Cisco in THE CISCO KID AND THE LADY.❚

Return of the Fly (1959) 80m. **½ D: Edward L. Bernds. Vincent Price, Brett Halsey, David Frankham, John Sutton, Dan Seymour, Danielle De Metz. Adequate sequel to THE FLY proves "like father, like son." Youth attempts to reconstruct his late father's teleportation machine and likewise gets scrambled with an insect. Followed six years later by CURSE OF THE FLY. CinemaScope.▼❚

Return of the Frontiersman (1950) C-74m. **½ D: Richard Bare. Gordon MacRae, Rory Calhoun, Julie London, Jack Holt, Fred Clark. Easygoing yarn of sheriff's son falsely accused of murder.❚

Return of the Scarlet Pimpernel, The (1938-British) 88m. ** D: Hans Schwartz. Barry K. Barnes, Sophie Stewart, Margaretta Scott, James Mason, Francis Lister, Anthony Bushell. Far below stunning original, with lower production values and less-than-stellar cast in costumer set in 1790s London and Paris. Original British running time: 94m.

Return of the Texan (1952) **88m.** ** D: Delmer Daves. Dale Robertson, Joanne Dru, Walter Brennan, Richard Boone, Robert Horton. Flabby Western about Robertson et al. fighting to save his ranch.

Return of the Vampire, The (1943) **69m.** ** D: Lew Landers. Bela Lugosi, Frieda Inescort, Nina Foch, Roland Varno, Miles Mander, Matt Willis. Lugosi plays a vampire in wartorn London (with a werewolf assistant!) in limp attempt to capitalize on previous success as Dracula. Final scene is memorable, though.▼●)

Return of the Whistler, The (1948) **63m.** **½ D: D. Ross Lederman. Michael Duane, Lenore Aubert, Richard Lane, James Cardwell, Ann Doran. The final *Whistler* series entry, about Duane's efforts to find his fiancée, who's been kidnapped and put in an asylum by a man who claims that she's already his wife. Intriguing Cornell Woolrich story.

Return to Paradise (1953) **C-100m.** ** D: Mark Robson. Gary Cooper, Roberta Haynes, Barry Jones, Moira MacDonald. Lackluster South Sea tale of beach bum Cooper in love with native girl; loosely based on James Michener's story. Filmed in Samoa.▼●

Return to Peyton Place (1961) **C-122m.** ** D: Jose Ferrer. Carol Lynley, Jeff Chandler, Eleanor Parker, Mary Astor, Robert Sterling, Luciana Paluzzi, Brett Halsey, Gunnar Hellstrom, Tuesday Weld, Bob Crane. Muddled follow-up to PEYTON PLACE suffers from faulty direction, and, save for stalwarts Astor and Parker, miscasting. Followed by TV movie MURDER IN PEYTON PLACE. CinemaScope.▼●

Return to Sender (1963-British) **63m.** ** D: Gordon Hales. Nigel Davenport, Yvonne Romain, Geoffrey Keen, William Russell, John Horsley. Programmer action tale of revenge, from Edgar Wallace yarn of industrialist's plot to ruin a D.A.'s career and life.

Return to Treasure Island (1954) **C-75m.** ·*½ D: E. A. Dupont, Tab Hunter, Dawn Addams, Porter Hall, James Seay, Harry Lauter. Poor updating of Stevenson novel, with student Hunter vying with crooks for buried treasure.❿

Return to Treasure Island (1954-Australian) SEE: **Long John Silver**

Return to Yesterday (1940-British) **69m.** **½ D: Robert Stevenson. Clive Brook, Anna Lee, Dame May Whitty, Hartley Power, Milton Rosmer, David Tree. Brook is improbably cast as one of Hollywood's biggest stars, who while vacationing in England becomes nostalgic for the days he spent at a seaside community theater and returns there to join the troupe in its latest production. Modest but engaging comedy with an ideal cast. Based on Robert Morley's play *Goodness, How Sad*.

Reunion in France (1942) **104m.** ** D: Jules Dassin. Joan Crawford, John Wayne, Philip Dorn, Reginald Owen, Albert Bassermann, John Carradine, Henry Daniell. Glossy romance, with Frenchwoman Crawford believing fiancé Dorn is a Nazi collaborator; she hides (and falls for) American flyer Wayne. Propaganda elements date badly. Watch for Ava Gardner as a salesgirl.▼●

Reunion in Reno (1951) **79m.** **½ D: Kurt Neumann. Mark Stevens, Peggy Dow, Gigi Perreau, Frances Dee, Leif Erickson. Diverting comedy of Perreau deciding to divorce her parents so she won't be in the way.

Reunion in Vienna (1933) **98m.** *** D: Sidney Franklin. John Barrymore, Diana Wynyard, Frank Morgan, May Robson, Eduardo Ciannelli, Una Merkel, Henry Travers. Too-literal adaptation of Robert Sherwood's dated stage play depends on its stars' considerable charm to come across. Barrymore provides most of the film's life with hilarious performance as exiled nobleman who returns to Vienna and tries to rekindle romance with Wynyard under the nose of her tolerant husband (Morgan).

Reveille With Beverly (1943) **78m.** ** D: Charles Barton. Ann Miller, William Wright, Dick Purcell, Franklin Pangborn, Larry Parks. Miller plays a versatile disk jockey throwing "big show" for servicemen. Jazz fans will shoot that rating higher, since guest stars include Frank Sinatra, Mills Brothers, Bob Crosby, Count Basie, and Duke Ellington.

Revenge of Frankenstein, The (1958-British) **C-91m.** *** D: Terence Fisher. Peter Cushing, Francis Matthews, Eunice Gayson, Michael Gwynn, Lionel Jeffries, John Welsh. Sequel to THE CURSE OF FRANKENSTEIN is quite effective with the good doctor still making a new body from others, ably assisted by hunchback dwarf and young medical student. Thought-provoking script has fine atmosphere, especially in color. Followed by THE EVIL OF FRANKENSTEIN.▼●

Revenge of the Creature (1955) **82m.** ** D: Jack Arnold. John Agar, Lori Nelson, John Bromfield, Nestor Paiva, Robert B. Williams. OK sequel to CREATURE FROM THE BLACK LAGOON destroys much of that film's mystery and terror by removing Gill Man from Amazonian home and placing him in Florida oceanarium. Clint Eastwood has his first screen role as lab technician. 3-D.▼●

Revenge of the Dead (1958) **69m.** BOMB D: Edward D. Wood, Jr. Duke Moore, Kenne Duncan, Paul Marco, Tor Johnson, John Carpenter, Valda Hansen, Jeannie Stevens, Criswell. Long-lost sequel to BRIDE OF THE MONSTER (and to a lesser extent, PLAN 9 FROM OUTER SPACE) doesn't reach the same heights of lunacy, but is still dreadful enough to tickle any bad-movie fan. "Ghosts" have been sighted in East L.A., so cops Moore and Marco are once more shoved into action; the trail leads to phony mystic Dr. Acula (Duncan, who really looks like he's in a trance). The incomparable Criswell again narrates the proceedings, this time from a coffin. Sat unreleased for *25 years* because Wood couldn't pay the lab bill! Retitled NIGHT OF THE GHOULS. ▼●▮

Revenge of the Pirates (1951-Italian) **95m.** ** D: Primo Zeglio. Maria Montez, Milly Vitale, Jean-Pierre Aumont, Saro Urzi, Paul Muller, Robert Risso. Aumont and Montez (offscreen husband and wife) try to spark this trite swashbuckler of wicked governor hoarding stolen gold, with Robin Hood of the seas coming to rescue.

Revenge of the Zombies (1943) **61m.** *½ D: Steve Sekely. John Carradine, Robert Lowery, Gale Storm, Veda Ann Borg, Mantan Moreland, Mauritz Hugo. Low-budget mad doctor saga, with Nazi Carradine experimenting on human guinea pigs on swampy Southern estate. Moreland's comic relief saves the day.

Revolt at Fort Laramie (1957) **C-73m.** ** D: Lesley Selander. John Dehner, Frances Helm, Gregg Palmer, Don Gordon, Robert Keys. Grade-B Western of internal rivalries of North-South soldiers at government fort during Civil War. Look for Harry Dean Stanton in his film debut.

Revolt in the Big House (1958) **79m.** **½ D: R. G. Springsteen. Gene Evans, Robert Blake, Timothy Carey, John Qualen. Career criminal Evans, sentenced to 20 years in a maximum security prison, plans a breakout. Despite a few brutal touches, this can't compare to classic breakout pictures, but some on-location (Folsom) shooting helps. ▮

Revolt of Mamie Stover, The (1956) **C-92m.** **½ D: Raoul Walsh. Jane Russell, Richard Egan, Joan Leslie, Agnes Moorehead, Jorja Curtright, Jean Willes, Michael Pate. Gorgeous Jane, in glorious color, is Honolulu-based "saloon singer" in 1941. Weak plot; Jane sings "Keep Your Eyes on the Hands." CinemaScope.

Revolt of the Zombies (1936) **65m.** *½ D: Victor Halperin. Dorothy Stone, Dean Jagger, Roy D'Arcy, Robert Noland, George Cleveland. Boring horror film, set in WW1 Cambodia, with weak-willed Jagger discovering secret by which humans can be transformed into zombies. ▼▮

Reward, The (1965) **C-92m.** **½ D: Serge Bourguignon. Max von Sydow, Yvette Mimieux, Efrem Zimbalist, Jr., Gilbert Roland, Emilio Fernandez, Henry Silva, Rodolfo Acosta. Promising premise and good cast led astray in static Western: group of bounty hunters turn on each other, as greed for larger share of reward money goads them into conflict. CinemaScope.

Rhapsody (1954) **C-115m.** **½ D: Charles Vidor. Elizabeth Taylor, Vittorio Gassman, John Ericson, Louis Calhern, Michael Chekhov. Three-cornered romance among rich Taylor, violinist Gassman, and pianist Ericson: melodic interludes bolster soaper. Script by Fay and Michael Kanin. ▼▮

Rhapsody in Blue (1945) **139m.** *** D: Irving Rapper. Robert Alda, Joan Leslie, Alexis Smith, Oscar Levant, Charles Coburn, Julie Bishop, Albert Basserman, Morris Carnovsky, Herbert Rudley, Rosemary DeCamp, Paul Whiteman, Hazel Scott. Hollywood biography of George Gershwin is largely pulp fiction, but comes off better than most other composer biopics, capturing Gershwin's enthusiasm for his work, and some of his inner conflicts. Highlight is virtually complete performance of title work. ▼▮

Rhino! (1964) **C-91m.** **½ D: Ivan Tors. Robert Culp, Harry Guardino, Shirley Eaton, Harry Mekela. Diverting African game-hunting nonsense, with an enthusiastic cast, good action scenes.

Rhodes (1936-British) **91m.** ** D: Berthold Viertel. Walter Huston, Oscar Homolka, Basil Sydney, Frank Cellier, Peggy Ashcroft, Renne De Vaux, Bernard Lee, Ndanisa Kumalo. Biography of Cecil Rhodes (Huston), who founded Rhodesia and opened up the Transvaal to British exploitation. Huston's performance is big, romantic, and hammy, but the movie is a justification for Rhodes' rape of Africa and the Boer War. Homolka's dour, crafty Kruger is more interesting than Huston's Rhodes. Aka RHODES OF AFRICA ▼

Rhubarb (1951) **95m.** *** D: Arthur Lubin. Ray Milland, Jan Sterling, Gene Lockhart, William Frawley, Elsie Holmes, Taylor Holmes, Leonard Nimoy. Eccentric Lockhart owns the Brooklyn Loons baseball team; he dies and leaves the club to his spunky pet cat. Spirited comedy, based on a famous story by H. Allen Smith. ▮

Rhythm of the Saddle (1938) **58m.** *** D: George Sherman. Gene Autry, Smiley Burnette, Pert Kelton, Peggy Moran, LeRoy Mason, Arthur Loft, Ethan Laidlaw, Eddie Acuff. Foreman Autry helps Moran, who's in danger of losing her rodeo contract to crooked nightclub owner Mason. Strong plotline, well directed, with burning barns and a terrific stagecoach race.

Rhythm on the Range (1936) **85m.** **½ D: Norman Taurog. Bing Crosby, Frances Farmer, Bob Burns, Martha Raye, Lucille Gleason, Samuel S. Hinds, Louis Prima, Leonid Kinskey. Spoiled N.Y.C. society girl runs away on the eve of her wedding and heads West, tangling with ranch hand Crosby along the way. Engaging, featherweight musical comedy includes Bing's beautiful rendition of "I Can't Escape From You." Extended performance of Johnny Mercer's "I'm an Old Cowhand (from the Rio Grande)" features an unbilled Louis Prima and the Sons of the Pioneers (including Roy Rogers). Remade as PARDNERS. ▼▮

Rhythm on the River (1940) 92m. *** D: Victor Schertzinger. Bing Crosby, Mary Martin, Basil Rathbone, Oscar Levant, Oscar Shaw, Charley Grapewin, William Frawley, Lillian Cornell, Wingy Manone. Breezy musical has Crosby ghostwriting music for Rathbone and meeting up with Martin, never dreaming that *she's* been hired to ghostwrite the lyrics. First-rate songs by Johnny Burke and James Monaco; director Schertzinger contributed "I Don't Want to Cry Any More." Billy Wilder cowrote the story. ▼●▶

Rhythm Romance SEE: **Some Like It Hot** (1939)

Rich and Strange (1932-British) 83m. **½ D: Alfred Hitchcock. Henry Kendall, Joan Barry, Betty Amann, Percy Marmont, Elsie Randolph. Kendall and Barry, married and bored, are given money and travel around the world; he has affair with a "princess," while she becomes romantically attached to an explorer. Fragmented, offbeat drama (until the finale). ▼●▶

Richard III (1912) 53m. *** D: James Keane. Frederick Warde, Robert Gemp, Albert Gardner, James Keane, George Moss, Howard Stuart, Virginia Rankin. Aging stage actor Warde is cast as Shakespeare's Richard, Duke of Gloster (*sic*), who hankers to become King of England in the 15th century. The oldest surviving feature film made in the U.S., it earned reams of publicity when it was unearthed in 1996; it was quite impressive in 1912, and is a real curio today. Must-viewing for film, theater, and Shakespeare buffs. The VHS and DVD include an extra six minutes of credits and a musical prologue composed by Ennio Morricone. ▼▶

Richard III (1955-British) C-155m. ***½ D: Laurence Olivier. Laurence Olivier, John Gielgud, Ralph Richardson, Claire Bloom, Alec Clunes, Cedric Hardwicke, Stanley Baker, Pamela Brown, Michael Gough. Elaborate if stagy version of Shakespeare's chronicle of ambitious 15th-century British king and his court intrigues. Some prints run 139m. VistaVision. ▼●▶

Rich Are Always With Us, The (1932) 73m. ** D: Alfred E. Green. Ruth Chatterton, Adrienne Dore, George Brent, Bette Davis, John Miljan, Robert Warwick, Berton Churchill. Wealthy woman (Chatterton) cannot fall out of love with irresponsible husband (Miljan), even after bitter divorce and new romance with Brent. Silly script. ▶

Richest Girl in the World, The (1934) 76m. *** D: William A. Seiter. Miriam Hopkins, Joel McCrea, Fay Wray, Reginald Denny, Henry Stephenson. Entertaining romantic comedy by Norman Krasna about millionairess wanting to make sure her next boyfriend loves her for herself, not for her money. Remade as BRIDE BY MISTAKE.

Rich, Young and Pretty (1951) C-95m. **½ D: Norman Taurog. Jane Powell,

Danielle Darrieux, Wendell Corey, Vic Damone, Fernando Lamas, Marcel Dalio, Una Merkel, Richard Anderson. Frivolous MGM musical with Powell in Paris, sightseeing and romancing, meeting mother Darrieux. Cowritten by Sidney Sheldon. ▼●▶

Ricochet Romance (1954) 80m. **½ D: Charles Lamont. Marjorie Main, Chill Wills, Pedro Gonzalez-Gonzalez, Rudy Vallee, Ruth Hampton. Another Main frolic, with the rambunctious gal hired as ranch cook but putting her two cents' worth into everything.

Ride a Crooked Mile (1938) 77m. **½ D: Alfred E. Green. Akim Tamiroff, Leif Erickson, Frances Farmer, Lynne Overman, John Miljan, J. M. Kerrigan. Tamiroff gives a bravura performance as a two-fisted Cossack who heads a gang of cattle thieves in contemporary America. After being reunited with his estranged son (Erickson), he is sent to jail and Erickson plots to free him. Odd but engrossing mix of crime drama and father-son angst; notable as the only screen pairing of Farmer (mostly wasted as a Russian singer) and her then-husband Erickson.

Ride a Crooked Trail (1958) C-87m. **½ D: Jesse Hibbs. Audie Murphy, Gia Scala, Walter Matthau, Henry Silva, Joanna Moore. Murphy plays a thief mistaken for a lawman in this otherwise average Borden Chase–scripted Western. Worth watching for Matthau's zesty performance as a bombastic, alcoholic judge. CinemaScope. ▶

Ride a Violent Mile (1957) 80m. *½ D: Charles Marquis Warren. John Agar, Penny Edwards, John Pickard, Sheb Wooley, Eva Novak. Trivial Western set in Civil War times about Southern blockade runners. Regalscope.

Ride Back, The (1957) 79m. *** D: Allen H. Miner. Anthony Quinn, Lita Milan, William Conrad, Ellen Hope Monroe, Louis Towers. Well-handled account of sheriff and prisoner who find they need each other's help to survive elements and Indian attacks. Title song sung by Eddie Albert. ▼▶

Ride Clear of Diablo (1954) C-80m. **½ D: Jesse Hibbs. Audie Murphy, Dan Duryea, Susan Cabot, Abbe Lane, Russell Johnson, Jack Elam, Denver Pyle. Cheerful gunslinger Duryea takes a liking to Murphy, a newly minted deputy seeking the cattle rustlers who killed his family. Unassuming, intelligent Western is a good showcase for its likable stars. ▼▶

Ride 'Em Cowboy (1942) 86m. **½ D: Arthur Lubin. Bud Abbott, Lou Costello, Dick Foran, Anne Gwynne, Johnny Mack Brown, Ella Fitzgerald, Douglass Dumbrille. Good combination of Western, comedy, and musical in A&C vehicle, with Ella and the Merry Macs singing tunes including "A Tisket A Tasket," Foran crooning "I'll Remember April." ▼●▶

Ride Him, Cowboy (1932) 55m. *½ D:

Fred Allen. John Wayne, Ruth Hall, Henry B. Walthall, Otis Harlan, Harry Gribbon, Frank Hagney. Duke, the wild palomino "miracle horse," is accused of murdering a rancher, so Wayne intercedes. The first of Wayne's Warner Bros. series is awkward at best; Hall is attractive but not much of an actress. Remake of a Ken Maynard silent (which is also source of much stock footage). Director is not the same-named radio star. ▼▶

Ride in the Whirlwind (1965) **C-83m.** **½ D: Monte Hellman. Cameron Mitchell, Jack Nicholson, Tom Filer, Millie Perkins, Katherine Squire, Rupert Crosse, Harry Dean Stanton. Nicholson coproduced and wrote the screenplay for this offbeat Western about three cowboys who find themselves wrongly pursued as outlaws. Neither as arty nor as intriguing as THE SHOOTING, which was filmed simultaneously. ▼▶●

Ride Lonesome (1959) **C-73m.** *** D: Budd Boetticher. Randolph Scott, Karen Steele, Pernell Roberts, James Best, Lee Van Cleef, James Coburn. Typically interesting Boetticher chamber-Western (with a Burt Kennedy script) about a tight-lipped bounty hunter who acquires unwanted companions while bringing in a wanted criminal. Unusually good supporting cast, including Coburn in his film debut. CinemaScope.▶

Ride Out for Revenge (1957) **79m.** *½ D: Bernard Girard. Rory Calhoun, Gloria Grahame, Lloyd Bridges, Vince Edwards. Tiresome account of gold-hungry men trying to dispossess Indians from their lands.▶

Ride, Ranger, Ride (1936) **63m.** ** D: Joseph Kane. Gene Autry, Smiley Burnette, Kay Hughes, Monte Blue, George J. Lewis, Robert Homans, Chief Thundercloud, Max Terhune, The Tennessee Ramblers. Ex-cavalryman Autry joins Lewis in the Texas Rangers and tries to prevent trouble with Indians, unaware that Army interpreter Blue is actually stirring things up. OK Autry vehicle actually set in the Old West for a change, but treatment of Indians is one-dimensional—and brutal. Gene sings the title tune and "Yellow Rose of Texas." ▼▶

Riders in the Sky (1949) **69m.** *** D: John English. Gene Autry, Gloria Henry, Pat Buttram, Mary Beth Hughes, Robert Livingston, Steve Darrell, Alan Hale, Jr., Tom London. Gene helps a friend (Darrell) who's being framed on a murder charge by crooked gambler Livingston. Memorable, atmospheric story inspired by the hit song offers a more mature Autry, whom some fans preferred and others did not.▶

Riders of Destiny (1933) **58m.** **½ D: Robert N. Bradbury. John Wayne, Cecilia Parker, Forrest Taylor, George Hayes, Al St. John, Heinie Conklin, Yakima Canutt. Wayne is an undercover investigator sent by the government to aid ranchers trying to recover water rights; builds up to suspenseful,

classic fast-draw showdown. First and best of Wayne's Lone Star Westerns for Monogram casts him as Singin' Sandy, with crooning supplied by director's son Bill Bradbury, twin brother of cowboy star Bob Steele. Dialogue, songs, situations sometimes trite and unintentionally hilarious, but sincere performances by likable cast (especially Parker) trump most criticism. ▼▶

Riders of the Deadline (1943) **72m.** ** D: Lesley Selander. William Boyd, Andy Clyde, Jimmy Rogers, Frances Woodward, William Halligan, Bob (Robert) Mitchum. When Texas Ranger on Mexican border is killed, Hopalong Cassidy poses as a Ranger in disrepute to become a confederate of the smugglers and exact justice. Action climax, filmed in Lone Pine, nearly makes up for other deficiencies. Mitchum was one of the few actors who could hold his own in scenes with Boyd. Reworking of Don "Red" Barry vehicle DESERT BANDIT (1941). ▼▶

Riders of the Purple Sage (1925) **56m.** *** D: Lynn Reynolds. Tom Mix, Beatrice Burnham, Arthur Morrison, Warner Oland, Fred Kohler, Harold Goodwin, Marian Nixon. Engrossing Zane Grey story filmed on beautiful locations, with Mix a Texas Ranger seeking scoundrel (Oland) who abducted his sister (Burnham). Fascinating twists in this tale, first filmed in 1918, again in 1931, 1941, and 1996 (for cable TV). Mix also filmed sequel, THE RAINBOW TRAIL, as done in 1918 and 1932.▼▶

Riders of the Timberline (1941) **59m.** **½ D: Lesley Selander. William Boyd, Andy Clyde, Brad King, Victor Jory, Eleanor Stewart, J. Farrell MacDonald, Tom Tyler. Hopalong Cassidy rides to the aid of old friend MacDonald, who's besieged by crooks while trying to run a logging camp. Fine action routines and splendid camerawork in big timber regions near Cedar Lake offset gratuitous musical interludes by Guardsmen Quartet and King, who looks good but adds zero as sidekick. Tyler, the heavy here, was concurrently part of the heroic *Three Mesquiteers* series.▼▶

Riders of the Whistling Pines (1949) **70m.** *** D: John English. Gene Autry, Patricia White (Barry), Jimmy Lloyd, Douglass Dumbrille, Damian O'Flynn, Clayton Moore, Leon Weaver, Jason Robards (Sr.), The Cass County Boys, The Pinafores. Gene helps the Forestry Service once he discovers that logging company owner Dumbrille is trying to dupe the government by hiding the existence of deadly moths in his trees. One of Gene's best even has an environmental message—though it involves the use of DDT. Fun to see future Lone Ranger Moore as a bad guy; Lloyd's wife (seen in a photograph) is a young Marilyn Monroe!▼▶

Riders of Vengeance SEE: **Raiders, The** (1952)

Riders to the Stars (1954) **C-81m.** **½ D:

Richard Carlson. William Lundigan, Herbert Marshall, Richard Carlson, Dawn Addams, Martha Hyer. Three men are trained to fly rockets to the borders of space to snare meteors, in order to find what keeps them from being turned to powder by cosmic rays. Uncharacteristically inaccurate science fiction from producer Ivan Tors; OK but tame.

Ride, Tenderfoot, Ride (1940) **66m.** ** D: Frank McDonald. Gene Autry, Smiley Burnette, June Storey, Mary Lee, Warren Hull, Forbes Murray, Joe Frisco. Gene runs a meatpacking company, which pits him against rival Storey; Hull is her shifty boyfriend. Very much played for laughs out West. Good songs, including the title tune.◗

Ride the High Country (1962) **C-94m.** **** D: Sam Peckinpah. Randolph Scott, Joel McCrea, Mariette Hartley, Ron Starr, Edgar Buchanan, R. G. Armstrong, Warren Oates, John Anderson, L. Q. Jones, James Drury. Literate, magnificent Western about two aged gunfighter pals who reflect on the paths their lives have taken while guarding gold shipment. Considered by some to be Peckinpah's finest film; breathtaking widescreen photography (by Lucien Ballard) and scenery, and flawless performances, with Buchanan notable as a drunken judge. Written by N. B. Stone, Jr. Hartley's first film, Scott's last. CinemaScope.▼◗◗

Ride the High Iron (1956) **74m.** *½ D: Don Weis. Don Taylor, Sally Forrest, Raymond Burr, Lisa Golm, Nestor Paiva, Mae Clarke. Korean veteran Taylor works for slick P.R. man Burr who makes his living keeping people's indiscretions out of the paper. Taylor tries to latch on to rich girl whose family Burr works for. Originally made for TV but shown theatrically.

Ride the Man Down (1952) **C-90m.** ** D: Joseph Kane. Brian Donlevy, Rod Cameron, Ella Raines, Barbara Britton, Chill Wills, Jack LaRue, J. Carrol Naish, Jim Davis. Lumbering account of ranchland feuding in old West.▼

Ride the Pink Horse (1947) **101m.** ***½ D: Robert Montgomery. Robert Montgomery, Wanda Hendrix, Thomas Gomez, Andrea King, Fred Clark, Art Smith, Rita Conde, Grandon Rhodes. Strong film noir of Montgomery coming to small New Mexican town during fiesta to blackmail gangster Clark, but romantic Hendrix and FBI agent Smith keep getting in his way. Taut script by Ben Hecht and Charles Lederer (from the Dorothy B. Hughes novel); super performance by Gomez as friendly carny. Remade for TV as THE HANGED MAN (1964).◗

Ride the Wild Surf (1964) **C-101m.** **½ D: Don Taylor. Fabian, Tab Hunter, Barbara Eden, Anthony Hayes, James Mitchum, Shelley Fabares. Formula beach boys tale, set in Hawaii; Jan and Dean sing the title song. It's not Shakespeare, but it *is* a cut above the usual BEACH PARTY shenanigans, and the surfing footage is great.▼◗

Ride, Vaquero! (1953) **C-90m.** **½ D: John Farrow. Robert Taylor, Ava Gardner, Howard Keel, Anthony Quinn, Kurt Kasznar, Ted de Corsia, Jack Elam. At the end of the Civil War, Mexican bandit Quinn tries to force new settlers Keel and Gardner off the land, but they don't scare easily. Then Quinn's adopted brother (Taylor) goes to work on their ranch. Star power helps an intriguing if not altogether satisfying script. Shot in Kanab, Utah, though it takes place in Texas!◗

Ridin' Down the Canyon (1942) **55m.** *** D: Joseph Kane. Roy Rogers, George "Gabby" Hayes, Buzzy Henry, Linda Hayes, Addison Richards, Lorna Gray (Adrian Booth), James Seay, Sons of the Pioneers. Hayes and kid brother Henry capture and sell wild horses to the government, but they are plagued by rustlers who take their orders over the radio from dude-ranch owners Richards and Gray. There's a lot to like in this fast-paced Rogers outing.▼◗

Riding High (1943) **C-89m.** *½ D: George Marshall. Dorothy Lamour, Dick Powell, Victor Moore, Gil Lamb, Cass Daley, Milt Britton and Band, Rod Cameron. Unmemorable songs, flat script, fair performances add up to dubious entertainment; Powell is obsessed with silver mine, while wooing Lamour.

Riding High (1950) **112m.** **½ D: Frank Capra. Bing Crosby, Coleen Gray, Charles Bickford, Margaret Hamilton, Frances Gifford, James Gleason, Raymond Walburn, William Demarest, Ward Bond, Clarence Muse, Percy Kilbride, Gene Lockhart, Douglass Dumbrille, Harry Davenport, Charles Lane, Frankie Darro. Musical remake of BROADWAY BILL follows it so closely that stock footage with some of the actors in their original parts is included from 1934 film. Crosby is racehorse owner whose nag has yet to come through. OK songs, Capra touch make this pleasing if unmemorable entertainment. Oliver Hardy is fun in rare solo appearance. Joe Frisco appears as himself.▼◗

Riding on Air (1937) **71m.** ** D: Edward Sedgwick. Joe E. Brown, Guy Kibbee, Florence Rice, Vinton Haworth, Anthony Nace, Harlan Briggs. Average Brown vehicle has him mixed up with smugglers and a wacky invention of a radio beam to control airplanes.▼◗

Riding Shotgun (1954) **C-74m.** **½ D: Andre de Toth. Randolph Scott, Wayne Morris, Joan Weldon, Joe Sawyer, James Millican, Charles Buchinsky (Bronson), James Bell, Fritz Feld, Howard Morris. Interesting HIGH NOON–like Western with Scott determined to nab outlaw Millican despite every effort by the citizenry of a Western town to get in his way. Wayne Morris is a striking presence as a silent rope-carrying townsman who is all too eager to partake in a lynching. ▶

Ridin' on a Rainbow (1941) 75m. *** D: Lew Landers. Gene Autry, Smiley Burncttc, Mary Lee, Carol Adams, Ferris Taylor, Georgia Caine, Byron Foulger, Ralf Harolde, Anthony Warde. Pert young Lee and her washed-up hoofer pop (Foulger) get mixed up with bank robbers; it's up to Gene and Frog to recover the money, since Gene convinced all the ranchers it was safe to put their cattle earnings in the bank. Pure entertainment; much of the action (and seven songs) takes place on a showboat. Songs include Lee's "I'm the Only One" and Autry's Oscar-nominated "Be Honest With Me." ▼▶

Riffraff (1935) 89m. **½ D: J. Walter Ruben. Jean Harlow, Spencer Tracy, Una Merkel, Joseph Calleia, Victor Kilian, Mickey Rooney. Comedy-drama doesn't always work, but worth viewing for stars playing married couple in fishing business who end up on wrong side of law. ▼▶

Riffraff (1947) 80m. *** D: Ted Tetzlaff. Pat O'Brien, Anne Jeffreys, Walter Slezak, Percy Kilbride, Jerome Cowan, George Givot, Jason Robards (Sr.). Fast-paced story of O'Brien foiling villains' attempts to take over oilfield in Panama. ▼◉▶

Rififi (1955-French) 115m. **** D: Jules Dassin. Jean Servais, Carl Mohner, Magali Noel, Robert Manuel, Perlo Vita (Jules Dassin). The granddaddy of all caper/heist movies, centering on quartet of French jewel thieves who find each other more dangerous than the cops. The burglary sequence itself is famous for being in complete silence. Scripted by director Dassin, Rene Wheeler, and Auguste Le Breton, from Le Breton's novel. On-screen title is RIFIFI CHEZ LES HOMMES. ▼▶

Right Approach, The (1961) 92m. **½ D: David Butler. Frankie Vaughan, Martha Hyer, Juliet Prowse, Gary Crosby, Jane Withers. Plucky minor film of Vaughan, a good-for-nothing who uses anything to get ahead. Adapted by Fay and Michael Kanin from a play by his brother Garson. CinemaScope. ▶

Right Cross (1950) 90m. **½ D: John Sturges. June Allyson, Dick Powell, Lionel Barrymore, Ricardo Montalban. Fairly compact account of boxing world, with sportswriter Powell and fighter Montalban in love with Allyson. One of Marilyn Monroe's early films.

Right of Way, The (1931) 65m. BOMB D: Frank Lloyd. Conrad Nagel, Loretta Young, Fred Kohler, William Janney, Snitz Edwards, George Pearce, Halliwell Hobbes. Married Canadian lawyer (Nagel) gets conked on the noggin, loses his memory, and falls for a beautiful girl (Young) in a lumber camp before remembering his true identity. Antediluvian soap opera is so stagy, stiffly acted, and loaded with risible

dialogue that it seems like a *parody* of a creaky early talkie. Based on a novel by Sir Gilbert Parker that was previously filmed in 1915 and 1920. ▶

Right to Live, The (1935) 69m. **½ D: William Keighley. Josephine Hutchinson, George Brent, Colin Clive, Peggy Wood, Henrietta Crosman, C. Aubrey Smith, Leo G. Carroll. After Clive is paralyzed in a plane accident, wife Hutchinson falls in love with his brother Brent and is accused of murder when Clive suddenly dies. Somber, well-acted adaptation of Somerset Maugham's play about euthanasia, *The Sacred Flame*, though the story is weakened by changing the original ending. ▶

Right to Romance, The (1933) 67m. ** D: Alfred Santell. Ann Harding, Robert Young, Nils Asther, Sari Maritza, Irving Pichel, Helen Freeman, Alden (Stephen) Chase, Delmar Watson. Overworked plastic surgeon Harding caters to the privileged class and desperately needs to enliven her life. Will she do so with wealthy devil-may-care pilot Young? Slow-moving soaper.

Riley the Cop (1928) 66m. **½ D: John Ford. J. Farrell MacDonald, Louise Fazenda, Nancy Drexel, David Rollins, Harry Schultz, Mildred Boyd, Ferdinand Schumann-Heink, Dell Henderson, Billy Bevan, Tom Wilson, Otto Fries. Irish N.Y.C. flatfoot who hasn't arrested anybody in 20 years is sent to Germany to retrieve a fugitive, but he spends most of his time romancing a fraulein in a Munich beer garden who turns out to be the sister of his nemesis! Boisterous blarney is minor Ford but offers an amusing showcase for character actor MacDonald. Silent with synchronized music and sound effects.

Rimfire (1949) 64m. **½ D: B. Reeves Eason. James Millican, Mary Beth Hughes, Reed Hadley, Henry Hull, Victor Kilian, "Fuzzy" Knight, Chris Pin Martin, George Cleveland, Margia Dean. Undercover U.S. Army officer Millican becomes new deputy in New Mexico town where a mysterious "ghost killer" is wreaking havoc. Slight but entertaining low-budget oater. ▶

Rim of the Canyon (1949) 70m. *** D: John English. Gene Autry, Nan Leslie, Thurston Hall, Clem Bevans, Walter Sande, Jock O'Mahoney (Mahoney), Francis McDonald, Alan Hale, Jr. Gene, playing his own father in early scenes, tracks down some outlaws, but not before they hide their loot. Twenty years later, Gene the son encounters the same outlaws, now out of jail, intent on recovering the stolen money in a ghost town. Different, more action-oriented Western for Autry with fewer songs. ▼▶

Ring, The (1927-British) 73m. *** D: Alfred Hitchcock. Carl Brisson, Lillian Hall-Davies, Ian Hunter, Harry Terry, Gordon Harker, Billy Wells, Tom Helmore. Boxers Brisson and Hunter battle over their love for the same woman. Standard scenario is uplifted by Hitchcock's keen eye for detail and imaginative use of visuals to communicate feelings and points of view. Written by Hitchcock and Alma Reville. ▼❱

Ring, The (1952) 79m. *** D: Kurt Neumann. Gerald Mohr, Rita Moreno, Lalo Rios, Robert Arthur, Art Aragon, Jack Elam. Neat little boxing yarn with a conscience: under the tutelage of fight manager Mohr, poor Chicano Rios tries his hand in the ring. Film offers a refreshingly nonstereotypical portrait of Mexican-Americans, plus a perceptive view of the fight racket. Scripted by Irving Shulman, based on his novel. ▼❱

Ring-a-Ding Rhythm! (1962-British) 78m. ** D: Richard Lester. Helen Shapiro, Craig Douglas, Felix Felton, Arthur Mullard, John Leyton, Chubby Checker, Del Shannon, Gary "U.S." Bonds, Gene Vincent, Gene McDaniels, Acker Bilk, The Temperance Seven. Shapiro and Douglas—whose characters are called Helen and Craig—organize a rock 'n' roll and Dixieland jazz show. Of interest only for the appearances of Bonds, Vincent, and company—although there's not one memorable song performed. Lester's first feature. British title: IT'S TRAD, DAD! ❱

Ringer, The (1952-British) 78m. *** D: Guy Hamilton. Herbert Lom, Mai Zetterling, Donald Wolfit, Greta Gynt, William Hartnell, Norman Wooland. Entertaining mystery from Edgar Wallace novel and play: The Ringer, an arch criminal, gets on the case of an unscrupulous lawyer involved in his sister's death. Filmed previously in 1931, and in 1938 as THE GAUNT STRANGER.

Ring of Fear (1954) C-93m. ** D: James Edward Grant. Clyde Beatty, Pat O'Brien, Mickey Spillane, Sean McClory, Marian Carr, John Bromfield. Offbeat murder yarn set at the Clyde Beatty circus; interesting for acting appearance by Spillane. Beatty plays himself. CinemaScope. ❱

Ring of Fire (1961) C-91m. **½ D: Andrew L. Stone. David Janssen, Joyce Taylor, Frank Gorshin, Joel Marston, Doodles Weaver. Assistant sheriff is held hostage by trio of young hoods. Highlight of film is climactic holocaust, including footage of a real Oregon forest fire.

Ringside Maisie (1941) 96m. ** D: Edwin L. Marin. Ann Sothern, George Murphy, Robert Sterling, Virginia O'Brien, Natalie Thompson, Maisie causes romantic complications at a boxer's training camp in this sticky and overlong entry. "Slapsy Maxie" Rosenbloom is fun as a punch-drunk pug. Costars Sothern and Sterling married two years later. ❱

Rings on Her Fingers (1942) 85m. **½ D: Rouben Mamoulian. Henry Fonda, Gene Tierney, Laird Cregar, Spring Byington, Marjorie Gateson, Iris Adrian, Clara Blandick, Mary Treen. Con artist Tierney falls for Fonda instead of fleecing him; standard romance with good cast hoping to repeat success of Fonda's THE LADY EVE. ❱

Rio (1939) 75m. ** D: John Brahm. Basil Rathbone, Victor McLaglen, Sigrid Gurie, Robert Cummings, Leo Carrillo, Billy Gilbert. Rathbone, serving ten-year prison term, suspects his wife (Gurie) is being unfaithful. His performance is sole virtue of this slick potboiler.

Rio Bravo (1959) C-141m. ***½ D: Howard Hawks. John Wayne, Dean Martin, Ricky Nelson, Angie Dickinson, Walter Brennan, Ward Bond, John Russell, Claude Akins, Bob Steele. Sheriff Wayne tries to prevent a killer with connections from escaping from the town jail, with only a drunken Dino, leggy Angie, gimpy Brennan, and lockjawed Ricky to help him. Quintessential Hawks Western, patronized by reviewers at the time of its release, is now regarded as an American classic; overlong, but great fun. Written by Leigh Brackett and Jules Furthman. Followed by EL DORADO; sort of remade as ASSAULT ON PRECINCT 13. ▼❍❱

Rio Conchos (1964) C-107m. *** D: Gordon Douglas. Richard Boone, Stuart Whitman, Tony Franciosa, Edmond O'Brien, Jim Brown. Post–Civil War Texas is the setting for this action-filled Western centering around a shipment of stolen rifles, and Boone taking on Franciosa. Brown is notable in his film debut, and there's a zesty performance by O'Brien. CinemaScope. ▼❱

Rio Grande (1950) 105m. *** D: John Ford. John Wayne, Maureen O'Hara, Ben Johnson, Harry Carey, Jr., Victor McLaglen, Claude Jarman, Jr., Chill Wills, J. Carrol Naish, Grant Withers, Pat Wayne. The last of director Ford's cavalry trilogy (following FORT APACHE and SHE WORE A YELLOW RIBBON), and the most underrated: a vivid look at the gentlemanly spirit of the cavalry during post–Civil War days . . . and the difficult relationship between an estranged father (commander Wayne) and his son (new recruit Jarman). Beautifully shot by Bert Glennon and Archie Stout, with lovely theme by Victor Young, songs by Sons of the Pioneers (including Ken Curtis). Also shown in computer-colored version. ▼❍❱

Rio Rita (1929) C/B&W-103m. **½ D: Luther Reed. Bebe Daniels, John Boles, Don Alvarado, Dorothy Lee, Bert Wheeler, Robert Woolsey, Georges Renavent. Historically fascinating, but cinematically archaic, version of the Ziegfeld-produced Broadway musical smash, about the bandit called "Kinkajou" being pursued in a Mexican border town by merry band of singing Texas Rangers. A straightforward recording of the stage show, the film creaks along, though some of the production numbers are quite lavish for their time, with the last 30m. in early two-strip Technicolor. Film debuts of Wheeler and Woolsey, who played their roles in the Broadway show. Original running time 135m. Loosely remade with Abbott and Costello in 1942. ◗

Rio Rita (1942) **91m.** **½** D: S. Sylvan Simon. Bud Abbott, Lou Costello, Kathryn Grayson, John Carroll, Tom Conway, Barry Nelson. Vintage Broadway musical brought up to date, with Nazis invading Western ranch where Bud and Lou work; some good music helps this one. Previously filmed in 1929 with Wheeler and Woolsey. ▼◗●

Riot in Cell Block 11 (1954) **80m.** **** D: Don Siegel. Neville Brand, Emile Meyer, Frank Faylen, Leo Gordon, Robert Osterloh. Realistic, powerful prison drama still packs a punch. Among the contemporary themes in this 1954 film is "media manipulation," with prisoners trying to use press for leverage. Actually shot at Folsom State Prison. ▼◗

Riot in Juvenile Prison (1959) **71m.** BOMB D: Edward L. Cahn. Jerome Thor, Marcia Henderson, Scott Marlowe, John Hoyt, Dick Tyler, Dorothy Provine, Ann Doran. Programmer fully explained by title. ◗

Riptide (1934) **90m.** **** D: Edmund Goulding. Norma Shearer, Robert Montgomery, Herbert Marshall, Mrs. Patrick Campbell, Skeets Gallagher, Ralph Forbes, Lilyan Tashman, Helen Jerome Eddy. Silly but entertaining story of vivacious Shearer marrying stodgy British Lord (Marshall), then becoming involved in scandal with Montgomery. Don't miss opening scene where stars are dressed as giant insects for costume party! That's Walter Brennan as a chauffeur; Bruce Bennett is an extra at the bar at Cannes. ▼◗

Rise and Fall of Legs Diamond, The (1960) **101m.** **** D: Budd Boetticher. Ray Danton, Karen Steele, Elaine Stewart, Jesse White, Simon Oakland, Robert Lowery, Warren Oates. Snappy chronicle of Depression-days gangster, well balanced between action gun battles and Danton's romancing flashy dolls (like young Dyan—billed Diane—Cannon). Outstanding photography by Lucien Ballard. ▼◗

Rise and Shine (1941) **93m.** **½** D: Allan Dwan. Jack Oakie, Linda Darnell, George Murphy, Walter Brennan, Sheldon Leonard, Donald Meek, Ruth Donnelly, Milton Berle, Donald MacBride, Raymond Walburn. Oakie has field day as dumb football player abducted by crooks so team won't win big game. Often unconsciously funny. Adapted by Herman J. Mankiewicz from James Thurber's *My Life and Hard Times*.

Rise of Catherine the Great, The SEE: **Catherine the Great**

Rising of the Moon, The (1957-U.S.-Irish) **81m.** **½** D: John Ford. Maureen Connell, Eileen Crowe, Cyril Cusack, Donal Donnelly, Frank Lawton, Jack MacGowran,

Denis O'Dea, Jimmy O'Dea, Maureen Potter, Noel Purcell, Tony Quinn. Spirited anthology oozes Ford's trademark blarney and features three stories: "The Majesty of the Law" (about the relationship between a police inspector and the man he must arrest); "A Minute's Wait" (spotlighting passengers passing through a rural train station); and "1921" (the best of the lot, centering on an Irish nationalist who is about to be executed). Each tale is introduced by Tyrone Power and features actors from Dublin's Abbey Theatre. ◗

Risk, The (1960-British) **81m.** *** D: Roy and John Boulting. Tony Britton, Peter Cushing, Ian Bannen, Virginia Maskell, Donald Pleasence, Thorley Walters, Kenneth Griffith, Spike Milligan. Tense drama of spies chasing scientist who has secret formula to combat plague. Good direction, cast. Original British title: SUSPECT. ▼◗

River, The (1951-Indian) **C-99m.** **** D: Jean Renoir. Patricia Walters, Nora Swinburne, Arthur Shields, Radha, Adrienne Corri, Esmond Knight, narrated by June Hillman. Immensely moving, lyrical adaptation of Rumer Godden novel about English children growing up in Bengal. One of the great color films, a total triumph for cinematographer Claude and director Jean Renoir. Scripted by Godden and Renoir. ▼◗●

River Lady (1948) **C-78m.** ** D: George Sherman. Yvonne De Carlo, Dan Duryea, Rod Cameron, Helena Carter, Lloyd Gough, Florence Bates. Typical De Carlo vehicle about riverboat queen trying to buy her man when she can't win him with love; colorful and empty. ◗

River of No Return (1954) **C-91m.** **½** D: Otto Preminger. Robert Mitchum, Marilyn Monroe, Rory Calhoun, Tommy Rettig, Murvyn Vye, Douglas Spencer. Mitchum rescues Calhoun and Monroe from leaky raft; Calhoun returns the favor by stealing his horse and abandoning them (and Mitchum's young son) to hostile Indians. Dialogue leaves a lot to be desired, but it's worth watching Mitchum and Monroe at her most beautiful—not to mention some gorgeous locations (seen to best advantage in CinemaScope). ▼◗●

River's Edge, The (1957) **C-87m.** *** D: Allan Dwan. Ray Milland, Anthony Quinn, Debra Paget, Byron Foulger. Melodrama about heel (Milland), his ex-girlfriend (Paget), and her husband (Quinn) trying to cross Mexican border with suitcase of money. Ray has never been nastier. CinemaScope. ◗

River's End (1930) **74m.** **½** D: Michael Curtiz. Charles Bickford, Evalyn Knapp, J. Farrell MacDonald, ZaSu Pitts, Walter McGrail, David Torrence, Junior Coghlan, Tom Santschi. Bickford delivers a two-fisted performance in a dual role as a wanted man who takes the place of a lookalike Royal Canadian Mountie who cap-

[578]

tured him but then died in a blizzard. Good trick photography highlights this James Oliver Curwood story. Filmed before in 1920, remade in 1940 with Dennis Morgan.

Road Back, The (1937) 97m. ** D: James Whale. Richard Cromwell, John King, Slim Summerville, Andy Devine, Barbara Read, Louise Fazenda, Noah Beery, Jr., Lionel Atwill. The German soldiers from ALL QUIET ON THE WESTERN FRONT find postwar life at home full of frustrations. Heavy-handed sequel to the Erich Maria Remarque classic; interesting to watch but unsatisfying. Summerville repeats his role from the 1930 original.

Roadblock (1951) 73m. **½ D: Harold Daniels. Charles McGraw, Joan Dixon, Lowell Gilmore, Louis Jean Heydt, Milburn Stone. Insurance investigator's growing attachment to a money-hungry woman leads him to crime. Typical film noir formula, smoothly executed. ▶

Road Gang (1936) 61m. **½ D: Louis King. Donald Woods, Kay Linaker, Carlyle Moore, Jr., Joseph Crehan, Henry O'Neill, Addison Richards, Marc Lawrence. Woods is a Chicago reporter who causes trouble for racketeers and crooked politicos and winds up in a brutal Southern chain gang for his efforts. Derivative but effective and absorbing programmer, scripted by Dalton Trumbo. ▶

Road House (1948) 95m. *** D: Jean Negulesco. Ida Lupino, Cornel Wilde, Celeste Holm, Richard Widmark, O. Z. Whitehead, Robert Karnes. Psychotic roadhouse owner Widmark deludes himself into thinking he "owns" singer Lupino; when she falls for his childhood friend and employee (Wilde), sparks fly in this entertaining melodrama. Ida even gets to sing, introducing the standard "Again." ▼▶

Roadhouse Murder, The (1932) 72m. **½ D: J. Walter Ruben. Eric Linden, Dorothy Jordan, Bruce Cabot, Phyllis Clare, Roscoe Ates, Purnell Pratt, Gustav von Seyffertitz, David Landau, Roscoe Karns. Cub reporter tries to grab headlines by implicating himself in a homicide he stumbled upon so he can write exclusive stories about the case . . . then the evidence that would clear him is stolen. Implausible but absorbing little thriller foreshadows Fritz Lang's BEYOND A REASONABLE DOUBT.

Roadhouse Nights (1930) 71m. **½ D: Hobart Henley. Helen Morgan, Charles Ruggles, Fred Kohler, Jimmy Durante, Lou Clayton, Eddie Jackson, Fuller Mellish, Jr., Tammany Young, Joe King. Reporter Ruggles poses as a tippler to track down a gangster who is using a country inn as a base for his rum-running operation. Fascinating if crudely filmed early talkie is notable for Morgan's glorious singing, and for the presence of Durante (in his film debut) performing routines with his vaudeville partners Clayton and Jackson. Story by Ben Hecht.

Road Show (1941) 87m. **½ D: Hal Roach, Gordon Douglas, Hal Roach, Jr. Adolphe Menjou, Carole Landis, John Hubbard, Charles Butterworth, Patsy Kelly, George E. Stone. Offbeat comedy of young man, wrongfully committed to an insane asylum, escaping and joining up with traveling carnival; some bright moments in inconsequential film. Cowritten by Harry Langdon. ▼▶

Road to Bali (1952) C-90m. *** D: Hal Walker. Bob Hope, Dorothy Lamour, Bing Crosby, Murvyn Vye, Ralph Moody. Only color ROAD film has lush trappings, many guest stars and good laughs, as Bob and Bing save Dorothy from evil princess and jungle perils. Carolyn Jones has a bit. ▼▶

Road to Denver, The (1955) C-90m. **½ D: Joseph Kane. John Payne, Lee J. Cobb, Skip Homeier, Mona Freeman, Ray Middleton, Lee Van Cleef, Andy Clyde, Glenn Strange. In the wake of the Civil War, two brothers wind up in the same town on opposite sides of the law. Good cast in a competent but rather ordinary Western.

Road to Eternity, The (1959-Japanese) 183m. ***½ D: Masaki Kobayashi. Tatsuya Nakadai, Michiyo Aratama, Kokinji Katsura, Jun Tatara, Michio Minami, Ryohei Uchida, Kenjiro Uemura, Keiji Sada, Minoru Chiaki, Kei Sato. In this second in Kobayashi's three-part epic (following NO GREATER LOVE and succeeded by A SOLDIER'S PRAYER), military conscript Kaji (Nakadai) is seen in training and eventually in battle. While surrounded by hostility and violence, he strains to preserve his humanity. Highlights include Koji's poignant one-night reunion with his wife (Aratama) and an unforgettable final, extended battle sequence. Scripted by Kobayashi and Zenzo Matsuyama, based on a six-volume novel by Junpei Gomikawa. Aka THE HUMAN CONDITION II. Grandscope. ▶

Road to Glory, The (1936) 95m. *** D: Howard Hawks. Fredric March, Warner Baxter, Lionel Barrymore, June Lang, Gregory Ratoff, Victor Kilian. Solid production, direction, and acting make more of script (cowritten by William Faulkner) than is really there. Hardened officer Baxter finds his father (Barrymore) serving in his unit in WW1 France. Romantic subplot involves officer March and nurse Lang. Unrelated to same-titled film directed by Hawks in 1926. Remake of 1932 French film LES CROIX DE BOIS, using some of its battle footage. ▶

Road to Hong Kong, The (1962) 91m. **½ D: Norman Panama. Bob Hope, Bing Crosby, Joan Collins, Dorothy Lamour, Robert Morley, Walter Gotell, Peter Sellers. Final ROAD picture was the first in a decade, and while it's fun it lacks the carefree spirit of its predecessors; Bob and Bing are con men who become involved in international intrigue—and space travel! Sellers has a hilarious cameo; Lamour appears briefly as herself. Look fast for the Bob Crosby Band. Filmed in England. ▼●)

Road to Morocco (1942) **83m.** **★★★** D: David Butler. Bing Crosby, Dorothy Lamour, Bob Hope, Dona Drake, Anthony Quinn, Vladimir Sokoloff, Monte Blue, Yvonne De Carlo. Typically funny ROAD picture, with Bing selling Bob to slave-trader in mysterious Morocco, both going after princess Lamour. Bing sings "Moonlight Becomes You." ▼●)

Road to Paradise (1930) **74m.** **★★★** D: William Beaudine. Loretta Young, Jack Mulhall, Raymond Hatton, George Barraud, Kathlyn Williams, Fred Kelsey, Purnell Pratt. Young plays two roles in this clever, enjoyable concoction: Mary Brennan, a good-hearted straight-arrow orphan raised by two kindly but crooked gents; and Margaret Waring, her wealthy, educated double. Could they possibly be related? And what about Mary's special ability to read minds? ▶

Road to Rio (1947) **100m.** **★★★** D: Norman Z. McLeod. Bing Crosby, Bob Hope, Dorothy Lamour, Gale Sondergaard, Frank Faylen, The Wiere Brothers. Bob and Bing are musicians trying to wrest Dorothy from sinister aunt Sondergaard. Very funny outing in series. Songs: "But Beautiful," "You Don't Have to Know the Language," sung with guests The Andrews Sisters. ▼▶

Road to Singapore (1940) **84m.** **★★½** D: Victor Schertzinger. Bing Crosby, Dorothy Lamour, Bob Hope, Charles Coburn, Judith Barrett, Anthony Quinn, Jerry Colonna, Monte Blue, Arthur Q. Bryan. Bing and Bob swear off women, hiding out in Singapore; then they meet saronged Lamour. First ROAD film is not the best, but still fun. ▼●)

Road to Utopia (1945) **90m.** **★★★** D: Hal Walker. Bing Crosby, Bob Hope, Dorothy Lamour, Hillary Brooke, Douglass Dumbrille, Jack LaRue, Jim Thorpe. Bob and Bing in the Klondike with usual quota of gags, supplemented by talking animals, Dorothy's song "Personality," Robert Benchley's dry commentary. ▼●)

Road to Yesterday, The (1925) **110m.** **★★★** D: Cecil B. DeMille. Joseph Schildkraut, Jetta Goudal, Vera Reynolds, William Boyd, Julia Faye. Criss-crossed couples in romantic tangle are contrasted with 17th-century ancestors, who play out similar story against colorful period setting. DeMille at his best: lavish, hokey, always entertaining. ▼▶

Road to Zanzibar (1941) **92m.** **★★½** D: Victor Schertzinger. Bing Crosby, Bob Hope, Dorothy Lamour, Una Merkel, Eric Blore. Weaker ROAD series entry, still amusing, with Bob and Bing circus performers traveling through jungle with Lamour and Merkel, looking for diamond mine. ▼●)

Roaring City (1951) **58m.** **★★½** D: William

Berke. Hugh Beaumont, Edward Brophy, Richard Travis, Joan Valerie, Wanda McKay, Rebel Randall, William Tannen. Tough-talking Beaumont, whose "sideline is trouble," is hired to place bets on a fixed fight, and then is paid to impersonate the husband of a mystery woman. Entertaining low-budget noir, intended to be shown as two half-hour TV episodes. ▶

Roaring Timber SEE: **Come and Get It**

Roaring Twenties, The (1939) **104m.** **★★★** D: Raoul Walsh. James Cagney, Priscilla Lane, Humphrey Bogart, Gladys George, Jeffrey Lynn, Frank McHugh, Joe Sawyer. Army buddies Cagney, Bogart, and Lynn find their lives intertwining dramatically after WW1 ends. Cagney becomes big-time prohibition racketeer in largely hackneyed script punched across by fine cast, vivid direction. Also shown in computer-colored version. ▼●)

Roar of the Crowd (1953) **C-71m.** **★½** D: William Beaudine. Howard Duff, Helene Stanley, Louise Arthur, Harry Shannon, Minor Watson, Don Haggerty. Hackneyed auto-racing tale chronicling the trials of driver Duff and his quest to compete in the Indianapolis 500. Top auto racers of the period appear as themselves.

Roar of the Dragon (1932) **69m.** **★★★** D: Wesley Ruggles. Richard Dix, Gwili Andre, Edward Everett Horton, Arline Judge, ZaSu Pitts, C. Henry Gordon. In Manchuria, fearless riverboat captain Dix becomes a bandit chieftain's #1 pain in the neck (and pain in the ear—Dix bites it off), so the bandit's forces lay siege to the hotel where Dix and many innocents are trapped. Pre-Code carnage overstuffs this 69-minute bag, from hot lead, flying knives, and an immolation to a mad-as-hell Horton on the business end of a machine gun!

Robbers' Roost (1955) **C-82m.** **★½** D: Sidney Salkow. George Montgomery, Richard Boone, Sylvia Findley, Bruce Bennett, Peter Graves, Tony Romano, Warren Stevens, William Hopper, Stanley Clements, Leo Gordon. Ranch owner Bennett hires two rival rustlers to protect his herd. Weak remake of Zane Grey Western filmed before in 1933, made worse by Romano's songs. ▶

Robbery Under Arms (1957-British) **C-83m.** **★★** D: Jack Lee. Peter Finch, Ronald Lewis, Laurence Naismith, Maureen Swanson, David McCallum. Quiet account of romance and robbery set in 19th-century Australia. ▼▶

Robe, The (1953) **C-135m.** **★★½** D: Henry Koster. Richard Burton, Jean Simmons, Victor Mature, Michael Rennie, Richard Boone, Jay Robinson, Dawn Addams, Dean Jagger, Jeff Morrow, Ernest Thesiger. Earnest but episodic costume drama from Lloyd C. Douglas novel about Roman centurion who presides over Christ's crucifixion. Burton's Oscar-nominated performance seems stiff and superficial today, while Mature (as his slave Demetrius) comes off quite well! Famed as first movie in CinemaScope, though it was simultaneously shot "flat." Sequel: DEMETRIUS AND THE GLADIATORS. ▼○◗

Roberta (1935) **106m.** *** D: William A. Seiter. Irene Dunne, Fred Astaire, Ginger Rogers, Randolph Scott, Helen Westley, Claire Dodd, Victor Varconi, Candy Candido. The story of this famous Jerome Kern–Otto Harbach musical creaks and groans, but "supporting" characters Astaire and Rogers make up for it in their exuberant dance numbers. You can try counting how many times Scott says "swell," or try to spot young Lucille Ball in fashion-show sequence to get through the rest. Songs include "I Won't Dance," "Lovely to Look At," "Smoke Gets in Your Eyes," and "Yesterdays." Based on the Alice Duer Miller novel *Gowns By Roberta*. Remade as LOVELY TO LOOK AT. ▼○◗

Robin and the 7 Hoods (1964) **C-123m.** *** D: Gordon Douglas. Frank Sinatra, Dean Martin, Sammy Davis, Jr., Bing Crosby, Peter Falk, Barbara Rush, Victor Buono, Sig Ruman, Allen Jenkins, Hans Conried, Jack LaRue, Edward G. Robinson. Rat Pack's final fling is amusing transposition of the merrie legend to 1928 Chicago, with gangleader Sinatra surprised to find he's something of a local hero. No classic, but good-looking and easy to take; Crosby is adroit as gang's elder statesman. Cahn-Van Heusen songs include "My Kind of Town," "Style," "Mr. Booze." Produced in 2010 as a stage musical. Panavision. ▼○◗

Robin Hood (1922) **127m.** ***½ D: Allan Dwan. Douglas Fairbanks, Wallace Beery, Sam De Grasse, Enid Bennett, Paul Dickey, William Lowery, Roy Coulson, Billie Bennett, Willard Louis, Alan Hale. Fairbanks is typically athletic, and charismatic, in this rousing action-adventure. Here, the Earl of Huntingdon/Robin Hood falls for "Lady" Marian and heads off to the Crusades with Richard the Lion-Hearted (Beery); he returns to England upon learning of the treachery of Prince John (De Grasse). Makes an interesting contrast to Errol Flynn's THE ADVENTURES OF ROBIN HOOD; Hale plays Little John in both films. Story is credited to Elton Thomas, Fairbanks' nom de plume. ▼◗

Robin Hood of El Dorado, The (1936) **86m.** **½ D: William Wellman. Warner Baxter, Ann Loring, Margo, Bruce Cabot, J. Carrol Naish. Pseudobiography of Mexican bandit Joaquin Murietta, who turns to crime to avenge his wife's murder. Well made, on beautiful locations, but fools around too much for its dramatic moments to be truly effective. ◗

Robin Hood of Texas (1947) **71m.** ** D:

Lesley Selander. Gene Autry, Lynne Roberts, Sterling Holloway, Adele Mara, James Cardwell, John Kellogg, The Cass County Boys. Gene and his friends track modern-day bank robbers to a dude ranch after they are suspected of the holdup themselves. Gene's last picture for Republic after 13 years is not one of his best. ▼◗

Robin Hood of the Pecos (1941) **59m.** ** D: Joseph Kane. Roy Rogers, George "Gabby" Hayes, Marjorie Reynolds, Cy Kendall, Leigh Whipper, Sally Payne, Eddie Acuff, Jay Novello, Robert Strange, William Haade, Roscoe Ates. Roy and Gabby organize night riders in post–Civil War Texas to combat villainous Kendall and his carpetbagger militia. Good cast in an overly familiar story set during the Reconstruction Era. ▼◗

Robinson Crusoe (1952) SEE: **Adventures of Robinson Crusoe**
Robinson Crusoeland SEE: **Utopia**
Robinson Crusoe on Mars (1964) **C-109m.** **½ D: Byron Haskin. Paul Mantee, Vic Lundin, Adam West. Surprisingly agreeable reworking of the classic Defoe story, with Mantee as stranded astronaut, at first accompanied only by a monkey. "Friday" turns out to be a similarly trapped alien. Beautifully shot in Death Valley by Winton C. Hoch; film's intimate nature helps it play better on TV screens than most widescreen space films. Techniscope. ▼○◗

Robot Monster (1953) **63m.** BOMB D: Phil Tucker. George Nader, Gregory Moffett, Claudia Barrett, Selena Royle, John Mylong. Gorilla in diving helmet wipes out entire Earth population save one family and Nader, then spends most of film's running time lumbering around Bronson Canyon trying to find them. One of the genuine legends of Hollywood: embarrassingly, hilariously awful . . . and dig that bubble machine with the TV antenna! Originally in 3-D (except for the dinosaur stock footage from ONE MILLION B.C. and LOST CONTINENT). Aka MONSTER FROM MARS. ▼○◗

Robot vs. the Aztec Mummy, The (1958-Mexican) **65m.** BOMB D: Rafael Portillo. Ramón Gay, Rosa Arenas, Crox Alvarado, Luis Aceves Castañeda, Arturo Martínez, Jorge Mondragón. A gleeful mad scientist has built a robot with a dead body inside to battle the treasure-guarding mummy of an Aztec warrior and seize said treasure. Reasonably well produced, but an incoherent mess that moves about as rapidly as its shambling mummy. Features lengthy flashbacks from LA MOMIA AZTECA and LA MALDICIÓN DE LA AZTECA (both 1957). ▼◗

Rob Roy, the Highland Rogue (1954) **C-85m.** *½ D: Harold French. Richard Todd, Glynis Johns, James Robertson Justice, Michael Gough, Finlay Currie, Jean Taylor-Smith. Disney's dreariest British film casts Todd as leader of Scottish clan planning uprising against England's King George in 18th century. Turgid and unrewarding. Story told much better in 1995 version. ▼▶

Rocco and His Brothers (1960-Italian) **180m.** ***½ D: Luchino Visconti. Alain Delon, Renato Salvatori, Annie Girardot, Katina Paxinou, Claudia Cardinale, Roger Hanin, Suzy Delair. Sweeping chronicle of familial loyalty and the tainting of innocence, chronicling the plight of idealistic, saintly Rocco (Delon) after he and his mother and brothers leave their rural southern Italian community and settle in Milan. Stunningly photographed by Giuseppe Rotunno. Restored to its original running time in 1991; beware many shorter, visually inferior prints and video versions. ▼●▶

Rockabye (1932) **67m.** *½ D: George Cukor. Constance Bennett, Joel McCrea, Paul Lukas, Jobyna Howland, Walter Pidgeon, Sterling Holloway. Other than offering a memorable shot of Bennett immersed in balloons, soaper about a morally ambiguous actress's love for her toddler is painful going. A curio for film buffs, but a minor credit for both star and director.

Rock-a-Bye Baby (1958) **C-103m.** *** D: Frank Tashlin. Jerry Lewis, Marilyn Maxwell, Connie Stevens, Baccaloni, Reginald Gardiner, James Gleason, Hans Conried. Good-natured schnook Jerry becomes full-time baby-sitter for movie sex-siren Maxwell, who doesn't want her public to know she's had triplets. Loose remake of Preston Sturges' THE MIRACLE OF MORGAN'S CREEK, with many funny moments. That's Lewis' son Gary playing Jerry as a boy in the musical flashback sequence. VistaVision. ▼▶

Rock All Night (1957) **63m.** ** D: Roger Corman. Dick Miller, Russell Johnson, Jonathan Haze, Abby Dalton, The Platters, Robin Morse. AIP quickie about a pair of killers taking refuge in a bar and terrorizing captive customers. OK Corman potboiler with better-than-average performances, and dig this—Johnson's one of the bad guys and Miller's the hero!▼

Rock Around the Clock (1956) **77m.** ** D: Fred F. Sears. Bill Haley and His Comets, The Platters, Tony Martinez and His Band, Freddie Bell and His Bellboys, Alan Freed, Johnny Johnston. Premise is slim (unknown band brought to N.Y.C. where they become famous) but picture is now a time-capsule look at the emergence of rock 'n' roll. Bill Haley and the Comets perform "See You Later Alligator," "Razzle Dazzle," and the title song; the Platters chip in with "Only You" and "The Great Pretender." Remade as TWIST AROUND THE CLOCK.▼▶

Rock Around the World (1957-British) **71m.** *½ D: Gerard Bryant. Tommy Steele, Patrick Westwood, Dennis Price, Tom Littlewood. Humdrum account of Tommy Steele's

rise in the singing profession. Originally titled THE TOMMY STEELE STORY.

Rock, Baby, Rock It (1957) **84m.** *½ D: Murray Douglas Sporup. Johnny Carroll and His Hot Rocks, Rosco Gordon and The Red Tops, The Five Stars, The Belew Twins, Don Coats and The Bon-Aires, Preacher Smith and The Deacons, The Cell Block Seven, Kay Wheeler. Teens vs. syndicate bookies in this silly period piece that's become a minor cult item, mostly because it was shot in Dallas and highlights performances by regional rock acts. For diehard fans of the genre only. ▼▶

Rocket Attack U.S.A. (1959) **71m.** BOMB D: Barry Mahon. Monica Davis, John McKay, Daniel Kern, Edward Czerniuk, Arthur Metrano. Spy attempts to uncover Russian missile plans; meanwhile, the dastardly Commies are planning to nuke N.Y.C. Perfectly awful Cold War melodrama with hilarious dialogue, atrocious performances, lots of stock footage.▼▶

Rocket Man, The (1954) **79m.** ** D: Oscar Rudolph. Charles Coburn, Spring Byington, Anne Francis, John Agar, George "Foghorn" Winslow, Beverly Garland. Campy fantasy of Winslow possessing a space gun that turns crooked people honest. Co-scripted by Lenny Bruce—so it's no wonder the villain is a politician, who's portrayed as a drunken, cigar-chomping chiseler. ▶

Rockets Galore SEE: **Mad Little Island**

Rocketship X-M (1950) **77m.** **½ D: Kurt Neumann. Lloyd Bridges, Osa Massen, Hugh O'Brian, John Emery, Noah Beery, Jr. Slightly better than average production of spaceship to moon that is thrown off-course to Mars. Nice photography, good acting. Mars sequences are color tinted. Video version contains new special effects shot in 1976.▼●▶

Rocket to the Moon SEE: **Cat-Women of the Moon**

Rocking Horse Winner, The (1949-British) **91m.** ***½ D: Anthony Pelissier. Valerie Hobson, John Howard Davies, John Mills, Ronald Squire, Hugh Sinclair, Charles Goldner, Susan Richards. Truly unique, fascinating drama based on D. H. Lawrence story; small boy has knack for picking racetrack winners, but complications set in before long. Beautifully done. Screenplay by the director.▼▶

Rockin' in the Rockies (1945) **63m.** ** D: Vernon Keays. The Three Stooges, Mary Beth Hughes, Jay Kirby, Tim Ryan, Gladys Blake, Vernon Dent. Mediocre grade-B musical comedy actually splits up the Stooges, with Moe playing straight (more or less) and Larry and Curly acting as a team, in a threadbare story of show biz hopefuls on a Western ranch. Only comes to life near the end with some specialty numbers, including one by Spade Cooley and his Western swing band.▶

Rockin' the Blues (1955) **66m.** ****** D: Arthur Rosenblum. Mantan Moreland, F. E. Miller, Connie Carroll, The Wanderers, The Harptones, The Hurricanes, The Five Miller Sisters, Pearl Woods, Linda Hopkins, Hal Jackson. Grade-Z production values hamper this intriguing curio, an all-black rhythm-and-blues show emceed by Jackson, with Moreland along for comic relief. Dance routines are generally awful, but much of the music is priceless; The Hurricanes' Army-life number is a real showstopper.▼

Rock Island Trail (1950) **C-90m.** ****½** D: Joseph Kane. Forrest Tucker, Adele Mara, Adrian Booth, Bruce Cabot, Chill Wills, Barbara Fuller, Grant Withers, Jeff Corey, Roy Barcroft, Pierre Watkin. Tucker plays a railroad pioneer overcoming numerous obstacles, particularly villainous steamboat operator Cabot, while trying to build a new rail line. Fairly entertaining Republic Western with a robust cast, knockdown, drag-out brawls, and better-than-usual Trucolor spicing up a familiar story.▼

Rock, Pretty Baby (1956) **89m.** ****** D: Richard Bartlett. Sal Mineo, John Saxon, Luana Patten, Edward C. Platt, Fay Wray, Rod McKuen, Shelley Fabares, George "Foghorn" Winslow. Prototype of rock 'n' roll entries of 1950s revolving around high school rock group's effort to win big-time musical contest.▼

Rock, Rock, Rock! (1956) **83m.** ****** D: Will Price. Tuesday Weld, Teddy Randazzo, Alan Freed, Frankie Lymon and The Teenagers, The Moonglows, Chuck Berry, The Flamingos, Johnny Burnette Trio, LaVern Baker, Cirino and The Bowties. Weld, in her film debut and barely out of her training bra, must raise $30 to buy a strapless evening dress for a prom! Filmed on a budget of $6.95—and it shows. But the rock 'n' rollers, particularly Chuck Berry, are lively. Lymon and The Teenagers sing "I'm Not a Juvenile Delinquent." Weld's singing voice was dubbed by Connie Francis. One of the teens is young Valerie Harper.▼▶

Rocky Mountain (1950) **83m.** ******* D: William Dieterle. Errol Flynn, Patrice Wymore, Scott Forbes, Guinn ("Big Boy") Williams, Dick Jones, Howard Petrie, Slim Pickens, Chubby Johnson, Buzz Henry, Sheb Wooley, Peter Coe, Yakima Canutt. Solid, unpretentious Western (from an Alan LeMay story) about a Confederate troop led by Flynn that saves a stagecoach from Indian attackers but may not be able to save itself. Filmed in New Mexico. ▼▶

Rodan (1956-Japanese) **C-70m.** ****** D: Ishiro Honda. Kenji Sawara, Yumi Shirakawa, Akihiko Hirata, Akio Kobori. Colossal pterodactyl hatches in mine, later goes on destructive rampage in Tokyo. Colorful comic book stuff, all too typical of Toho Studios' monster formula.▼●▶

Rodeo (1952) **C-70m.** ***½** D: William Beaudine. Jane Nigh, John Archer, Wallace Ford, Frances Rafferty, Gary Grey, Myron Healey, Fuzzy Knight. Clichéd account of spunky Nigh taking over the operation of a faltering rodeo and being romanced by bronco rider Archer.

Roger Touhy, Gangster (1944) **65m.** ****½** D: Robert Florey. Preston Foster, Victor McLaglen, Lois Andrews, Anthony Quinn, Kent Taylor, Henry (Harry) Morgan, Trudy Marshall, Kane Richmond. Unexceptional—if mostly factual—account of Chicago bootlegger who waged a turf war with Al Capone, and later masterminded a prison escape.

Rogue at Heart, A (1948-British) **87m.** ****½** D: Herbert Rawlins. Trevor Asquith, Celia Howard, Montgomery Jenkins, Margaret Sellers. Slight comedy about a wealthy cad (Asquith) who poses as a butler in order to get close to a young woman (Howard) with whom he's fallen in love. Pleasant enough; fine support from Sellers as a housekeeper with a fondness for the bottle.

Rogue Cop (1954) **92m.** ******* D: Roy Rowland. Robert Taylor, Janet Leigh, George Raft, Steve Forrest, Anne Francis, Robert F. Simon, Robert Ellenstein, Alan Hale, Jr., Vince Edwards. Dynamic account of crooked cop Taylor caught between loyalty to his brother and his gangster cohorts. Also shown in computer-colored version.

Rogue River (1950) **C-81m.** ****** D: John Rawlins. Rory Calhoun, Peter Graves, Frank Fenton, Ralph Sanford. Stepbrothers whose father is chief of police in a small Oregon lumber town lock horns after a robbery that divides the community. Minor yarn filmed on location. Graves' screen debut.

Rogue's March (1952) **84m.** ****** D: Allan Davis. Peter Lawford, Richard Greene, Janice Rule, Leo G. Carroll. Programmer-costumer set in India (via stock footage and rear projection scenes), with Lawford trying to redeem himself with regiment.

Rogues of Sherwood Forest (1950) **C-90m.** ****** D: Gordon Douglas. John Derek, Diana Lynn, George Macready, Alan Hale, Paul Cavanagh, Lowell Gilmore, Billy House, Lester Matthews, Billy Bevan. Routine swashbuckler about the son of Robin Hood, who bands together with the Merrie Men to battle the injustices meted out by King John (Macready). Hale plays Little John for the third time, following his stints with Douglas Fairbanks, Sr., and Errol Flynn. ▶

Rogue's Regiment (1948) **86m.** ****** D: Robert Florey. Dick Powell, Marta Toren, Vincent Price, Stephen McNally, Edgar Barrier, Henry Rowland. Contrived actioner about American agent Powell, who joins the French Foreign Legion in Indochina to hunt down Nazi bigwig McNally.

Rogues Tavern, The (1936) **70m.** ****** D:

Robert F. Hill. Wallace Ford, Barbara Pepper, Joan Woodbury, Clara Kimball Young, Jack Mulhall, John Elliott, Earl Dwire. Eloping detectives Ford and Pepper stop at an isolated tavern; all the other suspicious-looking guests have been mysteriously summoned there. Of course, a phantom killer starts knocking them off one by one, using the jaws of a dog head. Modestly entertaining poverty-row thriller hovers on the edge of being horror but never quite topples over. ▶

Roll On Texas Moon (1946) 67m. **½ D: William Witney. Roy Rogers, George "Gabby" Hayes, Dale Evans, Dennis Hoey, Elisabeth Risdon, Francis McDonald, Edward Keane, Bob Nolan and the Sons of the Pioneers. Roy tries to play peacemaker between cattle ranchers (like Gabby) and sheep ranchers (like Dale) and tries to rout the gang that's stirring up trouble between them. This film ushered in Roy's more serious, hard-action period under the direction of former serial director Witney, who would guide the rest of Roy's feature films. ▼▶

Romance (1930) 76m. ** D: Clarence Brown. Greta Garbo, Lewis Stone, Gavin Gordon, Elliott Nugent, Florence Lake, Clara Blandick. Garbo is miscast in this static, hokey early talkie about an Italian opera star who philosophizes about love and has a relationship with an inexperienced young priest (limply played by Gordon). ▼▶

Romance and Riches SEE: **Amazing Adventure**

Romance in Manhattan (1934) 78m. *** D: Stephen Roberts. Francis Lederer, Ginger Rogers, Arthur Hohl, Jimmy Butler, J. Farrell MacDonald, Helen Ware, Donald Meek, Sidney Toler. Chorus girl Rogers helps illegal alien Lederer, and romance blossoms, in this most enjoyable Capraesque comedy. ▼▶

Romance in the Dark (1938) 80m. ** D: H. C. Potter. Gladys Swarthout, John Barrymore, John Boles, Claire Dodd, Curt Bois. A womanizing tenor uses a naive young singer (Swarthout) in a scheme to distract his rival, but his plans backfire when he falls in love with her. Stylish treatment of trite material; more a showcase for funny Fritz Feld (as Boles' valet) than for opera star Swarthout.

Romance of Happy Valley, A (1919) 60m. **½ D: D. W. Griffith. Lillian Gish, Robert Harron, George Fawcett, Kate Bruce, George Nichols. A youth with sand in his shoes leaves Kentucky to seek riches and success in N.Y.C. Meanwhile, his sweetheart back home patiently awaits his sure return. Preachy but sincerely told piece of rural Americana features key members of Griffith's repertory troupe, champions country living as always, and exemplifies his ingenuous style. ▼

Romance of Rosy Ridge, The (1947) 105m. *** D: Roy Rowland. Van Johnson,

Thomas Mitchell, Janet Leigh, Marshall Thompson, Selena Royle, Charles Dingle, Dean Stockwell, Guy Kibbee, Jim Davis. Heartfelt post–Civil War tale, set in a Missouri farm community whose residents are still fighting the war. Farmer Mitchell casts suspicious eye on charming stranger Johnson, who is courting his daughter (Leigh, in her film debut). Fascinating, humanist script by soon-to-be-blacklisted Lester Cole (based on a story by MacKinlay Kantor). ▶

Romance on the High Seas (1948) C-99m. *** D: Michael Curtiz. Jack Carson, Janis Paige, Don DeFore, Doris Day, Oscar Levant, S. Z. Sakall, Fortunio Bonanova, Eric Blore, Franklin Pangborn. Sparkling, trivial romantic musical set on an ocean voyage, with Doris' star-making feature film debut, singing "It's Magic," "Put 'em in a Box." Easygoing fun. ▼●▶

Romance on the Range (1942) 63m. **½ D: Joseph Kane. Roy Rogers, George "Gabby" Hayes, Sally Payne, Linda Hayes, Edward Pawley, Harry Woods, Hal Taliaferro, Glenn Strange, Roy Barcroft, Sons of the Pioneers. New York socialite Linda Hayes falls for Roy, but he wants nothing to do with her—at first. Little does he dream that her business manager (Pawley) is behind a gang of fur thieves who murdered one of Roy's cowhand pals. Typical lightweight blend of story, music, action, and—yes, romance. Pat Brady (of the Pioneers) has a nice supporting role. ▼▶

Roman Holiday (1953) 119m. ***½ D: William Wyler. Audrey Hepburn, Gregory Peck, Eddie Albert, Tullio Carminati. Hepburn got first break and an Oscar as princess, yearning for normal life, who runs away from palace, has romance with reporter Peck. Screenplay by John Dighton and Ian McLellan Hunter, from an Oscar-winning story (written by blacklisted Dalton Trumbo and credited for almost 40 years to Hunter, who acted as his "front"). Utterly charming. Remade for TV in 1987 with Catherine Oxenberg and Tom Conti. ▼●▶

Romanoff and Juliet (1961) C-103m. *** D: Peter Ustinov. Peter Ustinov, Sandra Dee, John Gavin, Akim Tamiroff, Rik Von Nutter. Ustinov wrote, directed, and stars in this cold war satire with offspring of U.S. and Russian ambassadors falling in love. Italian locations substitute for mythical country which Ustinov rules. ▶

Roman Scandals (1933) 92m. *** D: Frank Tuttle. Eddie Cantor, Ruth Etting, Gloria Stuart, David Manners, Verree Teasdale, Alan Mowbray, Edward Arnold. Old-fashioned, enjoyable musical vehicle for Cantor to romp through as dreamer who is transported back to ancient Rome. Full of funny gags and delightful songs. Big Busby Berkeley production numbers include young Lucille Ball. ▼●▶

Roman Spring of Mrs. Stone, The (1961)

C-104m. *** D: Jose Quintero. Vivien Leigh, Warren Beatty, Lotte Lenya, Jill St. John, Jeremy Spenser, Coral Browne, Cleo Laine, Bessie Love, Jean Marsh. Middleaged actress retreats to Rome, buying a fling at romance from gigolo Beatty. Lenya, as Leigh's waspish friend, comes off best. Adapted from Tennessee Williams novella. Remade for cable TV in 2003.▼❿

Romantic Age, The (1949-British) **86m. **** D: Edmond T. Greville. Mai Zetterling, Hugh Williams, Margot Grahame, Petula Clark, Carol Marsh, Adrienne Corri. Art teacher Williams falls for flirtatious French schoolgirl Zetterling. Trifling; aka NAUGHTY ARLETTE.

Rome Adventure (1962) **C-119m. ***** D: Delmer Daves. Troy Donahue, Angie Dickinson, Rossano Brazzi, Suzanne Pleshette, Constance Ford, Chad Everett, Al Hirt, Hampton Fancher. Plush soaper with Pleshette as schoolteacher on Roman fling to find romance, torn between roué (Brazzi) and architect (Donahue). As Troy's mistress, Dickinson has some rare repartee. Lush Max Steiner score. Donahue and Pleshette married two years later.▼❿❿

Rome Express (1932-British) **94m. ***** D: Walter Forde. Conrad Veidt, Esther Ralston, Harold Huth, Gordon Harker, Donald Calthrop, Joan Barry, Cedric Hardwicke, Frank Vosper, Hugh Williams. Seminal mystery-thriller that spawned many imitations, including THE LADY VANISHES and NIGHT TRAIN TO MUNICH, among others. Entertaining, if slightly talky, tale of assorted group of passengers caught up in criminal activities aboard train. Remade as SLEEPING CAR TO TRIESTE.❿

Romeo and Juliet (1936) **126m. ***½** D: George Cukor. Norma Shearer, Leslie Howard, John Barrymore, Edna May Oliver, Basil Rathbone, C. Aubrey Smith, Andy Devine, Reginald Denny, Ralph Forbes. Well-acted, lavish production of Shakespeare's play about ill-fated lovers. Howard and Shearer are so good that one can forget they are too old for the roles. Not the great film it might have been, but a very good one.▼❿❿

Romeo and Juliet (1954-British) **C-140m. ***** D: Renato Castellani. Laurence Harvey, Susan Shentall, Flora Robson, Mervyn Johns, Bill Travers, Sebastian Cabot; introduced by John Gielgud. Sumptuously photographed in Italy, this pleasing version of Shakespeare's tragedy has the virtue of good casting.▼❿❿

Rome, Open City SEE: **Open City**

Roof, The (1956-Italian) **98m. **½** D: Vittorio De Sica. Gabriella Pallotta, Giorgio Listuzzi, Gastone Renzelli, Maria Di Rollo. Thoughtful neorealist account of a simple young married couple in overcrowded post-WW2 Rome, and their attempt to find a home for themselves. Original title: IL TETTO.▼

Roogie's Bump (1954) **71m. *½** D: Harold Young. Robert Marriot, Ruth Warrick, Olive Blakeney, Robert Simon, William Harrigan, David Winters. A bump on the arm of young Remington "Roogie" Rigsby (Marriot) results in his getting to pitch for the Brooklyn Dodgers. Slight kiddie fantasy, with more than a passing resemblance to ROOKIE OF THE YEAR. However, fans of Dem Bums will enjoy seeing Roy Campanella, Billy Loes, Carl Erskine, and Russ Meyer as Roogie's teammates.▼

Rookie, The (1959) **86m.** BOMB D: George O'Hanlon. Tommy Noonan, Pete Marshall, Julie Newmar, Jerry Lester, Joe Besser, Vince Barnett, Peter Leeds. Feeble Army comedy of draftee, tough sergeant, movie starlet, and other stereotypes set during 1940s. CinemaScope.

Room at the Top (1959-British) **118m. ****** D: Jack Clayton. Laurence Harvey, Simone Signoret, Heather Sears, Hermione Baddeley, Donald Wolfit, Ambrosine Philpotts, Donald Houston, Wendy Craig. Brilliant drama of ambitious Harvey determined to rise in the hierarchy of the factory that employs him; complications arise when he becomes involved with older, unhappily married Signoret. Trenchant and powerful adaptation of John Braine novel won Oscars for Signoret and screenwriter Neil Paterson. Followed by LIFE AT THE TOP and MAN AT THE TOP.▼❿❿

Room for One More (1952) **98m. ***** D: Norman Taurog. Cary Grant, Betsy Drake, Lurene Tuttle, George Winslow, John Ridgely. Grant and Drake are softhearted couple who can't resist adopting needy kids. Sentimental comedy retitled THE EASY WAY; basis for later TV series.❿

Room Service (1938) **78m. ***** D: William A. Seiter. Groucho, Chico and Harpo Marx, Lucille Ball, Ann Miller, Frank Albertson, Donald MacBride. Broadway farce about destitute producers trying to keep their play afloat—and avoid being evicted from their hotel room—is transformed by scenarist Morrie Ryskind into a vehicle for the Marx Bros. More conventional than their earlier outings, but still has a lot of funny material (and, thankfully, no intrusive songs). Remade as a musical, STEP LIVELY. MacBride reprises his Broadway role as the hothead trying to evict the brothers. Also shown in computer-colored version.▼❿❿

Rooney (1958-British) **88m. ***** D: George Pollock. John Gregson, Muriel Pavlow, Barry Fitzgerald, June Thorburn. Sprightly tale of Irish sanitation worker Gregson with an eye for the girls, trying to avoid marriage; Fitzgerald is bedridden geezer whom Rooney helps.▼

Rootin' Tootin' Rhythm (1937) **60m. **½** D: Mack V. Wright. Gene Autry, Smiley Burnette, Armida, Monte Blue, Al Clauser and His Oklahoma Outlaws, Hal

Taliaferro, Ann Pendleton, Charles King, Frankie Marvin. Gene and Smiley go after cattle rustlers but find themselves mistaken for two of the wanted men. Story takes a backseat to comedy and music. Gene sings "Mexicali Rose" for the first time on-screen.▼▶

Roots of Heaven, The (1958) C-131m. **½ D: John Huston. Errol Flynn, Juliette Greco, Trevor Howard, Eddie Albert, Orson Welles, Herbert Lom, Paul Lukas. Turgid melodramatics set in Africa, with conglomerate cast philosophizing over sanctity of elephants; loosely based on Romain Gary novel. CinemaScope.▶

Rope (1948) C-80m. *** D: Alfred Hitchcock. James Stewart, John Dall, Farley Granger, Cedric Hardwicke, Joan Chandler, Constance Collier, Douglas Dick. Two young men kill prep-school pal, just for the thrill of it, and challenge themselves by inviting friends and family to their apartment afterward—with the body hidden on the premises. Hitchcock's first color film was shot in ten-minute takes to provide a seamless flow of movement, but it remains today what it was then: an interesting, highly theatrical experiment. Inspired by the real-life Leopold-Loeb murder case, which later was depicted in COMPULSION and SWOON. Patrick Hamilton's play was adapted by Hume Cronyn and scripted by Arthur Laurents.▼▶●

Rope of Sand (1949) 104m. *** D: William Dieterle. Burt Lancaster, Paul Henreid, Corinne Calvet, Claude Rains, Peter Lorre, Sam Jaffe, John Bromfield, Mike Mazurki. Sturdy cast in adventure tale of smooth thief trying to regain treasure he hid away, with various parties interfering.▶

Rosalie (1937) 122m. ** D: W. S. Van Dyke. Eleanor Powell, Nelson Eddy, Frank Morgan, Edna May Oliver, Ray Bolger, Ilona Massey, Billy Gilbert. Elephantine MGM musical about romance between West Point cadet and mythical-kingdom princess. Living proof that money alone can't make a good movie. Cole Porter score includes "In the Still of the Night."▼▶

Roseanna McCoy (1949) 100m. ** D: Irving Reis. Farley Granger, Joan Evans, Charles Bickford, Raymond Massey, Richard Basehart, Aline MacMahon. Witless drama of Hatfield-McCoy feud, with young lovers from opposite sides of the fence rekindling old wounds.▼

Rose Bowl Story, The (1952) C-73m. ** D: William Beaudine. Marshall Thompson, Vera Miles, Richard Rober, Natalie Wood, Keith Larsen, Tom Harmon, Ann Doran, James Dobson, Jim Backus. Predictable B-movie yarn about romance of college football hero and the new Rose Bowl queen. ▼

Rose for Everyone, A (1965-Italian) C-107m. ** D: Franco Rossi. Claudia Cardinale, Nino Manfredi, Mario Adorf, Akim Tamiroff. Brazilian locale with NEVER ON SUNDAY plot. Girl brings happiness to many men and takes active interest in their private lives as well as their sexual lives. Nice locales, banal story.

Rose-Marie (1936) 110m. *** D: W. S. Van Dyke II. Jeanette MacDonald, Nelson Eddy, Reginald Owen, Allan Jones, James Stewart, Alan Mowbray, Gilda Gray. Don't expect the original operetta: story has opera star Jeanette searching for fugitive brother Stewart, as Mountie Nelson pursues the same man. The two fall in love, sing "Indian Love Call," among others. David Niven appears briefly as Jeanette's unsuccessful suitor. Retitled INDIAN LOVE CALL; previously filmed in 1928, then again in 1954.▼▶●

Rose Marie (1954) C-115m. **½ D: Mervyn LeRoy. Ann Blyth, Howard Keel, Fernando Lamas, Bert Lahr, Marjorie Main, Joan Taylor, Ray Collins. More faithful to original operetta than 1936 version, but not as much fun. Mountie Keel tries to "civilize" tomboy Blyth, but falls in love with her instead. Adventurer Lamas completes the triangle. Lahr sings "I'm the Mountie Who Never Got His Man" in comic highlight. CinemaScope.●

Rosemary (1958-German) 99m. **½ D: Rolf Thiele. Nadja Tiller, Peter Van Eyck, Gert Frobe, Mario Adorf, Carl Raddatz. Convincing study of famed post-WW2 Frankfurt prostitute (Tiller) who blackmailed industrialist; satirically sensational.

Rose of Washington Square (1939) 86m. **½ D: Gregory Ratoff. Tyrone Power, Alice Faye, Al Jolson, William Frawley, Joyce Compton, Hobart Cavanaugh, Louis Prima, Horace McMahon, Moroni Olsen. So-so musical with Faye as a thinly disguised Fanny Brice, who falls head over heels for cocky punk Power (a clone of Nicky Arnstein). Faye gets to sing Brice's signature song, "My Man," and the title number (a highlight), while Jolson reprises such old standbys as "Mammy" and "California, Here I Come."▼▶

Roses Are Red (1947) 67m. **½ D: James Tinling. Don Castle, Peggy Knudsen, Patricia Knight, Joe Sawyer, Edward Keane, Jeff Chandler, Charles McGraw, James Arness. Pretty nifty B picture about a crime boss who kidnaps the newly elected D.A. and replaces him with a look-alike ex-con (Castle in a dual role).▶

Rose Tattoo, The (1955) 117m. ***½ D: Daniel Mann. Anna Magnani, Burt Lancaster, Marisa Pavan, Ben Cooper, Virginia Grey, Jo Van Fleet. Magnani shines in Oscar-winning role as earthy, deluded widow in Gulf Coast city who's romanced by rambunctious truck driver Lancaster. Flavorful adaptation of Tennessee Williams play; cinematographer James Wong Howe also won an Oscar. VistaVision.▼▶●

Rotten to the Core (1965-British) **90m.**
*** D: John Boulting. Anton Rodgers, Eric Sykes, Charlotte Rampling, Ian Bannen, Avis Bunnage, Victor Maddern. Well-handled caper of ex-con trio joining forces with crook to carry off large-scale robbery. Panavision.

Rough and the Smooth, The SEE: **Portrait of a Sinner**

Roughly Speaking (1945) **117m.** ******* D: Michael Curtiz. Rosalind Russell, Jack Carson, Robert Hutton, Jean Sullivan, Alan Hale, Donald Woods, Ray Collins, Mona Freeman, Craig Stevens. Heartfelt biopic about spunky Louise Randall Pierson (Russell), her two very different husbands, and her plight through the ups and downs of the 20th century, all the way to WW2. Russell and Carson, as her easygoing husband number 2, are tops. Pierson scripted, based on her bestseller.▐

Rough Riders' Round-up (1939) **55m.** ******* D: Joseph Kane. Roy Rogers, Mary Hart (Lynne Roberts), Raymond Hatton, Eddie Acuff, William Pawley, Dorothy Sebastian, George Meeker, Guy Usher. After being mustered out as members of Teddy Roosevelt's Rough Riders at the end of the Spanish-American War, Rogers and his pals head for Arizona to join the Border Patrol. There they contend with outlaw Arizona Jack (Pawley), whose secret confederate (Meeker) works for Hart's father. Good entry in Roy's series of historical Westerns. Look for George Montgomery in a bit part as a telegrapher. ▼▐

Roughshod (1949) **88m.** ****½** D: Mark Robson. Robert Sterling, Claude Jarman, Jr., Gloria Grahame, Jeff Donnell, John Ireland, Myrna Dell, Martha Hyer. Intriguing oater in which Sterling and kid brother Jarman head West to start a ranch; they come upon a quartet of stranded saloon-hall dames, and face a trio of murderous escaped cons seeking vengeance.

Rough Shoot SEE: **Shoot First**

Rounders, The (1965) **C-85m.** ****½** D: Burt Kennedy. Glenn Ford, Henry Fonda, Sue Ane Langdon, Hope Holiday, Chill Wills, Edgar Buchanan, Kathleen Freeman. Agreeable comedy-Western from Max Evans' novel about two cowboys and an ornery horse was one of the sleepers of its year; nothing much happens, but cast and scenery make it a pleasant way to kill an hour-and-a-half. Panavision.▼▐

Round-Up Time in Texas (1937) **63m.** ***½** D: Joseph Kane. Gene Autry, Smiley Burnette, Maxine Doyle, LeRoy Mason, Earle Hodgins, Dick Wessel, Buddy Williams, Elmer Fain, Ken Cooper. Gene's strangest—and probably worst—Western finds him bringing horses to a South African diamond mine his brother has discovered. Horrible stereotypes abound, complete with Smiley in blackface. ▼▐

Roustabout (1964) **C-101m.** ****½** D: John

Rich. Elvis Presley, Barbara Stanwyck, Leif Erickson, Joan Freeman, Sue Ane Langdon. Elvis is a free-wheeling singer who joins Stanwyck's carnival, learns the meaning of hard work and true love. Stanwyck and supporting cast make this a pleasing Presley songer, with "Little Egypt" his one outstanding tune. Raquel Welch has a bit, and Teri Garr is one of the dancers. Techniscope.▼▐

Rovin' Tumbleweeds (1939) **62m.** ****½** D: George Sherman. Gene Autry, Smiley Burnette, Mary Carlisle, Douglass Dumbrille, Pals of the Golden West, William Farnum, Ralph Peters, Jack Ingram. Shades of MR. SMITH GOES TO WASHINGTON: after a disastrous flood in Green River, rancher-turned-radio-singer Autry gets elected to Congress with a flood control bill as his platform. One of Gene's early "environmental" Westerns, released shortly after the Capra classic. Gene also sings "Back in the Saddle." ▼▐

Roxie Hart (1942) **75m.** ****½** D: William Wellman. Ginger Rogers, Adolphe Menjou, George Montgomery, Lynne Overman, Nigel Bruce, Phil Silvers, Spring Byington, Iris Adrian, George Chandler. Fast-moving spoof of Roaring '20s, with Ginger as publicity-seeking dancer on trial for murder, Menjou her overdramatic lawyer. Hilarious antics make up for dry spells; scripted and produced by Nunnally Johnson. Previously filmed in 1927 as CHICAGO, also the title of later Broadway and movie musical.▼▐

Royal Affairs in Versailles (1954-French) **C-152m.** ****** D: Sacha Guitry. Claudette Colbert, Orson Welles, Jean-Pierre Aumont, Edith Piaf, Gérard Philipe, Jean Marais, Sacha Guitry, Micheline Presle, Daniel Gelin, Danielle Delorme. Impressive cast in static, leaden-paced chronicle of the Golden Age of the French monarchy. Guitry plays Louis XIV; also seen are D'Artagnan, Mme. de Pompadour, Moliere, Marie Antoinette, etc. Released in U.S. in 1957. Look fast for Brigitte Bardot. Retitled: AFFAIRS IN VERSAILLES.▼

Royal African Rifles, The (1953) **C-75m.** ****** D: Lesley Selander. Louis Hayward, Veronica Hurst, Michael Pate, Angela Greene. Adequate actioner set in Africa in 1910, with Hayward the British officer leading mission to recover cache of arms.

Royal Family of Broadway, The (1930) **82m.** *****½** D: George Cukor, Cyril Gardner. Fredric March, Ina Claire, Mary Brian, Henrietta Crosman, Charles Starrett, Arnold Korff, Frank Conroy. Delightful screen version of Edna Ferber–George S. Kaufman play about Barrymore-like theatrical family torn by conflict of show business tradition vs. "normal" private life. March is wickedly funny in his John Barrymore portrayal.

Royal Scandal, A (1945) **94m.** ****½** D: Ernst Lubitsch, Otto Preminger. Tallulah

Bankhead, Charles Coburn, Anne Baxter, William Eythe, Vincent Price, Mischa Auer. Comedy of manners about Catherine the Great of Russia promoting favored soldier Eythe to high rank; started by Lubitsch, "finished" by Preminger. Remake of Lubitsch's 1924 FORBIDDEN PARADISE. ▶

Royal Wedding (1951) **C-93m.** *** D: Stanley Donen. Fred Astaire, Jane Powell, Peter Lawford, Sarah Churchill, Keenan Wynn, Albert Sharpe. Pleasant MGM musical (written by Alan Jay Lerner) about brother and sister team who take their show to London at the time of Queen Elizabeth II's wedding, and find romance of their own. Highlights: Astaire's dancing on the ceiling and partnering with a hat-rack, and his dynamite duet with Powell, "How Could You Believe Me When I Said I Loved You (When You Know I've Been a Liar All My Life)?" Burton Lane/Alan Jay Lerner score also includes "Too Late Now." Donen's first solo directing credit. ▼●▶

Ruby Gentry (1952) **82m.** **½ D: King Vidor. Jennifer Jones, Charlton Heston, Karl Malden, Josephine Hutchinson. Turgid, meandering account of easy-virtue Southerner Jones marrying wealthy Malden to spite Heston, the man she loves. ▼▶

Ruggles of Red Gap (1935) **92m.** **** D: Leo McCarey. Charles Laughton, Mary Boland, Charlie Ruggles, ZaSu Pitts, Roland Young, Leila Hyams. Laughton is marvelous as staid English valet won in poker game by uncouth but amiable Westerner Ruggles and socially ambitious wife Boland and brought to the wild 'n' wooly American West; ZaSu is spinster he falls in love with. A completely winning movie. Harry Leon Wilson's story was filmed before in 1918 and 1923, then remade as FANCY PANTS. ▼●▶

Rulers of the Sea (1939) **96m.** **½ D: Frank Lloyd. Douglas Fairbanks, Jr., Will Fyffe, Margaret Lockwood, George Bancroft, Montagu Love, Alan Ladd, Mary Gordon, Neil Fitzgerald. Well-made drama of problems surrounding first steamship voyage across Atlantic.

Rules of the Game, The (1939-French) **106m.** **** D: Jean Renoir. Marcel Dalio, Nora Gregor, Mila Parely, Jean Renoir, Gaston Modot, Roland Toutain, Paulette Dubost, Julien Carette, Odette Talazac. Sublime, endlessly imitated film about romantic intrigues at a French country estate, both upstairs and downstairs. Renoir, who costars as Octave, used the façade of light comedy to satirize (and skewer) the bourgeoisie—their follies, rituals, and class distinctions—as Europe was about to go up in flames. His light touch, and extraordinarily fluid staging and camerawork, are what make the film still seem so fresh. Vilified on its initial release, it was severely cut, then rediscovered decades later and justly hailed as a masterpiece. Reconstructed in the 1960s. ▼●▶

Ruling Voice, The (1931) **71m.** *** D: Rowland V. Lee. Walter Huston, Loretta Young, Doris Kenyon, David Manners, John Halliday, Dudley Digges, Gilbert Emery, Willard Robertson. Gangster Huston rules the nation's underworld but starts to go soft when his innocent daughter returns from school abroad. Slows down in Loretta's scenes, but when Huston is on-screen it really hums.

Rumba (1935) **77m.** ** D: Marion Gering. George Raft, Carole Lombard, Margo, Lynne Overman, Gail Patrick, Akim Tamiroff, Iris Adrian. Weak follow-up to BOLERO, with Raft and Lombard in and out of love in silly, contrived story; most of their "dancing" actually done by Veloz and Yolanda.

Rumble on the Docks (1956) **82m.** ** D: Fred F. Sears. James Darren, Laurie Carroll, Michael Granger, Jerry Janger, Robert Blake, Edgar Barrier. Low-key waterfront corruption tale, with Darren the street-gang leader aiding racketeers. ▶

Runaround, The (1946) **86m.** **½ D: Charles Lamont. Rod Cameron, Ella Raines, Broderick Crawford, Frank McHugh, Samuel S. Hinds, George Cleveland. Clever little comedy-drama in which nervy private detective Cameron and bullying rival Crawford clash as they set out on the trail of runaway rich girl Raines.

Runaway, The (1961) **85m.** *** D: Claudio Guzman. Cesar Romero, Roger Mobley, Chick Chandler, Anita Page, Nacho Galindo, Lewis Martin, Frank Wolff. Streetwise, canine-loving Chicano, who's escaped from an orphanage, comes under the wing of kindly priest Romero. Heartfelt, refreshingly unsentimental boy-and-his-dog tale, produced independently and on a shoestring, was never released theatrically; it made its TV premiere in 2008. Also notable as an early credit for cinematographer Haskell Wexler.

Runaway Bus, The (1954-British) **74m.** ** D: Val Guest. Frankie Howerd, Margaret Rutherford, Petula Clark, George Coulouris, Toke Townley, Terence Alexander, Belinda Lee. Fog grounds all airplanes flying out of London, so bumbling bus driver Howerd (in his screen debut) is recruited to transport a diverse group of passengers to an alternate airport. Slight, forgettable comedy/caper film. ▼▶

Runaway Daughter SEE: Red Salute

Runaway Daughters (1956) **92m.** *½ D: Edward L. Cahn. Marla English, Anna Sten, John Litel, Adele Jergens, Lance Fuller, Mary Ellen Kaye, Gloria Castillo, Nicky Blair, Frank Gorshin. Parental angst drives three high-school girls to drift into trouble. Dull, dated, and overlong, this teen exploitation fare boasts a surprisingly geriatric cast. Remade for TV in 1994.

Run for Cover (1955) **C-93m.** **½ D: Nicholas Ray. James Cagney, Viveca Lindfors, John Derek, Jean Hersholt, Ernest Borgnine. Offbeat Western has ex-con Cagney becoming sheriff, while his embittered young companion (Derek) grows restive and antagonistic. Interesting touches cannot overcome familiar storyline. Retitled: COLORADO. VistaVision. ▶

Run for the Sun (1956) **C-99m.** *** D: Roy Boulting. Richard Widmark, Jane Greer, Trevor Howard, Peter Van Eyck, Carlos Henning. Third version of THE MOST DANGEROUS GAME has author Widmark and magazine writer Greer stumbling onto strange Mexican plantation run by mysterious Howard and Van Eyck. Engrossing, extremely well made film. SuperScope 235. ▶

Run for Your Money, A (1949-British) **83m.** *** D: Charles Frend. Donald Houston, Meredith Edwards, Moira Lister, Alec Guinness, Hugh Griffith, Joyce Grenfell. Delightful comic study of two Welsh miners having a spree in London. ▼▶

Running Man, The (1963-British) **C-103m.** *** D: Carol Reed. Laurence Harvey, Lee Remick, Alan Bates, Felix Aylmer, Eleanor Summerfield, Allan Cuthbertson. Harvey fakes his death to collect insurance money, but pursuing insurance investigator Bates forces him and wife Remick to go on the lam in Spain. Entertaining but not suspenseful enough. Panavision.

Running Wild (1927) **68m.** **½ D: Gregory La Cava. W.C. Fields, Mary Brian, Claude Buchanan, Marie Shotwell, Barney Raskle, Tom Madden, Frederick Burton. Fields (sporting his silent-film mustache) plays the ultimate milquetoast who undergoes a galvanizing change of personality when he chances to encounter a hypnotist. Fast, funny outing with the surefire satisfaction of seeing the worm turn. ▼

Running Wild (1955) **81m.** **½ D: Abner Biberman. William Campbell, Mamie Van Doren, Keenan Wynn, Kathleen Case, Jan Merlin, John Saxon. Straightforward drama of young cop Campbell going undercover to crack a teenage car-theft ring.

Run of the Arrow (1957) **C-86m.** **½ D: Samuel Fuller. Rod Steiger, Sarita Montiel, Brian Keith, Ralph Meeker, Jay C. Flippen, Charles Bronson, Olive Carey, Colonel Tim McCoy. Confederate soldier (played by Steiger with a broad Irish brogue!) cannot accept surrender to the North, aligns himself instead with Sioux Indians after submitting to a grueling test of endurance. Intriguing if not entirely satisfying, with choppy continuity. Angie Dickinson reportedly dubbed Montiel's voice. Video title: HOT LEAD. RKO-Scope.▼

Run Silent Run Deep (1958) **93m.** *** D: Robert Wise. Clark Gable, Burt Lancaster, Jack Warden, Brad Dexter, Nick Cravat, Mary LaRoche, Don Rickles, Eddie Foy III. Battle of wills between officers Gable and Lancaster on WW2 submarine is basis for

interesting drama. Script by John Gay, from a novel by Commander Edward L. Beach. One of the great WW2 "sub" pictures.▼▶

Rustler's Valley (1937) **61m.** ** D: Nate Watt. William Boyd, George Hayes, Russell Hayden, Stephen Morris (Morris Ankrum), Muriel Evans, Lee Colt (Lee J. Cobb). Cobb is crooked frontier lawyer behind bank robbery and also after pretty Evans and her valuable ranch. Pleasing Hopalong Cassidy Western has a strong cast but trite situations and slow, uninspired direction; not up to the series' usual high standard. Adapted from 1923 same-named novel by series creator Clarence E. Mulford. Remade five years later as LOST CANYON.▼▶

Ruthless (1948) **104m.** *** D: Edgar G. Ulmer. Zachary Scott, Louis Hayward, Diana Lynn, Sydney Greenstreet, Lucille Bremer, Martha Vickers, Raymond Burr. Scott steps on everyone to become big shot in this engrossing drama. Greenstreet is especially good as Southern tycoon.▶

Saadia (1953) **C-82m.** *½ D: Albert Lewin. Cornel Wilde, Mel Ferrer, Rita Gam, Cyril Cusack, Richard Johnson. Misfire; intellectual story of modernistic Moroccan ruler and doctor vying for love of superstitious native dancing girl. ▶

Sabaka (1953) **C-81m.** ** D: Frank Ferrin. Nino Marcel, Boris Karloff, Lou Krugman, Reginald Denny, Victor Jory, June Foray, Jay Novello, Lisa Howard, Peter Coe. By-the-numbers adventure with Marcel as Gunga Ram, a youthful hero who fights a cult of devil worshippers in India. GUNGA DIN it ain't. Aka THE HINDU. ▼▶

Sabotage (1936-British) **76m.** *** D: Alfred Hitchcock. Sylvia Sidney, Oscar Homolka, John Loder, Desmond Tester, Joyce Barbour. Elaborately detailed thriller about woman who suspects that her kindly husband (Homolka), a movie theater manager, is keeping something from her. Full of intriguing Hitchcock touches. Based on Joseph Conrad's *Secret Agent*, originally retitled A WOMAN ALONE for the U.S. ▼▶●

Sabotage Agent SEE: **Adventures of Tartu, The**

Saboteur (1942) **108m.** *** D: Alfred Hitchcock. Robert Cummings, Priscilla Lane, Norman Lloyd, Otto Kruger, Alan Baxter, Alma Kruger, Dorothy Peterson, Vaughan Glaser. Extremely offbeat wartime Hitchcock yarn about a munitions worker who's falsely accused of sabotage and forced to take it on the lam. Full of quirky touches, unusual supporting characters, and some outstanding set pieces, including famous Statue of Liberty finale . . . though actual story resolution is unfortunately abrupt. Screenplay by Peter Viertel, Joan Harrison, and Dorothy Parker.▼▶●

Saboteur, Code Name Morituri, The SEE: **Morituri**

Sabre Jet (1953) **C-96m.** **✶✶** D: Louis King. Robert Stack, Coleen Gray, Richard Arlen, Julie Bishop, Leon Ames, Amanda Blake, Reed Sherman, Kathleen Crowley, Jerry Paris. Routine Korean War story of fighter pilots heading off on their daily missions and the wives who await their return. Stack is one of the fliers; Gray is his estranged wife, who prefers a career as a reporter to that of a worrying spouse. Done in by too much extraneous footage of planes in flight.

Sabrina (1954) **113m.** **✶✶✶½** D: Billy Wilder. Humphrey Bogart, Audrey Hepburn, William Holden, John Williams, Francis X. Bushman, Martha Hyer, Nancy Kulp. Samuel Taylor's play *Sabrina Fair* is good vehicle for Hepburn as chauffeur's daughter romanced by aging tycoon Bogart to keep her from his playboy brother (Holden). Offbeat casting works in this fun film. Screenplay by Ernest Lehman, Billy Wilder, and Taylor. Remade in 1995. ▼○▶

Sabu and the Magic Ring (1957) **C-61m.** **✶½** D: George Blair. Sabu, Daria Massey, Vladimir Sokoloff, Robin Moore, William Marshall. Low-budget backlot Arabian Nights nonsense, with Sabu chasing thieves to regain stolen girl and priceless gem. Originally shot as two separate TV pilots.

Saddle and Spurs SEE: **Unexpected Guest**

Saddle Pals (1947) **72m.** **✶½** D: Lesley Selander. Gene Autry, Lynne Roberts, Sterling Holloway, Irving Bacon, Damian O'Flynn, Charles Arnt, Jean Van, Tom London, The Cass County Boys. Land corporation bad guys raise rents and try to drive people off their properties; Gene comes to the aid of Roberts and her sister. One of Gene's weakest films, with far too much time devoted to miscast sidekick Holloway, though there are two really good songs, "Amapola" and "You Stole My Heart." Remake of the Weaver Brothers and Elviry vehicle IN OLD MISSOURI (1940). ▶

Saddle the Wind (1958) **C-84m.** **✶✶✶** D: Robert Parrish. Robert Taylor, Julie London, John Cassavetes, Donald Crisp, Charles McGraw, Royal Dano. Well-acted Western of turned-good rancher (Taylor) fated to shoot it out with brother (Cassavetes). If you've ever wondered what a Western written by Rod Serling would be like, here's your chance. CinemaScope.▶

Saddle Tramp (1950) **C-77m.** **✶✶½** D: Hugo Fregonese. Joel McCrea, Wanda Hendrix, John Russell, John McIntire, Jeanette Nolan, Russell Simpson, Ed Begley, Jimmy Hunt, Antonio Moreno. Homey Western with McCrea a free spirit who takes on the responsibility of looking after four young boys and finding himself in the middle of a cattle-rustling scheme and a war between rival ranchers.

Sad Horse, The (1959) **C-78m.** **✶✶** D: James B. Clark. David Ladd, Chill Wills,

Rex Reason, Patrice Wymore. Tender, undemanding tale of a racehorse and a lonely boy (Ladd). CinemaScope.

Sadie McKee (1934) **92m.** **✶✶✶** D: Clarence Brown. Joan Crawford, Franchot Tone, Gene Raymond, Edward Arnold, Esther Ralston, Leo G. Carroll, Akim Tamiroff, Gene Austin. Solidly entertaining film follows serpentine story of working-girl Crawford and the three men in her life: smooth-talking Raymond, tipsy millionaire Arnold, earnest employer Tone. Beautifully paced, handsomely filmed. Song: "All I Do Is Dream of You," plus amusing rendition of "After You've Gone" by Austin, Candy Candido. ▼○▶

Sadie Thompson (1928) **97m.** **✶✶✶** D: Raoul Walsh. Gloria Swanson, Lionel Barrymore, Raoul Walsh, Blanche Frederici, Charles Lane, James Marcus. Fascinating, frequently high-powered version of W. Somerset Maugham's *Rain,* about a lusty, fun-loving prostitute who arrives in Pago Pago and tangles with stuffy, hypocritical reformer Barrymore while Marine Sgt. Walsh falls for her. Swanson, and especially Barrymore, are well cast. Unseen (except in archival showings) for many years, because the final reel decomposed years ago. Now the footage (about 8m.) has been re-created, using stills and the original title cards. Remade as RAIN, DIRTY GERTIE FROM HARLEM U.S.A., and MISS SADIE THOMPSON. ▼○▶

Sadist, The (1963) **91m.** **✶✶½** D: James Landis. Arch Hall, Jr., Helen Hovey, Richard Alden, Marilyn Manning. Taut little B picture about a psychotic punk who terrorizes three innocent people at a roadside gas station. Hall is distressingly believable as the psycho. Imaginatively shot by Vilmos (billed as William) Zsigmond. Retitled PROFILE OF TERROR. ▼▶

Sad Sack, The (1957) **98m.** **✶✶** D: George Marshall. Jerry Lewis, Phyllis Kirk, David Wayne, Peter Lorre, Gene Evans, Mary Treen. Disjointed comedy vaguely based on George Baker comic strip of Army misfit. Lorre appears as Arab in last part of film. VistaVision▼

Safari (1940) **80m.** **✶✶✶** D: Edward H. Griffith. Douglas Fairbanks, Jr., Madeleine Carroll, Tullio Carminati, Lynne Overman, Muriel Angelus, Billy Gilbert. Wealthy, spoiled prig Carminati and his fiancée Carroll hire Fairbanks as their guide for a hunting trip and sparks fly. Very enjoyable hokum with a dazzlingly beautiful couple in the leading roles, and pretty good use of stock footage for action scenes. "African" locale is clearly bogus, but what the heck....

Safari (1956-British) **C-91m.** **✶✶½** D: Terence Young. Victor Mature, Janet Leigh, John Justin, Roland Culver, Liam Redmond. Fierce jungle drama has Mature leading expedition against Mau Maus. Cast gives good performances. CinemaScope. ▶

Safari Drums (1953) **71m.** *½ D: Ford Beebe. Johnny Sheffield, Douglas Kennedy, Barbara Bestar, Emory Parnell, Smoki Whitfield, Leonard Mudie. Bomba the Jungle Boy enlists his animal friends to capture a murderous guide. Ultra low-budget stereotyped adventure. ▶

Safe at Home! (1962) **83m.** **½ D: Walter Doniger. Mickey Mantle, Roger Maris, William Frawley, Patricia Barry, Don Collier, Bryan Russell. Kid is pressured into lying to Little League pals about friendship with M&M. The stoic poetry of Jack Webb's acting pales beside that of Maris' in this kiddie time-capsule; leads, cameos by Whitey Ford and Ralph Houk make it a must for Yankee fans ... if no one else. ▼▶

Safecracker, The (1958-British) **96m.** ** D: Ray Milland. Ray Milland, Barry Jones, Jeannette Sterke, Ernest Clark, Melissa Stribling, Victor Maddern. Contrived story of burglar who almost goes straight, later forced to use his talents for war effort.

Safe in Hell (1931) **73m.** **½ D: William A. Wellman. Dorothy Mackaill, Donald Cook, Ralf Harolde, John Wray, Ivan Simpson, Victor Varconi, Nina Mae McKinney, Charles Middleton, Clarence Muse, Gustav von Seyffertitz. Remarkably frank and adult pre-Code drama about prostitute Mackaill, who believes she's killed one of her johns and flees to the remote island of Tortuga where she can't be extradited. Unfortunately, the island is populated by every form of slobbering lech and pervert imaginable. Extremely seamy tale pulls no punches, right up to its shocking conclusion ... but in some ways it's more astonishing than entertaining. ▶

Safety Last! (1923) **78m.** *** D: Fred Newmeyer, Sam Taylor. Harold Lloyd, Mildred Davis, Bill Strothers, Noah Young. Crackerjack silent comedy about go-getter Harold determined to make good in the big city includes his justly famous building-climbing sequence—still hair-raising after all these years. ▼▶

Saga of Anatahan, The SEE: **Anatahan**

Saga of Death Valley (1939) **55m.** *** D: Joseph Kane. Roy Rogers, George "Gabby" Hayes, Donald Barry, Doris Day, Frank M. Thomas, Jack Ingram, Hal Taliaferro. Roy vows vengeance on the outlaw gang that killed his father and abducted his brother years ago, unaware that his grown-up sibling (Barry) is now a member of that very gang (run by Thomas). One of Roy's best early vehicles, with a strong story and a star-making role for Barry. Music is supplied by a group including Johnny Bond, Frankie Marvin, and Jimmy Wakely. Leading lady Day is no relation to the later singing star. ▼▶

Saga of Gosta Berling, The SEE: **Atonement of Gosta Berling, The**

Saga of Hemp Brown, The (1958) **C-80m.** ** D: Richard Carlson. Rory Calhoun, Beverly Garland, John Larch, Russell Johnson.

Calhoun is bounced from Army, and seeks to find real crooks in just another Western. CinemaScope.

Sagebrush Trail (1933) **55m.** **½ D: Armand Schaefer. John Wayne, Nancy Shubert, Lane Chandler, Wally Wales (Hal Taliaferro), Yakima Canutt. Wrongly convicted of murder, Wayne infiltrates gang of outlaws to nab the real killer in this second of his Lone Star Western series. Has some nice touches, like an underwater sequence, but also some rough edges. Many scenes shot at the famous cave in Bronson Canyon only minutes above hectic Hollywood and Vine. Canutt doubles Duke in eye-popping stunts. Also available in computer-colored form as AN INNOCENT MAN. ▼▶

Sagebrush Troubador (1935) **58m.** ** D: Joseph Kane. Gene Autry, Barbara Pepper, Smiley Burnette, Fred Kelsey, Frank Glendon, Hooper Atchley, Julian Rivero. Gene gets involved in a murder mystery and protects Pepper from opportunistic relatives and friends who are after her gold mine. Standard B Western, notable only for Autry's first screen kiss (with Pepper). ▶

Saginaw Trail (1953) **57m.** ** D: George Archainbaud. Gene Autry, Smiley Burnette, Connie Marshall, Eugene Borden, Ralph Reed, Myron Healey, Gregg Barton. Offbeat Autry Western set in the Great Lakes area of 1827 as ranger captain Gene is called upon to stop Indian raiding parties who are driving away settlers. Unusual to see Gene in a period costume finishing off villain Borden in a sword fight. ▶

Sahara (1943) **97m.** ***½ D: Zoltan Korda. Humphrey Bogart, Bruce Bennett, J. Carrol Naish, Lloyd Bridges, Rex Ingram, Richard Nugent, Dan Duryea, Kurt Kreuger. Excellent actioner of British-American unit stranded in Sahara desert in the path of Nazi infantry; Bogie's the sergeant, with fine support by Naish and Ingram. Based on the 1937 Russian film THE THIRTEEN (and reminiscent of THE LOST PATROL); also made as NINE MEN and LAST OF THE COMANCHES; imitated many other times. Remade for cable-TV in 1995 with James Belushi. ▼◑

Saigon (1948) **94m.** ** D: Leslie Fenton. Alan Ladd, Veronica Lake, Luther Adler, Douglas Dick, Wally Cassell, Morris Carnovsky. Glossy Paramount caper about airmen stationed in Vietnam involved in robbery; only fair.

Sail a Crooked Ship (1962) **88m.** **½ D: Irving S. Brecher. Robert Wagner, Ernie Kovacs, Dolores Hart, Carolyn Jones, Frankie Avalon, Frank Gorshin, Harvey Lembeck. Bungled crime-caper comedy has hilarious moments, but not enough to make it a winner. Based on a Nathaniel Benchley novel. ▼▶

Sailing Along (1938-British) **80m.** **½ D: Sonnie Hale. Jessie Matthews, Barry MacKay, Jack Whiting, Roland Young, Alastair Sim, Athene Seyler, Noel Madison. Elfin

Matthews sparkles in a breezy but slight musical about a barge girl and her dream of becoming a big name in the theater. The dream comes true, but what to do about that chap waiting in the wings for her? Directed and cowritten by Matthews' real-life husband. ▼▶

Sail Into Danger (1957-Spanish-British) 72m. *½ D: Kenneth Hume. Dennis O'Keefe, Kathleen Ryan, James Hayter, Pedro de Cordoba, John Bull, Félix de Pommés. O'Keefe is blackmailed into assisting smuggler Ryan and her cronies in this limp action yarn.

Sailor Beware (1951) 108m. *** D: Hal Walker. Dean Martin, Jerry Lewis, Corinne Calvet, Marion Marshall, Robert Strauss, Vince Edwards; guest, Betty Hutton. Hilarious adventures of Martin & Lewis in the Navy. Induction scenes, boxing sequence are highlights in one of the team's funniest outings. James Dean can be glimpsed in the boxing scene. Remake of THE FLEET'S IN.▶

Sailor Beware! (1956) SEE: **Panic in the Parlor**

Sailor-Made Man, A (1921) 47m. **½ D: Fred Newmeyer. Harold Lloyd, Mildred Davis, Noah Young, Dick Sutherland. Harold plays a wealthy ne'er-do-well who must prove himself before his girlfriend's father will consent to their marriage. He joins the Navy and winds up in a Middle Eastern kingdom, where he has a series of gag-filled adventures. Lloyd's first official feature film (albeit one) is funny, but just a warm-up for better things to come.▶

Sailor of the King (1953-U.S.-British) 83m. *** D: Roy Boulting. Jeffrey Hunter, Michael Rennie, Wendy Hiller, Bernard Lee, Peter Van Eyck. Solid WW2 naval action story, based on C. S. Forester novel *Brown on Resolution*, with Hunter rising to challenge when opportunity arises to attack German raider. British title: SINGLE HANDED. Filmed before in 1935.▶

Sailor's Luck (1933) 79m. *** D: Raoul Walsh. James Dunn, Sally Eilers, Sammy Cohen, Frank Moran, Victor Jory, Esther Muir. Sailor Dunn woos feisty Eilers while on shore leave and has rowdy misadventures with two buddies. Boisterous pre-Code romp features an outrageously blatant gay character and a wild dance marathon climax. Jory is a hoot as Baron Portola.

Sailor Takes a Wife, The (1945) 91m. ** D: Richard Whorf. Robert Walker, June Allyson, Hume Cronyn, Audrey Totter, Eddie "Rochester" Anderson, Reginald Owen. Mild little comedy is summed up by title.

The Saint Leslie Charteris' literate, debonair detective has been the subject of an extremely popular British television show, but he never quite made it in the movies. From 1938 to 1942, RKO tried no less than three actors in the leading role. Louis Hayward seemed at home in THE SAINT IN NEW YORK, a smooth underworld saga with a bland leading lady (Kay Sutton) and a fine supporting cast (Sig Rumann as a ganglord, Jack Carson as a thug, etc.). Nevertheless, he didn't repeat the role; it went instead to suave George Sanders, who portrayed The Saint in five quickly made, entertaining mysteries, three of them with Wendy Barrie as leading lady, taking him from Palm Springs to London. The scripts were competent, but it was Sanders' usual offhand manner that kept them alive. In 1941 stage star Hugh Sinclair took a fling in THE SAINT'S VACATION but gave up after a second effort. Sanders left the series only to begin another, The Falcon, at the same studio, although without the main titles to inform viewers which series it was, one could hardly have told the difference. The Falcon continued through the 1940s, while the Saint came to a premature end in 1942. There was one revival attempt with Louis Hayward made in England in 1954, THE SAINT'S GIRL FRIDAY, which was no improvement over the original series. It took British television and Roger Moore to give real life to The Saint at last in the 1960s. Then, in 1997, Val Kilmer assumed the role on the big screen.

THE SAINT

Sainted Sisters, The (1948) 89m. **½ D: William Russell. Veronica Lake, Joan Caulfield, Barry Fitzgerald, William Demarest, George Reeves, Beulah Bondi. Fitzgerald's blarney is a bit overdone in this tale of two bad girls who go straight under his guidance.

Saint in London, The (1939) 72m. **½ D: John Paddy Carstairs. George Sanders, David Burns, Sally Gray, Henry Oscar, Ralph Truman. The Saint travels to England in pursuit of a counterfeiting gang and gets unwanted help from a scatterbrained socialite. Shot on location. ▼▶

Saint in New York, The (1938) 71m. *** D: Ben Holmes. Louis Hayward, Kay Sutton, Sig Rumann, Jonathan Hale, Frederick Burton, Jack Carson. First in the series and one of the best, with Hayward the smooth Robin Hood–like avenger hired to bump off six of the Big Apple's most rotten criminals. Extremely faithful adaptation of Leslie Charteris' novel; originally intended as American directorial debut of Alfred Hitchcock. ▼

[592]

Saint in Palm Springs, The (1941) **65m.**
**½ D: Jack Hively. George Sanders,
Wendy Barrie, Jonathan Hale, Paul Guilfoyle, Linda Hayes, Ferris Taylor. Murder
follows the Saint as he journeys West to deliver $200,000 worth of rare stamps to an
heir. Sanders' last appearance in the series,
which was coasting by this point.▼▶
Saint Joan (1957) **110m. **** D: Otto Preminger. Jean Seberg, Richard Widmark,
Richard Todd, Anton Walbrook, John Gielgud, Felix Aylmer, Harry Andrews, Barry
Jones, Finlay Currie, Bernard Miles, Margot
Grahame. Big-scale filming of Shaw's play
sounded large thud when released; some good
acting, but Seberg (who won her first film
role after a nationwide search), not suited to
film's tempo, throws production askew. Script
by Graham Greene. On-screen title is BER-
NARD SHAW'S SAINT JOAN. Also shown
in computer-colored version.▼▶
Saint Meets the Tiger, The (1943-British)
70m. ** D: Paul Stein. Hugh Sinclair, Jean
Gillie, Clifford Evans, Wylie Watson, Dennis Arundell. The Saint matches wits with
the gangster Tiger over a bogus gold mine
scheme in this minor entry. Loosely based
on Leslie Charteris' first *Saint* story.▼▶
Saint's Double Trouble, The (1940) **68m.**
**½ D: Jack Hively. George Sanders, Helene Whitney, Jonathan Hale, Bela Lugosi,
Donald MacBride, John F. Hamilton.
The Saint is on the trail of his lookalike, a
jewel thief who's smuggled diamonds in a
mummy from Cairo to Philadelphia. Passable entry with Sanders in a dual role. Lugosi is wasted as a dull-witted hood.▼▶
Saint's Girl Friday, The (1954-British)
68m. ** D: Seymour Friedman. Louis
Hayward, Naomi Chance, Sidney Tafler,
Charles Victor. Hayward, who played the
first Saint in 1938, returns in the last film
based on the debonair sleuth, tracking down
a gambling syndicate responsible for the
death of an ex-girlfriend. Original British
title: THE SAINT'S RETURN.
Saint Strikes Back, The (1939) **67m. *****
D: John Farrow. George Sanders, Wendy
Barrie, Jonathan Hale, Jerome Cowan,
Neil Hamilton, Barry Fitzgerald, Edward
Gargan. Sanders takes over the role of the
debonair Saint, adding his jaded persona to
the character as he helps the daughter of a
disgraced San Francisco policeman catch
the men who framed him. Superior B mystery, tightly directed. First in the series to
use Roy Webb's theme music, which was
later carried over to the Roger Moore TV
series.▼▶
Saint's Vacation, The (1941) **60m. **½**
D: Leslie Fenton. Hugh Sinclair, Sally
Gray, Arthur Macrae, Cecil Parker, Leueen
McGrath, Gordon McLeod. Sinclair picks
up the role of The Saint in this decent mystery (cowritten by Leslie Charteris himself)
about the search for a music box in Swit-

zerland containing secret codes coveted by
Axis spies. Made in England.▼▶
Saint Takes Over, The (1940) **69m. **½**
D: Jack Hively. George Sanders, Jonathan
Hale, Wendy Barrie, Paul Guilfoyle, Morgan Conway, Robert Emmett Keane. Fast-
moving entry has The Saint coming to the
aid of Inspector Fernack (Hale), who's being framed on bribery charges by racetrack
gambling racketeers.▼▶
Sallah (1965-Israeli) **C-105m. ***** D:
Ephraim Kishon. Haym Topol, Geula Noni,
Gila Almagor, Arik Einstein, Shraga Friedman, Esther Greenberg. Topol is amusing
as an Oriental Jew who emigrates to Israel
with his wife and seven children and is forever scheming to improve his lot. A modest,
lighthearted, thoroughly enjoyable satire.
▼
Sally (1929) **C/B&W-102m. **½** D: John
Francis Dillon. Marilyn Miller, Alexander Gray, Joe E. Brown, T. Roy Barnes,
Pert Kelton, Ford Sterling, Maude Turner
Gordon. Waitress who dreams of a dancing career catches the eye of a Long Island
playboy who's engaged to be married, to
someone he doesn't love. Genial if stagebound early talkie (with two-color Technicolor scenes) is a good showcase for
Ziegfeld dancing star Miller, and offers
an idea of what a Broadway musical must
have looked like in the 1920s. Based on the
play by Guy Bolton, Jerome Kern, Clifford
Gray, and P. G. Wodehouse; highlight of
the score is "Look for the Silver Lining."
Filmed before in 1925. ▶
Sally and Saint Anne (1952) **90m. **** D:
Rudolph Maté. Ann Blyth, Edmund Gwenn,
John McIntire, Palmer Lee (Gregg Palmer),
Hugh O'Brian, Jack Kelly, Frances Bavier,
King Donovan. Predictable, overly senti-
mental comedy about a blarney-filled Irish
clan, their feud with an ornery alderman,
and daughter Blyth's unwavering faith in
the title saint.
Sally, Irene and Mary (1938) **72m. **½** D:
William A. Seiter. Alice Faye, Tony Martin,
Fred Allen, Joan Davis, Marjorie Weaver,
Gregory Ratoff, Jimmy Durante, Louise
Hovick (Gypsy Rose Lee). Predictable
story of stage-struck girls trying to break
into show business, with good comedy
spots by Davis, pleasant songs from Faye
and Martin: "I Could Use a Dream," "This
Is Where I Came In." ▶
Sally of the Sawdust (1925) **91m. **½** D:
D. W. Griffith. W. C. Fields, Carol Dempster,
Alfred Lunt, Erville Alderson, Effie Shannon.
Pleasant yarn of sideshow con-man Fields
who tries to restore his ward (Dempster) to her
rightful place in society, knowing identity of
her wealthy grandparents. Interesting to see
W. C. in a silent film, particularly since one can
compare this to its remake, POPPY.▼▶
Sally's Irish Rogue SEE: **Poacher's
Daughter, The**

Salome (1953) **C-103m.** **½ D: William Dieterle. Rita Hayworth, Stewart Granger, Charles Laughton, Judith Anderson, Cedric Hardwicke, Maurice Schwartz. Great cast struggles with unintentionally funny script in biblical drama of illustrious dancer who offers herself to spare John the Baptist. Filmed before with Nazimova in 1923.▼❚

Salome, Where She Danced (1945) **C-90m.** BOMB D: Charles Lamont. Yvonne De Carlo, Rod Cameron, David Bruce, Walter Slezak, Albert Dekker, Marjorie Rambeau, J. Edward Bromberg. Ludicrous film provides some laughs while trying to spin tale of exotic dancer becoming Mata Hari–type spy. Nevertheless, this boosted De Carlo to stardom.▼❚

Salomy Jane (1914) **87m.** **½ D: Lucius Henderson, William Nigh. Beatriz Michelena, House Peters, Matt Snyder, William Nigh, Ernest Joy, Jack Holt. Early silent feature about Salomy Jane Clay (Michelena) and her father and their arrival in Hangtown, a 19th-century gold rush settlement. Based on a story by Bret Harte and play by Paul Armstrong, this primitive Western melodrama is of interest mostly as a curio. Remade in 1923 and (as WILD GIRL) in 1932. ❚

Salt of the Earth (1953) **94m.** ***½ D: Herbert Biberman. Juan Chacon, Rosaura Revueltas, Will Geer, Mervin Williams, Frank Talavera, Clinton Jencks, Virginia Jencks. Earnest film about Latino mine workers in New Mexico who go on strike—in spite of the tremendous hardships it causes. This film is particularly impressive considering its history—made under difficult conditions (and on a shoestring), with many nonprofessional actors, by blacklisted filmmakers. Produced by Paul Jarrico and written by Michael Wilson, two of Hollywood's more prominent blacklistees.▼❶❚

Salty O'Rourke (1945) **99m.** *** D: Raoul Walsh. Alan Ladd, Gail Russell, William Demarest, Stanley Clements, Bruce Cabot, Spring Byington. Lively tale of smooth con man Ladd aiming to clean up with jockey Clements, who turns out to be a large headache. Schoolteacher Russell steps in to foil Ladd's plans.

Saludos Amigos (1943) **C-43m.** *** D: Norman Ferguson, Bill Roberts, Jack Kinney, Hamilton Luske, Wilfred Jackson. Voices of Clarence Nash, Pinto Colvig, José Oliviera, Frank Graham. Vividly colored propaganda for the Pan American Union. The four segments (Donald Duck in "Lake Titicaca," the baby mail plane "Pedro," luscious "Aquarela do Brasil," and self-explanatory "El Gaucho Goofy") range from truly funny to strikingly artistic, melding live action with animation. Songs include "Brazil" and "Tico Tico." Trim but tasty salute to South America was followed two years later by THE THREE CABALLEROS. ▼❚

Salute (1929) **84m.** *½ D: John Ford. George O'Brien, Helen Chandler, William Janney, Stepin Fetchit, Frank Albertson, Joyce Compton, David Butler, Lumsden Hare, Ward Bond, Lee Tracy, John Wayne. Lumbering early talkie with Janney a new midshipman at Annapolis; his older brother (O'Brien) is a West Point cadet, and the two predictably quarrel. Fun to watch for film buffs, but fairly clunky, though location filming at Annapolis is a major asset. Young Wayne is prominently featured as a midshipman and even has some dialogue.

Salute to the Marines (1943) **C-101m.** **½ D: S. Sylvan Simon. Wallace Beery, Fay Bainter, Reginald Owen, Keye Luke, Ray Collins, Marilyn Maxwell, William Lundigan, Donald Curtis, Noah Beery, Sr., Rose Hobart, Bobby (Robert) Blake. OK WW2 propaganda with Beery in his element as a crusty Marine who reluctantly retires, then finds himself caught in a surprise attack on the Philippines. Some of Beery's adjectives for the Japanese must be heard to be believed. ❚

Salvatore Giuliano (1962-Italian) **125m.** ***½ D: Francesco Rosi. Frank Wolff, Salvo Randone, Federico Zardi, Pietro Cammarata, Fernando Cicero. Vivid, documentary-like drama, told in flashback, depicts the career of an infamous post-WW2 Sicilian criminal who rose through the ranks of organized crime, becoming a Mafia chieftain. This fact-based tale intricately weaves a story of political and governmental bureaucracy; it resulted in a real-life investigation of Mafia activities in Italy. Remade as THE SICILIAN.❚

Samar (1962) **C-89m.** ** D: George Montgomery. George Montgomery, Gilbert Roland, Ziva Rodann, Joan O'Brien, Nico Minardos, Mario Barri. Ordinary actioner has Roland as head of prison compound on a Philippine island who rejects inhumane treatment of prisoners and leads them on escape route.▼❚

Sammy Going South SEE: **Boy Ten Feet Tall, A**

Sammy the Way Out Seal (1962) **C-90m.** **½ D: Norman Tokar. Robert Culp, Jack Carson, Billy Mumy, Patricia Barry. Pretty funny sitcom for the kids about a seal who becomes Mumy's pet and wreaks havoc upon Culp and family. Shown as a feature in Europe, originally made as a two-part Disney TV show. ❚

Samson and Delilah (1949) **C-128m.** *** D: Cecil B. DeMille. Victor Mature, Hedy Lamarr, George Sanders, Angela Lansbury, Henry Wilcoxon, Olive Deering, Fay Holden, Russell (Russ) Tamblyn, George Reeves, Tom Tyler, Fritz Leiber, Mike Mazurki. With expected DeMille touches, this remains a tremendously entertaining film. Mature is surprisingly good as Samson, though his famous fight with lion is hopelessly phony; also difficult to swallow idea of Lansbury being Lamarr's *older* sister. Sanders supplies biggest surprise by underplaying his role as the Saran. This won Oscars for its Art Direction-Set Decoration and Costumes. Remade for TV in 1984 (with Mature as Samson's father) and 1996.▼●)

San Antone (1953) **90m.** ****½** D: Joseph Kane. Rod Cameron, Arleen Whelan, Forrest Tucker, Katy Jurado, Rodolfo Acosta, Bob Steele, Harry Carey, Jr. Offbeat Western tends to ramble, but story of Cameron and friends being victimized by despicable Tucker and bitchy Southern belle Whelan is intriguing.

San Antonio (1945) **C-111m.** ******* D: David Butler. Errol Flynn, Alexis Smith, S. Z. Sakall, Victor Francen, Florence Bates, John Litel, Paul Kelly. Elaborate Western has predictable plot but good production values as good guy Flynn tangles with cunning villains Francen and Kelly while romancing singer Smith. Screenplay by *The Searchers* novelist Alan LeMay and W. R. Burnett.▼)

San Antonio Rose (1941) **63m.** ****½** D: Charles Lamont. Robert Paige, Jane Frazee, Eve Arden, Lon Chaney, Jr., Shemp Howard, The Merry Macs, Richard Lane, Luis Alberni, Louis DaPron, Vernon Dent. Zippy Universal B musical about a group of entertainers who take over an abandoned roadhouse, unaware that a gangster competitor wants the property himself. Paige, Frazee, and the Macs handle the music (including "The Hut-Sut Song" and the title tune); Arden, Chaney, and Howard supply the laughs—the latter two as a faux Abbott and Costello. Packs more fun into an hour than most movies do in two.

Sanctuary (1961) **100m.** ****** D: Tony Richardson. Lee Remick, Yves Montand, Bradford Dillman, Harry Townes, Odetta, Howard St. John, Jean Carson, Reta Shaw, Strother Martin. Flat melodrama about a Southern governor's daughter (Remick) and her plight after she's raped by bootlegger Montand. Awkward adaptation (by James Poe) of William Faulkner's novels *Sanctuary* (previously filmed as THE STORY OF TEMPLE DRAKE) and *Requiem for a Nun*, and Ruth Ford's stage adaptation of the latter. CinemaScope.

Sand (1949) **C-78m.** ****** D: Louis King. Mark Stevens, Rory Calhoun, Coleen Gray, Charley Grapewin. Visually picturesque but dull account of show horse who turns wild. Retitled: WILL JAMES' SAND.

Sanders (1963-British) **C-83m.** ****** D: Lawrence Huntington. Richard Todd, Marianne Koch, Albert Lieven, Vivi Bach, Jeremy Lloyd. Loose adaptation of Edgar Wallace novel *Sanders of the River* follows police inspector's investigation of murder in an African hospital and discovery of hidden silver mine. Original British title DEATH DRUMS ALONG THE RIVER. Todd repeated role of Harry Sanders in 1964 COAST OF SKELETONS. Techniscope.

Sanders of the River (1935-British) **98m.** ******* D: Zoltan Korda. Paul Robeson, Leslie Banks, Nina Mae McKinney, Robert Cochran, Martin Walker. Dated adventure story (by Edgar Wallace) about river patrol officer maintains interest today, particularly for Robeson's strong presence and African location shooting. A fascinating relic of the sun-never-sets school of British imperialism. Sanders character revived in 1960s' SANDERS (DEATH DRUMS ALONG THE RIVER) and COAST OF SKELETONS.▼●)

San Diego, I Love You (1944) **83m.** ******* D: Reginald LeBorg. Jon Hall, Louise Allbritton, Edward Everett Horton, Eric Blore, Buster Keaton, Irene Ryan. Whimsical comedy of unconventional family trying to promote father Horton's inventions in San Diego. Allbritton is perky, Keaton memorable in delightful sequence as bored bus driver.

Sandpiper, The (1965) **C-116m.** ****½** D: Vincente Minnelli. Elizabeth Taylor, Richard Burton, Eva Marie Saint, Charles Bronson, Robert Webber, Torin Thatcher, Morgan Mason, Tom Drake. Ordinary triangle love affair. Beatnik Taylor in love with Burton, who is married to Saint. Nothing new, but beautiful California Big Sur settings help; so does Oscar-winning theme, "The Shadow of Your Smile." Written by Dalton Trumbo and Michael Wilson. Panavision.▼)

Sandra (1965-Italian) **105m.** ****½** D: Luchino Visconti. Claudia Cardinale, Jean Sorel, Michael Craig, Marie Bell, Renzo Ricci, Amalia Troiani. A small-town Italian beauty returns home with her American husband to attend a ceremony in memory of her Jewish father, who died in a concentration camp, setting off a series of emotional entanglements with her unfaithful mother and incestuous brother. Well acted but awfully soapy and melodramatic for Visconti.

Sands of Iwo Jima (1949) **110m.** ******* D: Allan Dwan. John Wayne, John Agar, Adele Mara, Forrest Tucker, Arthur Franz, Julie Bishop, Richard Jaeckel, Wally Cassell, Richard Webb. Enormously popular WW2 saga, with Wayne in one of his best roles as a tough Marine top-sergeant. Story and characters are pretty two-dimensional, and a bit worn from having been copied so many times since, but it's still good entertainment; use of authentic combat footage is striking. Wayne's first Oscar-nominated performance. The three surviving Marine vets who raised the American flag on Mt. Suribachi have small parts. Also shown in computer-colored version.▼●)

Sands of the Kalahari (1965-British) **C-119m. *** D: Cy Endfield. Stuart Whitman, Stanley Baker, Susannah York, Harry Andrews, Theodore Bikel, Nigel Davenport. Well-done story of plane crash survivors struggling through desert and battling simian inhabitants (and each other). Panavision. ▶

San Fernando Valley (1944) **74m. **½** D: John English. Roy Rogers, Dale Evans, Jean Porter, Andrew Tombes, Charles Smith, Edward Gargan, LeRoy Mason, Bob Nolan and the Sons of the Pioneers. Prideful ranch owner Evans brings in women to replace the ranch hands she fired, which leads to various complications. Some fans prefer more plot and action to production numbers with chorus girls, but this is still an enjoyable outing. Roy and Dale sing Gordon Jenkins' title tune. ▼▶

San Francisco (1936) **115m. ***½** D: W. S. Van Dyke II. Clark Gable, Jeanette MacDonald, Spencer Tracy, Jack Holt, Jessie Ralph, Ted Healy, Shirley Ross, Al Shean. Top-grade entertainment with extremely lavish production. Jeanette overdoes it a bit as the belle of San Francisco, but the music, Tracy's performance, and earthquake climax are still fine. Originally had footage of Golden Gate Bridge under construction; other rhythmically edited shots of S.F. were changed for later reissue. Script by Anita Loos. Also shown in computer-colored version. ▼▶

San Francisco Story, The (1952) **80m. ** D: Robert Parrish. Joel McCrea, Yvonne De Carlo, Sidney Blackmer, Richard Erdman, Florence Bates, Onslow Stevens. Tame Western actioner set in gold-rush days, with cleanup of city's criminal elements. ▶

Sangaree (1953) **C-94m. ** D: Edward Ludwig. Fernando Lamas, Arlene Dahl, Patricia Medina, Francis L. Sullivan, Charles Korvin, Tom Drake, Willard Parker. Lovers of 1950s kitsch will savor this corny, overheated period soaper in which honorable doctor Lamas, the son of a servant, comes to manage a colonel's estate amid much controversy. Lamas utters the word "fabulous," but not "marvelous." Based on a Frank G. Slaughter novel. Filmed in 3-D.

Sanjuro (1962-Japanese) **96m. *** D: Akira Kurosawa. Toshiro Mifune, Tatsuya Nakadai, Takashi Shimura, Yuzo Kayama, Reiko Dan. Sequel to YOJIMBO has shabby, wandering samurai Mifune aiding nine bumbling younger warriors in exposing corruption among the elders of their clan. Satirical comic-book actioner features a typically deadpan Mifune performance. Tohoscope. ▼▶

San Quentin (1937) **70m. **½** D: Lloyd Bacon. Pat O'Brien, Humphrey Bogart, Ann Sheridan, Veda Ann Borg, Barton MacLane. Warner Bros. formula prison film; convict Bogart's sister (Sheridan) loves O'Brien, who's captain of the guards. MacLane is memorable as tough prison guard. ▶

San Quentin (1946) **66m. **½** D: Gordon Douglas. Lawrence Tierney, Barton MacLane, Marian Carr, Harry Shannon, Carol Forman, Richard Powers (Tom Keene). Ex-con Tierney, organizer of a prison program which straightens out hardened criminals, goes into action when bad-boy MacLane abuses the system. Solid, if somewhat preachy, prison reform–oriented B film, introduced by Warden Lewis F. Lawes (20,000 YEARS IN SING SING).

Sanshiro Sugata (1943-Japanese) **79m. *** D: Akira Kurosawa. Susumu Fujita, Denjirô Ôkôchi, Yukiko Todoroki, Ryûnosuke Tsukigata, Takashi Shimura. Kurosawa's directorial debut is a lyrical, exciting coming-of-age tale centering on the education of a 19th-century student who becomes a master in the new fighting style of Judo. Originally released at 97m., cut to present length in 1944 due to Japanese government's wartime policies. Remade several times; Kurosawa directed a sequel released in 1945. ▶

Sansho the Bailiff (1954-Japanese) **125m. ****** D: Kenji Mizoguchi. Kinuyo Tanaka, Kisho Hanayagi, Kyoko Kagawa, Eitaro Shindo, Ichiro Sugai. Epic, poetic drama of 11th-century Japan, focusing on the tribulations of a family. Kindly father, a provincial governor, is exiled; children (Hanayagi, Kagawa) become slaves; mother (Tanaka) is sold as a prostitute. Haunting, with stunning direction and cinematography (by Kazuo Miyagawa). Original running-time: 130m. Aka THE BAILIFF. ▼▶

Santa Claus Conquers the Martians (1964) **C-80m. BOMB** D: Nicholas Webster. John Call, Leonard Hicks, Vincent Beck, Donna Conforti. Absurd low-budget fantasy (with a Milton Delugg score!) about Santa and two Earth children being abducted to Mars to help solve some of their domestic problems—like kids watching too much TV. One of the Martian tykes is Pia Zadora! Aka SANTA CLAUS DEFEATS THE ALIENS. ▼▶

Santa Fe (1951) **C-89m. ** D: Irving Pichel. Randolph Scott, Janis Carter, Jerome Courtland, Peter Thompson, John Archer, Warner Anderson, Roy Roberts, Jock Mahoney. Routine account of brothers in post–Civil War days, on opposite sides of the law. ▼▶

Santa Fe Marshal (1940) **66m. ** D: Lesley Selander. William Boyd, Russell Hayden, Marjorie Rambeau, Bernadene Hayes, Earle Hodgins, Britt Wood. Standard Hoppy Western emphasizes comedy and romance at expense of action and provides another excuse for Boyd to discard his trademark black garb for dude duds. Hodgins is a standout as fast-talking snake-oil con artist; there's also a wonderful jibe at singing cowboys: "This is one cowboy who never played a guitar, and never will." ▼▶

Santa Fe Passage (1955) **C-90m.** **
D: William Witney. John Payne, Faith
Domergue, Rod Cameron, Slim Pickens.
Routine wagon train westward; Indian attacks, love among the pioneers, etc.
Santa Fe Stampede (1938) **57m.** **½ D:
George Sherman. John Wayne, Ray Corrigan, Max Terhune, June Martel, William
Farnum, LeRoy Mason. Prospector pal of
fearless Three Mesquiteers strikes gold, but
when he's killed by claim jumpers, Wayne
is blamed. Swift story and direction adhere
to proven formula, highlighted by Mason as
ruthless and despicable villain. Title is completely meaningless. ▼●
Santa Fe Trail (1940) **110m.** ** D: Michael
Curtiz. Errol Flynn, Olivia de Havilland, Raymond Massey, Ronald Reagan, Alan Hale,
Guinn ("Big Boy") Williams, William Lundigan, Ward Bond, Van Heflin, Gene Reynolds,
John Litel, Charles Middleton. Lopsided picture can't make up its mind about anything:
what side it's taking, what it wants to focus on,
etc. Worthless as history, but amid the rubble
are some good action scenes as Jeb Stuart
(Flynn) and cohorts go after John Brown
(Massey). Reagan plays Flynn's West Point
classmate and romantic rival, George Armstrong Custer(!). Also shown in computer-
colored version. ▼●
Santiago (1956) **C-93m.** **½ D: Gordon
Douglas. Alan Ladd, Rossana Podesta,
Lloyd Nolan, Chill Wills, Paul Fix, L.Q.
Jones, Frank DeKova. Ladd and Nolan are
involved in gun-running to Cuba during fight
with Spain. Ladd becomes humane when he
encounters partisan Podesta. ▶
Saphead, The (1921) **78m.** **½ D: Herbert Blaché. Buster Keaton, William H.
Crane, Carol Holloway, Edward Connelly,
Irving Cummings, Beulah Booker. Buster
(in his feature-film debut) is shoehorned
into a pleasant but conventional plot about
a wealthy boob whose impending marriage
is imperiled when he's framed for a stock
swindle. Keaton is fine but not allowed to
express his unique comic personality. Based
on a Broadway play that was filmed once
before as THE LAMB (1915) with Douglas
Fairbanks. Villain Cummings later became
a top director at 20th Century-Fox. ▼●▶
Sapphire (1959-British) **C-92m.** *** D:
Basil Dearden. Nigel Patrick, Yvonne
Mitchell, Michael Craig, Paul Massie, Bernard Miles, Earl Cameron, Rupert Davies,
Yvonne Buckingham. When music student is
murdered, it is discovered she was passing as
white. Considered daring in its day, still absorbing today—both as entertainment and social comment. Fine performances. Story and
screenplay by Janet Green (with additional
dialogue by Lukas Heller). ▼▶
Saps At Sea (1940) **57m.** *** D: Gordon
Douglas. Stan Laurel, Oliver Hardy, James
Finlayson, Ben Turpin, Richard Cramer,
Harry Bernard. L&H comedy is short and

sweet: Ollie has breakdown working in
horn factory, tries to relax on a small boat
with Stan . . . and that's impossible. Cramer
is a memorable heavy. Harry Langdon was
one of the writers. ▼●
Saraband (1948-British) **C-95m.** ***
D: Basil Dearden. Stewart Granger, Joan
Greenwood, Flora Robson, Françoise Rosay,
Frederick Valk, Peter Bull, Anthony Quayle,
Michael Gough, Megs Jenkins, Christopher
Lee. Lavish, tearful romance with Greenwood
torn between royal responsibility and love for
young rogue. British title: SARABAND FOR
DEAD LOVERS. ▼
Saracen Blade, The (1954) **C-76m.** *½ D:
William Castle. Ricardo Montalban, Betta
St. John, Rick Jason, Carolyn Jones, Whit-
field Connor. Pretty bad 13th-century stuff,
with young man avenging death of father.
Unbelievable script traps cast.
Sarah and Son (1930) **76m.** ** D: Dorothy
Arzner. Ruth Chatterton, Fredric March,
Doris Lloyd, Philippe de Lacy. Chatterton,
obsessed with finding the son taken from her
years ago, enlists aid of lawyer March.
Saratoga (1937) **94m.** **½ D: Jack Con-
way. Clark Gable, Jean Harlow, Lionel Barrymore, Frank Morgan, Walter Pidgeon,
Una Merkel, Cliff Edwards, George
Zucco, Hattie MacDaniel, Margaret Hamilton. Harlow's last film—she died during
production—has stand-in Mary Dees doing
many scenes, but comes off pretty well, with
Jean as granddaughter of horse-breeder Bar-
rymore, Gable an influential bookie. ▼●
Saratoga Trunk (1945) **135m.** *½ D: Sam
Wood. Gary Cooper, Ingrid Bergman, Flora
Robson, Jerry Austin, John Warburton, Flor-
ence Bates. Elaborate but miscast, overlong
version of Edna Ferber's novel of New Or-
leans vixen Bergman and cowboy Cooper.
Unbearable at times. Made in 1943. ▼▶
Saskatchewan (1954) **C-87m.** **½ D:
Raoul Walsh. Alan Ladd, Shelley Winters,
J. Carrol Naish, Hugh O'Brian, Robert
Douglas, Richard Long, Jay Silverheels.
Cotton-candy Western about Ladd and fel-
low Canadian Mounties trying to prevent
Indian uprisings. ▼▶
Satan Bug, The (1965) **C-114m.** ***½ D:
John Sturges. George Maharis, Richard
Basehart, Anne Francis, Dana Andrews,
Edward Asner, Frank Sutton, John Larkin,
Henry Beckman. Overlooked little sus-
pense gem, loosely based on Alistair Mac-
Lean novel, detailing nerve-racking chase
after lunatic who's stolen flasks containing
horribly lethal virus from government lab.
Taut script (by Edward Anhalt and James
Clavell) and direction, stunning photography
by Robert Surtees. Panavision. ▼●▶
Satan Met a Lady (1936) **75m.** ** D: Wil-
liam Dieterle. Bette Davis, Warren Wil-
liam, Alison Skipworth, Arthur Treacher,
Winifred Shaw, Marie Wilson, Porter Hall.
Dashiell Hammett's *Maltese Falcon* in-

cognito; far below 1941 remake. William is private eye, Davis the mysterious client, Skipworth the strange woman searching for priceless artifact (here, a ram's horn). Filmed in 1931 and 1941 as THE MALTESE FALCON.▼▶

Satan Never Sleeps (1962) **C-126m.** ✶✶ D: Leo McCarey. William Holden, Clifton Webb, France Nuyen, Athene Seyler, Martin Benson, Edith Sharpe. Dreary goings-on of two priests holding fast when Communist China invades their territory. McCarey's last film. CinemaScope.▶

Satellite in the Sky (1956-British) **C-85m.** ✶✶½ D: Paul Dickson. Kieron Moore, Lois Maxwell, Donald Wolfit, Bryan Forbes, Jimmy Hanley. Spunky female reporter stows away aboard first British satellite rocket. Complications arise when bomb to be tested sticks to the side of the satellite and ticks away the moments to doom. Elaborate but unexciting. CinemaScope.▶

Saturday Night and Sunday Morning (1960-British) **90m.** ✶✶✶½ D: Karel Reisz. Albert Finney, Shirley Anne Field, Rachel Roberts, Norman Rossington. Grim yet refreshing look at angry young man, who in a burst of nonconformity alters the lives of girlfriends Field and Roberts. Superbly enacted. Script by Alan Sillitoe, from his novel. One of the first and best of Britain's "angry young men" dramas of the '60s.▼▶

Saturday Night Kid, The (1929) **62m.** ✶✶½ D: A. Edward Sutherland. Clara Bow, James Hall, Jean Arthur, Charles Sellon, Ethel Wales, Frank Ross, Edna May Oliver. Early-talkie remake of LOVE 'EM AND LEAVE 'EM (1926, which starred Evelyn Brent and Louise Brooks), with Bow giving a fairly restrained performance as a department store salesgirl in love with floorwalker Hall. In a strange bit of miscasting, Arthur plays her vampy sister, who's also sweet on Hall. Evocative of its era. Look for Jean Harlow in a bit part.

Saturday's Children (1940) **101m.** ✶✶½ D: Vincent Sherman. John Garfield, Anne Shirley, Claude Rains, Lee Patrick, George Tobias, Roscoe Karns, Dennie Moore, Elisabeth Risdon. N.Y.C.-based story of poor, hardworking Shirley, her dreamer-boyfriend Garfield, and what happens when they marry. Rains steals film as Shirley's sacrificing father. Based on Maxwell Anderson play previously filmed in 1929 and (as MAYBE IT'S LOVE) in 1935.▶

Saturday's Hero (1951) **111m.** ✶✶½ D: David Miller. John Derek, Donna Reed, Sidney Blackmer, Alexander Knox. Football player Derek wins a college scholarship, then discovers he isn't expected to spend much time in class. Pretty good attack on collegiate sports remains fairly timely; Reed is fine as love interest. Look quickly for Aldo Ray (in film debut).

Saturday's Heroes (1937) **60m.** ✶✶½ D:

Edward Killy. Van Heflin, Marian Marsh, Richard Lane, Alan Bruce, Minor Watson, Frank Jenks, Al St. John. Zippy little programmer about outspoken college football star's crusade against the hypocrites and bureaucrats who exploit amateur athletes. Biting indictment of the business of college football remains relevant today.

Saturday's Island SEE: **Island of Desire**

Savage, The (1952) **C-95m.** ✶✶½ D: George Marshall. Charlton Heston, Susan Morrow, Peter Hanson, Joan Taylor, Ted de Corsia. Heston is sincere and energetic as white man raised by the Indians and forced to choose sides when skirmishes break out.

Savage Drums (1951) **73m.** ✶✶ D: William Berke. Sabu, Lita Baron, H. B. Warner, Sid Melton, Steve Geray. U. S.-educated Sabu returns to the islands to put down local warfare; fair low-budgeter.▶

Savage Eye, The (1960) **68m.** ✶✶✶ D: Ben Maddow, Sidney Meyers, Joseph Strick. Barbara Baxley, Herschel Bernardi, Gary Merrill, Jean Hidey. Documentary-style drama of divorcee Baxley trying to start life anew in L.A.; contrived but intriguing.▼▶

Savage Guns, The (1962-U.S.-Spanish) **C-84m.** ✶✶½ D: Michael Carreras. Richard Basehart, Don Taylor, Alex Nicol, Paquita Rico, José Nieto, Fernando Rey, María Granada. Wounded gunslinger Basehart takes refuge at the ranch of newly married ex-Confederate officer Taylor, who has sworn off violence and settled down in Mexico. He stays to battle a ruthless land baron who hires killer Nicol to take over all the ranches in the area. Rare foray out West for Hammer Film vets Carreras and producer Jimmy Sangster has a standard SHANE-like story but is historically notable for being one of the earliest spaghetti Westerns (made two years before FISTFUL OF DOLLARS), and reputedly the first to be filmed in Almeria, Spain, where dozens of Euro-Westerns would be shot. Metroscope.

Savage Innocents, The (1960-Italian-French-British) **C-110m.** ✶✶½ D: Nicholas Ray. Anthony Quinn, Yoko Tani, Peter O'Toole, Marie Yang. Striking but uneven film about conflict of civilization vs. simple ways of Eskimo people. Quinn gives remarkable performance as native Eskimo; beautiful documentary-type location photography combined with studio work. O'Toole's voice is dubbed. Super Technirama 70.

Savage Mutiny (1953) **73m.** ✶½ D: Spencer Bennet. Johnny Weissmuller, Angela Stevens, Lester Matthews, Nelson Leigh, Paul Marion. Campy Cold War caper about *Jungle Jim* Weissmuller battling enemy agents while trying to relocate natives from their island to make way for A-bomb testing.

Savage Sam (1963) **C-103m.** ✶✶½ D: Norman Tokar. Brian Keith, Tommy Kirk,

Kevin Corcoran, Dewey Martin, Jeff York, Royal Dano, Marta Kristen. Sequel to Disney's OLD YELLER has Keith and country neighbors trying to rescue children who've been kidnapped by Indians. Savage Sam, canine son of Old Yeller, helps track down the tribe. Colorful but uneven.▼❶

Savage Wilderness SEE: **Last Frontier, The** (1956)

Sawdust and Tinsel (1953-Swedish) **92m.** **** D: Ingmar Bergman. Harriet Andersson, Ake Gronberg, Anders Ek, Gudrun Brost, Hasse Ekman, Annika Tretow. Sparks fly in this beautiful, allegorical film set in a small-time circus and focusing on the relationship between circus owner Gronberg and his oversexed mistress (Andersson). A key credit in Bergman's developing maturity as a filmmaker. Aka THE NAKED NIGHT.▼❶❸

Saxon Charm, The (1948) **88m.** *** D: Claude Binyon. Robert Montgomery, Susan Hayward, John Payne, Audrey Totter, Harry Morgan, Cara Williams, Harry Von Zell, Heather Angel. Well-acted but unconvincing study of ruthless producer, with Montgomery miscast in lead role. Still interesting, with fine work from playwright Payne, wife Hayward, and chanteuse Totter.

Say It in French (1938) **70m.** ** D: Andrew L. Stone. Ray Milland, Olympe Bradna, Irene Hervey, Janet Beecher, Mary Carlisle, Holmes Herbert, Walter Kingsford, Erik Rhodes. Milland has just married Bradna but has to keep it a secret, and pretend to be engaged to Hervey, to help his financially strapped parents. Forgettable farce based on a Viennese play.

Say It With Songs (1929) **85m.** *½ D: Lloyd Bacon. Al Jolson, Davey Lee, Marian Nixon, Holmes Herbert, Kenneth Thomson, Fred Kohler, Frank Campeau, John Bowers. Poor script hampers this tearjerker about a radio singer (Jolson) who winds up in prison, leaving behind loving wife Nixon and his son, "Little Pal" (Lee). Jolson sings "Used to You," "I'm in Seventh Heaven," and, of course, "Little Pal."❶❸

Sayonara (1957) **C-147m.** ***½ D: Joshua Logan. Marlon Brando, Ricardo Montalban, Miiko Taka, Miyoshi Umeki, Red Buttons, Martha Scott, James Garner. Romantic James Michener tale of Korean War pilot Brando falling in love with Japanese entertainer Taka; extremely well acted, with Oscar-winning support from Buttons and Umeki, and statuettes also going to the art direction–set decoration. Theme song by Irving Berlin. Paul Osborn wrote the screenplay. Technirama. ▼❶❸

Say One for Me (1959) **C-119m.** *½ D: Frank Tashlin. Debbie Reynolds, Bing Crosby, Robert Wagner, Ray Walston, Les Tremayne, Connie Gilchrist, Stella Stevens, Frank McHugh, Joe Besser, Sebastian Cabot. Bing plays a Broadway priest who

gets mixed up with a chorus girl (Debbie) and a TV charity show. Terribly contrived; no memorable music. CinemaScope. ❶

Scandal (1950-Japanese) **104m.** **½ D: Akira Kurosawa. Toshiro Mifune, Yoshiko Yamaguchi, Takashi Shimura, Yôko Katsuragi, Noriko Sengoku, Eitarô Ozawa. Successful painter, innocently snared in nasty gossip about a famous singer he chanced to meet but once, sues the sleazy magazine that has slandered him. Ozu-like study of the Americanization of Japan, a serious protest about man vs. media. Not entirely successful dramatically, but its caveat about the evils of paparazzi-driven celebrity journalism is timelier than ever. ▼❶

Scandal at Scourie (1953) **C-90m.** **½ D: Jean Negulesco. Greer Garson, Walter Pidgeon, Donna Corcoran, Agnes Moorehead, Arthur Shields. Tepid Garson-Pidgeon entry set in Canada, involving Protestant couple who shock community when they plan to adopt a Catholic child. ❶

Scandal, Inc. (1956) **79m.** *½ D: Edward Mann. Robert Hutton, Patricia Wright, Paul Richards, Robert Knapp, Claire Kelly, Nestor Paiva. Inept yarn involving a victimized movie star (Hutton) who's accused of killing a smarmy scandal-sheet writer.

Scandal in Paris, A (1946) **106m.** *** D: Douglas Sirk. George Sanders, Carole Landis, Akim Tamiroff, Signe Hasso, Gene Lockhart, Alan Napier, Alma Kruger. Stylish (though studio-bound) 18th-century story based on the memoirs of the notorious Frenchman Eugene Vidocq, whose life of crime reaches a crossroads when he encounters a young woman who idolizes him. Witty script was tailormade for Sanders. ▼❶

Scandal in Sorrento (1957-Italian) **C-92m.** *½ D: Dino Risi. Vittorio De Sica, Sophia Loren, Antonio Cifariello, Tina Pica. Listless sex romp of Loren romancing De Sica to make lover jealous. CinemaScope.

Scandal Sheet (1931) **77m.** **½ D: John Cromwell. George Bancroft, Kay Francis, Clive Brook, Lucien Littlefield, Jackie Searl. Usual triangle with a good twist. Editor Bancroft has the goods on Brook, the man his wife Francis plans to run off with.

Scandal Sheet (1952) **82m.** *** D: Phil Karlson. Broderick Crawford, Donna Reed, John Derek, Rosemary DeCamp, Henry O'Neill, Henry (Harry) Morgan, James Millican. Engrossing melodrama about an ambitious tabloid editor (Crawford) who accidentally kills his ex-wife (DeCamp), then finds hotshot reporter Derek investigating the story. Derek is miscast, but DeCamp has never been better and O'Neill is aces as a former prize-winning journalist who's now a hopeless alcoholic. Based on *The Dark Page*, a novel by Samuel Fuller. ❶

Scapegoat, The (1959-British) **92m.** **½ D: Robert Hamer. Alec Guinness, Bette

Davis, Nicole Maurey, Irene Worth, Peter Bull, Pamela Brown, Geoffrey Keen. Decent acting rescues a fuzzy script. French gentleman murders his wife, tries to involve his British lookalike in scheme. Davis has small but impressive role as the guilty Guinness' dope-ridden mother. Adapted by Hamer and Gore Vidal from a Daphne du Maurier novel. ❿

Scar, The SEE: **Hollow Triumph**

Scaramouche (1923) **123m.** *** D: Rex Ingram. Ramon Novarro, Lewis Stone, Alice Terry, Lloyd Ingraham, Julia Swayne Gordon, William Humphrey, Otto Matiesen, George Siegman (Siegmann). Freedom-loving lawyer Novarro becomes a spokesman for the downtrodden in pre-Revolutionary France. He naturally runs afoul of dastardly marquis Stone, who has murdered his best friend and whose money and power has attracted Terry, the woman he loves. Absorbing adaptation of the Rafael Sabatini novel, although it pales beside the 1952 remake (which also features Stone, in a supporting role). ❿

Scaramouche (1952) **C-118m.** ***½ D: George Sidney. Stewart Granger, Eleanor Parker, Janet Leigh, Mel Ferrer, Henry Wilcoxon, Lewis Stone, Nina Foch, Richard Anderson, Robert Coote. Excellent cast in rousing adaptation of Sabatini novel of illustrious ne'er-do-well who sets out to avenge friend's death, set in 18th-century France. Impeccably done. Highlight is climactic sword duel, one of the longest in swashbuckling history. Screenplay by Ronald Millar and George Froeschel. Filmed before in 1923. ▼◑❿

Scared Stiff (1945) **65m.** *½ D: Frank McDonald. Jack Haley, Ann Savage, Barton MacLane, Veda Ann Borg, Roger Pryor, George E. Stone, Lucien Littlefield. Inane comedy-chiller with Haley cast as an addle-brained reporter who becomes involved in a murder mystery and search for stolen antique chess pieces. Aka TREASURE OF FEAR. ▼❿

Scared Stiff (1953) **108m.** **½ D: George Marshall. Dean Martin, Jerry Lewis, Lizabeth Scott, Carmen Miranda, Dorothy Malone. Usual Martin and Lewis hijinks with duo on spooky Caribbean island inherited by Scott; Jerry and Carmen make a wild team. Remake of Bob Hope's THE GHOST BREAKERS. ▼◑❿

Scared to Death (1947) **C-65m.** *½ D: Christy Cabanne. Bela Lugosi, Douglas Fowley, Joyce Compton, George Zucco, Nat Pendleton, Angelo Rossitto, Molly Lamont. Lugosi's only color film is a dreadful, cheaply made chiller. Told from the point of view of a beautiful murder victim (Lamont), chronicling how she came to meet her demise. Lugosi plays Leonide, a hypnotist. ▼◑❿

Scarf, The (1951) **93m.** **½ D: E. A. Du-

pont. John Ireland, Mercedes McCambridge, James Barton, Emlyn Williams, Lloyd Gough, Basil Ruysdael. After escaping from a mental asylum, Ireland sets out to uncover the truth about the murder of his girlfriend. Capably handled melodrama with Barton offering a colorful turn as a crusty chicken farmer.

Scarface (1932) **90m.** ***½ D: Howard Hawks. Paul Muni, Ann Dvorak, George Raft, Boris Karloff, Karen Morley, Vince Barnett, Osgood Perkins, C. Henry Gordon. Powerful gangster film is the most potent of the 1930s, with Muni delivering emotionally charged performance as Capone-like mobster with more than just a soft spot for his sister (Dvorak). Raw, harsh, and brimming with unsubtle symbolism; five writers include Ben Hecht and W. R. Burnett. Filmed in 1931, release delayed by censors. Based on the book by Armitage Trail. The full title is SCARFACE, THE SHAME OF THE NATION. Remade in 1983. ▼◑❿

Scarface Mob, The (1962) **102m.** **½ D: Phil Karlson. Robert Stack, Keenan Wynn, Barbara Nichols, Pat Crowley, Neville Brand, Bruce Gordon. Feature version of a two-part *Desilu Playhouse* from 1959 that led to the hugely popular *Untouchables* TV series with Stack as racket-buster Eliot Ness, who sets out to break Chicago's underworld kingpin Al Capone. Still pretty potent (especially by TV standards) and blessed with the inimitable staccato narration of Walter Winchell.

Scarlet Angel (1952) **C-80m.** **½ D: Sidney Salkow. Yvonne De Carlo, Rock Hudson, Richard Denning, Amanda Blake. Neat little drama set in 1860 New Orleans, with De Carlo the dance-hall girl who assumes a dead woman's identity and goes West to stay with wealthy in-laws.

Scarlet Blade, The SEE: **Crimson Blade, The**

Scarlet Claw, The (1944) **74m.** ***½ D: Roy William Neill. Basil Rathbone, Nigel Bruce, Gerald Hamer, Arthur Hohl, Miles Mander, Ian Wolfe, Paul Cavanagh, Kay Harding. The ominous marshes of a French-Canadian village provide the setting for gruesome mutilation murders in this excellent *Sherlock Holmes* mystery, moodily photographed by George Robinson. Clearly the best of the series. ▼❿

Scarlet Clue, The (1945) **65m.** ** D: Phil Rosen. Sidney Toler, Benson Fong, Mantan Moreland, Helen Deveraux, Robert Homans, Virginia Brissac, Jack Norton, Stanford Jolley. One of the more bearable Monogram *Charlie Chan* entries, with Toler after spies who have stolen radar plans. ▼◑❿

Scarlet Coat, The (1955) **C-101m.** **½ D: John Sturges. Cornel Wilde, Michael Wilding, George Sanders, Anne Francis, Bobby Driscoll, Robert Douglas. Plucky costumer livened by cast and bright photography;

set in Colonial America, dealing with Major John Andre and Benedict Arnold spy capers. Partly shot in Sleepy Hollow, New York. CinemaScope. ▶

Scarlet Dawn (1932) **76m.** ✶✶ D: William Dieterle. Douglas Fairbanks, Jr., Nancy Carroll, Earle Fox, Lilyan Tashman, Sheila Terry, Betty Gillette, Frank Reicher, Arnold Korff, Guy Kibbee, Mae Busch. Fairbanks, a dashing officer in the Czar's army, is forced to flee after the Russian revolution in the company of his former servant (Carroll), whom he tries to seduce—and winds up marrying. Fairly interesting oddity, boosted by its attractive stars and an unusually handsome production. ▼

Scarlet Empress, The (1934) **110m.** ✶✶✶ D: Josef von Sternberg. Marlene Dietrich, John Lodge, Louise Dresser, Sam Jaffe, C. Aubrey Smith, Edward Van Sloan. Von Sternberg tells the story of Catherine the Great and her rise to power in uniquely ornate fashion, with stunning lighting and camerawork and fiery Russian music. It's a visual orgy; dramatically uneven, but cinematically fascinating. ▼▶

Scarlet Hour, The (1956) **95m.** ✶✶ D: Michael Curtiz. Carol Ohmart, Tom Tryon, Jody Lawrance, James Gregory, Elaine Stritch, E. G. Marshall, Edward Binns. Sluggish study of marital discord leading to murder. VistaVision.

Scarlet Letter, The (1926) **97m.** ✶✶✶ D: Victor Seastrom. Lillian Gish, Lars Hanson, Henry B. Walthall, Karl Dane, William H. Tooker, Marcelle Corday. Excellent, though liberal, adaptation of Hawthorne classic about Hester Prynne (Gish) who bears scar of adultery in Boston, having had clandestine affair with minister Hanson. Filmed several times in the silent era, and in 1934, 1973, 1979 (for TV), and 1995.

Scarlet Letter, The (1934) **70m.** ✶✶ D: Robert G. Vignola. Colleen Moore, Hardie Albright, Henry B. Walthall, Cora Sue Collins, Alan Hale, Virginia Howell, William Farnum, Betty Blythe. Slow, poorly directed, though not uninteresting version of the Nathaniel Hawthorne novel. Moore is miscast as Hester Prynne; Walthall repeats his role from the 1926 version as Roger Prynne. A real curio. ▼▶

Scarlet Pages (1930) **63m.** ✶✶ D: Ray Enright. Elsie Ferguson, Marian Nixon, John Halliday, Grant Withers, Daisy Belmore, William B. Davidson. Silent star Ferguson's lone talkie is a slight, predictable drama involving a celebrated woman lawyer who shrouds her past in secrecy. She's in for quite a surprise when she takes the case of a showgirl accused of murder. ▶

Scarlet Pimpernel, The (1935-British) **95m.** ✶✶✶½ D: Harold Young. Leslie Howard, Merle Oberon, Raymond Massey, Nigel Bruce, Bramwell Fletcher, Anthony Bushell, Joan Gardner, Melville Cooper. Excellent costumer with Howard leading double life, aiding innocent victims of French revolution while posing as foppish member of British society. Baroness Orczy's novel was scripted by Robert E. Sherwood, Sam Berman, Arthur Wimperis, and Lajos Biro; produced by Alexander Korda. Remade as THE ELUSIVE PIMPERNEL, and for TV in 1982. Also shown in computer-colored version. ▼▶

Scarlet River (1933) **54m.** ✶✶✶ D: Otto Brower. Tom Keene, Dorothy Wilson, Roscoe Ates, Edgar Kennedy, Betty Furness, Creighton Chaney (Lon Chaney, Jr.), Billy Butts, Yakima Canutt. Fun B movie about a troupe making a Western far from Hollywood, helping to save the female ranch owner from her greedy foreman. Canutt performs the horse-leaping stunt he famously repeated in STAGECOACH. Myrna Loy, Joel McCrea, Bruce Cabot, Rochelle Hudson, and Julie Haydon appear as themselves at the RKO commissary. A must for fans of movies about movies.

Scarlet Street (1945) **103m.** ✶✶✶ D: Fritz Lang. Edward G. Robinson, Joan Bennett, Dan Duryea, Margaret Lindsay, Rosalind Ivan. Meek, henpecked Robinson is pulled into world of crime and deception by seductive Bennett and her manipulative boyfriend Duryea. Stars and director of THE WOMAN IN THE WINDOW keep it interesting, but don't match earlier film. Dudley Nichols adapted this remake of Jean Renoir's LA CHIENNE. Also shown in computer-colored version. ▼▶

Scar of Shame, The (1927) **76m.** ✶✶✶ D: Frank Perugini. Harry Henderson, Norman Johnstone, Lucia Lynn Moses, William E. Pettus, Lawrence Chenault, Ann Kennedy, Pearl McCormack. Much heralded all-black melodrama about a refined, class-conscious young concert pianist and the damsel in distress he rescues from her weak-willed stepfather and a lust-filled con man. Standard story is elevated by its exploration of bigotry and class differences within the black community in America. One of several films produced by Philadelphia's Colored Players Film Corporation. ▼▶

Scene of the Crime (1949) **94m.** ✶✶ D: Roy Rowland. Van Johnson, Arlene Dahl, Gloria DeHaven, Tom Drake, Leon Ames, John McIntire, Donald Woods, Norman Lloyd, Jerome Cowan. Bland, talky film noir in which hard-boiled L.A. cop Johnson sets out to solve the murder of his ex-partner, who might have been on the take. ▶

Scent of Mystery SEE: **Holiday in Spain**

School for Love (1955-French) **72m.** ✶✶ D: Marc Allégret. Jean Marais, Brigitte Bardot, Isabelle Pia, Mischa Auer. Occasionally sensual flick with Bardot and Pia competing for Marais' affection. Original title: FUTERES VEDETTES. Retitled: JOY OF LOVING.

School for Scoundrels (1960-British) **94m.** *** D: Robert Hamer. Ian Carmichael, Terry-Thomas, Janette Scott, Alastair Sim, Dennis Price, Peter Jones, Edward Chapman. Wimpy Carmichael, about to lose the girl of his dreams to pushy Thomas, attends the title institute, where he learns "one-upmanship" and "gamesmanship." Clever, funny, veddy British satire. Full title on-screen is SCHOOL FOR SCOUNDRELS OR HOW TO WIN WITHOUT ACTUALLY CHEATING. Remade in 2006.▼▶

Scotland Yard Inspector (1952-British) **73m.** ** D: Sam Newfield. Cesar Romero, Lois Maxwell, Bernadette O'Farrell, Geoffrey Keen, Alistair Hunter, Peter Swanwick. Run-of-the-mill actioner with Romero assisting Maxwell in capturing her brother's killer. Original British title: LADY IN THE FOG.▶

Scotland Yard Investigator (1945) **68m.** ** D: George Blair. C. Aubrey Smith, Erich von Stroheim, Stephanie Bachelor, Forrester Harvey, Doris Lloyd, Eva Moore. Low-budget mystery wastes two leading players in routine art-theft tale.

Scott of the Antarctic (1948-British) **C-110m.** **½ D: Charles Frend. John Mills, Derek Bond, Harold Warrender, James Robertson Justice, Reginald Beckwith, Kenneth More, John Gregson, Christopher Lee. Unrelenting docudrama of determined British explorer Robert Falcon Scott (Mills), highlighting the details of his last expedition to the South Pole. This saga of bravery and endurance features an especially moving finale. Music by Vaughan Williams, who later used part of this score in his seventh symphony.▼▶

Scoundrel, The (1935) **78m.** *** D: Ben Hecht, Charles MacArthur. Noel Coward, Julie Haydon, Stanley Ridges, Martha Sleeper, Ernest Cossart, Eduardo Ciannelli, Alexander Woollcott, Lionel Stander. Fascinating Hecht-MacArthur original about a cynical, self-centered N.Y.C. publisher who toys with other people's lives—until his own existence is put on the line. Bizarre, sophisticated, indulgent—and unique. Coward, in his first starring film, puts over a challenging and unusual role. Famed critic/curmudgeon Woollcott plays one of the hangers-on, while Hecht and MacArthur have a funny flop-house cameo. Academy Award winner for Best Original Story.

Screaming Eagles (1956) **79m.** ** D: Charles F. Haas. Tom Tryon, Jan Merlin, Pat Conway, Martin Milner, Ralph Votrian, Paul Smith, Alvy Moore, Paul Burke, Jacqueline Beer, Robert Blake, Robert Dix, Edward G. Robinson, Jr., Mark Damon. Routine WW2 film spotlighting a diverse group of soldiers entrusted to capture a bridge on D-day. Of interest for cast of up-and-coming actors.▶

Screaming Mimi (1958) **79m.** ** D: Gerd Oswald. Anita Ekberg, Phil Carey, Harry Townes, Gypsy Rose Lee, Romney Brent, Red Norvo. Lurid low-budget melodrama about a woman who cracks up after being assaulted, takes a job as exotic dancer in Lee's nightclub but remains under the influence of a possessive psychiatrist. Strange, kinky film that sounds more interesting than it really is.▶

Screaming Skull, The (1958) **68m.** *½ D: Alex Nicol. John Hudson, Peggy Webber, Russ Conway, Tony Johnson, Alex Nicol. Hudson brings new wife Webber to his late first wife's remote home; soon she begins experiencing weird events centered on a phantom skull. Dreary but reasonably eerie toward the end, with a twist that's actually a surprise. Directorial debut for Nicol, who also plays a mentally retarded gardener. ▼▶

Scream in the Dark, A (1943) **53m.** **½ D: George Sherman. Robert Lowery, Marie McDonald, Edward Brophy, Elizabeth Russell, Wally Vernon, Hobart Cavanaugh, Jack La Rue. Fast-moving, lighthearted whodunit about adventures of reporter Lowery, who opens up a private detective business with photographer pal Brophy and gets mixed up in a baffling murder case. Based on Jerome Odlum's novel *The Morgue Is Always Open.*

Scream of Fear (1961-British) **81m.** *** D: Seth Holt. Susan Strasberg, Christopher Lee, Ann Todd, Ronald Lewis. Only wheelchair-bound Strasberg sees her father's corpse—while stepmom Todd insists he's on a trip. Good Hammer thriller written by Jimmy Sangster. Original British title: TASTE OF FEAR.▼▶

Scrooge (1935-British) **78m.** **½ D: Henry Edwards. Sir Seymour Hicks, Donald Calthrop, Robert Cochran, Mary Glynne, Oscar Asche, Maurice Evans. Faithful adaptation of *A Christmas Carol,* with an impressive Sir Seymour (who also cowrote the script) as Scrooge. Dickens' era brought colorfully to life.▼▶

Scudda Hoo! Scudda Hay! (1948) **C-95m.** ** D: F. Hugh Herbert. June Haver, Lon McCallister, Walter Brennan, Anne Revere, Natalie Wood. Any film with a title like that can't be all good, and it isn't; McCallister's life is devoted to two mules. Marilyn Monroe can be glimpsed in a canoe—it's her first film appearance.▶

Sea Around Us, The (1953) **C-61m.** *** Produced by Irwin Allen. Narrated by Theodor von Eltz and Don Forbes. Academy Award–winning documentary based on Rachel Carson's study of the history of the ocean, its fauna and life.▼▶

Sea Bat, The (1930) **69m.** ** D: Wesley Ruggles. Charles Bickford, Raquel Torres, Nils Asther, George F. Marion, John Miljan, Boris Karloff, Gibson Gowland, Edmund Breese. Primitive potboiler about an escaped convict (Bickford) posing as a priest, falling for island vamp Torres, and getting involved with pagan voodoo charms and rival sponge divers who are trying to capture a deadly stingray. Ripe hokum sparked by vividly shot action scenes.

Sea Chase, The (1955) **C-117m.** **½ D: John Farrow. John Wayne, Lana Turner, Tab Hunter, David Farrar, Lyle Bettger, James Arness, Claude Akins. Strange WW2 film, with Wayne as German (!) captain of fugitive ship with unusual cargo, assorted crew, plus passenger/girlfriend Turner. CinemaScope. ▼●▶

Sea Devils (1937) **88m.** ** D: Ben Stoloff. Victor McLaglen, Preston Foster, Ida Lupino, Donald Woods, Helen Flint, Gordon Jones. One of those brawling-can-be-fun formula films, with McLaglen and Foster as Coast Guard rivals and McLaglen's daughter (Lupino) a focal point of further conflict. Filmed and acted with zest, but script's stupidities all but sink it.▼

Sea Devils (1953-British) **C-91m.** ** D: Raoul Walsh. Yvonne De Carlo, Rock Hudson, Maxwell Reed, Denis O'Dea, Michael Goodliffe, Bryan Forbes. Smuggler Hudson becomes involved in the activities of British spy De Carlo in this unmemorable programmer set in the Napoleonic era. Filmed on and around the Channel Islands.▼▶

Sea Fury (1958-British) **72m.** ** D: C. Raker (Cy) Endfield. Stanley Baker, Victor McLaglen, Luciana Paluzzi, Gregoire Aslan, Francis de Wolff, Percy Herbert, Rupert Davies, Robert Shaw. Tug captain McLaglen is set to wed Paluzzi, but she's attracted to first mate Baker. Routine romantic adventure. Original running time: 97m.

Seagulls Over Sorrento SEE: **Crest of the Wave**

Sea Hawk, The (1924) **124m.** *** D: Frank Lloyd. Milton Sills, Enid Bennett, Lloyd Hughes, Wallace MacDonald, Marc McDermott, Wallace Beery, Frank Currier, Lionel Belmore, William Collier, Jr. Oily villain commits a murder and plants damning evidence on his half brother, then has him shanghaied to boot. After working as a galley slave, he escapes, finds refuge, and reinvents himself as Sakr-el-Bahr, a pirate king. Rousing, well-plotted adventure yarn from the Rafael Sabatini novel. The 1940 Errol Flynn movie is a remake in name only.▶

Sea Hawk, The (1940) **127m.** **** D: Michael Curtiz. Errol Flynn, Brenda Marshall, Claude Rains, Donald Crisp, Flora Robson, Alan Hale, Henry Daniell, Una O'Connor, Gilbert Roland. Top-notch combination of classy Warner Bros. costumer and Flynn at his dashing best in adventure on the high seas; lively balance of piracy, romance, and swordplay, handsomely photographed and staged, with rousing Erich Wolfgang Korngold score. Has nothing to do with the Sabatini novel, which was filmed faithfully in 1924. Restored for home video, with additional final scene intended for British audiences, in which Queen Elizabeth I offers morale-building war-time message. Beware of shorter prints. Also shown in computer-colored version.▼●▶

Sea Hornet, The (1951) **84m.** *½ D: Joseph Kane. Rod Cameron, Adele Mara, Adrian Booth, Chill Wills, Jim Davis, Richard Jaeckel, Ellen Corby, James Brown, Monte Blue. Run-of-the-mill stuff about deep-water divers and their women, with fireworks resulting when diver Cameron's partner is mysteriously killed.

Sealed Cargo (1951) **90m.** **½ D: Alfred L. Werker. Dana Andrews, Carla Balenda, Claude Rains, Philip Dorn, Onslow Stevens, Skip Homeier, Arthur Shields. Fishing boat captain Andrews tangles with Nazis attempting to supply war materials to U-boats lurking off the Newfoundland coast. Taut WW2 melodrama.

Sealed Lips (1942) **62m.** ** D: George Waggner. William Gargan, June Clyde, John Litel, Anne Nagel, Mary Gordon, Ralf Harolde, Joe Crehan. Pedestrian account of notorious gangster Litel forcing an innocent lookalike to serve his prison stretch; detective Gargan gets into plenty of scrapes when he discovers the deception. Litel works hard in dual role but Waggner's script is talky and his direction drab.

Sealed Verdict (1948) **83m.** ** D: Lewis Allen. Ray Milland, Florence Marly, Broderick Crawford, John Hoyt, John Ridgely. Far-fetched drama of Army lawyer who falls in love with traitorous woman he is supposed to prosecute in court; pretty dismal.

Seance on a Wet Afternoon (1964-British) **115m.** **** D: Bryan Forbes. Kim Stanley, Richard Attenborough, Patrick Magee, Nanette Newman, Judith Donner, Gerald Sim, Maria Kazan, Margaret Lacey. Gripping drama of crazed medium Stanley involving husband Attenborough in shady project. Brilliant acting, direction in this must-see film. Forbes adapted Mark McShane's novel and coproduced the film with Attenborough. Remade in Japan in 2000 as SÉANCE. ▼▶

Sea of Grass, The (1947) **123m.** **½ D: Elia Kazan. Katharine Hepburn, Spencer Tracy, Melvyn Douglas, Phyllis Thaxter, Robert Walker, Edgar Buchanan, Harry Carey. Plodding drama from Conrad Richter story of farmer-rancher feud over New Mexico grasslands. Walker stands out in hardworking but unsuccessful cast.▼▶

Sea of Lost Ships (1953) **85m.** ** D: Joseph Kane. John Derek, Wanda Hendrix, Walter Brennan, Richard Jaeckel. Standard fare of two Coast Guard men fighting over Hendrix.

Sea of Sand SEE: **Desert Patrol**

Search, The (1948) **105m.** **** D: Fred Zinnemann. Montgomery Clift, Ivan Jandl,

Aline MacMahon, Jarmila Novotna, Wendell Corey. Poignant drama of American soldier Clift caring for concentration camp survivor Jandl in postwar Berlin, while the boy's mother desperately searches all Displaced Person's Camps for him. Beautifully acted and directed; won a Best Story Academy Award for Richard Schweizer and David Wechsler and a special prize for Jandl for outstanding juvenile performance. Also shown in computer-colored version. Remade in 2014. ▼❱

Searchers, The (1956) **C-119m. ****** D: John Ford. John Wayne, Jeffrey Hunter, Vera Miles, Ward Bond, Natalie Wood, John Qualen, Harry Carey, Jr., Olive Carey, Antonio Moreno, Henry Brandon, Hank Worden, Ken Curtis, Lana Wood, Dorothy Jordan, Pat Wayne. Superb Western saga of Wayne's relentless search for niece (Wood) kidnapped by Indians, spanning many years. Color, scenery, photography all splendid, with moving, insightful Frank Nugent script to match (based on Alan Le-May's novel). And who could ever forget that final shot? Remade and imitated many times since (CARAVANS, WINTER-HAWK, GRAYEAGLE, etc.). VistaVision. ▼❱❱

Search for Beauty (1934) **78m. **½** D: Erle C. Kenton. Larry "Buster" Crabbe, Ida Lupino, Robert Armstrong, Gertrude Michael, James Gleason, Toby Wing, Bradley Page. Armstrong, just out of the pokey, hatches a new scheme to start a health and fitness magazine as an excuse to show off beautiful male and female bodies—and dupes athletes Crabbe and Lupino into fronting the enterprise. Amusing pre-Code piffle with Lupino in her bleached-blond phase. Watch for Ann Sheridan as "Texas Beauty Winner." ❱

Search for Bridey Murphy, The (1956) **84m. **½** D: Noel Langley. Teresa Wright, Louis Hayward, Nancy Gates, Kenneth Tobey, Richard Anderson. Strange account of woman under hypnosis with recollection of prior life; low-key telling to obtain realism makes it slow going. Based on a supposedly true (and then-topical) story. VistaVision. ▼

Search for Danger (1949) **62m. *½** D: Jack Bernhard. John Calvert, Albert Dekker, Myrna Dell, Douglas Fowley, Ben Welden. Low-budget *Falcon* mystery (last in the series), revolves around murderous gamblers who abscond with a fortune.

Search for Paradise (1957) **C-120m. **** D: Otto Lang. Visually sumptuous three-panel travelogue with Lowell Thomas and his Cinerama crew setting out to record the "last examples of traditional Oriental magnificence" before they are swept away by 20th-century technology: faraway temples, canyons, mountains, villages, and hidden valleys located "next door to nowhere." Up

until the finale, which is set in Katmandu, Nepal, and features Americans and Communist Chinese attending a coronation, film depicts a sweetly idealized 1950s world where there is no political or economic strife. Songs on the soundtrack (written by Dimitri Tiomkin and performed by Robert Merrill) might be right out of *South Pacific*. Restoration is presented in a curved screen simulation that replicates the feeling of seeing the film in its original presentation. Cinerama. ❱

Searching Wind, The (1946) **108m. **½** D: William Dieterle. Robert Young, Sylvia Sidney, Ann Richards, Dudley Digges, Douglas Dick, Albert Basserman. Talky but historically fascinating drama, scripted by Lillian Hellman and based on her play, about a deluded U.S. ambassador (Young) in Europe in the years before WW2. Socialite Richards is his wife, journalist Sidney the woman he really loves. Hellman's scenario mirrors, and condemns, the international politics that allowed Hitler to come to power.

Seas Beneath (1931) **89m. **½** D: John Ford. George O'Brien, Marion Lessing, Mona Maris, Walter C. Kelly, Warren Hymer, Gaylord (Steve) Pendleton, Walter McGrail, Larry Kent, Henry Victor, John Loder, William Collier, Sr. Early talkie is an interesting WW1 yarn about an American Q-boat "Mystery Ship" on a search-and-destroy mission against a German U-boat. Similar to, though not as grim as, Ford's MEN WITHOUT WOMEN, with taut action undercut by too much comedy relief and Lessing's poor performance as a German spy who bewitches Navy ace O'Brien. ❱

Sea Shall Not Have Them, The (1954-British) **93m. ** D: Lewis Gilbert. Dirk Bogarde, Michael Redgrave, Bonar Colleano, Jack Watling, Anthony Steel, Nigel Patrick, George Rose, Rachel Kempson, Nigel Green. After a British bomber makes a forced landing in mid-ocean during WW2, its crew awaits rescue in a dinghy. Uninspired wartime drama. ▼

Seaside Swingers (1964-British) **C-94m. *½** D: James Hill. John Leyton, Mike Sarne, Freddie and The Dreamers, Ron Moody, Liz Fraser. Group of teenagers working at seaside resort prepare for major talent contest which is to be the highlight of the summer season. Should have given them all the hook. Original British title: EVERY DAY'S A HOLIDAY. Techniscope. ▼

Season of Passion (1959-Australian) **93m. **½** D: Leslie Norman. Anne Baxter, John Mills, Angela Lansbury, Ernest Borgnine, Janette Craig. Tasteful study of human relationships; Mills and Borgnine are country workers who each year come to the city for their fling with Baxter and Lansbury. Based on Ray Lawlor's play, *Summer of the 17th Doll*.

Sea Wall, The SEE: **This Angry Age**

Sea Wife (1957-British) **C-82m.** *** D: Bob McNaught. Richard Burton, Joan Collins, Basil Sydney, Ronald Squire, Cy Grant. Disarming yarn of Burton and Collins surviving a torpedoed ship. He falls in love with her, not knowing she's a nun. Set during WW2. CinemaScope.▼◗

Sea Wolf, The (1941) **90m.** ***½ D: Michael Curtiz. Edward G. Robinson, John Garfield, Ida Lupino, Alexander Knox, Gene Lockhart, Barry Fitzgerald, Stanley Ridges. Bristling Jack London tale of brutal but intellectual sea captain Robinson battling wits with accidental passenger Knox, as brash seaman Garfield and fugitive Lupino try to escape. Script by Robert Rossen. Originally released at 100m. Remade many times (BARRICADE, WOLF LARSEN, etc.), as well as several silent versions. Also shown in computer-colored version.▼

Second Best Secret Agent in the Whole Wide World (1965-British) **C-96m.** **½ D: Lindsay Shonteff. Tom Adams, Veronica Hurst, Peter Bull, Karel Stepanek, John Arnatt. Snappy James Bondish entry, with virtue of satirical performance by Adams; he prevents the Russians from stealing scientist Stepanek's anti-gravity invention. Original British title: LICENSED TO KILL. Sequel: WHERE THE BULLETS FLY. ▼

Second Chance (1953) **C-81m.** **½ D: Rudolph Maté. Robert Mitchum, Linda Darnell, Jack Palance, Reginald Sheffield, Roy Roberts, Dan Seymour, Fortunio Bonanova, Milburn Stone. Two runaways—gambler's girlfriend Darnell and tainted prizefighter Mitchum—fall in love in Mexico. Complications arise when Palance arrives with orders to kill Darnell. OK melodrama. 3-D. ▼◗

Second Chorus (1940) **83m.** ** D: H. C. Potter. Fred Astaire, Paulette Goddard, Artie Shaw and his Orchestra, Charles Butterworth, Burgess Meredith. Routine musical comedy with Astaire and Meredith as musicians who want to join Shaw's band; they both have designs on Goddard. Not enough music and hardly any dancing, but what's there is fun. Fred and Paulette dance to "(I Ain't Hep to That Step but I'll) Dig It." ▼◗

Second Face, The (1950) **77m.** **½ D: Jack Bernhard. Ella Raines, Bruce Bennett, Rita Johnson, Jane Darwell, John Sutton. Concise study of the effects of plastic surgery on Raines, whose face has been scarred.▼

Second Fiddle (1938) **86m.** **½ D: Sidney Lanfield. Sonja Henie, Tyrone Power, Rudy Vallee, Edna May Oliver, Lyle Talbot, Brian Sisters, Mary Healy, Alan Dinehart, voice of Charles Lane. Contrived Henie musical of Power promoting Hollywood romance for Henie, falling in love himself. Irving Berlin's most uninspired score does include

the genuinely strange song—and production number—"Dancing Back to Back."▼

Second Greatest Sex, The (1955) **C-87m.** *½ D: George Marshall. Jeanne Crain, George Nader, Bert Lahr, Mamie Van Doren, Kitty Kallen, Keith Andes, Tommy Rall, Paul Gilbert, Jimmy Boyd. Second-rate musical up-dating of *Lysistrata,* about women out West protesting men's violence by going on sex strike. CinemaScope.

Second Honeymoon (1937) **79m.** **½ D: Walter Lang. Tyrone Power, Loretta Young, Stuart Erwin, Claire Trevor, Lyle Talbot. Power tries to win back ex-wife Young in pat marital farce with attractive cast.◗

Second Time Around, The (1961) **C-99m.** **½ D: Vincent Sherman. Debbie Reynolds, Andy Griffith, Steve Forrest, Juliet Prowse, Thelma Ritter, Isobel Elsom. Mild comic Western with widow Debbie moving to Arizona, becoming sheriff, tangling with suitors Griffith and Forrest. CinemaScope. ◗

Second Woman, The (1951) **90m.** **½ D: James V. Kern. Robert Young, Betsy Drake, John Sutton, Florence Bates, Morris Carnovsky, Henry O'Neill, Jean Rogers. Atmospheric psychological drama with architect Young becoming increasingly unstable as a result of his fiancée's death on the eve of their wedding. Is he a danger to himself and his new girlfriend Drake?▼◗

Secret Agent, The (1936-British) **86m.** **½ D: Alfred Hitchcock. John Gielgud, Madeleine Carroll, Robert Young, Peter Lorre, Percy Marmont, Lilli Palmer. Strange blend of comedy and thriller elements which don't quite mesh; Carroll and Gielgud are secret agents who pose as man and wife while on assignment in Switzerland to kill enemy spy. One of Hitchcock's oddest films. ▼◗

Secret Agent of Japan (1942) **72m.** ** D: Irving Pichel. Preston Foster, Lynn Bari, Noel Madison, Janis Carter, Sen Yung, Addison Richards, Frank Puglia, Ian Wolfe. Dated espionage film of soldier-of-fortune Foster working in the Pacific for England before Pearl Harbor. ◗

Secret Beyond the Door . . . (1948) **98m.** ** D: Fritz Lang. Joan Bennett, Michael Redgrave, Anne Revere, Barbara O'Neil, Natalie Schafer. Tedious Lang misfire along lines of Hitchcock's SUSPICION, with Bennett believing her husband is a demented murderer.▼◗

Secret Bride, The (1935) **64m.** **½ D: William Dieterle. Barbara Stanwyck, Warren William, Glenda Farrell, Grant Mitchell, Arthur Byron. State Attorney General William secretly weds governor's daughter Stanwyck, and summarily learns that her father may be taking bribes from a convicted embezzler. Tidy, well-acted drama.◗

Secret Command (1944) **82m.** *** D: A. Edward Sutherland. Pat O'Brien, Carole Landis, Chester Morris, Ruth Warrick, Wallace Ford. No-nonsense O'Brien tries to find source of sabotage in California shipyard during WW2. Good, fast moving espionage story. O'Brien also produced this film.

Secret File: Hollywood (1962) **85m.** BOMB D: Ralph Cushman. Robert Clarke, Francine York, Syd Mason, Maralou Gray, John Warburton. A Crown International classic. Clarke is a detective hired for a scandal magazine to investigate shady doings in Tinseltown. Utterly inept. ▼▶

Secret Fury, The (1950) **86m.** *** D: Mel Ferrer. Claudette Colbert, Robert Ryan, Jane Cowl, Paul Kelly, Vivian Vance, Philip Ober. Unknown person tries to drive Claudette crazy to prevent her marriage to Ryan. Exciting whodunit with twist ending.

Secret Garden, The (1949) **92m.** *** D: Fred M. Wilcox. Margaret O'Brien, Herbert Marshall, Dean Stockwell, Gladys Cooper, Elsa Lanchester. Young girl who comes to live at run-down Victorian estate finds abandoned garden, devotes herself to it and eventually changes the lives of everyone living there. Vividly atmospheric film with some color sequences. Based on the classic children's book by Frances Hodgson Burnett. Remade as a TV movie in 1987 and as a feature in 1993, as well as a Broadway musical. ▼▶

Secret Heart, The (1946) **97m.** **½ D: Robert Z. Leonard. Claudette Colbert, Walter Pidgeon, June Allyson, Lionel Barrymore, Robert Sterling, Patricia Medina, Marshall Thompson; narrated by Hume Cronyn. This is Allyson's film, as young girl obsessed with dead father, unable to accept stepmother Colbert. Film creates eerie mood, and acting is good, but it's offbeat and not for all tastes. ▶

Secret Invasion, The (1964) **C-95m.** *** D: Roger Corman. Stewart Granger, Mickey Rooney, Raf Vallone, Henry Silva, Edd Byrnes, Mia Massini. Good action, location photography, and direction in story of British Intelligence using criminals to work behind enemy lines in WW2 Yugoslavia. Panavision. ▶

Secret Land, The (1948) **C-71m.** *** Produced by Orville O. Dull. Narrated by Van Heflin, Robert Montgomery, Robert Taylor. Glossy but penetrating documentary study of Admiral Richard Byrd's exploratory missions to Antarctic.

Secret Life of Walter Mitty, The (1947) **C-110m.** **½ D: Norman Z. McLeod. Danny Kaye, Virginia Mayo, Boris Karloff, Fay Bainter, Ann Rutherford, Florence Bates, Thurston Hall. Formula comedy casts Danny as milquetoast who dreams of manly glory. Not much Thurber here, but daydream sequences are lots of fun, and so is Kaye's famous "Anatole of Paris" patter number. Young Robert Altman, smiling and smoking a cigarette, appears as an extra in a nightclub scene with Kaye. Remade in 2013. ▼●▶

Secret Mission (1942-British) **94m.** **½ D: Harold French. Hugh Williams, James Mason, Michael Wilding, Carla Lehmann, Nancy Price, Roland Culver, Karel Stepanek, Herbert Lom, Stewart Granger. Stiff-upper-lip WW2 drama in which three British spies and a free Frenchman (played by Mason!) sneak into occupied France to gather intelligence for an upcoming invasion. Well paced dramatically, but comical touches seem awkwardly out of place. ▼

Secret of Blood Island, The (1965-British) **C-84m.** ** D: Quentin Lawrence. Barbara Shelley, Jack Hedley, Charles Tingwell, Patrick Wymark. Woman agent Shelley parachutes into Malaya during WW2, ends up incognito in a prisoner-of-war camp. Mindless timekiller. Video title: P.O.W.: PRISONERS OF WAR. ▼

Secret of Convict Lake, The (1951) **83m.** **½ D: Michael Gordon. Glenn Ford, Gene Tierney, Ethel Barrymore, Zachary Scott, Ann Dvorak, Jeanette Nolan, Ruth Donnelly. Set in 1870s California, escaped prisoners hide out at settlement comprised largely of women; fine cast makes the most of script.

Secret of Dr. Kildare, The (1939) **84m.** **½ D: Harold S. Bucquet. Lew Ayres, Lionel Barrymore, Lionel Atwill, Laraine Day, Helen Gilbert, Nat Pendleton, Sara Haden, Samuel S. Hinds, Emma Dunn, Grant Mitchell, Walter Kingsford, Alma Kruger, Nell Craig, Marie Blake, Martha O'Driscoll, Donald Barry. The good doctor tries to cure a young woman of psychosomatic blindness while working equally hard to get stubborn Dr. Gillespie to take a vacation in this tidy episode. ▼▶

Secret of Dr. Mabuse, The SEE: **1,000 Eyes of Dr. Mabuse, The**

Secret of Madame Blanche, The (1933) **83m.** **½ D: Charles Brabin. Irene Dunne, Lionel Atwill, Phillips Holmes, Douglas Walton, Una Merkel, C. Henry Gordon, Jean Parker. Another MGM tearjerker in the MADAME X vein; Dunne is quite effective as a music-hall singer who loses her son to callous father-in-law Atwill when husband Holmes kills himself. Twenty years later, mother and son meet by accident and are involved in a murder. Contrived but well-made soaper.

Secret of My Success, The (1965-British) **C-99m.** *½ D: Andrew L. Stone. James Booth, Shirley Jones, Stella Stevens, Honor Blackman, Amy Dalby, Lionel Jeffries. Film certainly doesn't succeed. Naive boy is taken in by several crafty females on his road to maturity. Picturesque settings, variety of characterizations by Jeffries. Panavision.

Secret of the Blue Room (1933) **66m.** **½ D: Kurt Neumann. Lionel Atwill, Gloria Stuart, Paul Lukas, Edward Arnold, Onslow Stevens, William Janney. Atmospheric whodunit set in eerie European castle where Stuart's three suitors accept challenge to sleep in room from which several former occupants

mysteriously vanished. Cast makes this one worthwhile; remade as THE MISSING GUEST and MURDER IN THE BLUE ROOM. ▶
Secret of the Incas (1954) **C-101m. **½** D: Jerry Hopper. Charlton Heston, Robert Young, Nicole Maurey, Thomas Mitchell, Glenda Farrell, Yma Sumac. Good adventure of explorer searching for location of fabled treasure.
Secret of the Purple Reef, The (1960) **C-80m. **** D: William Witney. Jeff Richards, Margia Dean, Peter Falk, Richard Chamberlain, Robert Earle, Terence DeMarney. Programmer whose capable cast bounces the story along; siblings seek clues to their brother's disappearance in the Caribbean. CinemaScope.
Secret of the Telegian (1960-Japanese) **C-85m. **** D: Jun Fukuda. Koji Tsuruta, Akihiko Hirata, Yoshio Tsuchiya, Tadao Nakamaru, Yumi Shirakawa, Seizaburó Kawazu. Police are baffled by a series of murders in which the killer literally vanishes, but a reporter learns the villain has stolen a teleportation device and is seeking revenge on those who wronged him. Some interesting effects, but it's really just another of the crime/science fiction thrillers Toho alternated with giant monster adventures. Shown "flat" and in b&w in the U.S. Tohoscope. ▼
Secret of the Wastelands (1941) **66m. **½** D: Derwin Abrahams. William Boyd, Andy Clyde, Brad King, Barbara Britton, Soo Young, Douglas Fowley. Offbeat Hopalong Cassidy adventure has Western trio traveling with an archeological expedition in search of ancient Indian desert ruins. Instead, they find a mysterious "lost city" (think Shangri-La) populated by Chinese Americans. Based on a novel by Bliss Lomax (Harry Sinclair Drago). Two atypically strong women's roles in this final series entry for Paramount. ▼▶
Secret of the Whistler, The (1946) **65m. **** D: George Sherman. Richard Dix, Leslie Brooks, Mary Currier, Michael Duane, Mona Barrie, Ray Walker. Dix is an insane artist whose second wife suspects him of having killed her predecessor and fears she's his next victim. Nifty *Whistler* entry, with the customary ironic twist.
Secret of Treasure Mountain (1956) **68m. *½** D: Seymour Friedman. Valerie French, Raymond Burr, William Prince, Lance Fuller, Susan Cummings. Trivial tale of a hunt for buried gold in Apache territory; the catch is that the Indians have placed a curse on the treasure. Remake (with stock footage) of LUST FOR GOLD. ▼
Secret Partner, The (1961-British) **91m. **** D: Basil Dearden. Stewart Granger, Haya Harareet, Bernard Lee, Conrad Phillips. Fast-paced, atmospheric mystery about man trying to pull off ingenious scheme whereby he is accused of robbery. ▶

Secret People (1952-British) **87m. **** D: Thorold Dickinson. Valentina Cortesa, Serge Reggiani, Charles Goldner, Audrey Hepburn, Megs Jenkins, Irene Worth. Heavy-handed drama in which Cortesa and Reggiani attempt to assassinate the dictator responsible for her father's death. Hepburn registers as Cortesa's innocent kid sister.
Secrets (1933) **85m. **** D: Frank Borzage. Mary Pickford, Leslie Howard, C. Aubrey Smith, Blanche Friderici, Doris Lloyd, Herbert Evans, Ned Sparks. Saga follows two frontier settlers from youth to old age, and goes from light romance to soap opera to melodrama. Mary's screen swan song shows her great talent intact, but this episodic tale must have seemed old-fashioned (not to mention redundant) even in 1933. ▶
Secret Service of the Air (1939) **61m. **** D: Noel Smith. Ronald Reagan, John Litel, Ila Rhodes, James Stephenson, Eddie Foy, Jr., Rosella Towne. Reagan stars as Lt. Brass Bancroft, a pilot who joins the Secret Service and exposes a smuggling ring. Fast-paced Warner Bros. B entry, the first of a series of four. ▶
Secret Six, The (1931) **83m. **½** D: George Hill. Wallace Beery, Lewis Stone, Clark Gable, Jean Harlow, Johnny Mack Brown, Ralph Bellamy, Marjorie Rambeau, John Miljan. Hard-boiled gangster saga with powerhouse cast; sluggish at times, but worth seeing for milk-drinking racketeer Beery, aristocratic crime lord Stone, moll-with-a-heart-of-gold Harlow, et al. ▶
Secrets of an Actress (1938) **71m. **** D: William Keighley. Kay Francis, George Brent, Ian Hunter, Gloria Dickson, Isabel Jeans, Penny Singleton, Dennie Moore. Run-of-the-mill romantic melodrama with actress Francis attracting distraught Brent, an unhappily married architect.
Secrets of a Secretary (1931) **71m. **** D: George Abbott. Claudette Colbert, Herbert Marshall, Georges Metaxa, Mary Boland, Berton Churchill. Stiff drawing-room stuff, with Colbert finding ex-hubby Marshall blackmailing her new boss.
Secrets of a Soul (1926-German) **76m. **** D: G. W. Pabst. Werner Krauss, Ruth Weyher, Ilka Grüning, Jack Trevor, Pavel Pawlow, Hertha von Walther, Renate Brausewetter. Starkly directed exploration of the unconscious and the positive impact that psychoanalysis may have on curing mental illness. The scenario, based on a case history, shows how everyday (and not-so-everyday) events affect the life of happily married Krauss. Extended dream sequence and fantasy sequences are visual feasts. Only flaw is making the wonders of psychoanalysis a bit too pat. Karl Abraham and Hanns Sachs, the film's technical consultants, were colleagues of Sigmund Freud. Full title is SECRETS OF A SOUL: A PSYCHOANALYTIC FILM. ▼▶

Secrets of Life (1956) **C-75m.** *** D: James Algar. Narrated by Winston Hibler. Disney True-Life Adventure features closeup looks at plant life, insect life, sea creatures, and natural wonders like volcanoes. Wonderful footage includes time-lapse photography of plants set to a rousing bolero on the soundtrack. Climactic volcano sequence was originally shown in CinemaScope. ▼▶

Secrets of the Lone Wolf (1941) **67m.** **½ D: Edward Dmytryk. Warren William, Ruth Ford, Roger Clark, Victor Jory, Eric Blore, Thurston Hall, Fred Kelsey. Sturdy entry with the Lone Wolf's punctilious valet (Blore) thought to be his employer by some crooks who use him as part of a scheme to lift the Napoleon jewels.

Secrets of Women (1952-Swedish) **114m.** *** D: Ingmar Bergman. Anita Bjork, Karl-Arne Holmsten, Jarl Kulle, Maj-Britt Nilsson, Birger Malmsten, Eva Dahlbeck, Gunnar Bjornstrand. Episodic early Bergman drama about several women in a summer house who confide about their relationships with their men. Final sequence, with Dahlbeck and Bjornstrand trapped in an elevator, is most fascinating. ▼

Secret Ways, The (1961) **112m.** **½ D: Phil Karlson. Richard Widmark, Sonja Ziemann, Senta Berger, Charles Regnier. Much on-location shooting helps strengthen caper with Widmark as grim American sent into Communist Hungary to plan escape of pro-West refugee; from an Alistair MacLean novel.

Security Risk (1954) **69m.** ** D: Harold Schuster. John Ireland, Dorothy Malone, Keith Larsen, John Craven, Joe Bassett. Routine FBI-vs-Communist-agent; even Malone isn't diverting in this B thriller.

Seduced and Abandoned (1964-Italian) **118m.** ***½ D: Pietro Germi. Stefania Sandrelli, Saro Urzi, Lando Buzzanca, Leopoldo Trieste. Fast-paced, richly flavorful bedroom romp involving the fate of a Don Juan who manages to impregnate his fiancée's kid sister. A follow-up in spirit to Germi's DIVORCE—ITALIAN STYLE, this very funny film cleverly lampoons sexual tradition. ▼▶

See Here, Private Hargrove (1944) **100m.** *** D: Wesley Ruggles. Robert Walker, Donna Reed, Keenan Wynn, Robert Benchley, Bob Crosby, Grant Mitchell. Marion Hargrove's anecdotes of Army life make an amusing, episodic film; Benchley hilarious as Reed's garrulous dad. Sequel: WHAT NEXT, CORPORAL HARGROVE? ▶

Seekers, The (1954-British) **C-90m.** **½ D: Ken Annakin. Jack Hawkins, Glynis Johns, Noel Purcell, Inia Te Wiata, Laya Raki. Adequate adventure drama, set in the early 1800s, as British sailor Hawkins, along with his new wife and best friend, settles in New Zealand. The colorful location filming (especially among the Maoris) is a plus. Original U.S. title: LAND OF FURY. ▼▶

See My Lawyer (1945) **67m.** ** D: Edward F. Cline. Ole Olsen, Chic Johnson, Alan Curtis, Grace McDonald, Noah Beery, Jr., Franklin Pangborn, Edward S. Brophy. Last and least of Olsen and Johnson's movie vehicles, with the daffy duo at war with nightclub owner Pangborn—and aiding a trio of struggling lawyers. Tissue-thin plot serves only as framework for a variety of specialty acts, including Carmen Amaya and the (Nat) King Cole Trio.

Sellout, The (1952) **83m.** **½ D: Gerald Mayer. Walter Pidgeon, John Hodiak, Audrey Totter, Paula Raymond, Cameron Mitchell, Karl Malden, Everett Sloane, Thomas Gomez. Small-town newspaper editor Pidgeon finds himself in over his head when he tries to get the goods on corrupt sheriff Gomez. OK exposé drama. ▶

Seminole (1953) **C-87m.** **½ D: Budd Boetticher. Rock Hudson, Barbara Hale, Anthony Quinn, Richard Carlson, Hugh O'Brian, Russell Johnson, Lee Marvin, James Best. Capable cast in unusual drama about earnest cavalry lieutenant Hudson trying to help Indian tribe's efforts to remain free of white man law. ▶

Seminole Uprising (1955) **C-74m.** *½ D: Earl Bellamy. George Montgomery, Karin Booth, William Fawcett, Steve Ritch, Ed Hinton. Cavalryman Montgomery is sent to capture war-making Seminole chief Black Cat (Ritch)—because he is his half brother. Minor-league Western with all-too-obvious use of stock footage.

Senator Was Indiscreet, The (1947) **74m.** *** D: George S. Kaufman. William Powell, Ella Raines, Peter Lind Hayes, Arleen Whelan, Ray Collins, Hans Conried. Wit-playwright Kaufman's only directorial fling turns out quite well, with Powell as Senator whose diary causes embarrassment. Entertaining satire. ▼

Send Me No Flowers (1964) **C-100m.** *** D: Norman Jewison. Rock Hudson, Doris Day, Tony Randall, Clint Walker, Paul Lynde, Hal March, Edward Andrews, Patricia Barry. Hypochondriac Rock, convinced he has a short time to live, has Randall find new husband for wife Doris. Funny script by Julius J. Epstein; Lynde is a riot as aggressive cemetery plot salesman. ▼▶

Senechal the Magnificent (1957-French) **78m.** **½ D: Jacques Boyer. Fernandel, Nadia Gray, Georges Chamarat, Jeanne Aubert, Armontel, Robert Pizani. Fernandel is well cast as buffoon actor who, through mistaken identities and an ability to mimic, becomes a Parisian hit.

Senior Prom (1959) **82m.** *½ D: David Lowell Rich. Jill Corey, Paul Hampton, Barbara Bostock, Jimmy Komack, Tom Laughlin. The title tells all in this flimsy, mostly boring musical. The "guest stars" include Louis Prima, Keely Smith, Mitch Miller, Ed Sullivan, Connee Boswell, Bob Crosby, Les Elgart, and Freddy Martin.

Sensations SEE: **Sensations of 1945**

Sensations of 1945 (1944) 86m. **½ D: Andrew L. Stone. Eleanor Powell, Dennis O'Keefe, C. Aubrey Smith, Eugene Pallette, W. C. Fields, Cab Calloway, Sophie Tucker. Publicity-wise Powell shows press agent O'Keefe how to attract attention in this campy musical; one incredible number has her tap-dancing inside giant pinball machine! Fields' skit (his last appearance on film) is only fair. Retitled SENSATIONS.▼

Senso (1954-Italian) C-115m. **½ D: Luchino Visconti. Alida Valli, Farley Granger, Massimo Girotti, Heinz Moog. Carefully paced study of human emotions, chronicling the relationship between earthy, materialistic Austrian officer Granger and his aristocratic Italian mistress (Valli). An intriguing union of the neorealism of Visconti's earlier work and the lush romanticism often found in his later films. Retitled WANTON CONTESSA. English-language version, titled THE WANTON COUNTESS, features dialogue by Tennessee Williams and Paul Bowles!▼▶

Sentimental Journey (1946) 94m. ** D: Walter Lang. John Payne, Maureen O'Hara, William Bendix, Cedric Hardwicke, Glenn Langan, Mischa Auer, Connie Marshall. Maudlin yarn of dying actress O'Hara adopting little girl to give husband Payne a companion when she is gone; no holds barred here. Remade as THE GIFT OF LOVE and as a 1984 TV movie. ▶

Senza Pieta SEE: **Without Pity**

Separate Tables (1958) 99m. **** D: Delbert Mann. Burt Lancaster, Rita Hayworth, David Niven, Deborah Kerr, Wendy Hiller, Gladys Cooper, Cathleen Nesbitt, Rod Taylor, Felix Aylmer. Terence Rattigan's pair of romantic playlets set at English seaside resort are reworked here into superb drama in the GRAND HOTEL vein; Lancaster and Hayworth are divorced couple trying to make another go of it, Hiller is his timid mistress, Niven a supposed war hero, Kerr a lonely spinster dominated by mother Cooper. Bouquets all around, especially to Oscar winners Niven and Hiller. Screenplay by Rattigan and John Gay.▼▶▶

September Affair (1950) 104m. **½ D: William Dieterle. Joseph Cotten, Joan Fontaine, Françoise Rosay, Jessica Tandy, Robert Arthur, Fortunio Bonanova, Jimmy Lydon. Trim romance of married man Cotten and pianist Fontaine who find that they're listed as dead in plane crash and now have chance to continue their affair. Makes effective use of classical music and Walter Huston's recording of "September Song" (which once again became a hit).▼●

September Storm (1960) C-99m. BOMB D: Byron Haskin. Joanne Dru, Mark Stevens, Robert Strauss, Asher Dann, M. Jean-Pierre Kerien, Vera Valmont. Scheming fashion model joins a group of adventurers searching for buried treasure off the coast of Majorca. Film's only novelty is that it was shot in 3-D CinemaScope.

Sequoia (1934) 73m. **½ D: Chester Franklin. Jean Parker, Russell Hardie, Samuel S. Hinds, Paul Hurst. Girl living near national forest raises orphaned deer and mountain lion to be friends. Fascinating animal footage burdened by simplistic, often heavy-handed story. Reissued as MALIBU, also the name of book on which it's based.

Serenade (1956) C-121m. **½ D: Anthony Mann. Mario Lanza, Joan Fontaine, Sarita Montiel, Vincent Price, Joseph Calleia, Vince Edwards. James M. Cain novel becomes surface soaper of Lanza, the protégé of swank Fontaine, manipulated by manager Price and loved by earthy Montiel; spotty musical interludes.▼▶

Sergeant DeadHead (1965) C-89m. *½ D: Norman Taurog. Frankie Avalon, Deborah Walley, Eve Arden, Cesar Romero, Fred Clark, Buster Keaton, Gale Gordon, Harvey Lembeck. Bungling Army sergeant goes into space with a chimpanzee and undergoes personality change. Oh, that poor monkey. Also known as SERGEANT DEADHEAD, THE ASTRONUT. Panavision. ▶

Sergeant Madden (1939) 82m. ** D: Josef von Sternberg. Wallace Beery, Tom Brown, Alan Curtis, Laraine Day, Fay Holden, David Gorcey, Etta McDaniel, Horace McMahon. Director von Sternberg out of his element with standard Beery vehicle of policeman whose son alienates him, marries orphan girl he raised.

Sergeant Murphy (1938) 57m. ** D: B. Reeves Eason. Ronald Reagan, Mary Maguire, Donald Crisp, Ben Hendricks, William Davidson. Reagan stars in this forgettable programmer as a soldier who loves a talented horse. The sergeant of the title is the animal; Ronnie is a lowly private.

Sergeant Rutledge (1960) C-111m. *** D: John Ford. Jeffrey Hunter, Woody Strode, Constance Towers, Billie Burke, Carleton Young, Juano Hernandez, Willis Bouchey, Mae Marsh, Hank Worden, Jack Pennick. Arresting story of a black U.S. cavalryman on trial for rape and murder; his story is pieced together in flashback during his court-martial. Unusual subject matter for its time, solidly presented by Ford (with some occasionally awkward comic relief). Strode is commanding in the central role.▼▶

Sergeants 3 (1962) C-112m. **½ D: John Sturges. Frank Sinatra, Dean Martin, Sammy Davis, Jr., Peter Lawford, Joey Bishop, Ruta Lee, Henry Silva. Second reworking of GUNGA DIN is amusing, but not up to 1939 original. This time it's out West with the Rat Pack as cavalry sergeants. Davis can't eclipse Sam Jaffe as Gunga Din, though. Panavision.◗

Sergeant York (1941) **134m. ***½** D: Howard Hawks. Gary Cooper, Walter Brennan, Joan Leslie, George Tobias, Stanley Ridges, Margaret Wycherly, Ward Bond, Noah Beery, Jr., June Lockhart. Excellent story of pacifist Alvin York (Cooper) drafted during WW1, realizing purpose of fighting and becoming hero. Oscar-winning performance by Cooper in fine, intelligent film, balancing segments of rural America with battle scenes. John Huston was one of the writers. Also available in computer-colored version.▼◗●

Serpent of the Nile (1953) **C-81m. *½** D: William Castle. Rhonda Fleming, William Lundigan, Raymond Burr, Michael Ansara, Julie Newmar. Antony and Cleopatra, B-movie style; good for a few laughs, anyway. Producer Sam Katzman used leftover sets from Rita Hayworth's SALOME.

Servant, The (1963-British) **115m. ***½** D: Joseph Losey. Dirk Bogarde, James Fox, Sarah Miles, Wendy Craig, Catherine Lacey, Patrick Magee. Insidious story of moral degradation as corrupt manservant Bogarde becomes master of employer Fox; superb study of brooding decadence. Scripted by Harold Pinter.▼◗

Service De Luxe (1938) **85m. **** D: Rowland V. Lee. Constance Bennett, Vincent Price, Charles Ruggles, Mischa Auer, Joy Hodges, Helen Broderick. Easy-to-take but empty-headed froth about a woman who runs a service company that does just about anything its customers require. Price makes his film debut as man who finally breaks through Bennett's "strictly business" facade.

Set-Up, The (1949) **72m. ***½** D: Robert Wise. Robert Ryan, Audrey Totter, George Tobias, Alan Baxter, James Edwards, Wallace Ford. Gutsy account of washed-up fighter refusing to give up or go crooked; Ryan has never been better. Art Cohn's pungent screenplay was inspired by a narrative poem(!) by Joseph Moncure March. Photographed by Milton Krasner. Played out in real time—as you'll see by the clock shown in opening and closing shots.▼◗●

Seven Angry Men (1955) **90m. **** D: Charles Marquis Warren. Raymond Massey, Debra Paget, Jeffrey Hunter, James Best, Dennis Weaver, Dabbs Greer, Ann Tyrrell. Good historical drama of John Brown (Massey) and family fighting to free slaves during 1800s. Massey is fine in lead role, which he previously played in SANTA FE TRAIL.◗

Seven Brides for Seven Brothers (1954) **C-103m. ***** D: Stanley Donen. Howard Keel, Jane Powell, Jeff Richards, Russ Tamblyn, Tommy Rall, Virginia Gibson, Julie Newmeyer (Newmar), Ruta Kilmo-

nis (Lee), Matt Mattox. Rollicking musical perfectly integrates song, dance, and story: Keel's decision to get himself a wife (Powell) inspires his rowdy brothers to follow suit. Tuneful Johnny Mercer–Gene DePaul score (with Oscar-winning musical direction by Adolph Deutsch and Saul Chaplin), but it's Michael Kidd's energetic dance numbers that really stand out, with rare screen work by dancers Jacques D'Amboise and Marc Platt. The barn-raising sequence is an absolute knockout. Screenplay by Albert Hackett, Frances Goodrich, and Dorothy Kingsley, from a Stephen Vincent Benet story. Later a TV series and a Broadway musical. CinemaScope. ▼◗●

7 Capital Sins (1961-French-Italian) **113m. **** D: Jean-Luc Godard, Roger Vadim, Sylvaine Dhomme, Edouard Molinaro, Philippe De Broca, Claude Chabrol, Jacques Demy. Marie-Jose Nat, Dominique Paturel, Jean-Marc Tennberg, Perrette Pradier. Potpourri of directors and talents play out modern parables concerning anger, envy, gluttony, greed, laziness, lust, and pride. Aka SEVEN DEADLY SINS and LES SEPT PECHES CAPITAUX. Dyaliscope.▼

Seven Chances (1925) **56m. ***½** D: Buster Keaton. Buster Keaton, T. Roy Barnes, Snitz Edwards, Ruth Dwyer, Frankie Raymond, Jules Cowles. Buster will inherit a fortune if he's married by 7:00 that evening; a miscommunication with his girlfriend leads to his pursuit by thousands of would-be brides. The highlight: a furious chase down a hill in which Buster dodges dozens of oversized rolling boulders! One of Keaton's silent gems. That's young Jean Arthur as a switchboard operator. Remade as THE BACHELOR (1999). ▼◗●

Seven Cities of Gold (1955) **C-103m. **½** D: Robert D. Webb. Richard Egan, Anthony Quinn, Jeffrey Hunter, Rita Moreno, Michael Rennie. Average spectacle adventure has good cast and fair direction. "Roughneck" learns ways of God in search for fabled Indian treasure in Western U.S. CinemaScope.▼

Seven Days in May (1964) **118m. **** D: John Frankenheimer. Burt Lancaster, Kirk Douglas, Fredric March, Ava Gardner, Edmond O'Brien, Martin Balsam, George Macready, Whit Bissell, Hugh Marlowe. Absorbing, believable story of military scheme to overthrow the government. Fine cast includes Lancaster as the general planning the coup and Douglas as the colonel who discovers the plot, March as U.S. President; intelligent suspense in Rod Serling screenplay from Fletcher Knebel and Charles W. Bailey novel. John Houseman made his screen acting debut in small but crucial role. Remade for cable as THE ENEMY WITHIN. ▼◗●

Seven Days' Leave (1942) **87m. **½** D: Tim Whelan. Lucille Ball, Victor Mature,

Harold Peary, Ginny Simms, Peter Lind Hayes, Arnold Stang, Ralph Edwards. Mature is an Army private who will inherit $100,000 if he can marry heiress Ball. Sprightly musical comedy, featuring Freddy Martin and Les Brown's bands.▼◗

Seven Days to Noon (1950-British) **93m.** **** D: John Boulting. Barry Jones, Olive Sloane, Andre Morell, Sheila Manahan, Hugh Cross, Joan Hickson. Superbly paced thriller (from Paul Dehn and James Bernard's Oscar-winning story) about scientist threatening to explode atomic bomb in London if his demands are not met. Screenplay by Roy Boulting and Frank Harvey.

Seven Deadly Sins, The (1952-Italian-French) **124m.** **½ D: Eduardo De Filippo, Jean Dreville, Yves Allegret, Roberto Rossellini, Carlo Rim, Claude Autant Lara, Georges Lacombe. Gérard Philipe, Michele Morgan, Françoise Rosay, Isa Miranda, Paolo Stoppa, Eduardo De Filippo, Noel Noel, Viviane Romance, Henri Vidal. Episodic potpourri illustrating the seven major vices, with an eighth, "unknown" one thrown in for good measure. The best of the lot are "Gluttony," in which a piece of cheese comes between a man and the willing arms of a woman, and "Envy," in which a woman becomes jealous over her husband's pet cat. Also available in English-dubbed 83m. version.▼

711 Ocean Drive (1950) **102m.** **½ D: Joseph M. Newman. Edmond O'Brien, Joanne Dru, Otto Kruger, Barry Kelly, Dorothy Patrick, Donald Porter, Howard St. John, Sammy White, Bert Freed, Cleo Moore. Tidy racketeer yarn of the bookie syndicate in the U.S. with exciting climax at Hoover Dam.◗

7 Faces of Dr. Lao (1964) **C-100m.** *** D: George Pal. Tony Randall, Barbara Eden, Arthur O'Connell, John Ericson, Kevin Tate, Argentina Brunetti, Noah Beery, Jr., Minerva Urecal, John Qualen, Lee Patrick. Engaging fantasy of Western town brought to its senses by parables performed by mysterious traveling circus; tour de force for Randall, who plays six roles. William Tuttle won special Oscar for makeup creations. Based on Charles G. Finney's novel *The Circus of Dr. Lao.*▼◗

Seven Footprints to Satan (1929) **60m.** *** D: Benjamin Christensen. Thelma Todd, Creighton Hale, Sheldon Lewis, William V. Mong, Sojin, Laska Winters, Ivan Christy, DeWitt Jennings, Nora Cecil, Angelo Rossitto. Wild horror spoof about a man and his fiancée, who are abducted and taken to a spooky old house apparently run by Satan himself, with a torture chamber, a marauding gorilla, a dwarf hiding behind a sliding wall, and decadent socialites running around with guns. A surreal game-show–type challenge serves up a twist ending. Deliciously off-the-wall silent treat made in Hollywood by the distinguished Danish director of WITCHCRAFT THROUGH THE AGES.

Seven Hills of Rome (1958) **C-104m.** **½ D: Roy Rowland. Mario Lanza, Peggie Castle, Marisa Allasio, Renato Rascel, Rosella Como. Formula vehicle for Lanza, as a television star who retreats to Rome and falls in love; mellower than usual, with nice scenery and supporting cast. Technirama.▼◗

Seven Keys to Baldpate (1929) **73m.** *** D: Reginald Barker. Richard Dix, Miriam Seegar, Crauford Kent, Margaret Livingston, Joseph Allen, Lucien Littlefield, DeWitt Jennings. Engaging comedy-mystery about a novelist who tries to win a bet by writing an entire book in 24 hours while staying at a supposedly deserted mountain lodge. Early talkie moves briskly through its serpentine plot; Dix was never more buoyant. Based on George M. Cohan's play, adapted from an Earl Derr Biggers story; filmed before in 1916, 1917, and 1925, and again in 1935, 1947, and 1983 (as HOUSE OF THE LONG SHADOWS).▼◗

Seven Keys to Baldpate (1935) **80m.** **½ D: William Hamilton, Edward Killy. Gene Raymond, Margaret Callahan, Eric Blore, Grant Mitchell, Moroni Olsen, Erin O'Brien-Moore, Henry Travers, Walter Brennan. Moderately entertaining version of the oft-filmed comedy-mystery with writer Raymond confronted by a range of mysterious characters while holed up in a supposedly deserted inn. One debit: that annoying, piped-in music score. Remade again in 1947.

Seven Keys to Baldpate (1947) **66m.** **½ D: Lew Landers. Phillip Terry, Jacqueline White, Eduardo Ciannelli, Margaret Lindsay, Arthur Shields. Mystery writer finds plenty of real-life mystery at the Baldpate Inn, in this sixth go-round for the hardy George M. Cohan stage comedy (based on Earl Derr Biggers' book). Remade in 1983 as HOUSE OF THE LONG SHADOWS.▼◗

Seven Little Foys, The (1955) **C-95m.** *** D: Melville Shavelson. Bob Hope, Milly Vitale, George Tobias, Billy Gray, James Cagney. Pleasant biography of vaudevillian Eddie Foy and his performing family. Hope lively in lead role, Cagney guests as George M. Cohan; their table-top dance duet is the movie's high point. VistaVision.▼◗

Seven Men From Now (1956) **C-78m.** *** D: Budd Boetticher. Randolph Scott, Gail Russell, Lee Marvin, Walter Reed, John Larch, Donald Barry. Scott tracks down seven bandits who held up Wells Fargo station and killed his wife. Solid Western, first of seven from the Scott-Boetticher team, with a script by Burt Kennedy. Marvin is terrific.◗

Seven Miles From Alcatraz (1942) **62m.** **½ D: Edward Dmytryk. James Craig, Bonita Granville, Frank Jenks, Cliff Edwards, George Cleveland, Tala Birell, John Banner. Craig and Jenks break out of the "Rock" and hide out at a nearby lighthouse which is being used by Nazi spies. Which, then, is more important: America's freedom or their own? Medium-grade Hollywood propaganda in this OK B picture.▼

Seven Samurai (1954-Japanese) **141m.** **** D: Akira Kurosawa. Toshiro Mifune, Takashi Shimura, Yoshio Inaba, Ko Kimura, Seiji Miyaguchi, Minoru Chiaki. Classic film about 16th-century Japanese village which hires professional warriors to fend off bandits. Kurosawa's "far-east Western" has served as model for many films since, including American remake THE MAGNIFICENT SEVEN (a title once given this film for U.S. release). The complete 208m. version is even *more* impressive for its humanity as well as its powerful action sequences.▼●)

Seven Seas to Calais (1962-Italian) **C-102m.** **½ D: Rudolph Maté, Primo Zeglio. Rod Taylor, Keith Michell, Irene Worth, Anthony Dawson, Basil Dignam. Minor but entertaining swashbuckler with Taylor as Sir Francis Drake. CinemaScope.)

Seven Sinners (1936-British) **70m.** ** D: Albert de Courville. Edmund Lowe, Constance Cummings, Thomy Bourdelle, Henry Oscar, Felix Aylmer, Joyce Kennedy. Ersatz 39 STEPS, as a Yank detective and his Brit femme sidekick chase a gang of arms dealers who wreck trains to cover their tracks. Lowe, Cummings, and de Courville can't compare to Donat, Carroll, and Hitchcock, but at least there's one good full-size locomotive crash and a script by Frank Launder and Sidney Gilliatt. U.S. release title: DOOMED CARGO. ▼)

Seven Sinners (1940) **87m.** *** D: Tay Garnett. Marlene Dietrich, John Wayne, Albert Dekker, Broderick Crawford, Anna Lee, Mischa Auer, Billy Gilbert. Alluring Dietrich makes Wayne forget about the Navy for a while in this engaging action-love story with excellent supporting cast. Remade as SOUTH SEA SINNER.▼●)

Seven Sweethearts (1942) **98m.** **½ D: Frank Borzage. Kathryn Grayson, Van Heflin, Marsha Hunt, S. Z. Sakall, Cecilia Parker, Peggy Moran, Diana Lewis, Frances Rafferty, Carl Esmond, Isobel Elsom, Donald Meek, Louise Beavers. None of Sakall's seven daughters can marry until the eldest does . . . and that's pretentious, boyfriendless Hunt, a wannabe actress. Will reporter Heflin fall for her, or her youngest sister (Grayson)? Schmaltzy romance-with-music becomes more involving as it goes along.)

Seventeen (1940) **78m.** **½ D: Louis King. Jackie Cooper, Betty Field, Otto Kruger, Richard Denning, Peter Lind Hayes, Betty Moran, Ann Shoemaker, Norma Nelson. Cooper is delightful as teenager facing adolescent problems, in adaptation of Booth Tarkington story.

7th Cavalry (1956) **C-75m.** **½ D: Joseph H. Lewis. Randolph Scott, Barbara Hale, Jay C. Flippen, Jeanette Nolan, Frank Faylen. Scott plays an officer who must prove

that he didn't desert Custer at the Little Bighorn battle.▼)

Seventh Cross, The (1944) **110m.** *** D: Fred Zinnemann. Spencer Tracy, Signe Hasso, Hume Cronyn, Jessica Tandy, Herbert Rudley, Felix Bressart, Ray Collins, Alexander Granach, Agnes Moorehead, George Macready, Steven Geray, Kaaren Verne, George Zucco. Seven men escape from Nazi concentration camp and are pursued by the Gestapo. Exciting film makes strong statement about a cynic who regains hope when others risk their lives to save him. Tandy and Cronyn's first film together. An early winner for Zinnemann.▼)

7th Dawn, The (1964-British) **C-123m.** *½ D: Lewis Gilbert. William Holden, Susannah York, Capucine, Tetsuro Tamba, Michael Goodliffe. Dreary tale of personal and political conflict among WW2 allies— now adversaries—in postwar Malaya.▼)

7th Heaven (1927) **119m.** **½ D: Frank Borzage. Janet Gaynor, Charles Farrell, Ben Bard, David Butler, Marie Mosquini, Albert Gran. One of the most famous screen romances of all time does not hold up as perfectly as one would like; Gaynor won first Academy Award as Diane, mistreated Paris waif redeemed and revived by cocky sewer worker Chico (Farrell). His performance weakens film, as does terrible war subplot and finale. Still interesting, though; beautifully filmed, with lovely theme "Diane." Gaynor received her Oscar for this film, SUNRISE, and STREET ANGEL. Also won Oscars for Screenplay (Benjamin Glazer) and Director. Remade in 1937.▼)

Seventh Heaven (1937) **102m.** ** D: Henry King. Simone Simon, James Stewart, Jean Hersholt, Gregory Ratoff, Gale Sondergaard, J. Edward Bromberg, John Qualen. Stewart is miscast as a cocky Parisian street cleaner but still gives a good performance in this remake of the 1927 silent classic, with Simon appropriately waiflike as his true love, Diane. Starts well but soon becomes claustrophobic, and lacks the lyrical quality of the silent.)

Seven Thieves (1960) **102m.** ***½ D: Henry Hathaway. Edward G. Robinson, Rod Steiger, Joan Collins, Eli Wallach, Alexander Scourby, Michael Dante, Berry Kroeger, Sebastian Cabot. Taut caper of well-planned Monte Carlo heist, with excellent cast giving credibility to far-fetched premise. CinemaScope.▼)

Seventh Seal, The (1957-Sweden) **96m.** **** D: Ingmar Bergman. Max von Sydow, Gunnar Bjornstrand, Nils Poppe, Bibi Andersson, Bengt Ekerot. Sydow, a disillusioned knight on his way back from the Crusades, tries to solve the mysteries of life while playing chess game with Death, who has offered him a short reprieve. Spellbinding, one-of-a-kind masterpiece helped gain Bergman international acclaim. ▼●)

Seventh Sin, The (1957) **94m.** **½ D: Ronald Neame. Eleanor Parker, Bill Travers, Françoise Rosay, George Sanders, Jean-Pierre Aumont, Ellen Corby. Remake of W. Somerset Maugham's THE PAINTED VEIL has virtue of Parker's earnest performance as adulterous wife of a doctor who redeems herself during an epidemic; set in Hong Kong and inner China. CinemaScope.

Seventh Veil, The (1945-British) **95m.** ***½ D: Compton Bennett. James Mason, Ann Todd, Herbert Lom, Hugh McDermott, Albert Lieven. Superb psychological drama of pianist Todd, left as ward to her neurotic cousin Mason. Psychiatrist Lom uses hypnosis to enable Todd to regain her professional and personal sanity. All three stars are first-rate in one of the key British films of the 1940s. Muriel and Sydney Box's screenplay won an Oscar.▼●

Seventh Victim, The (1943) **71m.** *** D: Mark Robson. Tom Conway, Kim Hunter, Jean Brooks, Evelyn Brent, Elizabeth Russell, Hugh Beaumont, Erford Gage, Isabel Jewell, Barbara Hale. Offbeat Val Lewton chiller of innocent Hunter stumbling onto N.Y.C. group of devil-worshipers. Genuinely eerie.▼●]

7th Voyage of Sinbad, The (1958) **C-87m.** ***½ D: Nathan Juran. Kerwin Mathews, Kathryn Grant (Crosby), Richard Eyer, Torin Thatcher. Top-notch adventure/ fantasy pits hero Sinbad against unscrupulous magician (Thatcher) who has reduced Princess Grant to miniature size. Good pacing, eye-popping special effects by Ray Harryhausen (including famed duel with skeleton), music score by Bernard Herrmann. A winner all the way.▼●]

Seven Waves Away SEE: **Abandon Ship**

Seven Ways From Sundown (1960) **C-87m.** **½ D: Harry Keller. Audie Murphy, Barry Sullivan, Venetia Stevenson, John McIntire, Kenneth Tobey. Murphy is Texas ranger assigned to bring in seasoned killer Sullivan, with usual results.

Seven Wonders of the World (1956) **C-122m.** *** D: Ted Tetzlaff, Andrew Marton, Tay Garnett, Paul Mantz, Walter Thompson. What are the seven wonders of the modern world? Three-panel Cinerama travelogue, based on an idea by narrator and guide Lowell Thomas, features dazzlingly photographed images, filmed on an air voyage across five continents of cities great and small along with mountains, monuments, shrines, cathedrals, waterfalls, temples, gardens, volcanos, and deserts. The ultimate point is that there are so many wonders, both natural and human-made, that it would be impossible to choose seven. Restoration is presented in a curved screen simulation that replicates the feeling of seeing the film in its original presentation. Cinerama.]

Seven Year Itch, The (1955) **C-105m.** ***

D: Billy Wilder. Marilyn Monroe, Tommy (Tom) Ewell, Evelyn Keyes, Sonny Tufts, Victor Moore, Oscar Homolka, Carolyn Jones, Doro Merande, Robert Strauss. While Ewell's wife is vacationing in the country, wide-eyed Tom fantasizes about the sexpot who moves in upstairs. This film entered the ranks of pop culture when Marilyn stepped on a subway grating wearing a billowy white skirt... but writer-director Wilder had to skirt censorship issues in adapting George Axelrod's Broadway play, and the results are much tamer than the original (though still entertaining). Marilyn is delightful. Clever titles by Saul Bass. CinemaScope.▼●

Seven Years Bad Luck (1921) **64m.** *** D: Max Linder. Max Linder, Alta Allen, Ralph McCullough, Betty Peterson, F. B. Crayne, Chance Ward, Hugh Saxon, Thelma Percy. Bachelor Max, who is about to wed, breaks a mirror. Does this mean that he is fated to suffer the title malady? A series of nifty comic bits, including a mirror gag that predates the Marx Brothers and an attempt to board a train without paying a fare, highlight this funny, entertaining comedy. Linder also scripted; the first of his three U.S.-made features.]

Sex and the Single Girl (1964) **C-114m.** **½ D: Richard Quine. Natalie Wood, Tony Curtis, Lauren Bacall, Henry Fonda, Mel Ferrer, Fran Jeffries, Edward Everett Horton, Larry Storch, Stubby Kaye, Count Basie and Orchestra. Helen Gurley Brown's book shoved aside, title used to exploit fairly amusing tale of smut-magazine editor Curtis wooing notorious female psychologist Wood. Bacall and Fonda wrap it up as a battling married couple. Coscripted by Joseph Heller.▼●

Sex Kittens Go to College (1960) **94m.** BOMB D: Albert Zugsmith. Mamie Van Doren, Tuesday Weld, Mijanou Bardot (Brigitte's sister), Louis Nye, Martin Milner, Mickey Shaughnessy, Pamela Mason, (Norman) "Woo Woo" Grabowski, Jackie Coogan, John Carradine. Shockingly unfunny comedy; new head of college science department (Mamie, working very hard to convince us she's a genius) turns out to be an ex-stripper. Finding a movie with worse direction would be almost as impossible as finding another movie with a night club jazz combo fronted by *Conway Twitty*! Don't say you weren't warned.]

Sex Madness (1937) **52m.** BOMB D: Dwain Esper. Vivian McGill, Rose Tapley, Al Rigali, Stanley Barton (Mark Daniels), Linda Lee Hill, Charles Olcott. Small-town girl (McGill) comes to the big bad city and promptly contracts syphilis. Another trashy nugget from schlockmeister Esper, made on a budget of $5.00. In between the moralizing regarding "the awful truth about social diseases" there are hints of lesbianism and pedophilia. Indescribably, hilariously awful. Aka HUMAN WRECKAGE and THEY MUST BE TOLD. Beware alternate running times. ▼❿

Sexton Blake and the Hooded Terror (1938-British) **70m. ** D: George King. George Curzon, Tod Slaughter, Greta Gynt, Tony Sympson, Charles Oliver, Marie Wright, David Farrar, Norman Pierce. Blake was a popular Sherlock Holmes knockoff character aimed at a younger audience. Here, he's pitted against the Snake (evil, chuckling Slaughter), head of a crime organization called the Black Quorum. Slaughter plays it basically straight in this passable low-budget outing. ▼❿

Shack Out on 101 (1955) **80m. *** D: Edward Dein. Terry Moore, Frank Lovejoy, Lee Marvin, Keenan Wynn, Whit Bissell. Lee Marvin *is* Slob in this trash classic about the efforts of hash slinger Moore to combat Communism while juggling the lecherous advances of nearly all her co-stars. Absolutely one of a kind, with most of the action taking place on a single shabby set (Wynn's beanery). ▼❿

Shadowed (1946) **65m. *½ D: John Sturges. Anita Louise, Lloyd Corrigan, Michael Duane, Robert Scott (Mark Roberts), Doris Houck, Helen Koford (Terry Moore). Widower Corrigan finds himself menaced by crooks after he stumbles upon a corpse and a package of counterfeit plates while playing golf. Trite programmer is an early credit for director Sturges.

Shadow in the Sky (1951) **78m. **½ D: Fred M. Wilcox. Ralph Meeker, Nancy Davis (Reagan), James Whitmore, Jean Hagen, Gladys Hurlbut. Meeker is quite believable as shellshocked ex-G.I. trying to regain his sanity.

Shadow Man, The (1953-British) **75m. ** D: Richard Vernon. Cesar Romero, Kay Kendall, Edward Underdown, Victor Maddern, Simone Silva, Bill Travers. Saloon-keeper Romero falls for unhappily married Kendall, but then murder gets in his way. Standard action-programmer, with Maddern buoying the proceedings as Romero's limping underling. British version, titled STREET OF SHADOWS, runs 84m. ▼❿

Shadow of a Doubt (1943) **108m. ***½ D: Alfred Hitchcock. Teresa Wright, Joseph Cotten, Macdonald Carey, Patricia Collinge, Henry Travers, Wallace Ford, Hume Cronyn. Perceptive Americana intertwined with story of young girl who slowly comes to realize her beloved Uncle Charley is really the Merry Widow murderer; Cronyn steals film as nosy pulp-story fan, in his film debut. Scripted by Thornton Wilder, Alma Reville, and Sally Benson from Gordon McDonell's story. Remade in 1958 (as STEP DOWN TO TERROR) and for TV in 1991. ▼❶❿

Shadow of Fear (1955-British) **76m. ** D: Albert S. Rogell. Mona Freeman, Jean Kent, Maxwell Reed, Hugh Miller, Gretchen

Franklin. Flabby suspenser of Freeman realizing that her stepmother is planning to murder her as she did hubby; set in England. Original title: BEFORE I WAKE.

Shadow of the Thin Man (1941) **97m. *** D: W. S. Van Dyke II. William Powell, Myrna Loy, Barry Nelson, Donna Reed, Sam Levene, Alan Baxter. Nick and Nora probe murder at a race track and run into the usual assortment of shady characters in this agreeable fourth entry in the series, notable for famed future acting teacher Stella Adler in a rare film role (as a gambler's moll). Look fast for Ava Gardner walking by a car at the race track. ▼❶❿

Shadow of Zorro, The (1962-Italian) **C-84m. *½ D: Joaquin Romero Marchent. Frank Latimore, Maria Luz Galicia, Mario Felciani, Marco Tulli. Clumsy film with lackluster performance by Latimore in title role of Don Jose, who combats outlaws masked as Zorro. Aka ZORRO THE AVENGER. Totalscope. ▼

Shadow on the Wall (1950) **84m. *** D: Patrick Jackson. Ann Sothern, Zachary Scott, Gigi Perreau, Nancy Davis (Reagan), Kristine Miller, John McIntire, Barbara Billingsley. Clever noir-ish melodrama with young Perreau traumatized when she witnesses the murder of her adulterous stepmother. Davis has one of her best roles as a psychiatrist.

Shadow on the Window, The (1957) **73m. ** D: William Asher. Phil Carey, Betty Garrett, John Barrymore, Jr., Corey Allen, Jerry Mathers. Fair programmer; Garrett is held captive by robber-killers while cop husband Carey heads the search. DESPERATE HOURS lite. ❶

Shadow Returns, The (1946) **61m. *½ D: Phil Rosen. Kane Richmond, Barbara Reed, Tom Dugan, Joseph Crehan, Pierre Watkin, Robert Emmett Keane, Frank Reicher, Rebel Randall. Crimefighter Lamont Cranston dons the mask of "The Shadow" once again to investigate a case of stolen jewels and a secret formula for making plastics. Drab and static mystery is the first and worst of three *Shadow* B movies produced by Monogram in 1946, based on Walter B. Gibson's pulp character. Followed by BEHIND THE MASK.

Shadows (1922) **91m. **½ D: Tom Forman. Lon Chaney, Marguerite De La Motte, Harrison Ford, John Sainpolis, Walter Long, Buddy Messinger, Priscilla Bonner. In a small fishing community, the spouse of a much-coveted young woman (De La Motte) is lost at sea. She marries the town's new minister, who soon learns that the husband is still alive. Somewhat predictable melodrama of jealousy and faith is uplifted by Chaney's adroit performance as Yen Sin, a Chinese "heathen" who has a strong impact on the villagers. ▼❿

Shadows (1960) **87m. *** D: John Cassavetes. Hugh Hurd, Lelia Goldoni, Ben Carruthers, Anthony Ray, Rupert Crosse, Tom Allen (Reese). Cassavetes' first film as director, an improvisational, groundbreaking, independently made effort about a light-skinned black girl (Goldoni) who becomes involved with a Caucasian (Ray). Formless, crude, but strikingly realistic, with great use of N.Y.C. locations. Look fast for Cassavetes, Gena Rowlands, Seymour Cassel, and Bobby Darin. ▼●▶

Shadows in the Night (1944) **67m.** **½ D: Eugene J. Forde. Warner Baxter, Nina Foch, George Zucco, Minor Watson, Lester Matthews, Ben Welden, Edward Norris. Is Foch really having deadly nightmares or is one of her greedy relatives trying to bump her off? Dr. Ordway is called in to investigate in one of the better *Crime Doctor* entries.

Shadows Over Chinatown (1946) **61m.** *½ D: Terry Morse. Sidney Toler, Mantan Moreland, Victor Sen Yung, Tanis Chandler, Bruce Kellogg, John Gallaudet. More routine sleuthing as Charlie Chan probes an insurance scam in San Francisco. One of the later (and lesser) *Chan* entries. ▼▶

Shadow Strikes, The (1937) **61m.** *½ D: Lynn Shores. Rod La Rocque, Lynn Anders, James Blakely, Walter McGrail, Bill Kellogg, Cy Kendall, Kenneth Harlan. Lamont Cranston, secretly the cloaked Shadow, investigates a murder at a manor while disguised as a lawyer. Murky, dull, and talky. First of two *Shadow* movies with La Rocque; here the character out of cloak seems more like Philo Vance than he did on the radio or in the pulps. Followed by INTERNATIONAL CRIME. ▼▶

Shaggy Dog, The (1959) **104m.** **½ D: Charles Barton. Fred MacMurray, Jean Hagen, Tommy Kirk, Annette Funicello, Tim Considine, Kevin Corcoran, Cecil Kellaway, Alexander Scourby. Disney's first slapstick comedy has fine fantasy premise (a boy who turns into a sheepdog through ancient spell) but sluggish script. Some good gags, but not up to later Disney standard. Jack Albertson has bit part as reporter. Sequels: THE SHAGGY D.A. and a 1987 TV movie, THE RETURN OF THE SHAGGY DOG. Remade in 2006 and for TV in 1994. Also shown in computer-colored version. ▼●▶

Shaka Zulu SEE: **Mark of the Hawk, The**

Shakedown (1950) **80m.** **½ D: Joseph Pevney. Howard Duff, Peggy Dow, Brian Donlevy, Bruce Bennett, Peggie Castle, Anne Vernon, Lawrence Tierney. Fast-paced but familiar chronicle of ambitious photographer Duff, who uses any and all means—starting with blackmail—to get ahead. Look for Rock Hudson as a doorman.

Shakedown, The (1959-British) **92m.** ** D: John Lemont. Terence Morgan, Hazel Court, Donald Pleasence, Bill Owen, Harry H. Corbett. Cheesy crime yarn about a cocky small-time racketeer who sets up a photography studio and modeling school as a front for a blackmail scheme. Enjoyably bad, with one of the worst (read funniest) title songs ever warbled on screen.

Shake Hands With the Devil (1959) **110m.** ***½ D: Michael Anderson. James Cagney, Don Murray, Dana Wynter, Glynis Johns, Michael Redgrave, Cyril Cusack, Sybil Thorndike, Richard Harris. Gripping drama of war-torn Ireland in 1920s, with American student trying to stay aloof, but, drawn by circumstances, he joins rebel army led by iron-willed Cagney. Strikingly filmed on location. ▼▶

Shake, Rattle & Rock! (1956) **72m.** ** D: Edward L. Cahn. Touch (Mike) Connors, Lisa Gaye, Sterling Holloway, Fats Domino, Joe Turner, Tommy Charles, Margaret Dumont, Raymond Hatton. Sub-par 1950s rock film with standard plot about adults trying to put the lid on kids' music, benefitting from presences of Domino, Turner, and veteran character actors. Partially remade in 1994 for cable TV.▼

Shakespeare Wallah (1965-Indian) **115m.** *** D: James Ivory. Shashi Kapoor, Felicity Kendal, Geoffrey Kendal, Laura Liddell, Madhur Jaffrey, Utpal Dutt. Playboy Kapoor, who has an actress-mistress, romances Felicity Kendal, a member of a two-bit English theatrical company touring Shakespeare in India. Simple, poignant drama.▼▶

Shall We Dance (1937) **116m.** ***½ D: Mark Sandrich. Fred Astaire, Ginger Rogers, Eric Blore, Edward Everett Horton, Ann Shoemaker, Jerome Cowan, Harriet Hoctor. Lesser Astaire-Rogers is still top musical, with Gershwin's "Let's Call the Whole Thing Off," "They All Laughed," and "They Can't Take That Away from Me" holding together flimsy plot about dance team pretending to be wed. ▼●▶

Shame (1962) SEE: **Intruder, The** (1962)
Shameless Old Lady, The (1965-French) **94m.** *** D: Rene Allio. Sylvie, Malka Ribovska, Victor Lanoux, Etienne Bierry. Bertolt Brecht story charmingly brought to the screen. Sylvie is terrific as old woman who lives alone and follows a drab and uneventful routine until there is a strange turnabout in her relationships with others.▼

Shamrock Handicap, The (1926) **66m.** **½ D: John Ford. Janet Gaynor, Leslie Fenton, Willard Louis, J. Farrell MacDonald, Claire McDowell, Louis Payne, Brandon Hurst. Ford lays on the blarney in this likable but predictable melodrama-romance that spotlights the affection between an Irish lass (Gaynor), the lone daughter of a kindly nobleman, and a young son of Erin (Fenton) who heads off to America to work as a jockey. Of note for the way Ford contrasts life in Ireland and the U.S. Based on a story by Peter B. Kyne.

Shamrock Hill (1949) **62m.** ** D: Arthur Dreifuss. Peggy Ryan, Ray McDonald, Trudy Marshall, Rick Vallin, John Litel, Mary Gordon. A lass of Irish descent favors a special spot to tell fairy tales to local children, but a disdainful builder is about to wipe out her little corner of paradise with a new TV station. What else can she do but seek help from the leprechauns who live on the hill? The movie industry's terror over the advent of television is overt in this obscure musical whimsy. Ryan and McDonald got married four years later. ▼❶

Shane (1953) **C-118m.** **** D: George Stevens. Alan Ladd, Jean Arthur, Van Heflin, (Walter) Jack Palance, Brandon de Wilde, Ben Johnson, Edgar Buchanan, Emile Meyer, Elisha Cook, Jr. Former gunfighter Ladd comes to defense of homesteaders and is idolized by their son. Palance is unforgettable in role of creepy hired gunslinger. Classic Western is splendid in every way. Breathtaking cinematography by Loyal Griggs won an Oscar. Screenplay by A. B. Guthrie, Jr., from the Jack Schaefer novel. Arthur's final film. Shot in 1951. Later a brief TV series. ▼❶❸

Shanghai (1935) **75m.** *½ D: James Flood. Loretta Young, Charles Boyer, Warner Oland, Fred Keating, Charles Grapewin, Alison Skipworth. Dreary drama of American girl falling in love with mysterious Boyer, who turns out to be (gasp!) Eurasian. Two good stars can't save this turgid outing.

Shanghai Chest, The (1948) **56m.** *½ D: William Beaudine. Roland Winters, Mantan Moreland, Jim Ryan, Victor Sen Yung, Deannie Best, Tristram Coffin, John Alvin, Russell Hicks, Pierre Watkin. An executed criminal appears to have returned from the dead when his fingerprints are found at the scene of several murders. Weak *Charlie Chan* mystery. ❶

Shanghai Cobra, The (1945) **64m.** ** D: Phil Karlson. Sidney Toler, Benson Fong, Mantan Moreland, Walter Fenner, James Cardwell, Joan Barclay, James Flavin, Addison Richards. Charlie Chan is hired by the government to probe a series of murders in which the victims are allegedly killed by a snake bite. Middling entry, although par for the Monogram series. ▼❶❸

Shanghai Express (1932) **80m.** *** D: Josef von Sternberg. Marlene Dietrich, Anna May Wong, Warner Oland, Clive Brook, Eugene Pallette, Louise Closser Hale. Dated but prime Dietrich vehicle, grandly photographed by Lee Garmes (who won an Oscar). Marlene is Shanghai Lily, Brook her old flame, Oland a cruel war lord, Wong a spunky partisan, in Jules Furthman–scripted yarn of train ride through China during civil warfare. Remade as PEKING EXPRESS. ▼❶❸

Shanghai Gesture, The (1941) **98m.** ** D: Josef von Sternberg. Gene Tierney, Walter Huston, Victor Mature, Ona Munson, Maria Ouspenskaya, Phyllis Brooks, Albert Bassermann, Eric Blore, Mike Mazurki. Slow, overblown drama of Huston discovering daughter Tierney in Oriental gambling setup. Intriguing direction somehow never makes it. The mural is by artist (and actor) Keye Luke! ▼❶❸

Shanghai Story, The (1954) **99m.** ** D: Frank Lloyd. Ruth Roman, Edmond O'Brien, Richard Jaeckel, Barry Kelley, Whit Bissell. Tawdry yet intriguing little film about Americans trapped by Red Chinese. ❶

Sharkfighters, The (1956) **C-73m.** *½ D: Jerry Hopper. Victor Mature, Karen Steele, James Olson, Philip Coolidge, Claude Akins. Bland account of Mature et al. seeking some way to repel the man-killing fish. CinemaScope.

She (1935) **95m.** *** D: Irving Pichel, Lansing C. Holden. Helen Gahagan, Randolph Scott, Helen Mack, Nigel Bruce, Gustav von Seyffertitz. Escapist adventure on a grand scale, from H. Rider Haggard's story of expedition seeking Flame of Eternal Life, which has been given to one all-powerful woman. Gahagan's cold personality is major drawback, but film is still fun, with outstanding Max Steiner score. Some prints run 89m. Previously filmed in 1917 and 1926, remade several times. Also available in computer-colored version. ▼❶❸

She (1965-British) **C-106m.** **½ D: Robert Day. Ursula Andress, John Richardson, Peter Cushing, Bernard Cribbins, Christopher Lee, Andre Morell. Effective refilming of H. Rider Haggard's fantasy of love-starved eternal queen, seeking the reincarnation of her long-dead lover. The two leads certainly are attractive. Followed by THE VENGEANCE OF SHE. Hammerscope. ▼❶❸

She Couldn't Say No (1940) **62m.** ** D: William Clemens. Roger Pryor, Eve Arden, Cliff Edwards, Clem Bevans, Vera Lewis, Alexis Smith. Flat comedy featuring Arden as a lawyer who shows her mettle when circumstances force her to oppose her boyfriend in court.

She Couldn't Say No (1954) **89m.** *½ D: Lloyd Bacon. Robert Mitchum, Jean Simmons, Arthur Hunnicutt, Edgar Buchanan, Wallace Ford, Raymond Walburn, Pinky Tomlin. Silly fluff about wealthy, misguided young Simmons, who shows up in Progress, Arkansas, with a scheme to shower its citizens with free money; Mitchum is out of his element as the town doctor. A real dud. ▼

She Couldn't Take It (1935) **75m.** *** D: Tay Garnett. George Raft, Joan Bennett, Billie Burke, Walter Connolly, Lloyd Nolan, Franklin Pangborn, Alan Mowbray, Donald Meek, Wallace Ford. Fast-paced social comedy of bootlegger Raft impressing his henpecked cell mate Connolly (in stir on an income-tax-evasion rap). Upon release, Connolly appoints Raft his family guardian, causing rivalry with his madcap daughter Bennett.

She-Creature, The (1956) **77m.** ****** D: Edward L. Cahn. Marla English, Tom Conway, Chester Morris, Ron Randell, Frieda Inescort, Cathy Downs, El Brendel, Jack Mulhall, Frank Jenks. Bizarre blend of CREATURE FROM THE BLACK LAGOON and THE SEARCH FOR BRIDEY MURPHY. Evil hypnotist uses mesmerized assistant to call back the murderous ghost of the sea creature of which she is a reincarnation. Slow and preposterous but effectively moody, with one of Paul Blaisdell's more memorable monsters, which he also plays. Really odd cast. Remade as CREATURE OF DESTRUCTION and again for cable in 2001.▶

She Demons (1958) **80m.** BOMB D: Richard E. Cunha. Irish McCalla, Tod Griffin, Victor Sen Yung, Rudolph Anders, Gene Roth. Three men and sexy, spoiled McCalla are stranded on an island inhabited by Nazi criminals, a mad scientist, and the title creatures. Too boring to be funny; even McCalla's request to "give me some privacy while I undress" doesn't help.▼▶

She Devil (1957) **77m.** BOMB D: Kurt Neumann. Mari Blanchard, Jack Kelly, Albert Dekker, John Archer. Blanchard is injected with fruit fly serum in effort to cure her of TB; already rotten, she can now physically adapt to any look and survive fatal injuries. Based on a story by Stanley G. Weinbaum. Regalscope.

She Done Him Wrong (1933) **66m.** ******** D: Lowell Sherman. Mae West, Cary Grant, Gilbert Roland, Noah Beery, Rochelle Hudson, Rafaela Ottiano, Louise Beavers. West repeats her stage role of Diamond Lil in Gay '90s spoof. Grant is invited by Mae to come up and see her sometime—he does, fireworks result. Mae sings "Frankie and Johnny" and "Easy Rider" in her best film, which she coscripted from her Broadway hit.▼▶

Sheep Has Five Legs, The (1954-French) **95m.** ******* D: Henri Verneuil. Fernandel, Delmont, Françoise Arnoul, Paulette Dubost. Fernandel's tour de force, playing an old wine-grower and each of his five sons who have gathered together for a family reunion.▼▶

Sheepman, The (1958) **C-85m.** ******* D: George Marshall. Glenn Ford, Shirley MacLaine, Leslie Nielsen, Mickey Shaughnessy, Edgar Buchanan. Modest, entertaining comedy-Western with Ford battling Nielsen for sheep herds and MacLaine, though not always in that order. Shaughnessy is typically amusing. Written by genre vets William Bowers and James Edward Grant. CinemaScope.▶

She Gets Her Man (1945) **74m.** ******* D: Erle C. Kenton. Joan Davis, Leon Errol,

William Gargan, Vivian Austin, Russell Hicks, Donald MacBride. Hilarious slapstick whodunit with daughter of legendary female police chief hired to stop crime wave in city. Davis and Errol make marvelous duo in this fast-moving farce.

She Gods of Shark Reef (1958) **C-63m.** BOMB D: Roger Corman. Bill Cord, Don Durant, Lisa Montell, Jeanne Gerson, Carol Lindsay. Location filming in Hawaii does nothing for this confusing tale of brothers Cord and Durant shipwrecked on isolated isle inhabited only by pearl-diving native women.▼▶

She Had to Say Yes (1933) **66m.** ****½** D: Busby Berkeley, George Amy. Loretta Young, Winnie Lightner, Lyle Talbot, Regis Toomey, Hugh Herbert, Ferdinand Gottschalk. Strange, raw, racy story about a clothing company with "customer girls," whose job is to entertain out-of-town buyers. Toomey suggests drawing on the steno pool to give the buyers a change but doesn't want his fiancée (Young) involved. Loretta is very good as a good girl who learns the ropes overnight. Berkeley's first (co-) directing credit; the steno pool is full of his chorines, including Toby Wing.

Sheik, The (1921) **80m.** ******* D: George Melford. Rudolph Valentino, Agnes Ayres, Adolphe Menjou, Walter Long, Lucien Littlefield, George Waggner. Ayres, a "civilized" woman, falls completely under the spell of desert chieftain Valentino. The silent film that helped create the Valentino legend is hokey and campy, but still entertaining. It's easy to see why women went crazy for the Latin star. Racist/imperialist angle of the story is equally fascinating. Followed by SON OF THE SHEIK.▼▶

She Loved a Fireman (1937) **57m.** ****½** D: John Farrow. Dick Foran, Ann Sheridan, Robert Armstrong, Eddie Acuff, Veda Ann Borg. Wiseguy fireman Foran gets into hot water with captain Armstrong when he starts dating his sister (Sheridan) but proves himself worthy in the clinch. Standard Warner Bros. action fare, handled with gusto.

She Loves Me Not (1934) **83m.** ******* D: Elliott Nugent. Bing Crosby, Miriam Hopkins, Kitty Carlisle, Lynne Overman, Henry Stephenson, George Barbier, Warren Hymer. Hopkins is ebullient (and hilarious) as a nightclub performer running from murder scene who hides out with college man Crosby in his Princeton dorm. Gets funnier as it goes along, and introduces "Love in Bloom" to boot. Based on Howard Lindsay's play. Remade as TRUE TO THE ARMY and HOW TO BE VERY, VERY POPULAR.

She Married Her Boss (1935) **90m.** ****½** D: Gregory La Cava. Claudette Colbert, Melvyn Douglas, Edith Fellows, Michael Bartlett, Raymond Walburn, Jean Dixon. That's what she did, and nothing much happens until tipsy butler Walburn staggers in. Good stars with fair script by usually reliable Sidney Buchman.

Shenandoah (1965) **C-105m.** ******* D: Andrew V. McLaglen. James Stewart, Doug McClure, Glenn Corbett, Patrick Wayne, Rosemary Forsyth, Katharine Ross, Tim McIntire, Paul Fix, Denver Pyle, George Kennedy, James Best, Harry Carey, Jr., Dabbs Greer, Strother Martin. Rousing, well-acted saga of Virginia widower indifferent to War between the States until his family is involved. Sentimental drama captures heartbreak of America's Civil War. Basis for later Broadway musical. Ross' film debut.▼●❶

Shepherd of the Hills (1941) **C-98m.** ******* D: Henry Hathaway. John Wayne, Betty Field, Harry Carey, Beulah Bondi, James Barton, Samuel S. Hinds, Marjorie Main, Ward Bond, Marc Lawrence, John Qualen. Beautifully mounted production of Harold Bell Wright story about Ozark mountain folk, and a man who lives his life in the shadow of a curse: the promise to kill the man who abandoned his mother. Wayne is excellent, and surrounded by fine character actors, with unusual roles for Lawrence and Main. Fuzzy Knight sings a sentimental song ("Happy Hunting Ground") as he did in the not dissimilar THE TRAIL OF THE LONESOME PINE. Exquisitely shot by Charles Lang, Jr. and W. Howard Greene; filmed before in 1919 and 1928, then remade in 1963.▼❶

She Played With Fire (1957-British) **95m.** ****½** D: Sidney Gilliatt. Jack Hawkins, Arlene Dahl, Dennis Price, Bernard Miles, Ian Hunter, Malcolm Keen, Geoffrey Keen, Patrick Holt, Christopher Lee, Greta Gynt. Insurance investigator Hawkins is sent to a country estate to check out a fire-damage claim, only to find that the man of the house (Price) is married to his ex-lover (Dahl). Matters quickly grow more complicated in this fairly intriguing yarn. Original British title: FORTUNE IS A WOMAN.❶

Sheriff of Fractured Jaw, The (1959-British) **C-103m.** ****½** D: Raoul Walsh. Kenneth More, Jayne Mansfield, Henry Hull, William Campbell, Bruce Cabot, Robert Morley. Innocuous Western spoof with Englishman More handed job of sheriff in war-torn town, which he handles surprisingly well. CinemaScope.▼❶

Sheriff of Tombstone (1941) **54m.** ******* D: Joseph Kane. Roy Rogers, George "Gabby" Hayes, Elyse Knox, Addison Richards, Sally Payne, Harry Woods, Zeffie Tilbury, Jay Novello, Hal Taliaferro. Disreputable Tombstone mayor Richards wants a mine owned by Knox's grandmother and hires an outlaw to do his dirty work . . . but mistakes former Dodge City sheriff Rogers for that very outlaw! Engaging story with neat twists. Novello has a scene-stealing dual

role as a Wells Fargo manager and a Mexican bandit.▼❶

Sherlock Holmes Sherlock Holmes has been portrayed on film more often—and by more different people—than any other fictional character. The eminent John Barrymore played the detective in a 1922 silent film. Others have included Arthur Wontner (who starred in a series of five modest British films in the 1930s), Reginald Owen (who played Holmes one year after appearing as Watson opposite Clive Brook), Raymond Massey, Christopher Lee, and Peter Cushing. In the 1980s Jeremy Brett starred in a handsome and scrupulously faithful series of Holmes adventures filmed for British television. But there was only one American-made movie series featuring this world-famous sleuth, and it was launched quite inadvertently in 1939 when (by some genius of casting) Basil Rathbone and Nigel Bruce were signed to play Sherlock Holmes and Dr. Watson in an adaptation of Sir Arthur Conan Doyle's *Hound of the Baskervilles*; its immediate success prompted a follow-up, THE ADVENTURES OF SHERLOCK HOLMES, that same year. These were beautiful, atmospheric productions, faithful to the spirit of Doyle's stories. Three years later, at a new studio (Universal), the series resumed with SHERLOCK HOLMES AND THE VOICE OF TERROR, updating the Doyle tales to have Holmes battling the Nazis. The 12 "modern" films never captured the flavor of the initial two (THE SCARLET CLAW came closest), but they were always worth seeing for the performances of the two stars: Rathbone—smooth, cunning, seldom caught by surprise; and Bruce—talkative, bumbling, never close to fully understanding the situation at hand. Mary Gordon made token appearances as Holmes' landlady, Mrs. Hudson, and Dennis Hoey appeared in several films as Scotland Yard Inspector Lestrade, who usually managed to get in the way. Holmes was at his best battling wits with Professor Moriarty, played in various episodes by George Zucco, Lionel Atwill, and Henry Daniell. Every episode ended with a stirring ode by Holmes to the glory of England, America, Canada, or some comparable topic, in keeping with the war-time flag-waving nature of Hollywood films. Seldom faithful to Doyle, later episodes like DRESSED TO KILL wearing thin, dialogue often awkward (S. H. IN WASHINGTON, for example), the Sherlock Holmes series relied on Rathbone and Bruce for enjoyment, and they never failed.

SHERLOCK HOLMES

The Hound of the Baskervilles (1939)
The Adventures of Sherlock Holmes (1939)
Sherlock Holmes and the Voice of Terror (1942)
Sherlock Holmes and the Secret Weapon (1942)

Sherlock Holmes in Washington (1943)
Sherlock Holmes Faces Death (1943)
The Spider Woman (1944); aka Sherlock Holmes and the Spider Woman
The Scarlet Claw (1944)
The Pearl of Death (1944)
The House of Fear (1945)
The Woman in Green (1945)
Pursuit to Algiers (1945)
Terror by Night (1946)
Dressed to Kill (1946)

Sherlock Holmes (1922) **85m.** *½ D: Albert Parker. John Barrymore, Roland Young, Carol Dempster, Louis Wolheim, Gustav von Seyffertitz, William Powell, Percy Knight, Hedda Hopper, Reginald Denny. In helping a prince out of a jam, the great detective finds himself locking horns with nefarious Dr. Moriarty (von Seyffertitz). Woefully dull silent drama squanders perfect casting of the principal characters. Adapted from William Gillette's play based on Arthur Conan Doyle's stories. ▶

Sherlock Holmes (1932) **68m.** **½ D: William K. Howard. Clive Brook, Ernest Torrence, Miriam Jordan, Alan Mowbray, Herbert Mundin, Reginald Owen. Genteel, stylish approach to Holmes, set in modern-day London; pleasing but subdued. Torrence is a most enjoyable Moriarty.

Sherlock Holmes and the Secret Weapon (1942) **68m.** *** D: Roy William Neill. Basil Rathbone, Nigel Bruce, Lionel Atwill, Kaaren Verne, William Post, Jr., Dennis Hoey, Mary Gordon, Holmes Herbert. Holmes is hired to protect the inventor of a new bombsight from the deadly clutches of Moriarty (Atwill). Exciting entry with Hoey scoring as the comically maladroit Inspector Lestrade. Also shown in computer-colored version. ▼▶●

Sherlock Holmes and the Spider Woman SEE: **Spider Woman, The**

Sherlock Holmes and the Voice of Terror (1942) **65m.** **½ D: John Rawlins. Basil Rathbone, Nigel Bruce, Evelyn Ankers, Reginald Denny, Thomas Gomez, Henry Daniell, Montagu Love. First entry in the Universal Rathbone-Bruce series is probably the least impressive, but still enjoyable once you accept the premise of Victorian Holmes (with a particularly risible haircut) battling Nazi saboteurs in WW2 England. Excellent supporting performances by Gomez (in his film debut) and Ankers. ▶

Sherlock Holmes and the Woman in Green SEE: **Woman in Green, The**

Sherlock Holmes Faces Death (1943) **68m.** *** D: Roy William Neill. Basil Rathbone, Nigel Bruce, Hillary Brooke, Milburn Stone, Arthur Margetson, Halliwell Hobbes, Dennis Hoey. The deductive master and his blundering companion check into a mansion for convalescing war officers where a series of murders occurs. Very amusing entry replete

with a strange clock tower, a subterranean crypt, and a human chessboard. Look for Peter Lawford in a bit as a sailor. ▼▶●

Sherlock Holmes in Washington (1943) **71m.** **½ D: Roy William Neill. Basil Rathbone, Nigel Bruce, Marjorie Lord, Henry Daniell, George Zucco, John Archer, Gavin Muir. Holmes and Watson are off to D.C. in search of some hidden microfilm in this cheeky entry notable for its strong WW2 propaganda content and Watson's fascination with American bubble gum. ▼▶

Sherlock, Jr. (1924) **45m.** **** D: Buster Keaton. Buster Keaton, Kathryn McGuire, Ward Crane, Joseph Keaton, Erwin Connolly. Keaton reached his pinnacle with this brilliant and hilarious story of a hapless projectionist who walks right into the screen and takes part in the imaginary detective drama unfolding. Sublime study of film and fantasy, which has undoubtedly influenced countless filmmakers such as Woody Allen, Jacques Rivette, even Buñuel. ▼▶●

She's a Soldier Too (1944) **67m.** ** D: William Castle. Beulah Bondi, Lloyd Bridges, Nina Foch, Percy Kilbride, Shelley Winters, Ida Moore. OK B film with cabdriver Bondi helping out soldier Bridges.

She's Back on Broadway (1953) **C-95m.** **½ D: Gordon Douglas. Virginia Mayo, Steve Cochran, Gene Nelson, Frank Lovejoy, Patrice Wymore. Fading Hollywood star returns to Broadway, finds dealing with director Cochran her biggest challenge. Good cast in slick but predictable musical drama. ▶

She's Got Everything (1937) **73m.** ** D: Joseph Santley. Gene Raymond, Ann Sothern, Victor Moore, Helen Broderick, Parkyakarkus, Billy Gilbert, William Brisbane, Solly Ward, Jack Carson. Wealthy Sothern's father has died and left her penniless. What's a girl to do? Why not take a job as secretary to Raymond, the richest bachelor in N.Y.C.? Predictable romantic comedy with Broderick and Moore, slumming from Astaire & Rogers, lending much-needed support. ▶

She's Working Her Way Through College (1952) **C-101m.** **½ D: H. Bruce Humberstone. Virginia Mayo, Ronald Reagan, Gene Nelson, Don DeFore, Phyllis Thaxter, Patrice Wymore, Roland Winters. Reworking of THE MALE ANIMAL diminishes the role of the professor (played by Reagan), showcasing Mayo instead, as a burlesque star who tries to bury her past and pursue a college education. Pleasant but minor musical. ▶

She Went to the Races (1945) **86m.** ** D: Willis Goldbeck. James Craig, Frances Gifford, Ava Gardner, Edmund Gwenn, Sig Ruman, Reginald Owen. Mild romantic comedy in which scientist Gifford's colleagues develop a system for beating the horses; along the way, she falls for horse owner Craig. Buster Keaton briefly appears as a bellboy.

She-Wolf of London (1946) 61m. ** D: Jean Yarbrough. Don Porter, June Lockhart, Sara Haden, Jan Wiley, Lloyd Corrigan. Amidst a series of London murders, mousy Lockhart becomes convinced she is the werewolf responsible. Silly and predictable. No connection to later TV series. ▼⦆

She Wore a Yellow Ribbon (1949) C-103m. ***½ D: John Ford. John Wayne, Joanne Dru, John Agar, Ben Johnson, Harry Carey, Jr., Victor McLaglen, Mildred Natwick, George O'Brien, Arthur Shields, Tom Tyler, Noble Johnson, Francis Ford. Wayne gives one of his all-time best performances as an aging cavalry captain on the eve of retirement, heading a last patrol across the southwest desert as all-out Indian war looms. Beautifully filmed in Technicolor by Oscar-winning Winton Hoch, with breathtaking, painterly shots of Monument Valley. Frank S. Nugent and Laurence Stallings' script (from two short stories by James Warner Bellah) is a bit top-heavy with climaxes, but it's still a great film. Second of Ford's cavalry trilogy, following FORT APACHE and followed by RIO GRANDE. ▼●⦆

She Wouldn't Say Yes (1945) 87m. ** D: Alexander Hall. Rosalind Russell, Lee Bowman, Adele Jergens, Charles Winninger, Harry Davenport, Percy Kilbride, Darren McGavin. Self-assured psychiatrist Russell likes to think she's in control of her life—until cartoonist Bowman takes a shine to her and won't take no for an answer. Starts well but becomes silly and contrived.⦆

She Wrote the Book (1946) 72m. ** D: Charles Lamont. Joan Davis, Jack Oakie, Mischa Auer, Kirby Grant, John Litel, Jacqueline de Wit, Gloria Stuart. OK comedy about prim professor Davis posing as author of torrid bestseller. Fun for Davis fans, but not one of her best vehicles.

Shield for Murder (1954) 80m. **½ D: Edmond O'Brien, Howard W. Koch. Edmond O'Brien, John Agar, Marla English, Carolyn Jones, Claude Akins. Tidy, tough yarn of crooked detective involved in theft-murder, trying to keep his loot and avoid capture.

Shine On Harvest Moon (1938) 55m. **½ D: Joseph Kane. Roy Rogers, Mary Hart (Lynne Roberts), Stanley Andrews, William Farnum, Lulu Belle and Scotty, Frank Jaquet, Chester Gunnels. Pretty good early Rogers vehicle in which local ranchers suspect that Farnum is still in cahoots with no-good rustler Andrews, even though that partnership broke up long ago. It all leads up to a rousing fight finale. Roy sings two especially nice tunes, "Let Me Build a Cabin" and "The Man in the Moon Is a Cowboy." ▼⦆

Shine On Harvest Moon (1944) 112m. **½ D: David Butler. Ann Sheridan, Jack Carson, Dennis Morgan, Irene Manning, S.

Z. Sakall, Marie Wilson, The Step Brothers. Lives of great entertainers Nora Bayes and Jack Norworth make for fairly entertaining musical. Finale in color.

Shining Hour, The (1938) 80m. **½ D: Frank Borzage. Joan Crawford, Margaret Sullavan, Robert Young, Melvyn Douglas, Fay Bainter, Allyn Joslyn, Hattie McDaniel, Frank Albertson. N.Y.C. nightclub performer Crawford marries into Wisconsin farm family, leading to emotional fireworks. Crawford and Sullavan (as her sister-in-law) provide interesting contrast in this overwrought soap opera. ▼⦆

Shining Victory (1941) 80m. **½ D: Irving Rapper. James Stephenson, Geraldine Fitzgerald, Donald Crisp, Barbara O'Neil, Montagu Love, Sig Ruman. Handsome production of A. J. Cronin play about ultra-dedicated research psychologist who can't even see that his new assistant is in love with him. Very watchable but not terribly inspiring. Publicity from the time insists that Bette Davis makes a walk-on appearance as a nurse; just try to find her!

Ship Ahoy (1942) 95m. **½ D: Edward Buzzell. Eleanor Powell, Red Skelton, Virginia O'Brien, Bert Lahr, John Emery, Tommy Dorsey Orchestra, Frank Sinatra, Jo Stafford. Nonsensical plot of Skelton thinking U.S. agent is working for Axis; shipboard yarn has some salty dancing and singing, good Dorsey numbers featuring drummer Buddy Rich. ▼●⦆

Shipmates Forever (1935) 124m. **½ D: Frank Borzage. Dick Powell, Ruby Keeler, Lewis Stone, Ross Alexander, Eddie Acuff, Dick Foran, John Arledge. Singer Powell is manipulated by admiral father Stone into entering Annapolis. Middling military musical. Reissued at 108m.⦆

Ship of Fools (1965) 149m. **** D: Stanley Kramer. Vivien Leigh, Oskar Werner, Simone Signoret, Jose Ferrer, Lee Marvin, Jose Greco, George Segal, Elizabeth Ashley, Michael Dunn, Charles Korvin, Lilia Skala. GRAND HOTEL at sea in pre-WW2 days. Superb cast including Leigh, in her last film, as disillusioned divorcée, Werner and Signoret as illicit lovers, Marvin as punchy baseball player. Penetrating drama, when not a soaper. Script by Abby Mann from Katherine Anne Porter's novel; won Oscars for Cinematography (Ernest Laszlo) and Art Direction. ▼●⦆

Ship of Lost Men (1929-German-French) 121m. **½ D: Maurice Tourneur. Marlene Dietrich, Fritz Kortner, Robin Irvine, Vladimir Sokoloff, Gaston Modot, Boris de Fast, Feodor Chaliapin (Jr.). A transatlantic aviatrix's plane crashes at sea. Saved by a passing boat, she's horrified to find she's the lone woman aboard a vessel jammed with "lost men": miscreants with terrible pasts and no futures. Luminously photographed; Dietrich's last silent, and Tourneur's, too. ▼⦆

[620]

Ships With Wings (1942-British) **89m.** ★★★ D: Sergei Nolbandov. John Clements, Leslie Banks, Jane Baxter, Ann Todd, Basil Sydney, Edward Chapman, Hugh Williams, Michael Wilding, Michael Rennie, Cecil Parker. Sterling, patriotic WW2 drama spotlighting the importance of aircraft carriers in battling the Nazis; romantic subplot has pilot Clements falling for an admiral's daughter.▼

Ship That Died of Shame, The (1955-British) **91m.** ★★★ D: Basil Dearden. Richard Attenborough, George Baker, Bill Owen, Virginia McKenna, Roland Culver, Bernard Lee, Ralph Truman. Crew of British gunboat reteams after WW2 and uses the same vessel for smuggling purposes, until "it" begins to rebel at their increasingly grimy exploits. Fine cast in offbeat drama. Retitled PT RAIDERS and cut to 78m.◗

Ship Was Loaded, The (1957-British) **81m.** ★★ D: Val Guest. David Tomlinson, Peggy Cummins, Alfie Bass, Ronald Shiner. Inconsequential zaniness involving impersonations and shenanigans in Her Majesty's Navy. Retitled: CARRY ON ADMIRAL. CinemaScope.▼◗

Shiralee, The (1957-British) **99m.** ★★½ D: Leslie Norman. Peter Finch, Elizabeth Sellars, Dana Wilson, Rosemary Harris, Tessie O'Shea, Sidney James, George Rose. Rough-hewn Australian swagman takes daughter away from unfaithful wife to accompany him on his wanderings. Moving portrayal of their relationship compensates for diffuse, episodic nature of film. On-location scenery helps, too. Remade as a TV miniseries.

Shock (1946) **70m.** ★★ D: Alfred L. Werker. Vincent Price, Lynn Bari, Frank Latimore, Anabel Shaw, Michael Dunne, Reed Hadley. A woman becomes traumatized after witnessing a murder—and the psychiatrist who takes her case just happens to be the killer. Intriguing premise, so-so result. ▼◗

Shock Corridor (1963) **C/B&W-101m.** ★★★ D: Samuel Fuller. Peter Breck, Constance Towers, Gene Evans, James Best, Hari Rhodes. Journalist Breck gets admitted to mental institution to unmask murderer, but soon goes crazy himself. Powerful melodrama with raw, emotional impact. Fuller also produced and wrote the script; imaginative photography by Stanley Cortez. Three sequences are in color. ▼◗

Shocking Miss Pilgrim, The (1947) **C-85m.** ★★ D: George Seaton. Betty Grable, Dick Haymes, Anne Revere, Allyn Joslyn, Gene Lockhart, Elizabeth Patterson. Labored story of 1870s Boston woman in business world. Fair Gershwin score includes "For You, For Me, For Evermore."◗

Shockproof (1949) **79m.** ★★★ D: Douglas Sirk. Cornel Wilde, Patricia Knight, John Baragrey, Esther Minciotti, Howard St. John. Parole officer Wilde is lured into love affair with parolee Knight which threatens to destroy him. Stylish film noir, co-written by Samuel Fuller, which unfortunately cops out at the end.◗

Shock Treatment (1964) **94m.** ★★ D: Denis Sanders. Stuart Whitman, Carol Lynley, Roddy McDowall, Lauren Bacall, Olive Deering, Ossie Davis, Donald Buka, Bert Freed, Douglass Dumbrille. Out-of-work actor (Whitman) goes undercover at state mental asylum to discover whereabouts of murderer McDowall's supposed million-dollar stash. Odd, unsatisfying melodrama. CinemaScope.

Shoeshine (1946-Italian) **93m.** ★★★★ D: Vittorio De Sica. Rinaldo Smerdoni, Franco Interlenghi, Anniello Mele, Bruno Ortensi, Pacifico Astrologo. A brilliant, haunting neorealist drama about two youngsters struggling to survive in war-scarred Italy; they become involved with black marketeering and are sent to reform school. This deservedly won a special Oscar—before Best Foreign Film prizes were awarded. Screenplay by Sergio Amidei, Adolfo Franci, Cesare G. Viola, and Cesare Zavattini. ▼◗

Shoot First (1952-British) **88m.** ★★½ D: Robert Parrish. Joel McCrea, Evelyn Keyes, Herbert Lom, Marius Goring, Roland Culver, Laurence Naismith, Joan Hickson. Routine espionage tale with McCrea as an American colonel in England, who believes he accidentally killed a man, and becomes involved with spies. Screenplay by Eric Ambler. Originally titled: ROUGH SHOOT.

Shooting High (1940) **65m.** ★★ D: Alfred E. Green. Gene Autry, Jane Withers, Marjorie Weaver, Robert Lowery, Kay Aldridge, Jack Carson, Hobart Cavanaugh. Gene is persuaded to appear in a movie that's being shot in his hometown; meanwhile, he also must settle a family feud and capture some bank robbers. Autry shares center stage with energetic child star Withers in this weak musical Western, Gene's only film away from home base, Republic Pictures.▼◗

Shoot-Out at Medicine Bend (1957) **87m.** ★★½ D: Richard L. Bare. Randolph Scott, James Craig, Angie Dickinson, Dani Crayne, James Garner, Gordon Jones, Myron Healey. Ex-Army captain Scott and his men go undercover disguised as Quakers to find out who sold faulty ammo that resulted in the death of his brother. Minor but entertaining Scott oater has the look and feel of a Warner Bros. TV Western of the era.◗

Shoot the Piano Player (1960-French) **81m.** ★★★★ D: François Truffaut. Charles Aznavour, Marie Dubois, Nicole Berger, Michele Mercier, Albert Remy. Atmospheric early Truffaut gem. Aznavour is marvelous as a former concert pianist who traded on his fame and now plays in rundown Parisian cafe. His ambitious girlfriend wants him to resume his career, but he gets involved with gangsters and murder instead. This film, more than any other, reflects the influence of Hollywood low-budget melodramas on Truffaut and his cinematic style. Dyaliscope. ▼●▶

Shoot the Works (1934) 82m. **½ D: Wesley Ruggles. Jack Oakie, Ben Bernie, Dorothy Dell, Alison Skipworth, Roscoe Karns, Arline Judge, William Frawley, Lew Cody, Paul Cavanagh. Plot-heavy but entertaining musical about ne'er-do-well sideshow owner Oakie who aspires to be a songwriter. Best song: "With My Eyes Wide Open I'm Dreaming." Based on Gene Fowler and Ben Hecht's play *The Great Magoo*. Look for young Ann Sheridan as Cody's secretary. Remade as SOME LIKE IT HOT (1939).

Shoot to Kill (1947) 64m. ** D: William Berke. Russell Wade, Susan Walters (Luana Walters), Edmund MacDonald, Douglas Blackley, Vince Barnett. The bodies of a mobster *and* a D.A. are found in a crashed car after a police pursuit; what can the explanation be? Implausible C-grade crime drama is loaded with complications (including flashbacks within flashbacks), double-double-crosses, dual identities, and other dippy twists.

Shop Around the Corner, The (1940) 97m. ***½ D: Ernst Lubitsch. Margaret Sullavan, James Stewart, Frank Morgan, Joseph Schildkraut, Sara Haden, Felix Bressart, William Tracy, Charles Smith. The ultimate in sheer charm, a graceful period comedy about coworkers in a Budapest notions shop who don't realize that they are lonelyhearts penpals. Superbly scripted by Samson Raphaelson, from Nikolaus Laszlo's play *Parfumerie*. Later musicalized as IN THE GOOD OLD SUMMERTIME, brought to Broadway as *She Loves Me*, remade as YOU'VE GOT MAIL. Also shown in computer-colored version. ▼●▶

Shop on Main Street, The (1965-Czech) 128m. **** D: Jan Kadar, Elmar Klos. Josef Kroner, Ida Kaminska, Han Slivkova, Frantisek Holly, Martin Gregor. Potent, poignant drama set in WW2 Czechoslovakia, where an old Jewish woman loses her small button shop, and depends on man who takes it over to shield her from further persecution. Oscar winner as Best Foreign Film. Originally titled THE SHOP ON HIGH STREET. ▼●▶

Shopworn (1932) 72m. ** D: Nick Grinde. Barbara Stanwyck, Regis Toomey, ZaSu Pitts, Lucien Littlefield, Clara Blandick. Standard Depression soaper with Toomey's rich family rejecting working girl Stanwyck, who shows 'em and becomes famous star. ▶

Shopworn Angel, The (1938) 85m. *** D: H. C. Potter. Margaret Sullavan, James Stewart, Walter Pidgeon, Hattie McDaniel, Sam Levene, Nat Pendleton. Stewart and Sullavan are always a fine pair, even in this fairly routine soaper. Naive soldier falls in love with loose-moraled actress, who gradually softens under his influence. Beautifully done, including Slavko Vorkapich's masterful opening WW1 montage. Remake of 1929 film with Gary Cooper and Nancy Carroll; filmed again as THAT KIND OF WOMAN. ▼▶

Shore Leave (1925) 74m. **½ D: John S. Robertson. Richard Barthelmess, Dorothy Mackaill, Ted McNamara, Nick Long, Marie Shotwell, Arthur Metcalf. Appealing if sometimes slow-moving romantic comedy with Barthelmess at his best as reluctant seaman Bilge Smith; Mackaill is a dressmaker, approaching old-maidhood, who's out to make him captain of her schooner. Later musicalized as HIT THE DECK and FOLLOW THE FLEET. ▼▶

Short Cut to Hell (1957) 87m. **½ D: James Cagney. Robert Ivers, Georgann Johnson, William Bishop, Murvyn Vye, Yvette Vickers, Jacques Aubuchon. Generally taut remake of THIS GUN FOR HIRE with coldhearted killer Ivers seeking vengeance against the men who stiffed him, being befriended by tough but sympathetic Johnson. Only fling at directing by Cagney, who makes a pre-credit introduction on camera. VistaVision.

Shotgun (1955) C-81m. ** D: Lesley Selander. Sterling Hayden, Zachary Scott, Yvonne De Carlo, Guy Prescott, Angela Greene. Unremarkable Western with sheriff Hayden vs. culprit Scott; De Carlo is the half-breed girl they love. ▼▶

Shot in the Dark, A (1964) C-101m. **** D: Blake Edwards. Peter Sellers, Elke Sommer, George Sanders, Herbert Lom, Tracy Reed, Burt Kwouk, Graham Stark, Andre Maranne, Turk Thrust (Bryan Forbes). Second Inspector Clouseau comedy is far and away the funniest, with the great detective convinced gorgeous Sommer is innocent of murder despite all evidence to the contrary. Gaspingly hilarious farce never slows down for a second, with memorable scene in a nudist colony. Script by Edwards and William Peter Blatty; fine Henry Mancini score. Series debuts of Lom, Kwouk, Stark, and Maranne; last Clouseau film (excluding 1968's INSPECTOR CLOUSEAU, made by other hands) until THE RETURN OF THE PINK PANTHER in 1975. Panavision. ▼●▶

Should Ladies Behave (1933) 87m. **½ D: Harry Beaumont. Lionel Barrymore, Alice Brady, Conway Tearle, Katharine Alexander, Mary Carlisle, William Janney. Flighty Brady and crotchety Barrymore are unhappily married and forced to face the reality of their lives when her oft-married sister and a rakish artist pay them a visit. Occasionally entertaining (albeit predictable) comedy-drama, scripted by Sam and Bella Spewack from Paul Osborn's play *The Vinegar Tree*.

Show, The (1927) 76m. *** D: Tod Browning. John Gilbert, Renée Adorée, Lionel Barrymore, Edward Connelly, Gertrude Short, Andy MacLennan. A Hungarian carnival is the setting for this tale of love, jealousy, and revenge centering on the amorous entanglements of circus sideshow lothario Gilbert. Stylishly directed silent features some bizarre imagery and striking scenes that make it look like a dry run for Browning's FREAKS. Based on the novel *The Day of Souls* by Charles Tenney Jackson.

Show Boat (1929) 118m. ** D: Harry A. Pollard. Laura La Plante, Joseph Schildkraut, Emily Fitzroy, Otis Harlan, Alma Rubens, Jack McDonald, Jane La Verne, Stepin Fetchit, Matthew "Stymie" Beard. Clunky adaptation of Edna Ferber's 1926 novel of life and love on a Mississippi showboat, as riverboat leading lady Magnolia Hawks (La Plante) falls for charming but irresponsible gentleman-gambler Gaylord Ravenal (Schildkraut). Silent film with extended talkie sequences cries out for the Broadway score, heard only in snippets. Still fascinating for buffs. Remade in 1936 and 1951. ●

Show Boat (1936) 113m. *** D: James Whale. Irene Dunne, Allan Jones, Helen Morgan, Paul Robeson, Charles Winninger, Hattie McDaniel. Entertaining treatment of Jerome Kern–Oscar Hammerstein II musical (filmed before in 1929) mixes music, sentiment, and melodrama, with enough great moments to make up for the rest: Robeson doing "Old Man River," Morgan singing her unforgettable "Bill," etc. Originally an Edna Ferber novel; Hammerstein also wrote the screenplay. Filmed again in 1951. ▼●▶

Show Boat (1951) C-107m. *** D: George Sidney. Kathryn Grayson, Ava Gardner, Howard Keel, Joe E. Brown, Marge and Gower Champion, Robert Sterling, Agnes Moorehead, Leif Erickson, William Warfield. MGM's Technicolor valentine to this old-fashioned musical about life on a Mississippi show boat; acted with sincerity, stylishly shot and staged. Gardner makes a beautiful and poignant Julie. Timeless Jerome Kern–Oscar Hammerstein II songs include "Bill" (lyrics by P. G. Wodehouse), "Can't Help Lovin' That Man," "Make Believe," "Old Man River." ▼●▶

Show Business (1944) 92m. **½ D: Edwin L. Marin. Eddie Cantor, Joan Davis, George Murphy, Nancy Kelly, Constance Moore. If you like Cantor or Davis you'll enjoy this vaudeville musical entirely supported by them. Followed by IF YOU KNEW SUSIE. ▼●▶

Showdown, The (1940) 64m. **½ D: Howard Bretherton. William Boyd, Russell Hayden, Britt Wood, Morris Ankrum, Jane (Jan) Clayton, Roy Barcroft, Eddie Dean, Kermit Maynard. Phony baron (with phony accent) attempts to cheat friend of Hopalong Cassidy on a deal for choice trotting-horses. Title derives from clever poker sequence; there are also some socko action scenes. For once, Hayden as young sidekick gets the girl; he also married Clayton in real life. ▼▶

Showdown (1963) 79m. **½ D: R. G. Springsteen. Audie Murphy, Kathleen Crowley, Charles Drake, Harold Stone, Skip Homeier, Strother Martin, L.Q. Jones. Tough Western yarn with drifters Murphy and Drake abducted by outlaw gang who force them to help convert stolen securities into cash.

Showdown at Abilene (1956) C-80m. ** D: Charles Haas. Jock Mahoney, Martha Hyer, Lyle Bettger, David Janssen, Grant Williams, Ted de Corsia. Standard Western with ex-sheriff/Civil War vet Mahoney returning to the title town. He's "seen enough guns and shooting" and only wants peace—he doesn't even wear a gun—but is forced to take sides in a farmer-cattleman conflict.

Showdown at Boot Hill (1958) 72m. ** D: Gene Fowler, Jr. Charles Bronson, Fintan Meyler, Robert Hutton, John Carradine, Carole Mathews. Unpretentious Western of bounty killer Bronson trying to collect reward money. Regalscope. ▼▶

Show Girl in Hollywood (1930) 77m. ** D: Mervyn LeRoy. Alice White, Jack Mulhall, Blanche Sweet, Ford Sterling, John Miljan, Virginia Sale, Lee Shumway, Herman Bing. Routine tale of aspiring Broadway singer (Kewpie-doll White, in her brief fling at movie stardom) who goes West to make it big in pictures. Enlivened by some interesting behind-the-scenes glimpses of the Warner Bros. studio during the very early days of talkies. Al Jolson, Loretta Young, and others have uncredited cameos. Some sequences originally in two-strip Technicolor. ▶

Show Off, The (1926) 82m. *** D: Malcolm St. Clair. Ford Sterling, Claire McDowell, C. W. Goodrich, Lois Wilson, Louise Brooks, Gregory Kelly. Engaging comedymelodrama about Aubrey Piper (Sterling), an unabashed braggart; his narcissism is played in sharp contrast to the very real difficulties faced by his fiancée (Wilson) and her family. Brooks puts forth a raw charm in a girl-next-door supporting role. Nice location filming in Philadelphia; based on the play by George Kelly. Remade in 1930 as MEN ARE LIKE THAT (with Hal Skelly), 1934, and 1946. ▼▶

Show-Off, The (1934) 80m. **½ D: Charles Reisner. Spencer Tracy, Madge Evans, Henry Wadsworth, Grant Mitchell, Lois Wilson, Clara Blandick, Claude Gillingwater. Tracy brings his own brand of disarming brashness to the role of Aubrey Piper, the incurable braggart whose constant scheming causes no end of trouble for his wife and her family. Snappy version of George Kelly's play.

Show-Off, The (1946) 83m. **½ D: Harry Beaumont. Red Skelton, Marilyn Maxwell, Marjorie Main, Virginia O'Brien, Eddie "Rochester" Anderson, George Cleveland, Leon Ames, Marshall Thompson, Jacqueline White. Amusing if low-key Skelton vehicle casts the amiable clown as windbag Aubrey Piper, who courts Maxwell—and drives the rest of her family crazy with his reckless braggadocio. Based on the oft-filmed play by George Kelly. ▼

Show of Shows, The (1929) 128m. ** D: John G. Adolfi. John Barrymore, Beatrice Lillie, Loretta Young, Richard Barthelmess, Frank Fay, Myrna Loy, Alice White, Chester Morris, Dolores Costello, Winnie Lightner, Ted Lewis and Orchestra, Nick Lucas, Douglas Fairbanks, Jr., Rin Tin Tin, many others. Warners' contribution to the studios' early talkie all-star revues is no better or worse than the others. Overlong and unimaginatively shot, but retains considerable historical value. Fay is a wry master of ceremonies for a variety of musical, dramatic, and comedy sketches, highlighted by Barrymore doing a scene from *Henry VI*, Rin Tin Tin "introducing" a lavish Chinese fantasy with Loy, Lightner performing "Singing in the Bathtub" with a male chorus dressed as bathing girls, and a prophetically titled number called "Motion Picture Pirates." Most of it was originally filmed in two-strip Technicolor. ○▶

Show People (1928) 82m. ***½ D: King Vidor. Marion Davies, William Haines, Dell Henderson, Paul Ralli, Harry Gribbon, Polly Moran. Delightful silent comedy about a girl from the sticks who tries to crash Hollywood—and succeeds, but not as she expected to. Davies' best movie vehicle confirms her comic talent, and offers a lively glimpse behind the scenes of moviemaking. Some amusing guest-star cameos include director Vidor, who plays himself in the closing scene. ▼○▶

Show Them No Mercy! (1935) 76m. *** D: George Marshall. Rochelle Hudson, Cesar Romero, Bruce Cabot, Edward Norris, Edward Brophy, Warren Hymer. Young couple accidentally stumbles into hideaway of kidnappers who aren't counting on the resourcefulness of the FBI. Solid gangster saga from the G-men era, well cast, with an unforgettable burst of violence at the finale. Remade in a Western setting as RAWHIDE (1951). ▼▶

Shriek in the Night, A (1933) 66m. **½ D: Albert Ray. Ginger Rogers, Lyle Talbot, Arthur Hoyt, Purnell Pratt, Harvey Clark. Ultra-cheap but interesting B-picture whodunit, reuniting Ginger and Lyle from THE THIRTEENTH GUEST as rival reporters on a murderer's trail; starts with a bang and then simmers down. ▼▶

Shrike, The (1955) 88m. **½ D: Jose Ferrer. June Allyson, Jose Ferrer, Joy Page,

Edward Platt, Mary Bell. Allyson almost succeeds in change of pace title role, playing ultranag who has driven her theater director husband (Ferrer) into a nervous breakdown. Based on Joseph Kramm's play.

Sh! The Octopus (1937) 54m. *½ D: William McGann. Hugh Herbert, Allen Jenkins, Marcia Ralston, John Eldredge, George Rosener, Brandon Tynan. Dimwit detective Herbert and simpleton sidekick Jenkins tangle with crooks and octopi at an eerie lighthouse in this harebrained reworking of the oft-filmed stage play *The Gorilla*. ▶

Shut My Big Mouth (1942) 71m. ** D: Charles Barton. Joe E. Brown, Adele Mara, Victor Jory, Fritz Feld, Lloyd Bridges, Forrest Tucker, Pedro de Cordoba. Meek Joe goes West and innocently gets mixed up with gang of outlaws. ▼

Side Show (1931) 64m. **½ D: Roy Del Ruth. Winnie Lightner, Charles Butterworth, Evalyn Knapp, Donald Cook, Guy Kibbee, Matthew Betz. Lightner stars as a circus performer and jack-of-all-trades in love with carnival barker Cook, who runs off with her cute younger sister Knapp. Piquant portrait of life under the big top is an amusing showcase for Lightner's delightful singing, dancing, and clowning. ▶

Side Street (1929) 74m. ** D: Malcolm St. Clair. Tom Moore, Owen Moore, Matt Moore, Emma Dunn, Kathryn Perry, Frank Sheridan, Arthur Housman. Corny melodrama (written by the director) about three Irish-American siblings (played by the real-life Moore brothers): a cop, a doctor, and unbeknownst to the others, a gangster. Static early talkie with a few lively moments, including an electrifying dance by an uncredited George Raft in a party scene.

Side Street (1949) 83m. *** D: Anthony Mann. Farley Granger, Cathy O'Donnell, James Craig, Paul Kelly, Edmon Ryan, Paul Harvey, Jean Hagen, Charles McGraw, Adele Jergens, Harry Bellaver, Whit Bissell. Story of part-time postman Granger impulsively stealing a wad of money, and finding himself involved with gangsters and murder, is bolstered by striking N.Y.C. locations and stark cinematography by Joseph Ruttenberg. The chase finale is a highlight. ▶

Sidewalks of London (1938-British) 84m. *** D: Tim Whelan. Charles Laughton, Vivien Leigh, Rex Harrison, Tyrone Guthrie, Larry Adler. Laughton is superb as a busker (street entertainer), with Leigh almost matching him as his protegée, who uses and abuses all in her quest for success as a stage star (a character not unlike Scarlett O'Hara!). Top entertainment . . . until ill-conceived final sequence. Original British title: ST. MARTIN'S LANE. ▼▶

Sidewalks of New York (1931) 74m. ** D: Jules White, Zion Myers. Buster Keaton,

Anita Page, Cliff Edwards, Frank Rowan. Nowhere near Keaton's silent-film classics, but this talkie vehicle has some funny moments as witless young millionaire tries to reform tough street gang.▼◐)

Siege at Red River, The (1954) **C-81m.** ****½ D:** Rudolph Maté. Van Johnson, Joanne Dru, Richard Boone, Milburn Stone, Jeff Morrow. Predictable Western set during Civil War days with an Indian attack finale.◗

Siege of Pinchgut SEE: **Four Desperate Men**

Siege of Sidney Street, The (1960-British) **94m. ** D:** Robert Baker, Monty Berman. Donald Sinden, Nicole Berger, Kieron Moore, Peter Wyngarde. Based on real incident, this film traces account of anarchists in 1910 London, with climactic confrontation between hundreds of cops and battling criminals. Screenwriter Jimmy Sangster plays Winston Churchill. Shot in Dublin. Dyaliscope.◗

Siege of Syracuse (1962-Italian) **C-97m. *½ D:** Pietro Francisci. Rossano Brazzi, Tina Louise, Enrico Maria Salerno, Gino Cervi. No less than Archimedes defends Syracuse from invading armada by use of giant mirrors that make ships burst into flames. Despite that, it's routine. Dyaliscope.

Siege of the Saxons (1963-British) **C-85m. **½ D:** Nathan Juran. Janette Scott, Ronald Lewis, Ronald Howard, John Laurie, Mark Dignam. Colorful escapism about King Arthur's daughter trying to protect her kingdom, and her right to marry the knight she chooses, from takeover by nefarious Edmund of Cornwall.

Siegfried SEE: **Die Nibelungen**

Sierra (1950) **C-83m. **½ D:** Alfred E. Green. Audie Murphy, Wanda Hendrix, Dean Jagger, Burl Ives, Sara Allgood, James Arness, Anthony (Tony) Curtis. Capable cast elevates story of son and father on the lam from the law, trying to prove dad's innocence of crime. Remake of 1938 film FORBIDDEN VALLEY. Murphy and Hendrix were then married in real life.◗

Sierra Baron (1958) **C-80m. ** D:** James B. Clark. Brian Keith, Rick Jason, Rita Gam, Mala Powers, Steve Brodie. Western set in 19th-century California and Mexico has virtue of pleasing scenery, marred by usual land-grabbing shoot-out plot. CinemaScope.

Sierra Passage (1951) **81m. *½ D:** Frank McDonald. Wayne Morris, Lola Albright, Alan Hale, Jr., Roland Winters. Quickie oater with Morris on manhunt for father's murderer.

Sierra Stranger (1957) **74m. *½ D:** Lee Sholem. Howard Duff, Dick Foran, Barton MacLane, Gloria McGhee. Tame dust-raiser of Duff intervening in a lynching, romancing McGhee.

Sierra Sue (1941) **64m. **½ D:** William Morgan. Gene Autry, Smiley Burnette, Fay McKenzie, Frank M. Thomas, Robert Homans, Earle Hodgins, Dorothy Christy, Kermit Maynard, Rex Lease. Gene believes that spraying chemicals is the best way to control a "devil weed" that's killing off cattle, but he's got to convince rancher Homans—and his pretty daughter McKenzie, to whom Gene and Smiley both take a shine. Gene sings one of his biggest hits, "Be Honest With Me" (which earned him an Oscar nomination as cowriter), in this pleasant outing.▼

Sign of the Cross, The (1932) **125m. **½ D:** Cecil B. DeMille. Fredric March, Elissa Landi, Claudette Colbert, Charles Laughton, Ian Keith, Vivian Tobin, Nat Pendleton, Joe Bonomo. Well-meaning but heavy-handed account of Christians seeking religious freedom in Rome under Emperor Nero. Very slow going, despite fine work by March as Marcus Superbus, Laughton as Nero, and especially Colbert as alluring Poppaea. Reissued in 1944 at 118m. with many cuts of sexy and sadistic scenes and a nine-minute WW2 prologue added. Restored version on video includes an intermission/entr'acte. ▼◗

Sign of the Gladiator (1959-Italian) **C-84m. *½ D:** Vittorio Musy Glori. Anita Ekberg, Georges Marchal, Folco Lulli, Chelo Alonso, Jacques Sernas. Gladiator allows himself to be captured by queen of Syria so he can win her confidence. Not so hot. Dyaliscope.

Sign of the Pagan (1954) **C-92m. **½ D:** Douglas Sirk. Jeff Chandler, Jack Palance, Ludmilla Tcherina, Rita Gam, Jeff Morrow, Alexander Scourby. Uneven script hampers story of Attila the Hun threatening Rome; Sirk's stylish direction helps somewhat. CinemaScope.

Sign of the Ram (1948) **84m. **½ D:** John Sturges. Susan Peters, Alexander Knox, Peggy Ann Garner, Dame May Whitty, Phyllis Thaxter, Ron Randell, Allene Roberts. Well-wrought drama of crippled wife using ailment to hamstring husband and children. Comeback film for wheelchair-bound Peters, who was severely injured in a 1944 hunting accident; sadly this was also her final feature.

Sign of Zorro, The (1960) **91m. *½ D:** Norman Foster, Lewis R. Foster. Guy Williams, Henry Calvin, Gene Sheldon, Britt Lomond, George J. Lewis, Lisa Gaye. Several episodes of Disney's *Zorro* TV show pasted together; clumsy continuity undermines what charm the series had to offer.▼

Signpost to Murder (1965) **74m. **½ D:** George Englund. Stuart Whitman, Joanne Woodward, Edward Mulhare, Alan Napier, Joyce Worsley, Murray Matheson. Escapee from prison for criminally insane seeks shelter in home of woman whose husband is away. Contrived plot mars thriller but strong performances help. Panavision.◗

Silence, The (1963-Swedish) **95m.** ***½ D: Ingmar Bergman. Ingrid Thulin, Gunnel Lindblom, Håkan Jahnberb, Birger Malmsten. Stark, forceful symbolic narrative of two sisters who stop at a hotel in a North European city. One sister (Thulin) is a frustrated lesbian with no future, the other (Lindblom) a free-loving mother of a 10-year-old boy. The last in Bergman's trilogy on faith, following THROUGH A GLASS DARKLY and WINTER LIGHT.▼●▶

Silent Conflict (1948) **61m.** *½ D: George Archainbaud. William Boyd, Andy Clyde, Rand Brooks, Virginia Belmont, Earle Hodgins, James Harrison. Brooks is drugged and hypnotized by bogus doctor Hodgins to turn over proceeds (in gold) of Bar 20 cattle sale. Premise is contrived and weak; story drags, action flags. Lone Pine landscape exteriors are the lone plus. Reissued as TRIGGER TALK.▼▶

Silent Death SEE: **Voodoo Island**
Silent Duel, A SEE: **Quiet Duel, The**
Silent Enemy, The (1930) **84m.** ***½ D: H. P. Carver. Remarkable blend of documentary footage and a fictional story—in the tradition of GRASS and CHANG—about the Ojibwe Indian tribe of New York State, which faces starvation. Climactic caribou run is one of the most astonishing sights you'll ever witness. Silent film is preceded by an introductory speech by Chief Yellow Robe, who plays the tribal leader. Full title: THE SILENT ENEMY: AN EPIC OF THE AMERICAN INDIAN.▶

Silent Enemy, The (1958-British) **92m.** **½ D: William Fairchild. Laurence Harvey, Dawn Addams, John Clements, Michael Craig. British Naval frogmen, headed by Harvey, are assigned to combat enemy counterpart during WW2; underwater sequences well handled, with some pre-THUNDERBALL gimmicks.▼

Silent Witness (1932) **73m.** ** D: Marcel Varnel, R. L. Hough. Lionel Atwill, Greta Nissen, Weldon Heyburn, Helen Mack, Bramwell Fletcher. Stagy but pretty interesting courtroom drama with Atwill trying to protect his son from murder charge by taking blame himself.

Silent World, The (1956-French-Italian) **C-86m.** *** D: Jacques Yves-Cousteau, Louis Malle. Academy Award–winning documentary of an account of an expedition above and—most memorably—below the sea's surface by Captain Cousteau and his divers and crew. Dated in some ways, with an uncomfortable sequence involving the slaughtering of sharks. Still a milestone documentary, and Malle's first film.▶

Silken Affair, The (1957-British) **96m.** **½ D: Roy Kellino. David Niven, Genevieve Page, Ronald Squire, Wilfrid Hyde-White, Beatrice Straight. Droll little comedy of meek accountant Niven sparked by saucy Page into some fast bookkeeping manipulations.

Silk Express, The (1933) **61m.** **½ D: Ray Enright. Neil Hamilton, Sheila Terry, Arthur Byron, Guy Kibbee, Dudley Digges, Arthur Hohl, Allen Jenkins, Harold Huber, Robert Barrat, Douglass Dumbrille. A series of murders occurs aboard a train chartered by Hamilton to deliver silk to New York and break up a monopoly on the fabric maintained by a group of greedy businessmen. High-speed whodunit showcasing Warner's prolific stock company of character actors.▶

Silk Stockings (1957) **C-117m.** *** D: Rouben Mamoulian. Fred Astaire, Cyd Charisse, Janis Paige, Peter Lorre, George Tobias, Jules Munshin, Joseph Buloff, Barrie Chase. Words, music, dance blend perfectly in stylish remake of Garbo's NINOTCHKA. This time Charisse is cold Russian on Paris mission, Astaire the movie producer man-about-town who warms her up. Score by Cole Porter includes "All of You" and "Stereophonic Sound"; Mamoulian's final film. CinemaScope.▼●▶

Silly Billies (1936) **64m.** ** D: Fred Guiol. Bert Wheeler, Robert Woolsey, Dorothy Lee, Harry Woods, Ethan Laidlaw, Chief Thunderbird, Delmar Watson, Willie Best, Tommy Bond. Slow-moving comedy with Wheeler and Woolsey as "painless" dentists in the Old West. A funny action climax can't rescue this one.

Silver Blaze (1937-British) **71m.** **½ D: Thomas Bentley. Arthur Wontner, Lyn Harding, Ian Fleming, Judy Gunn, Eve Gray, Lawrence Grossmith. It's Sherlock Holmes to the rescue upon the disappearance of a racehorse and murder of its trainer. Moderately entertaining mystery; this was Wontner's final appearance as Sir Arthur Conan Doyle's legendary sleuth. Aka MURDER AT THE BASKERVILLES.▼▶

Silver Canyon (1951) **71m.** *** D: John English. Gene Autry, Pat Buttram, Gail Davis, Jim Davis, Bob Steele, Terry Frost, Edgar Dearing. Gene and Pat play Union scouts during Civil War days who are assigned to track down Confederate Jim Davis and his guerrilla raiders. Good later Autry vehicle.▶

Silver Chalice, The (1954) **C-144m.** ** D: Victor Saville. Virginia Mayo, Pier Angeli, Jack Palance, Paul Newman, Walter Hampden, Joseph Wiseman, Alexander Scourby, Lorne Greene, E. G. Marshall, Natalie Wood. Newman's screen debut is undistinguished in story of Greek who designs framework for cup used at Last Supper. This is the film Newman once apologized for in a famous Hollywood trade ad. From the Thomas Costain novel; Greene's first film, too. CinemaScope.▼●▶

Silver City (1951) **C-90m.** ** D: Byron Haskin. Edmond O'Brien, Yvonne De Carlo, Richard Arlen, Gladys George,

Barry Fitzgerald. Capable cast is above this mishmash set in the mining area of the West, with usual rivalry over gals and ore. ▶

Silver Cord, The (1933) 74m. **½ D: John Cromwell. Irene Dunne, Joel McCrea, Laura Hope Crews, Frances Dee, Eric Linden. Very much a photographed stage play (by Sidney Howard), but interesting for its look at a self-absorbed woman (Crews) who attempts to dominate her sons' lives completely—not counting on the strength of her new daughter-in-law (Dunne), a career woman with a mind of her own. Both Dunne and Dee are first-rate.

Silver Dollar (1932) 84m. **½ D: Alfred E. Green. Edward G. Robinson, Bebe Daniels, Aline MacMahon, Robert Warwick, Jobyna Howland. True story (though names are changed) of self-made silver tycoon H. A. W. Tabor, who helped build Denver from mining camp to a thriving city. One of America's great sagas, hampered by unimaginative presentation.

Silver Fleet, The (1942) 88m. *** D: Vernon Campbell Sewell, Gordon Wellesley. Ralph Richardson, Googie Withers, Esmond Knight, Beresford Egan, Frederick Burtwell, Kathleen Byron. Dutchman (Richardson) who runs a shipyard appears to be cooperating with Nazi invaders when in fact he's playing a dangerous game of sabotage, invoking the name of Piet Hein, a Dutch hero of the 1600s. Richardson is in prime form in this still-potent WW2 flag-waver, and the story never runs out of surprises. An early production of The Archers (Michael Powell and Emeric Pressburger). ▶

Silver Horde, The (1930) 75m. **½ D: George Archainbaud. Evelyn Brent, Joel McCrea, Louis Wolheim, Jean Arthur, Raymond Hatton, Blanche Sweet, Gavin Gordon. Rugged version of Rex Beach's brawling novel about the struggle for control of Alaska's burgeoning salmon fishing industry. McCrea is young fisherman torn between shady lady Brent and debutante Arthur, resulting in a memorable catfight between the two. Dated action yarn bolstered by good cast and fine documentary-style location work. ▼▶

Silver Lode (1954) C-80m. **½ D: Allan Dwan. John Payne, Lizabeth Scott, Dan Duryea, Dolores Moran, Emile Meyer, Harry Carey, Jr., Morris Ankrum, Stuart Whitman, Alan Hale, Jr. A Western town's respected citizen (Payne) is accused of thievery and murder on his wedding day by a slimy U.S. "marshal" (Duryea). So-so melodrama is a fascinating relic of its era as both a HIGH NOON variation and an obvious allegory of HUAC/McCarthyist hypocrisy. The action unfolds on July 4, and the villain is named "McCarty"! ▼▶

Silver on the Sage (1939) 68m. **½ D: Lesley Selander. William Boyd, George Hayes, Russell Hayden, Ruth Rogers, Stanley Ridges, Frederick Burton. When Bar 20 cowpunchers get fleeced by shrewd operators, Hopalong Cassidy goes undercover as a gambler to recover stolen herd, apprehend wrongdoers, and clear framed, impetuous sidekick Hayden. Ridges plays lawbreaking twins who always have an alibi for each other. Somewhat suspenseful story adapted from 1935 book *On the Trail of the Tumbling T* by Clarence E. Mulford. ▼▶

Silver Queen (1942) 80m. ** D: Lloyd Bacon. George Brent, Priscilla Lane, Bruce Cabot, Lynne Overman, Eugene Pallette, Guinn Williams. Post-Civil War tinsel of devoted girl raising money for father; hubby throws it away on "worthless" silver mine. ▼

Silver River (1948) 110m. **½ D: Raoul Walsh. Errol Flynn, Ann Sheridan, Thomas Mitchell, Bruce Bennett, Tom D'Andrea, Barton MacLane, Monte Blue. Union soldier Flynn, unfairly court-martialed, climbs the ladder of success wrong by wrong, ruthlessly getting everything he wants, from power and wealth to a friend's wife (Sheridan). Last of the Flynn-Walsh collaborations tends toward talk more than usual but its rise-and-fall story holds interest.

Silver Spurs (1943) 68m. *** D: Joseph Kane. Roy Rogers, Smiley Burnette, John Carradine, Phyllis Brooks, Jerome Cowan, Joyce Compton, Bob Nolan and the Sons of the Pioneers. Irresponsible ranch owner Cowan falls into the clutches of Carradine, who is trying to dupe him out of his oil-rich land while Cowan flirts with easterner Brooks. Ranch foreman Rogers saves the day. Unusually strong cast for a Rogers movie; moves at a crackling pace. ▼▶

Silver Streak, The (1934) 72m. *½ D: Thomas Atkins. Sally Blane, Charles Starrett, Hardie Albright, William Farnum, Irving Pichel, Arthur Lake. High-speed train journey is undertaken to deliver iron lungs to epidemic-stricken Nevada town. Derailed by wooden performances and leaden pace although climactic race against time is very exciting; no relation to 1976 film. ▼

Silver Whip, The (1953) 73m. **½ D: Harmon Jones. Dale Robertson, Rory Calhoun, Robert Wagner, Kathleen Crowley, Lola Albright. Occasionally actionful Western of outlaws vs. stage line. ▶

Simba (1928) 83m. **½ D: (none credited). Rambling, occasionally interesting "dramatic record" of famed husband-and-wife adventurers Martin and Osa Johnson, and their 15,000-mile trek through the wilds of Africa. Much of the footage now seems overly familiar. The full title is SIMBA, THE KING OF BEASTS. ▼▶

Simba (1955-British) C-99m. ***½ D: Brian Desmond Hurst. Dirk Bogarde, Virginia McKenna, Basil Sydney, Donald Sinden. Fine cast in story of young man arriving in Kenya only to find brother killed by Mau Maus. Some grisly scenes. ▼❶

Simon and Laura (1956-British) **C-91m.** **½ D: Muriel Box. Peter Finch, Kay Kendall, Muriel Pavlow, Ian Carmichael, Maurice Denham. Spunky farce involving Finch and Kendall, a married acting couple whose TV image contradicts their violent off-screen battles. VistaVision. ❶

Simon of the Desert (1965-Mexican) **45m.** **** D: Luis Buñuel. Claudio Brook, Silvia Pinal, Hortensia Santovena, Enrique Alvarez Felix. Hilarious parable about a bearded ascetic who plops himself atop a pillar to communicate with God better. Could only have been made by one filmmaker; even by Buñuel's standards, the ending of this one is pretty wild. ▼❶

Sinbad the Sailor (1947) **C-117m.** *** D: Richard Wallace. Douglas Fairbanks, Jr., Maureen O'Hara, Anthony Quinn, Walter Slezak, George Tobias, Jane Greer, Mike Mazurki, Sheldon Leonard. Tongue-in-cheek swashbuckler, with lavish color production. Great fun. ▼❶❶

Sincerely Yours (1955) **C-115m.** BOMB D: Gordon Douglas. Liberace, Joanne Dru, Dorothy Malone, William Demarest, Richard Eyer, Lurene Tuttle. Remake of George Arliss' THE MAN WHO PLAYED GOD becomes a ludicrous vehicle for Liberace. Camp classic written by Irving Wallace, with the star's brother George serving as musical adviser. ▼❶❶

Since You Went Away (1944) **172m.** ***½ D: John Cromwell. Claudette Colbert, Jennifer Jones, Joseph Cotten, Shirley Temple, Monty Woolley, Hattie McDaniel, Agnes Moorehead, Craig Stevens, Keenan Wynn, Nazimova, Robert Walker, Lionel Barrymore. Tearjerker supreme with Colbert at her valiant best. Story of family suffering through WW2 with many tragedies and complications dates a bit, but still is very smooth film. Producer David O. Selznick wrote the screenplay, from Margaret Buell Wilder's book. Beautifully photographed by Lee Garmes and Stanley Cortez. Max Steiner's score won an Oscar. Film debuts of Guy Madison (then an actual sailor, in the role of sailor Harold Smith) and John Derek (an extra). Video version runs 177m. with overture, intermission/entr'acte. ▼❶❶

Sing and Like It (1934) **72m.** **½ D: William A. Seiter. ZaSu Pitts, Pert Kelton, Edward Everett Horton, Nat Pendleton, Ned Sparks, John Qualen, Stanley Fields. Mobster Pendleton goes soft when he hears Pitts singing a song about her mother in rehearsal for an amateur play and determines to get her into a Broadway show by forcing himself into partnership with "the mad genius of the theater" (Horton). Never as funny as it ought to be, though with cast of great comic actors it has its moments.

Sing and Swing (1963-British) **75m.** ** D:

Lance Comfort. David Hemmings, Veronica Hurst, Jennifer Moss, John Pike. Virtue of modest musical is Hemmings in lead role of messenger boy who joins pals in combo; they record a song, and find their musical career in full sway. Originally titled LIVE IT UP.

Singapore (1947) **79m.** **½ D: John Brahm. Fred MacMurray, Ava Gardner, Roland Culver, Richard Haydn, Spring Byington, Thomas Gomez, Porter Hall. Alluring drama of trader/pearl smuggler MacMurray returning to Singapore after a five-year absence, recalling his previous romantic relationship with Gardner. He thinks she was killed during a Japanese bombing attack, but she really was a victim of amnesia. The characters in this seem to be very loosely modeled after those in CASABLANCA. Remade as ISTANBUL. ▼

Sing, Baby, Sing (1936) **87m.** *** D: Sidney Lanfield. Alice Faye, Adolphe Menjou, Gregory Ratoff, Ted Healy, Patsy Kelly, Tony Martin. Pleasant musicomedy stolen by Menjou as John Barrymore prototype involved with publicity-seeking Faye. Songs: "When Did You Leave Heaven?," "You Turned the Tables on Me," title tune. The Ritz Brothers are quite good in their feature-film debut. ❶

Sing Boy Sing (1958) **90m.** ** D: Henry Ephron. Tommy Sands, Lili Gentle, Edmond O'Brien, John McIntire, Nick Adams, Diane Jergens, Josephine Hutchinson, Jerry Paris, Regis Toomey. A teen idol and Elvis Presley clone (Sands) is manipulated by his cold-hearted manager (O'Brien) and kept apart from his roots. Muddled relic of its era, which purports to expose the evils of rock 'n' roll and show biz (in between Sands' endless musical numbers). Sands' film debut; based on 1957 TV play *The Singin' Idol*. CinemaScope. ❶

Singer Not the Song, The (1961-British) **C-129m.** **½ D: Roy (Ward) Baker. Dirk Bogarde, John Mills, Mylene Demongeot, Eric Pohlmann. Offbeat, sluggish yarn set in Mexico involving conflict of Catholic priest and local bandit to control the town, with Demongeot in love with the clergyman. CinemaScope. ▼

Singing Blacksmith, The (1938) **95m.** *** D: Edgar G. Ulmer. Moishe Oysher, Miriam Riselle, Florence Weiss, Anna Appel, Ben-Zvi Baratoff, Michael Goldstein, Herschel Bernardi. Colorful Yiddish-language musical comedy–drama, set in czarist Russia, with Oysher in excellent voice as the title character, a lover of dance, drink, and song. Bushy-haired, 15-year-old Bernardi plays "Young Yankl." Scripted by David Pinski and based on his play *Yankl der Schmid.* ▼

Singing Cowboy, The (1936) **56m.** **½ D: Mack V. Wright. Gene Autry, Smiley Burnette, Lois Wilde, Lon Chaney, Jr., Ann Gillis, Earle Hodgins, Harvey Clark, John

Van Pelt. Cowhand Autry becomes (what else?) a singing cowboy on a TV hookup to raise money for paralyzed Gillis' operation. Screwy but fun, with surprising emphasis on television in this mid-1930s film.▌

Singing Fool, The (1928) **101m.** **½ D: Lloyd Bacon. Al Jolson, Betty Bronson, Josephine Dunn, Arthur Housman, Davey Lee, Edward Martindel, Helen Lynch, Robert Emmett O'Connor. Part-talkie follow-up to THE JAZZ SINGER is potent melodrama, with Jolson as a songwriter/performer whose domestic life is in turmoil. Jolson's high-energy acting style will either delight or revolt. Songs include "It All Depends on You," "I'm Sitting on Top of the World," "There's a Rainbow 'Round My Shoulder," and "Sonny Boy" (which Jolson sings to Davey Lee).●▌

Singing Guns (1950) **C-91m.** *½ D: R. G. Springsteen. Vaughn Monroe, Ella Raines, Walter Brennan, Ward Bond, Billy Gray. Minor happenings in the old West with singer Monroe in straight role.

Singing Hill, The (1941) **75m.** ** D: Lew Landers. Gene Autry, Smiley Burnette, Virginia Dale, Mary Lee, Spencer Charters, George Meeker. Gene saves yet another ranch for still another wacky, madcap big-city girl (Dale) from one more conniving cattle broker (Meeker). Overlong Western screwball comedy has nine tunes (including "The Singing Hills") but not enough action.▌

Singing Kid, The (1936) **85m.** ** D: William Keighley. Al Jolson, Sybil Jason, Edward Everett Horton, Lyle Talbot, Allen Jenkins, Beverly Roberts, Claire Dodd. Jolson plays a Broadway star who loses his voice and recuperates in the country, where he takes in a young girl—and finds romance. A star vehicle if there ever was one, and recommended only for Jolson fans. Musical appearances by Cab Calloway, Wini Shaw, and The Yacht Club Boys. Highlight of the Harold Arlen–E.Y. Harburg score: "I Love to Singa."●▌

Singing Marine, The (1937) **106m.** **½ D: Ray Enright. Dick Powell, Doris Weston, Lee Dixon, Hugh Herbert, Jane Darwell, Allen Jenkins, Larry Adler, Veda Ann Borg, Jane Wyman. Title tells all in this slight but pleasant musical about painfully shy Marine Powell becoming a singing sensation, with resulting rivalries and complications.

Singing Vagabond, The (1935) **54m.** **½ D: Carl Pierson. Gene Autry, Ann Rutherford, Smiley Burnette, Barbara Pepper, Niles Welch, Grace Goodall, Henry Roquemore, Allan Sears, Warner Richmond, Frank LaRue, Charlie King. Cavalry plainsmen Gene and Smiley rout out a band of white renegades supplying horses and guns to the Indians, save their tarnished reputations, and find time to rescue a troupe of Eastern entertainers. Solid entertainment, with stock footage from Tim McCoy's 1926 WAR PAINT.▌

Singin' in the Rain (1952) **C-102m.** **** D: Gene Kelly, Stanley Donen. Gene Kelly, Debbie Reynolds, Donald O'Connor, Jean Hagen, Cyd Charisse, Millard Mitchell, Douglas Fowley, Madge Blake, Rita Moreno. Perhaps the greatest movie musical of all time, fashioned by Betty Comden and Adolph Green from a catalogue of Arthur Freed–Nacio Herb Brown songs. The setting is Hollywood during the transition to talkies, with Hagen giving the performance of a lifetime as Kelly's silent screen costar, whose voice could shatter glass. Kelly's title number, O'Connor's "Make 'Em Laugh," are just two highlights in a film packed with gems. Later a Broadway musical.▼●▌

Single Handed SEE: **Sailor of the King**

Single Standard, The (1929) **73m.** ** D: John S. Robertson. Greta Garbo, Nils Asther, John Mack Brown, Dorothy Sebastian, Lane Chandler. Greta is a San Francisco debutante, a free soul who breaks convention and has an affair with artist Asther. Pretty silly stuff, but Garbo is as beautiful as ever. From an Adela Rogers St. Johns novel.▼●

Sing Me a Love Song (1936) **75m.** *½ D: Ray Enright. James Melton, Patricia Ellis, Hugh Herbert, ZaSu Pitts, Allen Jenkins, Nat Pendleton, Walter Catlett, Dennis Moore. Musical chestnut about a rich boy who takes a job in his own department store to learn how the other half lives. Among that other half is attractive Ellis. As for Metropolitan Opera tenor Melton, if acting may be said to be wooden, then he is a veritable lumberyard. Undistinguished score by Harry Warren and Al Dubin.

Sing Your Way Home (1945) **72m.** ** D: Anthony Mann. Jack Haley, Marcy McGuire, Glen Vernon, Anne Jeffreys, Donna Lee, Patti Brill, Nancy Marlow. Egocentric war correspondent Haley, anxious to get back to N.Y.C., finds himself chaperoning a group of spunky young people on the high seas. Corny musical, of (slight) interest as a relic of its era. Look fast for Lawrence Tierney as a reporter.

Sing Your Worries Away (1942) **71m.** ** D: A. Edward Sutherland. June Havoc, Bert Lahr, Buddy Ebsen, Patsy Kelly, Sam Levene, Margaret Dumont, The King Sisters, Alvino Rey. Mild musical comedy as the theatrical world and racketeers clash.▼

Sing, You Sinners (1938) **88m.** *** D: Wesley Ruggles. Bing Crosby, Fred MacMurray, Donald O'Connor, Elizabeth Patterson, Ellen Drew, John Gallaudet. Gambling gay-blade Crosby can't face responsibility, despite prodding of brother MacMurray. Fine film with "I've Got a Pocketful of Dreams" and memorable "Small Fry" number featuring young O'Connor.▌

Sinister Hands (1932) **65m.** ** D: Armand Schaefer. Jack Mulhall, Phyllis Barrington, Crauford Kent, Mischa Auer. After a wealthy man is knifed during a lights-out séance, the cops learn that most of the people present might have a motive. Quite routine, a bit reminiscent of THE THIRTEENTH CHAIR, but enlivened a bit by the occult subplot and Auer's presence as Indian Swami Yomurda.

Sinister Journey (1948) 59m. ** D: George Archainbaud. William Boyd, Andy Clyde, Rand Brooks, Elaine Riley, John Kellogg, Stanley Andrews. Hopalong Cassidy and Bar 20 saddle pals take jobs on a railroad to subvert murderous outlaws and clear a wrongly accused ex-convict gone straight. Not enough action in the series' misguided bow to film noir style. Reissue title: TWO GUN TERRITORY.▼▶

Sinister Urge, The (1960) 75m. BOMB D: Edward D. Wood, Jr. Kenne Duncan, Duke Moore, Carl Anthony, Jean Fontaine, Dino Fantini, Jeanne Willardson. Dedicated cops Duncan and Moore set out to smash the "smut picture racket," which is run by a brassy blonde who writes with a four-foot quill pen. One of Wood's least-known works demonstrates with complete conviction how photos of plump women in their underwear are the principal cause of juvenile deliquency. Aka THE YOUNG AND THE IMMORAL.▼▶

Sink the Bismarck! (1960-British) 97m. *** D: Lewis Gilbert. Kenneth More, Dana Wynter, Carl Mohner, Laurence Naismith, Geoffrey Keen, Karel Stepanek, Michael Hordern. Good WW2 film based on fact. Exciting sea battles as British Navy starts deadly hunt for famed German war vessel. Script by Edmund H. North. CinemaScope.▼▶

Sinner, The SEE: **Desert Desperados**

Sinners' Holiday (1930) 60m. **½ D: John G. Adolfi. Grant Withers, Evalyn Knapp, James Cagney, Joan Blondell, Lucille LaVerne, Noel Madison. Predictable melodrama is interesting to watch, as period piece (with good Coney Island atmosphere) and as film debuts for Cagney and Blondell, re-creating stage roles in support of stars Withers and Knapp. Story involves romance, murder, and overprotective mother (LaVerne) who runs penny arcade.▶

Sinner's Holiday (1947) SEE: **Christmas Eve**

Sinners in Paradise (1938) 65m. ** D: James Whale. John Boles, Madge Evans, Bruce Cabot, Marion Martin, Gene Lockhart, Nana Bryant, Milburn Stone, Donald Barry. Plane crash survivors are stranded on tropic island where mysterious Boles lives as a recluse. Starts great, but peters out.▼▶

Sinners in the Sun (1932) 70m. ** D: Alexander Hall. Carole Lombard, Chester Morris, Adrienne Ames, Cary Grant, Walter Byron, Alison Skipworth, Rita La Roy, Ida Lewis. Lovely Lombard learns that money isn't all in this slick, typical triangle; Grant has a bit role.

Sin of Harold Diddlebock, The (1947) 90m. **½ D: Preston Sturges. Harold Lloyd, Frances Ramsden, Jimmy Conlin, Raymond Walburn, Edgar Kennedy, Arline Judge, Lionel Stander, Rudy Vallee. Fascinating idea of updating Lloyd's 1920s character to show what's happened to that go-getter doesn't fulfill its promise. Aimless comedy can't top opening sequence from THE FRESHMAN (1925), despite enthusiasm of fine cast. Reedited to 79m. and reissued in 1950 as MAD WEDNESDAY.▼▶

Sin of Madelon Claudet, The (1931) 73m. *** D: Edgar Selwyn. Helen Hayes, Lewis Stone, Neil Hamilton, Robert Young, Cliff Edwards, Jean Hersholt, Marie Prevost, Karen Morley, Charles Winninger, Alan Hale, Frankie Darro. First-rate, fast-moving soaper in the MADAME X vein, about a woman who sacrifices everything so her illegitimate son (Young) will have a good life. Hayes won an Oscar portraying woman who goes from bumpkin to Parisian sophisticate to suffering mother to haggard streetwalker—and she's terrific.▼▶

Sin of Nora Moran, The (1933) 65m. **½ D: Phil Goldstone. Zita Johann, Alan Dinehart, Paul Cavanagh, Claire Du Brey, John Miljan, Henry B. Walthall, Cora Sue Collins. Surprisingly interesting Poverty Row cheapie with supernatural overtones, told in flashback, about a hard-luck woman (Johann, who's excellent) who falls in love with the wrong man and makes the ultimate sacrifice for him. More notable for its ambitions than its achievements, with great use of stock footage and a wall-to-wall music score, unusual for 1933. Best known today for its iconic one-sheet poster image.▼▶

Sin Ship, The (1931) 65m. ** D: Louis Wolheim. Louis Wolheim, Mary Astor, Ian Keith, Hugh Herbert. Tough-guy ship captain Wolheim crudely dismisses women, but his attitude changes when he spies Astor—who is not what she seems. So-so programmer is of note as Wolheim's final screen role and his only directorial credit.

Sins of Jezebel (1953) C-74m. *½ D: Reginald LeBorg. Paulette Goddard, George Nader, John Hoyt, Eduard Franz. Embarrassing low-budget costumer with Goddard miscast in title role.▼▶

Sins of Lola Montès, The SEE: **Lola Montès**

Sins of Rachel Cade, The (1961) C-124m. **½ D: Gordon Douglas. Angie Dickinson, Peter Finch, Roger Moore, Woody Strode, Rafer Johnson, Juano Hernandez, Mary Wickes, Scatman Crothers. Turgid melodrama set in Belgian Congo with Dickinson a missionary nurse involved in romance and native conflicts.▶

Sins of Rome (1954-Italian) 75m. ** D: Riccardo Freda. Ludmilla Tcherina, Massimo Girotti, Gianna Maria Canale, Yves Vincent. Rebel slave Spartacus (Girotti) incites fellow prisoners to fight Roman republic. Early Italian spectacle doesn't have cheaper look of later grinds. ▼▶

Sins of the Children (1930) 85m. ** D: Sam Wood. Louis Mann, Robert Montgomery, Elliott Nugent, Leila Hyams, Clara Blandick, Mary Doran. Maudlin family saga centering on a German-immigrant barber (Mann) who constantly sacrifices for his children, even though they disappoint him in various ways. First-class production values and Mann's fine performance make this bit of treacle tolerable. Based on a story by Elliott Nugent (who plays one of the children) and his father, J. C. Nugent. ▶

Sin Takes a Holiday (1930) 80m. **½ D: Paul L. Stein. Constance Bennett, Kenneth MacKenna, Basil Rathbone, Rita La Roy, Louis John Bartels, ZaSu Pitts. Upscale divorce lawyer MacKenna gets out of an embarrassing case through a quick marriage of convenience to plain-Jane secretary Bennett. Then she, alone on her "honeymoon" cruise, meets handsome stranger Rathbone and blossoms. Pleasantly blonde romantic comedy. ▼▶

Sin Town (1942) 75m. **½ D: Ray Enright. Constance Bennett, Broderick Crawford, Anne Gwynne, Ward Bond, Andy Devine, Leo Carrillo, Patric Knowles, Hobart Bosworth. Fast-moving actioner of town in uproar after newspaper editor is killed; good cast in above-average film. Richard Brooks was one of the writers.

Sioux City Sue (1946) 69m. *** D: Frank McDonald. Gene Autry, Lynne Roberts, Sterling Holloway, Richard Lane, Ralph Sanford, Cass County Boys. Singing cowboy Autry is sought after by Hollywood— but only as the voice of a cartoon donkey. Gene looks terrific in his first film after four years away from Hollywood during WW2. He sings well and has a great leading lady in Roberts, but Holloway isn't fit the sidekick role vacated by Smiley Burnette. Eight great songs, including the title tune. Remake of a 1939 Republic B movie, SHE MARRIED A COP. ▼▶

Siren of Atlantis (1948) 75m. BOMB D: Gregg Tallas. Maria Montez, Jean-Pierre Aumont, Dennis O'Keefe, Henry Daniell, Morris Carnovsky. Ridiculous hokum of soldiers Aumont and O'Keefe stumbling upon famed Lost Continent; Montez is the sultry queen. Despite the title, film takes place in the desert! Based on *L'Atlantide*, previously filmed in 1921 and 1932. Remade as JOURNEY BENEATH THE DESERT.

Siren of Bagdad (1953) C-77m. **½ D: Richard Quine. Paul Henreid, Patricia Medina, Hans Conried, Charlie Lung. Comedy-adventure of magician and friend trying to save dancing girls in slave market. Conried provides film's best moments.

Siren of the Tropics (1927-French) 86m. **½ D: Mario Nalpas, Henri Etiévant. Josephine Baker, Pierre Batcheff, Régina Dalthy, Regina Thomas, Georges Melchior. Baker is effervescent and uninhibited (even topless) in her first starring feature, as a native of Antilles who falls madly in love with a handsome Frenchman who comes to her village on an engineering project. She follows him back to France, where she's "discovered" and put onstage in a music hall! Silly vehicle is just an excuse to showcase La Baker, who is irresistible. Also features some eye-popping art deco sets. Luis Buñuel is credited as assistant director. ▶

Sirocco (1951) 98m. **½ D: Curtis Bernhardt. Humphrey Bogart, Marta Toren, Lee J. Cobb, Everett Sloane, Gerald Mohr, Zero Mostel, Nick Dennis, Onslow Stevens, Ludwig Donath, Harry Guardino, Jeff Corey. Bogart's company produced this slick if superficial paraphrase of CASABLANCA with Bogie as a gunrunner who's the unofficial boss of Damascus in 1925, vying with French military officer Cobb for the affections of Toren. A strong supporting cast adds flavor. ▼▶

Sis Hopkins (1941) 98m. **½ D: Joseph Santley. Judy Canova, Bob Crosby, Charles Butterworth, Jerry Colonna, Susan Hayward, Katharine Alexander. Fairly amusing comedy of country girl who comes to live with social uncle and attends girls' school. Even Canova is restrained!

Sister Kenny (1946) 116m. ***½ D: Dudley Nichols. Rosalind Russell, Alexander Knox, Dean Jagger, Philip Merivale, Beulah Bondi, Dorothy Peterson. Russell shines in title role, as Australian nurse who initiated treatment for polio. Engrossing drama is among the better Hollywood biopics. Scripted by Nichols, Knox, and Mary McCarthy, from Mary Kenny's autobiography, *And They Shall Walk.* ▼●

Sisters, The (1938) 98m. *** D: Anatole Litvak. Errol Flynn, Bette Davis, Anita Louise, Ian Hunter, Donald Crisp, Beulah Bondi, Jane Bryan, Lee Patrick, Mayo Methot, Laura Hope Crews, Dick Foran, Henry Travers, Patric Knowles, Alan Hale. Davis, Louise, and Bryan are sisters whose marital problems are traced in this lavish film; Bette's got the most trouble, of course, with unreliable husband Flynn in San Francisco, 1905. ▼▶

Sisters of Nishijin (1952-Japanese) 110m. ***½ D: Kozaburo Yoshimura. Yumiko Miyagino, Mitsuko Miura, Yuko Tsumura, Chieko Higashiyama. Family of Kyoto silk-weavers cannot adapt to industrialization; the father-patriarch kills himself, and his widow, daughters, and assistants try to carry on. Excellent tale of greed and courage.

Sisters of the Gion (1936-Japanese) 66m. *** D: Kenji Mizoguchi. Isuzu Yamada, Yôko Umemura, Benkei Shiganoya, Eitarô Shindô, Taizô Fukami, Fumio Okura. Incisive tale of a traditional geisha who takes on her younger, more independent sister as her apprentice, with tragic results.

A compassionate look at human cruelty and exploitation, as well as a fascinating portrait of pre-WW2 Japan in general and Kyoto's Red Light District in particular. Mizoguchi remade the film in 1953 as A GEISHA. ▼❱

Sit Tight (1931) 76m. **½ D: Lloyd Bacon. Winnie Lightner, Joe E. Brown, Paul Gregory, Claudia Dell, Lotti Loder, Hobart Bosworth, Frank Hagney, Snitz Edwards. Scrawny health spa employee Brown has a crush on his wisecracking boss (Lightner) and tries to impress her by becoming a pro wrestler. Peppy farce sprinkled with snappy pre-Code dialogue and scantily clad femmes. ❱

Sitting Bull (1954) C-105m. ** D: Sidney Salkow. Dale Robertson, Mary Murphy, J. Carrol Naish, Iron Eyes Cody, John Litel, Bill (William) Hopper. Sluggish Western about cavalry major Robertson, who is compassionate toward the Sioux and clashes with his superiors over their disregard for Indian rights. CinemaScope. ▼❱

Sitting Pretty (1933) 85m. **½ D: Harry Joe Brown. Ginger Rogers, Jack Oakie, Jack Haley, Thelma Todd, Gregory Ratoff, Lew Cody. First half is bouncy yarn of songwriters Oakie and Haley going Hollywood, meeting homespun Rogers, vamp Todd; remainder bogs down, rescued by finale "Did You Ever See a Dream Walking." ▼

Sitting Pretty (1948) 84m. ***½ D: Walter Lang. Robert Young, Maureen O'Hara, Clifton Webb, Richard Haydn, Louise Allbritton, Ed Begley. Webb is perfect as self-centered genius who accepts job as full-time babysitter in gossip-laden suburban town. Highly entertaining, followed by the MR. BELVEDERE comedies. ▼❱

Situation Hopeless—But Not Serious (1965) 97m. ** D: Gottfried Reinhardt. Alec Guinness, Michael Connors, Robert Redford, Anita Hoefer, Mady Rahl, Paul Dahlke. Odd little comedy, from a Robert Shaw novel, about German clerk Guinness holding two American (Redford, Connors) prisoners for years after WW2 has ended. Interesting characterization by Guinness, but a flat film.

Six Black Horses (1962) C-80m. ** D: Harry Keller. Audie Murphy, Dan Duryea, Joan O'Brien, George Wallace. O'Brien pays two men to take her across Indian lands, intending to murder gunman of duo who killed her husband. Mediocre Western with a Burt Kennedy script apparently left over from the Randolph Scott–Budd Boetticher series. ❱

Six Bridges to Cross (1955) 96m. *** D: Joseph Pevney. Tony Curtis, Julia (Julie) Adams, George Nader, Sal Mineo, Jay C. Flippen, Jan Merlin. Entertaining film about a cop's longtime relationship with a juvenile delinquent who grows up to be a high-class crook. Based on the infamous Brink's truck robbery; filmed on location

in Boston. Mineo's film debut. Title song sung by Sammy Davis, Jr.

6 Day Bike Rider (1934) 69m. **½ D: Lloyd Bacon. Joe E. Brown, Maxine Doyle, Frank McHugh, Lottie Williams. Intriguing gimmick has Brown trying to impress girlfriend by entering marathon race; good little comedy.

Six Hours to Live (1932) 78m. ** D: William Dieterle. Warner Baxter, Miriam Jordan, John Boles, George Marion, Halliwell Hobbes, Beryl Mercer, Irene Ware. Unusual story of diplomat Baxter, whose stubbornness at international trade conference leads to his murder. A scientist brings him back to life for six hours. Stodgy production spoils interesting idea.

Six in Paris (1965-French) C-93m. **½ D: Claude Chabrol, Jean Douchet, Jean-Luc Godard, Jean-Daniel Pollet, Eric Rohmer, Jean Rouch. Barbara Wilkin, Jean-François Chappey, Jean-Pierre Andréani, Barbet Schroeder, Nadine Ballot, Gilles Quéant, Claude Melki, Micheline Dax, Jean-Michel Rouzière, Joanna Shimkus, Philippe Hiquilly, Serge Davri, Stéphane Audran, Gilles Chusseau, Claude Chabrol. Mildly interesting collection of six vignettes, each named for a Parisian locale and involving everyday individuals, their communications and miscommunications. Best are the entries by Rouch (a bored wife looks for excitement, much to her regret); Godard (a young woman confronts her two lovers); and Chabrol (a boy literally tunes out his boorish parents). Not at all memorable, but still a must for French New Wave aficionados. ▼❱

Six Lessons From Madame La Zonga (1941) 62m. ** D: John Rawlins. Lupe Velez, Leon Errol, Helen Parrish, Charles Lang, William Frawley, Eddie Quillan, Shemp Howard. Good cast of professional laugh-getters in typical, silly outing; Leon goes Latin, and Lupe goes gold-digging after him in shipboard comedy. Title derived from popular song of the day.

Six of a Kind (1934) 62m. *** D: Leo McCarey. W. C. Fields, George Burns, Gracie Allen, Charlie Ruggles, Mary Boland, Alison Skipworth. George and Gracie drive Mary and Charlie crazy traveling westward on vacation; Fields as pool-playing sheriff adds to confusion. Zany, wonderful nonsense. ▼❱

16 Fathoms Deep (1948) C-82m. ** D: Irving Allen. Lon Chaney, Jr., Lloyd Bridges, Arthur Lake, Eric Feldary, Tanis Chandler, John Qualen, Dickie Moore. Harmless story of sponge fishing in Florida, with a pre-*Sea Hunt* Bridges appropriately cast as a diver. Chaney is the heavy here. In a 1934 version he played the hero.

633 Squadron (1964-British) C-101m. **½ D: Walter Grauman. Cliff Robertson, George Chakiris, Maria Perschy, Harry Andrews. Pretentious WW2 aviation film about the group's air mission to bomb German-run factory in Norway. Robertson and Chakiris are stiff-lipped throughout; script by James Clavell and Howard Koch. Panavision. ▼●▶

6,000 Enemies (1939) **62m. **½ D:** George B. Seitz. Walter Pidgeon, Rita Johnson, Paul Kelly, Nat Pendleton, Harold Huber, Grant Mitchell, John Arledge, Tom Neal. Above-average programmer with Pidgeon as a crusading D.A. who's framed by the mob and sentenced to prison, where he seemingly runs into every thug he ever convicted. Combination gangster and prison movie delivers the goods on both counts.

Sixty Glorious Years (1938-British) **C-95m. *** D:** Herbert Wilcox. Anna Neagle, Anton Walbrook, C. Aubrey Smith, Walter Rilla, Charles Carson. Neagle's follow-up to VICTORIA THE GREAT is a repeat of her fine performance as England's legendary queen; good production values. U.S. title: QUEEN OF DESTINY.

Skin Game, The (1931-British) **86m. ** D:** Alfred Hitchcock. Edmund Gwenn, Jill Esmond, John Longden, C. V. France, Helen Haye, Phyllis Konstam. Gwenn adds the only spark of life to this dull adaptation of the Galsworthy play about rivalry between neighboring landowners. Hitchcock claimed he didn't make it by choice, and one can believe it considering the many long, static dialogue scenes; very atypical of the Master. ▼▶

Skipalong Rosenbloom (1951) **72m. ** D:** Sam Newfield. "Slapsie" Maxie Rosenbloom, Max Baer, Jackie Coogan, Fuzzy Knight, Hillary Brooke, Jacqueline Fontaine, Raymond Hatton. Rootin' tootin', mush-mouthed and paunchy, itinerant lawman Rosenbloom takes on sheriff-killin' outlaw Butcher Baer. Amiably goofy spoof of B Westerns and TV commercials is best appreciated by dedicated genre fans. Others be warned: it's shamelessly corny, slow, and repetitious. Reissued as SQUARE SHOOTER (his gun barrels are square). ▼▶

Ski Party (1965) **C-90m. ** D:** Alan Rafkin. Frankie Avalon, Dwayne Hickman, Deborah Walley, Yvonne Craig, Robert Q. Lewis, Bobbi Shaw, Aron Kincaid. BEACH PARTY gang puts on some clothes in this one, but the shenanigans are the same. Guest star Lesley Gore sings "Sunshine, Lollipops and Rainbows." James Brown sings "I Got You." Panavision.▶

Skipper Surprised His Wife, The (1950) **85m. *½ D:** Elliott Nugent. Robert Walker, Joan Leslie, Edward Arnold, Spring Byington, Jan Sterling. Unsurprising comedy; weak material about sailor Walker running home like ship. Good cast wasted.

Skippy (1931) **85m. *** D:** Norman Taurog. Jackie Cooper, Robert Coogan, Mitzi Green, Jackie Searl, Willard Robertson, Enid Bennett, Donald Haines. Classic children's film from Percy Crosby's popular comic strip, following misadventures of Cooper, the local health inspector's son, and Coogan, the poor ragamuffin from Shantytown, as they try to scrape up three dollars for a dog license. Simple and dated, but with timeless innocent charm. Taurog (Cooper's uncle) won Best Director Oscar. Followed by a sequel, SOOKY.▶

Skirts Ahoy! (1952) **C-109m. **½ D:** Sidney Lanfield. Esther Williams, Joan Evans, Vivian Blaine, Barry Sullivan, Keefe Brasselle, Billy Eckstine, Dean Miller, Margalo Gillmore, Jeff Donnell, Keenan Wynn. Chipper cast can't buoy this musical of three WAVE recruits and their romantic entanglements. Blaine virtually recreates her GUYS AND DOLLS character; Debbie Reynolds and Bobby Van sparkle in a specialty song-and-dance routine. ▼▶

Ski Troop Attack (1960) **63m. ** D:** Roger Corman. Michael Forest, Frank Wolff, Wally Campo, Richard Sinatra, James Hoffman, Sheila Carol, Roger Corman. Wintry WW2 adventure with five U.S. soldiers on skis behind enemy lines in Germany. OK Corman low-budgeter. ▼▶

Skull, The (1965-British) **C-83m. **½ D:** Freddie Francis. Peter Cushing, Patrick Wymark, Christopher Lee, Nigel Green, Jill Bennett, Michael Gough, George Coulouris, Patrick Magee. Good cast lends needed support to questionable script (based on a Robert Bloch story) of skull of Marquis de Sade that has mysterious powers. Techniscope. ▼▶

Sky Above The Mud Below, The (1961-French) **C-90m. *** D:** Pierre-Dominique Gaisseau. Narrated by William Peacock. Academy Award–winning documentary showing variety of primitive life found within confines of Dutch New Guinea. ▼▶

Sky Commando (1953) **69m. *½ D:** Fred F. Sears. Dan Duryea, Frances Gifford, Michael Connors, Michael Fox. Limping account of the responsibilities of being an Air Force officer, with usual rash of hackneyed situations.

Sky Devils (1932) **89m. ** D:** A. Edward Sutherland. Spencer Tracy, William "Stage" Boyd, Ann Dvorak, George Cooper, Billy Bevan, Yola D'Avril. Two dumbbells try to avoid WW1 service in this disjointed, low-grade comedy; Dvorak is beautiful; leftover flying scenes from producer Howard Hughes' HELL'S ANGELS are impressive.

Sky Dragon, The (1949) **64m. BOMB D:** Lesley Selander. Roland Winters, Keye Luke, Mantan Moreland, Noel Neill, Tim Ryan, Iris Adrian, Elena Verdugo, Milburn Stone, Lyle Talbot, John Eldredge. The nadir and, appropriately, the end of the *Charlie Chan* series, an unbearable whodunit set on a plane bound for San Francisco.

Sky Full of Moon (1952) **73m. ** D:** Norman Foster. Carleton Carpenter, Jan Sterling,

Keenan Wynn, Elaine Stewart. Unassuming comedy of naive cowpoke falling in love with a not-so-innocent in Las Vegas. ▶

Skylark (1941) 94m. ***½ D: Mark Sandrich. Claudette Colbert, Ray Milland, Brian Aherne, Binnie Barnes, Walter Abel, Ernest Cossart, Grant Mitchell. Sophisticated romance with Aherne trying to take Claudette away from business-minded husband Milland. Stars are at their peak in this smooth adaptation of Samson Raphaelson play. ▶

Sky Liner (1949) 61m. *½ D: William Berke. Richard Travis, Pamela Blake, Rochelle Hudson, Steven Geray, Gaylord (Steve) Pendleton, Michael Whalen, Greg McClure, Lisa Ferraday. Some of the passengers on an airplane flight just may be killers, spies, and G-men. Thoroughly forgettable time-killer. ▶

Sky Murder (1940) 72m. ** D: George B. Seitz. Walter Pidgeon, Donald Meek, Kaaren Verne, Edward Ashley, Joyce Compton, Tom Conway. Pidgeon as detective Nick Carter decides to help refugee Verne in above-average private-eye yarn. ▶

Sky Pilot, The (1921) 69m. **½ D: King Vidor. Colleen Moore, John Bowers, David Butler, Harry Todd, James Corrigan, Donald MacDonald. Down-to-earth Northwestern about a do-gooder who single-handedly struggles to sway a sinful Canadian town to salvation. Naive D. W. Griffith-esque scenario, based on an 1899 novel, sics the righteous onto the unwilling with a fury, but Vidor (just starting out as a director) makes it work better than it should. Moore is miscast. Second lead Butler, as the ranch foreman, began a 40-year directing career in 1927. ▼▶

Skyscraper (1928) 71m. ** D: Howard Higgin. William Boyd, Alan Hale, Sue Carol, Alberta Vaughn, Wesley Barry. Riveters toil heroically high above city streets, but after work they fall prey to the eternal triangle below. Boyd (not yet Hopalong Cassidy), Carol (not yet Mrs. Alan Ladd), and Hale (not yet called Sr.) form the three sides. Late silent is helped by location shooting on steel girders over Manhattan, but the drama is less than riveting. ▼

Skyscraper Souls (1932) 99m. *** D: Edgar Selwyn. Warren William, Maureen O'Sullivan, Gregory Ratoff, Anita Page, Verree Teasdale, Norman Foster, Jean Hersholt, Wallace Ford, Hedda Hopper, Helen Coburn, Ed Brophy. Entertaining comedy-drama in the GRAND HOTEL mode (released four months earlier, also by MGM) about a ruthless empire-builder (well played by William) who manipulates stock prices and double-crosses lovers in his quest to control a 100-story office building. Potent pre-Code entertainment, much of it still pretty risqué. ▼▶

Skyscraper Wilderness SEE: **Big City, The** (1937)

Sky's the Limit, The (1943) 89m. *** D: Edward H. Griffith. Fred Astaire, Joan Leslie, Robert Benchley, Robert Ryan, Elizabeth Patterson, Marjorie Gateson. Fred's a flier on leave who meets photographer Leslie; Benchley's dinner speech, Astaire's "One For My Baby" and "My Shining Hour" make this worthwhile. ▼▶

Slander (1956) 81m. **½ D: Roy Rowland. Van Johnson, Ann Blyth, Steve Cochran, Marjorie Rambeau, Richard Eyer. Slick, superficial "inside study" of the smut magazines, focusing on their exclusive on a TV personality. ▶

Slattery's Hurricane (1949) 83m. **½ D: Andre de Toth. Richard Widmark, Linda Darnell, Veronica Lake, John Russell, Gary Merrill. Weather-pilot Widmark, in midst of storm, thinks back on his life; Darnell and Lake are his two loves. Interesting idea; coscripted by Herman Wouk, who later expanded it into a novel. ▶

Slaughter on Tenth Avenue (1957) 103m. *** D: Arnold Laven. Richard Egan, Jan Sterling, Dan Duryea, Julie Adams, Walter Matthau, Sam Levene, Charles McGraw, Mickey Shaughnessy. Well-handled waterfront racketeer exposé, set in N.Y.C. with good supporting cast.

Slaughter Trail (1951) C-78m. *½ D: Irving Allen. Brian Donlevy, Gig Young, Virginia Grey, Andy Devine, Robert Hutton, Terry Gilkyson. Cavalry officer Donlevy goes up against bandits who've been terrorizing the title trail. Blah Western, done in by Gilkyson's repetitive, indescribably awful musical narration. ▼

Slave, The (1963-Italian) C-102m. *½ D: Sergio Corbucci. Steve Reeves, Jacques Sernas, Gianna Maria Canale, Claudio Gora. Interminable Italian spectacle. Son of Spartacus learns story of father, vows vengeance. Good photography only asset. Aka SON OF SPARTACUS. CinemaScope. ▶

Slave Girl (1947) C-80m. **½ D: Charles Lamont. Yvonne De Carlo, George Brent, Broderick Crawford, Albert Dekker, Lois Collier, Andy Devine, Arthur Treacher. Tale of adventure with evil potentate holding Americans prisoner; not to be taken seriously (there's even a talking camel), enjoyable on that scale.

Slave Ship (1937) 92m. *** D: Tay Garnett. Warner Baxter, Wallace Beery, Elizabeth Allan, Mickey Rooney, George Sanders, Jane Darwell, Joseph Schildkraut. Rousing drama of slave ship rebellion with fine atmosphere, good Beery-Rooney teaming, plenty of action. ▶

Slaves in Bondage (1937) 70m. *½ D: Elmer Clifton. Lona Andre, Donald Reed, Wheeler Oakman, Florence Dudley, John Merton, Richard Cramer. Oakman and Dudley use a beauty salon as a front for a vice ring. Low-grade "exposé" seems more pasted together than edited, with uninspiring vaudeville acts and scantily clad, catfighting damsels tossed in for good measure. Aka CRUSADE AGAINST RACKETS. ▼◗

Slaves of Babylon (1953) **C-82m.** ** D: William Castle. Richard Conte, Linda Christian, Maurice Schwartz, Michael Ansara, Julie Newmar. Jumbled biblical adventure mixed with romance. Nebuchadnezzar faces army of Israelites led by shepherd.

Sleepers West (1941) **74m.** ** D: Eugene Forde. Lloyd Nolan, Lynn Bari, Mary Beth Hughes, Louis Jean Heydt, Edward Brophy, Don Costello, Ben Carter. Private eye Michael Shayne (Nolan) tries to protect a murder witness on a train to San Francisco in this tolerable suspenser. Remake of SLEEPERS EAST (1934), written by *Torchy Blane* creator Frederick Nebel. ◗

Sleeping Beauty (1959) **C-75m.** *** D: Clyde Geronimi. Voices of Mary Costa, Bill Shirley, Eleanor Audley, Verna Felton, Barbara Jo Allen (Vera Vague), Barbara Luddy. Walt Disney's most expensive and elaborate animated feature (at the time) is actually a simple, straightforward telling of the classic fairy tale, with music adapted from Tchaikovsky, and such memorable characters as Flora, Fauna, and Merryweather (the three good fairies) and the evil witch Maleficent. Highlight: the final, fiery confrontation between Maleficent and Prince Phillip. Strikingly designed (in widescreen) by artist Eyvind Earle. The villainess was later revived in live-action MALEFICENT (2014). Super Technirama. ▼●◗

Sleeping Car Murder, The (1965-French) **90m.** *** D: Costa-Gavras. Simone Signoret, Yves Montand, Pierre Mondy, Jean-Louis Trintignant, Jacques Perrin, Michel Piccoli, Catherine Allegret, Charles Denner. Quick-paced, atmospheric police-chasing-mad-killer movie. Nice photography by Jean Tournier; original action good but dubbing hurts. Based on a Sébastien Japrisot novel. Costa-Gavras' directorial debut. CinemaScope.

Sleeping Car to Trieste (1948-British) **95m.** *** D: John Paddy Carstairs. Jean Kent, Albert Lieven, Derrick de Marney, Paul Dupuis, Rona Anderson, David Tomlinson. The Orient Express is the setting for fine cat-and-mouse story of espionage agents competing for possession of "hot" political diary. Remake of ROME EXPRESS. ▼

Sleeping City, The (1950) **85m.** **½ D: George Sherman. Richard Conte, Coleen Gray, Peggy Dow, John Alexander, Alex Nicol, Richard Taber. Earnest depiction of corruption within a medical institution's walls was controversial upon its release. Its hero is a cop (Conte) who goes undercover to ferret out a killer and other evil doings at a N.Y.C. hospital.

Sleeping Tiger, The (1954-British) **89m.** *** D: Victor Hanbury (Joseph Losey). Alexis Smith, Dirk Bogarde, Alexander Knox, Hugh Griffith, Patricia McCarron, Billie Whitelaw. Well-done drama with Knox a psychiatrist who takes low-life criminal Bogarde into his home, much to the consternation of his wife (Smith, in one of her best roles); the result is sexual and emotional fireworks. Losey's first film made outside the U.S., where he was blacklisted; this accounts for the pseudonym. ▼◗

Sleep, My Love (1948) **97m.** *** D: Douglas Sirk. Claudette Colbert, Robert Cummings, Don Ameche, Hazel Brooks, Rita Johnson, George Coulouris, Keye Luke, Raymond Burr, Ralph Morgan. Familiar territory covered by excellent cast as Ameche tries to drive wife Claudette crazy; Cummings saves her. From a Leo Rosten novel. ◗

Slender Thread, The (1965) **98m.** **½ D: Sydney Pollack. Sidney Poitier, Anne Bancroft, Telly Savalas, Steven Hill, Edward Asner, Dabney Coleman. Interchange between stars is the whole film in an interesting idea that doesn't fulfill potential. Bancroft takes overdose of sleeping pills and calls crisis clinic for help; college student volunteer Poitier tries to keep her on phone while rescue is organized. Filmed on location in Seattle; written by Stirling Silliphant, music by Quincy Jones. Pollack's directorial debut. ▼◗

Slide, Kelly, Slide (1927) **76m.** **½ D: Edward Sedgwick. William Haines, Sally O'Neil, Harry Carey, Karl Dane, Junior Coghlin (Coghlan), Warner Richmond, Paul Kelly, Guinn Williams, Edward Brophy. Predictable but enjoyable union of fact, fiction, and myth, spotlighting Jim Kelly (Haines), a brash, Ruthian hurler-slugger who tries out for the New York Yankees and causes all sorts of tumult. This one features a couple of characters with prophetic names: a Yankee catcher named Munson (Carey) and a ragamuffin named Mickey Martin (Coghlin) who would be just a few years older than Yankee greats Mickey Mantle and Billy Martin. Several real-life major leaguers appear as themselves.

Slight Case of Larceny, A (1953) **71m.** ** D: Don Weis. Mickey Rooney, Eddie Bracken, Elaine Stewart, Marilyn Erskine. Low hijinks from Rooney and Bracken as two buddies who open a gas station, siphoning supplies from oil company's pipelines. ◗

Slight Case of Murder, A (1938) **85m.** ***½ D: Lloyd Bacon. Edward G. Robinson, Jane Bryan, Allen Jenkins, Ruth Donnelly, Willard Parker, John Litel, Edward Brophy, Harold Huber, Bobby Jordan, Margaret Hamilton. Robinson's in peak comedy form as gangster who goes straight when Prohibition ends. This hilarious adaptation of a play by Damon Runyon and Howard Lindsay has brewer Robinson going bankrupt in a rented summer house filled with characters and corpses. Remake: STOP, YOU'RE KILLING ME. ◗

Slightly Dangerous (1943) **94m.** ** D:

Wesley Ruggles. Lana Turner, Robert Young, Walter Brennan, Dame May Whitty, Eugene Pallette, Florence Bates, Alan Mowbray, Bobby (Robert) Blake. Slightly ridiculous comedy of waitress Turner who claims to be daughter of wealthy industrialist. Good cast in trivial piece of fluff. ▷

Slightly French (1949) 81m. **½ D: Douglas Sirk. Dorothy Lamour, Don Ameche, Janis Carter, Willard Parker, Adele Jergens. Sassy musical of con-artist director Ameche passing off Lamour as French star. ▷

Slightly Honorable (1940) 83m. **½ D: Tay Garnett. Pat O'Brien, Edward Arnold, Broderick Crawford, Ruth Terry, Alan Dinehart, Eve Arden, Claire Dodd, Evelyn Keyes, Phyllis Brooks, Janet Beecher. Adequate mystery with lawyers O'Brien and Crawford involved in strange murders with corrupt politician Arnold. ▼▷

Slightly Scarlet (1956) C-99m. **½ D: Allan Dwan. John Payne, Arlene Dahl, Rhonda Fleming, Kent Taylor, Ted de Corsia, Lance Fuller. Effective study (from a James M. Cain novel) of big-city corruption; Payne involved with dynamic sister duo (Fleming, Dahl). Arlene steals the show as tipsy ex-con sister. SuperScope. ▼▷

Slim (1937) 80m. **½ D: Ray Enright. Pat O'Brien, Henry Fonda, Stuart Erwin, Margaret Lindsay, Dick Purcell, John Litel, Jane Wyman. Interesting story of men who string high-voltage wire, with Lindsay the girl who comes between tough veteran O'Brien and novice Fonda. Good performances all around. A semi-remake of TIGER SHARK; remade as MANPOWER. ▷

Slim Carter (1957) C-82m. ** D: Richard Bartlett. Jock Mahoney, Julie Adams, Tim Hovey, William Hopper, Ben Johnson, Bill Williams, Barbara Hale. Mild goings-on of cad Mahoney becoming popular Western movie star, interacting with studio publicist Adams and orphan Hovey, who enters their lives.

Slime People, The (1962) 76m. BOMB D: Robert Hutton. Robert Hutton, Les Tremayne, Susan Hart, Robert Burton. Lumpy, lizardy people from beneath the Earth wall off L.A. with curtain of fog. Movie talks itself to death. ▼▷

Small Back Room, The (1949-British) 106m. ***½ D: Michael Powell, Emeric Pressburger. David Farrar, Jack Hawkins, Kathleen Byron, Anthony Bushell, Michael Gough, Leslie Banks, Cyril Cusack, Renee Asherson. Mature, powerful story of crippled munitions expert Farrar, who's frustrated by his infirmity and mindless government bureaucracy during WW2. Robert Morley appears unbilled. Beware of edited versions. Original U.S. title: HOUR OF GLORY. ▼▷

Smallest Show on Earth, The (1957-British) 80m. *** D: Basil Dearden. Bill Travers, Virginia McKenna, Margaret Ruther-

ford, Peter Sellers, Bernard Miles, Leslie Phillips. Charming, often hilarious comedy about a couple who inherit a run-down movie house and its three equally run-down attendants (Sellers, Rutherford, Miles). Lovely scene in which the three veterans express their love for silent films. ▼▷

Small Town Girl (1936) 108m. *** D: William Wellman. Janet Gaynor, Robert Taylor, Binnie Barnes, Lewis Stone, Andy Devine, James Stewart. Breezy romance about Gaynor trapping Taylor into marriage while he's drunk, then working to win him over when he's sober.

Small Town Girl (1953) C-93m. **½ D: Leslie Kardos. Jane Powell, Farley Granger, Ann Miller, S. Z. Sakall, Billie Burke, Bobby Van, Robert Keith, Nat King Cole, Fay Wray. Bland MGM musical pairing playboy Granger and apple-pie Powell, who meet when he's thrown in jail by her father for speeding through town. Van's human pogo-stick number and Miller's "I've Gotta Hear That Beat," with Busby Berkeley's disembodied orchestra, are highlights. ▼▷

Smart Alecks (1942) 60m. *½ D: Wallace Fox. Leo Gorcey, Huntz Hall, Bobby Jordan, Gabriel Dell, Stanley Clements, Sunshine Sammy Morrison, David Gorcey, Bobby Stone, Maxie Rosenbloom, Gale Storm, Roger Pryor, Walter Woolf King. The East Side Kids indulge in a little larceny to purchase some baseball uniforms in this undernourished entry. Slapsy Maxie gets laughs as dim-witted hood. ▼▷

Smart Blonde (1936) 59m. **½ D: Frank McDonald. Glenda Farrell, Barton MacLane, Winifred Shaw, Craig Reynolds, Addison Richards, Charlotte Winters, Jane Wyman. First of nine *Torchy Blane* films sets the pace and tone for the rest, with Farrell and MacLane amusing as the acerbic reporter and her irascible cop boyfriend working together on a murder case. Only series entry adapted directly from story by pulp author Frederick Nebel. ▷

Smartest Girl in Town, The (1936) 58m. **½ D: Joseph Santley. Gene Raymond, Ann Sothern, Helen Broderick, Eric Blore, Erik Rhodes. Ann mistakes wealthy Gene for a lowly male model and avoids him as she sets her sights on a rich husband. No surprises, but short and pleasant. ▷

Smart Girls Don't Talk (1948) 81m. ** D: Richard Bare. Virginia Mayo, Bruce Bennett, Helen Westcott, Robert Hutton, Tom D'Andrea. Dull drama of socialite Mayo forced to join up with racketeer.

Smart Money (1931) 90m. **½ D: Alfred E. Green. Edward G. Robinson, James Cagney, Margaret Livingstone, Evalyn Knapp, Noel Francis. Known as Cagney and Robinson's only costarring film, but Robinson really stars, as lucky barber who becomes big-time gambler. Cagney is fine as Robinson's crony; watch for Boris Karloff in a bit as a shady gambler.◗

Smart Set, The (1928) **80m.** ****½** D: Jack Conway. William Haines, Jack Holt, Alice Day, Hobart Bosworth, Coy Watson, Jr., Constance Howard. Typically brash silent-comedy vehicle for Haines casts him as an arrogant playboy who gets kicked off the American polo team and has to redeem himself.◗

Smart Woman (1931) **68m.** ******* D: Gregory La Cava. Mary Astor, Robert Ames, John Halliday, Edward Everett Horton, Noel Francis, Ruth Weston, Gladys Gale. Astor comes home from a trip to find hubby Ames slobbering all over gold digger Francis (with her crude mother in tow), so she decides to win him back by pretending to be having an affair of her own. Highly amusing, sophisticated comedy-drama of sexual politics.◗

Smart Woman (1948) **93m.** ******* D: Edward A. Blatt. Brian Aherne, Constance Bennett, Barry Sullivan, Michael O'Shea, James Gleason, Otto Kruger, Iris Adrian, Isobel Elsom, Selena Royle. Lawyer Aherne doesn't let love interfere with his determined attempt to prosecute crooked D.A. and other officials. Pretty big budget for an Allied Artists film; Alvah Bessie was one of the writers.◗

Smarty (1934) **64m.** ****** D: Robert Florey. Joan Blondell, Warren William, Edward Everett Horton, Frank McHugh, Claire Dodd. Blondell teases husband William so relentlessly he finally hits her, prompting her to seek a divorce, but her marriage to their friend (and divorce lawyer) Horton is just as doomed. Wearisome pre-Code comedy, co-adapted by F. Hugh Herbert from his play. Blondell never looked better, photographed here by her husband, George Barnes.◗

Smashing the Money Ring (1939) **57m.** ****** D: Terry Morse. Ronald Reagan, Margot Stevenson, Eddie Foy, Jr., Joe Downing, Charles D. Brown. Reagan, as Lt. Brass Bancroft, again cracks a gang of counterfeiters, as he did in CODE OF THE SECRET SERVICE. Passable programmer.◗

Smash-up: The Story of a Woman (1947) **103m.** ******* D: Stuart Heisler. Susan Hayward, Lee Bowman, Marsha Hunt, Eddie Albert, Carl Esmond, Carleton Young. Hayward is excellent as an insecure nightclub singer who gives up her career when she weds soon-to-be radio star Bowman . . . and finds herself helplessly mired in alcoholism. This was Hayward's breakthrough role after a decade in Hollywood, and it deservedly earned her her first Oscar nomination. Taut script by John Howard Lawson, from an original story by Dorothy Parker and Frank Cavett.▼◗

Smiles of a Summer Night (1955-Swedish) **108m.** ******** D: Ingmar Bergman. Ulla Jacobsson, Eva Dahlbeck, Margit Carlquist, Harriet Andersson, Gunnar Bjornstrand, Jarl Kulle. One of the finest romantic comedies ever made, a witty treatise on manners, mores, and sex during a weekend at a country estate in the late 19th century. Inspired the Broadway musical and subsequent film A LITTLE NIGHT MUSIC (as well as Woody Allen's A MIDSUMMER NIGHT'S SEX COMEDY).▼◗

Smiley (1956-Australian) **C-97m.** ****½** D: Anthony Kimmins. Ralph Richardson, Colin Petersen, John McCallum, Chips Rafferty, Reg Lye. Soft-treading narrative of young boy who wants a bicycle, becoming entangled with drug smugglers. Sequel: SMILEY GETS A GUN. CinemaScope.◗

Smiley Gets a Gun (1959-Australian) **C-89m.** ****** D: Anthony Kimmins. Sybil Thorndike, Keith Calvert, Bruce Archer, Chips Rafferty, Margaret Christensen. Easygoing account of young boy trying to win the right to have a gun. CinemaScope.

Smiling Ghost, The (1941) **70m.** ****½** D: Lewis Seiler. Wayne Morris, Brenda Marshall, Alexis Smith, Alan Hale, Lee Patrick, David Bruce, Helen Westley, Willie Best. Unemployed Morris hires himself out as a suitor to "kiss of death" heiress Smith, unaware that her past three beaus all suffered horrible fates. Marshall is a newshound determined to get to the bottom of the story. Genial cast keeps the laughs and chills bubbling along in this comic spooky-old-house mystery.◗

Smiling Lieutenant, The (1931) **88m.** ******* D: Ernst Lubitsch. Maurice Chevalier, Claudette Colbert, Miriam Hopkins, Charlie Ruggles, George Barbier, Hugh O'Connell, Elizabeth Patterson. Utterly charming Lubitsch confection about a Viennese lieutenant who's forced to marry the naive, mousy Princess of Flausenthurm (Hopkins) when in fact he's in love with violinist Colbert. Pretty racy for its time. Highlight: the leading ladies singing "Jazz Up Your Lingerie." Based on the operetta *The Waltz Dream*, which was filmed under that title in Germany in 1928. Lubitsch simultaneously shot a French-language version, LE LIEUTENANT SOURIANT, with the same cast. ◗◗

Smilin' Through (1932) **97m.** ******* D: Sidney Franklin. Norma Shearer, Fredric March, Leslie Howard, O. P. Heggie, Ralph Forbes. Sentimental romantic tale (with fantasy elements) about an embittered old man who lost his love on their wedding day but finds new reason to live when he must raise his orphaned niece (who looks exactly like his long-ago fiancée). Polished MGM production gets a bit pokey midway through but leads to satisfying finale. Director Franklin originally filmed this with Norma Talmadge in 1922; it was remade in 1941.▼◗

Smilin' Through (1941) **C-100m.** ****½** D:

Frank Borzage. Jeanette MacDonald, Gene Raymond, Brian Aherne, Ian Hunter, Francis Robinson, Patrick O'Moore. Glossy remake of sentimental story about romance and rivalry spreading over two generations; lacks conviction of 1932 version, though MacDonald and Raymond are a good match (they married in real life). ▼▶

Smoke Signal (1955) C-88m. **½ D: Jerry Hopper. Dana Andrews, Piper Laurie, Rex Reason, Milburn Stone, William Talman. At-times zesty Western involving Indian massacre and survivors' trek downstream to escape.

Smoky (1946) C-87m. *** D: Louis King. Fred MacMurray, Anne Baxter, Burl Ives, Bruce Cabot, Esther Dale, Roy Roberts. First-rate family film from Will James story of man's devotion to his horse. Previously filmed in 1933, then again in 1966.

Smugglers' Cove (1948) 66m. **½ D: William Beaudine. Leo Gorcey, Huntz Hall, Gabriel Dell, Billy Benedict, David Gorcey, Bennie Bartlett, Martin Kosleck, Paul Harvey, Amelita Ward. With Kosleck in the cast, you know there's bound to be some evil Germans, and in this one they're smugglers at a posh Long Island estate, foiled by the Bowery Boys. ▶

Smuggler's Gold (1951) 64m. ** D: William Berke. Cameron Mitchell, Amanda Blake, Carl Benton Reid, Peter Thompson. Adequate drama about deep-sea diver Mitchell coping with girlfriend's (Blake's) father who's in the smuggling game.

Smuggler's Island (1951) C-75m. ** D: Edward Ludwig. Jeff Chandler, Evelyn Keyes, Philip Friend, Marvin Miller. Undemanding adventure story of diver Chandler involved with Keyes and search for sunken gold.

Snafu (1945) 82m. ** D: Jack Moss. Robert Benchley, Vera Vague (Barbara Jo Allen), Conrad Janis, Nanette Parks, Janis Wilson, Marcia Mae Jones, Kathleen Howard, Jimmy Lloyd, Enid Markey, Eva Puig. Young Conrad Janis is sent home by Army because of his age, but he can't get used to civilian life again; mild comedy with Benchley fine as perplexed father.

Snake Pit, The (1948) 108m. ***½ D: Anatole Litvak. Olivia de Havilland, Mark Stevens, Leo Genn, Celeste Holm, Glenn Langan, Helen Craig, Leif Erickson, Beulah Bondi, Lee Patrick, Natalie Schafer, Ruth Donnelly, Frank Conroy, Minna Gombell, Ann Doran, Betsy Blair, Isabel Jewell. One of the first films to deal intelligently with mental breakdowns and the painstakingly slow recovery process. Gripping film set in mental institution lacks original shock value but still packs a good punch, with de Havilland superb. Screenplay by Frank Partos and Millen Brand, from the Mary Jane Ward novel. ▼▶

Sniper, The (1952) 87m. *** D: Edward Dmytryk. Adolphe Menjou, Arthur Franz, Marie Windsor, Richard Kiley, Mabel Paige. Excellent, realistically filmed drama of mentally deranged sniper (Franz) who can't help himself from killing unsuspecting women. Fine performances by all. ▶

Snorkel, The (1958-British) 74m. **½ D: Guy Green. Peter Van Eyck, Betta St. John, Mandy Miller, Gregoire Aslan. Van Eyck ingeniously murders wife and plots to do away with stepdaughter, when she discovers his gimmick. ▶

Snow Creature, The (1954) 70m. *½ D: W. Lee Wilder. Paul Langton, Leslie Denison, Teru Shimada, Rollin Moriyama. Yeti brought back from Himalayas languishes in customs while officials wrangle over whether it is cargo or a passenger. Dull film at least has virtue of being made for adults, though only kids may like it now. ▼▶

Snow Queen, The (1959) C-70m. ** D: Phil Patton. Art Linkletter, Tammy Marihugh, Jennie Lynn. Voices of Sandra Dee, Tommy Kirk, Patty McCormack, Paul Frees, June Foray. American live-action footage frames a lavish, stately Soviet animated feature from 1955 (directed by Lev Atamanov) based on the Hans Christian Andersen fairy tale about an icy snow queen whose heart is melted by the presence of true love. ▶

Snows of Kilimanjaro, The (1952) C-117m. *** D: Henry King. Gregory Peck, Susan Hayward, Ava Gardner, Hildegarde Neff, Leo G. Carroll. Peck finds his forte as renowned writer critically injured while on safari in Africa, trying to decide if he found any meaning to his past; based on Hemingway story. ▼▶

Snow White (1916) 63m. *** D: J. Searle Dawley. Marguerite Clark, Dorothy Cumming, Creighton Hale, Lionel Braham, Alice Washburn, Richard Barthelmess. Appealing fairy tale about Snow White (Clark), a lovely young princess who is ill treated by her evil stepmother. Still charming, with amusing depiction of the seven dwarfs. Apparently this made a lasting impression on Walt Disney, who chose the same story for his first feature-length film. ▶

Snow White and the Seven Dwarfs (1937) C-83m. **** D: David Hand. Voices of Adriana Caselotti, Harry Stockwell, Lucille LaVerne, Scotty Mattraw, Roy Atwell, Pinto Colvig, Otis Harlan, Billy Gilbert, Moroni Olsen. Walt Disney's groundbreaking animated feature film—the first of its kind—is still in a class by itself, a warm and joyful rendition of the classic fairy tale, enhanced by the vivid personalities of the seven dwarfs. Only a real-life Grumpy could fail to love it. Songs include "Whistle While You Work," "Heigh Ho," and "Some Day My Prince Will Come." ▼▶

Snow White and the Three Stooges (1961) C-107m. BOMB D: Walter Lang. Three Stooges, Patricia Medina, Carol

Heiss, Buddy Baer, Guy Rolfe, Edgar Barrier. Big mistake with skating star Heiss as Snow White, Three Stooges as . . . the Three Stooges. Comics aren't given much to do, despite title; rest of film is rather stodgy. Even kids won't be thrilled with it. CinemaScope.▼▶

Soak the Rich (1936) 87m. BOMB D: Ben Hecht, Charles MacArthur. Walter Connolly, Mary Taylor, John Howard, Alice Duer Miller, Ilka Chase, Lionel Stander. Tycoon's daughter goes to college, falls for the militant anticapitalist who kidnaps her. Hard to believe that a Hecht-MacArthur collaboration about campus radicals could be thoroughly unwatchable, but it's true. Miller, writer of *The White Cliffs of Dover* and member of the Algonquin Round Table, appears here as Miss Beasely.

So big! (1932) 80m. ** D: William A. Wellman. Barbara Stanwyck, George Brent, Dickie Moore, Guy Kibbee, Bette Davis, Mae Madison, Hardie Albright, Alan Hale. Disappointing adaptation of Edna Ferber's saga of an orphaned girl who becomes a schoolteacher in the midst of a farming community and raises her son to aspire to big things. Abrupt continuity and sudden aging of its lead character keep this from amounting to very much. Stanwyck and Davis are both in the final scene—but never appear on screen together! Filmed before in 1925, remade in 1953.

So Big (1953) 101m. *** D: Robert Wise. Jane Wyman, Sterling Hayden, Nancy Olson, Steve Forrest, Martha Hyer, Tommy Rettig. Superficial but engrossing Edna Ferber soaper/saga about teacher who brings up son to be self-sufficient. Filmed before in 1924 and 1932.

Society Doctor (1935) 63m. ** D: George B. Seitz. Chester Morris, Robert Taylor, Virginia Bruce, Billie Burke, Raymond Walburn, Henry Kolker, Donald Meek. Talky, hokey soaper of the various interactions among doctors, nurses, and patients in a hospital. Morris is the spirited, principled head intern who even gets to direct his own operation! Bruce is his nurse-girlfriend, who's loved by intern Taylor; Burke is a pampered patient.

Society Lawyer (1939) 77m. **½ D: Edwin L. Marin. Walter Pidgeon, Virginia Bruce, Leo Carrillo, Eduardo Ciannelli, Lee Bowman, Frances Mercer, Herbert Mundin. Snappy reworking of PENTHOUSE, with sharp-minded lawyer Pidgeon playing detective while going to the defense of a society pal accused of murder.

So Dark the Night (1946) 71m. **½ D: Joseph H. Lewis. Steven Geray, Micheline Cheirel, Eugene Borden, Ann Codee, Egon Brecher, Helen Freeman. Famous Parisian detective is put to work during his holiday in the French countryside. Impressively made B movie, something of a sleeper in its time,

suffers only for lack of charisma on the part of its (mostly unknown) cast.▶

So Dear to My Heart (1949) C-84m. ***½ D: Harold Schuster. Burl Ives, Beulah Bondi, Bobby Driscoll, Luana Patten, Harry Carey. Warm, nostalgic Disney film about young boy's determination to raise a black sheep and bring him to State Fair competition. Brimming with period charm and atmosphere; several animated sequences, too. Songs include "Lavender Blue (Dilly Dilly)." Screenplay by John Tucker Battle, from Sterling North's book *Midnight and Jeremiah*. ▼▶

Sodom and Gomorrah (1963-Italian) C-154m. **½ D: Robert Aldrich. Stewart Granger, Pier Angeli, Stanley Baker, Anouk Aimée, Rossana Podesta. Lavish retelling of life in biblical twin cities of sin. Strong cast, vivid scenes of vice, gore, and God's wrath, make this overly long tale of ancient Hebrews fairly entertaining.▼▶

So Ends Our Night (1941) 117m. ***½ D: John Cromwell. Fredric March, Margaret Sullavan, Frances Dee, Glenn Ford, Anna Sten, Erich von Stroheim, Allan Brett. Superior filmization of Erich Maria Remarque story of German (March) rejecting Nazi reign, fleeing his country with hot pursuit by Axis agents. Written by Talbot Jennings from Remarque's novel *Flotsam*.▼▶

So Evil My Love (1948) 109m. *** D: Lewis Allen. Ray Milland, Ann Todd, Geraldine Fitzgerald, Leo G. Carroll, Raymond Huntley, Martita Hunt, Hugh Griffith. Excellent study of corruption; scoundrel Milland drags innocent Todd into larceny at expense of Fitzgerald.

Sofia (1948) C-82m. ** D: John Reinhardt. Gene Raymond, Sigrid Gurie, Patricia Morison, Mischa Auer. Acceptable programmer with Raymond helping nuclear scientists escape grip of Russians in Turkey. Filmed in Mexico.▶

Soft Boiled (1923) 78m. **½ D: John G. Blystone. Tom Mix, Joseph Girard, Billie Dove, L. D. Shumway, Tom Wilson, Frank Beal. Tom Mix tries comedy, as young man with challenge to spend 30 days without losing his temper; enjoyable fluff, with typical Mix action finale.

Soft Skin, The (1964-French) 120m. *** D: François Truffaut. Françoise Dorléac, Jean Desailly, Nelly Benedetti. Moody tale of married businessman drawn into tragic affair with beautiful airline stewardess; smooth direction uplifts basic plot.▼▶

So Goes My Love (1946) 88m. **½ D: Frank Ryan. Myrna Loy, Don Ameche, Rhys Williams, Bobby Driscoll, Richard Gaines, Molly Lamont. Amusing period comedy of fortune-hunting Loy marrying oddball inventor Ameche.▶

Soldier and the Lady, The (1937) 85m. **½ D: George Nicholls, Jr. Anton Walbrook, Elizabeth Allan, Margot Grahame,

Akim Tamiroff, Fay Bainter, Eric Blore. Hollywoodized version of Jules Verne's oft-filmed tale of a Czarist courier sent to deliver critical plans to the army in Siberia. Visually impressive, with sweeping battle scenes, though most exteriors were lifted from previous European version of the film, which also starred Walbrook. Aka MICHAEL STROGOFF.

Soldier in the Rain (1963) **88m.** *** D: Ralph Nelson. Jackie Gleason, Steve McQueen, Tuesday Weld, Tony Bill, Tom Poston, Ed Nelson, John Hubbard, Adam West. Strange film wavers from sentimental drama to high comedy. Gleason is swinging sergeant, McQueen his fervent admirer. Script by Blake Edwards and Maurice Richlin from William Goldman's novel.▼▶

Soldier of Fortune (1955) **C-96m.** *** D: Edward Dmytryk. Clark Gable, Susan Hayward, Michael Rennie, Gene Barry, Tom Tully, Alex D'Arcy, Anna Sten. Gable is hired to find Susan's husband (Barry) held captive in Hong Kong. Rennie is good as police chief. Scripted by Ernest K. Gann, from his novel. CinemaScope.▼▶

Soldier of Love SEE: **Fan Fan the Tulip**

Soldier's Prayer, A (1961-Japanese) **190m.** ***½ D: Masaki Kobayashi. Tatsuya Nakadai, Yusuke Kawazu, Tamao Nakamura, Chishu Ryu, Taketoshi Naitô, Reiko Hitomi, Kyôko Kishida, Fujio Suga. Final installment of Kobayashi's three-part rumination on the horrors of WW2 (after NO GREATER LOVE and THE ROAD TO ETERNITY) is set in the waning days of the conflict. Here, Kaji (Nakadai) and other soldiers and civilians struggle to stay alive in the desolate Manchurian countryside. Meanwhile, Kaji wonders if his beloved wife is still living, and if he will ever find her. The finale is haunting...and fitting. Scripted by Kobayashi, Zenzo Matsuyama, and Koichi Inagaki, based on a six-volume novel by Junpei Gomikawa. Aka THE HUMAN CONDITION III. Grandscope.▶

Soldiers Three (1951) **87m.** *** D: Tay Garnett. Stewart Granger, Walter Pidgeon, David Niven, Robert Newton, Cyril Cusack, Greta Gynt, Robert Coote, Dan O'Herlihy. Boisterous action-adventure with light touch; GUNGA DIN–esque story has three soldiering comrades in and out of spats with each other as they battle in 19th-century India. Loosely based on stories by Rudyard Kipling.

Solid Gold Cadillac, The (1956) **99m.** *** D: Richard Quine. Judy Holliday, Paul Douglas, Fred Clark, John Williams, Arthur O'Connell, Hiram Sherman, Neva Patterson, Ray Collins; narrated by George Burns. Dazzling Judy in entertaining comedy of small stockholder in large company becoming corporate heroine by trying to oust crooked board of directors. George S. Kaufman–Howard Teichman play adapted by Abe

Burrows. Jean Louis earned an Oscar for the costumes. Last scene in color.▼▶

Solitaire Man, The (1933) **67m.** ** D: Jack Conway. Herbert Marshall, Mary Boland, Lionel Atwill, May Robson, Elizabeth Allan, Ralph Forbes, Lucile Gleason. On the verge of retiring and getting married, jewel thief Marshall has to return a valuable necklace without being detected. Claustrophobic, talky adaptation of a Sam and Bella Spewack play shot in long takes, with a hilariously improbable airplane sequence. Boland is very funny as a loudmouthed, nouveau riche American.

Solomon and Sheba (1959) **C-139m.** *** D: King Vidor. Yul Brynner, Gina Lollobrigida, George Sanders, Marisa Pavan, John Crawford, Alejandro Rey, Harry Andrews. Splashy spectacle with alluring Gina and stoic Brynner frolicking in biblical days. Tyrone Power died during filming in Spain, was replaced by Brynner, who refilmed Power's early scenes. Some long shots still show Power, not Brynner. Vidor's final film as director. Also shown at 120m. Super Technirama 70.▼▶

So Long at the Fair (1950-British) **90m.** *** D: Terence Fisher, Anthony Darnborough. Jean Simmons, Dirk Bogarde, David Tomlinson, Honor Blackman, Cathleen Nesbitt, Felix Aylmer, Andre Morell, Betty Warren. Atmospheric drama set during 1889 Paris Exposition with English woman searching for brother who's mysteriously vanished. Absorbing, well-made rendering of a famous "urban legend" tale that retains every bit of its eerie allure.

So Long Letty (1929) **64m.** *** D: Lloyd Bacon. Charlotte Greenwood, Claude Gillingwater, Grant Withers, Patsy Ruth Miller, Bert Roach, Marion Byron. Eccentric Greenwood swaps places with her neighbor's wife when her hubby's grouchy millionaire uncle (a hilarious Gillingwater) comes for a visit. Surprisingly sprightly early-talkie musical comedy, with Greenwood, who starred in the Broadway version for years, giving an inspired, tour-de-force performance. Also filmed in 1920.▶

Sombrero (1953) **C-103m.** *½ D: Norman Foster. Ricardo Montalban, Pier Angeli, Vittorio Gassman, Yvonne De Carlo, Nina Foch, Cyd Charisse, Jose Greco, Walter Hampden, Kurt Kasznar, Rick Jason. Strange, overwrought MGM melodrama with music intertwining three love stories in small Mexican village. One good dance number with Charisse.▶

Somebody Loves Me (1952) **C-97m.** ** D: Irving S. Brecher. Betty Hutton, Ralph Meeker, Adele Jergens, Robert Keith. Schmaltzy vaudeville biography of troupers Blossom Seeley and Benny Fields with no originality and not much entertainment, either.

Somebody Up There Likes Me (1956) **113m.** ***½ D: Robert Wise. Paul Newman, Pier Angeli, Everett Sloane, Eileen Heckart, Sal Mineo, Joseph Buloff, Robert Loggia, Steve McQueen, Dean Jones. Top biography of boxer Rocky Graziano's rise from N.Y.C. sidewalks to arena success with fine performance by Newman. Script by Ernest Lehman; cinematographer Joseph Ruttenberg won an Oscar. ▼O▶

Some Came Running (1958) **C-136m.** *** D: Vincente Minnelli. Frank Sinatra, Dean Martin, Shirley MacLaine, Martha Hyer, Arthur Kennedy, Nancy Gates. Slick adaptation of James Jones' novel about disillusionment in a small midwestern town in the late 1940s; more character study than narrative. MacLaine is especially good as luckless floozie who's stuck on Sinatra; Elmer Bernstein's music score also a standout. CinemaScope. ▼O▶

Some Like It Hot (1939) **65m.** **½ D: George Archainbaud. Bob Hope, Shirley Ross, Una Merkel, Gene Krupa, Rufe Davis, Bernard Nedell, Richard Denning, Frank Sully, Jack (J. Scott) Smart. Sideshow owner Hope repeatedly takes advantage of Ross to keep his show afloat. Pleasant enough comedy-drama based on a Gene Fowler–Ben Hecht play (filmed in 1934 as SHOOT THE WORKS), though we never understand why Ross puts up with Hope's wayward ways. Krupa's numbers are mediocre but the film introduces "The Lady's in Love With You." Retitled RHYTHM ROMANCE.▼

Some Like It Hot (1959) **119m.** **** D: Billy Wilder. Jack Lemmon, Tony Curtis, Marilyn Monroe, Joe E. Brown, George Raft, Pat O'Brien, Nehemiah Persoff, Joan Shawlee, Mike Mazurki. Legendary comedy by Wilder and I.A.L. Diamond about two musicians who witness the St. Valentine's Day Massacre and try to elude their pursuers by joining an all-girl band heading for Miami. Sensational from start to finish, with dazzling performances by Lemmon and Curtis, a memorably comic turn by Monroe as Sugar Kane, and Oscar-winning costumes by Orry-Kelly. Brown has film's now-classic closing line. Based on a 1935 French movie, FANFARE D'AMOUR. Basis for hit Broadway musical *Sugar.* ▼O▶

Something Always Happens (1934-British) **69m.** *** D: Michael Powell. Ian Hunter, Nancy O'Neil, Peter Gawthorne, John Singer, Muriel George, Barry Livesey, Naunton Wayne, George Zucco. Charming and frothy film about an unemployed car salesman (Hunter) who scores a big success in the gas station business, unaware that his girlfriend-secretary is the daughter of his rival. One of the best of Powell's British "quota quickies."

Something for the Birds (1952) **81m.** **½ D: Robert Wise. Patricia Neal, Victor Mature, Edmund Gwenn, Larry Keating. Mild romantic froth, with Mature and Neal on opposite sides of issue in lobbying for bird sanctuary protection. ▶

Something for the Boys (1944) **C-85m.** **½ D: Lewis Seiler. Carmen Miranda, Michael O'Shea, Vivian Blaine, Phil Silvers, Sheila Ryan, Perry Como, Glenn Langan, Cara Williams, Thurston Hall. Pleasant musical with diverting Cole Porter score, set on a Southern plantation inherited by a trio of unlikely cousins (Blaine, Silvers, Miranda), which has been recruited as a home for soldiers' wives. Film debuts of Rory Calhoun and Murray Hamilton. Look for Judy Holliday as a defense plant welder. ▶

Something in the Wind (1947) **89m.** **½ D: Irving Pichel. Deanna Durbin, Donald O'Connor, Charles Winninger, Helena Carter. Mild comedy of errors with Durbin as female disk jockey who sings, too. Easy to take, amusing. ▼▶

Something New (1920) **57m.** *** D: Nell Shipman, Bert Van Tuyle. Nell Shipman, Bert Van Tuyle, L. M. Wells, William McCormack. Modern technology meets the Old West in this action-packed tale of writer Shipman heading south of the border, where she's kidnapped by banditos . . . but she's no stereotypical damsel in distress. Scenes of Van Tuyle's "gas-wagon" (translation: car) zipping across sand and rocks and up and down mountains are still impressive. Only flaw: embarrassingly racist descriptions of Mexicans. ▼▶

Something of Value (1957) **113m.** *** D: Richard Brooks. Rock Hudson, Dana Wynter, Sidney Poitier, Wendy Hiller, Frederick O'Neal. Robert Ruark's novel transformed to screen, sharply detailing brutal Mau Mau warfare in Kenya. Hudson and Poitier are fine as British colonial farmer and his childhood friend; Hiller memorable as widow struggling to retain dignity and spirit. ▼▶

Something to Live For (1952) **89m.** **½ D: George Stevens. Joan Fontaine, Ray Milland, Teresa Wright, Douglas Dick, Rudy Lee. Turgid melodrama trying to be another THE LOST WEEKEND. Fontaine is alcoholic in love with Milland, but he's married. ▶

Something to Shout About (1943) **93m.** ** D: Gregory Ratoff. Don Ameche, Janet Blair, Jack Oakie, Cobina Wright, Jr., William Gaxton, Veda Ann Borg. Hackneyed backstage Broadway musical with good Cole Porter score (including "You'd Be So Nice to Come Home To"), specialty numbers by Hazel Scott, Teddy Wilson and His Orchestra. Look for Cyd Charisse (billed as Lily Norwood) in her feature debut.

Something to Sing About (1937) **93m.** ** D: Victor Schertzinger. James Cagney, Evelyn Daw, William Frawley, Mona Barrie, Gene Lockhart. Low-budget musical doesn't live up to its title, with Cagney the only real asset in this lightweight story of a N.Y. bandleader who goes to Hollywood.

Forgettable songs. Reissued at 82m. as BATTLING HOOFER. Also shown in computer-colored version. ▼●▶

Something Wild (1961) **112m.** **½ D: Jack Garfein. Carroll Baker, Ralph Meeker, Mildred Dunnock, Martin Kosleck, Jean Stapleton. Bizarre study of rape victim Baker falling in love with would-be attacker Meeker, coming to rational understanding with mother Dunnock. N.Y.C. location scenes perk melodramatic soaper. ▶

Somewhere I'll Find You (1942) **108m.** **½ D: Wesley Ruggles. Clark Gable, Lana Turner, Robert Sterling, Patricia Dane, Reginald Owen, Lee Patrick, Charles Dingle, Sara Haden, Rags Ragland, Van Johnson, Leonid Kinskey, Grady Sutton, Keye Luke. Turner and Gable are improbable as WW2 war correspondents, but their love scenes between battles are most convincing. Film debut of Keenan Wynn. ▼▶

Somewhere in Sonora (1933) **57m.** *½ D: Mack V. Wright. John Wayne, Henry B. Walthall, Shirley Palmer, Ann Faye, J. P. McGowan, Paul Fix. A friend asks Wayne to locate missing son (Fix), who was possibly abducted by bandits, taken to Sonora, and forced to ride with notorious "Brotherhood of Death." Dull remake of samenamed 1927 Ken Maynard silent. Fix was a fixture in Wayne movies throughout their careers. ▼▶

Somewhere in the Night (1946) **108m.** **½ D: Joseph L. Mankiewicz. John Hodiak, Nancy Guild, Lloyd Nolan, Richard Conte, Josephine Hutchinson, Fritz Kortner, Sheldon Leonard, Whit Bissell, Jeff Corey, Henry (Harry) Morgan. Satisfactory drama of amnesiac Hodiak trying to discover his true identity and getting mixed up with mobsters and murder; not up to later Mankiewicz efforts. ▶

Son-Daughter, The (1932) **79m.** *½ D: Clarence Brown. Helen Hayes, Ramon Novarro, Lewis Stone, Ralph Morgan, Warner Oland. Designed as a tender love story with tragic overtones set in San Francisco's Chinatown, this film plays more like farce, with dialogue that sounds like Chinese Damon Runyon. One of Hayes' most embarrassing performances.

Song Is Born, A (1948) **C-113m.** **½ D: Howard Hawks. Danny Kaye, Virginia Mayo, Hugh Herbert, Steve Cochran, Felix Bressart; guest stars Benny Goodman, Louis Armstrong, Charlie Barnet, Lionel Hampton, Tommy Dorsey. A group of dowdy intellectuals need to learn about jazz to write an intelligent entry for their upcoming encyclopedia. Watered-down remake of BALL OF FIRE (also directed by Hawks) does give Danny some good material, and enables a formidable array of jazz greats to do their stuff (including Benny Goodman, made up as one of the bookish profs). ▼●▶

Song of Arizona (1946) **68m.** ** D: Frank McDonald. Roy Rogers, George "Gabby" Hayes, Dale Evans, Lyle Talbot, Tommy Cook, Johnny Calkins, Sarah Edwards, Tommy Ivo, Michael Chapin, Dick Curtis, Edmund Cobb, The Robert Mitchell Boys Choir, Bob Nolan and the Sons of the Pioneers. Gabby runs the Half-a-Chance Boys' Ranch to help troubled youth, one of whom (Cook) has been hiding his outlaw father's stash for years. Roy is a successful graduate of the ranch, and returns there to help Cook choose the right path—but crooks are determined to get their hands on that money. Music swamps the story here. ▼▶

Song of Bernadette, The (1943) **156m.** ***½ D: Henry King. Jennifer Jones, William Eythe, Charles Bickford, Vincent Price, Lee J. Cobb, Anne Revere, Gladys Cooper. Overlong but excellent story of religious French girl in 1800s who sees great vision, incurs local wrath because of it. George Seaton adapted Franz Werfel's bestselling novel. Four Oscars include Best Actress, Cinematography (Arthur Miller), Score (Alfred Newman). That's Linda Darnell, unbilled, as the Virgin Mary. Video version runs 158m. with exit music. ▼●▶

Song of Freedom (1936-British) **80m.** **½ D: J. Elder Wills. Paul Robeson, Elizabeth Welch, George Mozart, Esme Percy, Arthur Williams, Robert Adams. Robeson plays stevedore-turned-concert-singer who journeys to Africa in search of his roots. Promising idea doesn't quite work, but Robeson is always worth watching. ▼▶

Song of India (1949) **77m.** ** D: Albert S. Rogell. Sabu, Gail Russell, Turhan Bey, Anthony Caruso, Aminta Dyne. Well-meaning Sabu releases jungle animals callously trapped by royal family; typical jungle escapist adventure. ▼

Song of Love (1947) **119m.** **½ D: Clarence Brown. Katharine Hepburn, Paul Henreid, Robert Walker, Henry Daniell, Leo G. Carroll, Gigi Perreau, Tala Birell, Henry Stephenson. Classy production but slowmoving story of Clara Schuman (Hepburn), her composer husband (Henreid), and good friend Brahms (Walker). ▼▶

Song of Nevada (1944) **75m.** ** D: Joseph Kane. Roy Rogers, Dale Evans, Mary Lee, Lloyd Corrigan, Thurston Hall, John Eldredge, Forrest Taylor, George Meeker, LeRoy Mason, Helen Talbot, Bob Nolan and the Sons of the Pioneers. Dale is smitten by slick New Yorker Eldredge, but Roy suspects he's got something more than marriage on his mind—for instance, the ranch she just inherited from her father. Plot takes a backseat to music in this entry, typical of Rogers' mid-'40s vehicles. ▼▶

Song of Russia (1943) **107m.** **½ D: Gregory Ratoff. Robert Taylor, Susan Peters, John Hodiak, Robert Benchley, Felix Bressart, Joan Lorring, Darryl Hickman.

[642]

MGM's attempt to do for Russia what MRS. MINIVER did for England; hokey but effective story of American conductor Taylor falling in love with Russian musician Peters. Then-topical attitude toward U.S.S.R. makes this an interesting piece.

Song of Scheherazade (1947) **C-106m. **** D: Walter Reisch. Yvonne De Carlo, Brian Donlevy, Jean-Pierre Aumont, Eve Arden, Philip Reed. Colorful tripe about Rimsky-Korsakov's true inspiration, a dancing girl (De Carlo). ▼

Song of Songs, The (1933) **90m. **½** D: Rouben Mamoulian. Marlene Dietrich, Brian Aherne, Lionel Atwill, Alison Skipworth, Hardie Albright, Helen Freeman. Naïve country girl Dietrich falls in love with sculptor Aherne, for whom she poses in the nude . . . but Atwill, a wealthy reprobate, manages to marry her. Humdrum story made worthwhile by good performances. Dietrich is luminous in her first Hollywood film *not* directed by Josef von Sternberg. ▼▶

Song of Surrender (1949) **93m. **** D: Mitchell Leisen. Wanda Hendrix, Claude Rains, Macdonald Carey, Andrea King, Henry O'Neill, Elizabeth Patterson, Eva Gabor. Mild turn-of-the-20th-century tale of young woman (Hendrix) and older husband Rains.

Song of Texas (1943) **69m. **½** D: Joseph Kane. Roy Rogers, Sheila Ryan, Barton MacLane, Harry Shannon, Pat Brady, Arline Judge, William Haade, Hal Taliaferro, Bob Nolan and the Sons of the Pioneers. Roy allows old-timer Shannon to fib to his daughter (Ryan) that he is half owner of Roy's ranch—but things get complicated when Ryan sells her dad's "half" to villain MacLane. Action-filled tale with wagon races, fires, and horse stampedes and such songs as "Mexicali Rose." ▼▶

Song of the Islands (1942) **C-75m. ***** D: Walter Lang. Betty Grable, Victor Mature, Jack Oakie, Thomas Mitchell, Hilo Hattie, George Barbier, Billy Gilbert. Mature (with sidekick Oakie) visits idyllic Pacific island and falls in love with Grable, but romance is hindered by feuding between their fathers. Buoyant Technicolor fluff, full of engagingly silly songs by Mack Gordon and Harry Owens. ▼▶

Song of the Open Road (1944) **93m. **** D: S. Sylvan Simon. Charlie McCarthy, Edgar Bergen, Jane Powell, W. C. Fields, Bonita Granville, Peggy O'Neill, Jackie Moran, Reginald Denny, Regis Toomey, Sammy Kaye and His Orchestra. Insipid tale of juvenile film star (Powell, in her screen debut) who rebels, runs away and joins the CCC (Civilian Conservation Corps), picking tomatoes and mingling with "regular" kids. Hard to take, except for specialty numbers and guest appearance by Fields and his longtime wooden nemesis, McCarthy.

Song of the Road SEE: End of the Road, The

Song of the South (1946) **C-94m. ***½** D: Wilfred Jackson (animation), Harve Foster (live-action). Ruth Warrick, James Baskett, Bobby Driscoll, Luana Patten, Lucile Watson, Hattie McDaniel, Glenn Leedy. Lonely, misunderstood little boy, living on a plantation in the Old South, finds his only happiness in the tales spun by Uncle Remus. Sentimental but moving story serves as framework for three terrific Disney cartoon sequences featuring Brer Rabbit, Brer Fox, and Brer Bear (based on writings of Joel Chandler Harris). Superb blend of live-action and animation, sincere performances (Baskett earned a special Academy Award for his), and tuneful songs including Oscar-winning "Zip a Dee Doo Dah" make this a treat. Available only on Japanese home media. ●

Song of the Thin Man (1947) **86m. **½** D: Edward Buzzell. William Powell, Myrna Loy, Keenan Wynn, Dean Stockwell, Philip Reed, Patricia Morison, Gloria Grahame, Jayne Meadows, Don Taylor, Leon Ames. Nick and Nora search for clues to a murder in the dark and mysterious atmosphere of N.Y.C. jazz clubs. Eleven-year-old Stockwell portrays Nick, Jr., in this sixth and final series entry, still amiable and entertaining thanks to the stars' chemistry. ▼▶●

Song o' My Heart (1930) **85m. **** D: Frank Borzage. John McCormack, Alice Joyce, Maureen O'Sullivan, Tommy Clifford, J. M. Kerrigan, J. Farrell MacDonald, John Garrick, Andrés de Segurola. Slowly paced early-talkie vehicle for fabled Irish tenor McCormack allows him to sing a varied repertoire of songs amidst a simple, sentimental story. O'Sullivan is winsome but stilted in her film debut, while McCormack, who's given little to do dramatically, is a natural on camera. Songs include "I Hear You Calling" and "The Rose of Tralee." Grandeur. ▼▶

Song to Remember, A (1945) **C-113m. **½** D: Charles Vidor. Cornel Wilde, Paul Muni, Merle Oberon, Stephen Bekassy, Nina Foch, George Coulouris, Sig Arno. Colorful but superficial biography of Chopin (Wilde) with exaggerated Muni as his mentor, lovely Oberon as George Sand; good music, frail plot. ▼▶●

Song Without End (1960) **C-141m. **½** D: Charles Vidor. Dirk Bogarde, Capucine, Genevieve Page, Patricia Morison, Ivan Desny, Martita Hunt, Lou Jacobi. Beautiful music (scoring won an Oscar) submerged by dramatics of composer Franz Liszt's life. Bogarde tries; settings are lavish. Vidor died during filming, George Cukor completed picture. CinemaScope. ▼▶●

Son of a Gunfighter (1965-U.S.-Spanish) **C-92m. **½** D: Paul Landres. Russ Tamblyn, Kieron Moore, James Philbrook, Fernando Rey, Maria Granada, Aldo Sambrell. Lots of action in handsomely shot Western filmed in Spain, with Tamblyn gunning for the outlaw he blames for the death of his mother: his own father! Tamblyn reprised his character 47 years later in DJANGO UNCHAINED, with daughter Amber playing "Daughter of a Son of a Gunfighter." CinemaScope. ◗

Son of Ali Baba (1952) **C-75m.** ** D: Kurt Neumann. Tony Curtis, Piper Laurie, Susan Cabot, Victor Jory, Hugh O'Brian. Caliph uses princess Laurie to obtain treasure of Ali Baba. After father is captured, son appears and wins hand of princess. Good sets, fair acting. ◗

Son of a Sailor (1933) **73m.** **½ D: Lloyd Bacon. Joe E. Brown, Jean Muir, Frank McHugh, Thelma Todd, Johnny Mack Brown, Sheila Terry. Typical Brown vehicle, with Joe E. cast as a skirt-chasing seabee-showoff who becomes involved with spies. Always-vivacious Todd lends fine support.

Son of Captain Blood, The (1962-U.S.-Italian-Spanish) **C-88m.** *½ D: Tulio Demicheli. Sean Flynn, Ann Todd, Alessandra Panaro, Jose Nieto, John Kitzmiller. Interesting only in that Errol Flynn's 23-year-old son plays the son of the character Errol portrayed in CAPTAIN BLOOD. Ann Todd sparkles as the lad's mother (Olivia de Havilland's character in the original). Otherwise, routine. Filmed in Spain, from a screenplay by Casey Robinson (who also penned the 1935 CAPTAIN BLOOD). CinemaScope. ▼

Son of Dracula (1943) **78m.** *** D: Robert Siodmak. Lon Chaney, Jr., Robert Paige, Louise Allbritton, Evelyn Ankers, Frank Craven, J. Edward Bromberg, Samuel S. Hinds. Mysterious gentleman named Alucard turns up in the Deep South to sample the local cuisine. One of Universal's most atmospheric chillers, with crisp acting, fine effects . . . and an unexpected finale. ▼●◗

Son of Dr. Jekyll, The (1951) **77m.** *½ D: Seymour Friedman. Louis Hayward, Jody Lawrance, Alexander Knox, Lester Matthews. Jekyll's son tries to discover and improve upon his father's formula; complications ensue. Poorly scripted, produced; cast manages to save film from complete ruin.

Son of Flubber (1963) **100m.** **½ D: Robert Stevenson. Fred MacMurray, Nancy Olson, Keenan Wynn, Tommy Kirk, Elliott Reid, Joanna Moore, Leon Ames, Ed Wynn, Charlie Ruggles, Paul Lynde, Jack Albertson. Silly, disjointed sequel to THE ABSENT MINDED PROFESSOR has new inventions—flubbergas, dry rain—and appropriate slapstick highlights, to compensate for uneven script. Helped, too, by cast full of old pros, especially Lynde as smug sportscaster. ▼●◗

Son of Frankenstein (1939) **99m.** *** D: Rowland V. Lee. Basil Rathbone, Boris Karloff, Bela Lugosi, Lionel Atwill, Josephine Hutchinson, Edgar Norton, Donnie Dunagan. Third in the series (after BRIDE) finds late doctor's son (Rathbone) attempting to clear family name by making the Monster "good." He should live so long. Lavishly made shocker is gripping and eerie, if a bit talky, with wonderfully bizarre sets by Jack Otterson and Lugosi's finest performance as evil, broken-necked blacksmith Ygor. Karloff's last appearance as the Monster. Look fast for Ward Bond(!) as a constable guarding Castle Frankenstein from angry villagers late in film. Sequel: THE GHOST OF FRANKENSTEIN. ▼●◗

Son of Fury (1942) **98m.** *** D: John Cromwell. Tyrone Power, Gene Tierney, George Sanders, Frances Farmer, Roddy McDowall, Kay Johnson, John Carradine, Elsa Lanchester, Harry Davenport, Dudley Digges, Ethel Griffies. Good costumer about aristocratic Sanders abusing nephew Power, who flees to desert isle to plan revenge; Tierney's on the island, too. Remade as TREASURE OF THE GOLDEN CONDOR. ▼◗

Son of India (1931) **73m.** **½ D: Jacques Feyder. Ramon Novarro, Conrad Nagel, Madge Evans, Marjorie Rambeau, C. Aubrey Smith, Mitchell Lewis, John Miljan, Nigel de Brulier. Atmospheric oddity charting the riches-to-rags-to-riches saga of young Indian jewel merchant Novarro (who, amusingly, speaks with a Spanish accent). Problems arise when he becomes romantically involved with a pretty young American (Evans).

Son of Kong, The (1933) **70m.** **½ D: Ernest B. Schoedsack. Robert Armstrong, Helen Mack, Victor Wong, John Marston, Frank Reicher, Lee Kohlmar. Disappointing sequel to KING KONG, hurriedly put together—and it shows. Armstrong is back as Carl Denham, who returns to Skull Island and discovers Kong's cute li'l offspring. Mostly comedic film has some good moments, and Willis O'Brien's effects are still superb. ▼●◗

Son of Lassie (1945) **C-102m.** **½ D: S. Sylvan Simon. Peter Lawford, Donald Crisp, June Lockhart, Nigel Bruce, William Severn, Leon Ames, Fay Helm, Donald Curtis, Nils Asther, Helen Koford (Terry Moore). War-themed sequel to popular LASSIE COME HOME with Lawford and Lockhart playing adult roles of McDowall and Taylor. Crisp and Bruce are now training dogs for the war effort and Lassie's son (both roles played here by talented collie Pal) accompanies pilot Lawford to Nazi-occupied Norway. ▼◗

Son of Monte Cristo, The (1940) **102m.** *** D: Rowland V. Lee. Louis Hayward, Joan Bennett, George Sanders, Florence Bates, Lionel Royce, Montagu Love, Ian Wolfe, Clayton Moore, Ralph Byrd, Rand Brooks, Henry Brandon. Nothing new in big-scale swashbuckler, but very well done with Hayward battling Sanders and vying for Bennett's hand. ▼●◗

Son of Paleface (1952) **C-95m.** ***½ D: Frank Tashlin. Bob Hope, Jane Russell, Roy Rogers, Douglass Dumbrille, Bill Williams, Harry Von Zell, Iron Eyes Cody. One of Hope's best; same basic set-up as THE PALEFACE, but the presence of Rogers gives this one a satirical punch the original doesn't have. Full of director-cowriter Tashlin's cartoonlike gags; the scene where Hope and Trigger share the same bed is an unheralded comedy classic. ▼●▶

Son of Robin Hood, The (1959-British) **C-81m.** ** D: George Sherman. Al (David) Hedison, June Laverick, David Farrar, Marius Goring, George Coulouris. Bland forest tale continuing the legend of merrie men led by Robin's descendant, actually his daughter (Laverick). CinemaScope. ▶

Son of Satan SEE: **Whip and the Body, The**

Son of Sinbad (1955) **C-88m.** *½ D: Ted Tetzlaff. Dale Robertson, Sally Forrest, Lili St. Cyr, Vincent Price. Limp Arabian Nights adventure has Sinbad, captured by caliph, forced to perform wonders to win freedom and save Baghdad from evil Tamerlane. Look fast for Kim Novak as one of the ladies garbed in full-length hooded capes. SuperScope. ▼

Son of the Sheik, The (1926) **72m.** *** D: George Fitzmaurice. Rudolph Valentino, Vilma Banky, Agnes Ayres, Karl Dane, Bull Montana. Sequel to THE SHEIK contains flavorful account of desert leader who falls in love with dancing-girl Banky. Handsomely mounted silent film is first-rate adventure/romance, with tongue slightly in cheek. Valentino plays a dual role in this, his last film. ▼●▶

Sons and Lovers (1960-British) **103m.** ***½ D: Jack Cardiff. Trevor Howard, Dean Stockwell, Wendy Hiller, Mary Ure, Heather Sears, William Lucas, Donald Pleasence, Ernest Thesiger. Grim D. H. Lawrence story of sensitive youth Stockwell egged on by mother to make something of his life, away from coal-mining town and drunken father. Script by Gavin Lambert and T.E.B. Clarke. Freddie Francis' rich cinematography won an Oscar. CinemaScope. ▶

Sons of Katie Elder, The (1965) **C-122m.** *** D: Henry Hathaway. John Wayne, Dean Martin, Martha Hyer, Michael Anderson, Jr., Earl Holliman, Jeremy Slate, James Gregory, George Kennedy, Paul Fix, Dennis Hopper, John Litel, Strother Martin. Typical Western with Duke, Holliman, Anderson, and Martin the rowdy sons of frontier woman, who set out to learn why she died broke. Film marked return to big screen for Wayne after first highly publicized cancer operation. Lively fun. Music score by Elmer Bernstein. Compare with 2005's FOUR BROTHERS. Panavision. ▼●▶

Sons of New Mexico (1949) **71m.** *** D: John English. Gene Autry, Gail Davis, Robert Armstrong, Dickie Jones, Frankie Darro, Irving Bacon, Russell Arms, Marie Blake, Clayton Moore. Spoiled brat Jones learns about cooperation and fair play from Gene, while crooked gambler Armstrong seeks vengeance since Jones' dad turned him in years earlier. One of Gene's standout Columbia Westerns, with gritty atmosphere and characters, terrific supporting cast, and superior production values. ▶

Sons of the Desert (1933) **69m.** ***½ D: William A. Seiter. Stan Laurel, Oliver Hardy, Charley Chase, Mae Busch, Dorothy Christy, Lucien Littlefield. L&H's best feature film; duo sneaks off to fraternal convention without telling the wives; then the fun begins, with Chase as hilariously obnoxious conventioneer. Also shown in computer-colored version. ▼●▶

Sons of the Pioneers (1942) **55m.** *** D: Joseph Kane. Roy Rogers, George "Gabby" Hayes, Maris Wrixon, Forrest Taylor, Bradley Page, Minerva Urecal, Bob Nolan and the Sons of the Pioneers. When Sheriff Gabby has rustler trouble, he sends back East for Rogers, the descendant of two tough sheriffs . . . but Roy turns out to be a peace-loving entomologist! One of Roy's very best from this period with an entertaining, tongue-in-cheek attitude. ▼▶

Sons o' Guns (1936) **82m.** ** D: Lloyd Bacon. Joe E. Brown, Joan Blondell, Eric Blore, Winifred Shaw, Robert Barrat, Beverly Roberts, Craig Reynolds. So-so comedy with music, with Brown a stage actor humbled into joining the Army during WW1; he romances fiery French girl and is accused of being a German spy.

Sooky (1931) **85m.** **½ D: Norman Taurog. Jackie Cooper, Robert Coogan, Jackie Searl, Enid Bennett, Helen Jerome Eddy, Willard Robertson. Middling sequel to SKIPPY with Cooper as Percy Crosby's comic-strip kid and scene-stealing Coogan as his best friend. Lightly comic, with some extra-sentimental scenes.

So Proudly We Hail! (1943) **126m.** *** D: Mark Sandrich. Claudette Colbert, Paulette Goddard, Veronica Lake, George Reeves, Sonny Tufts, Barbara Britton, Walter Abel. Flag-waving soaper of nurses in WW2 Pacific, headed by Colbert. Versatile cast, action scenes and teary romancing combine well in this woman's service story. Dated but still entertaining. ▼▶

So Red the Rose (1935) **82m.** **½ D: King Vidor. Margaret Sullavan, Walter Connolly, Randolph Scott, Elizabeth Patterson, Janet Beecher, Robert Cummings, Dickie Moore. Story of Sullavan patiently waiting for Scott to return from Civil War lacks punch but is well acted and generally enjoyable; Maxwell Anderson was one of the writers.

Sorority Girl (1957) **60m.** *½ D: Roger Corman. Susan Cabot, Dick Miller, Barbara Crane, Fay Baker, June Kenney, Barboura

O'Neill. Lumbering tale of angst and alienation, 1950s-style. The heroine (Cabot) is a wealthy but warped college coed; she can't fit in with the members of her sorority, so she lashes out at everyone around her. A female version of Calder Willingham's *End as a Man*, filmed that same year as THE STRANGE ONE. Remade in 1994 as CONFESSIONS OF A SORORITY GIRL and in 2000 as CONFESSIONS OF SORORITY GIRLS. ▼

Sorrowful Jones (1949) 88m. **½ D: Sidney Lanfield. Bob Hope, Lucille Ball, William Demarest, Mary Jane Saunders, Bruce Cabot, Thomas Gomez. Average racetrack comedy, actually a remake of LITTLE MISS MARKER and hardly as good. Remade as 40 POUNDS OF TROUBLE and again as LITTLE MISS MARKER in 1980. ▼◑

Sorry, Wrong Number (1948) 89m. *** D: Anatole Litvak. Barbara Stanwyck, Burt Lancaster, Ann Richards, Wendell Corey, Ed Begley, Leif Erickson, William Conrad. Overly complicated adaptation of famous radio thriller, but still a tense study of woman overhearing murder plan on telephone, discovering she's to be the victim. Stanwyck won an Oscar nomination for her bravura performance; adapted—or rather, expanded—by Lucille Fletcher, from her radio drama (which starred Agnes Moorehead). Remade for cable TV in 1989 with Loni Anderson. ▼◑

S.O.S. Iceberg (1933-U.S.-German) 86m. *** D: Dr. Arnold Fanck. Leni Riefenstahl, Sepp Rist, Gustav Diessl, Gibson Gowland, Max Holzboer, Walter Riml, Ernst Udet. Daring explorers trek to Greenland to rescue a colleague who wandered off but still may be alive; they in turn are stranded on a melting iceberg, inspiring one man's aviator-wife (Riefenstahl) to search for them by air. Vivid drama with many hair-raising scenes, shot on actual locations by mountain-film veteran Fanck. Second half is nearly silent, and filled with striking images. Simultaneously filmed American version, directed by Tay Garnett (and running 76m.) and featuring Rod La Rocque as the first explorer, is substantially different. It opens with entirely different exposition and features much more dialogue, until the climax. ◑

S.O.S. Pacific (1960-British) 92m. **½ D: Guy Green. Eddie Constantine, Pier Angeli, Richard Attenborough, John Gregson, Eva Bartok, Jean Anderson. Middling study of human nature when passengers on plane crash-land on nuclear-test island. ▼◑

So This Is Africa (1933) 65m. **½ D: Edward F. Cline. Bert Wheeler, Robert Woolsey, Raquel Torres, Esther Muir, Berton Churchill, Clarence Moorehouse, Henry Armetta. Wheeler & Woolsey play vaudevillians who go on a safari to film a jungle movie with the great Mrs. Martini Johnson (Muir). Typical W&W nonsense, though this film was noto-

rious for its censorship problems: Norman Krasna's script is filled to overflowing with sexual double entendres, even in this version, which was severely cut to satisfy Production Code standards. Some prints run 54m.

So This Is College (1929) 98m. **½ D: Sam Wood. Elliott Nugent, Robert Montgomery, Cliff Edwards, Sally Starr, Phyllis Crane, Dorothy Dehn, Max Davidson, Polly Moran, Joel McCrea. Agreeable curio about college seniors (and best pals) Nugent and Montgomery, who vie for the same campus cutie. See if you can spot Ward Bond as a USC football player, Grady Sutton as a football game spectator, and Ann Dvorak as a coed. ◑

So This Is Love (1953) C-101m. ** D: Gordon Douglas. Kathryn Grayson, Merv Griffin, Walter Abel, Rosemary DeCamp, Jeff Donnell. Glossy, empty biography of opera star Grace Moore, antiseptically played by Grayson. ▼◑

So This Is New York (1948) 79m. *** D: Richard Fleischer. Henry Morgan, Rudy Vallee, Bill Goodwin, Hugh Herbert, Leo Gorcey, Virginia Grey, Dona Drake. Cheaply filmed but hilarious adaptation of Ring Lardner's *The Big Town*. Morgan's wife inherits money and they decide to go to N.Y.C., encountering its strange ways. Ingenious, offbeat script by Carl Foreman and Herbert Baker; radio/TV star Morgan fares well in screen debut, helped by top supporting cast. ◑

So This Is Paris (1926) 68m. *** D: Ernst Lubitsch. Monte Blue, Patsy Ruth Miller, Lilyan Tashman, Andre Beranger, Myrna Loy, Sidney D'Albrook. Frothy Lubitsch silent; sophisticated romantic comedy of dancers Tashman and Berenger flirting with Dr. Blue and wife Miller. Entertaining, fast-moving, and funny. ▼◑

So This Is Paris (1954) C-96m. **½ D: Richard Quine. Tony Curtis, Gloria DeHaven, Gene Nelson, Corinne Calvet, Paul Gilbert, Allison Hayes, Mara Corday. Perky stars enliven this unmemorable musical of gobs on leave in France. Nelson also served as co-choreographer.

So This Is Washington (1943) 64m. ** D: Ray McCarey. Chester Lauck, Norris Goff, Alan Mowbray, Mildred Coles, Roger Clark, Sarah Padden, Matt McHugh, Jimmie Dodd, Barbara Pepper. Radio's Lum Edwards (Lauck) 'n' Abner Peabody (Goff) are convinced the government needs their help to win the war, using Abner's synthetic rubber invention (it was supposed to come out as licorice). Fourth screen comedy featuring the corn-fed radio duo from Pine Ridge, Arkansas, is topical, but their pickle-barrel flavor has diminished over the years. ▼◑

Soul of a Monster, The (1944) 61m. BOMB D: Will Jason. Rose Hobart, George Macready, Jim Bannon, Jeanne Bates.

Otherworldly Hobart has strange control over doctor Macready after reviving him when he was at death's door. A guaranteed sleep-inducer. ◗

Souls at Sea (1937) 92m. *** D: Henry Hathaway. Gary Cooper, George Raft, Frances Dee, Olympe Bradna, Henry Wilcoxon, Harry Carey, Robert Cummings, Joseph Schildkraut, George Zucco, Virginia Weidler. Fine actioner with Cooper and Raft struggling to save lives during ship tragedy; Cooper wrongly accused of irresponsibility. The stars make a good team here. ▼◗

Souls for Sale (1923) 90m. **½ D: Rupert Hughes. Eleanor Boardman, Richard Dix, Barbara La Marr, Frank Mayo, Mae Busch, Lew Cody, Snitz Edwards, William Haines, Dale Fuller, Aileen Pringle. Runaway bride Boardman stumbles onto a movie set and, amid many complications, tries her luck in the film business. Episodic drama-comedy-romance attempts to counteract the Tinseltown scandals then making headlines by portraying Hollywood as a community filled with hardworking, clean-living individuals. Of note for cameo appearances of several dozen screen luminaries, including footage of Charlie Chaplin directing A WOMAN OF PARIS and Erich von Stroheim directing Jean Hersholt in GREED. Hughes adapted the screenplay from his novel. ◗

Sound and the Fury, The (1959) C-115m. **½ D: Martin Ritt. Yul Brynner, Joanne Woodward, Margaret Leighton, Stuart Whitman, Ethel Waters, Jack Warden, Albert Dekker. Strange adaptation of William Faulkner novel becomes plodding tale of girl seeking independence from strict family rule in the South. CinemaScope. ◗

Sound Barrier, The SEE: **Breaking the Sound Barrier**

Sound Off (1952) C-83m. ** D: Richard Quine. Mickey Rooney, Anne James, John Archer, Sammy White. Too-often unimaginative Army comedy with Rooney a performer who's drafted and can't stop showing off. Written by Quine and Blake Edwards.

Sound of Fury, The SEE: **Try and Get Me!**

Sound of Music, The (1965) C-174m. ***½ D: Robert Wise. Julie Andrews, Christopher Plummer, Eleanor Parker, Peggy Wood, Richard Haydn, Anna Lee, Portia Nelson, Norma Varden, Marni Nixon. The children: Charmian Carr, Nicolas Hammond, Heather Menzies, Duane Chase, Angela Cartwright, Debbie Turner, Kym Karath. Call it corn if you like, but blockbuster Rodgers & Hammerstein musical based on Austria's real-life Von Trapp family, who fled their homeland in 1938 to escape from Nazi rule, pleased more people than practically any other film in history. Fine music, beautiful scenery help offset coy aspects of script. Five Oscars include Best Picture,

Director, Score Adaptation (Irwin Kostal), Editing (William Reynolds). Screenplay by Ernest Lehman, based on the Howard Lindsay–Russel Crouse Broadway show. Songs include "Do Re Mi," "Climb Ev'ry Mountain" and title tune. Roadshow version on video includes an intermission/entr'acte. Todd-AO ▼◗

Soup to Nuts (1930) 71m. **½ D: Benjamin Stoloff. Ted Healy, Charles Winninger, Frances McCoy, Lucile Browne, Stanley Smith, Hallam Cooley, Roscoe Ates, Billy Barty. Oddball early talkie about a shopkeeper in trouble and some neighborhood firemen; written by cartoonist Rube Goldberg. Chief point of interest today is film debut of Healy and his Stooges (Moe, Larry, and Shemp, along with Fred Sanborn). They provide the movie's highlight, doing their vaudeville routine. ◗

Southerner, The (1945) 91m. **** D: Jean Renoir. Zachary Scott, Betty Field, Beulah Bondi, J. Carrol Naish, Norman Lloyd, Bunny Sunshine, Jay Gilpin, Estelle Taylor, Percy Kilbride, Blanche Yurka. Superb drama of family struggling to make farmland self-supporting against serious odds. Renoir adapted George Sessions Perry's novel *Hold Autumn in Your Hand*. ▼◗

South: Ernest Shackleton and the Endurance Expedition (1919-British) 88m. ***½ D: Frank Hurley. Extraordinary document of the fabled 1915 Ernest Shackleton expedition to Antarctica and the stranded crew's efforts to save themselves. The story has been recounted and dramatized since then, but nothing can compare to this original, straightforward account—with startlingly clear footage that looks as if it was shot this morning. ▼◗

Southern Yankee, A (1948) 90m. *** D: Edward Sedgwick. Red Skelton, Brian Donlevy, Arlene Dahl, George Coulouris, Lloyd Gough, John Ireland, Charles Dingle, Joyce Compton. Hilarious Skelton comedy set during Civil War with Red a bumbling Yankee spy down South. Reminiscent of silent comedies, since Buster Keaton devised many of the film's gags. ▼◗

South of Algiers SEE: **Golden Mask, The**

South of Caliente (1951) 67m. **½ D: William Witney. Roy Rogers, Dale Evans, Pinky Lee, Douglas Fowley, Ric Roman, Leonard Penn, Willie Best, Pat Brady, George J. Lewis, Roy Rogers Riders. Dale must sell her favorite race horse to save her ranch from crooked trainer Fowley and hires Roy to transport the horse and eventually save the day. Trigger is prominently featured in this horse-heavy story, but Lee's antics detract. ▼◗

South of Pago Pago (1940) 98m. ** D: Alfred E. Green. Victor McLaglen, Jon Hall, Frances Farmer, Olympe Bradna, Gene Lockhart. Juvenile actioner of pirates stealing natives' supply of pearls, encountering local hostility.▼

South of Santa Fe (1942) **60m.** ****½ D:** Joseph Kane. Roy Rogers, George "Gabby" Hayes, Linda Hayes, Paul Fix, Judy Clark, Bobby Beers, Arthur Loft, Charles Miller, Sam Flint, Jack Kirk, Pat Brady, The Sons of the Pioneers. Eastern gangster Fix joins Roy and Gabby on the annual Ride of the Vaqueros in order to kidnap and ransom rich businessmen. Good story, with most of the action toward the end. Brady, later Roy's TV sidekick in the '50s, emerges here as a comic foil to Gabby.▼▶

South of St. Louis (1949) **C-88m.** ****½ D:** Ray Enright. Joel McCrea, Alexis Smith, Zachary Scott, Dorothy Malone, Douglas Kennedy, Alan Hale, Victor Jory. Three ranching partners (McCrea, Scott, Kennedy) fall into dispute over land, money, Civil War gun-running, and women. Unmemorable Western has good cast, fast pacing, and Technicolor on its side.▼▶

South of Suez (1940) **86m.** ****½ D:** Lewis Seiler. George Brent, Brenda Marshall, George Tobias, James Stephenson, Lee Patrick, Eric Blore, Miles Mander, Cecil Kellaway. Greedy Tobias kills mine owner Mander to gain possession of the Star of Africa diamond and frames foreman Brent, who flees to England, changes his name, and has a torrid romance with the murdered man's unwitting daughter. Engrossing little Warner Bros. B film with scene-stealing work by Tobias (in a rare villainous role) and Patrick as his wife.

South of the Border (1939) **71m.** ***** D:** George Sherman. Gene Autry, Smiley Burnette, June Storey, Lupita Tovar, Mary Lee, Duncan Renaldo, Frank Reicher, Alan Edwards, Claire Du Brey, William Farnum. Top Autry adventure has him and Smiley trying to discover the identity of foreign agents attempting to overthrow the government of Latin country Palermo. Along the way Gene also falls for Tovar. Expert blend of action and heartfelt romance, with ten songs, including the classic title tune and "Goodbye Little Darlin'." One of Gene's best. ▼▶

South Pacific (1958) **C-151m.** ****½ D:** Joshua Logan. Rossano Brazzi, Mitzi Gaynor, John Kerr, Ray Walston, Juanita Hall, France Nuyen, Tom Laughlin; voice of Giorgio Tozzi. Disappointing filmization of great Rodgers & Hammerstein show; adaptation of James Michener's moving vignettes about WW2 life on Pacific island needs dynamic personalities to make it catch fire, and they aren't here. Even location filming is lackluster. Adequate but hardly memorable. Songs include "Some Enchanted Evening," "There Is Nothing Like a Dame." Among the sailors and servicemen you'll spot John Gabriel, Ron Ely, Doug McClure, and James Stacy. Video version runs 157m. with overture, intermission/entr'acte, exit music;

Roadshow version on video runs 172m. with restored footage. Remade in 2001 for TV. Todd-AO. ▼●▶

South Riding (1938-British) **84m.** ***** D:** Victor Saville. Ralph Richardson, Edna Best, Edmund Gwenn, Ann Todd, John Clements, Marie Lohr, Milton Rosmer, Glynis Johns. Enjoyable drama from Winifred Holtby's novel about political and personal problems among a group of characters living in Yorkshire. Smoothly made and superbly acted by a flawless cast. Film debut of 15-year-old Johns, cast as Richardson's daughter. Original British running time: 90m.▼

South Seas Adventure (1958) **C-124m.** ***** D:** Francis D. Lyon, Walter Thompson, Basil Wrangell, Richard Goldstone, Carl Dudley. Three-panel Cinerama travelogue, spotlighting mini storylines in Hawaii, Tahiti, Tonga, Fiji, New Zealand, and Australia. Brimful of stunningly shot, still-dazzling scenery. 2012 restoration is presented in a curved screen simulation that replicates the feeling of seeing the film in its original presentation. Cinerama.▶

South Sea Sinner (1950) **88m.** **** D:** H. Bruce Humberstone. Macdonald Carey, Shelley Winters, Luther Adler, Frank Lovejoy, Liberace. Muddled melodrama involving fugitive from justice being intimidated by those on island who knew his past; Winters is blowsy cafe singer. Remake of 1940 SEVEN SINNERS.

South Sea Woman (1953) **99m.** ****½ D:** Arthur Lubin. Burt Lancaster, Virginia Mayo, Chuck Connors, Arthur Shields, Paul Burke. Murky tropical isle story of love and deceit with soldier Lancaster sparking with Mayo.▶

SOuthside 1-1000 (1950) **73m.** ****½ D:** Boris Ingster. Don DeFore, Andrea King, George Tobias, Barry Kelley, Morris Ankrum, Robert Osterloh. Solid documentary-style crime thriller centering on treasury agent DeFore's efforts to infiltrate counterfeiting ring and making surprising discovery about the identity of the gang leader. Minorleague T-MEN is pretty well done, aided by standout Russell Harlan location photography of L.A. and San Quentin prison.▼▶

Southward, Ho! (1939) **58m.** ****½ D:** Joseph Kane. Roy Rogers, George "Gabby" Hayes, Mary Hart (Lynne Roberts), Wade Boteler, Arthur Loft, Lane Chandler, Tom London. Following the Civil War, ex–Confederate soldiers Rogers and Hayes repair to Gabby's Texas ranch, co-owned by former Yankee colonel Boteler . . . but a militia made up of crooked Union soldiers runs roughshod over the territory. Meanwhile, Roy and the colonel's daughter (Hart) set off sparks. Enjoyable musical Western marks Roy and Gabby's first film together.▼▶

Southwest Passage (1954) **C-82m.** **** D:** Ray Nazarro. Joanne Dru, Rod Cameron, John Ireland, John Dehner, Guinn ("Big

Boy") Williams, Mark Hanna. Familiar tale of bank robber and gal joining up with settlers heading West, staving off Indian attack. Originally in 3-D. ▶

So Well Remembered (1947-British) 114m. *** D: Edward Dmytryk. John Mills, Martha Scott, Trevor Howard, Patricia Roc, Richard Carlson, Ivor Barnard. Author James Hilton narrates saga (adapted by John Paxton) of earnest newspaper editor (Mills) determined to improve living conditions in factory town, sidetracked by marriage to blindly ambitious woman (Scott). Very young Juliet Mills has bit part. ●▶

So Young, So Bad (1950) 91m. **½ D: Bernard Vorhaus. Paul Henreid, Catherine McLeod, Grace Coppin, Cecil Clovelly, Anne Francis, Rosita (Rita) Moreno, Anne Jackson, Enid Pulver. Humane psychiatrist Henreid takes on superintendent Clovelly and sadistic head matron Coppin at a correctional home for girls. Effective study of female juvenile delinquency.

So You Won't Talk (1940) 69m. ** D: Edward Sedgwick. Joe E. Brown, Frances Robinson, Vivienne Osborne, Bernard Nedell, Tom Dugan. Typical mistaken identity comedy with bookworm Brown, a dead ringer for notorious mobster. Rehash of THE WHOLE TOWN'S TALKING.

Space Children, The (1958) 69m. ** D: Jack Arnold. Michel Ray, Peggy Webber, Adam Williams, Jackie Coogan, Johnny Washbrook. Strange force brainwashes children into performing sabotage at Pacific nuclear test site. Antiwar film isn't up to Arnold's other '50s science-fiction classics, but is sufficiently offbeat to warrant a peek. VistaVision. ▶

Spaceflight IC-1 (1965-British) 65m. *½ D: Bernard Knowles. Bill Williams, Norma West, John Cairney, Linda Marlowe, Jeremy Longhurst. Dreary, talky film with no space thrills and little action, set aboard a spaceship between planets.

Space Master X-7 (1958) 71m. ** D: Edward Bernds. Bill Williams, Robert Ellis, Lyn Thomas, Paul Frees, Joan Barry, Thomas B. Henry, Moe Howard. A returning satellite brings with it a fast-growing fungus, dubbed "Blood Rust." Williams and Ellis track down the woman who is unknowingly spreading the deadly stuff. Routine but competent. Moe plays a cab driver. Regalscope.

Spaceways (1953-British) 76m. *½ D: Terence Fisher. Howard Duff, Eva Bartok, Andrew Osborn, Alan Wheatley. To prove Duff hasn't murdered Bartok's husband and stuffed him into a just-launched satellite, they go up to look on the next rocket, but that happens only at the very end of this slow movie. From a novel and radio play by Charles Eric Maine. ▼▶

Spanish Affair (1958-Spanish) C-95m.

** D: Don Siegel. Richard Kiley, Carmen Sevilla, Jose Guardiola, Jesus Tordesillas. Virtually a travelogue pegged on slight plot of Kiley, American architect, traveling in Iberia, falling in love with local girl; nice scenery, but hardly typical Siegel fare. VistaVision.

Spanish Cape Mystery, The (1935) 65m. **½ D: Lewis D. Collins. Helen Twelvetrees, Donald Cook, Berton Churchill, Frank Sheridan, Guy Usher. First *Ellery Queen* movie finds master sleuth (Cook) investigating murder at seaside resort and falling in love with primary suspect (Twelvetrees). Hokey denouement mars otherwise enjoyable whodunit.

Spanish Gardener, The (1956-British) C-95m. *** D: Philip Leacock. Dirk Bogarde, Maureen Swanson, Jon Whiteley, Cyril Cusack, Bernard Lee, Michael Hordern. When gardener befriends employer's young son, diplomat father becomes jealous. Intelligent and beautifully filmed adaptation of A. J. Cronin novel. VistaVision. ▶

Spanish Main, The (1945) C-100m. **½ D: Frank Borzage. Paul Henreid, Maureen O'Hara, Walter Slezak, Binnie Barnes, John Emery, Barton MacLane. Colorful escapism with swashbuckling pirate Henreid foiling villain Slezak, winning O'Hara. ●▶

Sparrows (1926) 84m. *** D: William Beaudine. Mary Pickford, Gustav von Seyffertitz, Roy Stewart, Mary Louise Miller, Charlotte Mineau, Spec O'Donnell. One of Mary's best silent pictures is a full-blooded melodrama about intrepid girl who struggles to protect band of younger orphans from their wicked captor. ▼●▶

Spartacus (1960) C-184m. ***½ D: Stanley Kubrick. Kirk Douglas, Laurence Olivier, Jean Simmons, Tony Curtis, Charles Laughton, Peter Ustinov, John Gavin, Nina Foch, Herbert Lom, John Ireland, Charles McGraw, Woody Strode, Joanna Barnes. Epic-scale saga with Douglas as a rebellious slave who leads a crusade for freedom against the forces of the Roman Empire. Overlength (particularly in fully restored version released in 1991) and some dramatic weaknesses are offset by Alex North's magnificent score, staggering battle scenes, and the delicious performances of Olivier, Laughton, and especially Ustinov, who won a Best Supporting Actor Oscar for his scene-stealing work. Oscars also went to Art Direction, Costume Design, and Russell Metty's Cinematography. Screenplay by Dalton Trumbo from the Howard Fast novel. Cut for 1967 reissue. In restored print, Anthony Hopkins dubbed Olivier's voice for notorious bathing scene with Curtis. Remade for cable TV in 2004, then later as a series. Super Technirama 70. ▼●▶

Spawn of the North (1938) 110m. *** D: Henry Hathaway. George Raft, Henry Fonda, Dorothy Lamour, Louise Platt, John Barrymore, Akim Tamiroff, Lynne

Overman. Action-packed film of Alaskan fisheries with good cast; Lamour surprisingly good. Barrymore amusing as talky newspaperman. The special photographic and sound effects earned a special Academy Award. Remade as ALASKA SEAS.▼◗

Speak Easily (1932) **82m.** *** D: Edward Sedgwick. Buster Keaton, Jimmy Durante, Ruth Selwyn, Thelma Todd, Hedda Hopper, Sidney Toler. Dimwitted professor Keaton gets involved with show troupe en route to Broadway. One of Keaton's best talkies, with Durante in good form, Todd a wonderful vamp, Toler an amusing stage manager. ▼◗

Special Agent (1935) **78m.** **½ D: William Keighley. Bette Davis, George Brent, Ricardo Cortez, Jack LaRue, Henry O'Neill, J. Carrol Naish. Crisp but formulaic programmer, with Brent an undercover IRS agent intent on bringing down Capone-like thug Cortez. Davis is Cortez' sharp-eyed bookkeeper. ◗

Special Delivery (1955) **86m.** ** D: John Brahm. Joseph Cotten, Eva Bartok, Niall MacGinnis, René Deltgen. Mild froth with Cotten on U.S. diplomatic staff posted in Iron Curtain country, dealing with an abandoned baby and curvaceous refugee Bartok.

Speckled Band, The (1931-British) **90m.** *½ D: Jack Raymond. Lyn Harding, Raymond Massey, Angela Baddeley, Nancy Price, Athole Stewart. Slow-as-molasses version of the Conan Doyle story, with Sherlock Holmes coming to the aid of a frightened girl (Baddeley), whose sister has been murdered. Interesting to see Massey cast as the sleuth, but this film is really boring. ▼◗

Specter of the Rose (1946) **90m.** *** D: Ben Hecht. Judith Anderson, Michael Chekhov, Ivan Kirov, Viola Essen, Lionel Stander. Uniquely individual melodrama by Hecht set in the world of ballet, with an unusual cast, including dancers, nonactors, and scene-stealing Chekhov. Fascinating (some might even say strange), though definitely not for all tastes. ▼

Speed (1936) **70m.** ** D: Edwin L. Marin. James Stewart, Wendy Barrie, Una Merkel, Ted Healy, Weldon Heyburn, Ralph Morgan, Patricia Wilder. Stewart enhances this star-building quickie (one of eight features he made in 1936) as a test-car driver who's developed a high-speed carburetor. Most of the racing action consists of blatant rear-projection and stock footage. ◗

Speed Crazy (1959) **75m.** BOMB D: William Hole, Jr. Brett Halsey, Yvonne Lime, Charles Willcox, Slick Slavin, Jacqueline Ravell, Baynes Barron, Jackie Joseph. Trashy, campy bottom-of-the-barrel programmer about a psychotic drifter who's "an accident looking for a place to happen." He's obsessed with fast cars, and keeps complaining that "everybody keeps crowding me."▼

Speed to Spare (1948) **57m.** ** D: William Berke. Richard Arlen, Jean Rogers, Richard Travis, Roscoe Karns, Nanette Parks. Arlen is OK as a stunt-car driver who decides to take it easy and become a driver for his friend's trucking company, only to find himself in more trouble. Acceptable programmer from the Paramount B factory of Pine-Thomas. ◗

Speedway (1929) **77m.** *½ D: Harry Beaumont. William Haines, Anita Page, Ernest Torrence, Karl Dane, John Miljan, Eugenie Besserer, Polly Moran. In his final silent film, Haines plays yet another overbearing, womanizing braggart who's in dire need of a comeuppance. Here, he's a race car driver who deserts his loyal mentor right before the big race in Indianapolis. Tries to mix wacky comedy, boy-chases-girl romance, and thrill-a-minute action but fails on all accounts. ◗

Speedy (1928) **86m.** *** D: Ted Wilde. Harold Lloyd, Ann Christy, Bert Woodruff, Brooks Benedict. Contrived but enjoyable comedy has Harold trying to save N.Y.C.'s last horse-drawn trolley, run by his girlfriend's grandfather, from extinction. Vivid N.Y.C. location work includes hair-raising chase scene, and appealing cameo by Babe Ruth as himself.▼◗

Spellbinder, The (1939) **69m.** ** D: Jack Hively. Lee Tracy, Barbara Read, Patric Knowles, Allan Lane, Linda Hayes, Morgan Conway, Robert Emmett Keane. Tracy plays yet another silver-tongued sharpie, here a crafty lawyer who revels in acquitting guilty crooks, until his daughter falls for one. The once-sprightly Tracy looks weary in this routine meller.

Spellbound (1945) **111m.** ***½ D: Alfred Hitchcock. Ingrid Bergman, Gregory Peck, Leo G. Carroll, John Emery, Michael Chekhov, Wallace Ford, Rhonda Fleming, Bill Goodwin, Regis Toomey. Absorbing tale of psychiatrist Bergman trying to uncover Peck's hangups; Dali dream sequences, innovative (and Oscar-winning) Miklos Rozsa score help Hitchcock create another unique film. Based on novel *The House of Dr. Edwardes* by Francis Beeding; screenplay by Ben Hecht. In original theatrical prints, a key gunshot was shown in color. Video version runs 118m. with overture and exit music. ▼◗

Spencer's Mountain (1963) **C-119m.** ** D: Delmer Daves. Henry Fonda, Maureen O'Hara, James MacArthur, Donald Crisp, Wally Cox, Veronica Cartwright, Victor French. Mawkish sudser about Wyoming landowner Fonda who keeps promising to build another family house. Good cast stuck with inferior script. Based on the Earl Hamner, Jr. novel; later developed into *The Waltons*. Panavision.▼◗

Sphinx, The (1933) **63m.** ** D: Phil Rosen. Lionel Atwill, Sheila Terry, Theodore Newton, Paul Hurst, Luis Alberni, Robert Ellis.

Atwill plays a police suspect whose only alibi is his deaf-mute twin brother. Passable low-budgeter. Remade in 1942 as PHANTOM KILLER. ▼▶

Spider, The (1945) 62m. ** D: Robert Webb. Richard Conte, Faye Marlowe, Kurt Kreuger, John Harvey, Martin Kosleck, Mantan Moreland, Walter Sande, Cara Williams, Ann Savage. Humdrum remake of the 1931 thriller of the same name, set in the French Quarter of New Orleans, with Conte as a private eye hired to help a carnival mindreader who fears she may be murdered.

Spider, The (1958) SEE: **Earth vs the Spider**

Spider and the Fly, The (1949-British) 87m. **½ D: Robert Hamer. Guy Rolfe, Nadia Gray, Eric Portman, Maurice Denham, James Hayter, Arthur Lowe. Effective drama of Gallic law enforcer and British crook teaming up to retrieve government document; good interplay between cast members.

Spider Baby (1964) 81m. **½ D: Jack Hill. Lon Chaney, Jr., Sid Haig, Jill Banner, Mantan Moreland, Beverly Washburn, Carol Ohmart. Not bad little chiller about the antics of a very unusual—and very sick—family. At its best it's both scary and funny. Chaney is the clan's chauffeur and sings the title song! The full title is SPIDER BABY OR, THE MADDEST STORY EVER TOLD. Aka THE LIVER EATERS. ▼▶

Spiders, The (1919-German) 137m. *** D: Fritz Lang. Carl de Vogt, Ressel Orla, Lil Dagover, Georg John, Bruno Lettinger. Intrepid explorer/adventurer de Vogt—an early cross between Indiana Jones and James Bond—vies with evil Spider cult for mystic Incan diamond. First two chapters ("The Golden Lake" and "The Diamond Ship") of never completed four-part serial abound with lost civilizations, human sacrifice, pirate treasure, and too many perils to count. Lang's obsession with a diabolical underworld foreshadows his DR. MABUSE films. An exciting curio; the earliest of Lang's films to survive. German title: DIE SPINNEN. ▼▶

Spider Woman, The (1944) 62m. *** D: Roy William Neill. Basil Rathbone, Nigel Bruce, Gale Sondergaard, Dennis Hoey, Mary Gordon, Arthur Hohl, Alec Craig. A mysterious villainess is responsible for a series of deaths in which the victims are driven to suicide after being bit by poisonous spiders. Rip-roaring entry with thrills to spare; one of the best in the *Sherlock Holmes* series. ▼▶

Spider Woman Strikes Back, The (1946) 59m. *½ D: Arthur Lubin. Brenda Joyce, Gale Sondergaard, Kirby Grant, Rondo Hatton, Milburn Stone, Hobart Cavanaugh. Pitiful waste of fine actress Sondergaard in campy thriller with zero relation to earlier *Sherlock Holmes* feature.

Spies (1928-German) 143m. ***½ D: Fritz Lang. Rudolf Klein-Rogge, Gerda Maurus, Willy Fritsch, Lupu Pick, Fritz Rasp. Silent spy thriller still packs a wallop as government agent Fritsch determines to thwart seemingly respectable Klein-Rogge, a wheelchair-bound master fiend with an uncanny resemblance to Lenin! One of Lang's early masterpieces, aka SPIONE. Restored in 2004, eclipsing 90m. prints that circulated for years. ▼▶

Spiral Road, The (1962) C-145m. *½ D: Robert Mulligan. Rock Hudson, Burl Ives, Gena Rowlands, Geoffrey Keen, Neva Patterson, Will Kuluva, Philip Abbott, Larry Gates, Karl Swenson. Jan de Hartog's novel about love, leprosy, and lunacy in the Dutch East Indies makes for an interminable moviegoing experience. Hudson is miscast as an atheistic, self-absorbed doctor. The various (non-white) natives are patronizingly portrayed. ▶

Spiral Staircase, The (1946) 83m. ***½ D: Robert Siodmak. Dorothy McGuire, George Brent, Ethel Barrymore, Kent Smith, Rhonda Fleming, Gordon Oliver, Elsa Lanchester, Rhys Williams, Sara Allgood. Superb Hitchcock-like thriller with unforgettable performance by McGuire as mute servant in eerie household which may be harboring a killer. Well scripted by Mel Dinelli, adapting Ethel Lina White's novel *Some Must Watch*. Remade in 1975. ▼▶

Spirit of Culver (1939) 89m. ** D: Joseph Santley. Jackie Cooper, Freddie Bartholomew, Tim Holt, Andy Devine, Gene Reynolds, Jackie Moran. All the usual prep-academy clichés adapted for military school setting with Cooper and Bartholomew predictable. Remake of 1932 film TOM BROWN OF CULVER.

Spirit of St. Louis, The (1957) C-138m. *** D: Billy Wilder. James Stewart, Patricia Smith, Murray Hamilton, Marc Connelly. Long but inventive presentation of Lindbergh's flight across the Atlantic is mainly a tour de force by Stewart, backed by good Franz Waxman music score. CinemaScope. ▼▶

Spirit of West Point, The (1947) 77m. ** D: Ralph Murphy. Doc Blanchard, Glenn Davis, Tom Harmon, Robert Shayne, Anne Nagel, Alan Hale, Jr., Bill Stern, Harry Wismer. Comic-book chronicle of "the touchdown twins," all-American football heroes Blanchard and Davis, and their years at West Point. Will they or won't they resign their West Point commissions to play pro ball? The boys (especially Blanchard) are far more believable on the gridiron than reciting lines. ▼▶

Spirit of Youth (1938) 66m. ** D: Harry Fraser. Joe Louis, Clarence Muse, Edna Mae Harris, Mae Turner, Cleo Desmond, Mantan Moreland, Clarence Brooks. Cliché-ridden, highly fictionalized biopic is worth seeing for Louis' presence in and out of the ring. He's ideally cast as "Joe Thomas," a poor young man who rises in the fight game. ▼◗

Spiritualist, The SEE: **Amazing Mr. X, The**

Spite Marriage (1929) 75m. *** D: Edward Sedgwick. Buster Keaton, Dorothy Sebastian, Edward Earle, Leila Hyams, William Bechtel. Keaton's last silent is also one of his most underrated, a very funny film about a pants-presser who becomes infatuated with a stage actress. Plottier than usual for Buster, but full of great set pieces. Remade as I DOOD IT. ▼◗●

Spitfire (1934) 88m. ** D: John Cromwell. Katharine Hepburn, Robert Young, Ralph Bellamy, Martha Sleeper, Sara Haden, Sidney Toler, High Ghere (Bob Burns). Bizarre, boring melodrama with Hepburn sorely miscast in one of her oddest roles: Trigger, a spirited, single-minded but superstition-laden Ozark tomboy who attracts married engineer Young. This one's only for the curious. ▼◗

Spitfire (1942-British) 117m. *** D: Leslie Howard. Leslie Howard, David Niven, Rosamund John, Roland Culver, Anne Firth, David Horne, J. H. Roberts, Derrick de Marney, Bernard Miles, Patricia Medina. Howard plays R.J. Mitchell, who developed the ace fighting plane Spitfire which later became one of the Allies' most valuable WW2 assets. Good biographical drama. Howard's last screen appearance. Original title: THE FIRST OF THE FEW. U.S. version cut to 90m. ▼◗

Splendor (1935) 77m. **½ D: Elliott Nugent. Miriam Hopkins, Joel McCrea, Paul Cavanagh, Helen Westley, Billie Burke, Katharine Alexander, David Niven. Familiar story of McCrea's family upset when he loves poor girl Hopkins instead of upperclass young lady; script by Rachel Crothers, from her play. ▼

Splendor in the Grass (1961) C-124m. *** D: Elia Kazan. Natalie Wood, Warren Beatty, Pat Hingle, Audrey Christie, Sean Garrison, Sandy Dennis, Phyllis Diller, Barbara Loden, Zohra Lampert, Gary Lockwood. Sentimental sudser by William Inge (who won an Oscar) about emotionally broken girl (Wood) rebuilding her life; set in late 1920s Midwest. Film debuts of Beatty, Dennis, and Diller; look for Inge as the minister. Remade for TV in 1981. ▼◗●

Split Second (1953) 85m. **½ D: Dick Powell. Stephen McNally, Alexis Smith, Jan Sterling, Keith Andes, Arthur Hunnicutt, Paul Kelly, Robert Paige, Richard Egan. Capable cast in odd suspenser about escaped convict (McNally) holding several people hostage in Nevada ghost town—though well aware it's a nuclear test site! Script by William Bowers and Irving Wallace. Powell's directorial debut. ▼◗

Spoilers, The (1942) 87m. **½ D: Ray

Enright. Marlene Dietrich, Randolph Scott, John Wayne, Margaret Lindsay, Harry Carey, Richard Barthelmess. Retelling of famous Yukon tale has good cast but thuds out as average Western, with Dietrich as stereotyped saloon gal. Previously filmed in 1914, 1923, and 1930, then again in 1955. ▼◗●

Spoilers, The (1955) C-84m. **½ D: Jesse Hibbs. Anne Baxter, Jeff Chandler, Rory Calhoun, Barbara Britton, Raymond Walburn. Fifth filming of Rex Beach's Klondike actioner; elaborate fight scene, better than ever.

Spoilers of the Forest (1957) C-68m. ** D: Joseph Kane. Rod Cameron, Vera Ralston, Ray Collins, Hillary Brooke, Edgar Buchanan. Another timberland Western, with Cameron a tree-cutting foreman, romancing Ralston. Filmed in Naturama.

Spoilers of the Plains (1951) 68m. *** D: William Witney. Roy Rogers, Penny Edwards, Gordon Jones, Grant Withers, Don Haggerty, House Peters, Jr., Fred Kohler, Jr., George Meeker, Foy Willing and the Riders of the Purple Sage. Here's something new: a Cold War Western. Using an oil-well operation as a blind, some bad guys representing an unnamed foreign power try to steal missiles intended for use in weather forecasting . . . until Roy gets involved. Plenty of action. ▼◗

Spook Busters (1946) 68m. ** D: William Beaudine. Leo Gorcey, Huntz Hall, Douglass Dumbrille, Tanis Chandler, Bobby Jordan, Gabriel Dell, Billy Benedict, David Gorcey, Charles Middleton, Bernard Gorcey. The Bowery Boys set up shop as exterminators and tangle with baddies in a spooky old country house. ▼◗

Spook Chasers (1957) 62m. *½ D: George Blair. Huntz Hall, Stanley Clements, David Gorcey, Jimmy Murphy, Percy Helton, Darlene Fields, Eddie LeRoy, Bill Henry. Yet another *Bowery Boys* crooks-posing-as-ghosts entry, with a surfeit of wheezy gags. ◗

Spooks Run Wild (1941) 69m. ** D: Phil Rosen. Bela Lugosi, Leo Gorcey, Huntz Hall, Bobby Jordan, Sunshine Sammy Morrison, Donald Haines, David Gorcey, Dave O'Brien, Dennis Moore, Dorothy Short, Angelo Rossitto. Tongue-in-cheek *East Side Kids* horror-comedy, with the boys encountering Lugosi in a spooky country mansion. Ad libs fly fast and furious, to Lugosi's obvious consternation. ▼◗

Sporting Blood (1931) 82m. **½ D: Charles Brabin. Clark Gable, Ernest Torrence, Madge Evans, Lew Cody, Marie Prevost, J. Farrell MacDonald. Minor but likable film about a thoroughbred horse and its various owners; Gable is a tough-guy gambler ("C'mere, woman," he says to Evans, grabbing her for a clinch). Beautifully photographed by Harold Rosson. ◗

Sport Parade, The (1932) 65m. **½ D: Dudley Murphy. Joel McCrea, Marian

Marsh, William Gargan, Walter Catlett, Robert Benchley, Skeets Gallagher. College teammates and buddies McCrea and Gargan eventually clash over the same woman. Story is lame, but director Murphy is full of ingenious visual ideas, and Benchley (in his feature-film debut) is great fun as a befuddled sportscaster who opens and closes the film. ▶

Spotlight Scandals (1943) **71m. ** D: William Beaudine. Billy Gilbert, Frank Fay, Harry Langdon, Betty Blythe, Iris Adrian, Henry King and His Orchestra, Herb Miller and His Orchestra, ("Wee") Bonnie Baker, Butch and Buddy, The Radio Rogues, Claudia Dell. Only at Monogram could Gilbert and Fay be billed over the title, playing—who else?—"Gilbert and Fay," a small-town barber and an out-of-work actor who team up to become vaudeville headliners in N.Y.C. Several acts, notably Baker singing her hit "Oh Johnny," enliven things between skits. ▼▶

Spring Fever (1927) **78m. **½ D: Edward Sedgwick. William Haines, Joan Crawford, George K. Arthur, George Fawcett, Eileen Percy, Edward Earle. Wiseguy shipping clerk Haines falls for heiress Crawford at a country club, where he poses as a wealthy golf champ. Pleasant, easygoing silent star vehicle. Remade in 1930 as LOVE IN THE ROUGH. ▶

Springfield Rifle (1952) **C-93m. **½ D: Andre de Toth. Gary Cooper, Phyllis Thaxter, David Brian, Lon Chaney, Jr., Paul Kelly, Phil Carey, Guinn Williams. Unmemorable Cooper fare, with Gary joining up with outlaws to determine who's stealing government arms. ▼▶

Spring in Park Lane (1948-British) **C-100m. *** D: Herbert Wilcox. Anna Neagle, Michael Wilding, Tom Walls, Peter Graves, Marjorie Fielding, Nigel Patrick. Sunny romantic comedy has Neagle falling in love with her wealthy uncle's footman (Wilding), who's not what he seems. This was one of England's all-time most popular films. Followed by MAYTIME IN MAYFAIR.

Spring Is Here (1930) **69m. **½ D: John Francis Dillon. Lawrence Gray, Alexander Gray, Bernice Claire, Louise Fazenda, Ford Sterling, Inez Courtney, Frank Albertson, Natalie Moorhead. Likably silly early talkie musical of young people, courting rituals, and meddlesome fathers, centering on wealthy, flaky Long Island damsel Claire and her two very different suitors. Based on an Owen Davis–Lorenz Hart–Richard Rodgers musical; there's one memorable tune: "With a Song in My Heart."

Spring Madness (1938) **80m. **½ D: S. Sylvan Simon. Maureen O'Sullivan, Lew Ayres, Ruth Hussey, Burgess Meredith, Ann Morriss, Joyce Compton, Jacqueline Wells (Julie Bishop), Frank Albertson. Collegiate romance between O'Sullivan and brainy Ayres, elevated by strong cast. Enjoyable fluff.

Spring Parade (1940) **89m. *** D: Henry Koster. Deanna Durbin, Robert Cummings, Mischa Auer, Henry Stephenson, Butch and Buddy, Anne Gwynne. Delightful Austrian fluff with Durbin romancing Cummings, working for baker S. Z. Sakall, dancing with wacky Auer, and singing, of course. ▶

Spring Reunion (1957) **79m. ** D: Robert Pirosh. Betty Hutton, Dana Andrews, Jean Hagen, James Gleason, Laura LaPlante, George Chandler, Irene Ryan. Potentially good soaper marred by low-budget production: Andrews and Hutton revive old memories at high school reunion and try to plan new future together; Hagen has some fine comic moments. Silent star LaPlante plays Hutton's mother.

Springtime for Henry (1934) **74m. *½ D: Frank Tuttle. Otto Kruger, Nancy Carroll, Nigel Bruce, Heather Angel, Herbert Mundin, Arthur Hoyt, Geneva Mitchell. An inveterate ladies' man meets his Waterloo in the person of a sweet and persuasive new secretary (Angel). Kruger seems to be terribly amused throughout this leaden comedy, which is more than can be said for us in the audience. Based on Benn W. Levy's play, which was a summer-stock perennial for aging actors.

Springtime in the Rockies (1937) **60m. ** D: Joseph Kane. Gene Autry, Smiley Burnette, Polly Rowles, Ula Love, Ruth Bacon, Jane Hunt, George Chesebro, Al Bridge, Tom London, Edward Hearn. Gene tries to help Eastern ranch owner (and animal husbandry expert) Rowles and winds up in the middle of nefarious sheep double-dealing and ranch mix-ups. Standard early outing for Autry. ▼▶

Springtime in the Rockies (1942) **C-91m. *** D: Irving Cummings. Betty Grable, John Payne, Carmen Miranda, Cesar Romero, Charlotte Greenwood, Edward Everett Horton, Jackie Gleason. Near-definitive 1940s Fox musical: Grable at her prettiest, Miranda at her silliest (doing a Brazilian "Chattanooga Choo Choo"), Technicolor at its lushest, and Harry James and His Music Makers at their best, with Helen Forrest introducing "I Had the Craziest Dream." The "plot"—about a bickering Broadway duo—is neither too tiresome nor too intrusive. Good fun all the way. ▼▶▶

Springtime in the Sierras (1947) **C-75m. *** D: William Witney. Roy Rogers, Jane Frazee, Andy Devine, Stephanie Bachelor, Hal Landon, Harry V. Cheshire, Roy Barcroft, Bob Nolan and the Sons of the Pioneers. Roy works to break up a gang that's violating the law by slaughtering game out of season. One of Roy's best, with the novelty of a woman (Bachelor) as the main villain. ▼▶

Spring Tonic (1935) **58m.** *½ D: Clyde Bruckman. Lew Ayres, Claire Trevor, Walter (Woolf) King, ZaSu Pitts, Jack Haley, Tala Birell, Sigfried (Sig) Rumann, Frank Mitchell, Jack Durant, Herbert Mundin. Runaway bride takes off for the hinterlands and runs afoul of local crazies—and a traveling circus. Dreadful screwball comedy; everything about this film is heavy-handed, even director Bruckman's reuse of gags he devised for Harold Lloyd and Buster Keaton in the silent era. Based on the play *The Man-Eating Tiger* by Ben Hecht and Rose Caylor.

Sputnik (1958-French) **85m.** ** D: Jean Dreville. Nöel-Nöel, Denise Grey, Nöel Roquevert, Mischa Auer. Mild Cold War spoof involving Russian missile experiment which has backfired and naive Frenchman caught in the Red trap. Retitled: A DOG, A MOUSE AND A SPUTNIK.▼

Spy Chasers (1955) **66m.** **½ D: Edward Bernds. Leo Gorcey, Huntz Hall, Bernard Gorcey, David (Gorcey) Condon, Bennie Bartlett, Leon Askin, Sig Ruman, Veola Vonn, Richard Benedict. The Bowery Boys help an exiled king and his daughter battle usurpers in this practiced farce.❋

Spy Hunt (1950) **75m.** **½ D: George Sherman. Howard Duff, Marta Toren, Robert Douglas, Philip Dorn, Walter Slezak. Diverting yarn of espionage agent planting microfilm secrets in panthers' collars; when they escape captivity, various sides of the law seek the animals. Based on a Victor Canning novel.

Spy in Black, The (1939-British) **82m.** *** D: Michael Powell. Conrad Veidt, Sebastian Shaw, Valerie Hobson, Marius Goring, June Duprez, Helen Haye, Cyril Raymond, Hay Petrie. Intriguing espionage melodrama set in WW1 Scotland with Veidt as German naval officer/spy and Hobson a charming double agent. Nice surprise twists in story, with bittersweet romance worked in. That's Bernard Miles as the desk clerk in the opening scene. Scripted by Emeric Pressburger and Roland Pertwee; first collaboration of Powell and Pressburger. Original U.S. title: U-BOAT 29.▼●❋

Spy Ring, The (1938) **61m.** **½ D: Joseph H. Lewis. William Hall, Jane Wyman, Jane Carleton (Esther Ralston), Robert Warwick, Leon Ames, Ben Alexander, Don Barclay. Spry spy games set at a military base, where Hall thwarts espionage agents who are after a top-secret anti-aircraft gun and still finds time to woo adorable Army brat Wyman and play in a big polo match. Cult director Lewis lavishes customary visual flair on minor but fun early assignment.

Spy Ship (1942) **62m.** **½ D: B. Reeves Eason. Craig Stevens, Irene Manning, Maris Wrixon, Michael Ames (Tod Andrews), Peter Whitney, John Maxwell, William Forrest, Keye Luke. It's for good reason that influential aviatrix Manning speaks out against U.S. entry into WW2: She's in cahoots with the Nazis. Lively Warner Bros. B melodrama perfectly mirrors its era.

Spy Who Came In from the Cold, The (1965) **112m.** ***½ D: Martin Ritt. Richard Burton, Claire Bloom, Oskar Werner, Peter Van Eyck, George Voskovec, Sam Wanamaker, Cyril Cusack, Michael Hordern, Bernard Lee. John le Carré's potent account of a Cold War spy's existence—minus glamorous trappings of movie cliché. Burton is excellent as embittered agent at the end of his career. Scripted by Paul Dehn and Guy Trosper.▼●❋

Square Jungle, The (1955) **86m.** **½ D: Jerry Hopper. Tony Curtis, Pat Crowley, Ernest Borgnine, Paul Kelly, Jim Backus. Overly-familiar boxing yarn with Curtis the fighter on the way up.

Square Ring, The (1953-British) **73m.** ** D: Michael Relph, Basil Dearden. Jack Warner, Kay Kendall, Joan Collins, Robert Beatty, Bill Owen, Maxwell Reed. Uninspired intertwining of events in lives of people involved in the fight game.

Square Shooter SEE: **Skipalong Rosenbloom**

Squaw Man, The (1914) **73m.** *** D: Cecil B. DeMille, Oscar C. Apfel. Dustin Farnum, Monroe Salisbury, Winifred Kingston, Mrs. A. W. Filson, Haidee Fuller, Princess Red Wing. Still-engrossing tug-at-your-heartstrings tale of straight-arrow British officer Farnum, who accepts the blame when his cousin "borrows" money from a widows and orphans fund. He heads for the U.S. and ends up out West, but his troubles are only beginning. DeMille's initial directorial credit also is of note as the first feature shot in Hollywood. Raymond Hatton and Hal Roach reportedly have small roles as townsfolk. DeMille remade this in 1918 and 1931. Followed by a sequel, THE SQUAW MAN'S SON (1917).❋

Squaw Man, The (1931) **105m.** *** D: Cecil B. DeMille. Warner Baxter, Lupe Velez, Eleanor Boardman, Charles Bickford, Roland Young, Paul Cavanagh, Raymond Hatton, Dickie Moore. DeMille's talkie version of the story he filmed before in 1914 and 1918 is slow to start, but picks up steam after English aristocrat Baxter flees to America and marries Indian Velez. Surprisingly restrained and unsentimental, with a moving finale.❋

Squeaker, The (1937-British) **77m.** *** D: William K. Howard. Edmund Lowe, Sebastian Shaw, Ann Todd, Tamara Desni, Robert Newton, Alastair Sim. Classy cast in first-rate Edgar Wallace mystery about disgraced inspector Lowe trying to reform and catch infamous jewelry fence known as "the Squeaker." Good, compact Alexander Korda production. Aka MURDER ON DIAMOND ROW.▼

Squeaker, The (1965-German) **95m. **½** D: Alfred Vohrer. Heinz Drache, Eddi Arent, Klaus Kinski, Barbara Rutting. Overly complex actioner with a variety of plots spinning from action of underworld selling off proceeds of diamond robbery. From an Edgar Wallace novel previously filmed in 1930 and 1937. Ultrascope.▼▶

Stablemates (1938) **89m. **** D: Sam Wood. Wallace Beery, Mickey Rooney, Arthur Hohl, Margaret Hamilton, Minor Watson, Marjorie Gateson. Sticky story of jockey Rooney and racetrack mentor Beery. All the stops out during the syrupy scenes.

Stagecoach (1939) **96m. ***** D: John Ford. Claire Trevor, John Wayne, Andy Devine, John Carradine, Thomas Mitchell, Louise Platt, George Bancroft, Donald Meek, Berton Churchill, Tim Holt, Tom Tyler, Chris-Pin Martin, Francis Ford, Jack Pennick. One of the great American films, and a landmark in the maturing of the Western, balancing character study (as disparate passengers travel together on the same stagecoach) and peerless action (in a lengthy Indian attack, featuring Yakima Canutt's famous stuntwork). Also the film that propelled John Wayne to genuine stardom. Mitchell won an Oscar as the drunken doctor, as did the music score. Script by Dudley Nichols, from Ernest Haycox's story "Stage to Lordsburg" (whose plot is reminiscent of Guy de Maupassant's *Boule de Suif*). Filmed in Ford's beloved Monument Valley on the Arizona-Utah border. Remade in 1966 and as a TVM in 1986. Also shown in computer-colored version.▼▶

Stagecoach War (1940) **60m. **** D: Lesley Selander. William Boyd, Russell Hayden, Julie Carter, Harvey Stephens, J. Farrell MacDonald, Britt Wood. Rival factions compete for stage line mail-carrying contract; Bar 20 mustangs are matched against purebred Morgans in decisive stage race. Hopalong Cassidy yarn has a preponderance of tight close-ups of Boyd, to no meaningful end. With one exception, gratuitous songs by The King's Men (cast as heavies!) are unwelcome.▼▶

Stage Door (1937) **92m. ***** D: Gregory La Cava. Katharine Hepburn, Ginger Rogers, Adolphe Menjou, Andrea Leeds, Gail Patrick, Constance Collier, Lucille Ball, Eve Arden, Ann Miller, Ralph Forbes, Franklin Pangborn, Jack Carson. Theatrical boarding house is setting for wonderful film, from Edna Ferber–George S. Kaufman play. Dynamite cast includes Hepburn as rich girl trying to succeed on her own, Menjou as propositioning producer, Leeds as hypersensitive actress, and several stars-to-be: Lucille Ball, Ann Miller, and Eve Arden. Scripted by Morrie Ryskind and Anthony Veiller.▼▶

Stage Door Canteen (1943) **132m. **½** D: Frank Borzage. Cheryl Walker, William Terry, Marjorie Riordan, Lon McCallister, Margaret Early, Michael Harrison (Sunset Carson). Wartime story of romance between soldier and hostess at N.Y.C.'s fabled canteen is filled with cameos, walk-ons, speeches, and musical numbers by an incredible battery of stars, including Katharine Hepburn, Harpo Marx, Paul Muni, Helen Hayes, Benny Goodman, Count Basie, Edgar Bergen. Many prints run 93m.▼▶

Stage Fright (1950) **110m. **½** D: Alfred Hitchcock. Marlene Dietrich, Jane Wyman, Michael Wilding, Richard Todd, Kay Walsh, Alastair Sim, Joyce Grenfell, Sybil Thorndike, Patricia Hitchcock. Drama student Wyman turns undercover sleuth when actress' husband is murdered; some exciting moments, but the Master misses on this one. Filmed in London with delightful British supporting cast; Marlene sings "The Laziest Gal in Town."▼▶

Stage Mother (1933) **87m. **½** D: Charles Brabin. Alice Brady, Maureen O'Sullivan, Ted Healy, Franchot Tone, Phillips Holmes. Widowed vaudevillian stakes everything on making her daughter a star. Brady is wonderful, and so is seedy backstage atmosphere. Songs include "Beautiful Girl," later immortalized in SINGIN' IN THE RAIN.

Stage Struck (1936) **86m. **½** D: Busby Berkeley. Dick Powell, Joan Blondell, Warren William, Frank McHugh, Jeanne Madden, The Yacht Club Boys, Carol Hughes, Craig Reynolds, Spring Byington, Jane Wyman. Passable 42ND STREET–inspired musical with Broadway producer William finagling harried dance director Powell into staging a show financed by wealthy, self-absorbed Blondell. Highlight is The Yacht Club Boys' insane "The Body Beautiful" number. Madden (playing the Ruby Keeler role) understandably remained obscure after this one.

Stage Struck (1958) **C-95m. **½** D: Sidney Lumet. Henry Fonda, Susan Strasberg, Joan Greenwood, Christopher Plummer, Herbert Marshall. Faded remake of MORNING GLORY retelling the ascent of Broadway-bound actress. Supporting cast hampered by unconvincing Strasberg in lead role and by unreal theater world atmosphere. Plummer's film debut.▼▶

Stage to Thunder Rock (1964) **C-82m. **** D: William F. Claxton. Barry Sullivan, Marilyn Maxwell, Lon Chaney, Jr., Scott Brady, John Agar, Keenan Wynn, Allan Jones. One of producer A. C. Lyles' humdrum Westerns with veteran stars; this one has Sullivan as a sheriff who's put in the position of having to arrest the outlaw family that raised him. Techniscope.

Stairway to Heaven SEE: **Matter of Life and Death, A**

Stakeout on Dope Street (1958) **83m. *½** D: Irvin Kershner. Yale Wexler, Jonathan Haze, Morris Miller, Abby Dalton, Her-

[655]

schel Bernardi. Trio of youths discover cache of heroin, believing their futures will now be uncomplicated; good premise poorly executed.

Stalag 17 (1953) **120m.** **★★★★** D: Billy Wilder. William Holden, Don Taylor, Otto Preminger, Robert Strauss, Harvey Lembeck, Richard Erdman, Peter Graves, Neville Brand, Sig Ruman, Ross Bagdasarian, Gil Stratton, Jr. The pinnacle of all WW2 P.O.W. films. Holden (in Oscar-winning performance) is super-cynical sergeant suspected of being Nazi spy. Wilder brilliantly blends drama with comedy to show monotonous, anxiety-ridden life of P.O.W.s. Wonderful comic relief by Strauss and Lembeck (repeating their Broadway roles), plus superb turn by Preminger as Nazi camp commander. Scripted by Wilder and Edwin Blum, from Donald Bevan and Edmund Trzcinski's play. ▼◐)

Stallion Road (1947) **91m.** **★★** D: James V. Kern. Ronald Reagan, Alexis Smith, Zachary Scott, Peggy Knudsen, Patti Brady, Harry Davenport. Dedicated veterinarian Reagan and novelist friend Scott vie for the affection of horse rancher Smith; low-key drama written by Stephen Longstreet. ◐

Stamboul Quest (1934) **88m.** **★★½** D: Sam Wood. Myrna Loy, George Brent, Lionel Atwill, C. Henry Gordon, Mischa Auer. Exotic combination of romance and intrigue with German spy Loy falling in love with American student Brent in WW1 Turkey. Herman Mankiewicz's script based on true story also filmed as FRAULEIN DOKTOR.

Stampede (1949) **78m.** **★★½** D: Lesley Selander. Rod Cameron, Gale Storm, Johnny Mack Brown, Don Castle, John Miljan. Good Western of range war between cattle ranchers. ◐

Stampede Fury SEE: **Strange Gamble**

Stand at Apache River, The (1953) **C-77m.** **★★** D: Lee Sholem. Stephen McNally, Julia (Julie) Adams, Hugh Marlowe, Jack Kelly, Hugh O'Brian. Title tells all.

Stand by for Action (1942) **109m.** **★★½** D: Robert Z. Leonard. Robert Taylor, Brian Donlevy, Charles Laughton, Walter Brennan, Marilyn Maxwell, Henry O'Neill, Chill Wills. We're still waiting. Good cast in standard drama-with-comic-touches in which up-by-his-bootstraps Navy officer Donlevy and silver-spoon-fed subordinate Taylor clash in the early days of WW2. ◐

Stand-In (1937) **91m.** **★★★** D: Tay Garnett. Leslie Howard, Humphrey Bogart, Joan Blondell, Alan Mowbray, Marla Shelton, C. Henry Gordon, Jack Carson. Enjoyable spoof of Hollywood, with stuffy banker Howard sent to assess dwindling fortunes of Colossal Pictures, becoming involved with perky stand-in Blondell and mercurial producer Bogart to save company from ruin. Sags in second half. ▼◐

Standing Room Only (1944) **83m.** **★★** D: Sidney Lanfield. Fred MacMurray, Paulette Goddard, Edward Arnold, Hillary Brooke, Roland Young, Anne Revere. Topical wartime comedy is now dated. MacMurray and Goddard can't find rooms, so they work as servants.

Stand Up and Cheer (1934) **69m.** **★★** D: Hamilton MacFadden. Warner Baxter, Madge Evans, James Dunn, Sylvia Froos, John Boles, Shirley Temple, Ralph Morgan, Aunt Jemima, Mitchell and Durant, Nick (Dick) Foran, Nigel Bruce, Stepin Fetchit. Dismal musical fantasy about big-time show producer Baxter being named Secretary of Amusement by the President, to chase the country's Depression blues. Tough sledding until Shirley Temple shows up with Dunn to perform "Baby Take a Bow" (which helped make her a star). Originally released at 80m. Also shown in computer-colored version. ▼◐

Stand Up and Fight (1939) **97m.** **★★** D: W. S. Van Dyke II. Wallace Beery, Robert Taylor, Florence Rice, Charles Bickford, Charley Grapewin, Selmer Jackson. OK Western with railroading pioneer Taylor meeting crisis after crisis, battling stubborn stage-rider Beery. James M. Cain was one of the writers. ◐

Stanley and Livingstone (1939) **101m.** **★★★** D: Henry King. Spencer Tracy, Nancy Kelly, Richard Greene, Walter Brennan, Charles Coburn, Cedric Hardwicke, Henry Hull, Henry Travers, Miles Mander. Elaborate production with Tracy as determined reporter who searches turn-of-the-20th-century Africa for missing missionary (Hardwicke). Entertaining drama with beautifully understated performance by Tracy. ▼◐

Star, The (1952) **89m.** **★★★½** D: Stuart Heisler. Bette Davis, Sterling Hayden, Natalie Wood, Warner Anderson, Minor Watson, June Travis. An Oscar-winning actress tries to deal with the fact that her career is over, her money is gone, and she must find some way to put her life together. Modest film, shot on locations all around L.A., has many moments of truth (and a typically compelling performance by Davis) to make up for its excesses. ▼◐

Star Dust (1940) **85m.** **★★½** D: Walter Lang. Linda Darnell, John Payne, Roland Young, Charlotte Greenwood, William Gargan, Mary Beth Hughes, Mary Healy, Donald Meek. Hokey, entertaining yarn about talent scout Young (from Amalgamated Studios) discovering star-struck Darnell and football player Payne. ◐

Stardust SEE: **Mad About Money**

Stardust on the Sage (1942) **65m.** **★★** D: William Morgan. Gene Autry, Smiley Burnette, Bill Henry, Edith Fellows, Louise Currie, Emmett Vogan, Roy Barcroft. Radio station owner Currie tries to get Gene to support her brother's mine, but he's hesitant to recommend the investment to his fellow cattlemen. Complications arise when the brother (Henry) admits that he's embezzled money to keep it going. Even some good songs can't rescue this one from mediocrity.▶

Star in the Dust (1956) **C-80m.** ** D: Charles Haas. John Agar, Mamie Van Doren, Richard Boone, Leif Erickson, Coleen Gray, James Gleason. Intriguing cast is wasted in this trite tale of sheriff Agar forced to fight his townfolk to retain law and order. Look for Clint Eastwood as a ranch hand. ▼

Star Is Born, A (1937) **C-111m.** ***½ D: William Wellman. Fredric March, Janet Gaynor, Adolphe Menjou, May Robson, Andy Devine, Lionel Stander, Franklin Pangborn. Two remakes haven't dimmed the glow of this drama about a self-destructive actor and the young movie hopeful he marries. March and Gaynor are at their best and 1930s flavor (captured in early Technicolor) is a plus; screenplay by Dorothy Parker, Alan Campbell, and Robert Carson was inspired in part by 1932 film WHAT PRICE HOLLYWOOD? Won an Oscar for Carson and director Wellman's original story and a special Oscar for W. Howard Greene's cinematography.▼●▶

Star Is Born, A (1954) **C-170m.** **** D: George Cukor. Judy Garland, James Mason, Charles Bickford, Jack Carson, Tom Noonan. Powerful semi-musical remake of the 1937 classic, with Garland and Mason at their peaks as doomed Hollywood star couple, she on the way up, he down. Incisive script by Moss Hart; great Harold Arlen–Ira Gershwin songs include spellbinding "The Man That Got Away" and the showstopping "Born in a Trunk" sequence by Leonard Gershe. Badly cut to 154m. after premiere engagements of 181m.; restored in 1983 to present length using still photos to cover missing bits of footage. CinemaScope.▼●▶

Starlift (1951) **103m.** ** D: Roy Del Ruth. Janice Rule, Dick Wesson, Ron Hagerthy, Richard Webb. Flimsy account of GI (Hagerthy) romancing an actress (Rule), allowing for scenes of movie stars entertaining troops. Cameos by Warner Bros. people like Cagney, Virginia Mayo, Ruth Roman, Doris Day, Gordon MacRae, etc.▶

Star Maker, The (1939) **80m.** **½ D: Roy Del Ruth. Bing Crosby, Louise Campbell, Laura Hope Crews, Ned Sparks, Ethel Griffies, Billy Gilbert. Crosby plays Gus Edwards, vaudeville impresario who turned talented youngsters into stars. Pleasant musical doesn't always stick to facts. Originally 94m.

Star of India (1954-British) **C-84m.** **½ D: Arthur Lubin. Cornel Wilde, Jean Wallace, Herbert Lom. So-so costumer, overly earnest. Wilde is Gallic nobleman trying to reestablish his rightful inheritance.

Star of Midnight (1935) **90m.** ** D: Stephen Roberts. William Powell, Ginger Rogers, Paul Kelly, Gene Lockhart, Ralph Morgan, Leslie Fenton, J. Farrell MacDonald. Flip, but not terribly funny, comedy-mystery in the THIN MAN vein, with a convoluted story that doesn't offer much involvement. Powell plays a lawyer who enjoys solving cases more than trying them in court.▼●▶

Star Packer, The (1934) **53m.** ** D: Robert N. Bradbury. John Wayne, Verna Hillie, George Hayes, Yakima Canutt, Billy Franey, Ed Parker. U.S. marshal Wayne enters town incognito to quell lawbreakers led by mysterious figure in this average Lone Star quickie Western. Hayes plays a character known as The Shadow. Besides his role as Wayne's Indian companion, Canutt performed stunts for almost everyone on camera.▼▶

Stars and Stripes Forever (1952) **C-89m.** **½ D: Henry Koster. Clifton Webb, Robert Wagner, Ruth Hussey, Debra Paget, Finlay Currie. Diverting, fictionalized biography of bandmaster John Philip Sousa, well played by Webb, with standard march tunes worked into plot nicely.▼▶

Stars Are Singing, The (1953) **C-99m.** **½ D: Norman Taurog. Rosemary Clooney, Anna Maria Alberghetti, Lauritz Melchoir, Fred Clark. Frothy musical with ridiculous plot-line of immigration authorities tracking down Alberghetti as contestant on TV talent show.

Stars in My Crown (1950) **89m.** ***½ D: Jacques Tourneur. Joel McCrea, Ellen Drew, Dean Stockwell, Alan Hale, Lewis Stone, Ed Begley, Amanda Blake, James Arness, Juano Hernandez. Gentle, moving story of a quiet but persuasive minister in rural 19th-century America; episodic film creates warm feeling for characters and setting. Prime Americana from Joe David Brown's popular novel. Also interesting for pre-*Gunsmoke* casting of Arness and Blake.▼▶

Stars Look Down, The (1939-British) **110m.** **** D: Carol Reed. Michael Redgrave, Margaret Lockwood, Edward Rigby, Emlyn Williams, Nancy Price, Cecil Parker, Linden Travers. Classic adaptation of A.J. Cronin's novel (coscripted by the author) about Welsh coal miners struggling against dangerous working conditions, and Redgrave as a collier's son who intends to run for office. Gripping all the way.▼▶

Stars Over Broadway (1935) **84m.** ** D: William Keighley. Pat O'Brien, Jane Froman, Jean Muir, James Melton, Frank McHugh, Phil Regan, Marie Wilson, Frank Fay. Washed-up promoter plays his last ace, transforming a singing bellboy into a broadcast sensation. Metropolitan Opera tenor Melton is moderately tolerable in his screen debut. First of but two film appearances by radio songbird Froman, who also can't act.

Warren and Dubin score introduces "September in the Rain," but only as an instrumental. Underbudgeted production numbers are valiantly staged by Busby Berkeley and Bobby Connolly. Jack Dempsey has a one-second cameo as himself.

Star Spangled Rhythm (1942) **99m.** ★★★ D: George Marshall. Bing Crosby, Ray Milland, Bob Hope, Veronica Lake, Dorothy Lamour, Susan Hayward, Dick Powell, Mary Martin, Alan Ladd, Paulette Goddard, Cecil B. DeMille, Arthur Treacher, Preston Sturges, Eddie Anderson, Robert Preston, William Bendix, many others. Paramount's silly but agreeable star-packed WW2 extravaganza, filled with songs and sketches. There's a slight plot, about a studio switchboard operator (Betty Hutton) and gate guard (Victor Moore); the latter has told his son (Eddie Bracken), a sailor, that he's the studio's boss. Better numbers include "(That Old) Black Magic," "Time to Hit the Road to Dreamland." ▼●)

Start Cheering (1938) **78m.** ★★★ D: Albert S. Rogell. Jimmy Durante, Walter Connolly, Joan Perry, Charles Starrett, Gertrude Niesen, Hal LeRoy, The Three Stooges, Broderick Crawford, Louis Prima. Snappy collegiate musical about rugged movie star Starrett going back to school, with cohorts Connolly and Durante tagging along. Modest, enjoyable film with plenty of specialty numbers, guest stars, songs. ▼

Star Without Light (1946-French) **88m.** ★★½ D: Marcel Blistène. Édith Piaf, Marcel Herrand, Jules Berry, Serge Reggiani, Mila Parély, Yves Montand. Modest, naïve hotel maid Piaf, blessed with a beautiful singing voice, is hired to dub a silent film star appearing in her first musical talkie. Melodramatic fluff, but well worth a look for Piaf's presence. Montand (who then was Piaf's lover) makes his screen debut as her jealous small-town boyfriend. Original title: ÉTOILE SANS LUMIÈRE.

Star Witness, The (1931) **68m.** ★★★ D: William Wellman. Walter Huston, Sally Blane, Chic Sale, Frances Starr, Grant Mitchell, Edward Nugent, Ralph Ince, Dickie Moore. Gritty, no-nonsense account of a family who witnesses a gangland battle and is terrorized to prevent them from testifying in court. Huston is the idealistic district attorney; Sale steals the film as the crotchety but resourceful grandfather.

State Fair (1933) **96m.** ★★★ D: Henry King. Janet Gaynor, Will Rogers, Lew Ayres, Sally Eilers, Norman Foster, Louise Dresser, Victor Jory, Frank Craven. Not just a Rogers vehicle, but slice of life '30s-style as farm family gets ready for annual outing to state fair: Mom's entering bake-off contest, Dad the pig contest, son and daughter looking for first love. Great atmosphere, good performances. Phil Stong's novel has been remade twice (so far!).

State Fair (1945) **C-100m.** ★★★ D: Walter Lang. Jeanne Crain, Dana Andrews, Dick Haymes, Vivian Blaine, Charles Winninger, Fay Bainter, Donald Meek, Frank McHugh, Percy Kilbride. Remake of the 1933 film is bright, engaging musical of family's adventures at Iowa State Fair; colorful, with fine Rodgers and Hammerstein songs (their only film score), including "That's for Me," "Grand Night for Singing," Oscar-winning "It Might As Well Be Spring." Retitled IT HAPPENED ONE SUMMER for TV. ▼●)

State Fair (1962) **C-118m.** BOMB D: Jose Ferrer. Pat Boone, Bobby Darin, Pamela Tiffin, Ann-Margret, Alice Faye, Tom Ewell, Wally Cox. Remake of sprightly 1945 musical is pretty bad. Faye came out of retirement to play Tiffin's mother—a bad mistake. Ewell even sings to a pig! Third-rate Americana. CinemaScope. ▼)

State of the Union (1948) **124m.** ★★★½ D: Frank Capra. Spencer Tracy, Katharine Hepburn, Angela Lansbury, Van Johnson, Adolphe Menjou, Lewis Stone, Raymond Walburn, Margaret Hamilton, Carl ("Alfalfa") Switzer, Charles Lane, Tor Johnson. Contemporary as ever, this literate comedy-drama (adapted from the Howard Lindsay–Russel Crouse play) casts Tracy as an industrialist who struggles to keep his integrity as he's swallowed into the political machinery of running for President. Hepburn is his wife and conscience, Lansbury a power-hungry millionairess backing the campaign, Van Johnson the sardonic campaign manager. Great entertainment. ▼●)

State Penitentiary (1950) **66m.** ★★ D: Lew Landers. Warner Baxter, Karin Booth, Robert Shayne, Richard Benedict, Onslow Stevens. Mediocre programmer with Baxter sentenced to the Big House for embezzlement, despite his claim of innocence.

State's Attorney (1932) **79m.** ★★★ D: George Archainbaud. John Barrymore, Helen Twelvetrees, William "Stage" Boyd, Ralph Ince, Jill Esmond, Albert Conti, Mary Duncan, C. Henry Gordon, Oscar Apfel, Leon Waycoff (Ames). Barrymore's the whole show as a flamboyant attorney with a flair for women and liquor; not much of a story, but there's some slick dialogue by Rowland Brown and Barrymore crony Gene Fowler. ▼)

State Secret (1950-British) **104m.** ★★★ D: Sidney Gilliat. Douglas Fairbanks, Jr., Glynis Johns, Herbert Lom, Jack Hawkins, Walter Rilla. American doctor tries to flee Middle European country after he discovers its real leader has been assassinated and replaced with a double. Intelligent and witty suspense yarn; screenplay by Gilliat, from a Roy Huggins novel. Originally released in U.S. as THE GREAT MANHUNT.

Station Six-Sahara (1964-British) **99m.** ★½ D: Seth Holt. Carroll Baker, Peter Van Eyck, Ian Bannen, Denholm Elliott, Biff

McGuire. Dreary yarn of five love-starved men who find something new to fight over when sexpot Baker and her estranged husband crash land at their desert oasis. Written by Bryan Forbes and Brian Clemens.

Station West (1948) **80m.** ******* D: Sidney Lanfield. Dick Powell, Jane Greer, Tom Powers, Steve Brodie, Gordon Oliver, Raymond Burr, Agnes Moorehead, Burl Ives, Guinn Williams, Regis Toomey. Entertaining adaptation of Luke Short story about undercover military intelligence officer Powell stirring up trouble in Western town to find who's behind series of gold robberies. Script (by Frank Fenton and Winston Miller) has sharp dialogue throughout. Originally released at 92m. Also shown in computer-colored version.▼

St. Benny the Dip (1951) **80m.** ****** D: Edgar G. Ulmer. Dick Haymes, Nina Foch, Roland Young, Lionel Stander, Freddie Bartholomew, Richard Gordon. Silly, rambling account of a trio of con artists and their plight after disguising themselves as priests in order to evade the law. Child star Bartholomew's final film.▼▶

Steamboat Bill, Jr. (1928) **71m.** ******* D: Charles F. Riesner. Buster Keaton, Ernest Torrence, Marion Byron, Tom Lewis, Tom McGuire. Buster plays a milquetoast who must prove his manhood to steamboat captain father (Torrence). Not one of Keaton's best silents, but there are great moments, and classic, eye-popping cyclone finale.▼▶❶

Steamboat 'Round the Bend (1935) **96m.** ******* D: John Ford. Will Rogers, Anne Shirley, Irvin S. Cobb, Eugene Pallette, Berton Churchill, John McGuire, Stepin Fetchit, Francis Ford, Pardner Jones, Charles Middleton. Enjoyable Ford/Rogers period piece of steamboat captain (Rogers) who pilots a ramshackle floating waxworks museum, from which he also dispenses highly alcoholic cure-all medicine. Shirley is particularly good as swamp girl taken in by Rogers. Churchill shines in comic role of river prophet "The New Moses." Climactic steamboat race is a gem. Released posthumously after Rogers' tragic death.▶

Steel Against the Sky (1941) **67m.** ****** D: A. Edward Sutherland. Alexis Smith, Lloyd Nolan, Craig Stevens, Gene Lockhart, Edward Ellis, Walter Catlett, Howard da Silva, Edward Brophy, Julie Bishop. Interesting cast is wasted in this slight melodrama-comedy involving tough hardhat Nolan, who vies with his brother (Stevens) for the love of the boss' daughter (Smith). Look for unbilled Jackie Gleason in a bit as a tipsy steelworker.

Steel Bayonet (1957-British) **84m.** ****** D: Michael Carreras. Leo Genn, Kieron Moore, Michael Medwin, Robert Brown. Military unit is ordered to defend deserted farmhouse/lookout base at all costs. Tame WW2 film set in Africa; watch for Michael Caine as a German soldier. Hammerscope.

Steel Cage, The (1954) **80m.** ****** D: Walter Doniger. Paul Kelly, Maureen O'Sullivan, Walter Slezak, John Ireland, Lawrence Tierney, Alan Mowbray, George E. Stone, Lyle Talbot. Pedestrian telling of life at San Quentin, despite good cast. Sequel to DUFFY OF SAN QUENTIN.

Steel Fist, The (1952) **73m.** ***½** D: Wesley Barry. Roddy McDowall, Kristine Miller, Harry Lauter, Rand Brooks. Quickie flick with McDowall involved in escape from Iron Curtain country; low production values.

Steel Helmet, The (1951) **84m.** *****½** D: Samuel Fuller. Gene Evans, Robert Hutton, Steve Brodie, James Edwards, Richard Loo, Sid Melton. Evans is a gutsy American sergeant caught in dizzying turn of events in early days of Korean war; solid melodrama written by Fuller, with surprisingly contemporary view of war itself.▼▶

Steel Jungle, The (1956) **86m.** ***½** D: Walter Doniger. Perry Lopez, Beverly Garland, Allison Hayes, Walter Abel, Ted de Corsia, Kenneth Tobey. Lukewarm account of prison life.

Steel Town (1952) **C-85m.** ****** D: George Sherman. Ann Sheridan, John Lund, Howard Duff, James Best, Nancy Kulp. Uninspired story of steelmaking and the personal problems of nephew of steel plant owner; Sheridan tries, but can't perk up this programmer.

Steel Trap, The (1952) **85m.** ****½** D: Andrew Stone. Joseph Cotten, Teresa Wright, Jonathan Hale, Walter Sande, Eddie Marr. Location filming on the streets of L.A. and New Orleans enhances this trim caper of bank officer Cotten, a husband and father, who's tired of his humdrum life. He decides to steal a million dollars from his place of employment and escape to Brazil . . . but naturally, there are complications.▶

Stella (1950) **83m.** ****½** D: Claude Binyon. Ann Sheridan, Victor Mature, David Wayne, Frank Fontaine. Screwball comedy and murder don't blend well in tale of nutty family trying to hide a corpse.

Stella (1955-Greek) **94m.** ****½** D: Michael Cacoyannis. Melina Mercouri, Yiorgo (George) Foundas, Alekos Alexandrakis, Voula Zouboulaki, Sophia Vembo, Tasso Kavadia. Brains (a meek writer) and brawn (a soccer star) compete for a bar singer who's caught in the middle and doesn't know what to do except keep playing her bouzouki. Second feature by the now renowned Cypriot writer-director was the first Greek film to attain international recognition. Mercouri's debut, as an earthy free spirit, instituted her exuberant screen persona. ▼▶

Stella Dallas (1937) **106m.** ******* D: King Vidor. Barbara Stanwyck, John Boles, Anne Shirley, Barbara O'Neil, Alan Hale, Tim Holt, Marjorie Main. Definitive soap opera (from Olive Higgins Prouty's novel) of woman who sacrifices everything for her daughter; Stanwyck gives one of her finest performances. Tear-jerking score by Alfred Newman. Filmed before in 1925; remade in 1990 as STELLA. ▼◐▶

Stella Maris (1918) **84m.** ***½ D: Marshall Neilan. Mary Pickford, Conway Tearle, Marcia Manon, Ida Waterman, Herbert Standing, Josephine Crowell, Gustav von Seyffertitz. Pickford is at her very best in dual roles, as a disabled heiress who lives in a fantasy world created by those who love her and an ugly-duckling orphan who is enslaved by a disturbed woman. Both characters fall for the same man. While it deals in stereotypes involving the privileged and downtrodden and the nature of good and evil, it offers a vivid portrait of the world as it was in 1918 and poignantly explores the need to love and be loved. Screenplay by Frances Marion. Remade in 1925 with Mary Philbin. ▼▶

Step by Step (1946) **62m.** ** D: Phil Rosen. Lawrence Tierney, Anne Jeffreys, Lowell Gilmore, George Cleveland. Patriotic programmer with Tierney a WW2 veteran uncovering Fascist agents in America.

Step Down to Terror (1958) **75m.** ** D: Harry Keller. Colleen Miller, Charles Drake, Rod Taylor, Josephine Hutchinson, Jocelyn Brando. Washed-out remake of Hitchcock's SHADOW OF A DOUBT, retells account of psycho-murderer returning to home town after long absence. Story remade again (for TV) under original title.

Step Lively (1944) **88m.** *** D: Tim Whelan. Frank Sinatra, George Murphy, Adolphe Menjou, Gloria DeHaven, Eugene Pallette, Anne Jeffreys, Walter Slezak. Brisk musical remake of ROOM SERVICE with producer Murphy wheeling and dealing to get his show produced. Engagingly frantic, with sharp dialogue, funny contribution by Slezak as the hotel manager. If you blink you'll miss (brunette) Dorothy Malone as switchboard operator in lobby. ▼▶

Step Lively, Jeeves! (1937) **69m.** **½ D: Eugene Forde. Arthur Treacher, Patricia Ellis, Robert Kent, Alan Dinehart, George Givot, Franklin Pangborn. Treacher is in top form as P. G. Wodehouse's droll English valet, who comes to America and gets mixed up with gangsters when two con men convince him he's Sir Francis Drake's missing heir. Amusing, if overplotted, follow-up to THANK YOU, JEEVES!, though not based on any Wodehouse story. ▶

Stepping Out (1931) **73m.** ** D: Charles Riesner. Charlotte Greenwood, Leila Hyams, Reginald Denny, Lilian Bond, Cliff Edwards, Merna Kennedy. When Greenwood and Hyams catch their husbands fooling around, they clean out their bank accounts and take off for Mexico to indulge in some fun of their own. Mild pre-Code farce is more silly than saucy, though buffs may be interested to know that much of it was shot at the homes of Denny, Buster Keaton, and John Gilbert. ▶

Stick to Your Guns (1941) **62m.** **½ D: Lesley Selander. William Boyd, Andy Clyde, Brad King, Jacqueline (Jennifer) Holt, Dick Curtis, Weldon Heyburn, Kermit Maynard, Charles Middleton. Pretty good Hopalong Cassidy entry has Bar 20 boys riding to rescue rancher rampaged by rustlers. Jack Holt's daughter (and sister of Tim Holt) and Ken Maynard's brother sadly have little to do, but the Jimmy Wakely Trio with Johnny Bond provide some good songs. Uncredited source was series creator Clarence E. Mulford's 1926 novel *Bar-20 Rides Again.* ▼▶

Stingaree (1934) **76m.** **½ D: William Wellman. Irene Dunne, Richard Dix, Mary Boland, Conway Tearle, Andy Devine, Henry Stephenson, George Barraud, Una O'Connor, Snub Pollard, Reginald Owen, Billy Bevan. In 1874 Australia, dashing music-loving bandit Dix falls in love with servant girl Dunne and helps her become a great opera star. Oddly entertaining hokum melds musical romance and Robin Hood in the outback, based on the stories of E. W. Hornung (*Raffles*). Dunne never sang better or looked lovelier; Boland is a hoot as a vain old crow who fancies herself a chanteuse. Filmed before as a serial in 1915. ▶

St. Louis Blues (1939) **87m.** *** D: Raoul Walsh. Dorothy Lamour, Lloyd Nolan, Tito Guizar, Jerome Cowan, Jessie Ralph, William Frawley. Showgirl Lamour deserts the Great White Way and her manager to appear incognito on a riverboat. Amusing and entertaining Paramount musical-comedy. TV title: BEST OF THE BLUES.

St. Louis Blues (1958) **93m.** ** D: Allen Reisner. Nat "King" Cole, Eartha Kitt, Ruby Dee, Pearl Bailey, Juano Hernandez, Cab Calloway, Ella Fitzgerald, Mahalia Jackson. Treacly dramatics interspersed with outstanding musical performances in this so-called biography of W. C. Handy (Cole, in his lone starring role), who composed the title tune. Billy Preston plays Handy as a boy. VistaVision.

St. Louis Kid, The (1934) **67m.** **½ D: Ray Enright. James Cagney, Patricia Ellis, Allen Jenkins, Robert Barrat, Addison Richards. Breezy Cagney vehicle casts him and Jenkins as truckdriving buddies who have a knack for getting into trouble—and wind up in the middle of a war between a dairy trust and angry farmers. ▶

St. Martin's Lane SEE: **Sidewalks of London**

Stolen Face (1952-British) **72m.** **½ D: Terence Fisher. Lizabeth Scott, Paul Henreid, Andre Morell, Susan Stephen, Mary Mackenzie, John Wood. Interesting but far-fetched drama of plastic surgeon Henreid transforming female convict into replica of the woman he loves but cannot have, unable to curb her sociopathic tendencies. ▼▶

Stolen Goods SEE: **Blue Steel**
Stolen Heaven (1938) 88m. **½ D: Andrew L. Stone. Gene Raymond, Olympe Bradna, Glenda Farrell, Lewis Stone, Porter Hall, Douglass Dumbrille, Joe Sawyer. Offbeat story of jewel thieves posing as musicians on the lam but having change of heart when they meet kindly maestro Stone.
Stolen Holiday (1937) 76m. *** D: Michael Curtiz. Claude Rains, Kay Francis, Ian Hunter, Alison Skipworth, Alexander D'Arcy, Betty Lawford, Walter Kingsford. Stylish, briskly paced tale of charming Russian swindler Rains marrying naïve French model Francis and luring her into his fraudulent financial schemes. Interesting fictionalized version of a real-life scandal, later retold using real names in STAVISKY (1974). ▶
Stolen Hours (1963) C-100m. **½ D: Daniel Petrie. Susan Hayward, Michael Craig, Diane Baker, Edward Judd, Paul Rogers. Hayward takes Bette Davis' DARK VICTORY, transplants it to contemporary England, in tale of woman with fatal illness trying to get as much out of life as she can. Original is far superior in all departments.▼▶
Stolen Identity (1952-Austrian-U.S.) 81m. *** D: Gunther (von) Fritsch. Donald Buka, Joan Camden, Francis Lederer, Adrienne Gessner, Hermann Erhardt, E. (Egon) von Jordan. Atmospheric thriller about a jealous concert pianist (Lederer), his captive wife (Camden), and how a taxi driver (Buka) with no identity papers inadvertently becomes involved with them. Stylishly filmed in Vienna, with shadowy images reminiscent of THE THIRD MAN. Produced by actor Turhan Bey. Simultaneously filmed in a German-language version with Gustav Fröhlich in the role played here by Buka.
Stolen Life, A (1946) 107m. **½ D: Curtis Bernhardt. Bette Davis, Glenn Ford, Dane Clark, Walter Brennan, Charlie Ruggles, Bruce Bennett, Peggy Knudsen. A twin takes her sister's place as the man they both love in this slick but far-fetched soaper with Bette in dual role; remake of 1939 film with Elisabeth Bergner.▼▶
Stooge, The (1953) 100m. **½ D: Norman Taurog. Dean Martin, Jerry Lewis, Polly Bergen, Eddie Mayehoff, Marion Marshall. Egocentric singer (Martin) learns the hard way just how important his stooge (Lewis) is to his success. Martin & Lewis go dramatic with middling results. Completed in 1951, not released for two years.▼▶
Stop! Look! and Laugh! (1960) 78m. **½ D: Jules White. The Three Stooges, Paul Winchell, Jerry Mahoney, Knucklehead Smiff, The Marquis Chimps, Officer Joe Bolton. Original Stooges' funniest sequences strung together by ventriloquist Paul Winchell and dummies is aimed at children. Much of it is familiar, but still amusing.▼▶

Stop Me Before I Kill! (1961-British) 109m. ** D: Val Guest. Claude Dauphin, Diane Cilento, Roland Lewis, Françoise Rosay. Turgid dramatics: mentally unhinged man's new marriage is threatened by his illness and his psychiatrist's yen for his wife. Originally titled THE FULL TREATMENT. Megascope. ▶
Stopover Tokyo (1957) C-100m. **½ D: Richard L. Breen. Robert Wagner, Joan Collins, Edmond O'Brien, Ken Scott. Lumbering spy tale, loosely based on John P. Marquand novel. On-location filming in Japan makes a pretty background, but flat characters remain. CinemaScope.▼
Stop, You're Killing Me (1952) C-86m. ** D: Roy Del Ruth. Broderick Crawford, Claire Trevor, Virginia Gibson, Sheldon Leonard, Margaret Dumont. Mild froth based on Damon Runyon story of racketeer Crawford going legitimate. Remake of A SLIGHT CASE OF MURDER.
Stork Club, The (1945) 98m. **½ D: Hal Walker. Betty Hutton, Barry Fitzgerald, Don Defore, Andy Russell, Iris Adrian, Robert Benchley. Hat-check girl Hutton mysteriously becomes wealthy in fanciful musicomedy, mainly for Betty's fans. She sings "Doctor, Lawyer, Indian Chief."▼▶
Storm at Daybreak (1933) 78m. ** D: Richard Boleslawski. Kay Francis, Nils Asther, Walter Huston, Phillips Holmes, Eugene Pallette, C. Henry Gordon, Louise Closser Hale, Jean Parker. Turgid triangle tale involving a Serbian mayor (Huston) whose wife (Francis) falls for his Hungarian officer friend (Asther) at the start of WW1. Ornately directed and photographed historical drama (adapted from a play) has the look and feel of a silent film.
Storm Center (1956) 86m. **½ D: Daniel Taradash. Bette Davis, Brian Keith, Kim Hunter, Paul Kelly, Joe Mantell, Kevin Coughlin, Edward Platt, Kathryn Grant. Kindly small-town librarian Davis is in a quandary when city council members demand that she remove from her shelves a book about communism. Thoughtful, well-intentioned period piece is a bit too melodramatic to be completely effective. Screenwriter Taradash's lone film as director. ▶
Storm Fear (1955) 88m. ** D: Cornel Wilde. Cornel Wilde, Jean Wallace, Dan Duryea, Lee Grant, Dennis Weaver, David Stollery, Steven Hill. Wounded bank robber Wilde and two partners take refuge in farm home of his honest but sickly brother Duryea. Snowstorm increases group tensions and suspense. Well-developed characters in Horton Foote's script are enhanced by good acting. Based on the novel by Clinton Seeley. ▶
Storm in a Teacup (1937-British) 87m. *** D: Victor Saville, Ian Dalrymple. Vivien Leigh, Rex Harrison, Sara Allgood, Cecil Parker, Arthur Wontner, Ivor Barnard.

Witty social comedy, set in a provincial Scottish village, with Harrison a journalist who reports on a pompous politician's cruel treatment of a widow who is unable to afford a dog-license fee. At the same time, he finds himself falling in love with the bureaucrat's daughter (Leigh).▼▶

Storm Over Asia (1928-Russian) 93m. ***½ D: V. I. Pudovkin. Valeri Inkizhinov, A. Dedinstev, V. Tzoppi, Paulina Belinskaya. Sweeping, visually stunning drama, set in 1920, about a Mongolian trapper, thrust out of his village after a dispute with an American fur trader, who becomes a Soviet partisan. Eventually, he's discovered to be a descendant of Genghis Khan, and is set up as a puppet Mongolian ruler by the British army of occupation. Filmed in Central Asia; especially memorable are the sequence in which the trapper is almost shot and the finale. Aka THE HEIR TO GENGHIS KHAN.▼▶

Storm Over Lisbon (1944) 86m. ** D: George Sherman. Vera Ralston, Richard Arlen, Erich von Stroheim, Otto Kruger, Eduardo Ciannelli, Mona Barrie. WW2 intrigue in Lisbon with nightclub performer Ralston siding with von Stroheim to get goods on American Arlen; only for those who wonder what CASABLANCA would've been like if it'd been made by Republic.

Storm Over the Nile (1955-British) C-113m. **½ D: Zoltan Korda, Terence Young. Anthony Steel, Laurence Harvey, James Robertson Justice, Mary Ure, Christopher Lee. Remake of THE FOUR FEATHERS (by the same director) with stock footage from the original) lacks class and flair, but story is still good; script by R.C. Sherriff. CinemaScope.▶

Storm Over Tibet (1952) 87m. ** D: Andrew Marton. Rex Reason, Diana Douglas, Myron Healey, Robert Karnes, Strother Martin, Harold Fong. Reason is an ex-WW2 pilot who journeys to Tibet and gets in plenty of hot water when he purloins a holy mask from a temple. German documentary footage of the Himalayas is used extensively in this Ivan Tors production.

Storm Rider, The (1957) 70m. ** D: Edward Bernds. Scott Brady, Mala Powers, Bill Williams, John Goddard, James Dobson, Olin Howlin, William Fawcett. Brady, a gunman with a secret, becomes immersed in a conflict between small-time ranchers and their greedy nemesis. Not bad; Bernds also cowrote the script. Regalscope.▶

Storm Warning (1951) 93m. **½ D: Stuart Heisler. Ginger Rogers, Ronald Reagan, Doris Day, Steve Cochran, Hugh Sanders, Lloyd Gough, Ned Glass. Feverish but engrossing story of a woman who discovers that her sister (Day) has married a loutish Ku Klux Klansman. Good cast, with Reagan in one of his better roles as a crusading D.A.; cowritten by Richard Brooks.▶

Stormy Waters SEE: **Remorques**

Stormy Weather (1943) 77m. **½ D: Andrew L. Stone. Lena Horne, Bill (Bojangles) Robinson, Cab Calloway and His Band, Katherine Dunham, Fats Waller, Dooley Wilson, The Nicholas Brothers. This musical offers a legendary lineup of black performers, with Lena singing title song, Fats performing "Ain't Misbehavin'," others doing what they do best. Only problem: the so-called story is told in fragments, through flashbacks, and doesn't make much sense. Robinson is too old to be paired romantically with Horne, but they're terrific just the same.▼▶

Story of Alexander Graham Bell, The (1939) 97m. *** D: Irving Cummings. Don Ameche, Loretta Young, Henry Fonda, Charles Coburn, Spring Byington, Gene Lockhart, Polly Ann Young. Ameche overacts at times in his famous title role, but entertaining version of inventor is given plush 20th Century-Fox presentation.▼▶

Story of a Love Affair (1950-Italian) 98m. *** D: Michelangelo Antonioni. Massimo Girotti, Lucia Bosé, Gino Rossi, Marika Rowsky, Ferdinando Sarmi. Antonioni's first feature, which he coscripted, is an engrossing tale of love, desire, and class distinction, and how they affect the human spirit. A young beauty of modest background (Bosé) is unhappily married to a corrupt, power-obsessed businessman. Her lover (Girotti) was once engaged to wed a high school friend who died just before the nuptials; the pair now contemplate murdering the husband. Antonioni offers a knowing portrayal of the sterile, idle rich that is found in his less conventionally plotted later work.▶

Story of Danny Lester, The SEE: **Bad Boy**

Story of Dr. Wassell, The (1944) C-140m. **½ D: Cecil B. DeMille. Gary Cooper, Laraine Day, Signe Hasso, Dennis O'Keefe, Paul Kelly, Philip Ahn, Barbara Britton. Story of real-life dedicated Navy doctor who saved fighting men in Java during WW2; slow-moving adaptation of the James Hilton book. Far from top-grade DeMille or Cooper.▼

Story of Esther Costello, The (1957-British) 103m. **½ D: David Miller. Joan Crawford, Rossano Brazzi, Heather Sears, Lee Patterson, Fay Compton, Bessie Love, Ron Randell. Socialite rehabilitates impoverished blind and deaf girl and promotes charity fund in her name. Interesting look at charity huckstering but melodrama is overwrought and often unintentionally funny.▼▶

Story of Floating Weeds, A (1934-Japanese) 87m. *** D: Yasujiro Ozu. Takeshi Sakamoto, Choko Iida, Hideo Mitsui, Reiko Yagumo, Yoshiko Tsubouchi, Tokkan Kozo (Tomio Aoki), Reiko Tani. A traveling acting troupe arrives in a small village. The leader (Sakamoto) visits an old flame, with whom he sired an illegitimate son years before. Absorbing drama has its merits but pales beside FLOATING WEEDS, Ozu's sublime 1959 remake.▶

[662]

Story of G.I. Joe, The (1945) 109m. ***½ D: William Wellman. Burgess Meredith, Robert Mitchum, Freddie Steele, Wally Cassell, Jimmy Lloyd. Meredith is superb as war correspondent Ernie Pyle living with Yank soldiers on front lines to report their stories; Mitchum's first outstanding film role as officer. Full title: ERNIE PYLE'S STORY OF G.I. JOE. ▼▶

Story of Gilbert and Sullivan, The SEE: **Great Gilbert and Sullivan, The**

Story of Gosta Berling, The SEE: **Atonement of Gosta Berling, The**

Story of Louis Pasteur, The (1936) 85m. ***½ D: William Dieterle. Paul Muni, Josephine Hutchinson, Anita Louise, Donald Woods, Fritz Leiber, Porter Hall, Akim Tamiroff. The achievements of the famous French scientist are chronicled in this engrossing film. Muni gives Oscar-winning performance; writers Sheridan Gibney and Pierre Collings also won. ▼▶

Story of Mankind, The (1957) C-100m. ** D: Irwin Allen. Ronald Colman, Cedric Hardwicke, Vincent Price; guest stars Hedy Lamarr, Groucho, Harpo, Chico Marx, Virginia Mayo, Agnes Moorehead, Francis X. Bushman, Charles Coburn, Marie Windsor, John Carradine, Dennis Hopper. Ambitious in concept, laughable in juvenile results. Henrik Van Loon book of highlights of man's history becomes string of clichéd costume episodes, badly cast, and packed with stock footage; the Marxes don't even appear together! Colman's last film.▶

Story of Molly X, The (1949) 82m. **½ D: Crane Wilbur. June Havoc, John Russell, Dorothy Hart, Connie Gilchrist, Cathy Lewis, Charles McGraw, Richard Egan, Isabel Jewell, Hal March. Havoc is earnest as the title character, a gang leader's widow who takes over for her deceased mate. What will happen after she lands in the slammer?

Story of Robin Hood and His Merrie Men, The (1952) C-83m. *** D: Ken Annakin. Richard Todd, Joan Rice, Peter Finch, James Hayter, James Robertson Justice, Martita Hunt, Hubert Gregg, Michael Hordern. Zesty, colorful retelling of the familiar story, filmed in England by Walt Disney with excellent cast. Not as personality oriented as other versions, but just as good in its own way. ▼▶

Story of Ruth, The (1960) C-132m. **½ D: Henry Koster. Elana Eden, Stuart Whitman, Tom Tryon, Peggy Wood, Viveca Lindfors, Jeff Morrow. Static biblical non-epic retelling story of woman renouncing her "gods" when she discovers true faith. CinemaScope. ▼▶

Story of Seabiscuit, The (1949) C-93m. ** D: David Butler. Shirley Temple, Barry Fitzgerald, Lon McCallister, Rosemary DeCamp, Donald MacBride, Pierre Watkin. Technicolor hokum with Fitzgerald as the toora-loora trainer who convinces Charles S. Howard (Watkin) that the title horse has real possibilities. Temple is Fitzgerald's niece, whose brother was killed in a racing accident. Never a great film, this is now rendered meaningless (if not downright ludicrous) by Laura Hillenbrand's book and the 2003 adaptation, SEABISCUIT. ▼▶

Story of Temple Drake, The (1933) 72m. ***½ D: Stephen Roberts. Miriam Hopkins, William Gargan, Jack La Rue, Sir Guy Standing, Florence Eldridge, Irving Pichel, Jobyna Howland, William Collier, Jr., Elizabeth Patterson, Louise Beavers. Flirtatious Southern belle Hopkins gets more than she bargained for one stormy night after a car wreck. This sizzling pre-Code adaptation of William Faulkner's *Sanctuary* is memorable for La Rue's stone-cold performance as Trigger, a sadistic thug. Highly controversial in its day. Watch for John Carradine as a courtroom spectator. Remade as SANCTUARY in 1961.

Story of the Last Chrysanthemum, The (1939-Japanese) 115m. ***½ D: Kenji Mizoguchi. Shôtarô Hanayagi, Kakuko Mori, Gonjurô Kawarazaki, Kôkichi Takada, Ryôtarô Kawanami. Brilliantly directed film about a young failed Kabuki actor who marries his family maid and leaves home to become successful, which happens after years of struggle through the sacrifices of his wife. Shot in extended, poetic takes, film is long but extremely accomplished. Aka THE STORY OF THE LATE CHRYSANTHEMUMS. ▼

Story of the Late Chrysanthemums, The SEE: **Story of the Last Chrysanthemum, The**

Story of Three Loves, The (1953) C-122m. *** D: Vincente Minnelli, Gottfried Reinhardt. Pier Angeli, Moira Shearer, Ethel Barrymore, Kirk Douglas, Farley Granger, Leslie Caron, James Mason, Agnes Moorehead, Zsa Zsa Gabor. Bittersweet trio of love stories, told as flashbacks involving passengers on ocean liner.▶

Story of Vernon and Irene Castle, The (1939) 93m. *** D: H. C. Potter. Fred Astaire, Ginger Rogers, Edna May Oliver, Walter Brennan, Lew Fields. Fred and Ginger take an unusual turn, downplaying their usual breezy comedy to portray America's hugely popular early-20th-century husband-and-wife dance team. Many fine period dance numbers and songs. This was the last Astaire-Rogers film until THE BARKLEYS OF BROADWAY ten years later. Incidentally, that's young Marge Champion (then known as Marjorie Belcher) as Irene's girlfriend. ▼▶

Story of Will Rogers, The (1952) C-109m. *** D: Michael Curtiz. Will Rogers, Jr., Jane Wyman, Carl Benton Reid, James Gleason, Mary Wickes, Eddie Cantor. One of few show biz biographies that rings true, with

Rogers Jr. faithfully portraying his father, rodeo star turned humorist; Wyman is his loving wife, Cantor appears as himself. ◗

Story on Page One, The (1959) 123m. ******* D: Clifford Odets. Rita Hayworth, Anthony Franciosa, Gig Young, Mildred Dunnock, Hugh Griffith, Sanford Meisner, Robert Burton. Lovers Hayworth and Young are accused of killing Rita's husband, hire Franciosa to represent them in court. Odets' stark film has high tension and sincere performances, although Dunnock's Mama portrayal is a bit much. CinemaScope.

Stowaway (1936) 86m. ****½** D: William A. Seiter. Robert Young, Alice Faye, Shirley Temple, Eugene Pallette, Helen Westley, Arthur Treacher. Predictable yet engaging shipboard story with Faye and Young romancing, Temple the incurably curious child. Shirley even speaks Chinese! Also shown in computer-colored version. ▼◗

Stowaway Girl (1957-British) 87m. ****½** D: Guy Hamilton. Trevor Howard, Elsa Martinelli, Pedro Armendariz, Donald Pleasence, Warren Mitchell. Trim, sensible romancer of middle-aged captain Howard's infatuation with Martinelli, who hid aboard his ship. Originally titled MANUELA.

Straight Is the Way (1934) 59m. ****½** D: Paul Sloane. Franchot Tone, May Robson, Karen Morley, Gladys George, Nat Pendleton, Jack La Rue, C. Henry Gordon. Film version of a play called *Four Walls* lives up to its stage title with a set-bound, pat story of ex-con Tone returning to his mother and friends in Jewish section of N.Y.C., choosing between two sides of the law. Tone as conflicted tough guy fails to impress. And that repetitious score—oy! Previously filmed in 1928.

Straight Place and Show (1938) 68m. ****** D: David Butler. The Ritz Brothers, Richard Arlen, Ethel Merman, Phyllis Brooks, George Barbier, Sidney Blackmer. The Ritzes help socialite Brooks enter her horse in a steeplechase race in this forgettable farce that only slows down for a couple of forgettable song numbers by Merman. Based on play *Saratoga Chips* by Damon Runyon and Irving Caesar. Keep an eye out for Willie Best and Lon Chaney, Jr. ◗

Strait-Jacket (1964) 89m. ****½** D: William Castle. Joan Crawford, Diane Baker, Leif Erickson, Anthony Hayes, Howard St. John, Rochelle Hudson, George Kennedy. Crawford served 20 years for axe murders; now, living peacefully with daughter Baker, murders start again and she's suspected. Crawford's strong portrayal makes this one of best in the BABY JANE genre of older-star shockers; script by Robert Bloch. The first person to be decapitated is Lee Majors, in his unbilled screen debut. And stick around to see the Columbia Pictures logo at the end. ▼◗●

Stranded (1935) 76m. ****** D: Frank Borzage.

Kay Francis, George Brent, Patricia Ellis, Donald Woods, Robert Barrat, Barton MacLane. Francis is a travelers' aid worker solving everybody's problems, tangling with band of racketeers. ◗

Strange Adventure, A (1932) 60m. ****** D: Phil Whitman. Regis Toomey, June Clyde, Lucille La Verne, Jason Robards, William V. Mong. CAT AND THE CANARY–style skullduggery as family and acquaintances of a much-hated millionaire gather to hear him reveal the contents of his will. Resolutely ordinary and yet still recommended for fans of hooded-killer-roams-the-halls cheapies. Dwight Frye and Fred "Snowflake" Toones have minor roles as suspect and servant, respectively. Aka THE WAYNE MURDER CASE.

Strange Adventure, A (1956) 70m. ***½** D: William Witney. Joan Evans, Ben Cooper, Marla English, Jan Merlin, Nick Adams. Armored-car thieves hold hostages in High Sierras hideout. Familiar but functional melodramatics.

Strange Affair of Uncle Harry, The (1945) 80m. ******* D: Robert Siodmak. George Sanders, Geraldine Fitzgerald, Ella Raines, Sara Allgood, Moyna MacGill, Samuel S. Hinds. Engrossing melodrama about mild-mannered Sanders falling in love, but unable to break from grip of domineering sister (Fitzgerald). Vivid, if not always believable, with unfortunate ending demanded by 1940s censorship. Produced by longtime Hitchcock associate Joan Harrison. Originally titled UNCLE HARRY. ▼◗

Strange Affection (1957-British) 84m. ****** D: Wolf Rilla. Richard Attenborough, Colin Petersen, Jill Adams, Terence Morgan. A teacher decides to take in a boy who's been accused of murdering his drunkard father. Decent British drama. Original British title: THE SCAMP.

Strange Bargain (1949) 68m. ****½** D: Will Price. Martha Scott, Jeffrey Lynn, Henry (Harry) Morgan, Katherine Emery, Richard Gaines, Henry O'Neill, Walter Sande. Adequate mystery yarn about a bookkeeper (Lynn), who's framed for murder; Scott is his devoted wife, Morgan the police lieutenant on the case. This star trio reprised their roles 38 years later for a sequel, *Strangest of Bargains*, which aired as an episode of the *Murder, She Wrote* TV series. ▼◗

Strange Bedfellows (1965) C-98m. ****½** D: Melvin Frank. Rock Hudson, Gina Lollobrigida, Gig Young, Terry-Thomas, Nancy Kulp. Hudson ambles through another marital mix-up comedy, this one with fiery Gina and lots of slapstick. Mild entertainment; filmed in London. ▼◗

Strange Cargo (1940) 113m. ******* D: Frank Borzage. Joan Crawford, Clark Gable, Ian Hunter, Peter Lorre, Albert Dekker, Paul Lukas, Eduardo Ciannelli. Intriguing allegorical film of prisoners escaping from

Devil's Island with Christ-like presence of Hunter. Not for all tastes, but there are fine, realistic performances and flavorful Franz Waxman score.▼▌

Strange Case of Doctor Rx, The (1942) **66m.** ** D: William Nigh. Patric Knowles, Lionel Atwill, Anne Gwynne, Mona Barrie, Shemp Howard, Samuel S. Hinds, Paul Cavanagh, Mantan Moreland. Fast-paced whodunit about hunt for mysterious title character, who murders criminals gotten off by unscrupulous attorney. Not particularly puzzling, but good cast helps.▌

Strange Case of Madeleine SEE: **Madeleine** (1950)

Strange Confession SEE: **Impostor, The**

Strange Confession (1945) **62m.** ** D: John Hoffman. Lon Chaney (Jr.), Brenda Joyce, J. Carrol Naish, Milburn Stone, Lloyd Bridges, Addison Richards, Mary Gordon. *Inner Sanctum* mystery is told in flashback as tortured Chaney recounts his experiences as a selfless research chemist whose work is exploited by drug manufacturer Naish. Slick B movie holds your interest but leads to a disappointing finale. Remake of THE MAN WHO CLAIMED HIS HEAD.▼▌

Strange Death of Adolf Hitler, The (1943) **72m.** ** D: James Hogan. Ludwig Donath, Gale Sondergaard, George Dolenz, Fritz Kortner, Ludwig Stossel, William Trenk, Merrill Rodin. During WW2, a minor German officer is unwillingly transformed via plastic surgery into Hitler's double. Dated, forgettable melodrama. Costar Kortner was one of the film's writers.

Strange Door, The (1951) **81m.** *½ D: Joseph Pevney. Charles Laughton, Boris Karloff, Sally Forrest, Richard Stapley, Michael Pate, Alan Napier, Paul Cavanagh. Laughton camps it up in this heavy-handed, obvious adaptation of a Robert Louis Stevenson story about a sadistic squire and his nefarious schemes. Karloff has a thankless role as a servant named Voltan.▼●

Strange Fascination (1952) **80m.** ** D: Hugo Haas. Hugo Haas, Cleo Moore, Mona Barrie, Rick Vallin, Karen Sharpe. A concert pianist's career—and luck—fall apart because of his obsessive love for a young blonde. Starts interestingly but descends into hollow melodrama. Produced, directed, and written by Haas.

Strange Gamble (1948) **61m.** *½ D: George Archainbaud. William Boyd, Andy Clyde, Rand Brooks, Elaine Riley, James Craven, Robert B. Williams. The Bar 20 threesome cracks a counterfeiting ring for the government. Presence of lovely Riley and Lone Pine exteriors help 66th and final Hopalong Cassidy feature film, but not nearly enough. Disappointing end of the trail for fine B-Western series. Reissued as STAMPEDE FURY.▼▌

Strange Holiday (1942) **62m.** ** D: Arch

Oboler. Claude Rains, Bobbie Stebbins, Barbara Bates, Paul Hilton, Tommy Cook, Martin Kosleck. Adaptation of Oboler's radio play about businessman who returns from vacation to find U.S. democracy overthrown. Unreleased until 1946. This was originally sponsored by General Motors and intended to be shown only to its employees!

Strange Illusion (1945) **80m.** ** D: Edgar G. Ulmer. James Lydon, Sally Eilers, Warren William, Regis Toomey. Intriguing but unconvincing melodrama, a B-movie update of *Hamlet*, with teenaged Lydon having doubts about smooth-talker (William) who's wooing widowed mother (Eilers). Typically bizarre Ulmer touches in this low-budget quickie.▼▌

Strange Impersonation (1946) **68m.** *** D: Anthony Mann. Brenda Marshall, William Gargan, Hillary Brooke, George Chandler, Ruth Ford, H. B. Warner, Lyle Talbot. Marshall gives a first-rate performance in this grade-B film noir about a research scientist whose face is horribly disfigured in a so-called accident. Plastic surgery enables her to unravel the mystery behind that incident and seek revenge. Perhaps the definitive Hillary Brooke movie.▼▌

Strange Interlude (1932) **110m.** *** D: Robert Z. Leonard. Norma Shearer, Clark Gable, May Robson, Maureen O'Sullivan, Robert Young, Ralph Morgan, Henry B. Walthall, Mary Alden. Talky Eugene O'Neill play becomes marathon of inner thoughts revealed only to audience in chronicle of Gable, Shearer, et al. growing old without resolving their problems. Engrossing film, with Shearer at her radiant best.▼▌

Strange Intruder (1956) **82m.** ** D: Irving Rapper. Edmund Purdom, Ida Lupino, Ann Harding, Jacques Bergerac, Gloria Talbott, Carl Benton Reid, Douglas Kennedy, Donald Murphy. Will catastrophe ensue when shell-shocked Korean War vet/ex-POW Purdom visits the family of his fallen comrade? So-so psychological drama starts off well, then becomes slow and talky.

Strange Justice (1932) **68m.** ** D: Victor Schertzinger. Marian Marsh, Reginald Denny, Richard Bennett, Norman Foster, Irving Pichel, Nydia Westman, Geneva Mitchell, Walter Brennan. Not so strange at all; pretty predictable stuff. Despicable Pichel blackmails his boss, wealthy Denny, who's been embezzling funds from his bank, and frames chauffeur Foster. Bennett is fun to watch as a blarney-filled, tousle-haired lawyer.

Strange Lady in Town (1955) **C-112m.** **½ D: Mervyn LeRoy. Greer Garson, Dana Andrews, Cameron Mitchell, Lois Smith, Walter Hampden, Nick Adams. Unsuccessful grand-scale soaper-Western. Set in 1880s, Garson is the doctor coming to Santa Fe, involved with Andrews, perplexed by outlaw brother Mitchell. CinemaScope.▌

Strange Love of Martha Ivers, The (1946) **116m.** ******* D: Lewis Milestone. Barbara Stanwyck, Kirk Douglas, Lizabeth Scott, Van Heflin, Judith Anderson, Darryl Hickman. Gripping melodrama, with Stanwyck bound to her husband by crime she committed long ago. Douglas' film debut.▼◑❿

Strange Love of Molly Louvain, The (1932) **72m.** ****½** D: Michael Curtiz. Ann Dvorak, Lee Tracy, Richard Cromwell, Guy Kibbee, Leslie Fenton, Frank McHugh, Evalyn Knapp, Charles Middleton. Seamy, overplotted pre-Code melodrama about unwed mother Dvorak and the various bad eggs she has a habit of falling for. Typically fast-paced Warner Bros. yarn, though more unpleasant than most.▼❿

Strange Mr. Gregory, The (1946) **63m.** ****** D: Phil Rosen. Edmund Lowe, Jean Rogers, Don Douglas, Marjorie Hoshelle, Robert Emmett Keane. Low-budget drama of magician who goes to any length to win love of married woman.❿

Strange One, The (1957) **100m.** ******* D: Jack Garfein. Ben Gazzara, George Peppard, Pat Hingle, Mark Richman, Geoffrey Horne, James Olson. Bizarre military school account of far-out Gazzara's peculiar hold over various underclassmen. Remarkably frank version of Calder Willingham's *End as a Man*, scripted by the author; also filmed as SORORITY GIRL. Film debuts of Gazzara and Peppard. Released on DVD in 2009 with added footage that had been deleted prior to the theatrical release.❿

Strange Ones, The SEE: **Les Enfants Terribles**

Stranger, The (1946) **95m.** ******* D: Orson Welles. Orson Welles, Loretta Young, Edward G. Robinson, Richard Long, Martha Wentworth. Fine study of escaped Nazi war criminal Welles sedately living in small Connecticut town, about to marry unsuspecting Young. Robinson nicely understates role as federal agent out to get him. Also shown in computer-colored version.▼◑❿

Stranger at My Door (1956) **85m.** ****½** D: William Witney. Macdonald Carey, Patricia Medina, Skip Homeier, Louis Jean Heydt, Stephen Wootton, Slim Pickens. Offbeat Western about clergyman jeopardizing his family's safety when he tries to reform an outlaw. Solid performances in this original script by Barry Shipman. Highlighted by some truly remarkable scenes with an untamed horse.❿

Stranger Came Home, A SEE: **Unholy Four, The**

Stranger From Venus SEE: **Immediate Disaster**

Stranger in Between (1952-British) **84m.** ******* D: Charles Crichton. Dirk Bogarde, Elizabeth Sellars, Kay Walsh, Jon Whiteley, Geoffrey Keen. Modest but very entertaining film about orphan boy who grows to understand murderer as both flee police

in England. Warm, compassionate performances. Original British title: HUNTED.❿

Stranger in My Arms, A (1959) **88m.** ****½** D: Helmut Kautner. June Allyson, Jeff Chandler, Sandra Dee, Charles Coburn, Mary Astor, Peter Graves, Conrad Nagel. Undemanding old-fashioned weeper, based on Robert Wilder novel. Chandler falls in love with Allyson, wife of Air Force buddy killed in Korean War. Astor is the domineering mother-in-law. Typical Ross Hunter sudser. CinemaScope.

Stranger in Town, A (1943) **67m.** ******* D: Roy Rowland. Frank Morgan, Richard Carlson, Jean Rogers, Robert Barrat, Porter Hall, Chill Wills, Donald MacBride, John Hodiak. Enjoyable Capra-esque tale about a Supreme Court justice (Morgan) who gets mixed up in a small town's corrupt politics while on a fishing vacation. Highly amusing second feature that skillfully satirizes serious issues and features a gang of crooked politicos worthy of a Preston Sturges film.❿

Stranger on Horseback (1955) **C-66m.** ****½** D: Jacques Tourneur. Joel McCrea, Miroslava, Kevin McCarthy, John McIntire, John Carradine, Nancy Gates, Emile Meyer, Robert Cornthwaite, Roy Roberts. Straight-arrow circuit court judge McCrea arrives in a small town controlled by McIntire, whose wastrel son McCarthy has gotten away with murder—until now. Well made, well acted, and builds up to an exciting shootout showdown, but ends much too abruptly. Based on a Louis L'Amour story. Filmed in Sedona, Arizona.❿

Stranger on the Prowl (1952-Italian) **82m.** ****½** D: Andrea Forzano (Joseph Losey). Paul Muni, Vittorio Manunta, Joan Lorring, Luisa Rossi, Aldo Silvani. Sullen drifter (Muni) forms a bond with a poor boy who has stolen a bottle of milk. Muni's underwritten character is a liability, but the influence of neorealism (and Henri Alekan's fluid camerawork) make this an interesting curio. Losey's first film after leaving the U.S., made with blacklisted screenwriter Ben Barzman.❿

Stranger on the Third Floor (1940) **64m.** ******* D: Boris Ingster. Peter Lorre, John McGuire, Margaret Tallichet, Charles Waldron, Elisha Cook, Jr. Reporter's testimony has convicted Cook in brutal murder case, but the newspaperman has second thoughts. Excellent sleeper, with one nightmare montage that's a knockout.▼◑❿

Strangers (1953-Italian) **97m.** ******* D: Roberto Rossellini. Ingrid Bergman, George Sanders, Paul Muller, Maria Mauban, Natalia Ray. Beautiful, meditative tale of married couple Bergman and Sanders trying to reconcile their faltering relationship while driving through Italy. Received dreadful reviews when first released, but was rediscovered (and labelled a masterpiece) by French filmmakers and critics. Video titles: VOYAGE IN ITALY and VOYAGE TO ITALY, running 83m.▼

Stranger's Hand, The (1954-British) 86m. ******* D: Mario Soldati. Trevor Howard, Alida Valli, Richard Basehart, Eduardo Ciannelli, Richard O'Sullivan, Stephen Murray. British espionage officer, going to Venice to meet schoolboy son, disappears. Intriguing suspense yarn, based on Graham Greene story, with top-notch performances. Filmed in Italy.

Strangers in Love (1932) 76m. ****** D: Lothar Mendes. Kay Francis, Fredric March, Stuart Erwin, Juliette Compton, Sidney Toler, George Barbier. Mild comedy; Francis is secretary who loves March, weakling playboy forced to impersonate twin brother to expose family fraud.▼

Strangers in the Night (1944) 56m. ****½** D: Anthony Mann. William Terry, Virginia Grey, Helene Thimig, Edith Barrett, Anne O'Neal. An eccentric old woman harbors a dark secret in her hilltop home on the California coast, and lures a wounded soldier (just back from combat) there on the promise of meeting her beautiful daughter. Intriguing story idea gets silly by the end, but it's still a pretty good B, full of the shadowy staging favored by young director Mann.◗

Strangers May Kiss (1931) 85m. ****** D: George Fitzmaurice. Norma Shearer, Robert Montgomery, Neil Hamilton, Marjorie Rambeau, Jed Prouty, Hale Hamilton, Henry Armetta, Irene Rich. Polished but ridiculous pre-Code soaper of Shearer in love with—and fooling herself into trusting—unreliable hypocrite Neil Hamilton. Film's conclusion is not to be believed. Montgomery is fine as Shearer's pal; young Ray Milland has a couple of lines as one of her admirers.◗

Strangers on a Train (1951) 101m. ******** D: Alfred Hitchcock. Farley Granger, Ruth Roman, Robert Walker, Leo G. Carroll, Patricia Hitchcock, Marion Lorne. Walker gives his finest performance as psychopath involved with tennis star Granger in "exchange murders." Lorne is unforgettable as doting mother; so is merry-go-round climax. First-class Hitchcock, based on a Patricia Highsmith novel and coscripted by Raymond Chandler. Remade as ONCE YOU KISS A STRANGER and the inspiration for THROW MOMMA FROM THE TRAIN. British version of film, now available, runs almost two minutes longer, has a different ending and franker dialogue in the first scene where Granger and Walker meet.▼◗❶

Stranger's Return, The (1933) 89m. *****½** D: King Vidor. Lionel Barrymore, Miriam Hopkins, Franchot Tone, Stuart Erwin, Irene Hervey, Beulah Bondi. A young woman, recently separated from her husband, leaves the city to stay at her grandfather's farm. Here she finds her roots, as well as a kindred spirit in neighboring farmer Tone, a college graduate. Why this rich, mature, beautifully made film isn't better known is a mystery. Phil Stong helped adapt his own novel for director Vidor.

Strangers When We Meet (1960) C-117m. ****½** D: Richard Quine. Kirk Douglas, Kim Novak, Ernie Kovacs, Barbara Rush, Walter Matthau, Virginia Bruce, Kent Smith. Expensive soaper with attractive stars; both are married, but fall in love with each other. Script by Evan Hunter, from his novel. CinemaScope.▼❶

Stranger Wore a Gun, The (1953) C-83m. ****** D: Andre De Toth. Randolph Scott, Claire Trevor, Joan Weldon, George Macready, Alfonso Bedoya, Lee Marvin, Ernest Borgnine, Pierre Watkin, Roscoe Ates. Scott works as a spy for Quantrill's Raiders but severs his ties after they murder and plunder their way through Lawrence, Kansas; he soon discovers that it won't be easy to escape his past. Poorly developed story relies on a sturdy cast to get by. Bedoya is spectacularly unfunny as a comic-relief villain. One of the first 3-D films, full of action aimed directly at the camera.▼❶

Strange Skirts SEE: **When Ladies Meet** (1941)

Strange Woman, The (1946) 100m. ****½** D: Edgar G. Ulmer. Hedy Lamarr, George Sanders, Louis Hayward, Gene Lockhart, Hillary Brooke. Lamarr offers one of her best performances as a shrewish young woman in 19th-century Maine who affects the lives of three very different men. Nicely directed by Ulmer; a rare instance in which he was allowed a Grade-A cast.▼❶

Strange World of Planet X, The SEE: **Cosmic Monster, The**

Strangler, The (1964) 89m. ******* D: Burt Topper. Victor Buono, David McLean, Ellen Corby, Jeanne Bates, Wally Campo, James (B.) Sikking. Buono gives fine performance as mother-dominated mad killer who strangles women and pitches a city into frenzy. Inspired by the real-life Boston Strangler killings.▼❶

Strangler of the Swamp (1946) 59m. ****½** D: Frank Wisbar. Rosemary La Planche, Robert Barrat, Blake Edwards, Charles Middleton, Effie Parnell, Nolan Leary. The ghost of wrongly lynched Middleton haunts a swamp near a hand-powered ferry, strangling his killers and their descendants. La Planche takes over the ferry when her grandfather is killed and falls for local boy Edwards, but the strangler threatens their lives. Moody, atmospheric, full of fog, it's far more cinematic than other horror films from bargain-basement PRC studio but still suffers from a low budget as well as a lethargic pace. Remake of Wisbar's more elaborate German film FAØHRMAN MARIA (1936).▼◗

Strangler's Morgue SEE: **Crimes of Stephen Hawke, The**

Stranglers of Bombay, The (1960-British) **81m.** **½ D: Terence Fisher. Andrew Cruickshank, Marne Maitland, Guy Rolfe, Paul Stassino, Jan Holden. Grisly story of fanatical Indian cult attempting to drive British from trading station. Good cast helped by tense direction. Megascope.▌

Strategic Air Command (1955) **C-114m.** **½ D: Anthony Mann. James Stewart, June Allyson, Frank Lovejoy, Barry Sullivan, Bruce Bennett, Rosemary DeCamp. Film only gets off the ground when Stewart does, as baseball player recalled to air force duty; Allyson is his sugary wife. VistaVision.▼●

Stratton Story, The (1949) **106m.** ***½ D: Sam Wood. James Stewart, June Allyson, Frank Morgan, Agnes Moorehead, Bill Williams, Jimmy Dykes, Bill Dickey. Stewart is fine as Monty Stratton, the baseball player whose loss of one leg did not halt his career; well played by good cast, including ballplayers Dykes and Dickey. Oscar winner for story (Douglas Morrow); screenplay by Morrow and Guy Trosper. Also shown in computer-colored version.▼▌

Strauss's Great Waltz SEE: **Waltzes From Vienna**

Strawberry Blonde, The (1941) **97m.** *** D: Raoul Walsh. James Cagney, Olivia de Havilland, Rita Hayworth, Alan Hale, Jack Carson, George Tobias, Una O'Connor, George Reeves. Cagney's dynamic in entertaining turn-of-the-20th-century story of dentist infatuated with gold digger Hayworth, and his subsequent marriage to de Havilland. Remade in 1948 as ONE SUNDAY AFTERNOON, the title of the 1933 Gary Cooper film of which *this* is a remake.▼▌

Strawberry Roan, The (1948) **C-76m.** *** D: John English. Gene Autry, Gloria Henry, Jack Holt, Dick Jones, Pat Buttram, Rufe Davis, Eddy Waller. Gene's first Cinecolor Western is the gentle story of Champion, a wild horse Gene captures on the range, and his attempts to escape the wrath of rancher Holt, whose son (Jones) was crippled attempting to break the animal. Future sidekick Buttram makes his first appearance in an Autry film. Gene sings the title song.▌

Stray Dog (1949-Japanese) **122m.** **** D: Akira Kurosawa. Toshiro Mifune, Takashi Shimura, Keiko Awaji. Classic Japanese film noir, most effective as a look at life in post-WW2 Tokyo. Mifune does well as a detective whose gun is stolen; he sets out on an odyssey to reclaim his weapon, and to seek out a killer. Although not as well known as RASHOMON, this film is just as important.▼●

Street Angel (1928) **102m.** *** D: Frank Borzage. Janet Gaynor, Charles Farrell, Guido Trento, Natalie Kingston, Henry Armetta. Italian girl fleeing from police joins traveling circus, meets and falls in love with young painter who finds her an inspiration. Follow-up to 7TH HEAVEN is actually much better; a delicate, beautifully photographed silent film. Gaynor won a Best Actress Oscar (shared for her performances in 7TH HEAVEN and SUNRISE).▼▌

Streetcar Named Desire, A (1951) **122m.** **** D: Elia Kazan. Marlon Brando, Vivien Leigh, Kim Hunter, Karl Malden. Stunning production of Tennessee Williams' play, with Brando as the animalistic Stanley Kowalski and Leigh as his wistful, neurotic sister-in-law, Blanche Dubois, pressed together in a grim New Orleans tenement. Oscars went to Leigh, Hunter, and Malden for their flawless performances, as well as for the art direction-set decoration—but it's Brando who left an indelible mark on audiences. Highly influential jazz score by Alex North. Rereleased in 1993 with 4m. of censored footage, playing up sexual tension between Blanche and Stanley, and Stella's carnal attraction to her husband. Remade twice for TV.▼●▌

Street Corner SEE: **Both Sides of the Law**

Street of Chance (1930) **75m.** **½ D: John Cromwell. William Powell, Jean Arthur, Kay Francis, Regis Toomey, Stanley Fields, Brooks Benedict, Betty Francisco. Powell is a big-time New York gambler who makes the mistake of cheating in order to dissuade his kid brother Toomey from following in his footsteps. Zesty gangster yarn with a winning cast, allegedly based on the exploits of notorious 1920s gambling king Arnold Rothstein. Director Cromwell has a cameo.

Street of Chance (1942) **74m.** **½ D: Jack Hively. Burgess Meredith, Claire Trevor, Sheldon Leonard, Frieda Inescort, Jerome Cowan, Louise Platt, Adeline De Walt Reynolds. Early, prototypical film noir from a Cornell Woolrich story about a man who suffers from amnesia and tries to find clues to his former identity. The opening sequences are dynamite.

Street of Shadows SEE: **Shadow Man, The**

Street of Shame (1956-Japanese) **96m.** ***½ D: Kenji Mizoguchi. Machiko Kyô, Ayako Wakao, Aiko Mimasu, Michiyo Kogure. The stories of various prostitutes in Dreamland, a Tokyo brothel, are sensitively handled in Mizoguchi's last completed film. Kyô is particularly memorable as a tough, cynical lady of the night; her scene with her father is a highlight.▼▌

Street of Sorrow, The SEE: **Joyless Street, The**

Street Scene (1931) **80m.** ***½ D: King Vidor. Sylvia Sidney, William Collier, Jr., David Landau, Estelle Taylor, Walter Miller, Beulah Bondi. Heartbreakingly realistic account of life in N.Y.C. tenements, and younger generation's desperation to get out. Elmer Rice's Pulitzer Prize–winning play (adapted by him) enhanced by fine performances, George Barnes' striking camerawork, Alfred Newman's classic music score. ▼▶

Streets of Laredo (1949) **C-92m.** ** D: Leslie Fenton. William Holden, Macdonald Carey, Mona Freeman, William Bendix, Stanley Ridges, Alfonso Bedoya. Muddled Western of outlaws Carey, Holden, and Bendix, and how the latter two come to be Texas Rangers; in fact, this is a remake of THE TEXAS RANGERS. Fans of THE TREASURE OF THE SIERRA MADRE will appreciate Bedoya's characterization.

Streets of New York (1939) **73m.** **½ D: William Nigh. Jackie Cooper, Martin Spellman, Marjorie Reynolds, Dick Purcell, George Cleveland, George Irving. Good programmer of an upright young man (Cooper) who admires Abraham Lincoln and must overcome adversity on the streets of N.Y.C.'s Hell's Kitchen. Aka THE ABE LINCOLN OF NINTH AVENUE.

Street With No Name, The (1948) **91m.** *** D: William Keighley. Mark Stevens, Richard Widmark, Lloyd Nolan, Barbara Lawrence, Ed Begley, Donald Buka. Fine movie based on actual F.B.I. case of agent uncovering head of city mob. Suspense well handled. Remade as HOUSE OF BAMBOO. ▼▶

Strictly Dishonorable (1931) **91m.** *** D: John M. Stahl. Paul Lukas, Sidney Fox, Lewis Stone, George Meeker, William Ricciardi, Sidney Toler, Carlo Schipa. Innocent Southerner (Fox) breaks up with her obnoxious Northern fiancé (Meeker) at a N.Y.C. speakeasy and goes home with a womanizing Italian opera singer (Lukas), with whom she falls madly in love. First, and faithful, screen adaptation of Preston Sturges' risqué Broadway hit is talky but never static, with charming performances and fluid direction. Funny to see Toler as a cop doing a thick Irish brogue. Remade in 1951.

Strictly Dishonorable (1951) **86m.** ** D: Melvin Frank, Norman Panama. Ezio Pinza, Janet Leigh, Millard Mitchell, Gale Robbins. Tame shenanigans of opera star Pinza marrying Leigh to save her reputation. Based on the Preston Sturges play, previously filmed in 1931.

Strictly in the Groove (1942) **60m.** **½ D: Vernon Keays. Mary Healy, Richard Davies, Leon Errol, Shemp Howard, Grace McDonald, Ozzie Nelson, Franklin Pangborn, Russell Hicks, Martha Tilton, Eddie Johnson, Jimmie Davis, Tim Ryan, Jimmy Wakely Trio, Spade Cooley, Leo Diamond, The Dinning Sisters. Davies defies his father by playing with a swing band and trying to save a failing Arizona hotel. Lively B musical with plenty of jive talk, musical numbers, specialty acts, and comedy from Errol, Howard, and Ryan.

Strike (1924-Russian) **73m.** ***½ D: Sergei Eisenstein. Grigori Alexandrov, Maxim Strauch, Mikhail Gomarov, Alexander Antonov, Judith Glizer. Eisenstein's debut feature is a still-powerful, vivid account of a 1912 factory workers strike in Czarist Russia and its violent suppression. An appropriate prelude to POTEMKIN; some prints run 82m. ▼▶

Strike Me Pink (1936) **100m.** *½ D: Norman Taurog. Eddie Cantor, Ethel Merman, Sally Eilers, Parkyakarkus, William Frawley, Brian Donlevy. One of Cantor's worst films, built around his run-in with racketeers at amusement park which he manages. Good slapstick chase finale, forgettable music numbers. ▼▶▶

Strike Up the Band (1940) **120m.** **½ D: Busby Berkeley. Mickey Rooney, Judy Garland, Paul Whiteman, June Preisser, William Tracy, Larry Nunn, Margaret Early, Ann Shoemaker. Rooney is leader of high school band hoping to compete in Paul Whiteman's nationwide radio contest. Typical Mickey-Judy fare, with good songs: "Our Love Affair" and an extended finale featuring the Gershwins' title tune. George Pal contributes a unique segment featuring a symphony performed by animated pieces of fruit (an idea apparently hatched by Vincente Minnelli). ▼▶▶

Strip, The (1951) **85m.** ** D: Leslie Kardos. Mickey Rooney, Sally Forrest, William Demarest, James Craig, Kay Brown, Louis Armstrong and His Orchestra, Tommy Rettig, Monica Lewis, Vic Damone. Rooney gives sincere performance as jazz drummer who becomes involved with gangster Craig while falling for wannabe movie actress Forrest. Routine film enlivened by great music of Armstrong (and band members Barney Bigard, Earl "Fatha" Hines, and Jack Teagarden).

Stripper, The (1963) **95m.** **½ D: Franklin Schaffner. Joanne Woodward, Richard Beymer, Claire Trevor, Carol Lynley, Robert Webber, Gypsy Rose Lee, Louis Nye, Michael J. Pollard. Aging stripper falls in love with teen-age boy in this OK filmization of William Inge's play A Loss of Roses. Director Schaffner's first movie. CinemaScope. ▼

Stromboli (1949-Italian) **81m.** *½ D: Roberto Rossellini. Ingrid Bergman, Mario Vitale, Renzo Cesana, Mario Sponza. Rambling dreariness with refugee Bergman marrying fisherman Vitale; even an erupting volcano doesn't jar this plodding film, which was boycotted in the U.S. because Bergman had left her husband (Petter Lindstrom) for Rossellini. Original 107m. version is now available, but is little improvement over U.S. release (which was edited by Alfred Werker and has a different ending). ▼

Stronger Than Desire (1939) **79m.** *** D: Leslie Fenton. Virginia Bruce, Walter Pidgeon, Lee Bowman, Ann Dvorak, Ilka Chase, Rita Johnson, Richard Lane, Ann Todd. Clever, engrossing drama involving ultra-busy lawyer Pidgeon, who neglects wife Bruce. As a result, they both find themselves susceptible to the persistent, amorous advances of others, resulting in complications... and disaster. Remake of EVELYN PRENTICE.▶

Stronghold (1951) 82m. *½ D: Steve Sekely. Veronica Lake, Zachary Scott, Arturo de Cordova, Rita Macedo. Pedestrian costumer set in 1860s, with Lake fleeing U.S. and becoming embroiled in Mexican revolution.▶

Strong Man, The (1926) 78m. *** D: Frank Capra. Harry Langdon, Priscilla Bonner, Gertrude Astor, Brooks Benedict, Arthur Thalasso, Robert McKim, William V. Mong. Baby-faced Langdon's best movie (and Capra's feature-film debut) casts him as a Belgian WW1 veteran who comes to America in search of the girl he corresponded with during the war. Many fine set pieces make this a memorable comedy; the star never fared as well again.▼O▶

Struggle, The (1931) 77m. **½ D: D. W. Griffith. Hal Skelly, Zita Johann, Evelyn Baldwin, Edna Hagan, Charlotte Wynters, Jackson Halliday. Griffith's final film as director is a somber drama chronicling the plight and fate of Skelly, an average Joe who is victimized by alcoholism and desperation. A notorious failure in its day, this was the nail in the coffin of Griffith's then-sagging career. Today it's a fascinating curio—and a reminder that THE LOST WEEKEND was not the first film to explore the ravages of alcoholism. Baldwin (who plays Skelly's sister) went on to become Griffith's second wife.▼▶

Student of Prague, The (1926-German) 95m. ***½ D: Henrik Galeen. Conrad Veidt, Werner Krauss, Agnes Esterhazy, Elizza La Porta, Ferdinand von Alten, Fritz Alberti, Sylvia Torf. Mephistophelean specter Krauss proffers a metaphysical platter of temptation to Faustian collegiate fencer Veidt. The prize is a buffet of wealth and women; the price, merely the mirror reflection of oneself. Then the gate to Hell slowly swings open.... Atmospheric chiaroscuro marks this eerie highlight of German expressionistic fantasy. Pretty cool, creepy movie. Filmed before in 1913, and again in 1935.▼▶

Student Prince, The (1954) C-107m. ** D: Richard Thorpe. Ann Blyth, Edmund Purdom, John Ericson, Louis Calhern, Edmund Gwenn. Romberg music, dubbed voice of Mario Lanza chief assets in venerable operetta about heir to throne sent to Heidelberg for one last fling, where he falls in love with barmaid Blyth. Filmed before (sans music) in 1919 and 1927. CinemaScope.▼O▶

Student Prince in Old Heidelberg, The (1927) 105m. **** D: Ernst Lubitsch. Ramon Novarro, Norma Shearer, Jean Hersholt, Gustav von Seyffertitz, Philippe de Lacy, Edgar Norton, George K. Arthur, Edythe Chapman. Silent version of Sigmund Romberg's famed operetta has youthful prince Novarro breaking out of his cloistered life—for the first time—and attending Heidelberg University, where he falls in love with a commoner, pretty barmaid Shearer. This is Lubitsch at his best, an absolute delight from start to finish, and truly the kind of charmer "they just don't make anymore." Also known as OLD HEIDELBERG. Previously filmed in 1919; remade (with music) in 1954.▼O

Student Tour (1934) 87m. *½ D: Charles F. Reisner. Jimmy Durante, Charles Butterworth, Maxine Doyle, Phil Regan, Florine McKinney, Betty Grable, Herman Brix (Bruce Bennett). Deservedly obscure MGM musical about college students on world tour with an incredibly clunky leading lady. Pretty bad, though it's fun to see young Grable, and the sight of coeds swimming in front of the Taj Mahal is nothing to sneeze at. Guest star Nelson Eddy sings silly Bolero-type number "The Carlo."

Studio Murder Mystery, The (1929) 63m. **½ D: Frank Tuttle. Neil Hamilton, Doris Hill, Warner Oland, Fredric March, Chester Conklin, Florence Eldridge, Eugene Pallette. There's no shortage of suspects when a philandering actor is murdered at a movie studio. Good cast and fascinating glimpses of the Paramount lot enhance this creaky early talkie.

Studs Lonigan (1960) 95m. **½ D: Irving Lerner. Christopher Knight, Frank Gorshin, Venetia Stevenson, Carolyn Craig, Jack Nicholson, Dick Foran. Interesting if not altogether successful adaptation of James T. Farrell's "notorious" novel about a restless, sexually active young man (Knight) in 1920s Chicago. Good period atmosphere, but script makes unfortunate compromises with 1960 taste and censorship. Nicholson is one of Studs' cronies; Foran is impressive as Studs' father. Scripted and produced by Philip Yordan. Basis for a 1979 TV miniseries.▼▶

Study in Scarlet, A (1933) 70m. **½ D: Edwin L. Marin. Reginald Owen, Anna May Wong, June Clyde, Alan Dinehart, John Warburton, Alan Mowbray, Warburton Gamble. Not-bad low-budget Sherlock Holmes outing (for which Owen wrote much of the dialogue), though it has virtually nothing to do with Conan Doyle story of the same name! Owen played Dr. Watson one year earlier in SHERLOCK HOLMES, while Mowbray, who's Inspector Lestrade here, turned up in the 1946 TERROR BY NIGHT.▼▶

Study in Terror, A (1965-British) C-94m. *** D: James Hill. John Neville, Donald Houston, Georgia Brown, John Fraser, Anthony Quayle, Barbara Windsor, Robert Morley, Cecil Parker, Frank Finlay, Kay Walsh, Judi Dench. Compact little thriller pits Sherlock Holmes against Jack the Ripper; violent, well paced, and well cast. For another version of Holmes vs. the Ripper, see MURDER BY DECREE.▼●▶

Stunt Pilot (1939) 62m. ** D: George Waggner. John Trent, Marjorie Reynolds, Milburn Stone, Jason Robards, Sr., Pat O'Malley. Not-bad "Tailspin Tommy" tale has him joining a movie studio as a flyer, encountering danger and murder.▼▶

Submarine (1928) 92m. *** D: Frank Capra. Jack Holt, Dorothy Revier, Ralph Graves, Clarence Burton, Arthur Rankin. First and best of the Capra-Holt-Graves action trilogy (FLIGHT and DIRIGIBLE followed). Graves and Holt are Navy buddies who fall for the same girl; when the former is trapped in a sub, the latter has to decide whether to rescue him. Familiar story, tautly presented, with excellent Joseph Walker photography. Silent with sound effects and music. Remade in 1937 as DEVIL'S PLAYGROUND.

Submarine Command (1951) 87m. **½ D: John Farrow. William Holden, Nancy Olson, William Bendix, Don Taylor. Predictable but acceptable post-WW2 account of naval military life; Olson is wholesome love interest.

Submarine Patrol (1938) 95m. **½ D: John Ford. Richard Greene, Nancy Kelly, Preston Foster, George Bancroft, Slim Summerville, John Carradine, J. Farrell MacDonald, Maxie Rosenbloom, Jack Pennick, Elisha Cook, Jr. Routine actioner with tough captain Foster revitalizing beat-up Splinter Fleet ship and demoralized crew for duty in WW1.

Submarine Raider (1942) 65m. ** D: Lew Landers. John Howard, Marguerite Chapman, Bruce Bennett, Warren Ashe, Eileen O'Hearn, Larry Parks, Forrest Tucker, Philip Ahn. Lively but far-fetched B picture about a U.S. sub shadowing a Japanese aircraft carrier on its way to a place called Pearl Harbor. Yes, they do manage to get a girl on the sub—the sole survivor of the killer carrier's unprovoked attack on a civilian yacht. Badly executed miniatures dampen the suspense.▼▶

Subterraneans, The (1960) C-89m. **½ D: Ranald MacDougall. Leslie Caron, George Peppard, Janice Rule, Roddy McDowall, Anne Seymour, Jim Hutton, Scott Marlowe. Glossy, superficial study of life and love among the beatniks, with pure cornball stereotype performances; MGM was not the studio for this one. Script by Robert Thom, from the Jack Kerouac novel. Music by Andre Previn, who also appears on screen along with such jazz artists as Gerry Mulligan, Carmen McRae, Art Pepper, Art Farmer, Shelly Manne. CinemaScope.

Subway in the Sky (1959-German) 85m. *½ D: Muriel Box. Van Johnson, Hildegarde Neff, Katherine Kath, Cec Linder, Albert Lieven, Edward Judd. Flabby caper of soldier Johnson in post-WW2 Berlin, involved in the black market; terrible waste of Neff's talents.

Success, The (1963-Italian) 103m. *** D: Dino Risi. Vittorio Gassman, Anouk Aimée, Jean-Louis Trintignant. Intelligent delineation by Gassman as businessman overwhelmed by success urge makes this drama worthy.

Success at Any Price (1934) 75m. *** D: J. Walter Ruben. Douglas Fairbanks, Jr., Genevieve Tobin, Frank Morgan, Colleen Moore, Edward Everett Horton, Allen Vincent. Interesting moral tract tracing the rise and fall of ruthless businessman Fairbanks as he crushes everyone who gets in his way—and loses sight of the one woman who loves him. Surprisingly contemporary, and still potent, though it reveals its stage origins.

Successful Calamity, A (1932) 72m. **½ D: John G. Adolfi. George Arliss, Mary Astor, Evalyn Knapp, Grant Mitchell, David Torrence, William Janney, Hardie Albright, Randolph Scott, Leon Waycoff (Ames). Wealthy world figure returns home after almost a year of traveling, anxious to spend time with his family—only to find them all too concerned with themselves to give him more than a passing nod. Ever-so-slight Arliss comedy hews strictly to formula, but it's a formula that works, and Arliss is charming as always.▶

Sudan (1945) C-76m. ** D: John Rawlins. Maria Montez, Jon Hall, Turhan Bey, Andy Devine, George Zucco, Robert Warwick. Queen Montez escapes evil prime minister Zucco with help of Hall and Bey in colorful but empty adventure-romance. Montez and Hall's last pairing.

Sudden Danger (1955) 85m. *½ D: Hubert Cornfield. Bill Elliott, Tom Drake, Beverly Garland, Lucien Littlefield, Minerva Urecal, Lyle Talbot, Frank Jenks. Homicide detective Elliott investigates the supposed suicide of a clothing manufacturer. Former Western star Elliott played the same character in four other films.▶

Sudden Fear (1952) 110m. *** D: David Miller. Joan Crawford, Jack Palance, Gloria Grahame, Bruce Bennett, Touch (Mike) Connors, Virginia Huston. Wealthy playwright Crawford discovers new husband Palance (an actor whom she once fired) is planning to kill her; she uses her writing skills to concoct a scheme to make him trip himself up. Solid suspense thriller with many neat twists.▼●▶

Suddenly (1954) 77m. ***½ D: Lewis Allen. Frank Sinatra, Sterling Hayden, James Gleason, Nancy Gates, Willis Bouchey, Kim Charney, Paul Frees, Christopher Dark, Charles Smith. Sinatra leads trio of paid assassins who take over house in small town where the President will pass on his way to a fishing trip. White-knuckle thriller, written by Richard Sale, with Sinatra excellent in thoroughly detestable role; rest of cast equally fine. "Suddenly," incidentally, is the name of the town. Also shown in computer-colored version. ▼●▶

Suddenly, It's Spring (1947) **87m.** ✶✶ D: Mitchell Leisen. Paulette Goddard, Fred MacMurray, Macdonald Carey, Arleen Whelan, Lillian Fontaine. Strained comedy about married couple Goddard and MacMurray refusing to divorce each other.

Suddenly, Last Summer (1959) **114m.** ✶✶✶½ D: Joseph L. Mankiewicz. Elizabeth Taylor, Katharine Hepburn, Montgomery Clift, Mercedes McCambridge, Albert Dekker. Fascinating if talky (though cleaned-up) Tennessee Williams yarn about wealthy Southern matriarch (Hepburn), her supposedly mad niece (Taylor), and a neurosurgeon (Clift); grandly acted. Adaptation by Williams and Gore Vidal. Remade for TV in 1992 with Maggie Smith. ▼●▶

Suds (1920) **67m.** ✶✶½ D: John Dillon. Mary Pickford, Albert Austin, Harold Goodwin, Rose Dione, Nadyne Montgomery, Darwin Karr. Mostly enjoyable change-of-pace silent-film vehicle for Pickford as a homely Cockney laundrywoman who pines for the gentleman who left off a shirt to be cleaned months ago and never returned. Combination of wistfulness, slapstick, and drama doesn't always work. ▼●▶

Suez (1938) **104m.** ✶✶✶ D: Allan Dwan. Tyrone Power, Loretta Young, Annabella, Henry Stephenson, Maurice Moscovich, Joseph Schildkraut, Sidney Blackmer, J. Edward Bromberg, Sig Ruman, Nigel Bruce, Miles Mander, George Zucco, Leon Ames. Power is 19th-century French architect (and dreamer) Ferdinand de Lesseps, who pursues a single-minded goal of building the Suez Canal; his real problem is choosing between aristocratic Loretta and down-to-earth Annabella. Entertaining and elaborate hokum which apparently bears no resemblance to history. Power and Annabella later wed in real life. ▶

Sugarfoot (1951) **C-80m.** ✶✶½ D: Edwin L. Marin. Randolph Scott, Adele Jergens, Raymond Massey, S. Z. Sakall, Arthur Hunnicutt. Above-par Scott Western. Randy is ex-Rebel officer who encounters his old adversary in Arizona. Retitled: SWIRL OF GLORY.

Suicide Battalion (1958) **79m.** BOMB D: Edward L. Cahn. Michael Connors, John Ashley, Jewell Lain, Russ Bender. Static WW2 non-actioner. Army duo goes on mission to destroy government records hidden in building basement at Pearl Harbor. ▼

Suicide Fleet (1931) **87m.** ✶✶½ D: Albert Rogell. William Boyd, Robert Armstrong, James Gleason, Ginger Rogers, Harry Bannister, Frank Reicher, Ben Alexander. Shooting-gallery barker Boyd, photographer Armstrong, and tour guide Gleason compete for the attention of Rogers (at her cutest), who runs the candy-booth conces-

sion at Coney Island. When WW1 breaks out, all three men enlist, and the sprightly film goes downhill; partially rescued by an exciting finale. ▶

Suicide Squadron SEE: **Dangerous Moonlight**

Sullivans, The (1944) **111m.** ✶✶✶ D: Lloyd Bacon. Anne Baxter, Thomas Mitchell, Selena Royle, Ward Bond, Bobby Driscoll, Addison Richards. Homey, patriotic but fictionalized story of the real-life Sullivan brothers of Waterloo, Iowa, who fought together in WW2. Knowing the outcome of this story makes it very sad to watch. The Sullivans are played by Edward Ryan, John Campbell, James Cardwell, John Alvin, and George Offerman, Jr. Aka THE FIGHTING SULLIVANS. ▼▶

Sullivan's Travels (1942) **90m.** ✶✶✶✶ D: Preston Sturges. Joel McCrea, Veronica Lake, Robert Warwick, William Demarest, Margaret Hayes, Porter Hall, Eric Blore, Robert Greig, Jimmy Conlin, Al Bridge, Franklin Pangborn. Tired of making fluff, movie director McCrea decides to do a "serious" film, O BROTHER, WHERE ART THOU?; to research it, he sets out with 10¢ in his pocket to experience life in "the real world." Slapstick and sorrow blend seamlessly in this landmark Hollywood satire, which grows more pertinent with each passing year. A unique achievement for writer-director Sturges. ▼●▶

Summer and Smoke (1961) **C-118m.** ✶✶✶½ D: Peter Glenville. Geraldine Page, Laurence Harvey, Una Merkel, John McIntire, Pamela Tiffin, Rita Moreno, Thomas Gomez, Earl Holliman, Casey Adams (Max Showalter), Lee Patrick. Spinster Page is in love with young doctor Harvey, but he's understandably not interested; vivid adaptation of Tennessee Williams play, set in 1916 in small Mississippi town, with torrid performances making up for frequent staginess. Atmospheric score by Elmer Bernstein. Panavision. ▼●▶

Summer Holiday (1948) **C-92m.** ✶✶½ D: Rouben Mamoulian. Mickey Rooney, Walter Huston, Frank Morgan, Agnes Moorehead, Butch Jenkins, Selena Royle, Marilyn Maxwell, Gloria De Haven, Anne Francis. Lavish musical remake of AH, WILDERNESS! with Rooney (who played the younger brother in 1935) as the young man coming of age. Extremely good-looking film, with exquisite use of Technicolor, but dramatically unexceptional—and not nearly as good as the earlier film. This version was made in 1946. ▼●▶

Summer Holiday (1963-British) **C-107m.** ✶✶ D: Peter Yates. Cliff Richard, Lauri Peters, David Kossoff, Ron Moody, The Shadows, Melvyn Hayes, Una Stubbs, Teddy Green, Jeremy Bulloch. Richard, Hayes, Green, and Bulloch travel through Europe on a bus in this silly but cheerful musical;

inauspicious directorial debut by Yates. CinemaScope.▶

Summer Interlude SEE: **Illicit Interlude**

Summer Love (1958) 85m. ** D: Charles Haas. John Saxon, Molly Bee, Rod McKuen, Judi Meredith, Jill St. John, George Winslow, Fay Wray, Edward Platt, Shelley Fabares, Troy Donahue. Sequel to ROCK, PRETTY BABY has Saxon et al. hired to perform at summer resort camp; perky performances.

Summer Madness SEE: **Summertime**

Summer Magic (1963) C-110m. **½ D: James Neilson. Hayley Mills, Burl Ives, Dorothy McGuire, Deborah Walley, Eddie Hodges, Una Merkel. Disney's rehash of MOTHER CAREY'S CHICKENS has McGuire as widow who raises family on a shoestring in rambling Maine house. Burl sings "The Ugly Bug Ball." Pleasant but forgettable.▼▶

Summer Maneuvers SEE: **Les Grandes Manoeuvres**

Summer of '64 SEE: **Girls on the Beach**

Summer Place, A (1959) C-130m. *** D: Delmer Daves. Richard Egan, Dorothy McGuire, Sandra Dee, Arthur Kennedy, Troy Donahue, Constance Ford, Beulah Bondi. Lushly photographed (by Harry Stradling) soaper of adultery and teenage love at resort house on Maine coast. Excellent Max Steiner score (the theme was a big hit); based on the Sloan Wilson novel.▼▶

Summerplay SEE: **Illicit Interlude**

Summer Stock (1950) C-109m. *** D: Charles Walters, Judy Garland, Gene Kelly, Eddie Bracken, Marjorie Main, Gloria De Haven, Phil Silvers, Hans Conried. Kelly's theater troupe takes over Judy's farm, she gets show biz bug. Thin plot, breezy Judy, frantic Silvers, chipper De Haven. Judy sings "Get Happy," Kelly dances on newspapers.▼▶

Summer Storm (1944) 106m. ** D: Douglas Sirk. George Sanders, Linda Darnell, Edward Everett Horton, Anna Lee, Hugo Haas, Sig Ruman. Darnell gives one of her best performances as a peasant who victimizes every man she meets. Dreary adaptation of Chekhov's "The Shooting Party" enlivened by Horton as an amoral Russian count.▶

Summertime (1955) C-99m. ***½ D: David Lean. Katharine Hepburn, Rossano Brazzi, Isa Miranda, Darren McGavin, Mari Aldon, Andre Morell. Lilting film of spinster vacationing in Venice, falling in love with married man. Hepburn's sensitive portrayal is one of her best. Screenplay by Lean and H. E. Bates, from Arthur Laurents' play *The Time of the Cuckoo*. Beautifully filmed on location by Jack Hildyard. Original British title: SUMMER MADNESS.▼▶

Summer With Monika (1953-Swedish) 96m. ***½ D: Ingmar Bergman. Harriet Andersson, Lars Ekborg, John Harryson, Georg Skarstedt, Dagmar Ebbesen, Ake Gronberg. A brief affair between two working-class youngsters, aggressive Andersson and boyish Ekborg, results in the birth of their baby and marriage. Simple storyline has been filmed before and since, but rarely with such sensitivity. Video title: MONIKA.▼▶

Sumurun (1920-German) 103m. **½ D: Ernst Lubitsch. Ernst Lubitsch, Pola Negri, Paul Wegener, Jenny Hasselqvist, Aud Egede Nissen, Harry Liedtke. Florid melodrama-comedy with Lubitsch offering a scene-stealing performance as a hunchback who's obsessed with a sultry dancer (Negri), his colleague in a minstrel show. Meanwhile, the title character (Hasselqvist), a member of a sheik's harem, longs for the traveling cloth merchant with whom she has fallen in love. Adapted by Lubitsch and Hanns Kräly from a pantomime by Friedrich Freska. Released in the U.S. as ONE ARABIAN NIGHT.▶

Sun Also Rises, The (1957) C-129m. *** D: Henry King. Tyrone Power, Ava Gardner, Mel Ferrer, Errol Flynn, Eddie Albert, Gregory Ratoff, Juliette Greco, Marcel Dalio, Henry Daniell, Robert Evans. Hemingway story of expatriates in Parisian 1920s has slow stretches; worthwhile for outstanding cast, especially Flynn as a souse. European and Mexican locations add flavor to tale of search for self-identity. Remade (poorly) for TV in 1984. CinemaScope.▶

Sunbonnet Sue (1945) 89m. ** D: Ralph Murphy. Gale Storm, Phil Regan, George Cleveland, Minna Gombell, Edna Holland, Raymond Hatton. B musical of the Gay '90s enhanced by bouncy Storm as songstress in father's lower N.Y.C. saloon.

Sun Comes Up, The (1949) C-93m. ** D: Richard Thorpe. Jeanette MacDonald, Lloyd Nolan, Claude Jarman, Jr., Lewis Stone, Dwayne Hickman. Colorful but overly sentimental story of young orphan and embittered widow who blames her son's dog, Lassie, for his death. MacDonald's last film.▼

Sunday Dinner for a Soldier (1944) 86m. *** D: Lloyd Bacon. Anne Baxter, John Hodiak, Charles Winninger, Anne Revere, Chill Wills, Bobby Driscoll, Jane Darwell. Winning film of family that invites soldier to dinner; they are repaid for their kindness; enjoyable comedy-drama.▶

Sunday in New York (1963) C-105m. *** D: Peter Tewksbury. Cliff Robertson, Jane Fonda, Rod Taylor, Robert Culp, Jim Backus. Entire cast bubbles in this Norman Krasna sex romp of virginal Fonda discovering N.Y.C. and love. Peter Nero's score is perky.▶

Sunday Punch (1942) 76m. **½ D: David Miller. William Lundigan, Jean Rogers, Dan Dailey (Jr.), Guy Kibbee, J. Carrol Naish, Connie Gilchrist, Sam Levene, Leo Gorcey, Rags Ragland. Brooklyn boardinghouse for boxers gets all shook up when the owner's pretty niece (Rogers) moves in and sets hearts fluttering. Adept cast socks over stereotypes with aplomb in enjoyable comedy-drama. Dane Clark makes his film debut under his real name, Bernard Zanville. Ava Gardner also has a bit.

Sundays and Cybèle (1962-French) **110m.** ***½ D: Serge Bourguignon. Hardy Kruger, Nicole Courcel, Patricia Gozzi, Daniel Ivernel. Intelligently told account of shell-shocked Kruger finding source of communication with the world via orphaned waif Gozzi, with tragic results. Splendidly realized, Oscar winner as Best Foreign Language Film. Filmed in Franscope.

Sundown (1941) **90m.** **½ D: Henry Hathaway. Gene Tierney, Bruce Cabot, George Sanders, Harry Carey, Joseph Calleia, Dorothy Dandridge, Reginald Gardiner. Tierney is surprisingly cast as native girl who assists British troops in Africa during WW2; fairly interesting, lushly photographed by Charles Lang, but it never scores. Also shown in computer-colored version. ▼▌

Sundowners, The (1950) **C-83m.** **½ D: George Templeton. Robert Preston, Cathy Downs, Robert Sterling, John Barrymore, Jr., Jack Elam, Chill Wills. Preston shines (and even sings!) in this Western about brothers on opposite sides of the law. A showcase for young Barrymore, as Sterling's impressionable sibling. Filmed in Texas; written and produced by Alan LeMay (*The Searchers*). ▼▌

Sundowners, The (1960) **C-133m.** **** D: Fred Zinnemann. Deborah Kerr, Robert Mitchum, Peter Ustinov, Glynis Johns, Dina Merrill, Chips Rafferty, Michael Anderson, Jr., Lola Brooks, Wylie Watson, Mervyn Johns. First-rate film of Australian family who travel to allow the husband to shear sheep at various ranches. Entire cast excellent, Kerr especially fine. Isobel Lennart adapted Jon Cleary's novel. Wonderfully filmed on location by Jack Hildyard. ▼●▌

Sun Never Sets, The (1939) **98m.** **½ D: Rowland V. Lee. Douglas Fairbanks, Jr., Basil Rathbone, Barbara O'Neil, Lionel Atwill, Virginia Field, C. Aubrey Smith. Enjoyable patriotic drama of British brothers trying to prevent outbreak of war in Africa. Well done, with top-notch cast.

Sunny (1930) **78m.** ** D: William A. Seiter. Marilyn Miller, Lawrence Gray, Joe Donahue, O. P. Heggie, Inez Courtney, Barbara Bedford, Clyde Cook. Standard 1920s Broadway nonsense about a British circus bareback rider who marries the wrong man to get to the right man in America. High-spirited Ziegfeld creation Miller, in the second of her three movies, is poorly served by harsh Vitaphone recording, but her ballet and tap numbers show what made her a star. Memorable Jerome Kern–Otto Harbach–Oscar Hammerstein II score includes "Who?" and the title song. Remade in 1941. ▌

Sunny (1941) **98m.** **½ D: Herbert Wilcox. Anna Neagle, Ray Bolger, John Carroll, Edward Everett Horton, Paul & Grace Hartman, Helen Westley. New Orleans society scion Carroll falls in love with circus performer Neagle; pleasant enough musical but nothing special. Bolger's dancing is the real treat. Jerome Kern–Oscar Hammerstein–Otto Harbach score includes "Who?" Filmed before in 1930 with Marilyn Miller. ▌

Sunny Side of the Street (1951) **C-71m.** *½ D: Richard Quine. Frankie Laine, Terry Moore, Jerome Courtland, Audrey Long. Moore has fickle notions over aspiring Laine in this low-grade musical, with guest stars such as Billy Daniels, Toni Arden.

Sunnyside Up (1929) **122m.** *** D: David Butler. Janet Gaynor, Charles Farrell, El Brendel, Marjorie White, Joe Brown, Frank Richardson, Jackie Cooper. Charming antique, quite impressive for early-talkie musical. Fluffy story of tenement girl Gaynor falling in love with wealthy Farrell sufficient excuse for DeSylva-Brown-Henderson songs: "I'm a Dreamer," "If I Had a Talking Picture of You," title tune, and bizarre production number to "Turn on the Heat."▼

Sunrise (1927) **94m.** **** D: F. W. Murnau. George O'Brien, Janet Gaynor, Bodil Rosing, Margaret Livingston, J. Farrell MacDonald. Exquisite silent film is just as powerful today as when it was made, telling simple story of farmer who plans to murder his wife, led on by another woman. Triumph of direction, camerawork, art direction, and performances, all hauntingly beautiful. Screenplay by Carl Mayer, from Hermann Suderman's story. Cinematographers Karl Struss and Charles Rosher won Oscars, as did the film for "artistic quality of production." Gaynor also won Best Actress Oscar (shared for her performances in 7TH HEAVEN and STREET ANGEL). Remade in Germany as THE JOURNEY TO TILSIT. Full title on-screen is SUNRISE—A SONG OF TWO HUMANS. ▼●▌

Sunrise at Campobello (1960) **C-143m.** *** D: Vincent J. Donehue. Ralph Bellamy, Greer Garson, Hume Cronyn, Jean Hagen, Ann Shoemaker, Alan Bunce, Tim Considine, Zina Bethune, Frank Ferguson, Lyle Talbot. Sincere story of President Franklin Delano Roosevelt, his battles in politics and valiant struggle against polio. Well acted; Bellamy (re-creating his Tony-winning stage role) and Garson *are* the Roosevelts. Script by Dore Schary, from his hit play. ▼●▌

Sunset Blvd. (1950) **110m.** **** D: Billy Wilder. Gloria Swanson, William Holden, Erich von Stroheim, Nancy Olson, Fred Clark, Jack Webb, Hedda Hopper, Buster Keaton, Cecil B. DeMille, Anna Q. Nilsson. Legendary Hollywood black comedy about faded silent-film star Norma Desmond

(Swanson), living in the past with butler (von Stroheim), who shelters hack screenwriter (Holden) as boyfriend. Bitter, funny, fascinating; Gloria's tour de force. Oscar winner for Best Screenplay (Wilder, Charles Brackett, D.M. Marshman, Jr.), Score (Franz Waxman), and Art Direction–Set Decoration. Later a Broadway musical.▼●▶

Sunset in El Dorado (1945) **65m. *** D: Frank McDonald. Roy Rogers, George "Gabby" Hayes, Dale Evans, Hardie Albright, Margaret Dumont, Roy Barcroft, Tom London, Stanley Price, Bob Nolan and the Sons of the Pioneers. Big city tour company worker Evans heads to the title town, where her grandmother was queen of the Golden Nugget gambling house. There, she dreams of her grandmother's adventures involving bad men who steal Gabby's claim and the cowboy (Rogers, naturally) who comes to her rescue. Very entertaining blend of music and Western action, and a real showcase for Dale. ▼▶

Sunset in the West (1950) **C-67m. **½ D: William Witney. Roy Rogers, Estelita Rodriguez, Penny Edwards, Gordon Jones, Will Wright, Pierre Watkin, William J. Tannen, Foy Willing and the Riders of the Purple Sage. Roy must help an aging sheriff by tracking down gun collector Watkin and the gun runners using a train to hide their spoils. Good action, uninspired songs.▼▶

Sunset in Wyoming (1941) **65m. *** D: William Morgan. Gene Autry, Smiley Burnette, Maris Wrixon, George Cleveland, Robert Kent, Sarah Edwards, Monte Blue. Gene's efforts to protect the environment and restore ecological balance when unscrupulous lumbermen strip a large forest (and expose a ranch community to severe flooding) make this an extremely timely film. Expert meld of songs, action, and romance make this a perfect example of an Autry film of the period.▶

Sunset on the Desert (1942) **63m. *** D: Joseph Kane. Roy Rogers, George "Gabby" Hayes, Lynne Carver, Frank M. Thomas, Beryl Wallace, Glenn Strange, Douglas Fowley, Fred Burns, Roy Barcroft, Sons of the Pioneers. Roy does double duty as good guy who returns home to help a family friend and as the henchman of crooked attorney Fowley, who is forcing ranchers off their property. Entertaining Western with Roy making the most of his dual role. ▼▶

Sunset Serenade (1942) **58m. *** D: Joseph Kane. Roy Rogers, George "Gabby" Hayes, Helen Parrish, Onslow Stevens, Joan Woodbury, Frank M. Thomas, Roy Barcroft, Jack Ingram, Bob Nolan and the Sons of the Pioneers. Roy, Gabby, and the Sons discover that Woodbury and Stevens have been plotting to swindle a ranch from its rightful heir, a baby who's cared for by guardian Parrish. Fast-paced Western with music, drama, and a good story.▼▶

Sunset Trail (1938) **69m. **½ D: Lesley Selander. William Boyd, George Hayes, Russell Hayden, Charlotte Wynters, Jane (Jan) Clayton, Robert Fiske, Maurice Cass. Commissioned by stage line, Hopalong Cassidy poses as timid Eastern milquetoast to catch murderer and secure dude ranch for widow and daughter. Nice mix of comedy, drama, and Western action, adapted from Clarence E. Mulford's 1928 novel *Mesquite Jenkins*. (Cass, as pompous pulp fiction writer, mocks Mulford, who was then publicly criticizing Boyd's sanitized interpretation of Hoppy.) Boyd clearly relishes role as tenderfoot. Clayton was then Mrs. Hayden.▼▶

Sun Shines Bright, The (1953) **90m. *** D: John Ford. Charles Winninger, Arleen Whelan, John Russell, Stepin Fetchit, Milburn Stone, Russell Simpson, Francis Ford, Grant Withers, Slim Pickens, Mae Marsh, Jane Darwell, Clarence Muse, Jack Pennick, Patrick Wayne. This was director Ford's favorite film, a picaresque remake of JUDGE PRIEST with Winninger involved in political contest in small Southern town. Fine array of Ford regulars in character roles. Video and TV version is 100m. print prepared by Ford but never released.▼▶

Sun Valley Serenade (1941) **86m. *** D: H. Bruce Humberstone. Sonja Henie, John Payne, Glenn Miller and His Orchestra, Milton Berle, Lynn Bari, Joan Davis, Dorothy Dandridge, The Nicholas Brothers. Light musicomedy with Henie a war refugee, Payne her foster parent, traveling with the Miller band and manager Berle to Sun Valley. Songs: "It Happened in Sun Valley," "In the Mood," "Chattanooga Choo-Choo," "I Know Why (And So Do You)."▼●

Superman and the Mole-Men (1951) **58m. ** D: Lee Sholem. George Reeves, Phyllis Coates, Jeff Corey, Walter Reed, J. Farrell MacDonald, Stanley Andrews. Reporters Clark Kent and Lois Lane go to small town to see the world's deepest oil well; instead, they discover that "mole-men" have climbed out of the well, from their home at the center of the Earth. This very low-budget feature served as a pilot for the long-running TV series *Adventures of Superman*, but it's more serious (and less fun) than the subsequent show—and we barely get to see Superman fly! But it's still great to see Reeves as the Man of Steel. Edited down and retitled *The Unknown People* to run as a TV *Superman* two-parter.▼●▶

Supernatural (1933) **64m. **½ D: Victor Halperin. Carole Lombard, Randolph Scott, Vivienne Osborne, H. B. Warner, Alan Dinehart, Beryl Mercer, William Farnum. Interesting little thriller—most unusual for its time—about a woman on Death Row who upon her execution transfers her personality to an innocent victim.▼▶

Super-Sleuth (1937) **70m. *** D: Ben

Stoloff. Jack Oakie, Ann Sothern, Edgar Kennedy, Eduardo Ciannelli, Joan Woodbury, Bradley Page. Inconsequential but very funny outing with Oakie as egocentric detective-movie star who tries to solve real-life murder mystery. Kennedy has plum supporting role as police detective. Remade as GENIUS AT WORK.

Surf Party (1964) **68m.** BOMB D: Maury Dexter. Bobby Vinton, Jackie De Shannon, Patricia Morrow, Kenny Miller. Teenagers meet and mate in Malibu. Waterlogged. ▼▶

Surgeon's Knife, The (1957-British) **75m.** ** D: Gordon Parry. Donald Houston, Adrienne Corri, Lyndon Brook. Tepid drama of doctor Houston implicated in criminal negligence, becoming involved in murder.

Surprise Package (1960-British) **100m.** **½ D: Stanley Donen. Yul Brynner, Mitzi Gaynor, Barry Foster, Eric Pohlmann, Noel Coward, George Coulouris. Versatile Brynner tries screwball comedy, not doing too badly as devil-may-care gambler planning big-time robbery; Gaynor is sprightly leading lady. Script by Harry Kurnitz, from the Art Buchwald novel. ▼▶

Surrender (1931) **69m.** ** D: William K. Howard. Warner Baxter, Leila Hyams, Ralph Bellamy, C. Aubrey Smith, Alexander Kirkland, William Pawley. During WW1, a French prisoner of war ingratiates himself into the castle home of a Prussian general and falls in love with his niece. Potent antiwar sentiments are undercut by silly dialogue and ineffectual performances; accepting Baxter as a Frenchman is a stretch. Anton Grot's sets and James Wong Howe's camerawork are exquisite.

Surrender (1950) **90m.** **½ D: Allan Dwan. Vera Ralston, John Carroll, Walter Brennan, Francis Lederer, Jane Darwell, Jeff York. Ralston is exotic if overdramatic playing everyone against each other; Republic Pictures' nicely mounted costumer.

Surrender—Hell! (1959) **85m.** ** D: John Barnwell. Keith Andes, Susan Cabot, Paraluman, Nestor de Villa. Predictable account of Andes rallying partisan forces to combat Japanese control of Philippines. Shot on location. ▶

Susana (1951-Mexican) **82m.** **½ D: Luis Buñuel. Rosita Quintana, Fernando Soler, Victor Manuel Mendoza, Matilde Palou. A voluptuous orphan of the storm, engagingly played by Quintana, undermines the loving fabric of the family that rescues her. Well handled and staged by Buñuel, until the cop-out finale. ▼▶

Susan and God (1940) **115m.** **½ D: George Cukor. Joan Crawford, Fredric March, Ruth Hussey, John Carroll, Rita Hayworth, Nigel Bruce, Bruce Cabot, Rose Hobart, Rita Quigley, Marjorie Main, Gloria De Haven. Crawford is satisfying as woman whose religious devotion

loses her the love of her family. Gertrude Lawrence fared better on stage. Screenplay by Anita Loos, based on Rachel Crothers' play. ▼▶

Susan Lenox: Her Fall and Rise (1931) **76m.** **½ D: Robert Z. Leonard. Greta Garbo, Clark Gable, Jean Hersholt, John Miljan, Alan Hale. A young woman flees from her loutish father—who wants to marry her off—and finds refuge with Gable, but circumstances keep them apart until the final clinch. Contrived melodrama made compelling by the ever-mesmerizing Garbo.

Susannah of the Mounties (1939) **78m.** **½ D: William A. Seiter. Shirley Temple, Randolph Scott, Margaret Lockwood, J. Farrell MacDonald, Moroni Olsen, Victor Jory. Mountie Scott raises orphan Shirley in this predictable but entertaining Temple vehicle. Also shown in computer-colored version. ▼▶

Susanna Pass (1949) **C-67m.** **½ D: William Witney. Roy Rogers, Dale Evans, Estelita Rodriguez, Martin Garralaga, Robert Emmett Keane, Lucien Littlefield, Douglas Fowley, David Sharpe, Foy Willing and the Riders of the Purple Sage. Crooked newspaperman Keane murders his brother to seize oil-rich deposits underneath a lake that's used as a fish hatchery. He doesn't count on Dale (a Ph.D. in marine biology) inheriting the lake, or on game warden Roy being concerned with fish conservation. Interesting environmentalist story leads up to exciting chase and showdown. ▼▶

Susan Slade (1961) **C-116m.** **½ D: Delmer Daves. Troy Donahue, Dorothy McGuire, Connie Stevens, Lloyd Nolan, Brian Aherne, Bert Convy, Kent Smith. Slick soaper, beautifully photographed by Lucien Ballard. McGuire pretends to be mother of daughter's (Stevens) illegitimate child. Donahue is Connie's true love. ▶

Susan Slept Here (1954) **C-98m.** **½ D: Frank Tashlin. Dick Powell, Debbie Reynolds, Anne Francis, Glenda Farrell, Alvy Moore. Screenwriter Powell agrees to look after high-spirited delinquent Reynolds in this "cute" sex comedy, which has the distinction of being the only film in history ever narrated by an Oscar statuette! ▼▶

Suspect, The (1944) **85m.** ***½ D: Robert Siodmak. Charles Laughton, Ella Raines, Dean Harens, Molly Lamont, Henry Daniell, Rosalind Ivan. Superb, Hitchcock-like thriller of henpecked London tobacconist Laughton planning to get his wife (Ivan) out of the way so he can pursue lovely Raines. Set in 1903.

Suspect SEE: **Risk, The** (1960)

Suspected Alibi SEE: **Suspended Alibi**

Suspended Alibi (1956-British) **64m.** *½ D: Alfred Shaughnessy. Patrick Holt, Honor Blackman, Andrew Keir, Valentine Dyall. Holt is involved in homicide via circumstantial evidence in this coincidence-laden drama. Retitled: SUSPECTED ALIBI. ▼

Suspense (1946) 101m. ** D: Frank Tuttle. Barry Sullivan, Belita, Albert Dekker, Bonita Granville, Eugene Pallette. Completely unsuspenseful story of ambitious heel who makes time with married ice-skating star Belita. Some nice visual touches, but leaden pacing, film noir clichés, and such musical highlights as "Ice Cuba" make this heavy going. Opening shot is the best thing in the movie! Script by Philip Yordan. ◗

Suspicion (1941) 99m. ***½ D: Alfred Hitchcock. Cary Grant, Joan Fontaine, Cedric Hardwicke, Nigel Bruce, Dame May Whitty, Isabel Jeans, Heather Angel, Leo G. Carroll. Fontaine won Oscar for portraying wife who believes husband Grant is trying to kill her. Suspenser is helped by Bruce as Cary's pal, but finale (imposed by the Production Code) leaves viewer flat. Scripted by Samson Raphaelson, Joan Harrison, and Alma Reville (Hitchcock's wife), from *Before the Fact* by Francis Iles (Anthony Berkeley). Remade as a TVM in 1987. Also shown in computer-colored version. ▼◗

Sutter's Gold (1936) 94m. **½ D: James Cruze. Edward Arnold, Lee Tracy, Binnie Barnes, Katharine Alexander, Addison Richards, Montagu Love, Harry Carey. Biography of John Sutter—initiator of California's gold rush—starts off well, bogs down midway through story. Arnold is always good, but he's fighting a mediocre script here. Look for Billy Gilbert as a Spanish general taken hostage.

Suzy (1936) 99m. ** D: George Fitzmaurice. Jean Harlow, Franchot Tone, Cary Grant, Lewis Stone, Benita Hume. Fine cast sinks in this soapy romantic spy drama set in WW1, with Grant as French flier who falls in love with Harlow. Brightest moment has Cary crooning "Did I Remember?" ▼◗

Svengali (1931) 82m. *** D: Archie Mayo. John Barrymore, Marian Marsh, Donald Crisp, Carmel Myers, Bramwell Fletcher, Luis Alberni. Absorbing tale of artist's obsession with young girl, Trilby, who becomes singing artist under his hypnotic spell. Prime Barrymore in interesting production with bizarre Paris sets by Anton Grot, memorable visual effects. Followed by THE MAD GENIUS. ▼◗

Svengali (1955-British) C-82m. **½ D: Noel Langley. Hildegarde Neff, Donald Wolfit, Terence Morgan, Noel Purcell, Alfie Bass. Lacks flair of earlier version of du Maurier's novel about mesmerizing teacher and his actress-pupil Trilby. Robert Newton, originally cast as Svengali, quit in mid-production but can still be seen in some long shots. ▼◗

Swamp Diamonds SEE: **Swamp Women**

Swamp Fire (1946) 69m. ** D: William H. Pine. Johnny Weissmuller, Virginia Grey, Buster Crabbe, Carol Thurston, Pedro De Cordoba, David Janssen. Blah melodrama in which psychologically scarred Weissmuller returns from Coast Guard service in WW2, and attempts to settle into his old life as a Louisiana river pilot. ▼◗

Swamp Water (1941) 90m. **½ D: Jean Renoir. Dana Andrews, Walter Brennan, Anne Baxter, Walter Huston, Virginia Gilmore, John Carradine, Ward Bond, Guinn ("Big Boy") Williams, Eugene Pallette, Joe Sawyer, Mary Howard. Renoir's first American film is moody but erratic thriller set in the Okefenokee. Trapper Andrews finds fugitive Brennan hiding in the swamp, tries to clear him of murder rap without letting on that he knows the man's whereabouts. Powerhouse cast, handsome production, weakened by cornball dialogue and miscasting of Brennan. Remade as LURE OF THE WILDERNESS. ◗

Swamp Women (1955) C-73m. *½ D: Roger Corman. Carole Mathews, Marie Windsor, Beverly Garland, Touch (Mike) Connors, Jil Jarmyn, Susan Cummings. Heavy-handed nonsense with New Orleans policewoman Mathews going undercover, hooking up with notorious trio of female crooks who escape from jail and head out after stolen diamonds. Fans of Windsor and Garland will not want to miss it. Retitled: SWAMP DIAMONDS, CRUEL SWAMP. ▼◗

Swan, The (1956) C-112m. *** D: Charles Vidor. Grace Kelly, Alec Guinness, Louis Jourdan, Agnes Moorehead, Jessie Royce Landis, Brian Aherne, Leo G. Carroll, Estelle Winwood. Mild Molnár comedy of manners has attractive cast but not much sparkle. Jourdan good as Kelly's suitor, but she's promised to prince Guinness. Filmed before in 1925 and (as ONE ROMANTIC NIGHT) in 1930. CinemaScope. ▼◗

Swanee River (1939) C-84m. **½ D: Sidney Lanfield. Don Ameche, Al Jolson, Andrea Leeds, Felix Bressart, Russell Hicks. Bio of Stephen Foster where every song he writes is cued by a line of dialogue; clichés fill the movie, but it's fun on that level. Jolson is terrific as E. P. Christy; minstrel numbers are exceptionally well done. Other Foster bios are HARMONY LANE and I DREAM OF JEANIE. ◗

Sweater Girl (1942) 77m. **½ D: William Clemens. Eddie Bracken, June Preisser, Phillip Terry, Nils Asther, Frieda Inescort, Betty Jane Rhodes, Johnnie Johnston. While rehearsing the annual college revue, Bracken and Preisser investigate the mysterious deaths of a couple of their fellow students. Moderately entertaining mix of mystery, comedy, and music. Previously made as COLLEGE SCANDAL (1935).

Swedenhielms (1935-Swedish) 88m. **½ D: Gustaf Molander. Gosta Ekman, Bjorn Berglund, Hakan Westergren, Tutta Rolf, Ingrid Bergman. Slow-moving but not uninteresting tale of poor but honorable scientist Rolf Swedenhielm (well acted by

Ekman), who's up for the Nobel Prize, and his careless, childish offspring. Bergman, in her third feature, plays the wealthy fiancée of Swedenhielm's youngest son—and her star appeal is obvious. ▼●

Sweeney Todd, The Demon Barber of Fleet Street (1936-British) **68m.** ** D: George King. Tod Slaughter, Bruce Seton, Stella Rho, Eve Lister, Ben Soutten, D.J. Williams. Not many chills in this adaptation of the George Dibdin-Pitt play (later one of the sources for the Broadway musical *Sweeney Todd* by Stephen Sondheim), but it does contain a quintessential eye-rolling performance by Britain's master of grand guignol, Tod Slaughter, playing the sadistic barber who dumps his customers into the cellar and turns them into meat pies. Photographed by Ronald Neame. Not released in the U.S. until 1939. ▼▶

Sweepings (1933) **80m.** ***½ D: John Cromwell. Lionel Barrymore, William Gargan, Gloria Stuart, George Meeker, Eric Linden, Gregory Ratoff, Franklin Pangborn. Compelling Edna Ferberish saga of self-made man who devotes his life to building giant department store, hoping that his four children will carry on his work. Fine acting, inventive direction and camerawork—plus montages by Slavko Vorkapich—make this something special. Remade as THREE SONS in 1939. ▶

Sweet Adeline (1935) **87m.** **½ D: Mervyn LeRoy. Irene Dunne, Donald Woods, Hugh Herbert, Ned Sparks, Joseph Cawthorn, Louis Calhern, Winifred Shaw. Combination of spy chase and operetta isn't always smooth, but Kern-Hammerstein songs like "Why Was I Born" and Dunne's know-how make this enjoyable. ▼▶

Sweet and Low-Down (1944) **75m.** **½ D: Archie Mayo. Benny Goodman and His Band, Linda Darnell, Jack Oakie, Lynn Bari, James Cardwell, Allyn Joslyn, Dickie Moore. Thin story of trombonist Cardwell, a young man with "rough talent" who makes it big in Goodman's orchestra—and with pert deb Darnell. However, the King of Swing and his boys really cook, from the opening credits on; the jam session sequence is especially hot. ▶

Sweet Bird of Youth (1962) **C-120m.** ***½ D: Richard Brooks. Paul Newman, Geraldine Page, Shirley Knight, Ed Begley, Rip Torn, Mildred Dunnock, Madeleine Sherwood, Philip Abbott, Corey Allen. Tennessee Williams' play, cleaned up for the movies, still is powerful drama. Newman returns to Southern town with dissipated movie queen Page, causing corrupt town "boss" Begley (who won an Oscar) to have him fixed proper. Glossy production with cast on top of material. Scripted by Brooks. Newman, Page, Sherwood, and Torn reprised their Broadway performances. Remade for TV in 1989 with Elizabeth Taylor. CinemaScope. ▼●▶

Sweet Ecstasy (1962-French) **75m.** *½ D: Max Pecas. Elke Sommer, Pierre Brice, Christian Pezy, Claire Maurier. Silly soaper about life among the wealthy, beautiful, decadent, selfish young on the Riviera. Sommer is a cynical sexpot with an endless supply of false eyelashes. CinemaScope. ▼▶

Sweetheart of Sigma Chi (1933) **73m.** ** D: Edwin L. Marin. Mary Carlisle, Buster Crabbe, Charles Starrett, Florence Lake, Eddie Tamblyn, Sally Starr, Ted Fio Rito and His Orchestra (with Leif Erickson, Betty Grable). Forgettable Monogram musical enrolls all-American Crabbe as a campus athlete who'd rather row his team to victory than give his fraternity pin to blonde co-ed Carlisle. Though still a nameless band soloist, Grable is easily recognizable doing "It's Spring Again." No relation to 1946 movie of the same name.

Sweetheart of the Campus (1941) **67m.** **½ D: Edward Dmytryk. Ruby Keeler, Ozzie Nelson, Harriet Hilliard, Gordon Oliver, Don Beddoe, The Four Spirits of Rhythm. Dancer Keeler and bandleader Ozzie start a nightclub on a college campus. Modest musical comedy, nothing to write home about, but consistently peppy and surprisingly enjoyable.

Sweethearts (1938) **C-114m.** *** D: W. S. Van Dyke II. Jeanette MacDonald, Nelson Eddy, Frank Morgan, Florence Rice, Ray Bolger, Mischa Auer, Herman Bing, Reginald Gardiner, Allyn Joslyn. Comedic rewrite of Victor Herbert's operetta features MacDonald and Eddy as blissfully married stage stars who are manipulated into having a spat by their producer (Morgan). Elaborate Technicolor production earned an Oscar for cinematographer Oliver T. Marsh. Screenplay by Dorothy Parker and Alan Campbell. ▼●

Sweetie (1929) **95m.** **½ D: Frank Tuttle. Nancy Carroll, Stanley Smith, Jack Oakie, Helen Kane, Stuart Erwin, William Austin, Charles Sellon. Chorus girl Carroll inherits a boy's school; the plot doesn't go much deeper than that. Delightful song numbers including "The Prep Step," Kane's "He's So Unusual," and Oakie's version of alma mater, "Alma Mammy." Overlong but well directed, without the arid stretches of silence that mar so many early talkies.

Sweet Music (1935) **100m.** **½ D: Alfred E. Green. Rudy Vallee, Ann Dvorak, Helen Morgan, Ned Sparks, Alice White, Allen Jenkins. Genuinely mediocre musical with bandleader Vallee and dancer Dvorak constantly at odds. A few good songs, but the real highlight is the slapstick shenanigans of the Frank & Milt Britton Band, here playing Rudy's musical aggregation.

Sweet Rosie O'Grady (1943) **C-74m.** **½ D: Irving Cummings. Betty Grable, Robert Young, Adolphe Menjou, Reginald Gardiner, Virginia Grey, Phil Regan. Pleasant musical of ex-burlesque star and exposé reporter. Menjou steals film as editor of *Police Gazette.* Previously filmed as LOVE IS NEWS; remade again as THAT WONDERFUL URGE. ◗

Sweet Smell of Success (1957) 96m. ***½ D: Alexander Mackendrick. Burt Lancaster, Tony Curtis, Marty Milner, Sam Levene, Barbara Nichols, Susan Harrison, Joe Frisco, Chico Hamilton Quintet. Searing Clifford Odets–Ernest Lehman script about ruthless, all-powerful columnist J. J. Hunsecker (Lancaster) and a smarmy press agent (Curtis) who'll do *anything* to curry his favor. Vivid performances, fine jazz score by Elmer Bernstein, outstanding camerawork by James Wong Howe that perfectly captures N.Y.C. nightlife. Later a Broadway musical. ▼◗●

Swindle, The (1955-Italian) 92m. **½ D: Federico Fellini. Broderick Crawford, Giulietta Masina, Richard Basehart, Franco Fabrizi. Absorbing Fellini tale, which he coscripted, about a trio of small-time crooks who go about fleecing peasants in Italy, each planning for a better life. The spotlight is on the eldest, a world-weary loser nicely played by Crawford. Not among the director's best; still an intriguing portrait of hope and desperation. Aka THE SWINDLERS. Original title: IL BIDONE. ▼◗

Swing Fever (1944) 80m. *½ D: Tim Whelan. Kay Kyser, Marilyn Maxwell, William Gargan, Lena Horne, Nat Pendleton. Musical misfire with Kyser a hick with hypnotic powers, who's conned into aiding greedy fight-manager Gargan. Look for Ava Gardner as a receptionist. ◗

Swing High, Swing Low (1937) 95m. ** D: Mitchell Leisen. Carole Lombard, Fred MacMurray, Charles Butterworth, Jean Dixon, Dorothy Lamour, Harvey Stephens, Anthony Quinn. Musical drama with cornball plot of musician MacMurray's rise and fall. Redeemed somewhat by good cast, glossy production. From the stage play *Burlesque,* made before as THE DANCE OF LIFE and remade as WHEN MY BABY SMILES AT ME. ▼◗

Swingin' Affair, A (1963) 85m. BOMB D: Jay O. Lawrence. William Wellman, Jr., Arline Judge, Sandra Gale Bettin, Dick Dale and The Deltones. Young Wellman boxes to subsidize his university vacation. Awful drama with surf music. Also known as A SWINGING AFFAIR.

Swingin' Along (1962) C-74m. BOMB D: Charles Barton. Tommy Noonan, Peter Marshall, Barbara Eden, Ray Charles, Roger Williams, Bobby Vee. The witless shenanigans of aspiring composer Noonan and manager Marshall—with musical "guest stars" to relieve the tedium. Aka DOUBLE TROUBLE. CinemaScope.

Swingin' Summer, A (1965) C-80m. *½ D: Robert Sparr. James Stacy, William Wellman, Jr., Quinn O'Hara, Martin West, Allan Jones, Raquel Welch. The Righteous Brothers, The Rip Chords, Gary Lewis and The Playboys, Jody Miller. Typically thin storyline (about three guys who open a dance hall) as an excuse for music numbers by various guest stars. Techniscope. ▼◗

Swing Parade of 1946 (1946) 74m. *½ D: Phil Karlson. Gale Storm, Phil Regan, The Three Stooges, Ed Brophy, Will Osborne and His Orchestra, Connee Boswell. Dreary Grade-B musical with enough plot for a 10-minute short. The Stooges add some life, as does Louis Jordan performing "Caledonia," but it's not enough. Auteurists take note: Nicholas Ray is credited with "additional dialogue." ▼◗

Swing Shift Maisie (1943) 87m. **½ D: Norman Z. McLeod. Ann Sothern, James Craig, Jean Rogers, Connie Gilchrist, John Qualen, Marta Linden, Donald Curtis, Kay Medford. Patriotic Maisie quits her dog act to help out the war effort at an aircraft factory, only to be accused of sabotage by a jealous "friend" who's trying to steal her beau. Keep an eye out for John Hodiak, Don Taylor, Kirk Alyn, and Jim Davis. ◗

Swing Time (1936) 103m. **** D: George Stevens. Fred Astaire, Ginger Rogers, Victor Moore, Helen Broderick, Eric Blore, Betty Furness. One of the best Astaire-Rogers films, with stars as dance team whose romance is hampered by Fred's engagement to girl back home (Furness). Fine support by Moore and Broderick, unforgettable Jerome Kern–Dorothy Fields songs "A Fine Romance," "Pick Yourself Up." Oscar-winning "The Way You Look Tonight." Astaire's Bojangles production number is a screen classic. ▼◗●

Swingtime Johnny (1944) 61m. *½ D: Edward Cline. The Andrews Sisters, Harriet Hilliard, Peter Cookson, Tim Ryan. Show biz performers desert the theater for work in munitions factory; puny B musical.

Swing Your Lady (1938) 79m. *½ D: Ray Enright. Humphrey Bogart, Frank McHugh, Louise Fazenda, Nat Pendleton, Penny Singleton, Allen Jenkins, Ronald Reagan, Weaver Bros. and Elviry. Bogart promotes wrestler Pendleton; embarrassing comedy is easily his worst starring effort. Reagan appears briefly as a sportswriter. ◗

Swirl of Glory SEE: **Sugarfoot**

Swiss Family Robinson (1940) 93m. *** D: Edward Ludwig. Thomas Mitchell, Edna Best, Freddie Bartholomew, Tim Holt, Terry Kilburn. Mitchell decides to move family to Australia for a purer life, but shipwreck strands them on a remote island where his three spoiled sons learn honest values. Excellent adaptation of Johann Wyss book boasts impressive special effects, strong performances, and much darker elements than the later Disney version. Uncredited opening narration by Orson Welles. ▼

Swiss Family Robinson (1960) **C-128m.**
***½ D: Ken Annakin. John Mills, Dorothy
McGuire, James MacArthur, Janet Munro,
Sessue Hayakawa, Tommy Kirk, Kevin
Corcoran. Rollicking entertainment Disney-
style, with shipwrecked family building island
paradise, neatly dispatching Hayakawa and
his pirate band. Pure escapism, larger than
life. Panavision.▼●▌
Swiss Miss (1938) **72m.** ** D: John Blystone. Stan Laurel, Oliver Hardy, Della
Lind, Walter Woolf King, Eric Blore, Adia
Kuznetzoff, Charles Judels. Contrived romantic story with music tries hard to sub-
merge L&H, but Stan and Ollie's scenes
save film, especially when Ollie serenades
his true love with Stan playing tuba.▼▌
Sword and the Rose, The (1953) **C-93m.**
***½ D: Ken Annakin. Richard Todd,
Glynis Johns, James Robertson Justice, Michael Gough, Jane Barrett. Colorful filming
of *When Knighthood Was in Flower,* with
Johns as Mary Tudor, who uses wiles and
power to kindle romance with Todd—but
runs afoul of villainous duke (Gough). Rich
period flavor, fine performance by Justice
as King Henry VIII. Filmed in England by
Walt Disney.▼●▌
Sword in the Desert (1949) **100m.** **½
D: George Sherman. Dana Andrews, Marta
Toren, Stephen McNally, Jeff Chandler,
Philip Friend. Interesting account of underground trail of European refugees during
WW2; fairly good suspenser.
Sword in the Stone, The (1963) **C-75m.**
**½ D: Wolfgang Reitherman. Voices of
Ricky Sorenson, Sebastian Cabot, Karl
Swenson, Junius Matthews. One of Dis-
ney's weakest animated features follows a
young boy named Wart, who is destined to
become King Arthur—with the considerable
help of Merlin the Magician. Mildly entertaining and fast moving, but dialogue heavy,
and full of "modern" references that remove
much of the magic and wonder from T. H.
White's story. Highlight: wizards' duel between Merlin and Madame Mim.▼●▌
Sword of Ali Baba, The (1965) **C-81m.**
** D: Virgil Vogel. Peter Mann, Jocelyn
Lane, Peter Whitney, Gavin MacLeod,
Frank Puglia. Outrageous remake of ALI
BABA AND THE FORTY THIEVES, using a great deal of footage from the 1944
film. Puglia repeats his role as Prince Cas-
sim from '44 version to link old and new
footage.
Sword of Lancelot (1963-British) **C-
116m.** **½ D: Cornel Wilde. Cornel Wilde,
Jean Wallace, Brian Aherne, George Baker.
Camelot comes alive, minus music, with
profuse action and splendid scenery. Some
may find Wilde's approach too juvenile,
overly sincere, and Aherne a bit too cavalier. Originally titled LANCELOT AND
GUINEVERE. Panavision.▼▌
Sword of Monte Cristo, The (1951) **C-**

80m. ** D: Maurice Geraghty. George
Montgomery, Paula Corday, Berry Kroeger,
William Conrad, Steve Brodie. Uninspired
adventure of woman who finds legendary
sword of Count with key to treasure in-
scribed on it. Army officer joins her in fight
against evil prime minister.▼
Sword of Sherwood Forest (1960-British)
C-80m. **½ D: Terence Fisher. Richard
Greene, Peter Cushing, Niall MacGinnis,
Richard Pasco, Jack Gwillim, Sarah Branch,
Nigel Green, Oliver Reed. Fair continuation
of Robin Hood saga as Earl of Newark plots
murder of Archbishop of Canterbury. Mega-
scope.▼▌
Sword of the Conqueror (1961-Italian)
C-85m. *½ D: Carlo Campogalliani. Jack
Palance, Eleonora Rossi-Drago, Guy
Madison, Carlo D'Angelo. Flabby epic not
livened by cast or sets; set in 6th-century
Byzantine empire days. CinemaScope.▼▌
Swordsman, The (1948) **C-81m.** ** D:
Joseph H. Lewis. Larry Parks, Ellen Drew,
George Macready, Edgar Buchanan. Parks
and Drew have Romeo-Juliet relationship
in 18th-century Scotland; OK costumer.▌
Swordsman of Siena, The (1961-Italian) **C-
97m.** ** D: Etienne Perier. Stewart Granger,
Sylva Koscina, Christine Kaufmann, Tullio
Carminati, Gabriele Ferzetti. Predictable
swashbuckler about 16th-century adventurer
with mixed loyalties who becomes involved
in Spanish underground movement. Good
cast saddled with tired script. Cinema-
Scope.▌
Sylvia (1965) **115m.** **½ D: Gordon Douglas. Carroll Baker, George Maharis, Joanne
Dru, Peter Lawford, Viveca Lindfors, Edmond O'Brien, Aldo Ray, Ann Sothern,
Lloyd Bochner, Paul Gilbert, Nancy Kovack. Baker's prelude to HARLOW casts
her as a poetess and flower aficionado; she's
set to wed wealthy Lawford, who hires a
private eye (Maharis) to dig into her past.
Intriguing story, from a Howard Fast novel,
would have been far more effective had it
been made a few years later, when Sylvia's
plight could have been depicted in greater
detail. Sothern is a standout as one of the
characters in her past.
Sylvia Scarlett (1935) **94m.** *** D: George
Cukor. Katharine Hepburn, Cary Grant,
Brian Aherne, Edmund Gwenn, Natalie
Paley, Dennie Moore. Offbeat, charming
comedy-drama; Hepburn and ne'er-do-well
father Gwenn take to the road when he gets
in trouble. She disguises as a boy as they
travel with Cockney Grant in touring show.
Most unusual film made interesting by performances of Hepburn and Grant in their
first film together. Also shown in computer-
colored version.▼●▌
Symbol of the Unconquered, The (1920)
59m. **½ D: Oscar Micheaux. Iris Hall,
Walter Thompson, Lawrence Chenault,
Mattie Wilkes, Louis Déan, Leigh Whip-

per. A light-skinned black woman (Hall) settles the homestead she's inherited from her grandfather and initiates a friendship with a young prospector who thinks she's white. Awkwardly paced and overly melodramatic, but a fascinating slice of cultural history. The primary villains are an equal-opportunity lot—a white swindler, an Indian fakir, and a self-hating mulatto who conceals his racial identity—and the scenes featuring the Ku Klux Klan (here called the Knights of the Black Cross) starkly contrast Griffith's THE BIRTH OF A NATION. Restored from a print found in Belgium's Cinémathèque Royale, with title cards describing the missing footage. Compare with Micheaux's WITHIN OUR GATES (1920). Full title is THE SYMBOL OF THE UNCONQUERED: A STORY OF THE KU KLUX KLAN.

Symphony of Six Million (1932) **94m. **½** D: Gregory La Cava. Irene Dunne, Ricardo Cortez, Anna Appel, Gregory Ratoff, Lita Chevret. Predictable but well-made Fannie Hurst soap opera has young doctor Cortez abandoning his Jewish-ghetto neighborhood, family, friends—and crippled sweetheart Dunne—to join Park Avenue set and make big money. **)**

Synanon (1965) **107m. **½** D: Richard Quine. Chuck Connors, Stella Stevens, Alex Cord, Richard Conte, Eartha Kitt, Edmond O'Brien, Chanin Hale, Alejandro Rey. Potentially powerful study of dope-addiction treatment via the Synanon House methods bogs down in pat romantic tale with stereotyped performances. **)**

Syncopation (1942) **88m. **** D: William Dieterle. Adolphe Menjou, Jackie Cooper, Bonita Granville, George Bancroft, Ted North, Todd Duncan, Frank Jenks, Rex Stewart, Connee Boswell, Hall Johnson Choir. Promising but pedestrian story of early jazz travels from New Orleans to Chicago, focusing on trumpeter Cooper (who's dubbed by Bunny Berigan). Good music throughout; at the very end, there's a jam session featuring Benny Goodman, Charlie Barnet, Gene Krupa, Harry James, Jack Jenny, Joe Venuti, and Alvino Rey. **)**

System, The (1953) **90m. **** D: Lewis Seiler. Frank Lovejoy, Joan Weldon, Bob Arthur, Jerome Cowan. Uneven scripting spoils this potentially good study of gambling syndicate in large metropolitan city. **)**

Tabu—A Story of the South Seas (1931) **82m. ***½** D: F. W. Murnau. Anna Chevalier, Matahi, Hitu, Jean, Jules, Kong Ah. Fascinating melding of ethnographic documentary and narrative, about pearl fisherman Matahi and his ill-fated love for young Chevalier, who's been deemed by the gods as taboo to all men. Shot in Tahiti in 1929, produced and scripted by Murnau and Robert Flaherty; the latter left the project in

mid-production because of differences in opinion with Murnau—who died in a car accident just prior to the film's premiere. Floyd Crosby's cinematography won an Academy Award.▼●)

Taffy and the Jungle Hunter (1965) **C-87m. **** D: Terry O. Morse. Jacques Bergerac, Manuel Padilla, Shary Marshall, Hari Rhodes. Unassuming tale of son of big game hunter who takes off for jungle adventures with pet elephant and chimp. ▼

Taggart (1964) **C-85m. **½** D: R. G. Springsteen. Tony Young, Dan Duryea, Peter Duryea, David Carradine, Jean Hale, Harry Carey, Jr., Bob Steele. Neat little action Western based on a Louis L'Amour novel with Young on a revenge hunt, pursued by gunslingers in Indian territory.

Tailor's Maid, The (1957-Italian) **C-92m. **½** D: Mario Monicelli. Vittorio De Sica, Marcello Mastroianni, Marisa Merlini, Fiorella Mari, Memmo Carotenuto, Raffaele Pisu. Saucy, inconsequential comedy about an amorous tailor. CinemaScope.

Tail Spin (1939) **84m. **** D: Roy Del Ruth. Alice Faye, Constance Bennett, Nancy Kelly, Joan Davis, Charles Farrell, Jane Wyman, Kane Richmond, Wally Vernon. Hackneyed saga of female flyers, with Faye (in a change-of-pace role) having to scrounge for pennies and face competition from socialite/aviatrix Bennett. Written by Frank "Spig" Wead. **)**

Taira Clan Saga (1955-Japanese) **C-110m. ***** D: Kenji Mizoguchi. Raizo Ichikawa, Ichijiro Oya, Yoshiko Kuga, Michiyo Kogure, Eijiro Yanagi, Tatsuya Ishiguro, Narutoshi Hayashi, Tamao Nakamura, Koreya Senda. A Kyoto samurai, publicly hailed for bravery at sea, learns he is but a pawn in a game between a corrupt emperor and the military. Historically accurate 12th-century epic about the rise of the shoguns is an elegy for honor long gone. Second of only two color films by the great director. ▼)

Take a Chance (1933) **84m. *½** D: Laurence Schwab, Monte Brice. James Dunn, Cliff Edwards, June Knight, Charles "Buddy" Rogers, Lillian Roth, Dorothy Lee. Awful adaptation of Broadway musical of the same name about carnival hucksters aiming for the big time. Redeemed ever so slightly by its score ("It's Only a Paper Moon," "Eadie Was a Lady," "New Deal Rhythm") and a campy, risqué number with "Ukulele Ike" Edwards.

Take a Giant Step (1959) **100m. **½** D: Philip Leacock. Johnny Nash, Estelle Hemsley, Ruby Dee, Frederick O'Neal, Ellen Holly, Beah Richards. Earnest but only partly successful account of black teen Nash's problems in a white world. Stagy adaptation of Louis S. Peterson's play benefits from good performances. **)**

Take a Letter, Darling (1942) **93m. *****

D: Mitchell Leisen. Rosalind Russell, Fred MacMurray, Constance Moore, Robert Benchley, Macdonald Carey, Dooley Wilson, Cecil Kellaway. Witty repartee as advertising exec Roz hires MacMurray as secretary, but relationship doesn't end there. Benchley is wry as Russell's game-playing business partner.

Take Care of My Little Girl (1951) **C-93m.** ** D: Jean Negulesco. Jeanne Crain, Dale Robertson, Mitzi Gaynor, Jean Peters, Jeffrey Hunter, George Nader, Helen Westcott. Overdramatic story of sorority life at college.

Take Her, She's Mine (1963) **C-98m.** ** D: Henry Koster. James Stewart, Sandra Dee, Audrey Meadows, Robert Morley, Philippe Forquet, John McGiver, Bob Denver, Irene Tsu. Obvious family comedy with Stewart the harried father of wild teenage daughter Dee. Predictable gags don't help. Script by Nunnally Johnson, from the Broadway hit by Phoebe and Henry Ephron; later ripped off by THE IMPOSSIBLE YEARS. Look for James Brolin in airport scene. CinemaScope. ▶

Take It Big (1944) **75m.** *½ D: Frank McDonald. Jack Haley, Harriet Hilliard, Ozzie Nelson and His Orchestra, Mary Beth Hughes, Richard Lane, Arline Judge, Lucile Gleason, Fuzzy Knight, Fritz Feld. Haley, the wrong end of a two-man horse act, mistakenly thinks he's inherited a Nevada dude ranch. Though he's the nominal star of this silly B musical, one's attention is drawn more to the parents of David and Ricky Nelson. The all-female rodeo team is a keen idea. ▼

Take It or Leave It (1944) **70m.** *½ D: Benjamin Stoloff. Phil Baker, Edward Ryan, Marjorie Massow (Madge Meredith), Stanley Prager, Roy Gordon, Phil Silvers. Claptrap hinged on lives of contestants on Baker's popular radio quiz show; uses clips from older pictures (featuring Alice Faye, Betty Grable, Al Jolson, and many others) to enliven the proceedings.

Take Me Out to the Ball Game (1949) **C-93m.** *** D: Busby Berkeley. Frank Sinatra, Esther Williams, Gene Kelly, Betty Garrett, Edward Arnold, Jules Munshin, Richard Lane, Tom Dugan. Contrived but colorful musical set in 1906, with Williams taking over Sinatra and Kelly's baseball team. "O'Brien to Ryan to Goldberg" and Kelly's "The Hat My Father Wore on St. Patrick's Day" are musical highlights. Reworking of THEY LEARNED ABOUT WOMEN (1930). ▼●▶

Take Me to Town (1953) **C-81m.** **½ D: Douglas Sirk. Ann Sheridan, Sterling Hayden, Philip Reed, Lee Patrick, Lane Chandler, Lee Aaker. Unpretentious Americana of saloon singer Sheridan on the lam, finding love with widowed preacher Hayden and his three children.

Take One False Step (1949) **94m.** **½ D: Chester Erskine. William Powell, Shelley Winters, Marsha Hunt, James Gleason, Sheldon Leonard, Dorothy Hart. Ex-flame Winters attempts to seduce now-married educator Powell, leading to his becoming a wanted man. OK mystery-drama, adapted by Erskine and Irwin Shaw from the novel by Shaw and his brother David.

Take the High Ground! (1953) **C-101m.** *** D: Richard Brooks. Richard Widmark, Karl Malden, Elaine Stewart, Steve Forrest, Carleton Carpenter, Russ Tamblyn, Jerome Courtland. Taut account of infantry basic training with on-location filming at Fort Bliss, Texas, helping.

Talent Scout (1937) **62m.** *½ D: William Clemens. Donald Woods, Jeanne Madden, Fred Lawrence, Rosalind Marquis, Charles Halton. Tacky B musical about a Hollywood talent scout (Woods) and the singer (Madden) he promotes to stardom. The only fun is anticipating the clichéd dialogue scene by scene.

Tale of Five Women, A (1951-British) **86m.** *½ D: Romollo Marcellini, Geza von Cziffra, Wolfgang Staudte, E. E. Reinert, Montgomery Tully. Bonar Colleano, Barbara Kelly, Anne Vernon, Lana Morris, Karen Humbold, Lily Kahn, Eva Bartok, Gina Lollobrigida. Magazine editor Kelly accompanies amnesiac RAF officer to visit lovers in five cities, hoping to jar his memory. Disappointingly dull multi-episode film. Originally titled A TALE OF FIVE CITIES, running 99m. ▼

Tale of Two Cities, A (1917) **70m.** *** D: Frank Lloyd. William Farnum, Jewel Carmen, Joseph Swickard, Herschell Mayall, Rosita Marstini. Ambitious silent-film version of Dickens story was a big hit in 1917, and it's easy to see why: Farnum is an appealing hero, production is first rate, and battle scenes are reminiscent of Griffith's INTOLERANCE. ▼▶

Tale of Two Cities, A (1935) **128m.** **** D: Jack Conway. Ronald Colman, Elizabeth Allan, Edna May Oliver, Reginald Owen, Basil Rathbone, Blanche Yurka, Isabel Jewell, Walter Catlett, Henry B. Walthall, H. B. Warner, Donald Woods. Dickens' panorama of the 1780s French Revolution becomes an MGM blockbuster, with Colman as carefree lawyer awakened to responsibility, aiding victims of the Reign of Terror. Stage star Blanche Yurka creates a memorable Mme. Defarge in her film debut. Tremendous cast in a truly lavish production. Written for the screen by W.P. Lipscomb and S.N. Behrman. Also shown in computer-colored version. ▼●▶

Tale of Two Cities, A (1958-British) **117m.** *** D: Ralph Thomas. Dirk Bogarde, Dorothy Tutin, Cecil Parker, Stephen Murray, Athene Seyler, Christopher Lee, Donald Pleasence, Ian Bannen. Faithful retelling of Dickens story in this well-made British production, with Bogarde a good Sydney Carton. Remade again for TV in 1980.▼

Tales of Hoffmann, The (1951-British) **C-133m.** **½ D: Michael Powell, Emeric Pressburger. Moira Shearer, Robert Rounseville, Leonide Massine, Robert Helpmann, Pamela Brown. Jacques Offenbach's fantasy opera of student who engages in bizarre dreams, revealing three states of his life. Striking and offbeat film, not for all tastes. Beware of shorter prints. Famous score conducted by Sir Thomas Beecham. ▼●◗

Tales of Manhattan (1942) **118m.** *** D: Julien Duvivier. Charles Boyer, Rita Hayworth, Henry Fonda, Ginger Rogers, Charles Laughton, Edward G. Robinson, Ethel Waters, Paul Robeson, Eddie "Rochester" Anderson, Thomas Mitchell, Cesar Romero, George Sanders. Charming film about the effect a dress tailcoat has on its various owners; five episodes, alternately amusing, poignant, ironic. Our favorite: down-and-out Robinson attending 25th class reunion. Pictorially stylish throughout; photographed by Joseph Walker. Video has 9m. W. C. Fields episode deleted from original theatrical release.▼◗

Tales of Robin Hood (1951) **60m.** *½ D: James Tinling. Robert Clarke, Mary Hatcher, Paul Cavanagh, Wade Crosby, Whit Bissell, Ben Welden. Ultra-cheap, by-the-numbers account of Robin (Clarke) and his merry band of outlaws battling the Sheriff of Nottingham. Originally an unsold TV pilot that was released to theaters.

Tales of Terror (1962) **C-90m.** *** D: Roger Corman. Vincent Price, Peter Lorre, Basil Rathbone, Debra Paget, Maggie Pierce, Leona Gage, Joyce Jameson. Four Edgar Allan Poe stories distilled by Richard Matheson into three-part film, with Lorre's comic performance as vengeful husband walling up adulterous wife the standout. Price appears in all three segments. Notable for its odd widescreen and color effects. Panavision.▼◗

Talk About a Stranger (1952) **65m.** *** D: David Bradley. George Murphy, Nancy Davis (Reagan), Billy Gray, Kurt Kasznar, Lewis Stone. A lonely boy tries to prove reclusive neighbor Kasznar killed his dog. Good use of California orchard locations, well-judged direction, and John Alton's moody photography result in a fine little B that deserves to be better known.

Talk of the Town, The (1942) **118m.** **** D: George Stevens. Jean Arthur, Ronald Colman, Cary Grant, Glenda Farrell, Edgar Buchanan, Charles Dingle, Rex Ingram, Emma Dunn, Tom Tyler, Lloyd Bridges. Intelligent comedy with brilliant cast; fugitive Grant hides out with unsuspecting professor Colman and landlady Arthur, and tries to convince legal-minded Colman there's a human side to all laws. Splendid

film written by Irwin Shaw and Sidney Buchman.▼◗

Tall, Dark and Handsome (1941) **78m.** **½ D: H. Bruce Humberstone. Cesar Romero, Virginia Gilmore, Charlotte Greenwood, Milton Berle, Sheldon Leonard, Stanley Clements, Marc Lawrence, Frank Jenks. Amusing Runyonesque gangster comedy about an underworld bigwig (Romero) who's really a softie, and who falls for naive Gilmore. Leonard is the heavy, a role Romero played in the remake, LOVE THAT BRUTE.◗

Tall Headlines SEE: **Frightened Bride, The**

Tall in the Saddle (1944) **87m.** *** D: Edwin L. Marin. John Wayne, Ella Raines, Ward Bond, Gabby Hayes, Elisabeth Risdon, Raymond Hatton, Paul Fix, Audrey Long. Fast-paced, entertaining Western with Wayne a cowhand who becomes involved in affairs of rancher Raines. Also shown in computer-colored version.▼◗

Tall Lie, The SEE: **For Men Only**

Tall Man Riding (1955) **C-83m.** **½ D: Lesley Selander. Randolph Scott, Dorothy Malone, Peggie Castle, John Dehner, Lane Chandler. Sturdy Western with Scott involved in outmaneuvering greedy ranchers during territorial land granting in Montana.◗

Tall Men, The (1955) **C-122m.** ** D: Raoul Walsh. Clark Gable, Jane Russell, Robert Ryan, Cameron Mitchell, Juan Garcia, Harry Shannon, Emile Meyer, Mae Marsh. Large-scale Western with Gable and Mitchell as ex-Rebels who sign on for Ryan's cattle drive, and in short order all three are fighting Indians, blizzards, and each other (over Russell, of course). Pretty dull, considering stars and director. CinemaScope.▼◗

Tall Story (1960) **91m.** **½ D: Joshua Logan. Anthony Perkins, Jane Fonda, Ray Walston, Marc Connelly, Anne Jackson, Murray Hamilton, Elizabeth Patterson, Bob Wright, Bart Burns, Gary Lockwood. Fast-moving froth about man-hungry coed Fonda (in film debut) falling in love with college basketball star Perkins. Based on Howard Lindsay–Russel Crouse play.▼◗

Tall Stranger, The (1957) **C-81m.** ** D: Thomas Carr. Joel McCrea, Virginia Mayo, Michael Ansara, Michael Pate. Standard fare of McCrea helping wagon convoy cross Colorado territory. Based on a Louis L'Amour novel. CinemaScope.

Tall T, The (1957) **C-78m.** *** D: Budd Boetticher. Randolph Scott, Richard Boone, Maureen O'Sullivan, Henry Silva, Skip Homeier, John Hubbard, Arthur Hunnicutt. Scott becomes involved with kidnapped O'Sullivan, and tries to undermine unity of outlaw gang holding them prisoner. Solid Western all the way, scripted by Burt Kennedy from an Elmore Leonard story.▼◗

Tall Target, The (1951) **78m.** *** D: Anthony Mann. Dick Powell, Paula Raymond, Adolphe Menjou, Marshall Thompson, Ruby Dee, Will Geer, Leif Erickson. Gripping film noir–ish suspense as detective Powell follows tip that Abraham Lincoln is going to be assassinated during 1861 train ride. Interestingly, Powell's character is named John Kennedy! ▶

Tall Texan, The (1953) **82m.** ****** D: Elmo Williams. Lloyd Bridges, Lee J. Cobb, Marie Windsor, Luther Adler, Syd Saylor. Good cast cannot uplift this standard Western about a group seeking out a gold deposit in Indian territory. A tale of greed and gold that just doesn't pan out. ▼▶

Tamahine (1963-British) **C-85m.** ****** D: Philip Leacock. Nancy Kwan, John Fraser, Dennis Price, Coral Browne, Dick Dentley, Derek Nimmo, Justin Lord, Michael Gough, James Fox, Allan Cuthbertson. Curious British comedy trifle, about a sheltered but uninhibited Polynesian girl upsetting the order of an upper-crust men's university, might have been retitled *Tamahine, Tell Me True,* since it plays just like a Tammy movie. Cute but forgettable, notable only for its cast. CinemaScope.

Tamango (1957-French) **C-98m.** ******* D: John Berry. Dorothy Dandridge, Curt Jurgens, Jean Servais, Roger Hanin, Guy Mairesse, Alex Cressan. Stirring historical drama in which newly enslaved black African Cressan stirs revolt while being transported to Cuba aboard a slave ship. Dandridge is excellent in the complex role of a slave who is ship captain Jurgens' mistress. Way ahead of its time, and ripe for rediscovery. Based on a novelette by Prosper Merimée. CinemaScope. ▼

Taming of the Shrew, The (1929) **66m.** ****** D: Sam Taylor. Mary Pickford, Douglas Fairbanks, Edwin Maxwell, Joseph Cawthorn, Clyde Cook, Geoffrey Wardell, Dorothy Jordan. Static version of Shakespeare classic, with wild Kate (Pickford) ardently pursued and "tamed" by swaggering, self-confident Petruchio (Fairbanks). Defeated by its lack of pacing and downright embarrassing performances, though it's undeniably fascinating to see Doug and Mary in their only costarring appearance. This bears the infamous credit, "By William Shakespeare, with additional dialogue by Sam Taylor." Original running time 73m. Newly scored—and shortened—in 1966. ▼●▶

Taming Sutton's Gal (1957) **71m.** ***½** D: Lesley Selander. John Lupton, Gloria Talbott, Jack Kelly, May Wynn, Verna Felton. Bank clerk Lupton goes on a hunting trip and winds up tangling with villainous Kelly. Tedious hokum. Naturama.

T.A.M.I. Show, The (1964) **100m.** ******* D: Steve Binder. The Rolling Stones, James Brown, Chuck Berry, Marvin Gaye, The Supremes, Jan and Dean, Gerry & The Pacemakers, Smokey Robinson & The Miracles, Lesley Gore, Billy J. Kramer & The Dakotas. Historic rock and r&b concert at the Santa Monica Civic Auditorium was covered by television cameras and kinescoped onto film by whiz-kid Binder. Invaluable document of music history, with great early Mick Jagger and electrifying footwork by Brown. (Two of those go-go dancers are Teri Garr and Toni Basil!) Originally 113m., with Beach Boys sequence that was later cut (although they're still visible in the finale). Title stands for Teenage Awards Music International. Followed by THE BIG T.N.T. SHOW; see also THAT WAS ROCK. James Brown's performance was re-created in GET ON UP (2014). ▼▶

Tammy and the Bachelor (1957) **C-89m.** ******* D: Joseph Pevney. Debbie Reynolds, Walter Brennan, Leslie Nielsen, Mala Powers, Fay Wray, Sidney Blackmer, Mildred Natwick, Louise Beavers. Unpretentious if cutesy romantic corn of country girl Reynolds falling in love with pilot Nielsen whom she's nursed back to health after plane crash. Followed by two sequels and a TV series. CinemaScope. ▼▶

Tammy and the Doctor (1963) **C-88m.** ****½** D: Harry Keller. Sandra Dee, Peter Fonda, Macdonald Carey, Beulah Bondi, Margaret Lindsay, Reginald Owen, Adam West. Sugary fluff involving homespun Tammy (Dee) courted by a doctor (Fonda, in his film debut); supporting cast adds touching cameos. ▼▶

Tammy Tell Me True (1961) **C-97m.** ****** D: Harry Keller. Sandra Dee, John Gavin, Virginia Grey, Beulah Bondi, Cecil Kellaway, Edgar Buchanan. Tired romance of girl coming to college for first time, makes name for herself by helping dean of women. Script and acting very uneven. ▶

Tampico (1944) **75m.** ****** D: Lothar Mendes. Edward G. Robinson, Lynn Bari, Victor McLaglen, Marc Lawrence, Mona Maris. Robinson uplifts this otherwise obvious WW2 spy yarn, about a supply-ship captain contending with espionage; Bari is the femme fatale who may or may not be the guilty party. ▶

Tanganyika (1954) **C-81m.** ****** D: Andre de Toth. Van Heflin, Ruth Roman, Howard Duff, Jeff Morrow. OK adventure of explorer attempting land claim in East Africa with numerous perils along the way.

Tangier (1946) **76m.** ****½** D: George Waggner. Maria Montez, Preston Foster, Robert Paige, Louise Allbritton, Kent Taylor, Sabu, J. Edward Bromberg, Reginald Denny. Limp intrigue in Tangier with vengeful dancer Montez; it isn't even in color.

Tangier Incident (1953) **77m.** ***½** D: Lew Landers. George Brent, Mari Aldon, Dorothy Patrick, Bert Freed. Tame actioner with Brent a federal agent hunting an espionage ring.

Tank Force (1958-British) **C-81m.** ***½** D:

Terence Young. Victor Mature, Leo Genn, Anthony Newley, Luciana Paluzzi. Clichéd dud of WW2 with assorted British prisoners escaping across Libyan desert. Originally titled NO TIME TO DIE. CinemaScope.

Tanks Are Coming, The (1951) **90m.** ****** D: Lewis Seiler. Steve Cochran, Philip Carey, Mari Aldon, Paul Picerni, Harry Bellaver, James Dobson, George O'Hanlon, Robert Horton. Stock characters and situations fill this WW2 yarn about the U.S. Army's 3rd Armored Division as it rolls into Germany in 1944. The equipment outshines the actors. Based on a story by Sam Fuller.▼🌓

Tanned Legs (1929) **71m.** ****½** D: Marshall Neilan. Arthur Lake, June Clyde, Dorothy Revier, Ann Pennington, Albert Gran, Allen Kearns, Sally Blane, Lloyd Hamilton. Among the better early-talkie musicals, this spirited (if occasionally clunky) curio chronicles the romantic shenanigans at a summer beach resort, with young Clyde setting out to reform her wayward parents while being romanced by Lake. Songs by Oscar Levant and Sidney Clare.

Tap Roots (1948) **C-109m.** ****½** D: George Marshall. Van Heflin, Susan Hayward, Boris Karloff, Julie Lunnor, Whitfield Connor, Ward Bond, Richard Long, Arthur Shields. Oddball venture into GWTW territory, with Van and Susan as lovers in progressive Mississippi county that says it will secede from the state if the state secedes from the Union! No big deal, but watchable, with Karloff as an Indian medicine man.

Tarantula (1955) **80m.** ******* D: Jack Arnold. John Agar, Mara Corday, Leo G. Carroll, Nestor Paiva, Ross Elliott, Eddie Parker. Scientist Carroll's new growth formula works a little *too* well, and pretty soon there's a humongous spider chewing up the countryside. One of the best giant-insect films, with fast pacing, convincing special effects, and interesting subplot detailing formula's effect on humans. That's Clint Eastwood as the jet squadron leader in final sequence.▼🌓

Taras Bulba (1962) **C-122m.** ****½** D: J. Lee Thompson. Tony Curtis, Yul Brynner, Christine Kaufmann, Sam Wanamaker, George Macready. Cardboard costumer of 16th-century Ukraine, centering on Cossack life and fighting. Nice photography (on location in Argentina) by Joe Mac-Donald and fine musical score by Franz Waxman. The Gogol novel was previously filmed in 1936 in France (TARASS BOULBA) and in 1939 in England (THE REBEL SON). Remade in Russia in 2009. Panavision.▼🌓

Tarawa Beachhead (1958) **77m.** ****½** D: Paul Wendkos. Kerwin Mathews, Julie Adams, Ray Danton, Karen Sharpe. Standard account of WW2 military assault with usual focus on problems of troops. 🌓

Target Earth (1954) **75m.** ****½** D: Sherman Rose. Richard Denning, Virginia Grey, Kathleen Crowley, Richard Reeves, Whit Bissell, Robert Roark, Steve Pendleton. People in deserted city trapped by invading robot force. Competently acted movie starts off beautifully but bogs down too soon.▼🌓

Target Unknown (1951) **90m.** ****** D: George Sherman. Mark Stevens, Alex Nicol, Robert Douglas, Don Taylor, Gig Young, Joyce Holden, James Best. Standard drama of American flyers shot down and becoming POWs in German-occupied France during WW2; Nazis use devious means to interrogate them. Young has interesting role as German-American Nazi officer. Remake of Army training film RESISTING ENEMY INTERROGATION (1944).

Target Zero (1955) **92m.** ****** D: Harmon Jones. Richard Conte, Charles Bronson, Chuck Connors, L.Q. Jones, Peggie Castle, Strother Martin. Unrewarding Korean War film, focusing on plight of Lt. Conte as he leads his platoon behind enemy lines. 🌓

Tarnished Angel (1938) **67m.** ****½** D: Leslie Goodwins. Sally Eilers, Lee Bowman, Ann Miller, Alma Kruger, Paul Guilfoyle, Cecil Kellaway. Broadway showgirl–nightclub hostess Eilers, on the lam and in need of cash, transforms herself into Sister Connie, a phony "girl revivalist." Moderately effective grade-B drama benefits from Miller's all-too-brief dancing and singing.

Tarnished Angels, The (1958) **91m.** *****½** D: Douglas Sirk. Rock Hudson, Dorothy Malone, Robert Stack, Jack Carson, Robert Middleton, Troy Donahue, William Schallert. Compelling adaptation of William Faulkner's fatalistic drama *Pylon,* set in 1930s, with Hudson as newspaperman drawn to barnstorming pilot Stack—his curious life-style and ethics, his put-upon wife, and his frustrated mechanic. CinemaScope.▼🌓

Tarnished Lady (1931) **83m.** ****½** D: George Cukor. Tallulah Bankhead, Clive Brook, Phoebe Foster, Osgood Perkins, Elizabeth Patterson. Bankhead marries Brook for his money but falls in love with him almost too late. Ornate triangle has good performances.

Tars and Spars (1946) **88m.** ****** D: Alfred E. Green. Alfred Drake, Janet Blair, Sid Caesar, Marc Platt, Jeff Donnell, Ray Walker. Humdrum musical with Coast Guard backdrop, based very loosely on real-life camp show created by servicemen, one of whom, Sid Caesar, makes his movie debut doing a hilarious war-movie spoof. A rare film appearance for Broadway star Drake.

Tartars, The (1961-Italian) **C-83m.** ****** D: Richard Thorpe. Orson Welles, Victor Mature, Folco Lulli, Liana Orfei. Welles' performance as Burundai, head of Tartar invasion of Volga River, plus appearance of

Mature, are only distinguishing features of otherwise routine spectacle. Totalscope. ▶

Tartu SEE: **Adventures of Tartu, The**

Tartuffe (1926-German) **63m. **½** D: F. W. Murnau. Emil Jannings, Werner Krauss, Lil Dagover, Lucie Höflich, Rosa Valetti, Hermann Picha, André Mattoni. Solemn adaptation of the Molière classic, in which a wife (Dagover) attempts to persuade her mate (Krauss) that boastfully honest Jannings is actually a fraud. A parallel story involves a greedy housekeeper who's scheming to murder her aged employer. Not Murnau's (or Jannings') best, but still well worth a look. Gérard Depardieu remade this as LE TARTUFFE (1984). ▼▶

Tarzan Several generations of movie buffs have regarded Johnny Weissmuller as the definitive Tarzan, though Edgar Rice Burroughs' jungle king has been portrayed by numerous others since 1918, when beefy Elmo Lincoln first swung onto the screen. There were other silent-film versions of the Tarzan tale, but the next film to make a major impact was the early talkie TARZAN THE APE MAN, which starred Olympic swimming hero Weissmuller. Though it wasn't particularly faithful to Burroughs' book, it was an entertaining, well-made film that captured the imagination of a Depression-era audience, and led to a string of equally entertaining sequels. Buffs generally cite TARZAN AND HIS MATE as the best of all. This and the other 1930s entries in this series were "class" films with fine production values, plenty of action, and strong supporting casts, led, of course, by lovely Maureen O'Sullivan as Jane. (The success of these films inspired other producers to try and cash in with their own Tarzan projects, most of which were second-rate endeavors, though they all starred good-looking men who, like Weissmuller, had been Olympic medal winners: Buster Crabbe, Herman Brix—later known as Bruce Bennett—and Glenn Morris.) The later MGM outings such as TARZAN'S NEW YORK ADVENTURE became more contrived, like other series films, with often-excessive comedy relief supplied by Cheetah the chimp, and family interest sparked by the arrival of Johnny Sheffield as Boy. When MGM lost interest in the series, Weissmuller continued making Tarzan movies for producer Sol Lesser at RKO, without O'Sullivan and without that MGM production sheen. Lex Barker took over the role in 1949, and the series became progressively more routine; Barker made his last jungle outing in 1953. Since then a number of people have played Tarzan, including Denny Miller (who starred in a 1959 remake of Weissmuller's 1932 film, filled with tinted stock footage from the original), Jock Mahoney (who also played supporting roles in two other Tarzan films), Mike Henry, and Gordon Scott, the latter faring best in some well-produced British-made adventure stories (including TARZAN'S GREATEST ADVENTURE, an excellent jungle tale shot in color, with young Sean Connery in the cast). Ron Ely took on the role for a Mexican-filmed TV series, and some of these episodes have been strung together into ersatz feature films. But the most recent theatrical ventures involving Tarzan have all been unusual: an unappealing animated spoof called SHAME OF THE JUNGLE featuring the voice of Johnny Weissmuller, Jr.; a live-action farce called TARZAN, THE APE MAN designed as a showcase for sexy Bo Derek; a television update, with tongue in cheek, called TARZAN IN MANHATTAN; and the most ambitious of them all, GREYSTOKE: THE LEGEND OF TARZAN, LORD OF THE APES, which purported to return to Edgar Rice Burroughs' original concept but (for all its dramatic success) deviated from the source in its own way. Compared to a film like GREYSTOKE, the old series films might look simplistic and even quaint—but they're unpretentious and certainly entertaining. And while generations still think of Johnny Weissmuller as the definitive Tarzan, each decade brings new interpretations of the timeless character—the latest in animated form from Disney.

TARZAN

Tarzan of the Apes (1918)
Tarzan the Ape Man (1932)
Tarzan the Fearless (1933)
Tarzan and His Mate (1934)
The New Adventures of Tarzan (1935)
Tarzan Escapes (1936)
Tarzan's Revenge (1938)
Tarzan and the Green Goddess (1938)
Tarzan Finds a Son! (1939)
Tarzan's Secret Treasure (1941)
Tarzan's New York Adventure (1942)
Tarzan Triumphs (1943)
Tarzan's Desert Mystery (1943)
Tarzan and the Amazons (1945)
Tarzan and the Leopard Woman (1946)
Tarzan and the Huntress (1947)
Tarzan and the Mermaids (1948)
Tarzan's Magic Fountain (1949)
Tarzan and the Slave Girl (1950)
Tarzan's Peril (1951)
Tarzan's Savage Fury (1952)
Tarzan and the She-Devil (1953)
Tarzan's Hidden Jungle (1955)
Tarzan and the Lost Safari (1957)
Tarzan's Fight for Life (1958)
Tarzan and the Trappers (1958)
Tarzan's Greatest Adventure (1959)
Tarzan, the Ape Man (1959)
Tarzan the Magnificent (1960)

Tarzan and His Mate (1934) 105m. ***½ D: Cedric Gibbons, Jack Conway. Johnny Weissmuller, Maureen O'Sullivan, Neil Hamilton, Paul Cavanagh, Forrester Harvey. Jane's jilted fiance (Hamilton) returns to the jungle with a rapacious ivory poacher (Cavanagh) and tries to get Tarzan to lead them to the elephant graveyard, but the native couple is having too much fun swinging. Opulent, action-packed entry codirected by MGM's famed art director Gibbons, and notable for pre-Code sexual candor and a distinct lack of clothes. Beware 95m. prints. ▼◑

Tarzan and the Amazons (1945) 76m. **½ D: Kurt Neumann. Johnny Weissmuller, Brenda Joyce, Johnny Sheffield, Henry Stephenson, Maria Ouspenskaya, Barton MacLane. Archeologists seeking to plunder Amazon treasures have to deal with Tarzan first in this amusing nonsense highlighted by the diminutive Ouspenskaya as the Amazon Queen! ◑

Tarzan and the Green Goddess (1938) 72m. *½ D: Edward Kull. Herman Brix (Bruce Bennett), Ula Holt, Frank Baker, Don Castello, Lewis Sargent. More juvenile jungle escapades, with an educated Ape Man. Derived from 1935's THE NEW ADVENTURES OF TARZAN serial, produced by Edgar Rice Burroughs' own company, and filmed on location in Guatemala. Contains footage not used in serial. ▼▶

Tarzan and the Huntress (1947) 72m. ** D: Kurt Neumann. Johnny Weissmuller, Brenda Joyce, Johnny Sheffield, Patricia Morison, Barton MacLane. Familiar bungle in the jungle about Tarzan fighting a zoologist (Morison) who's trying to make off with a menagerie. Weissmuller was tired by this time, and so were the plots. ◑

Tarzan and the Leopard Woman (1946) 72m. ** D: Kurt Neumann. Johnny Weissmuller, Brenda Joyce, Johnny Sheffield, Acquanetta, Edgar Barrier, Tommy Cook. Tarzan and Boy take on a murder cult, and almost pay with their lives. The series was becoming increasingly silly, though it's still fun by Saturday matinee standards. ◑

Tarzan and the Lost Safari (1957-British) C-84m. ** D: H. Bruce Humberstone. Gordon Scott, Yolande Donlan, Robert Beatty, Betta St. John, Wilfrid Hyde-White, George Coulouris. Color and widescreen spruce up this entry about the passengers of a plane that crashes in the jungle, who are pursued by savage Oparians. But Tarzan still speaks in monosyllables, and the story is pretty slow going. RKO-Scope. ◑

Tarzan and the Mermaids (1948) 68m. **½ D: Robert Florey. Johnny Weissmuller, Brenda Joyce, Linda Christian, John Lanenz, George Zucco, Fernando Wagner. Tarzan comes to the aid of a native (stunning Christian) who's being forced to wed a phony island "God" (Wagner) by evil highpriest Zucco. Outlandish, often campy outing filmed in Mexico. Weissmuller hung up his loincloth after this. ◑

Tarzan and the She-Devil (1953) 76m. *½ D: Kurt Neumann. Lex Barker, Joyce MacKenzie, Raymond Burr, Monique Van Vooren, Tom Conway. Boring hokum about ivory poachers led by seductive Van Vooren. Barker's last appearance as Tarzan. Burr is an exceptionally good heavy. ◑

Tarzan and the Slave Girl (1950) 74m. ** D: Lee Sholem. Lex Barker, Vanessa Brown, Robert Alda, Hurd Hatfield, Arthur Shields, Anthony Caruso, Denise Darcel. When a tribe of lion worshippers kidnaps Jane (Brown) and alluring half-breed Darcel, it's Tarzan, Cheetah, and friends to the rescue. ◑

Tarzan and the Trappers (1958) 74m. *½ D: Charles Haas, Sandy Howard. Gordon Scott, Eve Brent, Rickie Sorensen, Leslie Bradley. Cheaply made hokum about evil white hunters on an expedition to find a lost city filled with treasure. Edited together from three episodes of a Tarzan TV series that never got off the ground. ▼▶

Tarzan Escapes (1936) 89m. *** D: Richard Thorpe. Johnny Weissmuller, Maureen O'Sullivan, John Buckler, Benita Hume, William Henry, Herbert Mundin. Graphically violent (for its time), and energetically directed, this entertaining entry has Tarzan captured by a hunter who wants to put him on exhibition in England. This film was completely reshot and reworked when the original version proved too potent and bloodcurdling for preview audiences; as a result there are some plot holes in what might have been the best Tarzan movie of all. ▼◑

Tarzan Finds a Son! (1939) 90m. *** D: Richard Thorpe. Johnny Weissmuller, Maureen O'Sullivan, Johnny Sheffield, Ian Hunter, Frieda Inescort, Laraine Day, Henry Wilcoxon. The jungle lovers find a child whose parents were killed in a plane crash and fight his greedy relatives to adopt him in this diverting entry. This was to be O'Sullivan's final appearance as Jane, but the end was reshot so she could return (in TARZAN'S SECRET TREASURE). ▼◑

Tarzan Goes to India (1962-British) C-86m. **½ D: John Guillermin. Jock Mahoney, Mark Dana, Simi, Leo Gordon, Jai. At the request of a dying maharajah, Tarzan tries to save a herd of elephants imperiled by the construction of a dam. Location shooting helps. CinemaScope. ◑

Tarzan of the Apes (1918) 55m. **½ D: Scott Sidney. Elmo Lincoln, Enid Markey, True Boardman, Kathleen Kirkham, Gordon Griffith. The very first Tarzan film is a surprisingly watchable and straightforward telling of the Greystoke tale, though Lincoln looks like he's about 50 years old, with a beer belly to boot. ▼◑

Tarzan's Desert Mystery (1943) 70m. **½ D: William Thiele. Johnny Weissmuller, Nancy Kelly, Johnny Sheffield, Otto Kruger, Joseph Sawyer, Lloyd Corrigan, Robert

Lowery. Tarzan vs. Nazis, take two, with some evil Arabs and prehistoric creatures (including a giant spider) thrown in for good measure.▶

Tarzan's Fight for Life (1958) C-86m. ** D: H. Bruce Humberstone. Gordon Scott, Eve Brent, Rickie Sorensen, Jil Jarmyn, James Edwards, Woody Strode. The jungle do-gooder helps a medic fight superstitious natives and a conniving witch doctor. Cheesy series entry with the cast stomping around a studio jungle set. ▶

Tarzan's Greatest Adventure (1959-British) C-88m. *** D: John Guillermin. Gordon Scott, Anthony Quayle, Sara Shane, Niall MacGinnis, Scilla Gabel, Sean Connery. Honorable attempt to upgrade the series' quality, with Tarzan on the trail of diamond-hunting scoundrels (including a young Connery). A superior action yarn shot on location in Africa, more adult than most of its predecessors. Tarzan has a much expanded vocabulary in this one. ▶

Tarzan's Hidden Jungle (1955) 73m. ** D: Harold Schuster. Gordon Scott, Vera Miles, Peter Van Eyck, Jack Elam, Rex Ingram. Scott's debut as Tarzan is a competent, if unexciting, outing focusing on his battle with evil hunter Elam who tries to butcher half the animal kingdom. ▶

Tarzan's Magic Fountain (1949) 73m. **½ D: Lee Sholem. Lex Barker, Brenda Joyce, Evelyn Ankers, Albert Dekker, Alan Napier, Charles Drake, Henry Brandon. Barker's first series entry, and one of his most endurable, as Tarzan finds a secret valley where nobody ages—unless they leave. (Sound a bit like LOST HORIZON?) Too bad the rest of the Barker films weren't as good. Elmo Lincoln, the screen's first Tarzan, has a bit part.▶

Tarzan's New Adventure SEE: New Adventures of Tarzan, The

Tarzan's New York Adventure (1942) 72m. **½ D: Richard Thorpe. Johnny Weissmuller, Maureen O'Sullivan, Johnny Sheffield, Virginia Grey, Charles Bickford, Paul Kelly, Russell Hicks, Chill Wills. When Boy is snatched from the jungle by nasty circus owners, Tarzan swings into action across the seas and over the Brooklyn Bridge to retrieve him. Seems pretty original until you realize that KING KONG was made a decade earlier! Still, an amusing entry; Tarzan's first encounter with indoor plumbing is truly memorable. O'Sullivan's final appearance in the series. ▼●▶

Tarzan's Peril (1951) 79m. **½ D: Byron Haskin. Lex Barker, Virginia Huston, George Macready, Douglas Fowley, Dorothy Dandridge, Alan Napier. White gunrunners out to get Tarzan try to stir up trouble between warring tribes in this fairly respectable entry with an interesting supporting cast. Dandridge is excellent, if wasted in a small role.▶

Tarzan's Revenge (1938) 70m. ** D: D. Ross Lederman. Glenn Morris, Eleanor Holm, George Barbier, C. Henry Gordon, Hedda Hopper, George Meeker. Olympic decathlon champ Morris cavorts capably enough in this adventure about an evil African ruler who covets perky Holm (a champion swimmer herself). No other Tarzan film had the Ape Man off screen for such long stretches, however. But . . . Me Tarzan, you *Eleanor*?▼▶

Tarzan's Savage Fury (1952) 80m. ** D: Cyril Endfield. Lex Barker, Dorothy Hart, Patric Knowles, Charles Korvin, Tommy Carlton. Slackly handled entry about diamond thieves who trick Tarzan into being their guide.▶

Tarzan's Secret Treasure (1941) 81m. **½ D: Richard Thorpe. Johnny Weissmuller, Maureen O'Sullivan, Johnny Sheffield, Reginald Owen, Barry Fitzgerald, Tom Conway. Melodramatic entry about greedy gold seekers who try to dupe Tarzan into helping them. Tarzan and Jane's treehouse has become pretty elaborate by now.▼●▶

Tarzan's Three Challenges (1963) C-92m. **½ D: Robert Day. Jock Mahoney, Woody Strode, Ricky Der, Tsuruko Kobayashi, Earl Cameron. Tarzan protects a young heir to the throne in Thailand from his malevolent uncle in this picturesque entry that includes a wicked machete fight. The athletic Mahoney became deathly ill while filming in India—which is all too obvious from his dramatic weight loss during the course of the picture. Dyaliscope. ▶

Tarzan the Ape Man (1932) 99m. *** D: W. S. Van Dyke. Johnny Weissmuller, Maureen O'Sullivan, C. Aubrey Smith, Neil Hamilton, Doris Lloyd. British gentry meets jungle savagery when the daughter of an English hunter is captured by Tarzan and decides she prefers his primal charms to those of her upper-crust fiancé. The original Weissmuller-MGM *Tarzan* entry is a little starchy, but still holds up thanks to a plush production and vivid atmosphere (with jungle footage provided by TRADER HORN). Also shown in a computer-colored version.▼●▶

Tarzan, the Ape Man (1959) C-82m. BOMB D: Joseph Newman. Denny Miller, Joanna Barnes, Cesare Danova, Robert Douglas, Thomas Yangha. Take one blond UCLA basketball star (Miller), the production values of a pep rally, steal Johnny Weissmuller's famous yell and (tinted) footage of him swinging through the trees, add a pseudo African jazz score by Shorty Rogers, and what you have is a cheesy and inept effort by MGM to utilize safari footage from KING SOLOMON'S MINES for the umpteenth time.

Tarzan the Fearless (1933) 85m. *½ D: Robert Hill. Buster Crabbe, Jacqueline Wells (Julie Bishop), E. Alyn Warren, Edward Woods, Philo McCullough, Matthew Betz, Frank Lackteen, Mischa Auer. Feature version of a crude serial about a scientific expedition to find the lost city of Zar. Crabbe's Tarzan is even more tightlipped than Weissmuller's.▼▶

Tarzan the Magnificent (1960-British) C-88m. *** D: Robert Day. Gordon Scott, Jock Mahoney, Betta St. John, John Carradine, Alexandra Stewart, Lionel Jeffries, Earl Cameron. Tarzan captures a murderer and faces numerous perils trying to escort him to the police through the jungle. Similarly mature follow-up to TARZAN'S GREATEST ADVENTURE, with a strong supporting cast. Ironically, villain Mahoney would take over the lead role from Scott in the next entry.▶

Tarzan Triumphs (1943) 78m. *** D: William Thiele. Johnny Weissmuller, Frances Gifford, Johnny Sheffield, Stanley Ridges, Sig Ruman. First of the series made by RKO features stunning Gifford (who earlier starred as Edgar Rice Burroughs' JUNGLE GIRL in a Republic serial) as the princess of a lost city invaded by Nazi paratroopers. WW2 propaganda all the way, with Tarzan an incongruous participant, but still an entertaining and energetic programmer. Cheetah's curtain-closing bit with the Nazis' short-wave radio is not to be missed.▶

Task Force (1949) 116m. **½ D: Delmer Daves. Gary Cooper, Jane Wyatt, Wayne Morris, Walter Brennan, Julie London, Bruce Bennett, Stanley Ridges, Jack Holt. Well-made but unremarkable story of a Naval officer's career, tracing aircraft carrier development. Originally shown with some scenes in color.▼▶

Taste of Honey, A (1961-British) 100m. ***½ D: Tony Richardson. Rita Tushingham, Robert Stephens, Dora Bryan, Murray Melvin, Paul Danquah. Homely young girl who has affair with black sailor and becomes pregnant is cared for by homosexual friend. Shelagh Delaney's London and Broadway stage hit is poignant and uncompromising film with fine, sensitive performances. Screenplay by Delaney and Richardson.▼

Tattered Dress, The (1957) 93m. **½ D: Jack Arnold. Jeff Chandler, Jeanne Crain, Jack Carson, Gail Russell, George Tobias, Philip Reed. Slowly paced but watchable account of lawyer Chandler defending society man accused of murder; Crain is his sympathetic wife. CinemaScope.

Tattooed Stranger, The (1950) 64m. **½ D: Edward J. Montagne. John Miles, Patricia White (Barry), Walter Kinsella, Frank Tweddell, Rod McLennan, Henry Lasko, Arthur Jarrett, Jack Lord. The corpse of a tattooed woman is discovered in Central Park, and the NYPD—specifically, a scruffy veteran flatfoot (Kinsella) and a new-breed, college-educated rookie (Miles)—go into

action. Generally engrossing NAKED CITY–influenced police procedural benefits from colorful N.Y.C. location filming, particularly in Brooklyn and the Bronx.▶

Tawny Pipit (1944-British) 85m. **½ D: Bernard Miles, Charles Saunders. Bernard Miles, Rosamund John, Niall MacGinnis, Jean Gillie, George Carney, Christopher Steele, Lucie Mannheim, Wylie Watson, Ian Fleming. Slight but appealing story of some English villagers' fight to save the title rare breed of birds, who have nested in a nearby field. Miles and Saunders also scripted.

Taxi! (1932) 70m. **½ D: Roy Del Ruth. James Cagney, Loretta Young, George E. Stone, Dorothy Burgess, Guy Kibbee, Leila Bennett, Cotton Club Orchestra. Hokey but colorful Depression melodrama of warring N.Y.C. cab drivers, with Cagney fine as a hotheaded hack. Yes, that's George Raft as his dance-contest rival. Nothing can top Jimmy's opening bit in Yiddish!▶

Taxi (1953) 77m. ** D: Gregory Ratoff. Dan Dailey, Constance Smith, Neva Patterson, Blanche Yurka, Stubby Kaye. Mild little comedy of N.Y.C. cab driver Dailey trying to help an Irish girl find her husband. John Cassavetes' film debut. Look for a young Geraldine Page.

Taza, Son of Cochise (1954) C-79m. **½ D: Douglas Sirk. Rock Hudson, Barbara Rush, Gregg Palmer, Bart Roberts (Rex Reason), Morris Ankrum, Joe Sawyer. Actually two sons: one wants to live peacefully with the white man, the other thinks Geronimo has a better idea. Sirk's only Western is uneven follow-up to BROKEN ARROW—with Jeff Chandler popping in just long enough to die—but sweeping action scenes and sympathetic treatment of Indians help. 3-D.▶

Tea and Sympathy (1956) C-122m. *** D: Vincente Minnelli. Deborah Kerr, John Kerr, Leif Erickson, Edward Andrews, Darryl Hickman, Dean Jones, Norma Crane. Glossy but well-acted version of Robert Anderson play about prep school boy's affair with a teacher's wife, skirting homosexual issues. Both Kerrs give sensitive portrayals; they and Erickson re-create their Broadway roles. Scripted by the playwright. CinemaScope.▼●▶

Teacher's Pet (1958) 120m. *** D: George Seaton. Clark Gable, Doris Day, Gig Young, Mamie Van Doren, Nick Adams, Charles Lane. Self-educated city editor Gable clashes with journalism teacher Day in this airy, amusing comedy. Young is memorable as Doris' intellectual boyfriend. Written by Fay and Michael Kanin. VistaVision.▼●▶

Tea for Two (1950) C-98m. **½ D: David Butler. Doris Day, Gordon MacRae, Gene Nelson, Patrice Wymore, Eve Arden, Billy De Wolfe, S. Z. Sakall, Bill Goodwin, Virginia Gibson. Pleasant but unexceptional musical very loosely based on the stage play *No, No, Nanette* (which was filmed before in 1930 and 1940). Day bets uncle Sakall she can answer no to every question for the length of a weekend—in order to win her chance to star in a Broadway show. ▼●◗

Teahouse of the August Moon, The (1956) **C-123m.** ***½ D: Daniel Mann. Marlon Brando, Glenn Ford, Machiko Kyo, Eddie Albert, Paul Ford, Henry (Harry) Morgan. Outstanding comedy scripted by John Patrick from his hit play of Army officers involved with Americanization of post-WW2 Okinawa. A warm and memorable film. Paul Ford re-creates his Broadway role and nearly steals the show. Based on book by Vern J. Sneider. CinemaScope. ▼●◗

Tear Gas Squad (1940) **55m.** **½ D: Terry Morse. Dennis Morgan, John Payne, Gloria Dickson, George Reeves, Edgar Buchanan. Wiseguy nightclub crooner becomes a rookie cop to impress a girl from a police family. A romantic comedy with songs, *nothing* like what the title promises—until the three-quarters mark, when it shifts gears and becomes *every*thing the title promises!

Teckman Mystery, The (1954-British) **89m.** ** D: Wendy Toye. Margaret Leighton, John Justin, Meier Tzelniker, Roland Culver, George Coulouris, Michael Medwin. Justin is writer commissioned to do a biography of Medwin, presumably dead war hero, with surprising results. Capably acted.

Teenage Bad Girl SEE: **Bad Girl**

Teenage Cave Man (1958) **66m.** ** D: Roger Corman. Robert Vaughn, Darrah Marshall, Leslie Bradley, Frank De Kova. Vaughn, light years away from THE YOUNG PHILADELPHIANS or S.O.B., is the title character, a prehistoric adolescent hankering for greener pastures, in this AIP quickie with predictable "surprise" ending. Superama. ▼◗

Teen-Age Crime Wave (1955) **77m.** BOMB D: Fred F. Sears. Tommy Cook, Molly McCart, Sue England, Frank Griffin, James Bell, Kay Riehl. Adolescent hoodlums terrorize farm family after a robbery and shooting. Bad. ▼◗

Teenage Devil Dolls (1952) **58m.** BOMB D: B. Lawrence Price, Jr. Barbara Marks, Robert A. Sherry, Robert Norman, Elaine Lindenbaum, Joel Climenhaga, B. Lawrence Price, Jr. Yet another entry in the REEFER MADNESS school of filmmaking, about an insecure, discontented teen girl's (Marks) descent into drug addiction and crime. Presented as a case history and without dialogue; there's only narration and sound effects. Originally titled ONE-WAY TICKET TO HELL. ▼◗

Teenage Doll (1957) **68m.** ** D: Roger Corman. June Kenney, Fay Spain, Richard Devon, Dorothy Neumann. Title dish (Kenney) doesn't want to spend school nights at home in her room, gets involved with punk

peers. This above-average sleazy B won't obscure memory of Dreyer and Ozu, but is true to its era. ▼◗

Teen-age Millionaire (1961) **C/B&W-84m.** BOMB D: Lawrence Doheny. Jimmy Clanton, ZaSu Pitts, Rocky Graziano, Diane Jergens, Chubby Checker, Jackie Wilson, Dion, Marv Johnson, Bill Black, Jack Larson, Vicki Spencer, Sid Gould, Maurice Gosfield. Deadening musical about teenager Clanton, with a huge inheritance, who becomes a pop star. The rock acts are unusually and annoyingly tame here.

Teenage Monster (1958) **65m.** BOMB D: Jacques Marquette. Anne Gwynne, Gloria Castillo, Stuart Wade, Gil Perkins, Charles (Chuck) Courtney, Stephen Parker. In the Old West, radiation from a meteor causes a boy to grow into a hairy, muscular brute (Perkins), who is controlled by his mother (Gwynne)—for a while. Trivial combo of Western and sci-fi is too slight and dull to work on either level. Perkins was 50 when this was made! Aka METEOR MONSTER. ◗

Teen-age Rebel (1956) **94m.** **½ D: Edmund Goulding. Ginger Rogers, Michael Rennie, Betty Lou Keim, Mildred Natwick, Rusty Swope, Warren Berlinger, Lilli Gentle, Louise Beavers, Irene Hervey. Pat yet provocative film of divorcée Rogers, now remarried, trying to reestablish understanding with her daughter. CinemaScope. ◗

Teenagers From Outer Space (1959) **86m.** BOMB D: Tom Graeff. David Love, Dawn Anderson, Harvey B. Dunn, Bryant Grant, Tom Lockyear (Tom Graeff). Ridiculous sci-fi about alien youths who bring monster to Earth, shown as the shadow of a lobster! Very, very cheap; but still a camp classic. Besides directing and playing a small part, Graeff wrote, produced, photographed, and edited! ▼◗

Teenage Zombies (1957) **73m.** BOMB D: Jerry Warren. Don Sullivan, Katherine Victor, Steve Conte, Paul Pepper, Bri Murphy, Mitzi Albertson. Victor captures teenagers snooping around her island, imprisons them for experiments. Typically awful Warren horror film with long stretches in which nothing happens ... and incidentally, no teenage zombies! Remade as FRANKENSTEIN ISLAND. ▼◗

Telegraph Trail, The (1933) **54m.** ** D: Tenny Wright. John Wayne, Frank McHugh, Marceline Day, Otis Harlan, Yakima Canutt, Lafe McKee. Government scout Wayne escorts supply train threatened by Indians to camp where crew is constructing the first cross-country telegraph line through the western plains. Lesser-grade Warner Bros. B Western. Wayne's horse is named Duke—and gets second billing! ▼◗

Television Spy (1939) **58m.** **½ D: Edward Dmytryk. William Henry, Judith Barrett, William Collier, Sr., Richard Denning, John Eldredge, Dorothy Tree, Anthony Quinn, Minor Watson, Morgan Conway. Foreign agents attempt to steal an American scientist's revolutionary device called the Iconoscope. Plotted and paced like an elongated serial chapter; just as nonsensical and just as much fun.

Tell It to the Judge (1949) **87m.** **½ D: Norman Foster. Rosalind Russell, Robert Cummings, Gig Young, Marie McDonald, Harry Davenport, Douglass Dumbrille. Flyweight marital farce with Russell and Cummings in and out of love every ten minutes; enjoyable if you like the stars. ▼▶

Tell It to the Marines (1926) **103m.** *** D: George W. Hill. Lon Chaney, William Haines, Eleanor Boardman, Eddie Gribbon, Carmel Myers, Warner Oland, Mitchell Lewis. Chaney, playing against type, is superb as a tough but compassionate leatherneck who mentors an immature recruit (Haines). The story is predictable, and little more than a U.S. Marine Corps recruiting poster, but it's a treat to see Chaney acting without makeup. ▼▶

Tell No Tales (1939) **69m.** **½ D: Leslie Fenton. Melvyn Douglas, Louise Platt, Gene Lockhart, Douglass Dumbrille, Sara Haden, Florence George, Zeffie Tilbury. Editor tries to save his dying newspaper by capturing notorious kidnappers himself. Good B picture with some telling vignettes (particularly a black boxer's wake), though it doesn't hold up to the finish.

Tell-Tale Heart, The (1960-British) **81m.** **½ D: Ernest Morris. Laurence Payne, Adrienne Corri, Dermot Walsh, Selma Vaz Dias. Atmospheric Edgar Allan Poe yarn about a meek librarian who becomes obsessed, sexually and otherwise, with his pretty new neighbor—but she shows more of an interest in his charming and good-looking best friend. ▼▶

Tempest (1928) **102m.** *** D: Sam Taylor. John Barrymore, Camilla Horn, Louis Wolheim, George Fawcett, Ullrich Haupt, Michael Visaroff. Lushly filmed tale of Russian Revolution, with peasant Barrymore rising to rank of sergeant, controlling fate of princess (Horn) who had previously scorned him. ▼▶

Tempest (1959-Italian) **C-125m.** **½ D: Alberto Lattuada. Silvana Mangano, Van Heflin, Viveca Lindfors, Geoffrey Horne, Oscar Homolka, Robert Keith, Agnes Moorehead, Finlay Currie, Vittorio Gassman, Helmut Dantine. Turgid, disjointed costumer set in 18th-century Russia, loosely based on Pushkin novel about peasant uprising to dethrone Catherine the Great (Lindfors). Technirama.

Temptation (1946) **98m.** **½ D: Irving Pichel. Merle Oberon, George Brent, Paul Lukas, Charles Korvin, Lenore Ulric, Ludwig Stossel. Woman-with-a-past Oberon marries archeologist Brent, then falls in love with unscrupulous Korvin. Nothing new, but smoothly done.

Temptress, The (1926) **117m.** **½ D: Fred Niblo. Greta Garbo, Antonio Moreno, Roy D'Arcy, Marc MacDermott, Lionel Barrymore, Virginia Brown Faire. Garbo's second American film is dated curio about wicked woman who drives men to death and destruction, only to have her own life ruined by falling in love with Moreno. Adapted from Blasco-Ibanez; some prints run 95m. ▶

Ten Cents a Dance (1931) **80m.** *½ D: Lionel Barrymore. Barbara Stanwyck, Ricardo Cortez, Monroe Owsley, Sally Blane, Blanche Frederici. Dreary, slow-moving drama about a taxi dancer's unfortunate marriage to a worthless wimp, who turns out to be a crook and a cheat, as well. ▶

Ten Commandments, The (1923) **146m.** *** D: Cecil B. DeMille. Theodore Roberts, Charles de Roche, Estelle Taylor, Richard Dix, Rod La Rocque, Leatrice Joy, Nita Naldi, Agnes Ayres. Biblical story, told in compact form (but on a gargantuan scale—with several scenes in two-color Technicolor) is only first portion of this silent film. The rest is a modern-day parable involving two brothers, one a saint, the other a sinner—and it's anything but subtle. Still, it's good entertainment in the best DeMille style. Remade in 1956, for TV in 2006, and as an animated feature in 2007. ▼▶

Ten Commandments, The (1956) **C-220m.** **** D: Cecil B. DeMille. Charlton Heston, Yul Brynner, Anne Baxter, Edward G. Robinson, Yvonne De Carlo, Debra Paget, John Derek, Cedric Hardwicke, H.B. Warner, Henry Wilcoxon, Nina Foch, Martha Scott, Judith Anderson, Vincent Price, John Carradine, Woodrow (Woody) Strode. Vivid storytelling at its best. Biblical epic follows Moses' life from birth and abandonment through manhood, slavery, and trials in leading the Jews out of Egypt. Few subtleties in DeMille's second handling of this tale (first filmed in 1923) but few lulls, either. Parting of the Red Sea, writing of the holy tablets are unforgettable highlights. Oscar-winning special effects. Roadshow version on video runs 231m. with overture, intermission/ entr'acte, exit music. VistaVision. ▼●▶

Ten Days That Shook the World SEE: **October**

Ten Days to Tulara (1958) **77m.** BOMB D: George Sherman. Sterling Hayden, Grace Raynor, Rodolfo Hoyos, Carlos Muzquiz. Dud adventure account of Hayden et al. pursued across Mexico by police for the gold they carry.

Tender Comrade (1943) **C-102m.** **½ D: Edward Dmytryk. Ginger Rogers, Robert Ryan, Ruth Hussey, Patricia Collinge, Mady Christians, Kim Hunter, Jane Darwell. Rogers and friends live communally while their men are out fighting the war, a situation that caused this Dmytryk–Dalton Trumbo collaboration to be labeled as Communist propaganda by HUAC in later years. Some unbearable—and ironically, pro-American—speechifying, but occasionally fascinating as social history.▼

Tenderfoot, The (1932) 70m. **½ D: Ray Enright. Joe E. Brown, Ginger Rogers, Lew Cody, George Chandler, Allan Lane, Vivien Oakland. Brown's a naive cowboy who wants to back a Broadway show in the worst way—and does.▶

Tender Is the Night (1962) C-146m. **½ D: Henry King. Jennifer Jones, Jason Robards, Jr., Joan Fontaine, Tom Ewell, Jill St. John, Paul Lukas. Sluggish, unflavorful version of F. Scott Fitzgerald novel with Jones unsatisfactory as mentally unstable wife of psychiatrist Robards; Fontaine is her chic sister; set in 1920s Europe. CinemaScope.
▶

Tender Trap, The (1955) C-111m. **½ D: Charles Walters. Frank Sinatra, Debbie Reynolds, Celeste Holm, David Wayne, Carolyn Jones, Lola Albright, Tom Helmore, James Drury. Silly romp of swinging, set-in-his-ways N.Y.C. bachelor Sinatra, who meets his match in determined, marriage-minded Reynolds. A real time capsule of 1950s attitudes toward men, women, and sex. Impeccable support from Holm and Wayne; memorable Cahn–Van Heusen title tune. Julius J. Epstein adapted the Max Shulman and Robert Paul Smith play. Cinema-Scope. ▼▶

Tender Years, The (1948) 81m. ** D: Harold Schuster. Joe E. Brown, Richard Lyon, Noreen Nash, Charles Drake, Josephine Hutchinson. Warm drama of minister trying to protect dog his son is attached to; notable mainly for rare dramatic performance by Brown.▼

Ten Gentlemen From West Point (1942) 102m. *** D: Henry Hathaway. George Montgomery, Maureen O'Hara, John Sutton, Laird Cregar, Victor Francen, Harry Davenport, Ward Bond, Tom Neal, Ralph Byrd, Douglass Dumbrille. Early years of West Point, with focus on resentful commander Cregar, rivalry of cadets Montgomery and Sutton, and other assorted military film clichés; somehow, it's still entertaining.

Tennessee Champ (1954) C-73m. **½ D: Fred M. Wilcox. Shelley Winters, Keenan Wynn, Dewey Martin, Earl Holliman, Dave O'Brien. Good performances highlight average story of boxer who reforms crooked employer. The climactic fight features Charles (Bronson) Buchinsky.

Tennessee Johnson (1942) 103m. **½ D: William Dieterle. Van Heflin, Lionel Barrymore, Ruth Hussey, Marjorie Main, Charles Dingle, Regis Toomey, Grant Withers, Lynne Carver, Noah Beery, Sr., Morris Ankrum. Sincere historical drama of President

Andrew Johnson's rise and subsequent conflicts with Congress, given a glossy MGM production.

Tennessee's Partner (1955) C-87m. **½ D: Allan Dwan. John Payne, Rhonda Fleming, Ronald Reagan, Coleen Gray, Morris Ankrum. Offbeat little Western with Payne excellent in an unusual "heel" characterization, Reagan accidentally becoming his pal. Based on a Bret Harte story. Filmed in SuperScope.▼▶

Ten North Frederick (1958) 102m. *** D: Philip Dunne. Gary Cooper, Diane Varsi, Suzy Parker, Geraldine Fitzgerald, Tom Tully, Ray Stricklyn, Stuart Whitman, Barbara Nichols. Grasping wife (Fitzgerald) prods her husband (Cooper) into big-time politics, with disastrous results. He finds personal solace in love affair with much younger woman (Parker). Good performances in somewhat soapy adaptation of John O'Hara novel. CinemaScope.▼

Ten Seconds to Hell (1959) 93m. **½ D: Robert Aldrich. Jeff Chandler, Jack Palance, Martine Carol, Robert Cornthwaite, Dave Willock, Wesley Addy. Chandler and Palance are almost believable as Germans involved in defusing bombs in Berlin, while competing for Carol's affection. ▶

Tension (1949) 95m. **½ D: John Berry. Richard Basehart, Audrey Totter, Cyd Charisse, Barry Sullivan, Tom D'Andrea. Timid Basehart methodically plans to murder his wife's lover, only to have someone beat him to it in this intriguing melodrama.▶

Tension at Table Rock (1956) C-93m. ** D: Charles Marquis Warren. Richard Egan, Dorothy Malone, Cameron Mitchell, Billy Chapin, Angie Dickinson. Soapy Western with Egan on the lam for a murder committed in self-defense.

Ten Tall Men (1951) C-97m. **½ D: Willis Goldbeck. Burt Lancaster, Jody Lawrance, Gilbert Roland, Kieron Moore. Tongue-in-cheek Foreign Legion tale, with dynamic Lancaster pushing the action along.

Tenth Avenue Angel (1948) 74m. BOMB D: Roy Rowland. Margaret O'Brien, Angela Lansbury, George Murphy, Phyllis Thaxter, Warner Anderson, Rhys Williams, Barry Nelson, Connie Gilchrist. Capable cast is lost in terrible, syrupy script about eight-year-old tenement girl O'Brien, her attachment to ex-con Murphy, and how she learns various, obvious lessons about faith. Filmed in 1946.▶

Ten Thousand Bedrooms (1957) C-114m. ** D: Richard Thorpe. Dean Martin, Anna Maria Alberghetti, Eva Bartok, Dewey Martin, Walter Slezak, Paul Henreid, Jules Munshin, Marcel Dalio, Dean Jones. Dean's first film without Jerry Lewis seemed to spell doom for his career; it's a lightweight but overlong musical romance with Dino as a playboy hotel-manager in Rome. CinemaScope.▶

Tenth Victim, The (1965-Italian) **C-92m.**
*** D: Elio Petri. Marcello Mastroianni, Ursula Andress, Elsa Martinelli, Salvo Randone, Massimo Serato. Cult sci-fi of futuristic society where violence is channeled into legalized murder hunts. Here, Ursula hunts Marcello. Intriguing idea, well done. Based on Robert Sheckley's story "The Seventh Victim."▼▶

Ten Wanted Men (1955) **C-80m.** ****** D: Bruce Humberstone. Randolph Scott, Jocelyn Brando, Richard Boone, Skip Homeier, Leo Gordon, Donna Martell. Conventional Western programmer with cattleman Scott's dream of law and order smashed by ambitions of ruthless rival Boone.▼▶

Ten Who Dared (1960) **C-92m.** BOMB D: William Beaudine. Brian Keith, John Beal, James Drury, R. G. Armstrong, Ben Johnson, L. Q. Jones. Dreadful Disney film based on true story of Major John Wesley Powell's exploration of Colorado River in 1869; cast is drowned in clichés, while action is sparse. Forget it.▼▶

Teresa (1951) **102m.** ****** D: Fred Zinnemann. Pier Angeli, John Ericson, Patricia Collinge, Richard Bishop, Peggy Ann Garner, Ralph Meeker, Bill Mauldin, Edward Binns, Rod Steiger. Ambitious but slow-moving psychological drama of a sensitive young man (Ericson), saddled with a mother from hell, who meets and marries a sweet young Italian (Angeli) while fighting in Italy during WW2. Steiger plays a psychiatrist in his screen debut. See if you can spot Lee Marvin as a GI on board the ship returning to the U.S.

Terminal Station SEE: **Indiscretion of an American Wife**

Term of Trial (1962-British) **113m.** ****½** D: Peter Glenville. Laurence Olivier, Simone Signoret, Sarah Miles, Terence Stamp, Roland Culver, Hugh Griffith. Talky story of schoolmaster charged with assault by young Miles, and subsequent trial's effect on Olivier's wife, Signoret. Despite fine cast, a wearisome film. Miles' film debut.▶

Terrible Beauty, A SEE: **Night Fighters**
Terrible People, The (1960-German) **95m.** ****** D: Harald Reinl. Eddi Arent, Karin Dor, Elizabeth Flickenschildt, Fritz Rasp, Joachim Fuchsberger. Fair action story of condemned bank crook vowing to return from dead to punish those who prosecuted him. Retitled: HAND OF THE GALLOWS.▶

Terror, The (1963) **C-81m.** ****½** D: Roger Corman. Boris Karloff, Jack Nicholson, Sandra Knight, Dick Miller. Engaging chiller nonsense with Karloff the mysterious owner of a castle where eerie deeds occur; set on Baltic coast in 1800s. This is the legendary Corman quickie for which all of Karloff's scenes were shot in less than three days as the sets (from THE RA-

VEN) were being torn down around them! Vistascope.▼▶

Terror at Midnight (1956) **70m.** ****** D: Franklin Adreon. Scott Brady, Joan Vohs, Frank Faylen, John Dehner. Undynamic telling of Vohs being blackmailed and her law-enforcer boyfriend (Brady) helping out.

Terror By Night (1946) **60m.** ****½** D: Roy William Neill. Basil Rathbone, Nigel Bruce, Alan Mowbray, Dennis Hoey, Renee Godfrey, Mary Forbes. Sherlock Holmes dodges death at every turn while guarding a priceless diamond on a bullet-train en route from London to Edinburgh. Lesser, later entry does give Mowbray a fine supporting role. Also shown in computer-colored version.▼▶

Terror-Creatures From the Grave (1965-Italian) **85m.** ****** D: Ralph Zucker (Massimo Pupillo). Barbara Steele, Walter Brandt, Marilyn Mitchell (Mirella Maravidi), Alfred Rice (Alfredo Rizzo), Richard Garrett (Riccardo Garrone), Alan Collins (Luciano Pigozzi). In 1911 Italy, a lawyer (Brandt) is summoned to an isolated manor, only to discover that the man who sent for him has been dead a year, and his widow (Steele) is aloof. Soon the newcomer learns the castle was built over the graves of victims of the Black Plague; now those present at the man's death begin mysteriously dying, one by one. OK Italian horror, a bit tamer than most, but blessed with Steele's iconic presence.▶

Terror From the Year 5000 (1958) **74m.** ****** D: Robert J. Gurney, Jr. Ward Costello, Joyce Holden, Frederic Downs, John Stratton, Salome Jens, Fred Herrick. At an isolated lab in Florida, scientists succeed in "trading" objects with a future society via time travel; when this brings a radiation-scarred woman (Jens) from the future, trouble ensues. OK American International effort, more imaginative than most.▼▶

Terror House (1942) SEE: **Night Has Eyes, The**

Terror in a Texas Town (1958) **80m.** ****½** D: Joseph H. Lewis. Sterling Hayden, Sebastian Cabot, Carol Kelly, Eugene Martin, Ned Young, Victor Millan. Offbeat Western drama about Scandinavian whaler (Hayden) who comes to his father's farm in Texas, finds town terrorized by Cabot, who's forcing everyone to sell their oil-rich land. Incredible final showdown.▼▶

Terror in the Crypt (1964-Spanish-Italian) **82m.** ***½** D: Thomas Millar (Camillo Mastrocinque). Christopher Lee, José Campos, Audry Amber (Adriana Ambesi), Véra Valmont, Nela Conjiu, Ursula Davis. In 1911 Spain, a young man comes to a castle to research an ancestor of the Count (Lee) who was buried alive for being a witch, cursing her descendants. The visitor is drawn to the

Count's daughter, but she's more interested in a young woman left stranded at the castle. Serious, adult, well photographed, but slow and dull; this is yet another adaptation of J. Sheridan Le Fanu's *Carmilla*, and not really a horror movie. ▶

Terror in the Haunted House SEE: **My World Dies Screaming**

Terror Is a Man (1959) 89m. ** D: Gerry DeLeon. Francis Lederer, Greta Thyssen, Richard Derr, Oscar Keesee. On Blood Island, doctor (Lederer) experiments with panther to turn him into a human. Filmed in the Philippines, this sci-fi horror story comes to life in last third of picture. Clearly inspired by H. G. Wells' *The Island of Dr. Moreau*. Aka BLOOD CREATURE. ▼▶

Terror of the Tongs (1961-British) C-79m. **½ D: Anthony Bushell. Geoffrey Toone, Burt Kwouk, Brian Worth, Christopher Lee, Richard Leech. Atmospheric British thriller of ship captain searching for killers of daughter; eventually breaks entire Tong society in Hong Kong. Good acting but may be a little gruesome for some viewers. Released theatrically in b&w. ▶

Terror of Tiny Town, The (1938) 63m. *½ D: Sam Newfield. Billy Curtis, Yvonne Moray, Little Billy, John Bambury. If you're looking for a midget musical Western, look no further. A typical sagebrush plot is enacted (pretty badly) by a cast of little people, and the indelible impression is that of characters sauntering into the saloon *under* those swinging doors! ▼▶

Terror on a Train (1953-British) 72m. **½ D: Ted Tetzlaff. Glenn Ford, Anne Vernon, Maurice Denham, Victor Maddern. Tense little film of Ford defusing time bomb placed aboard train full of high explosives. Original British title: TIME BOMB.

Tess of the Storm Country (1922) 118m. *** D: John S. Robertson. Mary Pickford, Lloyd Hughes, Gloria Hope, David Torrence, Forrest Robinson, Jean Hersholt. Pickford is letter perfect in this engrossing version of Grace Miller White's novel about a God-fearing, self-sacrificing squatter who becomes romantically involved with the son of a wealthy stuffed shirt while her father is falsely accused of murder. Hersholt makes a formidable villain. Pickford also played Tess in 1914; remade in 1932 and 1960. ▼▶

Tess of the Storm Country (1960) C-84m. **½ D: Paul Guilfoyle. Diane Baker, Jack Ging, Lee Philips, Archie Duncan, Nancy Valentine, Bert Remsen, Wallace Ford. Leisurely paced reworking of the Grace Miller White novel set in Pennsylvania Dutch country. Here, Tess (Baker) becomes immersed in a dispute between farmers, Mennonites, and chemical plant operators who are polluting the environment. CinemaScope.

Testament of Dr. Mabuse, The (1933-

German) 111m. ***½ D: Fritz Lang. Rudolf Klein-Rogge, Otto Wernicke, Gustav Diessl, Karl Meixner. Criminal mastermind controls his underworld empire even while confined to an insane asylum! Fabled character from Lang's silent-film epic returns in less stylized but no less entertaining crime story—which even incorporates supernatural elements. Film was a subject of controversy during Nazi era. Lang returned to this character once more for THE 1,000 EYES OF DR. MABUSE in 1960, but other hands remade this script in 1962. Aka THE LAST WILL OF DR. MABUSE. Some prints run 75m. Retitled THE CRIMES OF DR. MABUSE. ▼▶

Testament of Orpheus, The (1959-French) 80m. ***½ D: Jean Cocteau. Jean Cocteau, Edouard Dermit, Henri Cremieux, Jean-Pierre Léaud, Alice Saprich, Françoise Christophe, Yul Brynner, Daniel Gélin, Maria Casarès, François Perier, Charles Aznavour, Pablo Picasso, Luis Miguel Dominguin, Lucia Bosé, Jean Marais, Brigitte Bardot, Roger Vadim, Claudine Auger. Cocteau's deeply personalized farewell is a catalogue of his philosophies and phantasies. Occasionally too artsy, his reverie has no storyline per se, just a succession of astonishingly dreamy images with a seemingly impossible cast. A few moments are in startling color. Third in his Orphic Trilogy after THE BLOOD OF A POET and ORPHEUS. Full title on-screen is THE TESTAMENT OF ORPHEUS OR DO NOT ASK ME WHY. ▼▶

Test Pilot (1938) 118m. *** D: Victor Fleming. Clark Gable, Myrna Loy, Spencer Tracy, Lionel Barrymore, Samuel S. Hinds, Marjorie Main, Gloria Holden, Louis Jean Heydt. Blend of romantic comedy and drama doesn't always work, but with those stars it's well worth watching. Tracy steals film as Gable's mechanic/pal in story of daredevils who try out new aircraft. Based on a Frank "Spig" Wead story. ▼▶

Tevye (1939) 96m. ***½ D: Maurice Schwartz. Maurice Schwartz, Rebecca Weintraub, Miriam Riselle, Leon Liebgold. Yiddish stage star Schwartz brightens the screen in his most famous role as Sholem Aleichem's famed Ukrainian dairyman; a crisis comes when one of his daughters wishes to wed a non-Jew. This touching, profound drama was later musicalized as FIDDLER ON THE ROOF. Filmed in Jericho, Long Island. Aka TEVYA. ▼▶

Texan Meets Calamity Jane, The (1950) C-71m. BOMB D: Ande Lamb. Evelyn Ankers, James Ellison, Jack Ingram, Lee "Lasses" White. Ankers is too subdued as famed cowgirl of yesteryear, involved in fight to prove claim to prosperous saloon.

Texans, The (1938) 92m. **½ D: James Hogan. Randolph Scott, Joan Bennett, May Robson, Walter Brennan, Robert Cummings, Robert Barrat. Post–Civil War Texas is setting for average Western with good cast.▼▶

Texans Never Cry (1951) **66m.** *** D: Frank McDonald. Gene Autry, Pat Buttram, Mary Castle, Russell Hayden, Gail Davis, Richard Powers (Tom Keene), Don Harvey, Roy Gordon, Kenne Duncan. When Texas lawman Autry tries to stop a plot by Powers that involves Mexican lottery tickets, a deadly gunman is hired to get Gene out of the way . . . and the gunman falls for Gene's girl! One of Gene's best later efforts, with a terrific brawl between Autry and Duncan, the title tune, and a reprised "Ride, Ranger, Ride."▶

Texas (1941) **93m.** *** D: George Marshall. William Holden, Glenn Ford, Claire Trevor, George Bancroft, Edgar Buchanan. High-level Western of two friends, one a rustler (Holden), the other a cattleman (Ford), competing for Trevor's affection.▼▶

Texas, Brooklyn and Heaven (1948) **76m.** ** D: William Castle. Guy Madison, Diana Lynn, James Dunn, Lionel Stander, Florence Bates, Roscoe Karns. Stale "comedy" of cowboy who falls in love with city girl who loves horses. Good cast helps a little.▼▶

Texas Carnival (1951) **C-77m.** ** D: Charles Walters. Esther Williams, Red Skelton, Howard Keel, Ann Miller, Paula Raymond, Keenan Wynn, Tom Tully, Glenn Strange, Hans Conried, Red Norvo Trio. Carny performers Williams and Skelton are mistaken for a Texas cattle baron and his daughter. Energetic cast cannot save this emptier-than-usual musical. ▼◑▶

Texas Cyclone (1932) **60m.** **½ D: D. Ross Lederman. Tim McCoy, Shirley Grey, John Wayne, Wheeler Oakman, Wallace MacDonald, Vernon Dent, Walter Brennan. Daredevil McCoy rides into lawless town and is mistaken for heroic rancher thought killed five years earlier. Interesting William Colt MacDonald story has twist ending and young Wayne as cigarette-smoking ranch hand. A very young Brennan plays an old coot of a sheriff. Script includes the immortal words "This town ain't big enough to hold the both of us . . . come a-shootin'!" Remade five years later as ONE MAN JUSTICE with Charles Starrett.▼▶

Texas Lady (1955) **C-86m.** ** D: Tim Whelan. Claudette Colbert, Barry Sullivan, Greg Walcott, Horace McMahon, John Litel. Genteel oater with Colbert lovely as crusading newspaper editor in old West. Mediocre script. SuperScope.▼

Texas Legionnaires SEE: **Man From Music Mountain** (1943)

Texas Masquerade (1944) **59m.** *** D: George Archainbaud. William Boyd, Andy Clyde, Jimmy Rogers, Don Costello, Mady Correll, Russell Simpson. Hopalong Cassidy impersonates eastern milquetoast to upend gang of "night riders" terrorizing ranchers who have oil on their property they don't know about. Boyd enjoyed ditching his customary dark duds to play dandies, which works especially well here. Swell entertainment. Shoot-out among the Joshua trees makes for arresting finale.▼▶

Texas Rangers, The (1936) **95m.** *** D: King Vidor. Fred MacMurray, Jack Oakie, Jean Parker, Lloyd Nolan, Edward Ellis, Bennie Bartlett, George ("Gabby") Hayes. Fine, elaborate Western about three comrades who rob stagecoaches, with two of them (MacMurray and Oakie) eventually becoming Rangers. Reworked as STREETS OF LAREDO. ▼▶

Texas Rangers, The (1951) **C-74m.** **½ D: Phil Karlson. George Montgomery, Gale Storm, Jerome Courtland, Noah Beery, Jr., William Bishop, John Litel, Douglas Kennedy, John Dehner, John Doucette, Jock O'Mahoney (Mahoney), Jim Bannon. Pretty good B Western with Montgomery and Beery as bandits who reform and join the Texas Rangers, then go undercover to get the goods on outlaw boss Sam Bass (Bishop). ▼

Texas Rangers Ride Again, The (1940) **68m.** ** D: James Hogan. Ellen Drew, John Howard, Akim Tamiroff, May Robson, Broderick Crawford, Anthony Quinn. Sequel is standard Western fare of lawmen involved with cattle rustlers in the modern-day West. Look fast for a young Robert Ryan.▼▶

Texas Terror (1935) **51m.** ** D: Robert N. Bradbury. John Wayne, Lucille Brown, LeRoy Mason, Fern Emmett, George Hayes, Jack Duffy. In the belief he's accidentally killed his best friend, anguished Texas lawman Wayne turns in his sheriff's badge for the solitary life of a prospector, until he meets the dead pal's sister. Formula low-budget Lone Star Western has Indians siding with protagonists against cattle-rustling and bank-robbing lawbreakers.▼▶

Texas Trail (1937) **59m.** *** D: David Selman. William Boyd, Russell Hayden, George Hayes, Judith Allen, Billy King, Alexander Cross. At outbreak of Spanish-American War in 1898, Hopalong Cassidy is called upon by U.S. Army to find and supply cavalry horses but encounters rustlers. In the finest series of B Westerns ever made, this picture is near the top of the list, with expert use of Paramount music library, visually stunning locations, including Red Rock Canyon and Sedona, and an unusually appealing heroine (with little to do). Nominally derived from 1922 Clarence E. Mulford novel *Tex.*▼▶

Thanks a Million (1935) **87m.** *** D: Roy Del Ruth. Dick Powell, Ann Dvorak, Fred Allen, Patsy Kelly, Alan Dinehart, Margaret Irving, Paul Whiteman and Orchestra, Yacht Club Boys. Very entertaining musical of crooner Powell running for governor, with help of wisecracking manager Allen, sweetheart Dvorak, and blustery politician Raymond Walburn. Good fun, with several breezy tunes and specialties by Whiteman and Yacht Club Boys. Script by Nunnally Johnson. Remade as IF I'M LUCKY.▶

Thanks for the Memory (1938) 77m. **½ D: George Archainbaud. Bob Hope, Shirley Ross, Charles Butterworth, Otto Kruger, Roscoe Karns, Hedda Hopper, Patricia Wilder, Laura Hope Crews, Eddie Anderson. Paper-thin romantic comedy (from a play by Albert Hackett and Frances Goodrich) reteams Hope and Ross, who sang the title tune in THE BIG BROADCAST OF 1938. Here, they're newlyweds who face a crisis: he's got to stop partying and finish his novel. Song highlight: "Two Sleepy People."▼▶

Thank You, Jeeves! (1936) 57m. **½ D: Arthur Collins. Arthur Treacher, Virginia Field, David Niven, Lester Matthews, Willie Best. Treacher is at peak form playing P.G. Wodehouse's impeccable butler; he and his master (Niven) become immersed in intrigue after crossing paths with mystery woman Field. Retitled: THANK YOU, MR. JEEVES; followed by STEP LIVELY, JEEVES.▶

Thank You, Mr. Moto (1937) 67m. *** D: Norman Foster. Peter Lorre, Pauline Frederick, Sidney Blackmer, Sig Rumann, John Carradine, Nedda Harrigan. Second series entry (possibly the best) involves the Oriental sleuth in a complicated case centering on seven scrolls which hold the key to hidden treasure of Genghis Khan.▶

Thank Your Lucky Stars (1943) 127m. *** D: David Butler. Eddie Cantor, Dennis Morgan, Joan Leslie; guest stars Humphrey Bogart, Bette Davis, Olivia de Havilland, Errol Flynn, John Garfield, Ida Lupino, Ann Sheridan, etc. Very lame plot (Cantor plays both himself and lookalike cabbie) frames all-star Warner Bros. show, with Davis singing "They're Either Too Young or Too Old," Flynn delightfully performing "That's What You Jolly Well Get," other staid stars breaking loose.▼●▶

That Certain Age (1938) 101m. **½ D: Edward Ludwig. Deanna Durbin, Melvyn Douglas, Jackie Cooper, Irene Rich, Nancy Carroll, John Halliday, Jack Searl. Deanna develops crush on her parents' houseguest, sophisticated Douglas, leaving boyfriend Cooper out in the cold—and saddled with responsibility for putting on amateur show. Silly script made bearable by stars.▼▶

That Certain Feeling (1956) C-103m. BOMB D: Norman Panama, Melvin Frank. Bob Hope, Eva Marie Saint, George Sanders, Pearl Bailey, Al Capp, Jerry Mathers. Incredibly bad Hope comedy with Bob as neurotic cartoonist; Sanders gives only life to stale film. Pearl sings title song. VistaVision.

That Certain Woman (1937) 93m. **½ D: Edmund Goulding. Bette Davis, Henry Fonda, Ian Hunter, Donald Crisp, Anita Louise, Minor Watson, Sidney Toler. Remake of Goulding's early talkie THE TRESPASSER (with Gloria Swanson) features Bette as a gangster's widow who's trying to start life afresh and finds herself in a romantic triangle with weak-willed playboy Fonda and lawyer Hunter. Well-acted soaper.▼▶

That Dangerous Age SEE: **If This Be Sin**

That Darn Cat! (1965) C-116m. *** D: Robert Stevenson. Hayley Mills, Dean Jones, Dorothy Provine, Roddy McDowall, Neville Brand, Elsa Lanchester, William Demarest, Frank Gorshin, Ed Wynn. Long but entertaining suspense comedy from Disney, about a cat that leads FBI man Jones on trail of kidnapped woman. Slapstick scenes and character vignettes highlight this colorful film. Remade in 1997.▼●▶

That Forsyte Woman (1949) C-114m. **½ D: Compton Bennett. Errol Flynn, Greer Garson, Walter Pidgeon, Robert Young, Janet Leigh, Harry Davenport. Rather superficial adaptation of John Galsworthy novel of a faithless woman (Garson) who finds herself attracted to her niece's fiancé; good-looking, but no match for the later BBC-TV series *The Forsyte Saga.*▼▶

That Funny Feeling (1965) C-93m. **½ D: Richard Thorpe. Sandra Dee, Bobby Darin, Donald O'Connor, Nita Talbot, Larry Storch, Leo G. Carroll, Robert Strauss. Funny only if you adore Darin and Dee, and even then story of footloose playboy and maid who pretends she lives in his apartment wears thin.▼

That Gang of Mine (1940) 62m. ** D: Joseph H. Lewis. Leo Gorcey, Bobby Jordan, Sunshine Sammy Morrison, Clarence Muse, Dave O'Brien, Joyce Bryant, Donald Haines, David Gorcey. Muggs (Gorcey) trains to be a thoroughbred jockey in this *East Side Kids* entry marked by director Lewis' expertise with galloping racing action.▼▶

That Girl From Paris (1936) 105m. **½ D: Leigh Jason. Lily Pons, Jack Oakie, Gene Raymond, Herman Bing, Mischa Auer, Frank Jenks, Lucille Ball. Breezy Pons vehicle. She flees Continental wedding and runs to America. Tuneful songs, fine supporting cast. A remake of STREET GIRL; remade as FOUR JACKS AND A JILL.▼

That Hagen Girl (1947) 83m. **½ D: Peter Godfrey. Ronald Reagan, Shirley Temple, Rory Calhoun, Lois Maxwell, Dorothy Peterson, Charles Kemper, Conrad Janis, Penny Edwards, Jean Porter, Harry Davenport. Obvious but fascinating time capsule about small-town small-mindedness, with teen Temple ostracized because gossips think she's illegitimate. Of interest for the casting of Temple and Reagan (playing a lawyer who supposedly is Shirley's father), and as a portrait of a time in which illegitimate children were victimized because of the circumstances of their births.▶

That Hamilton Woman (1941) **128m.** *** D: Alexander Korda. Vivien Leigh, Laurence Olivier, Alan Mowbray, Sara Allgood, Gladys Cooper, Henry Wilcoxon, Heather Angel, Halliwell Hobbes, Gilbert Emery. Olivier and Leigh—both breathtakingly beautiful—enact ill-fated historical romance of Lord Admiral Nelson and Lady Emma Hamilton in American-made film intended to spur pro-British feelings before the U.S. entered WW2. Vincent Korda's sets are incredibly opulent. P.S. This was Winston Churchill's favorite movie. Aka LADY HAMILTON. ▼●▶

That Kind of Woman (1959) **92m.** *** D: Sidney Lumet. Sophia Loren, Tab Hunter, George Sanders, Jack Warden, Keenan Wynn, Barbara Nichols. WW2 soldier Hunter and dishy Loren are attracted to each other on a train, but she's the mistress of elegant fatcat Sanders. Surprisingly adult comedy-drama for its era; excellent performances from all but Hunter, and even he's better than usual. Well shot by Boris Kaufman. Remake of THE SHOPWORN ANGEL, scripted by Walter Bernstein. Look for young Bea Arthur as a WAC. VistaVision.

That Lady (1955) **C-100m.** **½ D: Terence Young. Olivia de Havilland, Gilbert Roland, Paul Scofield, Dennis Price, Christopher Lee. Unemotional costumer set in 16th-century Spain, with de Havilland a widowed noblewoman involved in court intrigue. Scofield's film debut. CinemaScope.

That Lady in Ermine (1948) **C-89m.** **½ D: Ernst Lubitsch. Betty Grable, Douglas Fairbanks, Jr., Cesar Romero, Walter Abel, Reginald Gardiner, Harry Davenport. Entertaining if overblown musical of mythical European kingdom where Grable is a just-married princess; her ancestors magically come to life as Fairbanks' conquering army descends on her castle. Lubitsch died during production, which was completed by Otto Preminger. Script by Samson Raphaelson.▶

That Man From Rio (1964-French) **C-114m.** *** D: Philippe De Broca. Jean-Paul Belmondo. Françoise Dorleac, Jean Servais, Adolfo Celi, Simone Renant. Engaging spoof of Bond-type movies features Belmondo as hero, chasing double-crosser and thief in search for Brazilian treasure. Nice cinematography by Edmond Séchan complements fast-moving script. Enjoyed great international success and spawned many imitations.▼▶

That Midnight Kiss (1949) **C-96m.** **½ D: Norman Taurog. Kathryn Grayson, Mario Lanza, Jose Iturbi, Ethel Barrymore, Keenan Wynn, J. Carrol Naish, Jules Munshin.

Flimsy musical romance between Lanza and Grayson salvaged by pleasant musical interludes and glossy production.▼●▶

That Naughty Girl SEE: **Mam'zelle Pigalle**

That Night! (1957) **88m.** **½ D: John Newland. John Beal, Augusta Dabney, Malcolm Brodrick, Shepperd Strudwick, Rosemary Murphy. Straightforward account of writer suffering a heart attack, and the effect it has on his family.

That Night in Rio (1941) **C-90m.** **½ D: Irving Cummings. Alice Faye, Don Ameche, Carmen Miranda, S. Z. Sakall, J. Carrol Naish, Curt Bois, Leonid Kinskey, Frank Puglia. Standard 20th Century-Fox musical of mistaken identities, uses Miranda to best advantage; Maria Montez has a tiny role. Filmed before as FOLIES BERGÈRE, and again as ON THE RIVIERA.▶

That Night With You (1945) **84m.** ** D: William A. Seiter. Franchot Tone, Susanna Foster, David Bruce, Louise Allbritton, Jacqueline de Wit, Buster Keaton. OK vehicle for soprano Foster who connives her way to show biz break via producer Tone.

That's My Boy (1951) **98m.** ** D: Hal Walker. Dean Martin, Jerry Lewis, Marion Marshall, Eddie Mayehoff, Ruth Hussey, Polly Bergen, John McIntire. Ex-football star Mayehoff wants klutzy son Lewis to follow in his footsteps, induces Martin to coach him. Supposed comic idea is played straight, with very few laughs, maudlin situations . . . yet it was considered quite funny in 1951 when M&L were in their heyday. Later a TV series.▶

That's My Man (1947) **99m.** ** D: Frank Borzage. Don Ameche, Catherine McLeod, Roscoe Karns, Joe Frisco, John Ridgely, Kitty Irish, Frankie Darro. Nice-guy accountant Ameche buys a race horse that becomes a champ, but he turns into a heel and neglects his family in the process. Minor love story is lighthearted and offbeat, then turns into a maudlin and clichéd triangle tale about a man, a woman, and a horse.▶

That's Right—You're Wrong (1939) **93m.** **½ D: David Butler. Kay Kyser, Adolphe Menjou, May Robson, Lucille Ball, Dennis O'Keefe, Edward Everett Horton, Roscoe Karns, Moroni Olsen. Amiable film debut for popular radio band leader Kyser as he and his wacky crew are offered a Hollywood contract and get into all sorts of trouble in Tinseltown. Much of the humor (and music) is dated, but there's plenty to enjoy in the supporting cast, including gossip queens Sheilah Graham and Hedda Hopper as themselves.●

That's the Spirit (1945) **93m.** ** D: Charles Lamont. Peggy Ryan, Jack Oakie, June Vincent, Gene Lockhart, Johnny Coy, Andy Devine, Arthur Treacher, Irene Ryan, Buster Keaton. Whimsy is too studied in this syrupy fantasy of Oakie returning from heaven to make explanations to wife on Earth. Songs include "How Come You Do Me Like You Do?"

That Touch of Mink (1962) **C-99m.** ****½** D. Delbert Mann. Cary Grant, Doris Day, Gig Young, Audrey Meadows, John Astin, Dick Sargent. Attractive cast in silly piece of fluff with wealthy playboy Grant pursuing Day. Amusing at times, but wears thin; Astin is memorable as a creep with designs on poor Doris, and there's a clever sequence featuring Mickey Mantle, Roger Maris, Yogi Berra, and umpire Art Passarella. Panavision. **▼◖◗**

That Uncertain Feeling (1941) **84m.** ******* D: Ernst Lubitsch. Merle Oberon, Melvyn Douglas, Burgess Meredith, Alan Mowbray, Olive Blakeney, Harry Davenport, Sig Rumann, Eve Arden. Chic little Lubitsch comedy about married couple with problems, and their absurd pianist friend. Stolen hands down by Meredith as the musical malcontent. Filmed before (in 1925) by Lubitsch as KISS ME AGAIN. Also shown in computer-colored version. **▼◗**

That Way With Women (1947) **84m.** ****** D: Frederick de Cordova. Dane Clark, Martha Vickers, Sydney Greenstreet, Alan Hale, Craig Stevens. Tired reworking of George Arliss' THE MILLIONAIRE, with Greenstreet as wealthy man who plays Cupid for Clark and Vickers.

That Woman Opposite SEE: **City After Midnight**

That Wonderful Urge (1948) **82m.** ****½** D: Robert B. Sinclair. Tyrone Power, Gene Tierney, Arleen Whelan, Reginald Gardiner, Lucile Watson, Gene Lockhart, Gertrude Michael, Porter Hall. Fairly entertaining remake of LOVE IS NEWS about heiress getting back at nasty reporter. Power repeats his role from the 1937 film. **◗**

Their Own Desire (1929) **65m.** ****½** D: E. Mason Hopper. Norma Shearer, Robert Montgomery, Lewis Stone, Belle Bennett, Helene Millard. Shearer and Montgomery become amorously attached, only there's a complication: her father has left her mother for another woman, who happens to be Montgomery's mother! Interesting premise in this well-acted early talkie. **◗**

Thelma Jordon SEE: **File on Thelma Jordon, The**

Them! (1954) **94m.** *****½** D: Gordon Douglas. James Whitmore, Edmund Gwenn, Joan Weldon, James Arness, Onslow Stevens. First-rate '50s sci-fi about giant ant mutations running wild in the Southwest. Intelligent script (by Ted Sherdeman, from George Worthing Yates' story) extremely well directed, with memorable climax in L.A. sewers. Fess Parker has small but memorable role. Look fast for Leonard Nimoy at a teletype machine. **▼◖◗**

Theodora Goes Wild (1936) **94m.** *****½** D: Richard Boleslawski. Irene Dunne,

Melvyn Douglas, Thomas Mitchell, Thurston Hall, Rosalind Keith, Spring Byington. Dunne's first starring comedy is a delightful story about small-town woman who writes scandalous best-seller and falls in love with sophisticated New Yorker who illustrated the book. Lots of funny twists in this engaging farce, scripted by Sidney Buchman from a Mary McCarthy story. **▼◗**

Theodora, Slave Empress (1954-Italian) **88m.** ****** D: Riccardo Freda. Gianna Maria Canale, Georges Marchal, Renato Baldini, Henri Guisol, Irene Papas. Better-than-average production values are only asset in standard plot of hero thwarting plan of Roman generals to overthrow empress.

There Goes My Heart (1938) **84m.** ******* D: Norman Z. McLeod. Fredric March, Virginia Bruce, Patsy Kelly, Alan Mowbray, Nancy Carroll, Eugene Pallette, Claude Gillingwater, Harry Langdon, Arthur Lake. Typical '30s fluff about runaway heiress Bruce spotted by reporter March; good cast makes one forget trite storyline.

There Goes the Groom (1937) **65m.** ****** D: Joseph Santley. Burgess Meredith, Ann Sothern, Louise Henry, Mary Boland, Onslow Stevens, William Brisbane. Strained screwball comedy about newly rich Meredith suddenly courted by Sothern and her wacky family; a smile or two but little else.

There's Always a Price Tag (1957-French) **102m.** ****½** D: Denys de la Patelliere. Michele Morgan, Daniel Gelin, Peter Van Eyck, Bernard Blier. Morgan is excellent in DOUBLE INDEMNITY–type plot about wife who conspires to murder her husband, but film drags and loses credibility after promising start.

There's Always a Woman (1938) **82m.** ******* D: Alexander Hall. Joan Blondell, Melvyn Douglas, Mary Astor, Frances Drake, Jerome Cowan, Robert Paige, Thurston Hall. Fine blend of mystery and comedy as D.A. Douglas and detective-wife Blondell try to solve the same crime.

There's Always Tomorrow (1956) **84m.** ****½** D: Douglas Sirk. Barbara Stanwyck, Fred MacMurray, Joan Bennett, William Reynolds, Pat Crowley, Gigi Perreau, Jane Darwell. MacMurray is in a rut, at work and at home, making him particularly susceptible to old flame Stanwyck, who comes back into his life. Sudsy but well-acted soap opera, filmed before in 1934. **◗**

Therese Desqueyroux (1962-French) **107m.** ****½** D: Georges Franju. Emmanuele Riva, Philippe Noiret, Edith Scob, Sami Frey. Bored Riva tries to poison rich husband Noiret; she's acquitted in court, but still does not escape punishment. Riva stands out in this otherwise gloomy drama adapted from a François Mauriac novel.

Thérèse Raquin (1953-French-Italian) **103m.** ****½** D: Marcel Carné. Simone Signoret, Raf Vallone, Jacques Duby, Sylvie,

Roland Lesaffre, Maria Pia Casilio, Marcel André. Complications ensue when weary Signoret, saddled with a small-minded husband and a mother-in-law from hell, begins an affair with earthy truck driver Vallone. Melodrama of passion and obsession has the right pedigree—Carné and Charles Spaak adapted Émile Zola's novel—but lacks the necessary fire to make it memorable. Remade in 2014 as IN SECRET. ❑

There's Magic in Music (1941) **79m.** ** D: Andrew L. Stone. Allan Jones, Susanna Foster, Diana Lynn, Margaret Lindsay, Lynne Overman, Grace Bradley. Adequate showcase for Foster, an ex-burlesque singer who becomes an opera diva at a summer music camp.

There's No Business Like Show Business (1954) **C-117m.** **½ D: Walter Lang. Ethel Merman, Dan Dailey, Donald O'Connor, Marilyn Monroe, Johnnie Ray, Mitzi Gaynor, Hugh O'Brian, Frank McHugh. Gaudy (and seemingly interminable) hokum about a show-biz family, built around catalog of Irving Berlin songs. Entertaining if not inspired, with several expensive numbers designed to fill the wide screen. Merman and Dailey are fine, Marilyn's at her sexiest, and O'Connor is in top form throughout. Then there's Johnnie Ray deciding to become a priest.... CinemaScope.▼❑❍

There's One Born Every Minute (1942) **59m.** ** D: Harold Young. Hugh Herbert, Tom Brown, Peggy Moran, Guy Kibbee, Gus Schilling, Edgar Kennedy, Carl "Alfalfa" Switzer, Elizabeth Taylor. Contrived comedy of nutty family whose erstwhile head (Herbert) runs a pudding company. Notable as screen debut of 10-year-old Liz as junior member of the clan.

These Are the Damned (1963-British) **96m.** **½ D: Joseph Losey. Macdonald Carey, Shirley Anne Field, Viveca Lindfors, Alexander Knox, Oliver Reed, James Villiers. Odd film chronicling American Carey's confrontation with a Teddy Boy motorcycle gang in Weymouth—after which the scenario becomes a *Twilight Zone*– like sci-fi drama! Original British title: THE DAMNED. Hammerscope. ❑

These Glamour Girls (1939) **80m.** **½ D: S. Sylvan Simon. Lew Ayres, Lana Turner, Richard Carlson, Anita Louise, Marsha Hunt, Ann Rutherford, Mary Beth Hughes, Jane Bryan, Tom Brown. Turner is effective as nonsocialite who turns the tables on sneering girls at swank college weekend; naive but polished gloss. ❑

These Thousand Hills (1959) **C-95m.** *** D: Richard Fleischer. Don Murray, Richard Egan, Lee Remick, Patricia Owens, Stuart Whitman, Albert Dekker, Harold J. Stone, Royal Dano, Jean Willes. Quietly solid, adult Western, based on an A. B. Guthrie, Jr., novel, with Murray a determined young dreamer whose ambitions clash with his

loyalty to those who help him—in particular, much-abused dance-hall girl Remick. CinemaScope. ❑

These Three (1936) **93m.** **** D: William Wyler. Miriam Hopkins, Merle Oberon, Joel McCrea, Catherine Doucet, Alma Kruger, Bonita Granville, Marcia Mae Jones, Margaret Hamilton, Walter Brennan. Penetrating drama of two young women (Oberon, Hopkins) running girls' school, ruined by lies of malicious student Granville; loosely based on Lillian Hellman's *The Children's Hour*. Superb acting by all, with Granville chillingly impressive; scripted by the playwright. Remade in 1961 by same director as THE CHILDREN'S HOUR. ▼❍

These Wilder Years (1956) **91m.** **½ D: Roy Rowland. James Cagney, Barbara Stanwyck, Walter Pidgeon, Betty Lou Keim, Don Dubbins, Edward Andrews, Dean Jones, Tom Laughlin. Unusual to see Cagney in this kind of soap opera, about a man who wants to find his illegitimate son, and becomes involved with teenage unwed mother (Keim) through intervention of foundling home director Stanwyck. Look for young Michael Landon in pool room. ❑

They All Come Out (1939) **70m.** ** D: Jacques Tourneur. Rita Johnson, Tom Neal, Bernard Nedell, Edward Gargan, John Gallaudet, Addison Richards, Frank M. Thomas, George Tobias, Charles Lane. Can a hardened gang of crooks be rehabilitated in prison? Expanded from an MGM *Crime Does Not Pay* short, this film is fine when concentrating on the gang's bank robbery and escape but sags when the story moves to prison and the tone becomes insufferably sanctimonious.

They All Kissed the Bride (1942) **85m.** **½ D: Alexander Hall. Joan Crawford, Melvyn Douglas, Roland Young, Billie Burke, Allen Jenkins. Good stars in fairly amusing film of man being arrested for kissing bride at wedding.▼

They Call It Sin (1932) **75m.** ** D: Thornton Freeland. Loretta Young, David Manners, George Brent, Louis Calhern, Una Merkel, Elizabeth Patterson. Restless small-town girl is wooed by visiting New Yorker, and follows him to the big city, where she discovers he's engaged to another woman. Interesting at first, then increasingly silly and predictable, but the stars certainly are attractive. Merkel is fun as Loretta's perky pal.▼❑

They Came to Blow Up America (1943) **73m.** ** D: Edward Ludwig. George Sanders, Anna Sten, Ward Bond, Dennis Hoey, Sig Ruman, Ludwig Stossel, Robert Barrat. Overzealous espionage yarn designed for WW2 audiences, dated now. Good cast is only virtue. ❑

They Came to Cordura (1959) **C-123m.** **½ D: Robert Rossen. Gary Cooper, Rita Hayworth, Van Heflin, Tab Hunter, Richard Conte, Michael Callan, Dick York. Soapy oater set in 1916 Mexico. Cooper is Army officer accused of cowardice, sent to find five men worthy of Medal of Honor. Hayworth is shady lady he meets on the way. CinemaScope.▼●)

They Dare Not Love (1941) 76m. *½ D: James Whale. George Brent, Martha Scott, Paul Lukas, Egon Brecher, Roman Bohnen, Edgar Barrier. Good story idea submerged by silly script and Brent's miscasting as dashing Austrian prince, who tries to bargain with Gestapo officer Lukas on behalf of his country. Lloyd Bridges has small role as Nazi seaman.

They Died With Their Boots On (1941) 138m. *** D: Raoul Walsh. Errol Flynn, Olivia de Havilland, Arthur Kennedy, Charley Grapewin, Gene Lockhart, Anthony Quinn, Stanley Ridges, Sydney Greenstreet, Regis Toomey, Hattie McDaniel, Walter Hampden. Sweeping Hollywood version of Little Bighorn battle, with Flynn flamboyant as Custer. Fine vignettes amidst episodic buildup to exciting Last Stand climax. This being Errol and Olivia's final film together lends poignance to their farewell scene. Superb score by Max Steiner. Also shown in computer-colored version. ▼●)

They Drive By Night (1938-British) 83m. *** D: Arthur Woods. Emlyn Williams, Anna Konstam, Allan Jeayes, Ernest Thesiger, Antony Holles, Ronald Shiner. Gripping suspenser about a man who is just released from prison and finds himself wanted for the murder of a former girlfriend he found strangled with a silk stocking; he goes on the run to find the real killer. Moody Hitchcockian thriller highlighted by the marvelous Thesiger's scene-stealing portrayal of a gentlemanly sex maniac. ▼)

They Drive by Night (1940) 93m. ***½ D: Raoul Walsh. George Raft, Ann Sheridan, Ida Lupino, Humphrey Bogart, Gale Page, Alan Hale, Roscoe Karns. Marvelous melodrama of truck-driving brothers, Bogie and Raft, battling the dangers of the open road as well as a murder frame-up by Lupino. Unforgettable dialogue by Jerry Wald and Richard Macaulay. Partial reworking of BORDERTOWN. Also shown in computer-colored version.▼●)

They Gave Him a Gun (1937) 94m. **½ D: W. S. Van Dyke II. Spencer Tracy, Gladys George, Franchot Tone, Edgar Dearing, Charles Trowbridge, Cliff Edwards, Mary Lou Treen. Gun-shy hayseed Tone, who was taught "thou shalt not kill," changes dramatically when he fights in WW1. Tracy is his devoted pal, who later tries to save him from a life of crime. Dramatically obvious, and falls apart with the entrance of nurse George; still, the opening montage is striking, and the war-related scenes exceptional. ❿

They Got Me Covered (1943) 95m. ** D: David Butler. Bob Hope, Dorothy Lamour,

Lenore Aubert, Otto Preminger, Eduardo Ciannelli, Marion Martin, Donald MacBride, Walter Catlett, Donald Meek. Spy yarn (by Harry Kurnitz) set in Washington was topical at the time, awkward now; not up to Hope standards.▼●)

They Had to See Paris (1929) 83m. *** D: Frank Borzage. Will Rogers, Irene Rich, Owen Davis, Jr., Marguerite Churchill, Fifi D'Orsay, Rex Bell, Bob Kerr, Ivan Lebedeff, Edgar Kennedy. When simple mechanic from Claremore, Oklahoma (Rogers' real-life hometown), strikes it rich as part owner of an oil well, his wife insists that the family travel to Paris to improve themselves. Each member of the clan winds up having an adventure. Leisurely adaptation of Homer Croy's novel is primarily a vehicle for the lovable Rogers; he's right at home in his talkie debut. Originally released at 95m. ❿

They Knew What They Wanted (1940) 96m. *** D: Garson Kanin. Carole Lombard, Charles Laughton, William Gargan, Harry Carey, Frank Fay. Laughton and Lombard are excellent in this flawed adaptation by Robert Ardrey of Sidney Howard's play (filmed twice before). He's an Italian grape-grower in California who conducts correspondence with waitress and asks her to marry him. Fay is too sanctimonious for words as local priest. Watch for Karl Malden and Tom Ewell as rowdy guests at the pre-wedding party.▼

They Learned About Women (1930) 81m. *** D: Jack Conway, Sam Wood. Joseph T. Schenck, Gus Van, Bessie Love, Mary Doran, J. C. Nugent, Benny Rubin, Tom Dugan, Eddie Gribbon, Nina Mae McKinney. Enjoyable early-talkie musical is a precursor/variation of TAKE ME OUT TO THE BALL GAME. Real-life vaudeville stars Van and Schenck play a pair of baseball-playing vaudevillians. Schenck is set to marry nice-girl Love, but a vamp (Doran) gets in the way. ●

They Live by Night (1949) 95m. ***½ D: Nicholas Ray. Farley Granger, Cathy O'Donnell, Howard da Silva, Jay C. Flippen, Helen Craig. Director Ray's first film is sensitive, well-made story of young lovers who are fugitives from the law. Set in 1930s, it avoids clichés and builds considerable impact instead. Based on Edward Anderson's *Thieves Like Us*, remade in 1974 under that name. Also shown in computer-colored version.▼●)

They Loved Life SEE: **Kanal**

They Made Me a Criminal (1939) 92m. **½ D: Busby Berkeley. John Garfield, Claude Rains, Gloria Dickson, May Robson, Billy Halop, Huntz Hall, Leo Gorcey, Bobby Jordan, Gabriel Dell, Barbara Pepper, Ward Bond, Ann Sheridan. Garfield takes it on the lam when he thinks he's killed a reporter, stays out West with Robson and Dead End Kids. Enjoyable, with Rains miscast as a Dick Tracy type. Remake of THE LIFE OF JIMMY DOLAN. ▼O●

They Made Me a Fugitive (1947-British) 103m. *** D: Cavalcanti. Trevor Howard, Sally Gray, Griffith Jones, Rene Ray, Mary Merrall, Charles Farrell. Dilettante crook is double-crossed by his boss and seeks revenge while on the lam from police. Potent (yet little-known) British film noir packs a real punch, with no holds barred in terms of brutality (and refusal to provide a pat, happy ending). Strikingly photographed by Otto Heller. Look sharp and you'll spot young Peter Bull and Sebastian Cabot. Originally cut when released in U.S. as I BECAME A CRIMINAL; also trimmed for British reissue. Finally restored on video in 1999.▼D

They Meet Again (1941) 67m. *½ D: Erle C. Kenton. Jean Hersholt, Dorothy Lovett, Robert Baldwin, Neil Hamilton, Maude Eburne, Anne Bennett, Barton Yarborough, Arthur Hoyt. Boring entry in Hersholt's *Dr. Christian* series, with the good doctor attempting to prove the innocence of bank teller Yarborough, accused of pilfering $3,000. A real drag, except for little Leon Tyler's jive musical number during a birthday party, a real pip.▼D

They Met in Argentina (1941) 77m. *½ D: Leslie Goodwins, Jack Hively. Maureen O'Hara, James Ellison, Alberto Vila, Buddy Ebsen, Joseph Buloff. Hollywood embraces Pan America in this dismal musical; oil company representative Ellison goes South of the Border, where he mixes business with beautiful O'Hara.

They Met in Bombay (1941) 93m. **½ D: Clarence Brown. Clark Gable, Rosalind Russell, Peter Lorre, Jessie Ralph, Reginald Owen, Eduardo Ciannelli. Two jewel thieves team up in ordinary romantic comedy-actioner, spiced by Lorre as money-hungry cargo-ship captain. Look for Alan Ladd in a small role.▼D

They Must Be Told SEE: **Sex Madness**
They Passed This Way SEE: **Four Faces West**

They Rode West (1954) C-84m. **½ D: Phil Carlson. Robert Francis, Donna Reed, May Wynn, Phil Carey, Onslow Stevens, Roy Roberts, Jack Kelly. Better-than-average Western with young Army doctor Francis arriving at military outpost, battling hostile superior Carey while attempting to combat malaria epidemic on Indian reservation.

They Saved Hitler's Brain (1963) 74m. BOMB D: David Bradley. Walter Stocker, Audrey Caire, Carlos Rivas, John Holland, Dani Lynn, Marshall Reed, Nestor Paiva. Daughter of kidnapped scientist traces him to isle of Mandoras, where Nazis still flourish under the leadership of Hitler's still-living head. Unbelievably muddled plot results from intercutting 1950s studio potboiler,

beautifully photographed by Stanley Cortez (MAGNIFICENT AMBERSONS) with super-cheap 1960s footage involving completely different cast. Originally titled MADMEN OF MANDORAS.▼D

They Shall Have Music (1939) 101m. *** D: Archie Mayo. Jascha Heifetz, Joel McCrea, Andrea Leeds, Walter Brennan, Gene Reynolds, Marjorie Main, Porter Hall, Dolly Loehr (Diana Lynn), Terry Kilburn. Cornerstone of Samuel Goldwyn's efforts to bring classical music to the masses. Slum brat Reynolds' interest in the violin is sparked after hearing Heifetz in concert; the boy soon becomes a student at a settlement music school. Heifetz has five violin solos. Film debut of Lynn, as a young pianist. Music director Alfred Newman appears on-screen as a conductor. ▼O●

They Were Expendable (1945) 135m. **** D: John Ford. Robert Montgomery, John Wayne, Donna Reed, Jack Holt, Ward Bond, Louis Jean Heydt, Marshall Thompson, Leon Ames, Cameron Mitchell, Russell Simpson, Jack Pennick, Robert Barrat, Tom Tyler. One of the finest (and most underrated) of all WW2 films, based on the true story of America's PT boat squadron in the Philippines during the early days of the war. Moving, exquisitely detailed production (photographed by Joseph August) under Ford's distinctive hand, with real-life Naval officer Montgomery a convincing lead. Screenplay by Frank "Spig" Wead. Also shown in computer-colored version. ▼O●

They Were Sisters (1945-British) 110m. **½ D: Arthur Crabtree. Phyllis Calvert, James Mason, Hugh Sinclair, Anne Crawford, Peter Murray-Hill, Dulcie Gray, Barry Livesey, Pamela Kellino (Mason). Fresh approach to stock drama about three sisters with contrasting marriages and lives. Mason is tops as a sadistic husband; Kellino, then his real-life spouse, is cast as his daughter. Scripted by Roland Pertwee, who plays Sir Hamish.

They Were So Young (1954-German) 78m. *** D: Kurt Neumann. Scott Brady, Raymond Burr, Johanna Matz, Ingrid Stenn, Gisela Fackeldey, Kurt Meisel, Katharina Mayberg, Gert Fröbe. "They" are naïve European women recruited to become models in Rio de Janeiro, but instead are forced into white slavery. One of them (Matz) rebels, and it's American mining engineer Brady to the rescue. Well-made little melodrama. Aka VIOLATED and PARTY GIRLS FOR SALE. Original running time 95m. ▼D

They Who Dare (1953-British) C-101m. **½ D: Lewis Milestone. Dirk Bogarde, Denholm Elliott, Akim Tamiroff, Eric Pohlmann, David Peel. Effective WW2 actioner with good character delineation, tracing commando raid on German-controlled Aegean air fields.

They Won't Believe Me (1947) 95m. ***½

D: Irving Pichel. Susan Hayward, Robert Young, Jane Greer, Rita Johnson, Tom Powers, Don Beddoe, Frank Ferguson. Fine James Cain–type melodrama about a philanderer who gets involved with three women, leading to tragedy (and a terrific twist ending). Young excels in his unsympathetic role; Johnson does wonders with her scenes as his wife.▼●

They Won't Forget (1937) 95m. **** D: Mervyn LeRoy. Claude Rains, Gloria Dickson, Otto Kruger, Allyn Joslyn, Elisha Cook, Jr., Edward Norris. Electrifying drama begins when pretty high school student is murdered in Southern town. A man is arrested, and a big-time Northern lawyer takes the case, but everyone seems more interested in exploiting personal interests than in seeing justice triumph. No punches are pulled in this still-powerful film. Lana Turner plays the unfortunate girl, in her first important role. Script by Robert Rossen and Aben Kandel, from the book *Death in the Deep South* by Ward Greene; based on notorious 1913 incident later dramatized for TV as THE MURDER OF MARY PHAGAN.▼❶

Thief, The (1952) 85m. **½ D: Russell Rouse. Ray Milland, Rita Gam, Martin Gabel, Harry Bronson. Spy yarn set in N.Y.C. with a difference: no dialogue. Gimmick grows wearisome, script is tame.▼❶

Thief of Bagdad, The (1924) 155m. ***½ D: Raoul Walsh. Douglas Fairbanks, Julanne Johnston, Anna May Wong, Sojin, Snitz Edwards, Charles Belcher, Brandon Hurst. Fairbanks is unusually balletic (and ingratiating as ever) in this elaborate Arabian Nights pantomime, designed to instill a true sense of wonder. Quite long, but never dull; one of the most imaginative of all silent films, with awesome sets by William Cameron Menzies. Remade three times (so far).▼❶

Thief of Bagdad, The (1940-British) C-106m. **** D: Ludwig Berger, Tim Whelan, Michael Powell. Sabu, John Justin, June Duprez, Conrad Veidt, Rex Ingram, Miles Malleson, Mary Morris. Remarkable fantasy of native boy Sabu outdoing evil magician Veidt in Arabian Nights fable with incredible Oscar-winning Technicolor photography by Georges Perinal and Osmond Borradaile, special effects, and art direction. Ingram gives splendid performance as a genie; vivid score by Miklos Rozsa.▼❶

Thief of Baghdad (1961-Italian) C-90m. ** D: Arthur Lubin. Steve Reeves, Giorgia Moll, Arturo Dominici, Edy Vessel. Reeves searches for enchanted blue rose so he can marry Sultan's daughter. Nothing like Sabu version, but occasionally atmospheric. CinemaScope. ▼

Thief of Damascus (1952) C-78m. ** D: Will Jason. Paul Henreid, John Sutton, Jeff Donnell, Lon Chaney (Jr.), Elena Verdugo.

Jumbled costume spectacle featuring Aladdin, Sinbad, and Ali Baba out to liberate Damascus from conqueror Sutton; typical Sam Katzman quickie reuses footage from JOAN OF ARC!

Thieves Fall Out (1941) 72m. ** D: Ray Enright. Eddie Albert, Joan Leslie, Jane Darwell, Alan Hale, William T. Orr, John Litel, Anthony Quinn, Edward Brophy, Minna Gombell, Frank Faylen. Slight tale of ambitious Albert, the son of stuffy mattress manufacturer Hale, who finds trouble at every turn as he sets out to establish himself in business and wed the girl he loves. Darwell steals the film as Eddie's spunky grandmother.

Thieves' Highway (1949) 94m. *** D: Jules Dassin. Richard Conte, Valentina Cortese, Lee J. Cobb, Barbara Lawrence, Jack Oakie, Millard Mitchell, Joseph Pevney. Tough postwar drama of a returning vet seeking to avenge his trucker/father's treatment at the hands of a crooked fruit dealer in San Francisco. Masterfully directed; script by A. I. Bezzerides, from his novel. Only the ending seems pat.❶

Thieves' Holiday SEE: **Scandal in Paris, A**

Thing From Another World, The (1951) 87m. ***½ D: Christian Nyby. Kenneth Tobey, Margaret Sheridan, Robert Cornthwaite, Douglas Spencer, James Arness, Dewey Martin, William Self, George Fenneman. Classic blend of science-fiction and horror, loosely based on John W. Campbell, Jr.'s *Who Goes There?* Scientists at lonely Arctic outpost dig up alien (Arness) from the permafrost and must fight for their lives when it's accidentally thawed. Tense direction (often credited to producer Howard Hawks), excellent performances, eerie score by Dimitri Tiomkin. Screenplay by Charles Lederer. Watch out for 81m. reissue prints. Remade in 1982. Followed by a prequel in 2011. Also shown in computer-colored version. ▼❶

Things Happen at Night (1947-British) 79m. **½ D: Francis Searle. Gordon Harker, Alfred Drayton, Garry Marsh, Gwynneth Vaughan, Robertson Hare, Wylie Watson, Joan Young, Beatrice Campbell. Insurance investigator Harker arrives at the estate of pompous Drayton and finds himself and everyone in the house the victims of a prankish poltergeist. Brisk, funny little comedy that introduced to movies the concept of poltergeists. Harker and Drayton are fun as contrasting very-British types. Based on Frank Harvey's play *The Poltergeist.* ▼❶

Things to Come (1936-British) 92m. *** D: William Cameron Menzies. Raymond Massey, Cedric Hardwicke, Ralph Richardson, Maurice Braddell, Edward Chapman, Ann Todd. Stunning visualization of H. G. Wells' depiction of the future. Massey portrays leader of new world, Richardson despotic wartime ruler. Aloof but always interesting, enhanced by Menzies' sets. Vibrant music by Arthur Bliss; Wells himself wrote the screenplay. 1979 movie THE SHAPE OF THINGS TO COME, though taking the actual title of Wells' book, has nothing in common with this film.▼▶

Thing That Couldn't Die, The (1958) **69m.** ** D: Will Cowan. Andra Martin, William Reynolds, Robin Hughes, Carolyn Kearney, Jeffrey Stone. You never know what a dowsing rod will find. In this thriller, one finds the still living, decapitated head of a 15th-century devil worshipper who's looking for his body. Cheap, and looks it, but Hughes is good in title role.▶

Thin Ice (1937) **78m.** **½ D: Sidney Lanfield. Sonja Henie, Tyrone Power, Arthur Treacher, Joan Davis, Alan Hale, Raymond Walburn, Sig Rumann. Satisfactory Henie vehicle, with sly, dashing prince Power romancing commoner Sonja. A highlight: Davis singing "I'm Olga From the Volga."▼▶

Think Fast, Mr. Moto (1937) **66m.** *** D: Norman Foster. Peter Lorre, Virginia Field, Thomas Beck, Sig Rumann, Murray Kinnell, Lotus Long, J. Carrol Naish. Lorre's first appearance as Moto, the wily Japanese detective, sends him from San Francisco to Shanghai on a worldwide chase after diamond smugglers. Swift, entertaining mystery with Lorre most amusing as the bespectacled master of disguise.▶

The Thin Man One series stands apart from the others; its episodes were filmed two and three years apart, its stars were those of the major rank, and the films were not looked down at as Grade-B efforts. This was THE THIN MAN, a highly successful series launched quite unexpectedly in 1934 with a delightfully unpretentious blend of screwball comedy and murder mystery, from a story by Dashiell Hammett. William Powell and Myrna Loy starred as Nick and Nora Charles, a perfectly happy, sophisticated couple whose marriage never stood in the way of their having fun and going off on detective capers. This blithe, carefree portrayal of a modern American couple was beautifully handled by Loy and Powell, and audiences loved it. Five *Thin Man* films followed, from 1936 to 1947. None of them fully captured the essence of the original, although they retained much of the charm and had the infallible byplay of the two stars, aided by their dog Asta, who soon became a star in his own right. AFTER THE THIN MAN featured an up-and-coming actor named James Stewart as a suspect, and Sam Levene in the detective role played in the original by Nat Pendleton (and repeated in ANOTHER THIN MAN). ANOTHER THIN MAN also introduced Nick Charles, Jr., as a baby, who grew up in each successive film. SHADOW OF THE THIN MAN was next in the series,

and featured Nick and Nora sleuthing at the race track. THE THIN MAN GOES HOME presented Nick's parents (Harry Davenport and Lucile Watson), who never wanted him to be a detective in the first place. The final film, SONG OF THE THIN MAN, had Nick and Nora frequenting many jazz hangouts (à la *Peter Gunn*) for some offbeat sequences. While the original THIN MAN rated above its follow-ups, even the weakest entries were fresh and enjoyable, thanks mainly to the two stars. An attempt to rekindle that magic in the 1991 Broadway musical *Nick and Nora* failed miserably. (A 1957–59 TV series starred Peter Lawford and Phyllis Kirk.) By the way, "The Thin Man" really wasn't Powell—he was a character in the first film, played by Edward Ellis.

THE THIN MAN

The Thin Man (1934)
After the Thin Man (1936)
Another Thin Man (1939)
Shadow of the Thin Man (1941)
The Thin Man Goes Home (1944)
Song of the Thin Man (1947)

Thin Man, The (1934) **93m.** **** D: W. S. Van Dyke. William Powell, Myrna Loy, Maureen O'Sullivan, Nat Pendleton, Minna Gombell, Cesar Romero, Natalie Moorhead, Edward Ellis, Porter Hall. Nick and Nora investigate the disappearance of an inventor in this classic blend of laughs and suspense which marked the first pairing of what was to become one of the movies' great romantic teams. Shot in just two weeks by director Woody "One-Shot" Van Dyke and cinematographer James Wong Howe, this has gone on to become *the* sophisticated comedy-mystery par excellence, inspiring five sequels as well as countless imitations. Frances Goodrich and Albert Hackett adapted Dashiell Hammett's novel.▼▶

Thin Man Goes Home, The (1944) **100m.** *** D: Richard Thorpe. William Powell, Myrna Loy, Lucile Watson, Gloria De Haven, Anne Revere, Helen Vinson, Harry Davenport, Leon Ames, Donald Meek, Edward Brophy. Nick takes the family on a vacation to Sycamore Springs to visit his parents, but naturally winds up embroiled in a murder case. Leisurely entry, with even more comedy than usual.▼▶

Thin Red Line, The (1964) **99m.** *** D: Andrew Marton. Keir Dullea, Jack Warden, James Philbrook, Kieron Moore. Gritty adaptation of James Jones' novel about personal conflict during the bloody attack on Guadalcanal during WW2. Dullea is the sensitive, iconoclastic soldier and Warden is the brutal sergeant who won't leave him alone. Remade in 1998. CinemaScope.▶

Third Day, The (1965) **C-119m.** **½ D: Jack Smight. George Peppard, Elizabeth Ashley, Roddy McDowall, Arthur O'Connell, Mona Washbourne, Herbert Marshall, Robert Webber, Charles Drake, Sally Kellerman, Vincent Gardenia, Arte Johnson. Capable cast helps standard amnesia tale about Peppard's inability to remember events that have caused him to be accused of murder. Panavision. ❱

Third Finger, Left Hand (1940) **96m. **** D: Robert Z. Leonard. Myrna Loy, Melvyn Douglas, Raymond Walburn, Lee Bowman, Bonita Granville. Mediocre comedy with attractive stars. Loy dissuades romance by pretending to be married, so Douglas claims to be her husband! ❱

Third Key, The (1956-British) **96m. ***** D: Charles Frend. Jack Hawkins, John Stratton, Dorothy Alison, Geoffrey Keen, Ursula Howells. Exciting story of Scotland Yard, as Inspector Hawkins and rookie sergeant (Stratton) diligently pursue safecracking incident to its surprising conclusion. Original British title: THE LONG ARM.▼

Third Man, The (1949-British) **104m. ****** D: Carol Reed. Orson Welles, Joseph Cotten, (Alida) Valli, Trevor Howard, Bernard Lee, Wilfrid Hyde-White. Graham Greene's account of mysterious Harry Lime (Welles) in post-WW2 Vienna is a bona fide classic, with pulp-writer Cotten on a manhunt for Harry. Anton Karas' zither rendition of "The Third Man Theme" adds just the right touch; cinematographer Robert Krasker won an Oscar. Note: there are two versions of this film. The British version features introductory narration by director Reed; the American print is narrated by Cotten, and runs 93m. Little of substance was actually cut, but the film was tightened somewhat by coproducer David O. Selznick. Later on radio with Welles and on TV with Michael Rennie. Also shown in computer-colored version.▼◉❱

Third Man on the Mountain (1959) **C-105m. ***** D: Ken Annakin. James MacArthur, Michael Rennie, Janet Munro, James Donald, Herbert Lom, Laurence Naismith. Fine Disney adventure about Swiss boy (MacArthur) determined to climb the Matterhorn (here called the Citadel) who learns more than just mountain-climbing in his dogged pursuit. Look quickly to spot MacArthur's mother Helen Hayes in a cameo as tourist.▼◉❱

Third Secret, The (1964-British) **103m. **½** D: Charles Crichton. Stephen Boyd, Jack Hawkins, Richard Attenborough, Diane Cilento, Pamela Franklin, Paul Rogers, Alan Webb, Judi Dench. Police rule that a celebrated psychoanalyst has committed suicide. His 14-year-old daughter (Franklin) thinks otherwise, and convinces news commentator Boyd (who also was one of the doctor's patients) to investigate. Talky, episodic whodunit; Dench's screen debut. CinemaScope. ❱

Third Voice, The (1960) **79m. ***** D: Hubert Cornfield. Edmond O'Brien, Laraine Day, Julie London, Ralph Brooks, Roque Ybarra, Henry Delgado. Neat suspense film involving murder, impersonation, and double-crossing. CinemaScope.

Thirst (1949) SEE: **Three Strange Loves**

13 Fighting Men (1960) **69m. *½** D: Harry Gerstad. Grant Williams, Brad Dexter, Carole Mathews, Robert Dix, Richard Garland, Rayford Barnes, John Erwin. Minor film about Union soldiers fighting off Rebel troops to protect gold shipment. CinemaScope.

13 Frightened Girls (1963) **C-89m.** BOMB D: William Castle. Murray Hamilton, Joyce Taylor, Hugh Marlowe, Khigh Dhiegh. One of Castle's weirdest films (no mean feat), set in Swiss boarding school catering to daughters of diplomats; after trading bits of info they picked up from Daddy during the holidays, the girls decide to go off and do spy stuff. Castle held a worldwide talent search to find his "stars," for whom this was their first—and no doubt last—film. A side-splitting camp classic awaiting rediscovery.❱

13 Ghosts (1960) **C/B&W-88m. **½** D: William Castle. Charles Herbert, Donald Woods, Martin Milner, Jo Morrow, Rosemary DeCamp, Margaret Hamilton, John Van Dreelen. Typically tongue-in-cheek Castle spook opera, about nice, all-American family (with children named Buck and Medea!) that inherits a haunted house. Plenty of chills and chuckles, with Hamilton cleverly cast as sinister housekeeper. Some prints run 85m., minus footage of Castle introducing "Illusion-O"—movie patrons were given "ghost viewers" enabling them to see (or not see) the spirits. Remade in 2001. ▼◉❱

Thirteen Hours by Air (1936) **80m. **½** D: Mitchell Leisen. Fred MacMurray, Joan Bennett, ZaSu Pitts, John Howard, Bennie Bartlett, Grace Bradley, Alan Baxter, Ruth Donnelly, Dean Jagger. Dated but diverting tale of transcontinental flight, with romance, murder, and intrigue surrounding mysterious passengers.

13 Lead Soldiers (1948) **64m. **** D: Frank McDonald. Tom Conway, Maria Palmer, Helen Westcott, John Newland, Terry Kilburn, William Stelling. Ancient toy soldiers hold the key to buried treasure in this minor *Bulldog Drummond* yarn.

13 Rue Madeleine (1947) **95m. ***** D: Henry Hathaway. James Cagney, Annabella, Richard Conte, Frank Latimore, Walter Abel, Melville Cooper, Sam Jaffe. Gripping documentary-style WW2 story about the training of new O.S.S. operatives, their first overseas assignments, and the ferreting-out of a German enemy agent in their ranks. Good cast also includes young E. G. Marshall, Karl Malden, Red Buttons. ▼❱

Thirteenth Chair, The (1937) **67m.** **½ D: George B. Seitz. Dame May Whitty, Madge Evans, Lewis Stone, Elissa Landi, Thomas Beck, Henry Daniell, Janet Beecher, Ralph Forbes. A murder is committed, and various suspects come together for an evening of surprises in the company of a secretive medium (Whitty) and a persistent police inspector (Stone). Entertaining whodunit is based on a Bayard Veiller play, previously filmed in 1919 and 1929.

Thirteenth Guest, The (1932) **69m.** **½ D: Albert Ray. Ginger Rogers, Lyle Talbot, J. Farrell MacDonald, Paul Hurst, James C. Eagles. Guests are reassembled from dinner party that took place 13 years earlier—at which the host fell dead—in order to solve mystery of unnamed 13th guest to whom the deceased bequeathed his estate. Enjoyable antique chiller complete with hooded murderer. Remade as THE MYSTERY OF THE THIRTEENTH GUEST. ▼▶

Thirteenth Hour, The (1947) **65m.** **½ D: William Clemens. Richard Dix, Karen Morley, Mark Dennis, John Kellogg, Bernadene Hayes, Jim Bannon, Regis Toomey. A trucking company owner is suspected of murder when the cop he had a feud with turns up dead. Efficient entry in *The Whistler* series, and Dix's last movie.

13th Letter, The (1951) **85m.** **½ D: Otto Preminger. Linda Darnell, Charles Boyer, Michael Rennie, Constance Smith, Judith Evelyn. Interesting account of effect of series of poison pen letters on townsfolk, set in Canada. Remake of Henri Georges Clouzot's LE CORBEAU.

13 West Street (1962) **80m.** **½ D: Philip Leacock. Alan Ladd, Rod Steiger, Michael Callan, Dolores Dorn, Jeanne Cooper. Early version of DEATH WISH has Ladd out to get gang of hoodlums; taut actioner with most capable cast. Based on novel *The Tiger Among Us* by Leigh Brackett. ▶

Thirteen Women (1932) **73m.** ** D: George Archainbaud. Irene Dunne, Ricardo Cortez, Myrna Loy, Jill Esmond, Florence Eldridge, Kay Johnson. Silly tripe with Loy as a half-caste with hypnotic powers who has sworn revenge on sorority sisters who rejected her years ago in school. ▶

—30— (1959) **96m.** *½ D: Jack Webb. Jack Webb, William Conrad, David Nelson, Whitney Blake, Louise Lorimer, Joe Flynn, James Bell. Hackneyed, overwritten tale of a typical night on a big-city newspaper. Conrad chews the scenery as city editor, but the script's the main villain, abetted by atrocious music score. Title, by the way, is journalists' way of indicating "the end." ▼▶

Thirty Day Princess (1934) **75m.** **½ D: Marion Gering. Sylvia Sidney, Cary Grant, Edward Arnold, Vince Barnett, Lucien Littlefield. Lightly entertaining if formulaic fluff, with Sidney cast in two roles: a prin-

cess making a goodwill tour of the U.S. and an unemployed actress hired to impersonate her. Coscripted by Preston Sturges. ▶

30-Foot Bride of Candy Rock, The (1959) **75m.** ** D: Sidney Miller. Lou Costello, Dorothy Provine, Gale Gordon, Charles Lane, Jimmy Conlin, Peter Leeds. Lou Costello's only starring film without Bud Abbott is nothing much, mildly entertaining, with Provine enlarged to gigantic proportions. Released after Costello's death. ▼▶

39 Steps, The (1935-British) **87m.** **** D: Alfred Hitchcock. Robert Donat, Madeleine Carroll, Lucie Mannheim, Godfrey Tearle, Peggy Ashcroft, John Laurie, Wylie Watson. Classic Hitchcock mystery with overtones of light comedy and romance, as innocent Donat is pulled into spy-ring activities. Memorable banter between Donat and Carroll, who thinks he's a criminal, set style for sophisticated dialogue for years. John Buchan's novel was adapted by Charles Bennett and Alma Reville; additional dialogue by Ian Hay. Remade three times and later adapted to the Broadway stage. ▼●▶

39 Steps, The (1959-British) **C-93m.** **½ D: Ralph Thomas. Kenneth More, Taina Elg, Brenda de Banzie, Barry Jones, Reginald Beckwith, Sidney James, James Hayter. Young man is accidentally involved in murder and espionage and ensnares the aid of disbelieving young woman. More and Elg are delightful in this replica of 1935 classic; not nearly as good, but still entertaining. Remade in 1978 and as a 2008 TVM. ▼▶

Thirty Seconds Over Tokyo (1944) **138m.** *** D: Mervyn LeRoy. Van Johnson, Robert Walker, Spencer Tracy, Phyllis Thaxter, Scott McKay, Robert Mitchum, Don DeFore, Stephen McNally, Louis Jean Heydt, Leon Ames, Paul Langton, Bill Williams. Exciting WW2 actioner of first American attack on Japan with sturdy cast, guest appearance by Tracy as General Doolittle. Script by Dalton Trumbo. Oscar-winning special effects. ▼●▶

36 Hours (1964) **115m.** **½ D: George Seaton. James Garner, Eva Marie Saint, Rod Taylor, Werner Peters, Celia Lovsky, Alan Napier. Intriguing WW2 yarn with Garner as captured spy brainwashed into thinking the war is over begins well, but peters out fast. Taylor as German officer is interesting casting. Remade for cable TV as BREAKING POINT in 1989 with Corbin Bernsen. Also shown in computer-colored version. Panavision. ▼▶

36 Hours to Kill (1936) **66m.** **½ D: Eugene Forde. Brian Donlevy, Gloria Stuart, Douglas Fowley, Isabel Jewell, Stepin Fetchit, Julius Tannen, Warren Hymer. G-man Donlevy and reporter Stuart board a train to trap fugitive gangster Fowley. Zippy B-movie mix of crime, comedy, and romance. Based on a W. R. Burnett story, *Across the Aisle.*

[705]

30 Years of Fun (1963) 85m. **** Compiled by Robert Youngson. Charlie Chaplin, Buster Keaton, Laurel and Hardy, Harry Langdon, Sydney Chaplin, Charley Chase, etc. Without repeating from previous films, Youngson presents hilarious silent comedy footage. Included is rare sequence of Laurel and Hardy performing together for the first time in 1917's LUCKY DOG.

This Above All (1942) 110m. *** D: Anatole Litvak. Tyrone Power, Joan Fontaine, Thomas Mitchell, Nigel Bruce, Gladys Cooper, Sara Allgood, Phillip Merivale, Alexander Knox. Timely WW2 film shows its age, but is still good, with strong cast in Eric Knight tale of embittered soldier Power finding courage and love with patriotic Britisher Fontaine; adapted by R. C. Sherriff.▶

This Angry Age (1958-Italian-U.S.) C-111m. ** D: René Clement. Silvana Mangano, Anthony Perkins, Alida Valli, Richard Conte, Jo Van Fleet, Nehemiah Persoff. Ludicrous mishmash set in IndoChina with Van Fleet a stereotyped, dominating mother who's convinced that her children (Perkins and Mangano) can make their rice fields a going proposition. Originally titled THE SEA WALL. Technirama.

This Could Be the Night (1957) 103m. **½ D: Robert Wise. Jean Simmons, Paul Douglas, Anthony Franciosa, Joan Blondell, Neile Adams, ZaSu Pitts, J. Carrol Naish. Forced, frantic comedy of prim teacher Simmons working as secretary to gangster Douglas, who runs a nightclub; Franciosa is the young associate who romances her. CinemaScope.▼●▶

This Day and Age (1933) 85m. *** D: Cecil B. DeMille. Charles Bickford, Judith Allen, Richard Cromwell, Harry Green, Eddie Nugent, Ben Alexander, Bradley Page. Fascinating story of high-schoolers taking law into their own hands to pin mobster Bickford for murder of tailor Green. Hardly subtle, yet powerfully effective.▶

This Earth Is Mine (1959) C-125m. **½ D: Henry King. Rock Hudson, Jean Simmons, Dorothy McGuire, Claude Rains, Kent Smith, Anna Lee, Ken Scott. Disjointed soaper set in 1930s California vineyards about intertwining family romances, focusing on Hudson-Simmons love story. CinemaScope.

This Gun for Hire (1942) 80m. *** D: Frank Tuttle. Alan Ladd, Veronica Lake, Robert Preston, Laird Cregar, Tully Marshall, Marc Lawrence, Pamela Blake. Ladd came into his own as paid gunman seeking revenge on man who double-crossed him, with Lake as a fetching vis-à-vis. Script by W. R. Burnett and Albert Maltz, from Graham Greene's novel *A Gun For Sale*. Remade in 1957 (as SHORT CUT TO HELL) and for cable TV in 1991 (with Robert Wagner).▼●▶

This Happy Breed (1944-British) C-110m. ***½ D: David Lean. Robert Newton, Celia Johnson, John Mills, Kay Walsh, Stanley Holloway, Amy Veness, Alison Leggatt. Splendidly acted saga follows British family from 1919 to 1939 in this adaptation of Noel Coward play. Scripted by director Lean, cinematographer Ronald Neame, and coproducer Anthony Havelock-Allan. Unbilled Laurence Olivier provides opening narration. ▼▶

This Happy Feeling (1958) C-92m. *** D: Blake Edwards. Debbie Reynolds, Curt Jurgens, John Saxon, Alexis Smith, Estelle Winwood, Mary Astor, Troy Donahue, Joe Flynn. Most engaging cast gives zip to simple yarn of Reynolds enthralled by actor Jurgens, but sparked by suitor Saxon; Winwood fine as eccentric housekeeper. CinemaScope.▼

This Is Cinerama (1952) C-122m. *** D: No director credited. Hosted by Lowell Thomas. A movie milestone, this elaborate travelogue was designed to show off a three-camera widescreen image, projected onto a giant curved screen, with stereophonic sound. Quaint today but still fascinating. Highlights include a roller-coaster ride in Rockaway, N.Y., a performance of *Aida* at La Scala Opera House in Milan, and a paean to the beauty of America as seen from the air. Majestic score by Max Steiner and Roy Webb. 2012 restoration is presented in a curved-screen simulation that replicates the feeling of seeing the film in a theater. Cinerama.▶

This Island Earth (1955) C-86m. *** D: Joseph Newman. Jeff Morrow, Rex Reason, Faith Domergue, Russell Johnson, Lance Fuller, Douglas Spencer. Suspenseful, intelligent science fiction about scientists lured to mysterious project, only to find they've been recruited—or more appropriately, shanghaied—by aliens to help them defend their invasion-torn planet. Thoughtful and exciting, with excellent visuals; based on Raymond F. Jones' novel. Film is spoofed in MYSTERY SCIENCE THEATER 3000: THE MOVIE. ▼●▶

This Is My Affair (1937) 101m. *** D: William A. Seiter. Barbara Stanwyck, Robert Taylor, Victor McLaglen, Brian Donlevy, Sidney Blackmer, John Carradine, Sig Ruman. Exciting film of undercover man Taylor joining gang of robbers on order from President McKinley; Stanwyck is saloon singer who loves Taylor (they married in real life two years later).▶

This Is My Love (1954) C-91m. ** D: Stuart Heisler. Linda Darnell, Rick Jason, Dan Duryea, Faith Domergue, Hal Baylor, Jerry Mathers. Darnell and her sister Domergue (who's married to invalid Duryea) compete for affections of Jason in this murky soap-drama.

This Is the Army (1943) C-121m. *** D:

Michael Curtiz. George Murphy, Joan Leslie, Lt. Ronald Reagan, Sgt. Joe Louis, Kate Smith, George Tobias, Alan Hale, Charles Butterworth, Dolores Costello, Una Merkel, Stanley Ridges, Rosemary DeCamp, Frances Langford, Irving Berlin, many others. Soldiers who staged Irving Berlin's WW1 musical *Yip Yip Yaphank* reunite to mount similar WW2 effort; corny but enjoyable framework (with Warner Bros. cast) for filmed record of legendary 1940s show, a topical melange of songs and skits. P.S.: This is the film where George Murphy plays Ronald Reagan's father! Restored video version runs 125m. with overture and exit music. ▼❷

This Is the Life (1944) 87m. ** D: Felix E. Feist. Donald O'Connor, Peggy Ryan, Susanna Foster, Patric Knowles. Spunky cast of versatile performers with Foster torn between swank Knowles and performer O'Connor. Based on a play by Sinclair Lewis and Fay Wray!

This Is the Night (1932) 78m. **½ D: Frank Tuttle. Lily Damita, Charlie Ruggles, Roland Young, Thelma Todd, Cary Grant, Irving Bacon. Enjoyable if somewhat strained romantic comedy in the Lubitsch mold, set in Paris and Venice, with Young hiring Damita to pose as his wife to help cover up his amorous pursuit of Todd. Grant has a wonderful entrance (as Todd's athletic husband) in his feature debut. ❷

This Land Is Mine (1943) 103m. ** D: Jean Renoir. Charles Laughton, Maureen O'Hara, George Sanders, Walter Slezak, Kent Smith, Una O'Connor, Philip Merivale, George Coulouris, Nancy Gates. Meek French teacher Laughton, aroused by Nazi occupation, becomes hero. Patriotic wartime film is dated and disappointing today; written by Dudley Nichols. ▼❶❷

This Love of Ours (1945) 90m. **½ D: William Dieterle. Merle Oberon, Charles Korvin, Claude Rains, Carl Esmond, Sue England, Jess Barker, Harry Davenport, Ralph Morgan. Sudsy soaper of Korvin leaving wife Oberon, meeting 12 years later, falling in love again. Rains steals show in supporting role. Remade in 1956 as NEVER SAY GOODBYE.

This Man Is Mine (1934) 76m. ** D: John Cromwell. Irene Dunne, Ralph Bellamy, Constance Cummings, Kay Johnson, Sidney Blackmer, Charles Starrett, Vivian Tobin. Lightweight script does in this lesser Dunne vehicle, with Irene vying with Cummings for the love of Bellamy.

This Man Is News (1938-British) 77m. *** D: David MacDonald. Barry K. Barnes, Valerie Hobson, Alastair Sim, John Warwick, Garry Marsh. Framed newspaperman goes after jewel thieves in this crisp, stylish little comedy-thriller. Sequel: THIS MAN IN PARIS. ▼

This Man's Navy (1945) 100m. *** D: William Wellman. Wallace Beery, Tom Drake, James Gleason, Jan Clayton, Selena Royle, Noah Beery, Sr., Steve Brodie. Usual Beery service story nicely rehashed; Beery treats Drake as a son, gets vicarious pleasure out of his Navy career. ❷

This Marriage Business (1938) 70m. ** D: Christy Cabanne. Victor Moore, Allan Lane, Vicki Lester, Cecil Kellaway, Jack Carson, Richard Lane, Paul Guilfoyle. Whenever modest small-town judge Moore issues marriage licenses, the newlyweds are assured wedded bliss. Complications arise when hotshot N.Y. reporter Lane hypes him as a "cupid." Slight, forgettable programmer.

This Modern Age (1931) 76m. ** D: Nicholas Grinde. Joan Crawford, Pauline Frederick, Neil Hamilton, Monroe Owsley, Hobart Bosworth, Emma Dunn. Crawford falls for Hamilton, but his conservative parents don't take to the free-living lifestyle she and her expatriate mother (Frederick) espouse. Standard, predictable plot. ❷

This Rebel Age SEE: **Beat Generation, The**

This Rebel Breed (1960) 90m. **½ D: Richard L. Bare. Rita Moreno, Mark Damon, Gerald Mohr, Jay Novello, Eugene Martin, Tom Gilson, Diane (Dyan) Cannon, Al Freeman (Jr.). Above average drama about racial tensions in a multi-ethnic high school, with Moreno well cast as a Latina teen involved with an Anglo boy (which displeases her trouble-prone brother). Cannon is amusingly cast as a gang deb! Retitled THREE SHADES OF LOVE and THE BLACK REBELS, the latter with incongruous R-rated footage added. ▼❷

This Side of the Law (1950) 74m. ** D: Richard L. Bare. Viveca Lindfors, Kent Smith, Janis Paige, Monte Blue. Hokey script has Smith hired by crooked lawyer to impersonate missing wealthy man. ❷

This Sporting Life (1963-British) 129m. ***½ D: Lindsay Anderson. Richard Harris, Rachel Roberts, Alan Badel, William Hartnell, Colin Blakely, Arthur Lowe. Yorkshire coal miner "betters" himself by becoming professional rugby player. Powerful film (written by David Storey) about love, success, and disillusionment; also serves to illustrate what a grueling game rugby is. Film debut of Glenda Jackson. Originally 134m. ▼❶❷

This Strange Passion SEE: **El**

This Thing Called Love (1941) 98m. *** D: Alexander Hall. Rosalind Russell, Melvyn Douglas, Binnie Barnes, Allyn Joslyn, Gloria Dickson, Lee J. Cobb. Adult comedy of newlyweds who set up three-month trial run for their marriage. Stars' expertise puts it over.

This Time for Keeps (1942) 72m. ** D: Charles Riesner. Robert Sterling, Ann Rutherford, Guy Kibbee, Irene Rich, Virginia Weidler, Henry O'Neill, Dorothy Morris. Trouble ensues for newlyweds Rutherford

and Sterling when he goes to work for his father-in-law (Kibbee) in this marginally likable small-town family comedy. Second and last entry in an attempt by MGM to come up with another *Andy Hardy*–type series, based on characters created by Herman J. Mankiewicz for 1940's KEEPING COMPANY. Look for Ava Gardner in a bit part.
This Time for Keeps (1947) **C-105m.** ****½** D: Richard Thorpe. Esther Williams, Jimmy Durante, Lauritz Melchior, Johnnie Johnston, Xavier Cugat, Dame May Whitty, Sharon McManus. Slight MGM musical with Johnston falling for aquacade star Williams, neglecting to inform her that he's engaged. ▼❶
This Way Please (1937) **75m.** ****½** D: Robert Florey. Charles "Buddy" Rogers, Betty Grable, Mary Livingstone, Ned Sparks, Jim Jordan, Marion Jordan, Porter Hall, Lee Bowman, Rufe Davis. Second-string musical about movie theater usherette with a crush on bandleader Rogers; amusing specialty material by Davis, engaging moments with radio's Fibber McGee and Molly (Jim and Marion Jordan).
This Woman Is Dangerous (1952) **100m.** ****½** D: Felix E. Feist. Joan Crawford, Dennis Morgan, David Brian, Richard Webb, Sherry Jackson. In typical tough-girl role, Crawford finds true love after countless mishaps, including an eye operation.❶
Thoroughbreds Don't Cry (1937) **80m.** ****½** D: Alfred E. Green. Judy Garland, Mickey Rooney, Ronald Sinclair, Sophie Tucker, C. Aubrey Smith, Frankie Darro, Henry Kolker, Helen Troy. Fairly good racetrack story with jockey Rooney involved in crooked deals, young Garland adding some songs. Mickey and Judy's first film together. ▼❶
Those Calloways (1965) **C-131m.** ******* D: Norman Tokar. Brian Keith, Vera Miles, Brandon de Wilde, Walter Brennan, Ed Wynn, Linda Evans, Philip Abbott. Long, episodic but rewarding Disney film about an eccentric New England man (Keith) and his family, focusing on his determined efforts to use nearby lake for bird sanctuary before it's bought up by business interests. Film debut of Linda Evans. Music score by Max Steiner. ▼❶
Those Endearing Young Charms (1945) **81m.** ****½** D: Lewis Allen. Robert Young, Laraine Day, Ann Harding, Bill Williams, Marc Cramer, Anne Jeffreys, Lawrence Tierney. Surprisingly effective wartime romance finds salesgirl Day being wooed by boyish nice guy Williams and becoming interested in smooth-talking heel Young. Nothing special, but nicely played and sparked by some amusing Jerome Chodorov dialogue.
Those Magnificent Men in Their Flying Machines (1965) **C-132m.** ******* D: Ken Annakin. Stuart Whitman, Sarah Miles, James Fox, Alberto Sordi, Robert Morley, Gert Frobe, Jean-Pierre Cassel, Terry-Thomas, Irina Demick, Benny Hill, Flora Robson, Sam Wanamaker, Gordon Jackson, Millicent Martin, Red Skelton, Tony Hancock; narrated by James Robertson Justice. Long but enjoyable film of great 1910 London-to-Paris airplane race involving international conflicts, cheating, and romance. Skelton has funny cameo in amusing prologue, tracing history of aviation. Clever title caricatures and designs by Ronald Searle. Roadshow version on video runs 138m. with intermission/entr'acte.Todd-AO. ▼❶
Those Redheads From Seattle (1953) **C-90m.** ****** D: Lewis R. Foster. Rhonda Fleming, Gene Barry, Agnes Moorehead, Teresa Brewer, Guy Mitchell. Modestly produced musical nonsense set in gold-rush era with Moorehead the mother of four girls who takes her brood to Alaska. Originally in 3-D.
Those Three French Girls (1930) **73m.** ****** D: Harry Beaumont. Fifi D'Orsay, Reginald Denny, Cliff Edwards, Yola d'Avril, Sandra Ravel, George Grossmith, Edward Brophy. Britisher Denny hooks up with Yanks Edwards and Brophy in jail and embarks on a series of zany romantic escapades with those three sexy damsels of the title. Frivolous confection cowritten by P. G. Wodehouse, of some interest for song and dance interludes by Edwards, but mostly for pre-Code views of the young ladies revealing their frilly lingerie as often as possible.
Those Were the Days (1940) **76m.** ****** D: J. Theodore Reed. William Holden, Bonita Granville, Ezra Stone, Judith Barrett, Vaughan Glaser, Lucien Littlefield, Richard Denning. Light-hearted (and -headed) comedy from George Fitch's *Siwash* stories, with Holden as a college hellraiser (circa 1904) who woos judge's daughter Granville to avoid a jail sentence. We give it a C-minus. Alan Ladd has a small role as a student.
Thousand and One Nights, A (1945) **C-93m.** ******* D: Alfred E. Green. Cornel Wilde, Evelyn Keyes, Phil Silvers, Adele Jergens, Dusty Anderson, Dennis Hoey, Rex Ingram. Wilde is a genial, singing Aladdin in this slice of Technicolor escapism, with Silvers as his very contemporary sidekick. Keyes is fun as the impish genie who emerges from a magic lamp. Ingram (who played the genie in THE THIEF OF BAGDAD) has a throwaway role here as a giant. Look fast for Shelley Winters. ▼
Thousand Clowns, A (1965) **118m.** *****½** D: Fred Coe. Jason Robards, Barbara Harris, Martin Balsam, Barry Gordon, Gene Saks, William Daniels. Faithful adaptation by Herb Gardner of his Broadway comedy about society dropout who's being pressured to drop in again for the sake of young nephew who lives with him. Per-

fectly cast, filmed in N.Y.C., with Balsam's Oscar-winning performance as Robards' brother.▼●)

Thousand Eyes of Dr. Mabuse, The SEE: **1,000 Eyes of Dr. Mabuse, The**

Thousands Cheer (1943) **C-126m.** **½ D: George Sidney. Mickey Rooney, Judy Garland, Gene Kelly, Red Skelton, Eleanor Powell, Ann Sothern, Lucille Ball, Virginia O'Brien, Frank Morgan, Kathryn Grayson, Lena Horne, many others. Grayson lives with officer-father John Boles at Army base, falls for hotheaded private Kelly and decides to prepare an all-star show for the soldiers. Dubious plot is an excuse for specialty acts by top MGM stars.▼●)

Thou Shalt Not Kill (1961-Italian-French-Yugoslavian) **129m.** **½ D: Claude Autant-Lara. Laurent Terzieff, Horst Frank, Suzanne Flon, Mica Orlovic. Too-often sterile narrative dealing with trial of French conscientious objector, with side plot of German priest facing penalty for having killed Frenchman during WW2. Based on a true story, and quite controversial when released. Dyaliscope.

Threat, The (1949) **65m.** *** D: Felix Feist. Charles McGraw, Michael O'Shea, Virginia Grey, Julie Bishop, Robert Shayne, Anthony Caruso. Thug McGraw escapes prison, kidnaps cop and D.A. who put him away, plus singer he suspects of having squealed. Fast, rugged little "B" keeps action hopping until tough conclusion.▼)

Threat, The (1960) **66m.** ** D: Charles R. Rondeau. Robert Knapp, Linda Lawson, Lisabeth Hush, James Seay, Mary Castle, Barney Phillips. A cop (Knapp) kills a fabled hoodlum, then finds himself stalked by a mysterious man seeking vengeance. Aimless drama.

Three Ages (1923) **63m.** *** D: Buster Keaton, Edward F. Cline. Buster Keaton, Margaret Leahy, Wallace Beery, Joe Roberts, Horace Morgan, Lillian Lawrence. Buster's comic observations on the pursuit of a mate in the Stone Age, the Roman Empire, and modern times. Entertaining silent comedy, with Keaton making a memorable entrance atop a dinosaur.▼●)

3 Bad Men (1926) **92m.** ***½ D: John Ford. George O'Brien, Lou Tellegen, J. Farrell MacDonald, Tom Santschi, Frank Campeau. Three gruff outlaws become benevolent protectors of young woman whose father is killed during Western settlement period. Beautiful mixture of action, drama, comedy, and sentiment in one of Ford's best silents. An obvious variation on 3 GODFATHERS. Remade as NOT EXACTLY GENTLEMEN (1931).▼)

Three Bad Sisters (1956) **76m.** *½ D: Gilbert L. Kay. Marla English, Kathleen Hughes, Sara Shane, John Bromfield, Jess Barker, Madge Kennedy, Tony (Anthony) George. Bad indeed! Trashy melodrama

with zillionaire tycoon dying in plane crash. His three offspring—one ruthless, one sluttish, one merely "intense" and psychotic—become immersed in battle over his estate.▶

Three Blind Mice (1938) **75m.** **½ D: William A. Seiter. Loretta Young, Joel McCrea, David Niven, Stuart Erwin, Marjorie Weaver, Pauline Moore, Jane Darwell, Binnie Barnes. Familiar idea of three fortune-hunting girls going after well-heeled male prospects; slickly done. Remade, reworked many times.

Three Blondes in His Life (1960) **81m.** ** D: Leon Chooluck. Jock Mahoney, Greta Thyssen, Anthony Dexter, Jesse White, Valerie Porter. Occasionally tangy mystery with Mahoney a private eye determined to probe the death of his insurance investigator pal.▼)

Three Brave Men (1957) **88m.** **½ D: Philip Dunne. Ray Milland, Frank Lovejoy, Ernest Borgnine, Nina Foch, Dean Jagger, Virginia Christine, Edward Andrews, Andrew Duggan, Joseph Wiseman. Navy clerk Borgnine is fired as a security risk because of alleged Communist leanings; lawyer Milland tries to get him reinstated. Adapted by Dunne from Pulitzer Prize–winning articles by Anthony Lewis, courtroom drama is interesting but unexceptional. CinemaScope.▶

Three Broadway Girls SEE: **Greeks Had a Word for Them, The**

Three Caballeros, The (1945) **C-70m.** *** D: Norman Ferguson. Aurora Miranda, Carmen Molina, Dora Luz, voices of Sterling Holloway, Clarence Nash, José Oliviera, Joaquin Garay. Colorful Disney pastiche that followed 1940s Good Neighbor Policy by saluting Latin America, through the eyes of Donald Duck. Filled with infectious music (including "Baia," "You Belong to My Heart"), eye-popping visuals, amusing cartoon sequences, and clever combinations of live action and animation. Donald, José Carioca, and Panchito perform title song in a dazzling display of cartoon wizardry.▼●)

Three Came Home (1950) **106m.** ***½ D: Jean Negulesco. Claudette Colbert, Patric Knowles, Florence Desmond, Sessue Hayakawa, Sylvia Andrew, Phyllis Morris. Stunning performances by Colbert and Hayakawa make this a must. British and American families living on Borneo during WW2 are sent to prison camps by Japanese, but cultured officer Hayakawa takes an interest in authoress Colbert. Producer Nunnally Johnson adapted Agnes Newton Keith's autobiographical book.▼)

Three Cases of Murder (1955-British) **99m.** **½ D: Wendy Toye, David Eady, George More O'Ferrall. Alan Badel, Hugh Pryse, John Gregson, Elizabeth Sellars, Emrys Jones, Orson Welles, Maxwell Reed,

Richard Wattis; introduced by Eammon Andrews. Three offbeat murder stories; opener "In the Picture" is genuinely eerie, closer "Lord Mountdrago" (from Somerset Maugham story) has Welles in absorbing tale of a pompous British government official haunted by a rival.▼●

Three Cheers for the Irish (1940) **100m.** ** D: Lloyd Bacon. Thomas Mitchell, Dennis Morgan, Priscilla Lane, Alan Hale, Virginia Grey, Irene Hervey, Frank Jenks, William Lundigan. Mitchell is the whole show (and chews the scenery) as a stereotypically ornery N.Y.C. Irish beat cop who's forced into retirement. Daughter Lane falls for his replacement (Morgan), who—heaven help him—is a Scotsman.

Three Coins in the Fountain (1954) **C-102m.** *** D: Jean Negulesco. Clifton Webb, Dorothy McGuire, Jean Peters, Louis Jourdan, Maggie McNamara, Rossano Brazzi, Cathleen Nesbitt. Splashy romance yarn made ultra-pleasing by Rome locations. Three women make wishes for romance at Fountain of Trevi, spurring several amorous adventures. Won Oscars for Milton Krasner's photography and the Jule Styne–Sammy Cahn title tune (sung by Frank Sinatra). Remade by same director as THE PLEASURE SEEKERS; reworked for TV in 1990 as COINS IN THE FOUNTAIN. CinemaScope.▼●

Three Comrades (1938) **98m.** ***½ D: Frank Borzage. Robert Taylor, Margaret Sullavan, Franchot Tone, Robert Young, Guy Kibbee, Lionel Atwill. Beautifully poignant film of Erich Maria Remarque's tale of post-WW1 Germany, and three lifelong friends who share a love for dying Sullavan. Excellent performances all around; coscripted by F. Scott Fitzgerald.▼●

Three-Cornered Moon (1933) **77m.** *** D: Elliott Nugent. Claudette Colbert, Richard Arlen, Mary Boland, Wallace Ford, Hardie Albright, William Bakewell, Lyda Roberti. Spoiled family goes broke and has to face the Depression head-on. Smart mix of comedy and drama anticipates ingredients of classic screwball comedies. ●

Three Daring Daughters (1948) **C-115m.** **½ D: Fred M. Wilcox. Jeanette MacDonald, Jose Iturbi, Elinor Donahue, Ann B. Todd, Jane Powell, Edward Arnold, Larry Adler. Contrived musical comeback vehicle for MacDonald, as a divorcée whose daughters try to reunite her with her ex while she falls in love with Iturbi.▼●

Three Desperate Men (1951) **71m.** *½ D: Sam Newfield. Preston Foster, Virginia Grey, Jim Davis, Ross Latimer, William Haade, Monte Blue, Sid Melton. Two brothers set out to rescue their sibling, who's condemned to hang, in this meager Western. ●

Three Faces East (1930) **71m.** **½ D: Roy Del Ruth. Constance Bennett, Eric (Erich) von Stroheim, Anthony Bushell, William

Holden, William Courtenay, Charlotte Walker, Crauford Kent. WW1 drama pits master spies Bennett and von Stroheim against each other in a stately British home where he is the butler and she is visiting under false pretenses. But who's really a double agent? Creaky in some ways but the stars are compelling. Anthony Paul Kelly's play was filmed before in 1926 and again in 1940, as BRITISH INTELLIGENCE. ●

Three Faces of Eve, The (1957) **91m.** ***½ D: Nunnally Johnson. Joanne Woodward, David Wayne, Lee J. Cobb, Nancy Kulp, Vince Edwards; narrated by Alistair Cooke. Academy Award tour de force by Woodward as young woman with multiple personalities and three separate lives. Cobb is psychiatrist who tries to cure her. Johnson also produced and wrote the screenplay. CinemaScope.▼●

Three Faces West (1940) **79m.** **½ D: Bernard Vorhaus. John Wayne, Sigrid Gurie, Charles Coburn, Spencer Charters, Roland Varno, Russell Simpson. In Republic Pictures' take on THE GRAPES OF WRATH, North Dakota farmers are defeated by endless dust storms and contemplate a mass migration to Oregon's greener fields. Wayne is the glue holding the community together, Gurie a newly arrived Viennese refugee he's stuck on. Offbeat drama is worth a look. ▼●

Three for Bedroom C (1952) **C-74m.** ** D: Milton Bren. Gloria Swanson, Fred Clark, James Warren, Steve Brodie, Hans Conried, Margaret Dumont. Sadly uneven comedy of romance between movie star and scientist aboard transcontinental train heading to L.A. A derailment for Swanson after her SUNSET BLVD. triumph.▼

Three for Jamie Dawn (1956) **81m.** ** D: Thomas Carr. Laraine Day, Ricardo Montalban, Richard Carlson, June Havoc. Diverting story poorly executed, about jury members being pressured to swing a not-guilty verdict for the defendant.

Three for the Show (1955) **C-93m.** ** D: H. C. Potter. Betty Grable, Marge and Gower Champion, Jack Lemmon, Myron McCormick. Grable's dead husband (Lemmon) turns out to be very much alive in this weak musical remake of TOO MANY HUSBANDS. Dance numbers cleverly staged for widescreen by Jack Cole. CinemaScope. ▼●

Three Girls About Town (1941) **73m.** **½ D: Leigh Jason. Joan Blondell, Binnie Barnes, Janet Blair, John Howard, Robert Benchley, Eric Blore, Hugh O'Connell, Una O'Connor. Wacky but amusing comedy of three sisters encountering a corpse in N.Y.C. hotel and the frantic consequences. Blair's film debut; Lloyd Bridges, Larry Parks, and Bruce Bennett play three of Howard's fellow reporters.

Three Godfathers (1936) **82m.** *** D:

Richard Boleslawski. Chester Morris, Lewis Stone, Walter Brennan, Irene Hervey, Willard Robertson, Sidney Toler. Little-seen and underrated version of Peter B. Kyne's story (filmed twice before) about three bad guys who adopt a foundling in the desert. Beautifully shot and warmly acted. ◗

3 Godfathers (1949) **C-105m.** ★★★ D: John Ford. John Wayne, Pedro Armendariz, Harry Carey, Jr., Ward Bond, Mae Marsh, Jane Darwell, Ben Johnson, Mildred Natwick. Sturdy, sentimental, sometimes beautiful rendition of Peter B. Kyne's oft-filmed saga of three bandits who "adopt" a baby born in the desert. Final scene doesn't ring true, but Ford makes up for it in balance of film. Dedicated to the director's first star, Harry Carey, Sr. Remade for TV as THE GODCHILD and as a Japanese animated feature, TOKYO GODFATHERS. ▼◗

Three Guys Named Mike (1951) **90m.** ★★ D: Charles Walters. Jane Wyman, Van Johnson, Barry Sullivan, Howard Keel, Phyllis Kirk, Jeff Donnell. Enthusiastic (to the point of nausea) stewardess Wyman has her choice of the title trio of nice, handsome, eligible bachelors. Only in the movies. Scripted by Sidney Sheldon. ▼◗

Three Hearts for Julia (1943) **83m.** ★★ D: Richard Thorpe. Ann Sothern, Melvyn Douglas, Lee Bowman, Richard Ainley, Felix Bressart, Marta Linden, Reginald Owen. Only debonair Douglas could seem right as husband romancing his wife who is divorcing him, but he can't support whole film.

Three Hours to Kill (1954) **C-77m.** ★★★ D: Alfred L. Werker. Dana Andrews, Donna Reed, Dianne Foster, Stephen Elliott, Richard Webb, Carolyn Jones, Whit Bissell. Andrews plays stagecoach driver unjustly accused of killing fiancée's brother; he returns to find real killer. Tight, well done. ◗

365 Nights in Hollywood (1934) **74m.** ★★ D: George Marshall. James Dunn, Alice Faye, Frank Mitchell, Jack Durant, Grant Mitchell, John Bradford. Cheerfully mediocre musical about a girl (Faye, in her Jean Harlow look-alike period) who enrolls at a phony Hollywood talent school, where ex-big-shot director Dunn now teaches. Songwriter Richard Whiting appears briefly as himself. ▼◗

300 Spartans, The (1962) **C-114m.** ★½ D: Rudolph Maté. Richard Egan, Ralph Richardson, Diane Baker, Barry Coe, David Farrar, Donald Houston, Kieron Moore, Laurence Naismith. Events leading up to heroic Greek stand against the Persian Army at Thermopylae; strictly cardboard, despite Mediterranean locations filmed in widescreen by Geoffrey Unsworth. However, this did have a profound effect on Frank Miller, who later created the graphic novel *300*. CinemaScope. ◗

Three Husbands (1950) **78m.** ★★½ D: Irving Reis. Eve Arden, Ruth Warrick,

Howard da Silva, Vanessa Brown, Shepperd Strudwick, Billie Burke, Emlyn Williams, Jane Darwell. Pleasing comedy of three husbands trying to find out whether or not deceased playboy spent time with their wives. Undoubtedly inspired by the 1949 hit A LETTER TO THREE WIVES, and cowritten by Vera Caspary, who adapted the earlier film. ▼◗

Three Is a Family (1944) **81m.** ★★½ D: Edward Ludwig. Fay Bainter, Marjorie Reynolds, Charlie Ruggles, Helen Broderick, Arthur Lake, Hattie McDaniel, Jeff Donnell, Walter Catlett, Cheryl Walker. Above-par fluff of hectic homelife in apartment filled with family, friends, and new babies. ◗

Three Little Girls in Blue (1946) **C-90m.** ★★★ D: H. Bruce Humberstone. June Haver, George Montgomery, Vivian Blaine, Celeste Holm, Vera-Ellen, Frank Latimore, Charles Smith. Cheerful tale of three spunky sisters out to trap wealthy husbands; familiar plot with good tunes like "You Make Me Feel So Young." A remake of THREE BLIND MICE and MOON OVER MIAMI, set in turn-of-the-20th-century Atlantic City. Holm's film debut. ◗

Three Little Words (1950) **C-102m.** ★★★ D: Richard Thorpe. Fred Astaire, Vera-Ellen, Red Skelton, Arlene Dahl, Keenan Wynn, Gloria De Haven, Debbie Reynolds, Carleton Carpenter. Standard MGM musical about famous songwriters Kalmar and Ruby and their climb to fame; bouncy cast, fine tunes, including "Who's Sorry Now?," "Thinking of You," title song. Debbie plays Helen Kane, but the real Helen dubbed "I Wanna Be Loved by You." ▼◗

Three Lives of Thomasina, The (1964) **C-97m.** ★★★ D: Don Chaffey. Patrick McGoohan, Susan Hampshire, Karen Dotrice, Matthew Garber, Vincent Winter, Denis Gilmore, Laurence Naismith, Finlay Currie. Charming Disney film made in England from Paul Gallico's story about a heartless veterinarian, his daughter's devotion to her pet cat, and a mystical young woman with life-giving "powers." A winner. ▼◗

Three Loves Has Nancy (1938) **69m.** ★★ D: Richard Thorpe. Janet Gaynor, Robert Montgomery, Franchot Tone, Guy Kibbee, Claire Dodd, Reginald Owen. Silly screwball comedy with scatterbrained small-town Southerner Gaynor coming to N.Y.C. to search for her wayward fiancé, causing endless problems for writer Montgomery. ◗

Three Men From Texas (1940) **75m.** ★★★ D: Lesley Selander. William Boyd, Russell Hayden, Andy Clyde, Morris Ankrum, Morgan Wallace, Esther Estrella. A favorite among Hopalong Cassidy fans, this marks the series debut of comedy star Clyde; he steals the show as California Jack Carlson, who joins the Bar 20 boys traveling west as Texas Rangers to resolve a squabble over land grants. Production polish, flying fists, gunplay, rousing Victor Young score, and beautiful scenery surround a solid story. Cowboy costume purists object to lighter-than-usual shirt worn by Boyd. ▼●

Three Men in a Boat (1956-British) **C-84m.** *½ D: Ken Annakin. Laurence Harvey, Jimmy Edwards, David Tomlinson, Shirley Eaton, Jill Ireland, Martita Hunt, Adrienne Corri, Lisa Gastoni. Third filming of the Jerome K. Jerome book is a frantic, frequently annoying comedy about womanizer Harvey and bumbling pals Edwards and Tomlinson on a boat trip up the Thames. CinemaScope.▼

Three Men in White (1944) **85m.** ** D: Willis Goldbeck. Lionel Barrymore, Van Johnson, Marilyn Maxwell, Keye Luke, Ava Gardner, Alma Kruger, Rags Ragland, Nell Craig, Walter Kingsford. MGM continued to spot its young starlets in this extension of the *Dr. Kildare* series, revolving around efforts (once again) to decide who should be Dr. Gillespie's assistant. ▶

Three Men on a Horse (1936) **88m.** *** D: Mervyn LeRoy. Frank McHugh, Sam Levene, Joan Blondell, Teddy Hart, Guy Kibbee, Carol Hughes, Allen Jenkins, Edgar Kennedy, Eddie Anderson. First-rate comedy of timid McHugh who always picks winning racehorses; stagy but funny. Blondell's fun as Levene's Brooklynese girlfriend. Adapted from Broadway play by George Abbott and John Cecil Holm. ▼

3 Murderesses (1960-French) **C-96m.** **½ D: Michel Boisrond. Alain Delon, Mylene Demongeot, Pascale Petit, Jacqueline Sassard, Anita Ruf, Simone Renant. Most diverting cast in standard playboy yarn with Delon romancing trio of contrasting females. Originally titled WOMEN ARE WEAK.

Three Musketeers, The (1921) **118m.** *** D: Fred Niblo. Douglas Fairbanks, Marguerite De La Motte, Adolphe Menjou, Barbara La Marr, Leon Barry, George Siegmann, Eugene Pallette, Nigel de Brulier, Boyd Irwin, Mary MacLaren, Sidney Franklin, Charles Stevens. Robust period adventure with Fairbanks a hearty D'Artagnan, Alexandre Dumas' swashbuckling hero who joins the King's Musketeers, becomes pals with Athos, Porthos, and Aramis, and battles evil in the court of Louis XIII. De Brulier almost steals the film as Cardinal Richelieu. Great fun! Followed by THE IRON MASK. ▼●

Three Musketeers, The (1935) **90m.** ** D: Rowland V. Lee. Walter Abel, Paul Lukas, Ian Keith, Onslow Stevens, Ralph Forbes, Margot Grahame, Heather Angel. Dullest version of Dumas story, with Abel miscast as D'Artagnan.▼●

Three Musketeers, The (1939) **73m.** *** D: Allan Dwan. Don Ameche, The Ritz Brothers, Lionel Atwill, Binnie Barnes, Miles Mander, Gloria Stuart, Pauline

Moore, John Carradine, Joseph Schildkraut. Spirited musical, generally faithful to Dumas story; Ameche flavorful as D'Artagnan, Barnes lovely as Lady DeWinter, Ritz Brothers funny substitutes for unsuspecting musketeers.▼●

Three Musketeers, The (1948) **C-125m.** **½ D: George Sidney. Lana Turner, Gene Kelly, June Allyson, Van Heflin, Angela Lansbury, June Allyson, Van Heflin, Angela Lansbury, Robert Coote, Frank Morgan, Vincent Price, Keenan Wynn, Gig Young. Oddball, lavish production of Dumas tale with Kelly as D'Artagnan. Occasional bright moments, but continual change of tone, and Heflin's drowsy characterization as Athos, bog down the action. Lana makes a stunning Lady DeWinter.▼●▶

Three Must-Get-Theres, The (1922) **57m.** *** D: Max Linder. Max Linder, Frank Cooke, Caroline Rankin, Bull Montana, Harry Mann, Jobyna Ralston, Jack Richardson. Deft, funny parody of Douglas Fairbanks' THE THREE MUSKETEERS with Linder (who also scripted) playing Dart-in-Again, a young nobleman who at the outset barely can mount a horse. Nevertheless, he hooks up with the title trio (who are named Walrus, Octopus, and Porpoise). The comical swordplay is especially entertaining. The last of Linder's three U.S.-made movies was also his final feature film. ▶

Three Nuts in Search of a Bolt (1964) **C/B&W-80m.** *½ D: Tommy Noonan. Mamie Van Doren, Tommy Noonan, Ziva Rodann, Paul Gilbert, John Cronin, Peter Howard, T. C. Jones, Alvy Moore, Marjorie Bennett. Neurotic stripper Mamie and her two pals hire Noonan to act out their personalities for shrink Rodann, so they can receive psychoanalysis at a discount. Because of a couple of scenes in which Mamie plies her trade, this was considered to be quite risqué back in '64; today it's merely idiotic and would be hard-pressed to earn a PG-13 rating. Some stripper and nudie sequences in color although rest of film is b&w. Noonan also coproduced and coscripted.▼●

Three of a Kind SEE: **Cookin' Up Trouble**

Three on a Match (1932) **64m.** *** D: Mervyn LeRoy. Warren William, Joan Blondell, Bette Davis, Ann Dvorak, Humphrey Bogart, Lyle Talbot, Glenda Farrell, Dawn O'Day (Anne Shirley), Edward Arnold. Fine, fast-moving (and surprisingly potent) pre-Code melodrama of three girls who renew childhood friendship, only to find suspense and tragedy. Dvorak is simply marvelous. Remade as BROADWAY MUSKETEERS. ▼●

Three on a Ticket (1947) **64m.** ** D: Sam Newfield. Hugh Beaumont, Cheryl Walker, Paul Bryar, Ralph Dunn, Louise Currie, Gavin Gordon. Efficient low-budget *Michael Shayne* detective entry, revolving around a scramble to piece together a railway locker ticket which holds the key to a fortune in bank loot.

Three on the Trail (1936) **66m.** ******* D: Howard Bretherton. William Boyd, Jimmy Ellison, Onslow Stevens, Muriel Evans, George Hayes, William Duncan. Ellison is framed for murder while courting schoolmarm Evans. Fifth Hopalong Cassidy series entry deals with cattle rustling and stagecoach robbing while showcasing Hayes as Windy Halliday and making the most of the chemistry between Boyd and Ellison. Also capitalizes on spectacular Lone Pine location landscape. Loosely based on 1921 novel *Bar-20 Three* by series creator Clarence E. Mulford.▼●❶

3 Penny Opera, The (1931-German) **112m.** *****½** D: G. W. Pabst. Rudolph Forster, Lotte Lenya, Carola Neher, Reinhold Schunzel, Fritz Rasp, Valeska Gert. Fine musical satire chronicling activities of dashing gangster Forster, his cohorts, and antagonists, with Lenya outstanding as Pirate Jenny. From Bertolt Brecht's play, with music by Kurt Weill, adapted from John Gay's *The Beggar's Opera*. Remade many times since.▼●❶

3 Ring Circus (1954) **C-103m.** ****** D: Joseph Pevney. Dean Martin, Jerry Lewis, Joanne Dru, Zsa Zsa Gabor, Wallace Ford, Sig Ruman, Nick Cravat, Elsa Lanchester. So-so Martin and Lewis comedy has them as discharged servicemen up to trouble in a circus. Reissued in shorter version as JERRICO, THE WONDER CLOWN. Remade as ROUSTABOUT. VistaVision.

Three's a Crowd (1927) **61m.** BOMB D: Harry Langdon. Harry Langdon, Gladys McConnell, Cornelius Keefe, Brooks Benedict, Arthur Thalasso. Downtrodden Harry takes in a pregnant homeless woman and gives himself a chance at having a real family for the first time. Langdon's directorial debut—a surprisingly morose film for a silent comedy star—put his skyrocketing career on the skids. ▼❶

Three Sailors and a Girl (1953) **C-95m.** ****** D: Roy Del Ruth. Jane Powell, Gordon MacRae, Gene Nelson, Sam Levene, Jack E. Leonard. Bland musical of three gobs who invest ship's surplus funds in a musical show starring Powell. Based on George S. Kaufman's *The Butter and Egg Man.*❶

Three Secrets (1950) **98m.** ******* D: Robert Wise. Eleanor Parker, Patricia Neal, Ruth Roman, Frank Lovejoy, Leif Erickson. Sturdy melodrama; three women wait anxiously for word of which one's child survived plane crash. Remade for TV in 1999.▼❶

Three Shades of Love SEE: **This Rebel Breed**

Three Smart Girls (1936) **84m.** *****½** D: Henry Koster. Deanna Durbin, Binnie Barnes, Alice Brady, Ray Milland, Barbara Read, Mischa Auer, Nan Grey, Charles Winninger. Delightful musicomedy with Deanna's feature-film debut as matchmaking girl who brings long-divided parents back together. Songs: "Someone to Care for Me," "My Heart Is Singing." Sequel: THREE SMART GIRLS GROW UP.▼●❶

Three Smart Girls Grow Up (1939) **90m.** ******* D: Henry Koster. Deanna Durbin, Charles Winninger, Nan Grey, Helen Parrish, Robert Cummings, William Lundigan. Little Deanna still matchmaking for sisters, warming up stern father, singing "Because," winning over everyone in sight.▼●❶

Three Sons (1939) **73m.** ****** D: Jack Hively. Edward Ellis, William Gargan, Kent Taylor, J. Edward Bromberg, Katharine Alexander, Robert Stanton (Kirby Grant), Virginia Vale, Dick Hogan, Grady Sutton, Adele Pearce (Pamela Blake). Saccharine remake of SWEEPINGS, with Ellis replacing Lionel Barrymore as a self-made Chicago department store proprietor who assumes that his offspring will take over the business—until complications arise. Occasionally effective but too often wallows in forced sentiment. Gargan played the eldest son in the original; here, he's cast as Ellis' brother.

Three Steps North (1951) **81m.** ****** D: W. Lee Wilder. Lloyd Bridges, Lea Padovani, Aldo Fabrizi, William C. Tubbs, Dino Galvani, Adriano Ambrogi, Gianni Rizzo. Before being tossed into the brig for black-market activities, an American G.I. (Bridges) in WW2 Italy stashes away several million lira. After the war, he returns to recover the buried loot, becomes involved with an old flame, and gets embroiled in murder. Location filming helps this predictable mystery, with a solid performance by Bridges.❶

Three Stooges Go Around the World in a Daze, The (1963) **94m.** ****½** D: Norman Maurer. Three Stooges, Jay Sheffield, Joan Freeman, Walter Burke, Peter Forster. Even those who dislike the Stooges may enjoy this funny updating of Jules Verne's tale, replete with sight gags and world travel.▼❶

Three Stooges in Orbit, The (1962) **87m.** ****½** D: Edward Bernds. The Three Stooges, Carol Christensen, Edson Stroll, Emil Sitka. Nutty scientist Sitka invents a tanklike contraption that flies and floats. The Stooges accidentally launch it and run headlong into a few Martian invaders, with usual slapstick results for younger audiences.▼❶

Three Stooges Meet Hercules, The (1962) **89m.** ****½** D: Edward Bernds. The Three Stooges, Vicki Trickett, Quinn Redeker, George N. Neise. Time machine takes the Stooges back to era of Roman legions; they are trapped on galley ship, battle Cyclops, and wind up with chariot chase. Good slapstick for kids and fans.▼❶

Three Strange Loves (1949-Swedish) **84m.** ******* D: Ingmar Bergman. Eva Henning, Birger Malmsten, Birgit Tengroth, Mimi

Nelson, Hasse Ekman. Interesting early Bergman drama which foreshadows much of his future work. This one explores the dynamics of a three-cornered love relationship, from a distinctly female perspective, and examines the possibility of two women having the same personality. Bergman can be seen on camera as a train passenger. Aka THIRST.▼◗

Three Strangers (1946) **92m. ***½** D: Jean Negulesco. Sydney Greenstreet, Geraldine Fitzgerald, Peter Lorre, Joan Lorring, Robert Shayne, Marjorie Riordan. Greenstreet and Lorre team up with Fitzgerald as partners holding winning sweepstakes ticket under unusual circumstances. Bizarre John Huston–Howard Koch script makes fascinating viewing.◗

Three Stripes in the Sun (1955) **93m. **½** D: Richard Murphy. Aldo Ray, Phil Carey, Dick York, Chuck Connors, Mitsuko Kimura. Good film of Japan-hating American soldier Ray, who softens when he becomes involved with Japanese orphans and romances a pretty translator (Kimura). This based-on-fact account effectively mirrors postwar U.S.-Japanese relations. Murphy also scripted.◗

3:10 to Yuma (1957) **92m. ***½** D: Delmer Daves. Van Heflin, Glenn Ford, Felicia Farr, Leora Dana, Henry Jones, Richard Jaeckel, Robert Emhardt. Extremely suspenseful Western, one of the best of the 1950s. Farmer Heflin, needing the money, agrees to hold captured outlaw Ford until the train arrives, but Ford starts to psych him out. Gripping every step of the way, with memorable George Duning theme sung by Frankie Laine. Script by Halsted Welles from an Elmore Leonard story. Remade in 2007.▼◗◗

Three Texas Steers (1939) **57m. **½** D: George Sherman. John Wayne, Ray Corrigan, Max Terhune, Carole Landis, Ralph Graves, Billy Curtis, Roscoe Ates, Dave Sharpe. Mesquite County's Three Mesquiteers rescue Landis when crooks sabotage her impoverished circus to force sale of the ranch she inherited to double-dealing business manager Graves. Played for laughs; fast, lively, with several twists, but still a bit disappointing in view of the top cast. Corrigan doubles as the circus gorilla!▼◗

Three Violent People (1956) **C-100m. **½** D: Rudolph Maté. Charlton Heston, Anne Baxter, Gilbert Roland, Tom Tryon, Forrest Tucker, Elaine Stritch, Bruce Bennett, Barton MacLane. Adequately paced Western set in post-Civil War Texas; Heston, returning home with bride Baxter, is forced to fight carpetbaggers and deal with wife's shady past. VistaVision.▼◗

Three Wise Fools (1946) **90m. **** D: Edward Buzzell. Margaret O'Brien, Lionel Barrymore, Lewis Stone, Edward Arnold, Thomas Mitchell, Jane Darwell, Cyd Charisse. Intended as fanciful, this turns out mawkish with adorable O'Brien winning over three crusty old men.

Three Wise Girls (1932) **66m. **** D: William Beaudine. Jean Harlow, Mae Clarke, Walter Byron, Jameson Thomas, Marie Prevost, Andy Devine, Lucy Beaumont. Harlow plays a small-town girl who moves to N.Y.C. and quickly learns that all men are after just one thing. Strictly so-so, but interesting as Harlow's first starring vehicle, with Clarke giving a typically natural and believable performance as her big city mentor.◗

3 Worlds of Gulliver, The (1960-British) **C-100m. ***** D: Jack Sher. Kerwin Mathews, Jo Morrow, June Thorburn, Lee Patterson, Gregoire Aslan, Basil Sydney, Peter Bull. Hero is washed overboard and finds himself in the Land of Lilliput . . . but that's just the beginning. Well-made adventure/fantasy designed for kids, fun for older viewers, too. Fine special effects by Ray Harryhausen, charming Bernard Herrmann score.▼◗

Three Young Texans (1954) **C-78m. **** D: Henry Levin. Mitzi Gaynor, Keefe Brasselle, Jeffrey Hunter, Harvey Stephens, Dan Riss. Standard Western has Hunter pulling railroad robbery to prevent crooks from forcing his father to do same job, expected complications.

Thrill of a Romance (1945) **C-105m. **** D: Richard Thorpe. Van Johnson, Esther Williams, Frances Gifford, Henry Travers, Spring Byington, Carleton G. Young, Lauritz Melchior, Tommy Dorsey. Slight musical-romance with sweet Williams, abandoned by her businessman husband on their honeymoon, falling for war hero Johnson. ▼◗

Thrill of Brazil, The (1946) **91m. **½** D: S. Sylvan Simon. Evelyn Keyes, Keenan Wynn, Ann Miller, Allyn Joslyn, Tito Guizar. Pleasant South-of-the-border romance with music and spirited cast giving life to ordinary script.

Thrill of It All, The (1963) **C-108m. ***** D: Norman Jewison. Doris Day, James Garner, Arlene Francis, Edward Andrews, Reginald Owen, ZaSu Pitts, Elliott Reid. Enjoyable spoof of TV and commercials by Carl Reiner; good vehicle for Day as housewife-turned-TV-spokeswoman and Garner as her neglected husband. Reiner has a particularly funny series of cameos.▼◗

Throne of Blood (1957-Japanese) **108m. ****** D: Akira Kurosawa. Toshiro Mifune, Isuzu Yamada, Takashi Shimura, Minoru Chiaki. Graphic, powerful adaptation of *Macbeth* in a samurai setting. Gripping finale, with Taketoki Washizu (the Macbeth character, masterfully played by Mifune) attacked by arrows.▼◗

Through a Glass, Darkly (1961-Swedish) **91m. ***½** D: Ingmar Bergman. Harriet Andersson, Gunnar Bjornstrand, Max

[714]

von Sydow, Lars Passgard. Four-character drama about just-released mental patient, her husband, her father, and her younger brother who spend summer together on secluded island. Moody, evocative story of insanity—well-deserved Oscar winner, one of Bergman's best. The first in the filmmaker's "faith" trilogy, followed by WINTER LIGHT and THE SILENCE.▼●◗

Through the Back Door (1921) **90m.** ** D: Alfred E. Green, Jack Pickford. Mary Pickford, Gertrude Astor, Elinor Fair, Helen Raymond, Wilfred Lucas, John Harron, Adolphe Menjou. Minor Pickford vehicle with Mary a neglected daughter of wealth who is abandoned by her widowed mother when she remarries. Pickford is always watchable, but she's defeated by a hackneyed storyline. Her brother Jack codirected. ▼◗

Thunder Afloat (1939) **94m.** **½ D: George B. Seitz. Wallace Beery, Chester Morris, Virginia Grey, Clem Bevans, John Qualen, Regis Toomey. Above-average Beery vehicle of old salt pitted against rival (Morris) when he joins the Navy.

Thunderball (1965-British) **C-129m.** **½ D: Terence Young. Sean Connery, Claudine Auger, Adolfo Celi, Luciana Paluzzi, Rik Van Nutter, Martine Beswick, Bernard Lee, Lois Maxwell, Desmond Llewelyn, Roland Culver. Fourth James Bond film isn't as lively as the others. Plenty of gimmicks, and Oscar-winning special effects, as world is threatened with destruction, but film tends to bog down—especially underwater. Celi makes a formidable Bond villain. Remade 18 years later—with Connery—as NEVER SAY NEVER AGAIN. Panavision.▼●◗

Thunder Bay (1953) **C-102m.** *** D: Anthony Mann. James Stewart, Joanne Dru, Gilbert Roland, Dan Duryea, Jay C. Flippen, Henry (Harry) Morgan. Action-packed account of oil-drillers vs. Louisiana shrimp fishermen, with peppery cast. ▼◗

Thunder Below (1932) **67m.** **½ D: Richard Wallace. Tallulah Bankhead, Charles Bickford, Paul Lukas, Eugene Pallette, James Finlayson, Edward Van Sloan. Tallulah loves Lukas, but when husband Bickford goes blind, she can't bear to leave him. Melodramatic triangle story, well acted by all.

Thunder Birds (1942) **C-78m.** ** D: William Wellman. Gene Tierney, Preston Foster, John Sutton, Dame May Whitty, Reginald Denny, Jack Holt, George Barbier. Ultrapatriotic time capsule is an ode to the WW2 lyer/flying instructor. Freewheeling veteran aviator Foster and intern-turned-trainee Sutton (who's afraid of heights) compete for the affection of flirtatious Tierney.◗

Thunderbirds (1952) **98m.** **½ D: John H. Auer. John Derek, John Barrymore, Jr., Mona Freeman, Gene Evans. Fact-based tale of Native Americans who fought in the 45th Infantry Division during WW2.

Thunderbolt (1929) **91m.** *** D: Josef von Sternberg. George Bancroft, Fay Wray, Richard Arlen, Tully Marshall, Eugenie Besserer, James Spottswood, Fred Kohler. While on death row, gangster Bancroft plots to get revenge on Arlen, who stole his moll (Wray), by setting up a frame job to get him sent to the same jail. Von Sternberg's first talkie contains some of the expected visual flourishes and makes imaginative use of sound, but isn't in the same league as UNDERWORLD or THE BLUE ANGEL (1930).

Thundercloud SEE: Colt .45

Thunderhead—Son of Flicka (1945) **C-78m.** **½ D: Louis King. Roddy McDowall, Preston Foster, Rita Johnson, James Bell, Diana Hale, Carleton Young. Good, colorful attempt to repeat MY FRIEND FLICKA's success; doesn't match original, but it's enjoyable. Followed by GREEN GRASS OF WYOMING.◗

Thunderhoof (1948) **77m.** *** D: Phil Karlson. Preston Foster, Mary Stuart, William Bishop. Offbeat, symbolic three-character Western centering on the search for a beautiful wild stallion in the Mexican desert and the conflict that erupts between an older rancher (Foster) and his adopted son (Bishop) over the father's sultry young wife (Stuart). Strikingly directed and unusually ambitious for a B Western from Columbia. Originally released in sepiatone.◗

Thunder in Carolina (1960) **C-92m.** ** D: Paul Helmick. Rory Calhoun, Alan Hale, Jr., Connie Hines, John (Race) Gentry, Ed McGrath, Troyanne Ross. Dull programmer of stock car racing in the South, with Calhoun as a skirt-chasing driver. Video title: HARD DRIVIN'.▼◗

Thundering Jets (1958) **73m.** ** D: Helmut Dantine. Rex Reason, Dick Foran, Audrey Dalton, Barry Coe, Buck Class, Robert Dix, Lee Farr, Sid Melton, Gregg Palmer, Robert Conrad. Familiar chronicle of life at a U.S. Air Force pilot training school, with Reason the center of the story as a frustrated instructor. RegalScope.

Thunder in the City (1937-British) **86m.** *** D: Marion Gering. Edward G. Robinson, Luli Deste, Nigel Bruce, Constance Collier, Ralph Richardson, Arthur Wontner. Amusing film about a go-getting American promoter who visits England and gambles on a long shot: hitherto unknown mineral known as Magnelite, which he proceeds to "ballyhoo." Tailor-made for an ebullient Robinson.▼◗

Thunder in the East (1953) **98m.** **½ D: Charles Vidor. Alan Ladd, Deborah Kerr, Charles Boyer, Corinne Calvet, Cecil Kellaway, John Williams. Adequate, politically loaded adventure with gunrunner Ladd caught amid tension and rebellion in rural India. Kerr and Boyer uplift the proceedings as a refined blind woman who falls for

Ladd and a stubbornly pacifistic government official.

Thunder in the Sun (1959) **C-81m.** **½D: Russell Rouse. Susan Hayward, Jeff Chandler, Jacques Bergerac, Blanche Yurka, Carl Esmond, Fortunio Bonanova. Hayward is romanced by wagon train scout Chandler and Bergerac, head of French Basque immigrants on way to California.

Thunder in the Valley (1947) **C-103m.** **½ D: Louis King. Lon McCallister, Peggy Ann Garner, Edmund Gwenn, Reginald Owen. Usual tale of boy in love with his dog, cruel father who doesn't share his feelings; colorful but standard.

Thunder Island (1963) **65m.** ** D: Jack Leewood. Gene Nelson, Fay Spain, Brian Kelly, Miriam Colon, Art Bedard. A hit man is hired to kill the former dictator of a Latin country who's now living in exile on a nearby island. Unexceptional programmer cowritten by Jack Nicholson. CinemaScope.

Thunder of Drums, A (1961) **C-97m.** **½ D: Joseph M. Newman. George Hamilton, Luana Patten, Richard Boone, Charles Bronson, Richard Chamberlain, Slim Pickens. Better than average cast saves average story of new lieutenant having rough time in cavalry. CinemaScope.

Thunder on the Hill (1951) **84m.** *** D: Douglas Sirk. Claudette Colbert, Ann Blyth, Robert Douglas, Anne Crawford, Gladys Cooper. Nun Colbert can't believe visitor Blyth, about to be hanged, is murderess, sets out to prove her innocent; Cooper fine as Mother Superior. Sincere, interesting drama.

Thunder Over Arizona (1956) **C-75m.** ** D: Joseph Kane. Skip Homeier, Kristine Miller, George Macready, Wallace Ford. Undemanding minor Western showing the corruption and greed of people incited by a rich silver ore discovery. Filmed in widescreen Naturama.▼

Thunder Over Hawaii SEE: **Naked Paradise**

Thunder Over Mexico SEE: ¡Qué Viva México!

Thunder Over Tangier (1957-British) **66m.** *½D: Lance Comfort. Robert Hutton, Martin Benson, Derek Sydney, Lisa Gastoni. Passable account of movie stuntman Hutton accidentally becoming involved in a scheme involving forged passports. Original British title: MAN FROM TANGIER.

Thunder Over the Plains (1953) **C-82m.** ** D: Andre de Toth. Randolph Scott, Lex Barker, Phyllis Kirk, Henry Hull, Elisha Cook, Jr., Richard Benjamin, Charles McGraw, Fess Parker. Routine Western set in post-Civil War Texas, with Scott as Army officer sent to prevent carpetbaggers from harassing all.

Thunder Pass (1954) **76m.** ** D: Frank McDonald. Dane Clark, Andy Devine,

Dorothy Patrick, John Carradine, Raymond Burr. Usual story of resolute Army officer (Clark) pushing settlers onward in face of Indian attack.▼

Thunder Road (1958) **92m.** *** D: Arthur Ripley. Robert Mitchum, Gene Barry, Jacques Aubuchon, Keely Smith, James Mitchum. Rural bootlegger takes on Feds *and* the Mob in cult favorite that even today continues to play in drive-ins; for many this remains the definitive moonshine picture. Jim Mitchum makes screen debut playing Bob's *brother*; the elder Mitchum got a hit record out of the title tune, which he also wrote!▼●

Thunder Rock (1942-British) **112m.** *** D: Roy Boulting. Michael Redgrave, Barbara Mullen, Lilli Palmer, James Mason, Frederick Valk. Allegorical fable of discouraged newspaperman-turned-lighthouse keeper given renewed faith by visions of various drowned people. Excellent cast makes this most enjoyable; based on Robert Ardrey's play.

Thunderstorm (1956-Spanish) **81m.** *½ D: John Guillermin. Carlos Thompson, Linda Christian, Charles Korvin, Gary Thorne. Warmed-over trivia concerning Christian's provocative arrival in a small fishing village on the Spanish coast.

Thursday's Child (1943-British) **81m.** **½ D: Rodney Ackland. Sally Ann Howes, Wilfrid Lawson, Kathleen O'Regan, Eileen Bennett, Stewart Granger, Marianne Davis, Gerhardt Kempinski, Felix Aylmer. Melodramatic soap opera of 12-year-old girl from middle-class family who becomes child film star, to the detriment of all around her. Howes, making her film debut, is excellent as the level-headed youngster. Recommended mainly for buffs and fans of dashing Granger (in an early supporting role).▼

Tiara Tahiti (1962-British) **C-100m.** ** D: William (Ted) Kotcheff. James Mason, John Mills, Claude Dauphin, Herbert Lom. Mild comedy-drama involving Mason and Mills as former Army officers who have an old grudge to settle; establishment of a Tahiti resort hotel sets wheels in motion.▼●

Ticket of Leave Man, The (1937-British) **71m.** ** D: George King. Tod Slaughter, John Warwick, Marjorie Taylor, Frank Cochran, Robert Adair, Peter Gawthorne. Fiendish strangler and all-round criminal mastermind The Tiger (Slaughter) frames innocent Warwick for forgery, hoping to pursue singer Taylor, the convicted man's sweetie. OK barnstorming melodrama of the *very* old school with Slaughter in particularly ripe, leering form. Based on an 1866 play; a "ticket of leave man" is a prison parolee. Marred by dated Jewish character played by Cochran.

Ticket to Tomahawk, A (1950) **C-90m.** *** D: Richard Sale. Dan Dailey, Anne Baxter, Rory Calhoun, Walter Brennan,

Charles Kemper, Connie Gilchrist, Arthur Hunnicutt, Mauritz Hugo, Chief Yowlachie, Victor Sen Yung. Engaging comedy-Western about stagecoach company that hires gunslinger Calhoun to keep dreaded railroad from running on time. Good fun; one of the chorus girls with Dailey in a musical number is Marilyn Monroe. Filmed in Colorado.▼

Tickle Me (1965) **C-90m.** **½ D: Norman Taurog. Elvis Presley, Jocelyn Lane, Julie Adams, Jack Mullaney, Merry Anders, Connie Gilchrist. That's the only way to get any laughs out of this one: Elvis works at all-girl dude ranch singing his usual quota of songs. Written by Elwood Ullman and Edward Bernds, both of whom worked with The Three Stooges in better days. Panavision.▼)

Ticklish Affair, A (1963) **C-89m.** ** D: George Sidney. Shirley Jones, Gig Young, Red Buttons, Carolyn Jones, Edgar Buchanan. Amiable film of Navy commander Young falling in love with widow Jones; all it lacks is wit, sparkle, and a fresh script. Panavision.

Tide of Empire (1929) **72m.** *** D: Allan Dwan. Renée Adorée, George Duryea (Tom Keene), George Fawcett, William Collier, Jr., Fred Kohler, Harry Gribbon, Paul Hurst. Colorful, action-packed tale based on Peter B. Kyne's novel about gold seekers and bandits disrupting the lives of peaceful Spanish ranchers in old California. Lusty silent Western with synchronized music, sound effects, and some background vocals; interesting early use of zoom lenses.)

Tiefland (1954-German) **98m.** **½ D: Leni Riefenstahl. Leni Riefenstahl, Franz Eichberger, Bernard Minetti, Maria Koppenhofer, Luis Rainer. Blonde, dreamy shepherd Eichberger and arrogant marquis Minetti vie for Spanish dancer Riefenstahl. Atmospheric, visually poetic drama, even though the characters lack depth. Filmed between 1942 and 1945; editing wasn't completed until 1954.▼)

Tiger Bay (1933-British) **79m.** ** D: J. Elder Wills. Anna May Wong, Henry Victor, Rene Ray, Lawrence Grossmith, Victor Garland, Ben Soutten. Tacky grade-B melodrama is strictly a vehicle for the always-compelling Wong, as a nightclub owner/performer fiercely protective of her adoptive sister, a bleach-blond who's irresistible to the sailors that frequent Tiger Bay, "the home of all the riff-raff of the seven seas.")

Tiger Bay (1959-British) **105m.** *** D: J. Lee Thompson. John Mills, Horst Buchholz, Hayley Mills, Yvonne Mitchell, Megs Jenkins, Anthony Dawson. Lonely Cardiff child witnesses a murder and is abducted by the Polish sailor-killer. A poignant, sensitive, and very different police chase story. Hayley steals the film in first major acting role.▼)

Tiger Likes Fresh Blood, The (1964-French-Italian) **83m.** *** D: Claude Chabrol. Roger Hanin, Daniela Bianchi, Maria Mauban, Roger Dumas, Antonio Passalia, Jimmy Karoubi, Stéphane Audran. Chabrol's sly, tongue-in-cheek contribution to the '60s spy craze centers on an agent known as The Tiger (Hanin), who tries to protect a Turkish government official in Paris from being assassinated while wooing his sexy daughter. Followed by AN ORCHID FOR THE TIGER.

Tiger of Eschnapur, The (1958-German) **C-101m.** ** D: Fritz Lang. Debra Paget, Paul Hubschmid, Walther Reyer, René Deltgen, Luciana Paluzzi. Exotic dancer Paget is desired by dastardly maharajah Reyer, but she loves architect Hubschmid; meanwhile, Reyer's subjects are plotting revolution. Slow-moving, disappointing adventure-romance of interest mostly for Lang's participation. The first of the director's Indian diptych, followed by THE INDIAN TOMB; both were originally edited down to 95m., dubbed and released as JOURNEY TO THE LOST CITY.)

Tiger Shark (1932) **80m.** *** D: Howard Hawks. Edward G. Robinson, Richard Arlen, Zita Johann, J. Carrol Naish, Vince Barnett. Robinson gives rich, colorful performance as Portuguese tuna fisherman who marries wayward girl out of pity, then sees her fall in love with his best friend—a plot gambit Warner Bros. reused several times (SLIM, MANPOWER, etc.). Authentically filmed amid fisheries on Monterey coast.)

Tiger Walks, A (1964) **C-91m.** **½ D: Norman Tokar. Brian Keith, Vera Miles, Pamela Franklin, Sabu, Kevin Corcoran, Peter Brown, Una Merkel, Frank McHugh, Edward Andrews, Jack Albertson. Oddball Disney film about young girl (Franklin) whose compassion for tiger which has broken away from circus stirs controversy and political wheeling-and-dealing. Surprisingly bitter portrait of small-town America. Sabu's last film.▼)

Tight Little Island (1949-British) **82m.** **** D: Alexander Mackendrick. Basil Radford, Joan Greenwood, James Robertson Justice, Jean Cadell, Gordon Jackson, Wylie Watson, John Gregson; narrated by Finlay Currie. Hilarious, fast-paced comedy about WW2 ship sinking while loaded with whiskey and the antics of local Scottish islanders thirsting for its cargo. A solid hit. Scripted by Compton Mackenzie, the author of the novel, who has a small role as Captain Buncher. British title: WHISKY GALORE! Followed by MAD LITTLE ISLAND.▼)

Tight Shoes (1941) **68m.** ** D: Albert S. Rogell. Broderick Crawford, Binnie Barnes, John Howard, Anne Gwynne. Cast pushes hard to make this Damon Runyon yarn amusing at times: Crawford is big-shot crook who has big feet.

Tight Spot (1955) **97m.** ****** D: Phil Karlson. Ginger Rogers, Edward G. Robinson, Brian Keith, Lorne Greene, Katherine Anderson. Rogers, key witness at a N.Y.C. crime lord's upcoming trial, does a lot of high-volume BORN YESTERDAY–like verbal sparring with Keith, her police lieutenant bodyguard, in this slack crime melodrama based on a flop Broadway play. A double dose of disappointment for Eddie G. fans: His screen time is short, and he plays the uninteresting role of the prosecutor!◗

Tijuana Story, The (1957) **72m.** BOMB D: Leslie Kardos. Rodolfo Acosta, James Darren, Robert McQueeney, Jean Willes, Joy Stoner, Paul Newlan, George E. Stone, Michael Fox, Robert Blake. Turgid programmer, fact-based and set south of the border, with newspaperman Acosta waging war against a well-connected crime organization involved in drug dealing.◗

Tillie and Gus (1933) **58m.** *****½** D: Francis Martin. W.C. Fields, Alison Skipworth, Baby LeRoy, Edgar Kennedy, Jacqueline Wells (Julie Bishop), Clifford Jones, Barton MacLane, Clarence Wilson. Fields and Skipworth are perfectly matched as card hustlers in this very entertaining comedy, which also pits W.C. against Baby LeRoy for the first time. Nominal plot has them helping niece Wells win a crucial riverboat race.◗

Tillie's Punctured Romance (1914) **73m.** ****½** D: Mack Sennett. Charlie Chaplin, Marie Dressler, Mabel Normand, Mack Swain, Charles Bennett, Chester Conklin, Keystone Kops. A comic curio, the first full-length comedy feature film, with Dressler repeating stage role as farm girl fleeced by city-slicker Chaplin (appearing out of his usual character). Not terribly funny, or coherent, but there are good moments; mainly interesting for historical purposes. Dressler starred in a pair of sequels, TILLIE'S TOMATO SURPRISE and TILLIE WAKES UP.▼◗

Till the Clouds Roll By (1946) **C-137m.** ****½** D: Richard Whorf. Robert Walker, Van Heflin, Lucille Bremer, Dorothy Patrick, many guest stars including Judy Garland, Kathryn Grayson, Lena Horne, Tony Martin, Dinah Shore, Frank Sinatra, June Allyson, Angela Lansbury, Cyd Charisse, Virginia O'Brien. Soggy biography of songwriter Jerome Kern (Walker), uplifted by song numbers featuring some high-powered MGM talent. Highlights include Lansbury's "How D'Ya Like to Spoon With Me," Lena's "Why Was I Born?," Judy's "Look for the Silver Lining," and mini-production of *Show Boat*.▼◗

Till the End of Time (1946) **105m.** ******* D: Edward Dmytryk. Dorothy McGuire, Guy Madison, Robert Mitchum, Bill Williams, Tom Tully, William Gargan, Jean Porter, Ruth Nelson. Solid, sympathetic drama of three returning WW2 veterans was re-leased months before THE BEST YEARS OF OUR LIVES; the focus is on Madison falling for troubled war widow McGuire. Screenplay by Allen Rivkin, based on Niven Busch's novel *They Dream of Home*. Title song (based on Chopin's Polonaise in A-flat Major) was a big hit.▼◗

Till We Meet Again (1944) **88m.** ****** D: Frank Borzage. Ray Milland, Barbara Britton, Walter Slezak, Lucile Watson, Mona Freeman. Fair wartime drama of nun Britton helping pilot Milland return to Allied lines; elements don't always click in this one.

'Til We Meet Again (1940) **99m.** ****½** D: Edmund Goulding, Merle Oberon, George Brent, Pat O'Brien, Geraldine Fitzgerald, Binnie Barnes, Frank McHugh, Eric Blore, George Reeves. Overblown remake of ONE WAY PASSAGE recounts romance between suave crook Brent and fatally ill Oberon; McHugh repeats comedy-relief role from 1932 original.

Timberjack (1955) **C-94m.** ****** D: Joseph Kane. Vera Ralston, Sterling Hayden, David Brian, Adolphe Menjou, Hoagy Carmichael. Young man fights crooks taking over lumber mill who also killed his father. Harmless potboiler.

Timber Queen (1944) **66m.** ***½** D: Frank McDonald. Richard Arlen, Mary Beth Hughes, June Havoc, Sheldon Leonard, George E. Stone, Dick Purcell. Static programmer with pilot Arlen romancing Hughes while helping to keep her lumber company solvent.▼

Timbuktu (1959) **91m.** ****** D: Jacques Tourneur. Victor Mature, Yvonne De Carlo, George Dolenz, John Dehner, Marcia Henderson, James Foxx. Mature plays adventurer involved in African story of plot to overthrow government. Script is below average; cast is uneven.◗

Time Bomb (1953-British) SEE: **Terror on a Train**

Time in the Sun SEE: **¡Qué Viva México!**

Time Limit (1957) **96m.** ******* D: Karl Malden. Richard Widmark, Richard Basehart, Dolores Michaels, June Lockhart, Carl Benton Reid, Martin Balsam, Rip Torn, Kaie Deei (Khigh Dhiegh). Powerful drama involving military investigator Widmark's effort to determine if Basehart, suspected of collaborating with the enemy while a POW in North Korea, should go on trial for treason. Impressive location filming on Governors Island (in New York Harbor). Malden's sole foray behind the camera.◗

Time Machine, The (1960) **C-103m.** ******* D: George Pal. Rod Taylor, Alan Young, Yvette Mimieux, Sebastian Cabot, Tom Helmore, Whit Bissell, Doris Lloyd. H. G. Wells' fantasy reduced to comic book level, but still entertaining, with Taylor as single-minded turn-of-the-20th-century London scientist who invents time-travel device and has vivid experiences in the future. Oscar-winning special effects. Remade in 1978 (for TV) and 2002. ▼●◗

Time of Indifference (1964-Italian) 84m. ** D: Francesco Maselli. Rod Steiger, Shelley Winters, Claudia Cardinale, Paulette Goddard, Tomas Milian. Turgid melodrama of moral and social decay in Italy during late 1920s, focusing on one nouveau-poor family; from novel by Alberto Moravia. ▼

Time of Their Lives, The (1946) 82m. *** D: Charles Barton. Bud Abbott, Lou Costello, Marjorie Reynolds, Binnie Barnes, John Shelton, Gale Sondergaard, Jess Barker. Most unusual film for A&C, and one of their best. Costello and Reynolds are killed during Revolutionary times, and their ghosts haunt a country estate where (in the 20th century) Abbott and friends come to live. Imaginative, funny, and well done. ▼◗

Time of Your Life, The (1948) 99m. ** D: H. C. Potter. James Cagney, William Bendix, Wayne Morris, Jeanne Cagney, Broderick Crawford, Ward Bond, James Barton, Paul Draper, James Lydon, Gale Page, Richard Erdman. Uninspired version of William Saroyan's prizewinning morality play about the various characters who populate Nick's Saloon, Restaurant and Entertainment Palace, which is actually a waterfront dive. Interesting cast, but it just doesn't come together. ▼◗

Time Out for Love (1961-French-Italian) 91m. **½ D: Jean Valère. Jean Seberg, Maurice Ronet, Micheline Presle, Françoise Prevost. Sometimes-effective drama chronicling the coming-of-age of young Seberg, an American living in Paris, who falls in love with capricious Ronet. ▼

Time Out for Rhythm (1941) 75m. ** D: Sidney Salkow. Rudy Vallee, Ann Miller, Rosemary Lane, Allen Jenkins, The Three Stooges. Mediocre show-biz musical turns out to be a wonderful showcase for the Stooges, who do some of their best material (including the "Maja? Aha!" routine). One good production number, "Boogie Woogie Man," features Glen Gray and His Casa Loma Orchestra. ◗

Time Out of Mind (1947) 88m. ** D: Robert Siodmak. Phyllis Calvert, Robert Hutton, Ella Raines, Eddie Albert, Leo G. Carroll. Plodding period piece, set in 1889 New England, of girl in love above her station seeing her lover live unhappy life. From a Rachel Field novel.

Timeslip SEE: **Atomic Man, The**

Times Square Lady (1935) 69m. ** D: George B. Seitz. Robert Taylor, Virginia Bruce, Helen Twelvetrees, Isabel Jewell, Nat Pendleton, Pinky Tomlin, Henry Kolker, Raymond Hatton, Jack La Rue. When naïve Bruce inherits her father's Broadway businesses, crooked lawyer Kolker assigns Taylor to get control of them, but Taylor falls for her and double-crosses his boss. Pro-

grammer starts out promisingly but bogs down in clichés. Taylor's first lead role in a feature; Ward Bond has a bit as a murderous hockey player.

Time Table (1956) 79m. ** D: Mark Stevens. Mark Stevens, King Calder, Felicia Farr, Marianne Stewart, Wesley Addy, Alan Reed, Jack Klugman. Several plot twists only slightly enliven this small-scale account of a train heist, with overworked insurance investigator Stevens on the case. ◗

Time, the Place and the Girl, The (1946) C-105m. **½ D: David Butler. Dennis Morgan, Martha Vickers, Jack Carson, Janis Paige, S. Z. Sakall, Alan Hale, Florence Bates, Carmen Cavallero. Best thing about this flimsily plotted put-on-a-show musical is the Arthur Schwartz–Leo Robin score, including "A Gal in Calico" and "Rainy Night in Rio." No relation to 1929 musical of same name.

Time to Kill (1942) 61m. ** D: Herbert I. Leeds. Lloyd Nolan, Ralph Byrd, Heather Angel, Doris Merrick, Richard Lane. Michael Shayne (Nolan) versus counterfeiters of rare coins. Adequate entry in the series, sparked by Nolan's tough-guy performance. Though a Mike Shayne movie, it's based on a Raymond Chandler story; remade as THE BRASHER DOUBLOON.

Time to Love and a Time to Die, A (1958) C-132m. *** D: Douglas Sirk. John Gavin, Lilo Pulver, Jock Mahoney, Don DeFore, Keenan Wynn, Thayer David, Dana (Jim) Hutton, Klaus Kinski. Intensely dramatic love story set against background of WW2. German soldier on furlough from battle falls in love, inevitably must return to the trenches. Well-directed version of Erich Maria Remarque novel (with the author in a small role). Hutton's film debut. CinemaScope. ▼

Time Travelers, The (1964) C-82m. **½ D: Ib Melchior. Preston Foster, Philip Carey, Merry Anders, John Hoyt, Steve Franken. Spirited flashes of imagination heighten this sci-fi story about scientists who journey into the future and find their actions there will affect the past. Not bad, with downbeat ending; one of the first American films photographed by Vilmos Zsigmond. ▼

Time Without Pity (1956-British) 88m. *** D: Joseph Losey. Michael Redgrave, Alec McCowen, Ann Todd, Peter Cushing, Leo McKern, Renee Houston, Lois Maxwell, Joan Plowright. Tense thriller with an anti-capital punishment point-of-view, as alcoholic Redgrave has 24 hours to prove son McCowen's innocence on a murder rap. Scripted by Ben Barzman, from an Emlyn Williams play. ▼◗

Tingler, The (1959) 82m. **½ D: William Castle. Vincent Price, Judith Evelyn, Darryl Hickman, Philip Coolidge, Patricia Cutts. Preposterous but original shocker: coroner Price discovers that fear causes a creepy-crawly creature to materialize on people's spines; it can be subdued only by screaming. This is the infamous picture that got moviegoers into the spirit with vibrating gizmos under selected theater seats!—a gimmick director/producer Castle billed as "Percepto." Also noteworthy as likely the earliest film depicting an LSD trip. One critical sequence is in color.▼○▶

Tin Pan Alley (1940) **94m.** ******* D: Walter Lang. Alice Faye, Betty Grable, Jack Oakie, John Payne, Esther Ralston, Allen Jenkins, Nicholas Brothers, John Loder, Elisha Cook, Jr. Predictable plot of struggling pre-WW1 songwriters enlivened by Alfred Newman's Oscar-winning score and colorful numbers including "Sheik of Araby" with Billy Gilbert as sultan. Oakie is in top form. Remade as I'LL GET BY.▼

Tin Star, The (1957) **93m.** ******* D: Anthony Mann. Henry Fonda, Anthony Perkins, Betsy Palmer, Neville Brand, Lee Van Cleef, John McIntire, Michel Ray. Fledgling sheriff Perkins turns to bounty hunter Fonda to help combat outlaws preying on his town; solid, well-acted Western. Scripted by Dudley Nichols. VistaVision.▼▶

Tip-Off, The (1931) **73m.** ******* D: Albert Rogell. Eddie Quillan, Robert Armstrong, Ginger Rogers, Joan Peers, Ralf Harolde. Consistently clever, amusing little film with naïve Quillan earning boxer Armstrong's eternal gratitude by (inadvertently) saving him from a going-over by gangster Harolde. That comes in handy when Quillan falls in love with the mobster's moll. Armstrong is very funny as the prizefighter who's always groping for big words, which are supplied by his perky girlfriend Rogers.▼

Tip-Off Girls (1938) **61m.** ****½** D: Louis King. Mary Carlisle, Lloyd Nolan, Roscoe Karns, Larry (Buster) Crabbe, J. Carrol Naish, Evelyn Brent, Anthony Quinn, Benny Baker, Harvey Stephens. Racketeers employ alluring damsels in distress to flag down truckers on highways and then hijack their shipments. Crisp crime programmer.

Tip on a Dead Jockey (1957) **99m.** ******* D: Richard Thorpe. Dorothy Malone, Robert Taylor, Gia Scala, Martin Gabel, Jack Lord. Neat account of Taylor tied in with smuggling syndicate in Madrid, romancing Malone. Good Charles Lederer adaptation of Irwin Shaw story. CinemaScope.▶

Titanic (1943-German) **85m.** ****½** D: Herbert Selpin, Werner Klingler. Sybille Schmitz, Hans Nielsen, Karl Schönböck, Charlotte Thiele, Otto Wernicke. Little-seen German drama about the doomed ocean liner was made during WW2, so a German officer is depicted as the only brave, outspoken man on board, while the English owner pursues an "endless quest for profit." Creditable disaster film, although the script is no more inspired than later versions of the saga. Some shots were reused in A NIGHT TO REMEMBER. Banned in Germany in 1943 because the scenes of panic were considered too potent in the midst of wartime air raids.▼

Titanic (1953) **98m.** ******* D: Jean Negulesco. Clifton Webb, Barbara Stanwyck, Robert Wagner, Richard Basehart, Audrey Dalton, Thelma Ritter, Brian Aherne. Hollywoodized version of sea tragedy centers on shipboard story. Not bad, but events better told in A NIGHT TO REMEMBER . . . and more spectacularly in the 1997 film. Oscar-winning script by producer Charles Brackett, Walter Reisch, and Richard Breen.▼○▶

Titanic: Disaster in the Atlantic (1929-British-German) **99m.** ****** D: E. A. Dupont. German cast: Fritz Kortner, Elsa Wagner, Heinrich Schroth, Julia Serda, Elfriede Borodin, Lucie Mannheim, Franz (Francis) Lederer, Willi Forst. British cast: Franklin Dyall, Madeleine Carroll, Monty Banks, John Stuart, John Longden. Doomed ocean liner's first to final moments are dutifully chronicled, but in the peculiar guise of a roman à clef. Dupont's first talkie was shot once as a German silent, then in German and British sound versions, each with different casts and scripts. Adapted from Ernest Raymond's play *The Berg*, and more an experiment in early sound than a sound drama. Aka ATLANTIK and ATLANTIC.▼▶

Titfield Thunderbolt, The (1953-British) **C-84m.** ******* D: Charles Crichton. Stanley Holloway, George Relph, Naunton Wayne, John Gregson, Godfrey Tearle, Edie Martin, Hugh Griffith, Sid James, Jack MacGowran. Boisterous Ealing comedy about villagers who are attached to their antiquated railway line and run it themselves in competition with the local bus line. Lovely photography by Douglas Slocombe. Script by T.E.B. Clarke.▶

T-Men (1947) **92m.** ******* D: Anthony Mann. Dennis O'Keefe, Alfred Ryder, Charles McGraw, Wallace Ford, Mary Meade, June Lockhart. Semidocumentary-style story of undercover treasury agents trying to get to the bottom of counterfeit ring. Vividly exciting; director Mann and cameraman John Alton went out of their way to use unusual, effective lighting and compositions in this A-1 film.▼○▶

Toast of New Orleans, The (1950) **C-97m.** ****½** D: Norman Taurog. Kathryn Grayson, Mario Lanza, David Niven, Rita Moreno, J. Carrol Naish. Lanza plays fisherman transformed into operatic star. Rest of cast good, and Lanza sings "Be My Love."▼○▶

Toast of New York, The (1937) **109m.** ******* D: Rowland V. Lee. Edward Arnold, Cary Grant, Frances Farmer, Jack Oakie, Donald Meek, Clarence Kolb, Billy Gilbert, Stanley Fields. Arnold is in fine form as rags-to-riches businessman Jim Fisk in mid-19th century. Grant is his partner in hokey but entertaining biographical fiction; good show-case for spirited Farmer.▼O◗

Tobacco Road (1941) 84m. **½ D: John Ford. Charley Grapewin, Marjorie Rambeau, Gene Tierney, William Tracy, Elizabeth Patterson, Dana Andrews, Slim Summerville, Ward Bond, Grant Mitchell. Lightly entertaining but genuinely odd seriocomedy about "quaint" Georgia backwoods community; worthwhile mainly to see Grapewin repeating his stage role as cheerful ne'er-do-well Jeeter Lester. Adapted (and sanitized) by Nunnally Johnson from the long-running Broadway play by Jack Kirkland, based on Erskine Caldwell's novel.◗

To Beat the Band (1935) 67m. ** D: Ben Stoloff. Hugh Herbert, Helen Broderick, Roger Pryor, Fred Keating, Eric Blore, Phyllis Brooks, Ray Mayer, Joy Hodges. Strange, silly B musical with Herbert forced to marry a widow to collect an inheritance while trying to prevent a neighbor (Pryor) from committing suicide. Musical numbers feature vocals by young Johnny Mercer (who also wrote the score with Matty Malneck) and an incredible specialty dance by one Sonny Lamont.◗

To Bed ... or Not to Bed (1963-Italian) 103m. **½ D: Gian Luigi Polidoro. Alberto Sordi, Bernhard Tarschys, Inger Sjostrand, Ulf Palme. Saucy sex romp. Sordi expects to find free love on business trip to Stockholm, discovers home sweet home is best. Retitled: THE DEVIL.

To Be or Not to Be (1942) 99m. ***½ D: Ernst Lubitsch. Jack Benny, Carole Lombard, Robert Stack, Lionel Atwill, Felix Bressart, Sig Ruman, Tom Dugan, Helmut Dantine, Stanley Ridges. Benny has the role of a lifetime as "that great, great actor" Joseph Tura, whose Polish theater troupe is put out of business by invading Nazis—until they become involved in espionage and find their thespian skills being put to the ultimate test. Superb black comedy scripted by Edwin Justus Mayer; the opening gag with Dugan is a gem. Lombard's final film, released after her death. Remade in 1983.▼O◗

Tobor the Great (1954) 77m. *½ D: Lee Sholem. Charles Drake, Karin Booth, Billy Chapin, Taylor Holmes, Steven Geray. Scientist allows his genius grandson to become pals with the robot of the title, leading to complications when spies try to glom onto the plans; terrible acting and dialogue. A botched attempt at a heartwarming sci-fi comedy-thriller.▼O◗

Toby Tyler, or Ten Weeks with a Circus (1960) C-96m. **½ D: Charles Barton. Kevin Corcoran, Henry Calvin, Gene Sheldon, Bob Sweeney, Richard Eastham, James Drury. Likable Disney fare about a young boy who runs away to join the circus at the turn of the 20th century.▼O◗

To Catch a Thief (1955) C-106m. *** D: Alfred Hitchcock. Grace Kelly, Cary Grant,

Jessie Royce Landis, John Williams, Charles Vanel, Brigitte Auber. The French Riviera serves as picturesque backdrop for this entertaining (if fluffy) Hitchcock caper with Grant as reformed cat burglar suspected in new wave of jewel robberies. Chic and elegant in every way—and Kelly never looked more ravishing. Script (including much-imitated fireworks scene) by John Michael Hayes; Oscar-winning photography by Robert Burks. VistaVision.▼O◗

Today We Live (1933) 113m. ** D: Howard Hawks. Joan Crawford, Gary Cooper, Robert Young, Franchot Tone, Roscoe Karns. Stilted William Faulkner story of WW1 romance and heroism; despite star-studded cast, not much. Faulkner cowrote the screenplay. Torpedo attack scenes were directed by Richard Rosson. ▼◗

To Die in Madrid (1963-French) 87m. **** D: Frédéric Rossif. Narrated by John Gielgud, Irene Worth. Masterpiece in documentary filmmaking dealing with bloody civil war in Spain in which more than a million people died.

To Each His Own (1946) 122m. *** D: Mitchell Leisen. Olivia de Havilland, John Lund, Mary Anderson, Roland Culver, Phillip Terry, Griff Barnett. Well-turned soaper of unwed mother giving up baby, lavishing love on him as his "aunt" without revealing truth. Fine support by Culver as aging Olivia's beau. De Havilland won Best Actress Oscar. Lund's film debut.▼

Together Again (1944) 100m. *** D: Charles Vidor. Irene Dunne, Charles Boyer, Charles Coburn, Mona Freeman, Elizabeth Patterson. Little bit of nothing carried off beautifully by Dunne, widow mayor of small town, and Boyer, suave New Yorker whom she hires to sculpt a statue of her late husband; charming comedy.◗

To Have and Have Not (1944) 100m. ***½ D: Howard Hawks. Humphrey Bogart, Walter Brennan, Lauren Bacall, Hoagy Carmichael, Dan Seymour, Marcel Dalio, Dolores Moran, Sheldon Leonard. Hemingway's "worst novel" forms the basis for Hawks' version of CASABLANCA: tough skipper-for-hire Bogart reluctantly becomes involved with French Resistance, less reluctantly woos even tougher Bacall (in her film debut). Their legendary love scenes make the movie, but there are also solid performances, taut action, and a couple of songs. (Andy Williams was hired to dub Bacall's singing, but that's her voice, after all.) Super dialogue by William Faulkner and Jules Furthman; remade as THE BREAKING POINT and THE GUN RUNNERS. Also shown in computer-colored version. ▼O◗

To Hell and Back (1955) C-106m. *** D: Jesse Hibbs. Audie Murphy, Marshall Thompson, Charles Drake, Jack Kelly, Paul Picerni, Gregg Palmer, Brett Halsey, David Janssen, Art Aragon, Rand Brooks, Denver Pyle, Susan Kohner. Murphy (the most decorated soldier of WW2) stars in very good war film based on his autobiography, with excellent battle sequences depicting Murphy's often breathtaking heroic exploits. Clichés in script are overcome by Murphy and cast's easygoing delivery. CinemaScope.▼�

To Joy (1950-Swedish) **95m. **½** D: Ingmar Bergman. Stig Olin, Maj-Britt Nilsson, John Ekman, Margit Carlquist, Victor Seastrom (Sjöström), Birger Malmsten. Early Bergman drama offers a thematic prelude of what was to come from the filmmaker. Modest, occasionally insightful chronicle of Olin and Nilsson's failing marriage.▼▸

To Kill a Mockingbird (1962) **129m. ****** D: Robert Mulligan. Gregory Peck, Mary Badham, Philip Alford, John Megna, Brock Peters, Robert Duvall, Frank Overton, Rosemary Murphy, Paul Fix, Collin Wilcox, Alice Ghostley, William Windom; narrated by Kim Stanley. In a small Alabama town in the 1930s, lawyer Atticus Finch (Peck) defends a black man (Peters) accused of raping a white woman. Their father's innate decency affects his two motherless children as they learn about life, especially about that spooky house in the neighborhood. Peck won a well-deserved Best Actor Oscar; screenwriter Horton Foote received one as well. This outstanding film only gains in stature as time passes. One of the best of the 1960s. From the semiautobiographical novel by Harper Lee. Duvall makes his screen debut as Boo Radley. Produced by Alan J. Pakula, with a memorable score by Elmer Bernstein.▼●▸

Tokyo Chorus (1931-Japanese) **91m. ***½** D: Yasujiro Ozu. Tokihiko Okada, Emiko Yagumo, Hideo Sugawara, Hideko Takamine, Tatsuo Saito, Choko Iida, Takashi Sakamoto, Reiko Tani. Elegant, emotionally resounding social drama with comedic touches involves the everyday struggles of a Tokyo family, with the proud husband-father (Okada) losing his job after speaking out against an injustice. Ozu offers poignant commentary on the plight of the unemployed and movingly contrasts the carefree nature of childhood to the stresses of adult responsibility.▸

Tokyo Joe (1949) **88m. **½** D: Stuart Heisler. Humphrey Bogart, Florence Marly, Sessue Hayakawa, Alexander Knox, Jerome Courtland. Lesser Bogart film about American in postwar Tokyo pulled into smuggling and blackmail for the sake of his ex-wife and child.▼●▸

Tokyo Olympiad (1965) **C-170m. ****** D: Kon Ichikawa. Once compromised by edited versions that diminished its power, epic documentary about the 1964 Olympics is artistically mentionable in the same breath as Leni Riefenstahl's OLYMPIA—and without the Hitler baggage. Though Ichikawa had over a hundred Tohoscope cameras at his disposal, result is less a re-

portorial chronicle than a sensory agony/ecstasy portrayal set against panoramic crowd shots. Broad jumpers compete on a messy, muddy track and a lonely runner from Chad finds himself . . . somewhere . . . in downtown Tokyo. CinemaScope. ▼●▸

Tokyo Story (1953-Japanese) **134m. ***** D: Yasujiro Ozu. Chishu Ryu, Chieko Higashiyama, So Yamamura, Haruko Sugimura, Setsuko Hara. An elderly couple (Ryu, Higashiyama) visit their children in Tokyo, who are too busy living their lives and treat them tactlessly. Quietly powerful story of old age, the disappointments parents experience with their children, and the fears the young have of time passing. A masterpiece. Not shown in the U.S. until 1972.▼▸

Tokyo Twilight (1957-Japanese) **141m. ***½** D: Yasujiro Ozu. Setsuko Hara, Ineko Arima, Chishu Ryu, Isuzu Yamada, Teiji Takahashi, Masami Taura. An aura of profound sadness permeates this quietly devastating account of the secrets and lies that eat away at the core of an otherwise average Japanese family. The eldest daughter (Hara) is unhappily married; meanwhile, her younger sister (Arima) is harboring a terrible secret. Ozu (who scripted with Kôgo Noda) paints a vivid portrait of characters whose souls are tainted by their inability to share their feelings.▸

Tol'able David (1921) **94m. ***½** D: Henry King. Richard Barthelmess, Gladys Hulette, Ernest Torrence, Warner Richmond, Walter P. Lewis. A mild-mannered boy is forced to take his brother's place delivering the mail—and dealing with a trio of heinous criminals who've moved into their rural community. Beautifully crafted Americana, shot on location in Virginia. The finale is a rip-roaring piece of movie storytelling. Remade in 1930.▼●▸

Toll Gate, The (1920) **59m. **** D: Lambert Hillyer. William S. Hart, Anna Q. Nilsson, Jack Richardson, Joseph Singleton, Richard Headrick. One of Hart's best films, casting him as fleeing outlaw who stops to save young boy's life, becomes involved with the child's widowed mother.▼●▸

Toll of the Sea, The (1922) **C-54m. **** D: Chester M. Franklin. Anna May Wong, Kenneth Harlan, Beatrice Bentley, Baby Moran, Etta Lee, Ming Young. Lotus Flower (Wong), a gentle young Chinese woman, discovers an unconscious Caucasian American by the edge of the sea; the two soon marry, but there are complications. Poignant story of love, longing, and self-sacrifice offers a sharp-edged view of the racial attitudes of the era. Pioneering two-color Technicolor feature is exquisite to watch. The final sequence, which did not survive, was reshot at the Pacific Ocean in 1985 using a genuine two-color Technicolor camera.▼▸

Tomahawk (1951) **C-82m. **½** D: George Sherman. Yvonne De Carlo, Van Heflin,

Preston Foster, Jack Oakie, Alex Nicol, Tom Tully, Rock Hudson. Colorful Western spiked with sufficient action to overcome bland account of friction between Indians and the Army.▼❂

To Mary—With Love (1936) 86m. ** D: John Cromwell. Warner Baxter, Myrna Loy, Ian Hunter, Claire Trevor, Jean Dixon, Pat Somerset. Humdrum drama of Baxter and Loy enduring ups and downs over a decade of married life.

Tomb of Ligeia, The (1964-British) C-81m. *** D: Roger Corman. Vincent Price, Elizabeth Shepherd, John Westbrook, Derek Francis. In 1821 England, castle lord Price's late wife manifests herself all over the place, both as a cat and in new bride Shepherd. Super-stylish chiller with superb location work. The last of Corman's eight Poe adaptations; screenplay by Robert Towne. Filmed in Widescreen Colorscope.▼❂

Tomboy and the Champ (1961) C-92m. ** D: Francis D. Lyon. Candy Moore, Ben Johnson, Jesse White, Jess Kirkpatrick, Rex Allen. Mild B film about a young girl and her prize cow; strictly for children, who will probably enjoy it, despite standard plot devices.❂

Tom Brown of Culver (1932) 82m. **½ D: William Wyler. Tom Brown, H. B. Warner, Richard Cromwell, Slim Summerville, Ben Alexander, Sidney Toler, Russell Hopton, Andy Devine. Well-made but corny military-school picture has Tom Brown in namesake role of wayward boy who gets a scholarship to famed Indiana military academy during the Depression. Much of the film was shot on location. Tyrone Power (billed as Jr.) makes his screen debut here, and reportedly, Alan Ladd can be spotted in a bit. Remade as SPIRIT OF CULVER.

Tom Brown's School Days (1940) 86m. **½ D: Robert Stevenson. Cedric Hardwicke, Freddie Bartholomew, Gale Storm, Jimmy Lydon, Josephine Hutchinson, Billy Halop, Polly Moran. Occasionally overbaked but still entertaining, fast-paced account of life at a Victorian boys' school. Although most of cast is American, British flavor seeps through. Retitled: ADVENTURES AT RUGBY.▼❂

Tom Brown's Schooldays (1951-British) 93m. ***½ D: Gordon Parry. John Howard Davies, Robert Newton, Diana Wynyard, Hermione Baddeley, Kathleen Byron, James Hayter, John Charlesworth, John Forrest, Michael Hordern, Max Bygraves. Well-acted film of Victorian England school life with exceptional British cast and good direction. Noel Langley scripted, from Thomas Hughes' novel.

Tom, Dick and Harry (1941) 86m. ***½ D: Garson Kanin. Ginger Rogers, George Murphy, Alan Marshal, Burgess Meredith, Joe Cunningham, Jane Seymour, Phil Silvers. Spirited comic dilemma as wide-eyed Ginger chooses among three anxious suitors: sincere Murphy, wealthy Marshal, nonconformist Meredith. Silvers has hilarious role as obnoxious ice-cream man. Written by Paul Jarrico. Remade as THE GIRL MOST LIKELY.▼❂

Tom Jones (1963-British) C-129m. **** D: Tony Richardson. Albert Finney, Susannah York, Hugh Griffith, Edith Evans, Joyce Redman, Diane Cilento, Joan Greenwood, David Tomlinson, Peter Bull, David Warner; narrated by Micheál MacLiammoir. High-spirited adaptation of the Henry Fielding novel about a young man's misadventures and bawdy experiences in 18th-century England; rowdy, randy, and completely disarming. Academy Award winner as Best Picture, it also won Oscars for Richardson, who directed with great flair and imagination, screenwriter John Osborne, who caught the gritty flavor of the period to perfection, and composer John Addison, whose infectious score suits the picture to a tee. Film debuts of Lynn Redgrave and David Warner. Richardson cut the film by seven minutes for its 1989 reissue.▼❂

Tommy Steele Story, The SEE: **Rock Around the World**

Tomorrow at Seven (1933) 62m. **½ D: Ray Enright. Chester Morris, Vivienne Osborne, Frank McHugh, Allen Jenkins, Henry Stephenson, Grant Mitchell, Charles Middleton, Oscar Apfel. Writer Morris is penning a book about the "Black Ace," a notorious murderer. When will he strike again? "Tomorrow at seven," perhaps? Clever edge-of-your-seat mystery is entertaining most of the way; McHugh and Jenkins are in vintage form as a pair of comical cops.❂

Tomorrow at Ten (1963-British) 80m. **½ D: Lance Comfort. John Gregson, Robert Shaw, Alec Clunes, Alan Wheatley. Taut drama involving kidnapper who dies, leaving boy in house (whereabouts unknown) with time bomb set to explode.

Tomorrow Is Another Day (1951) 90m. **½ D: Felix E. Feist. Ruth Roman, Steve Cochran, Lurene Tuttle, Ray Teal, Morris Ankrum, Hugh Sanders. Frank little film of ex-con Cochran marrying dime-a-dance girl Roman, heading for California, thinking he's killed her old boyfriend.❂

Tomorrow Is Forever (1946) 105m. *** D: Irving Pichel. Claudette Colbert, Orson Welles, George Brent, Lucile Watson, Richard Long, Natalie Wood. Weepy rehash of *Enoch Arden*, with Welles as man listed dead in WW1 returning decades later with new face to find wife Colbert remarried to Brent. Bravura work by Welles with good support by Wood as his adopted daughter.▼❂

Tomorrow, the World! (1944) 95m. *** D: Leslie Fenton. Fredric March, Betty Field, Agnes Moorehead, Skippy Homeier, Joan Carroll. Homeier re-creates his knockout Broadway performance as a German-raised child adopted by his American uncle, who soon discovers that the boy is a rabid Nazi with a sinister mindset. Still-potent and thoughtful drama about tolerance. Scripted by Ring Lardner, Jr., and Leopold Atlas from the play by James Gow and Armand D'Usseau. ▼▶

Tomorrow We Live (1942) 64m. ** D: Edgar G. Ulmer. Ricardo Cortez, Jean Parker, Emmett Lynn, William Marshall, Roseanne Stevens, Ray Miller. In modern-day Arizona, gangster Cortez, known as The Ghost, develops an unwelcome interest in desert cafe waitress Parker, the daughter of old geezer Lynn, who's secretly in The Ghost's employ. Odd wartime melodrama is less a story than a series of incidents; weakened by a bad (and incessant) score. ▶

Tom Sawyer (1930) 86m. **½ D: John Cromwell. Jackie Coogan, Mitzi Green, Junior Durkin, Jackie Searl, Clara Blandick, Lucien Littlefield. Enjoyable but slow-moving adaptation of the Mark Twain classic. Coogan, Green, Durkin, and Searl are, respectively, Tom, Becky Thatcher, Huck Finn, and Sid Sawyer; they all repeated their roles the following year in HUCKLEBERRY FINN. Remade in 1938 (as THE ADVENTURES OF TOM SAWYER) and twice in 1973. ▼

Tom Sawyer, Detective (1938) 68m. **½ D: Louis King. Billy Cook, Donald O'Connor, Porter Hall, Phillip Warren, Janet Waldo, Elisabeth Risdon, William Haade. Pleasant little family film based on Mark Twain's novella that turns Tom (Cook) and Huck (O'Connor) into backwoods detectives.

tom thumb (1958) C-98m. ***½ D: George Pal. Russ Tamblyn, June Thorburn, Peter Sellers, Terry-Thomas, Alan Young, Jessie Matthews, Bernard Miles. Excellent children's picture with Tamblyn as tiny tom thumb, taken in by kindly couple but exploited by villainous Terry-Thomas and henchman Sellers. Charming Puppetoons sequences, Oscar-winning special effects, perfect Peggy Lee–Sonny Burke score. Filmed in England. ▼▶

Toni (1935-French) 90m. ***½ D: Jean Renoir. Charles Blavette, Celia Montalvan, Jenny Helia, Max Dalban. Italian quarry worker Blavette lives with Montalvan, but falls in love with farm girl Helia—who in turn is wooed away by swaggering foreman Dalban. Renoir coscripted this simple, touching drama, which he filmed in a style that influenced the Italian Neorealist movement of the 1940s. ▼

Tonight and Every Night (1945) C-92m. *** D: Victor Saville. Rita Hayworth, Janet Blair, Lee Bowman, Marc Platt, Leslie Brooks, Professor Lamberti, Florence Bates. Entertaining, brightly colored wartime musical of British theater that never misses a performance, despite bombings and personal hardships. Try spotting Shel-

ley Winters as one of the chorines. Story of the real-life theater also chronicled in MRS HENDERSON PRESENTS (2005). ▼▶

Tonight at 8:30 (1952-British) C-81m. *** D: Anthony Pélissier. Valerie Hobson, Stanley Holloway, Nigel Patrick, Ted Ray, Kay Walsh, Jack Warner, Jessie Royce Landis, Betty Ann Davies, Martita Hunt, Yvonne Furneaux. Compact anthology based on a trio of playlets from Noel Coward's *Tonight at 8:30*. "Red Peppers" involves squabbling husband-and-wife music hall performers; "Fumed Oak: An Unpleasant Comedy," the best of the lot, spotlights the sweet revenge of a much-put-upon husband-father (Holloway); "Ways and Means" centers on a freeloading couple in a Riviera villa. Original British title: MEET ME TONIGHT.

Tonight Is Ours (1933) 75m. **½ D: Stuart Walker. Claudette Colbert, Fredric March, Alison Skipworth, Arthur Byron, Paul Cavanagh, Ethel Griffies. Princess Colbert falls in love with commoner March, though she is already spoken for in a planned marriage. Colbert is luminously beautiful (photographed by Karl Struss) in this sexy, pre-Code romance that opens light and airy, then turns serious. Mitchell Leisen is credited as Associate Director. Based on Noel Coward's play *The Queen Was in the Parlour*, filmed under that name in 1927.

Tonight or Never (1931) 81m. ** D: Mervyn LeRoy. Gloria Swanson, Melvyn Douglas, Alison Skipworth, Ferdinand Gottschalk, Robert Greig, Boris Karloff. Stylishly mounted but stagebound romantic comedy about a flighty opera singer (Swanson) who's criticized because her performances lack passion. Swanson is beautifully costumed by Coco Chanel. Douglas' screen debut, re-creating his Broadway role. ▶

Tonight's the Night (1954-British) C-88m. *** D: Mario Zampi. David Niven, Yvonne De Carlo, Barry Fitzgerald, George Cole, Robert Urquhart. Good British cast bolsters appealing comedy about house in Ireland which natives claim is haunted. Original British title: HAPPY EVER AFTER.

Tonight We Raid Calais (1943) 70m. **½ D: John Brahm. Annabella, John Sutton, Lee J. Cobb, Beulah Bondi, Blanche Yurka, Howard da Silva, Marcel Dalio. Fast-paced if undistinguished WW2 tale of sabotage mission in France with good performances; written by Waldo Salt. ▶

Tonight We Sing (1953) C-109m. **½ D: Mitchell Leisen. David Wayne, Ezio Pinza, Roberta Peters, Anne Bancroft, Tamara Toumanova, Isaac Stern, Jan Peerce. Hodgepodge supposedly based on impresario Sol Hurok's life, allowing for disjointed string of operatic/musical interludes. Produced by George Jessel. ▶

Tonka (1958) C-97m. **½ D: Lewis R. Foster. Sal Mineo, Philip Carey, Jerome Courtland, Rafael Campos, H. M. Wynant,

Joy Page. Mineo stands out in this modest Disney film about an Indian brave's attachment to a wild horse, lone "survivor" of Little Bighorn battle, which he captures and tames. Weak resolution and cut-rate version of Custer's Last Stand detract from promising story. Retitled A HORSE NAMED COMANCHE.▼❿

Tony Draws a Horse (1950-British) **91m.** **½ D: John Paddy Carstairs. Cecil Parker, Anne Crawford, Derek Bond, Mervyn Johns, Barbara Murray, Edward Rigby, Anthony Lang, Sebastian Cabot. Dr. Parker and psychologist Crawford cannot agree on the proper method of rearing their 8-year-old son; his mischief ends up affecting their marriage and entire family. Occasionally funny but overly talky (not to mention outdated) satire.▼

Too Bad She's Bad (1955-Italian) **95m.** ** D: Alessandro Blasetti. Sophia Loren, Vittorio De Sica, Marcello Mastroianni, Lina Furia. Unremarkable little comedy about life and love among happy-go-lucky crooks, set in Rome.❿

Too Busy to Work (1932) **76m.** **½ D: John G. Blystone. Will Rogers, Marian Nixon, Dick Powell, Frederick Burton, Charles Middleton, Louise Beavers. A hobo named Jubilo rides the rails to California in search of the man who made off with his wife years ago. When he learns that she passed away, he manages to insinuate himself into the lives of the family members—including his own daughter. Agreeable entertainment for Rogers fans.❿

Too Hot to Handle (1938) **105m.** *** D: Jack Conway. Clark Gable, Myrna Loy, Walter Pidgeon, Leo Carrillo, Johnny Hines, Virginia Weidler. Gable and Pidgeon are rival newsreel photographers vying for aviatrix Loy in this fast-paced action-comedy; Gable's scene faking enemy attack on China is a gem.▼❿

Too Hot to Handle (1960-British) **C-92m.** ** D: Terence Young. Jayne Mansfield, Leo Genn, Carl Boehm, Christopher Lee, Barbara Windsor. Seamy study of chanteuse Mansfield involved with one man too many in the nightclub circuit. Aka PLAYGIRL AFTER DARK.▼❿

Too Late Blues (1962) **100m.** ** D: John Cassavetes. Bobby Darin, Stella Stevens, John Cassavetes, Rupert Crosse, Vincent Edwards, Cliff Carnell, Seymour Cassel. Somewhat pretentious drama about jazz musician Darin becoming involved with selfish Stevens. Score by David Raksin, with on-camera performances "doubled" by such jazz greats as Benny Carter, Shelly Manne, and Jimmy Rowles.❿

Too Late for Tears (1949) **99m.** **½ D: Byron Haskin. Lizabeth Scott, Don DeFore, Dan Duryea, Arthur Kennedy, Kristine Miller. Atmospheric but muddled drama detailing what happens when a bag filled with cash is dropped into the car of greedy bad-girl Scott and nice-guy husband Kennedy. Duryea is at his best as a heavy. Aka KILLER BAIT.▼❿

Too Many Crooks (1958-British) **85m.** **½ D: Mario Zampi. Terry-Thomas, George Cole, Brenda De Banzie, Sid James, Sydney Tafler. OK satire on racketeer films buoyed by Terry-Thomas' presence.▼❿

Too Many Girls (1940) **85m.** *** D: George Abbott. Lucille Ball, Richard Carlson, Eddie Bracken, Ann Miller, Hal LeRoy, Desi Arnaz, Frances Langford. Engaging Rodgers-Hart musical comedy with winning cast, sharp dialogue. Four boys are hired to keep an eye on footloose Lucy at Pottawatomie College in Stopgap, New Mexico. Stagy presentation of musical numbers seems to work fine here; Van Johnson is very noticeable as one of the chorus boys (it was his film debut, as well as Arnaz and Bracken's). Incidentally, this is where Lucy and Desi met.▼❿

Too Many Husbands (1940) **84m.** *** D: Wesley Ruggles. Jean Arthur, Fred MacMurray, Melvyn Douglas, Harry Davenport, Dorothy Peterson, Edgar Buchanan. Jean is married to Douglas when husband #1 (MacMurray), thought dead, turns up. Engaging farce from W. Somerset Maugham's play *Home and Beauty*. Remade as THREE FOR THE SHOW.❿

Too Many Winners (1947) **61m.** *½ D: William Beaudine. Hugh Beaumont, Trudy Marshall, Ralph Dunn, Claire Carleton, Charles Mitchell, John Hamilton. Sleuth Michael Shayne tries to take a vacation, but naturally gets entangled in crime solving instead. Final entry in cut-rate series.

Too Much Harmony (1933) **76m.** **½ D: A. Edward Sutherland. Bing Crosby, Jack Oakie, Grace Bradley, Judith Allen, Lilyan Tashman, Ned Sparks. Pleasant, if plotty, backstage musical with some good song numbers, including "Thanks," "The Day You Came Along."

Too Much, Too Soon (1958) **121m.** ** D: Art Napoleon. Dorothy Malone, Errol Flynn, Efrem Zimbalist, Jr., Ray Danton, Neva Patterson, Martin Milner, Murray Hamilton. But not enough, in sensationalistic tale of Diana Barrymore's decline. Flynn steals the show as John Barrymore.❿

Too Soon to Love (1960) **85m.** ** D: Richard Rush. Jennifer West, Richard Evans, Warren Parker, Ralph Manza, Jack Nicholson. Mildly interesting period piece about illicit teenage love, pregnancy, and abortion. An early credit for Nicholson and writer-director Rush.❿

Too Young to Kiss (1951) **91m.** **½ D: Robert Z. Leonard. June Allyson, Van Johnson, Gig Young, Paula Corday, Hans Conried. Allyson is fetching as pianist posing as child prodigy to get her big break falling in love with Johnson.❿

Too Young to Know (1945) **86m.** ** D: Frederick de Cordova. Joan Leslie, Robert Hutton, Rosemary DeCamp, Dolores Moran. Slick, empty drama of career girl Leslie torn between husband and job.

To Paris With Love (1955-British) **C-78m.** **½ D: Robert Hamer. Alec Guinness, Odile Versois, Vernon Gray, Elina Labourdette, Claude Romain, Jacques François, Austin Trevor. Middle-aged widower Guinness and son (Gray) try to marry each other off while on holiday in Paris. So-so comedy should amuse Guinness fans and Francophiles.▼❿

Topaze (1933) **78m.** *** D: (Harry) D'Abbadie D'Arrast. John Barrymore, Myrna Loy, Albert Conti, Luis Alberni, Reginald Mason, Jobyna Howland. Delightful film adapted from Marcel Pagnol's play about an impeccably honest but naive schoolteacher in France who unwittingly becomes a dupe for wealthy baron's business scheme. Barrymore is perfect. Remade as I LIKE MONEY.▼❿

Topaze (1951-French) **136m.** *** D: Marcel Pagnol. Fernandel, Hélène Perdrière, Pierre Larquey, Jacques Morel, Jacqueline Pagnol, Marcel Vallée, Jacques Castelot. Fernandel is in top form as the title character, a naive, exploited schoolteacher cruelly fired from his job, who finds himself merrily wallowing in corruption. Pagnol scripted, from his play; filmed in 1933, 1935, 1936 (by Pagnol), and 1960 (as I LIKE MONEY). Beware edited versions.▼

Top Banana (1954) **C-100m.** *** D: Alfred E. Green. Phil Silvers, Rose Marie, Danny Scholl, Judy Lynn, Jack Albertson, Joey Faye, Herbie Faye. Fascinating curio is literally a filmed version of Silvers' Broadway hit about a Milton Berle–like TV comic. Full of burlesque chestnuts, and filmed (believe it or not) in 3-D. Current prints run 84m., with some musical numbers deleted.▼❿

Top Gun (1955) **73m.** **½ D: Ray Nazarro. Sterling Hayden, William Bishop, Karin Booth, Regis Toomey, Rod Taylor, Denver Pyle. Hayden, unwelcome in his own home town because of his gunfighter past, must help defend it against outlaws. OK Western drama, somewhat reminiscent of HIGH NOON. ❿

Top Hat (1935) **99m.** **** D: Mark Sandrich. Fred Astaire, Ginger Rogers, Edward Everett Horton, Helen Broderick, Eric Blore, Erik Rhodes. What can we say? Merely a knock-out of a musical with Astaire and Rogers at their brightest doing "Cheek to Cheek," "Isn't This a Lovely Day to Be Caught in the Rain," "Top Hat, White Tie, and Tails," and the epic "Piccolino," and other Irving Berlin songs, as the duo goes through typical mistaken-identity plot. Wonderful support from rest of cast; that's Lucille Ball as the flower shop clerk. Scripted by Dwight Taylor and Allan Scott,

from a play by Alexander Farago and Aladar Laszlo. Originally 101m.; some prints are 93m. Later a stage musical.▼❿

Topkapi (1964) **C-120m.** **** D: Jules Dassin. Melina Mercouri, Peter Ustinov, Maximilian Schell, Robert Morley, Akim Tamiroff, Despo Diamantidou. First-rate entertainment of would-be thieves who plan perfect crime in Constantinople museum; lighthearted caper has inspired many imitations. Filmed in Istanbul, with Ustinov's delightful performance copping an Academy Award. Written by Monja Danischewsky, from Eric Ambler's novel *The Light of Day*; memorable score by Manos Hadjidakis.▼❿

To Please a Lady (1950) **91m.** **½ D: Clarence Brown. Clark Gable, Barbara Stanwyck. Adolphe Menjou, Roland Winters, Will Geer, Emory Parnell, Frank Jenks. Unremarkable love story of reporter Stanwyck and race-car driver-heel Gable.▼

Top Man (1943) **74m.** **½ D: Charles Lamont. Donald O'Connor, Susanna Foster, Peggy Ryan, Richard Dix, Anne Gwynne, Lillian Gish, Noah Beery, Jr., Samuel S. Hinds, Louise Beavers, Count Basie and His Orchestra, Borrah Minnevitch and His Harmonica Rascals. When his father is recalled into active service, teenaged O'Connor becomes the head of the family. Oddly comical Oedipal situation, with a sidebar pitch for high schoolers to volunteer at defense plants, is frequently interrupted by swell musical numbers. Surprising to see Gish in an absolutely ordinary wartime mom role.

Top of the World (1955) **90m.** ** D: Lewis R. Foster. Dale Robertson, Evelyn Keyes, Frank Lovejoy, Nancy Gates. Set in Alaska, movie revolves around jet pilot Robertson, his ex-wife Keyes, and her new boyfriend Lovejoy.

Top o' the Morning (1949) **100m.** **½ D: David Miller. Bing Crosby, Barry Fitzgerald, Ann Blyth, Hume Cronyn, John McIntire, Eileen Crowe. Crosby-Fitzgerald malarkey is wearing thin in this fanciful musical of Bing searching for thief hiding the Blarney Stone.

Topper (1937) **97m.** ***½ D: Norman Z. McLeod. Constance Bennett, Cary Grant, Roland Young, Billie Burke, Alan Mowbray, Eugene Pallette, Arthur Lake, Hedda Hopper. Delightful gimmick comedy with ghosts Grant and Bennett dominating life of meek Young; sparkling cast in adaptation of Thorne Smith novel, scripted by Jack Jevne, Eddie Moran, and Eric Hatch. Followed by two sequels, a TV series, and a 1979 TV remake starring Kate Jackson and Andrew Stevens. Also shown in computer-colored version (the first b&w film to be "colorized," in 1985).▼❿

Topper Returns (1941) **88m.** *** D: Roy Del Ruth. Joan Blondell, Roland Young, Carole Landis, Billie Burke, Dennis O'Keefe,

Patsy Kelly, Eddie "Rochester" Anderson. Topper helps ghostly Blondell solve her own murder in the last of this series, with hilarious results. Also shown in computer-colored version. ▼◉)

Topper Takes a Trip (1939) 85m. *** D: Norman Z. McLeod. Constance Bennett, Roland Young, Billie Burke, Alan Mowbray, Verree Teasdale, Franklin Pangborn. Cary Grant is missing (except in a flashback), but rest of cast returns for repeat success as Young is frustrated on Riviera vacation by ghostess Bennett. Also shown in computer-colored version. ▼

Top Secret Affair (1957) 100m. **½ D: H. C. Potter. Susan Hayward, Kirk Douglas, Paul Stewart, Jim Backus, John Cromwell. John P. Marquand's *Melville Goodwin, U.S.A.* becomes fair comedy, with most credit going to Hayward as fiery publisher who knows all about the past of Senate appointee (Douglas). ◗

Tops Is the Limit SEE: **Anything Goes** (1936)

Top Speed (1930) 71m. *** D: Mervyn LeRoy. Joe E. Brown, Bernice Claire, Jack Whiting, Frank McHugh, Laura Lee, Rita Flynn, Edwin Maxwell. Big-mouth bond clerk Brown and pal Whiting pose as millionaires at a fancy hotel to impress a couple of rich cuties. One of Brown's best vehicles, a funny musical comedy (from the show by Bert Kalmar, Harry Ruby, and Guy Bolton), with zippy production numbers, some racy gags, and a wild speedboat race finale.

Torch, The (1950-Mexican) 90m. ** D: Emilio Fernandez. Paulette Goddard, Pedro Armendariz, Gilbert Roland, Walter Reed. Mexican revolutionary captures town and falls for daughter of nobility. Rare English-language effort by Mexico's top director; a shame it isn't better. Remake of Fernandez's ENAMORADA (1946), with Armendariz repeating his role. Both films beautifully photographed by Gabriel Figueroa. ▼◗

Torch Singer (1933) 71m. *** D: Alexander Hall, George Somnes. Claudette Colbert, Ricardo Cortez, David Manners, Lyda Roberti, Baby LeRoy, Florence Roberts, Charley Grapewin, Cora Sue Collins. A poor unwed mother tries to make it on her own but finally has to give up her child. She then becomes a notorious nightclub chanteuse and secretly moonlights as the host of a radio show for kiddies, which she uses to try to find her child. Colbert was never better—by turns sweet, vulnerable, sexy, and sophisticated. (She also reveals the "dark side of the moon," the little-seen right side of her face.) Funny, sentimental pre-Code examination of women's roles in a man's world. Featured song: "Give Me Liberty or Give Me Love." ◗

Torch Song (1953) C-90m. **½ D: Charles Walters. Joan Crawford, Michael Wilding, Marjorie Rambeau, Gig Young, Henry (Harry) Morgan, Dorothy Patrick, Benny Rubin, Nancy Gates. Crawford is hard as nails as a Broadway musical star who chews up people for lunch—until she meets blind pianist Wilding, who isn't cowed by her. Glossy, often hilariously clichéd drama reminds us that It's Lonely At the Top. There's one absurd musical number in which Crawford appears in blackface! Her "clumsy" dance partner in the opening number is director Walters, a former dancer and choreographer. ▼◉)

Torchy Blane Glenda Farrell was one of the leading lights of the Warner Bros. stock company; she could always be counted on to add zip and zest to a film, especially if provided with good wisecracks by the screenwriters. Her reward was a series of her own, *Torchy Blane,* which was adapted from a series of pulp magazine stories by the prolific Frederick Nebel. Nebel's mystery-solving reporter was a man, and his name was Kennedy, but the gender switch worked. In every film, Torchy matches wits with police lieutenant Steve McBride, who never quite seems to understand what's going on. It's usually up to Torchy to solve the case at hand, which causes Steve certain embarrassment, since he and Torchy are engaged to be married. Barton MacLane's casting as McBride rescued him from playing the same harsh-mouthed bad guys over and over again, but his part wasn't well written enough to make him terribly endearing. Comic actor Tom Kennedy was cast as Gahagan, McBride's right hand and the dumbest cop ever to hit the screen (though the recurring character of the desk sergeant, played in most cases by George Guhl, just might be his equal). There is nothing to distinguish these quickly made B pictures except for the usual Warner Bros. pizzazz, and the snap of Glenda Farrell. The first film in the series, SMART BLONDE, is easily the best (and the only one to be based directly on a Nebel story); most of the others are quite forgettable. Lola Lane and Paul Kelly replaced Farrell and MacLane for one episode, TORCHY BLANE IN PANAMA; Jane Wyman and Allen Jenkins finished off the series in TORCHY BLANE . . . PLAYING WITH DYNAMITE.

TORCHY BLANE

Smart Blonde (1936)
Fly-Away Baby (1937)
Adventurous Blonde (1937)
Blondes at Work (1938)
Torchy Blane in Panama (1938)
Torchy Gets Her Man (1938)
Torchy Blane in Chinatown (1939)
Torchy Runs for Mayor (1939)
Torchy Blane . . . Playing With Dynamite (1939)

Torchy Blane in Chinatown (1939) **59m.** *½ D: William Beaudine. Glenda Farrell, Barton MacLane, Tom Kennedy, Patric Knowles, Henry O'Neill, James Stephenson. Torchy and fiancé Steve get mixed up with jade smuggling and murder in this tiresome and confusing series episode. Remake of a 1930 film, MURDER WILL OUT which itself was later remade in 1940. ▶

Torchy Blane in Panama (1938) **58m.** *½ D: William Clemens. Lola Lane, Paul Kelly, Tom Kennedy, Anthony Averill, Larry Williams, Betty Compson. Lane and Kelly temporarily replaced Glenda Farrell and Barton MacLane in this indifferent entry about New York bank robbers who flee to Panama on an ocean liner. ▶

Torchy Blane . . . Playing With Dynamite (1939) **59m.** ** D: Noel Smith. Jane Wyman, Allen Jenkins, Tom Kennedy, Sheila Bromley, Joe Cunningham, Eddie Marr. Wyman, who had a small part in the first Torchy Blane entry, plays the lead in this farcical final episode, in which she goes to jail undercover to get the goods on a crook. Jenkins, replacing Barton MacLane, is very funny. ▶

Torchy Gets Her Man (1938) **62m.** ** D: William Beaudine. Glenda Farrell, Barton MacLane, Tom Kennedy, Willard Robertson, George Guhl, John Ridgely, Tommy Jackson. Farrell and MacLane returned for this mostly comical addition to the series, with Torchy in hot pursuit of a counterfeiting gang. ▶

Torchy Runs for Mayor (1939) **58m.** **½ D: Ray McCarey. Glenda Farrell, Barton MacLane, Tom Kennedy, John Miljan, Frank Shannon, Joe Cunningham, Irving Bacon. Torchy digs up some dirt on corrupt politicians and you can guess the rest from the title. Pretty good series entry with some very snappy dialogue. ▶

Torment (1944-Swedish) **100m.** ***½ D: Alf Sjoberg. Mai Zetterling, Stig Jarrel, Alf Kjellin, Olof Winnerstrand. Schoolboy Kjellin and girl he falls in love with (Zetterling) are hounded by sadistic teacher Jarrel. Moody and evocative, with a script by Ingmar Bergman. Also known as FRENZY. ▼▶

Tormented (1960) **75m.** BOMB D: Bert I. Gordon. Richard Carlson, Juli Reding, Susan Gordon, Lugene Sanders, Joe Turkel, Lillian Adams. Low-budget hogwash of guilt-ridden pianist dubious over his forthcoming marriage to society woman. Weak ghost story. ▼▶

Torpedo Alley (1953) **84m.** ** D: Lew Landers. Dorothy Malone, Mark Stevens, Charles Winninger, Bill Williams. Typical Korean War actioner involving U.S. submarine offensives. Look fast for Charles Bronson as sub crew member. ▶

Torpedo Bay (1963-Italian-French) **91m.** **½ D: Charles Frend. James Mason, Lilli Palmer, Gabriele Ferzetti, Alberto Lupo, Geoffrey Keen. British and Italian naval crews meet on neutral territory during WW2; modest but fairly interesting drama.

Torpedo Run (1958) **C-98m.** **½ D: Joseph Pevney. Glenn Ford, Ernest Borgnine, Diane Brewster, Dean Jones. Sluggish WW2 revenge narrative of sub-commander Ford whose family was aboard Jap prison ship he had to blow up. CinemaScope ▼▶

Torrent (1926) **87m.** *** D: Monta Bell. Ricardo Cortez, Greta Garbo, Gertrude Olmstead, Edward Connelly, Lucien Littlefield, Tully Marshall, Mack Swain. Garbo stars in her first American film as a Spanish peasant girl who becomes a famous prima donna after being deserted by nobleman Cortez, whose life is ruled by his mother. A still entertaining tale of lost love, based on a Blasco-Ibanez novel. ▶

Torrid Zone (1940) **88m.** ***½ D: William Keighley. James Cagney, Ann Sheridan, Pat O'Brien, Andy Devine, Helen Vinson, Jerome Cowan, George Tobias, George Reeves. South-of-the-border comedy, action and romance with nightclub star Sheridan helping plantation owner O'Brien keep Cagney from leaving. Zesty dialogue (scripted by Richard Macauley and Jerry Wald) in this variation on THE FRONT PAGE. ●▶

Tortilla Flat (1942) **105m.** *** D: Victor Fleming. Spencer Tracy, Hedy Lamarr, John Garfield, Frank Morgan, Akim Tamiroff, Sheldon Leonard, Donald Meek, John Qualen, Allen Jenkins. Steinbeck's salty novel of California fishing community vividly portrayed by three top stars, stolen by Morgan as devoted dog lover. Also shown in computer-colored version. ▼●▶

To the Ends of the Earth (1948) **109m.** ***½ D: Robert Stevenson. Dick Powell, Signe Hasso, Ludwig Donath, Vladimir Sokoloff, Edgar Barrier. Fast-moving thriller of government agent tracking down narcotics smuggling ring has good acting and ironic ending.

To the Shores of Tripoli (1942) **C-86m.** **½ D: H. Bruce Humberstone. John Payne, Maureen O'Hara, Randolph Scott, Nancy Kelly, William Tracy, Maxie Rosenbloom, Iris Adrian. Spoiled rich boy Payne joins Marines with off-handed attitude, doesn't wake up until film's end. Routine. ▼▶

To the Victor (1948) **100m.** **½ D: Delmer Daves. Dennis Morgan, Viveca Lindfors, Victor Francen, Eduardo Ciannelli, Anthony Caruso, Tom D'Andrea, William Conrad, Dorothy Malone, Joseph Buloff, Bruce Bennett. Thought-provoking post-WW2 drama about an apolitical black marketer (Morgan) who becomes involved with a mystery woman (Lindfors) whose life is in danger. Richard Brooks' script attempts to deal with issues relating to war, peace, morality, and responsibility, but too many dull stretches do this in. Strikingly photographed on location in Paris and especially at Normandy's Omaha Beach.

Touch and Go (1955-British) **C-85m.** ****½** D: Michael Truman. Jack Hawkins, Margaret Johnston, Roland Culver, June Thorburn. Wry study of sturdy English family trying to overcome obstacles upsetting their planned emigration to Australia.

Touchez Pas au Grisbi (1954-French) **94m. ***½** D: Jacques Becker. Jean Gabin, René Dary, Jeanne Moreau, Dora Doll, Gaby Basset, Denise Clair, Michel Jourdan, Daniel Cauchy, Lino Ventura. An elegant French gangster who's pulled off a daring heist forsakes his plan to keep the loot under wraps in order to save the life of his impetuous best friend. As much an observation about a certain way of life as it is a crime thriller; unpretentious and skillfully made, with a typically commanding performance by the incomparable Gabin. Aka GRISBI. ▼D

Touch of Evil (1958) **111m. ****** D: Orson Welles. Charlton Heston, Orson Welles, Janet Leigh, Joseph Calleia, Akim Tamiroff, Marlene Dietrich, Dennis Weaver, Valentin de Vargas, Mort Mills, Victor Milian, Joanna Moore, Zsa Zsa Gabor. Narc Heston and corrupt cop Welles tangle over murder investigation in sleazy Mexican border town, with Heston's bride Leigh the pawn of their struggle. Fantastic, justifiably famous opening shot merely commences stylistic masterpiece, dazzlingly photographed by Russell Metty. Great Latin rock score by Henry Mancini; neat unbilled cameos by Joseph Cotten, Ray Collins, and especially Mercedes McCambridge. Originally released at 93m. Years later a 108m. preview print was unearthed and reissued. Then the film was reconstructed in 1998 by Walter Murch, using Welles' notes, to present length. ▼O

Touch of Larceny, A (1959-British) **93m. ***** D: Guy Hamilton. James Mason, George Sanders, Vera Miles, Oliver Johnston, William Kendall, Duncan Lamont. Ingenious comedy of officer who uses availability of military secrets to his advantage in off-beat plan.

Tough as They Come (1942) **61m. **** D: William Nigh. Billy Halop, Huntz Hall, Bernard Punsly, Gabriel Dell, Helen Parrish, Paul Kelly, Ann Gillis. Contrived *Little Tough Guys* tale about law student Halop trying to straighten out a crooked credit union.

Tougher They Come, The (1950) **69m. **** D: Ray Nazarro. Wayne Morris, Preston Foster, Kay Buckley, William Bishop, Frank McHugh, Gloria Henry, Mary Castle, Joseph Crehan. Lumbering lumberjack saga has two-fisted loggers Foster and Morris battling sabotage from traitorous foreman Bishop, who is secretly working for a rival lumber combine. Stock footage of real loggers and a raging forest fire are the best things on display here.

Toughest Gun in Tombstone (1958) **72m. **** D: Earl Bellamy. George Montgomery, Jim Davis, Beverly Tyler, Gerald Milton, Don Beddoe, Scotty Morrow, Harry Lauter, Lane Bradford. Standard low-budget fare with Montgomery going undercover to break up a gang of rustlers—including the likes of Ike Clanton and Johnny Ringo, the same men who murdered his wife. ▶

Toughest Man Alive, The (1955) **72m. **** D: Sidney Salkow. Dane Clark, Lita Milan, Ross Elliott, Myrna Dell, Syd Saylor, Anthony Caruso. Mild caper with Clark a U.S. agent who goes undercover as a gun runner to sniff out the culprits who are smuggling arms to Central America.

Toughest Man in Arizona (1952) **C-90m. **½** D: R. G. Springsteen. Vaughn Monroe, Joan Leslie, Edgar Buchanan, Victor Jory. While waging war on crime, marshal Monroe falls for girl with expected results. Weak Western vehicle for crooner Monroe.

Tough Guy (1936) **76m. **½** D: Chester Franklin. Jackie Cooper, Joseph Calleia, Rin Tin Tin, Jr., Harvey Stephens, Jean Hersholt, Edward Pawley, Mischa Auer. Cooper is a rich kid who runs away with Rinty because his father doesn't like the pooch. Calleia is a crook he meets along the way, and the two develop an unusual bond. Efficient, fast-moving blend of gunplay and tears.

Tovarich (1937) **98m. ***** D: Anatole Litvak. Claudette Colbert, Charles Boyer, Basil Rathbone, Anita Louise, Melville Cooper, Isabel Jeans, Morris Carnovsky. Boyer and Colbert, royal Russians who fled the Revolution with court treasury but nothing for themselves, are reduced to working as servants. Enjoyable but dated romantic comedy set in Paris. Based on a French play Americanized by Robert E. Sherwood.

Toward the Unknown (1956) **C-115m. ***** D: Mervyn LeRoy. William Holden, Lloyd Nolan, Virginia Leith, Charles McGraw, Murray Hamilton, Paul Fix, James Garner, L. Q. Jones, Karen Steele, Jon Provost. Intelligent, crisply filmed precursor to THE RIGHT STUFF spotlights tarnished air officer Holden, who cracked under pressure while a POW in Korea. He must overcome the skepticism of his fellow flyers as he attempts to reestablish himself as a test pilot. Filmed on location at California's Edwards Air Force Base. Garner's film debut. ▶

Tower of London (1939) **92m. **½** D: Rowland V. Lee. Basil Rathbone, Boris Karloff, Barbara O'Neil, Ian Hunter, Vincent Price, Nan Grey, Leo G. Carroll, John Sutton, Miles Mander, Donnie Dunagan. Muddled historical melodrama (not a horror film, as many believe), with Rathbone as unscrupulous, power-hungry Richard III and Karloff as his dutiful executioner Mord. Court intrigue leads to uninspired battle scenes. Same-named 1962 movie has little in common with this—except the historical figures. ▼❼

Tower of London (1962) **79m.** *½ D: Roger Corman. Vincent Price, Michael Pate, Joan Freeman, Robert Brown. Price gives his all as Richard III, who dispatches his rivals for the crown of England, but this is a far cry from Shakespeare, and not even up to par for director Corman. Has little in common with the 1939 film of the same name, in which Price played the Duke of Clarence. ▼❶

Town Like Alice, A (1956-British) **107m.** **½ D: Jack Lee. Virginia McKenna, Peter Finch, Maureen Swanson, Vincent Ball. Taut WW2 tale, well acted, about Japanese oppression of female British POWs in Malaysia. Based on Nevil Shute's novel, later remade as TV miniseries. Retitled: RAPE OF MALAYA.▼❶❶

Town on Trial (1956-British) **96m.** **½ D: John Guillermin. John Mills, Charles Coburn, Derek Farr, Barbara Bates, Alec McCowen. A murder investigation in a small British town, where there's no shortage of suspects. Low-key drama makes good use of natural locations. ❶

Town Tamer (1965) **C-89m.** ** D: Lesley Selander. Dana Andrews, Terry Moore, Pat O'Brien, Lon Chaney (Jr.), Bruce Cabot, Lyle Bettger, Coleen Gray, Barton MacLane, Richard Arlen, Richard Jaeckel, Sonny Tufts. As title indicates, Andrews cleans up community, and among the rubble are some veteran actors. Routine Western has minor nostalgia value, in light of the cast. Techniscope.

Town Went Wild, The (1944) **78m.** ** D: Ralph Murphy. Freddie Bartholomew, Jimmy Lydon, Edward Everett Horton, Tom Tully, Jill Browning, Minna Gombell. Fitfully amusing Poverty-Row comedy concerning two feuding families and the interesting possibility that their children were switched at birth. ▼❶

Town Without Pity (1961) **105m.** **½ D: Gottfried Reinhardt. Kirk Douglas, E. G. Marshall, Christine Kaufmann, Robert Blake, Richard Jaeckel, Frank Sutton, Barbara Rutting. Courtroom drama of G.I.s accused of raping German girl. Decent cast, but could have been better handled. Title song, sung by Gene Pitney, was a big hit. Filmed in Germany.▼❶

Toys in the Attic (1963) **90m.** **½ D: George Roy Hill. Dean Martin, Geraldine Page, Yvette Mimieux, Wendy Hiller, Gene Tierney, Larry Gates, Nan Martin. Timid adaptation (by James Poe) of Lillian Hellman play about man returning home to New Orleans with childlike bride; Page and Hiller are Martin's overprotective sisters. Panavision.▼❶

Toy Tiger (1956) **C-88m.** **½ D: Jerry Hopper. Jeff Chandler, Laraine Day, Tim Hovey, Cecil Kellaway, Richard Haydn, David Janssen. Pleasant remake of MAD ABOUT MUSIC with Hovey "adopting" Chandler as his father to back up tales to school chums about a real dad.

Toy Wife, The (1938) **95m.** ** D: Richard Thorpe. Luise Rainer, Melvyn Douglas, Robert Young, Barbara O'Neil, H. B. Warner, Alma Kruger, Libby Taylor. In the pre–Civil War South, lively belle Rainer weds lawyer Douglas even though Young would be a more suitable match. Inconsequential drama based on Ludovic Halévy and Henri Meilhac's play *Frou-frou* and Augustin Daly's American version. Previously filmed in 1914, 1917 (as A HUNGRY HEART, with Alice Brady), 1918, and 1923. ❶

Track of the Cat (1954) **C-102m.** ** D: William Wellman. Robert Mitchum, Teresa Wright, Tab Hunter, Diana Lynn, Beulah Bondi, Philip Tonge, William Hopper, Carl ("Alfalfa") Switzer. Tennessee Williams meets American Gothic in this unusually harsh drama about a household filled with bitterness, regret, and envy, and how the hunt for a killer cougar changes the dynamics of the family. A. I. Bezzerides adapted the story by Walter Van Tilburg Clark; William Clothier's "colorless" palette, and daring camera angles, are the film's strongest assets. ❶

Track the Man Down (1955-British) **75m.** ** D: R. G. Springsteen. Kent Taylor, Petula Clark, Renee Houston, George Rose. Dog-tracking background makes this standard Scotland Yard murder hunt above par. ❶

Trader Horn (1931) **120m.** *** D: W. S. Van Dyke II. Harry Carey, Edwina Booth, Duncan Renaldo, Olive Golden (Carey), Mutia Omoolu, C. Aubrey Smith. Early talkie classic filmed largely in African jungles still retains plenty of excitement in tale of veteran native dealer Carey encountering tribal hostility. Remade in 1973.▼

Trade Winds (1938) **90m.** *** D: Tay Garnett. Fredric March, Joan Bennett, Ralph Bellamy, Ann Sothern, Sidney Blackmer, Thomas Mitchell. Debonair detective March goes after murder suspect Bennett; by the end of the around-the-world chase, they fall in love and solve mystery. Director Garnett filmed background footage on round-the-world cruise, but the stars never left the studio! This is the film where Bennett went from blonde to brunette—and never went back.

Traffic in Souls (1913) **74m.** **½ D: George Loane Tucker. Jane Gail, Ethel Grandin, William Turner, Matt Moore, William Welsh, William Cavanaugh. Lurid drama about a pair of sisters and how they unwittingly become involved with a band of white slavers. The first and most famous of the "white slave" exploitation features that were popular during the 1910s; once highly controversial, but now a trashy, corny guilty pleasure. ▼❶

Tragedy of Othello: The Moor of Venice, The SEE: **Othello** (1952-Italian)

Trail Beyond, The (1934) 55m. **★★½** D: Robert N. Bradbury. John Wayne, Verna Hillie, Noah Beery, Noah Beery, Jr., Robert Frazer, Iris Lancaster, Earl Dwire. Wayne goes into northwest wilderness searching for mentor's missing niece and a gold mine. One of Wayne's better Lone Star efforts, based on James Oliver Curwood's novel *The Wolf Hunters*. Beautifully shot in what is now King's Canyon National Park by Archie Stout. Daredevil water leaps and stunts by Yakima Canutt, including one that misfired for all to see!▼❶

Trail Dust (1936) 77m. **★★★** D: Nate Watt. William Boyd, Jimmy Ellison, George Hayes, Stephen Morris (Morris Ankrum), Gwynne Shipman, Britt Wood. Hopalong Cassidy and cowhands compete against unscrupulous profiteers driving herds to drought-ridden area, desperate to acquire stock for food. Timely Dust Bowl story, faithfully adapted from same-named 1934 novel by Clarence E. Mulford. One of the series' finest efforts. ▼❶

Trail of '98, The (1928) 87m. **★★★** D: Clarence Brown. Dolores Del Rio, Ralph Forbes, Karl Dane, Harry Carey, Tully Marshall, George Cooper, Russell Simpson, Emily Fitzroy. Celebrated silent epic charting the effects of gold fever on various characters who leave home and embark on a grueling trek to Alaska during the Klondike gold rush of 1898. You can practically feel the bitter wind and freezing snow in this entertaining "Northern Western," with a vivid you-are-there quality and several spectacular scenes.❶

Trail of Robin Hood (1950) C-67m. **★★★** D: William Witney. Roy Rogers, Penny Edwards, Gordon Jones, Jack Holt, Emory Parnell, Clifton Young, Carol Nugent, Foy Willing and the Riders of the Purple Sage. Roy's final Trucolor Western has him rounding up a host of Western guest stars—Rex Allen, Allan "Rocky" Lane, Monte Hale, Tom Tyler, William Farnum, Ray "Crash" Corrigan, Kermit Maynard, Tom Keene—to help thwart Christmas tree rustlers. Delightful; the perfect Christmas Western.▼❶

Trail of the Lonesome Pine, The (1936) C-99m. **★★★** D: Henry Hathaway. Sylvia Sidney, Henry Fonda, Fred MacMurray, Fred Stone, Fuzzy Knight, Beulah Bondi, Spanky McFarland, Nigel Bruce. Classic story of feuding families and changes that come about when railroad is built on their land. Still strong today, with fine performances, and Fuzzy Knight's rendition of "Melody from the Sky." First outdoor film

in full Technicolor. Previously filmed in 1915.▼❶

Trail of the Vigilantes (1940) 78m. **★★½** D: Allan Dwan. Franchot Tone, Warren William, Broderick Crawford, Peggy Moran, Andy Devine, Mischa Auer, Porter Hall. Tone is Eastern law enforcer out West to hunt down outlaw gang; lively comedy-Western.

Trail Street (1947) 84m. **★★½** D: Ray Enright. Randolph Scott, Anne Jeffreys, Robert Ryan, George "Gabby" Hayes, Madge Meredith, Steve Brodie. Fast-paced Western in which Bat Masterson (Scott) takes on murderers, robbers, cattle rustlers, and other ornery critters in the town of Liberal, Kansas.▼❶

Trail to San Antone (1947) 67m. **★★** D: John English. Gene Autry, Peggy Stewart, Sterling Holloway, William Henry, Johnny Duncan, Tristram Coffin, Dorothy Vaughan, Ralph Peters, Cass County Boys. Gene tries to help a young jockey (Duncan) ride again in this odd Western entry. No real outlaws or excitement in one of Autry's later Republic Pictures vehicles. ▼❶

Train, The (1964) 133m. **★★★★** D: John Frankenheimer. Burt Lancaster, Paul Scofield, Jeanne Moreau, Michel Simon, Suzanne Flon, Wolfgang Preiss, Albert Remy. Gripping WW2 actioner of French Resistance trying to waylay train carting French art treasures to Germany. High-powered excitement all the way.▼❶❶

Traitor's Gate (1964-British-German) 85m. **★★★** D: Freddie Francis. Albert Lieven, Gary Raymond, Catherina von Schell (Catherine Schell), Margot Trooger, Klaus Kinski, Heinz Bernard, Eddi Arent, Edward Underdown. Suspenseful and entertaining Edgar Wallace thriller (adapted by Jimmy Sangster) about a meticulous plot to steal the crown jewels from the Tower of London by abducting a guard and replacing him with a look-alike escaped convict.

Tramp, Tramp, Tramp (1926) 62m. **★★½** D: Harry Edwards. Harry Langdon, Joan Crawford, Edwards Davis, Carlton Griffin, Alec B. Francis, Brooks Benedict, Tom Murray. Langdon made his feature debut in this tale of a hobo who enters a cross-country walking race to raise money for his father and impress the pretty daughter (Crawford) of a shoe manufacturer. Frank Capra was one of the writers of this cute comedy featuring some impressive stunt sequences.▼❶

Tramp, Tramp, Tramp (1942) 70m. **★½** D: Charles Barton. Jackie Gleason, Florence Rice, Jack Durant, Bruce Bennett. Meager comedy as Gleason and Durant, 4-F rejects, protect the homefront, becoming involved in murder caper.

Transatlantic Merry-Go-Round (1934) 92m. **★★** D: Ben Stoloff. Jack Benny, Nancy Carroll, Gene Raymond, Sidney Blackmer, Patsy Kelly, Mitzi Green, The Boswell Sisters. Whodunit set against musical story of oceangoing radio troupe led by Benny. Just fair, with some odd production numbers, and a plot resolution that's for the birds. But the Boswell Sisters are great.▼

Trans-Atlantic Tunnel (1935-British) **70m. **½ D: Maurice Elvey. Richard Dix, Leslie Banks, Madge Evans, Helen Vinson, C. Aubrey Smith, George Arliss, Walter Huston. Disappointing story about building of transatlantic tunnel bogs down in two-dimensional character conflicts. Futuristic sets are main distinction. Originally 94m. and titled THE TUNNEL.▼🅓

Transgression (1931) **70m. ** D: Herbert Brenon. Kay Francis. Paul Cavanagh, Ricardo Cortez, Nance O'Neil, Doris Lloyd, John St. Polis. Happily married Francis' husband is on assignment in India, so she heads off to Paris and is romanced by suave, assertive Cortez. Melodramatic soaper of guilt and recrimination.

Trap, The (1947) **68m. *½** D: Howard Bretherton. Sidney Toler, Mantan Moreland, Victor Sen Yung, Tanis Chandler, Larry Blake, Kirk Alyn, Rita Quigley, Anne Nagel. Toler's swan song as Charlie Chan, about a series of murders striking actors at Malibu beach.▼🅓

Trap, The (1959) **C-84m. **½** D: Norman Panama. Richard Widmark, Lee J. Cobb, Tina Louise, Earl Holliman, Carl Benton Reid, Lorne Greene. Turgid drama set in Southwest desert town, with gangsters on the lam intimidating the few townspeople.▼🅓

Trapeze (1956) **C-105m. *** D: Carol Reed. Burt Lancaster, Tony Curtis, Gina Lollobrigida, Katy Jurado, Thomas Gomez, Johnny Puleo. Moody love triangle with a European circus background; aerialists Lancaster and Curtis vie in the air and on the ground for Gina's attention. Nice aerial stunt work by various big top professionals. CinemaScope. ▼🅞🅓

Trapped (1949) **78m. **½** D: Richard Fleischer. Lloyd Bridges, Barbara Payton, John Hoyt, James Todd, Russ Conway, Robert Karnes. The FBI's hot on the trail of a gang of counterfeiters in this so-so thriller, done in the semi-documentary style typical of that era.▼🅓

Trapped by Boston Blackie (1948) **67m. **½** D: Seymour Friedman. Chester Morris, June Vincent, Richard Lane, Patricia White (Barry), Edward Norris, George E. Stone, Frank Sully. Blackie springs into action to clear himself when an expensive pearl necklace disappears from a party for which he was a security guard.

Trauma (1962) **92m. ** D: Robert Malcolm Young. John Conte, Lynn Bari, Lorrie Richards, David Garner, Warren Kemmerling. Heavy-handed chiller about Richards' attempt to recover lost memory of past horrors in spooky mansion.🅓

Traveling Saleslady (1935) **63m. **½** D:

Ray Enright. Joan Blondell, Glenda Farrell, William Gargan, Hugh Herbert, Grant Mitchell, Ruth Donnelly. Snappy programmer with Blondell helping to put over inventor Herbert's booze-flavored toothpaste in order to teach her stubborn father (a rival toothpaste manufacturer) a lesson.🅓

Traveling Saleswoman (1950) **75m. ** D: Charles F. Riesner. Joan Davis, Andy Devine, Adele Jergens, Chief Thundercloud. Davis and Devine mug it up as soap sales woman and fiancé in stale Western comedy.🅓

Tread Softly Stranger (1958-British) **90m. **½** D: Gordon Parry. Diana Dors, George Baker, Terence Morgan, Patrick Allen, Jane Griffiths, Joseph Tomelty. Sultry Dors comes between two brothers in a dreary British factory town in this atmospheric drama.🅓

Treasure Island (1934) **105m. ***½** D: Victor Fleming. Wallace Beery, Jackie Cooper, Lewis Stone, Lionel Barrymore, Otto Kruger, Nigel Bruce, Douglass Dumbrille. Stirring adaptation of Robert Louis Stevenson pirate yarn of 18th-century England and journey to isle of hidden bounty; Beery is a boisterous Long John Silver in fine film with top production values. Only flaw is a stiff Cooper as Jim Hawkins. Also shown in computer-colored version.▼🅓

Treasure Island (1950) **C-96m. ***½** D: Byron Haskin. Bobby Driscoll, Robert Newton, Basil Sydney, Walter Fitzgerald, Denis O'Dea, Ralph Truman, Finlay Currie. Vivid Disney version of Robert Louis Stevenson's classic, filmed in England, with Driscoll a fine Jim Hawkins and Newton *the* definitive Long John Silver. Changes the novel's original ending, but who's quibbling? ▼🅞🅓

Treasure of Fear SEE: **Scared Stiff** (1945)

Treasure of Lost Canyon, The (1952) **C-82m. ** D: Ted Tetzlaff. William Powell, Julia (Julie) Adams, Rosemary DeCamp, Charles Drake, Tommy Ivo. Mild Western, uplifted by Powell as old prospector. Youth uncovers treasure which causes unhappiness to all. From a Robert Louis Stevenson story.▼🅓

Treasure of Monte Cristo (1949) **79m. ** D: William Berke. Glenn Langan, Adele Jergens, Steve Brodie, Robert Jordan, Michael Whelan, Sid Melton. Jergens marries seaman Langan, a descendant of the Count of Monte Cristo, for his inheritance, then falls in love with him. Adequate programmer.🅓

Treasure of Pancho Villa, The (1955) **C-96m. *½** D: George Sherman. Rory Calhoun, Shelley Winters, Gilbert Roland, Joseph Calleia. Good cast wasted in plodding account of Calhoun and Roland's search for gold. SuperScope.▼

Treasure of Ruby Hills (1955) **71m. *½**

D: Frank McDonald. Zachary Scott, Carole Matthews, Barton MacLane, Dick Foran, Lola Albright, Gordon Jones, Raymond Hatton, Lee Van Cleef. Scott gets involved with scheming ranchers in an Arizona town; uninspired Western. ▶

Treasure of the Golden Condor (1953) C-93m. **½ D: Delmer Daves. Cornel Wilde, Constance Smith, Fay Wray, Anne Bancroft, Leo G. Carroll, Bobby (Robert) Blake. Predictable costumer set in 18th-century Latin America, with noble-born Wilde out to claim his fortune. Remake of SON OF FURY.▼▶

Treasure of the Sierra Madre, The (1948) **124m.** **** D: John Huston. Humphrey Bogart, Walter Huston, Tim Holt, Bruce Bennett, Barton MacLane, Alfonso Bedoya. Excellent adaptation of B. Traven's tale of gold, greed, and human nature at its worst, with Bogart, Huston, and Holt as unlikely trio of prospectors. John Huston won Oscars for Best Direction and Screenplay, and his father Walter won as Best Supporting Actor. That's John as an American tourist near the beginning, and young Robert Blake selling lottery tickets. Also shown in computer-colored version.▼▶

Tree Grows in Brooklyn, A (1945) **128m.** **** D: Elia Kazan. Dorothy McGuire, Joan Blondell, James Dunn, Lloyd Nolan, Peggy Ann Garner, Ted Donaldson, James Gleason, Ruth Nelson, John Alexander. Splendid, sensitive film from Betty Smith's novel about a bright young girl trying to rise above the hardships of her tenement life in turn-of-the-20th-century Brooklyn, New York. Perfect in every detail. Dunn won an Oscar as the father, an incurable pipe dreamer; Garner received a special Academy Award for her performance. Screenplay by Tess Slesinger and Frank Davis. An impressive Hollywood directorial debut by Kazan. Remade for TV in 1974 with Cliff Robertson and Diane Baker.▼▶

Trent's Last Case (1952-British) **90m.** **½ D: Herbert Wilcox. Michael Wilding, Margaret Lockwood, Orson Welles, Hugh McDermott. Superior cast in lukewarm tale of the investigation of businessman's death. Previously filmed (by Howard Hawks) in 1929.

Trial (1955) **105m.** *** D: Mark Robson. Glenn Ford, Dorothy McGuire, John Hodiak, Arthur Kennedy, Katy Jurado, Rafael Campos. Intelligent filming of Don Mankiewicz novel, scripted by the author. Courtroomer involves Mexican boy accused of murder, but actually tied in with pro- vs. anti-Communist politics. ▶

Trial, The (1962-French-Italian-German) **118m.** ***½ D: Orson Welles. Anthony Perkins, Jeanne Moreau, Romy Schneider, Elsa Martinelli, Orson Welles, Akim Tamiroff. Gripping, if a bit confusing, adaptation of Kafka novel of man in nameless country arrested for crime that is never explained to him. Not for all tastes.▼▶

Trial and Error (1962-British) SEE: **Dock Brief, The**

Trial of Mary Dugan, The (1929) **114m.** ** D: Bayard Veiller. Norma Shearer, Lewis Stone, H. B. Warner, Raymond Hackett, Lilyan Tashman, Olive Tell. Stagy adaptation of director Veiller's hit play about a "fallen woman" (Shearer, chewing up the scenery) accused of killing her wealthy lover. MGM's first all-talkie is historically interesting but stiff as a board and drags on forever. Remade in 1941 with Laraine Day.

Trial of Vivienne Ware, The (1932) **56m.** *** D: William K. Howard. Joan Bennett, Donald Cook, Richard "Skeets" Gallagher, ZaSu Pitts, Lilian Bond, Alan Dinehart, Herbert Mundin. Incredibly fast-moving courtroom yarn in which Bennett is defended by ex-beau Cook when she's accused of killing her faithless fiancé, while the trial is broadcast live on the radio! A virtual textbook of early '30s filmmaking techniques, chock-full of whip-pans, jump-cuts, wipes, dissolves, tilted camera angles, and a flashback-laden narrative jammed with mystery and comic relief, all in less than an hour. Possibly the speediest film ever made.

Trials of Oscar Wilde, The (1960-British) C-123m. *** D: Ken Hughes. Peter Finch, Yvonne Mitchell, John Fraser, Lionel Jeffries, Nigel Patrick, James Mason. Fascinating, well-acted chronicle of Oscar Wilde's libel suit against the Marquis of Queensberry and the tragic turn his life takes because of it. Finch is superb as the once brilliant wit; stylish widescreen photography by Ted Moore. Released at the same time as OSCAR WILDE with Robert Morley. Super Technirama 70.▼

Tribute to a Bad Man (1956) C-95m. *** D: Robert Wise. James Cagney, Don Dubbins, Stephen McNally, Irene Papas, Vic Morrow, Royal Dano, Lee Van Cleef. Cagney is the whole show in this Western about a resourceful, ruthless land baron using any means possible to retain his vast possessions. CinemaScope.▼▶

Trigger, Jr. (1950) C-68m. *** D: William Witney. Roy Rogers, Dale Evans, Pat Brady, Gordon Jones, Grant Withers, George Cleveland, Peter Miles, Foy Willing and the Riders of the Purple Sage. Villain Withers sets loose a killer horse in order to terrorize local ranchers into joining his protective association. A young boy (Miles), deathly afraid of horses, surmounts his fear and saves the day for Roy. Remarkable horse scenes and touching performances make it one of Roy's best . . . though Jones' oafish comedy relief is a debit.▼▶

Trigger Talk SEE: **Silent Conflict**

Trio (1950-British) **88m.** *** D: Ken Annakin, Harold French. James Hayter, Kathleen Harrison, Anne Crawford, Nigel Patrick, Jean Simmons, Michael Rennie. Following the success of QUARTET, three more diverting Somerset Maugham stories, "The Verger," "Mr. Knowall," and "Sanatorium." All beautifully acted.▼

Triple Deception (1956-British) **C-85m.** ** D: Guy Green. Michael Craig, Julia Arnall, Brenda De Banzie, Barbara Bates, David Kosoff, Geoffrey Keen, Gerard Oury, Anton Diffring, Eric Pohlmann. Adequate thriller in which sailor Craig is brought in by British and French authorities to impersonate his double, a member of a gang of counterfeiters who's just been killed in an auto accident. Original British title: HOUSE OF SECRETS. VistaVision. ▼

Triple Trouble (1950) **66m.** ** D: Jean Yarbrough. Leo Gorcey, Huntz Hall, Gabriel Dell, William Benedict, G. Pat Collins, Lyn Thomas, Bernard Gorcey, Paul Dubov, David Gorcey. The Bowery Boys are mistaken for robbers and try to catch the real culprits from behind prison bars in this wearisome entry.◗

Tripoli (1950) **C-95m.** ** D: Will Price. John Payne, Maureen O'Hara, Howard da Silva, Philip Reed, Grant Withers, Lowell Gilmore, Connie Gilchrist, Alan Napier. Good cast cannot save average script of U.S. Marines battling Barbary pirates in 1805; sole standout is da Silva.

Triumph of Sherlock Holmes, The (1935-British) **75m.** **½ D: Leslie Hiscott. Arthur Wontner, Ian Fleming, Lyn Harding, Leslie Perrins, Jane Carr, Charles Mortimer. Wontner and Fleming make a very acceptable team as Holmes and Watson in this minor British series entry about murder and a secret society among coal miners. Based on Conan Doyle's "The Valley of Fear." Original British running time: 84m.▼◗

Triumph of the Will (1935-German) **110m.** **** D: Leni Riefenstahl. Riefenstahl's infamous documentary on Hitler's 1934 Nuremberg rallies is rightly regarded as the greatest propaganda film of all time. Fascinating and (of course) frightening to see.▼◗

Trocadero (1944) **74m.** ** D: William Nigh. Rosemary Lane, Johnny Downs, Ralph Morgan, Dick Purcell, Sheldon Leonard, Marjorie Manners, Cliff Nazarro, Erskine Johnson, Dewey Robinson, Ida James, The Radio Rogues. Humdrum B musical about the ups and downs of a Hollywood nightclub. Simple story leaves ample room for songs by bandleaders Bob Chester, Eddie LeBaron, Wingy Manone, and Matty Malneck, plus amusing doubletalk by Nazarro and tableside pen-and-ink animation by Dave Fleischer.◗

Trojan Horse, The (1962-Italian) **C-105m.** **½ D: Giorgio Ferroni. Steve Reeves, John Drew Barrymore, Hedy Vessel, Juliette

Mayniel. Above-average production values and Barrymore's presence in role of Ulysses inflates rating of otherwise stale version of Homer's epic. Techniscope.▼◗

Trollenberg Terror, The SEE: **Crawling Eye, The**

Trooper Hook (1957) **81m.** **½ D: Charles Marquis Warren. Joel McCrea, Barbara Stanwyck, Earl Holliman, Susan Kohner, Sheb Wooley, Celia Lovsky. Woman scorned by whites for having lived with Indians and having child by the chief, begins anew with cavalry sergeant.◗

Troopship SEE: **Farewell Again**

Tropic Holiday (1938) **78m.** **½ D: Theodore Reed. Dorothy Lamour, Ray Milland, Martha Raye, Bob Burns, Tito Guizar. Silly musical set in Mexico, with perky performances by all.

Tropic Zone (1953) **C-94m.** *½ D: Lewis R. Foster. Ronald Reagan, Rhonda Fleming, Estelita, Noah Beery (Jr.). Blah actioner set in South America with Reagan fighting the good cause to save a banana plantation from outlaws.

Trottie True SEE: **Gay Lady, The**

Trouble Along the Way (1953) **110m.** **½ D: Michael Curtiz. John Wayne, Donna Reed, Charles Coburn, Sherry Jackson, Marie Windsor, Tom Tully, Leif Erickson, Chuck Connors. Unusually sentimental Wayne vehicle casts him as divorced man trying to maintain custody of his daughter (Jackson); he earns back self-respect by coaching football team for small Catholic school.▼◗

Trouble at 16 SEE: **Platinum High School**

Trouble for Two (1936) **75m.** *** D: J. Walter Ruben. Robert Montgomery, Rosalind Russell, Frank Morgan, Reginald Owen, Louis Hayward. Unique, offbeat black comedy of Montgomery and Russell joining London Suicide Club; based on Robert Louis Stevenson story.

Trouble in Paradise (1932) **83m.** **** D: Ernst Lubitsch. Miriam Hopkins, Kay Francis, Herbert Marshall, Charlie Ruggles, Edward Everett Horton, C. Aubrey Smith, Robert Grieg, Leonid Kinskey. Sparkling Lubitsch confection about two jewel thieves (Marshall and Hopkins) who fall in love, but find their relationship threatened when he turns on the charm to their newest (female) victim. This film is a working definition of the term "sophisticated comedy." Script by Samson Raphaelson and Grover Jones.◗▼

Trouble in Store (1953-British) **85m.** **½ D: John Paddy Carstairs. Margaret Rutherford, Norman Wisdom, Moira Lister, Megs Jenkins. Full of fun sight gags and good character actors, film traces ups and downs of naive department store worker. Wisdom's film debut.▼◗

Trouble in the Glen (1954-British) **C-91m.** ** D: Herbert Wilcox. Margaret Lockwood,

Orson Welles, Forrest Tucker, Victor McLaglen. Scottish-based drama of feud over closing of road that has been used for a long time. Average-to-poor script benefits from Welles. ▼▶

Troublemaker, The (1964) 80m. ** D: Theodore Flicker. Tom Aldredge, Joan Darling, Theodore Flicker, Buck Henry, Godfrey Cambridge, Al Freeman, Jr. Terribly dated, independently made comedy about a country bumpkin's adventures in N.Y.C.; interesting as an artifact of its time, made by the talented improvisational comedy troupe known as The Premise.

Trouble Makers (1948) 69m. ** D: Reginald LeBorg. Leo Gorcey, Huntz Hall, Gabriel Dell, Billy Benedict, David Gorcey, Helen Parrish, Fritz Feld, Lionel Stander, Frankie Darro, John Ridgely, Bennie Bartlett, Bernard Gorcey. The Bowery Boys pose as hotel bellboys to probe a murder. This was one of veteran character actor Stander's last films before being blacklisted. ▶

Trouble With Harry, The (1955) C-99m. *** D: Alfred Hitchcock. Edmund Gwenn, John Forsythe, Shirley MacLaine, Mildred Natwick, Mildred Dunnock, Jerry Mathers, Royal Dano. Offbeat, often hilarious black comedy courtesy Mr. Hitchcock and scripter John Michael Hayes about bothersome corpse causing all sorts of problems for peaceful neighbors in New England community. Gwenn is fine as usual, MacLaine appealing in her first film. Beautiful autumn locations, whimsical score (his first for Hitch) by Bernard Herrmann. VistaVision. ▼▶▶

Trouble With Women, The (1947) 80m. ** D: Sidney Lanfield. Ray Milland, Teresa Wright, Brian Donlevy, Rose Hobart, Charles Smith, Lewis Russell, Iris Adrian, Lloyd Bridges. Professor Milland announces that women like to be treated roughly; you can guess the rest of this tame comedy.

True Confession (1937) 85m. *½ D: Wesley Ruggles. Carole Lombard, Fred MacMurray, John Barrymore, Una Merkel, Porter Hall, Edgar Kennedy, Lynne Overman, Irving Bacon, Fritz Feld. Alarmingly unfunny "comedy" about pathological liar Lombard and the trouble she causes for herself and good-natured lawyer husband MacMurray when she confesses to a murder she didn't commit. Remade with Betty Hutton as CROSS MY HEART. ▶

True Heart Susie (1919) 93m. *** D: D. W. Griffith. Lillian Gish, Robert Harron, Clarine Seymour, Kate Bruce, Raymond Cannon, Carol Dempster, George Fawcett. Gish is wonderful as a plain farm girl who secretly sells her cow to send her sweetheart to college, but when he returns he becomes a minister and marries a scheming city girl. Will he learn the truth before it's too late? One of Griffith's most charmingly old-fashioned films, made with a warm innocence and purity of style that is truly refreshing. ▼▶

True Story of Jesse James, The (1957) C-92m. **½ D: Nicholas Ray. Robert Wagner, Jeffrey Hunter, Hope Lange, Agnes Moorehead, Alan Hale (Jr.), John Carradine, Alan Baxter, Frank Gorshin. Remake of 1939 Tyrone Power/Henry Fonda classic (JESSE JAMES) understandably lacks its star power, but there are enough offbeat Ray touches to keep things interesting (along with some stock footage from the original). Screenplay by Walter Newman. CinemaScope. ▶

True Story of Lynn Stuart, The (1958) 78m. **½ D: Lewis Seiler. Betsy Palmer, Jack Lord, Barry Atwater, Kim Spaulding. Modest, straightforward account of housewife Palmer posing as gun moll to trap gang.

True to Life (1943) 94m. *** D: George Marshall. Mary Martin, Franchot Tone, Dick Powell, Victor Moore, Mabel Paige, William Demarest, Ernest Truex. Engaging comedy of radio writer going to live with "typical" American family to get material for his soap opera. Not a musical, but boasts delightful Hoagy Carmichael–Johnny Mercer song "The Old Music Master."

True to the Army (1942) 76m. ** D: Albert S. Rogell. Allan Jones, Ann Miller, Judy Canova, Jerry Colonna. Zany nonsense erupts when military life and romance clash; loud WW2 escapism. This remake of SHE LOVES ME NOT was remade again as HOW TO BE VERY, VERY POPULAR.

True to the Navy (1930) 71m. ** D: Frank Tuttle. Clara Bow, Fredric March, Sam Hardy, Eddie Fetherston, Jed Prouty, Rex Bell. Silly early talkie about on-again, off-again romance between sailor March and soda-fountain waitress Bow. Buffs will get a kick out of it; Clara does one sexy dance number. Bow and Bell later married in real life.

Trumpet Blows, The (1934) 72m. ** D: Stephen Roberts. George Raft, Adolphe Menjou, Frances Drake, Sidney Toler, Edward Ellis, Nydia Westman, Katherine DeMille. Raft is oddly cast in this slight, forgettable yarn as an American-educated Mexican who returns to brother Menjou's ranch; their mutual affection for dancer Drake puts them at odds. Raft in matador gear somehow doesn't quite cut it.

Truth About Spring, The (1965-British) C-102m. *** D: Richard Thorpe. Hayley Mills, John Mills, James MacArthur, Lionel Jeffries, Harry Andrews, Niall MacGinnis, David Tomlinson. Skipper Mills introduces daughter Hayley to first boyfriend, MacArthur, in enjoyable film geared for young viewers. ▶

Truth About Women, The (1958-British) C-98m. **½ D: Muriel Box. Laurence

Harvey, Julie Harris, Diane Cilento, Mai Zetterling, Eva Gabor, Wilfrid Hyde-White, Christopher Lee, Ernest Thesiger. Multi-episode tale about playboy Harvey's flirtations; well mounted and cast, but slow-going.▼

Truth About Youth, The (1930) 67m. *½ D: William A. Seiter. Loretta Young, Conway Tearle, David Manners, Myrna Loy, J. Farrell MacDonald, Myrtle Stedman, Harry Stubbs. Loy adds the only spark of life to this wooden and dated tale of a callow young man (Manners) who is engaged to the sweet daughter (Young) of his guardian's housekeeper, but becomes infatuated with a seductive, gold-digging cabaret singer (Loy). Based on Henry V. Esmond's play *When We Were Twenty-One*, previously filmed in 1915 and 1921. ▶

Try and Get Me! (1950) 90m. *** D: Cyril Endfield. Frank Lovejoy, Kathleen Ryan, Richard Carlson, Lloyd Bridges, Katherine Locke, Adele Jergens, Renzo Cesara. Husband and father Lovejoy can't find a job, so he reluctantly helps slick Bridges in a series of robberies . . . but he isn't prepared for kidnapping and murder. Very impressive independent film noir indicts yellow journalism and lynch-mob violence, but doesn't let the criminals off the hook. Based on a true story that took place in California during the 1930s. Deserves to be better known. Originally shown as THE SOUND OF FURY.▼

Tugboat Annie (1933) 87m. **½ D: Mervyn LeRoy. Marie Dressler, Wallace Beery, Robert Young, Maureen O'Sullivan, Willard Robertson, Frankie Darro. Marie is skipper of the tugboat *Narcissus,* Beery her ne'er-do-well husband in this rambling, episodic comedy drama; inimitable stars far outclass their wobbly material. Followed by TUGBOAT ANNIE SAILS AGAIN, and a 1950s TV series.▶

Tugboat Annie Sails Again (1940) 77m. ** D: Lewis Seiler. Marjorie Rambeau, Alan Hale, Jane Wyman, Ronald Reagan, Clarence Kolb, Charles Halton. Airy comedy with predictable plot about Annie's job in jeopardy. Rambeau takes up where Marie Dressler left off; Reagan saves the day for her.

Tulsa (1949) C-90m. *** D: Stuart Heisler. Susan Hayward, Robert Preston, Pedro Armendariz, Lloyd Gough, Chill Wills, Ed Begley, Jimmy Conlin. Bouncy drama of cattlewoman Hayward entering the wildcat oil business to avenge the death of her father, losing her values along the way as she becomes blinded by her success.▼▶

Tumbleweed (1953) C-79m. ** D: Nathan Juran. Audie Murphy, Lori Nelson, Chill Wills, Lee Van Cleef. Bland oater with Murphy trying to prove he didn't desert wagon train under Indian attack.

Tumbleweeds (1925) 81m. ***½ D: King Baggot. William S. Hart, Barbara Bedford, Lucien Littlefield, J. Gordon Russell, Richard R. Neill. One of the screen's most famous Westerns, with Hart deciding to get in on the opening of the Cherokee Strip in 1889, particularly if pretty Bedford is willing to marry him and settle there. Land-rush scene is one of the great spectacles in silent films. Above running time does not include a poignant eight-minute introduction Hart made to accompany 1939 reissue of his classic. ▼▶▶

Tumbling Tumbleweeds (1935) 57m. *** D: Joe Kane. Gene Autry, Smiley Burnette, George Hayes, Lucile Browne, Edward Hearn, Charles King. Gene's first musical Western sets the stage for all that would follow—a traditional B Western with songs introduced naturally, enough riding and shooting to satisfy, and a dash of slapstick comedy from Burnette. Gene appears slightly uncomfortable in dialogue scenes but is totally at ease singing his hit song "That Silver Haired Daddy of Mine."▶▶

Tuna Clipper (1949) 79m. *½ D: William Beaudine. Roddy McDowall, Elena Verdugo, Ronald Winters, Rick Vallin, Dickie Moore. Flabby tale of youth (McDowall) who pushes himself into rugged fishing life to prove his worth.

Tunes of Glory (1960-British) C-106m. **** D: Ronald Neame. Alec Guinness, John Mills, Susannah York, Kay Walsh, Dennis Price, John Fraser, Duncan Macrae, Gordon Jackson, Allan Cuthbertson. Engrossing clash of wills in peacetime Scottish Highland regiment as popular, easygoing Lt. Col. (Guinness) is replaced by stiff-necked martinet (Mills). Outstanding performances by both men, each in a role more naturally suited to the other! Impressive bagpipe-driven score by Malcolm Arnold. Scripted by James Kennaway, from his novel. York's film debut. ▼▶▶

Tunnel, The SEE: **Transatlantic Tunnel**

Tunnel of Love, The (1958) 98m. *** D: Gene Kelly. Doris Day, Richard Widmark, Gig Young, Gia Scala. Bright comedy of married couple Widmark and Day enduring endless red tape to adopt a child. Good cast spices adaptation of Joseph Fields–Peter de Vries play. CinemaScope. ▼▶▶

Turnabout (1940) 83m. ** D: Hal Roach. John Hubbard, Carole Landis, Adolphe Menjou, Mary Astor, William Gargan, Joyce Compton, Verree Teasdale, Donald Meek. Unique, but incredibly bad comedy, risqué in its day, about husband and wife switching personalities and voices thanks to magic Buddha; from a story by Thorne Smith, later a short-lived TV series in the 1970s.

Turn Back the Clock (1933) 77m. *** D: Edgar Selwyn. Lee Tracy, Mae Clarke, Otto Kruger, George Barbier, Peggy Shannon, C. Henry Gordon, Clara Blandick. Fascinating Depression-era sleeper with an intriguing premise. Tracy is ideally cast as a middle-aged working man who gets to relive his life . . . and marry into wealth and power. Snappy script by director Selwyn and Ben Hecht. And watch for The Three Stooges! ▶

Turning Point, The (1952) 85m. **½ D: William Dieterle. William Holden, Alexis Smith, Edmond O'Brien, Ed Begley, Tom Tully, Don Porter, Ted de Corsia, Neville Brand, Carolyn Jones. Tough script by Warren Duff sparks this gritty if familiar drama. O'Brien is a crime-buster investigating big-city corruption; Holden, his boyhood friend, is a cynical reporter. Scenario was inspired by the Kefauver Committee hearings into organized crime.

Turn the Key Softly (1953-British) 83m. ** D: Jack Lee. Yvonne Mitchell, Terence Morgan, Joan Collins, Kathleen Harrison, Thora Hird, Geoffrey Keen. Film recounts incidents in lives of three women ex-convicts upon leaving prison; contrived dramatics.

Tuttles of Tahiti, The (1942) 91m. *** D: Charles Vidor. Charles Laughton, Jon Hall, Peggy Drake, Florence Bates, Mala, Alma Ross, Victor Francen. Laughton and family lead leisurely life on South Seas island, avoiding any sort of hard labor. That's it . . . but it's good. ▼●

12 Angry Men (1957) 95m. **** D: Sidney Lumet. Henry Fonda, Lee J. Cobb, Ed Begley, E. G. Marshall, Jack Klugman, Jack Warden, Martin Balsam, John Fiedler, George Voskovec, Robert Webber, Edward Binns, Joseph Sweeney. Brilliant film about one man who tries to convince 11 other jurors that their hasty guilty verdict for a boy on trial should be reconsidered. Formidable cast (including several character-stars-to-be); Lumet's impressive debut film. Script by Reginald Rose, from his television play. Remade for TV in 1997 and as **12** in Russia in 2007. ▼●

Twelve Hours to Kill (1960) 83m. ** D: Edward L. Cahn. Nico Minardos, Barbara Eden, Grant Richards, Art Baker, Russ Conway, Byron Foulger. On his first night in N.Y.C., immigrant Minardos witnesses a gangland hit; his life in peril from both the mob and a cop on the take, he flees to a tiny upstate village, where he's sheltered by Eden. So-so thriller from the pre–Witness Protection era, well photographed by Floyd Crosby. *Mary Tyler Moore Show* fans will enjoy seeing early appearances by Gavin MacLeod and Ted Knight (though they have no scenes together). ▶

Twelve O'Clock High (1949) 132m. **** D: Henry King. Gregory Peck, Hugh Marlowe, Gary Merrill, Millard Mitchell, Dean Jagger, Paul Stewart. Taut WW2 story of U.S. flyers in England, an officer replaced for getting too involved with his men (Merrill) and his successor who has same problem (Peck). Jagger won Oscar in supporting role; Peck has never been better. Written by

Sy Bartlett and Beirne Lay, Jr., from their novel. Later a TV series. ▼●

12 to the Moon (1960) 74m. BOMB D: David Bradley. Ken Clark, Michi Kobi, Tom Conway, Tony Dexter, John Wengraf, Anna-Lisa. International expedition to the moon encounters hostile aliens who freeze North America solid. An ambitious failure. ▶

Twentieth Century (1934) 91m. **** D: Howard Hawks. John Barrymore, Carole Lombard, Walter Connolly, Roscoe Karns, Etienne Girardot, Ralph Forbes, Charles Levison (Lane), Edgar Kennedy. Super screwball comedy in which egomaniacal Broadway producer Barrymore makes shopgirl Lombard a star; when she leaves him, he does everything he can to woo her back on lengthy train trip. Barrymore has never been funnier, and Connolly and Karns are aces as his long-suffering cronies. Matchless script by Ben Hecht and Charles MacArthur, from their play; later a hit Broadway musical, *On the Twentieth Century.* ▼▶

24 Hours of a Woman's Life SEE: **Affair in Monte Carlo**

24 Hours to Kill (1965-British) C-92m. **½ D: Peter Bezencenet. Mickey Rooney, Lex Barker, Walter Slezak, Michael Medwin, Helga Somerfeld, Wolfgang Lukschy. OK suspenser with Rooney marked for execution by Slezak's smuggling ring when his plane is forced to land in Beirut for 24 hours. Techniscope. ▼▶

20 Million Miles to Earth (1957) 82m. *** D: Nathan Juran. William Hopper, Joan Taylor, Frank Puglia, Thomas B. Henry, John Zaremba, Tito Vuolo, Bart Bradley (Braverman). First spaceship to Venus crashes into the sea off Sicily, with two survivors: pilot Hopper and a fast-growing Venusian monster that just wants to be left alone (but fights back when frightened). Climax takes place in the Colosseum in Rome. Intelligent script, fast pace, and exceptional special effects by Ray Harryhausen make this one of the best monster-on-the-loose movies ever. Unnamed monster is known as "the Ymir" to its fans. Also shown in a computer-colored version. ▼●

Twenty Million Sweethearts (1934) 89m. **½ D: Ray Enright. Dick Powell, Ginger Rogers, Pat O'Brien, Allen Jenkins, Grant Mitchell, The Mills Brothers. Contrived musical about unscrupulous promoter O'Brien building Powell into radio star, career coming between him and happy marriage to Ginger. Plot soon wears thin, as does constant repetition of Powell's "I'll String Along With You," but bright cast helps out. Two good songs by the Mills Brothers. Remade as MY DREAM IS YOURS.

20 Mule Team (1940) 84m. ** D: Richard Thorpe. Wallace Beery, Leo Carrillo, Marjorie Rambeau, Anne Baxter, Douglas Fowley. Minor Western of borax-miners in Arizona with usual Beery mugging and standard plot. Baxter's first film.

21 Days Together (1939-British) **75m.** ****½** D: Basil Dean. Vivien Leigh, Laurence Olivier, Hay Petrie, Leslie Banks, Francis L. Sullivan. John Galsworthy's play of lovers with three weeks together before man goes on trial for murder; Olivier and Leigh are fine in worthwhile, but not outstanding, film. Script by Graham Greene. Original title: 21 DAYS.●

Twenty Plus Two (1961) **102m.** ****** D: Joseph M. Newman. David Janssen, Jeanne Crain, Dina Merrill, Agnes Moorehead, Brad Dexter. Poor production values detract from potential of yarn with private eye Janssen investigating a murder, encountering a neat assortment of people. ▶

27th Day, The (1957) **75m.** ****½** D: William Asher. Gene Barry, Valerie French, Arnold Moss, George Voskovec. Imaginative sci-fi study of human nature with five people given pellets capable of destroying the world. Based on John Mantley's novel. ▼▶

20000 Leagues Under the Sea (1954) **C-127m.** ******** D: Richard Fleischer. Kirk Douglas, James Mason, Paul Lukas, Peter Lorre, Robert J. Wilke, Carleton Young. Superb Disney fantasy-adventure on grand scale, from Jules Verne's novel. 19th-century scientist Lukas and sailor Douglas get involved with power-hungry Captain Nemo (Mason) who operates futuristic submarine. Memorable action sequences, fine cast make this a winner. Won Oscars for Art Direction and Special Effects. First filmed in 1916. Remade in 1997 as both a miniseries and made-for-TV movie. CinemaScope. ▼▶▶

20,000 Pound Kiss, The (1963-British) **57m.** ****½** D: John Moxey. Dawn Addams, Michael Goodliffe, Richard Thorp, Anthony Newlands. Edgar Wallace tale of blackmail, with a most intricate plot.

20,000 Years in Sing Sing (1933) **81m.** ******* D: Michael Curtiz. Spencer Tracy, Bette Davis, Arthur Byron, Lyle Talbot, Warren Hymer, Louis Calhern, Grant Mitchell, Sheila Terry. Still-powerful prison drama has only teaming of Tracy and Davis. He's a hardened criminal, she's his girl. Based on Warden Lewis E. Lawes' book. Remade as CASTLE ON THE HUDSON. ▶

23 Paces to Baker Street (1956) **C-103m.** ******* D: Henry Hathaway. Van Johnson, Vera Miles, Cecil Parker, Patricia Laffan, Maurice Denham, Estelle Winwood. Absorbing suspenser filmed in London has blind playwright Johnson determined to thwart crime plans he has overheard. ▶

Twice Blessed (1945) **78m.** ****½** D: Harry Beaumont. Preston Foster, Gail Patrick, Lee Wilde, Lyn Wilde, Richard Gaines, Jean Porter, Marshall Thompson, Jimmy Lydon, Gloria Hope. Intriguing precursor to THE PARENT TRAP, involving the she-

nanigans of two very different twins who plot to reunite their divorced parents. Predictable but fun.

Twice Round the Daffodils (1962-British) **89m.** ****** D: Gerald Thomas. Juliet Mills, Donald Sinden, Donald Houston, Kenneth Williams, Jill Ireland, Nanette Newman. Mills is charming nurse in a male TB ward, trying to avoid romantic inclinations of her patients; expected sex jokes abound.

Twice-Told Tales (1963) **C-119m.** ******* D: Sidney Salkow. Vincent Price, Sebastian Cabot, Mari Blanchard, Brett Halsey, Richard Denning. Episodic adaptation of Hawthorne stories has good cast, imaginative direction, and sufficient atmosphere to keep one's interest. One of the TALES is an abbreviated HOUSE OF THE SEVEN GABLES, which also starred Price in the 1940 version. ▼▶▶

Twilight for the Gods (1958) **C-120m.** ****½** D: Joseph Pevney. Rock Hudson, Cyd Charisse, Arthur Kennedy, Leif Erickson, Charles McGraw, Ernest Truex, Richard Haydn, Wallace Ford. Ernest K. Gann book, adapted by the author, becomes turgid soaper of people on run-down vessel heading for Mexico, their trials and tribulations to survive when ship goes down.

Twilight in the Sierras (1950) **C-67m.** ****** D: William Witney. Roy Rogers, Dale Evans, Pat Brady, Estelita Rodriguez, Russ Vincent, George Meeker, Fred Kohler, Jr., Edward Keane, Pierce Lyden, House Peters, Jr., Foy Willing and the Riders of the Purple Sage. Roy is a parole officer working at a camp that rehabilitates parolees, one of whom (Vincent) is kidnapped by his former gang when they need help with a counterfeiting scheme. As if that weren't enough, Roy also tangles with a wild mountain lion in this average Trucolor Western. ▼▶

Twilight of Honor (1963) **115m.** ****½** D: Boris Sagal. Richard Chamberlain, Nick Adams, Joan Blackman, Claude Rains, Joey Heatherton, James Gregory, Pat Buttram, Jeanette Nolan. Routine drama of struggling lawyer who takes on murder case with assistance of older expert Rains. Look for Linda Evans in a bit part. Panavision. ▶

Twilight on the Rio Grande (1947) **71m.** ****** D: Frank McDonald. Gene Autry, Sterling Holloway, Adele Mara, Bob Steele, Charles Evans, Martin Garralaga, Howard J. Negley, George J. Lewis, Cass County Boys. When their partner is killed, Gene and the Cass County Boys get involved with crooks smuggling jewels across the Mexican border and a dancer (Mara) looking for her father's murderer. One of Gene's lesser post-WW2 Westerns, with everyone simply going through the motions. ▼▶

Twilight on the Trail (1941) **57m.** ****** D: Howard Bretherton. William Boyd, Andy Clyde, Brad King, Wanda McKay, Jack Rockwell, Norman Willis. Rangers

Hopalong Cassidy and his pals disguise themselves as tenderfoot detectives to help rancher trap a crooked foreman who's rustling cattle, which seem to vanish. Routine series entry with excess of outdoor scenes shot indoors. Some nice harmonizing by the Jimmy Wakely Trio, with songwriter Johnny Bond. Screenplay cowritten by character actress Ellen Corby; title taken from the song introduced in TRAIL OF THE LONESOME PINE. ▼▶

Twin Beds (1942) **85m.** ** D: Tim Whelan. Joan Bennett, George Brent, Mischa Auer, Una Merkel, Glenda Farrell, Ernest Truex, Margaret Hamilton, Cecil Cunningham. Life of newly married couple Bennett and Brent is constantly interrupted by wacky neighbor Auer; he easily steals the picture.

Twinkle and Shine SEE: **It Happened to Jane**

Twinkle in God's Eye, The (1955) **73m.** ** D: George Blair. Mickey Rooney, Coleen Gray, Hugh O'Brian, Joey Forman, Michael Connors. Simple yarn of clergyman Rooney trying to convert wrongdoers in Western town to God's faith via good humor. ▼

Twist All Night (1961) **78m.** BOMB D: William Hole, Jr. Louis Prima, June Wilkinson, Sam Butera and The Witnesses, Gertrude Michael, David Whorf. Stupid comedy about Prima's attempts to keep his nightclub going; sexy Wilkinson is his girlfriend. Sometimes shown with a nine-minute color prologue, TWIST CRAZE, directed by Allan David. Aka THE CONTINENTAL TWIST.

Twist Around the Clock (1961) **86m.** ** D: Oscar Rudolph. Chubby Checker, Dion, The Marcels, Vicki Spencer, Clay Cole, John Cronin, Mary Mitchell. Agent Cronin tries to book Twist performers; of course, by the finale, the dance is the rage of America. Dion performs "The Wanderer" and "Runaround Sue." Remake of ROCK AROUND THE CLOCK. ▼▶

Twist of Fate (1954-British) **89m.** ** D: David Miller. Ginger Rogers, Herbert Lom, Stanley Baker, Jacques Bergerac, Margaret Rawlings, Coral Browne, Lisa Gastoni, Ferdy Mayne. Turgid thriller in which Rogers is taken in by wealthy Baker, who lavishes her with gifts, which she accepts because she thinks marriage is in the offing. But she's unaware of the true nature of his business and his marital status. Original British title: BEAUTIFUL STRANGER. ▼

Two Against the World (1932) **70m.** **½ D: Archie Mayo. Constance Bennett, Neil Hamilton, Helen Vinson, Allen Vincent, Gavin Gordon, Walter Walker, Roscoe Karns, Alan Mowbray. Rich-girl Bennett, a humanist at heart despite the influence of her greedy, insensitive relations, is intrigued by lawyer Hamilton, who advocates for the poor. Thoughtful Depression-era

morality tale starts off nicely but wallows in soap opera when murder enters the picture.

Two Against the World (1936) **57m.** ** D: William McGann. Humphrey Bogart, Beverly Roberts, Linda Perry, Carlyle Moore, Jr., Henry O'Neill, Claire Dodd. Remake of FIVE STAR FINAL set in radio station is more contrived, not as effective. Retitled: ONE FATAL HOUR.

Two and Two Make Six (1961-British) **89m.** ** D: Freddie Francis. George Chakiris, Janette Scott, Alfred Lynch, Jackie Lane. Mild romantic yarn of A.W.O.L. soldier Chakiris falling in love with Scott.

Two Arabian Knights (1927) **92m.** **½ D: Lewis Milestone. William Boyd, Mary Astor, Louis Wolheim, Ian Keith, Michael Vavitch, M. (Michael) Visaroff, Boris Karloff, DeWitt Jennings. Fairly engaging paraphrase of WHAT PRICE GLORY about the adventures of two roughneck soldiers who have a buddy/rivalry relationship overseas during WW1. Stylishly designed by William Cameron Menzies and directed with visual flair by Milestone, who won the only Oscar awarded for Best Directing of a Comedy Picture, given the first year of the Academy Awards. Produced by Howard Hughes.

Two Daughters (1961-Indian) **114m.** ***½ D: Satyajit Ray. Anil Chatterjee, Chandana Bannerjee, Soumitra Chatterjee, Aparna Das Gupta, Sita Mukherji. A pair of episodes, adapted from the writings of Rabindranath Tagore, one good and the other superb. The former concerns the curious relationship between a postmaster and an orphan girl; the latter is the funny, gentle chronicle of what happens when a student rejects the woman his mother has chosen for his wife, deciding instead to marry the local tomboy. Ray scripted both stories. Originally released in India as part of a trilogy, running 171m. ▼

Two Dollar Bettor (1951) **72m.** **½ D: Edward L. Cahn. Steve Brodie, Marie Windsor, John Litel, Barbara Logan, Robert Sherwood, Barbara Bestar, Walter Kingsford, Carl Switzer, Barbara Billingsley. Naïve nice-guy Litel wins a two-dollar bet at the racetrack and becomes hooked on playing the ponies. Entertaining programmer with Windsor at her femme-fatale best. ▶

Two-Faced Woman (1941) **94m.** **½ D: George Cukor. Greta Garbo, Melvyn Douglas, Constance Bennett, Roland Young, Robert Sterling, Ruth Gordon, Frances Carson. Garbo's last film, in which MGM tried unsuccessfully to Americanize her personality. Attempted chic comedy of errors is OK, but not what viewer expects from the divine Garbo. Constance Bennett is much more at home in proceedings, stealing the film with her hilarious performance. ▼▶

Two Faces of Dr. Jekyll, The (1960-British) **C-88m.** ** D: Terence Fisher. Paul Massie, Dawn Addams, Christopher Lee, David

[739]

Kossoff, Francis De Wolff, Norma Marla. Uneven, sometimes unintentionally funny reworking of Stevenson story stresses Mr. and Mrs. relationship, plus fact that doctor himself is a weakling (and Hyde is suave and handsome!). Unfortunately, dialogue and situations are boring. Look for Oliver Reed as a bouncer. Originally shown in U.S. as HOUSE OF FRIGHT. Megascope. ▼❷

Two Fisted Law (1932) **64m.** ** D: D. Ross Lederman. Tim McCoy, John Wayne, Walter Brennan, Tully Marshall, Alice Day, Wheeler Oakman, Wallace MacDonald. Crook cheats intense cowpoke McCoy out of ranch after first rustling his cattle. Action-filled but ordinary Western with Wayne as a cowhand named Duke. Story by pulp writer William Colt MacDonald presages his later *Three Mesquiteers* series, which would also feature Wayne. ▼❷

Two Flags West (1950) **92m.** ** D: Robert Wise. Joseph Cotten, Linda Darnell, Jeff Chandler, Cornel Wilde, Dale Robertson, Jay C. Flippen, Noah Beery, Jr. Very uneven Civil War Western. Battle scenes of good quality mixed with unappealing script and weak performances.

Two for the Seesaw (1962) **119m.** **½ D: Robert Wise. Robert Mitchum, Shirley MacLaine, Edmon Ryan, Elisabeth Fraser. Well-acted but dated drama about the evolving relationship between two imperfect, vulnerable people: wandering Nebraska lawyer Mitchum and eccentric "born victim" Mac-Laine. Based on the William Gibson play. Panavision. ▼❶❷

Two for Tonight (1935) **61m.** **½ D: Frank Tuttle. Bing Crosby, Joan Bennett, Mary Boland, Lynne Overman, Thelma Todd, James Blakeley. Songwriter Crosby is forced to write musical play in one week. Entertaining slapstick musical with Boland as his mother, Bennett his girl.

Two Gals and a Guy (1951) **71m.** ** D: Alfred E. Green. Janis Paige, Robert Alda, James Gleason, Lionel Stander. Trials and tribulations of married vocal duo, caught up in the early days of TV performing; standard production.

Two Girls and a Sailor (1944) **124m.** *** D: Richard Thorpe. Van Johnson, June Allyson, Gloria DeHaven, Jose Iturbi, Jimmy Durante, Lena Horne, Donald Meek, Virginia O'Brien, Gracie Allen, Harry James and Xavier Cugat orchestras. Singing sisters Allyson and DeHaven operate a canteen for GIs, and become romantically linked with sailor-with-a-secret Johnson. Breezy entertainment, with many fine musical numbers (from Gracie Allen playing the piano to Lena Horne singing "Paper Doll"). Watch for Ava Gardner as a dancing showgirl and in the dream sequence. ▼❶❷

Two Girls on Broadway (1940) **71m.** ** D: S. Sylvan Simon. Lana Turner, George Murphy, Joan Blondell, Kent Taylor, Wal-

lace Ford. Sisters love same man (Murphy) but everything works out in this routine musical, sparked by snappy Blondell. Remake of THE BROADWAY MELODY. ❷

Two-Gun Lady (1955) **71m.** ** D: Richard H. Bartlett. Peggy (Peggie) Castle, William Talman, Marie Windsor, Earle Lyon, Robert Lowery, Ian MacDonald, Joe Besser, Barbara Turner. Why has the title character (Castle), the world's greatest trick-shot artist, brought her "big-time act" to a one-horse Western town? Modest Western is mostly all talk and little action. Turner, who plays Jenny, went on to become a writer-producer and is the mother of Jennifer Jason Leigh.

Two Gun Man from Harlem (1938) **61m.** **½ D: Richard C. Kahn. Herbert Jeffrey (Herb Jeffries), Margaret (Marguerite) Whitten, Clarence Brooks, Mantan Moreland, Stymie Beard, Spencer Williams, Jr., Mae Turner, Jesse Lee Brooks, Rose Lee Lincoln, Tom Southern, The Cats and the Fiddle, The Four Tones. The first of three affable low-budget all-black-cast oaters with singing cowboy Jeffrey cast as Bob Blake, a cowpoke who's wrongfully accused of murder. He ends up in Harlem, where he takes on an assumed identity and sets out to prove his innocence. Followed by HARLEM RIDES THE RANGE and THE BRONZE BUCKAROO. ▼❷

Two Guns and a Badge (1954) **69m.** ** D: Lewis D. Collins. Wayne Morris, Morris Ankrum, Beverly Garland, Roy Barcroft, William Phipps, Damian O'Flynn, I. Stanford Jolley, Robert J. Wilke, Chuck Courtney. Former jailbird Morris is thought to be a famed gunman who's come to the rescue of a beleaguered Western town. Familiar faces dot the cast of this routine oater.

Two Gun Territory SEE: **Sinister Journey**

Two Guys From Milwaukee (1946) **90m.** **½ D: David Butler. Dennis Morgan, Jack Carson, Joan Leslie, Janis Paige, S. Z. Sakall, Patti Brady. Silly story of European prince Morgan Americanized by cabdriver Carson; cast is so engaging it doesn't matter. Look for Humphrey Bogart and Lauren Bacall in cameos.

Two Guys From Texas (1948) **C-86m.** **½ D: David Butler. Dennis Morgan, Jack Carson, Dorothy Malone, Penny Edwards, Fred Clark, Forrest Tucker. Average musical about two vaudevillians who find themselves on a Texas ranch. Highlight is an animated sequence with Bugs Bunny and caricatures of Morgan and Carson. Remake of THE COWBOY FROM BROOKLYN.

Two-Headed Spy, The (1958-British) **93m.** *** D: Andre de Toth. Jack Hawkins, Gia Scala, Alexander Knox, Felix Aylmer, Donald Pleasence, Michael Caine, Laurence Naismith. Exciting true story of British spy (Hawkins) who operated in Berlin during WW2 is loaded with heart-stopping tension and suspense. Fine performances all around; one of Caine's earliest roles.

Two in a Crowd (1936) **85m.** ** D: Alfred E. Green. Joan Bennett, Joel McCrea, Henry Armetta, Alison Skipworth, Nat Pendleton, Reginald Denny, Andy Clyde, Donald Meek, Elisha Cook, Jr. Down-and-out McCrea and Bennett find a stolen $1,000 bill on New Year's Eve. Starts cute but quickly fizzles.

Two Kinds of Women (1932) **75m.** *** D: William C. deMille. Miriam Hopkins, Phillips Holmes, Wynne Gibson, Irving Pichel, Vivienne Osborne, Stuart Erwin, James Crane, Robert Emmett O'Connor. Entertaining pre-Code yarn about righteous South Dakota senator Pichel traveling to Manhattan on a crusade to declare that New York's values are not America's. His daughter tags along and, naturally, falls in love with the city's leading playboy-wastrel. Hopkins is dynamic as always, but Gibson almost steals the show as a party girl who blackmails Holmes. Full of inventive visual touches by deMille and cinematographer Karl Struss. Adapted from Robert E. Sherwood's play *This Is New York*.

Two Little Bears, The (1961) **81m.** ** D: Randall Hood. Eddie Albert, Jane Wyatt, Soupy Sales, Nancy Kulp, Brenda Lee. Harmless fable-comedy of Albert confused to discover that his two children turn into bears at night, cavorting around the house. CinemaScope. ▶

Two Lost Worlds (1950) **61m.** *½ D: Norman Dawn. Laura Elliott (Kasey Rogers), James Arness, Bill Kennedy, Gloria Petroff. Draggy story of shipwreck on uncharted island with prehistoric monsters; stock footage courtesy of such films as ONE MILLION B.C. and CAPTAIN FURY. Cast doesn't reach island until last 20 minutes; you may not wait that long. ▼▶

Two Loves (1961) **C-100m.** ** D: Charles Walters. Shirley MacLaine, Laurence Harvey, Jack Hawkins, Juano Hernandez, Nobu McCarthy. Plodding sudser set in New Zealand with spinster teacher MacLaine trying to decide between suitors Harvey and Hawkins. CinemaScope.

Two Men in Manhattan (1959-French) **85m.** *** D: Jean-Pierre Melville. Pierre Grasset, Jean-Pierre Melville, Christiane Eudes, Ginger Hall, Monique Hennessy, Jean Darcante. Imagine if Melville, who loved American films, had come to the U.S. to make one of his classic studies in film noir. That's exactly what he did with this thriller, much of it in English, about two French reporters in N.Y.C. (one of whom is played by Melville with hangdog cynicism) embroiled in a labyrinthine mystery while looking for a French U.N. diplomat who has disappeared. A stylish and entertaining ride through nocturnal, neon-lit Manhattan, set to a cool jazz beat. ▶

Two Mrs. Carrolls, The (1947) **99m.** **½ D: Peter Godfrey. Humphrey Bogart, Barbara Stanwyck, Alexis Smith, Nigel Bruce, Isobel Elsom. Shrill murder drama with Bogie as psychopathic artist who paints wives as Angels of Death, then kills them; Stanwyck registers all degrees of panic as the next marital victim. Filmed in 1945. Also shown in computer-colored version. ▼▶

Two Nights With Cleopatra (1953-Italian) **C-77m.** *½ D: Mario Mattoli. Sophia Loren, Alberto Sordi, Ettore Manni, Paul Muller, Nando Bruno, Alberto Talegalli, Gianni Cavalieri. Broad, broad farce about the randy but cautious queen of the Nile, whose lover from last night is always this morning's execution. What does it take to survive for a second evening? Well, more than we get in this "sex comedy" that is neither. Widely promoted nude scene by 19-year-old stunner Loren, who plays both brunette Cleo and her blonde double, reveals nothing. Very disappointing. Cowritten by Ettore Scola. ▼▶

Twonky, The (1953) **72m.** *½ D. Arch Oboler. Hans Conried, Gloria Blondell, Trilby Conried, Billy Lynn. Satirical sci-fi is misfire entertainment, when Conried's TV set actually takes charge of his life, possessed by a spirit from the future.

Two O'Clock Courage (1945) **68m.** ** D: Anthony Mann. Tom Conway, Ann Rutherford, Richard Lane, Lester Matthews, Roland Drew, Bettejane (Jane) Greer. Conway wakes up on a street corner with amnesia and finds himself the top suspect in a murder case, joins with cabbie Rutherford to solve mystery. Routine effort which looks and sounds like a typical *Saint* or *Falcon* entry, but is actually a remake of a 1936 film, TWO IN THE DARK. ▶

Two of a Kind (1951) **75m.** **½ D: Henry Levin. Edmond O'Brien, Lizabeth Scott, Terry Moore, Alexander Knox, Griff Barnett. Minor but ingenious crime drama in which orphan O'Brien, in cahoots with femme fatale Scott and shady attorney Knox, poses as the long-missing son of an older, filthy-rich couple. ▶

Two on a Guillotine (1965) **107m.** **½ D: William Conrad. Connie Stevens, Dean Jones, Cesar Romero, Parley Baer, Virginia Gregg. To receive inheritance from her late father (Romero), a stage illusionist, Connie must spend a week in his spooky mansion. Familiar plot with some scares. Panavision. ▶

Two Rode Together (1961) **C-109m.** **½ D: John Ford. James Stewart, Richard Widmark, Linda Cristal, Shirley Jones, Andy Devine, John McIntire, Mae Marsh, Henry Brandon, Anna Lee. Fair Western with Stewart as cynical marshal hired to rescue pioneers captured by the Comanches years ago; Widmark is cavalry officer who accompanies him. ▼●▶

Two Seconds (1932) **68m.** **½ D: Mervyn LeRoy. Edward G. Robinson, Vivienne Osborne, Preston Foster, J. Carrol Naish, Guy Kibbee, Berton Churchill. Offbeat and engrossing, if not entirely successful, melodrama tells Robinson's life as he sees it in two seconds it takes for him to die in electric chair. Often overplayed, sometimes unusually effective; a most interesting curio.▶

Two Sisters From Boston (1946) **112m.** *** D: Henry Koster. Kathryn Grayson, June Allyson, Lauritz Melchior, Jimmy Durante, Peter Lawford, Ben Blue. Grayson and Allyson go to work in Durante's Bowery saloon in this entertaining turn-of-the-20th-century musical; bright score helps.▼▶

Two Smart People (1946) **93m.** ** D: Jules Dassin. Lucille Ball, John Hodiak, Lloyd Nolan, Hugo Haas, Lenore Ulric, Elisha Cook, Jr. Conniving couple involved in art forgery; laughs don't come very often. Cowritten by Leslie Charteris.▶

Two Thousand Women (1944-British) **97m.** **½ D: Frank Launder. Phyllis Calvert, Flora Robson, Patricia Roc, Renee Houston, Reginald Purdell, Anne Crawford, Jean Kent, James McKechnie, Thora Hird, Dulcie Gray. A group of British women, housed in an internment camp in Occupied France, attempts to harbor some downed RAF flyers. Spirited but dated WW2 tale.

Two Tickets to Broadway (1951) **C-106m.** **½ D: James V. Kern. Tony Martin, Janet Leigh, Gloria De Haven, Eddie Bracken, Ann Miller, Barbara Lawrence, Smith and Dale, Bob Crosby. Modest musical involving Martin et al. trying to get on Crosby's TV show. Forget the hackneyed plot and enjoy the Jule Styne–Leo Robin score, along with old standards. Best bit: Crosby's musical spoof of brother Bing, "Let's Make Comparisons" (by Bob C. and Sammy Cahn).▼▶

Two Tickets to London (1943) **79m.** ** D: Edwin L. Marin. Michele Morgan, Alan Curtis, Barry Fitzgerald, C. Aubrey Smith. Passable drama of Curtis helped by Morgan in hunting down espionage agents.

Two Tickets to Paris (1962) **78m.** BOMB D: Greg Garrison. Joey Dee and The Starlighters, Gary Crosby, Kay Medford, Jeri Lynne Fraser, Lisa James, Charles Nelson Reilly. Engaged to be married teenagers Dee and Fraser sail for France, with each having a meaningless flirtation. Trifling musical comedy; originally released at 90m.

Two Way Stretch (1960-British) **87m.** *** D: Robert Day. Peter Sellers, Wilfrid Hyde-White, Lionel Jeffries, Liz Fraser, Maurice Denham, Bernard Cribbins, David Lodge. Wry shenanigans of Sellers et al. as prisoners who devise a means of escaping to commit a robbery and then return to safety of their cell.▼▶

Two Weeks in Another Town (1962) **C-107m.** *** D: Vincente Minnelli. Kirk Douglas, Edward G. Robinson, Cyd Charisse, George Hamilton, Claire Trevor, Daliah Lavi, Rossana Schiaffino, Constance Ford. Overly ambitious attempt to intellectualize Irwin Shaw novel, revolving around problems of people involved in movie-making in Rome. Reunites much of the talent from THE BAD AND THE BEAUTIFUL, footage from which is used as the film-within-a-film here. CinemaScope.▼▶

Two Weeks-With Love (1950) **C-92m.** **½ D: Roy Rowland. Jane Powell, Ricardo Montalban, Louis Calhern, Ann Harding, Debbie Reynolds, Carleton Carpenter. Powell fans will enjoy her role as daughter vacationing in Catskills proving to her parents that she's grown up. Reynolds sings "Aba Daba Honeymoon" with Carpenter.▼▶

Two Women (1960-Italian) **99m.** **** D: Vittorio De Sica. Sophia Loren, Raf Vallone, Eleanora Brown, Jean-Paul Belmondo. Loren deservedly won Oscar for heart-rending portrayal of Italian mother who, along with young daughter, is raped by Allied Moroccan soldiers during WW2. How they survive is an intensely moving story. Screenplay by Cesare Zavattini from an Alberto Moravia novel. Loren remade this in 1989 as a two-part Italian TVM.▼▶

Two Yanks in Trinidad (1942) **88m.** ** D: Gregory Ratoff. Brian Donlevy, Pat O'Brien, Janet Blair, Donald MacBride. Donlevy and O'Brien are hoods who join the Army, turning their talents to fighting the enemy; patriotic fervor rings hollow here.

Two Years Before the Mast (1946) **98m.** *½ D: John Farrow. Alan Ladd, Brian Donlevy, William Bendix, Esther Fernandez, Howard da Silva, Barry Fitzgerald, Albert Dekker, Darryl Hickman. Badly scripted story of Richard Henry Dana's (Donlevy) crusade to expose mistreatment of men at sea. Da Silva is standout as tyrannical captain.▼

Tycoon (1947) **C-128m.** **½ D: Richard Wallace. John Wayne, Laraine Day, Cedric Hardwicke, Judith Anderson, James Gleason, Anthony Quinn, Grant Withers. Wayne plays determined railroad builder in this overlong, but well-acted drama with fine cast.▼▶

Typhoon (1940) **C-70m.** **½ D: Louis King. Dorothy Lamour, Robert Preston, Lynne Overman, J. Carrol Naish, Chief Thundercloud, Jack Carson. Another Lamour sarong epic, typically romantic; Overman provides good comedy support.

Tyrant of the Sea (1950) **70m.** ** D: Lew Landers. Rhys Williams, Ron Randell, Valentine Perkins, Doris Lloyd, Lester Matthews, Terry Kilburn, William Fawcett. Undistinguished melodrama set in 1803. Napoleon is ready to invade England and only retired tough sea captain (Williams) can destroy French landing barges and save the country. Meanwhile, romance blossoms between young Lt. Randell and captain's daughter Perkins. ◗

Ugetsu (1953-Japanese) **96m. ***½** D: Kenji Mizoguchi. Machiko Kyô, Masayuki Mori, Kinuyo Tanaka, Sakae Ozawa. Eerie ghost story set in 16th-century Japan tells of two peasants who leave their families; one seeks wealth in the city and the other wishes to become a samurai warrior. Superbly photographed by Kazuo Miyagawa. Full title UGETSU MONOGATARI. ▼◗
Ugly American, The (1963) **C-120m. **½** D: George H. Englund. Marlon Brando, Sandra Church, Pat Hingle, Eiji Okada, Arthur Hill, Kukrit Pramoj, Jocelyn Brando. Brando is American ambassador to Asian country; his arrival stirs up pro-communist elements, leading to havoc. Political revelations of U.S. power struggle aren't meat for exciting film. Adapted by Stewart Stern from the William J. Lederer–Eugene Burdick book. ▼◗
Ulysses (1954-Italian) **C-104m. ** D: Mario Camerini. Kirk Douglas, Silvana Mangano, Anthony Quinn, Sylvie, Rossana Podesta. Hokey, lumbering costumer with Douglas as Ulysses, on his Odyssey home to Penelope after the Trojan War. Watch Kirk speak in dubbed Italian, then English. Seven writers are credited for this, including Ben Hecht and Irwin Shaw. ▼◗
Ulysses Against Hercules (1961-Italian) **C-99m. *½** D: Mario Caiano. Georges Marchal, Michael Lane, Alessandra Panaro, Gianni Santuccio. Childish blend of myth and muscleman antics with Hercules (Lane) sent to punish Ulysses (Marchal); special effects of bird-men not up to snuff. Aka ULYSSES AGAINST THE SON OF HERCULES. ◗
Umberto D (1952-Italian) **89m. **** D: Vittorio De Sica. Carlo Battisti, Maria Pia Casilio, Lina Gennari. Ex-bureaucrat on a meager fixed pension is about to be forced out into Rome streets with only his beloved mongrel to comfort him. De Sica is said to have considered this his greatest work, and he may have been right; subplot about Battisti's relationship with an unmarried, pregnant woman is as touching as predominant storyline. Shattering, all the way up to the tearjerking conclusion. Screenplay by Cesare Zavattini. ▼◗
Umbrellas of Cherbourg, The (1964-French) **C-91m. ***½** D: Jacques Demy. Catherine Deneuve, Nino Castelnuovo, Anne Vernon, Marc Michel, Ellen Farnen. Haunting music (score by Michel Legrand, lyrics by Demy) and gorgeous photography make this an outstanding romantic drama. All dialogue is sung. Followed by THE YOUNG GIRLS OF ROCHEFORT. ▼◗
Un Carnet de Bal (1937-French) **109m.**

**** D: Julien Duvivier. Marie Bell, Francoise Rosay, Louis Jouvet, Harry Baur, Pierre-Richard Willm, Raimu, Pierre Blanchar, Fernandel, Robert Lynen, Roger Legris. Wealthy widow travels to various locales, intent on looking up the former beaux who filled her dance card ("carnet de bal"). What she finds surprises her, and viewer is treated to a number of poignant vignettes (some ahead of their time) acted by the cream of 1930s France. Hugely successful, this was the inspiration for all the episodic films that followed. (Duvivier even reworked it in Hollywood in 1941 as LYDIA.) Coscripted by the director, from his story. Music by Maurice Jaubert.
Uncertain Glory (1944) **102m. ** D: Raoul Walsh. Errol Flynn, Jean Sullivan, Paul Lukas, Lucile Watson, Faye Emerson, Douglass Dumbrille, Dennis Hoey, Sheldon Leonard. Wavering script about French criminal Flynn deciding to give his life for his country. ▼◗
Unchained (1955) **75m. ** D: Hall Bartlett. Elroy "Crazylegs" Hirsch, Barbara Hale, Chester Morris, Todd Duncan, Johnny Johnston, Peggy Knudsen, Jerry Paris. Fair drama of life at prison farm at Chino, California; highlighted by Alex North–Hy Zarek theme song: "Unchained Melody." Saxophonist Dexter Gordon is seen briefly as a musician (though his playing was dubbed by Georgie Auld).
Uncle Harry SEE: **Strange Affair of Uncle Harry, The**
Uncle Moses (1932) **87m. **½** D: Aubrey Scotto, Sidney Goldin. Maurice Schwartz, Rubin Goldberg, Judith Abarbanel, Zvee Scooler, Mark Schweid, Rebecca Weintraub. Schwartz stars as the title character, a prosperous, patronizing, womanizing sweatshop proprietor who falls for the young daughter of one of his employees, as his workers threaten to go on strike. To say this Yiddish-language film is dramatically overwrought would be an understatement, but it remains intriguing as a mirror of the Jewish immigrant experience and life on N.Y.C.'s Lower East Side. Based on a novel by Sholem Asch; scripted by Schwartz. ▼
Uncle Silas SEE: **Inheritance, The** (1947)
Uncle Tom's Cabin (1927) **112m. *** D: Harry Pollard. James B. Lowe, Virginia Grey, Margarita Fisher, George Siegmann, Eulalie Jensen, Arthur Edmund Carew, Vivien Oakland, Lucien Littlefield, Gertrude Astor. Ingratiatingly heart-tugging (albeit occasionally overwrought) version of Harriet Beecher Stowe's famed abolitionist novel, which charts the plight of various slaves and slave owners in the Deep South prior to and during the Civil War. Sets out to humanize African Americans by depicting the heartlessness of slavery, yet also reflects its era with the worst kind of "dancin' darkie" stereotypes. ▼◗

[743]

Uncle Was a Vampire (1959-Italian-French) **C-85m.** *½ D: Steno (Stefano Vanzina). Renato Rascel, Sylva Koscina, Lia Zoppelli, Kai Fischer, Franco Scandurra, Christopher Lee. Penniless baron Rascel works as a bellboy in the hotel that used to be his family's castle. Pale, towering (and undead) uncle Lee arrives and vampirizes Rascel, who in turn puts the bite on pretty tourists. Forced comedy does not translate well, but Lee is impressive (though dubbed by another actor) and there's lots of beautiful coastal scenery. Ultrascope. ▼

Unconquered (1947) **C-146m.** **½ D: Cecil B. DeMille. Gary Cooper, Paulette Goddard, Howard da Silva, Boris Karloff, Cecil Kellaway, Ward Bond, Katherine DeMille, C. Aubrey Smith, Porter Hall, Mike Mazurki. Gargantuan DeMille colonists-vs.-Indians nonsense, one of his most ludicrous films but still fun. ▼

Undead, The (1957) **75m.** *** D: Roger Corman. Richard Garland, Pamela Duncan, Allison Hayes, Mel Welles, Billy Barty, Richard Devon, Bruno VeSota. One of Corman's best early films, coscripted by Charles Griffith. A scientist, investigating the possibility of reincarnation, manages to transport himself back into the Dark Ages. Lots of atmosphere and black humor, with a neat twist ending. ▼

Under California Stars (1948) **70m.** *** D: William Witney. Roy Rogers, Jane Frazee, Andy Devine, George Lloyd, Wade Crosby, Michael Chapin, House Peters, Jr., Bob Nolan and the Sons of the Pioneers. Roy plays himself, returning to his ranch after shooting a movie, but all is not well: someone kidnaps Trigger and holds him for a huge ransom. Entertaining yarn puts Roy's golden palomino in the spotlight again. ▼

Under Capricorn (1949-British) **C-117m.** ** D: Alfred Hitchcock. Ingrid Bergman, Joseph Cotten, Michael Wilding, Margaret Leighton, Cecil Parker. Stuffy costumer set in 19th-century Australia; Bergman is frail wife of hardened husband Cotten; Wilding comes to visit, upsetting everything. Leighton excellent in supporting role. One of Hitchcock's few duds. Remade as an Australian miniseries in 1983. ▼●

Undercover Doctor (1939) **66m.** **½ D: Louis King. Lloyd Nolan, Janice Logan, J. Carrol Naish, Heather Angel, Broderick Crawford, Robert Wilcox, Richard Denning. Satisfying crime programmer finds Naish firmly in his element as an alcoholic sawbones who goes to work for the mob; Nolan is the G-man hunting him down. Based on a story by F.B.I. chief J. Edgar Hoover.

Undercover Girl (1950) **83m.** ** D: Joseph Pevney. Alexis Smith, Scott Brady, Richard Egan, Gladys George, Regis Toomey. Smith in title role joins police to locate her father's killer; George in cameo is outstanding.

Undercover Maisie (1947) **90m.** ** D: Harry Beaumont. Ann Sothern, Barry Nelson, Mark Daniels, Leon Ames, Clinton Sundberg. The brassy chorine joins the police as a special agent in this routine finale to the series. ▶

Undercover Man (1942) **66m.** *½ D: Lesley Selander. William Boyd, Andy Clyde, Jay Kirby, Antonio Moreno, Nora Lane, Chris-Pin Martin. When Hopalong Cassidy visits the Gonzales hacienda in Mexico, a troublemaker tries to make each friend suspect the other of misdeeds, including border raids and robberies. Partial reworking of IN OLD MEXICO has too many slow, stage-bound scenes and unsubtle dialogue expounding President Roosevelt's "Good Neighbor" policy. Series debut of the unmemorable Kirby, as "Breezy," yet another would-be replacement for "Windy" (George Hayes). ▼

Undercover Man, The (1949) **85m.** *** D: Joseph H. Lewis. Glenn Ford, Nina Foch, James Whitmore, Barry Kelley, Howard St. John. Realistic drama of mob leader (loosely based on Al Capone) being hunted down by Secret Service men who hope to nail him on tax-evasion charge. Whitmore's film debut. ▶

Undercurrent (1946) **116m.** **½ D: Vincente Minnelli. Katharine Hepburn, Robert Taylor, Robert Mitchum, Edmund Gwenn, Marjorie Main, Jayne Meadows, Clinton Sundberg. Stale melodramatics of newly married Hepburn, whose husband (Taylor) is bitterly estranged from his brother; however, there's more to the story than she realizes. Saved only by the fine cast and usual high MGM production quality. ▼

Under 18 (1932) **79m.** ** D: Archie Mayo. Marian Marsh, Regis Toomey, Warren William, Anita Page, Norman Foster, Joyce Compton, J. Farrell MacDonald. Seeing what poverty has done to her sister's marriage, tenement teen Marsh won't marry trucker Toomey until he makes some money; then she gets involved with rich playboy William. Expected spice is missing from this bland romantic melodrama. One great scene: William has a wild party in his penthouse, replete with girls diving for jewels in a swimming pool! ▶

Under Fiesta Stars (1941) **64m.** **½ D: Frank McDonald. Gene Autry, Smiley Burnette, Carol Hughes, Frank Darien, Joseph Strauch, Jr., Pauline Drake, Ivan Miller, Sam Flint, John Merton. Rodeo star Autry and spoiled city girl Hughes jointly inherit a ranch and mining property; he wants to run it as his adoptive dad always did, but she wants to sell out and hooks up with some lawyers who use rougher tactics than she ever envisioned to get rid of Gene. OK Autry Western with a great two-men-on-one-horse fight at the end. Series debut for Strauch as Frog's sidekick Tadpole. ▼

[744]

Under Fire (1957) **78m.** ** D: James B. Clark. Rex Reason, Steve Brodie, Jon Locke, Harry Morgan, Robert Levin. Bland war tale about soldiers alleged to have deserted under enemy fire. Regalscope.

Underground (1941) **95m.** *** D: Vincent Sherman. Jeffrey Lynn, Philip Dorn, Kaaren Verne, Mona Maris, Frank Reicher, Martin Kosleck. Gripping story of German underground movement, with Dorn shielding his activities from loyal soldier-brother Lynn. Kosleck is definitive Nazi swine.▼▶

Under My Skin (1950) **86m.** **½ D: Jean Negulesco. John Garfield, Micheline Presle, Luther Adler, Orley Lindgren, Noel Drayton. Pensive study of troubled, crooked jockey Garfield, attempting to reform for the sake of son Lindgren and pretty widow Presle. Based on Ernest Hemingway's *My Old Man*; remade for TV in 1979 under that title.▶

Under Nevada Skies (1946) **69m.** ** D: Frank McDonald. Roy Rogers, Dale Evans, George "Gabby" Hayes, Douglass Dumbrille, Leyland Hodgson, Tristram Coffin, Rudolph Anders, LeRoy Mason, George J. Lewis, Bob Nolan and the Sons of the Pioneers. Strangers come to town in search of a jeweled crest that contains a map to a rich deposit of pitchblende, which is used to manufacture atomic bombs! In the midst of this plotty Rogers film there's an incongruous musical production number, "Sea Going Cowboy."▼▶

Under Pressure (1935) **70m.** *** D: Raoul Walsh. Victor McLaglen, Edmund Lowe, Florence Rice, Marjorie Rambeau, Charles Bickford, Sig Rumann. Lowe and McLaglen team up again, this time as "sand hogs" digging a tunnel under the East River from Brooklyn to Manhattan, brawling over reporter Rice and racing to beat Bickford and his crew, who are tunneling from the other direction. Fast, snappy action-comedy with an unusual setting and a great climax.

Under-Pup, The (1939) **81m.** **½ D: Richard Wallace. Gloria Jean, Robert Cummings, Nan Grey, Beulah Bondi, Virginia Weidler, Margaret Lindsay, C. Aubrey Smith, Billy Gilbert. Hokey but heartwarming tale of singing tenement child who attends exclusive summer camp as charity guest of a snobbish girls' club. Film debut for Gloria Jean, Universal Pictures' "successor" to Deanna Durbin. Originally released at 88m.

Undersea Girl (1957) **75m.** BOMB D: John Peyser. Mara Corday, Pat Conway, Dan Seymour, Florence Marly, Myron Healey. Corday is a reporter (and diver) who joins the police and the Navy in trying to track down a gang that's looted a sunken ship. Sunk is right.

Under Suspicion SEE: **Innocent Affair, An**

Under Ten Flags (1960-U.S.-Italian) **92m.**

**½ D: Duilio Coletti. Van Heflin, Charles Laughton, Mylene Demongeot, John Ericson, Cecil Parker, Liam Redmond, Alex Nicol. German attack-ship during WW2 uses a variety of dodges to elude British pursuers, in naval cat-and-mouse game, told from Axis point of view. Filmed in Italy.

Under the Gun (1950) **83m.** *** D: Ted Tetzlaff. Richard Conte, Audrey Totter, John McIntire, Sam Jaffe, Philip Pine, Shepperd Strudwick, Royal Dano. N.Y. racketeer winds up in a Florida prison camp—from which he's determined to escape. Original crime yarn enhanced by excellent location work and a strong supporting cast.

Under the Red Robe (1937-British) **82m.** **½ D: Victor Seastrom. Conrad Veidt, Raymond Massey, Annabella, Romney Brent, Sophie Stewart. Diverting costumer with Veidt as hero, Annabella lovely heroine, and Massey the cruel villain in story of French Cardinal Richelieu's oppression of the Huguenots. Offbeat sense of humor adds to film's enjoyment.▼▶

Under the Roofs of Paris (1930-French) **92m.** ***½ D: René Clair. Albert Prejean, Pola Illery, Gaston Modot, Edmond Greville, Paul Olivier. Mime and song, with a minimum of dialogue, tell the story in this wonderful film about two ordinary Parisians (Prejean, Greville) involved with the same woman (Illery). A groundbreaking link between silent and sound cinema; Lazare Meerson's sets are outstanding. Written by Clair.▼▶

Under the Yum Yum Tree (1963) **C-110m.** **½ D: David Swift. Jack Lemmon, Carol Lynley, Dean Jones, Edie Adams, Imogene Coca, Paul Lynde, Robert Lansing. Obvious sex comedy owes most of its enjoyment to Lemmon as love-hungry landlord trying to romance tenant Lynley who's living with her fiancé (Jones).▼▶

Undertow (1949) **71m.** **½ D: William Castle. Scott Brady, John Russell, Dorothy Hart, Peggy Dow, Bruce Bennett, Gregg Martell. Well-done if predictable film noir. WW2 vet Brady, just separated from the service, yearns for a quiet, peaceful future. Instead, he's framed on a murder rap. Appearing briefly as an unnamed detective is Rock Hudson, billed here as "Roc."▶

Under Two Flags (1936) **96m.** *** D: Frank Lloyd. Ronald Colman, Claudette Colbert, Victor McLaglen, Rosalind Russell, Gregory Ratoff, Nigel Bruce, Herbert Mundin, John Carradine, J. Edward Bromberg. Debonair legionnaire Colman is caught between two women (aristocratic Russell and camp follower Colbert), and the envy of jealous commandant McLaglen in this unbelievable but entertaining Foreign Legion story, from the book by Ouida (filmed before in 1916 and 1922). Originally ran 110m.

Underwater! (1955) **C-99m.** ** D: John

Sturges. Jane Russell, Gilbert Roland, Richard Egan, Lori Nelson, Jayne Mansfield. Standard skin-diving fare, with Roland and Egan seeking out treasure in the deep. Russell in a bathing suit is the main attraction. SuperScope.▼●

Underwater City, The (1962) C-78m. ** D: Frank McDonald. William Lundigan, Julie Adams, Roy Roberts, Carl Benton Reid, Chet Douglas, Paul Dubov. Mildly diverting sci-fi about engineer who builds experimental underwater city. Released theatrically in b&w.

Underwater Warrior (1958) 91m. **½ D: Andrew Marton. Dan Dailey, Claire Kelly, James Gregory, Ross Martin. On-location filming in the Philippines adds zest to narrative-style account of frogmen in action during closing days of WW2. CinemaScope.

Under Western Skies (1945) 57m. ** D: Jean Yarbrough. Martha O'Driscoll, Noah Beery, Jr., Leo Carrillo, Leon Errol, Irving Bacon, Ian Keith, Jennifer Holt. Silly, innocuous grade-B Universal musical about a traveling revue in the Old West that runs afoul of the townspeople at their latest stop.

Under Western Stars (1938) 65m. *** D: Joseph Kane. Roy Rogers, Smiley Burnette, Carol Hughes, Guy Usher, Tom Chatterton, Kenneth Harlan, Alden (Stephen) Chase. Roy's first starring vehicle finds him elected to Congress, where he attempts to draw attention to the plight of Western ranchers beset by dust-bowl conditions. (In fact, Roy sings "Dust.") Film's huge box-office success launched the career of the King of the Cowboys.▼●

Underworld (1927) 85m. **** D: Josef von Sternberg. George Bancroft, Clive Brook, Evelyn Brent, Larry Semon, Fred Kohler, Helen Lynch, Jerry Mandy. Landmark silent film may not have been the first gangster movie, but it created archetypes of the genre that continue to this day: colorful character names, slangy mob argot, and a glamorized, sympathetic portrayal of criminals. Former Chicago crime reporter Ben Hecht won an Oscar for his story of a drunken lawyer who becomes a mobster's mouthpiece and falls for his moll. Von Sternberg's impressionistic direction and Bert Glennon's cinematography create a seminal and stylish piece of cinema that is still remarkably entertaining.●

Underworld After Dark SEE **Big Town After Dark**

Underworld Informers (1965-British) 105m. *** D: Ken Annakin. Nigel Patrick, Catherine Woodville, Margaret Whiting, Colin Blakely, Harry Andrews, Frank Finlay. Tight, taut crime tale as Scotland Yard inspector Patrick must clear his name by bringing in notorious gangland leaders. Vivid atmosphere, fine acting by all. Original British title: THE INFORMERS.

Underworld Scandal SEE: **Big Town Scandal**

Underworld Story, The (1950) 90m. *** D: Cy Endfield. Gale Storm, Dan Duryea, Herbert Marshall, Mary Anderson, Michael O'Shea. Surprisingly effective gangster yarn of reporter joining small town newspaper and uncovering corruption; cast is uniformly good.▼●

Underworld U.S.A. (1961) 99m. **½ D: Samuel Fuller. Cliff Robertson, Dolores Dorn, Beatrice Kay, Robert Emhardt, Larry Gates. Robertson sees his father murdered and develops lifetime obsession to get even with the mob responsible. One of director Fuller's most visually striking films; unfortunately, his script goes astray and doesn't fulfill initial promise.▼●

Undying Monster, The (1942) 63m. **½ D: John Brahm. James Ellison, John Howard, Heather Angel, Bramwell Fletcher. OK chiller of a werewolf on the prowl around an English estate; nothing new, but atmospherically photographed by Lucien Ballard.▼●

Unearthly, The (1957) 73m. *½ D: Brooke L. Peters (Boris Petroff). John Carradine, Allison Hayes, Myron Healey, Sally Todd. Mad scientist Carradine's experiments in immortality have resulted only in a basement full of deformed morons. Don't you join them.▼●

Unearthly Stranger (1963-British) 78m. **½ D: John Krish. John Neville, Gabriella Licudi, Philip Stone, Patrick Newell, Jean Marsh, Warren Mitchell. A scientist, one of a team trying to find a way of using the power of the human mind to reach other planets, gradually comes to fear his charming wife may be an alien who's here to halt the research. Compact little film with only a few sets and a small cast; intelligent and serious, with occasionally sharp dialogue and well-drawn characters, but diminished by some heavy-handed editing and an overstated score.●

Une Parisienne SEE: **La Parisienne**

Unexpected Guest (1947) 61m. *½ D: George Archainbaud. William Boyd, Andy Clyde, Rand Brooks, Una O'Connor, John Parrish, Patricia Tate. Bar 20 boys accompany Clyde to claim inheritance, then watch as his relatives are murdered one by one at the hands of a dark-cloaked, masked villain. Focus is on mystery, not Western action, in this modest "old dark house" Hopalong Cassidy whodunit. Boyd spends too much time indoors and quickly changes out of his trademark dark outfit into light-colored civilian duds. Reissued as SADDLE AND SPURS.▼●

Unexpected Uncle (1941) 67m. ** D: Peter Godfrey. Anne Shirley, James Craig, Charles Coburn, Ernest Truex, Astrid Allwyn, Hans Conried. Fairly strained comedy-drama does at least prove a pleasant showcase for Shirley, as young woman with romantic entan-

[746]

glements aided by benevolent millionaire Coburn. Based on a novel by Eric Hatch (MY MAN GODFREY).

Unfaithful, The (1947) **109m.** **½ D: Vincent Sherman. Ann Sheridan, Lew Ayres, Zachary Scott, Eve Arden, Steven Geray, John Hoyt. Sheridan kills an intruder in her home—but is she telling the truth about what happened? Diluted post–WW2 rehash of THE LETTER. ▶

Unfaithfully Yours (1948) **105m.** **** D: Preston Sturges. Rex Harrison, Linda Darnell, Rudy Vallee, Barbara Lawrence, Kurt Kreuger, Lionel Stander, Robert Greig, Edgar Kennedy, Julius Tannen, Al Bridge. Brilliant Sturges comedy of symphony conductor Harrison, who suspects his wife of infidelity and considers three courses of action (including murder) during concert. Great moments from Vallee and Kennedy; often side-splittingly funny. Remade in 1984. ▼●)

Unfaithfuls, The (1960-Italian) **89m.** **½ D: Stefano Steno. Mai Britt, Gina Lollobrigida, Pierre Cressoy, Marina Vlady, Anna Maria Ferrero, Tina Lattanzi, Carlo Romano. Multifaceted film of life among rich, corrupt society of Rome. ▼

Unfinished Business (1941) **96m.** ** D: Gregory La Cava. Irene Dunne, Robert Montgomery, Preston Foster, Eugene Pallette, Dick Foran, Esther Dale, Walter Catlett. Ordinary romance about ambitious singer Dunne, loving Foster, marrying his brother Montgomery for spite—and promptly regretting it. Good cast wasted.

Unfinished Dance, The (1947) **C-101m.** **½ D: Henry Koster. Margaret O'Brien, Cyd Charisse, Karin Booth, Danny Thomas, Esther Dale. Sugar-sweet story of young dancer O'Brien whose idol is ballerina Charisse. Remake of French film BALLERINA (LA MORT DU CYGNE). ▶

Unforgiven, The (1960) **C-125m.** *** D: John Huston. Burt Lancaster, Audrey Hepburn, Audie Murphy, John Saxon, Charles Bickford, Lillian Gish, Doug McClure, Joseph Wiseman, Albert Salmi. Western set in 1850s Texas tells of two families at odds with Indians over Hepburn, whom the latter claim as one of theirs. Gish and Bickford are outstanding in stellar-cast story, with rousing Indian attack climax. Panavision. ▼●)

Unguarded Hour, The (1936) **90m.** **½ D: Sam Wood. Loretta Young, Franchot Tone, Lewis Stone, Roland Young, Jessie Ralph, Dudley Digges, Henry Daniell, Aileen Pringle. Young is being blackmailed and cannot prove an accused murderer's innocence without damaging her own reputation—and embarrassing her prosecutor husband. Intriguing story comes to silly conclusion, but cast maintains interest (though the three leads are not terribly convincing as British subjects). ▶

Unguarded Moment, The (1956) **C-95m.**

**½ D: Harry Keller. Esther Williams, George Nader, John Saxon, Edward Andrews, Les Tremayne, Jack Albertson. Mild drama of schoolteacher whose emotional stability is endangered by lusting pupil. Film noteworthy only for Williams' nonaquatic role; based on a story by Rosalind Russell! ▶

Unholy Four, The (1954-British) **80m.** *½ D: Terence Fisher. Paulette Goddard, William Sylvester, Patrick Holt, Paul Carpenter, Jeremy Hawk. Muddled drama of amnesiac Sylvester caught up in a murder plot. Original British title: A STRANGER CAME HOME. ▼▶

Unholy Garden, The (1931) **74m.** **½ D: George Fitzmaurice. Ronald Colman, Fay Wray, Estelle Taylor, Tully Marshall, Warren Hymer, Mischa Auer, Henry Armetta. Forgettable but very entertaining fluff with Colman an adventurer/thief in desert setting; murder, action, romance neatly blended, carried by Colman's effortless charm. Written by Ben Hecht and Charles MacArthur.

Unholy Night, The (1929) **94m.** ** D: Lionel Barrymore. Ernest Torrence, Dorothy Sebastian, Roland Young, Boris Karloff, Natalie Moorhead, Sidney Jarvis, Polly Moran, Sojin. With the murder of several members of their regiment, veterans from the Indian war gather at Young's London home to ferret out the murderer. Stagy Ben Hecht melodrama with much hamming, especially by unbilled Karloff.

Unholy Partners (1941) **94m.** *** D: Mervyn LeRoy. Edward G. Robinson, Edward Arnold, Laraine Day, Marsha Hunt, William T. Orr, Don Beddoe, Walter Kingsford. Intriguing premise: Robinson starts sensationalistic newspaper after WW1, is forced to bargain with underworld king Arnold. Day gives fine performance as E.G.'s girl Friday; Hunt sings "After You've Gone."

Unholy Three, The (1925) **86m.** **½ D: Tod Browning. Lon Chaney, Mae Busch, Matt Moore, Victor McLaglen, Harry Earles. In departure from horrific roles, Chaney plays sideshow ventriloquist who teams with strongman and midget to form underworld trio. Corny aspects of story can't mar fascination with basic idea, or Chaney's performance. Remade in 1930. ▼●)

Unholy Three, The (1930) **72m.** **½ D: Jack Conway. Lon Chaney, Lila Lee, Elliott Nugent, Harry Earles, John Miljan, Ivan Linow. Almost scene-for-scene remake of 1925 film was Chaney's only talkie; he's terrific, other players less so. Denouement rewritten for this remake to take advantage of sound. Midget Earles is largely incomprehensible. ▼●)

Unholy Wife, The (1957) **C-94m.** *½ D: John Farrow. Rod Steiger, Diana Dors, Tom Tryon, Beulah Bondi, Marie Windsor. Muddled melodrama about farmer's wife attempting to kill husband and mistakenly shooting someone else. ▼

[747]

Uninhibited, The (1965-Spanish) **C-104m.** ** D: Juan Antonio Bardem. Melina Mercouri, Hardy Kruger, James Mason, Didier Haudepin, Jose Maria Monpin. Good cast can't save muddled drama of troubled souls whose lives intertwine in picturesque seaside village on the Costa Brava.

Uninvited, The (1944) **98m.** ***½ D: Lewis Allen. Ray Milland, Ruth Hussey, Donald Crisp, Gail Russell, Cornelia Otis Skinner, Dorothy Stickney, Barbara Everest, Alan Napier. Eerie ghost suspenser about Russell disturbed by dead mother's specter; Milland and Hussey, new owners of haunted house, try to solve mystery. No trick ending in this ingenious film, which introduced Victor Young's melody "Stella by Starlight." Spooky cinematography by Charles Lang, Jr. Scripted by Dodie Smith and Frank Partos, from Dorothy Macardle's novel. ▼○●

Union Depot (1932) **68m.** *** D: Alfred E. Green. Douglas Fairbanks, Jr., Joan Blondell, Guy Kibbee, Alan Hale, David Landau, Frank McHugh. Fast-paced, eventful yarn that brings sharpie Fairbanks and stranded chorus girl Blondell together at a bustling train station where a hundred subplots crisscross. Great fun, brimming with early-1930s flavor. ●

Union Pacific (1939) **135m.** *** D: Cecil B. DeMille. Barbara Stanwyck, Joel McCrea, Robert Preston, Akim Tamiroff, Brian Donlevy, Anthony Quinn, Lynne Overman, Evelyn Keyes, Fuzzy Knight, J. M. Kerrigan, Regis Toomey. Brawling DeMille saga about building the first transcontinental railroad; McCrea the hero, Donlevy the villain, Stanwyck (with Irish brogue!) caught between McCrea and likable troublemaker Preston. Action scenes, including spectacular train wreck, Indian attack, and subsequent cavalry rescue via railroad flat cars are highlights. ▼○●

Union Station (1950) **80m.** **½ D: Rudolph Maté. William Holden, Nancy Olson, Barry Fitzgerald, Jan Sterling, Allene Roberts, Lyle Bettger. Dated police techniques, plus general implausibility, detract from well-made film about manhunt for kidnapper (Bettger) of young blind woman (Roberts). ▼●

Unknown, The (1927) **50m.** *** D: Tod Browning. Lon Chaney, Joan Crawford, Norman Kerry, Nick De Ruiz, John George. Wild and wooly silent Chaney chiller about a criminal on the lam who hides out in a gypsy circus and pretends he has no arms. Ultra-creepy, even by Browning's bizarre standards, with an unforgettable finale. ●●

Unknown, The (1946) **70m.** ** D: Henry Levin. Jim Bannon, Barton Yarborough, Karen Morley, Jeff Donnell, Robert Scott, Robert Wilcox. So-so entry in brief *I Love a Mystery* series with Bannon as Jack Packard,

Yarborough as Doc Young. This one involves oddball family, with amnesiac daughter Donnell coming home to see her deranged mother (Morley) after 20 years.

Unknown Guest (1943) **64m.** **½ D: Kurt Neumann. Victor Jory, Pamela Blake, Veda Ann Borg, Harry Hayden, Emory Parnell. Murder whodunit manages to create suspense and perk interest, largely due to Jory's performance in this programmer. ▼

Unknown Island (1948) **C-76m.** *½ D: Jack Bernhard. Virginia Grey, Philip Reed, Richard Denning, Barton MacLane. Boring story of adventurers searching for prehistoric monsters on strange island features men in dinosaur suits. ▼●

Unknown Man, The (1951) **86m.** **½ D: Richard Thorpe. Walter Pidgeon, Ann Harding, Barry Sullivan, Keefe Brasselle, Lewis Stone, Eduard Franz, Richard Anderson, Dawn Addams. Capable cast enhances this yarn of scrupulously honest lawyer Pidgeon and his strange triumph of justice upon discovering the guilt of his client in a murder trial.

Unknown Terror, The (1957) **77m.** ** D: Charles Marquis Warren. John Howard, Paul Richards, Mala Powers, May Wynn, Sir Lancelot. Unremarkable chiller set in South America, involving uncontrollable fungus. Regalscope.

Unknown World (1951) **74m.** ** D: Terrell O. Morse. Bruce Kellogg, Marilyn Nash, Victor Kilian, Jim Bannon. Overbaked relic of its era, with geologist Kilian and colleagues boring to the earth's core in a Cyclotram (mechanical mole). Their purpose: to find a haven from the A-bomb. Nash's character, that of an (at first) icy-cold "feminist" scientist, is alone worth the price of admission. Unabashedly moralistic screenplay by Millard Kaufman; music by Ernest Gold. ▼●

Unnatural (1952-German) **78m.** ** D: Arthur Maria Rabenalt. Hildegarde Neff, Erich von Stroheim, Carlheinz (Carl) Boehm, Harry Meyen, Rolf Henniger, Harry Halm. Too much talk and not enough chills do in this tale of demented professor von Stroheim, who has used artificial insemination to create alluringly beautiful Neff. A curio, mostly of interest to von Stroheim completists. Based on an oft-filmed novel by Hanns Heinz Ewers. Originally 92m. Full title is UNNATURAL...THE FRUIT OF EVIL. ●

Unseen, The (1945) **81m.** ** D: Lewis Allen. Joel McCrea, Gail Russell, Herbert Marshall, Phyllis Brooks, Isobel Elsom, Norman Lloyd. Man who made THE UNINVITED with Gail Russell tries similar venture but doesn't succeed. Governess Russell haunted again by strange mystery, but film haunted by very weak ending. Screenplay by Raymond Chandler and Hagar Wilde.

Unsinkable Molly Brown, The (1964) **C-128m.** *** D: Charles Walters. Deb-

[748]

bie Reynolds, Harve Presnell, Ed Begley, Jack Kruschen, Hermione Baddeley, Audrey Christie, Martita Hunt, Harvey Lembeck. Big, splashy, tuneful adaptation of Broadway musical. Debbie is energetically entertaining as backwoods girl who knows what she wants, eventually gets to be wealthiest woman in Denver in the late 1800s. Based on a true story! Meredith Willson score includes "I Ain't Down Yet," "Belly Up to the Bar, Boys." Video version runs 135m. with overture and exit music. Panavision. ▼○◗

Unsuspected, The (1947) **103m.** ****½** D: Michael Curtiz. Claude Rains, Joan Caulfield, Audrey Totter, Constance Bennett, Hurd Hatfield. Predictable melodrama with good cast; superficially charming radio star Rains has murder on his mind, with niece Caulfield the victim. ◗

Untamed (1929) **88m.** ****** D: Jack Conway. Joan Crawford, Robert Montgomery, Ernest Torrence, Holmes Herbert, John Miljan, Gwen Lee. Cornball early talkie with Crawford as Bingo, an oil heiress reared in the tropical wilds, who falls in love with poor boy Montgomery. ◗

Untamed (1940) **C-83m.** ***½** D: George Archainbaud. Ray Milland, Patricia Morison, Akim Tamiroff, William Frawley, Jane Darwell, Esther Dale. Milland is a brave doctor trying to get serum through a blizzard in this hokey remake of Clara Bow's MANTRAP.

Untamed (1955) **C-111m.** ******* D: Henry King. Tyrone Power, Susan Hayward, Agnes Moorehead, Richard Egan, Rita Moreno, John Justin. Quite vivid account of Boer trek through hostile South African country, with Power romancing Hayward. CinemaScope. ◗

Untamed Breed, The (1948) **C-79m.** ****** D: Charles Lamont. Sonny Tufts, Barbara Britton, William Bishop, Edgar Buchanan. Routine trials and tribulations of breeding cattle in old Texas, amid romance and gunplay.

Untamed Frontier (1952) **C-75m.** ****½** D: Hugo Fregonese. Joseph Cotten, Shelley Winters, Scott Brady, Suzan Ball. Range war between Texan cattle owners is basis for this Western improved by good cast.

Untamed Heiress (1954) **70m.** ***½** D: Charles Lamont. Judy Canova, Donald Barry, Taylor Holmes, George Cleveland, Chick Chandler, Jack Kruschen, Ellen Corby. Slight Canova vehicle involving an aged prospector who once loved Judy's late mother and a villain intent on pilfering the prospector's fortune.

Untamed Women (1952) **70m.** ***½** D: W. Merle Connell. Mikel Conrad, Doris Merrick, Richard Monahan, Mark Lowell, Midge Ware, Carol Brewster. Campy nonsense about Air Force flyers stranded on Pacific island ruled by strange women, last descendants of the Druids. Caveat emptor! ◗

Untamed Youth (1957) **80m.** BOMB D: Howard W. Koch. Mamie Van Doren, Lori Nelson, John Russell, Don Burnett, Eddie Cochran, Lurene Tuttle, Robert Foulk, Yvonne Lime, Jeanne Carmen, The Hollywood Rock and Rollers. Side-splitting camp masterpiece has sisters Mamie and Lori railroaded onto yucky prison work farm owned by hissably slimy Russell. You know something's wrong when Mamie sings four songs and Cochran only one. Best line: "Don't hit me in the mouth again! You'll break my dental plate!" ◗

Until They Sail (1957) **95m.** ****½** D: Robert Wise. Paul Newman, Joan Fontaine, Jean Simmons, Sandra Dee, Piper Laurie, Charles Drake, Patrick Macnee, Dean Jones. Soaper courtroom story set in WW2 New Zealand, with sisters (Fontaine, Simmons, Laurie, and Dee) involved in love, misery, and murder. From James Michener story. Dee's film debut. Eydie Gorme sings title song. CinemaScope. ▼◗

Unvanquished, The SEE: **Aparajito**

Unwed Mother (1958) **74m.** ***½** D: Walter Doniger. Norma Moore, Robert Vaughn, Diana Darrin, Billie Bird, Jeanne Cooper. Country girl Moore arrives in L.A. and is promptly seduced and impregnated by smarmy Vaughn. Unexciting programmer. ◗

Up From the Beach (1965) **99m.** ****½** D: Robert Parrish. Cliff Robertson, Red Buttons, Francoise Rosay, Irina Demick, Marius Goring, Slim Pickens, James Robertson Justice, Broderick Crawford. Static film of American sergeant Robertson involved with French civilians in love and war during Normandy invasion. CinemaScope.

Up Front (1951) **92m.** ****½** D: Alexander Hall. David Wayne, Tom Ewell, Marina Berti, Jeffrey Lynn, Richard Egan. Sometimes amusing WW2 comedy based on Bill Mauldin's cartoon characters Willie and Joe, and their military shenanigans. Sequel: BACK AT THE FRONT.

Up Goes Maisie (1946) **89m.** ****** D: Harry Beaumont. Ann Sothern, George Murphy, Hillary Brooke, Stephen McNally, Ray Collins, Jeff York, Paul Harvey. Maisie gets a job as secretary to a helicopter inventor and battles crooks who are trying to pilfer the patent. Stock series entry. ◗

Up in Arms (1944) **C-106m.** ****½** D: Elliott Nugent. Danny Kaye, Dana Andrews, Constance Dowling, Dinah Shore, Louis Calhern, Lyle Talbot, Margaret Dumont, Elisha Cook, Jr. Danny's first feature film (about a hypochondriac in the Army) doesn't wear well, biggest asset being vivacious Dinah Shore; Virginia Mayo is one of the chorus girls. Only those great patter songs— including "The Lobby Number" and "Melody in 4F"—hold up. Based on The Nervous Wreck, filmed before in 1926 and later with Eddie Cantor as WHOOPEE! ▼◗

Up in Central Park (1948) **88m.** ** D: William A. Seiter. Deanna Durbin, Dick Haymes, Vincent Price, Albert Sharpe, Tom Powers. Disappointing screen version of Broadway musical hit (minus many of its songs) about an Irish colleen in turn-of-the-20th-century N.Y.C. who helps expose the crooked Tammany Hall tactics of Boss Tweed (Price).▼❻

Up in Mabel's Room (1944) **76m.** *** D: Allan Dwan. Dennis O'Keefe, Marjorie Reynolds, Gail Patrick, Mischa Auer, Charlotte Greenwood, Lee Bowman. Engaging comedy of innocent O'Keefe embarrassed by presence of old flame (Patrick) in front of his wife (Reynolds). Based on a stage play filmed before in 1926; director and star reteamed in 1945 for GETTING GERTIE'S GARTER.▼❻

Up in Smoke (1957) **64m.** *½ D: William Beaudine. Huntz Hall, Stanley Clements, Eddie LeRoy, David Gorcey, Judy Bamber, Benny Rubin, Jack Mulhall. The Bowery Boys trash *Faust*, as Sach makes a pact with Satan in exchange for some sure bets at the track.❻

Up in the World (1956-British) **91m.** **½ D: John Paddy Carstairs. Norman Wisdom, Maureen Swanson, Jerry Desmonde, Colin Gordon, Lionel Jeffries. Typical Wisdom comedy, anticipating Jerry Lewis' solo vehicles. He's a bumbling window cleaner involved with aristocrats and kidnappers, and even gets to sing.❻

Up Periscope (1959) **C-111m.** **½ D: Gordon Douglas. James Garner, Edmond O'Brien, Andra Martin, Alan Hale, Carleton Carpenter, Frank Gifford. Garner is Navy lieutenant transferred to submarine during WW2, with usual interaction among crew as they reconnoiter Japanese-held island. WarnerScope.▼❻

Upperworld (1934) **72m.** *** D: Roy Del Ruth. Warren William, Mary Astor, Ginger Rogers, Dickie Moore, Andy Devine, J. Carrol Naish, Mickey Rooney, Sidney Toler. Rich businessman William, wed to Astor, becomes involved with burlesque performer Rogers—much to his regret. Entertaining Ben Hecht drama, uplifted by William's charm, Rogers' presence, marred only by an unsatisfying conclusion.❻

Upstairs and Downstairs (1959-British) **C-100m.** *** D: Ralph Thomas. Mylene Demongeot, Michael Craig, Anne Heywood, James Robertson Justice, Daniel Massey, Claudia Cardinale. Witty study of human nature: Craig marries boss' daughter (Heywood) and they must entertain firm's clients. Traces chaos of party-giving, and odd assortment of servants who come and go.❻

Upstream (1927) **60m.** *** D: John Ford. Nancy Nash, Earle Foxe, Grant Withers, Lydia Yeamans Titus, Emile Chautard, Raymond Hitchcock, Ted McNamara, Sammy Cohen, Jane Winton, Francis Ford. Amusing

comedy about the colorful tenants of a show-business boardinghouse and what happens when a hammy vaudevillian (Foxe) gets his big break: playing *Hamlet* in London. Breezy film may not have familiar Ford touches but it's still fun to watch. This long-lost silent was discovered in New Zealand and restored in 2010.❻

Up the Creek (1958-British) **83m.** **½ D: Val Guest. David Tomlinson, Wilfrid Hyde-White, Peter Sellers, Vera Day, Michael Goodliffe. Broad naval spoof à la MISTER ROBERTS, which leans too much on slapstick rather than barbs; Hyde-White is best as nonplussed admiral. Previously filmed as OH, MR. PORTER! Hammerscope.▼

Up the River (1930) **92m.** **½ D: John Ford. Spencer Tracy, Claire Luce, Warren Hymer, Humphrey Bogart, William Collier, Sr. Silly but disarmingly funny comedy about a pair of habitual convicts, played by Tracy (dynamic in his feature-film debut) and Hymer, and their efforts to help fellow inmate Bogart (in his *second* feature), who's fallen in love with female prisoner Luce. Notable for its confluence of great talents at the beginnings of their careers—but it's also fun to watch.❻

Up to His Ears (1965-French-Italian) **C-108m.** *** D: Philippe De Broca. Jean-Paul Belmondo, Ursula Andress, Maria Pacome, Valerie Lagrange, Jess Hahn. Wealthy young man decides to end his troubles by hiring a killer to do him in, then changes his mind. Energetic comedy runs hot and cold, but has many delicious moments. Beware of 94m. version.❻

Uptown New York (1932) **80m.** **½ D: Victor Schertzinger. Jack Oakie, Shirley Grey, Leon Waycoff (Ames), George Cooper, Raymond Hatton. Modest, occasionally entertaining soaper about young Grey, who's loved by successful but slimy surgeon Waycoff and decent, enterprising bubble-gum salesman Oakie.▼❻

Upturned Glass, The (1947-British) **89m.** *** D: Lawrence Huntington. James Mason, Pamela Kellino (Mason), Rosamund John, Ann Stephens, Henry Oscar, Morland Graham. Mason stars as a doctor who is driven to murder to avenge the death of his lover (John). Somber psychological thriller that starts slowly but builds suspensefully to a powerful conclusion. Mason coproduced; Kellino coscripted.❻

Uranium Boom (1956) **67m.** *½ D: William Castle. Dennis Morgan, Patricia Medina, William Talman, Tina Carver. Dull account of two ore prospectors striking it rich, but more concerned with who will win Medina's love.❻

Utah (1945) **78m.** **½ D: John English. Roy Rogers, George "Gabby" Hayes, Dale Evans, Peggy Stewart, Beverly Lloyd, Grant Withers, Hal Taliaferro, Bob Nolan and the Sons of the Pioneers. Musical star

Evans is willing to sell the ranch she's just inherited in Utah, since she needs an infusion of cash to keep her show going. Ranch foreman Rogers tries to make her see that Withers is going to cheat her on the deal. Would have been better without the intrusion of an *Oklahoma*-style finale. ▼▶

Utah Blaine (1957) **75m.** *½ D: Fred F. Sears. Rory Calhoun, Angela Stevens, Max Baer, Paul Langton. Undistinguished Western about Calhoun helping to overcome land-grabbing outlaws.

Utamaro and His Five Women (1946-Japanese) **95m.** **** D: Kenji Mizoguchi. Minosuke Bando, Kinuyo Tanaka, Kotaro Bando, Hiroko Kawasaki, Toshiko Iizuka. Stylized, beautifully made period piece about the life of 18th-century Japanese printmaker Utamaro Kitagawa and his intense relationships with the coterie of models that inspired him. Much more than a biography, this highly stylized film is one of the best ever made about artists and the creative process, as well as an evocative portrait of Japan's demimonde of the late 1700s. ▼

Utopia (1950-French) **80m.** *½ D: Leo Joannon. Stan Laurel, Oliver Hardy, Suzy Delair, Max Elloy. L&H's final film saddles the great comics with poor script and production, despite decent premise of the duo inheriting a uranium-rich island. Aka ATOLL K and ROBINSON CRUSOELAND. ▼▶

Vacation From Love (1938) **66m.** **½ D: George Fitzmaurice. Dennis O'Keefe, Florence Rice, June Knight, Reginald Owen, Edward Brophy, Truman Bradley, Andrew Tombes, Herman Bing, George Zucco. Saxophone player O'Keefe objects to Rice's marriage on a whim, even though he's never seen her before in his life, and ends up wedding her himself. Complications arise when he goes to work for her father. Flimsy but pleasant romantic comedy, made with wit and speed.

Vacation From Marriage (1945-British) **92m.** *** D: Alexander Korda. Robert Donat, Deborah Kerr, Glynis Johns, Ann Todd, Roland Culver, Elliot Mason. Donat and Kerr sparkle in story of dull couple separated by WW2, each rejuvenated by wartime romance. Johns is perky as Kerr's military friend. Clemence Dane won an Oscar for her original story. British version, titled PERFECT STRANGERS, ran 102m. ▶

Vagabond King, The (1930) **C-104m.** **½ D: Ludwig Berger. Dennis King, Jeanette MacDonald, Lillian Roth, Theresa Allen, Warner Oland, O. P. Heggie. First screen version of Rudolf Friml operetta about the short life of 15th-century itinerant poet and part-time outlaw François Villon, who became *le roi* of France for a single day. Lavish color production demonstrates King can sing, and how, but MacDonald is wasted as the niece of Louis XI. Roth is a standout, at her affecting best in the "Huguette Waltz." Bet-

ter than the 1956 remake. Story, sans music, filmed in 1927 (THE BELOVED ROGUE) and 1938 (IF I WERE KING).

Vagabond King, The (1956) **C-86m.** ** D: Michael Curtiz. Kathryn Grayson, Oreste, Rita Moreno, Cedric Hardwicke, Walter Hampden, Leslie Nielsen; narrated by Vincent Price. Bland remake of Rudolf Friml's operetta (filmed before in 1930), about poet-scoundrel François Villon. Oreste was touted as new musical star in 1956, but didn't quite make it. VistaVision.

Vagabond Lover, The (1929) **69m.** **½ D: Marshall Neilan. Rudy Vallee, Sally Blane, Marie Dressler, Charles Sellon, Norman Peck. Orchestra leader-crooner Vallee impersonates impresario; rich Dressler hires his band, and he falls for her niece (Blane). Pleasant musical-comedy antique is sparked by Dressler. ▼▶

Valentino (1951) **C-102m.** *½ D: Lewis Allen. Anthony Dexter, Eleanor Parker, Richard Carlson, Patricia Medina, Joseph Calleia, Lloyd Gough, Otto Kruger. Undistinguished, superficial biography of famed star of American silent films.

Valerie (1957) **84m.** *½ D: Gerd Oswald. Sterling Hayden, Anita Ekberg, Anthony Steel, Malcolm Atterbury. Unmemorable account (via flashbacks) of facts leading up to the wounding of Hayden's wife and death of her parents. ▶

Valiant Is the Word for Carrie (1936) **110m.** **½ D: Wesley Ruggles. Gladys George, Arline Judge, John Howard, Dudley Digges, Harry Carey, Isabel Jewell, Jackie Moran. Get out your handkerchief for this one, the epitome of 1930s soapers as selfless George devotes herself to orphan children. She earned an Oscar nomination for her performance.

Valley of Decision, The (1945) **119m.** *** D: Tay Garnett. Greer Garson, Gregory Peck, Donald Crisp, Lionel Barrymore, Preston Foster, Marsha Hunt, Gladys Cooper, Reginald Owen, Dan Duryea, Jessica Tandy, Barbara Everest, Marshall Thompson, Dean Stockwell. Polished adaptation of Marcia Davenport's novel about labor and class struggles in 1870 Pittsburgh, and a star-crossed relationship between a housemaid (Garson) and the son of a steel mill owner (Peck). ▼▶

Valley of Fire (1951) **64m.** *½ D: John English. Gene Autry, Gail Davis, Russell Hayden, Christine Larsen, Harry Lauter, Terry Frost, Barbara Stanley, Pat Buttram. Mayor Autry arranges for a wagon train of brides for the men in his town, but villains try to hijack the ladies and sell them to love-starved miners. Very unsatisfactory, though Gene does sing "On Top of Old Smoky." ▼▶

Valley of Head Hunters (1953) **67m.** *½ D: William Berke. Johnny Weissmuller, Christine Larson, Robert C. Foulk, Steven

Ritch, Nelson Leigh. Typical *Jungle Jim* entry with our fearless hero fighting bad guys who are trying to steal mineral deposit rights from an African tribe.

Valley of the Dragons (1961) 79m. *½ D: Edward Bernds. Cesare Danova, Sean McClory, Joan Staley, Danielle De Metz, Roger Til. A comet carrying a fragment of prehistoric Earth picks up two 19th-century men. Tawdry version of Jules Verne's novel *Off on a Comet*; laden with stock footage from ONE MILLION B.C. Remade as ON THE COMET. ▶

Valley of the Eagles (1951-British) 85m. **½ D: Terence Young. Jack Warner, John McCallum, Nadia Gray, Anthony Dawson, Mary Laura Wood, Christopher Lee, Naima Wifstrand. Above-par chase tale of Swedish scientist tracking down his wife and assistant who stole his research data and headed for the north country. Filmed in Lapland. ▼

Valley of the Giants (1938) C-79m. ** D: William Keighley. Wayne Morris, Claire Trevor, Charles Bickford, Alan Hale, Jack LaRue, Frank McHugh, Donald Crisp, John Litel. Stale actioner of Morris thwarting Bickford's attempt to rape Northern California of its redwoods, with saloon girl Trevor brightening the proceedings. Previously made in 1919 and 1927. Footage and storyline were later used in THE BIG TREES.

Valley of the Kings (1954) C-86m. ** D: Robert Pirosh. Robert Taylor, Eleanor Parker, Kurt Kasznar, Carlos Thompson. Meandering adventure yarn of excavations in Egypt for tombs of ancient pharaohs. ▼

Valley of the Sun (1942) 84m. *** D: George Marshall. Lucille Ball, Cedric Hardwicke, Dean Jagger, James Craig, Billy Gilbert, Antonio Moreno, Tom Tyler. Intrigue of the Old West with Indian agent (Jagger) pursued by fugitive scout (Craig). ▼

Valley of the Zombies (1946) 56m. *½ D: Philip Ford. Robert Livingston, Lorna Gray (Adrian Booth), Ian Keith, Thomas Jackson, LeRoy Mason, William Haade, Charles Trowbridge. No valley and no zombies in this Poverty-Row horror thriller, but there's blood-seeking Ormand Murks, by his own admission "a strange man." Back from the dead, he's a peculiar party with a passion for pickling—embalming victims from whom he's drained the blood. It's a Republic Picture, so its short running time is filled with gunfire and a car chase, but except for Keith, who's having a high old time, it's third-rate.

Value for Money (1955-British) C-90m. **½ D: Ken Annakin. John Gregson, Diana Dors, Susan Stephen, Derek Farr, Frank Pettingell, Ernest Thesiger, Donald Pleasence, Leslie Phillips. Quirky little comedy about a man from an industrial town in the North of England who inherits his father's factory—and his stingy ways—until he's swept off his feet by showgirl Dors. VistaVision. ▶

Vampire, The (1957) 74m. ** D: Paul Lan-

dres. John Beal, Coleen Gray, Dabbs Greer, Kenneth Tobey. Minor chiller with scientist turned into blood-seeker. Not without some merit; Beal is excellent. Retitled: MARK OF THE VAMPIRE. ●▶

Vampire, The (1957-Mexican) 95m. *½ D: Fernando Méndez. Abel Salazar, Ariadna Welter, Carmen Montejo, Germán Robles, José Luis Jiménez, Mercedes Soler, Alicia Montoya. Visiting an isolated estate, Salazar and Welter learn that a vampire lurks nearby, and she's his next target. Strongly influenced by Universal chillers, it's atmospheric (there's thick fog everywhere) but draggy and more than a little silly. The vampire (Robles) dresses like Lugosi in full bloom, with an unexpectedly hearty laugh. Sequel: THE VAMPIRE'S COFFIN. ▼▶

Vampire and the Ballerina, The (1960-Italian) 85m. ** D: Renato Poiselli. Hélène Rémy, Maria Luisa Rolando, Tina Bloriani, Walter Brandi, Isarco Ravaioli, John Turner (Gino Turini). Ballet troupe rehearses in an isolated manor, disregarding rumors of vampires in the area, until they begin to fall victim themselves. Tired, routine story is beautifully photographed, with an unusual master-slave relationship between the two vampires. Ghoulish climax inspired by HORROR OF DRACULA.

Vampire Bat, The (1933) 62m. **½ D: Frank Strayer. Lionel Atwill, Melvyn Douglas, Fay Wray, Dwight Frye, Maude Eburne, George E. Stone, Lionel Belmore. Good cast helps average story along. Atwill stars as mad doctor forced to kill townsfolk in search of "blood substitute." ▼▶

Vampire Over London SEE: **Mother Riley Meets the Vampire**

Vampire's Coffin, The (1958-Mexican) 82m. ** D: Fernando Méndez. Abel Salazar, Ariadna Welter, Germán Robles, Carlos Ancira, Yerye Beirute, Alicia Montoya. In this sequel to THE VAMPIRE (1957-Mexican), Count Lavud (Robles) returns from the grave to seek fresh victims, mostly in a spacious hospital and a wax museum. Salazar is fun as the excitable hero. Well photographed and drenched in Gothic atmosphere, movie is let down by an erratic pace and a drawn-out ending. ▶

Vampire's Ghost, The (1945) 59m. **½ D: Lesley Selander. John Abbott, Charles Gordon, Peggy Stewart, Grant Withers, Emmett Vogan, Adele Mara, Roy Barcroft. In Africa, bar owner Abbott is secretly a 400-year-old vampire, weary of his lonely life. He wants Stewart to join him in his undead existence but finds opposition from her family and friends. Intelligent script (cowritten by Leigh Brackett) that owes little to Bram Stoker and pretty good cast are offset by a slow pace, even at less than an hour.

Vampyr (1932-French-German) 73m. *** D: Carl Theodor Dreyer. Julian West (Baron

Nicolas de Gunzburg), Sybille Schmitz, Maurice Schutz, Henriette Gerard. Dreyer's stylized use of light, shadow, and camera angles takes precedence over the plot in this chilling vampire-in-a-castle tale. Based on the novella *Carmilla* by Sheridan Le Fanu; filmed several times later. Originally made in French, German, and English versions.▼O▶

Vanessa, Her Love Story (1935) 74m. ** D: William K. Howard. Helen Hayes, Robert Montgomery, Otto Kruger, May Robson, Lewis Stone. Soapy story of gypsy love with Hayes attracted to roguish Montgomery. Dated romance doesn't come off too well today. Hayes' last starring role until 1952's MY SON JOHN.

Vanishing American, The (1925) 109m. *** D: George B. Seitz. Richard Dix, Noah Beery, Lois Wilson, Malcolm McGregor, Nocki, Shannon Day. Powerful drama of a valiant early-20th-century Navajo (Dix), and how he and his fellow tribesmen and women are cruelly manipulated by corrupt government agent Beery. Hampered only by an overlong, boring prologue charting the history of the American West. Based on a novel by Zane Grey and filmed in Monument Valley. Remade in 1955.▼▶

Vanishing American, The (1955) 90m. ** D: Joseph Kane. Scott Brady, Audrey Totter, Forrest Tucker, Gene Lockhart, Jim Davis, Jay Silverheels. Mild, minor film about landgrabbers trying to take Navajo territory; loosely adapted from Zane Grey's novel.

Vanishing Prairie, The (1954) C-75m. *** D: James Algar. Narrated by Winston Hibler. Disney's second True-Life Adventure feature provides astonishing footage of animal life in the great plains, including the birth of a buffalo calf. Fine presentation with little Disney gimmickry; Academy Award winner.▼▶

Vanishing Virginian, The (1942) 97m. *** D: Frank Borzage. Frank Morgan, Kathryn Grayson, Spring Byington, Natalie Thompson, Douglas Newland, Mark Daniels, Juanita Quigley, Scotty Beckett, Dickie Jones, Louise Beavers. Sweet film full of nostalgia for the Old South (though it's set in the 20th century), based on Rebecca Yancey Williams' memoir of her father, a lifelong public servant in Lynchburg, Virginia. Works in elements of suffragette movement, women's rights, and the coming of Prohibition, but focuses mainly on the family, headed by the ever delightful Morgan. Also serves as a musical showcase for young Grayson. ▶

Vanquished, The (1953) C-84m. *½ D: Edward Ludwig. John Payne, Jan Sterling, Coleen Gray, Lyle Bettger, Ellen Corby. Bland little Western about corruption within a town's administration.

Varan, the Unbelievable (1958-Japanese-U.S.) 70m. *½ D: Ishirô Honda, Jerry Baerwitz. Myron Healey, Tsuruko Kobayashi, Kozo Nomura, Ayumi Sonoda. Typical Japanese rubber monster film except that creature defies clear definition. It's vaguely reptilian, but some insist it's a giant squirrel, since in Japanese prints it flies like a flying squirrel. Regardless, it stomps cities and scares the masses. Unbelievable is key word. Tohoscope. ▼▶

Variety (1925-German) 79m. ***½ D: E. A. Dupont. Emil Jannings, Lya de Putti, Warwick Ward, Maly Delschaft, Georg John, Kurt Gerron, Werner Krauss. Jannings offers a towering performance in this searing, grimly realistic drama about an aging high-wire artist, his pretty young partner (de Putti), and the handsome acrobat (Ward) who comes between them. Karl Freund's cinematography is superlative and features memorable shots from the swinging trapeze. Many versions of this film exist with various running times. ▼▶

Variety Girl (1947) 97m. **½ D: George Marshall. Mary Hatcher, Olga San Juan, DeForest Kelley, William Demarest, Frank Faylen, Frank Ferguson. Hatcher and San Juan head for Hollywood with hopes of stardom; flimsy excuse for countless Paramount guest stars, including Gary Cooper and Ray Milland. Bob Hope and Bing Crosby come off best in amusing golfing scene. Puppetoon segment in color.▼▶

Variety Lights (1950-Italian) 93m. **½ D: Federico Fellini, Alberto Lattuada. Peppino De Filippo, Carla Del Poggio, Giulietta Masina, John Kitzmiller, Dante Maggio, Checco Durante. Fellini's first film (though codirected) is a rather ordinary tale of the lovely Del Poggio struggling through small-town music halls to become a star. Some funny and touching scenes featuring the usual Fellini eccentrics.▼O▶

Varsity Show (1937) 81m. *** D: William Keighley. Dick Powell, Priscilla Lane, Fred Waring, Walter Catlett, Ted Healy, Rosemary Lane. Broadway producer agrees to stage a show at his alma mater; result is a parade of musical numbers, including fine specialties by Buck and Bubbles, and rousing finale staged by Busby Berkeley. Originally released at 121m.▶

Veils of Bagdad, The (1953) C-82m. **½ D: George Sherman. Victor Mature, Virginia Field, James Arness, Nick Cravat, Mari Blanchard. Standard Arabian nights costumer, with Mature zestier than most such cardboard heroes.

Velocity SEE: **Wild Ride, The**

Velvet Cage, The SEE: **Problem Girls**

Velvet Touch, The (1948) 97m. **½ D: John Gage. Rosalind Russell, Leo Genn, Claire Trevor, Sydney Greenstreet, Leon Ames, Frank McHugh, Martha Hyer. Satisfying murder mystery about a stage actress who commits perfect crime; good Leo Rosten script with a nifty ending. ▼O▶

Vendetta (1950) 84m. ** D: Mel Ferrer. Faith Domergue, George Dolenz, Hillary

Brooke, Nigel Bruce, Joseph Calleia, Hugo Haas. Florid but uneven costume melodrama about a woman who must avenge her family's honor when her father is murdered. Howard Hughes' expensive showcase for beautiful but inexperienced Domergue. Ferrer was film's fifth director, after Preston Sturges, Max Ophuls, Stuart Heisler, and Hughes.

Venetian Bird (1953-British) 90m. **½ D: Ralph Thomas. Richard Todd, Eva Bartok, John Gregson, George Coulouris, Margot Grahame, Walter Rilla, Sidney James. Good location filming adds to this taut thriller with hard-nosed gumshoe Todd trying to find a missing WW2 hero in Venice, ending up neck-deep in intrigue. U.S. title: THE ASSASSIN.

Vengeance (1937-Canadian) 61m. ** D: Del Lord. Lyle Talbot, Wendy Barrie, Wally Albright, Marc Lawrence, Eddie Acuff, Lucille Lund, Robert Rideout. Harmless little crime drama about police officer Talbot's act of cowardice during a bank robbery. He resigns from the force in shame and infiltrates the gang of sinister hoodlum Lawrence. Originally titled WHAT PRICE VENGEANCE. ▼❙

Vengeance Valley (1951) C-83m. ** D: Richard Thorpe. Burt Lancaster, Robert Walker, Joanne Dru, Sally Forrest, John Ireland, Carleton Carpenter, Hugh O'Brian. Sex in the West with Lancaster and Walker as battling brothers, Dru and Forrest their women. Walker plays slimy villain with gusto. ▼●❙

Vera Cruz (1954) C-94m. *** D: Robert Aldrich. Gary Cooper, Burt Lancaster, Denise Darcel, Cesar Romero, George Macready, Ernest Borgnine, Charles (Bronson) Buchinsky. Lumbering yet exciting Western set in 1860s Mexico with Cooper and Lancaster involved in plot to seize a stagecoach filled with Emperor Maximilian's gold. SuperScope. ▼●❙

Verboten! (1959) 93m. **½ D: Samuel Fuller. James Best, Susan Cummings, Tom Pittman, Paul Dubov, Dick Kallman, Steven Geray. American soldier falls in love with local girl in turbulent post-WW2 Germany. Pointed subject matter explored in unsubtle fashion by writer-director Fuller. ▼●❙

Verdict, The (1946) 86m. **½ D: Don Siegel. Peter Lorre, Sydney Greenstreet, Joan Lorring, George Coulouris, Arthur Shields, Rosalind Ivan, Holmes Herbert. Greenstreet and Lorre make the most of this "perfect crime" yarn, with Greenstreet as Scotland Yard inspector who's "retired" after he sends innocent man to gallows. Director Siegel's first feature. Remake of THE CRIME DOCTOR (1934). ❙

Vertigo (1958) C-128m. **** D: Alfred Hitchcock. James Stewart, Kim Novak, Barbara Bel Geddes, Tom Helmore, Henry Jones, Ellen Corby, Raymond Bailey, Lee Patrick. One of Hitchcock's most discussed films. Retired police detective Stewart, who has a fear

of heights, is hired by old school chum in San Francisco to keep an eye on his wife (Novak), eventually falls in love with his quarry ... and that's just the beginning; to reveal more would be unthinkable. Alec Coppel and Samuel Taylor scripted, from the novel *D'entre les morts* by Pierre Boileau and Thomas Narcejac. Haunting, dreamlike thriller, with riveting Bernard Herrmann score to match; a genuinely great motion picture that demands multiple viewings. VistaVision. ▼●❙

Very Edge, The (1962-British) 82m. ** D: Cyril Frankel. Richard Todd, Anne Heywood, Nicole Maurey, Jack Hedley, Barbara Mullen, Jeremy Brett, Maurice Denham, Patrick Magee. Pregnant Heywood is assaulted by sex pervert Brett, with unfortunate repercussions. Unsavory and unexciting thriller.

Very Honorable Guy, A (1934) 62m. **½ D: Lloyd Bacon. Joe E. Brown, Alice White, Robert Barrat, Alan Dinehart, Irene Franklin, Hobart Cavanaugh. Unlucky but honest gambler Brown sells his body to loony doc Barrat to pay a debt and agrees to kill himself in 30 days; then he goes on a winning streak. Wacky little comedy based on a Damon Runyon story. Songwriters Harry Warren and Al Dubin have funny cameos in the first scene. ❙

Very Important Person SEE: **Coming-Out Party**

Very Private Affair, A (1962-French-Italian) C-95m. ** D: Louis Malle. Brigitte Bardot, Marcello Mastroianni, Gregor von Rezzori, Eleonore Hirt, Dirk Sanders. Rather remote romantic drama in which Bardot plays a famous movie star (from Geneva) who is robbed of her privacy and retreats from the world. Mastroianni is her mom's former lover, a theater director now protecting Bardot. Flashy ending filmed against backdrop of the Spoleto Festival. Originally titled: LA VIE PRIVÉE. ▼

Very Special Favor, A (1965) C-104m. ** D: Michael Gordon. Rock Hudson, Leslie Caron, Charles Boyer, Walter Slezak, Dick Shawn, Larry Storch, Nita Talbot, Norma Varden, Jay Novello. Blah, forced farce with frustrated father Boyer asking notorious ladies' man Hudson to romance his stuffy analyst daughter (Caron). ❙

Very Thought of You, The (1944) 99m. **½ D: Delmer Daves. Dennis Morgan, Eleanor Parker, Dane Clark, Faye Emerson, Beulah Bondi, Henry Travers, William Prince, Andrea King. Heartfelt romance of soldier Morgan and sweet young Parker falling in love and marrying, despite interference from the more neurotic members of her dysfunctional family.

Vessel of Wrath SEE: **Beachcomber, The** (1938-British)

Vice Raid (1960) 71m. ** D: Edward L. Cahn. Mamie Van Doren, Richard Coogan, Brad Dexter, Frank Gerstle, Barry Atwater,

Carol Nugent. Tawdry vehicle for Van Doren, as a hooker out to frame a cop. Blander than usual, but film does allow for some campy humor. ▶

Vice Squad, The (1931) 80m. ** D: John Cromwell. Paul Lukas, Kay Francis, Helen Johnson (Judith Wood), Esther Howard, William B. Davidson. Lukas is excellent in tale of corrupt vice squad, but production needs a shot of adrenalin. Good potential dissipated by slow presentation. ▼

Vice Squad (1953) 87m. ** D: Arnold Laven. Edward G. Robinson, Paulette Goddard, K. T. Stevens, Porter Hall, Adam Williams, Edward Binns, Lee Van Cleef. So-so melodrama involving L.A. police captain Robinson and events surrounding a cop killing and planned bank robbery. ▶

Vice Versa (1948-British) 111m. *** D: Peter Ustinov. Roger Livesey, Kay Walsh, David Hutcheson, Anthony Newley, James Robertson Justice, Petula Clark, Patricia Raine, Joan Young. Entertaining comedy about Victorian stockbroker Livesey and his schoolboy son Newley, who change places after wishing on a magic stone. Parts of it are silly, but much of it is inspired and hilarious. Justice is great as a hypocritical headmaster; Ustinov also wrote the script. Predates the father-son "comedies" of the 1980s. ▼

Vicious Circle, The SEE: **Circle, The**

Vicki (1953) 85m. **½ D: Harry Horner. Jeanne Crain, Jean Peters, Elliott Reid, Casey Adams (Max Showalter), Richard Boone, Carl Betz, Aaron Spelling. Loose remake of I WAKE UP SCREAMING, with Boone the resolute cop convinced agent Reid killed chanteuse girlfriend Peters. Dramatic flair isn't always evident, but wait till you find out who the killer is. ▶

Victim (1961-British) 100m. ***½ D: Basil Dearden. Dirk Bogarde, Sylvia Sims, Dennis Price, Nigel Stock, Peter McEnery, Donald Churchill, Anthony Nicholls, Hilton Edwards, Norman Bird. Fine thriller with lawyer Bogarde risking reputation by trying to confront gang of blackmailers who caused death of his onetime lover. Considered daring at the time for treatment of homosexuality. Screenplay by Janet Green and John McCormick. ▼▶

Victoria the Great (1937-British) C/B&W-118m. *** D: Herbert Wilcox. Anna Neagle, Anton Walbrook, H. B. Warner, Walter Rilla, Mary Morris, C. V. France, Charles Carson, Felix Aylmer. Neagle is radiant as Queen Victoria in often-stodgy biopic emphasizing her romance with Prince Albert (Walbrook). Final reel, the jubilee celebration, is in Technicolor. Sequel: SIXTY GLORIOUS YEARS.

Victors, The (1963) 156m. *** D: Carl Foreman. George Hamilton, George Peppard, Vince Edwards, Eli Wallach, Melina Mercouri, Romy Schneider, Jeanne Moreau, Peter Fonda, Senta Berger, Elke Sommer, Albert Finney. Sprawling WW2 drama of Allied soldiers on the march through Europe, focusing on their loving and fighting. Good cast and direction overcome Foreman's ambling script. Originally released at 175m. Panavision.

Victory (1919) 63m. *** D: Maurice Tourneur. Jack Holt, Seena Owen, Wallace Beery, Ben Deely, Lon Chaney, Bull Montana, Laura Winston, George Nicholls. Holt is determined to live in solitude on a deserted Pacific isle, away from all the world's greed and evil; then a lonely, hard-luck woman (Owen) enters the scene. Intriguing story based on a Joseph Conrad novel, written by Jules Furthman and vividly realized by Tourneur. Chaney is well cast as a sniveling villain. Remade several times, most recently in 1995 with Willem Dafoe. ▶

Victory (1940) 78m. *** D: John Cromwell. Fredric March, Betty Field, Cedric Hardwicke, Jerome Cowan, Rafaela Ottiano, Sig Ruman. March is authentic in tale of loner whose idyllic island life is disrupted by band of cutthroats; flavorful adaptation of Joseph Conrad novel sags at the end. Filmed before in 1919 and in 1930 (as DANGEROUS PARADISE).

Victory at Sea (1954) 108m. *** Produced by Henry Salomon. Narrated by Alexander Scourby. Briskly edited version of popular TV documentary series, highlighting Allied fight during WW2. Excellent photography, rousing Richard Rodgers score. ▼▶

Victory through Air Power (1943) C-63m. *** D: H. C. Potter; animation directors Clyde Geronimi, Jack Kinney, James Algar. Fascinating time capsule produced by Walt Disney to support Major Alexander P. de Seversky's theory that the U.S. could win WW2 if it relied more on air power. Opens with an animated history of aviation, then turns to its propagandistic theme. A unique film in Disney's career that shows how effectively his artists could use the medium of animation to do more than simply entertain. Seversky is also quite effective as host and narrator. ▶

View From Pompey's Head, The (1955) C-97m. **½ D: Philip Dunne. Richard Egan, Dana Wynter, Cameron Mitchell, Marjorie Rambeau, Sidney Blackmer, Bess Flowers. Superficial gloss from Hamilton Basso novel about social and racial prejudice in small Southern town; Blackmer as aging novelist and Rambeau his wife come off best. CinemaScope.

View From the Bridge, A (1962-French) 110m. *** D: Sidney Lumet. Raf Vallone, Maureen Stapleton, Carol Lawrence, Jean Sorel, Morris Carnovsky, Harvey Lembeck, Vincent Gardenia. Effective adaptation of Arthur Miller drama set near Brooklyn waterfront, involving dock worker Vallone's rejection of wife Stapleton and suppressed love of niece Lawrence; Sorel is smuggled-in immigrant Lawrence loves. ▼

Vigilantes Return, The (1947) **C-67m.** **
D: Ray Taylor. Margaret Lindsay, Jon Hall,
Paula Drew, Andy Devine, Robert Wilcox,
Jack Lambert. Standard Western with marshal Hall sent to bring law and order to untamed town.
Vigil in the Night (1940) **96m.** *** D:
George Stevens. Carole Lombard, Brian
Aherne, Anne Shirley, Julien Mitchell,
Robert Coote, Brenda Forbes, Rhys Williams, Peter Cushing. Compelling drama
of provincial hospital life in England, with
outstanding work by Lombard as dedicated
nurse, Shirley as her flighty sister, Aherne as
doctor. Potentially corny script made credible and exciting by good cast, fine direction
pulling viewer into the story. ◗
Viking, The (1929) **C-90m.** **½ D: Roy
William Neill. Donald Crisp, Pauline
Starke, LeRoy Mason, Anders Randolph,
Richard Alexander, Harry Lewis Woods.
Crisp is imposing as legendary Norse explorer and outlaw Leif Ericsson in this
story of his discovery of the New World.
Interesting silent adventure may not be historically accurate but is lavishly produced
in striking two-strip Technicolor. ◗
Viking, The (1931-Canadian) **72m.** **½ D:
Varick Frissell, George Melford. Charles
Starrett, Louise Huntington, Arthur Vinton,
Captain Bob Bartlett. Stunning location
filming highlights this dramatically clunky
tale of seal hunting in Newfoundland. Of
note as Canada's first talkie and for the
presence of Bartlett, a legendary Arctic
explorer, playing a sealing ship captain. Director Frissell (listed in the credits as writer
and producer) and 26 others were killed by
an explosion on board the ship from which
they were filming. The story of the making
of the film is told in Victoria King's documentary WHITE THUNDER (2002). ▼◗
Vikings, The (1958) **C-114m.** **½ D:
Richard Fleischer. Kirk Douglas, Tony
Curtis, Ernest Borgnine, Janet Leigh, Alexander Knox, Frank Thring; narrated by Orson Welles. Big-name cast and on-location
photography in Norway and Brittany are
only standouts in routine Viking adventure,
sweepingly photographed by Jack Cardiff.
Technirama. ▼◗
Viking Women and the Sea Serpent
(1957) **66m.** BOMB D: Roger Corman.
Abby Dalton, Susan Cabot, Brad Jackson,
Richard Devon, Jonathan Haze. The title
ladies are held captive on an island. The
original title of this Grade-Z hokum is THE
SAGA OF THE VIKING WOMEN AND
THEIR VOYAGE TO THE WATERS OF
THE GREAT SEA SERPENT(!) By any
name, it stinks. ▼◗
Villa!! (1958) **C-72m.** *½ D: James B.
Clark. Brian Keith, Cesar Romero, Margia
Dean, Rodolfo Hoyos, Jr. Dull re-creation
of events in life of Mexican bandit (Hoyos).
CinemaScope.

Village of the Damned (1960-British) **78m.**
*** D: Wolf Rilla. George Sanders, Barbara Shelley, Michael Gwynne, Laurence
Naismith, John Phillips, Richard Vernon.
Fine adaptation of John Wyndham novel
(*The Midwich Cuckoos*) about blackout in
English village followed by birth of strange,
emotionless children. Eerie, well-made
chiller, followed by CHILDREN OF THE
DAMNED. Remade in 1995. ▼◗
Village of the Giants (1965) **C-80m.**
BOMB D: Bert I. Gordon. Tommy Kirk,
Johnny Crawford, Beau Bridges, Ronny
Howard, Tisha Sterling, Tim Rooney, Joy
Harmon. Poor special effects are just one
problem with this silly film about teenagers growing to tremendous heights. Based
on H. G. Wells story, refilmed by Gordon in
1976 as FOOD OF THE GODS. ▼◗
Village Tale (1935) **79m.** *** D: John
Cromwell. Randolph Scott, Kay Johnson,
Arthur Hohl, Robert Barrat, Janet Beecher,
Edward Ellis, Dorothy Burgess. Littleknown, well-acted adaptation of a Phil
Stong novel, focusing on unhappy wife
Johnson and her desire for bachelor Scott.
Highly unusual (for its time) in its depiction
of the underbelly of small-town life, filled
with gossip, prejudice, and hypocrisy.
Villain Still Pursued Her, The (1940)
66m. ** D: Edward F. Cline. Anita Louise,
Richard Cromwell, Hugh Herbert, Alan
Mowbray, Buster Keaton, Joyce Compton,
Billy Gilbert, Margaret Hamilton. Laughs
are few and far between in this full-length
spoof of old-time melodramas in which
boos and hisses are encouraged. Even piethrowing sequence is dull. Keaton adds
brightest moments. ▼◗
Vintage, The (1957) **C-92m.** ** D: Jeffrey
Hayden. Pier Angeli, Michele Morgan,
John Kerr, Mel Ferrer, Theodore Bikel, Leif
Erickson. Strangely cast melodrama set in
vineyard of France involving two brothers
on the lam. CinemaScope.
Violated (1955) SEE: **They Were So
Young**
Violence (1947) **72m.** *½ D: Jack Bernhard. Nancy Coleman, Michael O'Shea,
Sheldon Leonard, Peter Whitney, Emory
Parnell, Pierre Watkin, Frank Reicher, John
Hamilton. Potentially explosive story about
an organization called United Defenders
that purports to help WW2 veterans but
takes advantage of them instead. Unfortunately, this juicy material is bungled by
clumsy storytelling and some terrible performances. ◗
Violent Men, The (1955) **C-96m.** **½
D: Rudolph Maté. Glenn Ford, Barbara
Stanwyck, Edward G. Robinson, Dianne
Foster, Brian Keith, May Winn, Warner
Anderson, Lita Milan, Richard Jaeckel,
James Westerfield, Jack Kelly. Ford is a
Civil War veteran who takes up the good
fight against a bitter, greedy rancher (Rob-

inson), his scheming wife (Stanwyck), and slimy brother (Keith). Some good action sequences highlight this standard Western. CinemaScope ▼●▶

Violent Road (1958) **86m.** ****½** D: Howard W. Koch. Brian Keith, Dick Foran, Efrem Zimbalist, Jr., Merry Anders. Well-done programmer involving men driving explosives over bumpy road, allowing for each to reexamine his way of life. ▶

Violent Saturday (1955) **C-91m.** ******* D: Richard Fleischer. Victor Mature, Richard Egan, Stephen McNally, Virginia Leith, Tommy Noonan, Lee Marvin, Margaret (Maggie) Hayes, J. Carrol Naish, Sylvia Sidney, Ernest Borgnine, Brad Dexter. Effective study of repercussion on small Arizona town when bank robbers carry out a bloody holdup. CinemaScope. ▶

Violent Stranger (1957-British) **83m.** ****½** D: Montgomery Tully. Zachary Scott, Faith Domergue, Faith Brook, Peter Illing, Gordon Jackson, Kay Callard. Domergue, wife of condemned killer, sets out to find the real culprit. Not-bad little crime drama. Originally titled MAN IN THE SHADOW.

Violent Years, The (1956) **57m.** BOMB D: William M. Morgan (Franz Eichorn). Jean Moorehead, Barbara Weeks, Arthur Millan, Theresa Hancock, Joanne Cangi, Gloria Farr. Tawdry, preachy juvenile delinquency trash about a rich teen girl, ignored by her parents, who heads up a gang. Wooden acting all around. Scripted by Edward Wood, Jr. Aka FEMALE. ▼▶

V.I.P.s, The (1963-British) **C-119m.** ****½** D: Anthony Asquith. Elizabeth Taylor, Richard Burton, Louis Jourdan, Margaret Rutherford, Rod Taylor, Maggie Smith, Orson Welles, Linda Christian, Elsa Martinelli, Dennis Price, David Frost, Michael Hordern, Robert Coote. Glossy GRAND HOTEL plot, set in London airport. Everyone is terribly rich and beautiful; if you like watching terribly rich, beautiful people, fine. If not, it's all meaningless. Rutherford (who won an Oscar for this) is excellent, and so is Maggie Smith. Written by Terence Rattigan. Panavision. ▼●▶

Virginia (1941) **C-110m.** ****** D: Edward H. Griffith. Madeleine Carroll, Fred MacMurray, Sterling Hayden, Helen Broderick, Marie Wilson, Carolyn Lee. Well-mounted but tedious film of Southern woman (Carroll) who must sacrifice her property and herself in order to raise money to live. ▼

Virginia City (1940) **121m.** ****½** D: Michael Curtiz. Errol Flynn, Miriam Hopkins, Randolph Scott, Humphrey Bogart, Frank McHugh, Alan Hale, Guinn ("Big Boy") Williams, John Litel. Follow-up to DODGE CITY has big cast in lush Civil War Western, but tale of rebel spy Hopkins posing as dance hall girl doesn't live up to expectations; Bogart miscast as slimy Mexican bandido. ▼▶

Virginian, The (1914) **55m.** ******* D: Cecil B. DeMille. Dustin Farnum, Winifred Kingston, Jack W. Johnston, William Elmer, Monroe Salisbury, Sydney Deane. First of several screen versions of the venerable oater with Farnum (following his noteworthy turn in DeMille's THE SQUAW MAN) well cast as the title character, a tough cowpuncher who mixes with Steve, his naïve but lovable best pal; Trampas, a tinhorn gambler and bully; and Molly Wood, his town's upright new schoolmarm. DeMille's first solo credit as director; based on Owen Wister's novel (and the subsequent play by Wister and Kirke La Shelle), which Farnum had starred in a decade earlier. ▼▶

Virginian, The (1929) **90m.** ****½** D: Victor Fleming. Gary Cooper, Richard Arlen, Walter Huston, Mary Brian, Chester Conklin, Eugene Pallette. Owen Wister's novel becomes stiff but interesting Western, salvaged in good climactic shoot-out; Huston is slimy villain, and Cooper has one of his better early roles. Famous line: "If you want to call me that, *smile*." Filmed before in 1914 and 1923. Remade in 1946 and 2000 (for cable TV); also a hit TV series in the 1960s. Remade again for TV in 2014. ▼

Virginian, The (1946) **C-90m.** ****½** D: Stuart Gilmore. Joel McCrea, Brian Donlevy, Sonny Tufts, Barbara Britton, Fay Bainter, Henry O'Neill, William Frawley, Vince Barnett, Paul Guilfoyle. Remake of '29 classic Western follows story closely. Good, not great, results due to story showing its age. McCrea is hero, Donlevy the villain, Tufts a good-guy-turned-bad. ▼▶

Virgin Island (1958-British) **C-84m.** ****½** D: Pat Jackson. John Cassavetes, Virginia Maskell, Sidney Poitier, Colin Gordon. Leisurely study of author Cassavetes and bride Maskell moving to Caribbean isle; film lightly touches on racial issue.

Virgin Queen, The (1955) **C-92m.** ******* D: Henry Koster. Bette Davis, Richard Todd, Joan Collins, Herbert Marshall, Jay Robinson, Dan O'Herlihy, Rod Taylor. Davis is in full authority in her second portrayal of Queen Elizabeth I, detailing her conflicts with Walter Raleigh. CinemaScope. ▼▶

Virgin Spring, The (1960-Swedish) **88m.** ******* D: Ingmar Bergman. Max von Sydow, Brigitta Valberg, Gunnel Lindblom, Brigitta Pettersson. Brooding medieval fable of a deeply religious farming family whose daughter is raped and murdered by vagrants. Fascinating, beautifully made, an Oscar winner for Best Foreign Film. Remade as—or, more appropriately, ripped off by— LAST HOUSE ON THE LEFT. ▼●▶

Viridiana (1961-Spanish) **90m.** *****½** D: Luis Buñuel. Francisco Rabal, Silvia Pinal, Fernando Rey, Margarita Lozano. Powerful psychological study of novice nun Pinal, who loses her innocence when forced by Mother Superior to visit nasty uncle Rey. Near-perfect direction by a master filmmaker; solid performances by all. ▼▶

Virtue (1932) **68m.** *** D: Edward Buzzell. Carole Lombard, Pat O'Brien, Ward Bond, Shirley Grey, Mayo Methot, Jack La Rue, Willard Robertson. Fine comedy-drama about the romance of reformed streetwalker Lombard and taxi driver O'Brien, who has a thing against all women. Genuinely warm chemistry between the two stars and plenty of snappy pre-Code patter spark this film. Written by Robert Riskin. ▶

Virtuous Sin, The (1930) **82m.** BOMB D: George Cukor, Louis Gasnier. Walter Huston, Kay Francis, Kenneth MacKenna, Jobyna Howland, Paul Cavanagh. Laughably bad production with alluring Francis giving herself to Russian general Huston so he will exempt her husband from death sentence. A real turkey.

Visit, The (1964-German-French-Italian) **100m.** **½ D: Bernhard Wicki. Ingrid Bergman, Anthony Quinn, Irina Demick, Paolo Stoppa, Hans-Christian Blech, Romolo Valli, Valentina Cortese, Eduardo Ciannelli. Intriguing but uneven film parable of greed and evil; wealthy Bergman returns to European home town, offering a fantastic sum to the people there if they will legitimately kill her first seducer (Quinn). Actors struggle with melodramatic script; results are interesting if not always successful. Bowdlerized version of Friedrich Durrenmatt's play. Remade in 1992 as HYÉNES. CinemaScope. ▶

Visit to a Small Planet (1960) **85m.** **½ D: Norman Taurog. Jerry Lewis, Joan Blackman, Earl Holliman, Fred Clark, John Williams, Jerome Cowan, Lee Patrick, Gale Gordon, Buddy Rich. Gore Vidal satiric play becomes talky Lewis vehicle with Jerry the alien who comes to Earth to observe man's strange ways.

Vivacious Lady (1938) **90m.** *** D: George Stevens. James Stewart, Ginger Rogers, James Ellison, Beulah Bondi, Charles Coburn, Frances Mercer, Grady Sutton, Jack Carson, Franklin Pangborn, Hattie McDaniel, Willie Best. Overlong but entertaining comedy of professor Stewart marrying nightclub singer Rogers, trying to break the news to his conservative family and fiancée back home. Bondi is fun in amusing variation on her usual motherly role. ▼▶

Viva Las Vegas (1964) **C-86m.** **½ D: George Sidney. Elvis Presley, Ann-Margret, Cesare Danova, William Demarest, Jack Carter. Elvis and Ann-Margret are well teamed in this popular Presley vehicle, with Elvis a race car driver. Songs include "The Lady Loves Me," "What'd I Say?," "I Need Somebody to Lean On," "Come On, Everybody," and classic title tune. Teri Garr is one of the dancers. Panavision. ▼▶

Viva Maria! (1965-French-Italian) **C-119m.** ***½ D: Louis Malle. Brigitte Bardot, Jeanne Moreau, George Hamilton, Gregor Von Rezzori, Paulette Dubost. Rollicking tale of two beautiful entertainers/revolutionaries in Mexico has inconsistent first half, then takes off for hilarious finish. Lots of fun. Panavision. ▼▶

Viva Villa! (1934) **115m.** ***½ D: Jack Conway. Wallace Beery, Leo Carrillo, Fay Wray, Donald Cook, Stuart Erwin, George E. Stone, Henry B. Walthall, Joseph Schildkraut, Katherine DeMille. Viva Beery, in one of his best films as the rowdy rebel who led the fight for Madera's Mexican Republic. Ben Hecht's script plays with facts, but overall, film is entertaining. ▼●▶

Viva Zapata! (1952) **113m.** **** D: Elia Kazan. Marlon Brando, Jean Peters, Anthony Quinn, Joseph Wiseman, Margo, Mildred Dunnock. Vibrant film about Mexican peasant's rise to power and eventual Presidency. Brando is perfect in title role, Quinn equally fine in Oscar-winning performance as his brother. Script by John Steinbeck. ▼●▶

Vogues (1937) **C-108m.** ** D: Irving Cummings. Warner Baxter, Joan Bennett, Helen Vinson, Mischa Auer, Alan Mowbray, Jerome Cowan, Alma Kruger, Marjorie Gateson, Penny Singleton, Polly Rowles, Hedda Hopper, The Wiere Brothers. Minor musical with wealthy Bennett jilting stuffy, high-powered fiancé Mowbray and going to work as model at Baxter's fashion house. One good song, "That Old Feeling," plus an outstanding musical number, "Turn on That Red Hot Heat." Original title: VOGUES OF 1938. ▼▶

Voice in the Mirror (1958) **102m.** **½ D: Harry Keller. Richard Egan, Julie London, Arthur O'Connell, Walter Matthau, Troy Donahue, Mae Clarke. Effective, unpretentious account of Egan trying to combat alcoholism, with help of wife London. CinemaScope.

Voice in the Wind (1944) **85m.** *** D: Arthur Ripley. Francis Lederer, Sigrid Gurie, J. Edward Bromberg, J. Carrol Naish. Low-key drama of pianist Lederer haunted by Nazi oppression, later rekindling old love affair; unusual film, well acted.

Voice of Bugle Ann, The (1936) **70m.** **½ D: Richard Thorpe. Lionel Barrymore, Maureen O'Sullivan, Eric Linden, Dudley Digges, Spring Byington, Charles Grapewin. Bugle Ann is a very special foxhunting hound, lovingly raised by Missouri farmer Barrymore. Trouble comes when an antisocial, dog-hating sheepherder becomes his neighbor. Lionel's whole show in this slight but entertaining tale, based on a MacKinlay Kantor novel.

Voice of Merrill, The SEE: **Murder Will Out**

Voice of Terror SEE: **Sherlock Holmes and the Voice of Terror**

Voice of the Turtle, The (1947) **103m.**

***½ D: Irving Rapper. Ronald Reagan, Eleanor Parker, Eve Arden, Wayne Morris, Kent Smith. Delightful wartime comedy of what happens when dreamy young actress Parker (who's been hurt once too often in love) meets soldier-on-leave Reagan. Arden is at her peak as Parker's flighty friend. John van Druten adapted his own Broadway hit. Retitled ONE FOR THE BOOK. ▶

Voice of the Whistler (1945) **60m.** *** D: William Castle. Richard Dix, Lynn Merrick, Rhys Williams, James Cardwell, Donald Woods, Gigi Perreau. Haunting love story about an avaricious nurse who dumps her fiancé in order to marry a dying millionaire and finds herself a virtual prisoner. Not as suspenseful as the other *Whistler* entries, but just as gripping.

Volcano (1953-Italian) **106m.** ** D: William Dieterle. Anna Magnani, Rossano Brazzi, Geraldine Brooks, Eduardo Ciannelli. Slowly paced dramatics about two sisters involved with unprincipled diver.

Volga Boatman, The (1926) **120m.** **½ D: Cecil B. DeMille. William Boyd, Elinor Fair, Victor Varconi, Julia Faye, Theodore Kosloff, Robert Edeson, Arthur Rankin. Elaborate Hollywoodized version of the Russian Revolution, with Princess Fair loved by elitist prince/military officer Varconi until ragged peasant-turned-revolutionary-leader Boyd enters the picture. DeMille glorifies the cause of the oppressed peasants while depicting them as an animalistic horde; the pre-revolutionary aristocracy fares no better. Interesting to contrast this to the political films then coming out of the USSR. Boyd and Fair later were briefly married. Eugene Pallette is prominent among the revolutionary rabble. ▼▶

Volpone (1939-French) **80m.** *** D: Maurice Tourneur. Harry Baur, Louis Jouvet, Fernand Ledoux, Marion Dorian. A rich merchant (Baur) fakes his imminent demise in order to observe the reactions of those set to inherit his wealth. Fine adaptation of famed Ben Jonson comedy, with Baur perfect as Volpone and Jouvet matching him as his servant, Mosca. ▼

Voltaire (1933) **72m.** **½ D: John G. Adolfi. George Arliss, Margaret Lindsay, Doris Kenyon, Reginald Owen, Alan Mowbray, Douglass Dumbrille. Arliss offers another crafty, knowing portrayal as the writer, wit, and "great humanitarian of the 18th century" who was the conscience of his country in pre-revolutionary France. Arliss is the whole show.

Von Ryan's Express (1965) **C-117m.** *** D: Mark Robson. Frank Sinatra, Trevor Howard, Raffaella Carra, Brad Dexter, Sergio Fantoni, Edward Mulhare, James Brolin, Adolfo Celi, John Leyton, Vito Scotti. Exciting WW2 saga with Sinatra a POW colonel who leads daring escape by taking over freight

train that is transporting prisoners. Strong supporting cast helps. CinemaScope. ▼▶●

Voodoo Island (1957) **76m.** ** D: Reginald LeBorg. Boris Karloff, Beverly Tyler, Murvyn Vye, Elisha Cook, Jr. Boring horror-thriller has Karloff asked by businessmen to investigate strange doings on potential motel-island resort. Aka SILENT DEATH. ▶

Voodoo Man (1944) **62m.** ** D: William Beaudine. Bela Lugosi, John Carradine, George Zucco, Michael Ames (Tod Andrews), Henry Hall, Wanda McKay, Louise Currie. With touching devotion to zombie-wife, Lugosi performs harrowing experiments with unsuspecting girls to cure her. Campy B film. ▶

Voodoo Tiger (1952) **67m.** *½ D: Spencer Bennet. Johnny Weissmuller, Jean Byron, James Seay, Jeanne Dean, Robert Bray. Absurd *Jungle Jim* hodgepodge featuring gangsters, headhunters, Nazis and a museum curator all in pursuit of stolen art treasures.

Voodoo Woman (1957) **77m.** *½ D: Edward L. Cahn. Marla English, Tom Conway, Touch (Mike) Connors, Lance Fuller. Cheater-chiller with few scares in jungle lowjinks about deranged scientist changing English into a monster. ▼

Voyage in Italy SEE: **Strangers** (1953)
Voyage to Italy SEE: **Strangers** (1953)
Voyage to the Bottom of the Sea (1961) **C-105m.** *** D: Irwin Allen. Walter Pidgeon, Joan Fontaine, Robert Sterling, Barbara Eden, Michael Ansara, Peter Lorre, Frankie Avalon, Henry Daniell, Regis Toomey. Entertaining, colorful nonsense about conflicts aboard massive atomic submarine, with Pidgeon the domineering admiral trying to keep the Earth from being fried by a burning radiation belt. No deep thinking, just fun. Later a TV series. CinemaScope. ▼▶●

Voyage to the End of the Universe (1963-Czech) **81m.** **½ D: Jack Pollack (Jindrich Polak). Dennis Stephans, Francis Smolen, Dana Meredith, Irene Kova, Rodney Lucas, Otto Lack. Twenty-fifth-century space crew is threatened by mysterious, radioactive dark star. Surprise ending is no surprise. Originally titled IKARIE XB 1, running 90m. CinemaScope.

Wabash Avenue (1950) **C-92m.** *** D: Henry Koster. Betty Grable, Victor Mature, Phil Harris, Reginald Gardiner, James Barton, Margaret Hamilton. Bright, colorful period piece with scoundrel Mature trying to break up romance between saloon-owner Harris and his musical star, Grable. Enjoyable remake of Grable's 1943 vehicle CONEY ISLAND. ▶

WAC From Walla Walla, The (1952) **83m.** ** D: William Witney. Judy Canova, Stephen Dunne, George Cleveland, Elizabeth Slifer, June Vincent, Irene Ryan, Roy Barcroft, Allen Jenkins. Cornpone Canova accidentally joins the Army in this typical lowbrow comedy, with a cast of comedy pros. Look for Carl "Alfalfa" Switzer as a private.

Wackiest Ship in the Army?, The (1960) **C-99m.** *** D: Richard Murphy. Jack Lemmon, Ricky Nelson, John Lund, Chips Rafferty, Tom Tully, Joby Baker, Warren Berlinger, Patricia Driscoll. Comedy-drama sometimes has you wondering if it's serious or not; it succeeds most of the time. Offbeat WW2 story about broken-down sailing ship used as decoy doesn't make fun of the war, for a change, and is entertaining. Later a TV series. CinemaScope.▼●)

Wages of Fear, The (1953-French-Italian) **156m.** ***½ D: H. G. Clouzot. Yves Montand, Charles Vanel, Peter Van Eyck, Vera Clouzot, Folco Lulli, William Tubbs. Marvelous, gritty, and extremely suspenseful epic set in South America, chronicling the personalities of and relationships among four men involved in long-distance driving of trucks filled with nitroglycerine. Beware: many other shorter versions exist. Remade as SORCERER.▼●)

Wagon Master (1950) **86m.** *** D: John Ford. Ben Johnson, Joanne Dru, Harry Carey, Jr., Ward Bond, Alan Mowbray, Jane Darwell, James Arness, Jim Thorpe, Russell Simpson, Hank Worden, Francis Ford. Good Ford Western about two roaming cowhands who join a Mormon wagon train heading for Utah frontier. Fine showcase for young stars Johnson and Carey. Beautifully filmed. Inspired the later *Wagon Train* TV series. Also shown in computer-colored version.▼●)

Wagons Roll at Night, The (1941) **84m.** **½ D: Ray Enright. Humphrey Bogart, Sylvia Sidney, Eddie Albert, Joan Leslie, Sig Ruman, Cliff Clark, Charley Foy, Frank Wilcox. KID GALAHAD in circus trappings is OK, thanks to cast: Bogie's the circus manager, Sidney his star, Albert the hayseed turned lion tamer.▼)

Wagon Team (1952) **62m.** ** D: George Archainbaud. Gene Autry, Pat Buttram, Gail Davis, Dick Jones, Gordon Jones, Harry Harvey, George J. Lewis, Gregg Barton, John Cason, Pierce Lyden, The Cass County Boys. Gene joins a medicine show in order to find the men who stole an Army payroll. This gives him more chance to sing than usual in his later Columbia Westerns, but there isn't much else to recommend about this tired entry. One long fight scene is lifted from THE BIG SOMBRERO.▶

Waikiki Wedding (1937) **89m.** *** D: Frank Tuttle. Bing Crosby, Martha Raye, Shirley Ross, Bob Burns, Leif Erickson, Grady Sutton, Anthony Quinn. Light-hearted musical about a freewheeling "idea man" who finds himself in hot water when the winner of a beauty contest he cooked up, for public relations purposes, shows

up in Honolulu—and says she doesn't care for it. Raye's comedy dates badly, and the stars obviously never set foot in the islands, but it's all very pleasant. Score includes Oscar-winning "Sweet Leilani" and "Blue Hawaii," sung first by Bing and then in a delightful duet with Ross.▼)

Wait Till the Sun Shines, Nellie (1952) **C-108m.** *** D: Henry King. Jean Peters, David Wayne, Hugh Marlowe, Albert Dekker, Alan Hale, Warren Stevens. Nostalgic film of the hopes and disappointments of small town barber Wayne in the early 1900s. Produced by George Jessel.▶

Wake Island (1942) **87m.** *** D: John Farrow. Brian Donlevy, Robert Preston, Macdonald Carey, Albert Dekker, Walter Abel, Barbara Britton, William Bendix, Rod Cameron. Stirring war film of U.S.'s fight to hold Pacific island at outbreak of WW2. Nothing new here, but exciting and well done.▼)

Wake Me When It's Over (1960) **C-126m.** *** D: Mervyn LeRoy. Dick Shawn, Ernie Kovacs, Margo Moore, Jack Warden, Don Knotts. Entertaining comedy of hustling Shawn making the most of being stationed in the Far East by building a fancy hotel with Army supplies. Kovacs lends good support. CinemaScope.▶

Wake of the Red Witch (1949) **106m.** **½ D: Edward Ludwig. John Wayne, Gail Russell, Luther Adler, Gig Young, Adele Mara, Eduard Franz, Henry Daniell, Paul Fix. Rivalry between East Indies magnate and adventuresome ship's captain over pearls and a woman. Film is a bit confused, but nicely photographed by Reggie Lanning. Incidentally, Wayne took the name of his production company, Batjac, from this film's shipping firm. Also shown in computer-colored version.▼●)

Wake Up and Dream (1946) **C-92m.** ** D: Lloyd Bacon. June Haver, John Payne, Charlotte Greenwood, Connie Marshall, John Ireland, Clem Bevans, Lee Patrick. Moody film from Robert Nathan's story about girl determined to find brother missing from WW2.▶

Wake Up and Live (1937) **91m.** *** D: Sidney Lanfield. Alice Faye, Walter Winchell, Ben Bernie, Jack Haley, Patsy Kelly, Joan Davis, Grace Bradley, Warren Hymer, Ned Sparks, Walter Catlett. Fast-moving spoof of radio with battling Winchell and Bernie, mike-frightened singer Haley, and Faye singing "There's a Lull in My Life."▶

Walk a Crooked Mile (1948) **91m.** **½ D: Gordon Douglas. Louis Hayward, Dennis O'Keefe, Louise Allbritton, Carl Esmond, Onslow Stevens, Raymond Burr, Art Baker, Lowell Gilmore, Philip Van Zandt. Two heroes, a G-man (O'Keefe) and a Scotland Yard detective (Hayward), work together to battle subversives who are pilfering nuclear formulas. Unexceptional documentary-style melodrama was produced just as the House Un-American Activities Committee was holding hearings involving alleged pro-Communist content in Hollywood movies. Partly shot in San Francisco; bearded Burr offers a vivid performance as a Commie thug. ▶

Walk East on Beacon! (1952) 98m. **½ D: Alfred L. Werker. George Murphy, Finlay Currie, Virginia Gilmore, Karel Stepanek, Louisa Horton, Peter Capell. OK documentary-style drama, penned by Leo Rosten (and based on an article by J. Edgar Hoover), about FBI inspector Murphy's effort to thwart some Commie spies. Benefits from location filming in Boston but most interesting as a mirror of its era. Future filmmaker George Roy Hill appears in a small role as a scientist. ▶

Walking Dead, The (1936) 66m. *** D: Michael Curtiz. Boris Karloff, Edmund Gwenn, Marguerite Churchill, Ricardo Cortez, Barton MacLane, Warren Hull, Joe Sawyer. Karloff is framed and executed, but professor brings him back to life. As he regains his memory, he seeks out those who framed him. Good horror tale.●

Walking Hills, The (1949) 78m. *** D: John Sturges. Randolph Scott, Ella Raines, William Bishop, Edgar Buchanan, Arthur Kennedy, John Ireland, Jerome Courtland, Russell Collins, Josh White. Disparate group of men (and one unexpected woman) search for a wagon train loaded with gold that was abandoned a century earlier. Location filming in Death Valley and folksinger White's music add atmosphere to this gritty thriller. Title refers to windswept desert's ever-shifting mountains of sand. Written by Alan LeMay. ▶

Walking My Baby Back Home (1953) C-95m. **½ D: Lloyd Bacon. Donald O'Connor, Buddy Hackett, Janet Leigh, Scatman Crothers, George Cleveland, Lori Nelson. Confused musical comedy about Army buddies forming a Dixieland band; redeemed by Hackett's wacky humor.

Walking Nightmare, A SEE: Living Ghost, The

Walk in the Sun, A (1945) 117m. ***½ D: Lewis Milestone. Dana Andrews, Richard Conte, Sterling Holloway, George Tyne, John Ireland, Herbert Rudley, Norman Lloyd, Lloyd Bridges, Huntz Hall. Human aspect of war explored as American battalion attacks Nazi hideout in Italy; good character studies of men in war. Adapted by Robert Rossen from Harry Brown's novel. ▼●

Walk Into Hell (1956-Australian) C-93m. *½ D: Lee Robinson. Chips Rafferty, Francoise Christophe, Reginald Lye, Pierre Cressoy. Lumbering account of civilized Australians vs. native customs, filmed on location in New Guinea. Original title: WALK INTO PARADISE. ▼●

Walk Into Paradise SEE: Walk Into Hell
Walk Like a Dragon (1960) 95m. **½ D: James Clavell. Jack Lord, Nobu McCar-

thy, James Shigeta, Mel Tormé, Josephine Hutchinson, Rodolfo Acosta. Offbeat Western drama of Lord saving McCarthy from life of prostitution, taking her back to San Francisco, overcoming expected obstacles.

Walk on the Wild Side (1962) 114m. **½ D: Edward Dmytryk. Laurence Harvey, Capucine, Jane Fonda, Anne Baxter, Barbara Stanwyck. Lurid hodgepodge set in 1930s New Orleans, loosely based on Nelson Algren novel, of Harvey seeking lost love Capucine, now a member of bordello run by lesbian Stanwyck. Memorable titles by Saul Bass; fine score by Elmer Bernstein. ▼▶

Walk Softly, Stranger (1950) 81m. *** D: Robert Stevenson. Joseph Cotten, (Alida) Valli, Spring Byington, Paul Stewart, Jack Paar, Jeff Donnell, John McIntire. Cotten and Valli, who costarred in THE THIRD MAN, reteam in this well-told tale (which actually was shot before the Carol Reed classic) of a mysterious small-time gambler-thief whose worldview changes upon coming to a small Ohio town and hooking up with a wheelchair-bound heiress. ▼▶

Walk the Dark Street (1956) 73m. *½ D: Wyott Ordung. Chuck Connors, Don Ross, Regina Gleason, Vonne Godfrey, Eddie Kafafian, Ewing Brown, Ernest Dominy. THE MOST DANGEROUS GAME is played out on the streets of L.A. Dismayingly amateurish with little suspense or action; neither of the opponents ever fires his high-powered rifle! Location work is interesting, and Connors occasionally creepy. Director Ordung also produced and scripted.

Walk the Proud Land (1956) C-88m. *** D: Jesse Hibbs. Audie Murphy, Anne Bancroft, Pat Crowley, Charles Drake, Jay Silverheels. Sturdy scripting makes this oater attractive; Murphy is Indian agent trying to quell strife between redskins and settlers, with the capture of Geronimo (Silverheels) his major feat. CinemaScope. ▼▶

Wallflower (1948) 77m. *** D: Frederick de Cordova. Joyce Reynolds, Robert Hutton, Janis Paige, Edward Arnold, Jerome Cowan, Barbara Brown. Amusing comedy based on Broadway success; two stepsisters (Reynolds and Paige) vie for the same love.

Wall of Noise (1963) 112m. **½ D: Richard Wilson. Suzanne Pleshette, Ty Hardin, Dorothy Provine, Ralph Meeker, Simon Oakland, Murray Matheson. Turgid racetrack drama with adultery, not horses, the focal point. ▶

Walls Came Tumbling Down, The (1946) 82m. *** D: Lothar Mendes. Lee Bowman, Marguerite Chapman, Edgar Buchanan, Lee Patrick, J. Edward Bromberg. Detective Bowman goes to work when priest is murdered in fast-moving private eye film. ▶

Walls of Gold (1933) 74m. *½ D: Kenneth MacKenna. Sally Eilers, Norman Foster, Ralph Morgan, Rosita Moreno, Rochelle Hudson. Eilers does something to ruffle fiancé Foster, so to spite her he marries her sister, and she marries his uncle. Forget it.

Walls of Jericho, The (1948) **106m. ** D: John M. Stahl. Cornel Wilde, Linda Darnell, Anne Baxter, Kirk Douglas, Ann Dvorak, Marjorie Rambeau, Henry Hull, Colleen Townsend, Barton MacLane. Good cast tries to perk up story of ambitious lawyer in Jericho, Kansas, whose marital problems stand in the way of success; pretty dreary going most of the way.

Wall Street Cowboy (1939) **66m. **½** D: Joseph Kane. Roy Rogers, George "Gabby" Hayes, Raymond Hatton, Ann Baldwin, Pierre Watkin, Louisiana Lou, Craig Reynolds, Ivan Miller, Reginald Barlow, Jack Ingram. Roy enlists the aid of cattle rancher Watkin and his daughter (Baldwin) to save his cattle ranch from a crooked banker and mortgagor. Engaging Western with two sidekicks (Hayes and Hatton) touches upon Depression-era subjects of corrupt banking institutions and foreclosures; fun to watch Roy riding in a steeplechase and singing in a nightclub (wearing a coat and tie). ▼▶

Waltzes From Vienna (1934-British) **80m. ** D: Alfred Hitchcock. Jessie Matthews, Esmond Knight, Frank Vosper, Fay Compton, Edmund Gwenn, Robert Hale. Hitchcock made this ponderous costume drama about composers Johann Strauss and his son just before THE MAN WHO KNEW TOO MUCH set him on his path to become the master of suspense and later called it the "low ebb of my career." It's really not that bad, but it only comes to life during the musical sequences. Inspirations for songs are as corny as those in most Hollywood musical biopics. Original U.S. title: STRAUSS'S GREAT WALTZ.

Waltz King, The (1963) **C-95m. **½** D: Steve Previn. Kerwin Mathews, Brian Aherne, Senta Berger, Peter Kraus, Fritz Eckhardt. Moderately entertaining Disney musical biopic stars Mathews as Johann Strauss, Jr., with lots of good music. Filmed in Austria; shown in the U.S. as two-part TV show. ▶

Waltz of the Toreadors (1962-British) **C-105m. *** D: John Guillermin. Peter Sellers, Dany Robin, Margaret Leighton, John Fraser. Jean Anouilh's saucy sex romp gets top notch handling with Sellers as the retired military officer who still can't keep his eye off the girls. ▼▶

Wandering Shadow, The (1920-German) **67m. ** D: Fritz Lang. Mia May, Hans Marr, Harry Frank, Rudolf Klein-Rogge, Loni Nest. Muddled, predictable early Lang "mountain film"/melodrama involving the plight of an honorable woman (May) sexually entangled with a rich louse (Marr, who also plays the villain's brother). ▶

Wanted for Murder (1946-British) **102m. *** D: Lawrence Huntington. Eric Portman, Dulcie Gray, Derek Farr, Roland Culver, Stanley Holloway, Barbara Everest, Bonar Colleano, Jenny Laird, Kathleen Harrison, Wilfrid Hyde-White. Engaging, semi-Hitchcockian story with Portman, descendant of a professional hangman, obsessed by his ancestor, strangling young women in London. Alternately dramatic, suspenseful, and darkly humorous; Culver and Holloway as Scotland Yard men are a delight. Coscripted by Emeric Pressburger, from a stage play. ▶

Wanted! Jane Turner (1936) **67m. *** D: Edward Killy. Lee Tracy, Gloria Stuart, Judith Blake (Ann Preston), John McGuire, Frank M. Thomas, Paul Guilfoyle, Irene Franklin, Patricia Wilder, Barbara Pepper, Willard Robertson, Paul Fix. Tracy and Stuart have great chemistry as squabbling postal inspectors teaming to foil the killer of a mail truck driver. Entertaining and cleverly plotted.

Wanton Countess, The SEE: Senso

War Against Mrs. Hadley, The (1942) **86m. ** D: Harold Bucquet. Edward Arnold, Fay Bainter, Richard Ney, Sara Allgood, Spring Byington, Jean Rogers, Frances Rafferty, Dorothy Morris, Rags Ragland, Isobel Elsom, Van Johnson. Mild WW2 human-interest tale by George Oppenheimer about matron Bainter who refuses to participate in war support.

War and Peace (1956-U.S.-Italian) **C-208m. **½** D: King Vidor. Audrey Hepburn, Henry Fonda, Mel Ferrer, Vittorio Gassman, John Mills, Herbert Lom, Oscar Homolka, Anita Ekberg, Helmut Dantine, Barry Jones, Milly Vitale, Jeremy Brett, Wilfrid Lawson, Mai Britt. Tolstoy's sprawling novel fails to come alive in this overlong, oversimplified adaptation. Star-studded cast and spectacular battle scenes (directed by Mario Soldati) cannot compensate for clumsy script (by six writers, including Vidor) and some profound miscasting. Filmed far more successfully in 1968. VistaVision. ▼▶

War Arrow (1953) **C-78m. ** D: George Sherman. Maureen O'Hara, Jeff Chandler, Suzan Ball, John McIntire, Noah Beery, Charles Drake, Henry Brandon, Dennis Weaver, Jay Silverheels, James (Jim) Bannon. U.S. cavalry major Chandler contends with misguided superior officer McIntire as he trains Seminole Indians to fight the murderous Kiowa. There's precious little action in this talky Western. ▼▶

War Between the Planets (1965-Italian) **C-80m.** BOMB D: Anthony Dawson (Antonio Margheriti). Jack Stuart (Giacomo Rossi-Stuarti), Amber Collins (Ombretta Colli), Peter Martell, Halina Zalewska. Alien planet is on collision course with earth, but valiant efforts by scientific forces snatch victory from the jaws of boredom. Fun only if you like spaghetti sci-fi. Made at same time as other losers such as WAR OF THE PLAN-

ETS, WILD WILD PLANET, etc. Aka PLANET ON THE PROWL. ▼▶

War Drums (1957) **C-75m.** **½ D: Reginald LeBorg. Lex Barker, Joan Taylor, Ben Johnson, Stuart Whitman, Jeanne Carmen. Sufficiently bloody Western set in Civil War days of Indian uprisings against onslaught of gold miners. ▶

War-Gods of the Deep (1965-U.S.-British) **C-85m.** **½ D: Jacques Tourneur. Vincent Price, Tab Hunter, David Tomlinson, Susan Hart, John LeMesurier. Gill-men invade remote seacoast town. Actually, two films in one: establishing menace, first half has odd, almost poetic feel to it, but second half deteriorates, with shoddy underwater city. Tourneur's final feature. British title: THE CITY UNDER THE SEA. Colorscope. ▼▶

War Hunt (1962) **81m.** **½ D: Denis Sanders. John Saxon, Robert Redford, Charles Aidman, Sydney Pollack. Well-done Korean War story focusing on kill-happy soldier Saxon who tries to help an orphan boy. Redford and Pollack's film debuts.▶

War Is Hell (1963) **81m.** ** D: Burt Topper. Tony Russel, Baynes Barron, Tony Rich, Burt Topper. Korean War actioner with no new ideas to offer. Introduced by Audie Murphy.

Warlock (1959) **C-121m.** *** D: Edward Dmytryk. Richard Widmark, Henry Fonda, Anthony Quinn, Dorothy Malone, Dolores Michaels, Wallace Ford, Tom Drake, Richard Arlen, DeForest Kelley, Regis Toomey. Philosophical vigilante "sheriff" Fonda is hired to clean up the crime-infested Western town of Warlock. This sets off a complex storyline involving, among others, crippled Quinn, guilt-ridden Widmark, and embittered Malone. Literate, allegorical adult Western examines the lynch-mob mentality and the meaning of machismo. Forgotten, but worthy of rediscovery. Scripted by Robert Alan Aurthur. CinemaScope.▼▶

War Lord, The (1965) **C-123m.** *** D: Franklin Schaffner. Charlton Heston, Rosemary Forsyth, Richard Boone, Maurice Evans, Guy Stockwell, Niall McGinnis, James Farentino, Henry Wilcoxon, Michael Conrad. Intriguing, generally well-done adaptation of Leslie Stevens' *The Lovers*, with Heston as feudal knight invoking little-known law allowing him to have another man's bride on their wedding night. Title and medieval setting would seem to indicate sweeping spectacle . . . which this certainly isn't. Panavision.▼▶

War Lover, The (1962-British) **105m.** **½ D: Philip Leacock. Steve McQueen, Robert Wagner, Shirley Anne Field, Gary Cockrell, Michael Crawford, Al Waxman. John Hersey's thoughtful novel becomes superficial account of egocentric, psychotic WW2 pilot McQueen, who becomes unhinged when copilot Wagner begins a romantic re-

lationship with Field. Worth seeing for McQueen's edgy, riveting presence.▼▶

War Nurse (1930) **78m.** *** D: Edgar Selwyn. Robert Montgomery, June Walker, Robert Ames, Anita Page, ZaSu Pitts, Marie Prevost, Hedda Hopper, Helen Jerome Eddy, Eddie Nugent, Martha Sleeper. Frank, gritty account of the illicit affairs of American women serving as nurses in France during WW1, based on a risqué, anonymously published book. Sometimes melodramatic but earnest and quite powerful, with a climactic battle scene that pulls no punches. Standout photography by Charles Rosher.

War of the Colossal Beast (1958) **68m.** *½ D: Bert I. Gordon. Sally Fraser, Roger Pace, Dean Parkin, Russ Bender, Charles Stewart. Sequel to THE AMAZING COLOSSAL MAN finds our oversized hero alive but not well; his face is a mess, and so is his mind, leading to the inevitable low-budget rampage. Forget it. Last shot is in color.▼▶

War of the Planets (1965-Italian) **C-99m.** BOMB D: Anthony Dawson (Antonio Margheriti). Tony Russel, Lisa Gastoni, Massimo Serato, Franco Nero, Carlo Giustini. Light creatures attack Earth but are repelled. Cheap sets and plodding script make this a loser. ▶

War of the Satellites (1958) **66m.** ** D: Roger Corman. Dick Miller, Susan Cabot, Richard Devon, Robert Shayne, Eric Sinclair. Ruthless combination of THE DAY THE EARTH STOOD STILL and KRONOS has unseen aliens warning Earth to cease their space exploration, brainwashing scientist Devon to make sure it's done. The day after the U.S. Explorer satellite went up, Corman told a studio he could have a film ready in two months . . . and he did. Not so hot, but any movie with Dick Miller as a heroic scientist can't be *all* bad.

War of the Wildcats SEE: **In Old Oklahoma**

War of the Worlds, The (1953) **C-85m.** ***½ D: Byron Haskin. Gene Barry, Les Tremayne, Ann Robinson, Robert Cornthwaite, Henry Brandon, Jack Kruschen; narrated by Sir Cedric Hardwicke. Vivid, frightening adaptation of H. G. Wells' novel about a Martian invasion, transplanted from 19th-century England to contemporary USA. Dramatically sound and filled with dazzling, Oscar-winning special effects; superior sci-fi, produced by George Pal. Later a TV series. Remade three times in 2005 as WAR OF THE WORLDS, H. G. WELLS' THE WAR OF THE WORLDS, and H. G. WELLS' WAR OF THE WORLDS. ▼▶

War of the Zombies (1965-Italian) **C-85m.** ** D: Giuseppe Vari. John Drew Barrymore, Susy Anderson, Ettore Manni, Ida Galli. Rome sends best legionnaire to quell disturbance in Eastern province in clutches of mad priest (Barrymore). Production values somewhat better than usual. Aka NIGHT STAR GODDESS OF ELECTRA.

War Paint (1953) **C-89m.** **½ D: Lesley Selander. Robert Stack, Joan Taylor, Charles McGraw, Peter Graves, Keith Larsen, William Pullen, Richard Cutting, Douglas Kennedy, Walter Reed. Action-packed film of U. S. cavalry detachment overcoming danger and villainous attempts to prevent delivery of peace treaty to an Indian chief. ▶

Warpath (1951) **C-95m.** **½ D: Byron Haskin. Edmond O'Brien, Dean Jagger, Forrest Tucker, Harry Carey, Jr., Wallace Ford, Polly Bergen. Nifty action Western with O'Brien hunting down outlaws who killed his girlfriend; an Indian attack is thrown in for good measure.

Warrior and the Slave Girl, The (1958-Italian) **C-84m.** ** D: Vittorio Cottafavi. Ettore Manni, Georges Marchal, Gianna Maria Canale, Rafael Calvo. Unsubtle costumer set in ancient Armenia, with Canale the evil princess, subdued by Roman Manni. SuperCinescope.

Warrior Empress, The (1960-Italian) **C-87m.** ** D: Pietro Francisci. Kerwin Mathews, Tina Louise, Riccardo Garrone, Antonio Batistella, Enrico Maria Salerno. Senseless mixture of fantasy and adventure with Phaon (Mathews) falling in love with Sappho (Louise), overcoming treacherous Salerno. CinemaScope.

Warriors, The (1955-British) **C-85m.** **½ D: Henry Levin. Errol Flynn, Joanne Dru, Peter Finch, Patrick Holt, Yvonne Furneaux, Michael Hordern, Christopher Lee. Flynn's final swashbuckler casts him as British prince protecting French conquests (and lovely Dru) from attacks by Finch and his supporters. Well made but awfully familiar. British title: THE DARK AVENGER. CinemaScope.▼▶

Washington Masquerade, The (1932) **87m.** **½ D: Charles Brabin. Lionel Barrymore, Karen Morley, Diane Sinclair, Nils Asther, Reginald Barlow, William Collier, Sr., Hattie McDaniel. Barrymore offers a bravura performance as an outspoken, idealistic lawyer who's elected to the U.S. Senate, where he tangles with the power elite; he's also seduced by a Washington hostess with a hidden agenda. Occasionally talky but still timely exposé of political shenanigans and special interests.

Washington Melodrama (1941) **80m.** ** D: S. Sylvan Simon. Frank Morgan, Ann Rutherford, Kent Taylor, Dan Dailey, Jr., Lee Bowman, Fay Holden, Virginia Grey, Anne Gwynne, Sara Haden, Douglass Dumbrille. Lonely Washington insider Morgan, whose wife and daughter are endlessly traveling, innocently befriends a showgirl—who's then murdered. Modest B movie is aptly titled; young Dailey plays a slimy villain.

Washington Merry-Go-Round (1932) **79m.** **½ D: James Cruze. Lee Tracy, Constance Cummings, Alan Dinehart, Jane Darwell. Dry run for MR. SMITH GOES TO WASHINGTON

has idealistic young congressman Tracy out to do good for his Depression-ravaged constituents—only to find it ain't that easy, especially when he opposes an "important" appropriations bill. Remains surprisingly relevant today, with engaging performances and strong feel for the political arena, but peters out after great first half.

Washington Story (1952) **81m.** ** D: Robert Pirosh. Van Johnson, Patricia Neal, Louis Calhern, Sidney Blackmer, Elizabeth Patterson. Newspaperwoman Neal assigned to harass Congress selects young Congressman Johnson as her target; naturally, she falls in love with him. Romantic angle is better than political one—but neither is particularly interesting.

Wasp Woman, The (1960) **66m.** **½ D: Roger Corman. Susan Cabot, Fred (Anthony) Eisley, Barboura Morris, Michael Mark, William Roerick. Enjoyable Corman cheapie about cosmetics magnate Cabot, fearful of aging, using royal jelly from wasps to become young and beautiful. She also periodically turns into a wasp-monster that must kill. Minor camp classic; an unauthorized semi-remake, EVIL SPAWN, was made for video in 1987. Remade for TV in 1996.▼▶

Watch It, Sailor! (1961-British) **81m.** ** D: Wolf Rilla. Dennis Price, Liz Fraser, Irene Handl, Graham Stark, Marjorie Rhodes. Mildly amusing stage farce adapted to screen, with Price managing to outdo Fraser's mother (Rhodes), getting to the church on time.

Watch on the Rhine (1943) **114m.** ***½ D: Herman Shumlin. Bette Davis, Paul Lukas, Geraldine Fitzgerald, Lucile Watson, Beulah Bondi, George Coulouris, Donald Woods, Henry Daniell. Fine filmization of Lillian Hellman's timely WW2 play of German Lukas and wife Davis pursued and harried by Nazi agents in Washington. Lukas gives the performance of his career, which won him an Oscar; Bette somewhat overshadowed. Script by Dashiell Hammett. ▼▶

Watch the Birdie (1950) **70m.** **½ D: Jack Donohue. Red Skelton, Arlene Dahl, Ann Miller, Leon Ames, Pamela Britton, Richard Rober. Average Skelton comedy features him as photographer, silly father, and grandfather. Rest of cast is also good with routine material, reworking of Buster Keaton's THE CAMERAMAN.▼▶

Watch Your Stern (1960-British) **88m.** ** D: Gerald Thomas. Kenneth Connor, Eric Barker, Leslie Phillips, Joan Sims, Hattie Jacques. Amusing, obvious shenanigans on the seas, with Connor impersonating a scientist sent to perfect a torpedo.

Waterfront (1944) **66m.** *½ D: Steve Sekely. John Carradine, J. Carrol Naish, Maris Wrixon, Edwin Maxwell, Terry Frost. Low-grade espionage tale of Nazi agents Carradine and Naish murdering and blackmailing in WW2 San Francisco. ▼▶

Waterloo Bridge (1931) 81m. *** D: James Whale. Mae Clarke, Kent Douglass (Douglass Montgomery), Doris Lloyd, Frederick Kerr, Enid Bennett, Bette Davis, Ethel Griffies. Excellent early-talkie version of Robert E. Sherwood play, a tearjerker romance with an exceptional performance by Clarke as an American chorus-girl-turned-prostitute in WW1 London. Has a pre-Code grittiness missing from its glossier, more famous 1940 remake; remade again in 1956 as GABY. One of Davis' earliest screen roles. ▶

Waterloo Bridge (1940) 103m. ***½ D: Mervyn LeRoy. Vivien Leigh, Robert Taylor, Lucile Watson, Virginia Field, Maria Ouspenskaya, C. Aubrey Smith. Sentimental love story, well acted, of soldier and ballet dancer meeting during London air raid, falling in love instantly. Cleaned-up version of the Robert E. Sherwood play, with beautiful performance by lovely Leigh. Screenplay by S. N. Behrman, Hans Rameau, and George Froeschel. First filmed in 1931, remade as GABY. Also shown in computer-colored version. ▼●▶

Waterloo Road (1944-British) 76m. *** D: Sidney Gilliat. John Mills, Stewart Granger, Alastair Sim, Joy Shelton, Beatrice Varley, Alison Leggatt, Jean Kent. Enjoyable wartime drama about soldier who goes AWOL when he learns his wife has been seeing another man. Evocative of its period, with spry touches of humor.

Watusi (1959) C-85m. **½ D: Kurt Neumann. George Montgomery, Taina Elg, David Farrar, Rex Ingram, Dan Seymour. Fabricated sequel to KING SOLOMON'S MINES built around footage from the 1950 original, with Allan Quatermain's son Harry now in search of fabled diamond mines. Written by James Clavell.

Waxworks (1924-German) 83m. *** D: Paul Leni. Wilhelm (William) Dieterle, John Gottowt, Olga Belajeff, Emil Jannings, Conrad Veidt, Werner Krauss. Atmospheric German-expressionist classic in which three notorious figures in a waxworks exhibit come to life. The Baghdad story pales beside the sequences involving Jack the Ripper (Krauss) and Ivan the Terrible, with Veidt bringing that character to vivid life. ▼▶

Way Ahead, The (1944-British) 91m. ***½ D: Carol Reed. David Niven, Stanley Holloway, James Donald, John Laurie, Leslie Dwyer, Hugh Burden, Jimmy Hanley, Billy Hartnell, Raymond Huntley, Reginald Tate, Leo Genn, Penelope Dudley Ward, Renée Asherson, Raymond Lovell, Peter Ustinov, Trevor Howard. Exhilarating wartime British film showing how disparate civilians come to work together as a fighting unit; full of spirit and charm, with an outstanding cast, and fine script by Eric Ambler and Peter Ustinov. Film debut of Trevor Howard. Originally released in the U.S. in a

shortened, more serious version called THE IMMORTAL BATTALION (with an introduction by journalist Quentin Reynolds). Original British running time 116m. ▼▶

Way and the Body, The SEE: **Whip and the Body, The**

Way Down East (1920) 119m. *** D: D. W. Griffith. Lillian Gish, Richard Barthelmess, Lowell Sherman, Burr McIntosh, Kate Bruce, Mary Hay, Creighton Hale. The ultimate stage melodrama—with a city slicker despoiling the innocence of a virginal heroine, who then must pay the price. Executed with conviction by Griffith and a fine cast, building up to famous climax with Gish adrift on ice floes. Often shown in shorter versions; restored to 148m. by the Museum of Modern Art in 1985. Remade in 1935. ▼●▶

Way Down East (1935) 80m. *** D: Henry King. Rochelle Hudson, Henry Fonda, Russell Simpson, Slim Summerville, Spring Byington, Margaret Hamilton, Andy Devine. Sincere retelling of stage melodrama about a "woman with a past" in a tight-knit farm community, first filmed by D. W. Griffith. Nice location work; only the phony ice-floe finale disappoints.

Way Down South (1939) 61m. **½ D: Bernard Vorhaus. Bobby Breen, Alan Mowbray, Clarence Muse, Ralph Morgan, Edwin Maxwell, Steffi Duna, Sally Blane, Charles Middleton, Hall Johnson Choir. Hokey but fascinating musical curio (written by Muse and Langston Hughes!), set in the pre–Civil War South. Boy soprano Breen is the young master of a plantation, whose "happy" slaves are scheduled for sale by crooked lawyer Maxwell. ▼▶

Way for a Sailor (1930) 83m. ** D: Sam Wood. John Gilbert, Wallace Beery, Leila Hyams, Jim Tully, Polly Moran. Early talkie with silent-star Gilbert as devoted sailor who loses girl for the sea. Mostly a curio for early-talkie film buffs.

Wayne Murder Case, The SEE: **Strange Adventure, A** (1932)

Way of a Gaucho (1952) C-91m. ** D: Jacques Tourneur. Gene Tierney, Rory Calhoun, Richard Boone, Hugh Marlowe, Everett Sloane. Soaper set in 1870s Argentina of Tierney and Calhoun trying to make a go of life on the Pampas. ▶

Way of All Flesh, The (1940) 86m. ** D: Louis King. Akim Tamiroff, Gladys George, William Henry, Muriel Angelus, Berton Churchill, Roger Imhof. Hungarian immigrant Tamiroff toils as a bank clerk, becomes victimized when his boss sends him on a mission to deliver money to a client. Overly sentimental melodrama; remake of Emil Jannings 1927 silent film.

Way of the Strong, The (1928) 61m. **½ D: Frank R. Capra. Mitchell Lewis, Alice Day, Margaret Livingston, Theodore von Eltz, William Norton Bailey. Gruff, unscrupulous bootlegger Lewis falls in love with a virginal, blind street violinist; he can't bear the idea that she should know him by his ugly face, so he has her "feel" the features of his down-and-out café pianist (von Eltz). Predictable, formulaic, but quite watchable, with some pretty rugged scenes (and impressive use of a moving camera).

Way of Youth, The (1959-French) **81m.** ** D: Michel Boisrond. Françoise Arnoul, Lino Ventura, Bourvil, Alain Delon, Jean-Claude Brialy, Paulette Dubost, Madeleine LeBeau, Pierre Mondy, Sandra Milo. Greedy older woman manipulates teenager into becoming involved in the local black market. Good cast tries its best.

Way Out, The (1955-British) **90m.** BOMB D: Montgomery Tully. Gene Nelson, Mona Freeman, John Bentley, Michael Goodliffe, Sydney Tafler. Lumbering, sloppily made melodrama in which devoted wife Freeman comes to the aid of duplicitous husband Nelson, who has committed murder while in an alcoholic haze. Original British title: DIAL 999. ▼▶

Way Out West (1930) **70m.** **½ D: Fred Niblo. William Haines, Leila Hyams, Polly Moran, Cliff Edwards, Francis X. Bushman, Jr., Vera Marsh, Charles Middleton. Haines is pretty funny as a carnival con man forced to work on a ranch after he swindles some cowboys. Naturally, the pretty ranch owner falls for him. One of the star's better talkies, a Western spoof with snappy one-liners and a rootin'-tootin' gun-battle finale.

Way Out West (1937) **65m.** ***½ D: James W. Horne. Stan Laurel, Oliver Hardy, Sharon Lynn, James Finlayson, Rosina Lawrence, Stanley Fields, Vivien Oakland. Stan and Ollie are sent to deliver mine deed to daughter of late prospector, but crooked Finlayson leads them to wrong girl. One of their best features; moves well without resorting to needless romantic subplot. Another bonus: some charming musical interludes, and the boys perform a wonderful soft-shoe dance. Also shown in computer-colored version. ▼▶▶

Way to Love, The (1933) **80m.** *** D: Norman Taurog. Maurice Chevalier, Ann Dvorak, Edward Everett Horton, Minna Gombell, Nydia Westman, Douglass Dumbrille, John Miljan, Grace Bradley, Sidney Toler. Chevalier falls in love with Dvorak, who works on the wrong end of a knife-throwing act, in this pleasant romantic comedy with music; songs include title tune, "I'm a Lover of Paris."

Way to the Gold, The (1957) **94m.** ** D: Robert D. Webb. Jeffrey Hunter, Sheree North, Barry Sullivan, Neville Brand, Walter Brennan. Meandering buried-loot-hunt story. CinemaScope.

Way to the Stars, The (1945-British) **109m.** *** D: Anthony Asquith. Michael Redgrave, John Mills, Rosamund John, Douglass Montgomery, Stanley Holloway, Renée Asherson,

Felix Aylmer, Basil Radford, Bonar Colleano, Jr., Trevor Howard, Jean Simmons, Joyce Carey, David Tomlinson, Anthony Dawson. Sentimental portrait of life at a British airfield and its neighboring town during WW2, made just after the war's conclusion. Sincere performances by a top-notch cast nicely capture the stiff-upper-lip attitude and sacrifices of the period. Screenplay by Terence Rattigan, from a story by Rattigan and Anatole de Grunwald. Original U.S. title: JOHNNY IN THE CLOUDS. ▶

Wayward Bus, The (1957) **89m.** ** D: Victor Vicas. Joan Collins, Jayne Mansfield, Dan Dailey, Rick Jason. Low-brow version of John Steinbeck novel about interaction of passengers on bus in California. CinemaScope. ▶

Wayward Girl, The (1957) **71m.** *½ D: Lesley Selander. Marcia Henderson, Peter Walker, Whit Bissell, Ray Teal, Barbara Eden. Turgid nonsense about mother and stepdaughter vying for same lover, leading to murder. Naturama.

Wayward Girl, The (1959-Norwegian) **91m.** **½ D: Edith Carlmar. Liv Ullmann, Atle Merton, Rolf Søder, Tore Foss, Nana Stenersen. Moralistic romance tale of young lovers who seek refuge on a deserted farm, becoming involved with the returning owner. Primarily of note for the presence of Ullmann, in one of her first screen roles.

Wayward Wife, The (1953-Italian) **91m.** ** D: Mario Soldati. Gina Lollobrigida, Gabriele Ferzetti, Franco Interlenghi, Renato Baldini. Unimaginative, predictable film of blackmail. Lollobrigida, girl with a past, finds her marriage threatened.

Weak and the Wicked, The (1953-British) **81m.** **½ D: J. Lee Thompson. Glynis Johns, John Gregson, Diana Dors, Jane Hylton. Frank study of women's prison life, focusing on their rehabilitation.

Weaker Sex, The (1948-British) **89m.** ** D: Roy (Ward) Baker. Ursula Jeans, Cecil Parker, Joan Hopkins, Derek Bond, Thora Hird, Bill Owen. Jeans is staunch English housewife showing her patriotic zest during WW2; modest domestic comedy.

Weapon, The (1956-British) **81m.** **½ D: Val Guest. Steve Cochran, Lizabeth Scott, George Cole, Herbert Marshall, Nicole Maurey, Jon Whiteley. Minor but trim story of youngster who accidentally shoots his pal and runs away. SuperScope 235. ▶

We Are All Murderers (1952-French) **113m.** *** D: André Cayatte. Marcel Mouloudji, Raymond Pellegrin, Louis Seigner, Antoine Balpetre, Claude Leydu, Georges Poujouly. Powerful, potent anti–capital-punishment drama. Mouloudji plays a none-too-bright hood who was praised for killing during WW2, but now is condemned to death for murdering a cop; he and two other men await their fates on death row. Released in the U.S. in 1957.

We Are Not Alone (1939) 112m. **½ D:
Edmund Goulding. Paul Muni, Jane Bryan,
Flora Robson, Raymond Severn, Una
O'Connor, Henry Daniell, Montagu Love,
Cecil Kellaway, Alan Napier. Gentle English
country doctor, with a hardened, shrewish
wife and an adoring son, innocently takes
in a troubled young woman as governess,
leading to unforeseen conflicts and crises.
Muni is a pleasure to watch, as always, and
Bryan is surprisingly effective as the Austrian governess with whom he falls in love,
but the story is too pat. More interesting as a
cautionary parable for a world on the brink
of war, which is what author James Hilton
intended; he also cowrote the script.
Weary River (1929) 86m. **½ D: Frank
Lloyd. Richard Barthelmess, Betty Compson, William Holden, Louis Natheaux,
George (E.) Stone. Intriguing curio with
Barthelmess a hood who's sent to the pen,
where he begins a new career as a singer-
composer. Silent film with sound sequences
makes those transitions better than most
"part talkies" of the period. Title tune (performed by Barthelmess but voiced by
Johnny Murray) is repeated no fewer than
four times! ◗
Web, The (1947) 87m. *** D: Michael Gordon. Ella Raines, Edmond O'Brien, William Bendix, Vincent Price, Maria Palmer.
Tough bodyguard engages in murder, then
finds himself a patsy for boss' schemes.
Exciting melodrama, one of O'Brien's best
early roles.
Web of Evidence (1959-British) 88m. **½
D: Jack Cardiff. Van Johnson, Vera Miles,
Emlyn Williams, Bernard Lee, Jean Kent,
Ralph Truman, Leo McKern. Sincere drama
of Johnson in England finding clues to prove
his father innocent of murder. Original British title: BEYOND THIS PLACE.
Web of Passion (1959-French) C-94m. ***
D: Claude Chabrol. Antonella Lualdi, Madeleine Robinson, Bernadette Lafont, Jacques
Dacqmine, Jeanne Valerie, Jean-Paul Belmondo, André Jocelyn. Beguiling early Chabrol concoction in which he pillories upper-
class superficiality and overindulgence. The
setting is a country estate that is home to a dysfunctional family whose members are either
eccentric or downright neurotic. Right in the
middle of it all, someone is murdered! Henri
Decaë's crisp cinematography and Paul Mis-
raki's tongue-in-cheek music score are assets.
Belmondo plays a decadent slacker named
Laszlo Kovacs, which is also his character's
alias in BREATHLESS. Aka LEDA and À
DOUBLE TOUR. ◗
Wedding March, The (1928) 113m. ****
D: Erich von Stroheim. Erich von Stroheim,
Fay Wray, ZaSu Pitts, George Fawcett,
Maude George, George Nicholls, Cesare
Gravina. In pre-WW1 Vienna, a roguish
prince (played to perfection by von Stro-
heim) agrees to marry for money and po-

sition to help his family, then falls in love
with a poor but beautiful and crippled girl
(Wray). A masterpiece, blending romance
and irony, with an unforgettable finale . . .
though what we see is just the first half of
the film von Stroheim completed (the second no longer exists). One sequence in two-
color Technicolor. ▼
Wedding Night, The (1935) 84m. **½
D: King Vidor. Gary Cooper, Anna Sten,
Ralph Bellamy, Walter Brennan, Helen
Vinson, Sig Ruman. Study of romance and
idealism; unbelievable love yarn but entertaining. Producer Samuel Goldwyn's third
and final attempt to make Anna Sten a new
Garbo. ▼◗
Wedding Present (1936) 81m. *** D:
Richard Wallace. Cary Grant, Joan Bennett, George Bancroft, Conrad Nagel, Gene
Lockhart, William Demarest, Inez Courtney.
Underrated screwball comedy centering on
antics of irresponsible—and perpetually
engaged—reporters Grant and Bennett, who
drive boss Bancroft crazy yet somehow
always come up with the big story. But
Bennett takes up with wealthy Nagel when
Grant is appointed editor and becomes a tyrant. Thoroughly enjoyable farce with lots
of laughs.◗
Wedding Rehearsal (1932-British) 79m.
** D: Alexander Korda. Roland Young,
George Grossmith, John Loder, Wendy
Barrie, Joan Gardner, Merle Oberon, Maurice Evans. Lifelong bachelor nobleman
(Young) tries to circumvent his rich grandmother's demand that he take a wife by
scheming to marry off the eligible young
ladies on her list. Excellent cast enhances
Korda's first London Films production,
which strains to be a Lubitsch-like comedy
of manners but lacks the requisite panache.
Weddings and Babies (1958) 77m. **½
D: Morris Engel. Viveca Lindfors, John
Myhers, Chiarina Barile, Leonard Elliott,
Joanna Merlin. Thoughtful observance
of human behavior and emotions from
always-interesting filmmaker Engel. Photographer who earns his living filming
weddings and babies has vague dreams of
making "real" movies; his assistant and
girlfriend is anxious to have a wedding and
babies of her own. ▼◗
We Dive at Dawn (1943-British) 98m.
*** D: Anthony Asquith. John Mills, Eric
Portman, Niall MacGinnis, Reginald Purdell,
Louis Bradfield, Ronald Millar. First-rate
WW2 submarine saga, concentrating on
personalities of men in the crew as much as
on assignment to sink German battleship.
Nicely understated drama. ▼◗
Wee Geordie (1955-British) C-93m. ***½
D: Frank Launder. Bill Travers, Alastair
Sim, Norah Gorsen, Molly Urquhart, Fran-
cis De Wolff. Flavorful romp with Travers
a Scottish hammer thrower who goes to the
Olympics. Despite predictable sight gags

and romance, film makes one relish each situation. Original British title: GEORDIE.

Weekend at Dunkirk (1965-France-Italy) **C-101m.** ** D: Henri Verneuil. Jean-Paul Belmondo, Catherine Spaak, Georges Geret, Jean-Pierre Marielle, Pierre Mondy. Dull war film, based on well-known French novel, about four French soldiers on the Dunkirk Beach around evacuation time early in WW2. Franscope.

Week-end at the Waldorf (1945) **130m.** *** D: Robert Z. Leonard. Ginger Rogers, Lana Turner, Walter Pidgeon, Van Johnson, Edward Arnold, Phyllis Thaxter, Keenan Wynn, Robert Benchley, Leon Ames, Porter Hall, George Zucco, Xavier Cugat and His Orchestra. Several "typical" days in the life of the fabled Waldorf-Astoria Hotel. Ultra-glossy MGM remake of GRAND HOTEL weaves disparate characters' lives together. No resonance whatsoever, but good, slick entertainment, with Rogers and Pidgeon standing out in the attractive cast. ▼▶

Weekend for Three (1941) **61m.** ** D: Irving Reis. Dennis O'Keefe, Jane Wyatt, Philip Reed, ZaSu Pitts, Edward Everett Horton, Franklin Pangborn, Hans Conried. Hapless O'Keefe and manipulative wife Wyatt entertain her boorish old friend (Reed), who quickly proves to be the houseguest from hell. Considering cast and writers (Dorothy Parker and Alan Campbell, from a Budd Schulberg story), it's astonishing this isn't better than it is.

Week-end in Havana (1941) **C-80m.** *** D: Walter Lang. Alice Faye, Carmen Miranda, John Payne, Cesar Romero, Cobina Wright, Jr., George Barbier, Leonid Kinskey, Sheldon Leonard, Billy Gilbert. Typically entertaining, Technicolored 20th Century-Fox musical fluff with Payne showing Faye a good time in Havana for business purposes only, but falling in love with her instead. Miranda adds her usual zest. ▼▶

Week-end Marriage (1932) **66m.** ** D: Thornton Freeland. Loretta Young, Norman Foster, Aline MacMahon, George Brent, Vivienne Osborne, Roscoe Karns, J. Carrol Naish. Comedy courtship leads to drama when traditional Foster doesn't want wifey Young in the workplace. Pre-Code and pre–women's lib, especially a closing scene in which voice-of-reason physician Grant Mitchell reads Young the riot act for holding down a job! ▶

Week-end With Father (1951) **83m.** **½ D: Douglas Sirk. Van Heflin, Patricia Neal, Virginia Field, Gigi Perreau, Richard Denning. Pleasant frou-frou of widow and widower courting despite their children's interference.

Wee Willie Winkie (1937) **99m.** *** D: John Ford. Shirley Temple, Victor McLaglen, C. Aubrey Smith, June Lang, Michael Whalen, Cesar Romero, Constance Collier, Douglas Scott. Shirley and her widowed mother come to live at a British Army outpost in India, where the moppet works hard to win over her crusty grandfather, the Colonel (Smith), and is quickly adopted by a soft-hearted sergeant (McLaglen). One of Shirley's best vehicles, "inspired" (it says here) by the Rudyard Kipling story. Beware 77m. prints. Also shown in computer-colored version. ▼▶

Weird Tales (1919-German) **75m.** **½ D: Richard Oswald. Anita Berber, Conrad Veidt, Reinhold Schünzel, Hugo Döblin, Paul Morgan, Georg John. The title tells all in this surreal fantasy featuring several stories, hazily told, that seamlessly blend together; each involves plot twists, strange disappearances, murder, ghosts, illicit romances, or odd fates. Strange, decidedly not for all tastes, but worth a look, particularly if you're an Edgar Allan Poe fan. ▼

Weird Woman (1944) **64m.** **½ D: Reginald LeBorg. Lon Chaney, Jr., Anne Gwynne, Evelyn Ankers, Ralph Morgan, Lois Collier, Elizabeth Russell, Phil Brown. Chaney's ex-girlfriend objects to his tropic isle bride, connives to get even. Way-out entry in the *Inner Sanctum* series, based on Fritz Leiber's *Conjure Wife*; good fun, with Ankers' nice change-of-pace villainess. Remade as BURN, WITCH, BURN and WITCHES' BREW. ▼▶

Welcome Danger (1929) **115m.** *½ D: Clyde Bruckman, Malcolm St. Clair. Harold Lloyd, Barbara Kent, Noah Young, Charles Middleton, William Walling. Lloyd's first talkie is incredibly long and dreary, with bookish Harold as the son of a legendary San Francisco police chief who's recruited to help solve a series of puzzling Chinatown crimes. Occasional funny gags sink in the mire of a heavy-handed film. Alternate silent version also exists and is a definite improvement over the talkie, although still not in the same league as Lloyd's best comedies.

Welcome Stranger (1947) **107m.** *** D: Elliott Nugent. Bing Crosby, Barry Fitzgerald, Joan Caulfield, Wanda Hendrix, Frank Faylen, Elizabeth Patterson. Entertaining musical of Crosby filling in for vacationing doctor in small community, getting involved with local girl and lovely little town. ▼▶

We Live Again (1934) **82m.** ** D: Rouben Mamoulian. Fredric March, Anna Sten, Sam Jaffe, C. Aubrey Smith, Jane Baxter, Ethel Griffies. Cumbersome costumer with March a Russian nobleman in love with peasant girl Sten. Based on Leo Tolstoy's *Resurrection*, filmed several times before; Preston Sturges and Maxwell Anderson were among the writers.▶

Well, The (1951) **85m.** *** D: Leo Popkin, Russell Rouse. Richard Rober, Henry (Harry) Morgan, Barry Kelley, Christine

Larson, Maidie Norman, Ernest Anderson. Incisive study of crowd psychology, focusing on effects on townfolk when black child goes missing. Fine score by Dimitri Tiomkin.▼❶

Well-Digger's Daughter, The (1941-French) **142m.** ***½ D: Marcel Pagnol. Raimu, Fernandel, Josette Day, Charpin, George Grey. Naive Day is seduced and abandoned—with child—and peasant father Raimu isn't very pleased. Both touching and hilarious. Remade in 2011 by Daniel Auteuil. ▼

Well-Groomed Bride, The (1946) **75m.** ** D: Sidney Lanfield. Olivia de Havilland, Ray Milland, Sonny Tufts, James Gleason, Percy Kilbride. Fine cast suffers with ridiculous comedy of stubborn girl insisting on champagne for her wedding.

Wells Fargo (1937) **94m.** *** D: Frank Lloyd. Joel McCrea, Frances Dee, Bob Burns, Lloyd Nolan, Ralph Morgan, Johnny Mack Brown, Porter Hall, Robert Cummings, Harry Davenport. McCrea, struggling to build famous express service, loses love of his wife (Dee) in process. Large-scale Western is long, but filled with action. Originally released at 115m.

Went the Day Well? (1942-British) **92m.** ***½ D: Alberto Cavalcanti. Leslie Banks, Elizabeth Allan, Frank Lawton, Mervyn Johns, Basil Sydney, David Farrar, Marie Lohr, C.V. France, Thora Hird. Wartime melodrama laced with humor about Germans invading a rural British community. Too sly and well written to be dismissed as mere propaganda; a most intriguing time capsule. Screenplay by John Dighton, Angus MacPhail, and Diana Morgan from a Graham Greene story. And remember: this story, told as a flashback at the end of WW2, was actually made at its peak, when the outcome was far from certain.❶

We're Going to Be Rich (1938-British) **78m.** **½ D: Monty Banks. Gracie Fields, Victor McLaglen, Brian Donlevy, Coral Browne, Ted Smith, Gus McNaughton. Entertainer Fields finds herself in the midst of an African gold boom in this OK story with musical numbers; Donlevy and McLaglen in contrived rivalry supply much of the plot. ❶

We're in the Money (1935) **65m.** **½ D: Ray Enright. Joan Blondell, Glenda Farrell, Hugh Herbert, Ross Alexander, Hobart Cavanaugh, Phil Regan, Anita Kerry, Henry O'Neill, Lionel Stander, Man Mountain Dean. Blondell and Farrell make an irresistible team as scheming process servers out to trap wealthy playboy Alexander in a breach-of-promise suit, until Blondell falls in love with him. Typically screwy Warner Bros. gold-digging romp with the usual quota of wisecracks and some wild slapstick scenes.

We're No Angels (1955) **C-106m.** **½ D: Michael Curtiz. Humphrey Bogart, Aldo

Ray, Peter Ustinov, Joan Bennett, Basil Rathbone, Leo G. Carroll. Mild entertainment as three escapees from Devil's Island find refuge with French family and extricate them from various predicaments. Remade in 1989. VistaVision.▼❶

We're Not Dressing (1934) **77m.** *** D: Norman Taurog. Bing Crosby, Carole Lombard, George Burns, Gracie Allen, Ethel Merman, Leon Errol, Ray Milland. Musical *Admirable Crichton* with rich girl Lombard falling in love with sailor Crosby when entourage is shipwrecked on desert isle. Merman is man-chasing second fiddle, with Burns and Allen on tap as local expeditionists. Great fun; Bing sings "Love Thy Neighbor."▼❶

We're Not Married! (1952) **85m.** *** D: Edmund Goulding. Ginger Rogers, Fred Allen, Victor Moore, Marilyn Monroe, Paul Douglas, David Wayne, Eve Arden, Louis Calhern, Zsa Zsa Gabor, James Gleason, Jane Darwell, Eddie Bracken, Mitzi Gaynor, Lee Marvin. Fine froth served up in several episodes as five married couples discover their weddings weren't legal. Segments vary in quality but the top-notch cast generally delivers the goods. Written and produced by Nunnally Johnson. ▼❶

We're Rich Again (1934) **71m.** ** D: William A. Seiter. Edna May Oliver, Billie Burke, Marian Nixon, Reginald Denny, Joan Marsh, Larry "Buster" Crabbe, Grant Mitchell, Gloria Shea, Edgar Kennedy. Screwball farce with rich Denny about to marry into Marsh's once-wealthy family, having to put up with usual assortment of eccentric relatives, including polo-playing grandma Oliver (who steals the film). Amiable cast defeated by hopelessly silly story.

Werewolf, The (1956) **83m.** **½ D: Fred F. Sears. Steven Ritch, Don Megowan, Joyce Holden, Eleanore Tanin, Harry Lauter. A stranger in a mountain town is revealed to be a werewolf, created by unscrupulous scientists seeking a cure for radiation poisoning. Surprisingly tense, with attractive use of Big Bear Lake locations, and a good performance by Ritch.❶

Werewolf in a Girls' Dormitory (1961-Italian-Austrian) **84m.** BOMB D: Richard Benson (Paolo Heusch). Carl Schell, Barbara Lass, Curt Lowens, Maurice Marsac. Superintendent at school for problem girls doubles as a werewolf. Strictly bottom-of-the-barrel.▼❶

WereWolf of London (1935) **75m.** **½ D: Stuart Walker. Henry Hull, Warner Oland, Valerie Hobson, Lester Matthews, Spring Byington. The first film about werewolves is dated but still effective. Scientist Hull stumbles onto curse of lycanthropy and terrorizes London as a mad killer. Oland is fun as mysterious man who warns Hull of impending doom.▼❶

Westbound (1959) **C-72m.** **½ D: Budd

Boetticher. Randolph Scott, Virginia Mayo, Karen Steele, Michael Dante, Andrew Duggan, Michael Pate. Trim sagebrush tale of Yankee officer Scott organizing a stagecoach line to bring in gold from California. Slick and watchable, but no match for the superior Scott-Boetticher Westerns of the period. ❒

West 11 (1963-British) **93m.** *½ D: Michael Winner. Alfred Lynch, Kathleen Breck, Eric Portman, Diana Dors, Kathleen Harrison. Lumbering account of out-of-work Lynch agreeing to murder Portman's aunt, with the crime bringing about a reformation of his character.

Westerner, The (1940) **100m.** ***½ D: William Wyler. Gary Cooper, Walter Brennan, Fred Stone, Doris Davenport, Forrest Tucker, Chill Wills, Dana Andrews, Tom Tyler, Lillian Bond. Excellent tale of land disputes getting out of hand in the old West, with Brennan's mercurial Judge Roy Bean winning him his third Oscar. Tucker's film debut. Also shown in computer-colored version. ▼❒

Western Jamboree (1938) **57m.** *½ D: Ralph Staub. Gene Autry, Smiley Burnette, Jean Rouverol, Esther Muir, Joe Frisco, Frank Darien, Margaret Armstrong, Harry Holman, Kermit Maynard, Jack Ingram. Gene helps Darien pretend to own a dude ranch to impress his daughter and tangles with bad guys who are after helium located on the property. Inferior Autry vehicle with forgettable songs and villains that match the hackneyed plot. ▼❒

Western Pacific Agent (1950) **65m.** **½ D: Sam Newfield. Kent Taylor, Sheila Ryan, Mickey Knox, Morris Carnovsky, Robert Lowery, Sid Melton. Amoral hothead Knox, in dire need of money but unwilling to find himself a job, goes on a murder spree. Pleasingly ironic low-budget melodrama. ❒

Western Union (1941) **C-94m.** *** D: Fritz Lang. Robert Young, Randolph Scott, Dean Jagger, Virginia Gilmore, John Carradine, Slim Summerville, Chill Wills, Barton MacLane. Big-scale Western, in gorgeous Technicolor, focuses on renegade attempts to thwart Western Union on the last leg of its westward expansion in the 1860s. Entertaining, if not terribly inspired. ▼❒

Westfront 1918 (1930-German) **97m.** ***½ D: G. W. Pabst. Fritz Kampers, H. J. Moebis, Gustav Diessl, Gustav Püttjer, Jackie Monnier, Hanna Hoessrich, Vladimir Sokoloff. Pabst's first sound film is a bone-chilling, unrelentingly bleak—and ultimately pacifistic—account of German soldiers battling their French counterparts in the trenches during WW1. Without the benefit of modern special effects, Pabst creates a vividly realistic, horrifying view of war, and effectively contrasts the tedium and sudden bedlam universally experienced

by soldiers. Makes an intriguing doublebill with his KAMERADSCHAFT (1931). As powerful an antiwar statement as ALL QUIET ON THE WESTERN FRONT. ▼

West of Broadway (1931) **73m.** ** D: Harry Beaumont. John Gilbert, El Brendel, Lois Moran, Madge Evans, Ralph Bellamy, Frank Conroy, Gwen Lee, Hedda Hopper, Ruth Renick, Willie Fung, Kermit Maynard, John Miljan. Complications arise when wealthy, ailing WW1 vet Gilbert, jilted by his fiancée, hooks up with poor-but-honest Moran. So-so romantic tale; one more dud that helped kill silent star Gilbert's career.

West of Shanghai (1937) **64m.** ** D: John Farrow. Boris Karloff, Beverly Roberts, Ricardo Cortez, Gordon Oliver, Sheila Bromley, Vladimir Sokoloff, Richard Loo. Cheap programmer of Chinese warlord Karloff holding Cortez and others prisoner in a remote Chinese outpost. Karloff shines. Reworking of THE BAD MAN. ❒

West of Suez SEE: **Fighting Wildcats, The**

West of the Badlands SEE: **Border Legion, The**

West of the Divide (1934) **54m.** ** D: Robert N. Bradbury. John Wayne, Virginia Brown Faire, George Hayes, Lloyd Whitlock, Yakima Canutt, Lafe McKee. Cowhand Wayne returns to boyhood hometown, where his father was murdered and brother abducted; he poses as wanted man in hopes of trapping killer and locating long-lost little brother. Has all the rough edges and shoddiness of humble Lone Star efforts . . . but also some good stunts by Canutt. ▼❒

West of the Pecos (1945) **66m.** **½ D: Edward Killy. Robert Mitchum, Barbara Hale, Richard Martin, Thurston Hall, Rita Corday, Russell Hopton, Bill Williams, Harry Woods. Spirited Hale and her ailing father move from Chicago to wild and woolly Texas, where she encounters Pecos Smith (Mitchum), a two-fisted cowpoke battling corrupt "vigilantes." Entertaining Zane Grey B Western was released after THE STORY OF G.I. JOE, which elevated Mitchum to the A-list. Hale and Williams married a year after the film's release. Filmed before in 1934. ▼

West of Zanzibar (1928) **63m.** *** D: Tod Browning. Lon Chaney, Lionel Barrymore, Mary Nolan, Warner Baxter, Jacqueline Gadsdon. Crippled Chaney rules a jungle monarchy and lives for one thing: revenge on the man who ruined his life. His scheme: to despoil the man's beautiful young daughter (Nolan). Pat ending nearly mars seamy, bizarre story; remade as KONGO. Originally released at 69m. ▼❒

West of Zanzibar (1954-British) **C-84m.** ** D: Harry Watt. Anthony Steel, Sheila Sim, Edric Connor, Orlando Martins. Ivory hunters meet up with jungle obstacles and native tribes; Steel and Sim share the adventures. ▼

West Point (1927) 95m. **½ D: Edward Sedgwick. William Haines, Joan Crawford, William Bakewell, Neil Neely, Ralph Emerson, Leon Kellar. Flag-waving tribute to the famed military academy with Haines as a cocky cadet who finds love with Crawford and learns team spirit in time for the big Army-Navy football game. Formulaic silent star vehicle helped by location filming. ▶

West Point of the Air (1935) 100m. **½ D: Richard Rosson. Wallace Beery, Robert Young, Maureen O'Sullivan, Lewis Stone, James Gleason, Rosalind Russell, Robert Taylor. Master Sergeant Beery pushes reluctant son Young through Army airtraining for his own satisfaction. Good cast enlivens standard drama.

West Point Story, The (1950) 107m. **½ D: Roy Del Ruth. James Cagney, Virginia Mayo, Doris Day, Gordon MacRae, Gene Nelson, Alan Hale, Jr., Jack Kelly, Roland Winters. Silly but watchable musical about a Broadway director staging a revue at West Point. Wait till you hear "The Military Polka." Cagney hoofs in several numbers with Day and Mayo. ▼▶

West Side Story (1961) C-151m. **** D: Robert Wise, Jerome Robbins. Natalie Wood, Richard Beymer, George Chakiris, Rita Moreno, Russ Tamblyn, Tucker Smith, David Winters, Tony Mordente, Simon Oakland, John Astin. Vivid film adaptation of the landmark Broadway musical, updating Romeo and Juliet story to youth-gang atmosphere of late 1950s N.Y.C. Wood and Beymer lack charisma, but everything surrounding them is great: Robbins' choreography, Leonard Bernstein–Stephen Sondheim score (including "Maria," "America," and "Something's Coming"). Script by Ernest Lehman, from Arthur Laurents' play. Winner of 10 Academy Awards including Best Picture, Direction, Supporting Actor and Actress (Chakiris, Moreno), Cinematography, Costumes, Art Direction–Set Decoration, Editing, Scoring; Robbins earned a special award for his choreography. Roadshow version on video runs 154m. with intermission/entr'acte. Super Panavision 70. ▼●▶

Westward Ho (1935) 62m. **½ D: Robert N. Bradbury. John Wayne, Sheila Mannors (Bromley), Frank McGlynn, Jr., James Farley, Jack Curtis, Glenn Strange, Dickie Jones. When trail jumpers murder their parents, two brothers are separated and grow up on different tracks. Wayne is forced to organize vigilantes (black-shirted riders on white horses called The Singing Riders) to avenge his parents and find his abducted brother. Unknown baritone dubs Wayne in near-ludicrous serenade of Mannors against beautiful Lone Pine backdrop. ▶

Westward Ho the Wagons! (1956) C-90m. ** D: William Beaudine. Fess Parker, Kathleen Crowley, Jeff York, David Stollery, Sebastian Cabot, George Reeves, Juliette Compton, Iron Eyes Cody. Lackluster pioneer saga has Disney polish but no excitement as wagon train travels West. Four Mouseketeers from the *Mickey Mouse Club* appear—Karen Pendleton, Cubby O'Brien, Tommy Cole, and Doreen Tracy. CinemaScope. ▼▶

Westward Passage (1932) 73m. ** D: Robert Milton. Ann Harding, Laurence Olivier, Irving Pichel, ZaSu Pitts, Juliette Compton, Irene Purcell, Don Alvarado, Florence Lake, Edgar Kennedy, Ethel Griffies. Acting uplifts clichéd tale of Harding marrying charming but egocentric Olivier, a struggling writer. Film debut of child actress Bonita Granville.

Westward the Women (1951) 118m. *** D: William Wellman. Robert Taylor, Denise Darcel, Beverly Dennis, John McIntire, Hope Emerson, Lenore Lonergan, Julie Bishop, Marilyn Erskine. Intriguing Western with Taylor heading wagon train full of females bound for California to meet mail-order husbands. Based on a story by Frank Capra. Also shown in computer-colored version. ▼▶

Wetbacks (1956) C-89m. *½ D: Hank McCune. Lloyd Bridges, Nancy Gates, John Hoyt, Barton MacLane. Draggy tale of California skipper Bridges contending with baddies who force him to smuggle peasants into U.S. "Great Gildersleeve" Harold Peary plays a knife-wielding Mexican heavy! ▼▶

We the Living (1942-Italian) 174m. *** D: Goffredo Alessandrini. Alida Valli, Rossano Brazzi, Fosco Giachetti, Giovanni Grasso, Emilio Cigoli, Mario Pisu. Still involving, and now rediscovered, romantic drama of young Russian Valli, an anti-Communist who becomes involved with party official Giachetti in order to obtain medical treatment for fugitive lover Brazzi. Based on an Ayn Rand novel and banned soon after its release because its scenario is as anti-authoritarian as it is anti-Communist. Originally shown as two separate films (titled NOI VIVI and ADDIO KIRA). ▼●

Wet Parade, The (1932) 120m. **½ D: Victor Fleming. Walter Huston, Myrna Loy, Neil Hamilton, Lewis Stone, Dorothy Jordan, Robert Young, Jimmy Durante, Wallace Ford. Extremely long diatribe about the Devil's Brew which manages to be both anti-liquor and anti-Prohibition. First half features Stone as an alcoholic Southern gentleman; second half moves North to focus on Prohibition agents (including Durante, of all people!). Strange but interesting; script by John Lee Mahin, from the Upton Sinclair novel. ▶

We've Never Been Licked (1943) 103m. ** D: John Rawlins. Richard Quine, Noah Beery, Jr., Robert Mitchum, Anne Gwynne, Martha O'Driscoll. Jingoistic, melodramatic account of American youth brought up in Japan, and his involvement in WW2. ▼▶

We Were Dancing (1942) **94m.** ** D: Robert Z. Leonard. Norma Shearer, Melvyn Douglas, Gail Patrick, Marjorie Main, Reginald Owen, Connie Gilchrist, Sig Ruman. Hokey adaptation from Noel Coward's *Tonight at 8:30,* about princess running off with another man at her engagement party. Shearer et al. try, but material defeats them. Ava Gardner's first film; Shearer's last.◗

We Were Strangers (1949) **106m.** *** D: John Huston. Jennifer Jones, John Garfield, Pedro Armendariz, Gilbert Roland, Ramon Novarro. Intense, intriguing political drama of Garfield and Jones joining with the Cuban underground in a plot to overthrow the government. Well directed by Huston; Garfield is fine, but Roland steals the film as one of the revolutionaries. Scripted by Huston and Peter Viertel.◗

We Who Are Young (1940) **79m.** ** D: Harold S. Bucquet. Lana Turner, John Shelton, Gene Lockhart, Grant Mitchell, Henry Armetta, Jonathan Hale, Clarence Wilson. Turner marries Shelton though his company's policy forbids it; aimless comedy-drama.

What a Life (1939) **75m.** **½ D: Jay Theodore Reed. Jackie Cooper, Betty Field, John Howard, Janice Logan, Vaughan Glaser, Lionel Stander, Hedda Hopper, James Corner, Dorothy Stickney, Lucien Littlefield, Sidney Miller. The bittersweet trials and tribulations of Henry Aldrich, the world's biggest patsy and the world's worst student. Mildly likable schooldays saga. Billy Wilder and Charles Brackett adapted Clifford Goldsmith's Broadway play, which led to the *Henry Aldrich* series.

What a Way to Go! (1964) **C-111m.** *** D: J. Lee Thompson. Shirley MacLaine, Paul Newman, Robert Mitchum, Dean Martin, Gene Kelly, Bob Cummings, Dick Van Dyke, Reginald Gardiner, Margaret Dumont, Fifi D'Orsay. Lavish, episodic black comedy by Betty Comden and Adolph Green stars MacLaine as jinx who marries succession of men, each of whom promptly dies, leaving her even wealthier than before. Series of movie parodies is amusing, and performances are uniformly charming, especially Newman as obsessed painter and Kelly as egotistical film star. Based on a story by Gwen Davis. One of the dancers on boat deck is Teri Garr. CinemaScope.◗

What a Woman! (1943) **94m.** **½ D: Irving Cummings. Rosalind Russell, Brian Aherne, Willard Parker, Alan Dinehart, Ann Savage. Literary agent Russell sells film rights to spicy novel, and unwillingly becomes involved with its bookish author (Parker) in this lightweight comedy vehicle.

What a Woman! (1956-Italian) SEE: **Lucky to Be a Woman**

What Ever Happened to Baby Jane? (1962) **132m.** ***½ D: Robert Aldrich. Bette Davis, Joan Crawford, Victor Buono, Marjorie Bennett, Anna Lee. Far-fetched,

thoroughly engaging black comedy of two former movie stars; Joan's a cripple at the mercy of demented sister Baby Jane Hudson (Davis). Bette has a field day in her macabre characterization, with Buono a perfect match. Triggered a decade-long spate of older female stars in horror films. Script by Lukas Heller, from Henry Farrell's novel. Remade for TV in 1991 with Vanessa and Lynn Redgrave.▼◗

What Every Woman Knows (1934) **92m.** ***½ D: Gregory La Cava. Helen Hayes, Brian Aherne, Madge Evans, Lucile Watson, Dudley Digges, Donald Crisp. Charming, funny adaptation of James Barrie's play about a woman who is "the brains" behind her well-meaning but none-too-bright politician husband. Beautifully acted and surprisingly contemporary. Filmed before in 1921.

What Next, Corporal Hargrove? (1945) **95m.** **½ D: Richard Thorpe. Robert Walker, Keenan Wynn, Jean Porter, Chill Wills, Hugo Haas, William Phillips, Fred Essler, Cameron Mitchell. Hargrove (Walker) is in France with con-man buddy (Wynn) in OK sequel to SEE HERE, PRIVATE HARGROVE; trivial and episodic.

What—No Beer? (1933) **66m.** ** D: Edward Sedgwick. Buster Keaton, Jimmy Durante, Rosco (Roscoe) Ates, Phyllis Barry, John Miljan, Edward Brophy, Henry Armetta. Mediocre Prohibition comedy about dimwitted bootleggers Keaton and Durante; plot makes no sense, Durante is incredibly overbearing. Best scenes involve Buster and leading lady Barry. Keaton's last starring feature in America.▼◗

What Price Glory (1926) **120m.** *** D: Raoul Walsh. Victor McLaglen, Edmund Lowe, Dolores Del Rio, William V. Mong, Phyllis Haver, Leslie Fenton, Barry Norton. Boisterous rivalry between Capt. Flagg (McLaglen) and Sgt. Quirt (Lowe) centers on lovely Charmaine (Del Rio) when they go to France during WW1. Zesty comedy, with plenty of fireworks for lip-readers, abruptly turns grim as focus shifts to horrors of war, only to return to Flagg-Quirt hijinks for finale. Fine entertainment, from Laurence Stallings–Maxwell Anderson play; two main characters reappeared in a handful of follow-ups, none of them as good as this. Remade in 1952.▼◗

What Price Glory (1952) **C-111m.** **½ D: John Ford. James Cagney, Corinne Calvet, Dan Dailey, Robert Wagner, Marisa Pavan, James Gleason. Classic silent film becomes shallow Cagney-Dailey vehicle of battling Army men Flagg and Quirt in WW1 France.▼◗

What Price Hollywood? (1932) **88m.** *** D: George Cukor. Constance Bennett, Lowell Sherman, Neil Hamilton, Gregory Ratoff, Brooks Benedict. Soused movie director Sherman helps waitress Bennett

[772]

fulfill her ambition to become a movie star—while he sinks into alcoholic ruin. Surprisingly sharp-eyed look at Hollywood—both comic and dramatic—that served as inspiration for later A STAR IS BORN. From a story by Adela Rogers St. Johns.▼●▶

What Price Murder (1958-French) **105m.** **½ D: Henri Verneuil. Henri Vidal, Mylene Demongeot, Isa Miranda, Alfred Adam. Well-turned murder mystery of hubby and secretary planning to do away with wife.

What Price Vengeance SEE: **Vengeance**

What's New Pussycat (1965) **C-108m.** ** D: Clive Donner. Peter Sellers, Peter O'Toole, Romy Schneider, Capucine, Paula Prentiss, Woody Allen, Ursula Andress. Disturbed fashion editor O'Toole goes to psychiatrist Sellers for help with his romantic problems, but Sellers is even crazier than he. Woody Allen's first feature as actor and writer, and like many of his comedies, one sits through a lot of misfired gags to get to a few undeniable gems. Hit title song by Burt Bacharach and Hal David. Opening titles by Richard Williams.▼●▶

What the Birds Knew SEE: **I Live in Fear**

Wheeler Dealers, The (1963) **C-106m.** *** D: Arthur Hiller. Lee Remick, James Garner, Jim Backus, Phil Harris, Shelley Berman, Chill Wills, John Astin, Louis Nye. Funny, fast-moving spoof of Texas millionaires who play with investments just for fun. Garner also catches Lee Remick along the way. Panavision.▼▶

Wheel of Fortune SEE: **Man Betrayed, A**

When a Feller Needs a Friend (1932) **67m.** ** D: Harry Pollard. Jackie Cooper, Charles "Chic" Sale, Ralph Graves, Dorothy Peterson, Helen Parrish, Donald Haines. Mediocre tearjerker about a lame boy whose overprotective parents keep him from playing with the neighborhood kids . . . and his rambunctious uncle (Sale) who gives him gumption and shows him a good time.

When a Man Loves (1927) **112m.** **½ D: Alan Crosland. John Barrymore, Dolores Costello, Warner Oland, Sam De Grasse, Holmes Herbert, Stuart Holmes. Barrymore is at his most dashing in this costume drama about an 18th-century French swashbuckler who tries to save his beloved from being forced into a life of prostitution by her own brother (Oland, at his slimiest). Overlong but quite lavish reworking of *Manon Lescaut* features synchronized music and sound effects. Look fast for Myrna Loy.▶

When a Woman Loves (1959-Japanese) **C-97m.** **½ D: Heinosuke Gosho. Ineko Arima, Shin Saburi, Yatsuko Tan-ami, Nobuko Otowa. Utilizing flashbacks, film recalls love affair between Saburi and older man Arima, a war correspondent; sentimental weeper with almost enough class. Grandscope.

When Comedy Was King (1960) **81m.** **** Compiled by Robert Youngson. Charlie Chaplin, Buster Keaton, Laurel and Hardy, Ben Turpin, Fatty Arbuckle, Wallace Beery, Gloria Swanson. Second Youngson compilation of silent comedy clips has many classic scenes. Chaplin, Keaton, L & H, Keystone Kops, Charley Chase, and others shine in this outstanding film.▼●▶

When Hell Broke Loose (1958) **78m.** ** D: Kenneth G. Crane. Charles Bronson, Violet Rensing, Richard Jaeckel, Arvid Nelson, Eddie Foy III. Tired WW2 melodrama with con artist Bronson joining the Army to avoid prison; he romances Rensing, whose brother (Jaeckel) is a Nazi terrorist intent on assassinating Gen. Eisenhower.▼

When I Grow Up (1951) **80m.** *** D: Michael Kanin. Bobby Driscoll, Robert Preston, Martha Scott, Sherry Jackson, Charley Grapewin, Henry (Harry) Morgan. Effective low-key study of the generation gap, with Driscoll most appealing as a boy who finds that he and his grandfather have much in common.

When in Rome (1952) **78m.** **½ D: Clarence Brown. Van Johnson, Paul Douglas, Joseph Calleia, Mimi Aguglia, Tudor Owen. Tasteful yet unrestrained tale of con artist Douglas disguising himself as priest attending Holy Year pilgrimage in Italy; through American priest Johnson et al. he finds new faith.

When Ladies Meet (1933) **85m.** *** D: Harry Beaumont. Ann Harding, Robert Montgomery, Myrna Loy, Alice Brady, Frank Morgan. Harding and Loy meet and discuss the characters of a new book, unaware that they both love the same man . . . just like the characters in the novel. Talky but unusual, intelligent film. Remade in 1941.

When Ladies Meet (1941) **108m.** ** D: Robert Z. Leonard. Joan Crawford, Robert Taylor, Greer Garson, Herbert Marshall, Spring Byington. Attractive performers in plodding remake of 1933 movie based on Rachel Crothers' play. Authoress Crawford loves Marshall, who's married to Garson; Taylor loves Joan. Taylor and Garson try to bring life to film, but can't. Retitled STRANGE SKIRTS for TV.▼●▶

When Lovers Meet SEE: **Lover Come Back**

When My Baby Smiles at Me (1948) **C-98m.** **½ D: Walter Lang. Betty Grable, Dan Dailey, Jack Oakie, June Havoc, James Gleason, Richard Arlen. Strictly routine musical about burlesque team that breaks up when one member gets job on Broadway. Eventually they're reteamed, of course. Based on famous play *Burlesque*. Filmed before as THE DANCE OF LIFE and SWING HIGH, SWING LOW.

When Strangers Marry (1944) **67m.** *** D: William Castle. Robert Mitchum, Kim

[773]

Hunter, Dean Jagger, Neil Hamilton, Lou Lubin, Milton Kibbee. Cleverly directed film noir about sweet, innocent Hunter, whose new husband (Jagger) just may be a murderer. Mitchum, as her ex-boyfriend, exudes his trademark cool in his first important role. As good a B picture as you'll ever find. Reissued as BETRAYED. ◗

When's Your Birthday? (1937) **77m.** ****** D: Harry Beaumont. Joe E. Brown, Marian Marsh, Edgar Kennedy, Margaret Hamilton, Frank Jenks, Maude Eburne, Fred Keating. Slight, meandering slapstick with Brown trying his best as an astrology-obsessed prizefighter whose prowess depends on the position of the stars. ▼◗

When the Boys Meet the Girls (1965) C-**110m.** ****** D: Alvin Ganzer. Connie Francis, Harve Presnell, Herman's Hermits, Louis Armstrong, Liberace, Sue Ane Langdon, Fred Clark, Sam the Sham. Rehash of GIRL CRAZY, turned into a dull guest-star showcase. Panavision. ◗◗

When the Clouds Roll By (1919) **86m.** *******½ D: Victor Fleming. Douglas Fairbanks, Kathleen Clifford, Albert MacQuarrie, Ralph Lewis, Frank Campeau. Doug falls under the spell of an unscrupulous doctor who manipulates his psyche. Fairbanks cavorts about as the scenario veers off in surprising directions. Clever dream sequences include a scene in which Fairbanks walks on walls and the ceiling, predating Fred Astaire in ROYAL WEDDING. ▼◗

When the Daltons Rode (1940) **80m.** ******* D: George Marshall. Randolph Scott, Kay Francis, Brian Donlevy, Broderick Crawford, Andy Devine, Stuart Erwin, Frank Albertson, George Bancroft, Edgar Buchanan, Mary Gordon. Action-packed (if highly illogical) Western with nice comedic touches, relating how the Dalton brothers were railroaded into becoming desperadoes. Good cast plays to the hilt, with Devine especially amusing as a love object! Also loaded with eye-popping stunt work. ◗

When Thief Meets Thief SEE: **Jump for Glory**

When Tomorrow Comes (1939) **90m.** ******½ D: John M. Stahl. Irene Dunne, Charles Boyer, Barbara O'Neil, Nydia Westman, Onslow Stevens. Standard soapy story (by James M. Cain!) enhanced by leading players; Boyer loves Dunne, although he's already married. Remade twice as INTERLUDE.

When Willie Comes Marching Home (1950) **82m.** ******½ D: John Ford. Dan Dailey, Corinne Calvet, Colleen Townsend, William Demarest, Mae Marsh. Schmaltzy WW2 adventures of West Virginia youth Dailey, including interlude with French underground leader Calvet. ◗

When Worlds Collide (1951) C-**81m.** ******* D: Rudolph Maté. Richard Derr, Barbara Rush, Peter Hanson, Larry Keating, John Hoyt. Scientist tries to convince a doubting world that Earth is in path of rogue planet. Convince yourself this could happen and you'll have fun. Special effects (including submersion of Manhattan) won Oscar for this George Pal production. Based on the novel by Edwin Balmer and Philip Wylie. ▼◗◗

When You're in Love (1937) **104m.** ******½ D: Robert Riskin. Grace Moore, Cary Grant, Aline MacMahon, Thomas Mitchell, Emma Dunn. Overlong but enjoyable vehicle for opera star Moore who "hires" Grant as her husband. Some 98m. prints are missing film's highlight, where star sings "Minnie the Moocher." Celebrated screenwriter Riskin's only fling at directing.

Where Are My Children (1916) **65m.** ******½ D: Lois Weber, Phillips Smalley (both uncredited). Tyrone Power (Sr.), Helen Riaume, A. D. Blake, Marie Walcamp, Juan de la Cruz, Rena Rogers, Cora Drew. District Attorney Power laments that he has no children. Why is his wife unable to conceive? In the meantime, he prosecutes a man charged with illegally distributing birth control information to the poor and a doctor who performs abortions. Dramatically speaking, this is little more than an unabashed tearjerker, but Weber and Smalley (who also coscripted) deserve kudos for exploring an issue that remains controversial to this day. Reconstructed in 2000 from several incomplete U.S. and European release prints. ◗

Where Are Your Children? (1943) **73m.** *****½ D: William Nigh. Jackie Cooper, Patricia Morison, Gale Storm, Gertrude Michael, John Litel, Evelynne Eaton. Thoughtless study of juvenile delinquency. ◗

Where Danger Lives (1950) **84m.** ****** D: John Farrow. Robert Mitchum, Faith Domergue, Claude Rains, Maureen O'Sullivan. Dr. Mitchum finds himself deep in trouble when he falls hard for manipulative, desperate Domergue. Atmospheric, predictable, and forgettable potboiler. ◗

Where Do We Go From Here? (1945) C-**77m.** ******½ D: Gregory Ratoff. Fred MacMurray, June Haver, Joan Leslie, Gene Sheldon, Anthony Quinn, Carlos Ramirez, Otto Preminger, Fortunio Bonanova. Engaging but ultimately silly musical comedy about genie enabling MacMurray to travel backwards into American history. Ira Gershwin–Kurt Weill score includes wonderful mini-opera involving Christopher Columbus (Bonanova). Fred and June later married in real life. ◗

Where Love Has Gone (1964) C-**114m.** ******½ D: Edward Dmytryk. Bette Davis, Susan Hayward, Michael Connors, Jane Greer, Joey Heatherton, George Macready. Glossy drama of Heatherton killing mother Hayward's lover; Davis is the domineering grandmother, Greer is a sympathetic probation officer. Script by John Michael

Hayes, from Harold Robbins' novel. Techniscope.▼▶

Where No Vultures Fly SEE: **Ivory Hunter**

Where's Charley? (1952) **C-97m.** ✶✶✶ D: David Butler. Ray Bolger, Allyn Ann McLerie, Robert Shackleton, Mary Germaine, Horace Cooper, Margaretta Scott. Bolger re-creates Broadway role in musical adaptation of CHARLEY'S AUNT, as Oxford student whose face-saving impersonation of dowdy dowager leads to endless complications. Frank Loesser score includes "Once in Love With Amy." One of the principal dancers is Jean Marsh. Filmed in England.

Where the Boys Are (1960) **C-99m.** ✶✶½ D: Henry Levin. Dolores Hart, George Hamilton, Yvette Mimieux, Jim Hutton, Barbara Nichols, Paula Prentiss, Connie Francis, Frank Gorshin, Chill Wills. Notbad film about teenagers during Easter vacation in Ft. Lauderdale. Connie Francis, in her first film, is pretty good, and sings the hit title tune; other young players seen to good advantage. Nichols is hilarious as usual as a flashy blonde. Ineptly remade in 1984. CinemaScope.▼▶

Where the Hot Wind Blows! (1958-French-Italian) **120m.** ✶✶ D: Jules Dassin. Gina Lollobrigida, Pierre Brasseur, Marcello Mastroianni, Melina Mercouri, Yves Montand, Paolo Stoppa. Sure-fire cast is wasted in pedestrian drama of hypocrisy in a small Italian town. Lollobrigida is poverty-stricken wench who falls for engineer Mastroianni; Mercouri is judge's wife in love with thug Montand's son. Aka THE LAW.▼▶

Where There's Life . . . (1947) **75m.** ✶✶✶ D: Sidney Lanfield. Bob Hope, Signe Hasso, William Bendix, George Coulouris, Vera Marshe, George Zucco, Dennis Hoey, Harry Von Zell. Wacky comedy with fasttalking Manhattan radio DJ Hope, just about to be married, earmarked as new king of Barovia, and tangling with the country's enemies, along with its top military authority—who happens to be a woman (Hasso). Bendix is fun as Hope's foreverbellowing brother-in-law-to-be.▼▶

Where the Sidewalk Ends (1950) **95m.** ✶✶✶ D: Otto Preminger. Dana Andrews, Gene Tierney, Gary Merrill, Karl Malden, Bert Freed, Tom Tully, Ruth Donnelly, Craig Stevens, Neville Brand. While investigating a homicide, brutal N.Y.C. cop (Andrews) inadvertently kills a man, then tries to conceal his own guilt while continuing his search for murderer. Moody crime melodrama is a good illustration of film noir. Fine characterizations, pungent script by Ben Hecht from William Stuart's novel *Night Cry.* Oleg Cassini (film's costume designer and Tierney's thenhusband) has a cameo.▶

While the City Sleeps (1956) **100m.** ✶✶✶ D: Fritz Lang. Dana Andrews, Ida Lupino, Rhonda Fleming, George Sanders, Vincent Price, Thomas Mitchell, Sally Forrest, Howard Duff, James Craig, John Barrymore, Jr., Mae Marsh. Veteran cast and intertwining storylines keep interest in account of newspaper reporters and police on the track of a berserk killer. SuperScope.▼▶

While the Patient Slept (1935) **66m.** ✶✶½ D: Ray Enright. Aline MacMahon, Guy Kibbee, Lyle Talbot, Patricia Ellis, Allen Jenkins, Robert Barrat, Hobart Cavanaugh, Dorothy Tree, Henry O'Neill. A gaggle of greedy relations eagerly awaits the demise of an elderly, wealthy man. One of them is murdered, and it's up to nurse MacMahon and cop Kibbee to sniff out the culprit. Entertaining whodunit, based on a novel by Mignon G. Eberhart. MacMahon's and Kibbee's characters later appeared in THE PATIENT IN ROOM 18 and MYSTERY HOUSE, while the nurse is the chief sleuth in THE GREAT HOSPITAL MYSTERY.▶

Whip and the Body, The (1963-Italian) **C-91m.** ✶✶✶ D: Mario Bava. Daliah Lavi, Christopher Lee, Tony Kendall, Isli Oberon, Harriet Medin, Luciano Pigozzi, Dean Ardow. Soon after domineering Lee returns to his castle home and resumes his sadomasochistic relationship with sister-inlaw Lavi, he's murdered. But then he returns as a ghost—with a whip. Perhaps horror maestro Bava's best film, moody, beautiful and deceptively simple. Lee is excellent, despite being dubbed. Aka SON OF SATAN, THE WAY AND THE BODY, and NIGHT IS THE PHANTOM. Beware of shorter version called WHAT.▶

Whip Hand, The (1951) **82m.** ✶½ D: William Cameron Menzies. Elliott Reid, Carla Balenda, Raymond Burr, Edgar Barrier, Lurene Tuttle. Communists with germ-warfare intentions have taken over an abandoned resort town, but do these slimes *really* think they can tangle with Elliott Reid? Howard Hughes RKO Special is campy, but not campy enough.▶

Whiplash (1948) **91m.** ✶✶ D: Lewis Seiler. Dane Clark, Alexis Smith, Zachary Scott, Eve Arden, Jeffrey Lynn, S. Z. Sakall, Alan Hale, Douglas Kennedy, Ransom Sherman. Clark does his best John Garfield imitation in this by-the-numbers drama about a painterturned-prizefighter who falls hard for beautiful, troubled Smith.▶

Whipsaw (1935) **83m.** ✶✶½ D: Sam Wood. Myrna Loy, Spencer Tracy, Harvey Stephens, William Harrigan, Clay Clement. Tracy uses bad-girl Loy to lead him to band of thieves; predictable complications follow in familiar but well-done crime drama. ▶

Whirlpool (1934) **73m.** ✶✶½ D: Roy William Neill. Jack Holt, Jean Arthur, Donald Cook, Lila Lee, Allen Jenkins, Rita La Roy, John Miljan, Ward Bond. Not-bad vehicle for Holt, who's rock-solid as a carnival proprietor sent to prison for 20 years; upon his release, he does everything he can to protect the daughter he's never met. Script goes flat in second half. ▶

Whirlpool (1949) 97m. **½ D: Otto Preminger. Gene Tierney, Richard Conte, Jose Ferrer, Charles Bickford, Barbara O'Neil, Eduard Franz, Fortunio Bonanova, Constance Collier. Ruthless con artist Ferrer uses hypnosis and his powers of persuasion to get away with various crimes, implicating innocent Tierney, who's married to bow-tied psychiatrist Conte. Mildly subversive portrait of "perfect" postwar couple and their well-ordered life going awry seems obvious today, especially Ferrer's overripe performance. Written by Ben Hecht (using pseudonym) and Andrew Solt, from Guy Endore's novel. ▶

Whirlpool of Fate (1925-French) 71m. *** D: Jean Renoir. Catherine Hessling, Pierre Philippe (Pierre Lestringuez), Harold Levingston, Maurice Touzé, Georges Térof, Henriette Moret, Pierre Champagne, André Derain. After her father drowns, a waiflike girl (Hessling) is accosted by her loutish uncle. She runs away . . . and is exposed to the simple kindnesses and unrelenting cruelty of everyday life. The story (reminiscent of D. W. Griffith) meanders a bit, but Renoir's powerful visuals capture a range of human experience. Renoir's second feature, and first as sole director. Scripted by Lestringuez, who plays "Uncle Jeff," and partially filmed on the estate of Paul Cezanne. ▶

Whirlwind (1951) 70m. *** D: John English. Gene Autry, Smiley Burnette, Gail Davis, Thurston Hall, Harry Lauter, Dick Curtis, Gregg Barton. Postal inspector Autry has to smoke out the head of a crime syndicate (Hall). On-screen reunion with Burnette (who was called in when Pat Buttram suffered a serious injury) brings out the best in Gene. ▶

Whisky Galore! SEE: **Tight Little Island**

Whispering Chorus, The (1918) 86m. *** D: Cecil B. DeMille. Raymond Hatton, Kathlyn Williams, Edythe Chapman, Elliott Dexter, Noah Beery, Guy Oliver, John Burton, Tully Marshall, Gustav von Seyffertitz. Hatton, a lowly first assistant cashier for a contracting company, laments his lack of income . . . and temptation for larceny is all around him. Unexpected plot twists enliven this ironic drama filled with striking visual touches. Title refers to the voices inside our heads that tell us what to do and how to live. ▼▶

Whispering Ghosts (1942) 75m. ** D: Alfred L. Werker. Brenda Joyce, Milton Berle, John Shelton, John Carradine. Berle is effective as bumbling performer trying to live up to radio role as crackerjack detective. ▶

Whispering Smith (1948) C-88m. **½ D: Leslie Fenton. Alan Ladd, Brenda Marshall, Robert Preston, Donald Crisp, William Demarest, Fay Holden, Frank Faylen. Ladd is in his element (in this otherwise ordinary Western) as a soft-spoken but iron-willed railroad agent whose hot-headed best friend (Preston) becomes involved in shady dealings. ▶

Whispering Smith vs. Scotland Yard (1951-British) 77m. ** D: Francis Searle. Richard Carlson, Greta Gynt, Rona Anderson, Herbert Lom, Dora Bryan. Famed detective proves conclusively that suicide was actually well-staged murder. Good cast in below-average mystery. Stanley Baker has a bit as a reporter and Alan Wheatley appears as an attorney. Original British title: WHISPERING SMITH HITS LONDON.

Whistle at Eaton Falls, The (1951) 96m. **½ D: Robert Siodmak. Lloyd Bridges, Dorothy Gish, Carleton Carpenter, Murray Hamilton, Anne Francis, Ernest Borgnine, Doro Merande, Arthur O'Connell. Set in New Hampshire, this documentary-style film deals with labor relation problems in a small town when new plant manager has to lay off workers. Gish is factory owner in interesting supporting role.

Whistle Down the Wind (1961-British) 99m. ***½ D: Bryan Forbes. Hayley Mills, Alan Bates, Bernard Lee, Norman Bird, Elsie Wagstaffe. Fugitive murderer seeking refuge in a North Country barn is discovered by three children who think him to be Christ. Mills and Bates are excellent in this poignant, believable, and well-produced story of childhood innocence. Adapted from novel by Mary Hayley Bell (Hayley's mother). Forbes' directorial debut. Later a stage musical. ▼

The Whistler One of the most unusual—and one of the best—mystery series of the '40s was based on a popular radio show called *The Whistler*. The premise of the show, and at least one of the films, was a mysterious figure who walked along whistling a haunting tune. "I am the Whistler," he would say. "And I know many things." He would introduce the current mystery and reappear from time to time to bridge gaps from one setting to another. Veteran Richard Dix starred in all but one of the eight *Whistler* films, but he alternated from hero to villain in various entries. The one non-Dix film, THE RETURN OF THE WHISTLER, followed the radio format of the mysterious narrator with excellent results. That entry, and several others, had stories by Cornell Woolrich, while others were written by Eric Taylor; they were all tightly knit, engrossing little mysteries.

THE WHISTLER

The Whistler (1944)
Mark of the Whistler (1944)
Power of the Whistler (1945)
Voice of the Whistler (1945)

Mysterious Intruder (1946)
Secret of the Whistler (1946)
The 13th Hour (1947)
The Return of the Whistler (1948)

Whistler, The (1944) **59m.** *** D: William Castle. Richard Dix, Gloria Stuart, Alan Dinehart, Joan Woodbury, J. Carrol Naish, Byron Foulger. First entry in the series centers on Dix's desperate attempt to cancel the contract he had taken out on his own life. Tense and moody tale of fate sets the ironic tone for the rest. Naish shines as the principal hit man. ◗

Whistle Stop (1946) **85m.** ** D: Leonide Moguy. George Raft, Ava Gardner, Victor McLaglen, Tom Conway, Jorja Curtright, Florence Bates, Charles Drake. Unusually stupid Raft vehicle about his on-again, off-again, on-again relationship with Gardner, who wishes he would do something with his life. You may feel the same . . . but Ava *is* stunningly beautiful. ▼◗

Whistling in Brooklyn (1943) **87m.** **½ D: S. Sylvan Simon. Red Skelton, Ann Rutherford, Jean Rogers, "Rags" Ragland, Ray Collins, Henry O'Neill, William Frawley, Sam Levene. Skelton, again as radio sleuth "The Fox," gets mixed up in murder and impersonates the pitcher of a bearded baseball team playing the Dodgers at Ebbets Field. Manager Leo Durocher and his boys appear as themselves. ▼◗

Whistling in Dixie (1942) **74m.** *** D: S. Sylvan Simon. Red Skelton, Ann Rutherford, George Bancroft, Guy Kibbee. Red, as radio's "Fox," marries Ann, but their Southern honeymoon is interrupted by murder and mystery. Funny Skelton vehicle. ▼◗

Whistling in the Dark (1941) **77m.** *** D: S. Sylvan Simon. Red Skelton, Ann Rutherford, Virginia Grey, Conrad Veidt, "Rags" Ragland, Eve Arden. Faithful remake of 1933 film isn't as wacky as subsequent outings with Skelton as radio sleuth "The Fox," but still enjoyable; Red is held by fiendish Veidt and forced to spell out plans for "perfect murder." Followed by two sequels (see above). ▼◗

White Angel, The (1936) **92m.** ** D: William Dieterle. Kay Francis, Ian Hunter, Donald Woods, Nigel Bruce, Donald Crisp, Henry O'Neill. Lavish but unsuccessful biography of Florence Nightingale with Francis miscast in reworked history of 19th-century British nursing pioneer.

White Banners (1938) **88m.** *** D: Edmund Goulding. Claude Rains, Fay Bainter, Jackie Cooper, Bonita Granville, Henry O'Neill, Kay Johnson, James Stephenson. Bainter shines in this inspirational Lloyd C. Douglas tearjerker about a motherly mystery woman who arrives in a small Indiana town and eases herself into the lives of teacher-inventor Rains, his family, and schoolboy Cooper.

White Cargo (1942) **90m.** ** D: Richard Thorpe. Hedy Lamarr, Walter Pidgeon, Frank Morgan, Richard Carlson, Reginald Owen. Lamarr, in one of her best-known roles, is the seductive Tondelayo who entrances all at British plantation post in Africa, with Pidgeon the expeditionist who really falls for her. Exotic love scenes, corny plot. Previously filmed in 1929. ▼

White Christmas (1954) **C-120m.** ** D: Michael Curtiz. Bing Crosby, Danny Kaye, Rosemary Clooney, Vera-Ellen, Dean Jagger, Mary Wickes, Sig Ruman, Grady Sutton. Nice Irving Berlin score is unfortunately interrupted by limp plot of army buddies Crosby and Kaye boosting popularity of winter resort run by their ex-officer Jagger. "What Can You Do with a General" stands out as Berlin's least memorable tune. Partial reworking of HOLIDAY INN, not half as good. Later a Broadway musical. Title on-screen: IRVING BERLIN'S WHITE CHRISTMAS. First film released in VistaVision. ▼◗

White Cliffs of Dover, The (1944) **126m.** *** D: Clarence Brown. Irene Dunne, Alan Marshal, Van Johnson, Frank Morgan, C. Aubrey Smith, Dame May Whitty, Roddy McDowall, Gladys Cooper, Peter Lawford. American Dunne marries Britisher Marshal in patriotic WW1 romancer that boasts wonderful cast (including young Elizabeth Taylor). Slick but shallow. ▼◗

White Cradle Inn SEE: High Fury

White Feather (1955) **C-102m.** **½ D: Robert D. Webb. Robert Wagner, Jeffrey Hunter, Debra Paget, John Lund, Eduard Franz, Noah Beery (Jr.), Hugh O'Brian. Pat Western film with some good action scenes of government agent Wagner attempting to convince Indian tribe to move to reservation; Paget and Hunter are members of Cheyenne tribe who resist. CinemaScope. ◗

White Heat (1949) **114m.** ***½ D: Raoul Walsh. James Cagney, Virginia Mayo, Edmond O'Brien, Margaret Wycherly, Steve Cochran. Cagney returned to gangster films, older but forceful as ever, as psychopathic hood with mother obsession; Mayo is his neglected wife, O'Brien the cop out to get him. "Top of the World" finale is now movie legend. Written by Ivan Goff and Ben Roberts, from a Virginia Kellogg story. Also shown in computer-colored version. ▼◗

White Hell of Pitz Palü, The (1929-German) **95m.** ***½ D: Dr. Arnold Fanck, G. W. Pabst. Gustav Diessl, Leni Riefenstahl, Ernst Petersen, Ernst Udet, Mizzi Götzel, Otto Spring, Kurt Gerron. The most famous of Fanck's celebrated "mountain films," shot under extraordinary conditions (and without special effects), this stark melodrama charts the plight of a mountain climber (Diessl) who is haunted by the death of his wife during their Alpine honeymoon. He never stops searching for her, and a newly married couple (Riefenstahl, Petersen) decide to help him. Fanck directed the jaw-dropping outdoor scenes, Pabst the dramatic interiors. ▼▶

White Nights (1957-Italian) **94m. ***
D: Luchino Visconti. Maria Schell, Jean Marais, Marcello Mastroianni, Clara Calamai. Shy Mastroianni comes upon mysterious Schell, who's been dumped by sailor boyfriend Marais (or so it seems). A captivating, elaborately plotted love story, and a key film in Visconti's transition away from neorealism. Based on a Dostoyevsky story. Original running time 107m. Aka LE NOTTI BIANCHE. ▼▶

White Savage (1943) **C-75m. **½ D:** Arthur Lubin. Jon Hall, Maria Montez, Sabu, Don Terry, Turhan Bey, Thomas Gomez, Sidney Toler. Standard escapist fare, in glorious Technicolor, with island princess Montez trying to remove obstacles that bar marriage to shark-hunter Hall. Richard Brooks' first screenplay!

White Shadows in the South Seas (1928) **88m. ***
D: W. S. Van Dyke. Monte Blue, Raquel Torres, Robert Anderson. MGM's first sound film features stunning, Oscar-winning cinematography of the Marquesas Islands (now French Polynesia) welded to a story about the corrupting influence of Western civilization, with Blue as an alcoholic doctor who falls in love with native Torres and clashes with exploitative trader Anderson. Portions of the beautiful, documentary-style footage were shot under the supervision of Robert Flaherty, who fought with the studio over its emphasis on a melodramatic plot and left the production. ▶

White Sheik, The (1951-Italian) **86m. **½ D:** Federico Fellini. Alberto Sordi, Brunella Bova, Leopoldo Trieste, Giulietta Masina. Fellini's first solo film as director is a minor chronicle of the adventures of a provincial couple honeymooning in Rome and the wife's involvement with a cartoon hero, The White Sheik (Sordi). Remade, more or less, as THE WORLD'S GREATEST LOVER. ▼▶

White Sister, The (1923) **130m. *** D:** Henry King. Lillian Gish, Ronald Colman, Gail Kane, J. Barney Sherry, Charles Lane, Juliette La Violette, Signor Serena. Long but engrossing saga of an innocent woman who is victimized by her stepsister, then told that the love of her life (military officer Colman) has been killed. With this, she decides to become a nun. Lavish production filmed in Italy features a dramatic climax involving the eruption of Mt. Vesuvius! Colman's screen debut. Based on a then-popular novel and play; filmed before in 1915, remade in 1933. ▼▶

White Sister, The (1933) **110m. **½ D:** Victor Fleming. Helen Hayes, Clark Gable, Lewis Stone, Louise Closser Hale, May Robson, Edward Arnold. Dated but interesting remake of 1923 silent with Lillian Gish and Ronald Colman. Hayes is woman who enters convent when she thinks her lover has been killed in the war. Fine performances offset predictable story. ▼▶

White Slave Ship (1962-Italian) **C-92m. *½ D:** Silvio Amadio. Pier Angeli, Edmund Purdom, Armand Mestral, Ivan Desny. Childish hokum, set in 18th century, of rebellion aboard vessel carrying women to the colonies. Totalscope.

White Squaw, The (1956) **75m. *½ D:** Ray Nazarro. David Brian, May Wynn, William Bishop, Nancy Hale, Roy Roberts, Myron Healey, Paul Birch. Tedious Western with Wynn, a white woman residing on a Sioux reservation, becoming immersed in conflict with Indians and vengeance-seeking settler Brian. ▶

White Tie and Tails (1946) **81m. **½ D:** Charles Barton. Dan Duryea, William Bendix, Ella Raines, Clarence Kolb, Frank Jenks, John Miljan, Scotty Beckett. Breezy film with usual-villain Duryea in good comedy form as butler who pretends to be master of house while boss is away.

White Tiger (1923) **82m. **½ D:** Tod Browning. Priscilla Dean, Wallace Beery, Matt Moore, Raymond Griffith. Not a jungle thriller but a melodrama about a brother and sister separated for 15 years who meet again without recognizing each other. Partnered unknowingly with the criminal who murdered their father, the gang of three hides out in a mountain cabin, leading to a tense finale in which pasts are at last revealed. Touted in its time as more of the macabre from the Poe of the cinema, it's really a character-driven story about sibling devotion—although there is a sequence in a chamber of horrors. ▼▶

White Tower, The (1950) **C-98m. **½ D:** Ted Tetzlaff. Glenn Ford, (Alida) Valli, Claude Rains, Oscar Homolka, Cedric Hardwicke, Lloyd Bridges. Stunning location filming in the French Alps helps otherwise ordinary melodrama of various individuals of many nationalities, who attempt to scale a "monstrous, beautiful" mountain peak. Scripted by Paul Jarrico, from James Ramsey Ullman's bestseller. ▼▶

White Voices (1965-Italian) **C-93m. *** D:** Pasquale Festa Campanile, Massimo Franciosa. Paolo Ferrari, Sandra Milo, Anouk Aimée, Graziella Granata, Barbara Steele. Good lusty adventure à la TOM JONES concerns exploits of castrati singers who have retained high singing voices by means of operation. Techniscope.

White Warrior, The (1961-Italian) **C-86m. *½ D:** Riccardo Freda. Steve Reeves, Giorgia Moll, Renato Baldini, Gerard Herter. Tiring spectacle about tribal chieftain leading rebellion against advancing troops of Czar, set in 19th century. Dyaliscope. ▼▶

White Wilderness (1958) **C-73m. *** D:**

[778]

James Algar. Narrated by Winston Hibler. Typically good Disney True-Life feature takes a look at the Arctic region; highlight is extended sequence on lemmings and their yearly suicide ritual.▼▶

White Witch Doctor (1953) C-96m. **½ D: Henry Hathaway. Susan Hayward, Robert Mitchum, Walter Slezak, Timothy Carey. Bakuba territory is scene of diverse interests of nurse Hayward who wants to bring modern medicine to natives and adventurers Mitchum and Slezak bent on finding hidden treasure. ▶

White Woman (1933) 68m. ** D: Stuart Walker. Carole Lombard, Charles Laughton, Charles Bickford, Kent Taylor, Percy Kilbride, James Bell, Charles Middleton. Laughton's hamminess knows no bounds in this potboiler about the ruthless owner of a Malayan rubber plantation who marries a café singer (Lombard) facing deportation, who proceeds to cuckold him with his hunky overseer (Taylor). Sounds more fun than it is. Loosely remade in 1939 as ISLAND OF LOST MEN. ▶

White Zombie (1932) 73m. *** D: Victor Halperin. Bela Lugosi, Madge Bellamy, Joseph Cawthorn, Robert Frazer, John Harron, Brandon Hurst, Clarence Muse. Zombie master Lugosi menaces newlyweds on Haitian sugar plantation; eerie, unique low-budget chiller. Also shown in a computer-colored version. ▼▶

Who Done It? (1942) 75m. *** D: Erle C. Kenton. Bud Abbott, Lou Costello, Patric Knowles, Louise Allbritton, William Gargan, William Bendix, Mary Wickes, Don Porter, Thomas Gomez, Jerome Cowan, Ludwig Stossel. One of A&C's best finds the boys as would-be radio writers who pretend to be detectives when the network's president is murdered, and everyone believes them—including the killer! Great supporting cast is topped by Wickes as wise-cracking secretary and Bendix as real cop who's even dumber than Lou.▼▶

Who Done It? (1956-British) 85m. **½ D: Basil Dearden. Benny Hill, Belinda Lee, David Kossoff, Garry Marsh, George Margo, Ernest Thesiger. Hill's only star vehicle movie is a Red Skelton–type comedy about a novice private eye involved with foreign spies. No double-entendre jokes, but lots of slapstick, much of it labored and obvious. Best for kids.▼▶

Who Goes There? SEE: **Passionate Sentry, The**

Who Killed Doc Robbin? (1948) C-50m. ** D: Bernard Carr. Virginia Grey, Don Castle, George Zucco, Whitford Kane, Larry Olsen, Eilene Janssen, Gerard Perreau. Those ersatz Little Rascals are back in the second attempt (after CURLEY) by producer Hal Roach to rekindle the *Our Gang* magic. This time the kids try to rescue a handyman who's accused of murdering a local "mad scientist." A spooky mansion

and a huge gorilla give this threadbare comedy what little life it has. Retitled CURLEY AND HIS GANG IN THE HAUNTED MANSION for TV.▼▶

Who Killed Gail Preston? (1938) 60m. **½ D: Leon Barsha. Don Terry, Rita Hayworth, Robert Paige, Wyn Cahoon, Gene Morgan, Marc Lawrence, Arthur Loft. Minor whodunit with cop Terry investigating the murder of the title character, an unlikable singer.

Who Killed Teddy Bear (1965) 91m. *½ D: Joseph Cates. Sal Mineo, Juliet Prowse, Jan Murray, Elaine Stritch, Dan Travanty (Daniel J. Travanti). Sleazy, leering low-budget suspenser about psychopathic busboy Mineo preying on discotheque hostess Prowse. A waste of talent. ▶

Whole Town's Talking, The (1935) 95m. *** D: John Ford. Edward G. Robinson, Jean Arthur, Wallace Ford, Arthur Hohl, Edward Brophy, Arthur Byron, Donald Meek. Entertaining comedy with meek clerk Robinson a lookalike for notorious gangster; fine performances by E. G. and Arthur. Script by Jo Swerling and Robert Riskin, from a W. R. Burnett novel. Reworked as SO YOU WON'T TALK.▼▶

Whole Truth, The (1958-British) 84m. **½ D: John Guillermin. Stewart Granger, Donna Reed, George Sanders, Gianna Maria Canale. Good cast lends strength to fair plot of almost perfect attempt to pin murder of movie starlet on producer Granger. ▶

Whom the Gods Destroy (1934) 75m. *** D: Walter Lang. Walter Connolly, Robert Young, Doris Kenyon, Scotty Beckett, Rollo Lloyd, Hobart Bosworth, Gilbert Emery, Akim Tamiroff, Henry Kolker, Charles Middleton, Walter Brennan. Famous theatrical producer turns coward during the sinking of an ocean liner but is thought to have died a hero. He cannot face his family and friends, so he watches from afar as his son grows to manhood. Good storytelling (from a story by Albert Payson Terhune), with a great shipwreck sequence, and no fewer than five montages! Screenplay by Sidney Buchman.

Whoopee! (1930) C-93m. *** D: Thornton Freeland. Eddie Cantor, Eleanor Hunt, Paul Gregory, John Rutherford, Ethel Shutta. Antique movie musical sparked by Cantor's performance as a hyper-hypochondriac, and Busby Berkeley's wonderful production numbers. Cantor sings "Making Whoopee" and "My Baby Just Cares for Me"; the girl who sings the first chorus of the opening song is a very young Betty Grable. Filmed in two-color Technicolor. Filmed in 1926 as THE NERVOUS WRECK, then later remade as UP IN ARMS.▼▶

Who's Been Sleeping in My Bed? (1963) C-103m. **½ D: Daniel Mann. Dean Martin, Elizabeth Montgomery, Carol Burnett, Martin Balsam, Jill St. John, Richard Conte,

Louis Nye. Undemanding fluff about TV star Martin being urged altar-ward by fiancée Montgomery. Burnett, in her film debut, is his psychiatrist's nurse. Panavision.

Who's Got the Action? (1962) **C-93m.** ****½** D: Daniel Mann. Dean Martin, Lana Turner, Eddie Albert, Nita Talbot, Walter Matthau, Paul Ford, Margo, John McGiver, Jack Albertson. Strained froth of Turner combatting hubby Martin's horse-racing fever by turning bookie. Panavision. ▼▶

Who's Minding the Store? (1963) **C-90m.** ****½** D: Frank Tashlin. Jerry Lewis, Agnes Moorehead, Jill St. John, John McGiver, Ray Walston, Nancy Kulp, Francesca Bellini. Jerry Lewis vehicle with bumbling idiot (guess who?) set loose in department store. Great supporting cast in stereotyped comic foil roles, plus one good inventive bit. ▼▶

Who Was That Lady? (1960) **115m.** ******* D: George Sidney. Tony Curtis, Dean Martin, Janet Leigh, James Whitmore, John McIntire, Barbara Nichols, Joi Lansing. Spicy shenanigans move along at lively pace as Curtis and Martin pretend to be secret agents to confuse Tony's jealous wife Leigh; script by Norman Krasna, from his play.▶

Why Be Good? (1929) **81m.** ******* D: William A. Seiter. Colleen Moore, Neil Hamilton, Bodil Rosing, John St. Polis, Edward Martindel, Louis Natheaux, Lincoln Stedman. Department store salesgirl Moore loves dressing up and dancing in the hottest nightspots—but she's still a "good" girl. The boss' son thinks so, too, until his father plants a seed of doubt. Entertaining period piece with serious undertones about a young woman's need to be desirable without sacrificing her virtue. Art deco sets and a peppy Vitaphone score are further assets. ▶

Why Bother to Knock (1961-British) **88m.** ***½** D: Cyril Frankel. Elke Sommer, Richard Todd, Nicole Maurey, Scot Finch. Trashy smut about Todd traipsing around Europe giving out keys to his pals, with the girls all turning up unexpectedly. Original British title: DON'T BOTHER TO KNOCK.CinemaScope.

Why Change Your Wife (1920) **92m.** ******* D: Cecil B. DeMille. Gloria Swanson, Thomas Meighan, Bebe Daniels, Theodore Kosloff, Sylvia Ashton, Clarence Geldart, Lucien Littlefield. DeMille, Swanson, and Meighan's follow-up to MALE AND FEMALE, with Robert Gordon (Meighan) wed to prim, proper, constantly disapproving Beth (Swanson). Is it any wonder that he is attracted to pretty model Daniels? What are Beth's chances of winning back her hubby? Smart, enjoyable marital tale explores issues and pressures that remain strikingly contemporary. Based on a story by William deMille, Cecil B.'s brother, and a follow-up of sorts to OLD WIVES FOR NEW (1918) and DON'T CHANGE YOUR

HUSBAND (1919). Look for William (*Hopalong Cassidy*) Boyd as the young naval officer at the hotel.▶

Why Must I Die (1960) **86m.** ****** D: Roy Del Ruth. Terry Moore, Debra Paget, Bert Freed, Julie Reding. Similar to I WANT TO LIVE! except in quality. Moore is singer falsely convicted of murder.▶

Why Worry? (1923) **63m.** *****½** D: Fred Newmeyer, Sam Taylor. Harold Lloyd, Jobyna Ralston, John Aasen, Leo White, James Mason. Hilarious story of millionaire playboy Lloyd who stumbles into revolution-ridden country and inadvertently becomes involved. Packed with belly-laugh sight gags.▶

Wichita (1955) **C-81m.** ****½** D: Jacques Tourneur. Joel McCrea, Vera Miles, Lloyd Bridges, Wallace Ford, Peter Graves, Edgar Buchanan, John Smith, Keith Larsen, Jack Elam, Robert Wilke. Action-filled Western; good cast helps Wyatt Earp (McCrea) restore order to Western town overrun with outlaws. CinemaScope.▼▶

Wicked as They Come (1956-British) **94m.** ****** D: Ken Hughes. Arlene Dahl, Phil Carey, Herbert Marshall, David Kossoff. Dahl cavorts nicely in this minor story of a girl from the poor part of town involved with the wrong people.

Wicked City, The (1949-French) **76m.** ***½** D: Francois Villiers. Maria Montez, Jean-Pierre Aumont, Lilli Palmer, Marcel Dalio. Even exotic Montez can't spice lazy telling of unscrupulous woman and the gob she involves in her sordid life. Original title: HANS LE MARIN.

Wicked Darling, The (1919) **59m.** ******* D: Tod Browning. Priscilla Dean, Lon Chaney, Wellington Playter, Spottiswoode Aitken, Gertrude Astor, Kalla Pasha. "Gutter Rose" (Dean) pilfers a necklace, setting off a chain of events involving a brutal fellow pickpocket (Chaney) and a newly impoverished aristocrat (Playter). Chaney and Dean offer vivid performances in this atmospheric melodrama–morality tale. Lone surviving print of this long-lost film is shorter than original U.S. release version.▶

Wicked Lady, The (1945-British) **104m.** ****½** D: Leslie Arliss. Margaret Lockwood, James Mason, Patricia Roc, Griffith Jones, Michael Rennie, Felix Aylmer, Martita Hunt. Moderately entertaining costumer of unashamedly evil Lockwood destroying the lives of one and all while pairing with notorious highwayman Mason. Loaded with sexual innuendo. Arliss also scripted. Remade in 1983. ▼▶

Wicked Wife SEE: **Grand National Night**

Wicked Woman (1954) **77m.** ***½** D: Russell Rouse. Richard Egan, Beverly Michaels, Percy Helton, Evelyn Scott. Lumbering drama about no-good waitress leading assorted men astray.

Wide Blue Road, The (1957-Italian) **C-99m.**

[780]

***½ D: Gillo Pontecorvo. Yves Montand, Alida Valli, Francisco Rabal, Umberto Spadaro, Peter Carsten, Federica Ranchi, Terence Hill. Moving, robust slice of life about an insular Italian fishing village and one proud, stubborn man who continues to engage in dynamite fishing (even though it's illegal), which pits him against a Coast Guard lieutenant—and the community. Montand was never more charismatic. Pontecorvo's debut film (which he cowrote with Franco Solinas) pays homage to neorealism but charts its own course—in breathtaking color.▼▶

Wide Open Faces (1938) 67m. **½ D: Kurt Neumann. Joe E. Brown, Jane Wyman, Alison Skipworth, Lyda Roberti, Alan Baxter, Lucien Littlefield, Sidney Toler. Enjoyable Brown vehicle with top-notch supporting cast; innocent soda jerk mixed up with gangster. ▶

Wide Open Town (1941) 77m. *** D: Lesley Selander. William Boyd, Russell Hayden, Andy Clyde, Evelyn Brent, Victor Jory, Morris Ankrum, Bernice Kay (Cara Williams). Icy proprietress of Paradise Saloon is also a crime queen with bad men who do her bidding—until Hopalong Cassidy arrives on the scene. Remake of HOPALONG CASSIDY RETURNS, with Brent repeating her role and Ankrum changing sides. Better director, production values, and action, plus beautiful Lone Pine exteriors (which receive unprecedented screen credit) help this surpass the original, a good movie on its own. Hayden's last ride for Bar 20; debut of 15-year-old redhead Kay.▼▶

Widow, The (1955-Italian) 89m. ** D: Lewis Milestone. Patricia Roc, Anna Maria Ferrero, Massimo Serrato, Akim Tamiroff. Uneven soaper of Roc involved with lover Serrato, a sports car racer, who falls for Ferrero; film meanders.

Widow From Chicago, The (1930) 64m. ** D: Edward F. Cline. Alice White, Neil Hamilton, Edward G. Robinson, Frank McHugh, Lee Shumway. Robinson plays a beer baron targeted for revenge by White, whose brother he rubbed out, in this antiquated gangster film, interesting only for Robinson's pre-LITTLE CAESAR performance.

Wife, Doctor and Nurse (1937) 85m. **½ D: Walter Lang. Loretta Young, Warner Baxter, Virginia Bruce, Jane Darwell, Sidney Blackmer, Minna Gombell, Elisha Cook, Jr., Lon Chaney, Jr. Baxter is caught between two women, but seems uninterested in both. Bright comedy with expert cast.

Wife, Husband and Friend (1939) 80m. *** D: Gregory Ratoff. Loretta Young, Warner Baxter, Binnie Barnes, George Barbier, Cesar Romero, J. Edward Bromberg, Eugene Pallette. Renie Riano. Entertaining comedy about aspiring singer Young whose husband Baxter tries to show her up; fun, but better as EVERYBODY DOES IT. Pro-

duced and scripted by Nunnally Johnson, from a story by James M. Cain(!). ▶

Wife of Monte Cristo, The (1946) 80m. ** D: Edgar G. Ulmer. John Loder, Lenore Aubert, Charles Dingle, Eduardo Ciannelli, Eva Gabor, Martin Kosleck. Corruption in the medical profession proves a formidable match for the Count; standard low-budget swashbuckler.▼

Wife Takes a Flyer, The (1942) 86m. ** D: Richard Wallace. Joan Bennett, Franchot Tone, Allyn Joslyn, Cecil Cunningham, Chester Clute. Weak WW2 espionage comedy of Tone pretending to be Bennett's husband to escape from Holland.

Wife vs. Secretary (1936) 88m. **½ D: Clarence Brown. Clark Gable, Jean Harlow, Myrna Loy, May Robson, George Barbier, James Stewart, Hobart Cavanaugh. Perfect example of Hollywood gloss, with three top-notch stars towering over inferior material. Harlow is particularly good in tale of secretary who becomes invaluable to her boss (Gable), causing complications in both of their lives.▼

Wife Wanted (1946) 73m. ** D: Phil Karlson. Kay Francis, Paul Cavanagh, Robert Shayne, Veda Ann Borg. In her last film, Francis is film star innocently hooked up with lonely-heart crooks; low production values. ▶

Wild and the Innocent, The (1959) C-84m. **½ D: Jack Sher. Audie Murphy, Joanne Dru, Gilbert Roland, Jim Backus, Sandra Dee, George Mitchell, Peter Breck. Murphy and Dee make an engaging duo as trapper and untamed country girl involved in gunplay in town during July 4th holiday. CinemaScope.

Wild and the Willing, The (1962-British) 112m. ** D: Ralph Thomas. Virginia Maskell, Paul Rogers, Samantha Eggar, Ian McShane, John Hurt, Richard Warner. Life and love at a provincial university, with over-earnest attempt to be realistic and daring in story of student who seduces professor's wife.

Wild and Wonderful (1964) C-88m. **½ D: Michael Anderson. Tony Curtis, Christine Kaufmann, Larry Storch, Marty Ingels, Jacques Aubuchon, Jules Munshin. Empty slapstick froth involving French poodle movie star with Curtis and Kaufmann romancing.

Wild Blue Yonder, The (1951) 98m. **½ D: Allan Dwan. Wendell Corey, Vera Ralston, Forrest Tucker, Phil Harris, Walter Brennan, Harry Carey, Jr. Standard WW2 aviation yarn, saluting the B-29 bomber, detailing friendship of Corey and Tucker, rivalry for nurse Ralston, etc. And just for change of pace, Harris sings "The Thing."

Wild Boys of the Road (1933) 68m. *** D: William A. Wellman. Frankie Darro, Rochelle Hudson, Dorothy Coonan, Edwin

Philips, Ann Hovey, Arthur Hohl, Sterling Holloway. Darro, Philips, and Coonan are unable to find work during the Depression, so they ride the rails, panhandle, steal. Dated but still provocative Warner Bros. "social conscience" drama.❚

Wildcat, The (1921-German) **82m.** ***½ D: Ernst Lubitsch. Pola Negri, Victor Janson, Paul Heidemann, Wilhelm Diegelmann, Hermann Thimig, Edith Meller. Whimsical, visually innovative tongue-in-cheek tale of a frisky mountain wench (broadly played by Negri), the female member of a band of thieves, who becomes enamored of a lieutenant (Heidemann) who's been reassigned to a border fortress. The playful, surreal set design is a standout, as are Lubitsch's clever directorial touches. Written by Lubitsch and Hanns Kräly.❚

Wildcat (1942) **70m.** ** D: Frank McDonald. Richard Arlen, Arline Judge, Buster Crabbe, William Frawley, Arthur Hunnicutt, Elisha Cook, Jr. Arlen and Crabbe are rival oilmen in this Pine-Thomas production that's crammed with the usual quota of thrills and romance. ▼❚

Wildcat Bus (1940) **64m.** *½ D: Frank Woodruff. Fay Wray, Charles Lang, Paul Guilfoyle, Don Costello, Paul McGrath. Blah time-killer with Wray and her father operating a failing bus line, with unemployed rich boy Lang coming to their assistance. Poor in all departments.

Wild Cats on the Beach (1959-Italian) **C-96m.** **½ D: Vittorio Sala. Elsa Martinelli, Alberto Sordi, Georges Marchal, Antonio Cifariello. Quartet of love tales set at resort area of Côte D'Azur; varying in quality. Dyaliscope.

Wild Company (1930) **73m.** *½ D: Leo McCarey. H. B. Warner, Frank Albertson, Sharon Lynn, Joyce Compton, Claire McDowell, Bela Lugosi. Badly dated melodrama of flaming youth and generation gap; devil-may-care Albertson ignores parents' warnings about company he keeps, gets into trouble over underworld murder. Lugosi plays nightclub owner.

Wild for Kicks (1960-British) **92m.** ** D: Edmond T. Greville. David Farrar, Noelle Adam, Christopher Lee, Gillian Hills, Adam Faith, Shirley Anne Field, Peter McEnery, Oliver Reed. Sultry teen Hills, with a bad attitude, resents her father's pretty new French-born wife and summarily gets into all sorts of mischief. Not very good; of interest mainly as a period piece. Original British title: BEAT GIRL. ▼❚

Wild Geese Calling (1941) **77m.** ** D: John Brahm. Henry Fonda, Joan Bennett, Warren William, Ona Munson, Barton MacLane, Russell Simpson. Action and romance in 1890s Oregon and Alaska, but not enough of either.

Wild Girl (1932) **74m.** *** D: Raoul Walsh. Charles Farrell, Joan Bennett, Ralph Bellamy, Eugene Pallette, Irving Pichel, Minna Gombell, Morgan Wallace, Willard Robertson. Eccentric but enjoyable backwoods story, with Bennett an appealing tomboy ("I like trees better than men," she says. "They're straight"), Wallace a hissable villain. Presented as a photo album with characters identifying themselves and pages flipped to change scenes. Told mostly (but not always) in broad, tongue-in-cheek fashion. Based on Bret Harte's *Salomy Jane* stories. Filmed in California's Giant Forest Sequoia National Park.

Wild Gold (1934) **75m.** ** D: George Marshall. John Boles, Claire Trevor, Harry Green, Roger Imhof, Monroe Owsley, Ruth Gillette. Strange blend of comedy, melodrama, romance, and music in hodgepodge story of miner Boles infatuated with singer Trevor, facing irate husband, unexpected disaster in remote forest cabin. Uses stock footage from silent film THE JOHNSTOWN FLOOD.

Wild Guitar (1962) **87m.** BOMB D: Ray Dennis Steckler. Arch Hall, Jr., Nancy Czar, William Watters (Arch Hall, Sr.), Cash Flagg (Ray Dennis Steckler). Guitar-playing, motorcycle-riding Hall is exploited by a deceitful record executive. Perfectly awful melodrama. ▼❚

Wild Harvest (1947) **92m.** *½ D: Tay Garnett. Alan Ladd, Dorothy Lamour, Robert Preston, Lloyd Nolan, Richard Erdman, Allen Jenkins. Pretty dismal film of traveling grain-harvesters with Preston and Ladd rivaling for Lamour's love.

Wild Heart, The (1950-British) **C-82m.** ** D: Michael Powell, Emeric Pressburger. Jennifer Jones, David Farrar, Cyril Cusack, Sybil Thorndike, Edward Chapman, George Cole, Hugh Griffith, Esmond Knight. Muddled tale of strange Shropshire girl in late 19th century whose life is dominated by superstitions; she marries minister but is stirred by lusty squire. Beautiful location photography by Christopher Challis. Reedited from 110m. British release called GONE TO EARTH, which plays much better.

Wild Heritage (1958) **C-78m.** **½ D: Charles Haas. Will Rogers, Jr., Maureen O'Sullivan, Rod McKuen, Casey Tibbs, George Winslow, Gigi Perreau, Troy Donahue, John Beradino, Jeanette Nolan. Soaper involving events in the intertwining lives of two westward-bound pioneer families. CinemaScope.

Wild in the Country (1961) **C-114m.** **½ D: Philip Dunne. Elvis Presley, Hope Lange, Tuesday Weld, Millie Perkins, John Ireland, Gary Lockwood. Can *you* resist Elvis in a Clifford Odets script about a back-country hothead with literary aspirations? Clichéd if earnest, but an undeniable curiosity with some good performances, Elvis' among them. That's young Christina Crawford as Lockwood's girlfriend. CinemaScope. ▼❚

Wild Is the Wind (1957) **114m.** **½ D: George Cukor. Anna Magnani, Anthony Quinn, Anthony Franciosa, Dolores Hart, Joseph Calleia. Turgid soaper set in the West, with Quinn marrying the sister of his dead wife, not able to separate the two. Good acting helps script along. VistaVision.

Wild Man of Borneo, The (1941) **78m.** ** D: Robert B. Sinclair. Frank Morgan, Mary Howard, Billie Burke, Donald Meek, Marjorie Main, Connie Gilchrist, Bonita Granville, Walter Catlett, Phil Silvers, Dan Dailey. Good cast in weak sideshow comedy; Morgan masquerades as title character in one of his less memorable roles.

Wild North, The (1952) **C-97m.** ** D: Andrew Marton. Stewart Granger, Cyd Charisse, Wendell Corey, J. M. Kerrigan, Ray Teal. Undazzling account of accused murderer hunted by Mountie, with the expected proving of innocence before finale; Charisse is love interest. ▶

Wild One, The (1954) **79m.** ***½ D: Laslo Benedek. Marlon Brando, Mary Murphy, Robert Keith, Lee Marvin, Jay C. Flippen, Jerry Paris, Alvy Moore, Gil Stratton, Jr. *The* original motorcycle film with Brando's renowned performance as packleader raising Cain in small town; dated, but well worth viewing. Script by John Paxton, based on a story by Frank Rooney; produced by Stanley Kramer. ▼●▶

Wild on the Beach (1965) **77m.** *½ D: Maury Dexter. Frankie Randall, Sherry Jackson, Jackie & Gayle, Sonny & Cher, Sandy Nelson. Randall and Jackson fight over the rights to a beachhouse—and fall in love. Dreary comedy notable only for the appearance of Mr. and Mrs. Bono, and as Cher's screen debut. ▶

Wild Oranges (1924) **88m.** ***½ D: King Vidor. Frank Mayo, Virginia Valli, Ford Sterling, Nigel De Brulier, Charles A. Post. An embittered young widower wanders aimlessly in a sailboat until he discovers an isolated inlet on the Georgia coast inhabited by a frightened girl, her paranoid grandfather, and a crazed killer on the lam. Beautifully made, highly cinematic silent fable with a dreamlike and sensuous quality. Vidor adapted Joseph Hergesheimer's novel. ▶

Wild Orchids (1929) **102m.** **½ D: Sidney Franklin. Greta Garbo, Lewis Stone, Nils Asther. Standard love triangle with married Garbo falling for wealthy, charming Asther on a trip to Java. Garbo's charisma elevates typical soaper. Silent with music score. ▼▶

Wild Party, The (1929) **76m.** **½ D: Dorothy Arzner. Clara Bow, Fredric March, Shirley O'Hara, Marceline Day, Joyce Compton, Jack Oakie. Fascinating antique about dishy new prof at all-girls' school and his on-again, off-again relationship with a sexy student who thinks college is just a lark. Absolutely awful by any objective standards, but great fun to watch. Clara's talkie debut. ▼

Wild Party, The (1956) **81m.** *½ D: Harry Horner. Anthony Quinn, Carol Ohmart, Arthur Franz, Jay Robinson, Kathryn Grant (Crosby), Nehemiah Persoff, Paul Stewart. Blah attempt at naturalistic drama with Quinn the has-been football star going mildly berserk at a sleazy dance hall.

Wild Ride, The (1960) **63m.** *½ D: Harvey Berman. Jack Nicholson, Georgianna Carter, Robert Bean. Amateurish low-budgeter about a hedonistic hot-rodder who's as casual about killing people as he is about stealing his buddy's girlfriend. Worth seeing only if you're curious about this early Nicholson performance. Revised for 2000 release as VELOCITY. ▼▶

Wild River (1960) **C-110m.** ***½ D: Elia Kazan. Montgomery Clift, Lee Remick, Jo Van Fleet, Albert Salmi, Jay C. Flippen, James Westerfield, Barbara Loden. Clift plays Tennessee Valley Authority official trying to convince elderly Van Fleet to sell her property for new projects. Kazan's exquisite evocation of 1930s Tennessee—and moving romance between Clift and Remick—give this film its strength. Bruce Dern makes his film debut in supporting role. Adapted from novels by William Bradford Huie and Borden Deal by Paul Osborn. CinemaScope. ▶

Wild Seed, The (1965) **99m.** *** D: Brian Hutton. Michael Parks, Celia Kaye, Ross Elliott, Woodrow Chambliss, Eva Novak. Arty yet gripping story of runaway Kaye traveling to California, guided by road bum Parks.

Wild Stallion (1952) **C-72m.** ** D: Lewis D. Collins. Martha Hyer, Edgar Buchanan, Hugh Beaumont, Ben Johnson. Johnson is determined to capture the horse that once was his pet but escaped during an Indian raid in which his parents were killed. OK Western yarn, told mostly in flashback. ▶

Wild Strawberries (1957-Swedish) **90m.** **** D: Ingmar Bergman. Victor Sjostrom, Ingrid Thulin, Bibi Andersson, Gunnar Bjornstrand, Folke Sundquist, Bjorn Bjelvenstam, Max von Sydow. Elderly Stockholm professor reviews the disappointments of his life, while traveling by car to receive an honorary degree. Superb use of flashbacks and brilliant performance by Sjostrom make this Bergman classic an emotional powerhouse. Still a staple of any serious filmgoer's education. ▼●▶

Wild Westerners, The (1962) **C-70m.** *½ D: Oscar Rudolph. James Philbrook, Nancy Kovack, Duane Eddy, Guy Mitchell. Humdrum account of marshal and new wife overcoming obstacles to bring gold east for Yankee cause. ▼

Wild, Wild Planet, The (1965-Italian) **C-93m.** *½ D: Anthony Dawson (Antonio Margheriti). Tony Russell, Lisa Gastoni, Massimo Serato, Charles Justin, Franco Nero. Female alien uses robots to gain control of earth scientists by shrinking them. Fairly good ending does not redeem lackluster film. Made at same time as WAR OF THE PLANETS and other losers.●)

Wild Youth SEE: **Naked Youth**

Willie and Joe Back at the Front SEE: **Back at the Front**

Will James' Sand SEE: **Sand**

Will Success Spoil Rock Hunter? (1957) **C-94m.** ***½ D: Frank Tashlin. Tony Randall, Jayne Mansfield, Betsy Drake, Joan Blondell, John Williams, Henry Jones, Mickey Hargitay. Guest star, Groucho Marx. Clever satire uses George Axelrod play about ad man who tries to persuade glamorous star to endorse Stay-Put Lipstick as springboard for scattershot satire on 1950s morals, television, sex, business, etc. Director-writer Tashlin in peak form. CinemaScope.▼●)

Willy McBean and His Magic Machine (1965-Japanese) **C-94m.** **½ D: Arthur Rankin, Jr. Voices of Larry Mann, Billie Richards, Alfie Scopp, Paul Ligman. Puppet novelty item about mad professor and his time machine; OK for kids.▼

Wilson (1944) **C-154m.** ***½ D: Henry King. Alexander Knox, Charles Coburn, Geraldine Fitzgerald, Thomas Mitchell, Cedric Hardwicke, Vincent Price, Mary Anderson, Sidney Blackmer, Stanley Ridges, Eddie Foy, Jr., Francis X. Bushman. Superb biography of WW1-era President whose League of Nations idea became an obsession; one of Hollywood's solid films. Notorious box-office flop, even after winning five Oscars (including Lamar Trotti's script and Leon Shamroy's photography).▼)

Winchester '73 (1950) **92m.** ***½ D: Anthony Mann. James Stewart, Shelley Winters, Dan Duryea, Stephen McNally, Charles Drake, Millard Mitchell, John McIntire, Will Geer, Jay C. Flippen, Rock Hudson, Anthony (Tony) Curtis. Exceptional Western story of Stewart tracking down a man—and his stolen rifle—through series of interrelated episodes, leading to memorable shootout among rock-strewn hills. First-rate in every way, this landmark film was largely responsible for renewed popularity of Westerns in the 1950s. Script by Robert L. Richards and Borden Chase, from a story by Stuart N. Lake. Beautifully photographed by William Daniels; remade for TV in 1967.▼●)

Wind, The (1928) **88m.** **** D: Victor Seastrom. Lillian Gish, Lars Hanson, Montagu Love, Dorothy Cumming, Edward Earle, William Orlamond. Virgin Virginian Gish battles the elements in a barren dustbowl town—marrying on the rebound a man who disgusts her, shooting the lout who rapes her. Probably Gish's greatest vehicle— and one of the last great silents—with a splendidly staged climactic desert storm sequence. Written by Frances Marion, from Dorothy Scarborough's novel.▼●

Wind Across the Everglades (1958) **C-93m.** **½ D: Nicholas Ray. Burl Ives, Christopher Plummer, Gypsy Rose Lee, George Voskovec, Tony Galento, Emmett Kelly, Chana Eden, MacKinlay Kantor. Oddball cast in even odder story of boozy turn-of-the-20th-century Florida game warden (Plummer) who takes it upon himself to rid the area of poachers. Matchup of director Ray and writer-producer Budd Schulberg makes this a genuine curio. Peter Falk makes his film debut in a small role; rare out-of-makeup appearance by top clown Kelly. Filmed in the Everglades.

Wind Cannot Read, The (1958-British) **C-110m.** **½ D: Ralph Thomas. Dirk Bogarde, Yoko Tani, Ronald Lewis, John Fraser, Anthony Bushell, Michael Medwin. Tidy tale of Bogarde escaping from Japanese prison camp during WW2 to find his ailing wife Tani.

Windjammer: The Voyage of the Christian Radich (1958) **C-141m.** *** D: Bill Colleran, Louis de Rochemont III. Visually impressive, meticulously detailed three-panel "Cinemiracle" chronicle of a special training voyage of the Norwegian vessel S/S *Christian Radich* from Oslo to N.Y.C. (and beyond) by way of Madeira, Portugal, and the West Indies. Film is part travelogue, part seagoing adventure, part idyllic trip back in time. A high point: dazzling images of N.Y.C. created by Arthur "Weegee" Fellig that call to mind the opening of ON THE TOWN. Only flaw, and it is minor: the awkward "singing" and "dramatic" sequences featuring the youthful crew. Produced by Louis de Rochemont. Cinemiracle.❂

Windom's Way (1957-British) **C-108m.** *** D: Ronald Neame. Peter Finch, Mary Ure, Natasha Parry, Robert Flemyng, Michael Hordern, Gregoire Aslan. Dedicated doctor (Finch) working in Malayan village tries to encourage resistance to Communist takeover. Strong performances in this intelligent film.▼

Window, The (1949) **73m.** *** D: Ted Tetzlaff. Bobby Driscoll, Barbara Hale, Arthur Kennedy, Paul Stewart, Ruth Roman. Sleeper film less impressive now than in 1949; still good, with young Driscoll earning a special Academy Award for his performance as a little boy who witnesses a murder and is unable to convince his parents he's not lying. Parents' dialogue weakens credibility, but suspense still mounts; extremely well photographed (by William Steiner) and staged. Based on a story by Cornell Woolrich. Remade as THE BOY CRIED MURDER and CLOAK AND DAGGER (1984).▼)

Window in London, A SEE: **Lady in Distress**

Winds of the Wasteland (1936) **55m.** **½

D: Mack V. Wright. John Wayne, Phyllis Fraser, Douglas Cosgrove, Lane Chandler, Sam Flint, Robert Kortman. Two obsolete Pony Express riders buy a worthless stage line to run-down town but win a race that pays with a lucrative government mail contract. Climactic stagecoach race is exciting, but process-screen work betrays a limited budget. Look for Charles Locher (later Jon Hall) in a small part. ▼▶

Wing and a Prayer (1944) 97m. *** D: Henry Hathaway. Don Ameche, Dana Andrews, William Eythe, Charles Bickford, Cedric Hardwicke, Kevin O'Shea, Richard Jaeckel, Henry (Harry) Morgan, Richard Crane, Glenn Langan, Reed Hadley. Fine WW2 actioner of life aboard a Navy aircraft carrier in the South Pacific, just after Pearl Harbor, leading to the Battle of Midway, chronicling the development of U.S. military strategy. Ameche is especially good as the ship's tough flight commander. Excellent use is made of real combat footage. Full title is WING AND A PRAYER THE STORY OF CARRIER X. ▼▶

Winged Victory (1944) 130m. **½ D: George Cukor. Lon McCallister, Jeanne Crain, Edmond O'Brien, Don Taylor, Judy Holliday, Lee J. Cobb, Peter Lind Hayes, Red Buttons, Barry Nelson, Karl Malden, Gary Merrill, Martin Ritt, Kevin McCarthy. WW2 saga is less stirring today than in 1944, but graphic depiction of young men's training for pilot duty is still interesting. So is opportunity of seeing future stars early in their careers. Script by Moss Hart, from his play. Film debuts of Buttons, Merrill, Ritt, McCarthy, Keith Andes, Brad Dexter, Martin Balsam, Mario Lanza.

Wings (1927) 139m. **½ D: William A. Wellman. Clara Bow, Charles "Buddy" Rogers, Richard Arlen, Jobyna Ralston, Gary Cooper, El Brendel. One of the most famous silent films is, alas, not one of the best, despite rose-colored memories. Story of two all-American boys (in love with the same girl) who enlist in the Army Air Corps during WW1 is much too thin to sustain such a long movie. What's important here are the combat flying sequences, among the best in Hollywood history. First Oscar winner as Best Picture. ▼●▶

Wings in the Dark (1935) 77m. **½ D: James Flood. Cary Grant, Myrna Loy, Dean Jagger, Roscoe Karns, Hobart Cavanaugh, Bert Hanlon. Sky-writing stunt flier Loy falls for flier Grant, who's blinded in a gas explosion. Attractive performers left dangling without a script in this implausible soap opera; fine aerial photography. ▶

Wings of Eagles, The (1957) C-110m. **½ D: John Ford. John Wayne, Maureen O'Hara, Dan Dailey, Ward Bond, Ken Curtis, Edmund Lowe, Kenneth Tobey, Sig Ruman. Biography of Frank "Spig" Wead, pioneer WW1 aviator who later turned to

screenwriting (including AIR MAIL and THEY WERE EXPENDABLE for Ford) after an accident; first half is slapstick comedy, with no sense of period detail, then abruptly changes to drama for balance of film. Very mixed bag; film buffs will have fun watching Bond play "John Dodge," spoofing director Ford. ▼▶

Wings of the Hawk (1953) C-80m. **½ D: Budd Boetticher. Van Heflin, Julia (Julie) Adams, George Dolenz, Pedro Gonzales-Gonzales, Abbe Lane, Antonio Moreno, Noah Beery, Jr. In 1911 Mexico, gringo gold miner Heflin becomes newest member of a resistance group opposing the despotic Federales. The action (fistfights, hard riding, explosions) is all above average. Originally in 3-D.

Wings of the Morning (1937-British) C-89m. **½ D: Harold Schuster. Annabella, Henry Fonda, Leslie Banks, Irene Vanbrugh, Steward Rome, Helen Haye, Edward Underdown, John McCormack. Trifling story of gypsies, crucial horserace, blossoming love between Fonda and Annabella, initially disguised as a boy. Much ado about nothing. England's first Technicolor film still boasts beautiful pastel hues (by Ray Rennahan and Jack Cardiff) as major attraction, along with famed tenor McCormack doing several songs. ▼▶

Wings of the Navy (1939) 89m. ** D: Lloyd Bacon. George Brent, Olivia de Havilland, John Payne, Frank McHugh, John Litel, Victor Jory, Henry O'Neill, John Ridgely. Standard semidocumentary of pilots being trained for fighting while de Havilland is vied for by brothers Brent and Payne. Typical Warners prewar propaganda, but watchable. ▶

Winner Take All (1932) 68m. **½ D: Roy Del Ruth. James Cagney, Virginia Bruce, Marian Nixon, Guy Kibbee, Alan Mowbray, Dickie Moore. Minor but engaging Cagney vehicle with Jimmy as a thick-witted, cocky prizefighter torn between good girl Nixon and fickle society girl Bruce. Yes, that's George Raft in a split-second shot as a nightclub bandleader, in stock footage from the Texas Guinan movie QUEEN OF THE NIGHTCLUBS. ▶

Winning of Barbara Worth, The (1926) 89m. *** D: Henry King. Ronald Colman, Vilma Banky, Gary Cooper, Charles Lane, Paul McAllister, Clyde Cook. A man rescues an infant daughter after her mother dies in a sandstorm and raises her as his own. Years later, when she has grown to womanhood, he imports a team of experts to help him "tame the Colorado" and bring water to the desert. Chief engineer Colman falls in love with Barbara (Banky), which raises the ire of her lifelong friend (Cooper, in his first major role). Simple, well-executed story builds to a spectacular climactic flood sequence. Frances Marion adapted the Harold Bell Wright novel. ▶

Winning of the West (1953) **58m. **½ D:** George Archainbaud. Gene Autry, Smiley Burnette, Gail Davis, Richard Crane, Robert Livingston, House Peters, Jr., Gregg Barton, William Forrest, George Chesebro. Ranger Autry must bring outlaws who offer protection for a price to justice, but his kid brother (Crane) is mixed up with them. Sturdy tale, with Gene and Smiley harmonizing brightly on Burnette-written "Fetch Me Down My Trusty .45." ▼🄳

Winning Team, The (1952) **98m. **½ D:** Lewis Seiler. Doris Day, Ronald Reagan, Frank Lovejoy, Eve Miller, James Millican, Rusty Tamblyn. Biography of baseball pitching great Grover Cleveland Alexander focuses on his relationship with supportive wife whose "teamwork" helps Alexander through problems with alcoholism and lack of confidence. Reagan is fine as the Hall of Fame hurler and film boasts good reenactments of Alexander's legendary 1926 World Series heroics. Cameo appearances by real-life big leaguers Bob Lemon, Peanuts Lowrey, Hank Sauer, Gene Mauch, and others. ▼🄾🄳

Winning Ticket, The (1935) **69m. ** D:** Charles F. Riesner. Leo Carrillo, Louise Fazenda, Ted Healy, Irene Hervey, James Ellison, Luis Alberni, Akim Tamiroff. Thoroughly innocuous (and thoroughly mediocre) grade-B comedy about a lottery ticket and the squabbling that occurs over it. This cast deserves better.

Winslow Boy, The (1948-British) **117m. ***½ D:** Anthony Asquith. Robert Donat, Margaret Leighton, Cedric Hardwicke, Francis L. Sullivan, Frank Lawton, Basil Radford, Wilfrid Hyde-White, Ernest Thesiger. Superior courtroom melodrama from Terence Rattigan's play, headed by Donat as barrister defending innocent Naval cadet (Neil North) accused of school theft. Script by Rattigan and Anatole de Grunwald. Remade in 1999. ▼

Winter A-Go-Go (1965) **C-88m. ** D:** Richard Benedict. James Stacy, William Wellman, Jr., Beverly Adams, Jill Donohue, Julie Parrish. Lowbrow shenanigans at a ski resort run by Stacy for the young, affluent set. ▶

Winter Carnival (1939) **105m. **½ D:** Charles F. Riesner. Richard Carlson, Ann Sheridan, Helen Parrish, James Corner, Virginia Gilmore, Robert Walker, Joan Leslie, Peggy Moran. Contrived romance flick (cowritten by Budd Schulberg) set at Dartmouth College during festive weekend; Sheridan is divorcée in love with professor Carlson. Filmed partly at Dartmouth.

Winter Light (1963-Swedish) **80m. ***½ D:** Ingmar Bergman. Ingrid Thulin, Gunnar Bjornstrand, Max von Sydow, Gunnel Lindblom, Allan Edwall. A difficult film for non-Bergman buffs, this look at a disillusioned priest in a small village is the second of Bergman's trilogy on faith (the first,

THROUGH A GLASS DARKLY; the third, THE SILENCE). Powerful, penetrating drama. ▼🄾🄳

Winter Meeting (1948) **104m. **½ D:** Bretaigne Windust. Bette Davis, Janis Paige, James (Jim) Davis, John Hoyt, Florence Bates. Sluggish script of disillusioned poetess who loves embittered war hero, prevents well-acted film from achieving greater heights. Notable as only romantic lead for Jim Davis, better known for his Westerns and TV series *Dallas.* ▼🄳

Winterset (1936) **78m. **½ D:** Alfred Santell. Burgess Meredith, Margo, Eduardo Ciannelli, Paul Guilfoyle, John Carradine, Edward Ellis, Stanley Ridges, Myron McCormick, Mischa Auer. Meredith, in his screen debut, plays an idealistic young man determined to find the man responsible for a crime that was pinned on his father years ago. The three stars of Maxwell Anderson's impassioned, allegorical Broadway play re-create their roles in this stagebound but fascinating curio of a film. Based in part on the Sacco-Vanzetti case. Look for Lucille Ball. ▼🄳

Wintertime (1943) **82m. ** D:** John Brahm. Sonja Henie, Jack Oakie, Cesar Romero, Carole Landis, Cornel Wilde, S.Z. Sakall, Woody Herman. Henie gives her all to save uncle's hotel from bankruptcy. Innocuous, below par for her vehicles. ▼🄳

Wise Girl (1937) **70m. **½ D:** Leigh Jason. Miriam Hopkins, Ray Milland, Walter Abel, Henry Stephenson, Alec Craig, Guinn Williams, Margaret Dumont, James Finlayson. Pleasant screwball comedy about rich girl pretending to be poor in order to track down her late sister's kids, who are living with starving Greenwich Village artist.

Wishing Ring, The (1914) **55m. *** D:** Maurice Tourneur. Vivian Martin, Alec B. Francis, Chester Barnett, Gyp Williams, Simeon Wiltsie, Johnny Hines. Pickfordesque ingenue Martin is a preacher's daughter bent on reconciling an expelled college student with his estranged father, a British earl. A gypsy ring that might be magical helps tie the twain. Slender romantic fable, set in a bucolic England, is emotionally aggrandized by writer-director Tourneur's mastery of atmosphere. Quite appealing, and never saccharine. ▼

Wistful Widow of Wagon Gap, The (1947) **78m. **½ D:** Charles Barton. Bud Abbott, Lou Costello, Marjorie Main, George Cleveland, Gordon Jones, William Ching, Peter Thompson, Glenn Strange, Audrey Young. Unusual Western spoof for A&C, inspired by real-life law: Lou is accused of killing a man, and is required to take care of his wife (Main) and children (seven). He then becomes sheriff, convinced that no one will dare kill him. Some slow spots, but overall, fun. ▼🄳

Witchcraft (1964-British) **79m. ** D:** Don

Sharp. Lon Chaney (Jr.), Jack Hedley, Jill Dixon, Viola Keats. Standard plot of witch cult happenings in English village after grave of 300-year-old witch is unearthed.▶

Witchcraft Through the Ages (1922-Swedish) **104m.** *** D: Benjamin Christensen. Oscar Stribolt, Clara Pontoppidan, Karen Winther, Maren Pedersen. Visually stunning history of the occult, recreating actual incidents based on records of witch trials, demonic possessions, and torture by the Inquisition. Writer-director Christensen plays Satan himself in this genuinely scary, no-holds-barred silent film. A shortened version was released in 1968 featuring commentary by William S. Burroughs. Original title: HAØXAN. ▼▶

Witch Doctor SEE: **Men of Two Worlds**

Witches of Salem, The SEE: **Crucible, The**

Witching Hour, The (1934) **66m.** **½ D: Henry Hathaway. Sir Guy Standing, John Halliday, Judith Allen, Tom Brown, Olive Tell, William Frawley, Richard Carle. Gambler who wins by using clairvoyant powers and mind control accidentally hypnotizes his daughter's boyfriend into committing a murder, and tries to convince a lawyer to take the unusual case. Minor but well-made chiller with eerie atmosphere. Based on a play by Augustus Thomas that was previously filmed in 1916 and 1921.

Witch Woman, The SEE: **Parson's Widow, The**

With a Song in My Heart (1952) **C-117m.** *** D: Walter Lang. Susan Hayward, Rory Calhoun, David Wayne, Thelma Ritter, Robert Wagner, Una Merkel. Well-intentioned schmaltz based loosely on events in life of singer Jane Froman with Hayward earnest as songstress struggling to make comeback after crippling plane crash. Alfred Newman won an Oscar for Scoring. Froman dubbed Hayward's singing.▶

With Byrd at the South Pole (1930) **82m.** *** D: (none credited). Narrated by Floyd Gibbons. The title tells all in this fascinating document of U.S. Navy Rear-Admiral Richard E. Byrd, his crew, and their journey by sea from N.Y.C. to the Antarctic, culminating with his Polar flight. Film plays as part historical record, part promotional film hyping Byrd (complete with rah-rah narration in the final sequence). Despite this, it's still a remarkable film. William Van der Veer and Joseph T. Rucker's stunning cinematography earned an Academy Award.▼●▶

With Fire and Sword (1961-Italian) **C-96m.** *½ D: Fernando Cerchio. Jeanne Crain, John Drew Barrymore, Pierre Brice, Akim Tamiroff. Costume spaghetti about Cossacks vs. Poles; embarrassing minor epic. Retitled: DAGGERS OF BLOOD. Filmed in widescreen Euroscope.

Within Our Gates (1920) **79m.** *** D:

Oscar Micheaux. Evelyn Preer, Flo Clements, James D. Ruffin, Jack Chenault, William Smith, Charles D. Lucas. Controversial, no-holds-barred racial drama, which, along with Micheaux's THE SYMBOL OF THE UNCONQUERED, counterpoints Griffith's THE BIRTH OF A NATION. Story focuses on light-skinned Preer's various entanglements and efforts to raise money for an all-black school. Despite the melodramatic and sometimes confusing narrative, Micheaux pointedly lambastes not only white racism but blacks who forsake their roots. The lynching scenes are undeniably powerful. Restored from a print found in Spain, with one sequence missing. ▼▶

Within the Law (1923) **105m.** **½ D: Frank Lloyd. Norma Talmadge, Lew Cody, Jack Mulhall, Eileen Percy, Joseph Kilgour, Arthur F. Hull, Helen Ferguson. Shopgirl is framed for robbery and sent to prison by a heartless department store owner. She vows revenge, and gets it three years later when, after being freed, she woos the tycoon's gullible son. Formulaic but well done. A good vehicle for Talmadge; Joan Crawford starred in the 1930s remake, PAID. Remade again in 1939. Frances Marion adapted the play by Bayard Veiller. ▶

Within the Law (1939) **65m.** **½ D: Gustav Machatý. Ruth Hussey, Tom Neal, Paul Kelly, William Gargan, Paul Cavanagh, Rita Johnson, Samuel S. Hinds. Hussey is compelling as an innocent shopgirl framed for stealing who studies law in prison to plot revenge. Slick, compact version of Bayard Veiller's stage hit, previously filmed in 1917, 1923, and in 1931 (as PAID) with Joan Crawford.

Within These Walls (1945) **71m.** ** D: H. Bruce Humberstone. Thomas Mitchell, Mary Anderson, Edward Ryan, Mark Stevens, B. S. Pully, Edward Kelly, Harry Shannon. Fairly good but predictable prison drama with warden Mitchell faced with his own son as a prisoner.

Without Honor (1949) **69m.** ** D: Irving Pichel. Laraine Day, Dane Clark, Franchot Tone, Agnes Moorehead, Bruce Bennett. Good cast talks endlessly in melodrama of woman (Day) who may have killed lover (Tone).▶

Without Love (1945) **111m.** *** D: Harold S. Bucquet. Spencer Tracy, Katharine Hepburn, Lucille Ball, Keenan Wynn, Carl Esmond, Patricia Morison, Felix Bressart, Gloria Grahame. Tracy and Hepburn have never been livelier, but script (by Donald Ogden Stewart, from Philip Barry's play) lets them down in story of inventor and widow who marry for convenience, later fall in love. Wynn and Ball are excellent second leads.▼●▶

Without Pity (1948-Italian) **94m.** *** D: Alberto Lattuada. Carla Del Poggio, John Kitzmiller, Giulietta Masina, Folco Lulli,

Pierre Luigi. Moving neorealist classic about a black G.I. (Kitzmiller) and his love affair with a prostitute (Del Poggio) in liberated WW2 Italy. Superb supporting performance by Masina; film was cowritten by her husband, Federico Fellini. Originally titled: SENZA PIETA.

Without Reservations (1946) **107m.** *** D: Mervyn LeRoy. Claudette Colbert, John Wayne, Don DeFore, Anne Triola, Frank Puglia, Phil Brown, Thurston Hall, Louella Parsons, Dona Drake, Ruth Roman. Authoress Colbert meets perfect man to play hero in movie version of her new book: soldier Wayne. Engaging comedy-romance, with some amusing swipes at Hollywood, several surprise guest stars. Look fast for Raymond Burr during dance scene. ▼●)

Without Warning! (1952) **77m.** *** D: Arnold Laven. Adam Williams, Meg Randall, Edward Binns, Harlan Warde, John Maxwell, Angela Stevens, Byron Kane, Charles Tannen, Robert Shayne. Creepy character actor Williams shines in a rare starring role as a shy, lonely gardener with a penchant for plunging his shears into bottle-blonde bombshells who remind him of his former wife. Low-budget noir is a taut and trim little crime thriller, stylishly shot by Joseph F. Biroc, which presents an evocative look at a seedy '50s L.A. and such vanished parts of the city as Chavez Ravine before it was razed to make way for Dodger Stadium. ▶)

Witness Chair, The (1936) **64m.** *½ D: George Nicholls. Ann Harding, Walter Abel, Douglass Dumbrille, Frances Sage, Moroni Olsen, Margaret Hamilton. Faithful secretary Harding tries to take the rap for her boss, with whom she's secretly in love. Unbelievable courtroom drama/whodunit, polished but dull.

Witness for the Prosecution (1957) **114m.** **** D: Billy Wilder. Marlene Dietrich, Tyrone Power, Charles Laughton, Elsa Lanchester, John Williams, Henry Daniell, Una O'Connor, Ian Wolfe. Fantastically effective London courtroom suspenser from Agatha Christie play. Dietrich is peerless as wife of alleged killer (Power). Laughton at his best as defense attorney, and Lanchester delightful as his long-suffering nurse. Power's last completed film. Scripted by Wilder and Harry Kurnitz. Remade as a TVM. ▼●)

Witness in the Dark (1959-British) **62m.** *½ D: Wolf Rilla. Patricia Dainton, Conrad Phillips, Madge Ryan, Nigel Green, Enid Lorimer. Uncommonly obvious suspenser with murderer seeking to kill blind girl who was present when crime was committed. ▶)

Witness to Murder (1954) **83m.** *** D: Roy Rowland. Barbara Stanwyck, George Sanders, Gary Merrill, Jesse White, Claude Akins. Stanwyck sees neighbor Sanders strangle a woman, but can't convince detective Merrill. However, *Sanders* believes

her. . . . Unconvincing and rather shrill, but suspenseful and well acted, with striking photography (by John Alton). ▶)

Wives and Lovers (1963) **103m.** **½ D: John Rich. Janet Leigh, Van Johnson, Shelley Winters, Martha Hyer, Ray Walston, Jeremy Slate. Surface, slick entertainment; newly famous writer Johnson, wife Leigh and child move to suburbia. Literary agent Hyer on the make almost causes divorce; Winters is wise-cracking neighbor. Script by Edward Anhalt, from Jay Presson Allen's play.

Wives Never Know (1936) **75m.** **½ D: Elliott Nugent. Charlie Ruggles, Mary Boland, Adolphe Menjou, Vivienne Osborne, Claude Gillingwater, Louise Beavers. Flimsy tale of couple trying to awaken each other's love; Ruggles and Boland are always worth watching, and Menjou adds dash.

Wives Under Suspicion (1938) **69m.** **½ D: James Whale. Warren William, Gail Patrick, Constance Moore, William Lundigan, Ralph Morgan. B-movie remake of THE KISS BEFORE THE MIRROR (also directed by Whale) has D.A. William ruthlessly prosecuting a timid professor who killed his neglected wife when she strayed—failing to realize that his own matrimonial situation is becoming identical. Whale fared better the first time around. Gotta love William's abacus of miniature skulls representing state-executed men! ▼▶)

Wizard of Baghdad, The (1960) **C-92m.** ** D: George Sherman. Dick Shawn, Diane Baker, Barry Coe, John Van Dreelen, Robert F. Simon, Vaughn Taylor. Blah satire on costumers, with Shawn a lazy genie. CinemaScope. ▶)

Wizard of Oz, The (1925) **72m.** ** D: Larry Semon. Larry Semon, Dorothy Dwan, Mary Carr, Virginia Pearson, Bryant Washburn, Josef Swickard, Charles Murray, Oliver N. Hardy, Frank Alexander. Silent version of the L. Frank Baum classic by comedy star (and filmmaker) Semon is novel but rather dreary. A toymaker recounts the tale to his granddaughter; Dorothy is the missing Princess of Oz, which is ruled by the treacherous Prime Minister Kruel, who's opposed by Prince Kynd; the woodsman and scarecrow are romantic rivals for Dorothy; and there's plenty of labored slapstick. Worth a look if only to see a fairly slim Hardy as the woodsman. Dwan (who was married to Semon) makes a pert Dorothy. Beware various versions and running times. ▼▶)

Wizard of Oz, The (1939) **C/B&W-101m.** **** D: Victor Fleming. Judy Garland, Frank Morgan, Ray Bolger, Bert Lahr, Jack Haley, Billie Burke, Margaret Hamilton, Charley Grapewin, Clara Blandick, The Singer Midgets. A genuine American classic, based on L. Frank Baum's story of a Kansas girl who goes "Over the

Rainbow" to a land of colorful characters and spirited adventure. A perfect cast in the perfect fantasy, with Harold Arlen and E. Y. Harburg's unforgettable score. Just as good the fifteenth time as it is the first time. Won Oscars for "Over the Rainbow" and Herbert Stothart's scoring, plus a special miniature award for Judy. Previously filmed in 1925; remade as THE WIZ (set in N.Y.C.), OZ (Australia), for TV in 2005 with the Muppets, and reimagined as the 2007 miniseries *Tin Man*. A pair of sequels: JOURNEY BACK TO OZ and RETURN TO OZ.▼●)

Wolf Dog (1958-Canadian) **61m.** *½ D: Sam Newfield. Jim Davis, Allison Hayes, John Hart, Tony Brown, Austin Willis. Low-jinks about farm life in the north country involving land-hungry ranchers. Regalscope.

Wolf Larsen (1958) **83m.** **½ D: Harmon Jones. Barry Sullivan, Peter Graves, Gita Hall, Thayer David. Nicely done version of Jack London's *The Sea Wolf* with Sullivan effective as the tyrannical captain of the eerie ship.▼

Wolf Man, The (1941) **70m.** ***½ D: George Waggner. Lon Chaney, Jr., Evelyn Ankers, Claude Rains, Maria Ouspenskaya, Ralph Bellamy, Patric Knowles, Warren William, Bela Lugosi, Fay Helm. One of the finest horror films ever made: Larry Talbot (Chaney) is bitten by werewolf Lugosi, survives to carry the curse himself. Outstanding cast includes Rains as Chaney's oblivious father, Ankers as perplexed girl friend, Ouspenskaya as wizened gypsy woman who foretells his fate and attempts to care for him. Literate and very engrossing, with superb makeup by Jack Pierce, atmospheric music (re-used in many other Universal chillers) by Charles Previn and Hans J. Salter. Written by Curt Siodmak. Sequel: FRANKENSTEIN MEETS THE WOLF MAN. Remade in 2010. ▼●)

Wolf of New York (1940) **67m.** ** D: William C. McGann. Edmund Lowe, Rose Hobart, James Stephenson, Jerome Cowan, William Demarest, Maurice Murphy, Charles D. Brown, Edward Gargan, Ben Welden. Slick lawyer Lowe, a mouthpiece for crooked Stephenson, undergoes a change of character when a young ex-con, who's trying to go straight, is framed on a murder rap. OK crime tale is done in by some huge plot holes.

Woman and the Hunter (1957) **C-79m.** *½ D: George Breakston. Ann Sheridan, David Farrar, Jan Merlin, John Loder. Tedious love triangle set in the jungles of Kenya; Sheridan tries hard but material defeats all.

Woman-Bait SEE: **Inspector Maigret**

Woman Chases Man (1937) **71m.** **½ D: John G. Blystone. Miriam Hopkins, Joel McCrea, Charles Winninger, Ella Logan, Erik Rhodes, Broderick Crawford. Sometime hilarious, often strained screwball comedy with Hopkins trying to fleece wealthy McCrea, falling in love in the process.

Womaneater (1958-British) **70m.** *½ D: Charles Saunders. George Coulouris, Vera Day, Robert MacKenzie, Norman Claridge, Marpessa Dawn, Jimmy Vaughan. Mad scientist feeds women to a stolen Amazonian tree that he keeps in the dungeon of his British manor, hoping to derive a substance that will revive the dead. And they say that scientific research lacks imagination!▼)

Woman From Monte Carlo, The (1932) **70m.** ** D: Michael Curtiz. Lil Dagover, Walter Huston, Warren William, John Wray, George E. Stone, Robert Warwick. Exotic German star Dagover made her Hollywood debut in this creaky romantic melodrama and promptly hightailed it back to Europe. She's alluring as a Viennese beauty with a scarlet past whose marriage to French naval commander Huston is jeopardized by an accusation of adultery with young lieutenant William. Curtiz' stylish pictorial sense and a court-martial conclusion keep one watching. Based on a play that was filmed as THE NIGHT WATCH in 1928.)

Womanhandled (1925) **55m.** *** D: Gregory La Cava. Richard Dix, Esther Ralston, Edmund Breese, Cora Williams, Olive Tell, Margaret Morris, Tammany Young. In order to impress Ralston, who's obsessed with Old West manliness, wealthy New Yorker Dix heads west to make a man of himself—and is in for quite a few surprises. Cute comedy deftly parodies Western-style machismo. Originally 70m.; no complete version exists.)

Woman Hater (1949-British) **70m.** ** D: Terence Young. Stewart Granger, Edwige Feuillere, Ronald Squire, Mary Jerrold. Contrived battle of wits between confirmed bachelor and single girl leads to predictable romance.▼)

Woman in a Dressing Gown (1957-British) **93m.** *** D: J. Lee Thompson. Yvonne Mitchell, Anthony Quayle, Sylvia Syms, Andrew Ray, Carole Lesley. Excellent British drama about middle-aged man lured away from his unkempt wife by an attractive young woman at his office. Mature, intelligent, and moving.

Woman in Green, The (1945) **68m.** *** D: Roy William Neill. Basil Rathbone, Nigel Bruce, Hillary Brooke, Henry Daniell, Paul Cavanagh, Matthew Boulton, Eve Amber. Blackmail, hypnotism, and murdered women with their right forefingers missing are the disparate elements in this solid *Sherlock Holmes* outing, with sleek Brooke and suave Daniell a formidable pair of foes for Holmes and Watson. Aka SHERLOCK HOLMES AND THE WOMAN IN GREEN. Also shown in computer-colorized version.▼●)

Woman in Hiding (1949) **92m.** ** D: Mi-

[789]

chael Gordon. Ida Lupino, Howard Duff, Stephen McNally, Peggy Dow, John Litel, Joe Besser. Overdone dramatics do in this soaper about a factory owner (Lupino) whose greedy new husband (McNally) attempts to kill her. She sets out to nail him, and is helped by war-veteran drifter Duff. ▶

Woman in Question, The (1950-British) **89m.** *** D: Anthony Asquith. Jean Kent, Dirk Bogarde, John McCallum, Susan Shaw, Hermione Baddeley, Charles Victor, Duncan Macrae. As a cop investigates the slaying of a fortune teller, the various suspects' conflicting perceptions of the deceased emerge. Nifty whodunit, much of which is told in flashback; Kent is excellent as many different versions of the murder victim. Retitled: FIVE ANGLES ON MURDER.▼

Woman in Red (1935) **68m.** ** D: Robert Florey. Barbara Stanwyck, Gene Raymond, Genevieve Tobin, John Eldredge, Phillip Reed, Edward Van Sloan, Arthur Treacher, Gordon (Bill) Elliott. Routine courtroom drama of Stanwyck and Raymond marriage interrupted by charge that she's been seeing Eldredge.▶

Woman in the Dunes (1964-Japanese) **147m.** ***½ D: Hiroshi Teshigahara. Eiji Okada, Kyoko Kishida, Koji Mitsui, Hiroko Ito, Sen Yano. Entomologist Okada becomes trapped in a sandpit and the prisoner of Kishida. Moving, memorable allegory, with striking direction and cinematography (by Hiroshi Segawa).▼▶

Woman in the Moon (1929-German) **156m.** ** D: Fritz Lang. Klaus Pohl, Willy Fritsch, Gustav von Wangenheim, Gerda Maurus, Fritz Rasp. This lesser Lang effort, his last silent film, is about a spaceship and its trip to the moon. It's slow and way overlong, and it pales beside his brilliant METROPOLIS.▼

Woman in the Window, The (1944) **99m.** ***½ D: Fritz Lang. Joan Bennett, Edward G. Robinson, Dan Duryea, Raymond Massey, Bobby (Robert) Blake, Dorothy Peterson. High-grade melodrama about Robinson meeting subject of alluring painting (Bennett), becoming involved in murder and witnessing his own investigation. Surprise ending tops exciting film. Nunnally Johnson scripted. Look for *Our Gang* alumni Bobby Blake (as Robinson's son) and Spanky McFarland (as a scout in the newsreel). Also shown in computer-colored version. ▼▶●

Woman in White, The (1948) **109m.** *** D: Peter Godfrey. Eleanor Parker, Alexis Smith, Sydney Greenstreet, Gig Young, Agnes Moorehead, John Emery, John Abbott. Florid gothic thriller from Wilkie Collins book about strange household and tormented Parker. Remake of CRIMES AT THE DARK HOUSE. Remade in 1997 for British TV.

Woman Is a Woman, A (1961-French) **C-83m.** **½ D: Jean-Luc Godard. Jean-Paul Belmondo, Jean-Claude Brialy, Anna Karina, Noel Pacquin. Pert stripper Karina wants a baby; boyfriend Brialy is not interested in fatherhood, so she approaches his best friend (Belmondo). Occasionally spirited, self-indulgent trifle. Franscope. ▼▶

Woman I Stole, The (1933) **70m.** *** D: Irving Cummings. Jack Holt, Fay Wray, Noah Beery, Raquel Torres, Donald Cook, Edwin Maxwell. Holt is his usual he-man self as an oil baron in North Africa who makes a play for Wray, who's married to his buddy Cook, then decides he doesn't want her after all. Very amusing comic adventure with a surprisingly modern sense of camp. Tangy script by Jo Swerling.

Woman Obsessed (1959) **C-102m.** **½ D: Henry Hathaway. Susan Hayward, Stephen Boyd, Barbara Nichols, Dennis Holmes, Theodore Bikel, Ken Scott. Energetic stars try hard in Canadian ranch-life soaper of widow Hayward who marries Boyd, with predictable clashing and making up. CinemaScope. ▶

Woman of Affairs, A (1928) **96m.** *** D: Clarence Brown. Greta Garbo, John Gilbert, Lewis Stone, John Mack Brown, Douglas Fairbanks, Jr., Hobart Bosworth, Dorothy Sebastian. Smooth, entertaining late-silent with Garbo as reckless socialite who undertakes serious burden of making good her late husband's thefts. Fine cast; story is diluted from Michael Arlen's *The Green Hat.*▼●

Woman of Distinction, A (1950) **85m.** *** D: Edward Buzzell. Rosalind Russell, Ray Milland, Edmund Gwenn, Janis Carter, Francis Lederer. Minor but very enjoyable slapstick, as visiting professor Milland causes scandal involving college dean Russell. Energetic cast puts this over; brief guest appearance by Lucille Ball. ▶

Woman of Dolwyn SEE: **Last Days of Dolwyn, The**

Woman of Paris, A (1923) **91m.** *** D: Charles Chaplin. Edna Purviance, Adolphe Menjou, Carl Miller, Lydia Knott, Charles French. French girl Purviance is set to marry her sweetheart (Miller), but a misunderstanding causes her to move to Paris, where she becomes the mistress of wealthy Menjou. Chaplin's one attempt to make a serious film (without himself as star) was quite sophisticated for its time, and remains interesting, even moving, today. It was a box-office flop in 1923; Chaplin reedited it, but waited until 1977 to reissue it, with his newly composed music score. Chaplin does a cameo as a railway porter, but he's virtually unrecognizable.▼●▶

Woman of Rome (1954-Italian) **93m.** ** D: Luigi Zampa. Gina Lollobrigida, Daniel Gélin, Franco Fabrizi, Raymond Pellegrin, Pina Piovani. Overbaked melodrama of beautiful young Lollobrigida, her complex relationship with her mother, and the varied men with whom she becomes involved in pre-WW2 Rome. Alberto Moravia co-scripted this severely watered-down adaptation of his novel.▼

Woman of Straw (1964-British) **C-117m.** ****½ D:** Basil Dearden. Sean Connery, Gina Lollobrigida, Ralph Richardson, Johnny Sekka, Alexander Knox. Muddled suspenser of Connery and Lollobrigida plotting the "perfect murder" of old Richardson with ironic results.▼◑

Woman of the North Country (1952) **C-90m** **** D:** Joseph Kane. Gale Storm, Ruth Hussey, Rod Cameron, Jim Davis, John Agar, J. Carrol Naish. Predictable love and fight tale set in the mining lands; Storm's last film to date.

Woman of the River (1955-Italian) **C-92m.** **** D:** Mario Soldati. Sophia Loren, Gerard Oury, Lise Bourdin, Rik Battaglia. Seamy, gloomy account of Loren involved with passion and criminals. Still, this was the film that really got her career going.

Woman of the Rumor, The (1954-Japanese) **95m.** ****½ D:** Kenji Mizoguchi. Kinuyo Tanaka, Yoshiko Kuga, Tomoemon Otani, Eitaro Shindo. Melodramatic account of Geisha house operator Tanaka, whose lover really prefers her daughter. Minor Mizoguchi.

Woman of the Town, The (1943) **90m.** ***** D:** George Archainbaud. Claire Trevor, Albert Dekker, Barry Sullivan, Henry Hull, Marion Martin. First-class Western with Dekker as Bat Masterson, who must choose between love for dance-hall girl Trevor and law and order.▼◑

Woman of the Year (1942) **112m.** *****½ D:** George Stevens. Spencer Tracy, Katharine Hepburn, Fay Bainter, Dan Tobin, Reginald Owen, Roscoe Karns, William Bendix. First teaming of Tracy and Hepburn is a joy; Kate's a world-famed political commentator brought down to earth by sports reporter Tracy, whom she later weds. Unforgettable scene of Hepburn trying to understand her first baseball game. Oscar-winning screenplay by Ring Lardner, Jr., and Michael Kanin; later a hit Broadway musical. Remade for TV in 1976. Also shown in computer-colored version. ▼◐◑

Woman on Pier 13, The SEE: I Married a Communist

Woman on the Beach, The (1947) **71m.** ***½ D:** Jean Renoir. Robert Ryan, Joan Bennett, Charles Bickford, Nan Leslie, Walter Sande, Irene Ryan. Overheated melodrama wastes clever gimmick: Coast Guard officer isn't completely convinced his lover's husband is really blind. Loaded with laughable dialogue and sledgehammer music cues; easy to see why this was Renoir's American swan song. ◑

Woman on the Run (1950) **77m.** ***** D:** Norman Foster. Ann Sheridan, Dennis

O'Keefe, Robert Keith, Ross Elliott, Frank Jenks. Eyewitness to murder flees from cops, who need him to testify, so they hound his estranged wife. Great San Francisco locations, snappy screenplay by Foster and Alan Campbell. ▼◑

Woman Rebels, A (1936) **88m.** ***** D:** Mark Sandrich. Katharine Hepburn, Herbert Marshall, Elizabeth Allan, Donald Crisp, Doris Dudley, David Manners, Lucile Watson, Van Heflin. Hepburn is marvelous as young girl whose experiences in Victorian England lead to her crusading for Women's Rights. Well-mounted soap opera remains surprisingly timely.◑

Woman's Devotion, A (1956) **C-88m.** **** D:** Paul Henreid. Ralph Meeker, Janice Rule, Paul Henreid, Rosenda Monteros. Choppy mystery of artist Meeker and wife Rule, involved in a murder while in Mexico. Aka BATTLE SHOCK.▼

Woman's Face, A (1941) **105m.** ***** D:** George Cukor. Joan Crawford, Melvyn Douglas, Conrad Veidt, Osa Massen, Reginald Owen, Albert Bassermann, Marjorie Main, Donald Meek, Connie Gilchrist, Henry Daniell, Richard Nichols. Crawford has one of her most substantial roles in this exciting yarn of a scarred woman whose life changes when she undergoes plastic surgery. Taut climax spotlights villain Veidt. Originally filmed in 1938 in Sweden, as EN KVINNAS ANSIKTE, with Ingrid Bergman; script by Donald Ogden Stewart and Elliot Paul. Also shown in computer-colored version.▼◐◑

Woman's Secret, A (1949) **85m.** ****½ D:** Nicholas Ray. Maureen O'Hara, Melvyn Douglas, Gloria Grahame, Bill Williams, Victor Jory. Intriguing flashback drama of woman coming to hate singer she built up to success; good performances by two female stars. Just a bit too sloppy. Produced and scripted by Herman J. Mankiewicz, from a Vicki Baum novel. Director Ray married Grahame after film's completion. ▼◑

Woman's Vengeance, A (1947) **96m.** *****½ D:** Zoltan Korda. Charles Boyer, Ann Blyth, Jessica Tandy, Cedric Hardwicke, Mildred Natwick. Outstanding drama of philandering Boyer put on trial when his wife is found dead; brilliant cast gives vivid realistic performances. Script by Aldous Huxley, from his story.

Woman's World (1954) **C-94m.** ***** D:** Jean Negulesco. Clifton Webb, June Allyson, Van Heflin, Arlene Dahl, Lauren Bacall, Fred MacMurray, Cornel Wilde, Elliott Reid. Slick look at diverse personalities in the world of big business as automobile mogul Webb decides to meet the wives of the men he's considering for a big promotion. CinemaScope.▼◑

Woman They Almost Lynched, The (1953) **90m.** **** D:** Allan Dwan. John Lund, Joan Leslie, Audrey Totter, Brian Donlevy,

Ellen Corby, Minerva Urecal, Jim Davis. Civil War period film about refined young woman Leslie who comes to Western town and learns to tote gun; title tells the rest. ▶

Woman Wanted (1935) **68m. ** D: George B. Seitz. Maureen O'Sullivan, Joel McCrea, Lewis Stone, Louis Calhern, Edgar Kennedy, Adrienne Ames, Robert Greig. Unremarkable programmer has O'Sullivan hunted by police and mobsters, McCrea out to prove her innocence.

Woman Who Came Back, The (1945) **68m. ** D: Walter Colmes. John Loder, Nancy Kelly, Otto Kruger, Ruth Ford, Harry Tyler. Fair yarn of woman (Kelly) who is convinced she has received witches' curse from ancient forebear. ▼▶

Woman Who Dared, The SEE: **Le ciel est à vous**

Woman With No Name, The SEE: **Her Panelled Door**

Woman Without Love, A (1951-Mexican) **85m. ** D: Luis Buñuel. Julio Villareal, Rosario Granados, Tito Junco, Xavier Loya, Joaquín Cordero, Elda Peralta. An unhappily married woman has an affair with a young engineer. Years later, he wills his estate to her second son; could the boy possibly be his own? Buñuel said this commercial chore was his worst film and it's hard not to agree with him. A few expected surreal touches can't wash away the suds. From a Guy de Maupassant story. ▼▶

Women, The (1939) **132m. ***½** D: George Cukor. Joan Crawford, Norma Shearer, Rosalind Russell, Mary Boland, Joan Fontaine, Paulette Goddard, Lucile Watson, Marjorie Main, Virginia Weidler, Phyllis Povah, Ruth Hussey, Mary Beth Hughes, Virginia Grey, Hedda Hopper, Butterfly McQueen. All-star (and all-female) cast shines in this hilarious adaptation of Clare Boothe play about divorce, cattiness, and competition in circle of "friends." Crawford has one of her best roles as bitchy homewrecker. Fashion show sequence is in color; script by Anita Loos and Jane Murfin. Remade in 1956 (as THE OPPOSITE SEX) and in 2008. ▼▶●

Women Are Like That (1938) **78m. **½** D: Stanley Logan. Kay Francis, Pat O'Brien, Ralph Forbes, Melville Cooper. Smooth fluff: Francis is daughter of ad executive in love with copywriter O'Brien. ▶

Women Are Weak SEE: **3 Murderesses**

Women in Bondage (1943) **70m. ** D: Steve Sekely. Gail Patrick, Nancy Kelly, Gertrude Michael, Anne Nagel, Tala Birell, Alan Baxter, H. B. Warner. Exploitation patriotism hammering away at Nazi maltreatment of conquered people. Dates badly.

Women in His Life, The (1933) **74m. **½** D: George B. Seitz. Otto Kruger, Una Merkel, Ben Lyon, Isabel Jewell, Roscoe Karns, Irene Hervey, C. Henry Gordon, Samuel S. Hinds. Kruger hams it up in fine style as a brilliant, unethical criminal lawyer who drinks and womanizes because his wife ran out on him. When he takes on a murder case and learns the victim is his exwife, he cleans up his act and seeks justice. Fairly engrossing MGM programmer with a smashing, nick-of-time finale.

Women in the Wind (1939) **63m. ** D: John Farrow. Kay Francis, William Gargan, Victor Jory, Maxie Rosenbloom, Eddie Foy, Jr., Sheila Bromley, Eve Arden. Francis woos ace pilot Gargan to use his plane in a women's air derby in order to win money for her brother's operation; Gargan's jealous estranged wife tries to send Francis into a tailspin by entering the race herself. Trite programmer.

Women of All Nations (1931) **72m. ** D: Raoul Walsh. Victor McLaglen, Edmund Lowe, Greta Nissen, El Brendel, Fifi D'Orsay, Marjorie White, Bela Lugosi. Third pairing of McLaglen and Lowe as Sergeants Flagg and Quirt (following WHAT PRICE GLORY and THE COCK-EYED WORLD) is just an excuse for the stars to brawl, double-cross each other, and go after the local sexpots from Sweden to Constantinople. Loud, raucous one-note film. Lugosi, as a jealous Middle Eastern prince, has the best line: "Bar the gates and sharpen the knives."

Women of Devil's Island (1961-Italian) **C-95m. *½** D: Domenico Paolella. Guy Madison, Michele Mercier, Frederica Ranchi. Humdrum mini-epic with Madison helping aristocratic woman held prisoner on swampy island. CinemaScope. ▶

Women of Pitcairn Island, The (1956) **72m. *½** D: Jean Yarbrough. James Craig, Lynn Bari, John Smith, Arleen Whelan, Sue England, Carol Thurston. Low-budget garbage about families developing from people who remained on island after MUTINY ON THE BOUNTY. Regalscope.

Women's Prison (1955) **80m. ** D: Lewis Seiler. Ida Lupino, Jan Sterling, Cleo Moore, Audrey Totter, Phyllis Thaxter, Howard Duff, Mae Clarke, Gertrude Michael, Juanita Moore. Campy 1950s programmer, with Lupino as a vicious prison superintendent riding herd over a cast that no B movie lover could resist. ▶

Women Without Men SEE: **Blonde Bait**

Women Without Names (1940) **63m. **½** D: Robert Florey. Ellen Drew, Robert Paige, Judith Barrett, John Miljan, Fay Helm, John McGuire, Louise Beavers, Marjorie Main. Newlyweds are framed for a cop killing committed by her wanted ex-husband. After a politically ambitious assistant D.A. suppresses evidence that proves their innocence, she determines to bust out of prison. Stylishly directed caged-heat yarn with a rip-roaring, hair-pulling catfight and a tense ending. Remake of LADIES OF THE BIG HOUSE.

Wonder Bar (1934) **84m. **½** D: Lloyd

Bacon. Al Jolson, Kay Francis, Dolores Del Rio, Dick Powell, Ricardo Cortez, Louise Fazenda, Hugh Herbert, Hal LeRoy, Guy Kibbee. Very strange, often tasteless musical drama set in Paris nightclub with murder, romance, and Busby Berkeley's incredible "Goin' to Heaven on a Mule" production number. Full of outrageous racial stereotypes.●▶

Wonderful Country, The (1959) **C-96m.** **✽✽½ D:** Robert Parrish. Robert Mitchum, Julie London, Gary Merrill, Pedro Armendariz, Jack Oakie, Albert Dekker. Brooding Western involving Mitchum running guns along Mexico-Texas line, romancing London; script by Robert Ardrey. ▶

Wonderful World of the Brothers Grimm, The (1962) **C-129m.** **✽✽✽ D:** Henry Levin, George Pal. Laurence Harvey, Claire Bloom, Karl Boehm, Oscar Homolka, Martita Hunt, Jim Backus, Yvette Mimieux, Barbara Eden, Walter Slezak, Russ Tamblyn, Buddy Hackett, Beulah Bondi, Terry-Thomas. Fanciful adaptations of Grimm tales offset by OK look at famed brothers' lives. Best of all are Puppetoons sequences in toy shop, Hackett battling fire-breathing dragon. Colorful George Pal entertainment, with Oscar-winning costumes by Mary Wills, was originally shown in Cinerama. Roadshow version runs 135m. with overture, intermission/entr'acte, exit music. ▼●

Wonder Man (1945) **C-98m.** **✽✽✽ D:** H. Bruce Humberstone. Danny Kaye, Virginia Mayo, Vera-Ellen, Donald Woods, S. Z. Sakall, Allen Jenkins, Ed Brophy, Steve Cochran, Otto Kruger, Natalie Schafer. Kaye's fun as twins, the serious one forced to take the place of his brash entertainer brother when the latter is killed. Big, colorful production with Oscar-winning special effects. ▼●▶

Wonders of Aladdin, The (1961-U.S.-Italian) **C-93m.** **✽✽ D:** Henry Levin, Mario Bava. Donald O'Connor, Noelle Adam, Vittorio De Sica, Aldo Fabrizi. Few wonders to behold in this mild children's fantasy. CinemaScope.▼

Wooden Horse, The (1950-British) **101m.** **✽✽✽ D:** Jack Lee. Leo Genn, David Tomlinson, Anthony Steel, Peter Burton, David Greene, Anthony Dawson, Bryan Forbes, Peter Finch. Sturdy, exciting POW drama of men determined to tunnel their way out of Nazi prison camp using an exercise vaulting horse for cover. Based on Eric Williams' novel *The Tunnel Escape*.▼

Words and Music (1948) **C-119m.** **✽✽½ D:** Norman Taurog. Mickey Rooney, Tom Drake, June Allyson, Ann Sothern, Judy Garland, Gene Kelly, Lena Horne, Vera-Ellen, Cyd Charisse, Allyn Ann McLerie, Mel Tormé, Betty Garrett, Perry Como, Janet Leigh. Sappy, Hollywoodized biography of songwriters Rodgers (Drake) and Hart (Rooney) is salvaged somewhat by their wonderful mu-

sic, including Kelly and Vera-Ellen's dance to "Slaughter on Tenth Avenue." ▼●▶

Working Girls (1931) **77m.** **✽✽½ D:** Dorothy Arzner. Judith Wood, Dorothy Hall, Charles "Buddy" Rogers, Paul Lukas, Stuart Erwin, Frances Dee, Mary Forbes, Claire Dodd, Dorothy Stickney. Two sisters from the Midwest arrive in N.Y.C. and try to make good, though one of them is more brazen than the other when it comes to using men to achieve her goals. Raw performances by Hall and Wood give this a refreshing, un-Hollywood feel and make it an interesting chronicle of young women in the big city. Screenplay by Zoe Akins, from a play by Vera Caspary and Winifred Lenihan.

Working Man, The (1933) **74m.** **✽✽✽ D:** John G. Adolfi. George Arliss, Bette Davis, Hardie Albright,. Theodore Newton, Gordon Westcott, J. Farrell MacDonald. Charming comedy about a businessman who chances to meet the children of his late arch-rival—and determines to change their wastrel ways, even if it means competing with his own company. A much-improved remake of Arliss' silent film $20 A WEEK (1924); remade with Irvin S. Cobb as EVERYBODY'S OLD MAN (1936). ▶

World and the Flesh (1932) **75m.** **✽✽ D:** John Cromwell. George Bancroft, Miriam Hopkins, Alan Mowbray, George E. Stone. Labored drama of soldier-of-fortune Bancroft asking price of Hopkins to save her wealthy friends from Russian Revolution; moves very slowly.

World Changes, The (1933) **90m.** **✽✽✽ D:** Mervyn LeRoy. Paul Muni, Mary Astor, Aline MacMahon, Donald Cook, Alan Dinehart, Guy Kibbee, Margaret Lindsay, Henry O'Neill, Jean Muir. Extremely watchable Edna Ferber–like saga of farm boy Muni, who pursues his ambitions to Chicago in the late 1800s and becomes a meat-packing baron and multimillionaire—only to see his family life crumble before his very eyes. Astor is excellent as his selfish wife, MacMahon her usual tower of strength as his mother. Cast is brimming with familiar faces, including young Mickey Rooney and pre–*Charlie Chan* Sidney Toler.

World for Ransom (1954) **80m.** **✽✽ D:** Robert Aldrich. Dan Duryea, Gene Lockhart, Patric Knowles, Reginald Denny, Nigel Bruce, Marian Carr. Deliriously cheesy B movie (made to cash in on Duryea's then-popular *China Smith* TV series) about intrigue and espionage in Singapore. Pretty poor, but some stylish shots and veteran cast are definite assets. ▶

World Gone Mad, The (1933) **74m.** **✽✽ D:** Christy Cabanne. Pat O'Brien, Evelyn Brent, Neil Hamilton, Mary Brian, Louis Calhern, J. Carrol Naish, Buster Phelps, Richard Tucker. District attorney about to uncover stock swindle is framed and murdered; his intrepid reporter pal (who else but O'Brien) and the new D.A. (Hamilton) investigate. Then-topical programmer has its moments, but is too talky and meandering. Aka PUBLIC BE DAMNED. ▼▶

World in His Arms, The (1952) **C-104m.** *** D: Raoul Walsh. Gregory Peck, Ann Blyth, John McIntire, Anthony Quinn, Andrea King, Eugenie Leontovich, Sig Ruman. Unlikely but entertaining tale of skipper Peck romancing Russian Blyth, set in 1850s San Francisco and Alaska. ▼▶

World in My Corner (1956) **82m** **½ D: Jesse Hibbs. Audie Murphy, Barbara Rush, Jeff Morrow, John McIntire, Tommy Rall, Howard St. John. Murphy is poor boy who rises to fame via boxing, almost ruined by rich life with Rush standing by.

World Moves On, The (1934) **104m.** **½ D: John Ford. Madeleine Carroll, Franchot Tone, Reginald Denny, Stepin Fetchit, Lumsden Hare, Raul Roulien, Louise Dresser, Sig Ruman. Long but interesting family saga covering 100 years as Louisiana family is split, three sons heading business operations in England, France, Germany, experiencing tremendous changes from peaceful 19th century through WW1. ▶

World of Abbott and Costello, The (1965) **75m.** ** Narrated by Jack E. Leonard. Bud Abbott, Lou Costello, Marjorie Main, Bela Lugosi, Tom Ewell, others. Inept compilation of A&C footage, with curious selection of scenes, senseless narration. Still, there's "Who's on First?" and other fine routines. ▼▶

World of Apu, The (1959-Indian) **103m.** ***½ D: Satyajit Ray. Soumitra Chatterjee, Sharmila Tagore, Alok Chakravarty, Swapan Mukherji. Sadly poetic tale of the shy Apu (Chatterjee) marrying and fathering a child. Magnificently acted; last of the director's "Apu" trilogy. ▼▶

World of Henry Orient, The (1964) **C-106m.** ***½ D: George Roy Hill. Peter Sellers, Tippy Walker, Merrie Spaeth, Paula Prentiss, Angela Lansbury, Phyllis Thaxter, Tom Bosley. Marvelous comedy of two teenage girls who idolize eccentric pianist (Sellers) and follow him around N.Y.C. Bosley and Lansbury are superb as Walker's parents, with Thaxter appealing as Spaeth's understanding mother. Screenplay by Nunnally and Nora Johnson, from her novel. Panavision. ▼▶●

World of Suzie Wong, The (1960) **C-129m.** **½ D: Richard Quine. William Holden, Nancy Kwan, Sylvia Syms, Michael Wilding, Laurence Naismith. Holden's sluggish performance as American artist in love with prostitute Kwan doesn't help this soaper, lavishly filmed in Hong Kong. Script by John Patrick from Paul Osborn's Broadway play. ▼▶●

World Premiere (1941) **70m.** *½ D: Ted Tetzlaff. John Barrymore, Frances Farmer,

Eugene Pallette, Virginia Dale, Ricardo Cortez, Sig Ruman, Fritz Feld. Poor excuse for comedy involves idiotic producer Barrymore, jealous movie stars, outlandish publicity stunts, and Nazi saboteurs. A real waste.

World's Greatest Sinner, The (1962) **76m.** **½ D: Timothy Carey. Timothy Carey, Gil Baretto, Betty Rowland, James Farley, Gail Griffen, Tyde Rule, Grace De Carolis; narrated by Paul Frees. The great, eccentric character actor Carey gives his creepiest, most over-the-top performance in this crazed vanity project, which he wrote, produced, and directed. A disillusioned insurance salesman declares himself to be God, becomes an Elvis-like rock 'n' roll evangelist, and is enticed to run for president by a shady power broker. Technically crude but weirdly fascinating as a prescient, primal scream of rage against cults, religious and political opportunism, and celebrity worship. A very young Frank Zappa (billed simply as "Zappa") composed the score and a hilarious title song. ▶

World the Flesh and the Devil, The (1959) **95m.** **½ D: Ranald MacDougall. Harry Belafonte, Inger Stevens, Mel Ferrer. Belafonte and Stevens are only survivors of worldwide nuclear accident; their uneasy relationship is jarred by arrival of Ferrer. Intriguing film starts well, bogs down halfway through, and presents ridiculous conclusion. Best scenes are at beginning, when Belafonte is alone in an impressively deserted Manhattan. CinemaScope. ▼●▶

World Was His Jury, The (1958) **82m.** *½ D: Fred F. Sears. Edmond O'Brien, Mona Freeman, Karin Booth, Robert McQueeney. Routine account of ship's captain proven innocent of negligence in sea disaster. ▶

World Without End (1956) **C-80m.** **½ D: Edward Bernds. Hugh Marlowe, Nancy Gates, Nelson Leigh, Rod Taylor. Space flight headed for Mars breaks the time barrier and ends up on post-apocalyptic Earth in the 26th century. Pretty good sci-fi owes more than a little to H. G. Wells' *The Time Machine*. CinemaScope. ▼▶

World Without Sun (1964-French-Italian) **C-93m.** **** D: Jacques Cousteau. Excellent, Oscar-winning documentary of Cousteau and his oceanauts, creating an underwater adventure that challenges any fiction.

Worst Woman in Paris?, The (1933) **78m.** **½ D: Monta Bell. Benita Hume, Adolphe Menjou, Harvey Stephens, Helen Chandler, Margaret Seddon. Glossy Lubitsch-like comedy of chic Hume walking out on wealthy husband Menjou, returning to America, falling in love with naive young Stephens.

Wreck of the Hesperus, The (1948) **70m.** ** D: John Hoffman. Willard Parker, Edgar Buchanan, Patricia White (Barry). Loosely based on Longfellow poem, this low-budget flick suffers from lack of production values to enhance special effects of storms at sea. ◗

Wreck of the Mary Deare, The (1959-U.S.-British) **C-105m.** **½ D: Michael Anderson. Gary Cooper, Charlton Heston, Michael Redgrave, Emlyn Williams, Cecil Parker, Alexander Knox, Virginia McKenna, Richard Harris. Salvage boat skipper Heston boards an apparently abandoned freighter, finds hostile Captain Cooper aboard. What really happened to the *Mary Deare*? Stars outshine their material in Eric Ambler's adaptation of the novel by Hammond Innes. CinemaScope. ▼◗

Written on the Wind (1956) **C-99m.** *** D: Douglas Sirk. Rock Hudson, Lauren Bacall, Robert Stack, Dorothy Malone, Robert Keith, Grant Williams. Florid melodrama of playboy-millionaire Stack, his nymphomaniac sister Malone, and how they destroy themselves and others around them. Irresistible kitsch. Malone won Oscar for her performance. ▼◗

Wrong Arm of the Law, The (1963-British) **94m.** *** D: Cliff Owen. Peter Sellers, Lionel Jeffries, Bernard Cribbins, Davy Kaye, Nanette Newman, John Le Mesurier, Dennis Price, Michael Caine. Wacky comedy spoof has Australian trio being chased by police as well as crooks because they've been dressing as cops and confiscating loot from apprehended robbers. Some very funny moments. ▼◗

Wrong Man, The (1957) **105m.** *** D: Alfred Hitchcock. Henry Fonda, Vera Miles, Anthony Quayle, Harold J. Stone, Nehemiah Persoff, Peggy Webber. Unusual Hitchcock film done as semi-documentary, using true story of N.Y.C. musician (Fonda) falsely accused of robbery. Miles is excellent as wife who cracks under strain; offbeat and compelling. Written by Maxwell Anderson and Angus MacPhail. Look for Tuesday Weld in giggly bit. ▼◗◗

Wrong Rut, The SEE: Not Wanted

Wuthering Heights (1939) **103m.** **** D: William Wyler. Merle Oberon, Laurence Olivier, David Niven, Flora Robson, Donald Crisp, Geraldine Fitzgerald, Leo G. Carroll, Cecil Kellaway, Miles Mander, Hugh Williams. Stirring adaptation of Emily Brontë's novel stops at chapter 17, but viewers shouldn't despair: sensitive direction and sweeping performances propel this magnificent story of doomed love in pre-Victorian England. Haunting, a mustsee film. Gregg Toland's moody photography won an Oscar; script by Ben Hecht and Charles MacArthur. Remade in 1953, 1970, 1992, 2011, and in 2013 for cable TV. ▼◗◗

Wuthering Heights (1953-Mexican) **90m.** **½ D: Luis Buñuel. Irasema Dilian, Jorge Mistral, Lilia Prado, Ernesto Alonso, Luis Aceves Castaneda. Strikingly directed but

talky, overbaked, ultimately unsuccessful version of the Brontë classic: bitter, coldhearted former servant Mistral, now rich, returns to disrupt the life of true love Dilian, now married to another. ▼

Wyoming (1940) **89m.** ** D: Richard Thorpe. Wallace Beery, Leo Carrillo, Ann Rutherford, Marjorie Main, Lee Bowman, Joseph Calleia, Bobs Watson. OK oater with Beery and Carrillo fun as on-again, off-again outlaw pals tempted by honesty.

Wyoming (1947) **84m.** **½ D: Joseph Kane. William Elliott, Vera Ralston, John Carroll, "Gabby" Hayes, Albert Dekker, Virginia Grey. Not-bad Wild Bill Elliott Western of ranchers vs. homesteaders in Wyoming territory. ▼

Wyoming Kid, The SEE: Cheyenne

Wyoming Mail (1950) **C-87m.** **½ D: Reginald LeBorg. Stephen McNally, Alexis Smith, Ed Begley, Richard Egan, James Arness, Frankie Darro, Richard Jaeckel. Postal robbery in old West, with capable cast shining up script's dull spots.

Wyoming Outlaw (1939) **57m.** *** D: George Sherman. John Wayne, Ray Corrigan, Raymond Hatton, Donald Barry, Adele Pearce (Pamela Blake), LeRoy Mason, Charles Middleton, Elmo Lincoln, Yakima Canutt. Based on a true incident, then in the news, about a modern Robin Hood (Barry) who steals but also combats graft and corruption. One of the best of the *Three Mesquiteers* series, with Hatton filling Max Terhune's place in the trio. Sympathetic lawbreaker Barry is outstanding in breakthrough title role. Top action, crisp direction. ◗

Wyoming Renegades (1955) **C-73m.** *½ D: Fred F. Sears. Phil Carey, Gene Evans, Martha Hyer, William Bishop, Aaron Spelling. Confused Western portraying the story of ex-bandit Carey who wants to go straight. ◗

X-15 (1961) **C-106m.** ** D: Richard Donner. David McLean, Charles Bronson, Ralph Taeger, Brad Dexter, Mary Tyler Moore, Patricia Owens; narrated by Jimmy Stewart. Mild narrative of pilots testing the experimental space plane of the title, and their romantic and family lives. Unusual role for Bronson, even then. Panavision. ◗

X: The Man With the X-Ray Eyes (1963) **C-80m.** **½ D: Roger Corman. Ray Milland, Diana Van Der Vlis, Harold J. Stone, John Hoyt, Don Rickles. Not-bad little film about scientist Milland developing serum that enables him to see through things. He lives to regret it. Title on-screen is simply X. ▼◗

X The Unknown (1956-British) **80m.** **½ D: Leslie Norman. Dean Jagger, Leo McKern, William Lucas, Edward Chapman, Anthony Newley. Well-thought-out sci-fi production set in Scotland. Radioactive mud from Earth's center grows and kills anything in its path. Effective chiller written by Jimmy Sangster. ▼●)

Yank at Eton, A (1942) 88m. ** D: Norman Taurog. Mickey Rooney, Freddie Bartholomew, Tina Thayer, Ian Hunter, Edmund Gwenn, Alan Mowbray, Peter Lawford, Terry Kilburn. Rooney goes to school in England and it's a wonder he's not ejected immediately.)

Yank at Oxford, A (1938-U.S.-British) 100m. *** D: Jack Conway. Robert Taylor, Lionel Barrymore, Maureen O'Sullivan, Vivien Leigh, Edmund Gwenn. Attractive cast, including young Leigh, in familiar story of cocky American trying to adjust to Oxford, and vice versa. Remade in 1984 as OXFORD BLUES.

Yankee Buccaneer (1952) **C-86m.** **½ D: Frederick de Cordova. Jeff Chandler, Scott Brady, Suzan Ball, David Janssen. Standard pirate tale, buoyed by healthy cast.)

Yankee Clipper, The (1927) **81m.** *** D: Rupert Julian. William Boyd, Elinor Fair, Frank Coghlan, Jr., John Miljan, Walter Long, Louis Payne, Burr McIntosh, Julia Faye. Splendid 19th-century seagoing adventure, as clipper ships race full-sail from China to Boston to earn a coveted tea trade contract. En route: typhoon! No fresh water! Mutiny! And a woman on board! Realistic yet heightened drama has it all. Boyd, a favorite actor of the film's producer, Cecil B. De-Mille, was married to Fair at the time. ▼)

Yankee Doodle Dandy (1942) **126m.** **** D: Michael Curtiz. James Cagney, Joan Leslie, Walter Huston, Irene Manning, Rosemary DeCamp, Richard Whorf, Jeanne Cagney, S. Z. Sakall, Walter Catlett, Frances Langford, Eddie Foy, Jr., George Tobias. Cagney wraps up film in neat little package all his own with dynamic re-creation of George M. Cohan's life and times; he deservedly won Oscar for rare song-and-dance performance, as did music directors Ray Heindorf and Heinz Roemheld. Also shown in computer-colored version. ▼●)

Yankee Pasha (1954) **C-84m.** **½ D: Joseph Pevney. Jeff Chandler, Rhonda Fleming, Mamie Van Doren, Bart Roberts (Rex Reason), Lee J. Cobb, Hal March. Nicely paced costumer set in 1800s with Chandler crossing the ocean to France and beyond to find his true love, captured by pirates.

Yank in Indo-China, A (1952) **67m.** *½ D: Wallace Grissell. John Archer, Douglas Dick, Jean Willes, Don Harvey. Just adequate yarn of American pilots involved in guerilla warfare.

Yank in Korea, A (1951) **73m.** *½ D: Lew Landers. Lon McCallister, William "Bill" Phillips, Brett King, Larry Stewart, Lonnie Burr. Young recruit (McCallister) and veteran sergeant (Phillips) are the typical

members of a combat platoon in this corny war story.

Yank in the R.A.F., A (1941) **98m.** *** D: Henry King. Tyrone Power, Betty Grable, John Sutton, Reginald Gardiner, Donald Stuart, Richard Fraser. Power's only there so he can see London-based chorine Grable; they make a nice team. Songs: "Another Little Dream Won't Do Us Any Harm," "Hi-Ya Love." ▼)

Yank in Viet-Nam, A (1964) **80m.** ** D: Marshall Thompson. Marshall Thompson, Enrique Magalona, Mario Barri, Urban Drew. Low-budget topical actioner set in Saigon, with Marine Thompson attempting to help the South Vietnamese. Retitled: YEAR OF THE TIGER.

Yank on the Burma Road, A (1942) **67m.** **½ D: George B. Seitz. Laraine Day, Barry Nelson, Stuart Crawford, Keye Luke, (Victor) Sen Yung, Phillip (Philip) Ahn. Pre–Pearl Harbor, intrepid N.Y.C. cabbie Nelson agrees to oversee a truck convoy delivering medical supplies along the Burma Road to Chungking. He also mixes with American Day, whose German-born flier husband is fighting for the Japanese. Formulaic but nicely done relic of its era.

Yaqui Drums (1956) **71m.** *½ D: Jean Yarbrough. Rod Cameron, J. Carrol Naish, Mary Castle, Robert Hutton. Soggy account of rancher vs. criminal saloon owner in old West.

Yearling, The (1946) **C-128m.** ***½ D: Clarence Brown. Gregory Peck, Jane Wyman, Claude Jarman, Jr., Chill Wills, Margaret Wycherly, Henry Travers, Jeff York, Forrest Tucker, June Lockhart. Marjorie Kinnan Rawling's sensitive tale of a boy attached to a young deer was exquisitely filmed in Technicolor on location in Florida, with memorable performances. Oscar winner for Cinematography and Art Direction, and a special Oscar for newcomer Jarman. Beware 94m. reissue print. Remade as a TV movie in 1994. ▼●)

Years Between, The (1946-British) **100m.** **½ D: Compton Bennett. Michael Redgrave, Valerie Hobson, Flora Robson, Felix Aylmer, Dulcie Gray, Edward Rigby, James McKechnie. Sensitively handled drama about war widow Hobson, once a wife, now a career woman and member of Parliament who is about to remarry. Her world is turned upside down when word comes that her husband (Redgrave) is still alive. Based on a play by Daphne du Maurier. ▼

Yellow Balloon, The (1952-British) **80m.** **½ D: J. Lee Thompson. Andrew Ray, Kenneth More, Veronica Hurst, William Sylvester, Bernard Lee. Sensible suspenser of small boy who thinks he accidentally killed a chum and is exploited by cheap crook.

Yellow Cab Man, The (1950) **85m.** *** D: Jack Donohue. Red Skelton, Gloria De Haven, Walter Slezak, Edward Arnold, James

Gleason, Jay C. Flippen, Polly Moran. Fine Skelton romp with Red as would-be inventor of unbreakable glass, involved with gangsters and crooked businessman; Slezak is perfect as bad guy. ▼▶

Yellow Canary, The (1943-British) **98m.** **✱✱½** D: Herbert Wilcox. Anna Neagle, Richard Greene, Albert Lieven, Margaret Rutherford, Valentine Dyall. Above average WW2 spy drama with Neagle feigning Nazi loyalty to obtain secrets for the Allies.

Yellow Canary, The (1963) **93m.** BOMB D: Buzz Kulik. Pat Boone, Barbara Eden, Steve Forrest, Jack Klugman, Jesse White, Milton Selzer, John Banner, Jeff Corey, Harold Gould. If you've lain awake nights hoping to see Pat Boone as an obnoxious pop singer in a movie written by Rod Serling, your wish has come true. But don't fret; Pat turns into a nice guy when his infant son is kidnapped and he has to go rescue him. And you thought *The Twilight Zone* was just a TV show! CinemaScope.

Yellow Jack (1938) **83m.** **✱✱** D: George B. Seitz. Robert Montgomery, Virginia Bruce, Lewis Stone, Stanley Ridges, Henry Hull, Charles Coburn, Buddy Ebsen, Andy Devine, Henry O'Neill, Sam Levene, Alan Curtis, William Henry. Story of Dr. Walter Reed's determination to find cure for yellow fever is artificial, dramatically stale. Based on Sidney Howard play.

Yellow Mountain, The (1954) **C-78m.** **✱✱½** D: Jesse Hibbs. Lex Barker, Mala Powers, Howard Duff, William Demarest, John McIntire. Spirited Western programmer with "frenemies" Barker and Duff clashing over mining claims and pretty Powers. Demarest as an old sourdough adds an agreeable dash of comic relief.

Yellow Rolls-Royce, The (1964-British) **C-122m.** **✱✱✱** D: Anthony Asquith. Rex Harrison, Shirley MacLaine, Ingrid Bergman, Jeanne Moreau, Edmund Purdom, George C. Scott, Omar Sharif, Art Carney, Alain Delon, Roland Culver, Wally Cox. Slick Terence Rattigan drama involving trio of owners of title car, focusing on how romance plays a part in each of their lives; contrived but ever-so-smoothly handled. Panavision.▼▶

Yellow Rose of Texas, The (1944) **69m.** **✱✱** D: Joseph Kane. Roy Rogers, Dale Evans, Grant Withers, Harry Shannon, George Cleveland, William Haade, Weldon Heyburn, Hal Taliaferro, Tom London, Bob Nolan and the Sons of the Pioneers. Undercover insurance investigator Rogers joins Dale's showboat troupe to prove her father innocent of an express payroll robbery. Music-heavy Western, with production numbers interrupting the lightweight plot every few minutes. ▼▶

Yellow Sky (1948) **98m.** **✱✱✱** D: William A. Wellman. Gregory Peck, Anne Baxter, Richard Widmark, Robert Arthur, John Russell, Henry (Harry) Morgan, James Barton. Exciting Western with Peck heading a gang of thieves who come to a ghost town, where they confront tough, mysterious Baxter and her grandfather. Similar in atmosphere to Wellman's classic THE OX-BOW INCIDENT. Script by Lamar Trotti from a W. R. Burnett story. Remade as THE JACKALS.▼▶

Yellowstone (1936) **65m.** **✱✱½** D: Arthur Lubin. Henry Hunter, Judith Barrett, Andy Devine, Alan Hale, Ralph Morgan, Monroe Owsley, Raymond Hatton, Paul Harvey, Paul Fix. Nifty programmer of murder, greed, and stolen money buried in the title park. Ambitious direction and a solid supporting cast elevate this one.▼▶

Yellowstone Kelly (1959) **C-91m.** **✱✱½** D: Gordon Douglas. Clint Walker, Edward Byrnes, John Russell, Ray Danton, Claude Akins, Rhodes Reason, Warren Oates, Andra Martin. Rugged Western involving Indian uprising, with Walker the burly hero trying to keep peace; written by Burt Kennedy.▶

Yellow Ticket, The (1931) **81m.** **✱✱✱** D: Raoul Walsh. Elissa Landi, Laurence Olivier, Lionel Barrymore, Walter Byron, Sarah Padden, Mischa Auer, Boris Karloff. Colorful melodrama set in czarist Russia, with peasant girl Landi coming under lecherous eye of officer Barrymore. Handsome production, lusty storytelling add up nicely; Karloff has good bit as drunken orderly.

Yellow Tomahawk, The (1954) **C-82m.** **✱✱** D: Lesley Selander. Rory Calhoun, Peggie Castle, Noah Beery (Jr.), Warner Anderson, Peter Graves, Lee Van Cleef, Rita Moreno. Calhoun is Indian guide who goes to any length to prevent Indian attack on settlers.

Yes, My Darling Daughter (1939) **86m.** **✱✱½** D: William Keighley. Priscilla Lane, Fay Bainter, Roland Young, May Robson, Jeffrey Lynn, Genevieve Tobin, Ian Hunter. Everybody is enthused about young lovers running off together except young man in question (Lynn). Mildly amusing comedy.

Yes, Sir, That's My Baby (1949) **C-82m.** **✱✱½** D: George Sherman. Donald O'Connor, Charles Coburn, Gloria De Haven, Joshua Shelley, Barbara Brown. Flimsy musical of football-crazy O'Connor on college campus, rescued by spirit and verve of cast.

Yesterday's Enemy (1959-British) **95m.** **✱½** D: Val Guest. Stanley Baker, Guy Rolfe, Leo McKern, Gordon Jackson, David Oxley, Philip Ahn, Bryan Forbes. Mild WW2 actioner set in Burma. Megascope. ▶

Yesterday, Today and Tomorrow (1963-Italian) **C-119m.** **✱✱✱✱** D: Vittorio De Sica. Sophia Loren, Marcello Mastroianni, Tina Pica, Giovanni Ridolfi. Oscar winner for Best Foreign Film is impeccable trio of comic tales, with Loren playing three women who use sex in various ways to get what they want. Striptease for Marcello is among the most famous scenes in her career (and remains pretty steamy). Techniscope.▼◗

Yidl Mitn Fidl (1936-Polish) **92m.** ***½ D: Joseph Green, Jan-Nowina Przybylski. Molly Picon, Max Bozyk, Leon Liebgold, Simcha Fostel, Dora Fakiel. Splendid, unique Yiddish-language musical comedy, with a storyline not unlike that of YENTL, with Picon (who's charming) posing as a boy, so she can travel the countryside playing her fiddle. English translation: YIDL WITH HIS FIDDLE. Avoid the English-dubbed version, titled CASTLES IN THE SKY.▼◗

Yodelin' Kid From Pine Ridge (1937) **60m.** **½ D: Joseph Kane. Gene Autry, Smiley Burnette, Betty Bronson, LeRoy Mason, Charles Middleton, Russell Simpson, The Tennessee Ramblers, Jack Dougherty, Guy Wilkerson, Frankie Marvin, Fred "Snowflake" Toones. Autry, estranged from his father for years, returns home as part of a Wild West show, determined to prove himself by routing out long-suspected cattle rustlers. Good B-Western fare, with fine support from Middleton and Simpson. Gene performs "Sing Me a Song of the Saddle." ▼◗

Yojimbo (1961-Japanese) **110m.** **** D: Akira Kurosawa. Toshiro Mifune, Eijiro Tono, Seizaburo Kawazu, Isuzu Yamada, Hiroshi Tachikawa, Kyu Sazanka, Tatsuya Nakadai, Takashi Shimura. Superb tongue-in-cheek samurai picture, the plot of which resembles a Western; Mifune is perfection as samurai up for hire in town with two warring factions, both of whom he teaches a well-deserved lesson. Beautiful on all counts; the inspiration for FISTFUL OF DOLLARS and many other films. Later remade as LAST MAN STANDING. Sequel: SANJURO. Tohoscope. ▼●◗

Yokel Boy (1942) **69m.** *½ D: Joseph Santley. Albert Dekker, Joan Davis, Eddie Foy, Jr., Alan Mowbray. Silly slapstick satire on gangster movies.

Yolanda and the Thief (1945) **C-108m.** **½ D: Vincente Minnelli. Fred Astaire, Lucille Bremer, Frank Morgan, Leon Ames, Mildred Natwick, Mary Nash. Opulent musical fantasy about a con man (Astaire) who tries to convince rich convent-bred girl (Bremer) that he's her guardian angel. Unusual film that you'll either love or hate. Best musical number: "Coffee Time."▼●◗

You and Me (1938) **90m.** **½ D: Fritz Lang. Sylvia Sidney, George Raft, Barton MacLane, Harry Carey, Roscoe Karns, George E. Stone, Warren Hymer, Robert Cummings. Genuinely odd but likable film about an ex-con (Raft) who falls in love with Sidney and marries her, unaware that she's a former jailbird herself. Unusual mix of gangsterism, sentiment, Damon Runyonesque comedy, and music (by Kurt Weill)—with even some rhythmic dialogue! Story by Norman Krasna, screenplay by Virginia Van Upp.▼◗

You Belong to Me (1941) **94m.** ** D: Wesley Ruggles. Barbara Stanwyck, Henry Fonda, Edgar Buchanan, Roger Clark, Ruth Donnelly, Melville Cooper, Maude Eburne. Weak comedy of doctor Stanwyck and hubby Fonda who's wary of her male patients. Looks as though it was made in three days. Coscripted by Dalton Trumbo. Remade as EMERGENCY WEDDING. ◗

You Came Along (1945) **103m.** **½ D: John Farrow. Robert Cummings, Lizabeth Scott, Don DeFore, Charles Drake, Kim Hunter, Julie Bishop, Helen Forrest, Franklin Pangborn, Ruth Roman, Hugh Beaumont. Clowning, womanizing fliers Cummings, DeFore, and Drake set out across the U.S. on a bond-selling tour. Their guide is pretty Scott (in her film debut); she falls in love with Cummings, who's harboring a terrible secret. Effective drama captures the essence of its era; Cummings' character shares the same name (Bob Collins) and much the same personality as his character in the later TV sitcom *The Bob Cummings Show.*

You Can't Beat Love (1937) **62m.** ** D: Christy Cabanne. Preston Foster, Joan Fontaine, Herbert Mundin, William Brisbane, Alan Bruce, Paul Hurst. Slow, trivial story of eccentric playboy Foster dabbling in politics and tangling with mayor's daughter Fontaine. Of interest only for the presence of young Fontaine.

You Can't Cheat an Honest Man (1939) **78m.** ***½ D: George Marshall. W. C. Fields, Edgar Bergen, Constance Moore, James Bush, Mary Forbes, Thurston Hall, Edward Brophy, Grady Sutton, Eddie Anderson. Fields (as Larson E. Whipsnade) runs circus with interference from Bergen and Charlie McCarthy in frantic comedy classic with loads of snappy one-liners and memorable ping-pong game. Most of Fields' scenes were directed by Eddie Cline. ▼◗

You Can't Escape Forever (1942) **77m.** **½ D: Jo Graham. George Brent, Brenda Marshall, Gene Lockhart, Roscoe Karns, Eduardo Ciannelli, Paul Harvey, Don DeFore. Fast-paced comedy-drama involving bullheaded editor Brent, who conjures up newspaper headlines from hunches. Bulk of the story has him setting out to expose crime boss Ciannelli's black market activities. One of several remakes of Paul Muni's HI, NELLIE! ◗

You Can't Fool Your Wife (1940) **68m.** ** D: Ray McCarey. Lucille Ball, James Ellison, Robert Coote, Emma Dunn, Virginia Vale, Elaine Shepard. Ball and Ellison are dull married couple until hubby takes a fling and wife makes herself glamorous to win him back. Comedy filler, made palatable by Lucy's charms in dual role.▼

You Can't Get Away With Murder (1939) 78m. ** D: Lewis Seiler. Humphrey Bogart, Billy Halop, Gale Page, John Litel, Henry Travers, Harvey Stephens, Joe Sawyer, Eddie "Rochester" Anderson. Cocky punk Bogart takes angry, impressionable Halop under his wing, leading to plenty of complications. Overbaked melodramatics do this one in. Based on play *Chalked Out* by Jonathan Finn and Sing Sing warden Lewis E. Lawes. ▶

You Can't Have Everything (1937) 99m. *** D: Norman Taurog. Alice Faye, The Ritz Brothers, Don Ameche, Charles Winninger, Tony Martin, Louise Hovick (Gypsy Rose Lee), Arthur Treacher, Tip, Tap, and Toe. Good show-biz musical as Faye writes drama which only succeeds as musical. The Ritz Brothers have good material, Louis Prima adds music. ▶

You Can't Run Away From It (1956) C-95m. ** D: Dick Powell. June Allyson, Jack Lemmon, Charles Bickford, Paul Gilbert, Jim Backus, Stubby Kaye, Henny Youngman. Slight musical remake of IT HAPPENED ONE NIGHT with Lemmon the reporter, Allyson the madcap heiress. CinemaScope.

You Can't Take It With You (1938) 127m. ***½ D: Frank Capra. Jean Arthur, Lionel Barrymore, James Stewart, Edward Arnold, Mischa Auer, Ann Miller, Spring Byington, Eddie Anderson, Donald Meek, Halliwell Hobbes, Dub Taylor, Samuel S. Hinds, Harry Davenport, Charles Lane. George S. Kaufman–Moss Hart play about eccentric but blissfully happy household becomes prime Capracorn, not quite as compelling today as MR. DEEDS or MR. SMITH (due to Robert Riskin's extensive rewriting), but still highly entertaining. Oscar winner for Best Picture and Director. Remade as a TVM in 1979 and later as a TV series. ▼●▶

You for Me (1952) 71m. **½ D: Don Weis. Peter Lawford, Jane Greer, Gig Young, Paula Corday, Howard Wendell, Tommy Farrell, Elaine Stewart. Unpretentious fluff has Greer a no-nonsense nurse who becomes involved with doctor Young and playboy Lawford at the same time.

You Gotta Stay Happy (1948) 100m. **½ D: H. C. Potter. Joan Fontaine, James Stewart, Eddie Albert, Roland Young, Willard Parker, Percy Kilbride, Porter Hall. OK comedy about millionairess who runs off on wedding night to find new marriage. Could have been much better. ▼▶

You Know What Sailors Are! (1954-British) C-89m. ** D: Ken Annakin. Akim Tamiroff, Donald Sinden, Sarah Lawson, Naunton Wayne. Attempted Cold War spoof of British Navy officer, jokingly telling cohorts that salvaged scrap is a new secret weapon. ▶

You'll Find Out (1940) 97m. ** D: David Butler. Kay Kyser, Boris Karloff, Peter Lorre, Bela Lugosi, Dennis O'Keefe, Ginny Simms, Helen Parrish, Alma Kruger, Harry Babbitt, Ish Kabibble. Kay and his band spend the night in a debutante's haunted house with three suspicious characters on hand. Obvious and overlong, a real disappointment to anyone anxious to savor the Karloff/Lugosi/Lorre team; more suited for fans of Ish Kabibble. ▼●

You'll Never Get Rich (1941) 88m. *** D: Sidney Lanfield. Fred Astaire, Rita Hayworth, John Hubbard, Robert Benchley, Osa Massen, Frieda Inescort, Guinn ("Big Boy") Williams, Cliff Nazarro. Broadway star Astaire is drafted, so producer Benchley brings the show to training camp, where Fred does his best to win over chorus girl Hayworth. Witty banter, a Cole Porter score (including "So Near and Yet So Far"), and terrific dancing by the two stars make this breezy fun. ▼●▶

You May Be Next! (1936) 66m. **½ D: Albert S. Rogell. Ann Sothern, Lloyd Nolan, Douglass Dumbrille, John Arledge, Berton Churchill, Nana Bryant, Robert Middlemass. Radio engineer Nolan accidentally cuts off his station—and the police signal—during a show, which inspires bad guy Dumbrille to deliberately jam radio signals to help him carry out his criminal activities. Likable, fast-moving B movie, though the title has no discernible meaning. Sothern sings a couple of mediocre songs.

You Must Be Joking! (1965-British) C-100m. *** D: Michael Winner. Michael Callan, Lionel Jeffries, Terry-Thomas, Denholm Elliott, Wilfrid Hyde-White, James Robertson Justice, Bernard Cribbins, Gabriella Licudi. Engaging poke at British Army as zany psychologist (Jeffries) rounds up five weirdos to establish, via special testing, the "complete, quick thinking" exemplary British soldier. ▶

You Never Can Tell (1951) 78m. *** D: Lou Breslow. Dick Powell, Peggy Dow, Charles Drake, Joyce Holden, Frank Nelson, Albert Sharpe. Amusing fantasy of a murdered dog returning to Earth as a human (Powell) to find his killer. Holden is a delight as his sidekick—who used to be a horse. Storyline reversed in OH, HEAVENLY DOG! ▶

Young America (1932) 70m. ** D: Frank Borzage. Spencer Tracy, Doris Kenyon, Ralph Bellamy, Tom Conlon, Raymond Borzage, Beryl Mercer, Sarah Padden, Dawn O'Day (Anne Shirley), Louise Beavers. Odd little film about juvenile delinquents, a sympathetic judge (played rather eccentrically by Bellamy, who sports a peculiar hairstyle), and one particular boy (Conlon) who's unfairly targeted as a bad egg. Do-gooder Kenyon takes him into her home, to the chagrin of her husband (Tracy). Interesting at times, but more often maudlin and ineffectual. ▶

Young and Dangerous (1957) 78m. ** D: William F. Claxton. Mark Damon, Edward Binns, Lili Gentle, Ann Doran, Connie Stevens. Damon, a footloose youth, turns respectable for love of a nice girl. The usual. Regalscope.

Young and Innocent (1937-British) 80m. *** D: Alfred Hitchcock. Nova Pilbeam, Derrick de Marney, Percy Marmont, Edward Rigby, Mary Clare, Basil Radford. A Hitchcock thriller with charm and humor; young girl helps runaway man accused of murder to find proof of his innocence. Pleasant echoes of THE 39 STEPS; nightclub revelation scene is especially memorable. Based on a novel by Josephine Tey. ▼●》

Young and the Brave, The (1963) 84m. **½ D: Francis D. Lyon. Rory Calhoun, William Bendix, Richard Jaeckel, Richard Arlen, John Agar, Manuel Padilla, Jr., Robert Ivers. Satisfactory Korean War drama with escaped American POWs attempting to elude the North Korean "commies" with the assistance of a cute but tough orphan and his dog.

Young and the Damned, The SEE: **Los Olvidados**

Young and the Immoral, The SEE: **Sinister Urge, The**

Young and Wild (1958) 69m. *½ D: William Witney. Gene Evans, Scott Marlowe, Carolyn Kearney, Robert Arthur. Trashy account of thrill-seeking teenagers on the loose with a stolen car. Naturama.

Young and Willing (1943) 82m. **½ D: Edward H. Griffith. William Holden, Eddie Bracken, Barbara Britton, James Brown, Martha O'Driscoll, Robert Benchley, Susan Hayward. Perennial summer-stock comedy *Out of the Frying Pan* becomes naive but zany comedy of show biz hopefuls. ▼

Young at Heart (1954) C-117m. *** D: Gordon Douglas. Doris Day, Frank Sinatra, Gig Young, Ethel Barrymore, Dorothy Malone, Alan Hale, Jr. Musical remake of Fannie Hurst's FOUR DAUGHTERS with Sinatra romancing Day amid much tear-shedding. Slickly done. ▼》

Young Bess (1953) C-112m. *** D: George Sidney. Jean Simmons, Stewart Granger, Charles Laughton, Deborah Kerr, Cecil Kellaway, Leo G. Carroll, Kay Walsh. Splashy costumer with Simmons as Elizabeth I, Laughton repeating role of Henry VIII. Fine cast does quite well in historical setting. Simmons and Granger were then married in real life. ▼》

Young Bill Hickok (1940) 59m. *** D: Joseph Kane. Roy Rogers, George "Gabby" Hayes, Jacqueline Wells (Julie Bishop), John Miljan, Sally Payne, Monte Blue, Hal Taliaferro, Jack Ingram, Yakima Canutt. Roy, as the title character, tries to stop European agent Miljan from forcing California to secede in order to control its wealth. Civil War meets Republic Pictures fiction in this action-packed entertainment, with classic Canutt stunts, and Payne a standout as Calamity Jane. ▼》

Youngblood Hawke (1964) 137m. **½ D: Delmer Daves. James Franciscus, Genevieve Page, Suzanne Pleshette, Eva Gabor, Mary Astor, Lee Bowman, Edward Andrews, Don Porter. Clichéd but somehow compelling trash from Herman Wouk's novel about a naive Southerner who writes a novel and becomes the toast of N.Y.C. literary society—with several women vying for his attention. 》

Young Buffalo Bill (1940) 59m. **½ D: Joseph Kane. Roy Rogers, George "Gabby" Hayes, Pauline Moore, Hugh Sothern, Chief Thundercloud, Julian Rivero, Trevor Bardette, Gaylord (Steve) Pendleton, Wade Boteler. Army surveyors Roy and Gabby come up against baddies who are trying to wrest control of a secret gold mine in New Mexico territory. Average Rogers "historical" entry, with Roy supposedly playing real-life title character; some good action amidst the Vasquez and Red Rock locations. ▼》

Young Captives, The (1959) 61m. ** D: Irvin Kershner. Steven Marlo, Tom Selden, Luana Patten, Ed Nelson, Joan Granville, Dan Blocker. Lurid melodrama of newly-weds involved with psychopathic killer.

Young Cassidy (1965-British) C-110m. *** D: Jack Cardiff, John Ford. Rod Taylor, Julie Christie, Maggie Smith, Flora Robson, Michael Redgrave, Edith Evans, Jack MacGowran. Taylor's best role ever as the earthy intellectual Sean O'Casey, set in 1910 Dublin; filled with rich atmosphere and fine supporting players. 》

Young Daniel Boone (1950) C-71m. *½ D: Reginald LeBorg. David Bruce, Kristine Miller, Mary Treen, Don Beddoe, Damian O'Flynn. Boone (Bruce) helps to rescue two young women who were captured by Indians, but that's not the end of their troubles . . . or the viewer's.

Young Dillinger (1965) 102m. **½ D: Terry O. Morse. Nick Adams, Mary Ann Mobley, Robert Conrad, John Ashley, Victor Buono, John Hoyt, Reed Hadley. Adams gives force to chronicle of gangster John Dillinger, his rise and seemingly inevitable fall; sufficient gunplay. 》

Young Doctors, The (1961) 100m. *** D: Phil Karlson. Fredric March, Ben Gazzara, Dick Clark, Eddie Albert, Ina Balin, Aline MacMahon, Edward Andrews, Arthur Hill, George Segal, Rosemary Murphy, Barnard Hughes, Dick Button, Dolph Sweet; narrated by Ronald Reagan. Sturdy cast uplifts soaper set in large city hospital. Based on an Arthur Hailey novel. Segal's first film.

Young Don't Cry, The (1957) 89m. ** D: Alfred L. Werker. Sal Mineo, James Whitmore, J. Carrol Naish, Paul Carr. OK drama of loner youth Mineo who takes pity on an escaped murderer (Whitmore). Filmed in Savannah.

[800]

Young Dr. Kildare (1938) **81m.** **½ D: Harold S. Bucquet. Lew Ayres, Lionel Barrymore, Lynne Carver, Nat Pendleton, Jo Ann Sayers, Samuel S. Hinds, Emma Dunn, Walter Kingsford, Monty Woolley, Phillip Terry, Donald Barry. MGM's first episode in the adventures of Kildare, as he graduates from medical school and must decide between country practice with his father or the big city's Blair General Hospital. ▶

Younger Brothers, The (1949) **C-77m.** **½ D: Edwin L. Marin. Wayne Morris, Janis Paige, Bruce Bennett, Geraldine Brooks, Robert Hutton, Alan Hale, Fred Clark, Tom Tyler. OK Western of notorious Younger brothers and the incident that drives them to renewed violence and terror.

Younger Generation, The (1929) **88m.** **½ D: Frank Capra. Jean Hersholt, Lina Basquette, Ricardo Cortez, Rosa Rosanova, Rex Lease. Ethnic heart-tugger by Fannie Hurst about a Jewish family that suffers because of one son's determination to abandon his roots and break into N.Y.C. society. (Cortez played a similar role in SYMPHONY OF SIX MILLION.) Director Capra pulls out all the stops in this silent film with talkie sequences.

Youngest Profession, The (1943) **82m.** **½ D: Edward Buzzell. Virginia Weidler, Jean Porter, Edward Arnold, John Carroll, Agnes Moorehead, Scotty Beckett. Weidler and Porter are incurable (and obnoxious) autograph hounds in innocent little film with many MGM guest stars (including Lana Turner, William Powell, Robert Taylor, Greer Garson, and Walter Pidgeon). ▶

Youngest Spy, The SEE: **My Name Is Ivan**

Young Fury (1965) **C-80m.** **½ D: Christian Nyby. Rory Calhoun, Virginia Mayo, Lon Chaney (Jr.), John Agar, Richard Arlen, Linda Foster. Tired gunslinger returns home to discover son leading gang of young hellions. Standard formula plot highlighted by a cast chockfull of old stars. William Bendix's last film. Techniscope.

Young Guns, The (1956) **84m.** **½ D: Albert Band. Russ Tamblyn, Gloria Talbott, Perry Lopez, Walter Coy, Chubby Johnson, Scott Marlowe, Myron Healey. Ostracized because his father was a killer, rebellious young Tamblyn takes refuge in a mountain sanctuary for a gang of outlaw teens. Somber B Western cashing in on the '50s juvenile delinquency genre craze. ▶

Young Guns of Texas (1962) **C-78m.** **½ D: Maury Dexter. James Mitchum, Alana Ladd, Jody McCrea, Chill Wills. Second generation of movie stars perform satisfactorily in account of gold and girl hunt in old West, tied in with Indian raid. CinemaScope. ▶

Young Hellions SEE: **High School Confidential!**

Young Ideas (1943) **77m.** *½ D: Jules Dassin. Susan Peters, Herbert Marshall,

Mary Astor, Elliott Reid, Richard Carlson. Dismal comedy in which college students Peters and Reid try to break up the new marriage of mom Astor and professor Marshall. Watch for Ava Gardner in a bit. ▶

Young in Heart, The (1938) **90m.** ***½ D: Richard Wallace. Janet Gaynor, Douglas Fairbanks, Jr., Paulette Goddard, Roland Young, Billie Burke, Minnie Dupree, Richard Carlson. Refreshing comedy about wacky family of con artists going straight under influence of unsuspecting Dupree. Written by Paul Osborn and Charles Bennett from an I.A.R. Wylie novel. Also shown in computer-colored version. ▼▶

Young Jesse James (1960) **73m.** *½ D: William Claxton. Ray Stricklyn, Willard Parker, Merry Anders, Robert Dix, Emile Meyer, Jacklyn O'Donnell. Title tells all in this routine oater. CinemaScope.

Young Land, The (1959) **C-89m.** **½ D: Ted Tetzlaff. Pat Wayne, Yvonne Craig, Dennis Hopper, Dan O'Herlihy, Cliff Ketchum. Sincere Western of pre–Mexican War Texas. ▼▶

Young Lions, The (1958) **167m.** ***½ D: Edward Dmytryk. Marlon Brando, Montgomery Clift, Dean Martin, Hope Lange, Barbara Rush, Maximilian Schell, May Britt, Lee Van Cleef. One of the all-time best WW2 studies, adapted by Edward Anhalt from the Irwin Shaw novel. Martin and Clift play U.S. soldiers, Brando a confused Nazi officer; effectively photographed by Joe MacDonald, with Hugo Friedhofer's fine score. Cinema-Scope. ▼▶

Young Lovers, The (1950) SEE: **Never Fear**

Young Lovers, The (1964) **109m.** ** D: Samuel Goldwyn, Jr. Peter Fonda, Sharon Hugueny, Nick Adams, Deborah Walley, Beatrice Straight, Joseph Campanella, Kent Smith. Amateurish, meandering drama of college youths involved in romance.

Young Man With a Horn (1950) **112m.** *** D: Michael Curtiz. Kirk Douglas, Lauren Bacall, Doris Day, Juano Hernandez, Hoagy Carmichael, Mary Beth Hughes. Effective drama of trumpet-player Douglas compulsively drawn to music, with Bacall the bad girl, Day the wholesome one. Carl Foreman–Edmund H. North script adapted from Dorothy Baker's book, and inspired by Bix Beiderbecke's life; Harry James dubbed Douglas' licks. ▼▶

Young Man With Ideas (1952) **84m.** **½ D: Mitchell Leisen. Glenn Ford, Ruth Roman, Denise Darcel, Nina Foch, Donna Corcoran, Ray Collins, Sheldon Leonard. Modest comedy-drama about a young Montana lawyer who moves to California with his wife and kids for a fresh start and encounters various problems while studying for the state bar exam. ▶

Young Mr. Lincoln (1939) **100m.** ***½ D: John Ford. Henry Fonda, Alice Brady,

Marjorie Weaver, Donald Meek, Richard Cromwell, Eddie Quillan, Milburn Stone, Ward Bond, Francis Ford. Series of vignettes presents a portrait of Abraham Lincoln before he even thought of running for president, from his first courtship to an important courtroom showdown. Not so much a historical document as a slice of Americana, filtered through the sensibilities of director Ford and screenwriter Lamar Trotti. The early, episodic portion of the film, covering Abe Lincoln's formative years, includes some of Ford's most lyrical moments, luminously photographed by Bert Glennon. ▼◐◗

Young Mr. Pitt, The (1942-British) **118m.** ****½** D: Carol Reed. Robert Donat, Robert Morley, Phyllis Calvert, John Mills, Max Adrian. Long, only occasionally moving historical drama of young British prime minister during Napoleonic era; thinly veiled WW2 morale-booster. Written by Frank Launder and Sidney Gilliatt. ◗

Young One, The (1961-Mexican) **96m.** ***½** D: Luis Buñuel. Zachary Scott, Bernie Hamilton, Key Meersman, Graham Denton, Claudio Brook. Racist Scott, who has violated Lolita-like Meersman on an isolated island, must contend with the presence of on-the-run black jazz musician Hamilton. Turgid, much-too-obvious melodrama is a disappointment from Buñuel. ▼◗

Young People (1940) **78m.** ****** D: Allan Dwan. Shirley Temple, Jack Oakie, Charlotte Greenwood, Arleen Whelan, George Montgomery, Kathleen Howard. Show-biz team Oakie and Greenwood raise orphaned Shirley and try to settle down in this weak musical, a later and lesser Temple vehicle. Good dance routine at the finish. Also shown in computer-colored version. ▼◗

Young Philadelphians, The (1959) **136m.** ******* D: Vincent Sherman. Paul Newman, Barbara Rush, Alexis Smith, Brian Keith, Diane Brewster, Billie Burke, John Williams, Robert Vaughn, Otto Kruger, Adam West. Newman and Rush have memorable roles as poor lawyer who schemes to the top and society girl he hopes to win; Vaughn is hard-drinking buddy Newman defends on murder charge, Smith quite good as frustrated wife of attorney Kruger. ▼◗

Young Racers, The (1963) **C-87m.** ****** D: Roger Corman. Mark Damon, William Campbell, Patrick Magee, Luana Anders, Robert Campbell. Juvenile nonsense about sports car racing involving ex-racer turned exposé writer, trying to do a book on the sport. ◗

Young Savages, The (1961) **103m.** ******* D: John Frankenheimer. Burt Lancaster, Dina Merrill, John Davis Chandler, Shelley Winters, Telly Savalas, Edward Andrews, Chris Robinson, Pilar Seurat, Milton Selzer. Lancaster is idealistic D.A. battling all odds to see justice done in street-gang slaying; at times brutal, too often pat. Adapted by Edward Anhalt and JP Miller from Evan Hunt-

er's novel *A Matter of Conviction*. Savalas' film debut. ▼◐◗

Young Scarface SEE: **Brighton Rock**

Young Stranger, The (1957) **84m.** ******* D: John Frankenheimer. James MacArthur, James Daly, Kim Hunter, James Gregory, Marian Seldes, Whit Bissell. Excellent drama about a teenage boy's brush with delinquency and strained relationship with his wealthy, neglectful father. Surprisingly undated, sincere little film; MacArthur's impressive screen debut (and director Frankenheimer's, too). Frankenheimer also directed the TV play *Deal a Blow*, on which this was based. ◐◗

Young Swingers, The (1963) **71m.** BOMB D: Maury Dexter. Molly Bee, Rod Lauren, Gene McDaniels, Jack Larson, Jo Helton. Singer Lauren tries to keep nightclub operating, despite interference of greedy real estate agent Helton. Grade Z all the way. ◗

Young Tom Edison (1940) **82m.** ******* D: Norman Taurog. Mickey Rooney, Fay Bainter, George Bancroft, Virginia Weidler, Eugene Pallette, Victor Kilian. Inventor's early life depicted with flair by effective Rooney, who could tone down when he had to; followed by Spencer Tracy's EDISON, THE MAN. ▼◐◗

Young Widow (1946) **100m.** ****** D: Edwin L. Marin. Jane Russell, Marie Wilson, Louis Hayward, Faith Domergue, Kent Taylor, Penny Singleton, Cora Witherspoon. Soap opera was not Russell's forte and she can't support teary WW2 tale of woman who can't forget her late husband. Feature debut of Domergue.

Young Wives' Tale (1951-British) **78m.** ****½** D: Henry Cass. Joan Greenwood, Nigel Patrick, Derek Farr, Helen Cherry, Guy Middleton, Athene Seyler, Audrey Hepburn. Slight farce about the housing shortage in post-WW2 England, in which two couples are forced to live under the same roof. Hepburn plays a lodger who also resides in the house.

You Only Live Once (1937) **86m.** ******* D: Fritz Lang. Sylvia Sidney, Henry Fonda, William Gargan, Barton MacLane, Jean Dixon, Jerome Cowan, Margaret Hamilton, Ward Bond, Guinn ("Big Boy") Williams. Beautifully crafted drama about ex-convict Fonda trying to go straight, finding that fate is against him. Loosely based on the Bonnie and Clyde legend, but impressive on its own. ▼◗

Your Cheatin' Heart (1964) **99m.** ******* D: Gene Nelson. George Hamilton, Susan Oliver, Red Buttons, Arthur O'Connell, Rex Ingram. One of Hamilton's best roles, as legendary country-western singer Hank Williams, who couldn't cope with fame on the ole opry circuit; songs dubbed by Hank Williams, Jr. Oliver most effective as Hank's wife. Also shown in computer-colored version. Panavision. ◗

You're a Sweetheart (1937) **96m.** ** D: David Butler. Alice Faye, George Murphy, Ken Murray, Andy Devine, William Gargan, Charles Winninger, Donald Meek, Bobby Watson, Oswald, Casper Reardon. Routine musical with go-getter Murphy dreaming up publicity stunt for show which stars Faye. Title song became a standard. Remade in 1943 as COWBOY IN MANHATTAN.

You're in the Army Now (1941) **79m.** ** D: Lewis Seiler. Jimmy Durante, Phil Silvers, Donald MacBride, Jane Wyman, Regis Toomey, Joe Sawyer. Rather obvious service comedy, with Durante and Silvers trying hard to rise above their material. Some funny scenes, with finale copied from Chaplin's THE GOLD RUSH. Trivia note: features the longest kiss (between Toomey and Wyman) in screen history, clocked at 3 min., 5 sec.

You're in the Navy Now (1951) **93m.** ** D: Henry Hathaway. Gary Cooper, Jane Greer, Millard Mitchell, Eddie Albert, John McIntire, Ray Collins, Harry Von Zell, Lee Marvin, Jack Webb. Flat naval comedy set in WW2 with Cooper commanding a dumb crew on the U.S.S. *Teakettle* (the ship is outfitted with a steam engine). Film debuts for Marvin and Charles Buchinski (Bronson). Originally screened with the title U.S.S. TEAKETTLE.◗

You're My Everything (1949) **C-94m.** ** D: Walter Lang. Dan Dailey, Anne Baxter, Anne Revere, Stanley Ridges, Alan Mowbray, Selena Royle. Lumpy musical-romance of socialite Baxter and hoofer-husband Dailey, who become movie stars in the 1920s and '30s. Based on a story by George Jessel. Watch for Buster Keaton in Baxter's second "silent film."

You're Never Too Young (1955) **C-102m.** *** D: Norman Taurog. Dean Martin, Jerry Lewis, Diana Lynn, Raymond Burr, Nina Foch, Veda Ann Borg. Fast, funny remake of THE MAJOR AND THE MINOR (which also featured Lynn) with Jerry disguised as 12-year-old at a girls' school, involved in jewel robbery. Script by Sidney Sheldon. VistaVision.◗

You're Not So Tough (1940) **71m.** **½ D: Joe May. Billy Halop, Huntz Hall, Bobby Jordan, Gabriel Dell, Bernard Punsly, Nan Grey, Henry Armetta. Halop and his pals are drifters who end up working on a California farm beset by the usual villains. One of the better *Little Tough Guys* entries.

You're Only Young Once (1938) **78m.** **½ D: George B. Seitz. Lewis Stone, Cecilia Parker, Mickey Rooney, Fay Holden, Frank Craven, Ann Rutherford. Second *Andy Hardy* film, with Andy (Rooney) and his sister finding romance on a family vacation in Catalina. Energetic Eleanor Lynn makes a peppy partner for Rooney.◗

You're Telling Me! (1934) **67m.** ***½ D: Erle C. Kenton. W. C. Fields, Joan Marsh,

Larry "Buster" Crabbe, Louise Carter, Kathleen Howard, Adrienne Ames. Hilarious remake of Fields' silent film SO'S YOUR OLD MAN, with thin storyline (about a friendly foreign princess giving lowly, browbeaten Fields respectability in his home town) a perfect excuse for some of his funniest routines—including classic golf game.◗◗

You're Telling Me (1942) **60m.** *½ D: Charles Lamont. Hugh Herbert, Jane Frazee, Robert Paige, Richard Davies, Anne Gwynne, Mischa Auer, Ernest Truex. Tired comedy vehicle for Hugh as bumbler given job with radio advertising agency, involved with matchmaking on the side.

Your Past Is Showing (1957-British) **92m.** *** D: Mario Zampi. Terry-Thomas, Peter Sellers, Peggy Mount, Shirley Eaton, Dennis Price, Georgina Cookson, Joan Sims, Miles Malleson. Scandal-sheet publisher Price is literally blackmailing celebrities to death by threatening to expose their past and present indiscretions. Several eventually band together and plot to rid themselves of their problem. Sellers (cast as a television star) is a special treat in this amusing satire. Original British title: THE NAKED TRUTH.◗◗

You Said a Mouthful (1932) **75m.** **½ D: Lloyd Bacon. Joe E. Brown, Ginger Rogers, Preston Foster, Allen "Farina" Hoskins, Sheila Terry, Guinn Williams. One of Brown's better vehicles, about an inventor of unsinkable bathing suits who's mistaken for a celebrated marathon swimmer. Rogers is Joe E.'s pert leading lady.◗

Youth Runs Wild (1944) **67m.** ** D: Mark Robson. Bonita Granville, Kent Smith, Tessa Brind (Vanessa Brown), Lawrence Tierney, Jean Brooks, Dickie Moore. With parents and older siblings at war or in defense plants, teenagers do just what the title implies. Rare non-horror entry from producer Val Lewton is interesting as time capsule, routine as drama.

You Were Meant for Me (1948) **92m.** *** D: Lloyd Bacon. Jeanne Crain, Dan Dailey, Oscar Levant, Barbara Lawrence, Selena Royle. Nice combination of musical score and script of girl who marries band leader; their experiences in Depression are basis of film.◗

You Were Never Lovelier (1942) **97m.** ***½ D: William A. Seiter. Fred Astaire, Rita Hayworth, Adolphe Menjou, Leslie Brooks, Adele Mara, Xavier Cugat, Gus Schilling, Larry Parks. Astaire pursuing Hayworth via matchmaking father Menjou becomes lilting musical with such lovely Jerome Kern–Johnny Mercer songs as title tune, "Dearly Beloved," "I'm Old-Fashioned."◗◗◗

Zamba (1949) **75m.** *½ D: William Berke. Jon Hall, June Vincent, George Cooper, Jane Nigh, George O'Hanlon, Beau Bridges. Juvenile adventure story of boy raised by gorillas; rough going.

Zarak (1957-British) **C-99m.** **½ D: Terence Young. Victor Mature, Michael Wilding, Anita Ekberg, Bernard Miles, Finlay Currie. Hokum set in India with Mature the head of native outlaws, Wilding the British officer sent to get him. CinemaScope. ▶

Zaza (1939) **83m.** ** D: George Cukor. Claudette Colbert, Herbert Marshall, Bert Lahr, Helen Westley, Constance Collier, Genevieve Tobin, Walter Catlett. Colbert, doing her own singing, is the French music hall performer who falls for married Marshall, playing the role in his sleep. Remake of Gloria Swanson silent vehicle has well-mounted novelty value, but the drama simply never gets into gear.

Zazie dans le Metro (1960-French) **C-88m.** **½ D: Louis Malle. Catherine Demongeot, Philippe Noiret, Vittorio Caprioli, Hubert Deschamps, Carla Marlier. Superficial comedy, coscripted by Malle, about a bright but impish 12-year-old (Demongeot), who visits her female-impersonator uncle (Noiret) in Paris, and is intent on riding in the city's subway. ▼▶

Zebra in the Kitchen (1965) **C-93m.** **½ D: Ivan Tors. Jay North, Martin Milner, Andy Devine, Joyce Meadows, Jim Davis, Dorothy Green. Wholesome family fare of young North involved with wild pets and the city zoo's attempt to keep its inmates locked up. ▼▶

Zenobia (1939) **71m.** **½ D: Gordon Douglas. Oliver Hardy, Harry Langdon, Billie Burke, Alice Brady, James Ellison, Jean Parker, June Lang, Chester Conklin, Stepin Fetchit, Hattie McDaniel. Small-town doctor agrees to treat an ailing elephant—and the grateful pachyderm refuses to leave his side! Amiable comedy set in the Old South, with some dated (and mildly tol'able) subplots. This was Hardy's only starring venture without Stan Laurel, and he's quite good, in a fairly straight nonslapsticky performance. ▼

Zero for Conduct (1933-French) **44m.** **** D: Jean Vigo. Jean Daste, Robert le Flon, Louis Lefebvre, Constantin Kelber, Gerard de Bedarieux. Life in a French boarding school, where the authorities attempt to regiment the students—unsuccessfully. The kids are all wonderfully spontaneous; one of the best films ever about children among children. The inspiration for IF. . . . Written by the director. ▼▶

Zero Hour! (1957) **81m.** **½ D: Hall Bartlett. Dana Andrews, Linda Darnell, Sterling Hayden, Elroy "Crazylegs" Hirsch, Geoffrey Toone, Jerry Paris, Peggy King, John Ashley. Effective suspense story (based on Arthur Hailey teleplay) of potential airplane disaster when pilots are felled by ptomaine poisoning. Remade for TV in 1971 as TER-

ROR IN THE SKY, and then spoofed in 1980 as AIRPLANE! ▶

Ziegfeld Follies (1946) **C-110m.** *** D: Vincente Minnelli. William Powell, Judy Garland, Lucille Ball, Fred Astaire, Fanny Brice, Lena Horne, Red Skelton, Victor Moore, Virginia O'Brien, Cyd Charisse, Gene Kelly, Edward Arnold, Esther Williams. Variable all-star film introduced by Powell as Ziegfeld in heaven. Highlights are Brice-Hume Cronyn sketch, Astaire-Kelly dance, Moore-Arnold comedy routine, Skelton's "Guzzler's Gin," Horne's solo, Garland's "The Interview." Various segments directed by George Sidney, Roy Del Ruth, Norman Taurog, Lemuel Ayers, Robert Lewis, Merrill Pye. Filmed mostly in 1944. Video version runs 117m. with overture and exit music. ▼▶

Ziegfeld Girl (1941) **131m.** *** D: Robert Z. Leonard. James Stewart, Lana Turner, Judy Garland, Hedy Lamarr, Tony Martin, Jackie Cooper, Ian Hunter, Edward Everett Horton, Al Shean, Eve Arden, Dan Dailey, Philip Dorn, Charles Winninger. Large-scale musical drama opens brightly, bogs down into melodrama and preposterous subplots, as the lives of three girls (Turner, Garland, Lamarr) are changed by being recruited as Ziegfeld Follies girls. Busby Berkeley's "You Stepped Out of a Dream" is most famous number, but somewhat overshadowed by Judy's "I'm Always Chasing Rainbows," "Minnie From Trinidad." The MGM glitter has never been brighter. ▼●▶

Zombies of Mora Tau (1957) **70m.** *½ D: Edward L. Cahn. Gregg Palmer, Allison Hayes, Autumn Russell, Joel Ashley. Juvenile hodgepodge about zombies guarding diamonds hidden in a sunken ship off the African coast. ▼▶

Zombies on Broadway (1945) **68m.** ** D: Gordon Douglas. Wally Brown, Alan Carney, Bela Lugosi, Anne Jeffreys, Sheldon Leonard, Frank Jenks. Press agents Brown and Carney (cut-rate version of Abbott and Costello) search for zombie to use in nightclub stunt. Lugosi adds only spice as zombie expert. ▼●▶

Zoo in Budapest (1933) **85m.** ***½ D: Rowland V. Lee. Loretta Young, Gene Raymond, O. P. Heggie, Paul Fix, Wally Albright. Wonderfully whimsical love story set in famous Budapest zoo where Raymond, who has spent his life there, falls in love with runaway Young, who's hiding inside zoo grounds. Offbeat film bathed in romantic aura; beautifully photographed by Lee Garmes.

Zorba the Greek (1964) **146m.** ***½ D: Michael Cacoyannis. Anthony Quinn, Alan Bates, Irene Papas, Lila Kedrova, George Foundas. Brooding, flavorful rendering of Nikos Kazantzakis novel. Quinn is zesty in title role of earthy peasant, Bates his intellectual British cohort. Kedrova won an Oscar as a dying prostitute, as did cinematographer Walter Lassally and the art direction–set decoration. Memorable Mikis Theodorakis score. Scripted by the director. Later a Broadway musical.▼●▶

Zorro (1961-Spanish) **C-90m.** **½ D: Joaquin Luis Romero Marchent. Frank Latimore, Mary Anderson, Ralph Marsch, Howard Vernon. Foreign-made Western with salty flavor of old California; Latimore is appropriately zealous as Zorro. SuperScope.▼

Zotz! (1962) **87m.** ** D: William Castle. Tom Poston, Julia Meade, Jim Backus, Fred Clark, Cecil Kellaway, Margaret Dumont. Goofy attempt at humorous chiller with Poston a teacher who finds strange coin that gives him mystical power over others.▼▶

Zouzou (1934-French) **92m.** **½ D: Marc Allegret. Josephine Baker, Jean Gabin, Pierre Larquey, Yvette Leblon, Illa Meery, Madeleine Guitty. 42ND STREET meets FOOTLIGHT PARADE French-style, with Baker cast as a Creole laundress. In the best backstage musical tradition, she replaces a temperamental performer in a stage revue and captivates the crowd in a star-making turn. Overly familiar storyline is helped by fast pace, and engaging musical numbers: how can you top Baker, covered in feathers and perched on a swing?▼●▶

Zulu (1964-British) **C-138m.** *** D: Cy Endfield. Stanley Baker, Jack Hawkins, Ulla Jacobsson, Michael Caine, Nigel Green, James Booth; narrated by Richard Burton. True story about undermanned British forces trying to defend their African mission from attack by hordes of Zulu warriors. Dramatic elements tend toward cliché, but virtually half the film is taken up by massive battle, which is truly spectacular and exciting. Followed 15 years later by prequel, ZULU DAWN. Technirama.▼●▶

Index of Stars

This index includes only the films that appear in this book; therefore, what follows doesn't pretend to be a complete list of Mary Pickford's silent films or Ingrid Bergman's screen appearances. What's more, the index, like the book, ends in 1965.

The titles in each entry are in chronological order. Years are indicated in the reviews and are included here to distinguish between two films of the same title, whether they are remakes or have nothing to do with each other.

When an actor directs but doesn't act in a movie, this is indicated by "(dir)" after the title; if the actor does appear, the designation is "(also dir)."

The prefix "co-" means a collaboration. "Cameo" indicates a well-known actor taking a small role, sometimes as a joke; their names almost never appear in the opening credits of a film.

adapt	=	screenplay adaptation
app	=	appearance, not a performance (as in a documentary)
dir	=	director
mus	=	composer
narr	=	narrator
scr	=	screenplay
set dec	=	set decorator
sty	=	story
uncred	=	uncredited performance

Abbott and Costello (*Bud Abbott, Lou Costello*): One Night in the Tropics; Buck Privates; In the Navy; Hold That Ghost; Keep 'Em Flying; Ride 'Em Cowboy; Rio Rita (1942); Pardon My Sarong; Who Done It? (1942); It Ain't Hay; Hit the Ice; Lost in a Harem; In Society; Here Come the Co-Eds; The Naughty Nineties; Abbott and Costello in Hollywood; Little Giant; The Time of Their Lives; Buck Privates Come Home; The Wistful Widow of Wagon Gap; The Noose Hangs High; Abbott and Costello Meet Frankenstein; Mexican Hayride; Africa Screams; Abbott and Costello Meet the Killer Boris Karloff; Abbott and Costello in the Foreign Legion; Abbott and Costello Meet the Invisible Man; Comin' Round the Mountain; Jack and the Beanstalk; Lost in Alaska; Abbott and Costello Meet Captain Kidd; Abbott and Costello Go to Mars; Abbott and Costello Meet Dr. Jekyll and Mr. Hyde; Abbott and Costello Meet the Keystone Kops; Abbott and Costello Meet the Mummy; Dance With Me, Henry; *Costello without Abbott*: Bardelys the Magnificent (bit); The 30-Foot Bride of Candy Rock
Allyson, June: Best Foot Forward; Thousands Cheer; Girl Crazy (1943); Two Girls and a Sailor; Meet the People; Her Highness and the Bellboy; The Sailor Takes a Wife; Music for Millions; Two Sisters from Boston; Till the Clouds Roll By; The Secret Heart; High Barbaree; Good News; The Bride Goes Wild; The Three Musketeers (1948); Words and Music; Little Women (1949); The Stratton Story; The Reformer and the Redhead; Right Cross; Too Young to Kiss; The Girl in White; Battle Circus; Remains to Be Seen; The Glenn Miller Story; Executive Suite; Woman's World; Strategic Air Command; The Shrike; The McConnell Story; The Opposite Sex; You Can't Run Away from It; Interlude; My Man Godfrey (1957); Stranger in My Arms
Ameche, Don: Clive of India; Dante's Inferno; Ramona; Ladies in Love; One in a Million; Love Is News; Fifty Roads to Town; You Can't Have Everything; Love Under Fire; In Old Chicago; Happy Landing; Josette; Alexander's Ragtime Band; Gateway; The Three Musketeers (1939); Midnight; The Story of Alexander Graham Bell; Hollywood Cavalcade; Swanee River; Lillian Russell; Four Sons (1940); Down Argentine Way; That Night in Rio; Moon Over Miami; Kiss the Boys Goodbye; The Femi-

nine Touch; Confirm or Deny; Girl Trouble; The Magnificent Dope; Something to Shout About; Heaven Can Wait (1943); Happy Land; Wing and a Prayer; Greenwich Village; It's in the Bag!; So Goes My Love; Guest Wife; That's My Man; Sleep, My Love; Slightly French; A Fever in the Blood

Arliss, George: Disraeli; The Green Goddess; Old English; The Millionaire; Alexander Hamilton (also costy); The Man Who Played God; A Successful Calamity; The King's Vacation; The Working Man; Voltaire; The House of Rothschild; The Last Gentleman; The Iron Duke; Cardinal Richelieu; Trans-Atlantic Tunnel (cameo); East Meets West; Doctor Syn

Arthur, Jean: Cameo Kirby (1923); Seven Chances (bit); The Canary Murder Case; The Mysterious Dr. Fu Manchu; The Greene Murder Case; Street of Chance; Paramount on Parade; The Return of Dr. Fu Manchu; Danger Lights; The Silver Horde; Whirlpool (1934); The Most Precious Thing in Life; The Defense Rests; The Whole Town's Talking; Party Wire; Public Hero No. 1; Diamond Jim; The Public Menace; If You Could Only Cook; Mr. Deeds Goes to Town; The Ex-Mrs. Bradford; Adventure in Manhattan; The Plainsman (1936); More Than a Secretary; History Is Made at Night; Easy Living (1937); You Can't Take It With You; Only Angels Have Wings; Mr. Smith Goes to Washington; Too Many Husbands; Arizona; The Devil and Miss Jones; The Talk of the Town; The More the Merrier; A Lady Takes a Chance; The Impatient Years; A Foreign Affair; Shane

Astaire, Fred: Dancing Lady; Flying Down to Rio; The Gay Divorcee; Roberta; Top Hat; Follow the Fleet; Swing Time; Shall We Dance (1937); A Damsel in Distress; Carefree; The Story of Vernon and Irene Castle; Broadway Melody of 1940; Second Chorus; You'll Never Get Rich; Holiday Inn; You Were Never Lovelier; The Sky's the Limit; Yolanda and the Thief; Ziegfeld Follies; Blue Skies; Easter Parade; The Barkleys of Broadway; Three Little Words; Let's Dance; Royal Wedding; The Belle of New York; The Band Wagon; Daddy Long Legs; Funny Face; Silk Stockings; On the Beach; The Pleasure of His Company; The Notorious Landlady

Autry, Gene: In Old Santa Fe; Tumbling Tumbleweeds; Melody Trail; Sagebrush Troubadour; The Singing Vagabond; Red River Valley; Comin' Round the Mountain; The Singing Cowboy; Guns and Guitars; Oh, Susanna!; Ride, Ranger, Ride; The Big Show; The Old Corral; Git Along, Little Dogies; Round-Up Time in Texas; Rootin' Tootin' Rhythm; Yodelin' Kid from Pine Ridge; Public Cowboy No. 1; Boots and Saddles; Springtime in the Rockies; The Old Barn Dance; Gold Mine in the Sky; The Man From Music Mountain (1938); Prairie Moon; Rhythm of

the Saddle; Western Jamboree; Home on the Prairie; Mexicali Rose; Blue Montana Skies; Mountain Rhythm; Colorado Sunset; In Old Monterey; Rovin' Tumbleweeds; South of the Border; Rancho Grande; Shooting High; Gaucho Serenade; Carolina Moon; Ride, Tenderfoot, Ride; Melody Ranch; Rodeo Dough; Ridin' on a Rainbow; Back in the Saddle; The Singing Hill; Sunset in Wyoming; Under Fiesta Stars; Down Mexico Way; Sierra Sue; Cowboy Serenade; Heart of the Rio Grande; Home in Wyomin'; Stardust on the Sage; Call of the Canyon; Bells of Capistrano; Sioux City Sue; Trail to San Antone; Twilight on the Rio Grande; Saddle Pals; Robin Hood of Texas; The Last Round-Up; The Strawberry Roan; Loaded Pistols; The Big Sombrero; Riders of the Whistling Pines; Rim of the Canyon; The Cowboy and the Indians; Riders in the Sky; Sons of New Mexico; Mule Train; Cow Town; Beyond the Purple Hills; Indian Territory; The Blazing Sun; Gene Autry and the Mounties; Texans Never Cry; Whirlwind; Silver Canyon; The Hills of Utah; Valley of Fire; The Old West; Night Stage to Galveston; Apache Country; Barbed Wire; Wagon Team; Blue Canadian Rockies; Winning of the West; On Top of Old Smoky; Goldtown Ghost Riders; Pack Train; Saginaw Trail; Last of the Pony Riders

Bacall, Lauren: To Have and Have Not; Confidential Agent; Two Guys from Milwaukee (cameo); The Big Sleep (1946); Dark Passage; Key Largo; Young Man With a Horn; Bright Leaf; How to Marry a Millionaire; Woman's World; The Cobweb; Blood Alley; Written on the Wind; Designing Woman; The Gift of Love; Flame Over India; Shock Treatment (1964); Sex and the Single Girl

Ball, Lucille: The Bowery (bit); Broadway Thru a Keyhole (bit); Blood Money (bit); Roman Scandals; Nana (chorus); Bottoms Up (bit); The Affairs of Cellini; Murder at the Vanities (chorus); Bulldog Drummond Strikes Back; Kid Millions (chorus); Broadway Bill; The Whole Town's Talking; Roberta; Old Man Rhythm; Top Hat; The Three Musketeers; I Dream Too Much; Chatterbox (1936); Follow the Fleet; Winterset; That Girl From Paris; Stage Door; Joy of Living; Go Chase Yourself; Having Wonderful Time; The Affairs of Annabel; Room Service; Annabel Takes a Tour; Next Time I Marry; Beauty for the Asking; Panama Lady; Five Came Back; That's Right—You're Wrong; You Can't Fool Your Wife; Dance, Girl, Dance; Too Many Girls; A Girl, a Guy, and a Gob; Look Who's Laughing; Valley of the Sun; The Big Street; Seven Days' Leave; Du Barry Was a Lady; Thousands Cheer; Meet the People; Without Love; Ziegfeld Follies; The Dark Corner (1946); Two Smart People; Lover Come Back (1946); Easy to Wed; Lured; Her Husband's Affairs; Sorrowful Jones; Miss Grant Takes Richmond;

Easy Living (1949); A Woman of Distinction (cameo); Fancy Pants; The Fuller Brush Girl; The Magic Carpet; The Long, Long Trailer; Forever, Darling; The Facts of Life; Critic's Choice

Bardot, Brigitte: Act of Love; Royal Affairs in Versailles; Doctor at Sea; Les Grandes Manoeuvres; School for Love; Helen of Troy; Mam'zelle Pigalle; Please! Mr. Balzac; . . .And God Created Woman; The Bride Is Much Too Beautiful; La Parisienne; The Night Heaven Fell; Babette Goes to War; Come Dance With Me!; The Testament of Orpheus; A Very Private Affair; Love on a Pillow; Contempt; Dear Brigitte (cameo); A Ravishing Idiot; Viva Maria!

Barrymore, John: Raffles, The Amateur Cracksman; Dr. Jekyll and Mr. Hyde (1920); Sherlock Holmes; Beau Brummell (1924); Don Juan; When a Man Loves (1927); The Beloved Rogue; Tempest (1928); Eternal Love; The Show of Shows; Moby Dick (1930); Svengali (1931); The Mad Genius; Arsene Lupin; Grand Hotel; A Bill of Divorcement (1932); State's Attorney; Rasputin and the Empress; Topaze (1933); Reunion in Vienna; Dinner at Eight; Night Flight; Counsellor at Law; Long Lost Father; Twentieth Century; Romeo and Juliet (1936); Maytime; Bulldog Drummond Comes Back; Night Club Scandal; True Confession; Bulldog Drummond's Revenge; Bulldog Drummond's Peril; Romance in the Dark; Spawn of the North; Marie Antoinette (1938); Hold That Co-Ed; The Great Man Votes; Midnight (1939); The Great Profile; The Invisible Woman; World Premiere; Playmates

Barrymore, Lionel: America; The Temptress; The Bells; The Show; Love; Sadie Thompson; West of Zanzibar; Free and Easy; A Free Soul; The Yellow Ticket; Mata Hari (1931); Guilty Hands; Broken Lullaby; Arsene Lupin; Grand Hotel; The Washingon Masquerade; Rasputin and the Empress; Sweepings; Looking Forward; Dinner at Eight; The Stranger's Return; Night Flight; One Man's Journey; Christopher Bean; Should Ladies Behave; Treasure Island (1934); The Girl from Missouri; Mark of the Vampire; The Little Colonel; Public Hero No. 1; The Return of Peter Grimm; David Copperfield; Ah, Wilderness!; The Voice of Bugle Ann; The Road to Glory; The Devil-Doll; The Gorgeous Hussy; Camille; A Family Affair; Captains Courageous; Saratoga; Navy Blue and Gold; A Yank at Oxford; Test Pilot; You Can't Take It With You; Young Dr. Kildare; Let Freedom Ring; Calling Dr. Kildare; On Borrowed Time; The Secret of Dr. Kildare; Dr. Kildare's Strange Case; Dr. Kildare Goes Home; Dr. Kildare's Crisis; The Bad Man; The Penalty; The People vs. Dr. Kildare; Lady Be Good; Dr. Kildare's Wedding Day; Dr. Kildare's Victory; Calling Dr.

Gillespie; Dr. Gillespie's New Assistant; Tennessee Johnson; Thousands Cheer; Dr. Gillespie's Criminal Case; A Guy Named Joe; Three Men in White; Dragon Seed (narr); Since You Went Away; The Valley of Decision; Between Two Women; Three Wise Fools; The Secret Heart; It's a Wonderful Life; Duel in the Sun; Dark Delusion; Key Largo; Down to the Sea in Ships; Malaya; Right Cross; Bannerline; Lone Star (1952); Main Street to Broadway

Bellamy, Ralph: The Secret Six; Surrender (1931); West of Broadway; Forbidden; Young America; Rebecca of Sunnybrook Farm; Wild Girl; Parole Girl; Picture Snatcher; The Narrow Corner; Blind Adventure; Headline Shooter; Ace of Aces; This Man Is Mine; Spitfire (1934); Girl in Danger; Rendezvous at Midnight; The Wedding Night; Air Hawks; Hands Across the Table; The Man Who Lived Twice; The Awful Truth; The Crime of Doctor Hallet; Fools for Scandal; Boy Meets Girl; Carefree; Girls' School; Trade Winds; Let Us Live; Blind Alley; Coast Guard; His Girl Friday; Brother Orchid; Queen of the Mob; Dance, Girl, Dance; Ellery Queen, Master Detective; Footsteps in the Dark; Ellery Queen's Penthouse Mystery; Affectionately Yours; Dive Bomber; Ellery Queen and the Perfect Crime; Ellery Queen and the Murder Ring; The Wolf Man; The Ghost of Frankenstein; Lady in a Jam; Guest in the House; Delightfully Dangerous; Lady on a Train; The Court-Martial of Billy Mitchell; Sunrise at Campobello

Bennett, Constance: Son of the Gods; Three Faces East; Sin Takes a Holiday; The Easiest Way; The Common Law; Bought!; Lady With a Past; What Price Hollywood?; Two Against the World (1936); Rockabye; Our Betters; Bed of Roses (1933); After Tonight; The Affairs of Cellini; After Office Hours; Ladies in Love; Topper; Merrily We Live; Service De Luxe; Topper Takes a Trip; Tail Spin; Escape to Glory; Law of the Tropics; Two-Faced Woman; Sin Town; Paris Underground; Centennial Summer; The Unsuspected; Smart Woman (1948); Angel on the Amazon; As Young as You Feel

Bergman, Ingrid: Swedenhielms; Intermezzo (1936); Intermezzo (1939); Rage in Heaven; Adam Had Four Sons; Dr. Jekyll and Mr. Hyde (1941); Casablanca; For Whom the Bell Tolls; Gaslight (1944); The Bells of St. Mary's; Spellbound (1945); Saratoga Trunk; Notorious; Arch of Triumph; Joan of Arc; Under Capricorn; Stromboli; The Greatest Love; Strangers (1954); Fear (1954); Paris Does Strange Things; Anastasia (1956); Indiscreet (1958); The Inn of the Sixth Happiness; Goodbye Again (1961); The Visit; The Yellow Rolls Royce

Bogarde, Dirk: Esther Waters; Quartet; So Long at the Fair; The Blue Lamp; The

Woman in Question; The Stranger in Between; Penny Princess; The Gentle Gunman; Desperate Moment; Appointment in London; The Sleeping Tiger; Doctor in the House; They Who Dare; The Sea Shall Not Have Them; For Better, For Worse; Doctor at Sea; Simba (1955); Cast a Dark Shadow; The Spanish Gardener; Campbell's Kingdom; Doctor at Large; Night Ambush; A Tale of Two Cities (1958); The Wind Cannot Read; The Doctor's Dilemma; Libel; Song Without End; The Angel Wore Red; The Singer Not the Song; Victim; Damn the Defiant!; The Mind Benders; The Password Is Courage; I Could Go on Singing; Doctor in Distress; The Servant; Agent 8¾; King & Country; McGuire, Go Home!; Darling

Bogart, Humphrey: Up the River; A Devil With Women; Bad Sister; A Holy Terror; Big City Blues; Love Affair (1932); Three on a Match; Midnight (1934); The Petrified Forest; Bullets or Ballots; Two Against the World (1936); China Clipper; Isle of Fury; Black Legion; The Great O'Malley; Marked Woman; Kid Galahad (1937); San Quentin (1937); Dead End; Stand-In; Swing Your Lady; Crime School; Men Are Such Fools; Racket Busters; The Amazing Doctor Clitterhouse; Angels With Dirty Faces; King of the Underworld; The Oklahoma Kid; Dark Victory; You Can't Get Away With Murder; The Roaring Twenties; The Return of Doctor X; Invisible Stripes; Virginia City; It All Came True; Brother Orchid; They Drive by Night; High Sierra; The Wagons Roll at Night; The Maltese Falcon (1941); Across the Pacific; In This Our Life; All Through the Night; The Big Shot; Casablanca; Action in the North Atlantic; Thank Your Lucky Stars (cameo); Sahara (1943); Passage to Marseille; To Have and Have Not; Conflict (1945); Two Guys from Milwaukee (cameo); The Big Sleep (1946); Dead Reckoning; The Two Mrs. Carrolls; Dark Passage; Always Together (cameo); The Treasure of the Sierra Madre; Key Largo; Knock on Any Door; Tokyo Joe; Chain Lightning; In a Lonely Place; The Enforcer (1951); Sirocco; The African Queen; Deadline U.S.A.; Battle Circus; Beat the Devil; The Love Lottery (cameo); The Caine Mutiny; Sabrina (1954); The Barefoot Contessa; We're No Angels (1955); The Left Hand of God; The Desperate Hours (1955); The Harder They Fall

Borgnine, Ernest: China Corsair; The Whistle at Eaton Falls; The Mob; From Here to Eternity; The Stranger Wore a Gun; Johnny Guitar; Demetrius and the Gladiators; The Bounty Hunter; Vera Cruz; Bad Day at Black Rock; Marty; Run for Cover; Violent Saturday; The Last Command (1955); The Square Jungle; Jubal; The Catered Affair; The Best Things in Life Are Free; Three Brave Men; The Vikings; The Badlanders; Torpedo Run; The Rabbit Trap;

Season of Passion; Man on a String; Pay or Die; Go Naked in the World; Barabbas; McHale's Navy; The Flight of the Phoenix (1965)

Bow, Clara: Down to the Sea in Ships; Parisian Love; The Primrose Path; Free to Love; The Plastic Age; My Lady of Whims; Dancing Mothers; Mantrap; it; Hula; Wings; The Wild Party (1929); The Saturday Night Kid; Paramount on Parade; True to the Navy; Love Among the Millionaires; No Limit; Call Her Savage; Hoopla

Boyd, William: Why Change Your Wife (bit); The Affairs of Anatol; The Volga Boatman; The Road to Yesterday; The Yankee Clipper; The King of Kings; High Voltage; His First Command; The Painted Desert; Beyond Victory; Suicide Fleet; Carnival Boat; Men of America; Lucky Devils; Emergency Call; Hop-Along Cassidy; The Eagle's Brood; Call of the Prairie; Three on the Trail; Hopalong Cassidy Returns; Trail Dust; Borderland; Hills of Old Wyoming; North of the Rio Grande; Rustler's Valley; Hopalong Rides Again; Texas Trail; Partners of the Plains; Cassidy of Bar 20; Heart of Arizona; Bar 20 Justice; Pride of the West; In Old Mexico; The Frontiersman; Sunset Trail; Silver on the Sage; The Renegade Trail; Range War; Law of the Pampas; Santa Fe Marshal; The Showdown; Hidden Gold; Stagecoach War; Three Men from Texas; Doomed Caravan; In Old Colorado; Border Vigilantes; Pirates on Horseback; Wide Open Town; Stick to Your Guns; Riders of the Timberline; Twilight on the Trail; Outlaws of the Desert; Secrets of the Wasteland; Undercover Man (1942); Lost Canyon; Hoppy Serves a Writ; Border Patrol; The Leather Burners; Colt Comrades; Bar 20; False Colors; Riders of the Deadline; Texas Masquerade; Lumberjack; Mystery Man; Forty Thieves; Fool's Gold; The Devil's Playground; Unexpected Guest; Dangerous Venture; The Marauders; Hoppy's Holiday; Silent Conflict; The Dead Don't Dream; Sinister Journey; Borrowed Trouble; False Paradise; Strange Gamble; The Greatest Show on Earth (cameo)

Boyer, Charles: Captain Fracasse; The Man From Yesterday; Red-Headed Woman; Liliom (1930); Caravan; Private Worlds; Break of Hearts; Shanghai; Mayerling (1936); The Garden of Allah; Tovarich; Conquest; History Is Made at Night; Algiers; Love Affair (1939); When Tomorrow Comes; All This, and Heaven Too; Back Street (1941); Hold Back the Dawn; Appointment for Love; Tales of Manhattan; The Heart of a Nation (app); The Constant Nymph; Flesh and Fantasy; Gaslight (1944); Together Again; Confidential Agent; Cluny Brown; A Woman's Vengeance; Arch of Triumph; The First Legion; Thunder in the East; The 13th Letter;

The Happy Time; The Earrings of Madame de . . .; The Cobweb; Around the World in Eighty Days (1956; cameo); La Parisienne; Lucky to Be a Woman; The Buccaneer (1958); Maxime; Fanny (1961); The Four Horsemen of the Apocalypse (1962); Adorable Julia; Love Is a Ball; A Very Special Favor

Brando, Marlon: The Men; A Streetcar Named Desire; Viva Zapata!; Julius Caesar (1953); The Wild One; On the Waterfront; Desiree; Guys and Dolls; The Teahouse of the August Moon; Sayonara; The Young Lions; The Fugitive Kind; One-Eyed Jacks (also dir); Mutiny on the Bounty (1962); The Ugly American; Bedtime Story (1964); Morituri

Bronson, Charles (*billed as Charles Buchinski or Buchinsky until* Drum Beat): You're in the Navy Now; The People Against O'Hara; The Mob; Red Skies of Montana; My Six Convicts; The Marrying Kind (bit); Pat and Mike; Diplomatic Courier; Bloodhounds of Broadway (1952); House of Wax (1953); The Clown; Miss Sadie Thompson; Crime Wave; Riding Shotgun; Apache; Vera Cruz; Drum Beat; Big House, U.S.A.; Jubal; Run of the Arrow; Machine-Gun Kelly; Gang War; Showdown at Boot Hill; When Hell Broke Loose; Never So Few; The Magnificent Seven; Master of the World; A Thunder of Drums; X-15; Kid Galahad (1962); The Great Escape; 4 for Texas; The Sandpiper; Battle of the Bulge

Brooks, Louise: It's the Old Army Game; The Show Off (1926); A Girl in Every Port (1928); Beggars of Life; Pandora's Box; The Canary Murder Case; Diary of a Lost Girl; Prix de Beauté; God's Gift to Women; When You're in Love; Overland Stage Raiders

Brown, Joe E.: On With the Show; Painted Faces; Sally; Top Speed; Maybe It's Love; The Lottery Bride; Sit Tight; Broadminded; Local Boy Makes Good; Fireman, Save My Child (1932); The Tenderfoot; You Said a Mouthful; Elmer, the Great; Son of a Sailor; A Very Honorable Guy; The Circus Clown; 6 Day Bike Rider; Alibi Ike; Bright Lights (1935); A Midsummer Night's Dream; Sons o' Guns; Polo Joe; Earthworm Tractors; When's Your Birthday?; Riding on Air; Fit for a King; Wide Open Faces; The Gladiator; Flirting With Fate; Beware Spooks!; So You Won't Talk; Shut My Big Mouth; Joan of Ozark; The Daring Young Man; Chatterbox; Casanova in Burlesque; Pin Up Girl; The Tender Years; Show Boat (1951); Around the World in Eighty Days (1956; cameo); Some Like It Hot (1959); It's a Mad Mad Mad Mad World; The Comedy of Terrors

Brynner, Yul: Port of New York; The King and I; The Ten Commandments (1956); Anastasia; The Brothers Karamazov; The

Buccaneer (1958); The Journey; Solomon and Sheba; The Testament of Orpheus (cameo); The Sound and the Fury; Once More, With Feeling; Surprise Package; The Magnificent Seven; Escape from Zahrain; Taras Bulba; Kings of the Sun; Flight from Ashiya; Invitation to a Gunfighter; Morituri

Burton, Richard: The Last Days of Dolwyn; Her Panelled Door; Green Grow the Rushes; My Cousin Rachel; The Desert Rats; The Robe; Demetrius and the Gladiators (cameo); Prince of Players; The Rains of Ranchipur; Alexander the Great; Sea Wife; Bitter Victory; Look Back in Anger; The Bramble Bush; Ice Palace; The Longest Day; Cleopatra (1963); The V.I.P.s; Zulu (narr); Becket; The Night of the Iguana; What's New Pussycat (cameo); The Sandpiper; The Spy Who Came In from the Cold

Cagney, James: Sinner's Holiday (1930); Doorway to Hell; Other Men's Women; The Millionaire; The Public Enemy; Smart Money; Blonde Crazy; Taxi!; The Crowd Roars (1932); Winner Take All; Hard to Handle; Lady Killer; Picture Snatcher; The Mayor of Hell; Footlight Parade; Jimmy the Gent; He Was Her Man; Here Comes the Navy; St. Louis Kid; Devil Dogs of the Air; "G" Men; The Irish in Us; Frisco Kid; A Midsummer Night's Dream (1935); Ceiling Zero; Great Guy; Something to Sing About; Boy Meets Girl; Angels With Dirty Faces; The Oklahoma Kid; Each Dawn I Die; The Roaring Twenties; The Fighting 69th; Torrid Zone; City for Conquest; The Strawberry Blonde; The Bride Came C.O.D.; Captains of the Clouds; Yankee Doodle Dandy; Johnny Come Lately; Blood on the Sun; 13 Rue Madeleine; The Time of Your Life; White Heat; Kiss Tomorrow Goodbye; West Point Story; Come Fill the Cup; Starlift (cameo); What Price Glory (1952); A Lion Is in the Streets; Run for Cover; The Seven Little Foys; Love Me or Leave Me; Mister Roberts; Tribute to a Bad Man; These Wilder Years; Man of a Thousand Faces; Short Cut to Hell (dir, app); Shake Hands With the Devil; Never Steal Anything Small; The Gallant Hours; One, Two, Three

Chaney, Lon: The Wicked Darling; Victory (1919); The Penalty (1920); The Ace of Hearts (1921); Shadows (1922); Oliver Twist (1922); The Hunchback of Notre Dame (1923); He Who Gets Slapped; The Monster; The Unholy Three (1925); The Phantom of the Opera (1925); Tell It to the Marines; The Unknown (1927); Mockery; Laugh, Clown, Laugh; West of Zanzibar; The Unholy Three (1930)

Chaney, Lon Jr.: Girl Crazy; Bird of Paradise; Lucky Devils; Scarlet River; Sixteen Fathoms Deep; The Life of Vergie Winters; Accent on Youth; The Singing Cowboy; The Old Corral; Love Is News; Charlie Chan at the Olympics; This Is My Affair;

Born Reckless; Thin Ice; Charlie Chan on Broadway; Life Begins in College; Slave Ship (bit); Wife, Doctor and Nurse; Happy Landing (bit); Sally, Irene and Mary (bit); Mr. Moto's Gamble; Alexander's Ragtime Band (bit); Josette; Straight Place and Show (bit); Submarine Patrol (bit); Jesse James; Union Pacific; Frontier Marshal; Charlie Chan in City in Darkness; Of Mice and Men; One Million B.C.; North West Mounted Police; Man Made Monster; Billy the Kid; San Antonio Rose; Badlands of Dakota; The Wolf Man; The Ghost of Frankenstein; The Mummy's Tomb; Eyes of the Underworld; Frankenstein Meets the Wolf Man; Crazy House (cameo); Son of Dracula; Calling Dr. Death; Weird Woman; Cobra Woman; Ghost Catchers; The Mummy's Ghost; Dead Man's Eyes; House of Frankenstein; The Mummy's Curse; Here Come the Co-Eds; The Frozen Ghost; Strange Confession; House of Dracula; Pillow of Death; My Favorite Brunette; Albuquerque; The Counterfeiters; Abbott and Costello Meet Frankenstein; 16 Fathoms Deep; Captain China; Once a Thief; Inside Straight; Only the Valiant; Behave Yourself; Bride of the Gorilla; Flame of Araby; The Bushwhackers; Thief of Damascus; High Noon; Springfield Rifle; The Black Castle; Raiders of the Seven Seas; A Lion Is in the Streets; Jivaro; The Boy From Oklahoma; Casanova's Big Night; Passion; The Black Pirates; Big House, U.S.A.; Not as a Stranger; I Died a Thousand Times; The Indian Fighter; Manfish; Indestructible Man; The Black Sleep; Pardners; Daniel Boone, Trail Blazer; The Cyclops; The Defiant Ones; Money, Women and Guns; The Alligator People; The Devil's Messenger; The Haunted Palace; Face of the Screaming Werewolf; Law of the Lawless; Stage to Thunder Rock; House of the Black Death; Spider Baby; Witchcraft; Young Fury; Black Spurs; Town Tamer

Chaplin, Charles (*features only*): Tillie's Punctured Romance; The Kid (also dir, scr); A Woman of Paris (dir, scr, cameo); The Gold Rush (also dir, scr); The Circus (also dir, scr); Show People (cameo); City Lights (also dir, scr); Modern Times (also dir, scr); The Great Dictator (also dir, scr); Monsieur Verdoux (also dir, scr, mus); Limelight (also dir, scr, mus); A King in New York (also dir, scr, mus)

Chevalier, Maurice: Innocents of Paris; The Love Parade; Paramount on Parade (cameo): The Big Pond; The Smiling Lieutenant; One Hour With You; Make Me a Star (cameo); Love Me Tonight; The Way to Love; A Bedtime Story (1933); The Way to Love; The Merry Widow (1934); Folies Bergère (1935); Pièges; Man About Town (1947); My Seven Little Sins; Love in the Afternoon; Gigi; Count Your Blessings; Can-Can; A Breath of Scandal; Pepe;

Black Tights (narr); Fanny (1961); Jessica; In Search of the Castaways; A New Kind of Love (cameo); Panic Button; I'd Rather Be Rich

Clift, Montgomery: The Search; Red River; The Heiress; The Big Lift; A Place in the Sun; I Confess; From Here to Eternity; Indiscretion of an American Wife; Raintree County; The Young Lions; Lonelyhearts; Suddenly, Last Summer; Wild River; The Misfits; Judgment at Nuremberg; Freud

Colbert, Claudette: The Hole in the Wall; The Big Pond; The Smiling Lieutenant; Secrets of a Secretary; His Woman; The Man From Yesterday; Make Me a Star (cameo); The Phantom President; The Sign of the Cross; Tonight Is Ours; I Cover the Waterfront; Three Cornered Moon; Torch Singer; Four Frightened People; It Happened One Night; Cleopatra (1934); Imitation of Life (1934); The Gilded Lily; Private Worlds; She Married Her Boss; The Bride Comes Home; Under Two Flags; Maid of Salem; Tovarich; I Met Him in Paris; Bluebeard's Eighth Wife; Zaza; Midnight (1939); Drums Along the Mohawk; It's a Wonderful World; Boom Town; Arise, My Love; Skylark (1941); Remember the Day; The Palm Beach Story; So Proudly We Hail!; No Time for Love; Since You Went Away; Practically Yours; Guest Wife; Tomorrow Is Forever; Without Reservations; The Secret Heart; The Egg and I; Sleep My Love; Family Honeymoon; Bride for Sale; Three Came Home; The Secret Fury; Thunder on the Hill; Let's Make It Legal; Outpost in Malaya; Daughters of Destiny; Royal Affairs in Versailles; Texas Lady; Parrish

Colman, Ronald: The White Sister (1923); Her Night of Romance; Her Sister from Paris; Lady Windermere's Fan; Kiki; The Winning of Barbara Worth; Bulldog Drummond; Condemned; Raffles (1930); The Devil to Pay!; The Unholy Garden; Arrowsmith; Cynara; The Masquerader; Clive of India; The Man Who Broke the Bank at Monte Carlo; A Tale of Two Cities (1935); Under Two Flags; Lost Horizon (1937); The Prisoner of Zenda (1937); If I Were King; The Light That Failed; Lucky Partners; My Life with Caroline; The Talk of the Town; Random Harvest; Kismet (1944); The Late George Apley (1947); A Double Life; Champagne for Caesar (1950); Around the World in Eighty Days (cameo); The Story of Mankind

Cooper, Gary: The Eagle (bit); Old Ironsides (bit); The Winning of Barbara Worth; Wings; It; Lilac Time; The Virginian (1929); Paramount on Parade; Morocco; Fighting Caravans; City Streets (1931); His Woman; Make Me a Star (cameo); The Devil and the Deep; If I Had a Million; A Farewell to Arms (1932); Today We Live; Design for Living; Alice in Wonderland (1933); One Sunday Afternoon (1933); Operator 13;

Now and Forever (1934); The Wedding Night; The Lives of a Bengal Lancer; Peter Ibbetson; Desire; Hollywood Boulevard (1936; cameo); Mr. Deeds Goes to Town; The General Died at Dawn; The Plainsman (1936); Souls at Sea; The Adventures of Marco Polo; Bluebeard's Eighth Wife; The Cowboy and the Lady; Beau Geste (1939); The Real Glory; The Westerner; North West Mounted Police; Meet John Doe; Sergeant York; Ball of Fire; The Pride of the Yankees; For Whom the Bell Tolls; The Story of Dr. Wassell; Casanova Brown; Along Came Jones; Saratoga Trunk; Cloak and Dagger (1946); Variety Girl (cameo); Unconquered; Good Sam; The Fountainhead; It's a Great Feeling (cameo); Task Force; Bright Leaf; Dallas; You're in the Navy Now; Starlift (cameo); It's a Big Country; Distant Drums; High Noon; Springfield Rifle; Return to Paradise; Blowing Wild; Vera Cruz; Garden of Evil; The Court-Martial of Billy Mitchell; Friendly Persuasion; Love in the Afternoon; Ten North Frederick; Man of the West; The Hanging Tree; Alias Jesse James (cameo); They Came to Cordura; The Wreck of the Mary Deare; The Naked Edge

Cotten, Joseph: Citizen Kane; Lydia; The Magnificent Ambersons; Shadow of a Doubt; Journey Into Fear (1943; also coscr); Hers to Hold; Gaslight (1944); Since You Went Away; I'll Be Seeing You; Love Letters (1945); Duel in the Sun; The Farmer's Daughter (1947); Portrait of Jennie; The Third Man; Under Capricorn; Beyond the Forest; Two Flags West; Walk Softly, Stranger; September Affair; Half Angel; Peking Express; The Man With a Cloak; The Wild Heart (narr); Untamed Frontier; The Steel Trap; Othello (uncred); A Blueprint for Murder; Special Delivery; The Bottom of the Bottle; The Killer Is Loose; The Halliday Brand; Touch of Evil (uncred); From the Earth to the Moon; The Angel Wore Red; The Last Sunset; Hush... Hush, Sweet Charlotte

Crawford, Broderick: Woman Chases Man; Start Cheering; Ambush (1939); Undercover Doctor; Beau Geste (1939); Island of Lost Men; The Real Glory; Eternally Yours; Slightly Honorable; When the Daltons Rode; Seven Sinners; Trail of the Vigilantes; The Black Cat (1941); Tight Shoes; Badlands of Dakota; Larceny, Inc.; Broadway (1942); Sin Town; The Runaround; Black Angel; Slave Girl; The Flame; The Time of Your Life; Sealed Verdict; A Kiss in the Dark; Night Unto Night; Anna Lucasta (1949); All the King's Men (1949); Cargo to Capetown; Convicted; Born Yesterday (1950); The Mob: Scandal Sheet (1952); Lone Star (1952); Stop, You're Killing Me; Last of the Comanches; The Last Posse; Night People; Human Desire; Down Three Dark Streets; New York Confidential; Big House, U.S.A. (1955); Not as a Stranger;

The Swindle (1955); The Fastest Gun Alive; Between Heaven and Hell; The Decks Ran Red; Goliath and the Dragon; Convicts 4; A House Is Not a Home; Up From the Beach

Crawford, Joan: Tramp, Tramp, Tramp; The Boob; The Unknown (1927); Spring Fever; West Point; Across to Singapore; Our Dancing Daughters; Our Modern Maidens; Untamed (1929); Hollywood Revue of 1929; Montana Moon; Our Blushing Brides; Paid; Dance, Fools, Dance; Laughing Sinners; This Modern Age; Possessed (1931); Grand Hotel; Letty Lynton; Rain (1932); Today We Live; Dancing Lady; Sadie McKee; Forsaking All Others; Chained; No More Ladies; I Live My Life; The Gorgeous Hussy; Love on the Run (1936); The Last of Mrs. Cheyney (1937); The Bride Wore Red; Mannequin (1937); The Shining Hour; Ice Follies of 1939; The Women; Strange Cargo; Susan and God; When Ladies Meet (1941); A Woman's Face; They All Kissed the Bride; Reunion in France; Above Suspicion; Hollywood Canteen; Mildred Pierce; Humoresque; Possessed (1947); Daisy Kenyon; Flamingo Road; It's a Great Feeling (cameo); The Damned Don't Cry; Harriet Craig; Goodbye, My Fancy; This Woman Is Dangerous; Sudden Fear; Torch Song; Johnny Guitar; Female on the Beach; Queen Bee; Autumn Leaves; The Story of Esther Costello; The Best of Everything; What Ever Happened to Baby Jane?; The Caretakers; Strait-Jacket; I Saw What You Did

Crosby, Bing: King of Jazz; Reaching for the Moon; The Big Broadcast; College Humor; Too Much Harmony; Going Hollywood; We're Not Dressing; Here Is My Heart; She Loves Me Not; Mississippi; Two for Tonight; The Big Broadcast of 1936; Anything Goes (1936); Rhythm on the Range; Pennies from Heaven (1936); Waikiki Wedding; Double or Nothing; Sing, You Sinners; Doctor Rhythm; Paris Honeymoon; The Star Maker (1939); East Side of Heaven; Rhythm on the River (1940); Road to Singapore; If I Had My Way; Birth of the Blues; Road to Zanzibar; My Favorite Blonde (cameo); Holiday Inn; Road to Morocco; Star Spangled Rhythm; Dixie; The Princess and the Pirate (cameo); Going My Way; Here Come the Waves; Out of This World (voice); Road to Utopia; Duffy's Tavern; The Bells of St. Mary's; Blue Skies; Welcome Stranger; My Favorite Brunette (cameo); Road to Rio; Variety Girl (cameo); The Emperor Waltz; A Connecticut Yankee in King Arthur's Court; The Adventures of Ichabod and Mr. Toad (narr); Top o' the Morning; Riding High (1950); Mr. Music; Here Comes the Groom; Angels in the Outfield (1951; cameo); The Greatest Show on Earth (cameo); Son of Paleface (cameo); Just for You; Road to Bali; Little Boy Lost;

Scared Stiff (1953; cameo); White Christmas; The Country Girl; Anything Goes (1956); High Society (1956); Man on Fire (1957); Alias Jesse James (cameo); Say One for Me; Let's Make Love (cameo); High Time; Pepe (cameo); The Road to Hong Kong; Robin and the 7 Hoods

Curtis, Tony: Criss Cross; City Across the River; The Lady Gambles; Johnny Stool Pigeon; Woman in Hiding (voice); Francis; I Was a Shoplifter; Winchester '73; Sierra; Kansas Raiders; The Prince Who Was a Thief; Son of Ali Baba; Flesh and Fury; No Room for the Groom; Meet Danny Wilson (cameo); Houdini; All American; Forbidden (1953); Beachhead; Johnny Dark; The Black Shield of Falworth; So This Is Paris (1954); Six Bridges to Cross; The Purple Mask; The Square Jungle; Trapeze; The Rawhide Years; Mister Cory; The Sweet Smell of Success; The Midnight Story; The Vikings; Kings Go Forth; The Defiant Ones; The Perfect Furlough; Some Like It Hot (1959); Operation Petticoat; Pepe (cameo); Who Was That Lady?; The Rat Race (1960); Spartacus; The Great Impostor; The Outsider (1961); Taras Bulba; 40 Pounds of Trouble; The List of Adrian Messenger (cameo); Captain Newman, M.D.; Wild and Wonderful; Goodbye Charlie; Sex and the Single Girl; The Great Race; Boeing Boeing

Cushing, Peter: The Man in the Iron Mask (1939; bit); A Chump at Oxford; Vigil in the Night; The Howards of Virginia (bit); They Dare Not Love (bit); Hamlet (1948); Moulin Rouge (1952); The Black Knight; The End of the Affair (1955); Alexander the Great; Time Without Pity; The Curse of Frankenstein; The Abominable Snowman of the Himalayas; Horror of Dracula; The Revenge of Frankenstein; John Paul Jones; The Hound of the Baskervilles (1959); The Mummy (1959); Mania; The Risk; The Brides of Dracula; Sword of Sherwood Forest; Night Creatures; The Hellfire Club; Fury at Smugglers' Bay; The Naked Edge; The Man Who Finally Died; The Evil of Frankenstein; The Gorgon; Dr. Terror's House of Horrors; She (1965); The Skull; Dr. Who and the Daleks

Darnell, Linda: Hotel for Women; Day-Time Wife; Star Dust; Brigham Young—Frontiersman; The Mark of Zorro; Blood and Sand; Rise and Shine; The Loves of Edgar Allan Poe; City Without Men; The Song of Bernadette (uncred); Buffalo Bill; It Happened Tomorrow; Summer Storm; Sweet and Low-Down; Hangover Square; The Great John L.; Fallen Angel; Anna and the King of Siam; Centennial Summer; My Darling Clementine; Forever Amber; The Walls of Jericho; Unfaithfully Yours (1948); A Letter to Three Wives; Slattery's Hurricane; Everybody Does It; No Way Out (1950); Two Flags West; The 13th Letter;

The Guy Who Came Back; The Lady Pays Off; Island of Desire; Night Without Sleep; Blackbeard, the Pirate; Second Chance; Angels of Darkness; This Is My Love; Dakota Incident; Zero Hour!; Black Spurs

Davis, Bette: Bad Sister; Waterloo Bridge (1931); Hell's House; The Dark Horse; The Menace; The Man Who Played God; The Rich Are Always With Us; Cabin in the Cotton; Three on a Match; 20,000 Years in Sing Sing; Parachute Jumper; Ex-Lady; The Working Man; Bureau of Missing Persons; Fashions; The Big Shakedown; Jimmy the Gent; Fog Over Frisco; Housewife; Of Human Bondage (1934); Bordertown; Front Page Woman; Special Agent; Dangerous; The Girl from 10th Avenue; The Golden Arrow; The Petrified Forest; Satan Met a Lady; Kid Galahad (1937); Marked Woman; That Certain Woman; It's Love I'm After; Jezebel; The Sisters; The Private Lives of Elizabeth and Essex; Dark Victory; Juarez; The Old Maid; All This, and Heaven Too; The Letter (1940); The Little Foxes; The Great Lie; Shining Victory (cameo); The Bride Came C.O.D.; The Man Who Came to Dinner; In This Our Life; Now, Voyager; Watch on the Rhine; Thank Your Lucky Stars; Old Acquaintance; Mr. Skeffington; Hollywood Canteen; The Corn Is Green; Deception (1946); A Stolen Life; Winter Meeting; June Bride; Beyond the Forest; All About Eve; Another Man's Poison; Payment on Demand; Phone Call from a Stranger; The Star; The Virgin Queen; The Catered Affair; Storm Center; The Scapegoat; John Paul Jones; Pocketful of Miracles; What Ever Happened to Baby Jane?; The Empty Canvas; Dead Ringer; Where Love Has Gone; Hush . . . Hush, Sweet Charlotte; The Nanny

Day, Doris: Romance on the High Seas; My Dream Is Yours; It's a Great Feeling; Young Man with a Horn; West Point Story; Tea for Two; Storm Warning; Lullaby of Broadway; Starlift; On Moonlight Bay; I'll See You in My Dreams; The Winning Team; April in Paris; By the Light of the Silvery Moon; Calamity Jane; Lucky Me; Young at Heart; Love Me or Leave Me; Julie; The Man Who Knew Too Much (1956); The Pajama Game; Teacher's Pet (1958); The Tunnel of Love; It Happened to Jane; Pillow Talk; Midnight Lace; Please Don't Eat the Daisies; Lover Come Back (1961); That Touch of Mink; Billy Rose's Jumbo; The Thrill of It All; Move Over, Darling; Send Me No Flowers; Do Not Disturb

Dean, James: Fixed Bayonets (bit); Sailor Beware (bit); Deadline U.S.A. (bit); Has Anybody Seen My Gal? (bit); East of Eden; Rebel Without a Cause; Giant

de Havilland, Olivia: A Midsummer Night's Dream (1935); Alibi Ike; The Irish in Us; Captain Blood (1935); Anthony Adverse; The Charge of the Light Brigade (1936); Call It a Day; The Great Garrick;

It's Love I'm After; Gold Is Where You Find It; The Adventures of Robin Hood; Four's a Crowd; Hard to Get; Wings of the Navy; Dodge City; The Private Lives of Elizabeth and Essex; Gone With the Wind; Raffles (1940); My Love Came Back; Santa Fe Trail; Strawberry Blonde; Hold Back the Dawn; They Died with Their Boots On; The Male Animal; In This Our Life; Thank Your Lucky Stars (cameo); Princess O'Rourke; Government Girl; Devotion; The Well-Groomed Bride; To Each His Own; The Dark Mirror; The Snake Pit; The Heiress; My Cousin Rachel; That Lady; Not as a Stranger; The Ambassador's Daughter; The Proud Rebel; Libel; Light in the Piazza; Lady in a Cage; Hush . . . Hush, Sweet Charlotte

Dietrich, Marlene: The Joyless Street (extra); Ship of Lost Men; The Blue Angel (1930); Morocco; Dishonored; Shanghai Express; Blonde Venus; The Song of Songs; The Scarlet Empress; The Devil Is a Woman (1935); Desire; The Garden of Allah; Knight Without Armour; Angel (1937); Destry Rides Again; Seven Sinners; The Flame of New Orleans; Manpower; The Lady Is Willing; The Spoilers (1942); Pittsburgh; Follow the Boys (1944); Kismet (1944); Golden Earrings; A Foreign Affair; Jigsaw (1949; cameo); Stage Fright; No Highway in the Sky; Rancho Notorious; Around the World in Eighty Days (1956; cameo); The Montecarlo Story; Witness for the Prosecution; Touch of Evil (cameo); Judgment at Nuremberg; Black Fox (narr); Paris—When It Sizzles (cameo)

Douglas, Kirk: The Strange Love of Martha Ivers; I Walk Alone; Out of the Past; Mourning Becomes Electra; My Dear Secretary; The Walls of Jericho; A Letter to Three Wives; Champion; Young Man with a Horn; The Glass Menagerie (1950); Along the Great Divide; Ace in the Hole; Detective Story; The Big Sky; The Big Trees; The Bad and the Beautiful; The Story of Three Loves; The Juggler; Act of Love; 20000 Leagues Under the Sea; Ulysses (1954); The Racers; Man Without a Star; The Indian Fighter; Lust for Life; Top Secret Affair; Gunfight at the O.K. Corral; Paths of Glory; The Vikings; Last Train from Gun Hill; The Devil's Disciple; Strangers When We Meet; Spartacus; Town Without Pity; The Last Sunset; Lonely Are the Brave; Two Weeks in Another Town; The Hook (1963); The List of Adrian Messenger; For Love or Money (1963); Seven Days in May; In Harm's Way; The Heroes of Telemark

Douglas, Melvyn: Tonight or Never; Prestige; The Old Dark House; As You Desire Me; The Vampire Bat; Counsellor at Law; Dangerous Corner; Mary Burns, Fugitive; She Married Her Boss; Annie Oakley; The Lone Wolf Returns; And So They Were Married (1936); The Gorgeous Hussy; Theodora

Goes Wild; Captains Courageous; I Met Him in Paris; I'll Take Romance; Arsène Lupin Returns; There's Always a Woman; The Toy Wife; Fast Company; The Shining Hour; That Certain Age; Good Girls Go to Paris; Tell No Tales; Ninotchka; The Amazing Mr. Williams; Too Many Husbands; Third Finger, Left Hand; He Stayed for Breakfast; Two-Faced Woman; That Uncertain Feeling; This Thing Called Love; A Woman's Face; They All Kissed the Bride; We Were Dancing; Three Hearts for Julia; The Guilt of Janet Ames; Sea of Grass; Mr. Blandings Builds His Dream House; My Own True Love; A Woman's Secret; The Great Sinner; My Forbidden Past; On the Loose; Billy Budd; Hud; Advance to the Rear; The Americanization of Emily; Rapture

Dunne, Irene: Cimarron (1931); Bachelor Apartment; Consolation Marriage; Symphony of Six Million; Back Street (1932); Thirteen Women; No Other Woman; The Secret of Madame Blanche; The Silver Cord; Ann Vickers; If I Were Free; This Man Is Mine; Stingaree; The Age of Innocence (1934); Sweet Adeline; Roberta; Magnificent Obsession (1935); Show Boat (1936); Theodora Goes Wild; High, Wide, and Handsome; The Awful Truth; Joy of Living; Love Affair (1939); Invitation to Happiness; When Tomorrow Comes; My Favorite Wife; Penny Serenade; Unfinished Business (1941); Lady in a Jam; A Guy Named Joe; The White Cliffs of Dover; Together Again; Over 21; Anna and the King of Siam; Life with Father; I Remember Mama; Never a Dull Moment (1950); The Mudlark; It Grows on Trees

Durbin, Deanna: Three Smart Girls; One Hundred Men and a Girl; That Certain Age; Mad About Music; Three Smart Girls Grow Up; First Love (1939); Spring Parade; It's a Date; Nice Girl?; It Started with Eve; The Amazing Mrs. Holiday; Hers to Hold; His Butler's Sister; Christmas Holiday; Can't Help Singing; Lady on a Train; Because of Him; I'll Be Yours; Something in the Wind; Up in Central Park; For the Love of Mary

Eastwood, Clint: Revenge of the Creature (bit); Francis in the Navy; Lady Godiva (bit); Tarantula (bit); Never Say Goodbye (bit); Star in the Dust (bit); The First Traveling Saleslady; Away All Boats (bit); Escapade in Japan (bit); Lafayette Escadrille; Ambush at Cimarron Pass; Fistful of Dollars; For a Few Dollars More

Eddy, Nelson: Broadway to Hollywood (uncred); Student Tour; Naughty Marietta; Rose-Marie; Rosalie; The Girl of the Golden West; Sweethearts; Let Freedom Ring; Balalaika; New Moon; Bitter Sweet; The Chocolate Soldier; I Married an Angel; Phantom of the Opera; Knickerbocker Holiday; Make Mine Music (voice); Northwest Outpost

Fairbanks, Douglas: His Picture in the

Papers; The Mystery of the Leaping Fish; Intolerance (cameo); The Matrimaniac; Reaching for the Moon (1917); A Modern Musketeer; When the Clouds Roll By; The Mollycoddle; The Mark of Zorro (1920); The Nut (also coscr, prod); The Three Musketeers (1921); Robin Hood (also sty); The Thief of Bagdad (1924); Don Q, Son of Zorro; The Black Pirate; The Gaucho; Show People (cameo); The Iron Mask; The Taming of the Shrew (1929); Reaching for the Moon (1931); Mr. Robinson Crusoe; The Private Life of Don Juan; Ali Baba Goes to Town (cameo)

Fairbanks, Douglas Jr.: The Three Musketeers (1921; uncred); A Woman of Affairs; Our Modern Maidens; The Show of Shows; Loose Ankles; The Dawn Patrol (1930); Outward Bound; One Night at Susie's; Little Caesar; Chances; I Like Your Nerve; Union Depot; It's Tough to Be Famous; Love Is a Racket; Scarlet Dawn; Parachute Jumper; The Life of Jimmy Dolan; The Narrow Corner; Morning Glory; Captured; Catherine the Great; Success at Any Price; Mimi; Man of the Moment; Jump for Glory; The Prisoner of Zenda (1937); Joy of Living; The Rage of Paris; Having Wonderful Time; The Young in Heart; Gunga Din; The Sun Never Sets; Rulers of the Sea; Green Hell; Safari; Angels Over Broadway; The Corsican Brothers; Sinbad the Sailor; The Exile; The Fighting O'Flynn (also coscr); State Secret; Mister Drake's Duck

Faye, Alice: George White's Scandals (1934); 365 Nights in Hollywood; George White's Scandals (1935); Music Is Magic; Every Night at Eight; Poor Little Rich Girl; Sing, Baby, Sing; King of Burlesque; Stowaway; On the Avenue; Wake Up and Live; You Can't Have Everything; You're a Sweetheart; In Old Chicago; Sally, Irene and Mary; Alexander's Ragtime Band; Tail Spin; Hollywood Cavalcade; Barricade (1939); Rose of Washington Square; Lillian Russell; Little Old New York; Tin Pan Alley; That Night in Rio; The Great American Broadcast; Weekend in Havana; Hello Frisco, Hello; The Gang's All Here; Four Jills in a Jeep; Fallen Angel (1945); State Fair (1962)

Fields, W. C.: Sally of the Sawdust; It's the Old Army Game; Running Wild (1927); Her Majesty, Love; If I Had a Million; Million Dollar Legs (1932); International House; Tillie and Gus; Alice in Wonderland (1933); Six of a Kind; You're Telling Me! (1934); The Old Fashioned Way (also sty, as Charles Bogle); It's a Gift (also sty, as Charles Bogle); Mrs. Wiggs of the Cabbage Patch; David Copperfield (1935); Mississippi; The Man on the Flying Trapeze (also costy, as Charles Bogle); Poppy; The Big Broadcast of 1938; You Can't Cheat an Honest Man (also sty, as Charles Bogle);

My Little Chickadee (also coscr); The Bank Dick (also scr, as Mahatma Kane Jeeves); Never Give a Sucker an Even Break (also sty, as Otis Criblecoblis); Tales of Manhattan; Follow the Boys (1944); Song of the Open Road; Sensations of 1945

Flynn, Errol: In The Wake of the Bounty; The Case of the Curious Bride; Don't Bet on Blondes; Captain Blood (1935); The Charge of the Light Brigade (1936); Green Light; The Prince and the Pauper (1937); Another Dawn; The Perfect Specimen; The Adventures of Robin Hood; The Sisters; Four's a Crowd; The Dawn Patrol (1938); Dodge City; The Private Lives of Elizabeth and Essex; Virginia City; The Sea Hawk (1940); Santa Fe Trail; Footsteps in the Dark; Dive Bomber; They Died With Their Boots On; Desperate Journey; Gentleman Jim; Edge of Darkness; Thank Your Lucky Stars (cameo); Northern Pursuit; Uncertain Glory; Objective, Burma!; San Antonio; Never Say Goodbye (1946); Cry Wolf; Escape Me Never; Silver River; Adventures of Don Juan; It's a Great Feeling (cameo); That Forsyte Woman; Montana (1950); Rocky Mountain; Kim (1950); Adventures of Captain Fabian; Mara Maru; Against All Flags; The Master of Ballantrae (1953); Crossed Swords (1954); Let's Make Up; The Warriors (1955); Istanbul (1957); The Big Boodle; The Sun Also Rises; Too Much, Too Soon; The Roots of Heaven; Cuban Rebel Girls

Fonda, Henry: The Farmer Takes a Wife (1935); Way Down East (1935); I Dream Too Much; The Trail of the Lonesome Pine; The Moon's Our Home; Slim; Wings of the Morning; That Certain Woman; You Only Live Once; Blockade; I Met My Love Again; The Mad Miss Manton; Jezebel; Spawn of the North; Jesse James; The Story of Alexander Graham Bell; Let Us Live; Drums Along the Mohawk; Young Mr. Lincoln; The Grapes of Wrath; The Return of Frank James; Lillian Russell; Chad Hanna; The Lady Eve; Wild Geese Calling; You Belong to Me; Rings on Her Fingers; The Male Animal; The Magnificent Dope; The Big Street; Tales of Manhattan; The Ox-Bow Incident; The Immortal Sergeant; My Darling Clementine; The Fugitive (1947); Daisy Kenyon; The Long Night; Fort Apache; On Our Merry Way; Jigsaw (1949; cameo); Mister Roberts; War and Peace (1956); The Wrong Man; 12 Angry Men (1957); The Tin Star; Stage Struck (1958); Warlock (1959); The Man Who Understood Women; Advise & Consent; The Longest Day; How the West Was Won; Spencer's Mountain; The Best Man; Fail-Safe; Sex and the Single Girl; The Rounders (1965); In Harm's Way; Battle of the Bulge; The Dirty Game

Fontaine, Joan: No More Ladies; A Million to One; Quality Street; The Man Who Found Himself; You Can't Beat Love;

Music for Madame; A Damsel in Distress; Maid's Night Out; Blond Cheat; Gunga Din; Man of Conquest; The Women (1939); Rebecca; Suspicion; This Above All; The Constant Nymph; Jane Eyre (1944); Frenchman's Creek; The Affairs of Susan; From This Day Forward; Ivy; Letter from an Unknown Woman; Kiss the Blood Off My Hands; The Emperor Waltz; You Gotta Stay Happy; Born to Be Bad; September Affair; Darling, How Could You!; Othello (1952; cameo); Something to Live For; Ivanhoe (1952); Decameron Nights; Flight to Tangier; The Bigamist; Casanova's Big Night; Serenade; Beyond a Reasonable Doubt; Island in the Sun; Until They Sail; A Certain Smile; Voyage to the Bottom of the Sea; Tender Is the Night

Ford, Glenn: Heaven with a Barbed Wire Fence; Convicted Woman; Men Without Souls; Blondie Plays Cupid; The Lady in Question; Texas; So Ends Our Night; Go West, Young Lady; The Adventures of Martin Eden; Flight Lieutenant; Destroyer; Desperadoes; Gilda; A Stolen Life; Gallant Journey; Framed (1947); The Mating of Millie; The Loves of Carmen; The Return of October; The Man from Colorado; The Undercover Man (1949); Lust for Gold; Mr. Soft Touch; The Doctor and the Girl; The White Tower; Convicted; The Flying Missile; The Redhead and the Cowboy; Follow the Sun; The Secret of Convict Lake; Young Man with Ideas; The Green Glove; Affair in Trinidad; The Man from the Alamo; Terror on a Train; Plunder of the Sun; The Big Heat; Appointment in Honduras; Human Desire; The Americano; The Violent Men; Interrupted Melody; Blackboard Jungle; Trial; Ransom! (1956); Jubal; The Fastest Gun Alive; The Teahouse of the August Moon; 3:10 to Yuma (1957); Don't Go Near the Water; The Sheepman; Cowboy; Torpedo Run; Imitation General; It Started With a Kiss; The Gazebo; Cimarron (1960); Cry for Happy; Pocketful of Miracles; The Four Horsemen of the Apocalypse (1962); Experiment in Terror; The Courtship of Eddie's Father; Love Is a Ball; Advance to the Rear; Fate Is the Hunter; Dear Heart; The Rounders (1965)

Gabin, Jean: Zouzou; The Lower Depths (1936); Pépé Le Moko; Grand Illusion; Port of Shadows; La Bête Humaine; Le Jour Se Lève; Remorques; Moontide; The Impostor (1944); Le Plaisir; Touchez Pas au Grisbi; French Cancan; Deadlier Than the Male; La Traversée de Paris; Crime and Punishment (1956); The Case of Dr. Laurent; Inspector Maigret; Les Misérables (1958); Any Number Can Win

Gable, Clark: The Merry Widow (1925; extra); The Plastic Age (bit); The Johnstown Flood (bit); The Painted Desert; The Easiest Way; Dance, Fools, Dance; The Finger Points; The Secret Six; Laughing Sinners; A Free Soul; Night Nurse; Sporting Blood;

Susan Lenox: Her Fall and Rise; Possessed (1931); Hell Divers (1932); Polly of the Circus; Red Dust (1932); No Man of Her Own (1932); Strange Interlude; The White Sister; Hold Your Man; Night Flight; Dancing Lady; It Happened One Night; Men in White; Manhattan Melodrama; Chained; Forsaking All Others; After Office Hours; China Seas; The Call of the Wild (1935); Mutiny on the Bounty (1935); Wife vs. Secretary; San Francisco; Cain and Mabel; Love on the Run (1936); Parnell; Saratoga; Test Pilot; Too Hot to Handle (1938); Idiot's Delight; Gone With the Wind; Strange Cargo; Boom Town; Comrade X; They Met in Bombay; Honky Tonk; Somewhere I'll Find You; Adventure; The Hucksters; Homecoming; Command Decision; Any Number Can Play; Key to the City; To Please a Lady; Across the Wide Missouri; Callaway Went Thataway (cameo); Lone Star (1952); Never Let Me Go; Mogambo; Betrayed (1954); Soldier of Fortune; The Tall Men; The King and Four Queens; Band of Angels; Run Silent, Run Deep; Teacher's Pet (1958); But Not for Me; It Started in Naples; The Misfits

Garbo, Greta: The Atonement of Gosta Berling; The Joyless Street; Torrent; The Temptress; Flesh and the Devil; Love; The Mysterious Lady; A Woman of Affairs; The Kiss (1929); Wild Orchids; The Single Standard; Anna Christie; Anna Christie (German-language); Romance; Susan Lenox: Her Fall and Rise; Inspiration; Mata Hari (1932); Grand Hotel; As You Desire Me; Queen Christina; The Painted Veil (1934); Anna Karenina (1935); Camille; Conquest; Ninotchka; Two-Faced Woman

Gardner, Ava: Shadow of the Thin Man (bit); H.M. Pulham, Esq. (bit); Babes on Broadway (bit); This Time for Keeps (bit); We Were Dancing; Joe Smith, American; Kid Glove Killer; Calling Dr. Gillespie; Reunion in France; Sunday Punch (bit); Pilot #5 (bit); Lost Angel; DuBarry Was a Lady (bit); Ghosts on the Loose; Young Ideas; Hitler's Madman; Swing Fever; Two Girls and a Sailor; Three Men in White; Blonde Fever; Maisie Goes to Reno; Music for Millions; She Went to the Races; The Killers (1946); Whistle Stop; The Hucksters; Singapore; This Time for Keeps (1947; cameo); One Touch of Venus; The Bribe; East Side, West Side; The Great Sinner; My Forbidden Past; Pandora and the Flying Dutchman; Show Boat (1951); Lone Star (1952); The Snows of Kilimanjaro; Ride, Vaquero!; The Band Wagon (cameo); Mogambo; Knights of the Round Table; The Barefoot Contessa; Bhowani Junction; The Little Hut; The Sun Also Rises; The Naked Maja; On the Beach; The Angel Wore Red; 55 Days at Peking; Seven Days in May; The Night of the Iguana

Garfield, John: Four Daughters; Blackwell's Island; Juarez; They Made Me a

Criminal; Daughters Courageous; Dust Be My Destiny; Saturday's Children; Flowing Gold; East of the River; Castle on the Hudson; The Sea Wolf (1941); Out of the Fog; Tortilla Flat; Dangerously They Live; Air Force; Destination Tokyo; Thank Your Lucky Stars; The Fallen Sparrow; Between Two Worlds; Hollywood Canteen; Pride of the Marines; The Postman Always Rings Twice (1946); Nobody Lives Forever; Humoresque; Daisy Kenyon; Body and Soul (1947); Gentleman's Agreement; Force of Evil; We Were Strangers; Jigsaw (1949; cameo); Under My Skin; The Breaking Point; He Ran All the Way

Garland, Judy: Pigskin Parade; Thoroughbreds Don't Cry; Broadway Melody of 1938; Everybody Sing; Listen, Darling; Love Finds Andy Hardy; Babes in Arms; The Wizard of Oz (1939); Andy Hardy Meets Debutante; Little Nellie Kelly; Strike Up the Band; Babes on Broadway; Life Begins for Andy Hardy; Ziegfeld Girl; For Me and My Gal; Girl Crazy (1943); Presenting Lily Mars; Thousands Cheer; Meet Me in St. Louis; The Clock; The Harvey Girls; Till the Clouds Roll By; Ziegfeld Follies; Easter Parade; The Pirate; Words and Music; In the Good Old Summertime; Summer Stock; A Star Is Born (1954); Pepe (voice); Judgment at Nuremberg; Gay Purr-ee (voice); A Child Is Waiting; I Could Go On Singing

Garner, James: The Girl He Left Behind; Toward the Unknown; Shoot-Out at Medicine Bend; Sayonara; Darby's Rangers; Up Periscope; Cash McCall; The Children's Hour; Boys' Night Out; The Great Escape; The Thrill of It All; The Wheeler Dealers; Move Over, Darling; The Americanization of Emily; 36 Hours; The Art of Love

Garson, Greer: Goodbye, Mr. Chips (1939); Remember?; Pride and Prejudice (1940); Blossoms in the Dust; When Ladies Meet (1941); Mrs. Miniver; Random Harvest; Madame Curie; The Youngest Profession; Mrs. Parkington; Adventure; The Valley of Decision; Desire Me; Julia Misbehaves; That Forsyte Woman; The Miniver Story; The Law and the Lady; Julius Caesar (1953); Scandal at Scourie; Her Twelve Men; Strange Lady in Town; Pepe (cameo); Sunrise at Campobello

Gaynor, Janet: The Plastic Age (bit); The Johnstown Flood; The Shamrock Handicap; Seventh Heaven; Sunrise; Street Angel; Lucky Star; Sunny Side Up; Happy Days (cameo); The Man Who Came Back (1931); Delicious; One More Spring; The Farmer Takes a Wife (1935); Small Town Girl (1936); Ladies in Love; A Star Is Born (1937); Three Loves Has Nancy; The Young in Heart; Bernadine

Gielgud, John: Tne Good Companions (1933); The Secret Agent (1936); The Prime Minister; Julius Caesar (1953); Romeo and Juliet (1954); Richard III; Around the World

in Eighty Days (1956; cameo); The Barretts of Wimpole Street (1957); Saint Joan; To Die in Madrid (narr); Becket; The Loved One; Chimes at Midnight

Gilbert, John: Hell's Hinges; Monte Cristo; Cameo Kirby (1923); He Who Gets Slapped; The Merry Widow (1925); The Big Parade; La Boheme; Bardelys the Magnificent; Flesh and the Devil; The Cossacks; Show People (cameo); A Woman of Affairs; Desert Nights; Redemption; Way for a Sailor; Gentleman's Fate; The Phantom of Paris; West of Broadway; Downstairs; Fast Workers; Queen Christina; The Captain Hates the Sea

Gish, Lillian: Judith of Bethulia; The Birth of a Nation; Intolerance; Hearts of the World; A Romance of Happy Valley; True Heart Susie; Broken Blossoms; Way Down East (1920); Orphans of the Storm; The White Sister; La Boheme; The Scarlet Letter (1926); Annie Laurie; The Wind (1928); One Romantic Night; His Double Life; The Commandos Strike at Dawn; Top Man; Miss Susie Slagle's; Duel in the Sun; Portrait of Jennie; The Cobweb; Night of the Hunter; Orders to Kill; The Unforgiven (1960)

Goddard, Paulette: City Streets; The Mouthpiece; Pack Up Your Troubles; The Kid from Spain; Roman Scandals; Kid Millions; Modern Times; The Bohemian Girl; The Young in Heart; Dramatic School; The Women; The Cat and the Canary; The Ghost Breakers; The Great Dictator; North West Mounted Police; Second Chorus; Pot o' Gold; Hold Back the Dawn; Nothing But the Truth; The Lady Has Plans; Reap the Wild Wind; The Forest Rangers; The Crystal Ball; Star Spangled Rhythm; So Proudly We Hail!; Standing Room Only; I Love a Soldier; Kitty; The Diary of a Chambermaid (1946); Suddenly, It's Spring; Unconquered; An Ideal Husband (1948); On Our Merry Way; Hazard; Bride of Vengeance; Anna Lucasta; The Torch (also assoc prod); Babes in Bagdad; Vice Squad (1953); Sins of Jezebel; Paris Model; Charge of the Lancers; The Unholy Four; Time of Indifference

Grable, Betty: Movietone Follies of 1930 (bit); Whoopee!; Palmy Days (bit); The Greeks Had a Word for Them (bit); The Age of Consent (bit); Hold 'Em Jail; The Kid from Spain; Cavalcade; Child of Manhattan (bit); Melody Cruise; Sweetheart of Sigma Chi (1933); The Gay Divorcee; By Your Leave; Student Tour; Hips, Hips, Hooray (bit); The Nitwits; Old Man Rhythm; Pigskin Parade; Follow the Fleet; This Way Please; College Swing; Give Me a Sailor; Man About Town (1939); Million Dollar Legs (1939); Down Argentine Way; Tin Pan Alley; A Yank in the R.A.F.; I Wake Up Screaming; Moon Over Miami; Footlight Serenade; Song of the Islands; Springtime in the Rockies; Coney Island; Sweet Rosie

O'Grady; Four Jills in a Jeep; Pin Up Girl; Diamond Horseshoe; The Dolly Sisters; Do You Love Me? (bit); The Shocking Miss Pilgrim; Mother Wore Tights; That Lady in Ermine; When My Baby Smiles at Me; The Beautiful Blonde from Bashful Bend; Wabash Avenue; My Blue Heaven (1950); Call Me Mister; Meet Me After the Show; The Farmer Takes a Wife (1953); How To Marry a Millionaire; Three for the Show; How To Be Very, Very Popular

Granger, Stewart: Secret Mission; Thursday's Child; The Man in Grey; Love Story (1944); Man of Evil; Madonna of the Seven Moons; Waterloo Road; Caesar and Cleopatra; Captain Boycott; Blanche Fury; Saraband; Woman Hater; Adam and Evalyn; King Solomon's Mines (1950); Soldiers Three; The Light Touch; Scaramouche (1952); The Wild North; The Prisoner of Zenda (1952); Salome; Young Bess; All the Brothers Were Valiant; Beau Brummell (1954); Green Fire; Moonfleet; Footsteps in the Fog; The Last Hunt; Bhowani Junction; The Little Hut; Gun Glory; Harry Black and the Tiger; The Whole Truth; North to Alaska; The Secret Partner; Sodom and Gomorrah; Swordsman of Siena; The Secret Invasion; The Crooked Road

Grant, Cary: This Is the Night; Sinners in the Sun; Merrily We Go to Hell; Devil and the Deep; Blonde Venus; Hot Saturday; Madame Butterfly; She Done Him Wrong; The Eagle and the Hawk (1933); Gambling Ship; I'm No Angel; Alice in Wonderland (1933); Thirty Day Princess; Born to Be Bad; Kiss and Make-Up; Ladies Should Listen; Enter Madame; Wings in the Dark; The Last Outpost (1935); Sylvia Scarlett; Big Brown Eyes; Suzy; Wedding Present; Amazing Adventure; When You're in Love; Topper; The Toast of New York; The Awful Truth; Bringing Up Baby; Holiday (1938); Gunga Din; Only Angels Have Wings; In Name Only; His Girl Friday; My Favorite Wife; The Howards of Virginia; The Philadelphia Story; Penny Serenade; Suspicion; The Talk of the Town; Once Upon a Honeymoon; Mr. Lucky; Destination Tokyo; Once Upon a Time; None But the Lonely Heart; Arsenic and Old Lace; Without Reservations (cameo); Night and Day; Notorious (1946); The Bachelor and the Bobby-Soxer; The Bishop's Wife; Mr. Blandings Builds His Dream House; Every Girl Should Be Married; I Was a Male War Bride; Crisis (1950); People Will Talk (1951); Room for One More; Monkey Business (1952); Dream Wife; To Catch a Thief; The Pride and the Passion; An Affair to Remember; Kiss Them for Me; Indiscreet (1958); Houseboat; North by Northwest; Operation Petticoat; The Grass Is Greener; That Touch of Mink; Charade (1963); Father Goose

Guinness, Alec: Great Expectations (1946); Oliver Twist (1948); Kind Hearts and Coronets; A Run for Your Money; Last Holiday (1950); The Mudlark; The Lavender Hill Mob; The Man in the White Suit; The Promoter; The Captain's Paradise; The Malta Story; The Detective (1954); To Paris with Love; The Prisoner; The Ladykillers (1955); The Swan; All at Sea; The Bridge on the River Kwai; The Horse's Mouth (also adapt); The Scapegoat; Our Man in Havana; Tunes of Glory; A Majority of One; Damn the Defiant!; Lawrence of Arabia; The Fall of the Roman Empire; Situation Hopeless—But Not Serious; Doctor Zhivago

Harlow, Jean: The Saturday Night Kid (bit); The Love Parade (bit); Hell's Angels; City Lights (bit); Iron Man (1931); The Public Enemy; Platinum Blonde; The Secret Six; Three Wise Girls; The Beast of the City; Red-Headed Woman; Red Dust (1932); Hold Your Man; Dinner at Eight; Bombshell; The Girl from Missouri; Reckless (1935); China Seas; Riffraff (1935); Wife vs. Secretary; Suzy; Libeled Lady; Personal Property; Saratoga

Harrison, Rex: Men Are Not Gods; Storm in a Teacup; Sidewalks of London; The Citadel; Over the Moon; Night Train to Munich; Major Barbara; Blithe Spirit; Notorious Gentleman; Journey Together (uncred); Anna and the King of Siam; The Ghost and Mrs. Muir; The Foxes of Harrow; Escape (1948); Unfaithfully Yours (1948); The Long Dark Hall; The Four Poster; King Richard and the Crusaders; The Constant Husband; The Reluctant Debutante; Midnight Lace; The Happy Thieves; Cleopatra (1963); My Fair Lady; The Yellow Rolls-Royce; The Agony and the Ecstasy

Hayes, Helen: The Sin of Madelon Claudet; Arrowsmith; A Farewell to Arms (1932); The Son-Daughter; The White Sister; Another Language; Night Flight; Crime Without Passion (uncred); What Every Woman Knows; Vanessa: Her Love Story; My Son John; Anastasia; Third Man on the Mountain (uncred)

Hayward, Susan: Hollywood Hotel (bit); I Am the Law (bit); The Sisters (bit); Comet Over Broadway (bit); Girls on Probation; The Amazing Doctor Clitterhouse (bit); Beau Geste (1939); Adam Had Four Sons; Sis Hopkins; Among the Living; Reap the Wild Wind; The Forest Rangers; I Married a Witch; Star Spangled Rhythm; Change of Heart; Young and Willing; Jack London; The Fighting Seabees; The Hairy Ape; And Now Tomorrow; Deadline at Dawn; Canyon Passage; Smash-up: The Story of a Woman; They Won't Believe Me; The Lost Moment; Tap Roots; The Saxon Charm; Tulsa; House of Strangers; My Foolish Heart; I'd Climb the Highest Mountain; Rawhide; I Can Get It for You Wholesale; David and Bathsheba; With a Song in My Heart; The Snows of Kilimanjaro; The

Lusty Men; The President's Lady; White Witch Doctor; Demetrius and the Gladiators; Garden of Evil; Untamed (1955); Soldier of Fortune; I'll Cry Tomorrow; The Conqueror; Top Secret Affair; I Want to Live!; Woman Obsessed; Thunder in the Sun; The Marriage-Go-Round; Ada; Back Street (1961); I Thank a Fool; Stolen Hours; Where Love Has Gone

Hayworth, Rita (*billed as Rita Cansino until* Girls Can Play)**:** In Caliente (bit); Charlie Chan in Egypt; Dante's Inferno; Paddy O'Day; Meet Nero Wolfe; Girls Can Play; Paid to Dance; Who Killed Gail Preston?; Homicide Bureau; The Lone Wolf Spy Hunt; Only Angels Have Wings; Music in My Heart; Blondie on a Budget; Susan and God; The Lady in Question; Angels Over Broadway; The Strawberry Blonde; Affectionately Yours; Blood and Sand (1941); You'll Never Get Rich; My Gal Sal; Tales of Manhattan; You Were Never Lovelier; Cover Girl; Tonight and Every Night; Gilda; Down to Earth (1947); The Lady from Shanghai; The Loves of Carmen; Champagne Safari (app); Affair in Trinidad; Salome; Miss Sadie Thompson; Fire Down Below (1957); Pal Joey; Separate Tables; They Came to Cordura; The Story on Page One; The Happy Thieves; Circus World

Hepburn, Audrey: Laughter in Paradise (bit); Young Wives' Tale; The Lavender Hill Mob (bit); Secret People; Roman Holiday; Sabrina (1954); War and Peace (1956); Funny Face; Love in the Afternoon; Green Mansions; The Nun's Story; The Unforgiven (1960); Breakfast at Tiffany's; The Children's Hour; Charade (1963); Paris—When It Sizzles; My Fair Lady

Hepburn, Katharine: A Bill of Divorcement (1932); Christopher Strong; Morning Glory; Little Women (1933); Spitfire (1934); The Little Minister; Break of Hearts; Alice Adams; Sylvia Scarlett; Mary of Scotland; A Woman Rebels; Quality Street; Stage Door; Bringing Up Baby; Holiday (1938); The Philadelphia Story; Woman of the Year; Keeper of the Flame; Stage Door Canteen; Dragon Seed; Without Love; Undercurrent; The Sea of Grass; Song of Love; State of the Union; Adam's Rib; The African Queen; Pat and Mike; Summertime; The Rainmaker (1956); The Iron Petticoat; Desk Set; Suddenly, Last Summer; Long Day's Journey Into Night

Heston, Charlton: Dark City (1950); The Greatest Show on Earth; The Savage; Ruby Gentry; The President's Lady; Pony Express; Arrowhead; Bad for Each Other; The Naked Jungle; Secret of the Incas; The Far Horizons; The Private War of Major Benson; Lucy Gallant; The Ten Commandments (1956); Three Violent People; Touch of Evil; The Big Country; The Buccaneer (1958); The Wreck of the Mary Deare;

Ben-Hur (1959); El Cid; The Pigeon That Took Rome; Diamond Head; 55 Days at Peking; The Greatest Story Ever Told; Major Dundee; The Agony and the Ecstasy; The War Lord

Holden, William: Million Dollar Legs (1939); Golden Boy; Invisible Stripes; Those Were the Days; Our Town; Arizona; I Wanted Wings; Texas; The Remarkable Andrew; Meet the Stewarts; The Fleet's In; Young and Willing; Variety Girl (cameo); Blaze of Noon; Dear Ruth; Apartment for Peggy; The Man from Colorado; Rachel and the Stranger; The Dark Past; Miss Grant Takes Richmond; Dear Wife; Streets of Laredo; Father Is a Bachelor; Born Yesterday (1950); Sunset Blvd.; Union Station; Submarine Command; Force of Arms; Boots Malone; The Turning Point (1952); The Moon Is Blue; Stalag 17; Forever Female; Escape from Fort Bravo; Executive Suite; The Bridges at Toko-Ri; Sabrina (1954); The Country Girl; Love Is a Many-Splendored Thing; Picnic; Toward the Unknown; The Proud and Profane; The Bridge on the River Kwai; The Key (1958); The Horse Soldiers; The World of Suzie Wong; Satan Never Sleeps; The Counterfeit Traitor; The Lion; Paris—When It Sizzles; The 7th Dawn

Hope, Bob: The Big Broadcast of 1938; College Swing; Give Me a Sailor; Thanks for the Memory; Never Say Die; Some Like It Hot (1939); The Cat and the Canary (1939); Road to Singapore; The Ghost Breakers; Road to Zanzibar; Caught in the Draft; Nothing But the Truth; Louisiana Purchase; My Favorite Blonde; Road to Morocco; Star Spangled Rhythm; They Got Me Covered; Let's Face It; The Princess and the Pirate; Road to Utopia; Monsieur Beaucaire; My Favorite Brunette; Where There's Life; Variety Girl (cameo); Road to Rio; The Paleface; Sorrowful Jones; The Great Lover; Fancy Pants; The Lemon Drop Kid (1951); My Favorite Spy (1951); The Greatest Show on Earth (cameo); Son of Paleface; Road to Bali; Off Limits (1953); Scared Stiff (1953; cameo); Here Come the Girls; Casanova's Big Night; The Seven Little Foys; That Certain Feeling; The Iron Petticoat; Beau James; Paris Holiday; The Five Pennies (cameo); Alias Jesse James; The Facts of Life; Bachelor in Paradise; The Road to Hong Kong; Critic's Choice; Call Me Bwana; A Global Affair; I'll Take Sweden

Howard, Leslie: Outward Bound; Five and Ten; A Free Soul; Smilin' Through (1932); The Animal Kingdom; Secrets; Captured!; Berkeley Square; Of Human Bondage (1934); British Agent; The Scarlet Pimpernel; The Petrified Forest; Romeo and Juliet (1936); It's Love I'm After; Stand-In; Pygmalion; Intermezzo (1939); Gone With the Wind; Pimpernel Smith; 49th Parallel;

Spitfire (1942; also dir); In Which We Serve (voice)

Howard, Trevor: The Way Ahead; The Way to the Stars; Brief Encounter; The Adventuress; Green for Danger; So Well Remembered; They Made Me a Fugitive; The Passionate Friends; The Third Man; Golden Salamander; One Woman's Story; Outcast of the Islands; The Stranger's Hand; Gift Horse; The Heart of the Matter; The Cockleshell Heroes; Run for the Sun; Around the World in Eighty Days (1956; cameo); Pickup Alley; Stowaway Girl; The Key; The Roots of Heaven; Sons and Lovers; Malaga; The Lion; Mutiny on the Bounty (1962); Man in the Middle; Father Goose; Operation Crossbow; Von Ryan's Express; Morituri

Hudson, Rock: Fighter Squadron; Undertow; I Was a Shoplifter; Winchester '73; One-Way Street; Peggy; The Desert Hawk; Shakedown; Double Crossbones; Tomahawk; Bright Victory; Iron Man (1951); The Fat Man; Air Cadet; Has Anybody Seen My Gal?; Bend of the River; Scarlet Angel; Here Come the Nelsons; Horizons West; The Lawless Breed; Gun Fury; Seminole; The Golden Blade; Back to God's Country; Sea Devils (1953); Taza, Son of Cochise; Bengal Brigade; Magnificent Obsession (1954); Captain Lightfoot; All That Heaven Allows; One Desire; Never Say Goodbye (1956); Written on the Wind; Four Girls in Town (cameo); Giant; Battle Hymn; A Farewell to Arms (1957); Something of Value; The Tarnished Angels; Twilight for the Gods; This Earth Is Mine; Pillow Talk; The Last Sunset; Come September; Lover Come Back (1961); The Spiral Road; A Gathering of Eagles; Man's Favorite Sport?; Send Me No Flowers; Strange Bedfellows; A Very Special Favor

Huston, Walter: The Virginian (1929); Abraham Lincoln; The Virtuous Sin; The Criminal Code; The Star Witness; The Ruling Voice; A House Divided; The Woman From Monte Carlo; The Beast of the City; Law and Order (1932); The Wet Parade; Night Court; American Madness; Kongo; Rain (1932); Gabriel Over the White House; Hell Below; Storm at Daybreak; Ann Vickers; The Prizefighter and the Lady; Keep 'Em Rolling; Trans-Atlantic Tunnel; Rhodes; Dodsworth; Of Human Hearts; The Light That Failed; The Maltese Falcon (1941; cameo); The Devil and Daniel Webster; Swamp Water; The Shanghai Gesture; Always in My Heart; In This Our Life (cameo); Yankee Doodle Dandy; The Outlaw; Edge of Darkness; Mission to Moscow; The North Star; Dragon Seed; And Then There Were None; Dragonwyck; Duel in the Sun; The Treasure of the Sierra Madre; Summer Holiday (1948); The Great Sinner; The Furies

Hutton, Betty: The Fleet's In; Star Spangled Rhythm; Happy Go Lucky; Let's Face

It; The Miracle of Morgan's Creek; And the Angels Sing; Here Come the Waves; Incendiary Blonde; The Stork Club; Cross My Heart (1946); The Perils of Pauline; Dream Girl; Red, Hot and Blue; Annie Get Your Gun; Let's Dance; The Greatest Show on Earth; Sailor Beware (cameo); Somebody Loves Me; Spring Reunion

Jolson, Al: The Jazz Singer (1927); The Singing Fool; Say It With Songs; Mammy; Big Boy; Show Girl in Hollywood; Hallelujah I'm a Bum; Wonder Bar; Go Into Your Dance; The Singing Kid; Rose of Washington Square; Hollywood Cavalcade; Swanee River; Rhapsody in Blue (cameo); The Jolson Story (voice only); Jolson Sings Again (voice only)

Jones, Jennifer (Phylis Isley until 1944): New Frontier (1939); The Song of Bernadette; Since You Went Away; Love Letters (1945); Cluny Brown; Duel in the Sun; Portrait of Jennie; We Were Strangers; Madame Bovary (1949); The Wild Heart; Carrie (1952); Ruby Gentry; Indiscretion of an American Wife; Beat the Devil; Love Is a Many-Splendored Thing; Good Morning Miss Dove; The Man in the Gray Flannel Suit; The Barretts of Wimpole Street (1957); A Farewell to Arms (1957); Tender Is the Night

Karloff, Boris: The Last of the Mohicans (1920); The Bells; Old Ironsides; Two Arabian Nights; Behind That Curtain; The Unholy Night; The Sea Bat; The Criminal Code; Smart Money; The Public Defender; Cracked Nuts; I Like Your Nerve; Graft; Five Star Final; The Yellow Ticket; The Mad Genius; The Guilty Generation; Frankenstein; Tonight or Never; Behind the Mask; Scarface (1932); The Miracle Man; Night World; The Old Dark House (1932); The Mask of Fu Manchu; The Mummy (1932); The Ghoul (1933); The Lost Patrol; House of Rothschild; The Black Cat (1934); The Gift of Gab (cameo); Bride of Frankenstein; The Raven (1935); The Black Room; The Invisible Ray; The Walking Dead (1936); The Man Who Lived Again; Charlie Chan at the Opera; Night Key; West of Shanghai; The Invisible Menace; Mr. Wong Detective; Devil's Island; Son of Frankenstein; Mystery of Mr. Wong; Mr. Wong in Chinatown; The Man They Could Not Hang; Tower of London (1939); The Fatal Hour; British Intelligence; Black Friday; The Man with Nine Lives; Doomed to Die; Before I Hang; The Ape; You'll Find Out; The Devil Commands; The Boogie Man Will Get You; The Climax; House of Frankenstein (1944); The Body Snatcher; Isle of the Dead; Bedlam (1946); The Secret Life of Walter Mitty; Lured; Unconquered; Dick Tracy Meets Gruesome; Tap Roots; Abbott and Costello Meet Killer Boris Karloff; The Strange Door; The Black Castle; Abbott and Costello Meet Dr. Jekyll and Mr. Hyde; Sabaka; Voodoo

Island; The Haunted Strangler; Franken-stein 1970; The Raven (1963); Corridors of Blood; The Terror; Black Sabbath; The Comedy of Terrors; Bikini Beach (cameo); Die, Monster, Die!

Kaye, Danny: Up in Arms; Wonder Man; The Kid from Brooklyn; The Secret Life of Walter Mitty; A Song Is Born; It's a Great Feeling (cameo); The Inspector General; On the Riviera; Hans Christian Andersen; Knock on Wood; White Christmas; The Court Jester; Merry Andrew; Me and the Colonel; The Five Pennies; The Millionair-ess (cameo); On the Double; The Man from the Diner's Club

Keaton, Buster: The Saphead; Three Ages; Our Hospitality (also codir); Sherlock, Jr.; The Navigator (also codir); Seven Chances; Go West (1925; also codir); Battling But-ler (also codir); The General (also codir); College (1927); Steamboat Bill, Jr.; The Cameraman; Spite Marriage; The Holly-wood Revue; Free and Easy; Doughboys; Parlor, Bedroom and Bath; Sidewalks of New York; The Passionate Plumber; Speak Easily; What—No Beer?; An Old Spanish Custom; The Jones Family in Hollywood; Hollywood Cavalcade; The Villain Still Pur-sued Her; Li'l Abner (1940); Forever and a Day (1943); San Diego, I Love You; That's the Spirit; That Night With You; She Went to the Races (bit); God's Country; Boom in the Moon; The Lovable Cheat; In the Good Old Summertime; You're My Everything; Sun-set Blvd. (cameo); Limelight; Around the World in Eighty Days (1956; cameo); The Adventures of Huckleberry Finn; It's a Mad Mad Mad Mad World; Pajama Party; Beach Blanket Bingo; How to Stuff a Wild Bikini; Sergeant DeadHead

Keeler, Ruby: 42nd Street; Gold Diggers of 1933; Footlight Parade; Dames; Flirta-tion Walk; Go Into Your Dance; Shipmates Forever; Colleen; Ready, Willing and Able; Mother Carey's Chickens; Sweetheart of the Campus

Kelly, Gene: For Me and My Gal; Pilot # 5; DuBarry Was a Lady; Thousands Cheer; The Cross of Lorraine; Cover Girl; Christ-mas Holiday; Anchors Aweigh; Ziegfeld Follies; Living in a Big Way; The Pirate; The Three Musketeers (1948); Words and Music; Take Me Out to the Ball Game; On the Town (also codir); Black Hand; Summer Stock; An American in Paris; It's a Big Country; Love Is Better Than Ever (cameo); Singin' In the Rain (also codir); The Devil Makes Three; Brigadoon; Crest of the Wave; Deep in My Heart (cameo); It's Always Fair Weather; Invitation to the Dance (also dir); The Happy Road; Les Girls; The Tunnel of Love (dir); Marjorie Morningstar; Let's Make Love (cameo); Inherit the Wind; What a Way to Go!

Kelly, Grace: Fourteen Hours; High Noon; Mogambo; Dial M for Murder; Rear Win-dow; The Country Girl; Green Fire; The Bridges at Toko-Ri; To Catch a Thief; The Swan; High Society (1956)

Kerr, Deborah: Major Barbara; Love on the Dole; Courageous Mr. Penn; Hatter's Castle; The Day Will Dawn; The Life and Death of Colonel Blimp; Vacation from Marriage; The Adventuress; Black Narcis-sus; The Hucksters; If Winter Comes; Ed-ward, My Son; Please Believe Me; King Solomon's Mines (1950); Quo Vadis; The Prisoner of Zenda (1952); Thunder in the East; Young Bess; Julius Caesar (1953); Dream Wife; From Here to Eternity; The End of the Affair (1955); The Proud and Profane; The King and I; Tea and Sympa-thy; Heaven Knows, Mr. Allison; An Affair to Remember; Bonjour Tristesse; Separate Tables; The Journey; Count Your Blessings; Beloved Infidel; The Sundowners (1960); The Grass Is Greener; The Naked Edge; The Innocents; The Chalk Garden; The Night of the Iguana; Marriage on the Rocks

Ladd, Alan: Once In a Lifetime (bit); Tom Brown of Culver; Island of Lost Souls; Pig-skin Parade; The Last Train from Madrid (bit); All Over Town (bit); The Goldwyn Follies; Hitler—Beast of Berlin; Rulers of the Sea; Brother Rat and a Baby; Those Were the Days; Captain Caution; The How-ards of Virginia (bit); Victory (1940); The Black Cat (1941); Citizen Kane; Great Guns; The Reluctant Dragon; They Met in Bombay; Gangs, Inc.; Joan of Paris; This Gun for Hire; The Glass Key (1942); Lucky Jordan; Star Spangled Rhythm (cameo); China; And Now Tomorrow; Salty O'Rourke; Duffy's Tavern (cameo); The Blue Dahlia; O.S.S.; Two Years Before the Mast; Calcutta; Variety Girl (cameo); Wild Harvest; My Favorite Brunette (cameo); Saigon; Beyond Glory; Whispering Smith; The Great Gatsby (1949); Chicago Dead-line; Captain Carey, U.S.A.; Branded; Ap-pointment with Danger; Red Mountain; The Iron Mistress; Thunder in the East; Desert Legion; Shane; Botany Bay; Paratrooper; The Black Knight; Saskatchewan; Hell Below Zero; Drum Beat; The McConnell Story; Hell on Frisco Bay; Santiago; The Big Land; Boy on a Dolphin; The Deep Six; The Proud Rebel; The Badlanders; The Man in the Net; Guns of the Timber-land; All the Young Men; One Foot in Hell; Duel of Champions; 13 West Street; The Carpetbaggers

Lake, Veronica (*Constance Keane un-til 1941*): Forty Little Mothers (uncred); I Wanted Wings; Hold Back the Dawn (cameo); Sullivan's Travels; This Gun for Hire; The Glass Key (1942); I Married a Witch; Star Spangled Rhythm; So Proudly We Hail!; The Hour Before the Dawn; Bring on the Girls; Out of This World; Hold That Blonde; Miss Susie Slagle's; The Blue Dahlia; Ramrod; Saigon; The Sainted Sisters; Isn't It Romantic?; Slattery's Hurricane; Stronghold

Lamarr, Hedy: Ecstasy; Algiers; Lady of the Tropics; I Take This Woman; Boom Town; Comrade X; Come Live With Me; Ziegfeld Girl; H. M. Pulham, Esq.; Tortilla Flat; Crossroads; White Cargo; The Heavenly Body; The Conspirators; Experiment Perilous; Her Highness and the Bellboy; The Strange Woman; Dishonored Lady; Let's Live a Little; Samson and Delilah; A Lady Without Passport; Copper Canyon; My Favorite Spy (1951); Loves of Three Queens; The Story of Mankind; The Female Animal

Lancaster, Burt: The Killers (1946); Variety Girl (cameo); Brute Force; Desert Fury; I Walk Alone; All My Sons; Sorry, Wrong Number; Kiss the Blood off My Hands; Criss Cross; Rope of Sand; The Flame and the Arrow; Mister 880; Vengeance Valley; Jim Thorpe—All American; Ten Tall Men; The Crimson Pirate; Come Back, Little Sheba; South Sea Woman; From Here to Eternity; His Majesty O'Keefe; Apache; Vera Cruz; The Kentuckian; The Rose Tattoo; Trapeze; The Rainmaker (1956); Gunfight at the O.K. Corral; Sweet Smell of Success; Run Silent, Run Deep; Separate Tables; The Devil's Disciple; The Unforgiven (1960); Elmer Gantry; The Young Savages; Judgment at Nuremberg; Birdman of Alcatraz; A Child Is Waiting; The Leopard; The List of Adrian Messenger (cameo); Seven Days in May; The Train; The Hallelujah Trail

Langdon, Harry: Tramp, Tramp, Tramp (1926); Ella Cinders (cameo); The Strong Man; Long Pants; Three's a Crowd (also dir); The Chaser (also dir); Hallelujah I'm a Bum; Mad About Money; Atlantic Adventure; There Goes My Heart (uncred); Zenobia; Misbehaving Husbands; All-American Co-Eds; Spotlight Scandals; Block Busters (bit)

Lansbury, Angela: Gaslight (1944); National Velvet; The Picture of Dorian Gray; The Harvey Girls; The Hoodlum Saint; Till the Clouds Roll By; The Private Affairs of Bel Ami; If Winter Comes; Tenth Avenue Angel; State of the Union; The Three Musketeers (1948); The Red Danube; Samson and Delilah (1949); Kind Lady (1951); Mutiny; Remains to Be Seen; A Lawless Street; Key Man; The Purple Mask; Please Murder Me; The Court Jester; The Long Hot Summer (1958); The Reluctant Debutante; Season of Passion; A Breath of Scandal; The Dark at the Top of the Stairs; Blue Hawaii; The Four Horsemen of the Apocalypse (1962; uncred voice); All Fall Down; The Manchurian Candidate (1962); In the Cool of the Day; The World of Henry Orient; Dear Heart; The Greatest Story Ever Told; The Amorous Adventures of Moll Flanders; Harlow (Carroll Baker version)

Laughton, Charles: Piccadilly; Devil and the Deep; The Old Dark House (1932); Payment Deferred; The Sign of the Cross; If I Had a Million; Island of Lost Souls; The Private Life of Henry VIII; White Woman; The Barretts of Wimpole Street (1934); Ruggles of Red Gap; Les Misérables (1935); Mutiny on the Bounty (1935); Rembrandt; The Beachcomber (1938); Sidewalks of London; Jamaica Inn; The Hunchback of Notre Dame (1939); They Knew What They Wanted; It Started with Eve; The Tuttles of Tahiti; Tales of Manhattan; Stand by for Action; Forever and a Day; This Land Is Mine; The Man from Down Under; The Canterville Ghost; The Suspect (1944); Captain Kidd; Because of Him; The Paradine Case; Arch of Triumph; The Big Clock; The Girl from Manhattan; The Bribe; The Man on the Eiffel Tower; The Blue Veil; The Strange Door; O. Henry's Full House; Abbott and Costello Meet Captain Kidd; Salome; Young Bess; Hobson's Choice; The Night of the Hunter (dir); Witness for the Prosecution; Under Ten Flags; Spartacus; Advise & Consent

Laurel & Hardy: The Hollywood Revue of 1929 (cameos); Pardon Us; Pack Up Your Troubles (1932); The Devil's Brother; Sons of the Desert; Hollywood Party (cameos); Babes in Toyland (1934); Bonnie Scotland; The Bohemian Girl; Our Relations; Way Out West (1937); Pick a Star (cameos); Swiss Miss; Block-Heads; The Flying Deuces; A Chump at Oxford; Saps At Sea; Great Guns; A-Haunting We Will Go; Air Raid Wardens; Jitterbugs; The Dancing Masters; The Big Noise; Nothing But Trouble (1944); The Bullfighters; Utopia; *features with Oliver Hardy but without Stan Laurel*: The Wizard of Oz (1925); Zenobia; The Fighting Kentuckian; Riding High (1950)

Lee, Christopher: Corridor of Mirrors; One Night With You; Hamlet (1948; bit); My Brother's Keeper; Saraband; Scott of the Antarctic; The Gay Lady; Captain Horatio Hornblower; Valley of the Eagles; The Crimson Pirate; Babes in Bagdad; Moulin Rouge (1952); Innocents in Paris; That Lady; The Warriors (1955); Storm Over the Nile; The Cockleshell Heroes; Port Afrique; Private's Progress; Beyond Mombasa; Pursuit of the Graf Spee; Night Ambush; She Played With Fire; The Curse of Frankenstein; Bitter Victory; The Truth About Women; A Tale of Two Cities (1958); Horror of Dracula; Missile from Hell; The Hound of the Baskervilles (1959); The Man Who Could Cheat Death; The Mummy (1959); Uncle Was a Vampire; Too Hot to Handle (1960); Wild for Kicks; Horror Hotel (1960); The Two Faces of Dr. Jekyll; Corridors of Blood; The Hands of Orlac (1960); Terror of the Tongs; The Puzzle of the Red Orchid; Scream of Fear; Hercules in the Haunted World; Terror in the Crypt; Horror Castle; The Whip and the Body; The Devil-Ship Pirates; The Pirates of Blood River; Castle of the Living Dead; The Gorgon; Dr. Terror's House of Horrors; She (1965); The Skull; The Face of Fu Manchu

Leigh, Janet: The Romance of Rosy Ridge; If Winter Comes; Hills of Home; Words and Music; Act of Violence; Little Women (1949); The Doctor and the Girl; That Forsyte Woman; The Red Danube; Holiday Affair; Strictly Dishonorable; Angels in the Outfield (1951); Two Tickets to Broadway; It's a Big Country (cameo); Just This Once; Scaramouche (1952); Fearless Fagan; The Naked Spur; Confidentially Connie; Houdini; Walking My Baby Back Home; Prince Valiant; Living It Up; The Black Shield of Falworth; Rogue Cop; Pete Kelly's Blues; My Sister Eileen (1955); Safari; Jet Pilot; Touch of Evil; The Vikings; The Perfect Furlough; Who Was That Lady?; Psycho (1960); Pepe (cameo); The Manchurian Candidate (1962); Bye Bye Birdie; Wives and Lovers

Leigh, Vivien: Fire Over England; Dark Journey; Storm in a Teacup; A Yank at Oxford; Sidewalks of London; 21 Days Together; Gone With the Wind; Waterloo Bridge (1940); That Hamilton Woman; Caesar and Cleopatra; Anna Karenina (1948); A Streetcar Named Desire; The Deep Blue Sea; The Roman Spring of Mrs. Stone; Ship of Fools

Lemmon, Jack: It Should Happen to You; Phffft!; Three for the Show; Mister Roberts; My Sister Eileen (1955); You Can't Run Away from It; Fire Down Below; Operation Mad Ball; Cowboy; Bell, Book and Candle; Some Like It Hot (1959); It Happened to Jane; The Apartment; Pepe (cameo); The Wackiest Ship in the Army?; The Notorious Landlady; Days of Wine and Roses; Irma la Douce; Under the Yum Yum Tree; Good Neighbor Sam; How to Murder Your Wife; The Great Race

Lewis, Jerry: My Friend Irma; At War with the Army; My Friend Irma Goes West; That's My Boy; Sailor Beware; Road to Bali (cameo); Jumping Jacks; The Stooge; Scared Stiff (1953); The Caddy; Money from Home; Living It Up; Three Ring Circus; You're Never Too Young; Artists and Models; Pardners; Hollywood or Bust; The Delicate Delinquent; The Sad Sack; Rock-a-Bye Baby; The Geisha Boy; Li'l Abner (1959; cameo); Don't Give Up the Ship; Visit to a Small Planet; Raymie (sings title song); The Bellboy (also dir, scr); Cinderfella; The Ladies Man (1961; also dir, scr); The Errand Boy (also dir, coscr); It'$ Only Money; It's a Mad Mad Mad Mad World (cameo); The Nutty Professor (1963; also dir, coscr); Who's Minding the Store?; The Patsy (also dir, coscr); The Disorderly Orderly; The Family Jewels (also dir, coscr); Boeing Boeing

Lloyd, Harold: A Sailor-Made Man; Grandma's Boy; Dr. Jack; Safety Last!; Why Worry?; Girl Shy; Hot Water; The Freshman (1925); For Heaven's Sake (1926); The Kid Brother; Speedy; Welcom Danger; Feet First; Movie Crazy; The Cat's Paw; The Milky Way (1936); Professor Beware; The Sin of Harold Diddlebock

Lombard, Carole: The Johnstown Flood (bit); High Voltage; The Racketeer; Fast and Loose (1930); Man of the World; Ladies Man (1931); No One Man; Sinners in the Sun; Virtue; No More Orchids; No Man of Her Own (1932); From Hell to Heaven; Supernatural; The Eagle and the Hawk (1933); Brief Moment; White Woman; Bolero (1934); We're Not Dressing; Twentieth Century; Now and Forever (1934); Lady By Choice; The Gay Bride; Rumba; Hands Across the Table; Love Before Breakfast; The Princess Comes Across; My Man Godfrey (1936); Swing High, Swing Low; Nothing Sacred; True Confession; Fools for Scandal; Made For Each Other (1939); In Name Only; Vigil in the Night; They Knew What They Wanted; Mr. & Mrs. Smith (1941); To Be or Not to Be (1942)

Loren, Sophia: Variety Lights (bit); Anna (1951; bit); Quo Vadis (extra); Aida; Two Nights With Cleopatra; Attila; Gold of Naples; Woman of the River; Too Bad She's Bad; Scandal in Sorrento; Lucky to Be a Woman; Boy on a Dolphin; The Pride and the Passion; Legend of the Lost; Desire Under the Elms; The Key (1958); Houseboat; The Black Orchid; That Kind of Woman; Heller in Pink Tights; It Started in Naples; A Breath of Scandal; The Millionairess; Two Women; El Cid; Madame; Boccaccio '70; Five Miles to Midnight; The Condemned of Altona; Yesterday, Today and Tomorrow; The Fall of the Roman Empire; Marriage-Italian Style; Operation Crossbow; Lady L

Lorre, Peter: M (1931); The Man Who Knew Too Much (1934); Mad Love (1935); Crime and Punishment (1935); The Secret Agent (1936); Crack-Up (1937); Nancy Steele Is Missing!; Think Fast, Mr. Moto; Lancer Spy; Thank You, Mr. Moto; Mr. Moto's Gamble; Mr. Moto Takes a Chance; I'll Give a Million; Mysterious Mr. Moto; Mr. Moto's Last Warning; Mr. Moto in Danger Island; Mr. Moto Takes a Vacation; Strange Cargo; I Was an Adventuress; Island of Doomed Men; Stranger on the Third Floor; You'll Find Out; Mr. District Attorney (1941); The Face Behind the Mask; They Met in Bombay; The Maltese Falcon (1941); All Through the Night; Invisible Agent; The Boogie Man Will Get You; Casablanca; Background to Danger; The Constant Nymph; The Cross of Lorraine; Passage to Marseille; The Mask of Dimitrios; Arsenic and Old Lace; The Conspirators; Hollywood Canteen (cameo); Hotel

Berlin; Confidential Agent; Three Strangers; Black Angel; The Chase (1946); The Verdict (1946); The Beast With Five Fingers; My Favorite Brunette; Casbah; Rope of Sand; Quicksand; Double Confession; The Lost One (also dir); Beat the Devil; 20000 Leagues Under the Sea; Meet Me in Las Vegas (cameo); Congo Crossing; Around the World in Eighty Days (1956; cameo); The Buster Keaton Story; Silk Stockings; The Story of Mankind (cameo); Hell Ship Mutiny; The Sad Sack; The Big Circus; Holiday in Spain; Voyage to the Bottom of the Sea; Tales of Terror; Five Weeks in a Balloon; The Raven (1963); The Comedy of Terrors; Muscle Beach Party (cameo); The Patsy

Loy, Myrna: Ben-Hur (1926; bit); So This Is Paris (1926); Don Juan; When a Man Loves (1927); The Jazz Singer (1927); A Girl in Every Port (bit); Noah's Ark; The Desert Song (1929); The Black Watch; The Show of Shows; Renegades (1930); The Naughty Flirt; The Truth About Youth; The Devil to Pay!; Rebound; Consolation Marriage; Arrowsmith; Emma (1932); The Wet Parade; New Morals for Old; Love Me Tonight; Thirteen Women; The Mask of Fu Manchu; The Animal Kingdom; Topaze (1933); Scarlet River (cameo); The Barbarian; When Ladies Meet; Penthouse; The Prizefighter and the Lady; Night Flight; Men in White; Manhattan Melodrama; The Thin Man; Stamboul Quest; Evelyn Prentice; Broadway Bill; Wings in the Dark; Whipsaw; Wife vs. Secretary; Petticoat Fever; The Great Ziegfeld; To Mary—With Love; Libeled Lady; After the Thin Man; Parnell; Double Wedding; Man-Proof; Test Pilot; Too Hot to Handle (1938); Lucky Night; The Rains Came; Another Thin Man; I Love You Again; Third Finger Left Hand; Love Crazy; Shadow of the Thin Man; The Thin Man Goes Home; So Goes My Love; The Best Years of Our Lives; The Bachelor and the Bobby-Soxer; The Senator Was Indiscreet (cameo); Song of the Thin Man; Mr. Blandings Builds His Dream House; The Red Pony; If This Be Sin; Cheaper by the Dozen (1950); Belles on Their Toes; The Ambassador's Daughter; Lonelyhearts; From the Terrace; Midnight Lace

Lugosi, Bela: Renegades (1930); Dracula (1931); Fifty Million Frenchmen; Women of All Nations; The Black Camel; Broadminded; Murders in the Rue Morgue (1932); White Zombie; Chandu the Magician; Island of Lost Souls; The Death Kiss; International House; The Devil's in Love; The Black Cat (1934); The Gift of Gab (cameo); Mark of the Vampire; The Mysterious Mr. Wong; The Raven (1935); Murder by Television; Phantom Ship; The Invisible Ray; Postal Inspector; Son of Frankenstein; The Gorilla; Ninotchka; The Phantom Creeps; The Human Monster; The Saint's Double Trouble; Black Friday; You'll Find Out; The Devil

Bat; The Black Cat (1941); The Invisible Ghost; Spooks Run Wild; The Wolf Man; The Ghost of Frankenstein; Black Dragons; The Corpse Vanishes; Bowery at Midnight; Night Monster; Frankenstein Meets the Wolf Man; The Ape Man; Ghosts on the Loose; Return of the Vampire; Voodoo Man; Return of the Ape Man; One Body Too Many; The Body Snatcher; Zombies on Broadway; Genius at Work; Scared to Death (1947); Abbott and Costello Meet Frankenstein; Bela Lugosi Meets a Brooklyn Gorilla; Mother Riley Meets the Vampire; Glen or Glenda?; Bride of the Monster; The Black Sleep; Plan 9 From Outer Space

Lupino, Ida: Search for Beauty; Peter Ibbetson; Anything Goes (1936); One Rainy Afternoon; The Gay Desperado; Artists & Models (1937); Fight For Your Lady; The Lone Wolf Spy Hunt; The Lady and the Mob; The Adventures of Sherlock Holmes; The Light That Failed; They Drive by Night (1940); High Sierra; The Sea Wolf; Out of the Fog; Ladies in Retirement; Moontide; Life Begins at 8:30 (1942); Forever and a Day; The Hard Way (1943); Thank Your Lucky Stars; In Our Time; Hollywood Canteen; Pillow to Post; Devotion; The Man I Love (1946); Deep Valley; Escape Me Never; Road House (1948); Lust for Gold; Woman in Hiding; Outrage (1950; dir, coscr, cameo); Hard, Fast and Beautiful (dir, cameo); On the Loose (narr); On Dangerous Ground; Beware, My Lovely; Jennifer (1953); The Bigamist (also dir); Private Hell 36; Women's Prison; The Big Knife; While the City Sleeps; Strange Intruder

MacDonald, Jeanette: The Love Parade; The Vagabond King (1930); Paramount on Parade; Let's Go Native; Monte Carlo; The Lottery Bride; One Hour with You; Love Me Tonight; The Cat and the Fiddle; The Merry Widow (1934); Naughty Marietta; Rose-Marie (1936); San Francisco; Maytime; The Firefly; The Girl of the Golden West; Sweethearts; Broadway Serenade; New Moon; Bitter Sweet (1940); Smilin' Through (1941); I Married an Angel; Cairo (1942); Follow the Boys (1944; cameo); Three Daring Daughters; The Sun Comes Up

MacLaine, Shirley: The Trouble With Harry; Artists and Models; Around the World in Eighty Days (1956); The Sheepman; The Matchmaker; Hot Spell; Some Came Running; Ask Any Girl; Career; Ocean's Eleven (1960; cameo); Can-Can; The Apartment; All in a Night's Work; Two Loves; The Children's Hour; My Geisha; Two for the Seesaw; Irma la Douce; What a Way to Go!; The Yellow Rolls-Royce; John Goldfarb, Please Come Home

MacMurray, Fred: Grand Old Girl; The Gilded Lily; Car 99; Alice Adams; Hands Across the Table; The Bride Comes Home; The Trail of the Lonesome Pine; Thirteen Hours by Air; The Princess Comes Across;

The Texas Rangers (1936); Champagne Waltz; Maid of Salem; Swing High, Swing Low; Exclusive; True Confession; Cocoanut Grove; Sing, You Sinners; Men with Wings; Cafe Society (1939); Invitation to Happiness; Honeymoon in Bali; Remember the Night; Little Old New York; Too Many Husbands; Rangers of Fortune; Virginia; One Night in Lisbon; Dive Bomber; New York Town; The Lady Is Willing; Take a Letter, Darling; The Forest Rangers; Star Spangled Rhythm; Flight for Freedom; Above Suspicion; No Time for Love; Standing Room Only; And the Angels Sing; Double Indemnity; Practically Yours; Where Do We Go From Here?; Murder, He Says; Captain Eddie; Pardon My Past; Smoky (1946); Suddenly, It's Spring; The Egg and I; Singapore; On Our Merry Way; The Miracle of the Bells; An Innocent Affair; Family Honeymoon; Father Was a Fullback; Borderline (1950); Never a Dull Moment (1950); A Millionaire for Christy; Callaway Went Thataway; Fair Wind to Java; The Moonlighter; The Caine Mutiny; Pushover; Woman's World; The Far Horizons; The Rains of Ranchipur; At Gunpoint; There's Always Tomorrow; Gun for a Coward; Quantez; Day of the Bad Man; Good Day for a Hanging; The Shaggy Dog (1959); Face of a Fugitive; The Oregon Trail; The Apartment; The Absent Minded Professor; Bon Voyage!; Son of Flubber; Kisses for My President

March, Fredric: The Wild Party (1929); The Studio Murder Mystery; Sarah and Son; True to the Navy; Paramount on Parade; Laughter; The Royal Family of Broadway; My Sin; Dr. Jekyll and Mr. Hyde (1932); Merrily We Go to Hell; Make Me a Star (cameo); Smilin' Through (1932); The Sign of the Cross; Tonight Is Ours; The Eagle and the Hawk (1933); Design for Living; All of Me (1934); Death Takes a Holiday; Good Dame; Affairs of Cellini; The Barretts of Wimpole Street (1934); We Live Again; Les Misérables (1935); Anna Karenina (1935); The Dark Angel; Mary of Scotland; The Road to Glory; Anthony Adverse; A Star Is Born (1937); Nothing Sacred; The Buccaneer (1938); There Goes My Heart; Trade Winds; Susan and God; Victory (1940); So Ends Our Night; One Foot in Heaven; Bedtime Story (1941); I Married a Witch; The Adventures of Mark Twain (1944); Tomorrow, the World!; The Best Years of Our Lives; Another Part of the Forest; An Act of Murder; Christopher Columbus; Death of a Salesman; It's a Big Country; Man on a Tightrope; Executive Suite; The Bridges at Toko-Ri; The Desperate Hours (1955); Alexander the Great; The Man in the Gray Flannel Suit; Middle of the Night; Inherit the Wind; The Young Doctors; The Condemned of Altona; Seven Days in May

Martin, Dean (see Jerry Lewis for films

through 1956): Ten Thousand Bedrooms; The Young Lions; Some Came Running; Career; Rio Bravo; Who Was That Lady?; Bells Are Ringing; Ocean's Eleven (1960); Pepe (cameo); All in a Night's Work; Ada; Sergeants 3; Who's Got the Action?; Toys in the Attic; 4 for Texas; Who's Been Sleeping in My Bed?; What a Way to Go!; Robin and the 7 Hoods; Kiss Me, Stupid; The Sons of Katie Elder; Marriage on the Rocks

Marvin, Lee: You're in the Navy Now; Teresa (bit); Hong Kong; We're Not Married!; Diplomatic Courier; The Duel at Silver Creek; Hangman's Knot; Eight Iron Men; Seminole; The Glory Brigade; Down Among the Sheltering Palms; The Stranger Wore a Gun; The Big Heat; Gun Fury; The Wild One; Gorilla at Large; The Caine Mutiny; The Raid; Bad Day at Black Rock; Violent Saturday; Not as a Stranger; A Life in the Balance; Pete Kelly's Blues; I Died a Thousand Times; Shack Out on 101; Seven Men from Now; Pillars of the Sky; The Rack; Attack; Raintree County; The Missouri Traveler; The Comancheros; The Man Who Shot Liberty Valance; Donovan's Reef; The Killers (1964); Cat Ballou; Ship of Fools

Marx Bros.: all four: The Cocoanuts; Animal Crackers; Monkey Business (1931); Horse Feathers; Duck Soup; Groucho, Harpo, Chico only: A Night at the Opera; A Day at the Races; Room Service; At the Circus; Go West (1940); The Big Store; A Night in Casablanca; Love Happy; The Story of Mankind; Groucho only: The King and the Chorus Girl (sty & scr only); Copacabana; Mr. Music; Double Dynamite; A Girl in Every Port (1952); Will Success Spoil Rock Hunter?

Mason, James: The Mill on the Floss; The High Command; Fire Over England; The Return of the Scarlet Pimpernel; Hatter's Castle; The Night Has Eyes; Secret Mission; Thunder Rock; The Man in Grey; Man of Evil; Hotel Reserve; A Place of One's Own; They Were Sisters; The Seventh Veil; The Wicked Lady (1945); Odd Man Out; The Upturned Glass; Caught (1949); Madame Bovary (1949); The Reckless Moment; East Side, West Side; One-Way Street; The Desert Fox; Pandora and the Flying Dutchman; Lady Possessed; 5 Fingers; The Prisoner of Zenda (1952); Face to Face (1952); The Story of Three Loves; The Desert Rats; Julius Caesar (1953); Botany Bay; The Man Between; Charade (1953); Prince Valiant; A Star Is Born (1954); 20000 Leagues Under the Sea; Forever, Darling; Bigger Than Life; Island in the Sun; Cry Terror; The Decks Ran Red; North by Northwest; Journey to the Center of the Earth; A Touch of Larceny; The Trials of Oscar Wilde; The Marriage-Go-Round; Hero's Island; Lolita (1962); Escape from Zahrain; Tiara Tahiti; Torpedo Bay; The Fall of the Roman Empire; The Pumpkin Eater; Lord Jim; Genghis Khan; The Uninhibited

Mastroianni, Marcello: Les Miserables (1947); A Tale of Five Women; Too Bad She's Bad; Island Princess; House of Ricordi; Lucky to Be a Woman; The Tailor's Maid; The Most Wonderful Moment; White Nights (1957); Big Deal on Madonna Street; Where the Hot Wind Blows!; La Dolce Vita; Bell' Antonio; Divorce—Italian Style; La Notte; A Very Private Affair; 8 1/2; The Organizer; Yesterday, Today and Tomorrow; Marriage-Italian Style; The Man With the Balloons; Kiss the Other Sheik; Casanova '70; The Tenth Victim

Matthau, Walter: The Kentuckian; The Indian Fighter; Bigger Than Life; A Face in the Crowd; Slaughter on Tenth Avenue; King Creole; Voice in the Mirror; Onionhead; Ride a Crooked Trail; Gangster Story (also dir); Strangers When We Meet; Lonely Are the Brave; Who's Got the Action?; Island of Love; Charade (1963); Ensign Pulver; Fail-Safe; Goodbye Charlie; Mirage

Mature, Victor: The Housekeeper's Daughter; One Million B.C.; Captain Caution; No, No, Nanette; I Wake Up Screaming; The Shanghai Gesture; Song of the Islands; My Gal Sal; Footlight Serenade; Seven Days' Leave; My Darling Clementine; Moss Rose; Kiss of Death; Fury at Furnace Creek; Cry of the City; Easy Living (1949); Red, Hot and Blue; Samson and Delilah; Wabash Avenue; Stella; Gambling House; The Las Vegas Story; Something for the Birds; Million Dollar Mermaid; Androcles and the Lion; The Glory Brigade; Affair with a Stranger; The Robe; The Veils of Bagdad; Dangerous Mission; Demetrius and the Gladiators; The Egyptian; Betrayed; Chief Crazy Horse; Violent Saturday; The Last Frontier; Safari (1956); The Sharkfighters; Zarak; Pickup Alley; The Long Haul; China Doll; Tank Force; Escort West; Timbuktu; The Bandit of Zhobe; The Big Circus; Hannibal; The Tartars

McCrea, Joel: The Single Standard; So This Is College; Dynamite (1929); The Silver Horde; The Common Law; Girls About Town; The Lost Squadron; Bird of Paradise (1932); The Most Dangerous Game; The Sport Parade; Rockabye; Scarlet River (cameo); The Silver Cord; Bed of Roses (1933); One Man's Journey; Chance at Heaven; Gambling Lady; The Richest Girl in the World; Private Worlds; Our Little Girl; Barbary Coast; Splendor (1935); Woman Wanted; These Three; Two in a Crowd; Adventure in Manhattan; Come and Get It; Banjo on My Knee; Internes Can't Take Money; Woman Chases Man; Dead End; Wells Fargo; Three Blind Mice; Union Pacific; They Shall Have Music; Espionage Agent; He Married His Wife; Primrose Path; Foreign Correspondent; Reaching for the Sun; Sullivan's Travels; The Great Man's Lady; The Palm Beach Story; The More the Merrier; Buffalo Bill; The Great Moment; The Unseen (1945); The Virginian (1946); Ramrod; Four Faces West; South of St. Louis; Colorado Territory; Stars in My Crown; The Outriders; Saddle Tramp; Frenchie; Hollywood Story (cameo); Cattle Drive; The San Francisco Story; Shoot First; Lone Hand; Border River; Black Horse Canyon; Wichita; Stranger on Horseback; The First Texan; The Oklahoman; Trooper Hook; Gunsight Ridge; The Tall Stranger; Cattle Empire; Fort Massacre; The Gunfight at Dodge City; Ride the High Country

McQueen, Steve: Somebody Up There Likes Me; Never Love a Stranger; The Blob (1958); Never So Few; The Great St. Louis Bank Robbery; The Magnificent Seven; The Honeymoon Machine; Hell Is for Heroes; The War Lover; The Great Escape; Soldier in the Rain; Love with the Proper Stranger; Baby the Rain Must Fall; The Cincinnati Kid

Mifune, Toshiro: Drunken Angel; The Quiet Duel; Stray Dog; Scandal; Rashomon; The Idiot (1951); The Life of Oharu; Seven Samurai; I Live in Fear; Throne of Blood; The Lower Depths (1957); The Hidden Fortress; The Bad Sleep Well; Yojimbo; Sanjuro; Chushingura; High and Low; Red Beard

Milland, Ray: Piccadilly (extra); The Informer (1929; uncred); Way for a Sailor; The Bachelor Father; Strangers May Kiss (bit); Bought!; Ambassador Bill; Blonde Crazy; The Man Who Played God; Polly of the Circus (bit); But the Flesh Is Weak (bit); Payment Deferred; Bolero (1934); We're Not Dressing; Charlie Chan in London; The Gilded Lily; Four Hours to Kill!; The Glass Key (1935); Next Time We Love; The Return of Sophie Lang; The Big Broadcast of 1937; The Jungle Princess; Three Smart Girls; Bulldog Drummond Escapes; Easy Living (1937); Ebb Tide; Wise Girl; Her Jungle Love; Tropic Holiday; Men with Wings; Say It in French; Hotel Imperial; Beau Geste (1939); Everything Happens at Night; Irene; The Doctor Takes a Wife; Arise, My Love; Untamed (1940); I Wanted Wings; Skylark; The Lady Has Plans; Reap the Wild Wind; Are Husbands Necessary?; The Major and the Minor; Forever and a Day; The Crystal Ball; Lady in the Dark; Till We Meet Again; The Uninvited (1944); Ministry of Fear; Kitty; The Lost Weekend; The Well-Groomed Bride; California; The Imperfect Lady; The Trouble with Women; Golden Earrings; The Big Clock; So Evil My Love; Sealed Verdict; Miss Tatlock's Millions; Alias Nick Beal; It Happens Every Spring; A Woman of Distinction; A Life of Her Own; Copper Canyon; Close to My Heart; Circle of Danger; Night Into Morning; Rhubarb; Bugles in the Afternoon; Something to Live For; The Thief; Jamaica

Run; Let's Do It Again (1953); Dial M for Murder; The Girl in the Red Velvet Swing; A Man Alone (also dir); Lisbon (also dir); Three Brave Men; High Flight; The River's Edge; The Safecracker (also dir); Premature Burial; Panic in Year Zero! (also dir); X: The Man with the X-Ray Eyes

Mitchum, Robert: Hoppy Serves a Writ; Aerial Gunner; Border Patrol; Leatherburners; Colt Comrades; Bar 20; False Colors; The Human Comedy; We've Never Been Licked; Corvette K-225; The Dancing Masters; Riders of the Deadline; Cry "Havoc"; "Gung Ho!"; Johnny Doesn't Live Here Any More; When Strangers Marry; Girl Rush (1944); Thirty Seconds Over Tokyo; Nevada; The Story of G.I. Joe; West of the Pecos; Till the End of Time; Undercurrent; The Locket; Pursued; Crossfire; Desire Me; Out of the Past; Rachel and the Stranger; Blood on the Moon; The Red Pony; The Big Steal; Holiday Affair; Where Danger Lives; My Forbidden Past; His Kind of Woman; The Racket (1951); Macao; One Minute to Zero; The Lusty Men; Second Chance; Angel Face; White Witch Doctor; She Couldn't Say No; River of No Return; Track of the Cat; Not as a Stranger; Night of the Hunter; Man with the Gun; Foreign Intrigue; Bandido (1956); Heaven Knows, Mr. Allison; Fire Down Below (1957); The Enemy Below; Thunder Road; The Hunters; The Angry Hills; The Wonderful Country; Home From the Hill; The Sundowners (1960); Night Fighters; The Grass Is Greener; The Last Time I Saw Archie; Cape Fear (1962); The Longest Day; Two for the Seesaw; The List of Adrian Messenger (cameo); Rampage (1963); Man in the Middle; What a Way to Go!; Mister Moses

Monroe, Marilyn: Scudda Hoo! Scudda Hay!; Ladies of the Chorus; Love Happy; A Ticket to Tomahawk; The Asphalt Jungle; All About Eve; Right Cross; The Fireball; Hometown Story; As Young As You Feel; Love Nest; Let's Make It Legal; Clash by Night; We're Not Married!; Don't Bother to Knock; Monkey Business (1952); O. Henry's Full House; Niagara; Gentlemen Prefer Blondes; How to Marry a Millionaire; River of No Return; There's No Business Like Show Business; The Seven Year Itch; Bus Stop; The Prince and the Showgirl; Some Like It Hot (1959); Let's Make Love; The Misfits

Montgomery, Robert: The Single Standard (extra); So This Is College; Untamed (1929); Free and Easy; Their Own Desire; The Divorcee; The Big House; Our Blushing Brides; Love in the Rough; War Nurse; Inspiration; The Easiest Way; Strangers May Kiss; The Man in Possession; Private Lives; Lovers Courageous; But the Flesh Is Weak; Letty Lynton; Blondie of the Follies; Faithless; Hell Below; Made on Broadway; When Ladies Meet; Another Language;

Night Flight; Fugitive Lovers; The Mystery of Mr. X; Riptide; Hide-Out; Forsaking All Others; Biography of a Bachelor Girl; Vanessa: Her Love Story; No More Ladies; Petticoat Fever; Piccadilly Jim; Trouble for Two; The Last of Mrs. Cheyney (1937); Night Must Fall (1937); Ever Since Eve; Live, Love and Learn; The First Hundred Years; Yellow Jack; Three Loves Has Nancy; Fast and Loose (1939); The Earl of Chicago; Haunted Honeymoon; Mr. & Mrs. Smith (1941); Rage in Heaven; Here Comes Mr. Jordan; Unfinished Business; They Were Expendable; Lady in the Lake (also dir); Ride the Pink Horse (also dir); The Saxon Charm; June Bride; Once More My Darling (also dir); Eye Witness (also dir); The Gallant Hours (dir, narr)

Moreau, Jeanne: Julietta; Touchez Pas au Grisbi; Demoniaque; Elevator to the Gallows; Back to the Wall; The Lovers (1958); The Four Hundred Blows; Dangerous Liaisons 1960; 5 Branded Women; La Notte; A Woman Is a Woman (cameo); Jules and Jim; Eva; The Trial (1962); Bay of Angels; Banana Peel; The Fire Within; The Victors; Diary of a Chambermaid (1964); The Train; The Yellow Rolls-Royce; Viva Maria!; Chimes at Midnight

Muni, Paul: Scarface (1932); I Am a Fugitive from a Chain Gang; The World Changes; Hi, Nellie!; Bordertown; Black Fury; Dr. Socrates; The Story of Louis Pasteur; The Good Earth; The Life of Emile Zola; Juarez; We Are Not Alone; Hudson's Bay; The Commandos Strike at Dawn; Stage Door Canteen; A Song to Remember; Counter-Attack; Angel on My Shoulder; Stranger on the Prowl; The Last Angry Man

Murphy, Audie: Beyond Glory; Sierra; The Kid From Texas; Kansas Raiders; The Red Badge of Courage; The Cimarron Kid; The Duel at Silver Creek; Gunsmoke (1953); Column South; Tumbleweed; Ride Clear of Diablo; Drums Across the River; Destry; To Hell and Back; World in My Corner; Walk the Proud Land; The Guns of Fort Petticoat; Joe Butterfly; Night Passage; The Quiet American; Ride a Crooked Trail; The Gun Runners; No Name on the Bullet; The Wild and the Innocent; Cast a Long Shadow; Hell Bent for Leather; The Unforgiven (1960); Seven Ways from Sundown; Battle at Bloody Beach; Six Black Horses; Showdown; War Is Hell (app); Gunfight at Comanche Creek; The Quick Gun; Posse from Hell; Bullet for a Badman; Apache Rifles; Arizona Raiders

Newman, Paul: The Silver Chalice; Somebody Up There Likes Me; The Rack; The Helen Morgan Story; Until They Sail; The Long Hot Summer; The Left Handed Gun; Cat on a Hot Tin Roof; Rally 'Round the Flag, Boys!; The Young Philadelphians; From the Terrace; Exodus; The Hustler; Paris Blues; Sweet Bird of Youth; Hemingway's Adventures of a Young Man; Hud; A New Kind of Love; The Prize; What a Way to Go!; The Outrage (1964); Lady L

Niven, David: Cleopatra (1934; bit); Barbary Coast (extra); A Feather in Her Hat; Mutiny on the Bounty (1935; bit); Splendor (1935); Rose-Marie; Dodsworth; Thank You, Jeeves!; The Charge of the Light Brigade; Beloved Enemy; The Prisoner of Zenda (1937); Dinner at the Ritz; Bluebeard's Eighth Wife; Four Men and a Prayer; Three Blind Mice; The Dawn Patrol (1938); Wuthering Heights (1939); Bachelor Mother; The Real Glory; Eternally Yours; Raffles (1940); Spitfire (1942); The Way Ahead; A Matter of Life and Death; Magnificent Doll; The Perfect Marriage; The Bishop's Wife; The Other Love; Bonnie Prince Charlie; Enchantment; A Kiss in the Dark; A Kiss for Corliss; The Elusive Pimpernel; The Toast of New Orleans: Soldiers Three; Happy Go Lovely; Island Rescue; The Lady Says No; The Moon Is Blue; The Love Lottery; Tonight's the Night; Court Martial; The King's Thief; The Birds and the Bees; Around the World in Eighty Days (1956); Oh Men! Oh Women!; The Little Hut; My Man Godfrey (1957); The Silken Affair; Bonjour Tristesse; Separate Tables; Ask Any Girl; Happy Anniversary; Please Don't Eat the Daisies; The Guns of Navarone; The Conquered City; The Best of Enemies; The Road to Hong Kong (cameo); Guns of Darkness; 55 Days at Peking; The Pink Panther; Bedtime Story (1964); Lady L

Novak, Kim: The French Line (bit); Pushover; Phffft!; Son of Sinbad; 5 Against the House; The Man with the Golden Arm; Picnic; The Eddy Duchin Story; Jeanne Eagels; Pal Joey; Vertigo; Bell, Book and Candle; Middle of the Night; Strangers When We Meet; Pepe (cameo); The Notorious Landlady; Boys' Night Out; Of Human Bondage (1964); Kiss Me, Stupid; The Amorous Adventures of Moll Flanders

O'Brien, Pat: The Front Page (1931); Flying High; Consolation Marriage; Hell's House; Final Edition; American Madness; Virtue; Airmail; Bombshell; College Coach; Gambling Lady; Twenty Million Sweethearts; Here Comes the Navy; I Sell Anything; The Personality Kid; Flirtation Walk; Devil Dogs of the Air; In Caliente; Oil for the Lamps of China; The Irish in Us; Page Miss Glory; Stars Over Broadway; Ceiling Zero; I Married a Doctor; Public Enemy's Wife; China Clipper; The Great O'Malley; Slim; San Quentin (1937); Back in Circulation; Submarine D-1; Women Are Like That; Cowboy from Brooklyn; Boy Meets Girl; Garden of the Moon; Angels With Dirty Faces; Off the Record; The Kid From Kokomo; Indianapolis Speedway; Slightly Honorable; The Fighting 69th; Castle on the Hudson; 'Til We Meet Again;

Torrid Zone; Escape to Glory; Flowing Gold; Knute Rockne, All American; Two Yanks in Trinidad; Broadway; Flight Lieutenant; The Navy Comes Through; Bombardier; The Iron Major; His Butler's Sister; Marine Raiders; Secret Command; Having Wonderful Crime; Man Alive; Perilous Holiday; Crack-Up; Riffraff (1947); Fighting Father Dunne; The Boy With Green Hair; A Dangerous Profession; Johnny One-Eye; The Fireball; Criminal Lawyer (1951); The People Against O'Hara; Okinawa; Jubilee Trail; Ring of Fear; Inside Detroit; Kill Me Tomorrow; The Last Hurrah; Some Like It Hot (1959); Town Tamer

O'Connor, Donald: Men with Wings; Sing, You Sinners; Tom Sawyer, Detective; Million Dollar Legs (1939); Beau Geste (1939); On Your Toes; Private Buckaroo; Give Out Sisters; Get Hep to Love; Mister Big; Top Man; Chip Off the Old Block; This Is the Life; The Merry Monahans; Bowery to Broadway; Something in the Wind; Are You With It?; Feudin', Fussin' and A-Fightin'; Yes Sir That's My Baby; Francis; Curtain Call at Cactus Creek; The Milkman; Double Crossbones; Francis Goes to the Races; Singin' In the Rain; Francis Goes to West Point; I Love Melvin; Call Me Madam; Francis Covers the Big Town; Walking My Baby Back Home; Francis Joins the WACS; There's No Business Like Show Business; Francis in the Navy; Anything Goes (1956); The Buster Keaton Story; Cry for Happy; The Wonders of Aladdin; That Funny Feeling

O'Hara, Maureen: Jamaica Inn; The Hunchback of Notre Dame (1939); A Bill of Divorcement (1940); Dance, Girl, Dance; They Met in Argentina; How Green Was My Valley; To the Shores of Tripoli; Ten Gentlemen from West Point; The Black Swan; The Immortal Sergeant; This Land Is Mine; The Fallen Sparrow; Buffalo Bill; The Spanish Main; Sentimental Journey; Do You Love Me?; Sinbad the Sailor; The Homestretch; Miracle on 34th Street (1947); The Foxes of Harrow; Sitting Pretty (1948); The Forbidden Street; A Woman's Secret; Father Was a Fullback; Bagdad; Comanche Territory; Tripoli; Rio Grande; Flame of Araby; At Sword's Point; Kangaroo: The Australian Story; The Quiet Man; Against All Flags; The Redhead from Wyoming; War Arrow; Fire Over Africa; The Long Gray Line; The Magnificent Matador; Lady Godiva; Lisbon; Everything But the Truth; The Wings of Eagles; Our Man in Havana; The Deadly Companions; The Parent Trap; Mr. Hobbs Takes a Vacation; Spencer's Mountain; McLintock!; Battle of the Villa Fiorita

Olivier, Laurence: Friends and Lovers; The Yellow Ticket; Westward Passage; Perfect Understanding; I Stand Condemned; As You Like It; The Conquest of the Air;

Fire Over England; The Divorce of Lady X; Q Planes; Wuthering Heights (1939); 21 Days Together; Rebecca; Pride and Prejudice (1940); That Hamilton Woman; 49th Parallel; The Demi-Paradise; This Happy Breed (uncred narr); Henry V (1945; also dir, coadapt); Hamlet (1948; also dir); The Magic Box (cameo); Carrie (1952); The Beggar's Opera; Richard III (1955; also dir); The Prince and the Showgirl (also dir); The Devil's Disciple; The Entertainer; Spartacus; Term of Trial; Bunny Lake Is Missing; Othello (1965)

O'Sullivan, Maureen: Song o' My Heart; Just Imagine; A Connecticut Yankee; Tarzan the Ape Man; Skyscraper Souls; Okay, America!; Payment Deferred; Strange Interlude; Tugboat Annie; Stage Mother; Tarzan and His Mate; The Thin Man; The Barretts of Wimpole Street; David Copperfield; West Point of the Air; Cardinal Richelieu; The Flame Within; Woman Wanted; Anna Karenina (1935); The Bishop Misbehaves; The Voice of Bugle Ann; The Devil-Doll; Tarzan Escapes; A Day at the Races; The Emperor's Candlesticks; Between 2 Women; A Yank at Oxford; Port of Seven Seas; The Crowd Roars (1938); Spring Madness; Let Us Live; Tarzan Finds a Son!; Pride and Prejudice; Maisie Was a Lady; Tarzan's Secret Treasure; Tarzan's New York Adventure; The Big Clock; Where Danger Lives; Bonzo Goes to College; All I Desire; Mission Over Korea; Duffy of San Quentin; The Steel Cage; The Tall T; Wild Heritage; Never Too Late

Palance, Jack: Panic in the Streets; Halls of Montezuma; Sudden Fear; Shane; Second Chance; Arrowhead; Flight to Tangier; Man in the Attic; Sign of the Pagan; The Silver Chalice; Kiss of Fire; The Big Knife; I Died a Thousand Times; Attack; The Lonely Man; House of Numbers; The Man Inside; Ten Seconds to Hell; The Battle of Austerlitz; The Mongols; Barabbas; Sword of the Conqueror; Contempt; Once a Thief (1965)

Payne, John: Dodsworth; Hats Off; Fair Warning; College Swing; Garden of the Moon; Wings of the Navy; Indianapolis Speedway; Kid Nightingale; Star Dust; King of the Lumberjacks; Tear Gas Squad; Maryland; The Great Profile; Tin Pan Alley; The Great American Broadcast; Sun Valley Serenade; Week-End in Havana; Remember the Day; To the Shores of Tripoli; Footlight Serenade; Iceland; Springtime in the Rockies; Hello Frisco, Hello; The Dolly Sisters; Sentimental Journey; The Razor's Edge; Wake Up and Dream; Miracle on 34th Street (1947); Larceny; The Saxon Charm; El Paso; The Crooked Way; Captain China; The Eagle and the Hawk; Tripoli; Passage West; Crosswinds; Caribbean; Kansas City Confidential; The Blazing Forest; Raiders of the Seven Seas; The Vanquished; 99 River Street; Rails Into

Laramie; Silver Lode; Hell's Island; Santa Fe Passage; The Road to Denver; Tennessee's Partner; Slightly Scarlet; Hold Back the Night; Rebel in Town; The Boss; Bailout at 43,000; Hidden Fear

Peck, Gregory: Days of Glory; The Keys of the Kingdom; The Valley of Decision; Spellbound (1945); The Yearling; Duel in the Sun; The Macomber Affair; Gentleman's Agreement; The Paradine Case; Yellow Sky; The Great Sinner; Twelve O'Clock High; The Gunfighter; Only the Valiant; David and Bathsheba; Captain Horatio Hornblower; The Snows of Kilimanjaro; The World in His Arms; Roman Holiday; Man with a Million; The Purple Plain; Night People; The Man in the Gray Flannel Suit; Moby Dick (1956); Designing Woman; The Bravados; The Big Country; Pork Chop Hill; Beloved Infidel; On the Beach; The Guns of Navarone; To Kill a Mockingbird; Cape Fear (1962); How the West Was Won; Captain Newman, M.D.; Behold a Pale Horse; Mirage

Perkins, Anthony: The Actress; Friendly Persuasion; Fear Strikes Out; The Lonely Man; The Tin Star; Desire Under the Elms; This Angry Age; The Matchmaker; Green Mansions; On the Beach; Tall Story; Psycho (1960); Goodbye Again (1961); Phaedra; Five Miles to Midnight; The Trial (1962); A Ravishing Idiot; The Fool Killer

Pickford, Mary: Cinderella (1914); The Poor Little Rich Girl (1917); Rebecca of Sunnybrook Farm (1917); A Little Princess (1917); Stella Maris; Amarilly of Clothes-Line Alley; Daddy-Long-Legs; M'Liss; Heart o' the Hills; Pollyanna (1920); Suds; The Love Light; The Nut (uncred); Through the Back Door; Little Lord Fauntleroy (1921); Tess of the Storm Country (1922); Little Annie Rooney; Sparrows; My Best Girl; The Gaucho (cameo); Coquette; The Taming of the Shrew (1929); Secrets (1933)

Pidgeon, Walter: Showgirl in Hollywood; Going Wild; Kiss Me Again; The Hot Heiress; Rockabye; The Kiss Before the Mirror; Journal of a Crime; Big Brown Eyes; Saratoga; The Girl of the Golden West; The Shopworn Angel; Man-Proof; Too Hot to Handle (1938); Listen, Darling; Society Lawyer; 6,000 Enemies; Stronger Than Desire; Nick Carter—Master Detective; The House Across the Bay; It's a Date; Dark Command; Phantom Raiders; Flight Command; Sky Murder; Man Hunt; Blossoms in the Dust; How Green Was My Valley; Design for Scandal; Mrs. Miniver; White Cargo; The Youngest Profession (cameo); Madame Curie; Mrs. Parkington; Week-end at the Waldorf; Holiday in Mexico; The Secret Heart; If Winter Comes; Julia Misbehaves; Command Decision; The Red Danube; That Forsyte Woman; The Miniver Story; Quo Vadis (narr); Soldiers Three; The Unknown Man; Calling Bulldog Drummond; The Sellout; Million Dollar Mermaid; The Bad and the Beautiful; Scandal at Scourie; Dream Wife; Executive Suite; Men of the Fighting Lady; The Last Time I Saw Paris; Deep in My Heart; Hit the Deck; The Glass Slipper (narr); Forbidden Planet; These Wilder Years; The Rack; Voyage to the Bottom of the Sea; Advise & Consent; Big Red

Poitier, Sidney: No Way Out (1950); Cry, the Beloved Country (1951); Red Ball Express; Go, Man, Go!; The Blackboard Jungle; Good-bye, My Lady; Edge of the City; Something of Value; Band of Angels; The Mark of the Hawk; Virgin Island; The Defiant Ones; Porgy and Bess; All the Young Men; Paris Blues; Pressure Point; Lilies of the Field; The Long Ships; The Greatest Story Ever Told; The Bedford Incident; A Patch of Blue; The Slender Thread

Powell, Dick: Blessed Event; Too Busy to Work; The King's Vacation; 42nd Street; Gold Diggers of 1933; Footlight Parade; College Coach; Wonder Bar; Dames; Twenty Million Sweethearts; Happiness Ahead; Flirtation Walk; Gold Diggers of 1935; Page Miss Glory; Broadway Gondolier; Shipmates Forever; Thanks a Million; A Midsummer Night's Dream (1935); Colleen; Hearts Divided; Stage Struck (1936); Gold Diggers of 1937; On the Avenue; The Singing Marine; Varsity Show; Hollywood Hotel; The Cowboy From Brooklyn; Hard to Get; Going Places (1938); Naughty But Nice; Christmas in July; I Want a Divorce; In the Navy; Model Wife; Star Spangled Rhythm; Happy Go Lucky; True to Life; Riding High (1943); Meet the People; It Happened Tomorrow; Murder, My Sweet; Cornered; Johnny O'Clock; To the Ends of the Earth; Station West; Pitfall; Rogue's Regiment; Mrs. Mike; The Reformer and the Redhead; Right Cross; The Tall Target; Cry Danger; You Never Can Tell; Callaway Went Thataway (cameo); The Bad and the Beautiful; Split Second (1953; dir); Susan Slept Here; The Conqueror (dir); You Can't Run Away From It (dir); The Enemy Below (dir); The Hunters (dir)

Powell, Eleanor: George White's Scandals; Broadway Melody of 1936; Born to Dance; Broadway Melody of 1938; Rosalie; Honolulu; Broadway Melody of 1940; Lady Be Good; Ship Ahoy; Thousands Cheer; I Dood It; Sensations of 1945; Duchess of Idaho (cameo)

Powell, William: Sherlock Holmes (1922); Paid to Love; The Last Command (1928); The Canary Murder Case; The Greene Murder Case; Charming Sinners; Street of Chance; The Benson Murder Case; Paramount on Parade; For the Defense; Man of the World; Ladies' Man (1931); High Pressure; Jewel Robbery; One Way Passage; Lawyer Man; Man Killer; Double Harness; The Kennel Murder Case; Fashions; Manhattan Melodrama; The Key (1934); The

Thin Man; Evelyn Prentice; Star of Midnight; Reckless (1935); Escapade (1935); Rendezvous; The Great Ziegfeld; The Ex-Mrs. Bradford; My Man Godfrey (1936); Libeled Lady; After the Thin Man; The Last of Mrs. Cheyney (1937); The Emperor's Candlesticks; Double Wedding; The Baroness and the Butler; Another Thin Man; I Love You Again; Love Crazy; Shadow of the Thin Man; Crossroads (1942); The Youngest Profession (cameo); The Heavenly Body; The Thin Man Goes Home; Ziegfeld Follies; The Hoodlum Saint; Life With Father; Song of the Thin Man; The Senator Was Indiscreet; Mr. Peabody and the Mermaid; Take One False Step; Dancing in the Dark (1949); It's a Big Country (cameo); The Treasure of Lost Canyon; The Girl Who Had Everything; How to Marry a Millionaire; Mister Roberts

Power, Tyrone: Tom Brown of Culver; Flirtation Walk; Girls' Dormitory; Ladies in Love; Lloyd's of London; Love Is News; Cafe Metropole; Thin Ice; Second Honeymoon; Ali Baba Goes to Town (cameo); In Old Chicago; Alexander's Ragtime Band; Marie Antoinette (1938); Suez; Jesse James; Rose of Washington Square; Second Fiddle; The Rains Came; Day-Time Wife; Johnny Apollo; Brigham Young; The Mark of Zorro (1940); Blood and Sand (1941); A Yank in the R.A.F.; Son of Fury; This Above All; The Black Swan; Crash Dive; The Razor's Edge (1946); Nightmare Alley; Captain From Castile; The Luck of the Irish; That Wonderful Urge; Prince of Foxes; The Black Rose; American Guerilla in the Philippines; Rawhide; I'll Never Forget You; Diplomatic Courier; Pony Soldier; The Mississippi Gambler; King of the Khyber Rifles; The Long Gray Line; Untamed (1955); The Eddie Duchin Story; Abandon Ship!; The Rising of the Moon (app); The Sun Also Rises; Witness for the Prosecution

Presley, Elvis: Love Me Tender; Loving You; Jailhouse Rock; King Creole; G.I. Blues; Flaming Star; Wild in the Country; Blue Hawaii; Follow that Dream; Kid Galahad (1962); Girls! Girls! Girls!; It Happened at the World's Fair; Fun in Acapulco; Kissin' Cousins; Viva Las Vegas; Roustabout; Girl Happy; Tickle Me; Harum Scarum

Preston, Robert: King of Alcatraz; Illegal Traffic; Disbarred; Union Pacific; Beau Geste (1939); Typhoon; North West Mounted Police; Moon Over Burma; Lady From Cheyenne; Parachute Battalion; New York Town; The Night of January 16th; Reap the Wild Wind; This Gun for Hire; Wake Island; Star Spangled Rhythm; Night Plane From Chungking; Variety Girl (cameo); The Macomber Affair; Wild Harvest; Big City (1948); Blood on the Moon; Whispering Smith; Tulsa; The Lady Gambles; The Sundowners (1950); My Outlaw

Brother; When I Grow Up; Best of the Badmen; Cloudburst; Face to Face (1952); The Last Frontier (1956); The Dark at the Top of the Stairs; The Music Man; How the West Was Won; Island of Love; All the Way Home

Price, Vincent: Service De Luxe; The Private Lives of Elizabeth and Essex; Tower of London (1939); The Invisible Man Returns; The House of the Seven Gables; Green Hell; Brigham Young; Hudson's Bay; The Song of Bernadette; The Eve of St. Mark; Wilson; Laura; The Keys of the Kingdom; A Royal Scandal; Leave Her to Heaven; Shock (1946); Dragonwyck; The Web; Moss Rose; The Long Night; Up in Central Park; Abbott and Costello Meet Frankenstein (voice); The Three Musketeers (1948); Rogue's Regiment; The Bribe; Bagdad; Champagne for Caesar; The Baron of Arizona; Curtain Call at Cactus Creek; His Kind of Woman; Adventures of Captain Fabian; The Las Vegas Story; House of Wax (1953); Dangerous Mission; Casanova's Big Night; The Mad Magician; Son of Sinbad; The Vagabond King; Serenade; While the City Sleeps; The Ten Commandments (1956); The Story of Mankind; The Fly (1958); House on Haunted Hill; The Big Circus; The Bat; Return of the Fly; The Tingler; House of Usher; Master of the World; Pit and the Pendulum (1961); Queen of the Nile; Convicts 4; Confessions of an Opium Eater; Tales of Terror; Tower of London (1962); The Raven (1963); Diary of a Madman; Beach Party (cameo); Twice-Told Tales; The Comedy of Terrors; The Haunted Palace; The Last Man on Earth; The Masque of the Red Death; The Tomb of Ligeia; War-Gods of the Deep; Dr. Goldfoot and the Bikini Machine

Quinn, Anthony: The Plainsman (1936); Night Waitress; Swing High, Swing Low; Waikiki Wedding; The Last Train from Madrid; Daughter of Shanghai; The Buccaneer (1938); Dangerous to Know; Tip-Off Girls; Bulldog Drummond in Africa; King of Alcatraz; King of Chinatown; Union Pacific; Television Spy; Island of Lost Men; Road to Singapore; The Ghost Breakers; Parole Fixer; City for Conquest; The Texas Rangers Ride Again; Knockout (1941); Thieves Fall Out; Blood and Sand (1941); Bullets for O'Hara; They Died With Their Boots On; Larceny, Inc.; Road to Morocco; The Black Swan; The Ox-Bow Incident; Guadalcanal Diary; Buffalo Bill; Roger Touhy, Gangster; Irish Eyes Are Smiling; China Sky; Where Do We Go From Here?; Back to Bataan; California; Sinbad the Sailor; The Imperfect Lady; Black Gold (1947); Tycoon; The Brave Bulls; Mask of the Avenger; Viva Zapata!; The Brigand; The World in His Arms; Against All Flags; City Beneath the Sea; Seminole; Ride, Vaquero!; East of Sumatra; Blowing Wild; Angels of

Darkness; Ulysses (1954); Fatal Desire; Attila; La Strada; The Long Wait; The Magnificent Matador; The Naked Street; Seven Cities of Gold; Lust for Life; Man From Del Rio; The Wild Party (1956); The Hunchback of Notre Dame (1957); The River's Edge; The Ride Back; Wild Is the Wind; Hot Spell; The Buccaneer (1958; dir); The Black Orchid; Warlock (1959); Last Train from Gun Hill; The Savage Innocents; Heller in Pink Tights; Portrait in Black; The Guns of Navarone; Barabbas; Requiem for a Heavyweight; Lawrence of Arabia; The Visit; Behold a Pale Horse; Zorba the Greek; A High Wind in Jamaica; Marco the Magnificent

Raft, George: Side Street (1929; bit); Quick Millions; Palmy Days; Taxi! (bit); Dancers in the Dark; Scarface (1932); Night World; Winner Take All (bit); Madame Racketeer; Night After Night; Under-Cover Man; If I Had a Million; Pick-up (1933); The Midnight Club; The Bowery; All of Me (1934); Bolero (1934); The Trumpet Blows; Limehouse Blues; Rumba; The Glass Key (1935); Every Night at Eight; She Couldn't Take It; Souls at Sea; You and Me; Spawn of the North; The Lady's from Kentucky; Each Dawn I Die; I Stole a Million; Invisible Stripes; The House Across the Bay; They Drive by Night; Manpower; Broadway; Background to Danger; Follow the Boys; Nob Hill; Johnny Angel; Whistle Stop; Mr. Ace; Nocturne; Christmas Eve; Intrigue; Outpost in Morocco; Johnny Allegro; Red Light; A Dangerous Profession; Lucky Nick Cain; Loan Shark; I'll Get You; The Man from Cairo; Rogue Cop; Black Widow; A Bullet for Joey; Around the World in Eighty Days (1956; cameo); Some Like It Hot (1959); Jet Over the Atlantic; Ocean's Eleven (cameo); For Those Who Think Young (cameo)

Rains, Claude: The Invisible Man; The Clairvoyant; Crime Without Passion; The Man Who Reclaimed His Head; Mystery of Edwin Drood (1935); The Last Outpost (1935); Hearts Divided; Anthony Adverse; Stolen Holiday; The Prince and the Pauper; They Won't Forget; White Banners; Gold Is Where You Find It; The Adventures of Robin Hood; Four Daughters; They Made Me a Criminal; Juarez; Daughters Courageous; Mr. Smith Goes to Washington; Four Wives; Saturday's Children; The Sea Hawk (1940); Lady With Red Hair; Four Mothers; Here Comes Mr. Jordan; The Wolf Man (1941); Kings Row; Moontide; Casablanca; Forever and a Day; Phantom of the Opera (1943); Passage to Marseille; Mr. Skeffington; Strange Holiday; This Love of Ours; Caesar and Cleopatra; Notorious (1946); Angel on My Shoulder; Deception (1946); The Unsuspected; The Passionate Friends; Rope of Sand; Song of Surrender; The White Tower; Where Danger Lives; Sealed

Cargo; The Paris Express; Lisbon; This Earth Is Mine; The Lost World (1960); Battle of the Worlds; Lawrence of Arabia; Twilight of Honor; The Greatest Story Ever Told

Rathbone, Basil: The Last of Mrs. Cheyney (1929); Bishop Murder Case; A Notorious Affair; The Flirting Widow; Sin Takes a Holiday; David Copperfield (1935); Anna Karenina (1935); The Last Days of Pompeii (1935); A Feather in Her Hat; Kind Lady (1935); A Tale of Two Cities (1935); Captain Blood (1935); Private Number; Romeo and Juliet (1936); The Garden of Allah; Love From a Stranger (1937); Make a Wish; Confession (1937); Tovarich; The Adventures of Marco Polo; The Adventures of Robin Hood; If I Were King; The Dawn Patrol (1938); Son of Frankenstein; The Hound of the Baskervilles (1939); The Sun Never Sets; The Adventures of Sherlock Holmes; Rio; Tower of London (1939); Rhythm on the River; The Mark of Zorro (1940); The Mad Doctor; The Black Cat (1941); International Lady; Paris Calling; Fingers at the Window; Crossroads (1942); Sherlock Holmes and the Voice of Terror; Sherlock Holmes and the Secret Weapon; Sherlock Holmes in Washington; Above Suspicion; Sherlock Holmes Faces Death; Crazy House (cameo); The Spider Woman; The Scarlet Claw; Bathing Beauty; The Pearl of Death; Frenchman's Creek; The House of Fear (1945); The Woman in Green; Pursuit to Algiers; Terror by Night; Heartbeat; Dressed to Kill (1946); The Adventures of Ichabod and Mr. Toad; Casanova's Big Night; We're No Angels (1955); The Court Jester; The Black Sleep; The Last Hurrah; Pontius Pilate; The Magic Sword; Tales of Terror; The Comedy of Terrors

Reagan, Ronald: Love Is on the Air; Hollywood Hotel; Sergeant Murphy; Swing Your Lady; Cowboy From Brooklyn; Boy Meets Girl; Girls on Probation; Brother Rat; Going Places (1938); Accidents Will Happen; Secret Service of the Air; Dark Victory; Code of the Secret Service; Naughty But Nice; Hell's Kitchen; Angels Wash Their Faces; Smashing the Money Ring; Brother Rat and a Baby; An Angel From Texas; Murder in the Air; Knute Rockne, All American; Tugboat Annie Sails Again; Santa Fe Trail; The Bad Man; Million Dollar Baby (1941); Nine Lives Are Not Enough; International Squadron; Kings Row; Juke Girl; Desperate Journey; This Is the Army; Stallion Road; That Hagen Girl; The Voice of the Turtle; John Loves Mary; Night Unto Night; The Girl From Jones Beach; It's a Great Feeling (cameo); The Hasty Heart; Louisa; Storm Warning; Bedtime for Bonzo; The Last Outpost (1951); Hong Kong; The Winning Team; She's Working Her Way Through College; Tropic Zone; Law and Order (1953); Prisoner of War; Cattle Queen of Montana; Tennessee's Partner; Hellcats of the Navy; The Young Doctors (narr); The Killers (1964)

Reynolds, Debbie: June Bride; The Daughter of Rosie O'Grady; Three Little Words; Two Weeks-With Love; Mr. Imperium; Singin' In the Rain; Skirts Ahoy! (cameo); I Love Melvin; The Affairs of Dobie Gillis; Give a Girl a Break; Susan Slept Here; Athena; Hit the Deck; The Tender Trap; The Catered Affair; Meet Me in Las Vegas (cameo); Bundle of Joy; Tammy and the Bachelor; This Happy Feeling; The Mating Game; Say One for Me; It Started With a Kiss; The Gazebo; The Rat Race (1960); Pepe (cameo); The Pleasure of His Company; The Second Time Around; How the West Was Won; My Six Loves; Mary, Mary; The Unsinkable Molly Brown; Goodbye Charlie

Robeson, Paul: Body and Soul (1925); The Emperor Jones; Sanders of the River; Show Boat (1936); Song of Freedom; King Solomon's Mines (1937); Dark Sands; Big Fella; The Proud Valley; Tales of Manhattan

Robinson, Edward G.: The Hole in the Wall; Outside the Law (1930); The Widow from Chicago; Little Caesar; A Lady to Love; Smart Money; Five Star Final; The Hatchet Man; Two Seconds; Tiger Shark; Silver Dollar; The Little Giant; I Loved a Woman; Dark Hazard; The Man with Two Faces; The Whole Town's Talking; Barbary Coast; Bullets or Ballots; Thunder in the City; Kid Galahad (1937); The Last Gangster; A Slight Case of Murder; The Amazing Dr. Clitterhouse; I Am the Law; Confessions of a Nazi Spy; Blackmail (1939); Dr. Ehrlich's Magic Bullet; Brother Orchid; A Dispatch From Reuters; The Sea Wolf; Manpower; Unholy Partners; Larceny, Inc.; Tales of Manhattan; Destroyer; Flesh and Fantasy; Tampico; Mr. Winkle Goes to War; Double Indemnity; The Woman in the Window; Journey Together; Our Vines Have Tender Grapes; Scarlet Street; The Stranger (1946); The Red House; All My Sons; Key Largo; Night Has a Thousand Eyes; House of Strangers; It's a Great Feeling (cameo); Operation X; Actors and Sin; Vice Squad (1953); Big Leaguer; The Glass Web; Black Tuesday; The Violent Men; Tight Spot; A Bullet for Joey; Illegal; Hell on Frisco Bay; Nightmare (1956); The Ten Commandments (1956); A Hole in the Head; Seven Thieves; Pepe (cameo); My Geisha; Two Weeks in Another Town; A Boy Ten Feet Tall; The Prize; Good Neighbor Sam; Robin and the 7 Hoods (cameo); The Outrage (1964); Cheyenne Autumn; The Cincinnati Kid

Rogers, Ginger: Follow the Leader (1930); The Tip-Off; Suicide Fleet; Carnival Boat; The Tenderfoot; The Thirteenth Guest; Hat Check Girl; You Said a Mouthful; 42nd Street; Broadway Bad; Gold Diggers of 1933; Professional Sweetheart; A Shriek in the Night; Sitting Pretty (1933); Flying Down to Rio; Rafter Romance; Chance at Heaven; Finishing School; Twenty Million Sweethearts; Upperworld; The Gay Divorcee; Romance in Manhattan; Roberta; Star of Midnight; Top Hat; In Person; Follow the Fleet; Swing Time; Shall We Dance (1937); Stage Door; Having Wonderful Time; Vivacious Lady; Carefree; The Story of Vernon and Irene Castle; Bachelor Mother; 5th Ave. Girl; Primrose Path; Lucky Partners; Kitty Foyle; Tom, Dick and Harry; Roxie Hart; Tales of Manhattan; The Major and the Minor; Once Upon a Honeymoon; Tender Comrade; Lady in the Dark; I'll Be Seeing You; Week-End at the Waldorf; Heartbeat (1946); Magnificent Doll; It Had to Be You; The Barkleys of Broadway; Perfect Strangers (1950); Storm Warning; The Groom Wore Spurs; We're Not Married!; Monkey Business (1952); Dreamboat; Forever Female; Black Widow (1954); Twist of Fate; Tight Spot; The First Traveling Saleslady; Teen-age Rebel; Oh, Men! Oh, Women!; Harlow (Carol Lynley version)

Rogers, Roy: Rhythm on the Range (as singer); The Big Show; The Old Corral; The Old Barn Dance; Under Western Stars; Billy the Kid Returns; Come On, Rangers; Shine On Harvest Moon; Rough Riders' Round-Up; Southward, Ho!; Frontier Pony Express; In Old Caliente; The Arizona Kid; Jeepers Creepers; Saga of Death Valley; Days of Jesse James; Dark Command; Young Buffalo Bill; The Carson City Kid; The Ranger and the Lady; Colorado; Young Bill Hickok; The Border Legion; Robin Hood of the Pecos; Arkansas Judge; In Old Cheyenne; Sheriff of Tombstone; Nevada City; Bad Man of Deadwood; Jesse James at Bay; Red River Valley; Man from Cheyenne; South of Santa Fe; Sunset on the Desert; Romance on the Range; Sons of the Pioneers; Sunset Serenade; Heart of the Golden West; Ridin' Down the Canyon; Idaho; King of the Cowboys; Song of Texas; Silver Spurs; Man From Music Mountain (1943); Hands Across the Border; Cowboy and the Senorita; The Yellow Rose of Texas; Song of Nevada; San Fernando Valley; Lights of Old Santa Fe; Lake Placid Serenade (cameo); Utah; Bells of Rosarita; The Man from Oklahoma; Along the Navajo Trail; Sunset in El Dorado; Don't Fence Me In; Song of Arizona; Rainbow Over Texas; My Pal Trigger; Under Nevada Skies; Roll on Texas Moon; Home in Oklahoma; Heldorado; Apache Rose; Bells of San Angelo; Springtime in the Sierras; On the Old Spanish Trail; The Gay Ranchero; Under California Stars; Melody Time; Eyes of Texas; Night Time in Nevada; Grand Canyon Trail; The Far Frontier; Susanna Pass; Down Dakota Way; The Golden Stallion; Bells of Coronado; Twilight in the Sierras; Trigger, Jr.; Sunset in the West; North of the Great Divide; Trail of Robin Hood; Spoilers of the Plains; Heart of the Rockies; In Old Amarillo; South of Caliente; Pals of the Golden West; Son of Paleface; Alias Jesse James (cameo)

Rogers, Will: Happy Days (cameo); They Had to See Paris; A Connecticut Yankee; Ambassador Bill; Down to Earth; Too Busy to Work; State Fair (1933); Doctor Bull; Mr. Skitch; David Harum; Judge Priest; Life Begins at Forty; Doubting Thomas; Steamboat 'Round the Bend; In Old Kentucky

Rooney, Mickey: The Beast of the City; The Big Cage; The Life of Jimmy Dolan; Broadway to Hollywood; The Chief; The World Changes; I Like It That Way; Upperworld; Manhattan Melodrama; Hide-Out (1934); Chained; Blind Date (1934); Death on the Diamond; Reckless (1935); A Midsummer Night's Dream (1935); Ah, Wilderness!; Riffraff (1935); Little Lord Fauntleroy (1936); Down the Stretch; The Devil Is a Sissy; A Family Affair; Captains Courageous; The Hoosier Schoolboy; Slave Ship; Live, Love and Learn; Thoroughbreds Don't Cry; You're Only Young Once; Love Is a Headache; Judge Hardy's Children; Lord Jeff; Love Finds Andy Hardy; Boys Town; Stablemates; Out West With the Hardys; Huckleberry Finn (1939); The Hardys Ride High; Andy Hardy Gets Spring Fever; Babes in Arms; Judge Hardy and Son; Young Tom Edison; Andy Hardy Meets Debutante; Strike Up the Band; Andy Hardy's Private Secretary; Men of Boys Town; Life Begins for Andy Hardy; Babes on Broadway; The Courtship of Andy Hardy; A Yank at Eton; Andy Hardy's Double Life; Thousands Cheer; Girl Crazy (1943); The Human Comedy; Andy Hardy's Blonde Trouble; National Velvet; Love Laughs at Andy Hardy; Killer McCoy; Summer Holiday (1948); Words and Music; The Big Wheel; Quicksand (1950); He's a Cockeyed Wonder; The Fireball; My True Story (dir); My Outlaw Brother; The Strip; Sound Off; Off Limits (1953); All Ashore; A Slight Case of Larceny; Drive a Crooked Road; The Atomic Kid; The Bridges at Toko-Ri; The Twinkle in God's Eye; The Bold and the Brave; Francis in the Haunted House; Magnificent Roughnecks; Operation Mad Ball; Baby Face Nelson; A Nice Little Bank That Should Be Robbed; Andy Hardy Comes Home; The Last Mile (1959); The Big Operator; Platinum High School; The Private Lives of Adam and Eve (also codir); King of the Roaring 20s—The Story of Arnold Rothstein; Breakfast at Tiffany's; Everything's Ducky; Requiem for a Heavyweight; It's a Mad Mad Mad Mad World; The Secret Invasion; 24 Hours to Kill; How to Stuff a Wild Bikini

Russell, Jane: The Outlaw; Young Widow; The Paleface; His Kind of Woman; Double Dynamite; The Las Vegas Story; Macao;

Son of Paleface; Montana Belle; Road to Bali (cameo); Gentlemen Prefer Blondes; The French Line; Underwater!; Foxfire; The Tall Men; Gentlemen Marry Brunettes; Hot Blood; The Revolt of Mamie Stover; The Fuzzy Pink Nightgown

Russell, Rosalind: Evelyn Prentice; The President Vanishes; Forsaking All Others; The Night Is Young; West Point of the Air; Casino Murder Case; Reckless (1935); China Seas; Rendezvous; It Had to Happen; Under Two Flags; Trouble for Two; Craig's Wife; Night Must Fall (1937); Live, Love and Learn; Man-Proof; Four's a Crowd; The Citadel; Fast and Loose (1939); The Women (1939); His Girl Friday; Hired Wife; No Time for Comedy; This Thing Called Love; They Met in Bombay; The Feminine Touch (1941); Design for Scandal; Take a Letter, Darling; My Sister Eileen (1942); Flight for Freedom; What a Woman! (1943); Roughly Speaking; She Wouldn't Say Yes; Sister Kenny; The Guilt of Janet Ames; Mourning Becomes Electra; The Velvet Touch; Tell It to the Judge; A Woman of Distinction; Never Wave at a WAC; The Girl Rush (1955); Picnic; The Unguarded Moment (costy); Auntie Mame; A Majority of One; Five Finger Exercise; Gypsy

Ryan, Robert: The Ghost Breakers (bit); Queen of the Mob (bit); Golden Gloves; North West Mounted Police; The Texas Rangers Ride Again; The Feminine Touch; Bombardier; The Sky's the Limit; Behind the Rising Sun; The Iron Major; Gangway for Tomorrow; Tender Comrade; Marine Raiders; Trail Street; The Woman on the Beach; Crossfire; Berlin Express; Return of the Bad Men; The Boy With Green Hair; Act of Violence; Caught (1949); The Set-Up; The Secret Fury; I Married a Communist; Born to Be Bad; Hard, Fast and Beautiful (cameo); Best of the Badmen; Flying Leathernecks; The Racket (1951); On Dangerous Ground; Clash by Night; Beware, My Lovely; Horizons West; The Naked Spur; City Beneath the Sea; Inferno; Alaska Seas; About Mrs. Leslie; Her Twelve Men; Bad Day at Black Rock; Escape to Burma; House of Bamboo; The Tall Men; The Proud Ones (1956); Back from Eternity; Men in War; God's Little Acre; Lonelyhearts; Day of the Outlaw; Odds Against Tomorrow; Ice Palace; The Canadians; King of Kings (1961); The Longest Day; Billy Budd; The Crooked Road; The Dirty Game; Battle of the Bulge

Sanders, George: Things to Come (bit); Lloyd's of London; The Man Who Could Work Miracles; Love Is News; Slave Ship; Lancer Spy; International Settlement; Four Men and a Prayer; Mr. Moto's Last Warning; The Saint Strikes Back; Confessions of a Nazi Spy; The Saint in London; Nurse Edith Cavell; Allegheny Uprising;

The Saint's Double Trouble; Rebecca; The Saint Takes Over; Foreign Correspondent; Bitter Sweet; The Son of Monte Cristo; The Saint in Palm Springs; Rage in Heaven; Man Hunt; Sundown; The Gay Falcon; A Date with the Falcon; Son of Fury; The Falcon Takes Over; Tales of Manhattan; The Falcon's Brother; The Black Swan; Quiet Please Murder; This Land Is Mine; They Came to Blow Up America; Appointment in Berlin; Paris After Dark; The Moon and Sixpence; The Lodger (1944); Action in Arabia; Summer Storm; Hangover Square; The Picture of Dorian Gray; The Strange Affair of Uncle Harry; A Scandal in Paris; The Strange Woman; The Private Affairs of Bel Ami; The Ghost and Mrs. Muir; Lured; Forever Amber; The Fan; Samson and Delilah; All About Eve; I Can Get It for You Wholesale; Captain Blackjack; The Light Touch; Ivanhoe; Assignment: Paris; Call Me Madam; Strangers; Witness to Murder; King Richard and the Crusaders; Jupiter's Darling; Moonfleet; The Scarlet Coat; The King's Thief; Never Say Goodbye (1956); While the City Sleeps; That Certain Feeling; Death of a Scoundrel; The Seventh Sin; The Whole Truth; From the Earth to the Moon; That Kind of Woman; Solomon and Sheba; A Touch of Larceny; The Last Voyage; Bluebeard's Ten Honeymoons; Village of the Damned; Five Golden Hours; Operation Snatch; In Search of the Castaways; Cairo; A Shot in the Dark; The Amorous Adventures of Moll Flanders

Scott, Randolph: The Black Watch (bit); The Virginian (1929; extra); Dynamite (1929; bit); Born Reckless (1930; bit); A Successful Calamity; Hot Saturday; Murders in the Zoo; Supernatural; Cocktail Hour; Roberta; Village Tale; She (1935); So Red the Rose; Follow the Fleet; The Last of the Mohicans (1936); Go West Young Man; High, Wide, and Handsome; Rebecca of Sunnybrook Farm (1938); The Texans; Jesse James; Susannah of the Mounties; Frontier Marshal; Coast Guard; Virginia City; My Favorite Wife; When the Daltons Rode; Western Union; Belle Starr; Paris Calling; To the Shores of Tripoli; The Spoilers (1942); Pittsburgh; Bombardier; The Desperadoes; Corvette K-225; Gung Ho!; Belle of the Yukon; China Sky; Captain Kidd; Abilene Town; Badman's Territory; Home, Sweet Homicide; Trail Street; Gunfighters; Christmas Eve; Albuquerque; Coroner Creek; Return of the Bad Men; The Walking Hills; Canadian Pacific; The Doolins of Oklahoma; Fighting Man of the Plains; The Nevadan; Colt .45; The Cariboo Trail; Sugarfoot; Santa Fe; Fort Worth; Man in the Saddle; Carson City; Hangman's Knot; The Man Behind the Gun; The Stranger Wore a Gun; Thunder over the Plains; Riding Shotgun; The Bounty Hunter; Ten Wanted Men; Rage at Dawn;

Tall Man Riding; A Lawless Street; Seven Men from Now; 7th Cavalry; The Tall T; Shoot-Out at Medicine Bend; Decision at Sundown; Buchanan Rides Alone; Westbound; Ride Lonesome; Comanche Station; Ride the High Country

Sellers, Peter: Down Among the Z Men; Orders Are Orders; The Ladykillers (1955); The Man Who Never Was (voice); The Smallest Show on Earth; Your Past Is Showing; Up the Creek (1958); tom thumb; Man in a Cocked Hat; The Mouse That Roared; I'm All Right Jack; The Battle of the Sexes; Two Way Stretch; Never Let Go; The Millionairess; I Like Money (also dir); Only Two Can Play; Waltz of the Toreadors; The Dock Brief; The Road to Hong Kong (cameo); Lolita (1962); The Wrong Arm of the Law; Heavens Above!; Dr. Strangelove Or: How I Learned to Stop Worrying and Love the Bomb; The Pink Panther (1964); The World of Henry Orient; A Shot in the Dark; What's New Pussycat

Shearer, Norma: The Flapper (bit); Way Down East (1920; bit); He Who Gets Slapped; Lady of the Night; The Student Prince in Old Heidelberg; A Lady of Chance; The Trial of Mary Dugan; The Last of Mrs. Cheyney (1929); The Hollywood Revue of 1929; Their Own Desire; The Divorcee; Let Us Be Gay; Strangers May Kiss; A Free Soul; Private Lives; Strange Interlude; Smilin' Through (1932); Riptide; The Barretts of Wimpole Street (1934); Romeo and Juliet (1936); Marie Antoinette (1938); Idiot's Delight; The Women (1939); Escape (1940); We Were Dancing; Her Cardboard Lover

Sheridan, Ann: Search for Beauty (bit); Bolero (bit); Murder at the Vanities (chorus); Shoot the Works; Kiss and Make-Up (bit); The Notorious Sophie Lang; Ladies Should Listen; The Lemon Drop Kid (1934; bit); Mrs. Wiggs of the Cabbage Patch (bit); College Rhythm; Behold My Wife!; Limehouse Blues (bit); Enter Madame (bit); Rumba; Car 99; Mississippi; The Glass Key (1935); The Crusades (bit); Fighting Youth; The Great O'Malley; San Quentin (1937); The Footloose Heiress; Alcatraz Island; She Loved a Fireman; The Patient in Room 18; Mystery House; Little Miss Thoroughbred; The Cowboy from Brooklyn; Letter of Introduction; Broadway Musketeers; Angels with Dirty Faces; They Made Me a Criminal; Dodge City; Naughty But Nice; Winter Carnival; Indianapolis Speedway; The Angels Wash Their Faces; Castle on the Hudson; It All Came True; Torrid Zone; They Drive by Night; City for Conquest; Honeymoon for Three; Navy Blues; The Man Who Came to Dinner; Kings Row; Juke Girl; Wings for the Eagle; George Washington Slept Here; Edge of Darkness; Shine On, Harvest Moon; The Doughgirls; One More Tomorrow; The Unfaithful; The Trea-

sure of the Sierra Madre (cameo); Silver River; Good Sam; I Was a Male War Bride; Stella; Woman on the Run; Steel Town; Just Across the Street; Take Me to Town; Appointment in Honduras; Come Next Spring; The Opposite Sex; Woman and the Hunter

Sidney, Sylvia: City Streets (1931); An American Tragedy; Street Scene; Ladies of the Big House; Merrily We Go to Hell; Make Me a Star (cameo); Madame Butterfly; Pick-up (1933); Good Dame; Thirty Day Princess; Behold My Wife!; Accent on Youth; Mary Burns, Fugitive; The Trail of the Lonesome Pine; Fury (1936); Sabotage (1936); You Only Live Once; Dead End; You and Me; One Third of a Nation; The Wagons Roll at Night; Blood on the Sun; The Searching Wind; Mr. Ace; Love From a Stranger; Les Miserables (1952); Violent Saturday; Behind the High Wall

Simmons, Jean: The Way to the Stars; Caesar and Cleopatra; Great Expectations (1946); Black Narcissus; Hungry Hill; The Inheritance; Hamlet (1948); The Blue Lagoon (1949); Adam and Evalyn; So Long at the Fair; Cage of Gold; Trio; The Clouded Yellow; Angel Face; Androcles and the Lion; Young Bess; Affair with a Stranger; The Robe; The Actress; She Couldn't Say No; Demetrius and the Gladiators (uncred); The Egyptian; A Bullet Is Waiting; Desirée; Footsteps in the Fog; Guys and Dolls; Hilda Crane; This Could Be the Night; Until They Sail; The Big Country; Home Before Dark; This Earth Is Mine; Spartacus; The Grass Is Greener; All the Way Home; Life at the Top

Sinatra, Frank: Las Vegas Nights (singer); Ship Ahoy (singer); Reveille With Beverly (singer); Higher and Higher; Step Lively; Anchors Aweigh; Till the Clouds Roll By; It Happened in Brooklyn; The Miracle of the Bells; The Kissing Bandit; Take Me Out to the Ball Game; On the Town; Double Dynamite; Meet Danny Wilson; From Here to Eternity; Suddenly; Three Coins in the Fountain (sings title song); Young at Heart; Not as a Stranger; Guys and Dolls; The Tender Trap; The Man With the Golden Arm; Meet Me in Las Vegas (cameo); High Society (1956); Johnny Concho; Around the World in Eighty Days (1956; cameo); Pal Joey; The Pride and the Passion; The Joker Is Wild; Kings Go Forth; Some Came Running; A Hole in the Head; Never So Few; Can-Can; Ocean's Eleven (1960); Pepe (cameo); The Devil at 4 O'Clock; Sergeants 3; The Road to Hong Kong (cameo); The Manchurian Candidate (1962); The List of Adrian Messenger (cameo); A New Kind of Love (sings title song); Come Blow Your Horn; 4 for Texas; Robin and the 7 Hoods; None But the Brave (also dir); Von Ryan's Express; Marriage on the Rocks

Skelton, Red: Having Wonderful Time; Flight Command; The People vs. Dr. Kildare; Whistling in the Dark; Dr. Kildare's Wedding

Day; Lady Be Good; Ship Ahoy; Maisie Gets Her Man; Panama Hattie; Whistling in Dixie; Du Barry Was a Lady; I Dood It; Thousands Cheer; Whistling in Brooklyn; Bathing Beauty; Ziegfeld Follies; The Show-Off (1946); Merton of the Movies; The Fuller Brush Man; A Southern Yankee; Neptune's Daughter; The Yellow Cab Man; Three Little Words; Duchess of Idaho; Watch the Birdie; Excuse My Dust; Texas Carnival; Lovely to Look At; The Clown; Half a Hero; The Great Diamond Robbery; Susan Slept Here (cameo); Around the World in Eighty Days (1956; cameo); Public Pigeon No. One; Ocean's Eleven (1960; cameo); Those Magnificent Men in Their Flying Machines (cameo)

Slaughter, Tod: Maria Marten, or The Murder in the Red Barn; Sweeney Todd, The Demon Barber of Fleet Street; The Crimes of Stephen Hawke; The Ticket of Leave Man; It's Never Too Late to Mend; Sexton Blake and the Hooded Terror; The Face at the Window; Crimes at the Dark House; The Greed of William Hart

Stack, Robert: First Love (1939); The Mortal Storm; A Little Bit of Heaven; Nice Girl?; Badlands of Dakota; To Be or Not to Be (1942); Eagle Squadron; A Date with Judy; Miss Tatlock's Millions; Fighter Squadron; Mr. Music; Bullfighter and the Lady; My Outlaw Brother; Bwana Devil; War Paint; Sabre Jet; Conquest of Cochise; The Iron Glove; The High and the Mighty; House of Bamboo; Good Morning, Miss Dove; Great Day in the Morning; Written on the Wind; The Tarnished Angels; The Gift of Love; The Scarface Mob; John Paul Jones; The Last Voyage; The Caretakers

Stanwyck, Barbara: The Locked Door; Ladies of Leisure; Illicit; Ten Cents a Dance; Night Nurse; The Miracle Woman; Forbidden (1932); Shopworn; The Purchase Price; The Bitter Tea of General Yen; Ladies They Talk About; Baby Face; Ever in My Heart; Gambling Lady; The Secret Bride; Woman in Red; Red Salute; Annie Oakley; A Message to Garcia; The Bride Walks Out; His Brother's Wife; Banjo on My Knee; The Plough and the Stars; Internes Can't Take Money; This Is My Affair; Stella Dallas; Breakfast for Two; Always Goodbye; The Mad Miss Manton; Union Pacific; Golden Boy; Remember the Night; The Lady Eve; Meet John Doe; You Belong to Me; Ball of Fire; The Great Man's Lady; The Gay Sisters; Lady of Burlesque; Flesh and Fantasy; Double Indemnity; Hollywood Canteen; Christmas in Connecticut; My Reputation; The Bride Wore Boots; The Strange Love of Martha Ivers; California; The Two Mrs. Carrolls; Variety Girl (cameo); The Other Love; Cry Wolf; B.F.'s Daughter; Sorry, Wrong Number; The Lady Gambles; East Side, West Side; The File on Thelma Jordon; No Man of Her Own (1950); The

Furies; To Please a Lady; The Man With a Cloak; Clash by Night; Jeopardy; Titanic (1953); All I Desire; The Moonlighter; Blowing Wild; Witness to Murder (1954); Executive Suite; Cattle Queen of Montana; The Violent Men; Escape to Burma; There's Always Tomorrow; The Maverick Queen; Crime of Passion; Trooper Hook; Forty Guns; Walk on the Wild Side; Roustabout; The Night Walker

Steiger, Rod: Teresa; On the Waterfront; Oklahoma!; The Big Knife; The Court-Martial of Billy Mitchell; Jubal; Back from Eternity; The Unholy Wife; Run of the Arrow; Across the Bridge; Cry Terror!; Al Capone; Seven Thieves; The Mark; 13 West Street; Convicts 4; The Longest Day; Hands Over the City; Time of Indifference; The Pawnbroker; The Loved One; Doctor Zhivago

Stewart, James: The Murder Man; Next Time We Love; Rose-Marie (1936); Wife vs. Secretary; Small Town Girl (1936); Speed (1936); The Gorgeous Hussy; Born to Dance; After the Thin Man; Seventh Heaven; The Last Gangster; Navy Blue and Gold; Of Human Hearts; Vivacious Lady; The Shopworn Angel; You Can't Take It With You; Made for Each Other (1939); The Ice Follies of 1939; It's a Wonderful World; Mr. Smith Goes to Washington; Destry Rides Again; The Shop Around the Corner; The Mortal Storm; No Time for Comedy; The Philadelphia Story; Come Live With Me; Pot o' Gold; Ziegfeld Girl; It's a Wonderful Life; Magic Town; On Our Merry Way; Call Northside 777; Rope; You Gotta Stay Happy; The Stratton Story; Malaya; Winchester '73; Broken Arrow (1950); The Jackpot; Harvey; No Highway in the Sky; The Greatest Show on Earth; Bend of the River; Carbine Williams; The Naked Spur; Thunder Bay; The Glenn Miller Story; Rear Window; The Far Country; Strategic Air Command; The Man From Laramie; The Man Who Knew Too Much (1956); The Spirit of St. Louis; Night Passage; Vertigo; Bell, Book and Candle; Anatomy of a Murder; The FBI Story; The Mountain Road; X-15 (narr); Two Rode Together; The Man Who Shot Liberty Valance; Mr. Hobbs Takes a Vacation; How the West Was Won; Take Her, She's Mine; Cheyenne Autumn; Dear Brigitte; Shenandoah; The Flight of the Phoenix (1965)

Stockwell, Dean: The Valley of Decision; Anchors Aweigh; The Green Years; Home, Sweet Homicide; The Mighty McGurk; The Arnelo Affair; The Romance of Rosy Ridge; Song of the Thin Man; Gentleman's Agreement; The Boy With Green Hair; Deep Waters; Down to the Sea in Ships; The Secret Garden; Stars in My Crown; The Happy Years; Kim; Cattle Drive; Gun for a Coward; Compulsion; Sons and Lovers; Long Day's Journey Into Night; Rapture

Swanson, Gloria: Male and Female; Why Change Your Wife; The Affairs of Anatol; Beyond the Rocks; The Love of Sunya; Sadie Thompson; Queen Kelly; Indiscreet (1931); Tonight or Never; Perfect Understanding; Father Takes a Wife; Sunset Blvd.; Three for Bedroom C

Taylor, Elizabeth: There's One Born Every Minute; Lassie Come Home; Jane Eyre (1944); The White Cliffs of Dover; National Velvet; Courage of Lassie; Cynthia; Life With Father; A Date With Judy; Julia Misbehaves; Little Women (1949); Conspirator; The Big Hangover; Father of the Bride (1950); Quo Vadis (cameo); Father's Little Dividend; A Place in the Sun; Callaway Went Thataway (cameo); Love Is Better Than Ever; Ivanhoe (1952); The Girl Who Had Everything; Rhapsody; Elephant Walk; Beau Brummell (1954); The Last Time I Saw Paris; Giant; Raintree County; Cat on a Hot Tin Roof; Suddenly, Last Summer (1959); BUtterfield 8; Cleopatra (1963); The V.I.P.s; The Sandpiper

Taylor, Robert: Society Doctor; Times Square Lady; West Point of the Air; Broadway Melody of 1936; Magnificent Obsession (1935); Small Town Girl (1936); Private Number; His Brother's Wife; The Gorgeous Hussy; Camille; Personal Property; This Is My Affair; Broadway Melody of 1938; A Yank at Oxford; Three Comrades; The Crowd Roars (1938); Stand Up and Fight; Lucky Night; Lady of the Tropics; Remember?; Waterloo Bridge (1940); Escape (1940); Flight Command; Billy the Kid (1941); When Ladies Meet (1941); Johnny Eager; Her Cardboard Lover; Stand by for Action; Bataan; The Youngest Profession (cameo); Song of Russia; Undercurrent; High Wall; The Bribe; Ambush; Conspirator; Devil's Doorway; Quo Vadis? (1951); Westward the Women; Ivanhoe (1952); Above and Beyond; I Love Melvin (cameo); Ride, Vaquero!; All the Brothers Were Valiant; Knights of the Round Table; Valley of the Kings; Rogue Cop; Many Rivers to Cross; Quentin Durward; The Last Hunt; D-Day the Sixth of June; The Power and the Prize; Tip on a Dead Jockey; Saddle the Wind; The Law and Jake Wade; Party Girl (1958); The Hangman; The House of the Seven Hawks; Killers of Kilimanjaro; Miracle of the White Stallions; Cattle King; A House Is Not a Home; The Night Walker

Temple, Shirley: Out All Night; Stand Up and Cheer; Little Miss Marker (1934); Baby Take a Bow; Now and Forever (1934); Bright Eyes; The Little Colonel; Our Little Girl; Curly Top; The Littlest Rebel; Captain January; Poor Little Rich Girl; Dimples; Stowaway; Wee Willie Winkie; Heidi (1937); Ali Baba Goes to Town (cameo); Rebecca of Sunnybrook Farm (1938); Little Miss Broadway; Just Around the Corner; The Little Princess (1939); Susannah of the Mounties; The Blue Bird (1940); Young People; Kathleen; Miss Annie Rooney; Since You Went Away; I'll Be Seeing You; Kiss and Tell (1945); Honeymoon (1947); The Bachelor and the Bobby-Soxer; That Hagen Girl; Fort Apache; Mr. Belvedere Goes to College; Adventure in Baltimore; The Story of Seabiscuit; A Kiss for Corliss

Tierney, Gene: The Return of Frank James; Hudson's Bay; Tobacco Road; Belle Starr; Sundown; The Shanghai Gesture; Son of Fury; Rings on Her Fingers; Thunder Birds (1942); China Girl (1942); Heaven Can Wait (1943); Laura; A Bell for Adano; Leave Her to Heaven; Dragonwyck; The Razor's Edge (1946); The Ghost and Mrs. Muir; The Iron Curtain; That Wonderful Urge; Whirlpool (1949); Night and the City (1950); Where the Sidewalk Ends; The Mating Season; On the Riviera; The Secret of Convict Lake; Close to My Heart; Way of a Gaucho; Plymouth Adventure; Never Let Me Go; Personal Affair; Black Widow (1954); The Egyptian; The Left Hand of God; Advise & Consent; Toys in the Attic; The Pleasure Seekers

Tracy, Lee: Salute; Born Reckless (1930); Liliom (1930); The Strange Love of Molly Louvain; Love Is a Racket; Doctor X; Blessed Event; Washington Merry-Go-Round; The Half Naked Truth; Clear All Wires!; The Nuisance; Dinner at Eight; Turn Back the Clock; Bombshell; Advice to the Lovelorn; I'll Tell the World (1934); The Lemon Drop Kid (1934); Sutter's Gold; Wanted! Jane Turner; Criminal Lawyer (1937); Behind the Headlines; Crashing Hollywood; Fixer Dugan; The Spellbinder; Millionaires in Prison; The Pay Off; Power of the Press; Betrayal From the East; I'll Tell the World (1945); High Tide (1947); The Best Man (1964)

Tracy, Spencer: Up the River; Quick Millions; Sky Devils; Young America; The Painted Woman; Me and My Gal; 20,000 Years in Sing Sing; Face in the Sky; The Power and the Glory; Man's Castle; The Show-Off (1934); Looking for Trouble; Bottoms Up; The Murder Man; Dante's Inferno; Whipsaw; Riffraff (1935); Fury (1936); San Francisco; Libeled Lady; They Gave Him a Gun; Captains Courageous; Big City (1937); Mannequin (1937); Test Pilot; Boys Town; Stanley and Livingstone; I Take This Woman; Northwest Passage (Book I—Rogers' Rangers); Young Tom Edison (cameo); Edison, the Man; Boom Town; Men of Boys Town; Dr. Jekyll and Mr. Hyde (1941); Woman of the Year; Tortilla Flat; Keeper of the Flame; A Guy Named Joe; The Seventh Cross; Thirty Seconds Over Tokyo; Without Love; The Sea of Grass; Cass Timberlane; State of the Union; Edward, My Son; Adam's Rib; Malaya; Father of the Bride (1950); Father's Little Dividend; The People Against O'Hara; Pat and

Mike; Plymouth Adventure; The Actress; Broken Lance; Bad Day at Black Rock; The Mountain; Desk Set; The Old Man and the Sea; The Last Hurrah; Inherit the Wind; The Devil at 4 O'Clock; Judgment at Nuremberg; How the West Was Won (narr); It's a Mad Mad Mad Mad World

Turner, Lana: A Star Is Born (1937; bit); They Won't Forget; The Great Garrick; The Adventures of Marco Polo; Four's a Crowd; Love Finds Andy Hardy; Dramatic School; Calling Dr. Kildare; These Glamour Girls; Dancing Co-Ed; Two Girls on Broadway; We Who Are Young; Ziegfeld Girl; Dr. Jekyll and Mr. Hyde (1941); Honky Tonk; Johnny Eager; Somewhere I'll Find You; Slightly Dangerous; The Youngest Profession (cameo); DuBarry Was a Lady (cameo); Marriage Is a Private Affair; Keep Your Powder Dry; Week-End at the Waldorf; The Postman Always Rings Twice (1946); Green Dolphin Street; Cass Timberlane; Homecoming; The Three Musketeers (1948); A Life of Her Own; Mr. Imperium; The Merry Widow (1952); The Bad and the Beautiful; Latin Lovers (1953); Flame and the Flesh; Betrayed (1954); The Prodigal (1955); The Sea Chase; The Rains of Ranchipur; Diane; Peyton Place; The Lady Takes a Flyer; Another Time, Another Place; Imitation of Life (1959); Portrait in Black; By Love Possessed; Bachelor in Paradise; Who's Got the Action?; Love Has Many Faces

Valentino, Rudolph: The Four Horsemen of the Apocalypse (1921); Camille (1921); Beyond the Rocks; The Sheik; Blood and Sand (1922); The Eagle; Cobra (1925); The Son of the Sheik

Wayne, John: Brown of Harvard; Bardelys the Magnificent (bit); Mother Machree (bit); Four Sons (bit); Hangman's House (bit); The Black Watch (bit); Salute; Men Without Women; The Big Trail; Arizona; The Range Feud; Texas Cyclone; Two Fisted Law; The Life of Jimmy Dolan; Baby Face; Ride Him, Cowboy; The Big Stampede; Haunted Gold; The Telegraph Trail; Central Airport; Somewhere in Sonora; His Private Secretary; The Man From Monterey; Riders of Destiny; College Coach (bit); Sagebrush Trail; The Lucky Texan; West of the Divide; Blue Steel; The Man From Utah; Randy Rides Alone; The Star Packer; The Trail Beyond; The Lawless Frontier; 'Neath the Arizona Skies; Texas Terror; Rainbow Valley; The Desert Trail; The Dawn Rider; Paradise Canyon; Westward Ho; The New Frontier (1935); Lawless Range; The Lawless Nineties; King of the Pecos; The Lonely Trail; Winds of the Wasteland; California Straight Ahead; I Cover the War; Born to the West; Pals of the Saddle; Overland Stage Raiders; Santa Fe Stampede; Red River Range; Stagecoach (1939); Night Riders; Three Texas Steers; Wyoming Outlaw; New Frontier (1939); Allegheny Uprising; Dark Command; Three Faces West; The Long Voyage Home; Seven Sinners; A Man Betrayed; Lady From Louisiana; Shepherd of the Hills; Lady for a Night; Reap the Wild Wind; The Spoilers (1942); In Old California; Flying Tigers; Reunion in France; Pittsburgh; A Lady Takes a Chance; In Old Oklahoma; The Fighting Seabees; Tall in the Saddle; Flame of Barbary Coast; Back to Bataan; They Were Expendable; Dakota (1945); Without Reservations; Angel and the Badman; Tycoon; Fort Apache; Red River; 3 Godfathers; Wake of the Red Witch; The Fighting Kentuckian; She Wore a Yellow Ribbon; Sands of Iwo Jima; Rio Grande; Operation Pacific; Flying Leathernecks; The Quiet Man; Big Jim McLain; Trouble Along the Way; Island in the Sky (1953); Hondo; The High and the Mighty; The Sea Chase; Blood Alley; The Conqueror; The Searchers; The Wings of Eagles; Jet Pilot; Legend of the Lost; I Married a Woman (cameo); The Barbarian and the Geisha; Rio Bravo; The Horse Soldiers; The Alamo (1960; also dir); North to Alaska; The Comancheros; The Man Who Shot Liberty Valance; Hatari!; The Longest Day; How the West Was Won; Donovan's Reef; McLintock!; Circus World; The Greatest Story Ever Told (cameo); In Harm's Way; The Sons of Katie Elder

Welles, Orson: Swiss Family Robinson (1940; narr); Citizen Kane (also dir, coscr); Journey into Fear (1942); The Magnificent Ambersons (also dir, narr, adapt); Jane Eyre (1944); Follow the Boys (1944); Tomorrow Is Forever; Duel in the Sun (narr); The Stranger (1946; also dir, uncred coscr); The Lady from Shanghai (also dir, scr); Macbeth (1948; also dir) Black Magic (1949); Prince of Foxes; The Third Man; The Black Rose; The Little World of Don Camillo (narr of English-language prints); Othello (1952; also dir, uncred adapt); Trent's Last Case; Royal Affairs in Versailles; Trouble in the Glen; Mr. Arkadin (also dir, scr); Three Cases of Murder; Moby Dick (1956); Man in the Shadow; The Long Hot Summer; Touch of Evil (also dir, scr); The Roots of Heaven; The Vikings (narr); Compulsion; Ferry to Hong Kong; Crack in the Mirror; The Battle of Austerlitz; David and Goliath; King of Kings (1961; narr); Lafayette; The Tartars; The Trial (1962; also dir, adapt); The V.I.P.s; Marco the Magnificent; Chimes at Midnight (also dir; adapt); A King's Story (narr)

West, Mae: Night After Night; She Done Him Wrong (also sty); I'm No Angel (also scr); Belle of the Nineties (also scr); Goin' to Town (also scr); Klondike Annie (also scr); Go West, Young Man (also scr); Every Day's a Holiday (also scr); My Little Chickadee (also coscr); The Heat's On

Wheeler (Bert) **and Woolsey** (Robert): Rio

Rita (1929); The Cuckoos; Dixiana; Half Shot at Sunrise; Hook, Line and Sinker; Cracked Nuts; Caught Plastered; Peach-O-Reno; Girl Crazy (1932); Hold 'Em Jail; So This Is Africa; Diplomaniacs; Hips, Hips Hooray!; Kentucky Kernels; Cockeyed Cavaliers; The Nitwits; The Rainmakers; Silly Billies; Mummy's Boys; On Again—Off Again; High Flyers; *Wheeler only*: The Cowboy Quarterback; Las Vegas Nights

Widmark, Richard: Kiss of Death (1947); The Street With No Name; Road House (1948); Yellow Sky; Down to the Sea in Ships (1949); Slattery's Hurricane; Night and the City (1950); Panic in the Streets; No Way Out (1950); Halls of Montezuma; The Frogmen; Red Skies of Montana; Don't Bother to Knock; O. Henry's Full House; My Pal Gus; Destination Gobi; Pickup On South Street; Take the High Ground!; Hell and High Water; Garden of Evil; Broken Lance; A Prize of Gold; The Cobweb; Backlash (1956); Run for the Sun; The Last Wagon; Saint Joan; Time Limit; The Law and Jake Wade; The Tunnel of Love; The Trap (1959); Warlock (1959); The Alamo (1960); The Secret Ways; Two Rode Together; Judgment at Nuremberg; How the West Was Won; Flight From Ashiya; The Long Ships; Cheyenne Autumn; The Bedford Incident

William, Warren: Under Eighteen; The Woman from Monte Carlo; Beauty and the Boss; The Mouthpiece; The Dark Horse; Skyscraper Souls; Three on a Match; The Match King; Employees' Entrance; The Mind Reader; Gold Diggers of 1933; Goodbye Again (1933); Lady for a Day; Bedside; Upperworld; Smarty; Dr. Monica; The Dragon Murder Case; The Case of the Howling Dog; Cleopatra; Imitation of Life (1934); The Secret Bride; Living on Velvet; The Case of the Curious Bride; Don't Bet on Blondes; The Case of the Lucky Legs; Satan Met a Lady; The Case of the Velvet Claws; Stage Struck; Go West Young Man; Outcast; Madame X (1937); The Firefly; Arsene Lupin Returns; The First Hundred Years; Wives Under Suspicion; The Lone Wolf Spy Hunt; The Gracie Allen Murder Case; The Man in the Iron Mask; Day-Time Wife, The Lone Wolf Strikes; The Lone Wolf Meets a Lady; Lillian Russell; Trail of the Vigilantes; Arizona; The Lone Wolf Keeps a Date; The Lone Wolf Takes a Chance; Wild Geese Calling; Secrets of the Lone Wolf; The Wolf Man (1941); Counter-Espionage; One Dangerous Night; Passport to Suez; Strange Illusion; Fear; The Private Affairs of Bel Ami

Williams, Esther: Andy Hardy's Double Life; A Guy Named Joe; Bathing Beauty; Thrill of a Romance; Ziegfeld Follies; The Hoodlum Saint; Easy to Wed; Till the Clouds Roll By (cameo); Fiesta; This Time for Keeps (1947); On an Island With You;

Take Me Out to the Ball Game; Neptune's Daughter; Duchess of Idaho; Pagan Love Song; Texas Carnival; Callaway Went Thataway (cameo); Skirts Ahoy!; Million Dollar Mermaid; Dangerous When Wet; Easy to Love (1953); Jupiter's Darling; The Unguarded Moment; Raw Wind in Eden; The Big Show (1961)

Wood, Natalie: Happy Land (bit); Tomorrow Is Forever; The Bride Wore Boots; Driftwood; Miracle on 34th Street (1947); The Ghost and Mrs. Muir; Scudda Hoo! Scudda Hay!; Chicken Every Sunday; The Green Promise; Father Was a Fullback; No Sad Songs for Me; Our Very Own; Never a Dull Moment (1950); The Jackpot; Dear Brat (cameo); The Blue Veil; Just for You; The Rose Bowl Story; The Star; The Silver Chalice; One Desire; Rebel Without a Cause; The Searchers; The Burning Hills; A Cry in the Night; The Girl He Left Behind; Bombers B-52; Marjorie Morningstar; Kings Go Forth; Cash McCall; All the Fine Young Cannibals; Splendor in the Grass; West Side Story; Gypsy; Love With the Proper Stranger; Sex and the Single Girl; The Great Race; Inside Daisy Clover

Woodward, Joanne: Count Three and Pray; A Kiss Before Dying (1956); The Three Faces of Eve; No Down Payment; The Long Hot Summer; Rally 'Round the Flag, Boys!; The Sound and the Fury; The Fugitive Kind; From the Terrace; Paris Blues; The Stripper; A New Kind of Love; Signpost to Murder

Wyman, Jane: The Kid From Spain (bit); Elmer the Great (bit); All the King's Horses (bit); Rumba (bit); George White's Scandals (1935; chorus); King of Burlesque (bit); Polo Joe (bit); Anything Goes (1936; bit); Cain and Mabel (bit); Gold Diggers of 1937 (bit); My Man Godfrey (1936); Stage Struck (bit); The King and the Chorus Girl; Ready, Willing and Able (bit); Slim; The Singing Marine; Public Wedding; Over the Goal (bit); Wide Open Faces; He Couldn't Say No; Fools for Scandal (bit); The Spy Ring; The Crowd Roars (1938); Brother Rat; Tail Spin; The Kid from Kokomo; Kid Nightingale; Private Detective; Brother Rat and a Baby; An Angel From Texas; My Love Came Back; Tugboat Annie Sails Again; Honeymoon for Three; Bad Men of Missouri; You're in the Army Now; The Body Disappears; Larceny, Inc.; My Favorite Spy (1942); Footlight Serenade; Princess O'Rourke; Make Your Own Bed; The Doughgirls; Crime by Night; Hollywood Canteen (cameo); The Lost Weekend; One More Tomorrow; Night and Day; The Yearling; Cheyenne; Magic Town; Johnny Belinda (1948); A Kiss in the Dark; It's a Great Feeling (cameo); The Lady Takes a Sailor; Stage Fright; The Glass Menagerie (1950); Three Guys Named Mike; Here Comes the Groom; The Blue Veil; Starlift (cameo); The Story of Will Rogers; Just for You; Let's Do It Again (1953); So Big (1953); Magnificent Obsession (1954); Lucy Gallant; All That Heaven Allows; Miracle in the Rain; Holiday for Lovers; Pollyanna (1960); Bon Voyage!

Young, Loretta: Laugh, Clown, Laugh; The Show of Shows; Loose Ankles; Road to Paradise; The Truth About Youth; The Devil to Pay!; The Right Way; Show Girl in Hollywood (cameo); Big Business Girl; I Like Your Nerve; Platinum Blonde; The Ruling Voice; Taxi!; The Hatchet Man; Play-Girl (1932); Week-end Marriage; Life Begins; They Call It Sin; Employees Entrance; Grand Slam (1933); Zoo in Budapest; The Life of Jimmy Dolan; Midnight Mary; Heroes for Sale; She Had to Say Yes; The Devil's in Love; Man's Castle; House of Rothschild; Born to Be Bad; Caravan; Clive of India; Shanghai; The Call of the Wild (1935); The Crusades; The Unguarded Hour; Private Number; Ramona; Ladies in Love; Love Is News; Cafe Metropole; Love Under Fire; Wife, Doctor and Nurse; Second Honeymoon; Four Men and a Prayer; Three Blind Mice; Suez; Kentucky; The Story of Alexander Graham Bell; Wife, Husband and Friend; Eternally Yours; The Doctor Takes a Wife; He Stayed for Breakfast; Lady From Cheyenne; The Men in Her Life; Bedtime Story (1941); A Night to Remember (1943); China; Ladies Courageous; And Now Tomorrow; Along Came Jones; The Stranger (1946); The Perfect Marriage; The Farmer's Daughter (1947); The Bishop's Wife; Rachel and the Stranger; The Accused (1948); Mother Is a Freshman;

Come to the Stable; Key to the City; Cause for Alarm!; Half Angel; Paula; Because of You; It Happens Every Thursday

Young, Robert: The Black Camel; The Sin of Madelon Claudet; The Guilty Generation; Hell Divers (bit); The Wet Parade; New Morals for Old; Strange Interlude; The Kid from Spain; Men Must Fight; Today We Live; Hell Below; Tugboat Annie; The Right to Romance; Spitfire (1934); The House of Rothschild; Lazy River; Paris Interlude; Death on the Diamond; West Point of the Air; Calm Yourself; Red Salute; Remember Last Night?; The Bride Comes Home; It's Love Again; The Secret Agent (1936); The Bride Walks Out; The Longest Night; Stowaway; Married Before Breakfast; I Met Him in Paris; The Emperor's Candlesticks; The Bride Wore Red; Navy Blue and Gold; Three Comrades; The Toy Wife; Rich Man, Poor Girl; Josette; The Shining Hour; Honolulu; Maisie; Miracles for Sale; Northwest Passage; The Mortal Storm; Florian; Dr. Kildare's Crisis; Western Union; Lady Be Good; H. M. Pulham, Esq.; Joe Smith, American; Cairo; Journey for Margaret; Slightly Dangerous; Sweet Rosie O'Grady; Claudia; The Canterville Ghost; The Enchanted Cottage; Those Endearing Young Charms; Claudia and David; The Searching Wind; Lady Luck; They Won't Believe Me; Crossfire; Relentless; Sitting Pretty; Adventure in Baltimore; That Forsyte Woman; Bride for Sale; And Baby Makes Three; The Second Woman; Goodbye, My Fancy; The Half-Breed; Secret of the Incas

Index of Directors

What follows is a selection of major directors whose work is represented in this book. The index includes only the titles that appear in this volume; it doesn't pretend to offer a complete list of Michael Curtiz's European work or John Ford's silent features. What's more, the index, like the book, ends in 1965.

The titles in each entry are in chronological order. Years are indicated in the reviews and are included here to distinguish between two films of the same title, whether they are remakes or have nothing to do with each other.

The prefix "co-" means a collaboration. "Seq" means a director was responsible for one sequence in a feature film.

This index is meant to be a convenient, quick-reference guide and only deals with the individuals' work as directors. It does not indicate the other functions they may have performed on a given film, whether as actor, writer, producer, composer, cinematographer, or editor.

Texas, Brooklyn and Heaven; Johnny Stool Pigeon; Undertow; It's a Small World; The Fat Man; Hollywood Story; Cave of Outlaws; Fort Ti; Serpent of the Nile; Conquest of Cochise; Slaves of Babylon; Charge of the Lancers; The Battle of Rogue River; Jesse James vs. the Daltons; Drums of Tahiti; The Iron Glove; The Saracen Blade; The Law vs. Billy the Kid; Masterson of Kansas; The Americano; New Orleans Uncensored; The Gun That Won the West; The Houston Story; Macabre; House on Haunted Hill; The Tingler; 13 Ghosts; Homicidal; Mr. Sardonicus; Zotz!; The Night Walker; 13 Frightened Girls; The Old Dark House (1963); Strait-Jacket; I Saw What You Did

Clair, René: The Italian Straw Hat; Under the Roofs of Paris; Le Million; À Nous la Liberté; The Ghost Goes West; The Flame of New Orleans; I Married a Witch; Forever and a Day (seq dir); It Happened Tomorrow; And Then There Were None; Man About Town (1947); Beauties of the Night; Les Grandes Manoeuvres; Gates of Paris

Corman, Roger: Five Guns West; Apache Woman; Swamp Women; Day the World Ended; The Oklahoma Woman; Gunslinger; It Conquered the World; Not of This Earth (1957); Naked Paradise; Attack of the Crab Monsters; Rock All Night; Teenage Doll; Carnival Rock; Sorority Girl; The Saga of the Viking Women and Their Voyage to the Waters of the Great Sea Serpent; War of the Satellites; She Gods of Shark Reef; Machine-Gun Kelly; Teenage Cave Man; I, Mobster; A Bucket of Blood; The Wasp Woman; Ski Troop Attack; House of Usher; The Little Shop of Horrors (1960); The Last Woman on Earth; Atlas; Creature From the Haunted Sea; Pit and the Pendulum; The Intruder (1962); Premature Burial; Tales of Terror; Tower of London (1962); The Raven (1963); The Terror; X: The Man with the X-Ray Eyes; The Haunted Palace; The Young Racers; The Secret Invasion; The Masque of the Red Death; The Tomb of Ligeia

Cukor, George: The Virtuous Sin (codir); The Royal Family of Broadway (codir); Tarnished Lady; Girls About Town; One Hour With You (codir); What Price Hollywood?; A Bill of Divorcement (1932); Rockabye; Our Betters; Dinner at Eight; Little Women (1933); David Copperfield (1935); Sylvia Scarlett; Romeo and Juliet (1936); Camille; Holiday (1938); Zaza; The Women; Gone With the Wind (uncred codir); The Philadelphia Story; Susan and God; A Woman's Face; Two-Faced Woman; Her Cardboard Lover; Keeper of the Flame; Gaslight (1944); Winged Victory; Desire Me (uncred codir; no dir credit); A Double Life; Edward, My Son; Adam's Rib; Born Yesterday (1950); A Life of Her Own; The Model and the Marriage Broker; The Marrying Kind; Pat and Mike; The Actress; It Should Happen to You; A Star Is Born

(1954); Bhowani Junction; Les Girls; Wild Is the Wind; Heller in Pink Tights; Song Without End (uncred codir); Let's Make Love; The Chapman Report; My Fair Lady

Curtiz, Michael: Noah's Ark; Mammy; Bright Lights (1930); River's End; God's Gift to Women; The Mad Genius; The Woman From Monte Carlo; Alias the Doctor; The Strange Love of Molly Louvain; Doctor X; Cabin in the Cotton; 20,000 Years in Sing Sing; The Mystery of the Wax Museum; The Keyhole; Man Killer; Goodbye Again (1933); The Kennel Murder Case; Female; Mandalay; Jimmy the Gent; The Key (1934); British Agent; Black Fury; The Case of the Curious Bride; Front Page Woman; Little Big Shot; Captain Blood; The Walking Dead; The Charge of the Light Brigade; Stolen Holiday; Mountain Justice; Kid Galahad (1937); The Perfect Specimen; Gold Is Where You Find It; The Adventures of Robin Hood (codir); Four's a Crowd; Four Daughters; Angels with Dirty Faces; Dodge City; Daughters Courageous; The Private Lives of Elizabeth and Essex; Four Wives; Virginia City; The Sea Hawk (1940); Santa Fe Trail; The Sea Wolf; Dive Bomber; Captains of the Clouds; Yankee Doodle Dandy; Casablanca; Mission to Moscow; This Is the Army; Passage to Marseille; Janie; Roughly Speaking; Mildred Pierce; Night and Day; Life with Father; The Unsuspected; Romance on the High Seas; My Dream Is Yours; Flamingo Road; The Lady Takes a Sailor; Bright Leaf; Young Man with a Horn; The Breaking Point; Force of Arms; Jim Thorpe—All American; I'll See You in My Dreams; The Story of Will Rogers; The Jazz Singer (1953); Trouble Along the Way; The Boy From Oklahoma; The Egyptian; White Christmas; We're No Angels (1955); The Vagabond King (1956); The Scarlet Hour; The Best Things in Life Are Free; The Helen Morgan Story; King Creole; The Proud Rebel; The Hangman; The Man in the Net; The Adventures of Huckleberry Finn; A Breath of Scandal; Francis of Assisi; The Comancheros

DeMille, Cecil B.: The Squaw Man (1914; codir); The Virginian (1914); Carmen; The Cheat; Joan the Woman; The Whispering Chorus; Male and Female; Why Change Your Wife; The Affairs of Anatol; Manslaughter; The Ten Commandments (1923); The Road to Yesterday; The Volga Boatman; The King of Kings (1927); The Godless Girl; Dynamite (1929); Madam Satan; The Squaw Man; The Sign of the Cross; This Day and Age; Four Frightened People; Cleopatra (1934); The Crusades; The Plainsman (1936); The Buccaneer (1938); Union Pacific; North West Mounted Police; Reap the Wild Wind; The Story of Dr. Wassell; Unconquered; Samson and Delilah (1949); The Greatest Show on Earth; The Ten Commandments (1956)

De Sica, Vittorio: The Children Are Watching Us; Shoeshine; Bicycle Thieves; Miracle in Milan; Umberto D.; Indiscretion of an American Wife; Gold of Naples; The Roof; Two Women; Boccaccio '70 (seq dir); The Condemned of Altona; Yesterday, Today and Tomorrow; Marriage Italian Style

Dieterle, William: The Last Flight; Her Majesty Love; Man Wanted; Jewel Robbery; The Crash; Six Hours to Live; Scarlet Dawn; Lawyer Man; Grand Slam; The Devil's in Love; Fashions; Fog Over Frisco; Madame DuBarry; The Secret Bride; A Midsummer Night's Dream; Dr. Socrates; The Story of Louis Pasteur; The White Angel; Satan Met a Lady; The Great O'Malley; Another Dawn; The Life of Emile Zola; Blockade; Juarez; The Hunchback of Notre Dame (1939); Dr. Erlich's Magic Bullet; A Dispatch from Reuters; The Devil and Daniel Webster; Tennessee Johnson; Syncopation; Kismet (1944); I'll Be Seeing You; Love Letters; This Love of Ours; The Searching Wind; Portrait of Jennie; The Accused (1948); Rope of Sand; Paid in Full; Volcano; Dark City; September Affair; Peking Express; Boots Malone; Red Mountain; The Turning Point; Salome; Elephant Walk; Magic Fire; Omar Khayyam

Donen, Stanley: On the Town (codir); Royal Wedding; Singin' In the Rain (codir); Love Is Better Than Ever; Fearless Fagan; Give a Girl a Break; Seven Brides for Seven Brothers; Deep in My Heart; It's Always Fair Weather (codir); Funny Face; The Pajama Game (codir); Kiss Them for Me; Indiscreet (1958); Damn Yankees (codir); Once More, With Feeling; Surprise Package; The Grass Is Greener; Charade

Dreyer, Carl Theodor: The Parson's Widow; Leaves from Satan's Book; Michael (1924); Master of the House; The Passion of Joan of Arc; Vampyr; Day of Wrath; Ordet; Gertrud

Edwards, Blake: Bring Your Smile Along; He Laughed Last; Mister Cory; This Happy Feeling; The Perfect Furlough; Operation Petticoat; High Time; Breakfast at Tiffany's; Experiment in Terror; Days of Wine and Roses; The Pink Panther (1964); A Shot in the Dark; The Great Race

Eisenstein, Sergei M.: Battleship Potemkin; October; ¡Que Viva México!; Alexander Nevsky; Ivan the Terrible, Part One; Ivan the Terrible, Part Two

Fellini, Federico: Variety Lights (codir); The White Sheik; Love in the City (episode dir); I Vitelloni; La Strada; The Swindle (1955); Nights of Cabiria; La Dolce Vita; Boccaccio '70 (seq dir); 8½; Juliet of the Spirits

Fleming, Victor: When the Clouds Roll By; The Mollycoddle; Mantrap; Hula; Renegades; The Wet Parade; The White Sister; Bombshell; Treasure Island (1934); Reckless; The Farmer Takes a Wife; Captains Courageous; Test Pilot; The Wizard of Oz (1939); Gone With the Wind; Dr. Jekyll

and Mr. Hyde (1941); Tortilla Flat; A Guy Named Joe; Adventure; Joan of Arc

Ford, John: Just Pals; Cameo Kirby (1923); The Iron Horse; Lightnin'; The Shamrock Handicap; 3 Bad Men; The Blue Eagle; Upstream; Mother Machree; Four Sons (1928); Hangman's House; Riley the Cop; The Black Watch; Salute; Men Without Women; Born Reckless; Up the River; Seas Beneath; The Brat; Arrowsmith; Airmail; Flesh; Pilgrimage; Dr. Bull; The Lost Patrol; The World Moves On; Judge Priest; The Whole Town's Talking; The Informer (1935); Steamboat 'Round the Bend; The Prisoner of Shark Island; Mary of Scotland; The Plough and the Stars; Wee Willie Winkie; The Hurricane (1937); Four Men and a Prayer; Submarine Patrol; Stagecoach (1939); Young Mr. Lincoln; Drums Along the Mohawk; The Grapes of Wrath; The Long Voyage Home; Tobacco Road; How Green Was My Valley; They Were Expendable; My Darling Clementine; The Fugitive (1947); Fort Apache; 3 Godfathers; She Wore a Yellow Ribbon; When Willie Comes Marching Home; Wagon Master; Rio Grande; The Quiet Man; What Price Glory (1952); The Sun Shines Bright; Mogambo; The Long Gray Line; Mister Roberts (codir); The Searchers; The Wings of Eagles; The Rising of the Moon; Gideon of Scotland Yard; The Last Hurrah; The Horse Soldiers; Sergeant Rutledge; Two Rode Together; The Man Who Shot Liberty Valance; How the West Was Won (seq dir); Donovan's Reef; Cheyenne Autumn; Young Cassidy (codir)

Fuller, Samuel: I Shot Jesse James; The Baron of Arizona; The Steel Helmet; Fixed Bayonets!; Park Row; Pickup On South Street; Hell and High Water; House of Bamboo; Run of the Arrow; Forty Guns; China Gate; Verboten!; The Crimson Kimono; Underworld U.S.A.; Merrill's Marauders; Shock Corridor; The Naked Kiss

Griffith, D. W.: The Avenging Conscience; Judith of Bethulia; The Birth of a Nation; Intolerance; Hearts of the World; A Romance of Happy Valley; The Girl Who Stayed at Home; Broken Blossoms; True Heart Susie; The Love Flower; Way Down East (1920); Dream Street; Orphans of the Storm; America (1924); Isn't Life Wonderful; Sally of the Sawdust; Battle of the Sexes (1928); Abraham Lincoln; The Struggle

Hawks, Howard: A Girl in Every Port (1928); Fazil; The Dawn Patrol (1930); The Criminal Code; The Crowd Roars (1932); Scarface (1932); Tiger Shark; Today We Live; Twentieth Century; Barbary Coast; Ceiling Zero; The Road to Glory; Come and Get It (codir); Bringing Up Baby; Indianapolis Speedway; Only Angels Have Wings; His Girl Friday; Sergeant York; Ball of Fire; Air Force; Corvette K-225; The Outlaw (uncred codir); To Have and Have Not; The Big Sleep (1946); Red River; A Song Is Born; I Was a Male War Bride; The Thing From Another World (uncred codir); The Big Sky; O. Henry's Full House (episode dir); Monkey Business; Gentlemen Prefer Blondes; Land of the Pharaohs; Rio Bravo; Hatari!; Man's Favorite Sport?; Red Line 7000

Hitchcock, Alfred: The Pleasure Garden; The Lodger (1926); Downhill; Easy Virtue (1927); The Ring (1927); The Farmer's Wife; Champagne; The Manxman; Blackmail (1929); Juno and the Paycock; Murder!; The Skin Game (1931); Rich and Strange; Number Seventeen; Waltzes from Vienna; The Man Who Knew Too Much (1934); The 39 Steps (1935); The Secret Agent (1936); Sabotage; Young and Innocent; The Lady Vanishes (1938); Jamaica Inn; Rebecca; Foreign Correspondent; Mr. & Mrs. Smith (1941); Suspicion; Saboteur; Shadow of a Doubt; Lifeboat; Spellbound (1945); Notorious; The Paradine Case; Rope; Under Capricorn; Stage Fright; Strangers on a Train; I Confess; Dial M for Murder; Rear Window; To Catch a Thief; The Trouble with Harry; The Man Who Knew Too Much (1956); The Wrong Man; Vertigo; North by Northwest; Psycho (1960); The Birds; Marnie

Huston, John: The Maltese Falcon (1941); In This Our Life; Across the Pacific; The Treasure of the Sierra Madre; Key Largo; We Were Strangers; The Asphalt Jungle; The Red Badge of Courage; The African Queen; Moulin Rouge (1952); Beat the Devil; Moby Dick (1956); Heaven Knows, Mr. Allison; The Barbarian and the Geisha; The Roots of Heaven; The Unforgiven (1960); The Misfits; Freud; The List of Adrian Messenger; The Night of the Iguana

Kazan, Elia: A Tree Grows in Brooklyn; Sea of Grass; Boomerang! (1947); Gentleman's Agreement; Pinky; Panic in the Streets; A Streetcar Named Desire; Viva Zapata!; Man on a Tightrope; On the Waterfront; East of Eden; Baby Doll; A Face in the Crowd; Wild River; Splendor in the Grass; America, America

Kramer, Stanley: Not As a Stranger; The Pride and the Passion; The Defiant Ones; On the Beach; Inherit the Wind; Judgment at Nuremberg; It's a Mad Mad Mad Mad World; Ship of Fools

Kubrick, Stanley: Fear and Desire; Killer's Kiss; The Killing; Paths of Glory; Spartacus; Lolita (1962); Dr. Strangelove or: How I Learned to Stop Worrying and Love the Bomb

Kurosawa, Akira: Sanshiro Sugata; The Men Who Tread on the Tiger's Tail; The Most Beautiful; No Regrets for Our Youth; One Wonderful Sunday; Drunken Angel; The Quiet Duel; Stray Dog; Scandal (1950); Rashomon; The Idiot (1951); Ikiru; Seven Samurai; I Live in Fear; Throne of Blood; The Lower Depths (1957); The Hidden Fortress; The Bad Sleep Well; Yojimbo; Sanjuro; High and Low; Red Beard

La Cava, Gregory: Womanhandled; Running Wild (1927); His First Command; Smart Woman (1931); Symphony of Six Million; The Age of Consent (1932); The Half Naked Truth; Gabriel Over the White House; Bed of Roses; Gallant Lady; The Affairs of Cellini; What Every Woman Knows; Private Worlds; She Married Her Boss; My Man Godfrey (1936); Stage Door; 5th Ave. Girl; Primrose Path (1940); Unfinished Business; Lady in a Jam; Living in a Big Way

Lang, Fritz: The Spiders; Harakiri (1919); The Wandering Shadow; Four Around the Woman; Destiny (1921); Dr. Mabuse der Spieler (The Gambler); Dr. Mabuse, King of Crime; Die Nibelungen; Metropolis (1927); Spies; Woman in the Moon; M (1931); The Testament of Dr. Mabuse; Fury (1936); You Only Live Once; You and Me; The Return of Frank James; Western Union; Man Hunt (1941); Hangmen Also Die!; The Woman in the Window; Ministry of Fear; Scarlet Street; Cloak and Dagger (1946); Secret Beyond the Door; The House by the River; American Guerrilla in the Philippines; Rancho Notorious; Clash by Night; The Blue Gardenia; The Big Heat; Human Desire; Moonfleet; While the City Sleeps; Beyond a Reasonable Doubt; The Tiger of Eschnapur; The Indian Tomb; The 1,000 Eyes of Dr. Mabuse

Lean, David: In Which We Serve (codir); This Happy Breed; Blithe Spirit; Brief Encounter; Great Expectations (1946); Oliver Twist (1948); The Passionate Friends; Madeleine (1950); Breaking the Sound Barrier; Hobson's Choice; Summertime; The Bridge on the River Kwai; Lawrence of Arabia; Doctor Zhivago

LeRoy, Mervyn: Show Girl in Hollywood; Numbered Men; Top Speed; Little Caesar; Gentleman's Fate; Broadminded; Five Star Final; Local Boy Makes Good; Tonight or Never; High Pressure; The Heart of New York; Two Seconds; Big City Blues; Three on a Match; I Am a Fugitive From a Chain Gang; Hard to Handle; Elmer, the Great; Gold Diggers of 1933; Tugboat Annie; The World Changes; Hi, Nellie!; Heat Lightning; Happiness Ahead; Sweet Adeline; Oil for the Lamps of China; Page Miss Glory; I Found Stella Parish; Anthony Adverse; Fools for Scandal; Waterloo Bridge (1940); Escape; Blossoms in the Dust; Unholy Partners; Johnny Eager; Random Harvest; Madame Curie; Thirty Seconds Over Tokyo; Without Reservations; Homecoming; Little Women (1949); Any Number Can Play; East Side, West Side; Quo Vadis; Lovely to Look At; Million Dollar Mermaid; Latin Lovers; Rose Marie; Strange Lady in Town; Mister Roberts; The Bad Seed; Toward the Unknown; No Time for Sergeants; Home Before Dark; The FBI Story; Wake Me When It's Over; The Devil at 4 O'Clock; A Majority of One; Gypsy; Mary, Mary

Lubitsch, Ernst: I Don't Want to Be a Man; The Doll; The Oyster Princess; Sumurun; Anne Boleyn; The Wildcat; The Marriage Circle; Lady Windermere's Fan (1925); So This Is Paris (1926); The Student Prince in Old Heidelberg; Eternal Love; The Love Parade; Paramount on Parade (codir); Monte Carlo; Broken Lullaby; The Smiling Lieutenant; One Hour With You (codir); Trouble in Paradise; If I Had a Million (seq dir); Design for Living; The Merry Widow (1934); Angel (1937); Bluebeard's Eighth Wife; Ninotchka; The Shop Around the Corner; That Uncertain Feeling; To Be or Not to Be (1942); Heaven Can Wait (1943); A Royal Scandal (1945; codir); Cluny Brown; That Lady in Ermine

Lumet, Sidney: 12 Angry Men (1957); Stage Struck (1958); That Kind of Woman; The Fugitive Kind; A View From the Bridge; Long Day's Journey Into Night; Fail-Safe; The Pawnbroker; The Hill

Mankiewicz, Joseph L.: Dragonwyck; Somewhere in the Night; The Late George Apley; The Ghost and Mrs. Muir; Escape (1948); A Letter to Three Wives; House of Strangers; No Way Out (1950); All About Eve; People Will Talk (1951); 5 Fingers; Julius Caesar (1953); The Barefoot Contessa; Guys and Dolls; The Quiet American; Suddenly, Last Summer; Cleopatra (1963)

Mann, Anthony: Moonlight in Havana; Nobody's Darling; Strangers in the Night; Dr. Broadway; The Great Flamarion; Two O'Clock Courage; Sing Your Way Home; Strange Impersonation; The Bamboo Blonde; Desperate; Railroaded!; T-Men; Raw Deal (1948); Reign of Terror; Border Incident; Side Street; Winchester '73; The Furies; Devil's Doorway; The Tall Target; Bend of the River; The Naked Spur; Thunder Bay; The Glenn Miller Story; The Far Country; Strategic Air Command; The Man From Laramie; The Last Frontier (1956); Serenade; Men in War; The Tin Star; God's Little Acre; Man of the West; Cimarron (1960); El Cid; The Fall of the Roman Empire; The Heroes of Telemark

McCarey, Leo: Let's Go Native; The Kid from Spain; Duck Soup; Six of a Kind; Belle of the Nineties; Ruggles of Red Gap; The Milky Way (1936); Make Way for Tomorrow; The Awful Truth; Love Affair; Once Upon a Honeymoon; Going My Way; The Bells of St. Mary's; Good Sam; My Son John; An Affair to Remember; Rally 'Round the Flag, Boys!; Satan Never Sleeps

Micheaux, Oscar: Within Our Gates; The Symbol of the Unconquered; Body and Soul (1925); The Girl from Chicago; Murder in Harlem; Lying Lips

Milestone, Lewis: Two Arabian Knights; The Garden of Eden; The Racket (1928); All Quiet on the Western Front; The Front Page (1931); Rain (1932); Hallelujah I'm a Bum; The Captain Hates the Sea; Anything Goes (1936); The General Died at Dawn; Of Mice and Men (1939); Lucky Partners; My Life With Caroline; Edge of Darkness; The Purple Heart; A Walk in the Sun; The Strange Love of Martha Ivers; Arch of Triumph; No Minor Vices; The Red Pony; Halls of Montezuma; Kangaroo: The Australian Story; Les Miserables (1952); Melba; They Who Dare; The Widow; Pork Chop Hill; Ocean's Eleven (1960); Mutiny on the Bounty (1962)

Minnelli, Vincente: Cabin in the Sky; I Dood It; Meet Me in St. Louis; The Clock; Yolanda and the Thief; Ziegfeld Follies; Undercurrent; The Pirate; Madame Bovary (1949); Father of the Bride (1950); Father's Little Dividend; An American in Paris; The Bad and the Beautiful; The Story of Three Loves (seq dir); The Band Wagon (1953); The Long, Long Trailer; Brigadoon; The Cobweb; Kismet (1955); Lust for Life; Tea and Sympathy; Designing Woman; Gigi (1958); The Reluctant Debutante; Some Came Running; Home From the Hill; Bells Are Ringing; The Four Horsemen of the Apocalypse (1962); Two Weeks in Another Town; The Courtship of Eddie's Father; Goodbye Charlie; The Sandpiper

Mizoguchi, Kenji: Osaka Elegy; Sisters of the Gion; The Story of the Last Chrysanthemum; Utamaro and His Five Women; The Life of Oharu; Ugetsu; A Geisha; Sansho the Bailiff; Princess Yang Kwei-Fei; Taira Clan Saga; Street of Shame

Murnau, F. W.: The Haunted Castle; Nosferatu; Phantom; The Finances of the Grand Duke; The Last Laugh; Tartuffe; Faust; Sunrise: A Song of Two Humans; City Girl; Tabu—A Story of the South Seas

Ophuls, Max (*sometimes billed as Opuls*): De Mayerling à Sarajevo; The Exile; Letter from an Unknown Woman; Caught; The Reckless Moment; La Ronde; Le Plaisir; The Earrings of Madame de . . .; Lola Montès

Ozu, Yasujiro: Tokyo Chorus; I Was Born, But . . .; Passing Fancy; A Story of Floating Weeds; Late Spring; Early Summer; Tokyo Story; Early Spring; Tokyo Twilight; Equinox Flower; Good Morning; Floating Weeds; Late Autumn; The End of Summer; An Autumn Afternoon

Powell, Michael: Something Always Happens; The Phantom Light; Crown v. Stevens; The Edge of the World; The Spy in Black; The Lion Has Wings; The Thief of Bagdad (1940; codir); Contraband (1940); 49th Parallel; '. . . . . one of our aircraft is missing' (codir); [*all of Powell's films from here through 1957 were cowritten and codirected with* **Emeric Pressburger**]: The Life and Death of Colonel Blimp; A Canterbury Tale; I Know Where I'm Going!; A Matter of Life and Death; Black Narcissus; The Red Shoes; The Small Back Room; The Wild Heart; The Elusive Pimpernel; Tales

of Hoffman; Oh . . . Rosalinda!!; Pursuit of the Graf Spee; Night Ambush; Honeymoon (1959); Peeping Tom; The Queen's Guards
Preminger, Otto: Danger—Love at Work; Margin for Error; They Got Me Covered; In the Meantime, Darling; Laura; A Royal Scandal (1945; codir); Fallen Angel (1945); Centennial Summer; Forever Amber; Daisy Kenyon; That Lady in Ermine (credited to Ernst Lubitsch); The Fan (1949); Whirlpool (1949); Where the Sidewalk Ends; The 13th Letter; Angel Face; The Moon Is Blue; River of No Return; Carmen Jones; The Man With the Golden Arm; The Court-Martial of Billy Mitchell; Saint Joan; Bonjour Tristesse; Porgy and Bess; Anatomy of a Murder; Exodus; Advise & Consent; The Cardinal; In Harm's Way; Bunny Lake Is Missing
Ray, Nicholas: They Live by Night; A Woman's Secret; Knock on Any Door; In a Lonely Place; Born to Be Bad; Flying Leathernecks; On Dangerous Ground; The Lusty Men; Johnny Guitar; Run for Cover; Rebel Without a Cause; Hot Blood; Bigger Than Life; The True Story of Jesse James; Bitter Victory; Wind Across the Everglades; Party Girl (1958); The Savage Innocents; King of Kings (1961); 55 Days at Peking
Reed, Carol: The Stars Look Down; Girl in the News; Night Train to Munich; The Young Mr. Pitt; The Way Ahead; Odd Man Out; The Fallen Idol; The Third Man; Outcast of the Islands; The Man Between; A Kid for Two Farthings; Trapeze; The Key (1958); Our Man in Havana; The Running Man (1963); The Agony and the Ecstasy
Renoir, Jean: Whirlpool of Fate; Nana (1926); La Chienne; Boudu Saved From Drowning; Madame Bovary (1934); Toni; The Crime of Monsieur Lange; The Lower Depths (1936); Grand Illusion; La Marseillaise; La Bête Humaine; Rules of the Game; Swamp Water; This Land Is Mine; The Southerner; A Day in the Country; Diary of a Chambermaid (1946); The Woman on the Beach; The River (1951); The Golden Coach; Only the French Can; Paris Does Strange Things; Picnic on the Grass; Le Testament du Dr. Cordelier; The Elusive Corporal
Ritt, Martin: Edge of the City; No Down Payment; The Long Hot Summer; The Black Orchid; The Sound and the Fury; 5 Branded Women; Paris Blues; Hemingway's Adventures of a Young Man; Hud; The Outrage; The Spy Who Came in from the Cold
Rossellini, Roberto: Open City; Paisan; Germany Year Zero; Stromboli; Francesco—Giullare di Dio; The Greatest Love; The Seven Deadly Sins (seq dir); Machine to Kill Bad People; Strangers (1954); Fear (1954); Il Generale Della Rovere
Siegel, Don (*sometimes billed as Donald Siegel*): The Verdict (1946); Night Unto Night; The Big Steal; The Duel at Silver Creek; No Time for Flowers; Count the

Hours; China Venture; Riot in Cell Block 11; Private Hell 36; An Annapolis Story; Invasion of the Body Snatchers (1956); Crime in the Streets; Baby Face Nelson; Spanish Affair; The Lineup; The Gun Runners; Hound-Dog Man; Edge of Eternity; Flaming Star; Hell Is for Heroes; The Killers (1964)
Sirk, Douglas (*Detlef Sierck*): La Habañera; Hitler's Madman; A Scandel in Paris; Summer Storm; Thieves' Holiday; Lured; Sleep My Love; Slightly French; Shockproof; Mystery Submarine (1950); The First Legion; Thunder on the Hill; The Lady Pays Off; Week-end With Father; No Room for the Groom; Has Anybody Seen My Gal?; Meet Me at the Fair; Take Me to Town; All I Desire; Taza, Son of Cochise; Magnificent Obsession (1954); Sign of the Pagan; Captain Lightfoot; All That Heaven Allows; There's Always Tomorrow; Written on the Wind; Battle Hymn; Interlude (1957); The Tarnished Angels; A Time to Love and a Time to Die; Imitation of Life (1959)
Stevens, George: Bachelor Bait; Kentucky Kernels; The Nitwits; Alice Adams; Annie Oakley; Swing Time; Quality Street; A Damsel in Distress; Vivacious Lady; Gunga Din; Vigil in the Night; Penny Serenade; Woman of the Year; The Talk of the Town; The More the Merrier; I Remember Mama; A Place in the Sun; Something to Live For; Shane; Giant; The Diary of Anne Frank; The Greatest Story Ever Told
Sturges, Preston: The Great McGinty; Christmas in July; The Lady Eve; Sullivan's Travels; The Palm Beach Story; Hail the Conquering Hero; The Miracle of Morgan's Creek; The Great Moment; The Sin of Harold Diddlebock; Unfaithfully Yours (1948); The Beautiful Blonde From Bashful Bend; The French, They Are a Funny Race
Tashlin, Frank: The First Time; Son of Paleface; Marry Me Again; Susan Slept Here; Artists and Models; The Lieutenant Wore Skirts; The Girl Can't Help It; Hollywood or Bust; Will Success Spoil Rock Hunter?; Rock-a-Bye Baby; The Geisha Boy; Say One for Me; Cinderfella; Bachelor Flat; It's \$ Only Money; The Man From the Diner's Club; Who's Minding the Store?; The Disorderly Orderly; The Alphabet Murders
Tourneur, Jacques: Nick Carter, Master Detective; Phantom Raiders; Cat People (1942); I Walked with a Zombie; The Leopard Man; Days of Glory; Experiment Perilous; Canyon Passage; Out of the Past; Berlin Express; Easy Living (1949); Stars in My Crown; The Flame and the Arrow; Circle of Danger; Anne of the Indies; Way of a Gaucho; Appointment in Honduras; Stranger on Horseback; Wichita; Great Day in the Morning; Nightfall (1957); Curse of the Demon; The Fearmakers; Timbuktu; The Comedy of Terrors; War-Gods of the Deep
Ulmer, Edgar G.: People on Sunday (as-

sistant); Damaged Lives; The Black Cat; Green Fields; The Singing Blacksmith; The Light Ahead; Moon Over Harlem; Tomorrow We Live; Isle of Forgotten Sins; Jive Junction; Bluebeard; Strange Illusion; Club Havana; Detour; The Wife of Monte Cristo; Her Sister's Secret; The Strange Woman; Carnegie Hall; Ruthless; Pirates of Capri; The Man From Planet X; St. Benny the Dip; Loves of Three Queens (uncred); Murder Is My Beat; The Naked Dawn; Daughter of Dr. Jekyll; Hannibal; Beyond the Time Barrier; The Amazing Transparent Man; Journey Beneath the Desert

Van Dyke II, W. S.: The Lady of the Dugout; White Shadows in the South Seas; The Pagan; Trader Horn; Guilty Hands; The Cuban Love Song; Tarzan the Ape Man; Night Court; The Prizefighter and the Lady; Penthouse; Eskimo; Manhattan Melodrama; The Thin Man; Hide-Out; Forsaking All Others; Naughty Marietta; I Live My Life; Rose-Marie (1936); San Francisco; His Brother's Wife; The Devil Is a Sissy; Love on the Run; After the Thin Man; Personal Property; They Gave Him a Gun; Rosalie; Marie Antoinette (1938); Sweethearts; Stand Up and Fight; It's a Wonderful World; Andy Hardy Gets Spring Fever; Another Thin Man; I Take This Woman; I Love You Again; Bitter Sweet; Rage in Heaven; The Feminine Touch; Shadow of the Thin Man; Dr. Kildare's Victory; I Married an Angel; Cairo; Journey for Margaret

Vidor, King: The Sky Pilot; Wild Oranges; The Big Parade; La Boheme; Bardelys the Magnificent; The Crowd; Show People; Hallelujah; Not So Dumb; Billy the Kid (1930); Street Scene; The Champ (1931); Bird of Paradise (1932); Cynara; The Stranger's Return; Our Daily Bread; The Wedding Night; So Red the Rose; The Texas Rangers (1936); Stella Dallas; The Citadel; Northwest Passage; Comrade X; H. M. Pulham, Esq.; An American Romance; Duel in the Sun; On Our Merry Way; The Fountainhead; Beyond the Forest; Lightning Strikes Twice; Japanese War Bride; Ruby Gentry; Man Without a Star; War and Peace; Solomon and Sheba

Visconti, Luchino: Osessione; Bellissima; Senso; Of Life and Love (seq dir); White Nights (1957); Rocco and His Brothers; Boccaccio '70 (seq dir); The Leopard

von Sternberg, Josef: The Last Command (1928); The Docks of New York; Thunderbolt; The Blue Angel (1930); Morocco; Dishonored; An American Tragedy; Shanghai Express; The Scarlet Empress; The Devil Is a Woman; Crime and Punishment; The King Steps Out; Sergeant Madden; The Shanghai Gesture; Macao; Anatahan; Jet Pilot

von Stroheim, Erich: Blind Husbands; Foolish Wives; Greed; The Merry Widow (1925); The Wedding March; Queen Kelly; Hello, Sister! (codir)

Welles, Orson: *See* Index of Stars

Wellman, William A.: The Boob; Wings; Beggars of Life; Chinatown Nights; The Man I Love; Maybe It's Love; Other Men's Women; The Public Enemy; Night Nurse; The Star Witness; Safe in Hell; The Hatchet Man; Love Is a Racket; The Purchase Price; The Conquerors; Frisco Jenny; Central Airport; Lilly Turner; Midnight Mary; Heroes for Sale; Wild Boys of the Road; College Coach; Looking for Trouble; Stingaree; The President Vanishes; The Call of the Wild; The Robin Hood of El Dorado; Small Town Girl (1936); A Star Is Born (1937); Nothing Sacred; Men with Wings; Beau Geste (1939); The Light That Failed; Reaching for the Sun; Roxie Hart; The Great Man's Lady; Thunder Birds (1942); The Ox-Bow Incident; Lady of Burlesque; Buffalo Bill; This Man's Navy; The Story of G.I. Joe; Gallant Journey; Magic Town; The Iron Curtain; Yellow Sky; Battleground; The Happy Years; The Next Voice You Hear; Across the Wide Missouri; It's a Big Country (codir); Westward the Women; My Man and I; Island in the Sky (1953); The High and the Mighty; Track of the Cat; Blood Alley; Good-bye, My Lady; Darby's Rangers; Lafayette Escadrille

Whale, James: Hell's Angels; Journey's End (1930); Waterloo Bridge (1931); Frankenstein; Impatient Maiden; The Old Dark House; The Invisible Man; By Candlelight; The Kiss Before the Mirror; One More River; Remember Last Night; Bride of Frankenstein; Show Boat (1936); The Road Back; The Great Garrick; Wives Under Suspicion; Sinners in Paradise; Port of Seven Seas; The Man in the Iron Mask (1939); Green Hell; They Dare Not Love

Wilder, Billy: Mauvaise Graine (codir); The Major and the Minor; Five Graves to Cairo; Double Indemnity; The Lost Weekend; The Emperor Waltz; A Foreign Affair; Sunset Blvd.; Ace in the Hole; Stalag 17; Sabrina (1954); The Seven Year Itch; The Spirit of St. Louis; Love in the Afternoon; Witness for the Prosecution; Some Like It Hot (1959); The Apartment; One, Two, Three; Irma La Douce; Kiss Me, Stupid

Wise, Robert: The Curse of the Cat People (codir); Mademoiselle Fifi; The Body Snatcher; A Game of Death; Criminal Court; Born to Kill; Mystery in Mexico; Blood on the Moon; The Set-Up; Two Flags West; Three Secrets; The House on Telegraph Hill; The Day the Earth Stood Still (1951); The Captive City; Something for the Birds; The Desert Rats; Destination Gobi; So Big; Executive Suite; Helen of Troy; Tribute to a Bad Man; Somebody Up There Likes Me; This Could Be the Night; Until They Sail; Run Silent, Run Deep; I Want to Live!; Odds Against Tomorrow; West Side Story (codir); Two for the Seesaw; The Haunting (1963); The Sound of Music

Wood, Edward D. Jr.: Glen or Glenda; Jail

Bait (1954); Bride of the Monster; Plan 9 From Outer Space; Revenge of the Dead; The Sinister Urge

Wyler, William: The Love Trap; Hell's Heroes; A House Divided; Tom Brown of Culver; Counsellor at Law; The Good Fairy; The Gay Deception; These Three; Dodsworth; Come and Get It (codir); Dead End; Jezebel; Wuthering Heights (1939); The Westerner; The Letter (1940); The Little Foxes; Mrs. Miniver; The Best Years of Our Lives; The Heiress; Detective Story; Carrie (1952); Roman Holiday; The Desperate Hours (1955); Friendly Persuasion; The Big Country; Ben-Hur (1959); The Children's Hour; The Collector

Zinnemann, Fred: Kid Glove Killer; Eyes in the Night; The Seventh Cross; Little Mister Jim; My Brother Talks to Horses; The Search; Act of Violence; The Men; Teresa; High Noon; The Member of the Wedding; From Here to Eternity; Oklahoma!; A Hatful of Rain; The Nun's Story; The Sundowners (1960); Behold a Pale Horse